Best Books for
High School
Readers

Recent Titles in the
Children's and Young Adult Literature Reference Series
Catherine Barr, Series Editor

Best Books for Children: Preschool Through Grade 6, 9th Edition
Catherine Barr and John T. Gillespie

Literature Links to World History, K–12: Resources to Enhance and Entice
Lynda G. Adamson

A to Zoo: Subject Access to Children's Picture Books, 8th Edition
Carolyn W. Lima and Rebecca L. Thomas

Literature Links to American History, 7–12: Resources to Enhance and Entice
Lynda G. Adamson

Literature Links to American History, K–6: Resources to Enhance and Entice
Lynda G. Adamson

Celebrating Cuentos: Promoting Latino Children's Literature and Literacy in Classrooms and Libraries
Jamie Campbell Naidoo, Editor

The Family in Literature for Young Readers: A Resource Guide for Use with Grades 4 to 9
John T. Gillespie

Best Books for High School Readers, Grades 9–12: Supplement to the Second Edition
Catherine Barr

Best Books for Middle School and Junior High Readers, Grades 6–9: Supplement to the Second Edition
Catherine Barr

Rainbow Family Collections: Selecting and Using Children's Books with Lesbian, Gay, Bisexual, Transgender, and Queer Content
Jamie Campbell Naidoo

A to Zoo: Subject Access to Children's Picture Books, Supplement to the 8th Edition
Rebecca L. Thomas

Best Books for Children: Preschool Through Grade 6, Supplement to the 9th Edition
Catherine Barr

Best Books for High School Readers

GRADES 9–12
Third Edition

Catherine Barr

Children's and Young Adult Literature Reference

LIBRARIES UNLIMITED

AN IMPRINT OF ABC-CLIO, LLC
Santa Barbara, California • Denver, Colorado • Oxford, England

Copyright © 2013 by Catherine Barr

Library of Congress Cataloging-in-Publication Data

Barr, Catherine, 1951–
  Best books for high school readers : grades 9–12 / Catherine Barr. — Third edition.
      pages cm. — (Children's and young adult literature reference)
  Includes bibliographical references and indexes.
   ISBN 978-1-59884-784-0 (hardcover) 1. Young adult literature—Bibliography. 2. High school libraries—United States—Book lists. 3. Teenagers—Books and reading—United States. I. Title.
   Z1037.G4816   2013
   001.62'5—dc23   2013011585

ISBN: 978-1-59884-784-0

17 16 15 14 13   1 2 3 4 5

Libraries Unlimited
An Imprint of ABC-CLIO, LLC

ABC-CLIO, LLC
130 Cremona Drive, P.O. Box 1911
Santa Barbara, California 93116-1911

This book is printed on acid-free paper ∞
Manufactured in the United States of America

Contents

Literary History and Criticism

Language and Communication

Biography, Memoirs, Etc.

The Arts and Entertainment

History and Geography

Philosophy and Religion

Society and the Individual

Guidance and Personal Development

Physical and Applied Sciences

ix

CONTENTS

Recreation and Sports

Major Subjects Arranged Alphabetically

Preface

Librarians and other specialists in children's literature have available, through print and online sources, a large number of bibliographies that recommend books suitable for young people. Unfortunately, these sources vary widely in quality and usefulness. The Best Books series was created to furnish authoritative, reliable, and comprehensive bibliographies for use in libraries that collect materials for readers from preschool through grade 12. The series now consists of three volumes: *Best Books for Children, Best Books for Middle School and Junior High Readers*, and *Best Books for High School Readers*.

Best Books for High School Readers, Third Edition is a continuation of *Best Books for Middle School and Junior High Readers, Third Edition* (Libraries Unlimited, 2013), which covers books recommended for grades 6 though 9. The present volume, *Best Books for High School Readers*, supplies information on books recommended for readers in grades 9 through 12, or roughly ages 15 through 18.

As every librarian knows, reading levels are elastic. There is no such thing, for example, as a tenth-grade book. Instead there are only tenth-grade readers who, in their diversity, can represent a wide range of reading abilities and interests. This bibliography contains a liberal selection of entries that, one hopes, will accommodate readers in these four grades, and make allowance for their great range of tastes and reading competencies. By the ninth grade, a percentage of the books read should be at the adult level. Keeping this in mind, more than a third of the entries in this volume are adult books suitable for young adult readers (they are designated by a reading level usually of 10–12 within the entries and by S–Adult in the subject index). At the other end of the spectrum, there are also many titles that are suitable for younger readers (these are indicated by grade level designations such as 5–10, 6–10, 7–10, and so forth).

To be included in this bibliography, books must be suitable for at least two of the four grades (9–12) covered in this bibliography. There is, therefore, a slight duplication of titles in this book with those in *Best Books for Middle School and Junior High Readers*. For example, a book that is recommended for grades 7–10 will be found in both volumes. Librarians seeking a more comprehensive listing of books at the lower end of the reading level scale should also consult *Best Books for Middle School and Junior High Readers.*

In selecting books for inclusion, deciding on their arrangement, and collecting the information supplied on each, it was the editors' intention to reflect the current needs and interests of young readers while keeping in mind the latest trends and curricular emphases in today's schools.

General Scope and Criteria for Inclusion

Of the 12,699 titles listed in *Best Books for High School Readers, Third Edition*, 12,438 are individually numbered entries and 261 are cited within the annotations as additional recommended titles by the same author (often these are titles that are part of an extensive series — see "Additional Pointers for Users" later in the Preface). It should be noted that some series are so extensive that, because of space limitations, only representative titles are included.

Excluded from this bibliography are general reference works, such as dictionaries and encyclopedias, except for a few single-volume works that are so heavily illustrated and attractive that they can also be used in the general circulation collection. Also excluded are professional books for librarians and teachers and mass market series books.

For most fiction and nonfiction, a minimum of two recommendations were required from the current reviewing sources consulted for a title to be considered for listing. However, there were a number of necessary exceptions. For example, in some journals only a few representative titles from extensive nonfiction series are reviewed even though others in the series will also be recommended. In such cases a single favorable review was enough for inclusion. This also held true for some of the adult titles suitable for young adult readers where, it has been found, reviewing journals tend to be less inclusive than with juvenile titles. Depending on the strength of the review, a single positive one was sufficient for inclusion. As well as favorable reviews, additional criteria such as availability, currency, accuracy, usefulness, and relevance were considered.

Sources Used

A number of current and retrospective sources were used in compiling this bibliography. Book reviewing journals consulted were *Booklist, Library Media Connection* (formerly *Book Report), School Library Journal*, and *VOYA (Voice of Youth Advocates)*. To a much lesser degree other sources used include *Bulletin of the Center for Children's Books, Horn Book*, and *Horn Book Guide*. Reviews in issues of these journals were read and evaluated from July 2008 through early 2013, when this book's coverage ends.

Uses of This Book

Best Books for High School Readers was designed to help librarians and media specialists with four vital tasks: (1) evaluating the adequacy of existing collections; (2) building new collections or strengthening existing holdings; (3) providing reading guidance to young adults; and (4) preparing bibliographies and reading lists. To increase the book's usefulness, particularly in the preparation of bibliographies or suggested reading lists, titles are arranged under broad areas of interest or, in the case of nonfiction works, by curriculum-oriented subjects rather than by the Dewey Decimal classification (suggested Dewey classification numbers are nevertheless provided within nonfiction entries). The subject arrangement corresponds roughly to the one used in *Best Books for Children* and *Best Books for Middle School and Junior High Readers*. It is hoped that the Subject/Grade Level Index will help guide the user in this regard.

Audio and ebook versions are indicated with the symbols ⋂ and **e**. Lexile reading levels are also provided where available. Additional information about Lexile measures is available at lexile.com.

Arrangement

In the Table of Contents, subjects are arranged by the order in which they appear in the book. Following the Table of Contents is a listing of Major Subjects Arranged Alphabetically, which provides entry numbers as well as page numbers for easy access. Following the main body of the text, there are three indexes. The Author Index cites authors and editors, titles, and entry numbers (joint authors and editors are listed separately). The Title Index gives the book's entry number. Works of fiction in both of these indexes are indicated by (F) following the entry number. Finally, an extensive Subject/Grade Level Index lists entry numbers under hundreds of subject headings with specific grade-level suitability given for each entry. The following codes are used to identify general grade levels:

JS   (Junior–Senior High) suitable for junior high and senior high grades (grades 7 and up)

S   (Senior High) suitable usually only for senior high grades (grades 10–12)

S–Adult   (Senior High–Adult) written for an adult audience but suitable for high school collections (usually grades 10–12)

In each case, the user should consult the grade levels indicated within the entry for specific grade recommendations.

Entries

A typical entry contains the following information where applicable: (1) author, joint author, or editor; (2) title and subtitle; (3) specific grade levels given in parentheses; (4) adapter or translator; (5) indication of illustrations; (6) publication date; (7) publisher and price of hardbound edition (LB = library binding); (8) International Standard Book Number (ISBN) of hardbound edition; (9) paperback publisher (paper) and price (if no publisher is listed it is the same as the hardbound edition); (10) ISBN of paperback edition; (11) annotation; (12) awards; (13) audio version; (14) ebook version; (15) Lexile; (16) review citations; (17) Dewey Decimal classification number.

Review Citations

Review citations are given for nearly all books published and reviewed from 1985 through early 2013. These citations can be used to find more-detailed information about each of the books listed. The periodical sources identified are:

Book Report (BR)
Booklist (BL)
Booklist Online (BLO)
Bulletin of the Center for Children's Books (BCCB)
Horn Book (HB)
Horn Book Guide (HBG)
Library Media Connection (LMC)
School Library Journal (SLJ)
VOYA (Voice of Youth Advocates) (VOYA)

Additional Pointers for Users

For series that contain an extensive number of titles that are too numerous to list and for very prolific authors of recommended books, only a representative number of books are listed. Examples of this would be the mysteries of Sue Grafton, science fiction from writers such as Piers Anthony and Alan Dean Foster, and horror stories by Stephen King. For more complete listings of titles, it is suggested that the user consult book jobbers' catalogs (print or online), author or publisher Web sites, or the Web sites of such online booksellers as Amazon (amazon.com) and Barnes and Noble (bn.com).

All graphic novels are collected in one section, which includes graphic adaptations of classics such as *Moby Dick*.

Anthologies of short stories on a single subject are found under that subject (an anthology of science fiction short stories will be listed under "Science Fiction," for example), but general anthologies or collections by a singe author on diverse subjects are listed in the "Short Stories and General Anthologies" section.

Similarly, books of experiments and projects on a specific subject in science are placed under that subject, but general science project books are in the section "Physical and Applied Sciences — Experiments and Projects."

Books of criticism about individual authors, even though they contain some biographical information, are placed in the "Literary History and Criticism" section.

Books on World War II are found in the "World War II and Holocaust" section but books on internal conditions in the United States during this period are found in the United States history section under "World War II."

Books on the history of specific ethnic groups (for example, books that are historical accounts of African American slavery) are generally found in the "Ethnic Groups and Prejudice" section.

Books that contain material that might be objectionable to some readers (scenes of graphic sex, for example), usually include a note in the annotation indicating that the book is suitable for mature readers.

Acknowledgments

Many people were involved in the preparation of this bibliography. In particular, we are grateful to Barbara Ittner of Libraries Unlimited and to Christine McNaull, who makes production of this book possible. Thanks are also due to Kristina Strain and Jane Higgins for their contributions.

Catherine Barr

Literary Forms

Fiction

Adventure and Survival Stories

1 Aguiar, Nadia. *The Lost Island of Tamarind* (7–10). 2008, Feiwel & Friends $17.95 (978-031238029-8). Part mystery, part fantasy, part survival story, this tale tells of 13-year-old Maya and her two young siblings who survive a storm aboard their parents' marine research boat and end up in a fantasy world full of danger and magic. ℮ Lexile 880L (Rev: BLO 10/29/08; LMC 3–4/09; SLJ 10/1/08; VOYA 12/08)

2 Aiken, Joan. *Midnight Is a Place* (7–10). Series: Wolves Chronicles. 1974, Scholastic paper $2.95 (978-0-590-45496-4). In Victorian England, two young waifs are cast adrift in a hostile town when their guardian's house burns.

3 Allende, Isabel. *City of the Beasts* (9–12). Trans. by Margaret Sayers Peden. 2002, HarperCollins $19.99 (978-0-06-050918-7). Fifteen-year-old Alex gets more than he bargained for when he accompanies his grandmother on a trip into the Amazon jungle on a search for a mysterious "beast." (Rev: BL 11/15/02; HB 1–2/03; HBG 3/03; SLJ 11/02; VOYA 2/03)

4 Allende, Isabel. *Kingdom of the Golden Dragon* (7–12). 2004, HarperCollins $19.99 (978-0-06-058942-4). Yetis, high in the Himalayas, help 16-year-old Alexander in his fight against American corporate villains in this sequel to *City of the Beasts*. (Rev: BL 2/15/04; SLJ 4/04)

5 Asai, Carrie. *The Book of the Sword* (6–12). Series: Samurai Girl. 2003, Simon & Schuster paper $6.99 (978-0-689-85948-9). Heaven abandons her adoptive family when her brother is murdered in the middle of her arranged wedding and devotes herself to studying to be a samurai and avenging her brother. (Rev: SLJ 8/03)

6 Becker, Helaine. *Trouble in the Hills* (8–12). 2011, Fitzhenry & Whiteside paper $9.95 (978-1-55455-174-

3). Reckless after an argument with his father, Cam sets off into the mountains on his bike; nonstop adventure ensues as he has an accident, meets a girl who has escaped from kidnappers, and must deal with drug runners. (Rev: LMC 10/12; SLJ 6/12)

7 Bernardo, Anilú. *Jumping Off to Freedom* (7–10). 1996, Arte Publico paper $9.95 (978-1-55885-088-0). The story of four refugees, including teenage David, on a harrowing voyage from Cuba to Florida on a raft. (Rev: BL BL 5/1/96; SLJ 7/96; VOYA 6/96; VOYA 6/96)

8 Birch, Carol. *Jamrach's Menagerie* (10–12). 2011, Doubleday $26.95 (978-0-385-53440-6). London street urchin Jaffy is invited aboard a dangerous voyage to the East Indies for the purpose of ensnaring a spectacular dragon in this adventure/survival story set in the 19th century. ⌓ ℮ (Rev: BL 5/15/11; SLJ 8/11)

9 Bodeen, S. A. *The Compound* (7–12). 2008, Feiwel & Friends $16.95 (978-0-312-37015-2). Eli and members of his family have lived in an elaborate underground shelter for years, believing that the world as they knew it was destroyed. But was it? Or did Eli's wealthy father have other reasons for building the compound? (Rev: BL 4/15/08; SLJ 7/08)

10 Bodeen, S. A. *The Raft* (9–11). 2012, Feiwel & Friends $16.99 (978-0-312-65010-0). When the cargo plane she boarded at the last minute goes down in a storm between Hawaii and Midway, 15-year-old Robie finds herself adrift on shark-infested waters on a leaky raft with the injured copilot. ℮ Lexile HL680L (Rev: BLO 8/12; HB 9–10/12; LMC 3–4/13; SLJ 9/12)

11 Bowler, Tim. *Apocalypse* (10–12). 2005, Simon & Schuster $16.95 (978-1-4169-0370-3). Kit and his parents, forced to ground their sinking boat on an unknown island, find themselves among primitive villagers who regard Kit as a figure of evil. (Rev: BL 9/15/05; SLJ 10/05; VOYA 8/05)

12 Brand, Max. *Dan Barry's Daughter* (7–12). 1976, Amereon LB $25.95 (978-0-88411-516-8). Harry is an accused murderer who, though innocent, is forced to hide. One of many recommended westerns by this prolific author.

13 Brand, Max. *Way of the Lawless* (10–12). 1985, Warner paper $2.50 (978-0-446-32665-0). In this western by the prolific writer Brand, a basically decent young man finds himself on the wrong side of the law.

14 Bray, Libba. *Beauty Queens* (8–12). 2011, Scholastic $18.99 (978-0-439-89597-2). When a plane carrying teen pageant contestants crashes on a remote island, the survivors face big challenges — and learn a lot about themselves and each other in the process. YALSA Amazing Audiobooks Top Ten 2012. ∩ **e** Lexile HL690L (Rev: BL 5/1/11; HB 7–8/11; SLJ 7/11*; VOYA 6/11)

15 Brown, Sam. *The Trail to Honk Ballard's Bones* (9–12). 1990, Walker $17.95 (978-0-8027-4101-1). In this western adventure, Honk Ballard discovers that his new trail buddy is really a bank robber. (Rev: BL 1/15/90)

16 Bruchac, Joseph. *Wolf Mark* (7–12). 2011, Lee & Low $17.95 (978-1-60060-661-8). When Luke's father is kidnapped, Luke must use unusual abilities to rescue him; a fast-paced adventure combining Native American lore, supernatural elements, and high-tech devices. **e** Lexile 810L (Rev: BL 10/1/11; LMC 1–2/12*; SLJ 9/1/11)

17 Butler, William. *The Butterfly Revolution* (7–12). 1961, Ballantine paper $6.50 (978-0-345-33182-3). A frightening story of problems in a boys' camp told in diary form by one of the campers.

18 Caveney, Philip. *Prince of Explorers* (7–10). Illus. by Jonny Duddle. Series: Sebastian Darke. 2010, Delacorte $17.99 (978-038573469-1). Accompanied by tiny warrior Cornelius and snarky buffalope Max, Sebastian works his way through dense jungle to find the lost city of Mendip, facing danger at every turn. **e** (Rev: BLO 4/15/10; SLJ 5/10)

19 Caveney, Philip. *Prince of Pirates* (7–10). Series: Sebastian Darke. 2009, Delacorte $16.99 (978-038573468-4); LB $19.99 (978-038590466-7). In the second book in the series, Sebastian Darke and his sidekicks try out the pirate life and sail off in search of treasure. Lexile 830L (Rev: BL 4/1/09; VOYA 10/09)

20 Clancy, Tom. *Patriot Games* (9–12). 1987, Berkley paper $7.99 (978-0-425-10972-4). In this large adventure novel for better readers, hero Jack Ryan tries to prevent a terrorist plan to kidnap Princess Diana and Prince Charles. Other recommended Clancy novels include *Red Storm Rising* (1986) and *The Hunt for Red October* (1984). (Rev: BL 6/1/87; SLJ 11/87)

21 Clavell, James. *The Children's Story . . . But Not Just for Children* (9–12). 1981, Delacorte $7.95 (978-0-385-28135-5); paper $5.99 (978-0-440-20468-8). After a terrible war has been lost, thought control is introduced in the schools.

22 Clavell, James. *Noble House* (10–12). 1981, Dell paper $7.99 (978-0-440-16484-5). An action-filled story about a China trading firm in Hong Kong. Also use *Tai-Pan* (1983).

23 Cole, Stephen. *Thieves till We Die* (8–11). 2007, Bloomsbury $16.95 (978-1-59990-082-7). Nathaniel Coldhart sends his band of teen outlaws on another action-packed adventure (after 2006's *Thieves Like Us*), this time to steal a priceless sword. (Rev: BL 5/1/07; SLJ 5/07)

24 Cooney, Caroline B. *Flash Fire* (7–10). 1995, Scholastic paper $14.95 (978-0-590-25253-9). A girl's wish for a more exciting life comes true when a fire sweeps the wealthy Los Angeles neighborhood where she lives. (Rev: BL 11/1/95; SLJ 12/95; VOYA 12/95)

25 Cooney, Caroline B. *Flight No. 116 Is Down* (7–10). 1992, Scholastic paper $14.95 (978-0-590-44465-1). With a lightning pace, the author depicts the drama and human interest inherent in disaster. (Rev: BL 1/15/92; SLJ 2/92)

26 Coonts, Stephen. *Fortunes of War* (10–12). 1998, St. Martin's paper $7.99 (978-0-312-96941-7). A modern military thriller about two friends, one an American colonel in the Air Force and the other a Japanese fighter pilot, who find themselves on opposing sides when Japanese radicals attempt to take over Siberian oil fields. (Rev: BL 3/15/98; SLJ 9/98)

27 Craze, Galaxy. *The Last Princess* (9–12). 2012, Little, Brown $17.99 (978-031618548-6). In 2090 Princess Eliza escapes when rebels kill the British king and abduct two of his children, and Eliza disguises herself in an effort to rescue them. ∩ (Rev: BL 6/12; SLJ 7/12; VOYA 4/12)

28 Cummings, Priscilla. *The Journey Back* (7–10). 2012, Dutton $16.99 (978-052542362-1). Fourteen-year-old Digger Griswald has many adventures when he escapes from a juvenile detention center and heads toward home to protect his mother from his abusive father. **e** Lexile 810L (Rev: BL 12/1/12; LMC 5–6/13; SLJ 1/13)

29 Cussler, Clive. *Treasure* (9–12). 1989, Pocket paper $7.99 (978-0-671-70465-0). Adventurer Dirk Pitt combats terrorists to rescue hostages in a frozen wilderness in Greenland. (Rev: BL 3/15/88)

30 Dickinson, Patti. *Hollywood the Hard Way: A Cowboy's Journey* (9–12). 1999, Univ. of Nebraska paper $16.95 (978-0-8032-6619-3). Cowboy Jerry Van Meter bravely undertakes a solo 1,500-mile horseback ride in this story — based on truth — set in 1945. (Rev: SLJ 2/00)

31 Docherty, Jimmy. *The Ice Cream Con* (6–10). 2008, Scholastic $16.99 (978-0-545-02885-1). Jake, who lives in a bad section of Glasgow, is tired of getting mugged and spreads a rumor about a bodyguard called the Big Baresi in this fun, vulgar, action-packed story. (Rev: BL 5/1/08; SLJ 6/08)

32 Easton, Kelly. *Aftershock* (7–10). 2006, Simon & Schuster $16.95 (978-1-4169-0052-8). Mute and in shock after seeing his parents die in a car crash, Adam hitchhikes from Idaho to Rhode Island, his life flashing through his mind as he makes his way home. (Rev: BL 12/15/06; SLJ 12/06)

33 Forester, C. S. *The African Queen* (9–12). 1935, Little, Brown paper $13.95 (978-0-316-28910-8). An English spinster and a cockney male friend decide, as an act of revenge, to blow up a German boat in this novel set in Africa.

34 Forsyth, Frederick. *The Day of the Jackal* (9–12). 1971, Bantam paper $7.50 (978-0-553-26630-6). A rousing thriller about an attempted assassination of Charles de Gaulle.

35 Forsyth, Frederick. *The Devil's Alternative* (9–12). 1980, Bantam paper $6.99 (978-0-553-26490-6). The rescue of a man from drowning in the Mediterranean Sea begins a series of events that almost leads to nuclear disaster in this thriller.

36 Forsyth, Frederick. *The Dogs of War* (9–12). 1982, Bantam paper $6.99 (978-0-553-26846-1). An adventure story about greed and an attempt to seize power in a small West African country.

37 Forsyth, Frederick. *The Fist of God* (9–12). 1994, Bantam paper $6.99 (978-0-553-57242-1). Two British brothers who are espionage experts organize an elaborate mission to find a secret weapon that's in Saddam Hussein's possession. (Rev: BL 3/1/94)

38 Forsyth, Frederick. *The Odessa File* (9–12). 1983, Bantam paper $6.99 (978-0-553-27198-0). A German reporter infiltrates an organization of former Nazis and is discovered.

39 Freedman, Benedict, and Nancy Freedman. *Mrs. Mike* (7–12). 1968, Berkley paper $5.99 (978-0-425-10328-9). Based on a true story, this tells of Kathy, her love for her Mountie husband Mike, and her hard life in the Canadian Northwest.

40 Gann, Ernest K. *Fate Is the Hunter* (9–12). 1986, Simon & Schuster paper $14.00 (978-0-671-63603-6). A thrilling adventure story that was the basis of a successful movie.

41 Gilman, David. *The Devil's Breath* (7–12). Series: Danger Zone. 2008, Delacorte $16.99 (978-038573560-5); LB $19.99 (978-038590546-6). In this action-packed adventure tale, 15-year-old Max Gordon embarks on a search for his missing father in the Namibian desert; the first installment in a series. ☊ (Rev: BL 11/1/08; SLJ 10/1/08)

42 Gilman, David. *Ice Claw* (7–12). Series: Danger Zone. 2010, Delacorte $15.99 (978-0-385-73561-2); LB $18.99 (978-0-385-90547-3). During an extreme sports competition in the French Pyrenees, 15-year-old Max Gordon becomes embroiled in a complex plot involving a Basque monk and a potential ecological disaster. ℮ Lexile 810L (Rev: BL 2/15/10; SLJ 5/10)

43 Golden, Christopher, and Tim Lebbon. *The Sea Wolves* (7–10). Illus. by Greg Ruth. Series: Secret Journeys of Jack London. 2012, HarperCollins $16.99 (978-006186320-2). An action-packed story in which 18-year-old Jack London is captured by werewolf pirates. ℮ (Rev: BL 2/1/12; SLJ 2/12)

44 Golding, William. *Lord of the Flies* (8–12). 1999, Viking paper $15.00 (978-0-14-028333-4). When they are marooned on a deserted island, a group of English schoolboys soon lose their civilized ways.

45 Goodman, Joan Elizabeth. *Paradise* (7–12). 2002, Houghton Mifflin $16.00 (978-0-618-11450-4). The fictionalized story of Marguerite de la Rocque, who in 1536, after being left on Canada's Isle of Demons by her explorer uncle, struggled to survive along with her maid and the young man she loved. (Rev: BL 11/15/02; HBG 3/03; SLJ 12/02; VOYA 12/02)

46 Gross, Philip. *The Lastling* (8–12). 2006, Clarion $16 (978-0-618-65998-2). Melding themes of the environment, adventure, and personal growth, this exciting story is about Paris — a privileged 14-year-old on a hunting expedition in the Himalayas with her uncle — who befriends a 12-year-old monk-to-be named Tahr and sets in motion a horrifying episode with a young yeti. (Rev: LMC 2/07*; SLJ 12/06)

47 Haggard, H. Rider. *King Solomon's Mines* (9–12). 1982, Amereon LB $20.95 (978-0-89190-703-9). First published in 1885, this is a story of old-fashioned adventure and romance and the search for the source of King Solomon's wealth in Africa.

48 Haldeman, Joe. *Tool of the Trade* (9–12). 1988, Avon paper $3.95 (978-0-380-70438-5). A thriller about a Russian spy being pursued by both the CIA and the KGB. (Rev: BL 4/15/87)

49 Harper, Jo. *Delfino's Journey* (6–12). 2001, Texas Tech Univ. $15.95 (978-0-89672-437-2). Delfino and Salvador travel from Mexico to the United States in search of a new life but face many difficult challenges in this novel that interweaves Aztec folklore and information on illegal immigration. (Rev: BL 4/15/01; HBG 10/01)

50 Heacox, Kim. *Caribou Crossing* (10–12). 2001, Winter Wren paper $24.95 (978-0-944197-70-7). In this fast-paced thriller, environmentalists are pitted against big oil interests to save a fragile landscape in Alaska. (Rev: BL 8/01)

51 Hemingway, Ernest. *The Old Man and the Sea* (9–12). 1977, Macmillan $30.00 (978-0-684-15363-6). A deceptively simple novel about an old Gulf fisherman and his encounter with a giant marlin.

52 Herlong, M. H. *The Great Wide Sea* (6–10). 2008, Viking $16.99 (978-067006330-7). Not long after their mother's death, three brothers find themselves stranded on an island in the Bahamas when their unpredictable father disappears in an ocean storm. YALSA Top Ten 2010. Lexile 660L (Rev: BL 11/15/08; HB 1–2/09; SLJ 3/1/09)

53 Hesse, Karen. *Safekeeping* (8–11). 2012, Feiwel & Friends $17.99 (978-125001134-3). Radley, 17, is in Haiti when the American president is assassinated and martial law is imposed, with many dissenters imprisoned; she returns home to find her parents are gone, and she and a girl named Celia head overland toward Canada. ☊ ℮ Lexile 720L (Rev: BL 8/12; LMC 1–2/13; SLJ 8/12; VOYA 12/12)

54 Higson, Charlie. *The Dead* (9–12). Series: Enemy. 2011, Hyperion $16.99 (978-1-4231-3412-1). An action-packed, bloodthirsty prequel to *The Enemy* (2010) in which young Jack and Ed try to protect younger children from the chaos occurring in London as disease attacks everyone over the age of 16. ℮ Lexile HL670L (Rev: BL 8/11; LMC 10/11; SLJ 8/11)

55 Higson, Charlie. *The Enemy* (9–12). Series: Enemy. 2010, Hyperion $16.99 (978-1-4231-3175-5). In a new world where a virus has killed everyone over the age of 16, groups of teens struggle to survive and cooperate; an action-packed, thought-provoking novel. A sequel is *The Fear* (2012). ℮ Lexile HL590L (Rev: BL 5/15/10; LMC 10/10; SLJ 7/10)

56 Hinton, S. E. *The Outsiders* (7–10). 1967, Viking $17.99 (978-0-670-53257-5). Two rival gangs — the "haves" and "have-nots" — fight it out on the streets of an Oklahoma city. (Rev: BL 11/15/97)

57 Hinton, S. E. *Rumble Fish* (7–10). 1975, Dell paper $5.99 (978-0-440-97534-2). Rusty-James loses everything he loves most — including his brother.

58 Hinton, S. E. *Tex* (7–10). 1979, Dell paper $5.50 (978-0-440-97850-3). Tex and his 17-year-old older brother encounter problems with family, sex, and drugs.

59 Hinton, S. E. *That Was Then, This Is Now* (7–10). 1971, Viking $17.99 (978-0-670-69798-4). Bryon discovers that his "brother" Mark is a drug pusher.

60 Hobbs, Will. *The Big Wander* (7–10). 1992, Avon paper $5.95 (978-0-380-72140-5). Clay Lancaster, 14, and his brother Mike are on a "big wander," their last trip together before Mike goes away to college. (Rev: BL 10/15/92*; SLJ 11/92)

61 Hobbs, Will. *Far North* (7–12). 1996, Morrow $17.99 (978-0-688-14192-9). Fifteen-year old Gabe, his school roommate, and an elderly Native American are stranded in the Canadian wilderness. The boys survive even af-

ter the death of the wise old man. (Rev: BL 7/96; SLJ 9/96; VOYA 2/97)

62 Hobbs, Will. *Leaving Protection* (7–12). 2004, HarperCollins $19.99 (978-0-688-17475-0). An exciting novel about a 16-year-old boy, his work on an Alaskan salmon trawler, and the secret plans of its skipper. (Rev: BL 3/1/04; SLJ 4/04)

63 Hobbs, Will. *The Maze* (6–12). 1998, Morrow $19.99 (978-0-688-15092-1). After living in a series of foster homes and detention centers, Rick escapes to Canyonlands National Park in Utah where he is befriended by a loner who helps him find himself. (Rev: BL 9/1/98; HBG 3/99; SLJ 10/98; VOYA 2/99)

64 Hobbs, Will. *Wild Man Island* (7–10). 2002, HarperCollins LB $16.89 (978-0-06-029810-4); paper $5.99 (978-0-380-73310-1). An adventure story in which 14-year-old Andy becomes stranded on a remote Alaska island, faces many dangers, and tests his dead archaeologist father's theories about the earliest prehistoric immigrants to America. (Rev: BL 4/15/02; HB 7–8/02; HBG 10/02; SLJ 5/02; VOYA 6/02)

65 Holt, Victoria. *The Time of the Hunter's Moon* (9–12). 1984, Fawcett paper $5.99 (978-0-449-45094-9). In 19th-century England a young schoolteacher is caught up in romance, adventure, and mystery.

66 Hubert, Cam. *Dreamspeaker* (9–12). 1981, Avon paper $3.50 (978-0-380-56622-8). A boy who escapes from an institution finds friendship in a British Columbia forest.

67 Jinks, Catherine. *Evil Genius* (7–10). 2007, Harcourt $17.00 (978-0-15-205988-0). By age 13, Cadel's illegal computer hacking skills have landed him in the secretive Axis Institute for World Domination, where he's surrounded by aspiring villains but questions his own commitment to the cause. (Rev: BL 5/15/07; SLJ 7/07)

68 Jinks, Catherine. *Genius Squad* (7–10). 2008, Harcourt $17.00 (978-0-15-205985-9). In this fast-paced sequel to *Evil Genius* (2007), 15-year-old Cadel and his friend Sonja join teen computer hackers enlisted to expose an evil corporation. (Rev: BL 6/1–15/08; SLJ 6/08)

69 Jinks, Catherine. *The Genius Wars* (7–10). Series: Genius Trilogy. 2010, Harcourt $17 (978-015206619-2). The trilogy that began with *Evil Genius* (2007) and *Genius Squad* (2008) reaches an ingenious conclusion as Cadel, who has a new family with a police detective as stepfather, travels in search of Prosper English, determined to stop his evil plots. ☊ ℮ Lexile 750L (Rev: BL 10/15/10; HB 9–10/10; VOYA 10/10)

70 Johnson, Maureen. *Girl at Sea* (8–11). 2007, HarperTeen $15.99 (978-0-06-054144-6). Clio, 17, is crushed to learn she must spend the summer with her father and his girlfriend sailing on the Mediterranean, but soon discovers that she's part of a treasure hunt. (Rev: BCCB 10/07; BL 7/07; SLJ 6/07)

71 Kalpakian, Laura. *Caveat* (10–12). 1998, Blair $19.95 (978-0-89587-223-4). In this novel set in a small, drought-stricken California town in 1916, rainmaker Hank Beecham vows revenge when the city fathers refuse to pay him after his efforts result in life-destroying floods. (Rev: BL 6/1–15/98; SLJ 1/99)

72 Kelley, Ann. *Lost Girls* (8–12). 2012, Little, Brown $17.99 (978-0-316-09062-9). In 1974 a group of Amelia Earhart cadets and their young troop leader find themselves in severe difficulties on an island off the coast of Thailand in the face of a fierce storm. ℮ (Rev: LMC 8–9/12*; SLJ 9/12; VOYA 4/12)

73 Kerrigan, Philip. *Survival Game* (9–12). 1987, Avon paper $3.95 (978-0-380-70682-2). A simulated war game turns serious when a gunman begins picking off the participants. (Rev: SLJ 12/87)

74 Kessler, Cristina. *Trouble in Timbuktu* (7–12). 2009, Philomel $17.99 (978-039924451-3). The history and culture of the city of Timbuktu are an integral part of this novel about Malian twins Ahmed and Ayisha, who embark on a dangerous journey to foil the attempt of two American thieves trying to steal valuable ancient manuscripts. Lexile 900L (Rev: BL 12/15/08; LMC 8–9/09; SLJ 3/1/09; VOYA 6/09)

75 Kinch, Michael. *The Fires of New Sun* (8–12). Series: Blending Time. 2012, Flux paper $9.95 (978-07387307-6-9). After surviving their journey to Africa in the mid-21st century, teens Jaym, Reya, and D'Shay work against treason and violence to unite the native peoples. ℮ (Rev: BL 1/1/12; SLJ 4/12; VOYA 2/12)

76 King, Stephen. *The Girl Who Loved Tom Gordon* (9–12). 1999, Scribner $16.45 (978-0-684-86762-5). This is a vivid novel about the terrors experienced by a 9-year-girl who is lost in the Maine woods for nine days when she wanders away from her parents. (Rev: BL 4/1/99; SLJ 3/00; VOYA 8/99)

77 Klavan, Andrew. *If We Survive* (8–11). 2012, Thomas Nelson $14.99 (978-159554795-8). Revolution in a Central American country propels 16-year-old Will and his friends, who have just finished a Christian outreach mission, into a desperate bid to escape. ♫ ℮ (Rev: BL 11/15/12; SLJ 3/13)

78 Kress, Nancy. *Flash Point* (7–10). 2012, Viking $17.99 (978-067001247-3). Desperate for money to help with her sick grandmother and younger sister, 16-year-old Amy signs up for a reality TV show — and surprising stress. ℮ Lexile HL680L (Rev: BL 11/15/12; LMC 1–2/13; SLJ 2/13; VOYA 10/12)

79 L'Amour, Louis. *Bendigo Shafter* (9–12). 1983, Bantam paper $5.50 (978-0-553-26446-3). An old-fashioned western by a master of the genre. There are approximately 100 other westerns by this author available in paperback.

80 Lee, Tanith. *Piratica II: Return to Parrot Island* (7–10). Series: Piratica. 2006, Dutton $17.99 (978-0-525-

47769-3). The second action-packed installment in the series finds Art the pirate queen leaving her husband behind on dry land as she sails the seas on behalf of the government — and perhaps with the opportunity to vanquish old enemies. (Rev: BL 12/15/06; SLJ 4/07)

81 Leib, Franklin Allen. *The House of Pain* (10–12). 1999, Forge $23.95 (978-0-312-86616-7). In this legal thriller, a Vietnam veteran suffering from post-traumatic stress disorder rescues his goddaughter, 15-year-old Sally Collins, from kidnappers, and is then put on trial for his vigilante killings. (Rev: SLJ 5/99)

82 Lester, Alison. *The Snow Pony* (6–12). 2003, Houghton Mifflin $15.00 (978-0-618-25404-0). Fourteen-year-old Dusty's love for Snow Pony lightens the problems of her life in this novel set on an Australian cattle ranch. (Rev: BL 3/15/03; HBG 10/03; SLJ 4/03; VOYA 6/03)

83 London, Jack. *Best Short Stories of Jack London* (9–12). 1953, Amereon LB $20.95 (978-0-89190-656-8). These stories of action and adventure represent locales ranging from the South Seas to the Far North.

84 Lopez, Barry. *Winter Count* (9–12). 1982, Avon paper $4.95 (978-0-380-58107-8). This group of stories deals with survival in the wilds and man's battle with nature.

85 Lu, Marie. *Legend* (7–12). 2011, Putnam $17.99 (978-0-399-25675-2). In a future, dystopian California the lives of 15-year-old Day (who commits crimes to help the needy) and June (clever and privileged, with military training) intersect as she hunts for Day and uncovers scary secrets. ♫ ℮ Lexile HL710L (Rev: BL 10/15/11*; HB 11–12/11; LMC 1–2/12*; SLJ 10/1/11)

86 Ludlum, Robert. *The Bourne Identity* (9–12). 1984, Bantam paper $7.99 (978-0-553-26011-3). A man wakens to find that in spite of having no memory, he is the target of a killer's plot. Followed by *The Bourne Supremacy*.

87 McCaughrean, Geraldine. *The White Darkness* (7–10). 2007, HarperCollins $16.99 (978-0-06-089035-3). Symone is thrilled when her uncle Victor offers to take her on a trip to the South Pole, since her "hero" is Captain Laurence "Titus" Oates, who traveled there in 1911 as part of Robert Scott's expedition. But the trip — and her uncle's obsession — turn out to be more than she bargained for. Printz Award 2008. ♫ (Rev: BL 12/1/06; HB 3–4/07; SLJ 4/07)

88 McCormick, Patricia. *Sold* (9–12). 2006, Hyperion $15.99 (978-0-7868-5171-3). Thirteen-year-old Lakshmi describes her life after being sold into prostitution to help support her poor family in Nepal and her struggle to find hope and a better life. (Rev: BL 9/15/06; SLJ 9/06)

89 MacLean, Alistair. *Circus* (9–12). 1984, Amereon $24.95 (978-0-89190-672-8). In this spy thriller, an aerialist is sent on a secret mission by the CIA into Eastern

Europe. Other recommended adventures by MacLean include *Secret Ways* and *South by Java Head.*

90 MacPhail, Catherine. *Underworld* (7–10). 2005, Bloomsbury $16.95 (978-1-58234-997-8). Five British teens with very different personalities find themselves trapped in a cave on a remote Scottish island; adding to their predicament is their fear of a giant worm reputed to inhabit the caves. (Rev: BL 7/05; SLJ 7/05; VOYA 8/05)

91 Marsden, John. *Darkness, Be My Friend* (9–12). Series: Tomorrow. 1999, Houghton Mifflin $16.00 (978-0-395-92274-3). In this sequel to *A Killing Frost,* Ellie, Fi, and other teenage combatants continue their struggle against the forces that have invaded Australia. (Rev: BL 6/1–15/99; HBG 9/99; SLJ 7/99; VOYA 10/99)

92 Marsden, John. *The Dead of Night* (6–10). Series: Tomorrow. 1997, Houghton Mifflin $16.00 (978-0-395-83734-4). In this sequel to *Tomorrow, When the War Began* (1996), the teenage group continues its guerrilla activities against their enemy, a country that has invaded their homeland, Australia. (Rev: HBG 3/98; SLJ 11/97; VOYA 2/98)

93 Marsden, John. *A Killing Frost* (7–12). Series: Tomorrow. 1998, Houghton Mifflin $17.00 (978-0-395-83735-1). In this third episode of an adventure series about a group of Australian teens who fight an enemy that has occupied their country, five young people carry out a plan to sink a container ship. (Rev: BCCB 4/98; BL 5/15/98; HB 7–8/98; HBG 9/98; SLJ 6/98; VOYA 6/98)

94 Marsden, John. *The Other Side of Dawn* (8–12). Series: Tomorrow. 2002, Houghton Mifflin $16.00 (978-0-618-07028-2). Ellie's exploits are at the center of this action-packed seventh and final installment in the Tomorrow series, which leaves Ellie back home after peace has been declared, trying to adjust to postwar life. (Rev: BCCB 10/02; BL 10/15/02; HB 11/02; HBG 3/03; SLJ 10/02; VOYA 2/03)

95 Marsden, John. *Tomorrow, When the War Began* (8–12). 1995, Houghton Mifflin $16.00 (978-0-395-70673-2). A girl and her friends return from a camping trip in the bush to find that Australia has been invaded and their families taken prisoner. (Rev: BL 4/15/95; SLJ 6/95)

96 Marsden, John. *While I Live* (8–12). Series: Ellie Chronicles. 2007, Scholastic $16.99 (978-0-439-78318-7). Ellie is back on her farm after the upheavals of the Tomorrow series, but new violence soon disrupts her life again; knowledge of the previous series will enhance understanding of this new story arc. (Rev: BCCB 6/07; HB 5–6/07; LMC 10/07; SLJ 5/07)

97 Meltzer, Brad. *The Tenth Justice* (10–12). 1997, Morrow $23.00 (978-0-688-15089-1). Ben, a clerk for a Supreme Court justice, is being blackmailed and he thinks one of his friends is supplying information to the blackmailer in this thriller that also supplies lots of information about the Supreme Court. (Rev: BL 2/1/97; SLJ 11/97)

98 Meyer, L. A. *In the Belly of the Bloodhound: Being an Account of a Particularly Peculiar Adventure in the Life of Jacky Faber* (8–11). Series: Bloody Jack. 2006, Harcourt $17.00 (978-0-15-205557-8). Jacky Faber, girl pirate, is kidnapped along with her classmates from the Lawson Peabody School for Young Girls in Boston; they find themselves on a slave ship bound for North Africa and Jacky must devise an escape plan. Odyssey Honor Recording 2010. ∩ (Rev: BL 11/1/06; SLJ 1/07)

99 Meyer, L. A. *The Mark of the Golden Dragon: Being an Account of the Further Adventures of Jacky Faber, Jewel of the East, Vexation of the West, and Pearl of the South China Sea* (8–11). Series: Bloody Jack Adventure. 2011, Harcourt $16.99 (978-0-547751764-3). Thinking Jacky Faber is dead after a typhoon in the South China Sea in 1807, a heartbroken Jaimy Fletcher heads for London even as Jacky has various adventures also on her way there. ∩ e Lexile 1000L (Rev: BL 12/1/11)

100 Meyer, L. A. *Mississippi Jack: Being an Account of the Further Waterborne Adventures of Jacky Faber, Midshipman, Fine Lady, and the Lily of the West* (8–11). Series: Bloody Jack. 2007, Harcourt $17.00 (978-0-15-206003-9). Jacky has plenty of outsized adventures as she travels down the Mississippi in search of her true love in this latest installment. (Rev: BL 11/1/07; SLJ 12/07)

101 Meyer, L. A. *Rapture of the Deep: Being an Account of the Further Adventures of Jacky Faber, Soldier, Sailor, Mermaid, Spy* (7–12). Series: Bloody Jack Adventure. 2009, Harcourt $17 (978-0-15-206501-0). On her way to her wedding in 1806, Jacky is forced by the British Navy to head for the Caribbean to search for a sunken treasure ship. YALSA Amazing Audiobooks Top Ten 2011. ∩ (Rev: BL 9/1/09; SLJ 12/09)

102 Meyer, L. A. *Under the Jolly Roger: Being an Account of the Further Nautical Adventures of Jacky Faber* (7–10). Series: Bloody Jack. 2005, Harcourt $17.00 (978-0-15-205345-1). In this volume full of adventure, plucky 15-year-old Jacky Faber — last seen in *Bloody Jack* (2002) and *Curse of the Blue Tattoo* (2004) — travels from Boston to England in 1804 in search of her true love but ends up taking control of a British warship. (Rev: BL 8/05; SLJ 9/05; VOYA 8/05)

103 Meyer, L. A. *The Wake of the Lorelei Lee: Being an Account of the Further Adventures of Jacky Faber, on Her Way to Botany Bay* (8–11). Series: Bloody Jack Adventure. 2010, Harcourt $17 (978-054732768-6). Hopeful that she can start a profitable career with her new ship, Jacky arrives in London only to find herself accused of piracy and sentenced to servitude in Australia; the 8th volume in the series. YALSA Amazing

Audiobooks Top Ten 2012. 🎧 **e** Lexile 970L (Rev: BL 9/15/10; VOYA 8/10)

104 Miklowitz, Gloria D. *After the Bomb* (7–12). 1987, Scholastic paper $2.50 (978-0-590-40568-3). This novel describes the experiences of a group of young people after an atomic bomb falls on Los Angeles. (Rev: BL 6/15/86; SLJ 9/85; VOYA 8/85)

105 Miklowitz, Gloria D. *Camouflage* (8–10). 1998, Harcourt $16.00 (978-0-15-201467-4). When 14-year-old Kyle visits northern Michigan to spend a summer with his father, he becomes involved in a government-hating militia movement in which his father is a general. (Rev: BCCB 5/98; HBG 9/98; SLJ 4/98; VOYA 10/98)

106 Morris, Deborah. *Teens 911: Snowbound, Helicopter Crash and Other True Survival Stories* (7–12). 2002, Health Communications paper $12.95 (978-0-7573-0039-4). Five stories that portray teens facing emergencies (being stranded, in helicopter crashes, rescuing residents of burning houses, and so forth) are followed by postscripts and survival quizzes. (Rev: SLJ 2/03; VOYA 2/03)

107 Mowll, Joshua. *Operation Typhoon Shore* (8–12). Illus. by author, et al. Series: The Guild of Specialists. 2006, Candlewick $15.99 (978-0-7636-3122-2). In 1920, siblings Doug and Becca sail through a typhoon on their uncle's ship while seeking the gyrolabe that may offer a clue to their parents' disappearance; the second installment in the series. (Rev: BL 1/1–15/07; SLJ 3/07)

108 Mullin, Mike. *Ashfall* (8–12). 2011, Tanglewood $16.95 (978-1-933718-55-2). Alex, 15, goes on a dangerous search for his family after a supervolcano erupts in Yellowstone Park; this action-packed story combines survival, science fiction, and romance. **e** Lexile 750L (Rev: BL 10/1/11; HB 1–2/12; LMC 1–2/13; SLJ 11/1/11; VOYA 12/11)

109 Murray, Yxta Maya. *The Queen Jade* (11–12). 2005, HarperCollins $23.95 (978-0-06-058264-7). When Lola Sanchez's archaeologist mother goes missing in the Guatemalan jungle, Lola enlists an unlikely ally in the search — Erik, her mother's professional archrival; for mature teens. (Rev: BL 1/1–15/05)

110 Neri, G. *Surf Mules* (10–12). 2009, Putnam $16.99 (978-039925086-6). Logan and Z-boy, Southern California high school seniors facing an uncertain future, unwisely decide to risk driving marijuana to Florida. (Rev: BL 6/1–15/09; SLJ 6/1/09)

111 Nordhoff, Charles, and James N. Hall. *The Bounty Trilogy* (9–12). 1982, Little, Brown paper $21.95 (978-0-316-61166-4). An adventure story based on fact concerning a mutiny aboard the *Bounty* and its aftermath. The three individual books are *Mutiny on the Bounty, Men against the Sea,* and *Pitcairn's Island.* These books were originally published in 1932, 1934, and 1934, respectively.

112 Olshan, Matthew. *Finn* (8–12). 2001, Bancroft $19.95 (978-1-890862-13-8); paper $14.95 (978-1-890862-14-5). Teenage Chloe, who has suffered an abusive childhood, and a pregnant Hispanic girl set off to find new lives in a Huck Finn-like adventure full of insight and social commentary. (Rev: BL 4/1/01; SLJ 4/01; VOYA 4/01)

113 Paulsen, Gary. *Canyons* (7–10). 1991, Dell paper $5.99 (978-0-440-21023-8). Blennan becomes obsessed with the story of a young Indian boy murdered by white men 100 years before. (Rev: SLJ 9/90)

114 Paulsen, Gary. *The River* (5–10). 1991, Delacorte $15.95 (978-0-385-30388-0). In this sequel to *Hatchet*, Paulsen takes the wilderness adventure beyond self-preservation and makes teen Brian responsible for saving someone else. (Rev: BL 5/15/91)

115 Petrucha, Stefan. *Teen, Inc.* (8–10). 2007, Walker $16.95 (978-0-8027-9650-9). Jaiden, 14, is being raised by a corporation after being orphaned as a baby, and he's coming to discover that his "parent" is harming his community in this action-packed eco-thriller. (Rev: BL 12/1/07; SLJ 12/07)

116 Pfeffer, Susan Beth. *The Dead and the Gone* (8–12). 2008, Harcourt $17.00 (978-0-15-206311-5). A tilt in the moon's orbit sends Earth into environmental and social chaos, and Alex, Bri, and Julie must fend for themselves and find food, safety, and shelter when their parents disappear. (Rev: BL 5/15/08; SLJ 8/08)

117 Pratchett, Terry. *Nation* (7–10). 2008, HarperCollins $16.99 (978-0-06-143301-6). In this survival tale, a tidal wave leaves survivors of very different backgrounds to re-create civilization and consider what it is they treasure and why. (Rev: BL 8/08)

118 Preston, Douglas, and Lincoln Child. *Riptide* (10–12). 1998, Warner $25.00 (978-0-446-52336-3). A classic struggle between good and evil emerges in this adventure yarn after a group of treasure seekers tries to recover buried booty worth billions of dollars. (Rev: BL 5/15/98; SLJ 12/98; VOYA 12/98)

119 Puzo, Mario. *The Godfather* (10–12). 1969, Putnam $19.95 (978-0-399-10342-1). The story of a fictional crime family in New York led by Vito Corleone and then by his son Michael.

120 Rees, Celia. *Pirates!* (7–10). 2003, Bloomsbury $17.95 (978-1-58234-816-2). Horrified by the prospect of an arranged marriage to a plantation owner, teenage Nancy and a close slave friend run off and join a pirate crew in this swashbuckling adventure set in the 18th century. (Rev: BCCB 1/04; BL 12/15/03*; HBG 4/04; SLJ 10/03*)

121 Richards, Justin. *The Chaos Code* (7–10). 2007, Bloomsbury $16.95 (978-1-59990-124-4). Matt's father is missing, and Matt must travel through time and kingdoms to find him in this fast-paced tale. ○ (Rev: BL 10/15/07)

122 Rochman, Hazel, and Darlene Z. McCampbell, eds. *Leaving Home* (7–12). 1997, HarperCollins LB $16.89 (978-0-06-024874-1). These 16 stories by well-known writers describe various forms of leaving home, from immigration to a new country to running away or taking a trip. (Rev: BL 1/1–15/97; SLJ 3/97*)

123 Rodman, Sean. *Infiltration* (7–12). 2011, Orca LB $16.95 (978-155469986-5); paper $9.95 (9781554699858). Abandoned-buildings explorer Bex feels threatened when a newcomer devises a plan more dangerous and exciting than he could have imagined. ℮ Lexile HL570L (Rev: BL 10/15/11; SLJ 3/12)

124 Schrefer, Eliot. *The School for Dangerous Girls* (8–11). 2009, Scholastic $16.99 (978-054503528-6). Angela, 15, uncovers what is happening to the "hopeless cases" at her Colorado reform school in this suspenseful novel about cruelty and punishment. (Rev: BL 2/1/09; LMC 5–6/09; SLJ 2/1/09)

125 Shusterman, Neal. *Dissidents* (7–10). 1989, Little, Brown $13.95 (978-0-316-78904-2). A teenage boy joins his mother, the American ambassador in Moscow, and becomes involved in a spy caper. (Rev: BL 8/89; SLJ 10/89)

126 Simmons, Dan. *The Terror* (11–12). 2007, Little, Brown $25.99 (978-0-316-01744-2). This fictionalization of the disastrous Franklin expedition of the 1840s blends elements of horror and fantasy as it describes the shipwrecked men's efforts to survive in the Arctic; for mature teens. (Rev: BL 11/15/06)

127 Simmons, Kristen. *Article 5* (7–12). 2012, Tor $17.99 (978-076532958-5). In a postwar America where Moral Statutes have replaced the Bill of Rights, 17-year-old Ember, usually non-confrontational, is perplexed when her former boyfriend arrests her mother for noncompliance. ○ ℮ Lexile HL660L (Rev: BL 3/15/12; LMC 8–9/12; SLJ 5/1/12; VOYA 4/12)

128 Smith, Cotton. *Dark Trail to Dodge* (7–10). 1997, Walker $20.95 (978-0-8027-4158-5). Eighteen-year-old Tyrel Bannon faces unusual problems on his first cattle drive when rustlers attack and plan on taking no prisoners. (Rev: BL 6/1–15/97; VOYA 8/97)

129 Smith, Roland. *Peak* (8–11). 2007, Harcourt $17.00 (978-0-15-202417-8). Aptly named Peak joins his father in Tibet, where he may become the youngest person (at 14) to climb Mount Everest; this is an exciting, multilayered adventure story. ○ (Rev: BL 4/1/07; HB 5–6/07; SLJ 6/07)

130 Sullivan, Paul. *The Unforgiving Land* (7–10). 1996, Fireworks paper $9.99 (978-0-88092-256-2). A white trader gives guns and bullets to a group of Inuit, causing a breakdown in the delicate harmony between nature and humankind and destruction of the Inuit way of life. (Rev: VOYA 8/96)

131 Svee, Gary. *Incident at Pishkin Creek* (9–12). 1989, Walker $18.95 (978-0-8027-4095-3). Max Bass exaggerated in his advertisement for a bride, as poor Catherine O'Dowd discovers when she arrives in Montana. (Rev: BL 7/89)

132 Swarthout, Glendon, and Kathryn Swarthout. *Whichaway* (7–10). 1997, Rising Moon paper $6.95 (978-0-87358-676-4). A reissue of an exciting story about a boy whose character is tested when he is trapped with two broken legs on top of a windmill in an isolated area of Texas. (Rev: HBG 3/98; VOYA 2/98)

133 Sweeney, Joyce. *Free Fall* (9–12). 1996, Delacorte $15.95 (978-0-385-32211-9). Trapped in a cave in Ocala National Park, four boys plot their escape and in the process learn about themselves, their families, and personal tragedies. (Rev: BL 7/96; SLJ 11/96; VOYA 6/96)

134 Thomas, Lex. *Quarantine: The Loners* (10–12). 2012, Egmont $17.99 (978-160684329-1). A very nasty virus results in students being quarantined in a high school that is sealed under a giant dome with deliveries of food and supplies every two weeks; as time passes the teens split into warring gangs and chaos ensues. A sequel is *Quarantine: The Saints* (2013). ℮ Lexile HL620L (Rev: BL 5/15/12*; SLJ 6/12; VOYA 4/12)

135 Thompson, Julian. *A Band of Angels* (9–12). 1986, Scholastic $12.95 (978-0-590-33780-9). Jordan, his suitcase of money, and two friends hit the road to escape government agents who are searching for them. (Rev: BL 3/87; SLJ 8/86; VOYA 6/86)

136 Thompson, Julian. *The Grounding of Group Six* (8–12). 1983, Avon paper $3.99 (978-0-380-83386-3). Five 16-year-olds think they are being sent to an exclusive school but actually they have been slated for murder.

137 Townsend, John Rowe. *The Islanders* (7–10). 1981, HarperCollins $11.95 (978-0-397-31940-4). Two strangers washed up on a remote island are regarded as enemies by the inhabitants. ℮

138 Townsend, John Rowe. *Kate and the Revolution* (7–10). 1983, HarperCollins LB $12.89 (978-0-397-32016-5). A 17-year-old girl is attracted to a visiting prince and then the adventure begins.

139 Volponi, Paul. *Hurricane Song* (7–12). 2008, Viking $15.99 (978-0-670-06160-0). Miles and his father find themselves in the middle of the chaos following Hurricane Katrina when they head to the New Orleans Superdome for shelter. (Rev: BL 5/1/08; SLJ 8/08)

140 Westerfeld, Scott. *Leviathan* (7–10). Illus. by Keith Thompson. 2009, Simon & Schuster $19.99 (978-1-4169-7173-3). An exciting steampunk adventure set in an alternate 1914 and featuring Prince Alek, son of the assassinated Archduke Ferdinand and a member of the technologically innovative Clankers, and Deryn, a girl from opposing Darwinist England masquerading as a boy in order to fly on the giant airship *Leviathan*. ALA Notable Books 2010; YALSA Popular Paperbacks for Young Adults Top Ten 2011. **e** Lexile 790L (Rev: BL 8/09; HB 11–12/09; SLJ 9/09)

141 Wild, K. *Firefight* (7–10). 2009, Scholastic $16.99 (978-043987176-1). Super-strong Freedom Smith must defeat an evil gang of kidnappers; world travel, action, the supernatural, and even romance combine in this exciting story, a sequel to *Fight Game* (2007). Lexile HL640L (Rev: BLO 3/24/09; SLJ 8/09)

142 Williams, Michael. *The Genuine Half-Moon Kid* (7–10). 1994, Dutton $15.99 (978-0-525-67479-5). Like questing Jason in Greek mythology, 18-year-old South African Jay Watson sets out with some friends to find a yellow wood box left him by his grandfather. (Rev: BL 6/1–15/94)

143 Withers, Pam. *First Descent* (8–12). 2011, Tundra $17.95 (978-177049257-8). In this adventure-filled book, whitewater daredevil Rex, 17, succeeds in kayaking an uncharted Colombian river — and avoiding guerrillas and paramilitary forces — with the help of a native young woman named Myriam. **e** Lexile 830L (Rev: BL 10/15/11; SLJ 1/12; VOYA 12/11)

144 Zindel, Paul. *Reef of Death* (7–12). 1998, HarperCollins $15.95 (978-0-06-024728-7). A tale of terror about two teens, a monster creature that lives on an Australian reef, and a mad geologist who has a torture chamber on her freighter. (Rev: BL 3/1/98; HBG 9/98; SLJ 3/98; VOYA 4/98)

Animal Stories

145 Armstrong, William H. *Sounder* (6–10). 1969, HarperCollins LB $17.89 (978-0-06-020144-9); paper $5.99 (978-0-06-440020-6). The moving story of an African American sharecropper, his family, and his devoted coon dog, Sounder. A sequel is *Sour Land* (1971). Newbery Medal 1970.

146 Benchley, Peter. *Jaws* (8–12). 1974, Doubleday paper $6.99 (978-0-449-21963-8). The best-selling novel about a small Long Island town and the creature that became a threat to its beaches.

147 Benchley, Peter. *White Shark* (9–12). 1995, St. Martin's paper $6.50 (978-0-312-95573-1). An evil Nazi scientist creates a water-breathing superkiller that is sunk in a U-boat at the end of World War II and gets loose 50 years later. (Rev: BL 1/15/94; SLJ 11/94)

148 Brown, Paul. *Wolf Pack of the Winisk River* (6–12). 2009, Lobster paper $10.95 (978-189755010-6). Told

in free verse from a wolf's point of view, this story takes the reader into the life of a wolf pack. (Rev: BL 4/15/09; LMC 10/09; SLJ 12/09)

149 Burnford, Sheila. *Bel Ria* (7–12). 2006, Random House $17.95 (978-1-59017-211-7). Set in France during World War II, this is a novel about a poodle's amazing adventures.

150 Caras, Roger A. *Roger Caras' Treasury of Great Cat Stories* (9–12). 1990, Galahad Books $9.98 (978-0-88365-763-8). A fine collection of short stories from internationally known writers, all about the mysterious cat. (Rev: BL 4/1/87)

151 Evans, Nicholas. *The Horse Whisperer* (9–12). 1995, Delacorte $24.95 (978-0-385-31523-4). After a teenager loses her leg in a riding accident, her mother moves them to Montana, where the "horse whisperer," a man of mystical powers, tries to rebuild their lives. (Rev: BL 8/95*)

152 Gallico, Paul. *The Snow Goose* (7–12). 1941, Knopf $15.00 (978-0-394-44593-9); paper $9.99 (978-0-7710-3250-9). A hunchbacked artist and a young child nurse a wounded snow goose back to health, and it later returns to protect them in this large, illustrated 50th anniversary edition of the classic tale. (Rev: BL 9/15/92)

153 Grey, Zane. *The Wolf Tracker and Other Animal Tales* (10–12). 1984, Santa Barbara paper $7.95 (978-0-915643-01-1). This collection of tales includes four stories about animals and the outdoors.

154 Herriot, James. *James Herriot's Favorite Dog Stories* (10–12). 1996, St. Martin's $17.95 (978-0-312-14841-6). A collection of 10 stories written by the famous veterinarian and author. (Rev: SLJ 5/97)

155 Lackey, Mercedes. *Reserved for the Cat* (9–12). 2007, DAW $25.95 (978-0-7564-0362-1). In this fifth installment in the Elemental Masters Series the Elemental Spirit is a cat that represents Earth and telepathically communicates to a penniless ballet dancer named Ninette that impersonating a famous Russian ballerina will rid her of her troubles, so with no other alternatives Ninette takes the advice, not knowing that she will also put herself in grave danger. (Rev: BL 11/1/07)

156 O'Hara, Mary. *My Friend Flicka* (7–12). 1988, HarperCollins paper $6.00 (978-0-06-080902-7). This story about Ken McLaughlin and the filly named Flicka is continued in *Thunderhead, Son of Flicka*.

157 Peyton, K. M. *Darkling* (9–12). 1989, Doubleday $16.95 (978-0-385-26963-6). Jenny's unusual grandfather buys her a horse but it is her lover, Goddard, who gives her the help that this responsibility requires. (Rev: BL 5/1/90; SLJ 5/90; VOYA 6/90)

158 Schinto, Jeanne, ed. *The Literary Dog: Great Contemporary Dog Stories* (9–12). 1991, Grove Atlantic paper $15.00 (978-0-87113-504-9). Over 30 dog stories by such present-day writers as Doris Lessing and John Updike. (Rev: BL 9/1/90)

159 Stein, Garth. *The Art of Racing in the Rain* (9–12). 2008, HarperCollins $23.95 (978-0-06-153793-6). Certain that his next life will be in a man's body, Enzo the dog studies human behavior and becomes a player in his family's very serious human dramas. (Rev: BL 3/15/08)

160 Steinbeck, John. *The Red Pony* (9–12). 1986, Viking paper $12.00 (978-0-14-018739-7). These stories about a young boy growing up on a farm in California involve such elements as a loving family, a colt, and an old hired hand.

161 Stranger, Joyce. *A Guiding Star* (9–12). 2006, Severn $27.95 (978-0-7278-6364-5). Devastated by tragedy, a Scottish family rescues a golden retriever and her puppies from the wild and finds unexpected comfort in the dogs' companionship; a moving story that gives the dog's point of view. (Rev: BL 4/15/06)

162 Sullivan, Paul. *Legend of the North* (7–12). 1995, Fireworks paper $9.99 (978-0-88092-308-8). Set in northern Canada, this novel contains two narratives, the first about a young wolf's struggle for dominance within the pack, and the second about an elderly Inuit and his survival in the harsh tundra regions. (Rev: BL 1/1–15/96; VOYA 4/96)

163 Wilson, Susan. *One Good Dog* (9–12). 2010, St. Martin's $29.50 (978-031257125-2). The story of a man who has lost everything and finds himself caring for a mistreated pit bull named Chance is told from the points of view of both man and dog. ∩ (Rev: BL 2/1–15/10)

Classics

Europe

GENERAL AND MISCELLANEOUS

164 Agard, John. *The Young Inferno* (9–12). Illus. by Satoshi Kitamura. 2009, Frances Lincoln $19.95 (978-1-84507-769-3). In this updated, heavily illustrated version of Dante's *Inferno*, the hoodie-wearing protagonist tours Hell with Aesop and meets a variety of sinners, many of whom will be familiar to today's readers. (Rev: LMC 11–12/09; SLJ 8/09)

165 Camus, Albert. *The Plague* (10–12). 1948, Vintage paper $12.00 (978-0-679-72021-8). An allegory for mature readers that uses the bubonic plague as a symbol of the absurdity of life and each character as a different attitude towards it.

166 Davenport, Basil. *The Portable Roman Reader* (10–12). 1951, Viking paper $18.00 (978-0-14-015056-8).

A cross-section of writings from ancient Roman times by such authors as Plautus, Virgil, Seneca, and Terence. [870.8]

167 Dumas, Alexandre. *The Count of Monte Cristo* (8–12). 1996, Random House $25.95 (978-0-679-60199-9). The classic French novel about false imprisonment, escape, and revenge.

168 Dumas, Alexandre. *The Man in the Iron Mask* (9–12). 1976, Lightyear LB $27.95 (978-0-89968-146-7). This rousing French adventure story continues the exploits of the three Musketeers.

169 Dumas, Alexandre. *The Three Musketeers* (8–12). 1984, Dodd paper $5.95 (978-0-553-21337-9). A novel of daring and intrigue in France. Sequels are *The Man in the Iron Mask* and *Twenty Years After* (available in various editions).

170 Hugo, Victor. *The Hunchback of Notre Dame* (10–12). 1981, Buccaneer LB $31.95 (978-0-89966-382-1). The world of medieval Paris, from nobility to paupers, comes alive in this sprawling novel whose central characters are Quasimodo, a hunchback, and a gypsy named Esmeralda.

171 Kafka, Franz. *The Trial* (10–12). Trans. by Willa Muir and Edwin Muir. 1992, Knopf $17.00 (978-0-679-40994-6). A disturbing novel about a man who is arrested and fights charges about which he has no knowledge.

172 Maupassant, Guy de. *The Best Short Stories of Guy de Maupassant* (7–12). 1968, Amereon $26.95 (978-0-88411-589-2). The French master is represented by 19 tales including "The Diamond Necklace."

173 Remarque, Erich Maria. *All Quiet on the Western Front* (10–12). 1929, Little, Brown $24.95 (978-0-316-73992-4); paper $5.99 (978-0-449-21394-0). The touching story of four young German boys and their army life during World War I. (Rev: BL 6/1/88)

174 Sienkiewicz, Henryk. *Quo Vadis* (10–12). 1981, Amereon LB $29.95 (978-0-89190-484-7). The contrast between the hedonistic pagans and the early Christians is highlighted in this novel set in ancient Rome.

175 Verne, Jules. *Around the World in Eighty Days* (7–12). 1996, Puffin paper $4.99 (978-0-14-036711-9). Phileas Fogg and servant Passepartout leave on a world trip in this 1873 classic adventure. (Rev: SLJ 7/96)

176 Verne, Jules. *A Journey to the Center of the Earth* (7–12). 1984, Penguin paper $7.00 (978-0-14-002265-0). A group of adventurers enter the Earth through a volcano in Iceland. First published in French in 1864.

177 Verne, Jules. *Twenty Thousand Leagues Under the Sea* (7–12). 1990, Viking paper $5.99 (978-0-14-036721-8). Evil Captain Nemo captures a group of underwater explorers. First published in 1869. A sequel is *The Mysterious Island* (1988 Macmillan).

178 Voltaire, Francois M. *The Portable Voltaire* (10–12). Ed. by Ben Ray Redmen. 1949, Viking paper $18.00 (978-0-14-015041-4). A fine selection of Voltaire's works including the novel *Candide*.

179 Wallace, Lew. *Ben Hur* (10–12). 1987, Buccaneer LB $35.95 (978-0-89966-289-3). The story of a Jewish slave who escapes a life on the galleys and later is converted to Christianity after an encounter with Christ's healing powers.

GREAT BRITAIN AND IRELAND

180 Brontë, Charlotte, and Amy Corzine. *Jane Eyre, The Graphic Novel: Original Text* (7–10). Illus. by John M. Burns. Series: Classical Comics. 2009, Classical Comics paper $16.95 (978-190633247-1). Drawing directly from Brontë's text, this graphic-novel adaptation offers an appealing introduction to the story; back matter includes material on Brontë's life. (Rev: BL 3/1/09)

181 Carroll, Lewis. *Alice's Adventures in Wonderland* (5–12). Illus. by Iassen Ghiuselev. 2003, Simply Read $29.95 (978-1-894965-00-2). Interesting illustrations by Ghiuselev that interpret incidents and characters in a different way highlight this new edition of an old classic. (Rev: BL 2/1/04; SLJ 6/04)

182 Chaucer, Geoffrey, and Peter Ackroyd. *The Canterbury Tales: A Retelling* (11–12). Illus. by Nick Bantock. 2009, Viking $35 (978-067002122-2). Author Peter Ackroyd recasts Chaucer's well-known tales in modern prose, retaining keeping much of the wit and bawdy humor; for advanced students. **e** (Rev: BL 9/09)

183 Collins, Wilkie. *The Woman in White* (10–12). 1998, Oxford paper $8.95 (978-0-19-283429-4). This mystery story first appeared in 1860 and tells of a plot to illegally obtain the inheritance of the heroine of the novel.

184 Dickens, Charles. *Great Expectations* (8–12). 1998, NAL paper $4.95 (978-0-451-52671-7). The story of Pip and his slow journey to maturity and fortune.

185 Doyle, Arthur Conan. *The Adventures of Sherlock Holmes* (7–12). 1981, Avon paper $2.95 (978-0-380-78105-8). A collection of 12 of the most famous stories about this famous sleuth.

186 Doyle, Arthur Conan. *The Complete Sherlock Holmes: All 4 Novels and 56 Stories* (7–12). 1998, Bantam paper $13.90 (978-0-553-32825-7). In two volumes, all the stories and novels involving Holmes and his foil Watson.

187 Doyle, Arthur Conan. *The Hound of the Baskervilles* (9–12). 1983, Buccaneer LB $19.95 (978-0-89966-229-9). These are two of the many editions available of this Sherlock Holmes mystery about strange deaths on the moors close to the Baskerville estate.

188 Doyle, Arthur Conan. *Sherlock Holmes: The Complete Novels and Stories* (8–12). 1986, Bantam paper $6.95 (978-0-553-21241-9). A handy collection in two volumes of all the writings about Holmes and Watson. (Rev: BL 3/15/87)

189 Doyle, Arthur Conan. *The Sign of Four* (9–12). 1989, Buccaneer LB $15.95 (978-0-89966-230-5). This is one of the four full-length novels featuring Sherlock Holmes.

190 Doyle, Arthur Conan. *Tales of Terror and Mystery* (9–12). 1982, Buccaneer LB $16.95 (978-0-89966-429-3). From the creator of Sherlock Holmes, 13 stories of mystery and the supernatural.

191 Kipling, Rudyard. *Captains Courageous* (7–10). 1964, Amereon LB $20.95 (978-0-88411-818-3). The story of a spoiled teenager who learns about life from common fishermen who save him when he falls overboard from an ocean liner.

192 Kipling, Rudyard. *Kim* (10–12). 1997, Bantam paper $3.95 (978-0-553-21332-4). Beginning in Lahore, this novel follows a young street urchin through many adventures in British-controlled India.

193 Kipling, Rudyard. *The Portable Kipling* (9–12). Ed. by Irving Howe. 1982, Viking paper $18.00 (978-0-14-015097-1). This collection contains 28 short stories and a selection of 50 poems.

194 Klein, Lisa. *Ophelia* (9–12). 2006, Bloomsbury $16.95 (978-1-58234-801-8). A retelling of Shakespeare's *Hamlet* from Ophelia's perspective, describing her experiences, her love for Hamlet, and what happens after her perceived drowning. (Rev: BL 11/1/06; SLJ 2/07)

195 Stevenson, Robert Louis. *The Black Arrow* (7–12). 1998, Tor paper $3.99 (978-0-8125-6562-1). Set against the War of the Roses, this is an adventure story involving a young hero, Dick Shelton. First published in 1888.

196 Stevenson, Robert Louis. *Dr. Jekyll and Mr. Hyde* (7–12). 1990, Buccaneer LB $16.95 (978-0-89968-552-6). This 1886 horror classic involves a drug-induced change of personality. One of several editions.

197 Stevenson, Robert Louis. *The Strange Case of Dr. Jekyll and Mr. Hyde* (9–12). 1993, Oxford paper $5.95 (978-0-19-585429-9). An edition of this classic that includes comments by Joyce Carol Oates and engravings by Barry Moser. (Rev: BL 5/1/90)

198 Stoker, Bram. *Dracula* (10–12). 1985, Amereon LB $27.95 (978-0-88411-131-3). In epistolary form, this novel involves a baron who is a vampire and his mysterious castle in Transylvania.

199 Wilde, Oscar, and Ian Edginton. *The Picture of Dorian Gray* (8–12). Illus. by I. N. J. Culbard. 2009, Sterling paper $14.95 (978-141141593-5). This graphic-novel interpretation of the classic story will serve as an introduction for reluctant readers. (Rev: BL 4/1/09)

200 Woolf, Virginia. *To the Lighthouse* (10–12). 1992, Random House $20 (978-0-679-40537-5). One of Woolf's most famous novels about the Ramsay family and their problems.

United States

201 Bradbury, Ray. *Fahrenheit 451: The Authorized Adaptation* (9–12). Illus. by Tim Hamilton. 2009, Farrar $30.00 (978-080905100-7); paper $16.95 (978-080905101-4). A faithful graphic-novel adaptation of the classic novel about censorship. (Rev: BL 7/09; SLJ 9/09)

202 Cather, Willa. *Death Comes for the Archbishop* (10–12). 1927, Knopf paper $14.95 (978-0-679-72889-4). The story of two clergymen who founded missions and pioneered missionary work in the West, chiefly in New Mexico.

203 Cather, Willa. *My Antonia* (10–12). 1973, Houghton Mifflin paper $7.95 (978-0-395-75514-3). A novel set in Nebraska about pioneering Bohemian farmers and the courageous heroine, Antonia. First published in 1918.

204 Cather, Willa. *Willa Cather: Early Novels and Stories* (10–12). 1987, Library of America $40.00 (978-0-940450-39-4). This collection of stories and novels includes the full text of four novels including *My Antonia, The Song of the Lark,* and *O Pioneers!*

205 Cather, Willa. *Willa Cather: Later Novels* (10–12). 1990, Library of America $35.00 (978-0-940450-52-3). This omnibus volume includes such novels as *Death Comes for the Archbishop, The Lost Lady,* and *Lucy Gayheart.*

206 Cather, Willa. *Willa Cather: Stories, Poems, and Other Writings* (9–12). 1992, Library of America $35.00 (978-0-940450-71-4). This collection includes novellas, stories, and poems. (Rev: SLJ 8/92)

207 Cooper, James Fenimore. *The Last of the Mohicans* (8–12). 1986, Macmillan paper $4.95 (978-0-553-21329-4). This is the second of the classic Leatherstocking Tales. The others are *The Pioneers, The Prairie, The Pathfinder,* and *The Deerslayer* (all available in various editions). (Rev: BL 1/87)

208 Crane, Stephen. *The Red Badge of Courage* (8–12). 1991, Airmont paper $2.50 (978-0-8049-0003-4). The classic novel of a young man who explored the meanings of courage during the Civil War.

209 Faulkner, William. *Light in August* (10–12). 1967, Random House paper $13.00 (978-0-679-73226-6). A classic novel by Faulkner that deals with Joe Christmas, a part-black, and his fate at the hands of bigots.

210 Hawthorne, Nathaniel. *Tales and Sketches, Including Twice-Told Tales, Mosses from an Old Manse, and The Snow-Image; A Wonder Book for Girls and Boys; Tanglewood Tales for Girls and Boys, Being a Second Wonder Book* (10–12). 1982, Library of America $39.50 (978-0-940450-03-5). This volume contains all of Hawthorne's stories and sketches, arranged by publication date.

211 London, Jack. *The Call of the Wild, White Fang, and Other Stories* (9–12). 1993, Viking paper $7.95 (978-0-14-018651-2). In addition to two complete novels, this collection contains two other stories with settings in the Arctic.

212 London, Jack. *The Sea-Wolf* (7–12). 1958, Macmillan $15.95 (978-0-02-574630-5). Wolf Larsen helps a ne'er-do-well and a female poet find their destinies in the classic that was originally published in 1904.

213 Lovecraft, H. P. *Nyarlathotep* (8–12). Illus. by Chuck BB. 2009, Boom! $14.99 (978-193450665-3). A graphic and disturbing rendering of the horrifying 1920 prose poem. (Rev: BL 3/15/09; SLJ 7/09)

214 Poe, Edgar Allan. *The Collected Tales and Poems of Edgar Allan Poe* (9–12). 1992, Modern Library $20.00 (978-0-679-60007-7). This collection of Edgar Allan Poe's writings includes such well-known works as "The Raven" and "The Murders in the Rue Morgue" plus other short stories, poems, essays, and literary criticism. [818]

215 Poe, Edgar Allan. *The Complete Tales and Poems of Edgar Allan Poe* (9–12). 1938, Random House paper $16.00 (978-0-394-71678-7). In addition to 63 stories, this volume includes 53 poems and some nonfiction works.

216 Poe, Edgar Allan. *Edgar Allan Poe's Tales of Mystery and Madness* (7–12). Illus. by Gris Grimly. 2004, Simon & Schuster $17.95 (978-0-689-84837-7). Striking artwork brings to life four of Edgar Allan Poe's classic mystery tales, presented here in abridged form. (Rev: BL 10/15/04*; SLJ 10/04)

217 Sinclair, Upton, and Peter Kuper. *The Jungle* (7–12). Series: Classics Illustrated. 2010, Papercutz $9.99 (978-156163-404-0). Kuper's graphic-novel adaptation brings new life to Sinclair's 1906 classic about the meatpacking industry and the plight of immigrant workers. (Rev: BL 6/18/10; LMC 10/10)

218 Stowe, Harriet Beecher. *Uncle Tom's Cabin* (10–12). 1982, Buccaneer LB $27.95 (978-0-89966-378-4). The American classic about slavery and racial violence in the old South.

219 Twain, Mark. *The Adventures of Huckleberry Finn* (7–12). 1993, Random House $16.50 (978-0-679-42470-3). One of many editions of this classic.

220 Twain, Mark. *The Complete Short Stories of Mark Twain* (9–12). 1957, Bantam paper $6.95 (978-0-553-

21195-5). A total of 60 stories are included and arranged chronologically.

221 Twain, Mark. *A Connecticut Yankee in King Arthur's Court* (7–12). 1988, Morrow $25.99 (978-0-688-06346-7); paper $4.95 (978-0-553-21143-6). Through a time-travel fantasy, a swaggering Yankee is plummeted into the age of chivalry. First published in 1889. (Rev: BL 2/15/89)

222 Twain, Mark. *How Nancy Jackson Married Kate Wilson and Other Tales of Rebellious Girls and Daring Young Women* (10–12). Ed. by John Cooley. 2001, Univ. of Nebraska paper $16.95 (978-0-8032-9442-4). This is an unusual collection of Twain stories, all dealing with unconventional, bold, and resourceful heroines. (Rev: BL 8/01)

223 Twain, Mark. *A Murder, a Mystery, and a Marriage* (10–12). Ed. by Roy Blount Jr. Illus. by Peter De Seve. 2001, Norton $16.95 (978-0-393-04376-1). This is a minor work dealing with murder, greed, love, and a mysterious stranger in a small town called Deer Lick. (Rev: BL 8/01)

224 Twain, Mark. *The Prince and the Pauper* (7–12). 1996, Andre Deutsch $9.95 (978-0-233-99081-1); paper $2.50 (978-0-8049-0032-4). A king and a poor boy switch places in 16th-century England. First published in 1881.

225 Twain, Mark. *Pudd'nhead Wilson* (7–12). 1966, Airmont paper $2.50 (978-0-8049-0124-6). In the Midwest of over 100 years ago, a black servant switches her baby with a white couple's child to ensure that he gets a fair chance at life.

226 Twain, Mark. *Tom Sawyer Abroad [and] Tom Sawyer, Detective* (7–12). 1981, Univ. of California $50.00 (978-0-520-04560-6). Two sequels to *The Adventures of Tom Sawyer,* both involving Tom and Huck.

227 Wharton, Edith. *Novellas and Other Writings* (10–12). 1990, Library of America $45.00 (978-0-940450-53-0). This volume contains a memoir and eight novelettes, including *Summer* (1917) and *Ethan Frome* (1911).

228 Wolfe, Thomas. *Look Homeward, Angel* (10–12). 1997, Scribner Classics $30.00 (978-0-684-84221-9). This classic American novel tells about the childhood and youth of a southern boy, Eugene Gant.

Other Countries

229 Hudson, W. H. *Green Mansions: A Romance of the Tropical Forest* (10–12). 1982, Buccaneer LB $25.95 (978-0-89966-374-6). The haunting novel of a naturalist's encounter with the bird-girl, Rima, in a South American jungle.

Contemporary Life and Problems

General and Miscellaneous

230 Ackley, Amy. *Sign Language* (7–10). 2011, Viking $16.99 (978-0-670-01318-0). Reeling from her father's death from cancer, Abby, 12, slowly grows out of her grief and begins accepting her life after tragedy. ⋒ ℮ Lexile HL730L (Rev: BL 8/11; SLJ 9/1/11)

231 Ahern, Cecelia. *The Gift* (9–12). 2009, HarperCollins $19.99 (978-006170626-4). Businessman Lou Suffern is so focused on getting promoted that Christmas and family are the last thing on his mind, but his priorities are about to be challenged when the homeless man he hires to work in his company's mailroom invites himself into Lou's personal life. (Rev: BL 10/1/09)

232 Alenyikov, Michael. *Ivan and Misha* (11–12). 2010, Northwestern Univ. $18.95 (978-081012718-0). This insightful collection of short stories revolves around gay twin brothers who immigrated from Russia and now live in New York City; for mature readers. (Rev: BLO 9/1–15/10)

233 Alexander, Jill S. *The Sweetheart of Prosper County* (7–10). 2009, Feiwel & Friends $16.99 (978-0-312-54856-8). Funny characters populate this likable story about 15-year-old Austin, a girl who learns to look inward for the confidence to stand up to a boy who bullies her, and decides to enter a rooster in the local poultry competition. ⋒ Lexile 710L (Rev: BL 8/09; SLJ 9/09)

234 Almond, David. *Click* (7–10). 2007, Scholastic $16.99 (978-0-439-41138-7). Ten well-known authors collaborate to form this compelling well-crafted novel (written to support Amnesty International) about a character named George "Gee" Keane — a famous photojournalist but something of a mystery man. (Rev: BL 9/15/07; SLJ 10/07)

235 Altebrando, Tara. *The Best Night of Your (Pathetic) Life* (9–12). 2012, Dutton $16.99 (978-052542326-3). Mary and her team come to unsettling realizations about their longtime friends during their highly competitive senior week scavenger hunt. Lexile 860L (Rev: BLO 7/12; HB 7–8/12; SLJ 8/12; VOYA 8/12)

236 Anderson, Jodi Lynn. *Love and Peaches* (8–11). 2008, HarperTeen $16.99 (978-0-06-073311-7); LB $17.89 (978-0-06-073312-4). Friends Leeda, Murphy, and Birdie return to Darlington Orchard, where they face jilted boyfriends, inheritances, heartbreak, and goodbyes. (Rev: SLJ 4/1/09)

237 Anderson, Jodi Lynn. *Peaches* (8–11). 2005, HarperCollins LB $16.89 (978-0-06-073306-3). Three teenage girls from diverse backgrounds forge lasting bonds during a summer picking peaches in a Georgia orchard. (Rev: BL 10/1/05; SLJ 8/05; VOYA 2/06)

238 Anderson, Jodi Lynn. *The Secrets of Peaches* (9–12). Series: Peaches. 2006, HarperCollins $16.99 (978-0-06-073308-7). In this sequel that picks up where *Peaches* (2005) left off, Birdie, Murphy, and Leeda are starting their senior year in high school, each facing problems — family, relationships, and otherwise — with the help of the others. (Rev: SLJ 1/07)

239 Anderson, Mary. *The Unsinkable Molly Malone* (7–10). 1991, Harcourt $16.95 (978-0-15-213801-1). Molly, 16, sells her collages outside New York's Metropolitan Museum, starts an art class for kids on welfare, and learns that her boyfriend is rich. (Rev: BL 11/15/91; SLJ 12/91)

240 Andrews, Jesse. *Me and Earl and the Dying Girl* (8–11). 2012, Abrams $16.95 (978-1-4197-0176-4). High school loner Greg's life changes when he befriends Rachel, who is dying from leukemia, in this surprisingly humorous novel. YALSA Top Ten Best Fiction for Young Adults 2013. e Lexile 820L (Rev: BL 3/1/12*; SLJ 7/12)

241 Anhalt, Ariela. *Freefall* (10–12). 2010, Harcourt $17 (978-0-15-206567-6). Submissive, weak-kneed boarding school student Luke goes along with his best friend's fencing team hazing plan, with disastrous results. e Lexile HL590L (Rev: BL 12/15/09; SLJ 1/10; VOYA 10/09)

242 Anthony, Joelle. *The Right and the Real* (8–11). 2012, Putnam $17.99 (978-039925525-0). After she refuses to join her father's cult, 17-year-old Jamie is thrown out of her home and must fend for herself. e (Rev: BL 4/1/12; LMC 10/12; SLJ 5/1/12)

243 Antieau, Kim. *Ruby's Imagine* (6–10). 2008, Houghton Mifflin $16.00 (978-061899767-1). Ruby, 17, lives in New Orleans but is in tune with nature, and when Hurricane Katrina overwhelms the city Ruby heeds her grandmother rather than her instincts and ends up learning some family secrets. Lexile 540L (Rev: BL 11/15/08; LMC 3–4/09; SLJ 12/08)

244 Archer, Lily. *The Poison Apples* (7–10). 2007, Feiwel & Friends $16.95 (978-0-312-36762-6). Three 15-year-old girls — Molly, Reena, and Alice — who have been shipped off to boarding school are united in their hatred for their new stepmothers in this funny novel full of pop-culture references. (Rev: BL 10/15/07; SLJ 9/07)

245 Asher, Jay, and Carolyn Mackler. *The Future of Us* (8–12). 2011, Penguin $18.99 (978-1-59514-491-1). In 1996 Emma and Josh discover their future selves on Facebook and perhaps the chance to change their destinies. ⌒ e (Rev: BL 10/15/11*; HB 1–2/12; SLJ 11/1/11)

246 Ashton, Victoria. *Confessions of a Teen Nanny* (8–12). 2005, HarperCollins LB $16.89 (978-0-06-077524-7). Hired as a temporary nanny for an 8-year-old child prodigy, 16-year-old Adrienne finds herself being manipulated by her charge's older sister. (Rev: BL 8/05; SLJ 7/05)

247 Atkins, Catherine. *The File on Angelyn Stark* (9–12). 2011, Knopf $16.99 (978-0-375-86906-8); LB $19.99 (978-037596906-5). Troubled teen Angelyn works to put her abusive past behind her, finding herself unsettled when others offer support and guidance. e (Rev: BL 11/15/11; SLJ 11/1/11; VOYA 12/11)

248 Auster, Paul. *Auggie Wren's Christmas Story* (9–12). Illus. by ISOL. 2004, Henry Holt $17.50 (978-0-8050-7723-0). Auggie, a New York smoke-shop owner, tells a heartwarming Christmas fable. (Rev: BL 9/15/04)

249 Ayarbe, Heidi. *Freeze Frame* (9–12). 2008, HarperCollins $17.89 (978-006135174-7); LB $17.89 (978-006135174-7). A fatal shooting of which he cannot remember the details changes 15-year-old Kyle's life, leaving him filled with self-loathing as he tries to make sense of his actions. e Lexile 490L (Rev: BL 10/15/08; SLJ 2/1/09; VOYA 12/08)

250 Bailey, Em. *Shift* (7–11). 2012, Egmont $16.99 (978-160684358-1). Olive, who is recovering from a suicide attempt, is suspicious of new student Miranda and her apparent devotion to popular Katie; could Miranda be a shape-shifter? e (Rev: BLO 6/12; HB 5–6/12; LMC 8–9/12; SLJ 6/12)

251 Bailey, Roz. *Postcards from Last Summer* (11–12). 2006, Kensington paper $12.95 (978-0-7582-0567-4). Four young women from different backgrounds and lifestyles, and who have been friends since childhood, support one another through thick and thin in this novel set in the Hamptons; suitable for mature readers. (Rev: BL 8/06)

252 Baratz-Logsted, Lauren. *Secrets of My Suburban Life* (9–12). 2008, Simon & Schuster paper $6.99 (978-1-4169-5288-6). Ren is crushed when she and her father move to the suburbs after her mother dies; even worse, she thinks her father may be trolling for sex on the Internet with one of her own classmates. (Rev: BL 12/15/07; SLJ 2/08)

253 Barkley, Brad, and Heather Hepler. *Scrambled Eggs at Midnight* (7–10). 2006, Dutton $16.99 (978-0-525-47760-0). Unhappy with the nomadic life she lives with her mother, 15-year-old Calliope finds friendship and romance and learns about herself in the process. (Rev: BL 6/1–15/06; LMC 1/07; SLJ 5/06)

254 Barnholdt, Lauren. *Reality Chick* (9–12). 2006, Simon & Schuster paper $8.99 (978-1-4169-1317-7). Ally is part of a reality-TV show and discovers that her love life is now being nationally broadcast. (Rev: SLJ 9/06)

255 Barron, Sandra Rodriguez. *Stay with Me* (10–12). 2010, HarperCollins paper $14.99 (978-00616506-2-8). Five adults, bonded by a mysterious childhood event, reunite to try to discover their true identities in this mystery/romance novel. (Rev: BL 11/1–15/10)

256 Barry, Lynda. *One Hundred Demons* (10–12). 2002, Sasquatch $24.95 (978-1-57061-537-5). In a combination of autobiography and fiction, comic-book creator Lynda Barry exorcises some of the demons that have haunted her personal life. (Rev: BL 8/02)

257 Bates, Shelley. *Pocketful of Pearls* (9–12). 2005, Warner paper $12.99 (978-0-446-69491-9). Former college professor Matthew Nicholas takes a job as handyman for Dinah Traynell, a woman caught in the vise-like grip of a religious cult, in a compelling story of unhappiness and newfound trust. (Rev: BL 10/1/05)

258 Bauer, A. C. E. *Gil Marsh* (8–11). 2012, Random House $15.99 (978-037586933-4); LB $18.99 (978-037596933-1). Track star Gil, 17, travels to the grave of his friend (and former rival) Enko and considers the meaning of life and death in this retelling of the ancient story of Gilgamesh. **e** (Rev: BL 2/15/12; LMC 3–4/12; SLJ 2/12)

259 Bauer, Michael Gerard. *Don't Call Me Ishmael* (9–12). 2007, Greenwillow $16.99 (978-0-06-134834-1). Saddled with a ridiculous name, 14-year-old Ishmael is having a tough year at St. Daniel's Boys School until confident new boy James arrives and offers new perspectives in this funny novel narrated by Ishmael. (Rev: BL 11/15/07; SLJ 2/08)

260 Bauman, Beth Ann. *Jersey Angel* (10–12). 2012, Random House $15.99 (978-038574020-3); LB $18.99 (978-038590828-3). Angel, 17, enjoys perhaps too much freedom and slowly comes to realize that life is not all about fun. ∩ **e** (Rev: BL 5/1/12; HB 7–8/12; SLJ 6/12; VOYA 6/12)

261 Bauman, Christian. *In Hoboken* (9–12). 2008, Melville paper $15.95 (978-1-933633-47-3). This sharp and funny novel follows Thatcher Smith and his guitar to Hoboken, New Jersey, where he gets a job as a clerk at the local mental clinic and assembles a motley band that struggles to make meaningful music. (Rev: BL 3/15/08)

262 Behrens, Andy. *All the Way* (9–12). 2006, Dutton $15.99 (978-0-525-47761-7). After a boring, uneventful summer 17-year-old Ian decides to take a road trip with two friends to get up close with a hot girl he met in a chat group, and learns a lot about himself and love along the way. (Rev: SLJ 5/06)

263 Benway, Robin. *Audrey, Wait!* (8–11). 2008, Penguin $16.99 (978-159514191-0). Audrey's ex-boyfriend Even, a rock singer, writes a song about their breakup and she suddenly finds herself a reluctant celebrity. Lexile 760L (Rev: BL 8/08; SLJ 8/08)

264 Berwin, Margot. *Hothouse Flower and the Nine Plants of Desire* (11–12). 2009, Pantheon $24 (978-030737784-5). Ready for something new following her divorce, Lila Nova stumbles upon a unique Laundromat filled with exotic tropical plants and soon finds herself tangled in romance and adventure far from her Manhattan home; for mature readers. ∩ **e** (Rev: BL 4–5/09)

265 Bick, Ilsa J. *Draw the Dark* (9–12). 2010, Carolrhoda $16.95 (978-0-7613-5686-8). A multilayered story featuring 17-year-old Christian, who can paint others' thoughts and has nightmares about being a Jewish child in the 1940s. ∩ Lexile 790L (Rev: BL 10/1/10; LMC 11–12/10; SLJ 11/1/10; VOYA 12/10)

266 Bjorkman, Lauren. *My Invented Life* (10–12). 2009, Henry Holt $17.99 (978-0-8050-8950-9). In order to re-establish the closeness she once shared with her sister, whom she suspects is gay, high school junior Roz Peterson pretends she herself is a lesbian, and this ruse prompts many unexpected revelations about her classmates as well as herself. **e** (Rev: BL 10/15/09; SLJ 12/09; VOYA 12/09)

267 Blexbolex. *People* (4–12). Trans. from French by Claudia Bedrick. Illus. by author. 2011, Enchanted Lion $19.95 (978-1-59270-110-0). A stimulating look at the similarities and differences in our lives, pairing, for example, a contortionist and a plumber, a bystander and a rescuer, a partygoer and a hermit. (Rev: HB 9–10/11; SLJ 9/1/11)

268 Bloor, Edward. *A Plague Year* (8–11). 2011, Knopf $15.99 (978-0-375-85681-5); LB $18.99 (978-037595681-2). Ninth-grader Tom Coleman documents the impact on his small Pennsylvania town of September 11, 2001, a rash of meth addiction, and a July 2002 mining accident. **e** Lexile HL590L (Rev: BLO 10/1/11; SLJ 12/1/11)

269 Bodett, Tom. *Norman Tuttle on the Last Frontier: A Novel in Stories* (8–10). 2004, Knopf LB $17.99 (978-0-679-99031-4). In this coming-of-age story presented in interconnected episodes, klutzy Alaskan teenager Norman Tuttle experiences many firsts — first job, first date, first hunting expedition — and his relationship with his father evolves. (Rev: BL 12/1/04; SLJ 12/04; VOYA 12/04)

270 Bradley, Alex. *Hot Lunch* (9–12). 2007, Dutton $16.99 (978-0-525-47830-0). After disruptive behavior, Molly and Cassie are assigned to lunch preparation until they learn to get it right; the two finally learn to get along and to produce edible food. (Rev: BCCB 9/07; HB 9–10/07; SLJ 8/07)

271 Brande, Robin. *Fat Cat* (8–11). 2009, Knopf $16.99 (978-0-375-84449-2); LB $19.99 (978-0-375-94449-9). A science research project motivates overweight high school junior Cat to take on a prehistoric lifestyle and thereby lose pounds and for the first time attract male attention. ∩ **e** (Rev: BL 10/15/09; SLJ 1/10)

272 Brashares, Ann. *Forever in Blue: The Fourth Summer of the Sisterhood* (8–11). Series: The Sisterhood of the Traveling Pants. 2007, Delacorte $18.99 (978-0-385-72936-9). The four girls of *The Sisterhood of the Traveling Pants* are growing up, exploring love and life, and recognizing their ability to succeed without the pants in this final book in the series. ⋒ (Rev: BL 12/15/06; SLJ 2/07)

273 Brashares, Ann. *My Name Is Memory* (11–12). 2010, Riverhead $25.95 (978-159448758-3). Two lovers separated by chronological distance finally connect in this tantalizing, sometimes steamy novel reminiscent of Niffenegger's *The Time Traveler's Wife*; for mature teens. ⋒ ℮ (Rev: BL 3/1–15/10)

274 Brian, Kate. *Megan Meade's Guide to the McGowan Boys* (8–11). 2005, Simon & Schuster $14.95 (978-1-4169-0030-6). Megan does not want to move to South Korea with her military parents and chooses instead to stay with the McGowans, a family with seven sons, requiring adjustments all round. (Rev: BL 9/15/05; SLJ 11/05; VOYA 12/05)

275 Brody, Jessica. *52 Reasons to Hate My Father* (8–12). 2012, Farrar $16.99 (978-0-374-32303-5). Lexi, 18, can't wait to get her hands on her multimillion-dollar trust fund, but when she wrecks a brand-new Mercedes convertible her father decides it's time for her to learn the value of money — through performing menial jobs for a whole year. ℮ Lexile 790L (Rev: BL 7/12; SLJ 9/12; VOYA 8/12)

276 Brody, Jessica. *My Life Undecided* (7–10). 2011, Farrar $16.99 (978-0-374-39905-4). Famous for her bad decision-making skills, Brooklyn, 15, decides to start a blog and let her readers guide her through life. ℮ Lexile 840L (Rev: BLO 8/11; SLJ 6/11; VOYA 8/11)

277 Buckley, Kristen. *Thirteen Reasons Why* (8–11). 2007, Penguin $16.99 (978-1-59514-171-2). Clay Jenson describes his thoughts as he listens to cassette tapes bearing the voice of his dead classmate, Hannah, who describes events and circumstances that led to her suicide. ⋒ (Rev: BL 9/1/07; SLJ 11/07)

278 Buffie, Margaret. *Winter Shadows* (7–10). 2010, Tundra $19.95 (978-0-88776-968-9). High school senior Cass, unhappy and resentful of her stepmother, finds a diary written by Beatrice in the mid-19th century, who also is grappling with an unpleasant stepmother — and the two form a bond that transcends time. (Rev: BL 11/15/10; SLJ 12/1/10)

279 Burton, Rebecca. *Leaving Jetty Road* (8–11). 2006, Knopf $15.95 (978-0-375-83488-2). Three Australian high school girls decide to become vegetarians, a choice that affects each in a different way and becomes more critical as Lise has serious anorexia. (Rev: BL 6/1–15/06; LMC 10/06; SLJ 8/06)

280 Bushnell, Candace. *The Carrie Diaries* (9–12). 2010, HarperCollins $18.99 (978-006172891-4). Carrie Bradshaw's senior year of high school is the subject of this prequel that contains many of the themes (friendship, drinking, romance, writing) familiar from *Sex and the City*. ℮ (Rev: BL 5/15/10; SLJ 6/10; VOYA 8/10)

281 Cabot, Meg. *Being Nikki* (7–10). Series: Airhead. 2009, Scholastic $16.99 (978-054504056-3). Romance, suspense, and comedy (and a touch of science fiction) are intertwined in this second book about the ordinary teen whose brain has been transplanted into a famous model's body. ⋒ Lexile 800L (Rev: BL 4/15/09; SLJ 1/10)

282 Cabot, Meg. *Boy Meets Girl* (9–12). 2004, Avon paper $13.95 (978-0-06-008545-2). Told in a series of e-mails, phone messages, and journal articles, this delightful novel reveals life behind the scenes of a New York newspaper. (Rev: BL 1/1–15/04)

283 Cadnum, Michael. *Flash* (8–11). 2010, Farrar $16.99 (978-0-374-39911-5). On a tense day in Albany, California, five young people deal with various acute personal problems. (Rev: BL 5/1/10; HB 7–8/10; LMC 8–9/10; SLJ 6/10)

284 Calame, Don. *Beat the Band* (9–12). 2010, Candlewick $16.99 (978-0-7636-4633-2). Assigned to work with the dreaded "Hot Dog" Helen for a health class presentation on safe sex, 10th-grader Coop tries to recoup his rep by entering his musically challenged rock group in the "Battle of the Bands" competition. (Rev: BL 9/1/10; SLJ 12/1/10)

285 Caletti, Deb. *The Fortunes of Indigo Skye* (10–12). 2008, Simon & Schuster $15.99 (978-1-4169-1007-7). Indigo gets a huge tip ($2.5 million, in fact) from a customer at the Seattle restaurant where she works, but manages to stay down-to-earth in the aftermath. (Rev: BL 4/1/08; SLJ 4/08)

286 Caletti, Deb. *The Secret Life of Prince Charming* (8–11). 2009, Simon & Schuster $16.99 (978-141695940-3). Quinn, 17, and her sisters Sprout and Frances take a road trip to visit their father's former wives and girlfriends and to learn why men do the things they do. ⋒ Lexile 760L (Rev: BL 4/1/09; HB 7–8/09; SLJ 6/1/09; VOYA 10/09)

287 Caletti, Deb. *Wild Roses* (7–10). 2005, Simon & Schuster $15.95 (978-0-689-86766-8). Seventeen-year-old Cassie finds life with her stepfather — an unstable violinist and composer — difficult at the best of times, but things go from bad to worse when she falls for one of his music students. (Rev: BCCB 10/05; BL 10/1/05; SLJ 11/05*; VOYA 12/05)

288 Calloway, Cassidy. *Confessions of a First Daughter* (7–10). 2009, HarperTeen paper $8.99 (978-0-06-172439-8). Eighteen-year-old Morgan Abbott thinks that life as the First Daughter of the United States is trying enough as it is, but when her mother, the president, asks her to temporarily fill her shoes, Morgan finds that her life is about to get considerably more complicated. ℮ (Rev: BL 7/09; SLJ 12/09; VOYA 8/09)

289 Calonita, Jen. *Paparazzi Princess* (6–10). Series: Secrets of My Hollywood Life. 2009, Little, Brown $16.99 (978-0-316-03064-9). Finding it difficult to cope with the impending end of her long-running show, teen TV star Kaitlin spends time with two publicity-hungry party girls until she finally realizes that their life is not satisfying. (Rev: SLJ 6/1/09; VOYA 6/09)

290 Calonita, Jen. *Reality Check* (7–10). 2010, Little, Brown $16.99 (978-0-316-04554-4). The friendship between four Long Island teenage girls does not survive when a media executive scout offers them their own reality TV show. **e** Lexile HL690L (Rev: BL 4/15/10; SLJ 10/1/10; VOYA 8/10)

291 Calonita, Jen. *Secrets of My Hollywood Life: On Location* (7–12). 2007, Little, Brown $16.99 (978-0-316-15439-0). Kaitlin is a likable Hollywood starlet whose life gets tricky when she has to make a movie co-starring her ex-boyfriend and her biggest enemy. (Rev: SLJ 7/07)

292 Calonita, Jen. *Sleepaway Girls* (7–10). 2009, Little, Brown $16.99 (978-031601717-6). Samantha has the time of her life at summer camp as a counselor in training. Lexile 710L (Rev: BL 5/1/09; SLJ 6/1/09)

293 Cameron, W. Bruce. *A Dog's Purpose* (10–12). 2010, Forge $22.99 (978-076532626-3). Narrated by clever, introspective Bailey, this charming, often humorous story charts the dog's diverse life changes — from stray to family dog, from K-9 rescue animal back to stray. ∩ (Rev: BLO 7/10)

294 Campbell, Drusilla. *The Good Sister* (11–12). 2010, Grand Central paper $13.99 (978-04465357-8-6). Simone is on trial for attempting to murder her three children, and her sister Roxane tries, as always, to protect her in this novel that revisits the girls' difficult childhood and explores the tragedy of postpartum depression; for mature readers. **e** (Rev: BLO 9/1–15/10)

295 Candela, Margo. *Good-bye to All That* (11–12). 2010, Touchstone paper $14 (978-14165713-5-3). Twenty-five-year-old marketing assistant Raquel copes with flirtation, family drama, and a seriously cutthroat work environment in Hollywood; for mature readers. (Rev: BL 6/1–15/10)

296 Capote, Truman. *Other Voices, Other Rooms* (10–12). 1968, Random House paper $12.00 (978-0-679-74564-8). Capote's first success as an novelist deals with a rundown Louisiana mansion peopled with eccentrics as seen through the eyes of a young boy.

297 Carlson, Melody. *Glamour* (7–10). Series: On the Runway. 2011, Zondervan paper $9.99 (978-031071790-4). Erin and Paige are filming Fashion Week in the Bahamas for their reality TV show as romantic problems intrude, their friend Fran has cancer, and Mollie awaits the arrival of her baby. **e** (Rev: BL 4/15/11)

298 Carney, Jeff. *The Adventures of Michael MacInnes* (9–12). 2006, Farrar $17.00 (978-0-374-30146-0). In 1924, orphan Michael MacInnes arrives at a privileged

boys' boarding school full of plans for the future and an irreverent attitude. (Rev: LMC 4/07; SLJ 11/06)

299 Carr, Robyn. *Never Too Late* (11–12). 2006, MIRA paper $6.99 (978-0-7783-2297-9). Clare reexamines her life and the behavior of her husband following a car accident and, with the help of her sisters, is able to find love again after many disappointments; mature teens will identify with Clare's angry son. (Rev: BL 5/1/06)

300 Carter, Ernessa T. *32 Candles* (11–12). 2010, Amistad $24.99 (978-006195784-0). Readers follow African American Davie Jones through her unhappy childhood in rural Mississippi to her career as a lounge singer in Los Angeles in this novel for mature readers about growth and first love. ∩ **e** (Rev: BL 7/10)

301 Castellucci, Cecil. *Rose Sees Red* (9–12). 2010, Scholastic $17.99 (978-0-545-06079-0). In 1980s New York City, teen ballet dancers Rose and her Russian neighbor Yrena overcome Cold War differences to enjoy a night of adventure. Lexile HL630L (Rev: BL 6/10; LMC 8–9/10; SLJ 9/1/10)

302 Castellucci, Cecil. *The Year of the Beasts* (9–12). Illus. by Nate Powell. 2012, Roaring Brook $16.99 (978-159643686-2). Tessa, 15, has an easier time accepting her little sister's new boyfriend when she begins a clandestine romance of her own; a parallel story featuring a Medusa-like character is told in graphic novel chapters that alternate with the prose narrative. **e** Lexile HL640L (Rev: BL 3/1/12*; LMC 8–9/12; SLJ 6/12)

303 Castle, Jennifer. *The Beginning of After* (10–12). 2011, HarperTeen $17.99 (978-0-06-198579-9). High school senior Laurel faces many challenges after her parents and brother are killed in a car accident. Lexile 800L (Rev: BL 9/15/11; SLJ 11/1/11)

304 Castrovilla, Selene. *The Girl Next Door* (9–12). 2010, WestSide $16.95 (978-1-934813-15-7). Ever-successful Jesse, who should now be in his senior year, is instead battling lymphoma and, despite the grim survival rate, nurturing a bittersweet love affair with Samantha, the girl next door. (Rev: BL 7/10; SLJ 12/1/10)

305 Catton, Eleanor. *The Rehearsal* (11–12). 2010, Little, Brown $23.99 (978-031607433-9). In this inventive, intellectually challenging read, one girl's trauma — sexual abuse by her music teacher — becomes fodder for a nearby drama school's performance; for mature readers. **e** (Rev: BL 4/15/10*)

306 Chambers, Aidan. *Dying to Know You* (9–12). 2012, Abrams $16.95 (978-141970165-8). Dyslexic Karl, 18, enlists help from his girlfriend's favorite author in writing a lengthy, revealing letter. **e** Lexile HL720L (Rev: BL 4/15/12*; HB 5–6/12; SLJ 5/1/12*)

307 Chandler, Ann. *Siena Summer* (7–10). 2009, Orca paper $12.95 (978-189658017-3). Angela spends a summer in Italy and rescues a doomed horse that she later rides in Siena's annual race. (Rev: BL 5/1/09)

308 Chase, Paula. *Don't Get It Twisted* (7–10). Series: Del Rio Bay Clique. 2007, Dafina paper $9.95 (978-0-7582-1861-2). Friends (and enemies) gossiping, IMing, and flirting fill the pages of this second novel about freshman Mina and her friends, full of slick, slangy dialogue and pop-culture references. ⌒ (Rev: BL 1/1–15/08)

309 Cheripko, Jan. *Rat* (7–12). 2002, Boyds Mills $16.95 (978-1-59078-034-3). Fifteen-year-old Jeremy faces difficult choices in this novel that looks at moral questions against a backdrop of basketball. (Rev: HBG 10/03; SLJ 8/02)

310 Chiang, Ted. *The Lifecycle of Software Objects* (10–12). 2010, Subterranean $25 (978-159606317-4). Software tester Ana decides to train her capable, digital pet to live on its own in this novella that raises ethical questions about the role of artificial intelligence. (Rev: BL 7/10)

311 Citra, Becky. *Missing* (7–10). 2011, Orca paper $9.95 (978-1-55469-345-0). When her father gets a job at a ranch, 8th-grader Thea finds friends in an abused horse and in a classmate named Van who helps her unravel a mystery about a young girl who disappeared in the 1950s. ℮ Lexile 670L (Rev: BL 5/1/11; LMC 10/11; SLJ 9/1/11; VOYA 4/11)

312 Clark, Catherine. *Frozen Rodeo* (8–12). 2003, HarperCollins LB $16.89 (978-0-06-623008-5). What starts out as a dull summer has its high points for P.F. (Peggy Fleming) Farrell as she enjoys a teen romance, foils a robbery, and even finds time to help deliver her mother's baby. (Rev: BL 2/15/03; HBG 10/03; SLJ 3/03; VOYA 4/03)

313 Cochrane, Mick. *Fitz* (8–12). 2012, Knopf $16.99 (978-0-375-85683-9); LB $19.99 (978-037595683-6). Fifteen-year-old Fitz's volatile mix of bitterness and longing boils over, and he kidnaps the father he's never known at gunpoint. ⌒ ℮ Lexile 750L (Rev: BL 12/1/12; SLJ 12/12)

314 Cocks, Heather, and Jessica Morgan. *Messy* (9–12). 2012, Little, Brown $17.99 (978-0-316-09829-8). Talented Max McCormack gets a break when she's asked to ghostwrite a celebrity daughter's blog in this entertaining companion to *Spoiled* (2011). ⌒ ℮ Lexile 870L (Rev: BLO 7/12; SLJ 7/12; VOYA 6/12)

315 Cohen, Tish. *Little Black Lies* (8–12). 2009, Egmont $16.99 (978-1-60684-033-7); LB $19.99 (978-1-60684-046-7). When high school junior Sara Black allows her snobbish classmates to believe that she has just transferred to her upper-crust Boston school from London, England, this lie puts her father — the school's new janitor and obsessive-compulsive disorder victim — in a precarious position. and jeopardizes her relationship with him. ℮ (Rev: BL 11/1/09; SLJ 12/09; VOYA 12/09)

316 Cohn, Rachel. *Very LeFreak* (10–12). 2010, Knopf $16.99 (978-0-375-85758-4); LB $19.99 (978-0-375-95758-1). Very (short for Veronica) comes close to flunking out of Columbia because of her devotion to electronic media and her very active social and sexual life; an intervention sends her off to tech rehab. ⌒ ℮ (Rev: BL 11/1/09; HB 1–2/10; SLJ 1/10; VOYA 4/10)

317 Cohn, Rachel, and David Levithan. *Dash and Lily's Book of Dares* (9–12). 2010, Knopf $16.99 (978-0-375-86659-3); LB $19.99 (978-0-375-96659-0). Alone in Manhattan at Christmas time, lonely teens Dash and Lily carry on a kind of literary scavenger hunt/romance centered on the pages of a moleskin journal. ⌒ ℮ Lexile 860L (Rev: BL 11/1/10; HB 1–2/11; SLJ 10/1/10; VOYA 12/10)

318 Colasanti, Susane. *When It Happens* (9–12). 2006, Viking $17.99 (978-0-670-06029-0). In alternating chapters full of realistic dialogue, high school seniors Sara and Tobey talk about their initially unlikely relationship. (Rev: BL 4/15/06; SLJ 7/06)

319 Cole, Stephen. *Thieves Like Us* (8–11). 2006, Bloomsbury $16.95 (978-1-58234-653-3). Jonah Wish, a member of a gang of teenage thieves, finds himself questioning the morality of certain activities. (Rev: BL 4/1/06)

320 Coleman, Rowan. *The Home for Broken Hearts* (11–12). 2010, Gallery paper $15 (978-14391568-5-8). When Ellen Wood's husband dies and she takes boarders to help make ends meet, her life and her relationships with her 11-year-old son and her sister begin to change; for mature readers. (Rev: BL 9/1–15/10)

321 Collard, Sneed B, III. *Flash Point* (7–10). 2006, Peachtree $16.95 (978-156145385-6). Luther, a high school sophomore, has turned away from sports and is now interested in birds of prey and the environment but this new focus threatens to alienate many in his logging community; when his girlfriend's beloved falcon is shot, this fast-paced story becomes even more exciting. ℮ (Rev: SLJ 12/06)

322 Collins, Yvonne, and Sandy Rideout. *Introducing Vivien Leigh Reid: Daughter of the Diva* (7–10). 2005, St. Martin's $11.95 (978-0-312-33837-4). Sent to Ireland to spend the summer on the set of her actress mother's latest film, 15-year-old Leigh Reid wins a bit part in the movie, develops a crush on a costar, and finally begins to build a meaningful relationship with her mom. (Rev: BL 6/1–15/05; SLJ 9/05)

323 Collins, Yvonne, and Sandy Rideout. *The New and Improved Vivien Leigh Reid: Diva in Control* (7–10). 2007, Griffin paper $9.95 (978-0-312-35828-0). Despite her determination to make her life better, Leigh continues to face challenges in both her personal and professional lives in this third book in the series. (Rev: SLJ 3/07)

324 Collins, Yvonne, and Sandy Rideout. *Now Starring Vivien Leigh Reid: Diva in Training* (8–12). 2006, Griffin paper $9.95 (978-0-312-33839-8). In this sequel to the witty *Introducing Vivien Leigh Reid: Daughter of the Diva* (2005), 16-year-old Leigh lands a role in a soap opera and initially adopts a prima donna attitude that threatens her friendships and her job. (Rev: SLJ 1/06; VOYA 4/06)

325 Coman, Carolyn. *Many Stones* (7–12). 2000, Front St $15.95 (978-1-886910-55-3). A year after her sister was murdered there, Berry reluctantly travels with her father to South Africa to attend her memorial in this novel set during the proceedings of the Truth and Reconciliation Commission. (Rev: BL 11/1/00; HB 1–2/01; HBG 3/01; SLJ 11/00*; VOYA 2/01)

326 Conrad, Lauren. *L.A. Candy* (9–12). 2009, HarperCollins $17.99 (978-006176758-6). A frothy tale about two college-age teens who find themselves starring in a reality show as they settle into their lives in Los Angeles. **e** (Rev: BLO 7/2/09; SLJ 10/09)

327 Cook, Eileen. *Unraveling Isobel* (8–10). 2012, Simon & Schuster $16.99 (978-144241327-6). Isobel, 17, begins to worry she's losing her mind when she and her mother move to her new husband's spooky mansion. **e** Lexile HL700L (Rev: BL 3/1/12; HB 1–2/12; VOYA 2/12)

328 *Cool Like That* (7–10). Series: So for Real. 2010, Kensington paper $9.95 (978-07582344-2-1). Gia had high hopes for her relationship with Ricky while attending a summer program at Columbia but Ricky is being cautious and she soon finds herself intrigued by Rashad; the fourth in the series, this book stands alone. **e** (Rev: BL 2/1/10)

329 Cooney, Caroline B. *Janie Face to Face* (7–10). 2013, Delacorte $17.99 (978-038574206-1); LB $20.99 (978-037599039-7). In this series conclusion, Janie and her friends are dogged by a writer who's eager to tell the story of her kidnapping to the world. **e** Lexile HL660L (Rev: BL 12/15/12; SLJ 2/13)

330 Coriell, Shelley. *Welcome, Caller, This Is Chloe* (8–12). 2012, Abrams Amulet $16.95 (978-1-4197-0191-7). Chloe copes with problems at home and the sudden alienation of her two best friends by joining her school's failing radio station, where she is given her own show. **e** (Rev: SLJ 6/12)

331 Cornwell, Autumn. *Carpe Diem* (9–12). 2007, Feiwel & Friends $16.95 (978-0-312-36792-3). Sixteen-year-old Vassar, hitherto leading a well-planned life, suddenly finds herself whisked off to backpack through Southeast Asia with her artistic grandmother and having unexpected adventures. ♩ (Rev: BL 8/07; SLJ 11/07)

332 Corrigan, Eireann. *Ordinary Ghosts* (9–12). 2007, Scholastic $16.99 (978-0-439-83243-4). Emil, 16, is reeling from his mother's death and older brother's disappearance when he discovers a master key to the boarding school where he lives; this leads to a relationship with a new friend, Jade, who helps him deal with subsequent revelations. (Rev: BL 5/15/07; LMC 10/07; SLJ 6/07)

333 Costello, Emily. *Ski Share: VT (Vermont)* (9–12). 2006, Simon & Schuster paper $8.99 (978-1-4169-1466-2). Six very different teenagers ski, snowboard, work, party, blog, and sometimes fight during a three-month ski and work program at Killington; this fast-paced novel features sex, drinking, and bad language. (Rev: SLJ 5/06)

334 Couloumbis, Audrey. *Not Exactly a Love Story* (8–11). 2012, Random House $16.99 (978-0-375-86783-5); LB $19.99 (978-037596783-2). After his dog dies and his parents get divorced, 15-year-old Vinnie finds himself living in Long Island and conducting a rocky relationship with a cute girl. ♩ **e** (Rev: BL 12/1/12; LMC 5–6/13; SLJ 11/12; VOYA 12/12)

335 Crane, Dede. *Poster Boy* (8–12). 2009, Groundwood $17.95 (978-0-88899-855-2). When his younger sister is diagnosed with late-stage cancer, 16-year-old Gray Fallon's focus changes from parties and fun to an obsessive crusade against chemicals and toxins. Lexile 700L (Rev: BL 8/09; LMC 5–6/10; SLJ 12/09)

336 Craven, Margaret. *I Heard the Owl Call My Name* (7–12). 1973, Dell paper $6.99 (978-0-440-34369-1). A terminally ill Anglican priest and his assignment in a coastal Indian community in British Columbia. The nonfiction story behind this book is told in *Again Calls the Owl*.

337 Crew, Linda. *Brides of Eden: A True Story Imagined* (7–12). 2001, HarperCollins LB $15.89 (978-0-06-028751-1). Teenage Eva Mae Hurt describes the influence that magnetic preacher Joshua Creffield has on a group of women, who renounce their families and their everyday lives to follow his lead in this book based on fact, set in early 20th-century Oregon. (Rev: BCCB 2/01; BL 12/15/00; HB 3–4/01; HBG 10/01; SLJ 2/01; VOYA 6/01)

338 Crewe, Megan. *The Way We Fall* (9–12). 2012, Hyperion $16.99 (978-142314616-2). As a deadly virus threatens her small island community in Canada, 16-year-old Kaelyn struggles to help. ♩ **e** (Rev: BL 2/15/12; HB 3–4/12; LMC 5–6/12; SLJ 6/12; VOYA 2/12)

339 Crutcher, Chris. *Athletic Shorts: 6 Short Stories* (8–12). 1991, Greenwillow $18.99 (978-0-688-10816-8). These short stories focus on themes important to teens, such as sports, father-son friction, insecurity, and friendship. (Rev: BL 10/15/91; SLJ 9/91*)

340 Cunningham, Michael. *Specimen Days* (11–12). 2005, Farrar $24.00 (978-0-374-29962-0). Channeling Walt Whitman, Cunningham weaves together three inventive and genre-rich stories of New York City, set in the mid-1800s, the 1920s, and the future; for mature teens. (Rev: BL 5/1/05; SLJ 10/05)

341 Curtis, Vanessa. *Zelah Green: One More Little Problem* (7–10). 2012, IPG/Egmont paper $7.99 (978-14052405-4-3). Zelah Green, first seen in 2011 and still suffering from obsessive compulsive disorder, is back in this novel about the summer Caro moves in and stirs things up. ℮ (Rev: BL 3/1/12; VOYA 2/12)

342 Cushman, Kathryn. *Another Dawn* (9–12). 2011, Bethany paper $14.99 (978-07642082-5-6). Grace, a Christian with a belief in a natural lifestyle — and no vaccinations, must revisit her thinking when her son becomes ill. ☊ ℮ (Rev: BLO 12/1–15/10)

343 Cusick, John M. *Girl Parts* (9–12). 2010, Candlewick $16.99 (978-0-7636-4930-2). David's parents worry about their popular son's callous behavior and get him a special robot companion called Rose with unexpected results. ☊ Lexile HL590L (Rev: BLO 8/10; HB 9–10/10; LMC 10/10; SLJ 10/1/10; VOYA 10/10)

344 Dahl, Sophie. *Playing with the Grown-ups* (10–12). 2008, Doubleday $24.00 (978-0-385-52461-2). Kitty is a serious teenager who gradually learns she is more grown up than her artist mother will ever be. (Rev: BL 3/1/08)

345 Dalby, Robert. *A Piggly Wiggly Christmas* (10–12). 2010, Putnam $24.95 (978-039915677-9). *A Piggly Wiggly Christmas,* the fourth book set in the southern town of Second Creek, follows the organizers of a caroling event as they attempt to help their townfolk amid personal and economic turmoil. (Rev: BL 10/1–15/10)

346 Damico, Gina. *Croak* (7–10). 2012, Houghton Mifflin paper $8.99 (978-05476083-2-7). Lex, a 16-year-old with delinquent tendencies, discovers her uncle is the Grim Reaper when she goes to live with him for a summer in this novel that blends humor and mystery. ☊ ℮ (Rev: BL 3/15/12; SLJ 4/12; VOYA 12/11)

347 Daswani, Kavita. *Salaam, Paris* (9–12). 2006, Plume paper $14.00 (978-0-452-28746-4). Beautiful Tanaya Shah struggles to stay true to her Muslim heritage as she moves from India to Paris to the center of the New York fashion world. (Rev: BL 6/1–15/06)

348 Davis, Tanita S. *Happy Families* (9–12). 2012, Random House $16.99 (978-0-375-86966-2). Talented twins Justin and Ysabel cope with the fact that their father is happier living as a woman. ℮ (Rev: LMC 10/12; SLJ 5/1/12; VOYA 6/12)

349 De Gramont, Nina. *Every Little Thing in the World* (8–11). 2010, Simon & Schuster $16.99 (978-1-4169-8013-1). Sent to a summer camp in Canada, 16-year-olds Sydney, who has just discovered she is pregnant, and her friend Natalia explore Sydney's options. ℮ Lexile 870L (Rev: BL 3/15/10; SLJ 4/10)

350 de la Cruz, Melissa. *Girl Stays in the Picture* (8–12). 2009, Simon & Schuster $16.99 (978-141696096-6). Gossip columns, news items, and parodies of real celebrities enliven this story of teens on a movie shoot in Saint-Tropez. (Rev: BL 7/09; SLJ 8/09)

351 de la Peña, Matt. *We Were Here* (7–12). 2009, Delacorte $17.99 (978-0-385-73667-1); LB $20.99 (978-0-385-90622-7). Thoughtful 16-year-old Miguel escapes from a California juvenile detention center with two other teens, and they become friends as they struggle to find a way to live. ℮ (Rev: BL 9/1/09; HB 11–12/09; SLJ 12/09; VOYA 12/09)

352 De Vigan, Delphine. *No and Me* (8–11). 2010, Bloomsbury $16.99 (978-1-59990-479-5). A moving book set in Paris about 13-year-old Lou's decision to invite a vagrant 18-year-old girl into her home, a home that has been unhappy since the death of Lou's younger sister. (Rev: BL 8/10; LMC 8–9/10; SLJ 7/10)

353 Dean, Carolee. *Forget Me Not* (7–10). 2012, Simon & Schuster $16.99 (978-1-4424-3254-3). Aspiring actress Ally struggles with depression and self-loathing when a compromising photo of her goes viral in this novel written in verse and with a plot twist involving ghosts. ℮ Lexile HL720L (Rev: BLO 11/1/12; SLJ 12/12; VOYA 12/12)

354 Dean, Margaret Lazarus. *The Time It Takes to Fall* (10–12). 2007, Simon & Schuster $24.00 (978-0-7432-9722-6). Twelve-year-old Dolores, whose father works for NASA, wants to be an astronaut but the *Challenger* disaster has a big impact on her already rocky home life. (Rev: BL 12/15/06)

355 Dean, Zoey. *Girls on Film* (9–12). Series: The A-List. 2004, Little, Brown paper $8.99 (978-0-316-73475-2). A fast-paced novel of wealth, shopping, intrigue, and gossip in Beverly Hills, with Anna Percy having to decide between the unsuitable but attractive Ben and the suitable but less stimulating Adam, as well as coping with her recovering-addict sister Susan's arrival on the West Coast; a sequel to *The A-List* (2003). (Rev: SLJ 5/04)

356 Dean, Zoey. *Hollywood Is Like High School with Money* (10–12). 2009, Grand Central paper $13.99 (978-04466971-9-4). A light novel about a young woman whose job as an assistant to a movie executive wakes her up to the dog-eat-dog world of Hollywood. ℮ (Rev: BL 7/09)

357 Dean, Zoey. *How to Teach Filthy Rich Girls* (9–12). 2007, Warner $13.99 (978-0-446-69718-7). The charming, readable story of Megan, a Yale graduate between jobs who gets hired by a rich family to tutor their twin daughters well enough for them to get high SAT scores. (Rev: BL 6/1–15/07)

358 Deaver, Julie Reece. *Say Goodnight Gracie* (8–10). 1988, HarperCollins $15.00 (978-0-06-021418-0); paper $6.99 (978-0-06-447007-0). When her best friend Jimmy dies in an accident, Morgan struggles with her grief. (Rev: SLJ 2/88)

359 Delinsky, Barbara. *Not My Daughter* (11–12). 2010, Doubleday $25.95 (978-038552498-8). High-school principal Susan Tate is shocked to learn that her teenage daughter and friends have successfully made a pact to get pregnant; for mature readers. ⏺ ℮ (Rev: BL 12/1/09)

360 Dellasega, Cheryl. *nugrl90 (Sadie), Book 1* (9–12). Illus. by Karina LaPierre. 2007, Marshall Cavendish $15.99 (978-0-7614-5375-8); paper $6.99 (978-0-7614-5396-3). Fifteen-year-old Sadie blogs about her parents' divorce, her move to a new high school, and her new friends and classmates, who give her some new problems. (Rev: SLJ 1/08)

361 Denman, K. L. *Battle of the Bands* (9–12). Series: Orca Soundings. 2006, Orca $14.95 (978-1-55143-674-6). The Lunar Ticks — Jay, Kelvin, and Cia — are aiming high in this book for reluctant readers that combines three teen topics: rock music, romance, and competition. (Rev: SLJ 3/07)

362 Dessen, Sarah. *Along for the Ride* (9–12). 2009, Viking $19.99 (978-067001194-0). During her last summer before college, Auden learns about herself and falls in love while getting to know her father's new wife and baby. ⏺ ℮ Lexile HL750L (Rev: BL 4/15/09; HB 5–6/09; SLJ 6/1/09*; VOYA 6/09)

363 Devillers, Julia. *Lynn Visible* (7–10). 2010, Dutton $16.99 (978-0-525-47691-7). Lynn's 9th-grade classmates mock her flamboyant clothes until she is chosen as the "It Girl" for an online magazine. Lexile HL560L (Rev: BL 3/1/10; SLJ 4/10)

364 DeWoskin, Rachel. *Big Girl Small* (11–12). 2011, Farrar $25 (978-0-374-11257-8). Judy, 16, who is less than 4 feet tall and has a spectacular singing voice, finds that transferring to a performing arts school does not solve her problems — and she now faces an embarrassing scandal; for mature readers this offers a blend of humor and pathos. Alex Award 2012. (Rev: BL 2/1–15/11; SLJ 5/11)

365 Dexter, Pete. *Spooner* (10–12). 2009, Grand Central $26.99 (978-044654072-8). Irreverent and at times both funny and poignant, this faux-biography contains relationships that ring true, especially the one between difficult young protagonist Warren Spooner and his navy commander stepfather. ⏺ ℮ (Rev: BL 7/09)

366 Diaz, Alexandra. *Of All the Stupid Things* (9–11). 2009, Egmont $16.99 (978-1-60684-034-4); LB $19.99 (978-1-60684-066-5). Tara, Whitney, and Pinkie, in their senior year at high school, find their long-standing friendship threatened when Tara is attracted to new-girl Riley. ℮ (Rev: BLO 2/15/10; SLJ 4/10)

367 Divakaruni, Chitra Banerjee. *One Amazing Thing* (11–12). 2010, Hyperion $23.99 (978-140134099-5). Trapped in an Indian consulate in an unnamed American city in the aftermath of an earthquake, nine diverse strangers each tell a story from their lives; for mature readers. ⏺ (Rev: BL 1/1–15/10)

368 Doller, Trish. *Something Like Normal* (9–12). 2012, Bloomsbury $16.99 (978-1-59990-844-1). Travis, home from combat in Afghanistan, is already dealing with nightmares and flashbacks when he finds that his parents are divorcing and his ex-girlfriend is dating his brother; can a new friendship with Harper, a girl he dissed in middle school, bring him some solace? Best Fiction for Young Adults. ℮ (Rev: HB 5–6/12; LMC 10/12; SLJ 9/12; VOYA 4/12)

369 Doster, Stephen. *Lord Baltimore* (10–12). 2002, F. Blair $22.95 (978-0-89587-264-7). A naive young man sets off on a maturing, adventure-filled journey through Georgia, collecting strange characters as he goes. (Rev: BL 5/15/02)

370 Doyle, Brian. *Pure Spring* (9–12). 2007, Groundwood $16.95 (978-0-88899-774-6). Martin O'Boy, first introduced to readers in *Boy O'Boy*, now 15, tells a small lie that leads to bigger problems when he goes to work for the Pure Spring company in 1950s Ottawa. (Rev: BCCB 9/07; BL 7/07; HB 7–8/07*; SLJ 9/07; VOYA 10/07)

371 Doyle, Roddy. *A Greyhound of a Girl* (7–12). 2012, Abrams $16.95 (978-141970168-9). Covering several generations of an Irish family, this story features sassy 12-year-old Mary, her mother Scarlett, grandmother Emer, and Tansey, her great-grandmother, now a ghost. ℮ Lexile 500L (Rev: BL 3/15/12*; HB 5–6/12; LMC 8–9/12; SLJ 8/12)

372 Draper, Sharon M. *The Battle of Jericho* (7–10). 2003, Simon & Schuster $16.95 (978-0-689-84232-0). Sixteen-year-old Jericho is initially thrilled when he's asked to pledge for membership in the Warriors of Distinction club, but subsequent events turn chilling. (Rev: BL 6/1–15/03; HBG 4/04; SLJ 6/03; VOYA 8/03)

373 Draper, Sharon M. *Darkness Before Dawn* (8–12). Series: Hazelwood High. 2001, Simon & Schuster $16.95 (978-0-689-83080-8). Keisha Montgomery copes with many issues — the suicide of her ex-boyfriend, a new relationship, date rape, and more in this novel set at Hazelwood High. (Rev: BCCB 3/01; BL 1/1–15/01; HBG 10/01; SLJ 2/01; VOYA 8/01)

374 Draper, Sharon M. *Double Dutch* (7–10). 2002, Simon & Schuster $16.00 (978-0-689-84230-6). Eighth-graders Delia and Randy both have secrets — Delia can't read and Randy's father has disappeared, leaving him on his own. (Rev: BCCB 10/02; BL 9/1/02; HBG 10/02; SLJ 6/02; VOYA 8/02)

375 Draper, Sharon M. *Just Another Hero* (7–10). 2009, Simon & Schuster $16.99 (978-141690700-8). Bullying, family problems, drug addiction, thefts, and worries about school and college challenge the students introduced in *The Battle of Jericho* (2003) and *November Blues* (2007). ⏺ (Rev: BL 6/1–15/09; SLJ 7/1/09)

376 DuPrau, Jeanne. *Car Trouble* (7–10). 2005, Greenwillow LB $16.89 (978-0-06-073674-3). Seventeen-year-old Duff Pringle has various car and people adventures on the road from Virginia to a promised job in California. (Rev: BL 8/05; SLJ 10/05; VOYA 10/05)

377 Easton, Kelly. *To Be Mona* (8–11). 2008, Simon & Schuster $16.99 (978-141696940-2). Hampered by her life with a bipolar mother, 17-year-old Sage envies gorgeous class president Mona and overlooks friend Vern's devotion in favor of the attentions of the manipulative Roger; with an afterword about bipolar disorder and abusive relationships. **e** (Rev: BL 11/15/08; LMC 3–4/09; SLJ 1/1/09)

378 Easton, Kelly. *White Magic: Spells to Hold You* (8–11). 2007, Random House $15.99 (978-0-375-83769-2). After moving to Los Angeles, Chrissie befriends Yvonne (a self-proclaimed witch) and Karen, who welcome her to their coven in this book that is more about friendship than magic. (Rev: BL 6/1–15/07; HB 9–10/07; SLJ 12/07)

379 Efaw, Amy. *After* (9–12). 2009, Viking $17.99 (978-0-670-01183-4). Fifteen-year-old Devon must face the fact that she has had a baby and left it to die. ⌒ **e** (Rev: BL 8/09; LMC 11–12/09; SLJ 9/09; VOYA 8/09)

380 Ehrenberg, Pamela. *Ethan, Suspended* (7–10). 2007, Eerdmans $16.00 (978-0-8028-5324-0). After being suspended from school, Ethan is sent to live with his grandparents in inner-city Washington, D.C., where he's one of the very few white students and learns about segregation, poverty, making new friends, and falling in love. (Rev: BL 5/15/07; SLJ 7/07)

381 Ehrenberg, Pamela. *Tillmon County Fire* (9–12). 2009, Eerdmans paper $9.00 (978-080285345-5). Who set the fire that destroyed a valuable home in a small Appalachian town? A number of teens give their perspectives on this incident. Lexile 1060L (Rev: BL 4/15/09; SLJ 4/1/09)

382 Ehrenhaft, Daniel. *Friend Is Not a Verb* (7–10). 2010, HarperCollins $16.99 (978-0-06-113106-6). Music helps Henry (Hen) cope with a breakup with his girlfriend, a close friendship with Emma that may lead somewhere, and the mysterious disappearance and reappearance of his sister. ⌒ **e** (Rev: BL 3/1/10; SLJ 5/10)

383 Elkeles, Simone. *How to Ruin My Teenage Life* (7–10). Series: How to Ruin a Summer Vacation. 2007, Flux paper $8.95 (978-0-7387-1019-8). In this follow-up to *How to Ruin a Summer Vacation* (2006), Amy's life in Chicago with her Israeli father is full of irritating people, including her dad — who badly needs a girlfriend, her mother and her new husband and forthcoming baby, and a nerdy new guy in her apartment building. (Rev: SLJ 7/07)

384 Elkeles, Simone. *How to Ruin Your Boyfriend's Reputation* (8–12). 2009, Flux paper $9.95 (978-0-7387-1897-8). Seventeen-year-old Amy's scheme to spend some face time with her long-distance boyfriend lands her in boot camp with the Israeli Defense Force. **e** Lexile HL750L (Rev: SLJ 12/09; VOYA 2/10)

385 Ellis, Jamellah. *That Faith, That Trust, That Love* (10–12). 2003, Villard paper $12.95 (978-0-8129-6656-5). A young African American woman's new-found religious faith gives her strength to reassess her engagement and to look after her ailing mother. (Rev: BL 2/1/03)

386 Ellsworth, Loretta. *In a Heartbeat* (8–12). 2010, Walker $16.99 (978-0-8027-2068-9). Figure skater Eagan, 16, dies in a fall and her heart is given to ailing 14-year-old Amelia, a procedure that affects both girls as they describe in alternating chapters. **e** Lexile HL580L (Rev: BL 1/1–15/10; LMC 3–4/10; SLJ 2/10)

387 Epstein, Robin. *God Is in the Pancakes* (7–10). 2010, Dial $16.99 (978-0-803-73382-4). While working as a candy striper, 15-year-old Grace becomes friends with a man suffering from Lou Gehrig's disease, who eventually asks her to help him die. ⌒ **e** (Rev: BL 5/15/10; LMC 10/10; SLJ 5/10; VOYA 8/10)

388 Eslami, Elizabeth. *Bone Worship* (11–12). 2010, Pegasus paper $15.95 (978-16059807-4-4). Iranian American college dropout Jasmine stalls her father's plans to have her marriage arranged and learns a few things about him, herself, and what she wants out of life; for mature readers. **e** (Rev: BL 12/1/09)

389 Espinoza, Alex. *Still Water Saints* (11–12). 2007, Random House $23.95 (978-1-4000-6539-4). The 72-year-old owner of a shop selling mystical wares, herbs, and candles deals with the problems and tragedies of a small Southern California town. (Rev: BL 11/15/06)

390 Eyre, Lucy. *If Minds Had Toes* (10–12). 2007, Bloomsbury paper $12.95 (978-1-59691-300-4). Fifteen-year-old Ben finds himself in the middle of a dispute between Socrates and Wittgenstein — can ordinary people appreciate philosophy? (Rev: BL 11/15/06)

391 Ferre, Caridad. *Adios to My Old Life* (9–12). 2006, Pocket paper $9.95 (978-1-4165-2473-1). Much to her father's disapproval, Ali Montero is a finalist in a reality show to find the next Latin music star and finds love and friendship along the way. (Rev: BL 9/15/06)

392 Fifty Cent, and Laura Moser. *Playground* (7–10). 2011, Penguin $17.99 (978-1-59514-434-8). After a violent act, troubled and overweight black teen Butterball finds himself being egged on to perpetrate more violence by his peers. ⌒ **e** Lexile 900L (Rev: BLO 10/1/11; SLJ 11/1/11)

393 Finch, Susan. *The Intimacy of Indiana* (8–12). 2001, Tudor $5.95 (978-0-936389-79-0). Readers follow three teens through the trials of their senior year in high school in small-town Indiana — SATs, college finance, romance, drugs, and of course parents. (Rev: BL 7/01)

394 Fitch, Janet. *Paint It Black* (11–12). 2006, Little, Brown $24.99 (978-0-316-18274-4). When the son of a well-to-do pianist commits suicide, his wealthy mother and girlfriend — an artist's model and teen runaway — form an uneasy relationship; for mature teens. (Rev: BL 9/15/06)

395 Fitzgerald, Kitty. *Pigtopia* (11–12). 2005, Hyperion $22.95 (978-1-4013-5251-6). Jack, so badly disfigured that he lives among pigs in what he calls "the Pig Palace," finds a friend — and temporary happiness — in loner Holly, a neighboring teen; for mature teens. (Rev: BL 9/1/05)

396 Fitzpatrick, Huntley. *My Life Next Door* (9–12). 2012, Dial $17.99 (978-0-8037-3699-3). Privileged Samantha, 17-year-old daughter of a perfectionist politician, falls for neighbor boy Jase and his wild, loving family, and when tragedy strikes she must make a difficult choice. ∩ ℮ Lexile HL720L (Rev: HB 11–12/12; SLJ 6/12; VOYA 6/12)

397 Fleischman, Paul. *Seek* (7–12). 2001, Cricket $16.95 (978-0-8126-4900-0). For a school autobiography project, 17-year-old Rob makes a recording of important sounds in his life, including the voice of the father he never knew. (Rev: BCCB 11/01; BL 12/15/01; HB 11–12/01; HBG 3/02; SLJ 9/01*; VOYA 12/01)

398 Fletcher, Ralph. *One O'Clock Chop* (8–10). 2007, Henry Holt $16.95 (978-0-8050-8143-5). In 1973, 14-year-old Matt falls for his gorgeous first cousin Jazzy, who ends up breaking his heart. (Rev: BL 9/15/07; SLJ 10/07)

399 Flinn, Alex. *Diva* (8–11). 2006, HarperTempest $15.99 (978-0-06-056843-6). Caitlin (last seen in the 2005 *Breathing Underwater*) deals with her past abusive relationship, weight issues, troubles with her mom, and her dream of attending a performing arts school for opera. (Rev: BL 10/1/06; SLJ 11/06)

400 Fogelin, Adrian. *The Real Question* (7–10). 2006, Peachtree $15.95 (978-1-56145-383-2). Fisher Brown, 16, is just under too much pressure — from his counselor dad, academic stress, a sick dog, and so forth — and on an impulse he sets off to do an out-of-town roofing job with a carefree guy named Lonny. (Rev: LMC 3/07; SLJ 11/06)

401 Foley, John. *A Mighty Wall* (7–10). 2009, Flux paper $9.95 (978-073871448-6). Jordan's junior year in high school is all about rock climbing, friends, drinking, and sex—until an accident changes everything. ℮ (Rev: BL 3/1/09; SLJ 6/1/09)

402 Ford, Jeffrey. *The Shadow Year* (9–12). 2008, Morrow $25.95 (978-0-06-123152-0). In this amateur-detective novel written with a surrealist hand, young Mary and her friends may somehow be affecting the strange happenings in the suburbs as they rearrange figures on the toy model of the community in their basement. (Rev: BL 3/1/08)

403 Forman, Gayle. *If I Stay* (10–12). 2009, Dutton $16.99 (978-052542103-0). Seventeen-year-old Mia, critically injured in the crash that killed her parents, fights to survive, even as she reminisces, in first-person narrative, about people and events in her past, and wonders about her future in this fast-paced novel. ∩ Lexile 830L (Rev: BL 12/15/08; HB 7–8/09; SLJ 5/1/09*; VOYA 2/09)

404 Franco, Betsy. *Metamorphosis: Junior Year* (7–10). Illus. by Tom Franco. 2009, Candlewick $16.99 (978-0-7636-3765-1). After the sudden departure of his drug-addicted sister, high school junior, poet, and artist Ovid finds himself the sole focus of his suddenly overattentive parents in this contemporary novel that finds its inspiration in Roman mythology. ∩ Lexile HL740L (Rev: BL 9/1/09; SLJ 12/09; VOYA 2/10)

405 Frank, Hillary. *Better Than Running at Night* (10–12). 2002, Houghton Mifflin $17.00 (978-0-618-10439-0); paper $7.99 (978-0-618-25073-8). An entertaining portrayal of a freshman college student's growth in confidence about her romantic and academic life. (Rev: BCCB 10/02; BL 10/02*; HBG 3/03; LMC 4–5/03; SLJ 1/03; VOYA 2/03)

406 Franklin, Emily, and Brendan Halpin. *Tessa Masterson Will Go to Prom* (8–12). 2012, Walker $16.99 (978-080272345-1); paper $9.99 (978-08027235-9-8). The forthcoming prom is a catalyst to local scandal as high school senior Luke invites his best friend Tessa and she reveals she is in fact lesbian and intends to bring a female date. ℮ (Rev: BL 4/1/12; LMC 5–6/12; SLJ 4/12; VOYA 12/11)

407 Frederick, Heather Vogel. *Home for the Holidays* (6–10). 2011, Simon & Schuster $15.99 (978-144240685-8). The mother-daughter book club's girls cope with imperfections in their plans for relaxing holiday vacations. ℮ Lexile 840L (Rev: BLO 12/15/11; SLJ 10/1/11)

408 Fredericks, Mariah. *Crunch Time* (8–11). 2006, Simon & Schuster $15.95 (978-0-689-86938-9). Four members of a private SAT study group — who have formed emotional attachments as they study — find themselves under suspicion of cheating. (Rev: BL 1/1–15/06; SLJ 1/06; VOYA 12/05)

409 Freymann-Weyr, Garret. *After the Moment* (10–12). 2009, Houghton Mifflin $16.00 (978-061860572-9). When 17-year-old Leigh moves to Maryland to live with his father, stepmother, and stepsister, he finds himself entranced by a disturbed girl named Maia; set against the backdrop of the U.S. invasion of Iraq. (Rev: BL 6/1–15/09*; LMC 8–9/09; SLJ 5/1/09)

410 Freymann-Weyr, Garret. *The Kings Are Already Here* (7–10). 2003, Houghton $15.00 (978-0-618-26363-9). Phebe's love of ballet dominates her life until she travels to Geneva to visit her father and meets Nikolai, a 16-year-old refugee who is obsessed with chess.

(Rev: BL 2/15/03; HB 3–4/03; HBG 10/03; SLJ 4/03; VOYA 4/03)

411 Friedman, Aimee. *The Year My Sister Got Lucky* (7–10). 2008, Scholastic $16.99 (978-0-439-92227-2). When Katie and Michaela's parents move them from New York City to the Adirondacks, Katie is crushed and angry, while Michaela adapts and thrives. (Rev: BL 12/1/07; SLJ 3/08)

412 Friend, Natasha. *For Keeps* (8–11). 2010, Viking $16.99 (978-0-670-01190-2). Josie's life is changing as she navigates her junior year — she has a serious boyfriend, and her mother also has found someone; and then the father she has never met comes back to town and shakes things up. **e** (Rev: BL 1/1–15/10; HB 5–6/10; SLJ 4/10; VOYA 4/10)

413 Friesen, Gayle. *The Isabel Factor* (7–10). 2005, Kids Can $16.95 (978-1-55337-737-5). Anna's best friend Zoe breaks her arm and, for the first time in years, Anna finds herself running her own life. (Rev: BL 9/1/05; SLJ 11/05)

414 Gabriele, Lisa. *The Almost Archer Sisters* (11–12). 2008, Simon & Schuster paper $14.00 (978-074325586-8). After catching her husband in bed with her glamorous sister Beth, quiet Peachy decides to go to New York City alone to seduce Beth's boyfriend; for mature teens. (Rev: BL 9/1/08)

415 Garcia, Cristina. *Dreams of Significant Girls* (10–12). 2011, Simon & Schuster $16.99 (978-1-4169-7920-3). Three teen girls from different backgrounds — an Iranian princess, a German Canadian, and a Jewish Cuban America from New York — become friends as they spend summers at a Swiss boarding school in the 1970s. **e** Lexile 850L (Rev: BL 7/11; LMC 11–12/11*; SLJ 7/11)

416 Garfinkle, D. L. *Stuck in the 70's* (9–11). 2007, Putnam $16.99 (978-0-399-24663-0). Beautiful party girl Shay falls asleep in 2006 and awakens in the year 1978, where she meets smart, geeky Tyler, and they learn from one another; reluctant readers will enjoy this light novel. (Rev: BL 6/1–15/07; SLJ 6/07)

417 Gattis, Ryan. *Kung Fu High School* (11–12). 2005, Harcourt paper $13.00 (978-0-15-603036-6). Full of strong language and extreme violence, this is the story of a school that has been taken over by gangs, drug dealers, and martial arts experts. (Rev: BL 8/05; VOYA 2/06)

418 George, Madeleine. *Looks* (7–10). 2008, Viking $16.99 (978-067006167-9). High school seniors Meghan, who is fat, and Aimee, who is razor thin, form an unlikely alliance as they seek revenge against the popular and cruel Cara in this tense story. Best Books for Young Adults 2009. (Rev: BL 9/15/08*; HB 7–8/08; SLJ 5/08; VOYA 10/08)

419 Gilbert, Barbara Snow. *Paper Trail* (7–10). 2000, Front St $16.95 (978-1-886910-44-7). A thought-pro-voking story of a boy torn between family loyalties and connections to a cult known as the Soldiers of God. (Rev: BL 7/00; HB 7–8/00; HBG 9/00; SLJ 8/00)

420 Giles, Gail. *Dark Song* (7–11). 2010, Little, Brown $16.99 (978-0-316-06886-4). In this timely riches-to-rags story, well-heeled Ames's family lands on skid row, and the 15-year-old takes up with 22-year-old criminally inclined Marc. **e** Lexile HL570L (Rev: BL 9/1/10; SLJ 10/1/10; VOYA 10/10)

421 Going, K. L. *King of the Screwups* (7–12). 2009, Harcourt $17.00 (978-015206258-3). Straight athlete Liam's love of fashion and fun irks his strict father, so Liam moves in with his cross-dressing uncle — "Aunt Pete" — and tries to fit in in his new environment. Lexile HL690L (Rev: BL 4/15/09; SLJ 4/1/09*)

422 Gonzalez, Julie. *Wings* (8–11). 2005, Delacorte LB $17.99 (978-0-385-90253-3). A suspenseful story in which Ben is convinced he will someday sprout wings and take to the sky despite evidence to the contrary. (Rev: BCCB 4/05; BL 3/15/05; SLJ 8/05; VOYA 4/05)

423 Goobie, Beth. *Before Wings* (7–10). 2001, Orca $16.95 (978-1-55143-161-1). An absorbing story that centers on the counselors at a summer camp and on 15-year-old Adrien's past illness and present mystical experiences. (Rev: BL 3/15/01; HB 3–4/01; HBG 10/01; SLJ 4/01; VOYA 4/01)

424 Goobie, Beth. *The Lottery* (7–12). 2002, Orca $15.95 (978-1-55143-238-0). As the lottery winner, 15-year-old Sal must spend the year doing the bidding of a sinister student group, the Shadow Council. (Rev: BL 1/1–15/03; HBG 10/03; SLJ 3/03; VOYA 2/03)

425 Gore, Kristin. *Sammy's Hill* (9–12). 2004, Hyperion $23.95 (978-1-4013-5219-6). An entertaining story about the trials and tribulations of a young innocent on Capitol Hill, by the daughter of the former vice president. (Rev: BL 8/04)

426 Grace, Amanda. *In Too Deep* (7–11). 2012, Flux paper $9.95 (978-07387260-0-7). An effort to make her best friend Nick jealous backfires when high school senior Sam allows a rumor to proliferate. **e** Lexile 730L (Rev: BL 2/1/12; LMC 5–6/12; SLJ 3/12)

427 Graham, Hilary Weisman. *Reunited* (9–12). 2012, Simon & Schuster $16.99 (978-1-4424-3984-9). Three friends who have lost touch decide to join up on a cross-country road trip to see a final reunion concert by their favorite band — and have fun and revelations along the way. **e** Lexile 830L (Rev: BLO 7/12; SLJ 7/12)

428 Greene, Brian. *Icarus at the Edge of Time* (10–12). Illus. 2008, Knopf $19.95 (978-030726888-4). The tale of Icarus is told in a new futuristic setting of deep space — with black holes and gorgeous, mysterious galaxies shown in NASA and Hubble images; an inventive and appealing story presented on board rather than paper. (Rev: BL 9/1/08)

429 Greene, Jennifer. *Sparkle* (9–12). 2006, Harlequin paper $5.50 (978-0-373-88100-0). Sharp humor, strong characters, and emotionally lively writing mark this well-crafted story of the friendship that springs up between two women who each receive an unexpected inheritance from the town eccentric. (Rev: BL 7/06)

430 Griffin, Adele. *The Julian Game* (8–12). 2010, Penguin $16.99 (978-0-399-25460-4). Scholarship student Raye is eager to make friends at her elite school and agrees to help the popular Ella with Mandarin — and with an ill-advised Facebook attempt at revenge. e Lexile HL700L (Rev: BL 8/10; SLJ 10/1/10; VOYA 10/10)

431 Griffin, Paul. *The Orange Houses* (10–12). 2009, Dial $16.99 (978-080373346-6). Three New York teenagers deal with different challenges—impaired hearing, illegal immigrant status, and postwar stress. YALSA Top Ten 2010. Lexile HL610L (Rev: BL 5/1/09; SLJ 6/1/09; VOYA 10/09)

432 Grossman, Nancy. *A World Away* (9–12). 2012, Hyperion/Disney $16.99 (978-1-4231-5153-1). Amish 16-year-old Eliza takes a job as a nanny near Chicago and encounters for the first time everything from electricity, cell phones, and computers to makeup and shopping malls. ∩ e Lexile HL760L (Rev: LMC 3–4/13; SLJ 9/12; VOYA 8/12)

433 Gruen, Sara. *Ape House* (11–12). 2010, Spiegel & Grau $26 (978-038552321-9). Scientist Isabel would rather connect with her bonobo apes than most humans — until they escape and she has to deal with a motley assortment of her own kind, including an attractive but married reporter; for mature readers. ∩ e (Rev: BL 8/10)

434 Gurtler, Janet. *Who I Kissed* (8–11). 2012, Sourcebooks paper $9.99 (978-1-4022-7-054-3). When a boy she kissed dies of anaphylactic shock, Samantha finds herself isolated from her peers. e Lexile HL590L (Rev: BL 10/15/12; SLJ 11/12)

435 Haber, Melissa Glenn. *The Pluto Project* (7–10). 2006, Dutton $17.99 (978-0-525-47721-1). Alan Green acts cool and indifferent to cover up his emotions after his mother's death, but a new love interest and a spy game that turns realistic force him to confront his feelings. (Rev: BL 7/06; SLJ 7/06)

436 Hall, Barbara. *Tempo Change* (7–12). 2009, Delacorte $16.99 (978-038573607-7); LB $19.99 (978-038590585-5). High school sophomore Blanche hopes her band's gig at a music festival will help her meet her long-lost father. e (Rev: BL 7/09; SLJ 10/09)

437 Halperin, David. *Journal of a UFO Investigator* (11–12). 2011, Viking $25.95 (978-067002245-8). This entertaining coming-of-age novel features a teen UFO investigator dealing with bickering parents, skeptical friends, romantic complications — and aliens — in a small Pennsylvania town in the 1960s; for mature readers. ∩ (Rev: BL 1/1–15/11)

438 Halpern, Julie. *Don't Stop Now* (9–12). 2011, Feiwel & Friends $16.99 (978-0-312-64346-1). When a mutual friend fakes her own kidnapping, Lillian and Josh set out on a road trip to find her and explore their own relationship along the way. e Lexile 820L (Rev: BL 5/1/11; LMC 11–12/11; SLJ 7/11; VOYA 8/11)

439 Halpern, Julie. *Have a Nice Day* (8–12). 2012, Feiwel & Friends $16.99 (978-0-312-60660-2). After being treated for depression, Anna struggles to readjust to life outside a mental hospital — and to cope with her parents' failing marriage — in this sequel to 2007's *Get Well Soon*. e Lexile 870L (Rev: BL 11/1/12; LMC 3–4/13; SLJ 10/12)

440 Hand, Elizabeth. *Illyria* (10–12). 2010, Viking $15.99 (978-0-670-01212-1). In 1970s Yonkers teen cousins Maddy and Rogan, who are involved in a sexual relationship, are chosen to play roles in *Twelfth Night* that expose the difficulties of this first love. e Lexile HL790L (Rev: BL 5/15/10*; HB 7–8/10; LMC 10/10; VOYA 8/10)

441 Harper, Suzanne. *The Juliet Club* (8–12). 2008, Greenwillow $16.99 (978-006136691-8); LB $17.89 (978-006136692-5). In this light, modern-day Shakespearean tale set in Verona, Italy, six teens — three American and three Italian — study and perform scenes from *Romeo and Juliet* — that mirror the events of their own lives. Lexile 830L (Rev: BL 8/08; SLJ 7/08; VOYA 6/08)

442 Harrington, Laura. *Alice Bliss: A Novel* (10–12). 2011, Viking $25.65 (978-0-670-02278-6). When her father is missing in action in Iraq, 14-year-old Alice must take on a lot of the household chores from her stricken mother, and turns to her good friend Henry for support. e (Rev: BL 6/15/11; SLJ 7/11)

443 Hartman, Brett. *Cadillac Chronicles* (8–12). 2012, Cinco Puntos $16.95 (978-1-935955-41-2). On a mission to find his absent father, 16-year-old Alex sets off on a road trip with an elderly African American man named Lester. e Lexile HL650L (Rev: BL 12/15/12; SLJ 9/12*)

444 Harvey, Sarah N. *Plastic* (9–12). 2010, Orca $16.95 (978-1-55469-253-8). The focus on women's breasts will attract some reluctant readers to this story about 15-year-old Jack's concern about his friend who plans to have a "boob job." Lexile HL560L (Rev: BL 3/15/10; LMC 8–9/10; SLJ 7/10)

445 Hathaway, Jill. *Slide* (8–12). 2012, HarperCollins $17.99 (978-006207790-5). Vee has an ability to slide into the minds of others, and when she witnesses a murder in this way she struggles to solve this without revealing her secret. e (Rev: BL 4/1/12; HB 3–4/12; SLJ 3/12)

446 Hautman, Pete. *All-In* (7–10). 2007, Simon & Schuster $15.99 (978-1-4169-1325-2). Seventeen-year-old Denn, the poker prodigy last seen in *Stone Cold* (1998), finds his luck deserting him in this fast-action story. (Rev: BL 5/1/07; HB 7–8/07; SLJ 7/07)

447 Hautman, Pete. *Blank Confession* (8–11). 2010, Simon & Schuster $16.99 (978-1-4169-1327-6). Bullying, drugs, and violence are themes in this story about a 16-year-old named Shayne who walks into a police station and confesses to murder. (Rev: BL 10/1/10; SLJ 12/1/10)

448 Hautman, Pete. *What Boys Really Want* (8–11). 2012, Scholastic $17.99 (978-054511315-1). Adam borrows liberally from Lita's blog for his self-published advice book for boys, endangering their friendship. ℮ (Rev: BL 12/15/11; HB 3–4/12; VOYA 2/12)

449 Haworth-Attard, Barbara. *My Life from Air-Bras to Zits* (8–10). 2009, Flux paper $9.95 (978-0-7387-1483-7). Tenth-grader Teresa chronicles her life in this entertaining diary-style narrative by taking readers on an A to Z trip through her myriad social and domestic challenges. (Rev: SLJ 3/1/09)

450 Haycak, Cara. *Living on Impulse* (9–12). 2009, Dutton $16.99 (978-0-525-42137-5). Forced by her mother to get a job after she's caught shoplifting, 15-year-old Mia Morrow soon realizes that employment is the one stable factor in her otherwise tumultuous life. ℮ (Rev: BL 8/98; SLJ 12/09; VOYA 12/09)

451 Hazelwood, Robin. *Model Student: A Tale of Co-Eds and Cover Girls* (9–12). 2006, Crown $23.95 (978-0-307-33718-4). This insider's look at modeling follows 17-year-old Emily Woods as she frantically fights to keep up her grades while pursuing her supermodel dreams. (Rev: BL 6/1–15/06)

452 Hazuka, Tom. *Last Chance for First* (8–11). 2008, Brown Barn paper $8.95 (978-0-9798824-0-1). Robby, a high school junior, faces a lot of challenges: unfavorable comparisons with his older brother, an attraction to an unpopular girl, problems with his coach and a soccer teammate. . . . (Rev: BL 6/1–15/08; SLJ 9/08)

453 Headley, Justina Chen. *Girl Overboard* (7–11). 2008, Little, Brown $16.99 (978-0-316-01130-3). Super-rich Chinese American Syrah learns more about her family's heritage and about the satisfaction in helping others when she uses her family's power to help a sick friend. (Rev: BL 1/1–15/08; SLJ 2/08)

454 Heiligman, Deborah. *Intentions* (9–12). 2012, Knopf $16.99 (978-0375-86861-0); LB $19.99 (978-037596861-7). After hearing her rabbi committing infidelity, 15-year-old Rachel reconsiders her feelings about adults and about her own behavior. Sydney Taylor Book Award 2013. ℮ (Rev: BL 8/12*; SLJ 10/12; VOYA 6/12)

455 Henderson, Eleanor. *Ten Thousand Saints* (11–12). 2011, HarperCollins $26.99 (978-0-06-202102-1). Jude Keffy-Horn's life changes when his best friend Teddy dies of a drug overdose and Jude becomes involved in the Straight Edge punk scene in this novel set in late-1980s New York City; for mature readers. ℮ (Rev: BL 5/1/11; SLJ 8/11)

456 Hendrickson, Dave. *Cracking the Ice* (8–11). 2011, WestSide $16.95 (978-193481355-3). In 1968 African American Jessie Stackhouse confronts racism when he wins a hockey scholarship to a New Hampshire prep school. Lexile HL770L (Rev: BLO 12/15/11; LMC 8–9/12)

457 Henry, Patti Callahan. *Where the River Runs* (11–12). 2005, NAL paper $12.95 (978-0-451-21505-5). Meridy must revisit a tragedy in her youth in this novel set in South Carolina's Low Country; for mature teens. (Rev: BL 5/1/05)

458 Herbach, Geoff. *Nothing Special* (7–10). 2012, Sourcebooks paper $9.99 (978-1-4022-6-507-5). In this often funny sequel to *Stupid Fast* (2011), high school football player Felton Reinstein frets over the disappearance of his younger brother Andrew and sets out to find him. ℮ Lexile 630L (Rev: BL 6/12; SLJ 7/12; VOYA 6/12)

459 Hernandez, David. *No More Us for You* (9–12). 2009, HarperTeen $16.99 (978-006117333-2). California 17-year-olds Carlos and Isabel fall for each other in the wake of tragedy. ℮ (Rev: BL 1/1–15/09; SLJ 7/1/09; VOYA 2/09)

460 Hershey, Mary. *The One Where the Kid Nearly Jumps to His Death and Lands in California* (7–10). 2007, Penguin $15.99 (978-1-59514-150-7). Thirteen-year-old Stump, so named because one of his legs was amputated below the knee after a skiing accident, expects a difficult summer with his father and his new wife but in addition to dealing with his dad, he falls for a soap opera star and learns to swim. (Rev: BL 5/1/07; SLJ 3/07)

461 High, Linda Oatman. *Sister Slam and the Poetic Motormouth Road Trip* (8–12). 2004, Bloomsbury $16.95 (978-1-58234-948-0). Laura Rose Crapper, a.k.a. Sister Slam, and her friend Twig head for New York, where they meet a handsome boy named Jake. (Rev: BL 5/1/04; SLJ 5/04)

462 Hollings, Anastasia. *Beautiful World* (7–10). 2009, HarperTeen paper $8.99 (978-006143532-4). Amelia Warner wants a place in New York society and is determined to get it by hook or by crook in this first installment in a chick-lit series. ℮ (Rev: BL 7/09)

463 Holmes, Gina. *Crossing Oceans* (11–12). 2010, Tyndale paper $13.99 (978-14143330-5-2). With only months to live, a single mother returns home to face up to her past — and let her former boyfriend know he has a 5-year-old daughter — in this thoughtful, faith-based novel. ℮ (Rev: BL 5/1–15/10)

464 Holtwijk, Ineke. *Asphalt Angels* (8–12). Trans. by Wanda Boeke. 1999, Front St $15.95 (978-1-886910-24-9). When a homeless boy in the slums of Rio de Janeiro joins a street gang, the Asphalt Angels, for protection from corrupt police officers, pedophiles, and other homeless people, he finds himself being drawn into a life of crime. (Rev: BL 8/99; HBG 4/00; SLJ 9/99; VOYA 12/99)

465 Hopkins, Ellen. *Tilt* (10–12). 2012, Simon & Schuster $18.99 (978-1-4169-8330-9). Three teens — Mikayla, Shane, and Harley — describe their sexual and other relationships in this novel in verse that is a YA companion to the adult *Triangles* (2011). ⌒ ℮ Lexile HL620L (Rev: BL 7/12; SLJ 10/12; VOYA 10/12)

466 Houston, Pam. *Sight Hound* (11–12). 2005, Norton $23.95 (978-0-393-05817-8). Playwright Rae and her menagerie of pets are taken by surprise by a marriage proposal in this novel written from many points of view, including a dog's. (Rev: BL 11/15/04; SLJ 5/05)

467 Hubbard, Jennifer R. *The Secret Year* (9–12). 2010, Viking $16.99 (978-0-670-01153-7). Sixteen-year-old working-class Colt and rich Julia kept their affair a secret, which makes it hard for Colt to cope with his grief when she is killed in a crash. William C. Morris YA Debut Award Finalist 2012. Lexile HL650L (Rev: BL 12/1/09; SLJ 2/10)

468 Hubbard, Kirsten. *Wanderlove* (10–12). Illus. by author. 2012, Delacorte $17.99 (978-038573937-5); LB $20.99 (978-038590785-9). Young artist Bria, recovering from an unfortunate relationship, heads deep into the jungles of Central America with back-packer Rowan and his sister, eager to experience a new culture and get her creative juices flowing. ℮ (Rev: BL 4/1/12; LMC 8–9/12; SLJ 4/12)

469 Hughes, Mark Peter. *Lemonade Mouth* (8–11). 2007, Delacorte $15.99 (978-0-385-73392-2). Five teens in the band Lemonade Mouth take turns — tied together by a fan's comments — telling the story of their rise to fame (and their various stumbles) at Opoquonsett High in Rhode Island. (Rev: BCCB 6/07; BL 2/15/07; SLJ 5/07)

470 Huntley, Amy. *The Everafter* (8–11). 2009, Harper-Collins $16.99 (978-0-06-177679-3); LB $17.89 (978-0-06-177680-9). Working from the afterlife, 17-year-old Maddy Stanton attempts to unravel the mystery of how she met her untimely demise. ⌒ ℮ Lexile HL680L (Rev: BL 8/09; SLJ 12/09; VOYA 12/09)

471 Hutchinson, Shaun David. *The Deathday Letter* (10–12). 2010, Simon & Schuster paper $9.99 (978-1-4169-9608-8). After receiving a letter notifying him that he will die within 24 hours, 15-year-old Ollie and his two friends decide to try to fulfill his last wishes, some of which include driving, drugs, and sex. ℮ Lexile HL700L (Rev: BL 6/10; LMC 8–9/10; SLJ 11/1/10)

472 Hyland, M. J. *Carry Me Down* (9–12). 2006, Canongate $23.00 (978-1-84195-740-1). John Egan is a study in confusion — he is only 11 but he's nearly 6 feet tall and has a deep voice; he considers himself a good liar but can't understand why his father needs to tell lies — and his first-person narrative explains the threats of the adult world. (Rev: BL 2/15/06)

473 Jackson, Joshilyn. *Backseat Saints* (11–12). 2010, Grand Central $24.99 (978-044658234-6). When an airport gypsy tells troubled Rose to leave her abusive husband — or risk death — Rose listens, setting off a string of tense events; for mature readers. ⌒ ℮ (Rev: BL 4/15/10*)

474 Jackson, Lucy. *Posh* (9–12). 2007, St. Martin's $23.95 (978-0-312-36389-5). Told from multiple points of view, this novel is set at an elite private school in New York and is full of characters involved in various, often difficult, relationships. (Rev: BL 11/15/06; SLJ 1/07)

475 Jacobs, Kate. *Knit the Season* (9–12). Series: Friday Night Knitting Club. 2009, Putnam $24.95 (978-039915638-0). Set during the Christmas season, this heartwarming third installment follows the familiar, multigenerational characters as they deal with an impending marriage, a stalled romance, and life-changing decisions. ⌒ (Rev: BL 10/1/09)

476 Jacobson, Jennifer Richard. *Stained* (9–12). 2005, Simon & Schuster $16.95 (978-0-689-86745-3). A multilayered novel in which the disappearance of a young man who was sexually involved with a Roman Catholic priest is the most thought-provoking aspect. (Rev: BCCB 2/05; BL 4/1/05; HB 3–4/05; SLJ 3/05; VOYA 4/05)

477 James, Rebecca. *Beautiful Malice* (11–12). 2010, Bantam $25 (978-055380805-6). When grief-stricken, shy Katherine is befriended by emotionally troubled Alice, she slowly gains self-confidence — and a fresh perspective on her friend; for mature readers. (Rev: BL 6/1–15/10)

478 Jenkins, A. M. *Out of Order* (8–10). 2003, HarperCollins LB $16.89 (978-0-06-623969-9). Sophomore Colt relies on his good looks and athletic prowess to pull him through, but failing grades place him in the company of a brainy girl and his attitudes begin to change. (Rev: BL 9/1/03; HB 11–12/03; HBG 4/04; SLJ 9/03*; VOYA 10/03)

479 Jenkins, Jerry B. *Riven* (10–12). 2008, Tyndale $24.99 (978-1-4143-0904-0). In this Christian tale of reconciliation and redemption, troubled teenage Brady and failed preacher Thomas Carey come to rely on each other as their lives become increasingly chaotic. ⌒ ℮ (Rev: BL 6/1–15/08)

480 Johnson, Angela. *A Certain October* (7–12). 2012, Simon & Schuster $15.99 (978-0-689-86505-3). Scotty, 16, feels responsible when her classmate Kris dies in a train crash that Scotty and her younger, autistic brother survive. **e** Lexile 870L (Rev: BL 6/12; HB 9–10/12; LMC 8–9/12; SLJ 8/1/12*)

481 Johnson, Catherine. *Face Value* (9–12). 2006, Walker $16.95 (978-0-8027-8920-4). Lauren, 15, is pleased to have a modeling career ahead of her and is unaware that her guardian's anxiety stems from her worry that Lauren will follow the downward path of her dead mother, who was also a model. (Rev: BL 4/1/06; SLJ 9/06)

482 Johnson, Maureen. *The Last Little Blue Envelope* (8–11). 2011, HarperTeen $16.99 (978-0-06-197679-7). Eager to continue the scavenger hunt that will offer up clues to her late great aunt's personality, Ginny travels to London in this sequel to *13 Little Blue Envelopes* (2005). ⌒ **e** Lexile HL670L (Rev: BL 5/1/11; HB 5–6/11; SLJ 8/11; VOYA 4/11)

483 Johnson, Maureen. *Scarlett Fever* (8–10). 2010, Scholastic $16.99 (978-0-439-89928-4). In this follow-up to 2008's *Suite Scarlett,* life at the Hopewell Hotel has reverted to its usual humdrum pace, and 15-year-old Scarlett is desperate for something to break the ennui even as she handles various crises. ⌒ **e** Lexile 710L (Rev: BLO 12/8/09; HB 3–4/10; SLJ 1/10; VOYA 8/10)

484 Johnson, Maureen. *Suite Scarlett* (7–12). 2008, Scholastic $16.99 (978-0-439-89927-7). When Scarlett turns 15, she's "given" the Empire Suite in the family's rundown hotel to care for; the suite comes with Mrs. Amberson, an unusual long-term guest, and here this zany adventure involving four siblings begins. (Rev: BL 6/1–15/08)

485 Johnson, Maureen. *13 Little Blue Envelopes* (8–11). 2005, HarperCollins LB $17.89 (978-0-06-054142-2). On a trip through Europe following instructions left to her in 13 letters written by her Aunt Peg before her death, 17-year-old Ginny learns about Peg's past and about herself. (Rev: BL 9/15/05; SLJ 10/05; VOYA 10/05)

486 Jones, Carrie. *Girl, Hero* (7–10). 2008, Flux $16.95 (978-0-7387-1051-8). High school freshman Lili writes letters to John Wayne, confiding to this hero her worries about her perhaps-gay father, her mother's new boyfriend who likes to drink, her own romantic interests, school challenges, and so forth. Lexile HL700L (Rev: BLO 9/15/08; SLJ 1/1/09)

487 Jones, Patrick. *Chasing Tail Lights* (10–12). 2007, Walker $16.95 (978-0-8027-9628-8). Living in Flint, Michigan, 17-year-old Christy has no bright lights in her future — her father is dead, her oldest brother is in prison, Christy is looking after his daughter Bree, her mother's an alcoholic, and her brother Ryan is abusing her; yet Christy does find help. (Rev: BCCB 11/07; BL 9/15/07; LMC 1/08; SLJ 10/07)

488 Jones, Patrick. *Nailed* (9–12). 2006, Walker $16.95 (978-0-8027-8077-5). Bret's unconventional interests in music and theater cause difficulties for him both at home and at school. (Rev: BL 2/15/06; SLJ 5/06; VOYA 4/06)

489 Jones, Patrick. *Stolen Car* (8–12). 2008, Walker $16.99 (978-080279700-1). Enraged by the shabby behavior of the older boy for whom she neglected her friends, 15-year-old Danielle steals his car and takes off on a road trip with BFF Ashley. **e** (Rev: BL 11/15/08; LMC 1–2/09; SLJ 12/08; VOYA 2/09)

490 Jordan, Hillary. *When She Woke* (11–12). 2011, Algonquin $24.95 (978-1-56512-629-9). In a future where nonviolent criminals are melachromed (red for murder, yellow for a misdemeanor, and so forth), young Hannah undergoes an abortion to protect the leader of her church and wakes up to find herself red; she must flee north to find refuge. For mature readers. ⌒ **e** (Rev: BL 8/11*; SLJ 11/11)

491 Juby, Susan. *Another Kind of Cowboy* (8–11). 2007, HarperTeen $16.99 (978-0-06-076517-0). A horse story with a male protagonist, this novel set in Vancouver centers on Alex, who is 16 and questioning his sexuality, and on Cleo, a fellow dressage student who needs a friend. (Rev: BL 12/1/07; HB 1–2/08; SLJ 2/08)

492 Juby, Susan. *Getting the Girl: A Guide to Private Investigation, Surveillance, and Cookery* (8–10). 2008, HarperTeen $16.99 (978-006076525-5); LB $17.89 (978-006076527-9). Goodhearted Sherman Mack sets out to protect the reputations of girls in his school through a combination of sleuthing, persuasion, and ultimately standing up for his beliefs in this quirky first-person story. **e** (Rev: BL 10/1/08; HB 9–10/08; SLJ 11/1/08)

493 Kantor, Melissa. *The Breakup Bible* (8–10). 2007, Hyperion $15.99 (978-0-7868-0962-2). Jen turns to a book called *The Breakup Bible* after Max, the editor at her school's newspaper, dumps her for another girl. (Rev: BL 7/07)

494 Karasyov, Carrie, and Jill Kargman. *Bittersweet Sixteen* (7–10). 2006, HarperCollins $15.99 (978-0-06-077844-6). Laura learns who her true friends are when new girl Sophie starts at her school and everyone starts planning their 16th-birthday parties. (Rev: SLJ 10/06)

495 Karasyov, Carrie, and Jill Kargman. *Summer Intern* (7–12). 2007, HarperCollins $16.99 (978-0-06-115375-4). In this entertaining novel, hardworking Kira gets a summer internship at a national fashion magazine in New York City and learns about both fashion and office politics. (Rev: SLJ 6/07)

496 Kashyap, Keshni. *Tina's Mouth: An Existential Comic Diary* (9–12). Illus. by Mari Araki. 2012, Houghton Mifflin $18.95 (978-061894519-1). High school sophomore Tina, from an East Indian family adapting to a new life is Southern California, creates a Sartre-inspired diary for an English class assignment. (Rev: BL 1/1/12*; HB 5–6/12)

497 Kate, Lauren. *The Betrayal of Natalie Hargrove* (9–12). 2009, Penguin paper $9.99 (978-1-595-14265-8). Palmetto Princess shoo-in Natalie and her boyfriend Mike cook up a scheme to ensure that Mike, not the much-disliked Justin, is crowned Prince; naturally, the prank goes awry and Natalie and Mike find themselves embroiled in an increasingly dangerous coverup. (Rev: BL 9/15/09; LMC 11–12/09; VOYA 4/10)

498 Kaye, Amy. *The Real Deal: Unscripted* (7–12). 2004, Dorchester paper $5.99 (978-0-8439-5315-2). Claire juggles a potential Broadway career, a romance with a teen star, and the needs of her newfound half-sister, all under the glare of reality TV cameras. (Rev: SLJ 5/04)

499 Kelly, Tara. *Amplified* (9–12). 2011, Henry Holt $16.99 (978-080509296-7). Spoiled Jasmine, 17, gets kicked out of her home and heads to California to live her dream of being in a rock band. Lexile HL550L (Rev: BL 11/1/11)

500 Kephart, Beth. *Small Damages* (9–12). 2012, Philomel $17.99 (978-0-399-25748-3). Pregnant teen Kenzie is sent to Spain so no one will find out about her baby and is surprised to find friendship and comfort there. ℯ (Rev: BL 7/12; LMC 1–2/13; SLJ 7/12; VOYA 8/12)

501 Kephart, Beth. *Undercover* (7–10). 2007, HarperCollins $16.99 (978-0-06-123893-2). Sensitive soul Elisa writes love letters for boys to give to their girlfriends as she deals with problems at home and tries to find solace in nature and her love of ice skating; her growing friendship with Theo gives her hope. ⋒ (Rev: BL 10/15/07; SLJ 10/07)

502 Keplinger, Kody. *A Midsummer's Nightmare* (9–12). 2012, Little, Brown $17.99 (978-0-316-08422-2). Whitley, 18, is horrified to find out that her father has moved in with his fiancee — and her daughter and her son, the guy Whitley had a disastrous drunken lovemaking session with on the night of her graduation. ℯ (Rev: SLJ 7/12)

503 Kerney, Kelly. *Born Again* (9–12). 2006, Harcourt paper $14.00 (978-0-15-603145-5). Fourteen-year-old Melanie questions her faith when she reads Darwin's *Origin of the Species*. (Rev: BL 8/06; SLJ 2/07)

504 Kerr, M. E. *Deliver Us from Evie* (10–12). 1995, HarperTrophy paper $6.99 (978-0-06-447128-2). A multilayered story about the impact on the individual members of a Missouri farm family when 18-year-old Evie enters a lesbian relationship with the local banker's daughter. (Rev: BL 9/15/94; HB 1/95*)

505 Key, Watt. *Dirt Road Home* (7–10). 2010, Farrar $16.99 (978-0-374-30863-6). Eager to get out of the state home for juvenile delinquents, 14-year-old Hal tries to behave amid the pervasive gang violence and hopes that his father will quit drinking. ℯ Lexile HL540L (Rev: BL 6/10; HB 9–10/10; LMC 11–12/10; SLJ 11/1/10; VOYA 12/10)

506 Kiernan, Kristy. *Matters of Faith* (11–12). 2008, Berkley paper $14.00 (978-042522179-2). Eighteen-year-old Marshall's zealous girlfriend attempts to "cure" his sister of her life-threatening food allergy, with disastrous results. ℯ (Rev: BL 7/08)

507 Killian, Beth. *Life as a Poser* (10–12). Series: The 310. 2006, Pocket paper $9.95 (978-1-4165-2031-3). A teenage girl moves to Los Angeles and befriends spoiled young celebrities while working for her talent-agent aunt. (Rev: BL 7/06)

508 King, A. S. *Please Ignore Vera Dietz* (10–12). 2010, Knopf $16.99 (978-0-375-86586-2); LB $19.99 (978-0-375-96586-9). High school senior Vera Dietz trusted her friend Charlie, but he betrayed her and then died; now his ghost is asking her to clear his name. Printz Honor 2011. ⋒ ℯ (Rev: BL 11/15/10*; SLJ 12/1/10)

509 Kirby, Jessi. *In Honor* (9–12). 2012, Simon & Schuster $16.99 (978-144241697-0). Honor ends up on an impulsive road trip bound for California when her brother Finn is killed in Iraq. ℯ Lexile 850L (Rev: BLO 6/12; SLJ 5/1/12; VOYA 4/12)

510 Kittle, Katrina. *Reasons to Be Happy* (7–10). 2011, Sourcebooks paper $7.99 (978-1-4022-6-020-9). When her movie star parents spiral downward — her mother with cancer, her father with alcohol — Hannah's aunt takes her on a trip to Ghana, hoping to arrest Hannah's own descent into bulimia. ℯ Lexile 690L (Rev: BL 10/1/11; LMC 3–4/12; SLJ 12/1/11)

511 Klass, David. *Dark Angel* (8–11). 2005, Farrar $17.00 (978-0-374-39950-4). Seventeen-year-old Jeff's family has hidden the existence of his older brother, a murderer who has been in jail; when Troy is released and comes home to live, Jeff's life is turned upside down. (Rev: BL 9/15/05; SLJ 10/05; VOYA 10/05)

512 Kluger, Steve. *My Most Excellent Year: A Novel of Love, Mary Poppins, and Fenway Park* (8–12). 2008, Dial $16.99 (978-0-8037-3227-8). The freshman year of three diverse Boston-area teenagers is filled with romance, good works, sexual awakenings, sports, and more, as revealed in this collection of entries that includes letters, poems, e-mails, and other artifacts. (Rev: BL 3/15/08; SLJ 4/08)

513 Koertge, Ron. *Deadville* (9–12). 2008, Candlewick $16.99 (978-076363580-0). Ryan is compelled to re-evaluate the drug-riddled, isolated life he chose after his sister's death two years ago when he visits his comatose classmate Charlotte in the hospital. Lexile HL560L (Rev: BL 11/15/08; LMC 3–4/09; SLJ 11/1/08; VOYA 12/08)

514 Kokie, E. M. *Personal Effects* (9–12). 2012, Candlewick $16.99 (978-076365527-3). Matt, 17, makes surprising discoveries about his brother after T.J. is killed in Iraq. YALSA Amazing Audiobooks Top Ten 2013. ⋒

e (Rev: BL 10/15/12; HB 9–10/12; LMC 1–2/13*; SLJ 1/13; VOYA 8/12)

515 Konigsberg, Bill. *Out of the Pocket* (9–12). 2008, Dutton $16.99 (978-052547996-3). High school quarterback Bobby Framingham's homosexuality is suddenly revealed and the teen faces a range of reactions while also dealing with his father's cancer diagnosis. **e** Lexile HL710L (Rev: BL 9/1/08; SLJ 9/1/08)

516 Koss, Amy Goldman. *Poison Ivy* (7–10). 2006, Roaring Brook $16.95 (978-1-59643-118-8). Multiple voices tell the story of the mock trial of the three bullies who have been making unpopular Ivy's life a misery. (Rev: BL 2/15/06; SLJ 3/06; VOYA 4/06)

517 Kraft, Erik P. *Miracle Wimp* (8–11). Illus. by author. 2007, Little, Brown $16.99 (978-0-316-01165-5). In often humorous anecdotes with accompanying drawings, Tom Mayo describes a year of his high school life as he deals with school and bullies, makes friends, gets his license, and finds a girlfriend. (Rev: BL 6/1–15/07; SLJ 10/07)

518 Kraus, Daniel. *The Monster Variations* (8–12). 2009, Delacorte $16.99 (978-038573733-3); LB $19.99 (978-038590659-3). James remembers the summer he was 12 and the wave of violence that swept his small town, terrifying him and his friends. (Rev: BLO 6/1/09; LMC 10/09; SLJ 11/09)

519 Krauss, Nicole. *The History of Love* (11–12). 2005, Norton $23.95 (978-0-393-06034-8). The stories of Leo Gursky, a retired locksmith who once wrote a book about his love for Alma back in pre-Nazi Poland, and of lonely 14-year-old Alma intersect in this rich novel full of twists. (Rev: BL 3/15/05)

520 Kraut, Julie. *Slept Away* (7–10). 2009, LB $11.99 (978-038590661-6); paper $8.99 (978-038573737-1). Very urban Laney Parker, 15, has a hard time adapting when she is sent to a summer camp in the Pennsylvania countryside. (Rev: BL 7/09; SLJ 8/09)

521 Krusoe, Jim. *Iceland* (11–12). 2002, Archive paper $14.95 (978-1-56478-314-1). This offbeat novel follows typewriter repairman Paul through successive, strangely surreal medical and romantic encounters; for mature teens. (Rev: BL 5/15/02*)

522 Kuehnert, Stephanie. *I Wanna Be Your Joey Ramone* (11–12). 2008, Pocket paper $13.00 (978-141656269-6). Punk rocker's daughter Emily starts her own band and finds instant success in this fast-paced story of teenage rebellion, search for a missing mother, and redemption; for mature readers. **e** (Rev: BL 6/1–15/08)

523 LaBan, Elizabeth. *The Tragedy Paper* (7–12). 2013, Knopf $17.99 (978-037587040-8); LB $20.99 (978-037597040-5). A suspenseful story set in a private school with traditions that affect the students' studies

and romantic relationships. ∩ **e** (Rev: BL 11/15/12*; SLJ 2/13; VOYA 12/12)

524 LaCour, Nina. *The Disenchantments* (9–12). 2012, Dutton $16.99 (978-052542219-8). Colby thought he and his best friend Bev would tour with her band and then spend a year in Europe, but everything changes when she announces she is going to college in this music-filled novel. **e** Lexile 780L (Rev: BL 3/15/12*; HB 5–6/12; SLJ 1/12; VOYA 2/12)

525 Lamm, Drew. *Bittersweet* (8–11). 2003, Clarion $15.00 (978-0-618-16443-1). When Taylor's grandmother, who has essentially raised her, falls ill, artist Taylor suddenly finds she lacks creativity and is unsure of her other relationships. (Rev: BCCB 2/04; BL 11/15/03; HBG 4/04; SLJ 12/03; VOYA 12/03)

526 Langan, John. *Search for Safety* (7–12). Series: Bluford. 2006, Townsend paper $4.95 (978-1-59194-070-8). Sophomore Ben is new at Bluford High and must find someone to talk to about his abusive home life before it is too late; suitable for reluctant readers. (Rev: SLJ 7/07)

527 Langan, Paul. *The Fallen* (7–12). Series: Bluford. 2006, Townsend paper $4.95 (978-1-59194-066-1). Martin Luna starts his sophomore year at Bluford High with the goal of avoiding the gang conflicts that took his brother's life; suitable for reluctant readers. (Rev: SLJ 7/07)

528 Langan, Paul. *Shattered* (7–12). Series: Bluford. 2006, Townsend paper $4.95 (978-1-59194-069-2). When Darcy's ex-boyfriend returns to town, the 11th-grader must come to terms with her past; suitable for reluctant readers. (Rev: SLJ 7/07)

529 Larson, Kirby. *Hattie Big Sky* (7–10). 2006, Delacorte $17.99 (978-0-385-73313-7). Hattie Brooks, a 16-year-old orphan, inherits a Montana homestead from her uncle, and learns to farm the land and make a home for herself despite the many difficulties she faces. Newbery Honor 2007. (Rev: BL 9/1/06; SLJ 11/06*)

530 Laxer, Mark. *The Monkey Bible: A Modern Allegory* (11–12). Illus. 2010, Outer Rim $25 (978-096381080-9). A spiritual college student faces a crisis of faith and identity when he discovers he is half-man, half-ape in this thought-provoking novel. (Rev: BL 9/1–15/10)

531 Lecesne, James. *Absolute Brightness* (8–12). 2008, HarperTeen $17.99 (978-0-06-125627-1). A gay teenager disappears from a small New Jersey town in this multilayered, well-written novel. (Rev: SLJ 3/08; VOYA 4/08)

532 Lee, Wendy. *Happy Family* (9–12). 2008, Grove paper $14.00 (978-0-8021-7046-0). When Chinese immigrant Hua Wu becomes nanny to an adopted Chinese girl, she finds herself observing an unhappy family. (Rev: BL 4/15/08)

533 Lennon, Stella, and Melissa Kantor. *Invisible I* (7–10). Series: The Amanda Project. 2009, HarperCollins $16.99 (978-0-06-174212-5). Callie is facing enough problems at home when she finds herself implicated in defacing the vice principal's car. She is sure her friend Amanda was the perpetrator, but where is Amanda now? ☊ ℮ (Rev: BL 8/09; LMC 1–2/10; SLJ 9/09)

534 Lerangis, Peter. *wtf* (9–12). 2009, Simon & Schuster paper $8.99 (978-1-4169-1360-3). In alternate narratives, six teens describe an eventful and tense night in New York City where a drug deal gets complicated. ℮ (Rev: BL 10/15/09; SLJ 2/10; VOYA 12/09)

535 Levin, Adam. *The Instructions* (11–12). 2010, Mc-Sweeney's $29 (978-193478182-1). This tour de force of a debut novel features a troubled 10-year-old Jewish genius named Gurion ben-Judah Maccabee who, upon being kicked out of school for violence, enlists his treatment program cohorts in a messianic army; this long, funny and at the same time troubling, novel is suitable for mature, advanced readers. (Rev: BL 10/1–15/10)

536 Levithan, David. *Wide Awake* (8–11). 2006, Knopf $16.95 (978-0-375-83466-0). When a recount is demanded after a gay Jewish man is elected president, Duncan — with his boyfriend Jimmy — joins the millions who protest and learns a lot about himself, his beliefs and feelings. (Rev: BL 9/15/06; SLJ 9/06)

537 Lewis, Wendy. *Graveyard Girl* (7–10). 2000, Red Deer paper $7.95 (978-0-88995-202-7). While looking back at her high school yearbook, Ginger reminisces about her classmates and vignettes reveal their stories of marriage, achievement, and lost romance. (Rev: BL 1/1–15/01; SLJ 5/01; VOYA 6/01)

538 Linko, Gina. *Flutter* (7–12). 2012, Random House $16.99 (978-037586996-9); LB $19.99 (978-037596996-6). A suspenseful story about 17-year-old Emery, who suffers seizures that lead her into adventure and romance. ℮ (Rev: BL 11/15/12; LMC 1–2/13; SLJ 1/13; VOYA 8/12)

539 Linz, Cathie. *Big Girls Don't Cry* (9–12). 2007, Berkley paper $7.99 (978-0-425-21831-0). As a plus-size model's career winds down, she must move back to her small hometown and deal with her lingering low self-esteem and people who don't seem to want to let go of the past. (Rev: BL 9/15/07)

540 Lockhart, E. *The Disreputable History of Frankie Landau-Banks* (7–12). 2008, Hyperion $16.99 (978-0-7868-3818-9). In her sophomore year at Alabaster Prep, Frankie shakes up her boyfriend's all-male secret club, the Loyal Order of the Basset Hounds, and brings much-needed change to her elite boarding school; combining humor and social commentary, this is an appealing book full of wordplay. ☊ (Rev: BL 1/1–15/08; HB 5–6/08; LMC 10/08; SLJ 3/08)

541 Lockhart, E., et al. *How to Be Bad* (9–12). 2008, HarperTeen $16.99 (978-0-06-128422-9). Teenagers Jesse, Vicks, and Mel — each with her own problems — take a road trip to Miami and find out a lot about themselves on the way; told in alternating chapters in this interesting book written by three popular novelists. (Rev: BL 3/1/08; SLJ 5/08)

542 Lodato, Victor. *Mathilda Savitch* (10–12). 2009, Farrar $25 (978-0-374-20400-6). Grief-stricken after the death of her beloved 16-year-old sister, Mathilda sets out to confront the man she believes is responsible; however, the man she finds is not the heartless murderer that she expected in this often humorous novel. (Rev: BL 8/09; SLJ 2/10)

543 Lodge, Hillary Manton. *Plain Jayne* (10–12). 2010, Harvest paper $13.99 (978-07369269-8-0). After the death of her father, journalist Jayne is forced to regroup and turns to the nearby Amish community for a new perspective on life; there she also finds a new love. ℮ (Rev: BL 11/15/09)

544 Lowry, Brigid. *Guitar Highway Rose* (8–12). 2003, Holiday $16.95 (978-0-8234-1790-2). Set in Australia, this story of two teens who run away from home presents the voices of various characters including teachers, family, and friends. (Rev: BL 2/15/04; HBG 4/04; SLJ 12/03; VOYA 4/04)

545 Ludwig, Elisa. *Pretty Crooked* (7–10). 2012, HarperCollins $17.99 (978-0-06-206606-0). A newcomer to a prep school for wealthy kids, artist's daughter Willa tries to even the score by stealing from her well-heeled and often bullying classmates and distributing the spoils among the poorer ones. ℮ (Rev: BL 1/1/12; SLJ 7/12; VOYA 12/11)

546 Luongo, Julie. *The Hard Way* (9–12). 2008, Forge paper $13.95 (978-0-7653-1667-7). Creativity and a sense of humor keeps twenty-something Lucy Venier going as she flounders through a hodgepodge of bad jobs and bad men. (Rev: BL 4/15/08)

547 Lurie, April. *The Latent Powers of Dylan Fontaine* (8–12). 2008, Delacorte $15.99 (978-0-385-73125-6). Sixteen-year-old Dylan's problems include separated parents, a brother doing drugs, his own arrest for shoplifting, and his best friend Angie appearing unaware of his romantic interest; humor adds to the appeal of this story. (Rev: BL 4/1/08; SLJ 9/08)

548 Lyga, Barry. *The Astonishing Adventures of Fanboy and Goth Girl* (8–11). 2006, Houghton Mifflin $16.95 (978-0-618-72392-8). Fanboy confides in his friend Goth girl and creates his own comic book as a way of escaping the violence he experiences at school. (Rev: BL 9/1/06; SLJ 11/06)

549 Lynch, Chris. *Inexcusable* (9–12). 2005, Simon & Schuster $16.95 (978-0-689-84789-9). Keir, a senior in high school and football player, prides himself on being a "lovable rogue" and is used to rationalizing some of his less lovable activities, but can he convince himself of his innocence when he rapes Gigi? (Rev: BL 9/15/05*; SLJ 11/05*; VOYA 12/05)

550 Lynch, Chris. *Sins of the Fathers* (9–12). 2006, HarperCollins $16.99 (978-0-06-074037-5). Drew has been friends with Skitz and Hector since the first day of Catholic school and they have vowed to stick together no matter what. But when one of them faces being sent to public school and the other with serious problems of abuse from a priest, it's up to Drew to help them. (Rev: BL 8/06; SLJ 9/06)

551 McCall, Guadalupe Garcia. *Summer of the Mariposas* (7–12). 2012, Lee & Low $19.95 (978-1-60060-900-8). Magical realism and traditional Latin American folkloric characters combine with a family story as five sisters decide to return a drowned man's body to his family in Mexico. e Lexile 840L (Rev: BL 11/15/12; LMC 5–6/13; SLJ 11/12*; VOYA 12/12)

552 McCarthy, Tara. *Wouldn't Miss It for the World* (9–12). 2007, Simon & Schuster paper $13.00 (978-1-4165-0325-5). A lighthearted novel about June and Cash, bandmates in a rock group whose wedding trip to Belize with family and friends is full of the unexpected. (Rev: BL 8/07)

553 McCorkle, Jill. *Carolina Moon* (10–12). 1996, Algonquin $29.95 (978-1-56512-136-2). Quee opens a no-smoking clinic in Fulton, North Carolina, and finds that her staff and clients have a number of problems in addition to smoking in this novel that combines romance, mystery, and humor. (Rev: BL 5/1/98; SLJ 1/97)

554 McCullough, Kathy. *Don't Expect Magic* (7–11). 2011, Delacorte $17.99 (978-0-385-74012-8). Still reeling from her mother's death, Delaney, 15, moves to California to live with her dad, and is much surprised to learn that he is a fairy godmother — and that she may well have the same powers. But how will this impact her life? e Lexile 800L (Rev: LMC 3–4/12; SLJ 6/12; VOYA 2/12)

555 McDonald, Abby. *The Anti-Prom* (8–11). 2011, Candlewick $16.99 (978-0-7636-4956-2). Bliss, Jolene, and Meg, students who barely know each other, all arrive at the prom with different problems — but they offer support where they can. ⌒ e Lexile HL720L (Rev: BL 4/1/11; SLJ 6/11; VOYA 6/11)

556 McDonald, Abby. *Sophomore Switch* (9–12). 2009, Candlewick $17.99 (978-076363936-5). British Emily and California girl Tasha do a student exchange and try out each other's lifestyles in this entertaining and insightful novel. e Lexile HL780L (Rev: BL 2/15/09; LMC 8–9/09; SLJ 6/1/09)

557 MacDonald, Ann-Marie. *The Way the Crow Flies* (11–12). 2003, HarperCollins $26.95 (978-0-06-057895-4). In the early 1960s, an innocently happy

family finds that it must confront issues including former Nazis and sex abuse of an 8-year-old; for mature readers. (Rev: BL 9/1/03*)

558 McGhee, Alison. *Falling Boy* (10–12). 2007, Picador paper $13.00 (978-0-312-42592-0). Wheelchair-bound Joseph, 16, works in a Minneapolis bakery with Zap, 17, son of the bakery's owner; a troubled 9-year-old girl named Enzo comes in frequently and Zap spins for her stories about Joseph that turn him into a superhero. (Rev: BL 2/15/07; SLJ 4/07)

559 Mackler, Carolyn. *Guyaholic: A Story About Finding, Flirting, Forgetting, and the Boy Who Changes Everything* (10–12). 2007, Candlewick $16.99 (978-0-7636-2537-5). V (who we first met in 2004's *Vegan Virgin Valentine*) becomes sexually involved with Sam Almond, but her fear of forming a strong relationship prompts her to cheat; Sam takes off and V, recently disappointed by her mother yet again, decides to drive from New York to Texas to see her. (Rev: BL 9/15/07; SLJ 1/08)

560 Mackler, Carolyn. *Tangled* (9–12). 2010, HarperTeen $16.99 (978-0-06-173104-4). On vacation in the Caribbean teens Jena (inferiority complex) and Skye (beautiful but depressed) have complex interactions with brothers Dakota (an overconfident drinker) and Owen (insecure geek); told in alternating first-person narratives. e Lexile HL750L (Rev: BL 1/1–15/10; SLJ 1/10; VOYA 2/10)

561 McLaughlin, Emma, and Nicola Kraus. *The Real Real* (9–12). 2009, HarperTeen $16.99 (978-0-06-172040-6). In this fast-paced page-turner, high school senior Jesse accepts a role on a new reality TV series — trading all semblance of "normal life" for a $40 K scholarship — and ends up more servant than star, compromising her integrity for the sake of her career. (Rev: SLJ 7/1/09; VOYA 8/09)

562 McNally, John. *America's Report Card* (9–12). 2006, Free Press $24.00 (978-0-7432-5626-1). With her father in prison and her life in shambles, 17-year-old Jainey O'Sullivan writes a dark essay that catches the eye of a depressed employee of the National Testing Center who decides to find Jainey and rescue her. (Rev: BL 6/1–15/06)

563 McNally, John, ed. *The Student Body: Short Stories About College Students and Professors* (10–12). 2001, Univ. of Wisconsin paper $16.95 (978-0-299-17404-0). These short stories about college life by writers including Richard Russo and Stephen King are divided into two groups, from the students' point of view and from the teachers'. (Rev: BL 9/15/01)

564 McNeal, Laura. *Dark Water* (8–12). 2010, Knopf $16.99 (978-0-375-84973-2); LB $19.99 (978-0-375-94973-9). Troubled 15-year-old Pearl seduces a mute migrant worker and faces difficult choices when wildfires approach her California town and threaten her uncle's ranch. ℮ (Rev: HB 1–2/11; SLJ 10/1/10; VOYA 12/10)

565 McNeal, Laura, and Tom McNeal. *The Decoding of Lana Morris* (8–11). 2007, Knopf $15.99 (978-0-375-83106-5). Lana suffers through the circumstances of her foster home — four special needs kids, a foster father who behaves inappropriately — until she gets an art kit that appears to have magical powers. (Rev: BCCB 7–8/07; BL 4/1/07; SLJ 6/07)

566 McNicoll, Sylvia. *A Different Kind of Beauty* (7–10). 2004, Fitzhenry & Whiteside $15.95 (978-1-55005-059-2); paper $8.95 (978-1-55005-060-8). Elizabeth, who is training a puppy as a guide dog, and Kyle, whose diabetes has left him blind, attend the same high school without knowing each other. (Rev: SLJ 8/04; VOYA 8/04)

567 Madigan, L. K. *Flash Burnout* (9–12). 2009, Houghton Mifflin $16 (978-0-547-19489-9). Blake, 15, navigates high school with a feeling of optimism but has trouble when trying to juggle his new girlfriend Shannon and his best friend Marissa, who shares his love of photography. Best Books for Young Adults 2010. ♪ ℮ Lexile HL570L (Rev: BL 9/15/09*; SLJ 11/09)

568 Makkai, Rebecca. *The Borrower: A Novel* (10–12). 2011, Viking $25.95 (978-0-6700-2281-6). Children's librarian Lucy makes a risky decision when she rescues 10-year-old Ian from the fundamentalist parents who censor his reading and enroll him in antigay classes; an often humorous story about a love of books and a long road trip. ♪ ℮ (Rev: BL 5/1/11; SLJ 9/11)

569 Mancusi, Marianne. *Gamer Girl* (6–10). 2008, Dutton $16.99 (978-052547995-6). Manga drawing and the online game Fields of Fantasy help Maddy cope with her parents' divorce, unpopularity in her new school, and rejection by boys, but she eventually finds the courage to reach out to others. Lexile HL660L (Rev: BL 11/15/08; SLJ 1/1/09)

570 Mapson, Jo-Ann. *Solomon's Oak* (11–12). 2010, Bloomsbury $25 (978-160819330-1). A widow fostering a surly 14-year-old girl whose sister has disappeared receives help from a world-weary ex-cop with problems of his own in this novel about second chances; for mature readers. ♪ ℮ (Rev: BL 9/1–15/10)

571 Markham, Wendy. *Love, Suburban Style* (9–12). 2007, Warner paper $6.99 (978-0-446-61843-4). In this entertaining novel, actress Meg and her teenage daughter move back to the New York suburb in which Meg was raised, which seems unpromising until Meg finds that her new next-door neighbor is her old teenage crush. (Rev: BL 6/1–15/07)

572 Marks, Graham. *Radio Radio* (8–11). 2004, Bloomsbury paper $11.99 (978-0-7475-5939-9). A group of London club kids goes up against both the government and some unsavory competitors when they set up a pirate radio station. (Rev: BL 1/1–15/05; SLJ 1/05)

573 Marr, Maggie. *Secrets of the Hollywood Girls Club* (9–12). 2008, Crown $23.95 (978-0-307-34631-5). This light gossipy novel for celebrity addicts keeps absolutely no secrets. (Rev: BL 3/15/08)

574 Marsden, John. *Hamlet* (9–12). 2009, Candlewick $16.99 (978-0-7636-4451-2). This modernized version of the story emphasizes Hamlet's youth and typical teen anxieties. Lexile HL760L (Rev: SLJ 8/09; VOYA 12/09)

575 Marshall, Bev. *Walking Through Shadows* (11–12). 2002, MacAdam $25.00 (978-1-931561-05-1). In 1940s Mississippi, a girl with a humped back finds a generous employer and a young husband only to be murdered soon afterward; for mature readers. (Rev: BL 3/15/02; SLJ 8/02)

576 Martin, C. K. Kelly. *I Know It's Over* (9–12). 2008, Random House $16.99 (978-037584566-6); LB $19.99 (978-037594566-3). Starting with the bombshell of his ex-girlfriend's pregnancy and working backward, this story explores 16-year-old Nick's emotions and the various tensions he must deal with — including a gay best friend and divorced parents. ℮ (Rev: BL 11/15/08; SLJ 11/1/08)

577 Martinez, Jessica. *Virtuosity* (8–11). 2011, Simon & Schuster $16.99 (978-1-4424-2052-6). Carmen, 17, is a talented violinist and on the eve of an international competition she decides to tackle her dependence on anti-anxiety medication, her controlling mother, and her growing affection for her competitor Jeremy. ℮ Lexile HL710L (Rev: BL 12/1/11; LMC 1–2/12; SLJ 10/1/11)

578 Mass, Wendy. *Heaven Looks a Lot like the Mall* (7–10). 2007, Little, Brown $16.99 (978-0-316-05851-3). Thanks to a poorly aimed dodge ball, 16-year-old Tessa has a near-death experience and looks back on her life in free verse. (Rev: BL 10/15/07; SLJ 9/07)

579 Matlock, Curtiss Ann. *Little Town, Great Big Life* (11–12). 2010, MIRA paper $13.95 (978-07783278-8-2). In this conclusion to the Valentine series, reluctantly pregnant Belinda's family — and their pharmacy, an institution — prepare for their small town's centennial celebration.; for mature readers (Rev: BL 6/1–15/10)

580 Matson, Morgan. *Second Chance Summer* (7–12). 2012, Simon & Schuster $16.99 (978-1-4169-9067-3). When her father is diagnosed with pancreatic cancer, the family decides to spend the summer together at their Poconos lake house, and Taylor finds herself in the company of her former best friend and her first boyfriend after an absence of five years. ℮ Lexile 1020L (Rev: BL 8/12*; SLJ 7/12*; VOYA 8/12)

581 Maude, Rachel. *Poseur* (8–12). Series: Poseur. 2008, Little, Brown paper $9.99 (978-0-316-06583-2). Charlotte, Janie, Petra, and Melissa — who attend an expensive private school in Los Angeles — are assigned to work together on creating their own clothing line. (Rev: BL 3/3/08; SLJ 3/08)

582 Maynard, Joyce. *Labor Day* (11–12). 2009, Morrow $24.99 (978-006184340-2). An escaped convict charms his way into the lives of a 13-year-old boy and his emotionally vulnerable mother in this suspense-filled novel written from the perspective of young Henry; for mature readers. (Rev: BL 7/09)

583 Mechling, Lauren, and Laura Moser. *All Q, No A: More Tales of a 10th-Grade Social Climber* (9–12). Series: 10th-Grade Social Climber. 2006, Houghton Mifflin paper $7.99 (978-0-618-66378-1). In the sequel to *The Rise and Fall of a 10th-Grade Social Climber*, Mimi writes an exposé about a classmate's father for the school newspaper and gets in hot water. (Rev: SLJ 9/06)

584 Mechling, Lauren, and Laura Moser. *Foreign Exposure: The Social Climber Abroad* (7–10). 2007, Houghton Mifflin paper $8.99 (978-0-618-66379-8). Sixteen-year-old Mimi visits a friend in London and soon finds herself immersed in the celebrity gossip scene. (Rev: SLJ 6/07)

585 Meehl, Brian. *You Don't Know About Me* (9–12). 2011, Delacorte $17.99 (978-0-385-73909-2); LB $20.99 (978-038590771-2). Sixteen-year-old Billy, who has been homeschooled by his Christian mother, sets off on a geocaching expedition to find his Mark Twain scholar, and befriends a gay African American baseball player who decides to accompany him. 𝐞 Lexile HL650L (Rev: BL 5/1/11; SLJ 6/11; VOYA 6/11)

586 Meister, Ellen. *The Smart One* (10–12). 2008, Avon paper $13.95 (978-006112962-9). Bev Bloomrosen, the smart sister, house-sits for her parents over the summer and winds up involved in her sisters' troubles, unexpected romance, and a murder mystery in this entertaining novel. (Rev: BL 8/08)

587 Mellom, Robin. *Ditched: A Love Story* (9–12). 2012, Hyperion $16.99 (978-142314338-3). The morning after her disastrous senior prom, Justina has to work out exactly what went wrong and how to fix it; a funny tale about misunderstandings and bad decisions. 𝐞 (Rev: BLO 12/15/11; SLJ 2/12; VOYA 2/12)

588 Mendle, Jane. *Better Off Famous?* (7–12). 2007, St. Martin's paper $8.95 (978-0-312-36903-3). On a visit to New York from Alabama, 16-year-old Annie, a talented violinist, unexpectedly wins a part on a TV series and becomes an instant celebrity — and an instant brat. (Rev: SLJ 2/08)

589 Michaels, Jamie. *Kiss My Book* (9–12). 2007, Delacorte LB $10.99 (978-0-385-90493-3); paper $7.99 (978-0-385-73499-8). Ruby is a celebrated first-time author . . . until her plagiarism is discovered and she seeks obscurity in a tiny town under a new identity. (Rev: BL 10/1/07; SLJ 2/08)

590 Michaels, Rune. *Fix Me* (9–12). 2011, Atheneum $16.99 (978-141695772-0). An empty cage at the zoo provides a haven for Leia, a 16-year-old who has not recovered from her parents' deaths and whose twin brother is abusive. 𝛀 𝐞 Lexile 720L (Rev: BL 12/15/11; LMC 3–4/12; SLJ 2/12; VOYA 12/11)

591 Minter, J. *Inside Girl* (8–12). 2007, Bloomsbury paper $8.95 (978-1-59990-086-5). Flan, younger sister of popular Patch Flood of the Insiders series, tries to escape her high-society world by transferring to a public school, but soon her ultra-rich friends show up to blow her cover. (Rev: BL 7/07; SLJ 7/07)

592 Minter, J. *The Insiders* (9–12). 2004, Bloomsbury paper $8.95 (978-1-58234-895-7). A novel about upper-class Manhattan teens, their social lives, and how they spend their parents' money. (Rev: BL 5/15/04; SLJ 6/04)

593 Miranda, Megan. *Fracture* (8–12). 2012, Walker $17.99 (978-080272309-3). After a near-death experience, Delaney, 17, finds herself fascinated by and able to predict impending death. 𝐞 (Rev: BL 12/15/11; SLJ 2/12; VOYA 12/11)

594 Moeyaert, Bart. *Hornet's Nest* (8–10). Trans. from Dutch by David Colmer. 2000, Front St $15.95 (978-1-886910-48-5). Translated from Dutch, this is a fablelike story of Susanna's efforts to solve some of the problems in her life and her village. (Rev: BL 9/15/00; HB 11–12/00; HBG 3/01; SLJ 11/00)

595 Monroe, Mary Alice. *Time Is a River* (11–12). 2008, Pocket $25.00 (978-141654436-4). Affronted by her adulterous husband, breast cancer survivor Mia heads to a secluded mountain cabin for some fly fishing, reflection, self-affirmation, and eventual healing; for mature readers. (Rev: BL 7/08)

596 Moore, Terry. *Strangers in Paradise: High School* (10–12). Series: Strangers in Paradise. 1998, Abstract Studio paper $8.95 (978-1-892597-07-6). Francine and Katchoo become friends in high school, setting off the events chronicled in the adult Strangers in Paradise series. (Rev: BL 2/1/03)

597 Moriarty, Jaclyn. *The Murder of Bindy Mackenzie* (8–11). 2006, Scholastic $16.99 (978-0-439-74051-7). Humor and mystery are combined in this story about the precocious Bindy, whose perfectionism has lost her many friends; her growth through this story is shown in diary entries, assignments, and other documents. (Rev: BL 10/15/06; HB 1–2/07*; SLJ 1/07)

598 Moriarty, Laura. *The Rest of Her Life* (9–12). 2007, Hyperion $23.95 (978-1-4013-0271-9). A teenage girl accidentally kills a classmate and she and her family try to cope with the tragedy in this poignant novel. (Rev: BL 7/07)

599 Morris, Keith Lee. *The Dart League King* (11–12). 2008, Tin House $14.95 (978-097941988-1). Drugs and darts combine in this suspenseful novel about five interconnected characters who come together for a dart contest in their small town; for mature readers. (Rev: BL 9/15/08*)

600 Morris, Mary McGarry. *Light from a Distant Star* (10–12). 2011, Crown $25 (978-0-307-45186-6). Nellie, 13, tries to do the right thing in a dreadful situation when there is a murder in her small town and Nellie's testimony will be key; for mature readers. (Rev: BL 9/1/11; SLJ 11/11)

601 Mukherjee, Bharati. *Desirable Daughters* (11–12). 2002, Hyperion $24.95 (978-0-7868-6598-7). A woman from a traditional Hindu family abandons her comfortable San Francisco life and faces some startling developments, including her son's declaration that he is gay; for mature teens. (Rev: BL 2/1/02)

602 Murray, Paul. *Skippy Dies* (11–12). 2010, The tragicomic death of a boy who dies participating in a donut-eating contest leads to increasingly complex questions about the boy's associates and personal life; set in Dublin, this is a complex, multilayered novel suitable for mature readers. ∩ (Rev: BL 7/10; SLJ 4/11)

603 Murray, Yxta Maya. *Good Girl's Guide to Getting Kidnapped* (9–12). 2010, Penguin $16.99 (978-1-595-14272-6). Michelle was known as Princess P when she lived with her Mexican American gangster father; now with a foster parent she is succeeding academically and athletically — until the gang kidnaps her and a friend for ransom money; with street language and realistic violence. ℯ (Rev: BL 12/1/09; LMC 1–2/10; SLJ 2/10)

604 Myers, Edward. *Far from Gringo Land* (7–10). 2010, Clarion $17 (978-0-547-05630-2). Rick, a teenager from Colorado, gets more than he bargained for when he moves to Mexico for a summer job and experiences culture shock. ℯ Lexile 990 (Rev: BL 11/15/09; LMC 1–2/10; SLJ 12/09)

605 Myers, Walter Dean. *All the Right Stuff* (8–12). 2012, Amistad $17.99 (978-006196087-1). After his father is killed, 16-year-old Paul volunteers at a soup kitchen and there learns much about civil liberties while also building relationships with his Harlem neighbors. ∩ ℯ (Rev: BL 2/15/12; HB 5–6/12; SLJ 5/1/12; VOYA 4/12)

606 Myers, Walter Dean. *Carmen* (9–12). 2011, Egmont $16.99 (978-1-60684-115-0); LB $ (978-1-60684-192-1). Set in Spanish Harlem, this adaptation of Bizet's opera weaves in pop culture references while staying true to the original pacing and drama. ℯ (Rev: BL 4/15/11; HB 5–6/11; SLJ 5/11; VOYA 6/11)

607 Myers, Walter Dean. *Monster* (9–12). 1999, HarperCollins LB $17.89 (978-0-06-028078-9). Sixteen-year-old African American Steve, who is on trial for his role in a fatal robbery, uses film script and a journal to convey his anguish in this novel illustrated with black-and-white photographs. (Rev: BL 5/1/99; HB 5–6/99; HBG 9/99; SLJ 7/99; VOYA 8/99)

608 Na, An. *Wait for Me* (8–11). 2006, Penguin $15.99 (978-0-399-24275-5). Unable to meet her mother's expectations, Korean American high school senior Mina resorts to lies and plans for escape, but when Ysrael, with whom she has fallen in love, is blamed for Mina's actions she must make a difficult choice. (Rev: BL 3/15/06*; SLJ 7/06)

609 Nadol, Jen. *The Mark* (9–12). 2010, Bloomsbury $16.99 (978-1-59990-431-3). Cassie, 16, can tell if a person is about to die within the next 24 hours, a "gift" that she questions as she falls in love with a handsome philosophy student. ℯ Lexile 700L (Rev: BL 12/15/09; HB 5–6/10; LMC 3–4/10; SLJ 2/10)

610 Nadol, Jen. *The Vision* (9–12). 2011, Bloomsbury $16.99 (978-1-59990-597-6). In this sequel to *The Mark* (2010) 17-year-old Cassie takes a job in a funeral home to learn more about death and meets the attractive Zander, who is also a descendant of the Fates and whose activities give Cassie pause. ℯ Lexile HL690L (Rev: BL 11/1/11; SLJ 12/1/11; VOYA 12/11)

611 Nash, Naomi. *I Am So Jinxed!* (8–12). 2006, Dorchester paper $5.99 (978-0-8439-5405-0). Vick Marotti gives up her Goth girl ways and gets in a relationship with a cute senior guy, but things are still far from perfect in her life; a sequel to *You Are So Cursed!* (2004). (Rev: SLJ 5/06)

612 Naylor, Phyllis Reynolds. *Alice on Board* (9–12). Series: Alice. 2012, Atheneum $16.99 (978-1-4424-4588-8). After high school graduation, Alice and her friends spend the summer working on a Chesapeake Bay cruise ship. ℯ (Rev: BLO 4/15/12; HB 7–8/12; SLJ 7/12; VOYA 6/12)

613 Naylor, Phyllis Reynolds. *Incredibly Alice* (9–12). Series: Alice. 2011, Atheneum $16.99 (978-1-4169-7553-3). In her last semester of high school Alice deals with school and social concerns while anticipating college and worrying about her boyfriend. ℯ Lexile 820L (Rev: BL 5/1/11; HB 7–8/11; SLJ 7/11; VOYA 6/11)

614 Naylor, Phyllis Reynolds. *Intensely Alice* (9–12). Series: Alice. 2009, Simon & Schuster $16.99 (978-141697551-9). In this installment in the long series, Alice is 17 and facing the end of high school, the possibility of sex with her college-age boyfriend, and even the death of a friend. Lexile HL770L (Rev: BL 5/1/09; HB 7–8/09; VOYA 6/09)

615 Nelson, Blake. *Paranoid Park* (8–11). 2006, Viking $15.99 (978-0-670-06118-1). The narrator of this title, a 16-year-old skateboarder, is involved in the death of security officer and must deal with his feelings of confusion, fear, and the decision to confess or not. (Rev: BL 9/1/06; SLJ 11/06)

616 Ness, Patrick. *A Monster Calls* (7–10). Illus. by Jim Kay. 2011, Candlewick $16.99 (978-0-7636-5559-4). Thirteen-year-old Conor's mother is dying and he is plagued by nightmares; then one night a monster wakes him and tells him three hard-to-fathom stories, finally asking Conor for a story that embodies the truth; a moving story about facing loss. ALA Notable Books 2012; YALSA Top Ten Best Fiction for Young Adults 2012. ⌂ ℮ Lexile 730L (Rev: BL 7/11; HB 9–19/11; LMC 1–2/12*; SLJ 9/1/11*)

617 Newman, Nancy. *Disturbing the Peace* (11–12). 2002, Avon paper $13.95 (978-0-380-79839-1). Sarah, who teaches English as a second language to immigrants in New York City, becomes preoccupied with her search for her birth mother; for mature teens. (Rev: BL 1/1–15/02)

618 Nields, Nerissa. *Plastic Angel* (7–10). 2005, Scholastic $17.95 (978-0-439-70913-2). Thirteen-year-olds Randi and Gellie become friends despite their differences and form a band called Plastic Angel. (Rev: BL 8/05; SLJ 9/05; VOYA 2/06)

619 Nilsson, Per. *You and You and You* (9–12). Trans. by Tara Chase. 2005, Front St $16.95 (978-1-932425-19-2). Three characters — 12-year-old Anon, who believes his father is a god; 17-year-old Zarah, who is in a lonely and abusive relationship; and 20-year-old Nils, who is obsessed by death — are at the center of this offbeat, graphically sexual but compelling novel. (Rev: BL 7/05*; SLJ 8/05*)

620 Noël, Alyson. *Saving Zoë* (7–10). 2007, St. Martin's paper $8.95 (978-0-312-35510-4). Fifteen-year-old Echo's world fell apart when her older sister Zoë was murdered; when she gets Zoë's diaries, however, she discovers just how many risks her sister had been taking and is able to start healing herself and her family. (Rev: SLJ 12/07; VOYA date)

621 Nolan, Han. *When We Were Saints* (7–10). 2003, Harcourt $17.00 (978-0-15-216371-6). After his grandfather's death, Archie, 14, is overwhelmed by a need to find God and, with his religious friend Clare, sets off on a pilgrimage to the Cloisters in New York. (Rev: BL 10/1/03; HBG 4/04; SLJ 11/03; VOYA 12/03)

622 Nunez, Sigrid. *Salvation City* (10–12). 2010, Riverhead $25.95 (978-159448766-8). Young Cole finds himself orphaned by a flu pandemic, transplanted to a super-religious settlement in near-future postapocalyptic America, and grappling with guns, sexuality, and a lust for knowledge. ⌂ ℮ (Rev: BL 8/10)

623 Oaks, J. Adams. *Why I Fight* (8–12). 2009, Simon & Schuster $16.99 (978-141691177-7). Since the age of 12, Wyatt has been traveling with his drifter uncle named Spade and earning money with his fists. Lexile 770L (Rev: BL 4/15/09; SLJ 7/1/09; VOYA 6/09)

624 Ockler, Sarah. *Bittersweet* (9–12). 2012, Simon & Schuster $16.99 (978-144243035-8). Talented figure skater Hudson, 17, gave up skating after her parents divorced and has been helping her mother and brother at their family diner; but she is offered another chance at skating — and perhaps a scholarship — and must make

difficult choices. ⌂ ℮ Lexile 840L (Rev: BL 2/15/12; SLJ 5/1/12)

625 O'Connell, Tyne. *Pulling Princes* (7–10). 2004, Bloomsbury $16.95 (978-1-58234-957-2). Calypso Kelly, a 15-year-old from LA, finds it difficult to fit in at her posh English boarding school. (Rev: SLJ 12/04; VOYA 4/05)

626 O'Keefe, Susan Heyboer. *My Life and Death by Alexandra Canarsie* (7–10). 2002, Peachtree $14.95 (978-1-56145-264-4). Allie, a lonely teenager, finds a friend and a mystery when she starts going to strangers' funerals. (Rev: HBG 10/02; SLJ 9/02; VOYA 4/02)

627 Oliver, Lauren. *Before I Fall* (9–12). 2010, HarperCollins $17.99 (978-0-06-172680-4). As she relives — seven times — the day of her death in a car accident, high school senior Samantha gains insight into her life and the mistakes she has made. ⌂ ℮ Lexile 860L (Rev: BL 10/15/09; LMC 1–2/10; SLJ 4/10)

628 Oppel, Kenneth. *Half Brother* (7–10). 2010, Scholastic $17.99 (978-0-545-22925-8). In 1970s Canada 13-year-old Ben's psychologist father brings home a young chimp that will be raised as a member of the family. ⌂ ℮ Lexile 680L (Rev: BL 9/1/10; HB 9–10/10; LMC 11–12/10; SLJ 9/1/10*; VOYA 12/10)

629 Ostow, Micol. *So Punk Rock (and Other Ways to Disappoint Your Mother)* (8–12). Illus. by David Ostow. 2009, Flux paper $9.95 (978-073871471-4). This is a funny and affecting story about four New Jersey Jewish teens and the ways in which their band's success affects their lives. (Rev: BL 6/1–15/09*; SLJ 11/09)

630 Pancake, Ann. *Strange as This Weather Has Been* (9–12). 2007, Shoemaker & Hoard paper $14.95 (978-1-59376-166-0). Set in the mountains of West Virginia, this gripping novel features a family coping with the effects of destructive, environmentally harmful mining, and struggling with whether to fight the powerful mining companies. (Rev: BL 9/1/07)

631 Papademetriou, Lisa. *Drop* (7–12). 2008, Knopf $15.99 (978-037584244-3); LB $18.99 (978-037594244-0). Three Las Vegas teens band together to try to beat the system at the roulette tables, one to pay off gambling debts, one to escape family problems, and one to prove her mathematical theories in this tense, fast-paced novel. Lexile 690L (Rev: BL 12/1/08; LMC 3–4/09; SLJ 12/08; VOYA 4/09)

632 Pattillo, Beth. *Mr. Darcy Broke My Heart* (10–12). 2010, Guideposts paper $14.99 (978-08249479-3-4). Charged with presenting a paper at a Jane Austen seminar, Claire feels overwhelmed until an elderly Harriet Dalrymple presents her with a revelatory early draft of *Pride and Prejudice* and Claire comes to recognize some truths about her own romantic relationships. (Rev: BLO 1/1–15/10)

633 Pearce, Jackson. *Purity* (8–12). 2012, Little, Brown $17.99 (978-031618246-1). Shelby, 16, struggles to find balance between living a morally pure life and fulfilling her mother's dying wish to live "without restraint." ℮ (Rev: BL 5/1/12; LMC 8–9/12; SLJ 5/1/12)

634 Perkins, Mitali. *Extreme American Makeover* (7–10). Series: First Daughter. 2007, Dutton $16.99 (978-0-525-47800-3). Sixteen-year-old Sameera is the adopted Pakistani daughter of the Republican candidate for president and finds herself half enjoying and half hating efforts to make her over for public scrutiny. (Rev: BL 5/15/07; SLJ 6/07)

635 Perkins, Mitali. *White House Rules* (7–10). Series: First Daughter. 2008, Dutton $16.99 (978-0-525-47951-2). Sameera, the adopted Pakistani daughter of President Righton, livens up the White House with a blog (that readers can actually access), parties for her friends, and her thoughts on politics; the sequel to *Extreme American Makeover* (2007). (Rev: BL 2/1/08; SLJ 2/08)

636 Peterfreund, Diana. *Secret Society Girl* (10–12). Series: Secret Society Girl. 2006, Delacorte $23.00 (978-0-385-34002-1). Amy's college experience goes from typical to mysterious when she's asked to join a secret campus society. (Rev: BL 5/15/06)

637 Peters, Kimberly Joy. *Painting Caitlyn* (8–11). 2006, Lobster paper $9.95 (978-1-897073-40-7). Fourteen-year-old Caitlyn feels alone and depressed about her life until she starts dating an older boy named Tyler. But when Tyler starts controlling her and the relationship becomes abusive, Caitlyn must make a choice. (Rev: BL 9/15/06; SLJ 9/06)

638 Picardie, Justine. *Daphne* (10–12). 2008, Bloomsbury $24.95 (978-159691341-7). Part literary mystery, part biography of Daphne du Maurier and Branwell Brontë (brother of the famed Brontë sisters), this engrossing story includes a modern-day plotline that mirrors the gothic, suspenseful tone of du Maurier's work. ℮ (Rev: BL 7/08)

639 Picoult, Jodi. *House Rules* (11–12). 2010, Atria $28 (978-074329643-4). Told from multiple viewpoints, this story features Jacob Hunt, a teen with Asperger's syndrome who is accused of murder; for mature readers. ⌒ (Rev: BL 12/15/09)

640 Picoult, Jodi. *Sing You Home* (11–12). 2011, Atria $28 (978-143910272-5). Before they divorced, Zoe and Max stored embryos for future use and now Zoe, who just married her new love Vanessa, wants to use them to become a mother, but Max, backed by his church, sues her for custody of the embryos; for mature readers. ⌒ ℮ (Rev: BL 1/1–15/11)

641 Pierson, D. C. *The Boy Who Couldn't Sleep and Never Had To* (10–12). 2010, Vintage paper $14 (978-03074746-1-2). Darren and his best friend Eric, who never sleeps, become embroiled in an adventure that parallels the science fiction epic they are working on,

in this entertaining coming-of-age story. Alex Award 2011. (Rev: BL 12/15/09)

642 Pollack, Jenny. *Klepto: Best Friends, First Love, and Shoplifting* (8–11). 2006, Viking $16.99 (978-0-670-06061-0). In the early 1980s, Julie Prodsky, a 14-year-old drama major at New York's High School of Performing Arts, meets cool Julie Braverman and sets out on a career of "getting" rather than buying. (Rev: BL 2/15/06; SLJ 4/06)

643 Potter, Ryan. *Exit Strategy* (9–12). 2010, Flux paper $9.95 (978-0-73871-573-5). Zach aims to leave his depressed Detroit suburb (and his unhappy family) as soon as he can, but in the meantime the high schooler realizes that his friend Tank's wired behavior is due to steroids provided by the coach and that he is attracted to Tank's sister; a gritty novel with mature themes. ℮ Lexile HL790L (Rev: BL 2/15/10; LMC 5–6/10)

644 Poznanski, Ursula. *Erebos: It's a Game. It Watches You* (9–12). Trans. by Judith Pattinson. 2012, Annick $29.95 (978-1-55451-373-4); paper $19.95 (978-1-55451-372-7). A mysterious computer game plays a principal role in this exciting story about the manipulation of teenagers in London. ℮ Lexile NC640L (Rev: BL 3/1/12; HB 7–8/12; SLJ 7/12; VOYA 6/12)

645 Preller, James. *Before You Go* (7–10). 2012, Feiwel & Friends $16.99 (978-0-312-56107-9). Haunted by the death of his little sister, Jude, 16, is sent reeling when tragedy strikes again, lashing out at work and at his erstwhile love interest. ℮ Lexile 740L (Rev: BL 7/12; SLJ 10/12)

646 Prinz, Yvonne. *The Vinyl Princess* (7–11). 2010, HarperCollins $16.99 (978-0-06-171583-9). Allie, 16, blogs about music, collects vinyl, and works in a record store while dreaming of romance, which proves rocky. ℮ Lexile 850L (Rev: BL 11/1/09; LMC 3–4/10; SLJ 2/10)

647 Proimos, James. *12 Things to Do Before You Crash and Burn* (10–12). 2011, Roaring Brook $14.99 (978-1-59643-595-7). After the death of his father — a man of whom he was not fond — Hercules, 16, goes to stay with his uncle in Baltimore and is assigned 12 tasks; a funny story with elements of romance. ℮ Lexile HL540L (Rev: SLJ 12/1/11)

648 Pruett, Lynn. *Ruby River* (11–12). 2002, Grove $24.00 (978-0-87113-855-2). When Hattie's daughter's illicit affair becomes public, religious elements in their Alabama town boycott Hattie's truck stop; for mature teens. (Rev: BL 9/1/02)

649 Quick, Matthew. *Boy21* (9–12). 2012, Little, Brown $17.99 (978-031612797-4). In a rough town where he is the only white player on his high school's basketball team, Finley — who has his own problems — is asked to mentor a troubled newcomer from California. YALSA Top Ten Best Fiction for Young Adults 2013.

(Rev: BL 3/1/12; HB 5–6/12; LMC 1–2/12; SLJ 3/12; VOYA 12/11)

650 Quick, Matthew. *Sorta Like a Rock Star* (9–12). 2010, Little, Brown $16.99 (978-0-316-04352-6). Tirelessly optimistic despite her desperate condition, homeless teen Amber seeks to inspire and uplift those around her until she encounters an obstacle even she can't cope with. ∩ ℮ Lexile 1030L (Rev: BL 8/10; SLJ 5/10; VOYA 10/10)

651 Rallison, Janette. *How to Take the Ex Out of Ex-boyfriend* (7–10). 2007, Putnam $15.99 (978-0-399-24617-3). This funny novel follows Giovanna as she is torn between being loyal to her brother, who is running for student body president, and her boyfriend, the other candidate's campaign manager. (Rev: SLJ 7/07)

652 Randle, Kristen D. *Slumming* (8–11). 2003, Harper-Tempest LB $16.89 (978-0-06-001023-2). Three Mormon high school seniors decide to befriend the friendless and invite them to the school prom. (Rev: BCCB 9/03; BL 8/03; HB 7–8/03; HBG 4/04; SLJ 8/03; VOYA 8/03)

653 Ranulfo. *Joker* (9–12). 2006, HarperCollins $15.99 (978-0-06-054158-3). Matt, a 17-year-old Australian, faces family, friendship, and global problems in this novel that channels Shakespeare's *Hamlet*. (Rev: BL 10/1/06; HB 7–8/06; SLJ 9/06)

654 Rapp, Adam. *The Children and the Wolves* (9–12). 2012, Candlewick $16.99 (978-076365337-8). Privileged teen genius Bounce, 14, persuades her friends Wiggins and Orange to kidnap a 3-year-old girl, keeping her in a basement while they collect donations around the neighborhood. ∩ ℮ (Rev: BL 11/15/11*; HB 1–2/12; SLJ 2/12; VOYA 4/12)

655 Reisfeld, Randi. *Starlet* (9–12). 2007, Hyperion paper $8.99 (978-1-4231-0501-5). This is the lighthearted story of Jacey, a reality TV show winner who comes to understand the highs and lows of celebrity life. (Rev: SLJ 6/07)

656 Resau, Laura. *The Indigo Notebook* (7–10). 2009, Delacorte $16.99 (978-0-385-73652-7); LB $19.99 (978-0-385-90614-2). It's move number 15 (to Ecuador), and 15-year-old Zeeta is heartily tired of their itinerant life; helping an American teenager find his birth parents brings her interest as she becomes involved in a mysterious adventure that involves magical realism. (Rev: BL 11/1/09; SLJ 12/09)

657 Resau, Laura. *Red Glass* (7–10). 2007, Delacorte $15.99 (978-0-385-73466-0). Sixteen-year-old Sophie, a girl beset by trepidations, befriends 6-year-old Pablo, whose parents died trying to cross the border illegally, and decides to take him back to see his relatives in Mexico with life-changing results. (Rev: BL 9/15/07; SLJ 10/07)

658 Rettig, Liz. *My Desperate Love Diary* (8–12). 2007, Holiday House $16.95 (978-0-8234-2033-9). Wittily

written in diary format, this book tells the story of Kelly Ann, a 15-year-old British girl with family problems who finds herself obsessed with a boy who doesn't return her feelings, while a caring boy waits on the sidelines. (Rev: SLJ 7/07)

659 Reynolds, Marilyn. *Love Rules: True-to-Life Stories from Hamilton High* (8–12). Series: True-to-Life. 2001, Morning Glory $18.95 (978-1-885356-75-8); paper $9.95 (978-1-885356-76-5). Lynn, a white high school senior, learns about prejudice as she dates an African American football player and supports her lesbian friend Kit. (Rev: BL 8/01; HBG 3/02; SLJ 9/01; VOYA 10/01)

660 Rice, Luanne. *The Edge of Winter* (10–12). 2007, Bantam $24.00 (978-0-553-80527-7). Family, community, ecology, and history are intertwined in this story of teenager Mickey's efforts to rescue a snowy owl's habitat. ∩ (Rev: BL 1/1–15/07)

661 Rich, Naomi. *Alis* (9–12). 2009, Viking $16.99 (978-067001125-4). Set in a fictional historical time period, 14-year-old Alis, member of a conservative religious group called "The Community of the Book," runs away after she is ordered to marry a much older man, finding herself in even more peril outside of her community. ℮ Lexile 730L (Rev: BL 12/15/08; LMC 3–4/09; SLJ 3/1/09)

662 Ripslinger, Jon. *Derailed* (9–12). 2006, Llewellyn paper $8.95 (978-0-7387-0888-1). Stony, a star high school football player, must get help from an English tutor in order to stay on the team; his tutor, Robyn, deals with being a teenage mother in an abusive relationship, while also making Stony question his plans for the future. (Rev: BL 9/1/06)

663 Ritter, John H. *Under the Baseball Moon* (7–10). 2006, Philomel $16.99 (978-0-399-23623-5). Andy and his friend Glory lean on each other for support as they both pursue their dreams; he wants to be a famous musician and she wants to be a professional softball player. ∩ (Rev: BL 8/06*; SLJ 10/06)

664 Rivers, Karen. *What Is Real* (10–12). 2011, Orca paper $12.95 (978-1-55469-356-6). High school senior Dex escapes the burgeoning problems in his life by getting high with his dad, who grows marijuana. (Rev: BL 8/11; LMC 11–12/11; SLJ 9/1/11; VOYA 8/11)

665 Robbins, Kenneth. *City of Churches* (10–12). 2004, NewSouth $25.95 (978-1-58838-142-2). Cutting back and forth in time, this novel describes the return to their southern hometown of two men, one white and the other black, both of whom lost their fathers to racial violence. (Rev: BL 3/15/04)

666 Rodrigues, Carmen. *34 Pieces of You* (8–11). 2012, Simon & Schuster $16.99 (978-144243906-1). Three friends try to piece together the truth about Ellie's death from a drug and alcohol overdose. ℮ Lexile HL690L (Rev: BL 10/1/12; SLJ 1/13; VOYA 10/12)

667 Roesch, Mattox. *Sometimes We're Always Real Same-Same* (11–12). 2009, Unbridled Bks paper $15.95 (978-1-932961-87-4). Seventeen-year-old Cesar, a tough Los Angeles gang member, must come to grips with his relocation to remote Unalakleet, Alaska, where his cousin Go-Boy helps him acclimate to his new community and lifestyle; for mature readers. (Rev: BL 9/15/09; SLJ 11/09)

668 Rosoff, Meg. *Just in Case* (9–12). 2006, Random House $16.95 (978-0-385-74678-6). Saving his little brother from falling out a window prompts 15-year-old David to reexamine his life and assume a new identity in this novel in which Fate plays an active role. (Rev: BL 6/1–15/06; HB 9–10/06; SLJ 9/06)

669 Roth, Matthue. *Losers* (9–12). 2008, Scholastic paper $8.99 (978-054506893-2). Russian immigrant Jupiter Glazer struggles to find himself — and escape the rampant bullying in his new high school — as he bonds over music with an unlikely new friend. e Lexile 930L (Rev: BL 11/1/08*; LMC 3–4/09; SLJ 1/1/09)

670 Rottman, S. L. *Out of the Blue* (8–11). 2009, Peachtree $16.95 (978-1-56145-499-0). Newly moved to Minot Air Force Base in North Dakota, 15-year-old Stu Ballentyne is compelled to act when he witnesses child abuse first hand, and the experience draws him out of his loneliness and isolation. Lexile 660L (Rev: BL 12/1/09; SLJ 10/09)

671 Rubens, Michael. *Sons of the 613* (8–10). 2012, Clarion $16.99 (978-0-547-61216-4). Preparations for Isaac's bar mitzvah take an unusual turn when his parents take off for Italy, leaving him in the care of his older brother Josh. e (Rev: BL 11/15/12; SLJ 12/12; VOYA 10/12)

672 Rudetsky, Seth. *My Awesome/Awful Popularity Plan* (7–10). 2012, Random House $16.99 (978-037586915-0); LB $19.99 (978-037596915-7). Justin, who is gay, Jewish, and longing to become popular, agrees to some perilous ploys in this story full of believable self-deprecation and humor. (Rev: BL 1/1/12; VOYA 2/12)

673 Ruditis, Paul. *The Four Dorothys* (9–12). Series: Drama. 2007, Simon & Schuster paper $8.99 (978-1-4169-3391-5). Because of multiple influential parents, several cast members must share the leads in a Malibu high school's production of *The Wizard of Oz* — the wild turns of events that follow are hilariously narrated by a closeted gay Scarecrow. (Rev: BL 2/15/07; SLJ 7/07)

674 Ryan, Darlene. *Pieces of Me* (8–12). 2012, Orca paper $12.95 (978-14598008-0-9). Teenager Maddie, living on the streets, connects with a young man named Q, and together they find themselves looking after an abandoned 6-year-old boy. e Lexile HL580L (Rev: BL 10/1/12; SLJ 2/13; VOYA 10/12)

675 Ryan, Darlene. *Saving Grace* (7–12). 2006, Orca $14.95 (978-1-55143-668-5). Evie, 15, soon regrets

that she gave up her baby and persuades the child's father to help her kidnap Brianna (now named Grace) and head for a new life in Montreal. (Rev: SLJ 4/07)

676 Ryan, Jeanne. *NERVE* (9–12). 2012, Dial $17.99 (978-0-8037-3832-4). An online game called NERVE, which involves bizarre dares, eventually makes risk-taking Vee too uncomfortable. e (Rev: BL 10/1/12; LMC 3–4/13; SLJ 11/12; VOYA 12/12)

677 Sales, Leila. *Mostly Good Girls* (8–12). 2010, Simon & Schuster $16.99 (978-1-4424-0679-7). Witty, sometimes whiny Violet narrates this story of two private-school friends growing apart as they contend with boys, PSATs, and school politicking. e Lexile 820L (Rev: BL 10/15/10; SLJ 10/1/10*)

678 Schroeder, Lisa. *The Day Before* (8–10). 2011, Simon & Schuster $16.99 (978-1-4424-1743-4). Sixteen-year-old Amber, about to meet her birth parents for the first time, hopes for one last happy day at the beach — and there she meets Cade, a handsome teen also facing a crisis; a novel told in verse. e Lexile HL560L (Rev: BL 6/1/11; SLJ 8/11)

679 Schumacher, Julie. *The Unbearable Book Club for Unsinkable Girls* (8–11). 2012, Delacorte $16.99 (978-038573773-9); LB $19.99 (978-038590685-2). A mother-daughter book club provides the framework for 15-year-old Adrienne and her friends' adventures during a humid summer in Delaware. (Rev: BL 8/12; SLJ 6/12)

680 Schwartz, Lynne Sharon. *The Writing on the Wall* (11–12). 2005, Counterpoint $24.00 (978-1-58243-299-1). The shocking events of September 11, 2001, have particular impact on Renata, a New York librarian who has tried to bury her own tragic past; for mature teens. (Rev: BL 5/1/05)

681 Scott, Elizabeth. *Between Here and Forever* (8–12). 2011, Simon & Schuster $16.99 (978-1-4169-9484-8). Her beautiful older sister Tess is in a coma after a car accident and Abby, 17, is desperate to help her recovery — to the point of asking handsome Eli to spend time with Tess. e Lexile HL760L (Rev: BL 5/15/11; SLJ 6/11; VOYA 6/11)

682 Scott, Kieran. *This Is So Not Happening* (8–12). Series: He's So/She's So Trilogy. 2012, Simon & Schuster $16.99 (978-141699955-3). Ally tries to remain supportive of her boyfriend Jake when they learn that a summer fling with Chloe resulted in pregnancy. e Lexile HL670L (Rev: BL 7/12A; VOYA 4/12)

683 Scudamore, James. *The Amnesia Clinic* (11–12). 2007, Harcourt $23.00 (978-0-15-101265-7). In Ecuador, two 15-year-olds — British Anthony ("Anti") and his best friend Fabián — have powerful imaginations and enjoy bragging and telling stories; when Fabián reveals his hope that his mother is still alive, Anti fabricates a story about an amnesia clinic and they set off on a dangerous journey to find her; for mature teens. (Rev: BL 9/15/06)

684 Selwood, Jonathan. *The Pinball Theory of Apocalypse* (9–12). 2007, HarperCollins paper $13.95 (978-0-06-117387-5). Hysterical twists and turns punctuate this clever story of Isabel, an up-and-coming painter whose chaotic life in L.A. keeps getting more and more bizarre. (Rev: BL 6/1–15/07)

685 Senate, Melissa. *Theodora Twist* (8–11). 2006, Delacorte $15.95 (978-0-385-73301-4). Dora, a teen star with a wild past, moves in with average teen Emily and her family, with a reality show TV crew monitoring their every move. (Rev: BL 5/15/06; SLJ 2/07)

686 Sendak, Maurice. *My Brother's Book* (10–12). Illus. by author. 2013, HarperCollins $18.95 (978-006223489-6). Full of literary and artistic allusions, this free-verse story of two brothers is a tribute to Sendak's late brother Jack. (Rev: BL 12/1/12*; HB 1–2/13; SLJ 1/13)

687 Serros, Michele. *Honey Blonde Chica* (10–12). 2006, Simon & Schuster $14.95 (978-1-4169-1591-1). A sophomore at an upper-class prep school, Evie Gomez struggles with identity and friendship issues with her Latina peers. (Rev: BL 5/15/06; SLJ 8/06)

688 Serros, Michele. *Scandalosa!* (9–12). 2007, Simon & Schuster $15.99 (978-1-4169-1593-5). Evie Gomez's perfect life is endangered when her parents threaten to cancel her 16th birthday party if her grades don't improve, her boyfriend seems lukewarm about her, and she might fail her driving test; "chick lit" with a Southern California accent. (Rev: BL 9/15/07)

689 Shapiro, Anna. *Living on Air* (10–12). 2006, Soho $22.00 (978-1-56947-431-0). In the 1960s, 14-year-old Maude faces a dichotomy between her artistic home life in middle-class Levittown and the wealth of her friends at the privileged Bay Farm School. (Rev: BL 4/1/06)

690 Shepard, Sara. *Twisted* (9–11). Series: Pretty Little Liars. 2011, HarperTeen $16.99 (978-006208101-8). In the ninth book in the series, Aria, Hanna, Emily, and Spencer worry about what happened to them in Jamaica last spring while dealing with the usual rich bad-girl dramas in their everyday lives. e Lexile HL720L (Rev: BL 10/1/11; VOYA 10/11)

691 Shreve, Anita. *Testimony* (11–12). 2008, Little, Brown $25.99 (978-031605986-2). *Testimony* tells the story of a shocking prep school sex scandal, the events that preceded it, and the many lives that are ruined by the disastrous fallout; for mature readers. ⌒ e (Rev: BL 9/1/08*)

692 Shulman, Polly. *Enthusiasm* (7–10). 2006, Penguin $15.99 (978-0-399-24389-9). A romantic comedy of errors featuring Jane and Ashleigh, who are both fans of Jane Austen, who get roles in a play at the local boys' prep school. (Rev: BL 1/1–15/06*; SLJ 3/06; VOYA 4/06)

693 Simone, Ni-Ni. *No Boyz Allowed* (8–12). 2012, Kensington paper $9.95 (978-0-7582-4-193-1). Foster child Gem, 16, struggles to adjust as she moves into a new home and seeks new friends at school. e (Rev: BL 8/12; LMC 3–4/13; SLJ 11/12)

694 Sitomer, Alan Lawrence. *Hip-Hop High School* (10–12). 2006, Hyperion $16.99 (978-0-7868-5515-5). Theresa, or "Tee-Ay" — younger sister of Andre in *The Hoopster* (2005) — tries to focus on schoolwork as she deals with the peer pressure to conform at her inner-city high school. ⌒ (Rev: BL 5/1/06; LMC 10/06; SLJ 6/06)

695 Sittenfeld, Curtis. *American Wife* (10–12). 2008, Random House $26.00 (978-140006475-5). Based on the life of First Lady Laura Bush, this first-person fictional memoir captures a Wisconsin girl's unlikely rise to the White House and her struggle to come to grips with her husband's intimidating family and contentious politics. ⌒ e (Rev: BL 7/08*)

696 Smith, Andrew. *Ghost Medicine* (8–12). 2008, Feiwel & Friends $17.95 (978-0-312-37557-7). Following the death of his brother and then of his mother, 16-year-old Troy finds comfort in a camping trip, spending time with his friends, and practicing "ghost medicine," but also must deal with the bullying son of the sheriff. (Rev: LMC 3–4/09; SLJ 9/1/08)

697 Smith, Andrew. *Stick* (8–11). 2011, Feiwel & Friends $17.99 (978-0-312-61341-9). Stick is a tall, skinny 13-year-old who has a deformed ear and relies on his older brother Bosten for protection from bullies until Bosten's homosexuality is revealed and he must flee from their home. ⌒ e Lexile HL750L (Rev: BL 9/1/11; HB 1–2/12; SLJ 12/1/11)

698 Smith, Sherri L. *Sparrow* (7–10). 2006, Delacorte $15.95 (978-0-385-73324-3). Orphaned when she was little, African American teen Kendall searches for an estranged aunt after her grandmother dies but her search does not progress as she hoped. (Rev: BL 6/1–15/06; SLJ 10/06)

699 Smolinski, Jill. *The Next Thing on My List* (11–12). 2007, Crown $23.00 (978-0-307-35124-1). After a car accident leaves her 24-year-old passenger, Marissa, dead, hitherto aimless June Parker decides to complete the list of things Marissa wanted to do before she turned 25, one of which is becoming a Big Sister. ⌒ (Rev: BL 2/15/07)

700 Snadowsky, Daria. *Anatomy of a Boyfriend* (10–12). 2007, Random House $16.99 (978-0-385-73320-5). In frank and explicit terms, high school senior Dominique describes her relationship with her boyfriend Wes, the sex they have together, and their eventual breakup when they go to different colleges. (Rev: BL 11/15/06; SLJ 2/07)

701 Solwitz, Sharon. *Bloody Mary* (11–12). 2003, Sarabande paper $13.95 (978-1-889330-93-8). Hadley has to cope alone with her first period when her epileptic mother becomes absorbed in her new lover in this tense and absorbing story of crisis and change suitable for mature readers. (Rev: BL 7/03*)

702 Sonnenblick, Jordan. *Curveball: The Year I Lost My Grip* (8–10). 2012, Scholastic $17.99 (978-054532069-6). Former star athlete Pete, 13, finds a new outlet and a deepened connection to his ailing grandfather through photography. ⌒ ℮ Lexile 800L (Rev: BL 2/1/12*; LMC 5–6/12; SLJ 4/12*)

703 Spinelli, Jerry. *Smiles to Go* (6–10). 2008, HarperCollins $16.99 (978-0-06-028133-5). The discovery that protons decay unsettles high school freshman Will Tuppence, causing him to take a new look at all sorts of things, including his little sister Tabby and his best friends Mi-Su and BT. (Rev: BL 2/15/08; SLJ 5/08)

704 Spitz, Marc. *How Soon Is Never?* (11–12). 2003, Crown paper $13.00 (978-0-609-81040-8). Joe Green is a rock journalist who pines for the sounds he heard in high school and sets off for England to find their creators. (Rev: BL 8/03)

705 Standiford, Natalie. *How to Say Goodbye in Robot* (9–12). 2009, Scholastic $17.99 (978-0-545-10708-2). High school senior Bea Szabo has adopted the cold persona of "Robot Girl" to cope with family drama, but she is slowly drawn out of her isolation by her new friend Jonas, the issues facing him, and a late-night radio show they enjoy together. ⌒ ℮ Lexile HL560L (Rev: BL 11/1/09; HB 1–2/10; LMC 11/09; SLJ 10/09)

706 Staples, Suzanne Fisher. *Under the Persimmon Tree* (7–10). 2005, Farrar $17.00 (978-0-374-38025-0). The stories of Najmal, a brave young Afghani refugee, and Nusrat, an American woman helping with a refugee school, intersect as they wait for news of their loved ones in the chaos of the 2001 Afghan War. (Rev: BL 7/05*; SLJ 7/05; VOYA 10/05)

707 Steele, J. M. *The Taker* (8–11). 2006, Hyperion $15.99 (978-0-7868-4930-7). Carly's SAT scores are not good enough to get her into Princeton as her family expects, so she accepts an offer to cheat next time she takes the test, a decision that has wide-ranging repercussions. (Rev: BL 10/1/06; SLJ 12/06)

708 Steinbeck, John. *Cannery Row* (10–12). 1945, Viking paper $14.00 (978-0-14-018737-3). Like the author's earlier *Tortilla Flat* (1945), this novel deals with California workers, this time involving cannery employees and their friends.

709 Stork, Francisco X. *Last Summer of the Death Warriors* (8–12). 2010, Scholastic $17.99 (978-0-545-15133-7). This complex tale features 17-year-olds Pancho, who seeks to avenge his sister's death, and D.Q., who is dying of brain cancer, as they contemplate the meaning of being a "Death Warrior." ⌒ ℮ Lexile HL640L (Rev: BL 2/1/10*; HB 3–4/10; LMC 3–4/10; SLJ 3/10)

710 Strasser, Todd. *Famous* (7–12). 2011, Simon & Schuster $15.99 (978-1-4169-7511-3). Budding paparazzo Jamie, 16, must decide how much to reveal of what she has learned about starlet Willow Twine's life. ℮ Lexile 800L (Rev: BL 5/1/11; LMC 5–6/11; SLJ 5/11; VOYA 2/11)

711 Strohmeyer, Sarah. *Smart Girls Get What They Want* (8–11). 2012, HarperCollins $17.99 (978-0-06-195340-8). Smart girl Gigi and her sophomore friends set out to become popular with mixed results. ℮ Lexile HL820L (Rev: BLO 6/12; SLJ 7/12; VOYA 2/12)

712 Supplee, Suzanne. *Somebody Everybody Listens To* (8–11). 2010, Dutton $16.99 (978-0-525-42242-6). Plucky country-star wannabe Retta heads for Nashville and succeeds despite having to sleep in her car at first. ℮ Lexile 830L (Rev: BL 6/10; SLJ 10/1/10)

713 Sutherland, Tui T. *This Must Be Love* (7–10). 2004, HarperCollins LB $16.89 (978-0-06-056476-6). Shakespearean plots are interwoven in this tale of Helena and Hermia, best friends in a modern New Jersey high school, and the comedy of errors that is their romantic life. (Rev: BCCB 1/05; SLJ 9/04)

714 Tanen, Sloane. *Are You Going to Kiss Me Now?* (8–11). 2011, Sourcebooks paper $8.99 (978-1-4022-5-461-1). High school junior Fran wins an essay contest and sets off to travel to Africa to a charity event with five celebrities; but the plane crashes and she finds herself stranded on an island learning the assets and foibles of her companions. ℮ Lexile HL700L (Rev: BL 4/1/11; SLJ 6/11; VOYA 6/11)

715 Tanner, Haley. *Vaclav and Lena* (11–12). 2011, Dial $25 (978-1-4000-6931-6). Vaclav and Lena, who live in the Russian immigrant area of Brighton Beach, NY, meet as children, become best friends, plan a magic show, and assume they will be together forever; but then Lena is taken away and Vaclav must carry on alone; for mature readers. ⌒ ℮ (Rev: BL 5/1/11; SLJ 7/11)

716 Tanner, Mike. *Resurrection Blues* (10–12). 2005, Annick $19.95 (978-1-55037-897-9); paper $9.95 (978-1-55037-896-2). Rock and roll beckons to 18-year-old Flynn and he drops out of school to go on the road with a traveling band. (Rev: BL 8/05; SLJ 8/05; VOYA 10/05)

717 Tanzman, Carol M. *dancergirl* (8–10). 2011, HarlequinTeen paper $9.99 (978-03732104-0-4). Ali Ruffino initially enjoys her Internet fame as "dancergirl," but the story turns grimmer as she discovers a video camera outside her bedroom window. ℮ (Rev: BL 2/1/12; LMC 8–9/12; SLJ 3/12)

718 Tashjian, Janet. *The Gospel According to Larry* (7–10). 2001, Henry Holt $16.95 (978-0-8050-6378-3). When Josh (a.k.a. "Larry") publishes his anticonsumerism worldview on the Web, he develops a cult following and discovers the dark side of fame. (Rev: BCCB

1/02; BL 11/1/01; HB 1–2/02*; HBG 3/02; SLJ 10/01; VOYA 12/01)

719 Tashjian, Janet. *Larry and the Meaning of Life* (8–12). 2008, Henry Holt $16.95 (978-080507735-3). In this third book in the series, Josh/Larry falls in with a mysterious guru named Gus and finds himself having a series of bizarre adventures. ∩ Lexile 760L (Rev: BL 9/1/08; SLJ 12/08; VOYA 2/09)

720 Tashjian, Janet. *Vote for Larry* (7–10). 2004, Henry Holt $16.95 (978-0-8050-7201-3). In this sequel to *The Gospel According to Larry* (2001), our young hero decides to run for president of the United States. (Rev: BL 5/1/04; HB 7–8/04; SLJ 5/04; VOYA 6/04)

721 Taylor, Benjamin. *The Book of Getting Even* (9–12). 2008, Steerforth $23.95 (978-1-58642-143-4). This intelligent novel follows Gabriel Geismar as he copes with life by studying numbers and astrophysics. (Rev: BL 3/15/08)

722 Teller, Janne. *Nothing* (7–12). 2010, Simon & Schuster $16.99 (978-1-4169-8579-2). A group of 7th-grade students struggle to defuse a classmate's existential crisis in this compelling novel translated from Danish. Printz Honor 2011; Batchelder Honor 2011; ALA Notable Books 2011. ∩ e (Rev: BL 12/1/09*; LMC 3–4/10; SLJ 4/10)

723 Thomas, Jodi. *Somewhere Along the Way* (10–12). 2010, Berkley paper $7.99 (978-04252377-2-4). In this sequel to *Welcome to Harmony* (2010), Reagan settles into life in the Texas town and finds friendship as well as support from the quirky residents. (Rev: BLO 10/1–15/10)

724 Thomas, Valerie, and Stacy Kramer. *From What I Remember . . .* (9–12). 2012, Hyperion/Disney $16.99 (978-1-4231-5508-9). Valedictorian Kylie and her friends try to work out the events of the previous couple of days when Kylie wakes up in Mexico next to Max, with no idea how she got there. e (Rev: LMC 10/12; SLJ 5/1/12)

725 Tigelaar, Liz. *Pretty Tough* (7–12). 2007, Penguin paper $8.99 (978-1-59514-112-5). Krista and Charlie Brown are sisters but very different — one popular, one solitary; when they are both chosen for the soccer team they must work together. (Rev: BCCB 2/08; SLJ 9/07)

726 Toews, Miriam. *A Boy of Good Breeding* (9–12). 2006, Counterpoint paper $14.00 (978-1-58243-340-0). Meet Hosea Funk, the mayor of tiny Algren, Canada, and the people who make the town special. (Rev: BL 5/15/06)

727 Toews, Miriam. *Summer of My Amazing Luck* (10–12). 2006, Counterpoint paper $14.00 (978-1-58243-346-2). Uncertain about the identify of the father of her 9-month-old son, Lucy, a funny and vulnerable 18-year-old, is determined to find love and a happy life. (Rev: BL 7/06)

728 Townsend, Wendy. *Lizard Love* (6–12). 2008, Front St $17.95 (978-1-932425-34-5). Grace, a country girl living in Manhattan, is thrilled to discover a city pet store that is stocked with reptiles and that becomes a refuge from the pressures of school and life. (Rev: BL 5/1/08; SLJ 8/08)

729 Tracey, Rhian. *When Isla Meets Luke Meets Isla* (8–10). 2004, Bloomsbury paper $9.95 (978-0-7475-6344-0). Told from alternating points of view, this is the story of troubled teens Isla and Luke — a Scottish girl who has just moved to England and a son of a newly divorced, obsessive mother — and the support and affection they give to each other. (Rev: SLJ 2/04)

730 Trembath, Don. *Rooster* (9–12). 2005, Orca paper $7.95 (978-1-55143-261-8). Rooster risks failing to graduate from high school until he is persuaded to coach a bowling team of special-needs adults; the death of one of these bowlers is the catalyst that pushes him to succeed. (Rev: SLJ 1/06; VOYA 10/05)

731 Trevanian. *The Crazyladies of Pearl Street* (9–12). 2005, Crown paper $13.95 (978-1-4000-8037-3). In 1936, Ruby moves 6-year-old Jean-Luc LaPointe and 3-year-old Anne-Marie to Albany, New York, to be with the father who is supposed to be getting out of jail but never turns up; they find a home on Pearl Street in a depressed Irish neighborhood and for the following years, Jean-Luc dreams of a better life. (Rev: BL 3/15/05)

732 Trigiani, Adriana. *Viola in Reel Life* (7–10). 2009, HarperTeen $16.99 (978-0-06-145102-7). Ninth-grader Viola feels neglected after her parents, documentary filmmakers, send her to a boarding school while they film in Afghanistan; but after making friends and getting involved in activities, she warms to her new school and finds a potential new romantic interest. e Lexile 820L (Rev: BL 8/09; SLJ 9/09; VOYA 12/09)

733 Trigiani, Adriana. *Viola in the Spotlight* (7–10). 2011, HarperTeen $16.99 (978-0-06-145105-8). In this sequel to *Viola in Reel Life* (1999) Viola is back home in Brooklyn with her parents and looking forward to the summer, but things don't turn out as she expected and she has to find different ways to fill her days. e Lexile 730L (Rev: BL 6/1/11; SLJ 9/1/11; VOYA 8/11)

734 Trujillo, Carla. *What Night Brings* (11–12). 2003, Curbstone paper $15.95 (978-1-880684-94-8). Marci is only 11, but she is smart, alert, amusing about her family's various secrets (including drugs, homosexuality, and infidelity), and already aware that she prefers girls. (Rev: BL 3/15/03*)

735 Ulinich, Anya. *Petropolis* (11–12). 2007, Viking $24.95 (978-0-670-03819-0). Sasha, a Russian Jew who has grown up in a Siberian wasteland, sets off for America and a series of entertaining yet poignant adventures. (Rev: BL 12/15/06)

736 Valdes-Rodriguez, Alisa. *Haters* (10–12). 2006, Little, Brown $16.99 (978-0-316-01307-9). When she moves with her father from Taos to Orange County, California, 16-year-old Pasquala "Paski" Archuleta, who has psychic abilities, finds herself dealing with a whole new set of social problems. ⋒ (Rev: BL 11/1/06; LMC 4–5/07; SLJ 12/06)

737 van de Ruit, John. *Spud* (8–12). 2007, Penguin paper $16.99 (978-1-59514-170-5). Attending an elite boys boarding school in Australia in 1990, 13-year-old Spud describes in diary form his problems with his classmates and his family as well as his thoughts on Mandela's release from prison; the fast-paced humor of this novel will get readers past the unfamiliar vocabulary and sports. (Rev: BL 9/15/07; SLJ 12/07)

738 van de Ruit, John. *Spud — The Madness Continues . . .* (8–12). 2008, Penguin $16.99 (978-159514190-3). In this humorous sequel to *Spud* (2007), Spud is still at his South African boarding school and dealing with puberty, a changing voice, racism, and particularly useless adults. (Rev: BLO 10/1/08; LMC 3/08)

739 Vande Velde, Vivian. *Remembering Raquel* (8–11). 2007, Harcourt $16.00 (978-0-15-205976-7). In text, emails, and blogs, classmates and others remember Raquel, a high-school freshman who died in a car accident, and learn that there was more to her than met the eye; this will appeal to reluctant readers. (Rev: BL 11/15/07; HB 1–2/08; LMC 2/08; SLJ 12/07)

740 Vaught, Susan. *Freaks Like Us* (7–12). 2012, Bloomsbury $16.99 (978-159990872-4). Jason, a high schooler with schizophrenia, investigates when one of his fellow disturbed students disappears. ℮ Lexile 890L (Rev: BL 10/1/12; HB 9–10/12; LMC 1–2/13*; VOYA 12/12)

741 Velasquez, Gloria. *Ankiza* (7–12). Series: Roosevelt High School. 2000, Piñata $16.95 (978-1-55885-308-9); paper $9.95 (978-1-55885-309-6). African American Ankiza learns about prejudice when she starts dating a white boy. (Rev: SLJ 4/01; VOYA 8/01)

742 Vivian, Siobhan. *The List* (9–12). 2012, Scholastic $17.99 (978-054516917-2). Nobody knows who posts the list of the prettiest and ugliest girls in each grade at Mount Washington High School in September every year. ℮ Lexile 750L (Rev: BL 4/15/12; SLJ 3/12)

743 Volponi, Paul. *The Hand You're Dealt* (8–11). 2008, Atheneum $16.99 (978-1-4169-6935-8). A raw and gritty coming-of-age page-turner about grief, family, and Texas Hold 'Em poker, featuring Huck Porter, a young man determined to avenge his father. (Rev: BL 8/08)

744 Von Ziegesar, Cecily. *Gossip Girl* (10–12). 2002, Little, Brown paper $8.95 (978-0-316-91033-0). *Gossip Girl* is full of tales about the teens of Manhattan's Upper East Side indulging in sex, drugs, high fashion, and high drama. (Rev: BL 6/1–15/02; SLJ 6/02; VOYA 6/02)

745 Von Ziegesar, Cecily. *Only in Your Dreams* (10–12). Series: Gossip Girl. 2006, Little, Brown paper $9.99 (978-0-316-01182-2). Blair travels to London to see her boyfriend while Serena is pursuing a movie career, Nate's going to the Hamptons, and Dan and Vanessa start a hot summer romance. (Rev: BL 8/06)

746 Vrettos, Adrienne Maria. *Skin* (8–11). 2006, Simon & Schuster $16.95 (978-1-4169-0655-1). Fourteen-year-old Donnie tells the story of his parents' unhappy marriage and his older sister's death from anorexia. (Rev: BL 3/1/06; SLJ 6/06)

747 Waite, Judy. *Forbidden* (8–11). 2006, Simon & Schuster $16.95 (978-0-689-87642-4). As one of the Chosen girls in the True Cause cult led by Howard, 16-year-old Elinor does not question her life until Outsider Jaime appears. (Rev: BCCB 2/06; BL 4/15/06; SLJ 3/06)

748 Wallington, Aury. *Pop!* (10–12). 2006, Penguin $8.99 (978-1-59514-092-0). Marit, 17, wants to lose her virginity but becomes nervous every time things get physical so she decides to do it with her best friend Jamie, which complicates their friendship. (Rev: BL 9/15/06; SLJ 1/07)

749 Walls, Jeannette. *Half Broke Horses* (11–12). 2009, Scribner $25 (978-141658628-9). In this "true-life novel" the author of *The Glass Castle* (2005) tells the story of her maternal grandmother, an impressive character who trained horses at a young age, taught school, and ran a large ranch during hard times in the Southwest; for mature readers. ⋒ (Rev: BL 9/09*)

750 Walters, Eric. *Stuffed* (8–12). Series: Orca Soundings. 2006, Orca $14.95 (978-1-55143-519-0). Ian gets even more of a reaction than he bargained for when he and his friends boycott a fast-food restaurant. (Rev: SLJ 10/06)

751 Wasserman, Robin. *Hacking Harvard* (8–11). 2007, Simon & Schuster paper $8.99 (978-1-4169-3633-6). Eric, Max, and Schwarz set out to hack into Harvard's admissions computer system and get their classmate Clay (who is definitely not Harvard material) admitted to the university. (Rev: BL 1/1–15/08; SLJ 1/08)

752 Watson, Sasha. *Vidalia in Paris* (9–12). 2008, Viking $16.99 (978-067001094-3). Studying art in Paris, Vidalia Sloane is beguiled by wily, smooth-talking Marco, a wannabe art dealer who isn't afraid to bend the rules to get what he wants. ℮ Lexile HL710L (Rev: BL 11/15/08; SLJ 4/1/09; VOYA 12/08)

753 Weiner, Jennifer. *Best Friends Forever* (10–12). 2009, Atria $26.95 (978-074329429-4). This story of a high school reunion gone awry includes many flashbacks to friends Val and Addie's younger lives. ⋒ (Rev: BL 7/09)

754 Weingarten, Lynn. *The Secret Sisterhood of Heartbreakers* (8–11). 2012, HarperTeen $17.99 (978-006192618-1). Reeling from a bad breakup, Lucy is intrigued by the appearance of three magical girls who offer to cure her heartbreak. **e** (Rev: BLO 12/15/11; SLJ 3/12; VOYA 12/11)

755 Weingarten, Lynn. *Wherever Nina Lies* (8–12). 2009, Scholastic $16.99 (978-054506631-0). Ellie, 16, sets out on a road trip to find her missing older sister and encounters romance and mystery in this compelling read. YALSA Popular Paperbacks for Young Adults Top Ten 2011. Lexile HL780L (Rev: BL 2/15/09; SLJ 8/09)

756 Wells, Pamela. *The Heartbreakers* (9–12). 2007, Scholastic $16.99 (978-0-439-02691-8). A group of friends, who have all been dumped by their boyfriends, make a list of breakup rules to get them through. (Rev: BL 9/15/07; SLJ 3/08)

757 Wells, Rebecca. *Ya-Yas in Bloom* (11–12). 2005, HarperCollins $24.95 (978-0-06-019534-2). This follow-up to *The Divine Secrets of the Ya-Ya Sisterhood* (1996) collects vignettes about the origins and exploits of the sisterhood and introduces the next two generations of Ya-Yas; for mature teens. (Rev: BL 1/1–15/05; VOYA 10/05)

758 Whitaker, Alecia. *The Queen of Kentucky* (7–10). 2012, Little, Brown $17.99 (978-031612506-2). New high school freshman Ricki Jo tries to reinvent herself as Ericka but finds popularity elusive in this novel set in rural Kentucky. **e** Lexile 860L (Rev: BL 10/15/11; SLJ 1/12)

759 White, Ellen Emerson. *Long May She Reign* (9–12). Series: Meg Powers. 2007, Feiwel & Friends $17.95 (978-0-312-36767-1). In the fourth book in the series, Meg (the teenage daughter of America's first woman president) has survived her kidnapping, but not without physical and emotional wounds that make her first year of college challenging. (Rev: BL 10/15/07; SLJ 12/07)

760 Whitney, Daisy. *The Rivals* (9–12). 2012, Little, Brown $17.99 (978-031609057-5). Alex is now the leader of the student justice system trying to bring order to their privileged Themis Academy and faces obstacles as she tries to stop a ring of drug users; the sequel to *The Mockingbirds* (2010). **e** (Rev: BL 2/15/12; LMC 1–2/12; SLJ 2/12)

761 Willey, Margaret. *A Summer of Silk Moths* (7–10). 2009, Flux paper $9.95 (978-0-7387-1540-7). Seventeen-year-old Pete and Nora overcome their initial animosity as they realize sobering truths about their pasts in this contemplative story with a nature preserve setting. (Rev: BLO 11/16/09; LMC 11–12/09; SLJ 1/10)

762 Williamson, Debrah. *Singing with the Top Down* (10–12). 2006, NAL paper $12.95 (978-0-451-21926-8). When their parents are killed in a roller-coaster accident, glamorous aunt Nora takes 13-year-old Pauly Mahoney and her little brother, Buddy, on an improbable cross-country adventure to live with her in California. (Rev: BL 7/06)

763 Wingate, Lisa. *Never Say Never* (11–12). 2010, Bethany paper $14.99 (978-07642049-2-0). A motley crew of hurricane evacuees, from 69-year-old Donetta to 27-year-old Kai, wind up in Daily, Texas, where they find new experiences; a quirky Christian adventure story with a dollop of romance. (Rev: BL 2/1–15/10)

764 Winston, Sherri. *Acting: A Novel* (9–12). 2004, Marshall Cavendish $15.95 (978-0-7614-5173-0). Sixteen-year-old Eve struggles with her own sexual feelings amid the family upheaval when her twin sister announces her pregnancy. (Rev: BL 10/1/04; VOYA 6/05)

765 Wiseman, Rosalind. *Boys, Girls and Other Hazardous Materials* (7–10). 2010, Putnam $17.99 (978-0-399-24796-5). Freshman Charlie finds new and old friends in high school and learns about romance and social pressure while navigating bullies and cliques. **e** Lexile HL660L (Rev: BL 12/15/09; SLJ 1/10; VOYA 4/10)

766 Wittlinger, Ellen. *Blind Faith* (7–10). 2006, Simon & Schuster $15.95 (978-1-4169-0273-7). Her mother's grief following the death of her grandmother causes 15-year-old Elizabeth to struggle with questions of faith even as she finds some solace in the new boy across the street. (Rev: BL 6/1–15/06; HB 7–8/06; SLJ 9/06)

767 Wittlinger, Ellen. *Razzle* (7–12). 2001, Simon & Schuster $17.00 (978-0-689-83565-0). New on Cape Cod, Kenyon becomes friends with an offbeat girl named Razzle — until he falls for beautiful Harley — in this mutilayered and appealing novel. (Rev: BCCB 10/01; BL 11/1/01; HB 11–12/01; HBG 3/02; SLJ 9/01; VOYA 10/01)

768 Wizner, Jake. *Castration Celebration* (11–12). 2009, Random House $16.99 (978-037585215-2); LB $19.99 (978-037595215-9). Olivia has a wild summer (including sex and drugs) at a Yale drama camp, culminating in a production of her musical about castration; this lighthearted book is full of entertaining references. (Rev: BL 4/15/09; SLJ 4/1/09)

769 Wolff, Virginia Euwer. *True Believer* (7–12). Series: Make Lemonade. 2001, Simon & Schuster $17.00 (978-0-689-82827-0). Poverty and violence are continuing forces in this sequel to *Make Lemonade*, in which LaVaughn fosters her college ambitions and finds romance. YPL National Book Award 2001; Printz Honor 2002. ⌒ (Rev: BL 6/1–15/02; HB 1–2/01; HBG 10/01; SLJ 1/01; VOYA 4/01)

770 Wood, Maryrose. *My Life the Musical* (8–12). 2008, Delacorte $15.99 (978-0-385-73278-9). Emily and Philip, both 16, have seen the musical "Aurora" umpteen times; what will they do if the show closes? (Rev: BL 2/20/08; SLJ 5/08)

771 Woolston, Blythe. *Catch and Release* (10–12). 2012, Carolrhoda $17.95 (978-076137755-9). Two teens who survive a flesh-eating bacteria become unlikely friends and, feeling rejected because of their different injuries, embark on a fishing and road trip. **e** Lexile 690L (Rev: BL 1/1/12; LMC 5–6/12; SLJ 3/12)

772 Wroblewski, David. *The Story of Edgar Sawtelle* (11–12). 2008, Ecco $26.95 (978-006137422-7). When mute teen Edgar Sawtelle's father is murdered by his uncle, Edgar turns to the dogs on his small Wisconsin farm — as well as his own wits and a Shakespeare-style apparition of his dead father — to understand the crime; suitable for mature readers. ☊ **e** (Rev: BL 6/1–15/08)

773 Wunder, Wendy. *The Probability of Miracles* (7–12). 2011, Penguin $17.99 (978-1-59514-368-6). After seven years of battling cancer, 16-year-old Cam learns that nothing more can be done and heads with her mother and sister to Promise, Maine, where miracles are known to happen; a quirky, often funny novel. ☊ **e** Lexile HL800L (Rev: BL 12/1/11; LMC 3–4/12; SLJ 12/1/11*)

774 Wynne-Jones, Tim. *A Thief in the House of Memory* (7–10). 2005, Farrar $17.00 (978-0-374-37478-5). Sixteen-year-old Dec can barely recall the events surrounding his mother's sudden disappearance six years earlier until the death of an intruder in the family home reawakens forgotten memories. (Rev: BCCB 5/05; BL 3/1/05; HB 5–6/05; SLJ 4/05; VOYA 6/05)

775 Yandell, J. Belinda. *Small Change: The Secret Life of Penny Burford* (10–12). 2002, Cumberland House $14.95 (978-1-58182-304-2). A housewife secretly amasses a large amount of money for charity by collecting her husband's loose change. (Rev: BL 6/1–15/02)

776 Zadoff, Allen. *My Life, the Theater, and Other Tragedies* (7–12). 2011, Egmont $16.99 (978-1-60684-036-8). High school theater "technie" Adam is drawn to an attractive young actress and overcomes his shyness even as he begins to come to terms with his father's death two years before. ☊ **e** Lexile HL500L (Rev: BL 5/1/11; HB 5–6/11; SLJ 7/11; VOYA 4/11)

777 Zarr, Sara. *Once Was Lost* (8–10). 2009, Little, Brown $16.99 (978-0-316-03604-7). A 13-year-old girl is missing and 15-year-old Samara begins to question her faith. Best Books for Young Adults 2010. ☊ **e** (Rev: BL 11/15/09*; SLJ 11/09)

778 Zemser, Amy Bronwen. *Dear Julia* (7–10). 2008, Greenwillow $16.99 (978-0-06-029458-8); LB $17.89 (978-006029459-5). Two unlikely young women — Elaine, 16, and Lucinda — forge a friendship built on shared family quirks and their separate quests for fulfillment and renown in this lighthearted exploration of feminist themes. Lexile 780L (Rev: BL 9/1/08; SLJ 1/1/09; VOYA 2/09)

779 Zevin, Gabrielle. *Because It Is My Blood* (8–11). 2012, Farrar $17.99 (978-0-374-38074-8). In 2083, 17-year-old Anya is released from Liberty Children's Facility (after the events of 2011's *All These Things I've Done*) and must figure out what to do about her

back-stabbing, unreliable, criminally inclined family. ☊ **e** Lexile 640L (Rev: BL 8/12; SLJ 9/12; VOYA 8/12)

780 Zielin, Lara. *The Waiting Sky* (8–11). 2012, Putnam $16.99 (978-0-399-25686-8). Seventeen-year-old Jane is guilt-ridden when she leaves her alcoholic mother for the summer and goes to work with her brother's tornado-chasing team in this novel that also features potential romance. **e** (Rev: BL 10/1/12; HB 7–8/12; SLJ 8/1/12; VOYA 8/12)

781 Zindel, Lizabeth. *Girl of the Moment* (7–10). 2007, Viking $16.99 (978-0-670-06210-2). Being a celebrity's assistant isn't all it's cracked up to be, as Lily learns when she takes a job working for the ultra-famous, ultra-rich Sabrina Snow. (Rev: BL 3/15/07; SLJ 6/07)

Ethnic Groups and Problems

782 Abdel-Fattah, Randa. *Does My Head Look Big in This?* (7–10). 2007, Scholastic $16.99 (978-0-439-91947-0). Amal is a Muslim Palestinian growing up in Australia, where family, friends, and strangers all react in different ways to her decision to veil herself in the traditional hijab. (Rev: BCCB 9/07; BL 7/07; LMC 11–12/07; SLJ 6/07)

783 Abdel-Fattah, Randa. *Ten Things I Hate About Me* (7–10). 2009, Scholastic $16.99 (978-054505055-5). In this humorous story about fitting in and finding who you really are, 16-year-old Jamilah — known as Jamie at school — is a Lebanese Australian Muslim who isn't comfortable telling her friends who she really is and hides her identity by dying her hair blond and wearing blue contact lenses. Lexile HL720L (Rev: BL 12/1/08; SLJ 2/1/09; VOYA 6/09)

784 Acosta, Belinda. *Sisters, Strangers, and Starting Over* (11–12). 2010, Grand Central paper $13.99 (978-04465405-2-0). Planning Celeste's quinceañera celebration keeps her extended family together in spite of rapidly changing dynamics and turmoil, as well as questions about her mother's murder; for mature readers. (Rev: BL 6/1–15/10)

785 Adler, Emily, and Alex Echevarria. *Sweet 15* (7–10). 2010, Marshall Cavendish $16.99 (978-0-7614-5584-4). Destiny Lozada is not sure she wants to have a quinceañera but she also does not want to disappoint her Puerto Rican family. (Rev: BLO 3/1/10; LMC 8–9/10; SLJ 7/10)

786 Alegria, Malin. *Crossing the Line* (7–12). Series: Border Town. 2012, Scholastic/Point paper $5.99 (978-054540240-8). An appealing first novel in a series featuring Latina teen Fabiola and her younger sister Alexis as they deal with the family restaurant, small town life close to the Mexican border, school life, and a mystery. **e** Lexile 680L (Rev: BL 5/15/12; LMC 5–6/13*; SLJ 6/12)

787 Alegría, Malín. *Estrella's Quinceañera* (7–10). 2006, Simon & Schuster $14.95 (978-0-689-87809-1). Planning for her 15th birthday celebration, Mexican American Estrella finds herself balancing her hopes against reality. (Rev: BL 2/15/06; SLJ 4/06)

788 Alegría, Malín. *Sofi Mendoza's Guide to Getting Lost in Mexico* (10–12). 2007, Simon & Schuster $15.99 (978-0-689-87811-4). After sneaking out to a party near Tijuana, spoiled 17-year-old Sofi Mendoza is stopped at the border on her way home and learns that her green card is a fake; while she is stuck in Mexico she learns to appreciate her Mexican relatives and her parents' efforts on her behalf. (Rev: BCCB 7–8/07; BL 8/07; LMC 11–12/07; SLJ 6/07)

789 Allen, Paula Gunn. *Spider Woman's Granddaughters: Traditional Tales and Contemporary Writing by Native American Women* (10–12). 1989, Beacon paper $14.00 (978-0-449-90508-1). This is an engrossing collection of 24 traditional and modern stories by Native American women.

790 Alvarez, Julia. *Finding Miracles* (8–11). 2004, Knopf LB $17.99 (978-0-375-82760-0). Sixteen-year-old Milly Kaufman, rescued as a child from a strife-torn Latin American nation, is encouraged to return to her native country and learn more about her family roots. (Rev: BL 10/15/04; SLJ 10/04; VOYA 12/04)

791 Alvarez, Julia. *How the Garcia Girls Lost Their Accents* (10–12). 1991, Algonquin $18.95 (978-0-945575-57-3). This novel, told in reverse chronological order, tells how the four Garcia girls and their family became Americanized after leaving the Dominican Republic in the 1960s. (Rev: BL 8/05; SLJ 9/91)

792 Alvarez, Julia. *Yo!* (10–12). 1997, Algonquin $29.95 (978-1-56512-157-7). The 16 stories in this collection feature the family and friends of Yolanda Garcia, whose roots are in the Dominican Republic. (Rev: BL 9/15/96; SLJ 4/97)

793 Anaya, Rudolfo. *Bless Me, Ultima* (10–12). 1994, Warner paper $6.99 (978-0-446-60025-5). A novel about growing up Chicano in southeastern New Mexico during the 1940s.

794 Angell, Judie. *One-Way to Ansonia* (7–10). 2001, iUniverse paper $12.95 (978-0-595-15830-0). In novel format this is the story of a young Russian girl's experience in this country around the turn of the century; originally published in 1985. (Rev: BL 1/1/86; SLJ 12/85; VOYA 2/86)

795 Asim, Jabari. *A Taste of Honey* (11–12). 2010, Broadway paper $13 (978-07679197-8-4). In this collection of vivid, fast-paced stories, Asim weaves a rich tapestry of life in the fictional Midwest town of Gateway City, where a black family is grappling with racial limitation and family dynamics in 1967; for mature readers. (Rev: BL 3/1–15/10)

796 Augenbraum, Harold, and Ilan Stavans, eds. *Growing Up Latino: Memoirs and Stories* (9–12). 1993, Houghton Mifflin paper $15.00 (978-0-395-66124-6). The "Hispanic journey from darkness to light, from rejection to assimilation, from silence to voice," in 25 diverse, eloquent voices. (Rev: BL 2/1/93)

797 Baca, Jimmy Santiago. *A Glass of Water* (11–12). 2009, Grove $23 (978-080211922-3). Baca's novel about two immigrant brothers illustrates the tragic circumstances of life on the U.S./Mexico border; suitable for mature readers. (Rev: BL 9/09)

798 Baez, Annecy. *My Daughter's Eyes and Other Stories* (9–12). 2007, Curbstone paper $15.00 (978-1-931896-38-2). Fourteen interrelated stories concerning Dominican girls growing up in the Bronx in the late 20th century reveal such issues as overprotective fathers, hot-tempered mothers, developing sexual awareness, self-esteem, sexual abuse, and the political turmoil in the homeland. (Rev: BL 11/1/07; SLJ 11/07)

799 Bailey-Williams, Nicole. *A Little Piece of Sky* (7–12). 2002, Broadway paper $9.95 (978-0-7679-1216-7). Song Byrd is an African American girl who rises above her very difficult circumstances in this realistic and compelling novel. (Rev: VOYA 4/03)

800 Baldwin, James. *Go Tell It on the Mountain* (10–12). 1953, Knopf $14.95 (978-0-679-60154-8). A novel about a black boy growing up and his relationships with his father and his church.

801 Barrett, William E. *The Lilies of the Field* (8–12). 1988, Warner paper $5.99 (978-0-446-31500-5). A young black man, Homer Smith, helps a group of German nuns to achieve their dream.

802 Barth-Grozinger, Inge. *Something Remains* (8–11). Trans. by Anthea Bell. 2006, Hyperion $16.99 (978-0-7868-3880-6). This book is based on the true story of a 12-year-old Jewish boy named Erich Levi and what life was like for him and his family, dealing with prejudice and persecution, during Hitler's first years in power. (Rev: BL 9/1/06; SLJ 12/06)

803 Bates, Judy Fong. *Midnight at the Dragon Café* (11–12). 2005, Counterpoint paper $14.00 (978-1-58243-189-5). Through deceptively simple narration, a Chinese girl tells of her immigration to Canada in the 1950s and her family's painful, hidden secrets; for mature teens. (Rev: BL 2/1/05)

804 Bavati, Robyn. *Dancing in the Dark* (7–11). 2013, Flux paper $9.99 (978-073873477-4). Ditty's love of ballet leads her to defy the edicts of her ultra-Orthodox Jewish family and at age 17 must make a difficult final choice. ℮ Lexile HL750L (Rev: BL 2/15/13; LMC 8–9/13; SLJ 2/13; VOYA 2/13)

805 Bedford, Simi. *Yoruba Girl Dancing* (9–12). 1994, Viking paper $14.00 (978-0-14-023293-6). A semiautobiographical novel about a Nigerian girl's adjustment to life at an English boarding school in the 1950s. (Rev: BL 10/1/92; SLJ 3/93*)

806 Bennett, O. H. *The Colored Garden* (10–12). 2000, Laughing Owl paper $12.50 (978-0-9659701-9-8). Sarge, newly relocated to his grandparents' farm in Kentucky, tries to find out the story behind the grave marked "Kate" in an old slave cemetery. (Rev: BL 2/15/00)

807 Bertrand, Diane Gonzales. *Sweet Fifteen* (8–12). 1995, Arte Publico paper $9.95 (978-1-55885-133-7). While making a party dress for Stefanie Bonilla, age 14, Rita Navarro falls in love with her uncle and befriends her widowed mother, maturing in the process. (Rev: BL 6/1–15/95; SLJ 9/95)

808 Brainard, Cecilia Manguerra, ed. *Growing Up Filipino: Stories for Young Adults* (9–12). 2003, PALH paper $18.95 (978-0-9719458-0-7). These stories by Filipino American writers will comfort and delight teenagers of Filipino descent. (Rev: BL 4/15/03; SLJ 6/03)

809 Brown, Wesley, and Amy Ling, eds. *Imagining America: Stories from the Promised Land* (9–12). 1992, Persea paper $12.95 (978-0-89255-167-5). A multicultural anthology of 37 stories by distinguished writers about emigration to and migration within the United States during the 20th century. (Rev: BL 12/15/91*; SLJ 6/92)

810 Canales, Viola. *Orange Candy Slices and Other Secret Tales* (6–12). 2001, Arte Publico paper $9.95 (978-1-55885-332-4). Life on the Texas-Mexico border is the focus of this collection of coming-of-age short stories. (Rev: VOYA 6/02)

811 Carlson, Lori Marie, ed. *American Eyes: New Asian-American Short Stories for Young Adults* (8–12). 1994, Henry Holt $15.95 (978-0-8050-3544-5). These stories present widely varied answers to the question, What does it mean to Asian American adolescents to grow up in a country that views them as aliens? (Rev: BL 1/1/95; SLJ 1/95; VOYA 5/95)

812 Carlson, Lori Marie, ed. *Voices in First Person: Reflections on Latino Identity* (7–12). Illus. by Flavio Morais. 2008, Simon & Schuster $16.99 (978-141696212-0). This book explores the experiences of Latinos in America through a variety of fictional monologues, poems, and short stories focusing on themes of heartbreak, prejudice, identity, and pride. ℮ (Rev: BL 10/1/08; HB 7–8/08; LMC 11–12/08; SLJ 8/08; VOYA 8/08)

813 Chase, Paula. *So Not the Drama* (7–10). Series: Del Rio Bay Clique. 2007, Kensington paper $9.95 (978-0-7582-1859-9). Mina deals with issues of popularity and prejudice at her high school, where students of all races and many backgrounds intermingle but don't always get along. (Rev: BL 2/1/07)

814 Childress, Alice. *A Hero Ain't Nothin' but a Sandwich* (7–10). 2000, Putnam paper $5.99 (978-0-698-11854-6). Benjie's life in Harlem, told from many viewpoints, involves drugs and rejection. (Rev: BL 10/15/88)

815 Cisneros, Sandra. *House on Mango Street* (10–12). 1994, Random House $24.00 (978-0-679-43335-4); paper $9.95 (978-0-679-73477-2). The rich story of a young girl, Esperanza Cordero, growing up in a deprived Latino neighborhood in Chicago and aspiring to greater things. (Rev: SLJ 7/05)

816 Cofer, Judith Ortiz. *If I Could Fly* (7–10). 2011, Farrar $16.99 (978-0-374-33517-5). When 15-year-old Doris's mother moves back to Puerto Rico, and her father is often absent, the girl finds comfort in a neighbor's pigeons. ℮ Lexile 820L (Rev: BL 5/1/11; HB 5–6/11; SLJ 6/11; VOYA 6/11)

817 Cofer, Judith Ortiz. *An Island Like You* (7–12). 2008, Paw Prints paper $15.99 (978-1-4395-0880-0). Stories of Puerto Rican immigrant children experiencing the tensions between two cultures. (Rev: BL 2/15/95*; SLJ 7/95)

818 Cofer, Judith Ortiz. *The Latin Deli* (9–12). 1993, Univ. of Georgia $24.95 (978-0-8203-1556-0). At the heart of this collection of stories, essays, and poems is the conflict of Cofer's childhood as a first-generation immigrant. (Rev: BL 11/15/93*)

819 Coldsmith, Don. *The Long Journey Home* (10–12). 2001, Tor $24.95 (978-0-312-87617-3). Based indirectly on the career of Jim Thorpe, this novel tells the story of John Buffalo, a Native American athlete who strives for and receives recognition and fame. (Rev: BL 3/15/01)

820 Daswani, Kavita. *Indie Girl* (7–10). 2007, Simon & Schuster paper $8.99 (978-1-4169-4892-6). Indira, who lives in Los Angeles, is thrilled to get a job for a fashion editor (even if she's only babysitting) until she discovers the woman is prejudiced against Indians. (Rev: BL 10/15/07; SLJ 12/07)

821 Dole, Mayra Lazara. *Down to the Bone* (9–12). 2008, HarperTeen $16.99 (978-0-06-084310-6). Lauri, a gay teenager in conservative Cuban Miami, is kicked out of her home and her school for her lesbianism. (Rev: BL 3/15/08; SLJ 5/08)

822 Draper, Sharon M. *Fire from the Rock* (9–12). 2007, Dutton $16.99 (978-0-525-47720-4). In 1957, Sylvia Patterson is one of the first black students to enter the all-white Central High School in Little Rock, Arkansas; this novel gives her account of the civil rights struggle that took place in her town and provides historical background. (Rev: BL 8/07; SLJ 10/07)

823 Easton, Kelly. *Hiroshima Dreams* (7–10). 2007, Dutton $16.99 (978-0-525-47821-8). Lin's Japanese mother wants their family to be more American but when her grandmother, Obaachan, arrives from Japan, she reminds them of their heritage. (Rev: BL 9/15/07; SLJ 12/07)

824 Ellison, James W. *Finding Forrester* (7–12). 2000, Newmarket paper $9.95 (978-1-55704-479-2). This inspiring novel tells how a reclusive author helps a promising inner-city African American youth to develop his writing skills. (Rev: SLJ 9/01; VOYA 6/01)

825 Erdrich, Louise. *The Round House* (11–12). 2012, HarperCollins $27.99 (978-0-06-206524-7). After his mother is attacked on their reservation in North Dakota and becomes deeply depressed, 14-year-old Joe and his friends set off to find the perpetrator; for mature readers. Alex Award 2013. ∩ ℮ (Rev: 8/12*; SLJ 1/13*)

826 Esquivel, Laura. *Like Water for Chocolate: A Novel in Monthly Installments, with Recipes, Romances, and Home Remedies* (10–12). 1992, Doubleday $23.00 (978-0-385-42016-7); paper $11.95 (978-0-385-42017-4). Recipes introduce each chapter of this novel about a traditional Mexican family, where much of the domestic drama takes place in the kitchen. (Rev: BL 9/15/92)

827 Felin, M. Sindy. *Touching Snow* (8–10). 2007, Atheneum $16.99 (978-1-4169-1795-3). Karina, 13, and her two Haitian sisters are referred to social services when their stepfather brutally beats Enid, the oldest sister, in this novel that shows the tensions in an immigrant family and the often unfulfilled aspirations. (Rev: BL 5/15/07; HB 7–8/07; SLJ 9/07)

828 Flake, Sharon G. *Who Am I Without Him?* (6–12). 2004, Hyperion $15.99 (978-0-7868-0693-5). Funny, moving, and truthful, these 10 short stories deal with growing up black in today's society. (Rev: BL 4/15/04*; HB 7–8/04; SLJ 5/04; VOYA 6/04)

829 Flake, Sharon G. *You Don't Even Know Me: Stories and Poems About Boys* (7–10). 2010, Disney/Jump at the Sun $16.99 (978-1-4231-0014-0). In prose and free-verse poetry, African American teens talk about their experiences in all areas of life in this companion to *Who Am I Without Him?* (2007). ℮ (Rev: BL 12/15/09; SLJ 5/10)

830 Gaines, Ernest J. *The Autobiography of Miss Jane Pittman* (9–12). 1971, Bantam paper $5.99 (978-0-553-26357-2). This novel, supposedly the memoirs of a 110-year-old ex-slave, is a stirring tribute to survival and courage.

831 Gallo, Donald R., ed. *Join In: Multiethnic Short Stories by Outstanding Writers for Young Adults* (7–12). 1995, Bantam paper $5.99 (978-0-440-21957-6). Seventeen stories concerning the problems teenagers of various ethnic backgrounds have living in the United States. (Rev: BL 1/15/94; SLJ 11/93; VOYA 10/93)

832 Gardner, Mary. *Boat People* (9–12). 1995, Norton $21.00 (978-0-393-03738-8). A sympathetic fictional portrait of Vietnamese refugees in Galveston, Texas. (Rev: BL 2/15/95*)

833 Garland, Sherry. *Shadow of the Dragon* (6–12). 1993, Harcourt $10.95 (978-0-15-273530-2); paper $6.00 (978-0-15-273532-6). Danny Vo has grown up American since he emigrated from Vietnam as a child. Now traditional Vietnamese ways, the new American culture, and skinhead prejudice clash, resulting in his cousin's death. (Rev: BL 11/15/93*; SLJ 11/93; VOYA 12/93)

834 Gillan, Maria Mazziotti, and Jennifer Gillan, eds. *Growing Up Ethnic in America: Contemporary Fiction About Learning to Be American* (10–12). 1999, Penguin paper $16.95 (978-0-14-028063-0). Thirty-five stories by such writers as Amy Tan, Toni Morrison, and E. L. Doctorow explore the ethnic experience. (Rev: BL 9/15/99)

835 Gonzalez, Christina Diaz. *The Red Umbrella* (6–10). 2010, Knopf $16.99 (978-0-375-86190-1). Lucia and her brother are uprooted from their comfortable life in Cuba and sent to live in Nebraska during the Communist revolution of the 1960s. ℮ (Rev: BLO 7/10; LMC 8–9/10; SLJ 5/10; VOYA 6/10)

836 Guy, Rosa. *The Friends* (7–10). 1995, Random House paper $5.99 (978-0-440-22667-3). Phyllisia, a newcomer to Harlem, finds a friend in the unusual Edith Jackson; first published in 1973.

837 Guy, Rosa. *The Music of Summer* (9–12). 1992, Doubleday $12.95 (978-0-385-30704-8). Sarah, age 17, weighs the pain of peer pressure against the excitement of first love during one summer on Cape Cod. (Rev: BL 4/15/92; SLJ 2/92)

838 Hale, Janet Campbell. *The Owl's Song* (10–12). 1976, Avon paper $2.50 (978-0-380-00605-2). A Native American boy faces new problems when he leaves the reservation to live with a half-sister in Los Angeles.

839 Hamilton, Julia. *Other People's Rules* (10–12). 2000, St. Martin's $24.95 (978-0-312-26627-1). In this gripping novel for mature readers, 15-year-old Lucy enjoys the lifestyle of her aristocratic friend Sarah but later discovers ugly truths about Sarah's family. (Rev: BL 10/1/00)

840 Hamilton, Virginia. *A White Romance* (8–12). 1987, Scholastic paper $4.50 (978-0-590-13005-9). A formerly all-black high school becomes integrated and social values and relationships change. (Rev: SLJ 1/88; VOYA 2/88)

841 Hardrick, Jackie. *Imani in Never Say Goodbye* (9–12). 2004, Enlighten paper $15.00 (978-0-9706226-2-4). The life of 17-year-old Imani, a typical African American high school student, intersects with many others who have greater problems than she does. (Rev: BL 2/15/04; SLJ 4/04; VOYA 12/03)

842 Hayes, Rosemary. *Mixing It* (7–12). 2007, Frances Lincoln paper $7.95 (978-1-84507-495-1). Fatimah, a Muslim, rescues a boy from a church bombing and exposes her family to unwanted attention in this novel set in England. (Rev: BL 1/1–15/08)

843 Hazelgrove, William Elliot. *Tobacco Sticks* (9–12). 1995, Pantonne $18.95 (978-0-9630052-8-1). Racial tensions come to a peak in 1945 Richmond, Virginia, when 13-year-old Lee Hartwell's lawyer father defends an African American maid in court. (Rev: BL 7/95; SLJ 9/95)

844 Headley, Justina Chen. *Nothing but the Truth (and a Few White Lies)* (9–12). 2006, Little, Brown $16.99 (978-0-316-01128-0). High school sophomore Patty Ho arrives at Stanford University for math camp feeling like she doesn't fit in anywhere but she begins to see things differently as she struggles to bridge the cultural distances between the white and Asian life. (Rev: BCCB 6/06; LMC 1/07; SLJ 7/06)

845 Henderson, Bill, ed. *The Pushcart Book of Short Stories: The Best Stories from a Quarter-Century of the Pushcart Prize* (10–12). 2001, Pushcart $35.00 (978-1-888889-23-9). For better readers, this is an anthology of short stories from previous winners of the Pushcart Prize, including such writers as Tobias Wolff, Cynthia Ozick, and Richard Ford. (Rev: BL 10/15/01)

846 Hernandez, Irene B. *Across the Great River* (7–10). 1989, Arte Publico paper $9.95 (978-0-934770-96-5). The harrowing story of a young Mexican girl and her family, who enter the United States illegally. (Rev: BL 8/89; SLJ 8/89)

847 Hernandez, Irene B. *The Secret of Two Brothers* (7–10). 1995, Arte Publico paper $9.95 (978-1-55885-142-9). An action-packed story about two Mexican American boys who meet many challenges. Especially appealing to those whose first language is Spanish or for reluctant readers. (Rev: BL 10/1/95; SLJ 11/95)

848 Hernández, Jo Ann Yolanda. *White Bread Competition* (7–12). 1997, Arte Publico paper $9.95 (978-1-55885-210-5). The effects of winning a spelling bee on Luz Rios and her Hispanic American family in San Antonio are explored in a series of vignettes. (Rev: BL 1/1–15/98; SLJ 8/98; VOYA 4/98)

849 Hidier, Tanuja Desai. *Born Confused* (9–12). 2002, Scholastic $16.95 (978-0-439-35762-3). Dimple Lala, a 17-year-old of Indian heritage who has been doing her best to fit in in America, is less than thrilled by her parents' choice of a suitor in this well-written novel. (Rev: BL 12/15/02; HBG 10/03; SLJ 12/02; VOYA 2/03)

850 Hijuelos, Oscar. *Dark Dude* (9–12). 2008, Simon & Schuster $16.99 (978-141694804-9). Cuban American teen Rico runs away from his troubled Harlem life to a midwestern hippie farm. ◑ ℮ Lexile 980L (Rev: BL 11/1/08; LMC 1–2/09; SLJ 11/1/08; VOYA 10/08)

851 Hoffman, Alice. *Incantation* (9–12). 2006, Little, Brown $16.99 (978-0-316-01019-1). Living in Spain during the time of the Spanish Inquisition, Estrella and her family hide the fact that they're Jewish but when Estrella's best friend finds out and betrays her by telling others, there are horrific consequences. Sidney Taylor Book Honor 2007. (Rev: BL 9/1/06; SLJ 12/06*)

852 Houston, Jeanne Wakatsuki. *The Legend of Fire Horse Woman* (10–12). 2003, Kensington $23.00 (978-0-7582-0455-4). This heartwarming multigenerational novel chronicles the lives of Sayo, a Japanese-born woman who emigrates to America after marriage and is interned during World War II; her daughter, Hana; and granddaughter, Terri. (Rev: BL 11/15/03)

853 Irwin, Hadley. *Kim / Kimi* (7–10). 1987, Penguin paper $5.99 (978-0-14-032593-5). A half-Japanese teenager brought up in an all-white small town sets out to explore her Asian roots. (Rev: BL 3/15/87; SLJ 5/87; VOYA 6/87)

854 Jackson, Brian Keith. *The View from Here* (10–12). 1998, Pocket paper $14.00 (978-0-671-56896-2). Set in rural Mississippi in the 1960s, this emotion-charged novel, told from various points of view, tells of a black family's struggle to succeed. (Rev: BL 2/15/97; SLJ 3/97)

855 Jimenez, Francisco. *The Circuit: Stories from the Life of a Migrant Child* (5–10). 1997, Univ. of New Mexico paper $11.95 (978-0-8263-1797-1). Eleven moving stories about the lives, fears, hopes, and problems of children in Mexican migrant worker families. (Rev: BL 12/1/97)

856 Jimenez, Francisco. *Reaching Out* (7–12). 2008, Houghton Mifflin $16 (978-061803851-0). In this fictionalized autobiography young Jimenez struggles to rise beyond his immigrant migrant farm family and succeed in college. Belpré Honor 2009; ALA Notable Books 2009. ℮ Lexile 910L (Rev: BL 8/08*; LMC 1–2/09; SLJ 12/08; VOYA 10/08)

857 Johnson, Angela. *Toning the Sweep* (7–12). 1993, Scholastic paper $6.99 (978-0-590-48142-7). This novel captures the innocence, vulnerability, and love of human interaction, as well as the melancholy, self-discovery, and introspection of an African American adolescent. (Rev: BL 4/1/93*; SLJ 4/93*)

858 Johnson, Dedra. *Sandrine's Letter to Tomorrow* (9–12). 2007, Ig paper $14.95 (978-0-9788431-2-0). Sandrine narrates the stories of her struggles with both white and black racism, sexism, and a physically and emotionally abusive mother while coming of age as an intelligent, lighted-skinned African American young lady in New Orleans. (Rev: BL 10/15/07)

859 Jolin, Paula. *In the Name of God* (9–12). 2007, Roaring Brook $16.95 (978-1-59643-211-6). What leads someone to become an extremist? Jolin attempts to answer that question with the story of Nadia, who becomes an Islamic fundamentalist when her cousin is arrested by the Syrian police. (Rev: BL 4/15/07; LMC 8–9/07; SLJ 4/07)

860 Jordan, Dream. *Hot Girl* (7–10). 2008, St. Martin's paper $9.95 (978-031238284-1). Troubled 14-year-old

African American Kate's resolve to stick with her new foster family is threatened when smooth-talking Naleejah takes her in, gives her a makeover, and teaches her how to win her crush's affection. **ℇ** Lexile HL660L (Rev: BLO 11/19/08; SLJ 4/1/09; VOYA 12/08)

861 Kaldas, Pauline, and Khaled Mattawa, eds. *Dinarzad's Children: An Anthology of Contemporary Arab American Fiction* (9–12). 2004, Univ. of Arkansas paper $24.95 (978-1-55728-781-6). Stories about what it is like to be an Arab in today's America, by Arab Americans from around the country. (Rev: BL 11/15/04)

862 Karim, Sheba. *Skunk Girl* (7–10). 2009, Farrar $16.95 (978-037437011-4). Muslim Nina, 16, comes from the only Pakistani American family in town, and struggles with her parents' strict rules and expectations and her own hairiness. Lexile 840L (Rev: BL 4/15/09; SLJ 4/1/09; VOYA 4/10)

863 Kelley, William. *The Sweet Summer* (10–12). 2000, Westminster $19.95 (978-0-664-22224-6). A novel set in the 1940s about a white Army recruit who wins a position on an all-black boxing team. (Rev: BL 4/15/00)

864 Keltner, Kim Wong. *Buddha Baby* (11–12). 2005, Avon paper $12.95 (978-0-06-075322-1). Chinese American Lindsey Owyang has become curious about her heritage — and, despite her permanent boyfriend, about what it would be like to date a Chinese guy — in this rich and entertaining novel in which she recalls her childhood worries about being different. (Rev: BL 8/05)

865 Kincaid, Jamaica. *The Autobiography of My Mother* (9–12). 1996, NAL paper $14.00 (978-0-452-27466-2). Kincaid's essay *A Small Place* is expanded into this novel about a woman's search for identity as she searches for her mother. (Rev: BL 12/1/95*)

866 Krech, Bob. *Rebound* (8–11). 2006, Marshall Cavendish $16.99 (978-0-7614-5319-2). In a school where Polish kids wrestle and African American kids play basketball, a student named Ray Wisniewski challenges the status quo and tries out for basketball, dealing with racism on and off the court. (Rev: BL 9/1/06; LMC 2/07; SLJ 12/06)

867 Kwok, Jean. *Girl in Translation* (11–12). 2010, Riverhead $25.95 (978-159448756-9). In this immigrant coming-of-age story, Kwok tells the story — loosely based on her own experience — of Kim, who arrives in Brooklyn from Hong Kong, helps her mother at the sweatshops, and faces down hostility and discrimination at every turn; for mature readers. Alex Award 2011. ☊ **ℇ** (Rev: BL 4/1–15/10)

868 Lahiri, Jhumpa. *The Namesake* (11–12). 2003, Houghton Mifflin $24.00 (978-0-395-92721-2). A young Bengali American struggles to escape his heritage and the strange name his father has given him: Gogol. (Rev: BL 6/1–15/03; SLJ 11/03)

869 Laird, Elizabeth. *Kiss the Dust* (6–10). 1992, Penguin $6.99 (978-0-14-036855-0). A docunovel about a refugee Kurdish teen caught up in the 1984 Iran-Iraq War. (Rev: BL 6/15/92)

870 Lansdale, Joe R. *The Bottoms* (10–12). 2000, Mysterious $24.95 (978-0-89296-704-9). Reminiscent of *To Kill a Mockingbird,* this novel set in East Texas in the early 1930s features two white youngsters and their father, caught up in the racially motivated murder of a young black woman. (Rev: BL 6/1–15/00; SLJ 1/01)

871 Lee, Gus. *China Boy* (9–12). 1994, NAL paper $15.00 (978-0-452-27158-6). Kai — or "China Boy," as he is called by the neighborhood bullies — turns his life around when he learns to stand his ground and fight back. (Rev: BL 3/1/91)

872 Lee, Harper. *To Kill a Mockingbird* (8–12). 1977, HarperCollins $23.00 (978-0-397-00151-4). A lawyer in a small Southern town defends an African American man wrongfully accused of rape.

873 Lee, Marie G. *Necessary Roughness* (7–12). 1996, HarperCollins LB $14.89 (978-0-06-025130-7). Chan, a Korean American football enthusiast, and his twin sister, Young, encounter prejudice when their family moves to a small Minnesota community. (Rev: BL 1/1–15/97; SLJ 1/97; VOYA 6/97)

874 Lee, Marie Myung-Ok. *Somebody's Daughter* (11–12). 2005, Beacon $23.95 (978-0-8070-8388-8). Raised in a stern adoptive midwestern family, 19-year-old Sarah travels to Korea, her birth land, intent on discovering the truth of her past. (Rev: BL 2/15/05; SLJ 4/05; VOYA 8/05)

875 Levitin, Sonia. *Strange Relations* (8–11). 2007, Knopf $15.99 (978-0-375-83751-7). Fifteen-year-old Marne, from a secular Jewish family, visits her conservative Jewish relatives in Hawaii and comes to appreciate their differences. Sydney Taylor Book Award 2008. (Rev: BL 6/1–15/07; SLJ 5/07)

876 Lewis, Beverly. *The Covenant* (10–12). Series: Abram's Daughters. 2002, Bethany paper $12.99 (978-0-7642-2330-3). Leah, a plain and practical Amish girl, is a contrast to her more flighty sister Sadie, whose romance with an outsider only brings trouble. (Rev: BL 8/02)

877 Lipsyte, Robert. *The Brave* (8–12). 1991, HarperCollins paper $5.99 (978-0-06-447079-7). A Native American heavyweight boxer is rescued from drugs, pimps, and hookers by a tough but tender ex-boxer/New York City cop. (Rev: BL 10/15/91; SLJ 10/91*)

878 Lipsyte, Robert. *The Chief* (7–10). 1995, HarperCollins paper $6.50 (978-0-06-447097-1). Sonny Bear can't decide whether to go back to the reservation, continue boxing, or become Hollywood's new Native American darling. Sequel to *The Brave.* (Rev: BL 6/1–15/93; VOYA 12/93)

879 Lipsyte, Robert. *The Contender* (9–12). 1967, HarperCollins paper $6.99 (978-0-06-447039-1). A black teenager hopes to get out of Harlem through a boxing career. (Rev: BL 3/1/90)

880 Litman, Ellen. *The Last Chicken in America: A Novel in Stories* (9–12). 2007, Norton $23.95 (978-0-393-06511-4). These short stories explore the experiences of Russian Jewish immigrants living in Pittsburgh and their struggles to find happiness in their confusing new surroundings. (Rev: BL 9/1/07)

881 Lopez, Lorraine. *Soy la Avon Lady and Other Stories* (11–12). 2002, Curbstone paper $15.95 (978-1-880684-86-3). Eleven short stories explore life for Hispanic Americans of all ages; for mature teens. (Rev: BL 8/02)

882 López, Tiffany Ana, ed. *Growing Up Chicana/o* (9–12). 1995, Avon paper $12.95 (978-0-380-72419-2). This anthology presents the writings of 20 current Chicano authors, including Rudolfo Anaya and Sandra Cisneros, on multicultural issues. (Rev: BL 12/1/93)

883 Ly, Many. *Roots and Wings* (6–10). 2008, Delacorte $15.99 (978-0-385-73500-1). Fourteen-year-old Grace learns about her Cambodian heritage when she and her mother travel to Florida for her grandmother's funeral. (Rev: BL 3/15/08; SLJ 7/08)

884 Lynch, Janet Nichols. *Messed Up* (7–10). 2009, Holiday House $17.95 (978-082342185-5). Part Cheyenne, part Mexican R.D. tries to make it on his own when the only reliable adult in his life dies and he must navigate life in an unstable school and a violent neighborhood. Lexile 780L (Rev: BL 4/1/09; SLJ 8/09; VOYA 8/09)

885 McCall, Guadalupe Garcia. *Under the Mesquite* (7–10). 2011, Lee & Low $18.95 (978-1-60060-429-4). After Lupita's mother is diagnosed with cancer, the teen finds herself assuming greater responsibility for her seven younger siblings in this Mexican American family story told in verse; includes a glossary of Spanish terms. Belpré Author Award 2012; ALA Notable Books 2012; YALSA Top Ten Best Fiction for Young Adults 2012. **e** Lexile 990L (Rev: BL 10/1/11; LMC 1–2/12; SLJ 10/1/11)

886 McCall, Nathan. *Them* (9–12). 2007, Atria $25.00 (978-1-4165-4915-4). A black man is irritated by efforts to gentrify his Atlanta neighborhood as exemplified in his new, white next-door neighbors. (Rev: BL 9/1/07)

887 McDonald, Janet. *Brother Hood* (7–12). 2004, Farrar $16.00 (978-0-374-30995-4). Nate Whitely, a 16-year-old student at a prestigious boarding school, finds himself straddling two very different cultures as he seeks to remain loyal to his Harlem roots. (Rev: BL 9/1/04; SLJ 11/04; VOYA 2/05)

888 McMullan, Margaret. *Cashay* (7–10). 2009, Houghton Mifflin $15.00 (978-054707656-0). Cashay's younger sister is killed in gang-related violence in their housing project, and Cashay is helped by a white mentor as her mother returns to drug taking. **e** Lexile 700L (Rev: BLO 5/27/09; SLJ 8/09)

889 Magoon, Kekla. *Fire in the Streets* (6–10). 2012, Aladdin $15.99 (978-1-4424-2230-8). African American Maxie, 14, gets involved with the Black Panthers in this compelling novel set in 1968 Chicago. **e** Lexile 650L (Rev: BL 7/12*; HB 9–10/12; LMC 1–2/13*; SLJ 9/12)

890 Major, Clarence, ed. *Calling the Wind: Twentieth-Century African-American Short Stories* (9–12). 1993, HarperCollins paper $19.95 (978-0-06-098201-0). Includes stories by Langston Hughes, Zora Neale Hurston, James Baldwin, Toni Morrison, and dozens more. (Rev: BL 12/1/92*)

891 Major, Devorah. *Brown Glass Windows* (10–12). 2002, Curbstone paper $15.95 (978-1-880684-87-0). An African American family in San Francisco faces competing demands from the Vietnam vet father and the graffiti artist son in a thoughtful, lyrical novel. (Rev: BL 5/1/02)

892 Malkani, Gautam. *Londonstani* (11–12). 2006, Penguin $24.95 (978-1-59420-097-7). Indian teenagers living in London deal with sex, violence, religion, and tradition; language limits this to mature teens. (Rev: BL 5/15/06)

893 Marino, Jan. *The Day That Elvis Came to Town* (7–10). 1993, Avon paper $3.50 (978-0-380-71672-2). In this tale of southern blacks, Wanda is thrilled when a room in her parents' boarding house is rented to Mercedes, who makes her feel pretty and smart — and who once went to school with Elvis Presley. (Rev: BL 12/15/90*; SLJ 1/91*)

894 Martin, Joe. *Fire in the Rock* (10–12). 2001, Novello Festival $21.95 (978-0-9708972-1-3). Racism and the role of religion in a person's life are the themes of this novel about the friendship between Bo, a white preacher's kid, and Poolo, an African American. (Rev: BL 10/15/01; SLJ 5/02)

895 Martinez, Victor. *Parrot in the Oven: Mi Vida* (7–10). 1996, HarperCollins LB $16.89 (978-0-06-026706-3). Through a series of vignettes, the story of Manuel, a teenage Mexican American, unfolds as he grows up in the city projects with an abusive father and a loving mother. (Rev: BL 10/15/96; SLJ 11/96)

896 Meminger, Neesha. *Shine, Coconut Moon* (7–10). 2009, Simon & Schuster $16.99 (978-141695495-8). An Indian American girl realizes how vital her heritage is to her in the months following 9/11. Lexile HL740L (Rev: BL 2/15/09; SLJ 4/1/09)

897 Meriwether, Louise. *Daddy Was a Number Runner* (7–12). 1986, Feminist paper $16.59 (978-1-55861-442-0). The story of Frances, a black girl, growing up in Harlem during the Depression.

898 Mi Young Hur, Angela. *The Queens of K-Town* (9–12). 2007, MacAdam $23.00 (978-1-59692-244-0); paper $13.00 (978-5-7). Ten years after her traumatic emigration to New York from Korea, Cora Moon looks back at her difficult teenage years in a struggle for understanding. (Rev: BL 8/07)

899 Miklowitz, Gloria D. *The War Between the Classes* (7–10). 1986, Dell paper $4.99 (978-0-440-99406-0). A Japanese American girl finds that hidden prejudices and bigotry emerge when students in school are divided into four socioeconomic groups. (Rev: BL 4/15/85; SLJ 8/85; VOYA 6/85)

900 Min, Katherine. *Secondhand World* (9–12). 2006, Knopf $23.00 (978-0-307-26344-5). A heartbreaking story of a Korean American family that suffers the loss of a son, then further tragedy when angry, neglected teenage daughter Isa propels them into danger. (Rev: SLJ 10/06)

901 Mosley, Walter. *Fortunate Son* (10–12). 2006, Little, Brown $23.95 (978-0-316-11471-4). This powerful story traces the lives of interracial stepbrothers whose family bonds are tested by tragedy and hardship. ⌒ (Rev: BL 4/15/06*)

902 Mullane, Deirdre. *Crossing the Danger Water: Three Hundred Years of African-American Writing* (9–12). 1993, Doubleday paper $16.00 (978-0-385-42243-7). The history of African Americans is explored in their writings, narratives, letters, editorials, speeches, lyrics, and folktales, from U.S. colonial times to today. (Rev: BL 11/1/93) [810.8]

903 Murguia, Alejandro. *This War Called Love* (11–12). 2002, City Lights paper $11.95 (978-0-87286-394-1). A collection of poignant and often humorous stories about Hispanic Americans; for mature readers. (Rev: BL 8/02)

904 Myers, Walter Dean. *Autobiography of My Dead Brother* (8–11). Illus. by Christopher Myers. 2005, HarperCollins LB $16.89 (978-0-06-058292-0). In this compelling novel of teenage life in contemporary Harlem, Jessie watches helplessly as his friend Rise drifts away from him, dragged down in a whirlpool of drugs and crime. (Rev: BL 6/1–15/05; SLJ 8/05; VOYA 10/05)

905 Myers, Walter Dean. *Fast Sam, Cool Clyde, and Stuff* (7–10). 1995, Peter Smith $20.75 (978-0-8446-6798-0); paper $6.99 (978-0-14-032613-0). Three male friends in Harlem join forces to found the 116th Street Good People.

906 Myers, Walter Dean. *Slam!* (8–12). 1996, Scholastic paper $15.95 (978-0-590-48667-5). Although Slam is successful on the school's basketball court, his personal life has problems caused by difficulties fitting into an all-white school, a very sick grandmother, and a friend who is involved in drugs. (Rev: BL 11/15/96; SLJ 11/96; VOYA 2/97)

907 Myers, Walter Dean. *Street Love* (9–12). 2006, HarperCollins $15.99 (978-0-06-028079-6). In free verse, successful Damien, 17, and struggling Junice, 16, both African Americans from Harlem, describe the romance that flourishes despite their differences. (Rev: BL 10/1/06; HB 11–12/06; SLJ 11/06)

908 Myers, Walter Dean. *The Young Landlords* (7–10). 1979, Penguin paper $6.99 (978-0-14-034244-4). A group of African American teenagers take over a slum building in Harlem.

909 Na, An. *A Step from Heaven* (9–12). 2001, Front St $16.95 (978-1-886910-58-4). America has been portrayed as "heaven," but Young Ju finds life there difficult as she struggles to cope with the transition from life in Korea to life as an immigrant, and with the behavior of her unhappy and alcoholic father. (Rev: BCCB 7–8/01; BL 6/1–15/01*; HB 7–8/01*; HBG 10/01; SLJ 5/01*; VOYA 6/01)

910 Namioka, Lensey. *April and the Dragon Lady* (7–12). 1994, Harcourt $10.95 (978-0-15-276644-3). A Chinese American high school junior must relinquish important activities to care for her ailing grandmother and struggles with the constraints of a traditional female role. (Rev: BL 3/1/94; SLJ 4/94; VOYA 6/94)

911 Naylor, Gloria, ed. *Children of the Night: The Best Short Stories by Black Writers, 1967 to the Present* (9–12). 1996, Little, Brown $24.95 (978-0-316-59926-9). A short-story collection, balanced thematically, from the editorial hands of one of the finest black female writers. (Rev: BL 12/1/95)

912 Olsen, Sylvia. *The Girl with a Baby* (6–10). 2004, Sono Nis paper $7.95 (978-1-55039-142-8). A biracial girl of white and Indian parents wants to stay in school and raise her baby but finds it difficult. (Rev: BL 3/15/04; SLJ 7/04)

913 Olsen, Sylvia. *White Girl* (7–10). 2005, Sono Nis paper $8.95 (978-1-55039-147-3). When her mother marries a native Canadian, 15-year-old Josie feels anger at being moved to a reservation where she is taunted for being different, but she eventually works past her resentment and begins to appreciate the larger family of which she is now a part. (Rev: BCCB 9/05; BL 4/15/05*; SLJ 7/05; VOYA 6/05)

914 Osa, Nancy. *Cuba 15* (6–10). 2003, Delacorte $15.95 (978-0-385-72021-2). Violet Paz, who considers herself totally American, is surprised when her grandmother insists that she celebrate a traditional coming-of-age ceremony. (Rev: BL 7/03*)

915 Ostow, Micol. *Emily Goldberg Learns to Salsa* (8–11). 2006, Penguin $16.99 (978-1-59514-081-4). When Emily's grandmother dies, Emily visits Puerto Rico — where her mother grew up — for the first time, and is amazed by a culture so foreign to her yet part of her heritage. (Rev: BL 12/15/06; SLJ 1/07)

916 Padian, Maria. *Out of Nowhere* (9–12). 2013, Knopf $16.99 (978-037586580-0); LB $19.99 (978-037596580-7). Soccer plays a major role in this story of a gifted Somali player who joins the high school team when he migrates to a small town in Maine, where he meets many challenges. **e** Lexile HL670L (Rev: BL 2/15/13; LMC 8–9/13; SLJ 3/13*; VOYA 4/13)

917 Pagliarulo, Antonio. *A Different Kind of Heat* (7–10). 2006, Delacorte LB $9.99 (978-0-385-90319-6). Luz Cordero's anger about life in general and her brother's violent death in particular begins to abate when she finds friendship at the St. Therese Home for Boys and Girls and faces the truth. (Rev: BL 4/1/06; SLJ 12/06)

918 Parker, Linda Busby. *Seven Laurels* (9–12). 2004, Southeast Missouri State Univ. $35.00 (978-0-9724304-8-7). Set in a small town in Alabama, this novel tells the story of one black family's struggle for civil rights from the 1950s on. (Rev: BL 2/15/04)

919 Parks, Gordon. *The Learning Tree* (10–12). 1987, Fawcett paper $5.99 (978-0-449-21504-3). The story of a black boy's coming of age in a small town in Kansas in the 1920s.

920 Pellegrino, Marge. *Journey of Dreams* (6–10). 2009, Frances Lincoln $15.95 (978-1-84780-061-9). Eleven-year-old Tomasa's family is reunited in Arizona after escaping violent persecution in their Mayan village. Lexile 740L (Rev: BL 8/09; SLJ 8/09)

921 Perkins, Mitali. *Secret Keeper* (7–12). 2009, Delacorte $16.99 (978-038573340-3); LB $19.99 (978-038590356-1). In the mid -1970s, 16-year-old Asha Gupta and her family make a difficult move from India to the United States, where Indian tradition and Asha's dreams for herself clash when she meets the boy next door, and attempts to rescue her older sister from a horrible arranged marriage. **e** Lexile 800L (Rev: BL 12/15/08; SLJ 3/1/09)

922 Power, Susan. *The Grass Dancer* (9–12). 1995, Berkley paper $7.99 (978-0-425-14962-1). Anna Thunder, a Sioux living in North Dakota, is the central character in this novel that tells the generational stories of Anna's family. (Rev: BL 8/94; SLJ 5/95; VOYA 12/94)

923 Rebolledo, Tey Diana, and Eliana S. Rivero, eds. *Infinite Divisions: An Anthology of Chicana Literature* (9–12). 1993, Univ. of Arizona paper $24.95 (978-0-8165-1384-0). A collection that spans the history of prose and poetry by Mexican American women and the settlement of the "New World." (Rev: BL 6/1–15/93)

924 Reddi, Rishi. *Karma and Other Stories* (10–12). 2007, Ecco $23.95 (978-0-06-089878-6). Indian Americans struggle to balance tradition and new ways of life in this collection of appealing and thought-provoking stories. (Rev: BL 1/1–15/07)

925 Ridley, John. *A Conversation with the Mann* (11–12). 2002, Warner $24.95 (978-0-446-52836-8). In the late 1950s, African American comedian Jackie Mann aspires to stardom and acceptance by whites; for mature teens. (Rev: BL 5/1/02)

926 Roth, Matthue. *Never Mind the Goldbergs* (9–12). 2005, Scholastic $16.95 (978-0-439-69188-8). Hava Aaronson, a somewhat unconventional Orthodox Jewish girl from New York City, is selected to star in a television sitcom caricaturing a modern Orthodox Jewish family and must reexamine her own beliefs. (Rev: BCCB 4/05; SLJ 6/05)

927 Saenz, Benjamin Alire. *Sammy and Juliana in Hollywood* (9–12). 2004, Cinco Puntos $19.95 (978-0-938317-81-4). In the late 1960s in a tough barrio called Hollywood in Las Cruces, New Mexico, Sammy Santos faces problems ranging from the death of his girlfriend, poverty, racism, and the Vietnam War to unpopular dress codes. (Rev: BL 10/1/04; SLJ 9/04)

928 Santiago, Danny. *Famous All over Town* (10–12). 1984, NAL paper $14.00 (978-0-452-25974-4). An honest, realistic novel about a young Mexican American growing up in a California barrio. (Rev: BL 12/15/89)

929 Santiago, Eduardo. *Tomorrow They Will Kiss* (9–12). 2006, Back Bay paper $13.99 (978-0-316-01412-0). Three recent female immigrants from Cuba adjust to life in 1960s United States by watching soap operas and gossiping on their way to work. (Rev: SLJ 9/06)

930 Savage, Deborah. *Kotuku* (7–12). 2002, Houghton Mifflin $16.00 (978-0-618-07456-3). Struggling to recover from the death of her best friend, 17-year-old Wim throws herself into her job at a Cape Cod riding stable, but visitors from afar prompt her to delve into the mystery surrounding her Maori heritage. (Rev: BL 5/15/02; HBG 10/02; SLJ 3/02; VOYA 4/02)

931 Schorr, Melissa. *Goy Crazy* (8–11). 2006, Hyperion $15.99 (978-0-7868-3852-3). Rachel, a 15-year-old Jewish girl facing typical teen challenges, dates a popular basketball player from a Catholic school and hides this from her parents while at the same time questioning her own beliefs. (Rev: BL 10/1/06; SLJ 10/06)

932 Schraff, Anne. *The Stranger* (8–11). Series: Urban Underground. 2010, Saddleback Educational paper $8.95 (978-16165126-6-8). Meeting cute Naomi makes 16-year-old Ernesto's return to the barrio where he was born more palatable; suitable for reluctant readers. ∩ (Rev: BL 4/1/11; VOYA 4/11)

933 Sebestyen, Ouida. *On Fire* (7–12). 1985, Little, Brown $12.95 (978-0-87113-010-5). Tater leaves home with his brother Sammy and takes a mining job where he confronts labor problems in this sequel to the author's powerful *Words by Heart*. (Rev: BL 5/15/85; SLJ 4/85; VOYA 8/85)

934 Sharif, Medeia. *Bestest. Ramadan. Ever* (7–10). 2011, Flux paper $9.95 (978-0-7387-2-323-5). A coming-of-age story about Almira, a 16-year-old Muslim girl trying to balance her family's pressures and her longing to fit in at school. **e** Lexile 760L (Rev: BL 7/11; LMC 11–12/11; SLJ 11/1/11)

935 Shtern, Ludmilla. *Leaving Leningrad* (10–12). 2001, Univ. Press of New England $19.95 (978-1-58465-100-0). This autobiographical novel follows Tatyana from her childhood in Soviet Russia to her marriage and re-settlement in the United States. (Rev: BL 6/1–15/01)

936 Singer, Isaac Bashevis. *The Power of Light: Eight Stories for Hanukkah* (7–10). 1980, Avon paper $2.50 (978-0-380-60103-5). Eight stories of the Festival of Lights that span centuries of Jewish history.

937 Singer, Marilyn, ed. *Face Relations: 11 Stories About Seeing Beyond Color* (7–12). 2004, Simon & Schuster $17.95 (978-0-689-85637-2). This collection of 11 original short stories by well-known authors explores the issues of racial identity and race relations in American high schools. (Rev: BL 8/04*; SLJ 6/04; VOYA 8/04)

938 Skinner, Jose. *Flight and Other Stories* (10–12). 2001, Univ. of Nevada paper $15.00 (978-0-87417-359-8). These 14 lively coming-of-age stories deal with Latinos in the American Southwest. (Rev: BL 3/1/01)

939 Sprinkle, Patricia. *The Remember Box* (10–12). 2000, Zondervan paper $11.99 (978-0-310-22992-6). In this novel reminiscent of *To Kill a Mockingbird*, the setting is a small South Carolina town and 11-year-old Carly has an uncle, a minister, who is defending an innocent black man. (Rev: BL 10/1/00; SLJ 6/01)

940 Stepto, Michele, ed. *African-American Voices* (7–12). Series: Writers of America. 1995, Millbrook LB $23.90 (978-1-56294-474-2). Selections by W. E. B. Du Bois, Toni Morrison, Ralph Ellison, and others, plus traditional chants, speeches, and poetry. (Rev: BL 5/15/95; SLJ 3/95)

941 Stering, Shirley. *My Name Is Seepeetza* (5–10). 1997, Douglas & McIntyre paper $5.95 (978-0-88899-165-2). Told in diary form, this autobiographical novel about a 6th-grade Native American girl tells of her heartbreak at the terrible conditions at her school, where she is persecuted because of her race. (Rev: BL 3/1/97)

942 Stevens, Marcus. *Useful Girl* (10–12). 2004, Algonquin $24.95 (978-1-56512-366-3). In this novel involving Native Americans, two plots are developed: the first a contemporary story about young love, and the second, a historical story involving the death of a young Cheyenne girl. (Rev: BL 3/1/04; SLJ 6/04)

943 Straight, Susan. *Highwire Moon* (10–12). 2001, Houghton Mifflin $24.00 (978-0-618-05614-9). The harsh world of the migrant worker is revealed in this story of a young girl, Elvia, and her mother, Serafina, and their struggle to be reunited after Serafina is arrested and deported. (Rev: BL 7/01*; SLJ 12/01)

944 Tan, Amy. *The Joy Luck Club* (10–12). 1989, Putnam $24.95 (978-0-399-13420-3). Through the stories of group of four Chinese women in San Francisco and their daughters, Tan looks immigrants' adjustment to their new lives and cultures.

945 Taylor, Mildred D. *The Road to Memphis* (7–12). 1990, Dial $18.99 (978-0-8037-0340-7). Set in 1941, this is a continuation of the story of the Logans, a poor black southern family who were previously featured in *Roll of Thunder, Hear My Cry* and *Let the Circle Be Unbroken*. (Rev: BL 5/15/90; SLJ 1/90; VOYA 8/90)

946 Vaught, Susan. *Stormwitch* (7–10). 2005, Bloomsbury $16.95 (978-1-58234-952-7). Sixteen-year-old Ruba Cleo, transplanted in 1969 to a Mississippi Gulf Coast town from Haiti, wants to strike back at the racism and hostility she encounters by calling on the voodoo skills she learned in her native land. (Rev: BCCB 3/05; BL 2/15/05; SLJ 5/05; VOYA 2/05)

947 Volponi, Paul. *Rooftop* (8–11). 2006, Viking $15.99 (978-0-670-06069-6). As teen cousins Clay and Addison struggle to overcome their drug problems, Addison is shot dead by a white police officer and Clay must cope with the aftermath of the shooting. (Rev: BL 4/15/06*; SLJ 8/06)

948 Walker, Brian F. *Black Boy White School* (9–12). 2012, HarperTeen $17.99 (978-006191483-6). After a semester adapting to life at an elite prep school, 14-year-old African American Anthony "Ant" returns home to the ghettos of Cleveland to discover he no longer fits in there either. **e** (Rev: BL 1/1/12*; SLJ 4/12; VOYA 12/11)

949 Washington, Mary Helen, ed. *Memory of Kin: Stories About Family by Black Writers* (9–12). 1991, Doubleday paper $14.95 (978-0-385-24783-2). A wide-ranging collection of short stories and poetry dealing with the African American family experience. (Rev: BL 1/1/91; SLJ 7/91)

950 Woodson, Jacqueline. *Behind You* (7–12). 2004, Putnam $15.99 (978-0-399-23988-5). In this sequel to *If You Come Softly* (1998), Jeremiah, though dead from a policeman's bullet, watches over the people he left behind. (Rev: BL 2/15/04; HB 5–6/04; SLJ 6/04; VOYA 6/04)

951 Woodson, Jacqueline. *From the Notebooks of Melanin Sun* (6–10). 1995, Scholastic paper $5.99 (978-0-590-45881-8). A 13-year-old African American boy's mother announces that she loves a fellow student, a white woman. (Rev: BL 4/15/95; SLJ 8/95)

952 Wright, Bil. *When the Black Girl Sings* (7–10). 2008, Simon & Schuster $16.99 (978-1-4169-3995-5). When adopted Lahni (who has grown up in a white family and attended a mostly white private school) discovers gospel music, she also finds a new pride in her identity. (Rev: BL 2/1/08; SLJ 1/08)

953 Wright, Richard. *Native Son* (10–12). 1998, Harper-Collins paper $13.00 (978-0-06-092980-0). The tragic life of a black youth named Bigger Thomas who was raised in a Chicago slum.

954 Wright, Richard. *Rite of Passage* (7–12). 1994, HarperCollins paper $6.99 (978-0-06-447111-4). This newly discovered novella, written in the 1940s, concerns a gifted 15-year-old who runs away from his loving Harlem home and survives on the streets with a violent gang. (Rev: BL 1/1/94; SLJ 2/94; VOYA 4/94)

955 Wright, Richard. *Uncle Tom's Children: Five Long Stories* (9–12). 1938, Harper & Row paper $7.00 (978-0-06-081251-5). The five stories in this collection deal with racial conflicts in the South.

956 Wu, Fan. *Beautiful as Yesterday* (11–12). 2009, Atria $24 (978-141659889-3). Chinese American Mary Chang tries to make peace with her younger sister and her family history when her mother arrives from China; for mature readers. **e** (Rev: BL 7/09)

957 Yee, Paul. *Learning to Fly* (6–10). 2008, Orca $16.95 (978-155143955-6); paper $9.95 (978-155143953-2). Chinese immigrant Jason, 17, bonds with Native American "Chief"— and falls in with a pot-smoking crowd — to escape prejudice and feeling like an outsider in his small Canadian town. **e** Lexile HL540L (Rev: BL 10/1/08; LMC 3–4/09; SLJ 3/1/09; VOYA 10/08)

958 Yep, Laurence, ed. *American Dragons: Twenty-Five Asian American Voices* (7–12). 1995, HarperCollins paper $7.99 (978-0-06-440603-1). Autobiographical stories, poems, and essays about children whose parents come from China, Japan, Korea, and Tibet, struggling to find "an identity that isn't generic." (Rev: BL 5/15/93; SLJ 7/93; VOYA 10/93)

959 Yoo, Paula. *Good Enough* (7–10). 2008, HarperTeen $16.99 (978-0-06-079085-1). In her senior year of high school, Patti must juggle pressure to be the "Perfect Korean Daughter" with college applications, a crush on a musician, and racist comments from school bullies; reluctant readers will enjoy the humor. (Rev: BL 11/15/07; SLJ 2/08)

960 Yu, Michelle, and Kouji Seo. *China Dolls* (11–12). 2007, St. Martin's $22.95 (978-0-312-36280-5). Three young Chinese women living in New York City desire both love and successful careers. (Rev: BL 12/1/06)

961 Yunis, Alia. *The Night Counter* (10–12). 2009, Crown $24 (978-030745362-4). Original, heartwarming, and funny, this novel about a Lebanese grandmother who believes she is about to die is full of twists and surprises. **e** (Rev: BL 7/09)

962 Zabytko, Irene. *When Luba Leaves Home* (9–12). 2003, Algonquin $22.95 (978-1-56512-332-8). Interconnected stories portray the life of Luba, a Ukrainian college student in Chicago in the 1960s who lives at home and is active in her own community while long-

ing to be independent and become truly American. (Rev: BL 2/15/03; SLJ 6/03)

Family Life and Problems

963 Aciman, André. *Baby* (8–11). 2007, Front St $16.95 (978-1-59078-502-7). After her alcoholic mother disappears again, 15-year-old Baby finds herself in another foster home; this time, though, it turns out to be a real refuge, with an older couple who race sled dogs. (Rev: BL 9/1/07; SLJ 11/07)

964 Ackermann, Joan. *In the Space Left Behind* (7–10). 2007, HarperCollins $16.99 (978-0-06-072255-5). Fifteen-year-old Colm's mother has married for the third time and is threatening to sell the family home when Colm's long-lost father shows up and offers to pay $70,000 if Colm will accompany him on a cross-country road trip. (Rev: BL 10/1/07; SLJ 12/07)

965 Adler, C. S. *The Shell Lady's Daughter* (7–10). 2004, iUniverse paper $10.95 (978-0-595-33912-9). Kelly's mother has emotional problems and attempts suicide; first published in 1983.

966 Adoff, Jaime. *Jimi and Me* (8–11). 2005, Hyperion $15.99 (978-0-7868-5214-7). Struggling to recover from the shock of his father's brutal murder, Keith, a biracial teen who loves the music of Hendrix, moves from Brooklyn to Ohio and discovers that his father had another son, named Jimi. (Rev: BL 10/1/05; SLJ 9/05)

967 Altebrando, Tara. *Dreamland Social Club* (7–12). 2011, Dutton $16.99 (978-0-525-42325-6). Jane and her brother, who have been living in Europe with their father, return to the United States when they inherit a house on Coney Island and there they learn secrets about their dead mother. ○ **e** (Rev: BLO 5/1/11; LMC 11–12/11; SLJ 7/11; VOYA 6/11)

968 Amateau, Gigi. *Claiming Georgia Tate* (8–12). 2005, Candlewick $15.99 (978-0-7636-2339-5). When her beloved and protective grandmother dies, 12-year-old Georgia Tate finds herself at the mercy of her sexually abusive father in this novel set in the 1970s. (Rev: SLJ 6/05; VOYA 6/05)

969 Anderson, Catherine. *Always in My Heart* (11–12). 2002, NAL paper $7.99 (978-0-451-20666-4). The death of their oldest son destroys Ellie and Tucker's marriage, but their younger sons have a plan to bring them back together; for mature teens. (Rev: BL 8/02)

970 Anfousse, Ginette. *A Terrible Secret* (7–12). Trans. from French by Jennifer Hutchison. 2001, Lorimer paper $4.99 (978-1-55028-704-2). A new neighbor, Ben, helps Maggie to recover from the death of her Down syndrome brother. (Rev: SLJ 9/01)

971 Arcos, Carrie. *Out of Reach* (9–12). 2012, Simon & Schuster $16.99 (978-1-4424-4053-1). Rachel, 16, sets out to find her meth-addicted older brother, Micah. ⌒ ℮ Lexile HL650L (Rev: BL 10/15/12; SLJ 12/12)

972 Armstrong, Sarah. *Salt Rain* (11–12). 2006, Mac-Adam $22.00 (978-1-59692-173-3). Spending time at the family farm in northern Australia after her mother commits suicide, 14-year-old Allie tries to find the truth about her father. (Rev: BL 3/15/06)

973 Avasthi, Swati. *Split* (9–12). 2010, Knopf $16.99 (978-0-375-86340-0); LB $19.99 (978-0-375-96340-7). Sixteen-year-old Jace is thrown out by his abusive father and hopes to live with his older brother — who fled the violent situation five years earlier; both young men struggle to make a life together while worrying about what's happening to their mother in their absence. ℮ Lexile HL610L (Rev: BL 1/1–15/10; HB 5–6/10; SLJ 3/10)

974 Bacon, Charlotte. *Split Estate* (9–12). 2008, Farrar $25.00 (978-0-374-28183-0). This is a look at how a new environment and a traumatic event can change a family in surprising ways as the widower of a suicide victim takes his two teenage kids from New York City to his mother's ranch in Wyoming to escape the reminders of their loss. (Rev: BL 11/1/07)

975 Banks, Kate. *Walk Softly, Rachel* (7–10). 2003, Farrar $16.00 (978-0-374-38230-8). When Rachel, 14, reads her dead brother's diary she discovers that his life was not the ideal she had thought. (Rev: BL 10/15/03; HBG 4/04; SLJ 9/03*; VOYA 2/04)

976 Barkley, Brad, and Heather Hepler. *Jars of Glass* (7–10). 2008, Dutton $16.99 (978-052547911-6). Sisters Chloe, 15, and Shana, 15, react differently when their artist mother is suddenly committed to a mental institution and their father turns to alcohol to cope. ℮ (Rev: BLO 12/11/08; SLJ 12/08; VOYA 12/08)

977 Barnes, John. *Tales of the Madman Underground* (9–12). 2009, Viking $18.99 (978-067006081-8). Six days in the life of a teenager in a small Ohio town in the 1970s. Karl comes from a dysfunctional home and has a collection of dysfunctional friends from his therapy group, yet he manages to get by with humor. Printz Honor 2010. Lexile 1040L (Rev: BL 5/1/09; HB 9–10/09; SLJ 7/1/09*; VOYA 6/09)

978 Baron, Kathi. *Shattered* (8–10). 2009, WestSide $16.95 (978-1-934813-08-9). When Cassie's father, in a fit of rage at his own father, shatters her vintage violin on the day of her debut performance with the Chicago Youth Orchestra, the 14-year-old virtuoso heads for her grandfather's house and uncovers the disturbing genesis of her father's fury. Lexile HL660L (Rev: BLO 8/20/09; SLJ 12/09)

979 Barwin, Gary. *Seeing Stars* (6–12). 2002, Stoddart paper $7.95 (978-0-7737-6227-5). A quirky story about a boy who has been brought up in strange circumstances and who now wants the truth about his father and his family. (Rev: BL 7/02; SLJ 5/02)

980 Bauer, Cat. *Harley, Like a Person* (7–10). 2000, Winslow $16.95 (978-1-890817-48-0); paper $6.95 (978-1-890817-49-7). Unhappy with her distant mother and an alcoholic father, Harley Columba becomes convinced that she is an adopted child. (Rev: BL 6/1–15/00; HB 5–6/00; HBG 9/00; SLJ 5/00)

981 Bauer, Joan. *Backwater* (7–10). 1999, Putnam $18.99 (978-0-399-23141-4). When 16-year-old Ivy Breedlove begins working on her family history, the trail leads to the New York State Adirondacks and eccentric, talented Aunt Jo. (Rev: BL 5/15/99; HB 7–8/99; HBG 9/99; SLJ 6/99; VOYA 8/99)

982 Bauman, Beth Ann. *Rosie and Skate* (9–12). 2009, Random House $15.99 (978-038573735-7). Rosie and Skate, sisters who attend high school in New Jersey, deal with their father's alcoholism and incarceration in different ways. Lexile HL590L (Rev: BL 10/1/09*; SLJ 11/09)

983 Bedford, Deborah. *A Rose by the Door* (10–12). 2001, Warner paper $11.95 (978-0-446-67789-9). When Gemma appears on Bea's doorstep, claiming to be Bea's dead son's wife, Bea must make a choice. (Rev: BL 1/1–15/02)

984 Belton, Sandra. *Store-Bought Baby* (7–10). 2006, Greenwillow $15.99 (978-0-06-085086-9). The death of her adopted older brother forces Leah to face issues of love, jealousy, and what it means to truly be a family. (Rev: BL 5/1/06; HB 5–6/06; LMC 3/07; SLJ 6/06)

985 Benedict, Helen. *The Opposite of Love* (7–12). 2007, Viking $16.99 (978-0-670-06135-8). Seventeen-year-old Madge, who never knew her Jamaican dad and has an irresponsible illegal-alien British mom, faces prejudice in her Pennsylvania town but helps an abandoned black foster kid. (Rev: BL 9/1/07; SLJ 3/08)

986 Berne, Suzanne. *A Crime in the Neighborhood* (10–12). 1997, Algonquin $28.95 (978-1-56512-165-2). A hurt and confused girl who can't accept her father's desertion begins to analyze her family and neighborhood using the same methods as Sherlock Holmes. (Rev: BL 4/15/97; SLJ 12/97)

987 Berry, James. *A Thief in the Village and Other Stories* (7–12). 1988, Penguin paper $5.99 (978-0-14-034357-1). Nine stories about a teenager in Jamaica and everyday life on the Caribbean island. (Rev: BL 4/15/88)

988 Birdsall, Olivia. *Notes on a Near-Life Experience* (6–12). 2007, Delacorte $15.99 (978-0-385-73370-0). Mia is 15 when her parents separate and her life changes dramatically; although she finds it hard to cope at first, she does — with some help — adapt and is happy to spark some interest in her brother's friend Julian. (Rev: BCCB 3/07; SLJ 3/07)

989 Block, Stefan Merrill. *The Story of Forgetting: A Novel* (10–12). 2008, Random House $24.95 (978-1-4000-6679-7). Early-onset/familial Alzheimer's disease is the focus of this novel that is told from two different perspectives — of 17-year-old Seth and 20-year-old Abel. (Rev: SLJ 9/08)

990 Bondoux, Anne-Laure. *Life as It Comes* (7–10). Trans. by Y. Mauder. 2007, Delacorte $15.99 (978-0-385-90390-5). After their parents are killed in a car crash, two French sisters — 15-year-old Mado and 20-year-old Patty — find adapting to a new life difficult, especially when Patty becomes pregnant. (Rev: BCCB 4/07; BL 3/1/07; SLJ 3/07)

991 Bonosky, Phillip. *A Bird in Her Hair and Other Stories* (9–12). 1987, International paper $5.95 (978-0-7178-0661-4). A collection of short stories about the struggles of working people in Pennsylvania from the 1930s into the 1950s. (Rev: BL 2/15/88)

992 Booth, Coe. *Bronxwood* (10–12). 2011, Scholastic $17.99 (978-0-439-92534-1). In this sequel to *Tyrell (2006), the teen's violent father is out of prison and Tyrell struggles to make enough money to leave home while trying to look after his younger brother's uncertain future. YALSA Quick Picks for Reluctant Young Adult Readers 2012.* ℮ Lexile HL780L (Rev: BL 9/1/11; HB 11–12/11; SLJ 10/1/11; VOYA 2/12)

993 Booth, Coe. *Kendra* (10–12). 2008, Scholastic $16.99 (978-043992536-5). Fifteen-year-old Kendra turns to sex to fight the sting of her mother's abandonment. ℮ Lexile 770L (Rev: BL 11/1/08*; HB 11–12/08; SLJ 10/1/08*; VOYA 10/08)

994 Booth, Coe. *Tyrell* (9–12). 2006, Scholastic $16.99 (978-0-439-83879-5). After his father goes to jail, 15-year-old African American Tyrell lives in a homeless shelter in the Bronx with his mother and younger brother and struggles to make a new life for his family and avoid the temptation of selling drugs. (Rev: BL 11/15/06; HB 1–2/07; LMC 3/07; SLJ 11/06*)

995 Bradbury, Ray. *Dandelion Wine* (9–12). 1975, Bantam paper $6.50 (978-0-553-27753-1). A tender novel about one summer in the life of a 12-year-old boy growing up in a small Illinois town during 1928. A reissue.

996 Braff, Joshua. *Peep Show* (11–12). 2010, Algonquin paper $13.95 (978-15651250-8-7). Caught between two worlds, child of divorce David, 16, sides with his father, who owns a porn theater, failing to anticipate the difficulty of being separated from his mother, now a strict Hasidic Jew; for mature readers. ℮ (Rev: BL 5/15/10*)

997 Braff, Joshua. *Unthinkable Thoughts of Jacob Green* (11–12). 2004, Algonquin $22.95 (978-1-56512-420-2). In a wry and often funny first-person narrative, Jacob Green, son of a perfectionist Jewish father, describes his inner conflicts and ways of coping; for mature teens. (Rev: BL 7/04; SLJ 12/04; VOYA 2/05)

998 Bretton, Barbara. *Someone Like You* (11–12). 2005, Berkley paper $7.99 (978-0-425-20388-0). When folk singer Mark Doyle disappears one day, he leaves be-hind his wife and two young daughters, affecting their lives for decades to come. (Rev: BL 7/05)

999 Brew-Hammond, Nana Ekua. *Powder Necklace* (10–12). 2010, Washington Square paper $15 (978-14391261-0-3). Fifteen-year-old Lila struggles to adapt as she is shipped first from her mother's home in London to a provincial boarding school in her parents' homeland of Ghana and then to Manhattan to stay with her father and his family. (Rev: BL 2/1–15/10)

1000 Briant, Ed. *Choppy Socky Blues* (8–11). 2010, Flux paper $9.95 (978-0-73871-897-2). Fourteen-year-old Jason's interest in a girl fascinated with karate prompts him to approach his father, a martial arts teacher whom he has not seen since his parents' difficult divorce; set in England. (Rev: BL 4/15/10; LMC 8–9/10; SLJ 5/10; VOYA 10/10)

1001 Bridgers, Sue Ellen. *Home Before Dark* (7–10). 1998, Replica LB $29.95 (978-0-7351-0053-4). A migrant worker and his family settle down in a permanent home.

1002 Bridgers, Sue Ellen. *Notes for Another Life* (7–12). 1981, Replica $29.95 (978-0-7351-0044-2). A brother and sister cope with a frequently absent mother and a mentally ill father. (Rev: BL 9/1/85; SLJ 10/85; VOYA 4/86)

1003 Brooks, Kevin. *Martyn Pig* (7–10). 2002, Scholastic $16.95 (978-0-439-29595-6). When Martyn's abusive father dies during a drunken argument, Martyn and a friend dispose of the body, setting off a complicated, suspenseful, and often amusing string of events. (Rev: BCCB 9/02; BL 5/1/02; HBG 10/02; SLJ 5/02*)

1004 Brooks, Martha. *Mistik Lake* (9–12). 2007, Farrar $16.00 (978-0-374-34985-1). When Odella's long-absent, disturbed mother dies, Odella's Icelandic family moves past its long-kept secrets in this story set in Canada. ∩ (Rev: BL 10/1/07; HB 9–10/07; SLJ 9/07)

1005 Brown, Jennifer. *Perfect Escape* (9–12). 2012, Little, Brown $17.99 (978-0-316-18557-8). Kendra, 17, takes her older brother Grayson, who suffers from obsessive-compulsive disorder, with her when she sets off on a cross-country road trip, fleeing a cheating scandal. ℮ (Rev: BLO 6/12; LMC 8–9/12; SLJ 7/12; VOYA 4/12)

1006 Buffie, Margaret. *Out of Focus* (7–10). 2006, Kids Can $16.95 (978-1-55337-955-3); paper $6.95 (978-1-55337-956-0). Sixteen-year-old Bernie moves his alcoholic mother and younger siblings into a lake cabin in hopes of keeping the family together. (Rev: LMC 3/07; SLJ 10/06)

1007 Bunting, Eve. *Surrogate Sister* (7–10). 1984, HarperCollins LB $13.89 (978-0-397-32099-8). A 16-year-old girl copes with a pregnant mother who has offered to be a surrogate mother for a childless couple.

1008 Bunting, Eve. *Will You Be My Posslq?* (9–12). 1987, Harcourt $12.95 (978-0-15-297399-5). Without her parents' approval freshman Kyle asks her friend Jamie to become her posslq (person of opposite sex sharing living quarters). (Rev: BL 10/1/87; SLJ 10/87; VOYA 4/88)

1009 Burks, Cris. *Neecey's Lullaby* (11–12). 2006, Broadway paper $12.95 (978-0-7679-1983-8). In this bleak coming-of-age story set in Chicago's poverty-stricken South Side in the 1950s, Neecey tries desperately to protect her younger siblings from her mother's abuse and neglect; for mature teens. (Rev: BL 12/15/05)

1010 Caletti, Deb. *Honey, Baby, Sweetheart* (9–12). 2004, Simon & Schuster $15.95 (978-0-689-86765-1). Ann and Marie, a mother and daughter, get involved in a plan to reunite a friend with a lost love. (Rev: BL 5/15/04; SLJ 7/04)

1011 Calonita, Jen. *Belles* (7–12). 2012, Little, Brown $17.99 (978-031609113-8). Isabelle's world is upended when her ailing grandmother — her only guardian — is placed in a nursing home, and the 15-year-old is sent to live with distant relatives. ☊ ℯ Lexile 730L (Rev: BL 4/1/12; SLJ 4/12)

1012 Carey, Lisa. *Every Visible Thing* (10–12). 2006, Morrow $24.95 (978-0-06-621289-0). Lena is 15 and her brother Owen, 10, when their older brother disappears — leading to anger and nearly to tragedy. (Rev: BL 5/1/06; SLJ 8/06)

1013 Carlson, Melody. *Just Ask* (8–12). Series: Diary of a Teenage Girl. 2005, Multnomah paper $12.99 (978-1-59052-321-6). A family tragedy shakes the faith of 16-year-old Kim, who's been struggling to live a Christian life. (Rev: SLJ 12/05)

1014 Cart, Michael, ed. *Necessary Noise: Stories About Our Families as They Really Are* (9–12). Illus. by Charlotte Noruzi. 2003, HarperCollins LB $16.89 (978-0-06-027500-6). YA authors familiar to young readers tell stories of families struggling to cope with contemporary problems. (Rev: BCCB 7–8/03; BL 5/15/03*; HB 7–8/03; HBG 10/03; SLJ 6/03; VOYA 6/03)

1015 Chaltas, Thalia. *Because I Am Furniture* (8–12). 2009, Viking $16.99 (978-0-670-06298-0). This novel in verse tracks the development of 14-year-old Anke, the only one of the three siblings in her family to escape her father's abuse, as she gains sufficient confidence to challenge him. Best Books for Young Adults 2010. (Rev: LMC 8–9/09; SLJ 6/1/09; VOYA 4/09)

1016 Chapman, Karen B. *The Marino Mission: One Girl, One Mission, One Thousand Words* (9–12). 2005, Wiley paper $12.99 (978-0-7645-7831-1). Alexa reluctantly joins her marine biologist mother on a summer trip to Nicaragua, where she joins forces with a local boy to investigate the fate of a baby dolphin in this novel that introduces 1,000 SAT vocabulary words. (Rev: SLJ 7/05)

1017 Charlton-Trujillo, E. E. *Feels Like Home* (8–10). 2007, Delacorte $15.99 (978-0-385-73332-8). Two siblings in South Texas — 17-year-old Michelle (Mickey) and her older brother — come together after their father's death and, after some false starts, find a way to heal. (Rev: SLJ 7/07)

1018 Chayil, Eishes. *Hush* (8–12). 2010, Walker $16.99 (978-0-8027-2088-7). Gittel, 17 and soon to enter into an arranged marriage, is determined to disobey tradition and speak out about sex abuse in her Hasidic community, in memory of her friend who committed suicide several years before. YALSA Best Fiction for Young Adults; Sydney Taylor Book Honor 2011. ℯ (Rev: 10/15/10; LMC 1–2/11; SLJ 9/1/10; VOYA 12/10)

1019 Cheng, Andrea. *Brushing Mom's Hair* (7–10). Illus. by Nicole Wong. 2009, Boyds Mills $17.95 (978-1-59078-599-7). This novel in verse follows 15-year-old dancer Ann through her mother's ultimately successful battle with breast cancer. (Rev: BL 9/1/09; SLJ 10/09)

1020 Clarke, Judith. *One Whole and Perfect Day* (8–10). 2007, Front St $16.95 (978-1-932425-95-6). Lily, 16, finally gets what she longs for — a single day when her irritating and eccentric family comes together happily — in this gentle novel set in Australia. Printz Honor 2008. (Rev: BL 5/1/07; HB 5–6/07; SLJ 8/07)

1021 Clements, Andrew. *Things Hoped For* (8–11). 2006, Philomel $16.99 (978-0-399-24350-9). Gwen lives with her grandfather in New York City and studies violin at the Manhattan School of Music; when her grandfather disappears, Gwen teams up with Robert, a fellow music student, to solve the mystery. A sequel to *Things Not Seen* (2002). ☊ (Rev: BL 8/06; SLJ 11/06)

1022 Close, Jessie. *The Warping of Al* (9–12). 1990, HarperCollins $15.95 (978-0-06-021280-3). Al tries to cope with a domineering father and a subservient mother. (Rev: BL 1/1/91; SLJ 9/90)

1023 Cocks, Heather, and Jessica Morgan. *Spoiled* (9–12). 2011, Little, Brown $17.99 (978-0-316-09825-0). On the eve of her 16th birthday, spoiled Brooke contends with the surprise introduction of her father's love child, who is the same age; a story with humor and lots of Hollywood fashion. ☊ ℯ Lexile 850L (Rev: BL 7/11; SLJ 12/1/11; VOYA 8/11)

1024 Cohen, Tish. *The Truth About Delilah Blue* (10–12). 2010, HarperCollins paper $13.99 (978-00618759-7-7). Twenty-year-old Lila, living in Los Angeles and hoping to become a model, struggles to forge a new identity for herself as she copes with new information from her mother about her now-ill father. ℯ (Rev: BL 4/1–15/10)

1025 Cohn, Rachel. *Gingerbread* (9–12). 2002, Simon & Schuster $15.95 (978-0-689-84337-2). Cyd, a rebellious 16-year-old, is sent to New York to spend the summer with her father in this hip and entertaining novel written in the first person. (Rev: BCCB 4/02; BL 4/15/02; HBG 10/02; SLJ 2/02*; VOYA 4/02)

1026 Cohn, Rachel. *You Know Where to Find Me* (8–11). 2008, Simon & Schuster $15.99 (978-0-689-87859-6). Miles turns to drugs following her cousin Laura's suicide in this story full of complicated families and relationships. (Rev: BL 4/1/08; SLJ 3/08)

1027 Cole, Brock. *The Facts Speak for Themselves* (9–12). 1997, Front St $16.95 (978-1-886910-14-0). A ground-breaking, sexually explicit story about Linda and how the experiences in her life lead to murder. (Rev: BL 10/1/97; HBG 3/98; SLJ 10/97*; VOYA 12/97)

1028 Colebank, Susan. *Cashing In* (9–12). 2009, Dutton $16.99 (978-0-525-42151-1). After the death of her father, 18-year-old Reggie grapples with her mother's gambling addiction and her own reluctance to interfere. ℮ Lexile 720L (Rev: BLO 12/8/09; SLJ 1/10)

1029 Collins, Yvonne, and Sandy Rideout. *The Black Sheep* (8–12). 2007, Hyperion $15.99 (978-1-4231-0156-7). Sick of her boring Manhattan lifestyle, 15-year-old Kendra agrees to be on a reality show where she switches lives with Maya, who comes from a hippie family that's all about saving otters. (Rev: BL 5/15/07; SLJ 9/07)

1030 Coman, Carolyn. *Bee and Jacky* (9–12). 1998, Front St $14.95 (978-1-886910-33-1). This is a controversial novel about the emotional consequences of an incestuous relationship between a 17-year-old boy and his younger sister. (Rev: BL 10/1/98; HB 11–12/98; HBG 3/99; SLJ 11/98; VOYA 12/98)

1031 Connelly, Neil. *The Miracle Stealer* (9–12). 2010, Scholastic $17.99 (978-0-545-13195-7). Andi, 19, tries to protect her 6-year-old brother Daniel, who was miraculously rescued from a well and is now being touted as a miracle worker in his own right. ℮ Lexile 910L (Rev: BL 11/1/10*; HB 11–12/10; LMC 11–12/10; SLJ 12/1/10; VOYA 12/10)

1032 Conroy, Pat. *The Great Santini* (10–12). 1987, Bantam paper $7.99 (978-0-553-26892-8). This novel about family dynamics centers on a Marine captain who treats his family as he does his troops. (Rev: BL 2/15/91)

1033 Conway, Celeste. *The Melting Season* (9–12). 2006, Delacorte $15.95 (978-0-385-73339-7). Sixteen-year-old Giselle, who studies ballet at a private school, finally deals with her feelings toward her mother and her deceased father after meeting a boy named Will. (Rev: BL 11/15/06; SLJ 1/07)

1034 Cook, Gloria. *Leaving Shades* (11–12). 2010, Severn $28.95 (978-072786905-0). Eager to avenge her long-ago abandonment, self-righteous Beth finally meets her mother — and realizes she must prove herself to win the affection of her new family in this story set in Cornwall. (Rev: BLO 7/10)

1035 Cooley, Beth. *Shelter* (7–10). 2006, Delacorte $15.95 (978-0-385-73330-4). Lucy and her mother and little brother go from affluence to a homeless shelter after Lucy's father dies, and Lucy must learn to adjust to new circumstances and improve her life. (Rev: BCCB 1/07; BL 1/1–15/07; SLJ 12/06)

1036 Cooney, Caroline B. *Whatever Happened to Janie?* (6–10). 1993, Dell paper $5.50 (978-0-440-21924-8). Janie, 15, after discovering she's a missing child on a milk carton, returns to her birth family, which has been searching for her since her kidnapping at age three. Sequel to *The Face on the Milk Carton.* (Rev: BL 6/1–15/93; SLJ 6/93; VOYA 8/93)

1037 Corrigan, Eireann. *Splintering* (9–12). 2004, Scholastic $16.95 (978-0-439-53597-7). In a gripping free-verse novel, siblings Paulie and Jeremy give voice to their feelings about an attack on their family by a drug-crazed intruder. (Rev: BCCB 4/04; BL 4/1/04; SLJ 7/04; VOYA 8/04)

1038 Cramer, W. Dale. *Summer of Light* (9–12). 2007, Bethany paper $13.99 (978-0-7642-2996-1). An ironworker loses his job, becomes a stay-at-home dad, and is surprised how much he enjoys his life and his children. ♫ (Rev: BL 1/1–15/07)

1039 Dalton, Annie, and Maria Dalton. *Invisible Threads* (8–11). 2006, Delacorte LB $17.99 (978-0-385-90303-5). In alternating chapters, Carrie Ann describes her need to find her birth mother and Naomi, the birth mother, talks about her pregnancy and the decision to give up her baby. (Rev: BL 4/1/06; SLJ 4/06)

1040 Darrow, Sharon. *Trash* (8–11). 2006, Candlewick $16.99 (978-0-7636-2624-2). The sad story of two abandoned siblings—Sissy Lexie and Boy—who suffer through abuse, poverty, depression, and death; written in rhythmic prose and free verse. (Rev: BL 12/1/06; SLJ 10/06)

1041 Dave, Laura. *London Is the Best City in America* (11–12). 2006, Viking $24.95 (978-0-670-03756-8). Emmy returns to Scarsdale, New York, for her brother's wedding, only to find herself haunted by a past relationship as she helps her brother face his own angst; for mature readers. ♫ (Rev: BL 4/15/06)

1042 Davis, Deborah. *Not Like You* (10–12). 2007, Clarion $16.00 (978-0-618-72093-4). Fifteen-year-old Kayla struggles to find meaning and joy in her life as she moves from place to place with her alcoholic mother. (Rev: BCCB 7–8/07; BL 7/07; SLJ 9/07)

1043 Davis, Jill A. *Ask Again Later* (10–12). 2007, Farrar $23.95 (978-0-06-087596-1). When her mother is diagnosed with cancer, Emily quits her job, moves in with her mother, and becomes a receptionist in her father's law firm, and in so doing learns about her parents and herself. (Rev: BL 1/1–15/07)

1044 De Goldi, Kate. *The 10 p.m. Question* (7–12). 2010, Candlewick $15.99 (978-0-7636-4939-5). Frankie, 12, worries about many things until free-thinking Sydney, veteran of 22 schools, makes him question his priorities; set in New Zealand. ∩ Lexile 830L (Rev: BL 8/10*; HB 11–12/10; LMC 1–2/11; SLJ 9/1/10; VOYA 12/10)

1045 de la Garza, Beatriz. *Pillars of Gold and Silver* (9–12). 1997, Arte Publico paper $9.95 (978-1-55885-206-8). After her father is killed in the Korean War, young Blanca Estela and her mother move from California to Mexico in this story of a girl trying to fit into a new culture and make new friends. (Rev: BL 2/1/98; SLJ 7/98)

1046 Deberry, Virginia, and Donna Grant. *Far from the Tree* (10–12). 2000, St. Martin's $24.95 (978-0-312-20291-0). Four generations of African American women converge at the family's property in Prosper, North Carolina, and discover decades-old secrets. (Rev: BL 7/00; SLJ 3/01)

1047 Deedy, Carmen A. *The Last Dance* (7–10). 1995, Peachtree $16.95 (978-1-56145-109-8). A picture book for young adults that tells of the abiding love through the years of husband and wife Ninny and Bessie. (Rev: BL 1/1–15/96; SLJ 1/96)

1048 Dellasega, Cheryl. *Sistrsic92 (Meg)* (7–10). Illus. by Tyler Beauford. Series: Bloggrls. 2009, Marshall Cavendish $16.99 (978-0-7614-5456-4). When Meg's older, perfect sister Cara develops an eating disorder, plain, average Meg feels even more isolated from her family and confides her woes to her blog. (Rev: BL 10/1/09; SLJ 1/10; VOYA 2/10)

1049 Dermansky, Marcy. *Twins* (11–12). 2005, Morrow $21.95 (978-0-06-075978-0). Identical twin sisters have increasing difficulties as they go through high school; for mature teens. (Rev: BL 8/05)

1050 Dessen, Sarah. *What Happened to Goodbye* (8–12). 2011, Viking $19.99 (978-0-670-01294-7). After her parents' bitter divorce, 17-year-old Mclean has been living with her father, moving from town to town and reinventing herself in each location. ∩ Ɛ Lexile HL760L (Rev: BL 5/1/11; HB 7–8/11; SLJ 6/11; VOYA 6/11)

1051 Deuker, Carl. *Runner* (7–10). 2005, Houghton Mifflin $16.00 (978-0-618-54298-7). Living on a weather-beaten sailboat on Puget Sound with his alcoholic father, high school senior Chance Taylor gets mixed up in some shady dealings to help pay the family bills. (Rev: BL 6/1–15/05; SLJ 6/05; VOYA 8/05)

1052 Donnelly, Gabrielle. *The Little Women Letters* (10–12). 2011, Simon & Schuster $25 (978-1-4516-1718-4). Emma, Lulu, and Sophie are descendants of Josephine March, and a treasure trove of letters reveals how similar they are to the original girls in Alcott's classic. (Rev: BL 5/15/11; SLJ 8/11)

1053 Doody, Margaret Anne. *The Annotated Anne of Green Gables* (7–12). 1997, Oxford $49.95 (978-0-19-510428-8). A biography of Lucy Maud Montgomery and notes and annotations explaining references to the

places, people, and settings add to this edition of Montgomery's novel. (Rev: SLJ 3/98; VOYA 6/98)

1054 Dorfman, Joaquin. *Playing It Cool* (10–12). 2006, Random House $15.95 (978-0-375-83641-1). Sebastian, a manipulative and "cool" 18-year-old, switches identities with his friend Jeremy when they meet Jeremy's biological father; the charade turns serious when Sebastian's insecurities make it difficult for him to surrender the act. (Rev: BL 5/1/06; HB 5–6/06; LMC 10/06; SLJ 6/06*)

1055 Dowd, Siobhan. *Solace of the Road* (8–12). 2009, Random House $17.99 (978-0-375-84971-8); LB $20.99 (978-0-375-94971-5). Holly Hogan, 14, assumes an alter-ego and escapes from her London foster home to reunite with her mother in Ireland, learning a valuable lesson about herself along the way. ∩ Ɛ Lexile HL650L (Rev: BL 10/1/09*; SLJ 10/09)

1056 Draper, Sharon M. *Forged by Fire* (7–10). 1997, Simon & Schuster $16.95 (978-0-689-80699-5). Nine-year-old African American Gerald Nickelby must leave the comfort of his aunt's home to live with a neglectful mother, her daughter Angel, and husband Jordan, who is secretly sexually abusing young Angel. A companion volume to *Tears of a Tiger*. (Rev: BL 2/15/97; SLJ 3/97; VOYA 6/97)

1057 Dessen, Sarah. *The Truth About Forever* (9–12). 2004, Viking $16.99 (978-0-670-03639-4). Macy Queen hides her grief over her father's death and pretends that all is well. (Rev: BL 4/15/04; SLJ 6/04; VOYA 6/04)

1058 Durrow, Heidi W. *The Girl Who Fell from the Sky* (11–12). 2010, Algonquin $22.95 (978-156512680-0). After a tragedy involving her Danish mother and her siblings, young Rachel finds herself living with her African American grandmother in a black neighborhood in Portland, Oregon, where she faces new challenges; for mature readers. ∩ (Rev: BL 2/1–15/10)

1059 Elkeles, Simone. *How to Ruin a Summer Vacation* (8–10). 2006, Flux paper $8.95 (978-0-7387-0961-1). Amy, 16, enters a whole new world when she goes to Israel for the summer with her father and must share a room with a cousin she's neverr met. (Rev: SLJ 12/06)

1060 Enger, Leif. *Peace Like a River* (10–12). 2001, Atlantic Monthly $24.00 (978-0-87113-795-1). When his brother flees after killing two young men who were harassing his family, Reuben and his father and sister set out to find him. (Rev: BL 5/15/01*)

1061 Ephron, Delia. *Frannie in Pieces* (7–10). 2007, HarperCollins $16.99 (978-0-06-074716-9). Frannie, devastated by her father's death, discovers a magical jigsaw puzzle that he made before his death and that allows Frannie to see him again. ∩ (Rev: BL 11/1/07; SLJ 10/07)

1062 Erskine, Kathryn. *Quaking* (8–10). 2007, Philomel $16.99 (978-0-399-24774-3). Fourteen-year-old Matilda's resistance gradually breaks down as she settles into her new, Quaker foster home; community differences over antiwar protests threaten this new ease. (Rev: BL 5/1/07; HB 7–8/07; SLJ 7/07)

1063 Eulo, Elena Yates. *Mixed-Up Doubles* (8–11). 2003, Holiday $16.95 (978-0-8234-1706-3). In this poignant yet funny story of a tennis-playing family hit by divorce, middle child Hank, 14, narrates the effects on the children. (Rev: BCCB 7–8/03; BL 5/15/03; HBG 4/04; SLJ 7/03; VOYA 6/03)

1064 Flake, Sharon G. *Begging for Change* (7–12). 2003, Hyperion $15.99 (978-0-7868-0601-0). Raspberry resorts to stealing from a friend when her mother is hospitalized after being hit in the head and her addicted father reappears on the scene in this sequel to *Money Hungry* (2001). (Rev: BL 8/03*; HBG 4/04; SLJ 7/03; VOYA 6/03)

1065 Fleischman, Paul. *Rear-View Mirrors* (7–10). 1986, HarperCollins $12.95 (978-0-06-021866-9). After her father's death, Olivia relives through memory a summer when she and her estranged father reconciled. (Rev: BL 3/1/86; SLJ 5/86; VOYA 8/86)

1066 Fleming, Anne. *Anomaly* (11–12). 2006, Raincoast $24.95 (978-1-55192-831-9). Two sisters have a complicated relationship while growing up near Toronto, partially because one is an albino. (Rev: BL 8/06)

1067 Fletcher, Susan. *Eve Green* (11–12). 2004, Norton $23.95 (978-0-393-05988-5). Eve Green, adopted more than 20 years earlier by her Welsh grandparents, is still struggling to come to grips with her mother's suicide when Eve was only 8 years old. (Rev: SLJ 2/05)

1068 Fletcher, Susan. *Oystercatchers* (9–12). 2007, Norton $23.95 (978-0-393-06003-4). The beautifully, poetically written story of Moira, whose 16-year-old sister Amy has been in a coma for four years; Moira feels alternately guilty about Amy's accident and resentful for the negative effects she feels Amy has always had on her life. (Rev: BL 7/07; SLJ 8/07)

1069 Flinn, Alex. *Nothing to Lose* (7–12). 2004, HarperCollins $16.99 (978-0-06-051750-2). At age 17, Michael returns home after being a runaway for a year to find that his mother is on trial for the murder of his abusive father. (Rev: BL 3/15/04; HB 5–6/04; SLJ 3/04; VOYA 6/04)

1070 Forbes, Kathryn. *Mama's Bank Account* (7–10). 1968, Harcourt paper $11.00 (978-0-15-656377-2). The story, told in vignettes, of a loving Norwegian family and of Mama's mythical bank account.

1071 Forster, Gwynne. *If You Walked in My Shoes* (11–12). 2004, Kensington paper $14.00 (978-0-7582-0652-7). For Coreen, who as a teenager was a rape victim, and Frieda, the daughter who was a result of that rape and who was herself abused, a reunion causes anger and pain; for mature teens. (Rev: BL 11/15/04)

1072 Franklin, Emily. *The Other Half of Me* (9–12). 2007, Delacorte $15.99 (978-0-385-73445-5). Jenny, an artistic 16-year-old in a family full of athletes, goes in search of her anonymous sperm-donor father at the urging of her boyfriend Tate and discovers that she has a half-sister. (Rev: BL 11/1/07; SLJ 12/07)

1073 Freund, Diane. *Four Corners* (10–12). 2001, MacAdam $25.00 (978-0-9673701-8-7). When her mother has a nervous breakdown, 10-year-old Rainey and her four siblings are cared for by a flamboyant aunt who arrives with a wild daughter and a peculiar son. (Rev: BL 8/01)

1074 Freymann-Weyr, Garret. *Stay with Me* (10–12). 2006, Houghton Mifflin $16.00 (978-0-618-60571-2). Sixteen-year-old Leila, who has always been uncertain in her relationships with her older stepsisters, decides to investigate when one of them kills herself in this complex and well-written novel. (Rev: BL 3/1/06*; SLJ 4/06)

1075 Friend, Natasha. *Lush* (7–10). 2006, Scholastic $16.99 (978-0-439-85346-0). Thirteen-year-old Sam writes anonymous letters to an older student at school, sharing the truth about her family life and her father's alcoholism, and asking for advice. (Rev: BL 11/1/06; SLJ 12/06)

1076 Friesen, Gayle. *For Now* (9–12). 2007, Kids Can $16.95 (978-1-55453-132-5); paper $7.95 (978-1-55453-133-2). Eleventh-grader Jes, first seen in *Losing Forever* (2002), finds her life shaken up again when her mother announces she is pregnant. (Rev: BL 3/1/08; SLJ 1/08)

1077 Friesen, Gayle. *Losing Forever* (7–10). 2002, Kids Can $16.95 (978-1-55337-031-4). As her mother prepares to remarry, 9th-grader Jes is still coping with her parents' divorce, her changing relationships with her friends, and her beautiful soon-to-be stepsister. (Rev: BCCB 11/02; BL 1/1–15/03; HBG 3/03; SLJ 11/02; VOYA 2/03)

1078 Fullerton, Alma. *Walking on Glass* (9–12). 2007, HarperCollins $15.99 (978-0-06-077851-4). A teenage boy's journal, written in free verse, describes his feelings about his mother's coma (the result of a suicide attempt), and his anguish over whether to keep her alive with machines. (Rev: BL 11/1/06; SLJ 4/07)

1079 Galante, Cecilia. *The Sweetness of Salt* (9–12). 2010, Bloomsbury $16.99 (978-1-59990-512-9). High school graduate Julia has her immediate future mapped out until her estranged older sister Sophie turns up and reveals family secrets that force Julia to reassess. **e** Lexile 630L (Rev: LMC 10/10; SLJ 12/1/10; VOYA 12/10)

1080 Garsee, Jeannine. *Before, After, and Somebody in Between* (8–11). 2007, Bloomsbury $16.95 (978-1-59990-022-3). This is a problem novel in which 14-year-old Martha — smart, sensitive, and musically gifted — copes with an alcoholic mother, poverty and violence, foster care, and ill-advised sex but finds hope at the end of it all. (Rev: BL 8/07; SLJ 10/07)

1081 Garsee, Jeannine. *Say the Word* (9–12). 2009, Bloomsbury $16.99 (978-159990333-0). Seventeen-year-old Shawna's life is turned upside-down when she learns that her lesbian mother—who abandoned the family years ago—is ill and that her father is bitter and cold-hearted. Lexile HL580L (Rev: BL 4/1/09; SLJ 6/1/09; VOYA 6/09)

1082 Gayle, Mike. *Dinner for Two* (9–12). 2004, Pocket paper $13.00 (978-0-7434-7766-6). Dave learns he is 13-year-old Nicola's father in this breezy novel about complex relationships. (Rev: BL 6/1–15/04)

1083 Glover, Bonnie J. *Going Down South* (11–12). 2008, Oneworld paper $14.00 (978-034548091-0). When Daisy's 15-year-old daughter gets pregnant in 1960s Brooklyn, the family leaves its black middle-class neighborhood for Alabama, where Daisy's mother puts the family back together with sass and compassion. e (Rev: BL 6/1–15/08; SLJ 10/08)

1084 Going, K. L. *Saint Iggy* (8–11). 2006, Harcourt $17.00 (978-0-15-205795-4). Sixteen-year-old Iggy Corso, who lives in public housing with his drug-addicted parents, faces expulsion from school and decides to make something of himself. ∩ (Rev: BL 9/15/06; HB 11–12/06; SLJ 9/06)

1085 Goobie, Beth. *Who Owns Kelly Paddik?* (7–10). Series: Orca Soundings. 2003, Orca paper $7.95 (978-1-55143-239-7). Kelly, 15, slowly comes to realize that she is not alone as she recovers from the sexual abuse inflicted by her father. (Rev: SLJ 11/03)

1086 Gottlieb, Eli. *The Boy Who Went Away* (10–12). 1997, St. Martin's $21.95 (978-0-312-15070-9). An autobiographical novel set in New Jersey in 1967 about a teenage boy growing up in a family with a mentally ill older brother. (Rev: BL 12/15/96; SLJ 5/97)

1087 Grant, Vicki. *B Negative* (7–10). Series: Orca Soundings. 2011, Orca LB $16.95 (978-155469842-4); paper $9.95 (9781554698417). Eighteen-year-old Paddy discovers his blood type doesn't match his family's when he gets a physical prior to joining the army; for reluctant readers. e Lexile HL510L (Rev: BLO 2/15/11)

1088 Grant, Vicki. *Comeback* (6–10). Series: Orca Soundings. 2010, Orca LB $16.95 (978-1-55469-311-5); paper $9.95 (978-1-55469-310-8). Upset when her father's plane goes down, Ria runs away from her mother's home with her 5-year-old brother and faces many challenges; for reluctant readers. e Lexile HL550L (Rev: BL 4/15/10; SLJ 4/10)

1089 Griffin, Adele. *All You Never Wanted* (10–12). 2012, Knopf $16.99 (978-0-375-87082-8); LB $19.99 (978-037597082-5). Sisters Alex and Thea become antagonistic toward each other when their mother re-

marries and they are suddenly wealthy but neglected. e Lexile HL600L (Rev: BL 9/15/12*; LMC 3–4/13; SLJ 10/12*)

1090 Griggs, Vanessa Davis. *Ray of Hope* (11–12). 2011, Dafina paper $15 (978-07582596-0-8). Hellraising African American teens Sahara and Crystal get a surprise when their confident, wise, church-loving grandmother take charge of them; for mature readers. ∩ e (Rev: BL 12/1–15/10)

1091 Gruen, Sara. *Riding Lessons* (10–12). 2004, HarperTorch paper $7.99 (978-0-06-058027-8). A mother returns with her rebellious 15-year-old daughter to her parents' riding school in New Hampshire where her father is dying of Lou Gehrig's disease. (Rev: BL 4/1/04*)

1092 Guest, Judith. *Ordinary People* (10–12). 1982, Viking paper $14.00 (978-0-14-006517-6). The accidental death of one of two sons brings a family to crisis and disintegration. (Rev: BL 6/1/88)

1093 Gurtler, Janet. *If I Tell* (9–12). 2011, Sourcebooks paper $9.99 (978-1-4022-6-103-9). Mixed-race high-schooler Jaz is upset when she sees her stepfather-to-be kissing one of her friends. e Lexile HL500L (Rev: BL 10/1/11; LMC 1–2/12; SLJ 11/1/11)

1094 Haigh, Jennifer. *The Condition* (11–12). 2008, HarperCollins $25.95 (978-006075578-2). In this family drama for mature readers that spreads across 20 years, siblings Billy, Scott, and Gwen cope with their parents' inattention (and impending divorce), as well as Gwen's genetic disorder. ∩ e (Rev: BL 6/1–15/08)

1095 Hall, Barbara. *Dixie Storms* (7–12). 1990, Harcourt $15.95 (978-0-15-223825-4). Dutch's troubled relationships within her family worsen when cousin Norma comes to stay. (Rev: BL 5/1/90; SLJ 9/90)

1096 Hall, Barbara. *The Noah Confessions* (8–12). 2007, Random House $15.99 (978-0-385-73328-1). The compelling story of Lynnie, a 16-year-old girl who comes to terms with her family's secret past when she reads a letter written by her deceased mother. (Rev: SLJ 6/07)

1097 Halpin, Brendan. *Donorboy* (9–12). 2004, Villard $22.95 (978-1-4000-6277-5). Rosalind moves in with her sperm-donor father, whom she had never met, after her lesbian mothers are killed in a car crash. (Rev: BL 7/04; SLJ 4/05)

1098 Hamilton, Jane. *When Madeline Was Young* (9–12). 2006, Doubleday $22.95 (978-0-385-51671-6). A finely tuned psychological saga, spanning the years from the Vietnam War through the invasion of Iraq, that follows the Maciver family through many experiences, both difficult and joyful. ∩ (Rev: BL 7/06)

1099 Hamilton, Ruth. *A Parallel Life* (11–12). 2010, Severn $28.95 (978-072786886-2). Emotionally complex Harrie, 21, struggles to carry the weight of a dysfunctional family on her shoulders as she aspires to become a jeweler; for mature readers. (Rev: BL 6/1–15/10)

1100 Hamilton, Virginia. *Junius over Far* (9–12). 1985, HarperCollins $12.95 (978-0-06-022194-2). Fearful that grandfather is lonely as he approaches death on a Caribbean island, 14-year-old Junius and his father go to visit him. (Rev: BL 5/15/85; SLJ 8/85; VOYA 6/85)

1101 Harmon, Michael. *Skate* (7–10). 2006, Knopf $15.95 (978-0-375-87516-8). Facing foster care and separation from his younger brother Sammy, Ian takes Sammy and the two run away, heading across Washington State to find their long-absent father. (Rev: BL 11/15/06; SLJ 12/06)

1102 Harrison, Troon. *Goodbye to Atlantis* (7–10). 2002, Stoddart paper $7.95 (978-0-7737-6229-9). Stella, 14, whose mother died of cancer, initially resents being stuck with her father's girlfriend as a traveling companion. (Rev: BL 9/1/02; SLJ 4/02)

1103 Hart, Beth Webb. *Grace at Low Tide* (10–12). 2005, West Bow paper $14.99 (978-1-59554-026-3). Forced to retrench after a financial reverse, the DeLoach family trades its posh Charleston home for a modest cottage on South Carolina's Edisto Island; the faith of teenage daughter DeVeaux helps to lift family spirits as matters go from bad to worse. (Rev: BL 10/1/05)

1104 Hartnett, Sonya. *What the Birds See* (7–12). 2003, Candlewick $15.99 (978-0-7636-2092-9). A beautifully written complex story featuring three missing children and a lonely and fearful boy who is fascinated by three children who move in next door. (Rev: BCCB 3/03; BL 4/15/03; HB 5–6/03; HBG 10/03; SLJ 5/03; VOYA 6/03)

1105 Hathorn, Libby. *Thunderwith* (7–10). 1991, Little, Brown $15.95 (978-0-316-35034-1). This story of an unhappy 15-year-old girl and a beautiful dingolike dog she finds is set in the Australian rain forest. (Rev: BL 9/1/91; SLJ 5/91*)

1106 Hay, Elizabeth. *A Student of Weather* (10–12). 2001, Counterpoint $24.00 (978-1-58243-123-9). Beginning in 1930 in the prairies of Saskatchewan, the sibling rivalry between two sisters continues throughout their lives. (Rev: BL 11/15/00)

1107 Hernández, Jo Ann Yolanda. *The Throwaway Piece* (9–12). 2006, Piñata paper $9.95 (978-1-55885-353-9). Jewel has suffered through a string of her mother's abusive boyfriends, several foster homes, and a tough girl reputation, but her life starts to change when a wise English teacher gives her a tutoring assignment in math and she begins to understand the value of friendship and helping others. (Rev: SLJ 8/06)

1108 Heuler, Karen. *The Soft Room* (10–12). 2004, Livingston $25.00 (978-1-931982-31-3). The story of twin girls, one of whom is unable to feel pain, and their mutual affection and care. (Rev: BL 3/15/04*)

1109 Hilderbrand, Elin. *The Love Season* (11–12). 2006, St. Martin's $24.95 (978-0-312-32230-4). After her mother's death, Renata travels to Nantucket to meet her mysterious godmother, who must decide to either keep her secrets or confront her past; for mature teens. (Rev: BL 4/15/06)

1110 Hill, Ernest. *Cry Me a River* (10–12). 2003, Kensington $24.00 (978-0-7582-0276-5). African American Tyrone Stokes, released from prison only to find out that his 17-year-old son is on death row, sets out to prove Marcus's innocence. (Rev: BL 2/15/03)

1111 Hinton, S. E. *Taming the Star Runner* (7–12). 1989, Bantam paper $5.50 (978-0-440-20479-4). A tough delinquent is sent to his uncle's ranch to be straightened out and there he falls in love with Casey, who is trying to tame a wild horse named Star Runner. (Rev: BL 10/15/88; SLJ 10/88; VOYA 12/88)

1112 Hoffman, Alice. *At Risk* (10–12). 1988, Putnam paper $7.99 (978-0-425-11738-5). The happy life of the Farrell family is shattered when they discover that their 11-year-old daughter has AIDS. (Rev: SLJ 12/88)

1113 Holeman, Linda. *Raspberry House Blues* (6–10). 2000, Tundra paper $6.95 (978-0-88776-493-6). Poppy's search for her birth mother looks hopeful for a while when she spends a summer in Winnipeg. (Rev: SLJ 12/00; VOYA 2/01)

1114 Holt, Kimberly Willis. *Keeper of the Night* (6–10). 2003, Henry Holt $16.95 (978-0-8050-6361-5). Isabel, a 13-year-old who lives on Guam, tells the story of her mother's suicide and the family's subsequent grief. (Rev: BL 4/15/03; HB 5–6/03; HBG 10/03; SLJ 5/03*; VOYA 6/03)

1115 Hopkins, Ellen. *Burned* (9–12). 2006, Simon & Schuster $16.95 (978-1-4169-0354-3). Written in free verse, this novel tells the story of Pattyn, a Mormon teen confused by her father's abuse of her mother who finds refuge and acceptance while visiting her aunt's Nevada ranch. (Rev: BL 6/1–15/06; SLJ 7/06)

1116 Hopkins, Ellen. *Fallout* (9–12). 2010, Simon & Schuster $18.99 (978-1-4169-5009-7). This sequel to *Crank* (2004) and *Glass* (2007) focuses on Kristina's oldest children and the problems they face resulting from her addiction to crystal meth. ❷ (Rev: BL 6/10; LMC 11–12/10*; SLJ 9/1/10; VOYA 10/10)

1117 Howrey, Meg. *Blind Sight* (10–12). 2011, Pantheon $24.95 (978-0-307-37916-0). Seventeen-year-old Luke spends the summer in Los Angeles with the TV-star father he just met, and uses his college application essay to examine their relationship. (Rev: BL 3/1–15/11; SLJ 6/11)

1118 Hrdlitschka, Shelley. *Kat's Fall* (9–12). 2004, Orca paper $7.95 (978-1-55143-312-7). The news that his mother is going to be released from prison causes 15-year-old Darcy to revisit the incident in which his baby sister was dropped from a balcony. (Rev: SLJ 8/04; VOYA 12/04)

1119 Huston, Nancy. *Fault Lines* (11–12). 2008, Grove paper $14.00 (978-080217051-4). Four generations of one family are affected by an ugly secret that slowly comes to light through four young narrators, beginning in contemporary California and reeling backward to World War II Germany; for mature readers. ♫ (Rev: BL 8/08*)

1120 Hyde, Catherine Ryan. *Love in the Present Tense* (9–12). 2006, Doubleday $21.95 (978-0-385-51800-0). Mitch is 25 when his 18-year-old neighbor Pearl leaves her son, Leonard, with him and disappears in this story of complicated relationships and love. (Rev: BL 4/1/06; SLJ 10/06)

1121 Hyde, Catherine Ryan. *The Year of My Miraculous Reappearance* (7–10). 2007, Knopf $15.99 (978-0-375-83257-4). In the void created by her alcoholic mother with her constantly changing boyfriends, Cynnie, 13, treasures her relationship with her young brother; when he is taken away, Cynnie sinks into alcoholism herself. (Rev: BCCB 7–8/07; BL 3/1/07; LMC 4–5/07; SLJ 4/07)

1122 Iida, Deborah. *Middle Son* (10–12). 1996, Algonquin $29.95 (978-1-56512-119-5). The death of an older brother haunts Spencer in this novel about a Japanese American family in Hawaii. (Rev: BL 3/1/98; SLJ 1/97)

1123 Irving, John. *The World According to Garp* (10–12). 1997, Ballantine paper $14.00 (978-0-345-41801-2). A satirical novel that spans four generations and two continents.

1124 Jaffe, Sherril. *Ground Rules: What I Learned My Daughter's Fifteenth Year* (10–12). 1997, Kodansha $20.00 (978-1-56836-172-7). Told from a mother's point of view, this novel tells of the clash between the mother and her 15-year-old daughter, who becomes increasingly unhappy, uncooperative, and defiant. (Rev: SLJ 8/97)

1125 James, Brian. *The Heights* (8–12). 2009, Feiwel & Friends $16.99 (978-031236853-1). Privileged Catherine and her stepbrother Henry, a Mexican orphan, share a doomed passion for each other in this contemporary retelling of *Wuthering Heights* set in San Francisco. Lexile 900L (Rev: BL 5/1/09; HB 5–6/09; LMC 8–9/09; SLJ 7/1/09)

1126 James, Tania. *Atlas of Unknowns* (10–12). 2009, Knopf $24.95 (978-030726890-7). This novel describes the lives of two bright Indian sisters whose bond is stronger than the separation, deceptions, pain, and success they meet; set in both India and the United States, this is suitable for mature students. e (Rev: BL 4–5/09)

1127 Jarzab, Anna. *The Opposite of Hallelujah* (8–12). 2012, Delacorte $16.99 (978-038573836-1); LB $19.99 (978-038590724-8). Carolina uses untruths to cope with her confusion of her sister's decision to enter a convent, and years later to suddenly leave it. (Rev: BL 10/1/12*; VOYA 12/12)

1128 Johnson, Angela. *Heaven* (6–10). 1998, Simon & Schuster $16.00 (978-0-689-82229-2). Marley, a 14-year-old African American girl, is devastated when she learns that she is adopted and that the couple she has regarded as her mother and father are really her aunt and uncle. (Rev: BCCB 12/98; BL 9/15/98; HBG 3/99; SLJ 10/98; VOYA 2/99)

1129 Johnson, Peter. *What Happened* (7–12). 2007, Front St $16.95 (978-1-932425-67-3). A hit-and-run accident reveals long-concealed relationships between the parents of Duane on one side and Kyle and the unnamed narrator on the other side in this novel about troubled young people facing difficult choices. (Rev: BL 5/1/07; SLJ 6/07)

1130 Jones, Tayari. *Silver Spar-row* (10–12). 2011, Algonquin $19.95 (978-1-56512-990-0). A bigamist's two families, kept a secret from each other for decades, meet and begin a tentative friendship. ♫ e (Rev: BL 5/15/11; SLJ 7/11)

1131 Kearney, Meg. *The Girl in the Mirror: A Novel in Poems and Journal Entries* (7–12). Series: Karen and Michael Braziller Books. 2012, Persea paper $15 (978-0-89255-385-3). Poems and journal entries document Lizzie's grief over the death of her adoptive father and her search for her birth mother in this sequel to *The Secret of Me* (2007). (Rev: BLO 3/1/12; HB 7–8/12; SLJ 6/12; VOYA 6/12)

1132 Kearney, Meg. *The Secret of Me* (7–10). 2005, Persea $17.95 (978-0-89255-322-8). Lizzie, 14, is disappointed that her family won't discuss her adoption with her and her obsession with this secret affects her whole life; a novel told in verse. (Rev: BCCB 1/06; SLJ 1/06)

1133 Kennedy, Cate. *The World Beneath* (9–12). 2011, Black Cat $14.95 (978-080217071-2). An estranged and clueless father seeks to reconnect with his unhappy teenage daughter by way of a wilderness experience in this story set in Tasmania that tests both their relationship and their survival skills. Booklist Editors' Choice: Adult Books for Young Adults, 2011. ♫ e (Rev: BL 12/1–15/10*)

1134 Kephart, Beth. *House of Dance* (7–10). 2008, HarperTeen $16.99 (978-0-06-142928-6). Fifteen-year-old Rosie's grandfather is dying, and she decides to bring back his youth by throwing a party with ballroom dancing. (Rev: BL 6/1–15/08; SLJ 7/08)

1135 Kephart, Beth. *You Are My Only* (9–12). 2011, Egmont $16.99 (978-1-60684-272-0). Parallel narratives reveal the stories of a young woman growing up in lonely isolation, and the kidnapping fourteen years earlier that ruined her mother's life. e Lexile 800L (Rev: BL 10/1/11; SLJ 10/1/11)

1136 Khashoggi, Soheir. *Mirage* (9–12). 1997, Forge paper $6.99 (978-0-614-20507-7). A novel with the plight of a Middle Eastern Islamic woman at its heart, from an author who is a product of a similar culture. (Rev: BL 12/1/95*)

1137 Kiernan, Kristy. *Between Friends* (11–12). 2010, Berkley paper $15 (978-04252334-7-4). Single career woman Cora donates an egg to her barren friend Ali; fourteen years later she's coping with the possibility that she passed a hereditary disease onto the child in this complex family drama; for mature readers. (Rev: BL 3/1–15/10)

1138 King, Lily. *Father of the Rain* (11–12). 2010, Atlantic Monthly $24 (978-080211949-0). Daughter-of-divorce Daley, 11, copes with her father's disastrous new affair, drinking problem, and seemingly sudden lack of morals in this compelling portrait of a dysfunctional family; for mature readers. ℮ (Rev: BL 4/1–15/10)

1139 Klein, Norma. *Breaking Up* (7–10). 1981, Avon paper $2.50 (978-0-380-55830-8). While visiting her divorced father in California, Alison falls in love with her best friend's brother.

1140 Klein, Norma. *Going Backwards* (9–12). 1986, Scholastic paper $12.95 (978-0-590-40328-3). A wrenching story of a boy and his grandmother, who is suffering from Alzheimer's disease, that introduces the theme of mercy killing. (Rev: BL 10/15/86; SLJ 1/87; VOYA 2/87)

1141 Kneale, Matthew. *When We Were Romans* (10–12). 2008, Doubleday $23.95 (978-038552625-8). Nine-year-old Lawrence tells the story of his mother's flight from London (and her imagined stalker) to Rome as he witnesses the slow undoing of his family. ℮ (Rev: BL 7/08*; SLJ 9/08)

1142 Koertge, Ron. *Strays* (7–10). 2007, Candlewick $16.99 (978-0-7636-2705-8). After the death of his parents, 16-year-old Ted is placed in foster care and initially finds comfort in talking to animals but gradually learns to trust his roommates and other human beings. (Rev: BL 5/1/07; HB 7–8/07; SLJ 7/07)

1143 Kogler, Jennifer Anne. *Ruby Tuesday* (8–10). 2005, HarperCollins LB $16.89 (978-0-06-073957-7). The world of 13-year-old Ruby Tuesday Sweet is turned upside down when her father is arrested for the murder of a bookie. (Rev: BCCB 5/05; SLJ 4/05; VOYA 8/05)

1144 Koja, Kathe. *Going Under* (9–12). 2006, Farrar $16.00 (978-0-374-30393-8). In this story that parallels the myths of Persephone and Narcissus, teenager Hilly must resist a manipulative psychologist who wants to publish her journal and at the same time cope with the new distance between herself and her brother Ivan. (Rev: BL 9/1/06; HB 9–10/06; LMC 4/07; SLJ 11/07)

1145 Kraus, Daniel. *Rotters* (9–12). 2011, Delacorte $16.99 (978-0-385-73857-6); LB $19.99 (978-0-385-

90737-8). After his mother's death, Joey, 16, moves from Chicago to live in rural Iowa with the father he has never met; there he learns that his reclusive dad is a grave robber and is strangely attracted to this grizzly profession. Odyssey Award 2012. ⌒ ℮ (Rev: BLO 4/1/11; LMC 10/11*; SLJ 7/11; VOYA 6/11)

1146 Kring, Sandra. *Thank You for All Things* (11–12). 2008, Bantam paper $12.00 (978-038534120-2). Bright 11-year-old Lucy, who is curious about her missing father, dredges up some unpleasant family history; for mature teens. ℮ (Rev: BL 8/08)

1147 Kuipers, Alice. *Lost for Words* (8–12). 2010, HarperCollins $16.99 (978-0-06-142922-4). Sophie, 16, finally begins to move on from her sister's death with help from her journal, a new friend, and a kind therapist. ℮ Lexile HL650L (Rev: SLJ 5/10; VOYA 8/10*)

1148 Kwasney, Michelle D. *Blue Plate Special* (9–12). 2010, Chronicle $16.99 (978-0-8118-6780-1). An absorbing story of three generations of young women, told in alternating narratives. (Rev: BL 10/15/09; LMC 1–2/10; SLJ 12/09)

1149 Lancaster, Craig. *The Summer Son* (11–12). 2011, AmazonEncore paper $14.95 (978-19355972-4-7). An angry, 40-something man suffering a midlife crisis recalls his difficult youth when he returns to Montana to confront his violent, estranged father in this book best suited to mature readers. (Rev: BL 1/1–15/11)

1150 Landalf, Helen. *Flyaway* (9–12). 2011, Harcourt $16.99 (978-0-547-51973-9). Fifteen-year-old Stevie's Aunt Mindy gives her niece support when her mother goes to rehab for crystal meth addiction. ℮ Lexile HL720L (Rev: BL 10/15/11; SLJ 12/1/11)

1151 Lantz, Francess. *Someone to Love* (7–10). 1997, Avon $14.00 (978-0-380-97477-1). Sara's secure family life changes when her parents decide to adopt the yet-unborn child of Iris, an unmarried teen. (Rev: BL 4/15/97)

1152 Les Becquets, Diane. *Season of Ice* (8–12). 2008, Bloomsbury $16.95 (978-1-59990-063-6). When her father disappears one day, 17-year-old Genesis must deal not only with grief but also with helping to support her stepbrothers in this novel set in wintry northern Maine. (Rev: BL 1/1–15/08; HB 5–6/08; SLJ 4/08)

1153 London, Julia. *Summer of Two Wishes* (11–12). 2009, Pocket paper $7.99 (978-14165470-8-2). Macy, who is newly married to Wyatt, finds out that her beloved first husband Finn was not killed by the Taliban years ago but has been found alive and is on his way home; for mature readers. ⌒ (Rev: BL 9/09)

1154 Lopez, Jack. *In the Break* (11–12). 2006, Little, Brown $16.99 (978-0-316-00874-7). For mature teens, this is a story about surfing and about teens — Juan, Jamie, and Jamie's sister — who flee a bad situation only to find themselves in a tragic one. (Rev: BL 9/1/06; LMC 2/07; SLJ 2/07)

1155 Lowell, Pamela. *Returnable Girl* (9–12). 2006, Marshall Cavendish $16.99 (978-0-7614-5317-8). After a series of foster homes 13-year-old Ronnie finally has the chance to settle down but remains afraid to trust and still nurtures a longing for her real mother. (Rev: BL 11/15/06; SLJ 10/06)

1156 Lowry, Lois. *Find a Stranger, Say Goodbye* (7–10). 1978, Houghton Mifflin $18.00 (978-0-395-26459-1). A college-bound girl decides to find her natural mother.

1157 Lynch, Chris. *The Big Game of Everything* (7–10). 2008, HarperTeen $16.99 (978-006074034-4); LB $17.89 (978-006074035-1). Jock and his younger brother Egon spend a summer working at their grandfather's golf course and learn the importance of integrity versus material gain. Lexile 830L (Rev: BL 9/1/08; HB 9–10/08; SLJ 10/1/08; VOYA 8/08)

1158 McCandless, Sarah Grace. *The Girl I Wanted to Be* (9–12). 2006, Simon & Schuster paper $12.00 (978-0-7432-8518-6). Presley, 14, knows something is going on between her cousin Barry and her Aunt Betsi, who's come to live with Presley's family after a stint in rehab. (Rev: BL 4/15/06)

1159 McCord, Patricia. *Pictures in the Dark* (7–10). 2004, Bloomsbury $16.95 (978-1-58234-848-3). Set in the 1950s, this is the story of two sisters, one 12 and the other 15, and how their mother gradually sank into insanity. (Rev: BL 5/15/04; HB 7–8/04; SLJ 5/04)

1160 MacCullough, Carolyn. *Drawing the Ocean* (8–11). 2006, Roaring Brook $16.95 (978-1-59643-092-1). Sadie, a gifted 16-year-old artist, wants to fit in and be popular at her new school but finds it hard when her dead twin brother still haunts her and she's drawn to an outcast poet named Ryan. (Rev: BL 11/15/06; LMC 2/07; SLJ 2/07)

1161 MacCullough, Carolyn. *Stealing Henry* (9–12). 2005, Roaring Brook $16.95 (978-1-59643-045-7). Unable to tolerate her drunken stepfather's abuse, 17-year-old Savannah knocks him out with a frying pan and takes off with her 8-year-old half brother. (Rev: BCCB 3/05; BL 4/1/05*; SLJ 4/05; VOYA 4/05)

1162 McDonald, Janet. *Off-Color* (7–12). 2007, Farrar $16.00 (978-0-374-37196-8). When her single mother gets a job on the other side of Brooklyn, 15-year-old Cameron has to leave her white neighborhood and move to the projects, where she learns about diversity and a secret about her absentee father. (Rev: BL 8/07; SLJ 3/08)

1163 McDonald, Janet. *Spellbound* (7–12). 2001, Farrar $16.00 (978-0-374-37140-1). Despite enormous obstacles, 16-year-old African American mother Raven decides to enter a spelling bee in hopes of going to college. (Rev: BCCB 10/01; BL 11/1/01; HB 1–2/02; HBG 3/02; SLJ 9/01; VOYA 10/01)

1164 McEwan, Ian. *Atonement* (10–12). 2002, Doubleday $26.00 (978-0-385-50395-2). Set on an English country estate at which there is a family reunion, this novel for mature readers tells how an imaginative young girl can cause events to spin out of control. (Rev: BL 11/15/01*; SLJ 6/02)

1165 McInerney, Monica. *The Alphabet Sisters* (11–12). 2005, Ballantine paper $13.95 (978-0-345-47953-2). Three sisters return to Clare Valley, Australia, for their grandmother's 80th birthday and find themselves forced to get along; for mature teens. (Rev: BL 5/15/05)

1166 Mack, Tracy. *Birdland* (7–10). 2003, Scholastic $16.95 (978-0-439-53590-8). Jed's family has not recovered from the death of his brother Zeke, and Jed finds some comfort in videotaping their neighborhood and finding links to Zeke through the poems and journal he left. Sidney Taylor Book Honor 2003. (Rev: BL 10/15/03*; SLJ 10/03)

1167 McKinney-Whetstone, Diane. *Tempest Rising* (10–12). 1998, Morrow paper $12.00 (978-0-688-16640-3). After the death of their father and the mental collapse of their mother, three African American adolescent sisters are placed in a foster-home, where new relationships are built. (Rev: BL 2/15/98; SLJ 10/98)

1168 McMann, Lisa. *Dead to You* (9–12). 2012, Simon & Schuster $16.99 (978-144240388-8). After being abducted at age 7 and ending up in care, 16-year-old Ethan is reunited with his family and finds it difficult to cope, especially with the brother who doubts his identity. ∩ ℮ Lexile HL620L (Rev: BL 1/12; LMC 8–9/12; SLJ 4/12; VOYA 2/12)

1169 Manley, Frank. *The Cockfighter* (10–12). 1998, Coffee House $19.95 (978-1-56689-073-1). In this novel set in the rural South, the hatred that develops between a sensitive 13-year-boy and his crude, redneck father who raises cocks for illegal cockfighting erupts in a bloody climax. (Rev: BL 3/15/98; SLJ 10/98)

1170 Mapson, Jo-Ann. *The Owl and Moon Cafe* (11–12). 2006, Simon & Schuster paper $14.00 (978-0-7432-6641-3). Mariah and her daughter, Lindsay, move in with Mariah's mother, Allegra, and must face illness, romance, and unemployment the best they can in this entertaining novel for mature readers. (Rev: BL 5/15/06)

1171 Marchetta, Melina. *Saving Francesca* (8–10). 2004, Knopf LB $17.99 (978-0-375-92982-3). Unhappy with life at her new Australian high school, Francesca desperately needs the help and support of her mother, who is struggling with her own battle against depression. (Rev: BL 10/1/04; SLJ 9/04; VOYA 10/04)

1172 Marion, Stephen. *Hollow Ground* (10–12). 2002, Algonquin $23.95 (978-1-56512-323-6). Taft must deal with several problems including a long-absent father's sudden return to Zinctown, Tennessee. (Rev: BL 2/1/02)

1173 Martinez, Jessica. *The Space Between Us* (8–12). 2012, Simon & Schuster $16.99 (978-144242055-7).

Amelia, 17, has been looking after her irresponsible younger sister for years, and now finds herself reluctantly accompanying a pregnant Charly to Canada for a year. ℮ Lexile HL640L (Rev: BL 11/1/12; SLJ 4/13; VOYA 2/13)

1174 Mazer, Norma Fox. *After the Rain* (7–10). 1987, Avon paper $5.99 (978-0-380-75025-2). Rachel gradually develops a warm relationship with her terminally ill grandfather who is noted for his bad temper. (Rev: BL 5/1/87; SLJ 5/87; VOYA 6/87)

1175 Mazer, Norma Fox. *Downtown* (7–10). 1984, Avon paper $4.95 (978-0-380-88534-3). Pete, 15, the son of anti-war demonstrators who are in hiding, faces problems when his mother reappears and wants to be part of his life.

1176 Mazer, Norma Fox. *Missing Pieces* (7–10). 1995, Morrow $16.00 (978-0-688-13349-8). A 14-year-old seeks a missing part of her life by looking for a father who abandoned her. (Rev: BL 4/1/95; SLJ 4/95*; VOYA 5/95)

1177 Miles, Jackie Lee. *All That's True* (10–12). 2011, Sourcebooks paper $13.99 (978-14022408-5-0). After 13-year-old Andi's brother dies in a hazing incident, she must deal with her own reactions and those of her parents and her older sister. (Rev: BL 10/1–15/10)

1178 Miller-Lachmann, Lyn. *Dirt Cheap: A Novel* (9–12). 2006, Curbstone paper $15.95 (978-1-931896-29-0). A leukemia survivor works to stop development in a community riddled with cancers caused by a polluting chemical company in this eco-thriller. (Rev: SLJ 8/06)

1179 Minter, J. *Pass It On: An Insiders Novel* (9–12). Series: Insiders. 2004, Bloomsbury paper $8.95 (978-1-58234-954-1). In volume two of the series, Jonathan feels overwhelmed by all the secrets that have been entrusted to him, not the least of which is the fact that his father has cheated his friends' parents out of large sums of money. (Rev: SLJ 2/05; VOYA 4/05)

1180 Mitchell, Mary E. *Americans in Space* (11–12). 2009, St. Martin's $24.99 (978-031237245-3). Still reeling two years after the death of her husband, high school guidance counselor Kate Cavanaugh finds it a struggle to simply get through her day; to complicate matters, her 14-year-old daughter is exhibiting some disconcerting behavior; for mature readers. (Rev: BL 10/1/09)

1181 Monardo, Anna. *Falling in Love with Natassia* (11–12). 2006, Doubleday $23.95 (978-0-385-51466-8). When her 15-year-old daughter has her heart broken, Mary returns to comfort her after years of absence. (Rev: BL 5/15/06)

1182 Morgan, Robert. *This Rock* (10–12). 2001, Algonquin $24.95 (978-1-56512-303-8). Set in the rural South in the early 1920s, this novel tells of the bitter and protracted rivalry between brothers Muir and Moody Powell. (Rev: BL 7/01; SLJ 4/02)

1183 Mori, Kyoko. *One Bird* (8–12). 1996, Fawcett paper $6.50 (978-0-449-70453-0). A coming-of-age story set in Japan about 15-year-old girl Megumi, who loses her mother yet finds people who understand and love her. (Rev: BL 10/15/95; SLJ 11/95; VOYA 2/96)

1184 Moriarty, Jaclyn. *The Spell Book of Listen Taylor* (9–12). 2007, Scholastic $16.99 (978-0-439-84678-3). The adults in 12-year-old Listen's life are busy having affairs while she tries to magically reveal the secret of her father's girlfriend's family. (Rev: BL 10/1/07; HB 9–10/07; SLJ 11/07)

1185 Moskowitz, Hannah. *Invincible Summer* (9–12). 2011, Simon & Schuster paper $9.99 (978-1-4424-0-751-0). Over the course of four summers at the beach, Chase McGill and his family interact with the family next door, with romances and other entanglements. ℮ Lexile HL710L (Rev: BL 4/1/11; SLJ 4/11; VOYA 6/11)

1186 Murdoch, Emily. *If You Find Me* (8–12). 2013, St. Martin's paper $9.99 (978-1-250-03327-7). After years of living in an isolated camper deep in the woods, often left alone by their meth-addict mother, 14-year-old Carey and her mute younger sister Janessa find themselves whisked away by their father to live in bewildering luxury with his new family. ℮ (Rev: BL 3/15/13*; SLJ 2/13*; VOYA 2/13)

1187 Murray, Martine. *How to Make a Bird* (8–12). 2010, Scholastic $16.99 (978-0-439-66951-1). Manon, 17, travels from the Australian countryside to Melbourne, where she hopes to come to terms with family tragedies. ℮ (Rev: BL 4/15/10; LMC 8–9/10; SLJ 8/10)

1188 Myracle, Lauren. *Peace, Love, and Baby Ducks* (8–12). 2009, Dutton $16.99 (978-052547743-3). Privileged Atlanta teen sisters Anna and Carly deal with boys, looks, and emerging belief systems as they navigate family and school life. ∩ Lexile HL630L (Rev: BL 4/15/09; HB 7–8/09; SLJ 8/09; VOYA 8/09)

1189 Nelson, Jandy. *The Sky Is Everywhere* (8–11). 2010, Dial $17.99 (978-0-8037-3495-1). When Lennie's popular older sister suddenly dies, the 17-year-old struggles to fill her shoes — which include a fiancé and the lead role in Romeo and Juliet. ∩ ℮ (Rev: BL 1/1–15/10; HB 3–4/10; SLJ 3/10; VOYA 8/10)

1190 Noble, Elizabeth. *Things I Want My Daughters to Know* (9–12). 2008, Morrow $22.95 (978-0-06-112219-4). This uplifting heartbreaker follows four sisters through the year after their beloved mother's death from cancer. (Rev: BL 3/15/08)

1191 Oates, Joyce Carol. *Freaky Green Eyes* (7–10). 2003, HarperCollins LB $17.89 (978-0-06-623757-2). Franky, 15, recounts the tensions between her artist mother and her abusive, controlling father and the buildup to her mother's eventual disappearance. (Rev: BL 12/1/03; HB 11–12/03; HBG 4/04; SLJ 10/03; VOYA 10/03)

1192 Ockler, Sarah. *Fixing Delilah* (9–12). 2010, Little, Brown $16.99 (978-031605209-2). Seventeen-year-old Delilah discovers a painful family history of depression that makes her question the course of her own life. e Lexile 930L (Rev: BL 11/15/10; SLJ 11/1/10; VOYA 12/10)

1193 O'Dell, Tawni. *Fragile Beasts* (11–12). 2010, Crown $25 (978-030735168-5). After their father is killed in an accident, two teenaged boys are taken in by a wealthy town matriarch with a melancholy past and thereby avoid returning to the mother who abandoned them; this arresting tale suitable for mature readers is set in a western Pennsylvania coal town. (Rev: BL 2/1–15/10)

1194 Omololu, C. J. *Dirty Little Secrets* (7–10). 2010, Walker $16.99 (978-0-8027-8660-9). High school sophomore Lucy is determined to hide the fact that her mother is a hoarder, and when she finds her mother dead from an asthma attack amid the stacks of junk, Lucy decides to take drastic action. ∩ e Lexile 890L (Rev: BL 10/1509; LMC 3–4/10; SLJ 2/10)

1195 O'Neal, Barbara. *How to Bake a Perfect Life* (10–12). 2011, Bantam paper $15 (978-05533867-7-6). Ramona, a baker, finds herself looking after her daughter's difficult stepdaughter in this story about a family facing challenges. (Rev: BL 12/1–15/10)

1196 Paterson, Katherine. *Come Sing, Jimmy Jo* (6–10). 1985, Avon paper $3.99 (978-0-380-70052-3). The family decides it's time to include James in their singing group. (Rev: BL 9/1/87; SLJ 4/85)

1197 Paterson, Katherine. *Jacob Have I Loved* (6–10). 1980, HarperCollins LB $17.89 (978-0-690-04079-1); paper $6.99 (978-0-06-440368-9). A story set in the Chesapeake Bay region about the rivalry between two sisters. Newbery Medal 1981.

1198 Patterson, Janci. *Chasing the Skip* (7–10). 2012, Henry Holt $16.99 (978-0-8050-9391-9). Abandoned by her neglectful mother, 15-year-old Ricki finds herself chasing bail jumpers with the bounty hunter father she hardly knows. e Lexile HL620L (Rev: BL 10/15/12; LMC 3–4/13; SLJ 11/12)

1199 Paul, Dominique. *The Possibility of Fireflies* (7–10). 2006, Simon & Schuster $15.95 (978-1-4169-1310-8). Ellie, 14, lives with an abusive, alcoholic mother and a rebellious older sister but tries to make right choices and looks for support from a neighbor named Leo. (Rev: BL 11/15/06; SLJ 11/06)

1200 Pearson, Mary E. *A Room on Lorelei Street* (9–12). 2005, Henry Holt $16.95 (978-0-8050-7667-7). Overcome by the burden of caring for her alcoholic mother, troubled 17-year-old Zoe moves into a rented room and struggles to find some peace. (Rev: BL 6/1–15/05; SLJ 8/05; VOYA 6/05)

1201 Peck, Richard. *Father Figure* (7–10). 1996, Puffin paper $6.99 (978-0-14-037969-3). Jim and his younger brother are sent to live in Florida with a father they scarcely know.

1202 Pedersen, Laura. *The Big Shuffle* (11–12). 2006, Ballantine paper $13.95 (978-0-345-47956-3). College sophomore Hallie must take over family responsibilities (including the care of her nine younger siblings) when her father dies of a heart attack and her mother is hospitalized after a nervous breakdown; this sequel to *Beginners Luck* (2003) and *Heart's Desire* (2005) is for mature teens. (Rev: BL 9/1/06)

1203 Petterson, Per. *Out Stealing Horses* (9–12). Trans. by Anne Born. 2007, Graywolf $18.00 (978-1-55597-470-1). This is the beautifully written story of Trond, a Norwegian widower haunted by his past who returns to the remote cabin where, as a 15-year-old in 1948, he spent the summer. (Rev: BL 6/1–15/07)

1204 Pfeffer, Susan Beth. *Blood Wounds* (8–12). 2011, Harcourt $16.99 (978-0-547-49638-2). Willa's settled life begins to fall apart when her estranged biological father sets out on a murderous rampage. e Lexile HL620L (Rev: BL 9/15/11; SLJ 8/11; VOYA 12/11)

1205 Phillips, Suzanne. *Chloe Doe* (9–12). 2007, Little, Brown $16.99 (978-0-316-01413-7). Chloe, a 17-year-old prostitute, is arrested and sent to the Madeline Parker Institute for Girls, where therapy sessions reveal the harsh reasons she left home. (Rev: BL 5/15/07; LMC 11/07; SLJ 10/07)

1206 Piccoult, Jodi, and Dustin Weaver. *The Tenth Circle* (11–12). 2006, Atria $26.00 (978-0-7434-9670-4). Despite his troubled teenage years in Alaska, graphic artist Daniel Stone enjoys a quiet life in Maine with his wife and teenage daughter until his daughter accuses her ex-boyfriend of rape; for mature readers. (Rev: BL 12/1/05)

1207 Picoult, Jodi. *My Sister's Keeper* (10–12). 2004, Atria $25.00 (978-0-7434-5452-0). Thirteen-year-old Anna Fitzgerald decides not to donate a kidney to help her older sister, who has leukemia, and seeks legal assistance. (Rev: BL 1/1–15/04*; SLJ 1/05)

1208 Puchner, Eric. *Model Home* (11–12). 2010, Scribner $26 (978-074327048-9). Warren moves his endearing yet dysfunctional family to California, where a series of mishaps — from his own real estate foible to his daughter's rocky relationship — draws them deeper and deeper into crazy, though amusing, chaos. ∩ (Rev: BL 1/1–15/10)

1209 Quindlen, Anna. *Every Last One* (11–12). 2010, Random House $26 (978-140006574-5). Mary Beth copes with tragedy — and the task of rebuilding her likable family — in this engrossing novel suitable for mature readers. ∩ (Rev: BL 3/1–15/10)

1210 Quindlen, Anna. *Object Lessons* (9–12). 1992, Ivy paper $6.99 (978-0-8041-0946-8). Maggie, 12, learns important lessons in life during the summer of 1960 in her home in the Bronx. (Rev: BL 1/15/91; SLJ 9/91)

1211 Rabb, Margo. *Cures for Heartbreak* (10–12). 2007, Delacorte $15.99 (978-0-385-73402-8). Mia must deal with her mother's death and her father's heart attack, two tragedies that seem intertwined with her family's Judaism; this well-written novel effectively conveys Mia's sensitive yet humorous take on life. (Rev: BL 12/15/06; HB 3–4/07; SLJ 1/07*)

1212 Reinhardt, Dana. *The Things a Brother Knows* (9–12). 2010, Random House $16.99 (978-0-375-84455-3); LB $19.99 (978-0-375-94455-0). Former marine Boaz has returned from combat a changed young man, and 17-year-old Levi is sufficiently concerned about his behavior to follow him when he leaves home and sets out on a walking trip. Sydney Taylor Book Award 2011; YALSA Top Ten Best Fiction for Young Adults 2011. ℮ (Rev: BL 10/1/10*; SLJ 12/1/10*)

1213 Reynolds, Marilyn. *Baby Help: True-to-Life Series from Hamilton High* (8–12). Series: Hamilton High. 1998, Morning Glory $15.95 (978-1-885356-26-0); paper $8.95 (978-1-885356-27-7). Partner-abuse is explored in this novel about a teenage mother who is living with a difficult boyfriend and his unsympathetic mother. (Rev: BL 2/1/98; HBG 9/98; SLJ 3/98; VOYA 6/98)

1214 Reynolds, Marilyn. *Shut Up!* (8–12). 2008, Morning Glory $15.96 (978-193253893-9); paper $9.95 (978-193253888-5). Seventeen-year-old Mario desperately attempts to get help when he finds his brother is being abused by his aunt's boyfriend in this inspiring story of a strong family coping with conflict. ℮ (Rev: BL 11/15/08; SLJ 2/1/09; VOYA 12/08)

1215 Rice, Luanne. *The Deep Blue Sea for Beginners* (11–12). 2009, Bantam $26 (978-055380514-7). A multilayered story for mature readers about how a daughter tracks down her estranged mother on the island of Capri; this tale includes characters from *The Geometry of Sisters* (2009. ⌒ (Rev: BL 7/09)

1216 Rice, Luanne. *The Perfect Summer* (11–12). 2003, Bantam paper $7.50 (978-0-553-58404-2). Life changes dramatically for Bay McCabe and her children when husband and father Sean McCabe is accused of theft. (Rev: BL 8/03)

1217 Rice, Luanne. *Summer's Child* (11–12). 2005, Bantam paper $7.50 (978-0-553-58762-3). Lily and her daughter Rose, who has a congenital heart defect, live in Nova Scotia under the shadow of continuing fear that Lily's abusive husband will find them; for mature teens. (Rev: BL 6/1–15/05)

1218 Richter, William Harlan. *Dark Eyes* (9–12). 2012, Penguin $17.99 (978-159514457-7). Adopted from a Russian orphanage, feisty 16-year-old Wallis now lives with a wealthy family in New York but prefers life as a runaway searching for her birth mother and learning about her mobster father. ⌒ ℮ (Rev: BL 2/15/12*; LMC 8–9/12; SLJ 5/1/12; VOYA 4/12)

1219 Rottman, S. L. *Shadow of a Doubt* (7–10). 2003, Peachtree $14.95 (978-1-56145-291-0). Shadow is newly 15 and entering high school when his brother Daniel, who has been missing for years, reappears on the scene, suspected of murder. (Rev: BCCB 1/04; BL 11/15/03; HBG 4/04; SLJ 1/04; VOYA 12/03)

1220 Runyon, Brent. *Maybe* (10–12). 2006, Knopf $16.95 (978-0-375-83543-8). Brian, 16, tells about his life after losing his brother in a car accident, moving house, having troubles at a new school, dealing with sexual desires, and trying to form relationships with girls. (Rev: BL 8/06; SLJ 11/06)

1221 Ryan, Darlene. *Rules for Life* (7–12). 2004, Orca paper $7.95 (978-1-55143-350-9). Sixteen-year-old Izzy, whose mother died two years earlier, has difficulty coming to terms with her father's decision to remarry; suitable for reluctant readers. (Rev: BCCB 2/05; SLJ 3/05; VOYA 6/05)

1222 Sachar, Louis. *The Cardturner: A Novel About a King, a Queen, and a Joker* (9–12). 2010, Delacorte $17.99 (978-0-385-73662-6). Alton, 17, volunteers to help his rich, blind uncle with his games of bridge and learns the game and a lot more; optional passages allow non-bridge players to skip details of the game. ⌒ ℮ Lexile HL720L (Rev: BL 5/15/10*; HB 5–6/10; LMC 11–12/10; SLJ 6/10)

1223 Sachs, Marilyn. *Baby Sister* (7–10). 1986, Avon paper $3.50 (978-0-380-70358-6). Penny is torn between her admiration for her older sister and the realization that she is really selfish. (Rev: BL 2/15/86; SLJ 8/86; VOYA 8/86)

1224 Salinger, J. D. *Franny and Zooey* (10–12). 1961, Little, Brown $24.95 (978-0-316-76954-9); paper $5.99 (978-0-316-76949-5). A Glass family story in which Zooey Glass tries to help his sister Franny out of her depression.

1225 Sarsfield, Mairuth. *No Crystal Stair* (10–12). 1997, Stoddart $14.95 (978-1-896867-02-1). Set in a black community in Quebec during the 1940s, this is a story of a widow with three children and her fight to keep her family fed and together. (Rev: SLJ 10/97)

1226 Savage, Deborah. *Summer Hawk* (7–10). 1999, Houghton Mifflin $16.00 (978-0-395-91163-1). In this coming-of-age story, 15-year-old Taylor has trouble relating to her mother and father, shuns the company of Rail Bogart, the other smart kid in her school, and showers her attention and affection on a young hawk she rescues. (Rev: BCCB 6/99; BL 3/1/99; HBG 9/99; SLJ 4/99; VOYA 4/99)

1227 Scarbrough, George. *A Summer Ago* (10–12). 1986, St. Luke's $13.95 (978-0-918518-46-0). A gentle story about a teenage boy and summer spent in rural Tennessee in the early Depression years. (Rev: SLJ 2/87)

1228 Schrefer, Eliot. *The New Kid* (9–12). 2007, Simon & Schuster $25.00 (978-0-7432-9909-1). Gloomy but well-written, this novel follows teenager Humphrey as he tries to make friends at school after constantly moving from place to place with his nomadic and toxic family. (Rev: BL 8/07)

1229 Schumacher, Julie. *Black Box* (9–12). 2008, Delacorte $15.99 (978-038573542-1); LB $18.99 (978-038590523-7). When stoic high school freshman Elena's older sister Dora is hospitalized for depression, Elena takes it upon herself to look after Dora even as her family falls to pieces around her. **e** Lexile NC600L (Rev: BL 11/1/08; SLJ 8/08*; VOYA 12/08)

1230 Sebestyen, Ouida. *Far from Home* (7–10). 1980, Little, Brown $15.95 (978-0-316-77932-6). An orphaned boy is taken in by a couple who run a boardinghouse and there he uncovers secrets about his family's past.

1231 Sebold, Alice. *The Lovely Bones* (10–12). 2002, Little, Brown $21.95 (978-0-316-66634-3). Fourteen-year-old Susie Salmon, in heaven after being raped and murdered on her way home from school, watches over her grieving family with interest and humor and tracks the progress of the investigation into the crime. (Rev: BL 5/1/02; SLJ 10/02; VOYA 12/02)

1232 Sedlack, Robert. *The African Safari Papers* (11–12). 2003, Overlook paper $13.95 (978-1-58567-300-1). On safari with his dysfunctional and feuding parents, Richard recounts in journal form the troubled family relationships and his own preoccupations (mainly sex and drugs); for mature teens. (Rev: BL 9/1/03)

1233 Seigel, Andrea. *The Kid Table* (10–12). 2010, Bloomsbury $16.99 (978-1-59990-480-1). Ingrid, 16, and her five teenage cousins bring their various problems to the "kid table" at family gatherings; Ingrid's observations are perceptive about herself, her cousins, and the adults in this dysfunctional yet tight-knit group. **e** Lexile 950L (Rev: LMC 10/10; SLJ 11/1/10; VOYA 12/10)

1234 Shamsie, Kamila. *Broken Verses* (10–12). 2005, Harcourt paper $14.00 (978-0-15-603053-3). A 31-year-old Pakistani woman is pulled into a web of intrigue when she reads letters written in a code known only to her long-absent mother and her mother's lover, a poet believed to be dead. (Rev: BL 3/1/05; SLJ 6/05)

1235 Sheehan, Aurelie. *History Lesson for Girls* (10–12). 2006, Viking $23.95 (978-0-670-03767-4). Alison and Kate both have neglectful parents and complicated young lives, drawing them together as they try to sort things out in this novel set in the turbulent 1970s. (Rev: BL 5/15/06)

1236 Shelton, Sandi Kahn. *A Piece of Normal* (10–12). 2006, Crown $21.00 (978-1-4000-9731-9). For Lily Brown, a divorced mother of a young boy, life changes when her sister, Dana, reappears in her small town. (Rev: BL 5/1/06)

1237 Shepherd, Paul. *More Like Not Running Away* (11–12). 2005, Sarabande paper $14.95 (978-1-932511-28-4). In this prize-winning first novel, 12-year-old Levi Revel idolizes his often-violent father and is driven to the edge of madness by the endless murmur of voices only he can hear. (Rev: BL 10/1/05)

1238 Shimko, Bonnie. *Letters in the Attic* (7–12). 2002, Academy Chicago $23.50 (978-0-89733-511-9). Twelve-year-old Lizzie and her mother move to upstate New York after her father leaves home, and there Lizzie finds new attachments and a new understanding of her mother's behavior. (Rev: VOYA 4/03)

1239 Shreve, Anita. *Rescue* (10–12). 2010, Little, Brown $26.99 (978-031602072-5). EMT Pete Webster seeks out the alcoholic wife who left him years ago so she can help him save their daughter, Rowan, who has fallen into the same self-destructive behaviors. ☊ **e** (Rev: BL 9/1–15/10)

1240 Shreve, Porter. *When the White House Was Ours* (11–12). 2008, Houghton Mifflin paper $12.95 (978-061872210-5). His father continues to lose teaching jobs and 12-year-old Daniel Truitt's life has been in constant flux; now his delusional parents are dragging him to Washington, D.C., in hopes of starting a progressive school; an entertaining read for mature teens, this is set in 1976. (Rev: BL 8/08)

1241 Shusterman, Neal. *What Daddy Did* (7–10). 1991, Little, Brown paper $15.95 (978-0-316-78906-6). A young boy recounts the story of how his father murdered his mother and how he ultimately comes to understand and forgive him. (Rev: BL 7/91; SLJ 6/91)

1242 Silver, Marisa. *The God of War* (9–12). 2008, Simon & Schuster $23.00 (978-1-4165-6316-7). Ares tells the haunting story of his traumatic twelfth year as part of a little family living on the margins of a sanctuary for pelicans and fish. (Rev: BL 3/15/08)

1243 Simmons, Michael. *Vandal* (7–10). 2006, Roaring Brook $16.95 (978-1-59643-070-9). In a story laced with tragedy, 16-year-old guitar player Will struggles to forge a relationship with his destructive older brother. (Rev: BL 7/06; HB 7–8/06; LMC 11–12/06; SLJ 6/06)

1244 Slezak, Ellen. *All These Girls* (11–12). 2004, Hyperion $23.95 (978-0-7868-6742-4). After the death of Candy's mother, Candy, her aunt, and her great-aunt retreat to a remote corner of Michigan; a family drama for mature teens. (Rev: BL 8/04)

1245 Sloan, Holly Goldberg. *I'll Be There* (9–12). 2011, Little, Brown $17.99 (978-0-316-12279-5). Sam, a musically gifted 17-year-old, and his autistic younger brother Riddle have had rotten, isolated childhoods living with their unstable and criminal father, but when they meet Emily there seems to be room for help. **e**

Lexile 810L (Rev: BL 4/1/11; HB 7–8/11; LMC 10/11; SLJ 5/11*; VOYA 6/11)

1246 Smith, Anne Warren. *Sister in the Shadow* (7–10). 1986, Avon paper $2.75 (978-0-380-70378-4). In competition with her successful younger sister, Sharon becomes a live-in baby-sitter, with unhappy results. (Rev: BL 5/1/86; SLJ 5/86; VOYA 8/86)

1247 Sones, Sonya. *One of Those Hideous Books Where the Mother Dies* (7–12). 2004, Simon & Schuster $15.95 (978-0-689-85820-8). In this free-verse novel, a high schooler, after the death of her mother, is sent to live with her father, a famous movie actor whom she detests. (Rev: BL 5/1/04*; SLJ 8/04)

1248 Sonnenblick, Jordan. *Notes from the Midnight Driver* (8–11). 2006, Scholastic $16.99 (978-0-439-75779-9). Unhappy about his parents' separation, 16-year-old Alex drives drunk and ends up with a sentence of 100 hours of community service at a nursing home, during which he ends up learning some very valuable life lessons from an older man named Solomon. (Rev: BL 10/1/06; SLJ 10/06)

1249 Sparks, Beatrice, ed. *Finding Katie: The Diary of Anonymous, a Teenager in Foster Care* (7–10). 2005, Avon paper $5.99 (978-0-06-050721-3). In this angst-filled fictional diary, Katie, a teenager living on a California estate, makes it clear that money and privilege do nothing to ensure a happy life. (Rev: SLJ 10/05)

1250 Spollen, Anne. *The Shape of Water* (7–10). 2008, Flux paper $9.95 (978-0-7387-1101-0). Fifteen-year-old Magda initially grieves her artistic mother's death by committing arson and imagining talking fish. (Rev: BLO 6/17/08; SLJ 6/08)

1251 Steinbeck, John. *The Pearl* (9–12). 1993, Viking paper $9.00 (978-0-14-017737-4). The lives of a poor Mexican pearl fisher and his family change dramatically after he uncovers a fabulous pearl.

1252 Stevenson, Robin. *Escape Velocity* (7–10). 2011, Orca paper $12.95 (978-15546986-6-0). After her father has a stroke, 15-year-old Lou is sent to live with her mother, a writer who abandoned her when she was only a few days old. e Lexile HL630L (Rev: BL 12/1/11; LMC 1–2/12; SLJ 1/12)

1253 Stevenson, Robin. *A Thousand Shades of Blue* (9–11). 2008, Orca paper $12.95 (978-155143921-1). Sixteen-year-old Rachel's troubled family spends a year sailing through the Caribbean, where Rachel learns about secrets, trust, and sexuality. e Lexile NC600L (Rev: BL 1/1–15/09; SLJ 3/1/09; VOYA 12/08)

1254 Stork, Francisco X. *Irises* (9–12). Illus. by Francisco X. Stork. 2012, Scholastic $17.99 (978-0-545-15135-1). Kate, 18, and Mary, 16, are forced to make a difficult decision when their father dies and their mother is in a vegetative state. 🎧 e Lexile HL660L (Rev: BL 12/15/11; LMC 5–6/12; SLJ 12/1/11; VOYA 12/11)

1255 Suzuma, Tabitha. *Forbidden* (10–12). 2011, Simon & Schuster $16.99 (978-1-4424-1995-7). Siblings Maya, 16, and Lochan, 17, describe their torn feelings when they fall in love with each other after years of looking after their three younger siblings, neglected by their alcoholic mother. e (Rev: BL 6/1/11; LMC 10/11; SLJ 10/1/11; VOYA 8/11)

1256 Swanson, Julie A. *Going for the Record* (7–12). 2004, Eerdmans paper $8.00 (978-0-8028-5273-1). High school soccer star Leah Weiczynkowski finds herself torn between family responsibilities and her sports aspirations when her father is diagnosed with terminal cancer. (Rev: BL 9/1/04*; SLJ 8/04; VOYA 10/04)

1257 Sweeney, Aoibheann. *Among Other Things, I've Taken Up Smoking* (9–12). 2007, Penguin $23.95 (978-1-59420-130-1). A richly layered story of a girl raised on a secluded island off the Maine coast and the mysteries she uncovers about her family when she moves back to the mainland. (Rev: BL 6/1–15/07)

1258 Sweeney, Joyce. *Headlock: A Novel* (8–10). 2006, Henry Holt $16.95 (978-0-8050-8018-6). Kyle, 18, wants to become a professional wrestler but must put his dream aside when his grandmother becomes ill. (Rev: BL 11/1/06; SLJ 11/06)

1259 Thesman, Jean. *The Last April Dancers* (7–10). 1987, Avon paper $2.75 (978-0-380-70614-3). Catherine tries to recover from the guilt caused by her father's suicide through friendship and love of a neighboring boy. (Rev: BL 9/15/87; SLJ 10/87; VOYA 10/87)

1260 Thomas, Jacquelin. *Divine Confidential* (9–12). Series: Divine. 2007, Pocket $9.95 (978-1-4165-2719-0). Divine, who became a Christian in *Simply Divine* (2006), is now living in Georgia with her cousins and trying hard to remain a virgin and steer clear of other teen traps. (Rev: BL 2/1/07)

1261 Torres, Laura. *Crossing Montana* (7–10). 2002, Holiday $16.95 (978-0-8234-1643-1). Callie sets off on a journey across Montana in search of her missing grandfather, and in the process finds out the truth about her father's death. (Rev: BCCB 10/02; BL 8/02; HBG 10/02; SLJ 7/02; VOYA 8/02)

1262 Townsend, John Rowe. *Downstream* (9–12). 1987, HarperCollins LB $12.89 (978-0-397-32189-6). A teenage English boy finds himself in competition with his father for the affections of an attractive divorcée. (Rev: BL 7/87; SLJ 8/87; VOYA 6/87)

1263 Treadway, Jessica. *And Give You Peace* (10–12). 2001, Graywolf paper $14.00 (978-1-55597-315-5). A young woman sets out to discover why her father shot her sister and then himself in this story of a family tragedy. (Rev: BL 11/15/00)

1264 Trembath, Don. *The Popsicle Journal* (7–12). 2001, Orca paper $6.95 (978-1-55143-185-7). Fledgling journalist Harper Winslow finds himself torn between professional responsibility and family loyalty when his sister is involved in a DUI auto accident while his father is running for mayor. (Rev: SLJ 7/02; VOYA 4/02)

1265 Trollope, Joanna. *The Other Family* (11–12). 2010, Touchstone paper $15 (978-14391298-3-8). Chrissie is overwhelmed when her partner Richie dies and leaves key items to his long-estranged wife rather than to her and their three daughters; for mature readers. (Rev: BL 2/1–15/10)

1266 Trueman, Terry. *Cruise Control* (7–10). 2004, HarperCollins LB $16.89 (978-0-06-623961-3). High school senior Paul McDaniel is a star athlete, but he's filled with rage over his brother's disabilities and his father's desertion; a companion to *Stuck in Neutral* (2000). (Rev: BCCB 11/04; BL 3/15/05; SLJ 1/05; VOYA 10/04)

1267 Tyler, Anne. *Dinner at the Homesick Restaurant* (10–12). 1982, Knopf paper $14.00 (978-0-449-91159-4). This family story involves Pearl Tull, a woman deserted by her husband years before, and the lives of her three children.

1268 Underdahl, S. T. *The Other Sister* (7–12). 2007, Flux paper $8.95 (978-0-7387-0933-8). The happy, secure life of 15-year-old Josey Muller is turned upside down when her parents tell her that she has an older sister, conceived when they were in high school and given up for adoption. (Rev: SLJ 3/07)

1269 Valentine, Jenny. *Broken Soup* (9–12). 2009, HarperTeen $16.99 (978-006085071-5). Following her older brother's death, Rowan discovers things about his life that lead to growth and healing. Lexile HL730L (Rev: BL 2/15/09; HB 5–6/09; SLJ 4/1/09)

1270 van Diepen, Allison. *Street Pharm* (9–12). 2006, Simon & Schuster paper $6.99 (978-1-4169-1154-8). Ty Johnson is a 17-year-old drug dealer in Brooklyn who is pleased at first to have inherited his father's territory until problems mount and he realizes the dangerous direction in which he is headed; contains street slang and profanity. (Rev: SLJ 8/06)

1271 Velasquez, Gloria. *Rina's Family Secret* (8–12). Series: Roosevelt High School. 1998, Arte Publico paper $9.95 (978-1-55885-233-4). Puerto Rican teenager Rina cannot endure life with her alcoholic stepfather, and so moves in with her grandmother. Also use *Tyrone's Betrayal*. 2006, Arte Publico paper $9.95 (978-1-55885-233-4). Puerto Rican teenager Rina cannot endure life with her alcoholic stepfather, and so moves in with her grandmother. Also use *Tyrone's Betrayal* (2006). (Rev: BL 8/98; SLJ 10/98)

1272 Vida, Vendela. *Let the Northern Lights Erase Your Name* (10–12). 2007, Ecco $23.95 (978-0-06-082837-0). When her father dies, Clarissa learns he was not her biological father; her search for her mother, who vanished 14 years earlier, and the man who fathered her leads her to Lapland. (Rev: BL 12/1/06)

1273 Vincent, Zu. *The Lucky Place* (7–10). 2008, Front St $17.95 (978-1-932425-70-3). Cassie struggles with the reality of having a stepfather as well as an "Old Daddy," especially when her stepfather becomes ill. (Rev: BL 5/1/08; SLJ 5/08)

1274 Waldorf, Heather. *Grist* (7–10). 2006, Red Deer paper $9.95 (978-0-88995-347-5). Sixteen-year-old Charlie decides to spend the summer with her grandmother at Lake Ringrose, Ontario, and discovers some secrets about her past while there. (Rev: BL 11/1/06; SLJ 1/07)

1275 Wallace, Rich. *Perpetual Check* (8–11). 2009, Knopf $15.99 (978-037584058-6); LB $18.99 (978-037594058-3). Brothers Zeke and Randy face off against each other in chess while growing closer and making important discoveries about life. e Lexile 750L (Rev: BL 1/1–15/09; SLJ 2/1/09; VOYA 6/09)

1276 Warman, Jessica. *Breathless* (9–12). 2009, Walker $16.99 (978-0-8027-9849-7). Fifteen-year-old Katie's schizophrenic older brother overshadows her life even when she goes away to boarding school. Best Books for Young Adults 2010. (Rev: BL 7/09; SLJ 11/09)

1277 Waugh, Evelyn. *Brideshead Revisited* (10–12). 1993, Knopf $17.00 (978-0-679-42300-3). The famous novel for better readers about an English well-born family, their country house, Brideshead, and the army officer, Charles Ryder, who was billeted there. With an introduction by Frank Kermode.

1278 Wenner, Kate. *Dancing with Einstein* (10–12). 2004, Scribner $24.00 (978-0-7432-5164-8). The story of the troubled inner life of Marea, who had an unusual childhood living with her Holocaust survivor father who helped develop the atomic bomb. (Rev: BL 3/1/04*)

1279 Werlin, Nancy. *The Rules of Survival* (7–10). 2006, Dial $16.99 (978-0-8037-3001-4). Written as a letter to his younger sister Emmy, Matt tells the story of their abusive mother, their everyday struggles to stay safe, and their search for an adult who is willing to help free them from the situation. (Rev: BL 8/06; SLJ 9/06)

1280 White, Ellen Emerson. *The President's Daughter* (7–10). 2008, Feiwel & Friends paper $8.99 (978-0-312-37488-4). Meg Powers, 16, is not pleased when her mother runs for and wins the presidency; an update of a book first published in 1984. (Rev: BL 8/08)

1281 White, Ellen Emerson. *White House Autumn* (7–10). 1985, Avon paper $2.95 (978-0-380-89780-3). The daughter of the first female president of the United States feels her family is coming apart after an assassination attempt on her mother. (Rev: BL 11/1/85; SLJ 2/86; VOYA 4/86)

1282 Whitney, Kim Ablon. *See You Down the Road* (9–12). 2004, Knopf $15.95 (978-0-375-82467-8). Bridget, a 16-year-old girl, and her family are known as Travelers, people who live in trailers and make their living dishonestly. (Rev: BL 3/15/04*; SLJ 2/04; VOYA 12/03)

1283 Williams, Carol Lynch. *Glimpse* (8–11). 2010, Simon & Schuster $16.99 (978-1-4169-9730-6). In free verse, Williams tells the story of two sisters who together face the difficulties of living with an alcoholic, prostitute mother; when Lizzie attempts suicide, the younger Hope plumbs her memories of abuse. ❤ Lexile 630L (Rev: BL 4/15/10; LMC 10/10; SLJ 8/10)

1284 Williams, Suzanne Morgan. *Bull Rider* (7–10). 2009, Simon & Schuster $16.99 (978-141696130-7). Fourteen-year-old Cam enters a bull-riding competition to win prize money to help with his brother's rehabilitation from injuries suffered in Iraq. ❤ (Rev: BL 1/1–15/09; SLJ 4/1/09)

1285 Williamson, Debrah. *Paper Hearts* (9–12). 2007, NAL paper $14.00 (978-0-451-22142-1). Teenage runaway Chancy sneaks into 83-year-old Max's garage, and the two find solace and protection with one another in this beautifully detailed novel. (Rev: BL 8/07)

1286 Wilson, Budge. *Before Green Gables* (9–12). 2008, Putnam $22.95 (978-0-399-15468-3). A prequel novel detailing the twelve years of Anne Shirley's hardscrabble life before she got to Green Gables. (Rev: BL 3/15/08)

1287 Wingate, Lisa. *The Language of Sycamores* (9–12). 2005, NAL paper $12.95 (978-0-451-21392-1). Grappling with both job loss and the possible recurrence of her cancer, Karen Sommerfield returns to Missouri for a family reunion; there she rediscovers lost pleasures and connects with a neighbor child through music. (Rev: BL 12/1/04)

1288 Wingate, Lisa. *Tending Roses* (10–12). 2001, NAL paper $13.95 (978-0-451-20307-6). Christmas is going to be difficult for Kate this year — it is the first family reunion since her mother's death, and she must make arrangements to put her grandmother in a nursing home. (Rev: BL 5/15/01)

1289 Wolff, Virginia Euwer. *Make Lemonade* (7–12). Series: Make Lemonade. 1993, Henry Holt $17.95 (978-0-8050-2228-5). Rooted in the community of poverty, this story offers a penetrating view of the conditions that foster ignorance, destroy self-esteem, and challenge strength. (Rev: BL 6/1–15/93*; SLJ 7/93*; VOYA 10/93)

1290 Wong, Norman. *Cultural Revolution* (10–12). 1994, One World paper $10.00 (978-0-345-39648-8). In this story of two generations of a Chinese family, the first part focuses on Wei's childhood and family relationships in China; the second follows Wei's marriage and move to Hawaii, where he fathers two children, one of whom is gay and whose struggles are the focus of this part of the book. (Rev: VOYA 4/96)

1291 Woodrell, Daniel. *Winter's Bone* (11–12). 2006, Little, Brown $22.95 (978-0-316-05755-4). Sixteen-year-old Ree Dolly must try to wrench answers from her family of Ozarks farmers when her father disappears and becomes a wanted man. (Rev: BL 5/1/06; SLJ 8/06)

1292 Woodson, Jacqueline. *Miracle's Boys* (6–10). 2000, Putnam $15.99 (978-0-399-23113-1). Twelve-year-old African American LaFayette, growing up in a poor inner-city environment, is cared for by his oldest brother who is also responsible for the troubled middle brother, Charlie. (Rev: BL 2/15/00; HB 3–4/00; HBG 9/00; SLJ 5/00; VOYA 4/00)

1293 Wylie, Sarah. *All These Lives* (8–12). 2012, Farrar $17.99 (978-0-374-30208-5). On the assumption that she has nine lives, 16-year-old Dani aims to give her remaining ones to her twin sister Jena, who has leukemia. ❤ Lexile 800L (Rev: LMC 11–12/12*; SLJ 7/12; VOYA 8/12)

1294 Yansky, Brian. *My Road Trip to the Pretty Girl Capital of the World* (9–12). 2003, Cricket $16.95 (978-0-8126-2691-9). Simon's quest to find his birth parents introduces him to some offbeat characters and gives him a new appreciation of his adoptive home. (Rev: BL 11/15/03; HBG 4/04; SLJ 12/03)

1295 Zarr, Sara. *How to Save a Life* (8–12). 2011, Little, Brown $17.99 (978-0-316-03606-1). Seventeen-year-old Jill is still struggling to deal with her father's sudden death when her mother announces that she plans to adopt a baby and that the expectant Mandy will be coming to live with them until the delivery; told from the perspectives of the two troubled teens. YALSA Top Ten Best Fiction for Young Adults 2012. ∩ ❤ Lexile HL710L (Rev: BL 11/1/11*; HB 1–2/12; SLJ 12/1/11*; VOYA 12/11)

Physical and Emotional Problems

1296 Abadzis, Nick. *Boy Toy* (11–12). 2007, Houghton Mifflin $16.95 (978-0-618-72393-5). This story of an affair between a 12-year-old boy and his history teacher, Eve, includes graphic sex scenes; it is narrated by Josh when he is a high school senior and still has not overcome the aftermath of the affair's discovery. (Rev: BL 9/1/07; SLJ 10/07)

1297 Adoff, Jaime. *The Death of Jayson Porter* (10–12). 2008, Hyperion $15.99 (978-1-4231-0691-3). Despairing over his family's poverty, dysfunction, and addictions, Jayson attempts suicide but survives, injured but with new hope for the future. (Rev: BL 4/1/08; SLJ 3/08)

1298 Anderson, Laurie Halse. *Wintergirls* (9–12). 2009, Viking $17.99 (978-067001110-0). In an intense first-person narrative, 18-year-old Lia describes her feelings as she slides further into the depths of anorexia after her former best friend dies of another eating disorder. ∩ (Rev: BL 12/15/08*; HB 3–40/09; LMC 8–9/09; SLJ 2/1/09*; VOYA 4/09)

1299 Antieau, Kim. *Mercy, Unbound* (9–12). 2006, Simon & Schuster paper $6.99 (978-1-4169-0893-7). Fifteen-year-old Mercy's denial of her anorexia extends to a fantasy that she is an angel and has no need for nourishment. (Rev: BL 4/1/06; SLJ 6/06)

1300 Arnold, Elana K. *Sacred* (8–11). 2012, Delacorte $17.99 (978-038574211-5); LB $20.99 (978-037599042-7). Scarlett struggles with anorexia and depression after her older brother dies, and finds some solace in her beloved horse and a strange boy named Will. **e** (Rev: BL 10/15/12; SLJ 3/13; VOYA 2/13)

1301 Aronson, Sarah. *Head Case* (9–12). 2007, Roaring Brook $16.95 (978-1-59643-214-7). Frank becomes a quadriplegic after causing a fatal accident while driving drunk and must now deal with the reality of his forever-altered life. (Rev: BCCB 9/07; BL 7/07; SLJ 11/07)

1302 Ayarbe, Heidi. *Compulsion* (10–12). 2011, HarperCollins $16.99 (978-0-06-199386-2). Soccer star Jake, 17, tries to hide his obsessive compulsive disorder in this compelling novel that clearly describes the difficulties of living with this problem. (Rev: BL 3/15/11*; SLJ 6/11; VOYA 8/11)

1303 Barfoot, Joan. *Critical Injuries* (11–12). 2002, Counterpoint $25.00 (978-1-58243-208-3). A grievously injured woman and her jailed teen assailant look back at their lives and at the impact of the incident; for mature teens. (Rev: BL 7/02)

1304 Bennett, Cherie. *Searching for David's Heart: A Christmas Story* (10–12). 1988, Scholastic paper $4.50 (978-0-590-30673-7). Darcy's brother David dies after they have an argument and her guilt lessens only when she meets the boy who received David's heart.

1305 Bingham, Kelly. *Shark Girl* (7–10). 2007, Candlewick $16.99 (978-0-7636-3207-6). When she's attacked by a shark and loses an arm, 15-year-old Jane feels divorced from her former popular self and has trouble adjusting to her new life. (Rev: BL 5/1/07; SLJ 6/07)

1306 Blank, Jessica. *Almost Home* (10–12). 2007, Hyperion $15.99 (978-1-4231-0642-5). A sad, bleak, and effective novel about abused, neglected kids who have left their homes for the streets of Los Angeles. (Rev: BL 11/15/07; SLJ 12/07)

1307 Borris, Albert. *Crash into Me* (8–12). 2009, Simon & Schuster $16.99 (978-141697435-2). Four suicidal teenagers set off on a road trip planning to kill themselves when they reach their destination, but things change along the way. Lexile HL530L (Rev: BL 5/15/09; SLJ 8/09; VOYA 12/09)

1308 Brenna, Beverley. *Wild Orchid* (9–12). 2006, Red Deer paper $7.95 (978-0-88995-330-7). Taylor, 18, narrates her experiences with Asperger's Syndrome, a condition characterized by difficulty looking at people in the face; when she realizes this is making her search for a boyfriend tricky, she focuses on her other goals and discovers some new talents. (Rev: SLJ 6/06)

1309 Brothers, Meagan. *Debbie Harry Sings in French* (8–12). 2008, Henry Holt $16.95 (978-0-8050-8080-3). Johnny, who has struggled with alcohol and bullies who think he is gay, is encouraged by his girlfriend to pursue his passion and sing in drag. (Rev: BL 4/1/08; SLJ 9/08)

1310 Bryson, Bill. *Choices* (7–10). 2007, Roaring Brook $16.95 (978-1-59643-217-8). Kathleen finds herself switching between realities after her brother is killed on his way to pick her up; when she meets Luke, this "phase shifting" takes on more meaning. (Rev: BL 9/1/07; SLJ 10/07)

1311 Bunting, Eve. *Face at the Edge of the World* (9–12). 1985, Ticknor paper $6.95 (978-0-89919-800-2). Jed tries to find out the reasons behind the suicide of his friend Charlie, a gifted black student. (Rev: BL 8/85; SLJ 12/85; VOYA 8/85)

1312 Burak, Kathryn. *Emily's Dress and Other Missing Things* (9–12). 2012, Roaring Brook $17.99 (978-1-59643-736-4). In Amherst, Massachusetts, troubled Claire — devastated by her mother's suicide and the disappearance of her best friend — finds solace in Emily Dickinson's poetry and homestead. **e** Lexile HL550L (Rev: BL 10/15/12*; LMC 3–4/13*; SLJ 10/12; VOYA 12/12)

1313 Burgess, Melvin. *Smack* (10–12). 1998, Henry Holt paper $16.95 (978-0-8050-5801-7). This novel, which won Britain's Carnegie Medal, is a harrowing, provocative story of teen heroin addiction in Bristol during the 1980s. (Rev: BCCB 4/98; BL 4/15/98; HB 5–6/98; HBG 9/98; SLJ 5/98)

1314 Camus, Albert. *The Stranger* (10–12). 1988, Random House $25.00 (978-0-394-53305-6); paper $9.95 (978-0-679-72020-1). For better readers, this novel describes how a convicted murderer at last finds some meaning in life.

1315 Carlson, Melody. *Finding Alice* (10–12). 2003, WaterBrook paper $11.99 (978-1-57856-573-3). In this gripping novel, the title character struggles with the demons of paranoid schizophrenia. (Rev: BL 10/1/03*)

1316 Castan, Mike. *Fighting for Dontae* (6–12). 2012, Holiday $16.95 (978-082342348-4). A tough Mexican American kid with gang connections learns the value of kindness when he begins helping a severely disabled kid in his special education class. Lexile 750L (Rev: BL 7/12; LMC 3–4/13; SLJ 5/1/12*)

1317 Chappell, Crissa-Jean. *Total Constant Order* (7–10). 2007, HarperTeen $16.99 (978-0-06-088605-9). Plagued by obsessive-compulsive behavior, 9th-grader Frances (called Fin) finds some relief when she meets Thayer, who has ADD, and starts seeing a new therapist. (Rev: BL 11/15/07; SLJ 1/08)

1318 Clauser, Suzanne. *A Girl Named Sooner* (9–12). 1976, Avon paper $2.95 (978-0-380-00216-0). A neglected girl is given a home by a veterinarian and his wife.

1319 Clinton, Cathryn. *The Eyes of Van Gogh* (9–12). 2007, Candlewick $16.99 (978-0-7636-2245-9). Jude can relate to Van Gogh's depression as her mother moves them to yet another new town. (Rev: BCCB 7–8/07; BL 7/07; LMC 10/07; SLJ 7/07)

1320 Coburn, Jake. *Lovesick* (9–12). 2005, Dutton $16.99 (978-0-525-47383-1). In their first year at college, recovering alcoholic and scholarship student Ted and wealthy bulimic Erica are thrown together and fall in love. (Rev: BL 9/15/05; SLJ 12/05; VOYA 12/05)

1321 Coffelt, Nancy. *Listen* (8–11). 2009, WestSide $16.95 (978-1-934813-07-2). In alternating narratives, this compelling, fast-paced novel introduces 18-year-old orphan Will, whose lonely life intersects with those of troubled 14-year-old Kurt and middle-aged schizophrenic Carrie. Lexile HL770L (Rev: BL 9/1/09; SLJ 12/09)

1322 Cole, Barbara. *Alex the Great* (8–12). 1989, Rosen LB $12.95 (978-0-8239-0941-4). The events leading up to Alex's drug overdose are told first by Alex and then by her friend, Deonna. (Rev: VOYA 8/89)

1323 Cooner, Donna. *Skinny* (7–10). 2012, Scholastic $17.99 (978-0-545-42763-0). Obese Ever, 15, realizes that self-hatred is her biggest problem after gastric bypass surgery helps her drop over a hundred pounds. ☊ ℯ Lexile 670L (Rev: BL 10/15/12; LMC 1–2/13; SLJ 10/12; VOYA 8/12)

1324 Cormier, Robert. *The Bumblebee Flies Anyway* (7–12). 1983, Dell paper $4.99 (978-0-440-90871-5). A terminally ill boy and his gradual realization of his situation.

1325 Crane, E. M. *Skin Deep* (7–10). 2008, Delacorte $16.99 (978-0-385-73479-0). Andrea, 16, befriends a woman named Honora, who is dying of cancer but teaches the unhappy girl a lot about life. (Rev: BL 1/1–15/08; SLJ 5/08)

1326 Cronn-Mills, Kirstin. *Beautiful Music for Ugly Children* (9–12). 2012, Flux paper $9.99 (978-07387325-1-0). Music-loving Gabe, who was born a girl, faces many challenges when the truth is uncovered; includes some frank language. ℯ (Rev: BL 11/15/12; LMC 3–4/13; SLJ 1/13; VOYA 10/12)

1327 Crutcher, Chris. *Angry Management* (9–12). 2009, Greenwillow $16.99 (978-0-06-050247-8); LB $17.89 (978-0-06-050246-1). Anger is at the center of these three stories featuring "angry management" classes held by Mr. Nak (of *Ironman*) and starring other familiar Crutcher characters. ℯ Lexile HL730L (Rev: HB 11–12/09; SLJ 9/09; VOYA 8/09)

1328 Crutcher, Chris. *Chinese Handcuffs* (10–12). 2004, HarperCollins paper $7.99 (978-0-06-059839-6). A brutal novel about basketball, a young man trying to adjust to his brother's suicide, and a sexually abused girl; first published in 1989. (Rev: BR 9–10/89; SLJ 4/89; VOYA 6/89)

1329 Crutcher, Chris. *Deadline* (10–12). 2007, Greenwillow $16.99 (978-0-06-085089-0). Eighteen-year-old Ben decides not to tell anyone about his incurable leukemia and to make the most of his last year — joining his brother on the football team and dating his dream girl, Dallas Suzuki. (Rev: BL 9/1/07; SLJ 9/07)

1330 Cummings, Priscilla. *Blindsided* (6–10). 2010, Dutton $16.99 (978-0-525-42161-0). Natalie, 14, is losing her eyesight and struggles to accept this reality and learn special skills at her new school for the blind. ℯ Lexile 710L (Rev: BL 6/10; LMC 10/10; SLJ 7/10; VOYA 8/10)

1331 Davidson, Andrew. *The Gargoyle* (11–12). 2008, Doubleday $25.95 (978-038552494-0). In this tale of excess, pain, and self-loathing, a former porn star who is planning suicide gets an unexpected chance at love and redemption when an unlikely woman enters his life with a tale of reincarnation; for mature readers only. ☊ ℯ (Rev: BL 9/1/08)

1332 Davis, Amanda. *Wonder When You'll Miss Me* (11–12). 2003, Morrow $24.95 (978-0-688-16781-3). Faith, a troubled and lonely high school girl, loses weight after being sexually assaulted but finds that her inner "Fat Girl" won't leave her alone; suitable for mature readers. (Rev: BL 2/1/03; SLJ 8/03; VOYA 12/03)

1333 Davis, Rebecca Fjelland. *Jake Riley: Irreparably Damaged* (7–10). 2003, HarperCollins LB $16.89 (978-0-06-051838-7). Lainey, a farm girl, struggles to cope with her friend Jake, a 15-year-old with frightening emotional problems. (Rev: BL 9/1/03; HBG 10/03; SLJ 7/03; VOYA 10/03)

1334 de la Peña, Matt. *I Will Save You* (8–11). 2010, Delacorte $16.99 (978-038573827-9); LB $19.99 (978-038590719-4). Seventeen-year-old Kidd flees his group home and struggles to find a new life at the beach, but the past soon catches up with him; a tense and complex tale. (Rev: BL 12/15/10; LMC 5–6/11)

1335 Deaver, Julie Reece. *The Night I Disappeared* (9–12). 2002, Simon & Schuster paper $5.99 (978-0-7434-3979-4). Jamie's summer in Chicago includes institutionalization for mental illness and a realization that she was traumatized as a child. (Rev: BCCB 5/02; BL 5/1/02; SLJ 5/02)

1336 Denman, K. L. *Me, Myself and Ike* (7–10). 2009, Orca paper $12.95 (978-1-55469-086-2). Encouraged to commit suicide by his antagonistic companion Ike, who is in reality the result of a schizophrenia-induced hallucination, 17-year-old Kit, once popular and even-tempered, becomes increasingly insular and paranoid. **℮** (Rev: BL 11/1/09; SLJ 12/09; VOYA 12/09)

1337 Dewey, Jennifer Owlings. *Borderlands* (7–12). 2002, Marshall Cavendish $14.95 (978-0-7614-5114-3). When Jamie, an unhappy 17-year-old, is hospitalized after a suicide attempt she finds new friends and slowly comes to terms with her difficult relationship with her parents. (Rev: BL 9/1/02; HBG 10/02; SLJ 7/02)

1338 Diersch, Sandra. *Ceiling Stars* (7–12). Series: SideStreets. 2004, Lorimer paper $4.99 (978-1-55028-834-6). The close friendship of two high school girls is put to the test when one falls victim to mental illness and begins acting strangely; suitable for reluctant readers. (Rev: SLJ 1/05)

1339 Diezeno, Patricia. *Why Me? The Story of Jenny* (7–10). 1976, Avon paper $3.50 (978-0-380-00563-5). A young rape victim doesn't know how to cope.

1340 Dogar, Sharon. *Waves* (9–12). 2007, Scholastic $16.99 (978-0-439-87180-8). When his sister is hospitalized after an accident that leaves her in a coma, Hal mysteriously feels her emotions and thoughts. ∩ (Rev: BL 12/1/06; SLJ 5/07)

1341 Dorfman, Joaquin. *The Long Wait for Tomorrow* (9–12). 2009, Random House $16.99 (978-037584694-6); LB $19.99 (978-037594694-3). Star quarterback Kelly confounds his friends by suddenly changing his personality and claiming to have time-traveled from a mental institution. **℮** (Rev: BL 7/09; SLJ 12/09)

1342 Downham, Jenny. *Before I Die* (9–12). 2007, Random House $15.99 (978-0-385-75155-1). Tessa is determined to do all the rebellious-teenager things she can before she dies of leukemia in this story about family ties and life lessons. (Rev: BL 11/15/07; SLJ 11/07)

1343 Doyle, Malachy. *Georgie* (6–10). 2002, Bloomsbury $13.95 (978-1-58234-753-0). Georgie, 14, who has buried horrible memories under a cloak of isolation, slowly learns to trust his teacher and recovers his sanity. (Rev: BCCB 11/02; BL 9/1/02; SLJ 7/02; VOYA 12/03)

1344 Draper, Sharon M. *November Blues* (9–12). 2007, Atheneum $16.99 (978-1-4169-0698-8). November, a high school senior, discovers she is pregnant by Josh (who died in 2003's *The Battle of Jericho*), and she must deal with carrying a child as well as her grief and the changes to her future. Coretta Scott King Honor Book, 2008. (Rev: BL 10/15/07; LMC 11/07; SLJ 11/07)

1345 Draper, Sharon M. *Tears of a Tiger* (7–10). 1994, Atheneum $16.95 (978-0-689-31878-8). A star basketball player is killed in an accident after he and his friends drink and drive. The driver, who survives, is depressed and ultimately commits suicide. (Rev: BL 11/1/94; SLJ 2/95)

1346 Dreyer, Ellen. *The Glow Stone* (8–12). 2006, Peachtree $15.95 (978-1-56145-370-2). When 15-year-old Phoebe begins to suspect that her uncle's death was not an accident, she journeys into a metaphorical and actual cave. (Rev: SLJ 7/06)

1347 Edwards, Johanna. *The Next Big Thing* (8–12). 2005, Berkley paper $14.00 (978-0-425-20028-5). Kat, determined to lose weight to win the heart of her online boyfriend, lands a spot on a reality TV makeover show but finds in the end that she likes herself just the way she is. (Rev: SLJ 11/05)

1348 Ellison, Kate. *The Butterfly Clues* (9–12). 2012, Egmont $17.99 (978-160684263-8). Obsessive compulsive Lo, 16, investigates a murder that happened in her presence while she was visiting the neighborhood of her older brother's death. ∩ **℮** Lexile HL790L (Rev: BL 3/1/12*; LMC 1–2/12; SLJ 2/12*)

1349 Eugenides, Jeffrey. *Middlesex* (11–12). 2002, Farrar $26.00 (978-0-374-19969-2). An absorbing story about the experiences of a young hermaphrodite and his incestuous ancestors; for mature teens. (Rev: BL 6/1–15/02; SLJ 3/03)

1350 Ferris, Jean. *Invincible Summer* (9–12). 1987, Avon paper $3.50 (978-0-380-70619-8). The story of a friendship and later a love shared by two courageous teenagers, both suffering from leukemia. (Rev: SLJ 8/87)

1351 Fields, Terri. *After the Death of Anna Gonzales* (7–12). 2002, Henry Holt $16.95 (978-0-8050-7127-6). A collection of poems written by her friends reveals the terrible aftermath of a teenager's suicide. (Rev: BL 12/15/02; HBG 3/03; SLJ 11/02; VOYA 12/02)

1352 Fischer, Jackie Moyer. *An Egg on Three Sticks* (9–12). 2004, St. Martin's paper $12.95 (978-0-312-31775-1). A deeply affecting novel about a 13-year-old girl who watches her mother sink into insanity and depression. (Rev: BL 5/1/04*; SLJ 7/04)

1353 Flake, Sharon G. *Pinned* (8–12). 2012, Scholastic $17.99 (978-0-545-05718-9). Struggling reader and championship wrestler Autumn is determined to make inroads with the team's brilliant manager Adonis, who was born without legs, in this story about African American teens told in alternating chapters. ∩ **℮** Lexile HL460L (Rev: BL 10/15/12; HB 11–12/12; LMC 3–4/13; SLJ 9/12)

1354 Frank, E. R. *America* (10–12). 2002, Simon & Schuster $18.00 (978-0-689-84729-5). While in a hospital after attempting suicide, America angrily describes his childhood full of sexual abuse and other agonies. (Rev: BL 2/15/02; HB 3–4/02; HBG 10/02; SLJ 3/02*; VOYA 2/02)

1355 Fraustino, Lisa Rowe. *Ash* (9–12). 1995, Orchard LB $17.99 (978-0-531-08739-8). A 15-year-old recalls, in diary form, his older brother's slide into schizophrenia. (Rev: BL 4/1/95; SLJ 4/95; VOYA 5/95)

1356 Fraustino, Lisa Rowe, ed. *Don't Cramp My Style: Stories About That Time of the Month* (8–12). 2004, Simon & Schuster $15.95 (978-0-689-85882-6). This collection of stories about girls' menstrual periods includes fiction about different places, cultures, and times. (Rev: BL 3/1/04; HB 3–4/04; SLJ 4/04; VOYA 4/04)

1357 Galloway, Gregory. *The 39 Deaths of Adam Strand* (10–12). 2013, Dutton $17.99 (978-052542565-6). At the age of 16, bored and disenchanted with life, Adam has committed suicide 39 times, only to wake up unharmed after each attempt; will an act of charity end this cycle? **e** (Rev: BL 2/1/13*; SLJ 3/13; VOYA 2/13)

1358 Garden, Nancy. *Annie on My Mind* (10–12). 2007, Farrar paper $8 (978-0-374-40011-8). Two girls find that they love one another but are afraid to tell anyone of their love. For mature readers, this novel was first published in 1982.

1359 Garden, Nancy. *Endgame* (8–12). 2006, Harcourt $16 (978-0-15-205416-8). While awaiting his murder trial, 15-year-old Gray Wilton reveals in a series of interviews with his lawyer the extreme bullying, both physical and emotional, that finally drove him to take a gun to school. (Rev: SLJ 5/06*)

1360 Geus, Mireille. *Piggy* (6–10). Trans. by Nancy Forest-Flier. 2008, Front St $14.95 (978-159078636-9). Told in the first-person voice of 12-year-old Lizzy, who has autism, this story recounts the constant teasing Lizzy faces everyday until she forms an unlikely friendship with Peggy, which leads to complications of its own. Lexile HL390L (Rev: BLO 11/19/08; HB 1–2/09; LMC 1–2/09; SLJ 1/1/09)

1361 Going, K. L. *Fat Kid Rules the World* (8–12). 2003, Putnam $17.99 (978-0-399-23990-8). An unlikely but beneficial friendship develops between suicidal, 300-pound Troy and dropout punk rock guitarist Curt. (Rev: BCCB 6/03*; BL 5/15/03*; HB 7–8/03; HBG 10/03; SLJ 5/03*; VOYA 6/03)

1362 Gonzalez, Ann. *Running for My Life* (8–10). 2009, WestSide $16.95 (978-193481300-3). Andrea turns to running as a way to cope with her mother's schizophrenia, but still suffers from anxiety and nightmares. Lexile HL520L (Rev: BL 5/1/09; SLJ 7/1/09)

1363 Goobie, Beth. *The Dream Where the Losers Go* (7–12). 2006, Orca paper $8.95 (978-1-55143-455-1). Skey finds herself institutionalized after a suicide attempt, but she doesn't know what caused her actions, just that she travels in tunnels in both her sleep and waking hours; a disturbing but compelling book about the ways in which we survive traumas. (Rev: SLJ 6/06)

1364 Green, John. *The Fault in Our Stars* (9–12). 2012, Dutton $17.99 (978-052547881-2). Terminal cancer patient Hazel, 16, is brought out of her depression when she meets Gus at a support group. Odyssey Award 2013. ⌒ **e** Lexile 850L (Rev: BL 1/1/12*; HB 11–12/12; LMC 8–9/12*; SLJ 2/12*; VOYA 4/12)

1365 Griffin, Adele. *Where I Want to Be* (7–10). 2005, Penguin $15.99 (978-0-399-23783-6). In alternating chapters, teenage sisters Lily and Jane tell about their relationship and the mental illness that led to Jane's tragic death. (Rev: BCCB 3/05; BL 2/15/05*; HB 3–4/05; SLJ 4/05; VOYA 4/05)

1366 Hall, Rachel Howzell. *A Quiet Storm* (11–12). 2002, Scribner paper $13.00 (978-0-7432-2616-5). Stacey, younger than her sister Rikki by only 11 months, has been Rikki's protector since childhood, and as Rikki's mental imbalances worsen Stacey must balance her sister's needs with her own; for mature teens. (Rev: BL 9/1/02)

1367 Halpern, Julie. *Get Well Soon* (8–12). 2007, Feiwel & Friends $16.95 (978-0-312-36795-4). Anna is sent to a psychiatric hospital for her depression and anxiety, and in letters to her best friend—full of profanity, sarcasm, and humor—she describes her experiences there. (Rev: BL 10/15/07; LMC 4–5/08; SLJ 10/07)

1368 Halpin, Brendan. *Forever Changes* (8–11). 2008, Farrar $16.95 (978-037432436-0). Cystic fibrosis sufferer Brianna ponders the meaning of life, and the futility of planning a future she likely won't live to see. Lexile 890L (Rev: BL 10/15/08; SLJ 11/1/08; VOYA 6/08)

1369 Harrar, George. *Not as Crazy as I Seem* (7–10). 2003, Houghton Mifflin $15.00 (978-0-618-26365-3). Devon, 15, is frustrated by his obsessive-compulsive disorder and the different responses of his peers, his parents, and his doctor. (Rev: BL 2/15/03; HBG 10/03; SLJ 4/03; VOYA 6/03)

1370 Hautman, Pete. *Invisible* (7–10). 2005, Simon & Schuster $15.95 (978-0-689-86800-9). It's clear to the reader from the beginning that there's something odd about the friendship between 17-year-old Doug Hanson and his only friend Andy, and the mystery unravels as Doug's state of mind deteriorates through the course of the book. (Rev: BL 6/1–15/05; SLJ 6/05; VOYA 8/05)

1371 Hautman, Pete. *Sweetblood* (8–12). 2003, Simon & Schuster $16.95 (978-0-689-85048-6). Sixteen-year-old Lucy, an insulin-dependent diabetic, links her condition with her interest in vampires. (Rev: BL 5/1/03*; HB 7–8/03; HBG 10/03; SLJ 7/03; VOYA 10/03)

1372 Headley, Justina Chen. *North of Beautiful* (9–12). 2009, Little, Brown $16.99 (978-031602505-8). Friendship with Jacob, a Goth Chinese boy with a cleft lip scar, helps 16-year-old Terra, who feels flawed because of a birthmark on her cheek. Lexile 850L (Rev: BL 2/15/09; SLJ 2/1/09; VOYA 6/09)

1373 Hernandez, David. *Suckerpunch* (10–12). 2008, HarperCollins $16.99 (978-0-06-117330-1). Facing the possibility that their abusive father may return, Marcus and Enrique head off to find him with a gun in the glove compartment; gritty, vulgar, and raw, this novel captures the emotions of very disturbed teenagers. (Rev: BL 4/15/08; SLJ 8/08)

1374 Hoekstra, Molly. *Upstream: A Novel* (7–12). 2001, Tudor paper $15.95 (978-0-936389-86-8). This story of a 16-year-old girl's struggle with anorexia gives a clear idea of the psychological problems associated with this illness. (Rev: SLJ 12/01)

1375 Homes, A. M. *Jack* (9–12). 2008, Paw Prints $21.95 (978-1-4352-7664-2). Four years after his parents are divorced, Jack learns that his father is gay; originally published in 1989. (Rev: BL 12/1/89; SLJ 11/89; VOYA 2/90)

1376 Honenberger, Sarah Collins. *Catcher, Caught* (10–12). 2010, AmazonEncore paper $14.95 (978-19355971-0-0). Fifteen-year-old Daniel has leukemia and reading *The Catcher in the Rye* inspires him to rebel against his parents' insistence on alternative therapies. (Rev: BL 12/1–15/10)

1377 Howe, James. *The Watcher* (8–12). 1997, Simon & Schuster $16.00 (978-0-689-80186-0). The lives of three troubled teens converge in a horrific climax in this novel of child abuse. (Rev: BL 6/1–15/97; SLJ 5/97; VOYA 8/97)

1378 Hubbard, Jennifer R. *Try Not to Breathe* (9–12). 2012, Viking $16.99 (978-067001390-6). Hospitalized after attempting to commit suicide, sophomore Ryan returns home and resumes his lonely life until he makes friends with Nikki. ℮ (Rev: BL 2/15/12; HB 3–4/12; LMC 8–9/12; SLJ 1/12)

1379 Hughes, Monica. *The King's Shadow* (7–10). 2003, Fitzhenry & Whiteside paper $9.95 (978-1-55005-056-1). In spite of his leukemia, Mike goes on a secret hunting trip; originally published in 1983.

1380 Hull, Maureen. *The View from a Kite* (9–12). 2007, Nimbus $15.95 (978-1-55109-591-2). Gwen describes her life in one of the last tuberculosis sanitariums in Nova Scotia in the 1970s, giving information on the disease, her friends, and her many family troubles. (Rev: BL 5/1/07; SLJ 6/07)

1381 Hurwin, Davida Wills. *A Time for Dancing* (7–12). 1995, Puffin paper $6.99 (978-0-14-038618-9). A powerful story of two friends, one of whom is diagnosed with lymphoma. Their friendship becomes a story of saying good-bye and death. (Rev: BL 11/1/95*; SLJ 10/95; VOYA 12/95)

1382 Hyde, Catherine Ryan. *Diary of a Witness* (7–10). 2009, Knopf $16.99 (978-037585684-6). Will gets pushed to the breaking point by school bullies and the death of his younger brother. The story is told through entries in Will's friend Ernie's diary. Lexile HL510L (Rev: BLO 5/27/09; SLJ 9/09)

1383 James, Brian. *Life Is But a Dream* (7–10). 2012, Feiwel & Friends $16.99 (978-031261004-3). Artistic Sabrina, 16, is hospitalized for serious mental problems and things go from bad to worse when co-patient Alec persuades her to stop taking her medication. ℮ Lexile 740L (Rev: BL 4/15/12; SLJ 3/12)

1384 Jenkins, A. M. *Damage* (11–12). 2001, HarperCollins paper $8.99 (978-0-06-447255-5). Football-playing high school senior Austin tries to escape his depression through sex with his girlfriend. (Rev: BL 9/15/01*; HB 9–10/01; HBG 3/02; SLJ 10/01; VOYA 10/01)

1385 John, Antony. *Five Flavors of Dumb* (9–12). 2010, Dial $16.99 (978-0-8037-3433-3). Eighteen-year-old Piper, who is profoundly hearing impaired and whose younger sister requires expensive cochlear implants, becomes the manager of the school's popular rock band, Dumb. ℮ (Rev: SLJ 12/1/10; VOYA 2/11)

1386 Johnson, Angela. *Humming Whispers* (8–12). 1995, Orchard LB $16.99 (978-0-531-08748-0). Sophy, 14, reveals the impact of her 24-year-old sister Nicole's schizophrenia on the lives of those who love her. (Rev: BL 2/15/95; SLJ 4/95; VOYA 5/95)

1387 Johnson, Harriet McBryde. *Accidents of Nature* (8–11). 2006, Henry Holt $16.95 (978-0-8050-7634-9). Set in 1970, this is the story of Jean, a teen with cerebral palsy who attends a camp for the disabled and discovers new possibilities for living her life. ∩ (Rev: BL 7/06; LMC 1/07; SLJ 5/06*)

1388 Jonsberg, Barry. *Dreamrider* (8–11). 2008, Knopf $15.99 (978-0-375-84457-7). Overweight Michael, starting at a new school yet again, is bullied and miserable; the only respite he finds is in his "lucid dreams," which he can control — can he use his dreams to control life too? (Rev: BL 2/15/08; SLJ 7/08)

1389 Kata, Elizabeth. *A Patch of Blue* (10–12). 1983, Amereon $18.95 (978-0-89190-119-8). A blind girl finds love with a man who also has a number of personal problems.

1390 Keith, Lois. *A Different Life* (9–12). Series: Livewire. 1998, Women's paper $11.95 (978-0-7043-4946-9). In this moving novel, 15-year-old Libby adjusts to a crippling disease with the help of a handicapped social worker, a school chum named Jesse, and her own fortitude. (Rev: SLJ 7/98)

1391 Kesey, Ken. *One Flew over the Cuckoo's Nest* (10–12). 1963, Signet paper $9.99 (978-0-451-16396-7). This novel deals with the power struggle between a sane inmate and the head nurse in a mental institution; for mature teens.

1392 Knowles, Jo. *Lessons from a Dead Girl* (8–11). 2007, Candlewick $16.99 (978-0-7636-3279-3). When Leah dies in an accident, Laine recalls their complicated relationship, including Leah's blackmail, threatening to reveal their "practice" sexual encounters. (Rev: BL 12/1/07; LMC 1/08; SLJ 12/07)

1393 Koertge, Ron. *Stoner and Spaz* (8–12). 2002, Candlewick $15.99 (978-0-7636-1608-3). An unlikely romance between a 16-year-old boy with cerebral palsy and a girl who is constantly stoned brings benefits to both of them. (Rev: BCCB 3/02; BL 5/1/02*; SLJ 4/02)

1394 Koss, Amy Goldman. *Side Effects* (8–11). 2006, Roaring Brook $16.95 (978-1-59643-167-6). Isabelle, 15, is diagnosed with lymphoma and is scared that she might miss out on all the things she wants to do but she makes it through. (Rev: BL 9/15/06; SLJ 9/06)

1395 Lamb, Wally. *She's Come Undone* (10–12). 1998, Pocket paper $7.99 (978-0-671-02100-9). Delores Price is an observant youngster who faces many challenges and unfortunately tackles most of them with a helping of Mallomars, and a dollop of humor. (Rev: BL 8/92)

1396 Lange, Erin Jade. *Butter* (9–12). 2012, Bloomsbury $16.99 (978-1-59990-780-2). Sixteen-year-old "Butter," who weighs 423 pounds, decides to eat himself to death and plans to make a webcast of his last meal. ℮ Lexile HL770L (Rev: BL 10/15/12; LMC 1–2/13; SLJ 12/12*; VOYA 10/12)

1397 Lascarso, Laura. *Counting Backwards* (8–11). 2012, Atheneum $16.99 (978-1-4424-0690-2). Committed to a juvenile psychiatric correctional facility, Taylor, 16, eventually learns to deal with the problems posed by her alcoholic mother and distant, Seminole father. ℮ Lexile 730L (Rev: BLO 8/12; LMC 1–2/13; SLJ 9/12; VOYA 8/12)

1398 Levenkron, Steven. *The Best Little Girl in the World* (10–12). 1989, Warner paper $6.99 (978-0-446-35865-1). Francessa's desire to be perfect leads her into the world of anorexia.

1399 Lipsyte, Robert. *One Fat Summer* (7–12). 1991, HarperCollins paper $5.99 (978-0-06-447073-5). Bobby Marks is 14, fat, and unhappy in this first novel of three that traces Bobby's career through his first year of college. (Rev: BL 1/1–15/98)

1400 Littman, Sarah Darer. *Purge* (7–10). 2009, Scholastic $16.99 (978-054505235-1). Janie, 16, confronts her bulimia as well as other psychological problems while at a rehab facility for eating disorders. Lexile 950L (Rev: BLO 2/9/09; LMC 5–6/09; SLJ 7/1/09)

1401 McBay, Bruce, and James Heneghan. *Waiting for Sarah* (7–10). 2003, Orca paper $7.95 (978-1-55143-270-0). After becoming disabled in a car accident, Mike suffers from depression and withdrawal until he gets to know 8th-grader Sarah. (Rev: BL 9/15/03; SLJ 10/03; VOYA 12/03)

1402 McCormick, Patricia. *Cut* (7–10). 2000, Front St $16.95 (978-1-886910-61-4). In a hospital that treats teens with serious issues, including drugs and anorexia, Callie participates in group therapy and tries to face her own self-mutilation. (Rev: BL 1/1–15/01; HB 11–12/00; HBG 3/01; SLJ 12/00; VOYA 2/01)

1403 MacCready, Robin Merrow. *Buried* (9–12). 2006, Dutton $16.99 (978-0-525-47724-2). When her alcoholic mother disappears, high school senior Claudine's already unstable life unravels even further. (Rev: BL 10/1/06; SLJ 11/06)

1404 McDaniel, Lurlene. *Breathless* (7–10). 2009, Delacorte $10.99 (978-038573459-2); LB $13.99 (978-038590458-2). This moving story about a champion diver who learns he has bone cancer is told from his perspective and from those of three other teens who all struggle with Travis's desire for assisted suicide. (Rev: BL 7/09; SLJ 4/1/09)

1405 McDaniel, Lurlene. *How Do I Love Thee? Three Stories* (6–10). 2001, Bantam $9.95 (978-0-553-57154-7). Three dramatic stories combine young romance and critical illness with clever twists of plot. (Rev: BL 10/15/01; HBG 3/02; SLJ 11/01; VOYA 12/01)

1406 McDaniel, Lurlene. *Saving Jessica* (7–10). 1996, Bantam paper $4.99 (978-0-553-56721-2). When Jessica is stricken with kidney failure, her boyfriend, Jeremy, volunteers to donate one of his but his parents, fearful that he will die, refuse permission. (Rev: VOYA 4/96)

1407 Maclean, John. *Mac* (8–12). 1987, Avon paper $2.95 (978-0-380-70700-3). A high school sophomore's life falls apart after he is sexually assaulted by a doctor during a physical exam. (Rev: BL 10/1/87; SLJ 11/87)

1408 McNamara, Amy. *Lovely, Dark and Deep* (9–12). 2012, Simon & Schuster $16.99 (978-1-4424-3435-6). Emotionally withdrawn since the car accident that killed her boyfriend, Wren spends her senior year in self-imposed silence in the deep Maine woods, until she meets kind, persistent Cal, who is suffering from MS. (Rev: BL 11/15/12; LMC 3–4/13; SLJ 11/12)

1409 Manning, Sara. *Let's Get Lost* (10–12). 2006, Dutton $16.99 (978-0-525-47666-5). Isabel, 16, is into sex, drugs, stealing, and bullying, but behind her tough facade is a girl grieving for her mother. (Rev: BL 1/1–15/07; SLJ 10/06)

1410 Mathis, Sharon. *Teacup Full of Roses* (7–12). 1987, Puffin paper $5.99 (978-0-14-032328-3). For mature teens, a novel about the devastating effects of drugs on an African American family.

1411 Mazer, Harry, and Peter Lerangis. *Somebody, Please Tell Me Who I Am* (9–12). 2012, Simon & Schuster $15.99 (978-141693895-8). Traumatic brain injury from an explosion in combat leaves Ben in crisis, and his best friend and his fiancee react differently. ℮ (Rev: BL 2/15/12; HB 5–6/12; LMC 5–6/12*; SLJ 1/12; VOYA 12/11)

1412 Miller, Sarah. *Miss Spitfire: Reaching Helen Keller* (8–11). 2007, Atheneum $16.99 (978-1-4169-2542-2). A fictionalized account of Annie Sullivan's first experiences and struggles with her famous student. 🎧 (Rev: BL 8/07; LMC 11/07; SLJ 7/07)

1413 Mitchard, Jacquelyn. *All We Know of Heaven* (8–12). 2008, HarperTeen $16.99 (978-0-06-134578-4). Inspired by a true but almost unbelievable story, this novel centers on a girl who is mistaken for her dead best friend after a terrible car accident; Maureen has to deal not only with learning to walk and talk again, but also with her guilt about her friend Bridget's death. (Rev: BL 3/15/08; SLJ 6/08)

1414 Moix, Ana Maria. *Julia* (11–12). Trans. by Sandra Kingery. 2004, Univ. of Nebraska $55.00 (978-0-8032-3235-8); paper $20.00 (978-0-8032-8291-9). A disturbed young woman attempts suicide in hopes of eradicating her tortured past; for mature teens. (Rev: BL 9/1/04)

1415 Morgenroth, Kate. *Echo* (7–10). 2007, Simon & Schuster $15.99 (978-1-4169-1438-9). Justin finds it hard to cope with his brother's accidental death and on the one-year anniversary of the tragedy he relives the day — again and again. (Rev: BL 11/15/06; LMC 4–5/07; SLJ 2/07)

1416 Moskowitz, Hannah. *Break* (9–12). 2009, Simon & Schuster paper $8.99 (978-141698275-3). Jonah, 17, responds to the problems of his dysfunctional family with self-destructive risk taking. (Rev: BL 6/1–15/09*; SLJ 1/10)

1417 Mowry, Jess. *Babylon Boyz* (9–12). 1997, Simon & Schuster paper $16.00 (978-0-689-80839-5). In this novel for mature readers, three alienated boys — one homosexual, another with a severe heart condition, and the third fat — try to escape their squalid inner-city neighborhood called Babylon in Oakland, California. (Rev: BL 2/15/97; SLJ 9/97*; VOYA 6/97)

1418 Myers, Edward. *Ice* (9–12). 2005, Montemayor $12.95 (978-0-9674477-9-7). In this haunting novel, New Jersey teenagers Seth and Jenna struggle to come to grips with the loss of Frannie — Seth's girlfriend and Jenna's sister — in a car accident. (Rev: BL 12/1/05; SLJ 7/06)

1419 Myers, Walter Dean. *Sweet Illusions* (10–12). 1987, Teachers & Writers paper $8.95 (978-0-915924-15-8). Stories about teenage pregnancy from both male and female points of view. (Rev: BL 6/15/87; VOYA 8/87)

1420 Neenan, Colin. *Thick* (9–12). 2006, Brown Barn paper $6.95 (978-0-9746481-9-4). As 17-year-old Nick talks with his lawyer about the person he murdered, the reader learns that Nick is in a special-ed program, has an abusive, alcoholic father, and has been trying to help both his sister and a friend to escape their bad situations; for reluctant readers. (Rev: SLJ 5/06)

1421 Nolan, Han. *Born Blue* (10–12). 2001, Harcourt $17.00 (978-0-15-201916-7). Janie, a talented singer who has had a troubled childhood, changes her name to Leshaya and turns to sex, drugs, and the blues in this absorbing and thought-provoking novel. (Rev: BL 10/15/01; HB 1–2/02; HBG 3/02; SLJ 11/01*; VOYA 10/01)

1422 Nolan, Han. *Crazy* (7–10). 2010, Houghton Mifflin $17 (978-0-15-205109-9). Fifteen-year-old Jason's

mother has died and he must cope alone with his mentally ill father; fear of his father and for his own sanity are alleviated when his predicament is discovered and he is sent to foster care. (Rev: BL 8/10*; HB 11–12/10; SLJ 9/1/10)

1423 Oates, Joyce Carol. *After the Wreck I Picked Myself Up, Spread My Wings, and Flew Away* (7–10). 2006, HarperCollins $16.99 (978-0-06-073525-8). After her mother dies in a car crash, 15-year-old Jenna moves in with her aunt's family and struggles to cope with feelings of guilt and loss. ∩ (Rev: BL 7/06; LMC 4–5/07; SLJ 10/06)

1424 Oke, Janette, and Laurel Oke Logan. *Dana's Valley* (7–12). 2001, Bethany House paper $11.95 (978-0-7642-2451-5). Erin, 10 years old and part of a happy Christian family, has her faith tested when her beloved older sister is diagnosed with leukemia. (Rev: VOYA 2/02)

1425 Orr, Wendy. *Peeling the Onion* (8–12). 1997, Holiday $16.95 (978-0-8234-1289-1); paper $4.99 (978-0-440-22773-1). An automobile accident leaves Anna with a broken back, debilitating pain, physical and mental handicaps, and questions about what to do with her life. (Rev: BL 4/1/97; SLJ 5/97*; VOYA 10/97)

1426 Packer, Ann. *The Dive from Clausen's Pier: A Novel* (10–12). 2002, Knopf $24.00 (978-0-375-41282-0); paper $14.00 (978-0-375-72713-9). Mike's dive off Clausen's pier results in paralysis and also creates problems for his girlfriend, Carrie. (Rev: BL 3/15/02; SLJ 8/02)

1427 Peck, Richard. *Remembering the Good Times* (7–10). 1986, Bantam paper $5.50 (978-0-440-97339-3). A strong friendship between two boys and a girl is destroyed when one of them commits suicide. (Rev: BL 3/1/85)

1428 Peters, Julie Anne. *By the Time You Read This, I'll Be Dead* (9–12). 2010, Hyperion/Disney $16.99 (978-1-4231-1618-9). High school student Daelyn, who has been bullied for years and has tried to kill herself several times, makes new suicide plans even as a boy named Santana tries to connect with her. ∩ ℮ (Rev: HB 3–4/10; SLJ 5/10; VOYA 2/10)

1429 Pixley, Marcella. *Without Tess* (8–12). 2011, Farrar $16.99 (978-0-374-36174-7). Lizzie, 15, reflects on the life and death of her older sister Tess, whose fantasies as a child morphed into full-fledged mental illness as a teen. ℮ Lexile 790L (Rev: BLO 11/15/11; HB 1–2/12; LMC 1–2/12; SLJ 11/1/11*)

1430 Price, Charlie. *Lizard People* (9–12). 2007, Roaring Brook $16.95 (978-1-59643-190-4). Ben, whose mother has been admitted to a psychiatric hospital, befriends Marco, the son of another patient, only to discover a new problem in his life. (Rev: BCCB 10/07; BL 7/07; HB 11–12/07; LMC 11–12/07; SLJ 9/07)

1431 Price, Nora. *Zoe Letting Go* (9–12). 2012, Penguin $17.99 (978-1-595-14466-9). Reeling from the loss of a friend, and grappling with her own identity, Zoe spends six difficult weeks at a hospital for patients with eating disorders. **e** (Rev: BL 5/1/12; SLJ 7/12)

1432 Rapp, Adam. *Little Chicago* (10–12). 2002, Front St $16.95 (978-1-886910-72-0). Blacky is sexually abused by his mother's boyfriend and ridiculed by his peers in this disturbing and sexually explicit novel. (Rev: BL 8/02; HB 9–10/02; HBG 3/03; SLJ 8/02; VOYA 8/02)

1433 Rapp, Adam. *Punkzilla* (10–12). 2009, Candlewick $16.99 (978-076363031-7). Jamie, known as "Punkzilla," runs away from military school and decides to hitchhike across-country to visit his dying older brother; sexual encounters, crime, drugs, danger, and loneliness are all part of his journey. Printz Honor 2010. Lexile 1300L (Rev: BL 4/15/09*; LMC 10/09; SLJ 7/1/09)

1434 Rapp, Adam. *Under the Wolf, Under the Dog* (10–12). 2005, Candlewick $16.99 (978-0-7636-1818-6). Deeply shaken by the loss of his mother to cancer and his brother to suicide, 16-year-old Steve Nugent recounts, in often-humorous journal entries, the chain of events that ended in his commitment to a facility for suicidal and drug-addicted teens. (Rev: BL 11/15/04; SLJ 10/04; VOYA 12/04)

1435 Reed, Amy. *Clean* (9–12). 2011, Simon & Schuster $16.99 (978-1-4424-1344-3). Five teens in rehab take stock of their lives in this story told in a variety of formats. **e** (Rev: BL 10/1/11; SLJ 10/1/11; VOYA 8/11)

1436 Reid, P. Carey. *Swimming in the Starry River* (9–12). 1994, Hyperion $19.95 (978-0-7868-6005-0). In this chronicle of courage, frustration, and compassion, a father forges a powerful bond with his young child who has a debilitating disease. (Rev: BL 5/15/94)

1437 Ross, Jeff. *Coming Clean* (7–12). 2012, Orca LB $16.95 (978-145980332-9); paper $9.95 (978-145980331-2). Aspiring DJ Rob becomes caught up in a world of drugs and betrayal, with unhappy consequences; for reluctant readers. **e** Lexile HL500L (Rev: BLO 10/15/12; SLJ 4/13)

1438 Ruckman, Ivy. *The Hunger Scream* (7–10). 1983, Walker $14.95 (978-0-8027-6514-7). Lily starves herself to become a popular member of the in-crowd.

1439 Ryan, Darlene. *Five Minutes More* (7–10). 2009, Orca paper $12.95 (978-155469006-0). D'Arcy has trouble adjusting after the death of her father, who suffered from ALS; the idea that he killed himself makes everything worse. Lexile HL570L (Rev: BLO 4/14/09; VOYA 6/09)

1440 Saldin, Erin. *The Girls of No Return* (9–12). 2012, Scholastic $17.99 (978-054531026-0). Lida, 16, is forced to face the fallout from her dual friendships with two other troubled girls while participating in a wilderness school. **e** Lexile 770L (Rev: BL 2/1/12*; HB 1–2/12; LMC 3–4/12*; SLJ 4/12)

1441 Sanchez, Alex. *Bait* (7–10). 2009, Simon & Schuster $16.99 (978-141693772-2). When Diego ends up in juvenile court, his parole officer helps him get to the source of his anger problems—namely, being sexually abused by his stepfather. Lexile HL630L (Rev: BL 5/15/09; SLJ 7/1/09*; VOYA 8/09)

1442 Sanchez, Alex. *The God Box* (10–12). 2007, Simon & Schuster $16.99 (978-1-4169-0899-9). Can Paul be both gay and Christian? He struggles with his feelings for other boys, praying to be straight, until gay friend Manuel helps him reconcile his spirituality with his sexuality. (Rev: BL 10/1/07; SLJ 1/08)

1443 Sandell, Lisa Ann. *A Map of the Known World* (7–10). 2009, Scholastic $16.99 (978-054506970-0). After her brother Nate dies in a car crash, 14-year-old Cora becomes close to Nate's best friend, who survived the crash, and learns that there was an artistic, thoughtful side to Nate that she had never seen. Lexile 800L (Rev: BL 4/1/09; SLJ 6/1/09)

1444 Schindler, Holly. *A Blue So Dark* (8–11). 2010, Flux paper $9.95 (978-0-73871-926-9). When 15-year-old Aura's mentally ill mother finally enters a catatonic state of schizophrenia, Aura realizes she can't care for her on her own. **e** (Rev: BL 5/1/10*; LMC 8–9/10; SLJ 6/10)

1445 Schmidt, Tiffany. *Send Me a Sign* (8–12). 2012, Walker $16.99 (978-080272840-1). Superstitious 17-year-old Mia consults horoscopes and tarot cards when she is diagnosed with leukemia and allows them to guide her behavior. **e** (Rev: BL 10/15/12; SLJ 2/13)

1446 Scoppettone, Sandra. *Long Time Between Kisses* (7–10). 1982, HarperCollins $12.95 (978-0-06-025229-8). A 16-year-old brings together a victim of multiple sclerosis and his fiance.

1447 Scott, Elizabeth. *Love You Hate You Miss You* (9–12). 2009, HarperTeen $16.99 (978-006112283-5); LB $17.89 (978-006112284-2). Through therapy and journal entries, wayward teen Amy comes to terms with the death of her friend Julia and the destructiveness of her own behavior. (Rev: BL 4/1/09; HB 7–8/09; SLJ 6/1/09; VOYA 10/09)

1448 Scott, Elizabeth. *Miracle* (7–10). 2012, Simon & Schuster $16.99 (978-1-4424-1706-9). Megan, the sole survivor of an airplane crash, remains haunted by the ghosts of the four passengers who died, and finds herself unable to fit back into her old life in this portrait of a teen with emotional damage who eventually finds solace. **e** Lexile HL750L (Rev: BLO 6/12; LMC 11–12/12; SLJ 7/12)

1449 Scott, Virginia M. *Belonging* (9–12). 1986, Kendall Green paper $2.95 (978-0-930323-33-2). A 15-year-old girl must adjust to deafness caused by an attack of meningitis. (Rev: VOYA 4/88)

1450 Sheinmel, Courtney. *Positively* (6–10). 2009, Simon & Schuster $15.99 (978-141697169-6). This is 13-year-old Emmy's first-person account of coming to accept living with AIDS. (Rev: BL 7/09; SLJ 1/10)

1451 Spencer, Katherine. *Saving Grace* (8–11). 2006, Harcourt $15.00 (978-0-15-205740-4). Grace is emotionally lost and heading down a dangerous path after her brother, Matt, dies in a car accident. Help comes in the form of a girl named Philomena who guides her back to God. (Rev: BCCB 11/06; BL 1/1–15/07; SLJ 10/06)

1452 Stork, Francisco X. *Marcelo in the Real World* (9–12). 2009, Scholastic $17.99 (978-054505474-4). Marcelo, a 17-year-old with Asperger's syndrome, is thrown into the "real world" when he takes a job in the mailroom at his father's law firm and must make ethical decisions. YALSA Top Ten 2010. ∩ Lexile HL700L (Rev: BL 4/1/09; LMC 5–6/09; SLJ 3/1/09*)

1453 Stratton, Allan. *Leslie's Journal* (8–12). 2000, Annick $19.95 (978-1-55037-665-4); paper $8.95 (978-1-55037-664-7). A new teacher reads Leslie's journal and learns about her boyfriend's abusive behavior. (Rev: HBG 10/01; SLJ 4/01; VOYA 2/01)

1454 Strohmeyer, Sarah. *The Cinderella Pact* (9–12). 2006, Dutton $24.95 (978-0-525-94957-2). Coerced into a "Cinderella" weight loss pact, tabloid editor Nola Devlin fights to lose weight in time to present herself as her alter ego, that most slender and popular columnist, Belinda Apple. (Rev: BL 6/1–15/06)

1455 Tan, Shaun. *The Red Tree* (6–12). 2003, Simply Read $15.95 (978-0-9688767-3-2). This arresting picture book for older readers portrays a girl searching for meaning in a frightening world, with a glimmer of hope that grows as the book reaches its conclusion. (Rev: BL 5/1/03)

1456 Tashjian, Janet. *Fault Line* (8–12). 2003, Henry Holt $16.95 (978-0-8050-7200-6). Becky, 17, happy and enjoying doing comedy routines, finds her life changing when she falls for Kip, whose apparent self-confidence hides his abusive nature. (Rev: BL 9/1/03; HB 9–10/03; HBG 4/04; SLJ 10/03; VOYA 10/03)

1457 Taylor, Michelle A. *The Angel of Barbican High* (7–12). 2002, Univ. of Queensland paper $15.95 (978-0-7022-3251-0). Jez feels responsible for the death of her boyfriend and pours out her guilt in her poems, which reveal that she is close to suicide. (Rev: SLJ 8/02)

1458 Tokio, Mamelle. *More Than You Can Chew* (8–10). 2003, Tundra paper $9.95 (978-0-88776-639-8). Anorexic 17-year-old Marty Black faces an uphill struggle as she begins treatment for her eating disorder but tackles it with some humor. (Rev: BL 1/1–15/04; SLJ 6/04; VOYA 8/04)

1459 Toten, Teresa. *The Game* (7–12). 2001, Red Deer paper $7.95 (978-0-88995-232-4). A dramatic story about Dani, a suicidal girl who finds friendship and succor at a clinic for troubled adolescents. (Rev: BL 2/15/02; VOYA 4/02)

1460 Trembath, Don. *Lefty Carmichael Has a Fit* (8–12). 2000, Orca paper $6.95 (978-1-55143-166-6). When 15-year-old Lefty discovers that he is an epileptic, he develops a fearful, cautious lifestyle that his friends and family try to change. (Rev: BL 1/1–15/00; SLJ 2/00; VOYA 4/00)

1461 Trueman, Terry. *Inside Out* (7–10). 2003, HarperCollins LB $16.89 (978-0-06-623963-7). An absorbing story about a schizophrenic teenager who is held hostage in a robbery attempt. (Rev: BL 9/1/03; HBG 4/04; SLJ 9/03; VOYA 10/03)

1462 Trueman, Terry. *Life Happens Next* (8–12). 2012, HarperTeen $17.99 (978-006202803-7). Cerebral palsy sufferer Shawn, almost 15, forges a strong bond with Debi, who has Down syndrome, when the woman and her dog move in with his family; the sequel to *Stuck in Neutral* (2001). ∩ ℮ (Rev: BL 12/1/12; HB 11–12/12; VOYA 6/12)

1463 Trueman, Terry. *Stuck in Neutral* (6–10). 2000, HarperCollins LB $16.89 (978-0-06-028518-0). Fourteen-year-old Shawn, whose severe cerebral palsy does not hamper his great intelligence, fears that his father may be planning to put him out of his misery. (Rev: BL 7/00*; HB 5–6/00; HBG 10/00; SLJ 7/00; VOYA 12/00)

1464 Tullson, Diane. *Riley Park* (7–12). 2009, LB $16.95 (978-155469124-1); paper $9.95 (978-155469123-4). After a night of partying and fighting, friends Darius and Corbin are attacked in a park. Darius dies and Corbin is seriously injured. A suspenseful offering for reluctant readers. Lexile HL480L (Rev: BL 5/1/09; SLJ 10/09)

1465 Tullson, Diane. *Zero* (8–11). 2007, Fitzhenry & Whiteside paper $9.95 (978-1-55041-950-4). While at a boarding school for the arts, Kas becomes anorexic and manages to hide her problem from everyone until she nearly dies. (Rev: BL 4/15/07; SLJ 6/07)

1466 Vaught, Susan. *Trigger* (9–12). 2006, Bloomsbury $16.95 (978-1-58234-920-6). As he slowly recovers from a brain injury caused by a self-inflicted gunshot, Jeremy must piece together his former life and what led to the desperate act he can't recall. (Rev: BL 12/1/06; HB 9–10/06; LMC 2/07; SLJ 11/06)

1467 Waite, Judy. *Shopaholic* (6–10). 2003, Simon & Schuster $16.95 (978-0-689-85138-4). Unhappy Taylor, a British 14-year-old, allows herself to fall in with glamorous Kat's plans despite her reservations. (Rev: BL 5/1/03; HBG 10/03; SLJ 7/03; VOYA 8/03)

1468 Waldorf, Heather. *Tripping* (8–12). 2009, Red Deer paper $12.95 (978-088995426-7). Rainey, who has a prosthetic leg, sets off on an Outward Bound-type trip across Canada and learns about herself, her mother, and her fellow travelers. YALSA Popular Paperbacks for Young Adults Top Ten 2012. Lexile HL780L (Rev: BL 5/1/09; SLJ 5/1/09)

1469 Walker, Alice. *The Color Purple* (10–12). 1992, Harcourt $23.00 (978-0-15-119154-3). For better readers, the candid memoirs of Celie, her abuse, and eventual triumph.

1470 Watt, Alan. *Diamond Dogs* (10–12). 2000, Little, Brown $23.95 (978-0-316-92581-5). Seventeen-year-old Neil Garvin becomes a bully, like his father, but the boy's aggression leads to the death of one of the boys he has bullied. (Rev: BL 7/00)

1471 Weatherly, Lee. *Kat Got Your Tongue* (8–10). 2007, Random House $15.99 (978-0-385-75117-9). After being hit by a car, Kat doesn't remember who she is and struggles with her new identity and relationships with her mother and friends. (Rev: BL 8/07; SLJ 9/07)

1472 Wersba, Barbara. *Fat: A Love Story* (8–12). 1987, HarperCollins $11.95 (978-0-06-026400-0). Rita Formica, fat and unhappy, falls for rich, attractive Robert. (Rev: BL 6/1/87; SLJ 8/87; VOYA 6/87)

1473 White, Ruth. *Memories of Summer* (7–12). 2000, Farrar $16.00 (978-0-374-34945-5). Lyric is devastated when her older sister, Summer, must be hospitalized for her schizophrenia in this novel set in 1955. (Rev: BL 9/1/00; HB 9–10/00; HBG 3/01; SLJ 8/00*; VOYA 12/00)

1474 White, Ruth. *Weeping Willow* (7–10). 1992, Farrar paper $5.95 (978-0-374-48280-0). This uplifting novel conveying hill country life is about a girl who overcomes abuse to make her own way. (Rev: BL 6/15/92; SLJ 7/92)

1475 Wieringa, Tommy. *Joe Speedboat* (10–12). 2010, Black Cat paper $14.95 (978-08021707-2-9). Wheelchair-bound Frankie becomes an arm-wrestling champ under the management of the energetic, eccentric young Joe Speedboat. (Rev: BL 3/1–15/10)

1476 Wiess, Laura. *Such a Pretty Girl* (9–12). 2007, Pocket paper $12.00 (978-1-4165-2183-9). Meredith is terrified when her abusive father is released from prison after serving only three years. To make matters worse, her mother takes her father's side in this disturbing story. ⌂ (Rev: BL 4/15/07)

1477 Wilson, Dawn. *Saint Jude* (8–12). 2001, Tudor $15.95 (978-0-936389-68-4). Taylor, who is bipolar, makes friends and learns to cope with her illness while in an outpatient program at St. Jude Hospital. (Rev: BL 11/1/01; SLJ 11/01)

1478 Wingate, Lisa. *Drenched in Light* (9–12). 2006, NAL paper $13.95 (978-0-451-21848-3). A junior-high school guidance counselor's feelings of failure threaten to overwhelm her until she meets a very talented and special student. (Rev: BL 6/1–15/06)

1479 Wolf, Allan. *Zane's Trace* (9–12). 2007, Candlewick $16.99 (978-0-7636-2858-1). Zane, a 17-year-old epileptic Native American, believes he is responsible for his grandfather's death and sets off in his dead father's 1969 Plymouth Barracuda with the intention of killing himself on the grave of his schizophrenic mother. (Rev: BL 10/15/07; HB 9–10/07; LMC 11/07; SLJ 10/07)

1480 Wolff, Virginia Euwer. *Probably Still Nick Swansen* (7–12). 1988, Henry Holt $14.95 (978-0-8050-0701-5). Nick, a 16-year-old victim of slight brain dysfunction, tells his story of rejection and separation. (Rev: BL 11/15/88; SLJ 12/88; VOYA 6/89)

1481 Wolfson, Jill. *Cold Hands, Warm Heart* (8–10). 2009, Henry Holt $17.95 (978-080508282-1). When a 14-year-old gymnast dies, her organs are transplanted, affecting many people in profound ways. Lexile HL760L (Rev: BL 3/15/09; SLJ 5/1/09; VOYA 6/09)

1482 Woodruff, Joan L. *The Shiloh Renewal* (7–10). 1998, Black Heron $22.95 (978-0-930773-50-2). Sandy, who has been mentally and physically disabled since an automobile accident, tries to regain basic skills, recover from the brain trauma, and straighten out her life in this novel that takes place on a small farm near Shiloh National Park in Tennessee. (Rev: VOYA 12/98)

1483 Woodson, Jacqueline. *Beneath a Meth Moon* (8–11). 2012, Penguin $16.99 (978-039925250-1). After becoming hooked on crystal meth in the aftermath of Hurricane Katrina, Laurel, 15, now struggles to overcome her addiction. YALSA Quick Picks for Reluctant Young Adult Readers 2013. ⌂ ℮ Lexile HL730L (Rev: BL 12/15/11; HB 3–4/12; SLJ 2/12*)

1484 Yeomans, Ellen. *Rubber Houses* (6–12). 2007, Little, Brown $15.99 (978-0-316-10647-X). This novel in verse follows Kit's grief when her younger brother, with whom she shared a love of baseball, is diagnosed with and then dies of cancer. (Rev: BCCB 2/07; BL 1/1–15/07; SLJ 3/07)

1485 Young, Janet Ruth. *My Beautiful Failure* (8–11). 2012, Atheneum $16.99 (978-141695489-7). Billy Morrison, a high school sophomore whose father has suffered from severe depression, signs up to volunteer on a suicide hotline and soon finds himself fascinated by a regular young woman caller named Jenney. ℮ Lexile HL670L (Rev: BL 11/15/12; LMC 3–4/13; SLJ 2/13)

1486 Young, Janet Ruth. *The Opposite of Music* (9–12). 2007, Simon & Schuster $15.99 (978-1-4169-0040-5). Life changes for 15-year-old Billy's family when his father becomes seriously mentally ill and they must care for him and search for a cure. (Rev: BCCB 4/07; BL 3/1/07; SLJ 3/07)

1487 Zarr, Sara. *Sweethearts* (8–12). 2008, Little, Brown $16.99 (978-0-316-01455-7). Jenna has remade herself in an attempt to forget her troubled childhood, but when Cameron — who suffered abuse along with Jenna long ago — reappears in her life, her past seems to come back with him. ∩ (Rev: BL 1/1–15/08; HB 5–6/08; SLJ 4/08)

1488 Zevin, Gabrielle. *Memoirs of a Teenage Amnesiac* (6–10). 2007, Farrar $17.00 (978-0-374-34946-2). After a head injury, Naomi, a high school junior, can't remember anything that's happened since 6th grade and struggles with her present and past life, a new romance, and her parents' separation. (Rev: BL 9/1/07; SLJ 10/07)

Personal Problems and Growing into Maturity

1489 Abrams, Amir. *Crazy Love* (10–12). 2012, Kensington $9.95 (978-075827356-7). Talented high school senior Kamiyah loses interest in her college plans when her love for college student Sincere turns into obsession. e (Rev: BL 12/15/12; SLJ 2/13)

1490 Acito, Marc. *How I Paid for College: A Novel of Sex, Theft, Friendship and Musical Theater* (11–12). 2004, Broadway $21.95 (978-0-7679-1841-1). High school senior Edward and his friends will try just about anything to help the talented Edward pay for Juilliard in this offbeat, funny, and poignant novel set in the 1980s and featuring young men exploring their sexual identities; suitable for mature teens. (Rev: BL 8/04; SLJ 9/04)

1491 Adams, Lenora. *Baby Girl* (7–10). 2007, Simon & Schuster paper $6.99 (978-1-4169-2512-5). Sheree, a pregnant runaway, exchanges letters with her mother expressing anguish over her life, which has included neglect, drugs, and disappointment. (Rev: BL 3/1/07)

1492 Alexie, Sherman. *The Absolutely True Diary of a Part-Time Indian* (7–10). 2007, Little, Brown $16.99 (978-0-316-01368-0). Arnold Spirit, a teenager on the Spokane Indian reservation, expects obstacles when he switches to a privileged white school but finds there are challenges at home too. ∩ (Rev: BL 8/07; HB 1–2/08; LMC 1/08; SLJ 9/07)

1493 Allen, M. E. *Gotta Get Some Bish Bash Bosh* (7–10). 2005, HarperCollins LB $16.89 (978-0-06-073201-1). When he's dumped by his girlfriend Sandi, the 14-year-old narrator resolves to cultivate a brand-new image in this entertaining novel set in Britain. (Rev: BL 1/1–15/05; SLJ 4/05; VOYA 2/05)

1494 Alphin, Elaine Marie. *Simon Says* (8–12). 2002, Harcourt $17.00 (978-0-15-216355-6). Charles, a brooding 16-year-old artist, is determined to remain nonconformist when he starts attending a boarding school for the arts in this thoughtful novel. (Rev: BCCB 6/02; BL 4/15/02; HBG 10/02; SLJ 6/02)

1495 Anderson, Laurie Halse. *Prom* (9–12). 2005, Viking $16.99 (978-0-670-05974-4). High school senior Ashley couldn't care less about the upcoming prom, but she responds to her best friend's plea for help after the big event is jeopardized by an embezzling math teacher. (Rev: BL 1/1–15/05*; SLJ 2/05; VOYA 4/05)

1496 Anderson, Laurie Halse. *Speak* (8–12). 1999, Farrar $16.00 (978-0-374-37152-4). A victim of rape, high school freshman Mellinda Sordino finds that her attacker is again threatening her. Printz Honor 2000; Margaret A. Edwards Award 2009. (Rev: BL 9/15/99; HB 9–10/99; HBG 4/00; SLJ 10/99; VOYA 12/99)

1497 Anderson, Laurie Halse. *Twisted* (9–12). 2007, Viking $16.99 (978-0-670-06101-3). When he gets into trouble for vandalism, Tyler finally shakes off his "nerd" label and enjoys a new popularity, but things get out of hand when he's accused of a more serious crime. (Rev: BL 1/1–15/07; SLJ 5/07)

1498 Angel, Jodi. *The History of Vegas* (11–12). 2005, Chronicle $19.95 (978-0-8118-4625-7). Ten short matter-of-fact stories feature West Coast teens in unhappy situations — violence, drugs and alcohol use, eating and disorders, and so forth. (Rev: BL 7/05)

1499 *Annie's Baby: The Diary of Anonymous, a Pregnant Teenager* (6–10). 1998, Avon paper $5.99 (978-0-380-79141-5). In diary format, this is the story of 14-year-old Annie, her love for an abusive rich boyfriend, and her rape and subsequent pregnancy. (Rev: SLJ 7/98; VOYA 6/98)

1500 Ashley, Bernard. *Little Soldier* (8–12). 2002, Scholastic $16.95 (978-0-439-22424-6). Young Kaninda Bulumba is rescued from the incredible violence taking place in his native country only to find himself confronting gang violence in his new neighborhood in London. (Rev: BCCB 7–8/02; BL 5/1/02; HBG 10/02; SLJ 6/02*; VOYA 8/02)

1501 Atwood, Margaret. *Cat's Eye* (10–12). 1989, Doubleday paper $12.95 (978-0-385-49102-0). This is a novel about Elaine Risley who, at 50, has become a famous Canadian painter and who tells the reader the story of her life.

1502 Babcock, Joe. *The Tragedy of Miss Geneva Flowers* (11–12). 2005, Carroll & Graf paper $13.95 (978-0-7867-1520-6). Erick Taylor, an unhappy 16-year-old, is enchanted by the persona and life of a drag queen; unfortunately the lure of crystal meth is even stronger than that of the stage; for mature teens. (Rev: BL 4/15/05)

1503 Banks, Russell. *Rule of the Bone* (10–12). 1996, HarperTrade $13.95 (978-0-06-092724-0). The reader follows Chappie from his life in a trailer park to discovery of drugs, rejection by parents, petty crime, and decision to take on a new name, "Bone," and style of life; as a homeless teen he moves through a variety of experiences, including a trip to the mountains of Jamaica.

1504 Baratz-Logsted, Lauren. *Angel's Choice* (10–12). 2007, Simon & Schuster paper $6.99 (978-1-4169-2524-8). Upset about her breakup with Danny, 17-year-old Angel Hansen has sex — for the first time — with someone else and becomes pregnant; the story of the choices she faces is compelling. (Rev: SLJ 1/07)

1505 Barbieri, Heather. *Snow in July* (11–12). 2004, Soho $24.00 (978-1-56947-384-9). Eighteen-year-old Erin tries to hold things together for her older sister Meghan, who is a drug addict with two children, in this story set in Montana; for mature teens. (Rev: BL 9/15/04)

1506 Barkley, Brad, and Heather Hepler. *Dream Factory* (9–12). 2007, Dutton $16.99 (978-0-525-47802-7). In alternating chapters, Ella and Luke tell the story of their attraction to each other as they both work at Disney World, performing as Cinderella and Dale the chipmunk respectively. (Rev: BCCB 6/07; BL 7/07; SLJ 7/07)

1507 Baskin, Nora Raleigh. *All We Know of Love* (7–10). 2008, Candlewick $16.99 (978-076363623-4). Sixteen-year-old Natalie Gordon sets off on a bus trip from Connecticut to Florida to find the mother who abandoned her four years ago, and learns lessons about herself, and about love, along the way. Lexile NC660L (Rev: BL 10/15/08; SLJ 9/1/08; VOYA 8/08)

1508 Bathurst, Bella. *Special* (11–12). 2003, Houghton Mifflin paper $12.00 (978-0-618-26327-1). Set in rural England, this is an eloquent portrayal of the aspirations, temptations, insecurities, and cruelties typical of 13-year-old girls. (Rev: BL 3/15/03)

1509 Bauer, Cat. *Harley's Ninth* (9–12). 2007, Knopf $17.99 (978-0-375-93736-1). Harley, a young artist whom readers got to know in *Harley, Like a Person* (2000), fears she may be pregnant and anticipates the opening of her first exhibit in this novel that takes place over the course of a single day. (Rev: BCCB 6/07; BL 1/1–15/07; HB 3–4/07; SLJ 3/07)

1510 Beam, Matt. *Last December* (9–12). 2009, Front St $18.95 (978-1-59078-651-2). Steven is a troubled 15-year-old who struggles with and eventually learns to weather multiple stresses in his life; the book is told in notes to his unborn sister. Lexile NC1750L (Rev: BL 10/15/09; LMC 1–2/10)

1511 Beaudoin, Sean. *Going Nowhere Faster* (8–12). 2007, Little, Brown $16.99 (978-0-316-01415-1). Stan Smith, 17, has a high IQ and showed promise when he was younger but now spends his time working in a video store, inventing dreadful screenplay scenarios, avoiding his embarrassing hippie parents, and worrying about a stalker; a darkly comic story with a satisfying resolution. (Rev: BCCB 5/07; HB 5–6/07; SLJ 4/07)

1512 Beede, John R. *Climb On! Dynamic Strategies for Teen Success* (9–12). 2005, Sierra Nevada paper $12.95 (978-0-9765697-0-1). A motivational novel in which troubled 16-year-old Anna joins a rock climbing group and learns skills including endurance and persistence and about the value of positive change; hints are highlighted throughout. (Rev: SLJ 1/06)

1513 Bell, William. *Death Wind* (7–12). 2002, Orca paper $7.95 (978-1-55143-215-1). After running away from her unhappy home when she thinks she may be pregnant, Allie returns to find that a tornado has devastated her town. (Rev: SLJ 10/02; VOYA 12/02)

1514 Berg, Elizabeth. *Durable Goods* (9–12). 2003, Random House paper $13.95 (978-0-8129-6814-9). Katie, 12, narrates this tender, poignant, funny, totally believable coming-of-age story. (Rev: BL 4/15/93; SLJ 11/93*; VOYA 12/93)

1515 Berg, Elizabeth. *Joy School* (9–12). 1997, Random House $19.00 (978-0-679-44943-0); paper $11.95 (978-0-345-42309-2). Lonely 13-year-old Katie develops a crush on 23-year-old Jimmy and makes new friends after moving to Missouri. (Rev: BL 9/15/98)

1516 Berlin, Adam. *Headlock* (10–12). 2000, Algonquin $21.95 (978-1-56512-266-6). A tough, raw novel for mature readers that deals with a trip to Las Vegas by a young man with a violent temper and his cousin, a grossly obese professional gambler. (Rev: BL 4/1/00*)

1517 Bick, Ilsa J. *Drowning Instinct* (9–12). 2012, Carolrhoda/Lab $17.95 (978-076137752-8). Jenna, 16, a girl with a troubled background, recounts the story of her life and of her affair with teacher and coach Mitch Anderson. ♫ ℮ Lexile 710L (Rev: BL 2/15/12; LMC 5–6/12; SLJ 3/12; VOYA 6/12)

1518 Bigelow, Lisa Jenn. *Starting from Here* (9–12). 2012, Amazon Children's $16.99 (978-0-7614-6233-0). A stray dog helps 16-year-old Colby to recover from the two years since her mother's death, years in which her truck driver father has mostly been absent and she has struggled with school and a failed relationship with her first girlfriend. ℮ (Rev: BL 10/1/12; SLJ 12/12)

1519 Bildner, Phil. *Busted* (9–12). 2007, Simon & Schuster $15.99 (978-1-4169-2424-1). The students of Coldwater Creek High get up to all sorts of illegal and ill-advised activities in four interconnected short stories about a school gone wrong. (Rev: SLJ 8/07)

1520 Billerbeck, Kristin. *Perfectly Dateless* (8–12). 2010, Revell paper $9.99 (978-08007343-9-8). Can Daisy find a date in time for the prom despite her weird parents and her social ineptitude? A funny story about high school problems. ℮ (Rev: BL 7/10)

1521 Billingsley, ReShonda Tate. *With Friends Like These* (7–12). Series: African American Christian Teen Fiction. 2007, Pocket paper $9.95 (978-1-4165-2562-2). The four girls we first met in *Nothing but Drama* (2006) now become enemies in their efforts to get on a TV show. (Rev: BL 4/1/07)

1522 Blau, Jessica Anya. *The Summer of Naked Swim Parties* (9–12). 2008, HarperCollins paper $13.95 (978-0-06-145202-4). Fourteen-year-old Jamie finds her parents' naked pot-smoking pool parties more humiliating than exciting, but things are about to change in this coming-of-age novel. (Rev: BL 4/15/08)

1523 Block, Francesca Lia. *Blood Roses* (10–12). 2008, HarperCollins $15.99 (978-0-06-076384-8). Stories, many of them dark and magical, about powerful girls and women discovering and using their sexuality. (Rev: BL 4/15/08; SLJ 10/08)

1524 Block, Francesca Lia. *Echo* (8–12). 2001, HarperCollins LB $14.89 (978-0-06-028128-1). A series of interconnected stories set in glamorous Los Angeles follows the maturing of an unhappy young girl called Echo, who feels neglected by her talented parents and seeks attention where she can find it. (Rev: BCCB 10/01; BL 8/01; HB 9–10/01; HBG 3/02; SLJ 8/01; VOYA 10/01)

1525 Block, Francesca Lia. *Pink Smog: Becoming Weetzie Bat* (9–12). 2012, HarperTeen $17.99 (978-006156598-4). Thirteen-year-old Weetzie's life is thrown into turmoil when her father abruptly leaves her alcoholic mother in this prequel to the 1989 novel. e (Rev: BL 11/1/11*; HB 3–4/12; SLJ 1/12; VOYA 12/11)

1526 Block, Francesca Lia. *Violet and Claire* (10–12). 1999, HarperCollins LB $14.89 (978-0-06-027750-5). The story of two talented and very different friends whose relationship goes awry when sex and drugs enter their lives. (Rev: BL 9/1/99; HBG 4/00; SLJ 9/99)

1527 Block, Francesca Lia. *Wasteland* (9–12). 2003, HarperCollins LB $16.89 (978-0-06-028645-3). Lex commits suicide after he and his sister have sex in this novel with a twist about two affectionate siblings. (Rev: BCCB 11/03; BL 7/03; HB 11–12/03; HBG 4/04; SLJ 10/03; VOYA 2/04)

1528 Bloor, Edward. *Tangerine* (7–10). 1997, Harcourt $17.00 (978-0-15-201246-5); paper $4.99 (978-0-590-43277-1). Although he wears thick glasses, Paul is able to see clearly the people around him, their problems and their mistakes, as he adjusts to his new home in Tangerine County, Florida. (Rev: BL 5/15/97; SLJ 4/97; VOYA 8/97)

1529 Bloss, Josie. *Albatross* (8–11). Series: Band Geek. 2010, Flux paper $9.95 (978-0-73871-476-9). Tess, a 16-year-old French horn player lacking in self-confidence, falls for pianist Micah despite his abusive and manipulative behavior. Lexile HL680L (Rev: BLO 1/1–15/10; LMC 5–6/10; SLJ 3/10)

1530 Bloss, Josie. *Faking Faith* (7–10). 2011, Flux paper $9.95 (978-0-7387-2-757-8). Shunned after inappropriate postings on the Internet, Dylan seeks new friends on a fundamentalist network, creating a new version of herself named Faith. e Lexile HL790L (Rev: BLO 10/15/11; SLJ 12/1/11; VOYA 12/11)

1531 Blount, Patty. *Send* (8–10). 2012, Sourcebooks paper $8.99 (978-14022733-7-7). Dan, 18 years old and a former bully, has been trying to keep a low profile at school but comes into the limelight when he stops a beating. e Lexile HL550L (Rev: BLO 8/12; VOYA 12/12)

1532 Blume, Judy. *Summer Sisters* (10–12). 1998, Delacorte $21.95 (978-0-385-32405-2). An entertaining adult novel about the friendship of two girls and their experiences, worries, and emotions as they grow into maturity during six summers together. (Rev: BL 3/15/98; SLJ 6/98)

1533 Blume, Judy. *Tiger Eyes* (7–10). 1981, Dell paper $5.99 (978-0-440-98469-6). A girl struggles to cope with her father's violent death. (Rev: BL 7/88)

1534 Bock, Caroline. *Lie* (9–12). 2011, St. Martin's paper $9.99 (978-0-312-66-832-7). A group of Long Island teens enjoy attacking Latinos until an assault becomes too rough and they must revise their views and question their loyalty to each other. e Lexile HL610L (Rev: BL 11/15/11*; SLJ 9/1/11*; VOYA 10/11)

1535 Bognanni, Peter. *The House of Tomorrow* (10–12). 2010, Putnam $24.95 (978-039915609-0). Sheltered, home-schooled Sebastian must leave his isolated bubble when his grandmother suffers a stroke; and with the help of the Whitcomb family he discovers a totally new world. Alex Award 2011. ⌒ e (Rev: BL 3/1–15/10)

1536 Boock, Paula. *Dare Truth or Promise* (8–12). 1999, Houghton Mifflin $15.00 (978-0-395-97117-8). Two girls, Willa and Louise, attend a New Zealand high school and, though they are opposites in many ways, they fall in love. (Rev: BL 9/15/99; HB 9–10/99; HBG 4/00; SLJ 11/99; VOYA 10/99)

1537 Book, Rick. *Necking with Louise* (7–12). 1999, Red Deer paper $7.95 (978-0-88995-194-5). Set in Saskatchewan in 1965, this is a book of stories about Eric Anderson's 16th year, when he has his first date, plays in a championship hockey game, has a summer job, and reacts to his family and the land on which he lives. (Rev: BL 10/15/99*; SLJ 3/00)

1538 Borntrager, Mary Christner. *Rebecca* (7–12). 1989, Herald paper $8.99 (978-0-8361-3500-8). A coming-of-age novel about an Amish girl and her attraction to a Mennonite young man. (Rev: SLJ 11/89)

1539 Bottner, Barbara. *Nothing in Common* (7–10). 1986, HarperCollins $12.95 (978-0-06-020604-8). When Mrs. Gregori dies, both her daughter and Melissa Warren, a teenager in the household where Mrs. Gregori worked, enter a period of grief. (Rev: VOYA 2/87)

1540 Bowsher, Melodie. *My Lost and Found Life* (10–12). 2006, Bloomsbury $16.95 (978-1-58234-736-3). After her mother is accused of embezzling funds and vanishes, Ashlee's perfect, spoiled lifestyle is over and she must learn to take care of herself. (Rev: BL 11/15/06; SLJ 10/06)

1541 Brashares, Ann. *Girls in Pants: The Third Summer of the Sisterhood* (8–12). Series: Sisterhood of the Traveling Pants. 2005, Delacorte LB $18.99 (978-0-385-90919-8). It's summer again for the four friends and they manage to get together for a weekend before they leave for separate colleges; the pants continue their travels. (Rev: BL 12/15/04*; SLJ 1/05; VOYA 2/05)

1542 Brashares, Ann. *3 Willows: The Sisterhood Grows* (6–10). Series: Sisterhood. 2009, Delacorte $18.99 (978-038573676-3); LB $21.99 (978-038590628-9). The author of *The Sisterhood of the Traveling Pants* introduces Ama, Jo, and Polly, who are about to enter high school and face different but typical challenges. ☊ e Lexile 700L (Rev: BL 2/15/09; HB 3–4/09; LMC 5–6/09; SLJ 1/1/09)

1543 Brezenoff, Steve. *Brooklyn, Burning* (8–12). 2011, Carolrhoda/Lab $17.95 (978-0-7613-7526-5). Sixteen-year-old Kid, overcoming the loss of Felix who disappeared, establishes an important new relationship in Scout in this sexually ambiguous novel set among homeless young people in Brooklyn. e Lexile 760L (Rev: BL 9/1/11; HB 11–12/11; SLJ 9/1/11; VOYA 8/11)

1544 Brian, Kate. *Fake Boyfriend* (7–10). 2007, Simon & Schuster $16.99 (978-1-4169-1367-2). A fast-paced, humorous read about Vivi and Lane's efforts to help their friend Izzy, whose boyfriend has turned undependable just before the senior prom; they naturally turn to the Internet and MySpace. (Rev: SLJ 1/08)

1545 Brian, Kate. *Invitation Only* (9–12). Series: Private. 2006, Simon & Schuster paper $8.99 (978-1-4169-1874-5). Reed Brennan is pleased to win a scholarship to the privileged Easton Academy but finds navigating the social structure there challenging. (Rev: SLJ 1/07)

1546 Brian, Kate. *The V Club* (9–12). 2004, Simon & Schuster $14.95 (978-0-689-86704-0). Four members of the V (for Virginity) Club — formed by girls anxious to win a scholarship that will go to a candidate who exemplifies purity of soul, spirit, and body — confide their innermost thoughts as the competition intensifies. The paperback edition (2005) is titled *The Virginity Club*. (Rev: BCCB 6/04; BL 6/1–15/04; VOYA 8/04)

1547 Bridgers, Sue Ellen. *All We Know of Heaven* (10–12). 1996, Banks Channel $22.00 (978-0-9635967-4-1). For mature readers, this a shocking story, with finely drawn characters, about a love that eventually leads to betrayal, madness, and death. (Rev: BL 10/1/96; SLJ 1/97)

1548 Bridgers, Sue Ellen. *Keeping Christina* (7–10). 1998, Replica LB $29.95 (978-0-7351-0042-8). Annie takes sad newcomer Christina under her wing, but she turns out to be a liar and troublemaker, which creates conflicts with Annie's family, friends, and boyfriend. (Rev: BL 7/93; SLJ 7/93)

1549 Bridgers, Sue Ellen. *Permanent Connections* (8–12). 1998, Replica LB $29.95 (978-0-7351-0043-5). When Rob's behavior gets out of control, the teenager is sent to his uncle's farm to cool off. (Rev: BL 2/15/87; SLJ 3/87; VOYA 4/87)

1550 Briggs, Matt. *Shoot the Buffalo: A Novel* (10–12). 2005, Clear Cut paper $14.95 (978-0-9723234-7-5). This is the coming-of-age story of Aldous Bohm, who blames himself for the death of his sister when he was only 9; it is not until years later, when he has joined the army, that he begins to cope with this history. (Rev: SLJ 5/06)

1551 Brockett, D. A. *Stained Glass Rose* (10–12). 2002, Western Reflections paper $14.95 (978-1-890437-61-9). An elderly woman revisits the murder of a great friend and at the same time seeks to rekindle her bereaved grandson's interest in life. (Rev: VOYA 4/03)

1552 Brooks, Kevin. *Candy* (9–12). 2005, Scholastic $16.95 (978-0-439-68327-2). Joe, a fairly ordinary London teenager, finds himself drawn into a dark, new world after he loses his heart to a 16-year-old, drug-addicted prostitute named Candy. (Rev: BCCB 2/05; BL 2/1/05; SLJ 3/05; VOYA 4/05)

1553 Brooks, Kevin. *Kissing the Rain* (9–12). 2004, Scholastic $16.95 (978-0-439-57742-7). Moo, a fat, bullied British teen, witnesses a murder and finds himself torn between telling the truth and pleasing a cop who threatens to ruin Moo's father if he doesn't lie. (Rev: BL 2/15/04; SLJ 3/04; VOYA 4/04)

1554 Brooks, Martha. *Bone Dance* (9–12). 1997, Orchard LB $17.99 (978-0-531-33021-0). When Alex drives out to see the property her dead father has left her, she meets and becomes involved with Lonnie, stepson of the land's former owner. (Rev: BL 10/1/97; HBG 3/98; SLJ 11/97; VOYA 12/97)

1555 Brooks, Martha. *Traveling On into the Light* (7–12). 1994, Orchard LB $16.99 (978-0-531-08713-8). Stories about runaways, suicide, and desertion, featuring romantic, sensitive, and smart teenage outsiders. (Rev: BL 8/94; SLJ 8/94*; VOYA 10/94)

1556 Brooks, Martha. *True Confessions of a Heartless Girl* (9–12). 2003, Farrar $16.00 (978-0-374-37806-6). A pregnant teenager wreaks havoc in Pembina Lake, Canada, in this gritty novel. (Rev: BL 4/1/03; HB 5–6/03; HBG 10/03; SLJ 2/03; VOYA 6/03)

1557 Brown, Larry. *Joe* (9–12). 1991, Algonquin $19.95 (978-0-945575-61-0). Hard-drinking Joe helps turn around the life of a neglected teenager. (Rev: BL 8/91*)

1558 Browne, Jill Conner. *The Sweet Potato Queens' First Big Assed Novel* (11–12). 2007, Simon & Schuster $22.95 (978-0-7432-7827-0). This first novel by the author of the Sweet Potato Queens series of advice books explains how the queens met as unpopular high school students in 1968 and then follows them through their lives. (Rev: BL 11/15/06)

1559 Brugman, Alyssa. *Walking Naked* (7–12). 2002, Allen & Unwin $17.95 (978-1-86508-822-8). A tragic tale in which a member of a 10th-grade elite group finds peer pressure more important than her growing friendship with the class outcast. (Rev: BCCB 4/04; BL 2/1/04; HB 7–8/04; SLJ 7/04; VOYA 4/03)

1560 Bryant, Jen. *The Fortune of Carmen Navarro* (9–12). 2010, Knopf $16.99 (978-0-375-85759-1); LB $19.99 (978-0-375-95759-8). In this modern retelling of the opera set in Valley Forge, Pennsylvania, Carmen is a high school dropout hoping to become a famous singer and Ryan is a military cadet; the pair's friends seek to protect them when their mutual passion becomes evident. **e** (Rev: BL 12/1/10; SLJ 12/1/10)

1561 Brynie, Faith Hickman. *Someday This Pain Will Be Useful to You* (9–12). 2007, Farrar $16.00 (978-0-374-30989-3). Eighteen-year-old James, the well-read loner son of a much-married mother, tries to work out what he wants — from college, from personal relations, from life. (Rev: BL 9/1/07; SLJ 11/07)

1562 Buckhanon, Kalisha. *Conception* (9–12). 2008, St. Martin's $21.95 (978-0-312-33270-9). Hopes and questions arise from the spirit of the unborn child of 15-year-old Shivana who is dealing with decisions associated with an unwanted pregnancy. (Rev: BL 11/15/07)

1563 Bunting, Eve. *Doll Baby* (5–10). Illus. by Catherine Stock. 2000, Clarion $15.00 (978-0-395-93094-6). A simple, direct narrative in which 15-year-old Ellie explains how being pregnant and having a baby radically changed her life. (Rev: BL 11/1/00; HB 9–10/00; HBG 3/01; SLJ 10/00)

1564 Bunting, Eve. *If I Asked You, Would You Stay?* (8–10). 1984, HarperCollins LB $12.89 (978-0-397-32066-0). Two lonely people find comfort in love for each other.

1565 Burchill, Julie. *Sugar Rush* (10–12). 2005, HarperCollins LB $17.89 (978-0-06-077620-6). It is with trepidation that Kim leaves her privileged English school for a local one, but there she finds herself falling in love with Maria Sweet, a girl who wants to experience everything. (Rev: BL 9/1/05; SLJ 10/05; VOYA 6/05)

1566 Burd, Nick. *The Vast Fields of Ordinary* (9–12). 2009, Dial $16.99 (978-080373340-4). Dade, a gay teenager watching his parents move toward divorce, learns to be honest about his sexuality during the summer after his high school graduation. Stonewall Award 2010 . Lexile HL730L (Rev: BL 5/15/09; SLJ 6/1/09*; VOYA 10/09)

1567 Burgess, Melvin. *Doing It* (10–12). 2004, Henry Holt $15.95 (978-0-8050-7565-6). Three sex-obsessed teenage boys — Ben, Dino, and Jonathan — share with one another the joys, confusion, and heartbreak of their sexual exploits. (Rev: BL 6/1–15/04; HB 7–8/04; SLJ 6/04; VOYA 6/04)

1568 Burgess, Melvin. *Nicholas Dane* (9–12). 2010, Henry Holt $17.99 (978-0-8050-9203-5). When his mother dies of a heroin overdose, 14-year-old Nick ends up in an English boys' home where he experiences all kinds of horrors and abuse. (Rev: BL 11/1/10; SLJ 12/1/10)

1569 Bush, Penelope. *Alice in Time* (7–10). 2011, Holiday $17.95 (978-0-8234-2329-3). After falling from a merry-go-round, 14-year-old Alice wakes up in her 7-year-old body and gets a rare opportunity to reevaluate her life, her relationships with family members, and her own behavior. Lexile 830L (Rev: BL 4/1/11; SLJ 7/11)

1570 Cabot, Meg. *Pants on Fire* (8–12). 2007, HarperTempest $16.99 (978-0-06-088015-6). Katie, 16, is a bit loose with the truth, and a bit loose with the guys; when her former best friend Tommy — who exposed some cheaters in the past — returns to town she finds herself reviewing her behavior. ∩ (Rev: BL 5/1/07; SLJ 8/07)

1571 Calame, Don. *Swim the Fly* (9–12). 2009, Candlewick $16.99 (978-076364157-3). See a naked girl: This is the summer's goal for 15-year-old Matt and his friends Sean and Coop in this light and funny story that involves a lot of swimming. ∩ **e** Lexile HL620L (Rev: BL 3/15/09; SLJ 4/1/09; VOYA 8/09)

1572 Caletti, Deb. *The Nature of Jade* (9–12). 2007, Simon & Schuster $16.99 (978-1-4169-1005-3). Jade, 18, volunteers at the zoo in hopes of conquering her panic disorder and of meeting an attractive boy, who turns out to be a single father. (Rev: BCCB 2/07; BL 2/1/07; SLJ 5/07)

1573 Caletti, Deb. *The Queen of Everything* (8–12). 2002, Simon & Schuster paper $5.99 (978-0-7434-3684-7). Jordan's life is turned upside-down by her grandmother's death, her father's new romance, and her own sexual experimentation. (Rev: BCCB 1/03; BL 11/15/02; SLJ 11/02; VOYA 2/03)

1574 Camus, Albert. *The Fall* (10–12). Trans. by Justin O'Brien. 1957, Knopf paper $10.00 (978-0-679-72022-5). A challenging novel about a man who is trying to avoid judging himself through a life of inaction and evaluating others.

1575 Cantor, Jillian. *The Life of Glass* (7–12). 2010, HarperCollins $16.99 (978-0-06-168651-1). Melissa, 14, is still grieving for her father while she struggles to adjust to her mother's new beau, get along with her sister, and make sense of her feelings for her friend Ryan. **e** Lexile 860L (Rev: BL 12/15/09; SLJ 5/10; VOYA 6/10)

1576 Canty, Kevin. *Into the Great Wide Open* (11–12). 1997, Vintage paper $13.00 (978-0-679-77652-9). Kenny Kolodny, an unhappy, pot-smoking 17-year-old from a dysfunctional family finds comfort with Junie Williamson, a girl with her own troubles; for mature readers.

1577 Carr, Dennis, and Elise Carr. *Welcome to Wahoo* (8–11). 2006, Bloomsbury $16.95 (978-1-58234-696-0). Snooty socialite Victoria gets a taste of what it means to be an outsider when she is forced to transfer to a small-town high school in Nebraska. (Rev: BL 7/06; SLJ 6/06)

1578 Cart, Michael, ed. *How Beautiful the Ordinary: Twelve Stories of Identity* (11–12). 2009, HarperTeen $16.99 (978-0-06-115498-0). Twelve stories — by well-known authors including Ron Koertge, Francesca Lia Block, and Eric Shanower — explore diverse aspects of gay, lesbian, and transgender youth. (Rev: BL 10/15/09; SLJ 9/09; VOYA 12/09)

1579 Carter, Alden R. *Dogwolf* (7–10). 1994, Scholastic paper $13.95 (978-0-590-46741-4). In this coming-of-age novel, Pete realizes that a dogwolf that he's set free must be found and killed before it harms a human. (Rev: BL 1/1/95; SLJ 4/95; VOYA 2/95)

1580 Carter, Scott William. *The Last Great Getaway of the Water Balloon Boys* (8–11). 2010, Simon & Schuster $16.99 (978-1-4169-7156-6). Charlie, 16, unwisely renews a friendship with the wayward Jake and the two embark on a series of unfortunate adventures that involve theft, car racing, drug use, and violence. (Rev: BLO 4/1/10; LMC 5–6/10; SLJ 4/10)

1581 Cassidy, Anne. *Looking for JJ* (8–11). 2007, Harcourt $17.00 (978-0-15-206190-6). Alice was called Jennifer Jones during the disturbed childhood that came to an abrupt end when she murdered another child; now Alice, released from prison, hopes to lead a new life. ⌒ (Rev: BL 10/1/07; LMC 1/08; SLJ 10/07)

1582 Castellucci, Cecil. *Boy Proof* (7–10). 2005, Candlewick $15.99 (978-0-7636-2333-3). Sixteen-year-old Victoria, who prefers to be known as Egg, is smart, cool, and totally in control until Max Carter enters her life and breaks the shell. (Rev: BCCB 2/05; BL 2/15/05; HB 5–6/05; SLJ 4/05; VOYA 4/05)

1583 Castellucci, Cecil. *The Queen of Cool* (10–12). 2006, Candlewick $15.99 (978-0-7636-2720-1). At the age of 16, Libby suddenly finds she's bored with her life and her many friends and she signs up for an internship at the Los Angeles Zoo. (Rev: BL 2/15/06; SLJ 3/06)

1584 Chambers, Aidan. *NIK: Now I Know* (10–12). 1988, HarperCollins $13.95 (978-0-06-021208-7). Nik questions his religious beliefs but by a tortuous route recovers his faith. (Rev: BL 7/88; SLJ 8/88; VOYA 10/88)

1585 Chambers, Aidan. *Postcards from No Man's Land* (9–12). 2002, Dutton $19.99 (978-0-525-46863-9). A multilayered novel in which Jacob, grandson of a World War II soldier, experiences bewildering emotions

when he visits his grandfather's grave in Amsterdam. (Rev: BL 5/15/02; HB 7–8/02*; HBG 10/02; SLJ 7/02; VOYA 8/02)

1586 Chambers, Aidan. *This Is All: The Pillow Book of Cordelia Kenn* (9–12). 2006, Abrams $19.95 (978-0-8109-7060-1). Cordelia Kenn, 19, is pregnant and decides to write the story of her life to her unborn child, telling about her first love, her friends and family, her favorite teacher and mentor, her affair with an older man, and her frightening experience of being kidnapped. She also includes other jottings, lists, poetry and more to express her feelings and emotions. (Rev: BL 8/06; SLJ 11/06)

1587 Chan, Gillian. *Glory Days and Other Stories* (7–10). 1997, Kids Can $16.95 (978-1-55074-381-4). Five stories about young people at Elmwood High School, each of whom faces problems because of decisions that have been made. (Rev: BL 1/1–15/98; SLJ 10/97)

1588 Chan, Gillian. *Golden Girl and Other Stories* (7–10). 1997, Kids Can $14.95 (978-1-55074-385-2). Short stories about students in a high school, with details of their pleasures, pains, and concerns. (Rev: BL 9/15/97; SLJ 11/97)

1589 Chandler, Kristen. *Girls Don't Fly* (7–10). 2011, Viking $16.99 (978-067001331-9). After getting dumped by her boyfriend, Myra pours herself into cormorant research, hoping to win a trip to the Galapagos islands. ⌒ **e** Lexile HL590L (Rev: BL 10/15/11; HB 1–2/12; SLJ 1/12; VOYA 10/11)

1590 Chbosky, Stephen. *The Perks of Being a Wallflower* (9–12). 1999, MTV paper $12.00 (978-0-671-02734-6). In letter format, outsider Charlie writes about his freshman year in high school, his new, insightful, bohemian friends, his defiance of conformity, and his evolution into a man of action. (Rev: BL 2/15/99; SLJ 6/99; VOYA 12/99)

1591 Chin, Michael. *Free Throw* (7–12). 2001, PublishAmerica paper $24.95 (978-1-58851-166-9). Basketball and romance play major roles in the life of high school sophomore Mike Weaver. (Rev: VOYA 4/02)

1592 Choyce, Lesley. *Random* (9–12). 2011, Red Deer $12.95 (978-088995443-4). The title reflects the credo of Joe, 16, who is struggling to understand the meaning of life since the death of his parents four years earlier, and his realization that most of the people he is close to also feel angst. (Rev: BL 4/1/11; SLJ 6/11; VOYA 6/11)

1593 Christensen, Bryce. *Winning* (9–12). 2007, Whiskey Creek paper $12.95 (978-1-59374-797-8). Brad is a high-school football coach who must reevaluate his "winning is everything" philosophy in this well-written novel, narrated by Brad's uncle, David, who in his youth had to undergo a similar transformation. (Rev: BL 7/07)

1594 Clairday, Robynn. *Confessions of a Boyfriend Stealer* (8–11). 2005, Delacorte paper $7.95 (978-0-

385-73242-0). In entries from a blog, 16-year-old Gen, high school junior and aspiring documentary film-maker, describes her growing disillusion with her best friends CJ and Tasha. (Rev: BL 9/15/05; SLJ 9/05)

1595 Clark, Catherine. *The Alison Rules* (7–12). 2004, HarperCollins LB $16.89 (978-0-06-055981-6). Reeling from her mother's death, high school sophomore Alison retreats into herself and creates sets of rules to help her cope; the arrival of a new student called Patrick finally brings her out of her shell. (Rev: BL 10/15/04; SLJ 8/04; VOYA 12/04)

1596 Clark, Catherine. *Wurst Case Scenario* (10–12). 2001, HarperCollins LB $16.89 (978-0-06-029525-7). The sequel to *Truth or Dairy* chronicles the adventures of vegan Courtney in her freshman year at a small college in Wisconsin. (Rev: BL 9/1/01; HBG 10/02; SLJ 10/01; VOYA 12/01)

1597 Clarke, Judith. *Night Train* (8–11). 2000, Henry Holt $16.95 (978-0-8050-6151-2). Luke Leman, an Australian teenager, finds that he is cracking under scholastic and family pressures and thinks he might be going insane. (Rev: BCCB 5/00; BL 6/1–15/00; HBG 9/00; SLJ 5/00)

1598 Clayton, Colleen. *What Happens Next* (9–12). 2012, Little, Brown $17.99 (978-0-316-19868-4). Sixteen-year-old Cassidy "Sid" spirals downward after suffering a date rape, avoiding her friends and obsessing about her weight, until she meets Corey. ℮ (Rev: BL 10/15/12; HB 11–12/12; LMC 3–4/13; SLJ 10/12; VOYA 12/12)

1599 Clipston, Amy. *Roadside Assistance* (7–11). 2011, Zondervan paper $9.99 (978-0-310-71-981-6). Car lover Emily, 17, struggles with her loss of faith and feelings of inadequacy when her mother dies and she and her father move in with her wealthy aunt. ℮ (Rev: BL 5/1/11; SLJ 7/11; VOYA 6/11)

1600 Cohn, Rachel. *Pop Princess* (8–12). 2004, Simon & Schuster $15.95 (978-0-689-85205-3). Sixteen-year-old Wonder Blake has a wry understanding of the changes affecting her life when she is offered a recording contract. (Rev: BCCB 4/04; BL 1/1–15/04; SLJ 3/04; VOYA 8/04)

1601 Cohn, Rachel. *Shrimp* (9–12). 2005, Simon & Schuster $15.95 (978-0-689-86612-8). In this entertaining sequel to *Gingerbread* (2002), Cyd Charisse, just back in San Francisco after an exciting summer in New York City, determines to rekindle the romance with Shrimp, her former boyfriend and an avid surfer. (Rev: BCCB 2/05; BL 5/1/05; HB 3–4/05; SLJ 2/05; VOYA 6/05)

1602 Cohn, Rachel, and David Levithan. *Naomi and Ely's No Kiss List* (9–12). 2007, Knopf $16.99 (978-0-375-84440-9). The long-standing friendship between Naomi (girl) and Ely (boy) (both really good-looking) is put to the test when they become college freshmen and Naomi's boyfriend decides he'd prefer to be with Ely. (Rev: BL 8/07; SLJ 9/07)

1603 Colasanti, Susane. *Take Me There* (7–10). 2008, Viking $17.99 (978-0-670-06333-8). Three high school students in New York — Rhiannon, James, and Nicole — deal with family problems, school, and romantic entanglements in this compelling story told in three alternating narratives. (Rev: BL 8/08; SLJ 9/08)

1604 Colgan, Jenny. *The Boy I Loved Before* (11–12). 2005, St. Martin's paper $13.95 (978-0-312-33198-6). After wishing, at her best friend's wedding, the she could remake her life, 32-year-old Flora awakens the next day as a 16-year-old, with one month to make fresh choices — or revert to her adult life. (Rev: BL 2/15/05)

1605 Collier, Kristi. *Throwing Stones* (7–10). 2006, Henry Holt $16.95 (978-0-8050-7614-1). In the year 1923, Andy begins high school and dreams of being a basketball star like his late brother, hoping that it will help his parents cope with his death, but a bet could ruin his plan. (Rev: BL 9/1/06; SLJ 11/06)

1606 Collins, B. R. *The Traitor Game* (9–12). 2008, Bloomsbury $16.95 (978-159990261-6). When insecure underdog Michael's secret fantasy world is exposed to ridicule, he immediately blames his new friend, Francis, in this story that explores betrayal, bullying, and the paranoia of the bullied. Lexile 650L (Rev: BL 10/15/08*; LMC 8–9/08; SLJ 8/08; VOYA 10/08)

1607 Conroy, Pat. *The Lords of Discipline* (10–12). 1980, Bantam paper $7.99 (978-0-553-27136-2). An engrossing novel set in a military academy during the Vietnam War and involving four roommates and the fate of the institution's first black cadet.

1608 Conroy, Pat. *The Prince of Tides* (10–12). 1986, Houghton Mifflin $35.00 (978-0-395-35300-4). Tom, from the South Carolina tidewater areas, comes to New York to help his twin sister, a successful poet, who has attempted suicide. (Rev: SLJ 4/87)

1609 Cook, K. L. *The Girl from Charnelle* (9–12). 2006, Morrow $24.95 (978-0-06-082965-0). Sixteen-year-old Laura Tate narrates her story of entering adulthood in the 1960s, having to assume responsibility for the household after her mother abandons the family, and seeking some family secrets while generating some of her own. (Rev: BL 2/1/06; SLJ 6/06)

1610 Cooney, Caroline B. *Summer Nights* (7–12). 1992, Scholastic paper $3.25 (978-0-590-45786-6). At a farewell party, five high school girls look back on their school years and their friendship. (Rev: SLJ 1/89)

1611 Cormier, Robert. *Beyond the Chocolate War* (9–12). 1985, Dell paper $4.99 (978-0-440-90580-6). The misuse of power at Trinity High by Brother Leon and the secret society of Vigils is again explored in this sequel to *The Chocolate War* (1974). (Rev: BL 3/15/85; SLJ 4/85)

1612 Cormier, Robert. *The Chocolate War* (7–12). 1993, Dell paper $3.99 (978-0-440-90032-0). A chocolate sale in a boys' private school creates power struggles. Followed by *Beyond the Chocolate War.*

1613 Cormier, Robert. *The Rag and Bone Shop* (8–10). 2001, Delacorte $15.95 (978-0-385-72962-8). Shy, introverted 13-year-old Jason is a suspect in the murder of a 7-year-old girl in this dark and suspenseful story that features an ambitious and ruthless detective. (Rev: BCCB 12/01; BL 7/01; HB 11–12/01; HBG 3/02; SLJ 9/01; VOYA 10/01)

1614 Cormier, Robert. *Tunes for Bears to Dance To* (6–12). 1992, Dell paper $5.50 (978-0-440-21903-3). In a stark morality tale set in a Massachusetts town after World War II, Henry, 11, is tempted, corrupted, and redeemed. (Rev: BL 6/15/92; SLJ 9/92)

1615 Cormier, Robert. *We All Fall Down* (8–12). 1991, Dell paper $5.50 (978-0-440-21556-1). Random violence committed by four high school seniors is observed by the Avenger, who also witnesses the budding love affair of one of the victims of the attack. (Rev: BL 9/15/91*; SLJ 9/91*)

1616 Cox, Elizabeth. *Night Talk* (10–12). 1997, Graywolf $23.95 (978-1-55597-267-7). This story tells of the 40-year friendship, beginning in 1949, between an African American woman and her white female employer in Georgia and of a similar bond between their two daughters. (Rev: BL 10/15/97; SLJ 2/98)

1617 Cramer, W. Dale. *Levi's Will* (9–12). 2005, Bethany House paper $13.99 (978-0-7642-2995-4). Will Mullet, a young Amish man rejected by his father, leaves his Ohio home in 1943 and heads out on his own. (Rev: BL 6/1–15/05)

1618 Cronin, A. J. *The Citadel* (10–12). 1983, Little, Brown $16.95 (978-0-316-16158-9). An idealistic doctor finds he must battle with the establishment.

1619 Cronin, A. J. *The Keys of the Kingdom* (10–12). 1984, Little, Brown $16.45 (978-0-316-16189-3). An inspiring story about a young priest and his missionary work.

1620 Cross, Gillian. *Tightrope* (7–12). 1999, Holiday $16.95 (978-0-8234-1512-0). To take her mind off the hours she spends caring for her invalid mother, Ashley begins to hang out with a local street gang. (Rev: BCCB 12/99; BL 9/15/99; HBG 4/00; SLJ 10/99; VOYA 4/00)

1621 Crowe, Carole. *Waiting for Dolphins* (6–12). 2000, Boyds Mills $16.95 (978-1-56397-847-0). Still recovering from her father's death in a boating incident, Molly must also adjust to her mother's new love interest. (Rev: BL 3/1/00; HBG 9/00; SLJ 4/00; VOYA 6/00)

1622 Crutcher, Chris. *The Sledding Hill* (8–11). 2005, HarperCollins LB $17.89 (978-0-06-050244-7). Not even death can separate teenage friends Billy Bartholomew and Eddie Proffit in this thought-provoking novel that not only features author Crutcher but also a controversial novel called *Warren Peace.* (Rev: BL 5/1/05; SLJ 6/05; VOYA 6/05)

1623 Cumbie, Patricia. *Where People like Us Live* (7–12). 2008, HarperCollins $16.99 (978-0-06-137597-2). When her family moves to a depressed town in Wisconsin, Libby makes friends with a girl named Angie and soon discovers that Angie is being sexually abused by her stepfather. (Rev: BL 4/1/08; SLJ 6/08)

1624 Cupala, Holly. *Don't Breathe a Word* (10–12). 2012, HarperTeen $17.99 (978-006176669-5). Joy, 16 and suffering from severe asthma, flees from an abusive boyfriend and lives on the streets of Seattle. ℮ (Rev: BL 12/15/11; LMC 1–2/12*; VOYA 12/11)

1625 Danforth, Emily M. *The Miseducation of Cameron Post* (9–12). 2012, HarperCollins $17.99 (978-006202056-7). Gay teen Cameron Post is sent to a religious conversion therapy center in this coming of age story set in early 1990s Montana. ℮ Lexile 1120L (Rev: BL 12/15/11*; SLJ 3/12*; VOYA 12/11)

1626 Daoust, Jerry. *Waking Up Bees: Stories of Living Life's Questions* (7–12). 1999, Saint Mary's paper $6.95 (978-0-88489-527-5). In this collection of 10 short stories, young Christians find answers to life's dilemmas in their faith. (Rev: VOYA 4/00)

1627 Davidson, Dana. *Played* (9–12). 2005, Hyperion $16.99 (978-0-7868-3690-1). Ian Striver, a student at Cross High School, is challenged to get Kylie Winship to surrender her virginity and declare her love for him in three weeks or less. (Rev: BL 12/15/05; SLJ 6/06)

1628 Davis, Donald. *Thirteen Miles from Suncrest* (9–12). 1994, August House $22.95 (978-0-87483-379-9). The youngest child of a farm family comes of age in quaint Close Creek, North Carolina. This journal chronicles his life from 1910 to 1913. (Rev: BL 9/15/94; SLJ 1/95)

1629 Davis, Lane. *I Swear* (9–12). 2012, Simon & Schuster $16.99 (978-1-4424-3506-3). Leslie Gatlin commits suicide after being bullied by a group of vicious girls — and the teens responsible try to explain what motivated their behavior. ℮ Lexile HL730L (Rev: LMC 3–4/13; SLJ 10/12; VOYA 10/12)

1630 Davis, Tanita S. *A La Carte* (7–10). 2008, Knopf $15.99 (978-0-375-84815-5). African American high school senior Lainey hopes to become a celebrity vegetarian chef; when her best friend Simeon disappears with $500 of her money, Lainey is alone in the kitchen and with her thoughts. (Rev: BL 8/08)

1631 Davis, Will. *My Side of the Story* (10–12). 2007, Bloomsbury paper $14.95 (978-1-59691-294-6). With wry, honest humor, Jaz, a 16-year-old gay teen, relates the problems he encounters at school, at home, and in the pub. (Rev: BL 2/1/07)

1632 Dayton, Anne, and May Vanderbilt. *Emily Ever After* (9–12). 2005, WaterBrook paper $11.95 (978-1-4000-7042-8). Emily Hinton struggles to remain true to her Christian faith after she lands a job at a prestigious publishing company in New York City. (Rev: BL 5/1/05; SLJ 11/05)

1633 de la Cruz, Melissa. *The Au Pairs* (9–12). 2004, Simon & Schuster $14.95 (978-0-689-87066-8). Three girls from very different backgrounds spend their summer working as au pairs in New York's tony Hamptons, an experience that changes all three for the better. (Rev: BL 7/04; SLJ 6/04; VOYA 10/04)

1634 de la Cruz, Melissa. *Skinny-Dipping* (9–12). Series: The Au Pairs. 2005, Simon & Schuster $14.95 (978-1-4169-0382-6). In this sequel to the exploits of the three young ladies who like to party, *The Au Pairs* (2004), Mara is having second thoughts about dumping Ryan, who is now dating Eliza. (Rev: SLJ 7/05)

1635 de la Peña, Matt. *Mexican WhiteBoy* (9–12). 2008, Delacorte $15.99 (978-0-385-73310-6). Sixteen-year-old half-Mexican Danny Lopez searches for his identity while staying with his paternal Mexican family, and deals with a variety of issues, including his fear that he was responsible for his father's departure, an obsession with baseball, and a practice of cutting himself. (Rev: BL 8/08; SLJ 9/08)

1636 De Vries, Anke. *Bruises* (6–10). Trans. by Stacey Knecht. 1996, Front St $15.95 (978-1-886910-03-4). This novel, set in Holland, tells of the friendship between a sympathetic boy, Michael, and Judith, a disturbed, abused young girl. (Rev: BL 4/1/96; SLJ 6/96; VOYA 6/96)

1637 Dean, Carolee. *Comfort* (7–10). 2002, Houghton Mifflin $15.00 (978-0-618-13846-3). Fourteen-year-old Kenny persists in his dreams of making something of himself in spite of his mother's conflicting desires. (Rev: HBG 10/02; SLJ 3/02*; VOYA 4/02)

1638 Delaney, Mark. *Pepperland* (8–12). 2004, Peachtree $14.95 (978-1-56145-317-7). In this poignant coming-of-age novel set in 1980, 16-year-old Pamela Jean tries to cope with the pain of her mother's death from cancer. (Rev: BL 12/1/04; SLJ 11/04; VOYA 10/04)

1639 Deriso, Christine Hurley. . . . *Then I Met My Sister* (8–10). 2011, Flux paper $9.95 (978-0-7387-2-581-9). Summer learns important truths when she receives her dead sister Shannon's diary; it seems her sister wasn't as perfect as everyone thought. **e** Lexile HL680L (Rev: BL 5/1/11; SLJ 4/11; VOYA 4/11)

1640 Dessen, Sarah. *Dreamland* (8–10). 2000, Viking $16.99 (978-0-670-89122-1). After her sister runs away, Caitlin's life comes apart and she descends into drugs and sex. (Rev: BL 11/1/00*; HB 9–10/00; HBG 3/01; SLJ 9/00)

1641 Dessen, Sarah. *Just Listen* (8–11). 2006, Viking $17.99 (978-0-670-06105-1). Annabel is shunned by her friends after being seen in a compromising situation with her best friend's boyfriend. (Rev: BL 3/15/06; SLJ 5/06; VOYA 4/06)

1642 Dessen, Sarah. *Keeping the Moon* (6–10). 1999, Viking $17.99 (978-0-670-88549-7). Colie, a 15-year-old girl with little self-esteem, spends a summer with an eccentric aunt and finds a kind of salvation in a friendship with two waitresses and the love of a shy teenage artist. (Rev: BL 9/1/99; HBG 4/00; SLJ 9/99; VOYA 12/99)

1643 Dessen, Sarah. *Lock and Key* (8–12). 2008, Viking $18.99 (978-0-670-01088-2). After a life of experiencing abandonment, 17-year-old Ruby moves in with her older sister Cora and her husband, starts attending a private school, and slowly learns to trust others and make friends. (Rev: BL 2/1/08; SLJ 5/08)

1644 Dessen, Sarah. *Someone Like You* (7–12). 1998, Viking $17.99 (978-0-670-87778-2). Young Halley discovers that her best friend Scarlett is pregnant and Scarlett's boyfriend has been killed in an accident. (Rev: BL 5/15/98; HB 7–8/98; HBG 9/98; SLJ 6/98; VOYA 8/98)

1645 Dessen, Sarah. *That Summer* (7–12). 1996, Orchard LB $17.99 (978-0-531-08888-3). Haven is 15 and 5 feet 11, and to make matters worse, she has to be bridesmaid at her picture-perfect sister's wedding. (Rev: BL 10/15/96*; SLJ 10/96; VOYA 12/96)

1646 Douglas, Lola. *True Confessions of a Hollywood Starlet* (8–10). 2005, Penguin $16.99 (978-1-59514-035-7). Teen movie star Morgan Carter, on the mend from a drug overdose in Hollywood, adopts a new identity when she is sent to a midwestern high school in this credible and amusing novel. (Rev: BCCB 2/06; SLJ 12/05; VOYA 4/06)

1647 Dowd, Siobhan. *A Swift Pure Cry* (10–12). 2007, Random House $16.99 (978-0-385-75108-7). A 15-year-old girl hopes to hide her pregnancy from her family and her Irish village in this sometimes disturbing novel set in 1984 and based on a true story. (Rev: BCCB 6/07; BL 4/1/07; SLJ 4/07)

1648 Dower, Laura. *Rewind* (10–12). 2006, Scholastic paper $8.99 (978-0-439-70340-6). This novel starts with Cady's amazement when she sees Lucas slap Hope at the prom; complex flashbacks reveal more about the events of the previous six months and the underlying problems. (Rev: BL 2/15/06)

1649 Dragonwagon, Crescent, and Paul Zindel. *To Take a Dare* (9–12). 1982, HarperCollins $12.95 (978-0-06-026858-9). After three years of wandering, Chrysta must find herself.

1650 Draper, Sharon M. *Romiette and Julio* (6–10). 1999, Simon & Schuster $16.00 (978-0-689-82180-6). An updated version of Romeo and Juliet set in contemporary Cincinnati involving a Hispanic American boy, an African American girl, street gangs, and, in this case, a happy ending. (Rev: BL 9/15/99; HBG 4/00; SLJ 9/99; VOYA 12/99)

1651 Earls, Nick. *48 Shades of Brown* (10–12). 2004, Graphia paper $6.99 (978-0-618-45295-8). Smart and sensitive 16-year-old Dan, left in Australia in the care of his 22-year-old aunt when his parents move to Switzerland, finds himself increasingly obsessed with his aunt's roommate, Naomi. (Rev: BCCB 7–8/04; BL 7/04; HB 9–10/04; SLJ 6/04; VOYA 4/04)

1652 Eisen, Adrienne. *Making Scenes* (11–12). 2002, Alt-X paper $15.00 (978-0-9703517-0-8). In succeeding related chapters, a young college graduate describes her youth, her family, her bulimia, and her struggles with sex; for mature teens. (Rev: BL 3/1/02)

1653 Elderkin, Susan. *The Voices* (10–12). 2003, Grove $24.00 (978-0-8021-1757-1). In this gripping novel, the protagonist harks back to lessons he learned as a teen as he struggles to recover from a devastating and mysterious accident. (Rev: BL 9/15/03)

1654 Elkeles, Simone. *Leaving Paradise* (9–11). 2007, Flux paper $8.95 (978-0-7387-1018-1). This story is told in alternating points of view: that of Caleb, who went to prison for hitting and injuring Maggie in a car accident, and of Maggie herself. (Rev: BL 4/1/07; SLJ 7/07)

1655 Elliot, Jessie. *Girls Dinner Club* (11–12). 2005, HarperCollins LB $16.89 (978-0-06-059540-1). Three ethnically diverse Brooklyn high school students — Junie, Celia, and Danielle — get together weekly to cook dinner and discuss their latest romantic adventures; for mature readers. (Rev: BCCB 10/05; BL 3/1/05; SLJ 6/05; VOYA 10/05)

1656 Elliott, Stephen. *A Life Without Consequences* (10–12). 2001, MacAdam $25.00 (978-0-9673701-7-0). This is an explicit novel about Paul, a runaway from an abusive father, who lives in group homes beginning at age 14. (Rev: BL 8/01; SLJ 5/02)

1657 Emond, Stephen. *Happyface* (7–10). Illus. by author. 2010, Little, Brown $16.99 (978-0-316-04100-3). In this quirky journal-style offering, awkward, talented teen Happyface records his life — his painful past, his determination to make a fresh start, and the smile he wears to hide the truth. (Rev: LMC 11–12/09; SLJ 3/10; VOYA 6/10)

1658 Erian, Alicia. *Towelhead* (11–12). 2005, Simon & Schuster $22.00 (978-0-7432-4494-7). When her mother discovers that her boyfriend is abusing 13-year-old Jasira, she's sent to live with her Lebanese father, who seems repulsed by her puberty; when a neighbor sexually assaults her, she has nowhere to turn. For mature readers. (Rev: BL 2/15/05)

1659 Erlings, Fridrik. *Fish in the Sky* (9–12). Trans. from Icelandic by Bernard Scudder. 2012, Candlewick $16.99 (978-0-7636-5888-5). Josh Stephenson deals with everything from his parents' divorce to his first

dance, problems at school, and the arrival of his sexy 17-year-old cousin in the year after his 13th birthday. ⌒ 𝐞 (Rev: LMC 1–2/13*; SLJ 10/12)

1660 Esckilsen, Erik E. *The Last Mall Rat* (7–10). 2003, Houghton Mifflin $15.00 (978-0-618-23417-2). Bored and penniless, 15-year-old Mitch agrees to harass rude shoppers. (Rev: BL 4/1/03; HBG 4/04; SLJ 6/03; VOYA 6/03)

1661 Evans, Mari. *I'm Late: The Story of LaNeese and Moonlight and Alisha Who Didn't Have Anyone of Her Own* (7–12). Illus. by Varnette Honeywood. 2006, Just Us Bks $14.95 (978-1-933491-00-4). Using an authentic voice and effective line drawings, Evans interweaves stories about pregnancy, loneliness, and bad decisions as experienced by three African American teenagers and shows their growth as they learn to make better choices. (Rev: SLJ 7/06)

1662 Eyerly, Jeannette. *Someone to Love Me* (7–10). 1987, HarperCollins LB $11.89 (978-0-397-32206-0). An unpopular high school girl is seduced by the school's glamour boy and decides, when she finds she is pregnant, to keep the child. (Rev: BL 2/1/87; SLJ 4/87; VOYA 4/87)

1663 Fabry, Chris. *Almost Heaven* (11–12). 2010, Tyndale paper $13.99 (978-14143195-7-5). After losing his home, most of his family, and dedicated attention from his guardian angel, gifted mandolin player Billy fulfills himself by building a Christian radio station for his West Virginia valley; for mature readers. 𝐞 (Rev: BLO 10/1–15/10)

1664 Fehlbaum, Beth. *Courage in Patience* (11–12). 2008, Kunati $14.95 (978-160164156-4). Young teenager Ashley Asher narrates this distressing story of surviving sexual abuse; for mature teens. (Rev: BL 8/08)

1665 Fergus, Maureen. *Exploits of a Reluctant (but Extremely Goodlooking) Hero* (8–10). 2007, Kids Can $16.95 (978-1-55453-024-3). A nameless 13-year-old narrator records his comments on life on a tape recorder; this is a funny story about a self-centered kid who eventually learns a little about sensitivity. (Rev: HB 5–6/07; LMC 10/07; SLJ 4/07)

1666 Ferraro, Tina. *Top Ten Uses for an Unworn Prom Dress* (9–12). 2007, Delacorte $7.99 (978-0-385-73368-7). Nicolette buys a dress to go to the prom with Rascal Pasqual, but Rascal's former girlfriend returns to town and Rascal reneges, leaving Nicolette with a couple of problems. (Rev: SLJ 4/07)

1667 Ferrell, Monica. *The Answer Is Always Yes* (11–12). 2008, Dial $24.00 (978-0-385-33929-2). Underdog Matt suddenly and surprisingly becomes King of Club Kids when he's hired as a promoter in 1990s New York in this novel for mature teens. (Rev: BL 6/1–15/08*)

1668 Ferris, Jean. *Across the Grain* (8–12). 1993, Topeka LB $16.35 (978-0-7857-0723-3). Paige and his elder sister head to a community in the desert where they take jobs in a restaurant. (Rev: BL 11/15/90)

1669 Ferris, Jean. *Bad* (7–10). 1998, Farrar paper $4.95 (978-0-374-40475-8). Dallas gains self knowledge when she is sent to a women's correctional center for six months and meets gang members, drug dealers, a 14-year-old prostitute, and other unfortunates. (Rev: BL 10/1/98; SLJ 12/98; VOYA 2/99)

1670 Ferry, Charles. *A Fresh Start* (7–10). 1996, Proctor paper $8.95 (978-1-882792-18-4). This novel explores the problems of troubled teens in a summer-school program for young alcoholics. (Rev: SLJ 5/96; VOYA 10/96)

1671 Filichia, Peter. *What's in a Name?* (7–12). 1988, Avon paper $2.75 (978-0-380-75536-3). Rose is so unhappy with her foreign-sounding last name that she decides to change it. (Rev: BL 3/1/89; VOYA 4/89)

1672 Flack, Sophie. *Bunheads* (8–12). 2011, Little, Brown $17.99 (978-0-316-12653-3). Five years into her career with the Manhattan Ballet, 19-year-old Hannah begins to realize how much she's given up to be where she is, and meeting Jacob makes her question her sacrifices. **e** (Rev: BL 10/15/11; SLJ 10/1/11; VOYA 10/11)

1673 Fleischman, Paul. *Breakout* (9–12). 2003, Cricket $16.95 (978-0-8126-2696-4). Present and future are interwoven in the narratives of Del, a 17-year-old foster child whose bid for freedom is hampered by a giant traffic jam, and of Elena (Del eight years in the future), whose one-woman show features observations about life and freeway traffic. (Rev: BCCB 10/03; BL 12/15/03; HB 11–12/03; HBG 4/04; SLJ 9/03; VOYA 12/03)

1674 Fletcher, Christine. *Tallulah Falls* (8–11). 2006, Bloomsbury $16.95 (978-1-58234-662-5). At the age of 17, unhappy Tallulah (formerly known as Debbie) runs away from home looking for her older friend Maeve, who has bipolar disease and has left Oregon for Florida; on the way, Tallulah becomes stranded in Tennessee and finds a haven working in a veterinary clinic. (Rev: BL 4/1/06; SLJ 6/06)

1675 Flinn, Alex. *Breathing Underwater* (7–12). 2001, HarperCollins $18.99 (978-0-06-029198-3). In this harrowing account of domestic violence, the sins of the father are reflected in troubled teen Nick Andreas's savage treatment of his girlfriend, Caitlin. (Rev: BCCB 7–8/01; BL 8/01; HBG 10/01; SLJ 5/01; VOYA 6/01)

1676 Foer, Jonathan Safran. *Extremely Loud and Incredibly Close* (10–12). 2005, Houghton Mifflin $24.95 (978-0-618-32970-0). Delightful New Yorker Oskar, 9, inventively grapples with the 9/11 loss of his father while an intersecting story details his grandparents' survival of World War II Dresden, culminating in a novel celebrating triumph over great loss. (Rev: BL 2/1/05; SLJ 7/05)

1677 Foon, Dennis. *Double or Nothing* (6–12). 2000, Annick $17.95 (978-1-55037-627-2); paper $6.95 (978-1-55037-626-5). High school senior Kip feels secure that he has saved enough money for college until he meets King, a magician and con artist who takes advantage of Kip's love of gambling. (Rev: BL 8/00; HBG 9/00; SLJ 9/00)

1678 Ford, Michael Thomas. *Suicide Notes* (10–12). 2008, HarperTeen $16.99 (978-006073755-9); LB $17.89 (978-006073756-6). Sarcastic, flippant 15-year-old Jeff is forced out of denial about his sexuality after a suicide attempt lands him in a psychiatric hospital. **e** Lexile HL670L (Rev: BL 10/1/08; LMC 3–4/09; SLJ 2/1/09)

1679 Fowler, Therese. *Exposure* (11–12). 2011, Ballantine $25 (978-0-345-51553-7). Anthony and Amelia, 18 and 17, who come from very different backgrounds, find their relationship in big trouble — even with the law — when her father finds evidence of sexting; for mature readers. **e** (Rev: SLJ 6/11)

1680 Frame, Ronald. *The Lantern Bearers* (10–12). 2001, Counterpoint $24.00 (978-1-58243-155-0). A young boy soprano falls in love with a composer and then fakes a molestation story when the composer rejects him. (Rev: BL 10/15/01)

1681 Francis, Brian. *Fruit* (11–12). 2004, MacAdam $23.00 (978-1-931561-76-1). Peter, a young teen, struggles with body image (including mysteriously growing huge nipples) and his sexual identity before coming out of the closet in this appealing book suitable for mature readers. (Rev: BL 8/04)

1682 Franco, Betsy, ed. *Things I Have to Tell You: Poems and Writing by Teenage Girls* (7–12). Photos by Nina Nickles. 2001, Candlewick paper $8.99 (978-0-7636-1035-7). Teen girls reveal their aspirations, fears, and frustrations in this appealing collection of poems, stories, and essays. (Rev: BL 3/15/01; HB 5–6/01; HBG 10/01; SLJ 5/01; VOYA 10/01)

1683 Frank, Hillary. *I Can't Tell You* (9–12). 2004, Houghton Mifflin $16.00 (978-0-618-41202-0); paper $7.99 (978-0-618-49491-0). Jake swears off speaking after alienating his college roommate and best friend Sean in an argument about a girl, but he jots down his thoughts about life, love, and the agonies of adolescence on napkins and other scraps of paper. (Rev: BL 9/15/04; SLJ 12/04; VOYA 2/05)

1684 Fredericks, Mariah. *The True Meaning of Cleavage* (7–10). 2003, Simon & Schuster $15.95 (978-0-689-85092-9). High school freshman Jess describes her friend Sari's obsession with an older student in this novel of sexuality, betrayal, and self-image. (Rev: BCCB 3/03; BL 3/15/03*; HB 7–8/03; HBG 10/03; SLJ 2/03; VOYA 4/03)

1685 Freeman, Martha. *1,000 Reasons Never to Kiss a Boy* (7–10). 2007, Holiday $16.95 (978-0-8234-2044-

5). Sixteen-year-old Jane actually comes up with only 40+ reasons not to kiss boys before she gets over her first boyfriend and finds reasons to love and kiss again; a funny, light novel. (Rev: BL 8/07; SLJ 10/07)

1686 Freymann-Weyr, Garret. *My Heartbeat* (8–12). 2002, Houghton Mifflin $15.00 (978-0-618-14181-4). Fourteen-year-old Ellen is in love with James, but James and her older brother Link are also involved. (Rev: BCCB 5/02; BL 6/1–15/02; HB 5–6/02*; HBG 10/02; SLJ 4/02; VOYA 4/02)

1687 Friedman, Aimee. *French Kiss* (9–12). 2006, Scholastic paper $8.99 (978-0-439-79281-3). Worldly Alexa and her estranged friend Holly get back on track in Paris as Holly forgives Alexa's previous transgressions. (Rev: SLJ 7/06)

1688 Friel, Maeve. *Charlie's Story* (8–10). 1997, Peachtree $14.95 (978-0-561-45167-1). Charlie, who was abandoned by her mother as a child, now lives with her father in Ireland and, at age 14, is facing a group of bullies at school who accuse her of a theft and cause a terrible field hockey incident. (Rev: BL 1/1–15/98; VOYA 2/98)

1689 Friend, Natasha. *My Life in Black and White* (9–12). 2012, Viking $17.99 (978-067001303-6); paper $8.99 (978-067078494-3). Lexi must reevaluate her priorities when a car accident robs her of the beauty she has been accustomed to. (Rev: BL 6/12; SLJ 6/12; VOYA 6/12)

1690 Frizzell, Colin. *Chill* (7–10). 2006, Orca paper $8.95 (978-1-55143-507-7). Chill, a talented artist with a crippled leg, has a very low opinion of the new English teacher, Mr. Sfinkter, and shows this in a mural he paints at the front of the school; suitable for reluctant readers. (Rev: SLJ 3/07)

1691 Froese, Deborah. *Out of the Fire* (8–11). 2002, Sumach paper $7.95 (978-1-894549-09-7). Sixteen-year-old Dayle is badly burned at a riotous bonfire party and spends the painful months that follow reassessing her feelings about friends and family. (Rev: BL 7/02; SLJ 8/02)

1692 Frost, Helen. *Keesha's House* (6–10). 2003, Farrar $16.00 (978-0-374-34064-3). Keesha reaches out to other teens in trouble as they describe their problems in brief, poetic vignettes. (Rev: BL 3/1/03; HBG 10/03; SLJ 3/03*; VOYA 4/03)

1693 Fulton, John. *Retribution* (10–12). 2001, St. Martin's $23.00 (978-0-312-27680-5). These realistic short stories portray teenagers coping with situations and problems that required adult help. (Rev: BL 5/15/01)

1694 Furey, Leo. *The Long Run* (9–12). 2006, Shambhala $22.95 (978-1-59030-411-2). The rough-and-tumble lives of a group of spirited boys living at a grim Catholic orphanage in Newfoundland in the 1960s. (Rev: BL 9/1/06)

1695 Galante, Cecilia. *The Patron Saint of Butterflies* (6–10). 2008, Bloomsbury $16.95 (978-1-59990-249-4). Honey and Agnes are whisked away from the religious commune in which they have grown up and are amazed to discover the world that has always existed around them. (Rev: BL 4/15/08; SLJ 6/08)

1696 Gale, Emily. *Girl Out Loud* (7–10). 2012, Scholastic $17.99 (978-0-545-30438-2). Kass, a 15-year-old who is not pretty and has no particular talents, contends with her father's dramatic mood swings and desire for his daughter to be famous. e (Rev: BL 6/12; SLJ 7/12; VOYA 6/12)

1697 Gallagher, Liz. *The Opposite of Invisible* (8–10). 2008, Random House $15.99 (978-0-375-84152-1). Should Alice return the affections of popular, football-playing Simon or remain true to her friend Julian (Jewel), an artistic loner who also has feelings for her? ⌒ (Rev: BL 11/15/07; LMC 4–5/08; SLJ 5/08)

1698 Gallo, Donald R., ed. *Sixteen: Short Stories by Outstanding Writers for Young Adults* (9–12). 1984, Dell paper $5.50 (978-0-440-97757-5). This anthology of original short stories covers such subjects as friendship, love, and families.

1699 Garden, Nancy. *The Year They Burned the Books* (7–12). 1999, Farrar $17.00 (978-0-374-38667-2). High school senior Jamie Crawford's problems as editor of the school newspaper under attack by a right-wing group are compounded when she realizes that she is a lesbian and falling in love with Tessa, a new girl in school. (Rev: BL 8/99; HBG 4/00; SLJ 9/99; VOYA 12/99)

1700 Garfinkle, D. L. *Storky: How I Lost My Nickname and Won the Girl* (8–11). 2005, Penguin $16.99 (978-0-399-24284-7). In journal entries, 14-year-old Mike Pomerantz chronicles the troubles and unexpected joys of his first year in high school. (Rev: BCCB 5/05; BL 3/15/05; SLJ 3/05)

1701 Gayle, Mike. *My Legendary Girlfriend* (10–12). 2001, Broadway $21.95 (978-0-7679-0973-0); paper $12.95 (978-0-7679-0655-5). Everything Will has hoped and dreamed for has gone sour, and then he meets Kate, the previous renter of his apartment. (Rev: BL 6/1–15/02; SLJ 1/03)

1702 George, Madeleine. *The Difference between You and Me* (8–11). 2012, Viking $16.99 (978-067001128-5). Jesse, a 15-year-old lesbian and political activist, is having a secret relationship with Emily, who is student council vice president and dating a star football player; tensions rise as they take opposite sides on a new superstore. e Lexile 1020L (Rev: BL 3/15/12; HB 3–4/12; LMC 8–9/12; SLJ 6/12)

1703 Gervay, Susanne. *Butterflies* (8–11). 2011, Kane/Miller paper $6.99 (978-1-61067-043-2). Katherine, now nearly 18, was severely burned as a child and has undergone many surgeries; she has tried to live a normal life and questions whether one last operation will do the trick. Set in Australia. Lexile 540L (Rev: BLO 11/15/11; LMC 1–2/12; SLJ 11/1/11*)

1704 Gibson, Tanya Egan. *How to Buy a Love of Reading* (11–12). 2009, Dutton $25.95 (978-052595114-8). Set in an extremely competitive and wealthy community, this novel centers on stressed-out and "intellectually impoverished" 15-year-old Carley, whose parents decide to hire a live-in author to write a book for Carley; for mature readers. ⌒ (Rev: BL 4–5/09)

1705 Gilbert, Barbara Snow. *Broken Chords* (8–12). 1998, Front St $15.95 (978-1-886910-23-2). As she prepares for the piano competition that could lead to a place at Juilliard, Clara has doubts about the lifetime of sacrifice that a career in music would require. (Rev: BL 12/15/98; HB 11–12/98; HBG 3/99; SLJ 12/98; VOYA 2/99)

1706 Giles, Gail. *Right Behind You* (8–11). 2007, Little, Brown $15.99 (978-0-316-16636-2). Four years after killing a child by setting him on fire, 14-year-old Kip is released from a juvenile mental facility and must try to start over in a new place with a new name. (Rev: BL 10/15/07; LMC 1/08; SLJ 9/07)

1707 Gilmore, Susan Gregg. *Looking for Salvation at the Dairy Queen: A Novel* (11–12). 2008, Shaye Areheart $23.00 (978-0-307-39501-6). Catherine Grace Cline longs to get away from her small town in Georgia, but when she finally does escape she comes to recognize the benefits of Ringgold; for mature teens, this novel is set in the 1970s. (Rev: SLJ 3/08)

1708 Godden, Rumer. *An Episode of Sparrows* (7–10). 1993, Pan Books paper $16.95 (978-0-330-32779-4). In postwar London two waifs try to grow a secret garden. (Rev: SLJ 6/89)

1709 Goldblatt, Stacey. *Stray* (9–12). 2007, Delacorte $15.99 (978-0-385-73443-1). Sixteen-year-old dog lover Natalie is used to following her strict veterinarian mother's rules, but when a handsome intern named Carver comes to live with them, things change. (Rev: BL 5/1/07; SLJ 7/07)

1710 Goldman, Steven. *Two Parties, One Tux, and a Very Short Film About The Grapes of Wrath* (9–12). 2008, Bloomsbury $16.99 (978-1-59990-271-5). Realistic yet wildly funny, this is the story of high school student Mitchell and his friends and family. Lexile HL770L (Rev: SLJ 10/1/08*; VOYA 10/08)

1711 Goldstein, Jan. *All That Matters* (9–12). 2004, Hyperion $17.95 (978-1-4013-0110-1). After surviving a suicide attempt, Jennifer learns about life from her dying grandmother Gabby. (Rev: BL 9/1/04)

1712 Goobie, Beth. *Hello, Groin* (10–12). 2006, Orca $17.95 (978-1-55143-459-9). Sixteen-year-old Dylan is struggling to desire her boyfriend Cam and to deny her longings for her best friend Jocelyn and even for other girls; a library display is a catalyst in Dylan's acceptance of her sexuality. (Rev: SLJ 12/06)

1713 Goode, Laura. *Sister Mischief* (10–12). 2011, Candlewick $16.99 (978-0-7636-4640-0). Sixteen-year-old Jewish lesbian Esme falls in love with another member of her hip-hop group in this story set in conservative Holyhill, Minnesota. ℮ Lexile 850L (Rev: BL 6/1/11; SLJ 11/1/11*; VOYA 8/11)

1714 Goodman, Shawn. *Something Like Hope* (9–12). 2010, Delacorte $16.99 (978-0-385-73939-9); LB $19.99 (978-0-385-90786-6). African American Shavonne, 17, will soon be released from juvenile lock-up and must conquer her anger at her grim past and her current situation in order to succeed in the future. ℮ (Rev: BL 12/15/10*; SLJ 12/1/10)

1715 Grab, Daphne. *Alive and Well in Prague, New York* (7–10). 2008, HarperCollins $16.99 (978-0-06-125670-7). Matisse's father becomes ill and the family moves from Manhattan to a tiny town in upstate New York, resulting in culture shock and resentment until Matisse learns to appreciate her new school and surroundings. (Rev: BL 5/15/08; SLJ 6/08)

1716 Grace, Amanda. *But I Love Him* (8–12). 2011, Flux paper $9.95 (978-07387259-4-9). The compelling story of how A-student and track star Ann's life spirals downward after she falls for Connor, a young man with a troubled past. ℮ (Rev: BL 5/1/11; LMC 8–9/11; VOYA 4/11)

1717 Grant, Vicki. *Dead-End Job* (7–12). 2005, Orca paper $7.95 (978-1-55143-378-3). Frances finds her life coming apart at the seams after she meets an emotionally disturbed loner named Devin; suitable for reluctant readers. (Rev: SLJ 11/05)

1718 Grattan-Dominguez, Alejandro. *Breaking Even* (9–12). 1997, Arte Publico paper $11.95 (978-1-55885-213-6). This coming-of-age story set in the 1950s tells how 18-year-old Valentin Cooper, a Mexican American, leaves his family and pregnant girlfriend in their small West Texas town on a quest to find his father. (Rev: SLJ 4/98)

1719 Green, John. *An Abundance of Katherines* (9–12). 2006, Dutton $16.99 (978-0-525-47688-7). Colin Singleton, having just graduated and feeling like a fading child prodigy, has been dumped by his latest girlfriend named Katherine (coincidentally all of his girlfriends have had that name); his friend Hassan decides a road trip will cheer him up and they find themselves in Gutshot, Tennessee, where Colin works on a math theorem to prove the predictability of relationships and love. (Rev: BL 8/06; SLJ 9/06)

1720 Green, John. *Looking for Alaska* (9–12). 2005, Dutton $15.99 (978-0-525-47506-4). Sixteen-year-old Miles Halter leaves his home in Florida to attend an Alabama boarding school and is promptly entranced by a sexy but self-destructive girl named Alaska. Printz

Award, 2006. (Rev: BCCB 2/05*; HB 3–4/05; SLJ 2/05; VOYA 4/05)

1721 Green, John, and David Levithan. *Will Grayson, Will Grayson* (9–12). 2010, Dutton $17.99 (978-0-525-42158-0). The lives of two Will Graysons — one straight and one gay — intersect in this quirky and compelling novel that deals frankly with teen attractions and includes graphic language. Stonewall Honor 2011; YALSA Amazing Audiobooks Top Ten 2011; Odyssey Honor Recording 2011. ♫ **℮** Lexile 930L (Rev: BL 1/1–15/10*; HB 5=6/10; LMC 3–4/10; SLJ 3/10)

1722 Green, Julia. *Hunter's Heart* (9–12). 2007, Carolrhoda LB $16.95 (978-0-7613-9493-8). Simon, a 14-year-old loner obsessed with weapons, is tested emotionally when an older girl moves into the house next door. (Rev: LMC 10/07; SLJ 6/07)

1723 Greene, Constance C. *Monday I Love You* (7–10). 1988, HarperCollins $11.95 (978-0-06-022183-6). An overdeveloped bust is just one of the problems 15-year-old Grace faces. (Rev: BL 7/88; VOYA 8/88)

1724 Greenman, Catherine. *Hooked* (8–11). 2011, Delacorte $16.99 (978-0-385-74008-1); LB $19.99 (978-038590822-1). Thea's pregnancy brings new stress to her relationship with Will, which has survived his going to college and their moving in together. (Rev: BL 8/11; SLJ 10/1/11; VOYA 8/11)

1725 Greenway, Alice. *White Ghost Girls* (9–12). 2006, Grove paper $13.00 (978-0-8021-7018-7). Follows the sometimes dangerous activities of two teenage American sisters — Frankie and Kate, daughters of a war photographer who spends most of his time in Vietnam and of a mother who is absorbed in her painting — living in Hong Kong in 1967. (Rev: BL 11/15/05; SLJ 5/06)

1726 Griffin, Adele. *My Almost Epic Summer* (7–10). 2006, Penguin $15.99 (978-0-399-23784-3). Irene, 14, who is spending the summer babysitting, learns about friendship when she takes up with the beautiful and manipulative Starla. (Rev: BL 2/15/06; SLJ 4/06; VOYA 4/06)

1727 Grimes, Nikki. *Bronx Masquerade* (7–12). 2002, Dial $16.99 (978-0-8037-2569-0). Eighteen high school English students enjoy the weekly open-mike opportunity to express themselves in poetry and prose, revealing much about their lives and their maturing selves. (Rev: BCCB 3/02; BL 2/15/02; HB 3–4/02; HBG 10/02; SLJ 1/02; VOYA 2/02)

1728 Grisham, John. *A Painted House* (10–12). 2001, Doubleday $27.95 (978-0-385-50120-0). More a family story than a mystery, this Grisham novel tells about the problems of a 7-year-old boy growing up in rural Arkansas who is fearful of many things, including admitting that he has witnessed two vicious killings. (Rev: BL 2/1/01)

1729 Gurtler, Janet. *I'm Not Her* (9–12). 2011, Sourcebooks paper $9.99 (978-1-4022-5-636-3). Timid Tess feels inferior to her popular, beautiful, older sister Kristina, but when Kristina is diagnosed with bone cancer, Tess finds her own role within the family and her peers changing. **℮** (Rev: BL 6/1/11; SLJ 7/11; VOYA 8/11)

1730 Ha, Thu-Huong. *Hail Caesar* (10–12). 2007, Scholastic paper $7.99 (978-0-439-89026-7). John Miller, a high school senior and the "Caesar" of the title, meets his match in new student Eva, who, unlike every other girl in town, does not seem to be charmed by him; written by a teen. (Rev: BL 4/1/07; SLJ 5/07)

1731 Haddix, Margaret Peterson. *Just Ella* (7–12). 2008, Paw Prints $14.99 (978-1-4352-7937-7). The story of Cinderella after the ball, when she finds out that castle life with Prince Charming isn't all it's cut out to be, meets a social activist tutor, and rethinks her priorities in life; first published in 1999. (Rev: BL 9/1/99; SLJ 9/99; VOYA 12/99)

1732 Hale, Stephanie. *The Alpha Bet* (9–12). 2010, Flux paper $9.95 (978-0-7387-1574-2). Nerdy, sheltered science geek Grace starts her college career with a bang by pledging a sorority, but worries what will happen when the sisters find out she's only 16. **℮** Lexile 850L (Rev: BL 4/1/10; SLJ 5/10)

1733 Hall, Sarah. *The Electric Michelangelo* (9–12). 2005, HarperCollins paper $13.95 (978-0-06-081724-4). Trained as a tattoo artist in an English seaside town, Cyril Parks travels to America, sets up shop in Coney Island, and begins an unusual relationship with an enigmatic circus performer named Grace; for mature readers. (Rev: BL 10/15/05)

1734 Halpern, Julie. *Into the Wild Nerd Yonder* (9–12). 2009, Feiwel & Friends $16.99 (978-0-312-38252-0). With her old friends dabbling in partying and punk rock, Jess finds she has more in common with the "nerds," learning that true friendship transcends stereotypes. **℮** (Rev: BL 11/15/09; HB 11–12/09; SLJ 9/09)

1735 Halpin, Brendan. *How Ya Like Me Now* (7–10). 2007, Farrar $16.00 (978-0-374-33495-6). After his mom finally checks into rehab, Eddie moves to Boston to live with his aunt, uncle, and cousin Alex; there he deals with a totally new school and social environment and begins to blossom. (Rev: BL 5/1/07; SLJ 7/07)

1736 Hannah, Kristin. *Firefly Lane* (9–12). 2008, St. Martin's $23.95 (978-0-312-36408-3). Tully and Kate are followed from the beginning of their unlikely friendship through adulthood where Tully, the more independent and ambitious of the two, follows her goal toward a career as anchorwoman, obtaining jobs for both of them at a television station after which Kate is led to motherhood and Tully, to the ladder of success. (Rev: BL 12/15/07; SLJ 4/08)

1737 Hantz, Sara. *The Second Virginity of Suzy Green* (8–10). 2007, Llewellyn paper $9.95 (978-0-7387-1139-3). Suzy decides to turn over a new leaf when her sister dies and her family moves to a new town in

Australia, even joining her school's virginity club and befriending the good students. (Rev: BL 10/1/07; SLJ 12/07)

1738 Harazin, S. A. *Blood Brothers* (10–12). 2007, Delacorte $15.99 (978-0-385-73364-9). Seventeen-year-old Clay, who works as a medical technician, is astonished when his valedictorian friend Joey ends up on a respirator after overdosing on drugs. (Rev: BCCB 9/07; SLJ 11/07)

1739 Hardy, Mark. *Nothing Pink* (10–12). 2008, Front St $16.95 (978-193242524-6). Son of a Baptist minister, closeted gay Vincent, 15, finds himself between a rock and hard place when he falls in love with Robert. (Rev: BL 10/1/08; LMC 1–2/09; SLJ 3/1/09)

1740 Harmon, Michael. *Brutal* (9–12). 2009, Knopf $16.99 (978-037584099-9); LB $19.99 (978-037594099-6). Rebellious Poe, 16, is sent to live with a father she barely knows and makes friends with the outcasts at her new school. ∩ ℮ Lexile HL620L (Rev: BL 1/1–15/09; SLJ 6/1/09)

1741 Harrington, Hannah. *Speechless* (9–11). 2012, HarlequinTeen paper $9.99 (978-0-373-21-052-7). When her incessant gossiping catches up with her, Chelsea Knot takes a vow of silence. ℮ (Rev: BLO 9/15/12; SLJ 12/12; VOYA 10/12)

1742 Hartinger, Brent. *The Order of the Poison Oak* (7–10). 2005, HarperCollins LB $16.89 (978-0-06-056731-6). Anxious to escape the "gay kid" label, 16-year-old Russel Middlebrook and two of his friends sign up to be counselors at a summer camp for young burn victims; a sequel to *Geography Club* (2003). (Rev: BCCB 3/05; BL 1/1–15/05; SLJ 4/05; VOYA 4/05)

1743 Hartinger, Brent. *Split Screen: Attack of the Soul-Sucking Brain Zombies/Bride of the Soul-Sucking Brain Zombies* (9–12). 2007, HarperTempest $16.99 (978-0-06-082408-2). Using a two-books-in-one "flip" format with a casting call as the focus, Hartinger relates Russel's worries about coming out to his parents and Min's hopes that she'll find a new relationship (perhaps with Leah); an often humorous sequel to *Geography Club* (2003) and *The Order of the Poison Oak* (2005). (Rev: SLJ 3/07)

1744 Harvey-Fitzhenry, Alyxandra. *Waking* (7–10). 2006, Orca paper $8.95 (978-1-55143-489-6). Since her mother's suicide, 16-year old Beauty has withdrawn into herself, but a new classmate, Luna, manages to reach her and Beauty soon finds the confidence to paint again and to take hesitant steps toward love. (Rev: SLJ 7/06)

1745 Hassman, Tupelo. *Girlchild* (11–12). , Farrar $24 (978-037416257-3). Unhappy with life in a Reno trailer park with her bartender/alcoholic mother, Rory finds comfort in the library and the *Girl Scout Handbook*; for mature readers. Alex Award. ∩ ℮ (Rev: BL 2/1/12)

1746 Hawks, Robert. *The Twenty-Six Minutes* (6–10). 1988, Square One paper $4.95 (978-0-938961-03-1). Two teenage misfits join an anti-nuclear protest group. (Rev: SLJ 11/88; VOYA 4/89)

1747 Haworth-Attard, Barbara. *Theories of Relativity* (8–11). 2005, Henry Holt $16.95 (978-0-8050-7790-2). When his mother sends him packing to make room for her latest boyfriend, 16-year-old Dylan Wallace struggles to survive on the streets without resorting to a life of crime. (Rev: BL 11/1/05; SLJ 11/05; VOYA 2/06)

1748 Hazelgrove, William Elliot. *Ripples* (9–12). 1992, Pantonne paper $6.95 (978-0-9630052-9-8). Brenton, age 18, feels betrayed when his best friend steals his summer love. (Rev: BL 3/15/92)

1749 Head, Ann. *Mr. and Mrs. Bo Jo Jones* (7–12). 1973, Signet paper $4.99 (978-0-451-16319-6). The perennial favorite about two teenagers madly in love but unprepared for the responsibilities of parenthood.

1750 Hemphill, Stephanie. *Things Left Unsaid* (8–12). 2005, Hyperion $16.99 (978-0-7868-1850-1). In this powerful free-verse novel, good girl Sarah Lewis becomes bored with her predictable life and adopts defiant Robin's bad habits, until Robin attempts suicide and Sarah must review her priorities. (Rev: BCCB 7–8/05; BL 5/1/05; HB 5–6/05; SLJ 2/05; VOYA 10/04)

1751 Henson, Heather. *Making the Run* (9–12). 2002, HarperCollins LB $15.89 (978-0-06-029797-8). Unhappy with the restrictions of her small town, Lu turns to alcohol, drugs, and sex but is forced to confront her future when her best friend dies in a car crash. (Rev: BCCB 9/02; BL 4/15/02; HBG 10/02; SLJ 5/02; VOYA 8/02)

1752 Herbach, Geoff. *Stupid Fast* (8–11). 2011, Sourcebooks paper $9.99 (978-1-4022-5-630-1). Social outcast Felton's fortunes take a turn for the better when he discovers hitherto unimagined athletic ability, but problems do remain. ∩ ℮ Lexile 670L (Rev: BL 5/1/11; LMC 10/11; SLJ 8/11)

1753 Herrick, Steven. *Love, Ghosts, and Facial Hair* (9–12). 2004, Simon & Schuster paper $6.99 (978-0-689-86710-1). At age 16, Jack is an aspiring poet who falls in love with another soulful teenager, Annabel. Also use the sequel *A Place Like This* (2004). (Rev: BL 3/15/04*; SLJ 3/04; VOYA 6/04)

1754 Herrick, Steven. *The Wolf* (7–10). 2007, Front St $17.95 (978-1-932425-75-8). Sixteen-year-old Lucy, who lives in the shadow of her abusive father, and 15-year-old Jake, who comes from a loving household, find romance when they set out to discover whether the howling heard at night is a wolf or a dog. (Rev: BL 5/1/07; HB 5–6/07; SLJ 4/07*)

1755 High, Linda Oatman. *Planet Pregnancy* (7–12). 2008, Front St $16.95 (978-1-59078-584-3). Written in free verse, this is the story of 16-year-old Sahara, a teen from a small Texas town coping with pregnancy, her emotions, and the difficult decision she must make. (Rev: BL 8/08)

1756 Hills, Lia. *The Beginner's Guide to Living* (9–12). 2010, Farrar $16.99 (978-0-374-30659-5). Overwhelmed by his mother's death in an accident, 17-year-old Will feels isolated from his father and brother and is amazed to find himself falling hard for a girl called Taryn, who he met at the funeral. (Rev: BL 10/15/10; SLJ 12/1/10)

1757 Hite, Sid. *I'm Exploding Now* (8–12). 2007, Hyperion $16.99 (978-0-7868-3757-1). Sixteen-year-old Max Whooten is disgruntled with life until he travels from Manhattan to Woodstock to bury his cat on his aunt's property and there finds some interest in life; Max's diary entries are intense and often funny. (Rev: SLJ 11/07)

1758 Hobbs, Valerie. *Get It While It's Hot. Or Not* (9–12). 1996, Orchard LB $17.99 (978-0-531-08890-6). The pregnancy of her best friend forces Megan to rethink her relationships, particularly with boyfriend Joe, in a novel that also explores themes involving friendship, freedom of the press, and mother-daughter relations. (Rev: BL 10/15/96; SLJ 10/96; VOYA 12/96)

1759 Hobbs, Valerie. *Letting Go of Bobby James, Or How I Found My Self of Steam* (9–12). 2004, Farrar $16.00 (978-0-374-34384-2). Abandoned by her husband at a Florida gas station, 16-year-old Jody takes a job at a nearby diner and tries to make a better life for herself. (Rev: BL 7/04; SLJ 9/04)

1760 Hoffmann, Kerry Cohen. *Easy* (10–12). 2006, Simon & Schuster $15.95 (978-1-4169-1425-9). This is the story of Jessica, a 16-year-old girl who becomes sexually promiscuous as she copes with her parents' divorce; for mature readers. (Rev: BL 7/06; SLJ 8/06)

1761 Holeman, Linda. *Mercy's Birds* (6–10). 1998, Tundra paper $5.95 (978-0-88776-463-9). Fifteen-year-old Mercy lives a life of loneliness and hurt as she cares for a depressed mother and an alcoholic aunt while working after school in a flower shop. (Rev: BL 12/15/98; SLJ 3/99; VOYA 12/98)

1762 Holland, Isabelle. *The Man Without a Face* (7–10). 1972, HarperCollins paper $5.99 (978-0-06-447028-5). Charles's close relations with his reclusive tutor lead to a physical experience.

1763 Hopkins, Cathy. *Mates, Dates, and Cosmic Kisses* (6–10). 2003, Simon & Schuster paper $5.99 (978-0-689-85545-0). Teen anxieties about dating, friendship, and making decisions fill this funny novel about Izzy's attraction to a boy — and how her friends help her cope. (Rev: BL 2/1/03; SLJ 4/03)

1764 Hopkins, Cathy. *Mates, Dates, and Inflatable Bras* (6–10). 2003, Simon & Schuster paper $4.99 (978-0-689-85544-3). Lucy, 14, is concerned about her lack of development but, with the help of her friends, she is able to accept herself and even attract a cute boy. Other

titles in this series include *Mates, Dates, and Designer Divas* (2003). (Rev: BL 2/1/03; SLJ 4/03)

1765 Hopkins, Ellen. *Tricks* (10–12). 2009, Simon & Schuster $18.99 (978-1-4169-5007-3). Five unhappy teens, now prostitutes, grapple with their pasts and their identities as they navigate the high-stakes underbelly of Las Vegas; told in separate verse narratives. Lexile HL590L (Rev: BL 8/09; SLJ 10/09; VOYA 4/10)

1766 Hornby, Nick. *Slam* (9–12). 2007, Putnam $19.99 (978-0-399-25048-4). When skateboarding, Sam, 15, finds out he's going to be a father (and break his mother's heart), he turns to his sports hero TH, who gives him (imaginary?) insight into the future. ∩ (Rev: BCCB 12/07; BL 8/07*; SLJ 10/07)

1767 Horner, Emily. *A Love Story: Starring My Dead Best Friend* (9–12). 2010, Dial $16.99 (978-080373420-3). In the wake of her best friend's death, 17-year-old Cass copes with grief, confusion about her sexual identity, and a need to memorialize Julia. e (Rev: BL 6/10; HB 7–8/10; SLJ 7/10; VOYA 10/10)

1768 Howe, Norma. *Blue Avenger and the Theory of Everything* (8–10). Series: Blue Avenger. 2002, Cricket $17.95 (978-0-8126-2654-4). David Schumacher (a.k.a. Blue Avenger) faces a dilemma as he seeks to save his girlfriend from eviction. (Rev: BCCB 7–8/02; BL 5/15/02; HBG 3/03; SLJ 7/02; VOYA 12/02)

1769 Howe, Norma. *God, the Universe, and Hot Fudge Sundaes* (7–10). 1986, Avon paper $2.50 (978-0-380-70074-5). A 16-year-old girl would like to share her mother's born-again faith but can't.

1770 Howell, Simmone. *Notes from the Teenage Underground* (8–11). 2007, Bloomsbury $16.95 (978-1-58234-835-3). Gem, 17, sets out to make an original film but has problems with her friends and makes discoveries about herself along the way. (Rev: BL 6/1–15/07; SLJ 4/07)

1771 Howells, Amanda. *The Summer of Skinny Dipping* (8–12). 2010, Sourcebooks paper $8.99 (978-1-4022-3862-8). Mia, 16, feels out of place at her cousins' beach house in the Hamptons until she meets Simon, the boy next door. e Lexile HL740L (Rev: BL 5/1/10; SLJ 5/10)

1772 Hrdlitschka, Shelley. *Dancing Naked* (7–12). 2001, Orca $6.95 (978-1-55143-210-6). Finding herself pregnant after her first sexual encounter, 16-year-old Kia walks away from an abortion at the last minute and must draw on her inner strength to deal with the consequences of that decision. (Rev: BL 3/15/02; SLJ 3/02*)

1773 Hrdlitschka, Shelley. *Disconnected* (7–12). 1999, Orca paper $6.95 (978-1-55143-105-5). The lives of Tanner, a hockey-playing teen who has recurring dreams of trying to escape an underwater attacker, and Alex, a boy escaping his father's abuse, connect in a most unusual way. (Rev: BL 4/1/99; SLJ 6/99; VOYA 6/99)

1774 Hrdlitschka, Shelley. *Sister Wife* (9–12). 2008, Orca paper $12.95 (978-155143927-3). A 15-year-old girl born into a polygamist sect faces her impending arranged marriage to an older man as she struggles with her faith and typical teen desires. (Rev: BL 12/15/08; LMC 5–6/09; SLJ 4/1/09)

1775 Hubbard, Jenny. *Paper Covers Rock* (9–12). 2011, Delacorte $16.99 (978-0-385-74055-5); LB $19.99 (978-037598954-4). In 1982 North Carolina 16-year-old Alex faces difficult choices after a friend drowns and a fellow student, Glenn, urges him to act against the English teacher who may have witnessed the incident and who recognizes Alex's writing talent. ⌒ ℮ Lexile 920L (Rev: BL 7/11; HB 7–8/11; SLJ 6/11*)

1776 Hunter, Travis. *On the Come Up* (9–12). 2011, Kensington paper $9.95 (978-0-7582-4-252-5). Growing up in inner-city Atlanta, African American DeMarco opts for the comfort of juvenile detention until he realizes that his baby brother needs his help even as his twin sister Jasmine is facing problems from their mother's alcoholic boyfriend. ℮ (Rev: BL 12/1/11; SLJ 12/1/11)

1777 Hunter, Travis. *Two the Hard Way* (10–12). 2010, Kensington paper $9.95 (978-07582425-0-1). In his senior year of high school, Romeo struggles to stay straight and out of trouble in order to get out of the violent, impoverished Atlanta neighborhood where he grew up, even as he worries about his older brother Kwame, recently released from prison, and their beloved Nana. ℮ Lexile HL670L (Rev: BL 8/10)

1778 Hurley, Valerie. *St. Ursula's Girls Against the Atomic Bomb* (11–12). 2003, MacAdam $19.00 (978-1-931561-55-6). In this offbeat novel, 18-year-old Raine, who is more interested in changing the world than in her studies, develops a close relationship with her guidance counselor; for mature teens. (Rev: BL 11/15/03; VOYA 6/04)

1779 Huser, Glen. *Stitches* (7–10). 2003, Groundwood paper $9.95 (978-0-88899-578-0). Disfigured Chantelle and much-bullied Travis support each other through the difficult years of junior high school. (Rev: BCCB 2/04; HB 11–12/03*; HBG 4/04; SLJ 12/03; VOYA 4/04)

1780 Huser, Glen. *Touch of the Clown* (7–10). 1999, Groundwood $15.95 (978-0-88899-343-4). Neglected sisters Barbara and Livvy get a new lease on life when they meet the eccentric Cosmo, who runs a teen clown workshop. (Rev: SLJ 11/99; VOYA 10/99)

1781 *Into the Widening World: International Coming-of-Age Stories* (9–12). 1995, Persea paper $12.95 (978-0-89255-204-7). The innocence and daring of youth are elegantly captured in this anthology of brilliant voices from 22 countries. (Rev: BL 1/1/95; SLJ 8/95; VOYA 5/95)

1782 Iversen, Jeremy. *21* (10–12). 2005, Simon & Schuster paper $6.99 (978-0-689-87623-3). Bret recounts the excesses of his 21st birthday party — held at his fraternity — and details of his adolescent soul searching; for mature teens. (Rev: BCCB 4/05; BL 4/1/05; SLJ 4/05)

1783 Jackson, Sheneska. *Caught Up in the Rapture* (10–12). 1996, Simon & Schuster $21.00 (978-0-634-81487-7). Street life in South Central Los Angeles is the subject of this novel about Jazmine Deems, who wants to be a singer, and her gangsta-rapper boyfriend known as the X-Man. (Rev: SLJ 8/96)

1784 Jacoby, M. Ann. *Life After Genius* (11–12). 2008, Grand Central $24.99 (978-044619971-1). Math genius Mead is about graduate from college at the age of 18 when he decides not to continue and struggles to find life's meaning. (Rev: BL 9/15/08)

1785 Jahn-Clough, Lisa. *Me, Penelope* (8–10). 2007, Houghton Mifflin $16.00 (978-0-618-77366-4). Penelope (called Lopi) is trying to lose her virginity, and her good friend Toad helps her out while also helping Lopi make sense of her difficult past. (Rev: BL 4/1/07; HB 5–6/07; SLJ 7/07)

1786 James, Brian. *A Perfect World* (7–10). 2004, Scholastic $16.95 (978-0-439-67364-8). Haunted by the suicide of her father, Lacie Johnson follows mindlessly in the footsteps of her best friend Jenna, but when she meets Benji and falls in love, she realizes that Jenna is not a real friend at all. (Rev: BL 1/1–15/05; SLJ 1/05)

1787 Jimenez, Francisco. *Breaking Through* (6–12). 2001, Houghton Mifflin $16.00 (978-0-618-01173-5). In this sequel to *The Circuit: Stories from the Life of a Migrant Child* (2001), 14-year-old Francisco recounts his efforts to improve his lot in life and describes his school and romantic experiences. (Rev: BCCB 1/02; BL 9/1/01; HB 11–12/01; HBG 3/02; SLJ 9/01; VOYA 12/01)

1788 Johnson, Angela. *The First Part Last* (6–12). 2003, Simon & Schuster $15.95 (978-0-689-84922-0). Sixteen-year-old single-parent Bobby is overwhelmed and exhausted, but he loves his baby daughter. (Rev: BL 9/1/03*; HB 7–8/03; HBG 10/03; SLJ 6/03*; VOYA 6/03)

1789 Johnson, Angela. *Sweet, Hereafter* (8–11). 2010, Simon & Schuster $16.95 (978-0-689-87385-0). African American teen Shoogy (Sweet) has left her home and moved into a cabin with Curtis when the army summons him for another tour in Iraq, a prospect he cannot face; the final volume in the trilogy that began with *Heaven* (1998) and *The First Part Last* (2003). ℮ Lexile 750L (Rev: BL 12/1/09; HB 3–4/10; LMC 5–6/10; SLJ 1/10)

1790 Johnson, J. J. *The Theory of Everything* (9–12). 2012, Peachtree $16.95 (978-1-56145-623-9). A moving and multilayered story about 15-year-old Sarah and the turmoil in her life after the death of her best friend Jamie. Lexile HL560L (Rev: BLO 10/15/12; SLJ 10/12)

1791 Johnson, J. J. *This Girl Is Different* (9–12). 2011, Peachtree $16.95 (978-1-56145-578-2). After being home-schooled by her hippie mother, Evie decides to attend public school before heading to Cornell and challenges both the school and herself. Lexile HL530L (Rev: BL 5/1/11; SLJ 7/11)

1792 Johnson, Kathleen Jeffrie. *Parallel Universe of Liars* (10–12). 2002, Roaring Brook $15.95 (978-0-7316-1746-3). Lonely, overweight, and attuned to all the sex going on around her, 15-year-old Robin allows encounters with an adult neighbor and is drawn to a biracial boy called Tri. (Rev: BCCB 12/02; BL 9/15/02; HBG 3/03; LMC 1/03; SLJ 12/02; VOYA 12/02)

1793 Johnson, LouAnne. *Muchacho* (8–12). 2009, Knopf $15.99 (978-0-375-86117-8); LB $18.99 (978-0-375-96117-5). A serious girlfriend and his love of reading are two major factors in stopping Mexican American high school junior Eddie Corazon's slide into juvenile delinquency. YALSA Amazing Audiobooks Top Ten 2011. ♫ Lexile 1250L (Rev: LMC 11–12/09; SLJ 9/09; VOYA 12/09)

1794 Johnson, Varian. *My Life as a Rhombus* (10–12). 2008, Flux paper $9.95 (978-0-7387-1160-7). African American high school senior Rhonda learns that the girl she is tutoring is pregnant, bringing back memories of her own pregnancy and abortion at age 14. (Rev: BL 12/1/07)

1795 Johnson, Varian. *Saving Maddie* (10–12). 2010, Delacorte LB $19.99 (978-0-385-90708-8). College-age preacher's kid Maddie returns to her southern hometown where her rebellious ways and provocative clothes do not make her popular, but her childhood friend Joshua, son of a preacher, recognizes her unhappiness and stands by her. ℮ Lexile HL590L (Rev: BL 4/15/10; LMC 5–6/10; SLJ 2/10)

1796 Jones, Jada. *Holding Back* (6–10). Series: Juicy Central. 2012, Saddleback Educational paper $8.95 (978-16165177-5-5). This title in the series suitable for reluctant readers features African American Nishell, 16, who is conflicted about her longing for Jackson. Also in this series set in an inner-city high school is *Keepin' Her Man* (2012). ℮ Lexile HL350L (Rev: BL 4/1/12)

1797 Jones, Patrick. *Cheated* (7–12). 2008, Walker $16.95 (978-0-8027-9699-8). This disturbing story about a teenager surrounded by people who cheat — and worse— spirals downward into drunken violence. (Rev: BL 3/15/08; SLJ 4/08)

1798 Jones, Patrick. *Things Change* (8–11). 2004, Walker $16.95 (978-0-8027-8901-3). Johanna, age 16, has her first boyfriend, Paul, a disturbed boy, in this novel about dating, violence, and the problems of falling in love. (Rev: BL 5/1/04; SLJ 5/04; VOYA 6/04)

1799 Jonsberg, Barry. *Am I Right or Am I Right?* (7–10). 2007, Knopf $15.99 (978-0-375-83637-4). Calma, 16, has a lot to cope with: her friend Vanessa, who is being abused; her long-absent father's return; her mother's behavior; and her crush on the gorgeous Jason. The interesting format and Calma's humor lighten the drama. (Rev: BL 1/1–15/07; SLJ 2/07)

1800 Jordan, Dream. *Bad Boy* (9–12). 2012, St. Martin's/Griffin paper $9.99 (978-031254997-8). Foster child Kate, 15, contends with returning to a group home after a year with a happy family and is vulnerable to handsome Percy, missing the signs of impending abuse. ℮ (Rev: BLO 7/12; LMC 5–6/12)

1801 Joyce, Graham. *TWOC* (8–12). 2007, Viking $16.99 (978-0-670-06090-0). Matt's brother, who taught Matt how to steal cars (TWOC equals "take without consent"), dies in a car accident. When he appears as a ghost to Matt, Matt becomes so difficult that he is sent to a camp for troubled teens for a life-changing weekend. (Rev: BL 4/1/07; SLJ 3/07)

1802 Juby, Susan. *Alice, I Think* (8–12). 2003, HarperTempest LB $16.89 (978-0-06-051544-7). Alice, a quirky 15-year-old who has been homeschooled, enters public school and narrates in her diary all her new experiences. (Rev: BCCB 9/03; BL 8/03; HB 7–8/03; HBG 10/03; SLJ 7/03; VOYA 8/03)

1803 Juby, Susan. *Alice MacLeod, Realist at Last* (8–11). 2005, HarperCollins LB $16.89 (978-0-06-051550-8). It's an eventful summer for unconventional 16-year-old Alice McLeod, who breaks up with her boyfriend, gets and loses jobs, attracts three new male admirers, and sees her activist mom packed off to jail — all with dark good humor. (Rev: BL 4/15/05; HB 9–10/05; SLJ 9/05)

1804 Kantner, Seth. *Ordinary Wolves* (10–12). 2004, Milkweed $22.00 (978-1-57131-044-6). This is a coming-of-age novel about Cutuk's rocky road to adulthood growing up in an Alaskan wilderness with a back-to-the-land father and siblings. (Rev: BL 5/1/04*; SLJ 2/05)

1805 Kaplow, Robert. *Alessandra in Between* (8–12). 1992, HarperCollins LB $13.89 (978-0-06-023298-6). A young heroine has a lot on her mind, including her grandfather's deteriorating health, her friendships, and an unrequited love. (Rev: BL 9/15/92; SLJ 9/92)

1806 Kaplow, Robert. *Me and Orson Welles* (10–12). 2003, MacAdam $18.50 (978-1-931561-49-5). Set in the late 1930s, this is the entertaining story of a 17-year-old who manages to land a role in an Orson Welles play and learns a lot about life during the experience. (Rev: BL 9/1/03; SLJ 12/03; VOYA 4/04)

1807 Kaslik, Ibi. *Skinny* (10–12). 2006, Walker $16.95 (978-0-8027-9608-0). Giselle, the older daughter of immigrants from Hungary, is a recovering anorexic who also struggles with issues of sexuality, death, and self-esteem. (Rev: BL 12/15/06; LMC 2/07; SLJ 11/06)

1808 Katcher, Brian. *Almost Perfect* (9–12). 2009, Delacorte $17.99 (978-0-385-73664-0); LB $20.99 (978-0-385-90620-3). Eighteen-year-old high school senior

Logan is devastated when he learns that the new class-mate to whom he is attracted is actually a transgendered male who is in transition to become a female. Stonewall Award 2011 . **e** Lexile HL620L (Rev: BLO 12/8/09; SLJ 12/09; VOYA 2/10)

1809 Katcher, Brian. *Playing with Matches* (8–11). 2008, Delacorte $15.99 (978-0-385-73544-5). Katcher combines humor and a serious teen dilemma in this story of geeky 17-year-old Leon who gets involved with Melody, who bears facial scars resulting from an accident, but then drops her to date the popular Amy. (Rev: BL 8/08)

1810 Kehoe, Stasia Ward. *Audition* (7–11). 2011, Viking $17.99 (978-0-670-01319-7). Sara, 16, leaves her rural Vermont home to study ballet and becomes involved in an unfortunate affair with a dancer and choreographer; this coming-of-age novel offers many details of the world of dance. **e** (Rev: BL 11/1/11; SLJ 10/1/11; VOYA 10/11)

1811 Kennen, Ally. *Beast* (8–12). 2006, Scholastic $16.99 (978-0-439-86549-4). Stephen, 17, has faced many challenges — a criminal father, a series of foster families, arrest for theft and arson — and now he must rid himself of the huge crocodile his father gave him; this suspenseful novel full of dark humor is set in Britain. (Rev: LMC 2/07; SLJ 11/06)

1812 Kerr, M. E. *Gentlehands* (7–12). 1990, HarperCollins paper $5.99 (978-0-06-447067-4). Buddy Boyle wonders if the grandfather he has recently grown to love is really a Nazi war criminal in this novel set on the eastern tip of Long Island.

1813 Kerr, M. E. *Night Kites* (9–12). 1987, Harper-Trophy paper $5.99 (978-0-06-447035-3). Erick's life seems to be falling apart when he discovers that his older brother has AIDS and he unwillingly has an affair with his best friend's girlfriend. (Rev: BL 4/1/86; SLJ 5/86; VOYA 6/86)

1814 Kerr, M. E. *The Son of Someone Famous* (7–10). 1991, HarperCollins paper $3.95 (978-0-06-447069-8). In chapters alternately written by each, two teenagers in rural Vermont write about their friendship and their problems.

1815 Kerr, M. E. *What I Really Think of You* (7–10). 1982, HarperCollins $13.00 (978-0-06-023188-0); paper $3.50 (978-0-06-447062-9). The meeting of two teenagers who represent two kinds of religion — the evangelical mission and the TV pulpit. (Rev: BL 9/1/95)

1816 Ketchum, Liza. *Blue Coyote* (7–12). 1997, Simon & Schuster $16.00 (978-0-689-80790-9). High school junior Alex Beekman denies that he is gay, but, in time, he realizes the truth about himself. (Rev: BL 6/1–15/97; SLJ 5/97; VOYA 8/97)

1817 Kidd, Chip. *The Cheese Monkeys: A Novel in Two Semesters* (10–12). 2001, Scribner $24.00 (978-

0-7432-1492-6). This is an excellent novel about the first year of college during which the hero discovers the world of graphic design. (Rev: BL 9/1/01*)

1818 Kincaid, Nanci. *As Hot as It Was You Ought to Thank Me* (9–12). 2005, Little, Brown paper $12.95 (978-0-316-00914-0). When Berry Jackson's father vanishes from Pinetta, Florida, one searing summer, her very identity as "the principal's daughter" seems endangered; Berry's wry narration reveals strong, quirky characters and her own resilience. (Rev: BL 12/15/04)

1819 King, A. S. *Ask the Passengers* (9–12). 2012, Little, Brown $17.99 (978-0-316-19468-6). High school senior Astrid rebels against the narrow-minded strictures of her small Pennsylvania town and her inattentive parents and shares her excess love with passengers on planes overhead even as she questions her own sexuality. 🎧 **e** Lexile HL630L (Rev: BL 9/15/12*; HB 1–2/13; LMC 3–4/13; SLJ 10/12*; VOYA 10/12)

1820 King, A. S. *Everybody Sees the Ants* (9–12). 2011, Little, Brown $17.99 (978-0-316-12928-2). Lucky Lindeman,15, finds solace in thinking about his grandfather, MIA since the Vietnam War, as he deals with constant bullying and adult lack of understanding. YALSA Top Ten Best Fiction for Young Adults 2012. **e** Lexile HL710L (Rev: BL 8/11*; HB 1–2/12; LMC 1–2/12; SLJ 10/1/11*)

1821 Kingsolver, Barbara. *The Bean Trees. 10th Anniversary ed.* (10–12). 1997, HarperFlamingo $19.95 (978-0-06-017579-5); paper $7.99 (978-0-06-109731-7). A poor young woman, heading west from her home, adopts a 2-year-old Cherokee girl and makes friends with an unusual widow.

1822 Kizer, Amber. *Seven Kinds of Ordinary Catastrophes* (10–12). 2011, Delacorte $16.99 (978-0-385-73432-5). Gert Garibaldi, 16, tackles such vexing questions as school, family, friends, jobs, and sex — how? who with? when? — in this sassy sequel to *One Butt Cheek at a Time* (2008). **e** (Rev: BLO 6/15/11; SLJ 2/1/09)

1823 Klass, David. *Home of the Braves* (8–12). 2002, Farrar $18.00 (978-0-374-39963-4). Joe's plans for his senior year in high school are changed by the arrival of a Brazilian student who threatens Joe's position as soccer star and steals his would-be girlfriend too. (Rev: BCCB 12/02; BL 9/1/02; HB 1–2/03; HBG 3/03; SLJ 9/02)

1824 Klauss, Lucas. *Everything You Need to Survive the Apocalypse* (9–12). 2012, Simon & Schuster $16.99 (978-144242388-6). Fifteen-year-old Phillip's certainties about life evaporate when he meets Evangelical Christian Rebekah. **e** Lexile HL510L (Rev: BL 2/15/12*; LMC 5–6/12; SLJ 1/12; VOYA 12/11)

1825 Knowles, Jo. *Jumping Off Swings* (9–12). 2009, Candlewick $16.99 (978-076363949-5). In alternating narratives, this novel describes the repercussions of a single sexual encounter that leaves Ellie pregnant. (Rev: BL 7/09; SLJ 8/09)

1826 Knowles, John. *Peace Breaks Out* (10–12). 1997, Bantam paper $5.99 (978-0-553-27574-2). During the 1945-46 school year a former student who is suffering from wartime trauma returns to his private prep school as a teacher. A sequel to *A Separate Peace.*

1827 Koertge, Ron. *The Arizona Kid* (8–12). 1989, Avon paper $3.99 (978-0-380-70776-8). Teenage Billy discovers that his uncle Wes is gay and learns about rodeos as well as the nature of love when he meets an outspoken girl named Cara. (Rev: BL 5/1/88; SLJ 6/88; VOYA 10/88)

1828 Koertge, Ron. *Boy Girl Boy* (8–11). 2005, Harcourt $16.00 (978-0-15-205325-3). Longtime friends Elliot, Teresa, and Larry find that their lives and their relationships change dramatically with high school graduation. (Rev: BL 9/1/05*; VOYA 12/05)

1829 Koja, Kathe. *Buddha Boy* (6–10). 2003, Farrar $16.00 (978-0-374-30998-5). Justin is intrigued by "Buddha Boy," a new student whose appearance and beliefs make him the target of bullies. (Rev: BL 2/15/03; HB 5–6/03; HBG 10/03; SLJ 2/03; VOYA 4/03)

1830 Koja, Kathe. *Headlong* (9–12). 2008, Farrar $16.95 (978-037432912-9). When punk rocker Hazel transfers to Lily's upscale, preppy boarding school, it forces Lily to see her school — and her life of privilege — in a new light. Lexile 920L (Rev: BL 11/15/08; SLJ 11/1/08; VOYA 8/08)

1831 Koja, Kathe. *Kissing the Bee* (9–12). 2007, Farrar $16.00 (978-0-374-39938-2). Dana loves Emil, who is dating Dana's best friend Avra, in this emotional story interwoven with Dana's research into the behavior of bees for her senior science project. (Rev: BL 9/15/07; SLJ 12/07)

1832 Koja, Kathe. *Straydog* (7–10). 2002, Farrar $16.00 (978-0-374-37278-1). Rachel, a lonely teenager who enjoys writing, is devastated when her favorite dog at the animal shelter is put to sleep, and her anger affects the people closest to her. (Rev: BL 4/15/02; HB 5–6/02; HBG 10/02; SLJ 4/02; VOYA 6/02)

1833 Korman, Gordon. *The Juvie Three* (7–10). 2008, Hyperion $15.99 (978-142310158-1). Troubled kids Terence, Arjay, and Gecko are given a second chance by a kindhearted social worker named Doug; when Doug ends up comatose the three band together to conceal his absence from the authorities. ∩ Lexile NC730L (Rev: BL 11/15/08; LMC 1–2/09; SLJ 12/08; VOYA 10/08)

1834 Kramon, Justin. *Finny* (10–12). 2010, Random House paper $15 (978-08129802-3-3). In this plucky coming-of-age story, we follow willful, independent Delphine (aka Finny) from age 14 to her mid-30s, watching episodes in her life — sometimes happy, sometimes hard — unfold. ℮ (Rev: BL 4/1–15/10)

1835 Krinsky, Natalie. *Chloe Does Yale* (11–12). 2005, Hyperion $19.95 (978-1-4013-0107-1). Based on the author's personal experiences, this novel introduces Chloe Carrington, a Yale senior who writes a sex advice column for the school newspaper; for mature teens. (Rev: BL 2/1/05)

1836 Kuehnert, Stephanie. *Ballads of Suburbia* (11–12). 2009, Pocket paper $13 (978-14391028-2-4). Troubled teens find solace in drugs, alcohol, self-abuse, music, and each other in this gripping and realistic novel suitable for mature readers. ℮ (Rev: BL 7/09)

1837 Kurland, Morton L. *Our Sacred Honor* (7–12). 1987, Rosen LB $12.95 (978-0-8239-0692-5). A story from two points of view about a pregnant teenage girl, her boyfriend, and their decision for abortion. (Rev: SLJ 6/87)

1838 Kyi, Tanya Lloyd. *My Time as Caz Hazard* (8–12). 2004, Orca paper $7.95 (978-1-55143-319-6). Caz Hazard — who faces problems at home and at school — strikes up a friendship with Amanda and is drawn into a series of antisocial activities, one of which leads to the suicide of a classmate. (Rev: SLJ 3/05; VOYA 2/05)

1839 LaCour, Nina. *Hold Still* (9–12). 2009, Dutton $17.99 (978-0-525-42155-9). After her best friend commits suicide, Caitlin comes to terms with this devastating act through reading her friend's diary and finding comfort in new friends. ∩ ℮ Lexile HL770L (Rev: BL 10/15/09; LMC 1–2/10; ∩ SLJ 12/09)

1840 Lamott, Anne. *Imperfect Birds* (11–12). 2010, Riverhead $25.95 (978-159448751-4). In this stirring novel of redemption and unconditional love, 17-year-old Rosie Ferguson lives in a world of sex, lies, and substance abuse until she hits rock bottom and both she and her parents must face the fact that Rosie needs serious help. ∩ ℮ (Rev: BL 2/1–15/10)

1841 Lane, Dakota. *The Orpheus Obsession* (10–12). 2005, HarperCollins LB $17.89 (978-0-06-074174-7). Anooshka Stargirl, who leads a pretty bleak life in a small New York town with her unstable mother, becomes obsessed with a 21-year-old singer named Orpheus. (Rev: BL 9/15/05; SLJ 9/05; VOYA 10/05)

1842 Larimer, Tamela. *Buck* (7–10). 1986, Avon paper $2.50 (978-0-380-75172-3). The friendship between runaway Buck and Rich is threatened when Buck becomes friendly with Rich's girlfriend. (Rev: BL 4/87; SLJ 6/87; VOYA 4/87)

1843 LaRochelle, David. *Absolutely, Positively Not* (7–10). 2005, Scholastic $16.95 (978-0-439-59109-6). A funny and sensitive first-person portrayal of a 16-year-old's efforts to deny his homosexuality. (Rev: BL 7/05*; SLJ 9/05; VOYA 10/05)

1844 Laser, Michael. *Cheater* (7–10). 2008, Dutton $16.99 (978-0-525-47826-3). When Karl is drawn into a secret cheating ring at his high school, he is found out by the evil assistant principal and faces challenges to his morality from all sides. (Rev: BL 3/1/08; SLJ 5/08)

1845 Le Guin, Ursula K. *Very Far Away from Anywhere Else* (7–10). 2004, Harcourt paper $6.95 (978-0-15-205208-9). In his friendship for Natalie, Owen finds the fulfillment he seeks; first published in 1976.

1846 Leavitt, Martine. *My Book of Life by Angel* (9–12). 2012, Farrar $17.99 (978-0-374-35123-6). Angel, 16, becomes determined to escape her life of drugs and prostitution in this novel in verse set in Vancouver. **e** Lexile 990L (Rev: BL 10/1/12*; HB 11–12/12; LMC 1–2/13; SLJ 10/12*; VOYA 10/12)

1847 Lehrman, Robert. *Juggling* (10–12). 1982, Harper-Collins $11.50 (978-0-06-023818-6). An explicit novel about a teenager and his love for soccer and his first sexual encounters. (Rev: BL 3/87)

1848 Leitch, Will. *Catch* (9–12). 2005, Razorbill paper $7.99 (978-1-59514-069-2). For Tim Temples, the summer after high school graduation — featuring a boring job, a romance with an older woman, and his older brother's mysterious decline — turns out to be a time for rethinking his future. (Rev: BCCB 11/05; BL 12/1/05; SLJ 11/05; VOYA 12/05)

1849 Lenhard, Elizabeth. *Chicks with Sticks (Knitwise)* (7–10). Series: Chicks with Sticks. 2007, Dutton $16.99 (978-0-525-47838-6). Now in their final year of high school (and in the final book of the series), the knitting friends must deal with family problems and plans for the future; includes four knitting projects. (Rev: BL 11/1/07; SLJ 12/07)

1850 Leon, Peggy. *Mother Country* (10–12). 2003, Permanent $26.00 (978-1-57962-095-0). After the death of her grandmother, 13-year-old orphan Mala falls under the care of her Serbian American extended family in the small copper mining town of Taylor, Nevada, circa 1950. (Rev: BL 11/15/03)

1851 Les Becquets, Diane. *Love, Cajun Style* (8–11). 2005, Bloomsbury $16.95 (978-1-58234-674-8). Romance seems to be in the air in Lucy Beauregard's Louisiana town, spicing her interest in Dewey, son of the artist who has just opened an art gallery. (Rev: BL 9/15/05*; SLJ 10/05; VOYA 10/05)

1852 Lester, Joan Steinau. *Black, White, Other: In Search of Nina Armstrong* (7–10). 2011, Zondervan $15.99 (978-0-310-72763-7). Nina, 15, learns about her great-great-grandmother's escape from slavery even as she herself struggles with her multiracial background and her parents' divorce. **e** (Rev: BL 10/15/11; SLJ 12/1/11; VOYA 8/11)

1853 Letts, Billie. *The Honk and Holler Opening Soon* (10–12). 1998, Warner $22.00 (978-0-446-52158-1). A story of love, hope, and humanity revolving around Caney Paxton, a crippled Vietnam veteran, and a cast of memorable characters he attracts at his restaurant in rural Oklahoma. (Rev: BL 5/1/98; SLJ 1/99)

1854 Leveen, Tom. *Party* (9–12). 2010, Random House $16.99 (978-0-375-86436-0); LB $19.99 (978-0-375-96436-7). In multiple narratives, 11 teens describe their experiences at an end-of-the-year party that involves drinking, sex, a fight, and generally wild behavior. **e** (Rev: BL 5/1/10; SLJ 4/10; VOYA 8/10)

1855 Levithan, David. *The Realm of Possibility* (9–12). 2004, Random House LB $17.99 (978-0-375-82845-4). In this appealing but challenging free-verse novel, students at the same high school tell of their relationships, heartaches, goals, and triumphs in a series of interconnected stories. (Rev: BL 9/1/04; SLJ 9/04; VOYA 8/04)

1856 Levithan, David, and Daniel Ehrenhaft, eds. *21 Proms* (9–12). 2007, Scholastic paper $8.99 (978-0-439-89029-8). Proms of all kinds — from the very good to the amazingly bad, some featuring the supernatural and others swank banquets — are portrayed in this collection of 21 stories by well-known authors. (Rev: BCCB 7–8/07; LMC 10/07; SLJ 5/07)

1857 Lieberman, Leanne. *Gravity* (10–12). 2008, Orca paper $12.95 (978-155469049-7). Fifteen-year-old Orthodox Jew Ellie struggles with faith, family dysfunction, and her growing attraction to Lindsay in this coming-of-age story. **e** Lexile 680L (Rev: BL 10/1/08; SLJ 4/1/09; VOYA 12/08)

1858 Lin, Ed. *Waylaid* (11–12). 2002, Kaya paper $12.95 (978-1-885030-32-0). Brought up in a seedy New Jersey motel, the son of Taiwanese immigrants observes life and plans for sexual experiences; for mature teens. (Rev: BL 8/02*)

1859 Linker, Julie. *Disenchanted Princess* (8–10). 2007, Simon & Schuster paper $8.99 (978-1-4169-3472-1). West's father is in prison and West is sent from her ritzy life in Beverly Hills to remote Possum Grape, Arkansas, to live with her aunt's family. (Rev: BL 7/07; SLJ 8/07)

1860 Lion, Melissa. *Upstream* (9–12). 2005, Random House LB $17.99 (978-0-385-70877-7). Amid the rich natural beauty of her home in Alaska, Marty has been blinded to almost everything by the death of her boyfriend, but a new friendship with Katherine helps Marty to confront the truth about the tragedy. (Rev: BL 6/1–15/05; SLJ 7/05; VOYA 6/05)

1861 Lisle, Janet Taylor. *Sirens and Spies* (7–10). 2003, Aladdin paper $4.99 (978-0-689-84457-7). Elsie discovers that her beloved music teacher, originally from France, was an accused collaborator who had a child by a German soldier; originally published in 1985. (Rev: BL 5/15/85; SLJ 8/85; VOYA 12/85)

1862 Littke, Lael. *Loydene in Love* (8–10). 1986, Harcourt $13.95 (978-0-15-249888-7). A high school junior from a small town gets a different view of life when she visits Los Angeles for the summer. (Rev: BL 2/15/87; SLJ 3/87)

1863 Littman, Sarah Darer. *Want to Go Private?* (7–10). 2011, Scholastic $17.99 (978-0-545-15146-7). Shy, insecure Abby retreats to Chezteen.com for solace, and there meets the attractive and sexy Luke; this cautionary tale contains graphic sexual emails. ℮ Lexile HL750L (Rev: BL 9/15/11; SLJ 11/1/11)

1864 Lockhart, E. *The Boyfriend List* (8–11). 2005, Delacorte LB $17.99 (978-0-385-90238-0). After her disastrous social life triggers a series of panic attacks, 15-year-old Ruby consults a psychiatrist. (Rev: BCCB 3/05; BL 4/1/05; SLJ 4/05)

1865 Lockhart, E. *Dramarama* (8–12). 2007, Hyperion $15.99 (978-0-7868-3815-8). Sarah and her gay friend Demi find their true selves and the fun of musical theater at drama camp. (Rev: BL 4/1/07; SLJ 7/07)

1866 Lockhart, E. *The Treasure Map of Boys* (9–12). 2009, Delacorte $15.99 (978-038573426-4); LB $18.99 (978-038590437-7). Ruby Oliver, who appeared in the humorous *The Boyfriend List* (2005) and *The Boy Book* (2006), has boy troubles again; the Seattle 16-year-old also deals with her mother, therapy, and running a school bake sale. ∩ Lexile 790L (Rev: BLO 4/24/09; SLJ 9/09; VOYA 10/09)

1867 Logsted, Greg. *Something Happened* (9–12). 2008, Simon & Schuster paper $8.99 (978-141696561-9). After the death of his father, 13-year-old Billy finds solace in his warm, empathetic 8th-grade teacher, Miss Gale, but their relationship quickly evolves into something less appropriate. (Rev: BL 11/15/08; SLJ 3/1/09; VOYA 4/09)

1868 London, Kelli. *Cali Boys* (8–11). 2012, Kensington paper $9.95 (978-0-7582-6129-8). A fast-paced story involving two African American girls in Los Angeles: teen model Kassidy, who attracts boys like fleas, and Jacobi, who is creative and does well academically but is less successful in other areas. ℮ (Rev: SLJ 5/1/12; VOYA 6/12)

1869 Loughery, John, ed. *First Sightings: Stories of American Youth* (9–12). 1993, Persea paper $12.95 (978-0-89255-187-3). An anthology of 20 dramatic stories about children and teens by John Updike, Philip Roth, Alice Walker, Joyce Carol Oates, and others. (Rev: BL 4/15/93)

1870 Love, D. Anne. *Defying the Diva* (7–10). 2008, Simon & Schuster $16.99 (978-1-4169-5209-1). When Haley publishes a piece about diva Camilla in the school newspaper's gossip column, Camilla retaliates with force, leaving Haley friendless. (Rev: BL 3/15/08; SLJ 5/08)

1871 Lowry, Brigid. *Things You Either Hate or Love* (8–11). 2006, Holiday $16.95 (978-0-8234-2004-9). The funny, compelling story of 15-year-old Georgia, a creative misfit whose quest to earn enough money for a concert ticket leads to valuable learning experiences in life and love; set in Australia, this novel includes journal entries that discuss Georgia's weight problems. (Rev: BL 4/15/06; SLJ 4/06)

1872 Lowry, Lois. *A Summer to Die* (7–10). 1977, Houghton Mifflin $16.00 (978-0-395-25338-0). Meg is confused and dismayed by her older sister's death. (Rev: BL 7/88)

1873 Lubar, David. *Dunk* (8–12). 2002, Clarion $15.00 (978-0-618-19455-1). Over the course of a summer, troubled young Chad learns a lot about himself and his anger. (Rev: BCCB 12/02; BL 9/1/02; HB 11–12/02; HBG 3/03; SLJ 8/02*)

1874 Lubar, David. *Sleeping Freshmen Never Lie* (8–11). 2005, Dutton $16.99 (978-0-525-47311-4). Aspiring writer Scott Hudson chronicles the highs and lows of his freshman year in high school. (Rev: BCCB 10/05; BL 5/15/05; SLJ 7/05*; VOYA 6/05)

1875 Luna, Louisa. *Brave New Girl* (10–12). 2001, MTV paper $11.95 (978-0-7434-0786-1). Doreen, a 14-year-old who hides her vulnerability under a facade of toughness, is raped by her sister's 21-year-old boyfriend, a crime that goes unpunished; for mature teens. (Rev: BL 4/15/01; VOYA 2/02)

1876 Luper, Eric. *Big Slick* (9–12). 2007, Farrar $16.00 (978-0-374-30799-8). Sixteen-year-old Andrew Lang's addiction to poker gets him into trouble. (Rev: BL 10/1/07; SLJ 12/07)

1877 Mac, Carrie. *The Beckoners* (9–12). 2004, Orca $16.95 (978-1-55143-309-7). Fifteen-year-old Zoe Anderson, the new girl in school, agrees to join a brutal, bullying girls' gang, if only to protect herself from becoming one of its victims; as the gang's misdeeds become progressively more outrageous, Zoe is finally forced to take a stand against it. (Rev: BL 11/15/04; SLJ 12/04; VOYA 2/05)

1878 Mac, Carrie. *Crush* (8–12). 2006, Orca $14.95 (978-1-55143-521-3); paper $7.95 (978-1-55143-526-8). While spending the summer with her older sister Joy in New York City, Hope discovers some surprises about both Joy (drug use and a live-in boyfriend) and herself (an apparent crush on a lesbian babysitting client); for reluctant readers. (Rev: SLJ 8/06)

1879 McBride, Susan. *The Debs: Love, Lies, and Texas Dips* (9–12). 2009, Delacorte $12.99 (978-038590509-1); paper $9.99 (978-038573520-9). The Houston debutantes first seen in *The Debs* (2008) face a variety of problems involving rivalry and jealousy among themselves as they attend etiquette classes. ℮ (Rev: BLO 6/16/09)

1880 McCafferty, Megan. *Charmed Thirds* (11–12). 2006, Crown $21.00 (978-1-4000-8042-7). This third volume in the series — after *Sloppy Firsts* (2001) and *Second Helpings* (2003) — sees witty Jessica Darling through her academic and social adventures at Columbia University; for mature teens. (Rev: BL 3/15/06; SLJ 6/06)

1881 McCafferty, Megan. *Sloppy Firsts* (10–12). 2001, Crown paper $10.95 (978-0-609-80790-3). All the angst of the teen years is beautifully captured in this story of 16-year-old Jess, who struggles to find meaning in her life after her brother dies of a drug overdose and her best friend moves away; for mature teens. (Rev: VOYA 4/02)

1882 McCaffrey, Kate. *In Ecstasy* (9–12). 2009, Annick $21.95 (978-1-55451-175-4); paper $12.95 (978-1-55451-174-7). Best friends Sophie and Mia head down diverging paths after an experience with Ecstasy yields lessons one friend heeds and the other ignores. Lexile HL630L (Rev: BL 12/1/09; SLJ 1/10; VOYA 609)

1883 McCullers, Carson. *The Heart Is a Lonely Hunter* (10–12). 1993, Modern Library $17.95 (978-0-679-42474-1). A deaf-mute is the central character in this challenging novel about several lonely individuals who seek companionship.

1884 McDaniel, Lurlene. *Prey* (10–12). 2008, Delacorte $10.99 (978-0-385-73453-0). For mature teens, this is the story of a handsome freshman boy's affair with his gorgeous female history teacher and the stresses that affect both of them. (Rev: SLJ 3/08; VOYA 4/08)

1885 McDaniel, Lurlene. *Telling Christina Goodbye* (6–10). 2002, Bantam paper $4.99 (978-0-533-57087-4). Tucker, who had been driving recklessly, is the only person uninjured in the accident that kills Christina. (Rev: BL 3/15/02; SLJ 7/02)

1886 MacDonald, Caroline. *Speaking to Miranda* (7–10). 1992, HarperCollins LB $13.89 (978-0-06-021103-5). Set in Australia and New Zealand, Ruby, 18, leaves her boyfriend, travels with her father, and gradually decides to explore the mysteries of her life: Who was her mother? Who is her family? Who is she? (Rev: BL 12/15/92*; SLJ 10/92)

1887 McDonald, Janet. *Harlem Hustle* (8–11). 2006, Farrar $16.00 (978-0-374-37184-5). When he raps, Eric is known as "Hustle" (and he hustles on the street, too, stealing), in this novel about a young man struggling to make it against tough odds. (Rev: BL 12/1/06; HB 9–10/06; SLJ 10/06*)

1888 McDonald, Joyce. *Swallowing Stones* (7–10). 1997, Bantam paper $4.99 (978-0-440-22672-7). When Michael accidentally kills a man with his rifle, he and his friend decide to hide the gun and feign ignorance. (Rev: BL 10/15/97; SLJ 9/97; VOYA 12/97)

1889 McDonell, Nick. *Twelve* (11–12). 2002, Grove $23.00 (978-0-8021-1717-5). Drugs, sex, and violence feature prominently in this tale about wealthy prep-school kids written by a 17-year-old; for mature teens. (Rev: BL 6/1–15/02; VOYA 12/02)

1890 MacKall, Dandi Daley. *Crazy in Love* (8–12). 2007, Dutton $16.99 (978-0-525-47780-8). Seventeen-year-old Mary Jane finally gets together with Jackson House and the two become an item; soon, however, Mary-Jane must decide whether to have sex with Jackson, recognizing that saying no might jeopardize their relationship. (Rev: SLJ 2/07)

1891 Mackey, Weezie Kerr. *Throwing Like a Girl* (7–10). 2007, Marshall Cavendish $16.99 (978-0-7614-5342-0). Ella adjusts to her new home in Dallas by playing on a softball team and dating a senior named Nate. (Rev: BL 3/15/07; SLJ 5/07)

1892 Mackler, Carolyn. *The Earth, My Butt, and Other Big Round Things* (7–10). 2003, Candlewick $15.99 (978-0-7636-1958-9). Virginia, a privileged New York 15-year-old, struggles with her weight, her lack of self confidence, her family, the absence of her best friend, and her aspiring boyfriend. (Rev: BL 9/1/03; HB 9–10/03; HBG 4/04; SLJ 9/03)

1893 Mackler, Carolyn. *Vegan Virgin Valentine* (8–12). 2004, Candlewick $16.99 (978-0-7636-2155-1). High school senior Mara Valentine, a classic overachiever, is right on schedule with her short-term goals for her future when Vivian comes to live with Mara's family. (Rev: BL 6/1–15/04; SLJ 8/04; VOYA 10/04)

1894 MacLean, Christine Kole. *How It's Done* (9–12). 2006, Flux $15.95 (978-0-7387-1029-7). Eighteen-year-old Grace rebels against the strict rules of her fundamentalist parents and becomes involved with an older man. (Rev: SLJ 1/07)

1895 McNaughton, Janet. *To Dance at the Palais Royale* (7–10). 1999, Stoddart paper $5.95 (978-0-7736-7473-8). The story of the loneliness and growing maturity of Aggie Maxwell who leaves her home in Scotland at age 17 to become a domestic servant with her sister in Toronto. (Rev: SLJ 5/99; VOYA 10/99)

1896 McVoy, Terra Elan. *Pure* (8–11). 2009, Simon & Schuster $16.99 (978-141697872-5). When one girl in their group of friends breaks the promise symbolized by her purity ring, 15-year-old Tabitha is shocked and forced to examine her friendship and her faith. Lexile 970L (Rev: BL 4/1/09; SLJ 9/09)

1897 Maguire, Gregory. *Oasis* (7–10). 1996, Clarion $15.00 (978-0-395-67019-4). This story of grief and guilt involves 13-year-old Hand, his adjustment to his father's sudden death, and his mother's efforts to save the motel her husband had managed. (Rev: BL 9/15/96; SLJ 11/96; VOYA 2/97)

1898 Mahy, Margaret. *The Catalogue of the Universe* (8–12). 1987, Scholastic paper $2.75 (978-0-590-42318-2). Through their friendship, Angela, who longs to meet her absent father, and Tycho, who believes he is physically ugly, find tenderness and compassion. (Rev: BL 3/15/86; SLJ 4/86; VOYA 12/86)

1899 Maillard, Keith. *Running* (9–12). 2005, Brindle & Glass paper $11.95 (978-1-897142-06-6). In the 1950s John Dupre is a student at a military academy, loves life and running, and hopes to become a writer; John is also conflicted about his sexual identity and calls himself a "boy-girl." (Rev: BL 9/15/05)

1900 Makris, Kathryn. *A Different Way* (7–10). 1989, Avon paper $2.95 (978-0-380-75728-2). A newcomer in a Texas high school wonders if acceptance by the in-crowd is worth the effort. (Rev: BL 10/15/89)

1901 Malloy, Brian. *Twelve Long Months* (8–12). 2008, Scholastic $17.99 (978-0-439-87761-9). Molly meets many challenges when she moves from a Minnesota high school to Columbia University, including finding out that the boy she loves is gay. (Rev: BL 8/08; SLJ 8/08)

1902 Mandabach, Brian. . . . *Or Not?* (7–10). 2007, Llewellyn $16.95 (978-0-7387-1100-3). From her 8th-grade classmates' point of view, Cassie is a contrarian — she rejects cell phones but loves vinyl records, she won't shave her legs, nor will she stand for the Pledge of Allegiance, and above all she's against the U.S. reaction to 9/11. (Rev: BL 9/15/07; SLJ 3/08)

1903 Manning, Sara. *French Kiss* (8–11). Series: Diary of a Crush. 2006, Penguin paper $6.99 (978-0-14-240632-8). Edie, a 16-year-old English teen, falls in love with Dylan, a brooding art student, in this first volume in a trilogy. (Rev: BL 7/06)

1904 Margolis, Leslie. *Fix* (7–12). 2006, Simon & Schuster paper $6.99 (978-1-4169-2456-2). Two sisters take different stands when their mother wants them to get nose jobs. (Rev: SLJ 10/06)

1905 Marineau, Michele. *Lean Mean Machines* (7–12). 2001, Red Deer paper $7.95 (978-0-88995-230-0). Canadian teen Jeremy Martucci befriends Laure, the new girl at his high school, but senses she's keeping a painful secret. (Rev: SLJ 11/01; VOYA 8/01)

1906 Marino, Peter. *Dough Boy* (7–10). 2005, Holiday House $16.95 (978-0-8234-1873-2). Fifteen-year-old Tristan, a child of divorce, is unfazed by his weight until Kelly, the health-obsessed daughter of his mother's boyfriend, starts picking on him. (Rev: BL 11/15/05; SLJ 11/05; VOYA 2/06)

1907 Martin, C. K. Kelly. *The Lighter Side of Life and Death* (9–12). 2010, Random House $16.99 (978-0-375-84588-8); LB $19.99 (978-0-375-95588-4). Mason and Kat are best friends until they have sex after a drunken party; Kat becomes distant while Mason, 16, starts a relationship with an older woman. (Rev: BL 3/15/10*; SLJ 8/10)

1908 Mason, Bobbie Ann. *In Country* (9–12). 1986, HarperCollins paper $13.00 (978-0-06-091350-2). This understated novel deals with a teenage girl and her gradual acceptance of the death of her father in the Vietnam War. (Rev: BL 8/85; SLJ 2/86)

1909 Matthews, Phoebe. *Switchstance* (7–10). 1989, Avon paper $2.95 (978-0-380-75729-9). After her parents' divorce, Elvy moves in with her grandmother and

forms friendships with two very different boys. (Rev: VOYA 2/90)

1910 Mayer, Melody. *Friends with Benefits: A Nannies Novel* (9–12). 2006, Delacorte LB $10.99 (978-0-385-90301-1); paper $8.95 (978-0-385-73284-0). Kylie, Lydia, and Esme are a trio of friends who each hold a nanny position and each have respective crises to solve, whether it's with their bosses, boyfriends, family members, or each other; also use *Have to Have It* (2006). (Rev: SLJ 6/06)

1911 Mazer, Anne, ed. *Working Days: Stories About Teenagers and Work* (6–12). 1997, Persea paper $9.95 (978-0-89255-224-5). An anthology of 15 varied, multicultural short stories about teenagers at their jobs. (Rev: BL 7/97; HBG 3/98; SLJ 9/97; VOYA 12/97)

1912 Mazer, Harry. *The Girl of His Dreams* (9–12). 1987, Avon paper $2.95 (978-0-380-70599-3). Willis Pierce is now 18 and into running while also being intent on his new girlfriend Sophie. Pierce was first introduced in Mazer's *The War on Villa Street*. (Rev: BL 9/15/87; SLJ 1/88; VOYA 12/87)

1913 Mazer, Harry. *Hey, Kid! Does She Love Me?* (7–12). 1986, Avon paper $2.95 (978-0-380-70025-7). Stage-struck Jeff falls in love with a woman who was once an aspiring actress in this romance that contains some sexually explicit language.

1914 Mazer, Harry. *I Love You, Stupid!* (9–12). 1983, Avon paper $3.50 (978-0-380-61432-5). In this sequel to *The Dollar Man*, 17-year-old Marcus and friend Wendy experiment with sex and find love. (Rev: BL 6/87)

1915 Mazer, Norma Fox, and Harry Mazer. *Bright Days, Stupid Nights* (7–10). 1993, Bantam paper $3.50 (978-0-553-56253-8). Charts the course of four youths who are brought together for a summer newspaper internship. (Rev: BL 6/15/92; SLJ 7/92)

1916 Mechling, Lauren, and Laura Moser. *The Rise and Fall of a 10th Grade Social Climber* (9–12). 2005, Houghton Mifflin paper $7.99 (978-0-618-55519-2). Newly transplanted to New York after her parents separate, 15-year-old Mimi Shulman bets a longtime friend that she can get the most popular girls in her 10th-grade class to accept her. (Rev: BCCB 5/05; BL 4/15/05; SLJ 6/05; VOYA 6/05)

1917 Medina, Nico. *The Straight Road to Kylie* (9–12). 2007, Simon & Schuster paper $8.99 (978-1-4169-3600-8). Realistic dialogue and hilarious situations pepper this novel about Jonathan, a gay 17-year-old who regrets hiding his lifestyle as part of a bargain with a rich girl. (Rev: SLJ 7/07)

1918 Meno, Joe. *Hairstyles of the Damned* (11–12). 2004, Akashic paper $14.95 (978-1-888451-70-2). Two teenagers — Brian and Gretchen — bond through punk rock and their anger at the world in this novel written in the first person and set in Chicago in 1990; strong language restricts this to mature teens. (Rev: BL 9/15/04; SLJ 2/05)

1919 Merullo, Roland. *The Talk-Funny Girl* (11–12). 2011, Crown $23 (978-0-307-45292-4). Raised by isolated parents who speak their own hybrid dialect and follow a sadistic cult, abused young Marjorie finally finds some comfort when she starts working for a gentle stonemason; for mature readers. Alex Award 2012. **e** (Rev: BL 6/15/11; SLJ 11/11)

1920 Miller-Lachmann, Lyn. *Hiding Places* (8–12). 1987, Square One paper $4.95 (978-0-938961-00-0). Mark runs away from his suburban home and ends up in a shelter in New York City. (Rev: SLJ 5/87)

1921 Miller, Mary Beth. *On the Head of a Pin* (9–12). 2006, Button $16.99 (978-0-525-47736-5). A prom queen is accidentally shot at a party, and the resulting cover-up exposes the characters of the three boys involved. (Rev: BL 2/15/06*; SLJ 4/06; VOYA 4/06)

1922 Millner, Denene, and Mitzi Miller. *Hotlanta* (9–12). 2008, Scholastic paper $8.99 (978-0-5450030-9). African American sisters Lauren and Sydney are twins but do not always agree; in alternating narratives they describe their luxurious lifestyle, their social lives, and their reactions to their father's release from prison. (Rev: BL 8/08; SLJ 5/08)

1923 Mitchell, Todd. *The Secret to Lying* (9–12). 2010, Candlewick $17.99 (978-0-7636-4084-2). Fifteen-year-old James transfers to a boarding school for gifted students and decides to reinvent himself, a plan that is initially successful but also involves lying, cutting himself, and self-destructive behavior. Lexile HL730L (Rev: BL 6/10; LMC 8–9/10; SLJ 6/10)

1924 Mlynowski, Sarah. *Ten Things We Did (and Probably Shouldn't Have)* (9–12). 2011, HarperTeen $16.99 (978-0-06-170124-5). April and Violet get to live the 16-year-old dream: a semester of independent living with no parental supervision in this at-times cautionary but never didactic tale. ⌒ **e** (Rev: BL 5/1/11; SLJ 8/11; VOYA 8/11)

1925 Moeyaert, Bart. *Bare Hands* (9–12). Trans. by Davi Colmer. 1998, Front St $14.95 (978-1-886910-32-4). A provocative novel about a boy's confused feelings when his actions provoke a neighboring farmer, who is courting the boy's single mother, into killing the boy's dog. (Rev: BL 12/15/98; HBG 9/99; SLJ 2/99; VOYA 6/99)

1926 Moore, Lorrie. *A Gate at the Stairs* (11–12). 2009, Knopf $25 (978-037540928-8). A wide-ranging and compelling novel about college student Tassie as she navigates through a year of school and personal growth during which she also cares for a biracial adoptee. ⌒ **e** (Rev: BL 7/09)

1927 Moore, Peter. *Caught in the Act* (8–11). 2005, Viking $16.99 (978-0-670-05990-4). Honor student Ethan Lederer is having trouble keeping his grades up and his problems multiply when he falls for Lydia, a Goth-type

who turns out to be alarmingly manipulative. (Rev: BCCB 6/05; BL 3/1/05; HB 3–4/05; SLJ 5/05; VOYA 4/05)

1928 Moranville, Sharelle Byars. *The Snows* (7–10). 2007, Henry Holt $16.95 (978-0-8050-7469-7). The stories of four 16-year-old characters in the Snow family (Jim, Cathy, Jim's daughter Jill, and Jill's daughter Mona), spanning the years 1931 to 2006 and describing key events in their adolescent lives, come together at a funeral. (Rev: BL 8/07; LMC 2/08; SLJ 9/07)

1929 Moriarty, Jaclyn. *The Year of Secret Assignments* (8–12). 2004, Scholastic $16.95 (978-0-439-49881-4). A rollicking year in the lives of three Australian high school girls — Lydia, Emily, and Cassie — is chronicled in their correspondence with male pen pals at a rival school. (Rev: BCCB 4/04; BL 1/1–15/04; HB 3–4/04; SLJ 3/04; VOYA 6/04)

1930 Moriarty, Laura. *The Center of Everything* (10–12). 2003, Hyperion $22.95 (978-1-4013-0031-9). Readers share the maturing of Evelyn Bucknow, a girl learning to cope with her young mother, with a new and retarded baby sister, and with new relationships outside her family. (Rev: BL 7/03; SLJ 12/03; VOYA 12/03)

1931 Morris, Winifred. *Liar* (7–10). 1996, Walker $15.95 (978-0-8027-8461-2). Fourteen-year-old Alex starts life over on his grandparents' farm in Oregon, but there are many obstacles, including school bullies, a hostile principal, and an unloving grandfather. (Rev: BL 12/1/96; SLJ 1/97; VOYA 12/96)

1932 Moskowitz, Hannah. *Gone, Gone, Gone* (8–12). 2012, Simon & Schuster paper $9.99 (978-14424075-3-4). September 11 and the sniper shootings in the District of Columbia area form a backdrop for this story about teens Craig and Lio, their personal problems, and their potential romantic relationship. Stonewall Honor Book 2013. **e** (Rev: BL 4/1/12; VOYA 4/12)

1933 Moyer, Kermit. *The Chester Chronicles* (9–12). 2010, Permanent Press $28 (978-157962194-0). Sixteen episodes relate coming-of-age experiences of Chet Patterson, an Army brat used to constant moves; set in the late 1950s and early 1960s. **e** (Rev: BL 12/15/09*)

1934 Munson, Sam. *The November Criminals* (11–12). 2010, Doubleday $23.95 (978-038553227-3). The novel's protagonist, a disaffected high school pot dealer, struggles with problems both mundane (filling out college applications, keeping a girlfriend at arm's length) and extraordinary (trying to solve a classmate's murder) in this book suitable for older teens. (Rev: BL 2/1–15/10)

1935 Murdoch, Patricia. *Exposure* (8–12). Series: Orca Soundings. 2006, Orca $14.95 (978-1-55143-523-7). Revenge is the theme of this story about a girl who uses incriminating photographs to get back at a classmate who has been tormenting her; for reluctant readers. (Rev: SLJ 10/06)

1936 Murdock, Catherine Gilbert. *Front and Center* (7–10). Series: Dairy Queen. 2009, Houghton Mifflin $16 (978-0-618-95982-2). Now in her junior year, basketball star D.J. is pressured by adults to choose the "right" college and navigates a tricky social life in this well-written, final volume in the trilogy. ∩ **e** Lexile 980L (Rev: BL 10/1/09; HB 9–10/09; SLJ 9/09; VOYA 12/09)

1937 Murdock, Catherine Gilbert. *The Off Season* (7–10). 2007, Houghton Mifflin $16.00 (978-0-618-68695-7). The unconventional D.J., first introduced to readers in 2006's *Diary Queen,* is now a junior in high school and must juggle work on her family's diary farm, playing on her school football team, and her first boyfriend. ∩ (Rev: BCCB 9/07; BL 4/15/07; HB 7–8/07; SLJ 4/07*)

1938 Murphy, Claire Rudolf. *Free Radical* (7–10). 2002, Clarion $15.00 (978-0-618-11134-3). Luke, a baseball star in Fairbanks, Alaska, is stunned when his mother turns herself in for her role in a fatal bombing more than 30 years before. (Rev: BCCB 6/02; BL 3/15/02; HBG 10/02; SLJ 3/02; VOYA 6/02)

1939 Myers, Walter Dean. *Crystal* (9–12). 1990, Bantam paper $5.95 (978-0-440-80157-3). A beautiful young black model finds success hard to handle. (Rev: BL 6/1/87; SLJ 6/87; VOYA 4/88)

1940 Myers, Walter Dean. *Dope Sick* (9–12). 2009, HarperTeen $16.99 (978-006121477-6); LB $17.89 (978-006121478-3). Seventeen-year-old African American Lil J encounters a mysterious old man who makes him question his chosen life of drugs, crime, and chaos. ∩ **e** Lexile HL720L (Rev: BL 11/15/08; HB 3–4/09; LMC 8–9/09; SLJ 4/1/09*; VOYA 4/09)

1941 Myers, Walter Dean. *Lockdown* (7–10). 2010, Amistad $16.99 (978-0-06-121480-6); LB $17.89 (978-0-06-121481-3). Determined not to sink deeper into a criminal life, 14-year-old African American Reese tries to control his behavior during his time at a juvenile corrections facility. Coretta Scott King Author Honor 2011. ∩ Lexile 730L (Rev: BL 12/1/09; HB 3–4/10; SLJ 2/10; VOYA 2/10)

1942 Myers, Walter Dean. *Shooter* (7–12). 2004, HarperCollins $15.99 (978-0-06-029519-6). Told from many viewpoints, this is the story of a high school senior who commits suicide after shooting a star football player and injuring several others. (Rev: BL 2/15/04*; HB 5–6/04; SLJ 5/04; VOYA 6/04)

1943 Myers, Walter Dean. *Won't Know Till I Get There* (7–10). 1982, Penguin paper $5.99 (978-0-14-032612-3). A young subway graffiti artist is sentenced to help out in a senior citizens' home.

1944 Myracle, Lauren. *l8r, g8r* (9–12). Series: Internet Girls. 2007, Abrams $15.95 (978-0-8109-1266-3). Written in chat-room shorthand, this book in the Internet Girls trilogy continues the growing-up adventures of Maddie, Zoe, and Angela, who are now in their senior year and grappling with sex, college, and cliques. (Rev: BL 3/15/07; SLJ 6/07)

1945 Myracle, Lauren. *ttfn* (10–12). 2006, Abrams $15.95 (978-0-8109-5971-2). Angela, Zoe, and Madigan, now 16, continue to be friends and to share details of their lives through text messages in this sequel to *ttyl* (2004). (Rev: BL 4/1/06; SLJ 3/06)

1946 Myracle, Lauren. *ttyl* (6–10). 2004, Abrams $15.95 (978-0-8109-4821-1). This story of three 10th-graders and their lives is told through instant messages. (Rev: BL 5/15/04; SLJ 4/04; VOYA 6/04)

1947 Nair, Kamala. *The Girl in the Garden: A Novel* (11–12). 2011, Grand Central $24.99 (978-0-446-57268-2). A young woman unsure about her forthcoming marriage remembers a journey she took at the age of 10, from Minnesota to India to visit her mother's family, and the tragic events resulting from her discovery in a mysterious garden; for mature readers. ∩ (Rev: BL 3/1–15/11; SLJ 8/11)

1948 Naylor, Phyllis Reynolds. *Alice in the Know* (7–10). 2006, Simon & Schuster $15.95 (978-0-689-87092-7). Alice, now 16, must find work for the summer, longs for more family contact, and copes with the often embarrassing teen rites of passage. (Rev: BL 5/1/06; HB 7–8/06; SLJ 8/06)

1949 Naylor, Phyllis Reynolds. *Alice on Her Way* (7–10). 2005, Simon & Schuster $15.95 (978-0-689-87090-3). Alice, now almost 16 and hoping to get her driver's license, protests the idea of attending a sex class at church, but finds to her surprise that it's interesting and informative. (Rev: BL 7/05; SLJ 5/05; VOYA 8/05)

1950 Naylor, Phyllis Reynolds. *Almost Alice* (9–12). 2008, Simon & Schuster $16.99 (978-0-689-87096-5). One of Alice's friends gets pregnant in this 23rd novel in the series. (Rev: HB 7–8/08; SLJ 5/08)

1951 Naylor, Phyllis Reynolds. *Dangerously Alice* (7–11). Series: Alice. 2007, Simon & Schuster $15.99 (978-0-689-87094-1). Alice is worried that she's being labeled a prude at school but is reluctant to "go all the way" with her boyfriend Tony in this installment in the Alice series. (Rev: BL 4/1/07; HB 7–8/07; SLJ 8/07; VOYA 4/07)

1952 Nelson, Blake. *Destroy All Cars* (8–11). 2009, Scholastic $17.99 (978-054510474-6). Following 17-year-old James through his junior year, this novel describes his early obsessions with environmental threats and base consumerism (and his ex-girlfriend) and his gradual development of a less austere attitude. (Rev: BL 6/1–15/09)

1953 Nelson, Blake. *Rock Star, Superstar* (9–12). 2004, Penguin $16.99 (978-0-670-05933-1). As his rock music career begins to heat up, 16-year-old Pete fears that his newfound fame will jeopardize his budding romance with Margaret. (Rev: BL 11/1/04; SLJ 10/04)

1954 Nelson, R. A. *Days of Little Texas* (8–10). 2009, Knopf $16.99 (978-037585593-1); LB $19.99 (978-037595593-8). Ronald Earl, a 16-year-old evangelist, begins to question his faith as he becomes obsessed by the ghost of a girl he failed to cure in this well-written, thought-provoking novel. ⌐ (Rev: BL 6/1–15/09; SLJ 10/09)

1955 Nelson, Suzanne. *The Sound of Munich* (6–10). 2006, Penguin paper $6.99 (978-0-14-240576-5). While Siena studies in Munich, she looks for the individual who enabled her father to escape from East Germany. (Rev: SLJ 6/06)

1956 Newbery, Linda. *Sisterland* (8–12). 2004, Random House $15.95 (978-0-385-75026-4). This powerful story of love, anger, and guilt includes many generations and countries and revolves around Hilly, a contemporary British teen who is love with a Palestinian. (Rev: BL 3/1/04; HB 3–4/04; SLJ 4/04; VOYA 4/04)

1957 Niemi, Mikael. *Popular Music from Vittula* (10–12). Trans. by Laurie Thompson. 2003, Seven Stories $21.95 (978-1-58322-523-3). In a remote village in 1960s Sweden, 11-year-old Matti discovers the Beatles and the charms and angst of adolescence. (Rev: BL 10/15/03)

1958 Noël, Alyson. *Art Geeks and Prom Queens* (9–12). 2005, St. Martin's paper $8.95 (978-0-312-33636-3). No one is more surprised than geekish 16-year-old Rio when she's befriended by cheerleader Kristi, the most popular girl at Rio's new school, but she soon learns that friendships like Kristi's can be very fleeting. (Rev: BL 10/1/05; SLJ 11/05)

1959 Noël, Alyson. *Faking 19* (9–12). 2005, St. Martin's paper $8.95 (978-0-312-33633-2). Seventeen-year-old Alex reevaluates her life and her friendship with M. when she realizes she needs to pave the way for a meaningful future. (Rev: SLJ 9/05; VOYA 10/05)

1960 Nolan, Han. *Pregnant Pause* (8–12). 2011, Harcourt $16.99 (978-0-15-206570-6). Pregnant and married at 16, Elly learns that she needs to rely on herself rather than undependable adults. ℮ Lexile 820L (Rev: BL 8/11; SLJ 9/1/11*; VOYA 10/11)

1961 Norris, Shana. *Something to Blog About* (7–10). 2008, Abrams $15.95 (978-0-8109-9474-4). Libby is horrified when her 10th-grade classmate Angel posts Libby's diary entries on the Web for all to see, and it's all made worse by the fact that her mother is dating Angel's father. (Rev: BL 2/8/08; SLJ 5/08)

1962 Oates, Joyce Carol. *Two or Three Things I Forgot to Tell You* (9–12). 2012, HarperTeen $17.99 (978-0-06-211047-3). In their senior year at high school Merissa and Nadia, both hiding secrets, miss their friend Tink, who killed herself the year before. ℮ (Rev: BL 5/1/12; SLJ 10/12)

1963 O'Brien, Maureen. *b-mother* (9–12). 2007, Harcourt $24.00 (978-0-15-101398-2). At the age of 16, unhappy Hillary meets a seductive guy and becomes pregnant; she decides to give her son up for adoption but spends the next 18 years regretting her decision. (Rev: BL 11/1/06)

1964 O'Connell, Mary. *The Sharp Time* (10–12). 2011, Random House $17.99 (978-0-385-74048-7); LB $20.99 (978-0-375-98948-3). Eighteen-year-old Sandinista Jones's mother has just died and the grief-stricken girl finds some comfort through her job in a vintage shop and her friend Bradley even as she fantasizes about revenge against an abusive teacher. ℮ (Rev: BL 1/1/12*; SLJ 12/1/11)

1965 O'Connell, Rebecca. *Myrtle of Willendorf* (10–12). 2000, Front St $15.95 (978-1-886910-52-2). In this humorous but poignant novel, Myrtle, an overweight and lonely college student rooming with a sexually active beauty, finds solace in art. (Rev: BL 10/15/00; HB 9–10/00; HBG 3/01; SLJ 10/00; VOYA 12/00)

1966 O'Dell, Kathleen. *Bad Tickets* (9–12). 2007, Knopf $15.99 (978-0-375-83801-9). In Oregon in the summer of 1967, good Catholic girl Mary Margaret, 16, throws caution to the wind and follows her new friend Jane into a new way of life. (Rev: BCCB 6/07; BL 1/1–15/07; SLJ 4/07)

1967 O'Neill, Heather. *Lullabies for Little Criminals* (11–12). 2006, HarperPerennial paper $13.95 (978-0-06-087507-7). The story of preteen Baby, whose life is filled with crime, drugs, sex, neglect, and abuse; for mature teens. (Rev: BL 9/1/06)

1968 Paddock, Jennifer. *A Secret Word* (10–12). 2004, Simon & Schuster paper $13.00 (978-0-7432-4707-8). The story of three girlfriends, their coming of age, and their different destinies. (Rev: BL 4/1/04)

1969 Palmer, Liza. *Conversations with the Fat Girl* (9–12). 2005, Warner paper $12.95 (978-0-446-69395-0). Maggie's self-image is not improved when best friend and fellow traveler Olivia slims down and bags a neat fiancé. (Rev: BL 8/05)

1970 Pascal, Francine. *The Ruling Class* (8–11). 2004, Simon & Schuster $14.95 (978-0-689-87332-4). Brutally harassed by bullies at her new high school in Dallas, 16-year-old Twyla Gay briefly considers dropping out but decides instead to seek revenge. (Rev: BCCB 12/04; BL 1/1–15/05; SLJ 12/04)

1971 Paulsen, Gary. *The Island* (7–10). 1988, Orchard paper $17.95 (978-0-531-05749-0). A 15-year-old boy finds peace and a meaning to life when he explores his own private island. (Rev: BL 3/15/88; SLJ 5/88; VOYA 6/88)

1972 Paulsen, Gary. *Popcorn Days and Buttermilk Nights* (8–12). 1989, Penguin paper $4.99 (978-0-14-034204-8). Carley finds adventure after he is sent to his Uncle David's farm in Minnesota to sort himself out.

1973 Paulsen, Gary. *Sisters / Hermanas* (8–10). Trans. by Gloria de Aragón Andújar. 1993, Harcourt $10.95 (978-0-15-275323-8); paper $6.00 (978-0-15-275324-5). The bilingual story of two girls, age 14, in a Texas town, one an illegal Mexican immigrant prostitute, the other a superficial blond cheerleader. (Rev: BL 1/1/94; SLJ 1/94; VOYA 12/93)

1974 Pearson, Mary E. *The Miles Between* (9–12). 2009, Henry Holt $16.99 (978-080508828-1). Unhappy 17-year-old Destiny and three classmates from the exclusive Hedgerow Academy set off on a quest to find "one fair day," a day of justification. ⌒ (Rev: BL 7/09; SLJ 9/09)

1975 Pearson, Michael. *Shohola Falls* (10–12). 2003, Syracuse Univ. $24.95 (978-0-8156-0785-4). Finding himself suddenly on his own, young Tommy Blanks finds love in the unlikely setting of a Catholic-run juvenile facility to which he's committed after a minor theft. (Rev: BL 9/15/03)

1976 Peck, Dale. *Sprout* (10–12). 2009, Bloomsbury $16.99 (978-159990160-2). Sixteen-year-old Sprout, cynical, green-haired gay son of a drunk father, prepares for an essay contest and deals humorously with challenges at school and at home. Stonewall Honor 2010. Lexile 1060L (Rev: BL 5/15/09; HB 7–8/09; SLJ 6/1/09; VOYA 6/09)

1977 Peck, Richard. *Bed and Breakfast* (10–12). 1998, Viking paper $23.95 (978-0-670-87368-5). A novel about the lasting friendship between Lesley, Julia, and Margo that culminates in a reunion where the three are dramatically changed after a stay at an elegant bed-and-breakfast in London run by the mysterious Mrs. Smith-Porter. (Rev: BL 6/1–15/98; SLJ 8/98)

1978 Pedersen, Laura. *Beginner's Luck* (11–12). 2003, Ballantine paper $13.95 (978-0-345-45830-8). Discontented Hallie Palmer is only 16 but she's determined to take charge of her own life, runs away, and soon finds a home with the eccentric Stockton family; for mature teens. (Rev: BL 12/15/02; VOYA 6/03)

1979 Perrotta, Tom. *Joe College* (10–12). 2000, St. Martin's $23.95 (978-0-312-26184-9). This novel about Danny, a junior at Yale in 1980, tells about his school, hometown, friends, girlfriends, and his job at semester breaks working in his father's lunch wagon. (Rev: BL 9/1/00)

1980 Peters, Julie Anne. *grl2grl* (9–12). 2007, Little, Brown $11.99 (978-0-316-01343-7). A collection of 10 short, first-person stories that describe the experiences of young women exploring their sexual preferences. (Rev: BL 8/07; HB 9–10/07; SLJ 12/07)

1981 Peters, Julie Anne. *It's Our Prom (So Deal with It)* (8–11). 2012, Little, Brown $17.99 (978-031613158-2). Plans for the senior prom get interesting — and a bit fractious — when lesbian Azure and bisexual Luke

are appointed to the planning committee. ℮ (Rev: BL 4/15/12; LMC 8–9/12; SLJ 4/12; VOYA 4/12)

1982 Peterson, Lois. *Disconnect* (7–10). Series: Orca Currents. 2012, Orca LB $16.95 (978-145980144-8); paper $9.95 (978-145980143-1). Suitable for reluctant readers, this is the story of Daria, who depends heavily on her cell phone when she is moved far from her friends — with potentially fatal results. ℮ Lexile 430L (Rev: BL 10/15/12; LMC 5–6/13; SLJ 3/13; VOYA 2/13)

1983 Petrucha, Stefan. *Split* (7–10). 2010, Walker $16.99 (978-0-8027-9372-0). Wade has trouble dealing with the death of his mother, and as a high school senior develops two quite different and separate personalities; the serious Wade is skilled with computers while the wayward Wade is a musician who gets in debt to gangsters. Lexile HL610L (Rev: BL 2/15/10; LMC 5–6/10; SLJ 3/10)

1984 Philbrick, Rodman. *Freak the Mighty* (7–10). 1993, Scholastic paper $16.95 (978-0-590-47412-2). When Maxwell Kane, the son of Killer Kane, becomes friends with Kevin, a new boy with a birth defect, he gains a new interest in school and learning. (Rev: BL 12/15/93; SLJ 12/93*; VOYA 4/94)

1985 Phillips, Wendy. *Fishtailing* (7–12). 2010, Coteau paper $14.95 (978-15505041-1-8). Four teens — Natalie, Tricia, Kyle, and Miguel — with a range of problems describe their lives in first-person free verse writing assignments; these are accompanied by teacher critiques. (Rev: BL 10/15/10; LMC 3–4/11)

1986 Piper, Steffan. *Greyhound* (11–12). 2010, Amazon Encore paper $13.95 (978-09825550-9-5). On a cross-country bus trip from California to his grandparents' Pennsylvania town, 11-year-old Sebastien mulls over his recent abandonment and unhappy childhood, and encounters memorable characters along the way in this road trip bildungsroman; for mature readers. ℮ (Rev: BL 5/1–15/10)

1987 Pittard, Hannah. *The Fates Will Find Their Way* (11–12). 2011, Ecco $24.99 (978-0-06-199605-4). Attractive and popular Nora disappeared when she was 16, and even years later boys, then men, wonder about her fate and remember her; for mature readers. ⌒ ℮ (Rev: BL 12/1–15/10; SLJ 5/11)

1988 Platt, Kin. *Crocker* (7–10). 1983, HarperCollins $11.95 (978-0-397-32025-7). Dorothy is attracted to a new boy in school.

1989 Platt, Randall B. *The Cornerstone* (8–12). 1998, Catbird $21.95 (978-0-945774-40-2). Using flashbacks, this novel tells about the growth of a tough 15-year-old charity case at summer camp on a scholarship in 1944, where he meets a Navy man on medical leave who changes his life. (Rev: VOYA 2/99)

113

1990 Plum-Ucci, Carol. *What Happened to Lani Garver* (8–12). 2002, Harcourt $17.00 (978-0-15-216813-1). Claire, a popular 16-year-old who is battling private demons, finds support and a cause in a newly arrived, curiously androgynous student who disturbs her friends. (Rev: BCCB 11/02; BL 8/02; HBG 10/03; SLJ 10/02*; VOYA 12/02)

1991 Prose, Francine. *Touch* (10–12). 2009, Harper-Teen $16.99 (978-006137517-0); LB $17.89 (978-006137518-7). Maisie is conflicted about an incident on the school bus that some are calling sexual harassment and others are saying was all her idea. Lexile 820L (Rev: BL 4/15/09*; SLJ 6/1/09; VOYA 6/09)

1992 Prosek, James. *The Day My Mother Left* (6–12). 2007, Simon & Schuster $15.99 (978-1-4169-0770-1). Jeremy's mother leaves his family to be with another man, and over the next few difficult years Jeremy finds some comfort being outside and sketching birds. ⌂ (Rev: BCCB 2/07; BL 4/15/07; LMC 8–9/07; SLJ 3/07)

1993 Prue, Sally. *The Devil's Toenail* (7–10). 2004, Scholastic $16.95 (978-0-439-48634-7). Thirteen-year-old Stevie Saunders, still trying to recover from a brutal bullying incident that left him scarred, enters a new school determined to endear himself. (Rev: BCCB 9/04; BL 4/15/04; SLJ 8/04)

1994 Qualey, Marsha. *Just Like That* (9–12). 2005, Dial $16.99 (978-0-8037-2840-0). Hanna, 18, feels guilty about the death of two teens; after she meets and becomes romantically and sexually involved with Will, who also is connected to the tragedy, she is distressed to discover that he is only 14. (Rev: BL 8/05; SLJ 5/05; VOYA 6/05)

1995 Quigley, Sarah. *TMI* (7–10). 2009, Dutton $16.99 (978-052547908-6). Becca, 15, learns the hard way that blogs are not private and that gossip can hurt people deeply. (Rev: BL 4/1/09; VOYA 12/09)

1996 Quintero, Sofia. *Efrain's Secret* (8–11). 2010, Knopf $16.99 (978-0-375-84706-6). Latino star student Efrain, 17, turns to dealing drugs to earn tuition money for an Ivy League college. Lexile 780L (Rev: BL 3/1/10*; LMC 8–9/10; SLJ 6/10)

1997 Rainfield, Cheryl. *Scars* (8–11). 2010, WestSide $16.95 (978-1-93481332-4.). Kendra, now 15 and hiding her habit of cutting herself, was sexually abused when she was younger and is sure her attacker is following her; her deepening relationship with classmate Meghan gives her support. YALSA Quick Picks for Reluctant Young Adult Readers 2011. Lexile HL560L (Rev: BL 3/1/10; LMC 10/10; SLJ 5/10; VOYA 4/10)

1998 Rambach, Peggy. *Fighting Gravity* (10–12). 2001, Steerforth $19.00 (978-1-58642-023-9). For mature readers, this is the story of a 19-year-old Jewish college student and her love for a twice-married Catholic professor who has four children. (Rev: BL 4/1/01)

1999 Rapp, Adam. *The Buffalo Tree* (9–12). 1997, Front St $15.95 (978-1-886910-19-5). Sura, who has adjusted to his confined world in a juvenile detention center, learns about himself through sessions with a counselor. (Rev: BL 9/1/97; SLJ 6/97*; VOYA 8/97)

2000 Rapp, Adam. *Missing the Piano* (9–12). 1994, Viking $14.99 (978-0-670-95340-0). In his new military academy, Mike discovers racism and intimidation in this story about values, basketball, and friendship. (Rev: BL 6/1–15/94; SLJ 6/94)

2001 Reed, Don C. *The Kraken* (6–10). 1997, Boyds Mills paper $7.95 (978-1-56397-693-3). In Newfoundland in the late 1800s, a boy struggles to survive against the impersonal rich and the harsh environment. (Rev: BL 3/15/95; SLJ 2/95)

2002 Rees, Celia. *The Wish House* (10–12). 2006, Candlewick $15.99 (978-0-7636-2951-9). While on summer vacation, Richard, 15, meets the free-spirited Dalton family and their beautiful daughter Clio. He falls in love with Clio and experiences a wild summer learning about their uninhibited lifestyle, family betrayals, and secrets. (Rev: BL 9/1/06; SLJ 10/06)

2003 Reid, Kimberly. *My Own Worst Frenemy* (8–11). Series: Landgon Prep Academy. 2011, Kensington paper $9.95 (978-0-7582-6740-5). At a new exclusive school, street-savvy Chanti finds herself suspected of theft and must identify the real perpetrator and clear her own name. ℯ (Rev: SLJ 12/1/11)

2004 Reinhardt, Dana. *Harmless* (7–12). 2007, Random House $15.99 (978-0-385-74699-1). Anna and Emma have been friends forever when Mariah enters the picture and widens their horizons, leading them, however, into a lie that has wide repercussions. ⌂ (Rev: BCCB 2/07; BL 12/1/06; LMC 4–5/07; SLJ 3/07)

2005 Reynolds, Clay. *Monuments* (10–12). 2000, Texas Tech Univ $29.95 (978-0-89672-433-4). The story of 14-year-old Hugh Rudd, life in his small Texas town, and his journey to manhood. (Rev: BL 7/00)

2006 Reynolds, Marilyn. *Beyond Dreams* (9–12). 1995, Morning Glory $15.95 (978-1-885356-01-7); paper $8.95 (978-1-885356-00-0). Using alternate male and female voices, Reynolds presents short stories of teens in crisis. (Rev: BL 11/15/95; SLJ 9/95; VOYA 2/96)

2007 Reynolds, Marilyn. *But What About Me?* (9–12). Series: True-to-Life. 1996, Morning Glory $15.95 (978-1-885356-11-6); paper $8.95 (978-1-885356-10-9). Eighteen-year-old Erica is trying to remain true to herself while her boyfriend is spiraling down a path to self-destruction in this story of the trials of true love. (Rev: SLJ 10/96; VOYA 2/97)

2008 Reynolds, Marilyn. *Detour for Emmy* (8–12). 1993, Morning Glory paper $8.95 (978-0-930934-76-7). Emmy is a good student and a hunk's girlfriend, but her home life includes a deserter father and an alcoholic mother. Emmy's pregnancy causes more hardship when she keeps the baby. (Rev: BL 10/1/93; SLJ 7/93; VOYA 12/93)

2009 Reynolds, Marilyn. *If You Loved Me: True-to-Life Series from Hamilton High* (8–12). 1999, Morning Glory paper $8.95 (978-1-885356-55-0). Seventeen-year-old Lauren, born to a drug-addicted mother now deceased, vows to abstain from drugs and sex, but the latter is particularly difficult because of an insistent boyfriend. (Rev: BL 9/1/99; HBG 4/00; VOYA 2/00)

2010 Reynolds, Marilyn. *Telling: True-to-Life Series from Hamilton High* (7–10). 1996, Morning Glory paper $8.95 (978-1-885356-03-1). Twelve-year-old Cassie is confused and embarrassed when her adult neighbor makes sexual advances towards her. (Rev: BL 4/1/96; SLJ 5/96; VOYA 6/96)

2011 Reynolds, Marilyn. *Too Soon for Jeff* (8–12). 1994, Morning Glory $15.95 (978-0-930934-90-3); paper $8.95 (978-0-930934-91-0). Jeff's hopes of going to college on a debate scholarship are put in jeopardy when his girlfriend happily announces she's pregnant. Jeff reluctantly prepares for fatherhood. (Rev: BL 9/15/94; SLJ 9/94; VOYA 12/94)

2012 Rhue, Morton. *The Wave* (7–10). 1981, Dell paper $5.50 (978-0-440-99371-1). A high school experiment to test social interaction backfires when an elitist group is formed.

2013 Richards, Alexandra. *Back Talk* (9–12). 2007, Flux paper $8.95 (978-0-7387-1017-4). Gemma, a 16-year-old from Idaho, learns that New York is not all about glamour when she interns on a TV talk show for the summer. (Rev: SLJ 12/07)

2014 Rivers, Karen. *The Healing Time of Hickeys* (9–12). 2004, Raincoast paper $6.95 (978-1-55192-600-1). Haley Andromeda Harmony, a 16-year-old hypochondriac, expects wonders from her senior year in high school but instead encounters a seemingly endless series of disasters and illnesses that she relates to her diary with wry wit. (Rev: BL 8/04; SLJ 6/04; VOYA 8/04)

2015 Robar, Serena. *Giving Up the V* (10–12). 2009, Simon & Schuster paper $8.99 (978-1-4169-7558-8). Does she want to lose her virginity? And if so, who with? Spencer, 16, has birth control pills but is uncertain about her desires in this frank story. ℮ (Rev: BL 8/09; SLJ 7/1/09)

2016 Robbins, Maggie. *Suzy Zeus Gets Organized* (11–12). 2005, Bloomsbury $17.95 (978-1-58234-535-2). An inventive novella in verse about saucy, sexy Suzy Zeus, newly arrived in New York from Indiana and full of zest for life until romance goes wrong; for mature readers. (Rev: BL 3/1/05)

2017 Roche, Lorcan. *The Companion* (11–12). 2010, Europa paper $15 (978-19333728-4-6). Loquacious Irishman Trevor uses his talent for storytelling as he cares for — and inspires — a young man with muscular dystrophy in this funny, irreverent coming-of-age story for mature readers. (Rev: BL 6/1–15/10)

2018 Rosen, Renee. *Every Crooked Pot* (10–12). 2007, St. Martin's paper $10.95 (978-0-312-36543-1). This is the story of Nina Goldman — a girl born with a facial disfigurement and a strong-willed father — and how she navigates her adolescence. (Rev: BL 8/07; SLJ 11/07)

2019 Rosen, Roger, and Patra M. Sevastiades, eds. *Coming of Age: The Art of Growing Up* (9–12). 1994, Rosen LB $21.95 (978-0-8239-1805-8); paper $11.95 (978-0-8239-1806-5). This multicultural anthology of short fiction and essays confronts traditional — and more complex — coming-of-age issues. (Rev: BL 1/1/95; SLJ 1/95)

2020 Rosenberg, Liz. *Heart and Soul* (8–12). 1996, Harcourt $11.00 (978-0-15-200942-7). It is only when Willie helps a troubled Jewish classmate that she is able to straighten out her own problems. (Rev: BL 6/1–15/96; VOYA 8/96)

2021 Rosenberg, Liz. *17: A Novel in Prose Poems* (10–12). 2002, Cricket $16.95 (978-0-8126-4915-4). Readers follow Stephanie through the stages of first love, from initial excitement to final separation. (Rev: BCCB 2/03; BL 11/15/02; HBG 3/03; SLJ 11/02; VOYA 4/03)

2022 Rosenfield, Kat. *Amelia Anne Is Dead and Gone* (9–12). 2012, Dutton $17.99 (978-052542389-8). When a girl's body is found in a small town, this has repercussions on many lives including that of Becca, a teen who had been planning her own future. ℮ (Rev: BL 8/12; LMC 1–2/13; SLJ 8/1/12)

2023 Rottman, S. L. *Rough Waters* (7–12). 1998, Peachtree $14.95 (978-1-56145-172-2). After the deaths of their parents, teenage brothers Gregg and Scott move to Colorado to live with an uncle who runs a white-water rafting business. (Rev: BL 5/1/98; HBG 9/98; SLJ 8/98; VOYA 8/98)

2024 Ruby, Laura. *Bad Apple* (8–12). 2009, HarperTeen $16.99 (978-0-06-124330-1). Tola (Cenerentola) Riley, a high school junior, struggles to tell the truth when she and her art teacher are accused of having an affair. (Rev: BL 11/15/09; LMC 11–12/09; SLJ 12/09)

2025 Rumley, Crickett. *Never Sit Down in a Hoopskirt and Other Things I Learned in Southern Belle Hell* (8–11). 2011, Egmont paper $8.99 (978-1-60684-131-0). Rebellious Jane — back home in Bienville, Alabama, after being thrown out of her 13th boarding school — is unexpectedly chosen as one of her Gulf town's Magnolia Maids, where she helps empower other outsiders and gradually gains acceptance. ℮ (Rev: BL 5/1/11; SLJ 6/11; VOYA 4/11)

2026 Runyon, Brent. *Surface Tension: A Novel in Four Summers* (8–11). 2009, Knopf $16.99 (978-037584446-1); LB $19.99 (978-037594446-8). This novel records how Luke changes over the summers he spends at his family's lake cabin from the ages of 13 to 16. Lexile HL720L (Rev: BL 2/15/09; SLJ 4/1/09)

2027 Ryan, P. E. *In Mike We Trust* (8–12). 2009, HarperTeen $16.99 (978-006085813-1). Gay-but-closeted Garth, 15, tries to free himself from the complications created by lies cooked up by his exploitative Uncle Mike. Lexile HL690L (Rev: BL 2/15/09; SLJ 3/1/09)

2028 Ryan, P. E. *Saints of Augustine* (8–11). 2007, HarperTempest $16.99 (978-0-06-085810-0). Charlie and Sam's close friendship was abruptly severed a year ago but their respective problems — including Charlie's use of drugs and Sam's worries about his sexuality — finally bring them together again. (Rev: BL 7/07; SLJ 10/07)

2029 Ryan, Sara. *Empress of the World* (9–12). 2001, Viking $15.99 (978-0-670-89688-2). Nic struggles with her feelings when she falls in love with another girl. (Rev: BCCB 9/01; BL 7/01; HB 9–10/01; HBG 3/02; SLJ 7/01; VOYA 8/01)

2030 Ryan, Sara. *The Rules for Hearts* (10–12). 2007, Viking $16.99 (978-0-670-05906-5). Battle spends the summer before college in Portland, Oregon, in a house full of people including her estranged older brother Nick, and learns a lot about love and family. (Rev: BL 6/1–15/07; SLJ 4/07)

2031 Ryan, Tom. *Way to Go* (8–11). 2012, Orca paper $12.95 (978-145980077-9). Danny, 17, is pretty sure he is gay but aims to test this during a summer in his tiny Nova Scotia town. ℮ (Rev: BLO 6/12; LMC 11–12/12; SLJ 6/12)

2032 Saenz, Benjamin Alire. *He Forgot to Say Goodbye* (8–11). 2008, Simon & Schuster $16.99 (978-1-4169-6228-1). Ramiro, from the poor section of El Paso, becomes friends with privileged Jake, the two fatherless young men forming a bond that is stronger than class or circumstance. (Rev: BL 4/15/08)

2033 Sáenz, Benjamin Alire. *Last Night I Sang to the Monster* (9–12). 2009, Cinco Puntos $19.95 (978-1-933693-58-3). Zach, an 18-year-old alcoholic from a dysfunctional family, ends up in residential rehab facility and begins the slow path towards healing aided by art, writing, and his middle-aged roommate Rafael. YALSA Top Ten Best Fiction for Young Adults 2011. ⌒ ℮ Lexile HL490L (Rev: BL 9/15/09; HB 1–2/10; LMC 3–4/10; SLJ 10/09; VOYA 12/09)

2034 Saenz, Benjamin Alire . *Aristotle and Dante Discover the Secrets of the Universe* (9–12). 2012, Simon & Schuster $16.99 (978-144240892-0). A friendship between Dante and Ari changes the two 15-year-old Mexican American loners. Belpré Winner 2013; Printz Award 2013; ALA Notable Books 2013; ; Stonewall Book Awards; YALSA Best Fiction for Young Adults. Lexile 380 (Rev: BL 1/1/12; HB 3–4/12; SLJ 2/12*; VOYA 2/12)

2035 Saldana, Rene. *The Whole Sky Full of Stars* (8–12). 2007, Random House $15.99 (978-0-385-73053-2). Barry agrees to a risky boxing match to help pay off a friend's gambling debt — and to help his own family after his father's death. (Rev: BCCB 5/07; BL 3/15/07; SLJ 5/07)

2036 Salinger, J. D. *The Catcher in the Rye* (7–12). 1951, Little, Brown $25.95 (978-0-316-76953-2). For mature readers, the saga of Holden Caulfield and his three days in New York City. (Rev: BL 10/1/88)

2037 Sanchez, Alex. *Boyfriends with Girlfriends* (9–12). 2011, Simon & Schuster $16.99 (978-1-4169-3773-9). Lance is gay and Sergio is bisexual, and heterosexual Allie finds herself attracted to Sergio's lesbian friend Kimiko in this novel about teens exploring their sexual identities. ℮ Lexile HL620L (Rev: BL 3/1/11*; SLJ 4/11; VOYA 4/11)

2038 Sanchez, Alex. *Getting It* (9–12). 2006, Simon & Schuster $16.95 (978-1-4169-0896-8). Carlos, 15, secretly asks a gay classmate to give him a makeover so he can try and land the popular girl Roxie as his girlfriend, and in exchange he must help Sal form a Gay-Straight Alliance at their high school. (Rev: BL 9/15/06; SLJ 11/06)

2039 Sanchez, Alex. *Rainbow Boys* (9–12). 2001, Simon & Schuster $17.00 (978-0-689-84100-2). The challenges facing gay teenagers are the focus of this novel about acceptance. (Rev: BL 11/15/01; HBG 3/02; SLJ 10/01; VOYA 12/01)

2040 Sanchez, Alex. *Rainbow Road* (9–12). 2005, Simon & Schuster $16.95 (978-0-689-86565-7). Gay teens Jason, Kyle, and Nelson take a road trip to LA where Jason will speak at the opening of a high school for gay and lesbian teens, encountering a variety of interesting individuals along the way. The final novel in a trilogy. (Rev: BL 9/1/05; SLJ 10/05)

2041 Sanchez, Jenny Torres. *The Downside of Being Charlie* (9–12). 2012, Running Press paper $9.95 (978-07624440-1-4). Charlie may have lost 30 pounds but problems at home and romantic disappointments at school make his senior year difficult. ℮ (Rev: BL 8/12; LMC 1–2/13; SLJ 5/1/12; VOYA 6/12)

2042 Schabas, Martha. *Various Positions* (9–12). 2012, Farrar $17.99 (978-037438086-1). Sex-obsessed Georgia, 14, is thrilled to get into ballet school in Toronto but has trouble dealing with her fantasies and the other ballerinas. ℮ Lexile HL780L (Rev: BLO 2/1/12; SLJ 2/12; VOYA 12/11)

2043 Scheidt, Erica Lorraine. *Uses for Boys* (9–12). 2013, St. Martin's paper $9.99 (978-12500071-1-7). Lonely Anna slowly learns to rely on herself for courage and inspiration after one too many bad experiences with boys. ⌒ ℮ (Rev: BL 11/15/12*; VOYA 4/13)

2044 Schmidt, Gary D. *Trouble* (7–10). 2008, Clarion paper $16.00 (978-0-618-92766-1). A multilayered novel in which Henry's brother dies after being hit by a truck driven by a classmate, a Cambodian immigrant named Chay; Henry later finds himself accepting a ride from Chay and the two learn more about each other. (Rev: BL 3/1/08; SLJ 4/08)

2045 Schmitt, Richard. *The Aerialist* (10–12). 2000, Overlook $26.95 (978-1-58567-070-3). This first novel presents a gritty behind-the-scenes look at life in a traveling circus. (Rev: BL 11/15/00*)

2046 Schneider, Robyn. *Better than Yesterday* (10–12). 2007, Delacorte $15.99 (978-0-385-73345-8). Four students about to start their senior year at a prestigious boarding school struggle with life in the fast lane (including sex, drinking, and partying) and their parents' high expectations. (Rev: BCCB 5/07; BL 4/1/07; LMC 4–5/07; SLJ 4/07)

2047 Schraff, Anne. *To Catch a Dream* (6–10). Series: Urban Underground. 2010, Saddleback Educational paper $8.95 (978-16165126-9-9). Abel, 16, struggles to achieve his ambition of becoming a chef in the face of many obstacles. Lexile HL630L (Rev: BL 8/11)

2048 Schreck, Karen Halvorsen. *Dream Journal* (7–10). 2006, Hyperion $15.99 (978-1-4231-0105-5). Sixteen-year-old Livy's dream journal records the happy times before her mother became terminally ill, and before Livy tried to renew her friendship with Ruth with "fun" that turns into tragedy. (Rev: SLJ 11/06)

2049 Scott, Elizabeth. *Living Dead Girl* (10–12). 2008, Simon & Schuster $16.99 (978-141696059-1). A courageous 15-year-old girl describes the horrors of her five years as a captive, undergoing sexual and emotional abuse at the hands of a man called Ray who will then discard her as too old; a compelling and distressing story. ⌒ ⓔ Lexile 870L (Rev: BL 10/15/08*; HB 11–12/08; LMC 1–2/09; SLJ 10/1/08; VOYA 2/09)

2050 Scott, Elizabeth. *Something, Maybe* (8–11). 2009, Simon & Schuster $16.99 (978-141697865-7). Hannah — the child of a famous playboy and an Internet sex celebrity — is unsure about romance and about her relationship with her father. Lexile HL760L (Rev: BL 2/15/09; SLJ 5/1/09)

2051 Scott, Elizabeth. *Stealing Heaven* (7–10). 2008, HarperTeen $16.99 (978-0-06-112280-4). Dani, weary from the life of crime she and her mother have long lived, yearns for normalcy when they move to the town of Heaven. (Rev: BL 4/15/08; SLJ 8/08)

2052 Scott, Kieran. *Geek Magnet* (9–12). 2008, Putnam $16.99 (978-0-399-24760-6). KJ seems to attract the wrong type of guy and tries to get in with the popular crowd by becoming the stage manager for the high school play. (Rev: BL 5/15/08; SLJ 6/08)

2053 Scott, Kieran. *I Was a Non-Blonde Cheerleader* (7–10). 2005, Penguin $16.99 (978-0-399-24279-3). As a brunette, Annisa has a hard time fitting in at her new high school where almost everybody else is blond. (Rev: BL 1/1–15/05; SLJ 1/05; VOYA 4/05)

2054 Scott, Kieran. *A Non-Blonde Cheerleader in Love* (8–12). 2007, Putnam $16.99 (978-0-399-24494-0). Annisa's cheerleading squad goes coed in this sequel to *I Was a Non-Blonde Cheerleader* (2005) and *Brunettes Strike Back* (2006). (Rev: BL 8/07; SLJ 6/07)

2055 Selvadurai, Shyam. *Swimming in the Monsoon Sea* (8–11). 2005, Tundra $18.95 (978-0-88776-735-7). In Sri Lanka in 1980, Amrith's expected quiet summer is enlivened by the arrival from Canada of his cousin Niresh, a boy with whom he soon falls in love but who does not share his feelings. (Rev: BL 9/15/05*; SLJ 11/05)

2056 Seymour, Tres. *The Revelation of Saint Bruce* (7–12). 1998, Orchard paper $16.95 (978-0-531-30109-8). Because of his honesty, Bruce is responsible for the expulsion of several friends from school. (Rev: BL 10/15/98; HBG 3/99; SLJ 9/98; VOYA 2/99)

2057 Shanahan, Lisa. *The Sweet, Terrible, Glorious Year I Truly, Completely Lost It* (7–10). 2007, Delacorte $15.99 (978-0-385-75316-2). In this coming-of-age novel set in small-town Australia, 14-year-old Gemma deals with her emotional family, her sister's wedding, the school play, and shifting romantic attractions. (Rev: BL 8/07; SLJ 8/07)

2058 Shaw, Liane. *Fostergirls* (8–12). 2011, Second Story paper $11.95 (978-1-897187-90-6). Foster child Sadie, 15, is in her 13th home and determined to keep a low profile until she reaches 16 and can seek emancipation. (Rev: SLJ 12/1/11)

2059 Shaw, Susan. *Safe* (7–10). 2007, Dutton $16.99 (978-0-525-47829-4). Thirteen-year-old Tracy, whose mother died when she was 3, is overwhelmed by fears after she is raped by the older brother of a classmate. (Rev: BL 9/15/07; SLJ 12/07)

2060 Shaw, Tucker. *Confessions of a Backup Dancer* (8–12). 2004, Simon & Schuster paper $8.99 (978-0-689-87075-0). Seventeen-year-old Kelly Kimball, a talented dancer, suddenly finds herself thrust into a close relationship with pop diva Darcy Barnes; in this journal-like novel, Kelly dishes the dirt on Darcy and the diva's entourage. (Rev: BL 9/15/04; SLJ 8/04)

2061 Shea, John, and Michael Harmon. *A Kid from Southie* (9–12). 2011, WestSide $16.95 (978-1-934813-53-9). Irish American Aiden, 17, faces many difficulty choices in this gritty novel about a difficult family life, drugs and Mafia temptations, a biracial girlfriend, and the lure of a career in boxing. Lexile HL590L (Rev: BL 9/1/11; SLJ 9/1/11)

2062 Sheldon, Dyan. *Planet Janet* (6–10). 2003, Candlewick $14.99 (978-0-7636-2048-6). Janet pours out to her diary the frustrations she and her friend Disha face in their dealings with family and friends in this entertaining novel set in London. (Rev: BCCB 3/03; BL 3/15/03; HBG 4/04; SLJ 5/03)

2063 Sheppard, John. *Small Town Punk* (10–12). 2007, Ig paper $13.95 (978-0-9771972-5-5). In Sarasota, Florida, in the early 1980s, 17-year-old Buzz and his younger sister are living aimless lives — unhappy at school, working part-time jobs, doing drugs, and drinking; told in a series of interconnected, semiautobiographical stories. (Rev: BL 11/15/06)

2064 Shoup, Barbara. *Stranded in Harmony* (7–10). 1997, Hyperion LB $18.49 (978-0-7868-2284-3). Lucas, an 18-year-old popular senior in high school, is discontented until he meets and becomes friendly with an older woman. (Rev: BL 7/97; HBG 3/98; SLJ 6/97*)

2065 Shulman, Mark. *Scrawl* (7–10). 2010, Roaring Brook $16.99 (978-1-59643-417-2). Todd, an 8th-grade bully, gets caught vandalizing school property and is sentenced to detention and writing journal entries — which proves quite revealing. e Lexile 650L (Rev: BLO 8/10; LMC 11–12/10*; SLJ 11/1/10; VOYA 10/10)

2066 Siegel, Lee. *Who Wrote the Book of Love?* (11–12). 2005, Univ. of Chicago $24.00 (978-0-226-75700-1). A humorous look at the sexual ambitions of a young male narrator in the 1950s; for mature teens. (Rev: BL 5/1/05)

2067 Simon, Charnan. *Plan B* (8–12). Series: Surviving Southside. 2011, Lerner/Darby Creek LB $27.93 (978-076136149-7); paper $7.95 (9780761361633). High schoolers Lucy and Luke struggle with difficult decisions when Lucy becomes pregnant; suitable for reluctant readers. Lexile HL430L (Rev: BL 5/1/11; SLJ 4/11)

2068 Sinclair, April. *Coffee Will Make You Black* (9–12). 1994, Hyperion $19.95 (978-1-56282-796-0). Set in late 1960s Chicago, 11-year-old "Stevie" Stevenson's growth from child to woman parallels the growth of African American pride and equality. (Rev: BL 12/15/93)

2069 Singer, Marilyn. *The Course of True Love Never Did Run Smooth* (10–12). 1983, HarperCollins $12.95 (978-0-06-025753-8). A gay couple "come out" during a school production of *A Midsummer Night's Dream*. (Rev: BL 6/87)

2070 Singer, Marilyn, ed. *Stay True: Short Stories for Strong Girls* (7–12). 1998, Scholastic paper $16.95 (978-0-590-36031-9). There are 11 new short stories in this collection that explores the problems girls face growing up and how they discover inner strength. (Rev: BL 4/1/98; HB 3–4/98; SLJ 5/98; VOYA 4/98)

2071 Skovron, Jon. *Struts and Frets* (9–12). 2009, Abrams $16.95 (978-0-8109-4174-8). In this funny novel, Sammy, 17, is preoccupied with his band — is it good enough to enter that recording competition? — and with his girlfriend, who seems to be interested in getting physical. YALSA Popular Paperbacks for Young Adults Top Ten 2013. Lexile HL670L (Rev: BLO 10/9/09; SLJ 1/10; VOYA 2/10)

2072 Sloan, Brian. *Tale of Two Summers* (10–12). 2006, Simon & Schuster $15.95 (978-0-689-87439-0). Chuck and Hal have been best friends since they were five even though Chuck is straight and Hal is gay. Now they're 15 and must spend the summer apart but they talk online through a blog every day about things like Hal's summer fling with a French foreign exchange student who has a problem with drugs and Chuck's romance with a girl at summer theater camp. (Rev: BL 9/1/06; SLJ 9/06)

2073 Smith, Betty. *Joy in the Morning* (9–12). 1963, HarperCollins paper $6.50 (978-0-06-080368-1). Two young people face a number of problems when their families disown them after finding out about their marriage.

2074 Smith, D. James. *My Brother's Passion* (11–12). 2005, Permanent $22.00 (978-1-57962-107-0). Dave, a Korean American preteen, comes of age in the 70s and during and after his adored brother's tour in Vietnam witnesses shocking small-town cruelties that culminate in tragedy. (Rev: BL 2/15/05; SLJ 7/05)

2075 Smith, Jennifer E. *You Are Here* (8–11). 2009, Simon & Schuster $15.99 (978-141696799-6). Sixteen-year-old Emma, who has always felt detached from her family, discovers she had a twin brother who died when they were newly born; she and a friend Peter set off on a road trip to visit her brother's grave and learn about each other on the way. (Rev: BL 6/1–15/09; SLJ 8/09)

2076 Smith, Kirsten. *The Geography of Girlhood* (8–11). 2006, Little, Brown $16.99 (978-0-316-16021-6). High schooler Penny documents in verse her unhappy family, school, and friendship experiences, all overshadowed by her mother's abandonment when she was young. (Rev: BCCB 5/06; BL 2/1/06; SLJ 5/06)

2077 Soehnlein, K. M. *Robin and Ruby* (11–12). 2010, Kensington $24 (978-075823218-2). Robin, the protagonist of *The World of Normal Boys* (2000), returns to save his sister from a troubled boyfriend who's recently resurfaced, and explore his deepening affections for his best friend George, in this novel set against the high-stakes backdrop of 1980s AIDS paranoia; for mature readers. (Rev: BL 3/1–15/10)

2078 Sones, Sonya. *What My Mother Doesn't Know* (6–10). 2001, Simon & Schuster $17.00 (978-0-689-84114-9). Sophie, 14, expresses her feelings about falling in and out of love in a poetic narrative that is humorous and romantic. (Rev: BCCB 12/01; BL 11/1/01; HBG 10/02; SLJ 10/01; VOYA 10/01)

2079 Soto, Gary. *Accidental Love* (7–10). 2006, Harcourt $16.00 (978-0-15-205497-7). Something clicks when 14-year-old Marisa meets wimpy Rene and she is inspired to transfer to his school, where, despite complications, she finds herself blossoming socially and academically — and enjoying her first love. (Rev: BL 1/1–15/06; SLJ 1/06; VOYA 2/06)

2080 Soto, Gary. *Buried Onions* (8–12). 1997, Harcourt $17.00 (978-0-15-201333-2). A junior college dropout, 19-year-old Eddie is trying to support himself in this story set in the barrio of Fresno, California. (Rev: BL 11/15/97; HBG 3/98; SLJ 1/98; VOYA 10/97)

2081 Spanbauer, Tom. *Now Is the Hour* (11–12). 2006, Houghton Mifflin $26.00 (978-0-618-58421-5). Rigby can't wait to get away from the Iowa farm of his childhood, and when he finally does, he discovers his true sexual nature in this novel set in the 1960s; for mature teens only. (Rev: BL 5/1/06)

2082 Spencer, Katherine. *More Than Friends* (7–10). 2008, Harcourt paper $6.95 (978-01520574-6-6). Teenage Grace is determined to overcome the self-destructive behavior she adopted after her brother's death in this story with a romantic twist; a sequel to *Saving Grace* (2006). (Rev: BL 8/08; VOYA 4/08)

2083 Spinelli, Jerry. *Hokey Pokey* (7–12). 2013, Knopf $15.99 (978-037583198-0); LB $18.99 (978-037593198-7). Jack comes to the unwelcome realization that he is growing up and will soon be leaving the wonderful world of Hokey Pokey. ⌒ ℮ Lexile HL600L (Rev: BL 11/1/12; HB 5–6/13; LMC 5–6/13; SLJ 1/13*; VOYA 12/12)

2084 Spinelli, Jerry. *Jason and Marceline* (7–10). 2000, Little, Brown paper $6.99 (978-0-316-80662-6). Jason, now in the 9th grade, sorts out his feelings toward girls in general and Marceline in particular. Preceded by *Space Station Seventh Grade*. (Rev: BL 1/1/87; SLJ 2/87)

2085 Spinelli, Jerry. *Love, Stargirl* (7–10). 2007, Knopf $16.99 (978-0-375-81375-7). In this sequel to the 2000 novel, 15-year-old Stargirl has moved to Pennsylvania and writes letters to her former boyfriend Leo, describing her new life and the very varied friends she has made in her new home. ⌒ (Rev: BL 8/07; HB 9–10/07; SLJ 9/07)

2086 St. James, James. *Freak Show* (9–12). 2007, Dutton $18.99 (978-0-525-47799-0). A funny and honest story of Billy, a teenage drag queen who seeks acceptance from his peers at his new, conservative high school while remaining true to himself. (Rev: SLJ 6/07)

2087 Stampler, Ann Redisch. *Where It Began* (9–12). 2012, Simon & Schuster $16.99 (978-1-4424-2321-3). Waking up in hospital after a horrible car crash, high school student Gabby assumes she got drunk and drove her boyfriend's BMW into a tree, but she just can't remember any details. ℮ Lexile 1150L (Rev: LMC 5–6/12; SLJ 5/1/12; VOYA 2/12)

2088 Stevenson, Robin. *Inferno* (9–12). 2009, Orca paper $12.95 (978-155469077-0). A move from the city to a suburban high school leaves lesbian Dante dissatisfied and she struggles to find her balance when a new friend leaves town and a dropout's unconventional life seems attractive. (Rev: BL 6/1–15/09)

2089 Stevenson, Robin. *Out of Order* (8–11). 2007, Orca paper $8.95 (978-1-55143-693-7). Sophie, newly slim, is starting high school in a new town and is attracted to classmate Zelia's wild ways until Zelia attempts suicide in this novel about self-perception, sexual identity, and self-respect. (Rev: BL 1/1–15/08)

2090 Stinson, Loretta. *Little Green* (11–12). 2010, Hawthorne paper $15.95 (978-09790188-1-7). When troubled 16-year-old Janie hooks up with Paul, a drug-dealing biker, at an Oregon bar, she slowly comes to understand the peril of their relationship and the changes she must make in order to protect herself.; set in the 1970s this book is suitable for mature readers. (Rev: BL 6/1–15/10)

2091 Stinson, Susan. *Fat Girl Dances with Rocks* (9–12). 1994, Spinsters Ink paper $10.95 (978-1-883523-02-2). Char, 17 and overweight, struggles with her identity, the meaning of beauty, and her confusion when her best friend, Felice, kisses her on the lips. (Rev: BL 9/1/94; VOYA 5/95)

2092 Stone, Heather Duffy. *This Is What I Want to Tell You* (9–12). 2009, Flux paper $9.95 (978-073871450-9). Teenage twins Nadio and Noelle deal with romantic relationships and shifting friendships. ℮ (Rev: BL 1/1–15/09)

2093 Stork, Francisco X. *Behind the Eyes* (10–12). 2006, Dutton $16.99 (978-0-525-47735-8). Hector, 16, is a good student who comes from a struggling Mexican American family but after he seeks revenge for his brother's gang-related death he must attend a reform school in San Antonio. (Rev: BL 9/1/06; LMC 1/07; SLJ 10/06; VOYA)

2094 Strasnick, Lauren. *Nothing Like You* (8–10). 2009, Simon & Schuster paper $16.99 (978-1-4169-8264-7). After her mother's death, high school senior Holly Hirsch puts her self-worth aside to seek acceptance in the arms of a popular, handsome guy who hides their relationship from everyone he knows. ℮ (Rev: BL 9/15/09; SLJ 10/09)

2095 Strasser, Todd. *Boot Camp* (8–12). 2007, Simon & Schuster $15.99 (978-1-4169-0848-7). After several warnings about his behavior (dating a teacher), Garrett's parents decide to send the 15-year-old to a disciplinary boot camp; Garrett's descriptions of the mental and physical abuse he undergoes at this camp are realistic. (Rev: BL 8/07; LMC 11–12/07; SLJ 4/07)

2096 Strasser, Todd. *Can't Get There from Here* (7–12). 2004, Simon & Schuster $15.95 (978-0-689-84169-9). A teenage girl who has been thrown out by an abusive mother tries to survive on the streets of New York City. (Rev: BL 3/15/04; SLJ 3/04; VOYA 6/04)

2097 Strauss, Peggy Guthart. *Getting the Boot* (8–12). Series: Students Across the Seven Seas. 2005, Penguin paper $6.99 (978-0-14-240414-0). A light story about popular high school junior Kelly Brandt's summer as an exchange student in Italy. (Rev: BL 5/15/05; SLJ 8/05)

2098 Sullivan, J. Courtney. *Commencement* (11–12). 2009, Knopf $24 (978-030727074-0). Four girls meet at Smith College and though they have different personalities and goals, they form bonds that last until well after graduation; for mature readers. ∩ ℮ (Rev: BL 4–5/09)

2099 Summer, Jane. *Not the Only One: Lesbian and Gay Fiction for Teens* (7–12). 2004, Alyson paper $13.95 (978-1-55583-834-8). This revised edition includes 10 new stories featuring gay and lesbian teens. (Rev: BL 12/15/04; VOYA 2/05)

2100 Sumner, Melanie. *The School of Beauty and Charm* (10–12). 2001, Algonquin $23.95 (978-1-56512-286-4). After the sudden death of her brother, teenage Louise runs away and joins a circus in this story for mature readers. (Rev: BL 8/01; SLJ 3/02)

2101 Supplee, Suzanne. *Artichoke's Heart* (7–10). 2008, Dutton $16.99 (978-0-525-47902-4). Overweight Rosemary is trying to deal with kids at school teasing her when her mother is diagnosed with cancer. (Rev: BL 5/1/08; SLJ 8/08)

2102 Swann, Maxine. *Serious Girls* (11–12). 2003, St. Martin's $23.00 (978-0-312-28802-0). Teen friends Maya and Roe search for meaning in their lives and fall into difficult sexual relationships in the process; for mature teens. (Rev: BL 10/1/03; VOYA 6/04)

2103 Sweeney, Joyce. *Waiting for June* (8–11). 2003, Marshall Cavendish $15.95 (978-0-7614-5138-9). High school senior Sophie is pregnant, reluctant to disclose the identity of the father, and in danger in this complex, suspenseful novel. (Rev: BL 9/1/03; HBG 4/04; SLJ 10/03; VOYA 4/04)

2104 Tan, Shaun. *Lost and Found: Three by Shaun Tan* (5–10). Illus. by author. 2011, Scholastic $21.99 (978-0-545-22924-1). A beautifully illustrated collection of three stories first published in Australia and dealing with loss. ALA Notable Books 2012. (Rev: BL 4/1/11; HB 5–6/11; SLJ 4/11*)

2105 Taylor, Michelle. *What's Happily Ever After, Anyway?* (9–12). 2004, Brown Barn paper $10.95 (978-0-9746481-3-2). Sixteen-year-old Miranda and her boyfriend, Keith, face a tough decision when she discovers that she is pregnant. (Rev: SLJ 2/05)

2106 Tharp, Tim. *The Spectacular Now* (8–12). 2008, Knopf $16.99 (978-037585179-7); LB $19.99 (978-037595179-4). Part comedic, part poignant, this novel explores the often reckless life of Sutter, a high school party boy, and the hurt and denial driving him. ∩ ℮ Lexile HL790L (Rev: BL 11/15/08; SLJ 12/08)

2107 Thesman, Jean. *Couldn't I Start Over?* (7–10). 1989, Avon paper $2.95 (978-0-380-75717-6). Grow-

ing up in a caring family situation, teenager Shiloh still faces many problems in her coming of age. (Rev: BL 11/15/89; VOYA 2/90)

2108 Thompson, Julian. *Philo Fortune's Awesome Journey to His Comfort Zone* (8–12). 1995, Hyperion $16.95 (978-0-7868-0067-4). A story of a youth who discovers the possibilities of the man he might become. (Rev: BL 5/1/95; SLJ 5/95; VOYA 2/96)

2109 Tibensky, Arlaina. *And Then Things Fall Apart* (9–12). 2011, Simon & Schuster paper $9.99 (978-1-4424-1-323-8). Keek, 15, finds comfort in Plath's *The Bell Jar* as she struggles to cope with her parents' divorce, her problems with her boyfriend, and a case of chicken pox. ℮ Lexile 930L (Rev: BL 9/15/11; SLJ 12/1/11; VOYA 8/11)

2110 Todd, Pamela. *The Blind Faith Hotel* (8–12). 2008, Simon & Schuster $16.99 (978-141695494-1). After getting caught shoplifting, defiant 14-year-old Zoe is assigned community service at a nature center and finally comes to appreciate her new surroundings in the rural Midwest, aided by a budding romance with fellow miscreant Todd. ℮ Lexile 780L (Rev: BL 10/15/08; SLJ 12/08; VOYA 2/09)

2111 Toews, Miriam. *A Complicated Kindness: A Novel* (10–12). 2004, Counterpoint $23.00 (978-1-58243-321-9). Sixteen-year-old Nomi Nichol, increasingly uncomfortable living in a repressive Mennonite community in Canada, tries to lose herself in drugs and dreams of escape to New York City. (Rev: BL 9/15/04; SLJ 4/05)

2112 Torres, Laura. *November Ever After* (8–12). 1999, Holiday $16.95 (978-0-8234-1464-2). Still recovering from her mother's death, 16-yer-old Amy discovers that her best friend, Sara, is a lesbian and in love with a girl in her class. (Rev: BL 12/1/99; HBG 4/00; SLJ 1/00)

2113 Townley, Roderick. *Sky: A Novel in 3 Sets and an Encore* (7–10). 2004, Simon & Schuster $16.95 (978-0-689-85712-6). Angered by his father's opposition to his interest in jazz, 15-year-old Sky runs away from home and moves in with the blind jazz pianist whose life he saved. (Rev: BL 8/04; SLJ 7/04)

2114 Trueman, Terry. *7 Days at the Hot Corner* (8–11). 2007, HarperTempest $16.99 (978-0-06-057494-9). The "hot corner" of the title is third base, Scott's position on the varsity baseball team, which is threatened when Scott fears he may have contracted AIDS while tending to an injured teammate and friend who is gay. (Rev: BCCB 4/07; BL 2/1/07; SLJ 4/07)

2115 Tullson, Diane. *Blue Highway* (9–12). 2004, Fitzhenry & Whiteside $9.95 (978-1-55005-124-7). High school student Truth is bound to her friend Skye by a traumatic childhood incident, and together the two slip deeper into an alcoholic haze until Truth wakes up to what's happening to her life. (Rev: BL 11/15/04; SLJ 12/04; VOYA 2/05)

2116 Tullson, Diane. *Edge* (7–10). 2003, Fitzhenry & Whiteside paper $6.95 (978-0-7737-6230-5). Tired of being bullied, Marlie Peters, 14, joins a group of other outcast students only to realize that they are involved in a dangerous plot. (Rev: BL 3/1/03; SLJ 10/03; VOYA 6/03)

2117 Uhlig, Richard. *Last Dance at the Frosty Queen* (10–12). 2007, Knopf $15.99 (978-0-375-83967-2). Arty wants to leave his tiny Kansas hometown as soon as he graduates from high school, but when he meets Vanessa he is less resentful of his many ties (including sexual, monetary, and familial) to Harker City; for mature teens. (Rev: BL 7/07; SLJ 11/07)

2118 Uppal, Priscila. *The Divine Economy of Salvation* (11–12). 2002, Algonquin $24.95 (978-1-56512-365-6). As Sister Angela looks back at her childhood in a Catholic girls' school and the cliques and jealousies that existed, she reassesses her role in a violent incident; for mature teens. (Rev: BL 8/02)

2119 Vail, Rachel. *Gorgeous* (7–10). Series: Avery Sisters Trilogy. 2009, HarperTeen $16.99 (978-0-06-089046-9). Ninth-grader Allison longs to be attractive and is stunned when she becomes a finalist in a teen magazine model contest. **e** Lexile 740L (Rev: BL 8/09; HB 7–8/09; SLJ 7/1/09; VOYA 8/09)

2120 Vail, Rachel. *If We Kiss* (7–10). 2005, HarperCollins LB $16.89 (978-0-06-056915-0). Fourteen-year-old Charlie struggles with feelings of guilt after she kisses Kevin, who just happens to be her best friend's steady. (Rev: BCCB 5/05; BL 3/15/05; HB 7–8/05; SLJ 5/05)

2121 Vail, Rachel. *Lucky* (7–10). 2008, HarperTeen $16.99 (978-0-06-089043-8). Fourteen-year-old Phoebe's family has never had to worry about money, so when her mother loses her job, Phoebe's new reality changes how she looks at the world and how her friends look at her. (Rev: BL 3/1/08; SLJ 4/08)

2122 Vail, Rachel. *You, Maybe: The Profound Asymmetry of Love in High School* (8–11). 2006, HarperCollins $15.99 (978-0-06-056917-4). Smart, secure teen Josie's confidence is shattered when a boy she casually "hooks up" with gains her trust and then breaks her heart. (Rev: BL 5/1/06; HB 5–6/06; SLJ 7/06)

2123 van Diepen, Allison. *Snitch* (7–10). 2007, Simon & Schuster paper $6.99 (978-1-4169-5030-1). Julia is reluctantly caught up in the world of gang violence when she falls in love with a Crip in this cautionary tale. (Rev: BL 1/1–15/08)

2124 Vande Velde, Vivian. *Curses, Inc.: And Other Stories* (6–10). 1997, Harcourt $16.00 (978-0-15-201452-0). In the title story in this collection of tales with surprise endings, Bill Essler thinks he has found the perfect way to get even with his girlfriend, who humiliated him, by utilizing a web site, Curses, Inc. (Rev: SLJ 6/97*; VOYA 6/97)

2125 Vasey, Paul. *A Troublesome Boy* (9–12). 2012, Groundwood $16.95 (978-1-55498-154-0); paper $9.95 (978-1-55498-155-7). In 1959 Ireland 14-year-old Teddy is sent off to an abusive Catholic boarding school where his closest friend commits suicide. **e** (Rev: BL 5/15/12; LMC 11–12/12; SLJ 8/1/12)

2126 Vaught, Susan. *Big Fat Manifesto* (9–12). 2008, Bloomsbury $16.95 (978-1-59990-206-7). Jamie doesn't like being fat, but she writes a column for her school paper defending the obese and ostracized and discussing her boyfriend's decision to have bariatric surgery. (Rev: BL 12/15/07; LMC 2/08; SLJ 1/08)

2127 Vaught, Susan. *Going Underground* (9–12). 2011, Bloomsbury $16.99 (978-1-59990-640-9). Del, now 17 and working as a gravedigger when not in school, has lived in a state of withdrawal since being found guilty of "sexting" three years before. **e** Lexile 870L (Rev: BL 10/1/11; LMC 1–2/12*; SLJ 12/1/11)

2128 Vega, Denise. *Rock On: A Story of Guitars, Gigs, Girls, and a Brother (Not Necessarily in That Order)* (8–12). 2012, Little, Brown $17.99 (978-031613310-4). Orion Taylor, 16, is just starting to feel optimistic about himself and his future as a musician but his older brother's unexpected return from college upsets this new worldview. **e** (Rev: BL 3/15/12; SLJ 3/12)

2129 Velasquez, Gloria. *Tommy Stands Alone* (7–10). 1995, Arte Publico paper $9.95 (978-1-55885-147-4). An engaging story about a Latino gay teen who is humiliated and rejected but finds understanding from a Chicano therapist. (Rev: BL 10/15/95; SLJ 11/95; VOYA 12/95)

2130 Verdelle, A. J. *The Good Negress* (9–12). 1995, Algonquin $29.95 (978-1-56512-085-3). Neesey, 13, returns to Detroit from her grandmother's in the South and rages internally over family obligations and a desire for white people's education. (Rev: BL 2/15/95; SLJ 10/95)

2131 Violi, Jen. *Putting Makeup on Dead People* (8–12). 2011, Hyperion $16.99 (978-142313481-7). Donna takes an internship at a funeral home as a way of working through her father's death and she finds the science and art of the job fascinating. **e** Lexile HL820L (Rev: BL 10/15/11; LMC 10/11; VOYA 6/11)

2132 Vivian, Siobhan. *Same Difference* (8–11). 2009, Scholastic $16.99 (978-054500407-7). Sixteen-year-old Emily takes a summer art course in Philadelphia and finds many differences from — and similarities to — her life in privileged suburbia. Lexile HL740L (Rev: BL 5/1/09; SLJ 5/1/09; VOYA 6/09)

2133 Vlautin, Willy. *Lean on Pete* (10–12). 2010, HarperPerennial paper $13.99 (978-00614565-3-4). Homeless 15-year-old Charley finds a friend in an aging racehorse, and relays the story of his troubled life as he and the horse travel together searching for a safe haven. **e** (Rev: BL 4/15/10*)

2134 Volponi, Paul. *Black and White* (9–12). 2005, Viking $15.99 (978-0-670-06006-1). Marcus and Eddie — best friends, stars of their high school basketball team, and African American and white respectively — find their friendship put to the test when they commit a robbery and only one of them is caught. (Rev: BCCB 6/05; BL 9/1/05*; SLJ 6/05)

2135 Volponi, Paul. *Crossing Lines* (7–12). 2011, Viking $16.99 (978-0-670-01214-5). Adonis is protective of his status as a football player and realizes too late that he could have acted to protect transgendered Alan from the cruelty of others. **e** Lexile 810L (Rev: BL 5/1/11; SLJ 11/1/11; VOYA 4/11)

2136 Volponi, Paul. *Homestretch* (7–10). 2009, Simon & Schuster $16.99 (978-1-4169-3987-0). When his father's behavior becomes unbearable after his mother is killed in an accident, high school senior Gas runs away and finds work at a horse track with the help of young Mexicans, a group his bigoted father blamed for his mother's death. (Rev: BL 9/15/09; SLJ 12/09)

2137 Volponi, Paul. *Rikers High* (8–11). 2010, Viking $16.99 (978-0-670-011070-). Martin attends high school at Rikers Island while he is waiting for his trial date; this book gives a good description of life in jail and will appeal to male reluctant readers. YALSA Quick Picks for Reluctant Young Adult Readers 2011. **e** Lexile 790L (Rev: BL 12/1/09; LMC 3–4/10; SLJ 1/10)

2138 Von Ziegesar, Cecily. *Because I'm Worth It* (10–12). Series: Gossip Girl. 2003, Little, Brown paper $8.99 (978-0-316-90968-6). The soap opera continues as Dan, Vanessa, and Serena all have successes but Nat is caught using drugs and Blair is still trying to get into Yale and risks becoming entangled with an older man. (Rev: SLJ 2/04)

2139 Von Ziegesar, Cecily. *Nothing Can Keep Us Together* (10–12). Series: Gossip Girl. 2005, Little, Brown $9.99 (978-0-316-73509-4). In the eighth volume of this series, the regular cast of characters prepares for high school graduation and what lies beyond. (Rev: BL 12/1/05)

2140 Walker, Melissa. *Small Town Sinners* (9–12). 2011, Bloomsbury $16.99 (978-1-59990-527-3). A series of events causes high school junior Lacey to question the evangelical Christian values she was raised with. **e** (Rev: SLJ 12/1/11)

2141 Walker, Paul R. *The Method* (8–12). 1990, Harcourt $14.95 (978-0-15-200528-3). A candid novel about a 15-year-old boy, his acting aspirations, and his sexual problems. (Rev: BL 8/90; SLJ 6/90)

2142 Wallace, Rich. *Losing Is Not an Option* (6–10). 2003, Knopf $15.95 (978-0-375-81351-1). Nine stories follow Ron, a high school athlete, through coming-of-age experiences including family problems, budding sexual attractions, and competition with his peers.

(Rev: BL 8/03; HB 9–10/03; HBG 4/04; SLJ 9/03; VOYA 10/03)

2143 Wallace, Rich. *One Good Punch* (9–12). 2007, Knopf $15.99 (978-0-375-81352-8). During his senior year, Michael, a talented writer and track star, must make a tough decision when his friend leaves drugs in his locker and Michael is faced with the blame and expulsion from school. (Rev: BL 9/1/07)

2144 Walters, Eric. *Sketches* (7–10). 2008, Viking $15.99 (978-0-670-06294-2). Runaway Dana, 14, finds solace at Sketches, an art center for homeless teens in Toronto. (Rev: BL 1/1–15/08; SLJ 4/08)

2145 Waltman, Kevin. *Nowhere Fast* (8–12). 2002, Scholastic paper $7.99 (978-0-439-41424-1). After stealing a car for joyriding, teenagers Gary and Wilson become entrapped in the activities of a former teacher with a dangerous agenda. (Rev: BL 2/1/03; SLJ 4/03; VOYA 4/03)

2146 Wartski, Maureen C. *My Name Is Nobody* (7–10). 1988, Walker $15.95 (978-0-8027-6770-7). A victim of child abuse survives a suicide attempt and is given a second chance by a tough ex-cop. (Rev: BL 2/1/88; SLJ 3/88; VOYA 4/88)

2147 Wasserman, Robin. *Lust* (8–11). Series: Seven Deadly Sins. 2005, Simon & Schuster paper $7.99 (978-0-689-87782-7). In an entertaining opening volume of a soap-opera-like series, several sex-obsessed high school seniors in a small California town ruthlessly scheme to win the girl or guy of their dreams. (Rev: BL 12/1/05; SLJ 1/06)

2148 Watson, Sterling. *Sweet Dream Baby* (11–12). 2002, Sourcebooks $22.00 (978-1-4022-0017-5). In 1950s Florida, young Travis's obsession with his beautiful and wild 16-year-old Aunt Delia has shocking results; for mature teens. (Rev: BL 10/1/02)

2149 Weaver, Beth Nixon. *Rooster* (7–12). 2001, Winslow $16.95 (978-1-58837-001-3). In the 1960s, 15-year-old Kady is growing up in a confusing mix of poverty at home on a struggling orange grove, a devoted but disabled neighboring child, and a wealthy boyfriend who introduces her to marijuana. (Rev: BL 7/01; HB 7–8/01; HBG 10/01; SLJ 6/01; VOYA 2/02)

2150 Weaver, Will. *Full Service* (7–10). 2005, Farrar $17.00 (978-0-374-32485-8). Paul, a sheltered Christian 15-year-old, discovers hippies, alcohol, and sex when he takes a job at a gas station in the summer of 1965. (Rev: BL 9/1/05; SLJ 11/05; VOYA 10/05)

2151 Weinheimer, Beckie. *Converting Kate* (7–10). 2007, Viking $16.99 (978-0-670-06152-5). Her parents' divorce and her father's death have led Kate, 16, to question her faith in the religious sect in which she has grown up, and a move to Maine exposes her to a world outside her strict upbringing. (Rev: BCCB 3/07; BL 3/1/07; SLJ 4/07)

2152 Wersba, Barbara. *Beautiful Losers* (9–12). 1988, HarperCollins $11.95 (978-0-06-026363-8). The concluding volume in the trilogy about teenaged Rita Formica and her love for Arnold, who is twice her age. Also use *Love Is the Crooked Thing* (1987). (Rev: BL 3/15/88; SLJ 3/88)

2153 Wersba, Barbara. *Wonderful Me* (9–12). 1989, HarperCollins $12.95 (978-0-06-026361-4). Seventeen-year-old Heidi Rosenbloom spends the summer making money dog walking and coping with the worshipful attention of a mentally unstable English teacher. A sequel to *Just Be Gorgeous* (1988). (Rev: BL 5/1/89; SLJ 4/89; VOYA 6/89)

2154 West, Nathanael. *Miss Lonelyhearts* (10–12). 1933, Liveright paper $8.95 (978-0-8112-0215-2). Loneliness is the main theme in this novel about a man who writes a lonelyhearts column for a newspaper.

2155 Whack, Rita Coburn. *Meant to Be* (11–12). 2002, Villard paper $11.95 (978-0-375-75809-6). Set in late 1970s Chicago, this is the story of a young African American woman with high career and romantic ambitions who must resolve family tensions. (Rev: BL 2/15/02)

2156 White, Michael J. *Weeping Underwater Looks a Lot Like Laughter* (10–12). 2009, Putnam $24.95 (978-039915590-1). Seventeen-year-old George struggles to navigate his status as the new kid in an Iowa high school, his first crush on a beautiful girl, and the crush that girl's sister has on him in this humorous, emotional story. e (Rev: BL 2/1–15/10)

2157 Whittenberg, Allison. *Life Is Fine* (8–12). 2008, Delacorte $15.99 (978-0-385-73480-6). Samara, a sad, neglected 15-year-old, develops a crush on a substitute teacher who introduces her to poetry. (Rev: BL 1/1–15/08; SLJ 2/08)

2158 Wieler, Diana. *RanVan: The Defender* (7–12). 1997, Douglas & McIntyre $16.95 (978-0-88899-270-3). Orphaned Rhan Van, who lives with his grandmother in a city apartment, begins hanging out in bad company and soon finds he is vandalizing school and private property. (Rev: BL 2/1/98; SLJ 3/98)

2159 Wilhelm, Doug. *Falling* (7–10). 2007, Farrar $17.00 (978-0-374-32251-9). Two troubled teens — Matt, whose first year in high school is ruined by his brother's heroin addiction, and Katie — connect through the Internet in this coming-of-age story set in Vermont. (Rev: BL 3/15/07; SLJ 7/07)

2160 Wilkins, Ebony Joy. *Sellout* (7–10). 2010, Scholastic $17.99 (978-0-545-10928-4). Socially uncertain African American NaTasha's parents have moved her to a privileged high school in New Jersey, but a summer with her grandmother in Harlem and volunteering at a crisis center in the Bronx help her adjust her preconceptions. e Lexile 720L (Rev: BL 9/1/10; LMC 10/10; SLJ 8/10)

2161 Wilkinson, Lili. *The Not Quite Perfect Boyfriend* (8–11). 2012, IPG/Allen & Unwin paper $8.99 (978-17423776-5-0). A lighthearted story about Australian Midge, 16, who invents a boyfriend. e (Rev: BL 3/15/12; SLJ 2/12)

2162 Williams-Garcia, Rita. *Jumped* (9–12). 2009, HarperTeen $16.99 (978-006076091-5); LB $17.89 (978-006076092-2). Leticia is unsure whether to speak up about Dominique's plans to "jump" another girl after school in this story about high school tensions and violence. ∩ e Lexile HL600L (Rev: BL 2/1/09; HB 3–4/09; LMC 8–9/09; SLJ 3/1/09)

2163 Williams, Carol Lynch. *Waiting* (8–11). 2012, Simon & Schuster $16.99 (978-144244353-2). Still grieving for her older brother Zach, London seeks comfort from two quite different boys, knowing she must make a choice; a novel told in free verse. e (Rev: BL 7/12; HB 7–8/12; SLJ 6/12; VOYA 6/12)

2164 Williams, Lori Aurelia. *Shayla's Double Brown Baby Blues* (7–12). 2003, Pulse $17.00 (978-0-689-85670-9). In this sequel to *When Kambia Elaine Flew in from Neptune* (2000), 13-year-old Shayla must cope with problems including the arrival of a new half-sister, her friend Kambia's traumatic and abusive past, and her friend Lemm's alcoholism. (Rev: BL 7/01; HB 9–10/01; SLJ 8/01)

2165 Williams, Lori Aurelia. *When Kambia Elaine Flew in from Neptune* (7–12). 2001, Pulse paper $17.00 (978-0-689-84593-2). In this first-person narrative, 12-year-old Shayla adjusts to the unhappy departure from the family of her older sister and finds escape in her friendship with an imaginative girl named Kambia. (Rev: BL 2/15/00)

2166 Williams, Margaret. *Haverstraw* (10–12). 2004, Avocet paper $12.95 (978-0-9725078-1-3). Set in the early 20th century, this is a quiet story of a girl who leaves her comfortable home in Quebec City to live with her brutish father on a poor farm in upper New York State. (Rev: BL 4/15/04)

2167 Wilson, Budge. *Sharla* (7–10). 1998, Stoddart paper $6.95 (978-0-7736-7467-7). A run-in with a polar bear, adjusting to a new school, trying to make friends, and getting used to severe weather are some of the problems 15-year-old Sharla faces when she moves with her family from Ottawa to Churchill, a small community in northern Manitoba. (Rev: SLJ 8/98)

2168 Wilson, Jacqueline. *Kiss* (7–10). 2010, Roaring Brook $16.99 (978-1-59643-242-0). At age 14, Sylvie has always assumed that she will eventually marry her best friend Carl, but with high school things change and Carl appears to be more interested in his new friend Paul. ∩ e Lexile HL680L (Rev: BL 2/1/10; HB 3–4/10; LMC 5–6/10; SLJ 3/10)

2169 Wilson, Martin. *What They Always Tell Us* (9–12). 2008, Delacorte $15.99 (978-038573507-0); LB $18.99

(978-038590500-8). In Tuscaloosa, Alabama, two brothers — James, a successful senior hoping to be accepted to Duke, and Alex, a junior who is recovering from a foolish, perhaps suicidal act with the help of Nathen — navigate their daily lives. **e** (Rev: BL 11/15/08; HB 9–10/08; LMC 10/08; SLJ 9/1/08; VOYA 12/08)

2170 Wimsley, Jim. *Dream Boy* (10–12). 1995, Algonquin $29.95 (978-1-56512-106-5). Nathan — bookish and slight and sexually abused by his father — moves to a farm, where he meets and falls in love with Roy, the outgoing, popular boy next door. (Rev: BL 9/15/95; SLJ 3/96; VOYA 2/96)

2171 Winter, Kathleen. *Annabel* (11–12). 2011, Black Cat paper $14.95 (978-08021708-2-8). Winter tells a grim tale of a hermaphrodite struggling to live up to his male gender assignment; for mature readers. **e** (Rev: BL 10/1–15/10)

2172 Withrow, Sarah. *What Gloria Wants* (7–10). 2005, Groundwood paper $6.95 (978-0-88899-692-3). Gloria always seems to be a step behind her best friend Shawna, so Gloria initially exults when she is first to land a boyfriend. (Rev: BCCB 11/05; BL 12/1/05; HB 1–2/06; SLJ 2/06; VOYA 12/05)

2173 Wittlinger, Ellen. *Hard Love* (8–12). 1999, Simon & Schuster paper $8.00 (978-0-689-84154-5). Two outsiders, John, a high school junior and fan of "zines," and Marisol, a self-proclaimed virgin lesbian, form an unusual relationship in this well-crafted novel that explores many teenage problems. (Rev: BL 10/1/99*; HB 7–8/99; HBG 9/99; SLJ 7/99; VOYA 8/99)

2174 Wittlinger, Ellen. *Parrotfish* (9–12). 2007, Simon & Schuster $16.99 (978-1-4169-1622-2). Angela becomes Grady in this story of a transgendered high school junior who must explain his new identity to family and friends. (Rev: BCCB 9/07; BL 4/15/07; HB 7–8/07; LMC 11–12/07; SLJ 9/07)

2175 Wittlinger, Ellen. *Sandpiper* (8–12). 2005, Simon & Schuster $16.99 (978-0-689-86802-3). Her promiscuous past has severely tarnished 16-year-old Sandpiper's reputation, but when she develops a friendship with Walker, both troubled teens begin to make some important discoveries about the ways in which the past is shaping their future. (Rev: BL 6/1–15/05; SLJ 7/05; VOYA 8/05)

2176 Wittlinger, Ellen. *Zigzag* (8–12). 2003, Simon & Schuster $16.95 (978-0-689-84996-1). A summer cross-country car trip with her recently widowed aunt and two cousins poses many challenges for 17-year-old Robin. (Rev: BL 9/1/03; HB 7–8/03; HBG 4/04; SLJ 8/03; VOYA 10/03)

2177 Wizner, Jake. *Spanking Shakespeare* (10–12). 2007, Random House $15.99 (978-0-375-84085-2). Shakespeare Shapiro, 17, is used to embarrassment and uses his own self-deprecation to comic effect as

he writes frankly about his life and the people in it. ♫ (Rev: SLJ 11/07)

2178 Wolff, Tobias. *Old School* (10–12). 2003, Knopf $22.00 (978-0-375-40146-6). A fascinating and insightful story set in 1960 of a talented youth from a deprived background who is struggling to fit in and succeed at a private school known for its literary excellence. (Rev: BL 9/1/03*; SLJ 4/04)

2179 Wright, Bil. *Putting Makeup on the Fat Boy* (7–10). 2011, Simon & Schuster $16.99 (978-1-4169-3996-2). Gay teen Carlos is on track for a career as a makeup artist but first must contend with a jealous boss, his sister's thuggish boyfriend, and his own crush on a boy at school. YALSA Popular Paperbacks for Young Adults Top Ten 2013. **e** Lexile 820L (Rev: BL 9/1/11; LMC 1–2/12; SLJ 7/11)

2180 Wright, Bil. *Sunday You Learn How to Box* (10–12). 2000, Scribner paper $12.00 (978-0-684-85795-4). This first novel, set in an inner-city housing project in Connecticut, is about a 14-year-old African American boy, Louis Bowman — his feelings, his past, his family, and his budding homosexuality. (Rev: BL 2/15/00; SLJ 9/00)

2181 Wyatt, Melissa. *Funny How Things Change* (9–12). 2009, Farrar $16.95 (978-037430233-7). After high school 17-year-old Remy must decide whether to accompany his girlfriend to Pennsylvania, where she will attend college, or stay in West Virginia and work in a garage; additional factors are his love for his mountain town and his interest in a visiting artist. Lexile HL690L (Rev: BL 3/15/09; SLJ 4/1/09; VOYA 6/09)

2182 Yang, J. A. *Exclusively Chloe* (6–10). 2009, Penguin paper $7.99 (978-014241226-8). A "makeunder" allows 16-year-old Chinese American Chloe to escape the constant attention her adoptive parents' celebrity has imposed on her. (Rev: BL 7/09)

2183 Yates, Bart. *Leave Myself Behind* (11–12). 2003, Kensington $23.00 (978-0-7582-0348-9). Mystery and gay romance are interwoven in this compelling story of a gay teenager who moves with his difficult mother to a house full of secrets. (Rev: BL 2/15/03)

2184 Yee, Lisa. *Absolutely Maybe* (7–10). 2009, Scholastic $16.99 (978-043983844-3). This is a mostly humorous tale about high school junior Maybe (short for Maybelline, her mother's favorite mascara), who leaves her soon-to-be-married-again mother's home and heads for California to search for her biological father. **e** Lexile HL570L (Rev: BL 12/1/08; HB 3–4/09)

2185 Young-Stone, Michele. *The Handbook for Lightning Strike Survivors* (11–12). 2010, Crown $24 (978-030746447-7). Lightning strikes — which hit Becca at the age of 8 and kill Buckley's mother when he is 13 — have profound impacts on these young people's lives; for mature readers. (Rev: BL 3/1–15/10)

2186 Zalben, Jane Breskin. *Water from the Moon* (8–10). 1987, Random House paper $4.99 (978-0-440-22855-4). Nicky Berstein, a high school sophomore, tries too hard to make friends and is hurt in the process. (Rev: BL 5/15/87; SLJ 5/87; VOYA 8/87)

2187 Zarr, Sara. *Story of a Girl* (10–12). 2007, Little, Brown $16.99 (978-0-316-01453-3). Deanna, now 16, is still paying for getting caught having sex when she was 13. ⌒ (Rev: BCCB 5/07; BL 3/1/07; SLJ 1/07)

2188 Zeller, Florian. *Julien Parme* (10–12). Trans. by William Rodarmor. 2008, Other $23.95 (978-159051280-7). Dramatic, disaffected Julien runs away from home in this compelling French coming-of-age story with a Salingeresque flavor. (Rev: BL 6/1–15/08)

2189 Zephaniah, Benjamin. *Gangsta Rap* (9–12). 2004, Bloomsbury paper $7.95 (978-1-58234-886-5). Expelled from his London school, 15-year-old Ray is given one last chance to redeem himself when he teams up with friends Prem and Tyrone to form a rap music group that, against all odds, wins a lucrative recording contract. (Rev: BL 6/1–15/04; HB 7–8/04; SLJ 2/05; VOYA 2/05)

2190 Zindel, Bonnie, and Paul Zindel. *A Star for the Latecomer* (7–10). 1980, HarperCollins $12.95 (978-0-06-026847-3). When her mother dies, Brooke is freed of the need to pursue a dancing career.

2191 Zindel, Lizabeth. *The Secret Rites of Social Butterflies* (7–10). 2008, Viking $16.99 (978-0-670-06217-1). At her new girls' school in New York City, Maggie breaks into the popular clique and soon finds that betrayal is her new friends' pastime. (Rev: BL 5/15/08)

2192 Zolotow, Charlotte, ed. *Early Sorrow: Ten Stories of Youth* (8–12). 1986, HarperCollins $12.95 (978-0-06-026936-4). This excellent collection of 12 adult stories about growing up is a companion piece to *An Overpraised Season* (o.p.), another anthology about adolescence. (Rev: BL 10/1/86; SLJ 1/87; VOYA 2/87)

2193 Zulkey, Claire. *An Off Year* (9–12). 2009, Dutton $16.99 (978-0-525-42159-7). Arriving at college for the first time, 18-year-old Cecily decides she's not ready and heads back home to spend a year reviewing her options. Best Books for Young Adults 2010. ℮ (Rev: BL 8/1/09; SLJ 11/09)

2194 Zusak, Markus. *Underdogs* (7–10). 2012, Scholastic $19.99 (978-054535442-4). This volume featuring brothers Cameron and Ruben Wolfe collects three novels: *The Underdog, Fighting Ruben Wolfe,* and *Getting the Girl.* ℮ Lexile HL610L (Rev: BLO 2/15/12; LMC 5–6/12)

World Affairs and Contemporary Problems

2195 Abelove, Joan. *Go and Come Back* (8–10). 1998, Puffin paper $5.99 (978-0-14-130694-0). The story of two female anthropologists studying a primitive Peruvian Indian village, written from the perspective of Alicia, one of the village teenagers. (Rev: BL 3/1/98; SLJ 3/98*; VOYA 10/98)

2196 Adoff, Jaime. *Names Will Never Hurt Me* (7–10). 2004, Dutton $16.99 (978-0-525-47175-2). As their high school marks the first anniversary of the shooting death of a fellow student, four very different teenagers express their feelings about school, their classmates, and themselves. (Rev: BCCB 4/04; BL 4/1/04; HB 7–8/04; SLJ 4/04; VOYA 4/04)

2197 Akinti, Peter. *Forest Gate* (11–12). 2010, Free Press paper $14 (978-14391721-7-9). In this gripping novel set in the London slums, teens James and Meina — who saw her parents tortured and murdered in her native Somalia — seek to overcome their violent backgrounds and find stability in their love for each other; for mature readers. (Rev: BL 1/1–15/10)

2198 Bell, Julia. *Dirty Work* (10–12). 2008, Walker $16.95 (978-0-8027-9741-4). Oksana, a Russian teenager hoping to find a better life in the West, and Hope, a privileged English girl, are kidnapped and delivered to a prostitution ring. (Rev: BL 12/15/07; LMC 3/08; SLJ 3/08)

2199 Benaïssa, Slimane. *The Last Night of a Damned Soul* (11–12). Trans. by Janice and Daniel Gross. 2004, Grove $24.00 (978-0-8021-1780-9). After his father's death, Arab American Raouf is drawn into the world of Muslim fundamentalism and terrorism. (Rev: BL 9/15/04)

2200 Brown, Jennifer. *Hate List* (9–12). 2009, Little, Brown $16.99 (978-0-316-04144-7). Valerie and her boyfriend Nick created a list of classmates' names to vent frustration about school bullying, but in the aftermath of her boyfriend's attack on the school, their list is turned against Val as she grapples with her own guilt and grief. Best Books for Young Adults 2010. ℮ Lexile HL760L (Rev: BL 9/1/09; SLJ 10/09; VOYA 12/09)

2201 Bryher. *Visa for Avalon* (11–12). 2004, Paris paper $15.00 (978-1-930464-07-0). First published in 1965, this story of a couple hoping to escape to a land called Avalon when "the Movement" forces them out of their home mirrors the predicament faced by many during World War II. (Rev: BL 10/15/04)

2202 Budhos, Marina. *Ask Me No Questions* (7–10). 2006, Simon & Schuster $16.95 (978-1-4169-0351-2). Fourteen-year-old Nadira describes the legal and emotional upheavals her family faces as Bangladeshis living illegally in the United States. (Rev: BCCB 3/06; BL 12/15/05*; HB 3–4/06; SLJ 4/06; VOYA 2/06)

2203 Burstyn, Varda. *Water Inc* (9–12). 2004, Verso $25.00 (978-1-85984-596-7). A plot to control the United States' water supply is foiled by a plucky team of environmentalists. (Rev: BL 8/04)

2204 Carlson, Melody. *Crystal Lies* (9–12). 2004, WaterBrook paper $12.99 (978-1-57856-840-6). Glennis's life is turned upside down when her son becomes addicted to crystal methamphetamine. (Rev: BL 10/1/04)

2205 Castaneda, Omar S. *Among the Volcanoes* (7–10). 1996, Bantam paper $4.50 (978-0-440-91118-0). Set in a remote Guatemalan village, this story is about a Mayan woodcutter's daughter, Isabel, who is caught between her respect for the old ways and her yearning for something more. (Rev: BL 5/15/91; SLJ 3/91)

2206 Collins, Pat Lowery. *The Fattening Hut* (8–12). 2003, Houghton Mifflin $15.00 (978-0-618-30955-9). Fourteen-year-old Helen sets off on a dangerous journey, running away from the tropical tribe that requires her to undergo female circumcision before her impending marriage. (Rev: BL 11/1/03; HBG 4/04; SLJ 11/03; VOYA 2/04)

2207 Cooney, Caroline B. *Diamonds in the Shadow* (8–12). 2007, Delacorte $15.99 (978-0-385-73261-1). Jared and Mopsy have different experiences when their family hosts a refugee family from Sierra Leone. (Rev: BL 9/1/07; SLJ 9/07)

2208 Covington, Dennis. *Lasso the Moon* (7–10). 1996, Bantam $20.95 (978-0-385-30991-2). After April and her divorced doctor father move to Saint Simons Island, April takes a liking to Fernando, an illegal alien from El Salvador being treated by her father. (Rev: BL 1/15/95; SLJ 3/95; VOYA 4/95)

2209 Cowan, Jennifer. *Earthgirl* (8–11). 2009, Groundwood $17.95 (978-088899889-7); paper $12.95 (978-088899890-3). A fast-food lunch tossed out a window spurs 16-year-old Sabine to environmental activism and she starts a successful blog and becomes involved in a relationship with Vray, a passionate eco-warrior. (Rev: BL 6/1–15/09; SLJ 6/1/09*)

2210 Craig, Colleen. *Afrika* (7–12). 2008, Tundra paper $9.95 (978-0-88776-807-1). Kim, a 13-year-old who has grown up in Canada, travels to South Africa with her journalist mother, a white South African, to cover the Truth and Reconciliation Commission hearings; while there she learns about her father's African roots and finds out why her mother left him. (Rev: BL 6/1–15/08; SLJ 7/08)

2211 Cross, Gillian. *Where I Belong* (9–12). 2011, Holiday $17.95 (978-0-8234-2332-3). Somali refugee Khadija, 13, works as a runway model in London to earn money to ransom her brother from his kidnappers. Lexile 650L (Rev: BL 5/1/11; LMC 10/11*; SLJ 6/11; VOYA 6/11)

2212 Dixon, Peter. *Hunting the Dragon* (8–12). 2010, Hyperion $15.99 (978-1-4231-2498-6). Eighteen-year-old Billy becomes a passionate defender of the rights of dolphins after working on a tuna boat. (Rev: LMC 8–9/10; SLJ 6/10)

2213 Doherty, Berlie. *The Girl Who Saw Lions* (6–12). 2008, Roaring Brook $16.95 (978-1-59643-377-9). Abela, 9, and Rosa, 13, tell their contrasting stories in alternating chapters. Abela is an AIDS orphan in Tanzania, whose uncle plans to sell her for adoption in England; in London, Rosa is unhappy when she learns that her single-parent mother plans to adopt a child. (Rev: BL 2/15/08; SLJ 7/08)

2214 Eggers, Dave. *What Is the What: The Autobiography of Valentino Achak Deng* (11–12). 2006, McSweeney's $26.00 (978-1-932416-64-0). This is the disturbing fictionalized memoir of a "Lost Boy" from Sudan who manages to survive unspeakable horrors and make it to the United States only to find himself facing new perils. (Rev: BL 11/15/06)

2215 Ellis, Deborah, and Eric Walters. *Bifocal* (7–10). 2007, Fitzhenry & Whiteside $18.95 (978-1-55455-036-4). When a Muslim student is arrested, suspected of being a terrorist, his school is abuzz, and various groups take sides. (Rev: BL 1/1–15/08; SLJ 3/08)

2216 Farish, Terry. *The Good Braider* (8–12). 2012, Amazon Children's $17.99 (978-0-7614-6267-5). Viola, 16, remembers in free-verse poems her difficult experiences in Sudan, harrowing escape overland to Egypt, and being received as a refugee in Portland, Maine. **e** Lexile HL630L (Rev: BL 7/12*; HB 9–10/12; LMC 1–2/13; SLJ 9/12*; VOYA 10/12)

2217 Flake, Sharon G. *Bang!* (9–12). 2005, Hyperion $16.99 (978-0-7868-1844-0). Fearful of losing another son to urban violence, Mann's father abandons teenage Mann and a friend at a remote campsite in imitation of an African coming-of-age ritual. (Rev: BL 7/05; SLJ 10/05; VOYA 12/05)

2218 Flegg, Aubrey. *The Cinnamon Tree* (7–10). 2002, O'Brien paper $7.95 (978-0-86278-657-1). The horror of the injuries inflicted by landmines is brought to life in this story of a girl who loses a leg and goes on to teach others about the dangers of these weapons. (Rev: BL 8/02; SLJ 8/02)

2219 Freirich, Roy. *Winged Creatures* (9–12). 2008, St. Martin's paper $13.95 (978-0-312-37895-0). This emotional story explores the surprising impact that a fateful diner shooting has made on its various survivors and their respective ways of coping. (Rev: BL 12/1/07; SLJ 4/08)

2220 Gomez, Iris. *Try to Remember* (11–12). 2010, Grand Central paper $13.99 (978-04465561-9-4). In 1970s Miami Gabriela's family worries constantly about deportation back to Colombia while Papi's mental illness gets worse, Mami despairs about her menial work, and Gabriela's movements are limited; for mature readers. **e** (Rev: BL 4/1–15/10)

2221 Griffin, Paul. *Ten Mile River* (8–12). 2008, Dial $16.99 (978-0-8037-3284-1). Ray, 14, and José, 15, live together in an abandoned building in west Harlem and survive on odd jobs and what they can steal; when they meet the lovely Trini, complications of romance and opportunity test their friendship. (Rev: BL 6/1–15/08; SLJ 9/08)

2222 Guest, Jacqueline. *War Games* (7–10). 2009, Orca $16.95 (978-155277036-8); paper $9.95 (978-155277035-1). His strict soldier father is in Afghanistan, and 15-year-old Ryan enjoys a freer life and ample access to computer war games while at the same time recognizing the dangers his father faces. (Rev: BL 6/1–15/09; SLJ 12/09)

2223 Halaby, Laila. *West of the Jordan* (10–12). 2003, Beacon paper $13.00 (978-0-8070-8359-8). Four Arab cousins — all young women — have been brought up in very different circumstances and have very different aspirations. (Rev: BL 6/1–15/03; SLJ 10/03)

2224 Hassan, Michael. *Crash and Burn* (9–12). 2013, HarperCollins $18.99 (978-006211290-3). Steven "Crash" Crashinsky tells the story of his 10 years knowing David "Burn" Burnett — years that night have predicted the day when Crash stops Burn from attacking their school with guns and explosives. e Lexile 1050L (Rev: BL 1/13*; SLJ 5/13)

2225 Henry, April. *Torched* (8–11). 2009, Putnam $16.99 (978-039924645-6). Ellie, 16, is recruited by the FBI to infiltrate and report on an ecoterrorism group, the Mother Earth Defenders; action, romance, and an environmental message combine for an exciting read. Lexile HL710L (Rev: BL 2/15/09; SLJ 4/1/09)

2226 Hentoff, Nat. *The Day They Came to Arrest the Book* (7–10). 1983, Dell paper $5.50 (978-0-440-91814-1). Some students at George Mason High think *Huckleberry Finn* is a racist book.

2227 Ho, Minfong. *Rice Without Rain* (7–12). 1990, Lothrop $17.99 (978-0-688-06355-9). Jinda, a 17-year-old girl, experiences personal tragedy and the awakening of love in this novel set during revolutionary times in Thailand during the 1970s. (Rev: BL 7/90; SLJ 9/90)

2228 Hopkins, Ellen. *Crank* (8–12). 2004, Simon & Schuster paper $6.99 (978-0-689-86519-0). In this debut novel written in verse, Hopkins introduces readers to Kristina Snow and how the high school junior became addicted to crystal meth. (Rev: BL 11/15/04; SLJ 11/04; VOYA 2/05)

2229 Hopkins, Ellen. *Glass* (10–12). 2007, Simon & Schuster $16.99 (978-1-4169-4090-6). In this sequel to *Crank* (2004), Kristina has now given birth to the child who was conceived when she was raped, and she returns to drugs and abusive men. (Rev: BL 10/1/07; SLJ 9/07)

2230 Hower, Edward. *A Garden of Demons* (10–12). 2003, Ontario Review $22.95 (978-0-86538-106-3).

An evocative novel set in Sri Lanka that juxtaposes terrorist threats and environmental aspirations. (Rev: BL 1/1–15/03)

2231 James, Brian. *Tomorrow, Maybe* (7–12). 2003, Scholastic paper $6.99 (978-0-439-49035-1). Living a hard life on the streets of New York, 15-year-old Gretchen, a.k.a. Chan, finds a purpose when she takes charge of an 11-year-old in the same predicament. (Rev: LMC 10/03; SLJ 6/03; VOYA 8/03)

2232 Kass, Pnina Moed. *Real Time* (9–12). 2004, Clarion $15.00 (978-0-618-44203-4). This chilling story of a suicide bomb attack on an Israeli bus is told from the viewpoints of bus passengers and their friends and loved ones. Sidney Taylor Book Award 2004. (Rev: BL 2/1/05; HB 1–2/05; SLJ 10/04; VOYA 2/05)

2233 Kemal, Yasher. *Memed, My Hawk* (10–12). 1993, HarperCollins paper $12.00 (978-0-00-217112-0). This tragic story, set in southern Turkey, takes place in an area where feudal conditions still exist.

2234 Kilbourne, Christina. *They Called Me Red* (8–12). 2008, Lobster $10.95 (978-189707388-9). This is a dark story about human trafficking in which an American teen is sold by his Vietnamese stepmother into a Cambodian brothel after his father dies. (Rev: BLO 12/30/08)

2235 Lalami, Laila. *Hope and Other Dangerous Pursuits* (10–12). 2005, Algonquin $21.95 (978-1-56512-493-6). Stories of four Moroccans who risk their lives to get across the Strait of Gibraltar to Spain reveal much about the circumstances in Morocco and the individuals' often unreasonable expectations of their destinations. (Rev: BL 8/05; SLJ 12/05)

2236 LaMarche, Phil. *American Youth* (9–12). 2007, Random House $21.95 (978-1-4000-6605-6). A 9th-grade boy is involved in a deadly shooting and his mother wants him to keep his involvement a secret; he's shunned at school and takes up with the American Youth, a vigilante group of teens that vandalizes homes. (Rev: BL 2/15/07; SLJ 5/07)

2237 Levithan, David. *Love Is the Higher Law* (8–12). 2009, Knopf $15.99 (978-037583468-4); LB $18.99 (978-037593468-1). Three New York City teens — Claire, Peter, and Peter's potential boyfriend Jasper — witness the events of September 11, 2001, and become close as they deal with the experience. (Rev: BL 6/1–15/09; LMC 11–12/09; SLJ 9/09)

2238 Levitin, Sonia. *The Return* (6–10). 1987, Fawcett paper $5.99 (978-0-449-70280-2). Seen from the viewpoint of a teenage girl, this is the story of a group of African Jews who journey from Ethiopia to the Sudan to escape persecution. (Rev: BL 4/15/87; SLJ 5/87; VOYA 6/87)

2239 Liggett, Cathy. *Beaded Hope* (10–12). 2010, Tyndale paper $12.99 (978-14143321-2-3). Three women and a pregnant teen, each with recent troubles on their minds, travel on a mission trip to South Africa where they meet a single mother with AIDS and are moved to help the community by selling their beaded jewelry in the United States. (Rev: BL 2/1–15/10)

2240 Livaneli, O. Z. *Bliss* (11–12). 2006, St. Martin's $23.95 (978-0-312-36053-5). Meryem is raped by her uncle and when she fails to hang herself in humiliation, her cousin Cemal is ordered to take her away and kill her in this novel set in Turkey; instead the two end up on a sailboat with a former professor and their eyes are opened to a different way of life. (Rev: BL 9/1/06; SLJ 3/07)

2241 Ludington, Max. *Tiger in a Trance* (11–12). 2003, Doubleday $24.00 (978-0-385-50704-2). An absorbing story of life, love, community, and drug use among fans of the Grateful Dead. (Rev: BL 8/03; SLJ 4/04)

2242 Lynch, Janet Nichols. *Peace Is a Four-Letter Word* (7–10). 2005, Heyday paper $9.95 (978-1-59714-014-0). The carefully ordered life of high school cheerleader Emily Rankin is shattered when a history teacher inspires her to get involved in the peace movement on the eve of the Gulf War. (Rev: BL 10/1/05; SLJ 10/05)

2243 Lynn, Tracy. *Rx* (9–12). 2006, Simon & Schuster paper $6.99 (978-1-4169-1155-5). From stealing an initial bottle of Ritalin, Thyme's familiarity with prescription drugs increases until she is supplying many classmates with their chosen medications. (Rev: BL 3/1/06; SLJ 3/06)

2244 McCormick, Patricia. *Purple Heart* (9–12). 2009, HarperTeen $16.99 (978-006173090-0); LB $17.89 (978-006173091-7). In Iraq Private Matt Duffy must cope with both his own traumatic brain injury and his suspicion that the Army is covering something up. ∩ (Rev: BL 7/09; LMC 11–12/09; SLJ 11/09)

2245 McDaniel, Lurlene. *Baby Alicia Is Dying* (8–10). 1993, Bantam paper $4.99 (978-0-553-29605-1). In an attempt to feel needed, Desi volunteers to care for HIV-positive babies and discovers a deep commitment in herself. (Rev: BL 10/1/93; SLJ 7/93; VOYA 8/93)

2246 Martin, Nora. *Perfect Snow* (8–12). 2002, Bloomsbury $16.95 (978-1-58234-788-2). Ben feels strong and confident when he participates in the violent intolerance of the local white supremacists until he meets Eden, a new — and Jewish — girl at school, in this novel set in a small Montana community. (Rev: BL 8/02; SLJ 9/02)

2247 Matthews, Tom. *Like We Care* (11–12). 2004, Bancroft $23.95 (978-1-890862-36-7). High-schoolers Todd and Joel head a boycott of everything marketed to teenagers — candy, cigarettes, even TV — putting them in the center of a media frenzy in this satirical novel suitable for mature teens. (Rev: BL 8/04; SLJ 11/04; VOYA 12/04)

2248 Meyer, Adam. *The Last Domino* (10–12). 2005, Penguin $16.99 (978-0-399-24332-5). A frightening story of school violence in which manipulative Daniel exploits Travis's unhappiness about his older brother's suicide. (Rev: BL 9/1/05; SLJ 11/05; VOYA 8/05)

2249 Michener, James A. *Legacy* (10–12). 1987, Fawcett paper $6.99 (978-0-449-21641-5). A contemporary novel about an army officer involved with the Contras in Nicaragua. (Rev: BL 8/87)

2250 Miller-Lachmann, Lyn. *Gringolandia* (9–12). 2009, Curbstone $16.95 (978-193189649-8). When 17-year-old Daniel's father is released by Pinochet in 1986 and travels from Chile to Wisconsin to join his family, the repercussions of his years of torture affect his health and the lives of Daniel and his activist girlfriend Courtney. (Rev: BL 7/09; HB 11–12/09; LMC 10/09; SLJ 4/1/09)

2251 Naqvi, H. M. *Home Boy* (11–12). 2009, Crown $23 (978-030740910-2). In this story of immigration and identity, three young Pakistani men take an unwise roadtrip right after 9/11 and find themselves locked up in the Metropolitan Detention Center; for mature teens. (Rev: BL 9/09)

2252 Nelson, Blake. *They Came from Below* (7–12). 2007, Tor $17.95 (978-0-7653-1423-9). Steve and Dave initially seem to be two cute boys, but Emily and Reese come to realize that they are actually creatures from another world intent on persuading humans to save the oceans from pollution. (Rev: BCCB 9/07; SLJ 8/07)

2253 Newman, Leslea. *October Mourning: A Song for Matthew Shepard* (8–12). 2012, Candlewick $15.99 (978-0-7636-5807-6). In a novel consisting of 68 poems, Newman tells from multiple perspectives the story of the savage beating and subsequent death of gay 21-year-old Matthew Shepard in 1998. Stonewall Honor 2013. ∩ (Rev: BL 9/15/12*; HB 9–10/12; LMC 3–4/13*; SLJ 11/12)

2254 Nye, Naomi Shihab. *Going Going* (7–10). 2005, Greenwillow LB $16.89 (978-0-06-029366-6). Angered by the exodus of small businesses from her hometown, 16-year-old Florrie launches a grassroots campaign against the giant chain stores that she believes are responsible. (Rev: BCCB 7–8/05; BL 4/1/05; HB 7–8/05; SLJ 5/05; VOYA 10/05)

2255 Orenstein, Denise Gosliner. *Unseen Companion* (10–12). 2003, HarperCollins LB $16.89 (978-0-06-052057-1). Four Alaskan teenagers explore in first-person narratives the impact on their lives of the imprisonment of a boy of mixed race who hit a white teacher. (Rev: BCCB 11/03; BL 10/15/03*; SLJ 1/04; VOYA 12/03)

2256 Paulsen, Gary. *Sentries* (8–12). 1986, Penguin paper $3.95 (978-0-317-62279-9). The stories of four different young people are left unresolved when they are all wiped out by a superbomb. (Rev: BL 5/1/86; SLJ 8/86; VOYA 8/86)

2257 Perera, Anna. *Guantanamo Boy* (7–12). 2011, Albert Whitman $17.99 (978-080753077-1). Based on a true story, this novel is about 15-year-old Khalid's experiences when he — a normal British Muslim teen — is captured during a visit to relatives in Pakistan and turned over to the U.S. authorities as a possible terrorist. ℮ Lexile 900L (Rev: BL 9/1/11*; LMC 11–12/11*)

2258 Perez, Ashley Hope. *The Knife and the Butterfly* (10–12). 2012, Carolrhoda $17.95 (978-076136156-5). For mature readers, this is a graphic story of gang members in Houston and the way they are treated in jail. ℮ (Rev: BL 2/1/12; LMC 5–6/12; SLJ 2/12)

2259 Picoult, Jodi. *Nineteen Minutes* (10–12). 2007, Atria $26.00 (978-0-7434-9672-8). In 19 minutes, a boy who has been bullied at school kills 10 and wounds 19; a compelling and thought-provoking story. (Rev: BL 1/1–15/07)

2260 Pitcher, Annabel. *My Sister Lives on the Mantelpiece* (7–10). 2012, Little, Brown $17.99 (978-031617690-3). Ten-year-old Jamie's family has fallen apart in the aftermath of his sister's death in a terrorist bombing, and his only friend seems to be a Muslim friend named Sunya — something he must keep secret from his father. ALA Notable Books 2013. ∩ ℮ (Rev: BL 9/15/12*; LMC 8–9/12; SLJ 8/1/12*)

2261 Pressler, Mirjam. *Let Sleeping Dogs Lie* (9–12). Trans. by Erik J. Macki. 2007, Front St $16.95 (978-1-932425-84-0). In 1995, wealthy 18-year-old Johanna discovers that her German family's fortune was stolen from Jews by her Nazi grandfather. Sidney Taylor Book Honor 2008. (Rev: BL 2/15/08; SLJ 2/08)

2262 Prose, Francine. *After* (8–10). 2003, HarperCollins LB $17.89 (978-0-06-008082-2). A school district hires an over-the-top crisis counselor to impose order in the name of safety after a massacre at a nearby high school. (Rev: HB 5–6/03; HBG 10/03; SLJ 5/03; VOYA 6/03)

2263 Purcell, Kim. *Trafficked* (9–12). 2012, Viking $16.99 (978-067001280-0). Hannah, 17, jumps at the chance to leave Moldova for the United States, not realizing the hard life of forced servitude ahead of her. ℮ (Rev: BL 2/1/12; HB 7–8/12; SLJ 2/12; VOYA 4/12)

2264 Rachlin, Nahid. *Jumping over Fire* (9–12). 2006, City Lights paper $12.95 (978-0-87286-452-8). During Khomeini's rise to power, the privileged family of Nora and her adopted brother Jahan must flee from their oil business in southern Iran and continue their lives in the United States, where, as the two maturing children struggle to rid themselves of an incestuous relationship, they grow apart — Nora toward American freedoms and Jahan toward Iranian patriotism. (Rev: BL 3/1/06; SLJ 8/06)

2265 Rand, Ayn. *Anthem* (10–12). 1999, Plume paper $13.95 (978-0-452-28125-7). A short novel set in the future about an individual fighting a powerful collective state.

2266 Rees, Celia. *This Is Not Forgiveness* (9–12). 2012, Bloomsbury $17.99 (978-1-59990-776-5). Beautiful and rebellious (anarchist) Caro comes between 17-year-old Jamie and his older brother Rob, who is suffering psychological and physical damage from military service in Afghanistan, in this story of politics, war, and love. ℮ (Rev: BL 11/15/12; LMC 1–2/13; SLJ 11/12)

2267 Rochman, Hazel, ed. *Somehow Tenderness Survives: Stories of Southern Africa* (8–12). 1988, HarperCollins $12.95 (978-0-06-025022-5); paper $5.99 (978-0-06-447063-6). Ten stories by such writers as Nadine Gordimer about growing up in South Africa. (Rev: BL 8/88; SLJ 12/88; VOYA 12/88)

2268 Rosen, Roger, and Patra McSharry, eds. *Border Crossings: Emigration and Exile* (8–12). Series: Icarus World Issues. 1992, Rosen LB $21.95 (978-0-8239-1364-0); paper $8.95 (978-0-8239-1365-7). Twelve fiction and nonfiction selections that illustrate the lives of those affected by geopolitical change. (Rev: BL 11/1/92)

2269 Ruby, Lois. *Skin Deep* (8–12). 1994, Scholastic paper $14.95 (978-0-590-47699-7). Dan, the frustrated new kid in town, falls in love with popular senior Laurel, but he destroys their relationship when he joins a neo-Nazi skinhead group. (Rev: BL 11/15/94*; SLJ 3/95; VOYA 12/94)

2270 Sallis, Eva. *The Marsh Birds* (11–12). 2006, Allen & Unwin paper $14.95 (978-1-74114-600-4). Young Dhurgham is separated from his Iraqi family in Damascus, Syria, and must fend for himself, suffering abuse and facing an uncertain future in New Zealand and Australia, where he is regarded as a potential terrorist; for mature teens. (Rev: BL 9/1/06; SLJ 11/06)

2271 Schaeffer, Frank. *Baby Jack* (10–12). 2006, Carroll & Graf $25.95 (978-0-7867-1716-3). An upper-class couple is shocked when their son joins the Marines and is killed while serving overseas. (Rev: BL 9/1/06)

2272 Scott, Paul. *Staying On* (10–12). 1979, Avon paper $3.50 (978-0-380-46045-8). Mr. and Mrs. Smalley decide to stay on in India after the country gains independence.

2273 Sitomer, Alan Lawrence. *Homeboyz* (7–10). 2007, Hyperion $16.99 (978-1-4231-0030-0). When his little sister Tina is gunned down by gang members, 17-year-old Teddy quickly seeks revenge and ends up arrested for attempted homicide in this novel that looks at the causes of inner-city violence; the third volume in the trilogy that started with *The Hoopster* (2005) and *Hip-Hop High School* (2006). (Rev: BL 7/07; LMC 10/07; SLJ 8/07)

2274 Sleator, William. *Test* (7–10). 2008, Abrams $16.95 (978-0-8109-9356-3). In a near-future United States, Ann discovers that a test that high school students must pass is part of a larger, corrupt government plan. (Rev: BL 5/1/08; SLJ 7/08)

2275 Solzhenitsyn, Alexander. *One Day in the Life of Ivan Denisovich* (10–12). 1984, Bantam paper $4.99

(978-0-553-24777-0). A harrowing short novel about life in a Stalinist labor camp in Siberia.

2276 Steinbeck, John. *Tortilla Flat* (10–12). 1962, Penguin paper $10.00 (978-0-14-004240-5). The life of some poor but carefree friends in Monterey, California, during the 1930s.

2277 Strasser, Todd. *If I Grow Up* (7–10). 2009, Simon & Schuster $16.99 (978-141692523-1). This story follows DeShawn's life in the projects from the ages of 12 to 28, and his efforts to resist the lure of gangs. **e** Lexile 650L (Rev: BL 1/1–15/09; LMC 8–9/09; SLJ 2/1/09; VOYA 12/08)

2278 Stratton, Allan. *Borderline* (8–11). 2010, HarperTeen $16.99 (978-0-06-145111-9); LB $17.89 (978-0-06-145112-6). In this culturally charged thriller, young Muslim Sami copes with faith-based bullying at school and his father's increasingly cold behavior, until his family is groundlessly accused of terrorism by the FBI. **e** Lexile HL560L (Rev: BL 1/1–15/10; SLJ 3/10)

2279 Temple, Frances. *Grab Hands and Run* (6–12). 1993, Orchard LB $16.99 (978-0-531-08630-8). Jacinto opposes the oppressive government of El Salvador. When he disappears, his wife, Paloma, and their son, 12-year-old Felipe, try to escape to freedom in Canada. (Rev: BL 5/1/93*; SLJ 4/93*)

2280 Trumbo, Dalton. *Johnny Got his Gun* (10–12). 1970, Bantam paper $6.99 (978-0-553-27432-5). This anti-war novel is also a moving tribute to the human instinct to survive.

2281 Tyler, Anne. *Digging to America* (9–12). 2006, Knopf $24.95 (978-0-307-26394-0). This novel traces the delicate cultural threads and bonds of friendship that grow and weave within and between an all-American family and an Iranian American family as they adopt and raise Korean infants. (Rev: BL 2/15/06*; SLJ 7/06)

2282 Updike, John. *Terrorist* (11–12). 2006, Knopf $25.00 (978-0-307-26465-7). Eighteen-year-old Ahmad's obsession with Islam draws him inexorably into a tangled and dangerous web. (Rev: BL 3/15/06)

2283 Wilson, Edward O. *Anthill* (11–12). 2010, Norton $24.95 (978-039307119-1). Raff Cody explores the lush Alabama woods as a boy and fights for that same land as a young lawyer. (Rev: BL 2/1–15/10)

2284 Woods, Brenda. *Emako Blue* (7–10). 2004, Penguin $15.99 (978-0-399-24006-5). After Emako, a talented singer, is mistakenly killed in a drive-by shooting in Los Angeles, her surviving friends — Eddie, Jamal, and Monterey — share their thoughts about what she meant to them. (Rev: BL 7/04; SLJ 7/04)

2285 Woodsmall, Cindy. *When the Heart Cries* (9–12). 2006, WaterBrook paper $13.99 (978-1-4000-7292-7). Mennonite Paul Waddell asks Amish Hannah Lapp to marry him, but Hannah's father is Old Order Amish and refuses to let his daughter marry outside the sect. (Rev: BL 1/1–15/07)

2286 Zenatti, Valérie. *A Bottle in the Gaza Sea* (7–12). Trans. by Adriana Hunter. 2008, Bloomsbury $16.95 (978-1-59990-200-5). A Jewish girl in Israel puts a message in a bottle that is thrown into the sea and makes its way to Naïm, a Palestinian in Gaza; Tal and Naïm correspond and develop a relationship despite the wide gulf between their peoples. Sidney Taylor Book Award 2009. (Rev: BL 4/1/08; SLJ 5/08)

Fantasy

2287 Aamodt, Donald. *A Name to Conjure With* (9–12). 1989, Avon paper $3.50 (978-0-380-75137-2). A reluctant participant embarks on a quest with a bumbling sorcerer. (Rev: BL 8/89; VOYA 10/89)

2288 Aaron, Rachel. *The Spirit Eater* (10–12). Series: Legend of Eli Monpress. 2011, Orbit paper $13.99 (978-03160690-8-3). This third installment in the fast-paced series has master thief Eli and his party traveling to the far north in search of Storn, the wizard who made Nico's coat. ☊ **e** (Rev: BL 1/1–15/11)

2289 Aaron, Rachel. *Spirit Rebellion* (10–12). Series: Legend of Eli Monpress. 2010, Orbit paper $7.99 (978-03160691-1-3). This follow-up to *The Spirit Thief* (2010) finds Miranda heading for a mysterious kingdom to prevent Eli from stealing a legendary artifact. (Rev: BLO 11/1–15/10)

2290 Aaron, Rachel. *The Spirit Thief* (10–12). Series: Legend of Eli Monpress. 2010, Orbit paper $7.99 (978-03160690-5-2). In his quest to steal $1 million in gold, master thief and magician Eli Monpress kidnaps the king of Mellinor, and is pursued by the sorceress Miranda; the first installment of a fantasy trilogy. (Rev: BLO 11/1–15/10)

2291 Abbey, Lynn. *Sanctuary: An Epic Novel of Thieves' World* (11–12). Series: Thieves' World. 2002, Tor $27.95 (978-0-312-87517-6). A rich saga full of intrigue about the city of Sanctuary and efforts to guard its secrets; for mature teens. (Rev: BL 4/15/02)

2292 Abbey, Lynn. *Unicorn and Dragon* (10–12). 1988, Avon paper $3.50 (978-0-380-75567-7). A fantasy set in 11th-century England that pits Druid magic against Norman sorcery. (Rev: SLJ 6/87)

2293 Abbey, Lynn, ed. *Turning Points* (10–12). Series: Thieves' World. 2002, Tor $25.95 (978-0-312-87491-9). The city featured in *Sanctuary* (2002) and its people are the focus of this stand-alone volume of short stories. (Rev: BL 11/15/02)

2294 Abbott, Ellen Jensen. *Watersmeet* (7–10). 2009, Marshall Cavendish $16.99 (978-076145536-3). Abisina, 14, learns to love those who are different from her when she travels to Watersmeet, a more diverse environment than her home of Vranille. (Rev: BLO 3/11/09; LMC 8–9/09; SLJ 8/09; VOYA 8/09)

2295 Abraham, Daniel. *A Betrayal in Winter* (9–12). 2007, Tor $24.95 (978-0-7653-1341-6). Interesting characters populate this sequel to A Shadow in Summer, in which the ruler's sons must fight to the death to see who will succeed the father. (Rev: BL 8/07)

2296 Adams, Richard. *Tales from Watership Down* (7–12). 1996, Avon paper $7.99 (978-0-380-72934-0). Nineteen tales keep readers abreast of developments on Watership Down and provide information on the exploits of El-ahrairah, the rabbit folk hero. (Rev: BL 9/1/96; SLJ 1/97)

2297 Adams, Richard. *Watership Down* (7–12). 1996, Scribner $30.00 (978-0-684-83605-8); paper $16 (978-0-7432-7770-9). In this fantasy first published in 1974, a small group of male rabbits sets out to find a new home.

2298 Adlington, L. J. *Cherry Heaven* (8–11). 2008, Greenwillow $16.99 (978-0-06-143180-7). In a strange world where cities and towns war against each other and hide disturbing secrets, three girls tell about their lives — one as a slave, two sisters as new citizens of the town of Meander. A companion to *The Diary of Pelly D*. (Rev: BCCB 6/08; BL 12/15/07; HB 3–4/08; LMC 10/08; SLJ 3/08)

2299 Aguirre, Ann. *Outpost* (9–12). 2012, Feiwel & Friends $17.99 (978-0-312-65009-4). In this followup to 2011's *Enclave*, Deuce finds herself volunteering for patrol in order to gain respect from her peers. ⌒ **e** Lexile 760L (Rev: BL 11/1/12; SLJ 10/12; VOYA 10/12)

2300 Aguirre, Ann, and Jaclyn Dolamore, et al. *Corsets and Clockwork: 13 Steampunk Romances* (8–11). Ed. by Trisha Telep. 2011, Running Press paper $9.95 (978-0-7624-4-092-4). With contributions by such authors as Tessa Gratton, Frewin Jones, and Caitlin Kittredge, this is a strong collection of steampunk romances. **e** (Rev: BL 5/1/11; SLJ 6/11; VOYA 6/11)

2301 Aidinoff, Elsie V. *The Garden* (9–12). 2004, HarperTempest $17.89 (978-0-06-055606-8). This is a fine reworking of the Garden of Eden story complete with the Serpent and conversations with God. (Rev: BL 3/1/04; HB 7–8/04; SLJ 8/04)

2302 Alexander, Alma. *Cybermage* (7–10). Series: Worldweavers. 2009, Eos $17.99 (978-006083961-1). Thea tackles new challenges at Wandless Academy, including new powers, old friends, and mysteries; the third volume in the trilogy. **e** (Rev: BLO 2/2/09; SLJ 8/09)

2303 Alexander, Alma. *Gift of the Unmage* (7–10). Series: Worldweavers Trilogy. 2007, HarperTeen $16.99 (978-0-06-083955-0). Thea, the seventh child of two seventh children, unexpectedly shows no magical abili-

ty until Grandma Spider uncovers her power as a dream weaver and Thea enters Wandless Academy for remedial magic. (Rev: BCCB 6/07; BL 3/1/07; SLJ 8/07)

2304 Alexander, Alma. *Spellspam* (7–10). Series: Worldweavers. 2008, Eos $17.99 (978-0-06-083958-1). E-mails that cast spells on unsuspecting people are endangering computer users around the world; can Thea use her magic to stop them? (Rev: BL 2/8/08; SLJ 7/08)

2305 Allen, Justin. *Year of the Horse* (9–12). 2009, Overlook paper $12.95 (978-1-59020-273-9). A diverse, multiethnic group faces a perilous journey as they band together to avenge a nefarious deed perpetrated decades earlier by an unearthly bandit in this action-packed fantasy set in the Old West. (Rev: BL 9/15/09; SLJ 12/09)

2306 Anderson, Jodi Lynn. *Tiger Lily* (8–11). 2012, HarperTeen $17.99 (978-0-06-200325-6). In Neverland Tiger Lily, 15, must choose between her tribe's wishes and her burgeoning crush on Peter Pan. ⌒ **e** Lexile 850L (Rev: BL 4/15/12; SLJ 7/12*; VOYA 2/12)

2307 Anderson, R. J. *Faery Rebels: Spell Hunter* (7–10). 2009, HarperCollins $16.99 (978-006155474-2). The fairy world of Oakenwyld is dying and a hunter named Knife sets out to save the Oakenfolk, involving herself with humans in the process. (Rev: BL 7/09; SLJ 8/09; VOYA 8/09)

2308 Anthony, Piers. *Air Apparent* (9–12). 2007, Tor $24.95 (978-0-7653-0410-0). The Magic of Xanth series continues with the disappearance of Good Magician Humfrey's son, Hugo, setting in motion a series of adventures through multiple Xanths involving a variety of colorful characters who find that they themselves are players in a grand scheme linked with the origins of time. (Rev: BL 10/1/07)

2309 Anthony, Piers. *Being a Green Mother* (10–12). Series: Incarnations of Immortality. 1987, Ballantine paper $5.95 (978-0-345-32223-4). In this installment in the series, Orb falls in love with a man who might be Satan. (Rev: BL 10/15/87; VOYA 6/88)

2310 Anthony, Piers. *Demons Don't Dream* (9–12). Series: Xanth Saga. 1994, Tor paper $5.99 (978-0-8125-3483-2). An interactive video game transports a 16-year-old boy to the infamous land of Xanth. (Rev: BL 12/15/92; VOYA 8/93)

2311 Anthony, Piers. *Faun and Games* (9–12). 1997, St. Martin's $23.95 (978-0-312-86162-9). In this Xanth novel, Forrest Faun consults Good Magician Humfrey to find a suitable creature to adopt his neighboring tree. (Rev: BL 9/1/97; VOYA 4/98)

2312 Anthony, Piers. *For Love of Evil* (10–12). 1990, Avon paper $7.99 (978-0-380-75285-0). The penultimate volume (number 6) of the Incarnations of Immortality series. In this episode Satan is the protagonist. (Rev: BL 9/1/88)

2313 Anthony, Piers. *Golem in the Gears* (10–12). 1986, Ballantine paper $6.99 (978-0-345-31886-2). In this ninth Xanth novel, Grundy the Golem sets out to find the lost dragon of Princess Ivy. (Rev: BL 2/15/86; SLJ 5/86; VOYA 6/86)

2314 Anthony, Piers. *Man from Mundania* (9–12). 1989, Avon paper $5.99 (978-0-380-75289-8). A Xanth novel that completes the trilogy begun with *Vale of the Vole* and continued in *Heaven Cent*. (Rev: BL 9/89; VOYA 12/89)

2315 Anthony, Piers. *A Spell for Chameleon* (10–12). 1987, Ballantine paper $6.99 (978-0-345-34753-4). This is the introductory Xanth novel where the reader first meets the young hero Bink and his quest to find magical powers. Two others in this extensive series are: *Castle Roogna* and *The Source of Magic* (both 1987).

2316 Anthony, Piers. *Wielding a Red Sword* (10–12). 1987, Ballantine paper $6.99 (978-0-345-32221-0). In the fourth book of the Incarnations of Immortality series, Mym is forced to do Satan's work and finds it impossible to stop. For better readers. (Rev: BL 9/1/86)

2317 Anthony, Piers. *With a Tangled Skein* (10–12). 1985, Ballantine paper $6.99 (978-0-345-31885-5). In this volume in the Incarnations of Immortality series, Niobe sets out to avenge her lover's death. An earlier volume was *On a Pale Horse* (1986).

2318 Armstrong, Kelley. *The Awakening* (7–10). Series: Darkest Powers. 2009, HarperCollins $17.99 (978-006166276-8); LB $18.89 (978-006166280-5). This sequel to *The Summoning* (2008) finds Chloe on the run and enlisting the help of other teens who have supernatural powers. ⌒ ℯ Lexile HL630L (Rev: BL 4/1/09; SLJ 9/09; VOYA 8/09)

2319 Armstrong, Kelley. *The Calling* (7–11). Series: Darkness Rising. 2012, HarperCollins $17.99 (978-006179705-7). Native American Maya and her friends, now aware of their supernatural powers, are being pursued by evil adults in this action-packed second volume in the series. ⌒ ℯ Lexile HL570L (Rev: BL 2/1/12; SLJ 5/1/12; VOYA 12/1/12)

2320 Ashby, Amanda. *Fairy Bad Day* (7–10). 2011, Penguin paper $7.99 (978-0-14-241-259-6). Emma Jones, a sophomore at Burtonwood Academy, is mortified to be assigned to the task of fairy slaying instead of dragon slaying, especially when the new dragon killer-in-training turns out to be a very attractive young man. ℯ Lexile 920L (Rev: BL 8/11; SLJ 8/11; VOYA 6/11)

2321 Ashby, Amanda. *Zombie Queen of Newbury High* (8–12). 2009, Penguin paper $7.99 (978-014241256-5). Mia accidentally turns her fellow high school students into flesh-eating zombies and escapes only with the help of handsome Chase, who works for the Department of Paranormal Containment. ℯ Lexile HL810L (Rev: BL 4/1/09; SLJ 6/1/09; VOYA 2/09)

2322 Ashley, Mike, ed. *The Mammoth Book of Fantasy* (9–12). Series: Mammoth. 2001, Carroll & Graf paper $11.95 (978-0-7867-0917-5). From Victorian authors like George Macdonald to present-day masters, this is an excellent collection of thrilling fantasies and a fine overview of the genre. (Rev: BL 10/1/01)

2323 Ashton, Brodi. *Everbound* (9–12). Series: Everneath. 2013, HarperCollins $17.99 (978-006207116-3). Nikki must ally herself with untrustworthy Cole, an Everliving, in order to rescue Jack from the Everneath in this second volume in the trilogy. ⌒ ℯ (Rev: BL 2/15/13; SLJ 5/13; VOYA 12/12)

2324 Ashton, Brodi. *Everneath* (9–12). 2012, HarperCollins $17.99 (978-006207113-2). In this story that draws on the myth of Hades and Persephone, 17-year-old Nikki gets a chance to leave the immortal world of Everneath and return to the Surface for six months. ⌒ ℯ Lexile HL590L (Rev: BL 1/12; SLJ 5/1/12; VOYA 12/11)

2325 Asprin, Robert. *Dragons Wild* (9–12). 2008, Ace paper $14.00 (978-0-441-01470-5). Griffen McCandles and his sister Valerie head for New Orleans after discovering they are actually dragons who will soon be able to use their powers, and that lots of other dragons want them dead. (Rev: BL 4/1/08)

2326 Atwater-Rhodes, Amelia. *Hawksong* (7–10). 2003, Delacorte $9.95 (978-0-385-73071-6). A gripping fantasy about two young leaders who seek to end the long war between their peoples — avian shapeshifters and serpent shapeshifters — and are prepared to consider marriage for the sake of peace. (Rev: HBG 4/04; SLJ 8/03*; VOYA 6/03)

2327 Atwater-Rhodes, Amelia. *Poison Tree* (9–12). 2012, Delacorte $15.99 (978-0-385-73754-8); LB $18.99 (978-0-385-90672-2). This complex paranormal tale includes vampires, shapeshifters, and witches as Alysia (a human) and Sarik (a human/tiger) work as mediators for SingleEarth, a peace-making organization. ℯ Lexile 940L (Rev: BL 6/12; LMC 11–12/12; SLJ 8/1/12)

2328 Augarde, Steve. *Celandine* (7–10). 2006, Random House $16.95 (978-0-385-75048-6). Celandine escapes the cruel boarding school she attends during World War I and returns to the village of the little people, the Various, that live near her family's farm where she discovers her special powers. (Rev: BL 8/06; SLJ 11/06)

2329 Augarde, Steve. *Winter Wood* (7–10). Series: The Touchstone Trilogy. 2009, Random House $17.99 (978-038575074-5); LB $20.99 (978-038575075-2). Midge moves to Mill Farm and finally meets her great-aunt Celandine, who holds the key to the fate of the Various, a race of tiny winged people; the final volume in the trilogy, following *The Various* (2004) and *Celandine* (2006). Lexile 750L (Rev: BL 4/1/09; SLJ 6/1/09; VOYA 8/09)

2330 Augarde, Steve. *X-Isle* (7–10). 2010, Random House $17.99 (978-038575193-3). After a cataclysmic flood, young Baz and Ray find themselves on an island that purportedly offers survival and a future but in fact turns out to be an evil society run by the fanatical Preacher John; it's up to Baz and Ray to ensure their future. e (Rev: BL 6/10; LMC 10/10; SLJ 8/10)

2331 Avi. *The Man Who Was Poe* (7–10). 1991, Avon paper $6.99 (978-0-380-71192-5). When Edmund goes out to search for his missing mother and sister, he encounters Edgar Allan Poe in disguise as detective Auguste Dupin. (Rev: BL 10/1/89; SLJ 9/89; VOYA 2/90)

2332 Bach, Richard. *Jonathan Livingston Seagull* (10–12). 1970, Avon paper $6.99 (978-0-380-01286-2). Because of his unusual love of flying, Jonathan is treated as an outsider.

2333 Bacigalupi, Paolo. *The Drowned Cities* (9–12). 2012, Little, Brown $17.99 (978-031605624-3). Friends Mahlia and Mouse take turns being the savior and the saved as they risk their lives escaping from the war-torn Drowned Cities; this postapocalyptic novel is a companion to 2010's *Ship Breaker* and also features the bioengineered Tool. ∩ e Lexile HL690L (Rev: BL 3/1/12*; HB 5–6/12; LMC 8–9/12; SLJ 5/1/12)

2334 Baker, E. D. *The Wide-Awake Princess* (7–10). 2010, Bloomsbury $16.99 (978-1-59990-487-0). Annie, Sleeping Beauty's little sister, is left wide awake when the rest of the castle falls into its 100-year slumber, so it's up to her to save the day. Lexile 890L (Rev: BLO 4/15/10; LMC 8–9/10; SLJ 6/10)

2335 Baker, Kage. *The Bird of the River* (10–12). 2010, Tor $25.99 (978-076532296-8). When half-siblings Eliss and Alder climb aboard a river maintenance barge, their paths quickly diverge: Alder jumps ship, while Eliss becomes an indispensable lookout for a young assassin. (Rev: BL 7/10)

2336 Baker, Kage. *The House of the Stag* (10–12). 2008, Tor $24.95 (978-076531745-2). Gard fights against the enslavement of his people and eventually becomes a powerful, vicious ruler who surprisingly chooses good in the end; for strong readers. e (Rev: BL 9/15/08)

2337 Baker, Kage. *Mother Aegypt and Other Stories* (11–12). 2004, Night Shade $27.00 (978-1-892389-75-6). An engrossing collection of 13 engaging fantasy stories for strong, mature teen readers. (Rev: BL 7/04)

2338 Balog, Cyn. *Fairy Tale* (7–10). 2009, Delacorte $16.99 (978-038573706-7); LB $19.99 (978-038590644-9). Morgan learns that her long-term boyfriend is a fairy changeling and does not belong in her world. (Rev: BL 5/15/09; LMC 10/09; SLJ 12/09)

2339 Balog, Cyn. *Sleepless* (7–10). 2010, Delacorte $16.99 (978-0-385-73848-4). Romance and fantasy blend in this novel about a Sandman called Eron whose contract is up and who must return to human form; he is reluctant to hand over care of his beloved Julia's nightly sleep to Griffin, her recently deceased boyfriend. e (Rev: LMC 10/10; SLJ 8/10)

2340 Banner, Catherine. *The Eyes of a King* (7–11). Series: The Last Descendants. 2008, Random House $16.99 (978-0-375-83875-0). An intricate and many-layered fantasy in which teenaged Leo discovers that the true ruler of Malonia has been exiled to England. (Rev: BL 5/15/08; SLJ 8/08)

2341 Baratz-Logsted, Lauren. *Little Women and Me* (6–10). 2011, Bloomsbury $16.99 (978-1-59990-514-3). Present-day teen Emily March finds herself drawn into another world when she begins reading Louisa May Alcott's *Little Women*. e Lexile 830L (Rev: BL 11/15/11; LMC 3–4/12; SLJ 10/1/11; VOYA 12/11)

2342 Barker, Clive. *Days of Magic, Nights of War* (7–12). Series: Abarat. 2004, HarperCollins $24.99 (978-0-06-029170-9). In the second installment in the series, Candy Quackenbush makes discoveries about herself and the islands of Abarat as she tries to stay one step ahead of the Lord of Midnight. (Rev: BL 9/1/04; SLJ 11/04)

2343 Barlough, Jeffrey E. *Bertram of Butter Cross* (9–12). 2007, Gresham & Doyle paper $14.95 (978-0-9787634-0-4). Terrifying creatures prey on a village in this fantasy novel that melds mysterious happenings with Victorian sensibilities. (Rev: BL 8/07)

2344 Barnes, Jennifer Lynn. *Nobody* (7–12). 2013, Egmont $17.99 (978-160684321-5). Claire, 15, has always kept a low profile and spent her life alone until she meets Nix, an attractive 17-year-old who has been sent to kill her but is now questioning why the Society has labeled Claire as dangerous. ∩ e Lexile HL710L (Rev: BL 1/13; LMC 5–6/13; SLJ 2/13)

2345 Barnes, Jennifer Lynn. *Tattoo* (8–11). 2007, Delacorte LB $11.99 (978-0-385-90363-9); paper $7.99 (978-0-385-73347-2). Four 15-year-old girls buy temporary tattoos and discover each of them now has a superpower that will help the quartet battle an ancient force that plans to create mayhem at their school dance. (Rev: BCCB 3/07; BL 1/1–15/07; SLJ 1/07)

2346 Barrett, Neal. *The Treachery of Kings* (10–12). 2001, Bantam paper $6.50 (978-0-553-58196-6). Among the strange characters in this fantasy are the Newlies, animals who have become humans, and a king who must imitate the sleep of the dead for months at a time. (Rev: BL 7/01; VOYA 6/02)

2347 Barrett, Tracy. *Dark of the Moon* (7–10). 2011, Harcourt $16.99 (978-0-547-58132-3). The story of the minotaur is told from the perspective of his 15-year-old sister Ariadne, a lonely girl destined to be a goddess. e Lexile 920L (Rev: BL 10/15/11; SLJ 8/11; VOYA 12/11)

2348 Barrett, Tracy. *King of Ithaka* (7–10). 2010, Henry Holt $16.99 (978-0-8050-8969-1). At the age of 16,

Telemachos sets off from Ithaka to find his long-departed father Odysseus in this action-packed novel. **e** Lexile 830L (Rev: BL 10/1/10; LMC 11–12/10; SLJ 11/1/10; VOYA 12/10)

2349 Barron, T. A. *The Eternal Flame* (7–10). Series: Great Tree of Avalon. 2006, Philomel $19.99 (978-0-399-24213-7). This final book in the trilogy follows Tamwyn, Elli, and Scree as they make their final, dramatic efforts to fend off the evil Rhita Gawr. (Rev: BL 9/1/06; SLJ 11/06)

2350 Barron, T. A. *The Fires of Merlin* (7–10). Series: Lost Years of Merlin. 1998, Putnam $20.99 (978-0-399-23020-2). A complex sequel to *The Seven Songs of Merlin,* in which young Merlin once again faces the threat of the dragon Valdearg, who is preparing to conquer the land of Fincayra. (Rev: BL 9/1/98; HBG 3/99; SLJ 3/99; VOYA 2/99)

2351 Barron, T. A. *The Great Tree of Avalon* (6–12). Series: Great Tree of Avalon. 2004, Penguin $19.99 (978-0-399-23763-8). The fate of Avalon, which the Lady of the Lake has prophesied will be destroyed by the Dark Child, rests in the hands of two 17-year-old boys: Tamwyn and Scree. (Rev: BL 9/1/04*; SLJ 10/04)

2352 Barron, T. A. *The Lost Years of Merlin* (7–10). Series: Lost Years of Merlin. 1996, Putnam $19.99 (978-0-399-23018-9). The author has created a magical land populated by remarkable creatures in this first book of a trilogy about the early years of the magician Merlin. (Rev: BL 9/1/96; SLJ 9/96; VOYA 10/96)

2353 Barron, T. A. *Merlin's Dragon* (7–10). Series: Merlin's Dragon Trilogy. 2008, Philomel $19.99 (978-039924750-7). Basil, a lizard-like creature with magical powers, sets off to track down Merlin and warn him of impending doom and, at the same time, find others like himself in this latest installment in Barron's Merlin saga. The second volume is *Doomraga's Revenge* (2009). Lexile 820L (Rev: BL 9/1/08; SLJ 9/1/08; VOYA 8/08)

2354 Barron, T. A. *The Mirror of Merlin* (7–10). Series: Lost Years of Merlin. 1999, Putnam $20.99 (978-0-399-23455-2). Young Merlin faces a deadly disease and confronts his future self as he continues his dangerous search for his sword. (Rev: BL 10/1/99; HBG 4/00; SLJ 10/99; VOYA 2/00)

2355 Barron, T. A. *The Seven Songs of Merlin* (7–10). Series: Lost Years of Merlin. 1997, Putnam $19.99 (978-0-399-23019-6). In this sequel to *The Lost Years of Merlin,* Emrys, who will become Merlin, must travel to the Otherworld to save his mother who has been poisoned. (Rev: BL 9/1/97; HBG 3/98; SLJ 9/97)

2356 Barron, T. A. *Shadows on the Stars* (7–10). Series: Great Tree of Avalon. 2005, Philomel $19.99 (978-0-399-23764-5). In the year 1002 Tamwyn, Elli, and Scree set off on separate quests to conquer the evil Rhi-

ta Gawr and save Avalon in this sequel to *Child of the Dark Prophecy* (2004). (Rev: BL 9/15/05; SLJ 12/05)

2357 Barron, T. A. *The Wings of Merlin* (7–10). Series: Lost Years of Merlin. 2000, Philomel $21.99 (978-0-399-23456-9). In this, the concluding volume of the saga, Merlin faces his most difficult decision. (Rev: BL 10/1/00; HBG 3/01; SLJ 11/00; VOYA 12/00)

2358 Beagle, Peter S. *The Last Unicorn* (9–12). 1991, NAL paper $15.00 (978-0-451-45052-4). A beautiful unicorn sets off to find others of her species.

2359 Beagle, Peter S. *The Line Between* (9–12). 2006, Tachyon paper $14.95 (978-1-892391-36-0). The ten fantasy stories in this book are light and clear, and laced with humor, intelligence and sheer human kindness. (Rev: BL 7/06)

2360 Beagle, Peter S., ed. *The Secret History of Fantasy* (10–12). 2010, Tachyon paper $15.95 (978-18923919-9-5). Stephen King, T. C. Boyle, Terry Bisson, and Francesca Lia Block are among the writers featured in this anthology. (Rev: BL 9/1–15/10)

2361 Becker, Tom. *Darkside* (7–10). 2008, Scholastic $16.99 (978-0-545-03739-6). Darkside is a dangerous and magical underground London that Jonathan discovers is connected to his family (specifically, his mentally troubled father) in mysterious ways. (Rev: BL 2/1/08; SLJ 5/08)

2362 Bedford, Martyn. *Flip* (7–10). 2011, Random House $16.99 (978-0-385-73990-0); LB $19.99 (978-038590808-5). Alex, 14, is shocked when he wakes up in the body of Flip, an athlete and his complete opposite, and struggles to understand this switch and to find a way back to his former self and his family. ∩ **e** Lexile HL740L (Rev: BL 5/1/11; HB 5–6/11; LMC 10/11*; SLJ 6/11*; VOYA 4/11)

2363 Bell, Clare. *Ratha and Thistle-Chaser* (7–12). 2007, Penguin paper $8.99 (978-0-14-240944-2). Further adventures of the clan of intelligent cats and their search for new land in this continuation (first published in 1990) of *Ratha's Creature* (1983) and *Clan Ground* (1984). (Rev: BL 2/1/90; SLJ 6/90; VOYA 6/90)

2364 Bell, Hilari. *Forging the Sword* (7–10). Series: Farsala Trilogy. 2006, Simon & Schuster $17.99 (978-0-689-85416-3). The final book in the Farsala trilogy finds Jiaan, Kavi, and Soraya fighting the Hrum with magic and a newly forged sword. (Rev: BL 12/15/06; SLJ 3/07)

2365 Bell, Hilari. *The Last Knight: A Knight and Rogue Novel* (8–10). 2007, HarperCollins $16.99 (978-0-06-082503-4). Eighteen-year-old Sir Michael Sevenson, a throwback knight errant, and 17-year-old Fisk, his squire, have many adventures as they tangle with the less-noble-than-they-initially-thought Lady Ceciel; the narration alternates between the honest knight and the slippery squire in this blend of fantasy, adventure, and mystery, with humor and "magica" thrown in. (Rev: BL 10/1/07; HB 9–10/07; LMC 2/08; SLJ 9/07)

2366 Bell, Hilari. *Traitor's Son* (7–12). Series: Raven Duet. 2012, Houghton Mifflin $16.99 (978-054719621-3). In this companion to *Trickster's Girl* (2011) set in 21st-century Alaska, Raven and Jase struggle to stop the bio-plague threatening the world's survival, requiring Jase to embrace his Native American roots. **e** Lexile 840L (Rev: BL 2/15/12; SLJ 3/12; VOYA 2/12)

2367 Bell, Hilari. *Trickster's Girl* (7–10). 2010, Houghton Mifflin $16 (978-0-547-19620-6). Humans have caused untold damage to the ecosystem and terrorism is rife, so in the year 2098, 15-year-old Kelsa hopes to use her magic to heal these ills. (Rev: BL 12/15/10; SLJ 12/1/10)

2368 Bemis, John Claude. *The White City* (7–10). Series: Clockwork Dark. 2011, Random House $17.99 (978-037585568-9); LB $20.99 (978-037595568-6). Fans of the series will enjoy this steampunk finale set in Chicago's White City in 1893. **e** Lexile 810L (Rev: BL 8/11)

2369 Bemis, John Claude. *The Wolf Tree* (7–10). Series: Clockwork Dark. 2010, Random House $16.99 (978-0-375-85566-5); LB $19.99 (978-0-375-95566-2). A Darkness is spreading over the land and Ray Cobb and the remaining Ramblers must cross into the Gloaming and try to stop the Gog's evil machine; the second book in the series. **e** (Rev: BL 10/1/10; SLJ 12/1/10)

2370 Benjamin, Curt. *The Prince of Dreams* (10–12). 2002, DAW $23.95 (978-0-7564-0089-7). Llesho, who is coming to grips with his powers, struggles to free his brothers and his land of Thebin in this sequel to *The Prince of Shadows* (2001). (Rev: BL 9/15/02)

2371 Bennardo, Charlotte, and Natalie Zaman. *Sirenz* (8–10). 2011, Flux paper $9.95 (978-0-7387-2-319-8). Having made a deal with Hades, 17-year-old fashionistas Shar and Meg become Sirens and must lure a fashion designer into the Underworld. **e** (Rev: BL 6/1/11; SLJ 11/1/11)

2372 Bennett, Cherie. *Love Never Dies* (7–10). Series: Teen Angels. 1996, Avon paper $3.99 (978-0-380-78248-2). In this fantasy, a teen angel is sent back to earth to help a rock star bent on self-destruction. (Rev: VOYA 6/96)

2373 Bennett, Holly. *The Bonemender's Choice* (7–10). Series: Bonemender. 2007, Orca paper $8.95 (978-1-55143-718-7). Gabrielle and her elfen husband race to rescue young Matthieu and Madeline from pirates and from a spreading affliction called the Gray Veil in this third book in the series. (Rev: BL 11/1/07; SLJ 12/07)

2374 Bennett, Holly. *The Bonemender's Oath* (7–12). 2006, Orca paper $8.95 (978-1-55143-443-8). Gabrielle faces a new threat as she heads home from the war in this satisfying sequel to *The Bonemender* (2005). (Rev: SLJ 2/07)

2375 Bennett, Holly. *Shapeshifter* (7–10). 2010, Orca paper $12.95 (978-1-55469-158-6). Sive uses her shapeshifting ability to become a deer in the mortal world and escape from the evil Far Doirche, who seeks to exploit her magical voice; a fantasy based on an ancient Irish legend. Lexile 910L (Rev: BL 6/10; LMC 11–12/10; SLJ 10/1/10; VOYA 8/10)

2376 Bennett, Holly. *The Warrior's Daughter* (7–10). 2007, Orca paper $8.95 (978-1-55143-607-4). With its roots in Irish mythology, this tale about the courageous daughter of a famous warrior will satisfy readers in search of adventure; a pronunciation guide helps with the many Gaelic names. (Rev: LMC 8–9/07; SLJ 6/07)

2377 Berg, Carol. *Song of the Beast* (11–12). 2003, NAL paper $7.99 (978-0-451-45923-7). A musician emerges from a long jail sentence determined to discover the reason for his imprisonment in this appealing fantasy with a Celtic flair. (Rev: BL 5/15/03)

2378 Berk, Ari. *Death Watch* (9–12). Series: Undertaken Trilogy. 2011, Simon & Schuster $17.99 (978-141699115-1). After his father's death, 17-year-old Silas starts to learn more about his strange heritage in this creepy Gothic story; the first volume in a series. **e** (Rev: BL 10/15/11; LMC 3–4/12; SLJ 2/12; VOYA 12/11)

2379 Berman, Steve, ed. *Magic in the Mirrorstone* (8–11). 2008, Mirrorstone $14.95 (978-0-7869-4732-4). Fifteen authors — among them Holly Black and Nina Kiriki Hoffman — contribute fantasy stories on topics that interest teens (bullies, friendship, cheating boyfriends, and so forth). (Rev: BL 2/15/08; SLJ 3/08)

2380 Bernobich, Beth. *Passion Play* (11–12). 2010, Tor $24.99 (978-076532217-3). Fifteen-year-old Ilse runs away from home when she learns her father plans to marry her to an older man, but when she arrives in the city of Tiralien she ends up in even deeper trouble; for mature readers. **e** (Rev: BL 9/1–15/10)

2381 Berry, Liz. *The China Garden* (8–12). 1996, HarperCollins paper $7.99 (978-0-380-73228-9). Mysterious occurrences involving villagers who appear to know Clare and a handsome young man on a motorcycle happen when she accompanies her mother to an estate named Ravensmere. (Rev: BL 3/15/96; SLJ 5/96; VOYA 6/96)

2382 Bertagna, Julie. *Exodus* (6–10). 2008, Walker $16.95 (978-0-8027-9745-2). In 2100, when the rising waters of global warming threaten her island world, 15-year-old Mara persuades her people to journey to the new sky cities and seek refuge there; but when they arrive they find only rejection. (Rev: BL 2/15/08; SLJ 3/08)

2383 Bertagna, Julie. *Zenith* (6–10). 2009, Walker $16.99 (978-080279803-9). In a world nearly obliterated by global warming, Mara seeks out higher ground with a group of refugees; a sequel to *Exodus* (2008). Lexile 820L (Rev: BL 2/15/09*; SLJ 7/1/09)

2384 Bishop, Toby. *Airs beneath the Moon* (9–12). 2006, Ace paper $6.99 (978-0-441-01462-0). Fourteen-year-old Larkyn, a farm girl, saves a winged colt when its mother dies and is taken with the colt to the Academy of the Air, where she faces prejudice and danger. (Rev: BL 12/15/06)

2385 Bisson, Terry. *Talking Man* (10–12). 1987, Avon paper $2.95 (978-0-380-75141-9). For better readers, this is a fantasy involving godlike creatures and their relations with humans. (Rev: BL 10/1/86)

2386 Black, Holly. *Black Heart* (8–11). Series: Curse Workers. 2012, Simon & Schuster $17.99 (978-144240346-8). In this third volume in the series Cassel, who has strong transformation powers in a world in which magic is illegal, must choose between the Feds and the Mob, challenging his passion for Lila. ∩ e Lexile HL680L (Rev: BL 2/15/12; SLJ 4/12)

2387 Black, Holly. *Ironside: A Modern Faery's Tale* (9–12). 2007, Simon & Schuster $16.99 (978-0-689-86820-7). In this multilayered sequel to *Tithe* (2002), Roiben is crowned king of the Unseelie Court and Kaye and her friend Corny find themselves embroiled in faery disputes. (Rev: BL 5/15/07; SLJ 7/07)

2388 Black, Holly. *The Poison Eaters and Other Stories* (9–12). 2010, Big Mouth $17.99 (978-1-931520-63-8). Vampires, fairies, unicorns, romance, and magic are all found in this collection of 12 dark stories. e Lexile HL760L (Rev: BLO 12/15/09; HB 5–6/10; SLJ 2/10; VOYA 4/10)

2389 Black, Holly. *Red Glove* (7–10). Series: Curse Workers. 2011, Simon & Schuster $17.99 (978-1-4424-0339-0). Cassel, 17, faces several challenges: he must cope with Lila, who is cursed to love him; he must try to solve his older brother's murder; and he must decide whether to work for the Feds or the Mob; the sequel to *White Cat* (2010). ∩ e Lexile HL660L (Rev: BL 4/1/11; SLJ 5/11; VOYA 6/11)

2390 Black, Holly. *Tithe: A Modern Faerie Tale* (8–12). 2002, Simon & Schuster $16.95 (978-0-689-84924-4). Sixteen-year-old Kaye's adventures include rescuing a knight, Roiben, and being caught up in the battles between faerie kingdoms. (Rev: BL 2/15/03; HBG 3/03; SLJ 10/02)

2391 Black, Holly. *Valiant: A Modern Tale of Faerie* (8–11). 2005, Simon & Schuster $16.95 (978-0-689-86822-1). In this dark fantasy featuring drugs and homeless teens in New York City, 17-year-old Val becomes involved with trolls and faeries. (Rev: BL 7/05; SLJ 6/05)

2392 Black, Holly. *White Cat* (7–10). Series: The Curse Workers. 2010, Simon & Schuster $17.99 (978-1-4169-6396-7). Cassel is a member of a family of curse workers — illegal practitioners who can change fate — but

have they now turned on him? The first installment in a series. e Lexile HL700L (Rev: BL 4/1/10; LMC 10/10; SLJ 6/10)

2393 Black, Holly, and Justine Larbalestier, eds. *Zombies vs. Unicorns* (9–12). 2010, Simon & Schuster $16.99 (978-1-4169-8953-0). Which is better — zombies or unicorns? Twelve entertaining stories fuel this important debate in a well-designed anthology. ∩ e Lexile 860L (Rev: BL 9/1/10; LMC 1–2/11; SLJ 10/1/10*)

2394 Black, Jenna. *Glimmerglass* (8–11). 2010, St. Martin's paper $9.99 (978-03125759-3-9). On a quest to find her father in Avalon, 16-year-old Dana enters a realm sandwiched between modern London and the fairy world, encountering danger and romance. e Lexile 880L (Rev: BLO 7/10; VOYA 10/10)

2395 Blackman, Malorie. *Naughts and Crosses* (8–11). 2005, Simon & Schuster $15.95 (978-1-4169-0016-0). Callum, a 15-year-old, pale-skinned Naught in a world dominated by the dark-skinned Crosses, falls in love with Sephy, daughter of the Cross politician for whom Callum's mother works. (Rev: BL 6/1–15/05*; SLJ 6/05; VOYA 8/05)

2396 Blake, Kendare. *Anna Dressed in Blood* (8–12). 2011, Tor $17.99 (978-0-7653-2865-6). Successful ghost hunter Cas, 17, surprisingly finds love when he meets a murderous teen ghost named Anna. e Lexile HL690L (Rev: BL 6/1/11; LMC 3–4/12*; SLJ 11/1/11*)

2397 Block, Francesca Lia. *Dangerous Angels* (9–12). Series: Weetzie Bat. 1998, HarperCollins $11.99 (978-0-06-440697-0). A collection of five Weetzie Bat books: dark, modern fairy tales set in Los Angeles. (Rev: BL 10/1/98)

2398 Block, Francesca Lia. *I Was a Teenage Fairy* (8–12). 1998, HarperCollins LB $14.89 (978-0-06-027748-2). Barbie Marks, at 16 a successful model, sorts herself out with the help of a fairy named Mab, after her father leaves and she is molested by a photographer. (Rev: BL 10/15/98; HB 11–12/98; HBG 3/99; SLJ 12/98*; VOYA 10/98)

2399 Block, Francesca Lia. *Psyche in a Dress* (11–12). 2006, HarperCollins $16.89 (978-0-06-076373-2). A modern free-verse interpretation of Psyche's story; for sophisticated, mature readers. (Rev: BL 9/1/06; SLJ 8/06)

2400 Block, Francesca Lia, and Carmen Staton. *Ruby* (9–12). 2006, HarperCollins $21.95 (978-0-06-084057-0). Ruby's magical abilities lead her to believe she and Orion, a famous actor, are meant to fall in love with each other. (Rev: BL 4/15/06; SLJ 7/06)

2401 Blubaugh, Penny. *Serendipity Market* (6–10). 2009, HarperCollins $16.99 (978-006146875-9); LB $17.89 (978-006146876-6). Mama Inez calls on storytellers from all over the world to tell their tales and get the earth back on track. **e** (Rev: BL 3/15/09; SLJ 4/1/09; VOYA 8/09)

2402 Blumlein, Michael. *The Healer* (9–12). 2005, Prometheus $25.00 (978-1-59102-314-2). Fourteen-year-old Payne has unique healing powers in a world in which beings known as grotesques are considered inferior to humans. (Rev: BL 7/05; SLJ 10/05)

2403 Bosworth, Jennifer. *Struck* (7–10). 2012, Farrar $17.99 (978-037437283-5). Seventeen-year-old Mia's propensity for attracting lightning draws the attention of two competing cults in post-disaster Los Angeles. **e** (Rev: BL 5/1/12; HB 7–8/12; LMC 7–8/12; SLJ 6/12)

2404 Bracken, Alexandra. *Brightly Woven* (7–10). 2010, Egmont $16.99 (978-1-60684-038-2). A wizard named Wayland whisks 16-year-old weaver Sydelle off on an action-packed effort to stop a war in this fantasy that features magic, romance, and danger. **e** Lexile HL760L (Rev: BL 3/15/10; LMC 10/10; SLJ 4/10)

2405 Bradbury, Ray. *The Illustrated Man* (7–12). 1990, Bantam paper $7.50 (978-0-553-27449-3). A tattooed man tells a story for each of his tattoos.

2406 Bradbury, Ray. *Now and Forever: Somewhere a Band Is Playing and Leviathan '99* (9–12). 2007, Morrow $24.95 (978-0-06-113156-1). These brilliant recent stories by Bradbury, one a tale about a town of immortals in Arizona and the other an adaptation of the Moby Dick story occurring in outer space, will not disappoint readers. (Rev: BL 9/1/07)

2407 Bradley, Marion Zimmer. *The Mists of Avalon* (9–12). 2000, Ballantine $30.00 (978-0-345-44118-8); paper $16.95 (978-0-345-35049-7). A popular retelling of the Arthurian legend with a focus on Morgan le Fay, also known as Morgaine.

2408 Bradshaw, Gillian. *Dangerous Notes* (11–12). 2002, Severn $26.99 (978-0-7278-5757-6). Val's talent as a musician is threatened when she is arrested and must undergo "risk-assessment testing" because of the brain regeneration treatment she received as a child; for mature teens. (Rev: BL 1/1–15/02)

2409 Bray, Libba. *Going Bovine* (8–12). 2009, Delacorte $17.99 (978-0-385-73397-7); LB $20.99 (978-0-385-90411-7). After Cameron, 16, is diagnosed with "mad cow" disease, he finds himself transported by an angel of kinds who sends him on a quest to save mankind; similarities to Don Quixote will amuse readers who know the story. Printz Winner 2010. ⌒ Lexile HL680L (Rev: BL 8/09*; HB 9–10/09; SLJ 9/09; VOYA 8/09)

2410 Bray, Libba. *A Great and Terrible Beauty* (8–12). 2003, Delacorte LB $17.99 (978-0-385-90161-1). Gemma, a troubled student in London, learns to control her visions and enter the Realms, a place of magic, in this multilayered novel that combines fantasy, mystery, and romance with a look at 19th-century manners.

⌒ (Rev: BCCB 5/04; BL 11/15/03; SLJ 2/04; VOYA 4/04)

2411 Bray, Libba. *The Sweet Far Thing* (8–10). Series: Gemma Doyle. 2007, Delacorte $17.99 (978-0-385-73030-3). This final installment in the series finds Gemma wondering whom she can trust with the magic of the Realms even as the Realms themselves are transforming. ⌒ (Rev: BL 11/15/07; SLJ 1/08)

2412 Bray, Patricia. *Devlin's Luck* (10–12). 2002, Bantam paper $5.99 (978-0-553-58475-2). Convinced he has nothing left to live for, Devlin Stonehand happily takes on the dangerous responsibilities of defending the kingdom as the Chosen One. (Rev: BL 5/1/02; VOYA 8/02)

2413 Brennan, Herbie. *Ruler of the Realm* (7–10). Series: The Faerie Wars Chronicles. 2006, Bloomsbury $18.95 (978-1-58234-881-0). This action-packed third installment of the series that blends fantasy and science fiction has Queen Blue investigating an office of peace from the Faeries of the Night and Henry (a human) being abducted by aliens. (Rev: SLJ 2/07)

2414 Brennan, Sarah Rees. *The Demon's Lexicon* (9–12). 2009, Simon & Schuster $17.99 (978-141696379-0). The first book in a series about two brothers who have been on guard against demons and evil magicians since their father's mysterious death. The sequel is *The Demon's Covenant* (2010). Lexile HL830L (Rev: BL 4/15/09; HB 9–10/09; SLJ 7/1/09*; VOYA 4/10)

2415 Briceland, V. *The Buccaneer's Apprentice* (7–11). Series: The Cassaforte Chronicles. 2010, Flux paper $9.95 (978-0-73871895-8.). Escaping servitude, 17-year-old Nic has many adventures at sea in his quest to save the city of Cassaforte. Lexile 880L (Rev: BLO 3/1/10; LMC 8–9/10; SLJ 7/10)

2416 Briceland, V. *The Glass Maker's Daughter* (7–11). Series: The Cassaforte Chronicles. 2009, Flux paper $9.95 (978-073871424-0). Risa struggles to find her place in the medieval city of Cassaforte when she is not chosen to learn valuable enchantment secrets. Lexile 840L (Rev: BL 4/15/09; SLJ 7/1/09)

2417 Bridges, Robin. *The Gathering Storm* (7–10). 2012, Delacorte $17.99 (978-038574022-7); LB $20.99 (978-038590829-0). Romance, social mores, fantasy, and intrigue are combined in this story about 16-year-old Katerina, Duchess of Oldenburg, and her abilities as a necromancer. **e** (Rev: BL 2/1/12; LMC 3–4/12; SLJ 2/12)

2418 Briggs, Patricia. *Dragon Blood* (10–12). 2003, Berkley paper $7.99 (978-0-441-01008-0). In this sequel to *Dragon Bones*, protagonist Ward of Hurog, aided and abetted by his companion Oreg, a dragon, struggles to foil the nefarious plans of King Jakoven. (Rev: BL 1/1–15/03; VOYA 6/03)

2419 Brockenbrough, Martha. *Devine Intervention* (7–12). 2012, Scholastic $17.99 (978-0-545-38213-7). Jerome, 17, messes everything up, even in the afterlife where he is struggling to succeed as a guardian angel but risks losing the soul of 16-year-old Heidi. ❹ Lexile 810L (Rev: LMC 11–12/12; SLJ 6/12)

2420 Broecker, Randy. *Fantasy of the 20th Century: An Illustrated History* (9–12). 2001, Collectors $60.00 (978-1-888054-52-1). This eye-catching collection showcases the very best in 20th-century fantasy writing and art. (Rev: BL 1/1–15/02) [809.3]

2421 Brom. *The Child Thief* (11–12). Illus. 2009, Eos $26.99 (978-006167133-3). Egocentric Peter Pan is back in this reimagined scenario that explains young Peter's origins and why, about a thousand or so years later, he is gathering lost children from New York City to help him defeat the evil captain; for mature readers. (Rev: BL 9/09)

2422 Brom. *The Plucker* (9–12). 2005, Abrams $24.95 (978-0-8109-5792-3). In a riveting blend of horror and fairy tale, spirits inhabiting a young boy's toys do battle for the soul of the child. (Rev: BL 10/15/05; SLJ 2/06)

2423 Brooks, Terry. *Armageddon's Children* (9–12). Series: The Genesis of Shannara. 2006, Del Rey $26.95 (978-0-345-48408-6). Set in the future, this first book in the series envisions a dark world in which humans and elves must fend off mutants who have been damaged by the polluted environment. (Rev: BL 5/15/06; SLJ 8/06)

2424 Brooks, Terry. *Bearers of the Black Staff* (10–12). Series: Legends of Shannara. 2010, Del Rey $27 (978-034548417-8). Centuries after the apocalyptic end to the Genesis of Shannara trilogy, elves and humans are using their magic to restore peace to their homeland in the face of menacing outside threats. ❹ (Rev: BL 8/10)

2425 Brooks, Terry. *The Elf Queen of Shannara* (9–12). Series: Heritage of Shannara. 1993, Ballantine paper $6.99 (978-0-345-37558-2). Wren and her friend Garth must survive the perils of the jungle to find the Elves and then persuade them to return to the environmentally endangered Westlands. (Rev: BL 12/15/91)

2426 Brooks, Terry. *The Elves of Cintra* (9–12). 2007, Del Rey $26.95 (978-0-345-48411-6). This exciting sequel to Armageddon's Children follows the maturing human and elf children as they battle Demonkind. (Rev: BL 7/07)

2427 Brooks, Terry. *The Gypsy Morph* (9–12). Series: Genesis of Shannara. 2008, Del Rey $27.00 (978-0-345-48414-7). In the conclusion to the trilogy, magical powers promise to aid the survivors of the horrors of a world gone mad. 🎧 (Rev: BL 6/1–15/08*)

2428 Brooks, Terry. *A Princess of Landover* (10–12). Series: Magic Kingdom of Landover. 2009, Del Rey $26 (978-0-345-45852-0). This sequel to *Witches' Brew* (1995) finds 15-year-old heroine Mistaya returning home and, with the help of her magical allies, fending

off an evil magician's plan to unleash demons on the magical kingdom of Landover. (Rev: BL 6/1–15/09; SLJ 12/09)

2429 Brooks, Terry. *The Talismans of Shannara* (9–12). Series: Heritage of Shannara. 1993, Ballantine paper $6.99 (978-0-345-38674-8). With their quests fulfilled, Par, Walker Bob, and Wren are drawn back together to face the Shadowen in the final book of the Shannara saga. (Rev: BL 1/1/93)

2430 Brooks, Terry. *The Tangle Box* (9–12). 1995, Ballantine paper $6.99 (978-0-345-38700-4). This humorous fantasy concerns Ben Holiday, sovereign of the magic kingdom of Landover, and some exiled sorcerers seeking revenge upon the fairy folk. (Rev: BL 3/15/94; VOYA 8/94)

2431 Brooks, Terry. *The Wishsong of Shannara* (9–12). Series: Heritage of Shannara. 1988, Ballantine paper $6.99 (978-0-345-35636-9). In the concluding volume of the Shannara saga, a young girl finds she holds the power of the wishsong, a weapon that the Four Lands can use against their enemies. Preceded by *The Sword of Shannara* and *The Elfstones of Shannara*. (Rev: BL 4/1/85; SLJ 8/85; VOYA 12/85)

2432 Brown, Mary. *Pigs Don't Fly* (9–12). 1994, Baen paper $6.99 (978-0-671-87601-2). With her unknown father's magic ring, the daughter of a village whore sets out to seek her fortune, accompanied by an assortment of animal characters and a blind, amnesiac knight. (Rev: BL 3/1/94; VOYA 10/94)

2433 Brown, Simon. *Inheritance* (10–12). Series: Keys of Power. 2003, DAW paper $7.99 (978-0-7564-0162-7). Sibling rivalry is at the heart of this fantasy saga in which the four children of the failing queen of Grenda Lear are entrusted with the four Keys of Power. (Rev: BL 9/15/03; VOYA 6/04)

2434 Browne, N. M. *The Story of Stone* (9–12). 2005, Bloomsbury $17.95 (978-1-58234-655-7). Nela, an archaeologist, discovers a mysterious black stone that allows her to look into the distant past and observe the interaction between two very different clans. (Rev: BL 10/15/05; SLJ 11/05; VOYA 10/05)

2435 Browne, N. M. *Warriors of Alavna* (7–10). 2002, Bloomsbury $16.95 (978-1-58234-775-2). This historical fantasy pits 15-year-olds Dan and Ursula against invaders in Roman Britain. A sequel is *Warriors of Camlann* (2003). (Rev: BCCB 10/02; SLJ 1/03; VOYA 2/03)

2436 Bruchac, Joseph. *Wabi: A Hero's Tale* (7–10). 2006, Dial $16.99 (978-0-8037-3098-4). A white great horned owl named Wabi has the power to transform himself into a human being and falls in love with an Abenaki girl named Dojihla. (Rev: BL 2/15/06; SLJ 4/06*; VOYA 4/06)

2437 Bryan, Kathleen. *The Golden Rose* (9–12). 2008, Tor paper $14.95 (978-0-7653-1329-4). Fantasy of magic, court intrigue and drama as Averil, duchess of Quitaine, travels to her evil uncle to be married to a nobleman so she can breed an heir for the kingdom. (Rev: BL 3/1/08)

2438 Buffie, Margaret. *The Finder* (6–10). Series: The Watcher's Quest. 2004, Kids Can $16.95 (978-1-55337-671-2). In the final volume of the trilogy, shape-changing heroine Emma Sweeny defies her training master and passes through a magical portal where she must get to four hidden power wands before they're found by the evil Eefa. (Rev: BL 10/15/04; SLJ 1/05; VOYA 2/05)

2439 Bujold, Lois McMaster. *Beguilement* (9–12). Series: The Sharing Knife. 2006, Eos $25.95 (978-0-06-113758-7). Dag and Fawn fall in love after Dag rescues Fawn from an evil demon called a malice that has destroyed her unborn child. (Rev: SLJ 10/06)

2440 Bujold, Lois McMaster. *Passage* (9–12). Series: Sharing Knife. 2008, Eos $25.95 (978-0-06-137533-0). Romance, adventure and magic as a young couple sets out to find a solution to the perilous split between their peoples. (Rev: BL 3/15/08)

2441 Bull, Emma. *Finder* (9–12). 1994, Tor $21.95 (978-0-312-85418-8). Set in Bordertown, just outside the Elflands, this is the story of a cop who exploits a finder's talents to track down a killer sorcerer. (Rev: BL 2/15/94; SLJ 6/95; VOYA 6/94)

2442 Bullen, Allexandra. *Wish* (8–11). 2010, Scholastic $17.99 (978-0-545-13905-2). Three magical dresses aid — and complicate — Olivia's efforts to recover from the death of her twin sister Violet. ℮ Lexile 1150 (Rev: BL 12/109; LMC 3–4/10; SLJ 1/10)

2443 Bunce, Elizabeth C. *A Curse as Dark as Gold* (7–10). 2008, Scholastic $17.99 (978-0-439-89576-7). Charlotte and her sister Rosie make a bargain with a man named Spinner to save themselves from a curse in this take on the Rumplestiltskin story. (Rev: BL 5/1/08; SLJ 5/08)

2444 Bunce, Elizabeth C. *Liar's Moon* (9–12). 2011, Scholastic $17.99 (978-054513608-2). A multilayered sequel to *Star Crossed* (2010) in which pickpocket Digger must prove that her friend Durrel Decath did not murder his wife. ℮ Lexile 840L (Rev: BLO 11/15/11; HB 11–12/11; SLJ 1/12)

2445 Bunce, Elizabeth C. *Star Crossed* (8–11). 2010, Scholastic $17.99 (978-0-545-13605-1). Fleeing after a job goes wrong, teen thief Digger takes on the persona of Celyn, a lady's maid, in this intricate fantasy full of political intrigue and magic. Lexile 820L (Rev: BL 11/15/10; LMC 11–12/10; SLJ 1/1/11; VOYA 2/11)

2446 Bunting, Eve. *The Lambkins* (7–10). Illus. by Jonathan Keegan. 2005, HarperCollins LB $16.89 (978-0-06-059907-2). Kyle's offer to help a woman with a flat tire goes awry when she kidnaps him and shrinks him to the size of a Coke bottle. (Rev: BL 8/05; SLJ 8/05)

2447 Burch, Heather. *Halflings* (9–12). Series: A Halflings Novel. 2012, Zondervan $14.99 (978-0-310-72818-4). Under siege from various bad guys, 17-year-old Nikki Youngblood is protected by three attractive male halflings — the children of angels and human women. ℮ (Rev: BL 5/15/12; SLJ 8/1/12)

2448 Burgis, Stephanie. *Renegade Magic* (6–10). Series: Kat, Incorrigible. 2012, Atheneum $16.99 (978-141699449-7). Kat, 12, struggles to get a grip on the magical talents she possesses in this fantasy set in 19th-century Bath, England, where the family has moved to find a suitable match for Kat's older sister. ℮ Lexile 790L (Rev: BL 3/15/12; SLJ 3/12)

2449 Butcher, Jim. *Proven Guilty* (9–12). Series: Dresden Files. 2006, Roc $23.95 (978-0-451-46085-1). Harry Dresden must determine who is using black magic and why in this follow-up to *Storm Front*. (Rev: BL 5/15/06)

2450 Cabot, Meg. *Insatiable* (11–12). 2010, Morrow $22.99 (978-006173506-6). Young soap opera writer Meena can see how people will die, but she does not realize that her new lover is a vampire. ♩ ℮ (Rev: BL 5/1–15/10)

2451 Cabot, Meg. *Underworld* (8–12). 2012, Scholastic $17.99 (978-054528411-0). John — the "deity of death" — takes Pierce to the Underworld, ostensibly to protect her from the Furies, but Pierce is determined to leave when she learns her family is in danger; the sequel to *Abandon* (2011). ♩ ℮ Lexile 850L (Rev: BL 6/12; SLJ 8/12; VOYA 8/12)

2452 Calhoun, Dia. *Avielle of Rhia* (8–11). 2006, Marshall Cavendish $16.99 (978-0-7614-5320-8). Princess Avielle of Rhia has the physical characteristics of Dredonians (fearful doers of magic) but when all of her royal family is murdered she must use her magic to save the people of Rhia, despite their hatred toward her. (Rev: BL 10/1/06; LMC 2/07; SLJ 11/06)

2453 Calhoun, Dia. *Firegold* (7–12). 1999, Winslow $15.95 (978-1-890817-10-7). A fantasy in which a 13-year-old boy is persecuted in his village because of his different looks and behavior and is forced to travel to the Red Mountains, home of fierce barbarians. (Rev: BL 5/15/99; SLJ 6/99; VOYA 8/99)

2454 Calhoun, Dia. *White Midnight* (9–12). 2003, Farrar $18.00 (978-0-374-38389-3). Rose, a diffident 15-year-old bondgirl who loves her home in the Valley, agrees to marry a neighboring "monster" in this fantasy set in the world seen in *Firegold* (1999). (Rev: BCCB 3/04; BL 9/15/03; LMC 3/04; SLJ 3/04; VOYA 12/03)

2455 Campbell, Alan. *Iron Angel* (9–12). 2008, Bantam $25.00 (978-0-553-38417-8). A dark fantasy adventure featuring angels, traitors, cruel gods and sorcerers, not to mention Deepgate, a city dangling over a black hole. (Rev: BL 4/15/08)

2456 Cann, Kate. *Possessed* (9–12). 2010, Scholastic $16.99 (978-0-545-12812-4). Sixteen-year-old Rayne escapes from her unsatisfactory mother and boyfriend in London and takes a job at a manor house only to find that she's in an even worse environment. Lexile 740L (Rev: BL 12/15/09; LMC 3–4/10; SLJ 2/10)

2457 Card, Orson Scott. *Enchantment* (9–12). 1999, Ballantine paper $6.99 (978-0-345-41688-9). A graduate student traveling in Russia finds a magical forest that takes him into a land of legend and fairy tales. (Rev: BL 3/1/99; SLJ 12/99)

2458 Card, Orson Scott. *Seventh Son* (10–12). 1993, Tor paper $5.99 (978-0-8125-3305-7). In this, the first volume of the Tales of Alvin Maker series, the author has created another world using early nineteenth-century America as a model. (Rev: BL 5/1/87; SLJ 12/87; VOYA 12/87)

2459 Card, Orson Scott. *Stonefather* (10–12). Illus. 2008, Subterranean $35.00 (978-159606194-1). An honest young man finds himself in a large city, realizes that he has magical powers, and navigates the world of unscrupulous characters who want to use him. (Rev: BL 8/08)

2460 Card, Orson Scott. *A War of Gifts: An Ender Story* (9–12). 2007, Tor $12.95 (978-0-7653-1282-2). This short novel features students at the International Fleet's Battle School rebelling against rules prohibiting religious and cultural expression. (Rev: BL 9/15/07; SLJ 2/08)

2461 Carey, Janet Lee. *Dragon's Keep* (7–10). 2007, Harcourt $17.00 (978-0-15-205926-2). Rosland discovers that she is part dragon and that she is destined to care for a brood of dragon children in this action-filled fantasy. ◠ (Rev: BCCB 5/07; BL 2/1/07; SLJ 4/07*)

2462 Carey, Janet Lee. *Dragonswood* (8–12). 2012, Dial $17.99 (978-080373504-0). Accused of witchcraft, Tess is offered protection by a mysterious warden in this fantastical romance set in 1192 and featuring dragons, humans, and fairies; a sequel to *Dragon's Keep* (2007). ℮ (Rev: BL 1/1/12; SLJ 1/12)

2463 Carey, Janet Lee. *Stealing Death* (7–10). 2009, Egmont $16.99 (978-1-60684-009-2); LB $19.99 (978-1-60684-045-0). After a tragic fire that kills his parents and brother, 17-year-old Kipp is on a mission to steal the sack in which the Gwali collects souls of the dead, hoping to keep his other loved ones from dying. Lexile 710L (Rev: BL 9/15/09; SLJ 9/09; VOYA 10/09)

2464 Carmody, Isobelle. *Alyzon Whitestarr* (7–10). 2009, Random House $17.99 (978-037583938-2); LB $20.99 (978-037593938-9). A concussion endows Alyzon Whitestarr with amazing abilities that will perhaps enable her to save her unusual family from disaster; set in Australia, this is a multilayered story full of mystery and romance. (Rev: BL 6/1–15/09; SLJ 11/09)

2465 Carmody, Isobelle. *Winter Door* (7–12). Series: Gateway Trilogy. 2006, Random House $16.95 (978-0-375-83018-1). In this second installment in the trilogy, Rage attempts to combat an unusually severe winter while also dealing with a bully; readers will want to read the first volume before tackling this one. (Rev: SLJ 7/06)

2466 Carriger, Gail. *Etiquette and Espionage* (9–12). 2013, Little, Brown $17.99 (978-031619008-4). This Victorian steampunk fantasy features the clever and exuberant Sophronia, who is happy to learn about espionage as well as etiquette. ◠ ℮ Lexile HL780L (Rev: BL 11/15/12*; HB 1–2/13; SLJ 3/13*; VOYA 2/13)

2467 Carson, Rae. *The Girl of Fire and Thorns* (8–12). 2011, Greenwillow $17.99 (978-0-06-202648-4). In a fantasy medieval world 16-year-old Elisa, a princess forced into an arranged marriage, grows into a strong woman worthy of the magical gem she carries in her navel. YALSA Top Ten Best Fiction for Young Adults 2012. ◠ ℮ Lexile 730L (Rev: BL 10/1/11; SLJ 8/11*)

2468 Carter, Aimee. *The Goddess Test* (9–12). 2011, HarlequinTeen paper $9.99 (978-0-373-21-026-8). In an echo of the Persephone story, Kate Winters makes a bargain with mysterious Henry in hopes of saving a girl's life but not realizing the compromises she must make. ℮ (Rev: BL 5/1/11; SLJ 7/11; VOYA 6/11)

2469 Cash, Steve. *The Meq* (11–12). 2005, Del Rey paper $13.95 (978-0-345-47092-8). When Z turns 12 in 1881, he learns of his heritage and fate as a Meq, a race living among humans; Z works to defeat the evil Fleur-du-Mal against a backdrop of richly detailed historical events at the turn of the 20th century; for mature teens. (Rev: BL 12/15/04)

2470 Cashore, Kristin. *Bitterblue* (9–12). 2012, Dial $19.99 (978-080373473-9). First seen as a child in *Graceling* (2008), Bitterblue is now 18 and queen of Monsea, struggling to heal her people from the ravages caused by her evil father. ◠ ℮ Lexile HL790L (Rev: BL 3/15/12; HB 5–6/12; LMC 10/12; SLJ 4/12*; VOYA 6/12)

2471 Cashore, Kristin. *Fire* (8–12). 2009, Dial $17.99 (978-0-8037-3461-6). A prequel to *Graceling*, this book focuses on the beautiful Fire, who, like the other inhabitants of the Dells, is part monster and has supernatural powers. ℮ Lexile 870L (Rev: BL 9/15/09*; HB 9–10/09; LMC 11–12/09; SLJ 8/09)

2472 Cashore, Kristin. *Graceling* (9–12). 2008, Harcourt $17.00 (978-015206396-2). Prince Po convinces Katsa — a talented fighter who's been subserviently using her powers on the brutal king's disloyal subjects — to stand up for herself in this exciting, romance-tinged story. ◠ Lexile 730L (Rev: BL 10/1/08*; HB 11–12/08; LMC 3–4/09; SLJ 10/1/08*)

2473 Cast, P. C., and Kristin Cast. *Lenobia's Vow* (8–11). Series: House of Night. 2012, St. Martin's $12.99 (978-

125000024-8). Sixteen-year-old Lenobia, posing as her dead half-sister, is on her way to marriage to a rich man in New Orleans in this romantic historical fantasy featuring an evil bishop, a handsome horse trainer, and vampyres. (Rev: BLO 3/15/12)

2474 Caveney, Philip. *Prince of Fools* (7–12). Series: Sebastian Darke. 2008, Delacorte $15.99 (978-0-385-73467-7). Would-be (but not very funny) jester Sebastian, 17 and half-elf, travels with his (quite funny) buffalope and the tiny Captain Cornelius, to the court of King Septimus in hopes of gaining employment; along the way they rescue a princess and find themselves embroiled in intrigue. (Rev: BL 3/15/08; SLJ 9/08)

2475 Chapman, Janet. *Tempting the Highlander* (11–12). Series: Highlander. 2004, Pocket paper $6.99 (978-0-7434-8630-9). Catherine, an abused wife and mother of two, finds herself falling in love with Robbie, who happens to be a time traveler from 13th-century Scotland; for mature teens. (Rev: BL 9/1/04)

2476 Charlton, Blake. *Spellwright* (10–12). 2010, Tor $24.99 (978-076531727-8). Dyslexic young wizard Nico struggles to discover his purpose in life as he fends off evil as well as the suspicions of his peers in this first installment in a series. (Rev: BL 2/1–15/10)

2477 Charnas, Suzy McKee. *The Kingdom of Kevin Malone* (7–10). 1993, Harcourt $16.95 (978-0-15-200756-0). This novel melds the world of the teenage problem novel with that of fantasy in a story that pokes gentle fun at the conventions of fantasy fiction. (Rev: BL 6/1–15/93; SLJ 1/94; VOYA 8/93)

2478 Chernenko, Dan. *The Bastard King* (11–12). Series: Sceptre of Mercy. 2003, NAL paper $14.95 (978-0-451-45914-5). A missing sceptre plays a central role in this story of adventure and strife featuring a youthful king, the first installment in a new series. (Rev: BL 3/1/03)

2479 Chernenko, Dan. *The Chernagor Pirates* (10–12). 2004, NAL paper $14.95 (978-0-451-45956-5). In this sequel to *The Bastard King* (2003), King Grus and Lanius, the king he opposes, are engaged in an ethical as well as military conflict. (Rev: BL 3/1/04)

2480 Childs, Tera Lynn. *Fins Are Forever* (9–12). 2011, HarperCollins $16.99 (978-0-06-191468-3). Lily, a half-mermaid girl, decides to give up her underwater throne and embrace her human side so that she can join her boyfriend Quince; a sequel to *Forgive My Fins* (2010). ∩ ℮ Lexile 770L (Rev: BL 7/11; SLJ 7/11)

2481 Childs, Tera Lynn. *Goddess Boot Camp* (7–10). 2009, Dutton $16.99 (978-052542134-4). Teenage Phoebe is a real goddess — a descendant of Nike — who first appeared in *Oh, My, Gods* (2008). Here she suffers through goddess boot camp on a Greek island. Lexile 710L (Rev: BLO 4/23/09; SLJ 7/1/09)

2482 Childs, Tera Lynn. *Sweet Venom* (7–10). 2011, HarperCollins $17.99 (978-006200181-8). Sixteen-year-old Grace discovers that she and her previously unknown sisters are descendants of Medusa charged with protecting humanity from all manner of mythological monsters. A sequel is *Sweet Shadows* (2012). ℮ Lexile 780L (Rev: BL 10/1/11; SLJ 2/12; VOYA 10/11)

2483 Chima, Cinda Williams. *The Demon King* (6–10). Series: Seven Realms. 2009, Hyperion $17.99 (978-1-4231-1823-7). A rich and varied fantasy featuring one-time thief Han Alister, owner of magic silver cuffs, and Princess Raisa, who rebels against many aspects of the royal court; their lives intersect as they face danger and challenge; the first installment in the series. ∩ ℮ Lexile 760L (Rev: HB 1–2/10; LMC 1–2/10; SLJ 12/09)

2484 Chima, Cinda Williams. *The Wizard Heir* (8–11). 2007, Hyperion $17.99 (978-1-4231-0487-2). When Seph's magical mishaps (he has had no wizard training) lead to a death, he's sent to a boys' school named the Havens, where he's offered training but at a cost Seph must reject; a companion to *The Warrior Heir* (2006). (Rev: BL 5/15/07; SLJ 12/07)

2485 Clare, Cassandra. *City of Glass* (8–11). Series: Mortal Instruments. 2009, Simon & Schuster $17.99 (978-141691430-3). Clary uncovers secrets about her family as she continues to seek a cure for her mother in this multilayered story; the third installment in the series. ∩ ℮ Lexile 760L (Rev: BL 3/1/09; SLJ 7/1/09; VOYA 4/09)

2486 Clare, Cassandra. *Clockwork Angel* (8–12). Series: The Infernal Devices. 2010, Simon & Schuster $19.99 (978-1-4169-7586-1). In Victorian England, 16-year-old Tessa Gray is kidnapped by the sinister Dark Sisters, who want to use her powers for their own diabolical purposes. ℮ Lexile HL780L (Rev: BL 8/10; LMC 1–2/11; SLJ 10/1/10; VOYA 8/10)

2487 Clare, Cassandra. *Clockwork Prince* (8–12). Series: The Infernal Devices. 2011, Simon & Schuster $19.99 (978-141697588-5). Tessa, 16, searches for answers about her identity and works to dismantle the clockwork army amid a richly imagined steampunk setting in this sequel to *Clockwork Angel* (2010). ∩ ℮ Lexile HL790L (Rev: BL 11/15/11; SLJ 1/12; VOYA 12/11)

2488 Clarke, Susanna. *Jonathan Strange and Mr. Norrell: A Novel* (9–12). 2004, Bloomsbury $27.95 (978-1-58234-416-4). In this sweeping novel set in early-19th-century England, two magicians — Gilbert Norrell and his pupil Jonathan Strange — set out to return magic to its former glory but soon clash over how to pull it off. (Rev: BL 7/04; SLJ 1/05)

2489 Clegg, Douglas. *The Lady of Serpents* (10–12). Series: Vampyricon. 2006, Ace $23.95 (978-0-441-01438-5). Dark and disturbing, the world of Vampyricon comes to life in this story of Aleric, the vampire featured in *The Priest of Blood* (2005). (Rev: BL 9/1/06)

2490 Clement-Davies, David. *Fell* (7–12). 2007, Abrams $19.95 (978-0-8109-1185-7). Alina travels through Transylvania with Fell, a wolf, to defeat Lord Vladeran and his dark powers in order to save the natural world; a sequel to *The Sight*. ⌂ (Rev: BL 10/15/07; SLJ 1/08)

2491 Clement-Moore, Rosemary. *Highway to Hell* (8–10). Series: Maggie Quinn: Girl vs. Evil. 2009, Delacorte $16.99 (978-038573463-9); LB $19.99 (978-038590462-9). Magic, legends, and religion mix while Maggie and Lisa are on vacation in south Texas. (Rev: BL 3/15/09; SLJ 4/1/09; VOYA 2/09)

2492 Coakley, Lena. *Witchlanders* (7–10). 2011, Atheneum $16.99 (978-1-4424-2004-5). Witchlander Ryder and Baen Prince Falpian are enemies but share a mystical bond as they struggle to spare the lives of their countrymen. e Lexile HL690L (Rev: BL 10/15/11; LMC 1–2/12; SLJ 12/1/11*; VOYA 8/11)

2493 Cochran, Molly, and Warren Murphy. *The Broken Sword* (10–12). 1997, Tor $24.95 (978-0-312-86283-1). Merlin and King Arthur are reincarnated in the 20th century as an old man and a teenager whose mission is to rescue the Holy Grail from a gang of villains. (Rev: SLJ 8/97)

2494 Coe, David B. *The Sorcerers' Plague* (9–12). 2007, Tor $25.95 (978-0-7653-1638-7). An elderly woman was the lone survivor in a village decimated by a plague as a child; she blames a group known as the Qirsi and, as punishment, intends to use blood magic to turn the plague on the Southlands where the Qirsi live. (Rev: BL 11/1/07)

2495 Coelho, Paulo. *The Alchemist* (9–12). 1993, HarperCollins $19.95 (978-0-06-250217-9). Parable about a boy who must learn to listen to his heart before he can find his treasure. (Rev: BL 5/1/93; SLJ 7/93)

2496 Colfer, Eoin. *Airman* (10–12). 2008, Hyperion $17.99 (978-1-4231-0750-7). Conor, who was born in a hot-air balloon in 1878, witnesses a murder and is thrown into a brutish prison, where he plans escape via flying machine; a multilayered fantasy full of adventure and intrigue. ⌂ (Rev: BL 2/1/08; SLJ 1/08)

2497 Collins, Suzanne. *Mockingjay* (6–12). Series: Hunger Games. 2010, Scholastic $17.99 (978-1-439-02351-1). Katniss has survived the Hunger Games and is now being asked to serve as a kind of poster girl for the rebels hoping to oust the evil President Snow. ⌂ e Lexile 800L (Rev: BLO 8/10*; HB 11–12/10; SLJ 10/1/10)

2498 Collodi, Carlo. *The Adventures of Pinocchio. Rev. ed.* (4–10). Trans. from Italian by M. A. Murray. Illus. by Roberta Innocenti. 2005, Creative Editions $19.95 (978-1-56846-190-8). Nineteenth-century European landscapes provide the backdrop for this appealing retelling of the classic story about the puppet that longed to become a little boy; a revision of the 1988 edition. (Rev: SLJ 12/05)

2499 Condie, Ally. *Crossed* (9–12). Series: Matched. 2011, Dutton $17.99 (978-0-525-42365-2). Cassia faces new dangers when she heads to the Outer Provinces looking for Ky in this sequel to *Matched* (2010). ⌂ e Lexile HL630L (Rev: BL 11/1/11; SLJ 12/1/11; VOYA 12/11)

2500 Condie, Ally. *Matched* (9–12). 2010, Dutton $17.99 (978-0-525-42364-5). The Society decides everything in Cassia's life — even her future husband — so why does her neighbor Ky also turn up on her match disk? (Rev: BL 9/15/10; SLJ 12/1/10)

2501 Condie, Ally. *Reached* (9–12). Series: Matched. 2012, Dutton $17.99 (978-0-525-42366-9). Cassia is working in Central, Ky is a pilot with the Rising, and Xander is a medical official as rebellion is in the air in this final volume in the compelling trilogy. ⌂ e Lexile 670L (Rev: BLO 11/15/12; SLJ 12/12; VOYA 2/13)

2502 Constable, Kate. *The Singer of All Songs* (7–10). Series: Chanters of Tremaris. 2004, Scholastic $16.95 (978-0-439-55478-7). In this impressive fantasy, Calwyn, a novice priestess, is able to control all things cold and uses this power to fight an evil sorcerer. (Rev: BL 2/1/04*; SLJ 4/04; VOYA 4/04)

2503 Constable, Kate. *The Tenth Power* (7–10). Series: Chanters of Tremaris. 2006, Scholastic $16.99 (978-0-439-55482-4). Mourning the loss of her nine powers of chantment, 18-year-old Calwyn returns to Antaris to discover she must go in search of the key to the mysterious tenth, healing, power. (Rev: BL 3/15/06; SLJ 3/06)

2504 Constable, Kate. *The Waterless Sea* (8–11). Series: Chanters of Tremaris. 2005, Scholastic $16.95 (978-0-439-55480-0). In the second volume of the trilogy, Calwyn and her friends travel to the desolate Merithuran Empire on a mission to rescue some children with magical powers. (Rev: BL 5/15/05; SLJ 8/05; VOYA 8/05)

2505 Constantine, Storm. *The Crown of Silence* (10–12). Series: Chronicle of Magravandias. 2001, Tor $27.95 (978-0-312-87329-5). This novel, the second of the series, tells how Shan, a peasant boy of 15, is taken to the local wizard to learn magic and manners. (Rev: BL 3/15/01)

2506 Cook, Dawn. *First Truth* (10–12). 2002, Berkley paper $7.99 (978-0-441-00945-9). Alissa sets out to be trained as a Master at the Hold, unaware that the evil Bailic has other intentions. (Rev: BL 5/15/02)

2507 Cook, Dawn. *Forgotten Truth* (10–12). 2003, Berkley paper $7.99 (978-0-441-01117-9). In this highly readable fantasy, Alissa, an eager student of magic able to switch form readily from human to beast, finds herself transported 400 years into the past. (Rev: BL 12/1/03)

2508 Cooney, Caroline B. *Prisoner of Time* (6–10). Series: Time Travel. 1998, Laurel Leaf paper $5.50 (978-0-440-22019-0). In this conclusion to the trilogy, there is again a contrast between the lifestyles of today and those of 100 years ago as a girl is rescued from an unsuitable marriage. (Rev: BL 6/1–15/98; HBG 3/02; SLJ 5/98; VOYA 6/98)

2509 Cooper, Louise. *Inferno* (9–12). 1989, Tor paper $3.95 (978-0-8125-0246-6). In this sequel to *Nemesis* (1989), Indigo must kill the demon she freed from the Tower of Regrets. (Rev: VOYA 4/90)

2510 Cornish, D. M. *Foundling* (7–10). Series: Monster Blood Tattoo. 2006, Penguin $18.99 (978-0-399-24638-8). Rossamund Bookchild, a foundling boy with a girl's name, sets off from the orphanage to his new job as a lamplighter and finds himself in a perilous world (called Half-Continent) full of monsters. (Rev: BL 4/1/06*; SLJ 7/06*)

2511 Cornish, D. M. *Lamplighter* (7–10). Series: Monster Blood Tattoo. 2008, Putnam $19.99 (978-0-399-24639-5). In the second book of the trilogy that began with *Foundling*, Rossamund Bookchild is joined in his lamplighting by Threnody and the two face even more danger. (Rev: BL 4/15/08; SLJ 7/08)

2512 Cremer, Andrea. *Nightshade* (7–11). 2010, Philomel $17.99 (978-0-399-25482-6). Werewolves Calla and Ren, both pack leaders, plan to marry, but when Shay, a human, arrives on the scene, Calla falls for him and risks everything. (Rev: BL 8/10; SLJ 12/1/10)

2513 Cremer, Andrea. *Rift* (7–11). Series: Nightshade. 2012, Philomel $18.99 (978-039925613-4). Ember wins her freedom from an arranged marriage when she joins the warrior branch of secret church society Conatus in this standalone prequel set in 1404 and featuring magic and romance. ⌒ 𝖊 Lexile HL790L (Rev: BL 8/12; SLJ 8/1/12; VOYA 10/12)

2514 Cremer, Andrea. *Rise* (7–11). Series: Nightshade. 2013, Philomel $18.99 (978-039915960-2). In this second prequel, a followup to 2012's *Rift*, 16-year-old Ember must appease former boyfriend Alistair while working with the handsome Barrow to escape supernatural forces. 𝖊 (Rev: BL 12/15/12; VOYA 4/13)

2515 Crichton, Michael. *Timeline* (9–12). 1999, Ballantine paper $17.99 (978-0-345-41762-6). In this fantasy novel, historians are sent back to France in 1357 and become involved in a war.

2516 Crispin, A. C. *The Paradise Snare* (9–12). 1997, Bantam paper $5.99 (978-0-553-57415-9). This is the first novel in a trilogy about the con man of *Star Wars* fame, Han Solo. The others are: *The Hunt Gambit* (1997) and *Rebel Dawn* (1997). (Rev: VOYA 12/98)

2517 Croggon, Alison. *The Crow: The Third Book of Pellinor* (7–10). Series: Pellinor. 2007, Candlewick $18.99 (978-0-7636-3409-4). Hem becomes a warrior in the fight against the Nameless One and goes in search of kidnapped Zelika in this third installment in the series. (Rev: BL 2/1/08; SLJ 2/08)

2518 Croggon, Alison. *The Naming* (7–10). 2005, Candlewick $17.99 (978-0-7636-2639-6). The life of 16-year-old Maerad, a slave, changes dramatically after she meets Cadvan, who tells her of her epic destiny. (Rev: BCCB 9/05; BL 5/1/05; SLJ 10/05*; VOYA 8/05)

2519 Croggon, Alison. *The Riddle: The Second Book of Pellinor* (7–10). Series: Pellinor. 2006, Candlewick $17.99 (978-0-7636-3015-7). In this second installment in the series, Maerad continues on her quest to find the Treesong, battling the Nameless One along the way, and discovering more about herself and her powers. (Rev: BL 11/1/06; LMC 4/07; SLJ 1/07)

2520 Croggon, Alison. *The Singing* (7–12). Series: Pellinor. 2009, Candlewick $19.99 (978-076363665-4). Maerad and her brother Hem combine their powers to retrieve the Treesong and conquer evil in this compelling final installment in the quartet. ⌒ 𝖊 Lexile 900L (Rev: BL 3/1/09; SLJ 5/1/09)

2521 Cross, Sarah. *Dull Boy* (7–10). 2009, Dutton $16.99 (978-052542133-7). Avery discovers he has superpowers and that there are others like him. Will they use their abilities for good or evil? Lexile 770L (Rev: BLO 4/14/09; SLJ 8/09)

2522 Cross, Sarah. *Kill Me Softly* (9–12). 2012, Egmont $17.99 (978-160684323-9). Mirabelle, 15, runs away from her godmother's to visit her parents' graves in Beau Rivage and learns that she is destined to live out the story of Sleeping Beauty. ⌒ 𝖊 Lexile HL720L (Rev: BL 4/1/12; LMC 10/12; SLJ 5/1/12)

2523 Cullum, J. A. *Lyskarion: The Song of the Wind* (9–12). 2001, Edge paper $13.95 (978-1-894063-02-9). Derwen, a wizard, has the task of finding the best of the children of Tamar and ensuring that the child becomes the greatest wizard ever. (Rev: BL 11/1/01; VOYA 8/02)

2524 Curley, Marianne. *The Named* (7–11). 2002, Bloomsbury $16.95 (978-1-58234-779-0). Ethan and Isabel time-travel through history on a difficult quest in this first volume of a multilayered trilogy recounting the battle against the Order of Chaos. (Rev: BL 11/15/02; SLJ 1/03)

2525 D'Lacey, Chris. *Fire Star* (7–12). Series: The Dragon Trilogy. 2007, Scholastic $15.99 (978-0-439-84582-3). David Rain faces a major dragon challenge in this conclusion to the trilogy; readers familiar with the earlier books will enjoy this most. (Rev: SLJ 4/07)

2526 D'Lacey, Chris. *Icefire* (7–12). Series: The Dragon Trilogy. 2006, Scholastic $14.99 (978-0-439-67245-0). In this action-packed sequel to *The Fire Within* (2005), David researches dragons for an essay that might win him a trip to the Arctic. (Rev: SLJ 11/06)

2527 Dann, Jack, ed. *The Dragon Book* (9–12). 2009, Ace $24.95 (978-044101764-5). A collection of 19 unique, atmospheric tales by contemporary fantasy writers including Garth Nix, Harry Turtledove, Bruce Coville, and Tanith Lee. (Rev: BL 11/15/09)

2528 Datlow, Ellen, and Terri Windling, eds. *The Beastly Bride: Tales of the Animal People* (10–12). Illus. by Charles Vess. 2010, Viking $19.99 (978-0-670-01145-2). Shape-changers are the focus of this collection of short stories featuring bears, deer, rats, fish, werewolves, and so forth. *e* (Rev: BLO 3/1/10; LMC 3–4/10; SLJ 5/10)

2529 Datlow, Ellen, and Terri Windling, eds. *Black Thorn, White Rose* (9–12). 1994, Avon $22.00 (978-0-688-13713-7). Variations of famous European folktales involving dwarves, witches, elves, and trolls, including a retelling of "Rumpelstiltskin." (Rev: BL 8/94; VOYA 4/95)

2530 Datlow, Ellen, and Terri Windling, eds. *Swan Sister: Fairy Tales Retold* (5–10). 2003, Simon & Schuster $16.95 (978-0-689-84613-7). Retellings by well-known authors of traditional stories are inventive and entertaining. (Rev: BCCB 11/03; BL 9/15/03; HBG 4/04; SLJ 12/03)

2531 Datlow, Ellen, ed. *Naked City: Tales of Urban Fantasy* (10–12). 2011, St. Martin's $25.99 (978-0-312-60431-8); paper $15.99 (978-0-312-38524-8). A collection of diverse, mainly paranormal, stories by writers including Holly Black, Melissa Marr, and 18 others. (Rev: SLJ 8/11)

2532 David, Peter. *Fall of Knight* (9–12). 2006, Ace $24.95 (978-0-441-01402-6). The King Arthur legend with a twist, this novel finds Gwen and Arthur selling Grail Ale (from the one and only Holy Grail) and trying to keep the Grail away from the Spear of Destiny. (Rev: BL 5/15/06)

2533 Davidson, Jenny. *The Explosionist* (8–12). 2008, HarperTeen $17.99 (978-0-06-123975-5); LB $18.89 (978-0-06-123976-2). Set in 1938 in an alternate Scotland (Napoleon won at Waterloo and spiritualists work with scientists), this is the story of Sophie, a 15-year-old girl whose message from a psychic medium sends her into a political firestorm. *e* Lexile 1010L (Rev: SLJ 10/1/08)

2534 Davies, Jocelyn. *A Beautiful Dark* (9–12). Series: Beautiful Dark Trilogy. 2011, HarperTeen $17.99 (978-0-06-199065-6). At her 17th birthday party, Skye meets two attractive boys who are complete opposites and who prompt her to examine her own nature and powers; this paranormal romance is the first installment in a series. *e* Lexile HL630L (Rev: BL 10/1/11; SLJ 12/1/11)

2535 Davies, Jocelyn. *A Fractured Light* (8–11). Series: Beautiful Dark Trilogy. 2012, HarperTeen $17.99 (978-006199067-0). Skye faces difficult decisions — to join the Rebellion with Asher or to try to redeem Devin, who betrayed her — in this turbulent sequel to 2011's *A Beautiful Dark*. *e* (Rev: BLO 11/1/12; SLJ 1/13)

2536 Davis, Bryan. *Starlighter* (7–10). Series: Dragons of Starlight. 2010, Zondervan paper $9.99 (978-03107183-6-9). When Jason's brothers disappear, he's forced to believe in the sinister dragons he always doubted, and he ventures into a mysterious realm where he meets Koren, a slave struggling to save mankind; the first installment in a series. *e* (Rev: BL 5/15/10; VOYA 8/10)

2537 Davis, Heather. *The Clearing* (8–11). 2010, Houghton Mifflin paper $8.99 (978-0-547-26367-0). Amy, 16, moves to rural Washington state to recover from an abusive relationship, and meets a mysterious 18-year-old boy stuck in 1944. *e* (Rev: BL 2/15/10; SLJ 5/10)

2538 de Alcantara, Pedro. *Backtracked* (8–11). 2009, Delacorte $15.99 (978-038573419-6); LB $18.99 (978-038590433-9). Tommy, a teenage drifter, travels through time while staying in New York City, experiencing the flu epidemic of 1918, the Depression, and World War II. *e* Lexile HL570L (Rev: BL 1/1–15/09; SLJ 6/1/09)

2539 de la Cruz, Melissa. *Blue Bloods* (9–12). 2006, Hyperion $15.99 (978-0-7868-3892-9). Humor mingles with horror as teen girls at an upper-class private school discover they are really "Blue Bloods," or vampires. (Rev: BL 5/15/06; SLJ 6/06)

2540 de Larrabeiti, Michael. *The Borribles* (10–12). 2005, Tom Doherty paper $6.99 (978-0-7653-5005-3). The Borribles are young children growing up wild in London who fight the police and ratlike creatures called the Rumbles; first published in 1984.

2541 de Lint, Charles. *Dingo* (7–10). 2008, Penguin $11.99 (978-0-14-240816-2). Miguel falls in love with a girl who happens to be an Aboriginal shape-shifter and who, along with her twin, is in danger and needs Miguel's help. (Rev: BL 5/15/08; SLJ 8/08)

2542 de Lint, Charles. *Eyes Like Leaves* (10–12). 2009, Subterranean $35 (978-159606282-5). Gods clash and humans suffer the consequences in this fantasy set in the Green Isles. (Rev: BL 10/15/09)

2543 de Lint, Charles. *A Handful of Coppers* (10–12). 2003, Subterranean $40.00 (978-1-931081-73-3). The 15 early stories by de Lint included in this anthology display his usual writing skill and may be unfamiliar to his many fans. (Rev: BL 2/1/03)

2544 de Lint, Charles. *Little (Grrl) Lost* (7–10). 2007, Viking $17.99 (978-0-670-06144-0). T.J., 14, misses her old friends and her horse after her family moves to the suburbs, but then she meets and befriends Elizabeth, a 16-year-old "Little" who is only 6 inches high but has an oversized personality. (Rev: BL 8/07; SLJ 11/07)

2545 de Lint, Charles. *Medicine Road* (10–12). 2004, Subterranean $35.00 (978-1-931081-96-2). In this fantasy, a red dog and a jackalope are given human shapes and 100 years to find mates. (Rev: BL 4/15/04)

2546 de Lint, Charles. *The Painted Boy* (7–12). 2010, Viking $18.99 (978-0-670-01191-9). Now a member of the Yellow Dragon Clan, part-dragon high-schooler Jay Li finds an Arizona barrio where he can do good work. (Rev: BL 12/1/10; SLJ 12/1/10)

2547 de Lint, Charles. *Trader* (10–12). 1997, Tor $24.95 (978-0-312-85847-6). Max Trader awakens to find that he has inexplicably traded bodies with a womanizing loser named Johnny Devlin. (Rev: BL 1/1–15/97; VOYA 8/97)

2548 de Lint, Charles. *Triskell Tales: 22 Years of Chapbooks* (10–12). 2000, Subterranean $40.00 (978-1-892284-78-5). This collection of stories and poems is arranged chronologically over a period of 22 years and shows the development of this fantasy writer. (Rev: BL 11/15/00)

2549 de Lint, Charles. *Widdershins* (9–12). 2006, Tor $27.95 (978-0-7653-1285-3). An intricate addition to de Lint's urban fantasies set in Newford, in which Lizzie Mahone finds her way into the spirit world and meets characters from previous books including Jilly Coppercorn and Geordie Riddell. (Rev: BL 3/15/06)

2550 Dean, J. David. *Ravennetus* (9–12). 1996, Pandea $21.95 (978-0-9646604-4-1). In this medieval fantasy, young Nelsyn is sent out into the world by two villains to find the secret power that will allow them to dominate the world. (Rev: BL 3/15/96)

2551 Deitz, Tom. *Fireshaper's Doom* (9–12). 1987, Avon paper $3.95 (978-0-380-75329-1). Because he accidentally caused the death of a faerie boy, Sullivan faces the wrath of the boy's mother in this sequel to *Windmaster's Bane*. (Rev: BL 11/15/87)

2552 Deitz, Tom. *Windmaster's Bane* (10–12). 1986, Avon paper $4.99 (978-0-380-75029-0). A man with second sight finds himself back in the time of legendary struggles involving the Celts. (Rev: BL 11/15/86)

2553 Dekker, Ted. *Chosen* (7–10). Series: The Lost Books. 2008, Thomas Nelson $12.99 (978-1-59554-359-2). A football game is used to choose four new forest guards who must find the seven lost Books of History. (Rev: BL 3/15/08)

2554 Del Vecchio, Gene. *The Pearl of Anton* (7–10). 2004, Pelican $16.95 (978-1-58980-172-1). In this complex, gripping fantasy, Jason inherits the Wizard's Stone when he turns 15, but the stone's powers cannot be realized until it is joined with the Pearl of Anton, which is hidden in a mountain cave and guarded by two fearsome beasts. (Rev: BL 6/1–15/04*; VOYA 10/04)

2555 Delany, Shannon. *Bargains and Betrayals* (7–10). Series: 13 to Life. 2011, St. Martin's paper $9.99 (978-03126091-6-0). Jessica struggles to maintain her equilibrium while locked away in a mental facility while Pietr makes an ill-advised agreement with the Russian mafia; for readers who have read the first two installments in the series. ℮ (Rev: BL 7/11)

2556 Delany, Shannon. *13 to Life* (7–10). Series: 13 to Life. 2010, St. Martin's paper $9.99 (978-0-312-60914-6). High school junior Jessica is still dealing with her mother's death in a car accident when strange events start happening in her town and she finds herself drawn to Pietr, the new guy at school, with whom she seems to share some kind of connection. ℮ (Rev: BL 6/10; SLJ 10/1/10)

2557 Derting, Kimberly. *The Pledge* (7–10). 2011, Simon & Schuster $16.99 (978-144242201-8). In a world where languages separate classes, 17-year-old Charlie learns that her linguistic abilities may be invaluable — and dangerous. (Rev: BL 12/1/11; SLJ 2/12)

2558 Desrochers, Lisa. *Last Rite* (9–12). Series: Personal Demons. 2012, Tor paper $9.99 (978-07653281-0-6). In this series closer, Frannie must decide between following the guidance of angel Gabe or demon Luc as she grapples with her supernatural powers. ⌒ ℮ (Rev: BLO 4/1/12; LMC 3–4/13)

2559 DeStefano, Lauren. *Sever* (9–12). Series: Chemical Garden. 2013, Simon & Schuster $17.99 (978-144240909-5). Readers of *Wither* and *Fever* will enjoy this final volume in the trilogy in which a "virus" kills people before their 25th birthdays. ℮ Lexile HL730L (Rev: BL 12/1/12)

2560 DeVita, James. *The Silenced* (8–12). 2007, HarperCollins $17.99 (978-0-06-078462-1). Under the new Zero Tolerance government, Marina attends a Youth Training Facility where she is educated under strict regulations but follows her heart and starts a resistance movement named the White Rose. (Rev: BL 6/1–15/07; SLJ 9/07)

2561 Dickinson, John. *The Cup of the World* (9–12). 2004, Random House LB $17.99 (978-0-385-75025-7). Sixteen-year-old Phaedra, the willful daughter of a widowed baron, rejects a number of noble would-be suitors and instead weds a mysterious knight, setting off a clash between good and evil. (Rev: BL 10/15/04; SLJ 9/04; VOYA 2/05)

2562 Dickinson, Peter. *Angel Isle* (7–10). 2007, Random House $17.99 (978-0-385-74690-8). Maja and her companions make an arduous journey to find the Ropemaker so he can use his magic to defy the Watchers; a sequel to *The Ropemaker* (2001). (Rev: BL 10/15/07; HB 11–12/07; LMC 1/08; SLJ 11/07)

2563 Dickinson, Peter. *Earth and Air* (9–12). 2012, Big Mouth $17.95 (978-1-6187-3058-9); paper $14.95 (978-1-6187-3-038-1). Six sometimes dark, occasionally comic stories feature mythical beasts linked with earth and air in this companion to *Water* (2002) and *Fire* (2009). ℮ Lexile NC1070L (Rev: BL 10/1/12; HB 11–12/12; SLJ 11/12)

2564 DiTocco, Robyn, and Tony DiTocco. *Atlas' Revenge: Another Mad Myth Mystery* (7–12). 2005, Brainstorm $19.95 (978-0-9723429-2-6); paper $11.95

(978-0-9723429-3-3). PJ Allen, a carefree college senior, is called upon to travel to the world of mythology to complete the legendary Twelve Labors of Hercules and solve a cryptic riddle in this fast-paced novel full of legendary characters and literary references. (Rev: SLJ 6/05)

2565 Dixon, Heather. *Entwined* (7–10). 2011, Greenwillow $17.99 (978-0-06-200103-0). In this dark version of a Grimm tale, Princess Azalea and her eleven sisters dance all night despite their mother's death, able to do so through the Keeper, whose intentions may not be kindly. ∩ e Lexile 740L (Rev: BL 2/1/11*; HB 5–6/11; SLJ 5/11; VOYA 4/11)

2566 Doherty, Robert. *Area 51: Nosferatu* (10–12). Series: Area 51. 2003, Dell paper $6.99 (978-0-440-23724-2). Past and present are interwoven in this exciting tale of aliens and vampires that provides alternate histories of many world events. (Rev: BL 7/03)

2567 Dolamore, Jaclyn. *Magic Under Glass* (7–10). 2010, Bloosmbury $16.99 (978-1-59990-430-6). Seventeen-year-old Nimira discovers that an automaton is in fact a trapped fairy prince and sets out to rescue him from the handsome sorcerer Hollin Parry. e Lexile HL680L (Rev: BL 10/15/09*; LMC 3–4/10; SLJ 3/10)

2568 Donaldson, Stephen R. *Lord Foul's Bane* (10–12). 1987, Ballantine paper $6.99 (978-0-345-34865-4). Thomas Covenant, a leper, finds himself in a magical world in this first volume of the Chronicles of Thomas Covenant the Unbeliever series. Others are *The Illearth War* and *The Power That Preserves*.

2569 Donohue, Keith. *The Stolen Child* (9–12). 2006, Doubleday $23.95 (978-0-385-51616-7). Henry lives with a group of changelings in the woods while a hobgoblin assumes Henry's place in his family. (Rev: SLJ 10/06)

2570 Douglass, Sara. *Crusader* (9–12). Series: The Wayfarer Redemption. 2006, Tor $27.95 (978-0-7653-1518-2). It's the Timekeeper demons versus the humans, who are clinging to safety in Sanctuary in this final installment of the series. (Rev: BL 5/15/06)

2571 Douglass, Sara. *Sinner* (11–12). Series: Wayfarer Redemption. 2004, Tor $26.95 (978-0-312-87046-1). Trouble is brewing once again in Tencendor among the humans, the bird people, and the Avar; for mature teens. (Rev: BL 9/15/04)

2572 Doyle, Marissa. *Bewitching Season* (7–10). 2008, Henry Holt $16.95 (978-0-8050-8251-7). Set during the reign of Queen Victoria, this novel about twins Persephone and Penelope as they ready for their London debut combines historical romance with mystery and a touch of fantasy. (Rev: BL 1/1–15/08; LMC 11–12/08; SLJ 3/08)

2573 *Dr. Ernest Drake's Dragonology: The Complete Book of Dragons* (5–12). 2003, Candlewick $18.99 (978-0-7636-2329-6). Presented as the recently discovered research of a 19th-century scientist, this richly illustrated volume presents a very realistic encyclopedia of dragon facts and figures. (Rev: BL 4/15/04; SLJ 4/04)

2574 Drake, David. *The Legions of Fire* (10–12). 2010, Tor $25.99 (978-076532078-0). In this action fantasy set in the world of Carce, two young men and two young women discover ominous clues that seem to foretell disaster for their city, which resembles an early Roman Empire. e (Rev: BL 5/1–15/10; SLJ 11/1/10)

2575 Duane, Diane. *The Book of Night with Moon* (9–12). 1997, Warner paper $12.99 (978-0-446-67302-0). An Evil has invaded the underground culture of the magical world beneath Grand Central Station, and four cats are dispatched to send the Evil back to the Darkness. (Rev: VOYA 4/98)

2576 Duane, Diane. *A Wizard Alone* (6–10). Series: Young Wizards. 2002, Harcourt $17.00 (978-0-15-204562-3). The sixth book in the series of Nita and Kit's adventures in magic finds wizard Kit working on his own while Nita mourns the death of her mother. (Rev: BL 11/15/02; HBG 3/03; SLJ 2/03; VOYA 4/03)

2577 Duey, Kathleen. *Skin Hunger* (7–10). Illus. by Sheila Rayyan. Series: A Resurrection of Magic. 2007, Atheneum $17.99 (978-0-689-84093-7). The story of Sadima, a teenage girl who can communicate with animals, as she lives with magician outlaws; interwoven with the story of Hahp, generations later, as he deals with attending a harsh wizardry school. ∩ (Rev: BL 6/1–15/07; HB 7–8/07; SLJ 11/07)

2578 Duncan, Dave. *The Alchemist's Code* (9–12). 2008, Ace paper $14.00 (978-0-441-01562-7). Venice's Council of Ten asks Nostradamus and his brash young apprentice Zeno to decode a ciphered message that will unmask a spy in this half-Sherlock Holmes, half magic novel. (Rev: BL 3/1/08)

2579 Dunkle, Clare B. *In the Coils of the Snake* (7–10). Series: Hollow Kingdom. 2005, Henry Holt $16.95 (978-0-8050-7747-6). When human girl Miranda learns she will not after all marry the new goblin king, she flees from the kingdom; this final volume in the trilogy is set 30 years after *Close Kin* (2004). (Rev: BL 1/1–15/06*; SLJ 10/05; VOYA 10/05)

2580 Durst, Sarah Beth. *Enchanted Ivy* (7–12). 2010, Simon & Schuster $16.99 (978-1-4169-8645-4). Sixteen-year-old Lily's special admission test for Princeton University, engineered by her alumnus grandfather, in fact qualifies her to enter a parallel world full of magical creatures. e (Rev: BLO 12/1/10; SLJ 12/1/10)

2581 Durst, Sarah Beth. *Ice* (7–10). 2009, Simon & Schuster $16.99 (978-1-4169-8643-0). The daughter of a scientist who studies polar bears in the Arctic, Cassie was raised believing that her mother was taken away by trolls; consequently, she agrees to marry the Polar Bear King if he will return her mother to her in this romantic fantasy. ☻ (Rev: BL 9/1/09; LMC 11–12/09; SLJ 12/09)

2582 Durst, Sarah Beth. *Vessel* (7–12). 2012, Simon & Schuster $16.99 (978-1-4424-2376-3). Sacrificial Liyana is abandoned by her clan when the goddess Bayla fails to take possession of her body, and she then finds herself facing new challenges in this exciting combination of fantasy, adventure, and romance. ☻ Lexile HL630L (Rev: BL 10/1/12*; LMC 1–2/13; SLJ 12/12)

2583 Eddings, David. *The Belgariad, Vol. I* (10–12). 2000, Del Rey paper $16.95 (978-0-345-45632-8). This volume contains the first three books about a magical world full of sorcery: *Pawn of Prophecy* (1982), *Queen of Sorcery* (1983), and *Magician's Gambit* (1983). Vol. II contains *Castle of Wizardry* (1983) and *Enchanters' End Game* (1984). (Rev: BL 4/15/00)

2584 Eddings, David. *Guardians of the West* (10–12). 1987, Ballantine paper $6.99 (978-0-345-35266-8). The beginning volume of a saga about King Garion. In this installment he sets out to save his son from an evil force. (Rev: BL 3/1/87)

2585 Elliott, Patricia. *Ambergate* (9–12). 2007, Little, Brown $16.99 (978-0-316-01060-3). Scuff, unsure of her own identity, is on the run from the agents of the Protector in this sequel to *Murkmere* (2006) that draws on British folklore. (Rev: BL 2/1/07; HB 1–2/07; LMC 10/07; SLJ 3/07)

2586 Ellis, Helen. *What Curiosity Kills* (8–11). Series: The Turning. 2010, Sourcebooks $14.99 (978-1-4022-3861-1). As 16-year-old Mary gradually turns into a cat she discovers that there are many cat people out at night and battles are looming between the domestic cats and the strays of New York City. ☻ Lexile HL700L (Rev: BL 5/15/10; LMC 10/10)

2587 Ende, Michael. *The Neverending Story* (7–12). Trans. by Ralph Manheim. 1984, Penguin paper $15.00 (978-0-14-007431-4). An overweight boy with many problems enters the magic world of Fantastica in this charming fantasy.

2588 Erikson, Steven. *The Bonehunters: A Tale of the Malazan Book of the Fallen* (9–12). 2007, Tor $27.95 (978-0-7653-1006-4); paper $16.95 (978-0-7653-1652-3). This original, compelling fourth book in the series features humans caught in the middle of a war among the gods. (Rev: BL 8/07)

2589 Estep, Jennifer. *Dark Frost* (7–10). Series: Mythos Academy. 2012, Kensington paper $9.95 (978-07582669-6-5). High school sophomore Gwen is on a mission to find the Helheim dagger and prevent Loki from unleashing havoc in this action-packed story with elements of romance and mythology. (Rev: BL 8/12)

2590 Ewing, Lynne. *Barbarian* (8–12). Series: Sons of the Dark. 2004, Hyperion $9.99 (978-0-7868-1811-2). Four gorgeous and immortal teens with magical powers escape slavery in the parallel universe of Nefandus and must deal with life in modern Los Angeles before fulfilling their destinies. (Rev: SLJ 10/04; VOYA 2/05)

2591 Ewing, Lynne. *Into the Cold Fire* (7–12). Series: Daughters of the Moon. 2000, Hyperion LB $9.99 (978-0-7868-0654-6). In this latest light-hearted tale about four Los Angeles girls with extraordinary powers, Serena is faced with a difficult choice: to succumb to the dark and seductive power of the Atrox or to remain loyal to her sister goddesses. (Rev: HBG 3/01; VOYA 6/01)

2592 Ewing, Lynne. *Outcast* (9–12). Series: Sons of the Dark. 2005, Hyperion $9.99 (978-0-7868-1813-6). The third volume in the series about four young aliens trying to fit in to contemporary America. (Rev: SLJ 6/05)

2593 Fallon, Jennifer. *Warrior* (9–12). Series: The Wolfblade Trilogy. 2006, Tor $25.95 (978-0-7653-0990-7). Damin, Marla Wolfblade's son, is being prepared to rule the kingdom when a group of sorcerers try to wrest his power from him. (Rev: SLJ 10/06)

2594 Fama, Elizabeth. *Monstrous Beauty* (9–12). 2012, Farrar $17.99 (978-0-374-37366-5). Alternating chapters tell two interconnected stories: one, the 1872 tale of a mermaid's love and the murders it precipitated; and the other a modern-day story of Hester's connection to the mermaid's ghost. Odyssey Honor Recording 2013. ∩ ☻ Lexile 780L (Rev: BL 9/15/12; SLJ 9/12; VOYA 12/12)

2595 Fantaskey, Beth. *Jessica's Guide to Dating on the Dark Side* (8–12). 2009, Harcourt $17.00 (978-015206384-9). Jessica learns she is a vampire princess when the Romanian boy to whom she was betrothed at birth shows up at her high school. ∩ ☻ Lexile 700L (Rev: BL 3/1/09; SLJ 3/1/09; VOYA 6/09)

2596 Farland, David. *The Lair of Bones* (11–12). Series: Runelords. 2003, Tor $27.95 (978-0-7653-0176-5). This adventure fantasy brings a violent confrontation between immortal Raj Athen; Prince Gaborn, the Earth King; and the Queen of the Reavers; violent content makes this suitable only for mature teens. (Rev: BL 11/15/03)

2597 Farley, Terri. *Seven Tears into the Sea* (7–10). 2005, Simon & Schuster paper $6.99 (978-0-689-86442-1). Working at her clairvoyant grandmother's seaside inn for the summer, 17-year-old Gwen becomes attracted to Jesse, a strange boy with secrets. (Rev: BCCB 4/05; BL 4/1/05; SLJ 6/05; VOYA 6/05)

2598 Federici, Debbie, and Susan Vaught. *L.O.S.T* (8–12). 2004, Llewellyn paper $9.95 (978-0-7387-0561-3). Fantasy and romance are intertwined in this fast-paced story about 17-year-old Bren, who is kidnapped by Jazz, 16-year-old Queen of the Witches, because she believes he is the long-prophesied Shadowalker. (Rev: SLJ 1/05)

2599 Ferrari, Mark J. *The Book of Joby* (9–12). 2007, Tor $27.95 (978-0-7653-1686-8). Nine-year-old Joby is unknowingly at the center of an ages-old bet between God and Lucifer in this novel, which also features reincarnated Arthurian characters. (Rev: BL 8/07)

2600 Fforde, Jasper. *The Last Dragonslayer* (7–10). Series: Chronicles of Kazam. 2012, Harcourt $16.99 (978-0-547-73847-5). Mystic retirement home manager Jennifer, 15, learns she's the last living dragonslayer in this captivating start to a series. (Rev: BL 8/12; SLJ 11/12*)

2601 Fforde, Jasper. *Shades of Grey: The Road to High Saffron* (10–12). 2010, Viking $25.95 (978-067001963-2). Eddie fully accepts that color is king in his society until he moves to East Carmine and falls in love with a Grey named Jane and has some amazing adventures. e (Rev: BL 12/15/09)

2602 Fine, Sarah. *Sanctum* (9–11). Series: Guards of the Shadowlands. 2012, Amazon Children's $17.99 (978-076146329-0); paper $9.99 (978-16110942-8-2). Desperate to rescue her best friend Nadia's soul from the Suicide Gates, 17-year-old Lela rejects the offer of Heaven when she dies soon afterward and heads to the dark city. e (Rev: BL 12/15/12; LMC 5–6/13; SLJ 10/12; VOYA 10/12)

2603 Finnin, Ann. *The Sorcerer of Sainte Felice* (7–10). 2010, Flux paper $9.95 (978-0-73872070-8.). Rescued from the stake by a Benedictine abbot, 15-year-old Michael de Lorraine becomes a wizard's apprentice in this novel set in turbulent 15th-century France. e (Rev: BL 6/10; LMC 10/10; SLJ 9/1/10; VOYA 6/10)

2604 Fisher, Catherine. *The Dark City* (8–11). Series: Relic Master. 2011, Dial $16.99 (978-0-8037-3673-3). Raffi, 16, travels with injured relic master Galen to the ruined city of Tasceron in search of an artifact that may save the world. e Lexile HL540L (Rev: BL 5/1/11; SLJ 7/11)

2605 Fisher, Catherine. *Incarceron* (8–12). 2010, Dial $17.99 (978-0-803-73396-1). In a future world, the daughter of the warden of a prison called Incarceron joins forces with an escaping prisoner in a tense adventure. ∩ e Lexile HL600L (Rev: BL 1/1–15/10*; HB 1–2/10*; LMC 1–2/10; SLJ 2/10)

2606 Fisher, Catherine. *Sapphique* (9–12). 2010, Dial $17.99 (978-080373397-8). Finn faces an uncertain future in the months after his escape from Incarceron, wondering if he will in fact be king of the Realm. ∩ Lexile HL570L (Rev: BL 10/1/10*; HB 1–2/11; SLJ 12/1/10)

2607 Fitzpatrick, Becca. *Hush, Hush* (9–12). 2009, Simon & Schuster $17.99 (978-1-4169-8941-7). High school sophomore Nora ignores her inner unease and warnings from others when she becomes attracted to Patch, who turns out to be a fallen angel who wants to become human. ∩ e Lexile HL640L (Rev: BL 10/15/09; LMC 1–2/10; SLJ 12/09)

2608 Flewelling, Lynn. *The Bone Doll's Twin* (10–12). 2001, Bantam paper $6.99 (978-0-553-57723-5). An fine epic in which Tobin, a female, is living in a time when highborn women are being murdered to ensure a male will mount the throne. (Rev: BL 10/1/01; VOYA 12/01)

2609 Flewelling, Lynn. *Hidden Warrior* (11–12). 2003, Bantam paper $6.99 (978-0-553-58342-7). A rich, multilayered story of a future queen whose guardian wizards decide to bring her up as a boy in an effort to ensure her safety. (Rev: BL 7/03)

2610 Flinn, Alex. *Beastly* (7–10). 2007, HarperTeen $16.99 (978-0-06-087416-2). Popular, snooty Kyle is transformed into a beast when he insults a classmate in this modern adaptation of "Beauty and the Beast." (Rev: BL 2/1/08; SLJ 11/07)

2611 Flinn, Alex. *Bewitching* (8–11). Series: Kendra Chronicles. 2012, HarperTeen $17.99 (978-006202414-5). Teen witch Kendra begins her life during the plague in 1666, when she and her brother outwit an evil witch in a gingerbread house, and goes on to participate in the *Titanic* disaster (the Little Mermaid), Versailles (the Princess and the Pea), and an evil stepsister story. e (Rev: BL 1/1/12; HB 3–4/12; SLJ 3/12; VOYA 12/11)

2612 Flinn, Alex. *A Kiss in Time* (7–10). 2009, HarperTeen $16.99 (978-006087419-3); LB $17.89 (978-006087420-9). A fractured and lively Sleeping Beauty tale in which Princess Talia of Euphrasia is awakened after 300 years by young American Jack. ∩ (Rev: BL 5/15/09; HB 7–8/09; SLJ 8/09; VOYA 6/09)

2613 Flint, Eric, and David Drake. *Fortune's Stroke* (10–12). 2000, Baen $24.00 (978-0-671-57871-8). Mixing times, cultures, and peoples, this is an action-filled alternate-world saga centered in 6th-century Byzantium. (Rev: BL 5/15/00; VOYA 2/01)

2614 Foon, Dennis. *The Dirt Eaters* (5–10). Series: Longlight Legacy Trilogy. 2003, Annick $19.95 (978-1-55037-807-8); paper $9.95 (978-1-55037-806-1). In this well-written first installment of a trilogy, 15-year-old Roan finds himself torn between the peaceful ways of his upbringing and a desire to avenge a murderous attack on his village. (Rev: SLJ 1/04; VOYA 2/04)

2615 Francis, Melissa. *Bite Me!* (9–12). 2009, HarperTeen paper $8.99 (978-0-06-143098-5). Mississippi high school senior AJ Ashe is trying her hardest to hide the fact that she is a vampire, but her efforts are complicated when she realizes that she may have inadvertently turned a classmate into a malevolent vampire during a drunken escapade. e (Rev: BL 10/1/09; SLJ 12/09)

2616 Frenette, Bethany. *Dark Star* (9–12). 2012, Hyperion $17.99 (978-142314665-0). The daughter of a superhero, 16-year-old Audrey has her own talents, which she uses in the fight against demons threatening Minneapolis. ⌒ ℮ (Rev: BL 10/15/12; LMC 1–2/13; SLJ 3/13; VOYA 12/12)

2617 Friesner, Esther. *Nobody's Princess* (6–10). 2007, Random House $16.99 (978-0-375-87528-1). The romantic, exciting, and dangerous childhood of Helen of Troy, whose face launched all those ships when she grew up. The sequel *Nobody's Prize* (2008) continues the story. (Rev: BCCB 7–8/07; BL 3/15/07; LMC 4–5/07; SLJ 7/07)

2618 Friesner, Esther. *Nobody's Prize* (8–12). 2008, Random House $16.99 (978-0-375-87531-1). Princess Helen of Sparta (the future Helen of Troy), longing for adventure, disguises herself as a boy and stows away on the *Argo* in this exciting sequel to *Nobody's Princess.* (Rev: BL 2/1/08; SLJ 6/08)

2619 Friesner, Esther. *Temping Fate* (7–10). 2006, Dutton $16.99 (978-0-525-47730-3). Unsuspecting teenager Ilana finds that her summer employer, Divine Relief Temp Agency, has genuine Greek gods and goddesses among its clientele. (Rev: BL 5/15/06; SLJ 8/06)

2620 Frost, James Bernard. *World Leader Pretend* (10–12). 2007, St. Martin's paper $13.95 (978-0-312-35223-3). The online multi-player strategy game The Realm plays an important part in the life of Xerxes Meticula, especially since his dot-com company collapsed and he's back home in his parents' basement. (Rev: SLJ 6/07)

2621 Frost, Mark. *The Paladin Prophecy* (7–10). 2012, Random House $17.99 (978-0-375-87045-3); LB $20.99 (978-037597045-0). Will West, a clever 15-year-old who tries to maintain a low profile, finds himself thrust into the midst of a centuries-old struggle between good and evil. ⌒ ℮ Lexile HL700L (Rev: BL 9/15/12; SLJ 10/12; VOYA 12/12)

2622 Funke, Cornelia. *Inkdeath* (8–12). 2008, Scholastic $24.99 (978-043986628-6). An old bookbinder brings characters both benevolent and evil to life in this plot-driven conclusion to Funke's popular trilogy. ⌒ Lexile 830L (Rev: BL 11/1/08*; HB 1–2/09; SLJ 12/08; VOYA 12/08)

2623 Funke, Cornelia. *Inkheart* (6–12). 2003, Scholastic $24.99 (978-0-439-53164-1). Twelve-year-old Meggie, the key character in this complex novel, is the daughter of a bookbinder who can release fictional characters from their books. (Rev: BL 9/1/03; HBG 4/04; SLJ 10/03; VOYA 12/03)

2624 Furey, Maggie. *Heart of Myrial* (7–12). Series: Shadowleague. 2000, Bantam paper $6.99 (978-0-553-57938-3). As catastrophic events threaten Myrial, a firedrake, a telepathic dragon, and a woman warrior seek to avert destruction. (Rev: VOYA 6/00)

2625 Gaiman, Neil. *Anansi Boys* (9–12). 2005, Morrow $26.95 (978-0-06-051518-8). To his surprise, Fat Charlie Nancy discovers that his father was Anansi, the West African trickster, and that he has a brother called Spider. (Rev: BL 8/05; SLJ 1/06)

2626 Gaiman, Neil. *The Graveyard Book* (6–10). Illus. by Dave McKean. 2008, HarperCollins $17.99 (978-006053092-1); LB $18.89 (978-006053093-8). After the murder of his family, a toddler wanders out of his house into a graveyard, where the residents agree to raise him and protect him from the killer. Newbery Medal 2009; Carnegie Medal; Hugo Best Novel Award 2009; ALA Notable Books 2009; Boston Globe–Horn Book Honor 2009. ⌒ ℮ (Rev: BL 9/15/08*; HB 11–12/08; SLJ 10/1/08)

2627 Gaiman, Neil. *M Is for Magic* (7–10). Illus. by Teddy Kristiansen. 2007, HarperCollins $16.99 (978-0-06-118642-4). This collection of previously published stories (many from *Fragile Things*) includes twisted fairy tales, stories based on myth and legend (from aliens to the Holy Grail), and quirky illustrations. (Rev: BCCB 9/07; BL 4/15/07; SLJ 8/07)

2628 Galloway, Priscilla. *Truly Grim Tales* (7–12). 1998, Random House paper $NIS (978-0-440-22728-1). Familiar folk tales get new twists in this collection. (Rev: BL 9/15/95; SLJ 9/95)

2629 Gansky, Alton. *The Prodigy* (9–12). 2001, Zondervan paper $12.99 (978-0-310-23556-9). The story of a boy who has the power to heal, and how this gift is exploited by others. (Rev: BL 6/1–15/01*)

2630 Garcia Marquez, Gabriel. *One Hundred Years of Solitude* (10–12). Trans. by Gregory Rabassa. 1995, Knopf $20.00 (978-0-679-44465-7). This novel of magic realism looks at the adventures and aspirations of generations of the Buendia family, of the town of Macondo.

2631 Garcia, Kami, and Margaret Stohl. *Beautiful Creatures* (9–12). 2009, Little, Brown $17.99 (978-0-316-04267-3). High school sophomore Ethan Wate's burning desire to escape his mundane southern hometown is dampened when spell caster Lena Duchannes and her peculiar family arrive on the scene in this contemporary romance with a gothic twist. ⌒ ℮ Lexile HL670L (Rev: BL 11/1/09; SLJ 12/09; VOYA 12/09)

2632 Garcia, Kami, and Margaret Stohl. *Beautiful Darkness* (9–12). 2010, Little, Brown $17.99 (978-031607705-7). In this sequel to the southern gothic *Beautiful Creatures* (2009), Lena pulls away from Ethan even as he struggles to save her from an uncertain fate. ℮ Lexile HL660L (Rev: BL 10/1/10; SLJ 1/1/11; VOYA 12/10)

2633 Gardner, Sally. *I, Coriander* (7–10). 2005, Dial $16.99 (978-0-8037-3099-1). In a fantasy full of the atmosphere of 17th-century England, Coriander is the daughter of a human father and a fairy princess. (Rev: BL 8/05; SLJ 9/05; VOYA 10/05)

2634 Gardner, Sally. *Maggot Moon* (7–12). Illus. by Julian Crouch. 2013, Candlewick $16.99 (978-

076366553-1). In a dystopian 1956 where the "impure" live in ghettos — grim but better than the camps — young Standish has knowledge that could bring down the Motherland. ⌒ ℮ Lexile 690L (Rev: BL 1/13*; HB 3–4/13*; SLJ 3/13; VOYA 2/13)

2635 Garfield, Henry. *Tartabull's Throw* (7–10). 2001, Simon & Schuster $15.00 (978-0-689-83840-8). A 19-year-old baseball player and a mysterious young woman called Cassandra are the principal characters in this multifaceted story set in 1967 that entwines baseball, werewolves, romance, and suspense. (Rev: BL 5/15/01; HBG 10/01; SLJ 6/01; VOYA 8/01)

2636 Gébler, Carlo. *The Bull Raid* (9–12). 2006, Egmont $22.95 (978-1-4052-1255-7). Every winter the men of Ulster are cursed with a pain akin to women's labor pains, all except for Cuchulainn who is half mortal, half immortal; he fights single-handedly to defend the town's famous Brown Bull against Queen Maeve of Connacht, who tries to use the men's incapacitation to her advantage. (Rev: SLJ 8/06)

2637 Gee, Maurice. *Salt* (7–10). 2009, Orca $18 (978-1-55469-209-5). This gripping, dark fantasy features Hari, a 17-year-old telepath who fights the oppressive ruling class that kidnapped his father; the first in a trilogy. Lexile 700L (Rev: LMC 1–2/10; SLJ 11/09)

2638 Gelder, Gordon Van, ed. *In Lands That Never Were* (9–12). 2004, Thunder's Mouth paper $16.95 (978-1-56858-314-3). A collection of fantasy stories from the *Magazine of Fantasy and Science Fiction*. (Rev: BL 9/1/04)

2639 George, Jessica Day. *Princess of the Midnight Ball* (6–10). 2009, Bloomsbury $16.99 (978-159990322-4). Galen, a young soldier at the end of a long war in a fictional 19th century, falls in love with a princess and saves her and her 11 dancing sisters by using his talent for knitting. ℮ Lexile 830L (Rev: BL 1/1–15/09; SLJ 4/1/09; VOYA 6/09)

2640 George, Jessica Day. *Sun and Moon, Ice and Snow* (7–10). 2008, Bloomsbury $16.95 (978-1-59990-109-1). Based on Norse myth, this is a story of a girl who lives in an ice palace with a white bear after being rejected by her mother. (Rev: BL 2/1/08; SLJ 3/08)

2641 Gibsen, Cole. *Katana* (7–10). 2012, Flux paper $9.95 (978-07387304-0-0). Rileigh, 17, comes to believe she is channeling the spirit of an ancient samurai, who provides her with guidance and the tools to break out of her very ordinary life. ℮ (Rev: BL 4/1/12; LMC 8–9/12; SLJ 3/12)

2642 Gier, Kerstin. *Ruby Red* (7–10). Trans. by Anthea Bell. 2011, Henry Holt $16.99 (978-0-8050-9252-3). Gwen, 16, is surprised to find that she carries the family's time-travel gene rather than her well-prepared cousin Charlotte, but she is soon having extraordinary adventures. ⌒ ℮ Lexile HL680L (Rev: BL 4/15/11; LMC 10/11; SLJ 6/11)

2643 Gilligan, Elizabeth. *The Silken Shroud* (10–12). 2004, DAW paper $6.99 (978-0-7564-0179-5). This sequel to *Magic's Silken Snare* (2003) continues the story of the quest for the body of Alessandra, murdered princess of the Rom. (Rev: BL 4/15/04)

2644 Gilman, Felix. *Thunderer* (9–12). 2007, Bantam $24.00 (978-0-553-80676-2). Arjun, a young man possessing magical abilities, witnesses a legendary great bird flying overhead and putting the cities of Ararat into a panic that is quickly calmed when *Thunderer,* an airship, captures the bird's power; in turn, the ruling elite vow to keep it under guard, but a shrewd Arjun is skeptical and journeys to discover the truth. (Rev: BL 12/1/07)

2645 Golden, Christopher. *The Boys Are Back in Town* (10–12). 2004, Bantam paper $12.00 (978-0-553-38207-5). Will James gets news from a friend whom he thought died 10 years before in this fantasy in which a teenage boy living in Will's house holds the key to these strange happenings. (Rev: BL 2/15/04*)

2646 Golden, Christopher. *The Lost Ones* (11–12). Series: The Veil. 2008, Bantam paper $12.00 (978-0-553-38328-7). This third and final, battle-filled installment in the series involves a daring plan on the part of Oliver and his sister, Collette, who as children of a myth and a human can remove the Veil that separates the human world from the mythological one; the earlier volumes, all suitable for mature teens, are *The Myth Hunters* (2006) and *The Borderkind* (2007). (Rev: BL 3/15/08)

2647 Golding, Julia. *The Glass Swallow* (7–10). 2011, Marshall Cavendish $17.99 (978-0-7614-5979-8). In a land where women cannot work, Rain hides her stained-glass designs; finally able to travel abroad, she finds herself in a chaotic country with some hope provided by a handsome falconer named Peri. ℮ Lexile 760L (Rev: BL 9/1/11; LMC 3–4/12; SLJ 11/11)

2648 Gonzalez, Ray. *The Ghost of John Wayne and Other Stories* (10–12). 2001, Univ. of Arizona $29.95 (978-0-8165-2065-7); paper $17.95 (978-0-8165-2066-4). These stories set in the U.S.-Mexican borderlands are filled with magic, ghosts, and visions. (Rev: BL 10/15/01)

2649 Goodkind, Terry. *Faith of the Fallen* (10–12). Series: Sword of Truth. 2000, Tor $27.95 (978-0-312-86786-7). In this sequel to *Soul of the Fire* (1999), our hero Richard is kidnapped by the Dark Sister Nicci, the emperor's mistress. (Rev: BL 8/00)

2650 Goodkind, Terry. *Wizard's First Rule* (9–12). 1994, Tor $27.95 (978-0-312-85705-9). With the sword of Truth, young Richard Cypher goes on a quest, encountering wizards, dragons, and other evils with a modern touch of ambiguity. (Rev: BL 9/1/94; VOYA 2/95)

2651 Goodman, Alison. *Eon: Dragoneye Reborn* (7–10). 2008, Viking $19.99 (978-067006227-0). A hypnotic tale about a 12-year-old girl who poses as a boy to compete to become the next apprentice to a dragon tamer, and who is pulled into the dangerous intrigues and political machinations of the Asian-inspired fantasy world in which the story takes place. (Rev: BL 12/15/08; LMC 5–6/09; SLJ 1/1/09)

2652 Goodman, Alison. *Eona* (7–10). Series: The Last Dragoneye. 2011, Viking $19.99 (978-0-670-06311-6). Eona (formerly disguised as a boy, Eon) faces both an internal struggle and a fierce battle for her homeland as she joins forces with the young Pearl Emperor; the sequel to *Eon* (2008). ∩ e Lexile 740L (Rev: BL 5/1/11; SLJ 7/11; VOYA 6/11)

2653 Gordon, Lawrence. *User Friendly* (7–10). Series: Ghost Chronicles. 1999, Karmichael paper $11.95 (978-0-9653966-0-8). Frank, a teenage ghost in limbo, contacts Eddie through the computer to get help to free himself and his friend, a runaway slave, from the purgatory in which they are living. (Rev: BL 1/1–15/99; SLJ 1/99)

2654 Gordon, Roderick, and Brian Williams. *Spiral* (7–10). Series: Tunnels. 2012, Scholastic $18.99 (978-054542961-0). Will, Chester, and Drake continue their struggle to prevent Earth's destruction even as the Styx institute "the phase," during which they use humans as egg incubators; new readers should tackle this series in order. e Lexile 910L (Rev: BLO 6/12; SLJ 1/13; VOYA 6/12)

2655 Goto, Hiromi. *Half World* (8–10). Illus. by Jillian Tamaki. 2010, Viking $16.99 (978-0-670-01220-6). Looking for her mother, 14-year-old Melanie Tamaki enters the Half World and finds herself in a gruesome realm of souls caught between life and death. e Lexile 710L (Rev: BL 3/1/10; HB 7–8/10; LMC 3–4/10; SLJ 4/10)

2656 Gourley, Susan. *The Keepers of Sulbreth* (10–12). 2010, Medallion paper $7.95 (978-16054206-5-3). Two young heroes attempt to restore order to Fuhark — where elves and humans once lived in harmony — in this multifaceted fantasy. (Rev: BL 1/1–15/10)

2657 Grant, K. M. *White Heat* (7–10). Series: The Perfect Fire. 2009, Walker $16.99 (978-0-8027-9695-0). In 13th-century France Raimon struggles to protect the mythical Blue Flame even as he worries about the fate of his love, Yolanda; the sequel to *Blue Flame* (2008). Lexile 820L (Rev: BL 3/15/10; HB 11–12/09; SLJ 1/10)

2658 Gray, Anne. *Rites of the Healer* (6–10). 2007, Sumach paper $11.95 (978-1-894549-59-2). This imaginative book tells the story of Dovella, a villager who is sent on a dangerous quest to find the source of a water supply shortage. (Rev: SLJ 3/08)

2659 Gray, Claudia. *Evernight* (8–11). 2008, HarperTeen $16.99 (978-0-06-128439-7). Bianca's new boarding school is populated with beautiful vampires,

and she and her boyfriend Lucas face danger as they uncover the school's secrets. (Rev: BL 5/15/08; SLJ 6/08)

2660 Gray, Claudia. *Fateful* (9–12). 2011, HarperTeen $17.99 (978-006200620-2). Aboard the *Titanic*, 17-year-old Tess, dreaming of a new life in America, is impressed by handsome Alec and does not imagine that he is actually a werewolf. e Lexile 770L (Rev: BL 7/11; HB 3–4/12; SLJ 1/12; VOYA 10/11)

2661 Gray, Claudia. *Hourglass* (9–12). Series: Evernight. 2010, HarperTeen $16.99 (978-0-06-128441-0). Teen vampire Bianca and her unlikely vampire-hunting love interest Lucas attempt to disguise the truth as they fight together in Manhattan's war between vampires and mortals; the third installment in the series. e Lexile 700L (Rev: BL 2/1/10; SLJ 3/10; VOYA 12/10)

2662 Gray, Claudia. *Spellcaster* (7–10). 2013, HarperTeen $17.99 (978-006196120-5). Nadia, Mateo, and Verlaine, high school seniors, are determined to save Captive's Sound from an evil sorceress. e (Rev: BL 12/15/12)

2663 Greenberg, Martin H., and Brittany A. Koren, eds. *Fantasy Gone Wrong* (9–12). 2006, DAW paper $7.99 (978-0-7564-0380-5). Many of these stories are twists on traditional fairy and folk tales that will surprise readers and stretch their imaginations. (Rev: BL 9/1/06)

2664 Grimsley, Jim. *The Ordinary* (10–12). 2004, Tor $24.95 (978-0-7653-0528-2). For better readers, this is a fantasy about two different cultures separated by a huge gate and the girl who travels in time to find the secret past of these kingdoms. (Rev: BL 4/15/04*)

2665 Grossman, Lev. *The Magician King* (10–12). 2011, Viking $26.95 (978-0-670-02231-1). Fed up with ruling Fillory, Quentin and his friend Julia set out on a cruise to the outer limits of their kingdom, and accidentally wind up back in dreaded reality; the sequel to *The Magicians* (2009). ∩ e (Rev: BL 8/11; SLJ 11/11)

2666 Habel, Lia. *Dearly, Departed* (7–10). 2011, Ballantine $16.99 (978-034552331-0). A steampunk fantasy involving zombies — set in the year 2195 but featuring a society more suited to Victorian England. ∩ e (Rev: BLO 11/15/11; SLJ 4/12)

2667 Hale, Shannon. *Book of a Thousand Days* (7–10). Illus. by James Noel Smith. 2007, Bloomsbury $17.95 (978-1-59990-051-3). As punishment for refusing to marry, Lady Saren and her servant Dashti are sentenced to seven years in a sealed tower, where Dashti writes in her diary about their imprisonment, her secret love for a lord, and their escape; based on a fairy tale from the Brothers Grimm. ∩ (Rev: BL 9/15/07; SLJ 10/07)

2668 Hale, Shannon. *Enna Burning* (8–11). Series: Books of Bayern. 2004, Bloomsbury $17.95 (978-1-58234-889-6). In this companion to *The Goose Girl*, Enna returns to her home in the forest and learns to wield the power of fire, but she must struggle to use that power wisely without risking her life or those of her people. (Rev: BL 9/15/04; SLJ 9/04; VOYA 12/04)

2669 Hale, Shannon. *Forest Born* (7–10). Series: Books of Bayern. 2009, Bloomsbury $17.99 (978-1-59990-167-1). An engaging addition to the series, this stand-alone volume follows a girl named Rin who comes to understand the value of her own special gifts as she and others struggle to defeat the evil Selia. **e** Lexile 800L (Rev: BL 12/15/09; HB 9–10/09; LMC 10/09; SLJ 9/09)

2670 Hale, Shannon. *The Goose Girl* (6–10). Series: Books of Bayern. 2003, Bloomsbury $17.95 (978-1-58234-843-8). Crown Princess Ani, who can talk to the animals, is betrayed by her guards and disguises herself as a goose girl until she can reclaim her crown. (Rev: BL 8/03; HBG 4/04; SLJ 8/03*; VOYA 10/03)

2671 Hale, Shannon. *River Secrets* (7–10). Series: Books of Bayern. 2006, Bloomsbury $17.95 (978-1-58234-901-5). Razo, a teenage soldier from Bazo, is surprised to learn he's being sent on a mission to Tira after the war, to help keep peace. But someone is trying to sabotage the peace and Razo must figure out who. A sequel to *The Goose Girl* (2003) and *Enna Burning* (2004). (Rev: BL 9/15/06; SLJ 10/06*)

2672 Hambly, Barbara. *Renfield: Slave of Dracula* (9–12). 2006, Berkley $23.95 (978-0-425-21168-7). In the tone of Bram Stoker's *Dracula,* Hambly tells the story of Renfield, the madman who served the bloodthirsty vampire. (Rev: BL 9/1/06)

2673 Hamilton, Kersten. *Tyger Tyger* (7–10). 2010, Clarion $17 (978-0-547-33008-2). The lives of Teagan Wylltson and her disabled brother change dramatically when their cousin Finn Mac Cumhaill arrives in Chicago and the three are drawn into a dangerous mission. (Rev: BL 11/1/10; SLJ 12/1/10*)

2674 Hamilton, Kiki. *The Faerie Ring* (7–10). 2011, Tor $17.99 (978-0-7653-2722-2). A street urchin steals a ring that carries remarkable power — and responsibility — in this action-filled mix of faerie fantasy and Victorian historical fiction. **e** (Rev: BL 10/15/11; SLJ 11/1/11)

2675 Hamilton, Virginia. *Justice and Her Brothers* (7–10). Series: The Justice Cycle. 1978, Scholastic paper $4.99 (978-0-590-36214-6). Four children with supernatural powers move in time in this complex novel. Sequels are *Dustland* (1980) and *The Gathering* (1981).

2676 Hancock, Karen. *The Light of Eidon* (10–12). Series: Legends of the Guardian King. 2003, Bethany paper $12.99 (978-0-7642-2794-3). In this artful blend of Christian allegory and fantasy, protagonist Abramm Kalladorne overcomes countless challenges in his search for spiritual truths. (Rev: BL 10/1/03*; VOYA 2/04)

2677 Hand, Cynthia. *Hallowed* (7–10). 2012, HarperTeen $17.99 (978-006199618-4). Part-angel Clara, 16, works to halt the predestined death of someone close to her as she contends with increasingly complex feelings toward her boyfriend Tucker. ∩ **e** (Rev: BL 1/1/12; VOYA 2/12)

2678 Hand, Cynthia. *Unearthly* (7–10). 2011, HarperTeen $17.99 (978-006199616-0). Sixteen-year-old Clara is a quarter-angel whose half-angel mother supports her in her efforts to fulfill her destiny, moving the family from California to Wyoming where Clara meets the boy she has seen in her visions; the first book in a series. ∩ **e** (Rev: BL 12/1/10; SLJ 1/1/11; VOYA 2/12)

2679 Hanley, Victoria. *The Healer's Keep* (7–12). 2002, Holiday $17.95 (978-0-8234-1760-5). A princess, a former slave girl, and their companions battle evil in a land full of magic. (Rev: BCCB 1/03; HBG 3/03; SLJ 12/02; VOYA 2/03)

2680 Hardinge, Frances. *The Lost Conspiracy* (6–10). 2009, HarperCollins $16.99 (978-006088041-5); LB $17.89 (978-006088042-2). In the strange world of Gullstruck Island, Hathin and her sister Arilou are on the run from a mysterious force killing off the Lost people. ALA Notable Books 2010. Lexile 970L (Rev: BL 5/15/09; HB 9–10/09; LMC 3–4/10; SLJ 9/09)

2681 Harness, Charles L. *Cybele, with Bluebonnets* (10–12). 2002, NESFA $21.00 (978-1-887668-41-5). Joseph falls in love with his chemistry teacher, Cybele, in high school, later comes to appreciate her mystical strength, and even after she has died feels her guidance in his life and work. (Rev: BL 11/1/02)

2682 Harris, Charlaine. *Dead to the World* (9–12). 2004, Berkley $19.95 (978-0-441-01167-4). Sookie Stackhouse discovers that a man she has just met has been robbed of his memory by a witch. (Rev: BL 4/15/04)

2683 Harris, Joanne. *Runemarks* (10–12). 2008, Knopf $18.99 (978-0-375-84444-7). Maddy discovers she has magical powers and that she will be crucial to the battle between Chaos and Order in this story that takes inspiration from Norse mythology. ∩ (Rev: BL 12/15/07; LMC 2/08; SLJ 1/08)

2684 Harrison, Kim. *Pale Demon* (11–12). Series: The Hollows. 2011, Eos $26.99 (978-006113806-5). In the ninth novel of the series, witch Rachel Morgan is traveling to San Francisco to clear her name of practicing black arts and finds herself on a road trip with Trent the elf plus Jenks the pixy and Ivy the vampire; for mature readers. ∩ **e** (Rev: BL 10/1–15/10)

2685 Harrison, M. John. *Viriconium* (9–12). 2005, Bantam paper $16.00 (978-0-553-38315-7). A collection of four classic novels and several stories set in the richly imagined mythical post-apocalyptic city of Viriconium and straddling the genres of fantasy and science fiction. (Rev: BL 9/15/05)

2686 Harrison, Mette Ivie. *The Princess and the Bear* (7–10). 2009, HarperTeen $17.99 (978-0-06-155314-1). This unlikely love story is told from the points of view of King Richon and Chala, human/animal shape-shifters whose bond grows as they try to end war in their kingdom. e Lexile 790L (Rev: SLJ 9/09; VOYA 8/09)

2687 Hartman, Rachel. *Seraphina* (9–12). 2012, Random House $17.99 (978-037586656-2); LB $20.99 (978-037596656-9). Half-human half-dragon Seraphina, a talented musician, hides her dragon side as the court is in turmoil after the suspicious death of Prince Rufus; the first volume in a series that combines high fantasy with romance and intrigue. William C. Morris Debut Award. ◠ e Lexile 760L (Rev: BL 5/15/12*; HB 7–8/12; LMC 11–12/12; SLJ 8/1/12*)

2688 Hartnett, Sonya. *The Ghost's Child* (8–12). 2008, Candlewick $16.99 (978-076363964-8). In this melancholic fantasy, elderly Matilda recounts the ill-fated romance of her youth to a mysterious young boy who turns out to have a connection to her past. ◠ Lexile 900L (Rev: BL 11/1/08*; LMC 3–4/09; SLJ 1/1/09; VOYA 2/09)

2689 Hartwell, David G. *Visions of Wonder* (9–12). 1996, St. Martin's $35.00 (978-0-312-86224-4); paper $24.95 (978-0-312-85287-0). An interesting anthology of 1990s science fiction and fantasy, plus several essays on various aspects of the genre. (Rev: VOYA 6/97)

2690 Harvey, Alyxandra. *Stolen Away* (8–12). 2012, Walker $17.99 (978-0-8027-2189-1). Jo concocts a daring scheme to rescue her friend Eloise, 17, who has been kidnapped by a tyrannical fairy ruler. e (Rev: LMC 5–6/12; SLJ 6/12; VOYA 4/12)

2691 Haydon, Elizabeth. *The Assassin King* (9–12). Series: Symphony of Ages. 2007, Tor $25.95 (978-0-7653-0565-7). A significant war is clearly on the horizon in this sixth installment in the series. (Rev: BL 1/1–15/07)

2692 Haydon, Elizabeth. *Elegy for a Lost Star* (9–12). Series: Symphony of Ages. 2004, Tor $27.95 (978-0-312-87883-2). War and conflict continue in this fifth installment in the series that started with *Rhapsody: Child of Blood* (1999). (Rev: BL 8/04)

2693 Healey, Karen. *Guardian of the Dead* (9–12). 2010, Little, Brown $17.99 (978-0-316-04430-1). At boarding school in New Zealand 17-year-old Ellie finds herself embroiled in a battle involving ancient Maori beings. ◠ e Lexile HL790L (Rev: BL 3/15/10; HB 7–8/10; LMC 10/10; SLJ 5/10; VOYA 6/10)

2694 Hearn, Julie. *Sign of the Raven* (7–10). 2005, Simon & Schuster $16.95 (978-0-689-85734-8). Living with his grandmother in London while his mother recovers from cancer, 12-year-old Tom finds a portal into an 18th-century world far different from his own. (Rev: BCCB 12/05; HB 1–2/06; SLJ 11/05; VOYA 10/05)

2695 Hellisen, Cat. *When the Sea Is Rising Red* (9–12). 2012, Farrar $16.99 (978-037436475-5). Faking her own death to escape from an arranged marriage, Felicita descends quickly from her sheltered aristocratic life

into the slums; romance, magic, and intrigue combine to make this a compelling read. e Lexile 810L (Rev: BL 3/1/12; LMC 8–9/12; SLJ 2/12; VOYA 2/12)

2696 Hemingway, Amanda. *The Sword of Straw* (9–12). 2006, Del Rey paper $12.95 (978-0-345-46080-6). Nathan Ward, a 14-year-old whose dreams take him to other worlds, wants to save a princess he sees trapped in a ruined city; a sequel to *The Greenstone Grail* (2005). (Rev: BL 3/15/06)

2697 Hendee, Barb, and J. C. Hendee. *Rebel Fay* (9–12). 2007, Roc $23.95 (978-0-451-46121-6). In the fifth in this horror fantasy series, half-human, half-elven Leesil and half-human, half-vampire Magiere, search for Leesil's elven mother, who's in prison. (Rev: BL 1/1–15/07)

2698 Hendee, Barb, and J. C. Hendee. *Sister of the Dead* (11–12). Series: The Noble Dead. 2005, NAL $7.99 (978-0-451-46009-7). In this sequel to *Thief of Lives* (2004) suitable for mature teens, Magiere, half-human and half-vampire, journeys with her half-elf friend Leesil in search of answers about their parentage. Also use *Rebel Fay* (2007). (Rev: BL 1/1–15/05)

2699 Hieber, Leanna Renee. *Darker Still* (7–10). 2011, Sourcebooks paper $8.99 (978-14022605-2-0). Magically talented Natalie, 17, falls in love with a man in a painting and becomes engrossed in his world in this story set in 1880. e Lexile 830L (Rev: BL 11/15/11; SLJ 1/12)

2700 Higgins, Wendy. *Sweet Evil* (10–12). 2012, HarperTeen paper $8.99 (978-0-06-208-561-0). Half demon, half angel Anna grows increasingly curious about her family past as she nears her 16th birthday. ◠ e (Rev: BLO 6/12; SLJ 7/12; VOYA 4/12)

2701 Hill, C. J. *Slayers* (7–10). 2011, Feiwel & Friends $16.99 (978-031261414-0). Tori, 16, learns that she is a dragon slayer and that she and her fellow campers are training for a real battle against the beasts. ◠ e Lexile 740L (Rev: BL 11/15/11; LMC 1–2/12; SLJ 2/12; VOYA 12/11)

2702 Hill, Laban Carrick. *Casa Azul: An Encounter with Frida Kahlo* (7–10). 2005, Watson-Guptill $15.95 (978-0-8230-0411-9). In this appealing novel, two country children roaming the streets of Mexico City in search of their mother are befriended by artist Frida Kahlo and introduced to the magical world in which she dwells. (Rev: BL 10/1/05; SLJ 9/05)

2703 Hill, Pamela Smith. *The Last Grail Keeper* (7–10). 2001, Holiday $17.95 (978-0-8234-1574-8). While visiting England with her mother, 16-year-old Felicity discovers she is an Arthurian "grail keeper" with magical powers. (Rev: BCCB 2/02; BL 11/15/01; HBG 3/02; SLJ 12/01; VOYA 6/02)

2704 Hill, Stuart. *Blade of Fire* (7–10). Series: The Icemark Chronicles. 2007, Scholastic $18.99 (978-0-439-84122-1). Charlemagne, the youngest child of Queen

Thirrin and Oskan Witchfather, is now an adult and finds himself at war with his own sister, who has joined the evil forces of Scipio Bellorum. (Rev: BL 3/15/07; LMC 8–9/07; SLJ 6/07)

2705 Hill, Stuart. *The Cry of the Icemark* (8–11). Series: The Icemark Chronicles. 2005, Scholastic $18.95 (978-0-439-68626-6). In this sprawling military fantasy, 13-year-old Thirrin succeeds her fallen father as ruler of Icemark and sets off to forge alliances with werewolves, vampires, and talking snow leopards to help her defend her tiny country. (Rev: BCCB 4/05; BL 2/15/05; SLJ 5/05; VOYA 6/05)

2706 Hindle, Lee J. *Dragon Fall* (9–12). 1984, Avon paper $2.95 (978-0-380-88468-1). The monsters Gabe creates for a toy company come alive and try to kill him.

2707 Hines, Jim C. *Goblin War* (9–12). 2008, DAW paper $7.99 (978-0-7564-0493-2). Part farce, part parody, this fantasy gives us a runty blue goblin hero prodded into danger by the forgotten god he worships. (Rev: BL 3/15/08)

2708 Hinwood, Christine. *The Returning* (9–11). 2011, Dial $17.99 (978-0-8037-3528-6). In a medieval time, Cam returns from war to his village missing one arm and with a strong desire to understand why his life was spared. Printz Honor 2012. e Lexile 670L (Rev: BL 5/1/11; HB 5–6/11; LMC 10/11; SLJ 6/11; VOYA 6/11)

2709 Hoban, Russell. *Soonchild* (9–12). Illus. by Alexis Deacon. 2012, Candlewick $15.99 (978-0-7636-5920-2). A struggling shaman concocts a potion to help his wife deliver her baby, which ends up opening mystical questions about faith, future, and destiny. (Rev: BL 8/12*; LMC 3–4/13; SLJ 9/12)

2710 Hobb, Robin. *Dragon Haven* (11–12). Series: Rain Wilds Chronicles. 2010, Eos $26.99 (978-006193141-3). Trouble stalks the Dragon Keepers as they desperately try to understand why their dragon hatchlings fail to thrive; the second installment in this series for mature readers. ∩ e (Rev: BL 5/15/10*)

2711 Hobb, Robin. *Dragon Keeper* (11–12). Series: Rain Wilds Chronicles. 2010, Eos $26.99 (978-006156162-7). A rich woman and a tribal girl grow close during their adventures sending endangered dragons to a better habitat; for mature readers. ∩ e (Rev: BL 12/1/09*)

2712 Hocking, Amanda. *Ascend* (9–12). Series: Trylle. 2012, St. Martin's paper $8.99 (978-12500063-3-2). Bound to marry Tove out of loyalty to her people, Wendy wrestles with her affections for Finn and Loki; the final volume in this paranormal romance trilogy. ∩ e Lexile HL670L (Rev: BL 3/15/12)

2713 Hocking, Amanda. *Switched* (9–12). 2012, St. Martin's paper $8.99 (978-12500063-1-8). At the age of 17, Wendy, whose mother tried to kill her 11 years before, learns she is in fact a trylle (troll) swapped for a human baby and is now being sought by her birth

mother. ∩ e Lexile HL740L (Rev: BL 12/1/11; LMC 5–6/12; SLJ 3/12; VOYA 2/12)

2714 Hocking, Amanda. *Torn* (9–12). 2012, St. Martin's paper $8.99 (978-12500063-2-5). Changeling troll princess Wendy returns to her home after the events of 2012's *Switched* only to be kidnapped by the Vittra, learning that their king is her father. ∩ e Lexile HL660L (Rev: BL 2/15/12; SLJ 3/12; VOYA 4/12)

2715 Hoeye, Michael. *Time to Smell the Roses: A Hermux Tantamoq Adventure* (7–10). Series: Hermux Tantamoq Adventures. 2007, Putnam $15.99 (978-0-399-24490-2). Our mouse detective must solve a mystery at Thorny End while planning his wedding to Linka Perflinger and dodging mutant bees. (Rev: BL 10/1/07)

2716 Hoffman, Alice. *Green Witch* (7–12). 2010, Scholastic $17.99 (978-0-545-14195-6). Seventeen-year-old Green — first seen in *Green Angel* (2003) — is tending her garden and listening to stories of other survivors of her ruined civilization while she hopes to find her lost love. e Lexile 740L (Rev: BL 1/1–15/10; LMC 3–4/10; SLJ 5/10)

2717 Hoffman, Alice. *The Red Garden* (10–12). 2011, Crown $25 (978-030739387-6). A series of linked stories follow the inhabitants of a Massachusetts town through two centuries, starting in colonial times, with a focus on a mysterious garden with red soil that produces only red plants. ∩ e (Rev: BL 10/1–15/10)

2718 Hoffman, Mary. *Stravaganza: City of Flowers* (7–10). Series: Stravaganza. 2005, Bloomsbury $17.95 (978-1-58234-887-2). In the final volume of the trilogy, Sky Meadows, a 17-year-old biracial Londoner, travels back in time to 16th-century Talia, where many of the characters become involved in multilayered intrigue. (Rev: BL 3/1/05; SLJ 5/05)

2719 Holder, Nancy, and Debbie Viguié. *Resurrection* (9–12). Illus. Series: Wicked. 2009, Simon & Schuster paper $9.99 (978-141697227-3). Witches Holly, Nicole, and Amanda tackle an evil threat in this fifth and final installment in the series. ∩ (Rev: BL 7/09; SLJ 10/09)

2720 Holdstock, Robert. *Celtika* (11–12). 2003, Tor $25.95 (978-0-7653-0692-0). Greek mythology and Merlin legend are intertwined in this fantasy full of adventure. (Rev: BL 3/15/03; VOYA 6/03)

2721 Hoobler, Dorothy, and Thomas Hoobler. *The Ghost in the Tokaido Inn* (6–12). 1999, Putnam $17.99 (978-0-399-23330-2). Set in 18th-century Japan, this is the story of 14-year-old Seikei, his dreams of becoming a samurai, and what happened after he saw a legendary ghost stealing a valuable jewel. (Rev: BL 6/1–15/99; HBG 4/00; SLJ 6/99; VOYA 10/99)

2722 Hopkinson, Nalo. *The Chaos* (9–12). 2012, Simon & Schuster $16.99 (978-141695488-0). Scotch, 16, must confront and make peace with her mixed heritage in order to stop the dangerous force that threatens her brother and the world. 𝒆 Lexile HL600L (Rev: BL 5/1/12*; LMC 10/12; SLJ 4/12)

2723 Horowitz, Anthony. *Necropolis* (7–12). Series: Gatekeepers. 2009, Scholastic $17.99 (978-043968003-5). Fifteen-year-old Scarlet joins the other four teens struggling to defeat the Old Ones. ⏾ (Rev: BLO 6/16/09)

2724 Horton, Rich, ed. *Fantasy: The Best of the Year, 2006 Edition* (9–12). 2006, Prime paper $13.95 (978-0-8095-5650-2). A collection of short stories by well-known writers such as Neil Gaiman and by newcomers to the genre. (Rev: BL 9/1/06)

2725 Houck, Colleen. *Tiger's Quest* (7–12). 2011, Sterling $17.95 (978-1-4027-8404-0). Back home in Oregon after her breakup with Ren, an immortal shape-shifting tiger, Kelsey tries to forget him — until he shows up at her house and then is kidnapped; Kelsey must return to India to rescue him. The sequel to *Tiger's Curse* (2011). ⏾ Lexile 720L (Rev: BL 6/1/11; SLJ 8/11)

2726 Hoving, Isabel. *The Dream Merchant* (8–12). Trans. from Dutch by Hester Velmans. 2005, Candlewick $17.99 (978-0-7636-2880-2). An action-packed, intricately plotted adventure involving three young people in time travel and a world of collective dreams called *umaya*. (Rev: SLJ 1/06; VOYA 12/05)

2727 Howard, Chris. *Rootless* (9–12). 2012, Scholastic $17.99 (978-054538789-7). In a future hard hit by climate change, trees are extinct — or so Banyan, a tree artist, thinks — but when he sees a picture of real, live tree with his father tied to it, his life takes a precipitous turn. ⏾ 𝒆 Lexile HL660L (Rev: BL 12/1/12; LMC 1–2/13; SLJ 1/13)

2728 Hoyt, Sarah A. *Ill Met by Moonlight* (10–12). 2001, Berkley $21.95 (978-0-425-00860-7). Shakespeare must contend with treachery, deceit, murder, and an affair with an elf, after his wife and infant daughter are spirited away by elves. (Rev: BL 10/1/01)

2729 Hubbard, Mandy. *Prada and Prejudice* (7–10). 2009, Penguin paper $8.99 (978-159514260-3). On a class trip to England, bumbling Callie has a bad fall and wakes up in the year 1815. She makes friends with Emily, a girl about to be forced into an unfortunate marriage, and gains the affections of a young duke. (Rev: BL 5/15/09; SLJ 7/1/09)

2730 Hubbard, Mandy. *Ripple* (7–11). 2011, Penguin $16.99 (978-1-59514-423-2). Since the drowning death of her boyfriend, 18-year-old Lexi has discovered that she is a siren, with the gift of luring men to their fates. 𝒆 (Rev: BL 9/15/11; SLJ 9/1/11)

2731 Huff, Tanya. *The Second Summoning: The Keeper's Chronicles #2* (7–12). 2001, DAW paper $7.99 (978-0-88677-975-7). Claire, a Keeper entrusted with

protecting Canada, allows an angel and a demon to enter with humorous results. (Rev: VOYA 12/01)

2732 Huff, Tanya. *Summon the Keeper* (9–12). Series: The Keeper's Chronicles. 1998, DAW paper $7.99 (978-0-88677-784-5). When she takes over the management of the Elysian Fields guesthouse, Claire discovers the Keeper upstairs asleep, which suggests there is a hole in the fabric of the universe. (Rev: VOYA 10/98)

2733 Hughes, Mark Peter. *A Crack in the Sky* (6–10). 2010, Delacorte $16.99 (978-0-385-73708-1). Eli, a 13-year-old with special powers, notices problems with his dome-city but his worries are ignored and his continuing investigations lead to him being sent for reeducation. 𝒆 Lexile 740L (Rev: BL 7/10; LMC 11–12/10; SLJ 10/1/10)

2734 Hughes, Monica, sel. *What If? Amazing Stories* (5–10). 1998, Tundra paper $6.95 (978-0-88776-458-5). Fourteen fantasy and science fiction short stories by noted Canadian writers are included in this anthology, plus a few related poems. (Rev: BL 2/15/99; SLJ 6/99; VOYA 6/99)

2735 Humphreys, Chris. *The Fetch* (9–12). 2006, Knopf $15.95 (978-0-375-83292-5). Fifteen-year-old Sky discovers runestones and meets his fetch, another self that can transcend space and time. (Rev: BL 7/06; HB 7–8/06; LMC 2/07; SLJ 12/06)

2736 Humphreys, Chris. *Vendetta* (8–11). Series: Runestone Saga. 2007, Knopf $15.99 (978-0-375-83293-2). Fifteen-year-old Sky March heads to Corsica to find a way to free his cousin Kristin from his evil Norwegian grandfather's spell. (Rev: BL 8/07; SLJ 1/08)

2737 Jablonski, Carla. *Silent Echoes* (7–10). 2007, Penguin $16.99 (978-1-59514-082-1). Lucy, a 19th-century spiritualist, is astonished when she finds herself communicating with Lindsay, a modern-day teenager, in this time travel novel that will have readers learning about life in the 1880s. (Rev: BCCB 4/07; BL 3/1/07; SLJ 3/07)

2738 Jacobs, John Hornor. *The Twelve-Fingered Boy* (9–12). 2013, Carolrhoda $17.95 (978-076139007-7). Serving two years in juvenile detention, 15-year-old Shreve discovers he has paranormal powers and he breaks out with similarly abled, 12-fingered roommate Jack. 𝒆 Lexile 650L (Rev: BL 1/13*; HB 3–4/13; SLJ 2/13)

2739 James, Syrie, and Ryan M. James. *Forbidden* (8–11). 2012, HarperTeen $8.99 (978-006202789-4). Happy to be settled in one place for her junior year, Claire finds herself having visions and learns, from new student Alec, that she is a half angel — and is in danger. 𝒆 (Rev: BL 2/1/12; SLJ 3/12; VOYA 4/12)

2740 Jenkins, A. M. *Night Road* (8–12). 2008, HarperTeen $16.99 (978-0-06-054604-5). Cole and Sandor, both hemovores (as these vampires prefer to be called), are assigned the project of helping young Gordon adjust to the difficult life of a vampire. (Rev: BL 5/15/08; SLJ 8/08)

2741 Jinks, Catherine. *The Reformed Vampire Support Group* (8–12). 2009, Houghton Mifflin $17.00 (978-015206609-3). Nina's support group for vampires is thrown for a loop when one member is killed by a stake through the heart; a funny take on the modern vampire genre. YALSA Top Ten 2010. ⌒ ℮ Lexile 750L (Rev: BL 1/1–15/09; HB 5–6/09; SLJ 3/1/09; VOYA 10/09)

2742 Johnson, Christine. *Claire de Lune* (8–10). 2010, Simon & Schuster $16.99 (978-1-4169-9182-3). Claire discovers that she is destined to become a werewolf and face terrible danger in this fast-paced fantasy. ℮ (Rev: BL 5/15/10; LMC 8–9/10; SLJ 4/10)

2743 Johnson, Kathleen Jeffrie. *A Fast and Brutal Wing* (8–11). 2004, Roaring Brook $16.95 (978-1-59643-013-6). In a series of e-mails, journal entries, and newspaper stories, three teens recount the mysterious and fantastic events that led to a Halloween disappearance. (Rev: BL 12/15/04; SLJ 12/04; VOYA 12/04)

2744 Jolin, Paula. *Three Witches* (9–12). 2009, Roaring Brook $17.99 (978-1-59643-353-3). Three girls from different cultural and religious backgrounds join together in hope of contacting their friend Trevor, who died in a car accident. ℮ (Rev: BL 8/09; SLJ 10/09)

2745 Jones, Darynda. *Death and the Girl Next Door* (9–12). 2012, St. Martin's paper $9.99 (978-0-312-62-520-7). Lorelei, a sophomore, finds herself at the center of a celestial battle in this first volume in a trilogy. ⌒ ℮ (Rev: BLO 10/15/12; SLJ 11/12)

2746 Jones, Diana Wynne. *Cart and Cwidder* (8–10). 1995, Greenwillow $15.00 (978-0-688-13360-3); paper $4.95 (978-0-688-13399-3). When his father dies, 11-year-old Moril becomes heir to the family's cwidder, a musical instrument that has magical powers.

2747 Jones, Diana Wynne. *Howl's Moving Castle* (7–12). 1986, Greenwillow $16.95 (978-0-688-06233-0). A fearful young girl is changed into an old woman and in that disguise moves into the castle of Wizard Howl. (Rev: BL 6/1/86; SLJ 8/86; VOYA 8/86)

2748 Jones, Diana Wynne. *Unexpected Magic: Collected Stories* (5–10). 2004, Greenwillow $16.99 (978-0-06-055533-7). An exciting anthology of 16 tales of mystery and magic by a master of fantasy. (Rev: BL 4/15/04; SLJ 9/04)

2749 Jones, Diana Wynne. *Year of the Griffin* (7–10). 2000, Greenwillow LB $15.89 (978-0-06-029158-7). Pirates, assassins, and plain old magic are among the challenges faced by students at Wizard's University — including Elda, griffin daughter of the wizard Derk — in this sequel to the humorous *Dark Lord of Derkholm* (1998). (Rev: BL 11/1/00; HB 11–12/00; HBG 3/01; SLJ 10/00; VOYA 12/00)

2750 Jones, Frewin. *Warrior Princess* (7–10). Series: Warrior Princess. 2009, Eos $16.99 (978-006087143-7). Branwen must choose between the pampered life of a princess and the dangerous life of a warrior in this action-paced story set in medieval Britain; the first in a series. Lexile 780L (Rev: BL 2/15/09; SLJ 2/1/09)

2751 Jones, J. V. *A Sword from Red Ice* (9–12). 2007, Tor $27.95 (978-0-7653-0634-0). The third story in the Sword of Shadows series takes place in a war-filled arctic environment where clans fight for dominance, but it is also a story of a group of extraordinary individuals fighting their own personal battles and unknowingly have the ability to save the world if they pull forces. (Rev: BL 10/1/07)

2752 Jones, Patrick. *The Tear Collector* (9–12). 2009, Walker $16.99 (978-0-8027-8710-1). In contemporary Michigan, 17-year-old Cassandra collects tears and brings them to the head of her vampire-like family that thrives on human suffering; but her loyalty to this way of life is threatened when she falls in love with human Scott and must make a difficult choice. Lexile HL670L (Rev: BL 9/1/09; SLJ 12/09; VOYA 12/09)

2753 Jordan, Robert. *Crossroads of Twilight* (10–12). Series: Wheel of Time. 2003, Tor $29.95 (978-0-312-86459-0). The 10th novel in this series follows the activities of a vast cast of characters as they move closer to a final, cataclysmic battle between good and evil. (Rev: BL 1/1–15/03)

2754 Jordan, Robert. *A Crown of Swords* (8–12). Series: Wheel of Time. 1996, Tor $29.95 (978-0-312-85767-7). In this seventh book of this series, Rand and his army of Aiel warriors prepare to do battle with the Dark One. (Rev: VOYA 2/97)

2755 Jordan, Robert. *Eye of the World* (10–12). 1990, Tor paper $6.99 (978-0-8125-1181-9). In this novel, the first of a series, a group of ordinary people flee from evil magic. (Rev: BL 10/1/89; VOYA 6/90)

2756 Jordan, Robert. *The Fires of Heaven* (10–12). Series: Wheel of Time. 1994, Tor paper $7.99 (978-0-8125-5030-6). This lengthy fifth volume in an epic saga set in a richly imagined world features thrilling battle scenes interspersed with comic relief. ⌒ (Rev: BL 10/1/93)

2757 Jordan, Robert. *Lord of Chaos* (9–12). Series: Wheel of Time. 1994, Tor $25.95 (978-0-312-85428-7). Rand al'Thor teaches magic to men while being pursued by the hostile Aes Sedai. Mat Cauthon is advised by dead generals and Nynaeve learns to restore magic. (Rev: BL 10/15/94; VOYA 5/95)

2758 Jordan, Robert. *The Shadow Rising* (9–12). Series: Wheel of Time. 1992, Tor $27.95 (978-0-312-85431-7). The fourth volume in the saga is ambitious, rich, and detailed. (Rev: BL 10/1/92*)

2759 Jordan, Robert. *Winter's Heart* (10–12). Series: Wheel of Time. 2000, Tor $29.95 (978-0-312-86425-

5). This ninth book in the Wheel of Time series (the eighth was *The Path of Daggers* in 1998), continues the struggle of good vs. evil in an epic fantasy format. (Rev: BL 11/1/00)

2760 Jordan, Sherryl. *Secret Sacrament* (8–12). 2001, HarperCollins LB $17.89 (978-0-06-028905-8). In an ancient time, Gabriel trains at the Citadel to become a healer, hoping to intervene in the violence that surrounds him. (Rev: BCCB 3/01; BL 2/15/01; HBG 10/01; SLJ 2/01; VOYA 6/01)

2761 Jordan, Sherryl. *Time of the Eagle* (7–10). 2007, Eos $16.99 (978-0-06-059554-8). As the daughter of Gabriel Eshban Vala (hero of the 2001 *Secret Sacrament*, Avala is a healer and the Chosen One, who must bring about the uprising of the persecuted Shinali people. (Rev: BL 5/15/07; LMC 11/07; SLJ 9/07)

2762 Jordan, Sophie. *Vanish* (8–12). 2011, HarperCollins $17.99 (978-0-06-193510-7). In this sequel to the paranormal romance *Firelight* (2010), draki Jacinda must make difficult choices when her human lover Will reappears on the scene. ⓔ (Rev: BL 10/1/11; SLJ 10/1/11)

2763 Jubert, Hervé. *Dance of the Assassins* (9–12). Trans. from French by Anthea Bell. Series: Devil's Dances. 2005, HarperCollins LB $17.89 (978-0-06-077718-0). In the opening volume of this trilogy, sorceress Roberta Morgenstern and rookie cop Clement Martineau travel to a series of virtual-reality theme parks modeled after historic cities in their quest to unravel a murder mystery. (Rev: BCCB 9/05; SLJ 12/05; VOYA 10/05)

2764 Kaaberbol, Lene. *The Shamer's War* (6–10). Series: The Shamer's Chronicles. 2006, Henry Holt $17.95 (978-0-8050-7771-1). The final volume in this action-packed series featuring a battle between Prince Nicodemus and his acquisitive relative Drakan. (Rev: HB 11–12/06; SLJ 1/07)

2765 Kagawa, Julie. *The Lost Prince* (8–12). 2012, HarlequinTeen paper $9.99 (978-0-373-21-057-2). Ethan, 17, finds himself risking his life to save Kenzie as the fey mount a menacing attack against humankind. ⌒ ⓔ (Rev: BL 11/1/12; LMC 5–6/13; SLJ 12/12)

2766 Kashina, Anna. *The Princess of Dhagabad* (10–12). 2000, Herodias $25.00 (978-1-928746-07-2). In this first volume of a trilogy, when a young princess opens a gift from her grandmother on her 12th birthday, her own personal djinn appears. (Rev: BL 6/1–15/00)

2767 Kate, Lauren. *Rapture* (8–11). Series: Fallen. 2012, Delacorte $17.99 (978-038573918-4); LB $20.99 (978-038590775-0). In this fourth book in the series, Luce and Daniel struggle to unravel the ancient mystery that threatens their love. ⌒ ⓔ (Rev: BL 8/12; VOYA 10/12)

2768 Kay, Guy Gavriel. *Ysabel* (10–12). 2007, Roc $24.95 (978-0-451-46129-2). Fifteen-year-old Ned visits a cathedral in France, meets Kate, and they become

entangled in an ancient love triangle between Celtic spirits. (Rev: BL 2/15/07)

2769 Kaye, Marilyn. *Demon Chick* (9–12). 2009, Henry Holt $16.99 (978-0-8050-8880-9). When Jessica, 16, realizes her mother has sold her to a demon named Brad in exchange for political gain, she plots to bring down her mother's plans for world domination— and to escape from Hell. ⓔ (Rev: BL 8/09; HB 9–10/09; LMC 11–12/09; SLJ 10/09)

2770 Kearney, Paul. *The Mark of Ran* (9–12). 2005, Bantam paper $12.00 (978-0-553-38361-4). In the opening volume of the Sea Beggars series, 15-year-old Rol Cortishane, accused of witchcraft and driven from his village, takes refuge in the tower sanctuary of family friend Michal Psellos. (Rev: BL 11/15/05)

2771 Keaton, Kelly. *A Beautiful Evil* (8–10). 2012, Simon & Schuster $16.99 (978-144240927-9). A descendant of Medusa, Ari struggles to sublimate the evil urges she feels as Athena comes to steal her secret powers. ⓔ Lexile 750L (Rev: BL 3/1/12; LMC 8–9/12; SLJ 5/1/12; VOYA 12/11)

2772 Kemp, Kenny. *I Hated Heaven: A Novel of Life After Death* (10–12). 1998, Alta Films $12.00 (978-1-892442-10-9). After his death, Tom Waring finds that Heaven will not allow him to fulfill his dying wish to return to earth once to tell his wife that heaven really exists. (Rev: BL 8/98; SLJ 12/98)

2773 Kennedy, James. *The Order of Odd-Fish* (7–12). 2008, Delacorte $15.99 (978-0-385-73543-8). A 13-year-old girl is transported to a strange world where she will play a key role in this involved tale full of absurdities and eccentricities. (Rev: BCCB 7–8/08; BL 8/08; LMC 8/08; SLJ 9/08)

2774 Kenner, Julie. *Demons Are Forever: Confessions of a Demon-Hunting Soccer Mom* (9–12). 2007, Berkley paper $14.00 (978-0-425-21538-8). Kate Connor leaves retirement to return to demon hunting but must also contend with her husband's ignorance of her career, her teenage daughter Allie's determination to follow in her footsteps, and the possibility that her ex — who died in an accident — is back in demon form. ⌒ (Rev: BL 6/07; SLJ 9/07)

2775 Kerner, Charlotte. *Blueprint* (9–12). Trans. by Elizabeth D. Crawford. 2000, Lerner LB $16.95 (978-0-8225-0080-3). Siri is a clone — or, as she prefers, "blueprint" — of her famous musician mother in this novel translated from German. (Rev: BL 9/15/00; HBG 3/01; SLJ 10/00; VOYA 12/00)

2776 Kerr, Katharine. *Darkspell* (10–12). 1994, Bantam paper $6.99 (978-0-553-56888-2). Three companions combat a group of evil sorcerers in this sequel to *Daggerspell*. (Rev: BL 9/1/87)

2777 Kerr, Katharine. *The Fire Dragon* (10–12). Series: Deverry. 2001, Bantam paper $6.99 (978-0-553-58247-5). This volume in the Deverry saga follows *The Black*

Raven (1999) and tells of the adventures of many souls who are reborn two centuries after their deaths. (Rev: BL 11/15/00)

2778 Kerr, Peg. *Emerald House Rising* (10–12). 1997, Warner paper $5.99 (978-0-446-60393-5). While struggling to master the skills of wizardry, Jena finds herself drawn to a mysterious nobleman named Morgan. (Rev: VOYA 8/97)

2779 Kessler, Jackie Morse. *Loss* (7–10). Series: Riders of the Apocalypse. 2012, Houghton Mifflin paper $8.99 (978-05477121-5-4). Tricked into becoming one of the Four Horsemen of the Apocalypse, Billy, 15, confronts Death in order to avoid his fate. **e** Lexile 850L (Rev: BL 3/1/12; SLJ 5/1/12)

2780 Keyes, Greg. *The Charnel Prince* (11–12). Series: Kingdoms of Thorn and Bone. 2004, Del Rey $23.95 (978-0-345-44067-9). In this sequel to *The Briar King* (2003), Crotheny is in the throes of a battle between good and evil forces, and the future of the monarchy is in danger. (Rev: BL 8/04)

2781 Keyes, J. Gregory. *The Shadows of God* (10–12). Series: Age of Unreason. 2001, Del Rey paper $15.00 (978-0-345-43904-8). An alternate history yarn in which the New World is trapped between Russia, which is ruled by a warlock, and Britain, which is determined to regain its colonies. (Rev: BL 4/15/01; VOYA 4/02)

2782 Kincy, Karen. *Other* (9–12). 2010, Flux paper $9.95 (978-0-7387-1919-1). In Washington State 17-year-old Gwen is an Other, a shapeshifter who hides her true nature, until a series of murders of Others forces her into action. YALSA Popular Paperbacks for Young Adults Top Ten 2011. (Rev: BL 6/1/10; LMC 10/10; SLJ 7/10)

2783 King, Stephen. *The Eyes of the Dragon* (9–12). 1987, NAL paper $7.99 (978-0-451-16658-6). In this tale of potions and evil magic, a king dies mysteriously and his older son is unjustly accused. (Rev: BL 11/1/86; SLJ 6/87; VOYA 8/87)

2784 King, Stephen. *Song of Susannah* (10–12). Series: Dark Tower. 2004, Scribner $30.00 (978-1-880418-59-8). This epic novel follows *The Wolves of Calla* (2003) in the Dark Tower series, and continues the story of the gunslingers that is concluded in *The Dark Tower* (2004). (Rev: BL 5/1/04)

2785 Kipling, Rudyard. *Kipling's Fantasy* (9–12). Ed. by John Brunner. 1992, Tor $17.95 (978-0-312-85354-9). Atmospheric tales of myth and horror, with rich language and image. (Rev: BL 10/15/92; SLJ 6/93)

2786 Kitanidis, Phoebe. *Glimmer* (9–12). 2012, HarperCollins $17.99 (978-006179928-0). Teens Elyse and Marshall wake up in each other's arms, both of them suffering from amnesia, and slowly come to realize that very bad things are happening in the town of Summer Falls, Colorado. **e** (Rev: BL 4/1/12; SLJ 5/1/12; VOYA 12/11)

2787 Kitanidis, Phoebe. *Whisper* (8–12). 2010, HarperCollins $16.99 (978-0-06-179925-9). Sisters Joy and Jessica both have the ability to hear others' thoughts, but they use this talent in quite different ways. (Rev: BLO 4/15/10; LMC 10/10; SLJ 6/10; VOYA 8/10)

2788 Kizer, Amber. *Meridian* (7–10). 2009, Delacorte $16.99 (978-0-385-73668-8); LB $19.99 (978-0-385-90621-0). After witnessing a traumatizing accident on her 16th birthday, Meridian's parents decide that it's time to inform their daughter that she is a Fenestra, an angel-like being who helps escort the dying to their final destinations. **e** Lexile HL590L (Rev: BL 2/15/10; SLJ 12/09; VOYA 2/10)

2789 Kizer, Amber. *Wildcat Fireflies* (7–10). 2011, Delacorte $16.99 (978-0-385-73971-9); LB $19.99 (978-038590803-0). In this sequel to 2009's *Meridian*, Tens and the title character continue their search for other half-angels or Fenestras, and finds a compelling case in Juliet, who they assist. **e** Lexile HL630L (Rev: BL 9/1/11; SLJ 8/11; VOYA 8/11)

2790 Klause, Annette Curtis. *Freaks: Alive on the Inside!* (10–12). 2006, Simon & Schuster $16.95 (978-0-689-87037-8). Brought up at Faeryland, a resort displaying people with "oddities" such as missing limbs and extra hair, normal 17-year-old Abel tries unsuccessfully to escape this life; set in the late 1890s, this is a mix of fantasy and reality. (Rev: BL 2/1/06*; SLJ 1/06; VOYA 12/05)

2791 Knox, Elizabeth. *Dreamhunter: Book One of the Dreamhunter Duet* (9–12). Series: Dreamhunter Duet. 2006, Farrar $19.00 (978-0-374-31853-6). Laura, a retiring 15-year-old, has inherited her father's gift as a dreamhunter, but her father has disappeared and she must draw on new reserves to continue his mission. (Rev: BL 4/1/06*; SLJ 3/06)

2792 Knox, Elizabeth. *Dreamquake: Book Two of the Dreamhunter Duet* (8–11). Series: Dreamhunter Duet. 2007, Farrar $19.00 (978-0-374-31854-3). Laura and her family are troubled by the government's dream-harvesting program in this follow-up to *Dreamhunter*. Printz Honor 2008. (Rev: BL 1/1–15/07; HB 3–4/07; SLJ 6/07)

2793 Knutsson, Catherine. *Shadows Cast by Stars* (8–11). 2012, Simon & Schuster $17.99 (978-1-4424-0191-4). In a future where plague has killed a large percent of the population, the blood of Native Americans, which has special properties, is much in demand and 16-year-old Cassandra and her family must flee to the Island, where Cassandra's special abilities come to the fore. **e** Lexile 670L (Rev: BL 5/15/12; LMC 10/12; SLJ 8/1/12; VOYA 6/12)

2794 Koertge, Ron. *Lies, Knives, and Girls in Red Dresses* (10–12). Illus. by Andrea Dezso. 2012, Candlewick $19.99 (978-0-7636-4406-2). Twenty-three free-verse fairy tales tell the true stories of Cinderella's stepsisters,

Bluebird's bride, Little Red Riding Hood, and others. (Rev: BL 6/12; LMC 10/12*; SLJ 7/12; VOYA 6/12)

2795 Kogler, Jennifer Ann. *The Death Catchers* (7–10). 2011, Walker $16.99 (978-080272184-6). Morgan le Fay descendant Lizzy with supernatural powers discovers that she must protect Drake, a popular senior at her school who is a descendant of King Arthur. **e** Lexile 800L (Rev: BL 5/1/11; LMC 8–9/11; SLJ 2/12; VOYA 8/11)

2796 Kolosov, Jacqueline. *The Red Queen's Daughter* (9–12). 2007, Hyperion $16.99 (978-1-4231-0797-2). Mary, 16, is the orphaned daughter of Katherine Parr and Henry VIII and has been raised as a lady-in-waiting/white witch; romance, fantasy, intrigue, and history are interwoven in this story of Mary's life at Queen Elizabeth's court. (Rev: BL 10/15/07; LMC 1/08; SLJ 12/07)

2797 Kontis, Alethea. *Enchanted* (9–12). 2012, Harcourt $16.99 (978-054764570-4). Sunday Woodcutter, seventh daughter of a seventh daughter, falls in love with a frog who turns out to be a prince despised by her family. YALSA Top Ten Best Fiction for Young Adults 2013. ∩ **e** Lexile HL770L (Rev: BL 7/12; HB 11–12/12; LMC 1–2/13; SLJ 6/12)

2798 Kostick, Conor. *Epic* (7–10). 2007, Viking $17.99 (978-0-670-06179-2). Readers who enjoy role-playing games will love this book, a fantasy that takes place on New Earth, where violence occurs only in the computer game Epic. (Rev: BL 3/1/07; SLJ 5/07)

2799 Kostick, Conor. *Saga* (7–10). 2008, Viking $18.99 (978-0-670-06280-5). The world of Saga is a virtual reality, role-playing game that has its players captive, and it is up to 15-year-old Ghost and Eric to stop the Dark Queen, who is using Saga to control New Earth. A sequel to *Epic*. (Rev: BL 5/15/08; SLJ 7/08)

2800 Krinard, Susan. *The Forest Lord* (10–12). 2002, Berkley paper $7.99 (978-0-425-18686-2). The Forest Lord needs a human mate to stop the extinction of the fairy people. (Rev: BL 10/1/02)

2801 Kristoff, Jay. *Stormdancer* (9–12). 2012, St. Martin's $24.99 (978-1-250-00140-5). Readers who persevere with this slow-to-start steampunk fantasy set in feudal Japan will enjoy the story of young Yukiko trying to save her people from evil. (Rev: BL 11/1/12; LMC 3–4/13; SLJ 12/12; VOYA 10/12)

2802 Kritzer, Naomi. *Fires of the Faithful* (10–12). 2002, Bantam paper $6.99 (978-0-553-58517-9). Eliana's music studies are set aside when she decides to lead a defense of the Old Way religion against the goddess worshippers who are terrorizing her people. (Rev: BL 9/1/02; VOYA 2/03)

2803 Kurland, Lynn. *My Heart Stood Still* (9–12). 2001, Berkley paper $7.99 (978-0-425-18197-3). A ghost who has haunted her castle for 600 years falls in love with the American businessman who buys and begins to restore it. (Rev: BL 9/15/01)

2804 Kurland, Lynn. *Star of the Morning* (9–12). Series: The Nine Kingdoms. 2006, Berkley paper $14.00 (978-0-425-21212-7). Black magic threatens the kingdom of Neroche, and Morgan of Melksham holds the power to defeat this threat; this first volume in a new fantasy series set in the Nine Kingdoms is also a story of romance. (Rev: BL 11/1/06)

2805 Kurtz, Katherine, and Deborah Turner Harris. *The Temple and the Crown* (10–12). 2001, Warner Aspect paper $6.99 (978-0-446-60854-1). The saga begun with *The Temple and the Stone* (1998) continues the story of the Templars, two members of the secret Cercle, and such historical characters as Robert the Bruce of Scotland and Philip the Fair of France. (Rev: BL 4/15/01; VOYA 8/01)

2806 Kushner, Ellen. *The Privilege of the Sword* (11–12). Series: Riverside. 2006, Bantam paper $14.00 (978-0-553-38268-6). Young Katherine is trained as a swordfighter by her uncle, the Mad Duke of Riverside, in this companion to *Swordspoint* (2003). (Rev: BL 8/06)

2807 L'Engle, Madeleine. *An Acceptable Time* (8–12). 1989, Farrar $18.00 (978-0-374-30027-2). Polly O'Keefe time-travels (as her parents did years before in the Time trilogy) but this time to visit a civilization of Druids that lived 3,000 years ago. (Rev: BL 1/1/90; SLJ 1/90; VOYA 4/90)

2808 Lackey, Mercedes. *Alta* (9–12). Series: The Dragon Jousters. 2004, DAW $24.95 (978-0-7564-0216-7). In this sequel to *Joust* (2003), young Vetch becomes indispensable in his land because he knows how to tame newly hatched dragons. (Rev: BL 3/15/04)

2809 Lackey, Mercedes. *Arrow's Fall* (10–12). 1987, Penguin paper $7.99 (978-0-88677-378-6). The last part of the Valdemar trilogy about Talia, the Queen's Own Herald. Preceded by *Arrows of the Queen* and *Arrow's Flight* (both 1987), this installment was published in 1988. (Rev: BL 1/15/88)

2810 Lackey, Mercedes. *Fiddler Fair* (9–12). 1998, Simon & Schuster paper $5.99 (978-0-671-87866-5). A collection of 12 fantastic stories that deal with such topics as televangelists, animals rights zealots, and old-fashioned men. (Rev: VOYA 10/98)

2811 Lackey, Mercedes. *Gwenhwyfar: The White Spirit* (10–12). 2009, DAW $25.95 (978-075640585-4). Although the dutiful Gwenhwyfar puts aside her own desires to become Arthur's queen, she proves herself a force to be reckoned with in the king's court as she battles to keep the throne from falling into conspiring hands. ∩ **e** (Rev: BL 10/15/09)

2812 Lackey, Mercedes. *Joust* (10–12). Series: The Dragon Jousters. 2003, DAW $24.95 (978-0-7564-0122-1). Young Vetch hopes to hatch a dragon and challenge the evil Tian, who have overrun and ruined his homeland. (Rev: BL 3/15/03*)

2813 Lackey, Mercedes. *Sanctuary* (9–12). Series: The Dragon Jousters. 2005, DAW $25.95 (978-0-7564-0246-4). In the final volume of the trilogy that started with *Joust* (2003) and *Alta* (2004), Kiron and his fellow jousters and dragons seek refuge from the evil Magi in the abandoned city called Sanctuary. (Rev: BL 5/1/05)

2814 Lackey, Mercedes. *The Serpent's Shadow* (10–12). 2001, DAW $24.95 (978-0-88677-915-3). Set in an alternative Victorian London touched with magic and romance, this novel features Maya, who must seek aid to prevent the destruction of London by the forces of Kali. (Rev: BL 2/15/01; VOYA 10/01)

2815 Lackey, Mercedes. *The Wizard of London* (10–12). Series: Elemental Masters. 2005, DAW $25.95 (978-0-7564-0174-0). In Victorian England, Lord Alderscroft, head of the British Elemental Masters Council, is reunited with a former lover who needs his help in a struggle to rescue two girls. (Rev: BL 10/15/05)

2816 Lackey, Mercedes, and James Mallory. *The Outstretched Shadow* (10–12). 2003, Tor $25.95 (978-0-7653-0219-9). Jaded with life as a young mage with high expectations, young Kellen is fascinated to find three books about forbidden magic, information that puts his life at risk. (Rev: BL 9/15/03; VOYA 12/03)

2817 Lackey, Mercedes, and James Mallory. *The Phoenix Endangered* (10–12). Series: Enduring Flame. 2008, Tor $27.95 (978-076531594-6). This second installment in the series finds young Tiercel and Harrier on a quest to find the Lake of Fire and defeat darkness; an entertaining fantasy full of humor and adventure. ⌒ (Rev: BL 9/15/08)

2818 Lackey, Mercedes, and Roberta Gellis. *This Scepter'd Isle* (10–12). 2004, Baen $25.00 (978-0-7434-7156-5). At the court of Henry VIII, there is evidence of elvish intervention in royal affairs. (Rev: BL 2/15/04)

2819 LaFevers, Robin. *Grave Mercy* (9–12). Series: His Fair Assassin. 2012, Houghton Mifflin $16.99 (978-054762834-9). Ismae, 17, escapes from an arranged marriage to a convent in Brittany in this tense and detailed fantasy set in the 15th century. *Grave Mercy* is the second book in the trilogy. **e** Lexile 850L (Rev: BL 1/1/12*; HB 3–4/12; LMC 11–12/12; SLJ 4/12*; VOYA 2/12)

2820 Lake, Nick. *Blood Ninja* (7–11). 2009, Simon & Schuster $16.99 (978-1-4169-8627-0). In 16th-century Japan teenage Taro is saved from certain death by a bite from a ninja vampire. **e** Lexile 870L (Rev: BL 12/1/09; SLJ 12/09; VOYA 2/10)

2821 Lally, Soinbhe. *A Hive for the Honeybee* (8–12). 1999, Scholastic paper $16.95 (978-0-590-51038-7). An allegory about life and work that takes place in a beehive with such characters as Alfred, the bee poet,

and Mo, a radical drone. (Rev: BL 2/1/99; HB 3–4/99; HBG 10/99; SLJ 5/99*; VOYA 4/99)

2822 Lanagan, Margo. *The Brides of Rollrock Island* (9–12). 2012, Knopf $17.99 (978-0-375-86919-8); LB $20.99 (978-0-375-96919-5). Magically gifted Misskaela discovers her gift for transforming seals into beautiful women in this lyrical fantasy. **e** Lexile 950L (Rev: BL 7/12*; HB 1–2/13; LMC 1–2/13; SLJ 9/12; VOYA 10/12)

2823 Lanagan, Margo. *Red Spikes* (10–12). 2007, Knopf $16.99 (978-0-375-84320-4). These ten unusual fantasy stories, some tinged with horror, are suitable for mature, advanced readers. (Rev: BL 10/1/07; HB 11–12/07; LMC 1/08; SLJ 10/07)

2824 Lanagan, Margo. *Tender Morsels* (10–12). 2008, Knopf $16.99 (978-037584811-7); LB $19.99 (978-037594811-4). Fifteen-year-old Liga and her two daughters are magically transported to a realm beyond the horrors they've encountered. Printz Honor 2009. ⌒ Lexile 950L (Rev: BL 8/08*; HB 9–10/08; SLJ 11/1/08*)

2825 Lang, Michele. *Lady Lazarus* (10–12). 2010, Tor paper $14.99 (978-07653231-7-0). A 20-year-old witch and the angel she has summoned must save the continent of Europe from Nazi wizards in this urban fantasy that features supernatural characters of all kinds. **e** (Rev: BL 9/1–15/10)

2826 Larbalestier, Justine. *Liar* (9–12). 2009, Bloomsbury $16.99 (978-1-59990-305-7). Her predisposition for lying calls 17-year-old Micah Wilkins's integrity into question when her boyfriend dies under mysterious circumstances. Lexile HL470L (Rev: BL 9/1/09; HB 11–12/09; LMC 10/09; SLJ 10/09; VOYA 12/09)

2827 Larbalestier, Justine. *Magic or Madness* (8–11). 2005, Penguin $16.99 (978-1-59514-022-7). Australian 15-year-old Reason resists the idea of magic until she is transported from her grandmother's home to New York City and finds herself tackling new realities. (Rev: BCCB 3/05; BL 3/15/05*; SLJ 3/05; VOYA 2/05)

2828 Larbalestier, Justine. *Magic's Child* (8–11). Series: Magic or Madness. 2007, Penguin $16.99 (978-1-59514-064-7). Reason, now 15, pregnant, and on her own, struggles with her magical abilities in this final installment in the trilogy. (Rev: BCCB 6/07; BL 4/15/07; SLJ 5/07)

2829 Laumer, Keith, ed. *Dangerous Vegetables* (9–12). 1998, Baen paper $5.99 (978-0-671-57781-0). A collection of fantastic stories, all dealing with plant life, by such well-known authors as Bradbury, Saberhagen, and John Christopher. (Rev: VOYA 6/99)

2830 Lawhead, Stephen R. *Merlin* (10–12). 1990, Avon paper $7.99 (978-0-380-70889-5). The story of how Merlin prepared the world for the arrival of Arthur. (Rev: VOYA 4/89)

2831 Lawrence, Michael. *A Crack in the Line* (8–12). Series: Withern Rise. 2004, HarperCollins $15.99 (978-0-06-072477-1). Still mourning his mother's death, 16-year-old Alaric discovers how to travel to an alternate reality where his mother is still alive. (Rev: BL 6/1–15/04*; SLJ 8/04)

2832 Lawrence, Michael. *Small Eternities* (9–12). Series: Withern Rise. 2005, Greenwillow $15.99 (978-0-06-072480-1). Two years after his mother's tragic, accidental death, 16-year-old Alaric finds himself transported to an alternate reality where his mother is still alive in this sequel to *A Crack in the Line* (2004). (Rev: BL 11/1/05; SLJ 3/06; VOYA 12/05)

2833 Lawrence, Michael. *The Underwood See* (8–11). Series: Withern Rise. 2007, Greenwillow $16.99 (978-0-06-072483-2). Readers of the previous books in the series (*The Crack in the Line* and *Small Eternities*, 2004 and 2005 respectively) will enjoy this final volume in which Naia, now pregnant, returns to the Underwood See to have her child there. (Rev: BL 5/15/07; SLJ 10/07)

2834 Le Guin, Ursula K. *Gifts* (6–10). 2004, Harcourt $17.00 (978-0-15-205123-5). In this engaging fantasy, Gry and Orrec, two Uplanders with supernatural abilities, are hesitant to use their awesome powers for fear that they will cause more harm than good. (Rev: BL 8/04*; SLJ 9/04; VOYA 12/04)

2835 Le Guin, Ursula K. *Powers* (8–12). Series: Annals of the Western Shore. 2007, Harcourt $17.00 (978-0-15-205770-1). The third book in the series continues the theme of a society based on slavery, with slave Gavir —who was kidnapped from his tribe as a child — running from his masters after his sister is raped. ⌒ (Rev: BL 10/1/07; HB 9–10/07; SLJ 9/07)

2836 Le Guin, Ursula K. *Voices* (7–10). 2006, Harcourt $17.00 (978-0-15-205678-0). Seventeen-year-old Memer resents the conquerors who oppress her land and ban books and writing and goes on a quest to get revenge; a thought-provoking companion to *Gifts*. ⌒ (Rev: BL 8/06; HB 9–10/06; LMC 3/07; SLJ 8/06*; VOYA)

2837 Le Guin, Ursula K. *A Wizard of Earthsea* (8–12). Series: Earthsea. 1968, Bantam paper $7.50 (978-0-553-26250-6). An apprentice wizard accidentally unleashes an evil power onto the land of Earthsea. Followed by *The Tombs of Atuan* and *The Farthest Shore*.

2838 Leavitt, Martine. *Keturah and Lord Death* (8–11). 2006, Front St $16.95 (978-1-932425-29-1). After Keturah becomes lost in the woods and encounters Lord Death she must use her storytelling skills to convince him to let her go and in the process he falls in love with her. (Rev: BL 9/15/06)

2839 Lebbon, Tim. *London Eye* (9–12). Series: Toxic City. 2012, PYR $16.95 (978-1-61614-680-1). In a postapocalyptic London, 17-year-old Jack and his friends and younger sister struggle to survive the vicious Choppers and hope to get news out to the rest of the world. ℮ (Rev: SLJ 9/12; VOYA 12/12)

2840 Lee, Tanith. *Mortal Suns* (10–12). 2003, Overlook $26.95 (978-1-58567-207-3). In the kingdom of Akhemony — a land reminiscent of ancient Greece — a queen gives birth to a beautiful daughter who has no feet. (Rev: BL 9/1/03)

2841 Leith, Valery. *The Riddled Night* (10–12). 2000, Bantam paper $13.95 (978-0-553-37939-6). This, the second Everien book, tells how Tash, the conqueror of Everien, wants to strengthen the Fire Houses to make weapons to fight the Clans. (Rev: BL 8/00)

2842 Lenahan, John. *Shadowmagic* (7–11). 2010, Independent paper $10.99 (978-1-90-554892-7). Conor is amazed to discover that he is a prince when he and his father are transported to Tir Na Nog and the Celtic past. ℮ (Rev: BL 2/1/10; SLJ 5/10)

2843 Levine, Gail Carson. *Ever* (6–10). 2008, HarperCollins $16.99 (978-0-06-122962-6). Olus, a god, is in love with Kezi, a human girl who is fated to be sacrificed to Admat, the god of oaths. (Rev: BL 4/1/08; SLJ 6/08)

2844 Levine, Gail Carson. *Fairest* (7–10). 2006, HarperCollins paper $17.00 (978-0-06-073408-4). An unattractive 15-year-old girl gains confidence as she comes to recognize her own strengths in this imaginative fairy tale. ⌒ (Rev: BL 7/06; SLJ 9/06)

2845 Levithan, David. *Every Day* (9–12). 2012, Knopf $16.99 (978-0-307-93188-7); LB $19.99 (978-0-375-97111-2). Sixteen year old A involuntarily changes personas nightly, always winding up as someone new in an unfamiliar place, until a romance interrupts the cycle. YALSA Top Ten Best Fiction for Young Adults 2013. ⌒ ℮ Lexile HL650L (Rev: BL 7/12*; HB 11–12/12; LMC 3–4/13*; SLJ 9/12; VOYA 12/12)

2846 Lewis, C. S. *Out of the Silent Planet* (10–12). 1996, Scribner Classics $22.00 (978-0-684-83364-4). This volume contains a trilogy of fantasy novels about a classic battle between good and evil.

2847 Lewis, Richard. *The Demon Queen* (8–11). 2008, Simon & Schuster $15.99 (978-1-4169-6226-7). Jesse, who appears to all to be a regular high-schooler, has a mysterious past that is made clear when it is revealed that he must fight a demon queen to save the world. (Rev: BL 5/15/08)

2848 Link, Kelly. *Pretty Monsters: Stories* (9–12). Illus. by Shaun Tan. 2008, Viking $19.99 (978-0-670-01090-5). A collection of strange stories with elements of horror, science fiction, and fantasy. (Rev: BL 9/15/08*; LMC 1–2/09; SLJ 10/1/08)

2849 Link, Kelly, and Gavin J. Grant, eds. *Steampunk! An Anthology of Fantastically Rich and Strange Stories* (8–12). Illus. 2011, Candlewick $22.99 (978-0-7636-

4843-5). History and technology blend in this collection of 14 steampunk stories by authors including Holly Black, Libba Bray, Garth Nix, and Cory Doctorow. **e** Lexile 940L (Rev: BL 11/1/11*; HB 9–10/11; LMC 3–4/12; SLJ 9/1/11*)

2850 Lipsyte, Robert. *The Chemo Kid* (9–12). 1992, HarperCollins $14.00 (978-0-06-020284-2). A high school junior gains superhuman strength after undergoing cancer treatments. (Rev: BL 3/1/92; SLJ 3/92)

2851 Lisle, Holly. *The Ruby Key* (6–10). Series: Moon & Sun. 2008, Scholastic $16.99 (978-0-545-00012-3). Genna and Danrith discover that the local nightlings have hatched an evil plan to do away with the nocturnal humans in their village in this first installment in the series. (Rev: BL 5/15/08; SLJ 6/08)

2852 Littlefield, Bill. *The Circus in the Woods* (6–10). 2001, Houghton Mifflin $15.00 (978-0-618-06642-1). Mystery and fantasy are combined in this quiet, reflective story about a 13-year-old girl who finds a strange circus in the Vermont woods where she spends her summers. (Rev: BCCB 12/01; HBG 10/02; SLJ 11/01; VOYA 12/01)

2853 Livingston, Lesley. *Darklight* (7–10). 2010, HarperCollins $16.99 (978-0-06-157540-2). In this sequel to *Wondrous Strange* (2009), actress Kelley is transported from New York to the Otherworld where she faces many challenges — including resurrecting her relationship with her beloved Sonny. Lexile 880L (Rev: BL 12/15/09; LMC 3–4/10; SLJ 2/10)

2854 Livingston, Lesley. *Wondrous Strange* (7–10). Series: Wondrous Strange. 2009, HarperCollins $16.99 (978-006157537-2). Kelley, 17, is acting in a New York City production of "A Midsummer Night's Dream" when she discovers she has a connection to a magic faerie world inhabited by mystical creatures. **e** Lexile 840L (Rev: BL 1/1–15/09; HB 3–4/09; SLJ 1/1/09; VOYA 4/09)

2855 Lo, Malinda. *Ash* (9–12). 2009, Little, Brown $16.99 (978-0-316-04009-9). In this Cinderella-esque tale, Ash falls in love not with the prince but with another female character, the King's huntress. **e** (Rev: BL 9/15/09; HB 11–12/09; LMC 11–12/09; SLJ 9/09; VOYA 10/09)

2856 London, Dena. *Shapeshifter's Quest* (7–10). 2005, Dutton $16.99 (978-0-525-47310-7). Syanthe, a shapeshifting teenager, ventures outside the forest that has always been her home on a mission to unravel the secret of the king's black magic. (Rev: BL 10/1/05; SLJ 10/05; VOYA 8/05)

2857 Lord, Karen. *Redemption in Indigo* (10–12). 2010, Small Beer paper $16 (978-19315206-6-9). In this modern adaptation of a Senegalese legend, the spirit of Patience has bestowed the Chaos Stick on the likable Paama, a female human, and the spirit of Chance tries

every trick in the book to win it back. ☊ **e** (Rev: BL 5/15/10*)

2858 Lowry, Lois. *Messenger* (6–10). 2004, Houghton Mifflin $16.00 (978-0-618-40441-4). In the Village where teenage Matty is a caregiver, the residents decide to build a wall to keep out undesirables in this fantasy filled with truth and symbolism. (Rev: BL 2/15/04*; HB 5–6/04; SLJ 4/04; VOYA 6/04)

2859 Lynch, Scott. *The Lies of Locke Lamora* (11–12). 2006, Bantam $23.00 (978-0-553-80467-6). Young Locke, an orphan on a far-flung world, must steal and deceive others in order to survive in this well-written and fascinating fantasy that includes some strong language. (Rev: BL 5/1/06)

2860 Maas, Sarah J. *Throne of Glass* (7–10). 2012, Bloomsbury $17.99 (978-1-59990-695-9). Teen assassin Celaena Sardothien has spent a year imprisoned in the salt mines when she is offered the chance to compete against soldiers and other men for the dubious privilege of being the king's champion — and for her eventual freedom. **e** Lexile HL790L (Rev: BL 9/1/12; LMC 1–2/13*; SLJ 12/12)

2861 Macaulay, David. *Baaa* (6–10). 1985, Houghton Mifflin paper $6.95 (978-0-395-39588-2). An allegory about the world after humans have left and intelligent sheep take control. (Rev: BL 9/1/85; SLJ 10/85)

2862 McBride, Lish. *Necromancing the Stone* (8–11). 2012, Henry Holt $16.99 (978-0-8050-9099-4). Having gained a conscience since 2010's *Hold Me Closer, Necromancer*, Sam returns to continue his work of sorting good from evil, still dogged by the evil Douglas. ☊ **e** Lexile HL720L (Rev: BL 12/1/12; SLJ 10/12)

2863 McBride, Regina. *The Fire Opal* (7–10). 2010, Delacorte LB $19.99 (978-0-385-90692-0). In late-16th-century Ireland, 14-year-old Maeve must retrieve a precious fire opal from the corpse goddess Uria in order to save the souls of her mother and sister. Lexile 970L (Rev: BL 5/15/10; LMC 8–9/10; SLJ 8/10)

2864 McCaffrey, Anne. *All the Weyrs of Pern* (9–12). Series: Pern. 1992, Tor paper $6.99 (978-0-345-36893-5). In this sequel to *Dragonsdawn*, human settlers of Pern rediscover their original landing site and revitalize a long-lost artificial intelligence system. (Rev: BL 10/1/91*)

2865 McCaffrey, Anne. *Nerilka's Story: A Pern Adventure* (9–12). Series: Pern. 1986, Ballantine paper $5.99 (978-0-345-33949-2). A young girl leaves her Hold to help nurse the sick stricken with a terrible plague. (Rev: BL 3/1/86; SLJ 5/86)

2866 McCaffrey, Anne, and Elizabeth Ann Scarborough. *Second Wave* (9–12). Series: Acorna's Children. 2006, HarperCollins $24.95 (978-0-06-052540-8). Khorri, daughter of Acorna and Aari, works with the android

Elviiz to search for the cause of the plague that has infected Khorri's parents. (Rev: SLJ 11/06)

2867 McCaffrey, Anne, and Todd McCaffrey. *Dragon Harper* (9–12). 2007, Del Rey $25.95 (978-0-345-48030-9). Apprentice Kinden is given the task of researching plagues of the past when a flu plague begins to kill thousands on Pern, while Dragonriders must ready themselves and their dragons for the imminent and deadly Thread. (Rev: BL 10/15/07; SLJ 1/08)

2868 McCaffrey, Todd. *Dragongirl* (10–12). Series: Dragonriders of Pern. 2010, Del Rey $26 (978-034549116-9). Young Fiona and her dragon Talenth are charged with recruiting and leading new dragons and riders as a mysterious plague ravages Pern. ⌒ ℮ (Rev: BL 5/1–15/10)

2869 MacCullough, Carolyn. *Always a Witch* (7–10). 2011, Clarion $16.99 (978-054722485-5). Witch Tamsin Greene travels back in time to 1887 to confront a villain and save her family in this sequel to *Once a Witch* (2009). ℮ Lexile HL800L (Rev: BLO 11/15/11; SLJ 2/12)

2870 MacCullough, Carolyn. *Once a Witch* (8–11). 2009, Clarion $16 (978-0-547-22399-5). Tamsin is bitter that her family's predisposition toward great talents has forsaken her, until a journey through time sets off a sinister chain of events and allows the edgy heroine to realize her true potential. ℮ Lexile HL790L (Rev: BL 10/1/09; SLJ 10/09; VOYA 10/09)

2871 McDonald, Sandra. *Diana Comet and Other Improbable Stories* (11–12). 2010, Lethe paper $15 (978-15902109-4-9). In this compelling collection of short stories, the lives of three quirky characters intersect as they navigate their fantastical world and its perils; for mature readers. (Rev: BL 6/1–15/10)

2872 Macela, Ann. *Wild Magic* (11–12). Series: Magic. 2009, Medallion paper $7.95 (978-19338369-9-7). Irenee, who finds ancient powerful pieces before they can be misused, and Jim, whose psychic powers help him fight crime, meet and together fight forces of evil; for mature readers. (Rev: BL 9/15/09)

2873 McGann, Oisín. *The Gods and Their Machines* (8–11). 2004, Tor $19.95 (978-0-7653-1159-7). Fantasy and allegory are blended in this story about Chamus, a teenage Altiman fighter pilot trainee, whose denigration of the people of nearby Bartokhin as ignorant religious fanatics is revised when a Bartokhrin girl helps him after his plane is forced to land near her home. (Rev: BL 12/15/04)

2874 McKillip, Patricia A. *The Bell at Sealey Head* (10–12). 2008, Ace $23.95 (978-044101630-3). Two different worlds coexist linked by a beautiful coastal house and an unseen ringing bell, and now the link is about to be revealed. (Rev: BL 9/1/08)

2875 McKinley, Robin. *Beauty: A Retelling of the Story of Beauty and the Beast* (9–12). 1978, HarperCollins

$16.99 (978-0-06-024149-0). From the standpoint of Beauty, this is the story of her quest in the forest where she encounters Beast. (Rev: BL 6/1/88)

2876 McKinley, Robin. *The Blue Sword* (7–10). 1982, Greenwillow $16.99 (978-0-688-00938-0). The king of Damar kidnaps a girl to help in his war against the Northerners. A prequel to *The Hero and the Crown*. Newbery Medal 1985. (Rev: BL 12/15/89)

2877 McKinley, Robin. *Dragonhaven* (8–11). 2007, Putnam $17.99 (978-0-399-24675-3). Jake, who lives on the dragon preserve at Smokehill National Park, rescues and cares for an orphaned dragon in this realistic novel with an environmental message. (Rev: BL 10/1/07; HB 9–10/07; LMC 3/08; SLJ 9/07)

2878 McKinley, Robin. *Pegasus* (8–11). 2010, Putnam $18.99 (978-0-399-24677-7). Human Princess Sylvi, 12, discovers she can communicate telepathically with Ebon, her personal pegasus, signaling a potential new era of rapprochement between the two species. (Rev: BL 10/1/10; LMC 3–4/11; SLJ 12/1/10)

2879 McKinley, Robin. *Rose Daughter* (6–12). 1997, Greenwillow $16.95 (978-0-688-15439-4). As in her award-winning *Beauty*, (1955) the author returns to the Beauty and the Beast fairy tale in this outstanding reworking of the traditional story. (Rev: BL 8/97; HBG 3/98; SLJ 9/97; VOYA 2/98) [398.2]

2880 McKinley, Robin, and Peter Dickinson. *Fire: Tales of Elemental Spirits* (6–10). 2009, Putnam $19.99 (978-0-399-25289-1). Five well-crafted tales illustrate contacts between humans and supernatural beings associated with fire; a companion to *Water: Tales of Elemental Spirits* (2002). ℮ (Rev: BL 9/1/09; HB 11–12/09; LMC 11–12/09; SLJ 9/09; VOYA 12/09)

2881 McLaughlin, Lauren. *Cycler* (9–12). 2008, Random House $17.99 (978-037585191-9); LB $20.99 (978-037595191-6). For four days each month 17-year-old Jill morphs into her male alter-ego, Jack — who's beginning to insist that he be given his freedom — and, on top of worrying about classes and prom and fitting in, Jill must cope with this bizarre situation. Lexile NC720L (Rev: BL 11/15/08; LMC 11–12/08; SLJ 8/08; VOYA 8/08)

2882 McLaughlin, Lauren. *(re)Cycler* (9–12). 2009, Random House paper $8.99 (978-0-375-85195-7). In this sequel to *Cycler* (2008), 17-year-old Jill is still turning into Jack for four days each month and with some trepidation heads off to New York to share an apartment with her friend Ramie, who is dating Jack. ℮ (Rev: BLO 7/16/09; SLJ 1/10)

2883 McMann, Lisa. *Fade* (8–11). Series: Wake Trilogy. 2009, Simon & Schuster $15.99 (978-141695358-6). This gripping sequel to 2008's *Wake* has the heroine, Janie, exploring more deeply her dream-catching abilities and using them to solve a dangerous case of student abuse. ℮ Lexile 570L (Rev: BL 12/1/08; SLJ 5/1/09)

2884 McMann, Lisa. *Gone* (8–11). Series: Wake Trilogy. 2010, Simon & Schuster $16.99 (978-1-4169-7918-0). Janie faces tough decisions about her future as she struggles with her alcoholic mother and her father, also a dream-catcher, surprisingly comes into her life when he is in a coma; the final volume in the trilogy that began with *Wake* (2008) and *Fade* (2009). **e** (Rev: BL 1/1–15/10; SLJ 2/10)

2885 McMann, Lisa. *Wake* (8–10). Series: Wake. 2008, Simon & Schuster $15.99 (978-1-4169-5969-4). Janie, 17, feels both cursed and blessed by her ability to enter and experience other people's dreams; then she begins to learn how to use her skill to help herself and others, including a boy named Cabel whose dreams include her. (Rev: BL 4/15/08; LMC 8//08; SLJ 3/08)

2886 McNaughton, Janet. *An Earthly Knight* (7–10). 2004, HarperCollins $15.99 (978-0-06-008992-4). In this romantic fantasy, 16-year-old Jennie in Scotland falls in love with an enchanted lord and their love is so strong that it shatters a powerful curse. (Rev: BL 2/15/04; SLJ 3/04)

2887 McNish, Cliff. *Angel* (7–10). 2008, Carolrhoda $16.95 (978-0-8225-8900-6). Freya's belief in angels has led her into trouble in the past; now, at the age of 14, she realizes that the angels are real. (Rev: BL 6/1–15/08; SLJ 6/08)

2888 McQuerry, Maureen Doyle. *The Peculiars* (7–12). 2012, Abrams/Amulet $16.95 (978-1-4197-0178-8). At the age of 18, long-fingered Lena sets out for Scree, a province where the Peculiars — including her long-lost father — may be living; on the journey she meets a young librarian and a handsome marshall. **e** (Rev: BL 5/15/12*; HB 7–8/12; LMC 11–12/12*; SLJ 11/12; VOYA 6/12)

2889 Madigan, L. K. *The Mermaid's Mirror* (8–10). 2010, Houghton Mifflin $16 (978-0-547-19491-2). Why does the sea call so strongly to Lena, even though her father, a former surfer, has forbidden her to swim in it? (Rev: BL 9/15/10*; SLJ 12/1/10)

2890 Mafi, Tahereh. *Shatter Me* (8–12). 2011, Harper-Teen $17.99 (978-006208548-1). An "undesirable" girl whose touch causes pain and death meets Adam, who is immune to her curse and gives her hope for a less violent future. ♠ **e** Lexile HL650L (Rev: BL 10/15/11; LMC 3–4/12; SLJ 2/12)

2891 Maguire, Gregory. *Son of a Witch* (9–12). 2005, Regan $26.95 (978-0-06-054893-3). Liir, 14, faces many mysteries — Was the witch Elphaba his mother? Does he have magical powers? How did he come to be in the Cloister of St. Glinda, wounded and amnesiac? — in this multilayered sequel to *Wicked* (1995). (Rev: BL 9/15/05; SLJ 3/06)

2892 Mahy, Margaret. *The Magician of Hoad* (9–12). 2009, Simon & Schuster $18.99 (978-1-4169-7807-7). Heriot has nightmares that begin to make sense as he is forced into service as the king's magician. **e** Lexile 1010L (Rev: BL 10/1/09; HB 11–12/09; LMC 1–2/10; SLJ 11/09)

2893 Maizel, Rebecca. *Infinite Days* (8–12). Series: Vampire Queen. 2010, St. Martin's paper $9.99 (978-0-312-64991-3). Lenah Beaudonte, a vampire whose humanity has been restored thanks to the sacrifice of her lover, Rhode, did not believe she would ever be 16 or fall in love again, but she is having those experiences until her past comes back to haunt her. (Rev: BL 7/10; SLJ 12/1/10)

2894 Malkin, Nina. *Swoon* (10–12). 2009, Simon & Schuster $17.99 (978-141697434-5). Seventeen-year-old Candice (Dice) moves to a Connecticut town and discovers that her cousin Penelope has been possessed by a man named Sin. As Sin seeks revenge for wrongs done to him in the colonial era, the entire town is affected. ♠ Lexile HL710L (Rev: BL 4/1/09; SLJ 6/1/09)

2895 Malley, Gemma. *The Declaration* (6–10). 2007, Bloomsbury $16.95 (978-1-59990-119-0). In a world where people exchange childlessness for immortality, Surplus Anna should never have been born and lives a life of servitude. ♠ (Rev: BL 11/15/07; SLJ 2/08)

2896 Mantchev, Lisa. *Eyes Like Stars* (8–12). Series: Théâtre Illuminata. 2009, Feiwel & Friends $16.99 (978-031238096-0). The magical Théâtre Illuminata — where characters from Shakespeare's plays materialize from thin air — has been Beatrice's home since infancy, and she is determined to save it by putting on a blockbuster. The sequels are *Perchance to Dream* (2010) and *So Silver Bright* (2011). ♠ Lexile HL740L (Rev: BL 5/15/09; LMC 10/09; SLJ 8/09; VOYA 8/09)

2897 Marchetta, Melina. *Finnikin of the Rock* (6–10). 2010, Candlewick $18.99 (978-0-7636-4361-4). In this rich, multilayered fantasy, 19-year-old Finnikin prepares to return from exile and, with the help of a mysterious young woman Evanjalin and other refugees, restore the kingdom of Lumatere to its former glory. YALSA Amazing Audiobooks Top Ten 2011. ♠ Lexile 820L (Rev: BL 3/1/10*; HB 5–6/10; LMC 5–6/10; SLJ 3/10)

2898 Marchetta, Melina. *Froi of the Exiles* (9–12). Series: Lumatere Chronicles. 2012, Candlewick $18.99 (978-076364759-9). Young Lumateren Guard Froi is sent on a deadly mission to the kingdom of Charyn, where he faces many challenges including a mentally unstable princess; a sequel to *Finnikin of the Rock* (2010). **e** Lexile HL770L (Rev: BL 2/15/12*; HB 5–6/12; SLJ 5/1/12; VOYA 6/12)

2899 Marillier, Juliet. *Cybele's Secret* (7–10). 2008, Knopf $16.99 (978-0-375-83365-6). Scholarly Paula, 17, accompanies her father on a trip to Istanbul to buy a treasured artifact, the remnant of a pagan cult, only to find herself in a dangerous and challenging position; a companion to *Wildwood Dancing* (2007). Best

Books for Young Adults 2009. ☊ (Rev: BL 7/08*; HB 11–12/08; LMC 11–12/08; SLJ 9/1/08; VOYA 12/08)

2900 Marillier, Juliet. *Daughter of the Forest* (9–12). Series: The Sevenwaters Trilogy. 2000, Tor $25.95 (978-0-312-84879-8). In this first book of a trilogy, young Sorcha must weave magical shirts to free her brothers, who have been turned into swans by a wicked stepmother. (Rev: BL 4/15/00*; VOYA 12/00)

2901 Marillier, Juliet. *Heart's Blood* (11–12). 2009, Roc $24.95 (978-045146293-0). In 12th-century Ireland young scribe Catrin seeks to free the crippled chieftain Anluan from a centuries-old curse; for mature readers. (Rev: BL 11/15/09)

2902 Marillier, Juliet. *Shadowfell* (7–10). 2012, Knopf $16.99 (978-0-375-86954-9); LB $19.99 (978-037596954-6). Neryn, a 15-year-old with magical powers that she has kept secret, learns that she alone can save her homeland of Alban from destruction. ℮ Lexile 730L (Rev: BLO 10/15/12; LMC 1–2/13; SLJ 12/12; VOYA 12/12)

2903 Marillier, Juliet. *Son of the Shadows* (10–12). Series: The Sevenwaters Trilogy. 2001, Tor $25.95 (978-0-312-84880-4). In this sequel to *Daughter of the Forest* (2000), evil again stalks the land of Sevenwaters in the shape of a tattooed outlaw. (Rev: BL 5/15/01; VOYA 12/01)

2904 Marillier, Juliet. *The Well of Shades* (9–12). Series: The Bridei Chronicles. 2007, Tor $27.95 (978-0-7653-0997-6). King Bridei sends his assassin/spy Faolon to find out who is threatening the kingdom in this gripping third installment of the fantasy set in 6th-century Scotland. (Rev: SLJ 7/07)

2905 Marillier, Juliet. *Wildwood Dancing* (8–11). 2007, Knopf $16.99 (978-0-375-83364-9). Five Transylvanian sisters live lives filled with magic, danger, and romance when they enter a portal into the Other Kingdom. (Rev: BCCB 3/07; BL 2/1/07; HB 3–4/07; LMC 4–5/07; SLJ 2/07*)

2906 Marks, Daniel. *Velveteen* (10–12). 2012, Delacorte $17.99 (978-038574224-5); LB $20.99 (978-037599051-9). Since her violent death at the age of 16, Velveteen has been rescuing lost souls in the City of the Dead, and illicitly haunting her murderer. ℮ (Rev: BL 10/15/12; LMC 1–2/13; SLJ 1/13; VOYA 12/12)

2907 Marks, Laurie J. *Water Logic* (9–12). 2007, Small Beer paper $16.00 (978-1-931520-23-2). Past and present collide as the Sainnites and Shaftal break a fragile peace in this third volume of the series. (Rev: BL 7/07)

2908 Marr, Melissa. *Carnival of Souls* (8–12). 2012, HarperCollins $17.99 (978-0-06-165928-7). When she falls in love with a daimon she's supposed to fight, Mallory, 17, learns important truths about her real heritage and destiny. ℮ (Rev: BL 8/12; SLJ 10/12)

2909 Marr, Melissa. *Faery Tales and Nightmares* (9–12). 2011, HarperCollins $14.99 (978-006185271-8). This collection of short tales set within the world of the Wicked Lovely series includes many characters who will be familiar to its fans; romance and fantasy abound. ☊ ℮ (Rev: BLO 10/15/11; SLJ 3/12)

2910 Marr, Melissa. *Fragile Eternity* (10–12). 2009, HarperCollins $16.99 (978-006121471-4); LB $17.89 (978-006121472-1). Aislinn is in love with Seth, a mortal, but is also attracted to Keenan, the faerie summer king, in this sequel to *Wicked Lovely* (2007). ℮ Lexile HL650L (Rev: BL 4/1/09; SLJ 6/1/09)

2911 Marr, Melissa. *Ink Exchange* (10–12). 2008, HarperTeen $16.99 (978-0-06-121468-4). Seventeen-year-old Leslie gets a tattoo in an effort to change her life for the better, only to find it connects her to the King of the Dark Court in this companion novel to *Wicked Lovely* (2007). ☊ (Rev: BL 6/1–15/08; SLJ 6/08)

2912 Marr, Melissa. *Wicked Lovely* (7–12). 2007, HarperTeen $16.99 (978-0-06-121465-3). Aislinn, who can see fairies, is faced with a very difficult choice that involves all of humanity and faerie when the Summer King asks her to be his queen. (Rev: SLJ 7/07)

2913 Marriott, Zoe. *Daughter of the Flames* (7–11). 2009, Candlewick $17.99 (978-076363749-1). Zira, who is part Ruan and part Sedorne, is caught up in a battle between the two tribes in this sweeping story. (Rev: BL 2/15/09; LMC 8–9/09; SLJ 8/09; VOYA 4/09)

2914 Marrone, Amanda. *Uninvited* (7–10). 2007, Simon & Schuster paper $8.99 (978-1-4169-3978-8). Jordan decides to clean up her act (really, her acting out with drugs and sex) when her vampire ex-boyfriend returns to haunt her. (Rev: BL 1/1–15/08; SLJ 11/07)

2915 Marsden, John. *Burning for Revenge* (8–12). Series: Tomorrow. 2000, Houghton Mifflin $17.00 (978-0-395-96054-7). Ellie and her four Australian friends attack an airfield held by the enemy in this continuing saga. (Rev: BL 10/1/00; HBG 3/01; SLJ 10/00)

2916 Marsden, John. *The Night Is for Hunting* (8–12). Series: Tomorrow. 2001, Houghton Mifflin $16.00 (978-0-618-07026-8). This sixth book in the Tomorrow series continues the action-packed story of a group of teenagers fighting to defend Australia against a band of invaders. (Rev: BCCB 2/02; BL 11/1/01; HBG 10/02; SLJ 10/01; VOYA 12/01)

2917 Martin, George R. R. *Quartet: Four Tales from the Crossroads* (10–12). Ed. by Christine Carpenito. 2001, NESFA $25.00 (978-1-886778-31-3). These four stories are excellent examples of Martin's mastery of the fantasy genre. (Rev: BL 4/15/01)

2918 Martinez, A. Lee. *Too Many Curses* (10–12). 2008, Tor paper $14.95 (978-076531835-0). A humble housekeeper turns heroine when her employer, a powerful wizard, dies leaving behind many angry cursed beings and a wicked sorceress who wants to take over the castle. ∩ (Rev: BL 9/1/08; SLJ 2/09)

2919 Massey, Misty. *Mad Kestrel* (9–12). 2008, Tor paper $14.95 (978-0-7653-1802-2). Awash with non-stop action, young Kestrel is literally at sea as a lady pirate who must save her captain without revealing her magical abilities. (Rev: BL 3/1/08)

2920 Melling, O. R. *The Book of Dreams* (7–12). Series: The Chronicles of Faerie. 2009, Abrams $19.95 (978-0-8109-8346-5). Dana, a 13-year-old who is half faerie, now lives unhappily in Canada but travels to the land of Faerie to find the Book of Dreams. Lexile 670L (Rev: BL 10/1/09; SLJ 8/09; VOYA 6/09)

2921 Melling, O. R. *The Light-Bearer's Daughter* (7–11). Series: Chronicles of Faerie. 2007, Abrams $16.95 (978-0-8109-0781-2). In a forest in the fairy realm, 12-year-old Dana embarks on a dangerous mission to deliver a message to the fairy High King; and in contemporary Ireland activists work to save the forest from developers. (Rev: BL 5/15/07)

2922 Melling, O. R. *The Summer King* (8–11). 2005, Abrams $16.95 (978-0-8109-5969-9). Laurel visits her grandparents in Ireland a year after her twin sister's death and discovers a hidden world of fairies, who enlist her help to save their kingdom. (Rev: BL 4/15/06; SLJ 8/06)

2923 Melling, Orla. *The Druid's Tune* (6–10). 1993, O'Brien paper $9.95 (978-0-86278-285-6). Peter, a Druid lost in the 20th century, involves two teenagers in a time-travel spell that sends them back to Ireland's Iron Age. (Rev: BL 2/15/93)

2924 Meno, Joe. *The Boy Detective Fails* (9–12). 2006, Akashi paper $14.95 (978-1-933354-10-1). Billy Argo is a successful boy detective until his sister commits suicide in this disturbing but compelling novel. (Rev: SLJ 9/06)

2925 Meyer, Stephenie. *Breaking Dawn* (9–12). Series: Twilight. 2008, Little, Brown $22.99 (978-031606792-8). Bella Swan marries handsome vampire Edward Cullen, but her connection with werewolf Jacob is still strong in this final volume in the popular series. ∩ **e** Lexile 690L (Rev: BLO 8/08; SLJ 10/1/08; VOYA 8/08)

2926 Michaelis, Antonia. *Dragons of Darkness* (9–12). Trans. from German by Anthea Bell. 2010, Abrams $18.95 (978-0-8109-4074-1). Magic and realism are interwoven in this story set in Nepal and featuring 14-year-old Christopher, a German searching for his older brother, and young prince Jumar; the two band together to destroy the dragons that have been disrupting the nation. Lexile 800L (Rev: BL 3/1/10*; SLJ 3/10; VOYA 2/10)

2927 Michaelis, Antonia. *Tiger Moon* (9–12). Trans. by Anthea Bell. 2008, Abrams $18.95 (978-081099481-2). In early 20th-century India, young Raka weaves a magical, compelling tale in an effort to escape a miser-

able arranged marriage. Batchelder Honor 2009; ALA Notable Books 2009. Lexile 820L (Rev: BL 10/15/08*; HB 11–12/08; LMC 5–6/09; SLJ 11/1/08*)

2928 Michaels, Kasey. *The Return of the Prodigal* (9–12). 2007, HQN paper $6.99 (978-0-373-77280-3). In this volume of the Beckets of Romney Marsh series, Rian is in France in spite of the British victory, being cared for by a beautiful French woman whose motives are questionable. (Rev: BL 9/15/07)

2929 Micklem, Sarah. *Wildfire* (11–12). 2009, Scribner $26 (978-074326524-9). When Firethorn defies her master Sir Galan and follows him into war, she is hit by lightning and loses her power of speech, after which she is hailed as a prophet; a sequel to *Firethorn* (2004), **e** (Rev: BL 7/09)

2930 Mieville, China. *Railsea* (9–12). Illus. by author. 2012, Del Rey $18 (978-034552452-2). Aboard the diesel train *Medes,* which carries a crew of moldywarpes (enormous molelike creatures) hunters, young orphan Sham interacts with characters including Captain Naphi, who lost her arm to a moldywarpe known as the Mocker-Jack. ∩ **e** (Rev: BL 5/15/12*)

2931 Miéville, China. *Perdido Street Station* (10–12). 2001, Ballantine paper $18.00 (978-0-345-44302-1). In an alternate version of Dickens's London, this novel for mature readers tells how a young scientist is trying to discover the secret of flight and instead raises the larva of a deadly snakemoth. (Rev: BL 2/15/01)

2932 Miles, Elizabeth. *Fury* (9–12). 2011, Simon & Schuster $17.99 (978-144242224-7). Three modern Furies turn up in Ascension, Maine, to sort out the lives of some problematic teens. ∩ **e** Lexile 750L (Rev: BLO 9/1/11; SLJ 2/12; VOYA 8/11)

2933 Miller, Kirsten. *All You Desire* (8–11). 2011, Penguin $17.99 (978-1-59514-323-5). Haven and Iain, both reincarnated, are in New York City on the trail of Beau Decker, a friend of Haven's who has gone missing; this sequel to *The Eternal Ones* (2010) has rich historical details. ∩ **e** (Rev: BL 10/1/11; SLJ 11/1/11)

2934 Miller, Kirsten. *The Eternal Ones* (8–11). 2010, Penguin $17.99 (978-1-595-14308-2). This suspenseful tale mixes fantasy, mystery, and romance as 17-year-old Haven faces discrimination because of her visions of previous lives and flees from small-town Tennessee to New York City. ∩ **e** Lexile HL760L (Rev: BL 6/10; LMC 11–12/10; SLJ 8/10)

2935 Mingle, Pamela. *Kissing Shakespeare* (7–12). 2012, Delacorte $17.99 (978-038574196-5); LB $20.99 (978-037599034-2). Kidnapped from her high school production of "The Taming of the Shrew," Miranda is whisked back to 1581 where her mission is to discourage young William Shakespeare from joining the priesthood. **e** (Rev: BL 9/15/12; SLJ 8/1/12; VOYA 10/12)

2936 Mitchard, Jacquelyn. *Look Both Ways* (7–10). Series: Midnight Twins. 2009, Penguin $16.99 (978-

159514161-3). Twins Merry and Mallory, who can "see" the future and the past, try to sort out their latest cryptic vision with the help of Native American friends. ∩ Lexile 710L (Rev: BL 2/15/09; SLJ 5/1/09)

2937 Mitchell, Todd. *The Traitor King* (7–10). 2007, Scholastic $16.99 (978-0-439-82788-1). Darren and Jackie discover their uncle in Maine is missing; their search for him leads them to family secrets, magical powers, and an alternate world. (Rev: BL 6/1–15/07; LMC 10/07; SLJ 5/07)

2938 Mlynowski, Sarah. *Gimme a Call* (7–10). 2010, Delacorte $17.99 (978-0-385-73588-9); LB $20.99 (978-0-385-90574-9). When Devi's boyfriend dumps her just before senior prom, she decides to rewrite her own present by summoning her 14-year-old self and attempting to avert her current problems from happening in this light novel with a time travel twist. ∩ e Lexile HL440L (Rev: BL 3/1/10; SLJ 3/10; VOYA 10/10)

2939 Modesitt, L. E., Jr. *Natural Ordermage* (9–12). 2007, Tor $27.95 (978-0-7653-1813-8). Part of the Recluce series, this novel follows Rahl and his adventures in the evil empire of Hamor. (Rev: BL 9/1/07)

2940 Modesitt, L. E., Jr. *Ordermaster* (9–12). Series: Recluce. 2005, Tor $27.95 (978-0-7653-1213-6). Lord Kharl nobly strives to maintain harmony in both his adoptive land and his homeland in this entry in the series. (Rev: BL 1/1–15/05)

2941 Modesitt, L. E., Jr. *The Soprano Sorceress* (9–12). 1997, Tor $25.95 (978-0-312-86022-6). Anna is transported in time to the land of Erde, where she can use her beautiful voice to create magic. (Rev: BL 2/1/97; VOYA 10/97)

2942 Moers, Walter. *Rumo and His Miraculous Adventures* (9–12). Trans. by John Brownjohn. 2006, Overlook $25.95 (978-1-58567-725-2). Imaginative adventure of half-deer, half-wolf Rumo, the Wolperting, who goes up against the mad King of Hel and his clockwork army. (Rev: BL 7/06)

2943 Mont, Eve Marie. *A Breath of Eyre* (8–10). 2012, Kensington paper $9.95 (978-07582694-8-5). Modern-day teen Emma finds herself trapped inside Jane Eyre's body after a lightning strike. e (Rev: BL 4/15/12; SLJ 4/12; VOYA 6/12)

2944 Moon, Elizabeth. *Against the Odds* (10–12). Series: Familias Regnant. 2000, Baen $24.00 (978-0-671-31961-8). In this, the last of the Familias Regnant saga, Esmay and Barin defeat a mutiny by followers of their late Nazi-like leader. (Rev: BL 12/1/00)

2945 Moore, Perry. *Hero* (8–11). 2007, Hyperion $16.99 (978-1-4231-0195-6). Thom, who hides his developing superpowers and his homosexual feelings from his once superhero father, joins the League as an apprentice. (Rev: BL 8/07; HB 9–10/07; LMC 11/07; SLJ 9/07)

2946 Morden, Simon. *The Lost Art* (7–10). 2008, Random House $16.99 (978-0-385-75147-6). The world has entered a new dark age, with books and knowledge locked away, and it is up to Va and Benzamir Michael Mahmood to rescue them in this fantasy with action, suspense and romance. (Rev: BL 5/15/08; LMC 4–5/08; SLJ 11/08)

2947 Moriarty, Jaclyn. *A Corner of White* (7–11). 2013, Scholastic $17.99 (978-054539736-0). Fourteen-year-old Madeleine, who lives in Cambridge, England, with her mother, and 15-year-old Elliot, who lives in the Kingdom of Cello, find they can communicate with each other by letters through a crack between their worlds, and share their concerns about their families. Boston Globe–Horn Book Honor 2013. ∩ e Lexile 800L (Rev: BL 2/15/13; HB 5–6/13; LMC 8–9/13; SLJ 5/13*; VOYA 6/13)

2948 Moulton, Courtney Allison. *Wings of the Wicked* (10–12). 2012, HarperCollins $17.99 (978-006200236-5). Ellie, 17, is Archangel Gabriel reincarnated and experiences both romance with her Guardian and preparation for fierce battle against evil. e Lexile HL730L (Rev: BL 2/1/12; SLJ 4/12)

2949 Mourlevat, Jean-Claude. *Winter's End* (9–12). Trans. from French by Anthea Bell. 2009, Candlewick $17.99 (978-0-7636-4450-5). Four teenagers escape their repressive boarding schools and, pursued by terrifying dog-men, set out on a dangerous mission to avenge the deaths of their parents. (Rev: BL 12/15/09*; LMC 11–12/09; SLJ 12/09)

2950 Mullin, Caryl Cude. *Rough Magic* (7–10). 2009, Second Story paper $9.95 (978-1-897187-63-0). This fantasy based on Shakespeare's *The Tempest* is presented in five acts and tells the story of three generations of Caliban's family. Lexile HL610L (Rev: BL 8/09; LMC 3–4/10)

2951 Murdock, Catherine Gilbert. *Princess Ben* (8–11). 2008, Houghton Mifflin $16.00 (978-0-618-95971-6). The princess of the title (whose full name is Benevolence) must take on new responsibilities when her parents and her uncle are killed and she learns magic secrets. (Rev: BL 5/15/08; SLJ 6/08)

2952 Murphy, Shirley Rousseau. *Cat Raise the Dead* (9–12). 1997, HarperCollins paper $6.99 (978-0-06-105602-4). Two intrepid cats, Joe Grey and Dulcie, investigate some burglaries and several disappearances at an old folks home in their seaside village in California. (Rev: VOYA 2/98)

2953 Myers, John Myers. *Silverlock and the Silverlock Companion* (10–12). 2004, NESFA $26.00 (978-1-886778-52-8). Silverlock voyages in the Commonwealth of Letters where he meets Orpheus, visits hell, and hears about the Alamo. (Rev: BL 3/15/04)

2954 Nance, Kathleen. *Spellbound* (11–12). 2003, Spell paper $6.99 (978-0-505-52486-7). In a romantic fan-

167

tasy set in New Orleans, Madeline meets a seductive minstrel from the land of Kaf; suitable for mature readers. (Rev: BL 6/1–15/03)

2955 Napoli, Donna Jo. *The Wager* (8–12). 2010, Henry Holt $16.99 (978-0-8050-8781-9). In 12th-century Sicily handsome Don Giovanni, 19, bets the devil he can go three years without bathing or changing his clothes; inspired by a traditional fairy tale. **e** Lexile HL580L (Rev: BL 5/1/10; HB 7–8/10; SLJ 5/10; VOYA 6/10)

2956 Neumeier, Rachel. *The City in the Lake* (8–11). 2008, Knopf $15.99 (978-0-375-84704-2). When Prince Cassiel disappears from the City in the Lake, so does the city's life and magic. Neill and Timou set off in search of him and learn about their heritage as they battle the forces that threaten the kingdom. (Rev: BL 5/15/08; SLJ 9/08)

2957 Nicholson, William. *Noman* (7–10). Series: Noble Warriors. 2008, Harcourt paper $14.00 (978-0-15-206005-3). In the third book of this unusually contemplative trilogy, Seeker, Morning Star and the Wildman search for a new leader. (Rev: BL 5/15/08; SLJ 8/08)

2958 Niffenegger, Audrey. *Her Fearful Symmetry* (11–12). 2009, Scribner $26.99 (978-143916539-3). When an aunt bequeaths 20-year-old twins Valentina and Julia a flat next to London's Highgate Cemetery, they become involved in an intricately woven tale of spirits, family secrets, and love lost and gained; for mature readers. ∩ (Rev: BL 9/09*)

2959 Niffenegger, Audrey. *The Three Incestuous Sisters* (11–12). 2005, Abrams $27.95 (978-0-8109-5927-9). For mature teens, this dark fairy tale about three sisters and the love affair that tears them apart is presented in a "novel in pictures." (Rev: BL 8/05) [813]

2960 Niffenegger, Audrey. *The Time Traveler's Wife* (11–12). 2003, MacAdam $25.00 (978-1-931561-46-4). An offbeat romance featuring a time-traveling husband and a normal wife who often find they are out of chronological order; for mature readers. (Rev: BL 9/1/03)

2961 Nigg, Joseph. *How to Raise and Keep a Dragon* (5–10). Illus. by Dan Malone. 2006, Barron's $18.99 (978-0-7641-5920-6). This whimsical guide to the care and feeding of dragons offers tips for selecting just the right type of dragon, finding the correct equipment and supplies, establishing good modes of communication, and training for competitions. (Rev: SLJ 11/06)

2962 Nix, Garth. *Superior Saturday* (8–11). Series: Keys to the Kingdom. 2008, Scholastic $17.99 (978-043970089-4). In this sixth installment in the series, Arthur is revealed as heir to the kingdom and must obtain the Sixth Key from the powerful Saturday in the face of many challenges. ∩ **e** Lexile 930L (Rev: BL 11/15/08; VOYA 8/08)

2963 Noel, Alyson. *Fated* (8–11). Series: Soul Seekers. 2012, St. Martin's/Griffin $18.99 (978-0-312-66485-5).

Daire, 16, learns the source of her bloody visions when she goes to live with her grandmother in Enchantment, New Mexico. ∩ **e** Lexile 1060L (Rev: BL 6/12; SLJ 7/12)

2964 Noël, Alyson. *Blue Moon* (8–11). Series: The Immortals. 2009, St. Martin's paper $9.99 (978-031253276-5). In this sequel to *Evermore* (2008), 600-year-old Damen's powers are weakening and 16-year-old Ever knows she must save him from the evil perpetrated by the newly arrived Roman. ∩ (Rev: BL 7/09)

2965 Noël, Alyson. *Evermore* (8–10). Series: The Immortals. 2009, St. Martin's $8.95 (978-031253275-8). The first book in the Immortals series introduces Ever, who finds she has supernatural powers as a result of the car crash that killed the rest of her family. Lexile 940L (Rev: BL 2/1/09; SLJ 4/1/09)

2966 Noël, Alyson. *Shadowland* (8–11). Series: The Immortals. 2009, St. Martin's $17.99 (978-0-312-59044-4). Girlfriend (Ever) and boyfriend (Damen) have achieved immortality but at a cost — they are never allowed to touch each other. Lexile 960L (Rev: BLO 11/17/09; SLJ 2/10)

2967 North, Pearl. *Libyrinth* (8–11). 2009, Tor $17.95 (978-076532096-4). In a distant future, Haly, who has the ability to hear books, finds herself between competing forces: the Libyrarians, who protect and preserve ancient books, and the Eradicants, who seek to destroy the printed word. (Rev: BLO 6/17/09; LMC 11–12/09; SLJ 9/09)

2968 Norton, Andre, and Jean Rabe. *A Taste of Magic* (9–12). 2006, Tor $24.95 (978-0-7653-1527-4). After the murder of their entire village, two youngsters set out to find the nobleman who endorsed the killing in this fantasy. (Rev: BL 11/15/06)

2969 Norton, Andre, and Lyn McConchie. *Ciara's Song: A Chronicle of Witch World* (9–12). 1998, Warner paper $6.50 (978-0-446-60644-8). After her family, which has a witch ancestry, is murdered by a mob, Ciara is raised by the powerful Tarnoor, and under his protection she discovers her magical healing powers and dangers that they hold for her. (Rev: BL 6/1–15/98; VOYA 12/98)

2970 Novik, Naomi. *Tongues of Serpents* (10–12). Series: Temeraire. 2010, Del Rey $25 (978-034549689-8). In this sixth installment of Novik's fantastical series, Temeraire and Laurence find themselves embroiled in a mission to safely transport dragon eggs through a land fraught with mutiny, betrayal, and thievery. ∩ (Rev: BL 6/1–15/10)

2971 Nylund, Eric. *All That Lives Must Die* (10–12). 2010, Tor paper $14.99 (978-07653230-4-0). Twins Eliot and Fiona — part devil, part deity — attend the challenging Paxington Institute and hone their powers as danger and intrigue surround them; a sequel to *Mortal Coils* (2009). (Rev: BL 7/10)

2972 Oliver, Lauren. *Pandemonium* (9–12). 2012, HarperCollins $17.99 (978-0061978-06-7). Grieving for her lost love Alex (*Delirium*, 2011), Lena is settling in among the Invalids who live in the Wilds when she meets Julian and happiness seems to be again within reach. ♩ **e** Lexile 760L (Rev: BL 11/1/11; HB 3–4/12; SLJ 3/12)

2973 Omololu, C. J. *Transcendence* (9–12). 2012, Walker $16.99 (978-080272370-3). A teen cello prodigy begins experiencing crippling visions in this foreboding supernatural mystery. **e** (Rev: BL 8/12; SLJ 6/12; VOYA 6/12)

2974 Oppel, Kenneth. *Starclimber* (6–10). 2009, HarperTeen $17.99 (978-006085057-9); LB $18.89 (978-006085058-6). Matt and Kate rocket into space aboard a Canadian spaceship in this exciting sequel to *Airborn* (2004) and *Skybreaker* (2005). **e** (Rev: BLO 6/16/09; SLJ 6/1/09*)

2975 Orgel, Doris. *The Princess and the God* (7–10). 1996, Orchard LB $16.99 (978-0-531-08866-1). A handsome retelling of the Cupid and Psyche myth in novel format, in which the power of pure love is shown conquering overwhelming obstacles. (Rev: BL 2/1/96; SLJ 4/96)

2976 Orwell, George. *Animal Farm* (9–12). 1983, NAL paper $9.99 (978-0-451-52634-2). A fantasy of world politics in which farm animals revolt to form a society in which everyone is meant to be equal.

2977 Owen, James A. *Here, There Be Dragons* (8–11). Series: Chronicles of Imaginarium Geographica. 2006, Simon & Schuster $9.99 (978-1-4169-1227-9). John, Jack, and Charles — English intellectuals who will one day be known as J. R. R. Tolkien, C. S. Lewis, and Charles Williams — sail to the Archipelago of Dreams to defeat the Winter King. (Rev: BL 12/15/06; LMC 2/07; SLJ 11/06)

2978 Owen, James A. *The Search for the Red Dragon* (8–11). Illus. by author. Series: Chronicles of the Imaginarium Geographica. 2008, Simon & Schuster $17.99 (978-1-4169-4850-6). In this sequel to *Here, There Be Dragons*, the caretakers of the Imaginarium must solve the mystery behind the disappearance of the Archipelago's children. (Rev: BL 4/15/08; SLJ 2/08)

2979 Page, Jan. *Rewind* (7–10). 2005, Walker $16.95 (978-0-8027-8995-2). When he is injured in an accident while playing drums onstage, Liam finds himself back in time watching his parents as teenagers, when they had a band whose drummer was killed. (Rev: BL 9/1/05; SLJ 11/05; VOYA 10/05)

2980 Palmer, Robin. *Little Miss Red* (7–11). 2010, Penguin paper $7.99 (978-0-14-241123-0). A frothy romantic fairy tale in which 16-year-old, Jewish Sophie, on her way to visit her grandmother in Florida, meets bad boy Jack, who is charming but somehow scary. Lexile 890L (Rev: BL 2/1/10; SLJ 2/10; VOYA 4/10)

2981 Paolini, Christopher. *Eldest* (8–11). Series: Inheritance. 2005, Knopf LB $24.99 (978-0-375-92670-9). Eragon continues his training as a Dragon Rider while his cousin Roran is under threat in this second installment in the trilogy. (Rev: BL 8/05; SLJ 10/05; VOYA 12/05)

2982 Paolini, Christopher. *Eragon* (7–12). Series: Inheritance. 2003, Knopf LB $20.99 (978-0-375-92668-6). A 15-year-old boy called Eragon finds a stone that hatches a magnificent blue dragon, drawing him into a series of dangerous adventures as the two hunt killers and in turn are hunted. (Rev: BL 8/03*; HBG 4/04; SLJ 9/03; VOYA 8/03)

2983 Paolini, Christopher. *Inheritance* (7–12). Series: Inheritance Cycle. 2011, Knopf $27.99 (978-037585611-2); LB $30.99 (978-037595611-9). Young Dragon Rider Eragon is forced to do battle with King Galbatorix in order to free Alagaesia in this lengthy final volume in the series. YALSA Amazing Audiobooks Top Ten 2013. ♩ **e** Lexile 1010L (Rev: BLO 11/1/11)

2984 Papademetriou, Lisa. *Siren's Storm* (9–12). 2011, Knopf $15.99 (978-037584245-0); LB $18.99 (978-037594245-7). Danger and mystery lurk even as 17-year-old Will mourns the death of his brother and is captivated by otherworldly newcomer Asia. (Rev: BL 8/11; SLJ 1/12; VOYA 8/01)

2985 Park, Paul. *A Princess of Roumania* (9–12). 2005, Tor $24.95 (978-0-7653-1096-5). Miranda, a princess of an alternate Romania, is sent by her aunt Aegypt to grow up in safety in contemporary Massachusetts, but the evil Baroness Ceaucescu's pursuit does not end and Miranda must travel through time and confront danger. (Rev: BL 7/05)

2986 Parks, Richard. *The Long Look* (10–12). 2008, Five Star $25.95 (978-159414704-3). The evil magician is not who he seems to be in this entertaining story of one man's attempt to change the future. (Rev: BL 9/1/08)

2987 Patterson, James. *Maximum Ride: School's Out — Forever* (7–10). 2006, Little, Brown $16.99 (978-0-316-15559-5). In this sequel to *The Angel Experiment* (2004), Max and her fellow bird-humans try to integrate into mainstream society but must overcome unexpected danger and betrayal. (Rev: BL 5/15/06; SLJ 8/06)

2988 Patton, Fiona. *The Golden Sword* (10–12). 2001, DAW paper $6.99 (978-0-88677-921-4). Four cousins organize a conspiracy that threatens to bring down the kingdom's ruling family in this well-told fantasy. (Rev: BL 8/01; VOYA 12/01)

2989 Pattou, Edith. *East* (6–10). 2003, Harcourt $18.00 (978-0-15-204563-0). A great white bear carries Rose away from home to her destiny in this romantic novelization of the East o' the Sun and West o' the Moon fairy tale. (Rev: BL 9/1/03*; HBG 4/04; SLJ 12/03; VOYA 12/03)

2990 Pauley, Kimberly. *Cat Girl's Day Off* (7–10). 2012, Lee & Low $17.95 (978-160060883-4). Natalie uses her ability to communicate with cats to solve a criminal celebrity impersonation case. **e** Lexile 660L (Rev: BL 5/1/12; SLJ 4/12; VOYA 6/12)

2991 Pauley, Kimberly. *Sucks to Be Me: The All-True Confessions of Mina Hamilton, Teen Vampire (Maybe)* (7–10). 2008, Mirrorstone $14.95 (978-078695028-7). Sixteen-year-old Mina must decide between staying human and becoming a vampire in this light, often funny story. **e** Lexile HL740L (Rev: BL 11/15/08; VOYA 10/08)

2992 Peacock, Kathleen. *Hemlock* (9–12). 2012, HarperCollins $17.99 (978-0-06-204865-3). While attempting to solve her best friend's murder, high school senior Mackenzie becomes haunted by ghosts and wary of the dangerous werewolf virus that has infected her town. **e** (Rev: BL 5/1/12; SLJ 7/12; VOYA 4/12)

2993 Pearce, Jackson. *As You Wish* (8–10). 2009, HarperTeen $16.99 (978-006166152-5). Upset when her boyfriend declares that he is gay, 16-year-old Viola accidentally summons a genie and her wish to be popular comes true. But does she prefer the genie to her new status? (Rev: BLO 5/15/09; SLJ 1/10; VOYA 8/09)

2994 Pearce, Jackson. *Fathomless* (8–11). 2012, Little, Brown $17.99 (978-0-316-20778-2). This dark remake of Hans Christian Andersen's "Little Mermaid" features Celia, a triplet who can read people's pasts, and a mermaid named Lo. **e** (Rev: BL 10/1/12; LMC 3–4/13; SLJ 12/12; VOYA 10/12)

2995 Peck, Dale. *The Drift House: The First Voyage* (8–11). 2005, Bloomsbury $16.95 (978-1-58234-969-5). The Oakenfield siblings are sent to live with their Uncle Farley in Canada, and when their uncle's ship-like home is swept away in a flood, they enjoy a magical journey on the Sea of Time. (Rev: BL 10/1/05; SLJ 11/05; VOYA 10/05)

2996 Peck, Dale. *The Lost Cities: A Drift House Voyage* (8–11). 2007, Bloomsbury $16.95 (978-1-58234-859-9). Siblings Susan and Charles, who first traveled the Sea of Time in *The Drift House: The First Voyage* (2005), are afloat again in this action-packed sequel, this time battling Vikings and a time jetty. (Rev: BL 4/1/07; SLJ 4/07)

2997 Peterfreund, Diana. *Rampant* (9–12). 2009, HarperTeen $17.99 (978-0-06-149000-2). Astrid learns she is destined to be a unicorn hunter, a dangerous and crucial calling that requires she remain a virgin. **e** Lexile 750L (Rev: BL 10/7/09; SLJ 8/09; VOYA 6/09)

2998 Pierce, Tamora. *Cold Fire* (6–10). Series: The Circle Opens. 2002, Scholastic $16.95 (978-0-590-39655-4). Daja is studying in the chilly northern city of Kugisko, where her ability to handle fire comes in handy but also draws her into a relationship with an arsonist.

(Rev: BL 9/1/02; HB 7–8/02; HBG 10/02; SLJ 8/02; VOYA 6/02)

2999 Pierce, Tamora. *Melting Stones* (6–10). 2008, Scholastic $17.99 (978-054505264-1). Evvy helps to save the Battle Islands from mysterious environmental ailments by using her magical powers. Ω **e** Lexile 590L (Rev: BLO 5/27/09; LMC 5–6/09; SLJ 12/08; VOYA 12/08)

3000 Pierce, Tamora. *Terrier* (7–10). 2006, Random House $18.95 (978-0-375-81468-6). Sixteen-year-old orphan Beka Cooper becomes a trainee (or Puppy) with the city guards (Dogs) and uses her magical abilities to good effect, relating her exploits in her journal. (Rev: BL 11/15/06; HB 1–2/07; SLJ 2/07*)

3001 Pierce, Tamora. *Trickster's Queen* (7–12). 2004, Random House LB $19.99 (978-0-375-81467-9). In this thrilling sequel to *Trickster's Choice*, Aly must call upon her magical powers to protect the Balitang children and ensure that one of them — Dove — ascends to the throne of the Copper Isles. (Rev: BCCB 10/04; BL 10/1/04; SLJ 9/04; VOYA 2/05)

3002 Pierce, Tamora. *The Will of the Empress* (8–11). 2005, Scholastic $17.99 (978-0-439-44171-1). Bowing to the will of the Empress of Namorn, Sandry, accompanied by her mage friends from the Winding Circle, embarks on a perilous journey to visit her cousin, the empress; this stand-alone novel comes after the Circle of Magic and The Circle Opens quartets. (Rev: BCCB 1/06; BL 11/15/05*; HB 11–12/05; SLJ 11/05; VOYA 10/05)

3003 Pike, Aprilynne. *Spells* (7–10). 2010, HarperTeen $16.99 (978-0-06-166806-7). In this sequel to *Wings* (2009), 16-year-old Laurel is studying at the faerie academy and feeling tensions between her two worlds and her romantic relationships. Ω (Rev: BL 3/15/10*; SLJ 8/10; VOYA 8/10)

3004 Plum, Amy. *Until I Die* (8–11). Series: Revenant Trilogy. 2012, HarperTeen $17.99 (978-006200404-8). In Paris, Kate and Vincent work against a dangerous supernatural power to maintain their affection for each other in this sequel to *Die for Me* (2011). Ω **e** (Rev: BLO 4/1/12; SLJ 6/12; VOYA 4/12)

3005 Pon, Cindy. *Silver Phoenix: Beyond the Kingdom of Xia* (9–12). 2009, Greenwillow $17.99 (978-006173021-4). Ai Ling faces danger as she searches for her missing father in this otherworldly adventure set in ancient China. Lexile 760L (Rev: BL 4/1/09*; SLJ 12/09)

3006 Popescu, Petru. *Birth of the Pack* (8–11). Series: Weregirls. 2007, Tor $12.95 (978-0-7653-1641-7). The members of the Weregirls soccer team find that they have magical powers to fight evil — and the mean girls at school. (Rev: BL 10/1/07; LMC 1/08; SLJ 12/07)

3007 Porter, Sarah. *Lost Voices* (7–10). 2011, Harcourt $16.99 (978-0-547-48250-7). During an attack by her abusive uncle, 14-year-old Luce falls from a cliff in an Alaskan fishing village and becomes a mermaid; in her new life she finds friendship but also horror as she learns how the mermaids extract vengeance against the humans who hurt them. ♩ ℮ Lexile 880L (Rev: BL 5/1/11; LMC 10/11*; SLJ 8/11; VOYA 10/12)

3008 Porter, Tracey. *Lark* (8–11). 2011, HarperTeen $15.99 (978-0-06-112287-3). After being kidnapped, raped, and murdered, 16-year-old Lark finds herself in limbo and seeks help from a young girl named Nyetta, who teams up with Lark's friend Eve and Eve's boyfriend. ℮ (Rev: BL 6/1/11; HB 5–6/11; LMC 8–9/11; SLJ 8/11; VOYA 8/11)

3009 Powell, Laura. *Burn Marks* (7–12). 2012, Bloomsbury $17.99 (978-1-59990-843-4). A story of discrimination against witchcraft set in an alternate London, England, and involving two teens from very different backgrounds. ℮ Lexile 770L (Rev: SLJ 7/12; VOYA 6/13)

3010 Pratchett, Terry. *A Hat Full of Sky* (6–10). 2004, HarperCollins $16.99 (978-0-06-058660-7). Witch-in-training Tiffany Aching battles a monster with help from the wee men and head witch Granny Weatherwax in the sequel to *The Wee Free Men*. Margaret A. Edwards Award 2011. (Rev: BCCB 5/04; BL 4/15/04; HB 7–8/04; SLJ 7/04; VOYA 6/04)

3011 Pratchett, Terry. *Unseen Academicals* (10–12). Series: Discworld. 2009, HarperCollins $25.99 (978-006116170-4). This fantasy is a humorous story of an unlikely group from Unseen University who are forced to learn how to play football. ♩ ℮ (Rev: BL 9/09)

3012 Pratchett, Terry. *Wintersmith* (7–10). 2006, HarperTempest $16.99 (978-0-06-089031-5). Tiffany Aching, a 13-year-old witch, must find a way to bring back spring, with the help of her friends the Wee Free Men, after the god of winter falls in love with her and will do anything to keep her in his frozen world. (Rev: BL 9/1/06; SLJ 11/06)

3013 Priest, Cherie. *Four and Twenty Blackbirds* (10–12). 2005, Tor paper $13.95 (978-0-7653-1308-9). In this chilling contemporary spin on the southern gothic novel, Eden, a girl of mixed race, leaves the Tennessee mountains where she's lived with her aunt and uncle and sets off on a journey to learn more about her familial roots. (Rev: BL 10/1/05)

3014 Priest, Cherie. *Wings to the Kingdom* (10–12). 2006, Tor paper $14.95 (978-0-7653-1309-6). Eden Moore tries to find out why all the ghosts at a local Civil War battlefield in Georgia are pointing at something in the distance in this sequel to *Four and Twenty Blackbirds* (2005). (Rev: BL 10/1/06)

3015 Pullman, Philip. *The Amber Spyglass* (7–12). Series: His Dark Materials. 2000, Knopf $19.95 (978-0-679-87926-8). Lyra and Will are key figures in the battle between good and evil in this final volume in

the prize-winning trilogy. (Rev: BL 10/1/00; HB 11–12/00; HBG 3/01; SLJ 10/00)

3016 Pullman, Philip. *The Golden Compass* (7–12). Series: His Dark Materials. 1996, Knopf $20.00 (978-0-679-87924-4). In this first book of a fantasy trilogy, young Lyra and her alter ego, a protective animal named Pantalaimon, escape from the child-stealing Gobblers and join a group heading north to rescue a band of missing children. (Rev: BL 3/1/96*; SLJ 4/96)

3017 Pullman, Philip. *Once Upon a Time in the North* (7–10). Illus. by John Lawrence. Series: His Dark Materials. 2008, Knopf $12.99 (978-0-375-84510-9). The story of how Lee Scoresby and bear Iorke Byrnison — of the His Dark Materials trilogy — met for the first time in an arctic frontier town; a board game is included with the book. ♩ (Rev: BL 5/15/08; LMC 10/08; SLJ 8/08; VOYA 4/08)

3018 Pullman, Philip. *The Subtle Knife* (7–12). Series: His Dark Materials. 1997, Random House $20.00 (978-0-679-87925-1). In this second volume of a trilogy, Will and Lyra travel from world to world searching for the mysterious Dust and Will's long-lost father. (Rev: BL 7/97; HBG 3/98; SLJ 10/97)

3019 Raedeke, Christy. *The Daykeeper's Grimoire* (7–10). Series: Prophecy of Days. 2010, Flux paper $9.95 (978-0-73871-576-6). Caity decodes a message she finds in a room in her parents' Scottish castle and is sent on a crucial mission that takes her around the world. ℮ (Rev: BL 5/15/10; LMC 8–9/10; SLJ 11/1/10)

3020 Randall, David. *Chandlefort: In the Shadow of the Bear* (7–12). 2006, Simon & Schuster $16.95 (978-0-689-87870-1). In this sequel to *Clovermead* (2004), the title character discovers she is really the royal Demoiselle Cerelune Cindertallow and the 13-year-old must learn a whole new way of living; a complex and multilayered fantasy. (Rev: SLJ 7/07)

3021 Randall, David. *Sorrel* (9–12). Series: In the Shadow of the Bear. 2007, Simon & Schuster $16.99 (978-0-689-87872-5). The further adventures of shape-shifting Clovermead, now 15, who sets off with Sorrel to fight Lord Ursus and his bear-priests. (Rev: BL 11/15/07; SLJ 2/08)

3022 Rapp, Adam. *The Copper Elephant* (9–12). 1999, Front St $16.95 (978-1-886910-42-3). In this fantasy set in a future world of chaos, Whensday Bluehouse manages to avoid dying in the mines where children work as slaves, but life on the run is dangerous and difficult. (Rev: BL 11/15/99; HB 1–2/00; HBG 4/00; SLJ 12/99; VOYA 4/00)

3023 Reeve, Philip. *A Darkling Plain* (7–10). Series: The Hungry City Chronicles. 2007, Eos $18.99 (978-0-06-089055-1). Cities are still gobbling one another up in this final installment in the Hungry City Chronicles, and the reappearance of the Stalker Fang threatens all human beings on Earth. (Rev: BL 7/07; HB 9–10/07; SLJ 6/07)

3024 Reilly, Matthew. *The 6 Sacred Stones* (9–12). 2008, Simon & Schuster $25.00 (978-0-7432-7054-0). Super-soldier Jack West Jr. and his team of adventurers are on a worldwide quest to locate the clue-holding Six Sacred Stones before Armageddon occurs, venturing to ancient sites from England's Stonehenge to sub-Saharan Africa to Three Gorges in China and engaging in action-packed adventures. (Rev: BL 12/15/07)

3025 Reiss, Kathryn. *Pale Phoenix* (7–10). 1994, Harcourt paper $3.95 (978-0-15-200031-8). Miranda Browne's parents take in an orphan girl who can disappear at will and who was the victim of a tragedy in a past life in Puritan Massachusetts. (Rev: BL 3/15/94; SLJ 5/94; VOYA 6/94)

3026 Rhodes, Jenna. *The Four Forges* (9–12). Series: The Elven Ways. 2006, DAW $23.95 (978-0-7564-0274-7). Elven groups are feuding, and escaped slave Grace and mixed-race Sevryn come together to fight the evil that is behind it all. (Rev: BL 5/15/06)

3027 Rhodes, Morgan. *Falling Kingdoms* (7–12). 2012, Penguin $18.99 (978-159514584-0). Princess Cleo finds she holds the fate of three kingdoms in her hands. ◯ ℮ (Rev: BL 10/15/12; LMC 1–2/13; SLJ 3/13)

3028 Rice, Patricia. *Mystic Warrior* (11–12). Series: Mystic Isle. 2009, Signet paper $7.99 (978-04512274-7-8). A misfit warrior with supernatural powers tries to control his anger, which has dire consequences for his surroundings. (Rev: BLO 7/09)

3029 Roberson, Jennifer. *Karavans* (9–12). 2006, DAW $25.95 (978-0-7564-0172-6). This is the well-written story of Audrun, whose family joins a "karavan" of refugees fleeing ruthless conquerors only to find themselves on the edge of even more danger. (Rev: BL 4/15/06)

3030 Roberts, Nora. *Key of Valor* (11–12). Series: Key Trilogy. 2004, Penguin paper $7.99 (978-0-515-13653-1). In the final book of a recommended trilogy that mixes romance and fantasy, plucky hairdresser Zoe Mc-Court seeks the final key needed to unlock the mystical box holding the souls of three Celtic demigoddesses; for mature teens. (Rev: BL 11/15/03; SLJ 3/04)

3031 Roberts, Nora, et al. *Once Upon a Rose* (10–12). 2001, Jove paper $7.99 (978-0-515-13166-6). An evil sorceress, a princess, a mute girl in war-torn Scotland, and a kingdom imprisoned in ice figure in the four novellas collected here by four different authors. (Rev: BL 10/1/01)

3032 Rochelle, Warren. *The Wild Boy* (10–12). 2001, Golden Gryphon $22.95 (978-1-930846-04-3). When the space-faring Lindauzi lose their companion race to the plague, the Crown Prince sets out to find a replacement species. (Rev: BL 8/01)

3033 Rogers, Mark E. *Samurai Cat Goes to the Movies* (9–12). 1994, Tor paper $10.95 (978-0-312-85744-8). Japanese feline Miowara and his nephew, Shiro, take on Hollywood and satirize assorted film classics. (Rev: BL 9/15/94; VOYA 4/95)

3034 Rossetti, Rinsai. *The Girl with Borrowed Wings* (7–12). 2012, Dial $17.99 (978-0-8037-3566-8). A Free shape-shifter brings new options to 17-year-old Frenenqer's tightly controlled life. ℮ Lexile 680L (Rev: BL 9/15/12*; HB 7–8/12; SLJ 12/12; VOYA 8/12)

3035 Rowen, Michelle. *Reign Check* (7–10). Series: Demon Princess. 2010, Walker $16.99 (978-080272093-1). Nikki (half-human and half-demon princess) contends with the unsettling prophesy that she will destroy the world as she also discovers that her best friend is training as a demon-slayer and that the attractive foreign-exchange student is in fact the faery king; the sequel to *Reign or Shine* (2009). ℮ (Rev: BL 5/15/10; SLJ 8/10)

3036 Rowling, J. K. *Harry Potter and the Deathly Hallows* (6–12). Illus. by Mary GrandPré. 2007, Scholastic $34.99 (978-0-545-01022-1). The seventh and final book in the series ties up all the plot threads and ends with an epilogue updating readers on the main characters 19 years later. Odyssey Honor Recording 2008; ALA Notable Books 2008. ◯ (Rev: BCCB 10/07; BL 8/07*; HB 9–10/07; SLJ 9/07)

3037 Rowling, J. K. *Harry Potter and the Half-Blood Prince* (5–12). Illus. by Mary GrandPré. 2005, Scholastic LB $34.99 (978-0-439-78677-5). In this sixth and penultimate volume, Harry, now 16, begins mapping a strategy to defeat the evil Lord Voldemort. (Rev: BL 8/05*; SLJ 9/05; VOYA 10/05)

3038 Rowling, J. K. *Harry Potter and the Order of the Phoenix* (4–12). 2003, Scholastic LB $34.99 (978-0-439-56761-9). Adolescence, adult hypocrisy, and the deadly threat of Voldemort and his evil supporters combine to make Harry's fifth year at Hogwarts as eventful as ever. (Rev: BL 7/03; HB 9–10/03; HBG 10/03; SLJ 8/03; VOYA 8/03)

3039 Russell, Barbara T. *The Taker's Stone* (7–12). 1999, DK $16.95 (978-1-78942-568-0). When 14-year-old Fischer steals some glowing red gemstones from a man at a campsite, he unleashes the terrible evil of Belial, some catastrophic weather, and the beginning of the end of the world. (Rev: VOYA 10/99)

3040 Russell, Randy. *Dead Rules* (9–12). 2011, HarperTeen $16.99 (978-0-06-198670-3). In this dark paranormal romance, Jana has died in a freak bowling accident and is now attending Dead School; how can she get her boyfriend Michael to join her? ℮ (Rev: BL 5/1/11; SLJ 8/11)

3041 Russon, Penni. *Breathe* (9–12). 2007, Greenwillow $16.99 (978-0-06-079393-7). In this sequel to *Undine* (2006), Undine struggles with her magical power and travels to Greece, where she learns more about her heritage. 🎧 (Rev: BL 2/15/07; HB 3–4/07; SLJ 1/07)

3042 Russon, Penni. *Undine* (9–12). 2006, Greenwillow LB $17.89 (978-0-06-079390-6). Not only does 16-year-old Undine have strange powers but she receives strange messages; with her friend Trout, she finds a link with *The Tempest* and sets off for the sea to find answers to her questions. (Rev: BL 2/15/06; SLJ 2/06*; VOYA 2/06)

3043 Saberhagen, Fred. *Gods of Fire and Thunder* (10–12). Series: Books of the Gods. 2002, Tor $24.95 (978-0-7653-0201-4). Saberhagen revisits Norse myths involving Valhalla in this installment in the series. (Rev: BL 8/02)

3044 Salvatore, R. A. *The Ancient* (9–12). 2008, Tor $25.95 (978-0-7653-1789-6). Reclusive young Bransen Garibond is searching for his father when he is drafted into the war against the villainous Ancient Baden. (Rev: BL 3/15/08)

3045 Salvatore, R. A. *Promise of the Witch-King* (9–12). 2005, Wizards of the Coast $27.95 (978-1-78693-823-7). In this sequel to *Servant of the Shard*, Jarlaxle Baenre, a dark elf, and Artemis Entreri, a human assassin wielding a vampire sword, team up to search for the source of the power of the Witch-King Zhengyi. (Rev: BL 10/15/05)

3046 Sanderson, Brandon. *Mistborn: The Final Empire* (9–12). 2006, Tor $27.95 (978-0-7653-1178-8). This coming-of-age fantasy features intrigue and action as the hero Kelsior plots his raid into the center of the Lord Ruler's palace to uncover the source of the evil one's power. (Rev: BL 7/06)

3047 Sanderson, Brandon. *The Well of Ascension* (9–12). 2007, Tor $27.95 (978-0-7653-1688-2). This exciting middle volume of the Mistborn trilogy features new ruler Vin and his tenuous hold on power. (Rev: BL 8/07)

3048 Sargent, Pamela. *Farseed* (7–10). Series: Seed Trilogy. 2007, Tor $17.95 (978-0-7653-1427-7). The offspring of the genetically engineered humans sent to the planet Home to create a new society have split into two factions in this second book in the trilogy. (Rev: BL 3/15/07; LMC 11–12/07; SLJ 10/07)

3049 Schultz, Mark. *Dinosaur Shaman: Nine Tales from the Xenozoic Age* (9–12). 1990, Kitchen Sink $29.95 (978-0-87816-117-1). These stories are set in the Xenozoic Age — a future time when humans and prehistoric beasts coexist — and describe the further adventures of Jack Tennrec and Hannah Dundee. (Rev: BL 9/1/91)

3050 Schwab, Victoria. *The Near Witch* (9–12). 2011, Hyperion $16.99 (978-1-4231-3787-0). When the children of the village of Near start to disappear, 16-year-old Lexi sets out to find the truth. ℮ Lexile 760L (Rev: BL 9/15/11; HB 9–10/11; SLJ 12/1/11; VOYA 10/11)

3051 Scott, Michael. *The Alchemyst: The Secrets of the Immortal Nicholas Flamel* (7–12). 2007, Delacorte $16.99 (978-0-385-73357-1). Fifteen-year-old twins Sophie and Josh find themselves caught up in a deadly, ancient struggle over a Codex, the Book of Abraham the Mage, that holds the promise of eternal youth. 🎧 (Rev: BL 5/1/07; LMC 10/07; SLJ 5/07)

3052 Scott, Michael. *The Necromancer* (8–12). Series: The Secrets of the Immortal Nicholas Flamel. 2010, Delacorte $18.99 (978-038573531-5); LB $21.99 (978-038590516-9). In this fourth, action-packed installment, twins Sophie and Josh help the dying Nicholas Flamel and his wife in their efforts to contain the monsters living on Alcatraz. 🎧 ℮ Lexile 780L (Rev: BLO 6/10; SLJ 8/10; VOYA 8/10)

3053 Scott, Michael. *The Sorceress* (7–10). Series: The Secrets of the Immortal Nicholas Flamel. 2009, Delacorte $17.99 (978-038573529-2); LB $20.99 (978-038590515-2). Twins Josh and Sophie, along with Nicolas Flamel, are still on the run in this third book in the series. Shakespeare, Billy the Kid, and Gilgamesh are some of the characters that pop up along the journey. Lexile 840L (Rev: BLO 4/24/09; SLJ 7/1/09)

3054 Selfors, Suzanne. *Coffeehouse Angel* (7–10). 2009, Walker $16.99 (978-0-8027-9812-1). Katrina helps a young man who turns out to be an angel, ready to grant her her heart's desire . . . once she figures out what that is. ℮ Lexile HL620L (Rev: BL 9/15/09; SLJ 8/09; VOYA 12/09)

3055 Selfors, Suzanne. *Saving Juliet* (7–10). 2008, Walker $16.95 (978-0-8027-9740-7). Mimi, a reluctant actress in her family's theater, is transported to medieval Verona, where she meets the real Juliet (and her Romeo). (Rev: BL 1/1–15/08; LMC 2/08; SLJ 3/08)

3056 Selfors, Suzanne. *The Sweetest Spell* (8–11). 2012, Walker $16.99 (978-0-8027-2376-5). Outcast Emmeline's life changes when she discovers she possesses the ability to make chocolate. ℮ (Rev: BL 9/15/12; LMC 10/12; SLJ 9/12; VOYA 4/12)

3057 Selzer, Adam. *I Kissed a Zombie, and I Liked It* (9–12). 2010, Delacorte LB $12.99 (978-0-385-90497-1); paper $7.99 (978-0-385-73503-2). Ambitious 18-year-old Ally Rhodes resists the peer pressure to "convert" to vampirism but instead falls in love with a zombie musician named Doug in this witty romance. ℮ Lexile 820L (Rev: BL 4/15/10; SLJ 1/10)

3058 Severin, Tim. *Odinn's Child* (9–12). 2006, Trafalgar paper $12.50 (978-0-330-42673-2). Gifted with his mother's clairvoyance and schooled in the customs and religion of the Vikings, Thorgils, son of a Norse chieftain, fights to fulfill his destiny in a world split by historic feuds and the introduction of a new Christianity into a traditional pagan culture. (Rev: BL 7/06)

3059 Shan, Darren. *Lord of the Shadows* (5–10). Series: Cirque du Freak. 2006, Little, Brown $15.99 (978-0-

316-15628-8). In the 11th book in the series, part-vampire Darren faces off against Steve Leopard, leader of the Vampaneze, in a battle to determine who will be the next Lord of the Shadows. (Rev: SLJ 9/06)

3060 Shan, Darren. *The Thin Executioner* (9–12). 2010, Little, Brown $17.99 (978-0-316-07865-8). Hoping despite evidence to the contrary to become an executioner like his father, Jebel Rum undertakes a quest for invincibility and must face many violent challenges; he is accompanied by a slave called Tel Hasani whom he intends to sacrifice. **e** Lexile 850L (Rev: BL 7/10; LMC 10/10; SLJ 7/10; VOYA 12/10)

3061 Shaw, Ali. *The Girl with the Glass Feet* (10–12). 2010, Henry Holt $24 (978-080509114-4). Young Ida Maclaird realizes she is slowly turning to glass, and she and lonely Midas Crook become romantically involved as they seek a cure in this novel full of magical realism on remote islands. (Rev: BL 10/15/09)

3062 Shepherd, Megan. *The Madman's Daughter* (9–12). 2013, HarperCollins $17.99 (978-006212802-7). In this dark story based on H. G. Wells's *The Island of Dr. Moreau*, 16-year-old Juliet travels to her father's island and finds intrigue and romance. ☊ **e** (Rev: BL 10/15/12; SLJ 2/13*)

3063 Sherman, Delia. *The Freedom Maze* (7–10). 2011, Big Mouth paper $9.95 (978-19315203-0-0). In 1960, 13-year-old Sophie finds herself transported back to 1860 Louisiana and is mistaken for a slave. ☊ **e** (Rev: BLO 11/15/11; HB 1–2/12; VOYA 10/11)

3064 Sherman, Josepha. *Windleaf* (7–12). 1993, Walker $14.95 (978-0-8027-8259-5). Count Thierry falls in love with half-faerie Glinfinial, only to have her father, the Faerie Lord, steal her away. (Rev: BL 11/1/93*; SLJ 12/93; VOYA 2/94)

3065 Shetterly, Will. *Elsewhere* (8–12). 1991, Harcourt $16.95 (978-0-15-200731-7). Set in Bordertown, between the real world and Faerie world, home to runaway elves and humans, this is a fantasy of integration, survival, and coming of age. (Rev: BL 10/15/91; SLJ 11/91)

3066 Shetterly, Will. *Nevernever* (8–12). 1993, Tor paper $4.99 (978-0-8125-5151-8). This sequel to *Elsewhere* (1991) shows Wolfboy trying to protect Florida, the heir of Faerie, from gangs of Elves out to get her, while one of his friends is framed for murder. (Rev: BL 9/15/93; SLJ 10/93; VOYA 12/93)

3067 Shinn, Sharon. *The Dream-Maker's Magic* (7–10). 2006, Viking $16.99 (978-0-670-06070-2). In this novel set in the same world as *The Safe-Keeper's Secret* (2004) and *The Truth-Teller's Tale* (2005), Kellen, who was brought up as a boy, matures and offers comfort to her deformed and abused friend Gryffin who turns out to be the new Dream-Maker. (Rev: BL 5/15/06; SLJ 7/06)

3068 Shinn, Sharon. *Gateway* (9–12). 2009, Viking $17.99 (978-0-670-01178-0). Walking under the Gateway Arch in St. Louis, Chinese American teen Daiyu finds herself whisked away to a parallel world where she is given a dangerous task; this exciting fantasy is sprinkled with romance. (Rev: BL 9/15/09; LMC 11–12/09*; SLJ 12/09)

3069 Shinn, Sharon. *The Safe-Keeper's Secret* (7–12). 2004, Viking $16.99 (978-0-670-05910-2). Truth and justice are themes in this fantasy about Fiona, a girl whose family has many secrets, and Reed, a boy without an identity, who was left as a baby with Fiona's mother. (Rev: BL 4/15/04; SLJ 6/04; VOYA 6/04)

3070 Shinn, Sharon. *The Shape-Changer's Wife* (9–12). 1995, Ace paper $6.99 (978-0-441-00261-0). Apprentice wizard Aubrey falls in love with his master's wife but wonders if she is really only one of his master's shape changes. (Rev: VOYA 2/96)

3071 Shinn, Sharon. *The Truth-Teller's Tale* (7–10). 2005, Viking $16.99 (978-0-670-06000-9). Twin sisters Eleda and Adele are mirror images — Eleda can neither tell nor hear a lie, while Adele can be trusted to keep secret anything she is told. (Rev: BCCB 9/05; BL 4/15/05*; SLJ 7/05; VOYA 8/05)

3072 Shirvington, Jessica. *Embrace* (10–12). 2012, Sourcebooks $16.99 (978-140226840-3). Violet, 17, finds herself in the midst of a sexually charged battle between good and evil in this story for mature readers. ☊ **e** Lexile HL670L (Rev: BL 3/1/12; SLJ 4/12; VOYA 2/12)

3073 Shirvington, Jessica. *Entice* (10–12). 2012, Sourcebooks $16.99 (978-1-4022-6843-4). Half-human, half-angel Violet, 17, tries to concentrate on her training when her old adversary Phoenix shows up, threatening to derail the relationships she's forged in his absence, especially with the attractive Lincoln. ☊ **e** Lexile HL720L (Rev: BL 11/1/12; SLJ 11/12; VOYA 12/12)

3074 Showalter, Gena. *Alice in Zombieland* (7–12). 2012, HarlequinTeen $18.99 (978-037321058-9). On her 16th birthday, Alice learns that her father was right and zombies do exist and she must avenge her family. ☊ **e** (Rev: BL 10/15/12)

3075 Showalter, Gena. *Intertwined* (7–10). 2009, Harlequin $15.99 (978-0-373-21002-2). Misdiagnosed as a schizophrenic, 16-year-old Aden Stone in fact has four souls with special powers living inside his body the complex plot involves vampires, werewolves, assorted magical beings, and a touch of romance. (Rev: BL 9/15/09; SLJ 12/09)

3076 Shusterman, Neal. *Duckling Ugly* (7–10). Series: Dark Fusion. 2006, Dutton $15.99 (978-0-525-47585-9). Apart from her ability to spell, Cara DeFido has no known attributes until she finds herself in a magic kingdom; her successes there prompt her to return home, however. (Rev: BL 2/1/06; SLJ 7/06)

3077 Shusterman, Neal. *Everwild* (7–10). Series: The Skinjacker Trilogy. 2009, Simon & Schuster $16.99 (978-1-4169-5863-5). Allie, Nick, and Mikey split up to pursue different and dangerous avenues in their quest to help the children of Everlost. (Rev: BLO 11/5/09; SLJ 12/09)

3078 Shwartz, Susan. *Suppose They Gave a Peace and Other Stories* (10–12). 2002, Five Star $23.95 (978-0-7862-4166-8). Ten diverse short stories merge genres in an intriguing blend. (Rev: BL 6/1–15/02)

3079 Simner, Janni Lee. *Bones of Faerie* (7–10). 2009, Random House $16.99 (978-037584563-5); LB $19.99 (978-037594563-2). In a world devastated by a war between faeries and humans, 15-year-old Liza finds herself in danger when she discovers she's gained faerie powers. e Lexile HL670L (Rev: BL 12/1/08; LMC 5–6/09; SLJ 4/1/09)

3080 Simner, Janni Lee. *Faerie Winter* (8–11). 2011, Random House $16.99 (978-0-375-86671-5); LB $19.99 (978-0-375-96671-2). The war between the fairy and human worlds has resulted in disaster for both sides and Liza, 16, learns that she may be able to help by stopping the Faerie Queen's evil plot; the sequel to *Bones of Faerie* (2009). e Lexile HL680L (Rev: BL 6/1/11; SLJ 11/1/11; VOYA 8/11)

3081 Simner, Janni Lee. *Thief Eyes* (7–10). 2010, Random House $16.99 (978-0-375-86770-8). While in Iceland with her father, 16-year-old Haley discovers that she is related to the Hallgerd of Icelandic mythology and that this relationship is linked with her mother's disappearance. (Rev: BL 4/1/10; LMC 8–9/10; SLJ 5/10)

3082 Singleton, Sarah. *Out of the Shadows* (8–10). 2008, Clarion $16.00 (978-061892722-7). A complicated plot makes knowledge of the time period's political and religious scheming necessary to fully understand this tale of friendship between a time-traveling faerie girl and a young Catholic teen in Elizabethan England. Lexile 770L (Rev: BL 12/1/08; LMC 3–4/09; SLJ 6/1/09)

3083 Sinisalo, Johanna. *The Dedalus Book of Finnish Fantasy* (9–12). Trans. by David Hackston. 2006, Dedalus paper $15.99 (978-1-903517-29-1). A high caliber sampler of Finnish literary fantasy from 1870 to 2003. (Rev: BL 7/06)

3084 Slade, Arthur. *The Hunchback Assignments* (7–10). 2009, Random House $15.99 (978-0-385-73784-5); LB $18.99 (978-0-385-90694-4). A complex steampunk adventure set in Victorian London in which 14-year-old Modo, a shape-shifting hunchback, joins the Permanent Association, an organization formed to fight the evil Clockwork Guild. ∩ (Rev: BL 8/09; LMC 11–12/09; SLJ 12/09)

3085 Slater, Adam. *Hunted* (7–10). 2011, Egmont $16.99 (978-1-60684-261-4). The barrier between the human world and a threatening underworld is de-

teriorating, and 14-year-old Callum, who is a "chime child," must fulfill his destiny. e Lexile 750L (Rev: BL 11/15/11; SLJ 12/1/11; VOYA 10/11)

3086 Smith, Andrew. *Passenger* (10–12). 2012, Feiwel & Friends $17.99 (978-1-250-00487-1). Jack and his friends return to their dark and dangerous alternate world in this sequel to 2010's *The Marbury Lens*. e Lexile HL720L (Rev: BL 10/1/12*; HB 1–2/13; SLJ 10/12)

3087 Smith, L. J. *The Initiation and the Captive, Part 1* (7–10). Series: The Secret Circle. 2008, HarperTeen paper $8.99 (978-006167085-5). Cassie discovers that she is part witch — and that there are others like her — when she and her mother move to New Salem, Massachusetts. (Rev: BLO 3/5/09)

3088 Smith, Sherwood. *Coronets and Steel* (10–12). 2010, DAW $24.95 (978-075640642-4). This urbanfantasy fairy tale set in Eastern Europe follows the journey of 23-year-old Kim who, while exploring her grandmother's past, discovers her own power to see ghosts. e (Rev: BL 9/1–15/10)

3089 Smith, Tara Bray. *Betwixt* (11–12). 2007, Little, Brown $16.99 (978-0-316-06033-2). Three teenagers with unusual abilities learn that they are part of a race of changelings in this dark, unsettling novel with some sexual situations. (Rev: BL 1/1–15/08; SLJ 3/08)

3090 Sniegoski, Thomas E. *Legacy* (8–11). 2009, Delacorte $15.99 (978-0-385-73714-2); LB $18.99 (978-0-385-90648-7). When his mother is killed, 18-year-old Lucas changes his mind and agrees to take on his father's role as Seraph City superhero and crime fighter. (Rev: BL 9/1/09; SLJ 12/09)

3091 Spiegler, Louise. *The Amethyst Road* (8–11). 2005, Clarion $16.00 (978-0-618-48572-7). In this cautionary futuristic novel, siblings Serena and Willow, half-Gorgio and half-Yulang, struggle to survive the violence of their urban neighborhood and the ostracism caused by their mixed blood. (Rev: BL 12/1/05; SLJ 11/05; VOYA 2/06)

3092 Spinner, Stephanie. *Damosel: In Which the Lady of the Lake Renders a Frank and Often Startling Account of Her Wondrous Life and Times* (6–10). 2008, Knopf $16.99 (978-037583634-3); LB $19.99 (978-037593634-0). Elegantly told, this Arthurian-based tale tells of the Lady of the Lake's magical creation of the sword Excalibur and the loyal support of Twixt, a dwarf jester in Arthur's court. e Lexile 830L (Rev: BL 10/1/08; LMC 3–4/09; SLJ 12/08; VOYA 2/09)

3093 Spotswood, Jessica. *Born Wicked* (8–12). 2012, Putnam $17.99 (978-039925745-2). In an alternate New England in 1900, 16-year-old Cate and her sisters Maura and Tess struggle to keep their witchcraft secret in the face of the threatening Brotherhood. e (Rev: BL 1/1/12; LMC 8–9/12; SLJ 4/12; VOYA 4/12)

3094 Stackpole, Michael A. *The New World* (9–12). 2007, Bantam paper $15.00 (978-0-553-38239-6). Set in a fantasy version of the European Renaissance, this final book in the Age of Discovery trilogy follows three siblings as they fight the forces of evil. (Rev: BL 7/07)

3095 Stackpole, Michael A. *A Secret Atlas* (10–12). 2005, Bantam paper $15.00 (978-0-553-38237-2). The family of the powerful Royal Cartographer of Nalenyr explores uncharted, sometimes magical lands, and defends against intrigue and sabotage at home, in the first of a series. (Rev: BL 3/1/05)

3096 Stahler, David, Jr. *Doppelganger* (9–12). 2006, HarperCollins $16.99 (978-0-06-087232-8). A young shape-shifting doppelganger discovers that life has a human boy, even a teen football star, is not without its problems. (Rev: SLJ 6/06)

3097 Stewart, Mary. *Mary Stewart's Merlin Trilogy* (9–12). 1980, Morrow $29.99 (978-0-688-00347-0). This fictionalized account of the story of King Arthur consists of three novels: *The Crystal Cave*, *The Hollow Hills*, and *The Last Enchantment*. On the same subject use the author's *The Wicked Day* (1984).

3098 Stewart, Sean, and Jordan Weisman. *Cathy's Ring: If Found, Please Call 650-266-8263* (8–11). Illus. by author. Series: Cathy. 2009, Running Press $17.95 (978-076243530-2). The page-turning final volume in the trilogy features the familiar format (doodles and designs on each page) and Cathy is still in love with an immortal and running from assassins. (Rev: BL 4/15/09; SLJ 6/1/09)

3099 Stiefvater, Maggie. *Forever* (7–10). Series: Wolves of Mercy Falls. 2011, Scholastic $17.99 (978-0-545-25908-8). Grace and Sam face new threats to their love as human-werewolf-wolf tensions escalate; the third book in the trilogy. ∩ e Lexile 770L (Rev: BL 9/15/11; SLJ 9/1/11)

3100 Stiefvater, Maggie. *Lament: The Faerie Queen's Deception* (9–12). Illus. by Julia Jeffrey. 2008, Flux paper $9.95 (978-073871370-0). Fantasy, danger, and romance are intertwined in this book about Deirdre, a 16-year-old harpist who meets the boy of her dreams only to discover that she has dangerous telekinetic powers, and that he has been sent by the Queen of Faeries to assassinate her. e (Rev: BL 12/1/08; VOYA 12/08)

3101 Stiefvater, Maggie. *Linger* (8–11). 2010, Scholastic $17.99 (978-0-545-12328-0). In this sequel to *Shiver* (2009), Sam is close to leaving his werewolf status and achieving humanity, but his girlfriend Grace is now suffering from illnesses that may be related to a wolf bite; at the same time a new wolf pack member called Cole threatens the group's stability. ∩ e Lexile 800L (Rev: BL 6/10; HB 7–8/10; LMC 10/10; SLJ 8/10; VOYA 8/10)

3102 Stiefvater, Maggie. *The Raven Boys* (9–12). Series: The Raven Cycle. 2012, Scholastic $17.99 (978-0-545-42492-9). Blue, 16, who can enhance the psychic experiences of others, meets students from a prestigious academy who are searching for the body of the sleeping king of Wales. ∩ e Lexile HL760L (Rev: BL 8/12*; HB 1–2/13; LMC 5–6/13; SLJ 10/12*)

3103 Stiefvater, Maggie. *The Scorpio Races* (8–12). 2011, Scholastic $17.99 (978-0-545-22490-1). The fictional island of Thisby is home to the famous Scorpio Races, in which 19-year-old Sean, riding a water horse, competes against Puck, the first girl to enter the race, who is riding a regular land horse. Printz Honor 2012; ALA Notable Books 2012; YALSA Top Ten Best Fiction for Young Adults 2012; Odyssey Honor Recording 2012. ∩ e Lexile 840L (Rev: BL 9/1/11*; HB 11–12/11*; LMC 3–4/12*; SLJ 11/1/11*)

3104 Stirling, S. M. *A Meeting at Corvallis* (9–12). 2006, Roc $25.95 (978-0-451-46111-7). After the fall of civilization, Oregon has been divided into three warring kingdoms that depend on ancient means to obtain their ends. (Rev: BL 8/06)

3105 Stirling, S. M. *On the Oceans of Eternity* (10–12). 2000, Penguin paper $7.99 (978-0-451-45780-6). In this last of a time-travel trilogy that started with *Island in the Sea of Time* (1998) and *Against the Tide of Years* (1999), the story of Nantucket being dragged back in time continues. (Rev: BL 4/1/00)

3106 Stone, Tamara Ireland. *Time Between Us* (7–12). 2012, Disney/Hyperion $17.99 (978-142315956-8). In 1995 Illinois 16-year-old Anna's ordinary life is changed forever when she meets Bennett, who has the ability to travel through space and time. ∩ e (Rev: BL 9/15/12; LMC 3–4/13; SLJ 2/13)

3107 Strahan, Jonathan, and Marianne S. J. Jablon, eds. *Wings of Fire* (10–12). 2010, Night Shade paper $15.95 (978-15978-01-8-7-4). A collection of 26 diverse dragon stories by well-known authors. (Rev: BLO 7/10; SLJ 10/1/10)

3108 Strahan, Jonathan, ed. *Under My Hat: Tales from the Cauldron* (9–12). 2012, Random House $16.99 (978-0-375-86830-6); LB $19.99 (978-037596830-3). Eighteen short stories about witches are written by well-known authors including Neil Gaiman, Garth Nix, and Jane Yolen. e (Rev: BL 10/1/12; LMC 3–4/13; SLJ 11/12; VOYA 10/12)

3109 Strieber, Whitley. *The Wild* (9–12). 1991, Tor paper $5.95 (978-0-8125-1277-9). Bob Duke stares at a wolf one day at a zoo, and its gaze seems to invade his soul. Soon Bob is transformed into a wolf and must flee the police. (Rev: BL 5/1/91*)

3110 Stross, Charles. *The Clan Corporate* (9–12). 2006, Tor $24.95 (978-0-7653-0930-3). A follow-up to *The Family Trade* (2004) and *The Hidden Family* (2005), with Miriam now on the run from her relatives and living in a world where she is again pursued — this time by the king. (Rev: BL 5/1/06)

3111 Stross, Charles. *The Merchants' War* (9–12). 2007, Tor $24.95 (978-0-7653-1671-4). Worldwalkers have the ability to move to alternate realities and Boston business journalist Miriam is one of them in this fourth successive book in the Merchant Princes Series that begins with an apparent attack of her betrothal to the Prince of Gruinmarkt, sparking a war and action-packed adventures for Miriam, who finds yet another world to escape to. (Rev: BL 10/1/07)

3112 Stroud, Jonathan. *The Amulet of Samarkand* (6–12). Series: The Bartimaeus Trilogy. 2003, Hyperion $17.95 (978-0-7868-1859-4). Nathaniel, an apprentice magician, plots to steal an amulet and sets powerful forces in motion in this fantasy set in London. (Rev: BL 9/1/03*; HB 11–12/03; HBG 4/04; SLJ 1/04; VOYA 12/03)

3113 Stroud, Jonathan. *The Golem's Eye* (7–12). Series: The Bartimaeus Trilogy. 2004, Miramax $17.95 (978-0-7868-1860-0). In this sequel to *The Amulet of Samarkand*, 14-year-old Nathaniel, a magician's apprentice, joins forces with the mischievous djinni Bartimaeus to foil the evil plot of a golem. (Rev: BL 8/04; SLJ 10/04)

3114 Stroud, Jonathan. *Heroes of the Valley* (6–10). 2009, Hyperion $17.99 (978-142310966-2). A rollicking fantasy about Halli Sveinsson, the young descendent of a legendary Nordic hero, who finds himself on an epic journey to avenge his uncle's death, in the process spawning his own, brand-new legend. ⌒ Lexile 770L (Rev: BL 12/1/08*; HB 1–2/09; LMC 8–9/09; SLJ 1/1/09*)

3115 Suma, Nova Ren. *Imaginary Girls* (9–12). Illus. by author. 2011, Dutton $17.99 (978-0-525-42338-6). After Chloe found a classmate drowned in the local reservoir, she went to live with her father; now, two years later, she returns to her upstate New York town to find that her classmate is alive and well and that Chloe's charismatic sister Ruby seems to have persuaded everyone that all is normal. ⌒ Lexile 840L (Rev: BL 5/1/11; LMC 11–12/11; SLJ 7/11*; VOYA 6/11)

3116 Sweeney, Joyce. *Shadow* (7–10). 1995, Bantam $20.95 (978-0-385-30988-2). Sarah's cat, Shadow, has mysteriously returned from the dead. Sarah and Cissy, the psychic housemaid, try to figure out why. (Rev: BL 7/94; SLJ 9/94; VOYA 10/94)

3117 Swendson, Shanna. *Don't Hex with Texas* (9–12). 2008, Ballantine paper $14.00 (978-0-345-49293-7). In this romantic fantasy novel, the impervious-to-magic Katie Chandler leaves her New York job at Magic, Spells, and Illusions Inc. to return home to Texas to protect Owen, the handsome wizard who is also her secret love interest. (Rev: BL 4/15/08)

3118 Swendson, Shanna. *Once Upon Stilettos* (9–12). 2006, Ballantine paper $13.95 (978-0-345-48127-6). Thanks to her immunity to magic, Katie lands a plum job as Merlin's personal assistant in New York City in this sequel to *Enchanted, Inc.* (2005). (Rev: BL 5/1/06)

3119 Tanigawa, Nagaru. *The Sigh of Haruhi Suzumiya* (9–12). Illus. by Noizi Ito. 2009, Little, Brown paper $8.99 (978-0-316-03879-9). In this followup to 2009's *The Melancholy of Haruhi Suzumiya,* the omnipotent protagonist decides to film a movie for the school's cultural festival, and her fellow SOS Brigade members have no choice but to follow along. (Rev: BLO 9/11/09; SLJ 3/10; VOYA 4/10)

3120 Tarr, Judith. *Lady of Horses* (10–12). 2000, Tor $25.95 (978-0-312-86114-8). For mature readers, this novel set in prehistoric times blends mythology and fantasy in the tale of Sparrow, a girl who can foretell the future, and a cult that worships the Horse Goddess. (Rev: BL 6/1–15/00)

3121 Tayler, Kassy. *Ashes of Twilight* (8–11). 2012, St. Martin's paper $9.99 (978-03126417-8-8). In this fast-paced dystopian novel set in the 2070s, 200 years after a comet hit the earth, 16-year-old Wren is a miner in a domed — and perhaps doomed — city. ⌒ ℮ (Rev: BL 11/15/12; LMC 3–4/13; SLJ 3/13; VOYA 4/13)

3122 Taylor, Laini. *Daughter of Smoke and Bone* (8–12). 2011, Little, Brown $18.99 (978-0-316-13402-6). Prague high-schooler Karou copes with the disappearance of the chimaera who've become her family. YALSA Top Ten Best Fiction for Young Adults 2012. ⌒ ℮ Lexile 850L (Rev: BL 9/1/11; HB 11–12/11*; LMC 1–2/12; SLJ 11/1/11*)

3123 Taylor, Laini. *Days of Blood and Starlight* (8–12). 2012, Little, Brown $18.99 (978-0-316-13397-5). Karou, betrayed by Akiva in *Daughter of Smoke and Bone* (2011), must decide what to risk to avenge her people. ⌒ ℮ Lexile HL800L (Rev: BL 11/15/12; HB 1–2/13; SLJ 12/12; VOYA 12/12)

3124 Taylor, Laini. *Silksinger* (7–10). Illus. by Jim Di Bartolo. Series: Dreamdark. 2009, Putnam $18.99 (978-0-399-24631-9). Full of fast-paced adventure, this second volume in the series has Magpie and the other fairies discovering long-lost clans as they try to save the world from destruction. ⌒ Lexile 870L (Rev: BLO 8/20/09; SLJ 9/09)

3125 Telep, Trisha, ed. *The Eternal Kiss: 13 Vampire Tales of Blood and Desire* (8–12). 2009, Running Press paper $9.95 (978-0-7624-3717-7). Vampires of all kinds populate these diverse stories featuring comedy, romance, violence, mystery, and so forth. (Rev: BL 9/1/09; SLJ 12/09)

3126 Thompson, Kate. *The Last of the High Kings* (7–10). 2008, Greenwillow $16.99 (978-0-06-117595-4). J.J. Liddy, introduced in *The New Policeman*, is now married and a father of four, one of whom is a fairy, having been traded for one of J.J.'s children at birth. (Rev: BL 5/15/08; SLJ 7/08)

3127 Thompson, Kate. *The New Policeman* (7–10). 2007, Greenwillow $16.99 (978-0-06-117427-8). J.J., hoping to grant his mother's wish for "more time," goes out into his Irish town to find out just where all the time has gone and discovers the land of eternal youth in this music-filled story. ALA Notable Books 2008. ∩ (Rev: BCCB 4/07; BL 2/1/07; HB 3–4/07; LMC 8–9/07; SLJ 3/07*)

3128 Tiernan, Cate. *A Chalice of Wind* (8–11). Series: Balefire. 2005, Penguin paper $6.99 (978-1-59514-045-6). Thais discovers that she has a twin — and that she is a witch — when her father dies and she is sent to live in New Orleans. (Rev: BL 9/1/05; SLJ 8/05)

3129 Tiernan, Cate. *Darkness Falls* (8–11). 2012, Little, Brown $17.99 (978-031603593-4). In this sequel to *Immortal Beloved* (2010), immortal Nastasya — now 450 years old — struggles to escape her inner darkness and to forget the past. ∩ **e** Lexile 760L (Rev: BL 12/15/11; SLJ 2/12)

3130 Tiernan, Cate. *Night's Child* (7–12). Series: Sweep. 2003, Penguin paper $7.99 (978-0-14-250119-1). In this 15th installment — a double-length, stand-alone novel — Moira, 15-year-old daughter of the powerful blood witch Morgan, learns about her heritage and faces danger and treachery as well as romance. (Rev: SLJ 2/04)

3131 Tiffany, Grace. *Ariel* (9–12). 2005, HarperCollins LB $17.89 (978-0-06-075328-3). A fanciful imagining of the events leading up to Shakespeare's *The Tempest*, centered on Ariel, the spirit whom Sycorax imprisoned in a tree. (Rev: BL 9/1/05*; SLJ 10/05; VOYA 10/05)

3132 Tolkien, J. R. R. *The Hobbit: Or, There and Back Again* (7–12). 1938, Houghton Mifflin $16.00 (978-0-395-07122-9); paper $7.99 (978-0-345-33968-3). In this prelude to *The Lord of the Rings*, the reader meets Bilbo Baggins, a hobbit, in a land filled with dwarfs, elves, goblins, and dragons.

3133 Tolkien, J. R. R. *The Lord of the Rings* (9–12). 1967, Ballantine paper $6.99 (978-0-345-33970-6). This combined volume includes all three books of the trilogy first published in 1954 and 1955. They are: *The Fellowship of the Ring, The Two Towers,* and *The Return of the King.*

3134 Tolkien, J. R. R. *The Silmarillion* (9–12). 1977, Ballantine paper $5.95 (978-0-345-32581-5). These modern legends deal with such subjects as the creation of the world.

3135 Tolkien, J. R. R. *Unfinished Tales of Numenor and Middle-Earth* (8–12). Ed. by Christopher Tolkien. 2001, Houghton Mifflin $26.00 (978-0-618-15404-3); paper $14.95 (978-0-618-15405-0). A collection of previously unpublished fantasy writings by this English master.

3136 Tomlinson, Heather. *Aurelie: A Faerie Tale* (7–10). 2008, Henry Holt $16.95 (978-080508276-0). As gifted friends Aurelie, Garin, and Netta come of age in their intricate, fantastical world, they cope with distance, physical struggles, familial obligations, and a complex and ill-fated love story. **e** Lexile 780L (Rev: BL 9/1/08; HB 9–10/08; SLJ 12/08)

3137 Tomlinson, Heather. *The Swan Maiden* (6–10). 2007, Henry Holt $16.95 (978-0-8050-8275-3). Swan maiden Doucette, who only discovers her natural magic in her teens, is in love with the shepherd Jaume, who must complete a series of trials to win her hand in this story based on French fairy tales. (Rev: BL 10/1/07; SLJ 12/07)

3138 Tomlinson, Heather. *Toads and Diamonds* (8–12). 2010, Henry Holt $16.99 (978-0-8050-8968-4). Perrault's classic tale is reimagined in a fictional Indian land, where stepsisters Diribani and Tana have very different experiences as they use the gifts bestowed on them by a goddess. **e** Lexile 820L (Rev: BL 2/15/10*; LMC 5–6/10; SLJ 7/10)

3139 Townsend, John Rowe. *The Fortunate Isles* (7–12). 1989, HarperCollins LB $13.89 (978-0-397-32366-1). Eleni and her friend Andreas seek the living god in this novel set in a mythical land. (Rev: BL 10/15/89; SLJ 10/89)

3140 Troop, Alan F. *The Dragon DelaSangre* (11–12). 2002, NAL paper $7.99 (978-0-451-45871-1). Peter and his father, dragons who can take human shape and are successful Florida entrepreneurs, are threatened with discovery; for mature teens. (Rev: BL 3/1/02*)

3141 Troop, Alan F. *The Seadragon's Daughter* (9–12). 2004, NAL paper $6.99 (978-0-451-46007-3). In this fast-paced sequel to *The Dragon DelaSangre* (2002) and *Dragon Moon* (2003), dragon hero Peter DelaSangre returns to defend his island — and himself — against attacks by the resurgent seadragons, who need male dragons to repopulate. (Rev: BL 12/15/04)

3142 Turtledove, Harry. *The Disunited States of America* (9–12). Series: Crosstime Traffic. 2006, Tor $24.95 (978-0-7653-1485-7). In a world in which states are individual countries that often wage wars against one another, Justin and Becky are trapped in Virginia when a quarantine is imposed. (Rev: BL 9/1/06)

3143 Turtledove, Harry. *Hitler's War* (11–12). 2009, Del Rey $27 (978-034549182-4). An alternate history full of interesting detail, fascinating characters, and exciting action; for mature readers. ∩ **e** (Rev: BL 7/09)

3144 Turtledove, Harry. *In at the Death: Settling Accounts* (9–12). 2007, Del Rey $26.95 (978-0-345-49247-0). This is the final volume of Turtledove's fantasy version of history, featuring very different twists to the Civil War, race relations and the Cold War. (Rev: BL 6/1–15/07)

3145 Turtledove, Harry. *In High Places* (10–12). Series: Crosstime Traffic. 2006, Tor $22.95 (978-0-7653-0696-8). Annette Klein, an 18-year-old Californian who travels with her family between alternate worlds, is captured by bandits and separated from her parents, making it doubtful she'll be able to return to her normal world. (Rev: BL 12/1/05)

3146 Turtledove, Harry. *Liberating Atlantis* (10–12). 2009, Roc $25.95 (978-045146296-1). Civil War seems certain in the United States of Atlantis in this concluding volume in the series. ☊ ℮ (Rev: BLO 12/15/09*)

3147 Turtledove, Harry. *Opening Atlantis* (9–12). 2007, Roc $24.95 (978-0-451-46174-2). Atlantis is an island halfway across the ocean between Europe and Terranova and contains natural resources that, over the centuries, become sources of conflict between the French, English, and Spanish and cause the founding Ratcliffe family to split into two warring factions. (Rev: BL 10/15/07)

3148 Turtledove, Harry. *West and East: The War That Came Early* (11–12). 2010, Del Rey $27 (978-034549184-8). Turtledove's alternate World War II history continues with this sequel to *Hitler's War* (2009) that follows Russian pilot Sergei and British Sergeant Alistair, among many others around the world; for mature readers. (Rev: BL 4/15/10*)

3149 Van Lowe, E. *Never Slow Dance with a Zombie* (7–10). 2009, Tor paper $8.99 (978-0-7653-2040-7). A satirically humorous zombie story in which 16-year-old Margot, who longs to be popular, gets her chance for stardom when nearly all her classmates are turned into zombies. ℮ Lexile 620L (Rev: BL 9/1/09; LMC 3–4/10; SLJ 1/10)

3150 Vande Velde, Vivian. *Conjurer Princess* (9–12). 1997, HarperCollins paper $4.99 (978-0-06-105704-5). Sixteen-year-old Lylene sets out to rescue her older sister, who has been abducted by a warlord on her wedding day. (Rev: VOYA 2/98)

3151 Vandervort, Kim. *The Northern Queen* (10–12). 2010, Hadley Rille $28.95 (978-098294671-8). In the sequel to *The Song and the Sorceress* (2009), Ki'leah, newly crowned Queen of Si'vad, must protect her kingdom from both internal and external threats. (Rev: BL 11/1–15/10)

3152 Vaughn, Carrie. *Voices of Dragons* (7–10). 2010, HarperTeen $16.99 (978-0-06-179894-8). When 17-year-old Kay is rescued from a fall by a friendly dragon named Artegal, the two attempt to negotiate a peace agreement between the warring realms of humans and dragons. ℮ Lexile HL690L (Rev: BL 1/1–15/10; SLJ 3/10; VOYA 8/11)

3153 Vaught, S. R., and J. B. Redmond. *Assassin's Apprentice* (7–12). Series: Oathbreaker. 2009, Bloomsbury paper $10.99 (978-1-59990-162-6). When young Aron is chosen to join an elite team of assassins — the Stone Brothers — his considerable aptitude for magic becomes apparent; the first volume in a two-part fantasy set in the world of Eyrie. ℮ Lexile 1020L (Rev: SLJ 6/1/09; VOYA 8/09)

3154 Vick, Helen H. *Walker's Journey Home* (7–10). 1995, Harbinger $14.95 (978-1-57140-000-0); paper $9.95 (978-1-57140-001-7). Walker leads the Sinagua Indians through treacherous challenges from both old enemies and new, and learns that greed and jealousy have been destructive forces throughout history. Sequel to *Walker of Time* (1993). (Rev: BL 8/95)

3155 Vinge, Joan D. *The Snow Queen* (10–12). 1989, Warner paper $6.99 (978-0-445-20529-1). When spring comes, the Snow Queen does not want to give up her throne.

3156 Vizzini, Ned. *The Other Normals* (9–12). 2012, HarperCollins $17.99 (978-0-06-207990-9). Sent off to summer camp to cure him of role-playing games, Perry instead discovers the World of the Other Normals and has fantastical adventures. ☊ ℮ Lexile 640L (Rev: BL 10/15/12; HB 9–10/12; LMC 3–4/13; SLJ 12/12)

3157 Voigt, Cynthia. *The Wings of a Falcon* (7–12). 1993, Scholastic $15.95 (978-0-590-46712-4). Two boys escape from a remote island and face danger and adventure in this multilayered tale that includes themes of friendship, romance, and heroism. (Rev: SLJ 10/93*; VOYA 12/93)

3158 Vonnegut, Kurt. *Slaughterhouse-Five: Or, The Children's Crusade, a Duty Dance with Death* (10–12). 1994, Bantam $23.95 (978-0-385-31208-0); paper $7.50 (978-0-440-18029-6). This is the surreal story of Billy Pilgrim who, after surviving the bombing of Dresden in World War II, spends time on the planet Trafalmador.

3159 Walton, Jo. *Among Others* (9–12). 2011, Tor $24.99 (978-076532153-4). Fantasy, science fiction, and coming-of-age story, this book, told in diary format, follows a 15-year-old girl with the ability to cast spells as she fights to escape her evil mother and reconnect with her estranged father, all the while drowning her troubles in her love of books. ℮ (Rev: BL 1/1–15/11)

3160 Wangerin, Walter, Jr. *The Book of the Dun Cow* (7–10). 1978, HarperCollins $12.95 (978-0-06-026346-1). A farmyard fable with talking animals that retells the story of Chanticleer the Rooster.

3161 Ward, James M. *Dragonfrigate Wizard Halcyon Blithe* (10–12). 2006, Tor $24.95 (978-0-7653-1254-9). In this sequel to *Midshipwizard Halcyon Blithe* (2005), wizard-warrior Blithe, 16, is now second-in-command and must take on a demonship. (Rev: BL 11/15/06)

3162 Ward, James M. *Midshipwizard Halcyon Blithe* (10–12). 2005, Tor $24.95 (978-0-7653-1253-2). Fantasy combines with seamanship aboard the *Sanguine*, a magical ship on the back of a sea dragon. (Rev: BL 9/1/05; SLJ 2/06)

3163 Ward, Rachel. *Numbers* (8–12). 2010, Scholastic $17.99 (978-0-545-14299-1). When Jem, 15, realizes that all the tourists in line for the London Eye Ferris wheel are scheduled to die that day, she and her friend

Spider take off, setting in motion a chain of events. ◯
e Lexile HL650L (Rev: BL 12/15/09; SLJ 1/10; VOYA 4/10)

3164 Warman, Jessica. *Between* (8–11). 2011, Walker $17.99 (978-0-8027-2182-2). Liz, newly 18, wakes up to find herself caught in the afterlife along with a loser named Alex, and together the two try to work out what caused their deaths. **e** Lexile HL620L (Rev: BL 9/15/11*; HB 9–10/11; LMC 1–2/12; SLJ 9/1/11; VOYA 10/11)

3165 Watt-Evans, Lawrence. *Dragon Weather* (10–12). Series: Obsidian Chronicles. 1999, Tor $25.95 (978-0-312-86978-6). Arlian, whose family was killed by dragons when he was only 11 years old, spends years plotting his revenge only to discover that he is part dragon himself. (Rev: VOYA 4/00)

3166 Watt-Evans, Lawrence. *A Young Man Without Magic* (10–12). 2009, Tor $27.99 (978-076532279-1). In the Walasian Empire, where sorcery translates into power, young Anrel Murau wants no part of either, but the death of a close friend inspires him to take action and jeopardize his own safety. **e** (Rev: BLO 10/1/09)

3167 Weatherly, L. A. *Angel Burn* (9–12). 2011, Candlewick $17.99 (978-0-7636-5652-2). In a world where angels are malevolent forces, Alex is sent to kill Willow, a half-angel with whom he falls in love. Also use *Angel Fire* (2011). **e** (Rev: BL 5/1/11; LMC 10/11; SLJ 9/1/11)

3168 Weis, Margaret. *The Dragon's Son* (9–12). Series: Dragonvald. 2004, Tor $25.95 (978-0-7653-0469-8). Two boys (twins, although one has a dragon for a father) become pawns in the struggle that runs through the trilogy of which this is the middle volume. (Rev: BL 7/04)

3169 Weis, Margaret, ed. *A Quest-Lover's Treasury of the Fantastic* (10–12). 2002, Warner Aspect paper $13.95 (978-0-446-67927-5). Quests form the core of this collection of excellent and varied short stories. (Rev: BL 5/15/02)

3170 Weiss, M. Jerry, and Helen S. Weiss, eds. *Dreams and Visions: Fourteen Flights of Fancy* (7–10). 2006, Tor $19.95 (978-0-7653-1249-5). A collection of 14 appealing fantasy short stories by writers including Joan Bauer and Tamora Pierce; includes short biographies of the authors. (Rev: BL 4/15/06; SLJ 4/06)

3171 Werlin, Nancy. *Extraordinary* (8–12). 2010, Dial $17.99 (978-0-8037-3372-5). Privileged Phoebe's best friend Mallory, and her mysterious half-brother Ryland, are both part fairy, and, as it turns out, they have secretive, sinister plans for their friend. ◯ (Rev: BL 7/10; HB 9–10/10; LMC 1–2/11; SLJ 10/1/10*; VOYA 10/10)

3172 Werlin, Nancy. *Impossible* (7–11). 2008, Dial $17.99 (978-0-8037-3002-1). Magic and reality are intertwined in this tale of 17-year-old Lucy, who becomes

pregnant after being raped by her date on prom night and decides to keep the baby even though she must rid herself and the unborn child of a curse. ◯ **e** (Rev: BL 7/08*; HB 9–10/08; SLJ 9/1/08*; VOYA 8/08)

3173 Weyn, Suzanne. *Reincarnation* (7–10). 2008, Scholastic $17.99 (978-0-545-01323-9). A fantasy in which a boy and girl are repeatedly reincarnated throughout history and manage to find each other over and over again although impediments to their love sadly also arise. (Rev: BL 6/1–15/08)

3174 White, Amy Brecount. *Forget-Her-Nots* (7–10). 2010, HarperTeen $16.99 (978-0-06-167298-9); LB $17.89 (978-0-06-167299-6). While at boarding school 14-year-old Laurel learns that her affinity with flowers — and her ability to affect the lives of others through them — is something she has inherited. **e** (Rev: BL 1/1–15/10; SLJ 3/10; VOYA 6/10)

3175 White, Kiersten. *Mind Games* (9–12). 2013, HarperTeen $17.99 (978-006213531-5). Sisters Annie and Fia have paranormal powers and struggle against forces that will use them for evil. ◯ **e** Lexile 770L (Rev: BL 12/15/12; SLJ 5/13)

3176 White, T. H. *The Book of Merlyn: The Unpublished Conclusion to "The Once and Future King"* (9–12). 1988, Univ. of Texas paper $16.95 (978-0-292-70769-6). An antiwar postscript to White's retelling of the Arthurian legend.

3177 White, T. H. *The Once and Future King* (10–12). 1958, Putnam $26.95 (978-0-399-10597-5). Beginning with *The Sword in the Stone* (1939), this omnibus includes all four of T. H. White's novels about the life and career of King Arthur. It was this version that became the basis for the musical Camelot.

3178 White, T. H. *The Sword in the Stone* (7–12). 1993, Putnam $24.99 (978-0-399-22502-4). In this, the first part of *The Once and Future King,* the career of Wart is traced until he becomes King Arthur.

3179 Whitfield, Kit. *In Great Waters* (11–12). 2009, Del Rey paper $15 (978-03454916-5-7). Power struggles amongst the mer-folk who guard coastal, fantastical Europe create drama in this original tale suitable for mature readers. (Rev: BL 11/15/09)

3180 Whitley, David. *The Midnight Charter* (7–10). 2009, Roaring Brook $16.99 (978-1-59643-381-6). In a society where lives are treated as a basic commodity, teens Lily and Mark — sold by their parents — take opposing attitudes to the prevailing system. ◯ **e** Lexile 790L (Rev: BL 8/09; LMC 1–2/10; SLJ 10/09)

3181 Whitman, Emily. *Radiant Darkness* (9–12). 2009, Greenwillow $16.99 (978-006172449-7); LB $17.89 (978-006178035-6). In this retelling of the myth, Persephone is in love with Hades and makes her own seasonal arrangement so she can spend part of the year with her mother, Demeter. (Rev: BL 5/15/09; SLJ 8/09; VOYA 8/09)

3182 Wignall, K. J. *Blood* (7–11). Series: Mercian Trilogy. 2011, Egmont $16.99 (978-1-60684-220-1). Sixteen-year-old Will has been a vampire for nearly 800 years and now in the 21st century meets an attractive young runaway named Eloise and starts to investigate his past; the first volume in a trilogy. **e** (Rev: BL 9/1/11; HB 11–12/11; SLJ 8/11*)

3183 Willingham, Bill. *Peter and Max: A Fables Novel* (10–12). Illus. Series: Fables. 2009, Vertigo $22.99 (978-140121573-6). Peter Piper has discovered that his brother Max is causing problems in the real world, and so Peter travels to Hamelin to end it; a prose addition to the series. ⌒ **e** (Rev: BL 9/15/09; SLJ 11/09)

3184 Willingham, Bill, and Mark Buckingham. *The Dark Ages: Fables 12* (11–12). Illus. Series: Fables. 2009, Vertigo $17.99 (978-140122316-8). Fragmentation after the war between the Fables leads to more dangerous instability in this well-crafted volume for mature readers. (Rev: BL 7/09)

3185 Wilson, N. D. *The Drowned Vault* (8–12). Series: Ashtown Burials. 2012, Random House $16.99 (978-0-375-86440-7); LB $19.99 (978-037596440-4). Cyrus and Antigone must evade the Transmortals and find Dr. Phoenix, regaining the Tooth of the Dragon; an action-packed sequel to *The Dragon's Tooth* (2011). ⌒ **e** (Rev: BL 9/15/12; LMC 1–2/13; SLJ 10/12)

3186 Wolfe, Gene. *Pirate Freedom* (9–12). 2007, Tor $24.95 (978-0-7653-1878-7). This is the story of a 17th-century pirate who travels through time to the present day, where he has become a priest, and longs to return to his past life. (Rev: BL 9/1/07)

3187 Wollman, Jessica. *Second Skin: Appearances Can Be Deceiving* (8–11). 2009, Delacorte $8.99 (978-038573601-5); LB $11.99 (978-038590581-7). Sam steals the invisible second skin that bestowed popularity on Kylie and discovers what it's like to be on top of the high school heap. (Rev: BL 5/15/09; SLJ 10/09)

3188 Wooding, Chris. *The Haunting of Alaizabel Cray* (9–12). 2004, Scholastic $16.95 (978-0-439-54656-0). In this fantasy thriller set in an alternate Victorian London, 17-year-old Thaniel Fox, a wych-hunter, joins forces with guardian Cathaline and a haunted young woman named Alaizabel to combat the forces of evil. (Rev: BL 8/04*; SLJ 8/04)

3189 Wrede, Patricia C. *Magician's Ward* (9–12). 1997, Tor $22.95 (978-0-312-85369-3). Teenager Kim, who is living with magician Mairelon in his London townhouse as his ward and apprentice, discovers that some wizards have disappeared and Mairelon's powers are mysteriously stolen. (Rev: BL 11/1/97; VOYA 4/98)

3190 Wrede, Patricia C. *Searching for Dragons* (6–10). Series: Enchanted Forest Chronicles. 1991, Harcourt $16.95 (978-0-15-200898-7). Cimorene goes on a quest with Mendanbar, king of the forest, to find the dragon

king Kazul by borrowing a faulty magic carpet from a giant. (Rev: BL 10/1/91; SLJ 12/91)

3191 Wrede, Patricia C. *Talking to Dragons* (6–10). Series: Enchanted Forest Chronicles. 1993, Harcourt $16.95 (978-0-15-284247-5). The fourth book in the series opens 16 years after *Calling on Dragons* with King Menenbar still imprisoned in his castle by a wizard's spells. (Rev: BL 8/93; VOYA 12/93)

3192 Wrede, Patricia C., and Caroline Stevermer. *The Mislaid Magician or Ten Years After* (7–10). 2006, Harcourt $17.00 (978-0-15-205548-6). Two cousins investigate a wizard's disappearance in this novel set in 1828 in a magical version of England; this sequel to *Sorcery and Cecelia* (2003) and *The Grand Tour* (2004) is told in the form of letters. (Rev: BL 1/1–15/07; SLJ 1/07)

3193 Wrede, Patricia C., and Caroline Stevermer. *Sorcery and Cecelia or the Enchanted Chocolate Pot* (10–12). 2003, Harcourt $17.00 (978-0-15-204615-6). In 19th-century England, Kate and Cecelia conduct a lively correspondence that describes their adventures, which often include magical aspects. (Rev: HBG 10/03; VOYA 6/03)

3194 Wurts, Janny. *Peril's Gate* (10–12). Series: Alliance of the Light. 2002, HarperCollins $27.95 (978-0-06-105220-0). The future of the land of Athera rests on the shoulders of Arithon, Master of Shadow. (Rev: BL 12/15/01; VOYA 2/03)

3195 Yancey, Rick. *Alfred Kropp: The Seal of Solomon* (8–11). 2007, Bloomsbury $16.95 (978-1-59990-045-2). Alfred, awkward high school sophomore and descendant of Sir Lancelot, has many adventures as he struggles to battle the forces of evil in this sequel to *The Extraordinary Adventures of Alfred Kropp* (2005). **e** (Rev: BL 5/15/07; SLJ 6/07)

3196 Yancey, Rick. *The Extraordinary Adventures of Alfred Kropp* (9–12). 2005, Bloomsbury $16.95 (978-1-58234-693-9). Excalibur, King Arthur's legendary sword, ends up in the hands of 15-year-old Alfred Kropp, changing his life in many action-packed and often violent ways. (Rev: BL 8/05; SLJ 10/05)

3197 Yansky, Brian. *Alien Invasion and Other Inconveniences* (9–12). 2010, Candlewick $15.99 (978-0-7636-4384-3). Most people die when the Sanginians take control of Earth, but high-schooler Jesse survives and develops his telepathic and other abilities until he feels able to save himself and others. ⌒ **e** Lexile 530L (Rev: BL 11/1/10; LMC 10/10; SLJ 2/1/11)

3198 Yolen, Jane. *The One-Armed Queen* (8–10). 1998, Tor $23.95 (978-0-312-85243-6). Scillia, the adopted daughter of Queen Jenna, is being groomed to rule when her younger brother decides that he should become king. (Rev: BL 10/1/98; VOYA 4/99)

3199 Yolen, Jane, ed. *Dragons and Dreams* (6–10). 1986, HarperCollins $12.95 (978-0-06-026792-6). A collection of 10 fantasy and some science fiction stories that can be a fine introduction to these genres. (Rev: SLJ 5/86; VOYA 6/86)

3200 Young, Moira. *Blood Red Road* (9–12). 2011, Simon & Schuster $17.99 (978-1-4424-2998-7). An action-packed story with a dollop of romance in which 18-year-old Saba and her younger sister set out to rescue Saba's kidnapped twin brother and find themselves facing incredible challenges. ⌒ ℮ Lexile HL460L (Rev: BL 5/1/11; LMC 10/11; SLJ 9/1/11)

3201 Young, Suzanne. *A Need So Beautiful* (9–12). 2011, HarperCollins $16.99 (978-0-06-200824-4). Charlotte realizes she's one of the Forgotten, put on this earth to do good deeds — and will fade away when the deeds are complete; as she resists this idea she is offered another alternative, but this involves difficult choices. ⌒ ℮ (Rev: BL 5/1/11; SLJ 8/11; VOYA 8/11)

3202 Young, Suzanne. *A Want So Wicked* (9–12). 2012, HarperCollins $17.99 (978-0-06-200826-8). Elise, 17, wakes up in the desert with no memory of her past and then realizes she can understand the experiences of strangers in his sequel to *A Need So Beautiful* (2011). ℮ Lexile HL640L (Rev: BLO 8/12; SLJ 7/12; VOYA 6/12)

3203 Yovanoff, Brenna. *The Space Between* (9–12). 2011, Penguin $17.99 (978-1-59514-339-6). In this paranormal romance Lucifer's daughter Daphne follows her brother Obie from Hell to Earth. ℮ Lexile HL760L (Rev: BL 10/1/11; HB 1–2/12; SLJ 12/1/11)

3204 Zafon, Carlos Ruiz. *The Shadow of the Wind* (10–12). Trans. by Lucia Graves. 2004, Penguin $24.95 (978-1-59420-010-6). This challenging novel set in Franco's Spain combines adventure, horror, and fantasy as young Daniel travels to the Cemetery of Forgotten Books to choose one he will save. (Rev: BL 3/1/04; SLJ 7/05)

3205 Zelazny, Roger. *Blood of Amber* (9–12). 1986, Avon paper $4.99 (978-0-380-89636-3). Merle Corey, hero of *Trumps of Doom* (1985), escapes from prison with the help of a woman who has many shapes. This is the seventh Amber novel. (Rev: BL 9/15/86; VOYA 2/87)

3206 Zelazny, Roger. *Trumps of Doom* (9–12). 1986, Avon paper $5.99 (978-0-380-89635-6). In this sixth Amber book, Merlin fights against mysterious foes from the worlds of Amber and Chaos. (Rev: BL 5/15/85)

3207 Zevin, Gabrielle. *Elsewhere* (7–10). 2005, Farrar $16.00 (978-0-374-32091-1). After dying of a head injury, 15-year-old Liz Hall does not adapt easily to afterlife in Elsewhere and at first spends a lot of time watching what's going on on Earth. (Rev: BL 8/05*; SLJ 10/05*)

3208 Zindell, David. *Lord of Lies* (9–12). 2008, Tor $27.95 (978-0-7653-1130-6). Prince Valashu fights to unite the free peoples of Ea against magical assassins and mercenary armies following the Great Red Dragon. (Rev: BL 3/15/08)

3209 Zink, Michelle. *Prophecy of the Sisters* (7–10). Series: Prophecy of the Sisters. 2009, Little, Brown $17.99 (978-031602742-7). Twins Lia and Alice, 16, are at the center of a battle against the fallen angel Samael in this complex fantasy set in the late 1800s. (Rev: BL 5/15/09; SLJ 1/10; VOYA 10/09)

3210 Zuckerman, Linda. *A Taste for Rabbit* (6–10). 2007, Scholastic $16.99 (978-0-439-86977-5). This fable of civilized animals can be disturbing in its violence as a group of rabbits begins selling its young to hungry foxes. (Rev: BL 11/15/07; HB 11–12/07; LMC 1/08; SLJ 11/07)

3211 Zuroy, Michael. *Second Death* (9–12). 1992, Walker $19.95 (978-0-8027-1181-6). A Special Intelligence Squad must track down the creator of a violent, zombie-like killer. (Rev: BL 2/15/92; SLJ 11/92)

Graphic Novels

3212 Abadzis, Nick. *Laika* (8–12). Illus. by author. 2007, Roaring Brook paper $17.95 (978-1-59643-101-0). A fictionalized account of the little dog named Laika, the first living creature launched into space by the Russians, and her trainer, Yelena Dubrovsky. (Rev: BL 9/1/07; SLJ 11/07)

3213 Abel, Jessica. *La Perdida* (10–12). Illus. by author. 2006, Pantheon $19.95 (978-0-375-42365-9). Carla travels to Mexico in hopes of connecting with her past and ends up in a dangerous circle of revolutionaries and criminals; in black and white, and in both English and Spanish. (Rev: BL 3/1/06*; SLJ 9/06)

3214 Abel, Jessica, and Gabe Soria. *Life Sucks* (9–12). 2008, First Second paper $19.95 (978-1-59643-107-2). Dave, a sensitive vampire (he only drinks Blood Brew or from the blood bank) stuck in a no-future job, falls for a Goth girl called Rosa. (Rev: BL 3/15/08; LMC 10/08)

3215 Abirached, Zeina. *A Game for Swallows: To Die, to Leave, to Return* (9–12). Illus. by author. 2012, Lerner/Graphic Universe LB $29.27 (978-076138568-4); paper $9.95 (9781575059419). Neighbors join Zeina and her brother as they wait tensely for their parents to return to the apartment during a night of bombardment in war-torn Beirut. Batchelder Honor 2013; ALA Notable Books 2013. ℮ Lexile GN680L (Rev: BL 8/12; HB 11–12/12; LMC 5–6/13; SLJ 9/12*)

3216 Abouet, Marguerite, and Clement Oubrerie. *Aya* (10–12). 2007, Drawn & Quarterly $19.95 (978-1-894937-90-0). In 1970s Ivory Coast, Aya is an intelligent girl who wants to become a doctor but remains friendly with the fun-oriented Adjoua and Bintou; this graphic novel gives a good portrait of life in the African country at that time. (Rev: BL 2/1/07; SLJ 3/07)

3217 Abouet, Marguerite, and Clément Oubrerie. *Aya of Yop City* (10–12). Illus. 2008, Drawn & Quarterly $19.95 (978-189729941-8). This story of Aya and her friends and family continues where *Aya* (2007) ended, and artfully blends the story of uncertain paternity and other social concerns with Ivory Coast culture; for mature readers. (Rev: BL 9/15/08; SLJ 1/09)

3218 Acheson, Alison. *House* (10–12). Illus. by author. 2007, Fantagraphics paper $12.95 (978-1-56097-855-8). In this wordless tale, three teens come across a house in the woods and try to escape a horrifying fate. (Rev: BL 9/1/07; SLJ 9/07)

3219 Aida, Yu. *Gunslinger Girl, Vol. 2* (10–12). Trans. from Japanese by Eiko McGregor. Illus. by author. Series: Gunslinger Girl. 2005, ADV paper $9.99 (978-1-4139-0233-4). The continuing manga adventures of a band of murderous young female cyborgs who are highly trained but have not totally forgotten their humanity. (Rev: SLJ 11/05)

3220 Akino, Matsuri. *Genju no Seiza* (9–12). 2006, TokyoPop paper $9.99 (978-1-59816-607-1). Kamishina, informed that he is the reincarnated ruler of the kingdom of Dhalashar, seeks revenge against those who were cruel to his friend Sato. (Rev: BL 10/15/06)

3221 Alexovich, Aaron. *Kimmie66* (8–12). Illus. by author. 2007, DC Comics paper $9.99 (978-1-4012-0373-3). In the technologically advanced 23rd century, Telly receives a suicide note from a friend — or is it from her friend's digital duplicate? (Rev: BL 1/1–15/08; SLJ 3/08)

3222 *All Star Comics: Archives, Vol. 11* (7–12). Illus. by Arthur Peddy and Bernard Sachs. Series: Archive Editions. 2005, DC Comics $49.95 (978-1-4012-0403-7). The final volume of the Archive Editions series continues the adventures of the Justice Society of America, a band of comic book superheroes that includes the Green Lantern, Flash, Wonder Woman, Atom, and Hawkman. (Rev: BL 7/05; SLJ 9/05)

3223 Allie, Scott, and Matt Dryer, eds. *Hellboy: Weird Tales, Vol. 1* (10–12). 2003, Dark Horse paper $17.95 (978-1-56971-622-9). Hellboy, a humanoid demon, is an agent who investigates such paranormal phenomena as ghosts, poltergeists, and other supernatural creatures. (Rev: BL 2/1/04)

3224 Allie, Scott, ed. *Buffy the Vampire Slayer: Omnibus Volume 2* (9–12). 2007, Dark Horse paper $24.95 (978-1-59307-826-3). This volume collects Buffy print comics that capture all the humor, irreverence, horror, and fun of the screen version, includes the graphic novel *Ring of Fire* and the miniseries *A Stake to the Heart*. (Rev: BL 11/1/07)

3225 Allie, Scott, ed. *The Dark Horse Book of Witchcraft* (9–12). 2004, Dark Horse $14.95 (978-1-59307-108-

0). This appealing blend of fact and fiction, presented in graphic novel format, explores various aspects of witchcraft. (Rev: BL 11/1/04)

3226 Allie, Scott, et al. *The Devil's Footprints* (10–12). 2003, Dark Horse paper $14.95 (978-1-56971-933-6). A graphic novel about a young man who must exorcise the demon that stalks his father's spirit. Also use *The Dark Horse Book of Hauntings* (2003), edited by Scott Allie. (Rev: BL 2/1/04)

3227 Altman, Steven-Elliot. *The Irregulars: . . . In the Service of Sherlock Holmes* (7–12). 2005, Dark Horse paper $12.95 (978-1-59307-303-9). In this suspenseful graphic novel, Holmes assigns the Baker Street Irregulars to find out who's responsible for a murder for which Dr. Watson has been charged. (Rev: BL 5/1/05)

3228 Andersen, Hans Christian, et al. *Science Fiction Classics* (9–12). Ed. by Tom Pomplun. Illus. by Hunt Emerson. Series: Graphic Classics. 2009, Eureka paper $17.95 (978-0978-791971). Stories by Andersen, Wells, Jules Verne, Arthur Conan Doyle, and E. M. Forster are among those illustrated in this effective collection in graphic novel format. (Rev: BL 6/1–15/09)

3229 Anderson, Kevin J., et al. *Veiled Alliances* (9–12). 2004, DC Comics $24.95 (978-1-56389-902-7). This graphic novel tells the story of some refugees from Earth and their life in the advanced civilization, the Ildaran Empire. (Rev: BL 2/1/04)

3230 Appignanesi, Richard. *A Midsummer Night's Dream* (8–12). Adapted by Richard Appignanesi. Illus. by Kate Brown. Series: Manga Shakespeare. 2008, Abrams paper $9.95 (978-0-8109-9475-1). A manga retelling of the comedy featuring fairies and lovers; illustrated by Kate Brown. (Rev: BL 3/15/08; SLJ 5/08)

3231 Aristophane. *The Zabime Sisters* (7–10). 2010, First Second paper $16.99 (978-1-59643-638-1). On the island of Guadeloupe, three teen sisters enjoy a summer day with adventures including smoking, sneaking a drink, stealing mangoes, and watching a fight. YALSA Great Graphic Novels Top Ten 2011. (Rev: BL 10/15/10; LMC 10/10; SLJ 11/10)

3232 Arni, Samhita. *Sita's Ramayana* (5–12). Illus. by Moyna Chitrakar. 2011, Groundwood $24.95 (978-155498145-8). With Patua scroll paintings, this graphic-novel retelling has Rama's beautiful wife as its main focus. ALA Notable Books 2012. (Rev: BL 9/15/11*; LMC 1–2/12*; SLJ 9/1/11*)

3233 Arnold, J. D. *BB Wolf and the 3 LPs* (9–12). Illus. by Rich Koslowski. 2010, Top Shelf paper $12.95 (978-16030902-9-2). Blues musician/farmer BB Wolf and his family are threatened by the ruthlessly greedy pigs in this racial allegory set in 1920s Mississippi and drawing on the life of a real blues player. YALSA's Great Graphic Novels for Teens 2011. (Rev: BLO 6/10; SLJ 7/10)

3234 Asakura, George. *A Perfect Day for Love Letters, Vol. 1* (10–12). Adapted by David Walsh. Illus. by author. 2005, Del Rey paper $10.95 (978-0-345-48266-2). The five love stories in this manga collection are loosely connected by the unifying love letters theme. (Rev: SLJ 9/05)

3235 Asamiya, Kia. *Dark Angel: The Path to Destiny* (8–12). Series: Dark Angel. 2000, CPM Comics paper $15.95 (978-1-56219-827-5). In this first volume of a series of graphic novels, a young swordsman named Dark travels through time and different worlds to complete his moral journey. (Rev: BL 12/1/00)

3236 Asamiya, Kia. *JUNK: Record of the Last Hero, Vol. 1* (9–12). Illus. by author. 2007, DrMaster paper $9.95 (978-1-59796-107-3). Hiro answers an online ad for JUNK and ends up receiving a gadget that gives him superpower abilities; can he use them wisely? (Rev: BL 8/07)

3237 Atangan, Patrick. *The Yellow Jar: Two Tales from Japanese Tradition, Vol. 1* (10–12). Illus. by author. 2003, NBM $12.95 (978-1-56163-331-9). "The Yellow Jar" and "Two Chrysanthemum Maidens" are told in beautiful graphic novel format. (Rev: BL 12/02; SLJ 4/03) [398.2]

3238 Austen, Jane, and Nancy Butler. *Sense and Sensibility* (9–12). Illus. by Sonny Liew. 2010, Marvel $19.99 (978-078514819-7). This graphic-novel adaptation of Austen's classic features fast-paced dialogue and softly colored period illustrations. (Rev: BL 2/15/11)

3239 Azzarello, Brian, et al. *For Tomorrow, Vol. 2* (9–12). Series: Superman: For Tomorrow. 2005, DC Comics $24.99 (978-1-4012-0715-1). In the second volume of the series, the superhero continues to search for the truth behind the cataclysmic event that resulted in the disappearance of millions of people from Earth. (Rev: BL 10/15/05; SLJ 5/06)

3240 Babra, Neil. *Hamlet* (9–12). Illus. by author. Series: No Fear Shakespeare Graphic Novels. 2008, Sterling paper $9.95 (978-1-4114-9873-0). Fear Shakespeare no longer! This graphic adaptation of one of the bard's most famous plays will appeal to reluctant readers without insulting their intelligence. (Rev: BL 4/15/08)

3241 Baillie, Liz. *My Brain Hurts, Vol. 1* (11–12). 2008, Microcosm paper $6.00 (978-1-934620-03-8). Fifteen-year-old Kate's brain is overloaded with issues of sexual identity, friendship, and pop culture as she navigates through high school. (Rev: BL 3/3/08)

3242 Baker, Kevin, and Danijel Zezelj. *Luna Park* (11–12). Illus. 2009, Vertigo $24.99 (978-140121584-2). A Russian immigrant with a brutal past and an increasingly grim future seeks to break free from violence, addiction, and poor choices in 1910 Brooklyn; for mature teens. (Rev: BL 11/15/09)

3243 Baron, Mike, and Steve Rude. *Nexus, Vol. 1* (10–12). Series: Nexus. 2005, Dark Horse $49.95 (978-1-59307-398-5). The first volume in this recommended series collects the early exploits of the unhappy superhero. (Rev: BL 12/15/05)

3244 Baron, Mike, and Steve Rude. *Nexus, Vol. 2* (9–12). 2006, Dark Horse $49.95 (978-1-59307-455-5). The intergalactic adventures of Nexus and Judah Maccabee are chronicled in this collection of 1983-1985 comic book issues. (Rev: BL 4/15/06)

3245 *Batman Black and White, Vol. 3* (9–12). 2007, DC Comics $24.99 (978-1-4012-1531-6). Thirty-three dramatic stories make up this anthology of Batman, all presented with moody black-and-white illustrations, contributed by the most popular modern writers and artists. (Rev: BL 7/07) [741.5]

3246 Beaupre, Stephen, and Steve Lafler. *40 Hour Man* (10–12). 2006, Manx Media paper $18.00 (978-0-9769690-0-6). The saga of a minimum-wage worker and his sometimes depressing, sometimes hilarious jobs, in an innovative format. (Rev: BL 8/06)

3247 Beddor, Frank, and Liz Cavalier. *Hatter M* (8–12). Illus. by Ben Templesmith. Series: Hatter M. 2008, Automatic Pictures paper $14.95 (978-098187370-1). Fans of Beddor's Looking Glass trilogy will enjoy this dark and complex story of Hatter Madigan and his search for Princess Alyss. (Rev: BL 1/1–15/09; VOYA 2/09)

3248 Beddor, Frank, and Liz Cavalier. *Hatter M, Vol. 3: The Nature of Wonder* (9–12). Illus. by Sami Makkonen. 2010, Automatic Pictures $24.99 (978-098187374-9). Royal Bodyguard Hatter Madigan heads for the American West in his search for Princess Alyss and has surreal adventures. (Rev: BL 2/15/11)

3249 Beechen, Adam. *Robin: Teenage Wasteland* (8–11). Illus. by Freddie Williams. 2007, DC Comics paper $17.99 (978-1-4012-1480-7). A collection of nine issues of well-written comic book stories featuring the boy wonder. (Rev: BL 1/15/08)

3250 Bell, Gabrielle. *Lucky* (11–12). 2006, Drawn & Quarterly $19.95 (978-1-897299-01-2). The author uses simple black-and-white drawings to tell of her life as an underemployed twenty-something living in New York — looking for accommodation, trying to find suitable work, and hoping to make her art pay. (Rev: BL 8/06)

3251 Benjamin. *Orange* (11–12). Illus. by author. 2009, Tokyopop paper $14.99 (978-142781463-0). A girl named Orange is brought back from the brink of suicide by a man who later kills himself. (Rev: BL 4/1/09)

3252 Bennett, Ian. *Leap Years* (10–12). 2005, Candle Light paper $17.95 (978-0-9743147-9-2). This amusing and thoughtful graphic novel tells how the life of high school sophomore Jake is transformed after he strikes up a friendship with an imaginary frog that's 6 feet tall. (Rev: BL 11/1/05)

3253 Biggs, Gina. *Red String, Vol. 1* (9–12). 2007, Dark Horse paper $12.95 (978-1-59307-624-5). A Japanese high school girl named Miharu is headed for an arranged marriage and instead of fighting the idea decides to give her groom a chance at winning her heart; a shojo manga created in the United States. (Rev: BL 8/07)

3254 Bishop, Debbie. *Black Tide: Awakening of the Key* (6–10). Illus. by Mike S. Miller. 2004, Angel Gate paper $19.99 (978-1-932431-00-1). In this gripping graphic novel, which collects the first eight issues of an ongoing comic book series, past and present collide when Justin Braddock embarks on a mission to solve a series of international murders. (Rev: BL 4/15/04)

3255 Black, Holly. *Kind* (10–12). Illus. by Ted Naifeh. Series: Good Neighbors. 2010, Scholastic $16.99 (978-043985564-8). Rue must choose between the human and faerie worlds in this taut trilogy conclusion. Lexile GN410L (Rev: BL 2/15/11; SLJ 5/1/11)

3256 Boyd, Andrew, and Ryan Yount. *Scurvy Dogs: Rags to Riches* (11–12). 2005, Ait paper $12.95 (978-1-932051-27-8). This volume collects all five published issues of the offbeat, independent comic book and adds commentary, character profiles, and interviews with the creators; for mature readers. (Rev: BL 4/15/05)

3257 Breathed, Berkeley. *Bloom County Library, Vol. 1: 1980–1982* (10–12). Illus. 2009, IDW $39.99 (978-160010531-9). The first installment in a series reintroducing the comic strip about the quirky residents of Bloom County, including Milo Bloom, Steve Dallas, Opus the Penguin, and Bill the Cat. (Rev: BLO 12/15/09)

3258 Brosgol, Vera. *Anya's Ghost* (7–12). Illus. by author. 2011, First Second paper $15.99 (978-159643552-0). Teenage Anya, embarrassed by her Russian immigrant family and failing to fit in at school, finds herself making friends with a ghost. YALSA Great Graphic Novels Top Ten 2012; ALA Notable Books 2012. (Rev: BL 3/15/11*; HB 7–8/11; SLJ 7/1/11*)

3259 Brown, Jeffrey. *Every Girl Is the End of the World for Me* (10–12). 2006, Top Shelf paper $8.00 (978-1-891830-77-8). Brown's relationships with five young women are the focus of his third graphic novel, which also documents his day-to-day life. (Rev: BL 4/15/06)

3260 Brown, Jeffrey. *Incredible Change-Bots* (8–12). 2007, Top Shelf paper $15.00 (978-1-891830-91-4). Change-Bots, who can morph from robots into vehicles, trash their own planet and then arrive on Earth with a continuing appetite for a fight in this funny, action-filled fantasy. (Rev: BL 11/15/07)

3261 Buchanan, Patrick J. *Town Boy* (9–12). Illus. by author. 2007, Roaring Brook paper $16.95 (978-1-59643-331-1). This sequel to *Kampung Boy* (2006) follows Mat as he and his family move from the rural Malaysian kampung to the town of Ipoh, where he attends a boarding school, makes multicultural friends, and has a social life. (Rev: BL 9/1/07; SLJ 9/07)

3262 Burns, Jason M. *The Sleepy Truth* (9–12). Illus. by Erik Valdez. 2007, Viper paper $9.95 (978-0-9793680-5-9). *The Sleepy Truth,* the town newspaper serving Sleepy Hollow, covers all the local news: aliens, hauntings, and monsters, reported on by a resourceful group of teenagers. (Rev: BL 2/1/08)

3263 Busiek, Kurt. *Local Heroes* (9–12). Illus. by Brent Anderson. Series: Astro City. 2005, Wildstorm paper $17.99 (978-1-4012-0284-2). Nine engaging vignettes about the ordinary people and superheroes of Astro City. (Rev: SLJ 1/06)

3264 Busiek, Kurt. *Shockrockets* (9–12). 2004, Dark Horse paper $14.95 (978-1-59307-129-5). In this futuristic fantasy, the Shockrockets — elite fighter pilots who work against crime, rebellions, and natural disasters — accept outsider Alejandro Cruz to help them fend off the threat of takeover by a military genius who's gone mad. (Rev: BL 11/1/04; SLJ 3/05)

3265 Byung-Jun, Byun. *Mijeong* (11–12). Trans. by Joe Johnson. Illus. 2009, NBM paper $19.95 (978-15616355-4-2). Mostly dark and gloomy, the stories in this graphic novel are still moving and visually arresting; for mature readers. (Rev: BL 7/09)

3266 Cadigan, Glen. *Titans Companion* (9–12). 2005, TwoMorrows paper $24.95 (978-1-893905-50-4). Published to mark the 25th anniversary of the New Teen Titans, superhero sidekick successors to the Teen Titans of the 1960s, this retrospective goes back to the very beginning. (Rev: BL 3/15/06)

3267 Callahan, James. *Rotting in Dirtville* (9–12). 2006, Gigantic paper $13.95 (978-0-9763038-2-4). Depressed and damaged teenagers are hardly surprised when giant robot zombies arrive in their town. (Rev: BL 8/06)

3268 Cammuso, Frank. *Max Hamm, Fairy Tale Detective, Vol. 1* (8–12). Series: Fairy Tale Detectives. 2005, Nite Owl paper $14.95 (978-0-9720061-4-9). Max Hamm, a pig, is also a private eye in a cycle of pulp-novel-style stories involving fairy tale characters and much clever wordplay. (Rev: BL 8/05; SLJ 11/05)

3269 Campbell, Bruce, et al. *Man with the Screaming Brain* (9–12). 2005, Dark Horse paper $13.95 (978-1-59307-397-8). In this graphic novel adaptation of Campbell's film of the same name, American industrialist William Cole goes behind the Iron Curtain on business but gets into serious trouble when he encounters a beautiful woman named Tatoya. (Rev: BL 11/15/05)

3270 Campbell, Ross. *Shadoweyes* (8–12). Illus. by author. 2010, SLG paper $14.95 (978-159362189-6). In a future dystopia called Dranac, African American Scout Montana morphs into a superhero but may never have the chance to revert to normal. YALSA Popular Paperbacks for Young Adults Top Ten 2011. (Rev: BL 9/15/10*; VOYA 10/10)

3271 Campbell, Ross. *Water Baby* (10–12). Illus. by author. 2008, DC Comics paper $9.99 (978-1-4012-1147-9). Brody, a bisexual surfing girl who has lost a leg to a shark, deals with her own nightmares and her deadbeat former boyfriend Jake in this graphic novel for mature readers. (Rev: BL 6/1–15/08; SLJ 7/08)

3272 Card, Orson Scott, and Mike Carey. *Ender's Shadow: Battle School* (10–12). Illus. by Sebastian Fiumara. 2009, Marvel $24.99 (978-078513596-8). A graphic novel adaptation of the classic science fiction tale about an orphan named Bean whose street smarts lead to a place at Battle School, where he befriends and competes with Ender Wiggin. Margaret A. Edwards Award 2008. (Rev: BLO 11/17/09*)

3273 Carey, Mike, and Grant Morrison. *Neil Gaiman's Neverwhere* (10–12). Illus. by Glenn Fabry and Frank Quitely. 2007, Vertigo paper $19.99 (978-1-4012-1007-6). This is an imaginative graphic novel version of Neil Gaiman's *Neverwhere,* the story of Richard Mayhew and his adventures in the subterranean world of London Below. (Rev: SLJ 7/07)

3274 Carey, Mike, and Louise Carey. *Confessions of a Blabbermouth* (7–12). Illus. by Aaron Alexovich. 2007, Minx paper $9.99 (978-1-4012-1148-6). Blabbermouth is the name of Tasha's blog, and it's an appropriate name for an effective tool that lets important people in her life know how she's feeling; a humorous, well-illustrated graphic novel. (Rev: LMC 1/08; SLJ 11/07)

3275 Carey, Mike, and Peter Gross. *Tommy Taylor and the Bogus Identity* (11–12). Illus. Series: The Unwritten. 2010, Vertigo paper $9.99 (978-14012256-5-0). Tom Taylor has not been thrilled to be regarded the model for the hero of his father's fantasy novels, but when he discovers he's not in fact Wilson Taylor's child he also begins wonders about his own unusual talents; a suspenseful story that skewers much of fantasy fiction and is the first of a series. (Rev: BL 12/15/09)

3276 Casey, Joe, and Charlie Adlard. *Codeflesh* (9–12). 2003, Ait paper $12.95 (978-1-932051-15-5). In this masked crime-fighter saga, bail bondsman Cameron Dalty dons a full-head mask to help catch the criminals. (Rev: BL 2/1/04)

3277 Casey, Joe, and Steve Parkhouse. *The Milkman Murders* (11–12). 2005, Dark Horse paper $12.95 (978-1-59307-080-9). In this horror graphic novel, for mature readers only, Barbara, a housewife dealing with a particularly difficult family, is pushed over the edge when she is assaulted by a milkman. (Rev: BL 4/15/05)

3278 Cassaday, John, et al. *Mike Mignola's Hellboy, Vol. 2* (10–12). Series: Weird Tales. 2004, Dark Horse paper $17.95 (978-1-56971-953-4). The second volume of the series collects 13 short stories about Hellboy and his investigations into paranormal phenomena. (Rev: BL 11/15/04; SLJ 7/05)

3279 Castellucci, Cecil. *Janes in Love* (9–12). Illus. by Jim Rugg. 2008, DC Comics paper $9.99 (978-140121387-9). In this tender, quirky comic, the Janes' love of art (and boys) spins a rich, believable background as the Janes navigate all the customary dramas of high school: romance, self-discovery, and family dysfunction; a sequel to 2007's *The Plain Janes.* (Rev: BL 10/1/08; HB 11–12/08; SLJ 11/08)

3280 Castellucci, Cecil, and Jim Rugg. *The Plain Janes* (9–12). Series: Minx. 2007, DC Comics paper $9.99 (978-1-4012-1115-8). The Plain Janes (who really are all named Jane) — a group of teenage outsiders — succeed in shocking their suburb with their public art displays. (Rev: BL 3/15/07; HB 7–8/07; LMC 10/07; SLJ 9/07)

3281 Chadwick, Paul. *Fragile Creature* (9–12). Series: Concrete. 2006, Dark Horse paper $12.95 (978-1-59307-464-7). In volume three of the series, the title character faces daunting new challenges when he is hired to perform special effects for a blockbuster science fiction movie. (Rev: BL 4/1/06; SLJ 9/06)

3282 Chadwick, Paul. *Killer Smile* (11–12). Series: Concrete. 2006, Dark Horse paper $12.95 (978-1-59307-469-2). Superhero Concrete must rescue his assistant, Larry, in this dark and action-packed fourth installment in the series. (Rev: BL 5/15/06)

3283 Chadwick, Paul. *Strange Armor* (9–12). Series: Concrete. 2006, Dark Horse paper $12.95 (978-1-59307-560-6). The sixth book in the revived Concrete series, this graphic novel tells of the origin of the character that was created in 1998 — a speech writer who is trapped in a powerful, massive stone-like being by aliens and seeks help from the CIA, NSA, and a beautiful researcher to better understand his new body. Also use *The Human Dilemma,* the seventh volume. (Rev: BL 9/15/06)

3284 Chadwick, Paul. *Think Like a Mountain: Concrete 5* (9–12). 2006, Dark Horse paper $12.95 (978-1-59307-559-0). The further adventures of Concrete involve an environmentally injured landscape. (Rev: BL 8/06)

3285 Chan, Queenie. *The Dreaming* (9–12). Series: Dreaming. 2005, TokyoPop paper $9.99 (978-1-59816-382-7). Identical twins Amber and Jeanie are thrilled to be accepted into an exclusive Australian boarding school, but they soon find themselves swept into a mystery when students begin to disappear; the first volume in a manga trilogy. (Rev: BL 12/1/05)

3286 Chantler, Scott. *The Annotated Northwest Passage* (8–12). Illus. by author. 2007, Oni $19.95 (978-1-932664-61-4). This action-packed graphic novel, set in northern Canada in 1755, tells of the fierce competition between the French, British, and other private interests to control the fur trade. (Rev: BL 8/07; SLJ 11/07)

3287 Chen, Jo. *The Other Side of the Mirror, Vol. 1* (10–12). Illus. by author. Series: The Other Side of the Mirror. 2007, TokyoPop paper $9.99 (978-1-4278-0316-0). Lou, a college-educated ne'er-do-well, and Sunny, a reluctant prostitute, become friends and lovers and together navigate the rough streets of New York City and the sad stories of their pasts. (Rev: BL 3/3/08)

3288 Clamp. *Tsubasa: Reservoir Chronicle, Vol. 1* (9–12). Trans. from Japanese by Anthony Gerard. Illus. by author. Series: Tsubasa: Reservoir Chronicle. 2004, Del Rey paper $10.95 (978-0-345-47057-7). Characters from other CLAMP manga series return in this story of teenage Sakura, princess of Clow and endowed with a mysterious power, and Syaoran, with whom she is in love; together the two set out on a quest to retrieve Sakura's dispersed memories. (Rev: SLJ 10/04)

3289 Clamp. *Wish* (9–12). 2002, TokyoPop paper $9.99 (978-1-59182-034-5). A graphic novel about a young surgeon and the angel he rescues. (Rev: BL 2/1/04)

3290 Colbert, C. C., and Tanitoc. *Booth* (11–12). Illus. 2010, First Second paper $19.99 (978-15964312-5-6). In graphic-novel form Colbert presents a fictionalized but thoroughly researched account of the life of John Wilkes Booth, Lincoln's assassin, from childhood to Confederate activist and actor. (Rev: BL 2/1–15/10; SLJ 5/10)

3291 Cole, Jack. *The Plastic Man: Archives, Vol. 7* (9–12). 2005, DC Comics $49.99 (978-1-4012-0410-5). The seventh volume of the Plastic Man series collects issues of the popular comic book from 1947. (Rev: BL 2/1/06)

3292 Cole, Jack. *The Plastic Man: Archives, Vol. 8* (9–12). 2006, DC Comics $49.99 (978-1-4012-0777-9). Volume 8 of the archives of Plastic Man includes light-hearted comics from the late 1940s, halfway through the series' 15 years, featuring the villain-battling hero who has the unique ability to stretch his body to any degree. (Rev: BL 11/1/06)

3293 Conami, Shoko. *Shinobi Life, Vol. 1* (8–11). Illus. by Vicente Rivera. 2008, Tokyopop paper $9.99 (978-142781111-0). Beni finds herself being shadowed by a very cute time-traveling ninja in this first installment in the series. (Rev: BLO 1/13/09)

3294 Cooke, Darwyn. *Ego and Other Tails: Batman* (9–12). 2007, DC Comics $24.99 (978-1-4012-1529-3). In *Ego,* one of the early Batman stories by Cooke included in this collection, Bruce Wayne recognizes his deepest fears in the form of a monstrous embodiment of his alter ego. (Rev: BL 8/07; SLJ 1/08) [741.5]

3295 Cooke, Darwyn, and Dave Stewart. *DC: The New Frontier, Vol. 2* (9–12). Series: DC: The New Frontier. 2005, DC Comics paper $19.99 (978-1-4012-0461-7). Contemporary adventures of superheroes including Green Lantern and the Martian Manhunter. (Rev: BL 5/15/05; SLJ 9/05)

3296 Crilley, Mark. *Brody's Ghost, Vol. 1* (7–12). Illus. by author. 2010, Dark Horse paper $6.99 (978-15958252-1-6). Brody's sad, directionless life changes when a teenage ghost enlists his aid to help her gain entrance into heaven. (Rev: BLO 9/1/10)

3297 Crilley, Mark. *Miki Falls: Summer* (7–12). Illus. by author. 2007, HarperTeen paper $7.99 (978-0-06-084617-X). This well-illustrated volume in the manga style follows Miki, a Japanese teen who falls in love with a superhuman entity. (Rev: SLJ 7/07)

3298 Crisse, Didier. *Luuna, Vol. 1* (9–12). Illus. by Nicolas Keramidas. Series: Luuna. 2009, Tokyopop paper $12.99 (978-142781412-8). Luuna sets off to find her totem and instead learns that her killer instinct will be released once each month — will she use it for good or evil? (Rev: BL 3/15/09)

3299 Dasgupta, Amit, and Neelabh. *Indian by Choice* (10–12). Illus. 2009, Wisdom Tree paper $19.95 (978-81832813-6-2). This graphic novel tells the story of U.S.-born Mandy's first visit to India, his family's homeland, and how he rediscovers his roots. **e** (Rev: BL 4–5/09)

3300 Davis, Jim. *Garfield: 30 Years of Laughs and Lasagna* (5–10). Illus. by author. 2008, Ballantine $35.00 (978-0-345-50379-4). A collection of the popular comic strip that centers on a grumpy, overweight cat. (Rev: BL 10/15/08; SLJ 1/09)

3301 Dawson, Mike. *Freddie and Me: A Coming-of-Age (Bohemian) Rhapsody* (9–12). 2008, Bloomsbury paper $19.95 (978-1-59691-476-6). In this autobiographical graphic novel memoir, the author explores his life through the lens of his long-time obsession with the UK rock band Queen. (Rev: BL 4/1/08; SLJ 5/08)

3302 De Crecy, Nicolas. *Glacial Period* (9–12). Trans. by Joe Johnson. 2007, NBM paper $14.95 (978-1-56163-483-5). In a frozen future, an intrepid group of explorers come across the Louvre and attempt to explain the strange objects they find there. (Rev: BL 2/15/07; SLJ 7/07)

3303 Deitch, Kim, and Simon Deitch. *The Boulevard of Broken Dreams* (11–12). 2002, Pantheon $21.00 (978-0-375-42191-4). An engrossing story of life at the pioneering Fontaine Talking Fables animation studio in New York in 1933; suited to mature teens. (Rev: BL 11/1/02; SLJ 8/03)

3304 Dembicki, Matt, ed. *Trickster: Native American Tales: A Graphic Collection* (8–12). Illus. 2010, Fulcrum Publishing paper $22.95 (978-1-55591-724-1). More than 20 Native American tales are presented in appealing graphic-novel format, illustrated by a variety of artists. ALA Notable Books 2011. (Rev: BL 5/1/10*; LMC 11–12/10; SLJ 5/10) [398.2]

3305 Dickens, Charles, and Loic Dauvillier. *Oliver Twist* (7–12). Illus. by Olivier Deloye. Series: Classics Illustrated Deluxe. 2012, Papercutz $24.99 (978-

159707308-0); paper $19.99 (978-15970730-7-3). With a French adapter and illustrator, this graphic-novel version of the story about Oliver's hard childhood reflects the original. (Rev: BL 4/15/12; SLJ 1/13)

3306 Dini, Paul, and Guillem March. *Gotham City Sirens Union* (10–12). Illus. 2010, DC Comics $19.99 (978-140122570-4). The three femmes fatales of Gotham City — Catwoman, Poison Ivy, and Harley Quinn — move in together, hoping for peace and quiet, but with a violent Batman impostor loose in the city, life is anything but. (Rev: BL 5/1–15/10)

3307 Dini, Paul, et al. *Paul Dini's Jingle Belle* (9–12). 2005, Dark Horse paper $12.95 (978-1-59307-382-4). Jingle Belle, Santa's teenage daughter, tries a number of schemes to increase her visibility. (Rev: BL 11/15/05)

3308 Ditko, Steve. *The Action Heroes Archives, v.2* (9–12). 2007, DC Comics $75.00 (978-1-4012-1346-6). When Spider-Man artist Ditko left Marvel and was hired by the smaller-budgeted Charlton Comics, what he lost in salary he gained in artistic and political freedom, and this is evident in his later stories of Captain Atom, Blue Beetle, and the Question that are collected in this archive. (Rev: BL 8/07) [741.5]

3309 Dixon, Chuck. *El Cazador* (9–12). Illus. by Steve Epting. 2007, Hyperion paper $12.99 (978-4-4231-0927-3). This compelling graphic novel set in 1687 tells the story of the Donessa Hidalgo, who becomes Lady Sin, a pirate captain, and sets out to rescue her family from Blackjack Tom. (Rev: SLJ 1/08)

3310 Dixon, Chuck. *Nightwing: On the Razor's Edge* (8–12). Illus. by Greg Land and Drew Geraci. 2005, DC Comics paper $14.99 (978-1-4012-0437-2). Robin, Batman's former sidekick, now takes on the superhero identity of Nightwing and must defend himself against his foes. (Rev: SLJ 11/05)

3311 Dixon, Chuck. *Way of the Rat: The Walls of Zhumar* (7–12). 2003, CrossGeneration paper $15.95 (978-1-931484-51-0). Boon has stolen a scholar's magic ring and the Book of Hell and is now being chased by villains in this fantasy set in Asia and enhanced by dynamic illustrations. (Rev: BL 2/1/03)

3312 Doran, Colleen. *A Distant Soil: The Gathering* (9–12). 2001, Image Comics paper $18.95 (978-1-887279-51-2). This is a classic graphic novel about siblings from another world. (Rev: BL 2/1/04)

3313 Dostoevsky, Fyodor, and David Zane Mairowitz. *Crime and Punishment* (10–12). Illus. by Alain Korkos. 2009, Sterling paper $14.95 (978-141141594-2). A graphic adaptation of the novel, set in present-day Russia and heavy on atmosphere and angst. (Rev: BL 5/1/09)

3314 Drake, Arnold. *The Doom Patrol Archives, Vol. 3* (9–12). 2006, DC Comics $49.99 (978-1-4012-0766-3). A collection of nine issues from the Doom Patrol's heyday in the 1960s. (Rev: BL 8/06)

3315 Dumas, Alexandre. *The Man in the Iron Mask* (9–12). Retold by Jim Pipe. Illus. by Penko Gelev. Series: Graphic Classics. 2007, Barron's $15.99 (978-0-7641-6055-4); paper $8.99 (978-0-7641-3779-2). An abridged, graphic-novel version of the classic adventure story; SAT vocabulary words are defined in footnotes that also add historical and other details. (Rev: SLJ 1/08)

3316 Dunning, John Harris. *Salem Brownstone: All Along the Watchtowers* (9–12). Illus. by Nikhil Singh. 2010, Candlewick $18.99 (978-0-7636-4735-3). This unusual, oversize graphic novel tells a gothic story of Salem Brownstone inheriting a mansion and a continuing struggle against dark forces. (Rev: BL 7/10*; LMC 11–12/10; SLJ 7/10; VOYA 8/10)

3317 Dysart, Joshua, and Cliff Chiang. *Neil Young's Greendale* (11–12). Illus. 2010, Vertigo $19.99 (978-140122820-0). Environmentally conscious 18-year-old Sun Green's charmed life unravels in the face of family drama in this vividly illustrated, political graphic novel inspired by Neil Young's rock opera; for mature teens. (Rev: BL 5/1–15/10; SLJ 7/10)

3318 Edginton, Ian. *H. G. Wells' The War of the Worlds* (9–12). Illus. by D'Israeli. 2006, Dark Horse $14.95 (978-1-59307-474-6). A well-written and brilliantly illustrated graphic novel adaptation of the H. G. Wells classic. (Rev: BL 6/1–15/06)

3319 Edginton, Ian, and D'Israeli. *The Great Game: Scarlet Traces* (9–12). 2007, Dark Horse $14.95 (978-1-59307-717-4). London of the early 20th century and Mars are the steampunk-type settings for this wartime detective story featuring an aging adventurer Robert Autumn and a news photographer Charlotte Hemming who are investigating disappearances of humans in the aftermath of *The War of the Worlds*. (Rev: BL 7/07; SLJ 9/07) [741.5]

3320 Eisner, Will. *The Best of the Spirit* (9–12). 2005, DC Comics paper $14.99 (978-1-4012-0755-7). Highlights from Eisner's The Spirit comic book series, which was published off and on between 1939 and 1952, are collected in this single paperback volume. (Rev: BL 2/1/06; SLJ 7/06)

3321 Eisner, Will. *Fagin the Jew* (10–12). Illus. by author. 2003, Doubleday paper $15.95 (978-0-385-51009-7). Eisner takes the character from *Oliver Twist* and envisions his youth. (Rev: BL 9/1/03; SLJ 1/04)

3322 Eisner, Will. *Will Eisner's The Spirit Archives, Vol. 12* (8–12). 2003, DC Comics $49.95 (978-1-4012-0006-0). This collection of comic strips covers the full 12-year career of the Spirit, a masked crime fighter. (Rev: BL 2/1/04)

3323 Eisner, Will. *Will Eisner's The Spirit Archives, Vol. 17* (9–12). 2005, DC Comics $49.99 (978-1-4012-0417-4). The 17th volume of the Spirit series showcases a dozen of the most celebrated stories from the

12-year run of Will Eisner's popular comic book. (Rev: BL 3/1/06)

3324 Eisner, Will. *Will Eisner's The Spirit Archives, Vol. 19* (9–12). Series: Spirit. 2006, DC Comics $49.99 (978-1-4012-0775-5). A collection of stories featuring The Spirit, the superhero from the 1940s. (Rev: BL 9/1/06)

3325 El Rassi, Toufic. *Arab in America* (9–12). 2008, Last Gasp paper $14.95 (978-0-86719-673-3). In this autobiographically based graphic novel, El Rassi thinks of himself as a normal American until his dark Arab beard begins to grow in 8th grade earning him threats and insults and a firsthand knowledge of the pervasive ignorance about Arabs and the Middle East. (Rev: BL 4/1/08)

3326 Eldred, Tim. *Grease Monkey* (9–12). 2006, Tor $27.95 (978-0-7653-1325-6). In this long sci fi graphic novel with elements of comedy and romance, Robin Plotnick, a young space cadet, is apprenticed to ace mechanic Mac Gimbensky, a talking gorilla, aboard the spaceship Fist of Earth. (Rev: BL 3/15/06; SLJ 7/06)

3327 Ellis, Warren, et al. *Ocean* (9–12). 2005, DC Comics paper $14.99 (978-1-4012-0849-3). In this graphic novel science fiction thriller, UN weapons inspector Nathan Kane journeys to a distant space station to investigate an alarming discovery. (Rev: BL 1/1–15/06; SLJ 5/06)

3328 Endo, Hiroki. *Eden: It's an Endless World! 1* (11–12). Trans. by Kumar Sivasubramanian. 2005, Dark Horse paper $12.95 (978-1-59307-406-7). In this futuristic graphic novel fantasy, a small band of survivors of a worldwide plague that has killed billions encounters intrigues and perils in its travels; for mature readers. (Rev: BL 1/1–15/06)

3329 Endo, Hiroki. *Eden: It's an Endless World! 2* (9–12). Trans. by Kumar Sivasubramanian. Series: Eden: It's an Endless World. 2006, Dark Horse paper $12.95 (978-1-59307-454-8). There's graphic gore and violence aplenty in volume two of this post-apocalyptic manga. (Rev: BL 3/15/06)

3330 Endo, Hiroki. *Eden: It's an Endless World! 3* (11–12). Trans. by Kumar Sivasubramanian. Series: Eden. 2006, Dark Horse paper $12.95 (978-1-59307-529-3). In a future militaristic world where violence abounds, the villains are cyber-augmented Aeon soldiers, part of a Propator organization fighting a group of guerrilla heroes still struggling to save the world and themselves; a manga for mature teens. Other volumes in this recommended series include *Eden: It's an Endless World! 4* (2006), in which we learn about the origins of the Japanese freedom fighter, Kenji. (Rev: BL 10/15/06)

3331 Endo, Hiroki. *Eden: It's an Endless World! 5* (10–12). Trans. by Kumar Sivasubramanian. Series: Eden. 2006, Dark Horse paper $12.95 (978-1-59307-634-4). Endo provides a character study of cyber-enhanced individuals separated from and trying to find their bodies while fiercely battling the evil world-dominating Aeon soldiers in this post-apocalyptic military science fiction series. (Rev: BL 12/15/06)

3332 Endo, Hiroki. *Tanpenshu 1* (10–12). Trans. by Kumar Sivasubramanian. 2007, Dark Horse $12.95 (978-1-59307-637-5). A collection of three manga stories featuring attractive young people dealing with violence, from the author known better for his science fiction. (Rev: BL 3/15/07)

3333 Englehart, Steve, et al. *Dark Detective: Batman* (9–12). 2006, DC Comics paper $14.99 (978-1-4012-0898-1). The authors go back to Batman's beginnings to give fans the story lines they enjoy most. (Rev: BL 5/15/06)

3334 Ennis, Garth, et al. *War Stories, Vol. 2* (10–12). 2006, DC Comics paper $19.99 (978-1-4012-1039-7). Four stories about the violence, heroism, and horror that accompany warfare, in graphic-novel format. (Rev: BL 4/15/06; SLJ 7/06)

3335 Espinosa, Rod. *Neotopia Color Manga* (6–12). Series: Neotopia. 2004, Antarctic paper $9.99 (978-1-932453-57-7). In the opening volume of the graphic novel series, Nalyn, a servant girl, takes over her spoiled mistress's responsibilities as grand duchess of Mathenia, but the going gets tough when Mathenia comes under attack from the evil empire of Krossos. (Rev: BL 12/1/04)

3336 Fies, Brian. *Whatever Happened to the World of Tomorrow?* (10–12). 2009, Abrams $24.95 (978-0-8109-9636-6). This unique graphic novel captures the feel of the 1939 World's Fair, complete with sepia tones, as a boy views "The Fantastic Future City of 2039," and it then follows him — and the development of technology — through 1975 and the final Apollo mission. (Rev: BLO 6/23/09; LMC 1–2/10)

3337 Fillbach, Matt, and Shawn Fillbach. *Roadkill* (10–12). Illus. by author. 2008, Dark Horse paper $9.95 (978-159582169-0). A trucker and his talking dog encounter flesh-eating zombies in a world inhabited by supernatural freaks; humor and horror are here in equal doses. (Rev: BLO 1/13/09)

3338 Fitzgerald, F. Scott, and Nunzio DeFilippis. *The Curious Case of Benjamin Button* (10–12). Illus. by Kevin Cornell. 2008, Quirk $15.95 (978-159474281-1). A graphic-novel adaptation of a story recently made into a movie starring Brad Pitt; lovely artwork adds to the charm of this tale of a baby born old. ℮ (Rev: BL 1/1–15/09; SLJ 1/09)

3339 Friedman, Aimee. *Breaking Up* (8–11). Illus. by Christine Norrie. 2007, Scholastic paper $8.99 (978-0-439-74867-4). Romance, sex, and fashion at the Georgia O'Keeffe School for the Arts. (Rev: BL 3/15/07; SLJ 3/07)

3340 Fujisawa, Tobru. *Rose Hip Zero* (9–12). Series: Rose Hip Zero. 2006, TokyoPop paper $9.99 (978-1-4278-0025-1). Kido, a cop, is fighting a terrorist cell in Japan with the reluctant and sexy Asakura, a girl who was trained to kill by the terrorists; the first volume in a new manga series. (Rev: BL 2/1/07)

3341 Fujishima, Kosuke. *Oh My Goddess! #27* (9–12). Trans. by Dana Lewis. Illus. by author. Series: Oh My Goddess. 2007, Dark Horse paper $10.95 (978-1-59307-788-4). Keiichi lives with five beautiful goddesses and this installment in the manga series continues their adventures. (Rev: BL 1/1–15/08)

3342 Fujishima, Kosuke. *Oh My Goddess! Colors* (8–12). Illus. by author. 2009, Dark Horse paper $19.95 (978-1595822550). Four classic manga stories each focus on a goddess — Belldandy, Urd, Skuld, and Peorth — in this oversized volume that includes a thorough encyclopedia of the series. (Rev: BL 6/1–15/09)

3343 Fujita, Maki. *Kids Joker, Vol. 1* (9–12). Trans. from Japanese by Kay Bertrand. Illus. by author. 2005, ADV paper $9.99 (978-1-4139-0162-7). Hotaru Yanagawa, a high school student, is determined to tag along with Yui, a young man who's part of a secret organization. (Rev: SLJ 7/05)

3344 Fukushima, Haruka. *Orange Planet, Vol. 1* (8–11). Illus. by author. 2009, Del Rey paper $10.99 (978-034551338-0). In this *shojo* manga, Rui finds herself the object of much male interest — from her contemporaries and from a teacher. (Rev: BLO 4/30/09; SLJ 9/09)

3345 Gaiman, Neil. *The Absolute Sandman, Vol. 1* (9–12). 2006, Vertigo $99.00 (978-1-4012-1082-3). The first of four volumes, this is a collection of issues 1-20 of "The Sandman" superhero comic with new coloring and newly published bonus material. (Rev: BL 10/15/06)

3346 Gaiman, Neil, and P. Craig Russell. *Murder Mysteries* (11–12). 2002, Dark Horse $13.95 (978-1-56971-634-2). A graphic novel adaptation of Gaiman's short story about two mysterious murders; for mature teens. (Rev: BL 9/1/02)

3347 Gallagher, Fred. *Megatokyo, Vol. 3* (9–12). Series: Megatokyo. 2005, Dark Horse paper $9.95 (978-1-59307-305-3). In the third volume of the manga series, romantic Piro and gamer geek Largo, stuck in Japan, continue to stir up trouble every way they turn. (Rev: BL 3/15/05)

3348 Gallagher, Fred, and Rodney Caston. *Megatokyo, Vol. 2* (11–12). 2004, Dark Horse paper $9.95 (978-1-59307-118-9). This graphic novel tells about two young geeks, Piro and Largo, and their pilgrimage to Japan. (Rev: BL 5/1/04; SLJ 8/04)

3349 Geary, Rick. *The Case of Madeleine Smith* (7–12). Illus. by author. Series: Treasury of Victorian Murder. 2006, NBM $15.95 (978-1-56163-467-5). Based on ac-

tual events in Victorian Glasgow, this story of an affair between an upper-class young woman and a merchant's son ends in murder. (Rev: BL 6/1–15/06; SLJ 9/06)

3350 Geary, Rick. *The Saga of the Bloody Benders* (9–12). 2007, NBM $15.95 (978-1-56163-498-9). From the Treasury of Victorian Murder series, this story takes place in the Kansas frontier along the Osage Trail where the Bender family runs an inn and grocery store and whose customers start vanishing in their travels. (Rev: BL 7/07) [364.1]

3351 Giallongo, Zack. *Broxo* (7–10). Illus. by author. 2012, First Second paper $16.99 (978-15964355-1-3). A multilayered graphic novel featuring Princess Zora, who is on a quest, and Broxo, a young warrior with no friends save his horned-beast companion Migo. (Rev: BL 9/15/12; LMC 3–4/13; SLJ 11/12; VOYA 10/12)

3352 Gibbons, Dave. *Thunderbolt Jaxon: From the World of Albion* (10–12). Illus. by John Higgins. 2007, Wildstorm paper $19.99 (978-1-4012-1257-5). British teens Jack, Billy, and Saf discover powerful Norse relics and unleash ancient powers and enmities. (Rev: LMC 1/08; SLJ 9/07)

3353 Giffen, Keith, and Alan Grant. *Holiday Hell: Lobo/The Authority* (11–12). 2006, DC Comics paper $17.99 (978-1-4012-0992-6). For mature comic book fans, this adventure involves Lobo, a Conan the Barbarian-type character; the Easter Bunny; a tyrannical Santa Claus; and a group of immensely powerful heroes known as "The Authority." (Rev: BL 9/15/06)

3354 Giffen, Keith, et al. *I Can't Believe It's Not the Justice League* (9–12). 2005, DC Comics paper $12.99 (978-1-4012-0478-5). The zany antics of such second-string superheroes as Mary Marvel, Blue Beetle, and the Elongated Man. (Rev: BL 1/1–15/06)

3355 Gipi. *Garage Band* (10–12). 2007, Roaring Brook paper $16.95 (978-1-59643-206-2). Four troubled teens — Guiliano, Stefano, Alberto, and Alex — promise to behave in return for the use of a garage for their band practice, but when their amplifier breaks and they cannot afford a new one, what will they do? (Rev: BCCB 7–8/07; BL 3/15/07; HB 5–6/07; LMC 8–9/07; SLJ 5/07)

3356 Gipi. *Notes for a War Story* (10–12). Illus. by author. 2007, Roaring Brook paper $16.95 (978-1-59643-261-1). A sad and scary story of young people caught up in an adults' war. (Rev: BCCB 11/07; BL 7/07; SLJ 7/08)

3357 Gore, Shawna, ed. *Creepy Archives, Vol. 1* (10–12). Illus. 2008, Dark Horse $49.95 (978-159307973-4). Here is a collection of *Creepy* issues known for their attention-getting covers and boundary-pushing content; the first in a series. (Rev: BL 9/1/08)

3358 *Green Lantern* (4–10). Series: Showcase Presents. 2005, DC Comics paper $9.99 (978-1-4012-0759-5). A collection of black-and-white reprints of the early comics about the handsome crime fighter. (Rev: SLJ 5/06)

3359 Gross, Milt. *He Done Her Wrong* (9–12). 2006, Fantagraphics paper $16.95 (978-1-56097-694-3). Milt Gross's wordless graphic novel from the early 1930s — one of the comics masterpieces of the 20th century — is presented anew in this attractive paperback edition. (Rev: BL 2/15/06)

3360 Hague, Michael. *In the Small* (7–10). Illus. by author. 2008, Little, Brown $12.99 (978-0-316-01323-9). In a flash of blue light, the people of the earth are shrunk to a height of six inches or less, changing their lives and leaving them vulnerable to animals — even the household cat; a teen brother and sister seem to offer the only path to salvation. (Rev: BL 3/15/08; SLJ 5/08)

3361 Hernandez, Gilbert. *Sloth* (10–12). 2006, DC Comics paper $19.99 (978-1-4012-0366-5). An effective graphic novel in which Miguel, a disaffected high school student in a small town who had sunk into a yearlong self-induced coma, comes back to life and indulges in a love triangle with friends Lita and Romeo. (Rev: BL 5/15/06; SLJ 1/07)

3362 Hernandez, Jaime. *Maggie the Mechanic: A Love and Rockets Book, Vol. 1* (10–12). Illus. by author. 2007, Fantagraphics paper $14.95 (978-1-56097-784-1). Today's YA readers will enjoy the adventures of the likable protagonists in this series of inventive science fiction comics first published in the 1980s. (Rev: SLJ 7/07)

3363 Heuvel, Eric. *A Family Secret* (7–12). Trans. from Dutch by Lorraine T. Miller. Illus. by author. 2009, Farrar $18.99. (978-0-374-32271-7). A contemporary teen learns from his grandmother about the Nazi occupation of the Netherlands and the difficult decisions that people had to make. (Rev: BL 9/15/09*; SLJ 5/10)

3364 Hicks, Faith Erin. *Friends with Boys* (8–12). Illus. by author. 2012, First Second paper $15.99 (978-15964355-6-8). After years of home-schooling, Maggie enters public high school where she must navigate all kinds of challenges, all the while accompanied by the ghost that haunts her. YALSA Great Graphic Novels Top Ten 2013. Lexile GN390L (Rev: BL 2/15/12; HB 5–6/12; LMC 8–9/12; SLJ 3/1/12*; VOYA 6/12)

3365 Higuri, You. *Angel's Coffin* (10–12). Illus. by author. 2008, Go! Comi paper $10.99 (978-193361768-8). History and the supernatural mix in this artfully rendered manga novel about the death of Austrian Crown Prince Rudolf in 1889. (Rev: BLO 12/8/08)

3366 Hinds, Gareth. *King Lear* (7–10). Illus. by author. 2007, Thecomic.com $30.00 (978-1-893131-07-1); paper $15.95 (978-1-893131-06-4). This graphic adaptation of the Shakespeare play brings visual drama to the abridged story, adding interest to pull in reluctant readers. (Rev: BL 2/1/08)

3367 Hinds, Gareth. *The Merchant of Venice* (8–12). Illus. by author. 2008, Candlewick $21.99 (978-0-7636-3024-9); paper $11.99 (978-0-7636-3025-6). Gray, moody illustrations of characters in modern dress combine with a pared-down story to make this a very engaging version of the play. (Rev: BL 3/15/08; SLJ 5/08)

3368 Hinds, Gareth. *The Odyssey* (7–12). 2010, Candlewick $24.99 (978-0-7636-4266-2). Rich illustrations enhance this faithful graphic-novel rendering of the amazing adventures of Odysseus. Lexile GN840L (Rev: BL 9/15/10*; HB 11–12/10; LMC 11–12/10; SLJ 11/10; VOYA 2/11)

3369 Hine, David, and Fabrice Sapolsky. *Spider-Man Noir* (10–12). Illus. by Carmine Di Giandomenico. 2009, Marvel paper $14.99 (978-078512923-3). In 1930s New York City a spider's bite transforms young Peter Parker into a crusader against crime and corruption. (Rev: BL 11/15/09*)

3370 Hino, Matsuri. *Captive Hearts, Vol. 2* (8–11). Illus. by author. Series: Captive Hearts. 2009, VIZ Media paper $8.99 (978-142151933-3). Megumi continues to do anything for Suzuka and her love in the second book in this manga series. (Rev: BLO 4/30/09)

3371 Holkins, Jerry, and Mike Krahulik. *Attack of the Bacon Robots! Penny Arcade 1* (11–12). Series: Penny Arcade. 2006, Dark Horse paper $12.95 (978-1-59307-444-9). Collects some of the zany — sometimes violent — adventures from the popular online comic strip for gamers. (Rev: BL 2/1/06)

3372 Hon, Creative. *Last Fantasy, Vol. 1* (10–12). Illus. by Yong-Wan Kwon. 2006, TokyoPop $9.99 (978-1-59532-526-6). Drei and Tian manage to mess up many times in this humorous adventure story where they search for treasure and meet up with ogres, monsters, dragons, centaurs and more. (Rev: BL 9/1/06; SLJ 7/06)

3373 Hornschemeier, Paul. *Mother, Come Home* (10–12). 2003, Dark Horse paper $14.95 (978-1-59307-037-3). The wrenching story of a 17-year-boy who must cope with the deaths of his mother and then his father. (Rev: BL 2/1/04*; SLJ 6/04)

3374 Hosseini, Khaled. *The Kite Runner* (10–12). Illus. by Fabio Celoni and Mirka Andolfo. 2011, Riverhead $19 (978-159448547-3). This graphic-novel version of the 2003 novel about Amir and his experiences in the turmoil that is Afghanistan both distills and extends the story. Also available in Arabic. (Rev: LMC 3–4/12; SLJ 11/11)

3375 Huddleston, Courtney, et al. *Decoy: Menagerie, Part 1* (9–12). 2005, Penny Farthing $19.95 (978-0-9719012-3-0). A collection of seven stories about an alien named Decoy who is locked in a symbiotic relationship with a wounded rookie cop, Bobby Luck, and their efforts to solve crimes in Dolphin City. (Rev: BL 11/1/05)

3376 Hughes, Richard E., and Ogden Whitney. *Herbie Archives; Vol. 1* (10–12). Illus. 2008, Dark Horse $49.95 (978-1-59307-987-1). A collection of the 1960s comics about chunky Herbie Popnecker and his supernatural lollipops and abilities to bend time and space and defeat monsters of all kinds. (Rev: BL 8/08) [741.5]

3377 Hugo, Victor. *The Hunchback of Notre Dame* (5–12). Retold by Michael Ford. Illus. by Penko Gelev. Series: Graphic Classics. 2007, Barron's $15.99 (978-0-7641-5979-4). The classic story about the misshapen bell ringer is presented in graphic-novel format. (Rev: SLJ 5/07)

3378 Hurd, Damon, and Tatiana Gill. *A Strange Day* (8–12). 2005, Alternative Comics paper $3.95 (978-1-891867-74-3). This appealing graphic novella tells a story of instant attraction between two teens who share the same tastes in music. (Rev: BL 5/1/05)

3379 Hwa, Kim Dong. *The Color of Earth* (10–12). Illus. by author. 2009, First Second paper $16.95 (978-159643458-5). This lovely coming-of-age manhwa set in rural Korea traces Ehwa's life from age 7 to 16 and her maturing from childhood into an adolescent interested in her own body and those of young men; she shares a close bond with her widowed mother, who runs a tavern and finds her own new love. (Rev: BL 6/1–15/09*; SLJ 9/09; VOYA 4/09)

3380 Igarashi, Daisuke. *Children of the Sea, Vol. 1* (7–12). Illus. by author. 2009, VIZ Media paper $14.99 (978-142152914-1). Fish are disappearing from aquariums around the world and strange children are simultaneously discovered living in the sea; young Ruka feels drawn to the aquarium and sets out to investigate. (Rev: BL 11/1/09*; VOYA 4/10)

3381 Ikezawa, Satomi. *Guru Guru Pon-Chan, Vol. 1* (5–12). Trans. from Japanese by Douglas Varenas. Illus. by author. 2005, Del Rey paper $10.95 (978-0-345-48095-8). In this whimsical shape-changing story, Ponta, a Labrador retriever puppy, nibbles on a newly invented "chit-chat" bone and turns into a human girl who comically retains doggy behavior. (Rev: SLJ 11/05)

3382 Ikezawa, Satomi. *Othello, Vol. 3* (10–12). Trans. from Japanese by William Flanagan. Illus. by author. 2005, Del Rey paper $10.95 (978-0-345-47998-3). Frequent appearances by her alter ego — the polar opposite of her primary personality — are complicating life for Yaya. (Rev: SLJ 9/05)

3383 Immonen, Kathryn, and Stuart Immonen. *Moving Pictures* (10–12). Illus. 2010, Top Shelf paper $14.95 (978-16030904-9-0). Parisian art curators struggle to protect the masterpieces they love during the Nazi occupation. (Rev: BL 5/1/10*)

3384 Inoue, Takehiko. *Real, Vol. 2* (10–12). Illus. by author. Series: Real. 2008, VIZ Media paper $12.99 (978-142151990-6). Athletic Kiyoharu, 14, is confined to a wheelchair after an illness and learns to cope with his limitations. (Rev: BL 3/1/09)

3385 Inzana, Ryan. *Ichiro* (7–10). Illus. by author. 2012, Houghton Mifflin $19.99 (978-054725269-8). Ichiro, son of an American soldier who died in battle and a Japanese mother, learns much about his heritage on a visit to his maternal grandfather in Hiroshima City. Lexile GN490L (Rev: BL 3/15/12; HB 3–4/12; LMC 11–12/12; SLJ 3/1/12)

3386 Inzana, Ryan. *Johnny Jihad* (10–12). 2003, NBM paper $9.95 (978-1-56163-353-1). A gripping and well-illustrated tale of a young American recruited into Islamic radicalism. (Rev: BL 8/03)

3387 Irwin, Jane, and Jeff Berndt. *Vogelein: Clockwork Faerie* (5–12). 2003, Fiery Studios paper $12.95 (978-0-9743110-0-5). A beautiful 17th-century mechanical fairy who is immortal but depends on others to wind her up stars in this graphic novel. (Rev: BL 11/1/03)

3388 Iwahara, Yuji. *King of Thorn, Vol. 1* (9–12). Illus. by author. Series: King of Thorn. 2007, TokyoPop paper $9.99 (978-1-59816-235-6). In a world where a virus is turning humans to stone, Kasumi awakes from suspended animation to search for a cure. (Rev: BL 10/1/07)

3389 Iwanaga, Ryoutaro. *Pumpkin Scissors, Vol. 1* (9–12). Trans. by Ikoi Hiroe. Illus. by author. Series: Pumpkin Scissors. 2007, Del Rey paper $10.95 (978-0-345-50119-6). Randel, whose powers come from a magic lantern, helps the Pumpkin Scissors unit fight off another band of soldiers in this first installment in the manga series. (Rev: BL 10/15/07; SLJ 3/08)

3390 Iwaoka, Hisae. *Saturn Apartments, Vol. 1* (9–12). Illus. by author. 2010, VIZ Media paper $12.99 (978-14215336-4-3). Humans have left Earth and moved to apartments in a large ring surrounding the planet, where a view is highly prized; young Mitsu takes over the important and dangerous job of window washing after his father's death. YALSA Great Graphic Novels Top Ten 2011. (Rev: BLO 9/1/10; SLJ 9/1/10)

3391 Jablonski, Carla. *Defiance* (7–10). Illus. by Leland Purvis. Series: Resistance. 2011, First Second paper $16.99 (978-15964329-2-5). Paul Tessier, 14, wants to join the French Resistance, and does work for them drawing maps, but he also feels he must look after his younger sister. Lexile GN300L (Rev: BL 6/1/11; HB 9–10/11; SLJ 9/1/11)

3392 Jablonski, Carla. *Resistance* (7–10). Illus. by Leland Purvis. Series: Resistance. 2010, First Second paper $16.99 (978-1-59643-291-8). Marie and Paul help Henri, who is Jewish, reunite with his deported parents in this graphic novel set in World War II. Sydney Taylor Book Honor 2011. Lexile GN190L (Rev: BL 3/15/10*; LMC 8–9/10; SLJ 5/10)

3393 Jablonski, Carla. *Victory* (7–10). Illus. by Leland Purvis. 2012, First Second paper $17.99 (978-

159643293-2). The Allies are in Normandy and the Tessier siblings are all working in the Resistance in this final volume in the trilogy, in which Paris is finally liberated. (Rev: BL 6/12; HB 7–8/12; LMC 11–12/12; SLJ 1/13; VOYA 8/12)

3394 Jansson, Tove. *Moomin: The Complete Tove Jansson Comic Strip, Book 2* (10–12). Illus. by author. 2007, Drawn & Quarterly $19.95 (978-1-897299-19-7). This volume collects comic strips written for adults in the 1950s and featuring the hippolike Scandinavians of the Moominvalley. (Rev: SLJ 1/08)

3395 Jansson, Tove, and Lars Jansson. *Moomin: The Complete Tove Jansson Comic Strip* (10–12). Illus. 2009, Drawn & Quarterly $19.95 (978-189729978-4). These comic strips based on the Moomin character are filled with time machines, funny situations, and down-to-earth life lessons; (Rev: BL 7/09; SLJ 9/09)

3396 Ji-Hyung, Song. *XS Hybrid* (10–12). Illus. by Song Ji Hyung. Series: XS Hybrid. 2007, Dark Horse paper $10.95 (978-1-59307-628-3). Hinchang finds he has romantic feelings for Mina as the two fight violent hybrid humans; also in this series is *Angel Virus* (2007) in which a dangerous virus is infecting gamers, transforming them into gang members on motorcycles. (Rev: BL 11/1/07)

3397 Johns, Geoff. *The Flash, Vol. 2: The Road to Flashpoint* (8–12). Illus. by Scott Kolins. 2012, DC Comics paper $14.99 (978-14012344-8-5). This title provides backstory on the Flash's biggest foe, Eobard Thawne, while also introducing a new villain whose motorcycle travels as fast as the hero's. (Rev: BLO 10/15/12)

3398 Johns, Geoff. *The Flash: The Secret of Barry Allen* (9–12). Illus. by Howard Porter and Livesay. 2005, DC Comics paper $19.99 (978-1-4012-0723-6). Wally West regains his memory of being the Flash in this volume and must make difficult choices about who to trust with his identity, and about information he receives in a letter from his dead predecessor, Barry Allen. (Rev: SLJ 3/06)

3399 Johns, Geoff. *Green Lantern, Vol. 1: Sinestro* (9–12). Illus. by Doug Mahnke. 2012, DC Comics $22.99 (978-140123454-6). Earth's Green Lantern, Hal Jordan, is stripped of his ring in this collection of the first six issues of the series. (Rev: BLO 6/12)

3400 Johns, Geoff. *Infinite Crisis* (7–12). 2006, DC Comics $24.99 (978-1-4012-0959-9). Adapted from the DC Comics miniseries, this is a novel of a nasty era for Superman, Batman, Wonderwoman, and other superheros known as the Justice League: already at odds with each other, being hunted down by cyborgs, and having to deal with parallel realities; fans familiar with DC back stories will appreciate this novel. (Rev: BL 11/15/06; SLJ 3/07)

3401 Johns, Geoff. *JSA: Black Reign* (7–12). Illus. by Rags Morales, et al. 2005, DC Comics paper $12.99

(978-1-4012-0480-8). In a setting reminiscent of present-day Iraq, superhero Black Adam fights for an unpopular cause and faces strong opposition from the people he's trying to help. (Rev: SLJ 11/05)

3402 Johns, Geoff, and Jeff Katz. *Blue and Gold* (6–12). Illus. by Norm Rapmund. 2008, DC Comics $24.99 (978-140121956-7). Booster Gold and Blue Beetle travel through time and encounter fellow superheroes in this engaging adventure. (Rev: BLO 2/9/09)

3403 Johns, Geoff, and Richard Donner. *Last Son: Superman* (10–12). Illus. 2008, DC Comics $19.99 (978-1-4012-1343-5). Elements from the films that Christopher Reeve made famous are captured in this tale that will satisfy fans as they see Superman struggle with his conflicted feelings for humanity and reluctantly turn to arch villains for help to save a Kryptonian boy. (Rev: BL 8/08; SLJ 11/08)

3404 Johnson, Nathan, and Matt Yamashita. *Ghostbusters: Ghost Busted* (6–10). Illus. by Chrissy Delk. 2008, Tokyopop $12.99 (978-142781459-3). Based on the 1984 movie about ghostbusting, this manga is filled with comedy, ghosts, and adventure. **e** (Rev: BL 1/1–15/09; LMC 8–9/09)

3405 Johnson, R. *Kikuo. Night Fisher* (9–12). 2005, Fantagraphics paper $12.95 (978-1-56097-719-3). This affecting coming-of-age graphic novel features Loren Foster, a boy who finds his new life in Hawaii challenging. (Rev: BL 11/1/05)

3406 Johnston, Anthony. *Wolverine: Prodigal Son* (9–12). Illus. by Wilson Tortosa. 2009, Del Rey paper $12.95 (978-034550516-3). A manga reimagining of the Wolverine story, with Logan as a contemporary teen who has lost his memory. (Rev: BL 3/1/09; SLJ 5/09)

3407 Jolley, Dan. *My Boyfriend Bites* (7–10). Illus. by Alitha E. Martinez. Series: My Boyfriend Is a Monster. 2011, Lerner/Graphic Universe LB $29.27 (978-076135599-1); paper $9.95 (978-076137078-9). In this light paranormal romance Vanessa discovers that her janitor boyfriend Jean-Paul has a hidden side. Lexile GN360L (Rev: BL 10/15/11)

3408 Jolley, Dan, and Tony Harris. *The Liberty Files* (9–12). 2004, DC Comics paper $19.95 (978-1-4012-0203-3). Batman is called in to help apprehend Jack the Grin, also known as the Joker. (Rev: BL 5/15/04)

3409 Jones, Frewin. *Lamia's Revenge: The Serpent Awakes* (8–11). Illus. by Alison Acton. Series: The Faerie Path. 2009, Tokyopop paper $7.99 (978-006145694-7). Teen faerie princess Tania sets out to rescue her mortal parents in this manga version. (Rev: BLO 4/30/09)

3410 Jones, Gerard. *Networked: Carabella on the Run* (9–12). Illus. by Mark Badger. 2010, NBM paper $12.99 (978-15616358-6-3). Carabella, a blue-skinned alien attending school on Earth, tries to warn her classmates about various Internet dangers in this suspenseful tale. (Rev: BL 9/15/10; LMC 1–2/11; SLJ 9/10)

3411 Joong-Ki, Park. *Shaman Warrior, Vol. 1* (7–12). Illus. by Park Joong Ki. 2007, Dark Horse paper $12.95 (978-1-59307-638-2). A battle-filled Korean manhwa tale featuring Shaman Warrior Master Yarong and his devoted servant Batu. (Rev: BL 8/07)

3412 Kalogridis, Laeta. *Pathfinder: An American Saga* (10–12). Illus. by Christopher Shy. 2006, Dark Horse paper $19.95 (978-1-59307-671-9). A Viking boy, the only survivor of a shipwreck, is raised by a Native American tribe; when the Vikings return and murder them, the boy sets out to avenge their deaths. (Rev: BL 11/1/06)

3413 Kanan, Nabiel. *The Birthday Riots* (10–12). 2002, NBM $14.95 (978-1-56163-299-2). The midlife crisis of a British political adviser and his sometimes-fractious relationship with his teenage daughter, Natalie, are the focus of this offbeat graphic novel. (Rev: BL 2/15/02)

3414 Kane, Bob, et al. *Batman in the Forties* (9–12). 2004, DC Comics paper $19.95 (978-1-4012-0206-4). This is a collection of early Batman strips from his beginnings in May 1939 to the introduction of Robin. (Rev: BL 5/15/04)

3415 Kanigher, Bob. *The Enemy Ace Archives, Vol. 2* (9–12). 2006, DC Comics $49.99 (978-1-4012-0776-2). Set in World War I and originally published in the 1960s and 1970s, the hero featured in these tales is a German fighter pilot, Hans von Hammer — a.k.a. Enemy Ace — who, although a merciless fighter, still laments the loss of young lives. (Rev: BL 12/1/06)

3416 Kanno, Aya. *Otomen, Vol. 1* (8–12). Illus. by author. 2009, VIZ Media paper $8.99 (978-1-4215-2186-2). Readers meet Asuka, a teenage boy who embraces his feminine side, in this first installment in the series. (Rev: BLO 2/9/09)

3417 Kawamura, Mika. *Panic X Panic, Vol. 1* (7–10). Illus. by author. 2010, Del Rey paper $10.99 (978-03455146-3-9). A race of evil demons locked up for millennia gets loose and begins to wreak havoc on mankind in this entertaining manga. (Rev: BLO 3/15/10)

3418 Kelly, Joe. *Four Eyes, Vol. 1: Forged in Flames* (9–12). Illus. by Max Fiumara. 2010, Image paper $9.99 (978-16070629-2-9). In gritty Depression-era New York City, Italian American Enrico, 10, seeks work as a dragon slayer, the profession that killed his father. **e** (Rev: BL 10/15/10)

3419 Kelly, Joe. *I Kill Giants* (9–12). Illus. by J. M. Ken Nimura. 2009, Image Comics paper $15.99 (978-160706092-5). This volume collects the first seven stories about a lonely and frightened but courageous girl named Barbara who battles the monsters in her life. (Rev: BLO 1/31/10*; VOYA 4/10)

3420 Kelly, Joe. *Justice League Elite, Vol. 1* (8–12). Illus. by Doug Mahnke and John Byrne. 2005, DC Comics paper $19.99 (978-1-4012-0481-5). Superman and other members of the Justice League clash with the rival Justice League Elite over strategies for dealing with evildoers. (Rev: BL 10/1/05; SLJ 11/05)

3421 Kelly, Joe, and Michael Turner. *Godfall* (9–12). Series: Superman. 2005, DC Comics paper $9.99 (978-1-4012-0236-1). The superhero is temporarily taken out of action when his memory is erased and he's trapped in the miniaturized city of Kandor. (Rev: BL 9/15/05)

3422 Kesel, Barbara. *Meridian: Flying Solo* (7–12). Series: Meridian. 2003, CrossGeneration paper $9.95 (978-1-931484-54-1). Sephie inherits her father's position as first minister of Meridian, a floating city, and must use her magical powers to battle an evil uncle. (Rev: BL 4/1/03)

3423 Ketcham, Hank. *Hank Ketcham's Complete Dennis the Menace: 1957–1958* (9–12). 2007, Fantagraphics $24.95 (978-1-56097-880-0). Classic 50's Dennis the Menace newspaper cartoons featuring middle-class themes and America's favorite mischievous boy. (Rev: BL 3/1/08)

3424 Khoury, George, and Eric Nolen-Weathington. *Kevin Maguire* (9–12). Series: Modern Masters. 2007, TwoMorrows $14.95 (978-1-893905-66-5). Maguire is known for his updated renderings of the Justice League comic book characters; this volume displays his talents and includes a personal interview. (Rev: BL 4/1/07)

3425 Kim, Derek Kirk. *Good as Lily* (10–12). Illus. by Jesse Hamm. 2007, DC Comics paper $9.99 (978-1-4012-1381-7). After she is hit on the head by a piñata, 18-year-old Grace Kwon confronts versions of herself in different phases of her life. (Rev: BL 10/1/07; SLJ 11/07)

3426 Kim, Jae-Hwan. *War Angels, Vol. 1* (9–12). Illus. by author. 2007, TokyoPop paper $9.99 (978-1-4278-0188-3). A vision of the future in which vicious warriors rule over humans, who have placed their faith in angels. (Rev: BL 11/1/07)

3427 Kindt, Matt. *Revolver* (11–12). Illus. 2010, Vertigo $24.99 (978-140122241-3). Young journalist Sam is caught between two parallel worlds — one a menial desk-job existence and the other just trying to survive in a nation in post-terrorist-attack shock; for mature readers. (Rev: BL 6/1–15/10; SLJ 9/1/10)

3428 Kindt, Matt. *3 Story: The Secret History of the Giant Man* (10–12). Illus. 2009, Dark Horse $19.95 (978-159582356-4). This intriguing graphic novel recounts the bizarre story of Craig Pressgang, a man who has grown so large that he is rendered incapable of interacting with other humans, leaving him completely alienated from those he loves. (Rev: BL 10/15/09)

3429 Kindt, Matt. *2 Sisters* (8–12). 2004, Top Shelf paper $19.95 (978-1-891830-58-7). In this graphic novel thriller, set in Europe during World War II, Elle, a volunteer ambulance driver, is recruited as a spy and dispatched on perilous missions behind enemy lines. (Rev: BL 11/1/04)

3430 Kinney-Petrucha, Maia, and Stefan Petrucha. *Breaking Down* (9–12). Illus. by Rick Parker. 2011, Papercutz $10.99 (978-159707245-8). A graphic-novel parody of the Twilight series. (Rev: BL 5/1/11; SLJ 9/1/11)

3431 Kirby, Jack. *Jack Kirby's Fourth World Omnibus, v.1* (9–12). 2007, DC Comics $49.99 (978-1-4012-1344-2). Volume one in DC's Fourth World series features the debuts of the four series it encompasses — New Gods, The Forever People, Mister Miracle, and Superman's Pal Jimmy Olsen — in chronological order as they originally appeared, and authored by the co-creator of Marvel's Hulk, X-men, and the Fantastic Four. (Rev: BL 7/07) [741.5]

3432 Kirishima, Takeru. *Kanna, Vol. 1* (9–12). Illus. by author. Series: Kanna. 2007, Go! Comi paper $10.99 (978-1-933617-55-8). Kagura's yet-to-be-born daughter materializes from the future, causing Kagura, a college student, to wonder what message she brings from his future self. (Rev: BL 11/1/07)

3433 Kiyuouki, Satoko. *Shoulder-A-Coffin Kuro, Vol. 2* (8–11). Illus. by author. Series: Shoulder-A-Coffin Kuro. 2008, Yen paper $10.99 (978-075952901-4). Little Kuro seeks to rid herself of her coffin as she travels through an eerie land and encounters creepy and dangerous characters; an unusual manga full of humor. (Rev: BLO 1/13/09; SLJ 5/09)

3434 Klein, Grady. *The Red Menace: The Lost Colony Book 2* (9–12). 2007, First Second paper $16.95 (978-1-59643-098-3). "Red Menace" refers to scalp-hunting Indians, a term used by a gun-toting, propaganda-spitting veteran General Sherman Krutch who still believes there's an "Injun problem." The story is best understood by those with a knowledge of 19th-century American history and the illustrations are stunning. (Rev: BL 8/07) [741.5]

3435 Klein, Grady. *The Snodgrass Conspiracy* (10–12). Series: Lost Colony. 2006, Roaring Brook paper $14.95 (978-1-59643-097-6). The opening volume in a series introduces readers to the 19th-century inhabitants of a mysterious island unknown to the rest of the world but full of aspects that may seem strangely familiar. (Rev: BL 3/15/06; SLJ 9/06)

3436 Knaak, Richard A. *Dragon Hunt* (7–10). Illus. by Jae-Hwan Kim. Series: Warcraft Sunwell. 2005, Tokyo-Pop paper $9.99 (978-1-59532-712-3). In the first volume of a graphic novel trilogy, Kalec, a shape-changing dragon, and Anveena race to reach the all-powerful Sunwell before the villainous Dar'khan can get to it. (Rev: BL 6/1–15/05; SLJ 7/05)

3437 Knauf, Charles, and Daniel Knauf. *The Eternals: To Slay a God* (9–12). Illus. by Daniel Acuna. 2009, Marvel paper $19.99 (978-078512978-3). There is trouble among the Eternals, superhumans created millions of years before, in this collection of the first six issues of the comic book. (Rev: BL 6/1–15/09)

3438 Kobayashi, Jin. *School Rumble, Vol. 1* (7–12). Adapted by William Flanagan. 2006, Del Rey paper $10.95 (978-0-345-49147-3). This romantic manga-style comedy features high school student Tsukamoto Tenma, who has a crush on the oblivious Karasuma Oji and is meanwhile the object of Harima Kenji's desires. (Rev: SLJ 7/06)

3439 Krueger, Jim. *Justice 1* (7–12). 2006, DC Comics $19.99 (978-1-4012-0969-8). Lex Luthor, the Riddler, and other villains join forces to eradicate the Justice League superheroes in this volume illustrated by the award-winning Alex Ross. (Rev: BL 11/15/06)

3440 Kubert, Joe. *Dong Xoai: Vietnam 1965* (9–12). 2010, DC Comics $24.99 (978-1-4012-2142-3). The 1965 battle over the village of Dong Xoia is the focus of this graphic-novel account that is fictional but conveys an accurate picture of the U.S. Special Forces that took part and of their adversaries. (Rev: BL 5/15/10; LMC 11–12/10)

3441 Kubert, Joe. *Edgar Rice Burroughs' Tarzan: The Joe Kubert Years, Vol. 1* (9–12). 2005, Dark Horse $49.95 (978-1-59307-404-3). This volume collects the first eight issues of *Tarzan* from DC Comics, as drawn by artist Joe Kubert. (Rev: BL 11/15/05)

3442 Kubert, Joe. *Edgar Rice Burroughs' Tarzan: The Joe Kubert Years, Vol. 2* (9–12). Series: Tarzan: The Joe Kubert Years. 2006, Dark Horse $49.95 (978-1-59307-416-6). Volume two in the Tarzan: The Joe Kubert Years series collects ten issues of the popular comic book from the early 1970s. (Rev: BL 3/15/06)

3443 Kubert, Joe. *Edgar Rice Burroughs' Tarzan: The Joe Kubert Years, Vol. 3* (9–12). 2006, Dark Horse $49.95 (978-1-59307-417-3). Joe Kubert wrote and illustrated Tarzan comics in the 1970s, and this reissue will please old fans and new readers alike. (Rev: BL 8/06)

3444 Kubert, Joe. *Yossel: April 19, 1943: A Story of the Warsaw Ghetto Uprising* (8–12). 2003, iBooks $24.95 (978-0-7434-7516-7). In this graphic novel, Yossel and his friends fight to the death against their Nazi oppressors. (Rev: BL 2/1/04; SLJ 7/04)

3445 Kurata, Hideyuki. *Train + Train, Vol. 1* (8–11). Illus. by Tomomasa Takuma. 2007, Go! Comi paper $10.99 (978-1-933617-18-3). On the way to school on the distant planet of Deloca, Reiichi Sakakusa meets a wild teen named Arena, who changes his life. (Rev: BL 8/07)

3446 Kusakabe, Rei. *Nephylym, Vol. 2* (8–12). Illus. by author. Series: Nephylym. 2008, DrMaster paper $9.99 (978-159796182-0). Sexy yet cute creatures team with humans to battle Noir, the personification of negativity. (Rev: BLO 2/9/09)

3447 Kusunoki, Kei, and Kaoru Ohashi. *Sengoku: Nights, Vol. 1* (9–12). Trans. from Japanese by Alethea Nibley. 2006, TokyoPop paper $9.99 (978-1-59532-945-5). Masoyoshi's teen life is changed forever when he learns that he is the reincarnation of a legendary female witch named Oni-hime and that he must deal with the evil curse that is linked to her past and his family. (Rev: SLJ 5/06)

3448 Kwitney, Alisa. *Token* (8–10). Illus. by Joelle Jones. 2008, DC Comics paper $9.99 (978-140121538-5). Jewish 15-year-old Shira and her widowed father struggle to cope with their changing lives — which include Shira's father's relationship with his secretary and her own romance with a young Spaniard — in 1980s Miami Beach. (Rev: BL 11/15/08; LMC 5–6/09)

3449 Kye, Seung-Hui. *Recast* (8–11). 2006, TokyoPop $9.99 (978-1-59816-664-4). JDs grandfather, a master magician, is in danger of assassination in this action-and humor-filled manga. (Rev: BL 2/1/07)

3450 L'Engle, Madeleine, and Hope Larson. *A Wrinkle in Time* (6–12). Illus. by Hope Larson. 2012, Farrar $19.99 (978-037438615-3). This graphic novel adaptation stays true to the breadth and spirit of L'Engle's original. YALSA Great Graphic Novels for Teens 2013. **e** Lexile 740L (Rev: BL 10/15/12*; LMC 5–6/13; SLJ 11/12)

3451 Lapham, David. *City of Crime: Batman* (11–12). 2006, DC Comics paper $19.99 (978-1-4012-0897-4). A dark story about Batman and Gotham City that starts with the deaths of six pregnant girls. (Rev: BL 9/1/06)

3452 Lapham, David. *Silverfish* (10–12). 2007, Vertigo $24.99 (978-1-4012-1048-9). Teenage Mia discovers a stash of money, a blood-covered knife, and her step-mother's address book, setting in motion a harrowing story. (Rev: BL 6/1–15/07)

3453 Larson, Hope. *Mercury* (9–12). 2010, Simon & Schuster $19.99 (978-1-4169-3585-8). With touch of magic realism, this graphic novel interweaves the stories of contemporary Tara and her ancestor Josey, and rumors of buried gold. (Rev: BL 11/1/09*; HB 3–4/10; LMC 11–12/10; SLJ 3/10; VOYA 12/09)

3454 Lash, Batton. *Mr. Negativity and Other Tales of Supernatural Law* (10–12). 2004, Exhibit A paper $15.95 (978-0-9633954-8-1). Two men who practice supernatural law take on the case of the man who is so pessimistic that he radiates negative energy. (Rev: BL 3/15/04)

3455 Lash, Batton. *The Vampire Brat and Other Tales of Supernatural Law* (10–12). 2001, Exhibit A paper $14.95 (978-0-9633954-7-4). This lighthearted romp features attorneys Alanna Wolff and Jeff Byrd and their unusual clients, who include a vampire, time-traveler, and a boy with a dual identity. (Rev: BL 2/1/02)

3456 Lasko-Gross, Miss. *A Mess of Everything* (11–12). Illus. 2009, Fantagraphics paper $19.99 (978-15609795-6-2). A sequel to the semi-autobiographic

Escape from "Special" (2007), this story deals with Melissa's experiences in high school — her friends, and her mistakes along the way to finding herself; for mature readers. (Rev: BL 4–5/09; SLJ SLJ 7/09)

3457 Lat. *Kampung Boy* (8–11). 2006, Roaring Brook paper $16.95 (978-1-59643-121-8). This funny and eloquent autobiographical graphic novel follows the childhood of a Muslim boy named Mat as he grows up in a small Malaysian town in the 1950s, giving details on the traditions of his kampung (village), and ending with his departure to attend a boarding school. (Rev: BL 9/15/06; SLJ 11/06*)

3458 Lee, So-Young. *Arcana, Vol. 1* (10–12). Trans. from Japanese by Youngju Ryu. Illus. by author. 2005, TokyoPop paper $9.99 (978-1-59532-481-8). In the opening volume of this fantasy manga, a young girl with magical powers roams the countryside with her wizard grandfather. (Rev: SLJ 11/05)

3459 Lee, Stan. *The Fantastic Four, Vol. 1* (5–10). Illus. by Jack Kirby. 2009, Marvel paper $24.99 (978-0-7851-3710-8). This volume collects the first 10 stories about the four who returned to Earth with superhuman abilities after being exposed to cosmic rays. (Rev: BLO 4/30/09)

3460 Lemire, Jeff. *The Nobody* (10–12). Illus. 2009, Vertigo $19.99 (978-140122080-8). Inspired by H. G. Wells's *The Invisible Man*, this graphic novel's bandaged stranger comes to a small town and causes tension that leads to violence; for mature readers. (Rev: BL 4–5/09; SLJ 11/09)

3461 Lemire, Jeff. *Out of the Deep Woods: Sweet Tooth 1* (10–12). Illus. 2010, Vertigo paper $9.99 (978-1-4012-2-696-1). A deer-like young boy is rescued from bounty hunters by a man who endeavors to build his trust. (Rev: BL 4/1–15/10; SLJ 9/1/10)

3462 Lia, Simone. *Fluffy* (11–12). Illus. 2008, Dark Horse $19.95 (978-1-59307-972-7). *Fluffy*, a graphic novel, details the emotional ups and downs of bachelor Michael and his bunny son as they figure out life and relationships; for mature readers. (Rev: BL 8/08)

3463 Little, Jason. *Shutterbug Follies* (10–12). 2002, Doubleday $24.95 (978-0-385-50346-4). In this graphic novel, 18-year-old Bea, who works in a New York City photo lab, sees a photograph of a naked female corpse and has some scary experiences. (Rev: SLJ 1/03)

3464 Loeb, Jeph. *Hulk, Vol. 1: Red Hulk* (6–12). Illus. by Ed McGuinness. Series: Hulk. 2009, Marvel paper $19.99 (978-078512882-3). Good old-fashioned superhero action for Marvel comics fans. (Rev: BL 4/15/09)

3465 Loeb, Jeph, and Tim Sale. *The Long Halloween: Absolute Batman* (9–12). 2007, DC Comics $75.00 (978-1-4012-1282-7). The Long Halloween series originally ran from Halloween 1993 to Halloween 1994, and it featured the cooperation of the police force and the DA with Batman against the Mob, but not without appearances of colorful villains the Joker and Catwoman. Consistent with the Absolute treatment, this volume includes early sketches and proposals, and creator interviews all bound together in hardcover with slipcase. (Rev: BL 7/07) [741.5]

3466 Lonergan, Jesse. *Flower and Fade* (11–12). 2007, NBM paper $13.95 (978-1-56163-496-5). Kyle and Erika, neighbors and both living unrewarding lives, drift into a relationship that does not appear to satisfy either of them; the black-and-white panels are presented in chapter-like sections and the text is written as a diary; for mature teens. (Rev: BL 6/1–15/07; SLJ 7/07)

3467 Love, Courtney, and D. J. Milky. *Princess Ai: Lumination, Vol. 2* (7–12). Trans. from Japanese by Kimiko Fujikawa and Yuki N. Johnson. Illus. by Misaho Kujiradou. 2005, TokyoPop paper $9.99 (978-1-59182-670-5). In volume two of the Princess Ai series, the title character, an aspiring rock star, turns ever more angelic as her music career begins to take off. (Rev: SLJ 11/05)

3468 Love, Jeremy. *Bayou, Vol. 1* (9–12). Illus. by author. 2009, DC Comics paper $14.99 (978-140122382-3). In this historical fantasy set in the South during the Depression, Lily, a white girl, is abducted, and her black friend Lee must brave a frightening parallel universe to rescue her. (Rev: BL 7/09)

3469 Lovecraft, H. P., and I. N. J. Culbard. *At the Mountains of Madness* (7–12). Illus. by I. N. J. Culbard. 2012, Sterling paper $14.95 (978-14027804-2-4). An effective graphic novel adaptation of Lovecraft's dark novel about an expedition to the Antarctic. (Rev: BL 3/15/12)

3470 Ma, Wing Shing. *Storm Riders: Invading Sun, Vol. 1* (8–12). 2003, ComicsOne paper $9.95 (978-1-58899-359-5). Martial arts and an alternate China are featured in this graphic novel about two expert fighters who set out to find their former master named Conquer. (Rev: BL 2/1/04)

3471 McCaffrey, Anne. *Dragonflight* (6–12). Adapted by Brynne Stephens. Series: Dragonriders of Pern. 1991, Eclipse Books $4.95 (978-1-56060-074-9). Book one of a three-part graphic novel based on *Dragonflight* from the Dragonriders of Pern series. (Rev: BL 9/1/91)

3472 McCann, Jim. *Return of the Dapper Men* (7–10). Illus. by Janet Lee. 2010, Archaia $24.95 (978-193238690-5). In a world where children live underground and robots inhabit houses overhead, time has stopped and is only restarted with the arrival of 314 Dapper Men. (Rev: BL 2/15/11*)

3473 McClintock, Norah. *I, Witness* (7–10). Illus. by Mike Deas. 2012, Orca paper $16.95 (978-15546978-9-2). Witnessing a murder poses questions for Boone — should he speak up or not? — and as things go from bad to worse, the conflicts deepen. Lexile HL270L (Rev: BL 11/15/12; SLJ 1/13; VOYA 2/13)

3474 McCloud, Scott. *The New Adventures of Abraham Lincoln* (7–10). 1998, Homage Comics paper $19.00 (978-1-887279-87-1). Time travel, an encounter with Abraham Lincoln, and an alien attempt to rule America are some of the adventures faced by a middle-school student when he is sent to detention. (Rev: BL 2/1/03)

3475 McCloud, Scott. *Zot! 1987–1991* (10–12). Illus. 2008, HarperCollins paper $24.95 (978-006153727-1). *Zot!* tells the story of two worlds through the interaction of Zot, a superhero teen from an alternate futuristic Earth, and Jenny, an ordinary, discontented girl from ours. (Rev: BL 9/1/08)

3476 McCreery, Conor, and Anthony Del Col. *Kill Shakespeare, Vol. 1* (9–12). Illus. by Andy Belanger. 2010, IDW paper $19.99 (978-16001078-1-8). An action-filled story featuring battles between Shakespeare's heroes and villains. (Rev: BL 11/15/10)

3477 McVeigh, Mark, and Ian Velez, eds. *Dead High Yearbook* (10–12). 2007, Dutton $18.99 (978-0-525-47783-9). High school horror stories told in sometimes grisly detail by different artists. (Rev: BCCB 5/07; BL 3/15/07; SLJ 5/07)

3478 Madison, Ivory. *Huntress: Year One* (10–12). Illus. by Cliff Richards. Series: Huntress. 2009, DC Comics paper $17.99 (978-140122126-3). Superhero Helena seeks revenge after her family is killed by the Mafia; an engaging and sometimes violent thriller. (Rev: BLO 3/24/09)

3479 Maeda, Mahiro. *Gankutsuou: The Count of Monte Cristo, Vol. 1* (10–12). Illus. by author. 2008, Del Rey paper $10.95 (978-034550520-0). This graphic-novel retelling of Dumas's classic story with a science fiction twist begins with a trip to another planet, where two young men meet a gothic version of the count of Monte Cristo and are drawn into a dangerous intrigue. (Rev: BL 12/1/08; SLJ 1/09)

3480 Marazano, Richard. *The Chimpanzee Complex, Vol. 1: Paradox* (7–12). Illus. by Jean-Michel Ponzio. 2009, Cinebook paper $13.95 (978-18491800-2-3). Young Sophia's astronaut mom becomes distracted by a sci-fi mystery: Buzz Aldrin and Neil Armstrong have returned from space more than 60 years after the Apollo XI mission. (Rev: BLO 3/15/10)

3481 Marder, Larry. *Beanworld: Wahoolazuma* (8–12). Illus. by author. Series: Beanworld. 2009, Dark Horse $19.95 (978-159582240-6). A collection of comics first published in the 1980s, *Wahoolazuma* features a world populated by beans who learn they are dependent on one another and on the environment. (Rev: BL 4/15/09)

3482 Marr, Melissa. *Sanctuary: Desert Tales, Vol. 1* (8–11). Illus. by Xian Nu Studio. Series: Wicked Lovely: Desert Tales. 2009, Tokyopop paper $9.99 (978-006149354-6). This first volume in a new manga trilogy is set in a world familiar to Marr's readers and features Rika, a faery living in the Mojave Desert who becomes involved with a mortal young man. **e** (Rev: BLO 6/16/09; SLJ 7/09)

3483 Martinson, Lars. *Tonoharu: Part One* (9–12). 2008, Pliant $19.95 (978-0-9801023-2-1). This fictional graphic novel about Dan Wells, an alienated American working in a Japanese high school, is based on the author's own experiences. (Rev: BL 3/15/08)

3484 Marz, Ron. *Crisis of Faith* (9–12). Series: The Path. 2003, CrossGeneration Comics paper $9.95 (978-1-59314-016-8). The illustrations are a major draw of this sometimes challenging graphic novel about a monk whose crisis of faith causes him to seek revenge against the gods and pits him against a boyhood friend. (Rev: BL 8/03)

3485 Marz, Ron. *Heaven and Earth* (9–12). Illus. by Luke Ross. Series: Samurai. 2007, Dark Horse paper $14.95 (978-1-59307-839-3). Shiro fights to save his kidnapped girlfriend in this comic set in 18th-century Japan and full of scantily clad women and bloody fights. (Rev: BL 1/1–15/08)

3486 Mashima, Hiro. *Fairy Tail, Vol. 1* (7–12). Trans. from Japanese by William Flanagan. Adapted by William Flanagan. Illus. by author. 2008, Del Rey paper $10.95 (978-0-345-50133-2). Lucy wants to join a wizards club called the Fairy Tail in this boisterous fantasy full of oddball characters; the first in a series. (Rev: SLJ 5/08)

3487 Matsumoto, Taiyo. *Gogo Monster* (10–12). Illus. 2009, VIZ Media $27.99 (978-142153209-7). In this manga tale, a young boy struggles to live in two worlds: a fantasy realm and one full of the reality of cruel classmates. (Rev: BL 12/1/09)

3488 Mechner, Jordan. *Solomon's Thieves* (6–10). Illus. by Pham LeUyen and Alex Puvilland. 2010, First Second paper $12.99 (978-1-59643-391-5). The very existence of the Knights Templar is threatened and they must fight for their lives and their treasure in early 14th-century France. (Rev: BL 4/15/10; LMC 8–9/10; SLJ 7/10)

3489 Mechner, Jordan, and A. B. Sina. *Prince of Persia: The Graphic Novel* (9–12). Illus. by LeUyen Pham. 2008, First Second paper $16.95 (978-15964320-7-9). Loosely based on the popular Prince of Persia video game, this tale weaves together the stories of the prince's origins and destiny through visual clues and a richly imagined color palette. (Rev: BL 9/1/08*; VOYA 8/08)

3490 Medley, Linda. *Castle Waiting* (9–12). 2006, Fantagraphics $29.95 (978-1-56097-747-6). In the castle home of Sleeping Beauty after she and her handsome prince have decamped for Happily-Ever-After, the princess's former ladies in waiting and new arrivals at the castle each recount fascinating stories of their own. (Rev: BL 3/15/06*; SLJ 9/06)

3491 Melville, Herman. *Moby Dick* (5–12). Retold by Sophie Furse. Illus. by Penko Gelev. Series: Graphic Classics. 2007, Barron's $15.99 (978-0-7641-5977-0). The classic story about the giant white whale is presented in graphic novel format. (Rev: SLJ 5/07)

3492 Messner-Loebs, William, and Sam Kieth. *Epicurus the Sage* (10–12). 2003, DC Comics paper $19.95 (978-1-4012-0028-2). Starring in this comic collection of stories is Greek philosopher Epicurus, who unaccountably finds himself teamed with Plato and a younger Alexander the Great in an exploration of some classic Greek myths. (Rev: BL 12/1/03*)

3493 Mignola, Mike. *Strange Places: Hellboy 6* (10–12). Series: Hellboy. 2006, Dark Horse paper $17.95 (978-1-59307-475-3). Hellboy travels under the sea to fight Bog Roosh, a fish-witch, in this latest dark tale about the demon. (Rev: BL 4/15/06)

3494 Mignola, Mike, and Guy Davis. *B.P.R.D.: Plague of Frogs* (9–12). Series: B.P.R.D. 2005, Dark Horse paper $17.95 (978-1-59307-288-9). Abe Sapien's amphibious origins come to light as the Bureau for Paranormal Research and Defense confronts a plague of frog-monsters. (Rev: BL 2/15/05)

3495 Mignola, Mike, and John Arcudi. *The Black Flame: B.P.R.D.5* (9–12). Series: B.P.R.D. 2006, Dark Horse paper $17.95 (978-1-59307-550-7). B.P.R.D. stands for the Bureau for Paranormal Research and Defense, and in this installment in the series its officers battle mutant frogs and their Nazi-like leader. (Rev: BL 8/06)

3496 Mignola, Mike, et al. *The Black Goddess* (9–12). Illus. Series: B.P.R.D. 2009, Dark Horse paper $17.95 (978-15958241-1-0). With Liz gone and their most powerful enemies banding together for a final, catastrophic attack, Abe, Kate, and Johann must determine the price of their souls as they decide where their loyalties lie - and whether the life of a friend is more valuable than the fate of the world. B.P.R.D.: The Black Goddess collects the second arc of the Scorched Earth trilogy, pulling together threads from the beginning of the series, with a twist that will shake the worlds of B.P.R.D. agents and readers alike. (Rev: BLO 10/1/09)

3497 Mignola, Mike, et al. *The Dead: B.P.R.D., Vol. 4* (9–12). 2005, Dark Horse paper $17.95 (978-1-59307-380-0). Mike Mignola, creator of Hellboy, teams with coauthor John Arcudi and artist Guy Davis for the fourth volume of the B.P.R.D. series, in which the Bureau for Paranormal Research and Defense makes an interesting discovery while moving into its new headquarters. (Rev: BL 10/15/05)

3498 Mignola, Mike, et al. *The Soul of Venice and Other Stories* (9–12). Ed. by Scott Allie. 2004, Dark Horse paper $17.95 (978-1-59307-132-5). In the second volume of the B.P.R.D. series, Hellboy's colleagues from the Bureau of Paranormal Research and Defense do battle with assorted evildoers in five different stories. (Rev: BL 9/1/04)

3499 Millar, Mark, and Peter Gross. *Chosen* (11–12). 2005, Dark Horse paper $9.95 (978-1-59307-213-1). Twelve-year-old Jodie Christianson recovers from a devastating accident to find that he now possesses miraculous powers, leading the boy to believe that he is the returned Jesus Christ. (Rev: BL 11/1/05)

3500 Miller, Frank, and Klaus Janson. *Absolute Dark Knight* (9–12). 2006, DC Comics $99.99 (978-1-4012-1079-3). The story of Batman's rise from retirement in Frank Miller's highly acclaimed *The Dark Knight Returns* (1986) is featured in this oversized slip-cased volume, which also includes its sequel, commentary from Miller, and preliminary sketches of the original book proposal in a 70-page appendix. (Rev: BL 10/15/06)

3501 Miller, John Jackson. *Star Wars: Knights of the Old Republic: Commencement, Vol. 1* (10–12). Illus. by Brian Ching and Travel Forman. 2006, Dark Horse paper $18.95 (978-1-59307-640-5). The events of this graphic novel take place about 4,000 years before the time readers know well, but the action-packed story will feel very familiar. (Rev: SLJ 3/07)

3502 Millionaire, Tony. *Billy Hazelnuts* (9–12). 2006, Fantagraphics $19.95 (978-1-56097-701-8). The creator of the Sock Monkey and Maakies comic characters makes his graphic novel debut with this offbeat tale about Becky, a girl scientist, and her friend, Billy, a creature fashioned by mice out of garbage. (Rev: BL 2/1/06)

3503 Millionaire, Tony. *Billy Hazelnuts and the Crazy Bird* (10–12). Illus. by author. 2010, Fantagraphics $19.99 (978-156097917-3). In this funny sequel to 2006's *Billy Hazelnuts,* our garbage-constructed hero embarks on a crazy quest to reunite a young owl with its mother, even as his charge chomps away at him. (Rev: BL 7/10)

3504 Mizuno, Ryo. *Record of Lodoss War: The Grey Witch — Birth of a New Knight* (7–12). Illus. by Yoshihiko Ochi. Series: Grey Witch Trilogy. 2000, CPM Comics $15.95 (978-1-56219-928-9). This graphic novel is the second volume of the Grey Witch Trilogy and tells how Pam struggles to learn the identity of his father in a universe where gods, goddesses, and goblins exist. (Rev: BL 12/1/00)

3505 Mochizuki, Minetaro. *Dragon Head, Vol. 1* (10–12). Trans. from Japanese by Alexis Kirsch. Illus. by author. 2006, TokyoPop paper $9.99 (978-1-59532-914-1). When the train he is riding home on derails in a tunnel, Aoki Teru is knocked unconscious and awakes to find that he is only one of three survivors and must find a way out. (Rev: SLJ 5/06)

3506 Modan, Rutu. *Jamilti and Other Stories* (11–12). Trans. by Noah Stollman. Illus. 2008, Drawn & Quarterly $19.95 (978-189729954-8). This book contains seven short stories that vary in plot but are united by Modan's artistic style and sharp characterization; for mature readers. (Rev: BL 9/15/08; SLJ 3/09)

3507 Moeller, Christopher. *Faith Conquers* (9–12). 2004, Dark Horse paper $17.95 (978-1-59307-015-1). Seasoned warrior Trevor Faith arrives on the planet Hotok to command the armed forces of the orthodox national church. Also use in this series *Sheva's War* (2004). (Rev: BL 5/15/04)

3508 Monroe, Kevin. *El Zombo Fantasma* (7–10). 2005, Dark Horse paper $9.95 (978-1-59307-284-1). In this eye-popping superhero graphic novel, Mexican wrestler El Zombo Fantasma, murdered for throwing a match, seeks to avoid eternal damnation by becoming guardian angel to a feisty 10-year-old and tracking down his own killer. (Rev: BL 3/15/05; VOYA 8/05)

3509 Moorcock, Michael, and Walter Simonson. *Michael Moorcock's Elric: The Making of a Sorcerer* (10–12). Series: Elric Saga. 2007, DC Comics paper $19.99 (978-1-4012-1334-3). This graphic novel serves as a prequel to the Melnibonian books, telling the story of Elric's succession to the throne of the empire. (Rev: BL 10/1/07)

3510 Moore, Alan. *Tom Strong: Book Six* (9–12). 2006, DC Comics $24.99 (978-1-4012-1108-0). With the help of original series artist Chris Sprouse, Moore gives us the sixth and final collection of superhero Tom Strong from the America's Best Comics line, this last one involving the world's end. (Rev: BL 12/1/06)

3511 Moore, Richard. *Boneyard, Vol. 2* (11–12). 2004, NBM paper $9.95 (978-1-56163-369-2). In this comic romp, cemetery owner Richard Paris, faced with a tax bill of more than half a million dollars, enlists the help of his monstrous tenants in raising the funds he'll need to pay the bill; for mature teens. (Rev: BL 12/1/03)

3512 Moore, Stuart, and Claude St. Aubin, et al. *Stuart Moore's Para* (10–12). 2007, Penny Farthing paper $19.95 (978-0-9719012-4-7). Stunning illustrations by a team of artists grace the pages of this thriller involving Sara Erie, who loses her father in a radioactive supercollider accident and cunningly gains access to investigate his death, which appears to have been violent and perhaps caused by supernatural forces. (Rev: BL 12/15/06)

3513 Mori, Kaoru. *A Bride's Story, Vol. 1* (10–12). Illus. by author. 2011, Yen $16.99 (978-031618099-3). Set in 19th-century Asia, this graphic novel with detailed illustrations features 20-year-old Amir, recently married to Karluk, 12 years her junior, and trying to make a new life for herself; the first volume in a series. YALSA Great Graphic Novels Top Ten 2012. (Rev: BL 6/1/11)

3514 Mori, Kaoru. *Shirley, Vol. 1* (7–10). Illus. by author. 2008, DC Comics paper $9.99 (978-1-4012-1777-8). Set in Edwardian England, this manga novel follows the life of an endearing 13-year-old orphan who gets a job as a maid for a cafe owner. (Rev: BLO 12/30/08)

3515 Morrison, Grant. *Seven Soldiers of Victory, Vol. 3* (9–12). 2006, DC Comics paper $14.99 (978-1-4012-

0976-6). DC Comics characters Zatanna, Klarion the Witchboy, Mister Miracle, Bulleteer and Frankenstein are featured in this third volume of the series. (Rev: BL 8/06)

3516 Morrison, Grant. *Vimanarama* (8–12). Illus. by Philip Bond. 2006, Vertigo paper $12.99 (978-1-4012-0496-9). In Bradford, England, Ali — 19-year-old son of Pakistani immigrants — and his arranged bride-to-be Sofia become embroiled in a battle against evil when an ancient spirit is released. (Rev: BL 2/1/06; SLJ 5/06)

3517 Morrison, Grant, and Duncan Fegredo. *Kid Eternity* (10–12). 2006, DC Comics paper $14.99 (978-1-4012-0933-9). This volume collects all three issues of Grant Morrison's comic book miniseries of 1991. (Rev: BL 4/1/06; SLJ 7/06)

3518 Morrison, Grant, and Frank Quitely. *WE3* (11–12). 2005, DC Comics paper $12.99 (978-1-4012-0495-2). Three former household pets, reprogrammed by the government into experimental weapons, escape their human captors and try to make their way home; violent, moving, and thought-provoking, this is for mature teens. (Rev: BL 7/05; SLJ 11/05)

3519 Morrison, Grant, et al. *Seven Soldiers of Victory, Vol. 1* (9–12). 2006, DC Comics paper $14.99 (978-1-4012-0925-4). In the first of three volumes, comic book artist Grant Morrison offers his vision of four second-string characters from the DC Comics stable. (Rev: BL 3/1/06; SLJ 9/06)

3520 Morrison, Grant, et al. *Seven Soldiers of Victory, Vol. 2* (9–12). 2006, DC Comics paper $14.99 (978-1-4012-0975-9). DC Comics characters the Shining Knight, the Guardian, Zatanna and Klarion the Witch Boy are featured here. (Rev: BL 5/15/06)

3521 Morvan, Jean David. *Wake, Vol. 6/7* (9–12). Illus. by Philippe Bucket. 2005, NBM paper $14.95 (978-1-56163-420-0). In this science fiction graphic novel, part of a multi-volume series, a human girl named Navee faces daunting challenges. (Rev: BL 4/15/05; SLJ 7/05)

3522 Morvan, Jean David. *Wake: Fire and Ash* (9–12). Illus. by Phillipe Buchet. 2001, NBM paper $9.95 (978-1-56163-267-1). The age-old struggle between good and evil takes center stage in this imaginatively illustrated story that pits Navee, a human girl, against an alien force from a world where mind control has replaced individual reason. (Rev: BL 4/15/01)

3523 Mowll, Joshua. *Operation Red Jericho* (8–11). Series: Guild Trilogy. 2005, Candlewick $15.99 (978-0-7636-2634-1). In this first volume of a trilogy set in the early 20th century, teens Becca and Doug MacKenzie search for their parents, who disappeared in China, and document their exciting adventures. (Rev: BL 11/15/05; SLJ 12/05)

3524 Mucci, Michael. *Dracula* (9–12). Illus. by Ben Caldwell. Series: All-Action Classics. 2008, Sterling paper $6.95 (978-1-4027-3152-5). A thrilling graphic adaptation of the classic vampire story that should attract reluctant readers. (Rev: BL 3/15/08)

3525 Mucha, Corinne. *Freshman: Tales of 9th Grade Obsessions, Revelations, and Other Nonsense* (7–10). Illus. by author. 2011, Zest paper $12.99 (978-09819733-6-4). Annie and her friends navigate the choppy waters of their freshman year at high school. (Rev: BLO 9/1/11; LMC 11–12/11)

3526 Murakami, Maki. *Kanpai! Vol. 1* (8–12). Trans. from Japanese by Christine Schilling. Illus. by author. 2005, TokyoPop paper $9.99 (978-1-59532-317-0). Yamada finds himself torn between his rigid training to be a monster guardian and his infatuation with attractive Taino Municipal Middle School classmate Nao. (Rev: SLJ 1/06)

3527 Muth, Jon. *Swamp Thing: Roots* (8–12). 1998, DC Comics paper $7.95 (978-1-56389-377-3). Visual images enhance this story of the supernatural elements that influence life in a small community. (Rev: BL 2/1/03)

3528 Myrick, Leland. *Missouri Boy* (9–12). 2006, Roaring Brook paper $16.95 (978-1-59643-110-2). A graphic novel depicting the author's boyhood and teen years growing up in a small town, recounting times with friends, problems with girls, tragedy, and more. (Rev: BL 9/15/06; VOYA)

3529 Nakaji, Yuki. *Zig Zag, Vol. 1* (9–12). Trans. from Japanese by Jonathan Lee. Illus. by author. 2007, TokyoPop paper $9.99 (978-1-4278-0308-5). Intricately detailed illustrations beautify this manga about Japanese teens united by their common love of flowers, as well as by their common teenage angst. (Rev: SLJ 3/08)

3530 Natsume, Yoshinori. *Batman: Death Mask* (9–12). Illus. by author. 2008, DC Comics paper $9.99 (978-140121924-6). This dark manga version of the Batman story will attract fans of Japanese comics. (Rev: BL 2/1/09)

3531 Neels, Betty. *Harlequin Pink: A Girl in a Million* (10–12). Illus. by Kako Itoh. 2005, Dark Horse paper $9.95 (978-1-59307-412-8). In this manga romance story, a nurse named Caroline falls in love with a handsome, wealthy doctor named Marius; written and illustrated in pink. (Rev: SLJ 5/06)

3532 Nelson, Arvid, and Eric Johnson. *The Lost Kings* (9–12). Series: Rex Mundi. 2006, Dark Horse paper $16.95 (978-1-59307-651-1). With a Holy Grail mystery, a secret society, and Knights Templar, this graphic novel set in an alternate 1933 Europe — in which the Catholic Church is the most powerful institution — will appeal to fans of *The Da Vinci Code*. (Rev: BL 9/15/06)

3533 Nelson, Arvid, and Juan Ferreyra. *Gate of God: Rex Mundi 6* (10–12). Illus. 2010, Dark Horse paper $17.99 (978-15958240-3-5). This sixth installment is the conclusion to the alternate history graphic novel series set in the 1930s, and provides lots of action, adventure, and a high body count as the hero, Julien Sauniere, searches for the Holy Grail in the mountains of France. (Rev: BL 2/1–15/10)

3534 Nicieza, Fabian. *A Stake to the Heart* (8–12). 2004, Dark Horse paper $12.95 (978-1-59307-012-0). Angel's efforts to help Buffy and Dawn cope with their parents' problems backfire in this graphic novel that precedes the events of the TV show. (Rev: BL 6/1–15/04)

3535 Nicolle, Malachai. *Axe Cop, Vol. 1* (9–12). Illus. by Ethan Nicolle. 2011, Dark Horse paper $14.99 (978-159582681-7). The wacky imaginings of 5-year-old Malachai (involving an axe-wielding policeman and a motley crew of superheroes, aliens, dinosaurs, werewolves, and so forth) are illustrated by his older brother in this stirring collection. YALSA Great Graphic Novels Top Ten 2012. (Rev: BL 3/15/11*)

3536 Nightow, Yasuhiro. *Trigun Anime Manga, Vol.1* (9–12). 2005, Dark Horse paper $14.95 (978-1-59307-105-9). In the first volume of a new graphic novel series set in a post-apocalyptic world and based on a Japanese television series, two insurance agents are dispatched to contact the outlaw known as Vash the Stampede and hopefully stem the flood of claims that seem to follow wherever he goes. (Rev: BL 5/1/05)

3537 Niles, Steve, and Kelley Jones. *Last Train to Deadsville* (11–12). 2005, Dark Horse paper $14.95 (978-1-59307-107-3). In this action-packed graphic novel for mature teens, supernatural detective Cal McDonald and sidekick Mo'lock try to rid a California town of demonic forces. (Rev: BL 5/1/05)

3538 Niles, Steve, and Scott Hampton. *Gotham County Line: Batman* (7–12). 2006, DC Comics paper $17.99 (978-1-4012-0905-6). Batman takes on a mysterious case of suburban murders, finds that logic (his usual method) is not leading to the solution this time, and must deal with the supernatural in this well-illustrated story. (Rev: BL 12/1/06)

3539 Nishiyama, Yuriko. *Harlem Beat* (8–12). 1999, TokyoPop paper $9.95 (978-1-892213-04-4). Created and produced in Japan, this graphic novel follows the adventures of an urban, teenage boy who loves basketball. (Rev: BL 2/1/03)

3540 No, Yee-Jung. *Visitor, Vol. 1* (7–10). Trans. from Japanese by Jennifer Hahm. Illus. by author. 2005, TokyoPop paper $9.99 (978-1-59532-342-2). On her first day at a new school, Hyo-Bin attracts a number of admirers, but she rebuffs them all, fearful that they could be harmed by the magical powers she's not yet learned to control. (Rev: SLJ 9/05)

3541 Novgorodoff, Danica. *Slow Storm* (11–12). Illus. by author. 2008, First Second $17.95 (978-1-59643-250-5). A tornado in a Kentucky town throws together a female firefighter searching for her place in life and a young Mexican immigrant on the run from the police in

this graphic novel with a literary feel and somber pictures. (Rev: BL 8/08; SLJ 9/08)

3542 Nowak, Naomi. *House of Clay* (9–12). Illus. by author. 2007, NBM paper $12.95 (978-1-56163-511-5). The outstanding artwork sets apart this graphic novel about a girl working in a sweatshop. (Rev: SLJ 3/08)

3543 Okamoto, Kazuhiro. *Translucent, Vol. 1* (6–10). Trans. by Heidi Plechl. Illus. by author. Series: Translucent. 2007, Dark Horse paper $9.95 (978-1-59307-647-4). Quiet 8th-grader Shizuka is slowly becoming invisible as a result of a strange disease called the Translucent Syndrome but Mamoru — a possible romantic interest? — and Keiko both help her cope and give her hope for the future. (Rev: BL 2/13/08)

3544 Okazaki, Takashi. *Afro Samurai* (10–12). Trans. by Greg Moore. Illus. by author. 2008, Tor paper $10.99 (978-076532123-7). Best for older teens because of violence and brief nudity, this is a complex manga story about a futuristic samurai's quest to best the warrior who murdered his father. (Rev: BL 12/1/08; LMC 5–6/09; SLJ 1/09)

3545 Oliver, Simon. *Gen13: 15 Minutes, Vol. 3* (9–12). Illus. by Carlo Barberi. 2008, DC Comics $14.99 (978-140122002-0). The members of Gen13 find themselves in New York City in this installment, but they are again in grave danger. (Rev: BLO 1/7/09)

3546 O'Malley, Bryan Lee. *Scott Pilgrim vs. the Universe, Vol. 5* (11–12). Illus. by author. Series: Scott Pilgrim. 2009, Oni paper $11.95 (978-193496410-1). Scott's relationship with Ramona is threatened by his own exes and her former boyfriends even as his band faces difficulties. (Rev: BL 4/1/09; SLJ 9/09)

3547 O'Malley, Bryan Lee. *Scott Pilgrim's Finest Hour* (10–12). Illus. by author. 2010, Oni paper $11.99 (978-19349643-8-5). This series finale delivers an epic and satisfying battle between Scott, Ramona, and Gideon Graves. (Rev: BL 9/15/10)

3548 Ono, Fuyumi. *Ghost Hunt, Vol. 3* (8–12). Trans. from Japanese by Akira Tsubasa. Illus. by Shiho Inada. 2006, Del Rey paper $10.95 (978-0-345-48626-4). Seventeen-year-old Naru and his paranormal detective agency investigate strange goings-on at the local high school. (Rev: SLJ 5/06)

3549 Ono, Natsume. *Not Simple* (10–12). Illus. by author. 2010, VIZ Media paper $14.99 (978-14215322-0-2). Brooding emotional issues are at play in this serious manga story about teen Ian's cross-country search for his missing sister. (Rev: BL 3/15/10)

3550 Panagariya, Ananth. *Applegeeks, Vol. 1: Freshman Year* (10–12). Illus. by Mohammad F. Haque. 2009, Dark Horse paper $14.95 (978-159582174-4). A collection of the first two years of the Webcomic starring college students Hawk and Jayce and their usual and unusual adventures. (Rev: BLO 6/17/09)

3551 Park, Sang-Sun. *The Tarot Café, Vol. 1* (11–12). Trans. by Sukhee Ryu. 2005, TokyoPop paper $9.99 (978-1-59182-555-5). The opening volume in the series introduces Pamela, a tarot card reader who offers help to a handful of supernatural beings that dwell in the human world; for mature teens. (Rev: BL 3/15/05)

3552 Pasko, Martin, and Matt Haley. *Superman Returns: The Movie and Other Tales of the Man of Steel* (9–12). 2006, DC Comics paper $12.99 (978-1-4012-0950-6). Adapted from the *Superman Returns* film, this graphic novel also includes scenes cut from the film version and a collection of other classic Superman stories, the origin tale originally presented in *The Amazing World of Superman, Metropolis Edition #1* among them. (Rev: BL 9/15/06)

3553 Patterson, James. *Maximum Ride, Vol. 1* (7–10). Illus. by NaRae Lee. Series: Maximum Ride. 2009, Yen paper $10.99 (978-075952951-9). A manga adaptation of the series by the same name, this story introduces readers to a group of mutant teenagers living in a dangerous world. e (Rev: BL 3/1/09; SLJ 5/09)

3554 Pedrosa, Cyril. *Three Shadows* (9–12). Illus. by author. 2008, Roaring Brook paper $15.95 (978-1-59643-239-0). A chilling story about a couple who try to save their young son from the shadows that have come to claim him. (Rev: BL 3/15/08)

3555 Pérez, George. *Wonder Woman: Destiny Calling, Vol. 4* (8–12). Illus. by author, et al. 2006, DC Comics paper $19.99 (978-1-4012-0943-8). Collects the last five issues of Wonder Woman, in which she investigates the death of her publicist, reveals much about her early home on Themyscira, and must rescue Earth from the god Hermes. (Rev: SLJ 11/06)

3556 Petersen, David. *Mouse Guard: Fall 1152* (7–12). Illus. by Philip Jacobs. 2007, Archaia Studios $24.95 (978-1-932386-57-8). The excellent art will draw readers into this story of about three mice — Saxon, Kenzie and Lieam — who, as part of the Mouse Guard, patrol the Mouse Territories borders, and battle to keep the inhabitants safe. (Rev: BL 9/1/07; LMC 1/08)

3557 Pini, Wendy. *ElfQuest: The Searcher and the Sword* (9–12). Series: ElfQuest. 2004, DC Comics $24.95 (978-1-4012-0183-8). Shuna, a human girl adopted by the elfin Wolfriders, seeks to bridge the gap between members of her race and the elves who've cared for her. (Rev: BL 8/04)

3558 Pini, Wendy, and Richard Pini. *ElfQuest: Archives, Vol. 1* (9–12). Series: ElfQuest. 2003, DC Comics $49.95 (978-1-4012-0128-9). These fantastic tales are reprinted from the comic books published in the late 1970s known as Elfquest. (Rev: BL 2/1/04)

3559 Pomplun, Tom, ed. *Adventure Classics, Vol. 12* (9–12). Series: Graphic Classics. 2005, Eureka paper $11.95 (978-0-9746648-4-2). Graphic novel adaptations of adventure stories and poems by such well-known authors as Alexandre Dumas, Zane Grey, and Rudyard Kipling are accompanied by short biographies of the writers and artists. (Rev: BL 10/1/05; SLJ 1/06; VOYA 4/06)

3560 Pomplun, Tom, ed. *Arthur Conan Doyle* (8–11). Series: Graphic Classics. 2005, Eureka paper $11.95 (978-0-9746648-5-9). This revised edition adds several non-Holmes stories to the collection. (Rev: BL 9/15/05; SLJ 11/05; VOYA 4/06)

3561 Pomplun, Tom, ed. *Gothic Classics, vol. 14* (8–12). Illus. by Anne Timmons, et al. Series: Graphic Classics. 2007, Eureka paper $11.95 (978-0-9787919-0-2). Poe, Austen, and Radcliffe are only three of the authors whose works are adapted here with effective illustrations. (Rev: BL 9/1/07; SLJ 9/07)

3562 Pomplun, Tom, ed. *Graphic Classics: Edgar Allan Poe* (8–12). 2006, Eureka paper $11.95 (978-0-9746648-7-3). This is a graphic novel collection of classic Poe stories. (Rev: BL 6/1–15/06; LMC 1/07)

3563 Pomplun, Tom, ed. *Mark Twain. 2nd ed.* (10–12). Illus. by Rick Geary. Series: Graphic Classics. 2007, Eureka paper $11.95 (978-0-9787919-2-6). Eight Twain stories are interpreted and illustrated by different artists. (Rev: SLJ 3/08)

3564 Pomplun, Tom, ed. *Rafael Sabatini* (9–12). Series: Graphic Classics. 2006, Eureka paper $11.95 (978-0-9746648-6-6). Graphic novel adaptations of eight stories by Sabatini, author of *Captain Blood* and *Scaramouche*. (Rev: BL 3/15/06)

3565 Pomplun, Tom, ed. *Robert Louis Stevenson* (9–12). Illus. by Michael Slack. Series: Graphic Classics. 2004, Eureka paper $9.95 (978-0-9746648-0-4). Six of Robert Louis Stevenson's most famous works, including *Kidnapped* and *The Strange Case of Dr. Jekyll and Mr. Hyde*, are presented in graphic novel format. (Rev: BL 9/15/04; VOYA 2/05)

3566 Pope, Paul. *Year 100: Batman* (9–12). 2007, DC Comics paper $19.99 (978-1-4012-1192-9). In 2039, the grandson of the former police commissioner of Gotham City is hunting for the murderer of a federal agent. Could the perpetrator be Batman, now a figure of legend? (Rev: BL 2/15/07)

3567 Porcellino, John. *Diary of a Mosquito Abatement Man* (11–12). 2005, Mano paper $12.00 (978-0-9765255-0-9). A fascinating memoir that follows on the events of *Perfect Example* (2001); for older teens. (Rev: BL 8/05)

3568 Porcellino, John. *Perfect Example* (10–12). 2001, Highwater $9.95 (978-0-9665363-5-5). All the wildly varied emotions of the passage from high school to college are captured in this account of one teenaged boy's experiences in 1980s suburbia. (Rev: BL 4/15/01; VOYA 8/01)

3569 Powell, Eric. *My Murderous Childhood (and Other Grievous Yarns)* (10–12). 2004, Dark Horse paper $13.95 (978-1-59307-194-3). Gross humor and sexy scenes are found in this graphic novel that deals with the muscular hero known as the Goon. Another in this series is *Rough Stuff* (2004). (Rev: BL 5/15/04)

3570 Powell, Eric, and Thomas Lennon. *Virtue and the Grim Consequences Thereof: The Goon 4* (9–12). 2006, Dark Horse paper $16.95 (978-1-59307-456-2). Volume four of the Goon series chronicles five high-octane adventures starring the title character. (Rev: BL 2/1/06)

3571 Powell, Nate. *Swallow Me Whole* (10–12). Illus. 2008, Top Shelf $20.95 (978-160309033-9). *Swallow Me Whole* is a graphic novel that skillfully portrays two teen step-siblings as they struggle with their mental illnesses. (Rev: BL 9/1/08; LMC 3–4/09; SLJ 1/09)

3572 Proust, Marcel. *Remembrance of Things Past: Part Three: Love of Swann, Vol. 1* (10–12). Illus. by Stéphane Heuet. 2007, NBM $16.95 (978-1-56163-513-9). Lovely watercolor illustrations bring to life this volume of Heuet's graphic novel adaptation of Proust's classic work. (Rev: SLJ 3/08)

3573 Pyle, Kevin. *Blindspot* (9–12). 2007, Henry Holt $13.95 (978-0-8050-7998-2). Dean and his new friends love to play war games in the woods — but the game takes an ominous turn when they discover a homeless man living there. (Rev: BL 3/15/07; HB 7–8/07; LMC 11–12/07; SLJ 7/07)

3574 Rabagliati, Michel. *Paul Goes Fishing* (9–12). Trans. by Helge Dascher. 2008, Drawn & Quarterly paper $19.95 (978-1-897299-28-9). The title sums up this warm hearted graphic novel filled with simple compelling moments and elegant pen cartoons. (Rev: BL 3/15/08)

3575 Rabagliati, Michel. *Paul Has a Summer Job* (9–12). 2003, Drawn & Quarterly $16.95 (978-1-896597-54-6). Paul, a discontented teen, takes a job as a camp counselor and finds romance and a new love of life in this graphic novel. (Rev: BL 2/1/03; SLJ 12/03; VOYA 10/03)

3576 Raicht, Mike, and Brian Smith. *The Stuff of Legend, Vol. 1: The Dark* (10–12). Illus. by Charles Paul Wilson. 2010, Villard paper $13 (978-03455210-0-2). A troupe of toys sets off to do battle with the Boogeyman when their keeper — a young boy — is kidnapped in this creepy thriller set during World War II. (Rev: BL 7/10; SLJ 7/10)

3577 Raymond, Alex. *Alex Raymond's Flash Gordon, Vol. 4* (9–12). Series: Flash Gordon. 2005, Checker paper $19.95 (978-1-933160-26-9). Volume four of the Flash Gordon series collects comic strips that first appeared in Sunday newspapers in the late 1930s and 1940. (Rev: BL 9/15/05)

3578 Raymond, Alex, and Don Moore. *Alex Raymond's Flash Gordon, Vol. 2* (8–12). 2004, Checker paper $19.95 (978-0-9741664-6-9). The second volume of the Flash Gordon series collects comic strips that first appeared in 1935 and 1936. (Rev: BL 10/1/04)

3579 Reed, Gary. *Mary Shelley's Frankenstein: The Graphic Novel* (7–10). Illus. by Frazer Irving. Series: Puffin Graphics. 2005, Penguin paper $10.99 (978-0-14-240407-2). This graphic novel adaptation accurately conveys the dominant themes of the classic. (Rev: BL 3/15/05; SLJ 9/05; VOYA 8/05)

3580 Reed, M. K. *Americus* (7–10). Illus. by Jonathan Hill. 2011, First Second $18.99 (978-159643768-5); paper $14.99 (978-15964360-1-5). On the verge of beginning high school, shy Neil finds the courage to stand up for what he likes when there is an effort to ban his favorite fantasy series from the local library. Lexile GN550L (Rev: BL 9/15/11; LMC 3–4/12*; SLJ 9/1/11)

3581 Reger, Rob, et al. *Emily the Strange: The Boring Issue, Vol. 1* (9–12). Illus. by Buzz Parker. Series: Emily the Strange. 2005, Dark Horse paper $7.95 (978-1-59307-323-7). Emily is a mysterious girl with dark hair, talking cats, an unusual slant on life, and a strong sense of humor. (Rev: BL 9/15/05)

3582 Robinson, Alex. *Too Cool to Be Forgotten* (10–12). Illus. 2008, Top Shelf paper $12.95 (978-189183098-3). Andy visits a hypnotherapist to cure his tobacco addiction and ends up traveling back in time to high school, when he has the chance to date his crush, say goodbye to his dying father, and decline that first offer of a cigarette. ⊖ (Rev: BL 6/1–15/08; LMC 1–2/09; SLJ 1/09)

3583 Robinson, James, and Tony Harris. *The Starman Omnibus 1* (10–12). Illus. 2008, DC Comics $49.99 (978-140121699-3). A collection of the comics featuring Jack Knight, son of a superhero, who suddenly and reluctantly finds himself inheriting his father's role; first in a series. (Rev: BL 9/1/08; LMC 1–2/09)

3584 Rodi, Rob. *Crossovers* (5–12). 2003, CrossGeneration paper $15.95 (978-1-931484-85-5). This graphic novel is an entertaining look at a suburban family whose members possess a unique power. (Rev: BL 2/1/04)

3585 Roman, Dave. *Agnes Quill: An Anthology of Mystery* (8–10). Illus. by John Ho. 2006, SLG paper $10.95 (978-1-59362-052-3). Agnes — a girl with the ability to speak to the dead — investigates the supernatural and the gory in this anthology, illustrated by four different artists. (Rev: BL 2/1/07)

3586 Rucka, Greg. *The Omac Project* (7–12). Illus. by Jesus Saiz and Cliff Richards. 2005, DC Comics paper $14.99 (978-1-4012-0837-0). Blue Beetle discovers that Max Lord, the millionaire who took over the surveillance camera Brother I, knows the identity of every superhero. (Rev: SLJ 5/06)

3587 Rucka, Greg, and Michael Lark. *The Quick and the Dead: Gotham Central* (7–12). 2006, Vertigo paper $14.99 (978-1-4012-0912-4). The police force of

Gotham is the central focus here — rather than the masked and caped hero who typically comes to their aid in crime-fighting — partially the Bat-Signal has been removed from police HQ following a dispute with Batman. (Rev: BL 12/15/06)

3588 Rucka, Greg, et al. *Bitter Rivals* (9–12). 2005, DC Comics paper $12.95 (978-1-4012-0462-4). In this brightly illustrated title from the Wonder Woman series, the comic book heroine seeks help from Batman in solving the murder of the leader of an anti-Wonder Woman protest group. (Rev: BL 3/15/05)

3589 Rucka, Greg, et al. *Eyes of the Gorgon: Wonder Woman* (9–12). Series: Wonder Woman. 2005, DC Comics paper $19.99 (978-1-4012-0797-7). In this riveting thriller, the Amazon heroine faces off against the deadly Medousa and her allies, who include Circe and Dr. Veronica Cale. (Rev: BL 3/15/06; SLJ 5/06)

3590 Rucka, Greg, et al. *Land of the Dead: Wonder Woman* (9–12). 2006, DC Comics paper $12.99 (978-1-4012-0938-4). Wonder Woman (Diana) faces problems new and old: her longtime enemy Medousa plus complications from her island home's new location near the U.S. coast. (Rev: BL 3/15/06; SLJ 7/06)

3591 Rucka, Greg, et al. *Wonder Woman: Down to Earth* (9–12). 2004, DC Comics paper $14.95 (978-1-4012-0226-2). Wonder Woman, now serving as ambassador from the Amazon island of Themyscria, seeks to promote the ideals of gender equality and peace. (Rev: BL 10/15/04)

3592 Rugg, Jim, and Brian Maruca. *Street Angel: The Princess of Poverty, Vol. 1* (11–12). Series: Street Angel. 2005, SLG paper $14.95 (978-1-59362-012-7). The opening volume in this entertaining series introduces its title character, a 12-year-old Hispanic American girl who fights foes ranging from ninjas to evil geologists using her skateboard and her knowledge of martial arts; for mature teens. (Rev: BL 9/1/05)

3593 Russell, P. Craig. *Conan and the Jewels of Gwahlur* (9–12). 2005, Dark Horse $13.95 (978-1-59307-491-3). Comic book artist P. Craig Russell offers his interpretation of one of author Robert E. Howard's stories about Conan the Barbarian. (Rev: BL 2/1/06)

3594 Ryukishi07. *Higurashi When They Cry: Abducted by Demons Arc, Vol. 1* (10–12). Illus. by Karin Suzuragi. 2008, Yen paper $10.99 (978-075952983-0). Keiichi tries to solve the mystery behind a string of gory murders in this manga adaptation of a computer game. (Rev: BLO 2/9/09; LMC 8–9/09; SLJ 3/09)

3595 Sacco, Joe. *Safe Area Gorazde* (11–12). 2000, Fantagraphics paper $19.95 (978-1-56097-470-3). A graphic novel depicting the conditions in a "safe area" during the recent unrest in Bosnia. (Rev: BL 2/1/03)

3596 Saenagi, Ryo. *Psychic Power Nanaki, Vol. 1* (7–12). Trans. from Japanese by Elina Ishikawa. Illus. by author. 2007, TokyoPop paper $9.99 (978-1-4278-0304-

7). In this well-illustrated manga book, a Japanese teen acquires psychic powers and uses them to investigate ghosts and supernatural phenomena. (Rev: SLJ 3/08)

3597 Sahara, Mizu. *The Voices of a Distant Star* (7–10). 2006, TokyoPop paper $9.99 (978-1-59816-529-6). When Mikako, 15, leaves Earth to travel through space and fight Tarsians (an alien race), she stays in contact with her boyfriend, Noboru, through text messages; but years pass and he must decide if he can wait for her any longer. (Rev: BL 11/1/06)

3598 Sakai, Stan. *Usagi Yojimbo, Vol. 24: Return of the Black Soul* (8–12). Illus. by author. 2010, Dark Horse paper $16.99 (978-15958247-2-1). The genesis of the demon spirit that has haunted samurai rabbit Usagi for years is finally revealed in this installment in the long-running series. (Rev: BL 12/15/10)

3599 Sakai, Stan. *Usagi Yojimbo: Glimpses of Death, Vol. 20* (8–11). Series: Usagi Yojimbo. 2006, Dark Horse $15.95 (978-1-59307-549-1). This newest installment in the series finds the samurai rabbit granting a dying man's last request and embarking on a danger-filled quest to deliver a mysterious package to the man's daughter. (Rev: BL 11/1/06)

3600 Sakai, Stan. *Usagi Yojimbo: Travels with Jotaro, Vol. 18* (8–12). 2004, Dark Horse paper $15.95 (978-1-59307-220-9). In the 18th volume of the series, the title character, a rabbit samurai in feudal Japan, encounters a series of adventures while traveling with Jotaro, who is Usagi's son but doesn't know it. (Rev: BL 9/15/04; SLJ 10/04)

3601 Sakuishi, Harold. *Beck: Mongolian Chop Squad, Vol. 1* (11–12). Trans. from Japanese by Stephen Paul. Illus. by author. 2005, TokyoPop paper $9.99 (978-1-59532-770-3). In this appealing manga, Yukio Tanaka, a 14-year-old nerd, finds his horizons broadened when the lovely Izumi and the exciting Ryusuke introduce him to the world of rock music. (Rev: SLJ 11/05)

3602 Sakura, Tsukuba. *Land of the Blindfolded* (8–11). 2004, DC Comics paper $9.95 (978-1-4012-0524-9). This manga designed primarily for girls tells of two Japanese high school friends (boy and girl) who become close as they decide how to use their conflicting super powers. (Rev: BL 2/15/05)

3603 Sala, Richard. *Cat Burglar Black* (7–10). Illus. by author. 2009, First Second paper $16.99 (978-159643144-7). K (Katherine), already quite skilled as a burglar, finds herself investigating the motives of an art theft group she has been working with. (Rev: BL 7/09; LMC 11–12/09; SLJ 11/09)

3604 Sala, Richard. *The Grave Robber's Daughter* (10–12). 2007, Fantagraphics paper $9.95 (978-1-56097-773-5). Judy Drood, the foul-mouthed detective heroine of *Mad Night* (2005), returns in a strange story of a town inhabited by teens and clowns. (Rev: BL 2/1/07; SLJ 5/07)

3605 Sala, Richard. *Mad Night* (10–12). 2005, Fantagraphics paper $16.95 (978-1-56097-681-3). Bodies, scares, and general silliness abound as coed detective Judy Drood and pal Kasper Keene investigate mysterious goings-on at Lone Mountain College. (Rev: BL 11/1/05)

3606 Schrag, Ariel, ed. *Stuck in the Middle: Seventeen Comics from an Unpleasant Age* (7–10). 2007, Viking $18.99 (978-0-670-06221-8). Is middle school really that bad? Yes, say these artists, who present their versions of this "unpleasant age" in various artistic styles. (Rev: BCCB 9/07; BL 3/15/07; LMC 11–12/07; SLJ 7/07)

3607 Schuiten, Francois, and Benoit Peeters. *The Invisible Frontier, Vol. 1* (10–12). Trans. by Joe Johnson. Series: Cities of the Fantastic. 2003, NBM $15.95 (978-1-56163-333-3). Suitable for mature teens, this comic fantasy recounts the adventures of novice mapmaker Roland in the state of Sodrovno's giant cartographic facility. (Rev: BL 12/15/02)

3608 Schweizer, Chris. *Crogan's Loyalty* (7–12). Illus. by author. 2012, Oni $14.99 (978-193496440-8). The Crogan brothers — Charlie and Will — are divided over the American Revolution, one a Loyalist and one a rebel. (Rev: BL 3/15/12*)

3609 Schweizer, Chris. *Crogan's March* (7–12). Illus. by author. Series: The Crogan Adventures. 2009, Oni $14.95 (978-1-934964-24-8). Peter Crogan is a legionnaire fighting for France in North Africa in 1912 in this action-packed addition to the legends of this unusual family. (Rev: BL 3/15/10*; SLJ 5/10)

3610 Schweizer, Chris. *Crogan's Vengeance* (7–12). Illus. by author. 2008, Oni $14.95 (978-193496406-4). Catfish Crogan and his crewmates fight off pirates on the high seas in this adventure tale set in 1701. (Rev: BL 1/1–15/09; SLJ 5/09)

3611 Seagle, Steven T., and Justin Norman. *Solstice* (9–12). 2005, Active Images paper $12.95 (978-0-9766761-1-9). In this striking graphic novel adventure tale, multimillionaire Russell Waterhouse and his son embark on a perilous journey to find the fountain of youth. (Rev: BL 10/1/05)

3612 Seo, Kouji. *Suzuka, Vol. 2* (10–12). Adapted by David Ury. Illus. by author. 2006, Del Rey paper $13.95 (978-0-345-48632-5). Yamato's attraction to the beautiful Suzuka, who works in his aunt's Tokyo spa, comes to naught until Yamato becomes ill and another girl shows interest in nursing him back to health. (Rev: SLJ 11/06)

3613 Serling, Rod, and Mark Kneece. *Death's-Head Revisited* (7–10). Illus. by Chris Lie. Series: Twilight Zone. 2009, Walker $16.99 (978-080279722-3); paper $9.99 (978-080279723-0). A faithful adaptation of an episode of the *Twilight Zone* television show in which a former concentration camp guard is judged by the souls of the people he murdered. (Rev: BL 3/1/09; SLJ 5/09)

3614 Sfar, Joann. *Klezmer: Book One, Tales of the Wild East* (11–12). Trans. by Alexis Siegel. 2006, First Second paper $16.95 (978-1-59643-198-0). A group of klezmer musicians, using the instruments left behind when their predecessors were murdered, travels through Eastern Europe in this appealing graphic novel suitable for mature teens. (Rev: BL 8/06)

3615 Sfar, Joann. *The Rabbi's Cat* (8–12). 2005, Pantheon $21.95 (978-0-375-42281-2). The entertaining and sophisticated adventures of a talking cat who lives with a rabbi and his daughter in 1930s Algeria. (Rev: BL 7/05; SLJ 3/06)

3616 Sfar, Joann. *The Rabbi's Cat 2* (9–12). 2008, Pantheon $22.95 (978-0-375-42507-3). The rabbi's cat accompanies the rabbi's cousin on his trek through the North African desert, meeting a fascinating melting pot of characters. (Rev: BL 4/1/08)

3617 Sfar, Joann. *Vampire Loves* (10–12). Trans. by Alexis Siegel. 2006, Roaring Brook paper $16.95 (978-1-59643-093-8). In this entertaining graphic novel, Ferdinand is a romantic and gentle young vampire from Lithuania. (Rev: BL 3/15/06; SLJ 7/06)

3618 Sfar, Joann, and Emmanuel Guibert. *The Professor's Daughter* (9–12). Trans. by Alexis Siegel. 2006, Roaring Brook paper $16.95 (978-1-59643-255-0). Lillian falls in love with an Egyptian mummy in this combination mystery/romance/time travel/humor story. (Rev: BCCB 7–8/07; BL 3/15/07; HB 7–8/07; SLJ 5/07)

3619 Shakespeare, William. *Julius Caesar* (8–12). Adapted by Richard Appignanesi. Illus. by Mustashrik. Series: Manga Shakespeare. 2008, Abrams paper $9.95 (978-081097072-4). Abridged text and expressive illustrations tell the story of the play with a manga twist. (Rev: BL 10/1/08*; SLJ 1/09) [741.5]

3620 Shakespeare, William. *Manga Shakespeare: Romeo and Juliet* (9–12). Ed. by Richard Appignanesi. Illus. by Sonia Leong. Series: Manga Shakespeare. 2007, Abrams paper $9.95 (978-0-8109-9325-9). Romeo and Juliet are transported to modern-day Tokyo in this abridged manga version of the play. (Rev: BL 3/15/07)

3621 Shakespeare, William, and John McDonald. *Macbeth: The Graphic Novel* (6–10). Illus. by Jon Haward. 2008, Classical Comics paper $16.95 (978-190633205-1). This dramatically illustrated, condensed version of the play is accompanied by background information to help students understand its plot, setting, characters and significance. (Rev: BL 1/1–15/09)

3622 Shakespeare, William, and Richard Appignanesi. *As You Like It* (8–10). Illus. by Chie Kutsuwada. 2009, Abrams paper $10.95 (978-081098351-9). A manga retelling of the play set in the forest of Arden. (Rev: BL 3/1/09; SLJ 3/09) [823]

3623 Shakespeare, William, and Steven Grant. *Hamlet* (8–10). Illus. by Tom Mandrake. Series: Classics Illustrated. 2009, Papercutz $9.95 (978-159707149-9). This graphic-novel adaptation gives an effective rendering of the key events and characters, and will be useful to supplement the play itself. (Rev: BL 6/1–15/09; LMC 10/09) [822]

3624 Shakespeare, William, et al. *The Tempest: The Graphic Novel; Original Text* (7–12). Illus. by Jon Haward. 2009, Classical Comics paper $16.95 (978-19063326-9-3). An effective graphic-novel version of the story about magic and adventure on a desert island. (Rev: BL 3/15/10*)

3625 Shanower, Eric. *Age of Bronze: Betrayal* (9–12). Illus. by author. Series: Age of Bronze. 2008, Image Comics $27.99 (978-1-58240-845-3); paper $17.99 (978-1-58240-755-5). Part three of the Trojan War in graphic format, this volume — like the others — features beautiful artwork and engaging storytelling. (Rev: BL 3/15/08; SLJ 5/08)

3626 Shanower, Eric. *A Thousand Ships: The Story of the Trojan War* (9–12). Series: Age of Bronze. 2001, Hungry Tiger $29.95 (978-1-58240-221-5); paper $19.95 (978-1-58240-200-0). Drawing on the legend and mythology of ancient Greece, Eric Shanower weaves a fast-paced graphic novel tale of the Trojan War, which is supplemented by such useful features as a glossary, bibliography, and genealogy charts. (Rev: BL 9/15/01; SLJ 2/06) [937]

3627 Shimizu, Aki. *Qwan, Vol. 1* (7–12). Trans. from Japanese by Mike Kief. Illus. by author. 2005, TokyoPop paper $9.99 (978-1-59532-534-1). This compelling graphic novel follows Qwan and his friend as they embark on a magical journey to uncover Qwan's destiny. (Rev: SLJ 7/05)

3628 Shimizu, Takashi, and Meimu. *Ju-On, Vol. 2* (10–12). Trans. by Andy Grossberg. 2006, Dark Horse $9.95 (978-1-59307-531-6). Fans of the movie *The Grudge* will enjoy this tale of death and disappearances. (Rev: BL 9/1/06)

3629 Shurei, Kouyo. *Alichino, Vol. 2* (9–12). Trans. from Japanese by Amy Forsyth. Illus. by author. 2005, TokyoPop paper $9.99 (978-1-59532-479-5). This exquisitely drawn manga, volume two of the Alichino series, explores the relationship of the Alichino with the Kusabi. (Rev: SLJ 11/05)

3630 Siddell, Thomas. *Orientation* (6–12). Illus. by author. Series: Gunnerkrigg Court. 2009, Archaia $26.95 (978-193238634-9). Antimony arrives at a creepy boarding school where things get odder every day in this webcomic collection, the first in a series. YALSA Great Graphic Novels for Teens 2010; Booklist Top 10 Graphic Novels for Youth. (Rev: BL 3/15/09*)

3631 Siddell, Thomas. *Research* (8–12). Illus. by author. Series: Gunnerkrigg Court. 2010, Archaia $26.95 (978-

193238677-6). Antimony Carver and her friend Kat discover more intriguing mysteries, including a tomb of ancient robots, as they explore their unusual boarding school; the second volume in the series. (Rev: BL 5/1/10)

3632 Siegel, Jerry, et al. *Superman in the Forties* (9–12). 2005, DC Comics paper $19.99 (978-1-4012-0457-0). A selection of stories from the first decade of Superman's comic book existence. (Rev: BL 12/1/05; SLJ 3/06)

3633 Sierra, Sergio A. *Frankenstein by Mary Shelley* (7–11). Illus. by Meritxell Ribas. Series: Dark Graphic Novel. 2012, Enslow LB $25.26 (978-076604084-7). A graphic-novel adaptation of the classic novel with woodcut-inspired art. (Rev: BL 9/15/12; SLJ 7/12; VOYA 10/12)

3634 Sievert, Tim. *That Salty Air* (11–12). Illus. by author. 2008, Top Shelf paper $10.00 (978-1-60309-005-6). A poor young couple who live by and depend on the sea are threatened by a giant squid; in black and white. (Rev: BL 5/1/08)

3635 Simmonds, Posy. *Tamara Drewe* (11–12). Illus. 2008, Houghton Mifflin paper $16.95 (978-054715412-1). Using both written word and art in this graphic novel loosely based on Hardy's *Far from the Madding Crowd*, Simmonds skillfully portrays a middle-class English country society shaken up by the arrival of a glamorous newspaper columnist; for mature readers. (Rev: BL 9/1/08*)

3636 Simone, Gail. *Wonder Woman: Ends of the Earth* (8–12). Illus. by Aaron Lopresti. 2010, DC Comics paper $14.99 (978-14012213-7-9). Wonder Woman goes head-to-head against a powerful lord at the edge of existence. (Rev: BL 5/1/10)

3637 Singer, Bryan, and Justin Gray. *Superman Returns: The Prequels* (7–12). 2006, DC Comics paper $12.99 (978-1-4012-1146-2). *Superman Returns,* the film, is enhanced by these stories that occur in the five years before his return to Earth and involve his adoptive mother Martha, his nemesis Lex Luthor, and his heartbroken love interest Lois Lane; they also bridge some scenes from the 1978 *Superman* film for a better continuity. (Rev: BL 12/1/06)

3638 Sizer, Paul. *B. P. M* (10–12). Illus. by author. 2008, Cafe Digital paper $15.99 (978-097685656-6). Roxy dreams of becoming a DJ in a top gay nightclub in this manga that's all about music and the club scene (the title stands for "beats per minute"). (Rev: BLO 4/30/09)

3639 Smart, Jamie. *Ubu Bubu: Filth* (11–12). Illus. 2009, SLG paper $12.95 (978-15936219-8-8). Full of anime-influenced artwork and dry British wit, this is the story of a destructive demon that inhabits the body of a kitten and attempts to bring about an apocalypse. (Rev: BL 11/15/09)

3640 Smith, Jeff. *The Art of Bone* (9–12). 2007, Dark Horse $39.95 (978-1-59307-441-8). An obvious pleaser for fans of Bone, a comic book that ended in 2004, this is a collection of many of the facets of artwork that went into the creation of the comic, from the ballpoint drawings originated from the 10-year-old Smith to artwork for promotional material. (Rev: BL 8/07) [741.5]

3641 Smith, Jeff. *Bone* (9–12). 2004, Cartoon paper $39.95 (978-1-888963-14-4). A massive volume containing the complete, and very popular, Bone fantasy saga. (Rev: BL 10/15/04)

3642 Smith, Jeff. *Old Man's Cave* (5–12). Illus. by author. Series: Bone. 2007, Scholastic $18.99 (978-0-439-70628-5); paper $9.99 (978-0-439-70635-3). Episode six of this series that combines goofy-looking characters with dramatic fantasy plots finds Phoney Bone and Thorn in grave danger. (Rev: BL 11/1/07)

3643 Smith, Jeff. *Shazam! The Monster Society of Evil* (7–12). 2007, DC Comics $29.99 (978-1-4012-1466-1). Young Billy Batson, an orphan living in unpleasant circumstances, only has to say Shazam to be transformed into Captain Marvel; but Billy is hampered by his own behavior and his younger sister and now faces an alien invasion and the Monster Society of Evil. (Rev: BL 10/15/07; SLJ 3/08)

3644 Smith, Jeff, and Tom Sniegoski. *Bone: Tall Tales* (6–12). 2010, Graphix $22.99 (978-0-545-14095-9). A collection of stories featuring the founder of Boneville, Big Johnson Bone, and his intrepid adventures. Lexile GN560L (Rev: BL 3/15/10; LMC 10/10; SLJ 7/10)

3645 Spears, Rick. *Dead West* (11–12). Illus. by Rob G. 2005, Gigantic paper $14.95 (978-0-9763038-1-7). This offbeat graphic novel blends the best of the horror and western genres in its tale of an ill-fated town that was built on the site of a Native American village. (Rev: BL 9/15/05; SLJ 11/05)

3646 Spears, Rick. *Teenagers from Mars* (10–12). Illus. by Rob G. 2005, Gigantic paper $19.95 (978-0-9763038-0-0). Three teenage comic book lovers in the small town of Mars declare war on the town's adults who've decided to rid their community of all vestiges of comics. (Rev: SLJ 9/05)

3647 Stanley, John. *Melvin Monster: The John Stanley Library* (6–12). Illus. 2009, Drawn & Quarterly $19.95 (978-189729963-0). Stanley's monster kid, Melvin, is funny and sympathetic in this reprinted comic book series. (Rev: BL 7/09; SLJ 11/09)

3648 Stanley, John, and Irving Tripp. *All Dressed Up: Little Lulu 10* (9–12). 2006, Dark Horse paper $9.95 (978-1-59307-534-7). Lulu, Annie, Tubby, and friends are in for more adventures in this installment in the classic comic series; also recommended are such volumes as *Late for School: Little Lulu 8, Leave It to Lulu: Little Lulu 12,* and *The Expert: Little Lulu 18.* (Rev: BL 8/06)

3649 Stanley, John, and Irving Tripp. *Color Special: Little Lulu* (7–12). 2006, Dark Horse paper $13.95 (978-1-59307-613-9). Little Lulu is back in vibrant color reproductions of selected stories from issues 4 through 86. (Rev: BL 10/1/06)

3650 Stanley, John, and Irving Tripp. *Letters to Santa* (9–12). Series: Little Lulu. 2005, Dark Horse paper $9.95 (978-1-59307-386-2). The attractions of Little Lulu, the girl with the curly black locks, have lasted more than 50 years; this sixth volume includes five issues dealing with the winter holidays. Also recommended are *Sunday Afternoon* (the fourth volume, 2004) and *Lulu's Umbrella Service* (the seventh volume, 2005). (Rev: BL 12/15/05)

3651 Stanley, John, and Irving Tripp. *Lulu Takes a Trip* (9–12). Series: Little Lulu. 2005, Dark Horse paper $9.95 (978-1-59307-317-6). Volume two of the Little Lulu series collects early stories from the classic comic strip. (Rev: BL 4/15/05)

3652 Stanley, John, and Irving Tripp. *Miss Feeny's Folly and Other Stories: Little Lulu 21* (6–12). Illus. 2009, Dark Horse paper $14.95 (978-15958236-5-6). This 21st volume continues the meticulous reprinting of the delightful Little Lulu series. (Rev: BL 12/1/09)

3653 Stassen, Jean-Philippe. *Deogratias: A Tale of Rwanda* (11–12). Trans. by Alexis Siegel. 2006, Roaring Brook paper $16.95 (978-1-59643-103-4). The unspeakable horrors of the Rwandan genocide of the early 1990s are revisited in this heartrending graphic novel. (Rev: BL 3/15/06; SLJ 7/06)

3654 Stathis, Pete. *Soul to Keep: Evenfall, Vol. 2* (11–12). 2007, Blue Feather paper $9.95 (978-1-4243-2632-7). Convinced that she's still alive, Phoebe Shankar nonetheless watches herself lying dead at the bottom of a canyon; she is at the beginning of a new struggle to escape and learn to live again; for mature teens. (Rev: BL 3/15/07)

3655 Stoker, Bram. *Dracula* (7–12). Adapted by Gary Reed. Illus. by Becky Cloonan. Series: Puffin Graphics. 2006, Puffin paper $10.99 (978-0-14-240572-7). A compelling graphic-novel version of the famous vampire story. (Rev: SLJ 3/06)

3656 Stokoe, James. *Wonton Soup: Space Trucker Opera* (10–12). Illus. by author. 2007, Oni paper $11.95 (978-1-932664-60-7). Yes, there are truckers in space, and they are wild, vulgar, combative gourmets, according to this humorous action-packed manga. (Rev: BL 1/1–15/08)

3657 Storrie, Paul D. *Made for Each Other* (7–10). Illus. by Eldon Cowgur. 2011, Lerner/Graphic Universe LB $29.27 (978-076135601-1); paper $9.95 (9780761370772). A saucy paranormal romance in graphic-novel format that features Maria and her new beau, Tom B. Stone, and a series of mysterious deaths.

Lexile GN340L (Rev: BL 5/1/11; LMC 10/11*; SLJ 7/1/11)

3658 Sturm, James. *James Sturm's America: God, Gold, and Golems* (10–12). 2007, Drawn & Quarterly $24.95 (978-1-897299-05-0). Three stories — "The Revival," "Hundreds of Feet Below Daylight," and "The Golem's Mighty Swing" — set in 1801, 1886, and the early 1920s, respectively, and tackling social issues including the yearning for a better life are rendered in graphic-novel format. (Rev: BL 3/15/07; SLJ 5/07)

3659 Sugisaki, Yukiro. *Rizelmine* (8–12). Trans. from Japanese by Alethea Nibley and Athena Nibley. Illus. by author. 2005, TokyoPop paper $9.99 (978-1-59532-901-1). Fifteen-year-old Iwaki Tomonori rejects the advances of robot-like Rizel, who's become his bride by government decree. (Rev: SLJ 11/05)

3660 Sumerak, Marc, and Fred Van Lente. *Wolverine: Tales of Weapon X* (8–12). Illus. by Mark Robinson. 2009, Marvel $14.99 (978-078513936-2). Six lively comics combine humor and adventure with details of Wolverine's past. (Rev: BLO 6/16/09)

3661 Suzuki, Yasushi. *Goths Cage* (9–12). Illus. by author. 2008, DrMaster $12.95 (978-159796157-8). The focus is on the artwork in these three dark fantasies loosely based on folk and fairy tales. (Rev: BLO 1/13/09)

3662 Tada, Kaoru. *Itazura na Kiss, Vol. 2* (7–10). Illus. by author. 2010, DMP paper $16.95 (978-15697013-6-2). Kotoko continues naively trying to get Naoki to fall for her as they graduate from high school and start college; the second volume in the series. (Rev: BLO 9/1/10)

3663 Tajima, Sho-U, and Eiji Otsuka. *Madara, Vol. 1* (11–12). 2004, DC Comics paper $9.95 (978-1-4012-0529-4). In this fantasy manga, the title character, badly maimed as a child, learns to function using mechanical limbs crafted by the villagers who rescue him; for mature teens only. (Rev: BL 2/1/05)

3664 Takada, Rie. *Gaba Kawa, Vol. 1* (8–12). Illus. by author. 2008, VIZ Media paper $8.99 (978-142152259-3). Rara is a high-school demon who falls in love with a human classmate in this funny yet sometimes disturbing story. (Rev: BLO 2/9/09)

3665 Takaya, Natsuki. *Phantom Dream, Vol. 1* (10–12). Trans. by Beni Axia Conrad. Illus. by author. 2009, Tokyopop paper $9.99 (978-142781089-2). Tamaki and Asahi learn that they come from warring families in this manga that combines romance and the supernatural. (Rev: BL 3/1/09)

3666 Takeuchi, Mick. *Bound Beauty* (8–11). Illus. by author. 2008, Go! Comi $10.99 (978-1-60510-008-1). This manga novel about a teenage matchmaker contains lots of great information about Japanese folklore, history, and traditions. (Rev: BLO 12/30/08)

3667 Talbot, Bryan. *The Tale of One Bad Rat* (9–12). 1995, Dark Horse $14.95 (978-1-56971-077-7). A classic graphic novel about a teenage runaway girl who is escaping an abusive father. (Rev: BL 2/1/04)

3668 Tamaki, Mariko. *Emiko Superstar* (8–12). Illus. by Steve Rolston. 2008, DC Comics paper $9.99 (978-140121536-1). Asian Canadian Emiko discovers she can use performance art to be someone completely different from the geeky teen she believes she is. (Rev: BL 12/1/08; LMC 5–6/09; SLJ 11/08)

3669 Tan, Shaun. *The Arrival* (6–12). Illus. by author. 2007, Scholastic $19.99 (978-043989529-3). This wordless graphic novel tells the moving story of a man who migrates to a new country hoping to build a new life. Boston Globe–Horn Book Special Citation 2008; ALA Notable Books 2008. (Rev: BL 9/1/07*; SLJ 9/07)

3670 Tan, Shaun. *Tales from Outer Suburbia* (7–12). Illus. by author. 2009, Scholastic $19.99 (978-054505587-1). These fifteen diverse short tales are beautifully illustrated with Tan's evocative artwork. ALA Notable Books 2010. Lexile 1100L (Rev: BL 12/1/08; HB 3–4/09; LMC 5–6/09; SLJ 3/1/09*; VOYA 6/09)

3671 TenNapel, Doug. *Bad Island* (6–10). Illus. by author. 2011, Graphix $24.99 (978-054531479-4); paper $12.99 (978-054531480-0). On a boat trip with his family, Reese finds himself washed up on an island inhabited by weird beings from a distant galaxy. (Rev: BL 3/15/11*; SLJ 11/1/11)

3672 Thomas, John Ira, and Carter Allen. *Man Is Vox: Barracudae* (9–12). 2003, Candle Light paper $9.95 (978-0-9743147-2-3). Our hero in a patched union suit and a store clerk join forces to further their various purposes in this graphic novel. (Rev: BL 2/1/04)

3673 Thomas, John Ira, and Jeremy Smith. *The Fairer Sex: A Tale of Shades and Angels, Vol. 1* (11–12). 2004, Candle Light paper $13.95 (978-0-9743147-5-4). In this gripping graphic novel mystery, homicide detectives Tom and Fred try to track down the woman responsible for gunning down multiple victims in a shooting at the local mall; for mature readers. (Rev: BL 10/1/04)

3674 Thomas, Roy, and Homer. *The Odyssey* (9–12). Illus. by Greg Tocchini. 2010, Marvel paper $19.99 (978-07851191-5-9). An effective graphic-novel account of some of Odysseus's adventures. (Rev: BLO 3/15/10)

3675 Thomas, Roy, et al. *The Monster of the Monoliths and Other Stories* (9–12). 2004, Dark Horse paper $15.95 (978-1-59307-024-3). Conan the barbarian faces wizards, witches, demons, and pirates in this collection of stories. (Rev: BL 3/15/04)

3676 Thomas, Roy, et al. *The Song of Red Sonja and Other Stories* (9–12). 2004, Dark Horse paper $15.95 (978-1-59307-025-0). This reprint from Marvel Comics continues the early adventures of Conan the Barbarian. (Rev: BL 5/15/04)

3677 Thompson, Craig. *Blankets* (11–12). 2003, Top Shelf paper $29.95 (978-1-891830-43-3). First love and loss are central to this coming-of-age story, a sequel to *Good-bye Chunky Rice* (1999); suitable for mature teens. (Rev: BL 6/1–15/03*; SLJ 4/04)

3678 Tinsley, Kevin, and Phil Singer. *Milk Cartons and Dog Biscuits* (7–12). 2004, Stickman Graphics paper $19.95 (978-0-9675423-4-8). People and elf-like creatures mingle in this adventure mystery about a state ranger who is searching for a runaway daughter. (Rev: BL 2/1/04)

3679 Tobe, Keiko. *With the Light: Raising an Autistic Child 1* (11–12). Trans. by Satsuki Yamashita. 2007, Yen paper $14.99 (978-0-7595-2356-2). In manga style, this is the story of a Japanese family learning to cope with a son's autism. (Rev: BL 9/15/07; SLJ 1/08)

3680 Tobe, Keiko. *With the Light: Raising an Autistic Child 2* (10–12). Trans. by Satsuki Yamashita. Illus. 2008, Yen paper $14.99 (978-075952359-3). In this second volume about an autistic child and the impact on the family, Hikaru is now in 4th grade and striving to cope with special-ed classes and social interactions. (Rev: BL 6/1–15/08*)

3681 Tolkien, J. R. R. *The Hobbit; or, There and Back Again* (5–10). Adapted by Charles Dixon. 1990, Eclipse Books paper $12.95 (978-0-345-36858-4). The classic story of Bilbo Baggins and his companions is introduced to reluctant readers in this full-color graphic novel. (Rev: BL 9/1/91)

3682 Tomori, Miyoshi. *A Devil and Her Love Song, Vol. 1* (8–12). Illus. by author. 2012, VIZ Media paper $9.99 (978-14215416-4-8). Maria's reputation precedes her at her new school but her angelic voice contradicts her overly frank behavior, attracting the attention of two boys. (Rev: BL 4/15/12; SLJ 7/1/12)

3683 Toume, Kei. *Kurogane, Vol. 1* (7–12). Trans. from Japanese by Akira Tsubasa. Adapted by Alex Kent. Illus. by author. 2006, Del Rey paper $10.95 (978-0-345-49203-6). Jintetsu, with a steel body and a talking sword, sets out to avenge his father's death in this story set in feudal Japan. (Rev: SLJ 9/06)

3684 Toyoda, Minoru. *Love Roma, Vol. 1* (8–11). 2005, Del Rey paper $10.95 (978-0-345-48262-4). This delightful manga chronicles the budding romance of teenagers Hoshino and Negishi. (Rev: BL 10/15/05; SLJ 1/06)

3685 Trondheim, Lewis. *Dungeon* (9–12). Illus. by Joann Sfar. 2004, NBM paper $14.95 (978-1-56163-401-9). In this French graphic novel import, a compelling blend of horror and heroic fantasy, Herbert the Duck is suddenly elevated from lowly messenger to the awesome responsibility of defending the Dungeon from outside attack. (Rev: BL 12/1/04)

3686 Trondheim, Lewis. *Harum Scarum* (10–12). Trans. from French by Kim Thompson. 1998, Fantagraphics paper $10.95 (978-1-56097-288-4). A graphic novel about McConey, who looks like a well-dressed pink rabbit, his friends, and magic powers that can turn a city's population (all animals) into self-destructing monsters. Also use for the same audience: *The Hoodoodad* (1998). (Rev: SLJ 2/99)

3687 Trondheim, Lewis. *Kaput and Zosky* (9–12). Illus. by Eric Cartier. 2008, Roaring Brook $13.95 (978-1-59643-132-4). Two inept aliens with universal dominion on their minds land on planet after planet and fail to meet their goal in a number of ways in this funny, bright comic book from France. (Rev: BL 3/15/08; SLJ 5/08)

3688 Trondheim, Lewis, and Manu Larcenet. *Astronauts of the Future, Vol. 1* (9–12). Trans. by Joe Johnson. Series: Astronauts of the Future. 2004, NBM paper $14.95 (978-1-56163-407-1). Talented and isolated young friends Gil and Martina find themselves facing off against the rest of the world, which is made up of either aliens or robots depending on the point of view. (Rev: BL 1/1–15/05)

3689 Truman, Timothy, and Mark Schultz. *Star Wars Omnibus: Emissaries and Assassins* (6–12). Illus. by Tim Bradstreet. 2009, Dark Horse paper $24.95 (978-159582229-1). A collection of comics based on movies *Episode I* and *II*, with different styles of artwork and featuring favorite characters. (Rev: BLO 5/27/09)

3690 Tsuda, Masami. *Castle of Dreams: Stories from the Kare Kano Creator* (8–12). Illus. Series: Sorcerer. 2009, Tokyopop paper $12.99 (978-142781227-8). Teenage romance, fantasy, and modern life mix in this collection of sweet stories. (Rev: BLO 2/9/09)

3691 Tsukiji, Toshihiko. *Maburaho, Vol. 1* (8–12). Trans. from Japanese by Kay Bertrand. Illus. by Miki Miyashita. 2005, ADV paper $9.99 (978-1-4139-0293-8). Kazuki, a hapless magician-in-training, is pursued by three female students who know that he is destined to father a child who'll become a powerful wizard. (Rev: SLJ 7/05)

3692 Tucci, Billy, and JC Vaughan. *Shi: Ju-Nen* (9–12). 2006, Dark Horse paper $12.95 (978-1-59307-451-7). Ana Ishikawa returns to Japan in hopes of finding respite from earlier adventures, but she soon finds herself caught up in a deadly confrontation between rival monk warriors from Kyoto and Nara. (Rev: BL 4/1/06)

3693 Turner, James. *I, Librarian: Rex Libris, Vol. 1* (9–12). 2007, SLG paper $14.95 (978-1-59362-062-2). Rex Libris, superhero and luminary of the International Order of Librarians, is a man with a long-term mission — to protect knowledge — in this humorous adventure. (Rev: BL 10/15/07)

3694 Type-Moon. *Fate/Stay Night* (8–11). Illus. by Dat Nishiwaki. Series: Fate/Stay Night. 2008, Tokyopop $9.99 (978-142781037-3). Emiya faces danger and evil forces in his ongoing fight for the powerful Holy Grail;

an action-packed manga with mythological references. (Rev: BLO 1/21/09)

3695 Ueda, Miwa. *Papillon, Vol. 1* (8–11). Illus. by author. 2008, Del Rey paper $10.95 (978-0-345-50519-4). High school student Ageha is always upstaged by her twin sister Hana in this manga novel until her sister steals the boy Ageha likes and she decides, with the encouragement of a friend and her school guidance counselor, that it's time to make a change. (Rev: BLO 12/8/08; SLJ 11/08)

3696 Ueda, Miwa. *Peach Girl* (9–12). 2000, TokyoPop paper $9.99 (978-1-59182-498-5). In this Japanese graphic novel, a young girl is shunned and maligned because she has dark skin. (Rev: BL 2/1/04)

3697 Urasawa, Naoki, et al. *Pluto, Vol. 1* (10–12). Illus. by author. 2009, VIZ Media paper $12.99 (978-142151918-0). Gesicht, a humanoid robot detective for Europol, investigates a serial murderer. (Rev: BLO 10/27/09*)

3698 Urrea, Luis Alberto. *Mr. Mendoza's Paintbrush* (9–12). Illus. by Christopher Carinale. 2010, Cinco Puntos paper $17.95 (978-1-933693-23-1). Mr. Mendoza's graffiti adorn the Mexican village of Rosario, portraying various social problems. (Rev: BL 5/1–15/10; HB 7–8/10; LMC 11–12/10; SLJ 7/10)

3699 Urushibara, Yuki. *Mushishi, Vol. 1* (8–12). Adapted by William Flanagan. Illus. by author. 2007, Del Rey paper $10.95 (978-0-345-49621-8). Mushi are parasitic, supernatural beings that invade human victims, and Ginko's job is to control them in this compelling manga. (Rev: SLJ 7/07)

3700 Valentino, Jim, and Kristen K. Simon, eds. *Fractured Fables* (9–12). Illus. 2010, Image/Silverline $29.99 (978-160706269-1). Sharp humor and bold illustrations spice up thirty classic fairy tales and nursery rhymes in this inventive collection. (Rev: BL 10/15/10; SLJ 7/1/11*)

3701 Varon, Sara. *Robot Dreams* (6–12). Illus. by author. 2007, Roaring Brook paper $16.95 (978-1-59643-108-9). Poor lonely Dog is very happy when Robot arrives, but Dog doesn't realize Robot can't go swimming in this appealing almost-wordless graphic novel that provides both humor and poignancy. ALA Notable Books 2008. (Rev: BL 8/07; LMC 11/07; SLJ 9/07)

3702 Vaughan, Brian K., and Niko Henrichon. *Pride of Baghdad* (11–12). 2006, DC Comics $19.99 (978-1-4012-1059-5). Lions that escaped from the Baghdad zoo during the Iraq War are the focus of this arresting graphic novel. (Rev: BL 8/06; SLJ 9/06)

3703 Vaughan, Brian K., and Tony Harris. *March to War: Ex Machina 4* (10–12). 2006, Wildstorm paper $12.99 (978-1-4012-0997-1). New York City may be under a terrorist attack as chaos reigns following a protest against the Iraq war. Will Mayor Hundred have to revert to superhero status to deal with the situation? For mature readers. (Rev: BL 2/1/07; SLJ 3/07)

3704 Vaughan, Brian K., and Tony Harris. *Smoke Smoke: Ex Machina 5* (11–12). 2007, DC Comics paper $12.99 (978-1-4012-1322-0). In this fifth volume, New York Mayor (and former superhero) Mitchell Hundred must cope with a rash of robberies and controversy about drug laws; for mature readers. (Rev: BL 4/15/07)

3705 Vaughan, Brian K., et al. *Cycles* (10–12). Series: Y: The Last Man. 2003, DC Comics paper $12.95 (978-1-4012-0076-3). Investigations continue into protagonist Yorick Brown's mysterious survival of a plague as he again confronts the Daughters of the Amazon and a new Israeli group; for mature teens. (Rev: BL 11/15/03; SLJ 2/04)

3706 Vaughan, Brian K., et al. *Girl on Girl, Vol. 6* (9–12). Series: Y: The Last Man. 2005, DC Comics paper $12.99 (978-1-4012-0501-0). In the sixth volume of Y: The Last Man collection, Yorick Brown, the last surviving human male on Earth, and his female escorts go in search of Ampersand, Brown's pet monkey that was abducted by a Japanese mercenary; also use *Paper Dolls*, volume 7, and *Kimono Dragons*, volume 8. (Rev: BL 1/1–15/06)

3707 Vaughan, Brian K., et al. *Safeword* (11–12). Series: Y: The Last Man. 2004, DC Comics paper $12.95 (978-1-4012-0232-3). Volume four of the series collects issues 18 to 23 of the post-apocalyptic road story. (Rev: BL 1/1–15/05)

3708 Vaughan, Brian K., et al. *Tag: Ex Machina, Book 2* (11–12). 2005, DC Comics paper $12.99 (978-1-4012-0626-0). In the second volume of Vaughan's Ex Machina graphic novel series, Mitchell Hundred, who possesses extraordinary powers, quits the police force to run for mayor of New York City; for mature readers. (Rev: BL 10/15/05; SLJ 5/06)

3709 Vaughan, Brian K., et al. *Whys and Wherefores* (9–12). Series: Y: The Last Man. 2008, Vertigo paper $14.99 (978-1-4012-1813-3). The last of ten installments in this action/drama/pop culture serial graphic novel. (Rev: BL 3/15/08)

3710 Veitch, Rick, and Alfredo Alcala. *Spontaneous Generation: Swamp Thing 8* (9–12). 2006, DC Comics paper $19.99 (978-1-4012-0793-9). The eighth volume of the Swamp Thing series contains some of the early issues created by Rick Veitch, who took over the comic from its original creator Alan Moore. (Rev: BL 2/1/06)

3711 Venditti, Robert, and Brett Weldele. *Flesh and Bone* (10–12). Illus. Series: The Surrogates. 2009, Top Shelf paper $14.95 (978-16030901-8-6). It is the year 2039 and wealthy people have avatars, or "surrogates," who go about their daily lives in their place, while revolution brews among those who can't afford this technology; a prequel to *The Surrogates* (2006). (Rev: BL 7/09; SLJ 11/09)

3712 Verheiden, Mark. *The American* (9–12). 2005, Dark Horse paper $14.95 (978-1-59307-419-7). Collected in this volume are several issues of the late-1980s comic book series featuring The American, a cynical government creation designed to foster the illusion of U.S. military invincibility. (Rev: BL 2/1/06)

3713 Vollmar, Rob, and Pablo G. Callejo. *Bluesman: Book Two* (10–12). Series: Bluesman. 2006, NBM paper $8.95 (978-1-56163-456-9). A gritty, atmospheric graphic novel about an African American blues singer accused of murder in early 20th-century Arkansas; the third volume also appeared in 2006. (Rev: BL 4/15/06; SLJ 9/06)

3714 Von Sholly, Pete. *Dead But Not Out! Pete Von Sholly's Morbid 2* (7–12). 2005, Dark Horse paper $14.95 (978-1-59307-289-6). Cheap horror movies are the target of this entertaining parody. (Rev: BL 3/15/05)

3715 Von Sholly, Pete. *Pete Von Sholly's Morbid* (10–12). 2003, Dark Horse paper $14.95 (978-1-59307-028-1). For mature readers, this is a graphic novel dealing with huge creatures, star-trekking, the living dead, and mad doctors and illustrated with processed photographs. (Rev: BL 2/1/04*)

3716 Wada, Shinji. *Crown* (9–12). Illus. by You Higuri. Series: Crown. 2008, Go! Comi paper $10.99 (978-160510005-0). This first volume in a series introduces Mahiro, whose long-lost brother and his friend show up to protect her from evil forces after her parents die in a car crash. (Rev: BL 3/1/09)

3717 Wagner, Matt. *Batman and the Monster Men 1* (9–12). 2006, DC Comics paper $14.99 (978-1-4012-1091-5). Set in an early time in the Batman saga (1940), this is the story of how gangsters become supervillains in the hands of mad scientist Hugo Strange and are genetically transformed into the monster men that plague Gotham City, driving Batman (still working alone) into action. (Rev: BL 10/1/06; LMC 4–5/07; SLJ 5/07)

3718 Waid, Mark. *Daredevil, Vol. 1* (9–12). Illus. by Paolo Rivera. 2012, Marvel $19.99 (978-078515237-8). Matt Murdock faces down a fresh slew of challenges as he realizes his past may have more impact on his present situation than he thought. YALSA Great Graphic Novels Top Ten 2013. (Rev: BL 4/15/12*)

3719 Waid, Mark. *Legion of Super-Heroes: Teenage Revolution* (8–11). Illus. by Barry Kitson. 2005, DC Comics paper $14.99 (978-1-4012-0482-2). In this comic book vision of the future, teenage superheroes rebel against their parents' utopian government. (Rev: BL 1/1–15/06; SLJ 3/06)

3720 Waid, Mark. *Ruse: Inferno of Blue* (7–12). Illus. by Butch Guice. 2002, CrossGeneration paper $15.95 (978-1-931484-19-0). Mystery, action, and magical powers abound in this graphic novel set in an alternate universe and starring detective Simon Archard and sidekick Emma Bishop. (Rev: BL 8/02)

3721 Waid, Mark, and Alex Ross. *Absolute Kingdom Come* (9–12). 2006, DC Comics $75.00 (978-1-4012-0768-7). Classic superheroes — Wonder Woman, Superman, Batman — must confront not only villains but also a new strain of superheroes in this collection from DC's Absolute series that combines stories with extra unpublished artwork and commentary. (Rev: BL 10/15/06)

3722 Watson, Andi. *Clubbing* (9–12). Illus. by Josh Howard. 2007, DC Comics paper $9.99 (978-1-4012-0370-2). As punishment for using a fake ID at a club in London's West End, Lottie is sent to stay with her grandparents in the country, where she expects to be mightily bored; with local boy Howard, however, Lottie soon ends up investigating a murder with supernatural aspects. (Rev: BL 9/1/07; SLJ 11/07)

3723 Wein, Len. *Secret of the Swamp Thing* (7–12). Illus. by Berni Wrightson. 2005, DC Comics paper $9.99 (978-1-4012-0798-4). A collection of the first ten issues of the original comics about the legendary hero called Swamp Thing. (Rev: SLJ 5/06)

3724 Weing, Drew. *Set to Sea* (8–12). Illus. by author. 2010, Fantagraphics $16.99 (978-160699368-2). After years of glorifying the sea in his mind, the unnamed main character of this simple fable suddenly finds himself aboard a clipper bound for Hong Kong. YALSA Great Graphic Novels Top Ten 2011. (Rev: BL 10/15/10*)

3725 Weissman, Steven. *White Flower Day* (9–12). 2003, Fantagraphics paper $14.95 (978-1-56097-514-4). Several weird young creatures who create mayhem are the stars of three different stories in this graphic novel. (Rev: BL 2/1/04)

3726 Wells, H. G. *The Invisible Man* (7–12). Retold by Terry Davis. Illus. by Dennis Calero. Series: Graphic Revolve. 2008, Stone Arch LB $23.93 (978-1-59889-831-6); paper $6.95 (978-1-59889-887-3). This somewhat altered retelling of Wells's story is concise and easy to understand. (Rev: SLJ 3/08)

3727 Wells, H. G. *The Time Machine* (7–12). Retold by Terry Davis. Illus. by Josée Alfonso and Ocampo Ruiz. Series: Graphic Revolve. 2008, Stone Arch LB $23.93 (978-1-59889-833-0); paper $6.95 (978-1-59889-889-7). Simpler in its retelling, this version of Wells's classic will attract a wide audience. (Rev: SLJ 3/08)

3728 Westerfeld, Scott, and Devin Grayson. *Shay's Story* (7–10). Illus. by Steven Cummings. Series: Uglies. 2012, Del Rey paper $10.99 (978-03455272-2-6). Shay must choose between the shallow perks of being beautiful and the realness of being an ordinary Ugly. Lexile GN510L (Rev: BL 3/15/12)

3729 Whedon, Joss. *MySpace Dark Horse Presents, Vol. 2* (11–12). Ed. by Zack Whedon. Illus. by Eric Canete. 2009, Dark Horse paper $19.95 (978-159582248-2). The second volume in this series features a collection of mysterious, romantic, and supernatural comic adventures by many different artists. (Rev: BLO 2/9/09)

3730 Whedon, Joss, and John Cassaday. *Astonishing X-Men: Gifted* (9–12). 2005, Marvel paper $14.99 (978-0-7851-1531-1). The opening volume of a new series featuring a struggle between good (a team of handsome young outcasts) and evil (a homicidal alien). (Rev: BL 3/15/05)

3731 Whedon, Joss, et al. *Tales of the Vampires* (9–12). 2004, Dark Horse paper $15.95 (978-1-56971-749-3). Screenwriter Joss Whedon, creator of *Buffy the Vampire Slayer*, weaves together an anthology of original vampire stories with a unifying tale of young vampire slayers in training. (Rev: BL 1/1–15/05)

3732 Whedon, Joss, et al. *Those Left Behind: Serenity 1* (9–12). 2006, Dark Horse paper $9.95 (978-1-59307-449-4). In this adventure, the captain and crew of the *Serenity* take on a scavenger mission that turns out to be not at all what it first seemed. (Rev: BL 2/1/06)

3733 White, James L., and Dalibor Talajic. *Hunter's Moon* (10–12). Illus. 2008, Boom! Studios paper $14.99 (978-193450622-6). African American Lincoln Greer takes his son Wendell on a hunting trip to the mountains, only to find himself framed for murder and ensnared in racial prejudice. (Rev: BL 6/1–15/08)

3734 White, Tracy. *How I Made It to Eighteen: A Mostly True Story* (9–12). Illus. by author. 2010, Roaring Brook $16.99 (978-159643454-7). Seventeen-year-old Stacy Black goes to a psychiatric hospital for help with her depression, anxiety, and eating disorders in this semi-autobiographical novel that combines both text sections and cartoon panels. **e** (Rev: BL 4/15/10; SLJ 11/10; VOYA 2/10)

3735 Williams, Rob. *Star Wars Rebellion: My Brother, My Enemy, Vol. 1* (8–12). Illus. by Brandon Badeaux. 2007, Dark Horse paper $14.95 (978-1-59307-711-2). This first volume in a new graphic novel series follows Luke Skywalker after he joins the rebellion and must decide whether to trust his old friend Tank, who is now an Imperial Officer. (Rev: BL 8/07)

3736 Willingham, Bill. *Robin: To Kill a Bird* (8–11). Illus. by Damion Scott. 2006, DC Comics paper $14.99 (978-1-4012-0909-4). In this Batman and Robin adventure, Robin learns to fight for himself as he's attacked by the Penguin's hit men. (Rev: BL 7/06)

3737 Willingham, Bill, and Mark Buckingham. *Arabian Nights (and Days)* (9–12). Series: Fables. 2006, Vertigo paper $14.99 (978-1-4012-1000-7). Sinbad leads an Arabian group to Fabletown to discuss an alliance against the Adversary in this volume of the series about fairy tale characters driven from their homes who have settled in Fabletown, in New York City. (Rev: BL 10/1/06; SLJ 1/07)

3738 Willingham, Bill, and Mark Buckingham. *The Good Prince* (9–12). Series: Fables. 2008, Vertigo pa-

per $17.99 (978-1-4012-1686-3). This 10th volume in the long series follows Fabletown's janitor, Flycatcher, as he seeks refuge from an oppressive emperor. (Rev: BL 4/1/08)

3739 Willingham, Bill, and Mark Buckingham. *1001 Nights of Snowfall* (9–12). Series: Fables. 2006, Vertigo $19.99 (978-1-4012-0367-2). Another beautifully illustrated book in the Fables series, this time involving Snow White endeavoring to help her fellow fairy tale characters out of exile while trying to beguile an Arabian sultan. (Rev: BL 10/1/06)

3740 Willingham, Bill, and Mark Buckingham. *Wolves* (11–12). Series: Fables. 2006, Vertigo paper $17.99 (978-1-4012-1001-4). Mowgli, Bigby (Big Bad Wolf), and Snow White hope for a happy ending in this eighth volume of the Fabletown tales. (Rev: BL 2/1/07; SLJ 7/07)

3741 Willingham, Bill, et al. *Fables: Legends in Exile* (11–12). 2003, DC Comics paper $9.95 (978-1-56389-942-3). This humorous graphic novel suitable for mature teens is peopled with refugees from fairy tales — including Jack of beanstalk fame, Snow White, Prince Charming, and Bigby (formerly Big Bad) Wolf — who suddenly find themselves faced with a perplexing mystery. (Rev: BL 2/1/03)

3742 Willingham, Bill, et al. *Fables: March of the Wooden Soldiers* (11–12). 2004, DC Comics paper $17.95 (978-1-4012-0222-4). In this fourth volume in the series, Boy Blue's romantic hopes soar when he encounters a grown-up Red Riding Hood, but doubts soon arise; for mature teens. Also recommended is the sixth volume, *Homelands* (2006). (Rev: BL 2/15/05)

3743 Willingham, Bill, et al. *Fables: Storybook Love* (11–12). 2004, DC Comics paper $14.95 (978-1-4012-0256-9). The third volume of the Fables series contains four more stories about fairy-tale characters who live in a section of New York City called Fabletown; for mature readers. (Rev: BL 7/04)

3744 Wilson, G. Willow, and M. K. Perker. *Cairo* (9–12). 2007, Vertigo $24.99 (978-1-4012-1140-0). Set in modern Cairo, this is an action-packed fantasy involving a drug smuggler, a female Israeli soldier, a young Lebanese American, an American reporter — and a hookah that is home to a powerful genie. (Rev: BL 9/15/07; SLJ 3/08)

3745 Windsor-Smith, Barry. *The Freebooters* (9–12). 2005, Fantagraphics $29.95 (978-1-56097-662-2). Gripping and humorous tales feature the ancient Freebooters, who first appeared in the short-lived *Storyteller* magazine. (Rev: BL 11/15/05)

3746 Winick, Judd. *Outsiders: Wanted* (10–12). 2005, DC Comics paper $14.99 (978-1-4012-0460-0). In volume three of the Outsiders graphic novel series, Nightwing, the leader of the team and a protégé of Batman, seems headed for a confrontation with his former mentor. (Rev: BL 1/1–15/06; SLJ 3/06)

3747 Winick, Judd. *Pedro and Me: Friendship, Loss, and What I Learned* (8–12). 2000, Henry Holt paper $16.00 (978-0-8050-6403-2). A graphic novel tribute to Pedro Zamora, an AIDS educator and actor who died of HIV complications at the age of 22. (Rev: BL 9/15/00; HB 11–12/00; HBG 3/01; SLJ 10/00)

3748 Wolfman, Marv. *The New Teen Titans Archives, Vol. 3* (7–12). 2006, DC Comics $49.99 (978-1-4012-1144-8). This collection includes the most popular stories from the 1980s comics that updated the 1960s tales about teen sidekicks of superheroes — Robin, Wonder Girl, Starfire, Cyborg, Raven, the Changeling, and Kid Flash. (Rev: BL 12/1/06)

3749 Won, Kim Kang. *I.N.U.V* (9–12). 2002, TokyoPop paper $9.99 (978-1-59182-001-7). In this graphic novel with Chinese characters, Sey discovers that the surly son of the family with whom she is staying is actually a girl. (Rev: BL 2/1/04)

3750 Wood, Brian. *DMZ: Body of a Journalist, Vol. 2* (11–12). Illus. by Riccardo Burchielli and Kristian Donaldson. Series: DMZ. 2007, Vertigo paper $12.99 (978-1-4012-1247-6). In this installment in the DMZ series, journalist Matty Roth is trapped in the war zone that is Manhattan and finds himself being used by each of the warring sides. (Rev: SLJ 7/07)

3751 Wood, Brian. *DMZ: On the Ground, Vol. 1* (11–12). Illus. by author and Riccardo Burchielli. Series: DMZ. 2006, Vertigo paper $9.99 (978-1-4012-1062-5). This compelling and sometimes disturbing graphic novel chronicling a war zone in a future U.S. will appeal to older teens. (Rev: SLJ 7/07)

3752 Wood, Brian. *DMZ: Public Works, Vol. 3* (11–12). Illus. by Riccardo Burchielli. Series: DMZ. 2007, Vertigo paper $12.99 (978-1-4012-1476-0). Grimy-looking cityscapes envelop this graphic novel, which continues the story of Matty Roth, a photojournalist who must go undercover and confront his own ethical limits. (Rev: SLJ 3/08)

3753 Wood, Brian, and Rob Goodridge. *Dirtbike Manifesto* (9–12). Series: Couriers. 2004, Ait paper $12.95 (978-1-932051-18-6). The Couriers, a young man and woman, deliver goods including drugs and weapons that no other bike messengers can. (Rev: BL 5/1/04)

3754 Wooding, Chris. *Pandemonium* (7–12). Illus. by Cassandra Diaz. 2012, Scholastic $22.99 (978-054525221-8); paper $12.99 (978-04398775-9-6). Peasant boy Seifer proves his merit when he's called on to impersonate the missing Prince Talon Pandemonium. Lexile GN460L (Rev: BL 3/15/12; LMC 5–6/12; SLJ 3/1/12*)

3755 Yagami, Yu. *Hikkatsu, Vol. 1* (6–10). Illus. by author. 2007, Go! Comi paper $10.99 (978-1-933617-29-9). A wacky manga story of a martial artist gone wild,

karate-chopping small electrical appliances. (Rev: BL 1/1–15/08)

3756 Yakin, Boaz. *Marathon* (9–12). Illus. by Joe Infurnari. 2012, First Second paper $16.99 (978-159643680-0). This graphic novel tells the story of the messenger Eucles who ran 26.2 miles to inform Athens about the progress of the Persian army — and provides a lot of backstory about Eucles's family and the turmoil of the time. Lexile GN700L (Rev: BL 5/15/12*; LMC 3–4/13; SLJ 7/1/12; VOYA 10/12)

3757 Yamada, Norie. *Someday's Dreamers, Vol. 1* (8–12). Trans. from Japanese by Jeremiah Bourque. Illus. by Kumichi Yoshizuki. 2006, TokyoPop paper $9.99 (978-1-59816-178-6). Yume is a "magic user" who is paid by the government to use her skills for the good of others. (Rev: SLJ 9/06)

3758 Yang, Gene Luen. *American Born Chinese* (10–12). 2006, Roaring Brook paper $16.95 (978-1-59643-152-2). Three separate tales, one about Jin (the only Chinese American student at his middle school student who's faced with racism and a crush on a Caucasian girl), one about the Monkey King (a Chinese folklore character who has great power but what's to be considered a god), and one about Danny (who deals with transferring schools because of the shame his visiting cousin Chin-Kee brings him), all converge with an unexpected ending. (Rev: BL 9/1/06; SLJ 9/06)

3759 Yang, Gene Luen. *The Eternal Smile* (9–12). Illus. by Derek Kirk Kim. 2009, First Second paper $16.95 (978-159643156-0). Three complex and engaging stories about imagination, fantasy, and reality; beautiful artwork enhances the text. (Rev: BL 3/1/09; LMC 8–9/09; SLJ 5/09)

3760 Yang, Gene Luen. *Prime Baby* (10–12). Illus. 2010, First Second paper $6.99 (978-15964361-2-1). Brilliant though jealous 8-year-old Thaddeus Fong fights his social insecurities with the help of patient space aliens in this richly imagined, spirited graphic novel with political undertones. (Rev: BL 3/1–15/10)

3761 Yang, Song. *Wild Animals, Vol. 1* (10–12). Illus. by author. 2008, Yen paper $10.99 (978-075952938-0). Expressive artwork punctuates this graphic novel that examines the life and growing awareness of a school boy during China's Cultural Revolution. (Rev: BL 12/1/08)

3762 Yolen, Jane. *Foiled* (6–10). Illus. by Mike Cavallaro. 2010, First Second paper $15.99 (978-1-59643-279-6). Reality morphs into fantasy (and black and white into color) when Aliera dons her fencing mask and wields her new ruby-handled foil; the first installment in a series. Lexile GN460L (Rev: BL 3/15/10; HB 7–8/10; LMC 8–9/10; SLJ 3/10)

3763 Yoshizaki, Mine. *Sgt. Frog, Vol. 1* (8–11). 2004, TokyoPop paper $9.99 (978-1-59182-703-0). In this *manga* work, a young brother and sister are dealing with an uninvited guest, an invader from another planet. (Rev: BL 3/15/04)

3764 Yune, Tommy. *From the Stars* (7–12). 2003, DC Comics paper $9.95 (978-1-4012-0144-9). When an alien ship crashes on earth, Roy Fokker signs up to be a test pilot and then learns a great deal about alien technology. (Rev: BL 2/1/04)

3765 Yuzuki, Jun. *Gakuen Prince, Vol. 1* (10–12). Trans. by Harumi Ueno. Illus. by author. 2009, Del Rey paper $10.99 (978-034550895-9). A new boy at a previously all-girls school, Azusa is pursued by packs of rapacious female students in this raunchy manga. (Rev: BLO 2/9/09; SLJ 5/09)

3766 Zeku, Toru. *Shiki Tsukai, Vol. 1* (9–12). Illus. by Yuna Takanagi. Series: Shiki Tsukai. 2007, Del Rey paper $10.95 (978-0-345-49925-7). Fourteen-year-old Akira uses magical powers and martial arts with the help of the beautiful Koyomi. (Rev: BL 11/1/07)

Historical Fiction and Foreign Lands

Prehistory

3767 Barnes, Steven. *Great Sky Woman* (9–12). 2006, Ballantine $24.95 (978-0-345-45900-8). Readers are transported to ancient Africa, where Frog Hopping and T'Cori climb Mount Kilimanjaro to save their tribe. (Rev: BL 5/15/06)

3768 Dann, John R. *Song of the Axe* (10–12). 2001, Tor $25.95 (978-0-312-86984-7). In this prehistoric epic set during the Ice Age, Agon is in love with Eena, who is raped by Ka, the foul Snake Man. (Rev: BL 4/15/01)

3769 Dickinson, Peter. *A Bone from a Dry Sea* (7–10). 1993, Dell paper $4.99 (978-0-440-21928-6). The protagonists are Li, a girl in a tribe of "sea apes" living four million years ago, and Vinny, the teenage daughter of a modern-day paleontologist. (Rev: BL 2/1/93; SLJ 4/93*)

3770 Levin, Betty. *Thorn* (7–10). 2005, Front St $16.95 (978-1-932425-46-8). Thorn, a young boy with an atrophied leg, is befriended by Willow but still feels uncomfortable and plans his escape. (Rev: BL 12/15/05; SLJ 1/06)

Ancient and Medieval History

GENERAL AND MISCELLANEOUS

3771 Cadnum, Michael. *Raven of the Waves* (7–10). 2001, Scholastic $17.95 (978-0-531-30334-4). In this gory tale set in the 8th century, 17-year-old Viking Lidsmod takes part in a bloodthirsty raid on an English community but later helps a boy who is taken captive.

(Rev: BL 4/1/01; HB 9–10/01; HBG 3/02; SLJ 7/01; VOYA 8/01)

3772 Gormley, Beatrice. *Poisoned Honey* (8–12). 2010, Knopf $16.99 (978-0-375-85207-7). Gormley reimagines the life of Mary Magdalene before she became a follower of Jesus Christ, with anecdotes about the evolution of Matthew the tax collector plus an author's note about various versions of Mary's story. ℮ Lexile HL780L (Rev: BL 5/15/10; LMC 5–6/10; SLJ 2/10)

3773 Holland, Cecilia. *The Serpent Dreamer* (9–12). 2005, Forge $24.95 (978-0-7653-0557-2). In the concluding volume of Cecelia Holland's trilogy on life in 10th-century Vinland, Corban, shunned by most tribe members, is taken in by the Wolf Clan and finds love with Epashti. (Rev: BL 11/1/05)

3774 Jacq, Christian. *The Stone of Light* (10–12). 2000, Pocket paper $16.00 (978-0-7434-0346-7). This novel, the beginning of a four-volume set, takes place in Egypt during the reign of Ramses the Great and is filled with intrigue, passion, and suspense. (Rev: BL 5/15/00)

3775 Lasky, Kathryn. *The Last Girls of Pompeii* (7–10). 2007, Viking $15.99 (978-0-670-06196-9). Julia and her slave (and best friend) Sura do not have bright futures in Pompeii but together they manage to escape the smothering ash of erupting Vesuvius. (Rev: BL 4/15/07; LMC 11–12/07; SLJ 8/07)

3776 McCaughrean, Geraldine. *Not the End of the World* (7–10). 2005, HarperCollins LB $17.89 (978-0-06-076031-1). A harrowing but thought-provoking story of what it was really like aboard Noah's ark, with terrified animals and humans unhinged by their circumstances. (Rev: BL 8/05; SLJ 8/05*; VOYA 8/05)

3777 Mahfouz, Naguib. *Akhenaten: Dweller in Truth* (10–12). Trans. by Tagreid Abu Hassabo. 2000, Doubleday paper $12.00 (978-0-385-49909-5). Mahfouz, the great contemporary Egyptian writer, has written a novel that takes place in ancient Egypt and tells how a young boy tries to uncover the truth about the dead pharaoh Akhenaten. (Rev: BL 3/15/00)

3778 Meyer, Carolyn. *Cleopatra Confesses* (9–12). 2011, Simon & Schuster $16.99 (978-1-4169-8727-7). Cleopatra narrates the eventful and dramatic story of her life, which includes bitter sibling rivalries; plenty of cultural and historical information is included. ℮ Lexile 920L (Rev: BL 7/11; SLJ 7/11)

3779 Miklowitz, Gloria D. *Masada: The Last Fortress* (7–10). 1998, Eerdmans $16.00 (978-0-8028-5165-9). The siege of Masada comes alive through the eyes of a young Jewish man and a Roman commander. (Rev: BCCB 10/98; BL 10/1/98; HBG 3/99; SLJ 12/98; VOYA 2/99)

3780 Moran, Katy. *Bloodline* (9–12). 2009, Candlewick $16.99 (978-076364083-5). Essa, who is of uncertain ancestry, must choose which king to serve and whom to fight for in this story set in Britain in the 7th century. Lexile 830L (Rev: BL 2/15/09; LMC 8–9/09; SLJ 5/1/09*)

3781 Napoli, Donna Jo. *Song of the Magdalene* (9–12). 1996, Scholastic $15.95 (978-0-590-93705-4). In biblical times Miriam, who suffers from seizures, is helped by a crippled young man who becomes her lover. After experiencing many difficulties, Miriam makes sense of her life when she meets the healer Joshua. (Rev: BL 10/1/96; SLJ 11/96; VOYA 2/97)

3782 Rice, Anne. *Christ the Lord: Out of Egypt* (9–12). 2005, Knopf $25.95 (978-0-375-41201-1). Told from the point of view of a 7-year-old Jesus, this novel chronicles the events of his early life. (Rev: BL 11/1/05; SLJ 12/05)

3783 Roberts, Judson. *Dragons from the Sea* (8–11). Series: Strongbow Saga. 2007, HarperCollins $16.99 (978-0-06-081300-0). In A.D. 845, a young Viking named Halfden, who is skilled at the longbow, joins the crew of the *Gull* and struggles to uphold his honor as he's involved in the violent invasion of France. (Rev: BL 5/15/07; SLJ 9/07)

3784 Roberts, Katherine. *I Am the Great Horse* (8–11). 2006, Scholastic $16.99 (978-0-439-82163-6). The life of Alexander the Great is related from the viewpoint of his famous horse, Bucephalus. (Rev: BL 10/15/06; SLJ 12/06)

3785 Shecter, Vicky Alvear. *Cleopatra's Moon* (7–10). 2011, Scholastic $18.99 (978-0-545-22130-6). Cleopatra's only daughter hopes for a royal future but her expectations are not realized in this compelling historical novel. 🎧 (Rev: BL 8/11; HB 9–10/11; LMC 11–12/11; SLJ 8/11; VOYA 10/11)

3786 Speare, Elizabeth George. *The Bronze Bow* (7–10). 1961, Houghton Mifflin paper $6.95 (978-0-395-13719-2). A Jewish boy seeks revenge against the Romans who killed his parents, but finally his hatred abates when he hears the messages and teachings of Jesus. Newbery Medal 1962. (Rev: BL 9/1/95)

3787 Zelitch, Simone. *Moses in Sinai* (10–12). 2001, Black Heron $23.95 (978-0-930773-59-5). An graceful retelling of the biblical story of Moses and the journey he led to Sinai. (Rev: BL 12/1/01)

GREECE AND ROME

3788 Beye, Charles Rowan. *Odysseus: A Life* (10–12). 2004, Hyperion $23.95 (978-1-4013-0024-1). This is a modern novel that retells the life of Odysseus based on a variety of sources. (Rev: BL 2/15/04)

3789 Bradshaw, Gillian. *The Sand-Reckoner* (9–12). 2000, Forge paper $14.95 (978-0-312-87581-7). This exciting historical novel deals with Archimedes' return to Syracuse after three years in Alexandria. (Rev: BL 4/1/00)

3790 Graves, Robert. *I, Claudius: From the Autobiography of Tiberius Claudius, Born b.c. 10, Murdered and Deified a.d. 54* (10–12). 1983, Modern Library paper $14.00 (978-0-679-72477-3). Born lame and with a stammer, Claudius surprised everyone by becoming an outstanding Roman emperor.

3791 Hoffman, Mary. *David* (9–12). 2011, Bloomsbury $16.99 (978-1-59990-700-0). Hoffman imagines the subject of Michelangelo's *David* as a naive 18-year-old stonecutter who is eager to be involved in the politics of the day and finds himself a center of attention after posing for the statue. 🅴 (Rev: BL 11/1/11; SLJ 12/1/11)

3792 Iggulden, Conn. *Emperor: The Field of Swords* (11–12). Series: Emperor. 2005, Delacorte $25.00 (978-0-385-33663-5). The projected penultimate volume in the series that started with *Emperor: The Gates of Rome* (2003), this focuses on Julius Caesar's political maneuverings and successful conquest of Britain. (Rev: BL 2/15/05)

3793 Iggulden, Conn. *Emperor: The Gates of Rome* (10–12). 2003, Delacorte $24.95 (978-0-385-33660-4). Caesar's youth, military training, and growing political acumen are the focus of this novel about the acquisition and use of power. (Rev: BL 11/15/02)

3794 McCullough, Colleen. *The Song of Troy* (10–12). 2001, Orion $27.50 (978-0-7528-1413-1). This is a fast-paced, thrilling retelling of the Trojan War story and the 10-year siege that ended with the fall of Troy. (Rev: BL 5/15/01)

3795 McLaren, Clemence. *Aphrodite's Blessings: Love Stories from the Greek Myths* (7–12). 2002, Simon & Schuster $16.00 (978-0-689-84377-8). The lot of women in ancient Greece comes to life in three stories, based on mythology, about Atalanta, Andromeda, and Psyche. (Rev: BL 3/1/02; HBG 10/02; SLJ 1/02; VOYA 4/02)

3796 Napoli, Donna Jo. *The Great God Pan* (7–10). 2003, Random House $15.95 (978-0-385-32777-0). A beautifully written novel about the life and aspirations of Pan, who was half man and half goat. (Rev: BL 4/15/03; SLJ 6/03)

3797 Napoli, Donna Jo. *Sirena* (7–12). 1998, Scholastic $15.95 (978-0-590-38388-2). This romantic expansion of the Greek myth of the Sirens describes the dilemma of an immortal mermaid who loves a mortal. (Rev: BL 1/1–15/03; HBG 3/99; SLJ 10/98; VOYA 12/98)

3798 Rao, Sirish, and Gita Wolf. *Sophocles' Oedipus the King* (7–10). Illus. by Indrapramit Roy. 2004, Getty $18.95 (978-0-89236-764-1). This retelling of Sophocles' tragic tale of Oedipus is highlighted by the striking illustrations of Indrapromit Roy. (Rev: BL 1/1–15/05)

3799 Renault, Mary. *The King Must Die* (10–12). 1958, Random House paper $11.00 (978-0-394-75104-7). A historical adventure story based on the legend of Theseus. Followed by *The Bull from the Sea* (1962). Also use: *The Mask of Apollo* (1988).

3800 Saylor, Steven. *Empire: The Novel of Imperial Rome* (10–12). 2010, St. Martin's $25.99 (978-0-312-38101-1). Saylor portrays the rise and fall of the Roman Empire through the life of one aristocratic family — the Pinarii — in this sequel to 2007's *Roma* that includes the Great Fire, military campaigns, and the insane whims of emperors. (Rev: BL 8/10)

3801 Saylor, Steven. *The Judgment of Caesar* (10–12). Series: Roma Sub Rosa. 2004, St. Martin's $24.95 (978-0-312-27119-0). Set at the time of Caesar and Pompey, this suspenseful mystery features Gordianus the Finder, a Roman citizen who has a gift for finding people and solving mysteries. Another title in this recommended series is *A Mist of Prophecies* (2002). (Rev: BL 5/1/04*)

3802 Sutcliff, Rosemary. *The Eagle of the Ninth* (7–12). 1993, Farrar paper $5.95 (978-0-374-41930-1). A reissue of the historical novel about the Roman legion that went to battle and disappeared.

MIDDLE AGES

3803 Alder, Elizabeth. *The King's Shadow* (7–12). 1995, Bantam paper $5.50 (978-0-440-22011-4). In medieval Britain, mute Evyn is sold into slavery, but as Earl Harold of Wessex's squire and eventual foster son, he chronicles the king's life and becomes a storyteller. (Rev: BL 7/95; SLJ 7/95)

3804 Bell, Hilari. *Player's Ruse* (7–10). Series: Knight and Rogue. 2010, HarperTeen $17.99 (978-0-06-082509-6). Sir Michael and his squire Fisk visit a port town, Huckerston, in an effort to solve a maritime mystery and perhaps woo the fair Rosamund. Lexile 910L (Rev: BL 12/1/09; HB 1–2/10; SLJ 1/10; VOYA 2/10)

3805 Cadnum, Michael. *Forbidden Forest* (7–10). 2002, Scholastic $17.95 (978-0-439-31774-0). The story of Little John's entry into Robin Hood's band of merry men is told from John's point of view and combines realistic descriptions of medieval life with adventure and romance. (Rev: BL 4/15/02; HB 7–8/02; HBG 10/02; SLJ 6/02; VOYA 4/02)

3806 Cadnum, Michael. *In a Dark Wood* (7–10). 1998, Orchard LB $18.99 (978-0-531-33071-5). The story of Robin Hood as seen through the eyes of the sheriff of Nottingham and his young squire, Hugh. (Rev: BL 3/1/98; HB 3–4/98; HBG 9/98; SLJ 4/98; VOYA 8/98)

3807 Cadnum, Michael. *The King's Arrow* (7–10). 2008, Viking $16.99 (978-0-670-06331-4). This story of young Simon, a nobleman who is present during the shooting of King William II with an arrow, will bring the harsh and intriguing Middle Ages to life for its readers. (Rev: BL 12/15/07; HB 3–4/08; LMC 10/08; SLJ 3/08)

3808 Calmann, Marianne. *Avignon* (10–12). 2000, Allison & Busby paper $14.95 (978-0-7490-0446-0). The plague, a case of amnesia, and Jewish-Christian rela-

tions are three elements in this adult romance set in the city of Avignon during 1346. (Rev: BL 2/1/00)

3809 Coats, J. Anderson. *The Wicked and the Just* (9–12). 2012, Harcourt $16.99 (978-054768837-4). In 13th-century Wales an English girl named Cecily slowly comes to understand the Welsh people and their animosity toward the English. **e** Lexile 780L (Rev: BL 4/1/12; HB 3–4/12; SLJ 5/1/12*; VOYA 2/12)

3810 Cornwell, Bernard. *Sword Song: The Battle for London* (9–12). 2008, HarperCollins $25.95 (978-0-06-088864-0). Protagonist warrior Uhtred has conflicting loyalties, having been born a Saxon and raised by Vikings, but under the charge of King Alfred, heroically fights to protect London from Viking invasion. (Rev: BL 11/15/07)

3811 Coulter, Catherine. *Lord of Falcon Ridge* (9–12). 1995, Berkley paper $7.99 (978-0-515-11584-0). In this conclusion to the trilogy, set in Britain in A.D. 922, Cleve and Chessa meet and fall in love as he transports her to her intended husband and she's pursued by a kidnapper. (Rev: BL 1/15/95; SLJ 9/95)

3812 Coventry, Susan. *The Queen's Daughter* (9–12). 2010, Henry Holt $16.99 (978-0-8050-8992-9). Set in 12th-century Europe, this novel focuses on the life of Joan, daughter of Henry II of England and Eleanor Aquitaine, and provides lots of details of court life and the expectations of a princess of the time. Lexile 690L (Rev: BL 4/15/10; LMC 8–9/10; SLJ 7/10)

3813 Cushman, Karen. *The Midwife's Apprentice* (7–12). 1995, Clarion $13.00 (978-0-395-69229-5). A homeless young woman in medieval England becomes strong as she picks herself up and learns from a midwife to be brave. (Rev: BL 3/15/95*; SLJ 5/95)

3814 Decker, Timothy. *Run Far, Run Fast* (8–12). Illus. by author. 2007, Front St $17.95 (978-1-59078-469-3). In 14th-century Europe a young girl's mother tells her to "run far, run fast" to escape the plague; the stark illustrations and simple text add to the setting and the tension. (Rev: BL 9/15/07; SLJ 1/08)

3815 Goodman, Joan Elizabeth. *Peregrine* (7–10). 2000, Houghton Mifflin $16.00 (978-0-395-97729-3). Fifteen-year-old Lady Edith, who has lost her husband and baby, escapes her problems by going on a pilgrimage from England to the Holy Land. (Rev: BL 4/1/00; HBG 9/00; SLJ 5/00; VOYA 6/00)

3816 Grant, K. M. *Blue Flame* (7–10). Series: Perfect Fire. 2008, Walker $16.99 (978-080279694-3). Young lovers Raimon and Yolanda's religious differences suddenly become cause for conflict when a powerful beacon of Christ reappears in 13th-century France. Lexile 890L (Rev: BL 10/15/08*; HB 11–12/08; LMC 1–2/09; SLJ 12/08; VOYA 2/09)

3817 Gregory, Philippa. *Changeling* (9–12). Illus. by Fred van Deelen. Series: Order of Darkness. 2012, Simon & Schuster $18.99 (978-1-4424-5344-9). In 1453

Luca Vero, 17, is sent on a mission to identify heretics and other threats to Christendom; he meets up with a young abbess named Isolde who joins him in adventures across Europe. ⌒ 𝖊 Lexile 820L (Rev: BLO 7/12; LMC 3–4/13; SLJ 10/12; VOYA 8/12)

3818 Grey, Christopher. *Leonardo's Shadow: or, My Astonishing Life as Leonardo da Vinci's Servant* (7–10). 2006, Simon & Schuster $16.95 (978-1-4169-0543-1). Fifteen-year-old Giacomo, a servant to the great Leonardo da Vinci, wards off the artist's creditors while also trying to uncover the truth about his own origins. (Rev: BL 8/06; SLJ 10/06)

3819 Hatcher, John. *The Black Death: A Personal History* (10–12). 2008, Da Capo $27.50 (9780306815713). In this fictional story rooted in fact, the Black Death is ravaging feudal Walsham, England, and its residents speculate about God and eternity as they struggle to bury their dead and carry on with life. 𝖊 (Rev: BL 6/1–15/08)

3820 Jinks, Catherine. *Babylonne* (8–12). 2008, Candlewick $18.99 (978-076363650-0). Sixteen-year-old Babylonne, daughter of Pagan Kidrouk, escapes her arranged marriage to an old man by teaming up with a priest in a daring journey through the 13th-century French countryside. (Rev: BL 10/15/08; HB 1–2/09; LMC 3–4/09; SLJ 12/08; VOYA 2/09)

3821 Jinks, Catherine. *Pagan in Exile* (9–12). 2004, Candlewick $15.99 (978-0-7636-2020-2). Squire Pagan accompanies Lord Roland to his castle in France in this sequel to *Pagan's Crusade* (2003), and describes the political and religious turmoil he finds there. (Rev: BCCB 2/04; BL 1/1–15/04; HB 5–6/04; VOYA 4/04)

3822 Jinks, Catherine. *Pagan's Vows* (8–10). 2005, Candlewick $16.99 (978-0-7636-2021-9). Seventeen-year-old Pagan Kidrouk, squire to Lord Roland, joins his master at the Abbey of St. Martin where they are to begin training as monks, but Pagan soon finds that he has trouble adjusting to all the rules of his new life. (Rev: BL 10/1/04; SLJ 9/04; VOYA 10/04)

3823 Karr, Kathleen. *Fortune's Fool* (7–12). 2008, Knopf $15.99 (978-0-375-84816-2). Set in 14th-century Germany, this story of a court jester in search of a new master is full of medieval flavor and humor. (Rev: BL 3/1/08; SLJ 7/08)

3824 McKenzie, Nancy. *Grail Prince* (10–12). 2003, Del Rey paper $14.95 (978-0-345-45648-9). After the death of Arthur, young Galahad sets out on a quest to locate the Holy Grail; a multilayered sequel to *Queen of Camelot* (2002). (Rev: BL 12/1/02; VOYA 6/03)

3825 McKenzie, Nancy. *Guinevere's Gamble* (6–10). Series: Chrysalis Queen Quartet. 2009, Knopf $16.99 (978-0-375-84346-4); LB $19.99 (978-0-375-94346-1). In the second installment in the series, Guinevere, 13, uses her wit to battle Morgan le Fey's conniving, sinister nature as she progresses toward maturity and

eventual queendom. 𝖊 Lexile 780L (Rev: SLJ 10/09; VOYA 10/09)

3826 Medeiros, Teresa. *Fairest of Them All* (10–12). 1995, Bantam paper $5.99 (978-0-553-56333-7). When the fair Holly de Chaste discovers that her father has offered her as the prize in a tournament of knights, she decides to disguise her beauty to foil the wedding plans. (Rev: SLJ 3/96)

3827 Morressy, John. *The Juggler* (7–10). 1996, Henry Holt $16.95 (978-0-8050-4217-7). In this adventure story set in the Middle Ages, a young man regrets the bargain he has made with the devil to become the world's greatest juggler in exchange for his soul. (Rev: SLJ 6/96; VOYA 8/96)

3828 Napoli, Donna Jo. *Hush: An Irish Princess' Tale* (8–11). 2007, Atheneum $16.99 (978-0-689-86176-5). Melkorka, an Irish princess, is captured by Russian slave traders and refuses to speak in this present-tense story set in the 10th century. (Rev: BL 11/1/07; SLJ 12/07)

3829 Pargeter, Edith. *The Heaven Tree Trilogy* (9–12). 1993, Warner $24.95 (978-0-446-51708-9). *The Heaven Tree* (1960), *The Green Branch* (1962), and *The Scarlet Seed* (1963) make up this trilogy about a medieval British family of artisans and their power-hungry benefactors. (Rev: BL 10/1/93*)

3830 Reeve, Philip. *Here Lies Arthur* (7–10). 2008, Scholastic $17.99 (978-0-545-09334-7). The story of King Arthur is told from the viewpoint of young Gwyna, a peasant girl given shelter by Myrddin, the Merlin figure. ALA Notable Books 2009. (Rev: BL 8/08*; LMC 3–4/09*)

3831 Sauerwein, Leigh. *Song for Eloise* (8–10). 2003, Front St $15.95 (978-1-886910-90-4). In the Middle Ages, an unhappy wife falls for a passing troubadour in a rich text full of historical detail. (Rev: BL 12/1/03; HBG 4/04; SLJ 12/03; VOYA 4/04)

3832 Temple, Frances. *The Beduins' Gazelle* (7–10). 1996, Orchard LB $16.99 (978-0-531-08869-2). In this 14th-century adventure, a companion piece to *The Ramsey Scallop*, young scholar Etienne becomes involved in the lives of two lovers when he goes to Fez to study at the university. (Rev: BL 2/15/96; SLJ 4/96*; VOYA 12/96)

3833 Temple, Frances. *The Ramsay Scallop* (7–10). 1994, Orchard LB $19.99 (978-0-531-08686-5). In 1299, 14-year-old Elenor and her betrothed nobleman are sent on a chaste pilgrimage to Spain and hear the stories of their fellow travelers. (Rev: BL 3/15/94*; SLJ 5/94; VOYA 4/94)

3834 Thal, Lilli. *Mimus* (8–11). Trans. by John Brownjohn. 2005, Annick $19.95 (978-1-55037-925-9); paper $9.95 (978-1-55037-924-2). Prince Florin is taken captive and made a jester when the kingdom of Vinland overpowers Moltovia in this novel of the Middle Ages. (Rev: BL 9/1/05*; SLJ 12/05*; VOYA 2/06)

3835 Thomson, Sarah L. *The Dragon's Son* (7–12). 2001, Scholastic $17.95 (978-0-531-30333-7). This historical novel, based on Welsh legends about King Arthur, tells the stories of family members and others who were involved in Arthur's life. (Rev: BCCB 7–8/01; BL 5/1/01; HBG 10/01; SLJ 7/01; VOYA 6/01)

3836 Tingle, Rebecca. *Far Traveler* (7–10). 2005, Penguin $18.99 (978-0-399-23890-1). In this historical novel set in 10th-century England, 16-year-old Aelfwyn flees when her uncle, West Saxon King Edward, tells her she must marry one of his allies or enter a convent. (Rev: BCCB 3/05; BL 2/1/05; SLJ 2/05; VOYA 8/05)

3837 Tomlinson, Theresa. *The Forestwife* (8–12). 1995, Orchard LB $17.99 (978-0-531-08750-3). A Robin Hood legend with Marian as the benevolent Green Lady of the forest. (Rev: BL 3/1/95*; SLJ 3/95; VOYA 5/95)

3838 Wein, Elizabeth E. *A Coalition of Lions* (7–12). Series: The Winter Prince. 2003, Viking $16.99 (978-0-370-03618-2). In the 6th century, a princess named Goewin travels from Britain to Africa on her way to an arranged marriage, in this absorbing sequel to *The Winter Prince* (1993). (Rev: BCCB 4/03; BL 2/15/03; SLJ 4/03)

Africa

3839 Achebe, Chinua. *Things Fall Apart* (10–12). 1992, Knopf paper $9.95 (978-0-385-47454-2). A proud Ibo leader, Okonkwo, sees his fortunes rise and fall and watches the disintegration of his village.

3840 Adichie, Chimamanda Ngozi. *Purple Hibiscus* (11–12). 2003, Algonquin $23.95 (978-1-56512-387-8). In Nigeria, Kambili, 15, and her older brother Jaja experience a new way of life when they visit their aunt's home and escape their father's brutally repressive influence; suitable for mature teens. (Rev: BL 9/15/03; SLJ 12/03)

3841 Atta, Sefi. *Everything Good Will Come* (11–12). 2005, Interlink $24.95 (978-1-56656-570-7). Two girl-friends come of age in Nigeria in 1971, struggling in a society that oppresses women. (Rev: BL 3/1/05)

3842 Badoe, Adwoa. *Between Sisters* (8–12). 2010, Groundwood $18.95 (978-0-88899-996-2); paper $12.95 (978-0-88899-997-9). Sixteen-year-old Ghanaian Gloria dreams of escaping a life of illiteracy, poverty, and AIDS in this poignant story, eventually befriending a young doctor who teaches her to read. (Rev: BL 10/1/10; HB 11–12/10; SLJ 10/1/10; VOYA 12/10)

3843 Combres, Élisabeth. *Broken Memory: A Novel of Rwanda* (9–12). Trans. by Shelley Tanaka. 2009, Groundwood $17.95 (978-0-88899-892-7). Inspired by interviews with survivors and narrated by 14-year-old

Emma, who was just 5 when she witnessed the murder of her mother by Hutu soldiers, this fictionalized account of the 1994 Rwanda genocide and its aftermath recounts the young woman's struggle to come to terms with her traumatic past and move forward with her life. Lexile 890L (Rev: BL 9/1/09; LMC 11–12/09; SLJ 12/09)

3844 Dow, Unity. *Far and Beyon'* (9–12). 2002, Aunt Lute paper $11.95 (978-1-879960-64-0). A young girl growing up in Botswana must battle a culture filled with AIDS and sexual abuse. (Rev: BL 5/1/02)

3845 Drew, Eileen. *The Ivory Crocodile* (10–12). 1996, Coffee House $21.95 (978-1-56689-042-7). A novel about a young American woman who grew up in Africa and later returns to teach English in an isolated bush post, but finds she cannot escape her white skin and her Western heritage. (Rev: BL 5/1/96; SLJ 3/97)

3846 Gien, Pamela. *The Syringa Tree: A Novel* (10–12). 2006, Random House $24.95 (978-0-375-50755-7). A compelling story of South Africa under apartheid, in which 6-year-old Lizzy's doctor father delivers a black baby and Lizzy helps to keep her a secret. (Rev: BL 6/1–15/06; SLJ 11/06)

3847 Glass, Linzi Alex. *The Year the Gypsies Came* (8–11). 2006, Henry Holt $16.95 (978-0-8050-7999-9). An elderly Zulu watchman turns out to be young Emily's strongest anchor in this moving story about a 12-year-old in 1960s Johannesburg, whose life is changed when a family of Australian vagabonds arrives, bringing additional tensions. (Rev: BL 3/1/06; SLJ 5/06)

3848 Habila, Helon. *Measuring Time* (11–12). 2007, Norton paper $13.95 (978-0-393-05251-0). Twin Nigerian brothers go different ways — one to brutal warfare, the other (afflicted with sickle-cell disease) to become a writer and recorder of his people's history. (Rev: BL 12/1/06)

3849 Habila, Helon. *Waiting for an Angel* (11–12). 2003, Norton $23.95 (978-0-393-05193-3). A compelling novel, suitable for mature teens, that paints a chilling picture of one man's struggle against oppression in 1990s Nigeria. (Rev: BL 1/1–15/03)

3850 Kingsolver, Barbara. *The Poisonwood Bible* (10–12). 1998, HarperFlamingo $26.00 (978-0-06-017540-5). A challenging novel about preacher Nathan Price and his family, including four daughters, who move from America to the Belgian Congo in 1959. (Rev: BL 8/98)

3851 McDaniel, Lurlene. *Angel of Hope* (7–10). 2000, Bantam paper $8.95 (978-0-553-57148-6). In this sequel to *Angel of Mercy,* Heather returns from missionary work in Uganda and, in her place, her younger, spoiled sister, Amber, continues the work in Africa. (Rev: BL 5/1/00; HBG 9/00)

3852 Mankell, Henning. *Shadow of the Leopard* (10–12). Trans. from Swedish by Anna Paterson. 2009, Annick $19.95 (978-1-55451-200-3); paper $10.95 (978-1-55451-199-0). Sofia, last seen in *Secrets in the Fire* (2003) when she had lost her legs in a landmine accident, is now married with three children and living in a Mozambique village; her discovery that her husband Armando is having an affair sets off a chain of events. (Rev: BL 12/1/09*; SLJ 12/09)

3853 Matar, Hisham. *In the Country of Men* (11–12). 2007, Dial $22.00 (978-0-385-34042-7). A challenging novel set in Libya in 1979, in which young Suleiman comes to recognize the dangers of living under such an oppressive regime. ∩ (Rev: BL 12/1/06; SLJ 6/07)

3854 Matthee, Dalene. *Fiela's Child* (9–12). 1992, Univ. of Chicago paper $13.95 (978-0-226-51083-5). A white boy in South Africa, who has been raised by a black family, is suddenly at age 12 claimed by a white family as its own. (Rev: BL 5/1/86)

3855 Naidoo, Beverley. *Burn My Heart* (7–12). 2009, Amistad $15.99 (978-006143297-2); LB $16.89 (978-006143298-9). In the turbulent Kenya of the 1950s, the tenuous friendship of a privileged white boy and a disenfranchised black boy — whose family has been accused of arson — unravels against a dramatic backdrop of prejudice and racial inequality. Lexile 740L (Rev: BL 10/1/08*; LMC 8–9/09; SLJ 2/1/09*; VOYA 4/09)

3856 Nanji, Shenaaz. *Child of Dandelions* (7–12). 2008, Front St $17.95 (978-1-932425-93-2). In 1972, the privileged life of 15-year-old Sabine, member of a wealthy Indian family, is turned upside down when President Idi Amin gives all Indians 90 days to leave the country. (Rev: BL 6/1–15/08; SLJ 5/08)

3857 Oron, Judie. *Cry of the Giraffe* (9–12). 2010, Annick $21.95 (978-1-55451-272-0); paper $12.95 (978-1-55451-271-3). Thirteen-year-old Wuditu and her Ethiopian Jewish family travel to Sudan in hopes of finding a way to get to Israel but Wuditu is separated from her family and must return to Ethiopia alone, where she becomes a slave; a grim story that mirrors the experiences of many in the 1980s. (Rev: BLO 10/15/10; SLJ 12/1/10)

3858 Powers, J. L. *This Thing Called the Future* (10–12). 2011, Cinco Puntos $16.95 (978-1-933693-95-8). In a shantytown in contemporary South Africa, 14-year-old Khosi is torn between her mother's ambitions for her as a modern girl and her grandmother's traditional beliefs. ☻ Lexile 710L (Rev: BL 6/1/11; HB 7–8/11; LMC 10/11; SLJ 5/11)

3859 Robert, Na'ima B. *Far from Home* (7–12). 2012, Frances Lincoln paper $8.99 (978-18478000-6-0). The turbulent history of the country now called Zimbabwe is illustrated in stories set in 1964 and 2000. (Rev: BLO 10/15/12; LMC 5–6/13; SLJ 2/13)

3860 Sabatini, Irene. *The Boy Next Door* (11–12). 2009, Little, Brown $23.99 (978-031604993-1). Sabatini tells a story set in Zimbabwe of a black girl and white boy

who become attached despite their differences and separate only to reunite several years later; for mature readers. ∩ ☻ (Rev: BL 9/15/09)

3861 Schrefer, Eliot. *Endangered* (8–12). 2012, Scholastic $17.99 (978-0-545-16576-1). Initially resentful of her mother's involvement with a Congolese bonobo sanctuary, 14-year-old Sophie comes to understand and appreciate the work when she spends the summer there, and when civil war breaks out she flees into the jungle with a young ape. ☻ Lexile 900L (Rev: BL 11/15/12; HB 1–2/13; LMC 1–2/13; SLJ 12/12; VOYA 12/12)

3862 Slovo, Gillian. *Red Dust* (10–12). 2002, Norton $25.95 (978-0-393-04148-4). Set in South Africa during the Truth and Reconciliation Commission hearings, this courtroom thriller involves the case of an apartheid killer. (Rev: BL 12/15/01)

3863 Stolz, Joelle. *The Shadows of Ghadames* (6–10). 2004, Random House LB $17.99 (978-0-385-73104-1). In late-19th-century Libya, Malika dreads the restricted life her 12th birthday will bring, but her father's two wives defy convention and nurse a wounded man back to health within the women's community, opening new horizons for Malika. (Rev: BL 12/1/04*; SLJ 11/04)

3864 Stratton, Allan. *Chanda's Secrets* (9–12). 2004, Annick $8.95 (978-1-55037-835-1). The devastating impact of AIDS in sub-Saharan Africa is poignantly conveyed in the gripping first-person story of 16-year-old Chanda, whose life is crumbling around her as the insidious disease spreads through her village and family. (Rev: BCCB 10/04; BL 7/04; SLJ 7/04) [813.54]

3865 Stratton, Allan. *Chanda's Wars* (8–12). 2008, HarperTeen $17.99 (978-0-06-087262-5). Chanda, the African AIDS orphan introduced in *Chanda's Secret*, tracks down her younger brother and sister after they are kidnapped and forced to become vicious child soldiers. (Rev: BL 12/1/07; HB 3–4/08; SLJ 3/08)

3866 Watson, Christie. *Tiny Sunbirds, Far Away* (10–12). 2011, Other paper $15.95 (978-159051-466-5). Blessing, 12, copes with life after her parents' separation, living in a new town on the Niger Delta and worrying about her brother, who has become a boy soldier. ∩ (Rev: BL 4/1/11; SLJ 8/11)

3867 Wein, Elizabeth E. *The Lion Hunter* (7–10). Series: The Mark of Solomon. 2007, Viking $16.99 (978-0-670-06163-1). To escape threats made against his aristocratic family, Telemakos (half-Ethiopian grandson of Britain's King Artos) and his young sister Athena are sent to a new community where new friendships are not what they seem in this first volume in a series set in 6th-century Africa and drawing on the author's preceding Arthurian-Aksumite cycle, which ended with *The Sunbird* (2004). (Rev: BL 6/1–15/07; HB 7–8/07; SLJ 9/07)

3868 Wein, Elizabeth E. *The Sunbird* (7–12). Series: The Winter Prince. 2004, Viking $16.99 (978-0-670-03691-

2). Telemakos, grandson of noblemen, undertakes a perilous journey to the African kingdom of Aksum to find those responsible for allowing the plague to enter the kingdom in this third volume in the saga. (Rev: BL 6/1–15/04; HB 3–4/04; SLJ 5/04; VOYA 4/04)

3869 Williams, Michael. *Now Is the Time for Running* (7–12). 2011, Little, Brown $17.99 (978-0-316-07790-3). Deo's soccer skills prove to be the 14-year-old's salvation — and that of his mentally disabled brother — as they flee violence in Zimbabwe and seek a new life in South Africa. e Lexile 650L (Rev: BL 9/15/11; HB 7–8/11; LMC 10/11; SLJ 9/1/11*)

3870 Zemser, Amy Bronwen. *Beyond the Mango Tree* (6–12). 1998, Greenwillow $14.95 (978-0-688-16005-0). Trapped in her home by a domineering mother, Sarina, a 12-year-old white American girl living in Liberia, befriends a gentle African boy named Boima. (Rev: BL 11/1/98; HB 11–12/98; HBG 3/99; SLJ 10/98; VOYA 4/99)

Asia and the Pacific

3871 Ali, Thalassa. *Companions of Paradise* (10–12). Series: Paradise. 2007, Bantam paper $14.00 (978-0-553-38178-8). In this final book in the trilogy that began with *A Singular Hostage* and continued with *A Beggar at the Gate* (2004), it's 1841 and Englishwoman Mariana Givens, now in Afghanistan, is being urged to divorce her Muslim husband and marry a British officer. (Rev: BL 2/15/07; SLJ 8/07)

3872 Ali, Thalassa. *A Singular Hostage* (10–12). 2002, Bantam paper $13.95 (978-0-553-38176-4). An Englishwoman becomes the savior of a young orphan in this novel full of historical detail of 19th-century India. (Rev: BL 10/1/02; SLJ 4/03)

3873 Ballard, J. G. *Empire of the Sun: A Novel* (9–12). 1984, Buccaneer $16.95 (978-1-56849-663-4). After the Japanese capture Shanghai in World War II, 11-year-old Jim is separated from his parents and spends time in an internment camp.

3874 Ballard, John H. *SoulMates: A Novel to End World Hunger, with an Introduction by Mother Theresa and The Gandhi Foundation* (9–12). 1998, World Citizens $19.95 (978-0-932279-06-4); paper $14.95 (978-0-932279-05-7). Teenager MacBurnie King discovers a whole new world when she and her father begin working in a mission in India and encounter disease, hunger, caste injustice, and monsoon rains. (Rev: HBG 9/98; SLJ 6/98; VOYA 8/98)

3875 Binstock, R. C. *Tree of Heaven* (9–12). 1995, Soho $22.00 (978-1-56947-038-1). Two lovers try to escape doom during the Japanese invasion of China in the 1930s. (Rev: BL 8/95; SLJ 10/95)

3876 Bobis, Merlinda. *The Solemn Lantern Maker* (10–12). 2009, Delta paper $14 (978-0-385-34113-4). Life is cheap in the slums of Manila, and when 6-year-old Noland brings home an American woman who has been shot, he soon finds himself suffering at the hands of his own government. e (Rev: SLJ 12/09)

3877 Bosse, Malcolm. *The Examination* (8–12). 2008, Paw Prints $17.95 (978-1-4352-4634-8). During the Ming Dynasty, two very different Chinese brothers try to understand one another as they travel to Beijing, where one brother hopes to pass a government examination. (Rev: BL 11/1/94*; SLJ 12/94)

3878 Bosse, Malcolm. *Tusk and Stone* (6–10). 1995, Front St $15.95 (978-1-886910-01-0). Set in 7th-century India, this story tells about a young Brahman who is separated from his sister and sold to the military as a slave, goes on to gain recognition and fame for his skills and bravery as a warrior, and ultimately discovers his true talents and nature as a sculptor and stonecarver. (Rev: BL 12/1/95; VOYA 2/96)

3879 Busfield, Andrea. *Born Under a Million Shadows* (11–12). 2010, Henry Holt paper $14 (978-08050906-1-1). In Kabul after the fall of the Taliban, 11-year-old Fawad's life changes after his mother gets a job working for three Americans; for mature readers. (Rev: BL 2/1–15/10; SLJ 2/10)

3880 Chang, Eileen. *Love in a Fallen City* (9–12). 2006, New York Review $14.95 (978-1-59017-178-3). A collection of six stories about life for teens and young adults in post-World War II China. (Rev: BL 10/15/06)

3881 Chen, Da. *Brothers* (9–12). 2006, Crown $25.00 (978-1-4000-9728-9). The two brothers of the title lead different lives due to their births: Tan is the legitimate son of a Chinese general, and Shento, the illegitimate, grows up in an orphanage. The two do not meet until they are both caught up in the Cultural Revolution. (Rev: BL 8/06; SLJ 9/06)

3882 Chen, Ran. *A Private Life* (10–12). Trans. by John Howard Gibbon. 2004, Columbia $24.50 (978-0-231-13196-4). A coming-of-age story about a sensitive, gawky Chinese girl living through childhood and first love during the Cultural Revolution and the demonstrations in Tiananmen Square. (Rev: BL 4/15/04)

3883 Choi, Sook N. *Year of Impossible Goodbyes* (6–10). 1991, Houghton Mifflin $16.00 (978-0-395-57419-5). An autobiographical novel of two children in North Korea following World War II who become separated from their mother while attempting to cross the border into South Korea. (Rev: BL 9/15/91; SLJ 10/91*)

3884 Clarke, Judith. *The Winds of Heaven* (8–12). 2010, Henry Holt $16.99 (978-080509164-9). In 1950s Australia Clementine and her cousin Fan come from very different backgrounds and have similarly divergent lives. e Lexile 910L (Rev: BL 10/15/10; HB 9–10/10; VOYA 8/10)

3885 Clavell, James. *Shogun: A Novel of Japan* (10–12). 1983, Delacorte paper $7.99 (978-0-440-17800-2). The story of an English sea captain in his adventures in feudal seventeenth-century Japan.

3886 Doshi, Tishani. *The Pleasure Seekers* (11–12). 2010, Bloomsbury paper $15 (978-16081927-7-9). This saga follows three generations of the Patel family, who live in Madras, India, as they deal with challenges including cross-cultural marriage and leaving home to study in England; for mature readers. **e** (Rev: BL 9/1–15/10)

3887 Farooki, Roopa. *Bitter Sweets* (9–12). 2007, St. Martin's $24.95 (978-0-312-36052-8). Lies are built upon lies in this crisply written novel about members of an east Indian family who conveniently avoid convention in order to get what they want. (Rev: BL 8/07; SLJ 11/07)

3888 Feiyu, Bi. *Three Sisters* (11–12). 2010, Houghton Mifflin $24 (978-015101364-7). In Communist China in the 1970s and 1980s three sisters from a small village use different strategies to escape from their confining boundaries; for mature, advanced readers. (Rev: BL 7/10)

3889 Fermine, Maxence. *Snow* (10–12). Trans. by Chris Mulhern. 2003, Atria $15.00 (978-0-7434-5684-5). In the late 19th century, a young Japanese poet enamored of white is encouraged to consult an artist who will give him an appreciation of color. (Rev: BL 12/15/02)

3890 Finn, Mary. *Anila's Journey* (9–12). 2008, Candlewick $16.99 (978-076363916-7). Talented 14-year-old orphan Anila — half Indian, half Irish — lands a job aboard a naturalist's river expedition and forges a sense of identity and belonging as she faces down sexist taunting in this tale set in 18th-century India. (Rev: BL 10/1/08; LMC 3–4/09; SLJ 1/1/09; VOYA 2/09)

3891 Foxlee, Karen. *The Anatomy of Wings* (9–12). 2009, Knopf $16.99 (978-037585643-3); LB $19.99 (978-037595643-0). Jennifer searches for answers about her older sister's death and her own losses in this lyrical story set in Australia in the 1980s; for sophisticated readers. **e** Lexile 710L (Rev: BL 1/1–15/09*; HB 3–4/09; LMC 5–6/09; SLJ 7/1/09; VOYA 4/09)

3892 Frazier, Angie. *Everlasting* (8–10). 2010, Scholastic $17.99 (978-0-545-11473-8). In 1885 independent-minded 17-year-old Camille sets off across Australia in search of her long-lost mother, whose existence her father revealed before the shipwreck that killed him. **e** Lexile 790L (Rev: LMC 10/10; SLJ 9/1/10; VOYA 6/10)

3893 Garland, Sherry. *Song of the Buffalo Boy* (7–10). 1992, Harcourt paper $6.00 (978-0-15-200098-1). Loi, the spurned daughter of an American G.I. and a disgraced Vietnamese woman, escapes to Ho Chi Minh City to avoid an arranged marriage. (Rev: BL 4/15/06)

3894 Gately, Roberta. *Lipstick in Afghanistan* (11–12). 2010, Gallery paper $15 (978-14391913-8-5). Gately brings her own experience to this novel about a volunteer nurse in post 9/11 Afghanistan who befriends an Afghani widow and romances an American serviceman; for mature readers. (Rev: BL 10/1–15/10)

3895 Golden, Arthur. *Memoirs of a Geisha* (10–12). 1997, Knopf $26.95 (978-0-375-40011-7); paper $14.00 (978-0-679-78158-5). This novel, set in Japan during the 1930s and 1940s, is about a young girl who is sold into slavery by her father and becomes an accomplished geisha. (Rev: BL 9/1/97)

3896 Gordon, Katharine. *The Palace Garden* (10–12). 2000, Severn House $26.00 (978-0-7278-5600-5). In Madore, India, in 1898, Zeena, who is betrothed to an evil older man, falls in love with a young Scottish officer. (Rev: BL 10/15/00)

3897 Gratz, Alan. *Samurai Shortstop* (8–11). 2006, Dial $15.99 (978-0-8037-3075-5). Even though the samurai traditions have been outlawed, 16-year-old Toyo is educated in the ancient ways and applies his discipline to the game of baseball in this novel set in 1890 Tokyo). ∩ (Rev: BL 4/15/06*; LMC 11–12/06; SLJ 7/06)

3898 Grenville, Kate. *The Secret River* (9–12). 2006, Canongate $24.00 (978-1-84195-797-5). William and his wife are sent to Australia as a punishment for a crime William has committed, and they struggle to build a life there among the aborigines. ∩ (Rev: BL 4/15/06; SLJ 10/06)

3899 Gunesekera, Romesh. *Reef* (9–12). 1995, New Press $20.00 (978-1-56584-219-9). This coming-of-age story tells of defiance and growth during the Marxist rebellion in Sri Lanka in 1962. (Rev: BL 1/15/95; SLJ 4/95)

3900 Guo, Xiaolu. *Twenty Fragments of a Ravenous Youth* (11–12). Illus. 2008, Doubleday $22.95 (978-038552592-3). Fenfang trades the isolation of her small village for Beijing, where she encounters violence, resentment, and poverty as she struggles to make a living; for mature readers. **e** (Rev: BL 7/08)

3901 Hartnett, Sonya. *Stripes of the Sidestep Wolf* (10–12). 2005, Candlewick $16.99 (978-0-7636-2644-0). Stuck in a dying Australian town, 23-year-old Satchel O'Rye sees hope for reversing the town's fortunes when he spots what he believes to be an animal long thought to be extinct. (Rev: BCCB 3/05; BL 3/1/05; SLJ 3/05; VOYA 6/05)

3902 Haugaard, Erik C. *The Revenge of the Forty-Seven Samurai* (7–12). 1995, Houghton Mifflin $16.00 (978-0-395-70809-5). In a true story set in feudal Japan, a young servant is a witness to destiny when his master meets an unjust death. (Rev: BL 5/15/95; SLJ 4/95)

3903 Herrick, Steven. *By the River* (9–12). 2006, Front St $16.95 (978-1-932425-72-7). Harry, 14, is torn between escaping the small Australian town he calls home and staying to honor his mother and best friend who died there. (Rev: BL 8/06; SLJ 7/06)

3904 Herrick, Steven. *Cold Skin* (8–12). 2009, Front St $18.95 (978-159078572-0). The murder of a pretty girl sets an Australian town on edge in this story set just after World War II. (Rev: BL 4/15/09; SLJ 5/1/09)

3905 Herrick, Steven. *The Simple Gift* (8–10). 2004, Simon & Schuster paper $14.95 (978-0-689-86867-2). In this compelling free-verse novel told in three voices, Australian 16-year-old Billy escapes an unhappy family life and takes up residence in an abandoned freight car where he finds both friendship and love. (Rev: BL 8/04; SLJ 9/04; VOYA 2/05)

3906 Hesse, Hermann. *Siddhartha* (10–12). 1982, Bantam paper $5.99 (978-0-553-20884-9). An inspiring story set in India about a young man's journey to a state of peace and holiness. First published in 1923.

3907 Hoobler, Dorothy, and Thomas Hoobler. *In Darkness, Death* (7–10). 2004, Putnam $16.99 (978-0-399-23767-6). Set in 18th-century Japan like the authors' previous *The Ghost in the Tokaido Inn* (1999), this novel tells how 14-year-old Seikei and his adopted father set out to discover who murdered a powerful warlord. (Rev: BL 5/1/04; SLJ 3/04; VOYA 4/04)

3908 Hosseini, Khaled. *The Kite Runner* (11–12). 2003, Riverhead $24.95 (978-1-57322-245-7). The relationship between two Afghani boys — one wealthy, one a servant — is the central focus of this compelling novel covering events in the last quarter of the 20th century. (Rev: BL 7/03; SLJ 11/03)

3909 Howell, Simmone. *Everything Beautiful* (10–12). 2008, Bloomsbury $16.99 (978-159990042-1). Rebellious 16-year-old Riley escapes from her despised Christian summer camp — along with paraplegic Dylan — for a vision quest in the Australian desert in this tough-talking first-person narrative. e (Rev: BL 10/1/08; LMC 3–4/09; SLJ 1/1/09)

3910 Hua, Yu. *Cries in the Drizzle* (9–12). 2007, Anchor paper $13.95 (978-0-307-27999-6). The middle son of three, Sun Guanglin is sent away to live with another family when he is six, and his homecoming six years later coincides with his family losing their house to a fire and he in turn becomes an outcast with a unique view of all that goes on in his world and society's during the reign of Mao. (Rev: BL 10/15/07)

3911 Jones, Lloyd. *Mister Pip* (9–12). 2007, Dial $24.00 (978-0-385-34106-6). This is the beautifully written story of Matilda and her schoolfriends, who find refuge in reading Dickens' Great Expectations as life in their war-torn island collapses around them. (Rev: BL 6/1–15/07)

3912 Jones, Nalini. *What You Call Winter* (9–12). 2007, Knopf $22.95 (978-1-4000-4276-0). These beautifully written stories about families living in a Catholic town in India explore issues both challenging and profound. (Rev: BL 8/07)

3913 Kadohata, Cynthia. *A Million Shades of Gray* (7–12). 2010, Simon & Schuster $16.99 (978-1-4169-1883-7). In 1975 Vietnam, Y'Tin, 13, survives a massacre and is able to find his favorite elephant, Lady, and take her deep into the jungle, but the stress of this flight lingers with him for years. e Lexile 700L (Rev: BL 12/1/09; SLJ 3/10; VOYA 2/10)

3914 Kim, Eugenia. *The Calligrapher's Daughter* (11–12). Illus. 2009, Henry Holt $26 (978-0-8050-8912-7). In the early part of the 20th century, during the brutal Japanese occupation of Korea, a young woman's life reflects the tumultuous political and social atmosphere of her homeland after she flees an arranged marriage; for mature readers. (Rev: BL 7/09; SLJ 12/09)

3915 Kirino, Natsuo. *Real World* (11–12). Trans. by Philip Gabriel. 2008, Knopf $22.95 (978-030726757-3). Four teenage girls struggling through summer cramming classes in suburban Tokyo are inexplicably sympathetic toward a matricidal boy named Toshi in this dark coming-of-age story. e (Rev: BL 7/08; SLJ 12/08)

3916 Knight, Dominic. *Disco Boy* (10–12). 2010, IPG/Bantam $22.95 (978-174166626-7). Paul is a self-conscious, 25-year-old Australian DJ and law school grad, still living with his parents and looking for love in this funny, touching novel about finding one's place in the world. (Rev: BL 2/1–15/10)

3917 Lovett, Li Miao. *In the Lap of the Gods* (10–12). 2010, Leapfrog/LeapLit paper $15.95 (978-19352481-3-2). In the shadow of the Three Gorges Dam, widowed scavenger Liu discovers an abandoned child and, despite numerous consequences, decides to adopt her. (Rev: BL 10/1–15/10)

3918 McCormick, Patricia. *Never Fall Down* (9–12). 2012, HarperCollins $17.99 (978-006173093-1). A moving novel based on the life of Cambodian peace advocate Arn Chorn-Pond, starting with his capture by the Khmer Rouge in 1975 and continuing through his time as a child soldier and escape to Thailand. YALSA Top Ten Best Fiction for Young Adults 2013. e Lexile 710L (Rev: BL 3/1/12*; HB 5–6/12; SLJ 5/1/12*; VOYA 12/12)

3919 McCullough, Colleen. *The Thorn Birds* (10–12). 1998, Avon paper $7.99 (978-0-380-01817-8). A family saga covering 1915 through 1969 in the lives of the Clearys of Australia.

3920 McFerrin, Linda Watanabe. *Namako: Sea Cucumber* (10–12). 1998, Coffee House paper $14.95 (978-1-56689-075-5). Ellen, who is part Scottish and part Japanese, suffers culture shock when her parents uproot her from her comfortable American suburban existence and move to a Japanese countryside. (Rev: BL 7/98; SLJ 1/99)

3921 McKay, Sharon E. *Thunder over Kandahar* (7–12). Photos by Rafal Gerszak. 2010, Annick LB $21.95 (978-1-55451-267-6); paper $12.95 (978-1-55451-266-

9). Two Afghan teens, Yasmine and Tamanna, are from very different backgrounds but become friends as they flee the Taliban. ∩ (Rev: BL 12/1/10; SLJ 12/1/10)

3922 Manivong, Laura. *Escaping the Tiger* (9–12). 2010, HarperCollins $15.99 (978-0-06-166177-8). Twelve-year-old Vonlai Sirivong and his family escape from Communist Laos in 1982 only to find new miseries in a UN refugee camp in Thailand; based on experiences of the author's husband. Lexile 750L (Rev: BL 1/1–15/10; LMC 5–6/10; SLJ 3/10)

3923 Marchetta, Melina. *Jellicoe Road* (9–12). 2008, HarperTeen $17.99 (978-006143183-8); LB $18.89 (978-006143184-5). Seventeen-year-old Taylor leads the Underground Community — a student faction that battles the Cadets (led by the attractive Jonah) and the Townies — and hopes to unlock her mother's secret identity in this melodramatic tale that combines mystery and romance and is infused with its Australian environment. Printz Winner 2009. ∩ **e** Lexile 820L (Rev: BL 11/1/08; HB 11–12/08; SLJ 12/08; VOYA 12/08)

3924 Marchetta, Melina. *Looking for Alibrandi* (8–10). 1999, Orchard LB $17.99 (978-0-531-33142-2). In this novel set in Sydney, Australia, teenage Josie Alibrandi is torn between her family's cultural ties to Italy and her Australian environment. (Rev: BL 2/15/99; HB 5–6/99; HBG 9/99; SLJ 7/99; VOYA 6/99)

3925 Meekings, Sam. *Under Fishbone Clouds* (11–12). 2010, St. Martin's $24.99 (978-031262279-4). In 20th-century China, Jinyi and Yuying struggle to sustain their love through war, cultural upheavals, famine, and other hardships; for mature readers. (Rev: BL 10/1–15/10*)

3926 Millard, Glenda. *A Small Free Kiss in the Dark* (7–10). 2010, Holiday House $16.95 (978-0-8234-2264-7). When war strikes unexpectedly, four unlikely allies — 12-year-old runaway Skip, homeless man Billy, 6-year-old Max, and teen mother Tia — flee their Australian city. Lexile 840L (Rev: BL 3/1/10; LMC 10/10; SLJ 3/10)

3927 Min, Anchee. *Empress Orchid* (11–12). 2004, Houghton Mifflin $24.00 (978-0-618-06887-6). This fictionalized life of China's last empress — Tzu Hsi, or Orchid — sympathetically and evocatively describes her impoverished childhood and ascent to a position of power; for mature teens. (Rev: BL 11/15/03*)

3928 Min, Anchee. *The Last Empress* (11–12). 2007, Houghton Mifflin $25.00 (978-0-618-53146-2). In this sequel to *Empress Orchid* (2004), China's Empress Tzu Hsi puts her nation's needs before her own. ∩ (Rev: BL 1/1–15/07)

3929 Mohan, Suruchi. *Divine Music* (11–12). 2009, Bayeux paper $19.95 (978-18974110-6-3). In 1970s India a young music student becomes aware of the double-standard imposed on women in her culture when she finds herself romantically involved with her married music teacher; for mature readers. (Rev: BLO 10/1/09)

3930 Newton, Robert. *Runner* (7–10). 2007, Knopf $15.99 (978-0-375-83744-9). Set in Australia in 1919, this novel is about 15-year-old Charlie and his dangerous efforts to lift himself and his mother from poverty. (Rev: BCCB 7–8/07; BL 4/15/07; SLJ 4/07)

3931 Qamar, Amjed. *Beneath My Mother's Feet* (7–10). 2008, Atheneum $16.99 (978-1-4169-4728-8). Fourteen-year-old Nazia's life changes dramatically when her family's economic well-being spirals downward and she finds herself cleaning houses in this novel set in Karachi, Pakistan. (Rev: BL 8/08; SLJ 7/08)

3932 Rees, Douglas. *Smoking Mirror: An Encounter with Paul Gauguin* (9–12). Series: Art Encounters. 2005, Watson-Guptill $15.95 (978-0-8230-4863-2). Joe Sloan, a 15-year-old Mexican American, travels to Tahiti in the 1890s and develops a friendship with French artist Paul Gauguin in this compelling story that interweaves fact and fiction. (Rev: BL 3/15/05; SLJ 3/05)

3933 Rippin, Sally. *Chenxi and the Foreigner* (10–12). 2009, Annick $21.95 (978-155451173-0); paper $10.95 (978-155451172-3). Anna visits China in 1989 and has an affair that opens her eyes to the Chinese government's reach and power over its citizens. (Rev: BL 4/15/09; SLJ 7/1/09)

3934 Sayres, Meghan Nuttall. *Anahita's Woven Riddle* (8–12). 2006, Abrams $16.95 (978-0-8109-5481-6). In early-20th-century Iran, Anahita, a teenage nomad, resists an arranged marriage and seeks a mate who can solve the riddles woven into her wedding carpet. (Rev: SLJ 1/07)

3935 Schaffner, M. A. *War Boys* (11–12). 2002, Welcome Rain $25.00 (978-1-56649-244-7). A coming-of-age story set in the Philippines in the Vietnam era and featuring a 14-year-old boy living on a naval base and enjoying Explorer Scouts exercises in the jungle; for mature teens who are good readers. (Rev: BL 6/1–15/02)

3936 Scott, Joanna C. *The Lucky Gourd Shop* (10–12). 2000, MacMurray & Beck $27.00 (978-1-878448-01-9). Set in Korea, this is a moving novel about an orphan girl who marries a man with a terrible secret past. (Rev: BL 7/00*)

3937 See, Lisa. *Snow Flower and the Secret Fan* (11–12). 2005, Random House $21.95 (978-1-4000-6028-3). In 19th-century China, two women from different backgrounds who were friends as young people start to drift apart when each gets married. (Rev: BL 7/05)

3938 Sheth, Kashmira. *Keeping Corner* (7–12). 2007, Hyperion $15.99 (978-0-7868-3859-2). A 12-year-old widow, Leela is forced to mourn in her family's home for a year but dreams of reforms that would allow her to get an education and a career in this story set in 1918 India. (Rev: BL 10/15/07; LMC 1/08; SLJ 12/07)

3939 Sheth, Kashmira. *Koyal Dark, Mango Sweet* (8–11). 2006, Hyperion $15.99 (978-0-7868-3857-8). At the age of 16, Jeeta, who lives in Mumbai (formerly Bombay), finds many of the traditions that preoccupy her mother to be old-fashioned and inappropriate. (Rev: BL 4/1/06; SLJ 4/06)

3940 Sijie, Dai. *Balzac and the Little Chinese Seamstress* (10–12). Trans. by Ina Rilke. 2001, Knopf $18.00 (978-0-375-41309-4). Two delightful young men are ordered into the Chinese countryside during the Cultural Revolution and find conditions are as bad as expected. (Rev: BL 9/15/01; SLJ 11/01)

3941 Sparrow, Rebecca. *The Year Nick McGowan Came to Stay* (8–11). 2008, Knopf $15.99 (978-0-375-84570-3). When Nick comes to live with her family after being kicked out of boarding school, Rachel finds out that under his cool, unapproachable exterior is a boy with serious problems; set in Australia in the late 1980s. (Rev: BL 4/15/08; SLJ 5/08)

3942 Staples, Suzanne Fisher. *Haveli: A Young Woman's Courageous Struggle for Freedom in Present-Day Pakistan* (9–12). 1993, Knopf $18.00 (978-0-679-84157-9); paper $4.99 (978-0-679-86569-8). This novel, a sequel to *Shabanu,* presents the issue of a woman's role in traditional Pakistani society, intrigue, tough women characters, and fluid writing. **℮** (Rev: BL 6/1–15/93*; VOYA 12/93)

3943 Staples, Suzanne Fisher. *The House of Djinn* (7–12). 2008, Farrar $16.95 (978-0-374-39936-8). Set in Pakistan, this family drama (and follow-up to 1989's *Shabanu* and 1993's *Haveli*) about Mumtaz and Jameel, young cousins who are ordered to marry, shows the conflicts between generations in traditional Pakistani families. (Rev: BL 2/15/08; SLJ 4/08)

3944 Tharoor, Shashi. *Riot: A Love Story* (10–12). 2001, Arcade $24.95 (978-1-55970-605-6). This novel for better readers describes how the parents of Priscilla Hart travel in India to investigate the death of their daughter and discover the depth of Hindu-Muslim conflicts. (Rev: BL 8/01)

3945 Toer, Pramoedya Ananta. *All That Is Gone* (9–12). Trans. by Willem Samuels. 2004, Hyperion $23.95 (978-1-4013-6663-6). Eight interconnected stories, many narrated by the same man, chronicle life in the little city of Brora in Java. (Rev: BL 2/1/04*)

3946 Tschinag, Galsan. *The Blue Sky* (9–12). Trans. from German by Katharina Rout. 2006, Milkweed $24 (978-1-57131-055-2). In 1950s Mongolia a young Tuva shepherd boy reflects on the harshness of life and watches the changes affecting his people under the Communist regime; this autobiographical novel is translated from German. (Rev: BL 10/1/06; SLJ 12/06)

3947 Venkatraman, Padma. *Island's End* (7–10). 2011, Putnam $16.99 (978-0-399-25099-6). Uido, 15, copes with the threats facing her people, who inhabit an island in the Bay of Bengal, and tries to provide the spiritual

guidance they expect from her. Lexile 800L (Rev: BL 9/15/11*; LMC 11–12/11; SLJ 8/11*; VOYA 10/11)

3948 Xinran. *Sky Burial* (11–12). Trans. by Julia Lovell and Esther Tyldesley. 2005, Doubleday $18.95 (978-0-385-51548-1). Wen, a young Chinese widow, travels to Tibet to find out more about her husband Kejun's death in this story of differing cultures in the mid-20th century. (Rev: BL 7/05)

3949 Yep, Laurence. *Mountain Light* (8–12). 1997, HarperCollins paper $8.99 (978-0-06-440667-3). Yep continues to explore life in 19th-century China through the experience of a girl, Cassia, her father and friends, and their struggle against the Manchus in this sequel to *The Serpent's Children* (1984). (Rev: BL 9/15/85; SLJ 1/87; VOYA 12/85)

Europe and the Middle East

3950 Abi-Ezzi, Nathalie. *A Girl Made of Dust* (10–12). 2009, Grove $24 (978-080211895-0). Set in Lebanon during the Israeli invasion, this story of war is told from the perspective of 9-year-old Christian Maronite Ruba, who has trouble understanding the reasons for the upheaval. **℮** (Rev: BL 4–5/09)

3951 Ahern, Cecelia. *The Book of Tomorrow* (11–12). 2011, HarperCollins $21.99 (978-0-06-170630-1). When her father commits suicide, privileged Irish 16-year-old Tamara and her mother go to live with relatives in the country, and Tamara finds comfort in a mysterious library book; for mature readers. ∩ **℮** (Rev: BL 12/1–15/10; SLJ 4/11)

3952 Aiken, Joan. *Lady Catherine's Necklace* (10–12). 2000, St. Martin's $21.95 (978-0-312-24406-4). The noted British novelist has written a charming sequel to Jane Austen's *Pride and Prejudice* that deals with Lady Catherine de Bourgh, her necklace, and a kidnapping. (Rev: BL 4/1/00)

3953 Almond, David. *Raven Summer* (7–12). 2009, Delacorte $16.99 (978-0-385-73806-4); LB $19.99 (978-0-385-90715-6). War and violence are at the heart of this novel set in northern England during the Iraq War, in which teenage Liam copes with an abandoned child, a Liberian refugee, and a prejudiced bully. **℮** Lexile HL480L (Rev: BL 9/15/09*; HB 11–12/09; LMC 11–12/09; SLJ 12/09; VOYA 12/09)

3954 Alsanea, Rajaa. *Girls of Riyadh* (9–12). Trans. by Marilyn Booth. 2007, Penguin $24.95 (978-1-59420-121-9). Returning home to the oppressive environment of Riyadh proves difficult for four Saudi girlfriends who had freedom while studying abroad in the U.S. (Rev: BL 6/1–15/07)

3955 Archibald, Malcolm. *Pryde and the Infernal Device* (10–12). 2009, Severn $27.95 (978-0-7278-6719-3). The young engineer we met in *Pryde's Rock* (2007) is now investigating, with his future bride Kate, the possibility that his employer may be in cahoots with Napoleon; for mature readers. (Rev: BL 2/1/09)

3956 Archibald, Malcolm. *Pryde's Rock* (10–12). 2007, Severn $28.95 (978-0-7278-6459-8). In 1803, a young engineer is sent to a remote English coast to persuade the townspeople that a lighthouse should be built there; in doing so, he learns about his mysterious youth. (Rev: BL 1/1–15/07)

3957 Arslan, Antonia. *Skylark Farm* (9–12). Trans. by Geoffrey Brock. 2007, Knopf $23.95 (978-1-4000-4435-1). Based on her own family's experiences, the author traces an Armenian family's struggles during the genocide of World War I; the town's men are killed and the remaining family members endure forced marches, hunger, and abuse in an order to survive. (Rev: BL 1/1–15/07)

3958 Bajoria, Paul. *The God of Mischief* (7–10). Illus. by Bret Bertholf. 2007, Little, Brown $16.99 (978-0-316-01091-7). Orphans Mog and Nick, the twin discovered in *The Printer's Devil* (2005), are sent to live with their uncle, Sir Septimus Cloy, at Kniveacres Hall and there have further spooky adventures and investigate their past; this series is set in early-19th-century England. (Rev: BL 1/1–15/07; HB 1–2/07; SLJ 3/07)

3959 Banks, Iain. *The Crow Road* (11–12). 2008, MacAdam $25.00 (978-1-59692-306-5). Young, self-involved Prentice McHoan of Glasgow searches for answers to his life questions about love, family, and religion in this often humorous novel suitable for mature readers. ⌂ (Rev: BL 8/08)

3960 Baratz-Logsted, Lauren. *The Education of Bet* (8–11). 2010, Houghton Mifflin $16 (978-0-547-22308-7). In 19th-century England 16-year-old Elizabeth poses as her brother Will, who has joined the army, and takes his place at boarding school, hoping to gain an education but also facing quite a few challenges. (Rev: BL 5/1/10; SLJ 12/1/10)

3961 Baratz-Logsted, Lauren. *The Twin's Daughter* (7–11). 2010, Bloomsbury $16.99 (978-1-59990-513-6). Thirteen-year-old Lucy Sexton's peaceful, privileged life in Victorian London is upset when her mother's identical twin sister turns up, starting a series of events that ends in murder. ℮ Lexile 910L (Rev: BL 9/1/10; LMC 10/10; SLJ 12/1/10; VOYA 12/10)

3962 Barlow, John. *Eating Mammals: Three Novellas* (10–12). 2004, Perennial paper $12.95 (978-0-06-059175-5). Three novellas give readers a fascinating — and sometimes dark — view of life in rural Yorkshire during the Victorian era. (Rev: BL 8/04; SLJ 1/05)

3963 Barnes, Julian. *Arthur and George* (9–12). 2006, Knopf $24.95 (978-0-307-26310-0). Barnes's two characters are taken from the lives of Sir Arthur Conan Doyle of Sherlock Holmes fame, and George Edalji, an English lawyer of Indian descent; when their paths

cross after George is accused of a horrible crime. (Rev: SLJ 6/06)

3964 Barratt, Mark. *Joe Rat* (7–10). 2009, Eerdmans paper $9 (978-0-8028-5356-1). In 19th-century London orphan Joe escapes his bleak future in the sewers by choosing to trust his new friend Bess Farleigh and a madman who gives the two sanctuary. (Rev: HB 1–2/10; SLJ 10/09)

3965 Baugh, Carolyn. *The View from Garden City* (11–12). 2008, Forge $24.95 (978-076531657-8). In this stereotype-busting novel, the often heartbreaking story of arranged marriage and female circumcision in the Islamic world is told through the stories of six Egyptian women; for mature readers. ℮ (Rev: BL 7/08)

3966 Beaufrand, Mary Jane. *Primavera* (8–10). 2008, Little, Brown $16.99 (978-0-316-01644-5). While Sandro Botticelli uses Flora's sister Domenica as inspiration for his painting "Primavera," Flora plots an escape from her powerful family and a future in a convent. (Rev: BL 1/1–15/08; LMC 1/08; SLJ 2/08)

3967 Benjamin, Melanie. *Alice I Have Been* (11–12). 2010, Delacorte $25 (978-0-385-34413-5). This fictionalized account of the life of Alice Liddell Hargreaves, the young girl who served as the inspiration for Lewis Carroll's Alice, recounts her childhood experiences with the author and the impact that relationship had on the rest of her life; for mature readers. (Rev: BL 10/15/09; SLJ 2/10)

3968 Bennett, Veronica. *Angelmonster* (10–12). 2006, Candlewick $15.99 (978-0-7636-2994-6). A well-written novel based on the dramatic life of Mary Wollstonecraft Shelley, who at age 16 was seduced by poet Percy Shelley and later wrote *Frankenstein*. (Rev: BL 7/06; LMC 2/07; SLJ 8/06)

3969 Bennett, Veronica. *Cassandra's Sister* (9–12). 2007, Candlewick $16.99 (978-0-7636-3464-3). An 18-year-old Jane (Jenny) Austen, in need of a husband, is the focus of this novel that is written in Austen's style and will be enjoyed by fans of Austen and of historical fiction. (Rev: BL 10/1/07; LMC 1/08; SLJ 12/07)

3970 Berdoll, Linda. *Mr. Darcy Takes a Wife* (10–12). 2004, Sourcebooks paper $16.95 (978-1-4022-0273-5). For mature readers, this is a bawdy, enjoyable sequel to Jane Austen's *Pride and Prejudice*. (Rev: BL 4/15/04)

3971 Blackwell, Lawana. *The Maiden of Mayfair* (9–12). Series: Victorian Tales of London. 2001, Bethany paper $11.99 (978-0-7642-2258-0). In this Victorian romance, Sarah Matthews, a ward in a foundling home, is rescued by a rich widow who thinks Sarah may be her granddaughter. (Rev: BL 3/1/01; VOYA 8/01)

3972 Bradbury, Jennifer. *Wrapped* (7–10). 2011, Atheneum $16.99 (978-1-4169-9007-9). In early 19th-century England 17-year-old debutante Agnes discovers a jackal in an Egyptian mummy and becomes embroiled in international intrigue. ⌒ e Lexile 860L (Rev: BL 5/1/11; LMC 8–9/11*; SLJ 6/11; VOYA 6/11)

3973 Bronsky, Alina. *Broken Glass Park* (11–12). Trans. by Tim Mohr. 2010, Europa paper $15 (978-19333729-6-9). In this fast-paced novel translated from German, Russian-born 17-year-old Sacha, who is now living in the projects in Berlin, cares for her siblings and plots revenge after her stepfather murders her mother; for mature readers. (Rev: BLO 2/1–15/10)

3974 Burgis, Stephanie. *A Most Improper Magick* (6–10). Series: Unladylike Adventures of Kat Stephenson. 2010, Templar paper $5.99 (978-1848770072). Romance, historical fiction, literary allusions, and humor are interwoven in this story, set in England in the early 19th century, about 12-year-old Kat who seeks to use her magic powers to help her siblings. e Lexile 740L (Rev: BL 2/15/10; LMC 11–12/10; SLJ 12/1/10)

3975 Cadnum, Michael. *Peril on the Sea* (7–10). 2009, Farrar $16.95 (978-037435823-5). Sherwin, an 18-year-old crew member on Captain Fletcher's *Vixen*, is charged with recording the captain's memoirs as they fight the Spanish Armada in 1588. (Rev: BL 4/15/09; VOYA 10/09)

3976 Cahill, Susan, ed. *For the Love of Ireland: A Literary Companion for Readers and Travelers* (10–12). 2001, Ballantine paper $14.95 (978-0-345-43419-7). A collection of short stories by established authors including Joyce and Swift, plus many by today's writers, all of which describe a particular region in Ireland. (Rev: BL 3/1/01)

3977 Cameron, Sharon. *The Dark Unwinding* (7–12). 2012, Scholastic $17.99 (978-0-545-32786-2). Katharine Tulman, 17, faces various challenges when she arrives at her uncle's estate in 1852, initially prepared to commit him to an asylum. e Lexile 890L (Rev: BLO 9/15/12; HB 11–12/12; LMC 1–2/13; SLJ 12/12; VOYA 12/12)

3978 Carroll, Susan. *The Huntress* (9–12). 2007, Ballantine paper $13.95 (978-0-345-49061-2). Cat must use her powers to protect her Irish territory as well as the thrones of England and France against an evil coven of witches. (Rev: BLO 7/17/07)

3979 Carter, Anne Laurel. *The Shepherd's Granddaughter* (7–12). 2008, Groundwood $17.95 (978-0-88899-902-3). Palestinian Amani, 15, witnesses the heartbreak and destruction of displacement firsthand in this story of the volatile Israeli-Palestinian conflict. e (Rev: BLO 10/7/08; LMC 5–6/09; SLJ 12/08)

3980 Chisholm, P. F. *A Surfeit of Guns* (10–12). 1997, Walker $20.95 (978-0-8027-3304-7). An adventure yarn set in 1592, based on real-life Englishman Sir Robert Carey, whose efforts to trace stolen arms leads him to the court of James VI at Dumfries, Scotland. (Rev: BL 5/1/97; SLJ 1/98)

3981 Coleman, Rowan. *The Accidental Mother* (9–12). 2007, Pocket paper $14.00 (978-1-4165-3270-5). London career woman Sophie must rise above her self-absorption as her oldest friend dies and leaves her with custody of her two young daughters. (Rev: BL 9/1/07)

3982 Collins, Pat Lowery. *Hidden Voices: The Orphan Musicians of Venice* (8–10). 2009, Candlewick $17.99 (978-076363917-4). Set in an orphanage where composer Antonio Vivaldi teaches, this story is about three of his young students — Anetta, Rosalba, and Luisa — and their differing aspirations. Lexile 1040L (Rev: BL 4/15/09; HB 7–8/09; LMC 8–9/09; SLJ 5/1/09; VOYA 6/09)

3983 Connery, Tom. *Honour Redeemed* (10–12). Series: Markam of the Marines. 2000, Regnery $21.95 (978-0-89526-255-4). Swashbuckling adventure during the wars of the French Revolution and Napoleon, starring Lieutenant George Markam, the hero of the first installment in this series, *A Shred of Honour* (1999), and the third, *Honour Be Damned* (2000). (Rev: BL 3/15/00)

3984 Cook, Gloria. *Pengarron Rivalry* (11–12). Series: Pengarron. 2004, Severn $28.95 (978-0-7278-6075-0). Kelynen and her brother Luke clash over their family's estate, and Kelynen finds herself falling in love with Sir Rafe in this novel set in 1780. (Rev: BL 11/15/04)

3985 Cooney, Caroline B. *Enter Three Witches* (8–11). 2007, Scholastic $16.99 (978-0-439-71156-2). A novel based on Shakespeare's play *Macbeth* in which the action centers on 14-year-old Lady Mary, ward of Lord and Lady Macbeth. (Rev: BCCB 5/07; BL 3/1/07; HB 5–6/07; LMC 10/07; SLJ 5/07)

3986 Cooper, Michelle. *A Brief History of Montmaray* (7–10). 2009, Knopf $16.99 (978-0-375-85864-2); LB $19.99 (978-0-375-95864-9). On the invented island nation of Montmaray in 1936, Sophie FitzOsborne, niece to the rather nutty king, lives in a castle with her family and starts a diary in which she records the struggle to escape Nazi domination; romance, conspiracy, ghosts, murder — they're all here. ⌒ e Lexile 1000L (Rev: BL 9/15/09*; HB 11–12/09; LMC 10/09; SLJ 12/09; VOYA 4/10)

3987 Cooper, Michelle. *The FitzOsbornes in Exile* (9–12). 2011, Knopf $17.99 (978-0-375-85865-9); LB $20.99 (978-037595865-6). After fleeing from their fictional kingdom when the Nazis attacked in *A Brief History of Montmaray* (2009), the FitzOsbornes settle in England and are introduced into society even as they work to regain their nation. ⌒ e Lexile 1010L (Rev: BL 5/1/11; HB 5–6/11; SLJ 5/11; VOYA 8/11)

3988 Cooper, Patrick. *I Is Someone Else* (10–12). 2006, Delacorte $16.95 (978-0-385-73269-7). Set in 1966, this is the graphic yet compelling story of British teen Stephen and his adventure-laden quest through Turkey and beyond to find his runaway older brother. (Rev: BCCB 5/06; BL 4/15/06; HB 3–4/06; LMC 3/06; SLJ 8/06)

3989 Crowley, Suzanne. *The Stolen One* (8–12). 2009, Greenwillow $17.99 (978-006123200-8); LB $18.89 (978-006123201-5). Could Kat, an orphan, really be Mary Seymour, the daughter of Katherine Parr and Thomas Seymour? This tale of romance and court intrigue, set in Elizabethan England, is full of historical detail. Lexile HL740L (Rev: BL 5/1/09; HB 7–8/09; SLJ 8/09; VOYA 4/09)

3990 Crowther, Yasmin. *The Saffron Kitchen* (11–12). 2007, Penguin $23.95 (978-0-670-03811-4). A moving story of an Iranian woman, married to an Englishman, who returns to Iran to face her past; for mature teens. ⌒ (Rev: BL 11/15/06)

3991 Cullen, Lynn. *I Am Rembrandt's Daughter* (8–12). 2007, Bloomsbury $16.95 (978-1-59990-046-9). The daughter of the famous artist feels adrift when her mother dies, leaving only her poor, unconventional father to raise her; Rembrandt's art and times are revealed in this compelling story. (Rev: BCCB 9/07; BL 4/15/07; LMC 1/08; SLJ 8/07)

3992 Cummins, Jeanine. *The Outside Boy* (10–12). 2010, NAL paper $15 (978-04512294-8-9). Family secrets begin to spill out after young Christy's Grandda dies, leaving Christy to ponder his identity in this evocative, detailed Irish story about the Pavee, a nomadic group of gypsies. ℮ (Rev: BL 5/15/10*)

3993 Dennis, Mary Ellen. *The Landlord's Black-Eyed Daughter* (9–12). 2007, Five Star $26.95 (978-1-59414-575-9). This wonderful adaptation of Alfred Noyes' The Highwayman features thief Rand Remington, who is so moved by a book written by Elizabeth Wyndham that he endeavors to meet her, and they fall in love in spite of numerous obstacles. (Rev: BL 7/07)

3994 Dent, Grace. *Diary of a Chav* (8–11). 2008, Little, Brown $16.99 (978-031603483-8). Fifteen-year-old Shiraz is already a bit of a trouble-maker when things go awry both at home and with her friends. ℮ Lexile 1090L (Rev: BLO 3/16/09; SLJ 12/08; VOYA 12/08)

3995 Dent, Grace. *Posh and Prejudice* (10–12). Series: Diary of a Chav. 2009, Little, Brown paper $7.99 (978-0-31603-484-5). In this humorous sequel to *Diary of a Chav* (2008), British teen Shiraz is now in the 6th form at school and finds herself caught between the limited opportunities afforded by her working-class upbringing and the equally unappealing prospect of attending college. ℮ Lexile 1160L (Rev: BLO 10/27/09; SLJ 12/09; VOYA 2/10)

3996 Dickinson, Peter. *Shadow of a Hero* (7–12). 1995, Doubleday $20.95 (978-0-385-30976-9). Letta's grandfather fights for the freedom of Varina, her family's Eastern European homeland. Living in England, she becomes interested in Varina's struggle. (Rev: BL 9/15/94*; SLJ 11/94; VOYA 10/94)

3997 Dines, Carol. *The Queen's Soprano* (9–12). 2006, Harcourt $17.00 (978-0-15-205477-9). Based on a real 17th-century character, this story features 17-year-old Angelica Voglia, a girl with a wonderful voice who faces numerous obstacles in conservative Rome. (Rev: BL 2/15/06; SLJ 5/06)

3998 Doherty, Berlie. *Treason* (8–12). 2012, IPG/Andersen paper $9.99 (978-18493912-1-4). William, a Catholic, is appointed a page to Henry VIII's son Edward and must hide his faith as he tries to save his father from execution. Lexile 760L (Rev: BLO 3/15/12; SLJ 3/12*)

3999 Donovan, Anne. *Being Emily* (11–12). 2010, Canongate $12.95 (978-184767125-7). With Emily Brontë as a role model, teenage artist Fiona navigates the prickly drama of grief, ungrateful siblings, and a gorgeous crush in working-class Glasgow; for mature readers. (Rev: BL 7/10)

4000 Dowd, Siobhan. *Bog Child* (8–11). 2008, Random House $16.99 (978-0-385-75169-8). Set in 1981 in politically troubled Northern Ireland, this richly told story weaves together two historical eras through 18-year-old Fergus, who finds the body of a girl in the peat bogs — apparently murdered perhaps 2000 years before — and begins to dream of her past. (Rev: BL 8/08; SLJ 8/08)

4001 Du Maurier, Daphne. *Jamaica Inn* (9–12). 1977, Avon paper $4.95 (978-0-380-00072-2). A suspenseful yarn set on the coast of England during the days of pirates. Also use *Frenchman's Creek* (1971) and *Mary Anne* (1971).

4002 Du Maurier, Daphne. *My Cousin Rachel* (9–12). 1952, Bentley LB $20 (978-0-8376-0413-8). A rich historical novel about a young man who is beginning to believe his new wife is a murderer.

4003 Dunlap, Susanne. *Anastasia's Secret* (8–11). 2010, Bloomsbury $16.99 (978-1-59990-420-7). The Russian Revolution is on the horizon as young Anastasia falls in love with one of the royal guards; historical details add to this story of doomed romance. (Rev: BL 2/1/10; LMC 3–4/10; SLJ 3/10)

4004 Dunlap, Susanne. *The Musician's Daughter* (8–11). 2009, Bloomsbury $16.99 (978-159990332-3). Fifteen-year-old viola virtuoso Theresa Maria gets a boost from her godfather — who conveniently turns out to be composer Franz Joseph Haydn — as she struggles to support her family after her father's murder. ℮ Lexile 950L (Rev: BL 11/1/08*; LMC 5–6/09; SLJ 5/1/09; VOYA 2/09)

4005 Eberstadt, Fernanda. *Rat* (11–12). 2010, Knopf $25.95 (978-030727183-9). In this gritty novel appropriate for older teens, bold-spirited 15-year-old Celia, who calls herself "Rat," lives in the south of France with her mother and an orphaned 9-year-old Algerian boy named Morgan; when her mother's new boyfriend sexually abuses the boy, Rat escapes with Morgan to London to search for the father she never knew. ℮ (Rev: BL 2/1–15/10)

4006 Elliott, Patricia. *The Pale Assassin* (7–10). 2009, Holiday House $17.95 (978-0-8234-2250-0). Pampered aristocrat Eugénie, 15, must leave behind her posh lifestyle to flee an arranged marriage and the turmoil of the French Revolution in this historical adventure full of political intrigue. Lexile 840L (Rev: BL 10/1/09*; SLJ 12/09)

4007 Faqir, Fadia. *The Cry of the Dove* (9–12). 2007, Grove paper $14.00 (978-0-8021-7040-8). This is the beautifully written story of Salma, a disgraced 16-year-old Bedouin girl who is imprisoned for years after giving birth out of wedlock; Salma escapes from prison and starts a new life in England, but she dreams of someday returning to find her daughter. (Rev: BL 8/07)

4008 Forester, C. S. *Mr. Midshipman Hornblower* (10–12). 1984, Little, Brown paper $13.00 (978-0-316-28912-2). This is one of a series of adventure stories about a courageous British seaman as he climbs the ranks. Some others are: *Admiral Hornblower in the West Indies*, *Lieutenant Hornblower*, and *Lord Hornblower*.

4009 Forster, E. M. *A Room with a View* (10–12). 1911, Kessenger $24.95 (978-1-4191-0311-7). On a visit to Italy, Lucy Honeychurch gets involved in a conflict of the classes when she meets and is attracted to lower-class George Emerson.

4010 Frost, Helen. *The Braid* (7–10). 2006, Farrar $16.00 (978-0-374-30962-6). Set in 1850, this moving tale of two Scottish sisters who become separated — Jeannie moving to Canada with her parents and younger siblings and Sarah staying behind with their grandmother — is told in narrative poems in alternating voices. (Rev: BL 6/1–15/06; HB 11–12/06; LMC 3/07; SLJ 10/06*)

4011 Gaughen, A. C. *Scarlet* (9–12). 2012, Walker $17.99 (978-080272346-8). Will Scarlet is a girl in Robin Hood's band and is willing to risk her life to save him when he is in danger. (Rev: BL 4/15/12*; LMC 3–4/12*; SLJ 2/12; VOYA 12/11)

4012 Giardino, Vittorio. *A Jew in Communist Prague: Rebellion* (10–12). Trans. from French by Joe Johnson. 1998, NBM paper $11.95 (978-1-56163-209-1). A novel in which the story and emotions are conveyed through text and drawings. This is the third in a series of novels about the hardships suffered by Jonas in Russian-occupied Prague. The others are *Loss of Innocence* and *Adolescence*. (Rev: BL 7/98; SLJ 2/99)

4013 Gill, Elizabeth. *Paradise Lane* (11–12). 2010, Severn $28.95 (978-072786832-9). When a deathbed confession by wealthy Annabel's father throws her privileged life — and impending propitious marriage — into chaos, Annabel sets out to uncover the truth about her history; this novel set in turn-of-the-20th-century Britain is suitable for mature readers. (Rev: BL 3/1–15/10)

4014 Gill, Elizabeth. *Snow Hall* (11–12). 2010, Severn $28.95 (978-072786942-5). In England in the early 20th century, Lorna Robson inherits a mansion and must struggle to find the resources to restore it; for mature readers. ⌒ (Rev: BL 12/1–15/10)

4015 Gooden, Philip. *Mask of Night* (10–12). 2004, Carroll & Graf $24.00 (978-0-7867-1312-7). Shakespeare's acting company, the Chamberlain's Men, are in Oxford when one of his friends is found dead backstage in this historical mystery. (Rev: BL 2/15/04*)

4016 Gormley, Beatrice. *Salome* (9–12). 2007, Knopf $17.99 (978-0-375-83908-5). The biblical story of the seductress who asked for the head of John the Baptist, with the viewpoint alternating between Salome herself and John the Baptist. (Rev: BL 2/15/07; LMC 8–9/07; SLJ 7/07)

4017 Gould, Sasha. *Cross My Heart* (8–12). 2012, Delacorte $17.99 (978-038574150-7); LB $20.99 (978-037599007-6). Laura gives up her studies at the convent to determine what really happened to her drowned sister in this story set in 16th-century Venice. Lexile HL700L (Rev: BL 4/15/12; LMC 8–9/12; SLJ 4/12; VOYA 2/12)

4018 Grant, K. M. *How the Hangman Lost His Heart* (7–12). 2007, Walker $16.95 (978-0-8027-9672-1). Alice is on a mission — to bury the head of her Uncle Frank, who was executed and beheaded for treason — and danger and romance won't stop her in this funny, action-packed tale set in England in 1746 and inspired by the fate of one of the author's ancestors. (Rev: BL 11/15/07; SLJ 12/07)

4019 Gray, Keith. *Ostrich Boys* (8–12). 2010, Random House LB $20.99 (978-0-375-95843-4). When Ross, 15, dies in an accident, his three best friends decide to take his ashes from England to the village of Ross in Scotland for the burial he would have wanted, encountering many challenges along the way. ⌒ Lexile HL630L (Rev: BL 2/1/10; LMC 5–6/10; SLJ 2/10)

4020 Gregson, Julia. *Band of Angels* (10–12). 2010, Touchstone $16 (978-143910113-1). In this adventure-filled novel, young Catherine disobeys her family to join up with Florence Nightingale's "band of angels," and encounters danger, harsh truths, and romance during the Crimean War. ℮ (Rev: BL 4/1–15/10)

4021 Guene, Faiza. *Kiffe Kiffe Tomorrow* (9–12). Trans. by Sarah Adams. 2006, Harcourt paper $13.00 (978-0-15-603048-9). Told in a sharp, painful and funny first-person, Doria, a 15-year-old Muslim girl, fights to break free of the circumstances she fears will imprison her in the grim Paris housing projects where she lives. (Rev: BL 6/1–15/06)

4022 Harper, Karen. *The Irish Princess: A Novel* (10–12). 2011, NAL paper $15 (978-0-451-23282-3). A novel full of politics, romance and intrigue, featuring Elizabeth Fitzgerald (Gera) and her time at the court of King Henry VIII. ℮ (Rev: SLJ 6/11)

4023 Harris, Jane. *The Observations* (11–12). 2006, Viking $24.95 (978-0-670-03773-5). A domestic servant living in Scotland in 1863 discovers her mistress' cruel intentions toward her, and seeks revenge; for mature teens. (Rev: BL 4/15/06)

4024 Hassinger, Peter W. *Shakespeare's Daughter* (7–12). 2004, HarperCollins $15.99 (978-0-06-028467-1). An assortment of historical figures make appearances, including papa, in this story about the 14-year-old daughter of William Shakespeare. (Rev: BL 3/1/04; SLJ 4/04)

4025 Hawes, Louise. *The Vanishing Point* (8–10). 2004, Houghton Mifflin $17.00 (978-0-618-43423-7). In this appealing historical novel that imagines the adolescence of Italian Renaissance artist Lavinia Fontana, young Vini resorts to subterfuge to get her father to let her paint in his studio. (Rev: BL 11/1/04; SLJ 12/04; VOYA 12/04)

4026 Hearn, Julie. *Ivy* (8–10). 2008, Atheneum $17.99 (978-1-4169-2506-4). In 19th-century London, Ivy struggles with addiction to laudanum as she earns a living as a model for a pre-Raphaelite painter. (Rev: BL 6/1–15/08; SLJ 7/08)

4027 Hemingway, Ernest. *For Whom the Bell Tolls* (10–12). 1996, Scribner $27.50 (978-0-684-83048-3); paper $14.00 (978-0-684-80335-7). A tale of romance and adventure set in the Spanish Civil War.

4028 Hemphill, Stephanie. *Sisters of Glass* (6–10). 2012, Knopf $16.99 (978-037586109-3); LB $19.99 (978-037596109-0). In 14th-century Murano, Italy, two daughters of a glassmaker grow apart after the death of their father and his request that the younger marry a nobleman; a romantic tale written in verse. (Rev: BL 4/15/12*; HB 3–4/13; LMC 10/12; SLJ 5/1/12; VOYA 4/12)

4029 Hendry, Frances Mary. *Quest for a Maid* (8–10). 1992, Farrar paper $6.95 (978-0-374-46155-3). The story of an 8-year-old princess and her maid who travel to Britain during the 13th century. (Rev: BL 7/90)

4030 Heuston, Kimberley. *Dante's Daughter* (10–12). 2003, Front St $16.95 (978-1-886910-97-3). Historical fact and fiction are interwoven in this richly detailed story, narrated by the daughter of Dante, that traces her life from childhood in an unhappy family through her bid to become an artist in her own right. (Rev: BCCB 3/04; BL 1/1–15/04; HBG 4/04; LMC 3/04; SLJ 2/04*; VOYA 4/04)

4031 Hilton, James. *Good-bye Mr. Chips* (9–12). 1962, Little, Brown $17.95 (978-0-316-36420-1). A loving tribute, in novel form, to a tough but excellent teacher in an English private school. First published in 1934.

4032 Hinton, Nigel. *The Road from Home* (6–10). 2009, Sourcebooks paper $13.99 (978-1-4022-2461-4). Eleven-year-old Leo leaves his native Poland in 1870 and

sets out for America, encountering many adventures on the way. (Rev: BLO 12/1/09; LMC 1–2/10; SLJ 11/09)

4033 Hoffman, Mary. *The Falconer's Knot* (8–11). 2007, Bloomsbury $16.95 (978-1-59990-056-8). Silvano, 16, is suspected of murder when Angelica's husband is stabbed in this multilayered mystery set in Renaissance Italy. (Rev: BCCB 6/07; BL 3/15/07; LMC 8–9/07; SLJ 4/07)

4034 Holub, Josef. *An Innocent Soldier* (8–11). Trans. by Michael Gofmann. 2005, Scholastic $16.99 (978-0-439-62771-9). Pressed into Napoleon's army for the ill-fated Russian campaign, Adam, a teenage farmhand, is selected as a personal servant by Konrad, an officer from a wealthy family, and the two develop a strong friendship. Batchelder Award, 2006. (Rev: BL 11/15/05; SLJ 12/05; VOYA 2/06)

4035 Hooper, Mary. *Newes from the Dead* (9–12). 2008, Roaring Brook $15.95 (978-1-59643-355-7). A servant girl who was hanged for infanticide awakens on a surgeon's table in this grisly historical mystery based on an actual event in 1650. (Rev: BL 5/1/08; SLJ 5/08)

4036 Hooper, Mary. *The Remarkable Life and Times of Eliza Rose* (10–12). 2006, Bloomsbury $16.95 (978-1-58234-854-4). Eliza Rose, 15, struggles on the streets of 1670 London until she becomes a companion to Nell Gwyn, mistress of the king, and learns the truth about her real parents. (Rev: BL 9/15/06; SLJ 12/06; VOYA)

4037 Hooper, Mary. *Velvet* (6–10). 2012, Bloomsbury $16.99 (978-159990912-7). In Victorian London, Velvet Groves, a 16-year-old orphan, is thrilled to find an alternative to the steam laundry where she has been toiling but does not realize that her new position assisting a famous spiritualist also has pitfalls. ☊ ⲉ Lexile 1000L (Rev: BL 11/15/12; LMC 1–2/13*; SLJ 1/13; VOYA 8/12)

4038 Hunter, Mollie. *The King's Swift Rider* (7–12). 1998, HarperCollins $16.95 (978-0-06-027186-2). A fast-paced historical novel about a young Scot, Martin Crawford, who became Robert the Bruce's page, confidante, and spy. (Rev: BL 9/15/98; HB 1–2/99; HBG 3/99; SLJ 12/98)

4039 Hunter, Mollie. *You Never Knew Her as I Did!* (7–10). 1981, HarperCollins $13.95 (978-0-06-022678-7). A historical novel about a plan to help the imprisoned Mary, Queen of Scots, to escape from prison.

4040 Jebreal, Rula. *Miral* (11–12). Trans. by John Cullen. 2010, Penguin paper $15 (978-01431161-9-6). This complex and thoughtful novel follows the life of Miral, a young woman growing up in a West Bank orphanage after the 1948 war, and provides a human perspective on the Arab-Israeli conflict; for mature readers. (Rev: BLO 7/10)

4041 Jiji, Jessica. *Sweet Dates in Basra* (10–12). 2010, Avon paper $14.99 (978-00616893-0-7). Iraqi Jew Sharif acquires an ill-fated fascination with Kathmiya, a traditional Muslim girl seeking the safety of an arranged marriage in WWII-era Iraq, where the shadow of Hitler adds to the suspense. ♫ ℯ (Rev: BL 5/1–15/10)

4042 Jocelyn, Marthe. *Folly* (8–12). 2010, Random House $15.99 (978-0-385-73846-0). In alternating sequences set in late-19th-century London, this book tells the stories of homeless, unmarried Mary Finn and of the son she must send to the Foundling Hospital so that he will have a chance for a decent future. Lexile 850L (Rev: BL 4/15/10; HB 5–6/10; LMC 8–9/10; SLJ 7/10)

4043 Jones, Sadie. *The Outcast* (9–12). 2008, HarperCollins $24.95 (978-0-06-137403-6). In post-World War II England, after witnessing his mother's accidental death, 10-year-old Lewis goes from traumatized to destructive and eventually lands in prison, after which he struggles to release his demons, determined to make a new life for himself. (Rev: BL 11/15/07)

4044 Kashua, Sayed. *Let It Be Morning* (9–12). Trans. from Hebrew by Miriam Shlesinger. 2006, Black Cat paper $13 (978-0-8021-7021-7). A young Arab man moves back to his village in Israel; when the government isolates the village from the rest of the country, strife grows within its confines. (Rev: SLJ 9/06)

4045 Kirkwood, Gwen. *Heart of the Home* (11–12). 2011, Severn $28.95 (978-072786963-0). A Scottish dairy farm provides the setting for this story about young Avril, who must give up her dreams of university education to return to the farm, and her love for Dean, whose mother is intent on breaking up their relationship; for mature readers. (Rev: BLO 1/1–15/11)

4046 Klein, Lisa. *Lady Macbeth's Daughter* (7–12). 2009, Bloomsbury $16.99 (978-1-59990-347-7). This re-imagining of Shakespeare's *Macbeth* is delivered in alternating chapters by Lady Macbeth and Albia, Macbeth's banished daughter. ℯ Lexile 730L (Rev: BL 8/09; LMC 11–12/09; SLJ 12/09; VOYA 2/10)

4047 Kolosov, Jacqueline. *A Sweet Disorder* (7–12). 2009, Hyperion $16.99 (978-1-4231-1245-7). Sixteen-year-old seamstress Miranda hopes to avoid an unfavorable arranged marriage by winning the favor of Queen Elizabeth I. Lexile 1080L (Rev: SLJ 12/09; VOYA 12/09)

4048 Kuijer, Guus. *The Book of Everything* (8–11). 2006, Scholastic $16.99 (978-0-439-74918-3). Thomas, a 9-year-old living in Amsterdam in 1951, strives to be happy in spite of his difficult, deeply religious father in this compelling and often humorous novel. (Rev: BCCB 5/06; BL 6/1–15/06; HB 7–8/06; LMC 10/06; SLJ 7/06)

4049 Laird, Elizabeth. *The Betrayal of Maggie Blair* (8–11). 2011, Houghton $16.99 (978-0-547-34126-2). In 17th-century Scotland, Maggie, 16, escapes being executed for witchcraft but must still deal with danger amid the political and religious turmoil of the time.

ℯ Lexile 840L (Rev: BL 4/15/11; HB 9–10/11; SLJ 4/11*; VOYA 4/11)

4050 Lalwani, Nikita. *Gifted* (9–12). 2007, Random House $23.95 (978-1-4000-6648-3). Rumi, a child of Indian immigrants born in Wales, is a math whiz whose scores get her into Oxford University at age 14, but her lack of social skills proves to be a problem even she can't solve. (Rev: BL 8/07; SLJ 10/07)

4051 Lasky, Kathryn. *Ashes* (6–12). 2010, Viking $16.99 (978-0-670-01157-5). In 1932 Berlin, Gabriella, 13, watches as Hitler's rise affects society, she is pressured to join the Hitler Youth, her sister dates a Nazi, and her astrophysicist father helps his friend Einstein. ℯ Lexile 770L (Rev: BL 1/1/10*; HB 3–4/10; SLJ 2/10; VOYA 4/10)

4052 Lawlor, Laurie. *The Two Loves of Will Shakespeare* (8–11). 2006, Holiday $16.95 (978-0-8234-1901-2). This well-written story imagines the wild love life of young William Shakespeare, based on historical records. (Rev: BL 4/15/06; SLJ 6/06)

4053 Le Clezio, J. M. G. *Wandering Star* (11–12). Trans. by C. Dickson. 2004, Curbstone paper $15.00 (978-1-931896-11-5). A young woman who has survived the Holocaust and made her way to Jerusalem meets a Palestinian girl who is being displaced by the Jews. (Rev: BL 9/15/04)

4054 Levine, Anna. *Freefall* (7–12). 2008, Greenwillow $16.99 (978-006157654-6); LB $17.89 (978-006157656-0). Eighteen-year-old Aggie is determined to do her compulsory service in the Israeli army as a soldier, not stuck in an office job, in this apolitical story with a touch of romance. Sydney Taylor Book Honor 2009. ℯ Lexile HL600L (Rev: BL 10/15/08; HB 1–2/09; SLJ 1/1/09)

4055 Libby, Alisa M. *The King's Rose* (8–11). 2009, Dutton $17.99 (978-052547970-3). A well-written account of the tragic life of Catherine Howard, the doomed fifth wife of King Henry VIII, full of court intrigue. ℯ Lexile HL810L (Rev: BL 3/1/09; LMC 5–6/09; SLJ 5/1/09; VOYA 6/09)

4056 Lisson, Deborah. *Red Hugh* (6–12). 2001, O'Brien paper $7.95 (978-0-86278-604-5). A exciting tale of 16th-century Ireland's Hugh Roe O'Donnell, a teen whose life is endangered when he is caught up in clan violence. (Rev: BL 12/1/01; SLJ 12/01)

4057 Little, Melanie. *The Apprentice's Masterpiece: A Story of Medieval Spain* (10–12). 2008, Annick $19.95 (978-1-55451-117-4). In first-person, free-verse narratives 15-year-old Ramon, a Jew who has converted to Christianity, and Muslim Amir describe their lives in the chaotic time of the Spanish Inquisition. (Rev: BL 6/1–15/08; SLJ 7/08)

4058 Llewellyn, Richard. *How Green Was My Valley* (9–12). 1983, Amereon LB $35.95 (978-0-88411-936-

4). The enduring saga of a Welsh mining town and of the Morgan family who live and work there.

4059 Llywelyn, Morgan. *1916* (10–12). 1998, St. Martin's $24.95 (978-0-312-86101-8). Fifteen-year-old Ned becomes a courier for the rebels in this epic novel set in Ireland at the time of the Easter Rebellion in 1916. (Rev: BL 4/15/98; SLJ 8/98)

4060 Longshore, Katherine. *Gilt* (9–12). 2012, Viking $17.99 (978-067001399-9). Kitty Tylney must learn to cope with palace intrigue when her best friend Cat Howard marries King Henry VIII. ⌒ **e** Lexile HL660L (Rev: BL 4/15/12)

4061 Lowe, Keith. *Tunnel Vision* (10–12). 2001, Pocket paper $12.95 (978-0-7434-2352-6). To win a bet, Andy travels the entire London Underground system with his pal Brian within a 24-hour period in this suspenseful, engaging novel. (Rev: BL 9/15/01)

4062 McCall Smith, Alexander. *Espresso Tales* (9–12). Series: 44 Scotland Street. 2006, Anchor paper $13.95 (978-0-307-27597-4). This entertaining collection of interconnected stories, first printed as a serial novel in *The Scotsman*, about the residents of an Edinburgh street pokes fun at Scottish culture and contemporary manners; the sequel to *44 Scotland Street* (2005). ⌒ (Rev: SLJ 11/06)

4063 McCaughrean, Geraldine. *Cyrano* (7–10). 2006, Harcourt $16.00 (978-0-15-205805-0). McCaughrean retells the classic tale of Cyrano de Bergerac, a famous swordsman and romantic poet with a very large nose, who lets a fellow French soldier use his poems and letters to win the love of Roxanne, the woman he secretly loves. (Rev: BL 9/15/06; SLJ 10/06)

4064 MacColl, Michaela. *Prisoners in the Palace: How Princess Victoria Became Queen with the Help of Her Maid, a Reporter, and a Scoundrel* (7–12). 2010, Chronicle $16.99 (978-0-8118-7300-0). Liza Hastings, a 17-year-old orphan, finds work as a lady's maid to 16-year-old Princess Victoria in 1835, the year before Victoria becomes queen, and helps her employer navigate the ins and outs of court life. (Rev: BL 8/10; LMC 1/2/11; SLJ 12/1/10*)

4065 McGowan, Anthony. *The Knife that Killed Me* (10–12). 2010, Delacorte LB $19.99 (978-0-385-90716-3). In a depressed area of Leeds, England, Paul Vardeman is struggling to find his place in his school's social structure and finds himself seduced by the power of a knife handed to him by a gang leader. **e** Lexile HL720L (Rev: BL 3/15/10*; LMC 8–9/10; SLJ 6/10)

4066 MacKall, Dandi Daley. *Eva Underground* (8–11). 2006, Harcourt $17.00 (978-0-15-205462-5). In 1978, Eva Lott's father moves her from her high school life in Chicago to Communist Poland, where she initially rebels but later meets a young political activist named Tomek and develops a strong affection for him and an

understanding of the oppression he is fighting. (Rev: BL 3/1/06; SLJ 6/06)

4067 MacLaverty, Bernard. *The Anatomy School* (10–12). 2002, Norton $25.95 (978-0-393-05052-3). A thoughtful teenager in 1960s Belfast, shy Martin struggles to deal with his bossy mother, his schoolfriends, and the influence of the Catholic church. (Rev: BL 4/1/02)

4068 Madoc, Gwen. *Keeping Secrets* (11–12). 2008, Severn $27.95 (978-072786667-7). In the 1930s in Wales two young women, first cousins, fall in love with the same forbidden man and the repercussions reveal many hidden family secrets; for mature readers. ⌒ (Rev: BL 9/1/08)

4069 Mallet, Nathalie. *The Princes of the Golden Cage* (9–12). 2007, Night Shade paper $7.99 (978-1-59780-090-7). Heirs to the Ottoman throne are being murdered, and one of the brothers is under suspicion and must discover the real killer before he is punished for crimes he didn't commit. (Rev: BL 8/07)

4070 Marsh, Katherine. *Jepp, Who Defied the Stars* (8–10). 2012, Hyperion $16.99 (978-1-4231-3500-5). Jepp, a 15-year-old dwarf in 16th-century Europe, struggles to find a life that rewards his intelligence and longing for love. ⌒ **e** Lexile 1010L (Rev: BL 11/15/12; LMC 3–4/13; SLJ 12/12*; VOYA 4/13)

4071 Masson, Sophie. *The Madman of Venice* (7–10). 2010, Delacorte $17.99 (978-0-385-73843-9). In the early 17th century young Ned travels to Venice with his employer and his daughter Celia; there they investigate piracy and a disappearance as the two young people fall for each other. Lexile 740L (Rev: BLO 7/10; LMC 11–12/10; SLJ 8/10; VOYA 12/10)

4072 Mayhew, Margaret. *The Little Ship* (10–12). 2004, Severn $27.99 (978-0-7278-6026-2). The lives of three teenage English boys change dramatically when they meet Anna Stein, a young Jewish refugee, in this novel set in pre-World War II England. (Rev: BL 3/1/04)

4073 Meyer, Carolyn. *Duchessina: A Novel of Catherine de' Medici* (9–12). Series: Young Royals. 2007, Harcourt $17.00 (978-0-15-205588-2). The hardships and dangers in Catherine's life are not sugarcoated in this exciting novel full of intrigue and romance. (Rev: BL 4/15/07; SLJ 10/07)

4074 Meyer, Carolyn. *In Mozart's Shadow* (7–12). 2008, Harcourt $17.00 (978-0-15-205594-3). The fictionalized story of Wolfgang's older sister, Nannerl, who was also a talented musician but remains virtually unknown. (Rev: BL 4/15/08; SLJ 6/08; VOYA 4/08)

4075 Meyer, Carolyn. *Loving Will Shakespeare* (8–11). 2006, Harcourt $17.00 (978-0-15-205451-9). Follows Anne Hathaway's difficult life until her marriage to William Shakespeare. (Rev: BL 9/15/06; LMC 3/07; SLJ 10/06; VOYA)

4076 Meyer, Carolyn. *The True Adventures of Charley Darwin* (9–12). 2009, Houghton Mifflin $17.00 (978-015206194-4). This fictionalized, first-person account of the early years of Charles Darwin offers romance, humor, and adventure as well as details of his scientific interests. Lexile 1060L (Rev: BL 1/1–15/09; LMC 8–9/09; SLJ 1/1/09; VOYA 4/09)

4077 Michaels, Kasey. *A Reckless Beauty* (9–12). 2007, HQN paper $6.99 (978-0-373-77216-2). Set during the Napoleonic wars, this novel features a girl who follows her brother to the battlefield in disguise and falls in love with the spy he entrusts to protect her. (Rev: BL 8/07)

4078 Mosse, Kate. *The Winter Ghosts* (10–12). 2011, Putnam $24.95 (978-039915715-8). Freddie Watson is touring the French Pyrenees while recovering from the death of his brother in World War I when he comes across a quaint village with a ghostly history, and a mysterious woman who helps him heal and promptly disappears. ◯ e (Rev: BL 1/1–15/11)

4079 Nadin, Joanna. *Paradise* (9–12). 2012, Candlewick $16.99 (978-076365713-0). Billie Paradise, 16, inherits a seaside house from her grandmother and moves there with her mother and little brother, then learning some secrets about her mother's past and her father's identity. (Rev: BL 12/1/12; SLJ 2/13; VOYA 2/13)

4080 Nahai, Gina B. *Caspian Rain* (9–12). 2007, MacAdam $25.00 (978-1-59692-251-8). Set in Tehran during the last years of the shah's reign, this is the moving story of Bahar, a teenage girl who marries a cruel man and who, along with their daughter, is virtually imprisoned by him. (Rev: BL 8/07)

4081 Napoli, Donna Jo. *Breath* (8–12). 2003, Simon & Schuster $16.95 (978-0-689-86174-1). Salz, a sickly youth, seems to be immune to the sufferings of the people of Hameln in this reinterpretation of the Pied Piper story that conveys much of the atmosphere of 13th-century Europe. (Rev: BL 9/15/03; HBG 4/04; SLJ 11/03; VOYA 12/03)

4082 Newbery, Linda. *Set in Stone* (10–12). 2006, Random House $16.95 (978-0-385-75102-5). In 1898 England, Samuel Godwin is hired to tutor a daughter of Ernest Farrow and soon uncovers shocking secrets about the wealthy family and their governess Charlotte. (Rev: BL 9/1/06; LMC 2/07; SLJ 2/07)

4083 Nicholson, Christopher. *The Elephant Keeper* (11–12). 2009, Morrow $24.99 (978-006165160-1). In 18th-century England young Tom Page is so devoted to an elephant named Jenny that his relationship with his sweetheart suffers; for mature readers. (Rev: BL 7/09)

4084 O'Brien, Anne. *The Virgin Widow* (10–12). 2010, NAL paper $15 (978-04512312-9-1). Set in England in the late 15th century, this historical romance is a fictionalized account of the life of Anne Neville and her romance with the man who would become Richard III, king of England. (Rev: BL 11/1–15/10)

4085 Odiwe, Jane. *Mr. Darcy's Secret* (9–12). 2011, Sourcebooks paper $14.99 (978-14022452-7-5). In this sequel to *Pride and Prejudice* Elizabeth discovers that her new husband may have some hidden secrets. e (Rev: BL 12/1–15/10)

4086 Oldfield, Pamela. *The Birthday Present* (11–12). 2010, Severn $27.95 (978-072786839-8). In this coming-of-age novel best suited to older teens and set in 1890s London, young music-hall singer Rose Paton finds herself entangled in the dramas of the wealthy Bennley siblings, including the fatally ill Marie; for mature readers. (Rev: BLO 2/1–15/10)

4087 Orczy, Emmuska. *The Scarlet Pimpernel* (10–12). 1984, Buccaneer LB $19.95 (978-0-89966-508-5). An English fop is actually a leader of a group that helps aristocrats flee the French Revolution in this novel first published in 1905. Others in the series are *The Triumph of the Scarlet Pimpernel, The Way of the Scarlet Pimpernel,* and *The Adventures of the Scarlet Pimpernel.*

4088 Orlev, Uri. *The Lady with the Hat* (7–10). Trans. by Hillel Halkin. 1995, Houghton Mifflin $16.00 (978-0-395-69957-7). Yulek, a concentration camp survivor, encounters anti-Semitism on her return to Poland, while another Jewish girl, hidden from the Nazis, wants to be a nun. (Rev: BL 3/15/95; SLJ 5/95)

4089 Ortiz, Michael J. *Swan Town: The Secret Journal of Susanna Shakespeare* (7–10). 2006, HarperCollins LB $16.89 (978-0-06-058127-5). Shakespeare's teenage daughter Susanna writes in her diary about her current circumstances and her literary and acting ambitions, revealing much about Elizabethan life. (Rev: BL 2/15/06; SLJ 3/06; VOYA 2/06)

4090 Pasternak, Boris Leonidovich, et al. *Doctor Zhivago* (10–12). Trans. by Manya Harari and Max Hayward. 1991, Knopf $20.00 (978-0-679-40759-1). Using the Russian Revolution as a backdrop, this celebrated novel is about the life of a Russian doctor, poet, and intellectual during the first three decades of the 20th century.

4091 Peet, Mal. *Life: An Exploded Diagram* (9–12). 2011, Candlewick $17.99 (978-0-7636-5227-2). Spanning the years between World War II and 9/11, this compelling saga follows the romance of working-class Clem and his wealthy girlfriend Frankie as they face political upheavals including the Cuban missile crisis from the vantage point of England. Boston Globe–Horn Book Honor 2012. ◯ e Lexile 820L (Rev: BL 9/15/11*; HB 11–12/11; LMC 3–4/12*; SLJ 10/1/11*)

4092 Perera, Anna. *The Glass Collector* (8–12). 2012, Albert Whitman $17.99 (978-080752948-5). A Zabbaleen (garbage collectors and recyclers) living on the outskirts of Cairo, 15-year-old Aaron is a glass collector until he is caught stealing and is shunned by his family and villagers, leaving him with difficult options for survival. Lexile 990L (Rev: BL 2/15/12; LMC 8–9/12; SLJ 3/12; VOYA 2/12)

4093 Pignat, Caroline. *Greener Grass* (7–10). 2009, Red Deer paper $12.95 (978-088995402-1). In 1847, 14-year-old Kit's family is threatened by the Irish potato famine. When she loses her job as a kitchen maid, escaping to Canada may be her only hope. Canada Council for the Arts Governor General's Literary Award 2009. Lexile 650L (Rev: BL 4/15/09*; LMC 5–6/09; VOYA 6/09)

4094 Pitkeathley, Jill. *Cassandra and Jane: A Jane Austen Novel* (10–12). Illus. 2008, HarperCollins paper $13.95 (978-006144639-9). Cassandra Austen's voice is heard in this novel depicting her strong relationship with her sister Jane and how dreams, disappointments, and family expectations shaped their lives. ℮ (Rev: BL 9/15/08)

4095 Pratchett, Terry. *Dodger* (8–12). 2012, HarperCollins $17.99 (978-0-06-200949-4); LB $18.89 (978-006200950-0). Street urchin Dodger, 17, meets a mysterious girl, gets to know Charles Dickens, and thwarts the barbaric barber Sweeny Todd in this caper set in an alternative Victorian London. Printz Honor 2013. ⌒ ℮ Lexile 1210L (Rev: BL 10/15/12*; HB 11–12/12; LMC 3–4/13; SLJ 11/12*)

4096 Quick, Barbara. *A Golden Web* (7–10). 2010, HarperCollins $16.99 (978-0-06-144887-4). In 14th-century Italy, 15-year-old Alessandra rebels against the arranged marriage that awaits her and, disguised as a boy, studies anatomy at the university. ℮ (Rev: BL 4/15/10; LMC 5–6/10; SLJ 5/10)

4097 Ravel, Edeet. *Ten Thousand Lovers* (11–12). 2003, HarperPerennial paper $12.95 (978-0-06-056562-6). A young couple struggles to cling to love despite their opposing political stances in this moving novel set in Israel in the 1970s; for mature readers. (Rev: BL 9/15/03)

4098 Rees, Celia. *The Fool's Girl* (8–11). 2010, Bloomsbury $16.99 (978-1-59990-486-3). Violetta and Feste go to London to retrieve from Malvolio a stolen holy relic; they meet William Shakespeare, who joins the quest and includes elements of *Twelfth Night*. ℮ Lexile HL780L (Rev: BL 4/15/10; LMC 10/10; SLJ 8/10; VOYA 10/10)

4099 Rees, Celia. *Sovay* (7–10). 2008, Bloomsbury $16.99 (978-159990203-6). In this fictional tale rooted in history, beautiful 17-year-old Sovay abandons her pastime as a highwayman and becomes caught up in the danger and intrigue surrounding the French Revolution as she endeavors to clear her father's name. ⌒ ℮ Lexile 810L (Rev: BLO 11/6/08; LMC 1–2/09; SLJ 10/1/08; VOYA 8/08)

4100 Rees, Elizabeth M. *The Wedding: An Encounter with Jan van Eyck* (8–11). Series: Art Encounters. 2005, Watson-Guptill $15.95 (978-0-8230-0407-2). In this novel set in 15th-century Bruges and channeling Jan van Eyck's *The Arnolfini Portrait*, 14-year-old Giovanna falls in love with a troubador called Angelo

even as her father plans her marriage to a wealthy man. (Rev: BL 9/15/05; SLJ 9/05)

4101 Reeves, Amy Carol. *Ripper* (10–12). 2012, Flux paper $9.95 (978-073873072-1). Volunteering at the Whitechapel Hospital in the east end of London in 1888, 17-year-old Abbie discovers the identity of Jack the Ripper; an exciting historical mystery with a fantasy component. ℮ (Rev: BLO 6/12; LMC 8–9/12; SLJ 5/1/12; VOYA 2/12)

4102 Reynolds, Abigail. *Mr. Darcy's Obsession* (11–12). 2010, Sourcebooks paper $14.99 (978-1-4022-4-092-8). This "alternate-history" Austen story explores what might have happened to Elizabeth Bennett and Darcy had Elizabeth's father died; for mature readers. ℮ (Rev: BL 9/1–15/10)

4103 Robert, Na'ima B. *From Somalia, with Love* (7–10). 2009, Frances Lincoln $15.95 (978-184507831-7); paper $7.95 (978-184507832-4). Safia, a 14-year-old Muslim girl, has grown up in East London and finds her whole life changing when her father arrives from Somalia after a 12-year absence with different expectations. (Rev: BL 7/09; SLJ 7/1/09)

4104 Robertson, R. Garcia y. *White Rose* (9–12). 2004, Forge $25.95 (978-0-312-86994-6). Following *Lady Robyn* (2001) and *Knight Errant* (2002), this entertaining trip through time has Robyn caught up in the War of the Roses and pregnant with the child of the future King Edward IV; for mature teens. (Rev: BL 10/1/04; VOYA 4/05)

4105 Rosoff, Meg. *The Bride's Farewell* (11–12). 2009, Viking $24.95 (978-0-670-02099-7). Faced with the stifling prospect of life as a housewife in mid-19th-century England, Pell's adventures begin when she runs off on her wedding day to attend the Salisbury Horse Fair; for mature readers. Alex Award 2010. (Rev: BL 8/09; SLJ 12/09)

4106 Rosoff, Meg. *What I Was* (9–12). 2008, Viking $23.95 (978-0-670-01844-4). A 100-year-old man simply referring to himself as "H" tells the story of a beach shack loner boy, Finn, whom he met while escaping his phys-ed class in his hated boarding school on the coast of England in the 1960s, and the idyllic relationship they shared until tragedy parted them. (Rev: BL 12/1/07; SLJ 6/08)

4107 Scott, Amanda. *The Secret Clan: Abducted Heiress* (10–12). 2001, Warner paper $5.99 (978-0-446-61026-1). A vivid Scottish setting, a strong-willed heroine, a dashing hero, a touch of fantasy, and the interesting times of King James all add to this historical romance. (Rev: BL 9/15/01)

4108 Sedgwick, Marcus. *Midwinterblood* (9–12). 2013, Roaring Brook $17.99 (978-159643800-2). Seven linked stories, told in reverse chronological order, are set on a Scandinavian island and feature two main characters, tales of love and death, Vikings, vampires, ghosts, and a rare orchid. **e** Lexile 770L (Rev: BL 12/1/12*; HB 3–4/13*; SLJ 3/13)

4109 Seraji, Mahbod. *Rooftops of Tehran* (11–12). 2009, NAL paper $15 (978-04512268-1-5). Set in Iran during the Shah's regime, this is the story of young love, joy, accidental betrayal to the secret police, and heartbreak experienced by Pasha, a 17-year-old boy; for mature readers. ∩ **e** (Rev: BL 4–5/09)

4110 Shaw, Rebecca. *A Country Affair* (10–12). Series: Barleybridge. 2006, Three Rivers paper $12.95 (978-1-4000-9820-0). In the hills of Yorkshire, 19-year-old Kate accepts her poor exam results and instead of studying to be a vet works instead as a receptionist in a vet's office. (Rev: BL 2/15/06)

4111 Shimony, Abner. *Tibaldo and the Hole in the Calendar* (10–12). 1997, Springer-Verlag $21.00 (978-0-387-94935-2). Using both real and fictitious characters, this novel describes events in 1582 when the Gregorian calendar was adopted and the problem this causes for 11-year-old Tibaldo, who will lose his birthday as a result. (Rev: SLJ 3/98)

4112 Simoen, Jan. *What About Anna?* (9–12). Trans. by John Nieuwenhuizen. 2002, Walker $16.95 (978-0-8027-8808-5). Anna's life in Eastern Europe is haunted by the ethnic violence that claimed the life of her half-brother Michael. (Rev: BL 5/1/02; HB 7–8/02; HBG 10/02; SLJ 6/02; VOYA 6/02)

4113 Smith, Dodie. *I Capture the Castle* (9–12). 1998, St. Martin's paper $13.95 (978-0-312-20165-4). A classic, witty story of coming of age featuring 17-year-old Cassandra and the rest of her zany family who live in a rundown English castle. Originally published in 1948.

4114 Smith, Michael Marshall. *The Servants* (9–12). 2007, Earthling $30.00 (978-0-9795054-0-9). Set in Brighton, England, this intricately detailed novel follows 11-year-old Mark, who discovers ghosts in the servants' quarters of his new house and must interact with them to help his own family. (Rev: BL 7/07)

4115 Sole, Linda. *Kathy* (9–12). 2004, Severn $26.99 (978-0-7278-5869-6). In London during World War I, a nurse-trainee falls in love with a doctor. (Rev: BL 2/1/04)

4116 Sole, Linda. *The Rose Arch* (10–12). 2001, Severn $25.99 (978-0-7278-5651-7). An old-fashioned romance set in late-19th-century France about a convent-raised girl and her love for the son of her guardian. (Rev: BL 9/15/01)

4117 Stone, Irving. *Lust for Life: The Novel of Vincent van Gogh* (10–12). 1954, NAL paper $17.00 (978-0-452-26249-2). A lengthy fictionalized biography of the Dutch painter, Vincent van Gogh.

4118 Strauss, Victoria. *Passion Blue* (7–10). 2012, Amazon Children's $18.99 (978-0-7614-6230-9). Giulia, 17, the illegitimate daughter of a count in 15th-century

Italy, learns how to mix paints and create art, discovering to her surprise that she enjoys the creative life possible inside the convent where she has been sent. **e** (Rev: BL 12/1/12; SLJ 11/12; VOYA 12/12)

4119 Sturtevant, Katherine. *The Brothers Story* (9–12). 2009, Farrar $16.99 (978-0-374-30992-3). In the 17th century, during a "Great Frost," 15-year-old Kit heads for London in hopes of finding the wherewithal to support his "simple" twin brother Christy. **e** Lexile 920L (Rev: BL 11/1/09*; HB 11–12/09; LMC 5–6/10; SLJ 1/10)

4120 Sutcliff, Rosemary. *Bonnie Dundee* (10–12). 1990, Peter Smith $21.50 (978-0-8446-6363-0). An adventure story set in Scotland during the war between King James and William and featuring a 17-year-old hero.

4121 Sutcliff, Rosemary. *The Shining Company* (7–12). 1990, Farrar paper $6.95 (978-0-374-46616-9). A novel set in early Britain about a young man who with his friends confronts the enemy Saxons. (Rev: BL 6/15/90; SLJ 7/90)

4122 Tanner, Janet. *Tucker's Inn* (9–12). 2004, Severn $26.99 (978-0-7278-6022-4). In this gothic romance set in England during the French Revolution, Flora become involved with a mysterious stranger, known as the Lynx, who saves French aristocrats from the guillotine. (Rev: BL 2/1/04)

4123 Tel, Jonathan. *Arafat's Elephant* (10–12). 2002, Counterpoint paper $14.00 (978-1-58243-183-3). A rich collection of short stories about the Jews and Arabs who are fighting over Jerusalem. (Rev: BL 12/15/01)

4124 Thompson, Kate. *Creature of the Night* (9–12). 2009, Roaring Brook $17.95 (978-159643511-7). Bobby and his mother move from the slums of Dublin to a haunted house in the Irish countryside. Lexile HL670L (Rev: BL 4/1/09*; HB 5–6/09; SLJ 8/09; VOYA 2/10)

4125 Thompson, Ricki. *City of Cannibals* (9–12). 2010, Front St $18.95 (978-1-59078-623-9). Dell travels to London, where she falls in love with a young monk and learns to be a puppeteer in this story set in 1536. Lexile HL660L (Rev: BL 1/1–15/10; HB 5–6/10; LMC 8–9/10; SLJ 3/10)

4126 Town, Florida Ann. *With a Silent Companion* (7–12). 2000, Red Deer paper $7.95 (978-0-88995-211-9). Beginning in 1806, this novel based on fact tells how a young Irish girl hides her identity and becomes a "man" to pursue a medical career. (Rev: BL 4/15/00; VOYA 6/00)

4127 Turnbull, Ann. *Forged in the Fire* (9–12). 2007, Candlewick $16.99 (978-0-7636-3144-4). Susanna and Will, of 2004's *No Shame, No Fear,* have been apart for three years and wish to marry, but the plague means they must wait even longer in this novel set in 17th-century England. (Rev: BCCB 6/07; BL 4/15/07; HB 5–6/07; LMC 10/07; SLJ 7/07)

4128 Updike, John. *Gertrude and Claudius* (10–12). 2000, Knopf $23.00 (978-0-375-40908-0). A fascinating novel that presents the personalities and the events that occurred before the opening of Shakespeare's *Hamlet*. (Rev: BL 1/1–15/00; SLJ 8/00)

4129 Uris, Leon. *Exodus* (9–12). 1958, Bantam paper $7.99 (978-0-553-25847-9). A moving novel about Jewish immigration to Israel after World War II. Also use *The Haj* (1984).

4130 Van Rijckeghem, Jean-Claude, and Pat Van Beirs. *A Sword in Her Hand* (7–10). Trans. by John Nieuwenhuizen. 2011, Annick $21.95 (978-1-55451-291-1); paper $12.95 (978-1-55451-291-1). The Count of Flanders is disappointed when his child turns out to be a girl, and Marguerite must endure his disdain while trying to make a good life for herself; full of details of the Middle Ages, this novel is based on the real Marguerite (1348–1405). **e** Lexile 550L (Rev: BL 6/1/11; LMC 11–12/11; SLJ 11/1/11)

4131 Vande Velde, Vivian. *The Book of Mordred* (8–11). 2005, Houghton Mifflin $18.00 (978-0-618-50754-2). A multilayered account of Mordred's acts, seen through the eyes of three women who know him well. (Rev: BL 9/15/05; SLJ 10/05; VOYA 10/05)

4132 Wallace, Karen. *The Unrivalled Spangles* (7–10). 2006, Simon & Schuster $16.95 (978-1-4169-1503-4). Ellen and Lucy Spangle, teenaged circus performers in 19th-century England, long to live new lives outside of the three rings. (Rev: BL 12/1/06; SLJ 12/06)

4133 Walsh, Jill Paton. *Grace* (9–12). 1992, Farrar paper $5.95 (978-0-374-42792-4). A novel based on the life of Grace Darling, the young English woman who became a hero when she rowed out from a lighthouse in 1838 to save shipwreck survivors. (Rev: BL 6/15/92; SLJ 7/92*)

4134 Welsh, T. K. *Resurrection Men* (9–12). 2007, Dutton $16.99 (978-0-525-47699-3). In 1830 London, a young Italian orphan named Victor works as a driver for "resurrection men" — undertakers who steal corpses from fresh graves to sell to medical researchers — and learns that children are being deliberately infected with cholera. (Rev: SLJ 2/08)

4135 Weyn, Suzanne. *Distant Waves: A Novel of the Titanic* (8–11). 2009, Scholastic $17.99 (978-054508572-4). Spiritualism and science intersect in this novel featuring Jane, 16-year-old daughter of a spirit medium, and inventor Nikola Tesla, who are traveling aboard the *Titanic*. Lexile 790L (Rev: BL 4/15/09*; LMC 10/09; SLJ 9/09)

4136 Whelan, Gerard. *The Guns of Easter* (6–10). 2000, O'Brien paper $7.95 (978-0-86278-449-2). Twelve-year-old Jimmy Conway grapples with the reasons for, and impact of, the violence erupting in Ireland in the early 20th century. (Rev: BL 3/1/01)

4137 Whelan, Gerard. *A Winter of Spies* (6–10). 2002, O'Brien paper $6.95 (978-0-86278-566-6). The story of the Conway family, begun in *The Guns of Easter* (2000), continues in this novel as 11-year-old Sarah sees spies and counterspies all around her in 1920 Dublin. (Rev: BL 6/1–15/02)

4138 Whelan, Gloria. *Parade of Shadows* (7–10). 2007, HarperCollins $15.99 (978-0-06-089028-5). Julia learns about the harsh realities of 1907 Turkish-occupied Syria while traveling across the country with her British father. (Rev: BL 11/15/07; SLJ 10/07)

4139 Whyte, Jack. *Saxon Shore* (10–12). 1998, St. Martin's $26.95 (978-0-312-86596-2). In this book, the third of a series about King Arthur, Merlin adopts Arthur to assure his safety until Arthur becomes king, and in a series of adventures rallies forces to support him. (Rev: BL 6/1–15/98; SLJ 4/99)

4140 Wiseman, Eva. *The Last Song* (8–12). 2012, Tundra $17.95 (978-088776979-5). In the late 15th century 14-year-old Isabel faces family and romantic dilemmas during the Spanish Inquisition. **e** (Rev: BL 4/15/12; SLJ 4/12)

4141 Wiseman, Eva. *Puppet* (7–12). 2009, Tundra $17.95 (978-088776828-6). A Jewish boy is forced into giving false witness in this story based on an actual case of anti-Semitic violence in Hungary in 1883. **e** Lexile HL660L (Rev: BL 2/15/09; SLJ 3/1/09)

4142 Woods, Janet. *The Coal Gatherer* (9–12). 2007, Severn $27.95 (978-0-7278-6546-5). While gathering sea coal in the northeast coast of Victorian England, Callie Ingram meets Patricia who is staying with her uncle while recuperating from pneumonia, and although they come from very different backgrounds, they become longtime friends; however, Callie must deal with the unfairness in her life after Patricia returns to the excitement of London. (Rev: BL 10/1/07)

4143 Wulf, Linda Press. *The Night of the Burning: Devorah's Story* (7–10). 2006, Farrar $16.00 (978-0-374-36419-9). Devorah and her younger sister Nechama are the only survivors left in their Polish town after a pogrom but are rescued and taken to a safe community in South Africa. They begin to build a new life and find happiness when they are adopted by families there. (Rev: BL 8/06; SLJ 1/07)

4144 Yolen, Jane, and Robert J. Harris. *The Queen's Own Fool: A Novel of Mary, Queen of Scots* (10–12). 2000, Philomel paper $7.99 (978-0-698-11918-5). Fiction and fact are interwoven in this novel about a 12-year-old girl who becomes a court fool for Mary, Queen of Scots. (Rev: BL 4/1/00; HB 5–6/00; HBG 9/00; SLJ 6/00; VOYA 6/00)

Latin America and Canada

4145 Alvarez, Julia. *In the Time of the Butterflies* (9–12). 1994, Algonquin $29.95 (978-1-56512-038-9). Follows the real-life struggles of the Mirabel sisters from girlhood to womanhood as they struggle under, and ultimately resist, the Trujillo dictatorship in the Dominican Republic. (Rev: BL 7/94)

4146 Berry, James. *Ajeemah and His Son* (10–12). 1994, HarperTrophy paper $4.99 (978-0-06-440523-2). Ajeemah and his 18-year-old son Atu are captured in Nigeria at the beginning of the 19th century and taken as slaves to Jamaica, where their experiences are very different.

4147 Brooks, Martha. *Queen of Hearts* (7–10). 2011, Farrar $16.99 (978-0-374-34229-6). In early 1940s Canada, tuberculosis hits a family and the three children are sent to a sanitarium, where young Marie-Claire experiences first love. ALA Notable Books 2012. **e** Lexile HL710L (Rev: BL 6/1/11; HB 7–8/11; LMC 11–12/11; SLJ 7/11*; VOYA 2/11)

4148 Cardenas, Teresa. *Old Dog* (7–12). Trans. by David Unger. 2007, Groundwood $16.95 (978-0-88899-757-9); paper $8.95 (978-0-88899-836-1). Seventy-year-old Cuban slave Perro Viejo helps to shelter 10-year-old runaway slave Aisa on the sugar plantation where Perro has lived a difficult life since childhood. (Rev: BL 12/15/07)

4149 Collison, Linda. *Star-Crossed* (7–10). 2006, Knopf $16.95 (978-0-375-83363-2). After her father's death in 1760, Patricia stows away on a ship bound for Barbados to claim his estate; there she finds romance and learns a valuable trade. (Rev: BL 9/15/06; SLJ 12/06)

4150 Danticat, Edwidge. *The Farming of Bones* (10–12). 1998, Soho $23.00 (978-1-56947-126-5). An emotion-charged historical novel about the people of Haiti and the Dominican Republic in which Amabelle, an aging Haitian woman, recalls the terrible massacre of 1937 and what happened to her and the man she loved. (Rev: BL 8/98; SLJ 11/98)

4151 Diaz, Junot. *The Brief Wondrous Life of Oscar Wao* (9–12). 2007, Riverhead $24.95 (978-1-59448-958-7). This is the brilliantly written story of a Dominican, Oscar Wao, and his family as they struggle under Trujillo's brutal dictatorship. (Rev: BL 7/07)

4152 Engle, Margarita. *The Lightning Dreamer* (7–12). 2013, Harcourt $16.99 (978-054780743-0). This novel in free verse tells the story of 19th-century Cuban abolitionist poet Gertrudis Gómez de Avellaneda, known as Tula, describing her teen years and her hatred of injustice. **e** (Rev: BL 2/15/13*; HB 5–6/13; SLJ 6/13; VOYA 4/13)

4153 Hamilton, Harriet. *Ribbons of the Sun* (9–12). 2006, Brown Barn paper $8.95 (978-0-9768126-2-3). Rosa, a 12-year-old girl from a traditional Indian village in Mexico, is sold as a servant and faces hardships and abuse until, pregnant, she finds refuge in a mission. (Rev: BL 11/1/06; SLJ 11/06)

4154 Hearn, Julie. *Hazel* (9–12). 2009, Simon & Schuster $17.99 (978-1-4169-2504-0). Having disgraced her upper-class family by participating in a suffragist protest in 1913 London, Hazel Mull-Dare, 13, is sent into exile on a Caribbean sugar plantation where she is forced to confront the racial inequities that have allowed her family to enjoy generations of privilege. **e** (Rev: BL 9/1/09; HB 11–12/09; SLJ 12/09; VOYA 2/10)

4155 Herbstein, Manu. *Brave Music of a Distant Drum* (11–12). 2012, Red Deer paper $12.95 (978-08899547-0-0). His mother's story of slavery and hardship affects her estranged son Zacharias, awakening him to harsh realities; for mature readers, this is a YA version of *Ama: A Story of the Atlantic Slave Trade* (2001). (Rev: BL 2/1/12; LMC 8–9/12; SLJ 5/1/12)

4156 Hiatt, Shelby. *Panama* (10–12). 2009, Houghton Mifflin $16.00 (978-054719600-8). This novel combines material on the building of the Panama Canal with an affair between a 15-year-old American girl, daughter of an engineer, and an older Spaniard named Federico who introduces her to new socioeconomic ideas and to sex. (Rev: BL 7/09; LMC 1–2/10; SLJ 12/09; VOYA 12/09)

4157 Jefferson, Joanne K. *Lightning and Blackberries* (7–10). 2008, Nimbus paper $10.95 (978-155109654-4). In 1774 Nova Scotia 17-year-old Elizabeth longs for independence but knows she must settle for marriage and domesticity until she meets an Acadian woman who widens her horizons. **e** (Rev: BLO 11/11/08; VOYA 10/08)

4158 Jocelyn, Marthe. *Mable Riley: A Reliable Record of Humdrum, Peril, and Romance* (5–10). 2004, Candlewick $15.99 (978-0-7636-2120-9). This is a charming, humorous diary set in 1901 by a 14-year-old girl who accompanies her sister when she becomes a teacher in Stratford, Ontario. (Rev: BL 3/1/04; HB 5–6/04; SLJ 3/04; VOYA 6/04)

4159 Kositsky, Lynne. *Claire by Moonlight* (7–10). 2005, Tundra paper $9.95 (978-0-88776-659-6). History and romance are interwoven in this story of 15-year-old Claire's struggle to return to Acadia with her brother and sister after their deportation in the 1750s. (Rev: BL 7/05; SLJ 10/05)

4160 Lake, Nick. *In Darkness* (10–12). , Bloomsbury $17.99 (978-1-59990-743-7). After the earthquake in Haiti, 15-year-old Shorty lies under rubble reviewing his own violent life, the disappearance of his twin sister, and the history of his nation. Printz Award 2013. (Rev: BL 1/1/12; SLJ 12/12*)

4161 Landman, Tanya. *The Goldsmith's Daughter* (9–12). 2009, Candlewick $16.99 (978-076364219-8).

Itacate, an Aztec girl, faces many challenges even before the arrival of the Spanish. (Rev: BL 7/09*; LMC 11–12/09)

4162 Limón, Graciela. *Song of the Hummingbird* (6–10). 1996, Arte Publico paper $12.95 (978-1-55885-091-0). The conquest of the Aztec Empire by Cortes is told through the experiences of Huizitzilin (Hummingbird), a descendent of Mexican kings. (Rev: VOYA 8/97)

4163 McCarthy, Cormac. *All the Pretty Horses* (10–12). 1992, Knopf $27.50 (978-0-394-57474-5); paper $13.00 (978-0-679-74439-9). The story of two young boys who venture into Mexico in 1950 and take jobs on a ranch working with horses.

4164 Mikaelsen, Ben. *Tree Girl* (7–12). 2004, HarperTempest $16.99 (978-0-06-009004-3). Through the first-person narrative of Mayan teenager Gabriela Flores, the reader experiences the civil war in Guatemala. (Rev: BL 2/15/04; SLJ 4/04; VOYA 6/04)

4165 Montoya, Maceo. *The Scoundrel and the Optimist* (11–12). 2009, Bilingual $28 (978-193101065-8); paper $18 (978-19310106-7-2). When abusive Filastro is nearly killed in a skirmish with police and gangsters — and undergoes a personal transformation, his son Edmund nurses him back to physical and emotional health; the humor balances the violence in this coming-of-age tale suitable for mature readers. (Rev: BL 12/1/09)

4166 Morrissey, Donna. *Kit's Law* (10–12). 2001, Houghton Mifflin paper $13.95 (978-0-618-10927-2). Fourteen-year-old Kit is living in a remote Newfoundland village with her mother and grandmother in the 1950s when her life suddenly falls apart because of love, hidden secrets, and family intrigue. (Rev: BL 4/1/01)

4167 Noël, Michel. *Good for Nothing* (8–11). 2004, Douglas & McIntyre $18.95 (978-0-88899-478-3). In this powerful coming-of-age novel set in northern Quebec in the late 1950s and early 1960s, 15-year-old Nipishish, part Algonquin and part white, struggles to find his own identity. (Rev: BL 1/1–15/05; SLJ 1/05; VOYA 2/05)

4168 O'Dell, Scott. *The King's Fifth* (7–10). 1966, Houghton Mifflin $17.00 (978-0-395-06963-9). In a story told in flashbacks, Esteban explains why he is in jail in the Mexico of the Conquistadors. Also use *The Hawk That Dare Not Hunt by Day* (1975).

4169 Porter, Pamela. *I'll Be Watching* (7–12). 2011, Groundwood $18.95 (978-1-55498-095-6); paper $12.95 (978-15549809-6-3). Four orphans struggle to make their own way in 1941 Saskatchewan in this inspiring story told in verse. e (Rev: BL 10/1/11; HB 11–12/11; LMC 1–2/12; SLJ 9/1/11)

4170 Resau, Laura, and Maria Virginia Farinango. *The Queen of Water* (8–12). 2011, Delacorte $16.99 (978-0-385-73897-2); LB $19.99 (978-038590761-3). Virgin-

ia, 7, is sent by her poor Quechua Indian family to be an indentured servant to a mestizo family; there she learns some skills and puts up with a certain amount of abuse, but can she ever go back home? (Rev: BL 2/15/11*; HB 7–8/11; SLJ 6/11*)

4171 Rothman, Claire Holden. *The Heart Specialist: A Novel* (10–12). 2011, Soho $25 (978-1-56947-945-2). At the turn of the 20th century, Agnes White overcomes being labeled "weird" and "unladylike" to become one of the world's most celebrated female doctors in this inspiring story based on the life of Canadian Maude Abbott. (Rev: SLJ 8/11)

4172 Schmidt, C. A. *Useful Fools* (10–12). 2007, Dutton $18.99 (978-0-525-47814-0). After his mother is killed in a bombing by Peru's Shining Path revolutionary movement and his family life spirals further downward, 15-year-old Alonso decides to join the guerrillas; will this move separate him further from his love, the privileged Rosa? (Rev: BL 9/1/07; SLJ 9/07)

4173 Temple, Frances. *Taste of Salt: A Story of Modern Haiti* (7–12). 1992, Orchard LB $17.99 (978-0-531-08609-4). A first novel simply told in the voices of two Haitian teenagers who find political commitment and love. (Rev: BL 8/92; SLJ 9/92*)

4174 Trottier, Maxine. *Three Songs for Courage* (10–12). 2006, Tundra $16.95 (978-0-88776-745-6). Set in Ontario in 1956, this book tells the story of 16-year-old Gordon, who seeks revenge after his brother is murdered. (Rev: BL 5/15/06; LMC 1/07; SLJ 9/06)

4175 Weber, Lori. *If You Live Like Me* (7–10). 2009, Lobster $14.95 (978-189755012-0). After a series of moves, Cheryl learns to love Newfoundland and her new neighbor, Jim, only to learn that she can finally return to Montreal. (Rev: BL 4/15/09; SLJ 6/1/09)

4176 Whelan, Gloria. *The Disappeared* (8–12). 2008, Dial $16.99 (978-0-8037-3275-9). Silvia tries to save her brother Eduardo when he is imprisoned for protesting against the government in Argentina in the 1970s. (Rev: BL 4/15/08; LMC 10/08*; SLJ 7/08)

4177 Wilder, Thornton. *The Bridge of San Luis Rey* (10–12). 1967, Perennial paper $11.00 (978-0-06-092986-2). This is the story of the five people who were killed when Peru's San Luis Rey bridge collapsed on July 14, 1714.

Polar Regions

4178 Farr, Richard. *Emperors of the Ice: A True Story of Disaster and Survival in the Antarctic, 1910–13* (10–12). Illus. 2008, Farrar $19.95 (978-037431975-5). In this journal-style fiction rooted in history, Apsley Cherry-Garrard, one of the men in Robert Scott's ill-fated Antarctic expedition, provides a glimpse into their struggle for survival. ∩ Lexile 1050L (Rev: BL 9/1/08; HB 11–12/08; SLJ 12/08; VOYA 8/08)

United States

NATIVE AMERICANS

4179 Anaya, Rudolfo. *Serafina's Stories* (9–12). 2004, Univ. of New Mexico $22.95 (978-0-8263-3569-2). In a story reminiscent of the Arabian Nights, 15-year-old Serafina, a Pueblo Indian held captive by the Spaniards who control 17th-century New Mexico, tells stories to the Spanish governor in exchange for the release of her fellow captives. (Rev: SLJ 3/05)

4180 Borland, Hal. *When the Legends Die* (9–12). 1963, Bantam paper $5.99 (978-0-553-25738-0). At the death of his parents, a young Native American boy must enter the world of the white man. (Rev: BL 11/1/87)

4181 Bruchac, Joseph. *Geronimo* (7–10). 2006, Scholastic $16.99 (978-0-439-35360-1). Geronimo's fictional adopted grandson narrates the tragic story of Geronimo's final surrender and the subsequent treatment of his people in this well-researched novel. (Rev: BL 3/15/06; SLJ 4/06)

4182 Bruchac, Joseph. *Turtle Meat and Other Stories* (9–12). 1992, Holy Cow paper $12.95 (978-0-930100-49-0). Abenaki writer Bruchac presents mythic, historical, and contemporary stories with wit and a fine sense of character. (Rev: BL 11/15/92; SLJ 12/92)

4183 Carvell, Marlene. *Sweetgrass Basket* (7–10). 2005, Dutton $16.99 (978-0-525-47547-7). Mohawk sisters Mattie and Sarah describe the abuse they endure at the Carlisle Indian Industrial School at the turn of the 20th century. (Rev: BL 8/05*; SLJ 12/05)

4184 Chibbaro, Julie. *Redemption* (9–12). 2004, Simon & Schuster $16.95 (978-0-689-85736-2). Set in the early 16th century, this is the story of 12-year-old Lily from England and how she found a home and family with an Indian tribe in the northeast forests. (Rev: BL 5/15/04; HB 7–8/04; SLJ 8/04)

4185 Creel, Ann Howard. *Under a Stand Still Moon* (6–10). 2005, Brown Barn paper $8.95 (978-0-9746481-8-7). In this captivating story set among the ancient Anasazi of the American Southwest, a young girl uses her magical powers to preserve her people's way of life. (Rev: SLJ 11/05)

4186 Foster, Sharon Ewell. *Abraham's Well* (9–12). 2006, Bethany paper $12.99 (978-0-7642-2887-2). In 1838, Armentia, part Cherokee, part African, is forced to walk the thousand-mile Trail of Tears to land set aside in Oklahoma; when she gets there she's sold into slavery. (Rev: BL 1/1–15/07)

4187 Gall, Grant. *Apache: The Long Ride Home* (7–10). 1988, Sunstone paper $9.95 (978-0-86534-105-0). Pedro was only nine when Apache raiders kidnapped him and renamed him Cuchillo. (Rev: BL 9/15/87)

4188 Hausman, Gerald. *The Coyote Bead* (7–12). 1999, Hampton Roads paper $11.95 (978-1-57174-145-5).

With the help of his grandfather and Indian magic, a young Navajo boy evades the American soldiers who killed his parents. (Rev: SLJ 1/00; VOYA 4/00)

4189 Highwater, Jamake. *Legend Days* (7–10). Series: Ghost Horse. 1984, HarperCollins $12.95 (978-0-06-022303-8). This story about a young Indian girl begins a moving trilogy about three generations of Native Americans and their fate in a white man's world. Followed by *The Ceremony of Innocence* and *I Wear the Morning Star*.

4190 Homstad, Daniel W. *Horse Dreamer* (7–12). 2001, PublishAmerica paper $27.95 (978-1-58851-042-6). A historical adventure in which 16-year-old Zakarias, son of a white father and a Dakota mother, serves as a scout for the army in the early 1860s until he is captured by renegade Dakotas and decides to join their cause. (Rev: VOYA 4/02)

4191 La Farge, Oliver. *Laughing Boy* (9–12). 1981, Buccaneer LB $24.95 (978-0-89966-367-8). A touching novel first published in 1929 about two young Navahos and the love they feel for each other.

4192 Landman, Tanya. *I Am Apache* (8–12). 2008, Candlewick $17.99 (978-076363664-7). When 14-year-old Apache Siki witnesses her brother's death at the hands of brutal Mexican raiders in the late 19th century, she vows to avenge him by earning her stripes as a daring, if unlikely, warrior. Lexile 860L (Rev: BL 10/1/08; LMC 3–4/09; SLJ 8/08; VOYA 12/08)

4193 Medawar, Mardi O. *Witch of the Palo Duro: A Tay-Bodal Mystery* (10–12). 1997, St. Martin's $21.95 (978-0-312-17065-3). Set in the Wild West of 1866, this murder mystery involves Kiowa Indians, the ghosts of their forefathers, and the sudden death of the wife of their chief. (Rev: BL 9/15/97; SLJ 4/98)

4194 Rees, Celia. *Sorceress* (7–11). 2002, Candlewick $15.99 (978-0-7636-1847-6). Agnes, a Native American who is beginning college, researches Mary Newbury, first seen in *Witch Child* (2001), and discovers a connection that results in a vision quest. (Rev: BL 1/1–15/03; HB 1–2/03; HBG 3/03; SLJ 12/02; VOYA 4/03)

4195 Spooner, Michael. *Last Child* (8–11). 2005, Henry Holt $16.95 (978-0-8050-7739-1). Rosalie, who is part Mandan and part Scottish American, is caught up in the conflicts between the Native Americans and the whites in 1837 North Dakota. (Rev: BL 9/1/05; SLJ 11/05; VOYA 8/05)

4196 Yeahpau, Thomas M. *X-Indian Chronicles: The Book of Mausape* (10–12). 2006, Candlewick $16.99 (978-0-7636-2706-5). The sometimes hard and discouraging lives of young Native Americans uncertain of their role in today's world are presented in a collection of gritty stories. (Rev: BCCB 3/07; BL 2/1/07; HB 11–12/06; LMC 3/07)

DISCOVERY AND EXPLORATION

4197 Glancy, Diane. *Stone Heart* (10–12). 2003, Overlook $21.95 (978-1-58567-365-0). Native American heroine Sacajawea comes alive as she narrates this fictionalized account of the Lewis and Clark expedition. (Rev: BL 1/1–15/03)

4198 Kudlinski, Kathleen. *My Lady Pocahontas* (7–10). 2006, Marshall Cavendish $16.95 (978-0-7614-5293-5). This fictional account of the life of Pocahontas from the time of the Jamestown settlement until her death focuses on her strength and inner conflicts. (Rev: BL 5/1/06; LMC 11–12/06; SLJ 12/06)

4199 Schneider, Paul. *Brutal Journey: The Epic Story of the First Crossing of North America* (10–12). 2006, Henry Holt $26.00 (978-0-8050-6835-1). The intense, true story of a band of Spaniards who become dependent on and are eventually enslaved by Native Americans as they journey across North America circa 1528. (Rev: BL 4/15/06) [973.1]

COLONIAL PERIOD AND FRENCH AND INDIAN WARS

4200 Allende, Isabel. *Zorro* (11–12). 2005, HarperCollins $25.95 (978-0-06-077897-2). Allende retells the legend of Zorro as the complex story of a Spanish-Shoshone boy who becomes a champion of the oppressed in 18th-century California. (Rev: BL 2/15/05*)

4201 Baker, Calvin. *Dominion* (9–12). 2006, Grove $24.00 (978-0-8021-1829-5). At the end of the 17th century, freed slave Jasper Merian seeks to build a life for himself and his sons, one free, one a slave. (Rev: BL 7/06)

4202 Bruchac, Joseph. *Pocahontas* (6–12). 2003, Harcourt $17.00 (978-0-15-216737-0). Pocahontas and John Smith take turns describing the relationship between the Jamestown colonists and the Powhatan Indians. (Rev: BL 9/15/03; HBG 4/04; SLJ 5/04; VOYA 4/04)

4203 Chance, Megan. *Susannah Morrow* (10–12). 2002, Warner $24.95 (978-0-446-52953-2). Susannah arrives in Salem at the height of the morality crusade and her finery only enhances suspicions when she is accused of witchcraft. (Rev: BL 8/02)

4204 Hemphill, Stephanie. *Wicked Girls: A Novel of the Salem Witch Trials* (7–12). 2010, HarperCollins LB $16.99 (978-0-06-185328-9). Three of the Salem accusers relate the story of the false testimony and resulting deaths in alternate verse voices. **e** Lexile 700L (Rev: BL 6/10*; HB 7–8/10; LMC 10/10; SLJ 8/10; VOYA 10/10)

4205 Johnston, Mary. *To Have and to Hold* (9–12). 1976, Lightyear LB $18.95 (978-0-89968-149-8). In this historical novel first published in 1900, a young girl escapes an intolerable situation by fleeing to Virginia with a cargo of brides.

4206 Kent, Kathleen. *The Wolves of Andover* (10–12). 2010, Little, Brown $24.99 (978-031606862-8). Unmarried at 23 in 17th-century Massachusetts, Martha Allen leaves her home to work as a servant to her cousin and finds both danger and romance when she meets a mysterious man who might have been involved with the death of Charles I. ∩ (Rev: BL 10/1–15/10)

4207 Kilian, Michael. *Major Washington* (10–12). 1998, St. Martin's $25.95 (978-0-312-18131-4). A novel that fictionalizes the life of George Washington during the period from 1753-1755, when he made three journeys into the Allegheny wilderness to spy on the French. (Rev: BL 1/1–15/98; SLJ 1/99)

4208 Larsen, Deborah. *The White* (11–12). 2002, Knopf $22.00 (978-0-375-41359-9). A young woman captured by the Shawnee in pre-Revolutionary America chooses to stay with the Indians despite opportunities to flee to her own people; for mature teens. (Rev: BL 6/1–15/02)

4209 Lasky, Kathryn. *Beyond the Burning Time* (7–12). 1994, Scholastic paper $14.95 (978-0-590-47331-6). In this docunovel that captures the ignorance, violence, and hysteria of the Salem witch trials, Mary, 12, tries to save her mother, accused of witchcraft. (Rev: BL 10/15/94; SLJ 1/95; VOYA 12/94)

4210 Noyes, Deborah. *Angel and Apostle* (11–12). 2005, Unbridled $24.95 (978-1-932961-10-2). This promising first novel suitable for mature readers tells the story of Pearl, the illegitimate daughter of Hester Prynne of Nathaniel Hawthorne's *The Scarlet Letter*. (Rev: BL 10/15/05)

4211 Rinaldi, Ann. *A Stitch in Time* (7–10). Series: Quilt Trilogy. 1994, Scholastic paper $13.95 (978-0-590-46055-2). This historical novel set in 18th-century Salem, Massachusetts, concerns the tribulations of a 16-year-old girl and her family. (Rev: BL 3/1/94; SLJ 5/94; VOYA 4/94)

4212 Steinmetz, Karen. *The Mourning Wars* (7–10). 2010, Roaring Brook $18.99 (978-1-59643-290-1). In 1704 young Eunice Williams is seized by Mohawk Indians and adopted by Atironta and Kenniontie, whose daughter has died; she soon adjusts to her new life and must make a difficult choice when her father finally comes looking for her. Based on a true story. **e** Lexile 910L (Rev: BL 6/10; LMC 11–12/10; SLJ 11/1/10; VOYA 10/10)

REVOLUTIONARY PERIOD AND THE YOUNG NATION (1775–1809)

4213 Amateau, Gigi. *Come August, Come Freedom: The Bellows, the Gallows, and the Black General Gabriel* (8–12). 2012, Candlewick $16.99 (978-0-7636-4792-6). A fictionalized biography of the brave blacksmith

239

who inspired rebellion in post-Revolution Richmond, Virginia. **e** Lexile 900L (Rev: BL 10/1/12; SLJ 11/12)

4214 Anderson, Joan. *1787* (7–10). 1987, Harcourt $14.95 (978-0-15-200582-5). The story of a teenager who became James Madison's aide during the 1787 Constitutional Convention in Philadelphia. (Rev: BL 5/87; VOYA 12/87)

4215 Anderson, Laurie Halse. *Chains* (7–10). 2008, Simon & Schuster $16.99 (978-141690585-1). Hoping to gain her freedom — and learn the whereabouts of her missing sister — slave Isabel decides to spy for the rebels in American Revolution-era New York City. ALA Notable Books 2009. ♪ **e** Lexile 780L (Rev: BL 11/1/08*; HB 11–12/09; LMC 1–2/09; SLJ 10/1/08; VOYA 10/08)

4216 Anderson, Laurie Halse. *Fever 1793* (6–10). 2000, Simon & Schuster $16.00 (978-0-689-83858-3). Matilda must find the strength to go on when her family is killed by yellow fever in a 1793 outbreak in Philadelphia. Margaret A. Edwards Award 2009. (Rev: BCCB 10/00; BL 10/1/00; HB 9–10/00; HBG 3/01; SLJ 8/00*)

4217 Anderson, M. T. *The Astonishing Life of Octavian Nothing, Traitor to the Nation: The Kingdom on the Waves, Vol. 2* (10–12). 2008, Candlewick $22.99 (978-0-7636-2950-2). In this continuation of the widely acclaimed first book, the promise of freedom offered to African Americans entices Octavian to enter the Loyalist Navy and fight the Patriots. (Rev: BL 6/1–15/08; SLJ 9/08)

4218 Anderson, M. T. *The Astonishing Life of Octavian Nothing, Traitor to the Nation: The Pox Party, Vol. 1* (10–12). 2006, Candlewick $17.99 (978-0-7636-2402-6). Follows the life of an African American boy named Octavian as he grows up in a Boston household before and during the Revolutionary War, apparently gaining a good education but also being used in an experiment to determine the aptitude of Africans. Winner, 2006 National Book Award for Young People's Literature. Boston Globe–Horn Book Honor 2007. ♪ (Rev: BL 9/1/06; HB 9–10/06; SLJ 10/06; VOYA)

4219 Bradley, Kimberly Brubaker. *Jefferson's Sons* (7–10). 2011, Dial $17.99 (978-0-8037-3499-9). Tells the story of the children Thomas Jefferson fathered with Sally Hemings and their aspirations for freedom. ALA Notable Books 2012. ♪ **e** Lexile 600L (Rev: BL 9/15/11; HB 1–2/12; LMC 1–2/12; SLJ 10/1/11*)

4220 Fast, Howard. *April Morning* (9–12). 1961, Bantam paper $5.99 (978-0-553-27322-9). A short novel about the first days of the American Revolution as experienced by a 15-year-old boy.

4221 Hughes, Pat. *Five 4ths of July* (8–10). 2011, Viking $16.99 (978-0-670-01207-7). Relates the experiences of 14-year-old Jake from 1777 to 1781 as war affects all aspects of his life. Lexile 710L (Rev: BL 5/1/11; LMC 11–12/11; SLJ 6/11; VOYA 8/11)

4222 Morgan, Robert. *Brave Enemies* (11–12). 2003, Algonquin $24.95 (978-1565123564). In the Revolutionary War, 16-year-old Josie, who has been traveling as a man, meets and marries a preacher but must continue her disguise; suitable for mature teens. (Rev: BL 8/03)

4223 Rinaldi, Ann. *Taking Liberty: The Story of Oney Judge, George Washington's Runaway Slave* (7–12). 2002, Simon & Schuster $16.95 (978-0-689-85187-2). An elderly Oney looks back on her life as Martha's personal slave, her initial acceptance of her lot, and her final decision to trade comfort for freedom. (Rev: HBG 3/03; SLJ 1/03; VOYA 2/03)

4224 Rinaldi, Ann. *Wolf by the Ears* (8–12). 1991, Scholastic $13.95 (978-0-590-43413-3). Harriet Hemings — the alleged daughter of Thomas Jefferson and his slave mistress — faces moral dilemmas in regard to freedom, equal rights, and her future. (Rev: BL 2/1/91; SLJ 4/91)

4225 Rosenburg, John. *First in War: George Washington in the American Revolution* (7–10). 1998, Millbrook LB $25.90 (978-0-7613-0311-4). This second part of the fictionalized biography of George Washington covers his career from 1775, when he was elected commander-in-chief, to the end of 1783, when he resigned from his military duties. (Rev: HBG 9/98; SLJ 7/98; VOYA 4/99)

NINETEENTH CENTURY TO THE CIVIL WAR (1809–1861)

4226 Charbonneau, Eileen. *Honor to the Hills* (8–10). 1996, Tor $18.95 (978-0-312-86094-3). Returning to her home in the Catskill Mountains in 1851, 15-year-old Lily Woods finds that her family is involved in the Underground Railroad. (Rev: VOYA 6/96)

4227 Crimmins, Jerry. *Fort Dearborn* (9–12). 2006, Northwestern Univ $27.95 (978-0-8101-2296-3). A taut historical novel dramatizing the politics, customs, and conflicts of the first organized settlement in Chicago, circa 1807-1812, including the massacre at Fort Dearborn as witnessed by two young boys, one white, one Indian, and their fathers. (Rev: BL 7/06)

4228 Draper, Sharon M. *Copper Sun* (9–12). 2006, Simon & Schuster $16.95 (978-0-689-82181-3). A moving story — full of historical detail — of the sufferings of Amari, captured in her village in Africa and taken to America, where she is bought as a gift for a plantation owner's son, and of her eventual bid for freedom. Coretta Scott King Author Award, 2007. (Rev: BL 2/1/06*; SLJ 1/06*; VOYA 2/06)

4229 Ferris, Jean. *Into the Wind* (9–12). Series: American Dreams. 1996, Avon paper $3.99 (978-0-380-78198-0). In this romantic historical novel set in 1814, 17-year-old Rosie sets sail on a ship engaged to fight the British Navy. (Rev: SLJ 9/96)

4230 Jensen, Lisa. *The Witch from the Sea* (10–12). 2001, Beagle Bay paper $16.95 (978-0-9679591-5-3).

A Boston girl who is part Native American disguises herself as a boy to live the life of a sailor in this romantic adventure set in 1823. (Rev: BL 8/01)

4231 Krisher, Trudy. *Uncommon Faith* (7–10). 2003, Holiday $17.95 (978-0-8234-1791-9). The year 1837-1838 is a time of change in Millbrook, Massachusetts, and 10 of the residents narrate their experiences in a collage that connects the reader to the townspeople and to the history. (Rev: BL 10/15/03; HBG 4/04; SLJ 10/03*; VOYA 10/03)

4232 LaFoy, Leslie. *Jackson's Way* (10–12). 2001, Bantam paper $5.99 (978-0-553-58313-7). In this historical romance, Jackson Stennett, with the help of his company's beautiful manager, investigates the family business and finds skullduggery and love in New York City in 1838. (Rev: BL 9/15/01)

4233 Moses, Shelia P. *I, Dred Scott* (8–11). Illus. by Bonnie Christensen. 2005, Simon & Schuster $16.95 (978-0-689-85975-5). In this fictionalized account, Dred Scott, born a slave, chronicles the ultimately unsuccessful 11-year legal battle to win his freedom. (Rev: BCCB 4/05; BL 3/15/05; SLJ 2/05; VOYA 4/05)

4234 Noble, Diane. *The Sister Wife* (11–12). 2010, Avon paper $12.99 (978-00619622-2-6). In this evenhanded look at the beginnings of polygamy set in the mid-19th century, Noble tells the story of Mary Rose, a recent covert to Mormonism, who is dismayed when her husband is advised to take a second wife; for mature readers. (Rev: BL 6/1–15/10)

4235 Paterson, Katherine. *Lyddie* (9–12). 1991, Dutton $18.99 (978-0-525-67338-5). The life and hard times of a young girl growing up in the mid-19th century. (Rev: BL 1/1/91*; SLJ 2/91*)

4236 Paulsen, Gary. *Nightjohn* (6–12). 1993, Delacorte $15.95 (978-0-385-30838-0). Told in the voice of Sarny, 12, Paulsen exposes the myths that African American slaves were content, well cared for, ignorant, and childlike, and that brave, resourceful slaves easily escaped. (Rev: BL 12/15/92)

4237 Preus, Margi. *Heart of a Samurai: Based on the True Story of Nakahama Manjiro* (7–11). Illus. 2010, Abrams $15.95 (978-0-8109-8981-8). This is a fictionalized version of the true story of Manjiro, the 14-year-old Japanese boy rescued from the sea by an American whaling ship in 1841; he becomes known as the first Japanese to set foot in the United States and must make many adjustments. Newbery Honor 2011; ALA Notable Books 2011. (Rev: BL 7/10*; HB 9–10/10; LMC 1–2/11; SLJ 9/1/10*)

4238 Prince, Bryan. *I Came as a Stranger: The Underground Railroad* (7–12). 2004, Tundra paper $15.95 (978-0-88776-667-1). This account tells what happened after the runaway slaves reached Canada and contains material both about famous leaders and about ordinary people involved in the Underground Railroad. (Rev: BL 5/1/04; SLJ 6/04) [971.1]

4239 Rinaldi, Ann. *Mine Eyes Have Seen* (8–12). 1998, Scholastic paper $16.95 (978-0-590-54318-7). The story of the raid at Harper's Ferry is retold through the eyes of John Brown's daughter Annie. (Rev: BL 2/15/98; HBG 9/98; SLJ 2/98; VOYA 4/98)

4240 Salerni, Dianne K. *We Hear the Dead* (8–11). 2010, Sourcebooks paper $12.99 (978-1-4022-3092-9). Explorer Elisha Kane falls in love with beautiful "spiritualist" Maggie Fox in this story based on actual events in the mid-19th century. **e** Lexile 1070L (Rev: BL 4/15/10; LMC 8–9/10; SLJ 6/10)

4241 Schwartz, Virginia Frances. *If I Just Had Two Wings* (6–10). 2001, Stoddart $15.95 (978-0-7737-3302-2). Accompanied by a friend and her two children, a young slave named Phoebe makes a daring escape to Canada and freedom via the Underground Railroad. (Rev: BL 12/1/01; SLJ 12/01; VOYA 12/01)

4242 Siegelson, Kim L. *Honey Bea* (7–10). 2006, Hyperion $15.99 (978-0-7868-0853-3). Beatrice, a young slave in Louisiana, relies on the magic of bees as her work in the master's house leads to discoveries about her past. (Rev: BL 4/15/06)

4243 Styron, William. *The Confessions of Nat Turner* (10–12). 1994, Modern Library paper $14.00 (978-0-679-73663-9). Based on fact, this powerful novel tells of the life of the black slave who led a rebellion at age 31.

4244 Tinti, Hannah. *The Good Thief* (11–12). 2008, Dial $25.00 (978-038533745-8). Despairing orphan Ren's purported long-lost younger brother turns out to be a con-man in this darkly comedic book set in 19th-century New England; for mature readers. Alex Award 2009. ∩ **e** (Rev: BL 6/1–15/08*)

4245 Torrey, Michele. *Voyage of Midnight* (8–11). 2006, Knopf $15.95 (978-0-375-82382-4). In the early 19th century, orphan Philip joins his uncle's crew and is shocked to find that his uncle is a slave trader; when the crew and slaves are blinded by a disease, Philip takes matters into his own hands and steers the ship back to Africa. (Rev: BL 12/15/06; SLJ 1/07)

4246 Vida, Nina. *The Texicans* (10–12). 2006, Soho $23.00 (978-1-56947-434-1). A rich, multilayered story about immigrants struggling to make their way in mid-19th-century Texas, a time of cholera outbreaks, Indian troubles, and new settlements. (Rev: SLJ 11/06)

4247 Watts, Leander. *Wild Ride to Heaven* (9–12). 2003, Houghton Mifflin $16.00 (978-0-618-26805-4). Hannah's father sells her to two men, but the plucky protagonist with the two strangely unmatched eyes manages to escape in this story set in 1800s New York state. (Rev: BL 11/1/03; HBG 4/04; SLJ 11/03; VOYA 4/04)

4248 Wilson, Diane Lee. *Black Storm Comin'* (7–10). 2005, Simon & Schuster $16.95 (978-0-689-87137-5). Son of a white father and a freed-slave mother, 12-year-old Colton Westcott joins the Pony Express in an effort to make sure his mother and siblings finally make it to the West Coast. (Rev: BL 8/05*; SLJ 7/05; VOYA 10/05)

THE CIVIL WAR (1861–1865)

4249 Brooks, Geraldine. *March* (9–12). 2005, Viking $24.95 (978-0-670-03335-5). Styled like a 19th-century novel, this explores the imagined life of Captain March, the father in Alcott's *Little Women*. (Rev: BL 2/1/05; SLJ 7/05)

4250 Brown, Dee Alexander. *The Way to Bright Star* (10–12). 1998, Forge $24.95 (978-0-312-86612-9). An adventure story, set in the American frontier during the Civil War, about Ben Butterfield, his friends, and the dangers they confront on a wagon train traveling through war-torn territory. (Rev: BL 5/1/98; SLJ 3/99)

4251 Brown, Linda Beatrice. *Black Angels* (9–12). 2009, Putnam $16.99 (978-0-399-25030-9). Toward the end of the Civil War, three children — two black and one white — become unlikely companions and bond over the violence they've witnessed. **e** Lexile 840L (Rev: BL 9/1/09; LMC 11–12/09; SLJ 1/10)

4252 Bruchac, Joseph. *March Toward the Thunder* (7–10). 2008, Dial $16.99 (978-0-8037-3188-2). In this story of a Canadian Indian who enters the Civil War with the Irish Brigade, readers are introduced to many important figures, issues, and lessons of the war. (Rev: BL 4/15/08; SLJ 7/08)

4253 Collier, James Lincoln, and Christopher Collier. *With Every Drop of Blood: A Novel of the Civil War* (6–10). 1994, Dell paper $5.99 (978-0-440-21983-5). A Civil War docunovel about Johnny, a young Confederate soldier, and Cush, a black Union soldier who captures him. Together, the two experience the horrors of war and bigotry. (Rev: BL 7/94; SLJ 8/94; VOYA 12/94)

4254 Elliott, L. M. *Annie, Between the States* (7–11). 2004, HarperCollins LB $16.99 (978-0-06-001211-3). As the Civil War rages around her northern Virginia home, 15-year-old Annie finds her feelings about the North-South conflict evolving. (Rev: BL 12/1/04; SLJ 11/04)

4255 Ernst, Kathleen. *Ghosts of Vicksburg* (6–10). 2003, White Mane paper $8.95 (978-1-57249-322-3). Jamie and Elisha, 15-year-old Union Army soldiers from Wisconsin, experience the horrors of war as their forces march to Mississippi. (Rev: SLJ 12/03)

4256 Frazier, Charles. *Cold Mountain* (10–12). 1997, Atlantic Monthly $24.00 (978-0-87113-679-4). In this best-selling novel set during Civil War times, a soldier deserts and treks through the wilderness to Cold Mountain, where two women, Ruby and Ada, are trying to eke out a living. (Rev: BL 6/1–15/97; SLJ 11/97)

4257 Gibbons, Kaye. *On the Occasion of My Last Afternoon* (10–12). 1998, Avon paper $13.00 (978-0-380-73214-2). This novel, set before and during the Civil War, tells of the childhood of a Southern belle, her marriage to a Northern doctor, and her transformation from a self-absorbed child to a loving, mature wife and mother. (Rev: BL 5/15/98; SLJ 9/98)

4258 Gindlesperger, James. *Escape from Libby Prison* (10–12). 1996, Burd Street $24.95 (978-0-942597-97-4). Fictional characters and figures from history are interwoven in this novel about the escape of 109 Union officers from the gruesome hell known as Libby Prison during the Civil War. (Rev: SLJ 2/97)

4259 Gourley, Catherine. *The Horrors of Andersonville: Life and Death Inside a Civil War Prison* (9–12). 2010, Lerner LB $38.60 (978-0-7613-4212-0). Gourley draws on primary sources including soldiers' memoirs to tell the story of the Confederate prisoner-of-war camp and the dreadful conditions there. Lexile 990L (Rev: BL 3/1/10; LMC 8–9/10; SLJ 4/10)

4260 Greenberg, Martin H., and Charles G. Waugh, eds. *Civil War Women II: Stories by Women About Women* (7–10). 1997, August House paper $9.95 (978-0-87483-487-1). A collection of short stories by such female writers as Louisa May Alcott and Edith Wharton that deal with women's lives during the Civil War. (Rev: SLJ 8/97)

4261 Hart, Lenore. *Becky: The Life and Loves of Becky Thatcher* (9–12). 2008, St. Martin's $24.95 (978-0-312-37327-6). This novel takes the characters from Twain's works into adulthood during the Civil War. Becky Thatcher is on a quest to find her Union soldier husband Sid after reading his mysterious letter, getting assistance from Huck Finn, reuniting with Tom, and resuming the past conflicts and bonds they shared. (Rev: BL 12/1/07)

4262 Hughes, Pat. *Guerrilla Season* (7–12). 2003, Farrar $18.00 (978-0-374-32811-5). This multilayered novel clearly conveys the confusion that Matt, 15, feels in the face of the approaching violence of the Civil War. **e** (Rev: BL 8/03; HBG 4/04; SLJ 11/03; VOYA 12/03)

4263 Johnson, Charles. *Soulcatcher and Other Stories* (10–12). 2001, Harvest paper $12.00 (978-0-15-601112-9). Based on solid research, these 12 short stories dramatize various aspects of slavery and its cruelty. (Rev: BL 3/1/01)

4264 Jones, Madison. *Nashville 1864: The Dying of the Light* (10–12). 1997, Sanders $17.95 (978-1-879941-35-9). This novel, set during the Civil War, tells of 12-year-old Steven who, with his slave, Dink, sets out to locate his father who is fighting on the Confederate side. (Rev: SLJ 1/98)

4265 Joslyn, Mauriel Phillips. *Shenandoah Autumn: Courage Under Fire* (6–10). 1999, White Mane paper $8.95 (978-1-57249-137-3). During the Civil War, young Mattie and her mother, though afraid of the Union troops around their Virginia home, save a wounded Confederate soldier and return him to his companions. (Rev: BL 5/1/99)

4266 Kantor, MacKinlay. *Andersonville* (10–12). 1955, World Pub. paper $23.00 (978-0-452-26956-9). A realistic, harrowing novel about the prisoners and guards in the notorious southern prison during the Civil War.

4267 Klein, Lisa. *Two Girls of Gettysburg* (7–10). 2008, Bloomsbury $16.99 (978-159990105-3). The voices of two young women — quiet, dutiful Lizzie and frivolous Rosanna — are woven together to tell the story of the Battle of Gettysburg. Lexile 830L (Rev: BL 9/1/08; SLJ 11/1/08; VOYA 12/08)

4268 Meriwether, Louise. *Fragments of the Ark* (9–12). 1995, Pocket paper $10.00 (978-0-671-79948-9). Based on a true account, this historical novel is about a group of slaves who escaped to join Union forces and the bigotry they faced from their "rescuers." (Rev: BL 2/15/94; SLJ 11/94)

4269 Mitchell, Margaret. *Gone with the Wind* (9–12). 1936, Avon paper $6.50 (978-0-380-00109-5). The magnificent Civil War novel about Scarlett O'Hara and her family at Tara.

4270 Moreau, C. X. *Promise of Glory* (10–12). 2000, Tor $24.95 (978-0-312-87272-4). Authentic historical characters are re-created in this novel about the battle at Antietam Creek in Maryland, the bloodiest battle of the Civil War. (Rev: BL 9/15/00)

4271 Moss, Marissa. *A Soldier's Secret: The Incredible True Story of Sarah Edmonds, a Civil War Hero* (7–12). Illus. 2012, Abrams $16.95 (978-1-4197-0427-7). This novel drawing on her own journals and correspondence tells the story of the woman who served in various capacities for the Union Army in the Civil War using the name of Frank Thompson. e Lexile 860L (Rev: BL 11/15/12; LMC 3–4/13; SLJ 11/12)

4272 Myers, Anna. *Assassin* (7–12). 2005, Walker $16.95 (978-0-8027-8989-1). The events surrounding the assassination of Abraham Lincoln are explored in this fictionalized account, narrated in alternating chapters by a teenage White House seamstress and assassin John Wilkes Booth. (Rev: BL 10/1/05; SLJ 12/05; VOYA 10/05)

4273 Myers, Walter Dean. *Riot* (7–12). 2009, Egmont $16.99 (978-1-60684-000-9); LB $19.99 (978-1-60684-042-9). Set in New York City in the summer of 1863, this story presented in screenplay format follows Claire, a biracial teen who lives amidst the chaos, ethnic tension, and anxiety of the Civil War and the riots that took place when Irish immigrants protested the draft. ⌒

e (Rev: BL 8/09*; LMC 11–12/09; SLJ 9/09; VOYA 12/09)

4274 Olmstead, Robert. *Coal Black Horse* (10–12). 2007, Algonquin $22.95 (978-1-56512-521-6). Fourteen-year-old Robey is witness to many horrors as he searches for his father on a Civil War battlefield in this well-written novel. (Rev: BL 1/1–15/07; SLJ 6/07)

4275 Peck, Richard. *The River Between Us* (7–12). 2003, Dial $16.99 (978-0-8037-2735-9). In 1861 Illinois, Tilly's family makes room for two young women of different complexions from the South. (Rev: BL 9/15/03*; HB 9–10/03; HBG 4/04; SLJ 9/03; VOYA 10/03)

4276 Reasoner, James. *Antietam* (10–12). Series: Civil War Battle. 2000, Cumberland House $22.95 (978-1-58182-084-3). This novel, part three of the eight-volume Civil War Battle series, uses the background of the Battle of Antietam to tell the story of the six young Brannon brothers and sisters. (Rev: BL 5/15/00; VOYA 12/00)

4277 Rinaldi, Ann. *Come Juneteenth* (8–11). 2007, Harcourt $17.00 (978-0-15-205947-7). The news of emancipation was slow to arrive to parts of Texas, and when it did, not everyone believed it, as readers will learn from this story of young slaves Luli and Sis Goose. (Rev: BCCB 9/07; BL 2/15/07; LMC 8–9/07; SLJ 5/07)

4278 Rinaldi, Ann. *In My Father's House* (7–10). 1993, Scholastic paper $14.95 (978-0-590-44730-0). A coming-of-age novel set during the Civil War about 7-year-old Oscie. (Rev: BL 2/15/93)

4279 Sappey, Maureen Stack. *Letters from Vinnie* (7–10). 1999, Front St $16.95 (978-1-886910-31-7). A novel that mixes fact and fiction to tell the story of the tiny woman who sculpted the large statue of Abraham Lincoln found in the Capitol Building in Washington. (Rev: BL 9/15/99; HBG 4/00; SLJ 11/99; VOYA 2/00)

4280 Severance, John B. *Braving the Fire* (7–12). 2002, Clarion $15.00 (978-0-618-22999-4). Jem finds war is far from the "glory" described by others in this coming-of-age story set in the realistic horrors of the Civil War. (Rev: BL 10/1/02; HBG 10/03; SLJ 11/02)

4281 Shaara, Jeff. *Gods and Generals* (10–12). 1996, Ballantine $25.00 (978-0-345-40492-3). This clever novel of the Civil War is told from the viewpoint of four important generals, Lee, Jackson, Hancock, and Chamberlin. (Rev: SLJ 8/97)

4282 Stone, Irving. *Love Is Eternal* (10–12). 1994, Buccaneer LB $27.95 (978-1-56849-556-9). A lengthy, rewarding novel about Lincoln's marriage to Mary Todd.

4283 West, Jessamyn. *The Friendly Persuasion* (9–12). 1982, Buccaneer LB $27.95 (978-0-89966-395-1). The pacifist views of the Quaker Birdwell family cause problems during the Civil War.

4284 Wilson, John. *Death on the River* (8–10). 2009, Orca paper $12.95 (978-1-55469-111-1). Jake, a young Union soldier, survives the horrors of Andersonville prison but then worries about the support he gets from a fellow prisoner. **e** Lexile 890 (Rev: BL 10/15/09; LMC 1–2/10; SLJ 11/09)

WESTWARD EXPANSION AND PIONEER LIFE

4285 Aldrich, Bess Streeter. *A Lantern in Her Hand* (9–12). 1983, Amereon LB $21.95 (978-0-88411-260-0). This novel, originally published in 1928, tells about a young bride and her husband who are homesteaders in Nebraska in 1865. A sequel is *A White Bird Flying.*

4286 Ammerman, Mark. *Longshot* (10–12). Series: The Cross and the Tomahawk. 2000, Horizon paper $11.99 (978-1-889651-65-1). Part of a series of novels about the Narragansett Indians, this one deals with an explorer-missionary and his Narragansett friend, who travel into the West in the mid-18th century to establish a settlement. (Rev: BL 6/1–15/00*)

4287 Berger, Thomas. *Little Big Man* (10–12). 1979, Dial paper $14.95 (978-0-385-29829-2). The amazing historical novel about Jack Crabb, who was a survivor of Custer's last stand.

4288 Blair, Clifford. *The Guns of Sacred Heart* (9–12). 1991, Walker $18.95 (978-0-8027-4123-3). Outlaws trying to free their leader, who is a prisoner at a remote mission school, are fought off by a marshal, a cowboy, and the school's staff and students. (Rev: BL 11/1/91; SLJ 5/92)

4289 Bonner, Cindy. *Lily* (9–12). 1992, Algonquin $17.95 (978-0-945575-95-5). An old-fashioned Western romance in which an innocent girl falls in love with a worldly guy from an outlaw family. (Rev: BL 9/1/92*; SLJ 12/92)

4290 Bowers, Terrell L. *Ride Against the Wind* (7–10). 1996, Walker $21.95 (978-0-8027-4156-1). Set in Eden, Kansas, in the late 1800s, this sequel to *The Secret of Snake Canyon* (1993) involves Jerrod Danmyer and his attachment to Marion Gates, daughter of his family's sworn enemies. (Rev: BL 12/15/96; VOYA 8/97)

4291 Bruchac, Joseph. *Sacajawea: The Story of Bird Woman and the Lewis and Clark Expedition* (7–10). 2000, Harcourt $17.00 (978-0-15-202234-1). Told in alternating chapters by Sacajawea and William Clark, this novel re-creates the famous cross-country journey of Lewis and Clark. (Rev: BL 4/1/00; HBG 9/00; SLJ 5/00)

4292 Charbonneau, Eileen. *Rachel LeMoyne* (10–12). Series: Women of the West. 1998, Forge $22.95 (978-0-312-86448-4). An adventure story, based on fact, about a mixed-blood Choctaw student who goes to Ireland to help famine victims, marries, and returns to America with her Irish husband to cross the frontier to settle in Oregon. (Rev: BL 5/15/98; SLJ 2/99; VOYA 12/98)

4293 Curtis, Jack. *Pepper Tree Rider* (9–12). 1994, Walker $19.95 (978-0-8027-4137-0). A subtle Western where a fast gun isn't always the answer; from the pen of the screenplay writer of *Gunsmoke.* (Rev: BL 5/1/94; SLJ 10/94)

4294 DeAndrea, William L. *Written in Fire* (9–12). 1995, Walker $19.95 (978-0-8027-3270-5). A mystery story set in the Wyoming Territory in the 1800s featuring Quinn Booker, a pulp fiction novelist who investigates the near-fatal shooting of his friend Lobo Blacke. (Rev: BL 1/1–15/96; VOYA 2/96)

4295 Doig, Ivan. *The Whistling Season* (11–12). 2006, Harcourt $25.00 (978-0-15-101237-4). Paul Milliron, in charge of schools in late 1950s Montana, looks back on his own 7th grade in a one-room school in 1910, the year in which Halley's Comet came and his motherless family got a housekeeper. (Rev: BL 12/15/05)

4296 Estleman, Loren D. *Journey of the Dead* (10–12). 1998, St. Martin's $21.95 (978-0-312-85999-2). A western for mature readers about Pat Garrett, Billy the Kid's killer, and how he is haunted by the ghost of the dead outlaw. (Rev: SLJ 10/98)

4297 Ferber, Edna. *Cimarron* (9–12). 1998, Amereon $28.95 (978-0-88411-548-9). The story of the fortunes of Yancey Cravat and his wife Sabra set against the days of the land rush of 1889 in Oklahoma. Also use: *Saratoga Trunk* (1986).

4298 Grey, Zane. *Riders of the Purple Sage* (9–12). 1990, Viking paper $12.00 (978-0-14-018440-2). This is probably the best known of Grey's westerns, a number of which are available in paperback. This one takes place in the wilderness of Utah in 1871.

4299 Hemphill, Helen. *The Adventurous Deeds of Deadwood Jones* (7–12). 2008, Front St $16.95 (978-159078637-6). Inspired by the true story of an African American cowboy, this book tells the story of Prometheus Jones, who rides a raffle-won horse away from racist-riddled Tennessee to adventure in the Wild West. **e** Lexile 720L (Rev: BL 10/1/08; HB 1–2/09; LMC 1–2/09; SLJ 12/08)

4300 Holt, Kimberly Willis. *The Water Seeker* (7–12). 2010, Henry Holt $16.99 (978-0-8050-8020-9). Young Amos travels the Oregon Trail with his father and takes on adult responsibilities out of necessity. Lexile 730L (Rev: BL 4/15/10; LMC 8–9/10; SLJ 7/10)

4301 Houston, James D. *Snow Mountain Passage* (10–12). 2001, Knopf $24.00 (978-0-375-41103-8). A gripping novel that reconstructs the drama and tragedy of the Donner party and its ill-fated trek west. (Rev: BL 4/1/01; SLJ 11/01)

4302 Kirkpatrick, Jane. *All Together in One Place* (10–12). 2000, WaterBrook paper $11.95 (978-1-57856-232-9). Faith and courage are key elements in this novel about pioneers on the Oregon Trail heading west in 1850. (Rev: BL 6/1–15/00*)

4303 Laxalt, Robert. *Dust Devils* (6–10). 1997, Univ. of Nevada paper $16.00 (978-0-87417-300-0). A Native American teenager named Ira sets out to retrieve his prize-winning horse that has been stolen by a rustler named Hawkeye. (Rev: BL 10/15/97; VOYA 12/98)

4304 Leigh, Ana. *The Lawman Said "I Do"* (11–12). 2006, Pocket paper $6.99 (978-0-7434-6996-8). In this compelling western romance suitable for mature teens, Colt Fraser, a former Confederate soldier bound for California, foils a stagecoach robbery, wins a temporary job as deputy in a small New Mexico town, and falls in love with the sheriff's daughter. (Rev: BL 12/1/05)

4305 McClain, Margaret S. *Bellboy: A Mule Train Journey* (6–10). 1989, New Mexico $17.95 (978-0-9622468-1-4). Set in California in the 1870s, this is the story of a 12-year-old boy and his first job on a mule train. (Rev: BL 3/1/90; SLJ 3/90)

4306 McDonald, Brix. *Riding on the Wind* (5–10). 1998, Avenue paper $5.95 (978-0-9661306-0-7). In frontier Wyoming during the early 1860s, 15-year-old Carrie Sutton is determined to become a rider in the Pony Express after her family's ranch has been chosen as a relay station. (Rev: SLJ 1/99)

4307 McKernan, Victoria. *The Devil's Paintbox* (8–12). 2009, Knopf $16.99 (978-037583750-0). Orphans Aiden, 15, and his younger sister Maddy face disease, death, and disasters as they travel with a wagon train from Kansas to Oregon in 1866. **e** Lexile 740L (Rev: BL 1/1–15/09; LMC 5–6/09; SLJ 2/1/09*; VOYA 4/09)

4308 McMurtry, Larry. *Lonesome Dove: A Novel* (9–12). 1985, Simon & Schuster paper $7.99 (978-0-671-68390-0). Two former Texas Rangers head north from the Mexican border to find fame and fortune in this fine western novel.

4309 Meyer, Carolyn. *Where the Broken Heart Still Beats: The Story of Cynthia Ann Parker* (7–12). 1992, Harcourt paper $7.00 (978-0-15-295602-8). A fictional retelling of the abduction of Cynthia Parker, who was stolen by Comanches as a child and lived with them for 24 years, first as a slave, then as a chief's wife. (Rev: BL 12/1/92; SLJ 9/92)

4310 Mitchell, Saundra. *The Springsweet* (7–10). 2012, Harcourt $16.99 (978-054760842-6). Tells the story of 17-year-old Zora's move from Baltimore to Oklahoma Territory in the late 1800s, and her adjustment to the hard life there — and to the knowledge that she has the power to find water underground. **e** (Rev: BLO 4/1/12; SLJ 4/12)

4311 Moore, Robin. *The Bread Sister of Sinking Creek* (7–10). 1990, HarperCollins LB $14.89 (978-0-397-32419-4). An orphaned 14-year-old girl becomes a servant in Pennsylvania during pioneer days. (Rev: BL 7/90; SLJ 4/90; VOYA 8/90)

4312 Nesbitt, John D. *Twin Rivers* (9–12). 1995, Walker $19.95 (978-0-8027-4152-3). This western, set in the Wyoming countryside, involves Clay Westbrook, a wrangler who must fight a challenge to the claim he has filed for 160 acres of land, and the Mexican girl he loves. (Rev: BL 1/1–15/96; VOYA 6/96)

4313 Nowak, Pamela. *Choices* (11–12). 2009, Five Star $25.95 (978-159414810-1). In 1876 Miriam reluctantly leaves boarding school and returns to her military family in the Dakota Territory, where she must endure the harsh treatment of her drug-addicted mother and prejudices that stifle her independence. (Rev: BL 10/1/09*)

4314 Parnham, I. J. *Miss Dempsey's School for Gunslingers* (9–12). 2005, Avalon $21.95 (978-0-8034-9690-3). Con games and corruption abound in Destiny, a frontier town where even the contest for Miss Destiny's hand is crooked. (Rev: BL 1/1–15/05)

4315 Riefe, Barbara. *Westward Hearts: The Amelia Dale Archer Story* (10–12). 1998, Forge $22.95 (978-0-312-86077-6). In the 1850s, Dr. Amelia Archer and her four granddaughters face hardships and danger as they travel by wagon trail west to Los Angeles, where she believes women have a chance to be recognized on their own merit. (Rev: SLJ 2/99)

4316 Schaefer, Jack. *Shane* (9–12). 1954, Houghton Mifflin $18.00 (978-0-395-07090-1). A stranger enters the Starret household and helps them fight an oppressive land baron.

4317 Snelling, Lauraine. *A Dream to Follow* (10–12). Series: Return to Red River. 2001, Bethany House paper $11.99 (978-0-7642-2317-4). This first installment in a new Christian-based historical series about the Bjorklund family of North Dakota (first seen in the Red River of the North series) features Thorliff and his college aspirations. (Rev: BL 8/01; VOYA 4/02)

4318 Snelling, Lauraine. *An Untamed Land* (9–12). Series: Red River of the North. 1996, Bethany House paper $9.99 (978-1-55661-576-4). This novel re-creates the experiences of the two Bjorklund brothers of Norway as they struggle to farm in the Dakota prairies, as told by the wife of the elder brother. (Rev: VOYA 8/96)

4319 Turner, Nancy E. *Sarah's Quilt: The Diary of Sarah Agnes Prine, 1906* (11–12). 2005, St. Martin's $24.95 (978-0-312-33262-4). The determined, twice-widowed Sarah deals with drought and thievery as she struggles to hold onto her Arizona ranch. (Rev: BL 3/1/05)

4320 Watson, Jude. *Impetuous: Mattie's Story* (9–12). Series: Brides of Wildcat County. 1996, Simon & Schuster paper $3.99 (978-0-614-15784-0). In this title in the Brides of Wildcat County series, tomboy Mattie comes to Last Chance, a California mining town, as a mail-order bride but decides she wants to be independent upon discovering that she can do anything a man can do. (Rev: VOYA 6/96)

4321 Wheeler, Richard S. *Second Lives: A Novel of the Gilded Age* (10–12). 1997, Forge $24.95 (978-0-312-86330-2). A novel about ordinary people, their aspirations, failures, and fulfillments, in Denver during the late 1880s. (Rev: SLJ 4/98)

4322 Whitson, Stephanie Grace. *Sixteen Brides* (10–12). 2010, Bethany paper $14.99 (978-07642051-3-2). Aghast to find they'd been promised as frontier brides, a group of women arrive on the Nebraska prairie and decide to overcome their troubled pasts by pooling their resources and building a house together. ⋒ ℮ (Rev: BL 4/1/10*)

4323 Wister, Owen. *The Virginian* (10–12). 1988, Viking paper $12.00 (978-0-14-039065-0). The classic novel of the American West first published in 1902 and containing the phrase "When you call me that, smile."

4324 Wolf, Allan. *New Found Land: Lewis and Clark's Voyage of Discovery* (7–12). 2004, Candlewick $18.99 (978-0-7636-2113-1). Seaman the dog, here called Oolum, is the primary narrator of this verse account of the famous expedition that draws heavily on such primary source documents as letters and journals. (Rev: BL 9/04; SLJ 9/04)

RECONSTRUCTION TO WORLD WAR I
(1865–1914)

4325 Bass, Ruth. *Sarah's Daughter* (8–10). 2007, Gadd $14.95 (978-0-9774053-4-3). When 14-year-old Rose's mother dies, she must look after her family and the farm while her father goes out carousing in this novel set in the 1800s. (Rev: BL 7/07)

4326 Bigsby, Christopher. *Beautiful Dreamer* (10–12). 2006, St. Martin's $21.95 (978-0-312-35583-8). When a white man is friendly to a black man, one is injured and the other lynched for it in this painful, disturbing story about the realities of life in Tennessee in the not-so-distant past. (Rev: BL 5/1/06; SLJ 7/06)

4327 Brewer, James D. *No Justice* (10–12). 1996, Walker $21.95 (978-0-8057-3283-2). Set along the Mississippi River during Reconstruction, this adult novel features an unlikely trio — a woman who makes a living entertaining gentlemen on riverboats, a former Union soldier, and a wounded Southern soldier — who join forces to solve a murder mystery. (Rev: SLJ 12/96)

4328 Burns, Olive Ann. *Cold Sassy Tree* (9–12). 1984, Ticknor $28.00 (978-0-89919-309-0). Fourteen-year-old Will has a crush on his grandfather's young bride in this novel set in turn-of-the-century Georgia. (Rev: BL 6/87)

4329 Carroll, Lenore. *One Hundred Girls' Mother* (10–12). 1998, Forge $24.95 (978-0-312-85994-7). An inspiring story, based on fact, about a mission director in San Francisco's Chinatown at the turn of the century and her efforts to save Chinese girls sold into slavery or prostitution. (Rev: BL 8/98; SLJ 11/98)

4330 Davies, Jacqueline. *Lost* (7–10). 2009, Marshall Cavendish $16.99 (978-076145535-6). Sixteen-year-

old Essie, who works in the Triangle Shirtwaist Factory in the early 1900s, must come to terms with losses in her life in this multilayered story. Lexile 680L (Rev: BL 3/15/09; LMC 8–9/09; SLJ 4/1/09; VOYA 8/09)

4331 Donnelly, Jennifer. *A Northern Light* (10–12). 2003, Harcourt $17.00 (978-0-15-216705-9). Set in upstate New York in 1906 against the backdrop of a murder that also inspired Dreiser's *An American Tragedy*, this story is about 16-year-old Mattie and the choice she must make between continuing her education and getting married. (Rev: BCCB 7–8/03; BL 5/15/04; HB 5–6/03; HBG 10/03; LMC 10/03; SLJ 5/03; VOYA 4/03)

4332 Faulkner, William. *The Reivers: A Reminiscence* (10–12). 1962, Random House paper $12.00 (978-0-679-74192-3). One of Faulkner's gentler novels, about an 11-year-old boy in small-town Mississippi in 1905.

4333 Godbersen, Anna. *The Luxe* (9–12). 2007, HarperTeen $17.99 (978-0-06-134566-1). Readers will discover that New York City society girls haven't changed much since 1899 in this juicy romance set in the Gilded Age. (Rev: BL 11/15/07; SLJ 12/07)

4334 Hale, Marian. *The Goodbye Season* (7–10). 2009, Henry Holt $16.99 (978-080508855-7). Sixteen-year-old Mercy Kaplan, daughter of a Texas sharecropper, struggles to make her way after her family dies in the 1918 flu epidemic. (Rev: BL 7/09; SLJ 10/09)

4335 Hatcher, Robin Lee. *A Matter of Character* (11–12). Series: Sisters of Bethlehem Springs. 2010, Zondervan paper $14.99 (978-03102580-7-0). Daphne decides to reveal the truth — that she's been writing dime novels under a pseudonym — when she encounters a man determined to clear the reputation of one of her characters in this faith-based romance set in 1918. (Rev: BL 6/1–15/10)

4336 Hesse, Karen. *Brooklyn Bridge* (7–12). 2008, Feiwel & Friends $17.95 (978-0-312-37886-8). Set in 1903 Brooklyn, this story alternates chapters about 14-year-old Joe, whose immigrant family manufactures America's first teddy bears, and abandoned children fending for themselves in the shadow of the Brooklyn Bridge; includes interesting final notes about the history of teddy bears. Sidney Taylor Book Award 2009. ⋒ (Rev: BL 8/08; SLJ 9/08)

4337 Kephart, Beth. *Dangerous Neighbors* (8–12). 2010, Egmont $16.99 (978-1-60684-080-1); LB $19.99 (978-1-60684-106-8). In 1876 during the Philadelphia Centennial Exhibition 17-year-old Katherine is contemplating suicide in her grief over her twin sister's death, but the celebration itself serves to bring her out of her despondency. ℮ Lexile 930L (Rev: BL 9/1/10; LMC 1–2/11; SLJ 10/1/10)

4338 LaFaye, A. *The Keening* (7–10). 2010, Milkweed $17 (978-1-57131-692-9). When 14-year-old Lyza's mother dies in the flu epidemic of 1918, her father begins acting strangely and Lyza learns that both she and her father can communicate with the dead. (Rev: BL 4/15/10; LMC 8–9/10; SLJ 6/10)

4339 Lavender, William. *Aftershocks* (9–12). 2006, Harcourt $17.00 (978-0-15-205882-1). In San Francisco in 1906, 14-year-old Jessie faces upheavals — an argument with her father over her wish to become a doctor, the discovery that her father has impregnated their Chinese maid, and a major earthquake. (Rev: BL 3/1/06; VOYA 4/06)

4340 Lerangis, Peter. *Smiler's Bones* (7–10). 2005, Scholastic $16.95 (978-0-439-34485-2). Lerangis brings alive the sad story, based on truth, of an Inuit boy named Minik, who, with his father and four others, was brought to New York City in the late 19th century by explorer Robert Peary. (Rev: BCCB 6/05; BL 4/1/05; SLJ 6/05; VOYA 8/05)

4341 Lowry, Lois. *The Silent Boy* (6–10). 2003, Houghton Mifflin $15.00 (978-0-618-28231-9). Young Katy, who has a comfortable existence as a doctor's daughter in early-20th-century New England, makes friends with a mentally backward boy and learns that there are tragedies in life. (Rev: BL 4/15/03; HB 5–6/03; HBG 10/03; SLJ 4/03)

4342 Marshall, Catherine. *Christy* (8–12). 1976, Avon paper $7.99 (978-0-380-00141-5). This story set in Appalachia in 1912 tells about a spunky young girl who goes there to teach. (Rev: BL 5/1/89)

4343 Morris, Lynn, and Gilbert Morris. *Toward the Sunrising* (10–12). 1996, Bethany House paper $10.99 (978-1-55661-425-5). A complex novel about a feisty Yankee woman doctor, Cheney Duvall, and her struggles in Charleston, South Carolina, during Reconstruction. (Rev: SLJ 8/96; VOYA 10/96)

4344 Morrison, Toni. *Beloved: A Novel* (10–12). 1987, Vintage paper $10.40 (978-1-4000-3341-6). This powerful novel deals with a runaway slave, Sethe, and the terrible past she has experienced.

4345 Napoli, Donna Jo. *Alligator Bayou* (7–10). 2009, Random House $16.99 (978-038574654-0). Based on a true event — a lynching of Sicilian immigrants in Louisiana in 1899 — this novel follows young Calogero, who is shut out of both black and white society. YALSA Top Ten 2010. Lexile HL430L (Rev: BL 2/15/09; LMC 8–9/09; SLJ 5/1/09; VOYA 4/09)

4346 Nowak, Pamela. *Chances* (9–12). 2008, Five Star $25.95 (978-1-59414-637-4). In 1876 Denver telegraph operator Sarah Donovan demonstrates that she is not afraid to overstep what was considered a woman's boundaries and stands up for everything and anything that she believes in, including the woman's suffrage movement. (Rev: BL 12/15/07)

4347 Richards, Jame. *Three Rivers Rising* (7–11). 2010, Knopf $16.99 (978-0-375-85885-7). Three characters caught up in the disaster tell their stories of survival fol-

lowing the 1889 Johnstown Flood. 🎧 Lexile HL780L (Rev: BL 4/15/10; LMC 8–9/10; SLJ 4/10)

4348 Sawyer, Kim Vogel. *In Every Heartbeat* (10–12). 2010, Bethany $19.99 (978-076420510-1); paper $14.99 (978-07642051-0-1). Three friends get scholarships to college in 1914, and cope with the competition, strife, and differing ambitions that opportunity brings in this novel with a Christian message. 🎧 (Rev: BL 8/10)

4349 Schmidt, Gary D. *Lizzie Bright and the Buckminster Boy* (7–12). 2004, Clarion $15.00 (978-0-618-43929-4). When Turner, son of a rigid minister, moves with his family to a small town in Maine during 1912, he doesn't fit in. Newbery Honor 2005; Printz Honor 2005. (Rev: BL 5/15/04*; SLJ 5/04)

4350 Shivers, Louise. *A Whistling Woman* (9–12). 1993, Longstreet $15.00 (978-1-56352-085-3). Set in North Carolina after the Civil War, this novel examines the relationship between a mother and daughter. (Rev: BL 8/93*)

4351 Sinclair, Upton. *The Jungle* (10–12). 1981, Bantam paper $5.95 (978-0-553-21245-7). This frequently brutal novel tells about working in the Chicago stockyards at the turn of the 20th century.

4352 Smith, Betty. *A Tree Grows in Brooklyn* (9–12). 1943, Buccaneer LB $21.95 (978-0-89966-303-6). The touching story of Francie Nolan growing up in a poor section of Williamsburg in Brooklyn during the early 1900s.

4353 Stewart, Elizabeth. *The Lynching of Louie Sam* (7–12). 2012, Annick $21.95 (978-1-55451-439-7); paper $12.95 (978-1-55451-438-0). In 1884, 15-year-old George Gillies witnesses a lynching and later worries that the young Native American was in fact innocent. 🄴 Lexile 840L (Rev: BL 12/15/12; LMC 3–4/13; SLJ 9/12)

4354 Tal, Eve. *Double Crossing: A Jewish Immigration Story* (7–10). 2005, Cinco Puntos $16.95 (978-0-938317-94-4). At the beginning of the 20th century, young Raizel and her Orthodox Jewish grandfather travel from Europe to New York only to find they are rejected by immigration officials. (Rev: BL 8/05*; SLJ 10/05; VOYA 4/06)

4355 Tall, Eve. *Cursing Columbus* (7–10). 2009, Cinco Puntos $16.95 (978-1-933693-59-0). In this sequel to *Double Crossing* (2005), 14-year-old Raizel and her younger brother Lemmel react in opposite ways to the challenges of being Ukrainian Jewish immigrants on the Lower East Side of Manhattan in 1908. 🄴 Lexile 500L (Rev: BL 10/15/09; LMC 5–6/10; SLJ 1/10)

4356 Taylor, Ardell L. D. *Whistling Girl* (10–12). 2001, Five Star $25.95 (978-0-7862-2854-6). In the 1880s, Anita Aldon, who lives on the family ranch in California, meets wealthy young John Vanderburg and love blossoms. (Rev: BL 12/15/00)

4357 Taylor, Kim. *Bowery Girl* (8–11). 2006, Viking $16.99 (978-0-670-05966-9). A realistic story about orphaned teen girls who resort to picking pockets and prostitution to survive in late-19th-century New York City. (Rev: BL 3/1/06; SLJ 3/06; VOYA 4/06)

4358 Taylor, Mildred D. *The Land* (7–12). 2001, Penguin $17.99 (978-0-8037-1950-7). In this prequel to *Roll of Thunder, Hear My Cry* (1976), Taylor weaves her own family history into a moving story of a young man of mixed parentage facing prejudice, cruelty, and betrayal during the time of Reconstruction. (Rev: BCCB 10/01; BL 8/01; HB 9–10/01; HBG 3/02; SLJ 8/01; VOYA 10/01)

4359 Welsh, T. K. *The Unresolved* (7–12). 2006, Dutton $15.99 (978-0-525-47731-0). The story of the *General Slocum* steamship disaster of 1904, told from the point of view of Mallory, the ghost of one of the victims. (Rev: SLJ 9/06)

4360 Wemmlinger, Raymond. *Booth's Daughter* (8–11). 2007, Boyds Mills $17.95 (978-1-932425-86-4). The niece of John Wilkes Booth, who assassinated Lincoln, and the daughter of famous actor Edwin Booth, Edwina must find an identity apart from her famous family in this novel set in the Gilded Age. (Rev: BCCB 6/07; BL 2/15/07; LMC 10/07; SLJ 9/07)

4361 Wilson, Diane Lee. *Firehorse* (7–10). 2006, Simon & Schuster $16.95 (978-1-4169-1551-5). Rachel, 15, living in 1872 Boston, loves horses and dreams of becoming a veterinarian, despite what her family and society thinks; when she saves a fire-station horse that has been severely burned, opportunities appear to open. (Rev: BL 10/15/06; LMC 4–5/07; SLJ 1/07)

4362 Wolf, Allan. *The Watch That Ends the Night: Voices from the Titanic* (9–12). 2011, Candlewick $21.99 (978-0-7636-37033). Free-verse poems express the points of view of diverse participants — from the captain, the shipbuilder, and millionaire John Jacob Astor to a refugee, a toddler, the ship rat, and the iceberg itself — as the *Titanic* approaches the end; includes extensive back matter. YALSA Amazing Audiobooks Top Ten 2013. ⌒ (Rev: BL 9/15/11*; HB 9–10/11; LMC 3–4/12*; SLJ 10/1/11; VOYA 10/11)

4363 Wright, Barbara. *Crow* (9–12). 2012, Random House $16.99 (978-037586928-0); LB $19.99 (978-037596928-7). Moses Thomas, 11, comes face to face with escalating racial tensions during his African American family's vacation to Wilmington, North Carolina, in 1898. ℮ (Rev: BL 2/1/12; HB 1–2/12*; LMC 3–4/12; SLJ 1/12; VOYA 12/11)

BETWEEN THE WARS AND THE GREAT DEPRESSION (1919–1941)

4364 Barnaby, Hannah. *Wonder Show* (7–10). 2012, Houghton Mifflin $16.99 (978-054759980-9). In Depression-era America Portia escapes from a Home for Wayward Girls and joins a traveling circus. Lexile 830L (Rev: BLO 4/15/12; HB 7–8/12; SLJ 8/12)

4365 Brewer, Sonny. *A Sound like Thunder* (9–12). 2006, Ballantine $23.95 (978-0-345-47633-3). Sixteen-year-old Rove is coming of age in 1941 Alabama as he watches his alcoholic father threaten a German American man, wonders about his mother's fidelity, nurtures an interest in a pretty girl, and finds solace in the boat he is rebuilding. (Rev: BL 5/15/06)

4366 Bryant, Jen. *Ringside, 1925: Views from the Scopes Trial* (6–10). 2008, Knopf $15.99 (978-037584047-0); LB $18.99 (978-037594047-7). A series of first-person free-verse poems brings to life the events of the Scopes Monkey Trial and the divisive, circus-like atmosphere it brought to town as citizens debated the teaching of evolution. (Rev: BLO 10/30/08; HB 5–6/08; LMC 4–5/08; SLJ 3/08; VOYA 6/08)

4367 Earley, Tony. *Jim the Boy* (9–12). 2000, Little, Brown $23.95 (978-0-316-19964-3). A gentle, nostalgic story set in a small town in North Carolina in 1934 about a 10-year-old boy, his mother, and the three uncles who are raising him. (Rev: BL 5/1/00; VOYA 12/00)

4368 Ellison, Ralph. *Invisible Man* (10–12). 1994, Modern Library $19.95 (978-0-679-60139-5); paper $12.00 (978-0-679-73276-1). This acclaimed novel depicts the experiences of a single black man during the Depression.

4369 Fergus, Jim. *The Wild Girl: The Notebooks of Ned Giles, 1932* (9–12). 2005, Hyperion $23.95 (978-1-4013-0054-8). In 1932, 17-year-old orphan Ned Giles joins an expedition to rescue a boy kidnapped by Apaches, and finds himself attracted to a wild Apache girl they find in a Mexican jail. (Rev: BL 4/15/05)

4370 Fitzgerald, F. Scott. *The Great Gatsby* (10–12). 1996, Simon & Schuster $25.00 (978-0-684-83042-1). The emptiness of the Jazz Age is conveyed in this novel about the mysterious Jay Gatsby and his love for Daisy.

4371 Flood, Nancy Bo. *No-Name Baby* (6–10). 2012, Namelos $18.95 (978-160898117-5). Fourteen-year-old Sophie blames herself when her little brother is born prematurely in this taut family drama set in the Midwest after World War I. ℮ (Rev: BL 5/1/12; SLJ 3/12)

4372 French, Albert. *Billy* (9–12). 2008, Paw Prints $24 (978-1-4352-4249-4). The tragedy of racism is underlined when 10-year-old Billy is tried as an adult in rural Mississippi for stabbing a 15-year-old girl in self-defense; set in the years preceding World War II, this was originally published in 1993. (Rev: BL 10/1/93*)

4373 Gabhart, Ann H. *Angel Sister* (10–12). 2011, Revell paper $14.99 (978-08007338-1-0). In this Christian novel set in the 1930s, young Kate, the middle child in a troubled family, rescues an abandoned 5-year-old-girl on the steps of a church. ℮ (Rev: BLO 1/1–15/11)

4374 Garlock, Dorothy. *The Edge of Town* (10–12). 2001, Warner $19.95 (978-0-446-52769-9). In a small town in Missouri in the 1920s, Julie looks after her five younger siblings and begins dating a decorated veteran of the Great War. (Rev: BL 4/15/01)

4375 Griffin, Molly Beth. *Silhouette of a Sparrow* (7–12). 2012, Milkweed $16.95 (978-157131701-8). In Minnesota for the summer of 1926, 16-year-old Garnet shocks her wealthy relatives by taking a job in a milliner's shop, where she meets and and falls in love with Isabella. 𝐞 (Rev: BL 9/15/12; VOYA 8/12)

4376 Hesse, Karen. *Out of the Dust* (6–12). 1997, Scholastic $16.95 (978-0-590-36080-7). In free verse, 15-year-old Billie Jo describes the tragedies that befall her family during the Dust Bowl years in Oklahoma. Newbery Medal, 1998. (Rev: HBG 3/98)

4377 Hesse, Karen. *Witness* (7–12). 2001, Scholastic paper $16.95 (978-0-439-27199-8). Hesse uses fictional first-person accounts in free verse to describe Ku Klux Klan activity in a 1924 Vermont town. (Rev: BCCB 11/01; BL 9/1/01; HB 11–12/01; HBG 3/02; SLJ 9/01*; VOYA 10/01)

4378 Honeyman, Kay. *The Fire Horse Girl* (8–12). 2013, Scholastic $17.99 (978-054540310-8). Born under the ominous sign of the Fire Horse in 1906, Jade Moon leaves China for America carrying false papers, and disguises herself as a boy while finding work in San Francisco's Chinatown. 𝐞 Lexile 660L (Rev: BL 1/13*; LMC 8–9/12; SLJ 1/13; VOYA 2/13)

4379 Ingold, Jeanette. *Hitch* (8–11). 2005, Harcourt $17.00 (978-0-13-204747-0). When he loses his job during the Great Depression, 17-year-old Moss Trawnley leaves home in search of his father and ends up in an interesting job with the Civilian Conservation Corps. (Rev: BCCB 9/05; BL 5/15/05; SLJ 8/05)

4380 Kennedy, William. *Ironweed* (10–12). 1983, Viking paper $14.00 (978-0-14-007020-0). This novel, part of the author's Albany (NY) cycle, is a tale of skid-row life during the Depression.

4381 Kerr, M. E. *Your Eyes in Stars* (9–12). 2006, HarperCollins LB $17.89 (978-0-06-075683-3). In a story that starts in upstate New York during the Depression and looks at prejudices, 14-year-old Jessica develops a strong friendship with Elisa, daughter of a German professor who's been hired to teach at nearby Cornell University. (Rev: BL 12/1/05*; SLJ 1/06)

4382 Knight, Arthur Winfield. *Johnnie D* (10–12). 2000, Tor $22.95 (978-0-312-86759-1). A fast-paced historical novel that deals with the last year in the life of legendary bank robber John Dillinger and with the social conditions in America during the Great Depression. (Rev: BL 3/15/00)

4383 Larkin, Jillian. *Diva* (9–12). Series: Flappers. 2012, Delacorte $17.99 (978-038574041-8); LB $20.99 (978-038590837-5). Romance, jazz, and danger abound in

this conclusion to the series featuring Clara, Lorraine, and Gloria in the exciting days of the 1920s. 🎧 𝐞 (Rev: BLO 9/15/12; VOYA 12/12)

4384 Laxalt, Robert. *Time of the Rabies* (7–12). 2000, Univ. of Nevada $16.00 (978-0-87417-350-5). Set in 1920s Nevada, this novella recalls a harrowing fight against a rabies epidemic. (Rev: VOYA 4/01)

4385 Lunievicz, Joseph. *Open Wounds* (9–12). 2011, WestSide $16.95 (978-1-934813-51-5). Growing up in the 1930s, Cid is able to overcome the nightmare of his childhood home and subsequent life in an orphanage when he goes to stay with a British cousin, where he becomes a fencer and fight choreographer. Lexile HL710L (Rev: BLO 8/11; LMC 1–2/10; SLJ 10/1/11)

4386 Luper, Eric. *Bug Boy* (8–12). 2009, Farrar $16.99 (978-0-374-31000-4). Set at the Saratoga Race Track during the Depression, this is the story of 15-year-old Jack, an apprentice jockey whose dreams of racing are almost sidetracked by shady characters and his own father's betrayal. 𝐞 (Rev: BL 9/1/09; SLJ 9/09)

4387 Marshall, Catherine. *Julie* (9–12). 1985, Avon paper $6.99 (978-0-380-69891-2). During the Depression, Julie and her family move to a small town in Pennsylvania where she finds fulfillment working on her father's newspaper.

4388 Myers, Anna. *Tulsa Burning* (8–10). 2002, Walker $16.95 (978-0-8027-8829-0). In 1921 Oklahoma, a 15-year-old boy helps an African American man who is injured during race riots. (Rev: BCCB 12/02; BL 10/1/02*; HBG 3/03; SLJ 9/02; VOYA 12/02)

4389 Myers, Walter Dean. *Harlem Summer* (7–10). 2007, Scholastic $16.99 (978-0-439-36843-8). The atmosphere of 1925 Harlem is strongly evoked in this story of 16-year-old Mark Purvis, an aspiring jazz saxophonist, who takes a job at the NAACP magazine *The Crisis* but soon becomes involved with mobsters. (Rev: BCCB 4/07; BL 2/1/07; HB 5–6/07; LMC 8–9/07; SLJ 3/07)

4390 Naylor, Phyllis Reynolds. *Blizzard's Wake* (7–12). 2002, Simon & Schuster $16.95 (978-0-689-85220-6). In a blizzard in 1941, 15-year-old Kate comes face to face with the man who caused her mother's death. (Rev: BCCB 1/03; BL 10/15/02; HBG 3/03; SLJ 12/02)

4391 O'Sullivan, Mark. *Wash-Basin Street Blues* (7–10). 1996, Wolfhound paper $6.95 (978-0-86327-467-1). In 1920s New York City, 16-year-old Nora is reunited with her two younger brothers but the reunion causes unforeseen problems. A sequel to *Melody for Nora* (1994). (Rev: BL 6/1–15/96)

4392 Prasad, Chandra. *Breathe the Sky* (10–12). 2009, Wyatt-MacKenzie $14.99 (978-193227939-9). This novelized account of the life of famed aviator Amelia Earhart focuses on her adult years and explores her fascination with flying and the accompanying celebrity, as well as her romance with the PR man who would further her career. (Rev: BL 10/1/09)

4393 Pratt, James Michael. *Ticket Home* (10–12). 2001, St. Martin's $23.95 (978-0-312-26633-2). The love between twin brothers is tested when they fall in love with the same woman in this novel that begins in Depression days in Oklahoma and ends during World War II. (Rev: BL 2/15/01)

4394 Preston, Caroline. *Gatsby's Girl* (10–12). 2006, Houghton Mifflin $24.00 (978-0-618-53725-9). Set in the 1920s, this is the fictional tale of the real-life first love of F. Scott Fitzgerald, Ginevra, who comes to regret marrying another man as she watches the rise of Fitzgerald's career from afar. (Rev: BL 4/15/06)

4395 Stuber, Barbara. *Crossing the Tracks* (7–12). 2010, Simon & Schuster $16.99 (978-1-4169-9703-0). In 1930s Missouri, 15-year-old Iris is sent to be a caregiver to an elderly woman and despite initial trepidation finds herself making a happy new home. **e** Lexile 680L (Rev: BL 7/10; LMC 10/10; SLJ 8/10; VOYA 10/10)

4396 Vernick, Shirley Reva. *The Blood Lie* (7–10). 2011, Cinco Puntos $15.95 (978-1-933693-84-2). In upstate New York in 1928 a Jewish teen named Jack is accused of killing a little girl as part of a blood sacrifice; based on a true story. Sydney Taylor Book Honor 2012. **e** Lexile 740L (Rev: BL 11/15/11; LMC 5–6/12; SLJ 11/1/11)

POST WORLD WAR II UNITED STATES
(1945–)

4397 Bauer, Marion Dane. *Killing Miss Kitty and Other Sins* (8–11). 2007, Clarion $16.00 (978-0-618-69000-8). Five interconnected stories about Claire, a girl growing up in the 1950s and exploring life and sexuality. (Rev: BCCB 9/07; BL 2/15/07; LMC 8–9/07; SLJ 5/07)

4398 Beard, Jo Ann. *In Zanesville* (11–12). 2011, Little, Brown $23.99 (978-0-316-08447-5). A witty and charming coming-of-age novel about an everyday girl struggling with friendship, family, and fitting in, set in the 1970s in small-town Illinois. Alex Award 2012. ⌒ (Rev: BL 3/1–15/11; SLJ 8/11)

4399 Berg, Elizabeth. *We Are All Welcome Here* (9–12). 2006, Random House $22.95 (978-1-4000-6161-7). Three women's lives are the root of this story set in Elvis's 1964 Tupelo, Mississippi: a paralyzed single white mother on welfare, her 13-year-old daughter, and her African American caregiver; and they deal with such issues as racism, poverty, social workers, and the burden of 24-hour care giving. (Rev: BL 9/15/05; SLJ 6/06)

4400 Blundell, Judy. *What I Saw and How I Lied* (8–12). 2008, Scholastic $16.99 (978-043990346-2). Fifteen-year-old Evie uncovers unsettling truths about her family while on vacation in Palm Beach in 1947. ⌒ **e** Lexile HL620L (Rev: BL 11/1/08*; SLJ 12/08; VOYA 2/09)

4401 Brown, Chris Carlton. *Hoppergrass* (7–10). 2009, Henry Holt $17.95 (978-080508879-3). This dark novel about 15-year-old Bowser's experiences in an institution for delinquent teens is set in 1969 Virginia. Lexile 850L (Rev: BL 4/15/09; SLJ 7/1/09)

4402 Burg, Shana. *A Thousand Never Evers* (7–12). 2008, Delacorte $15.99 (978-0-385-73470-7). African American Addie finds all aspects of life in her Mississippi town are affected by the civil rights movement of the 1960s. ⌒ (Rev: BL 4/15/08; LMC 4–5/08*; SLJ 7/08)

4403 Cady, Jack. *Rules of '48* (11–12). 2010, Night Shade paper $14.95 (978-15978-00-8-5-3). Cady portrays Louisville, Kentucky, as it was in 1948, when the town found itself in the midst of business and race-related clashes in this fictionalized memoir; for mature readers. (Rev: BL 1/1–15/10)

4404 Campbell, Bebe Moore. *Your Blues Ain't Like Mine* (10–12). 1992, Putnam paper $6.99 (978-0-345-40112-0). Todd Armstrong, a 15-year-old African American boy from Chicago, is murdered in 1950s Mississippi in this compelling story about segregation. (Rev: BL 1/15/93; SLJ 1/93)

4405 Carter, Betsy. *Swim to Me* (9–12). 2007, Algonquin $23.95 (978-1-56512-492-9). Set in Florida in the 1970s, this is the story of how a teenage girl escapes her miserable home life in Brooklyn by moving to Florida and making the best of the imperfect situation she finds there. (Rev: BL 8/07)

4406 Childress, Mark. *One Mississippi* (11–12). 2006, Little, Brown $24.95 (978-0-316-01211-9). Daniel moves from Indiana to Mississippi while in high school in 1973 and learns that race relations are different, complicated, and even violent in the South. (Rev: BL 5/1/06; SLJ 7/06)

4407 Crowe, Chris. *Mississippi Trial, 1955* (7–12). 2002, Penguin $17.99 (978-0-8037-2745-8). The story of the racist murder in 1955 of a 14-year-old black boy called Emmett Till is told through the eyes of Hiram, a white teenager. (Rev: BCCB 4/02; BL 2/15/02; HBG 10/02; SLJ 5/02; VOYA 4/02)

4408 Edwardson, Debby Dahl. *My Name Is Not Easy* (7–10). 2011, Marshall Cavendish $17.99 (978-0-7614-5980-4). Inupiaq Luke and his fellow students relate their difficult experiences adapting when they submit to cultural reeducation at a Catholic boarding school in the early 1960s. ⌒ **e** Lexile 830L (Rev: BL 9/15/11; SLJ 11/1/11*)

4409 Eidus, Janice. *The War of the Rosens* (9–12). 2007, Behler paper $15.95 (978-1-933016-38-2). Set in the Bronx in 1965, this novel follows two Jewish siblings as they must grapple with decisions of morality amid their bleak family lives. (Rev: BL 8/07)

4410 Epstein, Leslie. *San Remo Drive* (10–12). 2003, Other $26.00 (978-1-59051-066-7). This story of Hollywood in the 1950s portrays young people growing up in the rarefied environment of filmmakers. (Rev: BL 5/15/03*)

4411 Feldman, Ellen. *The Boy Who Loved Anne Frank* (9–12). 2005, Norton $23.95 (978-0-393-05944-1). Peter Van Pels hid with Anne Frank and died in the camps before liberation; Feldman re-imagines him as a survivor and immigrant to the United States, who denies his Jewish past until the edited *Diary*, play, and movie cause his new life to crumble. (Rev: BL 2/15/05)

4412 Guterson, David. *Snow Falling on Cedars* (10–12). 1994, Harcourt $25.00 (978-0-15-100100-2); paper $14.00 (978-0-679-76402-1). The murder trial of a Japanese American brings back memories of World War II and of young love between a journalist covering the trial and the accused's wife.

4413 Gwin, Minrose. *The Queen of Palmyra* (11–12). 2010, HarperCollins paper $14.99 (978-00618403-2-6). In 1960s Mississippi, neglected 11-year-old Florence is torn between her family's racist attitudes and her feelings for the black woman who raised her; for mature readers. (Rev: BL 3/1–15/10)

4414 Haigh, Jennifer. *Baker Towers* (10–12). 2005, Morrow $24.95 (978-0-06-050941-5). The five Novak children, of Italian and Polish heritage, grow up and leave their Pennsylvania home in the years after World War II — some enjoying more success than others — but the mining town still calls to them. (Rev: BL 11/1/04; SLJ 5/05)

4415 Hegedus, Bethany. *Between Us Baxters* (7–10). 2009, WestSide $17.95 (978-193481302-7). In late 1950s Georgia, 12-year-old Polly, from a struggling white family, and black 14-year-old Timbre Ann find their friendship threatened by the turmoil around them. Lexile 610L (Rev: BL 3/15/09; SLJ 5/1/09; VOYA 10/09)

4416 Hemphill, Helen. *Long Gone Daddy* (8–11). 2006, Front St $16.95 (978-1-932425-38-3). Set in the late 1960s, this is the story of Harlan, a 14-year-old funeral home worker who reconciles with his hard-line-preacher father when the two take a road trip to Las Vegas to transport Harlan's grandfather's body and collect their inheritance. (Rev: BL 5/1/06; HB 11–12/06; SLJ 7/06)

4417 Hilton, David E. *Kings of Colorado* (11–12). 2011, Simon & Schuster $24 (978-1-4391-8382-3). In 1963, after stabbing his abusive father, 13-year-old William is sent to a wretched boys reformatory in Colorado where the main activity is breaking wild mustangs; for mature readers. ∩ ℮ (Rev: BL 12/1–15/10; SLJ 5/11)

4418 Hostetter, Joyce Moyer. *Comfort* (6–10). 2009, Boyds Mills $17.95 (978-159078606-2). Ann Fay, although reluctant to leave her troubled family, goes to Warm Springs in Georgia to receive therapy for her polio. Lexile 680L (Rev: BLO 3/15/09; LMC 10/09; SLJ 5/1/09)

4419 Houston, Julian. *New Boy* (8–11). 2005, Houghton Mifflin $16.00 (978-0-618-43253-0). In the late 1950s, Rob Garrett, an African American teen from Virginia, is the first black student at a tony Connecticut prep school, where he learns about different forms of prejudice and watches civil rights developments in the South. (Rev: BL 11/15/05*; SLJ 3/06; VOYA 2/06)

4420 Howard, Ravi. *Like Trees, Walking* (11–12). 2007, Amistad $24.95 (978-0-06-052959-8). A moving fictional account of the lynching of a young man in Alabama in the early 1980s. (Rev: BL 12/1/06; SLJ 1/08)

4421 Huston, Charlie. *The Shotgun Rule* (9–12). 2007, Ballantine $21.95 (978-0-345-48135-1). Set during a California summer in the 1980s, this book tells the story of a group of white teenage male friends who, in the midst of misbehaving, come into conflict with three Hispanic brothers who steal their friend's bike. (Rev: BL 8/07)

4422 Joseph, Frank S. *To Love Mercy* (10–12). 2006, Mid-Atlantic Highlands paper $14.95 (978-0-9744785-3-1). In 1940s Chicago, a white boy and an African American boy form an unlikely friendship that reveals the racial tensions of the time. (Rev: BL 4/1/06)

4423 Kadohata, Cynthia. *Kira-Kira* (6–12). 2004, Simon & Schuster $15.95 (978-0-689-85639-6). Poverty, exploitation, and racial prejudice form a backdrop to this moving story of two Japanese American sisters growing up in a small Georgia town in the late 1950s and facing the older sister's death from lymphoma. Newbery Medal, 2005. (Rev: BCCB 1/04; BL 1/1–15/04; HB 3–4/04; SLJ 3/04; VOYA 8/04)

4424 Kidd, Sue Monk. *The Secret Life of Bees* (10–12). 2002, Viking $24.95 (978-0-670-89460-4). In 1964 Lily, a white teenager haunted by her mother's death, and Rosaleen, an African American servant close to Lily, flee from Lily's abusive father and find refuge at a black-operated honey business in South Carolina. (Rev: BL 12/1/01; SLJ 5/02; VOYA 8/02)

4425 Krisher, Trudy. *Fallout* (7–10). 2006, Holiday $17.95 (978-0-8234-2035-3). Growing up during the Cold War in a very conservative coastal town in North Carolina, Genevieve is struck by the ideas introduced by the outspoken Brenda Womper, a new student who has arrived from California. (Rev: BL 11/15/06; SLJ 11/06)

4426 Lester, Julius. *Guardian* (9–12). 2008, Amistad $16.99 (978-006155890-0); LB $17.89 (978-006155891-7). In the South in 1946 a white man and his 14-year-old son fail to act to stop the lynching of a black man falsely accused of raping and killing a white teenager. Best Books for Young Adults 2009. (Rev: BL 9/15/08; HB 11–12/08; SLJ 11/1/08; VOYA 2/09)

4427 Levchuk, Lisa. *Everything Beautiful in the World* (9–12). 2008, Farrar $16.95 (978-037432238-0). Emotionally numb, 17-year-old Edna escapes her mother's cancer and her father's icy neglect in the arms of her handsome though devious art teacher in this story set in 1980s New Jersey. Lexile 960L (Rev: BL 11/15/08; SLJ 1/1/09; VOYA 8/08)

4428 Levine, Ellen. *In Trouble* (8–12). 2011, Carolrhoda $17.95 (978-0-7613-6558-7). In 1950s New York two teens cope with pregnancies even as they deal with other difficulties including Jamie's father's imprisonment for refusing to name Communists. ℮ Lexile HL510L (Rev: BL 8/11; LMC 1–2/12; SLJ 8/11)

4429 Lurie, April. *Brothers, Boyfriends and Other Criminal Minds* (7–10). 2007, Delacorte $15.99 (978-0-385-73124-9). April is growing up in Brooklyn in the 1970s, and makes accommodations with the local Mafia partly to support her older brother. (Rev: BL 7/07; SLJ 10/07)

4430 McDermott, Alice. *After This* (9–12). 2006, Farrar $24 (978-0-374-16809-4). This a compelling saga that follows a family — Irish Catholics John and Mary, their four children, and an "aunt" — through the years from the end of World War II to the 1970s, a period that includes the new freedoms of the 1960s and the Vietnam War. (Rev: SLJ 2/07)

4431 MacEnulty, Pat. *Picara* (10–12). 2009, Livingston LB $27 (978-160489037-2); paper $16.95 (978-160489038-9). As the turbulent 1960s draw to a close, the death of the grandmother who has raised her prompts 14-year-old Eli to flee to St. Louis where she finds herself suddenly immersed in the counterculture in which her activist father is deeply engaged. (Rev: BL 10/15/09)

4432 McGuigan, Mary Ann. *Morning in a Different Place* (8–11). 2009, Front St $17.95 (978-159078551-5). Friendship between white Fiona and black Yolanda causes problems in 1963 New York. Lexile HL710L (Rev: BL 2/1/09; LMC 8–9/09; SLJ 3/1/09; VOYA 8/09)

4433 McLain, Paula. *A Ticket to Ride* (9–12). 2008, Ecco $24.95 (978-0-06-134051-2). After Jamie's guardian grandmother suffers a stroke, the 15-year-old is sent from California to the home of her uncle in Illinois where she is joined one summer in 1973 by her cousin Fawn, a 16-year-old girl who shows Jamie a bit of sexual knowledge accompanied by deep trouble. (Rev: BL 11/15/07; SLJ 5/08)

4434 Magoon, Kekla. *The Rock and the River* (6–10). 2009, Aladdin $15.99 (978-141697582-3). Fourteen-year-old Sam considers turning to violence and the Black Panthers when peaceful attempts to gain civil rights seem to fail in this novel set in 1968 Chicago. Coretta Scott King/John Steptoe New Talent Author Award Winner 2010; ALA Notable Books 2010; YALSA Amazing Audiobooks Top Ten 2011. ∩ Lexile HL550L (Rev: BL 2/1/09*; LMC 8–9/09; SLJ 2/1/09)

4435 Matthews, Kezi. *Scorpio's Child* (7–10). 2001, Cricket $15.95 (978-0-8126-2890-6). In South Carolina

in 1947, 14-year-old Afton has difficulty welcoming a taciturn, previously unknown uncle into her home despite her mother's pleas for compassion. (Rev: BCCB 10/01; BL 9/15/01; HB 1–2/02; HBG 3/02; SLJ 10/01; VOYA 4/02)

4436 Moranville, Sharelle Byars. *A Higher Geometry* (8–11). 2006, Henry Holt $16.95 (978-0-8050-7470-3). Fifteen-year-old Anna's love for mathematics sets her apart from her peers in this thoughtful novel about romance and identity in the rural Midwest of 1959. (Rev: BL 4/15/06; SLJ 6/06)

4437 Nelson, Vaunda Micheaux. *No Crystal Stair* (8–12). Illus. by R. Gregory Christie. 2012, Carolrhoda $17.95 (978-076136169-5). Nelson presents the fictionalized story of her great-uncle Lewis Michaux, a hugely influential Harlem bookseller during the mid-1930s. Boston Globe–Hornbook Fiction Award Winner 2012; Coretta Scott King Author Honor Book 2013. ℮ Lexile 850L (Rev: BL 2/1/12; HB 3–4/12*; LMC 5–6/12; SLJ 2/12*; VOYA 6/12)

4438 Neri, G. *Yummy: The Last Days of a Southside Shorty* (8–12). Illus. by Randy DuBurke. 2010, Lee Low paper $16.95 (978-158430267-4). Yummy, an 11-year-old African American with a sweet tooth, was a gang member in Chicago in the 1990s; this graphic novel based on documented sources describes his life on the streets, his shooting of a young girl, and his death at the hands of his own gang. Coretta Scott King Author Honor 2011; ALA Notable Books 2011; YALSA Great Graphic Novels Top Ten 2011; YALSA Quick Picks for Reluctant Young Adult Readers 2011. (Rev: BL 8/10*; HB 11–12/10; SLJ 9/10; VOYA 10/10)

4439 Noonan, Brandon. *Plenty Porter* (7–10). 2006, Abrams $16.95 (978-0-8109-5996-5). Set in 1950s Illinois, this is the story of 12-year-old Plenty, the 11th child of a sharecropper, who struggles to find a sense of belonging within her family and the secretive rural community in which they live. (Rev: BL 4/15/06; LMC 11–12/06; SLJ 8/06)

4440 Qualey, Marsha. *Too Big a Storm* (10–12). 2004, Dial $16.99 (978-0-8037-2839-4). In the 1960s, 18-year-old Brady is introduced into hippy lifestyles when she becomes friendly with Sally and Paul Cooper, two rebellious young people. (Rev: BL 5/15/04; SLJ 7/04)

4441 Robertson, Ray. *Moody Food* (11–12). 2006, Santa Fe Writers Project paper $15.00 (978-0-9776799-0-4). Inspired by the life of musician Gram Parsons, this novel, suitable for mature teens and set in Toronto in the 1960s, is full of drugs, rock-n-roll, and the American club scene of the time. (Rev: BL 9/1/06)

4442 Rowell, Rainbow. *Eleanor and Park* (9–12). 2013, St. Martin's $18.99 (978-125001257-9). In alternating narratives outsiders Eleanor (poor, new student, abusive stepfather) and Park (happy but immigrant family) describe their increasingly affectionate friendship, which they fear may never come to fruition; set in the 1980s. Boston Globe–Horn Book Award 2013. ∩ **e** (Rev: BL 1/13*; HB 5–6/13; SLJ 2/13*; VOYA 12/12)

4443 Sepetys, Ruta. *Out of The Easy* (10–12). 2013, Philomel $17.99 (978-039925692-9). At 17, Josie longs to escape 1950s New Orleans, where her mother works as a prostitute, and attend Smith College, but a murder investigation — and pure economics — dim her hopes. ∩ **e** Lexile HL590L (Rev: BL 2/15/13; HB 5–6/13; SLJ 3/13*)

4444 Sharenow, Robert. *My Mother the Cheerleader* (7–10). 2007, HarperCollins $16.99 (978-0-06-114896-5). Louise's mother pulls her out of school when young African American Ruby Bridges enrolls in their New Orleans school district in 1960. (Rev: BCCB 9/07; BL 7/07; LMC 10/07; SLJ 7/07)

4445 Stephenson, Lynda. *Dancing with Elvis* (9–12). 2005, Eerdmans $17.00 (978-0-8028-5293-9). In a Texas town during the late 1950s made turbulent by racial tensions, feisty 15-year-old Frankilee Baxter has trouble getting along with her foster sister Angel; realistic language may be a problem for some readers. (Rev: BL 11/15/05; SLJ 1/06; VOYA 4/06)

4446 Taniguchi, Yuko. *The Ocean in the Closet: A Novel* (11–12). 2007, Coffee House paper $14.95 (978-1-56689-194-3). In California in the 1970s, 9-year-old Helen is having a tough life (her father — a Vietnam vet with PTSD — seems unable to protect her from her unstable Japanese-born mother, who locks Helen and her little brother in a closet) until her Uncle Steve rescues her and she contacts her mother's family in Japan; for mature teens. (Rev: BL 4/15/07; SLJ 11/07)

4447 Tucker, Todd. *Over and Under* (9–12). 2008, St. Martin's $23.95 (978-0-312-37990-2). The tight friendship between two boys growing up in 1979 Indiana is strained by a strike at their fathers' workplace in this nostalgic coming-of-age story. Alex Award 2009. **e** (Rev: BL 6/1–15/08*)

4448 Vanliere, Donna. *The Angels of Morgan Hill* (9–12). 2006, St. Martin's $14.95 (978-0-312-33452-9). The Gables, a white family, take in young Milo, an African American, when his family's house is burned down by racists in this story set in 1947 Tennessee. ∩ (Rev: SLJ 10/06)

4449 Watkins, Steve. *Down Sand Mountain* (7–12). 2008, Candlewick $16.99 (978-0-7636-3839-9). A loss-of-innocence story set in 1966, simply yet beautifully told, in which a 12-year-old boy discovers the cruelty of racism in his small Florida hometown. (Rev: BL 8/08)

4450 Wolf, Elaine. *Camp* (7–10). 2012, Sky Pony $16.95 (978-161608657-2). In the early 1960s, 14-year-old Amy suffers bullying at Camp Takawanda for Girls but decides not to report this to her troubled home. ∩

e (Rev: BLO 9/15/12; LMC 1–2/13; SLJ 1/13; VOYA 12/12)

4451 Zafris, Nancy. *Lucky Strike* (10–12). 2005, Unbridled $23.95 (978-1-932961-04-1). In 1950s Utah quirky characters including young siblings Beth and Charlie stake their fortunes on discovering uranium. (Rev: BL 3/1/05)

Twentieth-Century Wars

WORLD WAR I

4452 Frost, Helen. *Crossing Stones* (7–12). 2009, Farrar $16.99 (978-0-374-31653-2). Siblings Muriel and Ollie and their friends Emma and Frank describe in heartfelt, evocative verse their experiences as the young men leave for World War I and Muriel and Emma take separate paths toward womanhood. ∩ (Rev: BL 10/1/09*; HB 11–12/09; LMC 11–12/09; SLJ 10/09; VOYA 10/09)

4453 Hamley, Dennis. *Without Warning: Ellen's Story, 1914-1918* (7–12). 2007, Candlewick $17.99 (978-0-7636-3338-7). World War I hits close to home for Ellen, whose brother is wounded and boyfriend is killed in the fighting; she later works as a nurse on the front, ministering to English soldiers and even a German prisoner of war. Although long, this first-person narrative is very readable. (Rev: BL 10/1/07; SLJ 2/08)

4454 Hemingway, Ernest. *A Farewell to Arms* (10–12). 1997, Scribner Classics $35.00 (978-0-684-83788-8). This love story set against the turmoil of World War I is considered to be one of Hemingway's finest works.

4455 Hylton, Sara. *Flirting with Destiny* (11–12). 2011, Severn $28.95 (978-072786949-4). Four privileged English girls find their lives much changed by the advent of World War I, for which they are ill prepared; for mature readers. ∩ (Rev: BL 12/1–15/10)

4456 Lottridge, Celia Barker. *Home Is Beyond the Mountains* (7–10). 2010, Groundwood $16.95 (978-0-88899-932-0). A moving story, based on the experiences of the author's aunt, about Assyrian children who become orphaned refugees during World War I. Lexile 680L (Rev: BL 4/15/10; LMC 8–9/10; SLJ 4/10)

4457 Morpurgo, Michael. *Private Peaceful* (7–12). 2004, Scholastic $16.95 (978-0-439-63648-3). Fifteen-year-old Thomas, who lied about his age to follow his beloved older brother into combat in World War I, reflects on the life he left behind in England and the horrors of life on the front lines. (Rev: BL 10/1/04*; SLJ 11/04; VOYA 12/04)

4458 Schroder, Monika. *My Brother's Shadow* (7–12). 2011, Farrar $16.99 (978-0-374-35122-9). In 1918 Berlin 16-year-old Moritz struggles to feed and care for his family even as he worries about their conflicting political views. **e** (Rev: BL 10/1/11; LMC 11–12/11*; SLJ 11/1/11)

4459 Sedgwick, Marcus. *The Foreshadowing* (8–11). 2006, Random House LB $18.99 (978-0-385-90881-8). Plagued by premonitions about her brother, 17-year-old Sasha signs up as a nurse so that she can look for him on the grim battlefields of World War I France. (Rev: BL 4/1/06*; SLJ 7/06)

4460 Slade, Arthur. *Megiddo's Shadow* (8–11). 2006, Random House $15.95 (978-0-385-74701-1). Edward, a 16-year-old Canadian, enlists in the army to avenge his brother's death and ends up fighting in a bloody battle against the Turks in this World War I novel. (Rev: BL 12/15/06; HB 11–12/06; SLJ 12/06*)

4461 Spilleben, Geert. *Kipling's Choice* (7–10). Trans. by Terese Edelstein. 2005, Houghton Mifflin $16.00 (978-0-618-43124-3). In this fictionalized biography of John Kipling, the son of the world-famous British author uses his father's influence to get into the army despite his poor eyesight, giving the teen a chance to do battle with the "barbaric Huns" in World War I. (Rev: BCCB 6/05; BL 5/15/05; SLJ 6/05; VOYA 12/05)

4462 Wilson, John. *And in the Morning* (8–12). 2003, Kids Can $16.95 (978-1-55337-400-8). This absorbing story of fighting in the trenches of World War I, told in diary form by a teenage boy, is enhanced by newspaper headlines and clippings. (Rev: BL 3/15/03; HBG 10/03; SLJ 6/03)

WORLD WAR II AND THE HOLOCAUST

4463 Atlema, Martha. *A Time to Choose* (8–12). 1995, Orca paper $7.95 (978-1-55143-045-4). While growing up in Holland under the Nazi occupation, 16-year-old Johannes tries to separate himself from his father, who is considered a collaborator. (Rev: VOYA 10/97)

4464 Bartoletti, Susan Campbell. *The Boy Who Dared* (6–12). 2008, Scholastic $16.99 (978-0-439-68013-4). This compelling story of a German teenager who was executed for resisting the Nazis is based on a true story. (Rev: BL 2/15/08; SLJ 5/08)

4465 Bass, Karen. *Summer of Fire* (9–12). 2010, Coteau paper $10.95 (978-15505041-5-6). Sent to spend the summer in Germany with her older sister, 16-year-old Del finds herself absorbed in the diary of another rebellious teen who lived in Hamburg during World War II. (Rev: BL 8/10)

4466 Benioff, David. *City of Thieves* (9–12). 2008, Viking $24.95 (978-0-670-01870-3). Seventeen-year-old Lev and 20-year-old Kolya brave incredible danger to achieve the nearly impossible task of finding a dozen eggs for the wedding of a Russian colonel's daughter during the Battle of Leningrad. Alex Award 2009. 🎧 (Rev: BL 4/15/08)

4467 Boulle, Pierre. *The Bridge over the River Kwai* (9–12). Trans. by Xan Fielding. 1954, Amereon $29.95 (978-0-89190-571-4). The thoughtful story of life in a Japanese prisoner-of-war camp and the building of a bridge that pits a British officer against his captors.

4468 Boyne, John. *The Boy in the Striped Pajamas: A Fable* (7–10). 2006, Random House $15.95 (978-0-385-75106-3). The 9-year old son of a Nazi commandant befriends a Jewish boy he meets through the fence of a concentration camp. (Rev: BL 7/06; HB 9–10/06; LMC 1/07; SLJ 9/06)

4469 Chan, Gillian. *A Foreign Field* (7–10). 2002, Kids Can $16.95 (978-1-55337-349-0). Friendship develops into love for 14-year-old Ellen and a young British pilot who is training at an air base near her home in Canada. (Rev: BCCB 12/02; BL 9/15/02; HBG 3/03; SLJ 11/02; VOYA 2/03)

4470 Chapman, Fern Schumer. *Is It Night or Day?* (6–10). 2010, Farrar $17.99 (978-0-374-17744-7). In 1938, 12-year-old Edith's German Jewish parents send her to Chicago where she leads a miserable, anxious life apart from her fondness for baseball; this story is based on the life of the author's mother. **e** (Rev: BL 2/1/10*; LMC 5–6/10; SLJ 5/10)

4471 Cheng, Andrea. *Marika* (7–12). 2002, Front St $16.95 (978-1-886910-78-2). Marika's earlier preoccupations disappear when the arrival of Nazis in 1944 Budapest changes her life. (Rev: BL 11/15/02; HB 11–12/02; HBG 3/03; SLJ 12/02; VOYA 2/03)

4472 Chotjewitz, David. *Daniel, Half Human: And the Good Nazi* (7–12). Trans. by Doris Orgel. 2004, Simon & Schuster $17.95 (978-0-689-85747-8). Daniel and Armin, best friends in Germany in the early 1930s, both admire Hitler, but their friendship is tested when Daniel learns that he is half-Jewish. Sidney Taylor Book Honor 2004. (Rev: BL 9/15/04; SLJ 12/04)

4473 Cookson, Catherine. *A Ruthless Need* (9–12). 2001, Center Point $29.95 (978-1-58547-066-2). During World War II, Geoff Fulton has a girlfriend named Janis, and then he meets Lizzie Gillespie and a love triangle begins. (Rev: BL 12/1/01)

4474 Cooper, Michelle. *The FitzOsbornes at War* (9–12). Series: Montmaray Journals. 2012, Knopf $17.99 (978-037587050-7); LB $20.99 (978-037597050-4). In this series conclusion, Sophie's journals continue to provide insight into the lives of the wealthy in wartime Britain. **e** Lexile 1010L (Rev: BL 11/15/12*; HB 9–10/12; VOYA 8/12)

4475 Craven, Margaret. *Walk Gently This Good Earth* (9–12). 1995, Buccaneer LB $21.95 (978-1-56849-646-7). The saga of an American family surviving the Depression and World War II.

4476 Dallas, Sandra. *Tallgrass* (9–12). 2007, St. Martin's $St. (978-0-312-36019-1). Life in her small Colorado town changes for bright 13-year-old Rennie when a Japanese internment camp is built there; the murder of a girl boosts the unrest to a new and scary level. ∩ (Rev: BL 1/1–15/07; SLJ 9/07)

4477 de Moor, Margriet. *Duke of Egypt* (10–12). Trans. by Paul Vincent. 2002, Arcade $24.95 (978-1-55970-546-2). A tragic but inspiring novel for mature readers that focuses on the persecution of the Gypsies in World War II and its aftermath. (Rev: BL 11/15/01)

4478 Dowswell, Paul. *The Auslander* (7–10). 2011, Bloomsbury $16.99 (978-1-59990-633-1). Thirteen-year-old Peter's Aryan features make him an attractive adoptee but when he settles into his new home in Berlin and membership in the Hitler Youth, he discovers his distaste for the Nazi party and, with his friend Anna, works against them. **e** Lexile 760L (Rev: BL 5/1/11; HB 9–10/11; LMC 8–9/11*; SLJ 9/1/11)

4479 Drucker, Malka, and Michael Halperin. *Jacob's Rescue: A Holocaust Story* (6–10). 1993, Dell paper $4.99 (978-0-440-40965-6). The fictionalized true story of two Jewish children saved from the Holocaust in Poland by "righteous Gentiles." (Rev: BL 2/15/93; SLJ 5/93)

4480 Dubis, Michael. *The Hangman* (10–12). 1998, Erica House paper $10.95 (978-0-9659308-6-4). The disturbing story of the Holocaust as experienced by Erik Byrnes, an SS officer whose assignment was to liquidate a ghetto outside of Vienna. (Rev: BL 12/15/98)

4481 Dudley, David L. *Caleb's Wars* (8–12). 2011, Clarion $16.99 (978-0-547-23997-2). In 1944 rural Georgia 15-year-old African American Caleb forms a friendship with a young German P.O.W. **e** Lexile HL600L (Rev: BL 10/1/11; SLJ 11/1/11; VOYA 10/11)

4482 Engle, Margarita. *Tropical Secrets: Holocaust Refugees in Cuba* (7–11). 2009, Henry Holt $16.95 (978-080508936-3). Paloma, a Cuban girl, and Daniel, a German Jew who fled to Cuba to escape the Nazis, become friends in this story told in verse. Sydney Taylor Book Award 2010. ∩ **e** Lexile 1170L (Rev: BL 1/1–15/09; LMC 10/09; SLJ 6/1/09*; VOYA 4/09)

4483 Fink, Ida. *A Scrap of Time: And Other Stories* (10–12). 1995, Northwestern Univ. paper $16.00 (978-0-8101-1259-9). These stories written by a Holocaust survivor are about the daily life of Polish Jews during World War II; first published in 1987. (Rev: BL 6/1/87)

4484 Friedman, Carl. *Nightfather* (9–12). Trans. by Arnold J. Pomerans and Erica Pomerans. 1994, Persea paper $7.95 (978-0-89255-210-8). The daughter of a Dutch Holocaust survivor describes how her father's constant reliving of his experiences affected the whole family in this moving autobiographical novel. (Rev: BL 6/1–15/98; SLJ 1/95)

4485 Friedman, D. Dina. *Escaping into the Night* (7–10). 2006, Simon & Schuster $14.95 (978-1-4169-0258-4). Based on true events, this is the story of Halina Rudowski's escape into the forest during a Nazi roundup

of Jews, and her subsequent efforts to survive. (Rev: BL 1/1–15/06; SLJ 3/06; VOYA 4/06)

4486 Gardam, Jane. *The Flight of the Maidens* (10–12). 2001, Carroll & Graf $25.00 (978-0-7867-0879-6). A novel about the bittersweet time between high school and college as experienced by three girls in an English village during World War II. (Rev: BL 7/01)

4487 Gille, Elizabeth. *Shadows of a Childhood: A Novel of War and Friendship* (9–12). Trans. by Linda Coverdale. 1998, New Press $23.00 (978-1-56584-388-2). Based on fact, this novel traces the complex story of a Jewish girl in France who survived World War II as a Gentile and her subsequent search for truth and her own identity. (Rev: BL 1/1–15/98; VOYA 12/98)

4488 Gleitzman, Morris. *Once* (7–10). 2010, Henry Holt $16.99 (978-0-8050-9026-0). After living in a Catholic orphanage for four years, young Felix, a Polish Jew, runs away to find his parents and experiences directly the horrors of the Holocaust. Sydney Taylor Book Honor 2011. ∩ **e** (Rev: BL 2/15/10; HB 3–4/10; SLJ 4/10)

4489 Gleitzman, Morris. *Then* (7–10). 2011, Henry Holt $16.99 (978-0-8050-9027-7). In 1942 Poland Felix, 10, and Zelda, 6, struggle to survive in the countryside after escaping from a train headed to a death camp; the sequel to *Once* (2010). Sydney Taylor Book Honor 2012. ∩ **e** (Rev: BL 4/15/11; HB 5–6/11; SLJ 6/11*)

4490 Gower, Iris. *Bomber's Moon* (10–12). 2009, Severn $28.95 (978-072786765-0). Set in Britain and Germany during World War II, this novel follows teens who experience fear, romance, death, and destruction. (Rev: BLO 7/09)

4491 Goyer, Tricia. *Night Song* (9–12). 2004, Moody paper $13.99 (978-0-8024-1555-4). The fates of a Jewish prisoner, a Nazi musician, an American doctor, and an Austrian woman come together at the Mauthausen concentration camp. (Rev: BL 9/1/04)

4492 Goyer, Tricia, and Mike Yorkey. *The Swiss Courier* (11–12). 2009, Revell paper $13.99 (978-08007333-6-0). Gabi Mueller, who is working for the United States as a spy, is assigned to rescue a German scientist in this fast-paced novel set in Hitler's Germany; for mature readers. (Rev: BL 10/15/09)

4493 Graber, Janet. *Resistance* (7–10). 2005, Marshall Cavendish $15.95 (978-0-7614-5214-0). In this suspenseful World War II novel, 15-year-old Marianne reluctantly joins her mother and brother in fighting for the French Resistance despite her fears that they will be found out by the German soldier billeted in their home. (Rev: BCCB 6/05; BL 5/15/05; SLJ 8/05)

4494 Greene, Bette. *Summer of My German Soldier* (10–12). 1973, Puffin paper $6.99 (978-0-14-130636-0). In World War II, Patty's family is not pleased when the young Jewish girl becomes involved with a German soldier who has escaped from a nearby Arkansas prison camp.

4495 Greif, Jean-Jacques. *The Fighter* (10–12). 2006, Bloomsbury $16.95 (978-1-58234-891-9). In a World War II concentration camp, a Polish Jew is forced to entertain Nazi soldiers by boxing with dying prisoners in this novel that describes the horror of the time and the sheer luck of most survivors. (Rev: BL 10/1/06; HB 11–12/06; LMC 2/07; SLJ 12/06)

4496 Hamamura, John Hideyo. *Color of the Sea* (10–12). 2006, St. Martin's $24.95 (978-0-312-34073-5). A poignant story of Japanese Americans in the turmoil after the bombing of Pearl Harbor, featuring young lovers Sam and Keiko who are separated by events. (Rev: BL 3/15/06)

4497 Harlow, Joan Hiatt. *Shadows on the Sea* (7–10). 2003, Simon & Schuster $16.95 (978-0-689-84926-8). Fourteen-year-old Jill, staying with her grandmother in Maine in 1942, finds a pigeon carrying a message in German and suspects U-boats may be close. (Rev: BL 9/15/03; HBG 4/04; SLJ 9/03)

4498 Heggen, Thomas. *Mister Roberts* (10–12). 1983, Buccaneer LB $16.95 (978-0-89966-445-3). The waste of war is one of the themes of this richly comic but also touching story of life on a supply ship during World War II.

4499 Heller, Joseph. *Catch-22* (10–12). 1995, Knopf $20.00 (978-0-679-43722-2). The much-praised World War II novel about the hypocrisy and stupidities that exist in our society.

4500 Hersey, John. *The Wall* (10–12). 1950, Knopf paper $17.00 (978-0-394-75696-7). A novel in diary form of a Jewish resident of the Warsaw Ghetto in World War II.

4501 Hunter, Bernice Thurman. *The Girls They Left Behind* (7–10). 2005, Fitzhenry & Whiteside paper $9.95 (978-1-55041-927-6). This coming-of-age novel, set in Toronto against the backdrop of World War II, paints a vivid portrait of what life was like for the teenage girls left behind on the home front. (Rev: BCCB 7–8/05; BL 5/15/05; SLJ 8/05; VOYA 8/05)

4502 Jenoff, Pam. *The Kommandant's Girl* (10–12). 2007, MIRA paper $13.95 (978-0-7783-2342-6). In Krakow in World War II, Emma and her young husband are both working for the underground resistance; but Emma is tested when her disguise brings her into close contact with an attractive Nazi Kommandant. (Rev: BL 2/15/07)

4503 Johnson, Jeannie. *Secret Sins* (9–12). 2007, Severn $28.95 (978-0-7278-6558-8). Forced out of her home after a bombing in England, Mary Anne Randall struggles to makes ends meet for her youngest son and herself while trying to help others who need it, but that is only part of the mysterious series of problems that arise for her in this novel. (Rev: BL 10/1/07)

4504 Keneally, Thomas. *Schindler's List* (10–12). 1993, Simon & Schuster paper $12.00 (978-0-671-88031-6). A mature novel that is a fictionalized treatment of the life of the German industrialist who saved the lives of many Jews during World War II.

4505 Kertesz, Imre. *Fateless* (9–12). Trans. by Christopher C. Wilson. 1992, Northwestern Univ. $68.00 (978-0-8101-1024-3); paper $19.95 (978-0-8101-1049-6). A Holocaust survival tale told from the viewpoint of a Hungarian Jewish teenager. (Rev: BL 9/15/92)

4506 Kositsky, Lynne. *The Thought of High Windows* (8–12). 2004, Kids Can $16.95 (978-1-55337-621-7). A Jewish refugee named Esther describes her experiences in France during World War II — lice and other discomforts, loneliness, longing for her family, her differences from the other refugees — and her involvement in the Resistance in this affecting novel based on true events. (Rev: HB 5–6/04; SLJ 5/04)

4507 Lourie, Richard. *A Hatred for Tulips* (9–12). 2007, Thomas Dunne $22.95 (978-0-312-34933-2). Joop, an old man living in modern Amsterdam, copes with feelings of guilt and anger for having been the one who betrayed Anne Frank and her family to the Nazis during World War II. (Rev: BL 6/1–15/07)

4508 McAuley, Amy. *Violins of Autumn* (9–12). 2012, Walker $16.99 (978-080272299-7). Adele, who has lied about her age, parachutes into occupied France and finds scary action, imprisonment, and romance. (Rev: BL 4/15/12; LMC 10/12; SLJ 6/12)

4509 McMorris, Kristina. *Letters from Home* (11–12). 2011, Kensington paper $15 (978-07582468-4-4). A sweeping saga told through letters about three young women whose lives take many unexpected twists and turns as they live, love, and work during World War II; for mature readers. **e** (Rev: BLO 1/1–15/11)

4510 Manley, Joan B. *She Flew No Flags* (7–10). 1995, Houghton Mifflin $16.00 (978-0-395-71130-9). A strongly autobiographical World War II novel about a 10-year-old's voyage from India to her new home in the United States and the people she meets on the ship. (Rev: BL 3/15/95; SLJ 4/95; VOYA 5/95)

4511 Mazer, Harry. *Heroes Don't Run: A Novel of the Pacific War* (7–10). 2005, Simon & Schuster $15.95 (978-0-689-85534-4). In this gripping sequel to *A Boy at War* (2001) and *A Boy No More* (2004), 17-year-old Adam Pelko lies about his age to join the U.S. Marines and fights in a climactic battle with the Japanese on Okinawa. (Rev: BL 5/15/05; SLJ 8/05; VOYA 8/05)

4512 Mazer, Harry. *The Last Mission* (7–10). 1981, Dell paper $5.50 (978-0-440-94797-4). An underage Jewish American boy joins the Air Corps and is taken prisoner by the Germans. (Rev: BL 5/1/88)

4513 Melnikoff, Pamela. *Prisoner in Time: A Child of the Holocaust* (6–10). 2001, Jewish Publication Soc. paper $9.95 (978-0-8276-0735-4). Melnikoff combines history, fantasy, and Jewish legend in this story of 12-year-old Jan, in hiding from the Nazis in 1942 Czechoslovakia. (Rev: BL 10/1/01; SLJ 12/01)

4514 Michener, James A. *Tales of the South Pacific* (9–12). 1986, Macmillan paper $6.99 (978-0-449-20652-2). This volume contains 18 short stories about the life of servicemen in the South Pacific during World War II. Several formed the basis of the popular musical.

4515 Orlev, Uri. *The Man from the Other Side* (6–10). Trans. by Hillel Halkin. 1991, Houghton Mifflin $16.00 (978-0-395-53808-1). The story of a teenager in Nazi-occupied Warsaw who helps desperate Jews despite his dislike of them. (Rev: BL 6/15/91*; SLJ 9/91*)

4516 Orlev, Uri. *Run, Boy, Run* (7–12). 2003, Houghton Mifflin $15.00 (978-0-618-16465-3). A Polish boy survives the Holocaust by pretending to be a Catholic in this harrowing book full of historical detail. (Rev: BCCB 12/03; BL 10/15/03*; HB 11–12/03; HBG 4/04; SLJ 11/03; VOYA 12/03)

4517 Patneaude, David. *Thin Wood Walls* (6–10). 2004, Houghton Mifflin $16.00 (978-0-618-34290-7). In this poignant tale set against the backdrop of an America reeling from the Japanese attack on Pearl Harbor, Joe Hanada and his Japanese American family feel the rising tide of prejudice and are eventually sent to an internment camp in California. (Rev: BL 9/15/04; SLJ 10/04; VOYA 12/04)

4518 Pausewang, Gudrun. *Traitor* (7–10). 2006, Carolrhoda $16.95 (978-0-8225-6195-8). Young Anna, a German girl whose family is involved in the Nazi movement, shelters a Russian soldier at great risk to herself in this novel set in 1944. (Rev: BL 12/1/06; SLJ 11/06)

4519 Peet, Mal. *Tamar* (8–12). 2007, Candlewick paper $8.99 (978-076364063-7). With parallel narratives set in Nazi-occupied Holland and 1995 England, this award-winning novel is about resistance fighters in World War II and the curiosity of a granddaughter on inheriting a box of memorabilia. ℮ (Rev: BL 2/1/07*; SLJ 4/07*)

4520 Peterson, Tracie. *Tidings of Peace* (10–12). 2000, Bethany House paper $9.99 (978-0-7642-2291-7). Four novellas set during World War II explore stories of Christian faith, including a Jewish war veteran's conversion and the reawakening of faith in a pregnant teenage girl. (Rev: VOYA 6/01)

4521 Polak, Monique. *What World Is Left* (7–12). 2008, Orca $12.95 (978-155143847-4). When 14-year-old Anneke and her Jewish family are taken from Holland to Theresienstadt, she suffers filthy, overcrowded conditions and the terror of the gas chambers while her artist father is charged with painting scenery that will make the town look hospitable to Red Cross inspectors, in this powerful book written in memoir format. (Rev: BL 12/15/08; LMC 5–6/09; SLJ 4/1/09)

4522 Ray, Karen. *To Cross a Line* (7–10). 1994, Orchard LB $16.99 (978-0-531-08681-0). The story of a 17-year-old Jewish boy who is pursued by the Gestapo and encounters barriers in his desperate attempts to

escape Nazi Germany. (Rev: BL 2/15/94; SLJ 6/94; VOYA 6/94)

4523 Riordan, James. *The Sniper* (9–12). 2009, Frances Lincoln paper $8.95 (978-1-84507-884-3). Teen sniper Tania Belova courageously defends Stalingrad against the invading Germans in this World War II novel based on a true story. (Rev: SLJ 1/10)

4524 Roth, Philip. *The Plot Against America: A Novel* (10–12). 2004, Houghton Mifflin $26.00 (978-0-618-50928-7). A chilling alternate history in which the ascent to the presidency in 1940 of Hitler sympathizer Charles Lindbergh strikes fear into the heart of the young Jewish narrator. (Rev: BL 8/04; SLJ 11/04)

4525 Ruby, Lois. *Shanghai Shadows* (7–10). 2006, Holiday $16.95 (978-0-8234-1960-9). Ilse and her Jewish family flee Vienna during the Nazi regime and settle in Japanese-occupied Shanghai, where they face many hardships and fears. (Rev: BL 11/1/06; SLJ 9/07)

4526 Saroyan, William. *The Human Comedy* (7–12). 1973, Dell paper $6.50 (978-0-440-33933-5). Homer Macauley is growing up during World War II in America, part of the everyday life that is the human comedy.

4527 Sasson, Jean. *Ester's Child* (10–12). 2001, Windsor-Brooke $24.95 (978-0-9676737-3-8). The paths of families cross in this rich historical novel that moves from the Warsaw ghetto during World War II to postwar Palestine and Lebanon. (Rev: BL 8/01*; SLJ 3/02)

4528 Sharenow, Robert. *The Berlin Boxing Club* (7–10). Illus. by author. 2011, HarperCollins $17.99 (978-0-06-157968-4). In 1936 Berlin 14-year-old Karl, from a nonobservant Jewish family, enjoys learning to box from the famous Max Schmeling even as he grapples with the horrors of Nazi oppression. YALSA Best Fiction for Young Adults; Sydney Taylor Award. Lexile 880L (Rev: BL 4/15/11; HB 5–6/11; SLJ 6/11*; VOYA 8/11)

4529 Shrayer-Petrov, David. *Autumn in Yalta* (10–12). 2006, Syracuse Univ. $24.95 (978-0-8156-0820-2). A collection of stories including a short novel about a boy who was evacuated from his city in Russia during World War II, based on the author's own experience; for strong teen readers. (Rev: BL 5/1/06)

4530 Sickels, Noelle. *The Medium* (9–12). 2007, Five Star $26.95 (978-1-59414-618-3). The granddaughter of a medium, Helen begins having visions at 13 but she does not accept it until she predicts the entrance of the United States into World War II and realizes that she can be of help to people whose lost soldiers she has contacted, much to the disapproval of the army. (Rev: BL 11/1/07)

4531 Smith, Sherri L. *Flygirl* (7–10). 2009, Putnam $16.99 (978-039924709-5). Even though she is black, Ida Mae manages to become a pilot in the WASP (Women Airforce Service Program) during World War

II. **e** Lexile 680L (Rev: BL 1/1–15/09*; HB 5–6/09; LMC 5–6/09; SLJ 2/1/09; VOYA 2/09)

4532 Tamar, Erika. *Good-bye, Glamour Girl* (7–10). 1984, HarperCollins LB $12.89 (978-0-397-32088-2). Liesl and her family flee from Hitler's Europe and Liesl must now become Americanized. (Rev: BL 1/1/85)

4533 Tsukiyama, Gail. *The Street of a Thousand Blossoms* (9–12). 2007, St. Martin's $24.95 (978-0-312-27482-5). Growing up in Tokyo, brothers Hiroshi and Kenji find their lives horribly interrrupted by the outbreak of World War II in this beautifully written novel. (Rev: BL 7/07)

4534 Twomey, Cathleen. *Beachmont Letters* (8–12). 2003, Boyds Mills $16.95 (978-1-59078-050-3). During World War II, 17-year-old Eleanor reaches out to a soldier through the letters that she writes him although she holds back those that deal with her own pain and suffering. (Rev: BL 3/1/03; HBG 10/03; SLJ 3/03)

4535 Uris, Leon. *Mila 18* (10–12). 1961, Bantam paper $7.99 (978-0-553-24160-0). A dramatic story involving the Warsaw Ghetto freedom fighters during World War II.

4536 Van Dijk, Lutz. *Damned Strong Love: The True Story of Willi G. and Stefan K.* (8–12). Trans. by Elizabeth D. Crawford. 1995, Henry Holt $15.95 (978-0-8050-3770-8). Nazi persecution of homosexuals, based on the life of Stefan K., a Polish teenager. (Rev: BL 5/15/95; SLJ 8/95)

4537 Vincenzi, Penny. *Forbidden Places* (11–12). 2010, Overlook $26.95 (978-159020356-9). Set in World War II England, this saga focuses on three women and their relationships with men and their families; for mature readers. (Rev: BL 9/1–15/10)

4538 Voorhoeve, Anne C. *My Family for the War* (7–12). Trans. by Tammi Reichel. Illus. 2012, Dial $17.99 (978-080373360-2). Ziska Mangold, 10, is rescued from Nazi Germany by a Jewish family in London, where she endures bullying and hardships and worries about the family she left behind. Batchelder Award 2013; ALA Notable Books 2013. **e** Lexile 900L (Rev: BL 4/15/12*; LMC 9–10/12; SLJ 5/1/12*)

4539 Wein, Elizabeth. *Code Name Verity* (9–12). 2012, Hyperion $16.99 (978-1-4231-5219-4). This compelling tale of bravery during World War II involves two women — Julie, tortured by the Gestapo as they try to extract the wireless codes she knows, and Maddie, a civilian pilot desperate to rescue her friend. Printz Honor 2013; Boston Globe–Horn Book Honor 2012; YALSA Amazing Audiobooks Top Ten 2013. **⌒ e** Lexile 1020L (Rev: BL 5/1/12*; HB 5–6/12; LMC 1–2/13*; SLJ 7/12*; VOYA 4/12)

4540 Whitney, Kim Ablon. *The Other Half of Life* (7–10). 2009, Knopf $16.99 (978-037585219-0); LB $19.99 (978-037595219-7). This moving story of Jewish refugees in 1939 is based on the true-life experiences of those aboard the MS *St. Louis,* which was denied entry to Cuba and the United States. Lexile HL730L (Rev: BL 4/15/09; LMC 10/09; SLJ 7/1/09; VOYA 6/09)

4541 Wiseman, Eva. *Kanada* (7–10). 2006, Tundra paper $9.95 (978-0-88776-729-6). Jutka, a young Hungarian Jew, loses her family at Auschwitz and barely survives herself; after she is released, she must decide whether to settle in Israel with a young man with whom she has fallen in love or to join relatives in Canada. (Rev: BL 2/15/07)

4542 Wiseman, Eva. *My Canary Yellow Star* (8–12). 2002, Tundra paper $7.95 (978-0-88776-533-9). Marta Weisz's privileged life as the daughter of a wealthy Jewish surgeon comes to an abrupt end when Hitler invades Hungary, but her life is spared through the efforts of Raoul Wallenberg. (Rev: BL 1/1–15/02; SLJ 6/02)

4543 Wouk, Herman. *The Caine Mutiny* (10–12). 1992, Little, Brown paper $14.00 (978-0-316-95510-2). The story of the conflict between the men and the possibly unstable captain who sailed aboard the minesweeper *Caine.*

4544 Wouk, Herman. *The Winds of War* (10–12). 1992, Little, Brown paper $6.99 (978-0-316-95516-4). This novel traces the effects of the beginning of World War II on the family of Commander Pug Henry. A sequel is *War and Remembrance.*

4545 Wulffson, Don. *Soldier X* (8–12). 2001, Viking $16.99 (978-0-670-88863-4). After a battle in World War II, a 16-year-old German boy switches uniforms with a dead Russian in a desperate effort to survive. (Rev: BCCB 3/01; BL 5/1/01; HB 7–8/01; HBG 10/01; SLJ 3/01; VOYA 4/01)

4546 Yolen, Jane. *The Devil's Arithmetic* (7–12). 1988, Puffin paper $6.99 (978-0-14-034535-3). This time-warp story transports a young Jewish girl back to Poland in the 1940s, conveying the horrors of the Holocaust. (Rev: BL 9/1/88; SLJ 11/88)

4547 Young, Sara. *My Enemy's Cradle* (9–12). 2008, Harcourt $24.00 (978-0-15-101537-5). In order to escape persecution in the Nazi-occupied Netherlands pregnant, blond, half-Jewish Cyrla pretends she is her now-deceased Gentile cousin and moves into a "breeding home" within the Lebensborn program in Munich. There the women are expected to breed Aryan babies for the master race, but Cyrla knows that her time is limited. (Rev: BL 11/1/07)

4548 Zusak, Markus. *The Book Thief* (10–12). 2006, Knopf $16.95 (978-037583100-3); LB $18.99 (9780375931000). In Nazi Germany, Death tells the story of Liesel, a young orphan and avid reader, who steals books and shares them with others including the Jewish man her foster parents are hiding. Printz Honor

2007. ♫ ℮ (Rev: BL 1/1/06; HB 3–4/06; LMC 3/06; SLJ 3/06*)

KOREAN, VIETNAM, AND OTHER WARS

4549 Amos, James. *The Memorial: A Novel of the Vietnam War* (10–12). 2001, iUniverse paper $18.95 (978-0-595-17440-9). For mature readers, a novel in the form of an agonizing remembrance of the war in Vietnam by a survivor; first published in 1989. (Rev: BL 6/1/89)

4550 Brown, Don. *Our Time on the River* (7–10). 2003, Houghton Mifflin $15.00 (978-0-618-31116-3). Two brothers learn more about each other on a canoe trip that precedes the older brother's departure to fight in Vietnam. (Rev: BL 4/1/03; HBG 10/03; SLJ 4/03)

4551 Burg, Ann. *All the Broken Pieces* (6–10). 2009, Scholastic $16.99 (978-054508092-7). Told in free verse, this is the story of a boy adopted from Vietnam in the 1970s and his conflicting emotions. ♫ Lexile HL680L (Rev: BL 2/15/09; HB 5–6/09; LMC 5–6/09; SLJ 5/1/09)

4552 Crist-Evans, Craig. *Amaryllis* (7–12). 2003, Candlewick paper $7.99 (978-0-7636-2990-8). Jimmy— who is facing problems at home including his alcoholic father's behavior—learns that his older brother Frank, off fighting in Vietnam, has become depressed and drug-addicted as a result of the war. (Rev: BCCB 1/04; BL 4/15/06; LMC 1/04; SLJ 4/05)

4553 Crocker, Gareth. *Finding Jack* (10–12). 2011, St. Martin's $23.99 (978-031262172-8). This is the moving story of a U.S. army sniper who stays behind after the Vietnam War, endangering his own life to rescue an injured scouting dog. ℮ (Rev: BL 1/1–15/11)

4554 Hillerman, Tony. *Finding Moon* (9–12). 1996, HarperCollins paper $7.99 (978-0-06-109261-9). In Vietnam in 1975, Moon Mathias, a newspaper editor, searches for the daughter of his younger brother, who died in the war. (Rev: BL 9/15/95*)

4555 House, Silas. *Eli the Good* (9–12). 2009, Candlewick $16.99 (978-0-7636-4341-6). Perceptive 10-year-old Eli copes with the changing family dynamics when his war-protesting aunt clashes with his Vietnam veteran father and his mother and sister disagree in this novel set in 1976. ♫ ℮ (Rev: BL 10/1/09; SLJ 1/10)

4556 Hughes, Dean. *Search and Destroy* (7–10). 2006, Simon & Schuster $16.95 (978-0-689-87023-1). Rick Ward, who joined the army during the Vietnam War to escape his home life, returns from a tour of duty unable to adjust to normal life. (Rev: BL 2/1/06; SLJ 1/06; VOYA 2/06)

4557 Karlin, Wayne, and Le Minh Khue, eds. *The Other Side of Heaven: Post-War Fiction by Vietnamese and American Writers* (10–12). 1995, Curbstone paper $17.95 (978-1-880684-31-3). A collection of short stories, many about the effects of the Vietnam War, written by Vietnamese and American writers. (Rev: BL 9/1/95; SLJ 4/96)

4558 Lee, Edward Jae-Suk. *The Good Man: A Novel* (10–12). 2005, BridgeWorks $21.95 (978-1-882593-94-1). Still haunted by sketchy memories of his war experiences, aging Korean War veteran Gabriel Guttman returns to his boyhood home in Montana. (Rev: BL 11/15/04; SLJ 7/05)

4559 Lynch, Chris. *I Pledge Allegiance* (8–11). Series: Vietnam. 2011, Scholastic $16.99 (978-054527029-8). Four friends make a pact to look out for each other at the start of the Vietnam War; this first volume in a series follows Morris, who joins the Navy. YALSA Quick Picks for Reluctant Young Adult Readers 2013. ℮ Lexile 860L (Rev: BL 10/15/11; LMC 11–12/11; SLJ 1/12; VOYA 2/12)

4560 Lynch, Chris. *Sharpshooter* (8–11). Series: Vietnam. 2012, Scholastic $16.99 (978-054527026-7). Ivan becomes a sharpshooter for the United States Army and works to halt the shipment of weapons from the north of Vietnam to the south. YALSA Quick Picks for Reluctant Young Adult Readers 2013. ℮ Lexile 850L (Rev: BL 3/1/12; SLJ 6/12; VOYA 8/12)

4561 Michener, James A. *The Bridges at Toko-Ri* (9–12). 1953, Fawcett paper $5.95 (978-0-449-20651-5). The story of a young navy pilot and his bombing missions over Korea during the early 1950s. (Rev: BL 10/1/88)

4562 Nelson, Theresa. *And One for All* (7–12). 1989, Scholastic paper $16.95 (978-0-531-05804-6). Wing faces the disapproval of his best friend, a pacifist, when he decides to sign up to fight in Vietnam. (Rev: BL 4/15/06; SLJ 9/97)

4563 O'Brien, Tim. *Going After Cacciato* (10–12). 1999, Broadway paper $13.00 (978-0-7679-0442-1). In this surreal novel, Private Cacciato's company follows him when he leaves the Vietnam War to walk to Paris. For better readers.

4564 Potok, Chaim. *I Am the Clay* (9–12). 1994, Fawcett paper $5.99 (978-0-449-22138-9). An injured orphan boy touches the hearts of a crusty Korean refugee and his more compassionate wife. (Rev: BL 4/1/92; SLJ 12/92)

4565 Rostkowski, Margaret I. *The Best of Friends* (7–12). 1989, HarperCollins $12.95 (978-0-06-025104-8). Three Utah teenagers have a growing interest in the Vietnam War and how it affects each of them. (Rev: BL 9/1/89; SLJ 9/89; VOYA 12/89)

4566 Smith, Andrew. *In the Path of Falling Objects* (10–12). 2009, Feiwel & Friends $17.99 (978-0-312-37558-4). Jonah, 16, and his younger brother Simon miss their older brother who is experiencing a miserable war in Vietnam; they take to the road and unfortunately hitch a ride with a violent killer. Best Books for Young Adults 2010. ♫ ℮ Lexile 840L (Rev: BL 11/1/09; SLJ 11/09)

4567 Soli, Tatjana. *The Lotus Eaters* (11–12). 2010, St. Martin's $24.99 (978-031261157-6). This novel follows the lives of two war photographers — Sam and Helen — who become involved while working in Vietnam and their separate relationships with the Vietnamese assistant Linh; for mature readers. ∩ **e** (Rev: BL 3/1–15/10)

4568 White, Ellen Emerson. *The Road Home* (8–12). 1995, Scholastic paper $15.95 (978-0-590-46737-7). This story re-creates a Vietnam War medical base in claustrophobic and horrific detail, and features army nurse Rebecca Phillips, from the Echo Company book series. (Rev: BL 1/15/95; SLJ 4/95; VOYA 4/95)

4569 White, Ellen Emerson. *Where Have All the Flowers Gone? The Diary of Molly Mackenzie Flaherty* (7–10). 2002, Scholastic paper $10.95 (978-0-439-14889-4). Molly, whose brother Patrick is off fighting in the Vietnam War, sees firsthand the casualties of the conflict while working in a Boston hospital. This book is a companion to the story of her brother, *The Journal of Patrick Seamus Flaherty, United States Marine Corps, Khe Sanh, Vietnam, 1968* (2002). (Rev: BL 4/15/06)

TWENTY-FIRST CENTURY CONFLICTS

4570 Eck, Matthew. *The Farther Shore* (9–12). 2007, Milkweed $22.00 (978-1-57131-057-6). This powerful novel written by a veteran of the Somalia conflict features three American soldiers trapped in a terrifyingly dangerous area in the African desert; their fear is palpable as they try desperately to escape. (Rev: BL 9/1/07)

4571 Leshem, Ron. *Beaufort* (9–12). Trans. by Evan Fallenberg. 2008, Delacorte $24.00 (978-0-553-80682-3). This award-winning first novel details the quick transformation of high-school-age soldiers given the punishing deployment of protecting northern Israel from terrorist fire at the ancient Crusader fortress of Beaufort where they are under the leadership of Erez Liberti, not much older than his charges. (Rev: BL 11/15/07)

4572 Myers, Walter Dean. *Sunrise over Fallujah* (8–11). 2008, Scholastic $17.99 (978-0-439-91624-0). Robin — nephew of Richie, the young black Vietnam War soldier in 1988's *Fallen Angels* — is serving in Operation Iraqi Freedom and now understands his uncle's reluctance to talk about his experiences. ∩ (Rev: BL 2/15/08; SLJ 4/08)

Horror Stories and the Supernatural

4573 Acosta, Marta. *Dark Companion* (9–12). 2012, Tor Teen $17.99 (978-076532964-6). Excited about transferring to an elite academy, orphan Jane discovers the administrators have an unsettling interest in her — and her blood. ∩ **e** (Rev: BL 7/12; LMC 3–4/13; VOYA 6/12)

4574 Adams, John Joseph, ed. *By Blood We Live* (10–12). 2009, Night Shade paper $15.95 (978-1-59780-156-0). This provocative collection presents 30 vampire tales written over the past 30 years by a diverse group of authors including Anne Rice, Neil Gaiman, and Stephen King. (Rev: BL 10/15/09; SLJ 12/09)

4575 Alender, Katie. *Bad Girls Don't Die* (7–10). 2009, Hyperion $15.99 (978-142310876-4). Alexis must determine why her little sister is possessed by the spirit of a child who died long ago. Lexile HL670L (Rev: BL 4/1/09; SLJ 8/09)

4576 Ansa, Tina McElroy. *Baby of the Family* (10–12). 1991, Harcourt paper $14.00 (978-0-15-610150-9). Lena McPherson was born with the magical ability to relate to ghosts. (Rev: SLJ 6/90)

4577 Armstrong, Kelley. *Counterfeit Magic* (10–12). Illus. 2011, Subterranean $25 (978-159606328-0). In this mystery/fantasy that shares a setting with two earlier books, Paige and her adopted daughter Savannah become entangled with the mafia of the supernatural world while investigating a murder. ∩ **e** (Rev: BL 12/1–15/10)

4578 Arthur, Artist. *Manifest* (7–11). Series: Mystyx. 2010, Kimani/Tru paper $9.99 (978-03738319-6-8). After her parents' divorce and her move to Connecticut, unhappy African American 15-year-old Krystal eventually finds two friends who also have supernatural powers and can help her in her quest to save an unhappy teen ghost. (Rev: BL 10/1/10; SLJ 9/1/10)

4579 Asimov, Isaac, et al, ed. *Devils* (9–12). 1987, NAL paper $3.50 (978-0-451-14867-4). A devilish collection of stories drawn from such sources as folklore and tales of horror.

4580 Asimov, Isaac, et al, ed. *Tales of the Occult* (9–12). 1989, Prometheus paper $26.98 (978-0-87975-531-7). A collection of 22 stories that explore such subjects as telepathy and reincarnation. (Rev: BL 4/1/89)

4581 Atwater-Rhodes, Amelia. *Persistence of Memory* (7–10). 2008, Delacorte $15.99 (978-038573437-0); LB $18.99 (978-038590443-8). Sixteen-year-old Erin has been treated for schizophrenia for most of her life, but after a two-year hiatus from her alter-ego Shevaun, she discovers she isn't mentally ill at all, but entwined with the soul of a 500-year-old vampire. **e** Lexile 860L (Rev: BL 12/1/08; LMC 5–6/09; SLJ 2/1/09)

4582 Atwater-Rhodes, Amelia. *Token of Darkness* (6–10). 2010, Delacorte $16.99 (978-0-385-73750-0). A strange spectral girl named Samantha has remained at Cooper's side since his car accident, but who is she and how can he help her in her quest for a physical presence? **e** Lexile 900L (Rev: BLO 11/19/10; LMC 5–6/10; SLJ 1/10)

4583 Baer, Marianna. *Frost* (8–11). 2011, HarperCollins $17.99 (978-0-06-179949-5). The arrival of an eccentric classmate named Celeste disrupts Leena's plans for a perfect senior year in this suspenseful modern gothic novel set in a boarding school. **e** (Rev: BL 9/1/11; SLJ 9/1/11; VOYA 10/11)

4584 Baldick, Chris, ed. *The Oxford Book of Gothic Tales* (9–12). 1992, Oxford paper $19.95 (978-0-19-286219-8). There are 37 stories by such masters as Poe, Hardy, Faulkner, and Hawthorne in this collection of gothic stories, many of which involve the supernatural.

4585 Barker, Clive. *The Thief of Always* (10–12). 1997, HarperCollins paper $4.50 (978-0-06-105769-4). Ten-year-old Harvey Swick is bored, but he soon learns that entertainment can come at a high price when a mysterious stranger offers a trip to the magical Holiday House.

4586 Barnes, Jennifer Lynn. *Every Other Day* (7–10). 2011, Egmont $17.99 (978-160684169-3). Sixteen-year-old Kali is an ordinary high school student who is transformed every other day into an efficient demon hunter. **e** (Rev: BL 1/1/12; LMC 3–4/12; SLJ 1/12)

4587 Barnes, Jennifer Lynn, and Sarah Rees Brennan, et al. *Enthralled: Paranormal Diversions* (8–11). Ed. by Melissa Marr and Kelley Armstrong. 2011, HarperCollins $17.99 (978-0-06-201579-2). Sixteen paranormal short stories include some unexpected and novel twists in this intriguing collection. **e** (Rev: BL 10/1/11; SLJ 10/1/11; VOYA 10/11)

4588 Barraclough, Lindsey. *Long Lankin* (8–11). 2012, Candlewick $16.99 (978-076365808-3). Cora and her younger sister go to live with their Aunt Ida in a remote English village in 1958 and find they are in danger from an ancient evil. ☊ **e** Lexile 890L (Rev: BL 4/15/12; HB 7–8/12; LMC 10/12; SLJ 8/12; VOYA 6/12)

4589 Beaudoin, Sean. *The Infects* (8–11). 2012, Candlewick $16.99 (978-0-7636-5947-9). Nero, 17, is distressed to find himself on a wilderness trek with other juvenile delinquents, but his predicament worsens when the counselors turn into aggressive zombies. ☊ **e** (Rev: BL 7/12; HB 9–10/12; LMC 3–4/13; SLJ 11/12; VOYA 8/12)

4590 Becker, Robin. *Brains: A Zombie Memoir* (11–12). 2010, Eos paper $13.99 (978-00619740-5-2). A troupe of zombies sets off to find the virus that caused their condition —and to end the war between the living and the undead — in this violent yet funny novel for mature readers. **e** (Rev: BL 6/1–15/10)

4591 Belkom, Edo Van, ed. *Be Afraid! Tales of Horror* (8–12). 2000, Tundra $6.95 (978-0-88776-496-7). Fifteen horror stories for and about teens feature sinister twists, hauntings, and violence. (Rev: BL 2/1/01; SLJ 3/01; VOYA 2/01)

4592 Benson, Amber, and Christopher Golden. *Accursed* (11–12). 2005, Del Rey paper $13.95 (978-0-345-47130-7). Charged with defending the soul of England

as Protectors of Albion, siblings William and Tamara Swift call on ghostly allies when dark forces threaten; set in Victorian England and suitable for mature teens. (Rev: BL 11/15/05)

4593 Betancourt, John Gregory, and Sean Wallace, eds. *Horror: The Best of the Year, 2006 Edition* (9–12). 2006, Prime paper $13.95 (978-0-8095-5648-9). With a brief introduction and an author's biography at the end of each selection, this is a collection of 17 well-written stories. (Rev: BL 7/06)

4594 Bick, Ilsa J. *Ashes* (7–10). 2011, Egmont $17.99 (978-1-60684-175-4). After electromagnetic pulses turn much of the surviving population into zombies, 17-year-old Alex and her companions find new threats to their survival. ☊ **e** Lexile HL730L (Rev: BL 9/15/11; HB 9–10/12; LMC 1–2/12*; SLJ 10/1/11)

4595 Bick, Ilsa J. *Shadows* (7–10). 2012, Egmont $17.99 (978-160684176-1). In this sequel to *Ashes* (2011), 17-year-old Alex discovers that the town of Rule is not the haven she thought and is populated by a variety of horrors. ☊ **e** Lexile HL730L (Rev: BLO 10/1/12; HB 9–10/12; SLJ 1/13)

4596 Black, Bekka. *iDrakula* (7–10). 2010, Sourcebooks paper $9.99 (978-14022446-5-0). This modern retelling of Dracula captures all the original's shock and drama via text messages, emails, and screenshots. **e** Lexile HL660L (Rev: BL 10/15/10; VOYA 12/10)

4597 Black, Yelena. *Dance of Shadows* (7–10). 2013, Bloomsbury $17.99 (978-159990940-0). Vanessa, 15, attends New York Ballet Academy and enjoys the dance while also seeking clues to the disappearance of her older sister, who was also a student there. **e** (Rev: BL 11/1/12; SLJ 1/13; VOYA 12/12)

4598 Blake, Kendare. *Girl of Nightmares* (8–12). 2012, Tor Teen $17.99 (978-0-7653-2866-3). In this sequel to 2011's *Anna Dressed in Blood*, ghost hunter Cas decides he must rescue Anna from the tortures she is suffering in hell on his account. ☊ **e** (Rev: BL 10/1/12; SLJ 11/12)

4599 Block, Francesca Lia. *The Frenzy* (9–12). 2010, HarperTeen $16.99 (978-0-06-192666-2). Something happened to Liv when she was 13, and now that she is 17 she finally comes to understand that she is a were-wolf and that both she and her family must learn to cope with this fact. (Rev: BL 9/1/10; SLJ 12/1/10)

4600 Block, Francesca Lia. *Pretty Dead* (9–12). 2009, HarperTeen $16.99 (978-006154785-0); LB $17.89 (978-006154786-7). Vampire Charlotte is just getting close to human Jared when William, the vampire who transformed her in 1925, comes back into her life. (Rev: BL 5/15/09; HB 1–2/10; SLJ 10/09; VOYA 10/09)

4601 Bradbury, Ray. *The Halloween Tree* (7–12). 1972, Knopf $19.95 (978-0-394-82409-3). Nine boys discover the true meaning — and horror — of Halloween.

4602 Bray, Libba, et al. *Vacations from Hell* (8–11). 2009, HarperTeen $16.99 (978-0-06-168873-7); paper $9.99 (978-0-06-168872-0). A collection of stories by well-known authors about teens whose vacations take scary turns. (Rev: BL 8/09; SLJ 8/09; VOYA 10/09)

4603 Brennan, Sarah Rees. *Unspoken* (7–12). Series: Lynburn Legacy. 2012, Random House $18.99 (978-0-375-87041-5); LB $21.99 (978-037597041-2). Kami recognizes that things are not quite as they seem in her English village when the boy she has talked to in her head for years turns up; the first volume in a paranormal romance. **e** (Rev: BL 8/12; HB 9–10/12; LMC 1–2/13; SLJ 10/12; VOYA 10/12)

4604 Brewer, Heather. *Tenth Grade Bleeds* (6–10). Series: The Chronicles of Vladimir Tod. 2009, Dutton $16.99 (978-0-525-42135-1). Half-vampire Vlad, now in 10th grade in the third volume in the series, is grappling with teen angst while at the same time fighting the supernatural forces seeking to destroy him. ∩ **e** Lexile 820L (Rev: SLJ 9/09; VOYA 6/09)

4605 Brooks, Max. *World War Z: An Oral History of the Zombie War* (11–12). 2006, Crown $24.95 (978-0-307-34660-5). Survivors and others take turns giving their accounts of the "the Crisis," when zombies attacked the human population in this humorous horror tale. ∩ (Rev: BL 8/06)

4606 Buckingham, Royce. *Vampire Academy* (10–12). 2007, Penguin paper $8.99 (978-1-59514-174-3). Seventeen-year-old best friends Lissa (a mortal vampire princess) and Rose (half-human/ half-vampire and Lissa's guardian-in-training) are captured and forced to return to St. Vladimir's Academy, where they face challenges including peer pressure, gossip, threats, and new relationships; for mature readers. (Rev: BL 9/1/07; SLJ 12/07)

4607 Bunting, Eve. *The Presence: A Ghost Story* (6–10). 2003, Clarion $16.00 (978-0-618-26919-8). Catherine, 17, who is still grieving over the death of a friend, finds solace in a handsome young man but at the same time senses that something isn't quite right. (Rev: BL 10/15/03; HBG 4/04; SLJ 10/03; VOYA 2/04)

4608 Butcher, Jim. *Death Masks* (11–12). 2003, NAL paper $7.99 (978-0-451-45940-4). Harry Dresden's diverse friends band together to help him in this exciting adventure involving flight from vampires and the theft of the Shroud of Turin. (Rev: BL 7/03)

4609 Butler, Octavia E. *Fledgling* (11–12). 2005, Seven Stories $24.95 (978-1-58322-690-2). After awakening from traumatic injuries to find that she is a 53-year-old vampire trapped in the body of a young girl, Shori Matthews struggles to learn what has happened to her; for mature readers. (Rev: BL 10/15/05)

4610 Cabot, Meg. *Twilight* (7–10). Series: The Mediator. 2005, HarperCollins LB $16.89 (978-0-06-072468-9). Suze, deeply in love with a ghost named Jesse, faces

a real dilemma when she discovers a way to give Jesse back his life that would mean losing him as a boyfriend; the sixth installment in the series. (Rev: SLJ 2/05)

4611 Cabot, Meg, et al. *Prom Nights from Hell* (10–12). 2007, HarperCollins $16.99 (978-0-06-125309-6). Five well-known YA authors — including Meg Cabot, Stephenie Meyer, and Lauren Myracle — each contribute a terrifying tale. (Rev: BL 5/15/07; SLJ 9/07)

4612 Caine, Rachel. *Ghost Town* (10–12). Series: Morganville Vampires. 2010, NAL $17.99 (978-045123161-1). This installment in the vampire series finds Claire fighting to save her community after widespread memory loss creates havoc. (Rev: BL 11/1–15/10)

4613 Cann, Kate. *Consumed* (9–12). 2011, Scholastic $16.99 (978-0-545-26388-7). Rayne reluctantly agrees to help restore order yet again when her supernatural powers are called upon in this sequel to *Possessed* (2010). Lexile HL710L (Rev: BL 5/1/11; SLJ 5/11)

4614 Card, Orson Scott. *Lost Boys* (10–12). 1993, Morrow paper $7.99 (978-0-06-109131-5). After a Mormon family, the Fletchers, moves to North Carolina, son Stevie starts to develop imaginary friends whose names mysteriously match those of children who have disappeared from the community. (Rev: BL 8/92)

4615 Carter, Dean Vincent. *The Hand of the Devil* (8–11). 2006, Delacorte LB $9.99 (978-0-385-90386-8); paper $7.95 (978-0-385-73371-7). Young journalist Ashley Reeves travels to an island in Britain's Lake District to investigate an unusual mosquito and finds himself in dire straits. (Rev: BL 10/1/06; LMC 2/07; SLJ 1/07)

4616 Cerf, Bennett, ed. *Famous Ghost Stories* (10–12). 1956, Amereon LB $26.95 (978-0-88411-146-7). This is a superior anthology of truly scary stories.

4617 Chadda, Sarwat. *Devil's Kiss* (7–10). 2009, Hyperion $17.99 (978-1-4231-1999-9). Fifteen-year-old Billi SanGreal is secretly a Templar Knight in training in this complex and compelling novel that features the Angel of Death on a rampage. ∩ Lexile HL620L (Rev: BL 10/15/09; LMC 1–2/10; SLJ 11/09)

4618 Chadda, Sarwat. *The Savage Fortress* (8–12). 2012, Scholastic $16.99 (978-0-545-38516-9). When Ash Mistry visits India he finds himself dragged into a battle with *rakshasas* (demons) from which he tries to save his uncle, his aunt, and finally his sister and all of mankind. ∩ **e** Lexile 660L (Rev: SLJ 1/13*)

4619 Chance, Karen. *Touch the Dark* (9–12). 2006, Roc paper $6.99 (978-0-451-46093-6). Clairvoyant Cassandra Palmer has been on the run for three years trying to save her own life while attempting to discover why so many — including the vampire senate — want her dead. (Rev: BL 6/1–15/06)

4620 Citra, Becky. *Never to Be Told* (6–12). 2006, Orca paper $7.95 (978-1-55143-567-1). A ghost story set in a small town called Cold Creek and featuring a 12-year-old girl named Asia who faces upheavals in her life. (Rev: SLJ 12/06)

4621 Clegg, Douglas. *The Queen of Wolves* (9–12). 2007, Ace $23.95 (978-0-441-01523-8). Vampyre Aleric raises an army of the undead to protect the living in this final volume of the Vampyricon trilogy. (Rev: BL 9/1/07)

4622 Clement-Moore, Rosemary. *Hell Week* (9–12). 2008, Delacorte $16.99 (978-0-385-73414-1). Maggie, now in college, learns that the members of one sorority share a strange magical power that brings success but at a terrible price; humorous asides about Greek life leaven the horror. (Rev: SLJ 2/08)

4623 Clement-Moore, Rosemary. *Prom Dates from Hell* (9–12). 2007, Delacorte $15.99 (978-0-385-73412-7). High school newspaper photographer Maggie, a girl with confidence and — as it happens — her grandmother's sixth sense, investigates strange events and smells preceding the senior prom. (Rev: BCCB 7–8/07; HB 5–6/07; SLJ 3/07)

4624 Clement-Moore, Rosemary. *Texas Gothic* (9–12). 2011, Delacorte $17.99 (978-0-385-73693-0); LB $20.99 (978-0-385-90636-4). Amy Goodnight, an 18-year-old member of a family of witches, meets Ben while house-sitting in Texas and their initial antipathy turns to romance in this paranormal story featuring ghosts. **e** Lexile 790L (Rev: BLO 6/21/11; HB 9–10/11; SLJ 8/11*)

4625 Cochran, Molly. *Legacy* (7–11). 2011, Simon & Schuster $17.99 (978-1-4424-1739-7). At a new school in Massachusetts, not far from Salem, 16-year-old half-witch and outsider Katy discovers that her family has a history here and that her powers may help save the town. **e** Lexile HL690L (Rev: BL 12/15/11; SLJ 12/1/11)

4626 Connolly, John. *The Gates* (10–12). 2009, Atria $24 (978-143917263-6). Weirdness abounds this in this comedic horror-fantasy as the neighborhood's adult population is inhabited by demons who are preparing for the Great Malevolence; fortunately for 11-year-old Samuel, the hapless demon who shows up in his bedroom takes a shine to him. ◯ **e** (Rev: BL 10/15/09)

4627 Cooney, Caroline B. *Night School* (7–10). 1995, Scholastic paper $3.50 (978-0-590-47878-6). Four California teens enroll in a mysterious night school course and encounter an evil instructor and their own worst character defects. (Rev: BL 5/1/95)

4628 Cray, Jordan. *Gemini 7* (6–10). 1997, Simon & Schuster paper $4.50 (978-0-689-81432-7). In this horror story, Jonah Lanier begins to realize that his new friend, Nicole, might be responsible for the mysterious disasters that are befalling his family and other friends. (Rev: SLJ 1/98)

4629 Cusick, Richie Tankersley. *The House Next Door* (6–12). 2002, Simon & Schuster paper $4.99 (978-0-7434-1838-6). Emma dares to spend a night in a haunted house and becomes caught up in a struggle to free a spirit from the past in this tale of supernatural suspense. (Rev: BL 1/1–15/02; SLJ 2/02; VOYA 6/02)

4630 Damico, Gina. *Scorch* (8–12). 2012, Houghton Mifflin $8.99 (978-054762457-0). Neophyte grim reaper Lex, 16, works to earn her stripes in this darkly comic sequel to *Croak* (2012). ◯ **e** (Rev: BLO 10/1/12; SLJ 4/13; VOYA 12/12)

4631 Davis, Heather. *Never Cry Werewolf* (7–10). 2009, HarperTeen $16.99 (978-006134923-2). At a "brat camp," willful 16-year-old Shelby meets an attractive young werewolf named Austin Bridges III. (Rev: BL 7/09; SLJ 12/09)

4632 de la Cruz, Melissa. *Witches of East End* (11–12). 2011, Hyperion $23.99 (978-140132390-5). Three female witches are called on to realize their hitherto hidden powers when their quiet town is besieged by violence and a girl disappears; for mature readers. **e** (Rev: BL 6/15/11; SLJ 8/11)

4633 de Lint, Charles. *The Blue Girl* (8–11). 2004, Penguin $17.99 (978-0-670-05924-9). Imogene, determined to turn over a new leaf at her new high school, strikes up an alliance with loner Maxine and meets the ghost of a former pupil, foreshadowing a struggle between an evil underworld and an inhospitable reality. (Rev: BL 11/15/04; SLJ 11/04; VOYA 12/04)

4634 Decker, Sherry. *Hook House and Other Horrors* (9–12). 2006, Silver Lake paper $12.95 (978-1-933511-09-2). A collection of horror and dark fantasy tales with well-developed characters. (Rev: SLJ 5/06)

4635 Dennard, Susan. *Something Strange and Deadly* (8–12). 2012, HarperCollins $17.99 (978-0-06-208326-5). In a 19th-century Philadelphia troubled by walking dead, gutsy 16-year-old Eleanor is determined to find her missing brother. **e** (Rev: SLJ 9/12; VOYA 4/12)

4636 Despain, Bree. *The Dark Divine* (7–11). 2009, Egmont $17.99 (978-1-60684-057-3); LB $20.99 (978-1-60684-065-8). Grace Divine, 16-year-old daughter of a pastor, and Daniel, a friend of her brother's who has returned to town, fall in love — and then Daniel reveals that he is a werewolf. ◯ **e** Lexile HL700L (Rev: BL 1/1–15/10; SLJ 5/10)

4637 Dimartino, Nick. *Seattle Ghost Story* (10–12). 1998, Rosebriar paper $12.95 (978-0-9653918-2-5). A horror story in which Billy Beck accidentally unleashes a deadly ghost that brings havoc to his quiet neighborhood. (Rev: SLJ 1/99)

4638 Diver, Lucienne. *Fangtastic* (8–12). Series: Vamped. 2012, Flux paper $9.95 (978-07387303-9-4). Gina, an undercover vampire federal agent, and her boyfriend Bobby investigate murders committed by a group of humans acting like vampires. ℮ Lexile 760L (Rev: BLO 2/15/12; SLJ 1/12; VOYA 2/12)

4639 Du Maurier, Daphne. *Echoes from the Macabre: Selected Stories* (9–12). 1977, Aeonian $25.95 (978-0-88411-543-4). Nine stories of suspense including the classic "The Birds."

4640 Duncan, Lois. *Locked in Time* (7–10). 1985, Dell paper $4.99 (978-0-440-94942-8). Nore's father marries into a family that somehow never seems to age. (Rev: BL 7/85; SLJ 11/85)

4641 Duncan, Lois. *Stranger with My Face* (7–10). 1984, Dell paper $5.50 (978-0-440-98356-9). A girl encounters her evil twin, who wishes to take her place.

4642 Duncan, Lois. *Summer of Fear* (7–10). 1976, Dell paper $5.50 (978-0-440-98324-8). An orphaned cousin who comes to live with Rachel's family is really a witch.

4643 Dunkle, Clare B. *The House of Dead Maids* (7–10). 2010, Henry Holt $15.99 (978-0-8050-9116-8). In this prequel to *Wuthering Heights,* 11-year-old Tabby arrives at the spooky Seldon House to be a nursemaid to the young Heathcliff (here called Himself) and learns about many previous housemaids who did not survive. ⌒ ℮ (Rev: BL 8/10; HB 11–12/10; LMC 11–12/10; SLJ 11/1/10; VOYA 12/10)

4644 Durst, Sarah Beth. *Drink, Slay, Love* (7–10). 2011, Simon & Schuster $16.99 (978-1-4424-2373-2). After a unicorn attack, teen vampire Pearl develops an uneasy amount of empathy for her victims. ⌒ ℮ (Rev: BL 9/15/11; SLJ 10/1/11)

4645 Edgerton, Leslie H., ed. *Monday's Meal* (10–12). 1997, Univ. of North Texas paper $14.95 (978-1-57441-026-6). A collection of 21 unique, often gruesome, horror stories, many of which are set in the French Quarter of New Orleans. (Rev: SLJ 1/98)

4646 Ee, Susan. *Angelfall* (9–12). 2012, Amazon Children's paper $6.99 (978-07614632-7-6). Penryn, 17, tries to rescue her wheelchair-bound sister and her schizophrenic mother but the apocalyptic angels that are taking over the world disrupt her plans. ⌒ ℮ (Rev: BL 9/15/12; SLJ 1/13; VOYA 12/12)

4647 Egan, Jennifer. *The Keep* (11–12). 2006, Knopf $24.00 (978-1-4000-4392-7). Danny travels to Eastern Europe to help his cousin fix up an old, mysterious castle and encounters a supernatural secret in this novel that will leave readers haunted and uneasy. (Rev: BL 5/1/06)

4648 Etchison, Dennis, et al, ed. *Gathering the Bones: Original Stories from the World's Masters of Horror* (11–12). 2003, Tor paper $15.95 (978-0-7653-0179-6). This collection of widely diverse horror fiction from the United States, Britain, and Australia is suitable only for mature readers. (Rev: BL 8/03)

4649 Evans, Justin. *The White De-vil* (11–12). 2011, HarperCollins $24.99 (978-006172827-3). American 17-year-old Andrew Taylor, who strongly resembles poet Lord Byron, finds himself an outcast when he arrives at the elite British boarding school — and he is the unwitting catalyst for some horrific events; for mature readers. ⌒ ℮ (Rev: BL 4/1/11*; SLJ 7/11)

4650 Fahy, Thomas. *Sleepless* (8–11). 2009, Simon & Schuster $15.99 (978-141695901-4). Emma and her friends are sleepwalking and having horrible nightmares. Could they be responsible for the deaths of some of their classmates? Lexile 710L (Rev: BLO 5/27/09; SLJ 12/09)

4651 Fahy, Thomas. *The Unspoken* (8–12). 2008, Simon & Schuster $15.99 (978-1-4169-4007-4). Allison escaped from a deadly cult years ago, but today she and other teenage survivors are facing mysterious and gory deaths. (Rev: BL 1/1–15/08; LMC 4–5/08; SLJ 4/08)

4652 Fleming, Candace. *On the Day I Died: Stories from the Grave* (7–10). 2012, Random House $16.99 (978-0-375-86781-1); LB $19.99 (978-0-375-96781-8). Teenage ghosts who died over the decades tell their stories to Mike Kowalski, who has strayed into a Chicago cemetery. ⌒ ℮ Lexile 720L (Rev: BL 5/15/12; LMC 11–12/12; SLJ 10/12)

4653 Fox, Andrew. *Bride of the Fat White Vampire* (9–12). 2004, Ballantine paper $14.95 (978-0-345-46408-8). The entertaining sequel to *Fat White Vampire Blues* finds vampire Jules back together again (after changing himself into 187 rats) and trying to get to the bottom of a mystery involving black vampires. (Rev: BL 8/04)

4654 Freedman, Dave. *Natural Selection* (9–12). 2006, Hyperion $21.95 (978-1-4013-0209-2). Huge, flying, meat-eating sting rays threaten Earth, and it's up to a small band of researchers to determine how to stop them. (Rev: BL 5/15/06)

4655 Gabhart, Ann H. *Wish Come True* (7–10). 1988, Avon paper $2.50 (978-0-380-75653-7). Lyssie receives as a gift a mirror that grants her wishes. (Rev: VOYA 6/89)

4656 Gantos, Jack. *The Love Curse of the Rumbaughs* (10–12). 2006, Farrar $17.00 (978-0-374-33690-5). A dark Gothic novel, this tale of adult albino twins and their unhealthy obsession with their dead mother is not for the faint of heart, but mature teens will find the plot compelling. ⌒ (Rev: BL 5/1/06; HB 7–8/06; SLJ 5/06)

4657 Garretson, Jerri. *The Secret of Whispering Springs* (7–12). 2002, Ravenstone paper $6.99 (978-0-9659712-4-9). A ghost and a mysterious stranger alert Cassie to potential danger, and a potential fortune, in this suspenseful adventure. (Rev: BL 8/02; SLJ 8/02)

4658 Gibson, Marley. *The Awakening* (7–10). Series: Ghost Huntress. 2009, Harcourt paper $8.99 (978-054715093-2). Newly moved from Chicago to a tiny town in Georgia, 16-year-old Kendall finds herself part of a ghost-hunting team that seeks to free Kendall's father of a troublesome spirit. (Rev: BL 5/15/09; LMC 10/09; SLJ 6/1/09)

4659 Gifaldi, David. *Yours Till Forever* (7–10). 1989, HarperCollins LB $13.89 (978-0-397-32356-2). In this easily read novel, a high school senior sees disturbing similarities between his friends and his dead parents. (Rev: BL 10/1/89; SLJ 11/89; VOYA 2/90)

4660 Gill, David Macinnis. *Soul Enchilada* (7–10). 2009, Greenwillow $16.99 (978-006167301-6); LB $17.89 (978-006167302-3). A quirky story in which 18-year-old Bug Smoot, whose prize possession is a 1958 Cadillac Biarritz, discovers that the car — and her soul — are part of a deal with the Devil made years before by her grandfather. Best Books for Young Adults 2010. (Rev: BL 11/15/08; SLJ 4/1/09)

4661 Golden, Christopher. *Poison Ink* (9–12). 2008, Delacorte LB $12.99 (978-0-385-90481-0); paper $8.99 (978-0-385-73483-7). Teenage angst and isolation are amplified as Sammi's friends abandon her after getting tattoos that seem to wield a negative, otherworldly influence. **e** (Rev: SLJ 10/1/08; VOYA 10/08)

4662 Golden, Christopher. *The Shell Collector* (10–12). 2006, Dance $30.00 (978-1-58767-114-2). A brief and suspenseful horror story set in a Massachusetts fishing town. (Rev: BL 3/15/06)

4663 Golden, Christopher. *Wildwood Road* (11–12). 2005, Bantam paper $12.00 (978-0-553-38208-2). For mature teens, this is a spooky horror story about a mysterious child whose constant appearances threaten to ruin a couple's lives. (Rev: BL 4/15/05)

4664 Gorog, Judith. *When Nobody's Home* (6–12). 1996, Scholastic paper $15.95 (978-0-590-46862-6). A collection of 15 terrifying (supposedly true) tales on the theme of baby-sitting. (Rev: BL 5/1/96; SLJ 4/96; VOYA 12/96)

4665 Grabien, Deborah. *New-Slain Knight* (9–12). 2007, St. Martin's $24.95 (978-0-312-37400-6). Ringan, a Scottish folk musician, and partner Penny take his violin prodigy niece Rebecca to a friend's home in Cornwall where they will vacation and play together in his band, but the house has some mysterious and dangerous effects on them, forcing them to find the truth. (Rev: BL 11/1/07)

4666 Grahame-Smith, Seth. *Abraham Lincoln: Vampire Hunter* (10–12). 2010, Grand Central $21.99 (978-044656308-6). Grahame-Smith tells the "true story" of Abraham Lincoln, revealed by a passage in Honest Abe's secret journal that outlines his lifelong campaign against vampires. ∩ Lexile 960L (Rev: BL 1/1–15/10)

4667 Grahame-Smith, Seth. *Pride and Prejudice and Zombies* (10–12). 2009, Quirk paper $12.95 (978-15947433-4-4). An entertaining mingling of disparate genres that has the ultra-mannered characters of *Pride and Prejudice* (much of Austen's text is kept) training

for combat and happily killing zombies. ∩ **e** (Rev: BL 4–5/09; SLJ 6/09)

4668 Grant, Mira. *Deadline* (11–12). 2011, Orbit paper $9.99 (978-0-316-08106-1). News anchor Shaun finds himself immersed in a breaking story when a CDC researcher pursued by zombies shows up at his door. ∩ (Rev: SLJ 7/11)

4669 Gray, Claudia. *Balthazar* (8–11). Series: Evernight. 2012, HarperTeen $17.99 (978-006196118-2). Rogue vampire Balthazar helps psychic Skye, who attended Evernight Academy, when she is threatened by vampire master Redgrave. (Rev: BL 3/1/12; SLJ 3/12; VOYA 2/12)

4670 Gray, Claudia. *Stargazer* (9–12). 2009, HarperTeen $16.99 (978-006128440-3); LB $17.89 (978-006128445-8). At Evernight, a boarding school for vampires, Bianca is torn between Balthazar and Lucas—and between the human realm and the world of the undead; a sequel to *Evernight* (2008). Lexile HL750L (Rev: BL 2/15/09; SLJ 5/1/09)

4671 Green, Simon R. *The Man with the Golden Torc* (9–12). 2007, Roc $23.95 (978-0-451-46145-2). An adventure-filled spy story about a supernatural being whose job is to protect human beings from their own bad dreams. (Rev: BL 6/1–15/07)

4672 Griffin, Bethany. *Masque of the Red Death* (9–12). 2012, Greenwillow $16.99 (978-006210779-4). Immune from a devastating plague, Araby is free to pursue romance and intrigue in this twist on Edgar Allen Poe's short story. **e** Lexile HL640L (Rev: BL 5/1/12; HB 5–6/12; SLJ 6/12)

4673 Hahn, Mary Downing. *Look for Me by Moonlight* (7–10). 1995, Clarion $16.00 (978-0-395-69843-3). A 16-year-old girl seeking friendship meets a boy whose attention has dangerous strings attached. (Rev: BL 3/15/95; SLJ 5/95)

4674 Hambly, Barbara, and Martin H. Greenberg, eds. *Sisters of the Night* (9–12). 1995, Warner paper $17.99 (978-0-446-67143-9). Fourteen original stories by such masters as Jane Yolan, Tanith Lee, and Larry Niven explore the world of the female vampire. (Rev: VOYA 4/96)

4675 Hamilton, Virginia. *Sweet Whispers, Brother Rush* (7–10). 1982, Putnam $21.99 (978-0-399-20894-2). A 14-year-old girl who cares for her older retarded brother meets a charming ghost who reveals secrets of her past.

4676 Harper, Suzanne. *The Secret Life of Sparrow Delaney* (7–10). 2007, Greenwillow $16.99 (978-0-06-113158-5). Sparrow is a reluctant psychic who must face up to her abilities when she begins seeing a ghost named Luke, the dead brother of a friend at school, who needs help. (Rev: BCCB 9/07; BL 7/07; SLJ 11/07)

4677 Harris, Charlaine. *Dead and Gone* (11–12). 2009, Ace $25.95 (978-044101715-7). In the latest installment of the series on which HBO's *True Blood* is based, barmaid Sookie Stackhouse investigates as werewolves follow vampires' lead in going public; for mature readers. ∩ (Rev: BL 4–5/09)

4678 Harris, Charlaine. *Dead as a Doornail* (11–12). Series: Southern Vampire Mysteries. 2005, Ace $22.95 (978-0-441-01279-4). Sookie, last seen in *Dead to the World* (2004), continues to lead a dangerous life — this time with the Were-people; for mature teens. (Rev: BL 5/1/05)

4679 Harris, Charlaine. *Definitely Dead* (11–12). Series: Southern Vampire Mysteries. 2006, Ace $23.95 (978-0-441-01400-2). When Sookie's vampire cousin is murdered, she must travel to New Orleans, leaving behind a new boyfriend — who happens to be a were-tiger. ∩ (Rev: BL 5/15/06)

4680 Harrison, Kim. *Once Dead, Twice Shy* (8–11). Series: Madison Avery. 2009, HarperTeen $16.99 (978-006171816-8). Madison joins angels, "timekeepers," and other supernatural beings when her soul hovers between life and death following a car crash. ℮ (Rev: BL 2/1/09; SLJ 7/1/09; VOYA 8/09)

4681 Hartwell, David G., ed. *The Screaming Skull and Other Great American Ghost Stories* (10–12). 1995, Tor $4.99 (978-0-8125-5178-5). A collection of 12 high-quality ghost stories by such writers as Edgar Allan Poe, F. Marion Crawford, Mark Twain, Nathaniel Hawthorne, Willa Cather, and Edith Wharton. (Rev: VOYA 4/96)

4682 Harvey, Alyxandra. *Hearts at Stake* (8–10). Series: Drake Chronicles. 2010, Walker $16.99 (978-0-8027-9840-4). This funny, coming-of-age vampire story — involving 15-year-old Solange (vampire queen to be), her seven protective older brothers, and her feisty mortal friend Lucy — is the first in a series. ℮ Lexile HL660L (Rev: BL 12/1/09; LMC 3–4/10; SLJ 3/10)

4683 Hawes, Louise. *Rosey in the Present Tense* (8–12). 1999, Walker $15.95 (978-0-8027-8685-2). After the death of his girlfriend, Rosey, 17-year-old Franklin can't stop living in the past until the ghost of Rosey and his family and friends help him accept his loss and begin to think of the present. (Rev: BL 4/1/99; HBG 9/99; SLJ 5/99; VOYA 10/99)

4684 Hawkins, Rachel. *Demonglass* (7–11). Series: Hex Hall. 2011, Disney/Hyperion $16.99 (978-1-4231-2131-2). Young demon Sophie must decide whether to live out her family legacy or have her magical powers removed. ∩ ℮ (Rev: BL 2/15/11; SLJ 7/11; VOYA 12/10)

4685 Hawkins, Rachel. *Hex Hall* (8–11). 2010, Hyperion $16.99 (978-142312130-5). When an attempt at casting a spell is unsuccessful, 16-year-old part-warlock Sophie is shipped off to a school for unruly supernaturally talented beings; a humorous and clever series starter. ∩ ℮ Lexile 790L (Rev: BL 3/15/10; VOYA 6/10)

4686 Hendee, Barb, and J. C. Hendee. *Dhampir* (11–12). 2003, NAL paper $7.99 (978-0-451-45906-0). Suitable for mature teens only, this is the story of Magiere and her companion Leesil, who is half elf, and their initially fraudulent but later for-real battles against vampires. (Rev: BL 1/1–15/03)

4687 Hendee, Barb, and J. C. Hendee. *Thief of Lives* (9–12). 2004, NAL paper $7.99 (978-0-451-45953-4). Magiere, a half-human-half-vampire female, is pressured to hunt down a vampire who has killed a councilman's daughter. (Rev: BL 1/1–15/04)

4688 Henry, Mark. *Battle of the Network Zombies* (11–12). 2010, Kensington paper $15 (978-07582252-6-9). In fashion-conscious zombie Amanda Feral's third adventure, a snarky sendup of reality TV, the undead owner of an ad company finds herself investigating the fame-seeking contestants she's living with in Minions Mansion — including a yeti stripper and a cross-dressing werewolf — in the murder of a promiscuous male wood-nymph named Johnny Birch. For mature readers. (Rev: BLO 2/1–15/10)

4689 Hightman, J. P. *Spirit* (6–10). 2008, HarperTeen $16.99 (978-006085063-0); LB $17.89 (978-006085064-7). Depraved, ghostly Old Widow Malgore haunts 1892 Blackthorne, Massachusetts, and newlyweds Tess and Tobias have their share of gruesome, eerie encounters as they explore the abandoned town and try to wrest Blackthorn's secret from its keeper. ℮ Lexile NC800L (Rev: BL 8/08; SLJ 9/1/08; VOYA 12/08)

4690 Hill, Will. *The Rising* (9–12). Series: Department 19. 2012, Penguin $18.99 (978-1-59514-407-2). A thrilling sequel in which Jamie and his vampire colleagues must ensure that Dracula does not return to power. ℮ (Rev: BLO 10/1/12; LMC 1–2/13; SLJ 12/12)

4691 Hines, T. L. *Waking Lazarus* (9–12). 2006, Bethany $18.99 (978-0-7642-0204-9). After falling under the ice and "dying" at the age of 8, Jude Allman has now grown into a recluse haunted by a clairvoyance that allows him to divine evil before it occurs. (Rev: BL 6/1–15/06)

4692 Hockensmith, Steve. *Dawn of the Dreadfuls* (10–12). 2010, Quirk paper $12.95 (978-15947445-4-9). Providing backstory to 2009's *Pride and Prejudice and Zombies*, Hockensmith explores the origin of the Bennett sisters' gifts as zombie killers. (Rev: BL 4–5/09)

4693 Hoffman, Nina Kiriki. *Spirits That Walk in Shadow* (8–11). 2006, Viking $17.99 (978-0-670-06071-9). In alternating narratives, roommates Kim and Jaimie describe their story; Jaimie, blessed with unusual powers, is determined to rid Kim of a tiresome "viri." (Rev: BL 11/1/06; SLJ 1/07)

4694 Holder, Nancy. *The Evil Within* (9–11). 2010, Penguin paper $9.99 (978-15951429-1-7). In this suspenseful sequel to *Possessions*, Lindsay returns to Marlwood Academy and makes chilling discoveries about activities there in the 19th century when the school was an asylum. **e** (Rev: BLO 6/10; VOYA 6/10)

4695 Holder, Nancy, and Debbie Viguié. *Crusade* (7–11). 2010, Simon & Schuster $16.99 (978-1-4169-9802-0). Jenn has trained at Spain's Salamanca Academy for vampire hunters and is now part of a teenage team battling power-hungry vampires. **e** (Rev: BL 9/15/10; SLJ 12/1/10)

4696 Holmes, Jeannie. *Blood Law* (11–12). 2010, Dell paper $7.99 (978-05535926-7-2). In small-town Mississippi, Alexandra Sabian, a vampire herself, is charged with keeping the peace between humans and vampires at a time when vampires start showing up murdered; a complex, violent novel for mature readers. **e** (Rev: BL 5/1–15/10)

4697 Holt, Simon. *Soulstice* (8–12). Series: The Devouring. 2009, Little, Brown $16.99 (978-0-316-03571-2). In this sequel to 2008's *The Devouring,* the evil Vours return, and Reggie — who can access the "fearscape" and retrieve human spirits — faces more demons in order to protect those she holds dear. **e** Lexile HL750L (Rev: SLJ 1/10; VOYA 2/10)

4698 Horowitz, Anthony. *Bloody Horowitz* (9–12). 2010, Philomel $12.99 (978-0-399-25451-2). A collection of gruesome stories, many with a technological twist. (Rev: BL 9/1/10; SLJ 12/1/10)

4699 Hubbard, Susan. *The Season of Risks* (10–12). Series: Ethical Vampire. 2010, Simon & Schuster paper $14 (978-14391834-2-7). Half-vampire Ari yearns for adulthood — and the chance to travel in elite political circles with fellow vampire presidential candidate Neil Cameron. (Rev: BL 7/10)

4700 Irwin, Stephen M. *The Dead Path* (10–12). 2010, Doubleday $26 (978-038553343-0). After an accident takes his wife and bestows him with second sight, Nicholas returns to his childhood home where he uncovers a woodland spirit that is killing local children. (Rev: BL 10/1–15/10)

4701 Jackson, Shirley. *The Haunting of Hill House* (9–12). 1984, Penguin paper $14.00 (978-0-14-007108-5). Four people decide to stay in Hill House to see if it is really haunted.

4702 Jacobs, Deborah Lynn. *Powers* (7–10). 2006, Roaring Brook $16.95 (978-1-59643-112-6). When Gwen meets Adrian they feel a powerful connection between themselves, and their powers — hers to see future tragedies and his to read others' minds — are increased; but can they learn to trust each other and work together? (Rev: BL 8/06; LMC 2/07; SLJ 10/06; VOYA)

4703 James, Ellie. *Shattered Dreams* (9–12). 2011, St. Martin's paper $9.99 (978-03126470-2-5). Sixteen-year-old Trinity moves to New Orleans to live with her aunt and finds herself haunted by visions of the future. **e** (Rev: BLO 11/15/11; SLJ 3/12; VOYA 12/11)

4704 Jay, Stacey. *Juliet Immortal* (9–12). 2011, Delacorte $17.99 (978-0-385-74016-6); LB $20.99 (978-038590826-9). Seven hundred years later, Romeo and Juliet are inhabiting other bodies in this gritty paranormal romance. ∩ **e** Lexile 770L (Rev: BL 9/15/11; SLJ 11/1/11; VOYA 10/11)

4705 Johnson, Maureen. *Devilish* (8–11). 2006, Penguin $16.99 (978-1-59514-060-9). Jane, a high school senior, finds out that her best friend Ally has sold her soul to a demon in exchange for popularity; Jane's efforts to help lead her into real danger. (Rev: BL 10/15/06; HB 11–12/06; SLJ 10/06)

4706 Johnson, Maureen. *The Name of the Star* (8–11). 2011, Putnam $16.99 (978-0-399-25660-8). A paranormal mystery/romance in which 18-year-old Rory arrives in London from Louisiana and discovers that she can see ghosts that may be involved in a series of horrific murders mirroring Jack the Ripper's 1888 killings. YALSA Popular Paperbacks for Young Adults Top Ten 2013. ∩ **e** Lexile HL710L (Rev: BL 9/1/11; HB 11–12/11; LMC 1–2/12; SLJ 9/1/11)

4707 Jones, Carrie, and Steven E. Wedel. *After Obsession* (9–12). 2011, Bloomsbury $17.99 (978-159990681-2). Besieged by violent dreams, Aimee forms a romantic bond with kindred spirit and half Navajo Alan, and together they set out to exorcise the evil that has taken over Alan's cousin Courtney. **e** Lexile HL570L (Rev: BL 9/15/11; SLJ 3/12)

4708 Jones, Stephen, ed. *The Mammoth Book of Best New Horror, Vol. 14* (11–12). 2003, Carroll & Graf paper $11.95 (978-0-7867-1217-5). Chilling tales by Ramsey Campbell, Neil Gaiman, and Stephen Gallagher are among those in this year's selection; for mature teens. (Rev: BL 11/1/03)

4709 Jones, Stephen, ed. *The Mammoth Book of Vampire Stories by Women* (10–12). Series: Mammoth. 2001, Carroll & Graf paper $11.95 (978-0-7867-0918-2). This is an excellent collection of vampire tales written over the years by women. (Rev: BL 11/15/01)

4710 Kade, Stacey. *Queen of the Dead* (8–12). 2011, Hyperion $16.99 (978-1-4231-3467-1). Ghost Alona is shocked to find that her parents are recovering from her death, while Will is becoming involved with a group of ghost-talkers; a sequel to *The Ghost and the Goth* (2010). **e** Lexile 810L (Rev: BL 7/11; SLJ 11/1/11)

4711 Kadrey, Richard. *Sandman Slim* (11–12). 2009, Eos $24.99 (978-006171430-6). After a long stint in hell, a tough-guy magician seeks revenge on the "Circle" responsible for putting him there; for mature readers. ∩ (Rev: BL 7/09)

4712 Kagawa, Julie. *The Immortal Rules* (7–10). Series: Blood of Eden. 2012, HarlequinTeen $18.99 (978-0-373-21051-0). Desperate to survive in the new world with few humans, Allison chooses to become a vampire but then must face the rabids. ∩ e (Rev: BL 4/15/12; LMC 10/12; SLJ 10/12)

4713 Kate, Lauren. *Fallen* (9–12). 2010, Delacorte $17.99 (978-0-385-73893-4). This tale of fallen angels involves 17-year-old Luce, who is sent to a boarding school after the mysterious death of her boyfriend, and the gorgeous Daniel, who also attends the same school and is strangely familiar. ∩ e Lexile 830L (Rev: BL 12/1/09; LMC 3–4/10; SLJ 1/10)

4714 Kelleher, Victor. *Del-Del* (7–12). 1992, Walker $17.95 (978-0-8027-8154-3). A family believes its son is possessed by an evil alien. (Rev: BL 3/1/92; SLJ 6/92)

4715 Kelly, Ronald. *Hell Hollow* (11–12). 2009, Cemetery Dance $40 (978-158767186-9). In this coming-of-age horror story, 12-year old Keith Bishop encounters a fugitive murderer while visiting his grandfather's Tennessee farm. (Rev: BL 11/15/09)

4716 Kemmerer, Brigid. *Storm* (10–12). Series: The Elemental. 2012, Kensington/KTeen paper $9.95 (978-0-7582-7281-2). A paranormal romance featuring high school junior Becca and brothers who have the ability to control the four elements. e (Rev: LMC 1–2/13; SLJ 9/12; VOYA 6/12)

4717 Kenyon, Nate. *Sparrow Rock* (11–12). 2010, Leisure paper $7.99 (978-08439637-7-9). A group of teenagers find themselves trapped in a bomb shelter as a nuclear holocaust takes place outside, and they face both external and internal challenges; for mature readers. e (Rev: BLO 5/1–15/10)

4718 King, Stephen. *Carrie* (10–12). 1974, Doubleday $29.95 (978-0-385-08695-0). Carrie, a teenager with telekenetic powers, takes horrible revenge on her tormentors.

4719 King, Stephen. *Cell* (9–12). 2006, Scribner $26.95 (978-0-7432-9233-7). In a world rendered mad by a single cell phone call, Clay Riddell, accompanied by 15-year-old Alice and bright 12-year-old Tom, seeks to survive and to set things to rights. (Rev: BL 1/1–15/06)

4720 King, Stephen. *Christine* (9–12). 1983, NAL paper $7.99 (978-0-451-16044-7). Arnie buys an old Plymouth that has mystical powers to possess and destroy.

4721 King, Stephen. *Cujo* (10–12). 1981, NAL paper $7.99 (978-0-451-16135-2). This is a horror story about a huge Saint Bernard that runs amok.

4722 King, Stephen. *The Dark Tower* (9–12). Series: Dark Tower. 2004, Scribner $35.00 (978-1-880418-62-8). A suspenseful finale to the long-running saga about the last gunslinger in the world. (Rev: BL 9/1/04)

4723 King, Stephen. *The Dead Zone* (9–12). 1979, NAL paper $7.99 (978-0-451-15575-7). A number of men named John Smith find themselves in the strange area known as The Dead Zone.

4724 King, Stephen. *Different Seasons* (10–12). 1998, NAL paper $7.99 (978-0-451-19712-2). Four short stories by this master of suspense and mystery.

4725 King, Stephen. *Dreamcatcher* (10–12). 2001, Scribner $28.00 (978-0-7432-1138-3). An ailing stranger stumbles into a hunting camp and explodes, releasing a monster that may herald an alien invasion. (Rev: BL 3/1/01)

4726 King, Stephen. *Everything's Eventual: 14 Dark Tales* (9–12). 2002, Scribner $28.00 (978-0-7432-3515-0). Fourteen horror stories by King with an introduction about the genre from the author.

4727 King, Stephen. *Firestarter* (9–12). 1980, NAL paper $7.99 (978-0-451-16780-4). A child is born with the incredible power to start fires.

4728 King, Stephen. *Four Past Midnight* (10–12). 1990, Viking paper $7.99 (978-0-451-17038-5). This book contains four horror stories bound to please those who enjoy chills with their reading.

4729 King, Stephen. *Just After Sunset* (10–12). 2008, Scribner $28.00 (978-141658408-7). A typical anthology of short stories from the master of horror. Alex Award 2009. ∩ e (Rev: BL 9/15/08)

4730 King, Stephen. *Lisey's Story* (9–12). 2006, Scribner $28.00 (978-0-7432-8941-2). Lisey Landon follows her dead husband's voice as she fights to save herself from the psychopath obsessed with possessing her husband's unpublished manuscripts. (Rev: BL 6/1–15/06)

4731 King, Stephen. *Night Shift* (10–12). 1978, Doubleday $30.00 (978-0-385-12991-6). Vampires and demons inhabit these horror stories by a master of the macabre. (Rev: BL 10/15/88)

4732 King, Stephen. *The Shining* (10–12). 1977, Doubleday $27.50 (978-0-385-12167-5). The Torrances take over a deserted hotel that is haunted by the spirits of the dead.

4733 King, Stephen. *Skeleton Crew* (9–12). 1985, Putnam paper $7.99 (978-0-451-16861-0). This is a collection of King's short fiction.

4734 King, Stephen. *The Stand* (10–12). 1990, Doubleday $45.00 (978-0-385-19957-5). This mammoth volume (over 1,100 pages) restores all the cuts made in the original 1978 edition. (Rev: BL 3/15/90)

4735 King, Tabitha, and Michael McDowell. *Candles Burning* (9–12). 2006, Berkley $24.95 (978-0-425-21028-4). Calley, a 7-year-old with supernatural abilities, becomes crucial to her southern family's security after her father is killed. (Rev: BL 5/15/06)

4736 Klause, Annette Curtis. *Blood and Chocolate* (9–12). 1997, Delacorte paper $4.99 (978-0-440-22668-0). Vivian, 16, is a lonely werewolf when she moves to a new school and she hopes that Aiden, a human boy, can learn to love her. (Rev: BL 6/1/97; HB 7/97; HBG 3/98; SLJ 8/97*; VOYA 8/97)

4737 Klause, Annette Curtis. *The Silver Kiss* (8–12). 1992, Bantam paper $5.50 (978-0-440-21346-8). A teenage girl, beset with personal problems, meets a silver-haired boy who is a vampire in this suspenseful, sometimes gory, novel. (Rev: BL 10/15/90; SLJ 9/90)

4738 Knight, Karsten. *Wildefire* (8–10). 2011, Simon & Schuster $16.99 (978-1-4424-2117-2). Ashline contends with life in a new boarding school, and the sudden realization that she's descended from Polynesian fire goddess Pele. ℮ Lexile 970L (Rev: BL 7/11; SLJ 12/1/11; VOYA 8/11)

4739 Koontz, Dean. *Brother Odd* (10–12). 2006, Bantam $27.00 (978-0-553-80480-5). In this third installment in the series, Odd is living in a monastery in the Sierra Nevada mountains and only he can see that the attached school is being invaded by evil ghosts. (Rev: BL 11/15/06)

4740 Koontz, Dean. *Forever Odd* (10–12). 2005, Bantam $27.00 (978-0-553-80416-4). In this sequel to *Odd Thomas* (2003), the appealing protagonist who can communicate with ghosts is drawn into a trap as he investigates the disappearance of a friend. (Rev: BL 11/15/05)

4741 Koontz, Dean. *Life Expectancy* (8–12). 2004, Bantam $27.00 (978-0-553-80414-0). Jimmy is stalked by a mad clown from the moment of his birth in this novel that spoofs cinematic and literary conventions. (Rev: BL 11/1/04)

4742 Koontz, Dean. *Odd Thomas* (10–12). 2003, Bantam $26.95 (978-0-553-80249-8). Odd Thomas, a 20-year-old fry cook in a California desert town, sees dead people — and talks to them too, unique gifts he uses to help track down the killers. (Rev: BL 12/15/03; SLJ 5/04)

4743 Koontz, Dean, and Kevin J. Anderson. *Prodigal Son* (11–12). 2005, Bantam paper $7.99 (978-0-553-58788-3). With Victor Frankenstein, now in biotechnology in 21st-century New Orleans, secretly striving to create a perfect "New Race," his first monster, Deucalion, seeks to thwart him; for mature teens. (Rev: BL 1/1–15/05)

4744 Krinard, Susan. *Chasing Midnight* (9–12). 2007, HQN paper $6.99 (978-0-373-77218-6). Set in 1920s Greenwich Village, this is the story of Allegra, a flapper/vampire who falls in love with a werewolf disguised as a wealthy mortal. (Rev: BL 9/15/07)

4745 Krinard, Susan. *Come the Night* (10–12). 2008, HQN paper $6.99 (978-037377315-2). A werewolf story and a tale of searching for one's identity combine in this romantic tale of forbidden love. ℮ (Rev: BL 9/15/08*)

4746 Lackey, Mercedes, and Rosemary Edghill. *Dead Reckoning* (7–10). 2012, Bloomsbury $16.99 (978-1-59990-684-3). In 1867 Texas 17-year-old Jeff Gallatin, a girl posing as a boy as she searches for her twin brother, joins up with a motley crew — including an independent-minded scientist inventor named Honoria Gibbons — to determine the source of a scourge of zombies. ℮ Lexile 960L (Rev: BL 8/12; LMC 10/12; SLJ 7/12; VOYA 4/12)

4747 Langston, Laura. *Exit Point* (8–12). 2006, Orca $14.95 (978-1-55143-525-1); paper $7.95 (978-1-55143-505-3). When Logan wakes up dead, he watches over his family in spirit form, and commits himself to saving his younger sister from abuse before he moves on forever; for reluctant readers. (Rev: SLJ 8/06)

4748 Larbalestier, Justine, and Sarah Rees Brennan. *Team Human* (9–12). 2012, HarperTeen $17.99 (978-0-06-208964-9). When Mel's best friend becomes obsessed with a vampire, Mel revisits her ideas about vampires in general; a funny novel set in a world where vampires are legal and responsible citizens. ⌂ ℮ Lexile HL650L (Rev: BL 7/12; HB 7–8/12; SLJ 11/12; VOYA 4/12)

4749 Lebbon, Tim. *Face* (11–12). 2002, Night Shade $25.00 (978-1-892389-19-0). After the Powell family picks up a hitchhiker, he begins to intrude on their lives in this tense and frightening story that includes sex and violence. (Rev: BL 1/1–15/02)

4750 Levin, Ira. *Rosemary's Baby* (10–12). 1997, NAL paper $7.99 (978-0-451-19400-8). Rosemary is pregnant and under the increased influence of witchcraft.

4751 Levy, Elizabeth. *The Drowned* (9–12). 1995, Hyperion $16.95 (978-0-7868-0135-0). A supernatural thriller with a demented mother who ritually drowns a teenager and a drowned victim who returns to life. (Rev: BL 12/1/95; SLJ 12/95)

4752 Lindsey, Mary. *Shattered Souls* (8–12). 2011, Philomel $16.99 (978-039925622-6). After she starts hearing voices, high school student Lenzi discovers she is a "Speaker" and can help the dead with unresolved issues. ℮ (Rev: BL 12/15/11; SLJ 1/12)

4753 Lucas, Tim. *The Book of Renfield: A Gospel of Dracula* (11–12). 2005, Touchstone paper $14.00 (978-0-7432-4354-4). Dr. Seward's study of Renfield, a minor character in Stoker's *Dracula*, forms the core of this documentary-like novel. (Rev: BL 6/1–15/05)

4754 Lumley, Brian. *Harry and the Pirates: Necroscope* (10–12). Series: Necroscope. 2009, Tor $23.95 (978-076532338-5). Harry's encounters with strange souls continue in this cleverly written story. (Rev: BL 7/09)

4755 Lumley, Brian. *The Source* (9–12). 1998, Tor paper $6.99 (978-0-8125-2127-6). In this, the third volume of the Necroscope series, scientists find in the Ural mountains the entrance to a world where vampires and other horrible creatures live. (Rev: VOYA 2/90)

4756 Maberry, Jonathan. *Dust and Decay* (9–12). 2011, Simon & Schuster $17.99 (978-1-4424-0235-5). In this sequel to 2010's *Rot and Ruin*, 15-year-old Benny and his friends head into the zombie areas of America and find both old and new dangers. ⌂ ℮ Lexile 770L (Rev: BL 8/11; SLJ 10/1/11)

4757 MacDonald, Caroline. *Hostilities: Nine Bizarre Stories* (7–10). 1994, Scholastic paper $13.95 (978-0-590-46063-7). A collection of nine tales with strange, unsettling themes and Australian locales. (Rev: BL 1/15/94; SLJ 3/94; VOYA 10/94)

4758 MacHale, D. J. *The Light* (6–10). Series: Morpheus Road. 2010, Aladdin $17.99 (978-1-4169-6516-9). A fast-paced fantasy thriller in which Marshall has frightening visions and is pursued by a figure called Gravedigger while he searches for his missing friend Coop. ⌂ ℮ (Rev: BLO 4/15/10; LMC 8–9/10; SLJ 5/10)

4759 McKay, Kristy. *Undead* (7–10). 2012, Scholastic $17.99 (978-0-545-38188-8). On a school trip to Scotland, four teens deal with various challenges after their companions turn into zombies. ⌂ ℮ Lexile HL630L (Rev: BL 10/15/12; LMC 1–2/13; SLJ 10/12)

4760 Mackel, Kathryn. *The Hidden* (9–12). 2006, West Bow paper $13.99 (978-1-59554-037-9). In this eerie tale, psychologist Susan Stone becomes involved with a strange young man implicated in a series of bizarre murders. (Rev: BL 6/1–15/06)

4761 McKinley, Robin. *Sunshine* (10–12). 2003, Berkley $23.95 (978-0-425-19178-1). Captured by vampires, Rae "Sunshine" Seddon uses her own magic to save herself and an out-of-favor vampire. (Rev: BL 10/15/03; VOYA 12/03)

4762 McMahon, Jennifer. *Don't Breathe a Word* (10–12). 2011, HarperCollins $14.99 (978-0-06-168937-6). Lisa walked away from her dysfunctional family at the age of 12, saying she was going to become queen of the fairy world, but 15 years later, her brother Sam, who was convinced she had been abducted, faces a series of mysterious occurrences that make him wonder if Lisa is still alive in this supernatural thriller. (Rev: BL 3/1–15/11; SLJ 7/11)

4763 McNally, Clare. *Stage Fright* (9–12). 1993, Tor paper $5.99 (978-0-8125-4839-6). Years after her lover and best friend were murdered, Hayley Seagel discovers that their ghosts have returned to help her and her friends fight a malevolent ghost. (Rev: VOYA 2/96)

4764 McNamee, Graham. *Beyond* (7–10). 2012, Random House $15.99 (978-0-385-73775-3); LB $18.99 (978-0-385-90687-6). Jane, 17, is accused of attempting suicide when really her shadow is trying to kill her. ℮ Lexile HL600L (Rev: BL 9/15/12; HB 11–12/12; SLJ 10/12; VOYA 12/12)

4765 McNeil, Gretchen. *Possess* (7–10). 2011, HarperCollins $17.99 (978-006206071-6). Fifteen-year-old exorcist Bridget must cope with many demonic challenges in this entertaining tale of possession. ℮ (Rev: BL 9/15/11; LMC 1–2/12; SLJ 3/12; VOYA 10/12)

4766 McNeil, Gretchen. *Ten* (8–11). 2012, HarperCollins $17.99 (978-0-06-211878-3). A teen house party on a remote island turns lethal and young Meg and Minnie must deal with the nightmare. YALSA Quick Picks for Reluctant Young Adult Readers 2013. ℮ (Rev: BL 10/1/12; SLJ 10/12; VOYA 8/12)

4767 McNeil, W. K., ed. *Ghost Stories from the American South* (9–12). 1985, August House paper $9.95 (978-0-935304-84-8). A collection of blood-curdlers from locales ranging from Virginia to Texas. (Rev: SLJ 12/85)

4768 Mahy, Margaret, and Susan Cooper. *Don't Read This! And Other Tales of the Unnatural* (7–10). 1998, Front St $15.95 (978-1-886910-22-5). Great stories of ghosts and the supernatural are included in this international collection that represents some of the top writers of scary fiction at work today. (Rev: BL 4/1/99; HBG 9/99; SLJ 7/99; VOYA 6/99)

4769 Mancusi, Mari. *Boys That Bite* (10–12). 2006, Berkley Jam paper $9.99 (978-0-425-20942-4). Sixteen-year old Sunshine McDonald accidentally gets the initiation vampire bite meant for her identical twin Rayne, which leads Sunshine into a battle against the dark forces that she must win in time for her senior prom; for mature teens. (Rev: SLJ 7/06)

4770 Marr, Melissa, et al. *Love Is Hell* (9–12). 2008, HarperTeen $16.99 (978-0-06-144305-3). Supernatural romance is the theme of these five short stories by writers including Justine Larbalestier and Scott Westerfeld. (Rev: SLJ 2/1/09)

4771 Martin, Eric B., ed. *The Campfire Collection: Spine-Tingling Tales to Tell in the Dark* (9–12). 2000, Chronicle paper $15.95 (978-0-8118-2454-5). A collection of 17 thrillers by such writers as Jack London, Edgar Allan Poe, and Tobias Wolff. (Rev: SLJ 1/01)

4772 Martinez, A. Lee. *Gil's All Fright Diner* (10–12). 2005, Tor paper $12.95 (978-0-7653-1471-0). Teenage Tammy — a.k.a. Mistress Lilith, Queen of the Night — is not pleased when her zombies are driven off by the arrival of vampire Earl and werewolf Duke in this comic supernatural story. (Rev: BL 5/15/05; SLJ 8/05)

4773 Masterton, Graham. *Blind Panic* (10–12). 2009, Severn $28.95 (978-072786820-6). Chaos ensues when the entire U.S. population is simultaneously stricken blind in this gripping thriller that features familiar characters Misquamacus (the ancient shaman) and charlatan-psychic Harry Erskine. (Rev: BL 10/15/09)

4774 Matheson, Richard. *Nightmare at 20,000 Feet* (11–12). 2002, Tor paper $14.95 (978-0-312-87827-6). Fourteen classic spine-chilling horror stories vary in theme; for mature teens. (Rev: BL 2/1/02)

4775 Matthews, L. S. *The Outcasts* (7–10). 2007, Delacorte $15.99 (978-0-385-73367-0). Five misfit students wonder why they have been chosen for a field trip to a mysterious estate — until they discover that they must endure surreal trials to make it back alive. (Rev: BL 11/15/07; SLJ 1/08)

4776 Meldrum, Christina. *Madapple* (9–12). 2008, Knopf $16.99 (978-0-375-85176-6). Was Aslaug the product of a virgin birth? When her mother dies, Aslaug goes to Maine to live with relatives she did not know she had; there she discovers dark secrets and is accused of murder. ∩ (Rev: BL 4/1/08; HB 5–6/08; SLJ 7/08*)

4777 Mertz, Stephen. *Night Wind* (10–12). 2002, Five Star $27.95 (978-0-7862-4353-2). Robin and her son flee her abusive husband only to find themselves in an even worse situation in this gripping tale of horror and romance with a touch of the mystic. (Rev: BL 9/1/02)

4778 Meyer, Stephenie. *Eclipse* (8–11). Series: Twilight. 2007, Little, Brown $18.99 (978-0-316-16020-9). Human teen Bella and vampire Edward continue their relationship in the face of opposition from werewolf Jacob (who's in love with Bella too) while Bella also faces decisions about college and her future. ∩ (Rev: BL 9/15/07; SLJ 10/07)

4779 Meyer, Stephenie. *New Moon* (8–11). Series: Twilight. 2006, Little, Brown $17.99 (978-0-316-16019-3). In this sequel to *Twilight* (2005), Bella laments boyfriend Edward's departure and engages in dangerous behavior. ∩ (Rev: BL 7/06; SLJ 8/06)

4780 Meyer, Stephenie. *The Short Second Life of Bree Tanner* (9–12). Series: Twilight Saga. 2010, Little, Brown $13.99 (978-031612558-1). Young vampire Bree, who played a minor role in *Eclipse* (2007) gains experience in battle (and romance) as she fulfills her destiny. ∩ ℮ Lexile 680L (Rev: BLO 7/10)

4781 Meyer, Stephenie. *Twilight* (9–12). Series: Twilight. 2005, Little, Brown $17.99 (978-0-316-16017-9). Seventeen-year-old Bella Swan, a new arrival in the rain-soaked city of Forks, Washington, falls quickly for fellow student Edward Cullen only to find he has dark secrets. (Rev: BL 11/15/05*; SLJ 10/05*; VOYA 10/05)

4782 Mignola, Mike, and Christopher Golden. *Baltimore: or, The Steadfast Tin Soldier and the Vampire* (9–12). 2007, Bantam $25.00 (978-0-553-80471-3). Vampires prey on the dead and dying on World War I's western front in this brilliantly written and illustrated book. (Rev: BL 8/07)

4783 Moore, Christopher. *Bite Me: A Love Story* (11–12). 2010, Morrow $23.99 (978-006177972-5). In this funny sequel to 2008's *You Suck,* vampire couple Tommy and Jody escape from the Rodin statue in which they were imprisoned and join up with a legion of vampire cats, much to the concern of Abby Normal and her boyfriend; for mature readers. ℮ (Rev: BL 2/1–15/10)

4784 Moore, Kelly, and Tucker Reed, et al. *Amber House* (9–12). 2012, Scholastic $17.99 (978-054543416-4). Sarah's explorations of her family's gothic Maryland estate lead to eerie contact with a distant ancestor in this effective ghost story. ∩ ℮ (Rev: BL 11/1/12; VOYA 12/12)

4785 Moore, Michael Scott. *Too Much of Nothing* (11–12). 2003, Carroll & Graf paper $13.00 (978-0-7867-1196-3). Eric, a ghost seeking a confrontation with his killer, reflects on his former life as a teenager. (Rev: BL 8/03)

4786 Moore, Peter. *Red Moon Rising* (7–10). 2011, Disney/Hyperion $16.99 (978-1-4231-1665-3). Dante "Danny" Gray is part vamp and part wulf, not a good combination in his world where vampyres are top, humans are in the middle, and werewolves are the lowest; now his wulf side seems to be coming to the fore . . . ℮ Lexile HL580L (Rev: BL 6/1/11; SLJ 11/1/11)

4787 Mullany, Janet. *Jane and the Damned* (11–12). 2010, Avon paper $13.99 (978-00619583-0-4). Jane Austen, now a vampire, must help defeat the French militia when they invade Bath, England. ℮ (Rev: BL 9/1–15/10)

4788 Myracle, Lauren. *Bliss* (9–12). 2008, Abrams $16.95 (978-081097071-7). Bliss, new girl at a fancy Atlanta school, uncovers some violent history in this scary tale with a backdrop of late-1960s culture. Lexile HL640L (Rev: BL 11/1/08*; LMC 3–4/09; SLJ 10/1/08; VOYA 12/08)

4789 Myracle, Lauren. *Rhymes with Witches* (8–11). 2005, Abrams $16.95 (978-0-8109-5859-3). Invited to join a super-popular clique at her high school, Jane is at first flattered but soon discovers that she's involved in something sinister. (Rev: BCCB 5/05; BL 3/15/05; SLJ 4/05)

4790 Nance, Andrew. *Daemon Hall* (7–10). Illus. by Coleman Polhemus. 2007, Henry Holt $16.95 (978-0-8050-8171-8). Three teenaged writers win a night at a haunted mansion with a horror writer, and each contestant must tell a spooky story by candlelight. Will all the contestants survive? (Rev: BCCB 6/07; BL 7/07; SLJ 12/07)

4791 Nance, Andrew. *Return to Daemon Hall: Evil Roots* (7–10). Illus. by Coleman Polhemus. 2011, Henry Holt $16.99 (978-0-8050-8748-2). In this follow-up to *Daemon Hall* (2007), author Tremblin holds another horror writing contest, this time in a supposedly safer location. ℮ Lexile HL690L (Rev: BLO 8/11; SLJ 8/11)

4792 Nayeri, Daniel, and Dina Nayeri. *Another Faust* (8–10). 2009, Candlewick $16.99 (978-0-7636-3707-1). In this well-written, Faustian tale, a wicked governess leads five siblings to exchange their souls for supernatural gifts. ∩ ℮ Lexile 740L (Rev: BL 9/15/09; LMC 10/09; SLJ 9/09; VOYA 8/09)

4793 Nayeri, Daniel, and Dina Nayeri. *Another Jekyll, Another Hyde* (7–10). 2012, Candlewick $17.99 (978-076365261-6). Wealthy teen Thomas Goodman-Brown is in danger of losing his mind and soul through his evil stepmother's machinations; the sequel to *Another Faust* (2009) and *Another Pan* (2010). ℮ (Rev: BL 2/1/12; SLJ 3/12; VOYA 4/12)

4794 Nelson, Marilyn, and Tonya C. Hegamin. *Pemba's Song: A Ghost Story* (7–10). 2008, Scholastic $16.99 (978-054502076-3). African American 14-year-old Pemba is aghast when her family relocates from Brooklyn to rural Connecticut, and unsettled when she starts having dreams about an 18th-century slave girl. Lexile 730L (Rev: BL 11/1/08; LMC 3–4/09; SLJ 12/08)

4795 Nixon, Joan Lowery. *Whispers from the Dead* (7–12). 1991, Bantam paper $4.99 (978-0-440-20809-9). After being saved from drowning, Sarah is able to communicate with dead spirits. (Rev: BL 9/15/89; SLJ 9/89; VOYA 12/89)

4796 Noyes, Deborah. *Gothic! Ten Original Dark Tales* (7–10). 2005, Candlewick $15.99 (978-0-7636-2243-5). Ten Gothic tales by contemporary authors embody the dark fantasy and the fairy tale aspects of the genre as well as offering supernatural horror plus humor. (Rev: BL 10/15/04; SLJ 1/05)

4797 Noyes, Deborah, ed. *The Restless Dead: Ten Original Stories of the Supernatural* (8–12). 2007, Candlewick $16.99 (978-0-7636-2906-9). Vampires, corpses, ghosts, and more appear in these scary stories by well-known YA authors. (Rev: BL 5/15/07; HB 9–10/07; LMC 11/07; SLJ 9/07)

4798 Olin, Sean. *Killing Britney* (10–12). 2005, Simon & Schuster paper $8.99 (978-0-689-87778-0). Britney Johnson finds her life turned upside down when someone starts killing those she loves; for mature readers. (Rev: BCCB 9/05; SLJ 7/05)

4799 Oppel, Kenneth. *Such Wicked Intent* (9–12). Series: The Apprenticeship of Victor Frankenstein. 2012, Simon & Schuster $16.99 (978-144240318-5). Mourning the death of his twin, Konrad, 16-year-old Victor, with his cousin and friend, find a way into the afterlife world of Chateau Frankenstein and create a new body for Konrad, which unfortunately is lacking a soul. ⌒ ℮ Lexile 730L (Rev: BL 6/12; HB 9–10/12; VOYA 8/12)

4800 Oppel, Kenneth. *This Dark Endeavor: The Apprenticeship of Victor Frankenstein* (8–12). 2011, Simon & Schuster $17.99 (978-1-4424-0315-4). In this first installment in a series set in the independent republic of Geneva in the 18th century, young Victor seeks a cure for his deathly ill twin brother, enlisting the help of an alchemist. ⌒ ℮ Lexile 690L (Rev: BL 6/1/11; HB 7–8/11; SLJ 10/1/11; VOYA 10/11)

4801 Pearce, Jackson. *Sisters Red* (8–12). 2010, Little, Brown $16.99 (978-0-316-06868-0). Sisters Scarlett and Rosie set out for revenge when a werewolf kills their grandmother and injures Scarlett; a retelling of the Little Red Riding Hood story with a twist that will appeal to fans of werewolves and vampires. (Rev: BL 4/15/10; HB 9–10/10; LMC 8–9/10; SLJ 5/10)

4802 Pendleton, Thomas. *Mason* (8–10). 2008, HarperCollins paper $8.99 (978-0-06-117736-1). Cruel and violent Gene terrorizes his brother Mason, as well as Mason's friends, until Mason begins to use his mind to retaliate. (Rev: BL 5/15/08)

4803 Perez, Marlene. *Dead Is a State of Mind* (7–10). Series: Nightshade. 2009, Graphia paper $7.99 (978-015206210-1). In this sequel to *Dead Is the New Black* (2008), 17-year-old Daisy and other residents of Nightshade, California — some of them with supernatural abilities — are shaken when a teacher at the high school is murdered. An entertaining combination of romance, mystery, and the paranormal. ℮ Lexile HL620L (Rev: BLO 1/7/09; SLJ 2/1/09)

4804 Phillips, Robert, ed. *Nightshade: 20th Century Ghost Stories* (9–12). 1999, Carroll & Graf paper $14.00 (978-0-7867-0808-6). Well-known authors including Isak Dinesen, Elizabeth Bowen, and Gabriel Garcia Marquez are represented in this collection of 27 tales of ghosts and the supernatural. (Rev: BL 5/15/99)

4805 Pines, T., ed. *Thirteen: 13 Tales of Horror by 13 Masters of Horror* (8–12). 1991, Scholastic paper $6.99 (978-0-590-45256-4). Popular horror writers' stories of revenge, lust, and betrayal. (Rev: BL 3/1/92)

4806 Poblocki, Dan. *The Nightmarys* (6–10). 2010, Random House $16.99 (978-0-375-84256-6). In this scary mystery story 7th-grader Timothy and his new classmate Abigail try to undo the curse on Abigail's family that is having an impact on them all. ℮ Lexile 680L (Rev: BL 8/10; LMC 11–12/10; SLJ 12/1/10)

4807 Pockell, Leslie, ed. *The 13 Best Horror Stories of All Time* (10–12). 2002, Warner paper $13.95 (978-0-446-67950-3). Classic tales including Poe's "Tell-Tale Heart" and LeFanu's "Green Tea." (Rev: BL 8/02)

4808 Poe, Edgar Allan. *The Cask of Amontillado* (8–12). Illus. by Gary Kelley. Series: Creative Short Stories. 2008, Creative Education LB $19.95 (978-1-58341-580-1). This chilling short story of revenge is accompanied by illustrations and brief biographical information about the author. (Rev: BL 4/30/08; SLJ 8/08)

4809 Polisar, Lisa. *The Ghost of Mary Prairie* (9–12). 2007, Univ. of New Mexico paper $18.95 (978-0-8263-4209-6). Jake sees a ghost one night on a baseball diamond in his town in Oklahoma and realizes that it is the spirit of a girl murdered years before. (Rev: BL 7/07; SLJ 8/07)

4810 Powell, Laura. *The Game of Triumphs* (9–12). 2011, Knopf $16.99 (978-0-375-86587-9); LB $19.99 (978-037596587-6). A complex tale of danger and intrigue surrounding a tarot card game in contemporary London;. (Rev: BL 8/11; LMC 11–12/11; SLJ 12/1/11)

4811 Preussler, Otfried. *The Satanic Mill* (7–10). 1987, Peter Smith $31.50 (978-0-8446-6196-4). A young apprentice outwits a strange magician in this fantasy first published in 1972. (Rev: BL 6/1–15/98)

4812 Priest, Cherie. *Boneshaker* (10–12). 2009, Tor paper $15.99 (978-07653184-1-1). Zeke is aware that his father is responsible for the zombies that roam the streets of lawless mid-19th-century Seattle; however, there are more bizarre discoveries to come about his parents' past in this atmospheric steampunk novel. (Rev: BL 10/15/09)

4813 Prill, David. *Dating Secrets of the Dead* (11–12). 2002, Subterranean $35.00 (978-1-931081-60-3). Humor and horror meld in the three offerings in this slim volume; for mature teens. (Rev: BL 8/02)

4814 Prose, Francine. *The Turning* (8–12). 2012, HarperTeen $17.99 (978-0-06-199966-6). In this gripping modern twist on *The Turn of the Screw,* Jackson finds himself looking after two children on a remote island where there are strange events. **e** (Rev: BL 8/12; SLJ 10/12; VOYA 8/12)

4815 Radford, Michelle. *Totally Fabulous* (7–10). 2009, HarperTeen paper $8.99 (978-006128531-8). British 14-year-old Fiona travels to New Jersey to spend time with her long-lost father and attend an ESP boot camp to hone her psychic powers. (Rev: BL 7/09)

4816 Reese, James. *The Strange Case of Doctor Jekyll and Mademoiselle Odile* (9–12). 2012, Roaring Brook $16.99 (978-159643684-8). In the laboratory of Dr. Jekyll in 1870s Paris 16-year-old Odile, from a long line of witches, tries to find a way to cure her sickly brother only to discover that the doctor is helping himself to her special salts, with unfortunate results. **e** Lexile 930L (Rev: BL 2/1/12; LMC 8–9/12*; SLJ 3/12)

4817 Rice, Anne. *Interview with the Vampire* (10–12). 1986, Ballantine paper $7.99 (978-0-345-33766-5). A 200-year-old vampire reveals every horrifying detail of his life. Rice has written other horror novels involving vampires.

4818 Richardson, E. E. *Devil's Footsteps* (8–11). 2005, Delacorte LB $17.99 (978-0-385-90279-3). Still troubled by his brother's disappearance at the hands of the Dark Man five years earlier, 15-year-old Bryan meets two other teens struggling with the effects of similar attacks. (Rev: BCCB 10/05; BL 5/1/05; SLJ 1/06)

4819 Rock, Peter. *The Bewildered* (11–12). 2005, MacAdam $23.00 (978-1-59692-112-2). Teens hired to steal copper wire discover an eerie zombie-like cult seemingly addicted to electricity; for mature teens. (Rev: BL 2/1/05)

4820 Rodriguez, Pedro. *Chilling Tales of Horror: Dark Graphic Short Stories* (7–10). Illus. by author. 2012, Enslow LB $30.60 (978-076604085-4). Seven classic horror stories including Maupassant's "The Hand" and Robert Louis Stevenson's "The Body Snatcher" are

given graphic-novel treatment here. (Rev: BL 8/12; SLJ 7/1/12)

4821 Rosati, Gina. *Auracle* (7–10). 2012, Roaring Brook $16.99 (978-1-59643-710-4). Her power to project astrally puts 17-year-old Anna in danger in this novel combining romance, suspense, and paranormal activity. **e** Lexile 890L (Rev: BL 9/15/12; HB 9–10/12; SLJ 12/12; VOYA 10/12)

4822 Ruby, Lois. *The Secret of Laurel Oaks* (7–10). 2008, Tor $16.95 (978-076531366-9). Siblings Lila and Gabe set out to solve the puzzle of who really poisoned the owner of Laurel Oaks Plantation in 1839; the narration alternates between Lila and Gabe and Daphne, the slave girl wrongly blamed for the murder. **e** Lexile 850L (Rev: BLO 10/30/08; LMC 5–6/09; SLJ 11/1/08; VOYA 12/08)

4823 Russell, Karen. *Swamplandia!* (11–12). 2011, Knopf $24.95 (978-030726399-5). In this suspenseful tale suitable for mature readers, 13-year-old Ava Bigtree, daughter of an alligator wrestling family, embarks on an otherworldly quest through the Everglades to save her family after her mother dies. ⌒ **e** (Rev: BL 10/1–15/10)

4824 Ryan, Alan, ed. *Haunting Women* (9–12). 1988, Avon paper $3.95 (978-0-380-89881-7). Fourteen horror stories written by such women as Shirley Jackson and Ruth Rendell. (Rev: BL 11/15/88; VOYA 2/89)

4825 Ryan, Carrie. *The Forest of Hands and Teeth* (9–12). 2009, Delacorte $17.99 (978-038573681-7); LB $20.99 (978-038590631-9). In this gory story, Mary faces terrifying flesh-eating zombies and the prospect of marriage to a man she does not love. ⌒ **e** Lexile 900L (Rev: BL 1/1–15/09; LMC 8–9/09; SLJ 5/1/09*)

4826 Salomon, Peter Adam. *Henry Franks* (9–12). 2012, Flux paper $9.99 (978-0-7387-3-336-4). With the help of his friend Justine, 16-year-old Henry begins to recover from the car crash that killed his mother and left him with mysterious scars and total amnesia in this novel that combines elements of horror and suspense. **e** (Rev: BL 9/15/12*; LMC 1–2/13; SLJ 12/12; VOYA 10/12)

4827 Saul, John. *Comes the Blind Fury* (9–12). 1990, Dell paper $6.99 (978-0-440-11475-8). An antique doll actually contains the evil spirit of a dead girl. Also use *Cry for the Strangers* (1986), *Suffer the Children,* and *When the Wind Blows.*

4828 Saul, John. *House of Reckoning* (10–12). 2009, Ballantine $26 (978-034551424-0). When teenaged Sarah finds herself in an oppressive foster home in the town where her drunken father is imprisoned, a troubled peer and mysterious teacher help her to overcome increasingly dire straits. ⌒ **e** (Rev: BL 9/09)

4829 Saul, John. *In the Dark of the Night* (10–12). 2006, Ballantine $25.95 (978-0-345-48701-8). While on vacation at a Wisconsin lake town, Eric, Kent, and Tad stumble across a carriage house with frightening secrets that invade their dreams. (Rev: BL 5/15/06; SLJ 11/06)

4830 Schreiber, Ellen. *Vampireville* (7–10). 2006, HarperCollins $15.99 (978-0-06-077625-1). Raven and her vampire boyfriend Alexander must get rid of the bad vampire twins Luna and Jagger before they sink their fangs into soccer star Trevor and try and take over the town of Dullsville. (Rev: BL 8/06; SLJ 11/06)

4831 Sedgwick, Marcus. *My Swordhand Is Singing* (9–12). 2007, Random House $15.99 (978-0-375-84689-2). Teenaged Peter and his father, Tomas, fight the undead of their European village with a vampire-slaying sword in this creepy story. (Rev: BL 11/15/07; SLJ 11/07)

4832 Sedgwick, Marcus. *White Crow* (8–12). 2011, Roaring Brook $15.99 (978-1-59643-594-0). Rebecca and her policeman father arrive in Winterfold, a town with disturbingly deep secrets, and begin to learn the scary truth. ∩ e Lexile 810L (Rev: BL 5/1/11; HB 7–8/11; LMC 8–9/12; SLJ 8/11*)

4833 Seigel, Andrea. *To Feel Stuff* (11–12). 2006, Harcourt paper $14.00 (978-0-15-603150-9). Elodie's mysterious maladies confine her to the Brown University infirmary, where she falls in love and discovers that she has some unusual abilities. (Rev: BL 5/1/06)

4834 Shan, Darren. *Blood Beast, Book 5* (7–10). Series: Demonata. 2007, Little, Brown $16.99 (978-0-316-00377-3). Grubbs worries that he too will become a werewolf in this gripping fifth installment in the series. (Rev: SLJ 2/08)

4835 Shan, Darren. *Demon Thief* (7–12). Series: Demonata. 2006, Little, Brown $15.99 (978-0-316-01237-9). An inventive horror story in which a boy who is able to construct windows from light discovers that demons live behind them. (Rev: SLJ 9/06)

4836 Shan, Darren. *Lord Loss* (9–12). Series: Demonata. 2005, Little, Brown $15.99 (978-0-316-11499-8). A teenager witnesses the brutal murder of his family by demons in the opening volume of a new Shan series. (Rev: BL 11/1/05; SLJ 11/05; VOYA 10/05)

4837 Shan, Darren. *Zom-B* (9–12). 2012, Little, Brown $14.99 (978-031621440-7). A zombie attack forces 11-year-old B, who struggles with Dad's racism, to join up with students previously disdained. ∩ e Lexile HL710L (Rev: BL 10/15/12; LMC 3–4/13; SLJ 1/13)

4838 Shepard, Leslie, ed. *The Dracula Book of Great Horror Stories* (10–12). 1977, Citadel $10.00 (978-0-8065-0565-7). Thirteen old-fashioned but still chilling horror stories.

4839 Shepard, Sara. *Ruthless* (9–12). Series: Pretty Little Liars. 2011, HarperTeen $17.99 (978-006208186-5). The spirit of Hanna, Spencer, Emily, and Aria's deceased friend Alison keeps intruding as the girls try to move on with their lives. e (Rev: BLO 1/19/12)

4840 Showalter, Gena. *Twisted* (10–12). Series: Intertwined. 2011, HarlequinTeen $18.99 (978-037321038-1). Teen vampires Aden and Victoria face incredible challenges in this third book in the series. e (Rev: BL 9/15/11; VOYA 10/11)

4841 Shusterman, Neal. *Bruiser* (8–12). 2010, HarperCollins $16.99 (978-0-06-113408-1). When Bronte, 16, starts dating the seemingly inappropriate Bruiser and her twin brother Tennyson comes to accept this, they are amazed to find that Bruiser absorbs all their physical and emotional pains; told from four perspectives. ∩ e Lexile 820L (Rev: BL 5/1/10; LMC 10/10; SLJ 8/10; VOYA 8/10)

4842 Shusterman, Neal. *Everfound* (7–10). Series: Skinjacker. 2011, Simon & Schuster $17.99 (978-1-4169-9049-9). An action-packed epic conclusion to the trilogy in which the fates of Everlost and the real world hang in the balance. ∩ e Lexile 910L (Rev: BL 5/1/11; HB 7–8/11; SLJ 6/11; VOYA 6/11)

4843 Shusterman, Neal. *Everlost* (7–10). Series: Skinjacker Trilogy. 2006, Simon & Schuster $16.95 (978-0-689-87237-2). Nick and Allie are killed in an automobile accident and end up in Everlost, a world for lost souls, where they must learn to survive. Nick accepts the situation but Allie will do anything to escape. (Rev: BL 9/15/06; SLJ 10/06*)

4844 Shusterman, Neal. *Full Tilt* (6–10). 2003, Simon & Schuster $16.95 (978-0-689-80374-1). A suspenseful drama in which 16-year-old Blake must tackle frightening rides at a mysterious carnival and face his own worst fears in order to save his daredevil older brother Quinn. (Rev: BCCB 9/03; BL 5/15/03; HB 7–8/03; HBG 10/03; SLJ 6/03; VOYA 10/03)

4845 Sigler, Scott. *Ancestor* (11–12). 2010, Crown $24.99 (978-030740633-0). On a small island in Lake Superior, two researchers endeavoring to engineer and clone an ancient human ancestor step into a genetic minefield in this action-packed thriller suitable for mature teens. ∩ e (Rev: BL 5/1–15/10)

4846 Singer, Nicky. *The Innocent's Story* (7–10). 2007, Holiday $16.95 (978-0-8234-2082-7). After dying in a suicide bomb attack, 13-year-old Cassina becomes a vapor and enters into the mind and hearts of living characters including her parents and the terrorists responsible for her death. (Rev: BL 5/15/07; SLJ 9/07)

4847 Singh, Sonia. *Ghost, Interrupted* (9–12). 2007, Avon paper $13.95 (978-0-06-089022-3). Anjali, an Indian American girl with psychic abilities, joins The Cold Spot, and hunts ghosts together with Scott, the owner, and telekinetic and attractive Coulter. (Rev: BL 12/1/06)

4848 Skovron, Jon. *Misfit* (8–11). 2011, Abrams $16.95 (978-1-4197-0021-7). Demon half-breed Jael discovers the truth about her identity when she receives a necklace that was her deceased mother's prized possession.

ℯ Lexile 660L (Rev: BLO 9/1/11; LMC 3–4/12; SLJ 10/1/11*; VOYA 10/11)

4849 Slater, Adam. *Skinned* (6–10). Series: The Shadowing. 2012, Egmont $16.99 (978-160684262-1). A tense story in which young Callum is pitted against a flesh-eating monster named Black Annis. ℯ (Rev: BLO 10/1/12; SLJ 2/13)

4850 Smith-Ready, Jeri. *Shift* (9–12). 2011, Simon & Schuster $17.99 (978-1-4169-9408-4). Aura is torn between her devotion to her ghost boyfriend Logan and her attraction to Zachary, even as she herself struggles to understand her own past; a sequel to *Shade* (2010). ☊ Lexile HL640L (Rev: BL 5/1/11; SLJ 9/1/11; VOYA 8/11)

4851 Smith, Cynthia Leitich. *Diabolical* (9–12). Series: Tantalize. 2012, Candlewick $17.99 (978-0-7636-5118-3). In this series finale told in alternating voices, former guardian angel Zachary and werewolf Kieren and others battle evil at a New England boarding school. ℯ (Rev: HB 1–2/12; SLJ 3/12; VOYA 2/12)

4852 Smith, Cynthia Leitich. *Eternal* (9–12). Series: Tantalize. 2009, Candlewick $17.99 (978-076363573-2). Miranda, a vampire princess, and Zachary, her guardian angel, find love in the tenuous and frightening world of the dead; a companion novel to *Tantalize* (2007). ☊ ℯ Lexile HL690L (Rev: BLO 2/9/09; HB 3–4/09; LMC 8–9/09; SLJ 7/1/09)

4853 Smith, Cynthia Leitich. *Tantalize* (9–12). 2007, Candlewick $16.99 (978-0-7636-2791-1). Seventeen-year-old Quince faces multiple challenges when her family's vampire-themed restaurant is the site of a murder. (Rev: BCCB 5/07; BL 3/1/07; HB 3–4/07; LMC 8–9/07; SLJ 5/07)

4854 Smith, Cynthia Leitich. *Tantalize: Kieren's Story* (9–12). Illus. by Ming Doyle. Series: Tantalize. 2011, Candlewick $19.99 (978-076364114-6). This graphic-novel spinoff from 2007's *Tantalize* tells the story of Kieren, a hybrid werewolf, and his relationship with mortal Quincie. YALSA Popular Paperbacks for Young Adults Top Ten 2011. (Rev: BL 6/1/11; LMC 1–2/12; SLJ 9/1/11; VOYA 10/11)

4855 Sokoloff, Alexandra. *The Harrowing* (11–12). 2006, St. Martin's $21.95 (978-0-312-35748-1). When a group of students stumble upon an old Ouija board and conjure up a ghost, their college experience becomes a nightmare. (Rev: BL 9/1/06; SLJ 11/06)

4856 Soto, Gary. *The Afterlife* (7–10). 2003, Harcourt $16.00 (978-0-15-204774-0). After he is stabbed to death, 17-year-old Chuy lingers long enough to watch the reactions of family and friends while getting to know some other ghosts. (Rev: BL 8/03*; HB 11–12/03; HBG 4/04; SLJ 11/03; VOYA 2/04)

4857 St. Crow, Lili. *Strange Angels* (8–11). Series: Strange Angels. 2009, Penguin paper $9.99 (978-

159514251-1). Dru's mother is dead and she was forced to kill her father, who was turned into a zombie, in this first book in the series populated by vampires, werewolves, and demons. ℯ Lexile HL810L (Rev: BL 5/15/09; SLJ 7/1/09)

4858 Stahler, David, Jr. *A Gathering of Shades* (7–10). 2005, HarperCollins LB $16.89 (978-0-06-052295-7). Sixteen-year-old Aidan, who moves to rural Vermont with his mother after his father's death, discovers that his grandmother is secretly feeding ghosts with a mixture of her own blood and spring water. (Rev: BCCB 5/05; BL 5/1/05; SLJ 8/05)

4859 Stall, Sam. *Suburban Legends: True Tales of Murder, Mayhem, and Minivans* (10–12). 2006, Quirk paper $15.95 (978-1-59474-051-0). Some dark, some funny, these more than 60 stories about spooky events in suburbia will hold readers' interest. (Rev: SLJ 11/06)

4860 Starkey, Dinah, ed. *Ghosts and Bogles* (5–10). 1987, David & Charles $17.95 (978-0-434-96440-6). A collection of 16 British ghost stories, each nicely presented with illustrations. (Rev: SLJ 9/87)

4861 Staub, Wendy Corsi. *Lily Dale: Awakening* (7–10). 2007, Walker $15.95 (978-0-8027-9654-7). At the age of 17, following her mother's accidental death and on a visit to the spiritualist community of Lily Dale, Calla discovers her psychic abilities. (Rev: BL 11/1/07; LMC 1/08; SLJ 11/07)

4862 Staub, Wendy Corsi. *Lily Dale: Connecting* (7–10). 2008, Walker $16.99 (978-0-8027-9785-8). Still in the spiritualist community of Lily Dale, Calla is preoccupied with romance and friendship even as she investigates her mother's death with the aid of the Internet and spirit guides; the third book in the series. ℯ Lexile 1230 (Rev: BL 2/1/09; SLJ 2/1/09)

4863 Stiefvater, Maggie. *Shiver* (9–12). 2009, Scholastic $17.99 (978-0-545-12326-6). A refreshing take on the supernatural/human romance fad, this well-written novel features a werewolf and the teenage girl who loves him. ☊ Lexile 740L (Rev: BL 8/09; HB 3–4/10; LMC 1–2/10; SLJ 10/09)

4864 Stivers, Valerie. *Blood Is the New Black* (9–12). 2007, Three Rivers paper $13.95 (978-0-307-35213-2). This spirited novel entertainingly follows Kate, an intern at a top fashion magazine who discovers that some of the staff members might be vampires. (Rev: BL 9/1/07)

4865 Stolarz, Laurie Faria. *Project 17* (7–10). 2007, Hyperion $15.99 (978-0-7868-3856-1). Five teenagers spend a spooky night at the ghost-filled Danvers State Insane Asylum. (Rev: BL 11/15/07; LMC 1/08; SLJ 12/07)

4866 Strand, Jeff. *A Bad Day for Voodoo* (7–10). 2012, Sourcebooks paper $8.99 (978-140226680-5). An annoying teacher whose leg is severed after Tyler, 16, pricks his voodoo doll is just the beginning of a funny action-packed adventure. **℮** Lexile HL730L (Rev: BLO 6/12; SLJ 6/12; VOYA 8/12)

4867 Straub, Peter. *A Dark Matter* (11–12). 2010, Doubleday $26.95 (978-038551638-9). Forty years after a small group of Wisconsin students fell under the sway of a mystic, novelist Lee Harwell attempts to unravel the strange occurrences of 1966 when an occult ritual resulted in the death of one student and the disappearance of another; for mature readers. (Rev: BL 10/1/09)

4868 Straub, Peter. *A Special Place: The Heart of a Dark Matter* (11–12). 2010, Pegasus paper $12.95 (978-16059810-2-4). This disturbing novella relays the backstory of serial murderer Keith Hayward — the focus of *A Dark Matter* (2010) — and describes Keith's education in the art of killing by his Uncle Till; for mature readers. (Rev: BL 7/10)

4869 Summers, Courtney. *This Is Not a Test* (9–12). 2012, St. Martin's/Griffin paper $9.99 (978-0-312-65-674-4). Of the six teens hiding in the high school during the zombie apocalypse, one — Sloane — is not sure she even wants to live. (Rev: BL 6/12; LMC 11–12/12; SLJ 10/12)

4870 Taylor, Laini. *Lips Touch Three Times* (8–12). Illus. by Jim Di Bartolo. 2009, Scholastic $16.99 (978-0-545-05585-7). Three supernatural short stories feature kisses that change lives. YALSA Top Ten 2010. ∩ **℮** Lexile 990L (Rev: BL 10/1/09*; SLJ 11/09)

4871 Turner, Joan Frances. *Dust* (10–12). 2010, Ace $24.95 (978-044101928-1). Chicago teenager Jessica Ann Porter is a thinking, feeling, and relatively contented zombie when a new virus appears and threatens both the living and the undead. ∩ (Rev: BL 9/1–15/10)

4872 Vande Velde, Vivian. *All Hallows' Eve: 13 Stories* (7–10). 2006, Harcourt $17.00 (978-0-15-205576-9). Thirteen chilling horror stories that take place on Halloween night feature teens and their encounters with vampires, killers, ghosts, and more. (Rev: BL 10/1/06; HB 9–10/06; LMC 4–5/07; SLJ 11/06)

4873 Viehl, Lynn. *Dead of Night* (8–11). Series: Youngbloods. 2012, Flux paper $9.95 (978-07387264-6-5). Catlyn Youngblood and her vampire boyfriend Jesse investigate a string of scary disappearances. **℮** (Rev: BLO 8/12; SLJ 8/12)

4874 Vincent, Rachel. *If I Die* (9–12). Series: Soul Screamers. 2011, HarlequinTeen paper $9.99 (978-03732103-2-9). Banshee Kaylee and needy Sabine band together to oust their hated new teacher before he discovers their supernatural gifts. ∩ **℮** (Rev: BL 12/15/11)

4875 Warrington, Freda. *Dracula the Undead* (9–12). 2009, Severn $28.95 (978-072786817-6). Told through letters and journal entries, this sequel to Bram Stoker's *Dracula* finds several of the characters returning to Transylvania seven years after the vampire's apparent

death only to find that their bloodthirsty adversary is back. (Rev: BL 10/15/09)

4876 Watts, Leander. *Beautiful City of the Dead* (8–11). 2006, Houghton Mifflin $16.00 (978-0-618-59443-6). Zee and her fellow heavy metal bandmates discover they have unsuspected powers and must battle the evil forces around them that want to take these powers away. (Rev: BL 9/15/06)

4877 Weldon, Phaedra. *Spectre* (11–12). 2008, Ace paper $14.00 (978-044101593-1). In this followup to *Wraith* (2007), Zoe, an investigator with paranormal abilities, copes with the sudden loss of her voice, her budding romance with Daniel, and a mysterious mission that turns out to be far more dangerous than she bargained for; for mature readers. **℮** (Rev: BL 6/1–15/08)

4878 Wellington, David. *Monster Island* (11–12). 2006, Thunder's Mouth paper $13.95 (978-1-56025-850-6). In the aftermath of a global disaster that has rendered most humans zombies, a band of teenage girl soldiers and a former UN arms inspector arrive in New York seeking medicine and ready for battle. (Rev: BL 3/15/06)

4879 Westall, Robert. *Shades of Darkness: More of the Ghostly Best Stories of Robert Westall* (7–12). 1994, Macmillan paper $11.95 (978-0-330-35318-2). Eleven eerie tales, not the guts-and-gore variety of supernatural fiction but haunting and insightful stories. (Rev: BL 4/15/94; SLJ 5/94; VOYA 8/94)

4880 Westerfeld, Scott. *The Last Days* (9–12). 2006, Penguin $16.99 (978-1-59514-062-3). In this sequel to *Peeps,* in which havoc reigns in New York City, five teens form a band that will play a key role in saving the world. (Rev: BL 9/1/06; SLJ 11/06)

4881 Westerfeld, Scott. *Peeps* (9–12). 2005, Penguin $16.99 (978-1-59514-031-9). Soon after he arrived in New York from Texas, college freshman Cal lost his virginity and in the process became the carrier of a parasite that causes vampirism; now he is in a key position to save the whole city. (Rev: BL 8/05; SLJ 10/05*)

4882 Westerfeld, Scott. *The Secret Hour* (6–10). Series: Midnighters. 2004, HarperCollins LB $17.89 (978-0-06-051952-0). In this exciting first volume, 15-year-old Jessica Day discovers that — like several others — she has special abilities to battle supernatural creatures. (Rev: SLJ 6/04; VOYA 4/04)

4883 Westerfeld, Scott. *Touching Darkness* (6–10). Series: Midnighters. 2005, HarperCollins LB $16.89 (978-0-06-051955-1). In volume two of the Midnighters series, five teens born at the stroke of midnight learn about the hidden past of their Oklahoma hometown and a frightening conspiracy that threatens them all. (Rev: SLJ 3/05)

4884 Westwood, Chris. *Calling All Monsters* (7–12). 1993, HarperCollins LB $14.89 (978-0-06-022462-2). Joanne is a huge fan of a horror writer, so when she starts seeing nightmare creatures from his books, she recognizes them. (Rev: BL 6/1–15/93; SLJ 7/93; VOYA 12/93)

4885 Whedon, Joss. *Fray* (10–12). Illus. by Karl Moline. 2003, Dark Horse paper $19.95 (978-1-56971-751-6). Melaka Fray, a vampire-fighting street kid in a grim, future Manhattan, finds herself leading a fight to save mankind. (Rev: SLJ 5/04)

4886 Whitcomb, Laura. *A Certain Slant of Light* (9–12). 2005, Houghton Mifflin paper $8.99 (978-0-618-58532-8). In this truly haunting romance, Helen — dead for 130 years — continues to exist in spirit form, but it's not until James comes along that anyone has been able to truly see her. (Rev: BL 11/15/05; HB 11–12/05; SLJ 9/05; VOYA 2/06)

4887 Whitcomb, Laura. *The Fetch* (9–12). 2009, Houghton Mifflin $17.00 (978-061889131-3). When Calder, a ghost who escorts souls from Earth to Heaven, interferes with a soul on Earth, he enters the body of Rasputin on the eve of the Russian Revolution and finds himself in league with the souls of Anastasia and Alexi Romanov in this complex and sophisticated novel that will raise questions about history and spirituality. ∩ Lexile 890L (Rev: BL 12/1/08; LMC 8–9/09; SLJ 3/1/09)

4888 White, Kiersten. *Supernaturally* (9–12). Series: Paranormalcy. 2011, HarperCollins $17.99 (978-0-06-198586-7). Evie finds herself in danger when she leaves the International Paranormal Containment Agency in this sequel to *Paranormalcy* (2010). ∩ **e** Lexile HL680L (Rev: SLJ 12/1/11; VOYA 8/11)

4889 Wiggins, Bethany. *Shifting* (7–10). 2011, Walker $16.99 (978-0-8027-2280-5). Troubled teen and shapeshifter Maggie Mae, who has been in numerous foster homes and has been arrested frequently for indecent exposure, starts at a new school in a new town — with perhaps a new romance — only to find herself threatened by malevolent Skinwalkers. **e** Lexile 720L (Rev: BL 10/15/11; LMC 1–2/12; SLJ 12/1/11; VOYA 10/11)

4890 Winnacker, Susanne. *The Other Life. Bk. 1* (7–10). Series: The Weepers. 2012, Marshall Cavendish $17.99 (978-0-7614-6275-0). In postapocalyptic Los Angeles more than three years after a rabies outbreak that drove survivors into underground bunkers, 15-year-old Sherry and 17-year-old Joshua rescue her family and find refuge from the Weepers (part humans, part animals) in Safe Haven. **e** Lexile 570L (Rev: BLO 5/16/12; LMC 1–2/13*; SLJ 7/12; VOYA 10/12)

4891 Winters, Ben H. *Sense and Sensibility and Sea Monsters* (10–12). Illus. 2009, Quirk paper $12.95 (978-15947444-2-6). The Dashwood women fight sea creatures and find true love in this mingling of horror and proper English manners. ∩ **e** (Rev: BL 9/15/09)

4892 Woon, Yvonne. *Life Eternal* (9–12). Series: Dead Beautiful. 2012, Hyperion $16.99 (978-142311957-9). Renee, 17, begins classes at a new school that will teach her how to kill the Undead even as she longs for her Undead boyfriend, Dante; the second book in the series. **e** Lexile HL740L (Rev: BLO 1/27/12; SLJ 4/12)

4893 Wright, Nina. *Sensitive* (8–10). 2007, Flux paper $9.95 (978-0-7387-1170-6). Cal and Easter, who have supernatural abilities, make contact with the dead and, more romantically, with each other in this novel set in ghost-filled St. Augustine, Florida; the sequel to *Homefree* (2006). (Rev: BL 11/1/07; SLJ 3/08)

4894 Yancey, Rick. *The Isle of Blood* (9–12). Series: The Monstrumologist. 2011, Simon & Schuster $17.99 (978-141698452-8). Dr. Warthrop and his assistant Will Henry receive a disgusting package that sets them off hot on the trail of their most diabolical monster yet; the third book in the series. YALSA Amazing Audiobooks Top Ten 2013. ∩ **e** Lexile 810L (Rev: BL 8/11*; HB 11–12/11)

4895 Yancey, Rick. *The Monstrumologist* (9–12). Series: The Monstrumologist. 2009, Simon & Schuster $17.99 (978-1-4169-8448-1). In 1888, 12-year-old Will Henry is an apprentice to Pellinore Warthrop, a scientist who hunts and studies real-life monsters. Printz Honor 2010. ∩ **e** Lexile 990L (Rev: BL 9/1/09*; LMC 11–12/09; SLJ 11/09)

4896 Yarbro, Chelsea Quinn. *In the Face of Death* (9–12). 2004, BenBella paper $14.95 (978-1-932100-29-7). In this novel that blends fantasy, history, and romance, a vampire named Madelaine leaves her home in London to travel to the U.S. to write a book about Indians in the mid-1800s. (Rev: BL 4/15/04)

4897 Yashinsky, Dan, ed. *Ghostwise: A Book of Midnight Stories* (7–12). 1997, August House $11.95 (978-0-87483-499-4). A collection of 35 short but chilling stories of the supernatural and ghosts. (Rev: BCCB 3/98; VOYA 2/98)

4898 Yovanoff, Brenna. *The Replacement* (9–12). 2010, Penguin $17.99 (978-159514337-2). Sixteen-year-old Mackie, who lives in a small town called Gentry that tries to ignore the supernatural beings that live underground, decides to challenge the status quo. (Rev: BL 9/1/10*; LMC 1–2/11; SLJ 12/1/10)

4899 Zafon, Carlos Ruiz. *The Midnight Palace* (9–12). Trans. by Lucia Graves. 2011, Little, Brown $17.99 (978-0-316-04473-8). Separated as infants and reunited in 1930s Calcutta as teens, twins Ben and Sheere face unanticipated dangers with the help of a secret society of orphans. ∩ **e** Lexile 1030L (Rev: BL 4/1/11; LMC 10/11*; SLJ 5/11; VOYA 4/11)

4900 Zafon, Carlos Ruiz. *The Watcher in the Shadows* (8–11). Trans. by Lucia Graves. 2013, Little, Brown $17.99 (978-031604476-9). After her family moves to an estate in Normandy owned by a toymaker, 15-year-old Irene starts to sense that all is not right. (Rev: BL 12/1/12; HB 5–6/13; LMC 8–9/12*)

4901 Zindel, Paul. *Loch* (7–10). 1994, HarperCollins LB $15.89 (978-0-06-024543-6). Lovable, though human-eating, creatures trapped in a Vermont lake become prey for a ruthless man. (Rev: BL 11/15/94; SLJ 1/95; VOYA 4/95)

Humor

4902 Acampora, Paul. *Defining Dulcie* (7–10). 2006, Dial $16.99 (978-0-8037-3046-5). Dulcie may only be 16 but she knows her own mind, and when her mother moves her to California following her janitor father's death, Dulcie drives home to Connecticut and lives with her janitor grandfather. (Rev: BL 4/1/06*; SLJ 4/06*; VOYA 4/06)

4903 Adams, S. J. *Sparks: The Epic, Completely True Blue, (Almost) Holy Quest of Debbie* (10–12). 2011, Flux paper $9.95 (978-0-7387-2-676-2). Sixteen-year-old lesbian Debbie, unhappy after her secret crush finds herself a guy, sets out to on a "holy quest" with two friends who have invented a Church of Blue. Stonewall Honor 2013. **e** (Rev: BLO 11/15/11; SLJ 11/1/11)

4904 Barnes, Derrick. *The Making of Dr. Truelove* (10–12). 2006, Simon & Schuster paper $7.99 (978-1-4169-1439-6). Full of humor and sexual innuendo, this is the story of 16-year-old Diego's efforts to retrieve the affection of the lovely Roxy through inventing a sex- and relationship-columnist called Dr. Truelove. (Rev: BCCB 2/07; SLJ 4/07)

4905 Barry, Max. *Company* (9–12). 2006, Doubleday $22.95 (978-0-385-51439-2). Poking fun at corporate life, this novel starts with a doughnut crisis, as viewed by a new hire on his first day, but continues with a surprising twist on the big picture. (Rev: SLJ 6/06)

4906 Benni, Stefano. *Margherita Dolce Vita* (9–12). Trans. by Anthony Shugaar. 2006, Europa paper $14.95 (978-1-933372-20-4). Margherita's family leads a simple life on the Italian countryside, but when a family with every modern convenience moves next door her family becomes enthralled with high-tech gadgetry; Margherita fights back against the consumerism and environmental damage. (Rev: BL 10/1/06)

4907 Bradley, Alex. *24 Girls in 7 Days* (8–11). 2005, Dutton $15.99 (978-0-525-47369-5). Dateless only two weeks before the senior prom, Jack is desperate, so desperate that two of his friends run a personal ad in the school paper in an effort to get Jack a date. (Rev: BL 1/1–15/05; SLJ 3/05; VOYA 2/05)

4908 Burnham, Niki. *Royally Jacked* (8–10). 2004, Simon & Schuster paper $5.99 (978-0-689-86668-5). Valerie, a 15-year-old product of divorce accompanies her father to live in a castle in Europe in this lively, humorous story. (Rev: BL 3/1/04; SLJ 2/04)

4909 Burnham, Niki. *Spin Control* (8–10). 2005, Simon & Schuster paper $5.99 (978-0-689-86669-2). Valerie is desperately unhappy when she's forced to leave Schwerinborg and her prince boyfriend and return to Virginia, but a reunion with an old boyfriend soon eases her pain in this sequel to *Royally Jacked* (2004). (Rev: SLJ 2/05)

4910 Cabot, Meg. *Airhead* (7–10). 2008, Scholastic $16.99 (978-0-545-04052-5). Feminist loner Em's brain is transplanted into the body of a famous model, allowing her to experience life as one of the beautiful people. (Rev: BL 4/15/08; SLJ 8/08)

4911 Cabot, Meg. *The Princess Diaries* (7–10). Series: Princess Diaries. 2000, HarperCollins LB $17.89 (978-0-06-029210-2). Fourteen-year-old Mia's diary reveals a fairly interesting life even before she learns that she is actually a royal princess, heir to the throne of Genovia. (Rev: BCCB 12/00; BL 9/15/00; HBG 3/01; SLJ 10/00; VOYA 4/01)

4912 Cabot, Meg. *Princess in Pink* (7–10). Series: Princess Diaries. 2004, HarperCollins $15.99 (978-0-06-009610-6). In this, the fifth volume of the Princess Diaries series, Mia celebrates her 15th birthday and her pregnant mom is about to give birth. (Rev: BL 4/15/04; SLJ 8/04)

4913 Cabot, Meg. *Princess in Training* (7–10). Series: Princess Diaries. 2005, HarperCollins $16.99 (978-0-06-009613-7). Princess Mia's current worries range from English and geometry, running for student council president, and her college boyfriend's expectations, to her new baby brother and the ecology of the Bay of Genovia. (Rev: BL 8/05; SLJ 6/05; VOYA 8/05)

4914 Cabot, Meg. *Princess on the Brink* (8–11). Series: Princess Diaries. 2007, HarperCollins $16.99 (978-0-06-072456-6). Princess Mia contemplates the pros and cons of having sex with her boyfriend in this continuation of the series. ∩ (Rev: BL 12/15/06)

4915 Cabot, Meg. *Ready or Not* (9–12). Series: All-American Girl. 2005, HarperCollins LB $16.89 (978-0-06-072451-1). Samantha is still dating the president's son in this sequel to *All-American Girl* (2002) but she's conflicted about having sex with him. (Rev: BL 9/15/05; SLJ 10/05)

4916 Capote, Truman. *Breakfast at Tiffany's: A Short Novel and Three Stories* (10–12). 1994, Modern Library $14.95 (978-0-679-60085-5); paper $11.00 (978-0-679-74565-5). In addition to this short novel about Holly Golightly, there are three short stories in this volume.

4917 Clarke, Will. *The Worthy: A Ghost's Story* (11–12). 2006, Simon & Schuster $23.00 (978-0-7432-7315-2). A fraternity pledge dies during hazing and comes back as a ghost seeking revenge in this fun romp through college life. ∩ (Rev: BL 5/15/06)

4918 Coupland, Douglas. *JPod* (11–12). 2006, Blooms-bury $24.95 (978-1-59691-104-8). Ethan works for a large video game company where he and his fellow "geeks" shirk hard work in favor of high-tech fun; meanwhile, his quirky family gets involved with a dangerous criminal underworld that is all too real; for mature readers. (Rev: BL 4/15/06*)

4919 Crawford, Brent. *Carter Finally Gets It* (7–10). 2009, Hyperion $15.99 (978-142311246-4). Clumsy freshman Will, who has ADD, attempts to talk to girls, cope with humiliation, and survive sports in this funny, believable account of high school from a hormone-crazed boy's perspective. ⌒ ℮ Lexile HL760L (Rev: BL 11/15/08; SLJ 3/1/09; VOYA 4/09)

4920 Davis, Donald. *Barking at a Fox-Fur Coat* (9–12). 1991, August House $19.95 (978-0-87483-141-2); paper $12.95 (978-0-87483-140-5). Seventeen original tales based on the author's childhood and family experiences in rural North Carolina, each highlighting a set of human foibles and ending with an ironic twist. (Rev: BL 10/15/91; SLJ 4/92)

4921 Dent, Grace. *LBD: Friends Forever!* (7–10). Series: LBD. 2006, Putnam $16.99 (978-0-399-24189-5). Claude enters a modeling contest while the girls are working and vacationing at Destiny Bay in the latest installment of the LBD (Les Bambinos Dangereuses) series. (Rev: SLJ 10/06)

4922 Evans, Red. *On Ice* (9–12). 2007, Kunati paper $19.95 (978-1-60164-015-4). This funny, original story is filled with unusual characters encountered by 12-year-old Eldridge and a famous banjo player who drive the corpse of another musician across the country to his proper burial site. (Rev: BL 9/1/07)

4923 Favorite, Eileen. *The Heroines* (9–12). 2008, Scribner $24.00 (978-1-4165-4810-2). Heroines of classic novels — Blanche DuBois, Scarlett O'Hara, Emma Bovary, and so forth — are boarders at a bed-and-breakfast, run by a Anne-Marie and her rebellious 13-year-old daughter Penny, where they are permitted to take a respite from the crises in their novels, but Penny gets fed up with Anne-Marie's coddling of the distraught women, becomes caught up in some of the characters' stories, and eventually finds herself in the psych ward. (Rev: BL 11/15/07)

4924 Geerling, Marjetta. *Fancy White Trash* (9–12). 2008, Viking $15.99 (978-0-670-01082-0). A humorous story about 15-year-old Abby, her out-of-control family — her mother and one of her sisters may be simultaneously pregnant by the same man — and her steadying friendship with gay neighbor Cody. Best Books for Young Adults 2009. (Rev: SLJ 10/1/08)

4925 Gerber, Michael. *Freshman* (10–12). 2006, Hyperion $16.99 (978-0-7868-3850-9). A satirical look at elite college admissions and campus life, in which Hart Fox accepts an assignment to look after the local mil-

lionaire's son in exchange for free tuition. (Rev: BL 4/1/06; SLJ 4/06)

4926 Gidwitz, Adam. *In a Glass Grimmly* (5–12). 2012, Dutton $16.99 (978-0-525-42581-6). Jack and Jill — and a lonely frog — brave many scary situations in this gory yet humorous fairy-tale companion to *A Tale Dark and Grimm* (2010). ALA Notable Books 2013. ⌒ ℮ Lexile 630L (Rev: HB 11–12/12; LMC 5–6/13*; SLJ 10/12*; VOYA 12/12)

4927 Gonzalez, Julie. *Imaginary Enemy* (6–10). 2008, Delacorte $15.99 (978-0-385-73552-0). Jane, 16, is shocked when her imaginary enemy, Bubba (whom she has blamed for any misbehavior since second grade), responds to one of her letters; a rich and funny novel. (Rev: BL 3/15/08)

4928 Gorey, Edward. *Amphigorey Again* (10–12). 2006, Harcourt $35.00 (978-0-15-101107-0). Character illustrations, sketches, and quirky humor are combined in a unique collection of previously unpublished work and stories by the talented Edward Gorey. (Rev: BL 9/15/06)

4929 Harmel, Kristin. *When You Wish* (7–10). 2008, Delacorte $15.99 (978-0-385-73475-2). Beck is tired of being a pop star and rebels against her manager mother by disguising herself and hopping on a bus to Florida. (Rev: BL 4/1/08; SLJ 5/08)

4930 Hautman, Pete. *Godless* (7–10). 2004, Simon & Schuster $15.95 (978-0-689-86278-6). Rebelling against his devoutly Catholic father, 16-year-old Jason Block and his best friend Shin create a religion of their own with the town's water tower as the deity. (Rev: BL 6/1–15/04*; HB 7–8/04; SLJ 8/04; VOYA 10/04)

4931 Hiaasen, Carl. *Star Island* (11–12). 2010, Knopf $26.95 (978-030727258-4). Things get complicated when out-of-control pop star Cherry Pye's body double is kidnapped, and the star's managers have to figure out a way to get the double back without Cherry finding out that she exists; for mature readers. ⌒ ℮ (Rev: BL 7/10)

4932 Ives, David. *Voss: How I Come to America and Am Hero, Mostly* (7–10). 2008, Putnam $17.99 (978-039924722-4). The hilarious misadventures of Voss, a 15-year-old immigrant, are populated with larger-than-life characters including gangsters, socialites, and crazy relatives, and are told in broken English through letters to a friend back home in Slobovia. (Rev: BL 12/1/08; LMC 1–2/09; SLJ 12/08)

4933 Jaffe, Michele. *Kitty Kitty* (9–12). 2008, Harper-Teen $16.99 (978-0-06-078111-8). Jas is in Italy with her father when her friends arrive just in time to help her solve a mystery involving the murder of a classmate; funny footnotes and lots of sarcasm add to the appeal. (Rev: BL 5/1/08; SLJ 8/08)

4934 Jennings, Patrick. *Barb and Dingbat's Crybaby Hotline* (9–12). 2007, Holiday House $16.95 (978-0-8234-2055-1). In a series of phone conversations in the mid-1970s, junior high students Barb and Jeff try to sort out Jeff's love life; the format will appeal to reluctant readers. (Rev: SLJ 2/08; VOYA 4/08)

4935 Juby, Susan. *Miss Smithers* (7–12). 2004, Harper-Collins LB $16.89 (978-0-06-051547-8). Told through journal articles and a zine, this is the story of Alice of *Alice, I Think* (2003) and how she enters a beauty contest in spite of her mother's opposition. (Rev: BL 5/1/04; HB 7–8/04; SLJ 10/04)

4936 Kinsella, Sophie. *Mini Shopaholic* (10–12). 2010, Dial $25 (978-038534204-9). In this followup to 2007's *Shopaholic and Baby,* the Brandons' toddler daughter, Minnie, begins exhibiting worrisome fashionista tendencies that create strife between Becky and Luke. ⌒ (Rev: BL 8/10)

4937 Kinsella, Sophie. *Shopaholic Ties the Knot* (10–12). 2003, Delta paper $10.95 (978-0-385-33617-8). Wedding bells are set to ring on the same day in two cities an ocean apart as Becky, of *Confessions of a Shopaholic* (2001) and *Shopaholic Takes Manhattan* (2002), tries to unravel another difficult situation. (Rev: BL 3/15/03)

4938 Koertge, Ron. *Where the Kissing Never Stops* (10–12). 1993, Avon paper $3.99 (978-0-380-71796-5). A candid, sometimes bawdy story about a 17-year-old boy, his love life, and his mother who is a stripper. (Rev: BL 11/1/86; SLJ 12/86; VOYA 12/86)

4939 Korman, Gordon. *Don't Care High* (7–10). 1986, Scholastic paper $2.50 (978-0-590-40251-4). A new student in a high school where apathy is so rife it's nicknamed Don't Care High decides to infuse some school spirit into the student body. (Rev: BL 10/15/85)

4940 Korman, Gordon. *Losing Joe's Place* (7–10). 1991, Scholastic paper $5.99 (978-0-590-42769-2). Three teenage boys take over an apartment for the summer with hilarious results. (Rev: BL 3/1/90; SLJ 5/90; VOYA 6/90)

4941 Kraft, Eric. *Taking Off: Book One of Flying, a Trilogy* (9–12). 2006, St. Martin's $23.95 (978-0-312-31884-0). Determined to fly from Long Island to New Mexico, 15-year-old Peter Leroy builds an aerocycle with a little help from his friends and a drawing from an unlikely magazine called the *Impractical Craftsman.* (Rev: BL 6/1–15/06)

4942 Kroese, Robert. *Mercury Falls* (11–12). 2010, AmazonEncore paper $14.95 (978-19355971-5-5). Religion journalist Christine Temetri gets the scoop of a lifetime when she runs across Galileo Mercury, an angel who inadvertently saves the Antichrist and must, with Christine's help, keep Lucifer from bringing about the Apocalypse; a funny, tongue-in-cheek tale suitable for mature readers. (Rev: BL 10/1–15/10)

4943 Lee, Linda Francis. *The Devil in the Junior League* (11–12). 2006, St. Martin's $22.95 (978-0-312-35495-4). When her husband takes off with another woman,

Frede (Fredericka) hires the best lawyer in Texas and ends up transforming his unsuitable wife into a Junior Leaguer. ⌒ (Rev: BL 8/06)

4944 Limb, Sue. *Girl, Barely 15: Flirting for England* (7–10). Series: Jess Jordan. 2008, Delacorte $15.99 (978-0-385-73538-4). Jess's class welcomes a group of French exchange students, and romance and hijinks ensue on a combined camping trip in this funny British import. (Rev: BL 1/1–15/08; SLJ 4/08)

4945 Limb, Sue. *Girl, Going on 17: Pants on Fire* (7–10). Series: Jess Jordan. 2006, Delacorte $15.95 (978-0-385-73218-5). Jess copes with love and school difficulties with her usual humor and fortitude. (Rev: BL 7/06; SLJ 9/06)

4946 Lockhart, E. *Fly on the Wall: How One Girl Saw Everything* (7–10). 2006, Delacorte LB $17.99 (978-0-385-90299-1). Gretchen Yee's wish to be a fly on the wall of the boys' locker room comes true and in the process she gains confidence and learns a lot about boys and friendship. (Rev: BCCB 4/06; BL 7/06; HB 3–4/06; SLJ 3/06)

4947 Lowry, Brigid. *Follow the Blue* (8–12). 2004, Holiday $16.95 (978-0-8234-1827-5). A delightful novel from Australia about 15-year-old Bec, who, with her two younger siblings, is left in the care of a dowdy housekeeper while her parents are away. (Rev: BL 5/1/04*; HB 7–8/04; SLJ 5/04)

4948 McCandless, Sarah Grace. *Grosse Pointe Girl: Tales from a Suburban Adolescence* (10–12). 2004, Simon & Schuster paper $12.00 (978-0-7432-5612-4). This hilarious novel tells about adolescence along with its humiliations and victories as experienced by Emma Harris, a privileged teenager in Grosse Point, Michigan. (Rev: BL 5/1/04)

4949 McFann, Jane. *Deathtrap and Dinosaur* (7–12). 1989, Avon paper $2.75 (978-0-380-75624-7). An unlikely pair works to force the departure of a disliked history teacher. (Rev: SLJ 10/89; VOYA 10/89)

4950 McGowan, Anthony. *Jack Tumor* (7–10). 2009, Farrar $17.95 (978-037432955-6). Funny and vulgar, this British novel features a teen boy named Hector and his brain tumor, Jack; Jack and Hector face an uncertain future and an interesting present as Jack tries to improve Hector's social life. (Rev: BL 6/1–15/09; SLJ 6/1/09)

4951 McLaughlin, Emma, and Nicola Kraus. *Nanny Returns* (11–12). 2009, Atria $25 (978-141658567-1). This sequel to *The Nanny Diaries* (2002) finds Nan settling into married life and a new job when an unexpected visitor from her past draws her back into the lives of the X family; for mature readers. (Rev: BL 10/1/09)

4952 MacLeod, Doug. *I'm Being Stalked by a Moon Shadow* (7–10). 2007, Front St $16.95 (978-1-59078-501-0). Seth, the son of hippies, falls in love with tough-girl Miranda, the daughter of an uptight neighbor in this funny Australian novel. (Rev: BL 10/1/07; SLJ 1/08)

4953 Manes, Stephen. *Comedy High* (7–10). 1992, Scholastic paper $13.95 (978-0-590-44436-1). A comic story of a new high school designed to graduate jocks, performers, gambling experts, and hotel workers. (Rev: BL 12/1/92; SLJ 11/92)

4954 Many, Paul. *These Are the Rules* (7–10). 1997, Walker $15.95 (978-0-8027-8619-7). In this hilarious first-person narrative, Colm tries to figure out the rules of dating, driving, girls, and getting some direction in his life. (Rev: BL 5/1/97; HBG 3/98; SLJ 5/97)

4955 Martin, Steve. *The Pleasure of My Company* (10–12). 2003, Hyperion $19.95 (978-0-7868-6921-3). Daniel Pecan Cambridge learns to put his phobias in second place in this entertaining novel. (Rev: BL 9/1/03*)

4956 Maxwell, Katie. *They Wear What Under Their Kilts?* (8–11). 2004, Dorchester paper $5.99 (978-0-8439-5258-2). Emily Williams, the 16-year-old American introduced in the riotous *The Year My Life Went Down the Loo*, is off to a Scottish sheep farm on a month-long work-study program. (Rev: BL 1/1–15/04)

4957 Meehl, Brian. *Suck It Up* (8–11). 2008, Delacorte $15.99 (978-0-385-73300-7). Sixteen-year-old Morning is an unlikely vampire — he drinks only blood substitute and is something of a nerd — but he is chosen to be the first of his kind to reveal his true nature to humans; romance and humor add to the appeal. (Rev: BL 3/1/08)

4958 Milligan, J. *Jack Fish: A Novel* (10–12). 2005, Soho $23.00 (978-1-56947-382-5). Jack Fish, a denizen of the deep, is assigned by the Elders of Atlantis to handle a sensitive mission on dry land in this funny look at life in New York City. (Rev: SLJ 6/05)

4959 Mlynowski, Sarah. *Frogs and French Kisses* (7–10). 2006, Delacorte $15.95 (978-0-385-73182-9). This funny, cleverly written sequel to *Bras and Broomsticks* (2005) features Rachel's efforts to control her family members' overuse of magic while she copes with the consequences. (Rev: BL 7/06; SLJ 9/06)

4960 Naylor, Phyllis Reynolds. *Alice Alone* (6–10). 2001, Simon & Schuster $15.00 (978-0-689-82634-4). Alice's story continues as she starts high school and deals with the misery of breaking up with her boyfriend. (Rev: BCCB 5/01; BL 5/15/01; HB 7–8/01; HBG 10/01; SLJ 6/01; VOYA 8/01)

4961 O'Brien, Gerry. *Planting Out: The Second Book of the Borough* (10–12). 2002, Colin Smythe $29.95 (978-0-86140-440-7). In the second entertaining book set in a fictional London borough, a vitally important microchip is lost and the corpse of the monastery's gardener hopes to rest in peace. (Rev: BL 1/1–15/02)

4962 Parkhurst, Carolyn. *Lost and Found* (11–12). 2006, Little, Brown $23.95 (978-0-316-15638-7). The diverse teams competing in a reality show called "Lost and Found" all find their relationships and aspirations challenged as the game proceeds; for mature teens. (Rev: BL 3/1/06; SLJ 9/06)

4963 Parks, Adele. *Larger Than Life* (11–12). 2003, Pocket paper $12.00 (978-0-7434-5760-6). An amusing British story of a steadfast love that begins to falter when Georgie finally gets to live with Hugh. (Rev: BL 8/03)

4964 Paulsen, Gary. *Harris and Me: A Summer Remembered* (6–10). 1993, Harcourt $16.00 (978-0-15-292877-3). A humorous story in which the 11-year-old narrator often gets the blame for mischief caused by troublemaker Harris. (Rev: BL 12/1/93*; SLJ 2/00; VOYA 2/94)

4965 Payne, C. D. *Revolting Youth* (10–12). 2000, Aivia $14.95 (978-1-882647-15-6). Fourteen-year-old Nick Twisp, in spite of good intentions, continues to create havoc in this hilarious sequel to *Youth in Revolt* (1993) that contains some explicit sex. (Rev: BL 10/15/00)

4966 Peck, Richard. *A Long Way from Chicago* (6–10). 1998, Dial $16.99 (978-0-8037-2290-3). Seven stories are included in this book, each representing a different summer from 1929 to 1935 that Joey spent visiting in Illinois with his lying, cheating, conniving, and thoroughly charming grandmother. (Rev: BCCB 10/98; BL 9/1/98; HB 11–12/98; HBG 3/99; SLJ 10/98*; VOYA 12/98)

4967 Peck, Richard. *A Year Down Yonder* (6–10). 2000, Dial $16.99 (978-0-8037-2518-8). In this 2001 Newbery Medal winner, 15-year-old Mary Alice visits her feisty, independent, but lovable Grandma Dowdel in rural Illinois during the Great Depression. A sequel to *A Long Way from Chicago* (1998). (Rev: BCCB 1/01; BL 10/15/00*; HB 11–12/00; HBG 3/01; SLJ 9/00; VOYA 12/00)

4968 Perry, Kate. *Project Date* (9–12). 2007, Zebra paper $4.99 (978-0-8217-8029-9). In this funny, clever novel, Mena risks losing her parents' approval as her attentions turn from the boyfriend they like to an exciting young man they most certainly won't like. (Rev: BL 7/07)

4969 Pratchett, Terry. *Going Postal* (8–12). Series: Discworld. 2004, HarperCollins $24.95 (978-0-06-001313-4). In this humorous and inventive 29th Discworld novel, career criminal Moist von Lipwig escapes hanging by accepting the job of postmaster for Ankh-Morpork, a job he intends to leave far behind as soon as he can. Margaret A. Edwards Award 2011. (Rev: BL 9/1/04; SLJ 2/05)

4970 Rennison, Louise. *A Midsummer Tights Dream* (7–10). Series: (Mis)adventures of Tallulah Casey. 2012, HarperCollins $17.99 (978-0-06-179936-5). In this sequel to *Withering Tights*, Tallulah begins a new school year full of hope and anticipation about dancing, boys, and saving her school's performing arts program. Lexile 660L (Rev: HB 9–10/12; SLJ 10/12; VOYA 12/12)

4971 Rennison, Louise. *Startled by His Furry Shorts: Confessions of Georgia Nicolson* (7–10). 2006, HarperTempest $16.99 (978-0-06-085384-6). Georgia, a British teenager, gives her hilarious views about dealing with boys, her family, having fun with friends, and getting stuck with a part in her school's play. ∩ (Rev: BL 10/15/06; SLJ 7/06)

4972 Rennison, Louise. *Then He Ate My Boy Entrancers: More Mad, Marvy Confessions of Georgia Nicolson* (7–10). 2005, HarperCollins $15.99 (978-0-06-058937-0). In her sixth volume of diaries, Georgia travels to and critiques the United States as well as cataloging her usual problems at home with friends, boyfriends, siblings, and cats. (Rev: BL 8/05; SLJ 8/05; VOYA 10/05)

4973 Rennison, Louise. *Withering Tights* (7–10). 2011, HarperTeen $16.99 (978-0-06-179931-0). Georgia Nicolson's British cousin Tallulah, 14, navigates a summer at performing arts camp where she worries about her ugly knees, makes new friends, and meets some interesting boys. ∩ **e** Lexile HL620L (Rev: BL 7/11; HB 9–10/11; SLJ 7/11; VOYA 8/11)

4974 Riggs, Bob. *My Best Defense* (6–10). 1996, Ward Hill paper $5.95 (978-1-886747-01-2). Sarcasm is the best defense of the narrator in this humorous story of a family and the unusual characters they attract. (Rev: SLJ 8/96; VOYA 10/96)

4975 Rosoff, Meg. *There Is No Dog* (9–12). 2012, Putnam $17.99 (978-039925764-3). God is a teenage boy named Bob in this tale full of dark humor. ∩ **e** (Rev: BL 11/15/11*; HB 1–2/12; LMC 8–9/12; SLJ 1/12; VOYA 12/11)

4976 Ross, Leonard Q. *The Education of H*Y*M*A*N K*A*P*L*A*N* (9–12). 1968, Harcourt paper $12.00 (978-0-15-627811-9). A series of hilarious stories about an immigrant Jew and his battle with the English language at night school.

4977 Ryan, Mary C. *Who Says I Can't?* (7–10). 1988, Little, Brown $12.95 (978-0-316-76374-5). Tessa decides to get revenge on a boy who shows too much ardor in his romancing. (Rev: SLJ 11/88)

4978 Sheldon, Dyan. *Confessions of a Hollywood Star* (7–10). 2006, Candlewick $208.00 (978-0-7636-3075-1). In this funny follow-up to *Confessions of a Teenage Drama Queen* (1999), Lola schemes to get a part in a Hollywood movie being filmed in her suburban New Jersey hometown. (Rev: BL 6/1–15/06; HB 7–8/06; LMC 11–12/06; SLJ 10/06)

4979 Shields, Gillian. *The Actual Real Reality of Jennifer James* (7–10). 2006, HarperCollins $16.99 (978-0-06-082240-8). Unpopular British high school student Jennifer James becomes a contestant on a TV reality

show in this funny story told through diary entries (with helpful definitions of British slang). (Rev: BL 5/15/06; SLJ 6/06)

4980 Shoup, Barbara. *Everything You Want* (9–12). 2008, Flux $16.95 (978-0-7387-1227-7). Would $50 million buy everything you want? Emma finds out when she wins the lottery and is forced to determine what she really wants in life. (Rev: BL 5/1/08)

4981 Sleator, William. *Oddballs* (8–12). 1995, Penguin paper $5.99 (978-0-14-037438-4). A collection of stories based on experiences from the author's youth and peopled with an unusual assortment of family and friends.

4982 Smith, Edwin R. *Blue Star Highway: A Tale of Redemption from North Florida, Vol. 1* (7–12). 1997, Mile Marker Twelve Publg. paper $9.95 (978-0-9659054-0-4). In this humorous novel, 14-year-old Marty Crane tells of the events in his life leading up to being sentenced to a detention home in 1962. (Rev: BL 2/15/99)

4983 Snow, Carol. *Just Like Me, Only Better* (11–12). 2010, Berkley paper $14 (978-04252324-8-4). Struggling young mom Veronica gets a big break when she's picked as star Haley Rush's celebrity double — but finds that balancing reality with stardom is far from easy street; for mature students. **e** (Rev: BL 4/1–15/10)

4984 Swendson, Shanna. *Enchanted, Inc* (9–12). 2005, Ballantine paper $12.95 (978-0-345-48125-2). Katie Chandler is 26, living in a New York City full of fairies, elves, and other magical beings, and — it turns out — valuable for the fact that she does not have any special powers. (Rev: BL 5/15/05; SLJ 9/05)

4985 Thompson, Julian. *Simon Pure* (10–12). 1987, Scholastic paper $3.50 (978-0-590-41823-2). Simon has some unusual but always hilarious adventures when he enters Riddle University. (Rev: BL 4/15/87; SLJ 3/87; VOYA 4/87)

4986 Townsend, Sue. *Adrian Mole: The Lost Years* (9–12). 1994, Soho $22.00 (978-1-56947-014-5). In this sequel to *The Secret Diary of Adrian Mole*, Adrian chronicles his struggle with the raging hormones of adolescence and his search for a suitable career. (Rev: BL 8/94; SLJ 1/95)

4987 Townsend, Sue. *The Secret Diary of Adrian Mole, Age Thirteen and Three Quarters* (9–12). 1984, Avon paper $5.99 (978-0-380-86876-6). The trials and tribulations of a young English boy as revealed through his hilarious diary entries. (Rev: BL 1/1–15/97)

4988 Trembath, Don. *A Fly Named Alfred* (7–10). 1997, Orca paper $6.95 (978-1-55143-083-6). In this sequel to *The Tuesday Cafe*, Harper Winslow gets into more trouble when he write an anonymous column in the school newspaper that enrages the school bully. (Rev: BL 8/97; SLJ 9/96)

4989 Vizzini, Ned. *Be More Chill: A Novel* (9–12). 2004, Hyperion $16.95 (978-0-7868-0995-0). Desperate to become cool and accepted by the school's elite, high school geek Jeremy Heere swallows a pill-sized super-computer that promises to help him achieve his goal but discovers that this quick fix has a downside; a funny novel that includes profanity and sex. (Rev: BL 8/04; SLJ 6/04; VOYA 6/04)

4990 Wersba, Barbara. *You'll Never Guess the End* (7–12). 1992, HarperCollins $14.00 (978-0-06-020448-8). A send-up of the New York City literary scene, rich dilettantes, and scientology. (Rev: BL 11/15/92; SLJ 9/92)

4991 Wibberley, Leonard. *The Mouse That Roared* (7–12). 1992, Buccaneer LB $27.95 (978-0-89966-887-1). To get foreign aid, the tiny Duchy of Grand Fenwick declares war on the United States.

4992 Wood, Maryrose. *Sex Kittens and Horn Dawgs Fall in Love* (7–10). 2006, Delacorte LB $17.99 (978-0-385-90296-0). To get closer to Matthew, the object of her affection, 14-year-old Felicia suggests that the two of them work together on a science fair project investigating the workings of love's "X-factor." (Rev: BL 11/15/05; SLJ 2/06)

4993 Zeitlin, Meredith. *Freshman Year and Other Unnatural Disasters* (8–11). 2012, Putnam $16.99 (978-039925423-9). Kelsey, 14, navigates a perilous freshman year at a new school in Manhattan; this humorous story is full of social and romantic missteps. ℮ (Rev: BL 4/15/12; SLJ 3/12; VOYA 4/12)

4994 Ziegler, Jennifer. *Alpha Dog* (8–11). 2006, Delacorte paper $7.99 (978-0-385-73285-7). When Katie learns to be alpha dog and control her adopted mutt, she also learns to assert herself with her mother and friends in this funny novel. (Rev: BL 7/06; LMC 10/06)

4995 Ziegler, Jennifer. *How Not to Be Popular* (7–10). 2008, Delacorte $15.99 (978-0-385-73465-3). When her family moves yet again, Sugar Magnolia (Maggie) ditches her usual effort to make friends and instead decides to become an outsider at school. (Rev: BL 4/1/08; SLJ 3/08)

Mysteries, Thrillers, and Spy Stories

4996 Abrahams, Peter. *Down the Rabbit Hole* (7–10). Series: Echo Falls. 2005, HarperCollins LB $17.89 (978-0-06-073702-3). Thirteen-year-old Ingrid Levin-Hill takes a page from her idol Sherlock Holmes and sets out to track down the murderer of an eccentric townswoman. (Rev: BCCB 4/05; BL 5/1/05*; SLJ 5/05; VOYA 6/05)

4997 Abrahams, Peter. *Into the Dark* (5–12). Series: Echo Falls. 2008, HarperCollins $15.99 (978-0-06-073708-5). Ingrid's grandfather, a World War II veteran, is a suspect in a murder committed using a World War II-era rifle. Can Ingrid solve the mystery and clear her grandfather's name? (Rev: BL 5/1/08; SLJ 3/08)

4998 Abrahams, Peter. *Reality Check* (8–11). 2009, HarperTeen $16.99 (978-006122766-0); LB $17.89 (978-006122767-7). Cody Laredo is already facing difficulties — a knee injury keeps him off the football team and ruins his chances of a college scholarship — when his rich girlfriend Clea disappears from her boarding school in Vermont and he sets off from Colorado to find her. ∩ ℮ (Rev: BL 7/09; SLJ 5/1/09; VOYA 4/09*)

4999 Adamson, Isaac. *Hokkaido Popsicle* (11–12). 2002, HarperPerennial paper $12.95 (978-0-380-81292-9). Teen reporter Billy Chaka investigates two possibly related deaths in this entertaining sequel to *Tokyo Suckerpunch* (2000). (Rev: BL 4/1/02; SLJ 10/02)

5000 Adamson, Isaac. *Kinki Lullaby* (9–12). 2004, HarperCollins paper $13.95 (978-0-06-051624-6). In the fourth, colorful book in the series, Billy Chaka investigates a mystery and a murder in the Osaka district of Japan. (Rev: BL 9/1/04; SLJ 2/05)

5001 Ahern, Cecelia. *There's No Place Like Here* (9–12). 2008, Hyperion $24.95 (978-1-4013-0188-0). This is the unique story of a woman who searches for missing people for a living and accidentally stumbles upon a community of missing people and things from many different places; in the process, the woman discovers important things about herself. (Rev: BL 9/1/07)

5002 Aidan, Pamela. *Duty and Desire: A Novel of Fitzwilliam Darcy, Gentleman* (9–12). 2006, Simon & Schuster paper $14.00 (978-0-7432-9136-1). *Duty and Desire* plays on the themes and characters of Jane Austen's *Pride and Prejudice,* with Darcy solving a mystery while daydreaming about Elizabeth Bennet. (Rev: BL 9/1/06)

5003 Allen, Conrad. *Murder on the Mauretania* (10–12). 2000, St. Martin's $23.75 (978-0-312-24116-2). A humorous mystery that involves a murder during the maiden voyage of the *Mauretania.* (Rev: BL 12/1/00)

5004 Alphin, Elaine Marie. *The Perfect Shot* (8–12). 2005, Carolrhoda LB $16.95 (978-1-57505-862-7). Brian, a high school basketball star, learns important lessons about justice, racial prejudice, and civic responsibility when his girlfriend's father is charged with the murder of his wife and two daughters and an African American teammate is arrested on trumped-up charges. (Rev: SLJ 10/05*; VOYA 12/05)

5005 Apone, Claudio. *My Grandfather, Jack the Ripper* (6–12). 2000, Herodias $19.00 (978-1-928746-16-4). Thirteen-year-old Andy Dobson, a clairvoyant Londoner, travels back in time — with the help of hallucinogenic drugs — to discover the true identity of the legendary murderer. (Rev: HBG 10/01; SLJ 6/01; VOYA 6/01)

5006 Archer, Jeffrey. *A Matter of Honor* (10–12). 1993, HarperCollins paper $7.99 (978-0-06-100713-2). For better readers, a tense thriller about a chase across Europe to secure a priceless icon. (Rev: BL 6/15/86)

5007 Arnold, Tedd. *Rat Life: A Mystery* (7–10). 2007, Dial $16.99 (978-0-8037-3020-5). Todd, 14, loves to write funny, crude stories to entertain his classmates until he befriends a Vietnam veteran named Rat; his writing takes on a new perspective while he also begins to uncover clues to an unsolved murder. (Rev: BL 5/1/07; SLJ 5/07)

5008 Arsenault, Emily. *In Search of the Rose Notes* (10–12). 2011, Morrow $14.99 (978-0-06-201232-4). Nora is forced to revisit the events surrounding her babysitter's death sixteen years ago when the young woman's bones are discovered. (Rev: SLJ 9/11)

5009 Ashford, Jeffrey. *A Fair Exchange Is Robbery* (10–12). 2003, Severn $26.99 (978-0-7278-5972-3). Gavin Penfold is accused of a crime he did not commit and sets out to expose the perpetrators in this thought-provoking novel. (Rev: BL 9/1/03)

5010 Asinof, Eliot. *Off-Season* (10–12). 2000, Southern Illinois Univ. $22.50 (978-0-8093-2297-8). In this murder mystery with a baseball setting, the hero, a major league pitcher, investigates the murder of his African American coach and uncovers a case of racism and corruption. (Rev: BL 4/1/00)

5011 Atkins, Charles. *Mother's Milk* (11–12). 2009, Severn $28.95 (978-072786795-7). The discovery of two dead teenagers and the disappearance of one of her patients, now the prime suspect, send forensic psychiatrist Barratt Conyers on a twisting search for the truth. (Rev: BL 10/1/09)

5012 Aubert, Rosemary. *Free Reign: A Suspense Novel* (10–12). 1997, BridgeWorks $21.95 (978-1-882593-18-7). A recluse rejoins society and experiences romance and extreme danger while investigating the meaning of a ringed hand placed in his garden. (Rev: BL 4/15/97; SLJ 10/97)

5013 Ayarbe, Heidi. *Wanted* (9–12). 2012, HarperCollins $17.99 (978-006199388-6). Michal, 17, takes big risks with her gambling business when she meets wealthy Josh Ellison. (Rev: BL 5/1/12; SLJ 6/12; VOYA 4/12)

5014 Bacus, K. C. *Calamity Jayne* (11–12). 2006, Dorchester paper $5.99 (978-0-505-52665-6). Followed by trouble wherever she goes, Tressa Jayne Turner gets involved in some serious difficulties when she accidentally takes someone else's car and discovers a large amount of cash and a corpse in its trunk; entertaining fare for mature teens. (Rev: BL 12/15/05)

5015 Bacus, Kathleen. *Calamity Jayne Rides Again* (9–12). 2006, Spell paper $6.99 (978-0-505-52669-4). Lovely if clumsy amateur detective Tressa "Calamity Jayne" Turner rides out again, this time to rescue Uncle Frank whose soft-frozen ice cream booth is being sys-

tematically sabotaged and to find her missing cousin Frankie. (Rev: BL 7/06)

5016 Bannister, Jo. *The Tinderbox* (11–12). 2006, Severn $27.95 (978-0-7278-6387-4). A father enters the frightening underworld of the homeless to find his daughter, who disappeared six years earlier. (Rev: BL 12/1/06)

5017 Barclay, Linwood. *Never Look Away* (11–12). 2010, Delacorte $25 (978-055380717-2). When average joe David becomes a suspect in his troubled wife's disappearance, he sets out to discover the truth — and clear his own name — in this engrossing family thriller suitable for mature readers. (Rev: BL 3/1–15/10)

5018 Barron, Sandra Rodriguez. *The Heiress of Water* (10–12). 2006, Rayo paper $13.95 (978-0-06-114281-9). Monica, a physical therapist in Connecticut, returns to El Salvador, the site of her mother's death by drowning years earlier, in an attempt to help a patient in a coma. (Rev: BL 8/06)

5019 Barron, Stephanie. *Jane and His Lordship's Legacy* (10–12). 2005, Bantam $24.00 (978-0-553-80225-2). Sleuth Jane Austen, mourning roguish Lord Harold's death, moves to Chawton Cottage with her mother and finds there is a body in the basement. (Rev: BL 2/15/05)

5020 Barron, Stephanie. *Jane and the Wandering Eye* (10–12). 1998, Bantam paper $5.99 (978-0-553-57817-1). Jane Austen turns sleuth when a theater manager is murdered in Bath and a portrait of an eye is found on the body. (Rev: SLJ 7/98)

5021 Beaufrand, Mary Jane. *The River* (8–12). 2010, Little, Brown $16.99 (978-0-316-04168-3). Ronnie, unhappy following her family's move from Portland to rural Oregon, is overwhelmed when the 10-year-old girl she has been babysitting drowns; suspicious about the circumstances, she sets out to discover what happened. Lexile HL730L (Rev: BL 12/15/09; HB 5–6/10; SLJ 2/10; VOYA 4/10)

5022 Bebris, Carrie. *The Intrigue at Highbury; or, Emma's Match* (10–12). Series: Mr. and Mrs. Darcy Mysteries. 2010, Tor $22.99 (978-076531848-0). In this Austen-flavored whodunit, Mr. Knightley agrees to help the Darcys to find the highwayman who robbed them, in return for help investigating the unexpected death of Frank Churchill's guardian, Edgar. (Rev: BL 3/1–15/10)

5023 Bebris, Carrie. *The Matters at Mansfield; or, The Crawford Affair* (10–12). Series: Mr. and Mrs. Darcy Mysteries. 2008, Forge $22.95 (978-0-7653-1847-3). Darcy and Elizabeth visit Mansfield Park in this murder mystery written in Austen's style. ⊕ (Rev: BL 8/08)

5024 Bebris, Carrie. *North by Northanger: or, The Shades of Pemberley* (9–12). Series: Mr. & Mrs. Darcy Mysteries. 2006, Forge $22.95 (978-0-7653-1410-9). Mr. Darcy and Elizabeth of *Pride and Prejudice* are the main characters in this mystery that also includes characters from *Northanger Abbey*. (Rev: BL 5/1/06)

5025 Beckett, Simon. *Written in Bone* (9–12). 2007, Delacorte $24.00 (978-0-385-34005-2). In this sequel to The Chemistry of Death set in the Hebrides, forensic anthropologist David Hunter examines a badly burned corpse and in the process discovers many of the islanders' hidden secrets. (Rev: BL 9/1/07)

5026 Beechey, Alan. *An Embarrassment of Corpses* (10–12). 1997, Thomas Dunne $22.95 (978-0-312-16936-7). A witty mystery set in London about serial murders investigated by a police detective and his nephew, a writer of children's books. (Rev: SLJ 5/98)

5027 Bell, Hilari. *Rogue's Home* (7–10). Series: Knight and Rogue. 2008, Eos $17.99 (978-0-06-082506-5). The second adventure in the series, this buddy story has the "knight" Mike and his sidekick squire Fisk returning to Fisk's hometown to investigate blackmail and arson. (Rev: BL 8/08; SLJ 9/08)

5028 Belmond, C. A. *A Rather Lovely Inheritance* (10–12). 2007, NAL paper $12.95 (978-0-451-22052-3). When Penny, a historical researcher, inherits part of her Aunt Penelope's estate, she also is faced with a family mystery which takes her traveling through Europe. (Rev: BL 11/15/06)

5029 Benjamin, Carol Lea. *The Dog Who Knew Too Much* (10–12). 1997, Walker $21.95 (978-0-8027-3312-2). With the help of her pit bull Dashiell, private investigator Rachel Alexander investigates the death of a young woman in Greenwich Village. (Rev: BL 9/1/97; VOYA 12/97)

5030 Benjamin, Carol Lea. *This Dog for Hire* (10–12). 1996, Walker $20.95 (978-0-8027-3292-7). Private investigator Rachel Alexander and her pit bull, Dashiell, are hired to track down a hit-and-run driver who killed a young New York artist. (Rev: SLJ 4/97; VOYA 2/97)

5031 Bennett, Jay. *Coverup* (8–10). 1992, Fawcett paper $5.99 (978-0-449-70409-7). Realizing his friend has killed a pedestrian on a deserted road after a party, Brad returns to the accident scene and meets a girl searching for her homeless father. (Rev: BL 11/1/91)

5032 Benoit, Charles. *Fall from Grace* (9–12). 2012, HarperTeen $17.99 (978-006194707-0). Naive, sheltered Sawyer finds himself taking surprising risks when an exotic new girl promises something more exciting than his current girlfriend. e Lexile HL810L (Rev: BL 5/1/12; HB 5–6/12; SLJ 6/12)

5033 Berk, Josh. *Guy Langman, Crime Scene Procrastinator* (9–12). 2012, Knopf $16.99 (978-037585701-0); LB $19.99 (978-037595701-7). A humorous mystery in which 16-year-old Guy and his best friend Anoop, along with other members of the school's forensics club, investigate a possible murder that may be related to Guy. ⌂ (Rev: BL 5/1/12; LMC 1–2/13; SLJ 6/12)

5034 Bilen, Tracy. *What She Left Behind* (9–12). 2012, Simon & Schuster paper $9.99 (978-1-4424-3951-1). Sara's brother committed suicide, her abused mother has disappeared, and her only solace is her friend Zach — but can he help when Dad kidnaps them both? e Lexile HL610L (Rev: LMC 10/12; SLJ 6/12; VOYA 4/12)

5035 Black, Veronica. *A Vow of Adoration* (10–12). 1997, St. Martin's $20.95 (978-0-312-18205-2). An English adventure mystery involving Sister Joan, her convent, and a murder on the Cornish moors. (Rev: SLJ 6/98)

5036 Blackman, Malorie. *Knife Edge* (11–12). Series: Black & White. 2007, Simon & Schuster $16.99 (978-1-4169-0018-4). The white father of black Sephy's unborn child was hanged in the book *Naughts and Crosses* (2005), set in a strictly racist land; now Sephy is in danger of being murdered by her former lover's brother; a very dark story for mature readers. (Rev: BL 7/07; HB 7–8/07; SLJ 9/07)

5037 Bohjalian, Chris. *The Double Bind* (11–12). 2007, Crown $25.00 (978-1-4000-4746-8). When a homeless man dies leaving behind a collection of photographs, young caseworker Laurel finds herself digging into the past — both his and her own. ⌂ (Rev: BL 12/15/06)

5038 Bond, Stephanie. *Body Movers* (11–12). Series: Body Movers. 2006, Mira $13.95 (978-0-7783-2333-4). Carlotta is suspected of murder when her former friend Angela is killed and Jack Terry takes on the case; humor and romance add to this engaging story suitable for mature teens. (Rev: BL 8/06)

5039 Bond, Stephanie. *5 Bodies to Die For* (11–12). Series: Body Movers. 2009, Harlequin paper $7.99 (978-07783270-5-9). In this fifth volume in the series Carlotta is dodging a serial killer and romantic entanglements; for mature readers ⌂ e (Rev: BL 4–5/09*)

5040 Bond, Stephanie. *6 Killer Bodies* (11–12). Series: Body Movers. 2009, MIRA paper $7.99 (978-07783270-7-3). Carlotta tracks a killer who leaves bracelet charms in the mouths of his victims; for mature readers. ⌂ e (Rev: BL 7/09)

5041 Bowler, Tim. *Frozen Fire* (7–10). 2008, Philomel $17.99 (978-0-399-25053-8). Set in a wintry England, this is a disquieting and complex story of a ghostlike boy whom Dusty suspects knows the whereabouts of her missing brother. (Rev: BL 5/15/08; SLJ 7/08)

5042 Bowler, Tim. *Storm Catchers* (6–10). 2003, Simon & Schuster $16.95 (978-0-689-84573-4). A multilayered, suspenseful story of the kidnapping of a 13-year-old girl on the Cornwall coast, her brother's agonized guilt, and the discovery of a dark family secret. (Rev: BL 9/1/03; HBG 4/04; SLJ 5/03; VOYA 8/03)

5043 Boyle, T. C. *When the Killing's Done* (10–12). 2011, Viking $26.95 (978-067002232-8). Environmental and business interests collide in this tense story about animal rights off the coast of Santa Barbara, with a family history intertwined. **e** (Rev: BL 12/1–15/10*)

5044 Bradbury, Jennifer. *Shift* (7–12). 2008, Atheneum $16.99 (978-1-4169-6219-9). Friends Chris and Win take a cross-country bike trip the summer after high school; but Win disappears in Montana and Chris becomes the focus of an FBI investigation. (Rev: BL 3/1/08)

5045 Bradley, Alan. *The Weed That Strings the Hangman's Bag* (9–12). 2010, Delacorte $24 (978-038534231-5). When a puppeteer is electrocuted in the middle of a performance at the local church, 11-year-old Flavia DeLuce is on the case; set in 1950s England. ∩ **e** (Rev: BL 2/1–15/10)

5046 Braun, Lilian Jackson. *The Cat Who Sang for the Birds* (10–12). 1998, Jove paper $7.99 (978-0-515-12463-7). In this part of the mystery series involving the sleuthing team of Jim Qwilleran and his cats, Koko the cat uses his talents to predict future events and helps Jim solve the mystery of the death of his elderly neighbor and the disappearance of a young artist. (Rev: BL 11/1/97; SLJ 8/98)

5047 Bray, Libba. *The Diviners* (9–12). 2012, Little, Brown $19.99 (978-0-316-12611-3). Seventeen-year-old flapper Evie's life picks up when her uncle's museum of the occult attracts a grisly and persistent murderer in this 1920s-era mystery and Evie is enlisted to help investigate, using her special abilities. YALSA Top Ten Best Fiction for Young Adults 2013; YALSA Amazing Audiobooks Top Ten 2013. ∩ **e** Lexile HL730L (Rev: BL 7/12*; HB 3–4/13; LMC 11–12/12*; SLJ 9/12*)

5048 Brewer, James D. *No Escape* (9–12). 1998, Walker $22.95 (978-0-8027-3318-4). Luke Williamson, Masey Baldridge, and Salina Tyner of the Big River Detective Agency are hired by the mayor of Memphis, Tennessee, to investigate embezzlement and the murders of fever victims at the beginning of the 1873 Yellow Fever epidemic. (Rev: VOYA 10/98)

5049 Brewer, James D. *No Remorse: A Masey Baldridge/Luke Williamson Mystery* (10–12). 1997, Walker $22.95 (978-0-8027-3302-3). Set after the end of the Civil War, this novel features riverboat captain/detective Luke Williamson and detective agency partners Masey Baldridge and Salina Tyner, who take on a case in which the widow of Williamson's competitor engages him to clear her son of his father's murder. (Rev: BL 8/97; VOYA 4/98)

5050 Brian, Kate. *Confessions* (9–12). Series: Private. 2007, Simon & Schuster paper $9.99 (978-1-4169-1876-9). Reed's boyfriend Josh is accused of murdering her former boyfriend and, convinced he is innocent, Reed starts an investigation in which she uncovers various secrets; this is the fourth installment in the series set at Easton Academy. (Rev: SLJ 9/07)

5051 Broach, Elise. *Desert Crossing* (9–12). 2006, Henry Holt $16.95 (978-0-8050-7762-9). Three teenagers find themselves engulfed in a mystery after finding a dead girl on a highway in New Mexico. (Rev: BL 6/1–15/06; LMC 1/07; SLJ 6/06)

5052 Brooks, Kevin. *Black Rabbit Summer* (9–12). 2008, Scholastic $17.99 (978-0-545-05752-3). When Pete and a group of high-school friends get together one last time over the summer, drugs and death come into the picture and change their friendship forever. (Rev: BL 5/1/08; SLJ 8/08)

5053 Browne, Ian. *The Da Vinci Mole: A Philosophical Parody* (9–12). 2006, BenBella paper $9.95 (978-1-932100-90-7). Mimicking the story lines of *The Da Vinci Code*, this suspenseful story, set in New York City, involves a curator — found dead at the Whitney Museum — who has left hidden riddles to find and decode, a task taken on by a modern art professor and the victim's French granddaughter. (Rev: SLJ 8/06)

5054 Bunkley, Anita. *Mirrored Life* (11–12). 2002, Kensington $24.00 (978-0-7582-0077-8). Sara Jane, an African American girl jailed at the age of 15, spends her time behind bars earning a cosmetology license; on her release she changes her name to Serena but her subsequent success brings her to the attention of someone from her past; for mature teens. (Rev: BL 10/15/02)

5055 Bunting, Eve. *The Haunting of Safe Keep* (7–10). 1985, HarperCollins LB $12.89 (978-0-397-32113-1). In this romantic mystery, two college friends work out their family problems while investigating strange occurrences where they work. (Rev: BL 4/15/85; SLJ 5/85; VOYA 8/85)

5056 Burgess, Melvin. *Sara's Face* (8–12). 2007, Simon & Schuster $16.99 (978-1-4169-3295-6). Wealthy rock star Jonathan Heat, whose obsession with plastic surgery has left him without a face, offers to pay for surgery for pretty teen Sara; could his motives be less than generous? (Rev: BL 5/15/07; SLJ 6/07)

5057 Burke, Jan. *Hocus* (10–12). 1997, Simon & Schuster $22.00 (978-0-684-80344-9). When her police hero husband is kidnapped by a group out to avenge murders that occurred years ago, sleuth/ reporter Irene Kelly must unravel the complicated, long-ago murder case and find the real killer in order to save him. (Rev: BL 5/1/97; SLJ 11/97)

5058 Burke, Morgan. *Last Call* (9–12). Series: The Party Room. 2005, Simon & Schuster paper $5.99 (978-0-689-87227-3). In the final volume of the trilogy, Kirsten Sawyer, now a student at NYU, looks into a student suicide that may really have been a murder. (Rev: SLJ 11/05)

5059 Butcher, A. J. *Spy High: Mission One* (7–10). 2004, Little, Brown paper $6.99 (978-0-316-73760-9). This thriller is set in the year 2060 and deals with a group of students at a school known as Spy High who are training to become secret agents. (Rev: BL 5/1/04; SLJ 7/04)

5060 Cabot, Meg. *Big Boned* (9–12). 2007, Avon paper $13.95 (978-0-06-052513-2). Just as the life of former rock star Heather Wells begins to improve after her mother made off with her earnings, she is caught up in the investigation of a New York College murder whose main suspect she aims to prove innocent. (Rev: BL 11/15/07)

5061 Cabot, Meg. *Size 12 Is Not Fat* (10–12). 2005, Avon paper $12.95 (978-0-06-052511-8). Heather Wells, former teen idol, turns detective after a number of coeds are found dead at the college where she works part-time as a residence hall director; for mature teens. (Rev: BL 11/15/05)

5062 Cadnum, Michael. *Seize the Storm* (7–10). 2012, Farrar $17.99 (978-037436705-3). On a yacht in the Pacific, Susannah and her family find a boat carrying two dead bodies and a large amount of cash, putting them directly in the sights of some very bad people. Lexile 980L (Rev: BL 6/12; HB 7–8/12; LMC 11–12/12; SLJ 8/1/12; VOYA 6/12)

5063 Cantor, Jillian. *The September Sisters* (7–12). 2009, HarperCollins $16.99 (978-006168648-1); LB $17.89 (978-006168649-8). Abigail's sister, missing for two years, is found dead in this story about grief, anger, suspicion, and loneliness. Lexile 850L (Rev: BL 2/1/09; SLJ 6/1/09; VOYA 6/09)

5064 Carey, Benedict. *The Unknowns* (6–10). 2009, Abrams $16.95 (978-081097991-8). A group of preteens sets out to solve a mystery on their island, home to a nuclear power plant. Their math teacher has left behind clues in the form of equations and geometry puzzles. Lexile 760L (Rev: BL 5/1/09; LMC 10/09; SLJ 10/09)

5065 Cargill, Linda. *Pool Party* (7–10). 1996, Scholastic paper $3.99 (978-0-590-58111-0). Sharon's beach party at a resort with a reputation for being haunted ends in murder. (Rev: SLJ 1/97)

5066 Carman, Patrick. *Dark Eden* (7–10). 2011, HarperCollins $17.99 (978-0-06-200970-8). A suspenseful story in which teenager Will learns unsettling secrets about a phobia-treatment center called Fort Eden. 🎧 ℯ (Rev: BL 11/15/11; LMC 11–12/11; SLJ 10/1/11; VOYA 8/11)

5067 Carman, Patrick. *Thirteen Days to Midnight* (7–10). 2010, Little, Brown $16.99 (978-0-316-00403-9). When his foster father dies in an accident, Jacob discovers that he has a unique power to ward off death but that this power is not without pitfalls; a suspenseful read. 🎧 Lexile 1010L (Rev: BL 5/1/10; LMC 8–9/10; SLJ 5/10)

5068 Carroll, James. *Secret Father* (10–12). 2003, Houghton Mifflin $25.00 (978-0-618-15284-1). Foolishly adventurous American teens add to the tension in this riveting novel set in Cold War Berlin. (Rev: BL 6/1–15/03)

5069 Casey, Donis. *Hornswoggled: An Alafair Tucker Mystery* (9–12). 2006, Poisoned Pen $24.95 (978-1-59058-309-8). In Oklahoma in the early 20th century, amateur detective Alafair is suspicious of her daughter Alice's beau. (Rev: SLJ 12/06)

5070 Cassidy, Anne. *Dead Time* (7–10). Series: Murder Notebooks. 2012, Walker $16.99 (978-080272351-2). Five years ago Rose's mother and Joshua's father disappeared and now the two step-siblings are investigating this and two potentially linked murders. ℯ Lexile 630L (Rev: BL 5/1/12; LMC 10/12; SLJ 5/1/12; VOYA 6/12)

5071 Cassidy, Anne. *Killing Rachel* (8–11). Series: Murder Notebooks. 2013, Walker $16.99 (978-080273416-7). Rose investigates the death of Rachel, a former classmate, even as she and Joshua continue the search for their missing parents. ℯ (Rev: BL 12/15/12; LMC 5–6/13; SLJ 4/13; VOYA 12/12)

5072 Causey, Toni McGee. *Bobbie Faye's (Kinda, Sorta, Not-exactly) Family Jewels* (11–12). 2008, St. Martin's paper $13.95 (978-031235450-3). In this second book about Bobbie Faye, the witty, feisty heroine must evade the FBI, Homeland Security, the Irish mob, and unsavory members of her own family as she tries to convince everyone she that doesn't know where the diamonds are hidden; for mature readers. ℯ (Rev: BL 6/1–15/08*)

5073 Chandler, Elizabeth. *Dark Secrets: Legacy of Lies* (6–12). Series: Dark Secrets. 2000, Pocket paper $4.99 (978-0-7434-0028-2). Megan, 16, has finally met her grandmother, but she still feels like an outsider and her frightening dreams become more and more intense. (Rev: BCCB 2/01; BL 2/1/01; SLJ 1/01; VOYA 12/00)

5074 Chesterton, G. K. *The Club of Queer Trades* (9–12). Series: Modern Voices. 2007, Hesperus paper $15.95 (978-1-84391-434-1). Six witty mysteries featuring the Club of Queer Trades and a cast of eccentric characters are solved by private detective Rupert Grant and his brother Basil, a talented retired judge; this volume also includes Chesterton's essay "A Defence of Detective Stories." (Rev: SLJ 3/08)

5075 Christie, Agatha. *Curtain* (9–12). 1975, Amereon $22.95 (978-0-88411-386-7). Hercule Poirot returns to the country manor of Styles, the site of his first case (*The Mysterious Affair at Styles*), to solve another murder. This is one of many suitable titles by Christie.

5076 Christie, Agatha. *Death on the Nile* (9–12). 1992, HarperCollins paper $5.99 (978-0-06-100369-1). Everyone on board the steamer sailing along the Nile envies Linnet Doyle — until she is murdered. One of many recommended mysteries involving Hercule Poirot.

5077 Christie, Agatha. *Evil Under the Sun* (9–12). 1991, Berkley paper $6.99 (978-0-425-12960-9). M. Poirot solves the mystery of the murder of beautiful Arlena Marshall. One of many suitable Poirot mysteries.

5078 Christie, Agatha. *Miss Marple: The Complete Short Stories* (9–12). 1985, Berkley paper $14.00 (978-0-425-09486-0). Miss Marple, the sleuth of St. Mary Mead, shines in this collection of 20 stories. (Rev: BL 12/15/85)

5079 Christie, Agatha. *Murder on the Orient Express* (9–12). 1991, HarperCollins paper $5.99 (978-0-06-100274-8). M. Poirot in one of his most famous cases, where each of the suspects appears to have a valid motive for murder.

5080 Christie, Agatha. *Ten Little Indians* (9–12). 1984, French paper $5.50 (978-0-573-61639-6). One of the earliest (1939) and best of this prolific writer's mysteries.

5081 Clancy, Tom. *Without Remorse* (10–12). 1993, Putnam $25.95 (978-0-399-13825-6). Vietnam vet John Kelly's revenge against the murderers of his 20-year-old girlfriend is an integral part of this complex thriller. (Rev: BL 6/1–15/93; SLJ 11/93)

5082 Clare, Alys. *Mist over the Water* (11–12). Series: Aelf Fen. 2010, Severn $28.95 (978-072786848-0). This Aelf Fen mystery set in Norman England follows the healer Lassair, 16, as she becomes embroiled in a mystery involving a monastery on Ely Island; for mature readers. ℮ (Rev: BL 12/1/09)

5083 Clare, Alys. *Out of the Dawn Light* (10–12). Series: Aelf Fen. 2009, Severn $27.95 (978-072786763-6). This blend of mystery and romance set in medieval England features 14-year-old Lassair, who finds herself embroiled in a dangerous quest for a magic crown. (Rev: BL 7/09)

5084 Clark, Carol Higgins. *Iced* (9–12). 1996, Warner paper $5.99 (978-0-446-60198-6). Los Angeles PI Regan Reilly, vacationing in Colorado, stumbles across a series of art thefts. (Rev: BL 5/15/95; SLJ 1/96)

5085 Clark, Mary Higgins. *Let Me Call You Sweetheart* (9–12). 1995, Simon & Schuster $7.50 (978-0-684-80396-8). Prosecutor Kerry McGrath scours the world of gem thieves, child stalkers, the Irish Mafia, and more to solve the murder of the beautiful Suzanne Reardon. (Rev: BL 4/1/95; SLJ 9/95)

5086 Clark, Mary Higgins. *Stillwatch* (9–12). 1997, Pocket paper $7.99 (978-0-671-52820-1). A TV documentary producer finds mystery and danger when she begins investigating a vice presidential candidate in Washington.

5087 Clark, Mary Higgins. *While My Pretty One Sleeps* (9–12). 1990, Pocket paper $7.99 (978-0-671-67368-0). While investigating a murder, our heroine becomes convinced that someone has been hired to kill her. (Rev: BL 4/1/89; VOYA 4/89)

5088 Clark, Mary Higgins, ed. *The International Association of Crime Writers Presents Bad Behavior* (8–12). 1995, Harcourt $20.00 (978-0-15-200179-7). Features many stories with young characters and less overt violence than adult fare. Includes works by Sara Paretsky, P. D. James, Lawrence Block, and Liza Cody. (Rev: BL 7/95)

5089 Clark, Robert. *Love Among the Ruins* (10–12). 2001, Norton $24.95 (978-0-393-02015-1). In the summer of 1968 in Minneapolis, two thoughtful teens fall in love, causing their parents to rethink their lives. (Rev: BL 6/1–15/01)

5090 Clement, Alison. *Twenty Questions: A Novel* (9–12). 2006, Atria $23 (978-0-7432-7266-7). June becomes involved with the family of a woman who was murdered in her small town and discovers just what the victim's family means to her. (Rev: SLJ 9/06)

5091 Coben, Harlan. *Hold Tight* (9–12). 2008, Dutton $26.95 (978-0-525-95060-8). A suspenseful, multilayered story involving a boy's suicide and another one's disappearance and parents' efforts to monitor what's going on through computer programs. (Rev: BL 3/1/08)

5092 Coben, Harlan. *Seconds Away* (8–11). Series: Mickey Bolitar. 2012, Putnam $18.99 (978-0-399-25651-6). In this sequel to 2011's *Shelter*, Mickey and friends Spoon and Ema must resolve two parallel mysteries, one involving the death of Mickey's father and the other the shooting of a classmate's mother. (Rev: BL 10/1/12; SLJ 11/12)

5093 Coben, Harlan. *Shelter* (8–12). 2011, Putnam $18.99 (978-0-399-25650-9). Myron Bolitar's nephew Mickey comes to live with him and finds himself embroiled in strange events relating to his father and to a classmate named Ashley. ☊ ℮ Lexile HL530L (Rev: BL 9/15/11; LMC 1–2/12*; SLJ 9/1/11)

5094 Coel, Margaret. *The Eagle Catcher* (10–12). 1987, University Pr. of Colorado $22.50 (978-0-87081-367-2); paper $6.50 (978-0-425-15483-0). When a tribal councilman is murdered, his young nephew is a prime suspect in this first book in a series of fine mysteries that feature Father John O'Malley and Arapaho lawyer Vicky Holden. (Rev: BL BL 5/1/00)

5095 Collins, Brandilyn, and Amberly Collins. *Final Touch* (8–12). Series: The Rayne Tour. 2010, Zondervan paper $9.99 (978-0-310-71933-5). On the very day her mother, rock star Rayne O'Connor, is to get remarried, teenage Shaley is abducted by a stalker. (Rev: BL 9/1/10; SLJ 12/1/10)

5096 Conwell, Kent. *Skeletons of the Atchafalaya* (10–12). 2003, Avalon $19.95 (978-0-8034-9628-6). A hurricane isolates private detective Tony Boudreaux in a house with a Louisiana family and at least one murderer in this tense thriller. (Rev: SLJ 1/04)

5097 Cook, Robin. *Sphinx* (9–12). 1983, NAL paper $7.99 (978-0-451-15949-6). Set in Egypt, this thriller involves a young art specialist from Boston and an antique statue in a tale of danger and romance.

5098 Cook, Robin. *Vital Signs* (10–12). 1992, Berkley paper $7.99 (978-0-425-13176-3). A medical thriller that combines murder and infertility therapy. (Rev: BL 11/15/90)

5099 Cooney, Caroline B. *If the Witness Lied* (7–10). 2009, Delacorte $16.99 (978-0-385-73448-6); LB $19.99 (978-0-385-90451-3). After their mother's death from cancer and their father's demise in an accident, siblings Smithy, Madison, and Jack must act to keep their toddler brother safe from their evil aunt and the threat of a reality TV show about their grief. **e** Lexile HL670L (Rev: BL 5/1/09; HB 5–6/09; LMC 8–9/09; SLJ 5/1/09; VOYA 6/09)

5100 Coonts, Stephen. *Hong Kong* (10–12). 2000, St. Martin's $25.95 (978-0-312-25339-4). In this novel of international intrigue, Admiral Jake Grafton defends his wife against a Hong Kong gangster. (Rev: BL 7/00)

5101 Cornwell, Patricia. *All That Remains* (10–12). 1992, Scribner $20.00 (978-0-684-19395-3). A whodunit about the baffling serial murders of five college-age couples. (Rev: BL 6/1/92; SLJ 12/92)

5102 Cornwell, Patricia. *Cruel and Unusual* (10–12). 1993, Scribner $21.00 (978-0-684-19530-8). An edge-of-your-seat thriller with plenty of action, a gripping plot, and a mind-boggling climax. (Rev: BL 4/15/93; SLJ 11/93)

5103 Cornwell, Patricia. *From Potter's Field* (10–12). 1995, Scribner $23.50 (978-0-684-19598-8). The Central Park (New York) murder of a young, homeless woman on Christmas sends medical examiner Scarpetta, her friend Captain Marino, and her niece on a chase that ends in the subway. (Rev: BL 5/1/95*)

5104 Cotterill, Colin. *Disco for the Departed* (9–12). Series: Dr. Siri. 2006, Soho $23 (978-1-56947-428-0). Dr. Siri returns in this mystery set in 1970s Laos, where a body has been found at a presidential home on the eve of a national celebration. (Rev: BL 5/1/06; SLJ 9/06)

5105 Cotterill, Colin. *The Merry Misogynist* (10–12). Series: Dr. Siri. 2009, Soho $24 (978-1-56947-556-0). Set in Laos in the 1970s, this sixth installment in the mystery series finds quirky coroner Dr. Siri Paiboun on the trail of a serial killer who is victimizing young women from rural villages. (Rev: SLJ 8/09)

5106 Coulter, Catherine. *KnockOut* (11–12). 2009, Putnam $26.95 (978-039915584-0). Married FBI agents Savich and Sherlock deal with psychic powers in this tense page-turner suitable for mature readers. ⌂ **e** (Rev: BL 4–5/09)

5107 Cox, Suzy. *The Dead Girls Detective Agency* (8–12). 2012, HarperTeen paper $8.99 (978-0-06-202-064-2). Charlotte, 16, wakes up in the Hotel Attlesa to find that she was murdered on the New York subway and

must find the perpetrator before she can pass to the Other Side. **e** (Rev: BL 10/1/12; SLJ 12/12; VOYA 6/12)

5108 Crichton, Michael. *Airframe* (10–12). 1996, Knopf $26.00 (978-0-679-44648-4). Casey Singleton leads an investigation into a mysterious airplane disaster in which three people are killed. (Rev: BL 11/15/96; SLJ 3/97)

5109 Crichton, Michael. *Prey* (10–12). 2002, Harper-Collins $26.95 (978-0-06-621412-2). An experiment using nanoparticles runs amok in this suspenseful thriller. (Rev: BL 12/1/02*; SLJ 5/03)

5110 Crider, Bill. *Murder Takes a Break* (9–12). 1997, Walker $21.95 (978-0-8027-3308-5). Tru Smith, a detective who hates to leave his home and computer, investigates the disappearance of a college student. (Rev: BL 10/15/97; VOYA 12/97)

5111 Curzon, Clare. *The Edge: A Superintendent Mike Yeadings Mystery* (10–12). 2007, St. Martin's $23.95 (978-0-312-34964-6). Could it be the missing 16-year-old boy who murdered the rest of his family in a manor house on the river Thames? (Rev: SLJ 3/08)

5112 Cussler, Clive. *Cyclops* (9–12). 1986, Pocket paper $7.99 (978-0-671-70464-3). A thriller involving hero Dirk Pitt and such elements as a missing blimp and a secret mission to the moon. (Rev: BL 1/15/86)

5113 Dain, Claudia. *A Kiss to Die For* (10–12). 2003, Leisure paper $6.99 (978-0-8439-5059-5). A tale of romance, adventure, and suspense featuring a hunt for a killer of young women in the Old West. (Rev: BL 3/15/03)

5114 Dams, Jeanne M. *Green Grow the Victims* (10–12). 2001, Walker $23.95 (978-0-8027-3355-9). Hilda Johansson, a housekeeper and amateur sleuth in early-20th-century South Bend, Indiana, is asked by her boss to look into the mysterious disappearance of city council candidate Dan Malloy, who also happens to be the uncle of her boyfriend. (Rev: BL 5/1/01)

5115 Davidson, Nicole. *Dying to Dance* (8–12). 1996, Avon paper $3.99 (978-0-380-78152-2). Carrie, a competitor on the ballroom-dance circuit, is suspected of murdering her archrival. (Rev: SLJ 7/96)

5116 Davis, Lindsey. *Alexandria* (10–12). Series: Marcus Didius Falco Mysteries. 2009, Minotaur $24.95 (978-0-312-37901-8). The 17th installment in the Marcus Didius Falco stories finds Roman private detective Falco in 1st-century Alexandria charged with solving the mystery of the dead librarian. (Rev: SLJ 12/09)

5117 Day, Marele. *The Disappearances of Madalena Grimaldi* (10–12). 1996, Walker $19.95 (978-0-8027-3277-4). Claudia, an Australian detective, is hired to find a missing teenage girl, while at the same time trying to solve the 30-year-old mystery of her own missing father. (Rev: SLJ 11/96)

5118 Delaney, Mark. *Of Heroes and Villains* (7–10). 1999, Peachtree paper $5.95 (978-1-56145-178-4). Using the world of comic books as a backdrop, this mystery features four teen sleuths known as the Misfits and the puzzle of a stolen film starring comic book hero Hyperman. (Rev: BL 7/99)

5119 Delinsky, Barbara. *The Secret Between Us* (9–12). 2008, Doubleday $25.95 (978-0-385-51868-0). Deborah Monroe and her daughter Grace must wrestle with increasing guilt after Grace accidentally hits a man who ran out in front of their car on a stormy night; the man turns out to be Grace's history teacher, who eventually dies, and Deborah delves into the causes behind the accident. (Rev: BL 10/15/07; SLJ 2/08)

5120 Derting, Kimberly. *The Body Finder* (7–12). 2010, HarperCollins $16.99 (978-0-06-177981-7). Violet's ability to sense the bodies of murdered people brings her anxious moments even as she is absorbed in her growing fascination with her best friend Jay; this suspenseful thriller, with a dollop of romance, contains language and sexual content that may limit the grade range. ℮ Lexile 940L (Rev: BL 10/15/09; LMC 3–4/10; SLJ 5/10)

5121 Deveraux, Jude. *Forever: A Novel of Good and Evil, Love and Hope* (10–12). 2002, Pocket paper $7.99 (978-0-671-01420-9). Darci Monroe, a young woman with psychic powers, is hired to help wealthy Adam Montgomery find information about the deaths of his parents in this tale that blends mystery, fantasy, and romance. (Rev: BL 10/15/02)

5122 Diggs, Anita D. *A Meeting in the Ladies Room* (10–12). 2004, Dafina $24.00 (978-0-458-20234-8). This mystery that involves the murder of a white publishing executive also explores the world of a group of black professionals in Manhattan's publishing world. (Rev: BL 3/1/04)

5123 Diotalevi, Dave. *Miracle Myx* (9–12). 2008, Kunati $24.95 (978-1-60164-155-7). Fourteen-year old insomniac Myx Amens is a reluctant detective who uses the peculiar skills garnered in his near-death experiences to help the police solve crimes. (Rev: BL 4/1/08)

5124 Doctorow, Cory. *Homeland* (8–12). 2013, Tor Teen $17.99 (978-076533369-8). In this sequel to *Little Brother* (2008), Marcus is at a Burning Man festival when he receives a USB drive holding the key to many documents revealing government treachery; can he pass on this information and retain his own job and security? ℮ Lexile 1060L (Rev: BL 1/13*; HB 5–6/13; SLJ 3/13)

5125 Doctorow, Cory. *Little Brother* (8–12). 2008, Tor $17.95 (978-0-7653-1985-2). A terrorist attack on the San Francisco of the not-too-distant future results in Marcus being detained by the Department of Homeland Security and organizing a group of hackers to fight the powers that be. (Rev: BL 4/1/08; SLJ 5/08)

5126 Downham, Jenny. *You Against Me* (8–12). 2011, Random House $16.99 (978-0-385-75160-5); LB $19.99 (978-038575161-2). Meeting — and liking — the sister of the young man who raped his younger sister Ellie complicates 18-year-old Mikey's life and his investigation of the crime. ℮ Lexile HL630L (Rev: BL 8/11*; HB 11–12/11; SLJ 11/1/11*; VOYA 10/11)

5127 Du Maurier, Daphne. *Rebecca* (9–12). 1938, Doubleday $20.00 (978-0-385-04380-9); paper $5.99 (978-0-380-00917-6). In this gothic romance, a timid girl marries a wealthy widower whose wife died mysteriously. Two other exciting novels by Du Maurier are *Hungry Hill* and *The Scapegoat*. (Rev: BL 6/1/88)

5128 Dumas, Margaret. *Speak Now* (10–12). 2004, Poisoned Pen $24.95 (978-1-59058-121-6). Charley Van Leeuwen, manager of a repertory theater company, returns from a yearlong working trip to London with a new husband, but things start to go terribly wrong when the couple finds a dead body in their hotel suite. (Rev: BL 9/1/04; SLJ 1/05)

5129 Dunant, Sarah. *Fatlands* (9–12). 1994, Penzler Books paper $21.00 (978-1-883402-82-2). Investigator Hannah Wolfe baby-sits for a famous scientist's daughter. When a bomb kills the child, Hannah believes it was meant for the scientist so she hunts for the killers. (Rev: BL 11/1/94*)

5130 Duncan, Lois. *Daughters of Eve* (7–10). 1979, Dell paper $4.99 (978-0-440-91864-6). A group of girls comes under the evil influence of the faculty sponsor of their club.

5131 Duncan, Lois. *Down a Dark Hall* (7–10). 1974, Little, Brown paper $5.50 (978-0-440-91805-9). From the moment of arrival, Kit feels uneasy at her new boarding school.

5132 Duncan, Lois. *Killing Mr. Griffin* (7–10). 1978, Dell paper $5.50 (978-0-440-94515-4). A kidnapping plot involving a disliked English teacher leads to murder. (Rev: BL 10/15/88)

5133 Duncan, Lois. *The Third Eye* (7–10). 1984, Little, Brown $15.95 (978-0-316-19553-9); paper $5.50 (978-0-440-98720-8). Karen learns that she has mental powers that enable her to locate missing children. (Rev: BL 7/87)

5134 Duncan, Lois. *The Twisted Window* (7–10). 1987, Dell paper $5.50 (978-0-440-20184-7). Tracy grows to regret the fact that she has helped a young man kidnap his 2-year-old half-sister. (Rev: BL 9/1/87; SLJ 9/87; VOYA 11/87)

5135 Dunker, Kristina. *Summer Storm* (10–12). Trans. by Margot Bettauer Dembo. 2011, AmazonCrossing paper $9.95 (978-16110903-0-7). In this taut psychological thriller a teen goes missing and the resulting search reveals many hidden secrets. ☊ ℮ (Rev: BL 10/15/11; SLJ 12/12)

5136 Dyja, Thomas. *The Moon in Our Hands* (11–12). 2005, Carroll & Graf $25.00 (978-0-7867-1505-3). A fictionalized account of Walter White, a light-skinned young African American recruited by the NAACP in 1918 to perform undercover investigations of lynching in the South; violence restricts this to mature teens. (Rev: BL 2/1/05)

5137 Ebisch, Glen. *Ghosts from the Past* (11–12). 2009, Avalon $23.95 (978-080349978-2). Young ghost hunter Marcie Ducasse finds herself with an additional death on her hands as she sets out to investigate the apparitions of three men who were hanged decades ago; for mature readers. (Rev: BL 10/15/09)

5138 Edwards, Grace. *If I Should Die* (10–12). 1977, Bantam paper $5.99 (978-0-533-57631-9). Former New York City cop Mali Anderson is drawn into a murder case that involves a crack cocaine operation and a journey through Harlem's rich cultural life. Part of a fine series. (Rev: BL 5/1/00)

5139 Ehrenhaft, Daniel. *Dirty Laundry* (8–11). 2009, HarperTeen $16.99 (978-006113103-5). A playful mystery about a teen actress who goes undercover at a New England boarding school in order to research a part, but becomes embroiled in the mystery of a missing student. **e** Lexile HL630L (Rev: BL 12/15/08; SLJ 3/1/09)

5140 Ehrenhaft, Daniel. *Drawing a Blank: or, How I Tried to Solve a Mystery, End a Feud, and Land the Girl of My Dreams* (8–11). Illus. by Trevor Ristow. 2006, HarperCollins $15.99 (978-0-06-075252-1). In this clever novel, with the narrative switching from first person to comic book panels, boarding school student Carlton travels to Scotland to solve a mystery and find his kidnapped father; footnotes are both informative and amusing. (Rev: BL 5/1/06; SLJ 6/06*)

5141 Epstein, Carole. *Perilous Relations: A Barbara Simons Mystery* (9–12). 1997, Walker $22.95 (978-0-8027-3309-2). Barbara Simons, who loves poking her nose into other people's business, has her hands full when she tries to solve the mystery surrounding the death of her former boss. (Rev: VOYA 4/98)

5142 Evanovich, Janet. *One for the Money* (9–12). 1994, Scribner $20.00 (978-0-684-19639-8). An out-of-work discount-lingerie buyer becomes a bounty hunter to earn money and is hired to find a wanted cop from her past. (Rev: BL 9/1/94*)

5143 Evenson, Brian. *The Open Curtain* (11–12). 2006, Coffee House $14.95 (978-1-56689-188-2). A murder mystery involving a young Mormon man who finds himself channeling Brigham Young's grandson, who committed murder in 1902; for mature teens. (Rev: BL 9/1/06)

5144 Feder, Harriet K. *Death on Sacred Ground* (6–10). Series: Vivi Hartman. 2001, Lerner $14.95 (978-0-8225-0741-3). Teen sleuth Vivi Hartman encounters a mystery at the funeral of an Orthodox Jewish girl who died on sacred Indian ground. (Rev: BCCB 3/01; BL 11/15/01; HBG 10/01; SLJ 3/01)

5145 Ferguson, Alane. *The Angel of Death: A Forensic Mystery* (9–12). 2006, Viking $16.00 (978-0-670-06055-9). Cameryn Mahoney's coroner father is training her to be a forensic pathologist, and Cameryn investigates the death of her high school English teacher while also fretting about her absent mother and about her attraction to a new boy. (Rev: BL 2/15/07; SLJ 9/06)

5146 Ferguson, Alane. *The Christopher Killer* (7–10). Series: Forensic Mystery. 2006, Viking $15.99 (978-0-670-06008-5). In this CSI-like story, a serial killer is on the loose and 17-year-old Cameryn, an aspiring forensic pathologist, helps her coroner father investigate. (Rev: BL 7/06; LMC 10/06; SLJ 8/06)

5147 Ferguson, Alane. *Circle of Blood* (9–12). Series: Forensic Mystery. 2008, Viking $15.99 (978-0-670-06056-6). A murdered girl is Cameryn's father's latest case in the coroner's office. How and why did she die? What did Cameryn's mother have to do with it? (Rev: BL 3/1/08; SLJ 3/08)

5148 Ferguson, Alane. *Overkill* (7–10). 1992, Avon paper $3.99 (978-0-380-72167-2). Lacey is seeing a therapist about nightmares in which she stabs her friend Celeste; when Celeste is found dead, Lacey is falsely arrested for the crime. (Rev: BL 1/1/93; SLJ 1/93)

5149 Ferguson, Alane. *Show Me the Evidence* (7–12). 1989, Avon paper $3.99 (978-0-380-70962-5). In this mystery story, a 17-year-old girl is fearful that her best friend might be involved in the mysterious deaths of several children. (Rev: BL 4/1/89; SLJ 3/89; VOYA 6/89)

5150 Ferraris, Zoe. *City of Veils* (10–12). 2010, Little, Brown $24.99 (978-031607427-8). Detective Osama Ibrahim investigates the death of a young filmmaker with the help of forensic expert Katya in this suspenseful novel that exposes the strictures of Saudi life. ∩ (Rev: BL 7/10)

5151 Ferraris, Zoe. *Finding Nouf* (10–12). 2008, Houghton Mifflin $24.00 (978-0-618-87388-3). A devout Muslim desert guide turns into a private eye when his wealthy client's daughter is found dead. Alex Award 2009. (Rev: BL 3/1/08)

5152 Fforde, Jasper. *The Fourth Bear* (11–12). Series: Nursery Crime. 2006, Viking $24.95 (978-0-670-03772-8). A grown-up mystery/fantasy full of humor and allusions to childhood figures: Red Riding Hood, Gingerbreadman, and Punch and Judy are all here as Jack Spratt investigates crime in the town of Reading. ∩ (Rev: BL 8/06)

5153 Fields, Terri. *Holdup* (6–10). 2007, Roaring Brook $16.95 (978-1-59643-219-2). Nine teen characters give their first-person accounts of the evening of a holdup of a fast-food restaurant. (Rev: BL 5/1/07; LMC 8–9/07; SLJ 4/07)

5154 Fleischman, A. S. *Danger in Paradise / Malay Woman* (10–12). 2010, Stark House paper $19.95 (978-19335862-8-1). Originally published in the 1950s, these two mysteries by children's author Sid Fleischman offer exotic glimpses into a world of espionage, seduction, and betrayal. (Rev: BL 8/10)

5155 Ford, G. M. *Cast in Stone* (10–12). 1996, Walker $21.95 (978-0-8027-3267-5). Marge contacts hardboiled Leo Waterman, a former flame and now a private investigator, to examine the mysterious circumstances surrounding the death of her son and his fiancee. (Rev: BL 4/1/96; SLJ 1/97)

5156 Ford, John C. *The Morgue and Me* (9–12). 2009, Viking $17.99 (978-067001096-7). Christopher has a summer job at a morgue and stumbles across a mystery involving the medical examiner and a suspicious dead body. e Lexile HL720L (Rev: BL 5/1/09; LMC 11–12/09; SLJ 8/09; VOYA 8/09)

5157 Fox, Janet. *Forgiven* (7–10). 2011, Penguin paper $8.99 (978-0-14-241-414-9). In San Francisco on a mission to clear her father's name, Kula is introduced into society, meets interesting men, uncovers current and past secrets, and experiences the 1906 earthquake. Lexile HL710L (Rev: BL 8/11; SLJ 9/1/11)

5158 Fredericks, Mariah. *The Girl in the Park* (8–12). 2012, Random House $16.99 (978-037586843-6); LB $19.99 (978-037589907-2). When the only person who believed in her is murdered, Rain, an outcast with a cleft palate, struggles to speak up for truth and justice. Lexile HL510L (Rev: BL 4/1/12; LMC 3–4/12; SLJ 5/1/12; VOYA 2/12)

5159 Fuerst, James W. *Huge* (10–12). 2009, Crown $23.95 (978-030745249-8). Eugene "Huge" Smalls is indeed small for his 12 years and compensates with his tough guy attitude and detective skills as he tries to solve a mystery at his grandma's nursing home. Ω e (Rev: BL 4–5/09*; SLJ 9/09)

5160 Gabbay, Tom. *The Berlin Conspiracy* (9–12). 2006, Morrow $24.95 (978-0-06-078785-1). Juxtaposed with events during the Kennedy administration (including his assassination), this novel takes place in a spy-infested Berlin, where a seasoned CIA agent must put a stop to an assassination that could lead to a catastrophic outcome. (Rev: SLJ 6/06)

5161 Galloway, Gregory. *As Simple as Snow* (9–12). 2005, Penguin $23.95 (978-0-399-15231-3). The teen narrator of this meandering, ambiguous, and yet compelling novel decides to find out why his quirky Goth girlfriend has vanished. (Rev: BL 1/1–15/05; SLJ 5/05)

5162 Gansky, Alton. *Dark Moon* (10–12). 2002, Zondervan paper $12.99 (978-0-310-23558-3). A mysterious red cloud on the moon causes consternation. (Rev: BL 10/1/02)

5163 Gardner, John. *Maestro* (9–12). 1993, Penzler Books $23.00 (978-1-883402-24-2). A multigenerational epic spanning 10 decades that focuses on a world-famous orchestra conductor who becomes a spy. (Rev: BL 9/1/93*)

5164 Gardner, Sally. *The Red Necklace* (9–12). 2008, Dial $16.99 (978-0-8037-3100-4). During the violence of the French Revolution, magician's assistant Yann meets the lonely daughter of a marquis and is caught up in a murder mystery. (Rev: BL 4/15/08; SLJ 5/08)

5165 Garretson, James D. *The Deadwood Conspiracy* (10–12). 1996, DeHart $19.95 (978-0-9649706-0-1). Complete with a surprise ending, this thrilling adult novel combines international intrigue, murder, romance, and a conspiracy involving top-ranking government officials. (Rev: SLJ 9/96)

5166 Gaus, P. L. *Clouds Without Rain* (10–12). 2001, Ohio Univ. $24.95 (978-0-8214-1379-1); paper $12.95 (978-0-8214-1380-7). A fascinating mystery (part of a series) involving the Ohio Amish and a local college professor who helps solve crimes. (Rev: BL 5/1/01)

5167 Gavin, Jamila. *See No Evil* (7–10). 2009, Farrar $16.95 (978-037436333-8). Nettie, 12, searches her family's London mansion for the secrets to her father's vast wealth after her tutor mysteriously disappears. (Rev: BL 5/1/09; SLJ 7/1/09; VOYA 2/09)

5168 Gear, Kathleen O'Neal, and W. Michael Gear. *The Visitant* (10–12). 1999, Forge $19.95 (978-0-312-86531-3). Anasazi history and modern archaeological methods feature in this mystery story involving the discovery of women's remains at a site in New Mexico. (Rev: BL 7/99; VOYA 2/00)

5169 George, Elizabeth. *The Edge of Nowhere* (8–12). 2012, Viking $18.99 (978-0-670-01296-1). Becca, a psychic 14-year-old who is on the run from her stepfather, must make her way by herself on a remote island near Seattle, where she meets a Ugandan orphan with a secret. Ω e Lexile HL800L (Rev: BL 7/12; LMC 3–4/13; SLJ 10/12; VOYA 10/12)

5170 Gerber, Linda. *Death by Bikini* (7–10). 2008, Penguin paper $7.99 (978-0-14-241117-9). A murder mystery complicates the romance between Aphra and Adam, a guest at the resort that Aphra's father runs. (Rev: BL 5/1/08; SLJ 8/08)

5171 Gerber, Linda. *Death by Denim* (7–10). Series: Death By. 2009, Penguin paper $7.99 (978-014241119-3). Sixteen-year-old Aphra and her mother, a CIA agent, race through Europe to escape the Mole and save Aphra's boyfriend, Seth. The third book after *Death by Bikini* and *Death by Latte* (both 2008). Lexile HL740L (Rev: BL 5/1/09; SLJ 6/1/09)

5172 Giles, Gail. *What Happened to Cass McBride?* (8–11). 2006, Little, Brown $16.99 (978-0-316-16638-6). When a cruel note from Cass pushes classmate David over the edge to suicide, David's older brother

Kyle takes Cass captive in this suspenseful novel. (Rev: BCCB 12/06; BL 1/1–15/07; LMC 4–5/07; SLJ 2/07)

5173 Gilman, Dorothy. *Mrs. Pollifax and the Hong Kong Buddha* (9–12). 1985, Fawcett paper $5.99 (978-0-449-20983-7). This unlikely CIA agent gets involved in a plan by terrorists to destroy Hong Kong. Another in this series is *Mrs. Pollifax on the China Station* (1983). (Rev: BL 11/1/85)

5174 Ginsberg, Debra. *Blind Submission* (11–12). 2006, Crown $23.95 (978-0-307-34604-9). A harried literary agency assistant, Angel Montgomery, receives a manuscript in segments via e-mail that contains unsettling similarities to her own life in this entertaining and suspenseful novel. (Rev: BL 9/15/06)

5175 Gist, Deeanne, and J. Mark Bertrand. *Beguiled* (11–12). 2010, Bethany paper $14.99 (978-07642062-8-3). Charleston provides the setting for this blend of romance and suspense about a female dog-walker and a male newspaper journalist who together try to discover the true identity of a modern-day Robin Hood; for mature readers. ∩ e (Rev: BL 2/1–15/10)

5176 Glidewell, Jeanne. *Leave No Stone Unturned* (9–12). 2008, Five Star $25.95 (978-1-59414-649-7). Soon-to-be-grandma Lexie Starr is forced to travel way out of her comfort zone when she discovers that her new son-in-law may be a murderer. (Rev: BL 4/1/08)

5177 Golden, Christopher, and Rick Hautala. *Throat Culture* (8–11). Series: Body of Evidence. 2005, Simon & Schuster paper $5.99 (978-0-689-86527-5). College sophomore Jenna Blake investigates the mysterious illness that has stricken her father's new bride. (Rev: BL 5/1/05; SLJ 7/05)

5178 Golding, Julia. *The Diamond of Drury Lane* (7–10). Series: Cat Royal Adventures. 2008, Roaring Brook $12.50 (978-1-59643-351-9). Catherine Royal, called Cat, lives with danger and intrigue in the Drury Lane theater in London in 1790. Her life is further complicated when she learns that a diamond is hidden somewhere in the theater. (Rev: BL 4/15/08; SLJ 6/08)

5179 Gonzales, Laurence. *Lucy* (11–12). 2010, Knopf $24.95 (978-030727260-7). Forced to flee the Congolese jungle, scientist Jenny and orphaned 14-year-old Lucy arrive in Chicago, where the truth about Lucy's heritage (she is half human and half bonobo) makes her the center of attention; for mature readers. ∩ e (Rev: BL 6/1–15/10)

5180 Goodman, Carol. *The Night Villa* (11–12). 2008, Ballantine paper $14.00 (978-034547960-0). Classics professor Sophie Chase travels to the island of Capri to solve two murder mysteries, one past and one present, in this exciting, clever, and romantic novel; for mature teens. ∩ (Rev: BL 8/08)

5181 Gordon-Smith, Dolores. *A Hundred Thousand Dragons* (10–12). 2010, Severn $28.95 (978-072786910-4). Home in England after World War II,

Jack Haldean has a chance meeting with an Arabian explorer that draws him into a web of mystery and adventure. e (Rev: BL 7/10)

5182 Gorman, Carol, and Ed Gorman, eds. *Felonious Felines* (10–12). 2000, Five Star $23.95 (978-0-7862-2672-6). There are 12 mystery stories in this collection, all dealing with cats in a variety of situations and locales. (Rev: BL 7/00)

5183 Grabenstein, Chris. *Mad Mouse* (11–12). 2006, Carroll & Graf $23.95 (978-0-7867-1760-6). A summer mystery at the Jersey Shore has rookie cop Danny Boyle on the alert for a sly sniper. (Rev: BL 5/1/06)

5184 Grace, C. L. *The Merchant of Death* (9–12). 1995, St. Martin's $19.95 (978-0-312-13124-1). In this mystery set in medieval Britain, healer Kathryn Swinbrooke and soldier Colum Murtagh must find a tax collector's murderer to recover the royal taxes stolen from him. (Rev: BL 6/1–15/95; SLJ 11/95)

5185 Grafton, Sue. *G Is for Gumshoe* (10–12). 1990, Henry Holt $25.00 (978-0-8050-0461-8). In this installment of the alphabet murders, Kinsey Millhone is involved in a missing persons case and a hired killer is out to get her. (Rev: BL 3/15/90; SLJ 9/90)

5186 Grafton, Sue. *M Is for Malice* (10–12). 1996, Henry Holt $25.00 (978-0-8050-3637-4). After detective Kinsey finds Guy Malek, missing heir to a huge fortune, the man is murdered in this part of Grafton's alphabet mystery series. (Rev: BL 9/15/96; SLJ 3/97)

5187 Grafton, Sue. *P Is for Peril* (10–12). 2001, Putnam $26.95 (978-0-399-14719-7). In this Kinsey Millhone mystery, part of a recommended series, a rich doctor is found dead and his ex-wife is among the suspects. (Rev: BL 3/15/01)

5188 Grant, Helen. *The Glass Demon: A Novel* (11–12). 2011, Bantam paper $15 (978-0-385-34420-3). Seventeen-year-old Lin's somewhat dysfunctional family spends a year in a crumbling German castle and faces a series of mysterious and scary deaths; for mature readers. (Rev: BL 5/15/11*; SLJ 8/11)

5189 Grant, Helen. *The Vanishing of Katharina Linden* (11–12). 2010, Delacorte $24 (978-038534417-3). In this suspenseful coming-of-age story, two adventure-seeking 10-year-olds set out to apprehend a real-live boogeyman, who's been kidnapping young girls from their German village; for mature readers. Alex Award 2011. ∩ e (Rev: BL 6/1–15/10)

5190 Grant, Vicki. *Quid Pro Quo* (7–10). 2005, Orca $16.95 (978-1-55143-394-3); paper $7.95 (978-1-55143-370-7). When his mother — newly graduated from law school — suddenly disappears, 13-year-old Cyril Floyd MacIntyre tries to unravel the mystery surrounding her disappearance. (Rev: SLJ 6/05)

5191 Gratz, Alan. *Something Rotten: A Horatio Wilkes Mystery* (9–12). 2007, Dial $16.99 (978-0-8037-3216-

2). In Denmark, Tennessee, teen Horatio Wilkes decides to find the murderer of his friend Hamilton Prince's father; a funny reworking of Shakespeare's *Hamlet.* ∩ (Rev: BCCB 11/07; BL 11/1/08; LMC 11–12/07; SLJ 1/08)

5192 Green, John. *Paper Towns* (9–12). 2008, Dutton $17.99 (978-0-525-47818-8). High school senior Quentin "Q" has been crazy about his neighbor Margo for years, and when she disappears he and his friends set out to investigate. ∩ (Rev: BL 12/1/08*; LMC 1–2/09*; SLJ 10/1/08)

5193 Green, Timothy. *Twilight Boy* (7–10). 1998, Northland LB $12.95 (978-0-87358-670-2); paper $6.95 (978-0-87358-640-5). Navajo folkways form the background of this gripping mystery about a boy who is haunted by the memory of his dead brother and an evil that is preying on his Navajo community. (Rev: BL 4/15/98; HBG 9/98; VOYA 8/98)

5194 Greene, Michele Dominguez. *Chasing the Jaguar* (7–10). 2006, HarperCollins $15.99 (978-0-06-076353-4). Strange dreams lead Martika, a Mexican American teenager living in Los Angeles, to discover she is descended from Mayan healers and has psychic powers that may help her solve a kidnapping. (Rev: BL 5/1/06; LMC 2/07; SLJ 7/06)

5195 Griffin, Paul. *Burning Blue* (8–12). 2012, Dial $17.99 (978-0-8037-3815-7). Jay Nazarro, a reclusive hacker since having a very public seizure, is determined to find out who threw acid in the face of popular, beautiful classmate Nicole in this compelling story. ℯ Lexile HL660L (Rev: BLO 1/13; HB 9–10/12; LMC 3–4/13*; SLJ 10/12; VOYA 8/12)

5196 Grisham, John. *The Client* (9–12). 1993, Doubleday $23.50 (978-0-385-42471-4). Mark Sway, 11, witnesses a Mafia lawyer's suicide, which puts him in danger from Barry the Blade and a politically ambitious U.S. attorney. (Rev: BL 2/1/93*; SLJ 7/93; VOYA 8/93)

5197 Grisham, John. *The Pelican Brief* (9–12). 1992, Doubleday $24.95 (978-0-385-42198-0). A law student runs for her life after discovering who murdered two supreme court justices. (Rev: BL 1/15/92)

5198 Grisham, John. *The Street Lawyer* (10–12). 1998, Doubleday $27.95 (978-0-385-49099-3); paper $7.99 (978-0-440-22570-6). In this fast-moving plot, a successful young lawyer's investigations raise serious questions about his firm's role in evicting homeless people during a cold winter. (Rev: BL 2/15/98; SLJ 6/98)

5199 Hahn, Mary Downing. *Mister Death's Blue-Eyed Girls* (8–11). 2012, Clarion $16.99 (978-0-547-76062-9). This scary story told from several perspectives describes the 1956 murder of two teenage girls in suburban Baltimore and the desperate rush to identify the

perpetrator. ∩ ℯ Lexile HL700L (Rev: BL 5/1/12; HB 7–8/12; SLJ 7/12; VOYA 10/12)

5200 Haig, Matt. *The Dead Fathers Club* (10–12). 2007, Penguin $23.95 (978-0-670-03833-6). Philip's dead father asks Philip to kill his murderer (Philip's Uncle Alan); Philip must decide what to do and his first-person narrative, inspired by *Hamlet,* is both humorous and poignant. ∩ (Rev: BL 12/1/06)

5201 Haines, Kathryn Miller. *The Girl Is Murder* (7–10). 2011, Roaring Brook $16.99 (978-1-59643-609-1). Still grieving for her mother, who committed suicide, 15-year-old Iris copes with moving from a life of luxury to an apartment and public school, and helps her detective father who lost a leg at Pearl Harbor; set in 1940s New York City. ∩ ℯ Lexile HL700L (Rev: BL 5/1/11; LMC 10/11*; SLJ 8/11*)

5202 Hall, Lynn. *Ride a Dark Horse* (7–10). 1987, Avon paper $2.95 (978-0-380-75370-3). A teenage girl is fired from her job on a horse-breeding farm because she is getting too close to solving a mystery. (Rev: BL 9/15/87; SLJ 12/87; VOYA 10/87)

5203 Halliday, Gemma. *Deadly Cool* (9–12). 2011, HarperTeen $8.99 (978-006200331-7). After hearing that her boyfriend Josh has been cheating on her with Courtney, Hartley is horrified to find Courtney dead in Josh's bedroom and sets out to prove his innocence; this riveting mystery is full of humor. ℯ (Rev: BL 12/1/11; SLJ 1/12; VOYA 8/11)

5204 Halliday, Gemma. *Social Suicide* (9–12). 2012, HarperTeen paper $8.99 (978-006200332-4). Hartley investigates the death of a cheating homecoming queen in this fast-paced sequel to *Deadly Cool* (2011). ℯ (Rev: BLO 6/12; SLJ 5/1/12; VOYA 6/12)

5205 Harmon, Michael. *The Chamber of Five* (9–12). 2011, Knopf $16.99 (978-0-375-86644-9); LB $19.99 (978-037596644-6). Rich kid Jason Weatherby is recruited to his private school's elite inner circle but soon discovers that he doesn't like its sinister activities. ℯ Lexile HL550L (Rev: BL 7/11; SLJ 7/11)

5206 Harrington, Kim. *Perception* (8–12). 2012, Scholastic $16.99 (978-054523053-7). Clare, the psychically gifted high schooler introduced in 2011's *Clarity,* investigates a classmate's disappearance and tries to choose between tall, dark Justin and Gabriel, attractive son of the new police detective. ℯ Lexile HL600L (Rev: BL 2/15/12; SLJ 3/12)

5207 Harris, Joanne. *Gentlemen and Players* (9–12). 2006, Morrow $24.95 (978-0-06-055914-4). Two teachers and a wannabe student at St. Oswald's, an English boys' school, relate a tale of aspirations, rumors, escalating incidents, and a death in this suspenseful novel. (Rev: BL 11/15/05*; SLJ 6/06)

5208 Harrison, Cora. *Writ in Stone* (10–12). 2009, Severn $27.95 (978-072786812-1). In 16th-century Ireland Mara seeks justice — and the motive of the killer — when a man is murdered in the village, perhaps in the place of her fiancé, the King? The fourth installment in the series. **e** (Rev: BL 11/15/09)

5209 Harrod-Eagles, Cynthia. *Fell Purpose* (11–12). Series: Detective Inspector Bill Slider Mysteries. 2010, Severn $28.95 (978-072786842-8). This entry in the series finds Slider investigating the murder of a well-heeled young woman whose secret life informs the violent circumstances of her death; for mature readers. **e** (Rev: BL 12/1/09)

5210 Hart, Carolyn. *Merry, Merry Ghost* (10–12). 2009, Morrow $24.99 (978-006087437-7). Second in a series, *Merry, Merry Ghost* marks the return of Bailey Ruth, a lovable yet often misguided spirit who helps a young orphan and solves the murder of his wealthy grandmother. (Rev: BL 9/15/09)

5211 Harvey, Alyxandra. *Haunting Violet* (7–10). 2011, Walker $16.99 (978-0-8027-9839-8). Violet, 16, is used to fraudulent seances conducted by her mother, but is startled when she actually starts seeing ghosts herself; set in Victorian England. **e** Lexile HL710L (Rev: BL 5/1/11; LMC 8–9/11; SLJ 11/1/11; VOYA 8/11)

5212 Hathaway, Robin. *The Doctor Digs a Grave* (10–12). 1998, St. Martin's $22.95 (978-0-312-18568-8). This mystery involves a sleuth cardiologist, Dr. Andrew Fenimore, the forgotten customs of the Lenape Indians, and the death of a young girl, whose body is found buried in an upright position facing east. (Rev: SLJ 10/98)

5213 Hautman, Pete, and Mary Logue. *Snatched* (7–10). Series: Bloodwater Mysteries. 2006, Philomel $15.99 (978-0-399-24377-6). High school students Roni and Brian investigate the mystery of the missing Alicia in this suspenseful novel that holds readers' interest. (Rev: BL 5/1/06; HB 7–8/06; SLJ 6/06)

5214 Healey, Karen. *The Shattering* (9–12). 2011, Little, Brown $17.99 (978-0-316-12572-7). Keri and her friends are endangered when they investigate a series of deaths in their New Zealand town and find clues indicating that witchcraft may be involved. ᴖ **e** Lexile HL790L (Rev: BL 10/1/11; LMC 1–2/12; SLJ 9/1/11)

5215 Healy, Erin. *Never Let You Go* (11–12). 2010, Thomas Nelson $21.99 (978-159554750-7). In this faith-based thriller, single mother Lexi is backed into a dangerous situation by one mishap after another — and it's only through hope, and one well-timed miracle, that she manages to persevere; for mature readers. ᴖ **e** (Rev: BLO 4/1–15/10)

5216 Henderson, Lauren. *Kiss Me Kill Me* (9–12). 2008, Delacorte $15.99 (978-0-385-73487-5). Can a first kiss be a killer? Scarlett, a British heiress, sets out to solve the mystery of the death of Dan McAndrew, who kissed her and then died. (Rev: BL 2/1/08; SLJ 3/08)

5217 Henderson, Lauren. *Kisses and Lies* (9–12). 2009, Random House $16.99 (978-038573489-9); LB $19.99

(978-038590486-5). British socialite Scarlett, whose crush, Dan, died mysteriously in *Kiss Me Kill Me* (2008), travels to Scotland to find his killer. (Rev: BL 5/1/09; SLJ 5/1/09)

5218 Henry, April. *Girl, Stolen!* (7–10). 2010, Henry Holt $16.99 (978-0-8050-9005-5). Things go from bad to worse when a young carjacker steals Cheyenne's mother's car — not realizing the blind, pneumonia-stricken teen is in the back seat. **e** Lexile HL700L (Rev: BL 9/15/10; SLJ 10/1/10)

5219 Henry, April. *The Night She Disappeared* (7–10). 2012, Henry Holt $16.99 (978-080509262-2). When Kayla disappears while delivering a pizza, Gabie realizes she was the intended victim and determines to uncover the truth. YALSA Quick Picks for Reluctant Young Adult Readers 2013. ᴖ **e** Lexile HL680L (Rev: BL 5/1/12; LMC 1–2/13*; SLJ 4/12)

5220 Hess, Joan. *Dear Miss Demeanor* (10–12). 1987, St. Martin's paper $5.99 (978-0-312-97313-1). In this first of a recommended series, Claire Malloy investigates the sudden death of the principal of the school at which she is a substitute teacher. (Rev: BL 5/1/00)

5221 Higgins, Jack. *The Eagle Has Flown* (9–12). 1990, Pocket paper $6.99 (978-0-671-72737-6). The sequel to *The Eagle Has Landed,* in which Devlin is asked by the Germans to parachute into England to free the formerly believed-dead Steiner. (Rev: BL 3/1/91)

5222 Hill, William. *The Vampire Hunters* (7–12). 1998, Otter Creek $19.95 (978-1-890611-05-7); paper $12.95 (978-1-890611-02-6). Members of a gang called the Graveyard Armadillos are convinced that Marcus Chandler is a vampire, and 15-year-old Scooter Keyshaw is determined to find the truth. (Rev: BL 10/15/98; SLJ 2/99)

5223 Hillerman, Tony. *The Best American Mystery Stories of the Century* (9–12). 2000, Houghton Mifflin $28.00 (978-0-618-01267-1). A 20th-century survey of the mystery story with contributions from such writers as Raymond Chandler, John Steinbeck, and Ellery Queen. (Rev: BL 4/1/00)

5224 Hillerman, Tony. *People of Darkness* (10–12). 1991, HarperCollins paper $7.99 (978-0-06-109915-1). Set in the Southwest, this mystery features Navajo police detective Jim Chee and gives rich background information about the culture of these Native Americans. Others in this series are *Listening Woman*, *The Blessing Way*, *Dance Hall of the Dead*, and *The Fly on the Wall.*

5225 Hillerman, Tony. *Talking God* (10–12). 1991, HarperCollins paper $7.99 (978-0-06-109918-2). The two Navajo police officers, Jim Chee and Joe Leaphorn, featured together in the author's earlier *A Thief of Time* and *Skinwalkers*, once more solve a puzzling, complex murder mystery set in New Mexico. (Rev: BL 5/1/89; SLJ 11/89; VOYA 10/89)

5226 Hillerman, Tony, ed. *The Mysterious West* (9–12). 1995, HarperCollins paper $7.99 (978-0-06-109262-6). This collection of 20 mystery and suspense stories with western themes features humor, action, and murder. (Rev: BL 10/1/94; SLJ 3/95)

5227 Hoag, Tami. *Deeper Than the Dead* (11–12). 2009, Dutton $26.95 (978-052595130-8). Set in 1985 in the sleepy town of Oak Knoll, California, this scary thriller thrusts four fifth-graders into the center of a hunt for a psychotic serial killer; for mature readers. ⌒ e (Rev: BL 10/15/09)

5228 Hoffman, William. *Tidewater Blood* (10–12). 1998, Algonquin $31.95 (978-1-56512-187-4). Charley LeBlanc, the black sheep of a wealthy plantation family in Virginia, is wrongfully accused of killing his mother and father and sets out to find the real murderer. (Rev: BL 2/1/98; SLJ 10/98)

5229 Hogan, Edward. *Daylight Saving* (7–10). 2012, Candlewick $16.99 (978-0-7636-5913-4). On a reluctant vacation at Leisure World, unhappy Daniel meets a strange girl called Lexi who has wounds that keep getting worse and a watch that runs backward. e (Rev: BL 11/1/12; HB 9–10/12; LMC 3–4/13; SLJ 11/12; VOYA 10/12)

5230 Horowitz, Anthony. *Eagle Strike* (7–12). Series: Alex Rider Adventure. 2004, Putnam $17.99 (978-0-399-23979-3). Alex Rider, the hero of many adventures, recognizes a famous Russian assassin while Alex is vacationing in France, and a new thriller begins. (Rev: BL 5/1/04; SLJ 3/04; VOYA 4/04)

5231 Horowitz, Anthony. *Point Blank* (6–10). Series: Alex Rider Adventure. 2002, Putnam $17.99 (978-0-399-23621-1). Alex, the young British spy, infiltrates an exclusive Swiss boarding school in this action-filled adventure. (Rev: BL 4/1/02; HBG 10/02; SLJ 3/02; VOYA 2/02)

5232 Horowitz, Anthony. *Scorpia* (8–11). Series: Alex Rider Adventure. 2005, Penguin $17.99 (978-0-399-24151-2). Teenage spy Alex Rider infiltrates a terrorist organization called Scorpia. (Rev: BL 2/1/05; SLJ 3/05; VOYA 4/05)

5233 Hrdlitschka, Shelley. *Tangled Web* (6–12). 2000, Orca paper $6.95 (978-1-55143-178-9). Telepathic twins Alex and Tanner again tangle with their former kidnapper in this fast-paced sequel to *Disconnected* (1999). (Rev: BL 10/15/00; SLJ 10/00; VOYA 12/00)

5234 Huston, Charlie. *Sleepless* (10–12). 2010, Ballantine $25 (978-034550113-4). When a plague of terminal insomnia strikes, a police officer assigned to bust a gang trafficking in the cure is further motivated by his stricken wife. ⌒ e (Rev: BLO 12/1/09)

5235 Hyland, Adrian. *Moonlight Downs* (9–12). 2008, Soho $24.00 (978-1-56947-483-9). After some studying at the University and working at various jobs, Tempest returns to her aboriginal neighborhood in the Northern Territory of Australia where she learns the leader of her tribe has been murdered, the killing seemingly involving sorcery, and she chooses to start her own investigation. (Rev: BL 10/1/07; SLJ 3/08)

5236 Jackson, Joshilyn. *The Girl Who Stopped Swimming* (9–12). 2008, Grand Central $23.99 (978-0-446-57965-0). Living a comfortable life in Florida with her husband, David, and their 13-year-old daughter, Shelby, Laurel Hamilton sets out to find the cause of the sudden death of Shelby's friend Molly, enlisting the help of her own sister whose arrival stirs up secrets from the past. (Rev: BL 12/1/07)

5237 Jackson, Shirley. *We Have Always Lived in the Castle* (9–12). 1962, Amereon LB $22.95 (978-0-89190-623-0); paper $14.00 (978-0-14-007107-8). Two sisters have become recluses after the arsenic poisoning of four members of their family.

5238 Jaffarian, Sue Ann. *The Curse of the Holy Pail* (11–12). Series: Odelia Grey. 2007, Llewellyn paper $13.95 (978-0-7387-0864-5). Odelia, an investigator who is neither young nor thin, takes on the mystery of the cursed lunch box. (Rev: BL 12/1/06)

5239 Jaffarian, Sue Ann. *Ghost a la Mode* (10–12). 2009, Midnight Ink paper $14.95 (978-07387138-0-9). *Ghost a la Mode* introduces divorcee Emma Whitecastle and her relative, the long-dead Granny Apples, who solve mysteries together beginning with clearing Granny of her husband's murder. (Rev: BL 9/09)

5240 Jaffe, Michele. *Ghost Flower* (9–12). 2012, Penguin paper $9.99 (978-15951439-6-9). Hired to impersonate a missing girl, runaway Eve contends with the eerie and unexpected appearance of the girl's ghost. e (Rev: BL 5/1/12; SLJ 3/12; VOYA 2/12)

5241 James, Bill. *Take* (9–12). 1994, Countryman $20.00 (978-0-88150-294-7). A small-time crook gets involved in a plan to steal a payroll, but the caper turns out to be much more than expected. (Rev: BL 5/15/94*)

5242 James, P. D. *An Unsuitable Job for a Woman* (10–12). 2001, Simon & Schuster paper $14.00 (978-0-7432-1955-6). For better readers, this English mystery first published in 1988 involves Cordelia Gray, who owns a detective agency. Some other titles are *Cover Her Face* (1987) and *Death of an Expert Witness* (1988).

5243 Jarzab, Anna. *All Unquiet Things* (9–12). 2010, Delacorte $17.99 (978-0-385-73835-4); LB $20.99 (978-0-385-90723-1). Neily and Audrey, students at a classy high school, join together to investigate the death of Carly, who was Neily's ex-girlfriend and whose murderer has been identified as Audrey's father. ⌒ e Lexile HL780L (Rev: BL 10/15/09; LMC 11–12/09; SLJ 2/10; VOYA 2/10)

5244 Johansen, Iris. *Eight Days to Live* (11–12). 2010, St. Martin's $27.99 (978-031236815-9). Jane MacGuire, adoptive daughter of Eve Duncan and an artist mysteriously targeted by a religious cult, seeks help as she receives death threats; for mature readers. (Rev: BL 2/1–15/10)

5245 Johansen, Iris. *Quicksand* (9–12). 2008, St. Martin's $26.95 (978-0-312-36806-7). Johansen borrows characters from earlier novels to enhance this suspense thriller about Eve Duncan's obsession for the ongoing search for her daughter's body, the strain it puts on her relationship with detective Joe Quinn, and the individuals (well-meaning and otherwise) who keep the search in motion. (Rev: BL 12/15/07)

5246 Jorgensen, Christine T. *Curl Up and Die* (10–12). 1997, Walker $21.95 (978-0-8027-3288-0). Stella Stargazer, writer of an astrology lovelorn column, tries to help a friend with romantic problems and finds herself involved in a case of blackmail and murder. (Rev: BL 12/15/96; SLJ 6/97)

5247 Jorgensen, Christine T. *Death of a Dustbunny: A Stella the Stargazer Mystery* (8–12). 1998, Walker $22.95 (978-0-8027-3315-3). An uncomplicated mystery in which sleuth Stella the Stargazer, who writes a combination astrology and advice-to-the-lovelorn column for a local newspaper, investigates the disappearance of her friend Elena Ruiz, an employee of the Dustbunnies housekeeping and nanny agency. (Rev: BL 4/15/98; VOYA 8/98)

5248 Jubert, Hervé. *Devil's Tango* (8–11). 2006, HarperCollins $16.99 (978-0-06-077720-3). Crime is virtually impossible in the futuristic city of Basle, Switzerland, thanks to tracers that monitor all parts of the city, but when a serial killer called the Baron of the Mists goes on a killing spree and can't be detected it's up to detective Roberta Morgenstern and her partner Clement to track him; this is a complex novel of suspense with elements of fantasy, science fiction, and romance. (Rev: BL 10/1/06; SLJ 2/07)

5249 Kaminsky, Stuart M. *Now You See It* (10–12). 2004, Carroll & Graf $25.00 (978-0-7867-1423-0). A mystery set in 1940s Hollywood in which a famous magician finds his life and his illusions in danger. (Rev: BL 10/1/04)

5250 Kane, Andrea. *The Girl Who Disappeared Twice* (11–12). 2011, Mira $24.95 (978-0-7783-2984-8). When her daughter is kidnapped, family court judge Hope must revisit the kidnapping of her twin sister 32 years before; a tense thriller with a fascinating team of investigators. ⌕ ℮ (Rev: BL 5/1/11; SLJ 7/11)

5251 Kane, Andrea. *Scent of Danger* (11–12). 2003, Pocket paper $7.99 (978-0-7434-4613-6). Romance and suspense abound in this entertaining novel about a daughter who works to save her sperm-donor father's perfume empire. (Rev: BL 2/1/03)

5252 Karas, Phyllis. *The Hate Crime* (7–10). 1995, Avon paper $3.99 (978-0-380-78214-7). A docunovel/ whodunit about a teen who scrawls the names of seven

concentration camps on a Jewish temple. (Rev: BL 12/1/95; VOYA 2/96)

5253 Kelly, Lauren. *Blood Mask* (11–12). 2006, Ecco $24.95 (978-0-06-111903-3). A teenage girl becomes entangled in her adoptive aunt's bizarre life in an upstate New York artists' colony in this novel written by Joyce Carol Oates using a pseudonym. (Rev: BL 4/15/06)

5254 Kenner, Julie. *Demon Ex Machina: Tales of a Demon-Hunting Soccer Mom* (11–12). 2009, Berkley paper $14 (978-04252296-4-4). Soccer-mom-turned-demon-hunter Kate enlists the help of her current and ex-husbands, as well as her surprisingly capable teenage daughter, to rid the sleepy hamlet of San Diablo, California of a growing number of demons; for mature readers. ℮ (Rev: BL 10/15/09)

5255 Kephart, Beth. *Nothing but Ghosts* (8–11). 2009, HarperCollins $17.95 (978-006166796-1); LB $18.89 (978-006166797-8). Katie, 16, in an effort to recover from her mother's death, works on the construction of a gazebo at a nearby estate and stumbles on a mystery that she investigates with some help from her art restorer father and fellow worker Danny. (Rev: BL 4/1/09; LMC 1–2/10; SLJ 7/1/09; VOYA 8/09)

5256 Kerr, M. E. *Fell* (8–12). 1987, HarperCollins paper $4.95 (978-0-06-447031-5). In a bizarre identity switch, a teenager from a middle-class background enters a posh prep school. Followed by *Fell Back* and *Fell Down*. (Rev: BL 6/1/87; SLJ 8/87; VOYA 10/87)

5257 Kerr, M. E. *Fell Down* (7–12). 1991, HarperCollins $15.00 (978-0-06-021763-1). Fell has dropped out of prep school but is haunted by the death of his best friend there, so he returns, to find kidnapping, murder, and obsession. (Rev: BL 9/15/91*; SLJ 10/91)

5258 King, Laurie R. *A Monstrous Regiment of Women* (10–12). 1995, St. Martin's $22.95 (978-0-312-13565-2). Sherlock Holmes's apprentice, Mary Russell, solves a case involving the strange deaths of several wealthy young women in Oxford. (Rev: BL 9/1/95; SLJ 2/96)

5259 King, Stephen. *Duma Key* (9–12). 2008, Scribner $28.00 (978-1-4165-5251-2). Building contractor Edgar Freemantle is in a job-site accident leaving him with many severe injuries — to both his brain and body — and after his wife divorces him he decides to rehabilitate on Florida's Duma Key where he discovers a mysterious history involving his new neighbor's family. (Rev: BL 12/1/07)

5260 Koontz, Dean. *The Darkest Evening of the Year* (9–12). 2007, Bantam $27.00 (978-0-553-80482-9). Amy Redwing has established a humane organization that rescues abused golden retrievers, heals them, and finds loving homes for them, but there is one mission where she and her boyfriend Bryan rescue a special dog named Nickie, a feat that opens up further confrontations with a list of evil characters. (Rev: BL 11/1/07)

5261 Koontz, Dean. *The Face* (11–12). 2003, Bantam $26.95 (978-0-533-80248-7). Ten-year-old Fric, son of a major movie star, is the target of a lunatic professor in this gripping thriller. (Rev: BL 5/15/03)

5262 Koontz, Dean. *Fear Nothing* (10–12). 1998, Bantam paper $7.99 (978-0-553-57975-8). A well-plotted thriller about a nocturnal person whose investigation of his father's death uncovers a sinister conspiracy involving experiments with animal intelligence. (Rev: SLJ 6/98; VOYA 6/98)

5263 Koontz, Dean. *The Husband* (11–12). 2006, Bantam $27.00 (978-0-553-80479-9). Mitch's wife is kidnapped and her ruthless captors demand a $2 million ransom in this complex thriller. ⌒ (Rev: BL 5/1/06)

5264 Koontz, Dean. *Velocity* (11–12). 2005, Bantam $27.00 (978-0-553-80415-7). A tense thriller in which a serial killer targets a bartender called Willy, selecting people Willy knows as his victims and planting evidence implicating Willy in the crimes; for mature teens. (Rev: BL 5/1/05; SLJ 9/05)

5265 Kress, Adrienne. *The Friday Society* (7–12). 2012, Dial $17.99 (978-080373761-7). In Edwardian England three talented teenage women meet by chance and join forces to solve a mystery. ℯ Lexile HL710L (Rev: BL 12/15/12; LMC 3–4/13; SLJ 2/13; VOYA 11–12/12)

5266 L'Engle, Madeleine. *Troubling a Star* (7–10). 1994, Farrar $19.00 (978-0-374-37783-0). Vicki Austin, 16, travels to Antarctica and meets a Baltic prince looking for romance, and the two try to solve a mystery involving nuclear waste. (Rev: BL 8/94; SLJ 10/94; VOYA 12/94)

5267 Lachtman, Ofelia Dumas. *The Summer of El Pintor* (7–10). 2001, Arte Publico paper $9.95 (978-1-55885-327-0). Sixteen-year-old Monica's father loses his job and the two move from their wealthy neighborhood to the barrio house in which her dead mother grew up, where Monica searches for a missing neighbor and discovers the truth of her past. (Rev: BL 8/01; SLJ 7/01; VOYA 12/01)

5268 Lachtman, Ofelia Dumas. *The Truth About Las Mariposas* (7–10). 2007, Arte Publico paper $9.95 (978-1-55885-494-9). While Caroline (called Caro) is spending the summer with Tía Matilde, helping her run her bed-and-breakfast in the tiny town of Two Sands, she stumbles on a mystery that could affect her aunt's livelihood. (Rev: BL 12/15/07)

5269 Landrigan, Linda, ed. *Alfred Hitchcock's Mystery Magazine Presents Fifty Years of Crime and Suspense* (9–12). 2006, Pegasus paper $16.95 (978-1-933648-03-3). The title says it all — 50 years of mystery are distilled into one rewarding volume. (Rev: SLJ 7/06)

5270 Lane, Andrew. *Rebel Fire* (7–10). Series: Sherlock Holmes: The Legend Begins. 2012, Farrar $16.99 (978-037438768-6). A teenaged Sherlock Holmes discovers that John Wilkes Booth is alive and living in England in

this action-packed tale that takes the young sleuth to the United States. ⌒ ℯ Lexile 920L (Rev: BL 5/1/12; HB 5–6/12; SLJ 4/12; VOYA 4/12)

5271 Laurie, Hugh. *The Gun Seller* (10–12). 1997, Soho $24.00 (978-1-56947-087-9). A British spoof of spy thrillers that moves at an exciting pace and involves not only Brits but CIA personnel, international arms dealers, and terrorists. (Rev: BL 4/15/97; SLJ 6/97)

5272 Lavender, Will. *Obedience* (9–12). 2008, Crown $24.00 (978-0-307-39610-5). Mary, Brian, and Dennis are among the Logic and Reasoning 204 students given a logic challenge by their professor to find Polly, a missing person, before she is murdered, but the trio soon find that assignment is invading their personal lives in creepy ways. ℯ (Rev: BL 12/15/07)

5273 Le Carré, John. *The Spy Who Came in from the Cold* (10–12). 1964, Coward-McCann paper $14.00 (978-0-7434-4253-4). One of the classic thrillers. This one is about Alec Leamus, a secret agent operating during the Cold War.

5274 Lee, Y. S. *The Body at the Tower* (8–12). Series: Agency. 2010, Candlewick $16.99 (978-076364968-5). Mary Quinn resorts to disguising herself as a boy to solve a murder in this second book in the series set in Victorian England. ⌒ ℯ (Rev: BL 12/15/10; SLJ 9/1/10; VOYA 10/10)

5275 Lee, Y. S. *A Spy in the House* (8–12). Series: Mary Quinn Mysteries. 2010, Candlewick $16.99 (978-0-7636-4067-5); paper $11.20 (978-1-4063-1516-5). Saved from hanging in 1850s London five years earlier, Mary Quinn, now 17, is part of an all-female detective agency and charged with tracing some missing cargo ships; this first installment in a series is full of Victorian details. ⌒ ℯ (Rev: BL 1/1–15/10; LMC 5–6/10; SLJ 4/10)

5276 Lehane, Dennis. *A Drink Before the War* (9–12). 1994, Harcourt $22.95 (978-0-15-100093-7). Patrick and Angelo are hired by two state senators to locate a black cleaning woman who filched several sensitive documents. (Rev: BL 11/15/94*)

5277 Lelic, Simon. *A Thousand Cuts* (10–12). 2010, Viking $24.95 (978-067002150-5). Detective Lucia May investigates a brutal shooting at a school in which a newly hired teacher kills three students, another teacher, and himself in this thought-provoking novel about bullying and retribution. (Rev: BL 2/1–15/10)

5278 Levien, David. *City of the Sun* (9–12). 2007, Doubleday $24.95 (978-0-385-52366-0). Private investigator Frank Behr takes on the case of the disappearance of 12-year-old Jamie Gabriel from his paper route in an Indianapolis suburb and despite the slim chance of finding him alive, the hunt leads to Mexico in this suspenseful novel. (Rev: BL 11/15/07)

5279 Levithan, David. *Every You, Every Me* (8–12). Illus. 2011, Knopf $16.99 (978-0-375-86098-0); LB $19.99

(978-037596098-7). Using a journal format including color photographs, this novel describes 16-year-old Evan's distress about the loss of his friend Ariel and his reactions when photographs of her start appearing in his locker and on his way home. **e** Lexile HL440L (Rev: BL 10/15/11; SLJ 10/1/11; VOYA 10/11)

5280 Lewin, Michael Z. *Underdog* (9–12). 1993, Mysterious $18.95 (978-0-89296-440-6). When homeless Jan Moro uncovers a police sting to catch thug Billy Cigar, his own entrepreneurial plan, which depends on Cigar's partnership, is endangered. (Rev: BL 10/1/93*)

5281 Lippman, Laura. *I'd Know You Anywhere* (11–12). 2010, Morrow $25.99 (978-006170655-4). Housewife Eliza looks back at her dreadful experiences when she was kidnapped at age 15 by a manipulative serial rapist; for mature readers. ⋒ **e** (Rev: BL 5/1/10*)

5282 Lisle, Janet Taylor. *Black Duck* (7–10). 2006, Philomel $15.99 (978-0-399-23963-2). In hopes of getting his story published, a teen boy interviews his elderly neighbor about the days of Prohibition and learns of lawlessness and mysterious events occurring in their Rhode Island town. ⋒ (Rev: BL 5/1/06; HB 7–8/06; LMC 1/07; SLJ 5/06*)

5283 Littke, Lael. *Lake of Secrets* (7–10). 2002, Henry Holt $16.95 (978-0-8050-6730-9). Carlene experiences strong and puzzling feelings of deja vu when she and her mother go to the town where Carlene's brother died 18 years earlier, before Carlene's birth. (Rev: BCCB 4/02; BL 3/1/02; HB 5–6/02; HBG 10/02; SLJ 3/02; VOYA 6/02)

5284 Littlefield, Sophie. *Hanging by a Thread* (10–12). 2012, Delacorte $16.99 (978-0-385-74104-0); LB $19.99 (978-037598982-7). Clare, a 16-year-old with a strong interest in fashion, uses her gift of seeing the lives of people through their clothes to investigate a series of murders in her California town. **e** (Rev: BL 5/1/12; LMC 11–12/12; SLJ 10/12)

5285 Littlewood, Ann. *Night Kill* (10–12). 2008, Poisoned Pen $24.95 (978-1-59058-504-7). *Night Kill* combines the thrill and danger of solving a murder mystery with a glimpse into the internal workings of a zoo. **e** (Rev: BL 8/08)

5286 Long, David Ryan. *Ezekiel's Shadow* (9–12). 2001, Bethany paper $10.99 (978-0-7642-2443-0). In this thriller, a famous horror writer is being stalked by someone who resembles one of the author's characters. (Rev: BL 1/1–15/01)

5287 Lott, Bret. *The Hunt Club: A Novel* (10–12). 1999, HarperCollins paper $5.99 (978-0-06-101390-4). In this murder mystery, 15-year-old Huger Dillard, his mother, and blind uncle are kidnapped and must fight for their lives. (Rev: SLJ 11/98)

5288 Lourey, Jess. *September Fair* (10–12). 2009, Midnight Ink paper $14.95 (978-07387187-2-9). When the newly elected Queen of the Dairy is killed at the fair, it

is up to reporter Mira James to solve the crime in this amusing tale of jealousy and dairy business. **e** (Rev: BL 9/09)

5289 Lovesey, Peter. *The Vault* (10–12). 2000, Soho $23.00 (978-1-56947-208-8). In this mystery set in Bath, England, Detective Peter Diamond is trying to solve an ugly crime while being pestered by an American professor who is searching for Mary Shelley's diary. (Rev: BL 8/00)

5290 Lucashenko, Melissa. *Killing Darcy* (8–10). 1998, Univ. of Queensland paper $13.95 (978-0-7022-3041-7). In this complex supernatural murder mystery set in New South Wales, 16-year-old Filomena uncovers a family murder, discovers a camera that can take pictures of the past, and is helped by a gay Aboriginal boy to solve the mystery. (Rev: SLJ 2/99)

5291 Lupton, Rosamund. *Sister* (11–12). 2011, Crown $24 (978-0-307-71651-4). When Bee refuses to believe her sister's death is a suicide, she plunges her family into a gripping search for trust, truth, and identity; for mature readers. ⋒ **e** (Rev: BL 5/1/11; SLJ 7/11)

5292 Lyga, Barry. *Game* (10–12). 2013, Little, Brown $17.99 (978-031612587-1). Seventeen-year-old Jazz, son of a serial killer, agrees to help the New York Police Department with their investigation of the Hat-Dog Killer in this sequel to *I Hunt Killers* (2012). ⋒ **e** (Rev: BL 2/1/13*; HB 5–6/13; SLJ 3/13; VOYA 6/13)

5293 Lyga, Barry. *I Hunt Killers* (9–12). 2012, Little, Brown $17.99 (978-031612584-0). Serial killer's son Jazz, 17, agrees to work with the police in solving a grisly murder case in his hometown. YALSA Quick Picks for Reluctant Young Adult Readers 2013. ⋒ **e** Lexile HL750L (Rev: BL 2/1/12; HB 5–6/12; SLJ 4/12; VOYA 4/12)

5294 Lynch, Chris. *Kill Switch* (9–12). 2012, Simon & Schuster $16.99 (978-141692702-0). Daniel's beloved grandfather begins to talk about a secret life as his dementia gets more serious, but he seems to be telling the truth and danger looms on the horizon. **e** Lexile HL690L (Rev: BL 3/1/12*; HB 3–4/12; LMC 8–9/12; SLJ 3/12; VOYA 8/12)

5295 McBride, Kristina. *One Moment* (9–12). 2012, Egmont $16.99 (978-160684086-3). Maggie's circle of friends unravels in the aftermath of her boyfriend's death while Maggie slowly remembers more about the event and comes to realize some truths about Joey. (Rev: BL 8/12; SLJ 8/12; VOYA 6/12)

5296 McCleary, Carol. *The Illusion of Murder* (10–12). 2011, Forge $24.99 (978-0-7653-2204-3). Adventure and mystery are combined in this story of Nellie Bly's attempt to beat Jules Verne's 80-day round-the-world trip. **e** (Rev: BL 4/1/11; SLJ 6/11)

5297 McClintock, Norah. *Dooley Takes the Fall* (8–12). 2008, Red Deer $12.95 (978-0-88995-403-8). Ryan Dooley, a 17-year-old with a record, is a suspect in two deaths and, to complicate matters, is attracted to the sister of one of the victims; eventually it seems that only he can clear himself. (Rev: BLO 6/17/08)

5298 McClintock, Norah. *Guilty* (9–12). 2012, Orca paper $12.95 (978-15546998-9-6). Finn struggles to understand his stepmother's murder when he learns the killer is the same person who killed his birth mother. ℮ Lexile HL560L (Rev: BL 5/1/12; SLJ 6/12; VOYA 8/12)

5299 McClintock, Norah. *Homicide Related* (9–12). 2009, Fitzhenry & Whiteside paper $12.95 (978-0-88995-431-1). Now living with his strict uncle, Ryan Dooley is recovering from his abuse of drugs and alcohol when his mother is found dead, supposedly from an overdose; Dooley decides to investigate. (Rev: BL 10/15/09; LMC 1–2/10; SLJ 12/09)

5300 McClintock, Norah. *Tell* (9–12). 2006, Orca $14.95 (978-1-55143-672-2); paper $8.95 (978-1-55143-511-4). For reluctant male teen readers, this is the story of David's relationship with his stepfather, who has been found murdered. Could David have done it? (Rev: LMC 3/07; SLJ 1/07)

5301 McClintock, Norah. *Victim Rights* (7–12). Series: Ryan Dooley Mystery. 2011, Red Deer paper $12.95 (978-0-88995-447-2). In this third volume in the series, Ryan's girlfriend accuses wealthy Parker Albright of rape and Ryan falls under suspicion when Parker is found dead. (Rev: BL 5/1/11; SLJ 5/11)

5302 McClure, Ken. *Tangled Web* (10–12). 2000, Simon & Schuster $25.00 (978-0-7432-0508-5). Genetic research and human cloning are subjects touched on in this novel about the murder of a 3-month-old girl. The setting is a small town in Wales. (Rev: BL 6/1–15/00)

5303 McDermid, Val. *The Grave Tattoo* (9–12). 2007, Minotaur $24.95 (978-0-312-33921-0). The discovery in England's Lake District of a 200-year-old body bearing tattoos from the South Pacific sends Wordsworth scholar Jane Gresham on a mission to prove that Fletcher Christian returned from Pitcairn Island to England to tell his adventures to Wordsworth; soon there is keen competition to find these valuable manuscripts. (Rev: SLJ 2/07)

5304 McDonnell, Margot. *Torn to Pieces* (8–11). 2008, Delacorte $15.99 (978-038573559-9); LB $18.99 (978-038590542-8). Anne, 17, discovers the horrifying truth about her mother's past in this occasionally violent teen thriller. ℮ Lexile NC510L (Rev: BL 11/1/08; SLJ 1/1/09)

5305 McGarrity, Michael. *Tularosa* (10–12). 1996, Norton $25.00 (978-0-393-03922-1). A private eye named Kevin Kerney travels to Tularosa, New Mexico, to investigate the strange disappearance of his godson, a soldier at the White Sands Missile Range. (Rev: BL 3/15/96; SLJ 1/97)

5306 McGovern, Cammie. *Eye Contact* (9–12). 2006, Viking $24.95 (978-0-670-03765-0). An autistic boy and his anxious mother are drawn into a mystery after the boy witnesses a murder. (Rev: BL 5/1/06)

5307 McGown, Jill. *Unlucky for Some: A Novel of Suspense* (9–12). 2005, Ballantine $22.95 (978-0-345-47655-5). Detectives Danny Lloyd and Judy Hill, with help from journalist Tony Baker, investigate a suspicious death that may be the work of a serial killer. (Rev: SLJ 7/05)

5308 Mackall, Dandi Daley. *The Silence of Murder* (8–12). 2011, Knopf $16.99 (978-0-375-86896-2); LB $19.99 (978-037596896-9). Hope defends her autistic brother when he is accused of murdering the baseball coach, and sets out to find the perpetrator. ☊ ℮ (Rev: BL 10/1/11; SLJ 11/1/11)

5309 McKevett, G. A. *Peaches and Screams* (9–12). 2002, Kensington $22.00 (978-1-57566-711-9). Private investigator Savannah Reid discovers that her little brother is in jail accused of murder in this mystery story with lots of family ties. (Rev: BL 11/15/01)

5310 McLoughlin, Jane. *At Yellow Lake* (7–10). 2012, Frances Lincoln paper $8.99 (978-18478028-7-3). Three troubled teens' story lines converge on a remote lake where they become the targets of kidnappers. ℮ (Rev: BLO 8/12; LMC 3–4/13)

5311 McMahon, Jennifer. *Island of Lost Girls* (9–12). 2008, HarperCollins paper $13.95 (978-0-06-144588-0). Rhonda, the lone witness to an abduction, closes in on the dark family secrets that tore her childhood apart in this coming-of-age mystery. (Rev: BL 3/15/08)

5312 McNab, Andy, and Robert Rigby. *Avenger* (7–12). 2007, Putnam $16.99 (978-0-399-24685-2). In this sequel to *Traitor* (2005) and *Payback* (2006), Danny, his grandfather Fergus, and his friend Elena pit their skills under Black Star, an evil computer expert. (Rev: SLJ 12/07; VOYA date)

5313 McNab, Andy, and Robert Rigby. *Meltdown* (8–11). 2008, Putnam $16.99 (978-0-399-24686-9). Danny and his secret agent grandfather Fergus investigate a new — and fatal — designer drug called Meltdown in this action-packed British story. (Rev: BL 7/08; SLJ 1/1/09)

5314 McNab, Andy, and Robert Rigby. *Payback* (10–12). 2006, Putnam $16.99 (978-0-399-24465-0). In this exciting sequel to *Traitor*, Danny aims to break into the British Ministry of Defense to get proof that his ex-SAS grandfather wasn't a traitor; a wave of suicide bombings in England make this task even more difficult. (Rev: BL 11/1/06; SLJ 12/06)

5315 McNamara, Mary. *The Starlet* (11–12). 2010, Simon & Schuster paper $15 (978-14391498-4-3). In this followup to 2008's *Oscar Season*, Juliette hopes to recover from Hollywood stress in Italy, and finds herself rescuing Mercy, a young, drugged-out actress, from a

Florence fountain; suspicious deaths add to the drama in this mystery suitable for mature readers. (Rev: BL 6/1–15/10)

5316 McNamee, Graham. *Bonechiller* (7–10). 2008, Random House $15.99 (978-038574658-8); LB $18.99 (978-038590895-5). High-schoolers Danny and Howie grapple with a merciless, bloodthirsty beast in this supernatural thriller set in the Canadian tundra. Lexile 580L (Rev: BL 11/1/08*; LMC 11–12/08; SLJ 1/1/09)

5317 Madison, Bennett. *Lulu Dark and the Summer of the Fox* (8–12). 2006, Sleuth paper $10.99 (978-0-595-14086-2). Lulu Dark's summer plans are ruined when she investigates the disappearances of her boyfriend and two actresses working on a movie in town — could her mother be involved? (Rev: BL 5/1/06; LMC 8–9/06; SLJ 8/06)

5318 Malone, Michael. *Red Clay, Blue Cadillac: Twelve Southern Women* (10–12). 2002, Sourcebooks paper $15.00 (978-1-57071-824-3). A collection of 12 compelling short stories featuring mystery, murder, and suspense in the South. (Rev: BL 2/1/02)

5319 Marks, Graham. *Missing in Tokyo* (10–12). 2006, Bloomsbury $16.95 (978-1-58234-907-7). London teen Adam travels to Japan to find his missing older sister and navigates Tokyo's criminal underworld with the help of a Japanese beauty named Aiko. (Rev: BL 5/1/06; SLJ 6/06)

5320 Marks, Graham. *Omega Place* (8–11). 2007, Bloomsbury $16.95 (978-1-59990-127-5). Paul, 17, runs away from home and joins a resistance group in London—Omega Place—that is bent on destroying the ubiquitous closed-circuit cameras that keep tabs on the nation's citizens. (Rev: BL 10/15/07; LMC 1/08; SLJ 4/08)

5321 Marks, Graham. *Zoo* (8–11). 2005, Bloomsbury paper $8.95 (978-1-58234-991-6). A complex and suspenseful adventure story in which 17-year-old Cam escapes from kidnappers only to find that he has a mysterious chip in his arm and his parents may have been involved in his capture. (Rev: BL 9/15/05; SLJ 10/05; VOYA 8/05)

5322 Maron, Margaret. *High Country Fall* (10–12). 2004, Mysterious $24.00 (978-0-89296-808-4). Judge Deborah Knott gets involved in a murder case in which the accused is a friend of her relatives. Part of a recommended series with this character. (Rev: BL 5/1/04*)

5323 Marrone, Amanda. *Devoured* (8–12). 2009, Simon & Schuster paper $9.99 (978-1-4169-7890-9). In this fast-paced murder mystery, 17-year-old Megan grapples with volatile politics at her summer job, her distant mother, and her dead twin sister's increasingly foreboding ghost. ℮ (Rev: BLO 8/20/09; SLJ 10/09)

5324 Massey, Sujata. *Shimura Trouble* (10–12). 2008, Severn $28.95 (978-0-7278-6601-1). Undercover agent Rei Shimura's family reunion in Hawaii runs into un-expected trouble with the Hawaiian mafia. (Rev: BL 3/1/08)

5325 Matas, Carol. *Past Crimes* (9–12). 2007, Key Porter paper $7.95 (978-1-55263-841-5). Nineteen-year-old Ros is unsure who she can trust after her husband is killed and her baby son Nate is kidnapped in this thriller with a historical subplot. (Rev: BL 8/07)

5326 Mazer, Norma Fox. *The Missing Girl* (9–12). 2008, HarperTeen $16.99 (978-0-06-623776-3). Eleven-year-old Autumn is kidnapped by a pedophile but eventually manages to escape and is reunited with her parents and four sisters in this gripping and tense story with good characterization. (Rev: BL 12/15/07; HB 5–6/08; SLJ 2/08)

5327 Michaels, Barbara. *Shattered Silk* (10–12). 1998, HarperCollins paper $7.50 (978-0-06-104473-1). When Karen sets up a boutique in Georgetown, she receives mysterious threats on her life. (Rev: BL 8/86; SLJ 2/87)

5328 Michaels, Barbara. *Stitches in Time* (9–12). 1998, HarperCollins paper $8.99 (978-0-06-104474-8). This novel weaves an incredible mystery based on a haunted quilt. (Rev: BL 5/1/95; SLJ 11/95)

5329 Michaels, Fern. *Plain Jane* (10–12). 2001, Kensington $24.00 (978-1-57566-673-0). In this romantic suspense story with a touch of the supernatural, psychotherapist Jane Lewis is hunting down a rapist. (Rev: BL 3/1/01)

5330 Michaels, Kasey. *Bowled Over* (9–12). 2007, Kensington paper $14.00 (978-0-7582-0884-2). Historical mystery writer Maggie Kelly is satisfied with her success as a writer and her life in general until peculiar events begin happening, in particular the appearance of two of her own fictitious characters in her life who eventually help her solve the murder that her father is arrested for. (Rev: BL 10/1/07)

5331 Michaels, Kasey. *High Heels and Homicide* (11–12). 2005, Kensington paper $14.00 (978-0-7582-0880-4). Regency romance author Maggie Kelly gets more than she bargained for when she heads to England to watch one of her books made into a film in this funny critique of the movie making; for mature teens. (Rev: BL 11/1/05)

5332 Michaels, Kasey. *Maggie Needs an Alibi* (10–12). 2002, Kensington $22.00 (978-1-57566-879-6). A humorous mystery in which the characters from a Regency novel emerge in contemporary New York and attempt to investigate incidents in their author's life. (Rev: BL 5/15/02)

5333 Michaels, Rune. *Genesis Alpha* (7–10). 2007, Atheneum $15.99 (978-1-4169-1886-8). Josh was a designer baby whose stem cells saved his older brother Max from cancer; now Max is accused of murder — is Josh in some way guilty too? (Rev: BCCB 9/07; BL 5/1/07; LMC 8–9/07; SLJ 7/07)

301

5334 Miles, Keith. *Murder in Perspective: An Architectural Mystery* (10–12). 1997, Walker $21.95 (978-0-8027-3298-9). A solid mystery with a sympathetic hero who has been wrongfully accused of murder and a glimpse at the world of architecture through appearances by Frank Lloyd Wright. (Rev: BL 2/15/97; VOYA 6/97)

5335 Miller, Linda Lael. *One Last Look* (11–12). 2005, Pocket paper $13.00 (978-0-7374-7050-5). Longing for some peace and quiet (and pregnant with his child), trouble-attracting attorney Clare Westbrook follows her fiancé, detective Tony Sonterra, to a new job in a small Arizona town; the last volume in a romantic suspense trilogy suitable for mature readers. (Rev: BL 10/1/05)

5336 Mitchard, Jacquelyn. *The Midnight Twins* (6–12). 2008, Penguin $16.99 (978-159514160-6). Identical twins Meredith and Mallory's eerie ability to communicate with each other forms the heart of this thrilling series starter. **e** (Rev: BL 7/08; LMC 11–12/08; SLJ 10/1/08)

5337 Mitchard, Jacquelyn. *Now You See Her* (8–11). 2007, HarperTempest $15.99 (978-0-06-111683-4). Is 15-year-old Hope telling the truth about her affair with the leading man in the school play? Was she truly abducted? Readers will have a hard time separating Hope's truth from the lies in this suspenseful psychological thriller. (Rev: BCCB 4/07; BL 2/15/07; SLJ 3/07)

5338 Mitchard, Jacquelyn. *What We Saw at Night* (8–12). 2013, Soho $17.99 (978-161695141-2). Three teens — Allie, Rob, and Juliet — are confined during the day because of a rare sensitivity to sunlight, and react by enjoying parkour at night — which leads them to witness a murder. ☊ **e** (Rev: BL 12/15/12; SLJ 2/13)

5339 Mitchell, Saundra. *Shadowed Summer* (8–12). 2009, Delacorte $15.99 (978-038573571-1); LB $18.99 (978-038590560-2). Iris, 14, accidentally contacts a ghost who pressures her to solve the mystery of his long-ago murder; her investigation uncovers unpleasant secrets about her Louisiana town. **e** Lexile 760L (Rev: BL 2/15/09; SLJ 4/1/09)

5340 Miyabe, Miyuki. *The Devil's Whisper* (9–12). Trans. by Deborah Stuhr Iwabuchi. 2007, Kodansha $24.95 (978-4-7700-3053-5). Sixteen-year-old Mamoru becomes tangled in mysterious goings-on and three deaths of young women, one of which involves his uncle, a taxi driver being charged with manslaughter, so when he comes to his uncles aid, Mamoru begins to unfold some of the mystery, including clues to his long-lost father's whereabouts. (Rev: BL 10/1/07)

5341 Moloney, James. *Black Taxi* (8–11). 2005, HarperCollins LB $16.89 (978-0-06-055938-0). When her grandfather is sent to jail for six months, 16-year-old Rosie Sinclair is appointed caretaker of his eye-catching black Mercedes; she enlists the help of her friends — one an attractive young man — when she starts getting threatening phone calls. (Rev: BCCB 5/05; BL 3/1/05; SLJ 3/05; VOYA 8/05)

5342 Montefiore, Santa. *Sea of Lost Love* (10–12). 2008, Simon & Schuster paper $15.00 (978-1-4165-4373-2). After her father's apparent suicide drowning in England, 21-year-old Celestria sets off for Italy where she uncovers his long-hidden secrets; this family saga combines mystery and romance. (Rev: BL 3/1/08)

5343 Morgenroth, Kate. *Jude* (9–12). 2004, Simon & Schuster $16.95 (978-0-689-86479-7). Still in shock from witnessing the murder of his drug-dealing father, 15-year-old Jude is tricked into pleading guilty to a crime he didn't commit to help advance his mother's political career. (Rev: BL 11/15/04; SLJ 11/04)

5344 Myers, Kate Kae. *The Vanishing Game* (8–12). 2012, Bloomsbury $16.99 (978-159990694-2). Is her twin brother still alive? Jocelyn, 17, is receiving mysterious communications, and she sets out with Jack's friend Noah to investigate. **e** (Rev: BL 5/1/12; LMC 3–4/12; SLJ 3/12)

5345 Nelson, R. A. *Breathe My Name* (10–12). 2007, Penguin $16.99 (978-1-59514-094-4). A compelling, often chilling story about an adopted teen whose birth mother tries to find her after serving time in prison for murdering her siblings and trying to kill her. (Rev: SLJ 3/08)

5346 Nevins, Francis M., and Martin H. Greenberg, eds. *Hitchcock in Prime Time* (10–12). 1985, Avon paper $9.95 (978-0-380-89673-8). This is a collection of 20 stories that formed the basis of some of Hitchcock's best television shows.

5347 Nikitas, Derek. *The Long Division* (11–12). 2009, Minotaur $24.99 (978-031236398-7). A 15-year-old boy, the mother who gave him up, a policeman, and other characters' story lines intertwine in this fast-paced novel about bad choices and inevitable outcomes; suitable for mature readers. (Rev: BL 9/15/09; SLJ 2/10)

5348 Nikitas, Derek. *Pyres* (9–12). 2007, St. Martin's $24.95 (978-0-312-36397-0). Fifteen-year-old Luc copes with the trauma of seeing her father shot and her mother's subsequent suicide attempts in this wonderfully written mystery. (Rev: BL 8/07; SLJ 1/08)

5349 Nixon, Joan Lowery. *A Candidate for Murder* (6–12). 1991, Dell paper $4.99 (978-0-440-21212-6). While Cary's father enters the political limelight, his daughter becomes embroiled in a series of strange events. (Rev: BL 3/1/91)

5350 Nixon, Joan Lowery. *The Dark and Deadly Pool* (7–12). 1989, Bantam paper $4.99 (978-0-440-20348-3). Mary Elizabeth becomes aware of strange happenings at the health club where she works. (Rev: BL 11/1/87; SLJ 2/88; VOYA 12/87)

5351 Nixon, Joan Lowery. *The Ghosts of Now* (7–10). 1984, Dell paper $4.99 (978-0-440-93115-7). Angie investigates a hit-and-run accident that has left her brother in a coma.

5352 Nixon, Joan Lowery. *The Other Side of Dark* (7–10). 1986, Dell paper $4.99 (978-0-440-96638-8). After waking from a four-year coma, Stacy is now the target of the man who wounded her and killed her mother. (Rev: BL 9/15/86; SLJ 9/86; VOYA 12/86)

5353 Nixon, Joan Lowery. *The Stalker* (9–12). 1985, Dell paper $4.50 (978-0-440-97753-7). In Corpus Christi, Jennifer sets out to prove the innocence of her friend, who has been accused of murder. (Rev: SLJ 5/85; VOYA 6/85)

5354 Nixon, Joan Lowery. *The Weekend Was Murder!* (6–10). 1992, Dell paper $4.99 (978-0-440-21901-9). A teen sleuth and her boyfriend attend a murder mystery enactment weekend and discover a real murder. (Rev: BL 2/15/92; SLJ 3/92)

5355 Norman, Hilary. *Ralph's Children* (11–12). 2008, Severn $27.95 (978-072786673-8). Four abused orphans bond as they secretly read *Lord of the Flies*, and as adults, decide to play their *Lord of the Flies* game to retaliate against perceived wrongdoing; for mature teens. (Rev: BL 9/1/08)

5356 Northrop, Michael. *Gentlemen* (10–12). 2009, Scholastic $16.99 (978-054509749-9). Mike, Mixer, and Bones suspect that their English teacher may be responsible for the disappearance of their friend Tommy. Lexile HL860L (Rev: BL 5/1/09; LMC 10/09; SLJ 8/09; VOYA 6/09)

5357 Nugent, Andrew. *Soul Murder* (10–12). 2009, Minotaur $24.95 (978-031253656-5). Irish police Superintendent Denis Lennon and Sergeant Molly Power investigate a murder at a boys' boarding school in this compelling and suspenseful novel. **e** (Rev: BL 7/09)

5358 Oldham, Nick. *Screen of Deceit* (11–12). 2008, Severn $27.95 (978-0-7278-6646-2). In this story for mature readers, 14-year-old Mark sets out to solve the puzzle of his drug-addicted sister's death and quickly finds himself between a rock and hard place: wear a wire for DCI Henry Christie, or let the bad guy go free. (Rev: BL 6/1–15/08)

5359 Orenstein, Denise Gosliner. *The Secret Twin* (7–10). 2007, HarperCollins $16.99 (978-0-06-078564-2). Skinny, sickly Noah, whose twin died at birth, is thrown for a loop when hearty Grace comes to take care of him after his grandmother's facelift in this suspenseful and complex novel. (Rev: BL 12/15/06; SLJ 3/07)

5360 Pagliarulo, Antonio. *The Celebutantes on the Avenue* (10–12). Series: Celebutantes. 2007, Delacorte paper $9.99 (978-0-385-73404-2). Wealthy 16-year-old triplets Lexington, Park, and Madison Hamilton are implicated in the death of a famous fashion editor and decide to investigate themselves. (Rev: BL 5/1/07; SLJ 6/07)

5361 Palmer, William J. *The Dons and Mr. Dickens: The Strange Case of the Oxford Christmas Plot* (10–12). 2000, St. Martin's $23.95 (978-0-312-26576-2). In this thriller set in Victorian times, Inspector Field seeks the help of Charles Dickens in solving the mystery of a gentleman murdered in an opium den. (Rev: BL 11/1/00)

5362 Pappano, Marilyn. *Heaven on Earth* (11–12). Series: Bethlehem. 2002, Dell paper $6.50 (978-0-440-23714-3). Romance blossoms between Melina and Sebastian as they search for runaway children in this stand-alone installment in the series set in Bethlehem, New York, a town guarded by angels; for mature teens. (Rev: BL 1/1–15/02)

5363 Paretsky, Sara. *Guardian Angel* (9–12). 1993, Dell paper $6.99 (978-0-440-21399-4). Intrepid female private eye V. I. Warshawski is involved with greedy Yuppies offloading risky bonds on Chicago seniors. (Rev: BL 12/1/91; SLJ 9/92)

5364 Parker, Robert B. *Chasing the Bear: A Young Spenser Novel* (7–10). 2009, Philomel $17.99 (978-039924776-7). An adult Spenser tells his girlfriend the story of being brought up by his rough-and-tumble father and uncles. ∩ **e** Lexile HL500L (Rev: BL 5/1/09; SLJ 8/09; VOYA 8/09)

5365 Pascal, Francine. *Fearless FBI: Kill Game* (8–11). Series: Fearless FBI. 2005, Simon & Schuster paper $7.99 (978-0-689-87821-3). Despite her unreliability, the FBI invites intrepid Gaia — of the earlier Fearless series — to try their boot camp training program. (Rev: BL 8/05; SLJ 6/05)

5366 Patrick, Cat. *Forgotten* (7–11). 2011, Little, Brown $17.99 (978-0-316-09461-0). London, 16, has memory problems caused by a traumatic event in her past — she "remembers" into the future and forgets everything each night until, with the help of her boyfriend she unravels the causes behind her problems. ∩ **e** Lexile HL720L (Rev: BL 4/1/11; LMC 10/11; SLJ 7/11)

5367 Patrick, Cat. *Revived* (7–11). 2012, Little, Brown $17.99 (978-0-316-09462-7). Daisy faces difficult decisions when she meets Audrey and Matt and starts to question the government's Revive program, which has brought her back from death repeatedly. ∩ **e** Lexile HL690L (Rev: BL 5/1/12; HB 5–6/12; LMC 8–9/12; SLJ 7/12; VOYA 4/12)

5368 Patterson, James, and Andrew Gross. *Judge and Jury* (10–12). 2006, Little, Brown $27.99 (978-0-316-01393-2). A Mafia trial, a heartless hitman, and a determined FBI agent make this an engaging read for fans of crime and mystery novels. (Rev: BL 5/1/06)

5369 Patterson, James, and Maxine Paetro. *10th Anniversary* (10–12). Series: Women's Murder Club. 2011, Little, Brown $27.99 (978-031603626-9). This tense thriller finds Sergeant Lindsay Boxer, Assistant DA Yuki Castellano, and reporter Cindy Thomas embroiled in mysterious cases involving young women, drugs, and crime in the San Francisco area. (Rev: BL 3/1–15/11)

5370 Patterson, James, and Peter de Jonge. *Beach Road* (11–12). 2006, Little, Brown $27.95 (978-0-316-15978-4). This legal thriller suitable for mature teens has lawyer Tom Dunleavy defending a young basketball star accused of murdering three of Tom's friends in the Hamptons. (Rev: BL 5/1/06)

5371 Peacock, Shane. *Eye of the Crow* (7–10). Series: The Boy Sherlock Holmes. 2007, Tundra $19.95 (978-0-88776-850-7). Named one of the *Booklist* Top Ten in Young Mysteries, this first book in the series begins in 1867, when Sherlock is 13 and accused of murder, launching his career of detective work. (Rev: BL 11/1/07; SLJ 11/07)

5372 Peacock, Shane. *Vanishing Girl* (7–10). Series: The Boy Sherlock Holmes. 2009, Tundra $19.95 (978-0-88776-852-1). The young daughter of a government official disappears, a ransom note arrives, and young Sherlock investigates in this fast-paced mystery full of Victorian atmosphere. e Lexile 810L (Rev: BLO 11/20/09; SLJ 2/10)

5373 Peloquin, Lili. *The Innocents* (8–10). 2012, Penguin $17.99 (978-159514582-6). When their mother remarries, sisters Alice and Charlie have different reactions to their new, wealthy surroundings and the secrets they uncover there. e (Rev: BL 10/15/12; LMC 1–2/13; SLJ 3/13)

5374 Pendergrass, Tess. *Dark of the Moon* (9–12). 2004, Five Star $26.95 (978-0-7862-5109-4). In this romantic, entertaining story, a librarian and a detective work on a case involving the murder of a politician's daughter. (Rev: BL 2/1/04)

5375 Penman, Sharon Kay. *The Queen's Man: A Medieval Mystery* (10–12). 1996, Henry Holt $20.00 (978-0-8050-3885-9). An intriguing mystery set in England during the time of Eleanor of Aquitaine and Richard Lionheart. (Rev: BL 11/1/96; SLJ 3/97)

5376 Penzler, Otto, ed. *Uncertain Endings* (10–12). 2006, Pegasus $23.95 (978-1-933648-16-3). A collection of (potentially frustrating) mystery stories that leave the reader guessing — and teach readers about the genre. (Rev: BL 12/1/06)

5377 Perrin, Kayla. *We'll Never Tell* (11–12). 2007, St. Martin's paper $13.95 (978-0-312-34016-2). A sorority pledge at the University of Buffalo is murdered; was the hazing partly responsible? (Rev: BL 1/1–15/07; SLJ 6/07)

5378 Perry, Anne. *Brunswick Gardens* (10–12). 1998, Fawcett $25.00 (978-0-449-90845-7); paper $6.99 (978-0-449-00318-3). A murder mystery set in Victorian England in which Inspector Pitt investigates the death of a woman noted as an agitator for women's rights. (Rev: SLJ 11/98)

5379 Pessl, Marisha. *Special Topics in Calamity Physics* (9–12). 2006, Viking $25.95 (978-0-670-03777-3). Blue Van Meer settles in as a high school senior at the St. Gallway School in this literary coming-of-age murder mystery structured as a syllabus for a Great Works of Literature class. (Rev: BL 6/1–15/06)

5380 Peters, Elizabeth. *Crocodile on the Sandbank* (10–12). 1975, Warner paper $6.99 (978-0-445-40651-3). Amelia Peabody, a wealthy and independent woman who is traveling in Egypt, finds herself involved in archaeology, villains, and a mystery in this novel that is part of a recommended series. (Rev: BL 5/1/00)

5381 Peters, Ellis. *The Holy Thief* (9–12). 1993, Mysterious $17.95 (978-0-89296-524-3). In this mystery set in medieval times, thievery and murder intrude upon Brother Cadfael's well-ordered monastery life. (Rev: BL 3/1/93; SLJ 7/93)

5382 Petrucha, Stefan. *Ripper* (8–10). 2012, Philomel $17.99 (978-039925524-3). In this exciting adventure set in 1895 New York, 14-year-old Carver is adopted by a detective who turns out to be a serial killer. e Lexile 710L (Rev: BL 3/1/12; HB 3–4/12; LMC 5–6/12; SLJ 3/12; VOYA 2/12)

5383 Phillips, Carly. *Sealed with a Kiss* (9–12). 2007, Harlequin paper $7.99 (978-0-373-77239-1). Molly Gifford and Daniel Hunter are reunited in this sequel to Cross My Heart; Daniel must move past the pain of Molly's rejection to help her clear her father's name. (Rev: BL 9/15/07)

5384 Phillips, Suzanne Marie. *Lindsey Lost* (7–10). 2012, Viking $16.99 (978-0-670-78460-8). Athletic Micah struggles to piece together what happened to his sister Lindsey, whose even greater athletic prowess may have made her a target for a murderer. e (Rev: BL 9/15/12; LMC 3–4/13; SLJ 10/12; VOYA 10/12)

5385 Pike, Christopher. *Chain Letter* (9–12). 1986, Avon paper $6.99 (978-0-380-89968-5). Six teenagers must perform acts of repentance in connection with the hit-and-run death of a man. (Rev: VOYA 8/86)

5386 Pike, Christopher. *Gimme a Kiss* (7–12). 1991, Pocket paper $4.50 (978-0-671-63682-1). A girl fakes her own death in a wild plot to get revenge. (Rev: BL 10/15/88; VOYA 4/89)

5387 Pike, Christopher. *Slumber Party* (7–10). 1985, Scholastic paper $5.99 (978-0-590-43014-2). Six teenage girls stranded in a winter vacation home experience mysterious occurrences that bring terror into their lives. (Rev: SLJ 12/86)

5388 Plum-Ucci, Carol. *The Body of Christopher Creed* (8–12). 2000, Harcourt $17.00 (978-0-15-202388-1). Torey and his friends are implicated in the disappearance of his classmate Chris, causing Torey to examine his life while trying to find Chris. (Rev: HBG 9/00; SLJ 7/00)

5389 Plum-Ucci, Carol. *Following Christopher Creed* (8–12). 2011, Harcourt $16.99 (978-0-15-204759-7). College student Mike begins researching the fate of Christopher Creed, uncovering one eerie similarity after another in this light, fast-paced read. A sequel to the award-winning *The Body of Christopher Creed* (2007). ⌒ e (Rev: BL 9/15/11; SLJ 9/1/11; VOYA 8/11)

5390 Plum-Ucci, Carol. *The Night My Sister Went Missing* (9–12). 2006, Harcourt $17.00 (978-0-15-204758-0). From his seat at the local police station, Kurt, 17, tries to uncover the truth about what happened to his missing 15-year-old sister Casey that night. Was she shot? Did she fall? Did she dive from the pier? (Rev: BL 10/15/06; SLJ 11/06)

5391 Plum-Ucci, Carol. *The She* (8–12). 2003, Harcourt $17.00 (978-0-15-216819-3). Evan, his brother, and a friend set out to find the truth behind the disappearance of Evan's parents years before. (Rev: BL 9/15/03*; SLJ 10/03; VOYA 12/03)

5392 Plum-Ucci, Carol. *Streams of Babel* (8–11). 2008, Harcourt $17.00 (978-0-15-216556-7). A Palestinian teenager working for the U.S. government uncovers a terrorist plot to poison drinking water that has already sickened and killed two people in New York. (Rev: BL 4/15/08; SLJ 7/08)

5393 Poirier, Mark Jude. *Modern Ranch Living* (11–12). 2004, Hyperion $23.95 (978-1-4013-0042-5). Sixteen-year-old fitness fanatic Kendra, her older brother, and a neighbor Merv find themselves working together to solve a mystery one hot Tucson summer; for mature teens. (Rev: BL 9/1/04)

5394 Powers, J. L. *The Confessional* (10–12). 2007, Knopf $16.99 (978-0-375-83872-9). There are many suspects to choose from when Mac, a student at a Catholic school in El Paso, Texas, is found murdered. (Rev: BCCB 9/07; LMC 10/07; SLJ 12/07)

5395 Preston, Douglas, and Lincoln Child. *The Ice Limit* (10–12). 2000, Warner $25.99 (978-0-446-52587-9). This absorbing, action-packed thriller involves a secret expedition to recover the world's largest meteorite from an island off the coast of Chile. (Rev: BL 5/15/00; SLJ 11/00; VOYA 12/00)

5396 Price, Charlie. *Desert Angel* (9–12). 2011, Farrar $16.99 (978-037431775-1). Angel, a 14-year-old who has had a tough life and is reluctant to trust others, flees into the desert to escape the man she believes killed her mother. e Lexile HL670L (Rev: BL 11/1/11; SLJ 2/12)

5397 Priestley, Chris. *The Dead of Winter* (7–10). 2012, Bloomsbury $16.99 (978-159990745-1). Michael finds himself in the midst of a spooky murder mystery unfolding in an isolated mansion in the middle of winter. (Rev: BL 3/1/12; LMC 3–4/12; SLJ 2/12; VOYA 2/12)

5398 Pronzini, Bill. *A Wasteland of Strangers* (10–12). 1997, Walker $21.95 (978-0-8027-3301-6). A swiftly plotted mystery in which scar-faced John Faith is wrongfully accused of murder and is sheltered by three women during an escape attempt. (Rev: BL 6/1–15/97; VOYA 2/98)

5399 Prowell, Sandra West. *The Killing of Monday Brown* (9–12). 1994, Walker $19.95 (978-0-8027-3184-5). Private eye Phoebe Siegel investigates a missing dealer in Native American artifacts. (Rev: BL 5/15/94*)

5400 Prowell, Sandra West. *When Wallflowers Die* (10–12). 1996, Walker $22.95 (978-0-8027-3254-5). An exciting mystery in which Phoebe Siegal finds her life is in danger when she begins an investigation of a murder that occurred years before. (Rev: BL 7/96; SLJ 2/97)

5401 Quinn, Spencer. *Thereby Hangs a Tail* (10–12). Series: Chet and Bernie Mysteries. 2010, Atria $25 (978-141658585-5). In this entertaining followup to *Dog on It* (2009), Bernie and Chet (Bernie's canine partner, who tells the story) investigate a missing show dog. ⌒ e (Rev: BL 12/1/09)

5402 Ravel, Edeet. *Held* (8–11). 2011, Annick $21.95 (978-155451283-6); paper $12.95 (978-15545128-2-9). Chloe, 17, is kidnapped on a vacation in Greece and held hostage by a kind abductor who makes her life quite comfortable — to the point that she finds herself attracted to him. e (Rev: BL 6/1/11; LMC 11–12/11)

5403 Read, Cornelia. *The Crazy School* (9–12). 2008, Grand Central $23.99 (978-0-446-58259-9). Madeline must enlist the help of rebellious pupils when she begins to uncover dark secrets in the boarding school for disturbed teenagers where she is employed and loses contact with the outside world. (Rev: BL 10/15/07)

5404 Reaver, Chap. *A Little Bit Dead* (8–12). 1992, Delacorte $15.00 (978-0-385-30801-4). When Reece saves an Indian boy from lynching by U.S. marshals, lawmen claim that Reece murdered one of the marshals and he must clear himself. (Rev: BL 9/1/92; SLJ 9/92)

5405 Reger, Rob, and Jessica Gruner. *The Lost Days* (7–10). Illus. by author. Series: Emily the Strange. 2009, HarperCollins $16.99 (978-006145229-1); LB $17.89 (978-006145230-7). Emily (first featured in graphic-novel form) has amnesia and uses her diary to sort out who she is. Lexile 870L (Rev: BL 5/1/09; SLJ 6/1/09)

5406 Reger, Rob, and Jessica Gruner. *Stranger and Stranger* (7–10). Illus. by author and Buzz Parker. Series: Emily the Strange. 2010, HarperTeen $16.99 (978-0-06-145232-1); LB $17.89 (978-0-06-145233-8). In a series of diary entries with manga-style cartoons, this quirky story follows Emily through a confusing cloning experience full of dark humor; a sequel to 2009's *The Lost Days*. Lexile 900L (Rev: BL 1/1–15/10; SLJ 1/10; VOYA 8/10)

5407 Reid, Kimberly. *Creeping with the Enemy* (8–12). Series: Langdon Prep. 2012, Kensington paper $9.95 (978-07582674-1-2). Chanti, 15, uses sleuthing skills she inherited from her undercover cop mom to investigate the disappearance of her friend Bethanie. (Rev: BL 5/1/12; SLJ 6/12)

5408 Reiken, Frederick. *Day for Night* (11–12). 2010, Little, Brown $24.99 (978-031607756-9). Historically and emotionally diverse characters propel this complex, ambitious psychological suspense novel that explores the underlying, often surprising connections between strangers; for mature readers. (Rev: BL 3/1–15/10)

5409 Renn, Diana. *Tokyo Heist* (7–10). 2012, Viking $17.99 (978-067001332-6). Aspiring manga artist Violet, 16, travels to Japan with her father to search for some missing Van Goghs. (Rev: BL 5/1/12; LMC 11–12/12; SLJ 6/12; VOYA 8/12)

5410 Riccio, Dolores Stewart. *Circle of Five* (11–12). 2003, Kensington paper $14.00 (978-0-7582-0300-7). A group of five Wiccan women have little success in their efforts to catch a murderer in this novel that mixes humor and suspense. (Rev: BL 3/1/03*)

5411 Riccio, Dolores Stewart. *The Divine Circle of Ladies Making Mischief* (11–12). 2005, Kensington paper $14.00 (978-0-7582-0986-3). A group of Wiccan crime fighters returns for a humorous third caper, led by Cass, a feisty entrepreneur who chats telepathically with her dog Scruffy. (Rev: BL 2/15/05)

5412 Riccio, Dolores Stewart. *Ladies Courting Trouble* (11–12). 2006, Kensington paper $14.00 (978-0-7582-0987-0). The five Wiccan women featured in *Circle of Five* (2003) must teach the minister's wife some arcane skills when the minister is a potential target. (Rev: BL 3/1/06)

5413 Rice, Luanne. *Last Kiss* (11–12). 2008, Bantam $25.00 (978-0-553-80512-3). When Nell's first love, Charlie, is mysteriously murdered, she hires a private investigator to solve the puzzle in this engrossing, multifaceted story for mature readers. ⋒ e (Rev: BL 6/1–15/08)

5414 Richardson, Nigel. *The Wrong Hands* (8–11). 2006, Knopf $15.95 (978-0-375-83459-2). Fourteen-year-old Graham has large, strange hands and an even bigger secret — with these hands, he can fly; when he rescues a baby and is considered a hero, this ability becomes harder for the British boy to conceal. ⋒ (Rev: BL 8/06; SLJ 10/06)

5415 Richmond, Michelle. *No One You Know* (10–12). 2008, Delacorte $23.00 (978-0-385-34013-7). Ellie is determined to regain control of the story of her sister's murder — which became a best-selling crime novel — in this incisive, travel-rich literary thriller. ⋒ e (Rev: BL 6/1–15/08*)

5416 Ripslinger, Jon. *Last Kiss* (8–12). 2007, Flux paper $9.95 (978-0-7387-1072-3). Billy, a simple farm boy, is the prime suspect when his girlfriend — from a wealthy and prominent family — is found murdered. (Rev: BL 11/1/07; SLJ 2/08)

5417 Ritari, Jacob. *Taroko Gorge* (10–12). 2010, Unbridled paper $15.95 (978-19360716-5-4). In this suspenseful novel set in a Taiwanese national park, two American journalists and a group of Japanese teens find themselves trapped as a cyclone bears down on the area. e (Rev: BL 5/1–15/10)

5418 Robb, Candace. *The Riddle of St. Leonard's: An Owen Archer Mystery* (10–12). 1997, St. Martin's $21.95 (978-0-312-16983-1). In England during 1369, Owen Archer is pressed into service for Sir Richard to investigate murders at St. Leonard's Hospital during a resurgence of the plague. (Rev: BL 9/15/97; SLJ 12/97)

5419 Roberts, Nora. *Tribute* (9–12). 2008, Putnam $26.95 (978-0-399-15491-1). Cilla knew restoring her grandmother's retreat in the Shenandoah Valley would take lots of time, money, and hard work but she didn't know just how far someone in her small town would go to keep past secrets buried. (Rev: BL 4/15/08)

5420 Roberts, Willo Davis. *Undercurrents* (7–10). 2002, Simon & Schuster $16.00 (978-0-689-81671-0). Fourteen-year-old Nikki is troubled when her father remarries only months after her mother's death and his new wife seems to be hiding facts about her unhappy past. (Rev: BCCB 4/02; BL 2/15/02; HBG 10/02; SLJ 2/02; VOYA 2/02)

5421 Robinson, Lynda S. *Eater of Souls* (10–12). 1997, Walker $21.95 (978-0-8027-3294-1). An engrossing mystery in which Lord Meren, King Tutankhamun's guru, tries to solve the mystery of Queen Nefertiti's death and becomes involved with a serial killer. (Rev: BL 4/15/97; SLJ 8/97; VOYA 4/98)

5422 Robinson, Lynda S. *Murder at the Feast of Rejoicing* (10–12). 1996, Walker $20.95 (978-0-8027-3274-3). An unusual murder mystery takes place on the Egyptian Nile at the time of Tutankhamun in this third book in the highly praised series featuring Lord Meren, confidant to the young pharaoh. (Rev: BL 1/1–15/96; SLJ 5/96)

5423 Roecker, Lisa, and Laura Roecker. *The Lies That Bind* (7–10). Series: The Liar Society. 2012, Sourcebooks paper $9.99 (978-14022702-4-6). Despite her dislike of secret societies, Kate becomes involved with the Sisterhood as part of her effort to solve the mystery of her friend Grace's death. e Lexile 840L (Rev: BL 12/15/12)

5424 Rollins, James. *Amazonia* (10–12). 2002, Morrow $24.95 (978-0-06-008906-1). Hoping to discover the fate of his missing father, Nathan travels deep into the Brazilian rain forest and encounters disease and other unseen forces in this fast-paced thriller. (Rev: BL 2/15/02)

5425 Roosevelt, Elliott. *Murder and the First Lady* (10–12). 1985, Avon paper $4.99 (978-0-380-69937-7). A mystery in which Eleanor Roosevelt serves as supersleuth.

5426 Roosevelt, Elliott. *Murder in the Oval Office* (10–12). 1990, Avon paper $4.99 (978-0-380-70528-3). First Lady Eleanor Roosevelt solves the murder of a congressman. (Rev: BL 12/15/88)

5427 Roosevelt, Elliott. *The White House Pantry Murder* (10–12). 1987, Avon paper $4.50 (978-0-380-70404-0). This is the fourth mystery involving Eleanor Roosevelt as sleuth. In this one, a body is found in a large White House refrigerator. (Rev: BL 12/15/86)

5428 Rose, Malcolm. *Final Lap* (8–12). 2007, Kingfisher paper $5.95 (978-0-7534-6005-4). Luke and his robot use their forensic skills in investigating sabotage at the Youth International Games. (Rev: SLJ 3/07)

5429 Ross, Jeff. *Dawn Patrol* (5–12). Series: Orca Sports. 2012, Orca paper $9.95 (978-1-4598-0062-5). Luca and Esme travel to Panama in search of their missing friend Kevin in this story for reluctant readers that features surfing and mystery. ☻ Lexile HL530L (Rev: LMC 11–12/12; SLJ 6/12)

5430 Roy, Lori. *Bent Road* (11–12). 2011, Dutton $25.95 (978-0-525-95183-4). Returning home to the town where her husband's sister mysteriously disappeared twenty years earlier, Celia struggles with ominous feelings and strange events; for mature readers, this is a tense psychological novel. ◐ ☻ (Rev: SLJ 6/11)

5431 Rozan, S. J. *Concourse* (10–12). 1995, St. Martin's paper $5.99 (978-0-312-95924-1). In this book, which is part of a series, Bill Smith and Lydia Chin, a Chinese American living in New York City's Chinatown, form a detecting partnership to solve a retirement home murder mystery. (Rev: BL 5/1/00)

5432 Runholt, Susan. *The Mystery of the Third Lucretia* (7–10). 2008, Viking $16.99 (978-0-670-06252-2). Two young artists are caught up in an international mystery when they pursue a painter who has forged a Rembrandt work; set in Minneapolis, London, and Amsterdam, this mystery combines art history with intrigue. (Rev: BL 5/1/08; SLJ 3/08)

5433 Russell, Kirk. *Dead Game* (10–12). 2005, Chronicle $23.95 (978-0-8118-5078-0). Marquez, the Fish and Game warden, is on the track of sturgeon poachers and kidnappers in this gripping ecothriller. (Rev: BL 8/05)

5434 Russell, Kirk. *Night Game* (11–12). 2004, Chronicle $23.95 (978-0-8118-4112-2). Department of Fish and Game officer John Marquez, introduced in *Shell Games* (2003), tracks down a murderous bear-poaching ring. (Rev: BL 9/15/04)

5435 Russell, Kirk. *Shell Games* (10–12). 2003, Chronicle $23.95 (978-0-8118-4186-3). Lieutenant Marquez finds his experience as a DEA agent is unexpectedly useful in his new job with the Department of Fish and Game. (Rev: BL 7/03)

5436 Saylor, Steven. *Last Seen in Massilia* (10–12). Series: Roma Sub Rosa. 2000, St. Martin's $23.95 (978-0-312-20928-5). An intriguing mystery story set in Rome in 49 B.C. during the civil war fought between Pompey and Julius Caesar, this is part of a recommended series of historical mysteries by Saylor. (Rev: BL 9/1/00)

5437 Scheier, Leah. *Secret Letters* (7–11). 2012, Disney/Hyperion $16.99 (978-142312405-4). Dora, 16, goes to London to seek the help of Sherlock Holmes, who may be her biological father, in recovering her cousin's stolen letters; she arrives in London to find that Holmes has died, but fortunately there is a handsome young detective who is willing to help. ☻ Lexile 880L (Rev: BL 5/1/12; LMC 10/12; SLJ 6/12; VOYA 6/12)

5438 Schmidt, Gary D. *First Boy* (7–10). 2005, Henry Holt $16.95 (978-0-8050-7859-6). With the help of kind neighbors, 14-year-old Cooper hopes to be able to live alone on his grandparents' farm, but questions about his missing parents seem linked to politics and the presidential elections. (Rev: BCCB 2/06; BL 9/15/05; HB 9–10/05; SLJ 10/05; VOYA 4/06)

5439 Schrefer, Eliot. *The Deadly Sister* (9–12). 2010, Scholastic $17.99 (978-0-545-16574-7). When Abby finds the body of her sister Maya's former boyfriend and her sister Maya's cell phone nearby, she is determined to find her missing sister and prove her innocent. ☻ Lexile HL720L (Rev: BL 6/10; LMC 10/10; SLJ 8/10)

5440 Schreiber, Joe. *Au Revoir, Crazy European Chick* (8–10). 2011, Houghton Mifflin $16.99 (978-0-547-57738-8). Perry's ho-hum night at the prom takes a turn when his frumpy exchange-student date turns out to be an undercover international assassin. ◐ ☻ Lexile 800L (Rev: BL 10/15/11*; HB 11–12/11; SLJ 8/11; VOYA 10/11)

5441 Schreiber, Joe. *Perry's Killer Playlist* (8–10). 2012, Houghton Mifflin $16.99 (978-0-547-60117-5). Touring Italy with his rock band, 18-year-old Perry finds himself embroiled in dangerous adventures in this action-packed sequel to *Au Revoir, Crazy European Chick* (2011). ◐ ☻ Lexile 850L (Rev: BLO 12/15/12; LMC 1–2/13; SLJ 12/12; VOYA 8/12)

5442 Scrimger, Richard. *From Charlie's Point of View* (7–10). 2005, Dutton $10.99 (978-0-525-47374-9). Fourteen-year-old Charlie is blind, but best friend Bernadette acts as his eyes, and together they set out to prove that Charlie's dad had nothing to do with a series of neighborhood ATM thefts. (Rev: BCCB 9/05; BL 5/1/05; SLJ 8/05)

5443 Sebestyen, Ouida. *The Girl in the Box* (9–12). 1988, Little, Brown $12.95 (978-0-316-77935-7). A high school girl is kidnapped by a masked man and kept prisoner in a damp, dark room. (Rev: BL 11/1/88; SLJ 10/88; VOYA 2/89)

5444 Sedgwick, Marcus. *Revolver* (7–10). 2010, Roaring Brook $16.99 (978-1-59643-592-6). In the early 20th century above the Arctic Circle, young Sig's father has been found frozen to death; Sig's sister and step-mother go for help and Sig is alone when a stranger bearing a Colt revolver arrives demanding gold he is owed. Printz Honor 2011; YALSA Top Ten Best Fiction for Young Adults 2011. ∩ ℮ Lexile 890L (Rev: BL 5/1/10; HB 3–4/10; LMC 5–6/10; SLJ 4/10)

5445 Seil, William. *Sherlock Holmes and the Titanic Tragedy: A Case to Remember* (10–12). 1996, Breese paper $14.95 (978-0-947533-35-9). Holmes and Watson are aboard the *Titanic* guarding a young secret agent who is transporting important submarine plans for the U. S. Navy. (Rev: SLJ 4/97)

5446 Shannon, John. *The Devils of Bakersfield* (9–12). 2008, Pegasus $25.00 (978-1-933648-29-3). This tenth book in the series brings Jack Liffey the thoughtful PI and his daughter, Maeve, to Bakersfield to face a storm of anti-Satanist hysteria. (Rev: BL 3/15/08)

5447 Sharratt, Mary. *The Vanishing Point* (9–12). 2006, Houghton Mifflin paper $12.95 (978-0-618-46233-9). In this well-researched historical mystery with a dash of gothic tension, Hannah travels to colonial Maryland to reunite with her sister and the evidence makes her doubt the report that her sister has died in childbirth. (Rev: BL 7/06)

5448 Shepard, Sara. *Flawless: A Pretty Little Liars Novel* (9–12). 2007, HarperTeen $16.99 (978-0-06-088733-9). Mystery and suspense add to the appeal of this sequel to *Pretty Little Liars* (2006), in which the girls are stalked by a mystery person who threatens to reveal their damaging secrets. (Rev: SLJ 7/07)

5449 Shepard, Sara. *Pretty Little Liars* (11–12). 2006, HarperTempest $16.99 (978-0-06-088730-8). Spencer, Emily, Aria, and Hanna are privileged teens who were once part of a five-strong friendship, but Alison disappeared and now the girls are receiving sinister messages from someone called "A"; this is a suspenseful story with a quick-moving plot. (Rev: SLJ 11/06)

5450 Shoemaker, Tim. *Code of Silence: Living a Lie Comes with a Price* (7–10). 2012, Zonderkidz $14.99 (978-031072653-1). Three 13-year-old witnesses to a violent crime must choose between remaining silent and coming forward to clear an innocent man. ℮ (Rev: BL 5/1/12*; SLJ 8/12)

5451 Siciliano, Sam. *The Angel of the Opera: Sherlock Holmes Meets the Phantom of the Opera* (9–12). 1994, Penzler Books $21.95 (978-1-883402-46-4). Sherlock Holmes's cousin is the narrator in this mystery that takes place at the Paris Opera house. (Rev: BL 5/15/94; SLJ 12/94)

5452 Simmons, Michael. *Finding Lubchenko* (7–10). 2005, Penguin paper $16.99 (978-1-59514-021-0). Evan Macalister, a 16-year-old slacker, steals high-value computer equipment from his father's business and sells it for spending cash, but he faces a moral dilemma when he discovers evidence that could clear

his father of murder charges on a laptop he's stolen; a funny, offbeat novel. (Rev: BCCB 7–8/05; SLJ 6/05; VOYA 12/04)

5453 Simmons, Michael. *The Rise of Lubchenko* (8–11). 2006, Penguin $16.99 (978-1-59514-061-6). in this sequel to *Finding Lubchenko* (2005), wealthy Evan Macalister is informed that his father's business partner is planning to smuggle a live smallpox virus into Europe. (Rev: BL 9/1/06; SLJ 9/06)

5454 Simpson, Marcia. *Sound Tracks* (10–12). 2001, Poisoned Pen $24.95 (978-1-890208-72-1). When Lisa Romero moves to Wrangell, Alaska, to manage a floating bookmobile, strange events occur, such as whales getting sick and the death of a marine biologist. (Rev: BL 6/1–15/01*)

5455 Singleton, Linda Joy. *Buried* (8–12). Series: Goth Girl Mysteries. 2012, Flux paper $9.95 (978-0-7387-1958-0). Thorn, a Goth high school student who has the ability to "find" lost objects, is newly living in Nevada when she becomes embroiled in a mystery involving a dead child; this paranormal mystery is a quick read. ℮ (Rev: SLJ 5/1/12; VOYA 2/12)

5456 Slater, Susan. *Thunderbird* (10–12). 2002, Intrigue $23.95 (978-1-890768-41-6). Tommy Spottedhorse is confronted with a disturbing mystery involving mutilated animals, UFOs, and his own girlfriend in this Ben Pecos story. (Rev: BL 1/1–15/02)

5457 Sloan, Kay. *The Patron Saint of Red Chevys: A Novel* (11–12). 2004, Permanent $21.95 (978-1-57962-104-9). Years after her mother was murdered in Mississippi, daughter Jubilee Starling, who has made a new life for herself in California, looks back and decides to investigate. (Rev: BL 6/1–15/04; SLJ 12/04)

5458 Smith, Scott. *The Ruins* (11–12). 2006, Knopf $24.95 (978-1-4000-4387-3). Two American couples on vacation in Mexico find themselves far out of their depth in this thriller suitable for mature teens. ∩ (Rev: BL 7/06; SLJ 12/06)

5459 Sniegoski, Tom. *Sleeper Code* (8–12). Series: Sleeper Conspiracy. 2006, Penguin paper $6.99 (978-1-59514-052-4). In this suspenseful adventure, Tom discovers that his narcolepsy is the result of government intervention and realizes he cannot trust anyone. (Rev: SLJ 8/06)

5460 Snyder, Keith. *Trouble Comes Back* (10–12). 1999, Walker $22.95 (978-0-8027-3338-2). Jason Keltner and his buddies Robert and Martin try to protect a drugged-out rock star's daughter. (Rev: BL 9/15/99; VOYA 2/00)

5461 Soos, Troy. *Burning Bridges* (9–12). 2004, Kensington paper $6.99 (978-0-7582-0624-4). In late 19th-century New York, passions run high regarding merging Manhattan and Brooklyn — even to the point of murder? (Rev: SLJ 12/04)

5462 Sorrells, Walter. *Club Dread* (8–11). 2006, Dutton paper $10.99 (978-0-525-47618-4). In this thrilling, action-packed sequel to *Fake I.D.* (2004), 16-year-old Chass has formed a band in San Francisco but witnesses a murder and becomes drawn into the investigation. (Rev: BL 1/1–15/06; SLJ 3/06)

5463 Sorrells, Walter. *Fake I.D.* (8–11). 2005, Dutton $12.99 (978-0-525-47514-9). On the run with her mother since she was a baby, 16-year-old Chastity Pureheart has only six days to find out what happened to her mother or face placement in foster care. (Rev: BL 5/1/05*; SLJ 6/05)

5464 Sorrells, Walter. *First Shot* (7–12). 2007, Dutton $16.99 (978-0-525-47801-0). In this taut teen thriller set at a New England boarding school, a young man named David Crandall is beset with problems: his own feelings of inadequacy; his mother's murder, his father's emotional and physical abuse, and above all the suspicion that his father is the murderer. (Rev: BL 9/15/07; SLJ 3/08)

5465 Sorrells, Walter. *The Silent Room* (8–11). 2006, Dutton $16.99 (978-0-525-47697-9). Oz is wrongly sent to an institution for wayward boys in a remote Florida swamp and hatches a desperate plot to escape after learning that he and his roommates are in danger. (Rev: BL 5/1/06; SLJ 7/06)

5466 Sorrells, Walter. *Whiteout* (7–12). Series: Hunted. 2009, Dutton $15.99 (978-0-525-42141-2). Sixteen-year-old Chass is determined to work out who's stalking herself and her mother rather than relocate yet again in this third installment in the series. **e** Lexile HL530L (Rev: BLO 8/20/09; SLJ 1/10; VOYA 10/09)

5467 Speart, Jessica. *Restless Waters* (11–12). 2005, Severn $28.95 (978-0-7278-6274-7). Now working in Hawaii, Fish and Wildlife agent Rachel Porter uncovers illegal animal trading in a fast-paced novel suitable for mature teens. (Rev: BL 7/05)

5468 Spiller, Robert. *The Witch of Agnesi* (10–12). 2006, Medallion paper $9.99 (978-1-932815-72-6). This suspenseful story involves the mysterious deaths of students competing in the Knowledge Boat competition and their teacher's efforts to find the culprit. (Rev: SLJ 11/06)

5469 Spradlin, Michael P. *To Hawaii, with Love* (7–10). Series: Spy Goddess. 2006, HarperCollins $15.99 (978-0-06-059410-7). This latest action-filled thriller has 15-year-old Rachel racing to recover an ancient Hawaiian artifact before it is seized by an evil foe. (Rev: BL 5/1/06)

5470 Squires, Susan. *No More Lies* (11–12). 2003, Spell paper $6.99 (978-0-505-52566-6). Psychiatrist Holland Banks, plagued by voices in her head, discovers she has a telepathic link with the investigative reporter who is dogging her footsteps; for mature teens. (Rev: BL 10/15/03)

5471 Steinbeck, Thomas. *In the Shadow of the Cypress* (10–12). 2010, Gallery $25 (978-143916825-7). When marine biologist Luke finds a 1906 diary mentioning ancient Chinese treasure lost along the California coast, he sets out to look for it and finds more than he anticipated. ∩ **e** (Rev: BL 4/1/10*)

5472 Steiner, Barbara. *Dreamstalker* (8–12). 1992, Avon paper $3.50 (978-0-380-76611-6). A girl wonders if she's psychic when her terrifying nightmares start coming true. (Rev: BL 3/15/92)

5473 Steiner, Barbara. *Spring Break* (7–10). 1996, Scholastic paper $3.99 (978-0-590-54419-1). Five high schoolers rent a haunted house where they contend with odd appearances and disappearances, arson, and a skeleton. (Rev: SLJ 12/96)

5474 Stewart, Sean. *Perfect Circle* (9–12). 2004, Small Beer paper $15.00 (978-1-931520-11-9). DK, a down-on-his-luck father who communicates with the dead, finds himself in the middle of a ghostly murder mystery. (Rev: BL 6/1–15/04)

5475 Strachan, Mari. *The Earth Hums in B Flat* (10–12). 2009, Canongate $24 (978-184767192-9). As she dreams, 12-year-old Gwenni happily glides above her Welsh village watching the people below until she spies something strange that causes her to seek answers and unravel lives. **e** (Rev: BL 4–5/09)

5476 Strasser, Todd. *For Money and Love* (9–12). Series: Mob Princess. 2007, Simon & Schuster paper $8.99 (978-1-4169-3533-9). Kate Blessing is a happy high school senior until things go wrong with her boyfriend and mob family and she has to take charge. (Rev: SLJ 9/07)

5477 Strasser, Todd. *Kill You Last* (9–12). 2011, Egmont $16.99 (978-160684024-5). Shelby's dad becomes a prime murder suspect when three of the girls he photographs for fashion disappear. ∩ **e** (Rev: BL 2/1/12; SLJ 2/12)

5478 Strasser, Todd. *Wish You Were Dead* (8–12). 2009, Egmont $16.99 (978-1-60684-007-8); LB $19.99 (978-1-60684-049-8). In this technology-filled thriller, Madison seeks the identity of a local killer — and her own cyberstalker — by unraveling clues in blog posts and Facebook conversations. ∩ **e** Lexile HL650L (Rev: BL 10/1/09; LMC 11–12/09; SLJ 10/09; VOYA 12/09)

5479 Sturman, Jennifer. *And Then Everything Unraveled* (7–10). 2009, Scholastic $16.99 (978-054508722-3). Delia Truesdale investigates her mother's disappearance at the same time as she tries to adapt to her new life in Manhattan with two very different aunts. **e** (Rev: BL 7/09; SLJ 8/09)

5480 Sturman, Jennifer. *The Hunt* (9–12). 2007, Red Dress Ink paper $13.95 (978-0-373-89570-0). With an intriguing and intermingled cast of characters this story involves Rachel who, amid celebrations of both a promising professional future and marital engagement, discovers the disappearance of her friend Hilary and sets out to find her, entangling herself in a perilous mystery. (Rev: BL 11/15/07)

5481 Sturman, Jennifer. *The Jinx* (10–12). 2005, Red Dress Ink paper $12.95 (978-0-373-89540-3). In this sequel to *The Pact* (2004), investment banker Rachel Benjamin's trip to Boston to do a little business and visit her boyfriend does not go as she expected. (Rev: BL 12/15/05)

5482 Sturman, Jennifer. *The Key* (10–12). 2006, Red Dress Ink paper $13.95 (978-0-373-89603-5). Investment banker and part-time sleuth Rachel Benjamin is accused of murdering her boss and works to clear her name. (Rev: BL 12/1/06)

5483 Tey, Josephine. *The Daughter of Time* (10–12). 1952, Macmillan paper $12.00 (978-0-684-80386-9). A classic mystery story that travels in time from the present to the reign of Richard III.

5484 Thrasher, Travis. *Admission* (10–12). 2006, Moody paper $12.99 (978-0-8024-8671-4). Jake sets out to solve a mystery involving old friends from his days (some of which he would rather forget) at a Christian college. (Rev: BL 4/15/06*)

5485 Thurlo, Aimée, and David Thurlo. *Enemy Way* (10–12). 1998, Forge $23.95 (978-0-312-85520-8). The geography on the Southwest figures prominently in this mystery involving Ella Clah of the Navajo police force, gang warfare, a murder, and skinwalkers, or Navajo witches. (Rev: BL 9/15/98; SLJ 1/99)

5486 Thurlo, Aimée, and David Thurlo. *Prey for a Miracle* (9–12). Series: Sister Agatha Mysteries. 2006, Minotaur $24.95 (978-0-312-32210-6). Sister Agatha and her Harley are at it again, this time trying to solve the mystery of a young mother's car accident and to raise money for the New Mexico convent. (Rev: SLJ 9/06)

5487 Unger, Lisa. *Fragile* (11–12). 2010, Crown $24 (978-030739399-9). When a teen girl goes missing in a quiet suburban town, the adults must sort out the web of secrets and hidden relationships of their own lives as they continue to search; for mature readers. ⌒ e (Rev: BL 7/10)

5488 Updale, Eleanor. *Montmorency and the Assassins* (7–10). 2006, Scholastic $16.99 (978-0-439-68343-2). Montmorency and Lord George Fox-Selwyn, plus some teen helpers, investigate bomb-planting anarchists in this Victorian mystery that ranges from London to Florence to New Jersey. (Rev: BL 3/15/06; SLJ 5/06; VOYA 2/06)

5489 Updale, Eleanor. *Montmorency's Revenge* (7–10). Series: Montmorency. 2007, Scholastic $16.99 (978-0-439-81373-0). Lord George Fox-Selwyn has been murdered, and this leads to the pursuit of revenge by his powerful group of friends in this fourth installment in the action-packed series. (Rev: BCCB 5/07; BL 7/07; HB 7–8/07; SLJ 8/07)

5490 Valentine, Jenny. *Me, the Missing, and the Dead* (9–12). 2008, HarperTeen $16.99 (978-0-06-085068-5). Sixteen-year-old Lucas, whose father has been missing for years, becomes obsessed with learning more about Violet, whose ashes were mysteriously left behind in a taxi; published in the U.K. as *Finding Violet Park*, this award-winning coming-of-age novel set in London blends humor, mystery, and magical realism. (Rev: BL 3/1/08; SLJ 4/08)

5491 Van Tine, Stuart M. *A Fine and Private War* (10–12). 2002, Force paper $24.95 (978-0-9717394-0-6). A fast-paced, high-tech story about wealthy families seeking to recover their offspring from a terrorist named Jinnah. (Rev: BL 6/1–15/02)

5492 Varrato, Tony. *Fakie* (7–10). 2008, Lobster paper $7.95 (978-1-897073-79-7). Danny and his mother, in the Witness Protection Program since Danny's father's murder, stay one step ahead of the bad guys in this suspenseful story. (Rev: BL 4/1/08)

5493 Vaughn, Carrie. *After the Golden Age* (10–12). 2011, Tor $24.99 (978-0-7653-2555-6). Called in to locate evidence for a tax evasion trial, forensic accountant Celia accidentally uncovers some unsettling truths about her superhero family and about her city. e (Rev: SLJ 6/11)

5494 Veryan, Patricia. *The Riddle of Alabaster Royal* (10–12). 1997, St. Martin's $23.95 (978-0-312-17121-6). Set in Regency England, this witty mystery novel involves Captain Jack Vesper and lovely Consuela Jones, who believes that her father was murdered on Vesper's estate. (Rev: SLJ 4/98)

5495 Vrettos, Adrienne Maria. *Sight* (8–10). 2007, Simon & Schuster $16.99 (978-1-4169-0657-5). Dylan, 16, is able to picture the details of the murders that took place in her town years before; when the killing begins again she must try to use her talent to bring the murderer to justice before the town splits apart. (Rev: BL 1/1–15/08; SLJ 3/08)

5496 Wager, Walter. *Kelly's People* (10–12). 2002, Tor $24.95 (978-0-312-30131-6). Five anti-terrorist agents track potential perpetrators in a tense and realistic story. (Rev: BL 4/15/02)

5497 Wahl, Mats. *The Invisible* (8–11). Trans. by Katarina E. Tucker. 2007, Farrar $17.00 (978-0-374-33609-7). A teenage Swedish boy named Hilmer is thought to be missing but has merely become invisible. Could neo-Nazis be responsible? (Rev: BCCB 4/07; BL 3/15/07; SLJ 4/07)

5498 Walton, Jo. *Farthing* (9–12). 2006, Tor $25.95 (978-0-7653-1421-5). A murder arranged by a group of Nazi sympathizers in 1949 England endangers Lucy and her Jewish husband, David, in this convincing and compelling alternate history. (Rev: BL 8/06; SLJ 12/06)

5499 Walton, Jo. *Ha'penny* (9–12). 2007, Tor $25.95 (978-0-7653-1853-4). In this sequel to *Farthing* (2006), Germany and Great Britain have made peace in 1949 and Britain has moved from democracy to fascist dictatorship; following Hitler's discriminatory philosophy, a new prime minister is threatened with assassination; Inspector Carmichael of Scotland Yard investigates a slew of conspirators while the plot thickens. (Rev: BL 10/1/07)

5500 Warman, Jessica. *Beautiful Lies* (9–12). 2012, Walker $17.99 (978-0-8027-2338-3). When Rachel disappears, her twin Alice is left to puzzle out the reasons why. e Lexile HL720L (Rev: BL 8/12; SLJ 9/12)

5501 Wasserman, Robin. *The Book of Blood and Shadow* (8–12). 2012, Knopf $17.99 (978-037586876-4); LB $20.99 (978-037596876-1). High school senior Nora's boyfriend is implicated in the murder of her best friend in this drama; a subplot involving a search for a mysterious divine communication device adds intrigue to this multilayered novel. ⌑ e Lexile 900L (Rev: BL 2/1/12; HB 3–4/12; LMC 5–6/12; SLJ 2/12)

5502 Way, Camilla. *The Dead of Summer* (9–12). 2008, Harcourt $23.00 (978-0-15-101370-8). Seven years after the fact and with psychological sharpness, Anita narrates the shocking story of the summer 1986 in London's Greenwich Park when she and two other outcast friends — spirited Kyle and space-case Dennis — explore the caves around the park and witness to menacing events. (Rev: BL 10/1/07)

5503 Webb, Betty. *The Koala of Death* (10–12). Series: Gunn Zoo. 2010, Poisoned Pen $24.95 (978-159058756-0). When zookeeper Teddy Bentley's coworker Kate is found murdered, Teddy finds herself struggling to fill Kate's shoes — and solve the crime — before the killer strikes again. ⌑ e (Rev: BL 6/1–15/10)

5504 Werlin, Nancy. *Black Mirror* (7–12). 2001, Dial $16.99 (978-0-8037-2605-5). Lonely Frances, 16, struggles with her Jewish-Japanese heritage and with her guilt and puzzlement over her brother's suicide in this intriguing and suspenseful novel set in a private boarding school. (Rev: BCCB 10/01; BL 9/15/01; HB 9–10/01; HBG 3/02; SLJ 9/01*; VOYA 10/01)

5505 Werlin, Nancy. *Double Helix* (9–12). 2004, Dial $16.99 (978-0-8037-2606-2). A thoughtful, exciting story about an 18-year-old who takes a job involving genetic engineering and discovers truths about himself and his family. (Rev: BL 2/1/04*; HB 5–6/04; SLJ 3/04; VOYA 4/04)

5506 Westerfeld, Scott. *So Yesterday* (7–12). 2004, Penguin $16.99 (978-1-59514-000-5). Two teenagers who help big companies identify coming trends in the consumer marketplace find themselves caught up in a mystery when their boss disappears. (Rev: BL 9/15/04; SLJ 10/04; VOYA 10/04)

5507 Wheat, Carolyn. *Tales out of School* (10–12). 2000, Crippen & Landru paper $16.00 (978-1-885941-48-0). Fascinating plots and memorable characters abound in this collection of 19 crime stories by this mystery story veteran. (Rev: BL 12/15/00)

5508 Whyman, Matt. *Icecore: A Carl Hobbes Thriller* (8–12). 2007, Simon & Schuster $16.99 (978-1-4169-4907-7). British Carl Hobbes, 17, hacks into the security system at Fort Knox — just to prove he can do it — and soon finds himself a prisoner at a maximum-security American site above the Arctic Circle — and that's just the beginning of the plot-driven adventure. (Rev: BCCB 2/08; SLJ 1/08)

5509 Wiesel, Elie. *The Sonderberg Case* (10–12). 2010, Knopf $25 (978-030727220-1). In this tense, mature courtroom drama, an ex-Nazi falls to his death in the Adirondack mountains. e (Rev: BL 4/1–15/10)

5510 Willey, Margaret. *Four Secrets* (7–10). Illus. by Bill Hauser. 2012, Carolrhoda $17.95 (978-0-7613-8535-6). Three teens accused of kidnapping a boy who was bullying them tell their story through journal entries. e Lexile 850L (Rev: BL 10/1/12*; HB 11–12/12; LMC 5–6/13; SLJ 12/12; VOYA 12/12)

5511 Williams, Carol Lynch. *The Chosen One* (7–10). 2009, St. Martin's $16.95 (978-031255511-5). In this compelling novel, 13-year-old Kyra is commanded to marry her uncle and plans a daring escape from the polygamous sect in which she has been raised. ⌑ Lexile HL480L (Rev: BL 2/15/09; HB 5–6/09; LMC 10/09; SLJ 7/1/09)

5512 Williams, Katie. *The Space Between Trees* (8–12). 2010, Chronicle $16.99 (978-0-8118-7175-4). Sixteen-year-old Evie, a loner given to making up stories, must grow up when the body of a classmate is found and she is drawn into the investigation. e Lexile 850L (Rev: BLO 4/1/10; LMC 8–9/10; SLJ 5/10)

5513 Windle, J. M. *Veiled Freedom* (11–12). 2009, Tyndale paper $13.99 (978-14143147-5-4). Two Americans — a female Christian relief worker and a Special Forces veteran — and an Afghani interpreter find themselves embroiled in political intrigue and unrest in Afghanistan; for mature readers. e (Rev: BL 4–5/09)

5514 Winslow, Emily. *The Whole World* (11–12). 2010, Delacorte $25 (978-038534288-9). American college students Polly and Liv meet while studying abroad at Cambridge University and become fast friends, but dark secrets are revealed when they both develop a crush on a male student who ends up dead; for mature readers. (Rev: BLO 2/1–15/10)

5515 Wolf, Jennifer Shaw. *Breaking Beautiful* (8–11). 2012, Walker $16.99 (978-080272352-9). Allie, 18, survived the accident that killed her boyfriend Trip, but she doesn't remember anything about it; however, she does know that Trip was not as perfect as he seemed.

e (Rev: BLO 4/15/12; LMC 3–4/12; SLJ 3/12; VOYA 2/12)

5516 Woods, Paula L., ed. *Spooks, Spies, and Private Eyes: Black Mystery, Crime, and Suspense Fiction* (9–12). 1995, Doubleday $22.95 (978-0-385-48082-6). Short mysteries by such African American writers as Richard Wright (*The Man Who Killed a Shadow*) and George Schuyler (*The Shoemaker Murder*). (Rev: BL 11/15/95)

5517 Wynne-Jones, Tim. *The Uninvited* (9–12). 2009, Candlewick $16.99 (978-076363984-6). NYU student Mimi Shapiro, recovering from an affair with a professor, retreats to her father's remote house in Canada and there discovers a hitherto-unknown half-brother and an unsettling intruder. Lexile HL630L (Rev: BL 5/1/09; HB 5–6/09*; LMC 8–9/09; SLJ 7/1/09; VOYA 6/09)

5518 Yancey, Richard. *The Highly Effective Detective* (9–12). Series: Teddy Ruzak Mysteries. 2006, Thomas Dunne $23.95 (978-0-312-34752-9). Security guard Teddy Ruzak embarks on his dream career — detective work — after receiving his inheritance, but must learn the ropes the hard way as he tries to solve cases in a Tennessee small town. **e** (Rev: BL 3/15/06; SLJ 6/06)

5519 Yovanoff, Brenna. *Paper Valentine* (9–12). 2013, Penguin $17.99 (978-159514599-4). Hannah and the ghost of her recently deceased friend Lillian form an unlikely crime-solving duo. **e** Lexile 970L (Rev: BL 12/15/12; HB 3–4/13; SLJ 2/13)

Romances

5520 Abu-Jaber, Diana. *Crescent* (11–12). 2003, Norton $24.95 (978-0-393-05747-8). Historical fantasy, contemporary fact, and passionate romance are combined in this rich story of a young couple living in America and sharing Iraqi roots. (Rev: BL 3/15/03)

5521 Ahern, Cecelia. *Rosie Dunne* (9–12). 2005, Hyperion $22.95 (978-1-4013-0091-3). Four decades of correspondence between Alex and his best friend Rosie reveal the pitfalls and triumphs of their intense relationship. (Rev: BL 1/1–15/05)

5522 Aidan, Pamela. *An Assembly Such as This: A Novel of Fitzwilliam Darcy, Gentleman* (9–12). 2006, Simon & Schuster paper $14.00 (978-0-7432-9134-7). Mr. Darcy (of *Pride and Prejudice*) tells his side of the story as he falls in love with Elizabeth Bennet. (Rev: BL 5/1/06)

5523 Alcott, Louisa May. *A Long Fatal Love Chase* (9–12). 1996, Dell paper $6.99 (978-0-440-22301-6). Written in 1866, this racy tale about Rosamond is melodramatic but intriguing, dramatizing the plight of women in oppressive times. (Rev: BL 9/15/95; SLJ 2/96)

5524 Allenbaugh, Kay, ed. *Chocolate for a Lover's Heart: Soul-Soothing Stories That Celebrate the Power of Love* (10–12). Series: Chocolate. 1999, Simon & Schuster paper $11.00 (978-0-684-86298-9). This collection of 49 stories tells how love conquers all and shines through in spite of misunderstandings, unfaithfulness, illness, or death. (Rev: SLJ 7/99)

5525 Anderson, Catherine. *My Sunshine* (11–12). 2005, Signet paper $7.99 (978-0-451-21380-8). Laura, living with brain damage from a swimming accident, accepts a job as a kennel keeper and her joie de vivre and skill with animals intrigue her boss, vet Isaiah Coulter; a warm novel suitable for mature teens. (Rev: BL 1/1–15/05)

5526 Anderson, Katie D. *Kiss and Make Up* (7–10). 2012, Amazon Children's $16.99 (978-0-761-46316-0). Sixteen-year-old Emerson can read people's minds through a kiss and sets out to rescue her academic career using this strategy, in the process finding a neat guy called Edwin. **Ω e** (Rev: BL 11/15/12; SLJ 11/12; VOYA 12/12)

5527 Arnold, Judith. *Meet Me in Manhattan* (11–12). 2010, Health Communications paper $13.95 (978-07573153-3-6). High school sweethearts Erika and Ted reconnect years later when they are both successful and working in Manhattan, but Ted wonders whether to give his heart again; for mature readers. **e** (Rev: BLO 9/1–15/10)

5528 Attenberg, Jami. *Instant Love* (9–12). 2006, Crown $21 (978-0-307-33782-5). Four young women search for love and romance, looking for maturity and self-knowledge as much as for mates. (Rev: SLJ 9/06)

5529 Balogh, Mary. *Slightly Tempted* (11–12). 2004, Dell paper $5.99 (978-0-440-24106-5). In the fourth installment in the popular Bedwyn family saga, 18-year-old Morgan meets and eventually wins the heart of Gervase Ashford as together they search for Morgan's brother, Alleyne, who's gone missing after the Battle of Waterloo; for mature teens. (Rev: BL 12/15/03)

5530 Baratz-Logsted, Lauren. *Crazy Beautiful* (7–10). 2009, Houghton Mifflin $16 (978-0-547-22307-0). This high school romance chronicles the unlikely attraction between the beautiful and popular Aurora and Lucius, the alienated loner who sports steel hooks after accidentally blowing his hands off in a mysterious accident. **e** Lexile 910L (Rev: BLO 8/20/09; SLJ 12/09; VOYA 12/09)

5531 Baratz-Logsted, Lauren. *How Nancy Drew Saved My Life* (11–12). 2006, Red Dress Ink paper $13.95 (978-0-373-89591-5). Charlotte takes a position as a nanny for a wealthy couple in Iceland and finds that her situation begins to mirror Jane Eyre's. (Rev: BL 9/1/06)

5532 Barnholdt, Lauren. *The Thing About the Truth* (9–12). 2012, Simon & Schuster $16.99 (978-1-4424-

3460-8). Lies and the complications they cause are at the heart of this novel about Kelsey and Isaac, both new students at Concordia Public with troubled histories; romance and drama are combined in the narratives told from alternating perspectives. **e** (Rev: SLJ 9/12; VOYA 8/12)

5533 Bat-Ami, Miriam. *Two Suns in the Sky* (8–12). 1999, Front St $15.95 (978-0-8126-2900-2). A docu-novel set in upstate New York during 1944 about the love between a Catholic teenage girl and a Jewish Holocaust survivor from Yugoslavia who is living in a refugee camp. (Rev: BL 4/15/99; HB 7–8/99; HBG 9/99; SLJ 7/99; VOYA 10/99)

5534 Belli, Gioconda. *The Scroll of Seduction* (11–12). 2006, Rayo $24.95 (978-0-06-083312-1). A professor tells his student-lover the story of Queen Juana and her doomed husband Philip, whose lives, he seems to hope, will in some ways mirror their own. (Rev: BL 8/06)

5535 Benjamin, Zelda. *Chocolate Secrets* (9–12). 2008, Avalon $21.95 (978-0-8034-9884-6). Alex (Juliet) Martinelli falls for fire fighter Mike (Romeo) Simone despite the long history of competition between the two families. (Rev: BL 4/1/08)

5536 Bennett, Jay. *I Never Said I Love You* (9–12). 1984, Avon paper $2.50 (978-0-380-86900-8). A boy must choose between fulfilling his father's wishes and the girl he loves.

5537 Bernardo, Anilú. *Loves Me, Loves Me Not* (7–10). 1998, Arte Publico $16.95 (978-1-55885-258-7). A teen romance that involves Cuban American Maggie, a basketball player named Zach, newcomer Justin, and Maggie's friend, Susie. (Rev: BL 1/1–15/99)

5538 Bertrand, Diane Gonzales. *Lessons of the Game* (7–10). 1998, Arte Publico paper $9.95 (978-1-55885-245-7). Student teacher Kaylene Morales is attracted to the freshman football coach but wonders if romance and her school assignments will mix. (Rev: BL 1/1–15/99; VOYA 10/99)

5539 Blackwell, Lawana. *The Jewel of Gresham Green* (11–12). 2008, Bethany paper $13.99 (978-076420511-8). Fourth in the *Gresham Cronicles*, this novel set in 1880s England tells the story of Jewel and her young daughter, who leave the dangers of the city for the safety of Gresham Green and wind up making a difference in the vicar's family. (Rev: BL 8/08)

5540 Blake, Michael. *Airman Mortensen* (9–12). 1991, Seven Wolves Publg $20.00 (978-0-9627387-7-7). The poignant summer romance between an 18-year-old airman awaiting court martial and the base commander's daughter is described in this story of the loss of innocence. (Rev: BL 10/1/91; SLJ 11/91)

5541 Blumenthal, Deborah. *The Lifeguard* (8–12). 2012, Albert Whitman $16.99 (978-080754535-5). A paranormal romance featuring 16-year-old Sirena, who is spending the summer at her aunt's beach house while

her parents divorce, and a handsome but mysterious lifeguard named Pilot. **e** Lexile 670L (Rev: BL 3/15/12; SLJ 4/12; VOYA 4/12)

5542 Bly, Stephen. *The Senator's Other Daughter* (9–12). Series: Belles of Lordsburg. 2001, Crossway paper $11.99 (978-1-58134-236-9). Grace Denison leaves her stuffy home and takes a job as a telegraph operator in a town in New Mexico in this romantic novel by the author of numerous Christian westerns. (Rev: BL 3/1/01)

5543 Bodwell, Teresa. *Loving Miranda* (11–12). Series: Zebra Historical Romance. 2005, Zebra paper $5.99 (978-0-8217-7816-6). The quiet ranch life of Mercy and Thaddeus is shattered by the sudden appearance of Mercy's sister, Miranda, and Benjamin Lansing. (Rev: BL 10/1/05)

5544 Bond, Stephanie. *Finding Your Mojo* (11–12). 2006, Avon paper $5.99 (978-0-06-082107-4). Taken into the witness protection program several years ago, Lorey is now Gloria and an attorney in Mojo, Louisiana . . . where the new town sheriff is the boy she loved as a teen. (Rev: BL 10/1/06)

5545 Boschee, Rebecca L. *Mulligan Girl* (10–12). 2010, Avalon $23.95 (978-080349992-8). Ren Edwards has every single girl's dream job, shopping at upscale stores to rate the service, but her personal life is lacking until she meets golf pro Adan Bennett. (Rev: BL 2/1–15/10)

5546 Brabant, Loretta. *Kiss and Tell* (11–12). 2009, Avalon $23.95 (978-080349974-4). Irresponsible Alexis is suddenly the guardian of her two nieces and is desperate to break into celebrity journalism when she becomes entangled with Max, a hugely popular jazz singer; for mature readers. (Rev: BL 9/15/09)

5547 Britton, Pamela. *Total Control* (9–12). 2007, HQN paper $6.99 (978-0-373-77242-1). When Benjamin's hero, NASCAR driver Todd Peters, breaks his second promise to pay a visit to the boy who is ill with leukemia, children's advocate Indi Wilcox will not stand for it and goes after Peters to make good, which leads to Benjamin's granted wish and more. (Rev: BL 10/1/07)

5548 Brockway, Connie. *Bridal Favors* (11–12). 2002, Bantam paper $6.99 (978-0-440-23674-0). An handsome, undercover spy lends his British estate to a pretty young lady in return for her silence long ago; for mature teens. (Rev: BL 9/15/02*)

5549 Brooks, Martha. *Two Moons in August* (7–12). 1992, Little, Brown $15.95 (978-0-316-10979-6). A midsummer romance in the 1950s between a newcomer to a small Canadian community and a 16-year-old girl who is mourning her mother's death. (Rev: BL 11/15/91*; SLJ 3/92*)

5550 Brown, Carolyn. *Come High Water* (10–12). 2010, Avalon $23.95 (978-080347766-7). Left to run her family's inn by herself, troubled 19-year-old Bridget O'Shea seeks help from wealthy, heartbroken Wyatt

Ferguson in this novel set in 1920 Huttig, Arkansas. (Rev: BL 6/1–15/10)

5551 Brown, Carolyn. *Evening Star* (9–12). 2007, Avalon $21.95 (978-0-8034-9866-2). In this book from the Oklahoma Drifters and Dreamers trilogy Tucker Anderson seems to come across one round of bad luck after another and while in his injured state his cousins provide him the services of Addison Carter, a female doctor who, like her uncooperative patient, is not afraid to voice her opinion as they get acquainted with one another. (Rev: BL 10/1/07)

5552 Brown, Carolyn. *From Wine to Water* (10–12). Series: Angels and Outlaws. 2011, Avalon $23.95 (978-080347706-3). Three cousins charged with escorting three women from Texas to Louisiana in 1836 get more than they bargained for with the high-spirited, sassy sisters; the first book in a new series. (Rev: BLO 1/1–15/11)

5553 Brown, Carolyn. *Sweet Tilly* (9–12). 2007, Avalon $21.95 (978-0-8034-9857-0). Set in the Ozarks in a bygone era, this is the story of headstrong Matilda, a maker of moonshine who falls for the sheriff who is trying to break up her illegal business. (Rev: BL 9/15/07)

5554 Burnham, Niki. *Fireworks: Four Summer Stories* (7–12). 2007, Scholastic paper $8.99 (978-0-439-90300-4). Well-written with believable characters, these stories of summer romances occur in varied locales and are sure to please a wide spectrum of readers. (Rev: SLJ 7/07)

5555 Buzo, Laura. *Love and Other Perishable Items* (9–12). 2012, Knopf $17.99 (978-0-375-87000-2); LB $20.99 (978-037597000-9). A 15-year-old girl working after school in a supermarket develops a crush on her college student supervisor in this compelling novel set in Sydney, Australia. **e** (Rev: BL 9/15/12; HB 1–2/13; SLJ 12/12; VOYA 12/12)

5556 Cabot, Meg. *Every Boy's Got One* (10–12). 2005, Avon paper $13.95 (978-0-06-008546-9). When Jane is asked to fly to Italy to serve as maid of honor for her best friend, Holly, she gladly agrees, only to discover that her chemistry with the best man is less than ideal in this fast-paced novel that relies on e-mails, blogs, and journal entries to tell much of the story. (Rev: BL 11/15/04; SLJ 4/05)

5557 Cabot, Meg. *Queen of Babble Gets Hitched* (9–12). 2008, Morrow $22.95 (978-0-06-085202-3). Lizzie's career is taking off and Jean-Luc has finally proposed, but she has lingering doubts: Is the prince really so charming — and why is she still gaga over the best man? (Rev: BL 3/15/08)

5558 Caldwell, Linda. *The Year of Living Famously* (9–12). 2004, Harlequin paper $12.95 (978-0-373-25075-2). Kyra marries an Irish movie star and finds out that fame is not all it's cracked up to be. (Rev: BL 10/1/04)

5559 Caletti, Deb. *The Six Rules of Maybe* (8–12). 2010, Simon & Schuster $16.99 (978-1-4169-7969-2). When Scarlet's beautiful older sister returns home with doting new husband Hayden in tow and a baby on the way, Scarlet finds herself increasingly drawn to Hayden. ∩ **e** Lexile 820L (Rev: BL 2/15/10; HB 5–6/10; SLJ 3/10)

5560 Caletti, Deb. *The Story of Us* (8–12). 2012, Simon & Schuster $16.99 (978-144242346-6). Teenage Cricket contends with the crises that seem to be converging in her personal life just before her mother's third attempt at marriage. **e** Lexile HL660L (Rev: BL 1/1/12*; HB 5–6/12; LMC 8–9/12; SLJ 3/12; VOYA 2/12)

5561 Calvert, Candace. *Disaster Status* (11–12). 2010, Tyndale paper $12.99 (978-14143254-4-6). In this suspenseful, faith-based story, fire chief Scott McKenna must cope with his hospitalized nephew Cody — and Cody's new orphan status — as well as romantic advances from Cody's nurse, as he reconciles his guilt over the accident; for mature readers. **e** (Rev: BL 4/1–15/10)

5562 Cann, Kate. *Grecian Holiday: Or, How I Turned Down the Best Possible Thing Only to Have the Time of My Life* (7–12). 2002, Avon paper $5.99 (978-0-06-447302-6). In addition to the beach, the food, and the drink, Kelly's vacation in Greece is a time of learning about herself, friendship, romance, and sex; for mature teens. (Rev: VOYA 2/03)

5563 Cann, Kate. *Ready? Love Trilogy #1* (8–12). 2001, HarperCollins paper $6.95 (978-0-06-440869-1). In the first book of a British romantic trilogy, 16-year-old Collette falls for Art, who is both rich and handsome, but she is troubled by his unrelenting pressure for physical intimacy. The sequels are *Sex* (2001) and *Go!* (2001). (Rev: HBG 10/02; SLJ 8/01; VOYA 10/01)

5564 Clark, Catherine. *Maine Squeeze* (9–12). 2004, HarperCollins paper $5.99 (978-0-06-056725-5). College-bound Colleen struggles to keep to her parents' 10 rules while her parents are away for the summer. (Rev: SLJ 8/04)

5565 Coble, Colleen. *Lonestar Homecoming* (10–12). 2010, Thomas Nelson paper $14.99 (978-15955473-4-7). Two adults with troubled pasts agree to a mutually beneficial marriage of convenience — but issues from their past lives keep getting in the way in this action-packed Christian romance. ∩ **e** (Rev: BL 4/1–15/10)

5566 Coffey, Jan. *Tropical Kiss* (8–11). 2005, HarperCollins paper $5.99 (978-0-06-076003-8). Morgan's summer on Aruba with her father turns out to be more fun than she expected, but the discovery that her dad may be in trouble casts a cloud over her enjoyment of a new friend and boyfriend. (Rev: SLJ 8/05)

5567 Cohn, Rachel, and David Levithan. *Nick and Norah's Infinite Playlist* (10–12). 2006, Knopf LB $18.99 (978-0-375-93531-2). Nick asks Norah to pretend to be his girlfriend just for a few minutes, but that brief start turns into a long night of discovery in this romance between two intelligent and funny teens who enjoy the same music. (Rev: BL 4/1/06; SLJ 5/06)

5568 Colasanti, Susane. *Waiting for You* (7–10). 2009, Viking $17.99 (978-067001130-8). Marisa learns about heartbreak when her handsome boyfriend's eye begins to wander and her parents' marriage falls apart. Lexile HL570L (Rev: BLO 3/24/09; SLJ 8/09; VOYA 8/09)

5569 Coleman, Jane Candia. *Desperate Acts* (10–12). 2001, Five Star $26.95 (978-0-7862-3210-9). Nan, an abused wife, and her daughter go on a vacation to a dude ranch where Nan falls in love with the ranch's sensitive owner. (Rev: BL 2/15/01)

5570 Converse, P. J. *Subway Girl* (9–12). 2011, Harper-Teen $16.99 (978-0-06-157514-3). The lives of a Chinese student of English and a (pregnant) American girl struggling to learn Chinese and deal with her predicament intersect in this story of friendship set in Hong Kong. ∩ ℮ (Rev: BL 5/1/11; LMC 3–4/11; SLJ 6/11; VOYA 4/11)

5571 Cooney, Caroline B. *Both Sides of Time* (6–10). 1997, Delacorte paper $4.99 (978-0-440-21932-3). Annie Lockwood, who has been yearning for love, suddenly finds herself in the 1890s, in a much more appealing era; however, traveling through time can lack romance. (Rev: BL 9/15/95; HB 11/95; HBG 3/02; SLJ 7/95)

5572 Crane, Caprice. *Stupid and Contagious* (9–12). 2006, Warner paper $12.95 (978-0-446-69572-5). A funny romantic comedy full of musical references, featuring two 20-somethings whose initial animosity turns to something closer on a road trip across the country. (Rev: BL 3/15/06)

5573 Criswell, Millie. *Mad About Mia* (11–12). 2004, Ballantine paper $6.99 (978-0-8041-1994-8). FBI agent Nick Caruso, who's posing as a nerdy author to investigate the Baltimore mob, hires unlikely bodyguard Mia DeNero to get closer to his quarry but soon finds himself falling under her spell; for mature teens. (Rev: BL 12/15/03)

5574 Crowley, Cath. *Graffiti Moon* (7–10). 2012, Knopf $16.99 (978-037586953-2); LB $19.99 (978-037596953-9). Obsessed with a graffiti artist named Shadow, Lucy fails to realize that Ed, a young man she disdains, is in fact the artist himself; set in Australia, this novel is told in alternating voices and includes poems by Ed's friend Leo, aka Poet. ∩ ℮ Lexile HL630L (Rev: BL 3/1/12; LMC 3–4/12; SLJ 2/12; VOYA 2/12)

5575 Cullars, Sharon. *Again* (11–12). 2006, Kensington $14.00 (978-0-7582-1370-9). Tyne, a black woman, and David, who is white, realize that their romantic relationship mirrors a love story of a century before; suitable for mature readers. (Rev: BL 5/1/06)

5576 Dailey, Janet. *A Capital Holiday* (9–12). 2001, Zebra paper $6.99 (978-0-8217-7224-9). Jocelyn, the

daughter of a widowed American president, disguises herself to get away from unwanted press attention and, in her new identity, falls in love. (Rev: BL 9/15/01)

5577 Davis, Leila. *Lover Boy* (7–12). 1989, Avon paper $2.95 (978-0-380-75722-0). Ryan finds that his racy reputation is keeping him from the girl he really loves. (Rev: SLJ 10/89; VOYA 8/89)

5578 de Oliveira, Eddie. *Johnny Hazzard* (10–12). 2005, Scholastic $16.95 (978-0-439-67361-7). At the age of 15, Texan Johnny finds new value in his usual summer in London with his father when he falls in love with an older British girl. (Rev: BL 9/15/05; SLJ 9/05; VOYA 2/06)

5579 Dellin, Genell. *Montana Gold* (11–12). 2006, HQN paper $5.99 (978-0-373-77153-0). Can a bullfighter and a bull rider find love? Chase and Elle must overcome injury and help Chase's son Shane before they can consider a future together in this sequel to *Montana Blue* (2005). (Rev: BL 4/15/06)

5580 Delsol, Wendy. *Stork* (7–11). 2010, Candlewick $15.99 (978-0-7636-4844-2). Romance and Norse mythology blend in this story of 16-year-old Kat, who returns to a Minnesota town and discovers some startling facts about herself while falling for the young man, Jack, who rescued her from a long-ago accident. A sequel is *Frost* (2011). ℮ Lexile 680L (Rev: BL 10/15/10; LMC 11–12/10; SLJ 1/1/11; VOYA 12/10)

5581 Desrochers, Lisa. *Personal Demons* (9–12). 2010, Tor paper $9.99 (978-07653280-8-3). Good and evil battle in this steamy novel involving high-school senior Frannie (a Catholic girl), Luc (a first level demon), and Gabe, an angel who aims to save Frannie's soul. ∩ (Rev: BLO 8/10)

5582 Dessen, Sarah. *This Lullaby* (8–12). 2002, Viking $16.99 (978-0-670-03530-4). Eighteen-year-old Remy's complex family life leads her to avoid deep romantic attachments until she meets Dexter. (Rev: BCCB 5/02; BL 4/1/02; HB 7–8/02; HBG 10/02; SLJ 4/02; VOYA 6/02)

5583 Deveraux, Jude. *Secrets* (9–12). 2008, Atria $25.95 (978-0-7434-3718-9). This long love story is filled with hairpin turns as Cassie grows and changes from victim to strong woman. (Rev: BL 4/15/08)

5584 Dokey, Cameron. *How Not to Spend Your Senior Year* (9–12). 2004, Simon & Schuster paper $5.99 (978-0-689-86703-3). Used to moving because she and her father are in the witness protection program, Jo usually keeps a low profile at school, but in her first day at a Seattle high school she attracts the attention of Alex Crawford in this light romantic comedy. (Rev: SLJ 3/04)

5585 Doyle, Marissa. *Courtship and Curses* (8–12). 2012, Henry Holt $17.99 (978-0-8050-9187-8). Magic, history, and romance are combined in this story about 18-year-old Sophie and her debut into society in Napoleonic Europe. **e** Lexile 820L (Rev: BL 9/15/12; LMC 11–12/12; SLJ 9/12; VOYA 12/12)

5586 Dufresne, John. *Deep in the Shade of Paradise* (10–12). 2002, Norton $25.95 (978-0-393-02020-5). Adlai falls in love with his cousin's fiancee only days before their wedding. (Rev: BL 1/1–15/02)

5587 Dyan, Sheldon. *The Crazy Things Girls Do for Love* (7–10). 2011, Candlewick $15.99 (978-076365018-6). Environmental concerns, humor, and romance intersect in this story about the arrival of gorgeous Cody — an advocate of vegan food, hemp clothing, and so forth — and the interest he arouses among the in-crowd (and all the other) girls. ∩ **e** (Rev: BL 10/1/11; SLJ 1/12)

5588 Earls, Nick. *After Summer* (10–12). 2005, Houghton Mifflin paper $6.99 (978-0-618-45781-6). A love story set in the Australian summer as Alex Delaney waits to hear if he has been accepted at university. (Rev: BL 7/05; SLJ 7/05; VOYA 10/05)

5589 Echols, Jennifer. *Major Crush* (8–12). 2006, Simon & Schuster paper $5.99 (978-1-4169-1830-1). Virginia wants to become the drum major in her high school band but finds she has competition in the form of the exasperating but very cute Drew. (Rev: SLJ 9/06)

5590 Elkeles, Simone. *Rules of Attraction* (10–12). 2010, Walker $16.99 (978-0-8027-2085-6). Opposites attract in this story about reckless Carlos Fuentes and studious Kiara, a professor's daughter, told in alternating narratives. Quick Pick for Reluctant Young Adult Readers. ∩ **e** Lexile HL680L (Rev: SLJ 5/10; VOYA 6/10)

5591 Emond, Stephen. *Winter Town* (9–11). Illus. by author. 2011, Little, Brown $17.99 (978-0-316-13332-6). Evan and Lucy have been friends forever — if only during Christmas vacations — but this year Lucy has morphed into a rebellious Goth and straight-laced Evan, who faces his own problems, is determined to get his old friend back. Lexile HL700L (Rev: BL 9/15/11; SLJ 12/1/11; VOYA 4/12)

5592 Eulberg, Elizabeth. *The Lonely Hearts Club* (7–10). 2010, Scholastic $17.99 (978-0-545-14031-7). Disillusioned with high school boys, Penny Lane Bloom starts a no-dating Lonely Hearts Club that proves very successful until a nice guy enters Penny's life and club rules are amended. Lexile HL640L (Rev: BL 1/1–15/10; SLJ 2/10)

5593 Evanovich, Janet, and Charlotte Hughes. *Full Bloom* (11–12). 2005, St. Martin's paper $7.99 (978-0-312-93430-9). A fast-paced, funny story of Annie Fortenberry's Peach Tree Bed and Breakfast, its offbeat residents, a dead body, and an attractive man named Wes Bridges. (Rev: BL 3/15/05)

5594 Evans, Richard Paul. *Finding Noel* (9–12). 2006, Simon & Schuster $19.95 (978-0-7432-8703-6). A heartwarming story about a man and woman, Mark

and Macy, who meet and connect immediately but must both deal with problems that have been troubling them before creating a lasting relationship. ∩ (Rev: BL 9/15/06)

5595 Fallon, Leigh. *The Carrier of the Mark* (8–12). 2011, HarperTeen paper $8.99 (978-00620278-7-0). An American student living in Ireland, Megan is drawn to a boy in her class and discovers that they share supernatural powers. ∩ **e** (Rev: BL 9/15/11; SLJ 2/12; VOYA 10/12)

5596 Feather, Jane. *Almost a Bride* (11–12). 2005, Bantam paper $6.99 (978-0-553-58755-5). Gambler Jack Fortescu, Duke of St. Jules, wins all the possessions of Frederick Lacey in a card game and hopes also to acquire his beautiful sister Arabella; a Regency romance with a strong heroine. (Rev: BL 3/15/05)

5597 Feather, Jane. *Bachelor List* (11–12). 2004, Bantam paper $6.99 (978-0-553-58618-3). London suffragette Constance Duncan finds herself falling under the spell of Max Ensor, a member of Parliament and outspoken opponent of giving women the vote; for mature teens. (Rev: BL 12/15/03)

5598 Feather, Jane. *Kissed by Shadows* (10–12). Series: Kiss. 2003, Bantam paper $5.99 (978-0-533-58308-9). This final installment in a trilogy set in 16th-century England and featuring Lady Philippa Nielson abounds in political and sexual intrigue. (Rev: BL 2/15/03)

5599 Fiedler, Lisa. *Dating Hamlet: Ophelia's Story* (9–12). 2002, Henry Holt $16.95 (978-0-8050-7054-5). With help from her friend Anne, Ophelia comes to Hamlet's rescue following the death of his father. (Rev: BL 9/15/02; HB 1–2/03; HBG 3/03; SLJ 11/02; VOYA 2/03)

5600 Fiedler, Lisa. *Romeo's Ex: Rosaline's Story* (8–11). 2006, Henry Holt $16.95 (978-0-8050-7500-7). A retelling of *Romeo and Juliet* from the point of view of Rosaline, Juliet's cousin and Romeo's first love. (Rev: BL 9/15/06; SLJ 11/06)

5601 Filichia, Peter. *Not Just Another Pretty Face* (7–10). 1988, Avon paper $2.50 (978-0-380-75244-7). A high school story in which the course of true love does not run smoothly for Bill Richards. (Rev: BL 3/1/88; SLJ 5/88)

5602 Foley, Gaelen. *Lord of Fire* (11–12). 2002, Ballantine paper $6.99 (978-0-449-00637-5). Lord Lucien Knight's reckless ways are tamed by young Alice despite his best intentions in this romance with a touch of spy story thrown in. (Rev: BL 1/1–15/02)

5603 Forman, Gayle. *Just One Day* (9–12). 2013, Dutton $17.99 (978-052542591-5). On a high school graduation present tour of Europe, Allyson finds her reliable life turned upside down when she meets Dutch actor Willem and throws caution to the winds. ∩ **e** Lexile HL750L (Rev: BL 1/13; SLJ 2/13*)

5604 Fortier, Anne. *Juliet* (11–12). 2010, Ballantine $25 (978-034551610-7). Julie Jacobs, 25, inherits a key to a safe-deposit box in Siena, Italy, and travels there only to discover a centuries-old feud and a handsome young man called Alessandro; a lively and suspenseful story for mature readers. ᛭ ☻ (Rev: BL 7/10)

5605 Fowler, Therese. *Souvenir* (9–12). 2008, Ballantine $21.95 (978-0-345-49968-4). Separated by circumstance, teen sweethearts Meg and Carson have taken different paths in life — he, a rock star and she, a successful doctor — but upon an unexpected reunion sixteen years after their parting, find that they are still attached in more ways than they expected. (Rev: BL 11/15/07)

5606 Frank, Lucy. *Will You Be My Brussels Sprout?* (7–10). 1996, Holiday $15.95 (978-0-8234-1220-4). In this continuation of *I Am an Artichoke,* Emily, now 16, studies the cello at a New York music conservatory and falls in love for the first time. (Rev: BL 4/15/96; SLJ 4/96; VOYA 10/96)

5607 Freitas, Donna. *The Survival Kit* (7–10). 2011, Farrar $16.99 (978-0-374-39917-7). Rose's mother recently died of cancer and the girl finds comfort in the "survival kit" her mother left behind, which leads her to a new romance. ☻ Lexile 850L (Rev: BL 10/1/11; HB 1–2/12; LMC 1–2/12; SLJ 11/1/11)

5608 Freud, Esther. *Love Falls* (9–12). 2007, HarperCollins paper $13.95 (978-0-06-134961-4). Lara is invited by her father, whom she barely knows, to vacation in Tuscany where she hopes to learn more about him and meet new people, which she does: the neighbors at the nearest villa are fellow British youth who spend their time seeking activities of the wealthy and one of them Kip, starts a romance with Lara. (Rev: BL 10/1/07)

5609 Friedman, Aimee. *A Novel Idea* (7–11). 2006, Simon & Schuster paper $5.99 (978-1-4169-0785-5). A light romantic comedy in which Norah's focus switches from her college resumé to the attractive James. (Rev: SLJ 2/06)

5610 Garcia Marquez, Gabriel. *Love in the Time of Cholera* (10–12). Trans. by Edith Grossman. 1988, Knopf $30.00 (978-0-394-56161-5). The story of a love that lasts for more than 50 years but is unrequited as the two people involved go their separate ways.

5611 Garvey, Amy. *Cold Kiss* (7–10). 2011, HarperTeen $17.99 (978-0-06-199622-1). When her boyfriend is killed in a car accident, Wren uses her supernatural abilities to bring him back to life, but things don't quite work out. ☻ (Rev: BLO 9/1/11; HB 1–2/12; SLJ 11/1/11; VOYA 10/11)

5612 Geras, Adele. *Pictures of the Night* (7–12). 1993, Harcourt $16.95 (978-0-15-261588-8). A modern version of *Snow White,* with the heroine an 18-year-old singer in London and Paris. (Rev: BL 3/1/93; SLJ 6/93)

5613 Geras, Adele. *The Tower Room* (7–12). 1992, Harcourt $15.95 (978-0-15-289627-0). The fairy tale *Rapunzel* is updated and set in an English girls' boarding school in the 1960s. (Rev: BL 2/15/92; SLJ 5/92)

5614 Gilson, Chris. *Crazy for Cornelia* (10–12). 2000, Warner $23.95 (978-0-446-52536-7). This is a humorous romantic novel involving a Fifth Avenue debutante and the new doorman in her building, struggling artist Kevin Doyle. (Rev: BL 2/15/00)

5615 Gist, Deeanne. *Maid to Match* (11–12). 2010, Bethany $19.99 (978-076420806-5); paper $14.99 (978-07642040-8-1). In this star-crossed love story, Mack and Tillie must fight their forbidden attraction for each other — for they're both servants in Vanderbilt's Biltmore Estate — and cope with sometimes demeaning, physically demanding work in an opulent environment; set in the late 19th century, this romance is suitable for mature readers. ᛭ ☻ (Rev: BL 6/1–15/10)

5616 Goldblatt, Stacey. *Girl to the Core* (7–10). 2009, Delacorte $16.99 (978-0-385-73609-1); LB $19.99 (978-0-385-90587-9). Molly grows more self-confident over the course of this book as the motherless 15-year-old learns valuable lessons about friendship and dating, partly through her exposure to the younger girls in the Girl Corps. (Rev: BL 9/15/09; SLJ 9/09)

5617 Gordon, Victoria. *Wolf in Tiger's Stripes* (11–12). 2010, Five Star $25.95 (978-159414844-6). Journalist Judith finds herself hoodwinked into following an expedition searching for the fabled Tasmanian tiger in this suspenseful romance suitable for mature readers. (Rev: BL 1/1–15/10)

5618 Greenfield, Jacquie. *Colorado Pride* (11–12). 2010, Five Star $25.95 (978-159414919-1). Wealthy womanizer Seth has taken custody of his orphaned 12-year-old niece Nicole when he falls for Nicole's counselor at an outreach camp for troubled kids in this Rocky Mountain romance; for mature teens. (Rev: BL 9/1–15/10)

5619 Griggs, Vanessa Davis. *Practicing What You Preach* (10–12). 2009, Kensington paper $15 (978-07582322-2-9). Complications arise when Melissa Anderson finds out that the seemingly perfect man she is dating is divorced; for readers who enjoy Christian romance. ᛭ ☻ (Rev: BL 4–5/09)

5620 Griggs, Winnie. *Whatever It Takes* (10–12). 2002, Leisure paper $5.99 (978-0-8439-5138-7). Thrust together by Maddy's desire to adopt a child, Maddy and Clay find their courtship is more than make-believe; a warm romance set in the late 19th century. (Rev: BL 10/1/02)

5621 Hahn, Mary Downing. *The Wind Blows Backward* (8–12). 1993, Clarion $16.00 (978-0-395-62975-8). Spencer's downward emotional spiral and Lauren's deep commitment evoke a fantasy love gone awry. (Rev: BL 5/1/93; SLJ 5/93)

5622 Hall, John. *Is He or Isn't He?* (9–12). 2006, HarperCollins paper $8.99 (978-0-06-078747-9). When handsome Max appears at the New York City high school of best friends Paige and Anthony, neither boyfriend seeker can tell if he's gay or straight, and by the time they learn his sexual orientation, they have each found other love interests. (Rev: SLJ 8/06)

5623 Han, Jenny. *The Summer I Turned Pretty* (7–10). 2009, Simon & Schuster $16.99 (978-141696823-8). The summer she is 15, Belly is finally noticed by two boys she's known all her life and finds that other boys are starting to appreciate her too. ∩ Lexile HL600L (Rev: BLO 5/28/09; SLJ 4/1/09*; VOYA 8/09)

5624 Handler, Daniel. *Why We Broke Up* (9–12). Illus. by Maira Kalman. 2011, Little, Brown $19.99 (978-0-316-12725-7). Min, 16 and a fan of old and foreign movies, breaks up with her jock boyfriend through a long letter — the text of the story — and a box of mementos. Printz Honor 2012. ∩ ℮ (Rev: BL 11/1/11*; HB 1–2/12*; LMC 1–2/12; SLJ 11/1/11*; VOYA 12/11)

5625 Hardy, Charlotte. *Sarah* (9–12). 2006, Severn $27.95 (978-0-7278-6379-9). Sarah Shaw flees a violent husband and finds work as a governess in a Yorkshire mansion only to find herself attracted to her young ward's father. (Rev: BL 6/1–15/06)

5626 Harper, Karen. *Down River* (11–12). 2010, MIRA paper $7.99 (978-07783274-7-9). Set in the Alaskan wilderness, this suspenseful romance suitable for older teens features lots of fast-paced adventure as Lisa and her ex-boyfriend Mitch fight to survive after Lisa is pushed into the white-rapids river. (Rev: BL 2/1–15/10)

5627 Harris, Lisa. *Blood Ransom* (11–12). Series: Mission Hope. 2010, Zondervan paper $14.99 (978-03103190-5-4). Surgeon Chad and medical consultant Natalie bond over helping young Joseph heal — physically and emotionally — from the wounds wrought by the slave traders in this romantic and suspenseful novel set in Africa. ∩ ℮ (Rev: BL 4/1/10*)

5628 Harrison, C. C. *Running from Strangers* (11–12). 2008, Five Star $25.95 (978-1-59414-709-8). Child advocate Allie Hudson tries to protect a little boy from being returned to his abusive parents and finds herself on the run and seeking help from an old boyfriend; a suspenseful romance featuring wild mustangs in high Colorado and suitable for mature readers. (Rev: BL 8/08)

5629 Hart, Bruce, and Carole Hart. *Sooner or Later* (8–12). 1978, Avon paper $2.95 (978-0-380-42978-3). In order to fool her 17-year-old boyfriend into thinking she is older than 13, Jessie begins an intricate pattern of lies.

5630 Hart, Bruce, and Carole Hart. *Waiting Games* (7–10). 1981, Avon paper $3.50 (978-0-380-79012-8).

Jessie and Michael are in love and must make difficult decisions about sex.

5631 Hauck, Rachel. *Dining with Joy* (11–12). 2010, Thomas Nelson paper $14.99 (978-15955433-9-4). Charming and witty, and in way over her head, Joy Ballard finds herself hosting a television cooking show; now all she needs to do is learn how to cook — and there's handsome chef Luke who may save the day; for mature readers. (Rev: BL 11/1–15/10)

5632 Hayes, Hunter. *A Pair Like No Otha'* (10–12). 2002, Avon paper $13.95 (978-0-380-81485-5). Successful Shemone and released convict Darnell have been friends since childhood and are now romantically involved. (Rev: BL 11/15/02)

5633 Heller, Jane. *Some Nerve* (9–12). 2006, Morrow $24.95 (978-0-06-059927-0). Hollywood writer Ann Roth volunteers at a hospital in hopes of getting an interview with a very private movie star. (Rev: BL 6/1–15/06)

5634 Henry, Patti Callahan. *Losing the Moon* (9–12). 2004, NAL paper $14.00 (978-0-451-21195-8). Amy finds that her son is romancing the daughter of the man who broke her heart many years before. (Rev: BL 5/1/04*)

5635 Henry, Patti Callahan. *The Perfect Love Song* (10–12). 2010, Vanguard $15.95 (978-159315616-9). After returning home and falling for local girls, musician brothers Jimmy and Jack must deal with Jimmy's sudden fame and face situations that demand difficult choices. ℮ (Rev: BL 10/1–15/10)

5636 Henry, Patti Callahan. *When Light Breaks* (11–12). 2006, NAL paper $12.95 (978-0-451-21834-6). Almost on the eve of her wedding to Peyton, Kara Larson listens to an elderly woman telling a story of love lost and remembers her own passion for Jack, a passion that will soon be resurrected by his reappearance; for mature teens. (Rev: BL 4/1/06)

5637 Herbsman, Cheryl Renee. *Breathing* (7–10). 2009, Viking $16.99 (978-067001123-0). Fifteen-year-old Savannah's asthma begins to ease when she meets gorgeous Jackson Channing in this romance set on the Carolina coast and using local dialect. (Rev: BL 4/1/09; SLJ 6/1/09; VOYA 8/09)

5638 Hilton, James. *Random Harvest* (10–12). 1982, Buccaneer LB $29.95 (978-0-89966-414-9). A highly romantic novel set in World War I days about an amnesia victim who has forgotten his first true love.

5639 Hobbs, Valerie. *Anything but Ordinary* (8–12). 2007, Farrar $16.00 (978-0-374-30374-7). High school sweethearts Bernie and Winifred are separated when Winifred goes off to college and Bernie stays behind; the distance between them increases when Winifred is "madeover" at school. (Rev: BCCB 5/07; BL 4/15/07; SLJ 3/07)

5640 Hodkin, Michelle. *The Evolution of Mara Dyer* (9–12). 2012, Simon & Schuster $17.99 (978-144242179-0). In this sequel to *The Unbecoming of Mara Dyer* (2011), 17-year-old Mara is in a psychiatric ward, questioning whether her evil ex-boyfriend Jude is really dead, hoping to convince her doctors that she is not schizophrenic, and relying on her new boyfriend, Noah. ℮ Lexile HL590L (Rev: BLO 10/15/12; SLJ 3/13)

5641 Hodkin, Michelle. *The Unbecoming of Mara Dyer* (9–12). 2011, Simon & Schuster $16.99 (978-1-4424-2176-9). In this paranormal romance, Mara, who has moved to Miami to forget her traumatic past, finds a new love interest but continues to experience unsettling visions and find clues that she might be responsible for murder. ℮ Lexile HL600L (Rev: BL 9/15/11; SLJ 11/1/11; VOYA 10/11)

5642 Hoffman, Alice. *The Third Angel* (9–12). 2008, Crown $25.00 (978-0-307-39385-2). A trio of love stories fill the pages of this book, all having a common setting — a haunted hotel in London — and the protagonist of each is a different young woman with her own unique story and time period. (Rev: BL 12/1/07)

5643 Hogan, Mary. *Pretty Face* (10–12). 2008, HarperTeen $16.99 (978-006084111-9); LB $17.89 (978-006084112-6). Overweight 16-year-old Haley travels to Italy on summer break, finding romance and self-acceptance in this girl-empowerment story. ℮ Lexile 620L (Rev: BL 8/08; SLJ 4/08; VOYA 8/08)

5644 Hood-Stewart, Fiona. *Silent Wishes* (11–12). 2003, MIRA paper $6.50 (978-1-55166-728-7). CEO Sylvia Hansen and colleague Jeremy Warmouth work together to find the identity of the traitor who is seeking to ruin both the company and Sylvia herself. (Rev: BL 9/15/03)

5645 Hughey, Carolyn. *Cupid's Web* (9–12). 2007, Avalon $21.95 (978-0-8034-9854-9). In this hilarious, lighthearted novel, Cassie has a number of suitors, including a man her pushy Italian mother is trying to foist on her because of his Italian background. (Rev: BL 9/15/07)

5646 Hyde, Catherine Ryan. *Chasing Windmills* (10–12). 2008, Doubleday $22.95 (978-0-385-52127-7). Eighteen-year-old Sebastian and 20-something Maria enjoy midnight subway rides together in this novel that channels *West Side Story*. (Rev: BL 3/15/08; SLJ 2/08)

5647 Jabaley, Jennifer. *Crush Control* (8–10). 2011, Penguin paper $9.99 (978-1-59514-424-9). Seventeen-year-old Willow, daughter of a "hip hypnotist," decides to borrow her mother's technique in an effort to make Max jealous, but things get complicated. ℮ (Rev: SLJ 12/1/11; VOYA 8/11)

5648 Jackson, Jane. *Heart of Stone* (11–12). 2010, Severn $27.95 (978-072786825-1). Young unwed mother Sarah reaches out to battle-scarred James for help in saving her father's granite quarry in this histori-cal romance set in 1840s Cornwall; for mature readers. (Rev: BL 1/1–15/10)

5649 Jacobs, Anna. *Saving Willowbrook* (11–12). 2009, Severn $28.95 (978-072786738-4). Ella Turner's life is already challenging when she discovers that her devious ex-husband plans to sell her lovely property to a cutthroat company, and she seeks to protect her sick daughter from him; a romance for mature readers. (Rev: BL 4–5/09)

5650 Jacobs, Holly. *Pickup Lines* (8–12). 2005, Avalon $21.95 (978-0-8034-9704-7). A comic romance in which teacher Mary Rosenthal and businessman Ethan Westbrook vie to win a pickup truck. (Rev: BL 4/1/05)

5651 Jacobs, Jenny. *Cold Hands, Warm Hearts* (11–12). 2010, Avalon $23.95 (978-080347775-9). Troubled single mom Char falls for charming Max as she copes with her ailing daughter Abby in this suspenseful yet tender romance; for mature readers. (Rev: BL 7/10)

5652 Jeffries, Sabrina. *Never Seduce a Scoundrel* (11–12). 2006, Pocket paper $6.99 (978-1-4165-1608-8). In Regency London, the unconventional Lady Amelia Plume and American soldier Lucas Winter maneuver around a secret that might harm her family; for mature teens. (Rev: BL 3/1/06)

5653 Johnson, Kathleen Jeffrie. *Dumb Love* (8–11). 2005, Roaring Brook $16.95 (978-1-59643-062-4). A funny romance in which high school student Carlotta aspires both to win the heart of Pete and to write a novel. (Rev: BL 9/15/05; SLJ 11/05)

5654 Johnson, RM. *Stacie and Cole* (10–12). 2007, Hyperion paper $8.99 (978-1-4231-0598-5). Sex, dating, loyalty, love, and friendship are the central themes in this novel about young African Americans growing into adulthood. (Rev: BL 3/1/08; SLJ 9/08)

5655 Jones, Jenny B. *There You'll Find Me* (7–10). 2011, Thomas Nelson paper $12.99 (978-1-59554-540-4). Eighteen-year-old Finley's quest for answers about faith and quiet time for practicing violin is interrupted by romance when she spends a summer in Ireland. ♫ ℮ Lexile HL560L (Rev: BL 11/15/11; SLJ 12/1/11)

5656 Judd, Wynonna, and LuAnn McLane. *Restless Heart* (11–12). 2011, NAL $25.95 (978-045122926-7). Judd's knowledge of the country music business sets apart this story of an aspiring country singer in Nashville who reconnects with her high school love just as her career takes off; for mature teens. ℮ (Rev: BLO 1/1–15/11)

5657 Jump, Shirley. *Pretty Bad* (10–12). 2007, Zebra paper $5.99 (978-0-8217-7949-1). A romantic comedy in which a fashion model reluctantly finds herself learning about the simple life. (Rev: BL 1/1–15/07)

5658 Kane, Andrea. *No Way Out* (10–12). 2001, Pocket paper $6.99 (978-0-7434-1275-9). In this romantic suspense novel, a second-grade teacher's concern over an emotionally abused child leads to political intrigue and involvement with the boy's uncle. (Rev: BL 9/15/01)

5659 Kantor, Melissa. *Confessions of a Not It Girl* (7–12). 2004, Hyperion $15.99 (978-0-7868-1837-2). Jan Miller has high hopes that love will come her way during her senior year in high school, but it's soon obvious that it won't be easy in this entertaining, true-to-life romantic comedy. (Rev: BL 6/1–15/04; HB 7–8/04; SLJ 4/04; VOYA 6/04)

5660 Kantor, Melissa. *The Darlings in Love* (7–10). 2012, Hyperion $16.99 (978-142312369-9). The three Darlings, 14-year-old best friends each in their first year of high school, share the triumphs and trials of first love; a sequel to *The Darlings Are Forever* (2011). **e** Lexile 810L (Rev: BL 1/1/12; SLJ 2/12)

5661 Kaplow, Robert. *Alessandra in Love* (8–10). 1989, HarperCollins LB $12.89 (978-0-397-32282-4). Alessandra's boyfriend turns out to be a self-centered disappointment. (Rev: BL 4/15/89; SLJ 4/89; VOYA 8/89)

5662 Kaufman, Jennifer, and Karen Mack. *A Version of the Truth* (9–12). 2008, Delacorte $24.00 (978-0-385-34019-9). The accidental death of Cassie's nasty, unscrupulous husband was actually a blessing to her, enabling her to find a job in the behavioral-sciences department at the university. Although she obtained the position through doctoring her resumé, she realizes the intelligence that had been stifled by her husband and falls in love with her boss. (Rev: BL 12/1/07)

5663 Kendrick, Beth. *Fashionably Late* (10–12). 2006, Pocket paper $13.00 (978-0-7434-9959-0). Bored with her humdrum life and humdrum boyfriend in Phoenix, Becca Davis sets out for Los Angeles, where she's determined to make a name for herself in the world of fashion. (Rev: BL 11/15/05)

5664 Kenneally, Miranda. *Stealing Parker* (8–12). 2012, Sourcebooks paper $8.99 (978-1-4022-7-187-8). Parker's happy life and balanced social relationships are turned upside down when her mother leaves her father for a woman in this multilayered novel. **e** (Rev: BL 9/15/12; LMC 5–6/13; SLJ 10/12; VOYA 12/12)

5665 Kennedy, Joanne. *One Fine Cowboy* (11–12). 2010, Sourcebooks paper $6.99 (978-14022367-0-9). This humorous romance features city girl Charlie and a Wyoming cowboy who are forced together when she is sent to his ranch to research horse-whisperers. **e** (Rev: BL 9/1–15/10)

5666 Kerr, M. E. *Someone Like Summer* (7–12). 2007, HarperTempest $15.99 (978-0-06-114100-3). Annabel, 17, falls in love with Esteban, an illegal alien working for her father, in this novel set in the Hamptons. (Rev: BCCB 9/07; BL 4/1/07; SLJ 11/07)

5667 Kindl, Patrice. *Keeping the Castle* (7–11). 2012, Viking $16.99 (978-067001438-5). Seventeen-year-old Althea must marry well to support her extended family and hold onto their rundown castle — but how to find a

suitable suitor? Set in 19th-century Yorkshire, this is a humorous take on classic Regency romances. **e** (Rev: BL 4/15/12*; HB 9–10/12; LMC 11–12/12; SLJ 6/12)

5668 Kirkwood, Gwen. *Children of the Glens* (10–12). 2004, Severn $28.95 (978-0-7278-6122-1). The farm is threatened by an unwise marriage in this third installment in the series about the Maxwell family's Scottish dairy farm, set in the early 1960s. (Rev: BL 11/1/04)

5669 Klasky, Mindy. *The Girl's Guide to Witchcraft* (11–12). 2006, Red Dress Ink paper $13.95 (978-0-373-89607-3). Jane, a quiet librarian, finds a store of witchcraft manuals and is amazed to find that the spells work — and bring her romance. (Rev: BL 10/15/06)

5670 Klein, Lisa. *Cate of the Lost Colony* (7–10). 2010, Bloomsbury $16.99 (978-1-59990-507-5). Lady Catherine (Cate), 14, is banished to Roanoke, Virginia, when she and Sir Walter Ralegh form an attachment; there, however, she meets a handsome Croatoan Indian named Manteo. (Rev: BL 9/15/10; LMC 10/10; SLJ 1/1/11; VOYA 12/10)

5671 Knudson, R. R. *Just Another Love Story* (7–10). 1983, Avon paper $2.50 (978-0-380-65532-8). Dusty takes up body building to help forget the girlfriend who has spurned him.

5672 Koertge, Ron. *Now Playing: Stoner and Spaz II* (8–12). 2011, Candlewick $16.99 (978-0-7636-5081-0). Cerebral palsy sufferer Ben struggles to wield a positive influence on his beautiful friend Colleen, who's battling drug addiction, even as he becomes reacquainted with his mother, enjoys his documentary film success, and spends time with fellow filmmaker AJ. A sequel to *Stoner and Spaz* (2002) 🎧 **e** Lexile HL580L (Rev: BL 8/11*; HB 9–10/11; SLJ 9/1/11; VOYA 8/11)

5673 Koja, Kathe. *The Blue Mirror* (9–12). 2004, Farrar $16.00 (978-0-374-30849-0). This story of first love that doesn't last tells of 17-year-old Maggy and her love for a beautiful but flawed boy named Cole. (Rev: BL 2/15/04; HB 5–6/04; SLJ 3/04; VOYA 4/04)

5674 Krovatin, Christopher. *Heavy Metal and You* (10–12). 2005, Scholastic $16.95 (978-0-439-73648-0). Sam, who attends a classy prep school in New York City, faces a difficult decision when girlfriend Melissa objects to his passion for heavy metal music. (Rev: BL 8/05*; SLJ 10/05; VOYA 10/05)

5675 Krulik, Nancy. *Ripped at the Seams* (9–12). 2004, Simon & Schuster paper $5.99 (978-0-689-86771-2). A romantic comedy series featuring a Minnesota 18-year-old named Sami who soon realizes that her dreams of immediate success in New York City were unrealistic. (Rev: SLJ 7/04)

5676 Kurland, Lynn. *If I Had You* (10–12). 2000, Berkley $7.99 (978-0-425-17694-8). In this tender medieval romance, Anne of Fenwyck, a cripple, falls in love with Robin de Piaget, who appears to reject her. (Rev: BL 9/15/00)

5677 Lachtman, Ofelia Dumas. *The Girl from Playa Bianca* (7–12). 1995, Arte Publico paper $9.95 (978-1-55885-149-8). A gothic romance in which a Mexican teenager and her young brother travel to Los Angeles in search of their father. (Rev: BL 11/15/95; SLJ 10/95; VOYA 12/95)

5678 Landvik, Lorna. *Welcome to the Great Mysterious* (10–12). 2000, Ballantine $23.00 (978-0-449-43881-7). New Yorker Geneva Jordan finds unexpected romance when she goes home to Minnesota for a month to care for her 13-year-old nephew who has Down's syndrome. (Rev: BL 10/15/00)

5679 Lane, Connie. *Dirty Little Lies* (10–12). 2004, Dell paper $6.50 (978-0-440-23747-1). Lacie Jo Baxter survives a kidnapping and becomes attracted to one of the men sent to protect her in this hilarious romantic comedy. (Rev: BL 2/15/04*)

5680 Lessman, Julie. *A Hope Undaunted* (11–12). Series: Winds of Change. 2010, Revell paper $14.99 (978-08007341-5-2). In 1929 Boston privileged Katie O'Connor finds herself working with poor but ambitious Luke McGee to help deprived children; for mature readers. (Rev: BLO 7/10)

5681 Levithan, David. *How They Met, and Other Stories* (9–12). 2008, Knopf $16.99 (978-0-375-84886-5). A collection of well-written short stories about love in all its teenage forms — straight, homosexual, unrequited, sweet, and not-so-sweet. (Rev: BL 12/15/07; LMC 2/08; SLJ 1/08)

5682 Lindner, April. *Catherine* (9–12). 2013, Little, Brown $17.99 (978-031619692-5). In this story that draws on *Wuthering Heights,* 17-year-old Chelsea learns of the love affair of the mother she thought died when she was young. ℯ (Rev: BL 9/15/12; LMC 3–4/13*; SLJ 2/13)

5683 Linz, Cathie. *Bad Girls Don't* (11–12). 2006, Berkley paper $7.99 (978-0-425-21284-4). A romantic comedy for mature teens in which bouncy Skye Wright — yoga teacher and belly dancer — wins the lottery, decides to restore a worn-out theater, and becomes involved with a hot cop. (Rev: BL 11/1/06)

5684 Linz, Cathie. *Luck Be a Lady* (11–12). 2010, Berkley Sensation paper $7.99 (978-04252378-3-0). After discovering that her mother is alive, librarian Megan West teams up with a detective to get to the bottom of why her entire family allowed her to believe that her mother was dead; a boisterous romance for mature readers. ℯ (Rev: BLO 10/1–15/10)

5685 Lon, Kiki. *Enter the Parrot* (8–12). Series: Got Kung Fu? 2009, Wild Rose paper $12.99 (978-160154459-9). Romance and mystery feature in this novel about 16-year-old Jade who is learning Cantonese and martial arts while hunting for her grandfather's missing parrot. (Rev: BL 7/09)

5686 Long, Ruth Frances. *The Treachery of Beautiful Things* (7–12). 2012, Dial $17.99 (978-0-8037-3580-4). Visiting the site where she saw her brother swallowed up by trees, 17-year-old Jenny is transported into the fairy realm where she finds danger and romance. ℯ Lexile HL690L (Rev: BL 9/15/12*; SLJ 10/12; VOYA 8/12)

5687 Love, Kathy. *Wanting Something More* (11–12). Series: Stepp Sisters. 2005, Zebra paper $5.99 (978-0-8217-7614-8). Marty recalls high school, where she and her sisters Abby and Ellie were not social successes, when she returns to her Maine hometown and finds she has attracted the attention of Nathaniel Peck; the final volume in a trilogy suitable for mature teens. (Rev: BL 7/05)

5688 Love, Kathy. *Wanting What You Get* (11–12). Series: Stepp Sisters. 2004, Zebra paper $5.99 (978-0-8217-7613-1). Ellie, a librarian lacking in self-confidence, and Mason, the popular and flirtatious town mayor, find themselves thrown together at a wedding; the second installment in a trilogy. (Rev: BL 11/1/04)

5689 Luntta, Karl. *Know It by Heart* (10–12). 2003, Curbstone paper $15.95 (978-1-880684-95-5). This teenage love story plays out in a tony Connecticut suburb torn apart by hatred and racism. (Rev: BL 9/1/03; VOYA 2/04)

5690 MacAlister, Katie. *Improper English* (11–12). 2003, Leisure paper $6.99 (978-0-8439-4985-8). Alix is determined to write a novel in this entertaining romance set in contemporary England. (Rev: BL 3/1/03)

5691 MacAlister, Katie. *Steamed* (11–12). 2010, Signet paper $7.99 (978-04512293-1-1). Dr. Jack Fletcher awakens in an airship captained by a woman in Victorian garb, and soon realizes that an experiment gone awry has landed him smack in the middle of his steampunk fantasies; for mature readers. ♩ ℯ (Rev: BL 2/1–15/10)

5692 McClymer, Kelly. *Getting to Third Date* (8–11). 2006, Simon & Schuster paper $5.99 (978-1-4169-1479-2). College advice columnist Katelyn is forced to take a dose of her own medicine and give her ex-boyfriends another chance. (Rev: BL 4/15/06)

5693 McDaniel, Lurlene. *Don't Die, My Love* (7–12). 1995, Bantam paper $4.99 (978-0-553-56715-1). A young couple, Julie and Luke, "engaged" since 6th grade, discover that Luke has Hodgkin's lymphoma. (Rev: BL 9/15/95; SLJ 10/95; VOYA 12/95)

5694 McDonald, Abby. *Getting Over Garrett Delaney* (9–12). 2012, Candlewick $16.99 (978-076365507-5). Sadie finally gets over her passion for Garrett when she realizes how one-sided this romance has been. ℯ (Rev: BL 2/15/12; SLJ 2/12; VOYA 2/12)

5695 McEachern, Shelagh. *Mr. Perfect* (9–12). 2004, Avalon $19.95 (978-0-8034-9644-6). When Verrick Grant moves to a new condo in Vancouver, she meets the impeccable and charming Lionel Parford and a gentle, sweet romance is the result. (Rev: BL 4/15/04)

5696 McGarry, Katie. *Pushing the Limits* (9–12). 2012, HarlequinTeen $17.99 (978-0-3732-1049-7). High school seniors Echo and Noah, both in therapy with their school's social worker, come to trust each other as they each explore the events that left them scarred. (Rev: BL 9/15/12; LMC 11–12/12; SLJ 9/12; VOYA 12/12)

5697 McKean, Erin. *The Secret Lives of Dresses* (9–12). 2011, 5 Spot paper $13.99 (978-04465557-2-2). When her beloved grandmother has a stroke, Dora takes over her vintage clothing store and finds friendship, romance, and some pesky relatives. **e** (Rev: BLO 12/10/10)

5698 McKelden, Shannon. *Venus Envy* (10–12). 2007, Forge paper $12.95 (978-0-7653-1585-4). A funny romance in which Venus, goddess of love, is stuck matchmaking on Earth; her toughest case is Rachel, who isn't interested in finding a man. (Rev: BL 12/15/06)

5699 McLaughlin, Emma, and Nicola Kraus. *Over You* (8–12). 2012, HarperTeen $17.99 (978-0-06-172043-7). Max, 17, runs a business helping dumped girls get over their exes but she suffers an attack of jitters when her own ex comes to town, prompting her to question her whole program. **e** Lexile 740L (Rev: BL 7/12; SLJ 12/12; VOYA 8/12)

5700 MacLean, Sarah. *The Season* (7–10). 2009, Orchard $16.99 (978-054504886-6). Lady Alexandra Stafford falls in love while solving a murder mystery in this traditional romance set in 1815 but featuring a feisty and independent heroine. Lexile 900L (Rev: BL 2/15/09; LMC 5–6/09; SLJ 6/1/09)

5701 Macpherson, Suzanne. *Hysterical Blondeness* (11–12). 2006, Avon paper $5.99 (978-0-06-077500-1). Patricia becomes a platinum blonde thanks to an experimental drug and finds that her life changes dramatically — and that she's torn between three men; for mature teens. (Rev: BL 9/1/06)

5702 Magorian, Michelle. *Not a Swan* (9–12). 1992, HarperCollins LB $17.89 (978-0-06-024215-2). During World War II, Rose, 17, and her two older sisters are evacuated to the English countryside, where Rose falls in love with a veteran who supports her efforts to become a writer. (Rev: BL 8/92)

5703 Mallery, Susan. *Sweet Spot* (10–12). Series: Bakery Sisters. 2008, HQN paper $6.99 (978-037377314-5). While running the family bakery and trying to forget the pain of the past, Nicole Keyes finds herself helping a foster boy and guarding her heart from his well-meaning, attractive coach; the second volume in a trilogy. **e** (Rev: BL 8/08)

5704 Mallory, Tess. *Highland Fling* (10–12). 2003, Dorchester paper $5.99 (978-0-505-52526-0). This romantic and humorous time-travel romp brings together in the Old West a handsome 7th-century Scotsman

and a gutsy 21st-century woman scientist. (Rev: BL 2/15/03)

5705 Mason, Sarah. *Party Girl* (11–12). 2005, Ballantine paper $12.95 (978-0-345-46956-4). Isabel Serranti, a British party planner, is reunited with a childhood tormentor when she's given the job of setting up a circus-themed gala at his family's estate; for mature teens. (Rev: BL 11/1/05)

5706 Mason, Sarah. *Playing James* (10–12). 2004, Ballantine paper $12.95 (978-0-345-46955-7). Holly, a reporter, is assigned to detective sergeant James Sabine who dislikes her in spite of the fact that Holly thinks she is falling in love with him. (Rev: BL 5/1/04)

5707 Mauser, Pat Rhoads. *Love Is for the Dogs* (7–10). 1989, Avon paper $2.50 (978-0-380-75723-7). Janna realizes that Brian, the boy next door, can be very desirable. (Rev: BL 4/15/89; SLJ 4/89)

5708 Meaney, Flynn. *The Boy Recession* (9–12). 2012, Little, Brown $17.99 (978-031610213-1). When budget cuts hit the town's high school and athlete players opt for private school, the sudden exodus provides opportunities for the remaining boys. **e** Lexile HL770L (Rev: BL 9/15/12; SLJ 8/1/12; VOYA 4/12)

5709 Mekler, Eva. *Sunrise Shows Late* (10–12). 1997, BridgeWorks $21.95 (978-1-882593-17-0). Manya, living in a displaced-persons camp in Germany after World War II, is attracted to two very different men and must make a choice. (Rev: BL 3/15/97; SLJ 7/97)

5710 Metzger, Barbara. *The Hourglass* (10–12). 2007, Signet paper $6.99 (978-0-451-22079-0). After bargaining with the devil for another chance at mortality, Ar — Earl of Ardeth, a knight from the Crusades — comes back to life during the Battle of Waterloo and meets a girl named Genie; and together, mostly in harmony, they search for the hourglass that is key to Ar's future. (Rev: BL 2/1/07)

5711 Michaels, Kasey. *Becket's Last Stand* (9–12). 2007, HQN paper $6.99 (978-0-373-77281-0). This is the final episode in the Romney Marsh Series, which involves a forbidden love between two adopted now-grown siblings whose family, the Beckets, prepare to protect themselves against their longtime enemy who will soon return to wreak revenge on them in England. (Rev: BL 10/15/07)

5712 Michaels, Kasey. *Beware of Virtuous Women* (9–12). Series: Romney Marsh. 2006, HQN paper $6.99 (978-0-373-77107-3). Eleanor Becket volunteers to pretend to be Jack Eastwood's wife and help him break up the British Red Men gang in early 19th-century England. (Rev: BL 5/15/06)

5713 Michaels, Kasey. *The Dangerous Debutante* (9–12). Series: Romney Marsh. 2006, HQN paper $6.99 (978-0-373-77151-6). Ethan Tanner, Earl of Aylesford, hopes to win the heart of beautiful Morgan Becket, one of the seven Becket orphans, in this installment in the historical romance series. (Rev: BL 4/15/06)

5714 Michaels, Kasey. *A Gentleman by Any Other Name* (11–12). Series: Romney Marsh. 2006, HQN paper $6.99 (978-0-373-77100-4). Smuggling is at the heart of this romance set in the time of Napoleon and featuring the young, beautiful, and intelligent Julia Carruthers and Chance Becket, whose child she looks after and who is trying to guard family secrets; for mature teens. (Rev: BL 4/1/06)

5715 Michaels, Kasey. *The Kissing Game* (10–12). 2003, Warner paper $5.99 (978-0-446-61085-8). This amusing regency romance tells the story of Lady Allegra Nesbitt, the fiercely independent daughter of a newly minted nobleman, and how she finds love with her London neighbor, Armand Gauthier. (Rev: BL 1/1–15/03)

5716 Michaels, Kasey. *Maggie by the Book* (10–12). 2003, Kensington $20.00 (978-1-57566-881-9). Humor, romance, and mystery are interwoven in this rollicking tale of a New York writer whose Regency characters have come to life; a sequel to *Maggie Needs an Alibi* (2002). (Rev: BL 7/03)

5717 Michaels, Kasey. *This Can't Be Love* (9–12). 2004, Zebra paper $6.99 (978-0-8217-7119-8). Molly Applegate, an extremely rich girl, trades places with a friend and takes a job babysitting for an attractive Broadway producer. (Rev: BL 3/15/04)

5718 Mills, Tricia. *Heartbreak River* (8–12). 2009, Penguin paper $8.99 (978-159514256-6). After her father's death in a whitewater rafting accident, 16-year-old Alex works through her grief and her fear of the water during a difficult summer in which she also struggles with her love for Sean. ℯ (Rev: BL 3/1/09; SLJ 4/1/09)

5719 *Mistletoe: Four Holiday Stories* (7–10). 2006, Scholastic paper $8.99 (978-0-439-86368-1). A collection of four different winter holiday stories about love by YA authors. (Rev: BL 11/1/06; SLJ 10/06)

5720 Montefiore, Santa. *Last Voyage of the Valentina* (10–12). 2006, Simon & Schuster paper $15.00 (978-0-7432-7686-3). Half-Italian and half-British, Alba, whose mother died soon after her birth, decides to travel to Italy in search of her family there in this novel that blends mystery and romance and alternates between wartime Italy and 1970s London. (Rev: BL 4/1/06)

5721 Morrill, Lauren. *Meant to Be* (7–12). 2012, Delacorte $17.99 (978-038574177-4); LB $20.99 (978-037599023-6). On a class trip to London, high school junior Julia finds herself spending unexpected time with class clown Jason; light mystery is combined with romance. ∩ ℯ (Rev: BL 11/1/12; SLJ 1/13; VOYA 2/13)

5722 Murdock, Catherine Gilbert. *Wisdom's Kiss: A Thrilling and Romantic Adventure, Incorporating Magic, Villainy, and a Cat* (7–10). 2011, Houghton Mifflin $16.99 (978-0-547-56687-0). The rebellious Princess Wisdom, a circus performer named Tips who attracts

her attention, and other colorful characters star in this tongue-in-cheek romantic fantasy set in the kingdom of Montagne. ∩ ℯ Lexile 1280L (Rev: BL 8/11*; HB 9–10/11; SLJ 10/1/11*; VOYA 10/11)

5723 Murray, J. J. *Original Love* (11–12). 2005, Kensington paper $15.00 (978-0-7582-1164-4). Peter Underhill, a 40-year-old white writer down on his luck, sets out to find his first love, an African American woman named Ebony Mills. (Rev: BL 10/1/05)

5724 Nance, Kathleen. *Jigsaw* (11–12). 2005, Leisure paper $6.99 (978-0-8439-5491-3). Romance, high technology, and terrorism are intertwined in this exciting story about Bella, who has created an artificial intelligence, and Daniel, who works for the National Security Agency; for mature teens. (Rev: BL 4/1/05)

5725 Napoli, Donna Jo. *The Smile* (8–11). 2008, Dutton $17.99 (978-052547999-4). In this story about the mysterious woman behind daVinci's Mona Lisa, we follow Monna Elisabetta through her tumultuous Italian youth and young womanhood, and her propitious meeting with the artist. Lexile 580L (Rev: BL 10/1/08; HB 11–12/08; LMC 1–2/09; SLJ 11/1/08; VOYA 12/08)

5726 Nathan, Melissa. *Persuading Annie* (10–12). 2004, Avon paper $12.95 (978-0-06-059580-7). Annie is still drawn to her ex, Jake, but the failing family business keeps getting in the way. (Rev: BL 7/04)

5727 Nathan, Melissa. *Pride, Prejudice, and Jasmin Field* (10–12). 2001, Avon paper $14.00 (978-0-06-018495-7). A modern and witty retelling of *Pride and Prejudice* with Jasmin Field playing the part of Elizabeth Bennet. (Rev: BL 5/1/01)

5728 Neale, Naomi. *Calendar Girl* (11–12). 2005, Dorchester paper $12.95 (978-0-8439-5470-8). Nan, disappointed in love and adrift, listens to sympathetic friends and takes steps to effect her own happiness in this humorous and realistic novel suitable for mature teens. (Rev: BL 1/1–15/05)

5729 Nicholson, William. *Rich and Mad* (8–12). 2010, Egmont $17.99 (978-1-60684-120-4). Seventeen-year-olds Maddy Fisher and Rich Ross yearn for love, and after their first attempts at relationships go awry, they find one another and form a deep bond that can only be expressed one way. (Rev: BLO 8/10; SLJ 12/1/10)

5730 Nilsson, Per. *Heart's Delight* (9–12). Trans. by Tara Chace. 2003, Front St $16.95 (978-1-886910-92-8). Full of jealousy, a 16-year-old boy looks back at a failed romance. (Rev: BCCB 2/04; BL 11/1/03*; HB 1–2/04*; HBG 4/04; LMC 3/04; SLJ 12/03; VOYA 4/04)

5731 Ockler, Sarah. *20 Boy Summer* (9–11). 2009, Little, Brown $16.99 (978-031605159-0). Anna's secret boyfriend, Matt, dies before she can tell her best friend (who is also Matt's sister) about their love. Lexile 940L (Rev: BL 5/1/09; SLJ 6/1/09; VOYA 10/09)

5732 O'Connell, Tyne. *True Love, the Sphinx and Other Unsolvable Riddles* (7–10). 2007, Bloomsbury $16.95 (978-1-59990-050-6). A ritzy school trip to Egypt brings together students from an American boys' school and an English girls' school in this romance that offers humor and informative travelogue. (Rev: BL 11/1/07; SLJ 3/08)

5733 Odiwe, Jane. *Lydia Bennet's Story: A Sequel to Pride and Prejudice* (10–12). 2008, Sourcebooks paper $12.95 (978-140221475-2). Jane Odiwe fills in the tale of the flirtatious Bennet sister Lydia and her life with Mr. Wickham. (Rev: BL 9/15/08)

5734 Odiwe, Jane. *Willoughby's Return* (10–12). 2009, Sourcebooks paper $14.99 (978-14022226-7-2). In this followup to *Sense and Sensibility,* now-married Marianne is sent into a spiral of self-doubt by the attractive Willoughby, who is now determined to get back in her good graces. (Rev: BL 11/15/09)

5735 Osterlund, Anne. *Aurelia* (7–12). 2008, Penguin paper $8.99 (978-0-14-240579-6). Princess Aurelia's life is in danger and she faces a marriage arranged by her father; can her childhood friend Robert save her? (Rev: BL 5/1/08)

5736 Parra, Nancy J. *The Bettin' Kind* (11–12). Series: Morgan Family Romance. 2005, Avalon $21.95 (978-0-8034-9736-8). Devastated when her brother loses her beloved horse to a professional gambler, Amelia Morgan is swept into a hasty marriage in an effort to remain close to the animal; for mature readers. (Rev: BL 10/1/05)

5737 Parra, Nancy J. *The Lovin' Kind* (10–12). Series: Morgan Family Romance. 2006, Avalon paper $21.95 (978-0-8034-9776-4). Beautiful Beth leaves her fiancé at the altar and instead travels from Wisconsin to Wyoming with the challenging Quaid Blair, proving along the way that she's more than just a pretty face. (Rev: BL 5/15/06)

5738 Parra, Nancy J. *Loving Lana* (11–12). 2003, Avalon $19.95 (978-0-8034-9617-0). Bored with life in Wyoming, Lana sets out to win a $2,000 reward for capturing a wild horse and in the process finds love with Taggart; for mature teens. (Rev: BL 10/15/03)

5739 Parra, Nancy J. *The Marryin' Kind* (9–12). Series: Morgan Family Romance. 2005, Avalon $21.95 (978-0-8034-9694-1). When her father insists that her marriage must precede any courting of her younger sisters, Maddie Morgan and her brother concoct a (temporary) solution in this historical romance. (Rev: BL 2/1/05)

5740 Parra, Nancy J. *A Wanted Man* (10–12). 2002, Avalon $19.95 (978-0-8034-3566-7). A feisty librarian sets off to rescue her younger brother Ethan, who was sent West on an orphan train, and finds romance in the process. (Rev: BL 9/15/02)

5741 Pearson, Joanna. *Rites and Wrongs of Janice Wills* (7–10). Illus. 2011, Scholastic $16.99 (978-0-545-

19773-1). Intellectually inclined 16-year-old Janice is persuaded to compete in the local beauty pageant, and learns about social relationships of all kinds. ∩ **e** Lexile 810L (Rev: BL 9/15/11; LMC 11–12/11; SLJ 7/11; VOYA 12/11)

5742 Pella, Judith. *Mark of the Cross* (9–12). 2006, Bethany paper $13.99 (978-0-7642-0132-5). The relationship between young Lady Beatrice and stable hand Philip is nearly thwarted by Philip's evil brother in this traditional Christian romance. (Rev: BL 4/15/06)

5743 Perkins, Stephanie. *Anna and the French Kiss* (9–12). 2010, Dutton $16.99 (978-0-525-42327-0). When Anna's romance-novelist father sends her to an elite American boarding school in Paris for her senior year of high school, she reluctantly goes, and meets an amazing boy who becomes her best friend, in spite of the fact that they both want something more. (Rev: BL 11/15/10; SLJ 12/1/10)

5744 Perkins, Stephanie. *Lola and the Boy Next Door* (8–12). 2011, Dutton $16.99 (978-0-525-42328-7). Lola, 17, who lives with her two fathers in San Francisco, finds herself torn between current boyfriend Max and former crush Cricket. ∩ **e** Lexile HL570L (Rev: BL 9/15/11; SLJ 10/1/11)

5745 Perl, Erica S. *Vintage Veronica* (9–12). 2010, Knopf $16.99 (978-0-375-85923-6); LB $19.99 (978-0-375-95923-3). Fifteen-year-old Veronica may be overweight but she also has good fashion sense and finds a job in a used-clothing store; there she finds unexpected romance. Lexile 710L (Rev: BL 2/15/10; SLJ 2/10)

5746 Peters, Julie Anne. *She Loves You, She Loves You Not . . .* (9–12). 2011, Little, Brown $17.99 (978-0-316-07874-0). Kicked out after her dad finds out she's a lesbian, 17-year-old Alyssa moves to Colorado to live with her estranged mother and struggles to make it on her own as a waitress. **e** Lexile HL510L (Rev: BL 5/1/11; LMC 10/11; SLJ 6/11; VOYA 8/11)

5747 Peterson, Tracie. *Controlling Interests* (10–12). 1998, Bethany House paper $8.99 (978-0-7642-2064-7). A love story that involves a modern, adult orphan, Denali Deveraux, who, though brilliant and successful, longs for the security and comfort of a family. (Rev: SLJ 2/99)

5748 Peterson, Tracie. *Embers of Love* (10–12). 2010, Bethany $19.99 (978-076420819-5); paper $14.99 (978-07642061-2-2). After calling off her marriage to Stuart, young Lizzie escapes to a logging town in Texas where she and her friend Deborah find love and intellectual challenge; this Christian romance is set in 1885. ∩ **e** (Rev: BL 9/1–15/10)

5749 Peterson, Tracie. *A Promise to Believe In* (11–12). Series: Brides of Gallatin County. 2008, Bethany $19.99 (978-076420586-6); paper $13.99 (978-076420148-6). This first volume in a romance trilogy set in Montana Territory begins with several tragedies that leave the three Gallatin sisters alone to run the family hotel and fend off the opposition; for mature readers. ∩ (Rev: BL 9/15/08*)

5750 Picoult, Jodi, and Samantha van Leer. *Between the Lines* (7–10). Illus. by Yvonne Gilbert. 2012, Simon & Schuster $19.99 (978-145163575-1). Delilah, 15, is delighted to discover the handsome fairy tale prince Oliver is an actual person who can communicate with her. ∩ e (Rev: BL 5/1/12; SLJ 8/1/12)

5751 Plain, Belva. *Eden Burning* (10–12). 1987, Dell paper $7.50 (978-0-440-12135-0). This is one of several recommended family sagas by the author of the popular *Evergreen* (1982) and *Random Winds*.

5752 Plumley, Lisa. *Josie Day Is Coming Home* (11–12). 2005, Zebra paper $6.50 (978-0-8217-7696-4). Las Vegas showgirl Josie Day saves a celebrity's life and receives a mansion in gratitude; the ramshackle place is in her Arizona hometown, where everyone believes rumors that she's a stripper. (Rev: BL 2/15/05)

5753 Plummer, Louise. *The Unlikely Romance of Kate Bjorkman* (7–10). 1997, Bantam paper $4.50 (978-0-440-22704-5). A brainy teen foils a beautiful, evil temptress and gets the man of her dreams. (Rev: SLJ 10/95; VOYA 12/95)

5754 Poppen, Nikki. *The Madcap* (11–12). 2010, Avalon $23.95 (978-080349987-4). Audacious (and very wealthy) Marianne, a 19-year-old from San Francisco, sets out to woo a noble but impoverished Brit away from his stiff, proper bride-to-be; for mature readers. (Rev: BLO 1/1–15/10)

5755 Putney, Mary Jo. *The Marriage Spell* (10–12). 2006, Ballantine $24.95 (978-0-345-44918-4). When Abby, a healer, helps Jack Langdon recover from an injury, he marries her, and their union leads to the use of Jack's magical powers to help break a spell; Regency romance and fantasy are skillfully combined. (Rev: BL 5/1/06)

5756 Quick, Amanda. *The River Knows* (11–12). 2007, Putnam $24.95 (978-0-399-15417-1). Humor and suspense abound in this historical romance about plucky Louisa Bryce, who transforms herself into an investigative reporter named I. M. Phantom. (Rev: BL 2/1/07)

5757 Rallison, Janette. *It's a Mall World After All* (8–11). 2006, Walker $16.95 (978-0-8027-8853-5). Charlotte is so busy trying to catch Bryant cheating on her friend that she doesn't notice what a nice guy Bryant's best friend Colton is. (Rev: BL 1/1–15/07; SLJ 12/06)

5758 Rallison, Janette. *Just One Wish* (7–11). 2009, Putnam $15.99 (978-039924618-0). Annika, 17, gets more than she bargained for (including romance) when she tries to get Steve Raleigh, a teen TV star, to visit her sick little brother. Lexile HL730L (Rev: BL 2/1/09; SLJ 5/1/09)

5759 Ramsay, Eileen. *Never Call It Loving* (10–12). 2001, Severn $25.99 (978-0-7278-5704-0). Fern Graham, a happily married writer, has an affair with opera star Pietro Petrungero, who is also married. (Rev: BL 7/01)

5760 Ray, Francis. *Only You* (9–12). 2007, St. Martin's paper $6.99 (978-0-312-94874-0). In this well-written romance, beautiful Sierra Grayson is focused on her career, but her life becomes complicated as her attentions turn to Blade Navarone, a wealthy builder. (Rev: BL 9/15/07)

5761 Raybourn, Deanna. *The Dead Travel Fast* (11–12). 2010, MIRA paper $13.95 (978-07783276-5-3). Visiting her friend Cosmina in Transylvania, author Theodora meets a disturbingly attractive count and learns more about the region when a servant girl is found dead with bite marks in her neck; a gothic romance for mature readers. e (Rev: BL 2/1–15/10)

5762 Reinhardt, Dana. *How to Build a House* (8–12). 2008, Random House $15.99 (978-0-375-84453-9). Harper sends a summer helping to build houses in Tennessee and learns that happiness is always possible. ∩ (Rev: BL 4/15/08; HB 7–8/08; SLJ 6/08—)

5763 Resau, Laura. *The Ruby Notebook* (7–11). 2010, Delacorte $16.99 (978-0-385-90615-9); LB $19.99 (978-0-385-73653-4). Recently arrived in France, 16-year-old Zeeta's relationship with her American boyfriend gets complicated when she's enchanted by gorgeous, mysterious Jean-Claude in this sequel to *The Indigo Notebook* (2009). e Lexile HL750L (Rev: BLO 8/10; SLJ 10/1/10; VOYA 12/10)

5764 Rice, Luanne. *Beach Girls* (9–12). 2004, Bantam paper $7.50 (978-0-553-58724-1). When Stevie's childhood friend Emma dies, Emma's daughter Nell looks to Stevie for guidance — and Emma's husband looks to her for comfort — in this romance suitable for mature teens, set at the seashore. (Rev: BL 8/04)

5765 Rice, Luanne. *Sandcastles* (9–12). 2006, Bantam $24.00 (978-0-553-80419-5). Artist Honor Sullivan fights to build a new life with her three daughters and her sculptor husband after he returns from six years in prison; for mature teens. (Rev: BL 6/1–15/06)

5766 Rice, Luanne. *True Blue* (11–12). 2002, Bantam paper $7.50 (978-0-553-58398-4). Rumer is nervous when she hears that Zeb, the man she loved who married her sister instead, is returning to Safe Harbor; for mature teens. (Rev: BL 8/02)

5767 Rice, Patricia. *The Wicked Wyckerly* (11–12). Series: Rebellious Sons. 2010, Signet paper $7.99 (978-04512307-1-3). Fitz Wyckerly lives a life of excess and irresponsibility — until his father and brother die suddenly, making him an earl overnight and leaving him with a pile of debt and the need to find a rich wife; this humorous romance is suitable for mature readers. e (Rev: BL 7/10)

5768 Roberts, Nora. *Birthright* (10–12). 2003, Berkley paper $7.99 (978-0-515-13711-8). An eminently readable suspenseful romance in which archaeologist Callie Dunbrook searches for the truth about her past; one of many recommended books by this prolific author, this is more suitable for mature teens. (Rev: BL 1/1–15/03)

5769 Roberts, Nora. *Blue Dahlia* (11–12). 2004, Berkley paper $7.99 (978-0-515-13855-9). Stella's life — and her job at a plant nursery — is complicated by her handsome coworker Logan and the ghost that's haunting her house. (Rev: BL 11/1/04)

5770 Roberts, Nora. *Born in Ice* (10–12). 1995, Jove paper $7.99 (978-0-515-11675-5). A readable romance about an Irish innkeeper and an American mystery writer. (Rev: SLJ 3/96)

5771 Roberts, Nora. *The Search* (11–12). 2010, Putnam $26.95 (978-039915657-1). Romance and suspense combine in this novel about independent Fiona, a dog trainer; for mature readers. ℮ (Rev: BL 4/1–15/10)

5772 Robinson, C. Kelly. *No More Mr. Nice Guy* (11–12). 2002, Villard paper $13.95 (978-0-375-76047-1). Mitchell is tired of his dating ineptitude and seeks advice from his friends; explicit sex scenes make this suitable only for mature readers. (Rev: BL 9/1/02)

5773 Rose, Elisabeth. *Instant Family* (11–12). 2010, Avalon $23.95 (978-080347784-1). Chloe is interested in single father Alex, but Chloe's half siblings, in her charge, and Alex's bratty daughter pose significant hurtles; for mature readers. (Rev: BL 10/1–15/10)

5774 Rose, Elisabeth. *Outback Hero* (11–12). 2009, Avalon $23.95 (978-080349982-9). Deceptions threaten to derail romance in this story of singer Stella Starr, traveling incognito in the Australian Outback, and Koologong resident Jonathan who hopes she will model clothing from his factory; for mature readers. (Rev: BL 12/15/09)

5775 Rosenthal, Lucy, ed. *Great American Love Stories* (9–12). 1988, Little, Brown $24.95 (978-0-316-75734-8). A collection of 28 stories and short novels that show the varied and changing faces of love. (Rev: BL 7/88)

5776 Rothenberg, Jess. *The Catastrophic History of You and Me* (8–11). 2012, Dial $17.99 (978-080373720-4). Brie, 16, dies of a broken heart when Jacob tells her he does not love her; in the afterlife she passes through the stages of grief, watches the actions of her family and friends, and eventually finds love and hope; humor blends with romance. ♫ ℮ (Rev: BL 2/15/12; SLJ 2/12; VOYA 4/12)

5777 Saberton, Ruth. *Katy Carter Wants a Hero* (11–12). 2010, IPG/Orion paper $11.95 (978-14091031-8-9). A funny story about English teacher Katy Carter, who is writing a romance novel even as her husband-to-be dumps her; for mature readers. ℮ (Rev: BL 12/1–15/10*)

5778 Saint James, Joycelyn. *One, Two, Three . . . Together* (11–12). 2010, Avalon $23.95 (978-080347762-9). When Liz's prima ballerina mother breaks her leg, Liz assumes responsibility for running her mom's dance studio — and discovers a pile of financial trouble, and one shining but unlikely way out — in this light romance for mature readers. (Rev: BLO 7/10)

5779 Sawyer, Kim Vogel. *A Hopeful Heart* (11–12). 2010, Bethany paper $14.99 (978-07642050-9-5). Socially awkward Tressa gains self-confidence, faith, and romance on the American frontier when her aunt sends her west to learn how to be a wife. ♫ ℮ (Rev: BL 6/1–15/10)

5780 Schindler, Nina. *An Order of Amelie, Hold the Fries* (9–12). Illus. by Robert Barrett. 2004, Annick paper $8.95 (978-1-55037-860-3). This clever and funny novel, told in a series of e-mails, text messages, and letters, traces the growing relationship between Tim and Amelie, who turns out to be a different girl than the one he thought she was. (Rev: BL 1/1–15/05; SLJ 1/05; VOYA 4/05)

5781 Schreck, Karen. *While He Was Away* (9–12). 2012, Sourcebooks paper $8.99 (978-140226402-3). Penelope, 18, is devastated when her boyfriend David leaves for Iraq and it takes her time to adjust to life without him. ℮ Lexile HL590L (Rev: BL 7/12; SLJ 6/12; VOYA 6/12)

5782 Schroeder, Lisa. *Chasing Brooklyn* (8–12). 2010, Simon & Schuster $15.99 (978-1-4169-9168-7). A year after Lucca died, his girlfriend — Brooklyn — and his brother Nico are still grappling with grief; when Gabe, who was driving that night, dies of an overdose, Brooklyn and Nico experience strange dreams and draw closer together; a moving novel told in verse. ℮ Lexile HL510L (Rev: BLO 11/17/09; SLJ 2/10; VOYA 4/10)

5783 Seilstad, Lorna. *Making Waves* (10–12). 2010, Revell paper $14.99 (978-08007344-5-9). It's 1895 and Marguerite Westing's independence and interests in astronomy and sailing have attracted only one, wealthy suitor; when she meets the attractive Trip Andrews she must choose between him and the riches that will save her whole family — a light, Christian romance. ℮ (Rev: BL 8/10)

5784 Sheinmel, Alyssa B. *The Beautiful Between* (9–11). 2010, Knopf $16.99 (978-0-375-86182-6). Shy Rapunzel-like Connelly 16, and cool prince-like Jeremy form a deep friendship as Jeremy shares his fears about his sister's leukemia and Connelly reveals her need to find out how her father died. ℮ (Rev: LMC 8–9/10; SLJ 5/10)

5785 Shinn, Sharon. *General Winston's Daughter* (7–10). 2007, Viking $16.99 (978-0-670-06248-5). Averie, whose father is a general in the Aebrian military, goes to visit a colonized land named Chiarrin and as she learns more about its culture, finds her views of many things in life — love, politics, even her father — are changing. (Rev: BL 8/07; SLJ 1/08)

5786 Showalter, Gena. *Playing with Fire* (11–12). 2006, HQN paper $6.99 (978-0-373-77129-5). Coffee shop worker Belle is suddenly transformed into Super Belle, controller of the four elements, and Super Belle in turn soon falls for Rome Masters, the secret agent sent to kill her; a humorous, quick-read romance for mature teens. (Rev: BL 9/15/06)

5787 Sierra, Patricia. *One-Way Romance* (7–10). 1986, Avon paper $2.50 (978-0-380-75107-5). A talented girl who does well with carpentry and track seems to be losing out with her boyfriend. (Rev: BL 8/86; SLJ 11/86; VOYA 12/86)

5788 Simonsen, Mary Lydon. *The Perfect Bride for Mr. Darcy* (11–12). 2011, Sourcebooks paper $14.99 (978-14022402-5-6). This retelling of *Pride and Prejudice* allows several minor characters to play larger roles in the future of Darcy and Elizabeth; for mature readers. e (Rev: BL 1/1–15/11)

5789 Smith-Brown, Fern. *Unforgettable* (9–12). 2000, GoldenIsle $21.95 (978-0-9666721-6-9). A romantic thriller about how a young woman vacationing in Maine becomes involved with an undercover agent tracking down arms smugglers. (Rev: BL 5/15/00)

5790 Smith, Emily Wing. *Back When You Were Easier to Love* (7–10). 2011, Dutton $16.99 (978-0-525-42199-3). When her boyfriend Zan leaves their Mormon community in Utah to attend college in California, a miserable Joy drives with Zan's best friend Noah to visit him, slowly shifting her affections along the way. e (Rev: BL 4/1/11; SLJ 7/11; VOYA 6/11)

5791 Smith, Jennifer E. *The Statistical Probability of Love at First Sight* (9–12). 2012, Little, Brown $17.99 (978-031612238-2). After falling in love on an airplane, Hadley and Oliver are brought back together by fate in this heady romance. Lexile 1060L (Rev: BL 2/1/12; HB 1–2/12; SLJ 1/12)

5792 Sneed, Tamara. *The Way He Makes Me Feel* (11–12). 2005, St. Martin's paper $6.99 (978-0-312-98731-2). On a bet, Dunston sets out to seduce Claire but then finds he's genuinely fond of her in this sexy romance suitable for mature teens. (Rev: BL 6/1–15/05)

5793 Snelling, Lauraine. *A Measure of Mercy* (10–12). Series: Home to Blessing. 2009, Bethany paper $13.99 (978-07642060-9-2). Astrid is a modern early 1900s young woman who plans to go to Chicago to become a doctor, but economic and romantic factors make this decision difficult in this faith-based novel, the first in a series. ∩ e (Rev: BLO 9/15/09)

5794 Sones, Sonya. *What My Girlfriend Doesn't Know* (7–10). 2007, Simon & Schuster paper $7.99 (978-0-689-87603-5). Popular Sophie falls for geeky Robin despite disapproval and disbelief from their friends in this stand-alone follow-up to *What My Mother Doesn't*

Know (2001), narrated by Robin in first-person free verse. (Rev: BL 4/1/07*; SLJ 6/07)

5795 Sparks, Nicholas. *The Choice* (9–12). 2007, Hachette $24.99 (978-0-446-57992-6). This romantic and poignant love story follows veterinarian Travis who falls for Gabby, his fiesty new neighbor, before tragedy turns their worlds upside down. (Rev: BL 9/15/07)

5796 Sparks, Nicholas. *Dear John* (11–12). 2006, Warner $24.99 (978-0-446-52805-4). John Tyree, a former soldier who's finally found the love of his life feels compelled to rejoin the army after 9/11, then worries about receiving a "Dear John" letter; for mature readers. (Rev: BL 10/1/06)

5797 Springer, Kristina. *The Espressologist* (7–10). 2009, Farrar $16.99 (978-0-374-32228-1). High school senior Jane's amazing ability to make matches among her coffeehouse customers doesn't extend to herself, but in the end . . . . e Lexile HL640L (Rev: BL 10/15/09; SLJ 9/09)

5798 Stanek, Lou W. *Katy Did* (8–12). 1992, Avon paper $2.99 (978-0-380-76170-8). A shy country girl and popular city boy fall in love, with tragic consequences. (Rev: BL 3/15/92)

5799 Steel, Danielle. *The House on Hope Street* (10–12). 2000, Delacorte $19.95 (978-0-385-33306-1). This standard Steel romantic novel involves a privileged woman, newly widowed, and her struggle to raise her family and still gain self-fulfillment. (Rev: BL 3/15/00)

5800 Steel, Danielle. *Leap of Faith* (10–12). 2001, Delacorte $19.95 (978-0-385-33296-5). Marie-Ange, a pampered orphan, is sent to Iowa to live with a wicked elderly aunt in this light romance. (Rev: BL 3/15/01; SLJ 11/01)

5801 Steel, Danielle. *The Promise* (10–12). 1978, Dell paper $6.99 (978-0-440-17079-2). A wealthy architect and a poor artist decide to marry in this romance. Other recommended titles by the author are *Once in a Lifetime*, *Now and Forever*, *Palomino*, *The Ring*, and *Season of Passion*.

5802 Steel, Danielle. *The Wedding* (10–12). 2000, Delacorte $26.95 (978-0-385-31437-4). In her 48th novel, the author combines a glamorous Hollywood setting with beautiful people and their amorous adventures and insecurities. (Rev: BL 2/1/00)

5803 Stepakoff, Jeffrey. *Fireworks over Toccoa* (11–12). 2010, St. Martin's $22.99 (978-031258158-9). On the eve of her husband's return from combat in World War II Lily meets Jake, a pyrotechnics expert in town to produce a show for the soldiers' homecoming, and falls in love for the first time; suitable for mature readers. ∩ (Rev: BL 2/1–15/10)

5804 Stewart, Sally. *Appointment in Venice* (10–12). 2003, Severn $26.99 (978-0-7278-6003-3). Sarah, a young Englishwoman, travels to Venice to work as a governess but rediscovers a lost love. (Rev: BL 10/15/03)

5805 Strohm, Stephanie Kate. *Pilgrims Don't Wear Pink* (7–10). 2012, Houghton paper $8.99 (978-054756459-3). History buff and fashionista Libby spends the summer working at a living history camp, where she meets a handsome, Shakespeare-quoting young man. **e** Lexile HL720L (Rev: BL 7/12; SLJ 5/1/12; VOYA 2/12)

5806 Sundin, Sarah. *A Distant Melody* (10–12). 2010, Revell paper $14.99 (978-08007342-1-3). Allie Miller is torn between her parents' wishes for her to marry her father's icy employee, and her own attraction to a less-than-perfect Air Force officer in this Christian romance set during World War II. (Rev: BL 2/1–15/10)

5807 Tahmaseb, Charity, and Darcy Vance. *The Geek Girl's Guide to Cheerleading* (9–12). 2009, Simon & Schuster paper $8.99 (978-141697834-3). Geeky Bethany decides to try cheerleading as a way to the heart of the attractive, sporty Jack. (Rev: BLO 6/19/09)

5808 Tanner, Janet. *Forgotten Destiny* (11–12). 2004, Severn $28.95 (978-0-7278-6095-8). A gothic romance involving a heroine with amnesia who is forced into a loveless and dangerous marriage. (Rev: BL 10/1/04)

5809 Tanner, Janet. *Seagull Bay* (10–12). 2010, Severn $28.95 (978-072786822-0). Taken in by her English Aunt Fran, Canadian orphan Dawn Stephens, 17, retreats into fantasies of future stardom until she meets Sandy, a man who absorbs her entirely; set in the 1960s. ∩ (Rev: BL 12/1/09)

5810 Tayleur, Karen. *Chasing Boys* (8–11). 2009, Walker $16.99 (978-080279830-5). El starts at a new school and finds that the boy of her dreams is already taken — by a "perfect" girl named Angelique. **e** Lexile 690L (Rev: BL 2/15/09; SLJ 6/1/09)

5811 Taylor, Janelle. *Dying to Marry* (11–12). 2004, Zebra paper $6.99 (978-0-8217-7464-9). When Lizbeth, a "Down Hill" girl, becomes engaged to Dylan, from "Up Hill," her very life is threatened and she must rely on Detective Lake for protection. (Rev: BL 10/15/04)

5812 Thomas, Abigail. *An Actual Life* (10–12). 1996, Algonquin $28.95 (978-1-56512-133-1). This novel tells of a young couple who married because of a pregnancy and of their eventual attractions to other possible partners. (Rev: BL 4/1/96; SLJ 3/97)

5813 Thomas, Jodi. *The Texan's Dream* (10–12). 2001, Jove paper $7.99 (978-0-515-13176-5). Kara O'Riley's relations with the ranch owner for whom she works become close in this historical western romance. (Rev: BL 10/15/01)

5814 Thomas, Jodi. *Texas Blue* (10–12). Series: Whispering Mountain. 2011, Berkley paper $7.99 (978-04252404-7-2). High-spirited Emily McMurray poses as a lowly ranch hand when her cousin sends along three men of marrying age, one of whom came to marry a rancher's daughter, but falls in love with the "ranch hand" instead. (Rev: BL 3/1–15/11)

5815 Thomas, Jodi. *When a Texan Gambles* (10–12). 2003, Penguin paper $7.99 (978-0-515-13629-6). In this charming western romance novel, plucky Sarah Andrews stands by her man — bounty hunter Sam Gatlin — when all others turn their backs on him. (Rev: BL 10/15/03*)

5816 Thompson, Alicia. *Psych Major Syndrome* (8–10). 2009, Hyperion $16.99 (978-1-4231-1457-4). Leigh, a serious-minded college freshman in California, wrestles with her relationships with friends and the opposite sex. (Rev: BL 10/15/09; SLJ 9/09)

5817 Thompson, Colleen. *Fatal Error* (11–12). 2004, Leisure paper $6.99 (978-0-8439-5421-0). Susan must enlist the help of former flame (and brother-in-law) Luke after her husband skips town. (Rev: BL 11/15/04)

5818 Thompson, Renee. *The Bridge at Valentine* (11–12). 2010, Tres Picos paper $14.95 (978-09745309-2-5). Farmer's daughter July falls for dreamy, introspective Rory in this 1890s Plains take on the Montagues and Capulets; for mature readers. (Rev: BL 8/10)

5819 Thornton, Elizabeth. *The Perfect Princess* (9–12). 2001, Bantam paper $6.50 (978-0-553-58123-2). In this Regency romance, Lady Rosamunde Devere visits Newgate Prison and is carried off by a dashing escaping prisoner. (Rev: BL 9/15/01)

5820 Tracy, Kristen. *Sharks and Boys* (7–12). 2011, Disney/Hyperion $16.99 (978-1-4231-4354-3). Worried that her boyfriend Wick is becoming involved with someone else, 15-year-old Enid sneaks onto a yacht he is sharing with a group of twins; a storm later sets them adrift and they must struggle to survive. **e** Lexile HL510L (Rev: BL 6/1/11; SLJ 6/11; VOYA 8/11)

5821 Trembath, Don. *A Beautiful Place on Yonge Street* (8–10). 1999, Orca paper $6.95 (978-1-55143-121-5). Budding writer Harper Winslow falls in love with Sunny Taylor when he attends a summer writing camp, and experiences all the angst that goes with it. (Rev: BL 3/1/99; SLJ 7/99; VOYA 6/99)

5822 Triana, Gaby. *Riding the Universe* (10–12). 2009, HarperTeen $16.99 (978-0-06-088570-0). Seventeen-year-old Chloé suddenly finds herself having to choose between Gordon, her chemistry tutor, and Rock, who has loved her since elementary school. **e** (Rev: BL 8/09; SLJ 8/09)

5823 Vega, Denise. *Fact of Life #31* (9–12). 2008, Knopf $16.99 (978-0-375-84819-3). Cat, known around school as a free spirit, has a new boyfriend: Manny, a popular jock. Will their romance survive or are they just too different? (Rev: BL 5/15/08)

5824 Veryan, Patricia. *Lanterns* (10–12). 1996, St. Martin's $23.95 (978-0-312-14640-5). This historical romance set in Sussex, England, in 1818, tells of Marietta

Warrington's struggles to keep the family together after her father's gambling debts drive them into poverty, and involves kidnapping, ancient treasure, sinister dealings, and true love. (Rev: BL 10/15/96; SLJ 3/97)

5825 Vogts, Deborah. *Seeds of Summer* (11–12). Series: Season of Tallgrass. 2010, Zondervan paper $12.99 (978-03102927-6-0). Rodeo queen Natalie must choose between faith and anger when she meets a handsome minister who wants to help her cope with bringing up her half siblings; set in rural Kansas this is suitable for mature readers. e (Rev: BL 7/10)

5826 Voigt, Cynthia. *Glass Mountain* (9–12). 1991, Harcourt $19.95 (978-0-15-135825-0). A wealthy New Yorker posing as a butler falls in love with his employer's fiancee. (Rev: BL 11/1/91; SLJ 4/92)

5827 Warner, Ann. *Dreams for Stones* (11–12). 2008, Samhain paper $14.00 (978-159998974-7). Vivid Alaskan scenery and strong emotions color this tale of broken and mended hearts and the struggle to become whole after loss. (Rev: BL 9/15/08)

5828 Wilkins, Kim. *Unclaimed Heart* (9–12). 2009, Penguin paper $8.99 (978-159514258-0). Constance is an adventurous 17-year-old British girl searching for her long-lost mother in this exciting romance set in the 18th century and featuring a sea voyage, stowaways, and Ceylon (now Sri Lanka). (Rev: BL 6/1–15/09)

5829 Williams, Kathryn. *Pizza, Love, and Other Stuff That Made Me Famous* (8–10). 2012, Henry Holt $16.99 (978-080509285-1). Sophie, 16, works hard to parlay her experiences in her Italian-Greek family's restaurant into success in a reality TV show while at the same time nurturing a crush for an adorable French chef. e Lexile 780L (Rev: BL 9/15/12; SLJ 8/1/12)

5830 Willig, Lauren. *The Betrayal of the Blood Lily* (10–12). Series: Pink Carnation. 2010, Dutton $25.95 (978-052595150-6). In her continuing research into 18th-century British spies, contemporary scholar Eloise Kelly investigates the life of rebellious Penelope Deveraux, who moves to India with her aloof, aristocratic husband and finds herself intrigued by their escort, Captain Alex Reid. ◠ e (Rev: BL 12/1/09)

5831 Willig, Lauren. *The Deception of the Emerald Ring* (11–12). Series: Pink Carnation. 2006, Dutton $21.95 (978-0-525-94977-0). Contemporary scholar Eloise Kelly finds a tale of romance and intrigue when she investigates the story of Letty Alsworthy, who elopes with her older sister's fiancé and then chases him to Ireland when he runs off to spy for the English during the early 19th century. ◠ (Rev: BL 8/06)

5832 Willig, Lauren. *The Mischief of the Mistletoe* (10–12). Series: Pink Carnation. 2010, Dutton $24.95 (978-052595187-2). A note on the wrapping of a Christmas pudding sets a young teacher and her new beau off on a spying adventure in this Regency romp. e (Rev: BL 9/1–15/10)

5833 Willig, Lauren. *The Orchid Affair* (9–12). Series: Pink Carnation. 2011, Dutton $25.95 (978-052595199-5). Newly minted spy Laura Grey is sent to Napoleonic France to be a governess and investigate political intrigue; there she spends time with the attractive Andre, deputy minister of police. ◠ e (Rev: BL 12/1–15/10)

5834 Wingate, Lisa. *Over the Moon at the Big Lizard Diner* (9–12). 2005, NAL paper $13.95 (978-0-451-21664-9). While in Texas working on an undercover mission involving dinosaur tracks, paleontologist Lindsey Atwood, a divorcee with an 8-year-old daughter, meets and falls in love with rancher Zach Truitt. (Rev: BL 10/15/05)

5835 Wittlinger, Ellen. *Lombardo's Law* (7–10). 1993, Morrow paper $4.95 (978-0-688-05294-2). The conventions of romance are thrown aside when sophomore Justine and 8th-grader Mike find themselves attracted to each other, despite obstacles. (Rev: BL 9/15/93; VOYA 12/93)

5836 Woods, Janet. *Edge of Regret* (10–12). 2008, Severn $27.95 (978-0-7278-6626-4). Set during the reign of Queen Victoria, this novel follows Kenna Mackenzie as she refuses an arranged marriage and is thrown out of her family's Edinburgh home with no concept of how to survive on the mean streets. (Rev: BL 4/15/08)

5837 Woods, Janet. *Salting the Wound* (11–12). 2010, Severn $28.95 (978-072786829-9). When Marianne tries to console her sister's spurned beau, she stumbles into the hold of his ship and is not discovered for days — setting in motion a series of misunderstandings and recriminations; this novel, set in 1850, is suitable for mature readers. ◠ (Rev: BL 12/1/09)

5838 Woodson, Jacqueline. *If You Come Softly* (7–10). 1998, Putnam $17.99 (978-0-399-23112-4). The story of the love between a black boy and a white girl, their families, and the prejudice they encounter. (Rev: BL 10/1/98; HBG 9/99; SLJ 12/98; VOYA 12/98)

5839 Wright, Deborah. *The History of Lucy's Love Life: In Ten and a Half Chapters* (9–12). 2008, Plume paper $14.00 (978-0-452-28914-7). Lucy is looking for something beyond what her love life with her boyfriend Anthony grants her, so she takes her ex-boss's time machine and expands her love encounters with individuals such as Casanova, Ovid, and Lord Byron, but each falls short of her expectations and each time she returns to her life in London to evaluate what she has. (Rev: BL 11/1/07)

5840 Zeises, Lara M. *The Sweet Life of Stella Madison* (8–11). 2009, Delacorte $16.99 (978-0-385-73146-1); LB $19.99 (978-0-385-90178-9). Stella, 17, becomes an intern for Baltimore's *Daily Journal* and, perhaps because of her foodie parents, is assigned to restaurant reviews; she is grateful for the help of the gorgeous Jeremy while fretting about her feelings toward her boyfriend Max. (Rev: BL 9/1/09; SLJ 7/1/09; VOYA 10/09)

329

5841 Ziegler, Jennifer. *Sass and Serendipity* (8–10). 2011, Delacorte $15.99 (978-0-385-73898-9); LB $18.99 (978-038590762-0). Gabby Rivera is sensible and down-to-earth whereas her sister Daphne is romantic and dreamy, and their views about their parents and about boys are equally different. **e** Lexile 710L (Rev: BL 7/11; SLJ 8/11)

Science Fiction

5842 Adams, Douglas. *The Long Dark Tea-Time of the Soul* (9–12). 1988, Pocket paper $6.99 (978-0-671-74251-5). Dirk Gently, private detective and slob first introduced in *Dirk Gently's Holistic Detective Agency*, returns in another hilarious series of misadventures. (Rev: BL 1/15/89)

5843 Adams, Douglas. *The Salmon of Doubt: Hitchhiking the Galaxy One Last Time* (9–12). Ed. by Christopher Cerf. 2002, Harmony $24.00 (978-1-4000-4508-2). A posthumous collection of Adams's diverse writings — essays, articles, and stories — including part of an unfinished Hitchhiker novel. (Rev: BL 4/15/02)

5844 Adams, John Joseph, ed. *Seeds of Change* (10–12). 2008, Prime $19.95 (978-0-8095-7310-3). *Seeds of Change* is an interesting compilation of science fiction stories, mostly by new authors, that center on a small change that affects the world in a big way. (Rev: BL 8/08; SLJ 11/1/08)

5845 Adams, John Joseph, ed. *Under the Moons of Mars: New Adventures on Barsoom* (7–12). Illus. 2012, Simon & Schuster $16.99 (978-144242029-8). An anthology of original stories featuring John Carter, the Earthman in Edgar Rice Burroughs's Barsoom series, by such authors as Tobias S. Buckell, David Barr Kirtley, and Garth Nix. **e** Lexile 1050L (Rev: BL 2/1/12; SLJ 5/1/12)

5846 Allen, Roger MacBride. *David Brin's Out of Time: The Game of Worlds* (7–12). Series: David Brin's Out of Time. 1999, Avon paper $4.99 (978-0-380-79969-5). Adam O'Connor, a mischievous high school student in the late 20th century, finds himself facing a whole new set of problems when he's yanked 350 years into the future. (Rev: VOYA 4/00)

5847 Allston, Aaron. *Betrayal* (9–12). Series: Star Wars: Legacy of the Force. 2006, Del Rey $25.95 (978-0-345-47734-7). The Star Wars saga continues as the Galactic Alliance struggles to control the rebellious Corellians. (Rev: BL 5/15/06)

5848 Anastasiu, Heather. *Glitch* (7–12). 2012, St. Martin's paper $9.99 (978-1-250-00-299-0). Zoe discovers a way to disconnect from her dystopia's mind-control software, and is suddenly forced to contend with emo-

tions — which include love. (Rev: BL 8/12; SLJ 11/12; VOYA 10/12)

5849 Anderson, Kevin J. *Dogged Persistence* (10–12). 2001, Golden Gryphon $25.95 (978-1-930846-03-6). Hard science and action subjects are combined in this collection of 18 stories for older teens by this well-known author. (Rev: BL 5/15/01)

5850 Anderson, Kevin J. *The Last Days of Krypton* (9–12). 2007, HarperEntertainment $25.95 (978-0-06-134074-1). The details of the final days of Krypton, Superman's birth planet, unfolds with his father Jor-El's efforts to persuade the authorities that space travel is needed, but unscrupulous General Zod hampers his scientific progress at every turn, resulting in the explosion of Krypton with the escape of only one infant. (Rev: BL 10/1/07)

5851 Anderson, Kevin J., ed. *War of the Worlds: Global Dispatches* (7–12). 1996, Bantam $22.95 (978-0-553-10352-6). This tribute to H. G. Wells's *War of the Worlds* features stories of Martian invasions that are either take-offs on the writing styles of such famous authors as Conrad, London, Verne, and Kipling, or the experiences of famous individuals, such as Teddy Roosevelt and Pablo Picasso, during a Martian invasion. (Rev: VOYA 10/96)

5852 Anderson, Poul. *Cold Victory* (10–12). 1985, Tor paper $2.95 (978-0-8125-3057-5). Six stories about the Psychotechnic League. Some other books by this master are: *Conflict, Fire Time*, and *A Midsummer Tempest*.

5853 Anderson, Poul. *Genesis* (10–12). 2000, Tor $23.95 (978-0-312-86707-2). Christian Brannock, immortalized through computer imprinting, embarks on a billion-year exploration of the stars. (Rev: BL 2/15/00; VOYA 6/00)

5854 Anderson, Taylor. *Crusade* (11–12). Series: Destroyermen. 2008, Roc $26.50 (978-045146230-5). A sequel to *Into the Storm* (2008), this novel set in an alternate world pits Lt. Commander Reddy and the Lemurian allies against the Grik, who are threatening a neighboring society; for mature teens who enjoy science fiction with a military flavor. (Rev: BL 9/1/08*)

5855 Anthony, Piers. *Split Infinity* (10–12). Series: Apprentice Adept. 1987, Ballantine paper $6.99 (978-0-345-35491-4). In this first part of the Apprentice Adept series, someone is trying to kill Stile on the planet Proton. Other titles are *Blue Adept* and *Juxtaposition*.

5856 Anthony, Piers. *Total Recall* (9–12). 1990, Avon paper $4.50 (978-0-380-70874-1). A novelization of the movie about a secret agent on Mars searching for his past. Also use *But What of Earth?* (Tor, 1989). (Rev: BL 8/89)

5857 Armstrong, Jennifer, and Nancy Butcher. *The Kindling* (7–10). Series: Fire-Us. 2002, HarperCollins LB $16.89 (978-0-06-029411-3). In 2007, after a virus has killed the adults, a small band of children join together in a Florida town and try to carry on with life. (Rev: BCCB 6/02; BL 4/15/02; HBG 10/02; SLJ 10/02)

5858 Asaro, Catherine. *Sunrise Alley* (10–12). 2004, Baen $24.00 (978-0-7434-8840-2). A fast-paced story in which biotech engineer Samantha Bryton agrees to help android Turner Pascal, who is on the run from the evil bioengineer Charon. (Rev: BL 8/04; SLJ 1/05)

5859 Asimov, Isaac. *Caves of Steel* (7–12). 1955, Spectra paper $6.99 (978-0-553-29034-9). A human and a robot combine forces in this science fiction classic to work together to help mankind. Part of Asimov's well-written Robot series. (Rev: BL BL 5/1/00)

5860 Asimov, Isaac. *Fantastic Voyage: A Novel* (8–12). 1966, Houghton Mifflin paper $6.99 (978-0-553-27572-8). Five people are miniaturized to enter the body of a sick man and save his life.

5861 Asimov, Isaac. *Forward the Foundation* (9–12). 1993, Bantam paper $6.99 (978-0-553-56507-2). The conclusion to Asimov's efforts to bind his various universes together into one vast future history. Part of the Foundation series. (Rev: BL 2/15/93; SLJ 3/94)

5862 Asimov, Isaac. *I, Robot* (10–12). 1991, Bantam paper $6.99 (978-0-553-29438-5). A collection about Dr. Susan Calvin and the robots she produces.

5863 Asimov, Isaac. *Nemesis* (9–12). 1990, Bantam paper $6.99 (978-0-553-28628-1). A space colony arrives at a planet only to find it is slated for destruction. (Rev: BL 8/89)

5864 Asimov, Isaac. *Prelude to Foundation* (10–12). 1989, Bantam paper $6.99 (978-0-553-27839-2). This novel links the Empire and Foundation series and supplies a chronology of novels in these two series as a guide to readers. (Rev: BL 4/1/88; VOYA 10/88)

5865 Asimov, Isaac, et al, ed. *Computer Crimes and Capers* (9–12). 1983, Academy Chicago paper $15.00 (978-0-89733-087-9). A lively anthology of stories featuring computers as masters, servants, or — sometimes — arch criminals.

5866 Asprin, Robert, and Peter J. Heck. *No Phule Like an Old Phule* (9–12). 2004, Berkley paper $7.99 (978-0-441-01152-0). In this humorous science fiction novel, Willard Phule must put up with a series of misadventures including a bungled kidnapping attempt and a celebrity canine named Barky the Environmental Dog. (Rev: BL 4/1/04)

5867 Atwood, Margaret. *The Handmaid's Tale* (10–12). 1998, Doubleday paper $12.95 (978-0-385-49081-8). A chilling look into the future where repression of women is rampant. For mature readers. (Rev: VOYA 12/86)

5868 Atwood, Margaret. *The Year of the Flood* (11–12). 2009, Doubleday $26 (978-038552877-1). After a pandemic decimates a city, survivors band together in a fragile environment ruled by a sinister government;

this novel intersects with the world of *Oryx and Crake* (2003) and is suitable for mature readers. ∩ ℯ (Rev: BL 7/09)

5869 Bacigalupi, Paolo. *Ship Breaker* (8–12). 2010, Little, Brown $17.99 (978-0-316-05621-2). In a future, chaotic Accelerated Age Nailer and his friend Pima come across a wealthy girl as they scavenge among wrecks on the beach; can they help her and keep her safe from her enemies? Printz Winner 2011; ALA Notable Books 2011; YALSA Top Ten Best Fiction for Young Adults 2011. ∩ Lexile HL690L (Rev: BL 5/15/10*; HB 7–8/10; LMC 8–9/10; SLJ 6/10)

5870 Bacigalupi, Paolo. *The Windup Girl* (10–12). 2009, Night Shade $24.95 (978-1-59780-157-7). This intricate science fiction novel is set in a grim Thailand of the future, where food is the most valuable asset, and the avaricious search for a new source of nutrition could jeopardize the future of the entire country. (Rev: SLJ 12/09)

5871 Baker, Kage. *Black Projects, White Knights: The Company Dossiers* (10–12). 2002, Golden Gryphon $24.95 (978-1-930846-11-1). Fourteen short stories about the adventures of time-traveling cyber-agents in search of treasures from the past. (Rev: BL 9/1/02)

5872 Baker, Kage, and John Barnes, et al. *Life on Mars: Tales from the New Frontier* (9–12). Ed. by Jonathan Strahan. 2011, Viking $19.99 (978-0-670-01216-9). With stories by such as authors as Cory Doctorow and Stephen Baxter, this is an excellent collection of twelve original stories about humans living on Mars. ℯ (Rev: BL 5/1/11; HB 5–6/11; LMC 10/11*; SLJ 7/11*; VOYA 6/11)

5873 Ball, Margaret. *Lost in Translation* (8–12). 1995, Baen $5.99 (978-0-671-87638-8). American teenager Allie flies to France to attend a university but lands in a fantasy world filled with spells of every kind, where people communicate through voice-bubbles and a group of terrifying monsters controls an important subterranean substance called landvirtue. (Rev: VOYA 4/96)

5874 Barnes, John. *Losers in Space* (9–12). 2012, Viking $18.99 (978-067006156-3). In 2129 nine celebrity-hungry teens stow away on a ship to Mars but get more than they bargained for. ℯ (Rev: BL 4/1/12; HB 3–4/12; LMC 10/12; SLJ 4/12; VOYA 4/12)

5875 Barnes, John. *The Merchants of Souls* (9–12). 2001, Tor $25.95 (978-0-312-89076-6). In this sequel to *Earth Made of Glass* (1998), Giraut Leones is persuaded to leave his planet to find ways to defeat an ugly criminal conspiracy. (Rev: BL 12/15/01)

5876 Barnes, John. *A Princess of the Aerie* (10–12). 2003, Warner Aspect paper $6.99 (978-0-446-61082-7). Best suited for mature teens because of its sexual content, this sequel to *The Duke of Uranium* recounts the adventures of 36th-century teen spy Jak Jinnaka as he discovers the duplicity of an ex-girlfriend who's set herself up as the despotic ruler of Greenworld. (Rev: BL 1/1–15/03)

5877 Barnes, John. *The Sky So Big and Black* (10–12). 2002, Tor $24.95 (978-0-7653-0303-5). At the age of 15, Teri is enjoying working as an ecoprospector on Mars and looking forward to taking her Full Adult test when a crisis erupts that challenges her skills and will. (Rev: BL 8/02; SLJ 12/02)

5878 Baron, Mike, and Steve Rude. *Nexus, Vol. 4* (10–12). 2006, Dark Horse $49.95 (978-1-59307-583-5). Classic science fiction stories feature aliens, superheroes, and all the other necessary elements; just one volume in a series recommended for young adult readers. (Rev: BL 9/1/06)

5879 Barrett, Neal. *Perpetuity Blues and Other Stories* (11–12). 2000, Golden Gryphon $21.95 (978-0-9655901-4-3). Science fiction stories with a southern flavor, for mature readers. (Rev: BL 5/15/00)

5880 Bear, Greg. *Moving Mars* (9–12). 1994, Tor paper $6.99 (978-0-8125-2480-2). A physicist on Mars links up with an artificial intelligence and a revolutionary woman determined to give her world a future. (Rev: BL 9/15/93; VOYA 4/94)

5881 Beaudoin, Sean. *Fade to Blue* (8–11). Illus. by author. 2009, Little, Brown $16.99 (978-031601417-5). Goth girl Sophie Blue's father disappears on her 17th birthday and she and her hunk friend Kenny Fade share a feeling they may be losing their minds in this quirky, dark yet funny novel that incorporates a comic book and involves a lab that may be infecting young people with software code. (Rev: BL 6/1–15/09; SLJ 10/09)

5882 BeauSeigneur, James. *In His Image* (10–12). Series: Christ Clone. 2003, Warner $18.95 (978-0-446-53125-2). In the first volume of a trilogy, skillful writing and plotting make plausible the tale of an Antichrist — Christopher Goodman — cloned from blood found on the shroud of Turin. (Rev: BL 1/1–15/03*)

5883 Beck, Ian. *Pastworld: A Mystery of the Near Future* (7–10). 2009, Bloomsbury $16.99 (978-1-59990-040-7). The year is 2050 and London has been turned into a Victorian theme park complete with a series of gruesome murders. **e** Lexile 880L (Rev: BL 11/15/09; LMC 11–12/09; SLJ 12/09)

5884 Bedford, K. A. *Hydrogen Steel* (10–12). 2007, Edge paper $19.95 (978-1-894063-20-3). An action-packed, multilayered mystery/sci fi story featuring a confused but plucky android named Zette. (Rev: SLJ 6/07)

5885 Benford, Gregory. *Worlds Vast and Various* (10–12). 2000, HarperCollins paper $14.50 (978-0-380-79054-8). This volume contains 12 thought-provoking short stories by one of the best science fiction writers. (Rev: BL 10/15/00)

5886 Benford, Gregory, ed. *Nebula Awards Showcase 2000: The Year's Best SF and Fantasy Chosen by the Science Fiction and Fantasy Writers of America* (9–12). 2000, Harcourt paper $14.00 (978-0-15-600705-4). Four prize-winning stories from 1998 are reprinted, with additional background material on science fiction publishing and authors. (Rev: BL 3/15/00)

5887 Blisson, Terry. *Pirates of the Universe* (10–12). 1996, Tor $22.95 (978-0-312-85412-6). Science fiction and a page-turning adventure yarn combine in this story of Gunter Glenn and his search for justice in a world gone mad. (Rev: BL 4/15/96; SLJ 10/96; VOYA 8/96)

5888 Boulle, Pierre. *Planet of the Apes* (7–12). 2001, Random House paper $6.99 (978-0-345-44798-2). Stranded on the planet Soror, Ulysse Merou discovers a civilization ruled by apes.

5889 Bova, Ben. *Jupiter* (10–12). 2001, Tor $24.95 (978-0-312-87217-5). Astrophysicist Grant Archer, dispatched by Earth's theocratic rulers to find out what's going on at a research station orbiting Jupiter, joins a manned mission to the planet's surface. (Rev: BL 1/1–15/01; VOYA 6/01)

5890 Bova, Ben. *Venus* (10–12). 2000, Tor $24.95 (978-0-312-87216-8). For hard science fiction fans, this novel tells how a sickly and despised second son of a wealthy family sets out to recover the body of his brother who was killed during the first attempt to land a man on Venus. (Rev: BL 4/1/00)

5891 Bracken, Alexandra. *The Darkest Minds* (8–12). 2012, Disney/Hyperion $17.99 (978-142315737-3). In a dystopian future where the few children who have survived are classified by their psychic abilities, 16-year-old Ruby escapes from a camp and faces many difficult choices. ◖ **e** Lexile 870L (Rev: BL 12/1/12; LMC 3–4/13; SLJ 3/13)

5892 Bradbury, Ray. *Bradbury Stories: 100 of His Most Celebrated Tales* (10–12). 2003, Morrow $29.95 (978-0-06-054242-9). Bradbury's selection of his own 100 best guarantees remarkable readability and many happy laughs. (Rev: BL 7/03)

5893 Bradbury, Ray. *Fahrenheit 451* (7–12). 1953, Ballantine paper $6.99 (978-0-345-34296-6). In this futuristic novel, book reading has become a crime.

5894 Bradbury, Ray. *The Martian Chronicles* (10–12). 1999, Simon & Schuster $24.95 (978-0-7838-8635-0). These interrelated short stories tell of the colonization of Mars.

5895 Bradbury, Ray. *The Martian Chronicles: The Fortieth Anniversary Edition* (10–12). 1950, Doubleday $15.95 (978-0-385-05060-9). Earth's efforts to colonize Mars are recounted in this collection of famous short stories. (Rev: BLO 8/18/08)

5896 Bradbury, Ray. *The October Country* (7–12). 1999, Avon $15.95 (978-0-380-97387-3). Ordinary people are caught up in unreal situations in these 19 strange stories.

5897 Breese, K. Ryer. *Future Imperfect* (10–12). 2011, St. Martin's paper $9.99 (978-0-312-64-151-1). Seventeen-year-old Ade, who is addicted to the visions he gets from banging his head hard, believes that a girl named Vauxhall will bring him love — and together they will change the world. ⌒ ℮ Lexile 1580L (Rev: BLO 5/1/11; SLJ 10/1/11; VOYA 4/11)

5898 Brin, David. *Otherness* (9–12). 1994, Bantam paper $6.99 (978-0-553-29528-3). Short fiction, essays, and commentaries that strive to define the term *otherness,* including stories about extraterrestrial contact and the limits of our perception of reality. (Rev: BL 8/94; VOYA 2/95)

5899 Brin, David. *The Postman* (9–12). 1985, Bantam paper $6.99 (978-0-553-27874-3). This novel deals with the aftermath of a nuclear war, when communication with survivors often depended on people like the Postman.

5900 Brin, David, and Kevin Lenagh. *Contacting Aliens: An Illustrated Guide to David Brin's Uplift Universe* (10–12). 2002, Bantam paper $14.95 (978-0-553-37796-5). The alien species of Brin's Uplift Universe are described and illustrated in this handy guide. (Rev: BL 5/15/02) [813]

5901 Brindley, John. *The Rule of Claw* (7–10). 2009, Carolrhoda $18.95 (978-158013608-2). In a land and time where mutants run wild, 15-year-old Ash is kidnapped by the Raptors and caught up in a war between two genetically altered races. Lexile HL740L (Rev: BLO 2/9/09; SLJ 5/1/09)

5902 Brooks, Kevin. *iBoy* (9–12). 2011, Scholastic $17.99 (978-0-545-31768-9). Tom, a 16-year-old with bits of an iPhone embedded in his brain, uses his newfound technological capabilities to help his friend Lucy, who was raped by a local gang. ℮ Lexile 850L (Rev: BL 9/1/11*; LMC 1–2/12*; SLJ 10/1/11; VOYA 12/11)

5903 Brooks, Terry. *Wizard at Large* (10–12). 1989, Ballantine paper $6.99 (978-0-345-36227-8). In this, the third book about the Magic Kingdom of Landover, High Lord Ben Holiday travels to Earth. Preceded by: *Magic Kingdom for Sale — Sold!* and *The Black Unicorn.* (Rev: BL 9/1/88; VOYA 4/89)

5904 Brown, Charles N., and Jonathan Strahan, eds. *The Locus Awards: Thirty Years of the Best in Science Fiction and Fantasy* (11–12). 2004, HarperCollins paper $15.95 (978-0-06-059426-8). Selected from past winners of the Locus Awards, the stories in this anthology represent the best in fantasy and science fiction writing over the past three decades; for mature teens. (Rev: BL 7/04; SLJ 3/05)

5905 Buckell, Tobias S., and Joe Monti, eds. *Diverse Energies* (9–12). 2012, Lee & Low $19.95 (978-160060887-2). Eleven dystopian stories written by YA authors including Ursula Le Guin and Ellen Oh feature diverse characters. ℮ (Rev: BL 11/1/12; LMC 5–6/13; SLJ 1/13; VOYA 12/12)

5906 Bujold, Lois McMaster. *A Civil Campaign: A Comedy of Biology and Manners* (10–12). 1999, Baen $24.00 (978-0-671-57827-5). In this deftly crafted intergalactic romance, brilliant military strategist Miles Vorkosigan mounts a campaign to win the heart of Ekaterin. (Rev: BL 9/1/99; VOYA 4/00)

5907 Bujold, Lois McMaster. *Komarr* (10–12). 1998, Pocket $22.00 (978-0-671-87877-1). Investigator Miles Vorkosigan's first case is to determine if the collision between a space freighter and a satellite was really an accident. (Rev: BL 5/15/98; VOYA 10/98)

5908 Burgess, Melvin. *Bloodsong* (10–12). 2007, Simon & Schuster paper $7.99 (978-1-4169-3616-9). Fifteen-year-old Sigurd, the son of Sigmund (of 2001's *Bloodtide*), overcomes many obstacles — including a genetically enhanced dragon — in his quest to unite his country in this violent futuristic story set in England and featuring human-animal and human-machine hybrids. (Rev: BL 9/1/07)

5909 Burroughs, Edgar Rice. *A Princess of Mars* (9–12). 1985, Ballantine paper $4.99 (978-0-345-33138-0). This is the beginning of a series of "space operas" involving John Carter on Mars. Some others are: *Gods of Mars, Warlord of Mars*, and *The Chessmen of Mars.*

5910 Butler, Octavia E. *Wild Seed* (11–12). 1980, Warner paper $6.50 (978-0-446-60672-1). Two very different immortal beings — Doro, who devours other beings, and Anyanwu, who prefers to love and heal — find their lives are intertwined throughout time.

5911 Bynum, Laura. *Veracity* (10–12). 2010, Pocket $25 (978-143912334-8). After her daughter is taken away, a mother must fight the dystopian society she had diligently served. ℮ (Rev: BL 12/1/09)

5912 Card, Orson Scott. *The Call of Earth* (9–12). Series: Homecoming Saga. 1994, Tor paper $6.99 (978-0-8125-3261-6). Teenagers are at the heart of this story featuring a sentient computer whose plans involve a return to Earth. (Rev: BL 11/15/92; VOYA 8/93)

5913 Card, Orson Scott. *Empire* (9–12). 2006, Tor $24.95 (978-0-7653-1611-0). A near-future thriller in which the president, vice president, and secretary of defense are killed and America enters a second civil war between red and blue states. (Rev: BL 10/1/06)

5914 Card, Orson Scott. *First Meetings: In the Enderverse* (6–12). 2003, Tor $17.95 (978-0-7653-0873-3). Contains the novella "Ender's Game," first published in 1977, and three other stories, one previously unpublished. (Rev: SLJ 1/04)

5915 Card, Orson Scott. *Hidden Empire* (10–12). 2009, Tor $24.99 (978-076532004-9). In this thrilling sequel to 2006's *Empire*, a cast of politicians, soldiers, and military advisers copes with conspiracy and imperialist politics in a plague-stricken futuristic Africa. ℮ (Rev: BL 11/15/09)

5916 Card, Orson Scott. *The Lost Gate* (9–12). 2011, Tor $24.99 (978-0-8653-2657-7). Danny is a powerful gatemage in a society where creating portals is forbidden, and his powers place him in danger. ∩ (Rev: BLO 2/28/13; SLJ 4/11)

5917 Card, Orson Scott. *The Memory of Earth: Homecoming, Vol. 1* (9–12). Series: Homecoming Saga. 1993, Tor paper $5.99 (978-0-8125-3259-3). A science fiction saga set on the planet Harmony, where a computer rules the population. (Rev: BL 1/1/92)

5918 Card, Orson Scott. *Pathfinder* (8–12). 2010, Simon & Schuster $18.99 (978-1-4169-9176-2). Thirteen-year-old Rigg can see the paths of others' pasts, and revelations after his father's death set him on a dangerous quest accompanied by friends who can bend time. ℮ (Rev: BL 11/1/10*; SLJ 12/1/10)

5919 Card, Orson Scott. *Ruins* (9–12). 2012, Simon & Schuster $18.99 (978-1-4169-9177-9). Rigg and his friends travel back 11,000 years to prevent the destruction of the Garden, a planet colonized by humans; a sequel to *Pathfinder* (2010). ∩ ℮ Lexile HL790L (Rev: BL 8/12*; HB 11–12/12; SLJ 11/12)

5920 Card, Orson Scott. *Shadow of the Giant* (10–12). Series: Ender. 2005, Tor $25.95 (978-0-312-85758-5). In a continuation of the saga, Bean and his fellow Battle School graduates, some of whom rule their own kingdoms, must face and work to resolve Earth's political turmoil. (Rev: BL 3/1/05)

5921 Card, Orson Scott. *Shadow of the Hegemon* (9–12). Series: Ender. 2000, Tor $25.95 (978-0-312-87651-7). In this sequel to *Ender's Shadow,* Bean is again the main character and he is faced with the mystery of who is kidnapping graduates of the Battle School. The next volume in the series is *Shadow Puppets* (2002). (Rev: BL 11/1/00; SLJ 6/01; VOYA 6/01)

5922 Card, Orson Scott. *Speaker for the Dead* (10–12). Series: Ender. 1986, Tor $21.95 (978-0-312-93738-6). Ender tries to prevent a war with a nonhuman intelligent race in this sequel to *Ender's Game.* (Rev: BL 12/15/85; VOYA 8/86)

5923 Card, Orson Scott, and Aaron Johnston. *Invasive Procedures* (9–12). 2007, Tor $25.95 (978-0-7653-1424-6). One scientist has created a dangerous virus and another has been hired by the government to stop him in this gripping adaptation of Card's original 1977 story, "Malpractice." (Rev: BL 8/07)

5924 Card, Orson Scott, ed. *Future on Ice* (9–12). 1998, Tor $24.95 (978-0-312-86694-5). A fine collection of 18 short stories by some of the most popular science fiction writers of the 1980s. (Rev: BL 9/15/98; SLJ 3/99; VOYA 4/99)

5925 Carey, Anna. *Eve* (10–12). 2011, HarperCollins $17.99 (978-006204850-9). Twelve years after the plague that decimated mankind, Eve learns the truth about her intended future and sets off into an unknown world, where she finds danger, friendship, and romance. ℮ Lexile 760L (Rev: BL 10/1/11; LMC 3–4/12; SLJ 1/12)

5926 Carman, Patrick. *Pulse* (7–12). 2013, HarperCollins $17.99 (978-006208576-4). In 2051 the United States is divided in two but a small group lives in the middle zone, including Faith and Dylan — who have the Pulse — and the brilliant Hawk. Can these three teens save the world from impending doom? ℮ Lexile HL820L (Rev: BL 12/15/12; SLJ 3/13; VOYA 12/12)

5927 Cart, Michael, ed. *Tomorrowland: 10 Stories About the Future* (7–10). 1999, Scholastic paper $15.95 (978-0-590-37678-5). Ten writers, including Ron Koertge, Lois Lowry, and Katherine Paterson, have contributed original stories to this anthology that reflect their concepts of the future. (Rev: BCCB 12/99; BL 8/99; HBG 4/00; SLJ 9/99; VOYA 12/99)

5928 Carver, Jeffrey A. *Eternity's End* (10–12). 2000, Tor $26.00 (978-0-312-85642-7). A space navigator doesn't realize that his captain has betrayed his ship and is in league with space pirates. (Rev: BL 12/1/00)

5929 Carver, Jeffrey A. *A Neptune Crossing* (9–12). 1995, Tor $5.99 (978-0-8125-3515-0). While doing survey work on Neptune's moon Triton, loner John Bandicut becomes a reluctant accomplice to aliens' efforts to save Earth. (Rev: BL 3/15/94; VOYA 12/94)

5930 Cass, Kiera. *The Selection* (7–10). 2012, HarperCollins $17.99 (978-006205993-2). In a dystopian future America with strict social structures America Singer is one of 35 young women competing to win the heart of Prince Maxon even though she is already in love with Aspen. ℮ Lexile HL680L (Rev: BL 5/1/12; SLJ 6/12)

5931 Castellucci, Cecil. *First Day on Earth* (7–10). 2011, Scholastic $17.99 (978-054506082-0). A brief, absorbing novel in which Mal, who has contended with an absent father and alcoholic mother, also believes he has been temporarily abducted by aliens and then returned to an uncertain Earth. ℮ Lexile HL540L (Rev: BL 10/1/11; HB 11–12/11; LMC 1–2/12*)

5932 Castro, Adam-Troy. *Spider-Man: Secret of the Sinister Six* (7–12). Illus. by Mike Zeck. 2002, BP $24.95 (978-0-7434-4464-4). Six supervillains attack New York City and Spider-Man comes to the rescue in this humorous and action-packed final installment in a trilogy. (Rev: SLJ 7/02)

5933 Cave, Patrick. *Sharp North* (9–12). 2006, Simon & Schuster $16.95 (978-1-4169-1222-4). Climate changes have dramatically changed the social order of future Great Britain, and adopted teen Miri attempts to unravel the mysteries of cloning in this compelling thriller. (Rev: BL 5/15/06; HB 7–8/06; LMC 2/07; SLJ 7/06)

5934 Cherryh, C. J. *Finity's End* (9–12). 1997, Warner paper $22.00 (978-0-446-57072-5). Fletcher, who has spent his first 17 years on Pell as a "stationer," is suddenly claimed by the crew of *Finity's End,* a space vehicle where his deceased mother once lived, and taken aboard to be a member of their community. (Rev: BL 8/97; VOYA 12/97)

5935 Cherryh, C. J. *The Pride of Chanur* (10–12). 1987, Phantasia $17.00 (978-0-932096-45-6). A human finds refuge on a spaceship operated by catlike beings. A sequel is *Chanur's Venture.*

5936 Cheva, Cherry. *DupliKate* (7–10). 2009, Harper-Teen $16.99 (978-0-06-128854-8). When 17-year-old Kate's online gaming avatar comes to life, the overbooked teen welcomes the extra set of hands — until her duplicate's wild nature and separate agenda begin to come through. ℮ (Rev: BL 12/1/09; SLJ 10/09)

5937 Clancy, Tom, and Steve Pieczenik. *Virtual Vandals* (7–12). Series: Net Force. 1999, Berkley paper $4.99 (978-0-425-16173-9). In 2025, after Matt Hunter and his computer friends attend an all-star virtual reality baseball game where terrorists shoot wildly at the stands, our hero and his pals set out to catch the culprits. Followed by *The Deadliest Game.* (Rev: BL 3/15/99)

5938 Clarke, Arthur C. *Childhood's End* (7–12). 1963, Ballantine paper $6.99 (978-0-345-34795-4). The overlords' arrival on Earth marks the beginning of the end for humankind.

5939 Clarke, Arthur C. *The Hammer of God* (9–12). 1994, Bantam paper $6.99 (978-0-553-56871-4). The struggle to avoid an asteroid on a collision course with Earth. (Rev: BL 4/15/93; VOYA 12/93)

5940 Clarke, Arthur C. *Rendezvous with Rama* (10–12). 1990, Bantam paper $6.99 (978-0-553-28789-9). Bill Norton and his crew set out to investigate a strange missile that has entered the earth's atmosphere.

5941 Clarke, Arthur C. *2010: Odyssey Two* (9–12). 1997, Ballantine paper $11.00 (978-0-345-41397-0). A team of scientists try to save the deserted spaceship *Discovery.*

5942 Clarke, Arthur C. *2061: Odyssey Three* (9–12). 1988, Ballantine paper $6.99 (978-0-345-35879-0). Heywood Floyd takes part in the space mission of landing on Halley's Comet. (Rev: BL 11/1/87)

5943 Clarke, Arthur C., and Gentry Lee. *Rama Revealed* (9–12). Series: Rama. 1995, Bantam paper $6.99 (978-0-553-56947-6). The fourth book of the series focuses on the New Eden colony, which is ruled by Nakamura, a dictator who overthrew the governess and wages war on the octospiders. (Rev: BL 12/1/93; VOYA 6/94)

5944 Clarke, Arthur C., and Stephen Baxter. *Firstborn* (9–12). 2007, Del Rey $25.95 (978-0-345-49157-2). A conclusion to the A Time Odyssey series finds Bisesa Dutt and her daughter emerging from hibernation hoping to solve Earth's dilemma as it is under attack of an ancient alien race, the Firstborn, who attempt to annihilate the planet with the Q-bomb. (Rev: BL 12/1/07)

5945 Clement, Hal. *The Essential Hal Clement, Vol. 3: Variations on a Theme by Sir Isaac Newton* (10–12). 2000, NESFA $25.00 (978-1-886778-08-5). For advanced science fiction fans, this volume contains reprints of two of Clement's best novels, *Mission of Gravity* from 1954 and *Star Light,* first published in 1971. (Rev: BL 11/1/00)

5946 Clements, Andrew. *Things Not Seen* (7–10). 2002, Putnam $16.99 (978-0-399-23626-6). Bobby, 15, suddenly becomes invisible and must deal with all the problems his "disappearance" causes. (Rev: BCCB 6/02; BL 4/15/02; HB 3–4/02; HBG 10/02; SLJ 3/02; VOYA 2/02)

5947 Collins, Paul. *The Skyborn* (8–11). 2005, Tor $17.95 (978-0-7653-1273-0). Accepted by the Earthborn after his ship *Colony* crashed on post-holocaust Earth, 14-year-old Welkin, born a Skyborn, learns the Earthborn are in danger from the Skyborn; a sequel to *The Earthborn* (2003). (Rev: BL 2/15/06)

5948 Collins, Suzanne. *Catching Fire* (9–12). Series: The Hunger Games. 2009, Scholastic $17.99 (978-043902349-8). Katniss and Peeta find unexpected challenges as they travel through Panem in this exciting sequel to *The Hunger Games* (2008). (Rev: BL 7/09; LMC 1–2/10; SLJ 9/09)

5949 Collins, Suzanne. *The Hunger Games* (7–12). 2008, Scholastic $17.99 (978-0-439-02348-1). A tense survival story set in a future dystopian North America, in which 16-year-old Kat is thrust into a fight to the death on live TV. ALA Notable Books 2009. ⌂ (Rev: BL 9/1/08*; HB 7–8/08; LMC 11–12/08*; SLJ 9/1/08*; VOYA 4/08)

5950 Crichton, Michael. *Jurassic Park* (9–12). 1990, Knopf $25.00 (978-0-394-58816-2). This thriller takes place in an amusement park on an island off Costa Rica where genetically engineered dinosaurs live. (Rev: BL 10/1/90; SLJ 3/91)

5951 Crockett, S. D. *After the Snow* (8–12). 2012, Feiwel & Friends $16.99 (978-031264169-6). In a new Ice Age 15-year-old Willo's family disappears and he sets off in the cold to find them, meeting a young girl called Mary and facing many dangers; in this postapocalyptic world with little government Willo speaks a fractured English. ℮ Lexile HL700L (Rev: BL 3/1/12; HB 3–4/12; LMC 8–9/12; SLJ 3/12*)

5952 Cross, Julie. *Tempest* (9–12). 2012, St. Martin's $17.99 (978-031256889-4). When his girlfriend is murdered, Jackson, 19, travels back in time to change the outcome, and discovers things aren't as easy as they seem. ℮ Lexile HL650L (Rev: BL 12/15/11; LMC 5–6/12; SLJ 2/12; VOYA 12/11)

5953 Czerneda, Julie E. *In the Company of Others* (7–12). 2001, DAW paper $7.99 (978-0-88677-999-3). Biologist Gail Smith embarks on the space ship Seeker to track down Aaron Pardell, whose help she needs in her mission to find and destroy a deadly life form called the Quill. (Rev: VOYA 2/02)

5954 Dashner, James. *The Scorch Trials. Bk. 2* (9–12). Series: Maze Runner Trilogy. 2010, Delacorte $17.99 (978-0-385-73875-0); LB $20.99 (978-0-385-90745-3). In this sequel to *The Maze Runner* (2009), Thomas and a group of other boys have escaped the horrors of the Maze and now seek an antidote to the insanity disease with which they are told they have been infected. ℮ (Rev: BL 1/1–15/11; SLJ 12/1/10)

5955 Datlow, Ellen, and Terri Windling, eds. *After: Nineteen Stories of Apocalypse and Dystopia* (9–12). 2012, Disney/Hyperion $16.99 (978-142314619-3). Nineteen well-developed stories about dire futuristic situations by well-known authors such as Katherine Langrish and Carol Emshiller are collected here. ℮ Lexile HL810L (Rev: BL 12/15/12; SLJ 3/13)

5956 Dedman, Stephen. *The Art of Arrow Cutting* (10–12). 1997, Tor $22.95 (978-0-312-86320-3). Mage, a young man who holds the power to perform miracles, is pursued by Tamenaga, a dead man who wants to possess this power. (Rev: VOYA 12/97)

5957 DeNiro, Alan. *Total Oblivion, More or Less* (11–12). 2009, Spectra paper $15 (978-05535925-4-2). Rampant plagues, slave traders, and marauders from the past are laying waste to America; but for 16-year-old Macy, the biggest danger of all may be posed by her conniving younger brother. For mature readers. ℮ (Rev: BL 10/15/09*)

5958 Denning, Troy. *Abyss* (10–12). Series: Star Wars: Fate of the Jedi. 2009, Del Rey $27 (978-034550918-5). The order of the Jedi is in danger of crumbling in this fast-paced Star Wars book (third in a series). (Rev: BL 7/09)

5959 Denning, Troy. *Vortex* (10–12). Series: Star Wars: Fate of the Jedi. 2010, Del Rey $27 (978-034550920-8). Converging plotlines are advanced in this sixth installment of the nine-part Star Wars series. (Rev: BL 11/1–15/10)

5960 Dick, Philip K. *Do Androids Dream of Electric Sheep?* (10–12). 1996, Ballantine paper $13.00 (978-0-345-40447-3). In the world of 2021, after a brutal war, androids have become so sophisticated that it is hard to distinguish them from humans. First published in 1968.

5961 Dick, Philip K. *Nick and the Glimmung* (7–10). 2008, Subterranean $35.00 (978-159606168-2). Diehard science fiction fans will enjoy this complex story

in which Dick travels from Earth to a more animal-friendly planet. (Rev: BL 3/1/09)

5962 Dickinson, Peter. *Eva* (8–12). 1990, Dell paper $5.50 (978-0-440-20766-5). When Eva wakes up after an accident she finds that she has retained her memory but been given the body of a chimpanzee. (Rev: HB 7/89; SLJ 4/89)

5963 Doctorow, Cory. *Pirate Cinema* (9–12). 2012, Tor $19.99 (978-0-7653-2908-0). In near-future Britain, 16-year-old filmmaker Trent's use of snippets of copyrighted material is forbidden and he joins a group of rebel artists and activists. ☊ ℮ Lexile 1090L (Rev: BL 6/12*; SLJ 10/12*; VOYA 4/13)

5964 Doyle, Larry. *Go, Mutants!* (10–12). 2010, Ecco $23.99 (978-006168655-9). J!m, a 17-year-old alien with blue skin, atomic ape Johnny, and their gooey sidekick Jelly band together to try to outwit bullies and win girls. (Rev: BL 6/1–15/10)

5965 Dozois, Gardner, ed. *Supermen: Tales of the Posthuman Future* (9–12). 2002, St. Martin's paper $17.95 (978-0-312-27569-3). This book contains 29 stories published between 1955 and 2000, all dealing with the next stages of human evolution. (Rev: BL 11/15/01)

5966 Dozois, Gardner, ed. *The Year's Best Science Fiction: Eleventh Annual Collection* (9–12). 1994, St. Martin's paper $17.95 (978-0-312-11104-5). The annual collection of outstanding sci-fi short stories. (Rev: BL 7/94; VOYA 2/95)

5967 Drake, David. *Lt. Leary, Commanding* (10–12). 2000, Baen $24.00 (978-0-671-57875-6). In this sequel to *With the Lightnings* (1998), Lieutenant Daniel Leary and his sidekick become involved in a political crisis on a distant planet. (Rev: BL 7/00)

5968 Drake, David, et al, ed. *The World Turned Upside Down* (9–12). 2005, Baen $24.00 (978-0-7434-9874-6). This fiction collection anthologizes seminal science fiction stories and writers, including Arthur C. Clarke and Isaac Asimov. (Rev: BL 12/1/04)

5969 Duane, Diane. *Omnitopia Dawn* (11–12). 2010, DAW $24.95 (978-075640623-3). Video game creator Dev Logan worries about hackers on the eve of a huge new expansion of his intricate, addictive online game, Omnitopia. ℮ (Rev: BL 8/10)

5970 Effinger, George Alec. *Budayeen Nights* (11–12). 2003, Golden Gryphon $24.95 (978-1-930846-19-7). The imagined Islamic city of Budayeen is the setting for a collection of stories featuring an offbeat cop and some equally questionable characters, many of them teens; for mature teens. (Rev: BL 9/1/03)

5971 Emerson, Kevin. *The Lost Code. Bk. 1* (8–10). Series: Atlanteans. 2012, HarperCollins $17.99 (978-0-06-206279-6). At a summer camp under a giant dome that allows survival in a world ravaged by environmental problems, Owen learns that he may be the descendant of an ancient race and may hold the key to Earth's salvation. ℮ Lexile HL730L (Rev: SLJ 7/12)

5972 Emshwiller, Carol. *The Mount* (10–12). 2002, Small Beer paper $16.00 (978-1-931520-03-4). Humans are the mounts for the alien hoots in this appealing novel about a young and ambitious mount named Charley. (Rev: BL 8/02; SLJ 6/03)

5973 Evans, Richard Paul. *Michael Vey: The Prisoner of Cell 25* (7–10). 2011, Simon & Schuster $17.99 (978-1-4516-6183-5). Michael, 14, has the power to produce electric shocks and is surprised to find that a lovely girl in his new school has similar powers — and then the two discover there is a deeper force at work. ⌒ ℮ (Rev: BLO 9/1/11; LMC 1–2/12; SLJ 11/1/11)

5974 Falkner, Brian. *The Assault* (7–12). 2012, Random House $17.99 (978-0-375-86946-4); LB $20.99 (978-0-375-96946-1). In 2030 a Recon Team Angel consisting of six teens modified to look like the aliens that are close to controlling the Earth infiltrates the enemy lines and discovers shocking secrets. ℮ (Rev: LMC 1–2/13; SLJ 1/13; VOYA 10/12)

5975 Falkner, Brian. *Brain Jack* (9–12). 2010, Random House $17.99 (978-0-375-84366-2); LB $20.99 (978-0-375-93924-2). In a near-future New York City, 14-year-old computer geek Sam Wilson manages to hack into the AT&T network and attracts attention from a government department. YALSA Popular Paperbacks for Young Adults Top Ten 2012. ℮ (Rev: BL 10/1/10; SLJ 12/1/10)

5976 Farmer, Nancy. *The Ear, the Eye and the Arm* (7–10). 1994, Orchard LB $19.99 (978-0-531-08679-7). In Zimbabwe in 2194, the military ruler's son, 13, and his younger siblings leave their technologically overcontrolled home and embark on a series of perilous adventures. (Rev: BL 4/1/94; SLJ 6/94; VOYA 6/94)

5977 Farmer, Nancy. *House of the Scorpion* (7–10). 2002, Simon & Schuster $17.95 (978-0-689-85222-0). Young Matt, who has spent his childhood in cruel circumstances, discovers he is in fact a clone of the 142-year-old ruler of Opium, a land south of the U.S. border. (Rev: BL 9/15/02; HB 11–12/02; HBG 3/03; SLJ 9/02)

5978 Farmer, Philip Jose. *The Gods of Riverworld* (10–12). Series: Riverworld. 1998, Ballantine paper $12.95 (978-0-345-41971-2). In this, the fifth and last of the recommended Riverworld series, people who lived on Earth in the past are resurrected.

5979 Farmer, Philip Jose. *The Magic Labyrinth* (10–12). Series: Riverworld. 1998, Ballantine paper $12.95 (978-0-345-41970-5). In this 4th installment in the saga, a battle begins between the resurrected humans and the Ethicals. Other volumes in this saga include *The Dark Design* (1984), and *To Your Scattered Bodies Go* (1985).

5980 Faust, Minister. *The Coyote Kings of the Space Age Bachelor Pad* (11–12). 2004, Del Rey paper $13.95 (978-0-345-46635-8). Two friends fight mysterious enemies for control of a power-giving device called a zodiascope; for mature teens. (Rev: BL 6/1–15/04)

5981 Fisher, Catherine. *Corbenic* (8–11). 2006, Greenwillow $16.99 (978-0-06-072470-2). Cal leaves his alcoholic mother to live with his uncle but on the train ride there is transported to a mythical place called Corbenic, where the fate of the Fisher King lies in his hands. (Rev: BL 8/06; HB 9–10/06; SLJ 11/06)

5982 Flint, Eric, and Ryk E. Spoor. *Boundary* (9–12). 2006, Baen $26 (978-1-4165-0932-5). When similar fossils are found in both Montana and on Phobos, the Mars moon, during research expeditions in both places, a group of young engineers and scientists embark on an intriguing adventure of discovery, solving scientific and linguistic puzzles along the way. (Rev: SLJ 6/06)

5983 Flynn, Michael. *Falling Stars* (9–12). 2001, Tor $25.95 (978-0-312-87443-8). In this sequel to *Rogue Star* (1998), an asteroid sent by aliens is only months away from Earth and a solution must be found quickly. (Rev: BL 3/1/01)

5984 Foster, Alan Dean. *Splinter of the Mind's Eye* (8–12). 1978, Ballantine paper $6.99 (978-0-345-32023-0). A novel about Luke Skywalker and Princess Leia of *Star Wars* fame and their battle against the Empire.

5985 Fukui, Isamu. *Truancy* (8–12). 2008, Tor $17.95 (978-0-7653-1767-4). Fifteen-year-old Tack joins a children's resistance movement called the Truancy that is bent on violently overthrowing the establishment. (Rev: BL 4/15/08; LMC 4–5/08; SLJ 6/08)

5986 Gerrold, David. *Blood and Fire* (8–12). 2004, BenBella paper $14.95 (978-1-932100-11-2). In this story that is a metaphor for the AIDS problem, a starship happens on another one, adrift in space, that contains blood worms, a deadly parasite. (Rev: BL 1/1–15/04)

5987 Gerrold, David. *Chess with a Dragon* (8–12). 1988, Avon paper $3.50 (978-0-380-70662-4). The entire human race becomes slaves of giant slugs and Yake must save them. (Rev: BL 6/15/87; SLJ 9/87)

5988 Gerrold, David. *Child of Earth* (9–12). 2005, BenBella paper $14.95 (978-1-932100-47-1). Twelve-year-old Kaer's family volunteers to migrate to the parallel world of Linna, where there are giant and beautiful horses — and unadvertised perils. (Rev: BL 6/1–15/05)

5989 Ghislain, Gary. *How I Stole Johnny Depp's Alien Girlfriend* (8–11). 2011, Chronicle $16.99 (978-0-8118-7460-1). Fourteen-year-old David, son of a French psychologist, falls for Zelda, a beautiful patient who believes she is an alien and who is devoted to Johnny Depp. ℮ Lexile HL570L (Rev: BL 6/1/11; LMC 8–9/11; SLJ 7/11; VOYA 6/11)

5990 Gibson, William. *Neuromancer* (10–12). 1994, Ace paper $7.99 (978-0-441-56959-5). In this variation on the Faust story, a computer expert sells his soul for money.

5991 Gideon, Melanie. *Pucker* (8–11). 2006, Penguin $16.99 (978-1-59514-055-5). Nicknamed "Pucker" by his classmates for the horrible burn scars on his face, 17-year-old Thomas Quicksilver has even larger issues to confront as he returns to his home world of Isaura on a mission to save his mother's life. (Rev: BL 4/15/06; SLJ 5/06)

5992 Gill, David Macinnis. *Black Hole Sun* (8–11). 2010, Greenwillow $16.99 (978-0-06-167304-7). In this action-packed novel set on a dystopian Mars, 16-year-old Durango and other mercenaries fight to protect mines at the South Pole. (Rev: BL 6/10*; SLJ 11/1/10)

5993 Gill, David Macinnis. *Invisible Sun* (8–11). 2012, Greenwillow $16.99 (978-006207332-7). Teens Durango and Vienne, mercenary soldiers, continue their adventures on Mars as they investigate his past in this action-packed stand-alone companion to *Black Hole Sun* (2010). **e** (Rev: BL 4/1/12; SLJ 5/1/12; VOYA 2/12)

5994 Golden, Christie. *Allies* (10–12). Series: Star Wars: Fate of the Jedi. 2010, Del Rey $27 (978-034550914-7). Luke and Ben decide to challenge Abeloth, the evil force that is threatening the young Jedi. ∩ **e** (Rev: BL 5/1–15/10)

5995 Golden, Christie. *Omen* (9–12). Series: Star Wars: Fate of the Jedi. 2009, Del Rey $27 (978-034550912-3). Second in a series, *Omen* opens with many Jedi mysteriously insane, and Luke and Ben trying to discover why, following Jacen, and getting closer to an unknown planet full of Sith. **e** (Rev: BL 4–5/09)

5996 Gould, Steven. *Reflex* (11–12). 2004, Tor $24.95 (978-0-312-86421-7). In this years-later sequel to *Jumper* (1992), a sinister group entraps and exploits Davy Rice, who can teleport from place to place, leaving his wife, her own teleporting ability born of the crisis, to find and rescue Davy; for mature teens. (Rev: BL 12/15/04)

5997 Gould, Steven. *7th Sigma* (10–12). 2011, Tor $24.99 (978-0-312-87715-6). In arid southwestern America, young Kimble Monroe has many adventures as he struggles with life among the "bugs" that are metal-eating machines. (Rev: BL 7/1/11; SLJ 8/11; VOYA 8/11)

5998 Gould, Steven. *Wild Side* (10–12). 1996, Tor $22.95 (978-0-312-85473-7). In this riveting science fiction novel, 18-year-old Charlie discovers a gateway to a parallel world that is a pollution-free, human-free Eden, where animals extinct on Earth still survive. (Rev: BL 3/15/96; VOYA 2/97)

5999 Grant, Michael. *BZRK* (9–12). 2012, Egmont $17.99 (978-1-60684-312-3). In a world of advanced nanotechnology, a group of teen hackers aim to stop the conjoined Armstrong twins from depriving humans of free will. ∩ **e** (Rev: BL 3/15/12*; LMC 10/12; SLJ 7/12)

6000 Grant, Michael. *Fear* (7–10). Series: Gone. 2012, HarperCollins $17.99 (978-006144915-4). This fifth installment in the series finds the young people of Perdido Beach threatened by the Darkness, heightening their ever-present fear. **e** Lexile HL610L (Rev: BL 2/1/12)

6001 Grant, Michael, and Katherine Applegate. *Eve and Adam* (7–10). 2012, Feiwel & Friends $17.99 (978-0-312-58351-4). After having her leg reattached following a car accident, Evening, daughter of a genetic engineering specialist, meets a boy named Solo and makes alarming discoveries. ∩ Lexile HL560L (Rev: BL 9/15/12; HB 1–2/13; LMC 3–4/13; SLJ 11/12; VOYA 10/12)

6002 Grant, Sara. *Dark Parties* (8–12). 2011, Little, Brown $17.99 (978-0-316-08594-6). Neva, 16, and her friend Sanna begin to question the need for their people to live enclosed in the Protectosphere that has covered the Homeland since the "Terror." **e** Lexile HL560L (Rev: BL 5/1/11; LMC 10/11; SLJ 12/1/11; VOYA 8/11)

6003 Haddix, Margaret Peterson. *Found* (6–12). Series: The Missing. 2008, Simon & Schuster $15.99 (978-1-4169-6227-4). Thirteen-year-old Jonah, who was adopted, receives strange notes referring to his past and discovers that, as babies, he and 35 other children traveled through time and arrived on an unpiloted airplane. ∩ (Rev: BL 5/1/08; LMC 4–5/08; SLJ 5/08)

6004 Haldeman, Joe. *Marsbound* (10–12). 2008, Ace $24.95 (978-0-441-01595-5). Carmen Dula has just graduated from high school when her family wins a chance to live on Mars, and while she knows it will be an adventure, Carmen has no idea what she is in for. **e** (Rev: BL 8/08)

6005 Harstad, Johan. *172 Hours on the Moon* (9–12). Trans. by Tara F. Chace. Illus. 2012, Little, Brown $17.99 (978-031618288-1). In 2019 three teenagers win a lottery to join a NASA mission to the moon, where they meet unexpected problems. **e** (Rev: BL 4/15/12; LMC 8–9/12; SLJ 4/12; VOYA 4/12)

6006 Hauge, Lesley. *Nomansland* (8–11). 2010, Henry Holt $16.99 (978-0-8050-9064-2). In a future dystopian world, members of a society of women discover a trove of fashion magazines , with unsettling results. ∩ (Rev: BL 5/15/10; HB 7–8/10; LMC 8–9/10; SLJ 8/10)

6007 Hautman, Pete. *The Obsidian Blade* (8–12). 2012, Candlewick $16.99 (978-076365403-0). After 13-year-old Tucker's parents disappear, he investigates the strange disks that hover in the air and is transported through time, visiting many civilizations. ∩ **e** Lexile 740L (Rev: BL 2/15/12*; HB 5–6/12; LMC 10/12; SLJ 6/12; VOYA 4/12)

6008 Hautman, Pete. *Rash* (9–12). 2006, Simon & Schuster $15.95 (978-0-689-86801-6). Bo, a 16-year old living in the late-21st-century "United Safer States of America," confronts a society preoccupied with safety at the expense of freedom and finds some solace in playing the violent game of football. ⌒ (Rev: BL 5/15/06; HB 5–6/06; SLJ 8/06)

6009 Hayden, Patrick Nielsen, ed. *New Skies: An Anthology of Today's Science Fiction* (7–12). 2003, Tor $19.95 (978-0-7653-0010-2). Short stories that were originally published in science fiction magazines include pieces by Orson Scott Card, Philip K. Dick, and Connie Willis. (Rev: BL 1/1–15/04)

6010 Heinlein, Robert A. *The Cat Who Walks Through Walls* (10–12). 1985, Ace paper $7.99 (978-0-441-09499-8). Colonel Colin Campbell and his wife travel through time to get help solving a murder mystery. (Rev: BL 8/85)

6011 Heinlein, Robert A. *The Door into Summer* (9–12). 1986, Ballantine paper $5.99 (978-0-345-33012-3). An inventor has an opportunity to look into the future in this science fiction novel.

6012 Heinlein, Robert A. *The Moon Is a Harsh Mistress* (10–12). 1996, St. Martin's $24.95 (978-0-312-86176-6); paper $14.95 (978-0-312-86355-5). For better readers, the story of a penal colony on the Earth's moon.

6013 Heinlein, Robert A. *The Star Beast* (7–10). 1977, Macmillan $15.00 (978-0-684-15329-2). A pet smuggled to Earth never seems to stop growing.

6014 Heinlein, Robert A. *Stranger in a Strange Land* (10–12). 1991, Ace paper $16.95 (978-0-441-78838-5). A young man from Mars comes to Earth and must learn our strange ways.

6015 Helfers, John, and Martin H. Greenberg, eds. *Future Americas* (10–12). 2008, DAW paper $7.99 (978-075640508-3). Themes ranging from ecology to criminal investigation to designer fetuses are examined in these thought-provoking stories from a variety of authors. **e** (Rev: BL 6/1–15/08)

6016 Herbert, Brian, and Kevin J. Anderson. *The Battle of Corrin* (9–12). Series: Dune. 2004, Tor $27.95 (978-0-7653-0159-8). This prequel to the classic *Dune* sets the stage on the planet Arrakis following a long battle between the Jihad and the machines. (Rev: BL 8/04)

6017 Herbert, Brian, and Kevin J. Anderson. *Dune: House Atreides* (9–12). 1999, Bantam paper $6.99 (978-0-553-58027-3). This prequel to the recommended Dune series describes the plots and schemes that lay the foundation of the saga. (Rev: BL 8/99; VOYA 4/00)

6018 Herbert, Brian, and Kevin J. Anderson. *Paul of Dune* (10–12). 2008, Tor $27.95 (978-0-7653-1294-5). Good on its own or as a link between *Dune* (1965) and *Dune: Messiah* (1970), this novel tells of Paul Muad-dib as the emperor and explains how he became the messiah. ⌒ **e** (Rev: BL 8/08)

6019 Herbert, Brian, and Kevin J. Anderson. *Sandworms of Dune* (9–12). 2007, Tor $27.95 (978-0-7653-1293-8). Clones and thinking machines do battle in this volume of the Dune prequel trilogy, which will interest Dune fans. (Rev: BL 6/1–15/07)

6020 Hickam, Homer. *Crater* (6–12). Series: Helium-3. 2012, Thomas Nelson $14.99 (978-1-595-54664-7). After a daring rescue, 16-year-old Crater Trueblood who has been a mine worker on the moon, is sent on a dangerous quest; set in the 22nd century. ⌒ **e** Lexile 910L (Rev: SLJ 5/1/12*)

6021 Hill, Will. *Department 19* (9–12). 2011, Penguin $17.99 (978-1-59514-406-5). Following his father's death and his mother's disappearance, Jamie, 16, finds out about a secret government agency that battles vampires and other supernatural entities; an action-packed mix of suspense and horror. **e** Lexile 940L (Rev: BL 5/1/11; SLJ 6/11)

6022 Hirsch, Jeff. *The Eleventh Plague* (7–10). 2011, Scholastic $17.99 (978-054529014-2). In the aftermath of the Collapse, 15-year-old Stephen warily enters a community that tries to emulate the pre-apocalyptic world. ⌒ **e** Lexile 790L (Rev: BL 9/1/11; LMC 1–2/12; SLJ 2/12)

6023 Hoffman, Eva. *The Secret* (11–12). 2002, Public Affairs $25.00 (978-1-58648-150-6). An adolescent clone named Iris is the heroine of this thought-provoking novel set in the near future; for mature teens. (Rev: BL 12/1/02)

6024 Hopkinson, Nalo. *Brown Girl in the Ring* (10–12). 1998, Warner paper $13.99 (978-0-446-67433-1). In this science fiction novel set in postmodern Toronto in the near future, Ti-Jeanne, living with her child and grandmother in urban squalor, must conquer her fears and find a way out of their dismal situation. (Rev: BL 5/15/98; SLJ 11/98; VOYA 8/98)

6025 Hopkinson, Nalo, and Uppinder Mehan, eds. *So Long Been Dreaming: Postcolonial Science Fiction and Fantasy* (11–12). 2004, Arsenal Pulp paper $19.95 (978-1-55I52-158-0). Science fiction and fantasy stories dealing with colonialization, of both alien and Earth societies; sex and violence limit this to mature teens. (Rev: BL 9/1/04)

6026 Horton, Rich, ed. *Science Fiction: The Best of the Year, 2006 Edition* (9–12). 2006, Prime paper $13.95 (978-0-8095-5649-6). The best of the genre in 2006 consists of alternate world fantasies, end-of-time set-ups, and other twists on reality that will keep SF fans turning the pages. (Rev: BL 9/1/06)

6027 Hughes, Monica. *Invitation to the Game* (7–10). 1991, Simon & Schuster paper $4.99 (978-0-671-86692-1). In 2154, a high school graduate and her friends face life on welfare in a highly robotic society and are invited to participate in a sinister government "game." (Rev: BL 9/15/91)

6028 Huxley, Aldous. *Brave New World* (10–12). 1998, HarperPerennial paper $13.95 (978-0-06-092987-9). A science fiction classic set in a future when science controls the life of mankind.

6029 Jablokov, Alexander. *The Breath of Suspension* (9–12). 1994, Arkham $22.95 (978-0-87054-167-4). Short stories with such themes as time-traveling detectives, a cyborg whale that explores Jupiter's atmosphere, and manmade alternate universes. (Rev: BL 8/94; VOYA 12/94)

6030 James, Nick. *Skyship Academy: The Pearl Wars* (7–10). 2011, Flux paper $9.95 (978-07387234-1-9). In 2095, when people either live in the Chosen Cities or the Fringe Towns, young Jesse and Cassius meet while searching for prized energy-full Pearls and wonder about the past. ∩ ℮ Lexile HL650L (Rev: BL 10/15/11; LMC 11–12/11; VOYA 10/11)

6031 Jeapes, Ben. *The Xenocide Mission* (7–10). 2002, Viking $15.95 (978-0-385-75007-3). A complex and exciting adventure set in the distant future in which humans and their quadruped companions must fight against ferocious aliens known as the Kin. (Rev: BCCB 6/02; BL 4/15/02; HBG 3/03; SLJ 6/02; VOYA 8/02)

6032 Jeschonek, Robert T. *My Favorite Band Does Not Exist* (9–12). 2011, Clarion $16.99 (978-0-547-37027-9). This unusual novel with horror and fantasy elements features 16-year-old Idea Deity, who believes that he is a character in a novel and will die in the 64th chapter; he creates a fictional underground rock band on the Internet called Youforia. But does Youforia actually exist? ℮ (Rev: BL 6/1/11; SLJ 9/1/11; VOYA 8/11)

6033 Jinks, Catherine. *Living Hell* (7–10). 2010, Houghton Mifflin $17 (978-0-15-206193-7). On a spaceship on a long journey to find a habitable planet, 17-year-old Cheney finds the peaceful routine turned on its head when they pass through a radiation field. ℮ Lexile 600L (Rev: BL 2/15/10; HB 3–4/10; SLJ 4/10; VOYA 6/10)

6034 John, Antony. *Elemental* (7–10). 2012, Dial $17.99 (978-080373682-5). Thomas, 16, copes with his seemingly powerless condition in a dystopia where everyone else represents either wind, water, fire, or earth. ℮ Lexile HL580L (Rev: BL 11/15/12; LMC 1–2/13; SLJ 1/13)

6035 Johnson, Elana. *Possession* (10–12). 2011, Simon & Schuster $16.99 (978-1-4424-2125-7). Rebellious Vi, 15, lives in a society ruled by Thinkers but is determined to control her own destiny; she must choose which direction to take and which young man to trust. ℮ Lexile HL580L (Rev: BL 6/1/11; LMC 11–12/11; SLJ 6/11)

6036 Jones, Diana Wynne. *Hexwood* (8–12). 1994, Greenwillow $16.00 (978-0-688-12488-5). A complex science fiction story about virtual realism, time manipulation, and a young girl who investigates the disappearance of guests at Hexwood Farm. (Rev: BL 6/1–15/94; SLJ 3/94; VOYA 10/94)

6037 Kacvinsky, Katie. *Awaken* (8–11). 2011, Houghton Mifflin $16.99 (978-0-547-37148-1). In 2060 Americans rarely leave their homes and everything takes place online; but 17-year-old Maddie finds herself targeted by a group, including the handsome Justin, that advocates disconnecting from the virtual world. ℮ Lexile HL700L (Rev: BL 4/1/11; LMC 10/11; SLJ 11/1/11; VOYA 4/11)

6038 Kacvinsky, Katie. *Middle Ground* (8–12). 2012, Houghton Mifflin $16.99 (978-054786336-8). In 2060 Los Angeles 17-year-old Maddie is sent to a detention center and must struggle to resist the reprogramming done there; a sequel to *Awaken* (2011). (Rev: BLO 11/1/12; SLJ 3/13; VOYA 10/12)

6039 Karpyshyn, Drew. *Path of Destruction: A Novel of the Old Republic* (9–12). 2006, Del Rey $25.95 (978-0-345-47736-1). Yoda's Rule of Two — "a master and an apprentice" — is the focus of this novel that provides a history of Darth Bane. (Rev: BL 9/1/06; SLJ 11/06)

6040 Kellerman, Faye, and Aliza Kellerman. *Prism* (9–12). 2009, HarperCollins $16.99 (978-006168721-1); LB $17.89 (978-006168722-8). A bus crash propels three high school students into a parallel universe in which illness and medicine are not recognized. ℮ (Rev: BL 7/09; SLJ 8/09)

6041 Kelly, James Patrick. *Burn* (9–12). 2005, Tachyon $19.95 (978-1-892391-27-8). In this literary science fiction novel, injured firefighter Spur becomes involved in the fight for the soul of his planet, which is named Walden for its dedication to the simple way of life. (Rev: BL 12/15/05)

6042 Kelly, James Patrick. *The Wreck of the Godspeed and Other Stories* (10–12). 2008, Golden Gryphon $24.95 (978-1-930846-51-7). This volume contains previously published science fiction short stories that evoke a surreal atmosphere through the strangeness of the settings while dealing with basic human emotions. (Rev: BL 8/08)

6043 Kenyon, Kay. *Maximum Ice* (10–12). 2002, Bantam paper $5.99 (978-0-553-58376-2). An action-packed tale of a starship's return to Earth to find it nearly covered in a strange substance and the remaining population living under the surface. (Rev: BL 2/1/02; VOYA 4/02)

6044 Khoury, Jessica. *Origin* (7–10). 2012, Penguin $17.99 (978-1-59514-595-6). Created by scientists striving to create a new immortal race, 17-year-old Pia escapes from her compound in the Amazon and meets Eio, from an indigenous tribe; as she falls in love with him she must take risks and make difficult choices. ℮ Lexile HL740L (Rev: BL 8/12; LMC 3–4/13; SLJ 10/12; VOYA 10/12)

6045 Kincaid, S. J. *Insignia* (8–12). 2012, HarperCollins $17.99 (978-0-06-209299-1). Virtual reality gamer Tom, 14, must submit to having a computer implanted in his brain when he becomes a pilot of drones fighting around the solar system. e Lexile HL750L (Rev: BL 7/12; SLJ 7/12*; VOYA 12/12)

6046 Klass, David. *Firestorm* (8–11). 2006, Farrar $17.00 (978-0-374-32307-3). A thrilling adventure about Jack who learns that he has special powers and was sent back from the future to save the dying planet. (Rev: BL 9/15/06; SLJ 9/06)

6047 Koontz, Dean. *Breathless* (10–12). 2009, Bantam $28 (978-055380715-8). In this trademark Koontz alien-encounter tale, two furry, pint-size beings arrive on Earth and set about applying their superhuman intelligence to the turmoil they encounter. (Rev: BL 11/15/09)

6048 Krokos, Dan. *False Memory* (8–11). 2012, Hyperion $17.99 (978-1-4231-4976-7). Miranda, 17, wakes up to find she has lost her memory — and that she can emit a strange energy that causes terror and suicide in those around her. e (Rev: BL 8/12; HB 9–10/12; LMC 1–2/13; SLJ 10/12; VOYA 8/12)

6049 L'Engle, Madeleine. *Many Waters* (7–10). 1986, Farrar $18.00 (978-0-374-34796-3). The Murry twins, from the author's Wrinkle in Time trilogy, time-travel to the Holy Land prior to the Great Flood. (Rev: BL 8/86; SLJ 11/86; VOYA 12/86)

6050 Lackey, Mercedes, and Eric Flint. *The Wizard of Karres* (9–12). 2004, Baen $22.00 (978-0-7434-8839-6). In this sequel to James Schmitz's *The Witches of Karres* (1966), Captain Pausert and his motley circus of a crew take the *Venture* on a new mission to save humanity. (Rev: BL 8/04; SLJ 11/04)

6051 Lancaster, Mike A. *The Future We Left Behind* (7–10). 2012, Egmont $16.99 (978-160684410-6). Long after the release of the Straker Tapes, Peter and Alpha learn that humans were indeed "upgraded" by aliens and that a new upgrade may be on the horizon. e (Rev: BL 11/1/12*; LMC 3–4/13; SLJ 3/13)

6052 Lancaster, Mike A. *Human.4* (7–10). 2011, Egmont $16.99 (978-160684099-3). Kyle, 15, was under hypnosis when humanity was upgraded, and he and his fellow three volunteers are invisible to the larger population. e Lexile 770L (Rev: BL 5/1/11)

6053 Landis, Geoffrey A. *Impact Parameter and Other Quantum Realities* (10–12). 2001, Golden Gryphon $24.95 (978-1-930846-06-7). A fine, varied assortment of 16 stories by the award-winning hard-science sf writer. (Rev: BL 10/15/01)

6054 Landis, Geoffrey A. *Mars Crossing* (9–12). 2000, Tor $24.95 (978-0-312-87201-4). Set in 2028, this space adventure tells of a manned mission to Mars that hopes to be the first to return to Earth safely after two earlier missions failed. (Rev: BL 12/1/00)

6055 Landon, Kristen. *The Limit* (8–11). 2010, Simon & Schuster $15.99 (978-1-4424-0271-3). When his family goes over its spending limit, 13-year-old Matt is sent to the Federal Debt Rehabilitation Agency, where his own living conditions are tolerable, but he recognizes that others are suffering and must be rescued. e (Rev: BL 10/1/10; SLJ 12/1/10)

6056 Lassiter, Rhiannon. *Shadows* (7–10). 2002, Simon & Schuster paper $4.99 (978-0-7434-2212-3). Raven, the superhacker introduced in *Hex*, faces new dangers as the government seeks to destroy her and her fellow mutants. The last volume in the trilogy is *Ghosts* (2002). (Rev: BL 4/15/02; SLJ 4/02)

6057 Lawrence, Louise. *Andra* (6–10). 1991, HarperCollins $14.95 (978-0-06-023685-4). This novel is set 2,000 years in the future, when humanity, having destroyed Earth's environment, lives in rigidly governed, sealed underground cities. (Rev: BL 5/1/91; SLJ 5/91)

6058 Lawrence, Theo. *Mystic City* (7–11). 2012, Delacorte $17.99 (978-038574160-6); LB $20.99 (978-037599013-7). In a dystopian Manhattan submerged by global warming, 18-year-old Aria Rose has lost her memory but is told that she is engaged to Thomas Foster, whose family has been engaged in a long-standing feud with her own. ⌒ e (Rev: BLO 10/15/12; LMC 5–6/13; SLJ 1/13; VOYA 12/12)

6059 Laybourne, Emmy. *Monument 14* (9–12). 2012, Feiwel & Friends $16.99 (978-0-312-56903-7). Six high school students from various social groups struggle to survive and protect the younger children in this postapocalyptic tale. ⌒ e Lexile HL590L (Rev: BL 6/12; HB 7–8/12; SLJ 11/12; VOYA 8/12)

6060 Layne, Steven L. *This Side of Paradise* (7–10). 2001, North Star $15.99 (978-0-9712336-9-0). Jack, a junior in high school, soon questions his father's motives for moving the family into a town called Paradise, where things are definitely not what they seem. (Rev: BL 2/1/02; SLJ 1/02; VOYA 2/02)

6061 Le Guin, Ursula K. *The Lathe of Heaven* (10–12). 1982, Bentley $14.00 (978-0-8376-0464-0); paper $5.50 (978-0-380-01320-3). In this novel set in the 21st century, a young man finds that his dreams are premonitions of events to come.

6062 Le Guin, Ursula K. *The Left Hand of Darkness* (7–12). 1969, Ace paper $7.99 (978-0-441-47812-5). An envoy is sent to the ice-covered planet Gethen where people can be either male or female at will.

6063 Le Guin, Ursula K., and Brian Attebery, eds. *The Norton Book of Science Fiction, 1960–1990* (9–12). 1993, Norton $29.95 (978-0-393-03546-9). The last three decades of North American science fiction are represented in 60 stories that focus on themes rather than on author reputation. (Rev: BL 10/1/93)

6064 Le Guin, Ursula K., and Brian Attebery, eds. *The Norton Book of Science Fiction: North American Sci-*

ence Fiction, 1960-1990 (9–12). 1993, Norton paper $36.60 (978-0-393-97241-2). This excellent collection includes more than 60 vintage science fiction short stories.

6065 Leiber, Fritz. *The Big Time* (10–12). 1976, Amereon LB $20.95 (978-0-88411-931-9). A young girl lives outside the confines of time on a space station.

6066 Leiber, Fritz. *The Dealings of Daniel Kesserich* (9–12). 1997, Tor $18.95 (978-0-312-85408-9). When George Kramer visits his friend John to comfort him after his wife's death, mysterious events begin to occur, including the disappearance of the wife's body. (Rev: BL 2/1/97; VOYA 8/97)

6067 Leicht, Martin, and Isla Neal. *Mothership* (9–12). 2012, Simon & Schuster $16.99 (978-144242960-4). At the Hanover School for Expecting Teen Mothers aboard an Earth-orbiting spaceship in 2074, Elvie discovers that her baby was fathered by an alien. ∩ e Lexile 890L (Rev: BL 7/12; LMC 1–2/13; SLJ 2/13; VOYA 8/12)

6068 Lerner, Edward M. *Fools' Experiments* (11–12). 2008, Tor $25.95 (978-076531901-2). *Fools' Experiments* is a clever, suspenseful science fiction novel that uses the possibilities of computer technology's evolution to chill and thrill; for mature readers. ∩ (Rev: BL 9/15/08)

6069 Levitin, Sonia. *The Goodness Gene* (9–12). 2005, Dutton $16.99 (978-0-525-47397-8). Cloning, euthanasia, and the environment are only three of the topics raised in this thought-provoking novel set in the year 2305 and featuring 16-year-old twins Will and Berk. (Rev: BL 9/1/05; SLJ 12/05; VOYA 10/05)

6070 Lewis, Jon S. *Invasion* (7–10). Series: C.H.A.O.S. 2011, Thomas Nelson $14.99 (978-159554753-8). After his parents die in a car crash, 16-year-old Colt is recruited by a secret organization that battles aliens. ∩ e Lexile HL760L (Rev: BL 5/1/11; VOYA 2/11)

6071 Lloyd, Saci. *The Carbon Diaries 2015* (9–12). 2009, Holiday House $17.95 (978-082342190-9). Teenager Laura documents daily life in London after climate change has led to carbon rationing and drastic changes in energy use. Lexile HL690L (Rev: BL 2/15/09; HB 5–6/09; SLJ 5/1/09*)

6072 Lloyd, Saci. *The Carbon Diaries 2017* (9–12). 2010, Holiday House $17.95 (978-0-8234-2260-9). In the aftermath of the global disaster seen in *The Carbon Diaries 2015,* new carbon rationing has been introduced in Great Britain, the population is abandoning London, and new right-wing political groups are in ascendance; these upheavals disrupt Laura Brown's studies and her punk group's tour of Europe. Lexile 690L (Rev: BL 2/15/10; HB 3–4/10; SLJ 4/10)

6073 Lloyd, Saci. *Momentum* (9–12). 2012, Holiday House $16.95 (978-082342414-6). In an energy-starved London inhabited by Citizens, privileged Hunter Nash

is fascinated by the lives of the Outsiders who live in the slums outside the city. e Lexile 750L (Rev: BL 9/15/12; HB 11–12/12; LMC 1–2/13; SLJ 1/13)

6074 Lo, Malinda. *Adaptation* (8–11). 2012, Little, Brown $17.99 (978-0-316-19796-0). Teens Reese and David are treated at a mysterious facility following a series of bizarre events and begin to realize they've been genetically altered in this science fiction thriller. e (Rev: BL 10/1/12; HB 11–12/12; LMC 3–4/13; SLJ 9/12)

6075 Locke, M. J. *Up Against It* (10–12). 2011, Tor $25.99 (978-076531515-1). On the asteroid colony of Phoecaea rocket-bike-riding teens expose a scheme by the Martian mob to gain control of the colony through the water supply, and cameras everywhere film the colonists for a reality TV show running back on Earth. (Rev: BL 3/1–15/11)

6076 Lore, Pittacus. *The Power of Six* (8–11). Series: Lorien Legacies. 2011, HarperCollins $17.99 (978-0-06-197455-7). In this sequel to *I Am Number Four* (2010) aliens John and Six, with human Sam, are on the run from authorities who think John is a terrorist while Marina, 17, who is in a Spanish convent and is in fact Number Seven, hopes to join them. ∩ e Lexile 840L (Rev: BL 7/11; SLJ 11/1/11)

6077 Lowry, Lois. *Son* (7–10). 2012, Houghton Mifflin $17.99 (978-0-547-88720-3). Set in the same world as *The Giver* (1993), this final volume in the quartet centers on 14-year-old Claire, who gives birth as a Birthmother and then is not given the pills that suppress emotion, leaving her missing her son. ∩ e Lexile 720L (Rev: BL 6/12*; HB 9–10/12; LMC 1–2/13; SLJ 9/12*)

6078 Lu, Marie. *Prodigy* (8–12). 2013, Putnam $17.99 (978-039925676-9). In this sequel to 2011's *Legend,* June and Day travel to Las Vegas and get involved in an assassination plot. ∩ e Lexile 780L (Rev: BL 12/15/12; HB 3–4/13; SLJ 2/13; VOYA 4/13)

6079 Lucas, George, and Chris Claremont. *Shadow Moon: First in the Chronicles of the Shadow War* (9–12). 1996, Bantam paper $5.99 (978-0-553-57285-8). Lucas of *Star Wars* fame and Claremont of Marvel Comics offer the first in a planned trilogy of sci-fi novels. (Rev: BL 10/1/95; VOYA 2/96)

6080 Luceno, James. *Labyrinth of Evil* (9–12). 2005, Del Rey $25.95 (978-0-345-47572-5). This prequel to the film *Revenge of the Sith* pits Jedi Knight Anakin Skywalker and Obi-Wan Kenobi against separatists, culminating in battle on the planet Coruscant. (Rev: BL 1/1–15/05)

6081 McAuley, Paul. *The Secret of Life* (10–12). 2001, Tor $25.95 (978-0-7653-0080-5). Biologist Mariella Anders goes to Mars to investigate the rumor that the Chinese have discovered life at the Red Planet's poles. (Rev: BL 5/15/01)

6082 McCafferty, Megan. *Bumped* (9–12). 2011, HarperCollins $16.99 (978-0-06-196274-5). In 2036 a virus has made most adults infertile and teen pregnancies are highly encouraged; twin 16-year-olds Melody and Harmony have conflicting ideas about being surrogate mothers. **e** (Rev: BL 5/1/11; LMC 10/11; SLJ 6/11; VOYA 4/11)

6083 McCaffrey, Anne. *The Chronicles of Pern: First Fall* (9–12). 1994, Ballantine paper $5.99 (978-0-345-36899-7). Five original stories by the author of the popular Pern series offer a glimpse into the early history of the Dragonriders. (Rev: BL 9/1/93; VOYA 4/94)

6084 McCaffrey, Anne. *The Crystal Singer* (10–12). 1985, Ballantine paper $6.99 (978-0-345-32786-4). This novel involves a crystal singer from the Planet Ballybran and the young girl he influences. (Rev: BL 12/15/87)

6085 McCaffrey, Anne. *Damia's Children* (9–12). 1993, Berkley paper $7.99 (978-0-441-00007-4). The saga of a telepathic/telekinetic family and alien contact, with teenage main characters. (Rev: BL 12/1/92; SLJ 11/93)

6086 McCaffrey, Anne. *The Dolphins of Pern* (9–12). Series: Dragonriders of Pern. 1995, Ballantine paper $6.99 (978-0-345-36895-9). Young Dragonrider T'lion rebuilds the world of Pern's ancient relationship with the "shipfish," dolphins that came to Pern with its early human settlers. (Rev: BL 9/15/94; VOYA 2/95)

6087 McCaffrey, Anne. *Dragonflight* (9–12). Series: Dragonriders of Pern. 1981, Ballantine paper $6.99 (978-0-345-33546-3). This is the first volume of the author's popular Dragonriders of Pern series. It is followed by *Dragonquest* and *White Dragon* (both 1986).

6088 McCaffrey, Anne. *Dragonsdawn* (9–12). 1989, Ballantine paper $6.99 (978-0-345-36286-5). A novel that takes place before the Dragonriders of Pern series. This describes how the planet Pern was colonized and the origins of the deadly Threadfall. (Rev: BL 9/1/88; VOYA 4/89)

6089 McCaffrey, Anne. *Freedom's Landing* (9–12). 1995, Putnam paper $7.99 (978-0-441-00338-9). The first volume in a series about survival and cooperation on an uncharted planet. (Rev: BL 5/15/98; SLJ 8/95)

6090 McCaffrey, Anne. *A Gift of Dragons* (10–12). 2002, Del Rey $15.95 (978-0-345-45635-9). Four stories — one previously unpublished — set on the planet Pern are accompanied by eye-catching illustrations. (Rev: BL 10/15/02; VOYA 4/03)

6091 McCaffrey, Anne. *Killashandra* (9–12). 1985, Ultramarine $25.00 (978-0-89366-187-8); paper $6.99 (978-0-345-31600-4). While visiting a neighboring planet, crystal singer Killashandra is kidnapped. (Rev: SLJ 2/86)

6092 McCaffrey, Anne. *Lyon's Pride* (9–12). 1995, Ace paper $7.99 (978-0-441-00141-5). An alliance between

humans and aliens searches for creatures that destroy indigenous life forms on any planet they inhabit. (Rev: BL 1/1/94; SLJ 9/94; VOYA 10/94)

6093 McCaffrey, Anne. *Moreta: Dragonlady of Pern* (9–12). Series: Dragonriders of Pern. 1984, Ballantine paper $6.99 (978-0-345-29873-7). The dragonriders of Pern are in danger from a mutated strain of influenza. (Rev: BL 12/15/87)

6094 McCaffrey, Anne, and Elizabeth Ann Scarborough. *Changelings* (9–12). Series: Twins of Petaybee. 2005, Del Rey $19.95 (978-0-345-47002-7). In the opening volume of the second Twins of Petaybee trilogy, shape-shifting twins Murel and Ronan are sent to live on a space station with a family friend. (Rev: BL 12/1/05)

6095 McCaffrey, Anne, and Elizabeth Ann Scarborough. *Maelstrom* (9–12). Series: Twins of Petaybee. 2006, Del Rey $23.95 (978-0-345-47004-1). In this sequel to *Changelings* (2005), the shape-shifting twins try to help inhabitants of another planet by bringing them to Petaybee. (Rev: BL 11/15/06; SLJ 3/07)

6096 McCaffrey, Anne, and Todd McCaffrey. *Dragon's Fire* (7–12). Series: Dragonriders of Pern. 2006, Del Rey $24.95 (978-0-345-48028-6). The series continues as the MacCaffreys return to Pern and as the colonists prepare for a phenomenon known as the Thread that follows the Red Star every 50 years and falls onto the planet killing all organic material that it touches; this preparation proves dangerous for the miners of explosive firestone and for the dragons who must chew it to burn the Thread from the sky. (Rev: BL 6/1–15/06; SLJ 8/06)

6097 McDevitt, Jack. *Time Travelers Never Die* (10–12). 2009, Ace $24.95 (978-044101763-8). Plucky protagonist Shel learns of his impending demise when he stumbles upon his father's time travel devices, and desperately searches for a way to change his future. (Rev: BL 11/15/09)

6098 McDonald, Ian. *Planesrunner* (8–11). Series: Everness. 2011, Prometheus $16.95 (978-161614541-5). When his physicist father is kidnapped, 14-year-old Everett finds a mysterious app on his computer that plunges him into a steampunk parallel world and threatening dark powers; the first book in the series. **e** (Rev: BL 2/1/12)

6099 McDonald, Steven E. *Waystation* (9–12). 2004, Tor $24.95 (978-0-7053-0485-6). The crew of the *Andromeda* encounters trouble on the planet Kantar. (Rev: BL 7/04)

6100 Malley, Gemma. *The Resistance* (9–12). 2008, Bloomsbury $16.99 (978-159990302-6). Teens Peter and Anna are working for the resistance, determined to restore the world's natural order and deliver it from the grips of Longevity — the drug that offers eternal life but renders unapproved reproduction a criminal act.

℮ Lexile 750L (Rev: BL 11/1/08; SLJ 12/08; VOYA 10/08)

6101 Mancusi, Marianne. *Razor Girl* (11–12). 2008, Love Spell paper $6.99 (978-050552780-6). An apocalyptic thriller combines with a tense romance in this story of survival in a world devastated by a Super Flu; for mature readers. (Rev: BL 9/15/08)

6102 Marino, Andy. *Unison Spark* (7–10). 2011, Henry Holt $16.99 (978-080509293-6). Living in a sub-canopy slum city, feisty 15-year-old Mistletoe meets Ambrose, 16-year-old heir to the Unison empire, and they discover strange similarities; together they investigate their pasts and realize they may play a key role in the future territory of Unison 3.0. **℮** Lexile 810L (Rev: BL 10/15/11; LMC 3–4/12; SLJ 3/12; VOYA 12/11)

6103 Mariz, Rae. *The Unidentified* (7–11). 2010, HarperCollins $16.99 (978-0-06-180208-9). Kid rejects the corporate, technology-based education system in which students learn by playing games in malls, and is drawn toward the underground activists called the Unidentified. **℮** Lexile HL740L (Rev: BL 9/15/10; SLJ 10/1/10; VOYA 12/10)

6104 Marley, Louise. *The Glass Harmonica* (7–12). 2000, Ace paper $16.00 (978-0-441-00729-5). In an appealing blend of science fiction, mystery, romance, and historical fiction, two related stories — one from the 18th century and the other from the not-so-distant future — feature young girls and a glass harmonica. (Rev: VOYA 2/01)

6105 Meyer, Marissa. *Cinder* (7–10). Series: Lunar Chronicles. 2012, Feiwel & Friends $17.99 (978-031264189-4). In a future New Beijing in a world ravaged by plague, a cyborg named Cinder, shunned because of her low status, attracts the attention of the handsome Prince Kai. ♩ **℮** Lexile 790L (Rev: BL 10/15/11; HB 1–2/12; LMC 3–4/12; SLJ 1/12; VOYA 12/11)

6106 Meyer, Marissa. *Scarlet* (7–10). Series: The Lunar Chronicles. 2013, Feiwel & Friends $17.99 (978-031264296-9). The lives of Scarlet and Cinder as Scarlet searches for her missing grandmother and Cinder escapes from jail, both of them wary of the wicked Lunar Queen Levana. ♩ **℮** Lexile 810L (Rev: BL 1/13*; HB 3–4/13; LMC 8–9/13*; SLJ 2/13; VOYA 6/13)

6107 Meyer, Stephenie. *The Host* (9–12). 2008, Little, Brown $25.99 (978-0-316-06804-8). This story is told from the point of view of an alien parasite called Wanderer, who has taken over the brain of 17-year-old Melanie and comes to love the people Melanie had cared for. ♩ (Rev: BL 3/1/08; SLJ 6/08)

6108 Mitchell, J. Barton. *Midnight City* (9–12). Series: The Conquered Earth. 2012, St. Martin's $17.99 (978-125000907-4). An alien invasion of Earth has killed all the human adults, and children — those with special powers — are the only hope for survival. ♩ **℮** (Rev: BLO 10/15/12; LMC 3–4/13; VOYA 12/12)

6109 Modesitt, L. E., Jr. *Chaos Balance* (10–12). Series: Saga of Recluce. 1997, St. Martin's $25.95 (978-0-312-86389-0); paper $6.99 (978-0-8125-7130-1). A complex story, combining science fiction and fantasy, of the travels of Nylan and his companion, Ayrlyn, as they seek a new home and peace. This is eighth in a series of challenging novels. (Rev: BL 9/15/97; SLJ 7/98; VOYA 2/98)

6110 Morrow, James, ed. *Nebula Awards 26: SFWA's Choices for the Best Science Fiction and Fantasy of the Year* (9–12). 1992, Harcourt paper $12.95 (978-0-15-665472-2). The best science fiction and fantasy stories of 1990. (Rev: BL 3/15/92)

6111 Morrow, James, ed. *Nebula Awards 27: SFWA's Choices for the Best Science Fiction and Fantasy of the Year* (9–12). 1993, Harcourt $24.95 (978-0-15-164935-8). The best science fiction stories of 1991, including a series of tributes to Isaac Asimov. (Rev: BL 3/15/93; VOYA 10/93)

6112 Morwood, Peter. *Star Trek: Rules of Engagement* (9–12). 1990, Pocket paper $4.99 (978-0-671-66129-8). Kirk and the *Enterprise* are sent to evacuate personnel from a politically dangerous planet. (Rev: BL 2/15/90; VOYA 6/90)

6113 Mullin, Mike. *Ashen Winter* (8–12). 2012, Tanglewood $17.95 (978-1-933718-75-0). More than six months after the volcano erupted in *Ashfall* (2011), Alex and Darla search for his parents amid the dangerous and dystopian wintry world. **℮** Lexile 730L (Rev: BL 8/12; LMC 1–2/13; SLJ 10/12; VOYA 10/12)

6114 Ness, Patrick. *The Ask and the Answer* (9–12). Series: Chaos Walking. 2009, Candlewick $18.99 (978-0-7636-4490-1). Alternating chapters follow teens Todd and Viola as they are separated by the brutal regime in New Prentisstown, a space colony inhabited by men who can hear others' thoughts; a sequel to *The Knife of Never Letting Go* (2008). ♩ **℮** Lexile 770L (Rev: BL 8/09*; HB 9–10/09; SLJ 1/10)

6115 Ness, Patrick. *The Knife of Never Letting Go* (8–12). Series: Chaos Walking. 2008, Candlewick $18.99 (978-076363931-0). Young Todd Hewitt realizes that there is a hole in the Noise — which makes the thoughts of men and animals audible — and sets off with his talking dog Viola to seek answers; the opening volume in a trilogy. Odyssey Award 2011; YALSA Top Ten Amazing Audiobooks for Young Adults. ♩ **℮** Lexile 860L (Rev: BL 9/1/08*; HB 11–12/08; LMC 3–4/09; SLJ 11/1/08; VOYA 10/08)

6116 Ness, Patrick. *Monsters of Men* (9–12). Series: Chaos Walking. 2010, Candlewick $18.99 (978-0-7636-4751-3). War is at the center of this conclusion to the trilogy involving Todd and Viola, who must make difficult decisions. ⌒ ℮ (Rev: BL 7/10*; HB 11–12/10; SLJ 9/1/10)

6117 Nissenson, Hugh. *The Song of the Earth* (10–12). 2001, Algonquin $24.95 (978-1-56512-298-7). This book, which has been called a masterpiece, presents a mock documentary about John First Baker, one of three genetically engineered children. (Rev: BL 4/15/01*)

6118 Niven, Larry. *Ringworld* (10–12). 1981, Ballantine paper $5.99 (978-0-345-33392-6). In this prize-winning book, four unique characters are sent to explore a distant place called Ringworld. A sequel is *The Ringworld Engineers* (1985).

6119 Nix, Garth. *A Confusion of Princes* (8–11). 2012, HarperCollins $17.99 (978-006009694-6). Khemri realizes that he must battle many other princes before he can gain stature, even as he meets Raine, a young woman who expands his horizons; a space opera with lots of fascinating details. ⌒ ℮ Lexile 1070L (Rev: BL 2/15/12; HB 5–6/12*; SLJ 6/12)

6120 Nix, Garth. *Shade's Children* (7–12). 1997, HarperCollins LB $15.89 (978-0-06-027325-5). In this science fiction novel, when a person reaches age 16, he or she is sent to the Meat Factory, where body parts are turned into hideous creatures. (Rev: BL 10/1/97; SLJ 8/97; VOYA 6/98)

6121 Norton, Andre. *Key Out of Time* (7–12). 1978, Ultramarine $25.00 (978-0-89366-186-1). Two Time Agents re-create the conflict that destroyed life on the planet Hawaika.

6122 Norton, Andre. *Time Traders II* (8–12). Series: Time Traders. 2001, Baen $24.00 (978-0-671-31968-7). This single volume contains two of Norton's Time Traders novellas: *Key Out of Time* and *The Defiant Agents*. (Rev: BL 2/1/01)

6123 Norton, Andre, and Martin H. Greenberg, eds. *Catfantastic* (9–12). 1989, NAL paper $6.99 (978-0-88677-355-7). A collection of 13 stories about cat-beings with unusual powers. (Rev: BL 7/89; VOYA 2/90)

6124 Nye, Jody Lynne. *View from the Imperium* (10–12). 2011, Baen paper $7.99 (978-14391343-0-6). This fast-paced, often humorous space opera follows the adventures of Ensign Thomas Innes Loche, who is enlisted to travel to the far reaches of the empire to inspect a military installation and runs into a band of dangerous space pirates. (Rev: BLO 3/1–15/11)

6125 Nylund, Eric. *Halo: The Fall of Reach* (10–12). 2001, Del Rey paper $6.99 (978-0-345-45132-3). Super-warriors, known as Spartans, face off against the forces of the Covenant in a battle that may hold the fate of humankind. (Rev: VOYA 4/02)

6126 O'Brien, Caragh M. *Birthmarked* (9–12). Series: Birthmarked Trilogy. 2010, Roaring Brook $16.99 (978-1-59643-569-8). As a midwife in her village outside the ramparts, 16-year-old Gaia must each month deliver the first three babies to the walled Enclave; she does not doubt the status quo until her parents are arrested, and she then sets out to rescue them and question the system. ℮ Lexile HL800L (Rev: BL 2/15/10; LMC 5–6/10; SLJ 5/10)

6127 O'Brien, Caragh M. *Prized* (9–12). Series: Birthmarked Trilogy. 2011, Roaring Brook $16.99 (978-159643570-4). Midwife Gaia and her baby sister find themselves in Sylum, a society where women — who form only 10 percent of the population — hold all the power, and Gaia there finds romance, danger, and scientific mysteries; a sequel to *Birthmarked* (2010). ⌒ ℮ Lexile HL680L (Rev: BL 12/1/11; SLJ 3/12; VOYA 12/11)

6128 O'Brien, Caragh M. *Promised* (9–12). Series: Birthmarked Trilogy. 2012, Roaring Brook $17.99 (978-159643571-1). Seventeen-year-old Gaia returns to the Enclave to find that girls there are being exploited as surrogate mothers; the final volume in the trilogy featuring romance, fantasy, and drama. ⌒ ℮ Lexile 730L (Rev: BL 10/1/12; SLJ 1/13)

6129 Oldham, June. *Found* (7–12). 1996, Orchard LB $17.99 (978-0-531-08893-7). In this novel set in the 21st century, Ren becomes lost in a bleak countryside, gets involved with three other misfits, and finds an abandoned baby. (Rev: BL 9/15/96; SLJ 10/96; VOYA 2/97)

6130 Oliver, Lauren. *Requiem* (9–12). 2013, HarperCollins $18.99 (978-006201453-5). This conclusion to the paranormal romance trilogy that began with *Delirium* (2011) and *Pandemonium* (2012) follows Lena and her fight for freedom and Hana and her preparations for a loveless marriage. ⌒ ℮ (Rev: BL 11/1/12; HB 3–4/13)

6131 Orwell, George. *1984* (10–12). 1950, Signet Classic paper $9.99 (978-0-451-52493-5). This prophetic novel published in 1945 tells of a future world where complete mind control is practiced.

6132 Osterlund, Anne. *Academy 7* (8–12). 2009, Penguin paper $8.99 (978-014241437-8). Aerin and Dane both attend the elite Academy 7 but come from very different worlds. They find themselves attracted to each other as they navigate the demands of school and political intrigue. Lexile 760L (Rev: BL 5/15/09; SLJ 9/09; VOYA 4/10)

6133 Patneaude, David. *Epitaph Road* (9–12). 2010, Egmont $16.99 (978-1-60684-055-9). In 2097 young Kellen, a 14-year-old boy in a population where males are restricted to a mere 5 percent, seeks to protect his rebellious father. ℮ Lexile HL720L (Rev: BL 1/1–15/10; LMC 10/10; SLJ 4/10)

6134 Pearson, Mary E. *The Adoration of Jenna Fox* (8–12). 2008, Henry Holt $16.95 (978-0-8050-7668-4). Jenna, 17, awakens from a coma to find her brain has been altered in this first-person narrative set in a not-too-distant future in which bioengineering has made great strides. ☊ (Rev: BL 3/1/08; SLJ 5/08)

6135 Pearson, Mary E. *The Fox Inheritance* (8–12). 2011, Henry Holt $16.99 (978-0-8050-8829-8). Two hundred and sixty years after their deaths, Locke and Kara are brought back to life in new bio-engineered bodies and set out to find their friend Jenna; a sequel to *The Adoration of Jenna Fox* (2008). ☊ ℯ Lexile 660L (Rev: BLO 9/15/11; HB 9–10/11; SLJ 9/1/11; VOYA 10/11)

6136 Perry, Steve, and Dal Perry. *Chris Bunch's The Gangster Conspiracy* (9–12). 2007, Roc paper $7.99 (978-0-451-46162-9). Interplanetary piracy, gangsters and outer space security firms are featured in this action-packed science fiction novel. (Rev: BL 7/07)

6137 Peterfreund, Diana. *For Darkness Shows the Stars* (7–12). 2012, HarperCollins $17.99 (978-006200614-1). This postapocalyptic retelling of Jane Austen's *Persuasion* features 18-year-old Elliot, a wealthy Luddite who looks after her family's threatened estate and takes care of their Reduced laborers while she longs for Kai, a Reduced whose love she once rejected. ℯ Lexile HL770L (Rev: BLO 6/12; HB 5–6/12; SLJ 6/12; VOYA 4/12)

6138 Pfeffer, Susan Beth. *Life as We Knew It* (7–10). 2006, Harcourt $17.00 (978-0-15-205826-5). Miranda, 16, describes the drastic changes in her life after a meteor hits the moon and causes major weather and other catastrophes on Earth. (Rev: BL 9/1/06; SLJ 10/06)

6139 Polansky, Steven. *The Bradbury Report* (10–12). 2010, Weinstein $24.95 (978-160286122-0). In this complex thriller set in 2071, Anna recognizes an escaped clone as her old boyfriend, and sets out to reunite the clone with his original. ℯ (Rev: BL 4/1/10*)

6140 Price, Lissa. *Starters* (7–10). 2012, Delacorte $17.99 (978-0-385-74237-5); LB $20.99 (978-037599060-1). Callie, 16, hires out her body for old people to experience youth again in this dystopian story fringed with dark consequences. ☊ ℯ (Rev: BL 3/15/12; LMC 10/12; SLJ 7/12; VOYA 12/12)

6141 Price, Susan. *The Sterkarm Handshake* (7–10). 2000, HarperCollins LB $18.89 (978-0-06-029392-5). Violent confrontations result when a 21st-century corporation makes inroads into the 16th-century Scottish Borders. (Rev: BL 10/1/00; HBG 3/01; SLJ 12/00)

6142 Priest, Cherie. *Clementine* (11–12). Series: Clockwork Century. 2010, Subterranean $25 (978-159606308-2). In this steampunk take on the Civil War, Confederate spy Belle Boyd has taken a job with the Pinkerton detective agency and must investigate who's threatening the *Clementine,* a blimp carrying needed supplies over the Rocky Mountains. ☊ ℯ (Rev: BLO 5/1–15/10)

6143 Reaves, Michael, and Steve Perry. *Death Star: Star Wars* (9–12). 2007, Del Rey $25.95 (978-0-345-47742-

2). This wonderful book speculates about the builders of the first imperial Death Star, including architects, military experts and eventual dissenters. (Rev: BL 9/1/07)

6144 Reed, Robert. *Marrow* (10–12). 2000, Tor $25.95 (978-0-312-86801-7). The Ship, on a journey of eons through the universe, is now in the Milky Way and a team must leave it to explore the surface of a dangerous planet. (Rev: BL 9/1/00)

6145 Reeve, Philip. *Infernal Devices* (7–10). Series: Hungry City Chronicles. 2006, HarperCollins $16.99 (978-0-06-082635-2). In this gripping third book of the post-apocalyptic series that started with *Mortal Engines*, adventure-seeking 15-year-old Wren is kidnapped and her parents must come to her rescue. (Rev: BL 5/15/06; HB 7–8/06; SLJ 6/06)

6146 Revis, Beth. *A Million Suns* (9–12). 2012, Penguin $18.99 (978-159514398-3). Elder and Amy must cope with chaos about the spaceship *Godspeed* as the passengers waken from their medicated states; romance and science fiction are combined in this tense sequel to *Across the Universe* (2011). ☊ ℯ Lexile HL760L (Rev: BL 12/1/11; HB 3–4/12; SLJ 2/12)

6147 Revis, Beth. *Shades of Earth* (9–12). 2013, Penguin $18.99 (978-159514399-0). Amy and Elder work to establish a new home on Centauri-Earth, even as they remain uncertain about the other residents of the planet; the final volume in the trilogy that began with *Across the Universe* (2011) and *A Million Suns* (2012). ☊ ℯ Lexile HL780L (Rev: BL 12/1/12; HB 1–2/13)

6148 Ringo, John. *East of the Sun, West of the Moon* (11–12). Series: The Council War. 2006, Baen $24.00 (978-1-4165-2059-7). A combination of space-age and archaic technologies make the battles and intrigue in this novel even more enjoyable; sexual situations may limit this to older readers. (Rev: BL 5/15/06)

6149 Ringo, John. *Live Free or Die* (11–12). 2010, Baen $26 (978-143913332-3). An unfriendly breed of extraterrestrials is at war with Earth, and an unlikely protagonist — Vermont native Tyler Vernon — saves the day; for mature readers. (Rev: BLO 1/1–15/10)

6150 Rivers, Karen. *X in Flight* (9–12). 2007, Raincoast $9.95 (978-1-55192-982-8). "X" is a teenage boy of mixed race who, amid relationship and family crises, finds out that he has the ability to fly. (Rev: SLJ 3/08)

6151 Roberts, Adam. *Salt* (11–12). 2002, Gollancz paper $14.95 (978-0-575-06897-1). Two tribes of Earth colonists battle over intermarriage on their new planet, a land of salty deserts; for mature teens. (Rev: BL 2/15/02)

6152 Robinson, Spider. *God Is an Iron and Other Stories* (10–12). 2002, Five Star $24.95 (978-0-7862-4162-0). A collection of short stories including the award-winning "Stardance," cowritten by Robinson's wife. (Rev: BL 5/1/02)

6153 Rosenblum, Gregg. *Revolution 19* (7–10). 2013, HarperTeen $17.99 (978-006212595-8). In 2051, after the robots took over, siblings Nick, Kevin, and Cass leave their wilderness community and try to rescue their parents from the bot-controlled city. e (Rev: BL 11/15/12; SLJ 5/13)

6154 Rossi, Veronica. *Under the Never Sky* (8–11). 2012, HarperCollins $17.99 (978-006207203-0). Aria, from a privileged community, and Peregrine, from a wasteland, must work together despite their differences if they are to survive; but the longer they know each other the closer they become. ☊ e Lexile HL580L (Rev: BL 2/15/12; HB 3–4/12; SLJ 3/12*; VOYA 12/11)

6155 Roth, Veronica. *Insurgent* (9–12). 2012, HarperCollins $17.99 (978-006202404-6). Readers who enjoyed the first book — *Divergent* (2011) — will appreciate 16-year-old Tris's continuing adventures in this complex and violent dystopian society. ☊ e Lexile HL710L (Rev: BL 3/15/12; SLJ 6/12; VOYA 6/12)

6156 Rowe, Rebecca K. *Forbidden Cargo* (9–12). 2006, Edge paper $14.95 (978-1-894063-16-6). Set in 2110, this story of artificial intelligence and genetically altered humans is both action-filled and thought-provoking. (Rev: SLJ 10/06)

6157 Rubenstein, Gillian. *Galax-Arena* (7–10). 1995, Simon & Schuster paper $15.00 (978-0-689-80136-5). A 13-year-old girl and 20 other children from Earth are removed to another planet and trained to perform dangerous acrobatic tricks. (Rev: BL 10/15/95*; SLJ 10/95)

6158 Rusch, Kristine Kathryn. *Stories for an Enchanted Afternoon* (9–12). 2001, Golden Gryphon $24.95 (978-1-930846-02-9). These 11 stories exploring alternate worlds and other eerie situations give readers an opportunity to sample this fine young writer's work. (Rev: BL 4/15/01)

6159 Russell, Eric Frank. *Entities: The Selected Novels of Eric Frank Russell* (10–12). Ed. by Rick Katze. 2001, NESFA $29.00 (978-1-886778-33-7). This anthology contains five novels by one of the great pioneers of science fiction. (Rev: BL 11/15/01)

6160 Ryan, Amy Kathleen. *Glow* (7–11). Series: Sky Chasers. 2011, St. Martin's $17.99 (978-0-312-59056-7). War breaks out between two pioneer spaceships over the issue of human reproduction. ☊ e Lexile 750L (Rev: BL 9/1/11; SLJ 9/1/11*; VOYA 10/11)

6161 Ryan, Amy Kathleen. *Spark* (7–11). 2012, St. Martin's/Griffin $17.99 (978-0-312-62135-3). Waverly's former fiance tries to belittle her contributions to the spaceship crew's safety in this sequel to *Glow* (2011). ☊ e (Rev: BLO 7/12; SLJ 11/12)

6162 Sagan, Nick. *Everfree* (10–12). 2006, Putnam $24.95 (978-0-399-15276-4). The final book of the trilogy that began with *Idlewild* (2003) and continued with *Edenborn* (2004) completes a futuristic fantasy world

in which "posthumans" revive cryogenically preserved humans, with disastrous results. ☊ (Rev: BL 5/1/06)

6163 Sampson, Jeff. *Havoc* (8–12). Series: Deviants. 2012, HarperCollins $17.99 (978-0-06-199278-0). Transformed into werewolves by a genetic experiment, Emily, 16, and her friends struggle to control their new powers and investigate the reason behind this change. e (Rev: SLJ 5/1/12; VOYA 12/11)

6164 Sargent, Pamela. *Alien Child* (8–12). 1988, HarperCollins $13.95 (978-0-06-025202-1). A teenage girl raised in an alien world discovers there is another human living in her complex. (Rev: BL 2/1/88; SLJ 4/88; VOYA 8/88)

6165 Sargent, Pamela, ed. *Nebula Awards 29: SFWA's Choices for the Best Science Fiction and Fantasy of the Year* (9–12). 1995, Harcourt paper $17.00 (978-0-15-600119-9). A collection of prize-winning science fiction and fantasy stories for the year 1993. (Rev: BL 4/15/95; SLJ 10/95)

6166 Sawyer, Robert J. *Iterations* (11–12). 2004, Red Deer paper $22.95 (978-0-88995-303-1). Mind-bending short stories by a master of science fiction. (Rev: BL 10/1/04)

6167 Sawyer, Robert J. *WWW: Wake* (10–12). 2009, Ace $24.95 (978-044101679-2). Hoping to break out of the darkness, 10th-grader Caitlin opts for experimental eye surgery and realizes afterward that she is seeing the World Wide Web instead of real life. e (Rev: BL 4–5/09)

6168 Scalzi, John. *Zoe's Tale* (10–12). Series: Old Man's War. 2008, Tor $24.95 (978-0-7653-1698-1). This addition to the trilogy is told from 15-year-old Zoe Perry's point of view as she helps defend the colony against an alien alliance. (Rev: BL 8/08)

6169 Scarrow, Alex. *Time Riders* (9–12). 2010, Walker $16.99 (978-0-8027-2172-3). Three teens join forces to travel through time and correct changes in history made by other time travelers. (Rev: LMC 11–12/10; SLJ 6/11)

6170 Schubert, Edmund R., and Orson Scott Card, eds. *Orson Scott Card's InterGalactic Medicine Show* (10–12). 2008, Tor paper $15.95 (978-076532000-1). Likening fantasy stories to an old-time medicine show, Schubert and Card present 17 new stories — 5 from the Ender series — that have appeared in Card's e-zine. e (Rev: BL 6/1–15/08)

6171 Sheehan, Anna. *A Long, Long Sleep* (8–12). 2011, Candlewick $16.99 (978-0-7636-5260-9). After 60 years in stasis, Rosalinda, still 16 years old, is awakened by a kiss to discover that she is in danger from a robot assassin. ☊ e Lexile HL670L (Rev: LMC 1–2/12; SLJ 12/1/11)

6172 Sheffield, Charles. *Cold As Ice* (9–12). 1993, Tor paper $4.99 (978-0-8125-1163-5). Nine sleeping infants nestled in pods and ejected from a doomed ship grow up to become the key to an extraordinary race. (Rev: BL 6/15/92*)

6173 Sheffield, Charles. *The Lady Vanishes and Other Oddities of Nature* (10–12). 2002, Five Star $25.95 (978-0-7862-4169-9). A collection of recent short stories drawing on physics. (Rev: BL 5/1/02)

6174 Shusterman, Neal. *UnWholly* (7–10). Series: Unwind Trilogy. 2012, Simon & Schuster $17.99 (978-1-4424-2366-4). The practice of harvesting organs from "troubled" teens continues in this thought-provoking second installment as Cam, totally constructed from grafted parts, begins to question the nature of humanity. ⌒ ℮ Lexile 860L (Rev: BL 7/12; HB 9–10/12; LMC 3–4/13; SLJ 9/12)

6175 Silverberg, Robert. *Phases of the Moon: Stories of Six Decades* (9–12). 2004, Subterranean $40.00 (978-1-931081-99-3). Covering the author's short fiction output for almost 50 years, this a fine collection that can serve as an introduction to the many talents of this sf writer. (Rev: BL 5/15/04)

6176 Silverberg, Robert. *To Be Continued: The Collected Stories of Robert Silverberg, Vol. 1* (9–12). 2006, Subterranean $35.00 (978-1-59606-061-6). This first volume of the collected works of Silverberg, who wrote close to 1,000 stories, focuses on science fiction. (Rev: BL 9/1/06)

6177 Silverberg, Robert, ed. *Robert Silverberg's Worlds of Wonder: Exploring the Craft of Science Fiction* (9–12). 1987, Warner $12.95 (978-0-446-39012-5). A collection of short science fiction plus a guide to science fiction writing. (Rev: BL 10/1/87; VOYA 2/88)

6178 Simmons, Dan. *Worlds Enough and Time* (10–12). 2002, Subterranean $40.00 (978-1-931081-54-2). Four stories and a screen treatment are accompanied by insightful introductions by the author. (Rev: BL 5/1/02)

6179 Skurzynski, Gloria. *The Revolt* (8–12). Series: The Virtual War Chronologs. 2005, Simon & Schuster $16.95 (978-0-689-84265-8). In this action-packed third volume in the series, Corgan flees to Florida to put an end to his battle with Brigand but is soon followed there by his violent enemy. (Rev: SLJ 7/05)

6180 Sleator, William. *The Boy Who Reversed Himself* (8–12). 1998, Puffin paper $5.99 (978-0-14-038965-4). Laura travels into the fourth dimension with her gifted neighbor and literally everything in her life becomes upside-down. (Rev: BL 10/15/86; SLJ 11/86; VOYA 6/87)

6181 Sleator, William. *House of Stairs* (7–10). 1991, Puffin paper $5.99 (978-0-14-034580-3). Five teenage orphans are kidnapped to become part of an experiment on aggression.

6182 Sleator, William. *Interstellar Pig* (7–10). 1996, Peter Smith $22.25 (978-0-8446-6898-7); paper $6.99

(978-0-14-037595-4). Barney plays an odd board game with strangers who are actually aliens from space.

6183 Sleator, William. *Parasite Pig* (7–10). 2002, Dutton $15.99 (978-0-525-46918-6). Barney and Katie continue playing the board game they began in *Interstellar Pig* and wind up on a planet called J'koot, threatened by crablike aliens with cannibal tendencies. (Rev: BCCB 2/03; BL 11/15/02; HB 11–12/02*; HBG 3/03; SLJ 10/02; VOYA 12/02)

6184 Sleator, William. *Singularity* (7–12). 1995, Puffin paper $6.99 (978-0-14-037598-5). Twin boys discover a playhouse on the property they have inherited that contains a mystery involving monsters from space and a new dimension in time. (Rev: BL 4/1/85; SLJ 8/85)

6185 Smibert, Angie. *Memento Nora* (8–11). 2011, Marshall Cavendish $16.99 (978-0-7614-5829-6). In a future where people are given pills that wipe out unpleasant memories, Nora and her friends create an underground comic that will allow them to save their experiences. ⌒ ℮ Lexile 670L (Rev: BL 6/1/11; HB 7–8/11; LMC 8–9/11; SLJ 4/11)

6186 Smith, Sherri L. *Orleans* (8–12). 2013, Putnam $17.99 (978-039925294-5). A dark multilayered tale set on the Gulf Coast, separated from the United States after the appearance of a deadly plague in the wake of ever-stronger hurricanes. ℮ Lexile HL750L (Rev: BL 2/1/13*; HB 3–4/13; SLJ 4/13; VOYA 2/13)

6187 Souders, J. A. *Renegade* (8–11). Series: The Elysium Chronicles. 2012, Tor Teen $17.99 (978-076553245-5). In the underwater utopia of Elysium 16-year-old Evelyn, Daughter of the People, is quite content until a surface dweller, Gavin, appears on the scene and turns her world upside down. ℮ Lexile HL690L (Rev: BL 12/15/12; SLJ 1/13)

6188 Spooner, Meagan. *Skylark* (9–12). 2012, Carolrhoda $17.95 (978-0-7613-8865-4). Sixteen-year-old Lark, exploited for her ability to provide constant power to the city, rebels and escapes only to find herself facing new dangers outside her domed home. ℮ (Rev: BL 10/1/12; LMC 3–4/13; SLJ 10/12)

6189 Stackpole, Michael A. *I, Jedi* (8–12). 1998, Random House paper $6.99 (978-0-553-57873-7). In order to find his wife, Corran must take a quick course at the Jedi Academy founded by Luke Skywalker and learn to use his hidden powers. (Rev: VOYA 12/98)

6190 Stasheff, Christopher. *A Wizard in a Feud* (10–12). 2001, Tor $22.95 (978-0-312-86674-7). Heroes Gar Pike and Alea travel to help a planet where basically decent people can't stop feuding. (Rev: BL 6/1–15/01; VOYA 12/01)

6191 Stasse, Lisa M. *The Forsaken* (9–12). 2012, Simon & Schuster $16.99 (978-1-4424-3265-9). In a dystopian future 16-year-old Alenna fails the Government Personality Profile Test and finds herself on a prison island full of conflict and danger. ℮ Lexile HL660L (Rev: BL 8/29/12; LMC 1–2/13; SLJ 8/1/12; VOYA 10/12)

6192 Steele, Allen. *The River Horses* (9–12). 2007, Subterranean $35.00 (978-1-59606-132-3). Three travelers learn to trust each other as they explore mysterious, unknown wilderness on their home planet. (Rev: BL 7/07)

6193 Stewart, Sean. *Dark Rendezvous* (9–12). 2004, Del Rey paper $7.50 (978-0-345-46309-8). Prequeling the film *Revenge of the Sith*, this *Clone Wars* series entry pits Jedi Master Yoda and several Knights against former disciple Count Dooku, who has embraced the Dark Side. (Rev: BL 12/15/04)

6194 Stirling, S. M. *The Sky People* (11–12). Series: Lords of Creation. 2006, Tor $24.95 (978-0-7653-1488-8). In this alternate history, Venus is habitable (albeit with dinosaurs and sabertooth tigers) and the Russians and Americans have set up separate, competing bases; but some important mysteries linger in this first installment in a new series. (Rev: BL 11/15/06)

6195 Strahan, Jonathan, ed. *The Starry Rift: Tales of New Tomorrows* (9–12). 2008, Viking $19.99 (978-0-670-06059-7). A collection of 16 stories by the best of today's science-fiction writers. After each story is brief information about the author and his or her thoughts on it. (Rev: BL 5/15/08; SLJ 6/08)

6196 Strieber, Whitley. *The Grays* (9–12). 2006, Tor $24.95 (978-0-7653-1389-8). The grays are aliens about to visit Earth to determine how their messenger — a human child who can receive their communications — is faring here. (Rev: BL 5/15/06)

6197 Strieber, Whitley. *2012: The War for Souls* (9–12). 2007, Tor $24.95 (978-0-7653-1896-1). Demonic aliens have infiltrated Earth for centuries, and the discovery of the physical existence of the soul leads to heightened conflicts in this exciting novel. (Rev: BL 8/07)

6198 Sutherland, Tui T. *So This Is How It Ends* (8–11). Series: Avatars. 2006, HarperCollins $16.99 (978-0-06-075024-4). Five teenagers are the only young people left in a future world, and their special powers will help them survive among crystal monsters and old, confused humans. (Rev: BCCB 2/07; BL 1/1–15/07; SLJ 11/06)

6199 Tenn, William. *Immodest Proposals: The Complete Science Fiction of William Tenn, Vol. 1* (10–12). Ed. by James A. Mann and Mary C. Tabasko. 2001, NESFA $29.00 (978-1-886778-19-1). For older readers, this is a collection of 33 ingenious, entertaining science fiction pieces by one of the masters. (Rev: BL 4/15/01)

6200 Testa, Dom. *The Cassini Code* (7–10). Series: Galahad. 2010, Tor paper $8.99 (978-07653607-9-3). The teens aboard starship *Galahad* must decide between returning to Earth and continuing on their mission even as they enter a deadly asteroid field. (Rev: BL 2/1/11)

6201 Testa, Dom. *The Comet's Curse* (7–10). Series: Galahad. 2009, Tor $16.95 (978-076532107-7). The first book in a six-part series, this sci-fi drama starts when a comet spews deadly dust, killing the adults on Earth and forcing 250 teens into space to colonize a safer planet. ℮ Lexile 840L (Rev: BL 12/15/08; LMC 8–9/09; SLJ 3/1/09; VOYA 4/09)

6202 Testa, Dom. *The Galahad Legacy* (7–10). Series: Galahad. 2012, Tor $16.99 (978-076532112-1). A rousing conclusion to the story of 251 teens venturing into space, in which they must make a difficult choice in the face of an alien race's offer. ℮ (Rev: BL 12/15/11*)

6203 Testa, Dom. *The Web of Titan* (7–10). Series: Galahad. 2010, Tor $16.99 (978-076532108-4). As they approach Saturn, the 251 teens aboard the *Galahad* contend with a mysterious illness and technological problems; the sequel to *The Comet's Curse* (2009). ℮ (Rev: BLO 5/15/10)

6204 Tolan, Stephanie S. *Welcome to the Ark* (7–10). 1996, Morrow $15.00 (978-0-688-13724-3). Science fiction and adventure combine in the story of four young people who are able to act for good or evil through telecommunications. (Rev: BL 10/15/96; SLJ 10/96; VOYA 4/97)

6205 Townsend, John Rowe. *The Creatures* (7–10). 1980, HarperCollins $12.95 (978-0-397-31864-3). Earth is dominated by creatures from another planet who believe in mind over emotion.

6206 Treggiari, Jo. *Ashes, Ashes* (7–10). 2011, Scholastic $17.99 (978-0-545-25563-9). In a postapocalyptic Manhattan, 16-year-old Lucy learns that her blood is of value to the dreaded Sweepers. ⌒ ℮ Lexile 810L (Rev: BLO 8/11; SLJ 8/11)

6207 Turtledove, Harry. *The Great War: American Front* (10–12). Series: The Great War. 1998, Del Rey $25.00 (978-0-345-40615-6). An alternate history set during the early 20th century, at the outbreak of World War I, in which Teddy Roosevelt allies his supporters with Germany and Woodrow Wilson joins with France and Great Britain, bringing a divided nation into trench warfare on U.S. soil. (Rev: BL 4/15/98*; SLJ 3/99; VOYA 12/98)

6208 Turtledove, Harry. *The Valley-Westside War* (10–12). 2008, Tor $24.95 (978-0-7653-1487-1). In post-nuclear Los Angeles, two teens struggle to overcome the prejudices of their warring principalities as they learn that even leaders make mistakes. (Rev: BL 6/1–15/08; SLJ 9/08)

6209 Turtledove, Harry, and Martin H. Greenberg, eds. *The Best Alternate History Stories of the 20th Century* (10–12). 2001, Del Rey paper $18.00 (978-0-345-43990-1). This is a superb collection of 14 stories that make a fine introduction to the alternate history genre. (Rev: BL 9/15/01; SLJ 3/02; VOYA 2/02)

6210 Turtledove, Harry, and Martin H. Greenberg, eds. *The Best Military Science Fiction of the 20th Century* (10–12). 2001, Del Rey paper $18.00 (978-0-345-43989-5). Thirteen science fiction stories with military themes by such writers as Orson Scott Card and Anne McCaffrey are included in this anthology. (Rev: BL 3/15/01)

6211 Ure, Jean. *Plague* (7–12). 1991, Harcourt $16.95 (978-0-15-262429-3). Three teenagers must band together to survive in a hostile, nearly deserted London after a catastrophe has killed almost everyone. (Rev: BL 11/15/91*; SLJ 10/91)

6212 Van Pelt, James. *Strangers and Beggars* (10–12). 2002, Fairwood paper $17.99 (978-0-9668184-5-1). The appealing and diverse stories in this collection offer science fiction combined with fantasy, mystery, and horror. (Rev: BL 7/02; VOYA 6/03)

6213 Verne, Jules. *Around the Moon* (8–12). 1968, Airmont paper $1.50 (978-0-8049-0182-6). An early science fiction relic about a trip to the moon. Also use *From the Earth to the Moon* (1984).

6214 Verne, Jules. *Master of the World* (9–12). 1979, Amereon $20.95 (978-0-89190-518-9). A scientist who has invented an amazing machine claims he is the master of the world. Originally published in 1904.

6215 Vonnegut, Kurt. *Cat's Cradle* (10–12). 1987, Delta paper $12.95 (978-0-385-33348-1). A mordantly humorous novel about a mythical island and the discovery of a weapon more powerful than the nuclear bomb.

6216 Waldrop, Howard. *Other Worlds, Better Lives: A Howard Waldrop Reader: Selected Long Fiction, 1989–2003* (10–12). 2008, Old Earth paper $15.00 (978-188296838-1). The seven novellas found in this book are fine examples of the author's skill and artistry as a writer of science fiction. (Rev: BL 9/15/08)

6217 Wallenfels, Stephen. *POD* (8–11). 2010, Namelos $18.95 (978-160898011-6); paper $9.95 (978-16089801-0-9). Told in alternate chapters, this is the story of two young people — 15-year-old Josh and 12-year-old Megs — who have different experiences in different cities when aliens attack the earth. **e** Lexile HL650L (Rev: BL 5/15/10; HB 7–8/10)

6218 Wasserman, Robin. *Crashed* (9–12). 2009, Simon & Schuster $16.99 (978-1-4169-7453-6). "Mech" — or synthetic human — Lia fights a conspiracy to destroy her and her kind in this sequel to 2008's *Skinned*. ∩ **e** Lexile HL770L (Rev: BLO 10/21/09; SLJ 1/10; ∩ VOYA 8/09)

6219 Wasserman, Robin. *Skinned* (9–12). 2008, Simon & Schuster $15.99 (978-141693634-3). Although 17-year-old Lia's body was destroyed in a car accident, her mind lives on in her new persona as a "mech"— a mechanical replica — and the previously popular and glamorous girl must cope with being ostracized and

isolated. **e** Lexile HL630L (Rev: BL 10/15/08; LMC 5–6/09; SLJ 1/1/09)

6220 Waugh, Charles G., and Martin H. Greenberg, eds. *Sci-Fi Private Eye* (9–12). 1997, Roc paper $5.99 (978-0-451-45582-6). Most of the nine stories in this collection, by such writers as Donald Westlake, Robert Silverberg, and Philip K. Dick, are mysteries with a science fiction twist. (Rev: VOYA 10/97)

6221 Weaver, Will. *The Survivors* (7–10). 2012, HarperTeen $17.99 (978-006009476-8). In a cabin in the Minnesota woods, 16-year-old Miles and his younger sister Sarah are struggling to survive after the volcanic eruptions disrupted society in *Memory Boy* (2001); Sarah's goat and Miles's memory prove invaluable until Miles's abilities are threatened. **e** (Rev: BL 2/15/12; SLJ 2/12)

6222 Weber, David. *Ashes of Victory* (10–12). 2000, Baen $24.00 (978-0-671-57854-1). This Honor Harrington novel continues the war between the Star Kingdom and the People's Republic of Haven. (Rev: BL 3/1/00)

6223 Weber, David. *The Excalibur Alternative* (10–12). 2002, Baen $21.00 (978-0-671-31860-4). Sir George Wincester with his company and family are transported from 1346 to the future, where they become slaves on primitive planets. (Rev: BL 12/1/01)

6224 Weber, David. *Honor Among Enemies* (9–12). 1996, Baen $21.00 (978-0-671-87723-1). Captain Honor Harrington is brought out of retirement by the Royal Manticoran Navy to lead a task force of interstellar vessels against pirates who are plundering merchant ships and ravaging their crews. (Rev: BL 6/1–15/96; VOYA 12/96)

6225 Weber, David. *Worlds of Weber: Ms. Midshipwoman Harrington and Other Stories* (10–12). 2008, Subterranean $45.00 (978-159606177-4). An interesting and lengthy compilation of Weber's short stories full of fascinating characters and science fiction adventure. (Rev: BL 9/1/08)

6226 Weber, David, and John Ringo. *March to the Sea* (10–12). 2001, Baen $24.00 (978-0-671-31826-0). In this sequel to *March Upcountry* (2001), Prince Roger and his marines must blast their way across alien landscapes to the planet's only spaceport. (Rev: BL 7/01)

6227 Weber, David, and John Ringo. *March Upcountry* (9–12). 2001, Baen $24.00 (978-0-671-31985-4). Prince Roger is sent on a war mission, but his ship is sabotaged and he makes a landing on a disputed planet. (Rev: BL 4/15/01*)

6228 Wells, Dan. *Partials* (8–12). 2012, HarperCollins $17.99 (978-006207104-0). The future of the human race rests in the hands of 16-year-old medical intern Kira in this post-apocalyptic thriller. ∩ **e** (Rev: BL 1/1/12; SLJ 4/12; VOYA 2/12)

6229 Wells, H. G. *First Men in the Moon* (7–12). 1993, Tuttle paper $7.95 (978-0-460-87304-8). The first men on the moon discover strange creatures living there.

6230 Wells, H. G. *The Food of the Gods* (10–12). 1978, Pendulum paper $2.95 (978-0-88301-314-4). This novel is set in a land where people do not stop growing.

6231 Wells, H. G. *The Invisible Man* (8–12). 1987, Buccaneer LB $21.95 (978-0-89966-377-7); paper $4.95 (978-0-553-21353-9). Two editions of many available of the story of a scientist who finds a way to make himself invisible.

6232 Wells, H. G. *The Time Machine* (7–12). 1984, Bantam paper $4.95 (978-0-553-21351-5). This is one of the earliest novels to use traveling through time as its subject.

6233 Wells, H. G. *The War of the Worlds* (7–12). 1988, Bantam paper $4.95 (978-0-553-21338-6). In this early science fiction novel, first published in 1898, strange creatures from Mars invade England.

6234 Wells, Robison. *Variant* (8–11). 2011, HarperTeen $17.99 (978-006202608-8). Benson, 17, is initially happy to have left a series of foster homes for Maxfield Academy but soon discovers that the school is a prison, the students are split into warring factions, and nothing is what it seems. A sequel is *Feedback* (2012). ⌒ e Lexile HL640L (Rev: BL 10/15/11; LMC 3–4/12)

6235 Westerfeld, Scott. *Extras* (7–10). Series: The Uglies. 2007, Simon & Schuster $16.99 (978-1-4169-5117-9). In the future world in which human worth is now based on celebrity, Aya, an Ugly and now an Extra, discovers the underside to her city while she chases popularity. (Rev: BL 1/1–15/08; HB 11–12/07; SLJ 1/08)

6236 Westerfeld, Scott. *Goliath* (7–10). Illus. by Keith Thompson. 2011, Simon & Schuster $19.99 (978-1-4169-7177-1). This finale to the steampunk trilogy that began with *Leviathan* (2009) centers on a Nikola Tesla invention, a weapon that could end World War I and bring Alek and Deryn together. ⌒ Lexile 790L (Rev: BL 8/11; HB 11–12/11; LMC 11–12/11; SLJ 9/1/11)

6237 Westerfeld, Scott. *Pretties* (8–11). Series: The Uglies. 2005, Simon & Schuster paper $6.99 (978-0-689-86539-8). In the sequel to *Uglies* (2005), Tally enjoys her transformation into a Pretty and the accompanying hedonistic lifestyle until she is reminded of her underlying purpose and faces real danger. (Rev: BL 9/15/05; SLJ 12/05; VOYA 10/05)

6238 Westerfeld, Scott. *Specials* (7–10). Series: The Uglies. 2006, Simon & Schuster $15.95 (978-1-4169-2165-3). Sixteen-year-old Tally (of *Uglies* and *Pretties,* 2004 and 2005 respectively) transforms yet again, this time becoming a Special, part of her government's high-powered commando unit that enforces adherence to the norms. ⌒ (Rev: BL 5/15/06; HB 9–10/06)

6239 Westerfeld, Scott. *Uglies* (7–10). Series: The Uglies. 2005, Simon & Schuster paper $6.99 (978-0-689-86538-1). In a futuristic dystopia, 15-year-old Tally is counting the days until she turns 16 and is transformed from ugly to pretty but events threaten this happening on schedule; a thought-provoking novel about the importance of image and ethics. (Rev: BCCB 2/05; BL 3/15/05*; SLJ 3/05; VOYA 6/05)

6240 White, Andrea. *No Child's Game: Reality TV 2083* (7–10). 2005, HarperCollins LB $16.89 (978-0-06-055455-2). In this chilling look at a future in which television is used to distract the populace from grim reality, five teens will live or die while reenacting a historic Antarctic expedition for the entertainment of the viewing audience. (Rev: BL 4/15/05; SLJ 7/05)

6241 Williams, Liz. *The Ghost Sister* (10–12). 2001, Bantam paper $5.99 (978-0-553-58374-8). Ethical questions are presented in this story about genetic engineering and a girl who is to be killed because she is different. (Rev: BL 5/15/01; VOYA 12/01)

6242 Williams, Sean. *The Resurrected Man* (10–12). 2005, Prometheus $25.00 (978-1-59102-311-1). Science fiction and mystery are blended in this late-21st-century thriller about detective Marylin Blaylock's efforts to track down a serial killer who's using flaws in the latest transportation technology to kidnap and murder victims. (Rev: SLJ 4/05)

6243 Williamson, Jack. *The Black Sun* (9–12). 1997, Tor $23.95 (978-0-312-85937-4). Carlos Mondragon, who always dreamed of space travel, stows away on the last of the quantum-wave starships. (Rev: VOYA 8/97)

6244 Willis, Connie. *Blackout* (11–12). 2010, Spectra $26 (978-055380319-8). Three researchers from the future (2060) travel back in time to 1940 London, where they face the perils of the Blitz, including evacuations, blackouts, and bombings. e (Rev: BL 2/1–15/10)

6245 Willis, Connie. *Impossible Things* (9–12). 1994, Bantam paper $6.50 (978-0-553-56436-5). In this second collection of her science fiction short stories, Willis presents 11 works, including award-winning "The Last of the Winnebagos," "Even the Queen," and "At the Rialto." (Rev: BL 12/15/93*; SLJ 3/95; VOYA 6/94)

6246 Willis, Connie, and Sheila Williams, eds. *A Woman's Liberation: A Choice of Futures by and About Women* (10–12). 2001, Warner Aspect paper $12.95 (978-0-446-67742-4). A recommended collection of speculative fiction by such women writers as Anne McCaffrey and Ursula Le Guin. (Rev: BL 8/01; VOYA 12/01)

6247 Wilson, Daniel H. *Robopocalypse* (10–12). 2011, Doubleday $25 (978-0-385-53385-0). Armageddon appears at hand in the near future when the robots that now outnumber humans rebel against their controllers. Alex Award 2012. ⌒ e (Rev: BL 5/15/11; SLJ 7/11)

351

6248 Wilson, F. Paul, and Matthew J. Costello. *Masque* (9–12). 1998, Warner $23.00 (978-0-446-51977-9). A high-tech adventure set in 2058 in which Kaze Glom secret agent Tristan, who is a mime — a cloned human being who can be transformed into a genetic copy of any human or creature — is tricked into bringing back a virus that destroys the Kaze Glom's entire mime population. (Rev: VOYA 8/98)

6249 Winters, Ben H. *Android Karenina* (10–12). 2010, Quirk paper $12.95 (978-15947446-0-0). Winters implants numerous robots, cyborgs, and other sci-fi elements into Tolstoy's classic tale of ill-fated love. (Rev: BL 6/1–15/10)

6250 Yancey, Rick. *The 5th Wave* (9–12). 2013, Putnam $18.99 (978-039916241-1). The aliens have killed 7 billion humans in four waves (electromagnetic pulse, tsunamis, plague, and implants of alien intelligence); now Cassie, 16, and other survivors must anticipate and resist the fifth wave, even as they wonder who they can trust. **e** Lexile HL690L (Rev: BL 2/1/13*; HB 5/6/13; SLJ 4/13)

6251 Yu, Charles. *How to Live Safely in a Science Fictional Universe* (11–12). 2010, Pantheon $24 (978-030737920-7). Charles, a bumbling time-machine repair man in a futuristic universe, seeks answers about his inventor father's disappearance; for mature readers. (Rev: BL 8/10)

6252 Zahn, Timothy. *Allegiance: Star Wars* (9–12). 2007, Del Rey $25.95 (978-0-345-47738-5). A look at the period between *A New Hope* and *The Empire Strikes Back,* in which a group of storm troopers turn into vigilantes to protect the Empire's citizens. (Rev: BL 10/15/06; SLJ 6/07)

6253 Zahn, Timothy. *Odd Girl Out* (10–12). Series: Quadrail. 2008, Tor $24.95 (978-076531733-9). The third in the Quadrail series, this book delivers action and adventure in an interstellar setting. ∩ **e** (Rev: BL 9/15/08)

6254 Zahn, Timothy. *The Third Lynx* (9–12). 2007, Tor $24.95 (978-0-7653-1732-2). This interstellar sequel of *Night Train to Rigel* involves private investigator Frank Compton and his assistant, Bayta, who are seeking an archeological relic in order to keep it out of the hands of the Modhri, a sinister mind who sends its mind-controlled "walkers" to steal it. (Rev: BL 11/1/07)

6255 Zelazny, Roger. *A Dark Traveling* (9–12). 1987, Avon paper $3.50 (978-0-380-70567-2). A fast-moving plot about parallel worlds highlights this Hugo Award-winning novella. (Rev: BL 4/1/87; SLJ 8/87; VOYA 8/87)

6256 Zettel, Sarah. *Quiet Invasion* (10–12). 2000, Warner Aspect $24.00 (978-0-446-52489-6). A colony of Venus and a conflict between humans and aliens are the subjects of this tension-filled adult yarn featuring scientist Helen Failia. (Rev: BL 1/1–15/00; VOYA 4/00)

6257 Zevin, Gabrielle. *All These Things I've Done* (9–12). Series: Birthright. 2011, Farrar $16.99 (978-0-374-30210-8). In this first volume in a trilogy, it is 2083 in a dilapidated New York City and 16-year-old Anya is trying to cope with her mafia family even as she works to clear herself of murder charges and meets a very interesting young man. Lexile HL630L (Rev: BL 9/15/11*; LMC 11–12/11; SLJ 11/1/11)

Sports

6258 Altman, Millys N. *Racing in Her Blood* (7–12). 1980, HarperCollins LB $12.89 (978-0-397-31895-7). A junior novel about a young girl who wants to succeed in the world of automobile racing.

6259 Averett, Edward. *The Rhyming Season* (9–12). 2005, Clarion $16.00 (978-0-618-46948-2). Brenda's finding her last year at school difficult — her older brother has died, her parents have separated, her favorite coach has left, the town is economically depressed — but she and the new poetry-loving coach succeed in taking the basketball team to success. (Rev: BL 9/1/05; SLJ 11/05)

6260 Bo, Ben. *Skullcrack* (7–12). 2000, Lerner LB $14.95 (978-0-8225-3308-5). Jonah, an avid surfer, travels with his father to Florida to be united with his twin sister who was put up for adoption at birth. (Rev: BL 6/1–15/00; HBG 9/00; SLJ 6/00)

6261 Carter, Alden R. *Bull Catcher* (7–10). 1997, Scholastic paper $15.95 (978-0-590-50958-9). High school friends Bull and Jeff seem to live for baseball and plan their futures around the sport, but one of them begins to move in a different direction. (Rev: BL 4/15/97; SLJ 5/97; VOYA 10/97)

6262 Carter, Alden R. *Love, Football, and Other Contact Sports* (8–11). 2006, Holiday House $16.95 (978-0-8234-1975-3). The football team at Argyle West High School is at the center of these entertaining short stories. (Rev: BL 3/15/06*; SLJ 6/06)

6263 Cohen, Joshua C. *Leverage* (10–12). 2011, Dutton $16.99 (978-0-525-42306-5). Diminutive gymnastics star Danny finds unlikely support against bullying in Kurt, the new football fullback who stutters. YALSA Top Ten Best Fiction for Young Adults 2012. ∩ **e** (Rev: BL 12/15/10*; LMC 5–6/11; SLJ 4/11; VOYA 2/11)

6264 Coy, John. *Crackback* (8–11). 2005, Scholastic $16.99 (978-0-439-69733-0). High school football player Miles Manning faces many challenges including difficult relationships with his father and his coach, girl problems, and whether to join his teammates in using steroids. (Rev: BL 9/1/05*; SLJ 12/05; VOYA 12/05)

6265 Crutcher, Chris. *The Crazy Horse Electric Game* (7–12). 1987, Greenwillow $16.99 (978-0-688-06683-

3). A motorboat accident ends the comfortable life and budding baseball career of a teenage boy. (Rev: BL 4/15/87; SLJ 5/87; VOYA 6/87)

6266 Crutcher, Chris. *Ironman* (8–12). 1995, Greenwillow $17.99 (978-0-688-13503-4). A psychological sports novel in which a 17-year-old carries an attitude that fuels the plot. (Rev: BL 3/1/95*; SLJ 3/95; VOYA 5/95)

6267 Crutcher, Chris. *Running Loose* (7–10). 1983, Greenwillow $18.99 (978-0-688-02002-6). A senior in high school faces problems when he opposes the decisions of a football coach. (Rev: BL 3/87)

6268 Crutcher, Chris. *Stotan!* (8–12). 2008, Harper-Tempest paper $7.99 (978-0-06-009492-8). A group of boys from different backgrounds but all close friends sign up for a brutally taxing physical program run by their school coach; first published in 1986. (Rev: BL 3/15/86; SLJ 5/86; VOYA 4/86)

6269 Crutcher, Chris. *Whale Talk* (8–12). 2001, Harper-Teen $15.95 (978-0-688-18019-5). Well-adjusted and academically able, T. J. is not into sports, which goes against the grain at his high school; he eventually is persuaded to form a swimming team and deliberately picks members from who buck the sports formula. ⌒ (Rev: BL 4/1/01; HB 5–6/01; SLJ 4/01)

6270 Deuker, Carl. *Gym Candy* (8–11). 2007, Houghton Mifflin $16.00 (978-0-618-77713-6). To improve his high school football performance, Mick begins using steroids ("gym candy") and suffers physical and emotional consequences. (Rev: BL 9/1/07; SLJ 10/07)

6271 Deuker, Carl. *Night Hoops* (7–11). 2000, Houghton Mifflin $15.00 (978-0-395-97936-5). When older brother Scott gives up basketball for music, Nick develops his own presence on the court. (Rev: BL 5/1/00; HB 5–6/00; HBG 9/00; SLJ 5/00)

6272 Deuker, Carl. *On the Devil's Court* (8–12). 1991, Avon paper $5.99 (978-0-380-70879-6). In this variation on the Faust legend, a senior high basketball star believes he has sold his soul to have a perfect season. (Rev: BL 12/15/88; SLJ 1/89; VOYA 4/89)

6273 Deuker, Carl. *Payback Time* (7–10). 2010, Houghton Mifflin $16 (978-0-547-27981-7). Student reporter Mitch finds himself in a tough situation as he investigates a potential football cheating scandal. **ℯ** (Rev: BL 9/1/10*; HB 11–12/10; SLJ 9/1/10; VOYA 12/10)

6274 Dygard, Thomas J. *Second Stringer* (6–12). 1998, Morrow $15.99 (978-0-688-15981-8). A star quarterback's knee injury gives second-stringer Kevin Taylor the opportunity of a lifetime during his senior year in high school. (Rev: BL 9/1/98; HBG 3/99; SLJ 12/98; VOYA 2/99)

6275 Esckilsen, Erik E. *Offsides* (6–10). 2004, Houghton Mifflin $15.00 (978-0-618-46284-1). Tom Gray, a top-notch soccer player, is proud of his Mohawk

heritage and when he moves to a new town where the school's mascot is an Indian, he refuses to play. (Rev: BL 9/1/04; SLJ 1/05; VOYA 12/04)

6276 Esckilsen, Erik E. *The Outside Groove* (7–10). 2006, Houghton Mifflin $16.00 (978-0-618-66854-0). Casey's family only cares about her brother and his stock-car racing career, ignoring all of her accomplishments, so she decides to start racing, finding out a lot of family secrets in the process. (Rev: BL 9/15/06)

6277 Flynn, Pat. *Alex Jackson: SWA* (6–10). 2002, Univ. of Queensland paper $13.50 (978-0-7022-3307-4). Alex flirts with physical danger and trouble with the police when he joins up with Skateboarders with Attitude. (Rev: SLJ 1/03)

6278 Flynn, Pat. *Out of His League* (9–12). 2008, Walker $16.95 (978-080279776-6). Australian exchange student Ozzie uses his rugby skills to lead the football team to victory for his Texas high school. Lexile 750L (Rev: BLO 8/08; SLJ 9/1/08)

6279 Foley, John. *Hoops of Steel* (10–12). 2007, Flux paper $8.95 (978-0-7387-0981-9). Jackson's school life is almost as complicated as his home life, which was destroyed by his father's alcoholism and violence; the basketball action will attract readers. (Rev: BL 3/15/07; SLJ 4/07)

6280 Galloway, Stephen. *Finnie Walsh* (10–12). 2001, Raincoast $16.95 (978-1-55192-372-7). Paul's friendship with Finnie, which centers around hockey, is forever changed when Paul's father is injured. (Rev: BL 5/1/01)

6281 Godfrey, Martyn. *Ice Hawk* (7–12). 1986, EMC paper $13.50 (978-0-8219-0235-6). An easy-to-read story about a young minor league hockey player who balks at unnecessary use of violence. (Rev: BL 2/1/87)

6282 Guest, Jacqueline. *Racing Fear* (7–10). Series: SideStreets. 2004, Lorimer paper $4.99 (978-1-55028-838-4). Trent and Adam are best friends and car racing buddies until an accident puts a strain on their friendship; suitable for reluctant readers. (Rev: SLJ 1/05)

6283 Halpin, Brendan. *Shutout* (8–10). 2010, Farrar $16.99 (978-0-374-36899-9). Amanda and Lena's long-standing friendship begins to fray when they enter high school and Lena makes the varsity soccer team while Amanda's sore heel disqualifies her. (Rev: BL 9/1/10*; SLJ 8/10)

6284 Hampshire, Anthony. *Fast Track* (6–12). Series: Redline Racing. 2006, Fitzhenry & Whiteside paper $6.95 (978-1-55041-570-4). For reluctant readers, this is an action-packed story with good car racing scenes. Also use *Full Throttle* and *On the Limit* (both 2006). (Rev: SLJ 2/07; VOYA)

6285 Heynen, Jim, ed. *Fishing for Chickens: Short Stories About Rural Youth* (9–12). 2001, Persea $19.95 (978-0-89255-264-1); paper $8.95 (978-0-89255-265-

353

8). Stories from 16 authors describe the realities of growing up in the country. (Rev: BL 9/15/01; HBG 3/02; SLJ 10/01; VOYA 10/01)

6286 Klass, David. *Danger Zone* (7–12). 1996, Scholastic paper $16.95 (978-0-590-48590-6). Jimmy Doyle, a young basketball star, tries to prove to himself as well as to his mostly African American teammates that he deserves a place on the American High School Dream Team. (Rev: BL 4/1/96; SLJ 3/96; VOYA 4/96)

6287 Lipsyte, Robert. *Raiders Night* (10–12). 2006, HarperTempest $15.99 (978-0-06-059946-1). Team co-captain Matt discovers the dark side of high school football, including drug abuse, corruption, and violent hazing rituals. (Rev: BL 5/15/06; SLJ 7/06)

6288 Lipsyte, Robert. *Yellow Flag* (8–11). 2007, HarperTeen $16.99 (978-0-06-055707-2). When his brother, a NASCAR driver, is injured, Kyle takes his place and does so well that he must decide whether to continue racing or instead pursue his love of music. (Rev: BL 9/1/07; SLJ 9/07)

6289 McKissack, Fredrick, Jr. *Shooting Star* (9–12). 2009, Simon & Schuster $16.99 (978-1-4169-4745-5). Steroids initially help Jomo build up his body, but the African American football player soon experiences mood swings that lead him to regret this drug use. **e** Lexile HL720L (Rev: BL 9/1/09; SLJ 9/09)

6290 MacLeod, J. E. *Waiting to Score* (9–12). 2009, WestSide $16.95 (978-193481301-0). Zack is a sensitive hockey player interested in Jane, a Goth girl who comes to see that he's not a sexist jock. (Rev: BL 5/15/09; SLJ 5/1/09; VOYA 10/09)

6291 Martino, Alfred C. *Over the End Line* (7–10). 2009, Harcourt $17 (978-0-15-206121-0). Jonny Fehey enjoys his celebrity when he scores a winning soccer goal during his senior year at high school, but the pleasure is brief when he realizes that the exchange student he has been seeing has been raped. **e** Lexile HL660L (Rev: BL 9/15/09; SLJ 9/09; VOYA 10/09)

6292 Martino, Alfred C. *Pinned* (9–12). 2005, Harcourt $17.00 (978-0-15-205355-0). Alternating chapters chronicle the lives of high school wrestlers Ivan Korske and Bobby Zane as they move toward a match against one another in the finals of the New Jersey State Wrestling Championship. (Rev: BCCB 4/05; BL 3/1/05; SLJ 2/05; VOYA 4/05)

6293 Myers, Walter Dean. *Game* (8–12). 2008, HarperTeen $16.99 (978-0-06-058294-4). Harlem born and bred, Drew hopes to become an NBA star, but the appearance of a talented white player on his team threatens his future. ⌒ (Rev: BL 2/1/08; SLJ 2/08)

6294 Myers, Walter Dean. *Hoops* (7–10). 1981, Dell paper $5.50 (978-0-440-93884-2). Lonnie plays basketball in spite of his coach, a has-been named Cal. Followed by *The Outside Shot* (1987).

6295 Norman, Rick. *Cross Body Block* (8–10). 1996, Colonial paper $9.95 (978-1-56883-060-5). An anguished story about a middle-aged football coach and his personal family tragedies, including the brutal death of a son. (Rev: VOYA 8/96)

6296 Peet, Mal. *Exposure* (9–12). 2009, Candlewick $18.99 (978-0-7636-3941-9). Soccer journalist Paul Faustino recounts the sorry story of star Otello's fall from grace in this novel loosely based on Shakespeare's *Othello*. (Rev: BL 8/09; SLJ 12/09)

6297 Peet, Mal. *Keeper* (9–12). 2005, Candlewick $15.99 (978-0-7636-2749-2). Looking back on his life in an interview, World Cup soccer star El Gato describes his humble beginnings in the rain forest and the ghost that trained him. (Rev: BL 8/05; SLJ 9/05)

6298 Peet, Mal. *The Penalty* (9–12). 2007, Candlewick $16.99 (978-0-7636-3399-8). Paul Faustino, a South American sports journalist, investigates the mysterious disappearance of a young soccer star in this multilayered novel full of South American history and occult traditions. (Rev: BL 9/1/07; SLJ 11/07)

6299 Powell, Randy. *Dean Duffy* (8–12). 1995, Farrar paper $5.95 (978-0-374-41698-0). A Little League baseball great has problems with his pitching arm and sees his career collapse. (Rev: BL 4/15/95; SLJ 5/95)

6300 Powell, Randy. *The Whistling Toilets* (7–10). 1996, Farrar paper $5.95 (978-0-374-48369-2). When Stan tries to help his friend Ginny with her tennis game, he finds that something strange is troubling the rising young tennis star. (Rev: BL 9/15/96; SLJ 10/96; VOYA 12/96)

6301 Romain, Joseph. *The Mystery of the Wagner Whacker* (7–12). 1997, Warwick paper $8.95 (978-1-895629-94-1). Matt, a baseball enthusiast, is upset at moving to a small Canadian town where the sport is all but unknown, but an accidental travel in time to 1928 changes the situation. (Rev: BL 7/98; SLJ 7/98)

6302 Staudohar, Paul D., ed. *Baseball's Best Short Stories* (9–12). 1997, Chicago Review paper $16.95 (978-1-55652-319-9). Baseball stories from such renowned authors as Zane Grey, Robert Penn Warren, and James Thurber. (Rev: BL 11/15/95)

6303 Strasser, Todd. *Cut Back* (7–12). Series: Impact Zone. 2004, Simon & Schuster paper $5.99 (978-0-689-87030-9). In this action-packed series installment, 15-year-old Kai faces off against his nemesis, Lucas Frank, in a surfing competition; a sequel is *Take Off* (2004). (Rev: BL 7/04; SLJ 8/04)

6304 Sweeney, Joyce. *Players* (6–12). 2000, Winslow $16.95 (978-1-890817-54-1). Corey, leader of the basketball team, is determined to find out who is sabotaging its chances of success. (Rev: BL 10/1/00; HBG 10/01; SLJ 9/00; VOYA 12/00)

6305 Tharp, Tim. *Knights of the Hill Country* (8–11). 2006, Knopf $16.95 (978-0-375-83653-4). In his senior year, Hampton, the star linebacker in a school and town that live for football, begins to deal with his uncertainties and realize that he is more than just an athlete. (Rev: BL 10/1/06; LMC 1/07; SLJ 9/06)

6306 Volponi, Paul. *The Final Four* (9–12). 2012, Viking $16.99 (978-067001264-0). The lives of four college basketball players intersect when their teams play in an NCAA Final Four match, each young man struggling with different ambitions and challenges. ℮ Lexile 870L (Rev: BL 2/15/12*; SLJ 3/12*; VOYA 4/12)

6307 Waltman, Kevin. *Learning the Game* (9–12). 2005, Scholastic $16.95 (978-0-439-73109-6). Nate is talked into committing a crime with his basketball teammates and wrestles with his guilty conscience in this compelling multilayered novel. (Rev: BL 9/1/05; SLJ 12/05; VOYA 10/05)

6308 Weaver, Will. *Checkered Flag Cheater* (8–11). Series: The Motor Novels. 2010, Farrar $16.99 (978-0-374-33062-8). Trace Bonham is having a successful stock-car racing career but suspects that someone is tinkering with his engine illegally. ℮ (Rev: BL 3/1/10; SLJ 5/10; VOYA 6/10)

6309 Weaver, Will. *Hard Ball* (7–12). 1998, HarperCollins LB $15.89 (978-0-06-027122-0). Billy Baggs discovers that his rival for the star position on the freshman baseball team is also his rival for the attention of the girl he is attracted to. (Rev: BL 1/1–15/98; HBG 9/98; SLJ 4/98; VOYA 6/98)

6310 Weaver, Will. *Saturday Night Dirt* (8–11). Series: Motor. 2008, Farrar $14.95 (978-0-374-35060-4). A racetrack in rural Minnesota is the setting for this story about a group of people who share a love of racing. (Rev: BL 3/1/08; SLJ 4/08)

6311 Weaver, Will. *Striking Out* (8–12). 1993, Harper-Collins paper $7.99 (978-0-06-447113-8). When Minnesota farmboy Billy Baggs picks up a stray baseball and fires it back to the pitcher, his baseball career begins, but his family isn't enthusiastic. (Rev: BL 11/1/93; SLJ 10/93; VOYA 12/93)

6312 Weaver, Will. *Super Stock Rookie* (8–11). Series: Motor Novels. 2009, Farrar $14.95 (978-037435061-1). High-schooler Trace wins a corporate sponsorship, giving him the chance to compete on the stock-car circuit, but is suspicious about the motives of Team Blu. Lexile HL720L (Rev: BL 2/15/09; SLJ 3/1/09; VOYA 6/09)

6313 Zadoff, Allen. *Food, Girls, and Other Things I Can't Have* (8–10). 2009, Egmont $16.99 (978-1-60684-004-7); LB $19.99 (978-1-60684-051-1). Overweight high school sophomore Andy Zansky finds his popularity soaring when he joins the football team but soon discovers that many pitfalls await him. ℮ Lexile

HL520L (Rev: BL 10/15/09; HB 11–12/09; LMC 11–12/09; SLJ 9/09; VOYA 10/09)

6314 Zusak, Markus. *Fighting Ruben Wolfe* (8–12). 2001, Scholastic $15.95 (978-0-439-24188-5). Two brothers, Ruben and Cameron, try to assist their struggling family by boxing under the direction of an unethical promoter. (Rev: BL 2/15/01; HB 3–4/01; HBG 10/01; SLJ 3/01; VOYA 4/01)

Short Stories and General Anthologies

6315 Abrahams, Peter. *Up All Night: A Short Story Collection* (7–12). 2008, HarperCollins $16.99 (978-0-06-137076-2). "What keeps you up all night?" Popular YA authors — including Libba Bray, David Levithan, and Patricia McCormick — contribute quite different answers to the question. (Rev: BL 4/1/08; SLJ 4/08)

6316 Aleichem, Sholem. *Tevye the Dairyman and The Railroad Stories* (9–12). Trans. by Hillel Halkin. 1987, Schocken paper $15.00 (978-0-8052-1069-9). Several of the 30 stories in this collection feature Tevye, the Russian Jew of "Fiddler on the Roof" fame.

6317 Allen, Jeffery Renard. *Holding Pattern* (11–12). 2008, Graywolf paper $16.00 (978-155597509-8). Strong characters and vivid settings burst to life in this collection of short stories suitable for mature readers. (Rev: BL 9/15/08*)

6318 Almond, Steve. *The Evil B. B. Chow and Other Stories* (11–12). 2005, Algonquin $21.95 (978-1-56512-422-6). Almond's edgy stories conjure love, lust, and a river trip on which Abraham Lincoln and Frederick Douglass get drunk together; for mature readers. (Rev: BL 2/15/05)

6319 Amnesty International. *Free? Stories About Human Rights* (9–12). 2010, Candlewick $17.99 (978-0-7636-4703-2). Short stories written by 14 popular YA authors (Eoin Colfer, Roddy Doyle, David Almond, and Rita Williams-Garcia, for example) are linked to articles from the United Nations Declaration of Human Rights. Lexile 750L (Rev: BL 2/15/10; LMC 5–6/10; SLJ 6/10)

6320 Angel, Ann, ed. *Such a Pretty Face: Short Stories About Beauty* (9–12). 2007, Abrams $18.95 (978-0-8109-1607-4). A collection of stories about girls dealing with the longing to be beautiful and the expectations that surround traditional beauty. (Rev: BL 7/07; HB 5–6/07; SLJ 1/08)

6321 Aspin, Diana. *Ordinary Miracles* (10–12). Series: Northern Lights Young Novels. 2003, Red Deer paper $7.95 (978-0-88995-277-5). Thirteen compelling short stories about teens' coming-of-age concerns in small Sky Falls, Canada, are linked through the memories of an elderly man who came to the community decades before. (Rev: SLJ 4/04; VOYA 2/04)

6322 Atta, Sefi. *News from Home* (11–12). 2010, Interlink paper $15 (978-15665680-3-6). Eleven moving stories portray the anxieties and challenges facing Nigerians both at home and as they move away seeking better opportunities; for mature readers. (Rev: BL 9/1–15/10)

6323 Atwood, Margaret. *The Tent* (9–12). 2006, Nan A. Talese $18 (978-0-385-51668-6). Atwood presents a collection of short works, mostly prose and a few pieces of poetry, which reflect on our times; includes her own line drawings throughout. (Rev: BL 11/15/05; SLJ 6/06)

6324 Banks, William H., ed. *Beloved Harlem: A Literary Tribute to Black America's Most Famous Neighborhood, from the Classics to the Contemporary* (11–12). 2005, Broadway paper $18.95 (978-0-7679-1478-9). Harlem's role as a center of African American culture is documented through excerpts from works of literature; for mature teens. (Rev: BL 7/05) [810.8]

6325 Bauer, Marion Dane, ed. *Am I Blue?* (8–12). 1995, HarperCollins paper $7.99 (978-0-06-440587-4). Sixteen short stories from well-known YA writers who have something meaningful to share about gay awareness and want to present positive, credible gay role models. (Rev: BL 5/1/94*; SLJ 6/94; VOYA 8/94)

6326 Bausch, Richard, ed. *Best New American Voices, 2008* (9–12). 2007, Harcourt paper $15.00 (978-0-15-603149-3). Short story writer and novelist Richard Bausch has compiled the writings in the 2008 volume of the Best New American Voices series, showcasing literature's future stars whose works have been gathered from writing programs and conferences across America; this volume's theme focuses on the importance of factors that link people to one another. (Rev: BL 10/1/07)

6327 Beattie, Ann. *The New Yorker Stories* (11–12). 2010, Scribner $30 (978-143916874-5). Forty-eight of Beattie's masterful stories — which deal with such universal themes as loneliness, family strife, and the consequences of violence — are presented in this collection for mature readers. (Rev: BL 8/10)

6328 Belleza, Rhoda, ed. *Cornered: 14 Stories of Bullying and Defiance* (8–11). 2012, Running Press paper $9.95 (978-0-7624-4-515-8). Fourteen stories explore the experience of being bullied from a variety of perspectives. (Rev: BL 8/12; LMC 1–2/13; SLJ 11/12)

6329 *Best-Loved Stories Told at the National Storytelling Festival* (9–12). 1991, National Storytelling Pr. paper $14.95 (978-1-879991-00-2). The 37 traditional stories collected here cover a wide range of ethnic backgrounds, genres, and colloquial voices. (Rev: BL 10/15/91)

6330 Black, Holly, and Cecil Castellucci, eds. *Geektastic: Stories from the Nerd Herd* (8–12). 2009, Little, Brown $16.99 (978-0-316-00809-9). A collection of short stories that will please fans of everything from Star Trek to Dungeon Maters, underlining some of the difficult sides of geekiness. YALSA Popular Paperbacks for Young Adults Top Ten 2012. ℮ (Rev: BL 9/09; HB 9–10/09; LMC 1–2/10; SLJ 8/09)

6331 Bloom, Harold. *Black American Prose Writers of the Harlem Renaissance* (10–12). Series: Writers of English: Lives and Works. 1994, Chelsea House $29.95 (978-0-7910-2203-0). Thirteen writers of the Harlem Renaissance, including Langston Hughes and Countee Cullen, are represented in this fine anthology.

6332 Boudinot, Ryan. *The Littlest Hitler* (11–12). 2006, Counterpoint $22.00 (978-1-58243-357-8). Confused, condemned, crushed and crazy characters populate this collection of witty short stories about people on the fringes of society. (Rev: BL 8/06)

6333 Boylan, Jennifer Finney, and Sarah Rees Brennan, et al. *Truth and Dare: 21 Tales of Heartbreak and Happiness* (9–12). Ed. by Liz Miles. 2011, Running Press paper $9.95 (978-0-7624-4-104-4). From authors including Gary Soto, Ellen Wittlinger, and Emma Donoghue come diverse stories about a wide range of teen experiences. (Rev: BL 4/1/11; SLJ 6/11; VOYA 6/11)

6334 Boyle, T. C. *The Human Fly and Other Stories* (10–12). 2005, Penguin $17.99 (978-0-670-06054-2); paper $9.99 (978-0-14-240363-1). This collection of short stories — many previously published for adults — includes many realistic young adult characters and is full of humor and surprises as well as some shocks. (Rev: BL 11/1/05; SLJ 11/05)

6335 Bradman, Tony, ed. *My Dad's a Punk: 12 Stories about Boys and Their Fathers* (7–10). 2006, Kingfisher paper $7.95 (978-0-7534-5870-9). The complexities of father/son relationships are explored in this collection of 12 short stories by writers including Ron Koertge and Tim Wynne-Jones. (Rev: BL 5/1/06; HB 7–8/06; SLJ 8/06)

6336 Brooks, Bruce. *All That Remains* (7–12). 2001, Simon & Schuster $16.00 (978-0-689-83351-9). Three darkly entertaining novellas tackle the topic of death and how young people cope with it. (Rev: BCCB 6/01; BL 5/1/01; HB 7–8/01; HBG 10/01; SLJ 5/01; VOYA 6/01)

6337 Busby, Cylin, ed. *First Kiss (Then Tell): A Collection of True Lip-Locked Moments* (7–10). 2008, Bloomsbury $15.95 (978-1-59990-199-2); paper $8.95 (978-1-59990-241-8). Popular YA authors including Jon Scieszka, David Levithan, Deb Caletti, and Justine Larbalestier describe their first kisses — some romantic, some sloppy, some embarrassing, some clumsy. (Rev: BL 2/1/08; SLJ 2/08)

6338 Capote, Truman. *A Christmas Memory, One Christmas, and The Thanksgiving Visitor* (10–12). 1996, Modern Library $13.95 (978-0-679-60237-8). Three short stories present Capote's memories of holidays of his youth. [818]

6339 Card, Orson Scott. *Keeper of Dreams* (9–12). 2008, Tor $27.95 (978-0-7653-0497-1). A masterful and varied collection of 22 science fiction and fantasy short stories heavy on mood and character. (Rev: BL 3/1/08; SLJ 7/08)

6340 Cart, Michael, ed. *Reckless: A Journal of Contemporary Voices, Vol. 4* (9–12). 2006, Delacorte $10.95 (978-0-385-73034-1). Stories of recklessness are told in verse, photograph, narrative, or drawing in this compilation dealing mostly with decision-making and the consequences thereof. (Rev: SLJ 6/06)

6341 Carter, Anne Laurel. *No Missing Parts and Other Stories About Real Princesses* (7–12). 2003, Red Deer paper $9.95 (978-0-88995-253-9). Ten thoughtful stories from Canada portray young women who rely on their own resources in difficult situations. (Rev: BL 5/1/03; SLJ 5/03; VOYA 10/03)

6342 Carver, Raymond, and Tom Jenks. *American Short Story Masterpieces* (10–12). 1987, Delacorte paper $7.50 (978-0-440-20423-7). The 36 stories reprinted here by such authors as Updike, O'Connor, Baldwin, and Malamud emphasize the realistic genre of writing.

6343 Charters, Ann, ed. *The Portable Sixties Reader* (10–12). 2003, Penguin paper $18.00 (978-0-14-200194-3). The many voices of the turbulent 1960s have been beautifully captured in this collection of writings by such diverse literary icons as James Baldwin, Rachel Carson, Thomas Merton, Alan Ginsburg, Susan Sontag, and Kate Millett. (Rev: BL 1/1–15/03) [810.8]

6344 Chekhov, Anton Pavlovich. *The Russian Master and Other Stories* (10–12). Trans. by Ronald Hingley. Series: World's Classics. 1999, Oxford paper $8.95 (978-0-19-283687-8). A collection of 11 short stories written by Chekhov between 1892 and 1899.

6345 Clarke, Judith. *Wolf on the Fold* (9–12). 2002, Front St $16.95 (978-1-886910-79-9). Fear, death, aging, war, divorce, and other hard topics are the focus of six short stories set in Australia. Winner of the Australian Children's Book of the Year award. (Rev: BL 9/1/02; HBG 10/02; SLJ 9/02)

6346 *Cowboy Stories* (7–12). Illus. by Barry Moser. 2007, Chronicle $16.95 (978-0-8118-5418-4). A collection of traditional western stories featuring cowboys, gunslingers, and lawmen by famous authors including Louis L'Amour and Elmer Kelton. (Rev: BL 9/15/07; SLJ 9/07)

6347 Crane, Milton, ed. *50 Great American Short Stories* (10–12). 1984, Bantam paper $5.99 (978-0-553-27294-9). This excellent anthology spans the entire history of American literature and represents the best work of many authors.

6348 Dahl, Roald. *Skin and Other Stories* (7–12). 2000, Viking $15.99 (978-0-670-89184-9). Selected from the author's short stories for adults, these 13 bizarre tales will also delight younger readers. (Rev: BL 10/1/00; HBG 3/01; VOYA 12/00)

6349 Danquah, Meri Nana-Ama, ed. *Shaking the Tree: A Collection of New Fiction and Memoir by Black Women* (10–12). 2003, Norton $24.95 (978-0-393-05067-7). This collection of recent writings by African American women displays their varied talents and concerns. (Rev: BL 8/03) [818]

6350 Datlow, Ellen, and Kelly Link, eds. *The Year's Best Fantasy and Horror, 2007: Twentieth Annual Collection* (9–12). 2007, St. Martin's $21.95 (978-0-312-36942-2). This wonderful collection of 37 fantasy and horror stories features great works from authors including Joyce Carol Oates and Christopher Harman. (Rev: BL 9/15/07)

6351 Datlow, Ellen, and Terri Windling, eds. *The Coyote Road: Trickster Tales* (9–12). 2007, Viking $19.99 (978-0-670-06194-5). A collection of 25 original trickster tales and poems by authors including Ellen Klages, Michael Cadnum, and Jane Yolen. (Rev: BL 9/15/07; SLJ 9/07)

6352 Datlow, Ellen, and Terri Windling, eds. *The Green Man: Tales from the Mythic Forest* (7–12). 2002, Viking $18.99 (978-0-670-03526-7). Mythical beings with special relevance to the natural world are portrayed in a collection of stories and poems. (Rev: BL 4/15/02; HBG 10/02; SLJ 7/02; VOYA 6/02)

6353 Deitz, Paula, ed. *Writes of Passage: Coming-of-Age Stories and Memoirs from the Hudson Review* (10–12). 2008, Ivan R. Dee $27.50 (978-1-56663-781-7). Twenty-one coming-of-age stories and ten memoirs from established and emerging writers are collected in this anthology from the *Hudson Review*. (Rev: BL 4/1/08) [813]

6354 Delany, Samuel R. *Aye, and Gomorrah* (10–12). 2003, Vintage paper $14.00 (978-0-375-70671-4). This collection of short stories, some featuring graphic sexual content, includes examples of the science fiction, fantasy, and horror genres. (Rev: BL 2/15/03)

6355 Didato, Thom, and Alexander Steele, eds. *The Gotham Writers' Workshop Fiction Gallery: Exceptional Short Stories Selected by New York's Acclaimed Creative Writing School* (10–12). 2004, Bloomsbury paper $14.95 (978-1-58234-462-1). A collection of short stories by writers including Anton Chekhov, T. C. Boyle, and Daniel Orozco. (Rev: SLJ 11/04)

6356 Edghill, Rosemary. *Paying the Piper at the Gates of Dawn* (10–12). 2003, Five Star $26.95 (978-0-7862-5345-6). A collection of appealing and varied fantasy and science fiction short stories. (Rev: BL 6/1–15/03)

6357 Elliott, Stephen, ed. *Politically Inspired: An Anthology of Fiction for Our Time* (11–12). 2003, MacAdam $21.00 (978-1-931561-58-7); paper $13.00 (978-1-931561-45-7). A broad range of modern-day concerns, from suburban malaise and the oppression of women and to rising crime and terrorism, are reflected in the contemporary fiction collected here; for mature teens. (Rev: BL 10/15/03)

6358 Ellis, Deborah. *Lunch with Lenin and Other Stories* (7–12). 2008, Fitzhenry & Whiteside $14.95 (978-155455105-7). This collection of uneven but nonetheless worthy short stories centers around the theme of drugs and drug addiction in different countries around the world. (Rev: BL 12/1/08; SLJ 2/1/09; VOYA 2/09)

6359 Engstrom, Elizabeth. *Suspicions* (11–12). 2002, Triple Tree paper $16.95 (978-0-9666272-9-9). A collection of short stories that entertain, provoke, and disturb; for mature teens. (Rev: BL 1/1–15/02)

6360 Estevis, Anne. *Down Garrapata Road* (6–12). 2003, Arte Publico paper $12.95 (978-1-55885-397-3). In this collection of closely linked short stories, Estevis paints an appealing portrait of life in a small Mexican American community in South Texas during the 1930s and 1940s. (Rev: BL 1/1–15/04)

6361 Evans, Danielle. *Before You Suffocate Your Own Fool Self* (11–12). 2010, Riverhead $25.95 (978-159448769-9). This compelling collection of short stories covers such universal themes as race, class, and coming-of-age; for mature readers. (Rev: BL 8/10)

6362 Faulkner, William. *Collected Stories of William Faulkner* (10–12). 1950, Random House paper $19.00 (978-0-679-76403-8). There are 42 short stories in this collection, many of which take place in Yoknapatawpha County, Mississippi.

6363 Fitzgerald, F. Scott. *The Short Stories of F. Scott Fitzgerald: A New Collection* (10–12). Ed. by Matthew J. Bruccoli. 1989, Scribner paper $18.00 (978-0-684-80445-3). This is the definitive collection of Fitzgerald's stories.

6364 Ford, Jeffrey. *The Empire of Ice Cream* (11–12). 2006, Golden Gryphon $24.95 (978-1-930846-39-5). A wide-ranging collection of well-written stories that are followed by comments by the author. (Rev: BL 3/15/06)

6365 Fox, Carol. *In Times of War: An Anthology of War and Peace in Children's Literature* (6–12). 2001, Pavilion $24.95 (978-1-86205-446-2). Educators in the United Kingdom, Belgium, and Portugal worked together on this anthology of fiction, memoirs, and poetry — most of which deals with World Wars I and II in Europe — that is presented in thematic groupings. (Rev: BL 4/15/01; SLJ 6/01)

6366 Frosch, Mary, ed. *Coming of Age in the 21st Century: Growing Up in America Today* (10–12). Series: Coming of Age. 2008, New Press paper $17.95 (978-159558055-9). Well-written short stories and selections taken from acclaimed novels and memoirs examine themes that deal with the interpersonal and societal issues of today's teens and young adults; the accompanying critical material may be less appealing to teen readers. (Rev: BL 8/08)

6367 Gallo, Donald R., ed. *What Are You Afraid Of? Stories About Phobias* (7–10). 2006, Candlewick $15.99 (978-0-7636-2654-9). This is a collection of short stories (by well-known authors) about a variety of phobias, how their victims' day-to-day lives are affected, and how they cope with their fears. (Rev: BL 9/1/06; SLJ 9/06)

6368 Garcia, Cristina, ed. *Bordering Fires: The Vintage Book of Contemporary Mexican and Chicana and Chicano Literature* (10–12). 2006, Vintage paper $13.95 (978-1-4000-7718-2). Collected by novelist García, this is an anthology of essays, fiction, and poetry by both well-known and emerging Mexican, Chicana, and Chicano writers from both sides of the Mexican-U.S. border. (Rev: BL 10/15/06; SLJ 2/07) [860.8]

6369 Gilchrist, Ellen. *I, Rhoda Manning, Go Hunting with My Daddy* (11–12). 2002, Little, Brown $25.95 (978-0-316-17358-2). Rhoda is just one of the many characters — both adult and teen — who will be familiar to Gilchrist readers in this collection of stories; for mature teens. (Rev: BL 5/15/02)

6370 Gilchrist, Ellen. *Nora Jane: A Life in Stories* (11–12). 2005, Little, Brown paper $14.95 (978-0-316-05838-4). Gilchrist's stories about the likable Nora Jane and her life are gathered in a single volume; for mature teens. (Rev: BL 6/1–15/05)

6371 Gioia, Dana, and R. S. Gwynn, eds. *The Art of the Short Story* (9–12). 2005, Pearson paper $18.95 (978-0-321-33722-1). This anthology of short fiction showcases the work of 52 great writers — including Margaret Atwood, Sandra Cisneros, Ha Jin, and Gustave Flaubert — and adds commentary and discussion of the elements of short fiction. (Rev: BL 4/15/05) [808.3]

6372 Glasrud, Bruce A., and Laurie Champion, eds. *The African American West: A Century of Short Stories* (10–12). 2000, Univ. Press of Colorado $29.95 (978-0-87081-559-1). Set in the American West, these 46 short stories are told from the standpoint of African Americans at various times and settings. (Rev: BL 2/15/00)

6373 Greenberg, Martin H., and Jim C. Hines, eds. *Heroes in Training* (9–12). 2007, DAW paper $7.99 (978-0-7564-0438-3). Young heroes-in-the-making are the subjects of these 13 stories by authors such as Esther Friesner and Sherwood Smith. (Rev: BL 9/1/07)

6374 Greenberg, Martin H., and John Helfers, eds. *Man vs. Machine* (9–12). 2007, DAW paper $7.99 (978-0-7564-0436-9). This multi-authored anthology features well-written, and often unsettling, short stories about humans' interactions with machines. (Rev: BL 6/1–15/07)

6375 Hartwell, David G., and Kathryn Cramer, eds. *Year's Best Fantasy 7* (9–12). 2007, Tachyon paper $14.95 (978-1-892391-50-6). This collection of fantasy short stories features some of the best fantasy writers, including Michael Moorcock and Dianna Wynne Jones. (Rev: BL 6/1–15/07)

6376 Hautman, Pete, ed. *Full House: Ten Stories about Poker* (9–12). 2007, Putnam $17.99 (978-0-399-24528-2). A collection of ten short stories about the popular game of poker. (Rev: BL 9/1/07; SLJ 9/07)

6377 Heggum, Lisa, ed. *All Sleek and Skimming* (10–12). 2006, Orca paper $17.95 (978-1-55143-447-6). A collection of more than 20 well-writtten stories, most by Canadian writers and in varied formats including a couple using a graphic novel style, about teenagers coping with both light and dark aspects of life. (Rev: BL 4/15/06; LMC 2/07; SLJ 5/06)

6378 Hemingway, Ernest. *The Complete Short Stories of Ernest Hemingway: The Finca Vigia Edition* (10–12). 1987, Scribner paper $20.00 (978-0-684-84332-2). This definitive collection of Hemingway's short stories numbers 49, including 7 that were never published before.

6379 Henry, O. *The Best Short Stories of O. Henry* (9–12). Ed. by Bennett A. Cerf and Van H. Cartmell. 1994, Modern Library $21.95 (978-0-679-60122-7). An excellent collection of short stories by this master of the surprise ending.

6380 Hillerman, Tony. *The Best of the West: An Anthology of Classic Writing from the American West* (9–12). 1991, HarperCollins paper $18.00 (978-0-06-092352-5). This collection of short fiction and nonfiction showcases classic and contemporary portrayals of the American West. [818]

6381 Hopkins, Ellen, et al. *Does This Book Make Me Look Fat?: Stories About Loving — and Loathing — Your Body* (7–12). Ed. by Marissa Walsh. 2008, Clarion $16.00 (978-054701496-8). A primarily fiction-based collection of essays and short stories by multiple YA authors that focus on various aspects of body image. (Rev: BL 12/15/08; LMC 3–4/09; SLJ 1/1/09; VOYA 2/09)

6382 Hopkinson, Nalo. *Skin Folk* (10–12). 2001, Warner paper $12.95 (978-0-446-67803-2). Drawing inspiration from Caribbean folklore, Hopkinson blends science fiction and realism in this collection of short stories. (Rev: BL 11/1/01; VOYA 2/02)

6383 Hurston, Zora Neale. *Novels and Stories* (10–12). 1995, Library of America $35.00 (978-0-940450-83-7). Four novels including *Their Eyes Were Watching God* are included, plus nine short stories. (Rev: BL 1/1/95)

6384 Jones, Stephen, ed. *Summer Chills: Strangers in Strange Lands* (9–12). 2007, Carroll & Graf paper $14.95 (978-0-7867-1986-0). This collection of short horror stories features 21 frightful tales from authors such as Karl Edward Wagner and Nancy Holder. (Rev: BL 7/07)

6385 Kafka, Franz. *The Metamorphosis and Other Stories* (10–12). Trans. by Joachim Neugroschel. 1993, Scribner paper $13.00 (978-0-684-80070-7). This is a collection of 30 macabre, highly original stories by the great European writer.

6386 Kelly, James Patrick, and John Kessel, eds. *Feeling Very Strange: The Slipstream Anthology* (9–12). 2006, Tachyon paper $14.95 (978-1-892391-35-3). A collection of the best of this genre, a combination of science fiction, fantasy, and realistic fiction. Writers include (among others) George Saunders, Jonathan Lethem, Karen Jay Fowler, Jeffrey Ford, Ted Chiang, Theodora Goss, and Benjamin Rosenbaum. (Rev: BL 5/15/06)

6387 Ketchin, Susan, and Neil Giordano, eds. *25 and Under: Fiction* (10–12). 1997, Norton $25.00 (978-0-393-04120-0). This is a collection of 15 stories that deal with such themes as sexuality, friendship, families, loneliness, addiction, and death, all written by authors age 25 or younger. (Rev: VOYA 6/98)

6388 Kilworth, Garry. *Moby Jack and Other Tall Tales* (9–12). 2006, PS Publishing $45.00 (978-1-904619-53-6). Myths, legends, fantasy, and adventure mix in these stories that will surprise and even shock their readers. (Rev: BL 5/1/06)

6389 Kraft, Eric. *On the Wing: Book 2 of Flying, a Trilogy* (9–12). 2007, St. Martin's $23.95 (978-0-312-36374-1). Often humorous, these three stories follow Peter Leroy and his childhood flying adventures, while showing his memory doesn't always jibe with what really happened. (Rev: BL 6/1–15/07)

6390 Kulka, John, and Natalie Danford, eds. *Best New American Voices, 2005* (10–12). 2004, Harcourt paper $14.00 (978-0-15-602899-8). This collection of diverse short stories introduces some of America's most promising new writers. (Rev: BL 9/15/04; SLJ 4/05)

6391 Kulpa, Kathryn, ed. *Something Like a Hero* (6–10). 1995, Merlyn's Pen paper $9.95 (978-1-886427-03-7). A collection of 11 short stories from different genres, reprinted from the national magazine of student writing *Merlyn's Pen*. (Rev: VOYA 2/96)

6392 Kyle, Aryn. *Boys and Girls Like You and Me* (11–12). 2010, Scribner $24 (978-141659480-2). A bleak, darkly rendered collection of stories for older teens, featuring mostly girls and young women protagonists who make universally bad choices while searching for meaning and identity in their lives; for mature readers. (Rev: BL 2/1–15/10)

6393 Lanagan, Margo. *White Time* (8–11). 2006, HarperCollins $15.99 (978-0-06-074393-2). From the author of Black Juice comes a thought-provoking collection of

10 short stories with topics on death, love, and more set in alternate realities. (Rev: BL 8/06; SLJ 11/06)

6394 Lange, Richard. *Dead Boys: Stories* (9–12). 2007, Little, Brown $21.99 (978-0-316-01736-7). Clever writing mixes with somber subjects in this collection of 12 short stories about young adult men whose lives are emotionally unsatisfying and empty. (Rev: BL 6/1–15/07)

6395 Le Clezio, J. M. G. *The Round and Other Cold Hard Facts* (11–12). Trans. by C. Dickson. 2003, Univ. of Nebraska $60.00 (978-0-8032-2946-4); paper $19.95 (978-0-8032-8007-6). Challenging short stories by this French writer feature teens seeking to escape depressing boundaries and finding danger instead. (Rev: BL 1/1–15/03)

6396 Levithan, David, ed. *This Is Push: A Push Anthology of New Work* (9–12). 2007, Scholastic paper $6.99 (978-0-439-89028-1). These 15 stories explore the darker side of adolescence, with abuse, psychological problems, disappointing friends and lovers, and neglectful parents some of their elements. (Rev: BCCB 4/07; BL 3/1/07; SLJ 5/07)

6397 Levithan, David, ed. *Where We Are, What We See: Poems, Stories, Essays, and Art from the Best Young Writers and Artists in America* (8–11). 2005, Scholastic paper $7.99 (978-0-439-73646-6). Winning entries in the Scholastic Art and Writing Awards program. (Rev: BL 9/15/05; SLJ 1/06) [810]

6398 Lewis, David Levering. *The Portable Harlem Renaissance Reader* (10–12). 1994, Viking paper $18.00 (978-0-14-017036-8). All kinds of writing genres, including fiction, memoir, poetry, and drama, are included in this overview of the great flowering of writing talent known as the Harlem Renaissance. [810.8]

6399 Little, Denise, ed. *The Magic Toy Box* (9–12). 2006, DAW paper $7.99 (978-0-7564-0379-9). A collection of short stories about toys that come to life — usually benevolently, to come to the aid of their owners, but sometimes with more sinister motives. (Rev: BL 8/06)

6400 Lombardo, Billy. *The Logic of a Rose: Chicago Stories* (9–12). 2005, BkMk paper $15.95 (978-1-886157-50-7). Short stories reveal sensitive young Petey's awareness of the world around him as he grows up in early 1970s Chicago. (Rev: BL 6/1–15/05)

6401 London, Jack. *The Portable Jack London* (8–12). Ed. by Earle Labor. 1994, Penguin paper $18.00 (978-0-14-017969-9). As well as several short stories and the full text of *The Call of the Wild,* this anthology contains some letters and general nonfiction. [818]

6402 Lord, Christine, ed. *Eighth Grade: Stories of Friendship, Passage and Discovery by Eighth Grade Writers* (6–12). Series: American Teen Writer. 1996, Merlyn's Pen paper $9.95 (978-1-886427-08-2). This is a group of short stories collected by *Merlyn's Pen*

magazine that were written by 8th-graders. Also in this series are *Freshman: Fiction, Fantasy, and Humor by Ninth Grade Writers* and *Sophomores: Tales of Reality, Conflict, and the Road,* plus eight other volumes (all 1996). Each is accompanied by an audiotape. (Rev: VOYA 6/98)

6403 Loughead, Deb, and Jocelyn Shipley, eds. *Cleavage: Breakaway Fiction for Real Girls* (8–12). 2009, Sumach paper $12.95 (978-1-894549-76-9). Fifteen diverse stories by Canadian writers explore the relationship between teen girls and their mothers, many with a focus on different perspectives of body image. (Rev: SLJ 2/1/09; VOYA 2/09)

6404 Lupoff, Richard A. *Claremont Tales II* (11–12). Series: Claremont Tales. 2002, Golden Gryphon $23.95 (978-1-930846-07-4). A varied short story collection for fans of fantasy, science fiction, mysteries, thrillers, and horror stories; for mature teens. (Rev: BL 2/15/02)

6405 McEwen, Christian, ed. *Jo's Girls: Tomboy Tales of High Adventure, True Grit and Real Life* (10–12). 1997, Beacon paper $30.50 (978-0-8070-6211-1). A well-edited collection of fiction and memoirs about girls who assume the role of tomboy by such writers as Annie Dillard, Ursula Le Guin, Toni Morrison, Colette, and Willa Cather. (Rev: BL 6/1–15/97; SLJ 3/98)

6406 McKinley, Robin, and Peter Dickinson. *Water: Tales of Elemental Spirits* (7–12). 2002, Putnam $18.99 (978-0-399-23796-6). Six captivating and imaginative stories feature magical sea-beings and the humans who love or fight them. (Rev: BL 4/15/02; HB 7–8/02; HBG 10/02; SLJ 6/02*; VOYA 6/02)

6407 MacLeod, Alexander. *Light Lifting* (11–12). 2011, Biblioasis paper $16.95 (978-18972319-4-4). This gritty collection of short stories, often violent and uncompromising, features protagonists who test the limits of the human body, spirit, and psyche; for mature readers (Rev: BLO 3/1–15/11)

6408 Marcus, Ben, ed. *The Anchor Book of New American Short Stories* (9–12). 2004, Anchor paper $13.00 (978-1-4000-3482-6). Selections by Lydia Davis, Stephen Dixon, Jhumpa Lahiri, and many others. (Rev: BL 8/04)

6409 Matheson, Richard. *Duel* (10–12). 2003, Tor paper $15.95 (978-0-312-87826-9). A varied collection of stories with elements of humor, fantasy, horror, and science fiction. (Rev: BL 12/15/02; VOYA 10/03)

6410 Mazer, Anne, ed. *A Walk in My World: International Short Stories About Youth* (9–12). 1998, Persea $17.95 (978-0-89255-237-5). Sixteen stories about young people from the pens of distinguished writers from around the world afford a powerful and lasting reading experience. (Rev: BL 1/1–15/99; HBG 3/99; SLJ 6/99; VOYA 4/99)

6411 Meno, Joe. *Bluebirds Used to Croon in the Choir* (11–12). 2005, Northwestern Univ $21.95 (978-0-

8101-5167-3). Seventeen offbeat short stories, many featuring young people in difficult situations; for mature teens. (Rev: BL 11/15/05)

6412 Mercado, Nancy E., ed. *Every Man for Himself: Ten Short Stories About Being a Guy* (10–12). 2005, Dial $16.99 (978-0-8037-2896-7). This collection includes a story told in comic book form, one about a boy's coming out, and others about triumphs, defeats, embarrassments, and other important experiences leading to adulthood. (Rev: BL 9/1/05; SLJ 9/05; VOYA 10/05)

6413 Messinger, Jonathan. *Hiding Out* (9–12). 2007, Featherproof paper $13.95 (978-0-9771992-3-5). Clever and at times profound, this collection of short stories features a wide variety of offbeat characters, all of whom have something interesting to relate (includes illustrations). (Rev: BL 9/15/07)

6414 Miller, Sue, ed. *Best New American Voices, 2007* (9–12). 2006, Harcourt paper $14.00 (978-0-15-603155-4). This volume features spirited and innovative short stories from authors with varied voices. (Rev: BL 10/1/06)

6415 Monson, Ander. *Other Electricities* (11–12). 2005, Sarabande paper $14.95 (978-1-932511-15-4). An interconnected collection of affecting and inventive stories set in a town on Michigan's Upper Peninsula and featuring many teen characters; for mature teens who are strong readers. (Rev: BL 5/1/05)

6416 Moon, Elizabeth. *Moon Flights* (9–12). 2007, Night Shade $24.95 (978-1-59780-109-6). Sixteen short stories of science fiction and fantasy make up this collection of the works of Moon, including an alternate World War I story and other military fiction, the author having been a marine herself. (Rev: BL 10/15/07)

6417 Mooney, Ben, ed. *You Never Did Learn to Knock: 14 Stories about Girls and Their Mothers* (7–10). 2006, Kingfisher paper $7.95 (978-0-7534-5877-8). Fourteen enjoyable stories about all types of mothers and the relationships — be they strained, loving, or complicated — they have with their daughters. (Rev: BL 4/15/06; LMC 8–9/06; SLJ 6/06)

6418 *More Best-Loved Stories Told at the National Storytelling Festival* (9–12). 1992, Storytelling Pr $24.95 (978-1-879991-09-5); paper $14.95 (978-1-879991-08-8). Stories featuring familiar folklore, family anecdotes, and tales from many cultures, with a brief note on each storyteller. (Rev: BL 11/15/92)

6419 Murphy, Mark. *House of Java* (10–12). 1998, NBM paper $8.95 (978-1-56163-202-2). A collection of short stories about the frequenters of a Seattle coffee shop and its neighborhood. (Rev: SLJ 8/98)

6420 Myers, Walter Dean. *What They Found: Love on 145th Street* (7–11). 2007, Random House $15.99 (978-0-385-32138-9). A collection of 15 interrelated stories about love of family among African Americans, many

dealing with poverty, drug addiction, incarceration, and other hardships. (Rev: BCCB 11/07; BL 7/07; SLJ 8/07)

6421 Na, An, and M. T. Anderson. *No Such Thing as the Real World: Stories About Growing Up and Getting a Life* (9–12). 2009, HarperTeen $16.99 (978-006147058-5); LB $17.89 (978-006147059-2). Short stories about young people facing the "real world" are written by An Na, M. T. Anderson, K. L. Going, Beth Kephart, Chris Lynch, and Jacqueline Woodson. (Rev: BL 7/09; SLJ 4/1/09)

6422 Naidoo, Beverley. *Out of Bounds: Seven Stories of Conflict and Hope* (6–10). 2003, HarperCollins LB $17.89 (978-0-06-050800-5). The seven stories in this book, with a foreword by Archbishop Desmond Tutu, look at the racism, apartheid, discrimination, and progress in South Africa from the 1950s to the present. (Rev: BL 2/15/03; HB 3–4/03*; HBG 10/03; SLJ 1/03; VOYA 6/03)

6423 Nix, Garth. *Across the Wall: A Tale of the Abhorsen and Other Stories* (7–10). 2005, HarperCollins LB $17.89 (978-0-06-074714-5). In this collection of short stories, Garth offers an eclectic mix of genres and settings — only the first is related to Abhorsen — suitable for a range of readers. (Rev: BL 6/1–15/05; SLJ 11/05; VOYA 10/05)

6424 November, Sharyn, ed. *Firebirds* (7–12). 2003, Putnam $19.99 (978-0-14-250142-9). An excellent collection of stories by authors who publish with the Firebird imprint, including Michael Cadnum, Garth Nix, and Meredith Ann Pierce. (Rev: BL 10/15/03; HBG 4/04; VOYA 12/03)

6425 November, Sharyn, ed. *Firebirds Rising: An Anthology of Original Science Fiction and Fantasy* (7–10). 2006, Penguin $19.99 (978-0-14-240549-9). Contributors to this anthology of 16 original stories include Tamora Pierce, Charles de Lint, Patricia A. McKillip, Kara Dalkey, and Tanith Lee. (Rev: BL 4/1/06; SLJ 4/06; VOYA 4/06)

6426 November, Sharyn, ed. *Firebirds Soaring: An Anthology of Original Speculative Fiction* (7–12). Illus. by Mike Dringenberg. Series: Firebirds. 2008, Penguin $19.99 (978-014240552-9). Nancy Springer, Nancy Farmer, Jane Yolen, Carol Emshwiller, and Kara Dalkey are among the authors of the 19 short stories included in this volume, diverse tales that reflect a number of genres. Lexile 820L (Rev: BL 1/1–15/09; LMC 5–6/09; SLJ 12/08)

6427 Noyes, Deborah, ed. *Sideshow: Ten Original Tales of Freaks, Illusionists, and Other Matters Odd and Magical* (9–12). Illus. 2009, Candlewick $16.99 (978-076363752-1). A creepy collection of short stories about the grotesque, the strange, and the spooky. Lexile 790L (Rev: BL 4/15/09; LMC 11–12/09; SLJ 7/1/09)

6428 Nye, Naomi Shihab. *There Is No Long Distance Now: Very Short Stories* (9–12). 2011, Greenwillow $17.99 (978-0-06-201965-3). Forty short stories written in poetic prose introduce adolescent characters around the world; they usually face problems but the stories are ultimately full of hope. ℮ Lexile 770L (Rev: BL 12/15/11; HB 11–12/11; SLJ 11/1/11*)

6429 Oates, Joyce Carol. *Small Avalanches and Other Stories* (9–12). 2003, HarperCollins LB $17.89 (978-0-06-001218-2). Stories of complicated young women, often making bad choices, make up this collection. (Rev: BL 3/15/03*; HBG 10/03; SLJ 7/03; VOYA 6/03)

6430 Oates, Joyce Carol, ed. *The Oxford Book of American Short Stories* (10–12). 1992, Oxford Univ $44.99 (978-0-19-507065-1); paper $19.95 (978-0-19-509262-2). An excellent collection of 56 stories by such authors as Poe, Hemingway, and Sandra Cisneros.

6431 O'Connor, Flannery. *Collected Works* (10–12). 1988, Library of America $35.00 (978-0-940450-37-0). As well as the novels *Wise Blood* and *The Violent Carry It Away,* this collection includes many short stories. (Rev: SLJ 1/89)

6432 O'Connor, Flannery. *The Complete Stories* (10–12). 1971, Farrar paper $15.00 (978-0-374-51536-2). This collection of short stories by one of the South's most famous writers is arranged chronologically.

6433 Ohlin, Alix. *Babylon and Other Stories* (9–12). 2006, Knopf $23.00 (978-0-375-41525-8). A collection of short stories about families and relationships, many with young protagonists. (Rev: BL 7/06)

6434 Pawlak, Mark, et al, ed. *Bullseye: Stories and Poems by Outstanding High School Writers* (9–12). 1995, Hanging Loose paper $15.00 (978-1-882413-12-6). A collection of poems and short narratives written by 68 teenagers, taken from the pages of the literary magazine *Hanging Loose.* (Rev: BL 2/1/96; SLJ 12/95)

6435 Peck, Richard. *Past Perfect, Present Tense* (5–12). 2004, Dial $16.99 (978-0-8037-2998-8). This anthology includes 11 previously published stories and two new ones, with comments on each story's inspiration and tips on writing fiction. (Rev: BL 4/1/04; HB 3–4/04; SLJ 4/04; VOYA 6/04)

6436 Penzler, Otto, ed. *The Vampire Archives: The Most Complete Volume of Vampire Tales Ever Published* (9–12). 2009, Vintage paper $25 (978-0-307-47389-9). Edgar Allan Poe, Stephen King, and Ray Bradbury are among the writers represented in this collection of more than 80 tales and poems. (Rev: SLJ 12/09)

6437 Phillips, Holly. *In the Palace of Repose* (10–12). 2005, Prime $29.95 (978-1-894815-58-1). Nine stories suitable for strong readers incorporate elements of fantasy, mystery, and the heroic. (Rev: BL 2/1/05)

6438 Porter, Katherine Anne. *The Collected Stories of Katherine Anne Porter* (10–12). 1965, Harcourt paper $16.00 (978-0-15-618876-0). This collection includes all the stories published previously in other books plus the addition of several others.

6439 Prasad, Chandra, ed. *Mixed: An Anthology of Short Fiction on the Multiracial Experience* (9–12). 2006, Norton paper $15.95 (978-0-393-32786-1). A thoughtful collection of short stories by and about people of mixed racial heritage that explores racial identity and the painful choices involved in a search for self-identity; each piece includes a short author biography and a commentary. (Rev: BL 7/06)

6440 Prescott, Peter S. *The Norton Book of American Short Stories* (10–12). 1988, Norton $29.95 (978-0-393-02619-1). An excellent survey of the American short story, with 70 examples beginning with Poe and Hawthorne and ending with some modern masters.

6441 Pullman, Philip, sel. *Whodunit? Detective Stories* (6–12). 2007, Kingfisher paper $6.95 (978-0-7534-6142-6). Pullman introduces this collection of stories — by the likes of Arthur Conan Doyle, Agatha Christie, Isaac Asimov, and Damon Runyon — with a history of the genre. (Rev: SLJ 11/07)

6442 Rabe, Jean, and Martin H. Greenberg, eds. *Pandora's Closet* (9–12). 2007, DAW paper $7.99 (978-0-7564-0437-6). In this wonderfully varied collection of 19 stories, the writers speculate on what magical items and garments might have been in Pandora's closet, and the effects of wearing them. (Rev: BL 8/07)

6443 Robison, Mary. *Tell Me* (11–12). 2002, Counterpoint paper $16.00 (978-1-58243-258-8). Family relationships are the focus of many of the 30 short stories in this collection; for mature teens. (Rev: BL 11/15/02)

6444 Robson, Claire, ed. *Outside Rules: Short Stories about Nonconformist Youth* (9–12). 2007, Persea paper $9.95 (978-0-89255-316-7). Teens who don't "fit in" with their peers are the subjects of each of the 14 well-written stories in this collection, authored by a mix of well-known and less-familiar writers. (Rev: SLJ 6/07)

6445 Rodriguez, Jason, ed. *Postcards: True Stories That Never Happened* (10–12). 2007, Villard $21.95 (978-0-345-49850-2). Each story in this multi-authored collection begins with a message from a real-life postcard found in an antique store; the writers imagine what happened before or after the postcard was sent, and the results are wonderfully creative. (Rev: LMC 3/08; SLJ 7/07)

6446 Rosen, Roger, and Patra M. Sevastiades, eds. *On Heroes and the Heroic: In Search of Good Deeds* (7–12). Series: Icarus World Issues. 1993, Rosen LB $21.95 (978-0-8239-1384-8); paper $11.95 (978-0-8239-1385-5). Nine fiction and nonfiction pieces explore the concepts of heroes and antiheroes. (Rev: BL 9/15/93; SLJ 1/94; VOYA 12/93)

6447 Rosen, Roger, and Patra McSharry, eds. *Teenage Soldiers, Adult Wars* (9–12). Series: Icarus World Issues. 1991, Rosen LB $21.95 (978-0-8239-1304-6); paper $11.95 (978-0-8239-1305-3). Short stories and essays by teenage soldiers in troubled areas around the world — from Northern Ireland to the Middle East — who express their frontline views of military conflict. (Rev: BL 6/15/91; SLJ 4/91)

6448 Roth, Philip. *Goodbye, Columbus, and Five Short Stories* (10–12). 1995, Modern Library paper $13.00 (978-0-679-74826-7). As well as the title story about young love, there are five other short stories in this collection.

6449 Salinger, J. D. *Nine Stories* (10–12). 1953, Little, Brown $24.95 (978-0-316-76956-3). A collection of Salinger's short fiction, mostly dealing with troubled youngsters.

6450 Salisbury, Graham. *Blue Skin of the Sea* (8–12). 1992, Delacorte $15.95 (978-0-385-30596-9). These 11 stories contain a strong sense of time and place, fully realized characters, stylish prose, and universal themes. (Rev: BL 6/15/92*; SLJ 6/92*)

6451 Sawyers, June S., ed. *The Best in Rock Fiction* (11–12). 2005, Hal Leonard paper $16.95 (978-0-634-08028-9). An anthology of short stories and novel excerpts exemplifying a "rock and roll sensibility," including work by T. C. Boyle, Sherman Alexie, Nick Hornby, and Don DeLillo. (Rev: BL 2/15/05)

6452 Scott, Whitney, ed. *Things That Go Bump in the Night: The Supernatural from the Horrific to the Hilarious* (11–12). Series: Black-and-White Anthology. 2004, Outrider paper $17.95 (978-0-9712903-1-0). An entertaining collection of diverse contemporary tales of the supernatural; for mature readers. (Rev: BL 9/15/04) [398.2]

6453 Sedaris, David, ed. *Children Playing Before a Statue of Hercules* (9–12). 2005, Simon & Schuster paper $14.95 (978-0-7432-7394-7). Sedaris's choices for this collection include short stories by Katherine Mansfield, Flannery O'Connor, Alice Munro, and Jhumpa Lahiri. (Rev: BL 5/1/05)

6454 Sedia, Ekaterina, ed. *Willful Impropriety: 13 Tales of Society, Scandal, and Romance* (9–12). 2012, Running Press paper $9.95 (978-07624443-0-4). A collection of romantic tales set in the Victorian era, many highlighting the social mores of the time and some using magic as a device. **e** (Rev: BLO 11/15/12; VOYA 12/12)

6455 Sherman, Josepha, ed. *Orphans of the Night* (6–10). 1995, Walker $16.95 (978-0-8027-8368-4). Brings together 11 short stories and two poems about creatures from folklore, most with teen protagonists. (Rev: BL 6/1–15/95; SLJ 6/95; VOYA 12/95)

6456 *Shining On: 11 Star Authors' Illuminating Stories* (7–10). 2007, Delacorte LB $11.99 (978-0-385-90470-4); paper $8.99 (978-0-385-73472-1). A collection of 11 short stories by well-known British and American

authors — Lois Lowry, Celia Rees, and Meg Cabot, among them — with the theme of growing up and dealing with problems. (Rev: BL 6/1–15/07; LMC 10/07; SLJ 4/07)

6457 Singer, Isaac Bashevis. *The Collected Stories of Isaac Bashevis Singer* (10–12). 1982, Farrar paper $18.00 (978-0-374-51788-5). This collection contains 47 short stories chosen by the author for inclusion.

6458 Singer, Marilyn. *Make Me Over: 11 Original Stories About Transforming Ourselves* (7–10). 2005, Dutton $17.99 (978-0-525-47480-7). Teenage transformations and the importance of relationships are themes of these stories by writers including Joseph Bruchac, Margaret Peterson Haddix, and Joyce Sweeney. (Rev: BL 9/15/05; SLJ 2/06)

6459 Singer, Marilyn, comp. *I Believe in Water: Twelve Brushes with Religion* (7–10). 2000, HarperCollins LB $15.89 (978-0-06-028398-8). Short stories by writers including Virginia Euwer Wolff and M. E. Kerr look at religion from varied viewpoints. (Rev: BL 10/1/00; HBG 3/01; SLJ 11/00; VOYA 4/01)

6460 Singleton, George. *Why Dogs Chase Cars* (11–12). 2004, Algonquin paper $14.95 (978-1-56512-404-2). For Mendal Dawes, growing up in South Carolina with an opinionated father can be funny, frustrating, and fortuitous; short stories for mature teens. (Rev: BL 8/04)

6461 Smiley, Jane, et al, ed. *Best New American Voices, 2006* (10–12). 2005, Harcourt paper $14.00 (978-0-15-602901-8). This collection of 15 short stories showcases the work of some of America's most promising new writers. (Rev: BL 10/1/05)

6462 Snyder, Scott. *Voodoo Heart* (9–12). 2006, Dial $24.00 (978-0-385-33841-7). A collection of offbeat stories in which lives change in the blink of an eye and everyone has a zany tale to tell. (Rev: BL 5/15/06)

6463 Soto, Gary. *Help Wanted* (7–10). 2005, Harcourt $17.00 (978-0-15-205201-0). In this collection of ten short stories, Soto explores the dreams and struggles of Mexican American teens living in central California. (Rev: BCCB 5/05; BL 5/1/05; HB 5–6/05; SLJ 5/05)

6464 Stirling, S. M. *Ice, Iron and Gold* (9–12). 2007, Night Shade $26.95 (978-1-59780-115-7). This is a collection of some of the most interesting works of Stirling, including military science fiction, fantasy, and imaginative juxtopositions of historical figures such as Pancho Villa, vice president to Theodore Roosevelt. (Rev: BL 10/15/07)

6465 Stolar, Daniel. *The Middle of the Night* (10–12). 2003, St. Martin's $23.00 (978-0-312-30409-6). Familiar situations and concerns are central to this collection of eight absorbing stories. (Rev: BL 5/15/03)

6466 Thompson, Holly, ed. *Tomo: Friendship Through Fiction — An Anthology of Japan Teen Stories* (7–10). 2012, Stone Bridge $14.95 (978-161172006-8). Thirty-six diverse stories — in prose, verse, and graphic art — were created by artists and writers who have a connection to Japan and published to benefit teens affected by the 2011 tsunami. (Rev: BL 4/15/12; LMC 1–2/13*; SLJ 5/1/12; VOYA 4/12)

6467 Thomsen, Brian M., ed. *A Yuletide Universe: Sixteen Fantastical Tales* (11–12). 2003, Warner paper $12.95 (978-0-446-69187-1). Christmas-themed short stories represent many genres, among them fantasy, mystery, science fiction, and westerns; recommended for mature teens because of violence. (Rev: BL 10/15/03*)

6468 Tolstoy, Leo. *Great Short Works of Leo Tolstoy* (10–12). 1967, Harper & Row paper $8.99 (978-0-06-083071-7). This is a collection of the major short works by Tolstoy including *The Death of Ivan Ilych* and *The Kreutzer Sonata.*

6469 Trelease, Jim. *Read All About It! Great Read-Aloud Stories, Poems, and Newspaper Pieces for Preteens and Teens* (9–12). 1993, Penguin paper $15.00 (978-0-14-014655-4). This anthology of good read-alouds comes from 52 authors and consists of fiction, poetry, and some nonfiction. [808.8]

6470 *Twice Told: Original Stories Inspired by Original Artwork* (7–10). Illus. by Scott Hunt. 2006, Dutton $19.99 (978-0-525-46818-9). Nine charcoal drawings by Scott Hunt were provided as inspiration to pairs of popular YA writers; the resulting short stories cover a wide range of styles and themes. (Rev: BL 2/15/06*; SLJ 4/06)

6471 Van Pelt, James. *The Last of the O-Forms and Other Stories* (9–12). 2005, Fairwood paper $17.99 (978-0-9746573-5-6). A diverse collection covering many genres including ghost stories, sports stories, and science fiction. (Rev: BL 8/05)

6472 Vapnyar, Lara. *There Are Jews in My House* (11–12). 2003, Pantheon $19.95 (978-0-375-42250-8). In this collection of six deftly drawn short stories, Vapnyar explores various aspects of Russian and Russian American life. (Rev: BL 11/15/03)

6473 Vonnegut, Kurt. *While Mortals Sleep: Unpublished Short Fiction* (11–12). 2011, Delacorte $27 (978-038534373-2). These sixteen unpublished short stories from the author of *Slaughterhouse-Five* are culled from Vonnegut's early career and show some of the cynicism of his later work. (Rev: BL 11/1–15/10)

6474 Warren, Robert Penn, and Albert Erskine, eds. *Short Story Masterpieces* (10–12). 1954, Dell paper $7.50 (978-0-440-37864-8). An international collection of 36 masterpieces of short fiction.

6475 Waters, Sarah, ed. *Dancing with Mr. Darcy: Stories Inspired by Jane Austen and Chawton House Library* (11–12). 2010, HarperCollins paper $13.99 (978-00619990-6-2). A collection of short stories from the Chawton House Library competition, featuring an eclectic mix of tales based on Jane Austen's characters, her stories, and her life; for mature readers. **e** (Rev: BL 9/1–15/10)

6476 Weiss, M. Jerry, and Helen S. Weiss, eds. *Big City Cool: Short Stories About Urban Youth* (7–12). 2002, Persea paper $8.95 (978-0-89255-278-8). A variety of urban settings and cultural and racial experiences are portrayed in these 14 stories, half of which have previously appeared in print. (Rev: BL 10/15/02; SLJ 11/02; VOYA 12/02)

6477 Welty, Eudora. *The Collected Stories of Eudora Welty* (10–12). 1980, Harcourt $38.00 (978-0-15-118994-6); paper $16.00 (978-0-15-618921-7). This omnibus volume contains stories from four previously published collections by one of America's great masters of the genre.

6478 White, Trudy. *Table of Everything* (7–12). 2001, Allen & Unwin paper $16.95 (978-1-86508-135-9). Australian writer White captivates readers with this collection of offbeat short stories. (Rev: VOYA 8/02)

6479 Wilde, Oscar. *The Portable Oscar Wilde. Rev. ed.* (10–12). Ed. by Richard Aldington and Stanley Weintraub. 1981, Viking paper $18.00 (978-0-14-015093-3). The collection contains plays including *The Importance of Being Earnest,* the novel *The Picture of Dorian Gray,* poems, letters, and quotations. [828]

6480 Williams, Sheila, ed. *Asimov's Science Fiction Magazine: 30th Anniversary Anthology* (9–12). 2007, Tachyon paper $14.95 (978-1-892391-47-6). This outstanding collection of 18 science fiction stories contains works by leading authors such as John Varley and Mike Resnick. (Rev: BL 7/07)

6481 Wilson, Kevin. *Tunneling to the Center of the Earth* (11–12). 2009, HarperPerennial paper $13.95 (978-00615790-2-8). A well-written collection of humorous and sometimes disturbing short stories suitable for mature readers. Alex Award 2010. (Rev: BL 4–5/09)

6482 Wolfe, Thomas. *The Complete Short Stories of Thomas Wolfe* (10–12). Ed. by Francis E. Skipp. 1987, Scribner paper $15.00 (978-0-02-040891-8). All of Wolfe's 55 short stories are reprinted in this volume.

6483 Yee, Paul. *What Happened This Summer* (7–10). 2006, Tradewind $10.95 (978-1-896580-88-3). A collection of nine short stories about Chinese Canadian teens and the particular tensions they face. (Rev: BL 11/1/06; LMC 4–5/07; SLJ 2/07)

6484 Yolen, Jane, and Patrick Nielsen Hayden, eds. *The Year's Best Science Fiction and Fantasy for Teens* (9–12). 2005, Tor $17.95 (978-0-7653-1383-6); paper

$12.95 (978-0-7653-1384-3). A winning collection of 11 outstanding fantasy and science fiction stories representing many subgenres and appropriate for young adults. (Rev: BL 6/1–15/05; SLJ 7/05; VOYA 10/05)

6485 Young, Mike. *Look! Look! Feathers* (10–12). 2011, Word Riot paper $16.95 (978-09779343-6-2). A collec-

tion of well-written, quirky stories set in Northern California and Oregon. ℮ (Rev: BLO 12/1–15/10)

6486 Zapata, Celia Correas de, ed. *Short Stories by Latin American Women: The Magic and the Real* (11–12). 2003, Modern Library paper $12.95 (978-0-8129-6707-4). A collection of stories full of realism, surrealism, and the unreal; for mature teens. (Rev: BL 12/1/02)

Plays

General and Miscellaneous Collections

6487 Allen, Laurie. *Comedy Scenes for Student Actors: Short Sketches for Young Performers* (9–12). 2009, Meriwether paper $17.95 (978-1-56608-159-7). This well-written collection of 31 comic two-person sketches includes a good mix of male and female parts. (Rev: SLJ 10/09; VOYA 12/10) [792.9]

6488 Bansavage, Lisa, and L. E. McCullough, eds. *111 Shakespeare Monologues for Teens: The Ultimate Audition Book for Teens, Vol. V* (7–12). Series: Young Actors. 2003, Smith & Kraus paper $11.95 (978-1-57525-356-5). Monologues ranging from 15 seconds to 2 minutes and chosen for the youthful speakers or topics of interest to young people are arranged in three sections: for female actors, for male actors, and for male or female; an introduction explains Shakespeare's language and rhythms. (Rev: SLJ 7/04) [808.82]

6489 Beard, Jocelyn A. *Scenes from Classic Plays, 468 B.C. to 1970 A.D.* (10–12). 1993, Smith & Kraus paper $11.95 (978-1-880399-36-1). These scenes, averaging three pages in length, are taken from the world's greatest plays, and each is introduced by a brief synopsis. (Rev: BL 6/1–15/94) [808.82]

6490 Beard, Jocelyn A., ed. *The Best Men's Stage Monologues of 1992* (9–12). 1993, Smith & Kraus paper $11.95 (978-1-880399-11-8). Monologues for men from outstanding 1992 theatrical works. (Rev: BL 6/1–15/93) [808.82]

6491 Beard, Jocelyn A., ed. *The Best Men's Stage Monologues of 1993* (9–12). 1994, Smith & Kraus paper $11.95 (978-1-880399-43-9). Includes 52 monologues from 1993 plays. (Rev: BL 4/1/94; VOYA 8/94) [808.82]

6492 Beard, Jocelyn A., ed. *The Best Women's Stage Monologues of 1992* (9–12). 1993, Smith & Kraus paper $11.95 (978-1-880399-10-1). Monologues for women from outstanding 1992 theatrical works. (Rev: BL 6/1–15/93) [808.82]

6493 Beard, Jocelyn A., ed. *The Best Women's Stage Monologues of 1993* (9–12). 1994, Smith & Kraus paper $11.95 (978-1-880399-42-2). Includes 58 monologues from 1993 plays. (Rev: BL 4/1/94; VOYA 8/94) [808.82]

6494 Beard, Jocelyn A., ed. *Monologues from Classic Plays 468 B.C. to 1960 A.D.* (9–12). 1993, Smith & Kraus paper $11.95 (978-1-880399-09-5). Monologues from early Greek, Roman, medieval, and Restoration plays and the modern works of Williams, Pinter, and Beckett. (Rev: BL 6/1–15/93) [808.82]

6495 Bert, Norman A., and Deb Bert. *Play It Again! More One-Act Plays for Acting Students* (8–12). 1993, Meriwether paper $14.95 (978-0-916260-97-2). This is a collection of 21 one-act plays and monologs for young actors. [812.008]

6496 Cerf, Bennett, and Van H. Cartmell, eds. *24 Favorite One-Act Plays* (10–12). 1958, Doubleday paper $14.95 (978-0-385-06617-4). An international collection of short plays — both comedies and tragedies — by such masters as Inge, Coward, and O'Neill. [808.82]

6497 Dabrowski, Kristen. *111 One-Minute Monologues* (9–12). 2004, Smith & Kraus $11.95 (978-1-57525-307-7). Aspiring teenage actors will find a wealth of audition material in this collection of 111 one-page monologues. (Rev: BL 8/04; SLJ 3/05) [812]

6498 Dabrowski, Kristen. *Teens Speak, Boys Ages 16 to 18: Sixty Original Character Monologues* (7–12). Series: Kids Speak. 2005, Smith & Kraus paper $11.95 (978-1-57525-415-9). A collection of brief, varied monologues for teenage boys from 16 to 18. Also in the series are *Teens Speak, Boys Ages 13 to 15: Sixty Origi-*

nal Character Monologues, Teens Speak, Girls Ages 16 to 18: Sixty Original Character Monologues, and *Teens Speak, Girls Ages 13 to 15: Sixty Original Character Monologues* (all 2005). (Rev: SLJ 7/05) [808.82]

6499 Dabrowski, Kristen. *Twenty 10-Minute Plays for Teens, Vol. 1* (9–12). Series: Young Actors. 2004, Smith & Kraus paper $14.95 (978-1-57525-405-0). Twenty short plays with roles for multiple characters deal with issues of interest to teens, from school life and sports to drinking, dating, and sexual identity. (Rev: SLJ 1/05) [812]

6500 Ellis, Roger, ed. *Audition Monologs for Student Actors II: Selections from Contemporary Plays* (8–12). 2001, Meriwether paper $15.95 (978-1-56608-073-6). Fifty monologues for both sexes from ages 10 to mid-20s are accompanied by scene-setting notes and acting tips. (Rev: SLJ 4/02)

6501 Ellis, Roger, ed. *Audition Monologs for Student Actors: Selections from Contemporary Plays* (9–12). 1999, Meriwether paper $15.95 (978-1-56608-055-2). One-person scenes for girls and boys offer many diverse roles, plus suggestions for the actor. (Rev: BL 2/1/00) [812]

6502 Ellis, Roger, ed. *International Plays for Young Audiences: Contemporary Works from Leading Playwrights* (7–12). 2000, Meriwether paper $16.95 (978-1-56608-065-1). The 12 short plays in this collection come from varied cultures and deal with situations of interest to young people. (Rev: SLJ 2/01)

6503 Ellis, Roger, ed. *More Scenes and Monologs from the Best New Plays: An Anthology of New Dramatic Writing from Professionally Produced Plays* (9–12). 2007, Meriwether paper $15.95 (978-1-56608-142-9). Ellis offers a range of interesting scenes of varying lengths, featuring characters from mid-teens to mid-20s and providing excellent tips on delivery, characterization, and staging. (Rev: SLJ 9/07) [812]

6504 Fairbanks, Stephanie S. *Spotlight: Solo Scenes for Student Actors* (7–12). 1996, Meriwether paper $14.95 (978-1-56608-020-0). This book contains 55 excellent one- to three-page monologues, some specifically for girls, others for boys, and others nonspecific. (Rev: BL 12/1/96; SLJ 5/97) [812]

6505 Fleischman, Paul. *Zap* (9–12). 2005, Candlewick $16.99 (978-0-7636-2774-4). Works by Shakespeare, Chekhov, Tennessee Williams, and Samuel Beckett are among those featured in this chaotic play in which the audience can "zap" any boring moments. (Rev: BL 9/15/05; SLJ 11/05) [812]

6506 Fugard, Athol. *Master Harold — and the Boys* (10–12). 1982, Knopf paper $12.00 (978-0-14-048187-7). A moving play set in South Africa that deals with relations between a white boy and his family's servants. [822]

6507 Gallo, Donald R., ed. *Center Stage: One-Act Plays for Teenage Readers and Actors* (7–12). 1990, HarperCollins $17.00 (978-0-06-022170-6); paper $8.99 (978-0-06-447078-0). A collection of 10 one-act plays especially written for this collection by such authors as Walter Dean Myers and Ouida Sebestyen. (Rev: BL 12/1/90; SLJ 9/90) [812]

6508 *Great Scenes for Young Actors* (7–12). Series: Young Actors. 1997, Smith & Kraus paper $14.95 (978-1-57525-107-3). A variety of scenes representing different forms of drama are reprinted from such playwrights as Arthur Miller, George S. Kaufman, Horton Foote, and Paul Zindel. (Rev: BL 3/1/99; SLJ 6/99) [808.82]

6509 Hamlett, Christina. *Humorous Plays for Teen-Agers* (7–10). 1987, Plays paper $12.95 (978-0-8238-0276-0). Easily read one-act plays for beginners in acting. (Rev: BL 5/1/87; SLJ 11/87) [812]

6510 Henderson, Heather H. *The Flip Side: 64 Point-of-View Monologs for Teens* (10–12). 1998, Meriwether paper $14.95 (978-1-56608-045-3). This is a collection of original, short monologues written for this anthology. (Rev: VOYA 10/99) [808.82]

6511 Horvath, John, et al, ed. *Duo! The Best Scenes for the 90's* (9–12). 1995, Applause Theatre paper $16.95 (978-1-55783-030-2). Some 130 scenes for two actors from productions by established playwrights of the 1980s and 1990s. (Rev: BL 4/15/95) [808.82]

6512 Houghton, Norris, ed. *Romeo and Juliet and West Side Story* (10–12). 1965, Dell paper $5.99 (978-0-440-97483-3). This combined edition affords an interesting comparison between the two versions of the same story. [808.1]

6513 Kamerman, Sylvia, ed. *The Big Book of Large-Cast Plays: 27 One-Act Plays for Young Actors* (5–10). 1994, Plays $12.95 (978-0-8238-0302-6). Thirty short plays on varied subjects, arranged according to audience appeal. (Rev: BL 3/15/95) [812]

6514 Kehret, Peg. *Encore! More Winning Monologs for Young Actors* (9–12). 1988, Meriwether paper $15.95 (978-0-916260-54-5). A collection of 63 short pieces suitable for recitations or auditions. (Rev: SLJ 8/88) [808.85]

6515 Kehret, Peg. *Tell It Like It Is: Fifty Monologs for Talented Teens* (9–12). 2007, Meriwether paper $15.95 (978-1-56608-144-3). A wide-ranging selection of scenes is offered in this volume, including simpler monologs for beginners and more challenging ones for advanced students. (Rev: SLJ 3/08)

6516 Kraus, Eric, ed. *Monologues from Contemporary Literature, Vol. 1* (9–12). 1993, Smith & Kraus paper $11.95 (978-1-880399-04-0). Monologues from such literary sources as Paul Theroux's *Chicago Loop*. (Rev: BL 6/1–15/93) [808.82]

367

6517 Krell-Oishi, Mary. *Perspectives: Relevant Scenes for Teens* (9–12). 1997, Meriwether paper $14.95 (978-1-56608-030-9). Problems in such areas as dating, teen pregnancy, family relationships, abortion, and homosexuality are explored in 23 original scenes for high school and college actors. (Rev: BL 10/1/97; SLJ 11/97) [812]

6518 Krell-Oishi, Mary. *Scenes Keep Happening: More Real-Life Snapshots of Teen Lives* (9–12). 2005, Meriwether paper $15.95 (978-1-56608-108-5). Fifty 5- to 10-minute acts featuring teens in diverse situations are grouped by girls, boys, and mixed casts. (Rev: SLJ 2/06) [812]

6519 Lamedman, Debbie. *The Ultimate Audition Book for Teens: 111 One-Minute Monologues, Vol. 4* (7–12). Series: Young Actors. 2003, Smith & Kraus paper $11.95 (978-1-57525-353-4). Monologues for both girls and boys give young actors ample opportunity to display their talent in a range of selections. (Rev: SLJ 4/03) [812]

6520 Lane, Eric, and Nina Shengold, eds. *Under Thirty: Plays for a New Generation* (9–12). 2004, Vintage paper $17.00 (978-1-4000-7616-1). This collection of plays will appeal to actors and audiences in their teens and twenties. (Rev: SLJ 4/05)

6521 Latrobe, Kathy Howard, and Mildred Knight Laughlin. *Readers Theatre for Young Adults: Scripts and Script Development* (7–12). 1989, Libraries Unlimited paper $22.00 (978-0-87287-743-6). A collection of short scripts based on literary classics, plus tips on how to do one's own adaptations. (Rev: BL 1/1/90) [808.5]

6522 Ratliff, Gerald L., and Theodore O. Zapel, eds. *Playing Contemporary Scenes: 31 Famous Scenes and How to Play Them* (8–12). 1996, Meriwether paper $16.95 (978-1-56608-025-5). A selection of scenes by contemporary playwrights, arranged according to age and gender. (Rev: VOYA 6/97) [812]

6523 Ratliff, Gerald L., ed. *Millennium Monologs: 95 Contemporary Characterizations for Young Actors* (8–12). 2002, Meriwether paper $15.95 (978-1-56608-082-8). High school thespians will appreciate this collection of monologues, which are arranged by theme, as well as the advice on auditions. (Rev: BL 3/15/03; SLJ 5/03) [792]

6524 Shengold, Nina, ed. *The Actor's Book of Contemporary Stage Monologues* (9–12). 1987, Penguin paper $15.00 (978-0-14-009649-1). A splendid collection of monologues from both well-known and obscure scripts. (Rev: SLJ 1/88; VOYA 4/88) [659.1]

6525 Slaight, Craig, and Jack Sharrar, eds. *Great Monologues for Young Actors* (9–12). Series: Young Actors. 2009, Smith and Kraus paper $14.95 (978-1-57525-408-1). Presenting a wide range of monologues, this volume also gives advice on presentation and contact information for those wishing to produce public performances. (Rev: SLJ 5/1/09) [808.82]

6526 Slaight, Craig, and Jack Sharrar, eds. *Great Scenes for Young Actors from the Stage* (9–12). 1991, Smith & Kraus paper $14.95 (978-0-9622722-6-4). A collection of 45 scenes from contemporary and classic theater, graded according to ability level and including a brief synopsis of each play. (Rev: BL 11/1/91) [808.82]

6527 Slaight, Craig, and Jack Sharrar, eds. *Multicultural Monologues for Young Actors* (9–12). 1995, Smith & Kraus paper $11.95 (978-1-880399-47-7). Includes 20 poems, plays, and other fiction, arranged by gender. Monologues represent various cultures and dramatic literatures, both contemporary and classic. Some strong language and mature themes. (Rev: BL 8/95; SLJ 9/95) [808.82]

6528 Slaight, Craig, and Jack Sharrar, eds. *Multicultural Scenes for Young Actors* (9–12). 1995, Smith & Kraus paper $11.95 (978-1-880399-48-4). Contemporary and classic materials for groups and pairs from a variety of cultural and dramatic literatures. Some strong language and mature themes. (Rev: BL 8/95) [808.82]

6529 Slaight, Craig, and Jack Sharrar, eds. *Short Plays for Young Actors* (8–12). 1996, Smith & Kraus paper $16.95 (978-1-880399-74-3). An impressive collection of short plays in a variety of genres, plus material on how to approach acting as a serious pursuit. (Rev: BL 9/15/96) [812]

6530 Smith, Marisa, ed. *Showtime's Act One Festival: The One-Act Plays 1994* (10–12). 1995, Smith & Kraus paper $16.95 (978-1-80039-996-9). This is a collection of 13 prize-winning one-act plays, some of which deal with teen situations. (Rev: BL 11/15/95; VOYA 6/96) [812]

6531 Steffensen, James L., Jr., ed. *Great Scenes from the World Theater* (10–12). 1972, Avon paper $5.95 (978-0-380-00793-6). A collection of 180 scenes ranging from Euripides to Albee. [808.82]

Geographical Regions

Europe

GREAT BRITAIN AND IRELAND

6532 Bolt, Robert. *A Man for All Seasons* (9–12). 1990, Vintage paper $9.00 (978-0-679-72822-1). The story in play form of the conflict between Sir Thomas More and Henry VIII. [822]

6533 Christie, Agatha. *The Mousetrap and Other Plays* (10–12). 1993, HarperCollins paper $7.50 (978-0-06-100374-5). Eight mystery thrillers, including *Witness for the Prosecution*. [822]

6534 Lipson, Greta Barclay, and Susan Solomon. *Romeo and Juliet: Plainspoken* (10–12). 1985, Good Apple paper $18.99 (978-0-86653-283-9). A modern-language version of *Romeo and Juliet* is given on one page and the Shakespeare version opposite. (Rev: SLJ 8/86) [822.3]

6535 McKeown, Adam. *Romeo and Juliet: Young Reader's Shakespeare* (5–10). Illus. by Peter Fiore. 2004, Sterling $14.95 (978-1-4027-0004-0). Faithful to the original, this retelling uses finely crafted prose and interweaves many of the best-known poetic stanzas. (Rev: BL 8/04; SLJ 10/04) [822.3]

6536 McKeown, Adam, retel. *Macbeth* (5–10). Retold by Adam McKeown. Illus. by Lynne Cannoy. Series: The Young Reader's Shakespeare. 2005, Sterling $14.95 (978-1-4027-1116-9). This conversational prose retelling includes an introduction to the play and incorporates many of the important poetic passages. (Rev: BL 3/1/05; SLJ 5/05) [822.3]

6537 Miles, Bernard. *Favorite Tales from Shakespeare* (7–10). 1993, Checkerboard $14.95 (978-1-56288-257-0). Shakespeare's most famous plays in a modern retelling. [822.3]

6538 *Othello* (9–12). 2005, Sourcebooks $19.95 (978-1-4022-0645-0); paper $14.95 (978-1-4022-0102-8). An audio CD that features recordings of scenes performed by well-known actors is included in this annotated full-text edition of the play; among additional features are essays on Shakespeare, an analysis of the play in popular culture, and interviews with actors and actresses. (Rev: SLJ 11/05*) [822]

6539 *Romeo and Juliet* (9–12). Series: The Sourcebooks Shakespeare. 2005, Sourcebooks $19.95 (978-1-4022-0644-3); paper $14.95 (978-1-4022-0101-1). An audio CD that features recordings of scenes performed by well-known actors is included in this annotated full-text edition of the play; among additional features are essays on Shakespeare, an analysis of the play in popular culture, and interviews with actors and actresses. (Rev: SLJ 11/05*) [822]

6540 Rosen, Michael. *Shakespeare's Romeo and Juliet* (7–10). Illus. by lane Ray. 2004, Candlewick $17.99 (978-0-7636-2258-9). Vivid, evocative illustrations and a conversational narrative accompany passages of Shakespeare in an appealing retelling of the popular story that includes references and glossaries. (Rev: BL 12/1/03; SLJ 2/04) [823]

6541 Stoppard, Tom. *Rosencrantz and Guildenstern Are Dead* (10–12). 1967, Grove paper $12.00 (978-0-8021-3275-8). In this play, there is a reworking of some of the situations found in *Hamlet* using two of Hamlet's friends as the central characters. [822]

6542 Thomas, Dylan. *Under Milk Wood: A Play for Voices* (10–12). 1954, New Directions paper $8.95 (978-0-8112-0209-1). This radio play about the people of a small Welsh village is also performed as a theater piece. [822]

6543 Wilde, Oscar. *The Importance of Being Earnest* (9–12). 1976, Avon paper $4.99 (978-0-380-01277-0). Mistaken identities is one of the dramatic ploys used in this comedy of manners. [822]

Other Countries

6544 Beckett, Samuel. *Waiting for Godot: Tragicomedy in 2 Acts* (10–12). 1954, Grove Press paper $12.00 (978-0-8021-3034-1). A difficult but rewarding play by the Irish playwright who lived in Paris. [842]

6545 Brecht, Bertolt, and Charles Laughton. *Galileo* (9–12). 1991, Grove Weidenfeld paper $6.95 (978-0-8021-3059-4). Brecht's play chronicles the clash between Italian scientist Galileo and the Roman Catholic Church over Galileo's theories about the solar system. [832]

6546 Chekhov, Anton Pavlovich. *The Plays of Anton Chekhov* (9–12). Trans. by Paul Schmidt. 1997, HarperCollins paper $15.95 (978-0-06-092875-9). These new translations capture the humor of Chekhov's plays. [891.7]

6547 Genet, Jean. *The Maids and Deathwatch: Two Plays* (10–12). Trans. by Bernard Frechtman. 1954, Grove paper $13.00 (978-0-8021-5056-1). This volume consists of two of Genet's most popular plays. [842]

6548 Goldoni, Carlo. *Villeggiatura: A Trilogy Condensed* (9–12). Trans. by Robert Cornthwaite. Series: Young Actors. 1995, Smith & Kraus paper $14.95 (978-1-880399-72-9). A three-act comedy of manners in 18th-century Italian court life, perfect for drama classes or theater groups. (Rev: BL 2/1/95; SLJ 4/95) [852]

6549 Goodrich, Frances. *The Diary of Anne Frank* (7–12). 1958, Dramatists Play Service paper $6.50 (978-0-8222-0307-0). This is the prize-winning play based on the diary. [812]

6550 Oates, Whitney J., and Eugene O'Neill, Jr. *Seven Famous Greek Plays* (10–12). 1950, Modern Library paper $9.00 (978-0-394-70125-7). A collection of the most famous plays from ancient Greece. [882.008]

6551 Perry, Mark. *A Dress for Mona* (7–12). 2002, Fifth Epoch $10.00 (978-1-931492-02-7). Iranian persecution of people of the Baha'i faith is illustrated in this moving play that features Mona, a 16-year-old who will die for her beliefs; staging advice and a pronunciation guide are among the aids provided. (Rev: VOYA 6/03)

6552 Shaffer, Peter. *Amadeus* (9–12). 1981, HarperCollins paper $11.00 (978-0-06-090783-9). A highly subjective view in dramatic format of the relationship between Mozart and Salieri. [822]

6553 Stein, Joseph, and Sheldon Harnick. *Fiddler on the Roof: Based on Sholem Aleichem's Stories* (9–12). 1990, Limelight paper $12.95 (978-0-87910-136-7). The script and lyrics of this musical set in prerevolutionary Russia. [812]

6554 Wasserman, Dale. *Man of La Mancha* (7–12). 1966, Random House paper $9.95 (978-0-394-40619-0). Based loosely on Cervantes's novel, this is a musical play of the adventures of Don Quixote and his servant Sancho Panza. [812]

United States

6555 Blinn, William. *Brian's Song* (9–12). 1983, Bantam paper $4.99 (978-0-553-26618-4). This edition is the screenplay of the television movie about the doomed football player Brian Piccolo. [808.1]

6556 Cassady, Marsh, ed. *Great Scenes from Minority Playwrights: Seventy-four Scenes of Cultural Diversity* (9–12). 1997, Meriwether paper $16.95 (978-1-56608-029-3). This work contains condensations of nine modern plays representing five minority groups and exploring insights into the various cultures and aspects of prejudice. (Rev: BL 10/1/97; SLJ 11/97) [812]

6557 Dove, Rita. *The Darker Face of the Earth* (9–12). 1994, Story Line paper $10.95 (978-0-934257-74-9). This verse play, based on the story of Oedipus and placed within the context of slavery, is set on a plantation in antebellum South Carolina. (Rev: BL 2/15/94*) [812.54]

6558 Gardner, Herb. *The Collected Plays* (9–12). 2000, Applause $27.95 (978-1-55783-394-5). Five plays include *A Thousand Clowns, I'm Not Rappaport,* and *Conversations with My Father,* and one screenplay. (Rev: BL 5/15/00) [812]

6559 Graham, Kristen, ed. *The Great Monologues from the Women's Project* (9–12). 1995, Smith & Kraus paper $7.95 (978-1-880399-35-4). Fifty-three monologues provide dramatic, funny, angry, and sexy performance opportunities. (Rev: BL 2/15/95) [808.82]

6560 Halline, Allan G., ed. *Six Modern American Plays* (10–12). 1966, McGraw-Hill paper $7.75 (978-0-07-553660-4). The six plays in this collection are *The Glass Menagerie, Mister Roberts, The Emperor Jones, The Man Who Came to Dinner, The Little Foxes,* and *Winterset.* [812]

6561 Hellman, Lillian. *Six Plays by Lillian Hellman* (9–12). 1979, Random House paper $15.00 (978-0-394-74112-3). This collection includes *Watch on the Rhine, The Little Foxes,* and *The Children's Hour.* [812]

6562 Kamerman, Sylvia, ed. *Plays of Black Americans: The Black Experience in America, Dramatized for Young People* (7–12). 1994, Plays paper $13.95 (978-0-8238-0301-9). Eleven dramas focus on the history of African Americans. (Rev: BL 5/15/95; SLJ 2/95) [812]

6563 McCullers, Carson. *The Member of the Wedding: A Play* (9–12). 1951, New Directions paper $9.95 (978-0-8112-0093-6). This play, based on the author's novel, tells of a young girl growing up in a southern town and searching for identity. [812]

6564 McCullough, L. E. *Plays of America from American Folklore for Young Actors* (7–12). Series: Young Actors. 1996, Smith & Kraus paper $14.95 (978-1-57525-040-3). Ten original short plays based on folk traditions are included, along with suggestions for staging and costumes. (Rev: BL 8/96; SLJ 8/96) [812]

6565 Miller, Arthur. *The Crucible* (10–12). 1987, Penguin paper $12.00 (978-0-14-048138-9). A powerful play that deals with the Salem witch trials of 1692. [812]

6566 Miller, Arthur. *Death of a Salesman* (10–12). 1949, Viking paper $12.00 (978-0-14-048134-1). The powerful drama of Willy Loman and his tragic end. (Rev: BL 2/15/91) [812]

6567 Nelson, Anne. *The Guys* (10–12). 2002, Random House paper $12.95 (978-0-8129-6729-6). This moving two-person play re-creates the horrors of September 11, 2001, as seen through the eyes of a journalist and a fire captain. (Rev: BL 8/02) [812]

6568 O'Neill, Eugene. *Long Day's Journey into Night* (10–12). 1956, Yale Univ. $9.00 (978-0-300-00807-4). A harrowing play about a night in lives of a theatrical family in their New England home in 1912. [812]

6569 Slaight, Craig, ed. *New Plays from A.C.T.'s Young Conservatory* (9–12). 1993, Smith & Kraus paper $19.95 (978-1-880399-25-5). Five contemporary plays written from the viewpoints of the young actors ages 13 to 22, who perform them. (Rev: BL 8/93; VOYA 8/93) [812]

6570 Slaight, Craig, ed. *New Plays from A.C.T.'s Young Conservatory, Vol. II* (10–12). 1996, Smith & Kraus paper $19.95 (978-1-880399-73-6). Mature in subject matter and language, this is a collection of four thought-provoking new plays (including a heart-breaker by Paul Zindel) for today's teens. (Rev: SLJ 7/96; VOYA 12/96) [812]

6571 Smith, Marisa, ed. *Seattle Children's Theatre: Six Plays for Young Audiences* (7–12). 1996, Smith & Kraus $21.95 (978-1-57525-008-3). A collection of six plays commissioned and performed by the Seattle Children's Theatre that explore adolescence, its problems and concerns. (Rev: BL 6/1–15/97; SLJ 6/97) [812]

6572 Smith, Ronn. *Nothing but the Truth* (7–10). 1997, Avon paper $4.99 (978-0-380-78715-9). This is a play version of Avi's novel about a 9th-grader whose suspension from school becomes a national issue. (Rev: VOYA 8/97) [812]

6573 Soto, Gary. *Nerdlandia: A Play* (8–12). 1999, Penguin paper $5.99 (978-0-698-11784-6). Young love causes transformations in nerdy Martin and cool Ceci in this hip play full of Spanish dialogue. (Rev: BL 10/1/99) [812.4]

6574 Thoms, Annie, ed. *With Their Eyes: September 11th: The View from a High School at Ground Zero* (7–12). Photos by Ethan Moses. 2002, HarperCollins paper $7.99 (978-0-06-051718-2). A collection of moving and dramatic monologues created after students at a high school near Ground Zero interviewed fellow students, faculty, and others about their experiences that day. (Rev: BL 9/1/02; SLJ 1/03) [812]

6575 Wasserstein, Wendy. *The Heidi Chronicles, and Other Plays* (10–12). 1990, Harcourt paper $13.00 (978-0-679-73499-4). A collection of plays from one of America's current playwrights noted for her good humor and depth of feeling. [812]

6576 Wilder, Thornton. *Our Town* (10–12). 1998, HarperCollins paper $9.00 (978-0-06-092984-8). Life in the town of Grover's Corners in New Hampshire as portrayed in the prize-winning play. [812]

6577 Williams, Tennessee. *The Glass Menagerie* (9–12). 1999, New Directions paper $7.95 (978-0-8112-1404-

9). A touching play in which a domineering mother persuades her son to help find a suitor for her crippled daughter. [812]

6578 Wilson, August. *Jitney* (10–12). 2001, Overlook paper $14.95 (978-1-58567-370-4). The adventure and misadventures of a group of African Americans involved in running a gypsy cab service are told in this engrossing play. [812]

6579 Wilson, August. *Joe Turner's Come and Gone: A Play in Two Acts* (10–12). 1988, New Am. Lib. paper $12.00 (978-0-452-26009-2). This is a fine addition to the cycle of plays by Wilson that explores black America during different decade intervals. [812]

6580 Wilson, August. *The Piano Lesson* (9–12). 1990, NAL paper $12.00 (978-0-452-26534-9). The Pulitzer Prize-winning play about an African American family in Pittsburgh in the 1930s. (Rev: BL 1/1/91) [812.54]

6581 Zindel, Paul. *The Effect of Gamma Rays on Man-in-the-Moon Marigolds* (9–12). 1971, HarperCollins $18.00 (978-0-06-026829-9). This play deals with a widow and her two daughters, one of whom finds fulfillment in a science project. (Rev: BL 10/15/88) [812]

371

Poetry

General and Miscellaneous Collections

6582 Alexander, Kwame. *Crush: Love Poems* (8–12). 2007, Word of Mouth paper $10.00 (978-1-888018-40-0). An anthology of varied poems about love. (Rev: SLJ 10/07) [811]

6583 Appelt, Kathi. *Poems from Homeroom: A Writer's Place to Start* (7–12). 2002, Henry Holt $16.95 (978-0-8050-6978-5). Poems that speak to the adolescent experience are accompanied by encouraging writing tips from the poet. (Rev: BL 11/15/02; SLJ 9/02) [811]

6584 Baker, Russell, ed. *The Norton Book of Light Verse* (10–12). 1986, Norton $29.95 (978-0-393-02366-4). An amusing collection that spans centuries and a large number of past and present writers. (Rev: BL 1/1/87) [821]

6585 Barnstone, Aliki, and Willis Barnstone. *A Book of Women Poets from Antiquity to Now. Rev. ed.* (9–12). 1992, Schocken paper $22.00 (978-0-8052-0997-6). This revised edition of the anthology first published in 1980 still offers representative writings by women of many cultures, but has broadened its selection of American poetry. [808.81]

6586 Bloom, Harold, ed. *Poets of World War I: Wilfred Owen and Isaac Rosenberg* (7–12). Series: Bloom's Major Poets. 2002, Chelsea LB $31.95 (978-0-7910-5932-6). This introduction to the work of these two poets includes four poems by each, with analysis. (Rev: SLJ 7/02) [821]

6587 Bowman, Catherine. *Word of Mouth* (10–12). 2003, Vintage paper $12.00 (978-0-375-71315-6). A stunning collection of contemporary poetry, including representative writings by Elizabeth Spires, Czeslaw Milosz, Lucille Clifton, Kevin Young, and Marilyn Chin. (Rev: BL 3/15/03) [811]

6588 Dore, Anita, ed. *The Premier Book of Major Poets* (10–12). 1996, Fawcett paper $11.00 (978-0-449-91186-0). This is a collection of English and American poetry from the Middle Ages to the present. [808.1]

6589 Eleveld, Mark, ed. *The Spoken Word Revolution Redux* (10–12). 2007, Sourcebooks $24.95 (978-1-4022-0869-0). With its accompanying CD, this book offers an overview of modern performance poetry, including slam and hip-hop; a companion volume to *The Spoken Word Revolution* (2004). (Rev: BL 5/1/07; SLJ 6/07) [811]

6590 Felleman, Hazel, ed. *Poems That Live Forever* (9–12). 1965, Doubleday $18.95 (978-0-385-00358-2). A collection of familiar poems arranged under subjects like love, friendship, and home. [821.08]

6591 Gilbert, Sandra M., et al, ed. *Mother Songs: Poems for, by, and About Mothers* (9–12). 1995, Norton $22.50 (978-0-393-03771-5). Poems by men and women for and about mothers. (Rev: BL 5/1/95) [811.008]

6592 Gordon, Ruth, ed. *Peeling the Onion* (8–12). 1993, HarperCollins $15.89 (978-0-06-021728-0). A collection of 66 poems with multilayered meanings by world-famous contemporary poets. (Rev: BL 6/1–15/93*; SLJ 7/93; VOYA 8/93) [808.81]

6593 Gordon, Ruth, sel. *Under All Silences: Shades of Love* (8–12). 1987, HarperCollins $13.00 (978-0-06-022154-6). Sixty-six love poems, dating from ancient Egypt to modern days. (Rev: BL 9/15/87; SLJ 10/87; VOYA 4/88) [808.1]

6594 Greenberg, Jan, ed. *Heart to Heart: New Poems Inspired by Twentieth-Century American Art* (5–10). 2001, Abrams $19.95 (978-0-8109-4386-5). This book contains specially commissioned poems from well-known writers to accompany some of the finest artworks of the 20th century. (Rev: BL 3/15/01*; HBG 10/01; SLJ 4/01*; VOYA 8/01) [811]

6595 Greenberg, Jan, ed. *Side by Side: New Poems Inspired by Art from Around the World* (8–12). 2008, Abrams $19.95 (978-0-8109-9471-3). Poems in many languages (with English translations) and inspired by art of all kinds are featured in this book that includes maps pinpointing each poet's country. (Rev: BL 5/1/08; SLJ 7/08) [811]

6596 Harmon, William. *The Top 500 Poems* (9–12). 1992, Columbia Univ. $34.95 (978-0-231-08028-6). A compilation of the 500 poems that appear most frequently in anthologies. (Rev: BL 4/1/93; SLJ 2/93) [821.008]

6597 Hemphill, Stephanie. *Your Own, Sylvia* (9–12). 2007, Knopf $17.99 (978-0-375-83799-9). A collection of poems, written from the fictional point of view of those who knew her, that give insight into the life and work of poet Sylvia Plath. Printz Honor 2008. (Rev: BCCB 5/07; BL 2/15/07; HB 3–4/07; LMC 4–5/07; SLJ 3/07) [811]

6598 Herrera, Juan Felipe. *CrashBoomLove* (9–12). 1999, Univ. of New Mexico $18.50 (978-0-8263-2113-8); paper $14.95 (978-0-8263-2114-5). A powerful narrative poem describes the alienation and anger felt by 16-year-old Cesar Garcia. (Rev: BL 2/1/00; SLJ 3/00) [811]

6599 Hill, Selma. *Bunny* (10–12). 2002, Bloodaxe paper $17.95 (978-1-85224-507-8). These poems take readers inside the mind of a troubled teenage girl flirting with depression and increasingly obsessed by morbid thoughts; recommended for mature teens. (Rev: BL 3/15/02) [821]

6600 Hollis, Jill, ed. *Love's Witness: Five Centuries of Love Poetry by Women* (9–12). 1993, Carroll & Graf paper $11.95 (978-0-7867-0030-1). This anthology of five centuries of love poetry by women reflects the similarities and differences of love through the ages. (Rev: BL 11/15/93) [821]

6601 Homer. *The Odyssey* (10–12). 1996, Farrar paper $10.00 (978-0-374-52574-3). These two editions represent the many available of this epic poem about the wanderings of Odysseus on his way home from the Trojan War. [883]

6602 Janeczko, Paul B., ed. *Looking for Your Name: A Collection of Contemporary Poems* (9–12). 1993, Orchard LB $17.99 (978-0-531-08625-4). A wide variety of poems by men and women about soldiers' war memories, family violence, gay/lesbian lives, sports, love, AIDS, suicide, and other aspects of life. (Rev: BL 1/15/93*) [811]

6603 Janeczko, Paul B., ed. *Stone Bench in an Empty Park* (5–12). 2000, Orchard LB $16.99 (978-0-531-33259-7). An inspired collection of haiku from a variety of poets, illustrated with stunning black-and-white pho-

tographs. (Rev: BCCB 6/00; BL 3/15/00*; HB 3–4/00; HBG 10/00; SLJ 3/00) [811]

6604 Janeczko, Paul B., ed. *Wherever Home Begins: 100 Contemporary Poems* (8–12). 1995, Orchard LB $17.99 (978-0-531-08781-7). One hundred poems that express various approaches to a sense of place. (Rev: BL 10/1/95; SLJ 11/95; VOYA 12/95) [811]

6605 Jay, Peter, ed. *The Sea! The Sea!* (9–12). 2006, Anvil paper $13.95 (978-0-85646-379-2). This anthology of varied poetry about the sea was published to mark the bicentennial of the Battle of Trafalgar. (Rev: BL 3/1/06) [808.81]

6606 Keillor, Garrison, ed. *Good Poems* (10–12). 2002, Viking $25.95 (978-0-670-03126-9). A cross section of outstanding English-language poems that Keillor originally selected to be read on air. (Rev: BL 8/02*; SLJ 3/03) [811]

6607 *Love Poems* (9–12). 1993, Knopf $12.50 (978-0-679-42906-7). Represented in this collection of classic love poems are such well-known poets as Robert Browning, W. B. Yeats, Robert Graves, Christina Rossetti, William Carlos Williams, and Pablo Neruda. [808.81]

6608 McCullough, Frances, ed. *Earth, Air, Fire, and Water. Rev. ed.* (9–12). 1989, HarperCollins $13.95 (978-0-06-024207-7). A collection of poems from many cultures that have been chosen for their specific appeal to young adults. (Rev: BL 5/15/89; SLJ 6/89; VOYA 8/89) [808.81]

6609 McCullough, Frances, ed. *Love Is Like a Lion's Tooth: An Anthology of Love Poems* (7–12). 1984, HarperCollins $12.95 (978-0-06-024138-4). A collection of love poems that span time from ancient days to the 20th century. [808.81]

6610 Mark, Jan, ed. *A Jetblack Sunrise: Poems About War and Conflict* (7–10). Illus. by John Yates. 2005, Hodder paper $8.99 (978-0-340-89379-1). This anthology of poems explores not only the barbarity and savagery of war but also the courage, selflessness, and valor that sometimes shine through. (Rev: BL 9/1/05) [808.9]

6611 Merrell, Billy. *Talking in the Dark* (9–12). 2003, Scholastic paper $7.99 (978-0-439-49036-8). This free-verse memoir, written at the age of 22, touches on a wide array of painful experiences, including parental divorce and remarriage, coming to terms with homosexuality, and a series of failed and new relationships, yet retains at its core a tone of hopefulness. (Rev: BL 12/1/03; SLJ 1/04; VOYA 4/04) [811]

6612 Mora, Pat. *Dizzy in Your Eyes: Poems About Love* (7–10). 2010, Knopf $15.99 (978-0-375-84375-4). Typical teen experiences with young love are covered in a collection of poems written in a wide variety of formats. ℮ (Rev: BL 11/15/09; LMC 1–2/10; SLJ 1/10) [811]

6613 Nye, Naomi Shihab. *Honeybee: Poems and Short Prose* (7–12). 2008, Greenwillow $16.99 (978-0-06-085390-5). A collection of poems and short pieces of prose that use honeybee imagery as a metaphor for human experiences and resilience. (Rev: BL 8/08; SLJ 3/08) [811]

6614 Nye, Naomi Shihab. *You and Yours* (9–12). 2005, BOA $22.95 (978-1-929918-68-3); paper $15.50 (978-1-929918-69-0). Nye's Palestinian American heritage informs this collection of poems that explores a wide array of topics and environments. (Rev: BL 8/05) [811]

6615 Nye, Naomi Shihab, sel. *Time You Let Me In: 25 Poets Under 25* (7–12). 2010, Greenwillow $16.99 (978-0-06-189637-8); LB $17.89 (978-0-06-189638-5). Diverse poems by young writers deal with contemporary themes both personal and political. (Rev: BL 1/1–15/10; SLJ 2/10) [811]

6616 Oliver, Mary. *A Poetry Handbook* (9–12). 1994, Harcourt paper $14.00 (978-0-15-672400-5). A handbook on the formal aspects and structure of poetry from a Pulitzer Prize-winning poet. (Rev: BL 7/94) [808.1]

6617 Parisi, Joseph, and Kathleen Welton, eds. *100 Essential Modern Poems by Women* (10–12). 2008, Ivan R. Dee $24.95 (978-1-56663-741-1). A lively and engaging collection of carefully chosen poems referencing the influence of the poets' lives upon their poetic styles and including lively profiles of the poets. (Rev: BL 3/1/08) [821]

6618 Parisi, Joseph, and Stephen Young, eds. *The Poetry Anthology, 1912-2002: Ninety Years of America's Most Distinguished Verse Magazine* (10–12). 2002, Ivan R. Dee $29.95 (978-1-56663-468-7). This anthology, published to mark the 90th anniversary of *Poetry* magazine, offers a retrospective sampling of the best poems to appear in its pages. (Rev: BL 10/15/02*) [811]

6619 Parisi, Joseph, ed. *100 Essential Modern Poems* (9–12). 2005, Ivan R. Dee $24.95 (978-1-56663-612-4). The former editor of *Poetry* magazine offers 100 of the greatest modern poems written in English, providing fascinating profiles of the authors. (Rev: BL 10/1/05; SLJ 6/06) [821]

6620 Paschen, Elise, and Rebekah Presson Mosby, eds. *Poetry Speaks Expanded: Hear Poets from Tennyson to Plath Read Their Own Work* (9–12). 2007, Sourcebooks $49.95 (978-1-4022-1062-4). This expanded second edition (following 2001's *Poetry Speaks*) now covers 47 poets, providing for each biographical information, an essay by a contemporary poet, representative verses; the three accompanying CDs include select readings. (Rev: BL 11/1/07; SLJ 1/08) [811]

6621 Pawlak, Mark, et al, ed. *Shooting the Rat: Outstanding Poems and Stories by High School Writers* (10–12). 2003, Hanging Loose $26.00 (978-1-931236-24-9); paper $16.00 (978-1-931236-23-2). This third anthology of poems by high school students that have

appeared in the pages of *Hanging Loose* magazine covers a broad spectrum of issues and includes frank sexual content. (Rev: BL 9/1/03; HBG 4/04; SLJ 10/03; VOYA 10/03) [810.8]

6622 Philip, Neil, ed. *War and the Pity of War* (6–12). 1998, Clarion $20.00 (978-0-395-84982-8). An outstanding collection of poetry from different times and cultures that explores the cruelty, bravery, and tragedy of war. (Rev: BL 9/15/98; HBG 10/99; SLJ 9/98; VOYA 2/99) [808.81]

6623 Pinsky, Robert, and Maggie Dietz, eds. *Americans' Favorite Poems: The Favorite Poem Project Anthology* (9–12). 1999, Norton $27.50 (978-0-393-04820-9). From John Keats to Lucille Clifton, this is a collection of poetry chosen by Americans of all ages. (Rev: BL 11/1/99) [808.81]

6624 Pinsky, Robert, and Maggie Dietz, eds. *Poems to Read: A New Favorite Poems Project Anthology* (10–12). 2002, Norton $27.95 (978-0-393-01074-9). A wide-ranging collection of poems selected by poetry lovers. (Rev: BL 6/1–15/02) [811]

6625 Rachel, T. Cole, and Rita D. Costello, eds. *Bend, Don't Shatter* (9–12). 2004, Soft Skull paper $7.95 (978-1-932360-17-2). Nearly 60 poems explore the coming-of-age experiences of young people who are gay, lesbian, bisexual, or transgendered. (Rev: BCCB 7–8/04; SLJ 1/05) [811]

6626 Rosenberg, Liz, and Deena November, eds. *I Just Hope It's Lethal: Poems of Sadness, Madness and Joy* (9–12). 2005, Houghton Mifflin paper $7.99 (978-0-618-56452-1). Editors Rosenberg and November, who have both suffered from depression, have compiled a collection of poems on mental problems by a wide variety of writers. (Rev: BL 11/15/05; SLJ 12/05; VOYA 2/06) [811]

6627 Rosenberg, Liz, ed. *Light-Gathering Poems* (6–12). 2000, Henry Holt $15.95 (978-0-8050-6223-6). An excellent anthology of high-quality poems, mainly from classic writers such as Byron and Frost but also from some newer voices. (Rev: BL 3/15/00; HB 5–6/00; HBG 9/00; SLJ 6/00; VOYA 6/00) [808.81]

6628 Rothenberg, Jerome, and Pierre Joris, eds. *Poems for the Millennium: The University of California Book of Modern and Postmodern Poetry, Vol. 2* (10–12). 1998, Univ. of California paper $34.95 (978-0-520-20864-3). An excellent international collection of poetry from post-World War II through the Cold War and its aftermath, representing a wide range of well-known poets and movements. (Rev: SLJ 12/98) [808.8]

6629 Rubin, Robert Alden. *Poetry Out Loud* (9–12). 1993, Algonquin paper $9.95 (978-1-56512-122-5). This is a selection of 100 poems specifically chosen for reading aloud. [821.008]

6630 Siegen-Smith, Nikki, comp. *Welcome to the World: A Celebration of Birth and Babies from Many Cultures* (10–12). 1996, Orchard $17.95 (978-0-531-36006-4). A collection of 20 international poems, each with a full-page photograph, that describe the pain and joy of childbirth and raising babies. (Rev: SLJ 10/96) [811]

6631 Strand, Mark, ed. *100 Great Poems of the Twentieth Century* (8–12). 2005, Norton $24.95 (978-0-393-05894-9). Pulitzer Prize-winning poet Strand offers his selection of the 100 best poems of the 20th century. (Rev: BL 5/15/05) [821]

6632 Vecchione, Patrice, ed. *Faith and Doubt: An Anthology of Poems* (8–12). 2007, Henry Holt $16.95 (978-0-8050-8213-5). Poems by authors of many faiths both challenge and embrace traditional religion; prayers, reflections, and supplications will appeal to readers with all sorts of spiritual lives. (Rev: BL 4/1/07; LMC 10/07; SLJ 6/07) [808.81]

6633 Vecchione, Patrice, ed. *Revenge and Forgiveness: An Anthology of Poems* (8–12). 2004, Henry Holt $16.95 (978-0-8050-7376-8). This anthology on war, violence, and the search for peace contains poems from many lands and times. (Rev: BL 3/15/04; HB 3–4/04; SLJ 7/04; VOYA 6/04) [808.81]

6634 Virgil. *The Aeneid of Virgil* (10–12). 1981, Bantam paper $4.95 (978-0-553-21041-5). One of several fine editions of the epic poem about the journey of Aeneas from Troy to Italy. [873]

6635 Waters, Fiona. *Poems from Many Cultures: Poetry Collection 4* (9–12). 2002, Evans $19.95 (978-0-237-52104-2). A diverse collection that reveals a wide range of cultures and experiences. (Rev: BL 3/15/02; SLJ 5/02) [808.81]

6636 Watson, Esther Pearl, and Mark Todd, sels. *The Pain Tree: And Other Teenage Angst-Ridden Poetry* (7–12). Illus. by Esther Pearl Watson and Mark Todd. 2000, Houghton Mifflin paper $6.95 (978-0-618-04758-1). Poems collected from teen Web sites and magazines and illustrated with paintings express a wide range of emotions. (Rev: HBG 9/00; SLJ 9/00; VOYA 6/00) [811]

6637 Willard, Nancy, ed. *Step Lightly: Poems for the Journey* (7–12). 1998, Harcourt paper $12.00 (978-0-15-202052-1). These works from the pens of about 40 poets represent the poems that the editor particularly loves. (Rev: BL 10/1/98; HBG 3/99; SLJ 11/98; VOYA 4/99) [811:008]

6638 Wright, Kristine, ed. *Poetically Correct* (10–12). 2000, Be-Mused Publications paper $17.95 (978-0-9704868-1-3). Twelve teens give voice to their innermost thoughts about such universal issues as love, alienation, friendship, and loneliness. (Rev: VOYA 12/01) [811]

Geographical Regions

Europe

GREAT BRITAIN AND IRELAND

6639 Auden, W. H. *Auden: Poems* (10–12). Ed. by Edward Mendelson. Series: Everyman's Library Pocket Poets. 1995, Knopf $12.50 (978-0-679-44367-4). This is a representative collection of Auden's poems that spans his entire career. [821]

6640 Barron, W. R., ed. *Sir Gawain and the Green Knight* (10–12). 1972, Viking paper $7.95 (978-0-14-044902-0). A fine edition of the medieval poem dealing with the testing of Gawain's courage. [821]

6641 *Beowulf: A New Verse Translation* (10–12). Trans. by Seamus Heaney. 2000, Farrar $25.00 (978-0-374-11119-9). The contemporary poet Seamus Heaney supplies a beautiful, lucid translation of the most famous and longest-surviving epic poem in Old English. (Rev: BL 2/15/00) [829]

6642 Coleridge, Samuel Taylor. *Samuel Taylor Coleridge* (6–10). Ed. by James Engell. Illus. by Harvey Chan. Series: Poetry for Young People. 2003, Sterling $14.95 (978-0-8069-6951-0). Biographical information introduces a sampling of Coleridge's most famous poems, which are accompanied by editorial notes and full-color illustrations. Also use *William Wordsworth* and *William Butler Yeats* (both 2003). (Rev: BL 4/1/03; HBG 4/04; SLJ 9/03) [821]

6643 Cook, Elizabeth, ed. *John Keats: The Major Works* (10–12). 2001, Oxford paper $18.95 (978-0-19-284063-9). This collection includes the poems published during Keats's lifetime, some published after his death, some unpublished ones, and some letters. [821]

6644 Duffy, Carol Ann. *Mrs. Scrooge: A Christmas Poem* (9–12). Illus. 2009, Simon & Schuster $12.99 (978-143917633-7). Ebenezer Scrooge's widow is swept away from her dogged anti-materialism protest by the ghosts of Christmas past, present, and future, who reveal the true meaning of the gifts we receive. (Rev: BL 11/15/09) [811]

6645 Eliot, T. S. *The Complete Poems and Plays, 1909–1950* (10–12). 1952, Harcourt $35.00 (978-0-15-121185-2). An omnibus volume of poetry and plays by the American-born writer who lived most of his life in England. [818]

6646 Eliot, T. S. *Eliot: Poems and Prose* (10–12). Series: Everyman's Library Pocket Poets. 1998, Knopf $12.50 (978-0-375-40185-5). A representative selection of the Nobel Prize winner's works. [818]

6647 Eliot, T. S. *Old Possum's Book of Practical Cats* (9–12). 1982, Harcourt $16.00 (978-0-15-168656-8); paper $8.00 (978-0-15-668570-2). Many of the poems in this delightful collection were used in the musical *Cats*. [821]

6648 Gardner, Helen, ed. *The New Oxford Book of English Verse, 1250–1950* (10–12). 1972, Oxford $57.95 (978-0-19-812136-7). The first edition of this anthology appeared in 1900, and it has continued to maintain its high standards in all subsequent editions. [821.08]

6649 Gillooly, Eileen, ed. *Robert Browning* (7–12). Illus. by Joel Spector. Series: Poetry for Young People. 2001, Sterling $14.95 (978-0-8069-5543-8). A fine, well-illustrated introduction to the works of the English poet that gives historical context, references, and explanations of terms. (Rev: HBG 10/01; SLJ 10/01) [811]

6650 Hughes, Ted. *Birthday Letters* (10–12). 1998, Farrar paper $12.00 (978-0-374-52581-1). Published shortly after his death, this collection of poems chronicles Hughes's sometimes tortured relationship with fellow poet Sylvia Plath. [821]

6651 Jones, Daniel, ed. *The Poems of Dylan Thomas. Rev. ed.* (10–12). 2003, Directions $34.95 (978-0-8112-1541-1). There are approximately 200 poems in this collection, arranged chronologically. [821]

6652 Keats, John. *Poems* (10–12). Series: Everyman's Library Pocket Poets. 1994, Knopf $12.50 (978-0-679-43319-4). This volume contains a good selection of the poetry of this English genius. [821]

6653 Lear, Edward. *The Owl and the Pussycat* (5–10). Illus. by Stephane Jorisch. Series: Visions in Poetry. 2007, Kids Can $16.95 (978-1-55337-828-0); paper $9.95 (978-1-55453-232-2). A charmingly illustrated version of Lear's classic poem using watercolor and ink. (Rev: SLJ 1/08) [821]

6654 Noyes, Alfred. *The Highwayman* (7–10). Illus. by Murray Kimber. Series: Visions in Poetry. 2005, Kids Can $16.95 (978-1-55337-425-1). In this beautifully illustrated Art Deco version of Noyes's immortal poem, the title character is transformed into a motorcycle-riding thief who roams the streets of New York City, while his beloved Bess is now a voluptuous glamour girl. (Rev: BL 5/1/05; SLJ 8/05; VOYA 10/05) [821]

6655 Opie, Iona, and Peter Opie. *I Saw Esau: The Schoolchild's Pocket Book* (7–12). 1992, Candlewick $19.99 (978-1-56402-046-8). Traces schoolyard folk rhymes to their roots. (Rev: BL 4/15/92*; SLJ 6/92) [821]

6656 Shakespeare, William. *The Essential Shakespeare* (9–12). Ed. by Ted Hughes. Series: Essential Poets. 1991, Ecco paper $8.00 (978-0-88001-314-7). Editor Ted Hughes has chosen representative selections of Shakespeare's poetry and other writings that illustrate his great versatility. [822.3]

6657 Thomas, Dylan. *A Child's Christmas in Wales* (10–12). 1997, Directions $10.95 (978-0-8112-1308-0); paper $6.00 (978-0-8112-1309-7). A poem that deals with the celebration of Christmas in a small Welsh town. [828]

6658 Woodring, Carl, and James Shapiro, eds. *The Columbia Anthology of British Poetry* (10–12). 1995, Columbia Univ. $52.50 (978-0-231-10180-6). A collection of major British poetry from Beowulf to the present. (Rev: SLJ 5/96) [821]

6659 Wordsworth, William. *Poems* (10–12). Series: Everyman's Library Pocket Poets. 1995, Knopf $12.50 (978-0-679-44369-8). This is a representative collection of Wordworth's poems spanning his writing career. [821]

United States

6660 Adoff, Arnold, ed. *I Am the Darker Brother: An Anthology of Modern Poems by Black Americans* (9–12). 1997, Simon & Schuster paper $4.99 (978-0-689-80869-2). This anthology of 64 poems by 29 African American poets of the 20th century explores the black person's role in American life. (Rev: BL 2/15/97; SLJ 5/97) [811.08]

6661 Alexander, Elizabeth. *Crave Radiance: New and Selected Poems, 1990–2010* (11–12). 2010, Graywolf $26 (978-1-55597-568-5). A collection of poems by the African American who wrote the inaugural poem for newly elected President Obama; for mature readers. (Rev: BL 10/1–15/10; SLJ 4/11) [811]

6662 Alexander, Elizabeth, and Marilyn Nelson. *Miss Crandall's School for Young Ladies and Little Misses of Color* (6–10). Illus. by Floyd Cooper. 2007, Boyds Mills $17.95 (978-1-59078-456-3). Told in poetry, this is the true story of a Connecticut teacher who founded a school for black girls in 1833 and faced cruel opposition. ALA Notable Books 2008. (Rev: BCCB 11/07; BL 10/1/07; HB 9–10/07; LMC 11–12/07; SLJ 9/07) [811]

6663 Angelou, Maya. *And Still I Rise* (10–12). 1978, Random House $13.00 (978-0-394-50252-6). A highly personalized volume of poetry by the author of such companion books of poetry as *Just Give Me a Cool Drink of Water 'fore I Die* (1971), *Oh Pray My Wings Are Gonna Fit Me Well* (1975), and *Shaker, Why Don't You Sing?* (1983). [811]

6664 Angelou, Maya. *Complete Collected Poems of Maya Angelou* (10–12). 1994, Random House $24.00 (978-0-679-42895-4). Love, travel, and age are among the topics discussed in this anthology. [811]

6665 Blum, Joshua, et al. *The United States of Poetry* (10–12). 1996, Abrams $29.95 (978-0-8109-3927-1). A collection of 80 poems from a variety of sources including famous poets, rappers, rockers, beats, and cowboys, all reflecting a fresh view of America in this handsomely illustrated book. (Rev: BL 5/15/96; SLJ 9/96) [811]

6666 Brooks, Gwendolyn. *In Montgomery* (10–12). 2003, Third World $22.95 (978-0-88378-232-3). In this posthumously published collection, Brooks delivers a message of hope from bleak settings. (Rev: BL 8/03) [811]

6667 Carlson, Lori Marie, ed. *Red Hot Salsa: Bilingual Poems on Being Young and Latino in the United States* (8–11). 2005, Henry Holt $14.95 (978-0-8050-7616-5). Poems in Spanish and English voice issues important to teens and the joys and sorrows of straddling two cultures. (Rev: BL 8/05; SLJ 8/05*) [811]

6668 Carruth, Hayden. *Toward the Distant Islands* (10–12). Ed. by Sam Hamill. 2006, Copper Canyon paper $17.00 (978-1-55659-236-2). This collection showcases many facets of Carruth's work. (Rev: BL 3/1/06) [811]

6669 Charara, Hayan, ed. *Inclined to Speak: An Anthology of Contemporary Arab American Poetry* (9–12). 2008, Univ. of Arkansas $59.95 (978-1-55728-866-0); paper $24.95 (978-1-55728-867-7). A collection of works by 39 poets, offering diverse points of view. (Rev: BL 4/1/08) [811]

6670 Clifton, Lucille. *Mercy* (11–12). 2004, BOA $22.00 (978-1-929918-54-6); paper $14.95 (978-1-929918-55-3). The African American poet explores such sensitive subjects as cancer, death, and the aftershocks from the 9/11 tragedy; for mature readers. (Rev: BL 9/15/04) [811]

6671 Clinton, Catherine, ed. *I, Too, Sing America: Three Centuries of African American Poetry* (6–10). 1998, Houghton Mifflin $22.00 (978-0-395-89599-3). This heavily illustrated volume of 36 poems by 25 authors traces the history of African American poetry, from Phillis Wheatley to Rita Dove. (Rev: BL 11/15/98; HBG 3/99; SLJ 11/98; VOYA 8/99) [712.2]

6672 Collins, Billy. *Horoscopes for the Dead* (10–12). 2011, Random House $24 (978-1-4000-6492-2). This whimsical collection of poems takes a fresh look at the time-tested themes of love, longing, life, and death. (Rev: SLJ 7/11) [811]

6673 Coval, Kevin. *Slingshots: (A Hip-Hop Poetica)* (10–12). 2006, EM paper $15.00 (978-0-9708012-4-1). The Chicago-based hip-hop poet explores questions of compassion and identity. (Rev: BL 3/15/06) [811]

6674 Crisler, Curtis L. *Tough Boy Sonatas* (10–12). Illus. by Floyd Cooper. 2007, Boyds Mills $19.95 (978-1-932425-77-2). Thirty-eight gritty poems, many with strong language and discussion of violence, about growing up poor and black in Gary, Indiana. (Rev: BCCB 4/07; BL 2/1/07; SLJ 3/07*) [811]

6675 Cummings, E. E. *100 Selected Poems by e. e. cummings* (9–12). 1959, Grove paper $11.00 (978-0-8021-3072-3). Many of cummings's best-known works appear in this slim volume. [811]

6676 Daniels, Jim, ed. *Letters to America: Contemporary American Poetry on Race* (9–12). 1995, Wayne State Univ. paper $24.95 (978-0-8143-2542-1). Accessible, readable poems that speak to race and racism. (Rev: BL 11/15/95) [811]

6677 DeDonato, Collete. *City of One: Young Writers Speak to the World* (7–12). 2004, Aunt Lute paper $10.95 (978-1-879960-69-5). In this moving collection of poetry from San Francisco-based WritersCorps, scores of young people give voice to their feelings about peace and violence. (Rev: BL 8/04; SLJ 8/04; VOYA 10/04) [810.8]

6678 Dickinson, Emily. *The Complete Poems of Emily Dickinson* (10–12). 1960, Little, Brown $32.50 (978-0-316-18414-4); paper $18.00 (978-0-316-18413-7). This definitive edition contains 1,775 poems and fragments. [811]

6679 Dickinson, Emily. *New Poems of Emily Dickinson* (9–12). Ed. by William H. Shurr. 1993, Univ. of North Carolina paper $20.00 (978-0-8078-4416-8). This collection of poetry comes from other writings such as letters where they had been hidden for years. (Rev: BL 9/15/93; SLJ 5/94) [811]

6680 Dove, Rita. *Mother Love* (9–12). 1995, Norton $17.95 (978-0-393-03808-8). Sonnets on the timeless tragedy of Demeter and Persephone. (Rev: BL 5/1/95*) [811]

6681 Dove, Rita. *Selected Poems* (9–12). 1993, Random House paper $12.00 (978-0-679-75080-2). Three collections of poetry by the U.S. poet laureate are gathered here into one volume: *The Yellow House on the Corner; Museum;* and the Pulitzer Prize-winning *Thomas and Beulah*. Dove's images draw on African American history and family experiences to illuminate today's world. (Rev: BL 10/15/93) [811]

6682 Dunbar, Paul Laurence. *The Complete Poems of Paul Laurence Dunbar* (7–12). 1980, Dodd paper $10.95 (978-0-396-07895-1). The definitive collection, first published in 1913, of this African American poet's work. [811]

6683 Dunbar, Paul Laurence. *In His Own Voice: The Dramatic and Other Uncollected Works of Paul Laurence Dunbar* (10–12). Ed. by Herbert Woodward Martin and Ronald Primeau. 2002, Ohio Univ. $49.95 (978-0-8214-1421-7); paper $22.95 (978-0-8214-1422-4). Essays, plays, poems, and short stories form the backbone of this collection of works by Dunbar. (Rev: BL 2/15/02) [811]

6684 Dungy, Camille T., ed. *Black Nature: Four Centuries of African American Nature Poetry* (10–12). 2009, Univ. of Georgia paper $24.95 (978-08203343-1-8). Perceptive essays introduce each section in this collection of poems about nature written by nearly 100 African Americans. (Rev: BL 2/1–15/10) [808.81]

6685 Frost, Robert. *Collected Poems, Prose, and Plays* (9–12). 1995, Library of America $35.00 (978-1-883011-06-2). There are several previously unpublished in this collections as well as plays and some prose selections. [818]

6686 Gardner, Joann, ed. *Runaway with Words: Poems from Florida's Youth Shelters* (6–12). 1996, Anhinga paper $14.95 (978-0-938078-47-0). Joy, anger, confusion, and fear are some of the emotions expressed in this collection of poems culled from writing workshops for teens in Florida's shelters. (Rev: BL 6/1–15/97) [811]

6687 Gibran, Kahlil. *The Prophet* (10–12). 1923, Knopf $15.00 (978-0-394-40428-8). A group of poems that deal with such subjects as love, good and evil, friendship, freedom, and death. [811]

6688 Gillan, Maria Mazziotti, and Jennifer Gillan, eds. *Unsettling America: An Anthology of Contemporary Multicultural Poetry* (9–12). 1994, Penguin paper $18.00 (978-0-14-023778-8). Features poets from various cultures and backgrounds, including Native American Joy Harjo, Hawaiian Garrett Hongo, and African American Rita Dove. (Rev: BL 10/1/94; SLJ 5/95) [811]

6689 Giovanni, Nikki. *The Collected Poetry of Nikki Giovanni, 1968–1998* (10–12). 2003, Morrow $24.95 (978-0-06-054133-0). This magnificent collection showcases three decades of Giovanni's poems plus notes, a biographical timeline, and an afterword by the author. (Rev: BL 12/15/03) [811]

6690 Giovanni, Nikki. *Quilting the Black-Eyed Pea* (10–12). 2002, Morrow $16.95 (978-0-06-009952-7). In this collection, Giovanni celebrates the lives of both her grandmother and fellow poet Gwendolyn Brooks, while also musing on topics that range widely (from Harry Potter to George W. Bush). (Rev: BL 12/15/02; VOYA 6/03) [811]

6691 Giovanni, Nikki. *The Selected Poems of Nikki Giovanni (1968-1995)* (9–12). 1996, Morrow $22.00 (978-0-688-14047-2). A rich synthesis of Giovanni's work that reveals the evolution of her poetic voice. (Rev: BL 12/15/95) [811]

6692 Giovanni, Nikki, ed. *The 100 Best African American Poems* (10–12). 2010, Sourcebooks $22.99 (978-140222111-8). Noted poet Nikki Giovanni brings together more than 100 of the best poems by African American writers. (Rev: BL 11/1–15/10) [811]

6693 Giovanni, Nikki, ed. *Shimmy Shimmy Shimmy Like My Sister Kate: Looking at the Harlem Renaissance Through Poems* (9–12). 1996, Henry Holt $17.95 (978-0-8050-3494-3). A collection of African American poetry that covers both the Harlem Renaissance with writers such as Langston Hughes as well as contemporaries including Ntozake Shange and LeRoi Jones. (Rev: BL 3/15/96; SLJ 5/96*; VOYA 10/96) [811]

6694 Glenn, Mel. *Jump Ball: A Basketball Season in Poems* (6–12). 1997, Dutton $15.99 (978-0-525-67554-9). In a series of poems, people involved in an inner-city high school are introduced, including basketball players, parents, teachers, and friends. (Rev: BL 10/15/97; SLJ 11/97*; VOYA 12/97) [811]

6695 Harper, Michael S., and Anthony Walton, eds. *The Vintage Book of African American Poetry* (10–12). 2000, Random House paper $14.00 (978-0-375-70300-3). A comprehensive collection of representative poems by 52 African American poets spanning more than two centuries. (Rev: BL 2/15/00) [811]

6696 Harris, Jana. *We Never Speak of It: Idaho-Wyoming Poems, 1889-90* (10–12). 2003, Ontario Review paper $14.95 (978-0-86538-109-4). These dramatic verse monologues in the voices of a schoolteacher and a handful of her pupils paint a revealing picture of pioneer life on the Idaho-Wyoming border in the late 19th century. (Rev: BL 3/1/03) [811]

6697 Hernandez Cruz, Victor, et al. *Paper Dance: 55 Latino Poets* (10–12). 1995, Persea $13.95 (978-0-89255-201-6). A collection of the work of 55 Hispanic American poets. [811.008]

6698 Herrera, Juan Felipe. *Laughing Out Loud, I Fly (A Caracajadas Yo Vuelo): Poems in English and Spanish* (6–10). 1998, HarperCollins $16.99 (978-0-06-027604-1). In this series of poems in both languages, the poet celebrates incidents in his childhood. Belpré Honor 2000. (Rev: SLJ 5/98; VOYA 6/99) [811]

6699 Holbrook, Sara. *Walking on the Boundaries of Change: Poems of Transition* (8–12). 1998, Boyds Mills paper $9.95 (978-1-56397-737-4). In this collection of 53 poems, the author explores the problems of being a teen with amazing insight into concerns and decisions. (Rev: VOYA 2/99) [811]

6700 Hollander, John, ed. *American Poetry* (4–10). Illus. by Sally Wern Comport. Series: Poetry for Young People. 2004, Sterling $14.95 (978-1-4027-0517-5). A colorful celebration of American life, containing 26 poems by well-known poets including Robert Frost, Walt Whitman, Maya Angelou, and Langston Hughes. (Rev: SLJ 8/04) [811]

6701 Hudson, Wade, ed. *Poetry from the Masters: The Pioneers* (6–12). Illus. by Stephan J. Hudson. 2003, Just Us Bks. paper $9.95 (978-0-940975-96-5). Two-page biographical profiles introduce 11 African Americans and their works; among them are Phillis Wheatley, Paul Laurence Dunbar, Countee Cullen, Langston Hughes, and Gwendolyn Brooks. (Rev: SLJ 2/04) [811]

6702 Hughes, Langston. *Vintage Hughes* (10–12). 2004, Vintage paper $9.95 (978-1-4000-3402-4). Three short stories are included with a selection of poems in this Vintage Reader edition. (Rev: BL 12/15/03) [811]

6703 *Is This Forever, or What? Poems and Paintings from Texas* (9–12). 2004, HarperCollins $24.99 (978-

0-06-051178-4). The many faces of the Lone Star State are beautifully portrayed in this appealing collection of poems and paintings by Texans; some are bilingual and many refer to Mexican heritage. (Rev: BL 7/04; HB 7–8/04; SLJ 7/04) [811]

6704 Johnson, Dave, ed. *Movin': Teen Poets Take Voice* (5–10). Illus. by Chris Raschka. 2000, Orchard $15.95 (978-0-531-30258-3); paper $6.95 (978-0-531-07171-7). An anthology of poems by teens who participated in New York Public Library workshops or submitted their work via the Web. (Rev: BL 3/15/00; HBG 10/00; SLJ 5/00; VOYA 6/00) [811]

6705 Knudson, R. R., and May Swenson, eds. *American Sports Poems* (7–12). 1988, Watts LB $19.99 (978-0-531-08353-6). An excellent collection that concentrates on such popular sports as baseball, football, and swimming. (Rev: BL 8/88; SLJ 11/88; VOYA 10/88) [811]

6706 Lauer, Brett Fletcher, and Aimee Kelley, eds. *Isn't It Romantic: 100 Love Poems by Younger American Poets* (10–12). 2004, Verse paper $19.95 (978-0-9746353-1-6). Love poems by 100 American poets born after 1960 are collected in this appealing and diverse anthology. (Rev: BL 1/1–15/05) [811]

6707 Le Guin, Ursula K. *Sixty Odd: New Poems* (9–12). 1999, Shambhala paper $14.00 (978-1-57062-388-2). A collection of poems by the popular science fiction author. (Rev: BL 3/15/99; SLJ 2/00) [811]

6708 Lewis, J. Patrick. *Freedom Like Sunlight: Praisesongs for Black Americans* (5–12). 2000, Creative $17.95 (978-1-56846-163-2). This collection of original poems pays tribute to such important African Americans as Sojourner Truth, Arthur Ashe, Rosa Parks, Marian Anderson, Malcolm X, and Langston Hughes. (Rev: BL 9/15/00*; HBG 3/01; SLJ 12/00) [811]

6709 Livingston, Myra Cohn, ed. *I Am Writing a Poem About . . . A Game of Poetry* (9–12). 1997, Simon & Schuster $16.00 (978-0-689-81156-2). These are the poems that resulted when students in the author's poetry-writing classes were asked to write poems using randomly selected words as inspirations. (Rev: BL 9/1/97; HBG 3/98; SLJ 10/97; VOYA 2/98) [811]

6710 Loewen, Nancy, ed. *Walt Whitman* (7–12). 1994, Creative Editions LB $23.95 (978-0-88682-608-6). A dozen selections from *Leaves of Grass* are juxtaposed with biographical vignettes and sepia photographs. (Rev: SLJ 7/94*) [811]

6711 Longfellow, Henry Wadsworth. *Poems and Other Writings* (9–12). 2000, Library of America $35.00 (978-1-883011-85-7). Included in this anthology of Longfellow's poems are "Hiawatha," "Evangeline," and "The Courtship of Miles Standish." [811]

6712 McLaughlin, Timothy P., ed. *Walking on Earth and Touching the Sky: Poetry and Prose by Lakota Youth at Red Cloud Indian School* (7–12). Illus. by S. D. Nelson. 2012, Abrams $19.95 (978-141970179-5). Poems and

poetic prose by Lakota students are divided into such chapters as "Natural World," "Native Thoughts," and "Family, Youth, and Dreams" and accompanied by rich paintings. (Rev: BL 5/1/12*; LMC 11–12/12*) [811]

6713 Marius, Richard, and Keith Frome, eds. *The Columbia Book of Civil War Poetry* (9–12). 1994, Columbia Univ. $39.95 (978-0-231-10002-1). An anthology of Civil War poetry, including famous songs and verses that appeared in newspapers by unknown writers. (Rev: BL 9/15/94; SLJ 11/94) [811.008]

6714 Marquis, Don. *Archyology: The Long Lost Tales of Archy and Mehitabel* (10–12). 1996, Univ. Press of New England $17.95 (978-0-87451-745-3). Light, humorous verse about Archy the cockroach and Mehitabel the cat. (Rev: BL 4/1/96; SLJ 2/97) [811]

6715 Meltzer, Milton, ed. *Hour of Freedom: American History in Poetry* (6–12). Illus. by Marc Nadel. 2003, Boyds Mills $16.95 (978-1-59078-021-3). Brief histories introduce many classic and some less-familiar poems — plus lyrics and speeches — that are grouped in chronological chapters, ranging from the colonial period to the 20th century. (Rev: BL 9/1/03; HBG 4/04; SLJ 7/03; VOYA 2/04) [811.54]

6716 Millay, Edna St. Vincent. *Edna St. Vincent Millay's Poems Selected for Young People* (7–10). 1979, HarperCollins $14.00 (978-0-06-024218-3). A fine selection of the poet's work, illustrated with woodcuts. [811]

6717 Mora, Pat. *My Own True Name: New and Selected Poems for Young Adults, 1984-1999* (6–12). 2000, Arte Publico paper $11.95 (978-1-55885-292-1). The Mexican American poet looks at her bilingual heritage, the beauty of the desert country in which she was raised, her love of language, and racial discrimination. (Rev: SLJ 7/00; VOYA 12/00) [811]

6718 Myers, Walter Dean. *Voices from Harlem: Poems in Many Voices* (7–10). 2004, Holiday House $16.95 (978-0-8234-1853-4). In this appealing collection of 54 poems, modeled on Edgar Lee Masters's *Spoon River Anthology*, Myers speaks in the diverse voices of imagined Harlem residents from many walks of life. (Rev: BCCB 12/04; BL 11/1/04*; HB 1–2/05; SLJ 12/04; VOYA 2/05) [811]

6719 Nash, Ogden. *I Wouldn't Have Missed It: Selected Poems of Ogden Nash* (9–12). 1975, Little, Brown $33.00 (978-0-316-59830-9). A selection of over 400 poems chosen by the poet's daughter after his death. [811]

6720 Nash, Ogden. *The Pocket Book of Ogden Nash* (9–12). 1991, Buccaneer LB $18.95 (978-0-89966-867-3). A fine collection of this writer's wittiest and most endearing poems. [811]

6721 Nelson, Marilyn. *Fortune's Bones: The Manumission Requiem* (7–12). 2005, Front St $16.95 (978-1-932425-12-3). Six poems celebrate the life of Fortune, a slave who died in 1798 but continued to serve his master, who rendered his bones and used Fortune's skeleton to teach anatomy. (Rev: BCCB 2/05; BL 11/15/04; HB 1–2/05; SLJ 12/04) [811]

6722 Nelson, Marilyn. *A Wreath for Emmett Till* (9–12). Illus. by Philippe Lardy. 2005, Houghton Mifflin $17.00 (978-0-618-39752-5). In this collection of 15 connected sonnets — in the form known as a heroic crown — Nelson remembers the 1955 lynching and the impact this tragic event had on the evolution of race relations in the United States. (Rev: BL 2/1/05*; SLJ 5/05) [811]

6723 Ortiz, Simon J. *Out There Somewhere* (10–12). 2002, Univ. of Arizona $35.00 (978-0-8165-2208-8); paper $17.95 (978-0-8165-2210-1). Ortiz's poetry gives voice to the disaffection among many Native Americans at the obstacles they face in carving out a place for themselves in mainstream society. (Rev: BL 3/15/02) [811]

6724 Parini, Jay. *The Columbia Anthology of American Poetry* (10–12). 1995, Columbia Univ. $39.95 (978-0-231-08122-1). This anthology gives a good representation to various schools of American poetry writing and a good sampling from women and minority groups. [811.008]

6725 Plath, Sylvia. *Ariel: The Restored Edition: A Facsimile of Plath's Manuscript, Reinstating Her Original Selection and Arrangement* (9–12). 2004, HarperCollins $24.95 (978-0-06-073259-2). This original version shows how Plath intended *Ariel* to appear. (Rev: BL 10/15/04) [811]

6726 Plath, Sylvia. *The Collected Poems* (10–12). 1992, HarperCollins paper $17.95 (978-0-06-090900-0). This collection contains 224 poems, including a selection of her very earliest work. Also use: *Crossing the River* (1971), a volume that contains the poet's last works. [811]

6727 Poe, Edgar Allan. *Complete Poems* (8–12). Ed. by Thomas Ollive Mabbott. 2000, Univ. of Illinois paper $25.00 (978-0-252-06921-5). This is an exhaustive collection of Poe's poems, totaling 101 works. [811]

6728 Rampersad, Arnold, and Hilary Herbold, eds. *The Oxford Anthology of African-American Poetry* (10–12). 2005, Oxford $45.00 (978-0-19-512563-4). An impressive anthology of poetry by African Americans. (Rev: BL 9/1/05) [811]

6729 Rampersad, Arnold, et al, ed. *The Collected Poems of Langston Hughes* (9–12). 1994, Knopf $35.50 (978-0-679-42631-8). A large collection of the African American poet's work. Hughes speaks in jazzlike rhythms of the pain of everyday life, Harlem street life, prejudice, Southern violence, and love. (Rev: BL 10/1/94*) [811]

6730 Reynolds, Jason, and Jason Griffin. *My Name Is Jason. Mine Too: Our Story. Our Way* (9–12). Illus. by authors. 2009, HarperCollins paper $12.99 (978-0-06-154788-1). Written in hip, gritty poetic prose, this book

chronicles the trials of two young men named Jason — one a painter and one a writer, one white and one black — as they learn the value of taking risks and cultivating friendships while finding their way in New York City. (Rev: SLJ 10/09; VOYA 8/09) [811]

6731 Rodriguez, Luis J. *My Nature Is Hunger: New and Selected Poems, 1989-2004* (9–12). 2005, Curbstone paper $14.95 (978-1-931896-24-5). In this collection of poetry, Luis Rodriguez, the son of Mexican immigrants, gives voice to his frustrations, anger, and hopes. (Rev: BL 8/05) [811]

6732 Roessel, David, and Arnold Rampersad, eds. *Poetry for Young People: Langston Hughes* (7–10). Illus. by Benny Andrews. 2006, Sterling $14.95 (978-1-4027-1845-8). An illustrated picture-book-format collection of 26 poems with a useful introduction, a biography, and notes. Coretta Scott King Illustrator Honor Award, 2007. (Rev: BL 2/1/06*; SLJ 5/06) [811]

6733 Rosenberg, Liz, ed. *The Invisible Ladder: An Anthology of Contemporary American Poems for Young Readers* (6–10). 1996, Henry Holt $19.95 (978-0-8050-3836-1). As well as an excellent anthology of modern American poetry, this volume provides commentary by the poets, photographs of them, and suggestions for using each of the poems. (Rev: BL 9/15/96; SLJ 2/97; VOYA 2/97) [811]

6734 Rylant, Cynthia. *Boris* (7–10). 2005, Harcourt $16.00 (978-0-15-205412-0). This collection of free-verse poems celebrates the life and times of Boris, a big, gray cat adopted from a humane shelter. (Rev: BCCB 4/05; BL 2/15/05; HB 5–6/05; SLJ 4/05; VOYA 4/05) [811]

6735 Rylant, Cynthia. *Soda Jerk* (7–12). 1990, Watts LB $16.99 (978-0-531-08464-9). A group of poems about the inhabitants of a small town, written from the viewpoint of a teenage soda jerk. (Rev: BL 2/15/90; SLJ 4/90; VOYA 6/90) [811]

6736 Rylant, Cynthia. *Something Permanent* (7–12). 1994, Harcourt $18.00 (978-0-15-277090-7). Combines Rylant's poetry with Walker Evans's photographs to evoke strong emotions of southern life during the Depression. (Rev: BL 7/94*; SLJ 8/94; VOYA 12/94) [811]

6737 Sandburg, Carl. *The Complete Poems of Carl Sandburg. Rev. ed.* (9–12). 1970, Harcourt $40.00 (978-0-15-100996-1). A collection of seven of the author's books of poetry, including *Chicago Poems* and *The People, Yes.* [811]

6738 Sandburg, Carl. *Selected Poems* (9–12). Ed. by George Hendrick and Willene Hendrick. 1996, Harcourt $16.00 (978-0-15-600396-4). This collection of Sandburg's poetry contains a number of poems not previously collected or published. [811]

6739 Schmidt, Elizabeth Hun, ed. *The Poets Laureate Anthology* (10–12). Illus. 2010, Norton $39.95 (978-

039306181-9). Short profiles introduce samples of each American poet laureate's work. (Rev: BL 10/1–15/10) [811]

6740 Sheeler, Jackie, ed. *Off the Cuffs: Poetry by and About the Police* (10–12). 2003, Soft Skull paper $16.00 (978-1-887128-81-0). This anthology interlaces poems protesting brutality and excessive force with paeans of praise for the important work done by the police. (Rev: BL 3/15/03) [811]

6741 Soto, Gary. *A Natural Man* (10–12). 1999, Chronicle paper $13.95 (978-0-8118-2518-4). These poems about the sometimes harsh reality of being a young Chicano in California will resonate with all teens. (Rev: SLJ 2/00) [811]

6742 Soto, Gary. *New and Selected Poems* (9–12). 1995, Chronicle paper $14.95 (978-0-8118-0758-6). This is a collection of the work of the Mexican American poet in which he expresses his innermost feelings and emotions. [811]

6743 Spires, Elizabeth. *I Heard God Talking to Me: William Edmondson and His Stone Carvings* (6–12). Illus. 2009, Farrar $17.95 (978-037433528-1). Poems celebrate the art of African American sculptor William Edmondson, who started carving tombstones in 1931 when he was in his 50s; with photographs of the artist and his works. (Rev: BL 2/1/09; SLJ 3/1/09*) [811]

6744 Stepanek, Mattie J. T. *Hope Through Heartsongs* (6–12). 2002, Hyperion $14.95 (978-0-7868-6944-2). Hope and courage are central to this third collection of poems by Mattie Stepanek, who died of muscular dystrophy in June 2004, less than a month before his 14th birthday. (Rev: SLJ 8/02; VOYA 8/02) [811]

6745 Stern, Gerald. *What I Can't Bear Losing: Notes from a Life* (10–12). 2003, Norton $24.95 (978-0-393-05818-5). Stern revisits pivotal periods in his life, including his rough-and-tumble childhood in Pittsburgh, encounters with anti-Semitism, love affairs, and experiences in the military; for mature teens. (Rev: BL 11/1/03) [811]

6746 Strickland, Michael R., ed. *My Own Song: And Other Poems to Groove To* (6–12). 1997, Boyds Mills $14.95 (978-1-56397-686-5). A collection of poems about music and its relationship to such subjects as love, cities, and birds. (Rev: BL 10/15/97; HBG 3/98; SLJ 12/97) [811]

6747 Suarez, Virgil, and Ryan G. Van Cleave, eds. *Like Thunder: Poets Respond to Violence in America* (10–12). 2002, Univ. of Iowa paper $19.95 (978-0-87745-792-3). More than 100 poets from diverse backgrounds speak out about such disturbing topics as child abuse, rape, gang shootings, and school violence. (Rev: BL 3/1/02*) [811]

6748 Tamblyn, Amber. *Free Stallion: Poems* (11–12). 2005, Simon & Schuster $14.95 (978-1-4169-0259-1). For mature readers, this is a frank collection of poems musing on the joys and agonies of teenage years and the developing sexuality. (Rev: SLJ 12/05)

6749 *Tell the World: Teen Poems from Writerscorps* (7–12). 2008, HarperTeen $16.99 (978-0-06-134505-0). Brief poems by teen participants in WritersCorps workshops are organized in chapters titled "Who We Are," "Where We're From," "What We Love," "What We Think," "How It Feels," and "Why We Hope." (Rev: SLJ 1/1/09) [811]

6750 Thayer, Ernest L. *Casey at the Bat* (5–10). Illus. by Joe Morse. Series: Visions in Poetry. 2006, Kids Can $16.95 (978-1-55337-827-3). The famous poem is reimagined in a contemporary setting, with a multicultural crowd and modern technology grounding the poem in the here-and-now. (Rev: SLJ 6/06) [811]

6751 Trethewey, Natasha. *Bellocq's Ophelia* (10–12). 2002, Graywolf paper $14.00 (978-1-55597-359-9). This collection of poems breathes life into the subject of an E. J. Bellocq photograph: a light-skinned African American prostitute in early-20th-century New Orleans. (Rev: BL 3/1/02) [811]

6752 Turner, Ann W. *Grass Songs: Poems* (7–12). 1993, Harcourt $16.95 (978-0-15-136788-7). Dramatic monologues in poetic form that express courage and despair, passion and loneliness, and the struggle to find a home in the wilderness. (Rev: BL 6/1–15/93; VOYA 8/93) [811]

6753 Turner, Ann W. *A Lion's Hunger: Poems of First Love* (8–12). 1999, Marshall Cavendish $15.95 (978-0-7614-5035-1). Written from a young woman's point of view, this is a collection of poems chronicling the joys and sorrows of first love. (Rev: BL 3/1/99; HBG 3/99; SLJ 1/99; VOYA 2/99) [811]

6754 Weatherford, Carole Boston. *Remember the Bridge: Poems of a People* (7–12). 2002, Putnam $17.99 (978-0-399-23726-3). This collection of poems celebrates African Americans from the era of slavery through today, with accompanying archival images. (Rev: BL 2/15/02; HBG 10/02; SLJ 1/02; VOYA 8/02) [811]

6755 Whitman, Walt. *Complete Poetry and Collected Prose* (10–12). 1982, Library of America $35.00 (978-0-940450-02-8); paper $17.95 (978-1-883011-35-2). This collection contains *Leaves of Grass*, plus all of Whitman's prose works. [818]

6756 Whitman, Walt. *Voyages: Poems by Walt Whitman* (7–12). 1988, Harcourt $15.95 (978-0-15-294495-7). An introductory biographical sketch is followed by 53 representative poems selected by Lee Bennett Hopkins. (Rev: BL 11/15/88; SLJ 12/88; VOYA 1/89) [811.3]

6757 Williams, Saul. *The Dead Emcee Scrolls: The Lost Teachings of Hip-Hop and Connected Writings* (9–12). 2006, Pocket paper $12.95 (978-1-4165-1632-3). Performance poet Saul Williams fuses hip-hop and poetry in this powerful collection. (Rev: BL 2/1/06) [811]

6758 Wong, Janet S. *Behind the Wheel* (7–12). 1999, Simon & Schuster $15.00 (978-0-689-82531-6). In a series of free-verse poems, the author explores individuals and their relationships within families. (Rev: BL 1/1–15/00*; HB 11–12/99; HBG 4/00; VOYA 2/00) [811]

6759 Young, Kevin. *Ardency: A Chronicle of the Amistad Rebels* (11–12). 2011, Knopf $27.95 (978-0-307-26764-1). Young provides a stirring series of poems chronicling the revolt that took place on the slave ship *Amistad*; for mature readers. (Rev: BL 2/1–15/11; SLJ 5/11) [811]

6760 Young, Kevin. *Dear Darkness* (11–12). 2008, Knopf $26.00 (978-030726434-3). This unique collection of poetry captures the Southern way of life, the sadness of death, and the sweet bizarreness of family; for mature teens. (Rev: BL 9/1/08) [811]

6761 Zucker, Rachel, and Arielle Greenberg, eds. *Starting Today: 100 Poems for Obama's First 100 Days* (11–12). 2010, Univ. of Iowa paper $20 (978-15872987-1-4). One hundred poems by a wide range of poets record Obama's first 100 days and reflect an initial blaze of hope and slowly mounting disappointment in the face of the continuing poor economy, two wars, and political gridlock. (Rev: BL 4/1–15/10) [811]

Other Regions

6762 Achebe, Chinua. *Collected Poems* (10–12). 2004, Anchor paper $12.00 (978-1-4000-7658-1). Nigerian-born novelist Achebe is also an accomplished poet, as this collection demonstrates. (Rev: BL 8/04) [821]

6763 Cole, Joanna, ed. *Best-Loved Folktales of the World* (7–12). 1982, Doubleday paper $17.00 (978-0-385-18949-1). A collection of 200 tales from around the globe, arranged geographically. [398.2]

6764 Dokey, Cameron. *Before Midnight: A Retelling of "Cinderella"* (6–10). Series: Once upon a Time. 2007, Simon & Schuster paper $5.99 (978-1-4169-3471-4). Dokey adds details to the Cinderella tale, explaining that the girl's father left her in his grief over his wife's death in childbirth. (Rev: SLJ 4/07)

6765 Dokey, Cameron. *Golden* (6–10). 2006, Simon & Schuster paper $5.99 (978-1-4169-0580-6). Obviously based on the Rapunzel fairy tale, but with several interesting twists on the original, this story tells of a bald Rapunzel whom her mother gave up to sorceress Melisande, who raised her as her own, having lost her own daughter Rue to a wizard who cursed her and imprisoned her in a magic tower. Rapunzel — in the midst of feelings of jealousy — leads the effort to save Rue before it is too late. (Rev: SLJ 8/06*)

6766 Dokey, Cameron. *Sunlight and Shadow* (6–10). Series: Once Upon a Time. 2004, Simon & Schuster paper $5.99 (978-0-689-86999-0). Mina — daughter of Pamina, the Queen of the Night, and of Sarastro, the Mage of the Day — falls in love with a prince called Tern and together the two face obstacles in this reworking of "The Magic Flute." (Rev: SLJ 11/04; VOYA 12/04)

6767 Engle, Margarita. *The Firefly Letters: A Suffragette's Journey to Cuba* (6–12). 2010, Henry Holt $16.99 (978-0-8050-9082-6). In alternating free-verse narratives Swedish suffragist Frederika Bremer, her teenage slave Cecilia, and a privileged 12-year-old daughter of a planter describe their lives and quite different experiences. Belpré Honor 2011; ALA Notable Books 2011. e Lexile NC1230L (Rev: BL 12/15/09; HB 3–4/10; LMC 11–12/09; SLJ 2/10) [813]

6768 Engle, Margarita. *The Surrender Tree: Poems of Cuba's Struggle for Freedom* (6–12). 2008, Henry Holt $16.95 (978-0-8050-8674-4). In free verse Engle describes the lives of residents of Cuba in the mid- to late-19th century who fought for freedom. Belpré Medal 2009; Newbery Honor 2009; ALA Notable Books 2009. (Rev: BL 3/15/08*; LMC 11–12/08) [811]

6769 Hamilton, Martha, and Mitch Weiss. *How and Why Stories: World Tales Kids Can Read and Tell* (5–10). 1999, August House $21.95 (978-0-87483-562-5); paper $12.95 (978-0-87483-561-8). This excellent collection of 25 pourquoi (how and why) stories from around the world also contains a useful introduction on folklore, plus tips on delivering each of the tales. (Rev: BL 5/15/00; HBG 3/00; SLJ 1/00) [398.2]

6770 Ji-Moon, Suh, and James A. Perkins, eds. *Brother Enemy: Poems of the Korean War* (10–12). Trans. by Suh Ji Moon and James A. Perkins. 2002, White Pine paper $16.00 (978-1-893996-20-5). This collection of moving poems revisits the horrors of Korea's mid-20th-century civil war that pitted brother against brother. (Rev: BL 9/1/02) [895.7]

6771 Liu, Siyu, and Orel Protopopescu. *A Thousand Peaks: Poems from China* (6–10). Illus. by Siyu Liu. 2002, Pacific View $19.95 (978-1-881896-24-1). Thirty-five translations of Chinese poems are accompanied by information giving historical and cultural context, the original in Chinese characters and pinyin transliteration, a literal translation, and black-and-white drawings. (Rev: BL 3/15/02; SLJ 2/02*) [895.1]

6772 MacDonald, Margaret Read. *Three Minute Tales: Stories from Around the World to Tell or Read When Time Is Short* (8–12). 2004, August House $24.95 (978-0-87483-728-5); paper $17.95 (978-0-87483-729-2). Brief tales that are easy to learn come with notes about sources and tips about effective telling. (Rev: BL 9/15/04; SLJ 10/04) [398.2]

6773 Nye, Naomi Shihab, ed. *The Space Between Our Footsteps: Poems and Paintings from the Middle East* (8–12). 1998, Simon & Schuster $21.95 (978-0-689-81233-0). More than 100 poets and artists from 19 countries in the Middle East are featured in this handsome volume of verse about families, friends, and everyday events. (Rev: BCCB 5/98; BL 3/1/98; HB 3–4/98; SLJ 5/98; VOYA 10/98) [808.81]

6774 Opie, Iona, and Peter Opie, eds. *The Classic Fairy Tales* (6–12). 1987, Oxford paper $19.99 (978-0-19-520219-9). The definitive retelling of 24 of the most popular fairy tales of all time. [398.2]

6775 Yolen, Jane, and Shulamith Oppenheim. *The Fish Prince and Other Stories* (7–12). Illus. by Paul Hoffman. 2001, Interlink $29.95 (978-1-56656-389-5); paper $15.00 (978-1-56656-390-1). An absorbing and informative collection of stories of mermaids and mermen from around the world, accompanied by black-and-white illustrations. (Rev: BL 11/15/01) [398.21]

Folklore and Fairy Tales

General and Miscellaneous

6776 Adams, Amanda. *A Mermaid's Tale* (11–12). 2006, Greystone $24.95 (978-1-55365-117-8). A collection of mermaid myths and mermaid lore, with rich illustrations by artists such as Arthur Rackham. (Rev: BL 9/15/06) [398.21]

6777 Creeden, Sharon. *Fair Is Fair: World Folktales of Justice* (9–12). 1995, August House $19.95 (978-0-87483-400-0). Thirty folktales, adapted from different times and places, relating to law and justice. (Rev: BL 5/15/95; SLJ 10/95) [398.2]

6778 De Caro, Frank, ed. *The Folktale Cat* (9–12). 1993, August House paper $14.95 (978-0-87483-303-4). An international collection of 51 classic and lesser-known feline folktales, with a discussion of the domestic cat's role in folklore. (Rev: BL 4/15/93; SLJ 11/93) [398.2]

6779 Dorson, Richard M., ed. *Folktales Told Around the World* (10–12). 1987, Univ. of Chicago paper $30.00 (978-0-226-15874-7). An international selection of folktales in authentic retellings and translations. [398.2]

6780 Goss, Theodora. *In the Forest of Forgetting* (9–12). 2006, Prime $24.95 (978-0-8095-5691-5). This collection of sixteen literary fairy tales features contemporary and sometimes funny characters involved in fractured fairy tale situations. (Rev: BL 6/1–15/06) [398.2]

6781 Hawes, Louise. *Black Pearls: A Faerie Strand* (9–12). Illus. by Rebecca Guay. 2008, Houghton Mifflin $16.00 (978-0-618-74797-9). Readers long past fairy-tale age are the audience for these retold stories, all familiar fairy tales with new — sometimes dark or odd — twists to them. (Rev: BL 4/15/08)

6782 Huygen, Wil. *Gnomes* (10–12). 2006, HNA Books $24.95 (978-0-8109-5498-4). Using a number of sources the author and illustrator have compiled a delightful book on gnomeology, first published in 1977. [398]

6783 Sadeh, Pinhas, ed. *Jewish Folktales* (9–12). 1989, Doubleday paper $16.00 (978-0-385-19574-4). This collection is distinguished by the worldwide coverage represented. (Rev: BL 11/1/89) [398.2]

6784 Schwartz, Howard, ed. *Leaves from the Garden of Eden: One Hundred Classic Jewish Tales* (10–12). Illus. by Kirstina Swarner. 2008, Oxford $34.95 (978-019533565-1). This large volume of diverse tales spans countries and traditions while explaining the common thread that makes them all Jewish. **e** (Rev: BL 9/15/08) [398]

6785 Tatar, Maria, ed. *The Annotated Classic Fairy Tales* (10–12). Trans. by Maria Tatar. 2002, Norton $35.00 (978-0-393-05163-6). A highly readable and well illustrated collection of 26 classic fairy tales retold in contemporary language and with notes on their original context, variations, and so forth. (Rev: BL 10/1/02; SLJ 2/03) [398.2]

6786 Vande Velde, Vivian. *Cloaked in Red* (7–10). 2010, Marshall Cavendish $15.99 (978-0-7614-5793-0). A collection of eight diverse stories that give new twists to the well-known tale. Lexile 920L (Rev: BL 9/15/10; LMC 11–12/10; SLJ 12/1/10; VOYA 10/10)

6787 Yolen, Jane, ed. *Favorite Folktales from Around the World* (9–12). 1988, Pantheon paper $18.00 (978-0-394-75188-7). This collection of 160 tales represents such diverse stories as American Indian legends and tales from the Brothers Grimm. (Rev: SLJ 12/86) [398]

Geographical Regions

Africa

6788 Abrahams, Roger D., ed. *African Folktales: Traditional Stories of the Black World* (7–12). 1983, Pantheon paper $18.00 (978-0-394-72117-0). A collection of about 100 tales from south of the Sahara. [398.2]

6789 Berry, Jack. *West African Folktales* (9–12). Ed. by Richard Spears. 1991, Northwestern Univ. paper $14.95 (978-0-8101-0993-3). Vivid folktales imparting basic life lessons collected over 35 years by a linguist who specialized in the spoken art of Sierra Leone, Ghana, and Nigeria. (Rev: BL 10/15/91) [398.2]

6790 McCall Smith, Alexander. *The Girl Who Married a Lion and Other Tales from Africa* (8–12). 2004, Pantheon $20.00 (978-0-375-42312-3). Traditional tales feature characterful animals and humans. (Rev: BL 11/1/04) [398.2]

6791 Offodile, Buchi. *The Orphan Girl and Other Stories: West African Folk Tales* (9–12). 2001, Interlink paper $15.00 (978-1-56656-375-8). From trickster tales to creation stories, this is a fine collection of folktales from West Africa, mainly from Nigeria. (Rev: BL 9/15/01) [398.2]

Asia and the Middle East

6792 Faurot, Jeannette L. *Asian-Pacific Folktales and Legends* (9–12). 1995, Simon & Schuster paper $12.00 (978-0-684-81197-0). This is a collection of 65 myths and folktales from eight East and South Asian countries, including China. [398.2]

6793 Livo, Norma J., and Dia Cha, eds. *Folk Stories of the Hmong: Peoples of Laos, Thailand, and Vietnam* (9–12). 1991, Libraries Unlimited LB $22.00 (978-0-87287-854-9). The unique culture and heritage of the Hmong people are celebrated in this collection of folktales. Includes an introduction to Hmong history. (Rev: BL 10/1/91) [398.2]

6794 Napoli, Donna Jo. *Bound* (7–12). 2004, Simon & Schuster $16.95 (978-0-689-86175-8). In this multilayered and thought-provoking Cinderella tale that draws on traditional Chinese elements, Xing Xing is mistreated by her stepmother and stepsister after the death of the girl's beloved father, but she escapes the cruel foot binding inflicted on her stepsister. (Rev: BL 12/1/04*; SLJ 11/04; VOYA 2/05)

6795 Nuweihed, Jamal Sleem. *Abu Jmeel's Daughter and Other Stories: Arab Folk Tales from Palestine and Lebanon* (10–12). 2002, Interlink paper $16.95 (978-1-56656-418-2). Twenty-seven fairly lengthy traditional folktales in which women play a prominent role are presented in a lively and enticing format. (Rev: BL 5/15/02) [398.2]

6796 Roberts, Moss. *Chinese Fairy Tales and Fantasies* (10–12). 1980, Pantheon paper $16.00 (978-0-394-73994-6). Culled from 25 centuries of folklore, this is a collection of 100 tales. [398]

6797 Yep, Laurence. *The Rainbow People* (7–10). 1989, HarperCollins $16.00 (978-0-06-026760-5); paper $6.99 (978-0-06-440441-9). The retelling of 20 Chinese folktales with illustrations by David Wiesner. (Rev: BL 4/1/89; SLJ 5/89) [398.2]

Australia and the Pacific Islands

6798 Flood, Bo, and Beret E. Strong. *Pacific Island Legends: Tales from Micronesia, Melanesia, Polynesia, and Australia* (6–12). Illus. by Connie J. Adams. 1999, Bess $22.95 (978-1-57306-084-4); paper $14.95 (978-1-57306-078-3). The ocean's impact on island life is a theme that runs through many of these tales, which are organized in geographical groupings with introductions on each area's culture and history. (Rev: HBG 4/00; SLJ 10/99) [398.2]

6799 Oodgeroo. *Dreamtime: Aboriginal Stories* (6–10). 1994, Lothrop $16.00 (978-0-688-13296-5). Traditional and autobiographical stories of aboriginal culture and its roots. Also examines current aboriginal life alongside white civilization. (Rev: BCCB 1/99; BL 10/1/94; SLJ 10/94) [398.2]

6800 Te Kanawa, Kiri. *Land of the Long White Cloud: Maori Myths, Tales and Legends* (7–12). 1997, Pavilion paper $17.95 (978-1-86205-075-4). A group of magical Maori folktales about sea gods, fairies, monsters, and fantastic voyages, retold by the famous opera singer from New Zealand. (Rev: BL 9/1/97) [398.2]

Europe

6801 Afanasév, Aleksandr. *Russian Fairy Tales* (7–12). 1976, Pantheon paper $18.00 (978-0-394-73090-5). This is a standard collection of traditional Russian tales. [398]

6802 Altom, Laura Marie. *Kissing Frogs* (11–12). 2004, Spell paper $5.99 (978-0-505-52568-0). In this humorous retelling of the Frog Prince fable, modern-day biologist Lucy Gordon faces tough choices when the frog she kisses is transformed into a prince. (Rev: BL 12/1/03*)

6803 Andersen, Hans Christian. *Tales and Stories* (9–12). 1980, Univ. of Washington paper $22.50 (978-0-295-95936-8). These 27 stories are retold for an adult audience. [398.2]

6804 Asbjörnsen, Peter Christen, and Jörgen Moe. *Norwegian Folk Tales* (9–12). Trans. by Pat Shaw and Carl Norman. 1982, Pantheon paper $14.00 (978-0-394-71054-9). About 25 Norwegian folktales are reprinted from an authoritative collection that first appeared in 1845. [398.2]

6805 Calvino, Italo, ret. *Italian Folktales* (9–12). Trans. by George Martin. 1956, Harcourt paper $25.00 (978-0-15-645489-6). A lively retelling of Italian folktales that include variations on such stories as Snow White and Cinderella. (Rev: BL 12/15/89) [398]

6806 D'Aulnoy, Madame. *Beauty and the Beast* (9–12). 2000, Creative Editions $17.95 (978-1-56846-129-8). Most remarkable for its stunning artwork, this retelling of the Beauty and the Beast legend will probably be of greatest interest to design students. (Rev: BL 11/15/00; HBG 10/01) [398.2]

6807 Delamare, David. *Cinderella* (7–12). 1993, Simon & Schuster paper $15.00 (978-0-671-76944-4). The familiar story is set in a locale much like Venice and enhanced by Delamare's paintings, both realistic and surreal. (Rev: BCCB 11/00; BL 9/15/93; SLJ 12/93) [398.2]

6808 Jacobs, Joseph, ed. *Celtic Fairy Tales* (10–12). 1968, Dover paper $7.95 (978-0-486-21826-7). One of the great collectors of folktales presents these from Ireland. Also use: *More Celtic Fairy Tales* (1968), *Indian Fairy Tales* (1969), and *English Fairy Tales* (Penguin, 1990). [398]

6809 McKinley, Robin. *The Outlaws of Sherwood* (9–12). 1988, Greenwillow $17.00 (978-0-688-07178-3). A reworking of the Robin Hood story in which our hero becomes a moody, self-doubting, somewhat ordinary man. (Rev: BL 12/15/88; SLJ 1/89; VOYA 4/89) [398.2]

6810 Markale, Jean. *King of the Celts: Arthurian Legends and Celtic Tradition* (9–12). Trans. by Christine Hauch. 1994, Inner Traditions paper $16.95 (978-0-89281-452-7). A survey of Arthurian lore in Celtic history that illustrates how the legends were misappropriated by propagandists of the courtly nobility. (Rev: BL 3/1/94) [942.01]

6811 Morpurgo, Michael. *Beowulf* (7–10). Illus. by Michael Foreman. 2006, Candlewick $17.99 (978-0-7636-3206-9). A retelling of the ancient story that does not leave out any gory details and that captures the atmosphere of the original through both prose and illustrations. (Rev: BL 3/1/07; LMC 4–5/07; SLJ 12/06) [398.2]

6812 Perrault, Charles. *Cinderella* (9–12). 2000, Creative Editions $17.95 (978-1-56846-130-4). The high quality of the illustrations are the main attraction of this retelling set in the Roaring '20s. (Rev: BL 11/15/00; HBG 10/01) [398.2]

6813 Phillips, Graham, and Martin Keatman. *King Arthur: The True Story* (9–12). 1994, Arrow paper $9.95 (978-0-09-929681-2). A scholarly examination of the Arthurian legend that attempts to document its roots and determine whether the king really existed. (Rev: BL 1/15/94) [942.01]

6814 Pyle, Howard. *The Story of King Arthur and His Knights* (8–12). 1973, Peter Smith $25.75 (978-0-8446-2766-3); paper $12.95 (978-0-486-21445-0). A retell-

ing that has been in print since its first publication in 1903. [398.2]

6815 Pyle, Howard. *The Story of Sir Launcelot and His Companions* (7–12). 1991, Dover paper $13.95 (978-0-486-26701-2). This book of episodes in the Arthurian legend is noteworthy because of the illustrations of Howard Pyle. [398.2]

6816 Raven, Nicky. *Beowulf: A Tale of Blood, Heat, and Ashes* (6–12). Illus. by John Howe. 2007, Candlewick $18.99 (978-0-7636-3647-0). This is a beautifully illustrated retelling of the epic story. (Rev: BL 11/15/07; SLJ 2/08) [398.2]

6817 Tolkien, J. R. R. *Sir Gawain and the Green Knight* (10–12). 1979, Ballantine paper $5.99 (978-0-345-27760-2). A retelling of three tales from the age of chivalry. [398]

6818 Weinreich, Beatrice Silverman. *Yiddish Folktales* (9–12). Trans. by Leonard Wolf. Series: Pantheon Fairy Tale and Folklore Library. 1988, Pantheon paper $18.00 (978-0-8052-1090-3). There are more than 200 selections in this volume from the world of Eastern European Jewry. [398.2]

6819 Wyly, Michael. *King Arthur* (7–10). Series: Mystery Library. 2001, Lucent LB $27.45 (978-1-56006-771-9). An engrossing account that explores the fact and fiction surrounding this legendary king and his knights. (Rev: BL 9/15/01) [942]

North America

GENERAL AND MISCELLANEOUS

6820 Currie, Stephen. *African American Folklore* (7–12). Series: Lucent Library of Black History. 2008, Gale/Lucent $32.45 (978-1-4205-0082-0). In chapters on folk stories, folk songs, jokes and rhymes, and roots and influences, Currie explores the genre. (Rev: SLJ 2/1/09) [398.08996]

6821 West, John O., ed. *Mexican-American Folklore* (9–12). 1988, August House paper $17.95 (978-0-87483-059-0). A collection of stories, proverbs, legends, and other forms of folklore reflecting the Mexican American culture. (Rev: BL 11/15/88) [398]

NATIVE AMERICANS

6822 Bierhorst, John. *The Way of the Earth: Native America and the Environment* (7–12). 1994, Morrow $15.00 (978-0-688-11560-9). Explores the mythologic and folkloric patterns of Native American belief systems. (Rev: BL 5/15/94; SLJ 5/94; VOYA 10/94) [179]

6823 Bruchac, Joseph. *Our Stories Remember: American Indian History, Culture, and Values Through Sto-*

rytelling (10–12). 2003, Fulcrum paper $16.95 (978-1-55591-129-4). Bruchac draws on the traditional folklore of many tribal groups to emphasize the importance of the storytelling tradition and the themes common to most Native American folk tales. (Rev: BL 4/15/03; SLJ 7/03; VOYA 10/03) [973.04]

6824 Erdoes, Richard, and Alfonso Ortiz, eds. *American Indian Myths and Legends* (10–12). 1984, Pantheon paper $18.00 (978-0-394-74018-8). From the entire North American continent, here is a collection of 160 tales from Native American folklore. [398.2]

6825 Philip, Neil, ed. *The Great Mystery: Myths of Native America* (8–12). 2001, Clarion $25.00 (978-0-395-98405-5). A collection of creation and other stories from many Native American tribes, organized by region. (Rev: BL 11/15/01; HBG 10/02; SLJ 11/01) [398.2]

6826 Pijoan, Teresa. *White Wolf Woman: Native American Transformation Myths* (7–12). 1992, August House paper $11.95 (978-0-87483-200-6). Drawn from a wide range of Indian tribes, a collection of 37 stories about animal and human transformations and connections. (Rev: BL 10/1/92) [398.2]

6827 Tingle, Tim. *Walking the Choctaw Road* (6–12). 2003, Cinco Puntos $16.95 (978-0-938317-74-6). A collection of stories that convey Choctaw traditions and culture, including experiences on the Trail of Tears. (Rev: BL 6/1–15/03; HBG 4/04; VOYA 2/04) [398.2]

6828 Van Etten, Teresa. *Ways of Indian Magic* (7–12). 1985, Sunstone paper $8.95 (978-0-86534-061-9). A fine retelling of six legends of the Pueblo Indians. [398.2]

6829 Van Etten, Teresa. *Ways of Indian Wisdom* (7–10). 1987, Sunstone paper $10.95 (978-0-86534-090-9). A collection of 20 Pueblo tales that reflect the Southeastern Indians' culture and customs. [398.2]

6830 Zitkala-Sa. *American Indian Stories, Legends, and Other Writings* (10–12). Ed. by Cathy N. Davidson and Ada Norris. 2003, Penguin paper $14.00 (978-0-14-243709-4). Published 65 years after her death, this collection of the writings of the late Sioux writer/activist Zitkala-Sa paints a poignant portrait of Native American life and lore. (Rev: BL 3/15/03) [398.2]

UNITED STATES

6831 Blair, Walter. *Tall Tale America: A Legendary History of Our Humorous Heroes* (10–12). 1987, Univ. of Chicago paper $17.95 (978-0-226-05596-1). Mike Fink, Davy Crockett, Johnny Appleseed, and Pecos Bill are only four of the many tall-tale heroes the reader meets in this collection of folktales. [398.2]

6832 Dance, Daryl Cumber, ed. *From My People: 400 Years of African American Folklore* (10–12). 2002, Norton $35.00 (978-0-393-04798-1). The cultural evolution of black America is beautifully documented in this collection of folktales, speeches, work songs, proverbs, sermons, and other representative examples of African American culture. (Rev: BL 1/1–15/02) [398.2]

6833 Lester, Julius. *Black Folktales* (9–12). 1991, Grove Atlantic paper $11.00 (978-0-8021-3242-0). A modern retelling with contemporary references to 12 African and African American folktales. [398.2]

6834 MacDonald, Margaret Read. *Ghost Stories from the Pacific Northwest* (10–12). Series: American Folklore. 1995, August House $24.95 (978-0-87483-436-9). A collection of folktales and ghost stories from Oregon, Washington, and British Columbia that are ideal for telling around a campfire. (Rev: SLJ 3/96) [398.2]

6835 Shepherd, Esther. *Paul Bunyan* (7–10). 1941, Harcourt paper $6.95 (978-0-15-259755-9). The tall-tale lumberjack is brought to life by the text and the stunning illustrations by Rockwell Kent. [398.2]

South and Central America

6836 Ashkenazi, Michael. *Handbook of Japanese Mythology* (10–12). Series: Handbooks of World Mythology. 2003, ABC-CLIO $75.00 (978-1-57607-467-1). After an extensive introduction to the nature of Shinto and Buddhist myths, more than 200 alphabetical entries explain major figures, themes, and concepts of Japanese mythology. (Rev: SLJ 4/04) [299]

6837 Kimmel, Eric A. *The Witch's Face: A Mexican Tale* (7–12). 1993, Holiday $15.95 (978-0-8234-1038-5). Kimmel uses a picture book format for this Mexican tale of a man who rescues his love from becoming a witch, only to lose her to his own doubt. (Rev: BL 11/15/93; SLJ 2/94) [398.22]

Mythology

General and Miscellaneous

6838 Berk, Ari. *The Runes of Elfland* (7–12). Illus. by Brian Froud. 2003, Abrams $25.00 (978-0-8109-4612-5). Brief stories and wonderful art highlighting the rune's significance and associations accompany each of 24 runes. (Rev: SLJ 5/04; VOYA 2/04) [398.2]

6839 Bingham, Ann. *South and Meso-American Mythology A to Z* (6–12). Series: Mythology A to Z. 2004, Facts on File $40.00 (978-0-8160-4889-2). A handsome and thorough guide to the legends and folklore of early civilizations in Central and South America. (Rev: BL 10/1/04; SLJ 2/05) [398.2]

6840 Echlin, Kim. *Inanna: From the Myths of Ancient Sumer* (7–12). Illus. by Linda Wolfsgruber. 2003, Groundwood $19.95 (978-0-88899-496-7). The stories of the powerful goddess Inanna and her adventures in love and war, based on 4,000-year-old sources. (Rev: BL 3/1/04; HBG 4/04; SLJ 3/04; VOYA 12/03) [398.2]

6841 Evslin, Bernard. *Pig's Ploughman* (7–12). 1990, Chelsea LB $19.95 (978-1-55546-256-7). In Celtic mythology, Pig's Ploughman is the huge hog who fights Finn McCool. (Rev: BL 8/90; SLJ 3/91) [398.2]

6842 Hamilton, Dorothy. *Mythology* (8–12). 1942, Little, Brown $27.95 (978-0-316-34114-1). An introduction to the mythology of Greece and Scandinavia, plus a retelling of the principal myths. [292]

6843 Harpur, James. *Celtic Myth: A Treasury of Legends, Art, and History* (8–12). Series: World Mythology. 2007, M.E. Sharpe LB $35.95 (978-0-7656-8102-7). A collection of artifacts of ancient Celtic culture, including myths (some violent), weapons, and artwork. (Rev: BL 12/15/07; LMC 2/08; SLJ 4/08) [299]

6844 Lavers, Chris. *The Natural History of Unicorns* (10–12). Illus. 2009, Morrow $26.99 (978-006087414-

8). This volume explores how different cultures throughout history have viewed this mythical animal. (Rev: BL 7/09) [398.24]

6845 Philip, Neil. *Mythology of the World* (8–12). 2004, Houghton Mifflin $24.95 (978-0-7534-5779-5). An excellent and thorough overview of world mythology, introducing readers to the plots and characters of myth and legend and examining the historical, cultural, and spiritual aspects of mythology. (Rev: BL 12/1/04; SLJ 10/04) [398.2]

Classical

6846 Aesop. *Aesop's Fables* (7–12). 1988, Scholastic paper $4.50 (978-0-590-43880-3). This is one of many editions of the short moral tales from ancient Greece. (Rev: BCCB 12/00) [398.2]

6847 Aesop. *The Fables of Aesop* (9–12). Trans. by Patrick Gregory and Justina Gregory. 1975, Gambit $13.95 (978-0-87645-074-1); paper $8.95 (978-0-87645-116-8). This book, one of many available editions, covers 100 of the fables and deletes the moralizing conclusions. [398.2]

6848 Cadnum, Michael. *Nightsong: The Legend of Orpheus and Eurydice* (7–10). 2006, Scholastic $16.99 (978-0-439-54535-8). The story of Orpheus traveling to the underworld to bring back his bride, Eurydice, only to lose her is retold as a novel. (Rev: BL 12/15/06; LMC 3/07; SLJ 4/07)

6849 Evslin, Bernard. *The Adventures of Ulysses: The Odyssey of Homer* (8–12). 1989, Scholastic paper $5.99 (978-0-590-42599-5). A modern retelling of the adventures of Ulysses during the 10 years he wandered after the Trojan War. [292]

6850 Evslin, Bernard. *The Furies* (7–12). 1989, Chelsea LB $19.95 (978-1-55546-249-9). In Greek mythology the Furies were three witches. This retelling also includes the story of Circe, the famous sorceress. (Rev: BL 12/15/89; SLJ 4/90) [398.21]

6851 Evslin, Bernard. *Heroes, Gods and Monsters of Greek Myths* (8–12). 1984, Bantam paper $5.99 (978-0-553-25920-9). The most popular Greek myths are retold in modern language. (Rev: SLJ 2/06) [292]

6852 Evslin, Bernard. *Ladon* (7–12). 1990, Chelsea LB $19.95 (978-1-55546-254-3). A splendid retelling of the Greek myth about the sea serpent called up by Hera to fight Hercules. (Rev: BL 8/90) [398.24]

6853 Evslin, Bernard. *The Trojan War: The Iliad of Homer* (8–12). 1988, Scholastic paper $2.95 (978-0-590-41626-9). The story of the 10-year war between the Greeks and the Trojans is retold for the modern reader. [292]

6854 Geras, Adele. *Ithaka* (10–12). 2006, Harcourt $17.00 (978-0-15-205603-2). This colorful retelling of Homer's *Odyssey* uses the viewpoint of young protagonists to make the story accessible to a teen audience. (Rev: BL 12/15/05; SLJ 2/06; VOYA 2/06)

6855 Grant, Michael. *Myths of the Greeks and Romans* (9–12). 1989, NAL paper $5.95 (978-0-317-02799-0). This collection of stories bridges the gap between these two similar mythologies. [292]

6856 Halam, Ann. *Snakehead* (9–12). 2008, Random House $16.99 (978-0-375-84108-8). Set in ancient Greece, this retelling of the myth of Perseus and his quest to find and kill Medusa will appeal to teens looking for an unusual fantasy. (Rev: BL 4/15/08; SLJ 7/08)

6857 Kindl, Patrice. *Lost in the Labyrinth* (6–10). 2002, Houghton Mifflin $16.00 (978-0-618-16684-8). Told by Xenodice, a 14-year-old princess and the younger sister of Ariadne, this is an expanded version of the legend of Theseus and the Minotaur. (Rev: BCCB 11/02; BL 1/1–15/03; HB 11–12/02; HBG 3/03; SLJ 11/02; VOYA 2/03)

6858 Lester, Julius. *Cupid* (10–12). 2007, Harcourt $17.00 (978-0-15-202056-9). The tale of Cupid and Psyche told as a meta-story, with humorous asides and anecdotes from the author. ⋒ (Rev: BCCB 3/07; BL 1/1–15/07; HB 1–2/07; LMC 3/07; SLJ 1/07)

6859 McBride-Smith, Barbara. *Greek Myths, Western Style: Toga Tales with an Attitude* (9–12). 1999, August House $14.95 (978-0-87483-524-3). These 16 Greek myths take on a new life when their locale is changed to wild and woolly Texas and their characters become contemporaries, e.g., Bacchus is a drunken womanizer. (Rev: HBG 3/99; SLJ 8/99) [398.2]

6860 Mikolaycak, Charles. *Orpheus* (9–12). 1992, Harcourt $19.95 (978-0-15-258804-5). A picture book version of the Orpheus myth that combines classical and romantic images that celebrate the human body. (Rev: BL 10/15/92; SLJ 9/92) [398.21]

6861 Spinner, Stephanie. *Quicksilver* (8–11). 2005, Knopf LB $17.99 (978-0-375-92638-9). Hermes, son of Zeus and quite a character in this incarnation, describes his participation in various well-known myths. (Rev: BCCB 4/05; BL 4/15/05; HB 3–4/05; SLJ 9/05; VOYA 4/05)

6862 Spinner, Stephanie. *Quiver* (7–12). 2002, Knopf LB $17.99 (978-0-375-91489-8). A deft retelling of the Greek myth of Atalanta, who will marry only a man who can outrun her. (Rev: BCCB 2/03; BL 1/1–15/03*; HB 1–2/03; HBG 3/03; SLJ 10/02; VOYA 12/02)

6863 Usher, Kerry. *Heroes, Gods and Emperors from Roman Mythology* (8–12). 1992, NTC LB $24.95 (978-0-87226-909-5). The origins of Roman mythology are given, accompanying retellings of famous myths. [292]

Humor and Satire

6864 Allen, Woody. *Without Feathers* (9–12). 1987, Ballantine paper $5.99 (978-0-345-33697-2). Sixteen humorous pieces plus two one-act plays are included in this collection. Also use: *Getting Even* (1971). [817]

6865 Asimov, Janet J. *Notes for a Memoir: On Isaac Asimov, Life, and Writing* (10–12). 2006, Prometheus $25.00 (978-1-59102-405-7). A collection of eclectic writings by the wife of the late science fiction writer Isaac Asimov. (Rev: BL 5/1/06) [813]

6866 Baker, Russell, ed. *Russell Baker's Book of American Humor* (9–12). 1993, Norton $30.00 (978-0-393-03592-6). More than 100 humorous pieces divided into 12 categories, such as "Shameless Frivolity" and "This Sex Problem." (Rev: BL 11/1/93) [818.02]

6867 Baldwin, James. *Nobody Knows My Name: More Notes of a Native Son* (10–12). 1961, Dial paper $12.00 (978-0-679-74473-3). A collection of essays about race relations and the relationship between a writer and society. [305.8]

6868 Barry, Dave. *Dave Barry's History of the Millennium (So Far)* (10–12). 2007, Putnam $22.95 (978-0-399-15437-9). A collection of Barry's end-of-the-year summations, cataloging key (often outrageous) events. (Rev: BL 9/1/07) [818]

6869 Bombeck, Erma. *At Wit's End* (9–12). 1986, Fawcett paper $5.99 (978-0-449-21184-7). A fine collection of pieces by one of America's favorite humorists. Also use: *Just Wait Till You Have Children of Your Own, If Life Is a Bowl of Cherries, What Am I Doing in the Pits?, The Grass Is Always Greener over the Septic Tank*, and *I Lost Everything in the Post-Natal Depression* (1986). [808.7]

6870 Bombeck, Erma. *Family: The Ties That Bind . . . and Gag!* (9–12). 1987, Fawcett paper $5.95 (978-0-449-21529-6). Bombeck writes humorously about family life and being a mother as she did in *Motherhood:*

The Second Oldest Profession (1983). (Rev: BL 8/87) [306.85]

6871 Boyd, Herb, ed. *The Harlem Reader: A Celebration of New York's Most Famous Neighborhood, from the Renaissance Years to the 21st Century* (10–12). 2003, Crown paper $15.00 (978-1-4000-4681-2). The many faces of Harlem emerge in this collection of essays and fiction by both well-established and lesser-known writers. (Rev: BL 4/15/03) [974.7]

6872 Brown, Larry. *Billy Ray's Farm* (10–12). 2001, Algonquin $22.95 (978-1-56512-167-6). The prize-winning southern author presents a number of outspoken, interesting essays on many topics. (Rev: BL 3/1/01) [813]

6873 Bryan, Sharon, and William Olsen, eds. *Planet on the Table: Poets on the Reading Life* (10–12). 2003, Sarabande paper $16.95 (978-1-889330-91-4). In this collection of essays, poets write about their reading habits and the importance of reading to their own art. (Rev: BL 2/15/03) [809.1]

6874 Childs, Craig. *The Animal Dialogues: Uncommon Encounters in the Wild* (9–12). 2007, Little, Brown $24.99 (978-0-316-06632-7). Childs tells interesting stories of unexpected encounters with animals ranging from a praying mantis to a mountain lion. (Rev: BL 12/15/07) [590]

6875 Coady, Roxanne, and Joy Johannessen, eds. *The Book That Changed My Life: Discover the Must-Read Books That Transformed 71 Remarkable Authors* (10–12). 2006, Gotham $17.50 (978-1-59240-210-6). This is a collection of 71 essays by well-known authors, such as Tomie dePaola, Elizabeth Berg, and Alice Hoffman, on their favorite books. (Rev: BL 9/15/06) [808]

6876 Cosby, Bill. *Love and Marriage* (9–12). 1990, Bantam paper $6.50 (978-0-553-28467-6). The comedian remembers his first attempts at love affairs and his experiences in marriage. (Rev: BL 4/15/89) [306.7]

6877 Couturier, Lisa. *The Hopes of Snakes: And Other Tales from the Urban Landscape* (9–12). 2005, Beacon $23.00 (978-0-8070-8564-6). In this collection of essays, Couturier celebrates encounters with nature in and around the cities of the northeastern United States. (Rev: BL 12/1/04; SLJ 6/05) [808]

6878 Eggers, Dave, and Michael Cart, eds. *The Best American Nonrequired Reading, 2002* (10–12). 2002, Houghton Mifflin paper $13.00 (978-0-618-24694-6). This wide-ranging collection of fiction, satire, and reportage explores the humor and angst of growing up. (Rev: BL 10/15/02) [818]

6879 Eggers, Dave, ed. *The Best American Nonrequired Reading, 2005* (11–12). Series: Best American. 2005, Houghton Mifflin $27.50 (978-0-618-57047-8); paper $14.00 (978-0-618-57048-5). For mature readers, this mixed bag of short fiction, magazine articles, and comics includes contributions from Al Franken, George Saunders, and William T. Vollmann. (Rev: BL 10/15/05) [818]

6880 Emerson, Ralph Waldo. *The Portable Emerson. Rev. ed.* (10–12). 1981, Penguin paper $18.00 (978-0-14-015094-0). This volume contains a generous sampling of Emerson's essays, plus 22 poems. [818]

6881 Fadiman, Anne, and Robert Atwan, eds. *The Best American Essays, 2003* (10–12). 2003, Houghton Mifflin paper $13.00 (978-0-618-34161-0). Essays in this edition cover such diverse topics as a 3-year-old girl's imaginary friend, the fall of France through the eyes of a child, and the plight of industrially farmed animals. (Rev: BL 10/15/03) [808]

6882 Huxley, Aldous. *Brave New World Revisited* (10–12). 1958, Harper & Row paper $10.00 (978-0-06-095551-9). A series of essays about the prophecies made in the author's novel *Brave New World* and how some have come to pass. [303.3]

6883 Keillor, Garrison. *Leaving Home: A Collection of Lake Woebegon Stories* (9–12). 1990, Penguin paper $14.00 (978-0-14-013160-4). A collection of stories and anecdotes about Lake Woebegon culled from monologues given on radio's "Prairie Home Companion." (Rev: SLJ 2/88; VOYA 4/88) [808.7]

6884 Kerouac, Jack. *Book of Sketches, 1952–54* (9–12). 2006, Penguin paper $18.00 (978-0-14-200215-5). Jack Kerouac's jottings from his years on the road offer valuable insights into the creative mind of the leader of America's Beat movement. (Rev: BL 3/15/06) [818]

6885 Kerr, Jean. *Please Don't Eat the Daisies* (9–12). 1994, Buccaneer LB $28.95 (978-0-568-49298-1). This is a humorous look at bringing up a family in suburbia. [808.7]

6886 Lightman, Alan, and Robert Atwan, eds. *The Best American Essays, 2000* (10–12). 2000, Houghton Mifflin paper $13.00 (978-0-618-03580-9). An excellent collection of 21 fine essays that deal with a variety of topics and ideas. (Rev: BL 10/1/00) [808]

6887 Macaulay, David. *Motel of the Mysteries* (10–12). 1979, Houghton Mifflin paper $13.00 (978-0-395-28425-4). A satire on archaeology and civilization that involves unearthing a motel in the year 4022. (Rev: BL 6/87) [817]

6888 McMorris, Megan. *Cat Women: Female Writers on Their Feline Friends* (9–12). 2007, Seal paper $14.95 (978-1-58005-203-0). Women writers who love cats contribute anecdotes about their furry companions. (Rev: BL 5/1/07) [636.8]

6889 Martin, Demetri. *This Is a Book* (10–12). Illus. 2011, Grand Central $24.99 (978-044653970-8). Fans of Martin from "The Daily Show" will appreciate his cutting, intelligent sense of humor in this collection of musings on history, pop culture, family and more. (Rev: BL 3/1–15/11) [818]

6890 Mash, Robert. *How to Keep Dinosaurs. Rev. ed.* (7–12). 2003, Weidenfeld & Nicolson $14.99 (978-0-297-84347-4). A tongue-in-cheek cleverly illustrated guide to the selection and care of your own pet prehistoric animal. (Rev: SLJ 4/04; VOYA 8/04)

6891 Menand, Louis, and Robert Atwan, eds. *The Best American Essays, 2004* (9–12). 2004, Houghton Mifflin $27.50 (978-0-618-35706-2); paper $14.00 (978-0-618-35709-3). Louis Menand, author of *The Metaphysical Club*, served as guest editor for this collection of essays by such diverse writers as James Agee, Laura Hillenbrand, Tennessee Williams, and Jonathan Franzen. (Rev: BL 10/15/04) [80]

6892 Nye, Naomi Shihab. *I'll Ask You Three Times, Are You OK? Tales of Driving and Being Driven* (10–12). 2007, Greenwillow $15.99 (978-0-06-085392-1). Nye presents interesting first-person narratives, based on her own experiences, that often center on encounters with strangers while traveling. (Rev: BL 8/07; SLJ 11/07)

6893 Orlean, Susan, and Robert Atwan, eds. *The Best American Essays, 2005* (11–12). 2005, Houghton Mifflin paper $14.00 (978-0-618-35713-0). Well-known writers represented in this volume for advanced readers include Jonathan Franzen, Ted Kooser, David Sedaris, and Cathleen Schine. (Rev: BL 10/1/05) [808]

6894 Paine, Thomas. *Rights of Man and Common Sense* (10–12). 1994, Knopf $17.00 (978-0-679-43314-9). This volume contains the basic writing of Thomas Paine including *Rights of Man*. [320]

6895 *The Paris Review Interviews, II* (10–12). 2007, Picador paper $16.00 (978-0-312-36314-7). Authors including William Faulkner, Toni Morrison, and Stephen King reveal details about their lives and their work in this fascinating compilation. (Rev: SLJ 1/08)

6896 Rich, Simon. *Ant Farm and Other Desperate Situations* (11–12). 2007, Random House paper $12.95

(978-1-4000-6588-2). Rich finds humor in the most dire situations in this collection of sketches, many of which appeared in the *Harvard Lampoon*. (Rev: BL 3/1/07) [818]

6897 Roberts, Cokie. *We Are Our Mothers' Daughters* (10–12). 1998, Morrow $19.95 (978-0-688-15198-0). This noted TV and radio news correspondent has written a series of personal essays on her relationship to her mother and family and the place of women and mothers in the world today. (Rev: BL 4/15/98; SLJ 8/98) [808]

6898 Rooney, Andrew A. *A Few Minutes with Andy Rooney* (9–12). 1982, Warner paper $4.95 (978-0-446-34766-2). This is a collection of short humorous pieces by the writer who gained prominence on television's "60 Minutes." Also use *And More by Andy Rooney* (1983). [808.7]

6899 Safire, William, ed. *Lend Me Your Ears: Great Speeches in History. Rev. ed.* ((9–12). 1997, Norton $39.95 (978-0-393-04005-0). Memorable speeches from across history and around the world are accompanied by Safire's own tips on making a great speech. [808.85]

6900 Sanders, Scott R. *Writing from the Center* (10–12). 1995, Indiana Univ $25.00 (978-0-253-32941-7). In this collection of 12 inspiring and penetrating essays, the author examines technology, community, love and strife within families, and the search for spiritual ground as seen through the eyes of a midwesterner. (Rev: SLJ 2/96) [808]

6901 Sante, Luc. *Kill All Your Darlings: Pieces, 1900-2005* (9–12). 2007, Yeti $17.95 (978-1-891241-53-6). Sante presents a collection of essays on pop culture icons in music, art, and politics and social customs, such as New Year's Eve and life in New York over the years. (Rev: BL 7/07) [306.0973]

6902 Slater, Lauren, and Robert Atwan, eds. *The Best American Essays, 2006* (10–12). 2006, Houghton Mifflin $28.00 (978-0-618-70531-3); paper $14.00 (978-0-618-70529-0). This is a collection of 20 moving personal essays on a variety of subjects, compiled from magazines such as *The New Yorker* and *Vanity Fair*. (Rev: BL 10/15/06) [808]

6903 Soto, Gary. *The Effects of Knut Hamsun on a Fresno Boy: Recollections and Short Essays* (10–12). 2000, Persea paper $12.95 (978-0-89255-254-2). This is a collection of 48 short autobiographical essays by this renowned Chicano writer, who muses on his child-

hood, his vocation, and his racial heritage. (Rev: BL 11/1/00) [811]

6904 Stewart, Jon, et al. *Earth (The Book): A Visitor's Guide to the Human Race* (10–12). Illus. 2010, Grand Central $27.99 (978-044657922-3). *The Daily Show* writers provide extraterrestrials with an irreverent guide to our planet and our dubious accomplishments. ⌒ (Rev: BLO 10/1–15/10) [818.5407]

6905 Thoreau, Henry David. *A Week on the Concord and Merrimack Rivers; Walden, or, Life in the Woods; The Maine Woods; Cape Cod* (10–12). 1985, Library of America $35.00 (978-0-940450-27-1). This volume contains the most important of Thoreau's writing, including *Walden*. [818]

6906 Twain, Mark. *The Innocents Abroad and Roughing It* (9–12). 1984, Library of America $35.00 (978-0-940450-25-7). This volume of Twain's works includes two travel books, *The Innocents Abroad* and *Roughing It*. [818]

6907 Twain, Mark. *Life on the Mississippi* (10–12). 1983, Buccaneer LB $25.95 (978-0-89966-469-9). A nonfiction account of life on the Mississippi, with many humorous passages. First published in 1874. [817]

6908 Twain, Mark. *Roughing It* (10–12). 1986, Buccaneer LB $25.95 (978-0-89966-524-5); paper $15.00 (978-0-14-039010-0). A humorous account first published in 1872 of a trip to California and Hawaii. [817]

6909 Wallace, David Foster, ed. *The Best American Essays, 2007* (9–12). 2007, Houghton Mifflin $28.00 (978-0-618-70926-7); paper $14.00 (978-0-618-70927-4). Mark Danner, Elaine Scarry, and Cynthia Ozick are only three of the writers featured in this collection of wide-ranging essays. (Rev: BL 10/15/07) [808]

6910 Woolf, Virginia. *The Virginia Woolf Reader* (10–12). Ed. by Mitchell A. Leaska. 1984, Harcourt paper $16.00 (978-0-15-693590-6). A generous selection from the works of Woolf including excerpts from novels, essays, short stories, letters, and diary entries. [828]

6911 Zaleski, Philip, ed. *The Best Spiritual Writing, 2002* (10–12). 2002, HarperSanFrancisco paper $15.95 (978-0-06-050603-2). For his 2002 anthology of the best in spiritual writing, editor Philip Zaleski has gathered together such diverse pieces as a tale of how a predominantly white Ohio community embraced its first black basketball coach and a portrait of Muslim pacifist Abdul Ghaffar Khan. (Rev: BL 9/15/02) [810.8]

Speeches, Essays, and General Literary Works

6912 Angelou, Maya. *Wouldn't Take Nothing for My Journey Now* (10–12). 1993, Random House $17.00 (978-0-679-42743-8). In this collection of inspiring essays, author/poet Maya Angelou muses on a wide variety of subjects, including domestic violence, respect, jealousy, and death. (Rev: BL 9/1/93; SLJ 5/94) [814]

6913 Davis, Jill, ed. *Open Your Eyes: Extraordinary Experiences in Faraway Places* (8–12). 2003, Viking $16.99 (978-0-670-03616-5). Ten writers, among them Lois Lowry and Harry Mazer, tell stories about how travel changed their lives. (Rev: BL 1/1–15/04; HBG 4/04; SLJ 1/04; VOYA 4/04) [910.4]

6914 Halliburton, Warren J., ed. *Historic Speeches of African Americans* (7–12). Series: African American Experience. 1993, Watts LB $24.00 (978-0-531-11034-8). Chronologically organized speeches by such leaders as Sojourner Truth, Frederick Douglass, Marcus Garvey, James Baldwin, Angela Davis, and Jesse Jackson. (Rev: BL 4/15/93; SLJ 7/93) [815]

6915 *Lines in the Sand: New Writing on War and Peace* (6–10). 2003, Disinformation paper $7.95 (978-0-9729529-1-0). More than 150 children from around the world have written essays, stories, and memoirs or drawn pictures calling for peace. (Rev: BL 2/1/04) [808.803]

6916 McIntire, Suzanne, ed. *The American Heritage Book of Great American Speeches for Young People* (7–12). 2001, Wiley paper $14.95 (978-0-471-38942-2). More than 100 key speeches by individuals ranging from politicians to athletes are provided in this single volume. (Rev: SLJ 12/01) [815.008]

6917 *Merlyn's Pen: Fiction, Essays, and Poems by American Teens* (6–12). 2001, Merlyn's Pen paper $15.95 (978-1-886427-50-1). This annual anthology of teen writings offers selected poetry, fiction, and essays written by students in middle school and high school. (Rev: VOYA 8/01)

6918 Meyer, Stephanie H., and John Meyer, eds. *Friends and Family* (6–12). Series: Teen Ink. 2001, Health Communications paper $12.95 (978-1-55874-931-3). This collection of fiction, poetry, and essays written by young people that appeared in *Teen Ink* magazine is organized by themes such as "Snapshots: Friends and Family" and "Out of Focus: Facing Challenges." (Rev: BL 1/1–15/02; SLJ 12/01) [810.8]

6919 Meyer, Stephanie H., and John Meyer, eds. *Love and Relationships* (6–12). Series: Teen Ink. 2002, Health Communications paper $12.95 (978-1-55874-969-6). In this collection of poems, essays, and photographs, teens give voice to their thoughts about love in all its many forms. ℮ (Rev: SLJ 8/02; VOYA 8/02) [810.8]

6920 Meyer, Stephanie H., and John Meyer, eds. *Teen Ink 2: More Voices, More Visions* (6–12). Series: Teen Ink. 2001, Health Communications paper $12.95 (978-1-55874-913-9). This collection of teen creativity includes poems, essays, short stories, and photographs that reflect their views on such themes as Family, Love, Friends, Challenges, Imagination, Fitting In, Memories, and School Days. ℮ (Rev: SLJ 8/01; VOYA 12/01)

6921 Remini, Robert V., and Terry Golway, eds. *Fellow Citizens: The Penguin Book of U.S. Presidential Addresses* (10–12). 2008, Penguin paper $16.00 (978-014311453-6). Well-respected historians Remini and Golway examine every presidential inaugural speech and comment on each one's eloquence and historical impact. (Rev: BL 8/08) [352.23]

6922 Roosevelt, Theodore. *Theodore Roosevelt's History of the United States: His Own Words, Selected and Arranged by Daniel Ruddy* (10–12). Ed. by Daniel Ruddy. 2010, HarperCollins $27.99 (978-006183432-5). The outspoken former president offers his frequently blunt opinions on everything from discrimination to history to Jefferson Davis in this collection of writings and speeches. ℮ (Rev: BLO 5/1–15/10) [973.91]

6923 Rosen, Roger, and Patra McSharry, eds. *East-West: The Landscape Within* (7–12). Series: World Issues. 1992, Rosen LB $21.95 (978-0-8239-1375-6); paper $11.95 (978-0-8239-1376-3). Short stories and nonfiction selections by diverse authors of varied nationalities on their cultures' beliefs and values, among them the Dalai Lama, Joseph Campbell, Lydia Minatoya, and Aung Aung Taik. (Rev: BL 12/15/92; SLJ 2/93) [909]

6924 Sedaris, David. *Dress Your Family in Corduroy and Denim* (8–12). 2004, Little, Brown $24.95 (978-0-316-14346-2). In this collection of 27 essays, David Sedaris mines humor from a series of incidents in his personal life, some of which were not at all funny when they happened. (Rev: SLJ 1/05) [813]

6925 Stavans, Ilan, ed. *The Norton Anthology of Latino Literature* (10–12). 2010, Norton $59.95 (978-039308007-0). This engaging collection of Latino literature spanning four centuries is an excellent resource for those who want to explore Latino poetry, letters, stories, and more. (Rev: BL 9/1–15/10) [810.8]

6926 Woolf, Virginia. *A Room of One's Own* (10–12). 1991, Harcourt $17.00 (978-0-15-178733-3). This is a modern classic by the great English novelist and essayist. [305.4]

6927 WritersCorps Youth. *Smart Mouth: Poetry and Prose by WritersCorps Youth* (7–12). 2000, San Francisco WritersCorps paper $12.95 (978-1-888048-05-6). This anthology offers multiple selections of both prose and poetry written by students who participated in the WritersCorps program. (Rev: VOYA 6/01)

Literary History and Criticism

General and Miscellaneous

6928 Bloom, Harold, ed. *Anton Chekhov* (10–12). Series: Bloom's Biocritiques. 2002, Chelsea House LB $35.00 (978-0-7910-6381-1). A biography of Chekhov is followed by a series of critical essays on his plays and fiction. [891.7]

6929 Currie, Stephen. *African American Literature* (7–10). Illus. Series: Lucent Library of Black History. 2011, Gale/Lucent LB $33.45 (978-142050383-8). Useful for researchers, this is a review of African American literature from the 1600s forward. (Rev: BL 2/1/12; SLJ 2/12) [810.9]

6930 Hahn, Daniel, and Leonie Flynn, eds. *The Ultimate Teen Book Guide* (7–12). 2008, Walker paper $16.95 (978-0-8027-9731-5). This well-organized guide contains more than 700 well-written reviews of teen fiction, nonfiction, classics and graphic novels. (Rev: SLJ 3/08)

6931 Kanigel, Robert. *Vintage Reading: From Plato to Bradbury, a Personal Tour of Some of the World's Best Books* (10–12). 1998, Bancroft paper $16.95 (978-0-9631246-7-8). In a series of essays, the author presents his personal choices of the world's best books, among them *Pride and Prejudice* and *Native Son*. (Rev: BL 2/15/98; SLJ 9/98) [807]

6932 Kappel, Lawrence, ed. *Autobiography* (9–12). Series: Literary Movements and Genres. 2001, Greenhaven paper $24.95 (978-0-7377-0672-7). This collection of essays explores various forms of personal narratives, with material on different aspects of this genre and how some authors blend fact and fiction. (Rev: BL 8/01; SLJ 10/01) [808.4]

6933 Knox, Bernard, ed. *The Norton Book of Classical Literature* (9–12). 1993, Norton $29.95 (978-0-393-03426-4). More than 300 pieces of classical literature, primarily Greek but also some Roman. (Rev: BL 2/15/93) [880]

6934 Tackach, James, ed. *Slave Narratives* (9–12). Series: Literary Movements and Genres. 2001, Greenhaven paper $24.95 (978-0-7377-0549-2). Critical essays discuss the origins and development of slave narratives, with material on important works in this genre and information on gender issues. (Rev: BL 8/01; SLJ 6/01) [808.4]

Fiction

General and Miscellaneous

6935 Barlowe, Wayne Douglas, and Neil Duskis. *Barlowe's Guide to Fantasy* (7–12). 1996, HarperCollins paper $19.95 (978-0-06-100817-7). Using double-page spreads, this handsome book covers the history of fantasy literature from ancient times to the present by highlighting 50 examples, among them *Beowulf*, *Wind in the Willows*, and *Mists of Avalon*. (Rev: VOYA 10/97)

6936 Clute, John, and John Grant, eds. *The Encyclopedia of Fantasy* (10–12). 1997, St. Martin's $75.00 (978-0-312-15897-2). This comprehensive research on fantasy literature and media includes material on authors, awards, movies, TV shows, themes, and articles on the fantasy literature of various countries. (Rev: BL 9/1/97; SLJ 8/97) [813]

6937 Cunningham, Jesse, ed. *Science Fiction* (9–12). Series: Literary Movements and Genres. 2002, Gale paper $36.20 (978-0-7377-0572-0). Explores the history and contemporary status of science fiction writing, with an emphasis on landmark writers and their creations. (Rev: BL 4/15/02) [808.3]

6938 Dickerson, Matthew, and David O'Hara. *From Homer to Harry Potter: A Handbook on Myth and Fantasy* (10–12). 2006, Brazos Press paper $19.99 (978-1-58743-133-3). An overview of the history of myths and fairy tales, from *Beowulf* to today, including modern fantasy stories and their influences. (Rev: BL 5/1/06) [809]

6939 Jones, Stephen, and Kim Newman, eds. *Horror: Another 100 Best Books* (9–12). 2005, Carroll & Graf paper $15.95 (978-0-7867-1577-0). In this collection of 100 essays, writers and critics single out their horror favorites, using a broad definition of the term *horror*. (Rev: BL 9/15/05) [808.83]

6940 Reid, Suzanne Elizabeth. *Presenting Young Adult Science Fiction* (7–12). Series: Twayne's United States Authors. 1998, Twayne $35.00 (978-0-8057-1653-5). This comprehensive introduction to science fiction describes the history of the genre, profiles such classical masters as Asimov, Bradbury, Heinlein, and Le Guin, and presents members of the new generation, among them Orson Scott Card, Pamela Service, Piers Anthony, and Douglas Adams. (Rev: SLJ 6/99) [808.3]

6941 Sorrentino, Paul M. *Student Companion to Stephen Crane* (9–12). Series: Student Companions to Classic Writers. 2005, Greenwood $39.95 (978-0-313-33104-6). Discusses the life, background, and writings of the 19th-century author known best for *The Red Badge of Courage*. (Rev: SLJ 5/06)

6942 Yolen, Jane. *Touch Magic: Fantasy, Faerie, and Folklore in the Literature of Childhood*. 2nd ed. (10–12). 2000, August House paper $11.95 (978-0-87483-591-5). This celebrated author has written a series of critical essays on the nature of fantasy and folklore and their lasting importance in literature for young people. (Rev: BL 5/15/00) [398]

Europe

Great Britain and Ireland

6943 Beetz, Kirk H. *Exploring C. S. Lewis' The Chronicles of Narnia* (10–12). 2001, Beacham paper $24.95 (978-0-933833-58-6). This is a critical examination of *The Chronicles of Narnia*, with material on characters, mythology, backgrounds, and literary importance. (Rev: SLJ 8/01) [823.009]

6944 Blom, Margaret Howard. *Charlotte Brontë* (10–12). 1977, Twayne $21.95 (978-0-8057-6673-8). A critical study of the life and works of the creator of *Jane Eyre*. [823.09]

6945 Bloom, Harold, ed. *Elizabeth Bennet* (10–12). Series: Bloom's Major Literary Characters. 2004, Chelsea House LB $40.00 (978-0-7910-7672-9). An analysis of the character and importance of the key figure in Jane Austen's *Pride and Prejudice*. (Rev: SLJ 9/04) [813]

6946 Bloom, Harold, ed. *King Arthur* (10–12). Series: Bloom's Major Literary Characters. 2003, Chelsea House LB $40.00 (978-0-7910-7670-5). Arthurian tales by Thomas Malory, Alfred Lord Tennyson, and T. H. White are dissected by scholars exploring such topics as spirituality, violence, treason, and the origins of the legends themselves. (Rev: SLJ 6/04) [813]

6947 Bloom, Harold, ed. *Thomas Hardy* (10–12). Series: Bloom's Major Novelists. 2003, Chelsea House LB $31.95 (978-0-7910-6348-4). This book covers the life of Hardy with an emphasis on his novels, their plots, construction, characters, and critical interpretations. [823.009]

6948 Bloom, Harold, ed. *The Victorian Novel* (10–12). Series: Bloom's Period Studies. 2004, Chelsea House $45.00 (978-0-7910-7678-1). The works of such authors as Dickens, the Brontës, Trollope, Thackeray, and Hardy are examined in this history of the Victorian novel. (Rev: SLJ 3/04) [820.9]

6949 Brontë, Charlotte. *Jane Eyre* (8–12). Ed. by Beth Newman. Series: Case Studies in Contemporary Criticism. 1964, St. Martin's paper $18.74 (978-031209545-1). An author biography is accompanied by brief critical comments, plot and theme analysis, and a list of characters.

6950 Crusie, Jennifer, ed. *Flirting with Pride and Prejudice: Fresh Perspectives on the Original Chick-Lit Masterpiece* (9–12). 2005, BenBella paper $14.95 (978-1-932100-72-3). This entertaining collection of thought-provoking essays explores various aspects of Jane Austen's *Pride and Prejudice*, including the suggestion that the classic novel provides a model for contemporary chick-lit fiction. (Rev: BL 10/1/05) [823]

6951 Dailey, Donna, and John Toniedi. *London* (9–12). Series: Bloom's Literary Places. 2005, Chelsea House LB $40.00 (978-0-7910-7841-9). This wide-ranging volume takes readers on a tour of London sites of literary significance, placing them in historical and social context. (Rev: SLJ 9/05) [823]

6952 Dickens, Charles. *The Annotated Christmas Carol: A Christmas Carol in Prose* (10–12). Illus. by John Leech. 2003, Norton $29.95 (978-0-393-05158-2). With many illustrations by a number of artists plus extensive quotations from many sources, this volume offers a biography of Dickens, discussion of the story's publication and reception, and the original text with many footnotes and supplementary facts. (Rev: SLJ 1/04) [823]

6953 Hornback, Bert G. *Great Expectations: A Novel of Friendship* (9–12). 1987, Twayne $29.00 (978-0-8057-7956-1). A critical analysis of this novel often studied in high school. (Rev: BL 5/15/87; SLJ 9/87) [823]

6954 Johnson, Claudia Durst, ed. *Issues of Class in Jane Austen's Pride and Prejudice* (10–12). Illus. Series: Social Issues in Literature. 2008, Gale/Greenhaven $36.20 (978-073774258-9); paper $24.95 (978-073774259-6). High schoolers studying *Pride and Prejudice* will find this collection of essays useful for reports and class discussions; also included are a chronology of Austen's life, discussion questions, and a bibliography. (Rev: BL 1/1–15/09) [823]

6955 Kelly, Richard. *Lewis Carroll* (9–12). 1990, Twayne $39.00 (978-0-8057-6988-3). A critical survey of Carroll's writings concentrating on the Alice books and *The Hunting of the Snark*. [828]

6956 Nelson, Harland S. *Charles Dickens* (10–12). 1981, Twayne $32.00 (978-0-8057-6805-3). This account focuses on five novels, including *David Copperfield, Oliver Twist,* and *Great Expectations*. [823.09]

6957 Saposnik, Irving S. *Robert Louis Stevenson* (10–12). 1974, Twayne $22.95 (978-0-8057-1517-0). Biographical information accompanies an analysis of Stevenson's works in several genres. [828]

6958 Shippey, T. A. *J. R. R. Tolkien: Author of the Century* (10–12). 2001, Houghton Mifflin $26.00 (978-0-618-12764-1). A thorough, critical analysis of Tolkien's books with particular emphasis on "the greatest book of the 20th century," *The Lord of the Rings*. (Rev: BL 5/15/01*) [823]

6959 Smyer, Richard I. *Animal Farm: Pastoralism and Politics* (9–12). 1988, Twayne paper $13.95 (978-0-8057-8030-7). A detailed analysis of this allegory that explains its structure and layers of meaning. (Rev: SLJ 8/88) [823.09]

6960 Tolkien, J. R. R. *The Shaping of Middle-Earth* (9–12). 1986, Houghton Mifflin $29.95 (978-0-395-42501-5). Background notes and information on the famous fantasy written by Tolkien and edited by his son. (Rev: BL 11/86; SLJ 3/87) [808.3]

6961 *Treasure Island and the Pirates of the 18th Century* (9–12). Series: Looking at Literature Through Primary Sources. 2004, Rosen LB $29.25 (978-0-8239-4507-8). After a brief biography of Robert Louis Stevenson, there is a plot summary plus information on 19th-century pirates and seafaring that is tied to specific passages. (Rev: BL 11/15/04) [823]

6962 Wagoner, Mary S. *Agatha Christie* (9–12). 1986, Twayne $22.95 (978-0-8057-6936-4). An analysis of this mystery story writer's works with an accompanying brief biography. (Rev: BL 2/1/87) [823]

6963 Watkins, Tony. *Dark Matter: Shedding Light on Philip Pullman's Trilogy* (11–12). 2006, InterVarsity paper $15.00 (978-0-8308-3379-5). An examination and critique, suitable for advanced teens interested in literature, of Pullman's popular His Dark Materials trilogy by a Christian reader. (Rev: BL 5/1/06) [823]

Other Countries

6964 Bloom, Harold, ed. *Hermann Hesse* (10–12). Series: Modern Critical Views. 2002, Chelsea House $45.00 (978-0-7910-7398-8). Besides biographical information on Hesse, this group of essays discusses his writing style, themes, characters, philosophy, and influences. (Rev: SLJ 9/03) [838]

6965 Prose, Francine. *Anne Frank: The Book, the Life, the Afterlife* (10–12). 2009, HarperCollins $24.99 (978-006143079-4). Francine Prose makes the case that Anne Frank was a skilled young writer, well aware of the darker aspects of the Holocaust, and that her diary has not been served well by later editing and portrayals on stage and film that portray her as a somewhat naive idealist. (Rev: BL 9/09*) [940.53]

United States

6966 Bail, Paul. *John Saul: A Critical Companion* (10–12). Series: Critical Companions to Popular Contemporary Writers. 1996, Greenwood $46.95 (978-0-313-29575-1). An extensive analysis of the works of John Saul, a famous writer of horror stories whose works include *Suffer the Children* and *Black Lightning*. (Rev: SLJ 10/96) [813]

6967 Baym, Nina. *The Scarlet Letter: A Reading* (10–12). 1986, Twayne $36.00 (978-0-8057-7957-8); paper $13.95 (978-0-8057-8001-7). An analysis of this novel, often studied in high school, plus an introduction to the life of its author, Nathaniel Hawthorne. (Rev: BL 7/86; SLJ 5/87) [813]

6968 Bishop, Rudine Sims. *Presenting Walter Dean Myers* (9–12). 1990, Twayne $28.00 (978-0-8057-8214-1). A profile of the life and work of this African American writer with an analysis of each of his most important books. (Rev: BL 10/15/90) [813]

6969 Bloom, Harold, ed. *Asian-American Writers* (10–12). Series: Bloom's Modern Critical Views. 2009, Bloom's Literary Criticism $45 (978-1-60413-401-8). Intended for students in advanced courses, this volume contains scholarly essays that examine Asian American fiction writers and how cultural identity is manifested in their writing. (Rev: SLJ 9/09)

6970 Bloom, Harold, ed. *George F. Babbitt* (10–12). Series: Bloom's Major Literary Characters. 2003, Chelsea House LB $40.00 (978-0-7910-7667-5). In addition to essays by contributors (including H. L. Mencken and Gore Vidal) on Sinclair Lewis and his work, this volume includes a character profile and a bibliography. (Rev: SLJ 5/04)

6971 Bloom, Harold, ed. *Truman Capote* (9–12). Series: Bloom's Modern Critical Views. 2003, Chelsea House LB $45.00 (978-0-7910-7397-1). Eight scholarly essays analyze Capote's key works and explore the influences of his life and times. (Rev: SLJ 2/04) [813]

6972 Bryfonski, Dedria, ed. *Peer Pressure in Robert Cormier's The Chocolate War* (9–12). Illus. Series: Social Issues in Literature. 2009, Gale/Greenhaven LB $37.30 (978-073774620-4); paper $25.70 (9780737746211). This collection of previously published articles focuses on the author and the themes prevalent in his work. Also in this series: *Violence in William Golding's Lord of the Flies* (2009). (Rev: BL 3/15/10) [813]

6973 Cady, Edwin H. *Stephen Crane* (10–12). 1980, Twayne $39.00 (978-0-8057-7299-9). An analysis of the short-lived author's work and career. [813.09]

6974 Campbell, Patricia J. *Presenting Robert Cormier. 2nd ed.* (9–12). 1989, Twayne $29.00 (978-0-8057-8212-7). A profile of this author and his work through the novel *Fade*. (Rev: BL 9/15/89; SLJ 12/89) [813.54]

6975 Cart, Michael. *Presenting Robert Lipsyte* (8–12). 1995, Twayne $29.00 (978-0-8057-4151-3). A probing look at Lipsyte's life and work. (Rev: BL 6/1–15/95; VOYA 6/96) [813]

6976 Colson, Mary. *The Story Behind Toni Morrison's The Bluest Eye* (9–12). Series: History in Literature. 2006, Heinemann LB $23.00 (978-1-4034-8212-9). Young fans of Morrison's novel will appreciate this critique of the book and its themes of racial identity and beauty; information on the author's life and how her experiences connect with those in the book aid comprehension. (Rev: BL 10/15/06; SLJ 4/07) [813.54]

6977 Crowe, Chris. *Presenting Mildred D. Taylor* (6–12). Series: United States Authors. 1999, Twayne $39.00 (978-0-8057-1687-0). As well as some biographical material, this book gives an analysis of Taylor's works, their historical context, and a history of racism and the civil rights movement in Mississippi. (Rev: BL 2/15/00; VOYA 6/00) [813]

6978 Daly, Jay. *Presenting S. E. Hinton. 2nd ed.* (9–12). 1989, Twayne $28.00 (978-0-8057-8211-0). A biography of this popular author plus an analysis of her work, including *Taming the Star Runner*. (Rev: BL 9/15/89; SLJ 3/90) [813.54]

6979 Doyle, Paul A. *Pearl S. Buck* (10–12). 1980, Twayne $22.95 (978-0-8057-7325-5). A critical study of this writer that covers such topics as plots, themes, and writing style. [813.09]

6980 Gates, Henry Louis, Jr, and K. A. Appiah. *Langston Hughes: Critical Perspectives Past and Present* (10–12). 1993, Amistad paper $14.95 (978-1-56743-029-5). The poetry and prose of Langston Hughes are critically appraised in this collection of reviews and essays by such leading literary lights as Carl Van Vechten, Richard Wright, James Baldwin, and Countee Cullen. [818]

6981 Gibson, Donald B. *The Red Badge of Courage* (10–12). 1988, Twayne $30.00 (978-0-8057-7961-5); paper $18.00 (978-0-8057-8014-7). Part of an extensive series from Twayne that provides in-depth analysis of the great works of literature. (Rev: SLJ 8/88) [813.09]

6982 Glenn, Wendy J. *Laurie Halse Anderson: Speaking in Tongues* (7–12). Illus. Series: Scarecrow Studies in Young Adult Literature. 2010, Scarecrow $40 (978-081087281-3). This well-researched volume analyzes the works of YA author Laurie Halse Anderson and includes excerpts from interviews, blog posts, and essays by the author. (Rev: BLO 1/1–15/10; VOYA 4/10) [813]

6983 Johnson-Feelings, Dianne. *Presenting Laurence Yep* (8–12). 1995, Twayne $35.00 (978-0-8057-8201-1). A biocritical study that uses material from the Chinese American's autobiography, *The Lost Garden*. (Rev: BL 12/15/95) [813]

6984 Johnson, Claudia Durst. *Understanding Adventures of Huckleberry Finn: A Student Casebook to Issues, Sources, and Historic Documents* (10–12). Series: Literature in Context. 1996, Greenwood $51.95 (978-0-313-29327-6). This work not only analyzes the novel, but also discusses censorship, racism, the life of Mark Twain, and the complex social and political issues of the time. (Rev: SLJ 12/96) [813]

6985 Johnson, Claudia Durst, ed. *Racism in Maya Angelou's I Know Why the Caged Bird Sings* (9–12). 2008, Gale LB $36.20 (978-0-7377-3901-5); paper $24.95 (978-0-7807-3773-0). Articles, many by university professors, explore the themes of Angelou's works and associated political and social issues. (Rev: BL 4/1/08; SLJ 4/08) [813]

6986 Jones, Patrick. *What's So Scary About R. L. Stine?* (9–12). Series: Scarecrow Studies in Young Adult Literature. 1998, Scarecrow $32.50 (978-0-8108-3468-2). An appreciation and critique of R. L. Stine's popular horror stories for young people. (Rev: SLJ 7/99) [813]

6987 Jones, Sharon S. *Critical Companion to Zora Neale Hurston: A Literary Reference to Her Life and Work* (10–12). Illus. 2009, Facts on File $75 (978-081606885-2). This is a comprehensive book detailing the life and work of Zora Neale Hurston including critical essays, influences, and photographs. (Rev: BL 4–5/09) [813]

6988 Jordan, Shirley M., ed. *Broken Silences: Interviews with Black and White Women Writers* (9–12). 1993, Rutgers $59.00 (978-0-8135-1932-6). Focuses on how African American and white women writers have depicted each other in their stories, with specific inquiries into each author's handling of race in her work. (Rev: BL 5/1/93) [810.9]

6989 Ladd, Andrew, and Karen Meyers. *Romanticism and Transcendentalism, 1800–1860* (9–12). Series: Backgrounds to American Literature. 2010, Chelsea House $40 (978-1-60413-486-5). An appealing, well-illustrated guide to the romantic and transcendentalist era in American literature with discussion of the foundations of the movement and some of the key writers involved, including Hawthorne and Melville. **e** (Rev: LMC 11–12/10) [810.9]

6990 Lathbury, Roger, and Karen Meyers. *Realism and Regionalism, 1860–1910* (9–12). Series: Backgrounds to American Literature. 2010, Chelsea House $40 (978-1-60413-487-2). An appealing, well-illustrated guide to realism and regionalism in American literature with discussion of the foundations of the movements, slave narratives, and some of the key writers involved, including Twain, James, Wharton, Crane, Sinclair, and Dreiser. **e** (Rev: LMC 11–12/10) [810.9]

6991 MacDonald, Gina. *James Clavell: A Critical Companion* (10–12). Series: Critical Companions to Popular Contemporary Writers. 1996, Greenwood $46.95 (978-0-313-29494-5). In addition to biographical information and general material on Clavell's writing, this book contains chapters on *King Rat, Shogun,* and other individual works. (Rev: SLJ 10/96) [813]

6992 MacRae, Cathi Dunn. *Presenting Young Adult Fantasy Fiction* (7–12). 1998, Twayne $35.00 (978-0-8057-8220-2). An excellent survey of current writers of fantasy plus in-depth interviews with Terry Brooks, Barbara Hambly, Jane Yolen, and Meredith Ann Pierce. (Rev: BL 1/1–15/99; VOYA 8/98) [813]

6993 Meyers, Karen. *Colonialism and the Revolutionary Period, Beginnings to 1800* (9–12). Series: Backgrounds to American Literature. 2010, Chelsea House $40 (978-1-60413-485-8). An appealing, well-illustrated guide to American literature in the early years of the nation with discussion of the historical context. **e** (Rev: LMC 11–12/10) [810.9]

6994 O'Connell, Jennifer, ed. *Everything I Needed to Know About Being a Girl I Learned from Judy Blume* (9–12). 2007, Pocket $23.00 (978-1-4165-3104-3). Women writers, including Meg Cabot and Kayla Perrin, celebrate the work of Judy Blume and the freedom and insight that her books brought to them as adolescents and sometimes as adults. (Rev: BL 6/1–15/07) [813.54]

6995 Pennell, Melissa McFarland. *Student Companion to Edith Wharton* (10–12). Series: Student Companions to Classic Writers. 2003, Greenwood $46.95 (978-0-313-31715-6). Introduces the life and works of the American writer, with critical analysis of her works, including *Ethan Frome* and *The Age of Innocence*. (Rev: SLJ 4/04) [8113]

6996 Perret, Patti. *The Faces of Science Fiction* (9–12). 1984, St. Martin's $35.00 (978-0-698-10348-1); paper $11.95 (978-0-685-10347-0). Photographs of 80 major science fiction and fantasy writers are given as well as comments on their work. (Rev: BL 2/15/85) [813]

6997 Pingelton, Timothy J. *A Student's Guide to Ernest Hemingway* (7–12). Series: Understanding Literature. 2005, Enslow LB $27.93 (978-0-7660-2431-1). Introduces Hemingway's life and works, with analysis of some of his best-known writings. (Rev: SLJ 10/05) [813]

6998 Rangno, Erik V. R., and Karen Meyers. *Contemporary American Literature, 1945 to Present* (9–12). Series: Backgrounds to American Literature. 2010, Chelsea House $40 (978-1-60413-489-6). With chapters on the 1950s, 1960s, contemporary poetry, new voices, the "postmodern moment," and millenial voices, this volume places the literature of this period in historical and social context. **e** (Rev: LMC 11–12/10) [810.0]

6999 Reed, Arthea J. S. *Norma Fox Mazer: A Writer's World* (9–12). Series: Scarecrow Studies in Young Adult Literature. 2001, Scarecrow LB $29.50 (978-0-8108-3814-7). The central themes and writing techniques of YA author Mazer are explored in this objective overview of her novels and short stories, which draws on interviews with the author as well as other sources. (Rev: BL 6/1–15/01; SLJ 6/01) [813]

7000 Reid, Suzanne Elizabeth. *Presenting Cynthia Voigt* (9–12). 1995, Twayne $35.00 (978-0-8057-8219-6). A biographical sketch of this popular author, followed by literary criticism in thematic chapters of 20 of Voigt's young adult novels. (Rev: BL 1/1/95; VOYA 4/96) [813]

7001 Reino, Joseph. *Stephen King: The First Decade, Carrie to Pet Sematary* (9–12). 1988, Twayne $39.00 (978-0-8057-7512-9). An analysis of King's most important works published from 1973 to 1983. (Rev: BL 2/15/88) [813]

7002 Russell, Sharon A. *Revisiting Stephen King: A Critical Companion* (9–12). Series: Critical Companions to Popular Contemporary Writers. 2002, Greenwood $46.95 (978-0-313-31788-0). Plots, characters, themes, and literary techniques in eight of King's novels are discussed. [813.009]

7003 Salvner, Gary M. *Presenting Gary Paulsen* (9–12). Series: Young Adult Authors. 1996, Macmillan $28.00 (978-0-8057-4150-6). After two chapters on the eventful life of Gary Paulsen, the author of more than 100 books for people of all ages, this book analyzes the major themes and subjects of his young adult novels. (Rev: VOYA 8/98) [813]

7004 Schultz, Jeffrey, and Luchen Li. *Critical Companion to John Steinbeck: A Literary Reference to His Life*

and Work (9–12). 2005, Facts on File $65.00 (978-0-8160-4300-2). This comprehensive volume offers a biography of Steinbeck, alphabetically arranged articles on his works, and information about people, places, and topics relating to his life and work. (Rev: BL 2/1/06; SLJ 2/06) [813]

7005 Showalter, Elaine, ed. *The Vintage Book of American Women Writers* (10–12). 2011, Vintage paper $17.95 (978-14000344-5-1). A rich anthology featuring the works of 79 American women writers who shaped the country's literary history, from Puritan poet to modern literary novelist. **e** (Rev: BL 1/1–15/11) [810.8]

7006 Stover, Leon. *Robert A. Heinlein* (9–12). 1987, Twayne $21.95 (978-0-8057-7509-9). An in-depth study of the science fiction of this acclaimed American writer. (Rev: BL 11/15/87) [813]

7007 Stover, Lois T. *Presenting Phyllis Reynolds Naylor* (9–12). 1997, Twayne $35.00 (978-0-8057-7805-2). In this scholarly work, the author presents a brief biography and an analysis of the Alice series, several novels, and other writings, showing how Naylor's life experiences are reflected in her major themes: how characters cope with family instability, how they develop a sense of self apart from family, and how they solve moral dilemmas. (Rev: SLJ 4/98; VOYA 10/98) [813]

7008 Stowe, Harriet Beecher. *The Annotated Uncle Tom's Cabin* (11–12). 2006, Norton $39.95 (978-0-393-05946-5). An annotated version of the classic novel, with illustrations spanning decades of images, and discussion of changes in social attitudes. (Rev: BL 2/1/07) [813]

7009 *A Student's Guide to Jack London* (7–12). Series: Understanding Literature. 2007, Enslow LB $20.95 (978-0-7660-2707-7). Provides summaries and critical analysis of London's most famous books as well as information on his life and beliefs. (Rev: BL 9/1/07) [813]

7010 Szumski, Bonnie, ed. *Readings on Edgar Allan Poe* (10–12). Series: Literary Companions. 1997, Greenhaven LB $26.20 (978-0-565-10589-1). The first essays explore Poe's many accomplishments, among them the perfection of the short story form and creation of the detective story, followed by critiques of his most popular works. (Rev: BL 12/15/97) [813.09]

7011 Trembley, Elizabeth A. *Michael Crichton: A Critical Companion* (10–12). 1996, Greenwood LB $29.95 (978-0-313-29414-3). A carefully researched book that gives a biography of Crichton plus an analysis of 10 of his most popular books, beginning with *The Andromeda Strain*. (Rev: VOYA 10/96) [813]

7012 Vincent, Bev. *The Road to the Dark Tower: Exploring Stephen King's Magnum Opus* (9–12). 2004, NAL paper $14.95 (978-0-451-21304-4). A useful companion to King's seven-volume Dark Tower series, with the story behind the writing of the series, a book-by-book analysis, and comments on links with other King novels. (Rev: BL 10/1/04) [813]

7013 Weidt, Maryann N. *Presenting Judy Blume* (9–12). 1989, Twayne $29.00 (978-0-8057-8208-0). A biography and a thorough analysis of Judy Blume's work with asides from both critics and Ms. Blume. (Rev: BL 11/1/89; VOYA 12/89) [813]

7014 Wiener, Gary, ed. *Readings on The Grapes of Wrath* (10–12). Series: Literary Companions. 1998, Greenhaven LB $220.96 (978-0-565-10955-4); paper $22.45 (978-1-56510-954-4). The saga of the Joad family is covered in this anthology that includes writings on the novel's creation, characters, themes, and structure,

and an evaluation of its merits and flaws. (Rev: BL 9/15/98) [813]

Other Regions and Countries

7015 Shea, George. *A Reader's Guide to Chinua Achebe's Things Fall Apart* (9–12). Series: Multicultural Literature. 2008, Enslow LB $23.95 (978-0-7660-2831-9). An examination of the important 1958 novel, with material on Achebe; for advanced readers. (Rev: BL 2/8/08) [823]

Plays and Poetry

General and Miscellaneous

7016 *Ancient Egyptian Literature* (10–12). Trans. by John L. Foster. 2001, Univ. of Texas paper $21.95 (978-0-292-72527-0). An amazing collection of poems, some of the first ever written and many translated from ancient Egyptian hieroglyphics. (Rev: BL 6/1–15/01) [893]

7017 Auslander, Joseph, and Frank Ernest Hill. *The Winged Horse: The Story of Poets and Their Poetry* (10–12). 1969, Haskell House LB $75.00 (978-0-8383-0328-3). This book, first published in 1928, gives a history of world poetry from its beginning to the early 20th century. [809.1]

7018 Chaucer, Geoffrey. *The Portable Chaucer. Rev. ed.* (10–12). Trans. by Theodore Morrison. 1975, Viking paper $17.00 (978-0-14-015081-0). An excellent collection of the works of Chaucer including selections from *The Canterbury Tales* and *Troilus and Cressida.* [821]

7019 Dabrowski, Kristen. *Ten-Minute Plays for Teens: Comedy, Vol. 8* (9–12). Series: Young Actors. 2006, Smith & Kraus paper $16.95 (978-1-57525-443-2). Twelve plays — each including two scenes and four monologues — deal with topics close to teen hearts and are supported by "Character Questions for Actors," "Playwright's Checklist," and a "Talk Back!" section with discussion questions. Also recommended is *Ten-Minute Plays for Teens: Drama. Vol. 9* (2006). (Rev: SLJ 4/07)

7020 Dante, Alighieri, and Mark Musa. *The Portable Dante* (10–12). 1995, Penguin paper $18.00 (978-0-14-243754-4). Contains complete verse translations of both the *Divine Comedy* and *La Vita Nuova.* [851]

7021 Deutsch, Babette. *Poetry Handbook: A Dictionary of Terms. 4th ed.* (7–12). 1981, Barnes & Noble paper $14.00 (978-0-06-463548-6). The standard introduction to the technical aspects of poetry through definitions of terms with examples. [808.1]

7022 Heaney, Seamus. *Opened Ground: Selected Poems, 1966-1996* (10–12). 1998, Farrar paper $16.00 (978-0-374-52678-8). The Nobel Prize winner's most important works are collected in this volume. [821]

7023 Housman, A. E. *The Collected Poems of A. E. Housman* (10–12). 1965, Henry Holt paper $16.00 (978-0-8050-0547-9). The authorized edition of the poems of this great English writer. [821]

7024 Ionesco, Eugene. *Four Plays* (10–12). Trans. by Donald M. Allen. 1958, Grove paper $13.00 (978-0-8021-3079-2). A collection of four of the most popular plays by this modern playwright. [842]

7025 Ionesco, Eugene. *Rhinoceros, and Other Plays* (10–12). Trans. by Derek Prouse. 1960, Grove paper $10.00 (978-0-8021-3098-3). Three plays, including *Rhinoceros,* by one of the leaders of the movement known as "theater of the absurd." [842]

7026 Lithgow, John, ed. *The Poet's Corner: The One-and-Only Poetry Book for the Whole Family* (7–12). 2007, Grand Central $24.99 (978-0-446-58002-1). Well-known poems by English and American poets are accompanied by conversational commentary, quotations, and other items of interest. ∩ (Rev: BL 10/15/07) [821.008]

7027 Milstein, Janet. *The Ultimate Audition Book for Teens: 111 One-Minute Monologues* (10–12). 2000, Smith & Kraus $11.95 (978-1-57525-236-0). An excellent resource for would-be actors who are looking for age-appropriate audition material, this collection of one-minute monologues is divided into comic and dramatic scenarios. (Rev: BL 1/1–15/01; SLJ 3/01) [812]

7028 Milton, John. *The Portable Milton* (10–12). 1949, Viking paper $18.00 (978-0-14-015044-5). A fine selection of Milton's prose and poetry, including such lengthy poems as *Paradise Lost* and *Paradise Regained*. [828]

7029 Nardo, Don, ed. *Readings on Medea* (9–12). Series: Literary Companion. 2000, Greenhaven paper $24.95 (978-0-7377-0402-0). The history of the famous Greek play is included in this collection, as well as material on its plot, characters, and themes. (Rev: BL 11/15/00) [882]

7030 Pomerance, Bernard. *The Elephant Man: A Play* (10–12). 1979, Grove paper $11.00 (978-0-8021-3041-9). The full text of the play that later became a successful motion picture based on a true story about the British medical phenomenon. [822]

7031 Smith, Helaine L. *Masterpieces of Classic Greek Drama* (9–12). Series: Greenwood Introduces Literary Masterpieces. 2005, Greenwood $49.95 (978-0-313-33268-5). Discusses plays by Aeschylus, Sophocles, Euripides, and Aristophanes. (Rev: SLJ 5/06) [882]

7032 Vecchione, Patrice, ed. *The Body Eclectic: An Anthology of Poems* (8–12). 2002, Henry Holt $16.95 (978-0-8050-6935-8). A collection of poems, both contemporary and classic, that look at parts of the body from serious, comic, tragic, reflective, and romantic points of view. (Rev: BL 7/02; HB 7–8/02; HBG 10/02; SLJ 8/02; VOYA 8/02) [808.81]

Europe

Great Britain

7033 Houle, Michelle M. *Modern British Poetry: "The World Is Never the Same"* (9–12). Illus. Series: Poetry Rocks! 2010, Enslow LB $34.60 (978-076603278-1). Eleven British poets including Alfred Lord Tennyson and Dylan Thomas are introduced to readers via pithy biographical sketches, excerpts, and literary analysis. (Rev: BL 3/15/10) [821]

7034 Johanson, Paula. *Early British Poetry: "Words That Burn"* (9–12). Series: Poetry Rocks! 2009, Enslow LB $34.60 (978-0-7660-3276-7). Chaucer, Spenser, Shakespeare, Donne, Milton, Blake, Wordsworth, and Keats are among the poets introduced in this volume that provides brief biographical information, two or more poems or excerpts, and discussion of themes and techniques. (Rev: BL 10/1/09; LMC 3–4/10) [821.009]

Shakespeare

7035 Bloom, Harold. *Shakespeare: The Invention of the Human* (10–12). 1998, Riverhead paper $20.00 (978-1-57322-751-3). In this thought-provoking study of Shakespeare's plays, Bloom underlines Shakespeare's

contribution to our understanding of human personality. (Rev: BL 10/1/98) [822.3]

7036 Bloom, Harold, ed. *Romeo and Juliet* (9–12). Series: Bloom's Guides. 2005, Chelsea House $30.00 (978-0-7910-8170-9). A critical analysis of the tale about ill-fated teen lovers, with essays that examine the characters and such topics as Shakespeare's treatment of adolescents. (Rev: SLJ 7/05) [822.3]

7037 Bloom, Harold, ed. *Shakespeare's Histories* (10–12). Series: Major Dramatists. 1999, Chelsea House $31.95 (978-0-7910-5241-9). Readings on *Richard III*, *Henry IV* (parts 1 and 2), and *Henry V*, for the advanced student of Shakespeare. (Rev: BL 4/1/00; SLJ 3/00) [822.3]

7038 Cahn, Victor L. *The Plays of Shakespeare: A Thematic Guide* (10–12). 2001, Greenwood $65.00 (978-0-313-30981-6). This book presents 19 thematic essays on Shakespeare's plays that treat such subjects as fate, honor, justice, love, money, and power. [822.3]

7039 Fallon, Robert Thomas. *A Theatergoer's Guide to Shakespeare* (10–12). 2001, Ivan R. Dee $29.95 (978-1-56663-342-0). The author gives a detailed plot summary of each of Shakespeare's plays with accompanying background material. (Rev: BL 4/15/01) [822]

7040 Ford, John R. *Twelfth Night: A Guide to the Play* (11–12). Series: Greenwood Guides to Shakespeare. 2005, Greenwood LB $75 (978-0-313-31700-2). A detailed guide to Shakespeare's play, including discussions of its context, sources, structure, themes, textual history, critical interpretations, and so forth. (Rev: SLJ 5/06)

7041 Gurr, Andrew, and John Orrell. *Rebuilding Shakespeare's Globe* (9–12). 1989, Routledge $25.00 (978-0-685-26528-4). A history of the project in London to rebuild the Globe as it was originally. [822.3]

7042 Lynch, Jack. *Becoming Shakespeare: The Unlikely Afterlife That Turned a Provincial Playwright into the Bard* (9–12). 2007, Walker $24.95 (978-0-8027-1566-1). The puritans shut down England's theaters soon after the death of Shakespeare in 1616; after nearly half a century of dormancy they were reopened and the literary and theatrical writings of Shakespeare were in need of revival. This book looks at the personalities and politics that were associated with the process of that revival during the next couple of centuries and the emergence of his status from a provincial playwright to the literary giant he is known as today. (Rev: BL 7/07) [822]

7043 Olster, Fredi, and Rick Hamilton. *A Midsummer Night's Dream: A Workbook for Students* (8–12). Series: Discovering Shakespeare. 1996, Smith & Kraus paper $19.95 (978-1-57525-042-7). The text of the play is presented in a double-page, four-column format that provides stage directions, scene description, and the original text, plus a version in the vernacular. Supplemental background material is also appended. (Rev: BL 1/1–15/97; SLJ 12/96; VOYA 2/97) [822.3]

7044 Olster, Fredi, and Rick Hamilton. *Romeo and Juliet: A Workbook for Students* (8–12). Series: Discovering Shakespeare. 1996, Smith & Kraus paper $19.95 (978-1-57525-044-1). This Shakespearean tragedy is presented in a four-column format that gives the original text, stage directions, scene descriptions, and a reworking into modern English. (Rev: BL 1/1–15/97; VOYA 2/97) [822.3]

7045 Olster, Fredi, and Rick Hamilton. *The Taming of the Shrew* (7–12). Series: Discovering Shakespeare. 1997, Smith & Kraus paper $19.95 (978-1-57525-046-5). This guide to Shakespeare's comedy uses a paraphrased text opposite the original script with details on stage directions. (Rev: BL 2/15/97; SLJ 6/97; VOYA 2/97) [822.3]

7046 Page, Philip, and Marilyn Pettit, eds. *Romeo and Juliet* (8–11). Series: Picture This! Shakespeare. 2005, Barron's paper $7.99 (978-0-7641-3144-8). This attractive title uses both straight text and cartoon characters to present not only the full text of Shakespeare's tragic romance but also notes on devices and related information. (Rev: BL 3/15/05; SLJ 9/05) [745.1]

7047 Rosenblum, Joseph. *Shakespeare* (10–12). Series: Magill's Choice. 1998, Salem $62.00 (978-0-89356-966-2). Following a brief biography, this volume gives summaries and critical analysis of Shakespeare's plays and poetry. [822.3]

7048 Shakespeare, William. *Poems* (10–12). Series: Everyman's Library Pocket Poets. 1994, Knopf $12.50 (978-0-679-43320-0). This is a representative collection of Shakespeare's poetry. [821]

7049 Shakespeare, William. *The Sonnets* (9–12). 1997, Cambridge Univ. paper $14.00 (978-0-521-55947-8). Each of Shakespeare's 154 sonnets is accompanied by a brief critical discussion of its theme and possible meanings. [821]

7050 Whalen, Richard F. *Shakespeare: Who Was He? The Oxford Challenge to the Bard of Avon* (9–12). 1994, Praeger $41.95 (978-0-275-94850-4). Probes the authorship of the works of Shakespeare and presents evidence suggesting the plays were written by others. (Rev: BL 11/1/94) [822.3]

7051 Woodford, Donna. *Understanding King Lear: A Student Casebook to Issues, Sources, and Historical Documents* (9–12). Series: Literature in Context. 2004, Greenwood $51.95 (978-0-313-31936-5). This guide uses period documents and literature to help readers get the most from *King Lear*. (Rev: SLJ 3/05) [822.3]

United States

7052 Abbotson, Susan C. W. *Student Companion to Arthur Miller* (9–12). Series: Student Companions to Classic Writers. 2000, Greenwood LB $46.95 (978-0-313-30949-6). Following a biographical section, there is a critical examination of each of Miller's plays. (Rev: SLJ 11/00) [812]

7053 Albee, Edward. *Who's Afraid of Virginia Woolf? A Play* (10–12). 1962, Atheneum paper $6.99 (978-0-451-15871-0). The searing play about a marriage on the rocks by one of America's finest contemporary playwrights. [812]

7054 Bloom, Harold, ed. *August Wilson* (10–12). Series: Bloom's Major Dramatists. 2002, Chelsea House LB $31.95 (978-0-7910-6362-0). The life and works of this major African American playwright are the subjects of this collection of critical essays. [812]

7055 Borus, Audrey. *A Student's Guide to Emily Dickinson* (7–12). Series: Understanding Literature. 2005, Enslow LB $27.93 (978-0-7660-2285-0). Introduces Dickinson's life and poetry, with discussion of key themes, how to analyze the poems, and a glossary of terms. (Rev: SLJ 10/05) [813]

7056 Dickinson, Emily. *Final Harvest: Emily Dickinson's Poems* (9–12). 1961, Back Bay paper $14.95 (978-0-316-18415-1). A collection of poems by one of the most widely read American poets. [811]

7057 Dunkleberger, Amy. *A Student's Guide to Arthur Miller* (7–12). Series: Understanding Literature. 2005, Enslow LB $27.93 (978-0-7660-2432-8). Combines biographical information and discussion of Miller's key works. (Rev: SLJ 10/05) [813]

7058 Ferlazzo, Paul J. *Emily Dickinson* (10–12). 1976, Twayne $39.00 (978-0-8057-7180-0); paper $4.95 (978-0-672-61511-5). Analyzes such subjects in Dickinson's poetry as love, death, and nature. [811.09]

7059 Gerber, Philip. *Robert Frost* (10–12). 1982, Twayne $39.00 (978-0-8057-7348-4). This book concentrates on an analysis of Frost's work but also covers his life and career. [811.09]

7060 Giovanni, Nikki. *Blues: For All the Changes* (10–12). 1999, Morrow $15.00 (978-0-688-15698-5). A collection of poems by Nikki Giovanni, a writer popular with young adults. (Rev: BL 3/15/99) [811]

7061 Hughes, Langston. *Poems* (10–12). 1999, Knopf $12.50 (978-0-375-40551-8). This is a selection of poems by this important African American writer. [811]

7062 Inge, William. *4 Plays* (10–12). 1979, Grove $13.50 (978-0-8021-3209-3). Four of Inge's best plays: *Picnic, Bus Stop, The Dark at the Top of the Stairs,* and *Come Back, Little Sheba.* [812]

7063 Kaufman, Moises, et al. *The Laramie Project* (10–12). 2001, Vintage paper $11.00 (978-0-375-72719-1). This docudrama script tells about the homophobia in Laramie, Wyoming, that resulted in the torture and murder of Matthew Shepard. (Rev: BL 9/1/01; SLJ 11/01) [812]

7064 Lansana, Quraysh Ali. *They Shall Run: Harriet Tubman Poems* (10–12). 2004, Third World $20.00 (978-0-88378-257-6). These poems pay tribute to famous African Americans, chiefly Harriet Tubman. (Rev: BL 2/15/04) [811]

7065 Llanas, Sheila Griffin. *Contemporary American Poetry: "Not the End, But the Beginning"* (9–12). Illus. Series: Poetry Rocks! 2010, Enslow LB $34.60 (978-076603279-8). Eleven American poets including Sylvia Plath, Allen Ginsberg, and Billy Collins are introduced in this title that includes pithy biographical sketches, excerpts, and literary critique. (Rev: BL 3/15/10) [811]

7066 MacGowan, Christopher, ed. *Poetry for Young People: William Carlos Williams* (6–12). Illus. by Robert

Crockett. 2004, Sterling $14.95 (978-1-4027-0006-4). Thirty-one poems by Williams plus biographical and critical material are included in this excellent collection. (Rev: BL 3/1/04) [811]

7067 Moss, Leonard. *Arthur Miller* (10–12). 1980, Twayne $21.95 (978-0-8057-7311-8). A thorough review of the components of each of Miller's plays, their themes, and structure. [812.09]

7068 Mueller, Melinda. *What the Ice Gets: Shackleton's Antarctic Expedition, 1914-1916* (10–12). 2000, Van West paper $14.00 (978-0-9677021-1-7). The second expedition of Sir Ernest Shackleton is recounted in this unusual book-length poem. (Rev: BL 10/15/00) [811]

7069 Shange, Ntozake. *For Colored Girls Who Have Considered Suicide/When The Rainbow Is Enuf: A Choreopoem* (9–12). 1977, Macmillan paper $9.00 (978-0-684-84326-1). The joys and sorrows of being a black woman are celebrated in this prize-winning play. [812]

Language and Communication

Signs and Symbols

7070 Grayson, Gabriel. *Talking with Your Hands, Listening with Your Eyes: A Complete Photographic Guide to American Sign Language* (9–12). 2003, Square One paper $26.95 (978-0-7570-0007-2). This excellent guide to American Sign Language makes extensive use of photographs to show readers not only how to begin and end each sign but also to illustrate the appropriate facial expression for each. (Rev: BL 1/1–15/03*; SLJ 8/03) [419]

7071 Lewis, Karen B., and Roxanne Henderson. *Sign Language Made Simple* (9–12). 1997, Doubleday paper $12.99 (978-0-385-48857-0). This book explains the development of sign language and gives a short course on how to master it. [419]

Words and Languages

7072 *The Art of Reading: Forty Illustrators Celebrate RIF's 40th Anniversary* (7–10). 2005, Dutton $19.99 (978-0-525-47484-5). To mark Reading Is Fundamental's 40th birthday, 40 illustrators choose a favorite children's book, talk about its importance, and create an image that captures the spirit of the book; a large, attractive volume. (Rev: BL 7/05; SLJ 8/05*) [745.6]

7073 Balistreri, Maggie. *Evasion-English Dictionary* (9–12). 2003, Melville House paper $12.95 (978-0-9718659-7-6). A brief look at the real meanings of favorite teen words such as "like" and "whatever." (Rev: SLJ 1/04)

7074 Casagrande, June. *Grammar Snobs Are Great Big Meanies: A Guide to Language for Fun and Spite* (8–12). 2006, Penguin paper $14.00 (978-0-14-303683-8). A lighthearted review of the rules of grammar, from prepositions and split infinitives to new conventions for e-mail and text messaging. (Rev: BL 4/1/06) [428]

7075 Espinasse, Kristin. *Words in a French Life: Lessons in Love and Language from the South of France* (7–12). 2006, Simon & Schuster $18.00 (978-0-7432-8728-9). Beef up French vocabulary with this collection of amusing stories by an American living in France combined with useful lists of words and phrases. (Rev: BL 4/15/06) [305.81]

7076 Fox, Margalit. *Talking Hands* (9–12). 2007, Simon & Schuster $27.00 (978-0-7432-4712-2). *New York Times* reporter Margalit Fox tells of her experience of accompanying a group of researchers — linguists, psychologists, and neurologists — as they visit a remote Bedouin village in Israel to document a sign language used over three generations for both the hearing and deaf. (Rev: BL 8/07) [419]

7077 Gorrell, Gena K. *Say What? The Weird and Mysterious Journey of the English Language* (7–12). 2009, Tundra paper $10.95 (978-0-88776-878-1). A clever

and often amusing history of the English language that emphasizes external influences and language's ability to change with the times, with word exercises and guessing games. (Rev: SLJ 1/10; VOYA 2/10) [420.9]

7078 Harrison, K. David. *The Last Speakers: The Quest to Save the World's Most Endangered Languages* (10–12). 2010, National Geographic $27 (978-142620461-6). A fascinating exploration of the world's disappearing languages and some of their last speakers. ⓔ (Rev: BLO 9/1–15/10) [408.9]

7079 Kennedy, John. *Word Stems: A Dictionary* (10–12). 1996, Soho paper $12.00 (978-1-56947-051-0). Supplies the word stems for common words used in English and gives definitions and language roots for each. (Rev: SLJ 5/97) [420]

7080 MacNeil, Robert, and William Cran. *Do You Speak American?* (10–12). 2005, Doubleday $23.95 (978-0-385-51198-8). An entertaining exploration of the continuing evolution of English as spoken by Americans, as well as the many regional, racial, and ethnic variants of the language. (Rev: BL 12/1/04; SLJ 6/05) [427]

7081 Muschell, David. *What in the Word? Origins of Words Dealing with People and Places* (9–12). 1996, McGuinn & McGuire paper $14.95 (978-1-881117-14-8). Explains the origins of real and imaginary person and place names. (Rev: BL 1/1/91) [422]

7082 Singh, Simon. *The Code Book: The Evolution of Secrecy from Mary, Queen of Scots, to Quantum Cryptography* (10–12). 1999, Doubleday paper $15.00 (978-0-385-49532-5). The history and nature of codes and cryptology are discussed with material on Mary, Queen of Scots, inventor and mathematician Charles Babbage, and the Navajo code-talkers of World War II. (Rev: BL 9/1/99) [652]

7083 Strunk, William, and E. B. White. *The Elements of Style. 4th ed.* (10–12). 1999, Allyn & Bacon $14.95 (978-0-205-31342-6); paper $7.95 (978-0-205-30902-3). A simple, direct guide to proper usage and composition. [808]

7084 Truss, Lynne. *Eats, Shoots and Leaves: The Zero Tolerance Approach to Punctuation* (9–12). 2004, Gotham $19.95 (978-1-59240-087-4). A witty plea for proper punctuation. (Rev: BL 6/1–15/04; SLJ 8/04) [428.2]

7085 vos Savant, Marilyn. *The Art of Spelling: The Madness and the Method* (10–12). 2000, Norton paper $12.95 (978-0-393-32208-8). As well as analyzing why some people cannot spell, the author describes spelling rules, gives tips on spelling methods and 500 problem words, and discusses changes in pronunciation and usage. (Rev: BL 8/00) [421]

7086 Wade, Nicholas. *The Science Times Book of Language and Linguistics* (10–12). 2000, Lyons $25.00 (978-1-55821-934-2). The current state of research on language — its purposes, origins, and uses — is explored in this collection of interesting columns from the *New York Times.* (Rev: BL 2/15/00) [400]

7087 Winchester, Simon. *The Professor and the Madman: A Tale of Murder, Insanity, and the Making of the Oxford English Dictionary* (10–12). 1998, HarperCollins $23.00 (978-0-06-017596-2). The story of the writing of the famous *Oxford English Dictionary* and the relationship between its editor, James Murray, and Dr. William Chester Minor, a major contributor and former Civil War doctor who was a patient in England's most famous insane asylum during their entire collaboration. (Rev: BL 8/98; SLJ 3/99) [410]

Writing and the Media

General and Miscellaneous

7088 Bauer, Marion Dane. *Our Stories: A Fiction Workshop for Young Authors* (6–10). 1996, Clarion paper $6.95 (978-0-395-81599-1). Using critiques of 30 selections by students, the author explores such writing techniques as character development, dialogue, and point of view. (Rev: BL 10/15/96; SLJ 12/96; VOYA 12/96) [808.3]

7089 Bush, Valerie Chow, ed. *Jump: Poetry and Prose by WritersCorps Youth* (6–12). 2001, WritersCorps $12.95 (978-1-888048-06-3). This collection of prose and poetry showcases the creativity of teenage members of the San Francisco-based WritersCorps youth writing program. (Rev: VOYA 6/02)

7090 Currie, Stephen, ed. *Terrorism* (7–10). Series: Writing the Critical Essay. 2005, Gale LB $29.95 (978-0-7377-3206-1). Opposing viewpoints on terrorism are combined with tips for writing a succinct essay on the subject. (Rev: BL 3/1/06) [363.32]

7091 Dunn, Jessica, and Danielle Dunn. *A Teen's Guide to Getting Published: Publishing for Profit, Recognition, and Academic Success. 2nd ed.* (9–12). 2006, Prufrock paper $14.95 (978-1-59363-182-6). This new edition of a handy guide to getting published covers freelance work, self-publishing, how to get feedback, and includes information on contests, writing camps, writer-support blogs, and so forth. (Rev: SLJ 12/06)

7092 Fish, Stanley. *How to Write a Sentence and How to Read One* (10–12). 2011, HarperCollins $19.99 (978-006184054-8). Fish emphasizes a sentence's potential for purpose and beauty in this interesting guide for advanced writing students. ℮ (Rev: BL 12/1–15/10) [808]

7093 Francis, Barbara. *Other People's Words: What Plagiarism Is and How to Avoid It* (6–12). Series: Issues in Focus Today. 2005, Enslow LB $31.93 (978-

0-7660-2525-7). Practical suggestions about avoiding plagiarism are accompanied by examples of plagiarism through history and current instances of "borrowing" ideas and words. (Rev: SLJ 12/05)

7094 Friedman, Lauri S., ed. *The Iraq War* (9–12). Series: Writing the Critical Essay, An Opposing Viewpoints Guide. 2008, Gale/Greenhaven $29.95 (978-0-7377-4037-0). Articles presenting opposing views about the war in Iraq are juxtaposed with chapters explaining how to write your own analytical essay — creating an outline, presenting theories and conclusions, using quotations, finding and citing information, and so forth. (Rev: SLJ 1/1/09) [956]

7095 Gevinson, Tavi, ed. *Rookie Yearbook One* (9–12). Illus. 2012, Drawn & Quarterly paper $29.95 (978-17704611-2-3). A collection of essays, how-to articles, interviews, photo editorials, and illustrations from the popular feminist online magazine *Rookie*. (Rev: BLO 11/15/12; SLJ 2/13) [305.2352]

7096 Jean, Georges. *Writing: The Story of Alphabets and Scripts* (7–12). Series: Discoveries. 1992, Abrams paper $12.95 (978-0-8109-2893-0). Traces the beginnings of writing from the development of alphabets to printing and bookmaking, emphasizing the technological rather than intellectual aspects of the process. (Rev: BL 7/92) [652.1]

7097 Jones, Diana Wynne. *Reflections: On the Magic of Writing* (8–12). 2012, Greenwillow $24.99 (978-006221989-3). This collection of 28 essays about Jones's life and works was compiled before the author's death and will be of interest to her fans, young and old; includes a foreword by Neil Gaiman. (Rev: BL 11/1/12; HB 1–2/13; SLJ 1/13) [823]

7098 Kennedy, George, and Daryl Moen, eds. *What Good Is Journalism? How Reporters and Editors Are Saving America's Way of Life* (9–12). 2007, Univ. of Missouri $37.50 (978-0-8262-1730-1); paper $19.95

(978-0-8262-1731-8). American journalism is criticized and its history explored in this collection of essays by journalism professors who point out how the public is changing its choice of news sources and how media is growing in emerging democracies. (Rev: BL 7/07) [070.4]

7099 Levine, Gail Carson. *Writing Magic: Creating Stories That Fly* (5–10). 2006, HarperCollins $16.99 (978-0-06-051961-2); paper $5.99 (978-0-06-051960-5). Well-known author Levine provides upbeat, practical tips on such topics as finding story ideas, character and plot development, and investigating the possibility of publication. (Rev: BL 12/15/06; SLJ 2/07*)

7100 Orr, Tamra. *Extraordinary Essays* (9–12). Series: F. W. Prep. 2005, Scholastic $31.00 (978-0-531-16761-8); paper $9.95 (978-0-531-17576-7). From choosing a suitable topic to researching, writing, and revising, this is a practical and well-organized guide that also provides advice on preparing for the SAT essay. (Rev: BL 2/1/06; SLJ 1/06; VOYA 4/06) [808.4]

7101 Rooke, Constance, ed. *Writing Life: Celebrated Canadian and International Authors on Writing and Life* (9–12). 2006, McClelland & Stewart paper $18.95 (978-0-7710-7625-1). Essays by 50 writers — Marilynne Robinson, Margaret Atwood and Michael Ondaatje among them — explore the art and craft of writing in this inspiring and revealing collection. (Rev: SLJ 10/06)

7102 Senn, Joyce. *The Young People's Book of Quotations* (5–10). 1999, Millbrook LB $39.90 (978-0-7613-0267-4). Beginning with "accomplishment" and ending with "zoos," this is a collection of 2,000 quotations of special interest to young people, arranged by topic. (Rev: BL 3/1/99*; SLJ 4/99) [082]

7103 Skinner, Jeffrey, and Lee Martin, eds. *Passing the Word: Writers on Their Mentors* (10–12). 2001, Sarabande paper $16.95 (978-1-889330-59-4). This collection of tributes by writers to the writers who inspired them should interest aspiring young authors. (Rev: BL 6/1–15/01) [810.9]

7104 Wolf, Allan. *Immersed in Verse: An Informative, Slightly Irreverent and Totally Tremendous Guide to Living the Poet's Life* (6–12). Illus. by Tuesday Mourning. 2006, Sterling LB $14.95 (978-1-57990-628-3). A humorous and inspirational guide for young people interested in writing poetry, this is full of helpful tips and ends with useful appendixes. (Rev: SLJ 6/06*)

Books and Publishing

7105 Barry, Lynda. *What It Is* (9–12). Illus. 2008, Drawn & Quarterly $24.95 (978-189729935-7). Comics illustrator Barry presents an array of scrapbook-style collages and text as she explores the creative process and

encourages teens with imaginative activities. (Rev: BL 6/1–15/08; SLJ 9/08) [741.5]

7106 Bettley, James, ed. *The Art of the Book: From Medieval Manuscript to Graphic Novel* (10–12). 2001, Abrams $49.50 (978-0-8109-6572-0). From the collection of books at London's Victoria and Albert Museum comes this handsome book with each chapter focusing on a different aspect of bookmaking, including illustrations, typography, poetry, and children's books. (Rev: BL 8/01; SLJ 9/01) [741.64]

7107 Collins, Paul. *The Book of William: How Shakespeare's First Folio Conquered the World* (10–12). 2009, Bloomsbury $25 (978-159691195-6). A fascinating glimpse at the history of the surviving copies of Shakespeare's first collected edition of plays. (Rev: BL 7/09) [016.8223]

7108 Garcia, John. *The Success of Hispanic Magazine* (7–10). Series: Success. 1996, Walker LB $16.85 (978-0-8027-8310-3). A behind-the-scenes look at the magazine business, from starting out to marketing research, staffing, sales, circulation, and distribution. Traces an article from initial conception to final version and publication. (Rev: BL 5/15/96; SLJ 4/96) [051]

7109 Gerard, Carolyn Forcheand Philip, ed. *Writing Creative Nonfiction* (10–12). 2001, Fitzhenry & Whiteside paper $18.99 (978-1-884910-50-0). From the book proposal to the finished product, this is a guide to writing in various formats and genres — journals, essays, biography, nature writing, and plotted narrative. (Rev: BL 4/1/01) [808]

7110 Harper, Timothy, and Elizabeth Harper. *Your Name in Print: A Teen's Guide to Publishing for Fun, Profit and Academic Success* (8–12). 2005, St. Martin's paper $13.95 (978-0-312-33759-9). The Harpers (father and daughter) offer alternating how-to advice on writing and getting published in a variety of formats. (Rev: BL 9/1/05; SLJ 11/05; VOYA 8/05) [808]

7111 Olmert, Michael. *The Smithsonian Book of Books* (9–12). 1992, Smithsonian $49.95 (978-0-89599-030-3). Celebrates the powerful link between readers and the printed page as it follows books from the days of scribes to moveable type to children's book illustration. (Rev: BL 9/1/92; SLJ 1/93*) [002]

7112 Osen, Diane, ed. *The Book That Changed My Life: Interviews with National Book Award Winners and Finalists* (10–12). 2002, Modern Library paper $13.95 (978-0-679-78351-0). Fifteen authors talk about the books that most deeply affected their lives and helped to lay the groundwork for their own writings. (Rev: BL 9/1/02) [810.9]

7113 Pennac, Daniel. *The Rights of the Reader* (9–12). Trans. by Sarah Adams. Illus. by Quentin Blake. 2008, Candlewick $17.99 (978-076363801-6). This new translation of the 1992 French celebration of reading features playful illustration as it emphasizes the joys of literature. (Rev: BL 10/15/08; HB 5–6/09*) [028]

7114 Rosinsky, Natalie M. *Graphic Content! The Culture of Comic Books* (6–10). Illus. Series: Pop Culture Revolutions. 2010, Compass Point LB $31.99 (978-0-7565-4241-2). The history of comics from Captain America to the modern world of Web comics is captured in this guide, which spotlights the medium's role in pop culture. (Rev: BL 4/1/10; SLJ 5/10) [780.9]

7115 Slate, Barbara. *You Can Do a Graphic Novel* (7–12). Illus. 2010, Penguin paper $19.95 (978-1-59257-955-6). In addition to advice on drawing, writing, and layout, this volume discusses the creative process, creative block, and creating characters and includes a chapter of students' work. (Rev: SLJ 5/10) [741.5]

Print and Other Media

7116 Baker, Nicholson, and Margaret Brentano. *The World on Sunday: Graphic Art in Joseph Pulitzer's Newspaper (1898–1911)* (9–12). 2005, Bulfinch $50.00 (978-0-8212-6193-4). Baker and his wife present representative examples of the graphic art that appeared in the pages of the *Sunday World*, Joseph Pulitzer's groundbreaking New York City newspaper. (Rev: BL 10/15/05) [071]

7117 *The Best American Magazine Writing, 2005* (10–12). 2005, Columbia paper $16.95 (978-0-231-13781-2). This anthology showcases 17 articles that won National Magazine awards in 2005. (Rev: BL 11/1/05) [818]

7118 Bowers, Rick. *Superman versus the Ku Klux Klan: The True Story of How the Iconic Superhero Battled the Men of Hate* (6–10). Illus. 2012, National Geographic $16.95 (978-142630915-1); LB $25.90 (978-142630917-5). Tells the story of the creation of the Superman comics alongside the evolution of the Klan, emphasizing Superman's fight against prejudice and other evils. e (Rev: BL 2/15/12; HB 3–4/12; SLJ 3/12*; VOYA 4/12) [741.5]

7119 Boynton, Robert S. *The New New Journalism: Conversations with America's Best Nonfiction Writers on Their Craft* (9–12). 2005, Vintage paper $13.00 (978-1-4000-3356-0). Some of today's leading literary journalists, including Jon Krakauer, Susan Orlean, Lawrence Weschler, and Jane Kramer, offer insights into how they do their job. (Rev: BL 2/15/05) [071]

7120 *Breaking News: How the Associated Press Has Covered War, Peace, and Everything Else* (9–12). 2007, Princeton $40.00 (978-1-56898-689-0). A survey of AP's coverage of the news — wars, trials, elections, disasters, sports — since 1846, with photographs. (Rev: BL 3/1/07) [070.4]

7121 Cohen, Daniel. *Yellow Journalism: Scandal, Sensationalism, and Gossip in the Media* (6–12). 2000, Twenty-First Century LB $22.90 (978-0-7613-1502-5). The history of tabloid journalism and sensation-driven media is the focus of this fascinating book that uses many modern cases as examples. (Rev: BL 5/15/00; SLJ 8/00) [302.23]

7122 Connolly, Sean. *Advertisements* (10–12). Series: Getting the Message. 2010, Smart Apple Media LB $34.25 (978-1-59920-345-4). Each volume in this series explores an area of mass communication and how it has changed over time. (Rev: LMC 1–2/10)

7123 Cooke, John Byrne. *Reporting the War: Freedom of the Press from the American Revolution to the War on Terrorism* (9–12). 2007, Palgrave $24.95 (978-1-4039-7515-7). Journalism (and history) students will appreciate Cooke's review of the waxing and waning threats to press freedom over the years. (Rev: BL 11/1/07) [070.4]

7124 Curry, George E., and William Sandifer, eds. *The Best of Emerge Magazine* (11–12). 2003, Ballantine paper $19.95 (978-0-345-46228-2). For mature teens, this collection spotlights a wide array of topics of interest to African Americans and others, including affirmative action, mandatory sentencing for drug-related crimes, Malcolm X, the murder of Emmett Till, and racism on the Internet. (Rev: BL 7/03) [305.896]

7125 Day, Nancy. *Sensational TV: Trash or Journalism?* (7–10). Series: Issues in Focus. 1996, Enslow LB $26.60 (978-0-89490-733-3). A history of tabloid journalism both in print and on TV, plus a discussion of present-day controversies surrounding it. (Rev: BL 4/1/96; SLJ 4/96; VOYA 6/96) [791.45]

7126 DeFalco, Tom. *Hulk: The Incredible Guide* (6–12). 2003, DK $24.99 (978-0-7894-9771-0). Full-color illustrations spanning 40 years of comics portray the Hulk's life and escapades in this oversize volume. Also use *X-Men: The Ultimate Guide* (2003). (Rev: BL 5/1/03) [741.5]

7127 Durham, M. Gigi. *The Lolita Effect: The Media Sexualization of Young Girls and What We Can Do About It* (10–12). 2008, Overlook $24.95 (978-1-59020-063-6). An alarming examination of how America's girls are suffering from a "Lolita effect" that sexualizes and demeans the way society views them — and the way girls view themselves. (Rev: BL 4/15/08) [305.42]

7128 Elish, Dan. *Screenplays* (6–10). Illus. Series: Craft of Writing. 2011, Marshall Cavendish LB $34.21 (978-160870501-6). This book made for aspiring filmmakers includes a brief history of film before delving deeper into the actual craft of creating a screenplay. (Rev: BL 10/1/11; VOYA 2/12) [808.2]

7129 Ellis, Sherry, and Laurie Lamson, eds. *Now Write! Screenwriting: Screenwriting Exercises from Today's Best Writers and Teachers* (10–12). 2011, Tarcher paper $14.95 (978-15854285-1-9). With essays by some of Hollywood's most successful screenwriters, this volume offers helpful tips on how to craft a screenplay, writing exercises, and advice on what to do with the script when it's finished. **e** (Rev: BL 1/1–15/11) [808.2]

7130 *Embedded in America: The Onion Ad Nauseam Complete News Archives, Vol. 16* (10–12). 2005, Three Rivers paper $18.95 (978-1-4000-5456-5). The 16th collection of the faux news in which The Onion specializes; for mature readers. (Rev: BL 11/15/05) [071]

7131 Ferrari, Michelle, and James Tobin, eds. *Reporting America at War* (10–12). 2003, Hyperion $25.95 (978-1-4013-0072-2). A collection of reminiscences from 11 war correspondents of past and present, including Edward R. Murrow, Walter Cronkite, and Peter Arnett. (Rev: BL 10/15/03) [070.4]

7132 Fingeroth, Danny. *Superman on the Couch* (9–12). 2004, Continuum paper $23.95 (978-0-8264-1540-0). A thoughtful, easy-to-read exploration of superheroes — male and female — and why they are popular and what they tell us about ourselves. (Rev: SLJ 8/04) [741.5]

7133 Goulart, Ron. *Comic Book Culture: An Illustrated History* (9–12). 2000, Collectors $49.95 (978-1-888054-38-5). This lavishly illustrated volume traces the history of the comic book from the mid-1930s through the late 1940s, with 400 examples including such staples as *Batman*. (Rev: BL 9/1/00; VOYA 12/00) [741.5]

7134 Handel, Sherry S., ed. *Blue Jean: What Young Women Are Thinking, Saying, and Doing* (9–12). 2001, Blue Jean paper $14.95 (978-0-9706609-1-6). Taken from the pages of *blue jean* magazine, the articles in this anthology were written and edited by teenage girls and cover a broad range of subjects, including racial discrimination, sexual violence, homelessness, and the creation of e-zines. (Rev: BL 6/1–15/01; SLJ 8/01; VOYA 4/02) [305.235]

7135 Harvey, Robert C. *The Art of the Comic Book: An Aesthetic History* (10–12). Series: Studies in Popular Culture. 1996, Univ. Press of Mississippi paper $30.00 (978-0-87805-758-0). An overview of the first century of comic books and the evolution of the art therein. (Rev: BL 1/1–15/96) [741.5]

7136 Herriman, George. *Krazy and Ignatz: "Love Letters in Ancient Brick."* (11–12). 2002, Fantagraphics paper $10.99 (978-1-56097-507-6). Comic characters Krazy Kat, Ignatz, and Offissa Pupp are brought to life once again in a volume of black-and-white strips that first ran in 1927 and 1928; for mature teens. (Rev: BL 2/1/03)

7137 Kallen, Stuart A. *Manga* (9–12). Illus. Series: Eye on Art. 2011, Gale/Lucent LB $33.45 (978-142050535-1). Serious students of manga will enjoy this history of

the art form that covers common characteristics and the acceptance of female artists who expanded comics for girls. (Rev: BL 11/1/11; SLJ 1/12) [741.5]

7138 Ketcham, Hank. *Hank Ketcham's Complete Dennis the Menace: 1953–1954* (9–12). 2006, Fantagraphics $24.95 (978-1-56097-725-4). This collection of the beloved exploits of the mischievous Dennis will entertain both old fans of and newcomers to the comic. (Rev: BL 5/1/06) [741.5]

7139 Ketcham, Hank. *Hank Ketcham's Complete Dennis the Menace: 1955-1956* (7–12). 2006, Fantagraphics $24.95 (978-1-56097-770-4). A collection of the funny cartoons about Dennis and his antics. (Rev: BL 1/1–15/07) [741.5]

7140 Mills, Eleanor, and Kira Cochrane, eds. *Journalistas: 100 Years of the Best Writing and Reporting by Women Journalists* (9–12). 2006, Carroll & Graf paper $14.95 (978-0-7867-1667-8). A fascinating collection of the best in reporting by women over the past century, touching on many important subjects, including the need to choose between career and family. (Rev: BL 11/1/05) [071]

7141 Morrison, Grant, et al. *Deus ex Machina* (11–12). 2003, DC Comics paper $19.95 (978-1-56389-968-3). The final issues of Morrison's Animal Man series, collected here, feature a protagonist who is able to assume the abilities of assorted creatures in his ongoing battle for animal rights; for mature teens. (Rev: BL 12/1/03) [741.5]

7142 Nadel, Dan, ed. *Art Out of Time: Unknown Comics Visionaries, 1900-1969* (9–12). 2006, Abrams $40.00 (978-0-8109-5838-8). A selection of almost-forgotten comic-strip art taken from newspapers and comic books. (Rev: BL 8/06) [741.5]

7143 Niemi, Robert. *History in the Media: Film and Television* (9–12). 2006, ABC-CLIO $85 (978-1-57607-952-2). Niemi explores the portrayal of history in film and television, commenting on accuracy in works by broad category — military history, sports history, music history, art history, crime history, and so forth. (Rev: SLJ 1/07)

7144 *The Onion Presents Homeland Insecurity: Complete News Archives, Vol. 17* (9–12). 2006, Three Rivers paper $18.95 (978-0-307-33984-3). Every article that appeared in The Onion between November 2004 and December 2005 is included, poking fun at the common stupidity of both public officials and the average Joe. (Rev: BL 10/1/06) [081]

7145 Pavlik, John V. *Journalism and New Media* (10–12). 2001, Columbia paper $17.50 (978-0-231-11483-7). This account looks at how telecommunications, computing, and traditional media are coming together and how this combination is changing journalism. (Rev: BL 7/01; SLJ 2/02) [070.4]

7146 Phillips, Peter, et al. *Censored 2003: The Top 25 Censored Stories* (10–12). 2002, Seven Stories paper $17.95 (978-1-58322-515-8). The authors spotlight 25 specific cases where corporate interests have persuaded major news organizations to overlook important stories. (Rev: BL 11/15/02) [909.83]

7147 Pilcher, Tim, and Brad Brooks. *The Essential Guide to World Comics* (9–12). 2006, Collins & Brown paper $19.95 (978-1-84340-300-5). A survey of the best of the genre from around the globe. (Rev: BL 2/15/06) [741.5]

7148 Pilger, John, ed. *Tell Me No Lies: Investigative Journalism That Changed the World* (10–12). 2005, Thunder's Mouth paper $18.95 (978-1-56025-786-8). A collection of important pieces of investigative journalism, each preceded by biographical information and a note giving context. (Rev: BL 9/15/05) [071]

7149 Rollins, Prentis. *The Making of a Graphic Novel* (7–12). Illus. by author. 2006, Watson-Guptill paper $19.95 (978-0-8230-3053-8). One side of this "double-sided flip book" contains the text of a graphic novel called *The Resonator*; the other side holds a detailed account of the construction of this novel and the inspirations for the designs. (Rev: SLJ 3/06) [741.5]

7150 Schulz, Charles M. *The Complete Peanuts: 1950 to 1952* (7–12). Ed. by Gary Groth. Series: Peanuts. 2004, Fantagraphics paper $28.95 (978-1-56097-589-2). The first volume in a series collecting the entire 50 years of this classic comic strip. (Rev: BL 4/1/04) [741.5]

7151 Segar, E. C. *I Yam What I Yam!: E.C. Segar's Popeye, Vol. 1* (7–12). 2006, Fantagraphics $29.95 (978-1-56097-779-7). An oversize volume collecting the first two years of the Popeye comic strip. (Rev: BL 1/1–15/07) [741.5]

7152 Seib, Philip. *Going Live: Getting the News Right in a Real-Time, Online World* (10–12). 2001, Rowman & Littlefield $24.95 (978-0-7425-0900-9). This book observes the news-gathering styles of various media and finds that slick presentations may be becoming more important than accuracy. (Rev: BL 2/15/01) [070.1]

7153 Serrin, Judith, and William Serrin. *Muckraking! The Journalism That Changed America* (10–12). 2002, New Press paper $25.00 (978-1-56584-681-4). Positive newspaper stories that addressed societal ills and helped individuals and causes are the focus of this collection. (Rev: BL 7/02) [306]

7154 Shapiro, Bruce, ed. *Shaking the Foundations: 200 Years of American Investigative Journalism* (10–12). 2003, Thunder's Mouth paper $15.95 (978-1-56025-433-1). Two centuries of investigative journalism are celebrated in this imposing collection of articles, book excerpts, essays, and memoirs from such diverse reporters as Nellie Bly, Ida B. Wells, Upton Sinclair, Jack Anderson, Ralph Nader, Bob Woodward, and Carl Bernstein. (Rev: BL 9/15/03) [070.4]

7155 Sites, Kevin. *In the Hot Zone: One Man, One Year, Twenty Wars* (10–12). 2007, HarperCollins paper $15.95 (978-0-06-122875-9). As a journalist for Yahoo! Internet's "The Hot Zone," Sites covered 20 wars in a single year; here he tells his story and those of many of the people he interviewed. (Rev: BL 10/15/07) [355]

7156 Streissguth, Thomas. *Media Bias* (8–12). Series: Open for Debate. 2006, Benchmark LB $27.95 (978-0-7614-2296-9). After a discussion of media bias in America (from the first newspaper in 1690), Streissguth illustrates how public opinion can be swayed. (Rev: SLJ 4/07) [302.23]

7157 Todd, Mark, and Esther Pearl Watson. *Whatcha Mean, What's a Zine? The Art of Making Zines and Mini-Comics* (9–12). 2006, Houghton Mifflin paper $12.99 (978-0-618-56315-9). This attractively designed book provides a wealth of information on creating and marketing "zines," or self-published magazines. (Rev: BL 7/06; LMC 1/07; SLJ 8/06*) [070.5]

7158 Vaughan, Brian K., et al. *Y: The Last Man* (11–12). 2003, DC Comics paper $12.95 (978-1-56389-980-5). This volume contains the first five adventure-filled issues of *The Last Man* comic book series featuring Yorick Brown, son of a U.S. congresswoman and sole survivor of a bizarre plague that has killed the rest of the world's men. (Rev: BL 2/1/03) [741.5]

7159 Wallace, Mike, and Beth Knobel. *Heat and Light: Advice for the Next Generation of Journalists* (10–12). 2010, Three Rivers paper $14 (978-03074646-5-1). Two seasoned TV journalists offer valuable advice on the changing world of journalism, the importance of objectivity, and the traditional skills that remain applicable in the new environment. (Rev: BL 7/10) [070.92]

7160 Willems, Mo. *You Can Never Find a Rickshaw When It Monsoons: The World on One Cartoon a Day* (11–12). 2006, Hyperion paper $12.99 (978-0-7868-3474-7). This collection of Willems's cartoon artwork features scenes he sketched 15 years ago while traveling around the world after he finished college. (Rev: BL 7/06) [818]

7161 Wright, Bradford W. *Comic Book Nation: Transforming American Culture* (10–12). 2001, Johns Hopkins $41.95 (978-0-8018-6514-5). With references to politics, social trends, and pop culture, this account traces the history of comic books in the United States over the past 60 years. (Rev: BL 4/1/01) [741.5]

Biography, Memoirs, Etc.

General and Miscellaneous

7162 Berson, Robin Kadison. *Young Heroes in World History* (7–12). 1999, Greenwood $57.95 (978-0-313-30257-2). Real people — of both sexes and many nationalities — who achieved amazing things before the age of 25 are profiled, with quotations and black-and-white illustrations. (Rev: SLJ 1/00; VOYA 4/00) [920.02]

7163 Claxton, Eve, ed. *The World's Best Memoir Writing: The Literature from St. Augustine to Nelson Mandela* (10–12). 2007, Sourcebooks paper $15.95 (978-1-4022-0975-8). Henry James, Charles Chaplin, Vladimir Nabokov, Peter O'Toole, Helen Keller — these are only a handful of the writers represented in this diverse collection. (Rev: BL 10/15/07) [920.02]

7164 Gifford, Clive. *1000 Years of Famous People* (6–10). 2002, Kingfisher $24.95 (978-0-7534-5540-1). Brief descriptions of famous men and women in sports, medicine, politics, the arts, and other fields are included in this large-format book that is organized by subject and provides historical overviews of each discipline. (Rev: BL 12/1/02; HBG 3/03; SLJ 2/03; VOYA 6/03) [920.02]

7165 Hatch, Robert, and William Hatch. *The Hero Project: How We Met Our Greatest Heroes and What We Learned from Them* (8–12). 2005, McGraw-Hill paper $16.95 (978-0-07-144904-5). Fascinating interviews with such luminaries as Jackie Chan, Lance Armstrong, Orson Scott Card, Yo-Yo Ma, and Jimmy Carter result from the Hatch brothers' "hero project," which started when William was only 11 years old. (Rev: BL 9/15/05; SLJ 1/06) [920]

7166 Ledbetter, Suzann. *Shady Ladies: Nineteen Surprising and Rebellious American Women* (9–12). 2006, Forge $24.95 (978-0-7653-0827-6). Nineteen very different women who showed their independence in the 19th and early 20th centuries are portrayed in conversational narrative. (Rev: SLJ 1/07)

7167 Rose, Phyllis, ed. *The Norton Book of Women's Lives* (9–12). 1993, Norton $30.00 (978-0-393-03532-2). This culturally and socially diverse anthology presents biographies of 61 20th-century women, among them Virginia Woolf, Anais Nin, and Kate Simon. (Rev: BL 9/15/93) [920.72]

Adventurers and Explorers

Collective

7168 Bledsoe, Karen E. *Daredevils of the Air: Thrilling Tales of Pioneer Aviators* (7–12). Series: Avisson Young Adult. 2003, Avisson paper $19.95 (978-1-888105-58-2). The Wright brothers, Eddie Rickenbacker, Bessie Coleman, and Beryl Markham are among the early flyers profiled in stories of exciting aerial exploits. (Rev: SLJ 1/04) [920]

7169 Doherty, Kieran. *Ranchers, Homesteaders, and Traders: Frontiersmen of the South-Central States* (6–10). 2001, Oliver LB $22.95 (978-1-881508-53-3). Seven important settlers — including Sam Houston, Daniel Boone, and Eli Thayer — are introduced with plenty of historical and geographical background material. (Rev: BL 5/1/02; HBG 10/02; SLJ 1/02) [976]

7170 French, Francis, and Colin Burgess. *Into That Silent Sea: Trailblazers of the Space Era, 1961–1965* (9–12). 2007, Univ. of Nebraska $29.95 (978-0-8032-1146-9). Yuri Gagarin, Alan Shepard, Gus Grissom, and Valentina Tereshkova are among the well-known astronauts featured in this volume that also introduces characters such as Dee O'Hara, a nurse who worked with the Mercury astronauts. (Rev: BL 4/15/07) [920]

7171 Gueldenpfennig, Sonia. *Women in Space Who Changed the World* (8–10). Illus. Series: Great Women of Achievement. 2012, Rosen LB $33.25 (978-144885998-6). Caroline Herschel, Valentina Tereshkova, and Sally Ride are among the 11 women — representing several nationalities — profiled in this collective biography. (Rev: BL 6/12) [920]

7172 Hardesty, Von. *Black Wings: Courageous Stories of African Americans in Aviation and Space History* (9–12). 2008, Smithsonian $21.95 (978-0-06-126138-1). An inspiring account of black pioneers in aviation and space exploration. (Rev: BL 4/1/08; SLJ 6/08) [629.13092]

7173 MacPhee, Ross D. E. *Race to the End: Amundsen, Scott, and the Attainment of the South Pole* (10–12). Illus. 2010, Sterling $27.95 (978-140277029-6). Numerous photographs and Arctic artifacts enhance this account of Scott's and Amundsen's heroic treks to the South Pole. (Rev: BL 4/1–15/10) [920]

7174 Miller, Brandon Marie. *Women of the Frontier: 16 Tales of Trailblazing Homesteaders, Entrepreneurs, and Rabble-Rousers* (6–10). Illus. Series: Women of Action. 2013, Chicago Review $19.95 (978-188305297-3). Tells the stories of 16 western women and their often grueling experiences. ℯ Lexile 1160L (Rev: BL 12/1/12; SLJ 2/13) [920]

7175 Murphy, Claire Rudolf, and Jane G. Haigh. *Gold Rush Women* (7–12). 1997, Alaska Northwest paper $16.95 (978-0-88240-484-4). A collective biography of several women in the late 19th century who went to the Yukon and Alaska, where they panned for gold, ran boarding houses, and worked as dance hall girls and prostitutes. (Rev: BL 8/97; SLJ 11/97*) [920]

7176 Plimpton, George, ed. *As Told at the Explorers Club: More Than Fifty Gripping Tales of Adventure* (10–12). 2003, Lyons $24.95 (978-1-59228-035-3). Diverse tales of adventure and misadventure make for great browsing. (Rev: BL 11/15/03) [910.4]

7177 Richie, Jason. *Spectacular Space Travelers* (6–10). Series: Profiles. 2001, Oliver LB $19.95 (978-1-881508-71-7). Three Soviet cosmonauts and four American astronauts are profiled in this volume that provides a brief history of the space race. (Rev: HBG 10/02; SLJ 4/02) [629.45]

Individual

BLEDSOE, LUCY JANE

7178 Bledsoe, Lucy Jane. *The Ice Cave: A Woman's Adventures from the Mojave to the Antarctic* (9–12). 2006, Univ. of Wisconsin $19.95 (978-0-299-21844-7). A woman writes about her adventures facing all kinds of dangers and extremely harsh conditions and hoping to gain a deeper understanding of the wild. (Rev: BL 9/15/06) [910.409]

BROWNSWORTH, CLAIRE

7179 Brownsworth, Claire. *Big World: A Girl's Own Adventure* (9–12). 2006, Allen & Unwin paper $14.95 (978-1-74114-308-9). Australian outdoor adventurer Claire Brownsworth shares her triumphs and mishaps with warm narrative (and 16 pages of photographs) as she rock climbs, surfs, bikes, and sails in places around the world. (Rev: SLJ 6/06) [921]

CAHILL, TIM

7180 Cahill, Tim. *A Wolverine Is Eating My Leg* (9–12). 1989, Random House paper $13.00 (978-0-679-72026-3). A fascinating travel writer tells about his adventures around the world in this continuation of *Jaguars Ripped My Flesh* (1987). (Rev: BL 2/15/89) [921]

COCHRAN, JACQUELINE

7181 Rich, Doris L. *Jackie Cochran: Pilot in the Fastest Lane* (9–12). 2007, Univ. Press of Florida $24.95 (978-0-8130-3043-2). Jackie Cochran (1906-1980), a colonel in the Air Force Reserve, was the first woman to break the sound barrier and the first to fly a bomber across the Atlantic. (Rev: BL 3/15/07) [921]

COOK, CAPTAIN JAMES

7182 Lawlor, Laurie. *Magnificent Voyage: An American Adventurer on Captain James Cook's Final Expedition* (7–12). 2002, Holiday $22.95 (978-0-8234-1575-5). This absorbing account of Captain Cook's ill-fated efforts to locate the Northwest Passage gives details of the various difficulties encountered and of Cook's violent death. (Rev: BL 1/1–15/03; HBG 10/03; SLJ 2/03; VOYA 4/03) [910]

D'ABOVILLE, GERARD

7183 D'Aboville, Gerard. *Alone: The Man Who Braved the Vast Pacific — and Won* (9–12). 1993, Arcade $21.95 (978-1-55970-218-8). Journal entries describe d'Aboville's solo crossing of the Pacific in a 26-foot rowboat. (Rev: BL 7/93) [920]

DRAKE, SIR FRANCIS

7184 Kelsey, Harry. *Sir Francis Drake: The Queen's Pirate* (10–12). 1998, Yale Univ. $60.00 (978-0-300-07182-5); paper $18.95 (978-0-300-08963-9). Much about Drake's character is revealed in this well-researched volume. (Rev: BL 9/15/98) [921]

7185 Whitfield, Peter. *Sir Francis Drake* (8–12). Series: British Library Historic Lives. 2004, New York Univ. $25.00 (978-0-8147-9403-6). Drake's great naval accomplishments are balanced against less admirable activities. (Rev: BL 10/15/04) [942.05]

EARHART, AMELIA

7186 Rich, Doris L. *Amelia Earhart: A Biography* (10–12). 1989, Smithsonian paper $16.95 (978-1-56098-725-3). This scholarly account of Earhart's life emphasizes her flying career and the personalities behind her fame. [921]

7187 Wels, Susan. *Amelia Earhart: The Thrill of It* (9–12). Illus. 2009, Running Press $35 (978-076243763-4). This photo-biography recounts Earhart's life and presents recent attempts to unravel the circumstances around her disappearance in 1937. (Rev: BL 10/1/09) [921]

7188 Winters, Kathleen C. *Amelia Earhart: The Turbulent Life of an American Icon* (9–12). Illus. 2010, Palgrave $25 (978-023061669-1). Winters provides an unsentimental look at Earhart's life and achievements, pointing out the pressures that were on her to succeed even as other female flyers were receiving less public attention. ❁ (Rev: BL 12/1–15/10) [921]

GRAHAM, ROBIN LEE

7189 Graham, Robin Lee, and Derek Gill. *Dove* (7–12). 1991, HarperCollins paper $13.00 (978-0-06-092047-0). A five-year solo voyage around the world and a tender romance with a girl the author met in Fiji. [921]

HILLARY, SIR EDMUND

7190 Crompton, Samuel Willard. *Sir Edmund Hillary* (6–12). Series: Great Explorers. 2009, Chelsea House $30 (978-1-60413-420-9). With photographs and journal excerpts, this biography gives an overview of the life of the mountaineer, his celebrated expeditions, his relationship with the Sherpa people, and other exploration taking place at that time. (Rev: LMC 3–4/10) [921]

JENKINS, PETER

7191 Jenkins, Peter. *A Walk Across America* (10–12). 2001, $14.00 (978-0-06-095955-5). This amazing book, first published in 1979, describes the author's trek with his dog from New York State to the Gulf of Mexico. It is followed by the account of a 3-year walk from New Orleans to Oregon in *The Walk West: A Walk Across America 2* (1982). [917.3]

LEWIS AND CLARK

7192 Ambrose, Stephen E. *Undaunted Courage: Meriwether Lewis, Thomas Jefferson, and the Opening of the American West* (10–12). 1996, Simon & Schuster $27.50 (978-0-684-81107-9). Though primarily a biography of Meriwether Lewis, this book also provides fascinating sketches of Thomas Jefferson, William Clark, Sacagawea, and other contemporaries. (Rev: BL 1/1–15/96; SLJ 6/96) [921]

7193 Crompton, Samuel Willard. *Lewis and Clark* (6–12). Series: Great Explorers. 2009, Chelsea House $30 (978-1-60413-418-6). With photographs and journal excerpts, this biography gives an overview of the lives of these two explorers, their celebrated expedition, their treatment of the native peoples, and other exploration taking place at that time. **e** (Rev: LMC 3–4/10) [920]

LINDBERGH, ANNE MORROW

7194 Winters, Kathleen C. *Anne Morrow Lindbergh: First Lady of the Air* (9–12). 2006, Palgrave $24.95 (978-1-4039-6932-3). Her husband's fame sometimes overshadows Anne Morrow Lindbergh's achievements in aviation; she was one of the first female pilots, the first female glider pilot, and a skilled radio operator. (Rev: BL 10/15/06) [921]

LINDBERGH, CHARLES

7195 Davies, R. E. *Charles Lindbergh: An Airman, His Aircraft, and His Great Flights* (9–12). 1997, Paladwr $30.00 (978-1-888962-04-8). Using many illustrations, including full paintings of his aircraft, this biography of Lindbergh is a gripping, human document. (Rev: VOYA 6/98) [921]

7196 Denenberg, Barry. *An American Hero: The True Story of Charles A. Lindbergh* (8–12). 1996, Scholastic paper $16.95 (978-0-590-46923-4). Beginning with Lindbergh's transatlantic flight, this fascinating biography then recounts the story of his early years followed by details about his multifaceted life. (Rev: BL 3/15/96*; SLJ 7/96; VOYA 6/96) [921]

7197 Giblin, James Cross. *Charles A. Lindbergh: A Human Hero* (6–12). 1997, Clarion $22.00 (978-0-395-63389-2). A book about the public and private life of one of America's heroes that deals with his pro-Nazi sympathies and anti-Semitism, the adoration he received for his transatlantic flight, and pity the public felt for the kidnapping and murder of his child. (Rev: BL 9/15/97; HBG 3/98; SLJ 11/97*; VOYA 6/98) [921]

MAGELLAN, FERDINAND

7198 Stefoff, Rebecca. *Ferdinand Magellan and the Discovery of the World Ocean* (7–12). 1990, Chelsea LB

$32.00 (978-0-7910-1291-8). Using many quotations from original sources, this is an engrossing account of the explorer and his voyage. (Rev: BL 6/15/90) [921]

MARKHAM, BERYL

7199 Gourley, Catherine. *Beryl Markham: Never Turn Back* (6–10). Series: Bernard Biography. 1997, Conari paper $11.95 (978-1-57324-073-4). An exciting biography of the unconventional Englishwoman who was the first person to fly the Atlantic from east to west. (Rev: BL 3/15/97; SLJ 5/97; VOYA 12/97) [921]

7200 Trzebinski, Errol. *The Lives of Beryl Markham* (10–12). 1995, Norton paper $12.00 (978-0-393-31252-2). A deft and intimate portrait of the aviator who made a pioneering transatlantic flight. (Rev: BL 3/15/97) [921]

MARTIN, JESSE

7201 Martin, Jesse. *Kijana: The Real Story* (9–12). 2005, Allen & Unwin paper $16.95 (978-1-74114-429-1). Jesse Martin, who at 18 became the youngest person to sail alone around the world, chronicles a subsequent global tour he undertook with his brother and three friends. (Rev: BL 11/1/05) [910.41]

MIKKELSEN, EINAR

7202 Mikkelsen, Einar. *Two Against the Ice: A Classic Arctic Survival Story and a Remarkable Account of Companionship in the Face of Adversity* (10–12). Trans. by Maurice Michael. 2003, Steerforth paper $14.95 (978-1-58642-057-4). An exciting, simply told story of the author's harrowing trip by dogsled, accompanied by Iver Iversen, to retrieve the diaries of earlier Greenland explorers. (Rev: BL 1/1–15/03) [919.8]

POLO, MARCO

7203 Freedman, Russell. *The Adventures of Marco Polo* (7–10). Illus. by Bagram Ibatoulline. 2006, Scholastic $17.99 (978-0-439-52394-3). Vivid illustrations accompany the descriptions of Marco Polo's exciting journey to Kublai Khan's court. (Rev: BL 10/15/06; HB 11–12/06; SLJ 11/06*) [910.4]

7204 Polo, Marco. *The Travels of Marco Polo* (10–12). 1958, Penguin paper $13.95 (978-0-14-044057-7). One of many editions of this account kept by Marco Polo of his travels in Asia in the 13th century. [915]

RALEIGH, SIR WALTER

7205 Aronson, Marc. *Sir Walter Ralegh and the Quest for El Dorado* (7–10). 2000, Clarion $20.00 (978-0-395-84827-2). The fascinating life and times of the colorful Elizabethan explorer, with illustrations, maps, and quotations from Sir Walter himself. (Rev: BL 8/00; HB 9–10/00; HBG 9/00; SLJ 7/00*) [942.05]

RIDE, SALLY

7206 Camp, Carole Ann. *Sally Ride: First American Woman in Space* (6–10). Series: People to Know. 1997, Enslow LB $20.95 (978-0-89490-829-3). A lively account of Sally Ride's work as an astronaut and astrophysicist, with material on her training, shuttle flight, and life in microgravity. (Rev: BL 1/1–15/98; HBG 3/98; SLJ 12/97) [921]

SACAGAWEA

7207 Waldo, Donna Lee. *Sacajawea* (10–12). 1979, Avon paper $9.99 (978-0-380-84293-3). A lengthy account of the Indian girl who accompanied the Lewis and Clark Expedition. [921]

SHACKLETON, SIR ERNEST

7208 Johnson, Rebecca L. *Ernest Shackleton: Gripped by the Antarctic* (6–10). Series: Trailblazer Biographies. 2003, Carolrhoda LB $30.60 (978-0-87614-920-1). Photographs, anecdotes, and quotations are sprinkled throughout this exciting account of Shackleton's youth and famous expeditions. (Rev: BL 6/1–15/03; HBG 10/03; SLJ 8/03; VOYA 8/03) [919.8]

7209 Riffenburgh, Beau. *Shackleton's Forgotten Expedition: The Voyage of the Nimrod* (8–12). 2004, Bloomsbury $25.95 (978-1-58234-488-1). This story of Shackleton's first expedition to the Antarctic aboard the *Nimrod* underlines its significant scientific and exploratory achievements. (Rev: BL 10/15/04) [919.8]

VESPUCCI, AMERIGO

7210 Fernandez-Armesto, Felipe. *Amerigo: The Man Who Gave His Name to America* (9–12). 2007, Random House $24.95 (978-1-4000-6281-2). The explorer who gave America its name is revealed to be a flamboyant man of many enthusiasms if not many actual successes; historical background adds appeal to this profile. ∩ (Rev: BL 6/1–15/07) [921]

VIESTURS, ED

7211 Viesturs, Ed, and David Roberts. *The Will to Climb: Obsession and Commitment and the Quest to Climb Annapurna — the World's Deadliest Peak* (9–12). 2011, Crown $26 (978-030772042-9). Viesturs describes his own ascents of mountains including Annapurna as well as the exploits of other climbers. ∩ ℮ (Rev: BL 9/15/11) [921]

WILKINS, HUBERT

7212 Maynard, Jeff. *Wings of Ice: The Mystery of the Polar Air Race* (10–12). 2010, IPG/Vintage $19.95 (978-174166934-3). Why have the accomplishments of Australian explorer (George) Hubert Wilkins been largely ignored? Maynard looks at his polar adventures in this exciting account. (Rev: BL 10/1–15/10) [921]

Artists, Authors, Composers, and Entertainers

7213 Adams, Maureen. *Shaggy Muses: The Dogs Who Inspired Virginia Wolf, Emily Dickinson, Elizabeth Barrett Browning, Edith Wharton, and Emily Bronte* (9–12). 2007, Ballantine $24.95 (978-0-345-48406-2). An interesting glimpse of the relationships between five female greats of literature — Browning, Woolf, Dickinson, Wharton, and Emily Brontë — and their respective dog companions tells how this relationship affected their writing, the dogs even showing up in their narratives at times. (Rev: BL 7/07) [820.9]

7214 Amend, Allison. *Hispanic-American Writers* (8–12). Series: Multicultural Voices. 2010, Chelsea House $35 (978-1-60413-312-7). Rudolfo Anaya, Julia Alvarez, and Sandra Cisneros are among the eight writers introduced in this volume that places them in historical and cultural context and examines major themes in their work. **e** (Rev: LMC 10/10; SLJ 9/1/10) [920]

7215 Andronik, Catherine M. *Wildly Romantic: The English Romantic Poets: The Mad, the Bad, and the Dangerous* (10–12). 2007, Henry Holt $16.95 (978-0-8050-7783-4). Students who consider poetry boring should get their hands on this book, which discusses the wild and often immoral lives of Wordsworth, Coleridge, Byron, Shelley, and Keats. Their poems are incorporated throughout. (Rev: BL 4/15/07; LMC 10/07; SLJ 4/07) [821]

7216 Austerlitz, Saul. *Another Fine Mess: A History of American Film Comedy* (10–12). Illus. 2010, Chicago Review paper $24.95 (978-15565295-1-1). More than 100 movie comics are included here in admiring profiles. **e** (Rev: BL 9/1–15/10) [920]

7217 Bearden, Romare, and Harry Henderson. *A History of African-American Artists: From 1792 to the Present* (9–12). 1993, Pantheon $65.00 (978-0-394-57016-7).

The lives and careers of 36 African American artists born before 1925 are part of this comprehensive history of African American art. Includes more than 300 black-and-white and color prints. (Rev: BL 10/15/93*) [920]

7218 Blum, David. *Quintet: Five Journeys Toward Musical Fulfillment* (10–12). 2000, Cornell $36.00 (978-0-8014-3731-1). This adult work profiles five individuals who have devoted their lives to classical music, including cellist Yo-Yo Ma, conductor Jeffrey Tate, pianist Richard Goode, and singer Birgit Nilsson. (Rev: BL 1/1–15/00) [920]

7219 Bollmann, Stefan. *Women Who Write* (9–12). Trans. by Helen Atkins. 2007, Merrell $24.95 (978-1-85894-375-6). Mary Wollstonecraft, Jane Austen, George Sand, Sylvia Plath, Marguerite Duras — these are only a few of the women writers introduced in this volume, each with a painting or photograph. (Rev: BL 6/1–15/07) [920]

7220 Bostrom, Kathleen Long. *Winning Authors: Profiles of the Newbery Medalists* (5–10). Series: Popular Authors. 2003, Libraries Unlimited $52.00 (978-1-56308-877-3). Report writers will find useful information on the authors who won this prestigious award, including quotations and material on experiences that relate to the winning books. (Rev: SLJ 6/04; VOYA 6/04) [920]

7221 Cahill, Susan, ed. *Writing Women's Lives: An Anthology of Autobiographical Narratives by Twentieth-Century American Women Writers* (9–12). 1994, HarperPerennial paper $18.00 (978-0-06-096998-1). A collection of autobiographical narratives by 20th-century women writers, including Jane Addams and Edith Wharton. (Rev: BL 4/15/94) [920]

7222 Cooke, Jon B., and John Morrow, eds. *Streetwise: Autobiographical Stories* (10–12). 2000, TwoMorrows $19.95 (978-1-893905-04-7). The lives of many famous comic-book artists, told in graphic form. (Rev: BL 2/1/03) [920]

7223 Davidson, Sue. *Getting the Real Story: Nellie Bly and Ida B. Wells* (6–10). 1992, Seal paper $8.95 (978-1-878067-16-6). A dual biography of two women who broke down barriers in journalism and how their different races shaped their individual stories. (Rev: BL 3/1/92; SLJ 7/92) [920]

7224 De Angelis, Gina. *Motion Pictures: Making Cinema Magic* (6–10). Series: Innovators. 2004, Oliver LB $21.95 (978-1-881508-78-6). Profiles eight inventors of motion picture technology, including Auguste and Louis Lumière, Lee de Forest, and Mike Todd. (Rev: BCCB 5/04; SLJ 9/04) [920]

7225 Earls, Irene. *Young Musicians in World History* (7–12). 2002, Greenwood $51.95 (978-0-313-31442-1). Thirteen musicians whose skills were recognized before the age of 25 are profiled, ranging from Bach and Beethoven to Louis Armstrong, Bob Dylan, and John Lennon. (Rev: LMC 2/03; SLJ 1/03) [780]

7226 Farrington, Lisa E. *Creating Their Own Image: The History of African-American Women Artists* (9–12). 2005, Oxford $75.00 (978-0-19-516721-4). Farrington profiles African American women artists, introduces their work, and discusses the challenges they faced. (Rev: BL 2/1/05) [704]

7227 Koolish, Lynda. *African American Writers: Portraits and Visions* (9–12). 2001, Univ. Press of Mississippi $45.00 (978-1-57806-258-4). This stylish collection features black-and-white photographs and brief accompanying profiles of influential African American writers including August Wilson, Lucille Clifton, Edwidge Danticat, and Sonia Sanchez. (Rev: BL 2/15/02) [810.9]

7228 Koopmans, Andy. *Filmmakers* (7–10). Series: History Makers. 2005, Gale LB $29.95 (978-1-59018-598-8). Profiles five of the world's most influential filmmakers — Alfred Hitchcock, Stanley Kubrick, Francis Ford Coppola, Spike Lee, and Peter Jackson. (Rev: BL 6/1–15/05) [920]

7229 Leiber, Jerry, et al. *Hound Dog: The Leiber and Stoller Autobiography* (10–12). Illus. 2009, Simon & Schuster $25 (978-141655938-2). Here is the story of songwriters Jerry Leiber and Mike Stoller, who wrote famous hits during the 1950s for the Coasters, Elvis, and many more. ℮ (Rev: BLO 4–5/09) [920]

7230 Mazer, Anne, ed. *Going Where I'm Coming From: Memoirs of American Youth* (8–12). 1995, Persea paper $7.95 (978-0-89255-206-1). Writers from different cultures talk about growing up and the incidents in their lives that helped to establish their identities. (Rev: BL 1/15/95; VOYA 5/95) [818]

7231 Nathan, Amy. *Meet the Dancers: From Ballet, Broadway, and Beyond* (6–12). 2008, Henry Holt $19.95 (978-0-8050-8071-1). Sixteen very different dancers describe their training and their careers, which run the gamut from Broadway to MTV. (Rev: BL 5/1/08; SLJ 4/08) [792.802]

7232 Otfinoski, Steven. *African Americans in the Performing Arts* (10–12). Illus. 2010, Facts on File $49.50 (978-081607838-7). Detailed profiles of landmark importance (Bill Cosby, Diana Ross, and Sidney Poitier, for example) and of lesser importance (Peg Leg Bates and Charley Pride, for example) are given in accessible language. ℮ (Rev: BL 10/1–15/10) [920]

7233 Otfinoski, Steven. *Native American Writers* (10–12). Series: Multicultural Voices. 2010, Chelsea House $35 (978-1-60413-314-1). Louise Erdrich and Sherman Alexie are among the ten writers introduced in this volume that places them in historical and cultural context and examines major themes in their work. ℮ (Rev: LMC 10/10; SLJ 8/10) [920]

7234 Ottaviani, Jim, and Janine Johnston. *Levitation: Physics and Psychology in the Service of Deception* (9–12). 2007, G. T. Labs paper $11.95 (978-0-9788037-0-4). The illusion trick of levitation is historically and pictorially defined here in this graphic novel, chronicling the three original 20th-century magicians — Maskelyne, then Kellar, then Thurston — who developed, refined, stole, or bought the "Levitation of Princess Karnac" and even revealed the trick to a few audience members who were persuaded to keep the secret, and they always did. Includes a diagram explaining the trick. (Rev: BL 7/07) [133.9]

7235 Plimpton, George, ed. *Playwrights at Work* (10–12). 2000, Random House paper $14.95 (978-0-679-64021-9). This collection of 16 interviews with authors from the pages of the *Paris Review* includes material on Thornton Wilder, Arthur Miller, Tennessee Williams, David Mamet, and Edward Albee. (Rev: BL 5/1/00) [920]

7236 Satter, James. *Journalists Who Made History* (7–12). Series: Profiles. 1998, Oliver LB $19.95 (978-1-881508-39-7). Ten journalists famous for their fearless reporting are profiled, including Horace Greeley, Ida Tarbell, Carl Bernstein and Bob Woodward, William Randolph Hearst, and Edward R. Murrow. (Rev: BL 10/15/98; SLJ 11/98) [920]

7237 Shreve, Susan Richards, ed. *Dream Me Home Safely* (10–12). 2003, Houghton Mifflin paper $13.00 (978-0-618-37902-6). Thirty-four American writers reveal details of their adolescence in this valuable collection of memoirs. (Rev: BL 10/15/03) [921]

7238 Sigafus, Kim, and Lyle Ernst. *Native Writers: Voices of Power* (8–12). Illus. Series: Native Trailblazers. 2012, 7th Generation paper $9.95 (978-0-977918-3-8-6). This collective biography includes profiles of contemporary Native American writers such as Sherman Alexie, Joseph Bruchac, and Louise Erdrich. (Rev: BL 11/1/12; SLJ 11/12) [920]

7239 Singer, Toba. *First Position: A Century of Ballet Artists* (9–12). 2007, Praeger $49.95 (978-0-275-98391-8). A collective biography featuring 15 dancers — among the well-known are Mikhail Baryshnikov, Margot Fonteyn, Rudolf Nureyev, and Anna Pavlova — with information on their lives and careers, artistic influences, dance partners, critical reception, and so forth. (Rev: BL 11/1/07) [920]

7240 Wenner, Jann S., and Joe Levy, eds. *The Rolling Stone Interviews* (9–12). 2007, Little, Brown paper $17.99 (978-0-316-00526-5). Phil Spector, Ray Charles, Oriana Fallaci, Jack Nicholson, Bill Clinton — these are only a few of the celebrities featured in *Rolling Stone* interviews collected in this 40th anniversary celebration. (Rev: BL 12/1/07) [080]

7241 Zucker, Carole. *In the Company of Actors: Reflections on the Craft of Acting* (10–12). 2000, Routledge $25.00 (978-0-415-92545-7). For mature theater fans, here are interviews with 16 Irish and British actors including Judi Dench, Alan Bates, Simon Callow, Nigel Hawthorne, Janet McTeer, and Eileen Atkins. (Rev: BL 1/1–15/00) [920]

Artists and Architects

ADAMS, ARTHUR

7242 Khoury, George, and Eric Nolen-Weathington. *Arthur Adams: Modern Masters, Vol. 6* (9–12). Series: Modern Masters. 2006, TwoMorrows paper $14.95 (978-1-893905-54-2). A look at the life and art of Arthur Adams, the award-winning comic book creator who became known in the mid-1980s for his Longshot series. (Rev: BL 4/1/06) [741.5]

ANDOE, JOE

7243 Andoe, Joe. *Jubilee City: A Memoir at Full Speed* (11–12). 2007, Morrow $22.95 (978-0-06-124031-7). In a collection of brief anecdotes artist Andoe gives the reader a glimpse into his reckless youth, his indulgence in alcohol and drugs, stays in jail, and so forth, before becoming more grounded as a professional and father; for mature teens. (Rev: BL 6/1–15/07) [921]

AUDUBON, JOHN JAMES

7244 Audubon, John James. *The Audubon Reader* (9–12). 2006, Everyman's Library $25.00 (978-1-4000-4369-9). Excerpts from the author's lively letters, journals, and other writings document his wide-ranging travels and zest for life. (Rev: BL 3/15/06) [598]

BAMA, JAMES

7245 Kane, Brian M. *James Bama: American Realist* (8–12). 2006, Flesk $34.95 (978-0-9723758-8-7). This is a tribute to James Bama, a triumphantly successful illustrator who did hundreds of paperback covers during the 1960s and 1970s as well as artwork for magazines, advertising, military, and sports publications. (Rev: BL 11/1/06) [759.13]

BOURGEOIS, LOUISE

7246 Greenberg, Jan, and Sandra Jordan. *Runaway Girl: The Artist Louise Bourgeois* (8–12). 2003, Abrams $19.95 (978-0-8109-4237-0). The life of the famous sculptor, with details of her youth and her difficult relations with her parents, is accompanied by many black-and-white and color photographs. (Rev: BL 4/15/03*; HB 7–8/03; HBG 10/03; SLJ 5/03*; VOYA 8/03) [730]

BOURKE-WHITE, MARGARET

7247 Rubin, Susan Goldman. *Margaret Bourke-White: Her Pictures Were Her Life* (6–12). 1999, Abrams $19.95 (978-0-8109-4381-0). An excellent biography of a courageous, highly disciplined photographer whose work remains a hallmark of quality in the field. (Rev: BL 11/1/99* ; HBG 4/00) [770]

BRAQUE, GEORGES

7248 Wilkin, Karen. *Georges Braque* (9–12). Series: Modern Masters. 1992, Abbeville paper $14.95 (978-0-89659-947-5). Examines the life, works, and style of the co-creator of Cubism. (Rev: BL 3/15/92) [921]

BYRNE, JOHN

7249 Cooke, Jon B., and Eric Nolen-Weathington, eds. *John Byrne: Modern Masters, Vol. 7* (9–12). 2006, TwoMorrows paper $14.95 (978-1-893905-56-6). A look at the work of "modern master" Byrne, who drew the X-Men and the Fantastic Four in the 1980s and also repopularized Superman comics. (Rev: BL 9/1/06) [921]

CANALETTO

7250 Rice, Earle, Jr. *Canaletto* (7–12). Series: Art Profiles for Kids. 2007, Mitchell Lane LB $29.95 (978-1-58415-561-4). Report writers will appreciate this thorough introduction to the artist's life and work, with interesting "FYI" sections and small color reproductions. (Rev: SLJ 1/08)

CATLIN, GEORGE

7251 Reich, Susanna. *Painting the Wild Frontier: The Art and Adventures of George Catlin* (7–12). 2008, Clarion $21.00 (978-0-618-71470-4). This excellent introduction to the artwork and life of George Catlin, a 19th-century painter of Native Americans, includes prints and photographs of his work and extensive back matter. (Rev: BL 6/1–15/08; SLJ 8/08) [921]

CÉZANNE, PAUL

7252 Rewald, John. *Cezanne: A Biography* (10–12). 1986, Abrams $75 (978-0-8109-0775-1). This handsome book tells the life story of the artist Paul Cezanne and reproduces many of his works. [921]

CHAGALL, MARC

7253 Kagan, Andrew. *Marc Chagall* (9–12). 1989, Abbeville paper $14.95 (978-0-89659-935-2). The life and work of this Russian Jewish painter whose faith and fantastic imagination dominated his work. (Rev: BL 12/15/89) [921]

CHONG, GORDON H.

7254 *The Success of Gordon H. Chong and Associates: An Architecture Success Story* (7–10). Series: Success. 1996, Walker $15.95 (978-0-8027-8307-3). The amazing rise of the contemporary American architect, with examples of his work. (Rev: BL 5/15/96; SLJ 9/96) [921]

COLAN, GENE

7255 Field, Tom. *Secrets in the Shadows: The Art and Life of Gene Colan* (9–12). 2005, TwoMorrows $44.95 (978-1-893905-46-7); paper $21.95 (978-1-893905-45-0). This eye-catching retrospective chronicles the long career of comic book artist Gene Colan. (Rev: BL 10/15/05) [741.5]

DALI, SALVADOR

7256 McNeese, Tim. *Salvador Dali* (9–12). 2006, Facts on File LB $35 (978-079108837-1). A well-researched introduction to the life, times, and cultural legacy of the artist. (Rev: SLJ 7/06) [921]

7257 Ross, Michael Elsohn. *Salvador Dali and the Surrealists: Their Lives and Ideas* (9–12). 2003, Chicago Review paper $17.95 (978-1-55652-479-0). This profile of the life and work of the Spanish-born painter and his fellow Surrealists is supplemented by period photographs and representative examples of their works. (Rev: BL 11/1/03; HBG 4/04; SLJ 12/03) [759.6]

DISNEY, WALT

7258 Jackson, Kathy Merlock, ed. *Walt Disney: Conversations* (9–12). Series: Conversations with Comic Artists. 2006, Univ. Press of Mississippi $50.00 (978-1-57806-712-1); paper $20.00 (978-1-57806-713-8). This collection of interviews and speeches offers useful insights into the man responsible for launching an empire. (Rev: BL 1/1–15/06) [791.43]

7259 Schickel, Richard. *The Disney Version: The Life, Times, Art, and Commerce of Walt Disney. 3rd ed.* (9–12). 1997, Ivan R. Dee paper $14.95 (978-1-56663-158-7). Chronicles the animator's rise from a job as a draftsman in Kansas City to control of an entertainment empire with a profound influence on America's popular culture. [921]

DITKO, STEVE

7260 Bell, Blake. *Strange and Stranger: The World of Steve Ditko* (10–12). Illus. 2008, Fantagraphics $39.95 (978-1-56097-921-0). With Ditko's forceful artwork and Bell's perceptive comments, this book provides comic fans with a wealth of information about the very private artist. (Rev: BL 8/08) [921]

7261 Ditko, Steve. *Strange Suspense: The Steve Ditko Archives* (9–12). Illus. 2009, Fantagraphics $39.99 (978-160699289-0). Idiosyncratic and sometimes blunt, this book features three dozen of Spider Man co-creator Steve Ditko's earliest works. (Rev: BL 11/15/09)

DRISKELL, DAVID C.

7262 McGee, Julie L. *David C. Driskell: Artist and Scholar* (9–12). 2006, Pomegranate $45.00 (978-0-7649-3747-7). The story of artist Driskell's progress from a one-room schoolhouse to recipient of doctoral degrees and awards recognizing both his artistic talents and his work on African American art will inspire young artists to look past simple creativity. (Rev: BL 2/1/07) [709.2]

ELLABBAD, MOHIEDDIN

7263 Ellabbad, Mohieddin. *The Illustrator's Notebook* (5–10). Trans. from French by Sarah Quinn. Illus. by author. 2006, Groundwood $16.95 (978-0-88899-700-5). In this fascinating journal printed from right to left, Egyptian-born illustrator Ellabbad reflects on the influences that led him to a life in art and offers valuable insights into Arabic cultural sensibilities. (Rev: SLJ 8/06)

GARCÍA-LÓPEZ, JOSÉ LUIS

7264 Nolen-Weathington, Eric, ed. *José Luis García-López: Modern Masters, Vol. 5* (9–12). Series: Modern Masters. 2005, TwoMorrows paper $14.95 (978-1-893905-44-3). Chronicles the life and work of Argentine-born José Luis García-López, one of the world's greatest comic book artists. (Rev: BL 10/15/05) [741.5]

GEHRY, FRANK

7265 Lazo, Caroline Evensen. *Frank Gehry* (7–10). Series: A&E Biography. 2005, Twenty-First Century LB $29.27 (978-0-8225-2649-0); paper $7.95 (978-0-8225-3388-7). Introduces the architect and his most famous structures, with full-color photos and reproductions. (Rev: SLJ 2/06) [921]

HERGÉ

7266 Farr, Michael. *The Adventures of Hergé: Creator of Tintin* (9–12). 2008, Last Gasp $29.95 (978-0-86719-679-5). A life of the Belgian artist and cartoonist who created 23 graphic novels following the adventures of a young reporter named Tintin. (Rev: BL 4/1/08; SLJ 3/08) [921]

HUNTER, CLEMENTINE

7267 Lyons, Mary E. *Talking with Tebe: Clementine Hunter, Memory Artist* (7–12). 1998, Houghton Mifflin $17.00 (978-0-395-72031-8). This richly illustrated book, which quotes extensively from taped interviews and is as much about social history as about painting, tells the story of the first illiterate, self-taught African American folk artist to receive national attention for her work. (Rev: BCCB 1/99; BL 8/98; HB 9–10/98; HBG 3/99; SLJ 9/98) [921]

KAHLO, FRIDA

7268 Bernier-Grand, Carmen T. *Frida: Viva la vida! Long Live Life!* (7–12). Illus. by Frida Kahlo. 2007, Marshall Cavendish $18.99 (978-0-7614-5336-9). Free-verse poems about the art and life of Frida Kahlo accompany reproductions of her artwork and photographs of the artist and her family; some poems deal with adult subjects such as a troubled marriage and a pregnancy loss. (Rev: BL 11/1/07; SLJ 12/07) [921]

KAMBALU, SAMSON

7269 Kambalu, Samson. *The Jive Talker* (11–12). 2008, Free Press $24.00 (978-1-4165-5931-3). Internationally known artist Kambalu tells the story of growing up poor in Malawi, of his father who was an educated man who loved words, and of his own struggle to find himself; for mature teens. **e** (Rev: BL 8/08) [921]

KANE, BOB

7270 Kane, Bob, and Tom Andrae. *Batman and Me* (9–12). 1989, Eclipse Books $40.00 (978-1-56060-016-9); paper $14.95 (978-1-56060-017-6). An autobiography of the creator of Batman, Robin, and other characters in the comics plus lots of illustrations. (Rev: BL 4/15/90) [921]

KIRBY, JACK

7271 Evanier, Mark. *Kirby: King of Comics* (9–12). 2008, Abrams $40.00 (978-0-8109-9447-8). In graphic novel format with original black-and-white art, this is a tribute to cartoonist Jack Kirby and his superheroes. (Rev: BL 3/15/08) [921]

7272 Kirby, Jack. *Kirby Five-Oh! Celebrating 50 Years of the "King" of Comics* (10–12). Ed. by John Morrow. Illus. 2008, TwoMorrows paper $19.95 (978-189390589-4). This admiring volume is filled with large layouts of the creator of *Iron Man*'s drawings including pencil originals, previously unpublished artwork, and accolades from many artists and authors. (Rev: BL 8/08) [921]

LANGE, DOROTHEA

7273 Acker, Kerry. *Dorothea Lange* (9–12). Series: Women in the Arts. 2004, Chelsea House LB $30.00 (978-0-7910-7460-2). The story of the great photographer of the Depression and the New Deal. (Rev: BL 3/15/04) [921]

LIN, MAYA

7274 Lashnits, Tom. *Maya Lin* (6–10). Series: Asian Americans of Achievement. 2007, Chelsea House LB $30.00 (978-0-7910-9268-2). This is an attractive biography of the designer of the Vietnam Veterans Memorial in Washington, D.C. (Rev: SLJ 8/07) [921]

MARSHALL, KERRY JAMES

7275 Marshall, Kerry James, et al. *Kerry James Marshall* (10–12). 2000, Abrams $29.95 (978-0-8109-3527-3). A beautifully illustrated volume on this great African American artist with essays by a number of people on his life and art. (Rev: BL 12/15/00) [921]

MCCAY, WINSOR

7276 Canemaker, John. *Winsor McCay: His Life and Art. Rev. ed.* (9–12). 2005, Abrams $45 (978-0-8109-5941-5). An excellent biography covering the life and art of Winsor McCay, detailing his achievements in comics, animation, advertising, and theater. (Rev: SLJ 5/06) [921]

MONET, CLAUDE

7277 Kallen, Stuart A. *Claude Monet* (7–10). Series: Eye on Art. 2008, Gale/Lucent $32.45 (978-1-4205-0074-5). This attractive Monet biography offers a compelling glimpse at the man behind the famed artwork, including his personal struggles, flaws, and volatile genius. (Rev: SLJ 6/1/09) [921]

MUYBRIDGE, EADWEARD

7278 Clegg, Brian. *The Man Who Stopped Time: The Illuminating Story of Eadweard Muybridge — Pioneer Photographer, Father of the Motion Picture, Murderer* (10–12). 2007, Joseph Henry $27.95 (978-0-309-10112-7). Eadweard Muybridge lived from 1830 to 1904 and is famous for his early photographic sequences — of horses and people in motion; but he's less well known for his dramatic private life. (Rev: BL 5/1/07) [921]

NOGUCHI, ISAMU

7279 Tiger, Caroline. *Isamu Noguchi* (6–12). Series: Asian Americans of Achievement. 2007, Chelsea House LB $30.00 (978-0-7910-9276-7). This is the fascinating story of Noguchi's search for an identity and a place to call home as well as his development into an internationally renowned sculptor. (Rev: SLJ 10/07) [921]

PEI, I. M.

7280 Rubalcaba, Jill. *I. M. Pei: Architect of Time, Place, and Purpose* (7–10). Illus. 2011, Marshall Cavendish $23.99 (978-0-7614-5973-6). Rubalcaba gives an interesting and well-designed overview of Pei's life and works, including reproductions of sketches and plans as well as photographs of buildings, with in-depth discussion of seven projects. (Rev: BL 11/1/11*; LMC 3–4/12; SLJ 10/1/11) [921]

PICASSO, PABLO

7281 Bernier-Grand, Carmen T. *Picasso: I the King, Yo el rey* (6–12). Illus. by David Diaz. 2012, Amazon Children's $19.99 (978-076146177-7). In free-style verse and dramatic images, Bernier-Grand profiles the famous artist. (Rev: BL 11/1/12; SLJ 1/13) [921]

7282 Leal, Brigitte, et al. *The Ultimate Picasso* (10–12). Trans. by Molly Stevens and Marjolijn de Jager. 2000, Abrams $95.00 (978-0-8109-3940-0). This expensive but definitive volume on the life and work of Picasso contains thought-provoking articles and 1,235 illustrations. (Rev: BL 12/15/00; SLJ 6/01) [921]

7283 McNeese, Tim. *Pablo Picasso* (9–12). Series: Great Hispanic Heritage. 2006, Facts on File LB $35 (9780791088432). A well-researched introduction to the life, times, and cultural legacy of the artist, with pictures from each period of his career. (Rev: SLJ 7/06)

REMBRANDT VAN RIJN

7284 Schwartz, Gary. *Rembrandt* (7–12). Series: First Impressions. 1992, Abrams $19.95 (978-0-8109-3760-4). This jargon-free, accessible biography presents Rembrandt with all his flaws and quirks. (Rev: BL 5/1/92; SLJ 6/92*) [921]

RIVERA, DIEGO

7285 Bernier-Grand, Carmen T. *Diego: Bigger Than Life* (7–10). Illus. by David Diaz. 2009, Marshall Cavendish $18.99 (978-076145383-3). The story of artist Diego Rivera's life is told using first-person free-verse poems; fact and fiction are defined in the informative back matter. Belpré Honor 2010; ALA Notable Books 2010. (Rev: BL 2/15/09; HB 5–6/09; LMC 8–9/09; SLJ 4/1/09) [921]

7286 Litwin, Laura Baskes. *Diego Rivera: Legendary Mexican Painter* (7–10). Series: Latino Biography. 2005, Enslow LB $31.93 (978-0-7660-2486-1). The life, art, and controversial politics of Mexican artist Diego Rivera are explored in this attractive and readable title. (Rev: BL 11/1/05; SLJ 4/06) [759.972]

7287 Rubin, Susan Goldman. *Diego Rivera: An Artist for the People* (6–10). Illus. 2013, Abrams $21.95 (978-081098411-0). With many examples of Rivera's paintings, drawings, and murals, this is an honest and acces-sible portrait of the Mexican artist. (Rev: BL 2/15/13*; SLJ 5/13*) [921]

ROWELL, GALEN

7288 Rowell, Galen. *Galen Rowell: A Retrospective* (9–12). 2006, Sierra Club $50.00 (978-1-57805-115-1). A beautiful collection of works by the accomplished landscape photographer and mountaineer (1940–2002), the first and only representation of his career; accompanying the 175 photographs are essays and commentaries by Rowell's friends and associates from the fields of mountaineering, conservation, photography, and publishing. (Rev: BL 10/1/06) [779]

SCHULKE, FLIP

7289 Schulke, Flip. *Witness to Our Times: My Life as a Photojournalist* (6–12). 2003, Cricket $19.95 (978-0-8126-2682-7). In this volume full of examples of his work, Schulke describes his early life and his career covering events of the 20th century including the space program and the civil rights movement. (Rev: BL 4/15/03; HBG 10/03; SLJ 6/03; VOYA 2/04) [070.4]

SCHULZ, CHARLES

7290 Inge, M. Thomas, ed. *Schulz: Conversations* (9–12). 2000, Univ. Press of Mississippi $50.00 (978-1-57806-304-8); paper $20.00 (978-1-57806-305-5). This collection of 16 interviews with the modest creator of Peanuts covers his biography, work, attitudes, and his philosophy of life. (Rev: BL 10/1/00) [921]

TIMM, BRUCE

7291 Nolen-Weathington, Eric, ed. *Bruce Timm* (9–12). Series: Modern Masters. 2004, TwoMorrows paper $14.95 (978-1-893905-30-6). Television animator/comic book artist Timm discusses the influences that helped to shape his distinctive style; this volume also includes a portfolio of his work. (Rev: BL 10/15/04) [741.5]

ULMANN, DORIS

7292 Jacobs, Philip Walker. *The Life and Photography of Doris Ulmann* (9–12). 2001, Univ. Press of Kentucky $40.00 (978-0-8131-2175-8). The people of Appalachia and rural African Americans were the main subjects of the pioneering American photographer whose life and work are chronicled in this handsome volume. (Rev: BL 2/15/01) [921]

VAN GOGH, VINCENT

7293 Bonafoux, Pascal. *Van Gogh: The Passionate Eye* (7–12). Series: Discoveries. 1992, Abrams paper $12.95 (978-0-8109-2828-2). An overview of the life and work of this disturbed Dutch painter. (Rev: BL 7/92) [921]

7294 Crispino, Enrica. *Van Gogh* (6–10). Illus. Series: Art Masters. 2008, Oliver LB $27.95 (978-193454505-

8). This insightful look at Van Gogh's work focuses more on the painter in the context of his times rather than providing a chronology of personal events. (Rev: BL 12/15/08; LMC 11–12/08) [921]

7295 Schapiro, Meyer. *Vincent van Gogh* (10–12). 2000, Abradale Press $19.98 (978-0-8109-8117-1). The life of van Gogh is detailed, with a generous use of quotations from his letters. [921]

7296 Whiting, Jim. *Vincent Van Gogh* (7–12). Series: Art Profiles for Kids. 2007, Mitchell Lane LB $29.95 (978-1-58415-564-5). Report writers will appreciate this thorough introduction to the artist's life and work, with interesting "FYI" sections and small color reproductions. (Rev: SLJ 1/08)

VESS, CHARLES

7297 Irving, Christopher, and Eric Nolen-Weathington. *Charles Vess* (9–12). Series: Modern Masters. 2007, TwoMorrows paper $14.95 (978-1-893905-69-6). Vess, winner of two World Fantasy Awards and two Eisner Awards, is known for the graphic novel *Spider-Man: Spirits of the Earth* as well as his collaborations with Neil Gaiman; this biography discusses his career and creative process and features an 8-page color section. (Rev: BL 5/1/07) [921]

WARHOL, ANDY

7298 Greenberg, Jan, and Sandra Jordan. *Andy Warhol, Prince of Pop* (8–12). 2004, Random House LB $18.99 (978-0-385-73056-3). Warhol had a successful career in commercial art before rising to fame as a pop icon; this volume covers his youth, early career, love of celebrity, and early death as well as his art and its lasting influence. (Rev: BCCB 12/04; BL 6/1–15/04*; HB 1–2/05; SLJ 11/04; VOYA 10/04) [709]

WRIGHT, FRANK LLOYD

7299 Adkins, Jan. *Frank Lloyd Wright* (7–12). Series: Up Close. 2007, Viking $16.99 (978-0-670-06138-9). The biographer does not gloss over the architect's infamously prickly nature but also emphasizes Wright's talent and his influence on building design. (Rev: BL 11/1/07; SLJ 11/07) [921]

7300 Fandel, Jennifer. *Frank Lloyd Wright* (7–12). Series: Xtraordinary Artists. 2005, Creative Education LB $21.95 (978-1-58341-378-4). This well-illustrated life of the visionary architect draws on comments from his students, contemporaries, and admirers. (Rev: SLJ 12/05) [921]

WYETH, ANDREW

7301 Wyeth, Andrew. *Andrew Wyeth, Autobiography* (10–12). 1995, Little, Brown paper $29.95 (978-0-8212-2569-1). This autobiography contains reproductions of 137 of Wyeth's paintings. (Rev: BL 11/15/95) [921]

Authors

ALCOTT, LOUISA MAY

7302 Reisen, Harriet. *Louisa May Alcott: The Woman Behind Little Women* (9–12). 2009, Henry Holt $26 (978-080508299-9). This lively biography describes the tumultuous childhood, varied careers, and struggles of the well-known author. ∩ (Rev: BL 10/1/09*) [921]

ALVAREZ, JULIA

7303 Alvarez, Julia. *Something to Declare* (10–12). 1998, Algonquin $32.95 (978-1-56512-193-5). In 24 autobiographical essays, the author presents her Dominican childhood, her family's immigration to the United States, her college years, writing, marriages, and return trips to her homeland. (Rev: BL 8/98; SLJ 4/99) [921]

7304 Aykroyd, Clarissa. *Julia Alvarez: Novelist and Poet* (7–10). Series: Twentieth Century's Most Influential Hispanics. 2007, Gale LB $32.45 (978-1-4205-0022-6). The poet's life and work, with many quotations from Alvarez and excerpts from her poems. (Rev: BL 2/15/08) [921]

ANGELOU, MAYA

7305 Angelou, Maya. *Letter to My Daughter* (11–12). 2008, Random House $25 (978-140006612-4). Angelou writes short stories, poems, and anecdotes of her life that serve as helpful advice and often warnings to the daughter she never had; for mature readers. ∩ ℮ (Rev: BL 9/15/08) [921]

7306 Gillespie, Marcia Ann, and Rosa Johnson Butler. *Maya Angelou: A Glorious Celebration* (9–12). 2008, Doubleday $30 (978-0-385-51108-7). Excerpts from interviews, photographs, and reproductions add to this inspiring biography. (Rev: BL 3/15/08; SLJ 8/08) [921]

7307 Shapiro, Miles. *Maya Angelou* (7–10). Series: Black Americans of Achievement. 1994, Chelsea LB $21.95 (978-0-7910-1862-0). A chronological narrative of the life of this amazing African American writer that describes her hardships and triumphs. (Rev: BL 6/1–15/94; SLJ 6/94) [921]

AUSTEN, JANE

7308 Locke, Juliane. *England's Jane: The Story of Jane Austen* (8–11). 2006, Morgan Reynolds LB $26.95 (978-1-931798-82-2). The parallels between Austen's life and novels are evident in this appealing biography. (Rev: BL 2/15/06; SLJ 2/06) [823]

7309 Wagner, Heather Lehr. *Jane Austen* (7–10). Series: Who Wrote That? 2003, Chelsea House LB $30.00 (978-0-7910-7623-1). Details of Austen's family life and education and of the mores of the time give insight into her humorous attitude toward society and romance. (Rev: SLJ 6/04) [921]

AVI

7310 Mercier, Cathryn M., and Susan P. Bloom. *Presenting Avi* (6–10). Series: Twayne's United States Authors. 1997, Macmillan $35 (978-0-8057-4569-6). This biography of the noted writer of books for children and young adults is divided into chapters based on roles he has assumed as a writer, including storyteller, stylist, magician, and historian, and explores his many beliefs about the significance of literature. (Rev: SLJ 6/98) [921]

BLAKE, WILLIAM

7311 Bedard, Michael. *William Blake: The Gates of Paradise* (9–12). 2006, Tundra $19.95 (978-0-88776-763-0). This satisfying, well-illustrated look at the life of William Blake, the 18th-century English artist, engraver, poet, and visionary includes background information on the industrialization taking place at the time. (Rev: BL 11/15/06; HB 1–2/07; LMC 4–5/07; SLJ 12/06) [921]

BRADSTREET, ANNE DUDLEY

7312 Gordon, Charlotte. *Mistress Bradstreet: The Untold Life of America's First Poet* (10–12). 2005, Little, Brown $27.95 (978-0-316-16904-2). The life and literary career of 17th-century Puritan poet Anne Dudley Bradstreet. (Rev: BL 3/1/05; SLJ 11/05) [811]

BRAY, ROSEMARY

7313 Bray, Rosemary L. *Unafraid of the Dark: A Memoir* (10–12). 1998, Random House $24 (978-0-679-42555-7); paper $14.00 (978-0-385-49475-5). The author recounts growing up in Chicago on welfare, developing an interest in the civil rights movement while in high school, winning a scholarship to Yale, and becoming an editor at the *New York Times Book Review*. She concludes with a strong statement, based on her childhood, against the 1996 welfare-reform bill. (Rev: BL 1/1–15/98; SLJ 6/98) [921]

BRENNAN, CHRISTINE

7314 Brennan, Christine. *Best Seat in the House: A Father, a Daughter, a Journey Through Sports* (9–12). 2006, Scribner $26 (978-0-7432-5436-6). A childhood and adolescence steeped in sports helped Brennan to realize her dream of a career in sports journalism. (Rev: BL 3/15/06) [070.4]

BRONTË FAMILY

7315 Dinsdale, Ann. *The Brontës at Haworth* (9–12). 2006, Antique Collectors Club $35.00 (978-0-7112-2572-5). The beauty of the Brontës' Yorkshire is clearly shown in this lovely book full of photographs that pro-

files members of the famous family and looks at their works. (Rev: BL 1/1–15/07) [823.809]

BROOKS, GWENDOLYN

7316 Hill, Christine M. *Gwendolyn Brooks: "Poetry Is Life Distilled"* (7–10). Series: African-American Biography Library. 2005, Enslow LB $31.93 (978-0-7660-2292-8). Poet Gwendolyn Brooks, the first African American to win the Pulitzer Prize, is profiled in accessible text with lots of photos and background information. (Rev: BL 11/1/05; SLJ 11/05) [811]

BROWN, RITA MAE

7317 Brown, Rita Mae. *Animal Magnetism: My Life with Creatures Great and Small* (10–12). Illus. 2009, Ballantine $25 (978-034551179-9). Brown fondly recounts memories of her family, friends, and their animals and focuses on the life-lessons they have taught her. ∩ (Rev: BL 10/15/09) [921]

BRYSON, BILL

7318 Bryson, Bill. *The Life and Times of the Thunderbolt Kid: A Memoir* (9–12). 2006, Broadway $25.00 (978-0-7679-1936-4). The author (who also wrote *A Short History of Nearly Everything*, *A Walk in the Woods*, and many other humorous works) recalls with fondness his childhood in 1950s Iowa. (Rev: SLJ 10/06) [921]

CARROLL, LEWIS

7319 Cohen, Morton Norton. *Lewis Carroll: A Biography* (10–12). 1995, Knopf paper $14.36 (978-0-679-74562-4). Illustrated with many of the drawings by Carroll, this is a fine biography of the author-mathematician. [921]

CATHER, WILLA

7320 Meltzer, Milton. *Willa Cather* (7–12). Series: Literary Greats. 2008, Lerner LB $33.26 (978-0-8225-7604-4). An easy-to-understand profile that describes Cather's upbringing on the plains and provides historical context. (Rev: BL 4/15/08; SLJ 6/08) [921]

COLLINS, SUZANNE

7321 Sapet, Kerrily. *Suzanne Collins* (7–10). Illus. Series: World Writers. 2012, Morgan Reynolds LB $28.95 (978-159935346-3). Sapet traces Suzanne Collins's life and work, discussing the plots and characters of the popular *Hunger Games*. (Rev: BL 11/1/12; SLJ 11/12; VOYA 12/12) [921]

CONROY, PAT

7322 Conroy, Pat. *My Losing Season* (10–12). 2002, Doubleday $26.00 (978-0-385-48912-6). Conroy describes his lifelong love of basketball and the lessons the game has taught him. (Rev: BL 8/02) [796.323]

CORMIER, ROBERT

7323 Campbell, Patty. *Robert Cormier: Daring to Disturb the Universe* (10–12). 2006, Delacorte $14.95 (978-0-385-73046-4). Examines the works of Robert Cormier, with information on his life, awards and honors, and his contributions to young adult literature. (Rev: BL 11/1/06; LMC 1/07; SLJ 2/07) [813]

COURLANDER, HAROLD

7324 Jaffe, Nina. *A Voice for the People: The Life and Work of Harold Courlander* (7–10). 1997, Henry Holt $16.95 (978-0-8050-3444-8). A biography of the famous collector of folktales from minority groups who was also a noted writer and storyteller. (Rev: BL 11/1/97; HBG 3/98; SLJ 12/97) [921]

CRUTCHER, CHRIS

7325 Davis, Terry. *Presenting Chris Crutcher* (6–10). 1997, Macmillan $29 (978-0-8057-8223-3). A warm biography of this important young adult author who combines sports stories with important themes such as tolerance and the meaning of friendship. (Rev: SLJ 6/98; VOYA 6/98) [921]

CUMMINGS, E. E.

7326 Reef, Catherine. *E. E. Cummings: A Poet's Life* (8–11). 2006, Clarion $21.00 (978-0-618-56849-9). In addition to Cummings's poetry, Reef looks at his difficult teen years and romantic relationships and at the culture of the time. (Rev: BL 11/15/06; HB 11–12/06; SLJ 3/07*) [921]

D'ANGELO, PASCAL

7327 Murphy, Jim. *Pick and Shovel Poet: The Journeys of Pascal D'Angelo* (6–12). 2000, Clarion $20.00 (978-0-395-77610-0). The story of the short, hard life of the Italian American poet who wrote an important autobiography about coming to the New World. (Rev: BCCB 12/00; BL 3/1/01; HB 1–2/01; HBG 3/01; SLJ 1/01; VOYA 2/02) [973.04]

DAHL, ROALD

7328 Dahl, Roald. *Boy: Tales of Childhood* (7–12). 1984, Farrar $17.00 (978-0-374-37374-0). The famous author's autobiography — sometimes humorous, sometimes touching — of growing up in Wales and spending summers in Norway. (Rev: BL 6/87) [921]

7329 Dahl, Roald. *More About Boy: Roald Dahl's Tales from Childhood* (6–12). Illus. by Quentin Blake. 2009, Farrar $24.99 (978-0-374-35055-0). This updated and expanded scrapbook-style version of Dahl's original autobiography *Boy* (1984) includes personal artifacts (report cards, photographs, letters, and so forth) as well as new anecdotes and a quiz. (Rev: HB 11–12/09; LMC 3–4/10; SLJ 1/10) [921]

7330 Gellety, LeeAnne. *Gift of Imagination: The Story of Roald Dahl* (7–10). 2006, Morgan Reynolds $26.95 (978-1-59935-026-4). Dahl's early life and career are detailed in this profile that includes many photographs, a timeline, and a bibliography of the author's works. (Rev: BL 11/1/06; SLJ 12/06) [823]

7331 Sturrock, Donald. *Storyteller: The Authorized Biography of Roald Dahl* (10–12). 2010, Simon & Schuster $30 (978-141655082-2). A highly readable profile that brings the author's oversized personality to life. ℮ (Rev: BL 9/1–15/10) [921]

DANZIGER, PAULA

7332 Krull, Kathleen. *Presenting Paula Danziger* (6–12). Series: United States Authors. 1995, Twayne $35.00 (978-0-8057-4153-7). Examines writer Danziger's personal problems, humorous teaching experiences, and group discussions of her books in six thematic chapters. (Rev: BL 9/1/95; VOYA 2/96) [921]

DIAKITE, BABA WAGUE

7333 Diakité, Baba Wagué. *A Gift from Childhood: Memories of an African Boyhood* (6–10). 2010, Groundwood $18.95 (978-0-88899-931-3). The author relates his childhood living with his grandparents in a village in Mali and recalls the wisdom and folklore he learned there along with many practical lessons. (Rev: BL 4/15/10; HB 7–8/10; LMC 8–9/10; SLJ 5/10) [921]

DICKENS, CHARLES

7334 Caravantes, Peggy. *Best of Times: The Story of Charles Dickens* (7–10). Series: Writers of Imagination. 2005, Morgan Reynolds LB $26.95 (978-1-931798-68-6). Examines the events in the author's life that led to his literary preoccupation with social injustices. (Rev: BL 8/05; SLJ 12/05) [823]

7335 Kaplan, Fred. *Dickens: A Biography* (10–12). 1998, Johns Hopkins $25.00 (978-0-8018-6018-8). A portrait of Dickens's life from youth with details of his various adult roles. [921]

7336 Smiley, Jane. *Charles Dickens* (10–12). 2002, Viking $19.95 (978-0-670-03077-4). In her insightful biography, Smiley traces Dickens's life through his work, beginning with essays he wrote for a monthly magazine. (Rev: BL 4/1/02) [921]

DICKINSON, EMILY

7337 Longsworth, Polly. *The World of Emily Dickinson* (9–12). 1990, Norton paper $19.95 (978-0-393-31656-8). This volume uses maps, drawings, and photographs to re-create the home, friends, and life of Emily Dickinson. [921]

7338 Meltzer, Milton. *Emily Dickinson* (8–11). Series: American Literary Greats. 2006, Lerner LB $31.93 (978-0-7613-2949-7). Dickinson's life story is interwoven with quotes from her poetry and excerpts from primary sources including letters. (Rev: BL 2/15/06; SLJ 6/06; VOYA 4/06) [811]

DINESEN, ISAK

7339 Dinesen, Isak. *Out of Africa and Shadows on the Grass* (10–12). 1989, Vintage paper $13.95 (978-0-679-72475-9). These two books, reprinted in one volume, tell of the author's experiences in Africa and her recollections of her servants. [921]

7340 Leslie, Roger. *Isak Dinesen: Gothic Storyteller* (8–12). 2004, Morgan Reynolds LB $23.95 (978-1-931798-17-4). Danish-born author Isak Dinesen, best known for *Out of Africa*, a memoir of her years spent in Kenya, is profiled in this engaging volume that emphasizes her battle with syphilis. (Rev: BL 4/1/04; SLJ 5/04) [921]

DOYLE, SIR ARTHUR CONAN

7341 Pascal, Janet B. *Arthur Conan Doyle: Beyond Baker Street* (7–12). 2000, Oxford $32.95 (978-0-19-512262-6). This biography of the creator of Sherlock Holmes tells how he was also a defender of those unjustly accused of crimes, a spiritualist, and a prolific author in various genres. (Rev: BL 2/15/00; HBG 9/00; SLJ 6/00) [921]

EDMONDS, WALTER D.

7342 Edmonds, Walter D. *Tales My Father Never Told* (9–12). 1995, Syracuse Univ. $29.95 (978-0-8156-0307-8). An author's memoir of his privileged New York upbringing by a demanding father and loving mother. (Rev: BL 3/15/95) [921]

ELLISON, RALPH

7343 Bishop, Jack. *Ralph Ellison* (9–12). 1987, Chelsea LB $21.95 (978-1-55546-585-8). A biography of the writer of the acclaimed novel *Invisible Man* and his struggle for acceptance in both black and white cultures. (Rev: BL 2/15/88; SLJ 6/88) [921]

EMERSON, RALPH WALDO

7344 Caravantes, Peggy. *Self-Reliance: The Story of Ralph Waldo Emerson* (7–10). Illus. Series: World Writers. 2010, Morgan Reynolds LB $28.95 (978-159935124-7). This chronological biography captures Emerson's life and work, and reveals his lack of self-esteem as a young adult. (Rev: BL 8/10; VOYA 10/10) [921]

FEIG, PAUL

7345 Feig, Paul. *Kick Me: Adventures in Adolescence* (10–12). 2002, Crown paper $12.95 (978-0-609-80943-3). In this collection of humorous essays about his youth, Feig, creator of the television show *Freaks and Geeks*, covers everything from his lack of success with

the opposite sex to a disastrous secret excursion into the world of cross-dressing. (Rev: BL 9/15/02; SLJ 2/03) [921]

7346 Feig, Paul. *Superstud; or, How I Became a 24-Year-Old Virgin* (11–12). 2005, Three Rivers paper $13.95 (978-1-4000-5175-5). The creator of the critically acclaimed *Freaks and Geeks* television program reveals the trials and tribulations of his early experiences with girls; for mature teens. (Rev: BL 6/1–15/05) [306.7]

FITZGERALD, F. SCOTT

7347 Boon, Kevin Alexander. *F. Scott Fitzgerald* (7–10). Series: Writers and Their Works. 2005, Benchmark LB $25.95 (978-0-7614-1947-1). *The Great Gatsby* is discussed in some detail in this overview of Fitzgerald's life and works. (Rev: SLJ 3/06) [921]

7348 Prigozy, Ruth. *F. Scott Fitzgerald* (10–12). Series: Overlook Illustrated Lives. 2002, Overlook $19.95 (978-1-58567-265-3). This brief, well-illustrated, and accessible biography focuses mainly on the author's life. (Rev: BL 7/02) [921]

FLEISCHMAN, SID

7349 Fleischman, Sid. *The Abracadabra Kid: A Writer's Life* (6–12). 1996, Greenwillow $16.99 (978-0-688-14859-1). The exciting autobiography of the famous author who was also a magician, gold miner, and World War II sailor. (Rev: BL 9/1/96*; SLJ 8/96*; VOYA 4/97) [921]

FRANZEN, JONATHAN

7350 Franzen, Jonathan. *The Discomfort Zone: A Personal History* (10–12). 2006, Farrar $22 (978-0-374-29919-4). Franzen recalls his childhood and adolescence, his rebellions against his parents, and his triumphs and failures. (Rev: SLJ 2/07) [921]

FRITZ, JEAN

7351 Fritz, Jean. *Homesick: My Own Story* (7–12). Illus. by Margot Tomes. 1982, Putnam $17.99 (978-0-399-20933-8). Growing up in the troubled China of the 1920s. (Rev: BL 2/1/89) [921]

FROST, ROBERT

7352 Caravantes, Peggy. *Deep Woods: The Story of Robert Frost* (7–10). 2006, Morgan Reynolds LB $26.95 (978-1-931798-92-1). An introduction to the poet's life and successful career. (Rev: BL 9/15/06; SLJ 6/06) [921]

GANTOS, JACK

7353 Gantos, Jack. *Hole in My Life* (8–12). 2002, Farrar $16.00 (978-0-374-39988-7). The gritty story of the author's experiences in prison after being convicted for drug smuggling — and his successful efforts to live a better life. (Rev: BCCB 5/02; BL 4/1/02; HB 5–6/02*; HBG 10/02; SLJ 5/02*; VOYA 6/02) [813.54]

GARCIA MARQUEZ, GABRIEL

7354 Garcia Marquez, Gabriel. *Living to Tell the Tale* (11–12). Trans. by Edith Grossman. 2003, Knopf $26.95 (978-1-4000-4134-3). In this first installment of what will be a three-volume memoir, recommended for mature teens only, author Gabriel Garcia Marquez interweaves recollections of his youth in Colombia with the contemporaneous history of his homeland. (Rev: BL 10/15/03*) [808]

GEISEL, THEODOR SEUSS

7355 Cohen, Charles D. *The Seuss, the Whole Seuss, and Nothing but the Seuss* (8–12). 2004, Random House $35.00 (978-0-375-82248-3). This oversize, abundantly illustrated book gives a profile of the great author/illustrator and an analysis of his ideas and work. (Rev: BL 3/15/04; SLJ 6/04) [921]

7356 Pease, Donald E. *Theodor Seuss Geisel* (10–12). Illus. Series: Lives and Legacies. 2010, Oxford $19.95 (978-019532302-3). A concise, engaging look at one of children's literature's greats, covering his childhood as well as his work and his adult experiences. **e** (Rev: BL 4/1–15/10) [921]

GILMAN, SUSAN JANE

7357 Gilman, Susan Jane. *Hypocrite in a Pouffy White Dress: Tales of Growing Up Groovy and Clueless* (10–12). 2004, Warner paper $12.95 (978-0-446-67949-7). A funny and totally recognizable memoir, detailing Gilman's life from a Jewish childhood in New York City's Upper West Side in the late 1960s and early 1970s through adolescence, adulthood, and marriage; for mature readers. (Rev: BL 9/1/04; SLJ 9/05) [974.7]

GOODWILLIE, DAVID

7358 Goodwillie, David. *Seemed Like a Good Idea at the Time: A Memoir* (10–12). 2006, Algonquin $23.95 (978-1-56512-465-3). The seemingly hapless Goodwillie describes his life since he failed to make the Cincinnati Reds team — working at a series of different jobs including as a writer, a private investigator, and a sports expert at Sotheby's auction house. (Rev: BL 2/15/06; SLJ 8/06) [921]

GORE, ARIEL

7359 Gore, Ariel. *Atlas of the Human Heart* (10–12). 2003, Seal paper $14.95 (978-1-58005-088-3). In this fascinating memoir, Ariel Gore, founder of *Hip Mama* magazine, describes her adventures on a three-year odyssey, starting at the age of 16, to the Far East and Europe. (Rev: BL 4/1/03) [305.235]

GROGAN, JOHN

7360 Grogan, John. *The Longest Trip Home* (11–12). 2008, Morrow $25.95 (978-006171324-8). This memoir explains the author of *Marley and Me*'s rejection and final acceptance of his Catholic faith; for mature readers. ∩ **e** (Rev: BL 9/15/08) [921]

GUY, ROSA

7361 Norris, Jerrie. *Presenting Rosa Guy* (9–12). 1988, Twayne $20.95 (978-0-8057-8207-3). A critical biography of the West Indian-born writer who has re-created Harlem life so vividly in her books for young adults. (Rev: SLJ 12/88; VOYA 12/88) [921]

HALEY, ALEX

7362 Shirley, David. *Alex Haley* (7–10). Series: Black Americans of Achievement. 1993, Chelsea LB $30.00 (978-0-7910-1979-5); paper $8.95 (978-0-7910-1980-1). The story of the African American writer who gave us the family saga *Roots*. (Rev: BL 2/15/94) [921]

HAMILTON, HUGO

7363 Hamilton, Hugo. *The Harbor Boys* (10–12). 2006, HarperCollins $24.95 (978-0-06-078467-6). Hamilton follows *The Speckled People* (2003), which told the story of his Irish childhood with a German mother and Irish father — each fiercely politically opinionated, with this account of his adolescent efforts to establish his own identity amid family quarrels and religious clashes between fishermen at his harbor job. (Rev: BL 10/1/06) [823]

HAMILTON, VIRGINIA

7364 Adoff, Arnold, and Kacy Cook, eds. *Virginia Hamilton: Speeches, Essays, and Conversations* (8–12). 2010, Scholastic $29.99 (978-043927193-6). This collection, edited by her husband and Kacy Cook, gives insight into the life and work of the popular, award-winning author of children's books. (Rev: BL 3/1/10; LMC 8–9/10; SLJ 3/10*; VOYA 4/10) [921]

HANSBERRY, LORRAINE

7365 Hansberry, Lorraine. *To Be Young, Gifted and Black* (9–12). 1970, NAL paper $6.99 (978-0-451-15952-6). An autobiographical collection of reminiscences, letters, and quotations from Hansberry's plays. [921]

7366 Sinnott, Susan. *Lorraine Hansberry: Award-Winning Playwright and Civil Rights Activist* (7–12). 1998, Conari paper $11.95 (978-1-57324-093-2). This story of the great African American playwright who grew up with a passion for theater and politics conveys a sense of the politics from the 1930s to the 1960s and the pressures of fame on an artist. (Rev: BL 2/15/99) [921]

HAWTHORNE, NATHANIEL

7367 Meltzer, Milton. *Nathaniel Hawthorne: A Biography* (6–12). 2006, Twenty-First Century LB $31.93 (978-0-7613-3459-0). Hawthorne had an event-filled life according to thisbiography that covers both triumphs and blemishes and puts the whole in historical context. (Rev: SLJ 11/06)

7368 Miller, Edwin Haviland. *Salem Is My Dwelling Place: A Life of Nathaniel Hawthorne* (9–12). 1991, Univ. of Iowa paper $24.95 (978-0-87745-381-9). Miller examines how the painfully shy 19th-century American writer gave voice to his inner torment through his writings, which include such classic novels as *The House of Seven Gables* and *The Scarlet Letter*. [921]

HEMINGWAY, ERNEST

7369 Reef, Catherine. *Ernest Hemingway: A Writer's Life* (8–12). Illus. 2009, Clarion $20.00 (978-061898705-4). With many quotations from Hemingway's contemporaries, Reef creates a vivid and balanced portrait of the author's complex life. ∩ (Rev: BL 6/1–15/09; SLJ 8/09) [921]

7370 Sandison, David. *Ernest Hemingway: An Illustrated Biography* (9–12). 1999, Chicago Review $24.95 (978-1-55652-399-1). A visually attractive, insightful biography organized into eight chronological chapters, combining biography, history, literature, and photography to show an amazingly talented yet tormented man. (Rev: SLJ 8/99) [921]

HENRY, MARGUERITE

7371 Collins, David R. *Write a Book for Me: The Story of Marguerite Henry* (7–10). Series: World Writers. 1999, Morgan Reynolds LB $23.95 (978-1-883846-39-8). A short, simple biography of the writer of such memorable books for young people as *King of the Wind*. (Rev: BL 3/15/99; SLJ 9/99; VOYA 10/99) [921]

HERBERT, FRANK

7372 Herbert, Brian. *Dreamer of Dune: The Biography of Frank Herbert* (10–12). 2003, Tor $27.95 (978-0-7653-0646-3). A loving but frank biography of the science fiction author by his son. (Rev: BL 2/15/03) [813]

HUGHES, LANGSTON

7373 Rummel, Jack. *Langston Hughes: Poet. Rev. ed.* (7–12). Series: Black Americans of Achievement. 2005, Chelsea House LB $30.00 (978-0-7910-8250-8). A revised edition of the highly readable and well illustrated biography of the African American poet and fiction writer, containing excerpts from his writings. (Rev: SLJ 11/05) [921]

7374 Wallace, Maurice. *Langston Hughes: The Harlem Renaissance* (8–12). Series: Writers and Their Works. 2007, Marshall Cavendish LB $27.95 (978-0-7614-

2591-5). Accessible analysis of Hughes's works is combined with information about his life and the environment in which he worked. (Rev: BL 2/1/08; SLJ 2/08) [921]

HURSTON, ZORA NEALE

7375 Boyd, Valerie. *Wrapped in Rainbows: The Life of Zora Neale Hurston* (10–12). 2003, Scribner $30.00 (978-0-684-84230-1). The extraordinary life of African American anthropologist/writer Zora Neale Hurston is chronicled in detail in this beautifully realized biography suitable for mature teens. (Rev: BL 12/15/02*) [921]

7376 Hemenway, Robert E. *Zora Neale Hurston: A Literary Biography* (10–12). 1977, Univ. of Illinois paper $16.95 (978-0-252-00807-8). As well as a fine biography, this volume includes an analysis of all of Hurston's works. [921]

7377 Hurston, Zora Neale. *Folklore, Memoirs, and Other Writings* (10–12). 1995, Library of America $35.00 (978-0-940450-84-4). In addition to Hurston's autobiography, *Dust Tracks on the Road,* and other personal writing, this volume includes a generous sampling of the African American folktales she collected. (Rev: BL 2/15/95) [818]

7378 Litwin, Laura Baskes. *Zora Neale Hurston: "I Have Been in Sorrow's Kitchen"* (7–10). 2007, Enslow LB $23.95 (978-0-7660-2536-3). Presents the life of legendary author and folklorist Zora Neale Hurston, including her childhood, her influences, and her remarkable career. (Rev: BL 6/1–15/07; SLJ 7/07) [921]

7379 Porter, A. P. *Jump at de Sun: The Story of Zora Neale Hurston* (7–12). 1992, Carolrhoda paper $8.95 (978-0-87614-546-3). A brief, easy-to-read biography that places Hurston within the context of the racism of her era. (Rev: BL 12/15/92; SLJ 1/93*) [921]

7380 Sapet, Kerrily. *Rhythm and Folklore: The Story of Zora Neale Hurston* (7–12). 2008, Morgan Reynolds LB $27.95 (978-1-59935-067-7). This vibrant biography of the author of *Their Eyes Were Watching God* contains plenty of personal quotes, full-page photographs, and complete back matter. (Rev: BL 6/1–15/08; SLJ 8/08) [921]

KAFKA, FRANZ

7381 Adler, Jeremy. *Franz Kafka* (10–12). Series: Overlook Illustrated Lives. 2002, Overlook $19.95 (978-1-58567-267-7). This brief, well-illustrated, and accessible biography focuses mainly on the author's life. (Rev: BL 7/02) [921]

KEROUAC-PARKER, EDIE

7382 Kerouac-Parker, Frankie Edith. *You'll Be Okay: My Life with Jack Kerouac* (10–12). 2007, City Lights paper $14.95 (978-0-87286-464-1). Kerouac's first

wife tells a fascinating tale of life amid the Beat generation. (Rev: BL 8/07) [921]

KERR, M. E.

7383 Nilsen, Alleen P. *Presenting M. E. Kerr. Rev. ed.*
(8–12). Series: Twayne's United States Authors. 1997,
Twayne $35.00 (978-0-8057-9248-5). A biography of
this popular young adult writer that also discusses her
works, with a detailed analysis of her five most popular
books. (Rev: SLJ 4/98; VOYA 4/98) [810]

KING, STEPHEN

7384 King, Stephen. *On Writing: A Memoir of the Craft*
(10–12). 2000, Scribner $25.00 (978-0-684-85352-9).
As well as recounting his life story, King gives good
advice to would-be writers in this interesting memoir.
(Rev: BL 7/00; SLJ 3/01) [921]

7385 Whitelaw, Nancy. *Dark Dreams: The Story of Stephen King* (7–10). Series: World Writers. 2005, Morgan
Reynolds $26.95 (978-1-931798-77-8). An inviting in-
troduction to King and to his writing, with lots of interesting anecdotes and snippets of his work. (Rev: BL
11/15/05; VOYA 2/06) [813]

KIRN, WALTER

7386 Kirn, Walter. *Lost in the Meritocracy: The Under-
education of an Overachiever* (11–12). 2009, Doubleday $24.95 (978-038552128-4). This is Kirn's account
of how he learned to coast through prestigious schools
by playing the system rather than pursuing knowledge.
e (Rev: BL 4–5/09) [921]

L'ENGLE, MADELEINE

7387 McClellan, Marilyn. *Madeleine L'Engle: Banned,
Challenged, and Censored* (8–12). Series: Authors of
Banned Books. 2008, Enslow LB $25.95 (978-0-7660-
2708-4). Why do some groups question if the author's *A
Wrinkle in Time* is appropriate for young readers? This
book examines the objections and the author's defense
of her award-winning book. (Rev: BL 4/1/08) [921]

LASKY, KATHRYN

7388 Brown, Joanne. *Presenting Kathryn Lasky* (9–12).
Series: Twayne's United States Authors. 1998, Twayne
$35.00 (978-0-8057-1677-1). An objective, lively biog-
raphy of this popular young adult author that illumi-
nates how her experiences have influenced her writing,
plus a critical analysis of her books. (Rev: SLJ 6/99)
[921]

LEE, HARPER

7389 Don, Katherine. *Real Courage: The Story of
Harper Lee* (7–10). Illus. Series: World Writers. 2012,
Morgan Reynolds LB $28.95 (978-159935348-7). An
interesting life of the woman who wrote only one novel,

but an enduring classic. (Rev: BL 11/1/12; SLJ 12/12;
VOYA 12/12) [921]

7390 Madden, Kerry. *Harper Lee* (7–12). Illus. Series:
Up Close. 2009, Viking $16.99 (978-067001095-0).
An introduction to the life and work of the reclusive
author of *To Kill a Mockingbird*. Lexile 1210 (Rev: BL
4/15/09; HB 3–4/09; SLJ 6/1/09) [921]

LONDON, JACK

7391 Stefoff, Rebecca. *Jack London: An American Original* (7–10). Series: Oxford Portraits. 2002, Oxford LB
$32.95 (978-0-19-512223-7). A profile of this Ameri-
can original, his life, his work, and his lasting importance. (Rev: BL 7/02; HBG 10/02; SLJ 8/02) [921]

MANZANO, JUAN FRANCISCO

7392 Engle, Margarita. *The Poet Slave of Cuba: A Biography of Juan Francisco Manzano* (7–10). Illus. by
Sean Quails. 2006, Henry Holt $16.95 (978-0-8050-
7706-3). This lyrical free-verse biography tells the story
of the poet born into slavery in Cuba in 1797, describing his early talent with languages and how it helped
him survived amazing brutality. Belpré Medal 2008;
ALA Notable Books 2008. (Rev: BL 2/15/06*; SLJ
4/06*) [811]

MCCOURT, FRANK

7393 McCourt, Frank. *Teacher Man* (9–12). 2005, Scribner $26.00 (978-0-7432-4377-3). With humor and elo-
quence, the author of *Angela's Ashes* (1996) recounts
his experiences as a teacher in the public schools of
New York City. (Rev: BL 9/15/05) [929]

MELVILLE, HERMAN

7394 Meltzer, Milton. *Herman Melville: A Biogra-
phy* (8–12). Series: American Literary Greats. 2005,
Twenty-First Century LB $31.93 (978-0-7613-2749-3).
Traces the writer's difficult life and links his struggles
to passages from his works, in particular *Moby Dick*.
(Rev: SLJ 1/06) [921]

MEYER, STEPHENIE

7395 Krohn, Katherine. *Stephenie Meyer: Dreaming
of Twilight* (6–12). Illus. Series: Lifeline Biographies.
2010, Lerner LB $33.26 (978-076135220-4). This at-
tractive biography draws on the archives of *USA Today*
to describe the author's life and publishing career. (Rev:
BL 9/1/10*) [921]

MILLER, ADAM DAVID

7396 Miller, Adam David. *Ticket to Exile* (11–12). 2007,
Heyday paper $14.95 (978-1-59714-065-2). African
American poet Miller tells the story of his arrest for
rape at the age of 19, when all he had done was pass a
note to a young white woman, and reflects on issues of

race and class in the South during the Depression. (Rev: BL 10/15/07) [811]

MILLER, ARTHUR

7397 Andersen, Richard. *Arthur Miller* (7–10). Series: Writers and Their Works. 2005, Benchmark LB $25.95 (978-0-7614-1946-4). *The Crucible* and *Death of a Salesman* are discussed in some detail in this overview of Miller's life and works. (Rev: SLJ 3/06) [921]

MOEHRINGER, J. R.

7398 Moehringer, J. R. *The Tender Bar* (11–12). 2005, Hyperion $23.95 (978-1-4013-0064-7). Pulitzer Prize-winning journalist Moehringer writes about growing up on Long Island and the male role models he found in a local bar; for mature teens. (Rev: BL 8/05) [070.92]

MORRISON, TONI

7399 Andersen, Richard. *Toni Morrison* (7–10). Series: Writers and Their Works. 2005, Benchmark LB $25.95 (978-0-7614-1945-7). *Sula* and *The Bluest Eye* are discussed in some detail in this overview of Morrison's life and works. (Rev: SLJ 3/06) [921]

7400 Haskins, Jim. *Toni Morrison: Telling a Tale Untold* (7–12). 2002, Millbrook LB $26.90 (978-0-7613-1852-1). Haskins adds discussion of each of Morrison's books to this account of her life and literary career. (Rev: BL 10/1/02; HBG 3/03; VOYA 12/02) [813]

NASH, OGDEN

7401 Parker, Douglas M. *Ogden Nash: The Life and Work of America's Laureate of Light Verse* (10–12). 2005, Ivan R. Dee $27.50 (978-1-56663-637-7). A readable profile of the playful poet. (Rev: SLJ 8/05) [921]

ORR, GREGORY

7402 Orr, Gregory. *The Blessing* (10–12). 2002, Council Oak $24.95 (978-1-57178-111-6). In this memoir of his troubled childhood, which included the accidental fatal shooting of his brother on a hunting trip, poet Orr searches for the factors that led him to a career in writing. (Rev: BL 10/15/02*) [921]

ORWELL, GEORGE

7403 Agathocleous, Tanya. *George Orwell: Battling Big Brother* (8–12). Series: Oxford Portraits. 2000, Oxford $32.95 (978-0-19-512185-8). A concise, well-written life of this fascinating English writer and his contributions to world literature. (Rev: BL 10/1/00; HBG 10/01) [921]

PEKAR, HARVEY

7404 Pekar, Harvey. *The Quitter* (9–12). Illus. by Dean Haspiel. 2005, Vertigo $19.99 (978-1-4012-0399-3).

Pekar tells the story of his troubled childhood and his tendency to quit anything in which he didn't excel. (Rev: BL 10/1/05; SLJ 3/06) [741.5]

POE, EDGAR ALLAN

7405 Meltzer, Milton. *Edgar Allan Poe* (6–12). 2003, Millbrook LB $31.90 (978-0-7613-2910-7). Poe's difficult life and literary accomplishments are described within the larger context of early 19th-century society in this well-illustrated and well-documented biography. (Rev: BL 11/15/03; HBG 4/04; VOYA 2/04) [818]

PULLMAN, PHILIP

7406 Yuan, Margaret Speaker. *Philip Pullman* (7–10). Series: Who Wrote That? 2005, Chelsea House LB $30.00 (978-0-7910-8658-2). In addition to profiling this author of award-winning books, this biography describes his writing methods. (Rev: BL 3/15/06; SLJ 5/06) [823]

RAND, AYN

7407 Britting, Jeffrey. *Ayn Rand* (9–12). Series: Overlook Illustrated Lives. 2005, Overlook $19.95 (978-1-58567-406-0). A useful introduction to the Russian-born writer's individualist beliefs and to her works. (Rev: SLJ 6/05) [921]

RAWLINGS, MARJORIE KINNAN

7408 Silverthorne, Elizabeth. *Marjorie Kinnan Rawlings: Sojourner at Cross Creek* (10–12). 1988, Overlook $24.95 (978-0-87951-308-5). This is the biography of the acclaimed author of such moving novels as *Cross Creek* and *The Yearling*. [921]

RICE, ANNE

7409 Rice, Anne. *Called Out of Darkness: A Spiritual Confession* (10–12). 2008, Knopf $23.95 (978-030726827-3). Author Anne Rice examines her loss of faith and her eventual path back to Catholicism; fans of her witch and vampire books will be interested in this memoir. ⌒ ℮ (Rev: BL 8/08) [921]

RIIS, JACOB

7410 Pascal, Janet B. *Jacob Riis: Reporter and Reformer* (8–11). Series: Oxford Portraits. 2006, Oxford LB $28.00 (978-0-19-514527-4). Riis's groundbreaking photography and journalism exposing 19th-century living and working conditions is explored in this well-balanced biography of the Danish American. (Rev: BL 6/1–15/06; SLJ 7/06) [921]

RIORDAN, RICK

7411 Sparks, Barry. *Rick Riordan* (7–10). Illus. Series: World Writers. 2012, Morgan Reynolds LB $28.95 (978-159935350-0). Sparks traces Riordan's life and work, discussing the plots and characters of popular works including the Percy Jackson series. (Rev: BL 11/1/12; SLJ 11/12) [921]

SALINGER, J. D.

7412 Slawenski, Kenneth. *J. D. Salinger* (9–12). 2011, Random House $27 (978-140006951-4). A thorough biography of the reclusive creator of Holden Caulfield. ⌒ e (Rev: BL 12/1–15/10*) [921]

SANDBURG, CARL

7413 Meltzer, Milton. *Carl Sandburg: A Biography* (5–10). 1999, Millbrook LB $31.90 (978-0-7613-1364-9). The story of a literary giant who, in addition to his poetry, is noted for nonfiction works including a biography of Abraham Lincoln. (Rev: BL 12/15/99; HBG 10/00; VOYA 6/00) [921]

SANDELL, LAURIE

7414 Sandell, Laurie. *The Impostor's Daughter: A True Memoir* (10–12). Illus. 2009, Little, Brown $24.99 (978-031603305-3). Sandell recounts her experiences growing up as the daughter of a highly deceptive father; the graphic-novel format conveys her own maturing. (Rev: BL 7/09) [921]

SEBESTYEN, OUIDA

7415 Monseau, Virginia R. *Presenting Ouida Sebestyen* (6–12). Series: United States Authors. 1995, Twayne $28.00 (978-0-8057-8224-0). Sebestyen's unorthodox writing habits enliven this text, with biographical information and detailed analysis of six novels. (Rev: BL 9/1/95) [921]

SHAKESPEARE, WILLIAM

7416 Bryson, Bill. *Shakespeare: The World as Stage* (8–12). 2007, HarperCollins $19.95 (978-0-06-074022-1). Bryson has created an unusual and enjoyable survey of Shakespeare's life and times, explaining his research as he goes and disproving earlier claims. ⌒ (Rev: BL 10/15/07) [921]

SHELLEY, MARY WOLLSTONECRAFT

7417 Hoobler, Dorothy, and Thomas Hoobler. *The Monsters: Mary Shelley and the Curse of Frankenstein* (11–12). 2006, Little, Brown $24.95 (978-0-316-00078-9). About the creative, troubled, complex woman from whose mind sprang the iconic novel *Frankenstein*; for mature teens. (Rev: BL 5/15/06) [921]

7418 Miller, Calvin Craig. *Spirit Like a Storm: The Story of Mary Shelley* (7–10). 1996, Morgan Reynolds LB $21.95 (978-1-883846-13-8). The life story of the fascinating, talented creator of *Frankenstein,* who was also the wife of poet Percy Bysshe Shelley. (Rev: BL 2/15/96; SLJ 3/96; VOYA 6/96) [921]

7419 Nichols, Joan Kane. *Mary Shelley: Frankenstein's Creator, First Science Fiction Writer* (10–12). Series: Barnard Biography. 1998, Conari paper $11.95 (978-1-57324-087-1). A compelling biography of the spirited rebel and talented author who was the creator of *Frankenstein* and the wife of the poet Shelley. (Rev: SLJ 2/99) [921]

SINGER, ISAAC BASHEVIS

7420 Noiville, Florence. *Isaac B. Singer: A Life* (9–12). Trans. from French by Catherine Temerson. 2006, Farrar $23 (978-0-374-17800-0). Noiville draws on memoirs of Singer's siblings, interviews, and Singer's own writings to present a profile of his life and work. (Rev: SLJ 2/07) [921]

SÍS, PETER

7421 Sís, Peter. *The Wall: Growing Up Behind the Iron Curtain* (7–10). Illus. by author. 2007, Farrar $18.00 (978-0-374-34701-7). This autobiographical picture book portrays Sis's childhood in Czechoslovakia and the impact of Soviet rule on life in the nation. Sibert Medal 2008; Boston Globe–Horn Book Honor 2008; Caldecott Honor 2008; ALA Notable Books 2008. (Rev: BL 9/1/07; SLJ 8/07) [943.7]

STEINBECK, JOHN

7422 Reef, Catherine. *John Steinbeck* (7–12). 1996, Clarion $17.95 (978-0-395-71278-8). A handsome photobiography that not only covers salient aspects of Steinbeck's life but also explores the themes and locales of his work. (Rev: BL 5/1/96; SLJ 3/96; VOYA 8/96) [921]

SWIFT, JONATHAN

7423 Aykroyd, Clarissa. *Savage Satire: The Story of Jonathan Swift* (9–12). 2006, Morgan Reynolds $26.95 (978-1-59935-027-1). A biography of the Anglo-Irish minister and writer who's best known as the author of *Gulliver's Travels*. (Rev: BL 11/1/06; SLJ 1/07) [921]

TERKEL, STUDS

7424 Terkel, Studs. *Touch and Go* (11–12). 2007, New Press $24.95 (978-1-59558-043-6). Terkel reviews his 95 years, from his childhood through his adolescence and on through his long career, with humor and with insight into others who affected his life. (Rev: BL 10/15/07) [921]

THOMPSON, HUNTER S.

7425 Wenner, Jann S., and Corey Seymour, eds. *Gonzo: The Life of Hunter S. Thompson* (11–12). 2007, Little, Brown $28.99 (978-0-316-00527-2). This oral biography — a collection of reminiscences about Thompson — reveals the journalist as his friends and others knew him, warts and all; for mature teens. (Rev: BL 11/1/07) [070.92]

THOREAU, HENRY DAVID

7426 Meltzer, Milton. *Henry David Thoreau* (8–11). Series: American Literary Greats. 2007, Lerner LB $31.93 (978-0-8225-5893-4). A clear examination of Thoreau's life and work, exploring his philosophy and wit and their continuing relevance today. (Rev: BL 6/1–15/07; SLJ 5/07) [818]

7427 Miller, Douglas T. *Henry David Thoreau: A Man for all Seasons* (9–12). Series: Makers of America. 1991, Replica $24.95 (978-0-7351-0220-0). This slim but insightful biography covers Thoreau's life and beliefs on civil liberty and nature. [921]

7428 Thoreau, Henry David. *Thoreau at Walden* (8–12). Illus. by John Porcellino. Series: Center for Cartoon Studies. 2008, Hyperion $16.99 (978-1-4231-0038-6); paper $9.99 (978-1-4231-0039-3). Using Thoreau's words and spare, clean illustrations, this is a graphic novel-style introduction to the philosopher's beliefs about leading a simple life. (Rev: BL 3/15/08; SLJ 3/08) [921]

TOLSTOY, LEO

7429 Heims, Neil. *Tortured Noble: The Story of Leo Tolstoy* (9–11). 2007, Morgan Reynolds LB $27.95 (978-1-59935-066-0). A detailed account of the life of Leo Tolstoy, including his privileged childhood, troubled youth, and religious interests, with discussion of the times in which he lived. (Rev: BL 8/07; SLJ 9/07) [921]

TWAIN, MARK

7430 Caravantes, Peggy. *A Great and Sublime Fool: The Story of Mark Twain* (7–10). Illus. Series: World Writers. 2009, Morgan Reynolds LB $28.95 (978-159935088-2). Well-chosen illustrations add to this informative survey of Twain's life and work. (Rev: BL 6/1–15/09; SLJ 7/1/09) [921]

7431 Howard, Todd, ed. *Mark Twain* (7–12). Series: People Who Made History. 2002, Gale paper $36.20 (978-0-7377-0897-4). Detailed essays that explore various aspects of Twain's life and writing are preceded by a general introductory that gives an overview of his life and times. (Rev: BL 4/1/02) [921]

7432 Neider, Charles, ed. *The Autobiography of Mark Twain* (10–12). 1990, HarperCollins paper $14.00 (978-0-06-092025-8). This is a well-edited version of the mass of material left by Twain to serve as his autobiography. [921]

7433 Rasmussen, R. Kent. *Mark Twain from A to Z: The Essential Reference to His Life and Writings* (9–12). Series: Literary A to Z. 1995, Facts on File $65.00 (978-0-8160-2845-0). This award-winning, comprehensive study of Twain's life and times contains nearly

1,300 entries that cover all important aspects of his life and works. (Rev: SLJ 3/96) [921]

7434 Ward, Geoffrey C. *Mark Twain* (8–12). 2001, Knopf $40.00 (978-0-375-40561-7). As well as a good text, this biography contains a treasure trove of photographs and other illustrations that depict the life and times of Mark Twain. (Rev: BL 10/15/01; SLJ 6/02) [921]

VONNEGUT, KURT

7435 Vonnegut, Kurt. *Conversations with Kurt Vonnegut* (10–12). Series: Literary Conversations. 1988, Univ. Press of Mississippi paper $22.00 (978-0-87805-358-2). A collection of interviews from various sources that reveal many facets of the life, character, and work of this amazing author. [921]

WHARTON, EDITH

7436 Wooldridge, Connie Nordhielm. *The Brave Escape of Edith Wharton: A Biography* (7–10). 2010, Clarion $20 (978-0-547-23630-8). Explaining the social structure of the Gilded Age, this biography reveals Wharton's own rebellion against conventions and shows how her experiences are reflected in those of her literary characters. (Rev: BL 10/1/10*; LMC 3–4/11; SLJ 9/1/10; VOYA 12/10) [921]

WHEATLEY, PHILLIS

7437 Jensen, Marilyn. *Phillis Wheatley: Negro Slave of Mr. John Wheatley of Boston* (9–12). 1987, Sayre LB $21.95 (978-0-87460-326-2). The story of a slave in Boston who became the first black poet in colonial America and gained sufficient fame to be invited to England to meet the king. (Rev: SLJ 12/87) [921]

WHEDON, JOSS

7438 Havens, Candace. *Joss Whedon: The Genius Behind Buffy* (10–12). 2003, BenBella paper $15.95 (978-1-932100-00-6). Teen fans of TV's *Buffy the Vampire Slayer* will enjoy this entertaining profile of its creator. (Rev: BL 5/15/03) [921]

WHITMAN, WALT

7439 Meltzer, Milton. *Walt Whitman: A Biography* (6–12). 2002, Millbrook LB $31.90 (978-0-7613-2272-6). This life story of the American poet emphasizes his place in the country's history. (Rev: BL 4/1/02; HB 9–10/02; HBG 3/03; SLJ 3/02; VOYA 6/03) [921]

7440 Reef, Catherine. *Walt Whitman* (7–12). 1995, Clarion $16.95 (978-0-395-68705-5). A biography of the 19th-century poet who sang of America and the self. (Rev: BL 5/1/95; SLJ 5/95) [921]

WILDER, LAURA INGALLS

7441 Zochert, Donald. *Laura: The Life of Laura Ingalls Wilder* (9–12). 1976, Avon paper $7.99 (978-0-380-01636-5). An honest, sympathetic biography of and tribute to the author of the Little House books. [921]

WILLIAMS, TENNESSEE

7442 Tracy, Kathleen. *Tennessee Williams* (9–12). Series: Poets and Playwrights. 2007, Mitchell Lane LB $24.95 (978-1-58415-427-3). A useful overview of Williams's life and works, with insight into his inspirations. (Rev: BL 4/1/07; SLJ 8/07) [921]

WOLFE, SWAIN

7443 Wolfe, Swain. *The Boy Who Invented Skiing: A Memoir* (9–12). 2006, St. Martin's $24.95 (978-0-312-31093-6). A childhood of neglect and abuse are followed by many adventures in the West in this engaging memoir. (Rev: SLJ 9/06) [921]

WOLFF, TOBIAS

7444 Wolff, Tobias. *This Boy's Life: A Memoir* (10–12). 1989, Atlantic Monthly paper $13.00 (978-0-8021-3668-8). This nonfiction work is an engrossing, entertaining look at the author's youth and adolescence. [921]

WOOLF, VIRGINIA

7445 Brackett, Virginia. *Restless Genius: The Story of Virginia Woolf* (7–12). Series: Writers of Imagination. 2004, Morgan Reynolds LB $23.95 (978-1-931798-37-2). Woolf's personal life — her relationship with Vita Sackville-West is touched on — and mental stability are the main focus of this brief, interesting biography that also discusses her writing and its influence. (Rev: BCCB 11/04; BL 10/1/04; SLJ 11/04) [921]

7446 Caws, Mary Ann. *Virginia Woolf* (10–12). Series: Overlook Illustrated Lives. 2002, Overlook $19.95 (978-1-58567-264-6). This brief, well-illustrated, and accessible biography focuses mainly on Woolf's life. (Rev: BL 7/02) [921]

7447 Mills, Cliff. *Virginia Woolf* (9–12). 2004, Chelsea House LB $30.00 (978-0-7910-7459-6). The personal and professional lives of this great English writer are covered with many quotations from a number of original sources. (Rev: BL 3/1/04) [921]

WRIGHT, RICHARD

7448 Hart, Joyce. *Native Son: The Story of Richard Wright* (6–10). Series: World Writers. 2002, Morgan Reynolds LB $23.95 (978-1-931798-06-8). This biography describes best-selling African American author Richard Wright's controversial works and his development as a writer. (Rev: BL 2/15/03; HBG 3/03; SLJ 4/03) [921]

7449 Levy, Debbie. *Richard Wright* (7–12). Series: Literary Greats. 2007, Lerner LB $33.26 (978-0-8225-6793-6). The life and times of the author of *Native Son* and *Black Boy*, with photographs and a timeline. (Rev: BL 12/1/07; SLJ 12/07) [921]

7450 Wright, Richard. *Black Boy: A Record of Childhood and Youth* (8–12). 1998, HarperCollins paper $13.95 (978-0-06-092978-7). The tortured boyhood of the great black writer growing up in the South. This autobiography is continued in *American Hunger* (1977). [921]

YEATS, WILLIAM BUTLER

7451 Allison, Jonathan, ed. *William Butler Yeats* (6–12). Illus. by Glenn Harrington. Series: Poetry for Young People. 2003, Sterling $14.95 (978-0-8069-6615-1). A handsomely illustrated collection of Yeats's poems, each introduced with commentary and followed by explanations of any challenging vocabulary. (Rev: BL 4/1/03; HBG 10/03; SLJ 2/03) [921]

ZINDEL, PAUL

7452 Forman, Jack Jacob. *Presenting Paul Zindel* (9–12). 1988, Twayne $20.95 (978-0-8057-8206-6). An analysis of both the life and works of this popular author whose trailblazing books have influenced the course of young adult literature. (Rev: BL 7/88; SLJ 9/88; VOYA 10/88) [921]

Composers

BACH, JOHANN SEBASTIAN

7453 Getzinger, Donna, and Daniel Felsenfeld. *Johann Sebastian Bach and the Art of Baroque Music* (6–12). Series: Classical Composers. 2004, Morgan Reynolds LB $26.95 (978-1-931798-22-8). This biography reviews Bach's life and times, emphasizing in particular his musical education and commitment and his love for this family. (Rev: BL 6/1–15/04; SLJ 8/04) [780]

BEETHOVEN, LUDWIG VAN

7454 Siepmann, Jeremy. *Beethoven: His Life and Music* (9–12). 2006, Sourcebooks $29.95 (978-1-4022-0751-8). An engaging account of Beethoven's life and contributions, bolstered by a CD of music, a chapter giving historical context, and profiles of key friends and colleagues. (Rev: SLJ 1/07)

BERNSTEIN, LEONARD

7455 Bernstein, Burton. *Leonard Bernstein: American Original: How a Modern Renaissance Man Transformed Music and the World During His New York Philharmonic Years, 1943–1976* (10–12). Ed. by Barbara B. Haws. Illus. 2008, HarperCollins $29.95 (978-0-06-153786-8). Revisiting a New York Philharmonic on the verge of bankruptcy and the unexpected young conductor who saved it, this portrait features an array of warm first-person stories about Leonard Bernstein from a variety of different authors. **e** (Rev: BL 6/1–15/08*; SLJ 3/09) [921]

7456 Lazo, Caroline Evensen. *Leonard Bernstein: In Love with Music* (7–12). 2002, Lerner LB $27.93 (978-0-8225-0072-8). This detailed portrait of Bernstein's life and musical accomplishments includes many black-and-white photographs. (Rev: BL 10/15/02; HBG 3/03; VOYA 12/02) [780]

7457 Rubin, Susan Goldman. *Music Was It: Young Leonard Bernstein* (5–10). Illus. 2011, Charlesbridge $19.95 (978-1-58089-344-2). A compelling account of the composer/conductor's youth through the age of 25 and his determination to succeed in music despite his father's resistance to the idea. ALA Notable Children's Book; Sydney Taylor Award. (Rev: BL 2/15/11*; HB 5–6/11; LMC 8–9/11; SLJ 3/1/11)

DVORAK, ANTONIN

7458 Horowitz, Joseph. *Dvorak in America* (6–12). 2003, Cricket $17.95 (978-0-8126-2481-6). Dvorak's life in the United States (he arrived from Prague in the 1890s) is the focus of this narrative, which also covers the composition of the New World symphony. (Rev: BL 6/1–15/03) [780]

GUTHRIE, WOODY

7459 Guthrie, Woody. *Bound for Glory* (10–12). 1943, Peter Smith $30.25 (978-0-8446-6178-0); paper $15.00 (978-0-452-26445-8). The saga of the man who grew up in poverty in the Oklahoma Dust Bowl and in time became one of America's most famous troubadours. [921]

7460 Partridge, Elizabeth. *This Land Was Made for You and Me: The Life and Songs of Woodie Guthrie* (6–12). 2002, Viking $21.99 (978-0-670-03535-9). The life, work, and times of the folk singer, from his childhood in the Dust Bowl to his death from Huntington's Disease. (Rev: BL 4/1/02; HB 3–4/02*; HBG 10/02; SLJ 4/02; VOYA 8/02) [782.42162]

7461 Yates, Janelle. *Woody Guthrie: American Balladeer* (6–10). 1995, Ward Hill LB $14.95 (978-0-9623380-0-7); paper $10.95 (978-0-9623380-5-2). Describes Guthrie's creative life and provides important historical information, including the many tragedies suffered by his family and his friendly relationship with labor, members of the Communist Party, and other musicians. (Rev: BL 2/1/95; SLJ 3/95) [921]

HANDEL, GEORGE FRIDERIC

7462 Getzinger, Donna, and Daniel Felsenfeld. *George Frideric Handel and Music for Voices* (6–10). Series:

Classical Composers. 2004, Morgan Reynolds LB $26.95 (978-1-931798-23-5). Handel's life and career are placed in historical context. (Rev: SLJ 11/04) [921]

JOPLIN, SCOTT

7463 Curtis, Susan. *Dancing to a Black Man's Tune: A Life of Scott Joplin* (9–12). 1994, Univ. of Missouri $34.95 (978-0-8262-0949-8). Curtis traces the life of Joplin, best known for his piano rag "The Entertainer," from his Texas origins through his success as a performer and composer to his troubled stay in Harlem and the failure of his opera, *Treemonisha*. (Rev: BL 5/1/94) [780]

MENDELSSOHN, FANNY

7464 Shichtman, Sandra H., and Dorothy Indenbaum. *Gifted Sister: The Story of Fanny Mendelssohn* (8–11). 2007, Morgan Reynolds LB $27.95 (978-1-59935-038-7). Fanny, the sister of the noted musician, was very talented herself and composed throughout her life; this biography shows how her life evolved under the social constraints of the early 1800s. (Rev: BL 9/15/07; SLJ 9/07) [921]

MOZART, WOLFGANG AMADEUS

7465 Siepmann, Jeremy. *Mozart: His Life and Music* (9–12). 2006, Sourcebooks $29.95 (978-1-4022-0752-5). An engaging account of Mozart's life and contributions, bolstered by a CD of music, a chapter giving historical context, and profiles of key friends and colleagues. (Rev: SLJ 1/07)

VIVALDI, ANTONIO

7466 Getzinger, Donna, and Daniel Felsenfeld. *Antonio Vivaldi and the Baroque Tradition* (6–10). Series: Classical Composers. 2004, Morgan Reynolds LB $26.95 (978-1-931798-20-4). The story of the rise and fall of this prolific composer as well as of his music world and the importance of Venice in this sphere. (Rev: BL 4/15/04; SLJ 6/04) [921]

Performers and Media Personalities

ALONSO, ALICIA

7467 Arnold, Sandra M. *Alicia Alonso: First Lady of the Ballet* (6–10). 1993, Walker LB $15.85 (978-0-8027-8243-4). Overcoming the lack of dance schools in her native Cuba and going blind in her 20s, Alicia Alonso became a prima ballerina and went on to teach, study, and perform in Cuba. (Rev: BL 12/15/93; SLJ 11/93; VOYA 2/94) [921]

ANDERSON, MARIAN

7468 Keiler, Allan. *Marian Anderson: A Singer's Journey* (9–12). 2000, Scribner paper $21.95 (978-0-252-07067-9). A moving biography of the quiet, modest, African American concert singer who nevertheless contributed significantly to breaking the barriers of segregation. (Rev: BL 2/1/00) [921]

ARMSTRONG, LOUIS

7469 Bradbury, David. *Armstrong* (10–12). 2004, Haus $22.95 (978-1-904341-47-5). This concise biography of Louis Armstrong deals with his life and legacy and, through sidebars, tells of his times and associates. (Rev: BL 2/15/04) [921]

BALANCHINE, GEORGE

7470 Gottlieb, Robert. *George Balanchine: The Ballet Maker* (8–12). 2004, HarperCollins $19.95 (978-0-06-075070-1). Balanchine's ballet talent was recognized at a young age; this biography follows his progress from St. Petersburg to New York and worldwide fame. (Rev: BL 11/1/04) [792.8]

7471 Taper, Bernard. *Balanchine: A Biography* (9–12). 1984, Times paper $29.95 (978-0-520-20639-7). A thrilling biography of the great choreographer who was also an amazing person and teacher. [921]

BEASTIE BOYS (MUSICAL GROUP)

7472 Light, Alan. *The Skills to Pay the Bills: The Story of the Beastie Boys* (9–12). 2006, Three Rivers paper $14.00 (978-0-609-60478-6). The Beastie Boys, three white Jewish boys from New York City, and their unlikely climb to rap music stardom are profiled here. (Rev: BL 1/1–15/06) [782.42164]

BEATLES (MUSICAL GROUP)

7473 *The Beatles Anthology* (9–12). 2000, Chronicle $60.00 (978-0-8118-2684-6). Based on extensive interviews with Paul, George, and Ringo, this massive tribute to the Beatles contains 1,300 photographs plus many original documents and letters. (Rev: BL 9/15/00) [921]

7474 Davies, Hunter. *The Beatles* (9–12). 2006, Norton paper $29.95 (978-0-393-32886-8). An in-depth look at the Beatles from childhood through the 1970s, first published in 1978. [920]

7475 DeWitt, Howard A. *The Beatles: Untold Tales* (9–12). 1985, Horizon paper $14.95 (978-0-938840-03-9). This is a fine behind-the-scenes look at the lads from Liverpool, based on more than 50 interviews. (Rev: SLJ 1/86) [921]

7476 Giuliano, Geoffrey, and Avalon Giuliano. *Revolver: The Secret History of the Beatles* (9–12). 2006, Trafalgar $24.95 (978-1-84454-160-7). This biography emphasizes the business and other pressures the Beatles had to withstand while maintaining their playful public image, and introduces some little-known trivia on the making of their music. (Rev: BL 10/1/06) [782.42166]

7477 Sawyers, June S., ed. *Read the Beatles: Classic and New Writings on the Beatles, Their Legacy, and Why They Still Matter* (8–12). 2006, Penguin paper $16.00 (978-0-14-303732-3). A compilation of articles and essays about the Beatles, by writers including Gloria Steinem, Allen Ginsberg, and Philip Glass. (Rev: BL 11/1/06) [920]

7478 Spitz, Bob. *Yeah! Yeah! Yeah!* (7–10). 2007, Little, Brown $18.99 (978-0-316-11555-1). A fluent history of the Beatles, with information on the group's beginnings, influences, growth, and worldwide legacy, enhanced by black-and-white photographs; from the author of the adult book *The Beatles* (2005). (Rev: BL 11/1/07; SLJ 12/07) [782.421]

BEIDERBECKE, BIX

7479 Berton, Ralph. *Remembering Bix: A Memoir of the Jazz Age* (9–12). 2000, Da Capo paper $12.60 (978-0-306-80937-8). A lively account of the legendary cornetist's brief career by a respected jazz writer and professor of jazz history. (Rev: BL 2/1/00) [921]

BELUSHI, JOHN

7480 Pisano, Judith Belushi, and Tanner Colby. *Belushi* (9–12). 2005, RuggedLand $29.95 (978-1-59071-048-7). The life and unique comedy talents of John Belushi are celebrated in this richly illustrated tribute from the comedian's widow, incorporating contributions from many show-biz personalities. (Rev: BL 10/15/05) [791.45]

BROKAW, TOM

7481 Brokaw, Tom. *A Long Way from Home: Growing Up in the American Heartland* (10–12). 2002, Random House $24.95 (978-0-375-50763-2). In this candid memoir, the NBC news anchor remembers his youth in South Dakota. (Rev: BL 10/15/02) [921]

CHAPLIN, CHARLIE

7482 Fleischman, Sid. *Sir Charlie: Chaplin, The Funniest Man in the World* (6–10). 2010, Greenwillow $19.99 (978-0-06-189640-8). This engaging profile covers Chaplin's life from his start in the slums of London through a Vaudeville career, success in Hollywood, and eventual move to Switzerland and relative obscurity. (Rev: BL 6/10*; LMC 11–12/10; SLJ 6/10; VOYA 6/10) [921]

7483 Schickel, Richard, ed. *The Essential Chaplin: Perspectives on the Life and Art of the Great Comedian* (10–12). 2006, Ivan R. Dee $27.50 (978-1-56663-682-7); paper $16.95 (978-1-56663-701-5). More than 30 writers, critics, and others with an interest give their views on Chaplin's fascinating film-making career. (Rev: SLJ 11/06)

CHARLES, RAY

7484 Duggleby, John. *Uh Huh! The Story of Ray Charles* (6–12). 2005, Morgan Reynolds LB $26.95 (978-1-931798-65-5). In addition to an account of Ray Charles's life and music, this volume reveals much about the social context of his times. (Rev: BL 6/1–15/05; SLJ 10/05) [921]

7485 Woog, Adam. *Ray Charles and the Birth of Soul* (7–12). 2006, Gale LB $28.70 (978-1-59018-844-6). Covering Charles's life from a child of poverty in Florida to the legendary soul musician, Woog touches on his mother's influence and chronicles the development of his talents and innovations despite his blindness. (Rev: SLJ 6/06)

CHO, MARGARET

7486 Tiger, Caroline. *Margaret Cho* (7–12). Series: Asian Americans of Achievement. 2007, Chelsea House LB $30.00 (978-0-7910-9275-0). This biography of the edgy Asian American comedian will appeal to all teenagers who feel marginalized or who simply appreciate Cho's brand of angry but hilarious humor. (Rev: BL 4/15/07) [921]

COBAIN, KURT

7487 Burlingame, Jeff. *Kurt Cobain: "Oh Well, Whatever, Nevermind"* (8–11). Series: American Rebels. 2006, Enslow $20.95 (978-0-7660-2426-7). The author has the inside scoop on the rocker's adolescence, and he delves into what influenced Cobain's troubled youth and sad death. (Rev: BL 1/1–15/07) [921]

7488 Cross, Charles R. *Heavier than Heaven: A Biography of Kurt Cobain* (10–12). 2001, Hyperion $24.95 (978-0-7868-6505-5). The life and legacy of Kurt Cobain, singer and songwriter of the rock band Nirvana, who committed suicide. (Rev: BL 7/01) [921]

7489 McDougall, Chros. *Kurt Cobain: Alternative Rock Innovator* (7–10). Illus. Series: Lives Cut Short. 2012, ABDO LB $23.95 (978-161783480-6). This profile includes first-person quotes, comments from insiders and critics, interesting sidebars, and relevant photographs. (Rev: BL 12/1/12) [921]

COSBY, BILL

7490 Smith, Ronald L. *Cosby: The Life of a Comedy Legend. Rev. ed.* (10–12). 1997, Prometheus $30.98 (978-1-57392-126-8). A serious, adult look at Cosby's life, from his early childhood through his climb to fame. The book ends with the tragic death of his son, Ennis. (Rev: BL 2/1/97; SLJ 11/97) [921]

CRONKITE, WALTER

7491 Cronkite, Walter. *A Reporter's Life* (10–12). 1996, Knopf $26.95 (978-0-394-57879-8). A memoir by one of America's most respected journalists, with material on the important stories he covered, including World War II, the Vietnam War, and the Apollo space program. (Rev: BL 11/1/96; SLJ 7/97) [921]

DE MILLE, AGNES

7492 Hasday, Judy L. *Agnes de Mille* (9–12). Series: Women in the Arts. 2004, Chelsea House LB $30.00 (978-0-7910-7457-2). The story of the great female choreographer, who was active both in ballet and the Broadway stage. (Rev: BL 3/15/04) [921]

DEGENERES, ELLEN

7493 Paprocki, Sherry Beck. *Ellen DeGeneres: Entertainer* (6–10). Series: Women of Achievement. 2009, Chelsea House $30 (978-1-60413-082-9). This is a balanced profile of the popular TV host and her impact on pop culture. (Rev: SLJ 5/1/09) [921]

DIXIE CHICKS

7494 Dickerson, James L. *Dixie Chicks: Down-Home and Backstage* (9–12). 2000, Taylor paper $16.95 (978-0-87833-189-5). The story of the popular country music stars and how they rose to stardom after years of obscurity. (Rev: BL 9/1/00) [921]

DOMINO, FATS

7495 Coleman, Rick. *Blue Monday: Fats Domino and the Lost Dawn of Rock 'n' Roll* (10–12). 2006, Da Capo $26.00 (978-0-306-81491-4). The author discusses his subject's life and career, arguing that Fats Domino is the true father of rock-and-roll. (Rev: BL 5/1/06) [781.42166]

DYLAN, BOB

7496 Roberts, Jeremy. *Bob Dylan: Voice of a Generation* (8–11). Series: Lerner Biographies. 2005, Lerner LB $27.93 (978-0-8225-1368-1). This evenhanded biography chronicles the folk singer's transformation from Bobby Zimmerman in small-town Minnesota to cultural icon. (Rev: BL 6/1–15/05) [921]

EDWARDS, HONEYBOY

7497 Edwards, David H. *The World Don't Owe Me Nothing: The Life and Times of Delta Bluesman Honeyboy Edwards* (10–12). 1997, Chicago Review $24.00 (978-1-55652-275-8). The biography of a black traveling country-blues musician that chronicles the brutality he suffered because of his class and color and recounts his experiences with gambling, romance, and classic blues artists over 65-plus years. (Rev: SLJ 5/98) [921]

EMINEM (MARSHALL MATHERS)

7498 Lane, Stephanie. *Eminem* (9–12). Series: People in the News. 2004, Gale LB $32.45 (978-1-59018-449-3). This is a frank profile of controversial rapper Eminem (born Marshall Mathers) and the violent and sexual images he favors in his lyrics. (Rev: BL 2/1/05) [782.4]

FARLEY, CHRIS

7499 Farley, Tom, and Tanner Colby. *The Chris Farley Show: A Biography in Three Acts* (10–12). 2008, Viking $26.95 (978-0-670-01923-6). A portrait of the fat comedian from Madison, Wisconsin, whose early death from drugs left some bittersweet memories. (Rev: BL 3/15/08) [921]

FITZGERALD, ELLA

7500 Stone, Tanya Lee. *Ella Fitzgerald* (7–10). Series: Up Close. 2008, Viking $16.99 (978-0-670-06149-5). The singer's hard work and exceptional voice are the main focus of this biography. (Rev: BL 2/1/08; SLJ 2/08) [782.421]

FREEMAN, MORGAN

7501 De Angelis, Gina. *Morgan Freeman* (7–12). Series: Black Americans of Achievement. 1999, Chelsea LB $30.00 (978-0-7910-4963-1). The life and career of the African American actor who has starred on Broadway, on television, and in movies. (Rev: HBG 4/00; SLJ 1/00) [791.43]

GOH, CHAN HON

7502 Goh, Chan Hon, and Cary Fagan. *Beyond the Dance: A Ballerina's Life* (6–12). 2002, Tundra LB $15.95 (978-0-88776-596-4). A readable account of Goh's childhood in Vancouver and rapid rise as a ballet dancer to become a prima ballerina with the National Ballet of Canada. (Rev: HBG 10/03; SLJ 4/03; VOYA 4/03) [921]

GOLDBERG, WHOOPI

7503 Blue, Rose, and Corinne J. Naden. *Whoopi Goldberg* (7–10). Series: Black Americans of Achievement. 1995, Chelsea LB $30.00 (978-0-7910-2152-1); paper $8.95 (978-0-7910-2153-8). A biography that tells how, in spite of great odds, this unusual comedian and actress rose to the top. (Rev: BL 3/15/95) [921]

HARRISON, GEORGE

7504 Rolling Stone, ed. *Harrison* (10–12). 2002, Simon & Schuster $29.95 (978-0-7432-3581-5). The late Beatle's life is celebrated in a well-illustrated blend of original content and interviews and articles that originally appeared in *Rolling Stone*. (Rev: BL 6/1–15/02) [921]

HENDRIX, JIMI

7505 Cross, Charles R. *Room Full of Mirrors: A Biography of Jimi Hendrix* (11–12). 2005, Hyperion $24.95 (978-1-4013-0028-9). Traces the brief life and career of rock guitarist Jimi Hendrix; for mature readers. (Rev: BL 6/1–15/05) [787.87]

7506 Willett, Edward. *Jimi Hendrix: "Kiss the Sky"* (7–10). Series: American Rebels. 2006, Enslow LB $20.95 (978-0-7660-2449-6). From the musician's childhood to his death at the age of 27, this biography does not shy away from describing Hendrix's destructive behavior, including the use of alcohol and drugs. (Rev: BL 2/1/07) [921]

HENSON, JIM

7507 Finch, Christopher. *Jim Henson: The Works* (9–12). 1993, Random House $40.00 (978-0-679-41203-8). Traces the career of the creator of the Muppets from local television in the 1950s through the triumph of *Sesame Street* and his experimental work. (Rev: BL 1/15/94) [921]

HERSH, KRISTIN

7508 Hersh, Kristin. *Rat Girl* (11–12). 2010, Penguin paper $15 (978-01431173-9-1). Throwing Muses founder Hersh chronicles her teenage experiences as her band found success, she was diagnosed with bipolar disorder, and she discovered she was pregnant; for mature readers. e (Rev: BL 8/10) [921]

HITCHCOCK, ALFRED

7509 Adair, Gene. *Alfred Hitchcock: Filming Our Fears* (7–10). Series: Oxford Portraits. 2002, Oxford LB $32.95 (978-0-19-511967-1). Hitchcock's youth in England is covered in addition to chronological details of his career from the silent movies through his classic creations. (Rev: HBG 3/03; SLJ 11/02) [921]

HOUSTON, WHITNEY

7510 Heppermann, Christine. *Whitney Houston: Recording Artist and Actress* (7–10). Illus. Series: Lives Cut Short. 2012, ABDO LB $34.22 (978-161783544-5). This profile includes first-person quotes, comments from insiders and critics, interesting sidebars, and relevant photographs. (Rev: BL 12/1/12; SLJ 12/12) [921]

JACKSON, MICHAEL

7511 George, Nelson. *Thriller: The Musical Life of Michael Jackson* (10–12). Illus. 2010, Da Capo $25 (978-030681878-3). Focusing more on Jackson's contributions to the music industry than on the scandals that plagued his later years, this book offers a well-researched look into the hardworking, barrier-busting King of Pop. (Rev: BL 6/1–15/10) [921]

JOHNSON, ROBERT

7512 Lewis, J. Patrick. *Black Cat Bone* (7–12). Illus. by Gary Kelley. 2006, Creative LB $19.95 (978-1-56846-194-6). A picture book for big kids, this story in poetry of blues musician Robert Johnson alludes to the legend that he sold his soul to the devil in exchange for some wicked skills on the guitar. (Rev: BL 1/1–15/07; LMC 8–9/07; SLJ 12/06*) [921]

7513 Wald, Elijah. *Escaping the Delta: Robert Johnson and the Invention of the Blues* (10–12). 2004, Harper-Collins $24.95 (978-0-06-052423-4). The blues pioneer's brief life is placed in social and cultural context. (Rev: BL 12/15/03*) [921]

JOPLIN, JANIS

7514 Angel, Ann. *Janis Joplin: Rise Up Singing* (9–12). 2010, Abrams $19.95 (978-0-8109-8349-6). This well-researched account of the short life of passionate, enigmatic Janis Joplin contains many photographs and quotations from friends and family. (Rev: BL 11/1/10*; LMC 1–2/11; SLJ 10/1/10*) [921]

KING, B. B.

7515 King, B. B., and Dick Waterman. *The B. B. King Treasures: Photos, Mementos and Music from B. B. King's Collection* (9–12). 2005, Bulfinch $40.00 (978-0-8212-5724-1). Photos, biographical information, memorabilia, and a CD of recordings and interview excerpts celebrate the life and musical contributions of the legendary musician. (Rev: BL 9/1/05) [921]

LANG, LANG

7516 Lang, Lang, and David Ritz. *Journey of a Thousand Miles: My Story* (10–12). Illus. 2008, Spiegel & Grau $24.95 (978-0-385-52456-8). Pianist Lang chronicles his youth in China and the supportive, though often tense relationship with his parents who sacrificed much for the son they had determined would become a star. ⌂ ℮ (Rev: BL 6/1–15/08; SLJ 1/09) [921]

7517 Lang, Lang, and Michael French. *Lang Lang: Playing with Flying Keys* (7–10). 2008, Delacorte $16.99 (978-0-385-73578-0). The internationally respected pianist recalls the stresses of his childhood, his unending training schedule, and his triumphs. (Rev: BL 6/1–15/08; SLJ 9/08) [921]

LANGSTAFF, JOHN

7518 Cooper, Susan. *The Magic Maker: A Portrait of John Langstaff, Creator of the Christmas Revels* (9–12). 2011, Candlewick $22.99 (978-076365040-7). An engaging portrait of the Revels founder and his passion for music. ⌂ ℮ (Rev: BL 9/15/11*; HB 11–12/11; SLJ 9/11) [921]

LATIFAH, QUEEN

7519 Allen, Amy Ruth. *Queen Latifah: From Jersey Girl to Superstar* (6–10). Illus. Series: Lifeline Biographies. 2012, Lerner/Twenty-First Century LB $34.60 (978-076134234-2). An attractive profile of the rap star with many quotations, photographs, and sidebars from *USA Today*. (Rev: BL 6/12; VOYA 6/12) [921]

LED ZEPPELIN (MUSICAL GROUP)

7520 Hoskyns, Barney. *Led Zeppelin IV* (8–12). 2006, Rodale $16.95 (978-1-59486-370-7). This profile of the rock band looks behind the scenes, especially at the making of its classic fourth album. (Rev: BL 11/15/06) [921]

LEE, BRUCE

7521 Little, John, ed. *Bruce Lee: The Celebrated Life of the Golden Dragon* (6–12). 2000, Tuttle $24.95 (978-0-8048-3230-4). Stunning photographs and excerpts from Lee's own writings paint an absorbing portrait of the late martial arts film star. (Rev: VOYA 8/01) [921]

LEE, SPIKE

7522 Haskins, Jim. *Spike Lee: By Any Means Necessary* (6–10). 1997, Walker LB $16.85 (978-0-8027-8496-4). Compiling previously published biographical material, the author has produced an interesting profile of this important African American filmmaker, including a behind-the-cameras view of each of Lee's 10 films. (Rev: BL 5/1/97; SLJ 6/97; VOYA 10/97) [921]

LENNON, JOHN

7523 Blaney, John. *John Lennon: In His Life* (10–12). Ed. by Valeria Manferto de Fabianis. Illus. 2010, Sterling paper $39.95 (978-88544044-9-6). The life and career of seminal rock musician John Lennon is revealed through many photographs and a narrative that covers his private and public life from a young age. (Rev: BL 11/1–15/10) [921]

7524 Greenberg, Keith Elliot. *December 8, 1980: The Day John Lennon Died* (11–12). Illus. 2010, Backbeat $24.99 (978-087930963-3). Bringing together facts from many first person accounts, Greenberg deftly paints a picture of a happy, relaxed, creative John Lennon and the mad, fanatical fan Mark David Chapman; for mature readers. (Rev: BL 10/1–15/10) [921]

7525 Henke, James. *Lennon Legend: An Illustrated Life of John Lennon* (10–12). 2003, Chronicle $40.00 (978-0-8118-3517-6). Highly illustrated and with facsimiles of Lennon artifacts plus a CD that includes an interview, this is a very attractive celebration of the Beatle's life. (Rev: SLJ 5/04) [921]

7526 Partridge, Elizabeth. *John Lennon: All I Want Is the Truth* (9–12). 2005, Viking $24.99 (978-0-670-05954-6). This appealing biography chronicles the late, great

Beatle's life from his birth during a Nazi air raid over Liverpool in October 1940 to his assassination in New York City in December 1980. (Rev: BL 10/1/05*; SLJ 10/05; VOYA 10/05) [782.42166]

7527 Wiener, Jon. *Come Together: John Lennon in His Time* (9–12). 1990, Univ. of Illinois $18.95 (978-0-252-06131-8). This biography gives many insights into the 1960s and the important issues of that time. [921]

LONG TACK SAM

7528 Fleming, Ann Marie. *The Magical Life of Long Tack Sam* (9–12). 2007, Riverhead paper $14.00 (978-1-59448-264-9). Long Tack Sam was a Chinese magician who performed all over the world in a career spanning both world wars. (Rev: BL 8/07) [921]

MA, YO-YO

7529 Worth, Richard. *Yo-Yo Ma* (6–10). Series: Asian Americans of Achievement. 2007, Chelsea House LB $30.00 (978-0-7910-9270-5). This attractive profile recounts the highlights of Ma's personal life and covers his career as a cellist and his work with young people. (Rev: SLJ 8/07) [921]

MADONNA

7530 Gnojewski, Carol. *Madonna: "Express Yourself"* (8–11). 2007, Enslow LB $25.95 (978-0-7660-2442-7). Covers the life and career of musical icon Madonna from childhood. (Rev: BL 8/07) [921]

7531 O'Brien, Lucy. *Madonna: Like an Icon* (9–12). 2007, HarperEntertainment $24.95 (978-0-06-089896-0). This is a comprehensive account of the career of the multi-talented performer who has proven herself adept in many areas. (Rev: BL 8/07) [921]

MARLEY, BOB

7532 Miller, Calvin Craig. *Reggae Poet: The Story of Bob Marley* (7–10). 2007, Morgan Reynolds LB $27.95 (978-1-59935-071-4). A look at the good and the bad about the late reggae musician, including his influential style, his drug use, and his difficult childhood; with photographs. (Rev: BL 11/15/07; SLJ 2/08) [921]

7533 Salewicz, Chris. *Bob Marley: The Untold Story* (10–12). Illus. 2010, Farrar $27 (978-086547999-9). Drawing on interviews with band mates, friends, and Marley himself, this biography tells of the culture, influence, and controversial legacy of the reggae star. (Rev: BL 4/1–15/10) [921]

7534 Taylor, Don. *Marley and Me: The Real Bob Marley* (9–12). 1995, Barricade paper $14.95 (978-1-56980-044-7). Marley's business manager sheds light on the complexities of this charismatic reggae musician's life. (Rev: BL 9/1/95) [921]

MCCARTNEY, PAUL

7535 Sounes, Howard. *Fab: The Life of Paul McCartney* (10–12). Illus. 2010, Da Capo $27.50 (978-030681783-0). Sounes's meticulously researched and impartial biography covers every aspect of McCartney's life from his start with the Beatles through his failed marriage to Heather Mills. (Rev: BL 10/1–15/10*) [921]

MCDANIEL, HATTIE

7536 Watts, Jill. *Hattie McDaniel: Black Ambition, White Hollywood* (9–12). 2005, HarperCollins $27.95 (978-0-06-051490-7). Explores the life and career of the African American actress and her struggle to improve opportunities for her race. (Rev: BL 9/15/05; SLJ 5/06)

MCKOY, MILLIE AND CHRISTINE

7537 Martell, Joanne. *Millie-Christine: Fearfully and Wonderfully Made* (10–12). 2000, John F. Blair paper $12.95 (978-0-89587-188-6). The story of conjoined African American twins Millie and Christine McKoy who were born slaves in 1851 and became entertainers who traveled with circus entrepreneur P. T. Barnum's shows and met Queen Victoria. (Rev: BL 1/1–15/00; SLJ 10/00) [921]

MONROE, MARILYN

7538 Lefkowitz, Frances. *Marilyn Monroe* (7–12). Series: Pop Culture Legends. 1995, Chelsea LB $21.95 (978-0-7910-2342-6); paper $8.95 (978-0-7910-2367-9). The story of the Hollywood star who, despite immense popularity, had a tragic life. (Rev: BL 8/95) [921]

7539 Owings, Lisa. *Marilyn Monroe: Hollywood Icon* (7–10). Illus. Series: Lives Cut Short. 2012, ABDO LB $34.22 (978-161783481-3). This profile includes first-person quotes, comments from insiders and critics, interesting sidebars, and relevant photographs. (Rev: BL 12/1/12; SLJ 12/12) [921]

OAKLEY, ANNIE

7540 Sayers, Isabelle S. *Annie Oakley and Buffalo Bill's Wild West* (9–12). 1981, Dover paper $9.95 (978-0-486-24120-3). Through a number of old photographs, the life of this sharp-shooter is re-created. [921]

PETTY, TOM

7541 Zollo, Paul. *Conversations with Tom Petty* (9–12). 2005, Omnibus $24.95 (978-1-84449-815-4). An indepth look at the life and career of rock musician Tom Petty. (Rev: BL 10/15/05) [782.421]

PRESLEY, ELVIS

7542 Guralnick, Peter. *Careless Love: The Unmaking of Elvis Presley* (10–12). 1999, Little, Brown $27.95 (978-0-316-33222-4); paper $17.95 (978-0-316-33297-2). This is the second, concluding volume of this definitive biography of the King, Elvis Presley. (Rev: BL 11/1/98*) [921]

7543 Guralnick, Peter. *Last Train to Memphis: The Rise of Elvis Presley* (9–12). 1994, Little, Brown $27.95 (978-0-316-33220-0); paper $17.95 (978-0-316-33225-5). This is the first part of the highly acclaimed biography of Elvis Presley. (Rev: BL 7/94) [921]

REEVE, CHRISTOPHER

7544 Finn, Margaret L. *Christopher Reeve: Actor and Activist* (6–10). 1997, Chelsea LB $32.00 (978-0-7910-4446-9); paper $8.95 (978-0-7910-4447-6). The story of the gallant film actor, his tragic accident, and the causes he champions. (Rev: HBG 3/98; VOYA 2/98) [921]

7545 Reeve, Christopher. *Still Me* (9–12). 1998, Random House paper $7.99 (978-0-345-43241-4). Reeve looks at his life and work today and at his life before his injury in 1995. [921]

ROBESON, PAUL

7546 Stewart, Jeffrey C., ed. *Paul Robeson: Artist and Citizen* (10–12). 1998, Rutgers paper $22.00 (978-0-8135-2511-2). A well-organized, skillfully designed collection of essays that offers an in-depth look at the famous African American performing artist, film actor, college athlete, political and civil rights activist, and government target, bringing out the complexity of Robeson's life and his many contributions. (Rev: BL 2/15/98; SLJ 2/99) [921]

RODRIGUEZ, ROBERT

7547 Marvis, Barbara. *Robert Rodriguez* (5–10). Series: A Real-Life Reader Biography. 1997, Mitchell Lane LB $15.95 (978-1-883845-48-3). This simple, attractive biography of the successful movie maker focuses on his problems growing up in a large family and clinging to his career dreams. (Rev: BL 6/1–15/98; HBG 3/98; SLJ 2/98) [921]

ROLLING STONES (MUSICAL GROUP)

7548 Greenfield, Robert. *Exile on Main Street: A Season in Hell with the Rolling Stones* (10–12). 2006, Da Capo $24.00 (978-0-306-81433-4). The story of a dissolute heroin- and dispute-laden summer (1971) at Keith Richards's Villa Nellcôte, during which the band still managed to make what was hailed as one of the greatest rock records of all time. (Rev: BL 10/1/06) [921]

7549 Rej, Bent. *The Rolling Stones in the Beginning* (9–12). 2006, Firefly $49.95 (978-1-55407-230-9). This photo-essay displays rare photographs by Bent Rej, who accompanied the Rolling Stones on an early European tour. ∩ (Rev: BL 10/1/06) [782.42166]

SANTANA, CARLOS

7550 Leng, Simon. *Soul Sacrifice: The Santana Story* (10–12). 2000, SAF-Helter Skelter paper $18.95 (978-0-946719-29-7). A story of influential guitarist Carlos Santana and of the music he and his group produced. (Rev: BL 5/1/00) [921]

SHAKUR, TUPAC

7551 Golus, Carrie. *Tupac Shakur: Hip-Hop Idol* (6–12). Illus. Series: Lifeline Biographies. 2010, Lerner LB $33.26 (978-076135473-4). This attractive biography draws on the archives of *USA Today* to give an unvarnished account of the rap star's life. (Rev: BL 9/1/10*) [921]

SIMONE, NINA

7552 Acker, Kerry. *Nina Simone* (9–12). Series: Women in the Arts. 2004, Chelsea House LB $30.00 (978-0-7910-7456-5). This account covers both the personal and professional lives of this great entertainer and singer. (Rev: BL 3/1/04) [921]

SMILEY, TAVIS

7553 Smiley, Tavis, and David Ritz. *What I Know for Sure: My Story of Growing Up in America* (9–12). 2006, Doubleday $23.95 (978-0-385-50516-1). A talk-show host for Black Entertainment Television (BET) and National Public Radio (NPR), Smiley revisits his childhood in Indiana and how he broke into broadcasting. (Rev: BL 9/1/06) [921]

SMITH, PATTI

7554 Smith, Patti. *Just Kids* (11–12). Illus. 2010, Ecco $27 (978-006621131-2). A cast of notable characters from the 1960s and 1970s creative scene in New York City populates this memoir by punk rocker/poet Patti Smith that chronicles both her own life and her relationship with photographer Robert Mapplethorpe; for mature readers. ∩ (Rev: BLO 2/1–15/10) [921]

SPECTOR, PHIL

7555 Brown, Mick. *Tearing Down the Wall of Sound: The Rise and Fall of Phil Spector* (9–12). 2007, Knopf $26.95 (978-1-4000-4219-7). Spector's trial was still under way when this biography was published, but the profile given will answer readers' questions about other facets of his life and career. (Rev: BL 6/1–15/07) [921]

449

STEWART, SHELLEY

7556 Stewart, Shelley, and Nathan Hale Turner. *The Road South* (11–12). 2002, Warner $23.95 (978-0-446-53027-9). African American radio personality Shelley Stewart tells how he struggled to overcome a childhood of violence, abuse, and poverty; for mature teens. (Rev: BL 7/02) [921]

WALLENDA, DELILAH

7557 Wallenda, Delilah, and Nan DeVicentis-Hayes. *The Last of the Wallendas* (9–12). 1993, New Horizon $22.95 (978-0-88282-116-0). Master highwire artist Karl Wallenda's granddaughter describes the fading charisma and finances of the circus in the United States from a personal perspective and presents her version of family squabbles. (Rev: BL 4/15/93) [921]

WINFREY, OPRAH

7558 Cooper, Ilene. *Up Close: Oprah Winfrey* (7–12). Series: Up Close. 2007, Viking $15.99 (978-0-670-06162-4). Cooper focuses on Winfrey's unhappy childhood and her philanthropic work when she became successful. (Rev: SLJ 5/07) [921]

Miscellaneous Artists

BARNUM, P. T.

7559 Barnum, P. T. *Barnum's Own Story* (7–12). 1962, Peter Smith $20.50 (978-0-8446-4001-3). The autobiography of the showman who could fool people like no one else. [921]

7560 Barnum, P. T. *Struggles and Triumphs* (10–12). 10-1, Ayer $53.95 (978-0-405-01651-6). An abridgment of the autobiography of one of America's first and greatest showmen. [921]

LANTZ, WALTER

7561 Lenburg, Jeff. *Walter Lantz* (7–10). Illus. Series: Legends of Animation. 2012, Chelsea House LB $34.95 (978-160413839-9). Profiles the man whose studio produced more than 800 cartoons, notably those featuring Woody Woodpecker. (Rev: BL 11/1/12) [921]

LASSETER, JOHN

7562 Lenburg, Jeff. *John Lasseter* (7–10). Illus. Series: Legends of Animation. 2012, Chelsea House LB $34.95 (978-160413840-5). Traces Lasseter's life and progress as an animator, from Disney to Pixar and *Toy Story*. (Rev: BL 11/1/12) [921]

Contemporary and Historical Americans

7563 Abdul-Jabbar, Kareem, and Alan Steinberg. *Black Profiles in Courage: A Legacy of African American Achievement* (10–12). 1996, HarperPerennial paper $13.00 (978-0-308-81341-0). An inspiring collection of profiles of 11 courageous African Americans, including Rosa Parks, Crispus Attucks, Frederick Douglass, and Harriet Tubman. (Rev: BL 10/15/96) [920]

7564 Adams, Katherine H., and Michael L. Keene. *After the Vote Was Won: The Later Achievements of Fifteen Suffragists* (11–12). 2010, McFarland paper $45 (978-07864493-8-5). Adams and Keene profile 15 suffragists and describe the challenges they faced after the 19th Amendment was ratified and the achievements of their later lives. (Rev: BLO 9/1–15/10) [920]

7565 Angelo, Bonnie. *First Mothers: The Women Who Shaped the Presidents* (10–12). 2000, Morrow paper $15.95 (978-0-06-093711-9). The story of 11 women who raised sons who became presidents of the United States. (Rev: BL 10/15/00) [920]

7566 Anthony, Carl Sferrazza. *America's First Families: An Inside View of 200 Years of Private Life in the White House* (9–12). 2000, Touchstone paper $18.00 (978-0-684-86442-6). This work gives a behind-the-scenes look at the home life of each of the presidents and their families. (Rev: BL 11/1/00) [920]

7567 Archer, Jules. *They Had a Dream* (10–12). 1996, Puffin paper $7.99 (978-0-14-034954-2). Biographies of Frederick Douglass, Marcus Garvey, Martin Luther King, Jr. and Malcolm X are accompanied by discussion of the history of the civil rights. [323]

7568 Bailey Hutchinson, Kay. *Leading Ladies: American Trailblazers* (7–12). 2007, HarperCollins $25.95 (978-0-06-113824-9). Pioneering American women in all walks of lives are celebrated in this collective biography that includes wives of presidents, activists, scientists, doctors, and journalists. (Rev: BL 12/1/07) [920]

7569 Brinkley, Alan, and Davis Dyer, eds. *The Reader's Companion to the American Presidency* (10–12). 2000, Houghton Mifflin $40.00 (978-0-395-78889-9). A collection of scholarly essays written by specialists, each of which deals with the life and accomplishments of a different United States president. (Rev: BL 2/1/00; SLJ 10/00) [920]

7570 Broadnax, Samuel L. *Blue Skies, Black Wings: African American Pioneers of Aviation* (9–12). 2007, Praeger $44.95 (978-0-275-99195-1). The accomplishments of the Tuskegee Airmen and other black pioneers of aviation are celebrated in this memoir/collection of profiles. (Rev: BL 4/1/07) [629.13092]

7571 Colman, Penny. *Elizabeth Cady Stanton and Susan B. Anthony: A Friendship That Changed the World* (7–10). Illus. 2011, Henry Holt $18.99 (978-0-8050-8293-7). Tells the story of the friendship between a married mother of five (Stanton) and an unmarried career woman (Anthony) and the impact they were to make on human rights in America. e Lexile 1180L (Rev: BL 6/1/11; LMC 10/11*; SLJ 5/11; VOYA 6/11) [920]

7572 Farquhar, Michael. *A Treasury of Foolishly Forgotten Americans: Pirates, Skinflints, Patriots, and Other Colorful Characters Stuck in the Footnotes of History* (9–12). 2008, Penguin paper $15.00 (978-0-14-311305-8). Thirty portraits of neglected notable Americans include murderers, evangelists, and spies. (Rev: BL 3/1/08) [973]

7573 Fawcett, Bill. *Oval Office Oddities: An Irreverent Collection of Presidential Facts, Follies, and Foibles* (9–12). 2008, HarperCollins paper $13.95 (978-0-06-134617-0). A lighthearted collection of trivia and facts about the presidents and their families, with funny illustrations and caricatures. (Rev: SLJ 6/08) [973.0099]

7574 Fleming, Thomas. *The Intimate Lives of the Founding Fathers* (10–12). 2009, Smithsonian $27.99 (978-0-06113-912-3). Fleming explores the home lives of George Washington, Ben Franklin, John Adams, Thomas Jefferson, Alexander Hamilton, and James Madison and the roles their wives played. ℮ (Rev: BL 10/15/09; LMC 5–6/10) [920]

7575 Gould, Lewis L. *American First Ladies: Their Lives and Their Legacy. 2nd ed.* (9–12). 2001, Routledge $125.00 (978-0-415-93021-5). This, the definitive work on the subject, give excellent biographical information on each of the first ladies through 2000. (Rev: BL 3/1/02; SLJ 8/96; VOYA 12/96) [920]

7576 Govenar, Alan. *Untold Glory* (10–12). 2007, Broadway paper $15.95 (978-0-7679-2117-6). This collective biography of 24 African Americans who succeeded in a variety of fields will include many figures new to readers; each profile includes a first-person account, with discussion of breaking racial barriers. (Rev: BL 2/1/07) [920]

7577 Hancock, Sibyl. *Famous Firsts of Black Americans* (7–12). 1983, Pelican $14.95 (978-0-88289-240-5). Biographies of 20 famous African Americans who have contributed in a unique way to our culture. [920]

7578 Hardy, Sheila Jackson, and P. Stephen Hardy. *Extraordinary People of the Civil Rights Movement* (9–12). Series: Extraordinary People. 2006, Children's Pr. LB $40 (978-0-516-25461-6). More than 50 important individuals and organizations are profiled in this volume that focuses on acts by ordinary people. (Rev: SLJ 2/07)

7579 Haskins, Jim, and Kathleen Benson. *African-American Religious Leaders* (7–10). Series: Black Stars. 2008, Wiley LB $24.95 (978-0-471-73632-5). Leaders of the black church in America since the days of slavery are profiled in this book that is organized in five chronological sections. (Rev: BL 2/1/08; SLJ 7/08) [277.3]

7580 Kallen, Stuart A. *Women of the Civil Rights Movement* (7–12). Series: Women in History. 2005, Gale LB $32.45 (978-1-59018-569-8). Women who made important contributions to the U.S. civil rights movement are celebrated in chapters devoted to organizations, protests, education, voting rights, radicals, and so forth. (Rev: SLJ 11/05) [920]

7581 Kennedy, Caroline. *Profiles in Courage for our Time* (10–12). 2002, Hyperion $23.95 (978-0-7868-6793-6). There are 14 chapters in this book, each focusing on a different recipient of the Profiles in Courage Award. Among them are Bob Woodward, Anna Quindlen, and Pete Hamill. (Rev: BL 3/15/02) [920]

7582 Kennedy, John F. *Profiles in Courage. Memorial Ed.* ((7–12). 1964, Perennial paper $7.00 (978-0-06-080698-9). Sketches of several famous Americans who took unpopular stands during their lives. (Rev: BL 4/87) [920]

7583 Kisseloff, Jeff. *Generation on Fire: Voices of Protest from the 1960s* (11–12). 2006, Univ. of Kentucky $34.95 (978-0-8131-2416-2). Kisseloff interviews 15 individuals who were fighters for or against various causes — racism, war, gay rights, women's rights, pollution, and so forth — during the turbulent 1960s; with photographs and historical overviews; suitable for mature teens. (Rev: BL 10/1/06) [303.48]

7584 McCullough, Noah. *The Essential Book of Presidential Trivia* (7–12). 2006, Random House paper $9.95 (978-1-4000-6482-3). Written by a 10-year-old presidential hopeful and historian, this book gives a short presidential biography per chapter, a "Did You Know?" section of trivia, and a black-and-white drawing for each. (Rev: SLJ 6/06)

7585 Morey, Janet Nomura, and Wendy Dunn. *Famous Hispanic Americans* (7–10). 1996, Dutton $16.99 (978-0-525-65190-1). Fourteen men and women of Hispanic heritage from science, sports, the arts, and other professions are featured in this collective biography. (Rev: BL 2/15/96; SLJ 2/96; VOYA 8/96) [920]

7586 Morgan, Edmund S. *American Heroes: Profiles of Men and Women Who Shaped Early America* (10–12). 2009, Norton $27.95 (978-039307010-1). Morgan sheds new light on some old truths in his essays about early America and its prominent individuals. ℮ (Rev: BL 4–5/09) [920]

7587 Morin, Isobel V. *Women of the U.S. Congress* (6–10). 1994, Oliver LB $19.95 (978-1-881508-12-0). Lists all the women who have served in Congress as of 1994 and provides political biographies of seven of them, citing their accomplishments and their different backgrounds and views. (Rev: BL 7/94; SLJ 5/94; VOYA 6/94) [920]

7588 Morin, Isobel V. *Women Who Reformed Politics* (7–12). 1994, Oliver LB $19.95 (978-1-881508-16-8). Describes the political activism of eight American women, including Abby Foster's abolition fight, Carrie Catt's suffrage battle, and Gloria Steinem's feminist crusade. (Rev: BL 10/15/94; SLJ 11/94; VOYA 2/95) [920]

7589 Newfield, Jack, ed. *American Rebels* (9–12). 2004, Thunder's Mouth paper $16.95 (978-1-56025-543-7). From Margaret Sanger to Bob Dylan and from Norman Mailer to Noam Chomsky, here is a series of miniature biographies of unconventional Americans whose contributions have changed our world in many fields of endeavor. (Rev: BL 1/1–15/04) [920]

7590 Peters, Margaret. *The Ebony Book of Black Achievement* (10–12). 1974, Johnson $10.95 (978-0-87485-040-6). This volume contains brief biographies of 26 African American men and women who have achieved in a number of fields. [920]

7591 Raphael, Ray. *Founders: The People Who Brought You a Nation* (10–12). Illus. 2009, New Press $35 (978-159558327-7). Raphael chooses seven notable people, three upper class and four middle class, whose significant contributions shaped the American Revolution. (Rev: BL 4–5/09) [920]

7592 Roberts, Cokie. *Founding Mothers: The Women Who Raised Our Nation* (10–12). 2004, Morrow $24.95 (978-0-06-009025-8). This collective biography that uses many original documents introduces heroines of the revolutionary period including Deborah Franklin (wife of Benjamin), Abigail Adams, Martha Washington, and Phillis Wheatley. (Rev: BL 3/15/04; SLJ 9/04) [920]

7593 Rodriguez, Robert, and Tamra Orr. *Great Hispanic-Americans* (6–12). 2005, Publications Int'l LB $15.98 (978-1-4127-1148-7). More than 50 Hispanic Americans from different walks of life are profiled in accessible text. (Rev: SLJ 1/06) [920]

7594 Schiff, Karenna Gore. *Lighting the Way: Nine Women Who Changed Modern America* (9–12). 2006, Hyperion $25.95 (978-1-4013-5218-9). Schiff, daughter of Al Gore, profiles nine 20th-century women who helped to shape America's social and political history. (Rev: BL 12/15/05) [920]

7595 Shetterly, Robert. *Americans Who Tell the Truth* (9–12). 2005, Dutton $18.99 (978-0-525-47429-6). With portraits, supplemented by quotes from his subjects, artist Robert Shetterly celebrates the lives of 50 Americans he deeply admires; included in his collection are such diverse figures as Chief Joseph, Mark Twain, Frederick Douglass, Rosa Parks, Noam Chomsky, and Cesar Chavez. (Rev: BL 4/1/05; SLJ 7/05) [920.073]

7596 Steele, Philip, and Marie Barrow Scoma. *The Family Story of Bonnie and Clyde* (10–12). 2000, Pelican paper $10.95 (978-1-56554-756-8). Heavily illustrated with photographs, this is the story of the two outlaws, their exploits, and their personal lives. (Rev: BL 3/15/00) [920]

7597 Streissguth, Thomas. *Legendary Labor Leaders* (7–12). Series: Profiles. 1998, Oliver LB $19.95 (978-1-881508-44-1). The eight labor leaders profiled in this collective biography are Samuel Gompers, Cesar Chavez, A. Philip Randolph, Jimmy Hoffa, Eugene Debs, William Haywood, Mother Jones, and John L. Lewis. (Rev: BL 10/15/98; SLJ 1/99) [920]

7598 Sullivan, Otha Richard. *African American Millionaires* (5–10). Series: Black Stars. 2004, Wiley $24.95 (978-0-471-46928-5). Tyra Banks and Oprah Winfrey are included here, but so are many names that may be unfamiliar to readers, such as William Alexander Leidesdorff and Annie Turnbo Malone. (Rev: SLJ 5/05) [920]

7599 Taylor, Kimberly H. *Black Abolitionists and Freedom Fighters* (6–10). 1996, Oliver LB $19.95 (978-1-881508-30-4). Profiles are given for eight African Americans who fought to end slavery, some well-known (including Nat Turner and Harriet Tubman) and others less familiar, such as Richard Allen and Mary Terrell. (Rev: SLJ 10/96) [920]

7600 Taylor, Kimberly H. *Black Civil Rights Champions* (6–12). 1995, Oliver LB $19.95 (978-1-881508-22-9). In separate chapters, seven civil rights leaders, including W. E. B. Du Bois, James Farmer, Ella Baker, and Malcolm X, are profiled, with a final chapter that gives thumbnail sketches of many more. (Rev: BL 1/1–15/96; SLJ 3/96; VOYA 6/96) [920]

7601 Thro, Ellen. *Twentieth-Century Women Politicians* (7–12). Series: American Profiles. 1998, Facts on File $25.00 (978-0-8160-3758-2). Beginning in the mid-20th century, this work features 10 women who were elected to important public offices, including Margaret Chase Smith, Geraldine Ferraro, Dianne Feinstein, Christine Todd Whitman, and Ann Richards. (Rev: BL 12/15/98) [920]

7602 Ungar, Harlow G. *Teachers and Educators* (7–10). Series: American Profiles. 1994, Facts on File $25.00 (978-0-8160-2990-7). This book profiles eight great American educators of the past, including John Dewey, Horace Mann, Emma Willard, Booker T. Washington, and Henry Barnard. (Rev: BL 7/95; VOYA 5/95) [920]

7603 Wong, Andrea, and Rosario Dawson. *Secrets of Powerful Women: Leading Change for a New Generation* (10–12). 2010, Hyperion paper $14.99 (978-14013411-1-4). Participants at 2008's Future Frontrunners Summit such as Congresswoman Jan Schakowsky and actress Fran Drescher recount for a teen audience their stories of succeeding as leaders. **e** (Rev: BLO 12/1/09) [920]

7604 Wood, Gordon S. *Revolutionary Characters: What Made the Founders Different* (9–12). 2006, Penguin $25.95 (978-1-59420-093-9). Eight founders are featured — George Washington, Benjamin Franklin, Thomas Jefferson, Alexander Hamilton, James Madison, John Adams, Thomas Paine, and Aaron Burr — with discussion of how their reputations have fluctuated throughout history, and describing their backgrounds, personalities, and philosophies. (Rev: BL 2/15/06; SLJ 8/06) [920]

7605 Zimmerman, Dwight Jon. *First Command: Paths to Leadership* (7–12). 2005, Vandamere $22.95 (978-0-918339-62-1). A collective biography of 23 American soldiers and marines who went on to become generals, focusing on their early commands and the leadership qualities that helped them advance. (Rev: SLJ 5/06)

Civil and Human Rights Leaders

ANTHONY, SUSAN B.

7606 Todd, Anne M. *Susan B. Anthony: Activist* (6–10). Series: Women of Achievement. 2009, Chelsea House $30 (978-1-60413-087-4). This concise and balanced profile is a good starting place for anyone researching the famous suffragette and her legacy. (Rev: SLJ 5/1/09) [921]

BAKER, ELLA

7607 Bohannon, Lisa Frederiksen. *Freedom Cannot Rest: Ella Baker and the Civil Rights Movement* (7–12). Series: Civil Rights Leaders. 2005, Morgan Reynolds LB $26.95 (978-1-931798-71-6). A well-illustrated and evenhanded introduction to the life and accomplishments of Ella Baker, a major — but often overlooked — player in the U.S. civil rights movement. (Rev: SLJ 12/05) [921]

BATES, DAISY

7608 Fradin, Judith Bloom, and Dennis Brindell Fradin. *The Power of One: Daisy Bates and the Little Rock Nine* (8–11). 2004, Clarion $19.00 (978-0-618-31556-7). A detailed profile of Daisy Bates, who as president of the Arkansas chapter of the NAACP played a pivotal role in the 1957 integration of Central High School in Little Rock. (Rev: BL 2/1/05; SLJ 4/05) [323]

BLACKWELL, UNITA

7609 Blackwell, Unita, and JoAnne Prichard Morris. *Barefootin': Life Lessons from the Road to Freedom* (9–12). 2006, Crown $23 (978-0-609-61060-2). The life story of a civil rights activist who came from humble roots and eventually became the first black woman to be mayor of a Mississippi town. (Rev: BL 6/1–15/06; SLJ 9/06) [921]

BROWN, JOHN

7610 Reynolds, David S. *John Brown, Abolitionist: The Man Who Killed Slavery, Sparked the Civil War, and Seeded Civil Rights* (8–12). 2005, Knopf $30.00 (978-0-375-41188-5). This insightful biography adds fuel to the continuing debate over what motivated the fiery abolitionist. (Rev: BL 2/1/05) [973.7]

CHAVEZ, CESAR

7611 Young, Jeff C. *Cesar Chavez* (7–10). Series: American Workers. 2007, Morgan Reynolds $27.95 (978-1-59935-036-3). The activist's early life and inspirations as well as his influence on labor practices are well presented in this easy-to-read biography. (Rev: BL 3/15/07; SLJ 4/07) [331.88]

CHILD, LYDIA MARIA

7612 Kenschaft, Lori. *Lydia Maria Child: The Quest for Racial Justice* (6–10). Series: Oxford Portraits. 2002, Oxford LB $32.95 (978-0-19-513257-1). Lydia Maria Child, an activist for civil rights in the early and middle 1800s, is also known for her literary career. (Rev: BL 3/1/03; HBG 3/03; SLJ 1/03) [303.48]

DIX, DOROTHEA

7613 Muckenhoupt, Margaret. *Dorothea Dix: Advocate for Mental Health Care* (9–12). Series: Oxford Portraits. 2004, Oxford LB $32.95 (978-0-19-512921-2). Dix was a tireless advocate on behalf of the mentally ill; this volume also describes her work as a teacher and nurse. (Rev: SLJ 7/04) [921]

DOUGLASS, FREDERICK

7614 Adler, David A. *Frederick Douglass: A Noble Life* (6–10). 2010, Holiday House $18.95 (978-0-8234-2056-8). With many quotations from Douglass's own writings, this generally admiring profile tells the story of his life and considerable achievements. (Rev: BL 6/10*; LMC 1–2/11; SLJ 9/1/10*) [921]

7615 Douglass, Frederick. *Autobiographies* (10–12). 1994, Library of America $35.00 (978-0-940450-79-0); paper $13.95 (978-1-883011-30-7). This single volume contains all of the autobiographical writings of Frederick Douglass. [921]

7616 Douglass, Frederick. *Narrative of the Life of Frederick Douglass, an American Slave* (10–12). 1982, Penguin paper $10.00 (978-0-14-039012-4). An autobiography that tells of the life of this former slave and abolitionist. [921]

7617 Meltzer, Milton, ed. *Frederick Douglass: In His Own Words* (8–12). 1995, Harcourt $22.00 (978-0-15-229492-2). An introduction to the articles and speeches of the great 19th-century abolitionist leader, arranged chronologically. (Rev: BL 12/15/94; SLJ 2/95) [305.8]

DU BOIS, W. E. B.

7618 Bolden, Tonya. *W. E. B. Du Bois: A Twentieth-Century Life* (7–10). Illus. Series: Up Close. 2008, Viking $16.99 (978-067006302-4). A look at the life of the complex African American leader, this will be helpful to report writers and others interested in important civil rights figures. (Rev: BL 2/1/09; HB 3–4/09; SLJ 1/1/09) [921]

7619 Hinman, Bonnie. *A Stranger in My Own House: The Story of W. E. B. Du Bois* (9–12). Series: Civil Rights Leaders. 2005, Morgan Reynolds LB $26.95 (978-1-931798-45-7). The personal story of the scholar and controversial civil rights leader is placed in interesting social and historical context. (Rev: BL 3/15/05; SLJ 7/05) [305.896]

7620 Marable, Manning. *W. E. B. Du Bois: Black Radical Democrat* (10–12). 1986, Twayne $28.95 (978-0-8057-7750-5). A compact biography of the great African American intellectual, humanitarian, and civil rights leader. (Rev: BL 11/1/86) [921]

FARRAKHAN, LOUIS

7621 Haskins, Jim. *Louis Farrakhan and the Nation of Islam* (7–12). 1996, Walker LB $16.85 (978-0-8027-8423-0). Beginning with a history of African American nationalism and the Nation of Islam, this biography places the life of Farrakhan within the movement for black solidarity. (Rev: BL 10/1/96; SLJ 1/97) [921]

FREEMAN, ELIZABETH

7622 Wilds, Mary. *MumBet: The Life and Times of Elizabeth Freeman: The True Story of a Slave Who Won Her Freedom* (7–12). 1999, Avisson LB $19.95 (978-1-888105-40-7). The story of MumBet (Elizabeth Freeman), a slave who sued for her freedom in Massachusetts in 1781 after hearing a reading of the Declaration of Independence and won, helping to set the legal precedents that ended slavery in New England. (Rev: BL 6/1–15/99; SLJ 6/99; VOYA 2/00) [921]

GARVEY, MARCUS

7623 Caravantes, Peggy. *Marcus Garvey: Black Nationalist* (6–10). Series: Twentieth Century Leaders. 2004, Morgan Reynolds LB $23.95 (978-1-931798-14-3). A biography of this black nationalist, Pan-Africanist, and exponent of black civil rights. (Rev: BL 2/15/04; HBG 4/04; SLJ 11/03; VOYA 6/04) [921]

7624 Cronon, E. David. *Black Moses: The Story of Marcus Garvey and the Universal Negro Improvement Association* (10–12). 1955, Univ. of Wisconsin paper $15.95 (978-0-299-01214-4). This vivid, detailed account traces the life of the Jamaica-born black leader. [921]

7625 Kallen, Stuart A. *Marcus Garvey and the Back to Africa Movement* (7–12). 2006, Gale LB $28.70 (978-1-59018-838-5). An excellent account of Garvey's contributions to the black pride and power movements, touching on his charisma but also on his deficiencies. (Rev: SLJ 8/06)

GRIMKE, ANGELINA

7626 Todras, Ellen H. *Angelina Grimke: Voice of Abolition* (9–12). 1999, Linnet LB $25.00 (978-0-208-02485-5). A handsome biography of the woman, born in Charleston in 1805, who became an outspoken foe of slavery and left the South for New England to work for the abolition of slavery and for women's rights. (Rev: BL 6/1–15/99; SLJ 5/99; VOYA 12/99) [921]

HAMER, FANNIE LOU

7627 Fiorelli, June Estep. *Fannie Lou Hamer: A Voice for Freedom* (5–10). Series: Avisson Young Adult. 2005, Avisson paper $19.95 (978-1-888105-62-9). Hamer's life, including her youth, are described and placed in the context of events in the United States at the time. (Rev: SLJ 2/06) [921]

HAYDEN, LEWIS

7628 Strangis, Joel. *Lewis Hayden and the War Against Slavery* (7–12). 1998, Shoe String LB $25.00 (978-0-208-02430-5). The dramatic story of the former slave who became an active abolitionist and a stationmaster on the Underground Railroad. (Rev: BL 2/15/99; HBG 9/99; SLJ 5/99; VOYA 10/99) [921]

KING, CORETTA SCOTT

7629 Rhodes, Lisa Renee. *Coretta Scott King: Civil Rights Activist* (7–12). Series: Black Americans of Achievement. 2005, Chelsea House LB $30.00 (978-0-7910-8251-5). This revised edition of King's life adds new photographs and information boxes to the description of her childhood, education, marriage, participation in the civil rights movement, and work after her husband's assassination. (Rev: SLJ 11/05) [921]

KING, MARTIN LUTHER, JR.

7630 Bolden, Tonya. *M. L. K: Journey of a King* (7–10). 2007, Abrams $19.95 (978-0-8109-5476-2). An inspiring biography of the civil rights leader that emphasizes his influences and legacy. (Rev: BCCB 3/07; BL 2/1/07; LMC 8–9/07; SLJ 2/07*) [921]

MALCOLM X

7631 Helfer, Andrew. *Malcolm X: A Graphic Biography* (10–12). Illus. by Randy DuBurke. Series: Novel Graphics. 2006, Hill & Wang $15.95 (978-0-8090-9504-9). A frank, graphic-novel profile of the controversial figure that places him in historical context. (Rev: BL 2/1/07; SLJ 5/07) [921]

7632 Malcolm X, and Alex Haley. *The Autobiography of Malcolm X* (7–12). 1999, Ballantine $20.00 (978-0-345-91536-8); paper $12.00 (978-0-345-91503-0). The story of the man who turned from Harlem drug pusher into a charismatic leader of his people. [921]

NICHOLS, CLARINA

7633 Eickhoff, Diane. *Revolutionary Heart: The Life of Clarina Nichols and the Pioneering Crusade for Women's Rights* (10–12). 2006, Beagle Bay paper $14.95 (978-0-9764434-4-5). The life and achievements of Clarina Nichols, a pioneer in the struggle for women's rights who has been largely overlooked in history books. (Rev: BL 2/15/06) [305.42]

PARKS, ROSA

7634 Parks, Rosa, and Jim Haskins. *Rosa Parks: My Story* (6–10). 1992, Dial $17.99 (978-0-8037-0673-6). This autobiography of the civil rights hero becomes an oral history of the movement, including her recollections of Martin Luther King, Jr., Roy Wilkins, and others. (Rev: BL 12/15/91; SLJ 2/92) [921]

RANDOLPH, A. PHILIP

7635 Miller, Calvin Craig. *A. Philip Randolph and the African-American Labor Movement* (7–10). Series: Civil Rights Leaders. 2005, Morgan Reynolds $26.95 (978-1-931798-50-1). The life and achievements of the founding president of the Brotherhood of Sleeping Car Porters. (Rev: BL 2/15/05; SLJ 5/05) [323]

RUSTIN, BAYARD

7636 Miller, Calvin Craig. *No Easy Answers: Bayard Rustin and the Civil Rights Movement* (7–10). Series: Civil Rights Leaders. 2005, Morgan Reynolds LB $26.95 (978-1-931798-43-3). Rustin's significant achievements in the field of civil rights are discussed along with his homosexuality, which was a large factor in his relative obscurity. (Rev: BL 2/1/05; SLJ 6/05; VOYA 8/05) [323]

STANTON, ELIZABETH CADY

7637 Sigerman, Harriet. *Elizabeth Cady Stanton: The Right Is Ours* (6–10). Series: Oxford Portraits. 2001, Oxford $32.95 (978-0-19-511969-5). The life of the pioneering suffragist, accompanied by photographs and historic documents such as newspaper articles and cartoons. (Rev: BL 12/15/01; HBG 3/02; SLJ 11/01; VOYA 2/02) [921]

TRUTH, SOJOURNER

7638 Whalin, Terry. *Sojourner Truth: American Abolitionist* (9–12). Series: Heroes of the Faith. 1998, Chelsea House $14.95 (978-0-7910-5034-7). Truth's life and work as an abolitionist are placed in historical context. (Rev: HBG 3/99) [921]

TUBMAN, HARRIET

7639 Lowry, Beverly. *Harriet Tubman: Imagining a Life* (10–12). 2007, Doubleday $26.00 (978-0-385-50291-7). Lowry draws on recognized sources to imagine the life of Tubman, a woman who did not leave her own account. (Rev: BL 2/1/07) [921]

WASHINGTON, BOOKER T.

7640 Washington, Booker T. *Up from Slavery: An Autobiography by Booker T. Washington* (7–12). 1963, Airmont paper $3.95 (978-0-8049-0157-4). The story of the slave who later organized the Tuskegee Institute. [921]

WELLS, IDA B.

7641 Fradin, Dennis Brindell, and Judith Bloom Fradin. *Ida B. Wells: Mother of the Civil Rights Movement* (5–10). 2000, Clarion $19.00 (978-0-395-89898-7). An inspiring biography of the African American who was born a slave and went on to become a school teacher, journalist, and an activist who fought for black women's right to vote and helped found the NAACP. (Rev: BL 2/15/00; HB 5–6/00; HBG 10/00; SLJ 4/00*) [921]

WOODHULL, VICTORIA

7642 Brody, Miriam. *Victoria Woodhull: Free Spirit for Women's Rights* (7–12). Series: Oxford Portraits. 2004, Oxford LB $32.95 (978-0-19-514367-6). Presenting historical and social context, this biography covers the American reformer's difficult childhood and complex adult life. (Rev: SLJ 2/05) [921]

7643 Havelin, Kate. *Victoria Woodhull: Fearless Feminist* (7–10). Series: Trailblazer Biographies. 2006, Twenty-First Century LB $30.60 (978-0-8225-5986-3). A concise, well-researched biography of the ardent suffragist who ran for U.S. president in 1872. (Rev: SLJ 11/06) [921]

Presidents and Their Families

ADAMS, JOHN

7644 Lukes, Bonnie L. *John Adams: Public Servant* (8–12). Series: Notable Americans. 2000, Morgan Reynolds LB $23.95 (978-1-883846-80-0). An excellent biography of the second president of the United States that reveals both his virtues and his flaws. (Rev: BL 12/1/00; HBG 3/01; SLJ 2/01) [921]

7645 McCullough, David. *John Adams* (10–12). 2001, Simon & Schuster $35.00 (978-0-684-81363-9). In this prize-winning biography, the author sees the second president of the United States as a blunt, thin-skinned, compassionate, intelligent man. (Rev: BL 3/1/01*) [921]

7646 Yoder, Carolyn P., ed. *John Adams The Writer: A Treasury of Letters, Diaries, and Public Documents* (7–10). 2007, Boyds Mills $16.95 (978-1-59078-247-7). Selected writings of the second president of the United States are drawn from speeches, diaries, letters, and other sources, providing a full picture of this important figure from his own words. (Rev: BL 12/1/07; LMC 1/08; SLJ 4/08) [793.4]

ADAMS, JOHN QUINCY

7647 Remini, Robert V. *John Quincy Adams* (11–12). Series: American Presidents. 2002, Henry Holt $20.00 (978-0-8050-6939-6). This frank and engaging biography of America's sixth president paints a portrait of a well-meaning son who was unable to live up to the legacy of his illustrious father. (Rev: BL 7/02) [921]

ARTHUR, CHESTER A.

7648 Karabell, Zachary. *Chester Alan Arthur* (10–12). Series: American Presidents. 2004, Henry Holt $20.00 (978-0-8050-6951-8). Arthur became the nation's leader after the assassination of Garfield in 1881. (Rev: BL 5/15/04) [921]

BUSH, GEORGE H. W.

7649 Anderson, Ken. *George Bush: A Lifetime of Service* (6–12). 2003, Eakin $16.95 (978-1-57168-663-3); paper $12.95 (978-1-57168-600-8). George Herbert Walker Bush, the 41st president, is profiled in this biography that gives insights into his relationship with his son, George W. Bush. (Rev: BL 1/1–15/03; HBG 10/03; SLJ 2/03) [921]

CLEVELAND, GROVER

7650 Graff, Henry. *Grover Cleveland* (10–12). 2002, Henry Holt $20.00 (978-0-8050-6923-5). A concise overview of the life and political career of the only American president elected to two non-consecutive terms in office. (Rev: BL 8/02) [921]

CLINTON, BILL

7651 Warshaw, Shirley Ann. *The Clinton Years* (9–12). Series: Presidential Profiles. 2004, Facts on File $85.00 (978-0-8160-5333-9). An overview of the major events of Bill Clinton's presidency is followed by more than 200 profiles of U.S. and world figures who played key roles during his administration. (Rev: SLJ 2/05) [921]

COOLIDGE, CALVIN

7652 Greenberg, David. *Calvin Coolidge* (9–12). Series: American Presidents. 2007, Times $20.00 (978-0-8050-6957-0). Greenburg presents an evenhanded profile of the president known as "Silent Cal" — who was actually a fairly skillful manipulator of public image. (Rev: BL 12/15/06) [973.91]

EISENHOWER, DWIGHT D.

7653 Ambrose, Stephen E. *Eisenhower: Soldier and President* (10–12). 1990, Simon & Schuster paper $18.00 (978-0-671-74758-9). An excellent one-volume biography of Eisenhower that includes his failures as well as his triumphs. [921]

7654 Wicker, Tom. *Dwight D. Eisenhower* (10–12). Series: American Presidents. 2002, Henry Holt $20.00 (978-0-8050-6907-5). A concise appraisal of the life and presidency of Dwight D. Eisenhower; useful for report writers. (Rev: BL 10/15/02) [921]

7655 Young, Jeff C. *Dwight D. Eisenhower: Soldier and President* (6–12). 2001, Morgan Reynolds LB $23.95

(978-1-883846-76-3). This well-written and interesting biography of the 34th president covers his life from boyhood, his career, and his personality. (Rev: BL 11/15/01; HBG 3/02; SLJ 2/02) [921]

GRANT, ULYSSES S.

7656 Mosier, John. *Grant* (9–12). Series: Great Generals. 2006, Palgrave $21.95 (978-1-4039-7136-4). Grant's accomplishments as a general are the focus of this accessible but detailed biography. ◯ (Rev: BL 6/1–15/06) [973.8]

7657 Rice, Earle, Jr. *Ulysses S. Grant: Defender of the Union* (8–11). Series: Civil War Leaders. 2005, Morgan Reynolds LB $26.95 (978-1-931798-48-8). A vivid portrait of Grant, who rose from humble beginnings in his native Ohio to achieve acclaim as a military leader and ascend to the highest office in the land. (Rev: BL 3/15/05; SLJ 11/05) [973.8]

7658 Smith, Jean Edward. *Grant* (10–12). 2001, Simon & Schuster paper $20.00 (978-0-684-84927-0). An outstanding biography of Ulysses S. Grant from his youth and career at West Point to his presidency and after. (Rev: BL 4/1/01) [921]

HARDING, WARREN G.

7659 Dean, John W. *Warren G. Harding* (10–12). Series: American Presidents. 2004, Henry Holt $20.00 (978-0-8050-6956-3). A useful biography of this often-overlooked president that depicts him as an innovative, intelligent, and conscientious man. (Rev: BL 1/1–15/04; SLJ 6/04) [921]

HARRISON, BENJAMIN

7660 Calhoun, Charles W. *Benjamin Harrison* (9–12). Series: American Presidents. 2005, Henry Holt $20.00 (978-0-8050-6952-5). Calhoun casts light on Harrison's background and little-known accomplishments. (Rev: BL 5/15/05) [973.8]

HAYES, RUTHERFORD B.

7661 Trefousse, Hans L. *Rutherford B. Hayes* (10–12). Series: American Presidents. 2002, Henry Holt $20.00 (978-0-8050-6908-2). A concise profile of America's 19th and often-overlooked president; useful for report writers. (Rev: BL 10/15/02) [921]

JACKSON, ANDREW

7662 Remini, Robert V. *Andrew Jackson* (10–12). Illus. Series: Great Generals. 2008, Palgrave $21.95 (978-023060015-7). This biography of Andrew Jackson focuses on his military skill and reasons for his actions, especially when fighting against the Creek and Seminole tribes. ◯ (Rev: BL 9/15/08) [921]

7663 Whitelaw, Nancy. *Andrew Jackson: Frontier President* (7–10). Series: Notable Americans. 2000, Morgan

Reynolds LB $23.95 (978-1-883846-67-1). A fine biography of an interesting, multifaceted man who overcame many obstacles to achieve prominence. (Rev: BL 11/1/00; HBG 3/01; SLJ 2/01) [921]

7664 Wilentz, Sean. *Andrew Jackson* (11–12). 2006, Henry Holt $20.00 (978-0-8050-6925-9). This biography emphasizes the seventh U.S. president's unflagging support for the common man, offering new insight for advanced history students. (Rev: BL 12/15/05) [973.5]

JEFFERSON, THOMAS

7665 Appleby, Joyce. *Thomas Jefferson* (10–12). Series: American Presidents. 2003, Henry Holt $20.00 (978-0-8050-6924-2). An appreciative look at Jefferson's life and presidency that offers insight into his political and social philosophies. (Rev: BL 1/1–15/03) [921]

7666 Ellis, Joseph J. *American Sphinx: The Character of Thomas Jefferson* (10–12). 1997, Knopf $29.95 (978-0-679-44490-9). This well-written study of Jefferson shows the human side of this great historical figure — a man who made mistakes, a man with debts, a man with family problems. (Rev: BL 1/1–15/97; SLJ 9/97) [921]

7667 Hitchens, Christopher. *Thomas Jefferson: Author of America* (9–12). Series: Eminent Lives. 2005, HarperCollins $21.95 (978-0-06-059896-9). A brief biography that succeeds in covering the essentials, highlighting Jefferson's contributions to the institution of democracy while admitting his weaknesses. (Rev: BL 4/15/05) [973.4]

7668 Mullin, Rita Thievon. *Thomas Jefferson: Architect of Freedom* (7–10). Series: Sterling Biographies. 2007, Sterling paper $5.95 (978-1-4027-3397-0). Report writers will find a wealth of information on the president's prolific and remarkable life, as well as drawings and photographs to enhance the text. (Rev: BL 4/1/07; SLJ 5/07) [973.4]

7669 Severance, John B. *Thomas Jefferson: Architect of Democracy* (7–12). 1998, Clarion $18.00 (978-0-395-84513-4). A thoughtful, well-rounded biography that focuses on Jefferson's accomplishments and his beliefs, with many quotations from his writings. (Rev: BL 9/1/98; HBG 3/99; SLJ 12/98; VOYA 4/99) [921]

7670 Whitelaw, Nancy. *Thomas Jefferson: Philosopher and President* (7–10). 2001, Morgan Reynolds LB $23.95 (978-1-883846-81-7). This concise and thorough biography, which covers Jefferson's strengths and weaknesses, will be useful for report writers. (Rev: HBG 3/02; SLJ 3/02) [921]

JOHNSON, LYNDON B.

7671 Goodwin, Doris Kearns. *Lyndon Johnson and the American Dream* (10–12). 1976, Harper & Row paper $17.95 (978-0-312-06027-5). For better readers, this is a biography of Johnson, that reveals the real man behind the power. [921]

7672 Woods, Randall B. *LBJ: Architect of American Ambition* (9–12). 2006, Free Press $35.00 (978-0-684-83458-0). The author paints a picture of the president through examining his personal and public personas, revealing a man whose political astuteness led to a lasting legacy. (Rev: BL 8/06) [921]

KENNEDY, JOHN F.

7673 Kaplan, Howard S. *John F. Kennedy* (5–10). Series: DK Biography. 2004, DK paper $4.99 (978-0-7566-0340-3). A heavily illustrated, attractive biography of Kennedy that offers broad historical background. (Rev: BL 6/1–15/04) [921]

7674 Spencer, Lauren. *The Assassination of John F. Kennedy* (6–10). Series: Library of Political Assassinations. 2001, Rosen LB $27.95 (978-0-8239-3541-3). This is a highly readable account of the assassination, its political buildup, and the social fallout. (Rev: BL 3/15/02; SLJ 6/02) [921]

LINCOLN, ABRAHAM

7675 Barter, James. *Abraham Lincoln* (7–12). Series: The Importance Of. 2003, Gale LB $32.45 (978-1-56006-965-2). This biography of Lincoln uses ample quotations from important sources and tries to evaluate Lincoln's importance by present-day standards. (Rev: BL 3/15/03) [921]

7676 Carwardine, Richard. *Lincoln: A Life of Purpose and Power* (9–12). 2006, Knopf $27.50 (978-1-4000-4456-6). Lincoln's innovations, principles, and politics are closely examined in this biography, with discussion of his status as the Great Emancipator and, in popular opinion, America's greatest president. (Rev: BL 1/1–15/06; SLJ 6/06) [921]

7677 Donald, David Herbert, and Harold Holzer, eds. *Lincoln in the Times: The Life of Abraham Lincoln as Originally Reported in the New York Times* (9–12). 2005, St. Martin's $29.95 (978-0-312-34919-6). For advanced students, this volume offers lots of fodder for reports and discussion. (Rev: BL 10/15/05) [973.7]

7678 Holzer, Harold. *Abraham Lincoln: The Writer* (6–10). 2000, Boyds Mills $16.95 (978-1-56397-772-5). Following a brief biography, this resource contains letters, excerpts from speeches, notes, debates, and inaugural addresses, each with explanatory introductions that connect the snippet to his life. (Rev: BL 5/1/00; HBG 9/00; SLJ 6/00) [921]

7679 Sandburg, Carl. *Abraham Lincoln: The Prairie Years and the War Years. illustrated ed.* (10–12). 1970, Harcourt paper $26.00 (978-0-15-602752-6). This one-volume work condenses Sandburg's esteemed longer work on the life of Lincoln. [921]

7680 Stone, Tanya Lee. *Abraham Lincoln* (5–10). Series: DK Biography. 2005, DK $14.99 (978-0-7566-0833-0); paper $4.99 (978-0-7566-0834-7). A heavily illustrated, attractive biography of Lincoln that offers broad historical background. (Rev: BL 6/1–15/04) [921]

LINCOLN, ABRAHAM AND MARY TODD

7681 Fleming, Candace. *The Lincolns: A Scrapbook Look at Abraham and Mary* (7–12). 2008, Random House LB $28.99 (978-0-375-93618-0). With a pleasing mix of narrative, documents, paintings and etchings, and political cartoons, this attractive volume provides a detailed life of both Abraham and Mary. Boston Globe–Horn Book Award 2009; ALA Notable Books 2009. (Rev: BL 9/15/08; LMC 1–2/09; SLJ 10/1/08*) [921]

MADISON, JAMES

7682 Wills, Garry. *James Madison* (10–12). 2002, Henry Holt $20.00 (978-0-8050-6905-1). Wills paints a portrait of America's fourth president as a well-meaning intellectual who was ill-equipped to lead his nation in war. (Rev: BL 3/1/02*) [921]

MCKINLEY, WILLIAM

7683 Phillips, Kevin. *William McKinley* (10–12). Series: American Presidents. 2003, Henry Holt $20.00 (978-0-8050-6953-2). High school report writers will appreciate this detailed biography of McKinley that makes a convincing case for reevaluating the widely held perception that the 25th president made few worthwhile contributions. (Rev: BL 7/03) [921]

MONROE, JAMES

7684 Hart, Gary. *James Monroe* (9–12). Series: American Presidents. 2005, Henry Holt $20.00 (978-0-8050-6960-0). Former U.S. Senator Gary Hart profiles America's fifth president, best remembered for his doctrine declaring the Western Hemisphere off-limits to European intervention. (Rev: BL 10/1/05) [973.5]

OBAMA, BARACK

7685 Mendell, David. *Obama: From Promise to Power* (10–12). 2007, Amistad $25.95 (978-0-06-085820-9). Written before Obama's successful presidential campaign, this book focuses on his rise in politics from the local level to the national level. 🎧 (Rev: BL 9/1/07) [921]

PIERCE, FRANKLIN

7686 Holt, Michael F. *Franklin Pierce* (10–12). Series: American Presidents. 2010, Times $23 (978-080508719-2). Holt examines the life and contributions of dark-horse president Franklin Pierce, who failed to achieve a second term in office thanks mostly to the divisive Kansas-Nebraska Act. (Rev: BL 3/1–15/10) [921]

POLK, JAMES K.

7687 Seigenthaler, John. *James K. Polk* (10–12). Series: American Presidents. 2004, Henry Holt $20.00 (978-0-8050-6942-6). An accessible biography of the honest, hard-working president whom most people consider a near-great. (Rev: BL 1/1–15/04) [921]

REAGAN, RONALD

7688 Young, Jeff C. *Great Communicator: The Story of Ronald Reagan* (6–10). Series: Twentieth-Century Leaders. 2003, Morgan Reynolds LB $23.95 (978-1-931798-10-5). Reagan's career is the main focus of this biography that includes many quotations and black-and-white photographs and deals objectively with the former president's strengths and weaknesses. (Rev: BL 6/1–15/03; HBG 10/03; SLJ 10/03; VOYA 12/03) [921]

ROOSEVELT, ELEANOR

7689 Hubbard-Brown, Janet. *Eleanor Roosevelt: First Lady* (6–10). Series: Women of Achievement. 2009, Chelsea House $30 (978-1-60413-076-8). This volume is a good source of basic information on former First Lady Eleanor Roosevelt and her influence on American culture. (Rev: SLJ 5/1/09) [921]

ROOSEVELT, FRANKLIN D.

7690 Brinkley, Alan. *Franklin Delano Roosevelt* (9–12). 2010, Oxford paper $12.95 (978-01997320-2-9). Personal and professional roles are both covered in this even-handed introduction to Roosevelt's life from childhood. (Rev: BL 12/15/09) [921]

7691 Devaney, John. *Franklin Delano Roosevelt, President* (6–10). 1987, Walker $12.95 (978-0-8027-6713-4). A detailed account of Roosevelt's personality and career. (Rev: SLJ 1/88; VOYA 12/87) [921]

7692 Jenkins, Roy. *Franklin Delano Roosevelt* (10–12). Series: American Presidents. 2003, Henry Holt $20.00 (978-0-8050-6959-4). A very readable and insightful biography that concentrates on Roosevelt's political career. (Rev: BL 10/15/03; SLJ 5/04) [921]

7693 Nardo, Don. *Franklin D. Roosevelt: U.S. President* (7–10). Series: Great Achievers: Lives of the Physically Challenged. 1995, Chelsea LB $14.95 (978-0-7910-2406-5). This biography stresses the physical challenges Roosevelt faced and the strong personality that allowed him to achieve great success. (Rev: SLJ 1/96) [921]

ROOSEVELT, THEODORE

7694 Auchincloss, Louis. *Theodore Roosevelt* (10–12). 2002, Times $20.00 (978-0-8050-6906-8). A sparkling short biography that catches the major events in Roosevelt's life and their significance. (Rev: BL 11/15/01) [921]

7695 Donald, Aida D. *Lion in the White House: A Life of Theodore Roosevelt* (9–12). 2007, Basic Bks $26.00 (978-0-465-00213-9). The 26th president is brought to life in this accessible biography. (Rev: BLO 9/19/07) [921]

7696 Marrin, Albert. *The Great Adventure: Theodore Roosevelt and the Rise of Modern America* (8–11). 2007, Dutton $30.00 (978-0-525-47659-7). Marrin provides excellent, balanced information on Roosevelt's life and political career, giving good background on the social and political mores of the time and covering the president's achievements and peculiarities. (Rev: BL 9/1/07; SLJ 12/07) [973.91]

TRUMAN, HARRY S

7697 Dallek, Robert. *Harry S. Truman* (10–12). Series: American Presidents. 2008, Times $22.00 (978-0-8050-6938-9). This biography of Harry Truman focuses on the struggles he faced during his presidency. ∩ ℮ (Rev: BL 8/08) [921]

7698 Fleming, Thomas. *Harry S Truman, President* (6–12). 1993, Walker LB $15.85 (978-0-8027-8269-4). The author of this uncritical biography of the former president had access to family photographs and documents. (Rev: BL 1/1/94; SLJ 12/93; VOYA 2/94) [921]

7699 McCullough, David. *Truman* (9–12). 1992, Simon & Schuster $32.00 (978-0-671-45654-2). A landmark biography of the 33rd president and his times. (Rev: BL 4/15/92*) [921]

VAN BUREN, MARTIN

7700 Widmer, Ted. *Martin Van Buren* (9–12). Series: American Presidents. 2005, Henry Holt $20.00 (978-0-8050-6922-8). A lively, very readable account of Van Buren's life and achievements. (Rev: BL 12/1/04) [973.5]

WASHINGTON, GEORGE

7701 Burns, James MacGregor, and Susan Dunn. *George Washington* (10–12). Series: American Presidents. 2004, Henry Holt $20.00 (978-0-8050-6936-5). A concise biography of the first president that concentrates on his political life and contributions. (Rev: BL 1/1–15/04) [921]

7702 Ellis, Joseph J. *His Excellency: George Washington* (9–12). 2004, Knopf $26.95 (978-1-4000-4031-5). Washington's complex character is the main focus of this biography that draws heavily on the president's correspondence. (Rev: BL 9/15/04; SLJ 3/05) [973.4]

7703 Flexner, James Thomas. *Washington, the Indispensable Man* (10–12). 1974, Little, Brown paper $17.95 (978-0-316-28616-9). Noted historian Flexner has written one of the best biographies of the first U.S. president. [921]

7704 Hort, Lenny. *George Washington* (5–10). Series: DK Biography. 2005, DK $14.99 (978-0-7566-0832-3); paper $4.99 (978-0-7566-0835-4). A heavily illustrated, attractive biography of the man born in Virginia. (Rev: BL 6/1–15/04) [921]

7705 Lengel, Edward G. *Inventing George Washington: America's Founder, in Myth and Memory* (10–12). 2011, HarperCollins $25.99 (978-006166258-4). Lengel turns a practiced, critical eye on the lore surrounding George Washington, systematically debunking fabrications and examining the roots of their creation. ℮ (Rev: BL 12/1–15/10) [973.4]

7706 Rosenburg, John. *First in Peace: George Washington, the Constitution, and the Presidency* (7–10). 1998, Millbrook LB $25.90 (978-0-7613-0422-7). The last of a trilogy about Washington, this installment describes the emergence of the new nation and the role played by the first president. (Rev: HBG 3/99; SLJ 1/99) [921]

7707 Yoder, Carolyn P., ed. *George Washington: The Writer: A Treasury of Letters, Diaries, and Public Documents* (7–10). 2003, Boyds Mills $16.95 (978-1-56397-199-0). Washington's speeches, letters, will, and other documents — many excerpted — reveal much about his life and career. (Rev: BL 3/15/03; HBG 10/03; SLJ 2/03; VOYA 12/03) [921]

WILSON, WOODROW

7708 Lukes, Bonnie L. *Woodrow Wilson and the Progressive Era* (6–10). Series: World Leaders. 2005, Morgan Reynolds LB $26.95 (978-1-931798-79-2). A chronological survey of Wilson's life from birth in 1856 through his death in 1924, with discussion of his achievements in light of the global events of the time. (Rev: SLJ 2/06) [921]

Other Government and Public Figures

ADAMS, SAMUEL

7709 Irvin, Benjamin H. *Samuel Adams: Son of Liberty, Father of Revolution* (9–12). Series: Oxford Portraits. 2002, Oxford LB $32.95 (978-0-19-513225-0). This well-researched profile of Samuel Adams, who worked feverishly for American independence and later served as governor of Massachusetts, sheds light on the life of a very private man. (Rev: BL 2/1/03; HBG 10/03; SLJ 2/03; VOYA 8/03) [921]

ARNOLD, BENEDICT

7710 Murphy, Jim. *The Real Benedict Arnold* (7–10). 2007, Clarion $20.00 (978-0-395-77609-4). An examination of Arnold's character reveals what may have led him to become a traitor. (Rev: BL 10/1/07; HB 1–2/08; LMC 2/08; SLJ 12/07) [921]

BRADLEY, BILL

7711 Jaspersohn, William. *Senator: A Profile of Bill Bradley in the U.S. Senate* (6–10). 1992, Harcourt $19.95 (978-0-15-272880-9). An in-depth photoessay about Congress in general and Senator Bradley of New Jersey in particular, showing how his sports career led to the Senate. (Rev: BL 7/92; SLJ 10/92) [921]

BUNCHE, RALPH

7712 Henry, Charles P. *Ralph Bunche: Model Negro or American Other?* (10–12). 1999, New York Univ. $60.00 (978-0-8147-3582-4). Bunche's lasting contributions in the diverse realms of statesmanship and civil rights are covered in detail. (Rev: BL 12/15/98) [921]

CLINTON, HILLARY RODHAM

7713 Abrams, Dennis. *Hillary Rodham Clinton: Politician* (6–10). Series: Women of Achievement. 2009, Chelsea House $30 (978-1-60413-077-5). Covering her youth, her university career, her marriage and political life with Bill Clinton, and her election to the Senate and run for the White House, this volume provides a balanced account. (Rev: LMC 10/09; SLJ 5/1/09) [921]

CODY, BUFFALO BILL

7714 Carter, Robert A. *Buffalo Bill Cody: The Man Behind the Legend* (10–12). 2000, Wiley paper $21.95 (978-0-471-07780-0). The many facets of Buffalo Bill Cody's talents as a scout, marksman, buffalo hunter, and showman are chronicled in this biography. (Rev: BL 10/15/00) [921]

CRAZY HORSE (SIOUX CHIEF)

7715 Freedman, Russell. *The Life and Death of Crazy Horse* (6–12). 1996, Holiday $24.95 (978-0-8234-1219-8). This biography of Crazy Horse tells an uncompromising story of bloody wars, terrible grief, tragedy, and the Sioux's losing battle to preserve their independence and their land. (Rev: BL 6/1–15/96*; SLJ 6/96*; VOYA 10/96) [921]

FRANKLIN, BENJAMIN

7716 Brands, H. W. *The First American: The Life and Times of Benjamin Franklin* (10–12). 2000, Doubleday paper $17.00 (978-0-385-49540-0). A highly readable biography about this multitalented American who amassed an amazing list of achievements. [921]

7717 Dash, Joan. *A Dangerous Engine: Benjamin Franklin, from Scientist to Diplomat* (6–10). Illus. by Dusan Petricic. 2006, Farrar $17.00 (978-0-374-30669-4). Franklin's keen interest in science and the development of new technology is emphasized in this lively

biography illustrated with pen-and-ink drawings. (Rev: BCCB 1/06; BL 3/1/06; HB 3–4/06; SLJ 2/06) [921]

7718 Gaustad, Edwin S. *Benjamin Franklin: Inventing America* (7–10). Series: Oxford Portraits. 2004, Oxford LB $32.95 (978-0-19-515732-1). The life and achievements of Benjamin Franklin are described using many quotations from Franklin's autobiography. (Rev: SLJ 2/05) [921]

7719 Lee, Tanja, ed. *Benjamin Franklin* (7–12). Series: People Who Made History. 2002, Gale LB $24.95 (978-0-7377-0898-1); paper $36.20 (978-0-7377-0899-8). After a general introduction to Franklin, his life, and his times, essays explore his talents, contributions, accomplishments, and his place in world history. (Rev: BL 4/1/02) [921]

7720 Miller, Brandon Marie. *Benjamin Franklin, American Genius: His Life and Ideas with 21 Activities* (7–12). Illus. 2009, Chicago Review paper $16.95 (978-1-55652-757-9). The life and times of Benjamin Franklin — inventor, publisher, scientist, founding father — are presented clearly and engagingly in this illustrated, large-format biography. (Rev: BL 12/15/09; SLJ 10/09) [921]

7721 Morgan, Edmund S. *Benjamin Franklin* (10–12). 2002, Yale $28.00 (978-0-300-09532-6). An absorbing and insightful biography that will also be useful for reports. (Rev: BL 8/02; SLJ 4/03) [921]

GERONIMO

7722 Barrett, S. M., ed. *Geronimo: His Own Story* (10–12). 1983, Irvington paper $15.95 (978-0-8290-0658-2). The memoirs of the Apache warrior Geronimo with valuable background information about his people and their culture. [921]

GOODE, W. WILSON

7723 Goode, W. Wilson, and Joann Stevens. *In Goode Faith: Philadelphia's First Black Mayor Tells His Story* (9–12). 1992, Judson $15.00 (978-0-8170-1186-4). Philadelphia's first African American mayor recounts his early life and candidly describes his turbulent political career. (Rev: BL 10/1/92) [921]

GREENE, NATHANAEL

7724 Carbone, Gerald M. *Nathanael Greene: A Biography of the American Revolution* (10–12). 2008, Palgrave $27.95 (978-0-230-60271-7). A fast-paced tour through the 44-year-long life of Nathanael Greene, one of Washington's top generals during the Revolutionary War. ℮ (Rev: BL 6/1–15/08) [921]

HOOVER, J. EDGAR

7725 Aronson, Marc. *Master of Deceit: J. Edgar Hoover and America in the Age of Lies* (9–12). Illus. 2012, Candlewick $25.99 (978-076365025-4). A frank profile of the longtime FBI chief and his personal and political relationships. 🎧 📖 Lexile 1090L (Rev: BL 4/15/12; HB 5–6/12; LMC 10/12; SLJ 3/12*; VOYA 4/12) [921]

7726 Geary, Rick. *J. Edgar Hoover: A Graphic Biography* (10–12). 2008, Hill & Wang $16.95 (978-0-8090-9503-2). Hoover's life gets a pulp-fiction-style graphic novel treatment in this biography that emphasizes the FBI director's manipulative style and places his actions in historical context. (Rev: BL 12/1/07; SLJ 3/08) [921]

INOUYE, DANIEL K.

7727 Slavicek, Louise Chipley. *Daniel Inouye* (6–10). Series: Asian Americans of Achievement. 2007, Chelsea House LB $30.00 (978-0-7910-9271-2). A useful profile of the first Japanese American elected to the U.S. Congress, with information on his family's arrival in Hawaii and Inouye's experiences in World War II. (Rev: SLJ 8/07) [921]

JACKSON, STONEWALL

7728 Brager, Bruce L. *There He Stands: The Story of Stonewall Jackson* (8–10). Series: Civil War Leaders. 2005, Morgan Reynolds LB $26.95 (978-1-931798-44-0). The life and military career of Stonewall Jackson, one of the Civil War's most skilled tacticians; photographs, reproductions, and maps complement the well-written text. (Rev: SLJ 11/05) [921]

7729 Davis, Donald A. *Stonewall Jackson* (10–12). 2007, Palgrave $21.95 (978-1-4039-7477-8). Covering Jackson's life from his youth through his military career, this is an informative and accessible biography. (Rev: BL 6/1–15/07) [973.7]

JARAMILLO, MARI-LUCI

7730 Jaramillo, Mari-Luci. *Madame Ambassador: The Shoemaker's Daughter* (10–12). 2002, Bilingual paper $15.00 (978-1-931010-04-7). In this inspiring autobiography, the former U.S. ambassador to Honduras chronicles her rise from a childhood of poverty to prominence as a civil rights advocate and diplomat. (Rev: BL 3/15/02) [921]

JONES, JOHN PAUL

7731 Brager, Bruce L. *John Paul Jones: America's Sailor* (7–10). 2006, Morgan Reynolds LB $26.95 (978-1-931798-84-6). The naval commander's life (flaws and attributes) and times are covered in well-organized text plus maps, timeline, sources, and a bibliography. (Rev: BL 7/06; SLJ 5/06) [921]

JOSEPH (NEZ PERCE CHIEF)

7732 Yates, Diana. *Chief Joseph: Thunder Rolling from the Mountains* (7–12). 1992, Ward Hill LB $14.95 (978-0-9623380-9-0); paper $10.95 (978-0-9623380-8-3). A sensitive distillation of the life and times of

Chief Joseph of the Nez Perce. (Rev: BL 12/15/92; SLJ 12/92) [921]

KENNEDY, ROBERT F.

7733 Aronson, Marc. *Robert F. Kennedy* (8–11). Series: Up Close. 2007, Viking $15.99 (978-0-670-06066-5). True to the series' title, this book looks at Robert F. Kennedy up close, examining his personal life more than his public achievements. (Rev: BCCB 6/07; BL 3/1/07; HB 3–4/07; SLJ 5/07) [921]

KERRY, JOHN

7734 Brager, Bruce L. *John Kerry: Senator from Massachusetts* (6–10). 2005, Morgan Reynolds LB $23.95 (978-1-931798-64-8). Kerry's life and military service are presented along with his career in politics and unsuccessful bid for the presidency in 2004. (Rev: SLJ 8/05) [921]

LEE, ROBERT E.

7735 Blount, Roy. *Robert E. Lee* (10–12). Series: Penguin Lives. 2003, Henry Holt $19.95 (978-0-670-03220-4). This well-written biography explores Lee's life, covering his much-vaunted reputation as a military leader and his personal political philosophy. (Rev: BL 4/1/03; SLJ 9/03) [921]

7736 Rice, Earle, Jr. *Robert E. Lee: First Soldier of the Confederacy* (8–10). Series: Civil War Leaders. 2005, Morgan Reynolds LB $26.95 (978-1-931798-47-1). Lee's childhood, adult life, and military career are covered; photographs, reproductions, and maps complement the well-written text. (Rev: SLJ 11/05) [921]

7737 Robertson, James I. *Robert E. Lee: Virginian Soldier, American Citizen* (7–10). 2005, Simon & Schuster $21.95 (978-0-689-85731-7). A rich and even-handed portrait of Robert E. Lee, including a number of excerpts from such primary sources as letters and diaries. (Rev: BL 11/15/05; SLJ 1/06; VOYA 10/05) [973.7]

MACARTHUR, DOUGLAS

7738 Frank, Richard B. *MacArthur* (9–12). Series: Great Generals. 2007, Palgrave $21.95 (978-1-4039-7658-1). MacArthur's adaptability, large ego, and uneven accomplishments are underlined in this readable biography of the controversial military figure. (Rev: BL 6/1–15/07) [921]

MARSHALL, GEORGE C.

7739 Gimpel, Lee. *Fighting Wars, Planning for Peace: The Story of George C. Marshall* (9–12). Series: World Leaders. 2005, Morgan Reynolds LB $26.95 (978-1-931798-66-2). A clear profile of the American soldier and diplomat and his importance to the world in the 20th century. (Rev: BL 1/1–15/06; SLJ 12/05) [973.918]

MARSHALL, THURGOOD

7740 Crowe, Chris. *Thurgood Marshall* (6–12). Series: Up Close. 2008, Viking $16.99 (978-0-670-06228-7). Using many quotations, Crowe covers Marshall's life, work as an NAACP lawyer, civil rights activism, and career on the Supreme Court. (Rev: BL 6/1–15/08) [921]

7741 Williams, Juan. *Thurgood Marshall: American Revolutionary* (10–12). 1998, Times paper $16.00 (978-0-8129-3299-7). A thorough biography of the African American lawyer who won *Brown* v. *Board of Education* and was named to the Supreme Court. (Rev: BL 8/98) [921]

MCCAIN, JOHN

7742 Kozar, Richard. *John McCain* (8–12). Series: Overcoming Adversity. 2002, Chelsea LB $30.00 (978-0-7910-6299-9). The story of the prominent U.S. politician and how he survived the ordeal of a POW camp in Vietnam. (Rev: BL 4/15/02; HBG 10/02) [921]

MCCARTHY, JOSEPH

7743 Giblin, James Cross. *The Rise and Fall of Senator Joe McCarthy* (8–12). 2010, Clarion $22 (978-0-618-61058-7). This well-researched biography of McCarthy includes photographs, quotes, and little-known facts to provide a complete portrait of the man and his life. Lexile 1400 (Rev: BL 10/15/09; HB 11–12/09; LMC 1–2/10; SLJ 12/09) [921]

MITCHELL, BILLY

7744 Miller, Roger G. *Billy Mitchell: Evangelist of Air Power* (9–12). Series: Shapers of America. 2007, OTTN LB $25.95 (978-1-59556-025-4). The story of how the perspicacious but controversial World War I general came to be known as "the father of the U.S. Air Force." (Rev: BL 2/15/08) [921]

NADER, RALPH

7745 Graham, Kevin. *Ralph Nader: Battling for Democracy* (6–12). 2000, Windom paper $9.95 (978-0-9700323-0-0). A readable biography of the man who has devoted his life to fighting for liberty and justice for all. (Rev: BL 12/1/00; SLJ 11/00) [921]

O'CONNOR, SANDRA DAY

7746 Herda, D. J. *Sandra Day O'Connor: Independent Thinker* (6–10). Series: Justices of the Supreme Court. 1995, Enslow LB $17.95 (978-0-89480-558-5). The story of the first female Supreme Court justice, including her personal life and some key decisions since becoming a Supreme Court member in 1981. (Rev: BL 2/15/96) [921]

PAINE, THOMAS

7747 Collins, Paul. *The Trouble with Tom: The Strange Afterlife and Times of Thomas Paine* (9–12). 2005, Bloomsbury $24.95 (978-1-58234-502-4). A witty account of the author's research into Tom Paine's life and the strange tale of his lost remains. (Rev: SLJ 3/06) [921]

7748 Kaye, Harvey J. *Thomas Paine: Firebrand of the Revolution* (6–10). 2000, Oxford LB $32.95 (978-0-19-511627-4). A readable, well-illustrated biography on the career, accomplishments, and lasting importance of this Revolutionary War personality, with material on the social and political conditions of the period. (Rev: BL 3/1/00; HBG 9/00; SLJ 4/00) [921]

PATTON, GEORGE S.

7749 Axelrod, Alan. *Patton* (9–12). Series: Great Generals. 2006, Palgrave $21.95 (978-1-4039-7139-5). A no-holds-barred portrait of the life and wartime achievements of the controversial World War II general. (Rev: BL 2/1/06) [355]

7750 Gitlin, Martin. *George S. Patton: World War II General and Military Innovator* (7–10). Series: Military Heroes. 2010, ABDO LB $32.79 (978-1-60453-964-6). A well-written and richly illustrated account of the life of the World War II commander, covering his childhood, education, military career, and his strengths and weaknesses. (Rev: BL 4/1/10; LMC 10/10; SLJ 4/10) [921]

PELOSI, NANCY

7751 Pelosi, Nancy. *Know Your Power: A Message to America's Daughters* (9–12). 2008, Doubleday $23.95 (978-0-385-52586-2). Pelosi combines information about her youth and rise to power with (fairly standard) advice on achieving one's dreams. **e** (Rev: BL 6/1–15/08) [921]

PERKINS, FRANCES

7752 Keller, Emily. *Frances Perkins: First Woman Cabinet Member* (8–12). 2006, Morgan Reynolds LB $27.95 (978-1-931798-91-4). Perkins, a social reformer, served as Secretary of Labor under Franklin D. Roosevelt; this thorough biography documents her achievements and covers her personal life. (Rev: SLJ 5/07) [921]

PICKETT, GEORGE EDWARD

7753 Gordon, Lesley J. *General George E. Pickett in Life and Legend* (10–12). 1998, Univ. of North Carolina $32.50 (978-0-8078-2450-4). The third wife of this Confederate general is a principal figure in this biography that will appeal to teens who enjoy the genre or who are interested in the Civil War. (Rev: BL 12/1/98) [921]

POCAHONTAS

7754 Woodward, Grace Steele. *Pocahontas* (10–12). Series: Civilization of the American Indian. 1969, Univ. of Oklahoma paper $19.95 (978-0-8061-1642-6). A vivid adult recreation of the life of the daughter of Chief Powhatan and her role in the history of the Jamestown settlement. [921]

POWELL, COLIN

7755 Brown, Warren. *Colin Powell* (7–10). Series: Black Americans of Achievement. 1992, Chelsea LB $30.00 (978-0-7910-1647-3). A nicely illustrated account of the African American general who distinguished himself during the Persian Gulf War. (Rev: BL 8/92) [921]

7756 Powell, Colin. *My American Journey* (10–12). 1995, Random House $25.95 (978-0-679-43296-8). The autobiography of the American hero who grew up in the South Bronx and later became chairman of the Joint Chiefs of Staff. (Rev: SLJ 2/96) [921]

SHARPTON, AL

7757 Mallin, Jay. *Al Sharpton: Community Activist* (6–12). Series: Great Life Stories. 2006, Watts LB $30.50 (978-0-531-13872-4). Mallin looks at Sharpton's personal and professional life from childhood to his bid for the presidency. (Rev: SLJ 3/07) [921]

SITTING BULL

7758 Vestal, Stanley. *Sitting Bull, Champion of the Sioux: A Biography. New ed.* (10–12). Series: Civilization of the American Indian. 1969, Univ. of Oklahoma paper $24.95 (978-0-8061-2219-9). An excellent and well-documented biography of the great Sioux chief who died in 1890. [921]

7759 Yenne, Bill. *Sitting Bull* (9–12). 2008, Westholme $29.95 (978-1-59416-060-8). An eloquent well-researched biography of the Lakota leader. (Rev: BL 4/15/08) [921]

WARREN, EARL

7760 Compston, Christine L. *Earl Warren: Justice for All* (7–10). Series: Oxford Portraits. 2002, Oxford $32.95 (978-0-19-513001-0). In addition to Warren's family life and career, this portrait presents his belief in the rule of law and his dealings with successive presidents. (Rev: BL 4/15/02; HBG 10/02; SLJ 6/02) [921]

Miscellaneous Persons

BARTON, CLARA

7761 Hamilton, Leni. *Clara Barton* (5–10). 1987, Chelsea LB $19.95 (978-1-55546-641-1). The story of the Civil War nurse and how she prepared for the founding of the American Red Cross. (Rev: BL 11/1/87) [921]

7762 Oates, Stephen B. *A Woman of Valor: Clara Barton and the Civil War* (10–12). 1994, Free Press paper $16.95 (978-0-02-874012-6). Known as the angel of the battlefield, this is the story of Clara Barton, her part in the Civil War, and the founding of the Red Cross. [921]

BILLY THE KID

7763 Cline, Don. *Alias Billy the Kid, the Man Behind the Legend* (8–12). 1986, Sunstone paper $12.95 (978-0-86534-080-0). The real story of Billy the Kid, clearing up many misconceptions. [921]

BLY, NELLIE

7764 Bankston, John. *Nellie Bly: Journalist* (7–10). Illus. Series: Women of Achievement. 2012, Chelsea House LB $35 (978-160413908-2). A balanced and thorough life of the reporter known for her investigative flair and round-the-world journey. (Rev: BL 6/12) [921]

7765 Marks, Jason. *Around the World in 72 Days: The Race Between Pulitzer's Nellie Bly and Cosmopolitan's Elizabeth Bisland* (9–12). 1993, Gemittarius paper $12.95 (978-0-9633696-2-8). An account of the 1889 publicity stunt by rival publishers sending two female reporters on a race to beat the fictional record of Jules Verne's Phileas Fogg. (Rev: BL 4/15/93) [921]

BOONE, DANIEL

7766 Faragher, John Mack. *Daniel Boone: The Life and Legend of an American Pioneer* (7–12). 1992, Henry Holt paper $18.00 (978-0-8050-3007-5). A biography of the complex frontier pioneer/politician/maverick. (Rev: BL 11/1/92*; SLJ 5/93*) [921]

BOOTH, JOHN WILKES

7767 Swanson, James L. *Chasing Lincoln's Killer: The Search for John Wilkes Booth* (7–12). Illus. 2009, Scholastic $16.99 (978-043990354-7). This engaging account of the hunt for John Wilkes Booth in the 12 days following Lincoln's assassination is adapted from the author's 2006 adult book, "Manhunt," but lacks source notes and bibliography. ∩ Lexile 980L (Rev: BL 12/1/08; LMC 5–6/09; SLJ 1/1/09*; VOYA 12/08) [921]

BRADLEY, GUY

7768 McIver, Stuart B. *Death in the Everglades: The Murder of Guy Bradley, America's First Martyr to Environmentalism* (10–12). 2003, Univ. Press of Florida $24.95 (978-0-8130-2671-8). The life of pioneering environmentalist Guy Bradley and his death for his cause (protecting egrets, herons, and other birds) are recounted in gripping detail. (Rev: BL 6/1–15/03) [333.95]

CARSON, KIT

7769 Quaife, Milo Milton, ed. *Kit Carson's Autobiography* (10–12). 1966, Univ. of Nebraska paper $12.95 (978-0-8032-5031-4). This autobiography dictated in the years 1856-57 gives fascinating details of the life of this famous hunter, trapper, and Indian fighter. [921]

COLVIN, CLAUDETTE

7770 Hoose, Phillip. *Claudette Colvin: Twice Toward Justice* (7–12). Illus. 2009, Farrar $19.95 (978-037431322-7). Readers will be inspired by the story of teenager Claudette Colvin, who was arrested when she refused to give up her seat on a bus months before Rosa Parks made her famous stand; with photographs and background information about the civil rights movement. Newbery Honor 2010; Sibert Honor 2010; ALA Notable Books 2010. Lexile 1000L (Rev: BL 2/1/09; LMC 8–9/09; SLJ 2/1/09*) [921]

CROCKETT, DAVY

7771 Groneman, William. *David Crockett: Hero of the Common Man* (10–12). 2005, Forge $19.95 (978-0-7653-1067-5). Groneman cuts through the haze of myth and folklore to present the real — and not always inspiring — story of the legendary frontiersman and Alamo defender. (Rev: BL 11/1/05) [973.5]

DAVIS, DONALD

7772 Davis, Donald. *See Rock City* (10–12). 1996, August House $22.95 (978-0-87483-448-2); paper $12.95 (978-0-87483-456-7). From his first day in kindergarten in 1948 through his sophomore year in college, this is the gentle, family-oriented autobiography of Donald Davis and his life in rural North Carolina. (Rev: SLJ 9/96) [921]

FRY, VARIAN

7773 McClafferty, Carla Killough. *In Defiance of Hitler: The Secret Mission of Varian Fry* (7–12). 2008, Farrar $19.95 (978-0-374-38204-9). This is the amazing story of a New York journalist who helped to save more than 2,000 — Jews and non-Jews — from Nazi-occupied France. (Rev: BL 6/1–15/08; SLJ 9/08) [921]

GALLAGHER, HUGH

7774 Gallagher, Hugh Gregory. *Black Bird Fly Away: Disabled in an Able-Bodied World* (10–12). 1998, Vandamere $21.95 (978-0-918339-44-7). The autobiography of Hugh Gallagher, who, after becoming crippled by polio in college, became a disabled rights activist, lobbied for the Architectural Barriers Act of 1968, and became known as the grandfather of the Americans with Disabilities Act. The work weaves in his reaction to his paralysis and the evolution of his own feelings about himself as a paraplegic and as a human being. (Rev: BL 5/15/98; SLJ 1/99) [921]

GRAHAM, BILLY

7775 Gibbs, Nancy, and Michael Duffy. *The Preacher and the Presidents: Billy Graham in the White House* (9–12). 2007, Center Street $26.99 (978-1-59995-734-0). This is an account of Graham's contacts with presidents since Truman. (Rev: BL 8/07) [921]

HAYES, ERNESTINE

7776 Hayes, Ernestine. *Blonde Indian: An Alaska Native Memoir* (11–12). 2006, Univ. of Arizona $32.95 (978-0-8165-2538-6); paper $16.95 (978-0-8165-2537-9). The author's difficult childhood and adolescence gave way to a rewarding adulthood centered on her Tlingit heritage, chronicled in this memoir that gives readers a look into native Alaskan life. (Rev: BL 9/1/06) [921]

HEARST, WILLIAM RANDOLPH

7777 Whitelaw, Nancy. *William Randolph Hearst and the American Century* (6–12). 1999, Morgan Reynolds $21.95 (978-1-883846-46-6). Hearst's eccentricities and lively, thrusting approach to life are well portrayed in this vivid biography. (Rev: BL 10/1/99; HBG 4/00; VOYA 6/00) [921]

JACOBS, JANE

7778 Lang, Glenna, and Marjory Wunsch. *Genius of Common Sense: Jane Jacobs and the Story of the Death and Life of Great American Cities* (7–12). 2009, Godine $17.95 (978-1-56792-384-1). Jane Jacobs fought against urban renewal projects she feared would do more harm to New York City than good, changing the way Americans view cities and city life. (Rev: BL 9/1/09; HB 7–8/09; SLJ 4/1/09) [921]

KELLER, HELEN

7779 Garrett, Leslie. *Helen Keller: Biography* (5–10). Series: DK Biography. 2004, DK paper $5.99 (978-0-7566-0339-7). Keller's struggles to conquer her physical disabilities and her worldwide recognition as a political activist and public speaker are covered in the usual rich DK format. (Rev: BL 6/1–15/04) [921]

7780 Herrmann, Dorothy. *Helen Keller: A Life* (10–12). 1998, Knopf paper $20.00 (978-0-226-32763-1). Herrmann captures Keller's successful struggle to overcome her physical disabilities and develop into a truly multidimensional adult and looks at the important role of her teacher, Annie Sullivan. (Rev: BL 7/98) [921]

7781 Keller, Helen. *The Story of My Life: The Restored Classic, Complete and Unabridged, Centennial Edition* (8–12). 2003, Norton $21.95 (978-0-393-05744-7). The autobiography of the blind and deaf women who overcame her handicaps through the help of a devoted teacher, Anne Sullivan. Originally published in 1903. [921]

7782 Lambert, Joseph. *Annie Sullivan and the Trials of Helen Keller* (6–12). Illus. by author. 2012, Disney/Hyperion $17.99 (978-142311336-2). Informative and poignant, this graphic-novel format biography uses words and images to show the relationship between Helen Keller and her teacher. YALSA Great Graphic Novels Top Ten 2013. (Rev: BL 3/15/12*; HB 5–6/12; LMC 10/12*; SLJ 5/1/12) [921]

KINGSLEY, ANNA MADGIGINE JAI

7783 Schafer, Daniel. *Anna Madgigine Jai Kingsley: African Princess, Florida Slave, Plantation Slaveowner* (10–12). 2003, Univ. Press of Florida $24.95 (978-0-8130-2616-9). This absorbing biography chronicles the incredible life of a Senegalese woman who was thrust into slavery in the early 19th century at the age of 13, married her American owner, and became manager of his plantation. (Rev: BL 5/15/03) [975.9]

KLECKLEY, ELIZABETH

7784 Rutberg, Becky. *Mary Lincoln's Dressmaker: Elizabeth Kleckley's Remarkable Rise from Slave to White House Confidante* (6–10). 1995, Walker $15.95 (978-0-8027-8224-3). The story of a slave, a fine seamstress, who was freed and became Mary Todd Lincoln's dressmaker. (Rev: BL 10/15/95; SLJ 12/95; VOYA 12/95) [921]

LONG LANCE, CHIEF BUFFALO CHILD

7785 Smith, Donald B. *Chief Buffalo Child Long Lance: The Glorious Impostor* (10–12). 2000, Red Deer paper $14.95 (978-0-88995-197-6). The incredible biography of a man who posed as a Native American hero and became famous — until he was found out. (Rev: BL 5/15/00*) [921]

LUCAS, JACK H.

7786 Lucas, Jack H., and D. K. Drum. *Indestructible: The Unforgettable Story of a Marine Hero at the Battle of Iwo Jima* (9–12). 2006, Da Capo $22.95 (978-0-306-81470-9). For his acts of bravery as a 17-year-old Marine in the Second World War, Lucas became the youngest soldier ever to receive the Medal of Honor. (Rev: SLJ 9/06)

MARTIN, LUTHER

7787 Kauffman, Bill. *Forgotten Founder, Drunken Prophet: The Life of Luther Martin* (10–12). Series: Lives of the Founders. 2008, ISI $25.00 (978-193385973-6). Kauffman brings to life Luther Martin who, as the Constitution was being written, argued against a centralized government, was harshly criticized, and went on as Maryland's attorney general to defend Samuel Chase and Aaron Burr. (Rev: BL 9/1/08) [921]

MORRIS, GOUVERNEUR

7788 Miller, Melanie. *An Incautious Man: The Life of Gouverneur Morris* (10–12). Series: Lives of the Founders. 2008, ISI $25.00 (978-193385972-9). Miller presents not only the role Morris played in the Constitutional Convention but also his work as a diplomat in France during the tumultuous times before and during the French Revolution. (Rev: BL 9/1/08) [921]

NISSEL, ANGELA

7789 Nissel, Angela. *Mixed: My Life in Black and White* (9–12). 2006, Villard paper $12.95 (978-0-345-48114-6). Growing up in West Philadelphia as the child of a black mother and white father, Nissel constantly questioned her sense of self in school, dating, and careers. (Rev: BL 2/1/06; SLJ 6/06)

ROSS, BETSY

7790 Miller, Marla R. *Betsy Ross and the Making of America* (10–12). 2010, Henry Holt $30 (978-080508297-5). This accessible portrait paints a vivid picture of Ross's life and times, showing the contributions of working men and women to the formation of a new nation. ∩ ℮ (Rev: BL 4/1–15/10) [921]

SABERI, ROXANA

7791 Saberi, Roxana. *Between Two Worlds: My Life and Captivity in Iran* (11–12). 2010, HarperCollins $25.99 (978-006196528-9). Journalist Roxana Saberi recounts the 100 days spent in an Iranian prison after her arrest in 2009, and the lessons she learned from her experience; for mature readers. (Rev: BL 4/1/10*) [921]

SITIKI

7792 Sitiki. *The Odyssey of an African Slave* (10–12). Ed. by Patricia C. Griffin. Illus. 2009, Univ. Press of Florida $24.95 (978-081303391-4). Griffin adds explanatory notes to the autobiography of an African slave named Sitki, who was captured in Africa at a young age and transported to America in the early 1800s. (Rev: BL 9/15/09) [306.3]

SMITH, JOSEPH

7793 Remini, Robert V. *Joseph Smith* (10–12). 2002, Viking $19.95 (978-0-670-03083-5). A balanced account of Smith's formative years and religious beliefs, placed in the context of the social environment of the time. (Rev: BL 9/1/02) [921]

SMITH, VENTURE

7794 Nelson, Marilyn. *The Freedom Business: Including a Narrative of the Life and Adventures of Venture, a Native of Africa* (9–12). Illus. by Deborah Dancy. 2008, Boyds Mills $18.95 (978-193242557-4). The story of

Venture Smith, an 18th-century slave, is told through evocative poetry and illustrations set alongside Venture's original account published in 1798. Lexile 1200L (Rev: BL 10/1/08; HB 11–12/08; LMC 1–2/09; SLJ 10/1/08) [921]

STEWART, BRIDGETT

7795 Stewart, Bridgett, and Franklin White. *No Matter What* (7–12). 2002, Blue/Black $12.99 (978-0-9652827-1-0). In diary form, Stewart relates the hardships of growing up poor in a shack in Georgia and the uphill battle she faced in her effort to get a full education. (Rev: BL 7/02) [921]

TILL, EMMETT

7796 Wright, Simeon, and Herb Boyd. *Simeon's Story: An Eyewitness Account of the Kidnapping of Emmett Till* (6–10). 2010, Chicago Review $19.95 (978-1-55652-783-8). Author Wright was just 12 years old when his cousin Till came from the North to visit relatives in Mississippi, and he gives real insight into the murder of the 14-year-old African American and the events that followed. (Rev: BL 2/1/10; SLJ 2/10; VOYA 12/09) [921]

WASHINGTON, JOHN

7797 Washington, John. *John Washington's Civil War: A Slave Narrative* (9–12). 2008, Louisiana State $36.95 (978-0-8071-3301-9); paper $16.95 (978-0-8071-3302-6). An account of Washington's life as house slave, laborer, and a slave under Union officers during the Civil

War; chapters end with public records and supporting evidence. (Rev: BL 3/15/08) [921]

WILKERSON, CATHY

7798 Wilkerson, Cathy. *Flying Close to the Sun: My Life and Times as a Weatherman* (9–12). 2007, Seven Stories $26.95 (978-1-58322-771-8). Wilkerson recounts her experiences as a leading member of the 1960s Weather Underground organization and describes her years on the run from the law and her later reevaluation of her movement's use of violence. (Rev: BL 9/15/07) [921]

WILLIAMS, STANLEY TOOKIE

7799 Williams, Stanley Tookie. *Blue Rage, Black Redemption* (11–12). 2007, Damamli $24.99 (978-1-4165-4449-4). Williams, cofounder of the infamous Crips gang in Los Angeles, was executed in 2005 after serving 24 years for murder; in this book, published posthumously, he talks about gang violence and his work to end it; for mature readers. (Rev: BL 10/1/07) [364.152]

YOUNG, CHARLES

7800 Shellum, Brian G. *Black Cadet in a White Bastion: Charles Young at West Point* (10–12). 2006, Univ. of Nebraska paper $16.95 (978-0-8032-9315-1). The life and achievements of Charles Young, who was born into slavery but became the third African American to graduate from the U.S. Military Academy at West Point and went on to become a colonel. (Rev: BL 2/15/06) [355]

467

Science, Medicine, Industry, and Business Figures

Collective

7801 Aaseng, Nathan. *Business Builders in Broadcasting* (7–10). Series: Business Builders. 2005, Oliver LB $24.95 (978-1-881508-83-0). From Morse and Marconi to Sarnoff and Rupert Murdoch, this is a useful overview of key figures in broadcasting. (Rev: SLJ 3/06) [920]

7802 Armstrong, Mabel. *Women Astronomers: Reaching for the Stars* (7–10). Series: Discovering Women in Science. 2008, Stone Pine paper $16.95 (978-0-9728929-5-7). Readers may be surprised to learn that women have been studying the skies since 2350 b.c. and that many of them made important discoveries; this volume has a browser-friendly format. (Rev: BL 4/1/08; SLJ 1/08) [508.2]

7803 Balchin, Jon. *Science: 100 Scientists Who Changed the World* (6–12). 2003, Enchanted Lion $18.95 (978-1-59270-017-2). Two-page chapters introduce 100 scientists and their accomplishments, grouped by century. (Rev: SLJ 1/04) [920]

7804 Bussing-Burks, Marie. *Influential Economists* (7–12). 2003, Oliver $19.95 (978-1-881508-72-4). The historical perspective of this book provides insights into economic theories and introduces some of the key people — including John Maynard Keynes and Milton Friedman — who have shaped the world's economy. (Rev: BL 3/1/03; HBG 10/03; SLJ 12/03) [920]

7805 Byrnes, Patricia. *Environmental Pioneers* (6–10). 1998, Oliver LB $19.95 (978-1-881508-45-8). This collective biography of early environmentalists includes profiles of John Muir, David Brower, Rachel Carson, Jay Darling, Rosalie Edge, Aldo Leopold, and Gaylord Nelson. (Rev: BL 9/15/98; SLJ 11/98) [920]

7806 Cooney, Miriam P. *Celebrating Women in Mathematics and Science* (6–10). 1996, National Council

of Teachers of Math paper $26.95 (978-0-87353-425-3). Covering ancient times to the present, this collective biography highlights the struggles and triumphs of women in the fields of mathematics and sciences. (Rev: SLJ 10/96) [920]

7807 Cullen, Katherine. *Science, Technology, and Society: The People Behind the Science* (8–11). Series: Pioneers in Science. 2006, Chelsea House $29.95 (978-0-8160-5468-8). Pioneers whose biographies appear in this volume include Marie Curie, Louis Pasteur, Guglielmo Marconi, Rachel Carson, and J. Robert Oppenheimer. Also use *Earth Science: The People Behind the Science* and *Marine Science: The People Behind the Science* (both 2006). (Rev: BL 4/1/06) [509]

7808 De Angelis, Gina, and David J. Bianco. *Computers: Processing the Data* (7–10). Series: Innovators. 2005, Oliver LB $24.95 (978-1-881508-87-8). Profiles of computer pioneers including Charles Babbage, Steve Wozniak, and Tim Berners-Lee are accompanied by explanations of the technology involved. (Rev: BL 12/1/05; SLJ 1/06) [004]

7809 Evans, Harold. *They Made America: From the Steam Engine to the Search Engine: Two Centuries of Innovators* (8–12). 2004, Little, Brown $40.00 (978-0-316-27766-2). For both browsing and research, this is an interesting and information-packed celebration of American inventiveness, focusing as much on the entrepreneurs as on the products. (Rev: BL 10/1/04) [609.2]

7810 Hall, Derek, ed. *Philosophy, Invention, and Engineering* (8–11). Illus. Series: Facts at Your Fingertips: Great Scientists. 2009, Brown Bear LB $24.95 (978-193383448-1). Aristotle, Thomas Edison, Alan Turing, and Jonas Salk are among the scientists profiled in this attractive and informative volume. (Rev: BL 10/1/09*; LMC 5–6/10) [920]

7811 Haskins, Jim. *Outward Dreams: Black Inventors and Their Inventions* (7–12). 1991, Walker LB $14.85

(978-0-8027-6994-7). Examines the lives and inventions of African American men and women did not receive recognition for their contributions until after the Civil War. (Rev: BL 5/15/91) [920]

7812 Henderson, Harry. *Larry Page and Sergey Brin: Information at Your Fingertips* (7–10). Illus. Series: Trailblazers in Science and Technology. 2012, Chelsea House LB $35 (978-160413676-0). Combining biography and science, this informative volume explores the lives and contributions of the Google founders. (Rev: BL 12/15/12) [920]

7813 Holmes, Madelyn. *American Women Conservationists: Twelve Profiles* (9–12). 2004, McFarland paper $35.00 (978-0-7864-1783-4). Profiles of 12 women who played a significant role in protecting America's natural resources include information on their youthful aspirations. (Rev: BL 9/1/04) [333.72]

7814 Leroy, Francis, ed. *A Century of Nobel Prize Recipients: Chemistry, Physics, and Medicine* (9–12). 2003, Marcel Dekker $159.95 (978-0-8247-0876-4). Nobel laureates are presented chronologically by discipline, with portraits, key data, and essays on their contributions. (Rev: SLJ 2/04) [920]

7815 Malone, John Williams. *It Doesn't Take a Rocket Scientist: Great Amateurs of Science* (9–12). 2002, Wiley $24.95 (978-0-471-41431-5). The lives of 10 amateur scientists — among them Gregor Mendel, Joseph Priestley, Michael Faraday, and Arthur C. Clarke — are examined in this collective biography. [920]

7816 Pile, Robert B. *Top Entrepreneurs and Their Business* (6–12). 1993, Oliver LB $19.95 (978-1-881508-04-5). The rags-to-riches stories of nine entrepreneurs, among them L. L. Bean, Walt Disney, and Sam Walton. With photographs. (Rev: BL 11/15/93; SLJ 1/94) [920]

7817 Rohmer, Harriet. *Heroes of the Environment: True Stories of People Who Are Helping to Protect Our Planet* (6–10). Illus. by Julie McLaughlin. 2009, Chronicle $16.99 (978-0-8118-6779-5). This book highlights 12 environmental crusaders — many of them teens or young adults — and their work to end pollution and industrial development from Appalachia to Alaska. (Rev: BLO 11/1/09; SLJ 1/10; VOYA 12/09) [920]

7818 Sapet, Kerrily. *Google Founders: Larry Page and Sergey Brin* (7–12). Illus. Series: Business Leaders. 2011, Morgan Reynolds LB $28.95 (978-159935177-3). This biography combines information about the founders of Google with details of the creation, amazing growth, and importance of its browser and related technology. (Rev: BL 11/15/11) [920]

7819 Shell, Barry. *Sensational Scientists: The Journeys and Discoveries of 24 Men and Women of Science* (8–11). 2006, Raincoast paper $15.95 (978-1-55192-727-5). Profiles of 24 scientists associated with Canada cover a wide range of interests. (Rev: BL 2/15/06) [509]

7820 Smith, Chris, and Marci McGrath. *Twitter: Jack Dorsey, Biz Stone and Evan Williams* (7–12). Illus. Series: Business Leaders. 2011, Morgan Reynolds LB $28.95 (978-159935179-7). Describes the founders of Twitter and the impact of this technology. (Rev: BL 11/15/11; VOYA 4/12) [920]

7821 Stux, Erica. *The Achievers: Great Women in the Biological Sciences* (9–12). Series: Avisson Young Adult. 2005, Avisson paper $19.95 (978-1-888105-70-4). Eight women who made significant contributions to the biological sciences are introduced with details of their careers and personalities. (Rev: BL 7/05) [570]

7822 Yount, Lisa. *A to Z of Women in Science and Math. Rev. ed.* (9–12). 2007, Facts on File $60.00 (978-0-8160-6695-7). The profiles in this updated work are well researched and highly readable. (Rev: BL 3/15/08) [920]

7823 Yount, Lisa. *Edward Pickering and His Women "Computers": Analyzing the Stars* (7–10). Illus. Series: Trailblazers in Science and Technology. 2012, Chelsea House LB $35 (978-160413664-7). Combining biography and science, this informative volume explores the lives and contributions of the talented women who helped Harvard astronomer Pickering. (Rev: BL 12/15/12) [920]

7824 Zach, Kim K. *Hidden from History: The Lives of Eight American Women Scientists* (6–12). 2002, Avisson paper $19.95 (978-1-888105-54-4). The important achievements of eight women who made often unacknowledged contributions to the sciences are accompanied by some personal details. (Rev: BL 12/1/02; SLJ 4/03; VOYA 12/03) [920]

Science and Medicine

AKELEY, CARL

7825 Kirk, Jay. *Kingdom Under Glass: A Tale of Obsession, Adventure, and One Man's Quest to Preserve the World's Great Animals* (10–12). 2010, Henry Holt $26 (978-080509282-0). A compelling profile of innovative turn-of-the-20th-century taxidermist Carl Akeley, who often ventured out into the field to personally bag his own trophies and who created the dioramas in the African Hall at New York's Museum of Natural History. (Rev: BL 10/1–15/10) [921]

AL-HAYTHAM, IBN

7826 Steffens, Bradley. *Ibn Al-Haytham: First Scientist* (8–11). Series: Profiles in Science. 2007, Morgan Reynolds $27.95 (978-1-59935-024-0). A Muslim who was born in A.D. 965 in the Middle East, Ibn al-Haytham made important contributions to science. (Rev: BL 12/1/06; SLJ 7/07) [921]

ARCHIMEDES

7827 Hasan, Heather. *Archimedes: The Father of Mathematics* (6–10). Series: The Library of Greek Philosophers. 2006, Rosen LB $33.25 (978-1-4042-0774-5). The importance of this ancient thinker is explained, and readers learn of his times and his influence. (Rev: SLJ 9/06)

ATANASOFF, JOHN V

7828 Smiley, Jane. *The Man Who Invented the Computer: The Biography of John Atanasoff, Digital Pioneer* (10–12). Series: Great Innovators. 2010, Doubleday $25.95 (978-038552713-2). A look into the earliest years of computer science, this fascinating biography examines the life and inventions of physicist John Atanasoff, who many believe invented the first computer. **e** (Rev: BL 9/1–15/10) [921]

BELL, ALEXANDER GRAHAM

7829 Gray, Charlotte. *Reluctant Genius: Alexander Graham Bell and the Passion for Invention* (9–12). 2006, Arcade $27.95 (978-1-55970-809-8). Bell's family life receives much attention in this look at the inventor and his times. (Rev: BL 8/06) [921]

7830 Shulman, Seth. *The Telephone Gambit: Chasing Alexander Graham Bell's Secret* (8–12). 2008, Norton $24.95 (978-0-393-06206-9). Did Bell really invent the telephone? History and science students will find this well-written investigation riveting. (Rev: BL 12/1/07) [921]

BONNER, JOHN TYLER

7831 Bonner, John Tyler. *Lives of a Biologist: Adventures in a Century of Extraordinary Science* (10–12). 2002, Harvard $33.00 (978-0-674-00763-5). Bonner's eminently readable autobiography recounts how he was drawn to a career in science, chronicles the impressive advances made in biology during his lifetime, and conveys good information about the scientific process. (Rev: BL 3/15/02) [921]

BOYLE, ROBERT

7832 Baxter, Roberta. *Skeptical Chemist: The Story of Robert Boyle* (8–11). 2006, Morgan Reynolds $26.95 (978-1-59935-025-7). Boyle's natural curiosity led to his developing an important methodology for scientific experimentation, and his biography will inspire students interested in both science and history. (Rev: BL 12/1/06; SLJ 1/07) [921]

BREAZEAL, CYNTHIA

7833 Brown, Jordan D. *Robo World: The Story of Robot Designer Cynthia Breazeal* (6–10). Series: Women's Adventures in Science. 2005, Watts LB $31.50 (978-0-531-16782-3). An interesting biography that blends personal information with scientific facts. (Rev: SLJ 2/06) [921]

CARSON, RACHEL

7834 Levine, Ellen. *Rachel Carson* (7–10). Series: Up Close. 2007, Viking $15.99 (978-0-670-06220-1). A well-documented biography of the groundbreaking environmentalist that provides details of her personal life as well as her career and of the obstacles she faced. (Rev: BL 2/15/07; HB 3–4/07; SLJ 4/07*) [921]

CARVER, GEORGE WASHINGTON

7835 Nelson, Marilyn. *Carver: A Life in Poems* (10–12). 2001, Front St $16.95 (978-1-886910-53-9). This is a fine biography of botanist and teacher George Washington Carver, told in easy-to-read free verse that is also moving. (Rev: BL 5/1/01; HB 9–10/01*; HBG 3/02; SLJ 7/01; VOYA 8/01) [921]

CHINN, MAY

7836 Haulsey, Kuwana. *Angel of Harlem* (9–12). 2004, Ballantine $19.95 (978-0-345-50870-6). A fictional first-person biography of Dr. May Chinn, who overcame adversity to become the first African American woman doctor in New York City; includes many details about the Harlem Renaissance and personalities of the time. (Rev: BL 9/1/04)

COPERNICUS, NICOLAUS

7837 Gingerich, Owen, and James MacLachlan. *Nicolaus Copernicus: Making the Earth a Planet* (9–12). 2005, Oxford LB $32.95 (978-0-19-516173-1). A thorough and insightful profile of Copernicus, the Polish astronomer who revolutionized world thinking about the solar system. (Rev: BL 12/1/05; SLJ 6/06) [520]

CRICK, FRANCIS

7838 Ridley, Matt. *Francis Crick: Discoverer of the Genetic Code* (9–12). Series: Eminent Lives. 2006, HarperCollins $19.95 (978-0-06-082333-7). A clear explanation of the problems facing the discoverer of the double helix, plus personal details of Crick's life and working style. (Rev: BL 4/1/06) [576.5]

CURIE FAMILY

7839 Henderson, Harry. *The Curie Family: Exploring Radioactivity* (7–10). Illus. Series: Trailblazers in Science and Technology. 2012, Chelsea House LB $35 (978-160413675-3). Combining biography and science, this informative volume explores the lives of Marie and Pierre Curie — and of their daughter Irene and her husband — and their important contributions in the study of radioactivity. (Rev: BL 12/15/12) [920]

CURIE, MARIE

7840 Koestler-Grack, Rachel A. *Marie Curie: Scientist* (6–10). Series: Women of Achievement. 2009, Chelsea House $30 (978-1-60413-086-7). This is a balanced profile that provides good basic information on Curie and her impact on the world of science. (Rev: SLJ 5/1/09) [921]

7841 McClafferty, Carla Killough. *Something Out of Nothing: Marie Curie and Radium* (7–10). 2006, Farrar $18.00 (978-0-374-38036-6). This readable biography examines Curie's personal life and her valuable contributions to scientific knowledge. (Rev: BL 3/1/06; SLJ 5/06*) [540]

7842 Quinn, Susan. *Marie Curie: A Life* (10–12). 1995, Simon & Schuster paper $21.00 (978-0-201-88794-5). A biography of the Polish-born scientist who won the Nobel Prize twice for her work with radium. [921]

7843 Yannuzzi, Della A. *New Elements: The Story of Marie Curie* (5–10). Illus. Series: Profiles in Science. 2006, Morgan Reynolds $26.95 (978-1-59935-023-3). More about the scientist's life than about the significance of her research, this introduction will be helpful to report writers. (Rev: BL 12/1/06; SLJ 1/07)

DARWIN, CHARLES

7844 Bowlby, John. *Charles Darwin: A Biography* (9–12). 1991, Norton paper $14.95 (978-0-393-30930-0). The story of the dedicated scientist, his many voyages to gather data, and the development of his theory of evolution. (Rev: BL 3/1/91) [921]

7845 Eldredge, Niles. *Darwin: Discovering the Tree of Life* (11–12). 2005, Norton $35.00 (978-0-393-05966-3). Eldredge, a leading evolutionary theorist and curator at New York's American Museum of Natural History, celebrates the life and revolutionary ideas of Charles Darwin; a well-illustrated volume. (Rev: BL 11/1/05) [576.8]

7846 Eldredge, Niles, and Susan Pearson. *Charles Darwin and the Mystery of Mysteries* (7–10). 2010, Flash Point LB $19.99 (978-1-59643-374-8). This engaging biography gives lots of information on Darwin's youth and private life as well as his research and the voyages of the *Beagle*. (Rev: BL 7/10; LMC 5–6/10; SLJ 6/10) [921]

DARWIN, CHARLES AND EMMA

7847 Heiligman, Deborah. *Charles and Emma: The Darwins' Leap of Faith* (8–12). 2009, Henry Holt $18.95 (978-080508721-5). The story of Charles Darwin and his relationship with his wife (and cousin) Emma; family letters and other primary sources document a loving marriage between two very different people. National Book Award Finalist, YALSA Nonfiction Winner 2010, Printz Honor 2010. ⌓ ℮ Lexile 1020L (Rev: BL 1/1–

15/09*; HB 1–2/09; LMC 8–9/09; SLJ 1/1/09*; VOYA 12/08) [920]

EDISON, THOMAS ALVA

7848 Israel, Paul. *Edison: A Life of Invention* (10–12). 1998, Wiley $50.00 (978-0-471-52942-2); paper $19.95 (978-0-471-36270-8). Edison's inventions and commercial enterprises are at the center of this biography that includes many reproductions of his drawings. (Rev: BL 10/1/98) [921]

7849 Stross, Randall. *The Wizard of Menlo Park: How Thomas Alva Edison Invented the Modern World* (10–12). 2007, Crown $24.95 (978-1-4000-4762-8). Stross looks at Edison's life from the point of view of fame — of the celebrity he attained and its attendant benefits and drawbacks. (Rev: BL 3/1/07) [621.3092]

EINSTEIN, ALBERT

7850 Brian, Denis. *Einstein: A Life* (10–12). 1996, Wiley paper $19.95 (978-0-471-19362-3). A well-researched profile that looks both at Einstein's life and personality. (Rev: BL 5/1/96) [921]

7851 Goldsmith, Donald, and Marcia Bartusiak, eds. *E = Einstein: His Life, His Thought, and His Influence on Our Culture* (10–12). 2007, Sterling $19.95 (978-1-4027-3787-9). With a large number of color illustrations, diagrams and cartoons, and plenty of sidebar features, this compilation of essays about Einstein's life and work offers thought-provoking and accessible material for both researchers and browsers. (Rev: BL 2/15/07) [530]

7852 Robinson, Andrew. *Einstein: A Hundred Years of Relativity* (9–12). 2005, Abrams $29.95 (978-0-8109-5923-1). An attractive celebration of Einstein's life and work, this volume includes useful resources for reports. (Rev: BL 10/15/05) [921]

7853 Severance, John B. *Einstein: Visionary Scientist* (7–12). 1999, Clarion $18.00 (978-0-395-93100-4). This book covers Einstein's academic theories as well as his private life and his celebrity. (Rev: BCCB 9/99; BL 9/1/99; HB 9–10/99; HBG 4/00; SLJ 9/99) [921]

7854 Strathern, Paul. *Einstein and Relativity* (10–12). 1999, Anchor paper $9.95 (978-0-385-49244-7). As well as an account of Einstein's life, this book explains the theory of relativity and how it changed scientific thinking. (Rev: BL 5/1/99) [921]

7855 Yeatts, Tabatha. *Albert Einstein: The Miracle Mind* (7–12). Series: Sterling Biography. 2007, Sterling LB $12.95 (978-1-4027-4950-6); paper $5.95 (978-1-4027-3228-7). Covers the life and scientific accomplishments of Albert Einstein, as well as his stand against racism and nuclear war. (Rev: BL 9/1/07) [921]

EUCLID

7856 Hayhurst, Chris. *Euclid: The Great Geometer* (6–10). 2006, Rosen LB $33.25 (978-1-4042-0497-3). The importance of this ancient thinker (who is called the father of geometry) is explained, and readers learn of his times and his influence. (Rev: SLJ 9/06) [921]

FARADAY, MICHAEL

7857 Ludwig, Charles. *Michael Faraday: Father of Electronics* (9–12). 1988, Herald $9.99 (978-0-8361-3479-7). The life of the scientist who worked on such inventions as the dynamo, the generator, and the transformer. [921]

7858 Russell, Colin A. *Michael Faraday: Physics and Faith* (8–12). Series: Oxford Portraits in Science. 2001, Oxford LB $32.95 (978-0-19-511763-9). The story of the inventor of the electric transformer and the dynamo is placed in interesting historical context. (Rev: HBG 10/01; SLJ 3/01) [921]

FARNSWORTH, PHILO

7859 Schatzkin, Paul. *The Boy Who Invented Television: A Story of Inspiration, Persistence and Quiet Passion* (10–12). 2002, TeamCom paper $16.95 (978-1-928791-30-0). A candid and absorbing portrait of Farnsworth and his technical genius from a young age. (Rev: BL 9/1/02) [921]

7860 Stashower, Daniel. *The Boy Genius and the Mogul: The Untold Story of Television* (9–12). 2002, Broadway $24.95 (978-0-7679-0759-0). Stashower celebrates the contributions of Idaho teenager Philo Farnsworth, who came up with the idea for a television-like "image dissector" but lacked the finances to turn his dream into a reality. (Rev: BL 3/15/02) [921]

FERMI, ENRICO

7861 Cooper, Dan. *Enrico Fermi: And the Revolutions of Modern Physics* (8–12). Series: Oxford Portraits in Science. 1999, Oxford $32.95 (978-0-19-511762-2). A readable biography of the Italian scientist who immigrated to the United States in 1939 and worked on the first atomic bomb. Some of the coverage of quantum and nuclear physics is challenging. (Rev: SLJ 6/99) [921]

FEYNMAN, RICHARD

7862 Henderson, Harry. *Richard Feynman: Quarks, Bombs, and Bongos* (7–10). Illus. Series: Makers of Modern Science. 2010, Chelsea House $35 (978-081606176-1). Feynman is known for his brilliance in the fields of particle physics and quantum mechanics, but this biography also tells readers about his personal life — and his love of bongo drums. (Rev: BL 6/1/11) [921]

FOSSEY, DIAN

7863 de la Bédoyère, Camilla, and Dian Fossey. *No One Loved Gorillas More: Dian Fossey, Letters from the Mist* (11–12). 2005, National Geographic $30.00 (978-0-7922-9344-6). Photographs, biographical narrative, and letters by Fossey herself tell the story of her life among the mountain gorillas of Rwanda. (Rev: BL 2/15/05) [599.8]

7864 Mowat, Farley. *Woman in the Mists: The Story of Dian Fossey and the Mountain Gorillas of Africa* (10–12). 1987, Warner paper $19.99 (978-0-446-38720-0). A naturalist and writer has created a stirring life of the zoologist whose study of gorillas was trailblazing. (Rev: BL 9/1/87; SLJ 2/88; VOYA 4/88) [921]

FRANCE, DIANE

7865 Hopping, Lorraine Jean. *Bone Detective: The Story of Forensic Anthropologist Diane France* (7–10). Series: Women's Adventures in Science. 2005, Watts LB $31.50 (978-0-531-16776-2). Part of the Women's Adventures in Science series, this compelling biography of Diane France traces the forensic anthropologist's life from her childhood in Colorado to her role in identifying victims of the 9/11 terrorist attacks. (Rev: BL 10/15/05; SLJ 2/06) [363.25]

FRANKL, VIKTOR EMIL

7866 Redsand, Anna S. *Viktor Frankl: A Life Worth Living* (9–12). 2006, Clarion $19.00 (978-0-618-72343-0). A look at the life of Viktor Frankl, his contributions to the field of psychiatry with his logotherapy approach, how he survived the Holocaust and dealt with the deaths of his wife and parents, and how he went on to write his acclaimed book *Man's Search for Meaning*. (Rev: BL 10/15/06; LMC 3/07; SLJ 12/06) [921]

FRANKLIN, ROSALIND

7867 Maddox, Brenda. *Rosalind Franklin: The Dark Lady of DNA* (10–12). 2002, HarperCollins $29.95 (978-0-06-018407-0). Maddox profiles the life and lasting scientific contributions of Rosalind Franklin, the chemist who played a vital — but generally overlooked — role in the unraveling of DNA's structure. (Rev: BL 10/15/02) [921]

7868 Polcovar, Jane. *Rosalind Franklin and the Structure of Life* (8–11). Series: Profiles in Science. 2006, Morgan Reynolds LB $26.95 (978-1-59935-022-6). Franklin had a small part in the discovery of DNA — she took the image that set Watson and Crick on the path to found the field of genetics; this profile looks at her advancement in a profession generally closed to women and at the competitive nature of the search for the double helix. (Rev: BL 12/1/06; SLJ 3/07) [921]

FREUD, SIGMUND

7869 Kramer, Peter D. *Freud: Inventor of the Modern Mind* (11–12). 2006, AtlasBooks $21.95 (978-0-06-059895-2). For advanced students, this evenhanded biography points out the influence that Freud, whether taken seriously now or not, has had on our culture and our literature. (Rev: BL 11/15/06) [921]

7870 Reef, Catherine. *Sigmund Freud: Pioneer of the Mind* (7–12). 2001, Clarion $19.00 (978-0-618-01762-1). Reef looks at Freud's life and career, showing the ways in which his ideas evolved over time and the initial rejection of many of his revolutionary thoughts. Sidney Taylor Book Award 2001. (Rev: BL 7/01; HB 7–8/01*; HBG 10/01; SLJ 8/01; VOYA 10/01) [921]

FUNG, INEZ

7871 Skelton, Renee. *Forecast Earth: The Story of Climate Scientist Inez Fung* (6–10). Series: Women's Adventures in Science. 2005, Watts LB $31.50 (978-0-531-16777-9). An interesting biography that blends personal information with scientific facts. (Rev: SLJ 2/06) [921]

GALILEO

7872 Boerst, William J. *Galileo Galilei and the Science of Motion* (6–10). Series: Great Scientists. 2003, Morgan Reynolds LB $26.95 (978-1-931798-00-6). Galileo's early insistence on adherence to scientific verification is emphasized in this detailed yet accessible biography that includes color period reproductions and a timeline. (Rev: BL 11/1/03; HBG 4/04; SLJ 12/03) [921]

GOODALL, JANE

7873 Greene, Meg. *Jane Goodall: A Biography* (9–12). Series: Greenwood Biographies. 2005, Greenwood LB $31.95 (978-0-313-33139-8). Goodall's personality is highlighted in this appealing biography. (Rev: SLJ 3/06) [921]

7874 Kozleski, Lisa. *Jane Goodall: Primatologist/Naturalist* (7–12). Series: Women in Science. 2003, Chelsea LB $30.00 (978-0-7910-6905-9). An absorbing biography that discusses the primatologist's personal life as well as her dedicated work with chimpanzees in Tanzania. (Rev: LMC 11–12/03; SLJ 7/03) [921]

HAMMEL, HEIDI

7875 Bortz, Fred. *Beyond Jupiter: The Story of Planetary Astronomer Heidi Hammel* (6–10). Series: Women's Adventures in Science. 2005, Watts LB $31.50 (978-0-531-16775-5). An interesting biography that blends personal information with scientific facts. (Rev: SLJ 2/06) [921]

HARRISON, JOHN

7876 Dash, Joan. *The Longitude Prize* (10–12). 2000, Farrar $16.00 (978-0-374-34636-2). This colorful — but quite technical — biography tells how 18th-century English clockmaker John Harrison developed instruments to help sailors determine their relative east-west position as they sailed the seas, sharply reducing the number of ships that foundered when their crews became disoriented. (Rev: BL 1/1–15/01; HB 11–12/00; HBG 3/01; SLJ 11/00; VOYA 2/01) [921]

HORNEY, KAREN

7877 Hitchcock, Susan Tyler. *Karen Horney: Pioneer of Feminine Psychology* (9–12). Series: Women in Medicine. 2004, Chelsea House LB $30.00 (978-0-7910-8025-2). A life of Karen Horney, an outspoken critic of Sigmund Freud's concentration on the male psyche. (Rev: SLJ 6/05) [921]

JEMISON, MAE

7878 Jemison, Mae. *Find Where the Wind Goes* (7–12). 2001, Scholastic $16.95 (978-0-439-13195-7). The fascinating autobiography of the first African American woman in space. (Rev: BL 11/1/01; HBG 10/01; SLJ 4/01; VOYA 8/01) [629.45]

JONES, THOMAS D.

7879 Jones, Thomas D. *Sky Walking: An Astronaut's Memoir* (9–12). 2006, HarperCollins $26.95 (978-0-06-085152-1). A frank and illuminating account of a career building to four flights on the space shuttle. (Rev: BL 1/1–15/06) [629.45]

KOEHL, MIMI

7880 Parks, Deborah. *Nature's Machines: The Story of Biomechanist Mimi Koehl* (6–10). Series: Women's Adventures in Science. 2005, Watts LB $31.50 (978-0-531-16780-9). An interesting biography that blends personal information with scientific facts. (Rev: SLJ 2/06) [921]

KÜBLER-ROSS, ELISABETH

7881 Worth, Richard. *Elisabeth Kübler-Ross: Encountering Death and Dying* (9–12). Series: Women in Medicine. 2004, Chelsea House LB $30.00 (978-0-7910-8027-6). The life and career of the psychiatrist who was a pioneer in the study of death and dying. (Rev: SLJ 6/05) [921]

LEAKEY FAMILY

7882 Bowman-Kruhm, Mary. *The Leakeys: A Biography* (9–12). Series: Greenwood Biographies. 2005, Greenwood LB $31.95 (978-0-313-32985-2). Lays out the contributions of three generations of the Leakey family to the world of anthropology, with good coverage of the individuals' personalities. (Rev: SLJ 3/06) [921]

7883 Henderson, Harry. *The Leakey Family: Unearthing Human Ancestors* (7–10). Illus. Series: Trailblazers in Science and Technology. 2012, Chelsea House LB $35 (978-160413674-6). Combining biography and science, this informative volume explores the lives and contributions of these anthropologists. (Rev: BL 12/15/12) [920]

LEVI-MONTALCINI, RITA

7884 Yount, Lisa. *Rita Levi-Montalcini: Discoverer of Nerve Growth Factor* (9–12). Series: Makers of Modern Science. 2009, Chelsea House LB $35.00 (978-081606171-6). A clear and thorough account of the long and eventful life of the Nobel-winning scientist who was born in Italy in 1909. (Rev: BLO 6/17/09) [921]

MAYER, MARIA GOEPPERT

7885 Ferry, Joseph. *Maria Goeppert Mayer: Physicist* (6–12). Series: Women in Science. 2003, Chelsea LB $30.00 (978-0-7910-7247-9). Ferry explores the life and achievements of Mayer, who won a Nobel Prize in 1963 for research into the atomic nucleus. (Rev: HBG 10/03; SLJ 10/03) [921]

MCCLINTOCK, BARBARA

7886 Cullen, J. Heather. *Barbara McClintock: Geneticist* (6–12). Series: Women in Science. 2003, Chelsea LB $30.00 (978-0-7910-7248-6). Cullen explores the life and achievements of McClintock, who won a Nobel Prize in 1983 for research in genetics that she conducted decades earlier. (Rev: HBG 10/03; SLJ 10/03) [921]

7887 Spangenburg, Ray, and Diane Kit Moser. *Barbara McClintock: Pioneering Geneticist* (8–11). Series: Makers of Modern Science. 2008, Chelsea House LB $29.95 (978-0-8160-6172-3). A biography of the 1983 winner of a Nobel Prize for her work on the genetics of maize. (Rev: BL 4/15/08) [576.5092]

MEAD, MARGARET

7888 Mark, Joan. *Margaret Mead: Coming of Age in America* (6–10). Series: Oxford Portraits in Science. 1999, Oxford $32.95 (978-0-19-511679-3). An introduction to the life and work of the pioneering anthropologist and her research with the peoples of the South Seas, particularly in Samoa. (Rev: BL 4/1/99; SLJ 3/99) [921]

MENDEL, GREGOR

7889 Edelson, Edward. *Gregor Mendel: And the Roots of Genetics* (7–10). Series: Oxford Portraits in Science. 1999, Oxford $34.99 (978-0-19-512226-8). Describes Mendel's life and his work on plant heredity and the study of genetics in the context of the social, scientific, and political events of his time. (Rev: SLJ 7/99) [921]

MERCATOR, GERARDUS

7890 Heinrichs, Ann. *Gerardus Mercator: Father of Modern Mapmaking* (5–12). Series: Signature Lives. 2007, Compass Point LB $31.93 (978-0-7565-3312-0). Scientific concepts are presented clearly in this profile that covers Mercator's life, with excerpts from his writing and a timeline that adds historical context. (Rev: SLJ 1/08)

MERIAN, MARIA SIBYLLA

7891 Todd, Kim. *Chrysalis: Maria Sibylla Merian and the Secrets of Metamorphosis* (11–12). 2007, Harcourt $27.00 (978-0-15-101108-7). Naturalist and artist Maria Sibylla Merian (1647-1717) made important strides in the study of insects but her work was not given the recognition it deserved; this book tells her life story and hopes to reinstate her status in the field of nature study. (Rev: BL 12/1/06) [508.092]

MONTAGNIER, LUC

7892 Yount, Lisa. *Luc Montagnier: Identifying the AIDS Virus* (7–10). Illus. Series: Trailblazers in Science and Technology. 2011, Chelsea House $35 (978-160413661-6). Yount provides a life of the famous French virologist and background information on the virus that came to light in the United States in the 1980s. (Rev: BLO 3/15/12) [921]

MUIR, JOHN

7893 Ehrlich, Gretel. *John Muir: Nature's Visionary* (10–12). 2000, National Geographic $35.00 (978-0-7922-7954-9). The story of the early conservationist and how he loved nature, fought to preserve it, and cofounded the Sierra Club. (Rev: BL 1/1–15/01) [921]

7894 Wadsworth, Ginger. *John Muir: Wilderness Protector* (6–12). 1992, Lerner LB $18.95 (978-0-8225-4912-3). Original photographs and Muir's letters, journals, and writings provide an overview of the conservationist's personal life, achievements, and contributions to the environmental movement. (Rev: BL 8/92) [921]

7895 Wilkins, Thurman. *John Muir: Apostle of Nature* (10–12). Series: Oklahoma Western Biographies. 1995, Univ. of Oklahoma paper $21.95 (978-0-8061-2797-2). An excellent biography of an American folk hero who loved the wilderness and fought to preserve it. (Rev: BL 10/15/95) [921]

NEWTON, SIR ISAAC

7896 Boerst, William J. *Isaac Newton: Organizing the Universe* (6–10). Series: Renaissance Scientists. 2004, Morgan Reynolds LB $26.95 (978-1-931798-01-3). A fine biography of Newton that includes good explanations of the laws of motion and excellent color reproductions of period paintings. (Rev: BL 2/1/04; SLJ 4/04) [921]

7897 Christianson, Gale E. *Isaac Newton and the Scientific Revolution* (8–12). Series: Oxford Portraits in Science. 1996, Oxford $32.95 (978-0-19-509224-0). A challenging biography that gives the scientist's life history plus detailed explanations of theories of gravity, relativity, and calculus. (Rev: BL 12/1/96; SLJ 1/97; VOYA 2/97) [921]

OPPENHEIMER, J. ROBERT

7898 Scherer, Glenn, and Marty Fletcher. *J. Robert Oppenheimer: The Brain Behind the Bomb* (6–10). Series: Inventors Who Changed the World. 2007, Enslow LB $33.27 (978-1-59845-050-7). The story of the physicist who shepherded the Manhattan Project, with discussion of the science involved and the key political and social factors. (Rev: BL 7/07; SLJ 11/07) [921]

PASCAL, BLAISE

7899 Connor, James A. *Pascal's Wager: The Man Who Played Dice with God* (10–12). 2006, HarperSanFrancisco $24.95 (978-0-06-076691-7). The short life of mathematician Blaise Pascal and his involvement with the Catholic Jansenist movement of the mid-17th century are the focus of this biography that covers Pascal's thinking about probability and the existence of God. (Rev: BL 10/1/06) [921]

PASTEUR, LOUIS

7900 Ackerman, Jane. *Louis Pasteur and the Founding of Microbiology* (7–12). Series: Great Scientists. 2004, Morgan Reynolds $26.95 (978-1-931798-13-6). Using his microscope, Pasteur developed the fields of immunology and microbiology and invented the pasteurization of milk. (Rev: BL 2/1/04; SLJ 4/04) [921]

7901 Robbins, Louise E. *Louis Pasteur and the Hidden World of Microbes* (8–12). Series: Oxford Portraits in Science. 2001, Oxford $34.99 (978-0-19-512227-5). A look at the life of the famous scientist, with glimpses of his personality as well as his research and discoveries. (Rev: BL 12/1/01; HBG 3/02; SLJ 12/01) [921]

PAULING, LINUS

7902 Hager, Tom. *Linus Pauling and the Chemistry of Life* (9–12). Series: Portraits in Science. 1998, Oxford $32.95 (978-0-19-510853-8). A profile of the multitalented giant who won the Nobel Prize in chemistry as well as the Nobel Peace Prize for his participation in the antiwar and disarmament movements. (Rev: BL 5/15/98; SLJ 8/98) [921]

RICHTER, CHARLES

7903 Hough, Susan Elizabeth. *Richter's Scale: Measure of an Earthquake, Measure of a Man* (11–12). 2007, Princeton $27.95 (978-0-691-12807-8). Richter (1900-1985), the famous seismologist generally regarded as eccentric (he was also a nudist and a poet), may have

had Asperger's syndrome according to research conducted by Hough; this is a compelling exploration of an interesting personality. (Rev: BL 12/1/06) [551.22092]

RUTHERFORD, ERNEST

7904 Pasachoff, Naomi. *Ernest Rutherford: Father of Nuclear Science* (6–12). Series: Great Minds of Science. 2005, Enslow LB $26.60 (978-0-7660-2441-0). The life and scientific career of the New Zealand-born physicist who helped to pave the way for the development of nuclear physics. (Rev: SLJ 8/05) [921]

7905 Reeves, Richard. *A Force of Nature: The Frontier Genius of Ernest Rutherford* (10–12). 2007, Norton $23.95 (978-0-393-05750-8). A lively portrait of the nuclear physicist, born in New Zealand, who won a Nobel Prize in 1908 and continued to make advances for years thereafter. (Rev: BL 12/1/07) [921]

SAGAN, CARL

7906 Head, Tom, ed. *Conversations with Carl Sagan* (10–12). 2005, Univ. Press of Mississippi paper $22.00 (978-1-57806-736-7). Sixteen interviews — from such diverse sources as *Rolling Stone, Psychology Today,* and *The Charlie Rose Show* — reveal much about the popular astrophysicist. (Rev: BL 12/1/05) [520]

SLOWINSKI, JOSEPH

7907 James, Jamie. *The Snake Charmer: A Life and Death in Pursuit of Knowledge* (10–12). Illus. 2008, Hyperion $24.95 (978-140130213-9). James explores the passion, personality, and tragic death of Joe Slowinski, a wildlife adventurer and herpetologist who died after being bitten by a deadly snake in the Burmese jungle. e (Rev: BL 7/08) [921]

SPILSBURY, SIR BERNARD

7908 Evans, Colin. *The Father of Forensics: The Groundbreaking Cases of Sir Bernard Spilsbury, and the Beginnings of Modern CSI* (9–12). 2006, Berkley paper $14.00 (978-0-425-21007-9). Forensics fans will enjoy this biography of Spilsbury, a celebrity in his day, and will be fascinated by the accounts of some of the crimes he helped to solve. (Rev: BL 8/06) [921]

TESLA, NIKOLA

7909 Aldrich, Lisa J. *Nikola Tesla and the Taming of Electricity* (8–11). Series: Modern Scientists. 2005, Morgan Reynolds LB $26.95 (978-1-931798-46-4). The life and many inventions — including radio — of the Croatian-born electrical engineer. (Rev: BL 5/1/05; SLJ 10/05; VOYA 10/05) [621.3]

TURING, ALAN

7910 Corrigan, Jim. *Alan Turing* (7–10). 2008, Morgan Reynolds LB $27.95 (978-1-59935-064-6). This biography of "the father of computer science" goes beyond his work in mathematics into his private life, discussing how his homosexuality affected his career. (Rev: BL 6/1–15/08) [921]

7911 Henderson, Harry. *Alan Turing: Computing Genius and Wartime Code Breaker* (7–10). Illus. Series: Makers of Modern Science. 2011, Chelsea House $35 (978-081606175-4). A fascinating, detailed life of the man whose childhood was lonely, whose education was difficult, and who went on to make amazing contributions to mathematics and science, especially in the area of computers; includes discussion of his homosexuality and his early death. (Rev: BL 6/1/11) [921]

7912 Leavitt, David. *The Man Who Knew Too Much: Alan Turing and the Invention of the Computer* (9–12). 2005, Norton $22.95 (978-0-393-05236-7). David Leavitt's unflinching biography of computer pioneer Alan Turing examines the British mathematician's accomplishments and also how his brilliant career and life were cut short by homophobia. (Rev: BL 10/15/05) [510]

WALKER, MARY

7913 Joinson, Carla. *Civil War Doctor: The Story of Mary Walker* (8–11). 2007, Morgan Reynolds LB $27.95 (978-1-59935-028-8). Walker studied medicine at a time when this was very unusual for a woman; she later served as a surgeon in the Union Army and in 1865 was the first woman to be awarded the Congressional Medal of Honor. (Rev: BL 1/1–15/07) [921]

WEGENER, ALFRED

7914 *Ending in Ice: The Revolutionary Idea and Tragic Expedition of Alfred Wegener* (9–12). 2006, Oxford $30.00 (978-0-19-518857-8). German meteorologist Wegener was the first to propose the theory of continental drift — an idea initially derided but later accepted; he died on a research expedition to Greenland in 1930. (Rev: BL 7/06) [551]

WEXLER, NANCY

7915 Glimm, Adele. *Gene Hunter: The Story of Neuropsychologist Nancy Wexler* (6–10). Series: Women's Adventures in Science. 2005, Watts LB $31.50 (978-0-531-16778-6). An interesting biography that blends personal information with scientific facts. (Rev: SLJ 2/06) [921]

WRIGHT, WILBUR AND ORVILLE

7916 Crompton, Samuel Willard. *The Wright Brothers: First in Flight* (6–12). Series: Milestones in American History. 2007, Chelsea House LB $35.00 (978-0-7910-9356-6). An accessible account of the lives of the two brothers and their contributions to aviation. (Rev: LMC 1/08; SLJ 10/07) [921]

7917 Martin, Michael J. *The Wright Brothers* (7–12). Series: The Importance Of. 2003, Gale LB $32.45 (978-

1-56006-847-1). With lengthy quotations from primary and secondary sources, this is a lively biography of Wilbur and Orville Wright and how they changed history at Kitty Hawk. (Rev: BL 6/1–15/03) [921]

Industry and Business

BEZOS, JEFF

7918 Scally, Robert D. *Jeff Bezos: Founder of Amazon and the Kindle* (7–12). Illus. Series: Business Leaders. 2011, Morgan Reynolds LB $28.95 (978-159935178-0). This biography combines information about Bezos with details of the creation, growth, and influence of Amazon and its e-books. (Rev: BL 11/15/11) [921]

BUFFETT, WARREN

7919 Johnson, Anne Janette. *Warren Buffett* (7–12). Series: Business Leaders. 2008, Morgan Reynolds LB $27.95 (978-1-59935-080-6). This biography of Buffett covers both the personal and professional milestones of his life in clear, accessible prose. (Rev: SLJ 10/1/08) [921]

CARNEGIE, ANDREW

7920 Edge, Laura B. *Andrew Carnegie: Industrial Philanthropist* (7–10). Series: Lerner Biography. 2004, Lerner LB $27.93 (978-0-8225-4965-9). The fascinating story of Carnegie's progress from poor Scottish immigrant to wealthy industrialist and generous philanthropist. (Rev: BL 6/1–15/04; SLJ 2/04) [936.2]

CHOO, JIMMY

7921 Sapet, Kerrily. *Jimmy Choo* (7–10). Illus. Series: Profiles in Fashion. 2010, Morgan Reynolds LB $28.95 (978-159935151-3). This intriguing biography chronicles the success of Malaysian-born footwear pioneer Jimmy Choo. (Rev: BL 10/1/10) [921]

GATES, BILL

7922 Aronson, Marc. *Bill Gates* (6–10). Illus. Series: Up Close. 2008, Viking $16.99 (978-067006348-2). This book provides an insightful and evenhanded glimpse into Bill Gates's world, from his ultra-competitive childhood to his business practices and philanthropic works. (Rev: BL 12/1/08) [921]

GATES, BILL AND MELINDA

7923 Isaacs, Sally. *Bill and Melinda Gates* (6–10). Series: Front-Page Lives. 2010, Heinemann-Raintree $38.93 (978-1-4329-3220-6). Using a headlines format that highlights events, Isaacs covers the Gates's lives from childhood and includes a timeline, glossary, and other useful back matter. (Rev: LMC 3–4/10) [921]

GOODYEAR, CHARLES

7924 Slack, Charles. *Noble Obsession: Charles Goodyear, Thomas Hancock, and the Race to Unlock the Greatest Industrial Secret of the Nineteenth Century* (10–12). 2002, Hyperion $24.95 (978-0-7868-6789-9). Goodyear's struggles to perfect his vulcanization process — making use of natural rubber practical — are chronicled in this excellent portrait full of accessible history and technological information. (Rev: BL 7/02) [921]

HARPER, MARTHA MATILDA

7925 Plitt, Jane R. *Martha Matilda Harper and the American Dream: How One Woman Changed the Face of Modern Business* (10–12). 2000, Syracuse Univ. $26.95 (978-0-8156-0638-3). This inspirational biography tells how Harper became a successful businesswoman in the early 20th century through a chain of beauty salons and America's first franchise network. (Rev: BL 6/1–15/00) [921]

HERSHEY, MILTON S.

7926 D'Antonio, Michael. *Hershey: Milton S. Hershey's Extraordinary Life of Wealth, Empire, and Utopian Dreams* (9–12). 2006, Simon & Schuster $25 (978-0-7432-6409-9). An entertaining look at the personal and business life of Milton S. Hershey, the candy company he founded, his beliefs, and his legacy. (Rev: BL 12/1/05; SLJ 5/06) [921]

JOBS, STEVE

7927 Blumenthal, Karen. *Steve Jobs: The Man Who Thought Different* (7–10). Illus. 2012, Feiwel & Friends $16.99 (978-125001557-0); paper $8.99 (978-12500144-5-0). Chronicles the life and career of the Apple founder, with details of his childhood, college days, work, faith, friendships, and death from pancreatic cancer. ALA Notable Books 2013. (Rev: BL 2/15/12*; HB 5–6/12; VOYA 6/12) [921]

7928 Imbimbo, Anthony. *Steve Jobs: The Brilliant Mind Behind Apple* (7–10). Illus. Series: Life Portraits. 2009, Gareth Stevens LB $34.00 (978-143390060-0). Photographs and anecdotes add interest to this profile of the inventive computer engineer. Lexile 980L (Rev: BL 4/1/09; LMC 8–9/09) [921]

JONES, CAROLINE

7929 Fleming, Robert. *The Success of Caroline Jones Advertising, Inc.* (7–10). Series: Success. 1996, Walker LB $16.85 (978-0-8027-8354-7). The story of Jones's rapid rise in the world of advertising. (Rev: BL 1/1–15/96; SLJ 4/96) [921]

LAUREN, RALPH

7930 Weatherly, Myra. *Business Leaders: Ralph Lauren* (7–12). 2008, Morgan Reynolds LB $27.95 (978-1-59935-084-4). This volume covers Lauren's successful career in the fashion industry. (Rev: SLJ 10/1/08) [921]

OCHS, ADOLPH S.

7931 Faber, Doris. *Printer's Devil to Publisher: Adolph S. Ochs of The New York Times* (10–12). 1996, Black Dome paper $8.95 (978-1-883789-09-1). A rags-to-riches story about the trailblazing journalist and how he ran *The New York Times,* with a behind-the-scenes look at the newspaper's role in covering such stories as the sinking of the *Titanic.* (Rev: SLJ 10/96) [921]

ORFALEA, PAUL

7932 Orfalea, Paul, and Ann Marsh. *Copy This! Lessons from a Hyperactive Dyslexic Who Turned a Bright Idea into One of America's Best Companies* (9–12). 2005, Workman $23.95 (978-0-7611-3777-1). The founder of Kinko's describes in entertaining fashion how he overcame the challenges of dyslexia and hyperactivity and gives advice on life and business success. (Rev: SLJ 9/05) [921]

PULITZER, JOSEPH, II

7933 Pfaff, Daniel W. *Joseph Pulitzer II and the Post-Dispatch: A Newspaperman's Life* (9–12). 1991, Pennsylvania State Univ. $69.00 (978-0-271-00748-9). This biography of the son of the newspaper empire's founder shows him to be an astute, principled journalist who helped establish the reputation of the St. Louis newspaper. (Rev: BL 9/15/91) [921]

RAY, RACHAEL

7934 Abrams, Dennis. *Rachael Ray: Food Entrepreneur* (6–10). Illus. Series: Women of Achievement. 2009, Chelsea House LB $30.00 (978-160413078-2). The popular TV personality and cookbook author is profiled here in appealing text with many interesting quotations. (Rev: BL 4/1/09; SLJ 5/1/09) [921]

ROCKEFELLER, JOHN D.

7935 Segall, Grant. *John D. Rockefeller: Anointed with Oil* (9–12). Series: Oxford Portraits. 2001, Oxford $32.95 (978-0-19-512147-6). One of America's giants of industry, John D. Rockefeller comes alive in this well-researched biography that chronicles his life from childhood and provides an excellent resource for students writing reports or simply curious about the man and his times. (Rev: BL 1/1–15/01; HBG 10/01; SLJ 3/01) [921]

STEWART, MARTHA

7936 Paprocki, Sherry Beck. *Martha Stewart: Lifestyle Entrepreneur* (6–10). Series: Women of Achievement. 2009, Chelsea House $30 (978-1-60413-083-6). Paprocki does not shy away from controversy in this evenhanded profile of the business and lifestyle maven and her impact on American culture. (Rev: SLJ 5/1/09) [921]

SUI, ANNA

7937 Darraj, Susan Muaddi. *Anna Sui* (7–10). Series: Asian Americans of Achievement. 2009, Chelsea House $30 (978-1-60413-570-1). Sui's devotion to fashion — and her success at creating an international company with interests in fragrance, cosmetics, and even cell phones — are documented here, with interesting sidebars on culture and business. (Rev: BL 5/15/10; SLJ 2/10) [921]

WALKER, MADAM C. J.

7938 Bundles, A'Lelia. *Madam C. J. Walker: Entrepreneur* (7–12). Illus. Series: Black Americans of Achievement. 2008, Chelsea House $30.00 (978-160413072-0). The story of the successful African American business-

woman, complete with photographs and background information. (Rev: BLO 1/13/09) [921]

WANG, VERA

7939 Todd, Anne M. *Vera Wang* (6–10). Series: Asian Americans of Achievement. 2007, Chelsea House LB $30.00 (978-0-7910-9272-9). This attractive profile recounts the highlights of Wang's personal life and covers her work for *Vogue* and Ralph Lauren before starting her own business. (Rev: SLJ 8/07) [921]

ZUCKERBERG, MARK

7940 Hasday, Judy L. *Facebook and Mark Zuckerberg* (7–12). Illus. Series: Business Leaders. 2011, Morgan Reynolds LB $28.95 (978-159935176-6). This biography profiles Facebook founder Mark Zuckerberg, emphasizing his youth and entrepreneurial spirit. (Rev: BL 11/15/11; VOYA 8/12) [921]

Sports Figures

Collective

7941 Friedman, Steve. *The Agony of Victory: When Winning Isn't Enough* (10–12). 2007, Arcade $26.00 (978-1-55970-851-7). Fourteen athletes describe their determination to win — and their discovery that the toll on health and mind often simply isn't worth it. (Rev: BL 9/1/07) [796.0922]

7942 Grange, Michael. *Basketball's Greatest Stars* (9–12). Illus. 2010, Firefly $35 (978-155407637-6). An eye-catching, photo-filled survey of the 50 greatest players, with biographical information and analysis of their strengths. (Rev: BL 9/1–15/10) [920]

7943 Halberstam, David. *The Teammates* (8–12). 2003, Hyperion $22.95 (978-1-4013-0057-9). The story of the lives and friendships of four Boston Red Sox players: Ted Williams, Dominic DiMaggio, Johnny Pesky, and Bobby Doerr. [920]

7944 Harris, Cecil, and Larryette Kyle-DeBose. *Charging the Net: A History of Blacks in Tennis from Althea Gibson and Arthur Ashe to the Williams Sisters* (9–12). 2007, Ivan R. Dee $26.95 (978-1-56663-714-5). This volume covers 100 years of African American tennis achievements and provides insight into the prejudice, politics, and economic problems these athletes faced. (Rev: BL 7/07; SLJ 10/07) [920]

7945 Hasday, Judy L. *Extraordinary Women Athletes* (6–12). Series: Extraordinary People. 2000, Children's Press LB $16.95 (978-0-516-27039-5). A collective biography of 45 women who have gained recognition in a wide variety of sports. (Rev: BL 10/1/00; VOYA 2/01) [920]

7946 Staples, Bill, and Rich Herschlag. *Before the Glory: 20 Baseball Heroes Talk About Growing Up and Turning Hard Times into Home Runs* (8–12). 2007, Health Communications paper $14.95 (978-0-7573-

0626-6). Twenty major-league players talk about their childhoods and relate anecdotes that influenced their future careers. (Rev: BLO 5/22/07) [796.357]

7947 Taggart, Lisa. *Women Who Win: Women Athletes on Being the Best* (9–12). 2007, Seal paper $14.95 (978-1-58005-200-9). Taggart profiles 10 women athletes — including a distance swimmer, a big-wave surfer, and a jockey — and gives their personal stories as well as details of their professional contributions. (Rev: SLJ 7/07) [920]

7948 Thompson, Neal. *Hurricane Season: A Coach, His Team, and Their Triumph in the Time of Katrina* (9–12). 2007, Free Press $26.00 (978-1-4165-4070-0). In the aftermath of Hurricane Katrina, the members of the John Curtis Christian School's football team made inspiring attempts to keep themselves on the field. (Rev: BL 7/07) [920]

Automobile Racing

PATRICK, DANICA

7949 Sirvaitis, Karen. *Danica Patrick: Racing's Trailblazer* (6–10). Illus. 2010, Lerner/Twenty-First Century LB $33.26 (978-076135222-8). Visually appealing graphics, excerpts from news stories, and back matter add heft to this well-written biography of racing icon Danica Patrick. (Rev: BL 9/1/10*) [921]

SCOTT, WENDELL

7950 Donovan, Brian. *Hard Driving: The Wendell Scott Story; The American Odyssey of NASCAR's First Black Driver* (10–12). Illus. 2008, Steerforth $25.95 (978-158642144-1). Scott, the first black man to compete in 1950s NASCAR racing, faced hate, verbal and physical abuse, and a lack of sponsors, yet he persevered, gaining respect and popularity. (Rev: BL 9/1/08*) [921]

Baseball

AARON, HANK

7951 Aaron, Henry, and Lonnie Wheeler. *I Had a Hammer* (9–12). 2007, HarperCollins paper $14.95 (978-0-06-137360-2). The saga of "Hammerin' Hank," who broke Babe Ruth's homerun record and continued to play baseball despite the racism surrounding him and the sport; this book was originally published in 1991. (Rev: BL 2/1/91) [796.357]

7952 Bryant, Howard. *The Last Hero: A Life of Henry Aaron* (10–12). Illus. 2010, Pantheon $29.95 (978-037542485-4). Aaron goes from rural, poor Alabama to breaking Babe Ruth's home run record in this athletic rags-to-riches biography that includes photos and statistics. ⋒ ℮ (Rev: BL 4/15/10*) [921]

ALOMAR, ROBERTO

7953 Macht, Norman L. *Roberto Alomar* (6–10). Series: Latinos in Baseball. 1999, Mitchell Lane LB $18.95 (978-1-883845-84-1). Using extensive interviews with Alomar, his family, friends, and colleagues, this profile of the famous Puerto Rican baseball player shows his strong self-discipline, work ethic, and close family ties. (Rev: BL 4/15/99; HBG 10/99; SLJ 5/99) [921]

BONDS, BARRY

7954 Pearlman, Jeff. *Love Me, Hate Me: Barry Bonds and the Making of an Antihero* (9–12). 2006, HarperCollins $25.95 (978-0-06-079752-2). A former *Sports Illustrated* writer takes on this prickly, complex, talented, and possibly drug-using sports personality. (Rev: BL 5/15/06) [921]

CLEMENTE, ROBERTO

7955 Santiago, Wilfred. *21: The Story of Roberto Clemente* (10–12). 2011, Fantagraphics $22.99 (978-1-56097-892-3). Full of historical detail, this biography uses a graphic-novel format to tell the story of this baseball legend. (Rev: BL 4/15/11; LMC 10/11; SLJ 7/11) [921]

COSTE, CHRIS

7956 Coste, Chris. *The 33-Year-Old Rookie: How I Finally Made It to the Big Leagues After Eleven Years in the Minors* (9–12). 2008, Ballantine $25.00 (978-1-4000-6686-5). The heartwarming story of a 33-year-old rookie who doggedly pursued — and achieved — his dream of playing in the major leagues. (Rev: BL 3/15/08) [921]

DIMAGGIO, JOE

7957 Cramer, Richard Ben. *Joe DiMaggio: The Hero's Life* (10–12). 2000, Simon & Schuster paper $16.00 (978-0-684-86547-8). For mature readers, this biography of baseball great Joe DiMaggio includes both his virtues and his faults. (Rev: BL 11/15/00) [92i]

7958 Johnson, Dick, and Glenn Stout. *DiMaggio: An Illustrated Life* (10–12). 1995, Walker $29.95 (978-0-8027-1311-7). Written before his death, this is a stirring biography of a baseball giant, with material on his life off the field and his impact on the game. (Rev: SLJ 6/96) [921]

KOUFAX, SANDY

7959 Gruver, Edward. *Koufax* (9–12). 2000, Taylor $24.95 (978-0-87833-157-4). An enlightening biography of Sandy Koufax, a humble, gracious baseball pitcher who became a Hall of Famer. (Rev: BL 5/15/00) [921]

LEACH, TERRY

7960 Leach, Terry, and Tom Clark. *Things Happen for a Reason: The True Story of an Itinerant Life in Baseball* (9–12). 2000, Frog $14.95 (978-1-58394-050-1). The ups and downs of life in the minor and major leagues are revealed through the experiences of Terry Leach, a pitcher who never became a star. (Rev: BL 5/15/00) [921]

MANTLE, MICKEY

7961 Berger, Phil. *Mickey Mantle* (10–12). Series: Biography. 1998, Park Lane $20.00 (978-0-517-20099-5). This comprehensive profile traces Mantle's rise to stardom and his struggle with alcoholism. [921]

MARTINEZ, PEDRO

7962 Lashnits, Tom. *Pedro Martinez* (6–10). Series: Great Hispanic Heritage. 2006, Chelsea House LB $30 (978-0-7910-8840-1). Baseball fans will enjoy this account of the Red Sox player's life and career. (Rev: SLJ 9/06) [921]

MATHEWS, EDDIE

7963 Mathews, Eddie, and Bob Buege. *Eddie Mathews and the National Pastime* (9–12). 1994, Douglas American Sports $22.95 (978-1-882134-41-0). Hall of Famer Mathews chronicles his life and baseball career, including anecdotes about Hank Aaron and Bob Uecker. (Rev: BL 9/15/94) [921]

MATSUI, HIDEKI

7964 Beach, Jerry. *Godzilla Takes the Bronx: The Inside Story of Hideki Matsui* (8–12). 2004, Taylor $24.95 (978-1-58979-113-8). A biography of the Japanese baseball player who joined the Yankees. (Rev: BL 3/15/04) [921]

MORRIS, JIM

7965 Morris, Jim, and Joel Engel. *The Oldest Rookie: Big-League Dreams from a Small-Town Guy* (9–12). 2001, Little, Brown $22.95 (978-0-316-59156-0). The amazing story of the ups and downs of Jim Morris, a boy in love with baseball, and how he finally made it to the majors. (Rev: BL 4/1/01*) [921]

ROBINSON, JACKIE

7966 Eig, Jonathan. *Opening Day: The Story of Jackie Robinson's First Season* (9–12). 2007, Simon & Schuster $26.00 (978-0-7432-9460-7). As the title says, this is the story of Robinson's first season, with the Brooklyn Dodgers in 1947, and the uphill personal battle he faced while playing excellent baseball. ∩ (Rev: BL 3/1/07) [921]

7967 Weidhorn, Manfred. *Jackie Robinson* (6–12). 1993, Atheneum LB $15.95 (978-0-689-31644-9). This biography of the African American legend who integrated baseball in 1947 focuses on the personal qualities of the boy, the man, and the athlete. (Rev: BL 3/15/94; SLJ 2/94; VOYA 4/94) [921]

RUTH, BABE

7968 Creamer, Robert W. *Babe: The Legend Comes to Life* (9–12). 1974, Simon & Schuster paper $14.00 (978-0-671-76070-0). A biography of Babe Ruth that covers both his professional baseball career and his private life. [921]

7969 Gilbert, Brother. *Young Babe Ruth: His Early Life and Baseball Career, from the Memoirs of a Xaverian Brother* (9–12). 1999, McFarland paper $29.95 (978-0-7864-0652-4). A former teacher of the boy who grew up to be Babe Ruth recounts memories of the baseball star's formative years. (Rev: BL 4/1/00) [921]

SOSA, SAMMY

7970 Muskat, Carrie. *Sammy Sosa* (6–10). Series: Latinos in Baseball. 1999, Mitchell Lane LB $18.95 (978-1-883845-92-6). This account of Sosa's life tells of his beginning as a poor shoeshine boy in the Dominican Republic and his rise in baseball to his record-setting home run at age 29. (Rev: BL 4/15/99; HBG 10/99; SLJ 5/99) [921]

WILLIAMS, TED

7971 Linn, Ed. *Hitter: The Life and Turmoil of Ted Williams* (9–12). 1993, Harcourt $23.95 (978-0-15-193100-2). Examines the baseball career of the legendary Boston Red Sox slugger, considered by many to be the greatest of all time. (Rev: BL 4/15/93) [921]

Basketball

AURIEMMA, GENO

7972 Auriemma, Geno, and Jackie MacMullan. *Geno: In Pursuit of Perfection* (9–12). 2006, Warner $25.95 (978-0-446-57764-9). The coach of the phenomenally successful UConn women's basketball team tells of coming to America with his parents at the age of 7 and of his lifelong struggle to succeed. (Rev: BL 1/1–15/06) [796.323]

BOGUES, TYRONE "MUGGSY"

7973 Bogues, Tyrone "Muggsy", and David Levine. *In the Land of the Giants* (9–12). 1994, Little, Brown $19.95 (978-0-316-10173-8). The autobiography of the Charlotte Hornets' "Muggsy" Bogues, the shortest basketball player in the NBA, tells of his poverty-stricken youth and convict father. (Rev: BL 11/1/94; SLJ 5/95) [921]

HASKINS, DON

7974 Haskins, Don, and Dan Wetzel. *Glory Road: My Story of the 1966 NCAA Basketball Championship and How One Team Triumphed Against the Odds and Changed America Forever* (10–12). 2006, Hyperion paper $14.95 (978-1-4013-0791-2). Haskins tells how he led the all-black Texas Western College basketball team to the NCAA championship in 1966. (Rev: BL 1/1–15/06) [796.323]

JAMES, LEBRON

7975 James, LeBron, and Buzz Bissinger. *Shooting Stars* (10–12). Illus. 2009, Penguin $26.95 (978-159420232-2). LeBron James describes his early life in Akron, Ohio, including the hardships that came with poverty and all the people who helped him succeed. ∩ (Rev: BL 9/09) [921]

7976 Morgan, David Lee, Jr. *LeBron James* (7–12). 2003, Gray & Company paper $14.95 (978-1-886228-74-0). The biography of the African American basketball superstar who came from a culture of poverty and drugs to reach the peak of the sports world. (Rev: BL 2/15/04; SLJ 6/04) [921]

JORDAN, MICHAEL

7977 Lovitt, Chip. *Michael Jordan* (6–10). 1998, Scholastic paper $4.50 (978-0-590-59644-2). This quick read, an update of the 1993 edition, traces Jordan's remarkable career from a young age to the end of the Chicago Bulls' 1998 season. (Rev: VOYA 4/99) [921]

7978 Williams, Pat, and Michael Weinreb. *How to Be Like Mike: Life Lessons About Basketball's Best* (10–12). 2001, Health Communications paper $12.95 (978-1-55874-955-9). Interviews with more than 1,400 people bring to life basketball great Michael Jordan, who has become a role model for many. (Rev: BL 9/1/01; SLJ 1/02) [921]

MING, YAO

7979 Ming, Yao, and Ric Bucher. *Yao: A Life in Two Worlds* (8–12). 2004, Miramax $22.95 (978-1-4013-5214-1). Yao Ming writes of his success in the NBA and also of the sharp contrast between the culture of his native China and that of the United States. (Rev: BL 9/1/04) [796.323]

NUNEZ, TOMMY

7980 Marvis, Barbara. *Tommy Nunez, NBA Referee: Taking My Best Shot* (6–10). 1996, Mitchell Lane paper $12.95 (978-1-883845-28-5). The story of the young-ster who grew up in the poverty of Phoenix's barrio to become the first Mexican American referee in the NBA. (Rev: BL 5/15/96; SLJ 3/96; VOYA 6/96) [921]

STARKS, JOHN

7981 Starks, John. *My Life: Don't Ever Give Up* (9–12). 2004, Sports Publishing $24.95 (978-1-58261-802-9). The NBA basketball star describes how he escaped the mean streets of Tulsa, Oklahoma, to become a top player for the New York Knicks. (Rev: BL 10/15/04) [796.323]

Boxing

ALI, MUHAMMAD

7982 Hauser, Thomas. *Muhammad Ali: His Life and Times* (9–12). 1992, Simon & Schuster paper $16.00 (978-0-671-77971-9). This biography traces Ali's con-tributions to boxing and to the betterment of his people through 1990. (Rev: BL 5/15/91) [921]

7983 *Muhammad Ali* (6–10). 1997, Random House $20.00 (978-0-517-20080-3). Using plenty of sidebars, quotations from his poetry, and photographs, this excel-lent biography, based on A&E cable TV's *Biography* show, traces the boxer's life from his days as a scrawny kid named Cassius Clay, Jr. to his becoming "the great-est," ending with the 1996 lighting of the Olympic torch in Atlanta. (Rev: VOYA 8/98) [921]

CARTER, RUBIN "HURRICANE"

7984 Hirsch, James S. *Hurricane: The Miraculous Jour-ney of Rubin Carter* (10–12). 2000, Houghton Mifflin paper $15.00 (978-0-618-08728-0). The story of the African American boxing champion and of his ordeal and fight for justice after being wrongly convicted of murdering three people. (Rev: BL 12/1/99) [921]

CHAVEZ, JESUS

7985 Pitluk, Adam. *Standing Eight: The Inspiring Story of Jesus "El Matador" Chavez, Who Became Light-weight Champion of the World* (10–12). 2006, Da Capo $24.95 (978-0-306-81454-9). The story of Chavez's ef-forts to make a life in the United States will appeal both to boxing fans and general readers. (Rev: SLJ 11/06) [921]

HAWKINS, DWIGHT

7986 Hawkins, Dwight, and Morrie Greenberg. *Survival in the Square* (7–10). 1989, Richards paper $5.95 (978-0-9622652-0-4). The story of an African American who overcame a physical handicap and became a boxing champion. (Rev: BL 11/15/89; VOYA 12/89) [921]

Football

BETTIS, JEROME

7987 Bettis, Jerome, and Gene Wojciechowski. *The Bus: My Life In and Out of a Helmet* (9–12). 2007, Double-day $23.95 (978-0-385-52061-4). Jerome Bettis ("The Bus") shares the story of his childhood in a rough neighborhood in Detroit, the support he received from his parents and coaches, and the life he found in profes-sional football. (Rev: BL 8/07) [921]

BRADY, TOM

7988 Pierce, Charles P. *Moving the Chains: Tom Brady and the Pursuit of Everything* (11–12). 2006, Farrar $23.00 (978-0-374-29923-1). A biography of the fa-mous Patriots quarterback by a writer at the *Boston Globe* Sunday magazine; for mature teens. (Rev: BL 9/1/06) [921]

BURRESS, PLAXICO

7989 Burress, Plaxico, and Jason Cole. *Giant: The Road to the Super Bowl* (10–12). Illus. 2008, HarperEnter-tainment $24.95 (978-0-06-169574-2). A likable ac-count of Burress's road to success, with insight into football in general and the New York Giants in particu-lar. (Rev: BLO 8/28/08) [921]

FAVRE, BRETT

7990 Funk, Joe, ed. *Favre: The Man, The Legend* (9–12). Illus. 2008, Triumph $27.95 (978-157243920-7). Here is a chronological account of Brett Favre's career in-cluding quotes from those who played with him and against him, statistics, and plenty of terrific photo-graphs. (Rev: BL 9/1/08) [921]

MANNING, PEYTON

7991 Crompton, Samuel Willard. *Peyton Manning* (7–10). Illus. Series: Football Superstars. 2008, Chelsea House LB $30 (978-079109605-5). Star quarterback Peyton Manning's childhood, school years, and early career are documented in this well-organized book with a chronology, statistics, and play-by-plays. (Rev: BLO 8/08) [921]

NGUYEN, DAT

7992 Nguyen, Dat, and Rusty Burson. *Dat: Tackling Life and the NFL* (9–12). 2005, A & M Univ $24.95 (978-1-58544-472-4). Dat Nguyen, the only Vietnamese American in the NFL, writes about the long and difficult road he traveled to make his mark in professional football. (Rev: BL 9/15/05) [796.332]

OHER, MICHAEL

7993 Lewis, Michael. *The Blind Side: Evolution of a Game* (9–12). 2006, Norton $24.95 (978-0-393-06123-9). Lewis combines discussion of the importance of left tackles in professional football with the story of Michael Oher, a poor boy with athletic ability who is adopted by a wealthy family that recognizes and nurtures his gifts. ∩ (Rev: BL 10/15/06) [796.332]

7994 Oher, Michael, and Don Yaeger. *I Beat the Odds: From Homelessness to The Blind Side and Beyond* (9–12). 2011, Gotham $26 (978-1-592-40612-8). Oher chronicles his unstable youth and describes how he found success on the football field. ∩ (Rev: BL 9/1/11; SLJ 4/11) [921]

PATERNO, JOE

7995 Pittman, Charlie, and Tony Pittman. *Playing for Paterno: One Coach, Two Eras . . . a Father's and Son's Recollections of Playing for JoPa* (9–12). 2007, Triumph $24.95 (978-1-60078-000-4). Joe Paterno has been the coach of the Penn State Nittany Lions for so long that there is now a book of tributes and memoirs by a father and a son who have both played for him during their respective eras — the late 1960s and the early 1990s. (Rev: BL 8/07) [921]

PICCOLO, BRIAN

7996 Morris, Jeannie. *Brian Piccolo: A Short Season. Special 25th anniversary ed.* (10–12). 1995, Bonus paper $12.95 (978-1-56625-024-5). The biography of Brian Piccolo, a running back for the Chicago Bears, who died of cancer at 28. [921]

SAYERS, GALE

7997 Sayers, Gale, and Fred Mitchell. *Sayers: My Life and Times* (9–12). 2007, Triumph $24.95 (978-1-57243-995-5). The Chicago Bears running back also known for his friendship with teammate Brian Piccolo (memorialized in the movie *Brian's Song*) expresses his thoughts about the game of football and footballers' responsibilities to the community. (Rev: BL 9/1/07) [921]

TUAOLO, ESERA

7998 Tuaolo, Esera, and John Rosengren. *Alone in the Trenches: My Life as a Gay Player in the NFL* (11–12). 2006, Sourcebooks $24.95 (978-1-4022-0505-7). Longtime NFL lineman Tuaolo Esera tells how he hid his homosexuality to protect his career in professional football; for mature readers. (Rev: BL 11/1/05) [796.332]

YOAST, BILL

7999 Yoast, Bill. *Remember This Titan: Lessons Learned from a Celebrated Coach's Journey* (9–12). 2005, Taylor $21.95 (978-1-58979-278-4). Yoast, replaced by an African American as head football coach at T. C. Williams High School in Alexandria, Virginia, in 1972, recounts how he worked with his successor, Herman Boone, to lead the newly integrated team to the state championship. (Rev: BL 10/1/05) [796.332]

Gymnastics

MILLER, SHANNON

8000 Miller, Claudia. *Shannon Miller: My Child, My Hero* (9–12). 1999, Oklahoma Univ. $9.95 (978-0-8061-3110-8). Told by her mother, this is the story of Shannon Miller, who overcame enormous odds, including painful injuries, to become a world champion gymnast and gold medal winner. (Rev: VOYA 10/99) [921]

SEY, JENNIFER

8001 Sey, Jennifer. *Chalked Up: Inside Elite Gymnastics' Merciless Coaching, Overzealous Parents, Eating Disorders, and Elusive Olympic Dreams* (9–12). 2008, Morrow $24.95 (978-0-06-135146-4). A disturbing memoir of unfulfilled dreams. (Rev: BL 4/1/08) [796.44]

Ice Skating and Hockey

HALL, GLENN

8002 Adrahtas, Tom. *Glenn Hall: The Man They Call Mr. Goalie* (10–12). 2003, Moyer Bell/Albion paper $16.95 (978-0-9709170-1-0). Glenn Hall, one of the most successful goalies in National Hockey League history and master of the "butterfly" style of goal tending, is candidly profiled in this absorbing biography. (Rev: BL 4/1/03) [921]

HAMILL, DOROTHY

8003 Hamill, Dorothy. *A Skating Life* (10–12). 2007, Hyperion $24.95 (978-1-4013-0328-0). The skating star tells all about her life — her parents' depression, her own unhappiness and failed marriages — and her career on the ice. (Rev: BL 9/1/07) [796.91]

KWAN, MICHELLE

8004 Koestler-Grack, Rachel A. *Michelle Kwan* (7–10). 2007, Chelsea House LB $30.00 (978-0-7910-9273-6). Details the accomplishments of figure skater Kwan and provides information about her training, competition, and her life off the ice. (Rev: BL 9/1/07) [920]

OHNO, APOLO ANTON

8005 Aldridge, Rebecca. *Apolo Anton Ohno* (7–10). Series: Asian Americans of Achievement. 2009, Chelsea House $30 (978-1-60413-565-7). Son of a Japanese father, Ohno has won medals as a speed skater at the Olympics. (Rev: SLJ 2/10) [921]

Tennis

ASHE, ARTHUR

8006 Ashe, Arthur, and Arnold Rampersad. *Days of Grace: A Memoir* (9–12). 1994, Random House paper $7.99 (978-0-345-38681-6). A memoir, concentrating on the 1980s, of the deceased African American tennis player who won the Davis Cup and died from AIDS. (Rev: BL 5/15/93*; SLJ 11/93) [921]

GIBSON, ALTHEA

8007 Gray, Frances Clayton, and Yanick Rice Lamb. *Born to Win: The Authorized Biography of Althea Gibson* (9–12). 2004, Wiley $35.00 (978-0-471-47165-3). The story of African American Gibson's remarkable achievements in tennis in the 1950s, a time when the sport was largely played by whites. (Rev: BL 9/1/04) [796.34]

MCENROE, PATRICK

8008 McEnroe, Patrick, and Peter Bodo. *Hardcourt Confidential: Tales from Twenty Years in the Pro Tennis Trenches* (10–12). 2010, Hyperion $25.99 (978-140132381-3). Tennis pro McEnroe serves up a collection of wry anecdotes from his career playing, observing, administrating, and commenting on professional tennis. (Rev: BL 6/1–15/10) [921]

Track and Field

JONES, MARION

8009 Jones, Marion. *On the Right Track: From Olympic Downfall to Finding Forgiveness and the Strength to Overcome and Succeed* (10–12). Illus. 2010, Simon & Schuster $25 (978-145161082-6). Olympic Gold Medalist Marion Jones recounts her rise to the pinnacle of her sport and the scandal and subsequent incarceration resulting from her use of performance-enhancing drugs. (Rev: BL 11/1–15/10) [921]

JOYNER-KERSEE, JACKIE

8010 Harrington, Geri. *Jackie Joyner-Kersee: Champion Athlete* (6–10). 1995, Chelsea LB $21.95 (978-0-7910-2085-2). Describes Joyner-Kersee's four Olympic championships, despite asthma attacks. (Rev: BL 10/1/95) [921]

LONGBOAT, TOM

8011 Batten, Jack. *The Man Who Ran Faster Than Everyone: The Story of Tom Longboat* (7–12). 2002, Tundra paper $12.95 (978-0-88776-507-0). A straightforward biography of the Onondaga Indian distance runner who won fame in the early 20th century. (Rev: BL 4/1/02; SLJ 6/02) [796.42]

THORPE, JIM

8012 Buford, Kate. *Native American Son: The Life and Sporting Legend of Jim Thorpe* (10–12). Illus. 2010, Knopf $35 (978-037541324-7). An in-depth look at the life of the great athlete, placing his importance in historical context and examining his personal struggles. e (Rev: BL 9/1–15/10) [921]

8013 Crawford, Bill. *All American: The Rise and Fall of Jim Thorpe* (8–12). 2004, Wiley $32.50 (978-0-471-55732-6). An in-depth look at the tumultuous life of the Native American athlete who triumphed on the world's playing fields but ultimately died in relative obscurity. (Rev: BL 11/15/04) [796]

8014 Wheeler, Robert W. *Jim Thorpe: World's Greatest Athlete* (9–12). 1981, Univ. of Oklahoma paper $19.95 (978-0-8061-1745-4). This biography traces the amazing career of the Native American athlete who won both the decathlon and the pentathlon at the 1912 Olympics. [921]

Miscellaneous Sports

ARMSTRONG, LANCE

8015 Coyle, Daniel. *Lance Armstrong's War: One Man's Battle Against Fate, Fame, Love, Death, Scandal, and a Few Other Rivals on the Road to the Tour de France* (8–12). 2005, HarperCollins $25.95 (978-0-06-073794-8). Traces Armstrong's winning 2004 season and reviews the daunting challenges the cyclist has had to overcome in his life. (Rev: BL 6/1–15/05) [796.6]

8016 Strickland, Bill. *Tour de Lance: The Extraordinary Story of Lance Armstrong's Fight to Reclaim the Tour de France* (10–12). Illus. 2010, Harmony $25.99 (978-030758984-2). Strickland tells the story of Armstrong's 2009 effort to make a comeback. **e** (Rev: BL 5/15/10*) [921]

EDERLE, GERTRUDE

8017 Dahlberg, Tim, and Brenda Greene, et al. *America's Girl: The Incredible Story of How Swimmer Gertrude Ederle Changed the Nation* (9–12). 2009, St. Martin's $25.99 (978-0-312-38265-0). The story of 20-year-old Gertrude Ederle's historic 1926 swim across the English Channel, not only the first woman to do so but beating the men's record by nearly two hours. (Rev: SLJ 12/09) [921]

FUSSELL, SAMUEL WILSON

8018 Fussell, Samuel Wilson. *Muscle: Confessions of an Unlikely Bodybuilder* (9–12). 1992, HarperCollins paper $13.95 (978-0-380-71763-7). How one man went from beanpole to bodybuilder after moving to New York City. Includes material on use and abuse of steroids in bodybuilding. (Rev: BL 1/15/91; SLJ 9/91) [646.7]

GARDNER, RULON

8019 Gardner, Rulon, and Bob Schaller. *Never Stop Pushing: My Life from a Wyoming Farm to the Olympic Medals Stand* (9–12). 2005, Carroll & Graf paper $14.95 (978-0-7867-1593-0). The inspiring story of Rulon Gardner, who won an Olympic gold medal in wrestling after hypothermia caused him to lose part of each foot. (Rev: BL 9/1/05) [796.812]

GUERRERO, EDDIE

8020 Guerrero, Eddie. *Cheating Death, Stealing Life* (9–12). 2005, World Wrestling Entertainment $26.00 (978-0-7434-9353-6). This inspirational autobiography chronicles the life of pro-wrestler Eddie Guerrero, his privileged childhood, early success, subsequent drug abuse, and eventual rehabilitation. (Rev: BLO 7/11/07) [921]

HAWK, TONY

8021 Hawk, Tony, and Sean Mortimer. *Hawk: Occupation, Skateboarder* (8–12). 2000, Regan paper $15.00 (978-0-06-095831-2). The biography of a man who, during a rebellious youth, discovered skateboarding and was determined to excel at it. [921]

8022 Peterson, Todd. *Tony Hawk: Skateboarder and Businessman* (8–11). Series: Ferguson Career Biographies. 2005, Ferguson LB $25.00 (978-0-8160-5893-8). Skateboarder Tony Hawk's childhood, skating career, and business achievements are all covered in this readable volume. (Rev: BL 9/1/05) [796.22]

LOPEZ, NANCY

8023 Sharp, Anne Wallace. *Nancy Lopez: Golf Hall of Famer* (6–10). Illus. Series: 20th Century's Most Influential Hispanics. 2008, Gale/Lucent LB $32.45 (978-142050060-8). Sharp highlights the various obstacles Lopez faced as she rose to prominence in a male-dominated sport in this appealing profile. (Rev: BL 9/1/08) [921]

MAY-TREANOR, MISTY

8024 May-Treanor, Misty, and Jill Lieber Steeg. *Misty: Digging Deep in Volleyball and Life* (10–12). Illus. 2010, Scribner $25 (978-143914854-9). Volleyball star May-Treanor details her wins, losses, injuries, and coach changes — as well as her mother's death from cancer — in this approachable sports autobiography. (Rev: BL 6/1–15/10) [921]

PARKIN, JOE

8025 Parkin, Joe. *A Dog in a Hat: An American Bike Racer's Story of Mud, Drugs, Blood, Betrayal, and Beauty in Belgium* (10–12). 2008, Velo paper $21.95 (978-193403026-4). Parkin tells the story of his life as a young American bike racer in Belgium who strove to fit in amid the stress of racing, the illegal drugs, and the fierce competition. (Rev: BL 9/1/08) [921]

PRADO, EDGAR

8026 Prado, Edgar, and John Eisenberg. *My Guy Barbaro: A Jockey's Journey Through Love, Triumph, and Heartbreak with America's Favorite Horse* (9–12). 2008, HarperCollins $25.95 (978-0-06-146418-8). Jockey Edgar Prado describes his rise from poverty and his remarkable friendship with the thoroughbred Barbaro, the undefeated Kentucky Derby winner who suffered a breakdown during the Preakness. (Rev: BL 3/1/08) [798.4]

SPITZ, MARK

8027 Foster, Richard J. *Mark Spitz: The Extraordinary Life of an Olympic Champion* (10–12). Illus. 2008, Santa Monica $24.95 (978-159580039-8). Mark Spitz's life, from his humble beginnings to Olympic glory, is detailed in this inspiring biography. (Rev: BL 9/1/08) [921]

STARK, PETER

8028 Stark, Peter. *Driving to Greenland* (9–12). 1994, Lyons $22.95 (978-1-55821-320-3). The author describes his adventures on skis, dogsled, and luge on mountains in Greenland and Iceland. (Rev: BL 9/1/94) [796.93]

TAYLOR, MARSHALL B.

8029 Balf, Todd. *Major: A Black Athlete, a White Era, and the Fight to Be the World's Fastest Human Being* (9–12). 2008, Crown $24.00 (978-0-307-23658-6). Marshall (commonly known as Major) Taylor was one of the — if not *the* — fastest bicycle racer of his time; he was also African American, and much of this book focuses on the discrimination he overcame. (Rev: BL 12/15/07; SLJ 4/08) [921]

WHITFIELD, SIMON

8030 Whitfield, Simon, and Cleve Dheensaw. *Simon Says Gold: Simon Whitfield's Pursuit of Athletic Excellence* (7–12). 2009, Orca paper $14 (978-1-55469-141-8). In this illustrated biography, Whitfield chronicles his successes, failures, and eventual rise to Olympic stardom. (Rev: BLO 11/20/09; SLJ 1/10; VOYA 6/10) [921]

ZAHARIAS, BABE DIDRIKSON

8031 Cayleff, Susan E. *Babe: The Life and Legend of Babe Didrikson Zaharias* (9–12). 1996, Univ. of Illinois $14.95 (978-0-252-06593-4). Looks at Babe Didrikson Zaharias, pro golfer and Olympic gold medalist, examining how she lived her life, her public persona, and her lesbianism. (Rev: BL 6/1–15/95) [921]

8032 Cayleff, Susan E. *Babe Didrikson: The Greatest All-Sport Athlete of All Time* (7–12). 2000, Conari paper $8.95 (978-1-57324-194-6). A candid, honest look at the life of this difficult, brash, competitive golf legend. (Rev: BL 10/1/00; VOYA 8/01) [921]

8033 Freedman, Russell. *Babe Didrikson Zaharias: The Making of a Champion* (6–12). 1999, Clarion $19.00 (978-0-395-63367-0). Although she was known to most for her golf career, this entertaining biography points out that Babe Didrikson Zaharias was also an Olympic athlete, a track star, leader of a women's amateur basketball team, and an entrepreneur. (Rev: BCCB 10/99; BL 7/99; HB 9–10/99; HBG 3/00; SLJ 7/99; VOYA 12/00) [921]

World Figures

Collective

8034 Axelrod-Contrada, Joan. *Women Who Led Nations* (7–10). Series: Profiles. 1999, Oliver LB $19.95 (978-1-881508-48-9). Corazon Aquino, Benazir Bhutto, and Golda Meir are among the seven women profiled in detail in this collective biography. (Rev: HBG 4/00; SLJ 10/99) [920]

8035 Baker, Rosalie F., and Charles F. Baker. *Ancient Egyptians: People of the Pyramids* (6–12). Series: Oxford Profiles. 2001, Oxford $55.00 (978-0-19-512221-3). Detailed biographies of key figures such as Nefertiti, Hatshepsut, Tutankhamen, and Ramses give plenty of background social and cultural information and are accompanied by sidebar features and black-and-white photographs. (Rev: BL 9/15/01; HBG 10/02; SLJ 11/01) [920.032]

8036 Benson, Sonia G. *Korean War: Biographies* (6–10). 2001, Gale LB $70.00 (978-0-7876-5692-8). A collection of 25 biographies of individuals — Koreans, Americans, and other nationalities — who participated in or affected the course of the Korean War. (Rev: BL 3/15/02; SLJ 5/02) [920]

8037 Coddon, Karin S., ed. *Black Women Activists* (9–12). Series: Profiles in History. 2004, Gale LB $36.20 (978-0-7377-2313-7). Mary Church Terrell, Sojourner Truth, Rosa Parks, Fannie Lou Hamer, and Winnie Mandela are among the 11 women profiled in this volume. (Rev: SLJ 11/04) [920]

8038 Dunn, Jane. *Elizabeth and Mary: Cousins, Rivals, Queens* (11–12). 2004, Knopf $30.00 (978-0-375-40898-4). For strong readers, this well-documented, well-illustrated, and well-written account of the two very different queens will be rewarding. (Rev: SLJ 5/04) [920]

8039 Hastings, Max. *Warriors: Portraits from the Battlefield* (9–12). 2006, Knopf $27.50 (978-1-4000-4441-2). British military historian Hastings celebrates the warrior spirit in profiles of 14 men and one woman who fought for their countries during the 19th and 20th centuries. (Rev: BL 12/15/05) [355]

8040 Phibbs, Cheryl Fisher, ed. *Pioneers of Human Rights* (8–11). Series: Profiles in History. 2005, Gale LB $36.20 (978-0-7377-2146-1). Among the figures profiled in this volume are Mohandas Gandhi, Frederick Douglass, Nelson Mandela, and Eleanor Roosevelt. (Rev: BL 7/05) [323]

8041 Pouy, Jean-Bernard. *The Big Book of Dummies, Rebels and Other Geniuses* (7–10). Illus. by Serge Bloch. 2008, Enchanted Lion $19.95 (978-159270103-2). This often funny, irreverently illustrated book showcases the unlikely, often chaotic beginnings of 26 prominent figures in art, science, literature, and history, from Charlemagne and Dumas to Pablo Picasso and Agatha Christie. (Rev: BLO 10/7/08; SLJ 9/1/08; VOYA 8/08) [920]

8042 Price-Groff, Claire. *Twentieth-Century Women Political Leaders* (7–10). Series: Global Profiles. 1998, Facts on File LB $25.00 (978-0-8160-3672-1). A look at 12 women political leaders in the second half of the 20th century: Golda Meir, Indira Gandhi, Eva Peron, Margaret Thatcher, Corazon Aquino, Winnie Mandela, Barbara Jordan, Violeta Chamorro, Wilma Mankiller, Gro Harlem Brundtland, Aung San Suu Kyi, and Benazir Bhutto. (Rev: SLJ 1/99) [920]

8043 Scandiffio, Laura. *Evil Masters: The Frightening World of Tyrants* (7–10). 2005, Annick $24.95 (978-1-55037-895-5); paper $12.95 (978-1-55037-894-8). Nero, Ivan the Terrible, Hitler, Stalin, and Saddam Hussein are five of the seven rulers profiled; an introduction discusses personality traits and the reasons why such men are able to assume power. (Rev: SLJ 1/06) [920]

8044 Scandiffio, Laura. *People Who Said No: Courage Against Oppression* (8–11). Illus. 2012, Annick $24.95 (978-1-55451-383-3); paper $14.95 (978-1-55451-382-6). Rosa Parks, Andrei Sakharov, and Aung San Suu Kyi are among the seven individuals profiled here, with historical sidebars and well-chosen photographs. (Rev: BL 11/15/12; SLJ 9/12)

8045 Traub, Carol G. *Philanthropists and Their Legacies* (7–12). Series: Profiles. 1997, Oliver LB $19.95 (978-1-881508-42-7). Profiles — warts and all — of nine of the world's greatest benefactors, including Alfred Nobel, Andrew Carnegie, Cecil Rhodes, George Eastman, and Will Kellogg. (Rev: BL 2/15/98; SLJ 2/98) [920]

8046 Waller, Maureen. *Sovereign Ladies: The Six Reigning Queens of England* (9–12). 2007, St. Martin's $29.95 (978-0-312-33801-5). Mary I, Elizabeth I, Mary II, Anne, Victoria, and Elizabeth II are the six queens (queens in their own right, not through marriage) profiled in this accessible volume that looks at their personal and political lives. (Rev: BL 4/1/07) [920]

8047 Young, Mitchell, ed. *Terrorist Leaders* (11–12). Series: Profiles in History. 2004, Gale LB $36.20 (978-0-7377-2649-7). After a section on Osama bin Laden, chapters organize biographies under state terrorists (Stalin, Pol Pot), liberation fighters (Menachem Begin, Yasir Arafat), and ideologists (the Unabomber, Timothy McVeigh). (Rev: SLJ 4/05) [920]

Africa

ANNAN, KOFI

8048 Meisler, Stanley. *Kofi Annan* (10–12). 2007, Wiley $30.00 (978-0-471-78744-0). This profile focuses mainly on Annan's professional life and his career at the United Nations, where he started work in 1962. (Rev: BL 1/1–15/07) [921]

BASHIR, HALIMA

8049 Bashir, Halima, and Damien Lewis. *Tears of the Desert: A Memoir of Survival in Darfur* (11–12). 2008, Ballantine $25.00 (978-0-345-50625-2). Bashir recounts her work as a doctor in Darfur during the civil war, the atrocities that took place, and her efforts to gain global recognition of this genocide; for mature readers. ⌒ ℮ (Rev: BL 8/08) [921]

CLEOPATRA

8050 Nardo, Don. *Cleopatra: Egypt's Last Pharaoh* (6–10). Series: The Lucent Library of Historical Eras. 2005, Gale LB $32.45 (978-1-59018-660-2). Presenting many quotations from ancient writings about Cleopatra, Nardo discusses their biases plus the importance of the

Egyptian leader's relationships with Julius Caesar and Marc Antony. (Rev: SLJ 11/05) [921]

8051 Sapet, Kerrily. *Cleopatra: Ruler of Egypt* (8–12). 2007, Morgan Reynolds LB $27.95 (978-1-59935-035-6). Presents the fascinating details of the life of the Egyptian queen, with descriptions of the cultural wealth of the ancient world, the role of women, and life along the Nile. (Rev: BL 6/1–15/07; SLJ 7/07) [921]

HANNIBAL

8052 Mills, Clifford W. *Hannibal* (6–10). Series: Ancient World Leaders. 2008, Chelsea House LB $30 (978-0-7910-9580-5). Mills covers the founding of Carthage and Hannibal's famous journey through the Alps and campaign against Rome. (Rev: SLJ 1/1/09) [921]

KORN, FADUMO

8053 Korn, Fadumo. *Born in the Big Rains: A Memoir of Somalia and Survival* (11–12). 2006, Feminist $23.95 (978-1-55861-531-1). After growing up with a series of serious health problems resulting from female circumcision at age 7, Korn aims to educate young African women so they can avoid this unnecessary and dangerous procedure; for mature teens. (Rev: BL 10/1/06) [392.109]

MAATHAI, WANGARI

8054 Maathai, Wangari. *Unbowed* (9–12). 2006, Knopf $24.95 (978-0-307-26348-3). The story of the struggles that Maathai, Kenya's deputy minister for the environment and natural resources, faced before she became a Nobel laureate and famed environmentalist. (Rev: BL 9/1/06) [921]

MANDELA, NELSON

8055 Cohen, David Elliot. *Nelson Mandela: A Life in Photographs* (10–12). Illus. 2010, Sterling $24.95 (978-140277707-3). Featuring more than 100 color photographs, a brief history of apartheid, and six of Mandela's historic speeches dating from the 1960s to the 1990s, this oversize volume rewards browsers and researchers. (Rev: BL 2/1–15/10) [921]

8056 Gaines, Ann. *Nelson Mandela and Apartheid in World History* (10–12). Series: In World History. 2001, Enslow $26.60 (978-0-7660-1463-3). This biography integrates personal stories about Nelson Mandela with a history of modern South Africa and the battle against apartheid. (Rev: BL 6/1–15/01; HBG 10/01) [921]

8057 Keller, Bill. *Tree Shaker: The Story of Nelson Mandela* (6–12). 2008, Kingfisher $16.95 (978-0-7534-5992-8). The accomplishments of the South African leader are related by a former *New York Times* Johannesburg bureau chief. An explanation of the history of apartheid helps readers to understand what Mandela was fighting for. (Rev: BL 11/1/07; SLJ 8/08) [921]

8058 Maharaj, Mac, and Ahmed Kathrada, eds. *Mandela: The Authorized Portrait* (9–12). 2006, Andrews McMeel $50.00 (978-0-7407-5572-9). A big and beautiful pictorial and narrative tribute — with contributions from world figures such as Bill Clinton, Desmond Tutu, and Kofi Annan — to the incredible life of Nelson Mandela. (Rev: BL 10/15/06) [968.06]

8059 Mandela, Nelson. *Mandela: An Illustrated Autobiography* (10–12). 1996, Little, Brown $29.95 (978-0-316-55038-3). In this beautifully illustrated autobiography, Nelson Mandela describes his lifelong battle against South Africa's system of racial oppression, including his 27 years as a political prisoner and his election as president in his country's first multiracial balloting. (Rev: BL 11/15/96) [921]

8060 Sawyer, Kem Knapp. *Nelson Mandela* (7–12). Illus. Series: Champion of Freedom. 2012, Morgan Reynolds LB $28.95 (978-159935167-4). A fascinating and detailed life of the South African leader who did so much to end apartheid. (Rev: BL 3/15/12; LMC 10/12; SLJ 5/1/12) [921]

8061 Smith, David James. *Young Mandela: The Revolutionary Years* (10–12). 2010, Little, Brown $27.99 (978-031603548-4). Smith paints a warts-and-all portrait of Mandela's activism up until his imprisonment. ⌒ ℮ (Rev: BL 10/1–15/10) [921]

MUBARAK, HOSNI

8062 Darraj, Susan Muaddi. *Hosni Mubarak* (8–12). Series: Modern World Leaders. 2007, Chelsea House LB $30.00 (978-0-7910-9280-4). Events in Egypt during Mubarak's presidency are the main focus of this profile. (Rev: SLJ 10/07) [921]

NEFERTITI

8063 Lange, Brenda. *Nefertiti* (6–12). Series: Ancient World Leaders. 2008, Chelsea House $30 (978-0-7910-9581-2). Full of illustrations that complement the text, this volume describes everyday life in ancient Egypt and the importance of religion and royalty as well as documenting what we know about the queen's life. (Rev: SLJ 3/1/09) [921]

TUTU, DESMOND

8064 Allen, John. *Rabble-Rouser for Peace: The Authorized Biography of Desmond Tutu* (9–12). 2006, Free Press $28.00 (978-0-7432-6937-7). Written by Archbishop Desmond Tutu's media secretary, this is the moving story of South Africa's champion of the apartheid resistance and fighter for peace and human rights. (Rev: BL 10/1/06) [921]

Asia and the Middle East

AHMADINEJAD, MAHMOUD

8065 Broyles, Matthew. *Mahmoud Ahmadinejad: President of Iran* (8–12). Series: Newsmakers. 2007, Rosen LB $31.95 (978-1-4042-1900-7). Readers are introduced to the president of Iran, whose provocative and challenging statements have enraged many and impressed others; Iran's current political climate and its history are covered as well. (Rev: BL 10/15/07) [955.05]

ARAFAT, YASIR

8066 Ferber, Elizabeth. *Yasir Arafat: The Battle for Peace in Palestine* (7–12). 1995, Millbrook $23.90 (978-1-56294-585-5). A balanced presentation of Arafat's political career. (Rev: BL 10/1/95; SLJ 12/95) [921]

AUNG SAN SUU KYI

8067 O'Keefe, Sherry. *Aung San Suu Kyi* (7–12). Illus. Series: Champion of Freedom. 2012, Morgan Reynolds LB $28.95 (978-159935168-1). A fascinating and detailed life of the daughter of the assassinated leader of Burma (Myanmar) and her commitment to human rights. (Rev: BL 3/15/12*; LMC 10/12; SLJ 6/12) [921]

DALAI LAMA

8068 Iyer, Pico. *The Open Road: The Global Journey of the Fourteenth Dalai Lama* (9–12). 2008, Knopf $24.00 (978-0-307-26760-3). Iver describes his experiences with the Dalai Lama and explores the paradoxical roles the Dalai Lama plays in the modern world. (Rev: BL 3/1/08) [921]

8069 Lama, Dalai. *My Spiritual Journey: Personal Reflections, Teachings, and Talks* (10–12). Trans. by Charlotte Mandell. Ed. by Sofia Stril-Rever. 2010, HarperOne $25.99 (978-006196022-2). The Dalai Lama's teachings, hopes, and concerns for people and the planet are collected here. ℮ (Rev: BL 10/1–15/10) [294.3]

8070 Talty, Stephan. *Escape from the Land of Snows: The Young Dalai Lama's Harrowing Flight to Freedom and the Making of a Spiritual Hero* (11–12). Illus. 2011, Crown $26 (978-030746095-0). A gripping account of the life of the current Dalai Lama, from young monk to courageous leader in Tibet's uprising against invading China and during his long exile. ⌒ ℮ (Rev: BL 1/1–15/11) [921]

GANDHI, INDIRA

8071 Dommermuth-Costa, Carol. *Indira Gandhi: Daughter of India* (7–12). Series: Lerner Biographies. 2001, Lerner LB $6.95 (978-0-8225-4963-5). A thorough profile that places Gandhi's life in historical context and provides a good history of modern India. (Rev: HBG 3/02; SLJ 3/02) [921]

GANDHI, MAHATMA

8072 Fischer, Louis. *Gandhi* (10–12). 1982, NAL paper $7.99 (978-0-451-62742-1). An admiring biography of the man who led India through nonviolent revolt to freedom. [921]

GENGHIS KHAN

8073 Rice, Earle, Jr. *Empire in the East: The Story of Genghis Khan* (7–11). Series: World Leaders. 2005, Morgan Reynolds LB $26.95 (978-1-931798-62-4). A life of Genghis Khan, who rose from obscurity to become leader of the Great Mongol Nation and ruler of vast territories that stretched from the Adriatic to the Pacific. (Rev: BL 8/05; SLJ 8/05) [950]

HO CHI MINH

8074 Duiker, William J. *Ho Chi Minh* (10–12). 2000, Hyperion $35.00 (978-0-7868-6387-7); paper $16.95 (978-0-7868-8701-9). A biography of the public and personal life of this Vietnamese leader. (Rev: BL 8/00) [921]

HUSSEIN, SADDAM

8075 Stewart, Gail B. *Saddam Hussein* (8–12). Series: Heroes and Villains. 2004, Gale LB $29.95 (978-1-59018-350-2). Ending before Saddam Hussein's capture by U.S. forces, this is a portrait of a ruthless dictator and his ascent to and maintenance of power. (Rev: SLJ 4/04) [921]

JUNDI, SAMI AL

8076 Al Jundi, Sami, and Jen Marlowe. *The Hour of Sunlight: One Palestinian's Journey from Prisoner to Peacemaker* (10–12). 2011, Nation paper $16.95 (978-15685844-8-5). The Palestinian founder of the Seeds of Peace program, which brings together Israeli and Palestinian teens in the Middle East, describes his stay in an Israeli prison and how it led him to change his politics and the course of his life. **e** (Rev: BL 1/1–15/11) [921]

KARZAI, HAMID

8077 Abrams, Dennis. *Hamid Karzai* (8–12). Series: Modern World Leaders. 2007, Chelsea House LB $30.00 (978-0-7910-9267-5). Karzai was sworn in as the first democratically elected president of Afghanistan in 2004, and since then has faced many challenges in the struggle to rebuild the war-torn country. (Rev: SLJ 10/07) [921]

KHAMENEI, ALI

8078 Murphy, John. *Ali Khamenei* (8–12). Series: Modern World Leaders. 2007, Chelsea House LB $30.00 (978-0-7910-9517-1). A look at the rise to power of Ali

Khamenei, who became the Grand Ayatollah of Iran upon Khomeini's death. (Rev: BL 4/10/08) [955.05]

KIM JONG IL

8079 Behnke, Alison. *Kim Jong Il's North Korea* (7–12). 2007, Lerner LB $38.60 (978-0-8225-7282-4). Extensive background about North Korea gives the reader a foundation for understanding Kim Jong Il's dictatorship. (Rev: BL 10/15/07; SLJ 11/07) [921]

KORDI, GOHAR

8080 Kordi, Gohar. *An Iranian Odyssey* (9–12). 1993, Serpent's Tail paper $13.95 (978-1-85242-213-4). A memoir of a blind Iranian-born woman, who, without financial or emotional support from her parents, graduated from Teheran University in 1970. (Rev: BL 1/15/93) [921]

MEIR, GOLDA

8081 Burkett, Elinor. *Golda* (9–12). 2008, HarperCollins $27.95 (978-0-06-078665-6). This profile focuses on Meir's role as a politician in the creation of the Jewish state. (Rev: BL 4/1/08) [921]

RIZAL, JOSE

8082 Arruda, Suzanne Middendorf. *Freedom's Martyr: The Story of José Rizal, National Hero of the Philippines* (6–12). Series: Avisson Young Adult. 2003, Avisson paper $19.95 (978-1-888105-55-1). A patriot and activist on behalf of the native peoples of the Philippines, Rizal was executed by the Spanish for treason in 1896 and remains the country's national hero. (Rev: SLJ 5/04) [921]

SASAKI, SADAKO

8083 Nasu, Masamoto. *Children of the Paper Crane: The Story of Sadako Sasaki and Her Struggle with the A-Bomb Disease* (9–12). Trans. by Elizabeth W. Baldwin and others. 1991, M.E. Sharpe $62.95 (978-0-87332-715-2). A personal account of the legacy of the Hiroshima bombing that describes the devastating decline of one child and the effects on her family and all Japan. (Rev: BL 12/15/91) [921]

SHEBA, QUEEN OF

8084 Lucks, Naomi. *Queen of Sheba* (6–12). Series: Ancient World Leaders. 2008, Chelsea House $30 (978-0-7910-9579-9). Lucks provides a glimpse into the past with this well-illustrated volume that documents what we know about the Queen of Sheba. (Rev: SLJ 3/1/09) [921]

TAJ AL-SALTANA

8085 al-Saltana, Taj. *Crowning Anguish: Memoirs of a Persian Princess from the Harem to Modernity, 1884–1914* (9–12). Trans. by Anna Vanzan and Amin Neshati.

Ed. by Abbas Amanat. 1993, Mage paper $17.95 (978-0-934211-36-9). An Iranian princess's memoirs of her life in a sheik's palace. (Rev: BL 9/15/93) [921]

TERESA, MOTHER

8086 Slavicek, Louise Chipley. *Mother Teresa: Caring for the World's Poor* (8–12). Series: Modern Peacemakers. 2007, Chelsea House LB $30.00 (978-0-7910-9433-4). An evenhanded profile of the Nobel Peace Prize winner, including the text of her acceptance speech. (Rev: SLJ 8/07) [921]

8087 Spink, Kathryn. *Mother Teresa: A Complete Authorized Biography* (9–12). 1997, HarperSanFrancisco paper $15.95 (978-0-06-251553-7). This authorized biography, written by a woman who for several years worked with Mother Teresa's Missionaries of Charity, chronicles the nun's life story from her birth in the Balkans to her death in Calcutta in 1997. (Rev: BL 11/1/97) [921]

8088 Teresa, Mother. *Mother Teresa: Come Be My Light; The Private Writings of the Saint of Calcutta* (9–12). 2007, Doubleday $22.95 (978-0-385-52037-9). Mother Teresa's personal thoughts and doubts are revealed in this collection of her letters and journal entries. (Rev: BL 10/1/07) [921]

Australia and the Pacific Islands

CONWAY, JILL KER

8089 Conway, Jill Ker. *The Road from Coorain* (10–12). 1990, Vintage paper $12.00 (978-0-679-72436-0). The youth and adolescence in Australia of the woman who would later be the president of Smith College. (Rev: VOYA 4/90) [921]

Europe

ALEXANDER THE GREAT

8090 Behnke, Alison. *The Conquests of Alexander the Great* (6–12). Series: Pivotal Moments in History. 2007, Twenty-First Century LB $38.60 (978-0-8225-5920-7). A thorough biography of Alexander's life and achievements, with background information on the time as well as details of battles, maps, a timeline, and key figures. (Rev: SLJ 9/07) [921]

BLAIR, TONY

8091 Hinman, Bonnie. *Tony Blair. Rev. ed.* (7–10). Series: Major World Leaders. 2006, Chelsea House $30.00 (978-0-7910-9216-3). An updated profile (to 2006, be-fore his resignation) of the leader of the British Labour Party who in 1997 became the youngest prime minister in nearly 200 years. (Rev: BL 1/1–15/07) [921]

CAESAR, AUGUSTUS

8092 Everitt, Anthony. *Augustus: The Life of Rome's First Emperor* (9–12). 2006, Random House $26.95 (978-1-4000-6128-0). After the assassination of Julius Caesar in 44 B.C. Gaius Octavius (later to be known as Caesar Augustus) became a contender for the Roman throne and proved himself by defeating Mark Antony in battle and converting Rome into a thriving empire. (Rev: BL 10/15/06) [921]

CATHERINE THE GREAT

8093 Alexander, John T. *Catherine the Great: Life and Legend* (10–12). 1989, Oxford paper $24.95 (978-0-19-506162-8). In a compelling narrative, the author traces the life of this amazing Russian leader who was born an obscure German princess. [921]

8094 Whitelaw, Nancy. *Catherine the Great and the Enlightenment in Russia* (8–12). Series: European Queens. 2004, Morgan Reynolds LB $26.95 (978-1-931798-27-3). The colorful life of the Russian empress from childhood in her native Germany to her pivotal role in leading her adopted country into full participation in the cultural and political life of Europe. (Rev: BL 12/15/04; SLJ 12/04) [921]

CHARLEMAGNE

8095 Wilson, Derek. *Charlemagne* (10–12). 2006, Doubleday $26.00 (978-0-385-51670-9). Introduces the significance of the reign of Charles the Great and his part in the spread of Christianity. (Rev: BL 5/1/06; SLJ 8/06) [921]

CLEISTHENES

8096 Parton, Sarah. *Cleisthenes: Founder of Athenian Democracy* (7–10). Series: Leaders of Ancient Greece. 2004, Rosen LB $33.25 (978-0-8239-3826-1). Information about Cleisthenes and his times is carefully couched in discussion of the sources used and the ways in which this material has been gathered and analyzed. (Rev: SLJ 9/04) [921]

CROMWELL, OLIVER

8097 Gaunt, Peter. *Oliver Cromwell* (10–12). Series: British Library Historic Lives. 2004, New York Univ. $25.00 (978-0-8147-3164-2). A compact, well-illustrated, and balanced profile of Cromwell, who altered the course of British history in the mid-17th century, clearly presenting historical and religious context. (Rev: BL 10/15/04; SLJ 4/05) [941.06]

DIANA, PRINCESS OF WALES

8098 Owings, Lisa. *Diana: The People's Princess* (7–10). Illus. Series: Lives Cut Short. 2012, ABDO LB $34.22 (978-161783545-2). This profile includes first-person quotes, comments from insiders and critics, interesting sidebars, and relevant photographs. (Rev: BL 12/1/12) [921]

DIDEROT, DENIS

8099 Stark, Sam. *Diderot: French Philosopher and Father of the Encyclopedia* (9–12). Series: Philosophers of the Enlightenment. 2005, Rosen LB $33.25 (978-1-4042-0418-8). Presents the life and achievements of Diderot, focusing on the Frenchman's work on the Encyclopédie, one of the Enlightenment's most significant books. (Rev: BL 11/1/05) [034]

ELEANOR OF AQUITAINE

8100 Sapet, Kerrily. *Eleanor of Aquitaine: Medieval Queen* (8–11). 2006, Morgan Reynolds $26.95 (978-1-931798-90-7). A look at the rise and fall of Eleanor of Aquitaine, who was Queen of France and then Queen of England during the Middle Ages. (Rev: BL 8/06; SLJ 8/06) [921]

8101 Weir, Alison. *Eleanor of Aquitaine: A Life* (10–12). 2000, Ballantine $28.00 (978-0-345-40540-1); paper $15.95 (978-0-345-43487-6). The biography of the 12th-century French queen who later became Queen of England and mother of Richard the Lionhearted. (Rev: BL 1/1–15/00) [921]

FRANK FAMILY

8102 Denenberg, Barry. *Shadow Life: A Portrait of Anne Frank and Her Family* (6–10). 2005, Scholastic $16.95 (978-0-439-41678-8). In this engaging title from the Shadow Life series, author Barry Denenberg tells the complete story of Anne Frank and her family from their earlier life in Frankfurt to their eventual transport to Nazi concentration camps. (Rev: BL 2/1/05*; SLJ 4/05; VOYA 4/05) [940.53]

FRANK, ANNE

8103 Frank, Anne. *The Diary of a Young Girl: The Definitive Edition* (7–12). Trans. by Susan Massotty. 1995, Doubleday $27.50 (978-0-385-47378-1). This edition contains all of the writings of Anne Frank, including some short passages in the diary that had been formerly suppressed. (Rev: BL 4/15/95) [921]

8104 Lee, Carol Ann. *Anne Frank and the Children of the Holocaust* (7–10). 2006, Viking $16.99 (978-0-670-06107-5). Lee describes Anne Frank's life before she went into hiding, providing historical context and stories of other children who suffered. (Rev: BL 10/1/06; HB 3–4/05; LMC 4–5/07; SLJ 12/06) [940.53]

8105 Lindwer, Willy. *The Last Seven Months of Anne Frank* (8–12). 1992, Doubleday paper $12.95 (978-0-385-42360-1). Moving testimony from six women interned in a concentration camp with Anne Frank tells of the tragic conclusion of the young diarist's life. (Rev: BL 3/15/91) [921]

8106 Metselaar, Menno, and Ruud van der Rol. *Anne Frank: Her Life in Words and Pictures* (6–12). Trans. by Arnold J. Pomerans. 2009, Flash Point $19.99 (978-1-59643-546-9); paper $12.99 (978-1-59643-547-6). Short excerpts from Anne Frank's diary are interspersed with news photos, scrapbook pages, and family history to paint a rich and harrowing picture of Nazism, World War II, and the Frank family's place in history. Sydney Taylor Book Honor 2010; ALA Notable Books 2010; Boston Globe–Horn Book nonfiction Honor 2010. (Rev: BL 11/1/09*; HB 1–2/11; LMC 11/09; SLJ 10/09) [921]

8107 Muller, Melissa. *Anne Frank: A Biography* (9–12). Trans. by Robert Kimber. 1998, Henry Holt paper $14.00 (978-0-8050-5997-7). In this supplement to Anne Frank's diary, the author includes new information about the Frank family and about possible betrayers of their hiding place, as well as insights into the character, personality, and quality of life of Anne's parents, relatives, and friends. (Rev: SLJ 4/99) [921]

HAVEL, VACLAV

8108 Duberstein, John. *A Velvet Revolution: Vaclav Havel and the Fall of Communism* (8–11). 2006, Morgan Reynolds $26.95 (978-1-931798-85-3). This profile of the magnetic Czech leader cleverly interweaves history with biographical information (includes photos and resource lists). (Rev: BL 7/06; SLJ 9/06) [921]

HIMMLER, HEINRICH

8109 Worth, Richard. *Heinrich Himmler: Murderous Architect of the Holocaust* (8–11). Series: Holocaust Heroes and Nazi Criminals. 2005, Enslow LB $27.93 (978-0-7660-2532-5). A profile of the career of the architect of Nazi Germany's lethally effective campaign against the Jews and other victims of the Holocaust. (Rev: BL 10/15/05; SLJ 1/06) [940.53]

HITLER, ADOLF

8110 Fuchs, Thomas. *The Hitler Fact Book* (10–12). 1990, Fountain paper $14.95 (978-0-9623202-9-3). All sorts of trivia about the dictator and the high German officials around him. (Rev: BL 3/1/90; SLJ 6/90) [921]

8111 Hitler, Adolf. *Mein Kampf* (11–12). Trans. by Ralph Manheim. 1998, Houghton Mifflin $40.00 (978-0-395-95105-7); paper $22.00 (978-0-395-92503-4). Hitler's blueprint for the Third Reich includes autobiographical reflections. [921]

8112 Kershaw, Ian. *Hitler, 1889–1936: Hubris* (10–12). 1999, Norton $35.00 (978-0-393-04671-7); paper

$21.95 (978-0-393-32035-0). As well as a biography, this account stresses historical issues, events, and circumstances surrounding Hitler's rise to power. (Rev: BL 1/1–15/99*) [92i]

8113 Toland, John. *Adolf Hitler* (10–12). 1976, Doubleday paper $23.00 (978-0-385-42053-2). A detailed biography of Hitler that is based on many documents and interviews with more than 250 people. [921]

JOAN OF ARC

8114 Spoto, Donald. *Joan: The Mysterious Life of the Heretic Who Became a Saint* (9–12). 2007, HarperCollins $24.95 (978-0-06-081517-2). Based on newly translated trial transcripts from the Middle Ages, this is a fresh look at Joan of Arc and how she was proclaimed a heretic and a saint by the same institution. (Rev: BL 10/1/06) [944]

JOHN PAUL II, POPE

8115 Behnke, Alison. *Pope John Paul II* (7–10). Series: A&E Biography. 2005, Lerner paper $7.95 (978-0-8225-3387-0). This very human portrait of Pope John Paul II traces his life and presents the views of his critics as well as his supporters. (Rev: BL 10/1/05; SLJ 9/05) [282]

8116 Flynn, Raymond. *John Paul II: A Personal Portrait of the Pope and the Man* (10–12). 2001, St. Martin's paper $14.95 (978-0-312-28328-5). A profile of Pope John Paul II by a former U.S. ambassador to the Vatican. (Rev: BL 4/15/01) [921]

8117 Mainardi, Alessandro. *The Life of Pope John Paul II . . . in Comics!* (7–10). Illus. by Werner Maresta. 2006, Papercutz $16.95 (978-1-59707-039-3); paper $9.95 (978-1-59707-057-7). A biography of the life of Pope John Paul II, told in graphic-novel format, covering his childhood, journey into priesthood, his accomplishments, and leadership as the Pope. (Rev: BL 10/1/06; LMC 4–5/07; SLJ 1/07) [921]

LENIN, VLADIMIR ILICH

8118 Naden, Corinne J., and Rose Blue. *Lenin* (6–10). Series: Importance Of. 2005, Gale $32.45 (978-1-59018-233-8). The life and political career of Vladimir Lenin, founder of the Russian Communist Party. (Rev: BL 6/1–15/04) [921]

MACHIAVELLI, NICCOLÒ

8119 King, Ross. *Machiavelli: Philosopher of Power* (11–12). 2007, HarperCollins $21.95 (978-0-06-081717-6). The great political thinker is revealed as a clever diplomat and keen observer while at the same time using others for his own ends; King places Machiavelli in historical context, giving the reader insight into the intrigues of the time. (Rev: BL 6/1–15/07) [921]

MARIE ANTOINETTE

8120 Lever, Evelyne. *Marie Antoinette: The Last Queen of France* (10–12). Trans. by Catherine Temerson. 2000, Farrar paper $16.95 (978-0-312-28333-9). Using memoirs and other primary documents, the author has written a fine biography of Marie Antoinette and an accurate picture of court life at Versailles. [921]

MARY, QUEEN OF SCOTS

8121 Lotz, Nancy, and Carlene Phillips. *Mary Queen of Scots* (7–10). Series: European Queens. 2007, Morgan Reynolds LB $27.95 (978-1-59935-040-0). Chronicling the life of Mary Queen of Scots and her involvement in politics, conspiracies, and religious conflict, this volume will be helpful for report writers. (Rev: BL 6/1–15/07; SLJ 9/07) [921]

MUSSOLINI, BENITO

8122 Bosworth, R. J. B. *Mussolini* (10–12). 2002, Oxford paper $24.95 (978-0-340-80988-4). A fascinating biography of the Italian dictator who used his power for selfish ends. (Rev: BL 6/1–15/02) [921]

NAPOLEON I

8123 Landau, Elaine. *Napoleon Bonaparte* (7–10). 2006, Twenty-First Century LB $27.93 (978-0-8225-3420-4). This biography of Bonaparte chronicles his most important milestones with the help of a timeline, map, quotations, and black-and-white photographs. (Rev: SLJ 6/06) [921]

NOSTRADAMUS

8124 Roberts, Russell. *The Life and Times of Nostradamus* (9–12). Series: Biography from Ancient Civilizations. 2008, Mitchell Lane LB $20.95 (978-1-58415-544-7). The myths and lore surrounding this mysterious figure — sometimes called a prophet — will intrigue readers and researchers. (Rev: BL 4/15/08) [133.3092]

PETER THE GREAT, CZAR OF RUSSIA

8125 Massie, Robert K. *Peter the Great: His Life and World* (10–12). 1980, Knopf paper $16.00 (978-0-345-29806-5). A lengthy but readable biography of the great Russian czar who founded the city that for centuries was the country's capital. [921]

PUTIN, VLADIMIR

8126 Putin, Vladimir, et al. *First Person: An Astonishingly Frank Self-Portrait by Russia's President* (10–12). Trans. by Catherine A. Fitzpatrick. 2000, Public Affairs paper $15.00 (978-1-58648-018-9). Although now out of date (coverage ends in early 2000), this biographical sketch assembled from a number of interviews gives valuable background information on this leader of the Russian state. (Rev: BL 5/1/00) [921]

8127 Streissguth, Thomas. *Vladimir Putin* (7–10). Series: A&E Biography. 2005, Lerner LB $29.27 (978-0-8225-2374-1); paper $7.95 (978-0-8225-9630-1). Putin's professional and political life take center stage in this biography that will be useful for report writers. (Rev: BL 9/1/05) [947.086]

ROMANOV, ANASTASIA

8128 Lovell, James Blair. *Anastasia: The Lost Princess* (9–12). 1991, Regnery Gateway $24.95 (978-0-89526-536-4). The story of the woman who claims to be the only surviving daughter of the last czar of Russia. (Rev: BL 8/91) [921]

SARKOZY, NICOLAS

8129 Abrams, Dennis. *Nicolas Sarkozy* (7–10). Illus. Series: Modern World Leaders. 2009, Chelsea House $30.00 (978-160413081-2). With many quotations from Sarkozy and others, Abrams covers the French president's private life and public achievements. (Rev: BL 6/1–15/09) [921]

SCHINDLER, OSKAR

8130 Fensch, Thomas, ed. *Oskar Schindler and His List: The Man, the Book, the Film, the Holocaust and Its Survivors* (9–12). 1995, Paul S. Eriksson $24.95 (978-0-8397-6472-4). Articles, essays, and interviews relating to the development of the book and the film *Schindler's List*. (Rev: BL 9/15/95) [921]

SCHOLL, HANS AND SOPHIE

8131 Axelrod, Toby. *Hans and Sophie Scholl: German Resisters of the White Rose* (7–12). Series: Holocaust Biographies. 2001, Rosen LB $31.95 (978-0-8239-3316-7). The Scholls, brother and sister, were arrested and executed for their role in organizing the group known as the White Rose, which worked to expose the Nazis' atrocities. (Rev: SLJ 6/01) [921]

SOCRATES

8132 Navia, Luis E. *Socrates: A Life Examined* (10–12). 2007, Prometheus $28.00 (978-1-59102-501-6). Navia uses primary and secondary sources — including the writings of Aristophanes and Plato — to create an account of Socrates' life and times. (Rev: BL 3/15/07; SLJ 4/07) [183]

SOLON

8133 Randall, Bernard. *Solon: The Lawmaker of Athens* (7–10). Series: Leaders of Ancient Greece. 2004, Rosen LB $33.25 (978-0-8239-3829-2). Information about Solon and his times is carefully introduced with discussion of the sources used and the ways in which this material has been gathered and analyzed. (Rev: SLJ 9/04) [921]

STALIN, JOSEPH

8134 Cunningham, Kevin. *Joseph Stalin and the Soviet Union* (9–12). 2006, Morgan Reynolds LB $26.95 (978-1-931798-94-5). This biography of Stalin provides a wealth of information including color illustrations, photos, glossary and a timeline. (Rev: BL 6/1–15/06; SLJ 6/06) [921]

8135 Radzinsky, Edvard. *Stalin: The First In-depth Biography Based on Explosive New Documents from Russia's Secret Archives* (10–12). Trans. by H. T. Willetts. 1996, Doubleday paper $16.95 (978-0-385-47954-7). Radzinsky's access to previously unavailable archival information makes this a vivid portrait of the iron-fist dictator. [921]

THEMISTOCLES

8136 Morris, Ian Macgregor. *Themistocles: Defender of Greece* (7–10). Series: Leaders of Ancient Greece. 2004, Rosen LB $33.25 (978-0-8239-3830-8). Information about Themistocles and his times is carefully couched in discussion of the sources used and the ways in which this material has been gathered and analyzed. (Rev: SLJ 9/04) [921]

VAN BEEK, CATO BONTJES

8137 Friedman, Ina R. *Flying Against the Wind: The Story of a Young Woman Who Defied the Nazis* (6–10). 1995, Lodgepole paper $11.95 (978-1-886721-00-5). The story of Cato Bontjes van Beek, who grew up in a progressive German household and was executed by the Nazis with her boyfriend for joining an underground movement. (Rev: BL 7/95; VOYA 4/96) [921]

VICTORIA, QUEEN

8138 Hibbert, Christopher. *Queen Victoria: A Personal History* (10–12). 2000, Basic paper $21.00 (978-0-306-81085-5). Using many original sources, including Victoria's letters and journals, the author has produced an intimate look at the life and reign of this long-serving British monarch. [921]

VLAD III, PRINCE OF WALLACHIA

8139 Florescu, Radu R. N., and Raymond T. McNally. *Dracula: Prince of Many Faces, His Life and His Times* (9–12). 1989, Little, Brown paper $16.95 (978-0-316-28656-5). The biography of the 15th-century Romanian prince who is the real man behind the vampire stories. [921]

WALLENBERG, RAOUL

8140 Borden, Louise W. *His Name Was Raoul Wallenberg: Courage, Rescue, and Mystery During World War II* (7–12). Illus. 2012, Houghton Mifflin $18.99 (978-061850755-9). A free-verse portrait of Wallenberg's life, his courageous efforts to save tens of thousands of Jews, and his mysterious disappearance in the hands of the Soviets; the many photographs, documents, and profiles will appeal to reluctant readers. Sydney Taylor Book Award 2013. Lexile 1080L (Rev: BL 9/15/11; HB 1–2/12; LMC 8–9/12*; SLJ 1/12; VOYA 2/12)

8141 Smith, Danny. *Lost Hero: Raoul Wallenberg's Dramatic Quest to Save the Jews of Hungary* (9–12). 2002, Trafalgar paper $13.00 (978-0-00-711117-6). This readable biography details Wallenberg's efforts to help thousands of Jews escape from the Nazis; a revised and updated edition. (Rev: BL 1/1–15/02) [921]

South and Central America, Canada, and Mexico

CALCINES, EDUARDO F.

8142 Calcines, Eduardo F. *Leaving Glorytown: One Boy's Struggle Under Castro* (7–10). 2009, Farrar $16.95 (978-037434394-1). The author writes of his childhood in Communist Cuba in the 1960s, the hardships that Castro's regime brought to Cuba, and how they affected one close family. ⌒ Lexile 800L (Rev: BL 4/1/09; SLJ 6/1/09*; VOYA 4/09) [921]

CARLOS THE JACKAL

8143 Follain, John. *Jackal: The Complete Story of the Legendary Terrorist, Carlos the Jackal* (11–12). 1998, Arcade $25.95 (978-1-55970-466-3). The life and times of Ilich Ramirez Sanchez, better known as international terrorist Carlos the Jackal, are explored in detail. (Rev: BL 11/15/98) [921]

CASTRO, FIDEL

8144 Foss, Clive. *Fidel Castro* (10–12). 2000, Sutton paper $9.95 (978-0-7509-2384-2). A short, readable introduction to Cuba and the ruler who has withstood America's opposition for nearly 50 years. (Rev: BL 8/00) [921]

8145 Geyer, Georgie Anne. *Guerrilla Prince: The Untold Story of Fidel Castro. 3rd rev. ed.* (10–12). 2001, Andrews McMeel paper $16.95 (978-0-7407-2064-2). This biography focuses on Castro's personality and pictures him as a paranoid megalomaniac. [921]

CHAVEZ, HUGO

8146 Jones, Bart. *Hugo: The Hugo Chavez Story from Mud Hut to Perpetual Revolution* (9–12). 2007, Steerforth $30.00 (978-1-58642-135-9). Venezuela's fascinating president is the focus of this interesting profile, which covers his deprived childhood, military training, political ambitions, concern for the poor, and controversial policies. (Rev: BL 9/1/07) [921]

8147 Marcano, Cristina, and Alberto Barrera Tyszka. *Hugo Chavez* (10–12). Trans. by Kristina Cordero. 2007, Random House $27.95 (978-0-679-45666-7). The controversial Venezuelan leader is placed in social and historical context in this lively biography that includes photographs, excerpts from his diary, and interviews. (Rev: BL 9/1/07) [921]

8148 Young, Jeff C. *Hugo Chavez: Leader of Venezuela* (6–12). 2007, Morgan Reynolds LB $27.95 (978-1-59935-068-4). Covers the life of Venezuela's leader from his childhood to the present, as well as his military career, brief imprisonment, presidency, and attitude toward the United States. (Rev: BL 8/07) [921]

GUEVARA, CHE

8149 Havelin, Kate. *Che Guevara* (7–12). Series: Biography. 2006, Twenty-First Century LB $27.93 (978-0-8225-5951-1). This is a brief but thorough profile of the revolutionary who had so much impact in his short life. (Rev: SLJ 3/07) [921]

8150 Kallen, Stuart A. *Che Guevara: You Win or You Die* (7–10). Illus. 2012, Lerner/Twenty-First Century LB $33.27 (978-082259035-4). A clear profile of Guevara's revolutionary ideals and activities. (Rev: BL 11/1/12; SLJ 10/12) [921]

8151 Miller, Calvin Craig. *Che Guevara: In Search of the Revolution* (7–10). 2006, Morgan Reynolds LB $26.95 (978-1-931798-93-8). A captivating biography of Che Guevara, with details on his personal life, his role as a revolutionary leader in Cuba, and the time he spent working with Castro. (Rev: BL 8/06; SLJ 3/07) [921]

8152 Uschan, Michael V. *Che Guevara, Revolutionary* (8–11). Series: The Twentieth Century's Most Influential Hispanics. 2006, Gale LB $31.20 (978-1-59018-970-2). A balanced profile of the socialist rebel who has become a popular icon. (Rev: BL 4/1/07) [921]

MENCHU, RIGOBERTA

8153 Kallen, Stuart A. *Rigoberta Menchú: Indian Rights Activist* (6–12). Series: The Twentieth Century's Most Influential Hispanics. 2006, Gale LB $32.45 (978-1-59018-975-7). A life of the Nobel laureate and advocate for human rights. (Rev: SLJ 9/07) [921]

8154 Schulze, Julie. *Rigoberta Menchú Túm: Champion of Human Rights* (8–12). Series: Contemporary Profile and Policy. 1998, John Gordon Burke $20.00 (978-0-934272-42-1); paper $12.95 (978-0-934272-43-8). This biography combines the life story of Nobel Peace Prize-winner Rigoberta Menchu Tum with the story of the struggle of the Mayan people for equality in Guatemala and throughout Central America. (Rev: BL 4/1/98) [921]

8155 Wagner, Heather Lehr. *Rigoberta Menchú Tum: Activist for Indigenous Rights in Guatemala* (8–12).

2007, Chelsea House LB $30.00 (978-0-7910-8998-9). An introduction to the life of the 1992 Nobel Peace Prize winner, from her impoverished childhood in a Mayan-K'iche community, through the murder of her activist parents and siblings, to her fight for the rights of indigenous people. (Rev: BL 6/1–15/07) [921]

ROMERO, OSCAR

8156 Wright, Scott. *Oscar Romero and the Communion of Saints* (10–12). Illus. 2010, Orbis paper $20 (978-15707583-9-3). Wright tells the life story of Oscar Romero, the Catholic archbishop of El Salvador who was assassinated in 1980. (Rev: BLO 12/1/09) [921]

Miscellaneous Interesting Lives

Collective

8157 Baggett, Jennifer, et al. *The Lost Girls: Three Friends, Four Continents, One Unconventional Detour Around the World* (10–12). 2010, HarperCollins $24.99 (978-006168906-2). Three young women in their 20s encounter plenty of adventure — as well as questions about leadership, teamwork, careers, and self-preservation — as they travel the world during a year off work. ℮ (Rev: BL 4/1–15/10) [920]

8158 Deng, Ayuel Leek, et al. *Courageous Journey: Walking the Lost Boys' Path from the Sudan to America* (11–12). Illus. 2008, New Horizon $24.95 (978-088282334-8). Deng and Ngor, refugees from Sudan's brutal civil war, tell the story of their harrowing survival and long journey to the United States; for mature teens. (Rev: BL 8/08) [920]

8159 Gilbreth, Frank B., and Ernestine Gilbreth Carey. *Cheaper by the Dozen.* Rev. ed. (8–12). 1963, Crowell paper $11.95 (978-0-06-008460-8). A biographical account of the Gilbreth family, whose 12 children were reared by a father who believed in time and efficiency applications even in the home. [920]

8160 Murphy, Bill. *In a Time of War: The Proud and Perilous Journey of West Point's Class of 2002* (10–12). Illus. 2008, Henry Holt $27.50 (978-0-8050-8679-9). Murphy follows the lives of several West Point graduates as they choose their specialties, form personal relationships, and are posted to combat zones. ℮ (Rev: BL 8/08) [920]

8161 Salsitz, Norman, and Amalie Petranker Salsitz. *Against All Odds: A Tale of Two Survivors* (9–12). 1991, Holocaust Publns $24.95 (978-0-89604-148-6); paper $12.95 (978-0-89604-149-3). In these recollections of the Holocaust by two Polish Jews who married after the war, similar tales of Nazi brutality, false identi-

ties, close escapes, and great endurance are told. (Rev: BL 9/15/91) [920]

8162 Silverwood, John, and Jean Silverwood. *Black Wave: A Family's Adventure at Sea and the Disaster That Saved Them* (10–12). 2008, Random House $25.00 (978-1-4000-6655-1). A dramatic account of a how the family's devastating wreck at sea turned into an event that pulled the family closer together. ⌒ ℮ (Rev: BLO 8/28/08; SLJ 9/08) [920]

8163 Sjoholm, Barbara, ed. *Steady as She Goes: Women's Adventures at Sea* (10–12). 2003, Seal paper $15.95 (978-1-58005-094-4). Women writers describe a variety of seagoing situations — some scary, some joyous, some athletic, some thought-provoking. (Rev: SLJ 5/04)

8164 Welch, Liz, et al. *The Kids Are All Right* (10–12). 2009, Harmony $24.99 (978-030739604-4). Four children, who are suddenly orphaned and split up, strive to keep in touch with each other and make sense of the tragedy that has befallen them; for mature readers. Alex Award 2010. (Rev: BL 9/15/09) [306.88]

8165 Yolen, Jane, and Heidi E. Y. Stemple. *Bad Girls: Sirens, Jezebels, Murderesses, Thieves and Other Female Villains* (7–10). Illus. by Rebecca Guay. 2013, Charlesbridge $18.95 (978-158089185-1). Twenty-six notorious women ranging from Delilah, Cleopatra, and Queen Mary to Calamity Jane, Bonnie Parker, and Typhoid Mary are introduced in an attractive combination of text and portraits. (Rev: BL 2/15/13*; SLJ 4/13) [920]

Individual

8166 Satrapi, Marjane. *Persepolis 2: The Story of a Return* (10–12). 2004, Pantheon $17.95 (978-0-375-

42288-1). Picking up from the comic-strip memoir *Persepolis* (2003), Satrapi recounts her time at school in Vienna, far from her home in Tehran, and her difficulties adjusting to adolescence in a very foreign country. (Rev: BL 8/04; SLJ 12/04) [741.5]

AFZAL-KHAN, FAWZIA

8167 Afzal-Khan, Fawzia. *Lahore with Love: Growing Up with Girlfriends, Pakistani-Style* (11–12). 2010, Syracuse Univ. paper $19.95 (978-08156092-4-7). Describing her life in Pakistan (and telling the story of her arrival and work in the United States), Afzal-Khan emphasizes the importance of female friendship in a country where women face so many challenges; for mature readers. (Rev: BL 4/1–15/10) [921]

AKBAR, SAID HYDER

8168 Akbar, Said Hyder, and Susan Burton. *Come Back to Afghanistan: A California Teenager's Story* (9–12). 2005, Bloomsbury $24.95 (978-1-58234-520-8). Said Hyder Akbar, son of Afghani immigrants to the United States, writes movingly about his visits to his parents' homeland in the wake of the fall of the Taliban government in late 2001. (Rev: BL 9/1/05; SLJ 12/05*) [921]

ALI, NUJOOD

8169 Ali, Nujood, and Delphine Minoui. *I Am Nujood, Age 10 and Divorced* (11–12). 2010, Three Rivers paper $12 (978-03075896-7-5). This is the extraordinary first-person story of a brave 10-year-old Yemeni girl, named *Glamour* magazine's Woman of the Year in 2008, who fled the husband three times her age who repeatedly raped and beat her — and headed straight for the courthouse; for mature readers. (Rev: BL 2/1–15/10) [921]

ALLISON, PETER

8170 Allison, Peter. *Whatever You Do, Don't Run: True Tales of a Botswana Safari Guide* (9–12). 2007, Lyons paper $16.95 (978-0-7627-4565-4). An entertaining story about how Allison took a job at a game camp in southern Africa and survived to become an experienced guide. (Rev: BL 9/15/07) [916.88304]

APPELT, KATHI

8171 Appelt, Kathi. *My Father's Summers: A Daughter's Memoir* (6–12). 2004, Henry Holt $15.95 (978-0-8050-7362-1). In a series of prose poems, Appelt paints a poignant portrait of her life growing up in Houston and the pain caused by the extended absences of her father. (Rev: BCCB 7–8/04; BL 6/1–15/04; SLJ 6/04; VOYA 6/04) [813]

ASHCRAFT, TAMI OLDHAM

8172 Ashcraft, Tami Oldham, and Susea McGearhart. *Red Sky in Mourning: A True Story of Love, Loss, and Survival at Sea* (10–12). 2002, Hyperion $23.95 (978-

0-7868-6791-2). In this moving memoir of survival and loss, the author recounts how a storm at sea swept her fiancé away, leaving her alone to pilot the damaged craft back to harbor. (Rev: BL 5/1/02) [910.9164]

AYERS, NATHANIEL

8173 Lopez, Steve. *The Soloist: A Lost Dream, an Unlikely Friendship, and the Redemptive Power of Music* (9–12). 2008, Putnam $25.95 (978-0-399-15506-2). Thirty years after Nathaniel Ayers experienced his first schizophrenic episode while studying classical bass at Julliard, *LA Times* columnist Steve Lopez finds him playing on a street corner and tries to help him. (Rev: BL 3/15/08) [921]

BAIEV, KHASSAN

8174 Baiev, Khassan, et al. *The Oath: A Surgeon Under Fire* (10–12). 2003, Walker $26.00 (978-0-8027-1404-6). A Chechnya doctor explains his support for his country in the face of great danger and offers insights into the republic's reasons for seeking independence from Russia. (Rev: BL 8/03) [947.5]

BAILEY, ELISABETH TOVA

8175 Bailey, Elisabeth Tova. *The Sound of a Wild Snail Eating* (10–12). 2010, Algonquin $19.95 (978-156512606-0). Bailey recounts how tending a snail distracted her from a debilitating virus and helped her to enjoy life's simple pleasures. (Rev: BL 10/1–15/10) [921]

BARAKAT, IBTISAM

8176 Barakat, Ibtisam. *Tasting the Sky: A Palestinian Childhood* (7–10). 2007, Farrar $16.00 (978-0-374-35733-7). A memoir of the author's war-torn youth, which included running from bomb attacks, living at detention centers, and uneven schooling. ALA Notable Books 2008. (Rev: BL 3/15/07; LMC 10/07; SLJ 5/07*) [921]

BARBER, CHARLES

8177 Barber, Charles. *Songs from the Black Chair: A Memoir of Mental Interiors* (11–12). 2005, Univ. of Nebraska $22.00 (978-0-8032-1298-5). Barber writes movingly about how the suicide of a close friend and Barber's own struggles with obsessive-compulsive disorder led him to become a psychiatrist; for mature teens. (Rev: BL 3/1/05) [921]

BARKER, ADELE

8178 Barker, Adele. *Not Quite Paradise: An American Sojourn in Sri Lanka* (11–12). Illus. 2010, Beacon $24.95 (978-080700061-8). Barker details her time spent teaching in Sri Lanka, from her life as a university professor to mundane aspects of everyday life to the civil unrest gripping the country; for mature readers. (Rev: BL 1/1–15/10) [921]

BEAH, ISHMAEL

8179 Beah, Ishmael. *A Long Way Gone: Memoirs of a Boy Soldier* (11–12). 2007, Farrar $22.00 (978-0-374-95191-7). This is the terrible story of Ishmael's time as a child soldier in Sierra Leone; happily at the age of 15 he was rescued by the United Nations, brought to the United States, and went on to graduate from Oberlin; for mature teens. ⌒ (Rev: BL 11/15/06) [921]

BEASLEY, SANDRA

8180 Beasley, Sandra. *Don't Kill the Birthday Girl: Tales from an Allergic Life* (9–12). 2011, Crown $25.95 (978-0-3075-8811-1). A fascinating memoir from a person with unusually wide-ranging allergies, detailing how these have affected her life (who dare she kiss? what to drink or eat at a party?). ℮ (Rev: SLJ 9/11) [921]

BECHDEL, ALISON

8181 Bechdel, Alison. *Fun Home: A Family Tragicomic* (11–12). 2006, Houghton Mifflin $19.95 (978-0-618-47794-4). In this excellent and moving graphic memoir, Allison Bechdel writes candidly about her lesbianism and her relationship with her father, who she later learned was gay; for mature teens. (Rev: BL 3/15/06) [921]

BEHR, HANS-GEORG

8182 Behr, Hans-Georg. *Almost a Childhood: Growing Up Among the Nazis* (9–12). Trans. by Anthea Bell. 2006, Trafalgar $24.95 (978-1-86207-781-2). The author tells of growing up surrounded by key figures in the Nazi regime, including Hermann Göring and Josef Goebbels, who were friends of his parents. (Rev: BL 8/06) [921]

BELL, MARGARET

8183 Bell, Margaret. *When Montana and I Were Young: A Frontier Childhood* (10–12). 2002, Univ. of Nebraska $30.00 (978-0-8032-1325-8). In this compelling memoir of a childhood on America's Great Plains frontier, Bell tells how she managed to hold on to both dignity and hope despite a series of daunting hardships. (Rev: BL 2/15/02) [921]

BELLIL, SAMIRA

8184 Bellil, Samira. *To Hell and Back: The Life of Samira Bellil* (11–12). Trans. by Lucy R. McNair. 2008, Univ. of Nebraska $19.95 (978-080321356-2). After years of life on the streets in a rough suburb of Paris, including degradation and rape, author Samira Bellil chose to be heard, not only for herself but for all abused women; for mature readers. (Rev: BL 9/15/08) [921]

BEN-ATAR, ROMA NUTKIEWICZ

8185 Ben-Atar, Roma Nutkiewicz, and Doron S. Ben-Atar. *What Time and Sadness Spared: Mother and Son Confront the Holocaust* (9–12). 2006, Univ. of Virginia $27.95 (978-0-8139-2513-4). In this searing Holocaust memoir co-written with her son, Roma Ben-Atar recalls the horrors of the Warsaw Ghetto and life in Nazi concentration camps. (Rev: BL 3/15/06) [940.53]

BERG, MARY

8186 Berg, Mary. *The Diary of Mary Berg: Growing Up in the Warsaw Ghetto* (10–12). 2007, Oneworld $25.00 (978-1-85168-472-4). Good readers will appreciate this intense diary — 12 notebooks that Berg kept during the terrible years she spent as a Jew in Hitler's Europe, partly in the Warsaw ghetto. (Rev: BL 2/1/07) [940.53]

BERNSTEIN, HARRY

8187 Bernstein, Harry. *The Invisible Wall: A Love Story That Broke Barriers* (9–12). 2006, Ballantine $22.95 (978-0-345-49580-8). Just before World War I an invisible wall existed on a street in Lancashire, England, dividing the Jews from the Christians, but the Jewish sister of the author ignores that barrier when she falls in love with a Christian boy and must keep it a secret in a place where religious tolerance has yet to exist. (Rev: BL 11/1/06; SLJ 6/07) [921]

BITTON-JACKSON, LIVIA

8188 Bitton-Jackson, Livia. *Hello, America* (9–12). 2005, Simon & Schuster $16.95 (978-0-689-86755-2). In the final installment of a trilogy about her life before, during, and after the Holocaust, the Czech-born author tells of her experiences as an 18-year-old immigrant to Brooklyn in 1951. (Rev: BL 1/1–15/05; SLJ 3/05; VOYA 4/05) [940.53]

BLANCO, JODEE

8189 Blanco, Jodee. *Please Stop Laughing at Me . . . One Woman's Inspirational Journey* (10–12). 2003, Adams paper $12.95 (978-1-58062-836-5). In this memoir of her school years, Blanco recounts the years of relentless bullying and torment she endured before corrective surgery for a physical deformity changed her appearance and outlook. (Rev: BL 3/15/03; SLJ 5/03) [305.235]

BONHOEFFER, DIETRICH

8190 Martin, Michael J. *Dietrich Bonhoeffer* (7–12). Illus. Series: Champion of Freedom. 2012, Morgan Reynolds LB $28.95 (978-159935169-8). Tells the story of the German theologian who opposed Nazi activities, conspired in a plot to assassinate Hitler, and died in a concentration camp in 1945. ℮ (Rev: BL 3/15/12*; LMC 10/12; SLJ 6/12) [921]

BOYLE, BRIAN

8191 Boyle, Brian, and Bill Katovsky. *Iron Heart: The True Story of How I Came Back from the Dead* (10–12). Illus. 2009, Skyhorse $24.95 (978-160239771-2). Brian Boyle survives a horrific car crash, a nearly fatal coma, and goes on to compete in an Iron Man triathlon. (Rev: BL 9/09) [921]

BRAITHWAITE, E. R.

8192 Braithwaite, E. R. *To Sir, with Love* (9–12). 1990, Jove paper $5.99 (978-0-515-10519-3). The inspiring story of a young black teacher from British Guiana and his class in a school in London's slums. [921]

BRILL, LEIGH

8193 Brill, Leigh. *A Dog Named Slugger* (10–12). 2010, BelleBooks paper $14.95 (978-09843256-5-8). In this inspiring memoir subtitled *The True Story of the Friend Who Changed My World,* Brill chronicles her struggle with cerebral palsy and celebrates the big-hearted dog — Slugger — who helped her cope with and accept her condition. **e** (Rev: BL 4/1–15/10) [921]

BROYARD, BLISS

8194 Broyard, Bliss. *One Drop: A True Story of Family, Race, and Secrets* (9–12). 2007, Little, Brown $24.99 (978-0-316-16350-7). After finding out at the age of 24 that her father Anatole, book reviewer for the *New York Times,* had concealed his black heritage, Bliss Broyard set out to learn about her family. (Rev: BL 8/07) [921]

BRUCK, EDITH

8195 Bruck, Edith. *Who Loves You Like This* (10–12). Trans. by Thoma Kelso. 2000, Paul Dry paper $14.95 (978-0-9664913-7-1). In this haunting memoir, Bruck recounts her tumultuous life after surviving the Holocaust. (Rev: VOYA 4/01) [853]

BUCKLEY, BRYAN AND UMBRELL, COLBY

8196 Sielski, Mike. *Fading Echoes: A True Story of Rivalry and Brotherhood from the Football Field to the Fields of Honor* (10–12). Illus. 2009, Berkley $24.95 (978-042522974-3). Sielski tells the story of two football stars, from opposing high school teams in Pennsylvania, who both join the military after 9/11 and fight in Iraq; their lives reflect much of the turmoil of the early 21st century. (Rev: BL 9/09) [921]

BUCKLEY, KRISTEN

8197 Buckley, Kristen. *Tramps Like Us: A New Jersey Tale* (9–12). 2007, Cyan $24.95 (978-1-905736-23-2). Although the facts of this funny memoir may seem outlandish, readers will greatly enjoy the stories of a childhood beset with adopted siblings, blended families, a larger-than-life mother, rat infestations, and underage drinking, just to name a few problem situations. (Rev: BL 3/1/07) [306]

BUFORD, BILL

8198 Buford, Bill. *Heat: An Amateur's Adventures as Kitchen Slave, Line Cook, Pasta-Maker, and Apprentice to a Dante-Quoting Butcher in Tuscany* (9–12). 2006, Knopf $25.95 (978-1-4000-4120-6). A funny and engaging book about the trials of becoming a cook. (Rev: SLJ 9/06)

BURAU, CAROLINE

8199 Burau, Caroline. *Answering 911: Life in the Hot Seat* (9–12). 2006, Borealis $19.95 (978-0-87351-569-6). A dispatcher's work is varied and comes with great responsibility; Burau recounts her own experiences and the reasons she chose this demanding career. (Rev: SLJ 1/07)

BURCH, JENNINGS MICHAEL

8200 Burch, Jennings Michael. *They Cage the Animals at Night* (9–12). 1984, NAL paper $6.99 (978-0-451-15941-0). The story of a youth from a broken home and of the many shelters and foster homes where he spent his childhood while his mother tried to cope with her mounting responsibilities. [921]

BUSBY, CYLIN AND JOHN

8201 Busby, Cylin, and John Busby. *The Year We Disappeared: A Father-Daughter Memoir* (9–12). 2008, Bloomsbury $16.99 (978-159990141-1). The sometimes violent true story of a Cape Cod policeman and his attacker is told here through the alternating voices of the policeman himself and his daughter, Cylin, who was 9 years old when the family was forced to go into hiding. **e** Lexile 940L (Rev: BL 9/1/08; HB 11–12/08; SLJ 10/1/08; VOYA 10/08) [921]

CANADA, GEOFFREY

8202 Canada, Geoffrey, and Jamar Nicholas. *Fist Stick Knife Gun: A Personal History of Violence* (7–12). Illus. by Jamar Nicholas. 2010, Beacon paper $14 (978-08070444-9-0). Using graphic novel format, the author presents 10 vignettes from his gritty urban childhood that are designed to show readers coping mechanisms for violence and instability. (Rev: BL 11/15/10; VOYA 12/10) [921]

CAPOTORTO, CARL

8203 Capotorto, Carl. *Twisted Head: An Italian American Memoir* (10–12). 2008, Broadway $23.95 (978-076792861-8). Vivid descriptions and skillful writing evoke Capotorto's experience growing up gay in the Bronx in the 1970s. (Rev: BL 9/1/08) [921]

CHAI, MAY-LEE

8204 Chai, May-Lee. *Hapa Girl* (11–12). 2007, Temple Univ. $25.00 (978-1-59213-615-5). The daughter of a Chinese American father and Irish American mother, Chai recalls the family's move from New York to South Dakota in 1979 and the racism that they met there; for mature readers. (Rev: BL 1/1–15/07) [921]

CHARLES, BRYAN

8205 Charles, Bryan. *There's a Road to Everywhere Except Where You Came From* (11–12). 2010, Open City paper $14 (978-18904475-7-1). Charles recounts his writing career from near unemployment to profitable yet unsatisfying financial writing and explains how surviving the 9/11 attacks led him to focus on his true love: creative writing; for mature readers. (Rev: BL 10/1–15/10) [921]

CHIN, STACEYANN

8206 Chin, Staceyann. *The Other Side of Paradise* (11–12). 2009, Scribner $24 (978-074329290-0). Jamaican-born Staceyann Chin is a well-known New York City political activist and performance artist whose poignant memoir depicts her horrible childhood and how she overcame her many setbacks and came out as a lesbian; for mature readers. (Rev: BLO 9/09) [921]

CHOI, ANNIE

8207 Choi, Annie. *Happy Birthday or Whatever: Track Suits, Kim Chee, and Other Family Disasters* (9–12). 2007, HarperCollins paper $13.95 (978-0-06-113222-3). Choi relates with great humor her struggles growing up in a Korean American family in Los Angeles with a mother who doesn't understand her. (Rev: BL 3/15/07) [974.7]

CHOQUETTE, SONIA

8208 Choquette, Sonia. *Diary of a Psychic: Shattering the Myths* (10–12). 2003, Hay $14.95 (978-1-4019-0192-9). In this memoir of her childhood and teenage years, spiritual teacher Sonia Choquette tells how she first discovered and developed her psychic abilities. (Rev: BL 8/03) [133.8]

COHEN, KERRY

8209 Cohen, Kerry. *Loose Girl: A Memoir of Promiscuity* (10–12). 2008, Hyperion $21.95 (978-1-4013-0349-5). Kerry Cohen's memoir details her eventual success in kicking the habit of dangerous sex. (Rev: BL 4/15/08) [921]

CONLON-MCIVOR, MAURA

8210 Conlon-McIvor, Maura. *FBI Girl: How I Learned to Crack My Father's Code* (9–12). 2004, Warner $23.00 (978-0-446-53310-2). In this engaging memoir going back to the 1960s, Conlon-McIvor writes about how she confused her father's unhappiness with his job. (Rev: BL 7/04) [363]

COOK, PAUL

8211 Cook, Paul. *Cooked in LA: I Shot for the Stars and Hit Bottom* (11–12). Illus. 2009, Kunati $24.95 (978-160164193-9). Drug and alcohol problems, combined with the pressures of trying to succeed in the entertainment business, cause Paul Cook to spiral out of control; for mature readers. (Rev: BL 4–5/09) [921]

COOPER, HELENE

8212 Cooper, Helene. *The House at Sugar Beach* (9–12). 2008, Simon & Schuster $26.00 (978-0-7432-6624-6). A near-fatal experience in Iraq prompts journalist Cooper to return to her native Liberia to find her adopted sister, revisiting painful childhood memories. ∩ (Rev: BL 4/1/08) [966.620]

CORYAT, SONJA HEINZE

8213 Coryat, Sonja Heinze. *Sunny, Ward of the State: Calamity Strikes a Family During the Great Depression* (10–12). 2004, PublishAmerica paper $27.95 (978-1-4137-1523-1). A poignant memoir of a harrowing childhood, much of it spent in institutions as a ward of the state. (Rev: SLJ 4/05) [921]

COX, LYNNE

8214 Cox, Lynne. *Grayson* (9–12). 2006, Knopf $18.95 (978-0-307-26454-1). A brief but moving account of the author's encounter with a young whale (whom she named Grayson) off the coast of California, an experience she says changed her life. (Rev: BL 5/1/06; SLJ 10/06) [797.29]

CRAVAN, ARTHUR

8215 Richardson, Mike, and Rick Geary. *Cravan* (10–12). 2005, Dark Horse $14.95 (978-1-59307-291-9). In this graphic novel-format biography, Mike Richardson and Rick Geary chronicle the stranger-than-fiction life of Arthur Cravan, a self-confessed con artist, forger, and thief. (Rev: BL 11/15/05; VOYA 2/06) [741.5]

CROSS, JUNE

8216 Cross, June. *Secret Daughter: A Mixed-Race Daughter and the Mother Who Gave Her Away* (9–12). 2006, Viking $24.95 (978-0-670-88555-8). A painful account by a woman who — because of race and societal taboos — was forced as a child to pretend she was not her mother's daughter. (Rev: BL 5/15/06) [921]

CRYSTAL, DAVID

8217 Crystal, David. *By Hook or by Crook: A Journey in Search of English* (9–12). 2008, Overlook $27.95 (978-1-59020-061-2). A fascinating reflection on the English language, with details of the author's quest to "collect"

British English accents and dialects. (Rev: BL 4/15/08) [400]

DAOUD, HARI

8218 Daoud, Hari. *The Translator: A Tribesman's Memoir of Darfur* (10–12). 2008, Random House $23.00 (978-1-4000-6744-2). Daoud, a Darfur tribesman driven into exile by Sudanese militia, became a UN translator for investigators of genocide and wrote eloquent stories about the victims of the violence. (Rev: BL 4/1/08) [962.404]

DARZNIK, JASMIN

8219 Darznik, Jasmin. *The Good Daughter: A Memoir of My Mother's Hidden Life* (11–12). 2011, Grand Central $24.99 (978-044653497-0). Darznik tells the story of her mother's difficult life in Iran; for mature readers. (Rev: BL 12/1–15/10) [921]

DAU, JOHN BUL

8220 Dau, John Bul, and Michael S. Sweeney. *God Grew Tired of Us* (10–12). 2007, National Geographic $26.00 (978-1-4262-0114-1). Dau tells how he lived apart from his family in refugee camps from the age of 13 until he arrived in the United States in 2001, one of 4,000 Lost Boys of Sudan; a moving story of survival against terrible odds, with moments of humor. (Rev: BL 2/15/07) [962.404]

DAVIS, MATTHEW

8221 Davis, Matthew. *When Things Get Dark: A Mongolian Winter's Tale* (11–12). 2010, St. Martin's $25.99 (978-031260773-9). Mongolian history, culture, and its changing identity are interwoven in this memoir of a Peace Corps teacher sent to live in a yurt in a small village for two years; there he finds himself struggling with the same issues of drinking and violence to which many Mongolian men fall prey; for mature readers. (Rev: BL 2/1–15/10) [921]

DEN HARTOG FAMILY

8222 den Hartog, Kristen, and Tracy Kasaboski. *The Occupied Garden: A Family Memoir of War-Torn Holland* (10–12). Illus. 2009, St. Martin's $24.95 (978-031256157-4). Using the photos, diaries, and letters of their grandparents, the authors recreate the daily effort it took to survive in Holland during World War II. e (Rev: BL 4–5/09) [921]

DONOFRIO, BEVERLY

8223 Donofrio, Beverly. *Riding in Cars with Boys: Confessions of a Bad Girl Who Makes Good* (10–12). 1992, Penguin paper $14.00 (978-0-14-015629-4). Donofrio describes her rebellious teens and her experiences as a single young mother. [921]

DOUGLAS, SCOTT

8224 Douglas, Scott. *Quiet, Please: Dispatches from a Public Librarian* (9–12). 2008, Da Capo $25.00 (978-0-7867-2091-0). This memoir in blogs pays homage to libraries and librarians — and their quirky patrons. (Rev: BL 4/1/08) [020.92]

DUGARD, JAYCEE

8225 Dugard, Jaycee. *A Stolen Life: A Memoir* (11–12). 2011, Simon & Schuster $24.99 (978-1-4516-2918-7). Dugard chronicles the 18 years she spent as the captive of Phillip Craig and Nancy Garrido, which included living in a tent in the back yard and giving birth to two daughters. YALSA Quick Picks for Reluctant Young Adult Readers 2012. (Rev: SLJ 11/11) [921]

DUMAS, FIROOZEH

8226 Dumas, Firoozeh. *Laughing Without an Accent: Adventures of an Iranian American, at Home and Abroad* (9–12). 2008, Villard $22.00 (978-0-345-49956-1). A warm and funny memoir by an Iranian woman, reflecting on her quirky family and her perspectives as child, wife, and mother. (Rev: BL 4/15/08) [910.4]

EBADI, SHIRIN

8227 Ebadi, Shirin, and Azedeh Moaveni. *Iran Awakening: A Memoir of Revolution and Hope* (10–12). 2006, Random House $24.95 (978-1-4000-6470-0). A former judge in Iran, Ebadi recalls the changes in her country that forced her and millions of others to leave the land they loved. (Rev: BL 5/1/06) [323.3]

EICHENGREEN, LUCILLE

8228 Eichengreen, Lucille. *From Ashes to Life: My Memories of the Holocaust* (9–12). 1994, Mercury House paper $17.95 (978-1-56279-052-3). A young girl's harrowing experiences in the Nazi death camps end with liberation, followed by survivor guilt and search for meaning. (Rev: SLJ 10/94) [921]

EIRE, CARLOS

8229 Eire, Carlos. *Learning to Die in Miami: Confessions of a Refugee Boy* (10–12). 2010, Free Press $26 (978-143918190-4). Picking up where his award-winning *Waiting for Snow in Havana* (2002) left off, Eire describes his arrival in America in 1962, his journey through foster homes, and living with an uncle in Chicago as he tries to assimilate to his new surroundings. e (Rev: BL 9/1–15/10) [921]

FLEMING, EDWARD

8230 Fleming, Edward. *Heart of the Storm: My Adventures as a Helicopter Rescue Pilot and Commander* (9–12). 2004, Wiley $24.95 (978-0-471-26436-1). This is an adventure-filled memoir of a veteran U.S. Air Force and Air National Guard rescue helicopter pilot. (Rev: BL 5/15/04) [921]

FRIEDMAN, CORY

8231 Patterson, James, and Hal Friedman. *Med Head: My Knock-Down, Drag-Out, Drugged-Up Battle with My Brain* (7–10). Illus. 2010, Little, Brown paper $8.99 (978-03160761-7-3). With an introduction, photographs, and question-and-answer sessions, this version of *Against Medical Advice,* intended for youth readers, tells the story of Cory Friedman's struggle to find a resolution to the obsessive-compulsive disorder and Tourette's syndrome making his young life so difficult. **e** (Rev: BLO 3/1/10; VOYA 6/10) [921]

FRIEDMAN, HANNAH

8232 Friedman, Hannah. *Everything Sucks: Losing My Mind and Finding Myself in a High School Quest for Cool* (9–12). 2009, Health Communications paper $12.95 (978-0-7573-0775-1). In this sassy, wry memoir, Hannah Friedman recounts her no-holds-barred campaign to gain popularity and her self-destructive behaviors (drugs, eating disorders, and superficiality). (Rev: SLJ 10/09; VOYA 10/09) [921]

FURIYA, LINDA

8233 Furiya, Linda. *Bento Box in the Heartland: My Japanese Girlhood in Whitebread America* (9–12). 2007, Seal paper $15.95 (978-1-58005-191-0). Furiya grew up in small-town Indiana in the 1960s, the only Asian girl in her school; her differences were underlined by the food she brought to school for lunch and the importance of food in her life is a continuing theme in this memoir that contains favorite recipes. (Rev: BL 1/1–15/07) [977.2]

GALLAGHER, TIM

8234 Gallagher, Tim. *Falcon Fever: A Falconer in the Twenty-first Century* (10–12). 2008, Houghton Mifflin $25.00 (978-0-618-80575-4). Gallagher intersperses details of a boyhood obsessed with hawks and falcons with information on the history of falconry. (Rev: BL 4/15/08) [921]

GAO, ANHUA

8235 Gao, Anhua. *To the Edge of the Sky: A Story of Love, Betrayal, Suffering and the Strength of Human Courage* (10–12). 2003, Overlook $27.95 (978-1-58567-362-9). Gao tells the courageous story of her struggle to survive and carve out a meaningful life for herself amid the political volatility of Maoist China. (Rev: BL 1/1–15/03) [951.05]

GARCIA, LUIS M.

8236 Garcia, Luis M. *Child of the Revolution: Growing up in Castro's Cuba* (10–12). 2007, Allen & Unwin paper $16.95 (978-1-74114-852-7). Garcia recalls his childhood in Cuba, the concerns he had at the time, and the new set of problems that assaulted him when the family received permission to leave the country. (Rev: BL 4/1/07) [972.9106]

GARNER, ELEANOR

8237 Garner, Eleanor Ramrath. *Eleanor's Story: An American Girl in Hitler's Germany* (7–12). 1999, Peachtree $15.95 (978-1-56145-193-7). The author recounts her family's struggle to survive in Germany during World War II. (Rev: BL 10/1/99*; HBG 4/00; SLJ 3/00) [940.54]

GHAHRAMANI, ZARAH

8238 Ghahramani, Zarah, and Robert Hillman. *My Life as a Traitor* (10–12). 2007, Farrar $23.00 (978-0-374-21730-3). Arrested when she was a university student in Tehran, Ghahramani was convicted of a variety of crimes (including speaking against the government) and was jailed and tortured; in this memoir, she reflects on her privileged childhood, on Iranian culture, and on her time in prison. (Rev: SLJ 2/08) [921]

GILDINER, CATHERINE

8239 Gildiner, Catherine. *After the Falls: Coming of Age in the Sixties* (10–12). 2010, Viking $25.95 (978-067002205-2). This second memoir (following 2001's *Too Close to the Falls*) describes Gildiner's life as she deals with high school cliques, gets a job, goes to college, and becomes personally involved in civil rights. **e** (Rev: BL 10/1–15/10) [921]

GOLDSWORTHY, ANNA

8240 Goldsworthy, Anna. *Piano Lessons* (10–12). 2010, St. Martin's $24.99 (978-031264628-8). This touching memoir documents how the author's childhood piano teacher helped shape her future. **e** (Rev: BL 9/1–15/10) [921]

GONZÁLEZ, RIGOBERTO

8241 Gonzalez, Rigoberto. *Butterfly Boy: Memories of a Chicano Mariposa* (10–12). 2006, Univ. of Wisconsin $24.95 (978-0-299-21900-0). Written in a clear eloquent style, this is an intense coming-of-age and coming-out memoir of a first-generation Mexican American. (Rev: BL 7/06) [921]

GRAY, AMY

8242 Gray, Amy. *Spygirl: True Adventures from My Life as a Private Eye* (10–12). 2003, Villard paper $12.95 (978-0-8129-7152-1). Gray blends the story of her experiences as a fledgling private investigator with humorous and poignant anecdotes from her personal life; for mature teens. (Rev: BL 9/15/03) [921]

GREENLAW, LAVINIA

8243 Greenlaw, Lavinia. *The Importance of Music to Girls* (10–12). 2008, Farrar $23.00 (978-0-374-17454-5). An appreciation of the role of music in the author's lfe — from classical through disco and punk. (Rev: BL 4/15/08) [921]

GREITENS, ERIC

8244 Greitens, Eric. *The Warrior's Heart: Becoming a Man of Compassion and Courage* (8–12). 2012, Houghton Harcourt $16.99 (978-0-547-86852-3). In this thought-provoking adaptation of the adult title *The Heart and the Fist* (2011), Greitens describes his adventures in various countries around the world and the circumstances that led him to become a Navy SEAL. e (Rev: SLJ 9/12) [921]

GRIMBERG, TINA

8245 Grimberg, Tina. *Out of Line: Growing Up Soviet* (8–12). 2007, Tundra $22.95 (978-0-88776-803-3). Grimberg, now a rabbi in Canada, recalls her life as a girl in a Jewish family in the Soviet Union in the 1960s and 1970s. (Rev: BL 12/1/07; SLJ 1/08) [305.2]

GUIDRY, JEFF

8246 Guidry, Jeff. *An Eagle Named Freedom: My True Story of a Remarkable Friendship* (10–12). 2010, Morrow $21.99 (978-006199435-7). The true story of a man's deep kinship with a rehabilitated bald eagle he met while volunteering at a wildlife rescue center. e (Rev: BLO 1/1–15/11) [921]

GURDON, MARTIN

8247 Gurdon, Martin. *Travels with My Chicken: A Man and His Companion Take to the Road* (9–12). 2005, Lyons paper $12.95 (978-1-59228-778-9). The British author of *Hen and the Art of Chicken Maintenance* (2004) chronicles the unique book-promotion tour he undertook with a chicken named Tikka; offbeat humor and wry perceptions. (Rev: BL 11/15/05) [914.104]

HALDER, BABY

8248 Halder, Baby. *A Life Less Ordinary* (10–12). Trans. by Urvashi Butalia. 2007, Penguin $21.95 (978-8-189-01367-7). Abused by her father and then by the man to whom she was married at the age of 12, the Indian author nonetheless found the courage to flee with her three children and find work as a maid; when she finally found a real home, she was encouraged to tell her story. (Rev: BL 5/15/07) [305.23]

HANCOCK, BILL

8249 Hancock, Bill. *Riding with the Blue Moth* (9–12). 2005, Sports Publishing $24.95 (978-1-59670-104-5). In this poignant memoir, Bill Hancock, coordinator of the annual NCAA March Madness basketball tournament, tells how a cross-country bicycle trip helped him — and his wife — to deal with the heartbreak of their son's death in an airplane crash. (Rev: BL 9/1/05) [796.6]

HAUTZIG, ESTHER

8250 Hautzig, Esther. *The Endless Steppe: Growing Up in Siberia* (7–12). 1968, HarperCollins paper $5.99 (978-0-06-447027-8). The autobiography of a Polish girl who, with her family, was exiled to Siberia during World War II. [921]

HENDERSON, JEFF

8251 Henderson, Jeff. *Cooked: From the Streets to the Stove, from Cocaine to Foie Gras* (10–12). 2007, Morrow $24.95 (978-0-06-115390-7). The author was in prison for drug dealing when he was assigned to the prison kitchen and found he had a real talent for cooking, eventually becoming a celebrity chef. ☊ (Rev: BL 3/15/07) [921]

HESTER, CHARLEY

8252 Hester, Charley. *The True Life Wild West Memoir of a Bush-Popping Cow Waddy* (9–12). 2004, Univ. of Nebraska paper $13.95 (978-0-8032-7346-7). A fascinating memoir of an exciting period in American history, by the great-great-grandfather of the editor. (Rev: BL 9/1/04) [978]

HIRSI ALI, AYAAN

8253 Hirsi Ali, Ayaan. *Infidel* (11–12). 2007, Free Press $26.00 (978-0-7432-8968-9). Hirsi Ali, known for her book *The Caged Virgin* (2006) and for the film for which Theo van Gogh was killed, tells her moving story of growing up in a strict Muslim family in Africa and Saudi Arabia, fleeing an arranged marriage, and fighting for the rights of Muslim women despite threats against her own life. ☊ (Rev: BL 2/15/07) [949.207]

HOBBES, ANNE

8254 Specht, Robert. *Tisha: The Story of a Young Teacher in the Alaska Wilderness* (9–12). 1984, Bantam paper $5.99 (978-0-553-26596-5). The heartwarming biography of a young schoolteacher who at age 19 began working in the tiny Alaska town of Chicken. [921]

HOCKENBERRY, JOHN

8255 Hockenberry, John. *Moving Violations: War Zones, Wheelchairs, and Declarations of Independence* (9–12). 1996, Hyperion paper $15.95 (978-0-7868-8162-8). Hockenberry — a paraplegic who covered the Middle East conflict for National Public Radio — tells how he managed to accomplish it from the confines of a wheelchair. (Rev: BL 6/1–15/95) [362.4]

HOLLOWAY, MONICA

8256 Holloway, Monica. *Driving with Dead People* (11–12). 2007, Simon & Schuster $23.00 (978-1-4169-4002-9). Holloway recalls her childhood obsession with death, her parents' divorce and her mother's neglect, and her emerging memories of her father's abuse; for mature teens. (Rev: BL 1/1–15/07) [972.2]

HOLLOWAY, NATALEE

8257 Holloway, Beth. *Loving Natalee: A Mother's Testament of Hope* (10–12). 2007, HarperCollins $24.95 (978-0-06-145227-0). The mother of Natalee Holloway, a girl who disappeared during a senior trip to Aruba, describes the horrible months afterward and the family's struggle to find out what happened to her. (Rev: SLJ 2/08) [921]

HOLMAN, JAMES

8258 Roberts, Jason. *A Sense of the World: How a Blind Man Became History's Greatest Traveler* (10–12). 2006, HarperCollins $26.95 (978-0-00-716106-5). The story of a world traveler who in the early 1800s became well known through his memoirs. (Rev: SLJ 9/06)

HUNTER-GAULT, CHARLAYNE

8259 Hunter-Gault, Charlayne. *To the Mountaintop: My Journey Through the Civil Rights Movement* (6–12). 2012, Roaring Brook $22.99 (978-1-59643-605-3). Journalist Hunter-Gault, one of two students who integrated the University of Georgia in 1961, describes her personal experiences against the backdrop of the entire civil rights movement. Lexile 1240L (Rev: BL 2/1/12*; HB 1–2/12; LMC 3–4/12; SLJ 12/1/11*) [921]

JACOBS, A. J.

8260 Jacobs, A. J. *The Know-It-All: One Man's Humble Quest to Become the Smartest Person in the World* (10–12). 2004, Simon & Schuster $25.00 (978-0-7432-5060-3). In this humorous alphabetically organized memoir, Jacobs tells how his mind was expanded — to the breaking point — by reading every volume of the *Encyclopaedia Britannica*; for mature readers. (Rev: BL 9/1/04; SLJ 2/05) [031]

JACOBSEN, RUTH

8261 Jacobsen, Ruth. *Rescued Images: Memories of a Childhood in Hiding* (6–12). 2001, Mikaya $19.95 (978-1-931414-00-5). The author, who was 8 years old when her family fled the Nazis and went into hiding in the Netherlands, relates memories evoked by family photographs, which are also included. (Rev: BCCB 2/02; BL 1/1–15/02; HBG 3/02; SLJ 1/02; VOYA 2/02) [921]

JENIFER, TREVON

8262 Jenifer, Trevon, and Alan Goldenbach. *Trevon Jenifer: From the Ground Up* (9–12). 2006, Sports Publishing $22.95 (978-1-59670-143-4). Born without legs, African American Trevon moved with his family to a mostly white suburb and decided to join the wrestling team, a decision that affected his entire life. (Rev: BL 9/1/06) [921]

JENKINS, MISSY

8263 Jenkins, Missy, and William Croyle. *I Choose to Be Happy: A School Shooting Survivor's Triumph Over Tragedy* (6–12). 2008, LangMarc paper $16.95 (978-1-880292-31-0). School shooting survivor Missy Jenkins documents the horrific events of December 1, 1997, in West Paducah, Kentucky, and the long road to hope and forgiveness. (Rev: SLJ 3/1/09; VOYA 6/09) [921]

JENSEN, K. THOR

8264 Jensen, K. Thor. *Red Eye, Black Eye* (10–12). Illus. by author. 2007, Alternative Comics paper $19.95 (978-1-891867-99-6). In 2001 cartoonist Jensen suddenly found himself without a job, an apartment, and a girlfriend and this upheaval galvanized him into action; he bought a 60-day bus pass and traveled across the country, staying with people he found on the Internet and the story is told here in graphic novel format. (Rev: BL 5/1/07; SLJ 9/07) [741.5]

JIANG LU, SHU

8265 Jiang Lu, Shu. *When Huai Flowers Bloom: Stories of the Cultural Revolution* (9–12). 2007, SUNY $25.00 (978-0-7914-7231-6). Jiang Lu interweaves stories of her difficult life as a girl during China's restrictive Cultural Revolution with stories she heard from her father and grandmother. (Rev: BL 10/15/07) [951.05]

JIANG, JI-LI

8266 Jiang, Ji-li. *Red Scarf Girl: A Memoir of the Cultural Revolution* (6–10). 1997, HarperCollins $17.99 (978-0-06-027585-3). An engrossing memoir of a Chinese girl, her family, and how their lives became a nightmare during Chairman Mao's Cultural Revolution of the late 1960s. (Rev: BL 10/1/97; SLJ 12/97; VOYA 6/98) [921]

JUETTE, MELVIN

8267 Juette, Melvin, and Ronald J. Berger. *Wheelchair Warrior: Gangs, Disability, and Basketball* (9–12). 2008, Temple Univ. $25.00 (978-1-59213-474-8). Skip the dense academic introduction and go right to the big heart of this inspirational story of the boy who grows from gang member to wheelchair athlete. (Rev: BL 3/1/08) [921]

JUNGER, SEBASTIAN

8268 Junger, Sebastian. *War* (11–12). 2010, Twelve $26.99 (978-044655624-8). Junger recounts his thrilling, dangerous experiences embedded with the Second Platoon, Battle Company, in eastern Afghanistan in this inside look at life in combat; for mature teens. ℮ (Rev: BL 3/1–15/10) [921]

KAMARA, MARIATU

8269 Kamara, Mariatu, and Susan McClelland. *The Bite of the Mango* (9–12). Illus. 2008, Annick paper $12.95 (978-155451158-7). A disturbing but hopeful memoir of a young woman who was maimed and raped during the civil war in Sierra Leone. ℮ (Rev: BL 1/1–15/09; SLJ 11/1/08*; VOYA 2/09) [921]

KANG, HYOK

8270 Kang, Hyok. *This Is Paradise: My New Korean Childhood* (10–12). 2006, Little, Brown paper $13.95 (978-0-316-72966-6). The author tells of his life as a boy in North Korea, where he and his family lived in constant fear and in danger of starvation and even execution before escaping to China in 1998. (Rev: BL 8/06) [921]

KANN, WENDY

8271 Kann, Wendy. *Casting with a Fragile Thread: A Story of Sisters and Africa* (11–12). 2006, Henry Holt $23.00 (978-0-8050-7956-2). A memoir about a girl growing up in colonial Rhodesia (now Zimbabwe) who endures her parents' divorce, father's suicide, and economic hardships before emigrating to the United States. (Rev: BL 4/15/06) [968.91]

KANTNER, SETH

8272 Kantner, Seth. *Shopping for Porcupine: A Life in Arctic Alaska* (10–12). Illus. 2008, Milkweed $28.00 (978-157131301-0). In this photo-filled volume Kantner shares poignant first-person stories from the Alaskan tundra that touch on environmental calamity, the displacement of Inuit elders, and the slow attrition of an ancient culture. (Rev: BL 6/1–15/08*) [921]

KARPEL, NINI

8273 Kaplan, Vivian Jeanette. *Ten Green Bottles: The True Story of One Family's Journey from War-Torn Austria to the Ghettos of Shanghai* (11–12). 2004, St. Martin's $24.95 (978-0-312-33054-5). Writing in the first-person voice of her mother, Nini Karpel, Kaplan recounts her family's grueling experiences in World War II, escaping from Nazi-occupied Austria to China, one of the few countries accepting Jewish refugees during this troubled period; for mature readers. (Rev: BL 10/1/04) [940.53]

KATIN, MIRIAM

8274 Katin, Miriam. *We Are on Our Own* (11–12). 2006, Drawn & Quarterly $19.95 (978-1-896597-20-1). In this gripping World War II memoir presented in graphic-novel format, animator Katin tells the harrowing story of her escape from Budapest with her mother; for mature readers. (Rev: BL 3/15/06) [741.5]

KEAT, NAWUTH

8275 Keat, Nawuth, and Martha Kendall. *Alive in the Killing Fields: The True Story of Nawuth Keat, a Khmer Rouge Survivor* (7–12). 2009, National Geographic $15.95 (978-1-4263-0515-3); LB $23.90 (978-1-4263-0516-0). In this stirring memoir, Cambodian Nawuth Keat provides a graphic, wrenching picture of the life of a young refugee and his struggle toward freedom. (Rev: BL 8/09; LMC 11–12/09; SLJ 10/09) [921]

KERMAN, PIPER

8276 Kerman, Piper. *Orange Is the New Black: My Year in a Women's Prison* (11–12). 2010, Spiegel & Grau $25 (978-038552338-7). Indicted ten years after her nonviolent crime, Kerman spends a year absorbing the engrossing — and often unexpectedly kind — culture of a federal women's prison; for mature readers. (Rev: BL 3/1–15/10) [921]

KLEIN, STEPHANIE

8277 Klein, Stephanie. *Moose: A Memoir of a Fat Camp* (10–12). 2008, Morrow $24.95 (978-006084329-8). With humor and pain, Klein describes her summer fat camp experience and speaks of how it had lasting effects on her adult life; for mature teens. ℮ (Rev: BLO 9/2/08; SLJ 11/08) [921]

KOHLER, DEAN ELLIS

8278 Kohler, Dean Ellis. *Rock 'n' Roll Soldier* (9–12). 2009, HarperTeen $16.99 (978-006124255-7). A memoir of the Vietnam War and the author's band, the Electrical Banana. ℮ (Rev: BL 7/09; SLJ 9/09) [921]

KOPELMAN, JAY

8279 Kopelman, Jay. *From Baghdad to America: Life Lessons from a Dog Named Lava* (9–12). 2008, Skyhorse $23.95 (978-160239264-9). In this followup to 2006's *From Baghdad, with Love,* Kopelman and his inspiring canine dog struggle with the transition to civilian life after the war. ⌒ (Rev: BL 7/08) [921]

KOR, EVA MOZES

8280 Kor, Eva Mozes, and Lisa Rojany Buccieri. *Surviving the Angel of Death: The Story of a Mengele Twin in Auschwitz* (6–10). 2009, Tanglewood $14.95 (978-1-933718-28-6). Kor tells the horrifying story of her treatment — with her twin sister — at the hands of Mengele in Auschwitz. (Rev: LMC 5–6/10; SLJ 5/10) [921]

KUEGLER, SABINE

8281 Kuegler, Sabine. *Child of the Jungle* (11–12). 2007, Warner $24.99 (978-0-446-57906-3). Daughter of German missionaries, Kuegler spent nine years of her childhood with the Fayu tribe in the Indonesian jungle, coping with giant spiders, snakes, and primitive living conditions; but her transition back to Western society also proved difficult; for mature readers. (Rev: BL 12/15/06) [995.1]

KUUSISTO, STEPHEN

8282 Kuusisto, Stephen. *Eavesdropping: A Life by Ear* (9–12). 2006, Norton $23.95 (978-0-393-05892-5). A collection of essays on growing up blind and traveling to distant places to "sight-see by ear." (Rev: BL 9/1/06) [921]

8283 Kuusisto, Stephen. *Planet of the Blind* (10–12). 1997, Doubleday $22.95 (978-0-385-31615-6); paper $11.95 (978-0-385-33327-6). The biography of a young man who coped with legal blindness and bouts of obesity and anorexia before he reached out for help, accepted his disability, and learned to trust a seeing eye dog. (Rev: BL 11/15/97; SLJ 5/98) [921]

LAMBKE, BRYAN

8284 Lambke, Bryan, and Tom Lambke. *I Just Am: A Story of Down Syndrome Awareness and Tolerance* (4–10). 2006, Five Star $14.99 (978-1-58985-020-0). In this compelling photoessay, a young adult with Down syndrome — with some help from his father — explains what it's like to live with this disability. (Rev: SLJ 10/06)

LAUREN, JILLIAN

8285 Lauren, Jillian. *Some Girls: My Life in a Harem* (11–12). 2010, Plume paper $15 (978-04522963-1-2). Lauren chronicles her time spent in the harem of Prince Jefri of Borneo: first exotic and exciting, the atmosphere grows increasingly paranoid and catty as Lauren vies for the prince's affections; for mature readers. (Rev: BL 3/1–15/10) [921]

LAWRENCE, CANDIDA

8286 Lawrence, Candida. *Fear Itself* (10–12). 2004, Unbridled $19.95 (978-1-932961-01-0). In her third soul-baring memoir, Lawrence looks back at her first marriage and the terrible price she paid for her involvement in the early years of the atomic age. (Rev: BL 10/15/04) [362.19]

LAWRENCE, SARAHLEE

8287 Lawrence, Sarahlee. *River House* (11–12). 2010, Tin House paper $16.95 (978-09825691-3-9). Returning to her family's rural Oregon environs after escaping to become a successful globe-trotting river guide, Lawrence settles in to build a log cabin and faces many hardships; for mature readers. **e** (Rev: BL 10/1–15/10) [921]

LEKUTON, JOSEPH LEMASOLAI

8288 Lekuton, Joseph Lemasolai. *Facing the Lion: Growing Up Maasai on the African Savanna* (5–12). 2003, National Geographic $15.95 (978-0-7922-5125-5). Lekuton, a member of a nomadic Masai tribe and now a teacher in Virginia, remembers his youth in Kenya. (Rev: BCCB 5/06; BL 9/15/03; HBG 4/04; LMC 11–12/06; SLJ 10/03*) [967.62]

LELEUX, ROBERT

8289 Leleux, Robert. *The Memoirs of a Beautiful Boy* (11–12). 2008, St. Martin's $23.95 (978-0-312-36168-6). With self-deprecating humor and an appealing world view, Leleux describes his coming-of-age teen years with a mother preoccupied with catching herself a rich man but aware enough to realize her son is gay. (Rev: BL 11/15/07) [818]

LERNER, GERDA

8290 Lerner, Gerda. *Fireweed: A Political Autobiography* (10–12). 2002, Temple Univ. $59.50 (978-1-56639-889-3). Lerner, an expert in women's history, looks back on her earlier life, including her youth in Austria, escape from fascism, immigration to the United States, membership in the Communist Party, and brushes with Hollywood blacklisting. (Rev: BL 4/15/02) [921]

LI, MOYING

8291 Li, Moying. *Snow Falling in Spring: Coming of Age in China During the Cultural Revolution* (7–12). 2008, Farrar $16.00 (978-0-374-39922-1). Moying Li tells the story of her childhood during the Great Leap Forward, followed by the shock of the Cultural Revolution, during which her mother was sent to the countryside and her father to a labor camp; Li's remarkable grandmother and Li's own love of literature nurtured her through this difficult time. (Rev: BL 2/15/08; SLJ 4/08) [951.05]

LUCAS, FRANK

8292 Lucas, Frank, and Aliya S. King. *Original Gangster: The Real Life Story of One of America's Most Notorious Drug Lords* (11–12). Illus. 2010, St. Martin's $25.99 (978-031254489-8). Lucas's view of the world was changed forever when at the age of 6 he watched his cousin murdered by a couple of hate-filled white men; in this confessional memoir suitable for mature readers, he owns up to his drug lord career with honesty and bluntness. ◠ **e** (Rev: BL 5/1–15/10) [921]

LUKAS, CHRISTOPHER

8293 Lukas, Christopher. *Blue Genes: A Memoir of Loss and Survival* (11–12). 2008, Doubleday $24.95 (978-

0-385-52520-6). Lukas writes of his family's struggle with depression and suicide and how it has affected them all; for mature readers. (Rev: BL 8/08) [616.85]

LUND, ERIC

8294 Lund, Doris. *Eric* (9–12). 1974, HarperCollins $16.95 (978-0-397-01046-2). The tragic story of a gifted young man and his fatal bout with leukemia, as told by his mother. [921]

MACDONALD, WARREN

8295 MacDonald, Warren. *A Test of Will: One Man's Extraordinary Story of Survival* (8–12). 2004, Douglas & McIntyre paper $14.95 (978-1-55365-064-5). The riveting story of Macdonald's survival after his legs were pinned under a massive rock on an island off Australia. (Rev: BL 9/15/04) [790.5]

MAI, MUKHTAR

8296 Mai, Mukhtar, and Marie-Therese Cuny. *In the Name of Honor* (11–12). Trans. by Linda Coverdale. 2006, Atria $24.00 (978-1-4165-3228-6). Gang-raped by four men as punishment for an act that did not take place, Mukhtar Mai sued her village tribal council before the Supreme Court of Pakistan and used the winnings to start a school for girls. (Rev: BL 10/15/06) [921]

MALARKEY, DON

8297 Malarkey, Don. *Easy Company Soldier: The Endless Combat of a Sergeant from World War II's "Band of Brothers"* (9–12). 2008, St. Martin's $24.95 (978-0-312-37849-3). Paratrooper Don Malarkey describes his days as an NCO of Easy Company, later famous as the Band of Brothers. (Rev: BL 4/1/08) [921]

MANN, REVA

8298 Mann, Reva. *The Rabbi's Daughter* (11–12). 2007, Dial $24.00 (978-0-385-34142-4). Daughter of one rabbi and granddaughter of another, Mann describes with humor her journey from one extreme — a promiscuous, drug-taking adolescence — to another — an arranged marriage to an orthodox Jew — before finding a calmer place; for mature teens. (Rev: BL 9/15/07) [305.48]

MANZOOR, SARFRAZ

8299 Manzoor, Sarfraz. *Greetings from Bury Park: Race, Religion, and Rock and Roll* (10–12). 2008, Vintage paper $13.95 (978-0-307-38802-5). Sixteen-year-old Pakistani-born Manzoor's love of Bruce Springsteen's music and lyrics helps him reconcile his relationship with his father and learn what being true to oneself really means. (Rev: BL 3/1/08) [942.085]

MARIC, VESNA

8300 Maric, Vesna. *Bluebird* (10–12). 2009, Soft Skull paper $14.95 (978-15937625-8-2). Sprinkling wit among the sorrow, Maric, a Bosnian teen living in England, describes life as a refugee and includes letters from her father describing the horrors at home. (Rev: BLO 9/15/09) [325.]

MASTERS, JARVIS JAY

8301 Masters, Jarvis Jay. *That Bird Has My Wings: The Autobiography of an Innocent Man on Death Row* (11–12). 2009, HarperOne $24.99 (978-006173045-0). Death-row inmate Masters's memoir eloquently recounts the unfortunate lead-up to his incarceration; suitable for mature readers. ℮ (Rev: BL 9/09) [921]

MATHEWS, DAN

8302 Mathews, Dan. *Committed: A Rabble Rouser's Memoir* (11–12). 2007, Atria $24.00 (978-1-4165-3955-1). Matthews's spirited memoir relates his work for PETA (People for the Ethical Treatment of Animals) and the accompanying problems he's had to deal with, tells about the various celebrities he has persuaded to join the cause, and discusses his homosexuality and how childhood bullying affected him; for mature teens. (Rev: BL 3/1/07) [179]

MAYOR, MIREYA

8303 Mayor, Mireya. *Pink Boots and a Machete: My Journey from NFL Cheerleader to National Geographic Explorer* (10–12). Illus. 2011, National Geographic $26 (978-142620786-0). Former Miami Dolphins cheerleader and current co-host of "National Geographic Wild," Mireya Mayor writes about her experiences in the wild and how we can protect our endangered lands and animals. (Rev: BL 3/1–15/11) [921]

MIRO, ASHA

8304 Miro, Asha. *Daughter of the Ganges* (9–12). 2006, Atria $24.00 (978-0-7432-8672-5). The author, who was born in India and adopted by Spanish parents, tells of returning to India in search of her birth parents and discovering a sister. (Rev: BL 5/15/06; SLJ 11/06) [362.73]

MONAQUE, MATHILDE

8305 Monaque, Mathilde. *Trouble in My Head: A Young Girl's Fight with Depression* (7–12). Trans. by Lorenza Garcia. 2009, Trafalgar paper $15.95 (978-009191723-4). A memoir of a French teen's struggle to overcome depression. (Rev: BL 4/1/09; SLJ 9/09) [921]

MONTANA-LEBLANC, PHYLLIS

8306 Leblanc, Phyllis Montana. *Not Just the Levees Broke: My Story During and After Hurricane Katrina* (10–12). 2008, Atria $20.00 (978-1-4165-6346-4). In this personal account of New Orleans during and after Katrina, Montana-Leblanc tells of her fears, anger, and bewilderment at the politics involved. ∩ **e** (Rev: BL 8/08) [921]

MOODY, ANNE

8307 Moody, Anne. *Coming of Age in Mississippi* (10–12). 1970, Dell paper $6.99 (978-0-440-31488-2). The story of a black girl growing up in the desperate poverty of rural Mississippi. [921]

MOORE, WES

8308 Moore, Wes. *Discovering Wes Moore* (7–12). Illus. 2012, Delacorte $15.99 (978-038574167-5); LB $18.99 (978-037599018-2). A memoir about two Wes Moores, one a Rhodes scholar and combat veteran and the other serving a life sentence for murder, who came from very similar backgrounds. ∩ **e** (Rev: BL 10/1/12; SLJ 3/13; VOYA 10/12)

MORTENSON, GREG

8309 Mortenson, Greg, and David Oliver Relin. *Three Cups of Tea: One Man's Mission to Fight Terrorism and Build Nations . . . One School at a Time* (9–12). 2006, Viking $25.95 (978-0-670-03482-6). Mortenson relates his efforts to build a school for a Pakistani village whose inhabitants nursed him back to health while on a climbing trip. (Rev: BL 3/15/06) [371]

MURRAY, LIZ

8310 Murray, Liz. *Breaking Night* (11–12). 2010, Hyperion $24.99 (978-078686891-9). Murray unflinchingly relates the story of her own childhood — cocaine-addicted parents, domestic instability, and life on the streets — in this straightforward, surprisingly unsentimental memoir for mature readers subtitled *A Memoir of Forgiveness, Survival, and My Journey from Homeless to Harvard.* Alex Award 2011. ∩ **e** (Rev: BL 8/10) [921]

NEMAT, MARINA

8311 Nemat, Marina. *Prisoner of Tehran: A Memoir* (11–12). 2007, Free Press $26.00 (978-1-4165-3742-7). Nemat tells the affecting story of her (minor in world terms) rebellion as a 16-year-old Catholic in Islamic Iran, her imprisonment and torture, rescue from execution by an interrogator who himself is assassinated, and eventual marriage and migration to Canada; suitable for mature teens. (Rev: BL 4/1/07) [955]

NEUFELD, JOSH

8312 Neufeld, Josh. *A Few Perfect Hours . . . and Other Stories from Southeast Asia and Central Europe* (11–12). 2004, Alternative Comics paper $12.95 (978-1-891867-79-8). An interesting graphic treatment of a travel memoir, describing backpacking through South-

east Asia and Central Europe; for mature readers. (Rev: BL 9/15/04) [741.5]

NGUYEN, BICH MINH

8313 Nguyen, Bich Minh. *Stealing Buddha's Dinner: A Memoir* (10–12). 2007, Penguin paper $24.95 (978-0-670-03832-9). Food is a recurrent theme in this memoir of the Vietnamese American author's youth in Michigan in the 1980s and her efforts to fit in to her new society while also viewing it with a writer's observant eye. (Rev: BL 1/1–15/07) [977.4]

NIVEN, JENNIFER

8314 Niven, Jennifer. *The Aqua Net Diaries: Big Hair, Big Dreams, Small Town* (10–12). Illus. 2010, Simon & Schuster $24 (978-141695429-3). Niven describes her high school years in rural Indiana in the 1980s, complete with irreverent fashion commentary and frank tales of less successful moments. (Rev: BLO 3/1–15/10) [921]

NORRIS, MICHELE

8315 Norris, Michele. *The Grace of Silence* (11–12). 2010, Pantheon $24.95 (978-030737876-7). NPR journalist Norris explores her African American family's history in this account of an investigation that took her to surprising places. (Rev: BL 9/1–15/10) [921]

NORTH, STERLING

8316 North, Sterling. *Rascal: A Memoir of a Better Era* (7–12). 1963, Dutton $16.99 (978-0-525-18839-1). Remembrances of growing up in Wisconsin in 1918 and of the joys and problems of owning a pet raccoon. Newbery Honor. (Rev: BL 9/1/89) [599.74]

NORTON, TREVOR

8317 Norton, Trevor. *Underwater to Get Out of the Rain: A Love Affair with the Sea* (9–12). 2006, Da Capo $25.00 (978-0-306-81487-7). The author, a marine biologist, writes of the mystique of the ocean as well as the plants, animals, and humans that live in and around it. (Rev: BL 5/1/06) [578.77]

NYE, NAOMI SHIHAB

8318 Nye, Naomi Shihab. *Never in a Hurry: Essays on People and Places* (10–12). 1996, Univ. of South Carolina paper $18.95 (978-1-57003-082-6). This collection of autobiographical essays on a variety of subjects reflects the people and places encountered by the author, a Palestinian American married to a Swedish American who has lived most of her life in San Antonio, Texas. (Rev: BL 8/96; SLJ 11/96) [921]

O'CONNOR, LARRY

8319 O'Connor, Larry. *Tip of the Iceberg* (10–12). 2002, Univ. of Georgia $24.95 (978-0-8203-2356-5). O'Connor describes his childhood in central Canada, in a place of long, hard winters and with a father of a wintry disposition that turns out to hide a secret. (Rev: BL 5/1/02) [971.064]

O'DELL, CAROL D.

8320 O'Dell, Carol D. *Mothering Mother: A Daughter's Humorous and Heartbreaking Memoir* (9–12). 2007, Kunati $19.95 (978-1-60164-003-1). Teens whose parents are pulled between caring for their own parents and spending time with their children may find some revelations in this well-told memoir. (Rev: BL 2/15/07) [306.874]

O'NEILL, MOLLY

8321 O'Neill, Molly. *Mostly True: A Memoir of Family, Food, and Baseball* (9–12). 2006, Scribner $25.00 (978-0-7432-3268-5). O'Neill's well-written memoir traces her childhood growing up with five younger brothers (including former Yankee Paul O'Neill) and her later experiences as the *New York Times* food writer. (Rev: BL 4/15/06) [641.3]

OPPENHEIMER, MARK

8322 Oppenheimer, Mark. *Wisenheimer: A Childhood Subject to Debate* (10–12). 2010, Free Press $25 (978-143912864-0). Oppenheimer manages to achieve success — despite being his teacher's worst nightmare — by joining the debate club in middle school and discovering his aptitude for language and logic; an exuberant and compelling memoir. (Rev: BL 3/1–15/10) [921]

OTOTAKE, HIROTADA

8323 Ototake, Hirotada. *No One's Perfect* (10–12). Trans. by Gerry Harcourt. 2000, Kodansha $19.95 (978-4-7700-2500-5). The story of a Japanese man who was born without arms or legs and how he has tried to lead a normal life, including playing basketball and football. (Rev: BL 9/1/00) [921]

PACHEN, ANI

8324 Pachen, Ani, and Adelaide Donnelly. *Sorrow Mountain: The Journey of a Tibetan Warrior Nun* (10–12). 2000, Kodansha $24.00 (978-1-56836-294-6). The autobiography of a brave Tibetan woman who suffered imprisonment and torture by the Chinese because she opposed their occupation of her country. (Rev: BL 1/1–15/00) [921]

PATTON, LARRY

8325 Kastner, Janet. *More Than an Average Guy* (9–12). 1989, Life Enrichment paper $8.95 (978-0-938736-25-7). An inspiring story of a boy who was born with cerebral palsy and of the family that loved him. (Rev: BL 5/15/89) [921]

PAYNE, LUCILLE M. W.

8326 Rice, Dorothy M., and Lucille Payne. *The Seventeenth Child* (7–12). 1998, Linnet LB $18.50 (978-0-208-02414-5). The story of an African American woman growing up in rural Virginia during the 1930s and 1940s, as recorded and edited by her daughter. (Rev: HBG 3/99; SLJ 1/99; VOYA 6/99) [921]

PAZIRA, NELOFER

8327 Pazira, Nelofer. *A Bed of Red Flowers: In Search of My Afghanistan* (11–12). 2005, Free Press paper $15.00 (978-0-7432-8133-1). The star of the movie *Kandahar* writes about the turbulent political and social backdrop to her youth in Afghanistan; for mature teens. (Rev: BL 8/05) [958.104]

PETERSON, BRENDA

8328 Peterson, Brenda. *I Want to Be Left Behind: Finding Rapture Here on Earth* (11–12). 2010, Da Capo $25 (978-030681804-2). Peterson's memoir about being raised a Southern Baptist explains her struggles to find common ground between radical evangelists and environmentalists. **e** (Rev: BL 12/1/09*) [921]

PHILLIPS, JOSEPH C.

8329 Phillips, Joseph C. *He Talk Like a White Boy: Reflections on Faith, Family, Politics and Authenticity* (10–12). 2006, Running Pr $22.95 (978-0-7624-2399-6). The author, an African American who grew up in Colorado, acted on *The Cosby Show,* and is now a conservative commentator, expresses his thoughts on "fitting in" within the black community. (Rev: BL 5/15/06) [921]

POOLE, ERIC

8330 Poole, Eric. *Where's My Wand? One Boy's Magical Triumph over Alienation and Shag Carpeting* (10–12). 2010, Putnam $24.95 (978-039915655-7). Poole navigates a minefield of family dysfunction, romantic obsession, and anxiety about his homosexuality in this amusing memoir of 1970s St. Louis. **e** (Rev: BL 4/1–15/10) [921]

PRESS, EYAL

8331 Press, Eyal. *Absolute Convictions: My Father, a City, and the Conflict That Divided America* (10–12). 2006, Henry Holt $26.00 (978-0-8050-7731-5). In this absorbing memoir, journalist Eyal Press writes about what it was like to grow up as the son of an abortionist during a time when the pro-life movement was becoming increasingly vocal and often violent. (Rev: BL 3/1/06) [363.4]

RAGUSA, KYM

8332 Ragusa, Kym. *The Skin Between Us: A Memoir of Race, Beauty, and Belonging* (9–12). 2006, Norton

$23.95 (978-0-393-05890-1). The daughter of an African American woman and an Italian American man remembers her youth and its contradictions. (Rev: BL 5/1/06) [974.7]

REICHL, RUTH

8333 Reichl, Ruth. *Tender at the Bone: Growing Up at the Table* (10–12). 1997, Broadway paper $13.00 (978-0-7679-0338-7). This entertaining autobiography by a woman who reviewed restaurants for *The New York Times* for many years tells how she became interested in food, describes some of her kitchen disasters, and gives a few mouth-watering recipes. (Rev: BL 2/15/98; SLJ 6/98) [921]

REID, KIM

8334 Reid, Kim. *No Place Safe: A Family Memoir* (11–12). 2007, Kensington paper $15.00 (978-0-7582-2052-3). As a 13-year-old African American girl in the late 1970s, the author found herself attending a privileged white school in Atlanta during a time of horrific murders of black boys and had to deal with conflicting loyalties; for mature teens. ∩ (Rev: BL 9/1/07) [303.324]

REISS, JOHANNA

8335 Reiss, Johanna. *The Upstairs Room* (7–10). 1972, HarperCollins $19.99 (978-0-690-85127-4); paper $6.99 (978-0-06-447043-8). The author's story of her years spent hiding from the Nazis in occupied Holland. Followed by *The Journey Back* (1976). (Rev: BL 3/1/88) [921]

RESTON, HILLARY

8336 Reston, James, Jr. *Fragile Innocence: A Father's Memoir of His Daughter's Courageous Journey* (9–12). 2006, Harmony $23 (978-1-4000-8243-8). Reston describes the struggles involved in dealing with a severely ill child and stresses the need for medical research and provisions for the disabled in the planning of national healthcare. (Rev: BL 2/1/06; SLJ 6/06) [921]

RHODES-COURTER, ASHLEY

8337 Rhodes-Courter, Ashley. *Three Little Words* (8–12). 2008, Atheneum $17.99 (978-1-4169-4806-3). A product of the U.S. foster care system describes her childhood with foster parents, some who were kind, others who were abusive; a disturbing story, explicitly told. (Rev: BL 1/1–15/08; LMC 2/08; SLJ 1/08) [362.73]

RICHARDS, SUSAN

8338 Richards, Susan. *Saddled: How a Spirited Horse Reined Me In and Set Me Free* (10–12). 2010, Harcourt $24 (978-054724172-2). Richards's powerful connection to her horse helps her recover from a troubled past and present filled with depression and alcoholism. ∩ e (Rev: BLO 1/1–15/11) [921]

ROBINSON, HOLLY

8339 Robinson, Holly. *The Gerbil Farmer's Daughter* (10–12). Illus. 2009, Harmony $23 (978-030733745-0). Holly Robinson's memoir is unusual as it turns from growing up as a military daughter to her father's secret, intense study of gerbils. (Rev: BL 4–5/09) [921]

RODRIGUEZ, GABY

8340 Rodriguez, Gaby, and Jenna Glatzer. *The Pregnancy Project* (8–11). 2012, Simon & Schuster $17.99 (978-144244622-9). From a family with a history of teen mothers, 17-year-old Gaby decided to make her senior project a fake pregnancy, recording the reactions of students, teachers, family, and friends; her story became a sensation. YALSA Quick Picks for Reluctant Young Adult Readers 2013. e Lexile 970L (Rev: BL 2/15/12; SLJ 4/12; VOYA 2/12) [306.874]

ROSEN, CHRISTINE

8341 Rosen, Christine. *My Fundamentalist Education: A Memoir of a Divine Girlhood* (9–12). 2006, Public Affairs $25.00 (978-1-58648-258-9). In this compelling and humorous memoir, Rosen recalls her experiences while attending a fundamentalist Christian school in Florida during the 1970s and 1980s. (Rev: BL 10/1/05) [277.59]

ROSEN, R. D.

8342 Rosen, R. D. *A Buffalo in the House: The True Story of a Man, an Animal, and the American West* (9–12). 2007, New Press $24.95 (978-1-59558-165-5). A tale without a happy ending about a buffalo named Charlie. (Rev: BL 4/1/07) [9778.9]

ROWLAND, MARY CANAGA

8343 Rowland, Mary Canaga. *As Long As Life: The Memoirs of a Frontier Woman Doctor* (9–12). 1994, Peak paper $11.95 (978-0-9641357-0-3). The memoirs of an early 19th-century doctor who braved the wilderness to treat wounds, pull teeth, and deliver babies. (Rev: BL 11/1/94) [610]

RUNYAN, BRENT

8344 Runyon, Brent. *The Burn Journals* (8–12). 2004, Random House LB $19.99 (978-0-375-82621-4). In this powerful memoir, Runyon recounts his journey to recovery from life-threatening burns suffered in a teenage suicide attempt. (Rev: BL 6/1–15/04; SLJ 11/04) [362.28]

SAMUELS, ALLISON

8345 Samuels, Allison. *Off the Record: A Reporter Lifts the Velvet Rope on Hollywood, Hip-Hop and Sports* (10–12). 2007, Amistad $24.95 (978-0-06-113766-2). *Newsweek* reporter Samuels, an African American, often reports on black celebrities and here talks about interviewing the stars. (Rev: BL 1/1–15/07) [921]

SANCHEZ, IVAN

8346 Sanchez, Ivan. *Next Stop: Growing Up Wild-Style in the Bronx* (11–12). Illus. 2008, Touchstone paper $14.00 (978-141656267-2). A violent memoir about the daily danger, crime, and sadness that Sanchez experienced while growing up in the Bronx; for mature teens. (Rev: BL 9/1/08) [921]

SARTOR, MARGARET

8347 Sartor, Margaret. *Miss American Pie: A Diary of Love, Secrets and Growing Up in the '70s* (11–12). 2006, Bloomsbury $19.95 (978-1-59691-200-7). Race relations, religion, and typical teen problems all figure in this reminiscence of 1970s Louisiana; for mature readers. (Rev: BL 3/15/06; SLJ 8/06) [305.235]

SATRAPI, MARJANE

8348 Satrapi, Marjane. *Persepolis: The Story of a Childhood* (10–12). 2003, Pantheon paper $17.95 (978-0-375-42230-0). In simple black-and-white drawings, the author chronicles her childhood in Iran between the ages of 10 and 14, during a time of revolution and turmoil. (Rev: BL 5/1/03; SLJ 8/03) [741.5]

SCHAFFER, DYLAN, AND SCHAFFER, ALFRED ALAN

8349 Schaffer, Dylan. *Life, Death and Bialys: A Father/Son Baking Story* (9–12). 2006, Bloomsbury $24.95 (978-1-59691-192-5). Schaffer agrees to attend a baking class with his dying father, although his father abandoned the family long ago; this funny and moving memoir chronicles their relationship and includes baking anecdotes. (Rev: BL 4/15/06; SLJ 2/07) [921]

SCHEERES, JULIA

8350 Scheeres, Julia. *Jesus Land* (11–12). 2005, Counterpoint $23.00 (978-1-58243-338-7). In this harrowing coming-of-age memoir suitable for older readers, Scheeres recounts how she and her adopted black brother helped each other through a soul-scarring fundamentalist Christian childhood and a stay in a brutal reform school in the Dominican Republic. (Rev: BL 9/1/05) [811]

SEATON, BILL

8351 Seaton, Bill. *My Seven Years in Captivity: Tails and Misadventures in the San Diego Zoo* (9–12). 2006, SP paper $10.95 (978-1-59025-902-3). In this appealing memoir, Seaton describes his years working as public relations director of the world-famous San Diego Zoo. (Rev: BL 1/1–15/06) [636.088]

SELLERS, HEATHER

8352 Sellers, Heather. *You Don't Look Like Anyone I Know: A True Story of Family, Face Blindness, and Forgiveness* (11–12). 2010, Riverhead $25.95 (978-159448773-6). A diagnosis of prosopagnosia — the inability to recognize faces — rescues Sellers from fear that she has inherited her parents' mental illnesses; for mature readers. 🎧 ℮ (Rev: BL 9/1–15/10) [921]

SHEFF, NIC

8353 Sheff, Nic. *Tweak: Growing Up on Methamphetamines* (10–12). 2008, Atheneum $16.99 (978-1-4169-1362-7). A 22-year-old heroin addict recalls his worst moments (including trading sex for drugs and stealing from his own family) and writes of his hope for a better future. (Rev: BL 11/15/07; SLJ 10/07) [362]

8354 Sheff, Nic. *We All Fall Down: Living with Addiction* (10–12). 2011, Little, Brown $17.99 (978-0-316-08082-8). This soul-baring sequel to *Tweak* (2008) documents Sheff's continuing difficulties with addictions and generally bad decision-making. (Rev: BL 2/15/11*; SLJ 4/11; VOYA 6/11) [362]

SIMMONS, RUSSELL

8355 Lommel, Cookie. *Russell Simmons* (7–10). Series: Hip-Hop Stars. 2007, Chelsea House LB $30.00 (978-0-7910-9467-9). Lommel includes lots of hip-hop history in this profile of the founder of Def Jam records. (Rev: BL 3/1/08) [921]

SMALL, DAVID

8356 Small, David. *Stitches* (10–12). Illus. 2009, Norton $24.95 (978-039306857-3). In graphic novel format, Small tells the sad tale of his youth in a joyless home and the surgery that rendered him mute for many years. Alex Award 2010; YALSA Top Ten 2010. (Rev: BL 7/09; SLJ 9/09) [921]

SMITHSON, RYAN

8357 Smithson, Ryan. *Ghosts of War: The True Story of a 19-Year-Old GI* (9–12). 2009, HarperCollins $16.99 (978-006166468-7); LB $17.89 (978-006166470-0). Smithson describes his decision after 9/11 to join the Army, basic training, his experiences in Iraq including worthwhile interactions with poverty-stricken Iraqi children and the night terrors he suffered afterward. (Rev: BL 7/09; SLJ 3/1/09*; VOYA 8/09) [921]

SOFFEE, ANNE THOMAS

8358 Soffee, Anne Thomas. *Snake Hips: Belly Dancing and How I Found True Love* (10–12). 2002, Chicago Review $22.95 (978-1-55652-458-5). A passion for belly dancing taught the author, who is half Lebanese, important lessons about herself and her romantic life; for mature teens. (Rev: BL 8/02) [793.3]

SOLOWAY, ELAINE

8359 Soloway, Elaine. *The Division Street Princess* (10–12). 2006, Syren paper $15.95 (978-0-929636-63-4). Soloway's memoir tells a moving story of a young daughter of Jewish immigrants navigating her way through a Chicago neighborhood full of tension and change. (Rev: BL 6/1–15/06) [973]

SONE, MONICA

8360 Sone, Monica. *Nisei Daughter* (9–12). 1987, Univ. of Washington paper $14.95 (978-0-295-95688-6). From a happy childhood in Seattle to a World War II relocation center as seen through the eyes of a Japanese American girl. [921]

SONTAG FAMILY

8361 Sontag, Rachel. *House Rules* (10–12). 2008, Ecco $24.95 (978-0-06-134122-9). The monster in this memoir closet is sometimes mommy and sometimes daddy and sometimes both and it takes a survivor to make it through. (Rev: BL 4/1/08; SLJ 9/08) [921]

ST. JOHN, LAUREN

8362 St. John, Lauren. *Rainbow's End: A Memoir of Childhood, War and an African Farm* (11–12). 2007, Scribner $25.00 (978-0-7432-8679-4). St. John describes her childhood on a Rhodesian farm called Rainbow's End, both a childhood wonderland and a place of danger — from nature and from terrorists; for mature teens. (Rev: BL 11/15/06) [968.91]

STEINER, MATTHEW

8363 Warren, Andrea. *Escape from Saigon: How a Vietnam War Orphan Became an American Boy* (5–12). 2004, Farrar $17.00 (978-0-374-32224-3). An inspiring account of a young Amerasian war orphan's long journey from Vietnam to a new and successful life in the United States; Long was part of the 1975 Operation Babylift and took the name of Matt Steiner when he was adopted by an American family. (Rev: BL 6/1–15/04*; SLJ 10/04) [959.704]

STRICKLAND, BILL

8364 Strickland, Bill. *Ten Points: A Father's Promise, a Daughter's Wish — How a Magical Season of Bicycle Riding Made It All Come True* (10–12). 2007, Hyperion $23.95 (978-1-4013-0258-0). A promise to his daughter sets the executive editor of *Bicycling* a bike-racing challenge that also prompts memories about his difficult childhood. (Rev: BL 6/1–15/07) [796.609]

STRINGER, LEE

8365 Stringer, Lee. *Sleepaway School: Stories from a Boy's Life* (10–12). 2004, Seven Stories $21.95 (978-1-58322-478-6). In this moving memoir, Stringer, an African American, writes about the three years he spent at a "sleepaway school" for troubled boys and the events that led to his being sent there. (Rev: BL 6/1–15/04; SLJ 11/04) [649.153]

SUBERMAN, STELLA

8366 Suberman, Stella. *When It Was Our War: A Soldier's Wife in World War II* (10–12). 2003, Algonquin $23.95 (978-1-56512-403-5). In this continuation of her autobiography, begun in *The Jew Store,* Suberman recounts her emotional experiences as a military wife during World War II. (Rev: BL 9/1/03; SLJ 5/04) [921]

SUKRUNGRUANG, IRA

8367 Sukrungruang, Ira. *Talk Thai: The Adventures of Buddhist Boy* (11–12). 2010, Univ. of Missouri $24.95 (978-082621889-6). Growing up in the Chicago suburbs in the 1980s, Thai American Ira Sukrungruang tries hard to reconcile his family's resistance to assimilation and his own need to fit in with his white suburban neighbors; this sometimes hilarious, sometimes painful memoir is suitable for mature readers. (Rev: BLO 2/1–15/10) [921]

SUNDQUIST, JOSH

8368 Sundquist, Josh. *Just Don't Fall: How I Grew Up, Conquered Illness, and Made It Down the Mountain* (10–12). 2010, Viking $25.95 (978-067002146-8). Sundquist lost a leg to cancer as an adolescent and describes with wry humor his struggles at home and at school, and his eventual success on the ski slopes, competing in the 2006 Paralympics in Italy. ⌒ ℮ (Rev: BLO 12/15/09) [921]

SUPERNAW, SUSAN

8369 Supernaw, Susan. *Muscogee Daughter: My Sojourn to the Miss America Pageant* (10–12). Series: American Indian Lives. 2010, Univ. of Nebraska $24.95 (978-080322971-6). The first Native American to win the title of Miss Oklahoma tells the story of her difficult youth and road to academic success, emphasizing the importance of the Native traditions inculcated by her grandmother and other mentors. (Rev: BL 9/1–15/10) [921]

SWADOS, ELIZABETH

8370 Swados, Elizabeth. *My Depression: A Picture Book* (8–12). 2005, Hyperion $16.95 (978-1-4013-0789-9). In a candid yet entertaining cartoon picture-book format, Swados reveals her struggles with severe depression. (Rev: BL 3/15/05) [818]

SWAN, ROBERT

8371 Swan, Robert, and Gil Reavill. *Antarctica 2041: My Quest to Save the Earth's Last Wilderness* (10–12). 2009, Broadway $24.99 (978-076793175-5). This book has two purposes: to give an account of the explorer's journey to the poles and to call attention to Antarctica's environmental needs. (Rev: BL 9/15/09) [577.5]

TALL, DEBORAH

8372 Tall, Deborah. *A Family of Strangers* (11–12). 2006, Sarabande $24.95 (978-1-932511-45-1). Brought up in a Jewish household silent about the past, Tall felt a need to know more about her family history and here recounts the journey that takes her to a shtetl in Ukraine. (Rev: BL 10/15/06) [814]

TAMM, JAYANTI

8373 Tamm, Jayanti. *Cartwheels in a Sari: A Memoir of Growing Up Cult* (10–12). 2009, Harmony $22.95 (978-030739392-0). With humor and frankness, the author writes of her life in a controlling popular cult from childhood to young adulthood when she broke free. (Rev: BL 4–5/09) [921]

TAMMET, DANIEL

8374 Tammet, Daniel. *Born on a Blue Day: Inside the Extraordinary Mind of an Autistic Savant* (10–12). 2007, Free Press $22.95 (978-1-4165-3507-2). The author, only 27 at the time he wrote this book, is an autistic savant with an incredible mastery of arithmetic and languages; this is a well-written account of his youth, education, and recognition that he is gay. (Rev: BL 1/1–15/07) [362.196]

THOMAS, CULLEN

8375 Thomas, Cullen. *Brother One Cell: An American's Coming of Age in South Korea's Prisons* (11–12). 2007, Penguin $24.95 (978-0-670-03827-5). Not long after finishing college, Cullen Thomas spent three and a half years in a South Korean prison for smuggling hashish into the country; this is the story of his confinement. (Rev: BL 3/15/07) [365.6]

TOINGAR, N. ESAIE

8376 Toingar, N. Esaie. *A Teenager in the Chad Civil War: A Memoir of Survival. 1982-1986* (10–12). 2006, McFarland paper $29.95 (978-0-7864-2403-0). Toingar chronicles his experiences as a teenager in the turmoil of Chad's civil war, the atrocities he witnessed, and his eventual escape. (Rev: BL 6/1–15/06) [967.4304]

TRUSSONI, DANIELLE

8377 Trussoni, Danielle. *Falling Through the Earth* (11–12). 2006, Henry Holt $23.00 (978-0-8050-7732-2). Trussoni's memoir of growing up with her hard-drinking father will resonate with many young adults; for mature readers. (Rev: BL 1/1–15/06) [810]

TWO TREES, JOE

8378 Kazimiroff, Theodore L. *The Last Algonquin* (10–12). 2008, Paw Prints $22.95 (978-1-4395-0242-6). The story of an Algonquin who was living off the land in a park in the Bronx during the 1920s, this was first published in 1982. [921]

UMRIGAR, THRITY N.

8379 Umrigar, Thrity. *First Darling of the Morning: Selected Memories of an Indian Childhood* (10–12). 2008, HarperCollins paper $14.95 (978-006145161-4). In this compelling coming-of-age memoir, Umrigar describes her middle-class childhood in India, a life-changing meeting and subsequent rebellion against her family, and her move to America where she is an author and university teacher. **e** (Rev: BL 9/1/08*) [921]

UNFERTH, DEB OLIN

8380 Unferth, Deb Olin. *Revolution: The Year I Fell in Love and Went to Join the War* (11–12). 2011, Henry Holt $23 (978-080509323-0). In 1987 Unferth and her boyfriend dropped out of college and went to join the revolutionaries in Central America, an idealistic journey that brought danger and disillusion; for mature readers. (Rev: BL 1/1–15/11) [921]

VAN MAARSEN, JACQUELINE

8381 van Maarsen, Jacqueline. *My Name Is Anne, She Said, Anne Frank: The Memoirs of Anne Frank's Best Friend* (9–12). Trans. by Hester Velmans. 2007, Arcadia $24.95 (978-1-905147-10-6). Jacqueline van Maarsen shares her remembrances of life in Amsterdam with Anne Frank as her best friend and confidant (Anne refers to her as "Jopie" in her famous diary) and of her own family's handling of their Jewish faith in order to survive Nazi occupation. (Rev: BL 7/07; SLJ 10/07) [940.53]

VASISHTA, MADAN

8382 Vasishta, Madan. *Deaf in Delhi: A Memoir* (10–12). 2006, Gallaudet Univ. paper $29.95 (978-1-56368-284-1). Eleven-year-old Vasishta lost his hearing after contracting mumps and typhoid; in a culture where a deaf person's future is very bleak, he nevertheless succeeded in getting a place at a photography school for the deaf in Delhi and later found employment as a professor. (Rev: SLJ 8/06) [921]

VEGA, MARTA MORENO

8383 Vega, Marta Moreno. *When the Spirits Dance Mambo* (9–12). 2004, Three Rivers paper $13.00 (978-1-4000-4924-0). Vega, of Puerto Rican heritage, writes fluently about coming of age in Spanish Harlem during the 1950s. (Rev: BL 11/15/04; SLJ 5/05) [974.7]

VINCENT, ERIN

8384 Vincent, Erin. *Grief Girl* (8–11). 2007, Delacorte $15.99 (978-0-385-73353-3). An account of how the author, then 14, and her siblings coped with the deaths of their parents in a car crash in 1983. (Rev: BCCB 4/07; BL 2/1/07; LMC 8–9/07; SLJ 2/07) [155.9]

WALD, ELIJAH

8385 Wald, Elijah. *Riding with Strangers: A Hitchhiker's Journey* (9–12). 2006, Chicago Review $22.95 (978-1-55652-605-3). Hitching around the country may be less dangerous than you thought. Wald mixes in history, tips, and views on American society in general in this account of a Boston-Seattle journey using his thumb. (Rev: BL 4/15/06; SLJ 6/06) [921]

WALKER, JERALD

8386 Walker, Jerald. *Street Shadows: A Memoir of Race, Rebellion, and Redemption* (11–12). 2010, Bantam $25 (978-055380755-4). Alternately grim and inspiring, this memoir describes reconciling a gritty, violent past as an African American youth on the South Side of Chicago with an increasingly stable life as a writer and college professor. (Rev: BL 11/15/09) [921]

WASDIN, HOWARD E.

8387 Wasdin, Howard E., and Stephen Templin. *I Am a SEAL Team Six Warrior: Memoirs of an American Soldier* (9–12). 2012, St. Martin's paper $7.99 (978-12500164-3-0). Wasdin describes the stamina and determination required to become an elite Navy SEAL, and attributes his abilities to his difficult childhood; a YA version of an adult book. ℯ Lexile 930L (Rev: BL 4/15/12; SLJ 8/1/12) [921]

WEINSTEIN, LAUREN

8388 Weinstein, Lauren. *Girl Stories* (7–10). 2006, Henry Holt paper $16.95 (978-0-8050-7863-3). Episodic graphic novel-format vignettes paint a vivid portrait of the author's 8th- and 9th-grade years. (Rev: BL 3/15/06; SLJ 7/06; VOYA 4/06) [741.5]

WELLS, JEFF

8389 Wells, Jeff. *All My Patients Have Tales: Favorite Stories from a Vet's Practice* (10–12). 2009, St. Martin's $24.95 (978-0-312-53739-5). Whether ministering to circus animals or the common house cat, this veterinarian recounts his adventures with humor and compassion. (Rev: BL 2/15/09; SLJ 9/09)

WHITE, SHANE

8390 White, Shane. *North Country* (9–12). 2005, NBM paper $13.95 (978-1-56163-435-4). In graphic novel format, this compelling memoir realistically recounts a painful childhood growing up in an abusive home in the Great Lakes/St. Lawrence River region. (Rev: BL 10/1/05; SLJ 11/05; VOYA 4/06) [741.5]

WILKS, BURREL LEE

8391 Wilks, Burrel Lee. *Tattoos on My Soul: From the Ghetto to the Top of the World* (11–12). 2006, Burrell Streetwise $29.95 (978-0-9768736-0-0). Wilks writes frankly about his past as a drug dealer and hustler and explains how he was able to turn away from crime and make something positive of his life; for mature teens. (Rev: BL 3/15/06) [332.6]

WILLIAMS, RITA

8392 Williams, Rita. *If the Creek Don't Rise: My Life out West with the Last Black Widow of the Civil War* (9–12). 2006, Harcourt $23.00 (978-0-15-101154-4). A fascinating account of a childhood as a black among whites (in Colorado), with an opinionated Civil War widow as a guardian. (Rev: BL 5/15/06; SLJ 8/06) [921]

WILSON, G. WILLOW

8393 Wilson, G. Willow. *The Butterfly Mosque: A Young American Woman's Journey to Love and Islam* (10–12). 2010, Atlantic Monthly $24 (978-080211887-5). Wilson, daughter of two atheists, tells the story of her conversion to Islam, her move to Cairo, and her romance with an Egyptian teacher. ℯ (Rev: BL 5/15/10*) [921]

WOLFF, MISHNA

8394 Wolff, Mishna. *I'm Down* (10–12). Illus. 2009, St. Martin's $23.95 (978-031237855-4). Wolff writes of her confusing childhood as a white girl who could never fit in while living in a black neighborhood with a father who wanted to be black. ♫ ℯ (Rev: BL 4–5/09; SLJ 6/09) [921]

WOODE, ANTON

8395 Kreck, Dick. *Anton Woode: The Boy Murderer* (9–12). 2006, Fulcrum paper $15.95 (978-1-55591-578-0). The true story of an 11-year-old boy who shot and killed a hunter in 1893 and was sentenced to prison for 25 years; details about the Colorado justice system and societal realities of the time add interest to the account. (Rev: SLJ 10/06)

WOODS, VANESSA

8396 Woods, Vanessa. *Bonobo Handshake: A Memoir of Love and Adventure in the Congo* (10–12). 2010, Gotham $26 (978-159240546-6). Woods tells the story of her and her husband's research in the Congo, trying to save the threatened bonobo ape as civil war boiled around them. ♫ ℯ (Rev: BL 5/1–15/10) [921]

YU, CHUN

8397 Yu, Chun. *Little Green: Growing Up During the Chinese Cultural Revolution* (7–10). 2005, Simon & Schuster $15.95 (978-0-689-86943-3). Chun Yu, who was born the year that China's Cultural Revolution began, recounts in poetry what life was like during one of the most tumultuous periods in Chinese history. (Rev: BL 1/1–15/05; SLJ 3/05; VOYA 10/05) [951.05]

ZAILCKAS, KOREN

8398 Zailckas, Koren. *Fury* (11–12). 2010, Viking $25.95 (978-067002230-4). The author of the memoir *Smashed* (2005) follows up her bestseller by examining the source of her deep-seated anger, sharing both personal stories and the results of extensive reading and research; for mature readers. (Rev: BL 9/1–15/10) [921]

ZENATTI, VALÉRIE

8399 Zenatti, Valérie. *When I Was a Soldier* (8–11). Trans. by Adriana Hunter. 2005, Bloomsbury $16.95 (978-1-58234-978-7). In this compelling memoir, Valérie Zenatti, an immigrant to Israel from France, chronicles her two years of compulsory service in the Israeli army. (Rev: BCCB 7–8/05; BL 5/1/05*; SLJ 5/05) [921]

The Arts and Entertainment

General and Miscellaneous

8400 Aronson, Marc. *Art Attack: A Short Cultural History of the Avant-Garde* (11–12). 1998, Clarion $24.00 (978-0-395-79729-7). Eminently readable, this overview traces the avant-garde movement from its mid-19th-century origins in Paris to today's post-avant-garde age and examines the interrelationships among culture, the arts, history, and politics. (Rev: BL 7/98) [700]

8401 Barcella, Laura. *The End: 50 Apocalyptic Visions from Pop Culture That You Should Know About . . . Before It's Too Late* (9–12). Illus. 2012, Zest paper $12.99 (978-0-9827322-5-0). An interesting survey of the various ways in which the end is manifested in movies, plays, art, music, and so forth. (Rev: SLJ 8/1/12) [001.9]

8402 Chadwick, Paul. *Depths: Concrete, Vol. 1* (9–12). Series: Concrete. 2005, Dark Horse paper $12.95 (978-1-59307-343-5). Early strips about the laid-back comic strip character are reprinted here along with previously uncollected pieces. (Rev: BL 10/15/05) [741.5]

8403 Herriman, George. *A Wild Warmth of Chromatic Gravy: Krazy and Ignatz, 1935-36* (9–12). 2005, Fantagraphics paper $19.95 (978-1-56097-690-5). Color arrives in this sixth volume of the collected Krazy Kat comic strip series, which showcases panels that first appeared in Sunday newspapers during the mid-1930s. (Rev: BL 10/15/05) [741.5]

8404 Ketcham, Hank. *Hank Ketcham's Complete Dennis the Menace: 1951–1952* (9–12). 2005, Fantagraphics $24.95 (978-1-56097-680-6). This hefty volume collects the first two years of cartoonist Hank Ketcham's popular Dennis the Menace comic strip, which celebrates the antics of everybody's favorite neighborhood brat. (Rev: BL 10/1/05; SLJ 2/06) [741.5]

8405 O'Kane, Bernard. *Treasures of Islam: Artistic Glories of the Muslim World* (8–12). 2007, Sterling $35.00 (978-1-84483-483-9). With about 170 color photographs, this handsome volume traces Islamic art and architecture from the 7th to 19th centuries and discusses political and religious aspects throughout. (Rev: BL 10/1/07) [709]

8406 Robson, David. *The Black Arts Movement* (7–12). Series: Lucent Library of Black History. 2008, Gale/Lucent $32.45 (978-1-4205-0053-0). Black nationalism, cultural influences, identity, and assimilation are all considered as factors in this overview of the movement that has had an impact in literature, music, and art. (Rev: SLJ 2/1/09) [700.89]

8407 Smith, Anna Deavere. *Letters to a Young Artist* (9–12). 2006, Vintage paper $13.00 (978-1-4000-3238-9). Anna Deavere Smith, an author and actress, offers some sage advice to would-be artists of all stripes. (Rev: BL 1/1–15/06; SLJ 4/06) [700]

8408 Tan, Shaun. *The Bird King: An Artist's Notebook* (7–12). Illus. by author. 2013, Scholastic $19.99 (978-054546513-7). A collection of fascinating sketches that show how an expert artist records his ideas. (Rev: BL 11/1/12*; SLJ 3/13; VOYA 4/13) [741.6]

8409 Waterhouse, Jo, and David Penhallow. *Concrete to Canvas: Skateboarders' Art* (10–12). 2006, Watson-Guptill paper $19.95 (978-0-8230-0887-2). Teenaged enthusiasts will appreciate this collection of sometimes angry, sometimes silly, sometimes meaningful art by other skateboarders. (Rev: BL 4/15/06) [700.9]

Architecture and Building

General and Miscellaneous

8410 Phillips, Cynthia, and Shana Priwer. *Ancient Monuments* (7–10). Illus. Series: Frameworks. 2008, Sharpe Focus LB $43.95 (978-076568123-2). A look at monuments in ancient Greece, Rome, China, Europe, and other regions, with discussion of the engineering feats involved as well as their beauty and significance. (Rev: BL 4/1/09; SLJ 9/09) [732]

8411 Rense, Paige, ed. *Architectural Digest: Hollywood at Home* (9–12). 2005, Abrams $40.00 (978-0-8109-5929-3). A fascinating peek inside the homes of stars from the earliest days of Hollywood to today's celebrities. (Rev: BL 11/1/05) [728.09]

8412 Vogel, Steve. *The Pentagon: A History; The Untold Story of the Wartime Race to Build the Pentagon — and to Restore It Sixty Years Later* (9–12). 2007, Random House $32.95 (978-1-4000-6303-1). This fascinating history of the five-sided building covers its design, construction, postwar role, 9/11 terrorist damage, and many other interesting social and cultural aspects. (Rev: BL 5/15/07) [355.60973]

History of Architecture

8413 Macaulay, David. *Mosque* (6–12). 2003, Houghton Mifflin $18.00 (978-0-618-24034-0). Macaulay follows a 16th-century mosque through initial design and planning, construction, and the uses of the finished structure and all its associated support buildings. (Rev: BL 10/1/03*; HB 11–12/03; SLJ 11/03*) [726]

8414 Macaulay, David. *Pyramid* (7–12). 1975, Houghton Mifflin $20.00 (978-0-395-21407-7); paper $9.95 (978-0-395-32121-8). In beautiful line drawings, the author describes how an ancient Egyptian pyramid was constructed. [726]

8415 Nardo, Don. *Artistry in Stone: Great Structures of Ancient Egypt* (6–10). Series: The Lucent Library of Historical Eras. 2005, Gale LB $32.45 (978-1-59018-661-9). Photographs, reproductions, and film and documentary stills illustrate this well-documented examination of massive ancient Egyptian structures such as the pyramids and the Sphinx. (Rev: SLJ 11/05) [932]

8416 Watkin, David. *A History of Western Architecture. 3rd ed.* (10–12). 2000, Watson-Guptill paper $40.00 (978-0-8230-2274-8). Beginning with ancient architecture like that of Egypt and Mesopotamia and continuing to he present, this history of the architecture of Europe and the United Sates is well illustrated and easily read. [720.9]

Painting, Sculpture, and Photography

General and Miscellaneous

8417 Adamowicz, Adam, et al. *New Recruits, Vol. 1* (9–12). 2006, Dark Horse paper $12.95 (978-1-59307-383-1). In this volume, Dark Horse showcases the work of five promising new comic book artists. (Rev: BL 2/15/06) [741.5]

8418 Aldana, Patricia, ed. *Under the Spell of the Moon: Art for Children from the World's Great Illustrators* (6–12). Trans. by Stan Dragland. 2004, Groundwood $25.00 (978-0-88899-559-9). Artwork by children's book illustrators from around the world celebrates children's literature and the work of the International Board on Books for Young People. (Rev: BL 12/15/04; SLJ 1/05) [741.6]

8419 Bitner, Jason, and Alex Kotlowitz. *LaPorte, Indiana* (9–12). 2006, Princeton Architectural paper $19.95 (978-1-56898-530-5). A collection of 200 portraits of LaPorte residents taken during the 1950s and 1960s. (Rev: BL 4/15/06) [977.2]

8420 Danziger, Danny. *Museum: Behind the Scenes at the Metropolitan Museum of Art* (9–12). 2007, Viking $27.95 (978-0-670-03861-9). An inside look at the workings of New York City's huge museum and at its treasures and many employees. (Rev: BL 5/15/07) [708]

8421 de Rynck, Patrick, ed. *How to Read a Painting: Lessons from the Old Masters* (8–12). 2004, Abrams $35.00 (978-0-8109-5576-9). Introduces readers to the symbols, themes, and motifs that aid understanding of the great masters' art; two-page spreads display 150 paintings and frescoes. (Rev: BL 12/15/04) [753]

8422 Ditko, Steve, et al. *Marvel Visionaries: Steve Ditko* (9–12). 2005, Marvel $29.99 (978-0-7851-1783-4). The work of longtime comic book artist Steve Ditko,

co-creator of Spider-Man, is showcased in this attractive volume. (Rev: BL 8/05) [741.5]

8423 Fillion, Susan. *Miss Etta and Dr. Claribel: Bringing Matisse to America* (8–12). Illus. 2011, Godine $18.95 (978-1-56792-434-3). Tells the story of two art-loving sisters responsible for introducing America to Picasso, Matisse, and many other artists from Europe, Asia, and Africa in the early 20th century; this well-designed book includes many illustrations and reproductions. (Rev: BL 10/1/11; HB 9–10/11; SLJ 9/1/11*) [709.2]

8424 Ganz, Nicholas. *Graffiti World: Street Art from Five Continents* (8–12). Ed. by Tristan Manco. 2004, Abrams $35.00 (978-0-8109-4979-9). Graffiti from around the world is organized by continent and then by artist, with more than 2,000 color photos showing the common themes and wonderful inventiveness of these artists. (Rev: BL 1/1–15/05; SLJ 5/05) [751.7]

8425 Geisel, Theodor Seuss. *The Early Works of Dr. Seuss, Vol. 1* (10–12). 2005, Checker paper $22.95 (978-0-9753808-9-5). A look at Seuss's early works including political cartoons, advertising layouts, and art for government pamphlets. (Rev: BL 11/1/05) [741.5]

8426 Hand, John Oliver. *National Gallery of Art: Master Paintings from the Collection* (8–12). 2004, Abrams $60.00 (978-0-8109-5619-3). Four hundred paintings from the National Gallery serve as the base for a satisfying review of European and American art. (Rev: BL 11/15/04) [750]

8427 Kallen, Stuart A. *Photography* (7–12). Series: Eye on Art. 2007, Gale LB $32.45 (978-1-59018-986-3). Tracing the history of the camera and of photography as an art form, this volume includes plenty of photographs that illustrate concepts and styles. (Rev: BL 11/1/07; LMC 2/08; SLJ 12/07) [770]

8428 Lehmann, Timothy R. *Manga: Masters of the Art* (11–12). 2005, Collins Design paper $24.95 (978-0-

06-083331-2). For mature manga fans, Lehmann offers interviews with 12 noted artists. (Rev: BL 12/15/05) [741.5]

8429 *Life: The Platinum Anniversary Collection* (7–12). 2006, Time-Life $29.95 (978-1-933405-17-9). This is a showcase of the best of 70 years of *Life* photography. (Rev: BL 11/15/06) [070.4]

8430 Masur, Louis P. *The Soiling of Old Glory: The Story of a Photograph That Shocked America* (9–12). 2008, Bloomsbury $24.95 (978-1-59691-364-6). One picture *is* worth a thousand words — in this case, a photograph taken during a race riot in Boston in 1976 of a young white man attacking a black man with a metal flagpole, from which hangs the American flag. (Rev: BL 3/15/08) [974.4]

8431 Moore, Alan. *DC Universe: The Stories of Alan Moore* (9–12). 2006, DC Comics paper $19.99 (978-1-4012-0927-8). This volume showcases some of comic book artist Alan Moore's earlier work for DC Comics. (Rev: BL 3/1/06) [741.5]

8432 Nairne, Sandy, and Sarah Howgate. *The Portrait Now* (9–12). 2006, Yale paper $40.00 (978-0-300-11524-6). The varied forms, subjects, and impacts of these portraits will inspire artists and casual browsers alike. (Rev: BL 4/15/06) [704.9]

8433 Raczka, Bob. *Unlikely Pairs: Fun with Famous Works of Art* (4–10). 2005, Millbrook LB $23.93 (978-0-7613-2936-7); paper $9.95 (978-0-7613-2378-5). Raczka pairs famous works from different eras and styles (Rodin's "The Thinker" appears to be considering a move on Klee's chessboard, for example); a closing catalog offers factual information. (Rev: SLJ 12/05) [750]

8434 Webb, Linda, ed. *Beatles Art: Fantastic New Artwork of the Fab Four* (9–12). 2006, Boxigami paper $29.95 (978-0-9754176-2-1). More than 100 works of art by contemporary artists are inspired by the Beatles themselves, their songs, and their performances. (Rev: SLJ 9/06)

History of Art

8435 Baskett, John. *The Horse in Art* (8–12). 2006, Yale $45.00 (978-0-300-11740-0). Representations of horses in both two- and three-dimensional art are presented here, from ancient Greek and Roman battle scenes to medieval, Renaissance, Baroque, 19th-century, and modern-day works, including pieces by Stubbs, Rubens, and Remington. (Rev: BL 11/1/06) [704.94]

8436 Belloli, Andrea. *Exploring World Art* (7–12). 1999, Getty Museum $27.50 (978-0-89236-510-4). Using examples from world art and artifacts, this work introduces a variety of media and images under such chap-

ter headings as "Daily Life" and "History and Myth." (Rev: BL 1/1–15/00; HBG 4/00; SLJ 4/00) [709]

8437 Cole, Bruce, and Adelheid M. Gealt. *Art of the Western World: From Ancient Greece to Post-Modernism* (9–12). 1989, Summit paper $22.00 (978-0-671-74728-2). Along with many full-color reproductions, this is a excellent compact survey of the history of Western art. [709]

8438 Gombrich, E. H. *The Story of Art. Rev. ed.* (9–12). 1995, Chronicle $49.95 (978-0-7148-3355-2); paper $29.95 (978-0-7148-3247-0). A revision of a comprehensive standard art book, with 443 color illustrations. (Rev: BL 10/1/95) [709]

8439 *The Guerrilla Girls' Bedside Companion to the History of Western Art* (10–12). 1998, Viking paper $20.00 (978-0-14-025997-1). An introductory overview of traditional art history is followed by chapters highlighting the work of female artists during each time period, with reproductions of "mistresspieces" that have been overlooked by traditional male critics. The Guerrilla Girls are a group of anonymous artists and art professionals who seek to expose racism, sexism, and homophobia in the art world. (Rev: SLJ 9/98) [709]

8440 Janson, H. W., and Anthony F. Janson. *History of Art. 6th ed.* (9–12). 2001, Abrams $95.00 (978-0-8109-3446-7). This is a basic, well-respected (but expensive) history of art that is particularly strong on coverage of 20th-century art. (Rev: BL 5/1/01) [709]

8441 Johnson, Paul. *Art: A New History* (10–12). 2003, HarperCollins $39.95 (978-0-06-053075-4). In a fresh, new look at the history of art, Johnson traces the cultural backdrop of artistic vision from the cave paintings of prehistory to the modern era. (Rev: BL 10/1/03*) [709]

8442 Khalili, Nasser D. *Islamic Art and Culture: A Visual History* (8–12). 2006, Overlook $60.00 (978-1-58567-839-6). This is a large and varied collection of examples of Islamic art, ranging from carpets and textiles, paintings, jewelry, and lacquer to calligraphy, metal work, scientific instruments, and weapons; a good introduction to the culture of Islam. (Rev: BL 11/1/06) [709]

8443 Little, Stephen. . . . *Isms: Understanding Art* (9–12). 2004, Universe $16.95 (978-0-7893-1209-9). An introduction to the major movements that have shaped the world of art, covering more than 50 "isms" and profiling key artists and works. (Rev: BL 12/15/04) [709]

8444 Mason, Antony. *A History of Western Art: From Prehistory to the 20th Century* (7–10). 2007, Abrams $22.50 (978-0-8109-9421-8). A sweeping overview of important sculpture, architecture, painting, and other works from Western culture from the ancient to the postmodern, presented in a pleasing, uncrowded design. (Rev: BL 2/1/08; SLJ 4/08) [709]

8445 Mason, Antony. *In the Time of Michelangelo: The Renaissance Period* (7–10). Series: Art Around the World. 2001, Millbrook LB $23.90 (978-0-7613-2455-

3). Full of full-color reproductions, this volume not only looks at the work of major artists of the Renaissance but also profiles artists in other parts of the world during the 15th and 16th centuries. Also use *In the Time of Renoir: The Impressionist Era* (2001). (Rev: HBG 10/02; SLJ 3/02) [709]

8446 Newhall, Beaumont. *The History of Photography: From 1839 to the Present Day. Rev. ed.* (10–12). 1982, Bulfinch paper $32.95 (978-0-87070-381-2). A history of photography that gives many prints representing the best from the past and present. [770.9]

8447 Opie, Mary-Jane. *Sculpture* (7–12). Series: Eyewitness Art. 1994, DK $16.95 (978-1-56458-613-1). A handsome book filled with color illustrations introducing the world of sculpture, its history, and its various forms and materials. (Rev: BL 12/1/94; SLJ 6/95; VOYA 5/95) [730]

8448 Robinson, Shannon. *Cubism* (6–12). Series: Movements in Art. 2005, Creative Education LB $31.35 (978-1-58341-347-0). A review of cubism from the works of Picasso and Braque through the movement's influence on sculpture and architecture, with large, clear reproductions. (Rev: SLJ 2/06)

8449 Roukes, Nicholas. *Humor in Art: A Celebration of Visual Wit* (10–12). 1997, Davis $32.50 (978-0-87912-304-8). With numerous black-and-white and color illustrations and a lively text, this book explores humor in art, with examples from artists both past and present. (Rev: SLJ 12/97) [701]

8450 Sandler, Martin W. *Photography: An Illustrated History* (6–12). 2002, Oxford $39.99 (978-0-19-512608-2). An overview of photography's major figures and developments, from its invention to new technologies, featuring many photographs. (Rev: BL 4/15/02; HBG 3/03; SLJ 6/02; VOYA 4/02) [770.9]

8451 *30,000 Years of Art: The Story of Human Creativity across Time and Space* (7–12). 2007, Phaidon $49.95 (978-0-7148-4789-4). Arranged chronologically, 1,000 beautifully reproduced pieces of art illustrate the evolution of creativity around the world. (Rev: BL 11/1/07) [700]

8452 *Treasures from the Art Institute of Chicago* (9–12). 2000, Art Institute of Chicago $75.00 (978-0-86559-182-0). More than 400 reproductions are the glory of this volume, which traces the history of world art through the holdings of the Art Institute of Chicago. (Rev: BL 12/15/00; SLJ 7/01) [709]

8453 Zuffi, Stefano. *The Cat in Art* (8–12). Trans. by Simon Jones. 2007, Abrams $35.00 (978-0-8109-9328-0). A survey of art featuring cats serves to introduce a wide variety of artists — from Raphael and Rembrandt to Picasso and Warhol — and art forms. (Rev: BL 5/1/07) [704.9]

Regions

Europe

8454 Adams, Laurie Schneider. *Italian Renaissance Art* (9–12). 2001, Westview paper $60.00 (978-0-8133-3691-6). This is an exquisite introduction to the people, places, and events associated with the art of the Italian Renaissance, with a focus on paintings but additional coverage of architecture and sculpture. (Rev: BL 5/15/01) [709.02]

8455 Brettell, Richard R. *Impression: Painting Quickly in France, 1860-1890* (10–12). 2001, Yale $55.00 (978-0-300-08446-7). Impressionism is explored in this beautiful book, with special material that shows the techniques employed by such artists as Manet, Monet, and van Gogh. (Rev: BL 3/15/01) [759.054]

8456 Gunderson, Jessica. *Gothic Art* (5–10). Series: Movements in Art. 2008, Creative Education $32.80 (978-1-58341-610-5). With good reproductions and clear historical context, Gunderson looks at the era of Gothic art. Also use *Realism* and *Romanticism* (both 2008). (Rev: SLJ 12/08) [709.02]

8457 Impelluso, Lucia. *Nature and Its Symbols* (8–12). Trans. by Stephen Sartarelli. 2004, Getty Museum paper $24.95 (978-0-89236-772-6). A helpful guide to the symbols found in European painters' depictions of the natural world from the 14th through the 17th centuries. (Rev: BL 12/15/04) [704.9]

8458 Marani, Pietro C. *Leonardo da Vinci: The Complete Paintings* (9–12). 2000, Abrams $85.00 (978-0-8109-3581-5). This enormous tome tracks only 31 paintings in all media, with exhaustive material on each work and a total of 295 illustrations, most of them colorplates. (Rev: BL 12/15/00) [759.5]

8459 Rebman, Renee C. *The Sistine Chapel* (7–10). Series: Building History. 2000, Lucent LB $28.70 (978-1-56006-640-8). This account includes material on Michelangelo's original creation, his conflicts with the Pope, and the recent restorations of the ceiling. (Rev: BL 9/15/00; HBG 3/01) [945]

United States

8460 Adams, Ansel. *Ansel Adams: Our National Parks* (9–12). 1992, Little, Brown paper $19.95 (978-0-8212-1910-2). A collection of photographs, essays, and letters. (Rev: BL 5/15/92) [770]

8461 Amaki, Amalia K., ed. *A Century of African American Art: The Paul R. Jones Collection* (8–12). 2004, Rutgers paper $29.95 (978-0-8135-3457-2). The work of 66 African American artists is showcased in this attractive volume that includes profiles and commentary. (Rev: BL 2/1/05) [704.03]

8462 Biel, Steven. *American Gothic: A Life of America's Most Famous Painting* (10–12). 2005, Norton $21.95 (978-0-393-05912-0). The history and multiple meanings of "American Gothic," one of this country's most iconic paintings. (Rev: BL 5/1/05) [759.13]

8463 Curtis, Edward S., and Christopher Cardozo. *Edward S. Curtis: The Women* (8–12). 2005, Bulfinch $35.00 (978-0-8212-2895-1). This stunning volume showcases 100 of photographer Edward S. Curtis's portraits of Native American women. (Rev: BL 4/1/05) [779]

8464 Glaser, Milton. *Art Is Work: Graphic Design, Interiors, Objects, and Illustration* (10–12). 2000, Overlook $85.00 (978-1-58567-069-7). The author uses his own work on book jackets, record covers, ad posters, and soup cans to illustrate the many sides of graphic, commercial art. (Rev: BL 12/15/00) [741.6]

8465 Jordan, Chris. *In Katrina's Wake: Portraits of Loss from an Unnatural Disaster* (9–12). 2006, Princeton Architectural $35.00 (978-1-56898-622-7). Artistic images of surfaces and objects both man-made and natural, full of irony, color, and confusion, make up this photo-essay on the aftermath of Hurricane Katrina. (Rev: BL 9/15/06) [976.04]

8466 Nesbitt, Peter T., and Michelle DuBois. *The Complete Jacob Lawrence* (10–12). 2000, Univ. of Washington $150.00 (978-0-295-97963-2). Though very expensive, this two-volume set is a magnificent tribute to one of the great African American artists. (Rev: BL 11/15/00) [759.13]

8467 Panchyk, Richard. *American Folk Art for Kids: With 21 Activities* (6–12). 2004, Chicago Review paper $16.95 (978-1-55652-499-8). This historical survey of American folk art is supplemented by detailed instruc-

tions for projects that readers can make for themselves. (Rev: BL 11/1/04; SLJ 11/04) [745]

8468 Sandusky, Phil. *Painting Katrina* (9–12). 2007, Pelican $19.95 (978-1-58980-477-7). Sandusky's luminous paintings of New Orleans before and after Katrina reveal both the extent of the destruction and the impact of paintings rather than TV reportage. (Rev: BL 10/15/07) [759.13]

8469 Slowik, Theresa J. *America's Art: Smithsonian American Art Museum* (8–12). 2006, Abrams $65.00 (978-0-8109-5532-5). An oversize volume showcasing some of the best-known works in the collection of the Smithsonian American Art Museum. (Rev: BL 3/15/06) [709]

8470 Smolan, Rick, and David Elliot Cohen. *America 24/7: 24 Hours, 7 Days: Extraordinary Images of One American Week* (9–12). 2003, DK $50.00 (978-0-7894-9975-2). In a single week, more than 25,000 professional and amateur photographers took digital photographs of life in America; the 1,000+ images published here show the diversity of everyday life. (Rev: SLJ 4/04) [779]

8471 Sneden, Robert Knox. *Images from the Storm: 300 Civil War Images by the Author of Eye of the Storm* (10–12). 2001, Free Press $50.00 (978-0-7432-2360-7). This is an outstanding collection of the paintings Robert Knox Sneden began while he was a Union soldier and reworked after the war. (Rev: BL 8/01*; SLJ 2/02) [973.7]

8472 Storr, Robert, et al. *Art 21: Art in the Twenty-first Century* (10–12). 2001, Abrams $65.00 (978-0-8109-1397-4). Twenty-one living artists of different generations, backgrounds, and artistic metiers are introduced in this overview of contemporary American visual artists. (Rev: BL 12/15/01) [709]

524

Decorative Arts

8473 Emert, Phyllis Raybin. *Art in Glass* (7–12). Series: Eye on Art. 2007, Gale LB $32.45 (978-1-59018-983-2). This book reviews the history of glassmaking from ancient times through Venetian glass to art nouveau and art deco to contemporary styles and techniques. (Rev: LMC 2/08; SLJ 12/07) [748]

8474 Kurin, Richard. *Hope Diamond: The Legendary Story of a Cursed Gem* (9–12). 2006, HarperCollins $24.95 (978-0-06-087351-6). The mystery and romance surrounding the famous diamond are captured in this account, which carefully traces its provenance. (Rev: BL 5/1/06) [736]

Music

General and Miscellaneous

8475 Barker, Hugh, and Yuval Taylor. *Faking It: The Quest for Authenticity in Popular Music* (10–12). 2007, Norton $25.95 (978-0-393-06078-2). The tension between commercial forces and authentic performance is discussed using musicians and musical groups including Nirvana, Elvis Presley, the Beatles, and Neil Young as examples. (Rev: BL 2/15/07) [781.6409]

8476 Evans, Roger. *How to Read Music: For Singing, Guitar, Piano, Organ, and Most Instruments* (8–12). 1979, Crown paper $10.00 (978-0-517-88438-6). An easily understood introduction to music notation and score reading for the beginner. [781.4]

8477 Laine, Kristen. *American Band: Music, Dreams, and Coming of Age in the Heartland* (9–12). 2007, Gotham $26.00 (978-1-59240-319-6). Follows the ups and downs of a small-town high school band — the Concord (Indiana) Marching Minutemen. (Rev: BL 9/15/07) [784.8]

8478 Levitin, David J. *This Is Your Brain on Music: The Science of a Human Obsession* (10–12). 2006, Dutton $24.95 (978-0-525-94969-5). Levitin offers an accessible survey of our relationship with music since the earliest days, reviewing how we perceive sounds, rhythms, pitches, and so forth, and how we retain musical memories. (Rev: SLJ 11/06)

8479 Sacks, Oliver. *Musicophilia: Tales of Music and the Brain* (9–12). 2007, Knopf $25.00 (978-1-4000-4081-0). Sacks discusses the amazing ways in which the brain processes music — and music influences thinking and imagining. (Rev: BL 9/1/07) [781]

History of Music

8480 Gilbert, Sara. *Play It Loud! The Rebellious History of Music* (6–10). Illus. Series: Pop Culture Revolutions. 2010, Compass Point LB $31.99 (978-0-7565-4243-6). This title discusses the history of music with a counterculture message, and profiles artists ranging from J. S. Bach to Tupac Shakur. (Rev: SLJ 5/10) [780.9]

8481 Kallen, Stuart A. *The History of Classical Music* (6–10). Series: Music Library. 2002, Gale LB $32.45 (978-1-59018-123-2). This overview covers classical music and composers starting with the Middle Ages, providing interesting excerpts from primary documents. Also use *The History of Jazz* (2002). (Rev: BL 11/1/02) [781.6]

8482 Scherer, Barrymore Laurence. *A History of American Classical Music* (9–12). 2007, Sourcebooks $29.95 (978-1-4022-1067-9). With its accompanying CD of 18 excerpts, this is a useful chronological guide to American classical music, intended for the layman. (Rev: BL 11/1/07) [781.6]

8483 Swafford, Jan. *The Vintage Guide to Classical Music* (9–12). 1992, Vintage paper $17.00 (978-0-679-72805-4). Chronological essays cover the lives and compositions of nearly 100 of the world's greatest composers. [781.6]

Jazz and Popular Music (Country, Rap, Rock, etc.)

8484 *American Popular Music: Blues* (9–12). Series: American Popular Music. 2005, Facts on File $67.00 (978-0-8160-5310-0). Part of an eight-volume set, this encyclopedia includes entries on blues artists, styles, genres, and so forth. (Rev: BL 4/15/06) [781.643]

8485 *American Popular Music: Rhythm and Blues, Rap, and Hip-Hop* (9–12). 2005, Facts on File $67.00 (978-0-8160-5315-5). This volume on rhythm and blues, rap and hip-hop is part of the American Popular Music set and provides information on artists, musical styles, and other relevant topics. (Rev: BL 4/15/06) [781.643]

8486 *American Popular Music: Rock and Roll* (9–12). 2005, Facts on File $67.00 (978-0-8160-5317-9). Artist biographies, descriptions of musical styles and other topics related to rock and roll are featured in this volume. (Rev: BL 4/15/06) [781.66]

8487 Aquila, Richard. *That Old Time Rock and Roll: A Chronicle of an Era, 1954-1963* (8–12). 1989, Schirmer $25.00 (978-0-02-870082-3). A history complete with important biographies from the first decade of rock. (Rev: BL 9/15/89) [784.5]

8488 Beaujon, Andrew. *Body Piercing Saved My Life: Inside the Phenomenon of Christian Rock* (9–12). 2006, Da Capo paper $16.95 (978-0-306-81457-0). Borrowing his book title from a slogan on a T-shirt showing Christ's wounds, Beaujon, journalist for *Spin* magazine, investigates the booming subculture of Christian rock that combines hard rock or ballads with fundamentalist evangelical Christian beliefs. (Rev: SLJ 8/06)

8489 Blush, Steven. *American Hair Metal* (9–12). 2006, Feral House paper $22.95 (978-1-932595-18-5). Hair bands — flamboyant, big-haired, Spandex-clad male rock musicians with no shortage of female groupies — are the focus of this collection of photographs and interviews with stars from such bands as KISS, Mötley Crüe, and Poison. (Rev: BL 10/15/06) [782.421]

8490 Bradley, Adam, and Andrew DuBois, eds. *The Anthology of Rap* (10–12). 2010, Yale $35 (978-030014190-0). An extensive anthology of rap lyrics, presented chronologically starting with "The Old School" (1978 to 1984). (Rev: BL 11/1–15/10) [782.421]

8491 Bradley, Lloyd. *This Is Reggae Music: The Story of Jamaica's Music* (10–12). 2001, Grove paper $18.00 (978-0-8021-3828-6). An overview that identifies and covers the origins and history of reggae, the personalities involved, and how it came to the U.S. and became commercialized. (Rev: BL 10/15/01) [782.4]

8492 Brown, Ethan. *Queens Reigns Supreme* (11–12). 2005, Anchor paper $13.00 (978-1-4000-9523-0). The music editor of *New York* magazine explores the links between the 1980s cocaine trade in Queens borough and the "gangsta" rap movement in popular music. (Rev: BL 12/1/05) [364.106]

8493 Burns, Kate, ed. *Rap Music and Culture* (9–12). Series: Current Controversies. 2008, Gale/Greenhaven $36.20 (978-0-7377-3964-0); paper $24.95 (978-0-7377-3965-7). More than 20 essays consider various

aspects of rapping, DJ-ing, break dancing, hip-hop, and graffiti and their contributions — as well as sometimes destructive messages — within African American culture. (Rev: SLJ 3/1/09) [306.4]

8494 Bynoe, Yvonne. *Encyclopedia of Rap and Hip Hop Culture* (9–12). 2005, Greenwood $69.95 (978-0-313-33058-2). Alphabetical entries cover all the elements of the hip-hop culture, such as the lyrics, instrumentals, break dancing, aerosol painting, and artists. (Rev: BL 6/1–15/06; SLJ 6/06)

8495 Cepeda, Raquel, ed. *And It Don't Stop* (11–12). 2004, Faber and Faber paper $15.00 (978-0-571-21159-3). The best in media coverage of hip-hop music and culture is collected in this volume suitable for mature readers. (Rev: BL 9/1/04) [782.42]

8496 Cooper, Kim, and David Smay, eds. *Bubblegum Music Is the Naked Truth: The Dark History of Prepubescent Pop, from the Banana Splits to Britney Spears* (10–12). 2001, Feral House paper $19.95 (978-0-922915-69-9). This book explores the music that is merchandised to preteens and young teens with articles on individual bands, record labels, and spinoffs to other media. (Rev: BL 9/15/01) [782.42166]

8497 Delancey, Morgan. *Dave Matthews Band: Step Into the Light.* Rev. 2nd ed. (7–12). 2001, ECW paper $16.95 (978-1-55022-443-6). In addition to a detailed history of the band, this revised edition includes interviews with band members. (Rev: VOYA 8/02) [782.42]

8498 Dutton, Monte. *True to the Roots: Americana Music Revealed* (11–12). 2006, Univ. of Nebraska $24.95 (978-0-8032-6661-2). Dutton interviews performers and bands that showcase a music genre known as Americana that is described as noncommercial, American-roots-based, and alternative country, it is also considered a state of mind. (Rev: BL 12/1/06) [781.642]

8499 Espejo, Roman, ed. *Should Music Lyrics Be Censored for Violence and Exploitation?* (9–12). Series: At Issue. 2008, Gale/Greenhaven LB $29.95 (978-0-7377-4064-6); paper $23.96 (978-0-7377-4065-3). Diverse articles present varying viewpoints on violent and negative lyrics and the harm they potentially cause. (Rev: SLJ 2/1/09) [303.3]

8500 Evans, Mike, ed. *Woodstock: Three Days That Rocked the World* (10–12). Illus. 2009, Sterling $35 (978-140276623-7). This pictorial tribute book features many photographs and recollections from fans and musicians who were at the famous concert. (Rev: BL 7/09) [781.66]

8501 Freeman, Phil, ed. *Marooned: The Next Generation of Desert Island Discs* (9–12). 2007, Da Capo paper $16.95 (978-0-306-81485-3). Following up on *Stranded* (1979), this collection of desert island choices includes an eclectic mix of old and new. (Rev: BL 8/07) [781.64]

527

8502 Fyfe, Andy. *When the Levee Breaks: The Making of Led Zeppelin IV* (10–12). 2003, Chicago Review paper $14.95 (978-1-55652-508-7). A behind-the-scenes look at the making of the influential rockers' best-selling album. (Rev: BL 10/1/03) [781.42166]

8503 Gioia, Ted. *The History of Jazz* (9–12). 1997, Oxford paper $19.95 (978-0-19-512653-2). The evolution of jazz and its key figures are covered in this well-researched volume. (Rev: BL 11/15/97) [781.65]

8504 Goldman, Vivien. *The Book of Exodus: The Making and Meaning of Bob Marley and the Wailers' Album of the Century* (9–12). 2006, Three Rivers paper $14.95 (978-1-4000-5286-8). A fascinating look at the history behind Marley's Exodus album of 1977. Goldman explains the artist's political and religious beliefs as well as the roots of reggae. (Rev: BL 4/15/06) [781.646092]

8505 Greenwald, Andy. *Nothing Feels Good: Punk Rock, Teenagers, and Emo* (10–12). 2003, St. Martin's paper $14.95 (978-0-312-30863-6). In this thoughtful analysis, a music historian profiles the rise of emo, an increasingly popular musical genre that some have described as emotionally charged punk rock. (Rev: BL 11/1/03) [782.42166]

8506 Gueraseva, Stacy. *Def Jam, Inc: Russell Simmons, Rick Rubin, and the Extraordinary Story of the World's Most Influential Hip-Hop Label* (11–12). 2005, Ballantine $23.95 (978-0-345-46804-8). The story behind the founding, growth, and financial ups and downs of the record label Def Jam. (Rev: BL 8/05; SLJ 11/05) [782.4]

8507 Higgins, Dalton. *Hip Hop World* (9–12). 2009, Groundwood $18.95 (978-0-88899-910-8); paper $10 (978-0-88899-911-5). This exploration of the genre of hip-hop discusses prevalent themes in the music and explains how the art form, now less socially relevant in the West, is becoming an increasingly popular and effective means of self-expression and social commentary in regions as diverse as Asia and the Middle East. (Rev: BL 11/1/09; SLJ 11/09) [782.421]

8508 Hirshey, Gerri. *Nowhere to Run: The Story of Soul Music* (9–12). 2006, Southbank paper $16.95 (978-1-904915-10-2). A history of soul music and practitioners such as James Brown, Aretha Franklin, and Michael Jackson; first published in 1984. [784.5]

8509 Kallen, Stuart A. *The History of Rock and Roll* (6–10). Series: Music Library. 2002, Gale LB $32.45 (978-1-59018-126-3). Beginning in the early 1950s, this account traces the history of rock and roll, profiles many musicians involved, and describes the unique characteristics of this form of music. (Rev: BL 3/15/03) [781.66]

8510 Kot, Greg. *Wilco: Learning How to Die* (10–12). 2004, Broadway paper $14.00 (978-0-7679-1558-8). The story of Wilco, an alt-country rock group that abandoned its record label to self-market the album it believed in. (Rev: BL 6/1–15/04; SLJ 10/04) [781.66]

8511 Kurutz, Steven. *Like a Rolling Stone: The Strange Life of a Tribute Band* (9–12). 2008, Broadway $23.95 (978-0-385-51890-1). This volume profiles the tribute bands that make a marginal living imitating famous bands. (Rev: BL 4/1/08) [782.42]

8512 Lang, Michael, and Holly George-Warren. *The Road to Woodstock: From the Man Behind the Legendary Festival* (9–12). Illus. 2009, Ecco $29.99 (978-006157655-3). One of the organizers of the rock event describes the planning for the festival and the aspects that just didn't work out. (Rev: BL 7/09) [781.66]

8513 Manning, Sean, ed. *The Show I'll Never Forget: 50 Writers Relive Their Most Memorable Concert-Going Experience* (10–12). 2007, Da Capo paper $16.95 (978-0-306-81508-9). R.E.M., Van Morrison, the Rolling Stones, Prince, Miles Davis, the Beatles, Billy Joel — these and many more performers are featured in these accounts of favorite concerts. (Rev: BL 1/1–15/07) [780.78]

8514 Marsalis, Wynton. *Jazz A B Z: An A to Z Collection of Jazz Portraits* (7–12). Illus. by Paul Rogers. 2005, Candlewick $24.99 (978-0-7636-2135-3). Arranged in alphabet-book format, this strikingly illustrated volume celebrates jazz and its best-known practitioners. (Rev: BL 1/1–15/06; SLJ 1/06*) [811]

8515 Marsalis, Wynton. *Marsalis on Music* (9–12). 1995, Norton $29.95 (978-0-393-03881-1). A manual that uses examples from jazz greats to teach the fundamentals of jazz and the elements of improvisation. Includes a CD. (Rev: BL 10/1/95) [780]

8516 Marsalis, Wynton, and Geoffrey C. Ward. *Moving to Higher Ground: How Jazz Can Change Your Life* (10–12). Illus. 2008, Random House $26.00 (978-1-4000-6078-8). Marsalis explains the important role jazz played and continues to play in his life, and discusses several genres of music in great detail. ℮ (Rev: BL 8/08*) [781.65]

8517 Morse, Tim. *Classic Rock Stories: The Stories Behind the Greatest Songs of All Time* (10–12). 1998, Griffin paper $12.95 (978-0-312-18067-6). A history of rock during the 1960s and 1970s, with insights into hit songs and the artists who recorded them, among them Paul McCartney, Mick Jagger, Rod Stewart, Elton John, and Alice Cooper, plus an update on where they are today. (Rev: SLJ 1/99) [781.66]

8518 Nichols, Travis. *Punk Rock Etiquette: The Ultimate How-To Guide for DIY, Punk, Indie and Underground Bands* (7–10). Illus. by author. 2008, Flash Point $10.95 (978-159643415-8). This irreverent guide delivers lots of laughs as well as some practical, sage advice. ℮ (Rev: BL 9/1/08; SLJ 12/08; VOYA 10/08) [781.6]

8519 Oliver, Richard, and Tim Leffel. *Hip-Hop, Inc: Success Strategies of the Rap Moguls* (9–12). 2006, Thunder's Mouth paper $14.95 (978-1-56025-732-5). Authors Richard Oliver and Tim Leffel chronicle the success stories of rap moguls Sean "Diddy" Combs, Percy "Master P" Millers, and Russell Simmons. (Rev: BL 3/1/06) [782.4]

8520 Pollock, Bruce. *By the Time We Got to Woodstock: The Great Rock 'n' Roll Revolution of 1969* (10–12). Illus. 2009, Backbeat paper $19.99 (978-08793097-9-4). Focusing mostly on 1969, Pollock discusses the impact of the music of the 1960s and the events he believes caused the end of that idealistic time. (Rev: BL 9/09) [781.6609]

8521 Raymer, Miles. *How to Analyze the Music of Paul McCartney* (8–12). Illus. Series: Essential Critiques. 2010, ABDO LB $22.95 (978-161613531-7). After an overview of McCartney himself and the Beatles' music, this book explains how to apply biographical and historical criticism to his music over the decades, with a particular focus on gender and historical themes. (Rev: BL 12/15/10) [782.42]

8522 Robertson, Brian. *Little Blues Book* (10–12). 1996, Algonquin paper $15.95 (978-1-56512-137-9). A history of the blues and blues singers covering the past 70 years, with numerous quotations from the artists and their songs. (Rev: SLJ 6/97) [782]

8523 Rose, Tricia. *Black Noise: Rap Music and Black Culture in Contemporary America* (9–12). 1994, Wesleyan Univ. paper $16.95 (978-0-8195-6275-3). An analysis of various facets of rap, including a discussion of hip-hop and the neglected recognition of women's role in rap. (Rev: BL 4/15/94) [782.42]

8524 Russell, Tony. *The Blues: From Robert Johnson to Robert Cray* (10–12). 1998, Schirmer paper $18.00 (978-0-02-864886-6). More than 400 blues musicians are profiled — 24 in depth — and lists highlight important recordings and festivals in the United States and Europe. [781.643]

8525 RZA, The, and Chris Norris. *The Wu-Tang Manual* (9–12). 2005, Riverhead paper $16.00 (978-1-59448-018-8). Two members of the Wu-Tang Clan recount the story of the rap group's climb to success in the 1990s and also discuss its philosophy. (Rev: SLJ 7/05)

8526 Shipton, Alyn. *A New History of Jazz* (9–12). 2001, Continuum $35.00 (978-0-8264-4754-8). The true history of jazz is revealed in this excellent account that offers several theories on the origins of jazz. (Rev: BL 9/1/01) [781.65]

8527 Soocher, Stan. *They Fought the Law: Rock Music Goes to Court* (11–12). 1998, Schirmer $25.00 (978-0-02-864731-9). Collisions of pop music and litigation — most of them relating to questions of copyright and liability — are explored in this survey of court cases, for teens with a serious interest in the subject. (Rev: BL 11/15/98) [781.66]

8528 Spitz, Marc. *Nobody Likes You: Inside the Turbulent Life, Time, and Music of Green Day* (9–12). 2006, Hyperion $23.95 (978-1-4013-0274-0). Years after its huge success with the album *Dookie,* just when it seemed this punk band's popularity was over, it had a major comeback with *American Idiot,* which hit No. 1 on the *Billboard* charts and stayed on the charts for 18 months. (Rev: BL 10/15/06) [782.42166]

8529 Stroff, Stephen M. *Discovering Great Jazz: A New Listener's Guide to the Sounds and Styles of the Top Musicians and Their Recordings on CDs, LPs, and Cassettes* (9–12). 1991, Newmarket $19.95 (978-1-55704-103-6). A description of the stylistic developments in the history of jazz, with recommendations for the best recorded performances from each period up to the 1990s. (Rev: BL 10/1/91) [781.65]

8530 Sullivan, Caroline. *Bye Bye Baby: My Tragic Love Affair with the Bay City Rollers* (10–12). 2001, Bloomsbury paper $14.95 (978-0-7475-4703-7). This is a memoir by a rabid fan of the Bay City Rollers and an account of the band's popularity during the 1970s. (Rev: BL 2/15/01) [782.421]

8531 Ward, Geoffrey C., and Ken Burns. *Jazz: A History of America's Music* (10–12). 2000, Knopf $65.00 (978-0-679-44551-7). This history of jazz (based on the PBS television series) focuses on such greats as Louis Armstrong, Duke Ellington, Charlie Parker, and Miles Davis. (Rev: BL 9/15/00; SLJ 6/01) [781.65]

8532 Whitehead, Kevin. *Why Jazz? A Concise Guide* (10–12). 2011, Oxford $17.95 (978-019973118-3). This very basic introduction to jazz provides a history of the genre from its beginnings to the modern period, as well as information on music theory and important figures in the jazz world. (Rev: BL 11/1–15/10) [781.65]

8533 Willman, Chris. *Rednecks and Bluenecks: The Politics of Country Music* (10–12). 2005, New Press $25.95 (978-1-59558-017-7). Willman, senior writer for *Entertainment Weekly,* explores the diversity of political views within the country music industry. (Rev: BL 11/1/05) [781.642]

Opera and Musicals

8534 Brener, Milton. *Opera Offstage: Passion and Politics Behind the Great Operas* (10–12). 1996, Walker $24.95 (978-0-8027-1313-1). For each of the 26 operas discussed, a full plot summary is provided, along with material on musical forms used in the opera and its sources, which may include history, mythology, literature, politics, even the everyday experiences of the composer. (Rev: SLJ 7/97) [782.1]

8535 Freeman, John W. *The Metropolitan Opera Stories of the Great Operas* (9–12). 1984, Norton $29.95 (978-0-393-01888-2). Plots are given for 150 great operas with accompanying biographical material on their composers. [782.1]

8536 Sondheim, Stephen, and James Lapine. *Into the Woods* (9–12). 1989, Theatre Communications paper $10.95 (978-0-930452-93-3). The text and lyrics of the prize-winning musical about fairy tale characters and what happens to their "happily ever after." (Rev: BL 9/1/89) [782.81]

Orchestra and Musical Instruments

8537 Bacon, Tony, and Paul Day. *The Ultimate Guitar Book* (9–12). 1991, Knopf paper $27.50 (978-0-375-70090-3). Richly illustrated, this overview traces the guitar's evolution from its origins in 16th-century Spain through today's electronically enhanced instruments. [787.87]

8538 Evans, Roger. *How to Play Guitar: A New Book for Everyone Interested in Guitar* (8–12). 1980, St. Martin's paper $9.95 (978-0-312-36609-4). An easily followed basic guidebook on how to play the guitar with information on such topics as buying equipment and reading music. [787.6]

8539 Fleming, Tom. *The Complete Guitar Course* (9–12). 2006, Reader's Digest $30 (978-0-7621-0662-2). Information on great guitarists and their instruments adds to this comprehensive introduction to scales, chords, and hand positions, as do good charts, lots of photographs, and a wide variety of pieces to learn. (Rev: SLJ 12/06)

8540 Monath, Norman. *How to Play Popular Piano in Ten Easy Lessons* (10–12). 1984, Simon & Schuster paper $12.00 (978-0-671-53067-9). A useful guide that requires a great deal of work on the part of the reader. [786.2]

Songs and Folk Songs

8541 Collins, Ace. *Stories Behind the Best-Loved Songs of Christmas* (9–12). 2001, Zondervan $15.99 (978-0-310-23926-0). These are the stories behind such pop Christmas songs as "Silver Bells" and "Have Yourself a Merry Little Christmas." (Rev: BL 10/1/01) [264]

8542 Hart, Mickey, and K. M. Kostyal. *Songcatchers: In Search of the World's Music* (10–12). 2003, National Geographic $30.00 (978-0-7922-4107-2). Period photographs enhance this clearly written overview of the "songcatchers," men and women who track down and record traditional music. (Rev: BL 6/1–15/03) [780]

8543 McNeil, Keith, and Rusty McNeil. *Moving West Songbook: With Historical Commentary* (7–10). 2003, $15.95 (978-1-878360-30-4). Historical information, anecdotes, illustrations, and guitar chords accompany this large-format selection of about 50 songs of the early to mid-19th century. (Rev: BL 7/03; SLJ 11/03) [782.42]

8544 McNeil, Keith, and Rusty McNeil, eds. *California Songbook with Historical Commentary* (6–10). 2001, WEM Records $15.95 (978-1-878360-27-4). Music, chords, lyrics, and background information are given for a large selection of songs that originated in California. (Rev: BL 8/01) [782.42]

8545 Sandburg, Carl. *The American Songbag* (7–12). 1970, Harcourt paper $35.00 (978-0-15-605650-2). A fine collection of all kinds of American folk songs with music and background notes from Mr. Sandburg. [784.7]

Theater, Dance, and Other Performing Arts

General and Miscellaneous

8546 Babinski, Tony. *Cirque du Soleil: 20 Years Under the Sun* (9–12). 2004, Abrams $50.00 (978-0-8109-4636-1). Cirque du Soleil's growth from a group of young street performers to an international concern is documented with beautiful photographs. (Rev: BL 1/1–15/05; SLJ 5/05) [791.3]

8547 Ellis, Roger. *The Complete Audition Book for Young Actors: A Comprehensive Guide to Winning by Enhancing Acting Skills* (9–12). 2004, Meriwether paper $17.95 (978-1-56608-088-0). This practical, well-written guide covers the selection and preparation of material for an audition, cold readings, musical theater, and other more general aspects of a job search, with practical exercises and lists of resources. (Rev: SLJ 7/04) [792.02]

Dance (Ballet, Modern, etc.)

8548 Anderson, Janet. *Modern Dance* (7–12). Series: World of Dance. 2003, Chelsea House LB $30.00 (978-0-7910-7644-6). Traces the history of modern dance, describing key personalities and innovations and looking at a modern dance class. (Rev: SLJ 3/04; VOYA 8/04) [792.8]

8549 Balanchine, George, and Francis Mason. *101 Stories of the Great Ballets* (7–12). 1975, Doubleday paper $16.00 (978-0-385-03398-5). Both the classics and newer ballets are introduced plus general background material such as a brief history of ballet. [792.8]

8550 Glass, Barbara S. *African American Dance: An Illustrated History* (9–12). 2007, McFarland $55.00 (978-0-7864-2816-8). A fascinating survey of African American dance, tracing its roots and development and profiling key dancers, including Josephine Baker and Chubby Checker. (Rev: BL 2/1/07) [792.8]

8551 Haskins, Jim. *Black Dance in America: A History Through Its People* (7–12). 1990, HarperCollins LB $14.89 (978-0-690-04659-5). Beginning with the dances brought from Africa by the slaves, this history moves to the present with the contributions of such people as Gregory Hines and Alvin Ailey. (Rev: BL 8/90; SLJ 6/90; VOYA 6/90) [792.8]

8552 Heth, Charlotte, ed. *Native American Dance: Ceremonies and Social Traditions* (9–12). 1993, Starwood paper $29.95 (978-1-56373-021-4). Celebrates Indian dance ceremonies and social traditions, past and present, throughout the Americas. Color photographs. (Rev: BL 4/1/93*) [394.3]

8553 Kuklin, Susan. *Reaching for Dreams: A Ballet from Rehearsal to Opening Night* (7–12). 2001, iUniverse paper $13.95 (978-0-595-17081-4). Using the introduction of a new ballet into the Alvin Ailey dance company's repetoire as a springboard, this is the account of the pangs of creation in the ballet world; first published in 1987. (Rev: BL 3/1/87; BR 11–12/87; SLJ 5/87; VOYA 12/87) [792.8]

8554 Rinaldi, Robin. *Ballet* (7–12). Series: World of Dance. 2003, Chelsea House LB $30.00 (978-0-7910-7640-8). Traces the history of ballet, describing key personalities and innovations and looking at a modern ballet class. (Rev: SLJ 3/04; VOYA 8/04) [792.8]

8555 Roseman, Janet Lynn. *Dance Masters: Interviews with Legends of Dance* (10–12). 2001, Routledge $65.00 (978-0-415-92951-6); paper $20.95 (978-0-415-92952-3). Fans of contemporary dance will be interested in these seven conversations with such dancers and choreographers as Mark Morris, Merce Cunningham, and Edward Villella. (Rev: BL 5/1/01) [792.8]

8556 Sonnenfeld, Sandi. *This Is How I Speak: The Diary of a Young Woman* (10–12). 2002, Impassio paper $15.00 (978-0-9711583-1-3). A year in the life of a graduate dance student at the University of Washington; includes social and academic issues, plus an attack by a friend's boyfriend. (Rev: BL 6/1–15/02) [818]

Motion Pictures

8557 *Amistad: "Give us Free": A Celebration of the Film by Steven Spielberg* (9–12). 1998, Newmarket paper $27.50 (978-1-55704-351-1). After reviewing the *Amistad* insurrection, this book focuses on the casting, producing, and shooting of the film. (Rev: SLJ 12/98) [791.43]

8558 Brackett, Leigh, and Lawrence Kasdan. *The Empire Strikes Back: The Illustrated Screenplay* (8–12). 1998, Ballantine paper $12.00 (978-0-345-42070-1). The shooting script for the second of the original *Star Wars* trilogy, with action direction and drawings of action scenes, preceded by an introduction that includes background and thoughts about the movie trilogy from the perspectives of people who were involved with the first release of the films. (Rev: SLJ 12/98) [791.43]

8559 Brin, David, ed. *King Kong Is Back! An Unauthorized Look at One Humongous Ape!* (10–12). 2005, BenBella paper $17.95 (978-1-932100-64-8). This collection of essays analyzes the cultural impact of King Kong, brought to the screen in three motion picture incarnations since 1933. (Rev: BL 11/1/05) [791.43]

8560 Burtt, Ben. *Star Wars Galactic Phrase Book and Travel Guide: Beeps, Bleats, and Other Common Intergalactic Verbiage* (7–12). 2001, Ballantine $8.00 (978-0-345-44074-7). A small-format, travel guide/phrase book that will fascinate devotees of Star Wars. (Rev: SLJ 12/01; VOYA 6/02) [791.43]

8561 Clee, Paul. *Before Hollywood: From Shadow Play to the Silver Screen* (7–12). 2005, Clarion $22.00 (978-0-618-44533-2). Early technologies and the reactions of early audiences are the focus of this fascinating account. (Rev: BCCB 7–8/05; HB 9–10/05; SLJ 7/05) [791.43]

8562 Cowie, Peter, ed. *World Cinema: Diary of a Day* (9–12). 1995, Overlook $29.95 (978-0-87951-573-7). An overview of filmmaking, with input from directors, producers, technicians, and performers. (Rev: BL 3/15/95) [791.43]

8563 Hamen, Susan E. *How to Analyze the Films of the Coen Brothers* (8–11). Illus. Series: Essential Critiques. 2012, ABDO LB $34.22 (978-161783454-7). Biographical information on the brothers is followed by analysis of films including *O Brother, Where Art Thou?* and *Fargo*. (Rev: BL 11/1/12) [791.4302]

8564 Harryhausen, Ray, and Tony Dalton. *The Art of Ray Harryhausen* (9–12). 2006, Billboard $50.00 (978-0-8230-8400-5). Pioneering animator Harryhausen, best known for his fantasy films, offers readers a look at a representative collection of drawings, storyboards, and photographs of models from his archives. (Rev: BL 2/15/06) [791.43]

8565 Hemming, Roy. *The Melody Lingers On: The Great Songwriters and Their Movie Musicals* (9–12). 1999, Newmarket paper $24.95 (978-1-55704-380-1). A look at the great Hollywood musicals that featured songs and lyrics of 10 great writers, including Berlin, Gershwin, Kern, Porter, and Rogers. (Rev: SLJ 8/99) [791.43]

8566 Hirshenson, Janet, and Jane Jenkins. *A Star Is Found: Our Adventures Casting Some of Hollywood's Biggest Movies* (9–12). 2006, Harcourt $25.00 (978-0-15-101234-3). The authors share their experiences casting movies for a variety of Hollywood directors, and emphasize that even the smallest role is important. (Rev: BL 11/15/06) [791.4302]

8567 Jones, Sarah. *Film* (7–10). Series: MediaWise. 2003, Smart Apple LB $28.50 (978-1-58340-256-6). The world of film making is clearly explained, with information on everything from initial concept to financing to the mechanics of production. (Rev: BL 10/15/03; SLJ 11/03) [791.43]

8568 Kay, Glenn, and Michael Rose. *Disaster Movies: A Loud, Long, Explosive, Star-Studded Guide to Avalanches, Earthquakes, Floods, Meteors, Sinking Ships, Twisters, Viruses, Killer Bees, Nuclear Fallout, and Alien Attacks in the Cinema!!!!* (9–12). 2006, Chicago Review paper $18.95 (978-1-55652-612-1). This guide to good, tolerable, and awful disaster movies (categorized under "So Bad It's Good") is lots of fun, with carnage ratings and a chapter dedicated to ridiculous disaster movie concepts. Color photographs and stills add interest. (Rev: SLJ 10/06)

8569 King, Emily. *A Century of Movie Posters: From Silent to Art House* (10–12). 2003, Barron's $39.95 (978-0-7641-5599-4). Hundreds of posters, in chronological and style groupings, are introduced by commentary. (Rev: BL 11/15/03) [791.43]

8570 Knoll, John. *Creating the Worlds of Star Wars: 365 Days* (10–12). 2005, Abrams $29.95 (978-0-8109-5936-1). Knoll describes the techniques used in making the "365 Days" series, with photos of concept art and props, dazzling panoramic views of film sets, and a CD-ROM with 360-degree shots. (Rev: SLJ 2/06) [791.43]

8571 Koenig, David. *Mouse Under Glass: Secrets of Disney Animation and Theme Parks* (10–12). 1997, Bonaventure Pr $23.95 (978-0-9640605-0-0). This is a chronological overview of Disney's 30 films, from "Snow White" through "The Hunchback of Notre Dame," giving background information (but no pictures) about each. (Rev: BL 1/1–15/97; SLJ 11/97) [791.43]

8572 Lace, William W. *Blacks in Film* (7–10). Illus. Series: Lucent Library of Black History. 2008, Gale/Greenhaven LB $32.45 (978-142050084-4). From the earliest appearances of African Americans in silent films through their roles in today's movies, this book covers how blacks have been depicted in the cinema; photographs add to the presentation. (Rev: BL 2/1/09; SLJ 2/1/09) [791.43089]

8573 Laverty, Paul. *Sweet Sixteen* (9–12). 2003, Screen-Press paper $9.95 (978-1-901680-67-6). This prize-winning screenplay relates the struggles of a Scottish teenager to escape a dysfunctional family environment and to create for his mother, sister, and nephew an idyllic life, safe from abuse. (Rev: BL 7/03) [302.7]

8574 McCaig, Iain. *Star Wars Visionaries* (7–10). 2005, Dark Horse paper $17.95 (978-1-59307-311-4). Artists who worked on *The Revenge of the Sith* showcase their individual artistic styles in this gallery of Star Wars scenarios. (Rev: BL 5/15/05; SLJ 11/05) [741.5]

8575 Miller, Frank, and Robert Rodriguez. *Frank Miller's Sin City: The Making of the Movie* (11–12). 2005, Troublemaker $30.00 (978-1-933104-00-3). A behind-the-scenes look at how Miller's graphic novel *Sin City* was made into a film; for mature teens. (Rev: BL 5/1/05) [791.43]

8576 Miller, Logan, and Noah Miller. *Either You're in or You're in the Way: Two Brothers, Twelve Months, and One Filmmaking Hell-Ride to Keep a Promise to Their Father* (10–12). 2009, HarperCollins $26.99 (978-006176314-4). The Miller twins recount their winning struggle to honor their late father by making a motion picture despite having no prior experience. (Rev: BL 4–5/09) [791.43]

8577 Miller, Ron. *Special Effects: An Introduction to Movie Magic* (7–10). 2006, Lerner LB $26.60 (978-0-7613-2918-3). Covers both the history of special effects and the techniques used today; boxed features discuss key figures and offer career advice. (Rev: BL 3/15/06; SLJ 6/06) [778.5]

8578 Morgan, David. *Knowing the Score: Film Composers Talk About the Art, Craft, Blood, Sweat, and Tears of Writing for Cinema* (10–12). 2001, HarperCollins paper $15.00 (978-0-380-80482-5). Sixteen composers of movie scores, including Philip Glass, Elmer Bernstein, and Bernard Herrmann, talk about their art, its problems, and its satisfactions. **e** (Rev: BL 1/1–15/01) [781.5]

8579 Morris, Mark, ed. *Cinema Macabre* (9–12). 2006, PS Publishing $45.00 (978-1-904619-44-4). Fifty horror writers — mostly British and some very well known — discuss in entertaining fashion their favorite films in this genre. (Rev: BL 3/15/06) [791.43]

8580 O'Connor, Mimi. *Reel Culture: 50 Classic Movies You Should Know About (So You Can Impress Your Friends)* (7–10). 2009, Zest paper $15.95 (978-0-9819733-1-9). A "cheat sheet" guide to 50 key movies (*Casablanca, Citizen Kane, Psycho,* and so forth) with interesting anecdotes and trivia as well as synopses and cast lists. Lexile 1230 (Rev: BL 1/1–15/10; SLJ 5/10; VOYA 2/10) [791.43]

8581 Osborne, Robert A. *75 Years of the Oscar: The Official History of the Academy Awards* (8–12). 2003, Abbeville $75.00 (978-0-7892-0787-6). A history of the Oscars through 2003, with asides about the ceremonies, winners, nominees, and the Academy of Motion Picture Arts and Sciences. [791.43]

8582 Patmore, Chris. *Moviemaking Course: Principles, Practice, and Techniques: the Ultimate Guide for the Aspiring Filmmaker* (9–12). Series: Barron's Educational. 2005, Barron's paper $19.99 (978-0-7641-3191-2). From preproduction through postproduction and on to marketing via film festivals and the Internet, this book explains the steps involved in making a short film in clear text with helpful color photographs. (Rev: SLJ 1/06) [791.43]

8583 Reynolds, Mike. *How to Analyze the Films of Spike Lee* (8–12). Illus. Series: Essential Critiques. 2010, ABDO LB $32.79 (978-161613530-0). Spike Lee's best-known films are deconstructed with an eye toward racial and identity issues. (Rev: BL 12/15/10) [791.43]

8584 Richards, Andrea. *Girl Director: A How-to Guide for the First-Time Flat-Broke Film Maker (and Video Maker)* (7–12). Illus. by Elizabeth McCallie. 2001, Alloy $17.95 (978-1-931497-00-8). Technical tips, inspiration, and instruction for would-be directors, with plenty of illustrations and other graphic elements. (Rev: BL 11/1/01; VOYA 6/01) [791.43]

8585 Rinzler, J. W. *The Making of Star Wars: The Empire Strikes Back* (9–12). Illus. 2010, Del Rey $85 (978-034550961-1). Rinzler provides an exhaustive account of the making of *The Empire Strikes Back* — complete with photographs, newspaper clippings, interviews, and archival records — in this thoroughly researched guide. (Rev: BL 6/1–15/10) [791.43]

8586 Salisbury, Mark. *Planet of the Apes: Re-Imagined by Tim Burton* (6–12). 2001, Newmarket $32.95 (978-1-55704-487-7); paper $22.95 (978-1-55704-486-0). A richly illustrated look behind the scenes at film director Tim Burton's recent remake of *The Planet of the Apes*. (Rev: VOYA 2/02)

8587 Sanello, Frank. *Reel v. Real: How Hollywood Turns Fact into Fiction* (10–12). 2003, Taylor paper $19.95 (978-0-87833-268-7). Sanello takes filmmakers to task for the ways in which they distort historical reality in the processing of transferring it to the screen. (Rev: BL 12/15/02) [791.43]

8588 Sansweet, Stephen J. *Star Wars Encyclopedia* (9–12). 1998, Ballantine $49.95 (978-0-345-40227-1). Made for browsing, this is an exhaustive, alphabetically arranged collection of data about *Star Wars* — characters, memorabilia, weapons, movies, books, toys, and planets. (Rev: SLJ 12/98) [791.43]

8589 Schwartz, Mark Evan. *How to Write: A Screenplay* (11–12). 2005, Continuum paper $14.95 (978-0-8264-1711-4). Schwartz, who teaches screenwriting at Loyola Marymount University, uses a screenplay to demonstrate the fundamentals of the craft. (Rev: SLJ 8/05)

8590 Smith, Marisa, and Amy Schewel, eds. *The Actor's Book of Movie Monologues* (9–12). 1986, Penguin paper $14.00 (978-0-14-009475-6). A collection of 80 monologues starting with *M* and ending with *The Breakfast Club*. (Rev: BL 11/1/86) [791.43]

8591 Vankin, Jonathan, and John Whalen. *Based on a True Story: Fact and Fantasy in 100 Favorite Movies* (9–12). 2005, Chicago Review $18.95 (978-1-55652-559-9). The facts behind many "true" stories are questioned in this interesting analysis of 100 movies. (Rev: SLJ 3/05) [791.43]

8592 Vaz, Mark Cotta. *The Art of The Incredibles* (8–12). 2004, Chronicle $40.00 (978-0-8118-4433-8). Many illustrations enhance this look at the making of the popular animated motion picture. (Rev: BL 10/15/04) [791.43]

8593 Wallace, Daniel. *Star Wars: The Essential Guide to Planets and Moons* (6–12). 1998, Del Rey paper $19.95 (978-0-345-42068-8). This volume provides fascinating information on 110 different planets and moons in the *Star Wars* universe, arranged alphabetically from Abregado-rae, a popular stop for smugglers, to Zhar, a gas-filled giant, covering each world's inhabitants, climate, language, points of interest, and history. (Rev: VOYA 6/99) [791.45]

Radio, Television, and Video

8594 Abbott, Stacey, ed. *Reading Angel: The TV Spin-Off with a Soul* (11–12). 2005, I. B. Tauris paper $14.95 (978-1-85043-839-7). Fans of *Angel*, the spin-off from *Buffy the Vampire Slayer* that ran for five seasons on television, will enjoy this retrospective; for mature teens. (Rev: BL 8/05) [791.45]

8595 Cartwright, Nancy. *My Life as a 10-Year-Old Boy* (9–12). 2000, Hyperion $19.95 (978-0-7868-6696-0). The author, who is the voice of Bart Simpson of "The Simpsons," presents a candid insider's look at this popular television program. (Rev: BL 9/15/00) [791.45]

8596 Castro, Adam-Troy. *My Ox Is Broken!: Roadblocks, Detours, Fast Forwards and Other Great Moments from TV's The Amazing Race* (9–12). 2006, BenBella paper $17.95 (978-1-932100-91-4). Fans of the reality show will enjoy reading this commentary, full of the sarcastic remarks they probably make while while watching it on TV. Interviews with many of the contestants add to the fun. (Rev: SLJ 9/06)

8597 Killick, Jane. *Babylon 5: The Coming of Shadows* (7–12). 1998, Ballantine paper $11.00 (978-0-345-42448-8). This is the second of a five-volume guide to this popular television series. (Rev: VOYA 12/98) [791.45]

8598 Owen, Rob. *Gen X TV: The Brady Bunch to Melrose Place* (10–12). 1997, Syracuse Univ. $29.95 (978-0-8156-0443-3). A history of popular television programs that shows not only how Gen Xers influenced network programming, but also how television affected their lives. (Rev: SLJ 2/98) [384.55]

8599 Phillips, Lisa A. *Public Radio: Behind the Voices; Profiles of Public Radio's Most Treasured Personalities* (9–12). 2006, CDS $25.00 (978-1-59315-143-0). This is the book for anyone who's ever wanted to know more about Terry Gross, Bob Edwards, or the "Car Talk" guys — and how they got into public radio. (Rev: BL 5/15/06) [791.4402]

8600 Rushfield, Richard. *American Idol: The Untold Story* (10–12). 2011, Hyperion $24.99 (978-140132412-4). Fans of the popular TV show will appreciate this candid look behind the scenes, which includes a rundown of some of the scandals and criticisms surrounding its production. ℮ (Rev: BL 1/1–15/11) [791.45]

8601 Schieffer, Bob. *Face the Nation: My Favorite Stories from the First 50 Years of the Award-Winning News Broadcast* (8–12). 2004, Simon & Schuster $26.95 (978-0-7432-6585-0). Highlights from the first 50 years of CBS's popular *Face the Nation*. (Rev: BL 9/1/04) [791.45]

8602 Shales, Tom, and James Andrew Miller. *Live from New York: An Uncensored History of Saturday Night Live* (10–12). 2002, Little, Brown $25.95 (978-0-316-78146-6). A collection of revealing behind-the-scenes memories from the show's stars, producers, writers, guest hosts, and staffers. (Rev: BL 10/1/02) [791.45]

8603 Siegel, Lee. *Not Remotely Controlled: Notes on Television* (9–12). 2007, Basic paper $14.95 (978-0-465-07810-3). What makes television so much a part of American culture? Siegel looks at the kinds of shows on offer and how they have evolved. (Rev: BL 7/07) [791.45]

8604 Stone, Brad. *Gearheads: The Turbulent Rise of Robotic Sports* (10–12). 2003, Simon & Schuster $23.00 (978-0-7432-2951-7). An insider's look at the phenomenon of robotic combat and its popularity with American television viewers. (Rev: BL 2/15/03) [796.15]

8605 Wilcox, Rhonda. *Why Buffy Matters: The Art of Buffy the Vampire Slayer* (11–12). 2005, I. B. Tauris paper $14.95 (978-1-84511-029-1). A scholarly look at the themes, symbolism, and characters of television's long-running *Buffy the Vampire Slayer*; for mature readers. (Rev: BL 12/15/05) [791.45]

Theater and Other Dramatic Forms

8606 Blumenthal, Eileen. *Puppetry: A World History* (9–12). 2005, Abrams $65.00 (978-0-8109-5587-5). The colorful history of puppetry from ancient Asia and Africa to the Muppets and *The Lion King*. (Rev: BL 9/1/05) [791.5]

8607 Caruso, Sandra, and Susan Kosoff. *The Young Actor's Book of Improvisation: Dramatic Situations from Shakespeare to Spielberg: Ages 12-16* (6–12). 1998, Heinemann paper $22.95 (978-0-325-00049-7). This work supplies hundreds of situations suitable for improvisation culled from all forms of literature, plays, and movie scripts, arranged by themes such as confrontation and relationships. (Rev: BL 9/15/98; SLJ 1/99) [793]

8608 Cassady, Marsh. *The Theatre and You: A Beginning* (9–12). 1992, Meriwether paper $17.95 (978-0-916260-83-5). A comprehensive introduction to theater as a performing art and craft, outlining five broad areas of study: theaters and stages, directing, design, acting, and theater history. (Rev: BL 11/1/92) [792]

8609 Halpern, Charna, et al. *Truth in Comedy: The Manual for Improvisation* (9–12). 1994, Meriwether paper $17.95 (978-1-56608-003-3). A thorough manual of comedic improvisation by three improv gurus. (Rev: BL 4/15/94) [792]

8610 Haskins, Jim, and Kathleen Benson. *Conjure Times: Black Magicians in America* (6–12). 2001, Walker LB $17.85 (978-0-8027-8763-7). The authors explore the substantial contributions of black performers to the early theater in America. (Rev: BL 7/01; HBG 3/02; SLJ 11/01; VOYA 4/02) [793.8]

8611 Kipnis, Claude. *The Mime Book* (7–12). 1988, Meriwether paper $16.95 (978-0-916260-55-2). One of the world's greatest mimes explains what it is and how it is done. [792.3]

8612 Lee, Robert L. *Everything About Theatre! The Guidebook of Theatre Fundamentals* (7–12). 1996, Meriwether paper $19.95 (978-1-56608-019-4). This excellent introduction to the backstage world includes material ranging from theater history to stagecraft, acting, and play production. (Rev: BL 12/1/96; SLJ 2/97) [792]

8613 McCullough, L. E. *Anyone Can Produce Plays with Kids: The Absolute Basics of Staging Your Own At-Home, In-School, Round-the-Neighborhood Plays* (9–12). Series: Young Actors. 1998, Smith & Kraus $14.95 (978-1-57525-151-6). McCullough offers solid advice on all aspects of staging plays — choosing the script, set construction, publicity, and so forth. (Rev: BL 2/1/99) [792]

8614 Nevraumont, Edward J, et al. *The Ultimate Improv: A Complete Guide to Comedy Improvisation* (9–12). 2001, Meriwether paper $17.95 (978-1-56608-075-0). This guide explores the arena of comedic improvisation and offers step-by-step advice to help interested students create well-rounded skits. (Rev: BL 2/15/02) [792.7]

8615 Stevens, Chambers. *Sensational Scenes for Teens: The Scene Studyguide for Teen Actors!* (7–10). Series: Hollywood 101. 2001, Sandcastle paper $14.95 (978-1-883995-10-2). Acting coach Stevens includes more than 30 scenes — both comedy and drama — suitable for two teen actors, with choices for boy-girl, boy-boy, and girl-girl combinations. (Rev: BL 5/15/01; SLJ 4/01) [812.6]

History and Geography

General History and Geography

Atlases, Maps, and Mapmaking

8616 Collinson, Claire, ed. *The First Civilizations to 500 BCE* (10–12). Series: Curriculum Connections: Atlas of World History. 2010, Black Rabbit LB $39.95 (978-1-933834-65-8). With extensive maps and concise text, this book covers the world from 2000 BCE to 500 BCE, looking at agriculture, the development of cities, the Bible lands, and the Bronze Age. Also by this editor: *The Classical World: 500 BCE to 600 CE* (2010). (Rev: LMC 8–9/10) [930]

8617 Jennings, Ken. *Maphead: Charting the Wide, Weird World of Geography Wonks* (10–12). 2011, Scribner $25 (978-1-4391-6717-5). Jeopardy record-setter Ken Jennings chronicles a lifetime of interest in maps and geography, and muses on America's geographic illiteracy, antique map collecting, and more. ⌂ (Rev: BL 7/1/11; SLJ 11/11) [912]

8618 Jouris, David. *All Over the Map: An Extraordinary Atlas of the United States* (8–10). 1994, Ten Speed paper $11.95 (978-0-89815-649-2). A U.S. atlas that explores the history of the names of towns and cities, including such places as Peculiar, Ding Dong, Vendor, and Joy. (Rev: BL 7/94) [910]

8619 Ross, Val. *The Road to There: Mapmakers and Their Stories* (7–10). 2003, Tundra $19.95 (978-0-88776-621-3). Mapmakers of different eras and nationalities, well-known figures such as Henry the Navigator and less familiar individuals, and the charts they created are featured in this interesting volume with period illustrations and many maps. (Rev: BCCB 1/04; BL 12/15/03; HBG 4/04; SLJ 12/03*) [912]

8620 Spilsbury, Louise, ed. *World Wars and Globalization: 1914–2010* (10–12). Series: Curriculum Connections: Atlas of World History. 2010, Black Rabbit LB $39.95 (978-1-933834-70-2). Useful, well-organized maps are accompanied by concise text and give students a clear view of global trends. (Rev: LMC 8–9/10) [909.82]

Paleontology

8621 Arduini, Paolo, and Giorgio Teruzzi. *Simon and Schuster's Guide to Fossils* (9–12). 1987, Simon & Schuster paper $14.00 (978-0-671-63132-1). In addition to a detailed description of the science of paleontology, this account, through photographs and text, identifies particular fossils and gives hints on how to collect them. (Rev: BL 5/1/87) [560.9]

8622 Barrett, Paul. *National Geographic Dinosaurs* (6–10). 2001, National Geographic $29.95 (978-0-7922-8224-2). This comprehensive and attractive guide provides a wealth of information about dinosaurs, their timeframe and evolution, individual species, and eventual extinction, with maps, fact boxes, and graphics. (Rev: BL 7/01; SLJ 10/01) [567.9]

8623 Cohen, Claudine. *The Fate of the Mammoth: Fossils, Myth, and History* (10–12). Trans. by William Rodarmor. 2002, Univ. of Chicago $30.00 (978-0-226-11292-3). Drawing on what has been learned from cave drawings, fossils, and frozen remains, paleontologist Stephen Jay Gould provides a comprehensive and well-illustrated overview of the mammoth. (Rev: BL 4/15/02) [569]

8624 Currie, Philip J., and Kevin Padian, eds. *Encyclopedia of Dinosaurs* (8–12). 1997, Academic $148.00 (978-0-12-226810-6). An adult reference book, written by scientists, with interesting, alphabetically arranged articles on dinosaurs, digs, and sites. (Rev: BL 11/1/97; SLJ 5/98) [567.9]

8625 Fiffer, Steve. *Tyrannosaurus Sue: The Extraordinary Saga of the Largest, Most Fought over T. Rex Ever Found* (10–12). 2000, W. H. Freeman paper $14.95 (978-0-7167-9462-2). This is the story of the discovery in 1990 of the largest Tyrannosaurus rex ever excavated and of the struggles and intrigues it produced. [567.9]

8626 Haines, Tim. *Walking with Dinosaurs: A Natural History* (9–12). 2000, BBC $30.00 (978-0-563-38449-6). This heavily illustrated book, part of a spinoff from a TV series, tells of the life cycle of an individual dinosaur living in its prehistoric environment. (Rev: BL 3/15/00) [567.9]

8627 Holmes, Thom. *Last of the Dinosaurs: The Cretaceous Period* (9–12). Illus. Series: Prehistoric Earth. 2009, Chelsea House $35.00 (978-081605962-1). Holmes provides a detailed discussion of our current knowledge about the dinosaurs that flourished during this time and what led to their extinction. (Rev: BL 3/15/09) [567]

8628 Holmes, Thom, and Laurie Holmes. *Feathered Dinosaurs: The Origin of Birds* (6–10). Illus. by Michael William Skrepnick. Series: Dinosaur Library. 2002, Enslow LB $26.60 (978-0-7660-1454-1). A well-organized introduction to these dinosaurs and their relationship to today's birds, with illustrations, graphic elements, a timeline of scientific discoveries, and a glossary. (Rev: BL 8/02; HBG 10/02; SLJ 10/02) [567.9]

8629 Holtz, Thomas R., Jr. *Dinosaurs: The Most Complete, Up-to-Date Encyclopedia for Dinosaur Lovers of All Ages* (5–12). Illus. by Luis V. Rey. 2007, Random $34.99 (978-0-375-82419-7). Paleontologist Holtz offers a well-organized overview of dinosaurs and everything dinosaur-related in a well-illustrated volume that will be appreciated by users of many ages (those not interested in cladistics, for example, may find just the information they need on dinosaur eggs). (Rev: HB 1/08; SLJ 12/07)

8630 Mitchell, W. I. T. *The Last Dinosaur Book* (9–12). 1998, Univ. of Chicago $35.00 (978-0-226-53204-2). In this well-researched study, Mitchell looks at our abiding interest in dinosaurs and the ways in which they appear in movies, comic strips, and earlier cultural media. (Rev: BL 11/15/98)

8631 Thompson, Ida. *The Audubon Society Field Guide to North American Fossils* (7–12). 1982, Knopf $19.95 (978-0-394-52412-2). An illustrated guide to the identification of North American fossils plus some background information on their formation. [560]

Anthropology and Evolution

8632 Angela, Alberto, and Piero Angela. *The Extraordinary Story of Human Origins* (9–12). Trans. by Gabriele Tonne. 1993, Prometheus $38.98 (978-0-87975-803-5). A comprehensive presentation of the still-growing body of knowledge of human evolution, including interesting speculations and conflicting claims. (Rev: BL 6/1–15/93) [573.2]

8633 Carroll, Sean B. *The Making of the Fittest: DNA and the Ultimate Forensic Record of Evolution* (11–12). 2006, Norton $25.95 (978-0-393-06163-5). Carroll uses anecdotes, pictures, charts, tables, and animal examples to explain evolution and the importance of the DNA code. (Rev: BL 10/1/06) [572.8]

8634 Crump, Donald J., ed. *Giants from the Past: The Age of Mammals* (7–10). 1983, National Geographic LB $12.50 (978-0-87044-429-6). A description of early animals, such as the mastodon, and how they evolved during the Ice Age. [569]

8635 Darwin, Charles. *The Darwin Reader. 2nd ed.* (10–12). 1996, Norton paper $20.60 (978-0-393-96967-2). The many faces of Charles Darwin are revealed in this collection of excerpts from the scientist's greatest works, including *Origin of Species*. [576.8]

8636 Deem, James M. *Faces from the Past: Forgotten People of North America* (6–10). Illus. 2012, Houghton Mifflin $18.99 (978-0-547-37024-8). A look at the human remains found in North America dating as far back as 10,500 years and moving forward to include a Mexican soldier killed in 1836, providing a fascinating mix of history and science. Lexile 1190L (Rev: BL 11/15/12*; HB 11–12/12; SLJ 12/12*) [599.9]

8637 Gibson, Phil, and Terri R. Gibson. *Natural Selection* (6–12). Series: Science Foundations. 2009, Chelsea House $35 (978-0-7910-9784-7). Following a review of Darwin and Mendel's importance in this field, this volume looks at artificial selection, natural selection, and

sexual selection, and discusses objections to Darwin's theory. (Rev: LMC 11–12/09) [576.8]

8638 Gordon, Sherri Mabry. *The Evolution Debate: Darwinism vs. Intelligent Design* (8–12). Series: Issues in Focus Today. 2009, Enslow LB $31.93 (978-0-7660-2911-8). Gordon provides an unbiased look at the debate over the teaching of Darwinism and intelligent design in American schools. (Rev: SLJ 4/1/09) [576.8]

8639 Johanson, Donald C., and Maitland Armstrong Edey. *Lucy: The Beginnings of Humankind* (10–12). 1981, Simon & Schuster paper $15.00 (978-0-671-72499-3). The story of the great anthropological find of bones of a hominid named Lucy who lived 3.5 million years ago. [599.93]

8640 Lauber, Patricia. *Who Came First? New Clues to Prehistoric Americans* (5–10). 2003, National Geographic $18.95 (978-0-7922-8228-0). An attractive, oversized volume that encompasses anthropology, archaeology, genetics, and linguistics in its discussion of the provenance of the peoples of the Americas. (Rev: BL 7/03*; HB 7–8/03; HBG 10/03; SLJ 8/03*) [970.01]

8641 Leakey, Richard E. *The Origin of Humankind* (10–12). Series: Science Masters. 1994, Basic paper $14.95 (978-0-465-05313-1). This is a summary of various theories involving evolution and their similarities and differences. (Rev: BL 10/1/94) [599.93]

8642 Leakey, Richard E., and Roger Lewin. *Origins Reconsidered: In Search of What Makes Us Human* (10–12). 1992, Doubleday paper $16.95 (978-0-385-46792-6). Leakey and Lewin look back at what has been learned about human origins and reflect on the characteristics that distinguish humans from other, closely related primates. (Rev: SLJ 6/93) [599.93]

8643 Naff, Clay Farris, ed. *Evolution* (7–12). Series: Exploring Science and Medical Discoveries. 2005, Gale LB $34.95 (978-0-7377-2823-1). This collection of writings documents the history of theories about human origins from ancient Greece to the 20th century. (Rev: SLJ 12/05)

8644 *Primitive Worlds: People Lost in Time* (9–12). 1973, National Geographic $8.95 (978-0-87044-127-1). The societies of several primitive peoples in Africa, New Guinea, and Central America are described. [306]

8645 Robertshaw, Peter, and Jill Rubalcaba. *The Early Human World* (8–12). Series: The World in Ancient Times. 2005, Oxford LB $32.95 (978-0-19-516157-1). Using primary sources and good illustrations, this volume looks at the world's earliest hominids and the evidence that they evolved from more primitive primates. (Rev: SLJ 6/05; VOYA 8/04) [599]

8646 Sarmiento, Esteban. *The Last Human: A Guide to Twenty-Two Species of Extinct Humans* (10–12). 2007, Yale $39.95 (978-0-300-10047-1). A field guide to human evolution, this volume looks chronologically at each of our ancestors, providing fictional scenarios to draw the reader in as well as eye-catching illustrations. (Rev: BL 2/15/07) [569.9]

8647 Scott, Eugenie C., and Glenn Branch, eds. *Not in Our Classrooms: Why Intelligent Design Is Wrong for Our Schools* (10–12). 2006, Beacon paper $14.00 (978-0-8070-3278-7). Experts in the fields of law, education, religion, and science discuss the tensions between the teaching of science and religion in American schools and caution against efforts to restrict science education in a world of increasing technology. (Rev: BL 10/15/06) [231.7]

8648 Smith, Cameron M., and Charles Sullivan. *The Top 10 Myths About Evolution* (9–12). 2006, Prometheus paper $12.00 (978-1-59102-479-8). Ten common misconceptions about evolution are identified, explained, and refuted. (Rev: BL 10/15/06) [576.8]

8649 Thorndike, Jonathan L. *Epperson v. Arkansas: The Evolution-Creationism Debate* (6–10). Series: Landmark Supreme Court Cases. 1999, Enslow LB $20.95 (978-0-7660-1084-0). This book examines the issues involved in this case of evolution versus creationism, traces the case from lower courts to the Supreme Court, and discusses the present-day impact of the court's decision. (Rev: BL 3/15/99) [116]

8650 Walker, Sally M. *Written in Bone: Buried Lives of Jamestown and Colonial Maryland* (7–11). Illus. 2009, Carolrhoda $22.95 (978-082257135-3). Walker explores how forensic anthropology has helped researchers to learn more about the hard realities of life in colonial America. ALA Notable Books 2010. Lexile NC1140L (Rev: BL 2/1/09; HB 5–6/09; LMC 10/09; SLJ 2/1/09*) [614]

8651 Walter, Chip. *Thumbs, Toes, and Tears and Other Traits That Make Us Human* (10–12). 2006, Walker $25.95 (978-0-8027-1527-2). Walter explores the traits that humans don't share with the rest of the animal kingdom — including the big toe, opposable thumb, and the abilities to laugh, kiss, and cry — as well as the impact of our larger brains. (Rev: BL 11/15/06) [599.93]

8652 Whitfield, Philip J. *Evolution* (10–12). Series: Living Universe. 2000, Gale $135.00 (978-0-02-865593-2). From Darwin's theory to modern generic research, this is a history of the study of evolution. (Rev: SLJ 8/01) [576.8]

Archaeology

8653 Ceram, C. W. *Gods, Graves, and Scholars: The Story of Archaeology. 2nd rev. ed.* (10–12). Trans. by E. B. Garside and Sophie Wilkins. 1967, Knopf paper $14.00 (978-0-394-74319-6). A classic history of archaeology that tells of the Rosetta Stone, the excavations at Ur, and more. [930.1]

8654 Echo-Hawk, Roger C., and Walter R. Echo-Hawk. *Battlefields and Burial Grounds: The Indian Struggle to Protect Ancestral Graves in the United States* (7–10). 1994, Lerner LB $22.60 (978-0-8225-2663-6); paper $8.95 (978-0-8225-9722-3). A solid discussion of the conflict over Indian graves that have been plundered in the name of scientific research. (Rev: BL 5/15/94; SLJ 7/94*) [393]

8655 Rubalcaba, Jill, and Peter Robertshaw. *Every Bone Tells a Story: Hominin Discoveries, Deductions, and Debates* (8–12). 2010, Charlesbridge $18.95 (978-1-58089-164-6). Rubalcaba and Robertshaw tell a compelling version of human prehistory by focusing on four landmark discoveries, and the questions they raised and answered. (Rev: BL 2/15/10; SLJ 3/10) [930.1]

8656 Ryan, Donald P. *Beneath the Sands of Egypt: Adventures of an Unconventional Archaeologist* (10–12).

Illus. 2010, Morrow $26.99 (978-006173282-9). This real-life story of the discovery of Hatshepsut's tomb crackles with the enthusiasm of an archaeologist who's passionate about his work. ℮ (Rev: BL 6/1–15/10) [932]

8657 Scheller, William. *Amazing Archaeologists and Their Finds* (6–10). 1994, Oliver LB $19.95 (978-1-881508-17-5). This work presents eight archaeologists' discoveries, including the walls of Troy, the tomb of King Tut, Jericho, and Incan ruins. (Rev: BL 11/1/94; SLJ 2/95; VOYA 2/95) [930.1]

8658 *Splendors of the Past: Lost Cities of the Ancient World* (9–12). 1981, National Geographic $19.95 (978-0-87044-358-9). A lavishly illustrated volume that deals with such historical sites as Pompeii, Angkor Wat, and those associated with the Hittite Empire. [930]

8659 Stiebing, William H. *Uncovering the Past: A History of Archaeology* (9–12). 1993, Prometheus $37.98 (978-0-87975-764-9). Surveys the history of archaeology and documents the discoveries of numerous explorers. (Rev: BL 3/1/93) [930.1]

World History and Geography

General

8660 Aronson, Marc. *Race: A History Beyond Black and White* (9–12). 2007, Simon & Schuster $18.99 (978-0-689-86554-1). From prehistoric man to the modern day, Aronson chronicles the story of racism in the western world. (Rev: BCCB 11/07; BL 10/15/07; HB 11–12/07; LMC 1/08; SLJ 12/07) [305.8009]

8661 Arthus-Bertrand, Yann. *Our Living Earth: A Story of People, Ecology, and Preservation* (6–12). Illus. by David Giraudon. 2008, Abrams $24.95 (978-081097132-5). Eye-catching aerial photographs of locations around the world reveal how people live, work, and relate to nature; statistics on sustainability and disparities will open readers' eyes to issues that affect the lives of millions on Earth. Lexile 1060L (Rev: BL 2/15/09; SLJ 1/1/09*; VOYA 12/08) [779]

8662 Badcott, Nicholas. *Pocket Timeline of Islamic Civilizations* (7–12). 2009, Interlink $13.95 (978-1-56656-758-9). An informative, eye-catching guide to the various achievements of Islamic civilizations from the 7th to the 20th century; includes color photographs and a detachable timeline. (Rev: LMC 3–4/10; SLJ 9/09)

8663 Beller, Susan Provost. *The History Puzzle: How We Know What We Know about the Past* (8–11). 2006, Lerner LB $26.60 (978-0-7613-2877-3). This concise overview of how archaeology and other methods allow historians to piece together the past includes sepia photographs, illustrations, and paintings. (Rev: BL 4/15/06; LMC 11–12/06; SLJ 5/06) [901]

8664 Beyer, Rick. *The Greatest Stories Never Told: 100 Tales from History to Astonish, Bewilder, and Stupefy* (6–12). 2003, HarperCollins $18.95 (978-0-06-001401-8). Browsers will enjoy this well-illustrated and well-researched chronological overview of historical tidbits. (Rev: VOYA 10/03)

8665 Boren, Mark Edelman. *Student Resistance: A History of the Unruly Subject* (10–12). 2001, Routledge $75.00 (978-0-415-92623-2); paper $19.95 (978-0-415-92624-9). This is a history of student resistance from the Renaissance to the present, with emphasis on the 1960s and the decades that follow. (Rev: BL 7/01) [378.1]

8666 Bouchard, Constance Brittain. *Knights in History and Legend* (10–12). 2009, Firefly $40 (978-1-55407-480-8). A large-format, highly illustrated guide to knights not only in Europe during the Middle Ages but also in Asia. (Rev: BL 12/15/09; LMC 5–6/10) [940.1]

8667 Cawthorne, Nigel. *Military Commanders: The 100 Greatest Throughout History* (6–12). 2004, Enchanted Lion $18.95 (978-1-59270-029-5). This chronology identifies the greatest military battles in world history and the men who led their forces to victory in those battles. (Rev: BL 6/1–15/04; SLJ 4/04) [355]

8668 Conlon, Faith, et al, ed. *A Woman Alone: Travel Tales from Around the Globe* (10–12). 2001, Seal paper $15.95 (978-1-58005-059-3). This is collection of 29 essays by women travels whose journeys involve six continents. (Rev: BL 11/15/01) [910.4]

8669 Davis, Paul K. *100 Decisive Battles: From Ancient Times to the Present* (9–12). 1999, ABC-CLIO paper $19.95 (978-0-19-514366-9). From the Battle of Megiddo in 1469 to Operation Desert Storm in 1991, this volume highlights 100 great battles. [904]

8670 De Porti, Andrea. *Explorers: The Most Exciting Voyages of Discovery — from the African Expeditions to the Lunar Landing* (8–12). 2005, Firefly $49.95 (978-1-55407-101-2). Rare archival photos document the history of exploration over the past 150 years, telling 53 stories of discovery — some well-known and others more obscure. (Rev: BL 12/1/05) [910.92]

8671 Diamond, Jared. *Collapse: How Societies Choose to Fail or Succeed* (10–12). 2004, Viking $29.95 (978-

0-670-03337-9). Diamond examines the factors that led to the decline of past civilizations and threaten to do the same in the foreseeable future. (Rev: BL 11/1/04; SLJ 6/05) [973]

8672 Durschmied, Erik. *Blood of Revolution: From the Reign of Terror to the Rise of Khomeini* (10–12). 2002, Arcade $25.95 (978-1-55970-607-0). This absorbing overview focuses on the key personalities and interesting events of two centuries of political revolution. (Rev: BL 2/1/02) [303.6]

8673 Feldman, Burton. *The Nobel Prize: A History of Genius, Controversy, and Prestige* (9–12). 2000, Arcade $29.95 (978-1-55970-537-0); paper $15.95 (978-1-55970-592-9). This is a comprehensive history of all of the Nobel Prizes — science, literature, social sciences, and so forth. (Rev: BL 12/1/00) [001.4]

8674 Galeano, Eduardo. *Mirrors: Stories of Almost Everyone* (11–12). Trans. by Mark Fried. Illus. 2009, Nation $25.95 (978-156858423-2). Using a variety of literary forms, Galeano tells stories of the world from the dawn of time to more current events and highlights both the beautiful and the horrific aspects of humanity. e (Rev: BL 4–5/09) [909]

8675 Gilkerson, William. *A Thousand Years of Pirates* (6–10). Illus. by author. 2009, Tundra $32.95 (978-0-88776-924-5). With interesting biographical sketches, maps, and beautiful illustrations, this is a sweeping survey of piratical activity across time and geography. (Rev: BL 12/15/09; SLJ 2/10; VOYA 2/10) [910.4]

8676 Gonick, Larry. *The Cartoon History of the Modern World: Part 1, From Columbus to the U.S. Constitution* (9–12). 2007, HarperCollins paper $17.95 (978-0-06-076004-5). Modern history can be fun with this informative survey that focuses mainly on Europe and North America, covering key developments and figures and with often sarcastic asides by ordinary citizens. (Rev: BL 1/1–15/07; SLJ 1/07) [741.5]

8677 Gonick, Larry. *The Cartoon History of the Modern World: Part II, from the Bastille to Baghdad* (10–12). 2009, HarperCollins paper $18.99 (978-0-06-076008-3). This final installment in Gonick's epic graphic history covers the years from the French Revolution to the wars in Iraq and Afghanistan. (Rev: BL 10/15/09; LMC 5–6/10; SLJ 11/09) [909.08]

8678 Hannigan, Des. *One People: Many Journeys* (8–12). 2005, Lonely Planet $40.00 (978-1-74104-600-7). Striking photographs from around the world capture the universality of the human experience and demonstrate the wide diversity of resources. (Rev: BL 1/1–15/06) [910]

8679 Haugen, David M., ed. *The Third World* (9–12). Series: Opposing Viewpoints. 2006, Gale LB $34.95 (978-0-7377-2965-8). Detailed essays tackle such topics as overpopulation, AIDS, hunger, globalization, de-

mocracy, and U.S. aid; for strong teen readers. (Rev: SLJ 2/07)

8680 Helphand, Kenneth I. *Defiant Gardens: Making Gardens in Wartime* (9–12). 2006, Trinity Univ. $34.95 (978-1-59534-021-4). A fascinating look at gardens created in the worst of circumstances. (Rev: BL 4/1/06) [635]

8681 Hoopes, James. *Oral History: An Introduction for Students* (10–12). 1979, Univ. of North Carolina paper $15.95 (978-0-8078-1344-7). This work explains the methodologies used in oral history collections and gives tips on how to put them into practice. [907]

8682 Huff, Toby. *An Age of Science and Revolutions: 1600–1800* (7–10). Series: Medieval and Early Modern World. 2005, Oxford $32.95 (978-0-19-517724-4). A sweeping overview of history in both the East and West from the beginning of the 17th century through the end of the 18th century, with color photographs, maps, profiles of key figures, and so forth. (Rev: BL 10/15/05; SLJ 7/06) [909]

8683 Jenkins, Mark, ed. *Worlds to Explore: Classic Tales of Travel and Adventure from National Geographic* (9–12). 2006, National Geographic $23.00 (978-0-7922-5487-4). This collection of *National Geographic* articles celebrates the wonders of travel in all the varied forms available from the 1890s to the 1950s. (Rev: BL 3/1/06) [910.9163]

8684 Konstam, Angus. *Scourge of the Seas: Buccaneers, Pirates and Privateers* (10–12). Series: General Military. 2007, Osprey $24.95 (978-1-84603-211-0). After defining pirates, privateers, and buccaneers, this book goes on to describe how they operated, their equipment and battle strategies, and so forth, also offering profiles of key figures. (Rev: SLJ 6/07) [364.164]

8685 Konstam, Angus, and Roger Michael Kean. *Pirates: Predators of the Seas* (9–12). 2007, Sterling $29.95 (978-1-60239-035-5). This is a colorful history of a colorful bunch of characters — from Blackbeard and Anne Bonney to the pirates found on oceans around the world today. (Rev: BL 5/1/07) [364.164]

8686 Kurlansky, Mark. *Salt: A World History* (10–12). 2002, Walker $28.00 (978-0-8027-1373-5). An interesting chronicle of the age-old commerce in salt, its uses, and its importance to a variety of communities. (Rev: BL 1/1–15/02*) [553.63]

8687 Leon, Vicki. *Uppity Women of the New World* (10–12). Series: Uppity Women. 2001, Conari paper $17.95 (978-1-57324-187-8). In this book there are profiles of 220 women — from explorers, spies, and religious leaders to criminals and pirates — who contributed to the establishment of colonies in the Americas, New Zealand, and Australia. (Rev: BL 3/1/01) [305.4]

8688 London, Charles. *One Day the Soldiers Came: Voices of Children in War* (11–12). 2007, HarperCollins paper $13.95 (978-0-06-124047-8). This is a harrowing account of the experiences of child soldiers in countries including Thailand, Myanmar, and Congo; for mature teens. (Rev: BL 9/1/07) [355]

8689 Mason, Phil. *How George Washington Fleeced the Nation: And Other Little Secrets Airbrushed from History* (10–12). 2010, Skyhorse $22.95 (978-161608075-4). This well-documented book irreverently points out some of the foibles of key figures in history. (Rev: BLO 7/10) [902]

8690 Murray, Sarah. *Moveable Feasts: From Ancient Rome to the 21st Century, the Incredible Journeys of the Food We Eat* (9–12). 2007, St. Martin's $24.95 (978-0-312-35535-7). An interesting history of the transportation of food around the globe, stretching back to ancient Rome and including everything from tea clippers to the Berlin Airlift to bananas traveling in refrigerated ships. (Rev: SLJ 3/08) [382]

8691 *National Geographic Expeditions Atlas* (9–12). 2000, National Geographic $40.00 (978-0-7922-7616-6). Using maps and photographs, this volume chronicles the many scientific expeditions, including some underwater ones, that have been financed by National Geographic. (Rev: BL 9/1/00) [910.4]

8692 Noland, David. *Travels Along the Edge* (10–12). 1997, Vintage paper $14.00 (978-0-679-76344-4). A world traveler describes 40 different adventure trips around the world with tips and detailed advice. (Rev: BL 9/1/97; SLJ 2/98) [910.2]

8693 Perry, James M. *Arrogant Armies: Great Military Disasters and the Generals Behind Them* (10–12). 1996, Wiley $32.50 (978-0-471-11976-0). This collection of failed military missions over the past two and a half centuries, such as Braddock's campaign during the French and Indian Wars and Gordon's loss of Khartoum in the Sudan, underlines the waste and horror of war. (Rev: SLJ 11/96) [900]

8694 Poole, Robert M., ed. *Nature's Wonderlands: National Parks of the World* (9–12). 1990, National Geographic $29.95 (978-0-87044-766-2). A photo-text tour of the national parks of the world with fuller coverage of those that are most important. (Rev: BL 5/1/90) [363.7]

8695 Prentzas, G. S. *The Marshall Plan* (8–12). Illus. Series: Milestones in Modern World History. 2011, Chelsea House LB $35 (978-160413460-5). With photographs, timelines, and maps, this volume explains the aid that the United States gave to Europe in the aftermath of World War II. **e** (Rev: BL 2/15/12) [338.91]

8696 Rushby, Kevin. *Hunting Pirate Heaven: In Search of the Lost Pirate Utopias of the Indian Ocean* (10–12). 2003, Walker $25.00 (978-0-8027-1423-7). Exciting, entertaining and informative, this is an account of the author's search for the Indian Ocean haunts of early privateers. (Rev: BL 10/15/03) [910]

8697 Sanna, Ellyn. *Nature's Wrath: Survivors of Natural Disasters* (6–12). Series: Survivors — Ordinary People, Extraordinary Circumstances. 2009, Mason Crest LB $24.95 (978-1-4222-0454-2). Sanna discusses our relationship with our planet and describes the experiences of survivors of tsunamis, hurricanes, and volcanoes. (Rev: SLJ 9/09)

8698 Scharfstein, Sol, and Dorcas Gelabert. *Chronicle of Jewish History: From the Patriarchs to the 21st Century* (10–12). 1997, KTAV paper $36.88 (978-0-8112-5606-3). Richly illustrated with more than 400 photographs and maps, this volume traces the story of the Jewish people from biblical times to the 1993 Oslo Agreement between Israel and the Palestine Liberation Organization. [909]

8699 Smith, Bonnie G. *Imperialism: A History in Documents* (6–12). Series: Pages from History. 2000, Oxford $39.95 (978-0-19-510801-9). This detailed account of how powerful nations spread their influence around the globe draws on many primary sources and includes eye-catching photographs and a useful timeline. (Rev: BL 11/15/00; HBG 10/01; SLJ 4/01) [325]

8700 Standage, Tom. *An Edible History of Humanity* (10–12). Illus. 2009, Walker $26 (978-080271588-3). Standage's overview explains how food supply has affected the evolution of civilization from ancient times to the present. **e** (Rev: BL 4–5/09) [394.12]

8701 Stewart, Robert. *Mysteries of History* (7–12). 2003, National Geographic $29.95 (978-0-7922-6232-9). Such controversial topics as Stonehenge, Napoleon's death, and Custer's Last Stand are presented with 16 others in this well-illustrated book. (Rev: BL 2/1/04; HBG 4/04) [902]

8702 Whitfield, Peter. *Cities of the World: A History in Maps* (9–12). 2005, Univ. of California $45.00 (978-0-520-24725-3). Maps dating from the Renaissance to the Victoria era show how some of the world's great cities have evolved over time and also provide clues to how those cities wanted to be perceived. (Rev: BL 12/1/05) [911.1]

8703 Wiesner-Hanks, Merry E. *An Age of Voyages, 1350–1600* (7–12). 2006, Oxford LB $32.95 (978-0-19-517672-8). Exploration from Europe to Asia, Africa, the Middle East, and the Americas is examined with many illustrations and extracts from primary sources, including letters and diaries, and text that discusses the accompanying discoveries, inventions, and social changes. (Rev: LMC 11–12/06; SLJ 7/06)

8704 Wojtanik, Andrew. *Afghanistan to Zimbabwe: Country Facts That Helped Me Win the National Geographic Bee* (5–12). 2005, National Geographic paper $12.95 (978-0-7922-7981-5). Facts and figures about the world's 192 independent countries are organized into three categories: Physical, Political, and Environmental/Economic. (Rev: SLJ 10/05; VOYA 8/05) [910]

Ancient History

General and Miscellaneous

8705 Allan, Tony. *Exploring the Life, Myth, and Art of Ancient Vikings* (8–11). Series: Civilizations of the World. 2011, Rosen LB $39.95 (978-144884833-1). A handsome, well-written survey of Viking history, mythology, and arts, with maps and color illustrations. **e** (Rev: BL 2/15/12; LMC 5–6/12) [948]

8706 Bauer, Susan Wise. *The History of the Ancient World: From the Earliest Accounts to the Fall of Rome* (10–12). 2007, Norton $29.95 (978-0-393-05974-8). This is an attractive and accessible chronologically arranged account of ancient history through the 3rd century A.D. with useful maps and graphs. (Rev: BL 1/1–15/07) [930]

8707 Fagan, Brian M., ed. *The Seventy Great Inventions of the Ancient World* (7–12). 2004, Thames & Hudson $40.00 (978-0-500-05130-6). This photo-filled volume explores inventions in categories ranging from hunting and farming to artwork and communications. (Rev: BL 12/1/04) [609]

8708 George, Charles, and Linda George. *Maya Civilization* (7–10). Illus. Series: World History. 2010, Gale/Lucent LB $33.45 (978-142050240-4). With a timeline, photographs, illustrations, and quotations, this survey of the Maya civilization is useful for report writers. (Rev: BL 2/1/11; LMC 5–6/11) [305.897]

8709 Haywood, John. *The Encyclopedia of Ancient Civilizations of the Near East and the Mediterranean* (8–12). 1997, M.E. Sharpe $95.00 (978-1-56324-799-6). Divided into three parts — ancient Near East and Egypt, the Greek world, and the Roman world — this adult narrative presents basic history and, through the use of sidebars, provides material on important places, cultural advances, scientific progress, religious practices, and military advances. (Rev: SLJ 8/98) [909]

8710 Laughton, Timothy. *Exploring the Life, Myth, and Art of the Maya* (8–11). Illus. Series: Civilizations of the World. 2011, Rosen LB $39.95 (978-144884832-4). A handsome, well-written survey of the Mayans' history, mythology, society, and arts, with maps and color illustrations. **e** (Rev: BL 2/15/12; LMC 5–6/12) [972.8]

8711 Leon, Vicki. *How to Mellify a Corpse and Other Human Stories of Ancient Science and Superstition* (9–12). 2010, Walker paper $17 (978-08027170-2-3). This funny, accessible book details fascinating, amazing, and often disturbing ancient-world trivia relating to politics, art, warfare, and science. (Rev: BL 6/1–15/10) [509.3]

8712 Mellor, Ronald, and Amanda H. Podany. *The World in Ancient Times: Primary Sources and Reference Volume* (6–12). Series: The World in Ancient Times. 2006, Oxford LB $32.95 (978-0-19-522220-3). More than 75 selections from poems, letters, inscriptions, and other accounts introduce civilizations and everyday life in ancient times. (Rev: SLJ 5/06) [930]

8713 Reinhard, Johan. *The Ice Maiden: Inca Mummies, Mountain Gods, and Sacred Sites in the Andes* (9–12). 2005, National Geographic $26.00 (978-0-7922-6838-3). A compelling account of the 1995 discovery of the Ice Maiden and what it revealed about the ancient civilization of the Incas. (Rev: BL 3/15/05) [985]

8714 Starr, Chester G. *A History of the Ancient World. 4th ed.* (9–12). 1991, Oxford $69.95 (978-0-19-506629-6). This comprehensive overview focuses primarily on the Greeks and Romans but also covers early civilizations in Mesopotamia, China, Egypt, and India. [930]

8715 Strapp, James. *Science and Technology* (7–10). Illus. Series: Inside Ancient China. 2009, Sharpe Focus LB $31.45 (978-076568169-0). Strapp looks at ancient Chinese inventions and innovations ranging from gunpowder and the compass to *feng shui*; includes maps, photographs, timelines, and drawings. (Rev: BL 2/15/09; SLJ 6/1/09) [609.31]

Egypt and Mesopotamia

8716 Cline, Eric H., and Jill Rubalcaba. *The Ancient Egyptian World* (5–10). Series: The World in Ancient Times. 2005, Oxford LB $32.95 (978-0-19-517391-8). An overview of ancient Egyptian history and culture, with chronologically arranged chapters covering religion, medicine, clothing, arts, and so forth and introducing key figures such as Hatshepsut, Tutankhamen, and Cleopatra. (Rev: SLJ 1/06) [932]

8717 Fletcher, Joann. *Exploring the Life, Myth, and Art of Ancient Egypt* (7–12). Series: Civilizations of the World. 2010, Rosen LB $39.95 (978-1-4358-5616-5). Daily life, mythology, arts, religion, and various aspects of preparing for the afterlife are covered in this well-designed book that includes illustrations and a list of Web sites. (Rev: BL 10/1/09; LMC 1–2/10)

8718 Giblin, James Cross. *Secrets of the Sphinx* (7–12). Illus. by Bagram Ibatoulline. 2004, Scholastic LB $17.95 (978-0-590-09847-2). Full of interesting facts and details of archaeological discoveries, this is a handsome, well-illustrated picture-book-format account of the mysteries that still surround the Sphinx and the facts that are known. (Rev: BL 9/15/04; HB 11–12/04; SLJ 11/04) [932]

8719 Hawass, Zahi. *Tutankhamun and the Golden Age of the Pharaohs* (8–12). 2005, National Geographic $35.00 (978-0-7922-3873-7). Companion to a traveling exhibit, this volume highlights the importance of items retrieved from Tutankhamen's tomb. (Rev: BL 6/1–15/05) [932]

8720 James, T. G. H. *Tutankhamun* (9–12). 2000, Friedman $60.00 (978-1-56799-032-4). This lavish book tells, in great photographs and an interesting text, about the discovery in 1922 of the famous tomb of the king buried 3,000 years ago. (Rev: BL 12/15/00) [932]

8721 Kallen, Stuart A. *Ancient Egypt* (7–12). Illus. Series: Understanding World History. 2011, ReferencePoint LB $27.95 (978-160152152-1). With information on the pyramids and the mysteries that surround their construction, this is a thorough overview of the culture of ancient Egypt and its legacy on art, medicine, religion, and so forth. (Rev: BL 10/1/11; LMC 9–10/12) [932.01]

8722 Nardo, Don. *Ancient Alexandria* (6–10). Series: A Travel Guide To. 2003, Gale LB $29.95 (978-1-59018-142-3). Readers are treated to a guidebook-style survey of ancient Alexandria's attractions, with a focus on weather, transport, hotels, shopping, festivals and sporting events, institutions, and people. (Rev: SLJ 6/03) [962]

8723 Nardo, Don. *Arts, Leisure, and Sport in Ancient Egypt* (6–10). Series: The Lucent Library of Historical Eras. 2005, Gale LB $32.45 (978-1-59018-706-7). Photographs, reproductions, and film and documentary stills illustrate this well-documented examination of the art and leisure activities of ancient Egyptians, from music and dance to hunting and fishing. Also use *Mummies, Myth, and Magic: Religion in Ancient Egypt* (2005). (Rev: SLJ 11/05) [932]

8724 Nardo, Don. *Peoples and Empires of Ancient Mesopotamia* (8–12). Series: Lucent Library of Historical Eras. 2008, Gale/Lucent $32.45 (978-1-4205-0101-8). This informative, well-illustrated volume describes ancient Mesopotamian society and politics, looking at urban and rural life, early systems of writing, and the successive empires of the region. Also use *Arts and Literature in Ancient Mesopotamia, Life and Worship in Ancient Mesopotamia,* and *Science, Technology, and Warfare of Ancient Mesopotamia* (all 2009). (Rev: SLJ 5/1/09)

8725 Podany, Amanda H., and Marni McGee. *The Ancient Near Eastern World* (8–12). Series: The World in Ancient Times. 2005, Oxford LB $32.95 (978-0-19-516159-5). Using primary sources and useful illustrations, this volume explores the ancient civilizations that flourished in the Fertile Crescent until the region was conquered by Alexander the Great in the 4th century B.C. (Rev: SLJ 6/05; VOYA 10/04) [935]

8726 Pollard, Justin, and Howard Reid. *The Rise and Fall of Alexandria: Birthplace of the Modern Mind* (9–12). 2006, Penguin $27.95 (978-0-670-03797-1). Rivaling ancient Rome and Athens, Alexandria was an intellectual and cultural giant in the ancient Mediterranean world, producing such scholars as Euclid and Eratosthenes and such institutions as the famous library. (Rev: BL 10/1/06) [932]

8727 Stetter, Cornelius. *The Secret Medicine of the Pharaohs: Ancient Egyptian Healing* (9–12). 1993, Quintessence paper $19.95 (978-0-86715-265-4). Uses Egyptian papyri to reconstruct ancient Egyptian medicine and explain it in a modern scientific context. Many color illustrations. (Rev: BL 9/15/93) [610]

Greece

8728 Baker, Rosalie F., and Charles F. Baker. *Ancient Greeks* (9–12). 1997, Oxford $55.00 (978-0-19-509940-9). Using the timespan of 700 to 200 B.C., this work profiles the lives and accomplishments of 37 prominent men and women of ancient Greece. (Rev: BL 8/97; SLJ 9/97) [938]

8729 Hamilton, Edith. *The Greek Way* (10–12). 1943, Norton paper $12.95 (978-0-393-31077-1). A discussion of the great works and writers of the golden age of Greece, including Pindar, Aristophanes, and Aeschylus. [880.9]

8730 Kirby, John T. *Classical Greek Civilization, 800–323 B.C.E.* (9–12). Series: World Eras. 2001, Gale $146.00 (978-0-7876-1707-3). This work covers the classical Greek period under such topics as the arts, class system, the family and social trends, and religion and philosophy. (Rev: BL 5/15/01) [938]

8731 Nardo, Don. *Women of Ancient Greece* (7–10). Series: World History. 2000, Lucent LB $32.45 (978-1-56006-646-0). The story of the place of women in ancient Greek society, how they lacked political rights and lived sheltered lives yet performed many important duties. (Rev: BL 6/1–15/00; HBG 3/01) [938]

8732 Roberts, Jennifer T., and Tracy Barrett. *The Ancient Greek World* (7–10). Series: The World in Ancient Times. 2004, Oxford LB $32.95 (978-0-19-515696-6). The authors take a lively and humorous approach to their carefully researched account of political and cultural life in ancient Greece. (Rev: SLJ 8/04) [938]

8733 Robinson, C. E. *Everyday Life in Ancient Greece* (7–12). 1933, AMS $45.00 (978-0-404-14592-7). The classic account, first published in 1933, of how people lived during various periods in ancient Greek history. [938]

8734 Stafford, Emma J. *Exploring the Life, Myth, and Art of Ancient Greece* (8–11). Illus. Series: Civilizations of the World. 2011, Rosen LB $39.95 (978-144884830-0). A handsome, well-written survey of ancient Greece's history, mythology, society, and arts, with maps and color illustrations. e (Rev: BL 2/15/12; LMC 5–6/12) [938]

8735 Strauss, Barry. *The Trojan War: A New History* (10–12). 2006, Simon & Schuster $27.00 (978-0-7432-6441-9). Professor Strauss examines *The Iliad* as a historically accurate work and makes the war of myth come alive for readers. (Rev: BL 9/1/06) [939]

8736 Wood, Michael. *In the Footsteps of Alexander the Great: A Journey from Greece to Asia* (9–12). 1997, Univ. of California paper $21.95 (978-0-520-23192-4). Published as a companion to the BBC series of the same name, this richly illustrated volume retraces the epic travels of the king of Macedonia. (Rev: BL 11/15/97) [938]

8737 Woodford, Susan. *The Parthenon* (6–10). 1983, Cambridge Univ. paper $19.00 (978-0-521-22629-5). A history of the famous temple in Athens and of the religion of ancient Greece. [938]

8738 Wright, Anne. *Art and Architecture* (7–10). Series: Inside Ancient Greece. 2007, M.E. Sharpe LB $31.45 (978-0-7656-8130-0). Focusing on practical and decorative art and architecture in ancient Greece, this volume describes in detail how art was produced during this time. (Rev: BL 10/15/07; LMC 2/08; SLJ 12/07) [709.38]

Middle East

8739 Palmer, Alan. *The Decline and Fall of the Ottoman Empire* (9–12). 1994, M. Evans $22.50 (978-0-87131-754-4). Traces the long decline of the Ottoman Empire from 1683 to 1922 and explores the impact of its legacy on contemporary Middle Eastern society. (Rev: BL 2/1/94) [958.1]

8740 Zeinert, Karen. *The Persian Empire* (7–10). Series: Cultures of the Past. 1996, Benchmark LB $29.93 (978-0-7614-0089-9). A brief history of the Persian Empire, with material on the kings Cyrus, Darius, and Xerxes, is followed by chapters on daily life, culture, religion, and lasting contributions the empire made to human achievement. (Rev: SLJ 3/97) [935]

Rome

8741 Allan, Tony. *Exploring the Life, Myth, and Art of Ancient Rome* (8–11). Illus. Series: Civilizations of the World. 2011, Rosen LB $39.95 (978-144884831-7). A handsome, well-written survey of ancient Rome's history, mythology, society, and arts, with maps and color illustrations. e (Rev: BL 2/15/12; LMC 5–6/12) [937]

8742 Baker, Rosalie F., and Charles F. Baker. *Ancient Romans: Expanding the Classical Tradition* (9–12). Series: Oxford Profiles. 1998, Oxford $55.00 (978-0-19-510884-2). Divided into five time periods spanning 400 B.C. to 350 A.D., this work recounts the history of Rome's rise to power through profiles of 39 notable Romans, including Virgil, Ovid, Julius Caesar, Constantine, Livia, and Spartacus. (Rev: BL 5/1/98; SLJ 8/98) [937]

8743 Davis, William Stearns. *A Day in Old Rome: A Picture of Roman Life* (9–12). 1959, Biblo & Tannen paper $24.00 (978-0-8196-0106-3). This account of the daily life, habits, and customs of ancient Romans first

appeared in 1925. A companion volume is *A Day in Old Athens* (1959). [937]

8744 Hamilton, Edith. *The Roman Way* (10–12). 1932, Norton paper $11.95 (978-0-393-31078-8). By examining the great writers and thinkers of ancient Rome, this book gives an interpretation of the life of the period. [870.9]

8745 Hinds, Kathryn. *Everyday Life in the Roman Empire* (7–10). 2009, Marshall Cavendish $29.95 (978-0-7614-4484-8). Hinds looks at society across the Roman Empire, examining in turn the court, the city, the countryside, and the church. (Rev: BL 4/1/10*; LMC 5–6/10; SLJ 12/09) [937]

8746 Macaulay, David. *City: A Story of Roman Planning and Construction* (6–10). 1974, Houghton Mifflin $18.00 (978-0-395-19492-8); paper $9.95 (978-0-395-34922-9). In text and detailed drawing, the artist explores an imaginary Roman city over approximately 125 years. [711]

8747 Matyszak, Philip. *Legionary: The Roman Soldier's Unofficial Manual* (10–12). Illus. 2009, Thames & Hudson $24.95 (978-0-500-25151-5). Intended to resemble a guidebook for prospective Roman legionnaires, this generously illustrated, meticulously researched volume outlines the expectations, duties, and martial tactics of those who devoted their lives to the protection of ancient Rome. (Rev: SLJ 11/09) [356.1]

8748 Mellor, Ronald, and Marni McGee. *The Ancient Roman World* (7–10). Series: The World in Ancient Times. 2004, Oxford LB $32.95 (978-0-19-515380-4). This attractive and accessible volume introduces readers to the history, people, and culture of ancient Rome, using many quotations and illustrations. (Rev: BL 4/1/04; SLJ 7/04) [937]

8749 Scarre, Chris. *Chronicle of the Roman Emperors: The Reign-by-Reign Record of the Rulers of Imperial Rome* (9–12). 1995, Thames & Hudson $34.95 (978-0-500-05077-4). The story of emperors from Augustus to Romulus Augustulus is told through surviving annals of classical historians, with photographs of ruins from their reigns. (Rev: BL 10/15/95) [937]

Middle Ages Through the Renaissance (500–1700)

8750 Aronson, Marc. *John Winthrop, Oliver Cromwell, and the Land of Promise* (7–10). 2004, Houghton Mifflin $20.00 (978-0-618-18177-3). In this fascinating historical study, Aronson explores the interrelationship between John Winthrop, 17th-century governor of the Massachusetts Bay Colony, and Oliver Cromwell, who led the successful Puritan revolt against Britain's King

Charles I. (Rev: BL 6/1–15/04; HB 7–8/04; SLJ 9/04) [974.4]

8751 Bishop, Morris. *The Middle Ages* (10–12). Series: American Heritage Library. 2001, American Heritage paper $17.00 (978-0-618-05703-0). This volume covers the period from Constantine's conversion in 312 A.D. to the end of the Hundred Years War in 1461. [940.1]

8752 Byrne, Joseph P. *Daily Life during the Black Death* (9–12). Series: Daily Life Through History. 2006, Greenwood $49.95 (978-0-313-33297-5). Readers learn about the effects of the plague in chapters that look at life at medical school, at home, in the village and on the manor, in the bishop's palace, and so forth. (Rev: SLJ 12/06)

8753 Crompton, Samuel Willard. *The Third Crusade: Richard the Lionhearted vs. Saladin* (7–12). Series: Great Battles Through the Ages. 2003, Chelsea House LB $30.00 (978-0-7910-7437-4). A useful survey of the First and Second Crusades is followed by details of the third campaign and portrayals of Richard and Saladin. (Rev: SLJ 5/04) [909.07]

8754 Davenport, John. *The Age of Feudalism* (8–11). Series: World History. 2007, Gale LB $32.45 (978-1-59018-649-7). A look at the feudal social and economic system in Europe, which lasted from the 5th century until the rise of nation-states. (Rev: BL 2/1/08) [940.1]

8755 Elgin, Kathy. *Elizabethan England* (6–12). Series: Costume and Fashion Source Books. 2009, Chelsea House $35 (978-1-60413-379-0). This volume looks at fashion and clothing in the Elizabethan area, describing the garb of men and women at court, the middle classes and professions, urban and rural residents, soldiers and sailors, and children. (Rev: LMC 11–12/09; SLJ 10-09) [391]

8756 Elgin, Kathy. *The Medieval World* (6–12). Series: Costume and Fashion Source Books. 2009, Chelsea House $35 (978-1-60413-378-3). This volume looks at the attire of men and women of various different walks of life in the Middle Ages. (Rev: LMC 11–12/09; SLJ 10/09) [391]

8757 Gies, Frances. *The Knight in History* (10–12). 1987, Harper & Row paper $14.95 (978-0-06-091413-4). The story of the beginnings, flowering, and decline of the institution of knighthood. [940.1]

8758 Gies, Joseph, and Frances Gies. *Life in a Medieval Castle* (10–12). 1979, HarperCollins paper $14.95 (978-0-06-090674-0). A Welsh castle is used as a model in this exploration of the feudal system and description of everyday life. [940.1]

8759 Hanawalt, Barbara. *The Middle Ages: An Illustrated History* (8–12). 1999, Oxford $37.99 (978-0-19-510359-5). A carefully researched account of the Roman Empire and its gradual fall, the rise of the church, its use of power, and feudal society, including such topics as castles, the Crusades, the Black Death, the rise of

guilds and universities, and the growth of the middle class. (Rev: BL 3/1/99; HBG 3/99; SLJ 4/99) [909.07]

8760 Hinds, Kathryn. *Everyday Life in the Renaissance* (7–10). 2010, Marshall Cavendish LB $42.79 (978-0-7614-4483-1). Hinds looks at society in the Renaissance, examining in turn the court, the city, the countryside, and the church. (Rev: LMC 5–6/10; SLJ 12/09) [940.21]

8761 Knight, Judson. *Middle Ages: Almanac* (6–10). Series: UXL Middle Ages Reference Library. 2000, Gale LB $70.00 (978-0-7876-4856-5). A comprehensive review of events around the world during the Middle Ages, with material on Africa and Asia as well as on Europe and the Middle East. Also use *Middle Ages: Biographies* and *Middle Ages: Primary Sources* (both 2000). (Rev: BL 4/1/01; SLJ 5/01) [940.1]

8762 Knight, Judson. *Middle Ages: Primary Sources* (8–12). 2000, U.X.L $70.00 (978-0-7876-4860-2). This book includes 19 entire or excerpted documents from the Middle Ages by such authors as Dante and Marco Polo. (Rev: BL 4/1/01; SLJ 5/01) [909.07]

8763 Lace, William W. *Elizabethan England* (8–12). 2005, Gale LB $31.20 (978-1-59018-655-8). The major issues and figures important in Queen Elizabeth I's reign — as well as the social, scientific, and geographic developments of the 1500s — are described in this book, with lots of color reproductions, a timeline, sidebars, and a further reading section. (Rev: SLJ 6/06)

8764 Leone, Bruno, ed. *The Middle Ages* (10–12). Series: History Firsthand. 2002, Gale LB $24.95 (978-0-7377-1073-1); paper $36.20 (978-0-7377-1074-8). Vivid eyewitness accounts re-create the history, social life, and culture of the Middle Ages. (Rev: BL 8/02) [940.1]

8765 McKitterick, Rosamond. *Atlas of the Medieval World* (9–12). 2005, Oxford $47.95 (978-0-19-522158-9). Chronicles developments on multiple fronts during the years between the fall of the Roman Empire and the 16th century, using detailed maps, diagrams, timelines, and other useful visual aids. (Rev: BL 9/1/05; SLJ 12/05)

8766 Nardo, Don. *Lords, Ladies, Peasants, and Knights: Class in the Middle Ages* (7–10). Series: The Lucent Library of Historical Eras — Middle Ages. 2006, Gale LB $28.70 (978-1-59018-928-3). Nardo describes the social classes of medieval Europe — from kings and popes down through knights and clergy to the peasants and serfs. (Rev: SLJ 4/07)

8767 Nicholson, Helen. *The Crusades* (10–12). Series: Greenwood Guides to Historic Events of the Medieval World. 2004, Greenwood $49.95 (978-0-313-32685-1). This broad overview of the Crusades explores all Christian campaigns during the medieval period that were directed against Muslims, pagans, and even other Christians who were judged guilty of heresy. (Rev: SLJ 1/05) [909.07]

8768 Obstfeld, Raymond, and Loretta Obstfeld, eds. *The Renaissance* (10–12). Series: History Firsthand. 2002, Gale paper $24.95 (978-0-7377-1079-3). Firsthand accounts are used to re-create the life, culture, history, and famous personalities of the Renaissance. (Rev: BL 12/15/02) [940.2]

8769 Stark, Rodney. *God's Battalions: The Case for the Crusades* (10–12). Illus. 2009, HarperOne $24.99 (978-006158261-5). In lively fashion, Stark presents newly discovered information that indicates that the Crusaders were not the avaricious, merciless opportunists that popular opinion maintains, but in fact many sacrificed wealth and exhibited higher moral standards than their contemporaries. ⌒ ℮ (Rev: BL 10/1/09*) [909.07]

8770 Thackeray, Frank W., and John E. Findling. *Events that Changed the World Through the Sixteenth Century* (9–12). 2001, Greenwood $55.00 (978-0-313-29079-4). This book highlights 10 important events of the 15th and 16th centuries, ending with a description of the defeat of the Spanish Armada. (Rev: BL 11/1/01) [909]

8771 Tuchman, Barbara Wertheim. *A Distant Mirror: The Calamitous 14th Century* (10–12). 1978, Knopf paper $17.95 (978-0-345-34957-6). A scholarly but accessible account of the political, social, and cultural life of the 14th century as experienced by a French feudal lord. [944]

8772 Wells, Peter S. *Barbarians to Angels: The Dark Ages Reconsidered* (9–12). 2008, Norton $24.95 (978-0-393-06075-1). Challenging the popular concept of the Dark Ages, Wells sees the time not as an interruption of civilization but as a cultural remaking. (Rev: BL 4/15/08) [940.1]

8773 White, Pamela. *Exploration in the World of the Middle Ages, 500-1500* (6–12). Series: Discovery and Exploration. 2005, Facts on File $40.00 (978-0-8160-5264-6). The expeditions of Marco Polo, the Vikings, and other explorers of the Middle Ages are chronicled in clear, informative text plus maps, illustrations, and excerpts from primary sources. (Rev: SLJ 8/05) [973]

8774 Zahler, Diane. *The Black Death* (8–12). Series: Pivotal Moments in History. 2009, Lerner LB $38.60 (978-0-8225-9076-7). Full-color illustrations and first-person accounts punctuate this well-written history of the 14th-century pandemic that killed nearly half of Europe's population. (Rev: SLJ 5/1/09) [614.5]

Eighteenth Through Nineteenth Centuries (1700–1900)

8775 Allport, Alan. *The Congress of Vienna* (8–12). Illus. Series: Milestones in Modern World History. 2011, Chelsea House LB $35 (978-160413497-1). Allport introduces the events that took place after the defeat of Napoleon and includes photographs and a timeline. (Rev: BL 2/15/12) [940.2]

8776 Damon, Duane. *Life in Victorian England* (9–12). 2005, Gale LB $28.70 (978-1-56006-391-9). Damon describes the many changes (principally social and industrial) that came with the Victorian era and their impact on each of the economic classes. (Rev: SLJ 6/06)

8777 Druett, Joan. *Island of the Lost: Shipwrecked at the Edge of the World* (9–12). 2007, Algonquin $24.95 (978-1-56512-408-0). The author drew on diaries, ship logs, and newspaper reports to tell this story of two ships that foundered in a storm in 1864; the crew of one ship not only survived but did well, creating a successful community and building a new boat, while the crew of the other did poorly and few survived. (Rev: BL 2/1/07; SLJ 4/07) [919.3]

8778 Frader, Laura L. *The Industrial Revolution: A History in Documents* (10–12). Series: Pages from History. 2006, Oxford LB $36.95 (978-0-19-512817-8). Letter, diaries, newspaper articles, and posters are only some of the primary documents used in creating this well-written, well-illustrated survey of the Industrial Revolution. (Rev: SLJ 12/06)

8779 Hicks, Peter. *Documenting the Industrial Revolution* (6–10). Series: Documenting History. 2010, Rosen LB $26.50 (978-1-4358-9670-3). Following an overview of Britain's position as the first industrial nation, this slim volume looks in turn at steam, coal, and iron; the factory system; the transport revolution and the importance of steam; urbanization; and the problems involved in such rapid progress; a rich variety of primary source materials add interest. ℮ (Rev: LMC 11–12/10) [330.941]

8780 Postma, Johannes. *The Atlantic Slave Trade* (9–12). 2003, Greenwood $51.95 (978-0-313-31862-7). From the 1400s to the final abolition of slavery in the New World in 1888, this is the history of the Atlantic slave trade and its influence on economic development. (Rev: SLJ 12/03) [326]

8781 Rediker, Marcus. *The Slave Ship: A Human History* (10–12). 2007, Viking $27.95 (978-0-670-01823-9). Rediker looks at life aboard the slave ships that sailed between Africa, Europe, and the Americas, exploring relationships among the captain, crew, and slaves. (Rev: BL 9/15/07) [306.3]

8782 Sommerville, Donald. *Revolutionary and Napoleonic Wars* (8–10). Series: History of Warfare. 1998, Raintree LB $29.97 (978-0-8172-5446-9). This well-illustrated book looks at the wars fought from the late-18th through mid-19th centuries, focusing primarily on the Americans and the French and their wars of independence and subsequent battles with other enemies. (Rev: HBG 3/99; SLJ 1/99) [909]

8783 Streissguth, Thomas. *The Napoleonic Wars: Defeat of the Grand Army* (9–12). Series: History's Great

Defeats. 2003, Gale LB $29.95 (978-1-59018-065-5). Napoleon's flaws — including a tendency to overestimate his own abilities and to underestimate those of his enemies — are underlined in this look at his defeats. (Rev: SLJ 1/04) [944.05]

Twentieth Century

General and Miscellaneous

8784 Buell, Hal. *Uncommon Valor, Common Virtue: Iwo Jima and the Photograph That Captured America* (9–12). 2006, NAL $28.95 (978-0-425-20980-6). The famous photograph of a flag-raising at Iwo Jima demonstrates just how meaningful this medium was and still is in war and in peace, claims the author, who has filled this book with other war photographs and information about war reporting. (Rev: BL 5/15/06) [940.54]

8785 Bussey, Jennifer A. *1940–1960* (9–12). Series: Events That Changed the World. 2004, Gale LB $36.20 (978-0-7377-1756-3). Introduces pivotal events during the turbulent decades between 1940 and 1960. (Rev: BL 4/1/04) [909.8]

8786 Crew, David F. *Hitler and the Nazis: A History in Documents* (8–12). 2006, Oxford $36.95 (978-0-19-515285-2). Government documents, propaganda, letters, articles, personal memoirs, and trial testimony reveal much about the growth, success, and eventual defeat of the Nazis. (Rev: SLJ 6/06)

8787 Filipovic, Zlata, and Melanie Challenger, eds. *Stolen Voices: Young People's War Diaries, from World War I to Iraq* (9–12). 2006, Penguin paper $14.00 (978-0-14-303871-9). Moving memoirs by young people (including Filipovic) recount experiences ranging from World War I Germany to the war in Iraq, each diary flanked by a historical introduction and an afterword. (Rev: BL 12/1/06) [949.7]

8788 Kaufman, Michael T. *1968* (7–12). Illus. 2009, Flash Point $22.95 (978-159643428-8). Drawing on *New York Times* articles, Kaufman chronicles the events of the tumultuous year that saw the escalation of the Vietnam War, assassinations in the United States, uprisings in Europe, and first pictures of Earth from space. Lexile NC1310L (Rev: BL 11/15/08; HB 1–2/09; LMC 3–4/09; SLJ 12/08; VOYA 10/08) [909.82]

8789 McEvoy, Anne. *The 1920s and 1930s* (6–12). Series: Costume and Fashion Source Books. 2009, Chelsea House $35 (978-1-60413-383-7). This volume looks at the attire of men and women of various different walks of life in the 1920s and 1930s, examining in particular the casual wear and sportswear. (Rev: LMC 11–12/09; SLJ 10/09) [391]

8790 Milo, Paul. *Your Flying Car Awaits: Robot Butlers, Lunar Vacations, and Other Dead-Wrong Predictions of the Twentieth Century* (10–12). 2009, HarperCollins paper $14.99 (978-00617246-0-2). Milo explains why many of the technological advances we expected never happened. **e** (Rev: BLO 12/1/09) [909.82]

8791 *National Geographic Eyewitness to the 20th Century* (9–12). 1998, National Geographic $40.00 (978-0-7922-7049-2). A record of the 20th century as recorded in *National Geographic* magazine, arranged by decades, each with a six-page introduction followed by outstanding illustrations. (Rev: SLJ 3/99) [909]

8792 Reynolds, David. *Summits: Six Meetings That Shaped the Twentieth Century* (11–12). 2007, Basic Bks $35.00 (978-0-465-06904-0). Advanced history students will enjoy this detailed examination of key diplomatic meetings — including those between Chamberlain and Hitler in 1938, Kennedy and Khrushchev in 1961, and Reagan and Gorbachev in 1985. (Rev: BL 11/1/07) [327.20904]

8793 Rooney, Anne. *The 1950s and 1960s* (6–12). Series: Costume and Fashion Source Books. 2009, Chelsea House $35 (978-1-60413-385-1). This volume looks at the attire of men and women of various different walks of life in the 1950s and 1960s, covering formal evening wear, leisure wear, work wear and uniforms, and accessories. (Rev: LMC 11–12/09; SLJ 10/09) [391]

8794 Steere, Deirdre Clancy. *The 1980s and 1990s* (6–12). Series: Costume and Fashion Source Books. 2009, Chelsea House $35 (978-1-60413-686-8). This volume looks at the attire of men and women of various different walks of life in the 1980s and 1990s, covering the new fashion trends, the clothing of average people, and the extreme fashions and celebrity culture. (Rev: LMC 11–12/09; SLJ 10/09) [391]

8795 Tuchman, Barbara Wertheim. *The Proud Tower: A Portrait of the World Before the War, 1890-1914* (10–12). 1966, Macmillan paper $15.95 (978-0-345-40501-2). This nonfiction work describes conditions in Europe and the events that led up to World War I. [909.82]

World War I

8796 Best, Nicholas. *The Greatest Day in History: How, on the Eleventh Hour of the Eleventh Day of the Eleventh Month, the First World War Finally Came to an End* (10–12). Illus. 2008, PublicAffairs $27.95 (978-158648640-2). Best interweaves personal accounts with profiles of the key figures involved in bringing World War I to its final end. **e** (Rev: BL 7/08) [940.3]

8797 Freedman, Russell. *The War to End All Wars: World War I* (6–10). 2010, Clarion $22 (978-0-547-02686-2). Freedman's photo-essay combines analysis of the key events and personalities of World War I with maps and personal stories drawn from letters and diaries. ∩ **e** Lexile 1220L (Rev: BL 3/1/10*; HB 7–8/10; LMC 10/10; SLJ 6/10) [940.3]

8798 Lawrence, T. E. *Seven Pillars of Wisdom: A Triumph* (10–12). 1935, Doubleday paper $19.95 (978-0-385-41895-9). From Lawrence of Arabia comes this account of the Arab revolt during World War I and of the national character of the countries involved. [940.4]

8799 Steele, Philip. *Documenting World War I* (6–10). Series: Documenting History. 2010, Rosen LB $26.50 (978-1-4358-9673-4). With many interesting primary source materials — posters, postage stamps, photographs, cartoons, quotations — this slim volume looks at the causes of the war, the strategies, the social impact, and the eventual peace. (Rev: LMC 11–12/10) [940.3]

8800 Stokesbury, James L. *A Short History of World War I* (9–12). 1981, Morrow paper $14.95 (978-0-688-00129-2). A brief but penetrating history of World War I that gives both political and military perspectives. [940.3]

8801 Stone, Norman. *World War One: A Short History* (10–12). Illus. 2009, Basic $25 (978-046501368-5). Stone offers a concise overview of World War I including the events leading to the war, the strategies employed by opposing sides, and the reasons for the failures. **e** (Rev: BL 4–5/09) [940.3]

8802 Tuchman, Barbara Wertheim. *The Guns of August* (10–12). 1988, Macmillan paper $14.95 (978-0-345-38623-6). The story of the negotiations that preceded World War I, how and why they failed, and the events of the first weeks of the war. [940.3]

8803 Tuchman, Barbara Wertheim. *The Zimmermann Telegram. New ed* (10–12). 1966, Macmillan paper $14.00 (978-0-345-32425-2). This work describes the attempts made by Germany to persuade Mexico to attack the United States during World War I. [940.3]

World War II and the Holocaust

8804 Ackerman, Diane. *The Zookeeper's Wife: A War Story* (9–12). 2007, Norton $23.95 (978-0-393-06172-7). In World War II Warsaw, Jan and Antonina Zabinski turned their damaged zoo into a refuge for both Jews and the Resistance, all under the guise of helping the director of the Berlin Zoo achieve Aryan perfection in the animal kingdom. (Rev: BL 8/07) [940.53]

8805 Allport, Allan. *The Battle of Britain* (8–11). Illus. Series: Milestones in Modern World History. 2012, Chelsea House LB $35 (978-160413920-4). With many eye-catching photographs this volume tells the story of the air battle between the German Luftwaffe and Britain's Royal Air Force in 1940. (Rev: BL 2/15/13) [940.54]

8806 Altman, Linda J. *Hidden Teens, Hidden Lives: Primary Sources from the Holocaust* (8–12). Series: True Stories of Teens in the Holocaust. 2010, Enslow LB $31.93 (978-076603271-2). In chapters such as "Plans and Preparations," "Secret Places," and "Hiding in Plain Sight," this is a fascinating collection of stories about teens who hid from the Nazis, their strategies, and their protectors; with photographs and news pictures. (Rev: BL 4/1/10) [940.53]

8807 Altshuler, David A. *Hitler's War Against the Jews: A Young Reader's Version of The War Against the Jews, 1933-1945, by Lucy S. Dawidowicz* (7–10). 1995, Behrman paper $14.95 (978-0-87441-298-7). The tragic story of Hitler's Final Solution and its aftermath. [940.54]

8808 Ambrose, Stephen E. *Citizen Soldiers: The U.S. Army from the Normandy Beaches to the Bulge to the Surrender of Germany, June 7, 1944-May 7, 1945* (9–12). 1997, Simon & Schuster paper $17.00 (978-0-684-84801-3). Beginning the day after the landing on the beaches of Normandy, this highly readable narrative traces the advance of U.S. armed forces toward the Rhineland. (Rev: BL 9/15/97) [940.54]

8809 Ambrose, Stephen E. *D-Day: June 6, 1944: The Climactic Battle of World War II* (9–12). 1994, Simon & Schuster $29.50 (978-0-671-67334-5). Long, detailed, immediate, and readable, this history is for teens who can't get enough of World War II drama. (Rev: BL 4/1/94) [940.54]

8810 Ambrose, Stephen E. *The Good Fight: How World War II Was Won* (7–12). 2001, Simon & Schuster $19.95 (978-0-689-84361-7). Historian Ambrose presents an appealing and well-written overview of World War II, from its origins through the Marshall Plan, with many photographs, fact boxes, and maps. (Rev: BL 7/01; HBG 10/01; SLJ 5/01; VOYA 6/01) [940.53]

8811 Bard, Mitchell G., ed. *The Holocaust* (7–12). Series: Turning Points in World History. 2001, Greenhaven LB $37.45 (978-0-7377-0576-8); paper $24.95 (978-0-7377-0575-1). The Jewish genocide in Nazi Germany is explored in an anthology of essays, each of which examines a different aspect of this terrible period in history. (Rev: BL 6/1–15/01) [940.54]

8812 Bard, Mitchell G., ed. *The Nuremberg Trial* (10–12). Series: History Firsthand. 2002, Gale LB $24.95 (978-0-7377-1075-5); paper $36.20 (978-0-7377-1076-2). The trials in which several Nazi war criminals were brought to justice are presented from various points of view through original documents, narratives, and reminiscences. (Rev: BL 8/02; SLJ 7/02) [940.54]

8813 Berland-Hyatt, Felicia. *Close Calls: Memoirs of a Survivor* (9–12). 1991, Holocaust paper $13.95 (978-0-89604-138-7). A survivor's account of the Holocaust. (Rev: BL 1/15/92) [921]

8814 Block, Gay, and Malka Drucker. *Rescuers: Portraits of Moral Courage in the Holocaust* (9–12). 1992, Holmes & Meier paper $29.95 (978-0-8419-1323-3). Profiles of 49 people who risked their lives to hide and protect Jews during the Holocaust. (Rev: BL 3/15/92) [940.53]

8815 Boisclaire, Yvonne. *In the Shadow of the Rising Sun* (10–12). 1997, Clearwood Publishers paper $14.95 (978-0-9649997-3-2). The horrifying, true story of U.S. Army Sergeant Robert Davis and how he and some colleagues survived inhuman treatment in Japanese prison camps in the Pacific. (Rev: VOYA 12/97) [940.54]

8816 Boraks-Nemetz, Lillian, and Irene N. Watts, eds. *Tapestry of Hope: Holocaust Writing for Young People* (6–12). 2003, Tundra $24.99 (978-0-88776-638-1). Two Holocaust survivors have collected fiction, poetry, drama, and nonfiction excerpts that detail the experiences of those who went into hiding, were sent to the camps, joined the resistance movement, and made their way to other countries. (Rev: BL 6/1–15/03; HBG 10/03; SLJ 8/03; VOYA 10/03) [810.8]

8817 Brenner, Hannelore. *The Girls of Room 28: Friendship, Hope, and Survival in Theresienstadt* (10–12). Trans. by John E. Woods. Illus. 2009, Schocken $26 (978-080524244-7). Ten detailed survivor stories of girls who endured the horrors of the Nazi concentration camp. 🎧 (Rev: BL 9/15/09) [940.53]

8818 Burgan, Michael. *Hiroshima: Birth of the Nuclear Age* (8–12). Series: Perspectives On. 2010, Marshall Cavendish LB $39.93 (978-0-7614-4023-9). Burgan provides a concise account of the developments that led up to the destruction of Hiroshima, and of the long aftermath; sidebars, photographs, and illustrations enhance the well-written text. (Rev: LMC 3–4/10; SLJ 2/10)

8819 Byers, Ann. *The Holocaust Camps* (8–12). Series: Holocaust Remembered. 1998, Enslow LB $18.95 (978-0894909955). This work traces the evolution of political prison camps to labor camps and eventually to death camps during the Nazi regime. (Rev: SLJ 12/98; VOYA 8/98) [940.54]

8820 Cherny, Andrei. *The Candy Bombers: The Untold Story of the Berlin Airlift and America's Finest Hour* (9–12). 2008, Putnam $29.95 (978-0-399-15496-6). This narrative focuses on the political impact in Washington, D.C. of the Berlin crisis and the 1948-1949 airlift. (Rev: BL 3/15/08) [943]

8821 Childers, Thomas. *Wings of Morning: The Story of the Last American Bomber Shot Down over Germany in World War II* (9–12). 1996, Perseus paper $18 (978-0-201-40722-8). A re-creation of the lives of the 12-man crew of the bomber Black Cat, the last air casualty over Germany in World War II. (Rev: BL 4/15/95*) [940.54]

8822 Churchill, Winston. *The Gathering Storm* (10–12). Series: Second World War. 1948, Houghton Mifflin paper $20.00 (978-0-395-41055-4). The first volume of Churchill's history of World War II traces the causes of war and Hitler's victories prior to Dunkirk. [940.53]

8823 Churchill, Winston. *The Grand Alliance* (10–12). Series: Second World War. 1950, Houghton Mifflin paper $20.00 (978-0-395-41057-8). Russia's entrance into the war and later that of the United States are the focus of this volume. [940.53]

8824 Churchill, Winston. *The Hinge of Fate* (10–12). Series: Second World War. 1950, Houghton Mifflin paper $20.00 (978-0-395-41058-5). The war in Africa and the planned invasion of Sicily are covered in this volume that spans January 1942 through May 1943. [940.53]

8825 Churchill, Winston. *Their Finest Hour* (10–12). Series: Second World War. 1949, Houghton Mifflin paper $20.00 (978-0-395-41056-1). The story of the Battle of Britain and the evacuations at Dunkirk is given here. [940.53]

8826 Churchill, Winston. *Triumph and Tragedy* (9–12). Series: Second World War. 1953, Houghton Mifflin paper $20.00 (978-0-395-41060-8). This, the last volume of Churchill's history of World War II, deals with the closing days of the war and the defeat of Germany and Japan. [940.53]

8827 Clive, A. Lawton. *Hiroshima* (6–12). 2004, Candlewick $18.99 (978-0-7636-2271-8). This powerful photoessay presents the history of the development and dropping of the first atom bomb, documenting with many quotations the misgivings of some of the key figures. (Rev: BL 7/04; SLJ 11/04) [940.54]

8828 Cox, Jeromy. *Holocaust: The Events and Their Impact on Real People* (6–12). 2007, DK $29.99 (978-0-7566-2535-1). Using DK's usual layout and accompanying DVD with narratives by Holocaust survivors and eyewitnesses, this volume provides a well-rounded overview of anti-Semitism in world history and of the events of the Holocaust itself. (Rev: BL 9/1/07; SLJ 8/07) [940.53]

8829 Deem, James M. *Kristallnacht: The Nazi Terror That Began the Holocaust* (8–12). Illus. Series: The Holocaust Through Primary Sources. 2011, Enslow LB $31.93 (978-076603324-5). Eyewitness accounts from Jews, Nazis, and others — old and young — tell the story of the atrocity that took place in 1938. (Rev: BL 10/1/11) [940.53]

8830 Del Calzo, Rick. *The Triumphant Spirit: Portraits and Stories of Holocaust Survivors, Their Messages of Hope and Compassion* (10–12). 1997, Spirit paper $29.95 (978-0-9655260-1-2). Black-and-white photographs are intertwined with narratives of more than 90 Holocaust survivors. (Rev: BL 3/15/97; SLJ 10/97) [940.54]

8831 Devaney, John. *America Fights the Tide: 1942* (6–10). 1991, Walker $17.95 (978-0-8027-6997-8). Using a diary format and anecdotal accounts, this volume focuses on the United States' entry into World War II in both the European and the Pacific theaters. (Rev: BL 10/15/91; SLJ 10/91) [940.54]

8832 Devaney, John. *America on the Attack: 1943* (6–10). Series: Walker's World War II. 1992, Walker LB $18.85 (978-0-8027-8195-6). This well-illustrated account describes America's active participation in World War II once the war effort got under way. (Rev: BL 12/1/92) [940.53]

8833 Downing, David. *The Origins of the Holocaust* (7–10). Series: World Almanac Library of the Holocaust. 2005, World Almanac LB $31.00 (978-0-8368-5943-0). Downing looks at the roots of anti-Semitism and the continuing persecution of the Jews over the centuries, connecting this history with the rise of the Nazi Party. (Rev: BL 10/15/05; SLJ 3/06) [940.53]

8834 Fantlova, Zdenka. *My Lucky Star* (10–12). 2001, Herodias $24.00 (978-1-928746-20-1). A Holocaust memoir in which a Czech Jewish woman tells of her survival of the Nazi death camps. (Rev: BL 4/15/01) [940.54]

8835 Filar, Marian, and Charles Patterson. *From Buchenwald to Carnegie Hall* (10–12). 2002, Univ. Press of Mississippi $35.00 (978-1-57806-419-9). In this touching memoir of Holocaust survival, Polish-born concert pianist Filar recounts his experiences as a young man in the Warsaw Ghetto and a series of Nazi concentration camps. (Rev: BL 1/1–15/02) [786.2]

8836 Fisch, Robert O. *Light from the Yellow Star: A Lesson of Love from the Holocaust* (7–12). 1996, Univ. of Minnesota $14.95 (978-1-885116-00-0); paper $9.95 (978-0-9644896-0-8). A biographical account that uses the author's abstract paintings to tell about his childhood in Budapest and his death camp experiences. (Rev: BL 4/15/96) [940.53]

8837 Friedman, Ina R. *The Other Victims: First-Person Stories of Non-Jews Persecuted by the Nazis* (7–12). 1995, Houghton Mifflin paper $7.99 (978-0-395-74515-1). This account deals with the other victims of the Holocaust — including Gypsies, homosexuals, dissenters, and some religious minorities. (Rev: BL 6/15/90; SLJ 4/90; VOYA 6/90) [940.53]

8838 Fuller, William, and Jack James. *Reckless Courage: The True Story of a Norwegian Boy Under Nazi Rule* (8–11). 2005, Taber Hall paper $13.95 (978-0-9769252-0-0). The true story of a Norwegian boy's participation in the resistance against his country's Nazi occupiers. (Rev: BL 9/15/05) [940.53]

8839 Galloway, Priscilla, ed. *Too Young to Fight: Memories from Our Youth During World War II* (6–12). 2000, Stoddart $22.95 (978-0-7737-3190-5). Eleven Canadian authors of books for young people describe what it was like growing up on the home front during World War II. (Rev: BL 5/1/00; SLJ 7/00) [940.53]

8840 Gies, Miep, and Alison L. Gold. *Anne Frank Remembered: The Story of Miep Gies, Who Helped to Hide the Frank Family* (8–12). 1987, Simon & Schuster paper $14.00 (978-0-671-66234-9). The story of the woman who helped the Frank family during World War II and of the Resistance movement in the Netherlands. (Rev: BL 4/1/87; SLJ 11/87; VOYA 12/87) [940.53]

8841 Gilbert, Martin. *The Holocaust: A History of the Jews of Europe During the Second World War* (10–12). 1986, Henry Holt paper $24.00 (978-0-8050-0348-2). Drawing on many original sources and interviews, this is a forceful chronicle of Hitler's rise to power, the final solution, and the liberation of the death camps. [940.53]

8842 Gilbert, Martin. *Kristallnacht: Prelude to Destruction* (9–12). Series: Making History. 2006, HarperCollins $21.95 (978-0-06-057083-5). The Night of Broken Glass is recalled by eyewitnesses and identified as the beginning of the Holocaust. (Rev: SLJ 10/06)

8843 Gottfried, Ted. *Displaced Persons: The Liberation and Abuse of Holocaust Survivors* (6–12). 2001, Twenty-First Century LB $29.90 (978-0-7613-1924-5). Survivors of the Holocaust went on to suffer many indignities and rejections, as Gottfried shows in this account of continued racism, displaced persons camps, and denial of shelter by countries including the United States. (Rev: BL 9/1/01; HBG 3/02) [940]

8844 Hastings, Max. *Overlord: D-Day and the Battle for Normandy* (10–12). 1985, Simon & Schuster paper $13.00 (978-0-671-55435-4). A history of the events surrounding the Allied landings in Normandy during World War II. [940.53]

8845 Hecht, Thomas T. *Life Death Memories* (9–12). 2002, Leopolis paper $24.95 (978-0-9679960-1-1). This powerful memoir recounts the story of a Jewish teenager who, with his mother, survives the Nazis' arrival in their Polish *shtetl*. (Rev: BL 5/1/02) [940.53]

8846 Hersey, John. *Hiroshima: A New Edition with a Final Chapter Written Forty Years After the Explosion* (10–12). 1985, Knopf $26.00 (978-0-394-54844-9); paper $6.50 (978-0-679-72103-1). Using the stories of six survivors, this is a devastating account of the atomic bombing of Hiroshima during World War II. [940.54]

8847 Heyes, Eileen. *Children of the Swastika: The Hitler Youth* (7–12). 1993, Millbrook LB $22.40 (978-1-56294-237-3). A study of the Hitler Youth's structure, purpose, impact on the war effort, and effects on the youth. (Rev: BL 2/15/93) [324.243]

8848 Hill, Jeff, ed. *The Holocaust* (7–12). 2006, Omnigraphics LB $65 (978-0-7808-0935-2). Provides primary sources that will help students researching the various stages of the Holocaust from its roots through the camps for displaced persons and the aftermath of the war. (Rev: SLJ 1/07)

8849 Hillesum, Etty. *Etty Hillesum: An Interrupted Life and Letters from Westerbork* (10–12). Trans. from Dutch by Arnold J. Pomerans. 1996, Henry Holt $27.50 (978-0-8050-4894-0). This inspiring book contains the diaries and letters of a Jewish woman who died in her mid-20s in the Holocaust. (Rev: SLJ 4/97) [940.54]

8850 Hillman, Laura. *I Will Plant You a Lilac Tree: A Memoir of a Schindler's List Survivor* (8–11). 2005, Simon & Schuster $16.95 (978-0-689-86980-8). In this inspiring true story of Holocaust survival, Hannelore escapes the Nazi gas chambers when her name is added to Schindler's list. (Rev: BCCB 7–8/05; BL 5/1/05*; HB 7–8/05; SLJ 9/05; VOYA 8/05) [940.5]

8851 Hodge, Deborah. *Rescuing the Children: The Story of the Kindertransport* (5–12). Illus. 2012, Tundra $17.95 (978-1-77049-256-1). Using first-person accounts, accessible text, and effective illustrations, this book tells the story of the 10,000 Jewish children rescued from the Nazis in 1939. (Rev: BL 12/1/12*; SLJ 11/12) [940.53]

8852 Hoyt, Edwin. *McCampbell's Heroes* (9–12). 1984, Avon paper $3.95 (978-0-380-68841-8). The story of the U.S. Navy's carrier fighters and their role in the Pacific area during World War II. Also use *Blue Skies and Blood: The Battle of the Coral Sea* (1989). [940.53]

8853 Kaiser, Reinhard. *Paper Kisses: A True Love Story* (9–12). Trans. from German by Anthea Bell. 2006, Other paper $13.95 (978-1-59051-181-7). Kaiser recounts the tragic story of a German man and Swedish woman who fell in love but were kept apart by World War II; the couple's letters and black-and-white photographs make the account more immediate. (Rev: SLJ 7/06)

8854 Leckie, Robert. *Okinawa: The Last Battle of World War II* (9–12). 1995, Viking paper $15.00 (978-0-14-017389-5). A history of the Battle of Okinawa with good background material on the war in the Pacific. (Rev: BL 4/15/95) [940.54]

8855 Levi, Primo. *Survival in Auschwitz* (10–12). Trans. by Stuart Woolf. 1995, Touchstone paper $14.00 (978-0-684-82680-6). A moving memoir of the author's 10 months in a concentration camp. Also use *The Reawakening*, the story of his journey home to Italy via the Soviet Union. [940.53]

8856 Lifton, Betty Jean. *A Place Called Hiroshima* (9–12). 1985, Kodansha $24.95 (978-0-87011-649-0). In this album of text and photographs, the author tells what has happened to Hiroshima and the survivors of the atomic attack 40 years after. (Rev: BL 10/1/85; SLJ 11/85) [940.54]

8857 Madison, James H. *World War II: A History in Documents* (7–12). Illus. Series: Pages from History. 2010, Oxford LB $39.95 (978-019516176-2). This volume provides a generous mix of primary sources from many countries — letters, speeches, posters, maps, songs, and so forth. (Rev: BL 9/15/10; SLJ 6/10) [940.5373]

8858 Mara, Wil. *Kristallnacht: Nazi Persecution of the Jews in Europe* (8–12). Series: Perspectives On. 2010, Marshall Cavendish LB $39.93 (978-0-7614-4026-0). Mara provides a concise account of the developments that led up to Kristallnacht and the long and terrible events that ensued; sidebars, photographs, and illustrations enhance the well-written text. (Rev: LMC 3–4/10; SLJ 2/10) [940.531]

8859 Maruki, Toshi. *Hiroshima No Pika* (7–10). 1982, Lothrop $17.99 (978-0-688-01297-7). One family's experiences during the day the bomb dropped on Hiroshima, told in text and moving illustrations by the author. (Rev: BL 3/87) [940.54]

8860 Meyers, Odette. *Doors to Madame Marie* (10–12). 1997, Univ. of Washington $30.00 (978-0-295-97576-4). A deeply moving memoir of a Jewish girl in wartime France who was sent to live in the countryside, pretending to be Catholic for safety's sake, and who returns to visit years later. (Rev: SLJ 12/97) [940.54]

8861 Miller, Donald L. *D-Days in the Pacific* (8–12). 2005, Simon & Schuster paper $16.00 (978-0-7432-6929-2). The Allied military offensives that finally brought an end to World War II in the Pacific are described in readable text with excellent illustrations. (Rev: BL 3/15/05) [940.54]

8862 Paldiel, Mordecai. *Saving the Jews: Amazing Stories of Men and Women Who Defied the 'Final Solution.'* (10–12). 2000, Schreiber $24.95 (978-1-887563-55-0). This contains 47 accounts of Gentiles from different parts of Europe who saved Jews during the Holocaust. (Rev: BL 11/15/00) [940.53]

8863 Rappaport, Doreen. *Beyond Courage: The Untold Story of Jewish Resistance During the Holocaust* (7–12). Illus. 2012, Candlewick $22.99 (978-076362976-2). Tells moving and unsettling stories of the ways in which Jews saved themselves and others, fighting back in Nazi-occupied Europe. Sidney Taylor Book Honor 2013. ⌒ Lexile 1030L (Rev: BL 7/12*; HB 11–12/12; LMC 1–2/13; SLJ 8/1/12*; VOYA 8/12) [940.53]

8864 Reich, Howard. *The First and Final Nightmare of Sonia Reich: A Son's Memoir* (10–12). 2006, Public Affairs $25.00 (978-1-58648-362-3). The author tells of the hardships his Jewish mother endured in Poland during the Second World War — and of her much-later collapse from the strain. (Rev: BL 5/15/06) [362.19.]

8865 Richman, Sophia. *A Wolf in the Attic: The Legacy of a Hidden Child of the Holocaust* (9–12). 2002, Haworth $49.95 (978-0-7890-1549-5); paper $24.95 (978-0-7890-1550-1). The author and her mother, both Jews, spent much of World War II in hiding in Poland. This is the daughter's story and tells what happened when they came to the United States in 1951. (Rev: BL 12/15/01) [940.53]

8866 Roleff, Tamara L., ed. *The Holocaust: Death Camps* (10–12). Series: History Firsthand. 2002, Gale LB $36.20 (978-0-7377-0883-7). Life in the Holocaust death camps is re-created in a series of contemporary narratives and reminiscences from various viewpoints. (Rev: BL 4/15/02; SLJ 3/02) [940.54]

8867 Ross, Bill D. *Iwo Jima: Legacy of Valor* (9–12). 1985, Random House paper $15.00 (978-0-394-74288-5). A day-by-day account of the 1945 battle against the Japanese. [940.54]

8868 Rubin, Susan Goldman. *Fireflies in the Dark: The Story of Friedl Dicker-Brandeis and the Children of Terezin* (5–10). 2000, Holiday $18.95 (978-0-8234-1461-1). A heartbreaking picture book that reproduces some of the artwork and writings of the children imprisoned at the Terezin concentration camp, where only 100 of 15,000 children survived. Sidney Taylor Book Honor 2000. (Rev: BCCB 11/00; BL 7/00*; HB 9–10/00; HBG 10/00; SLJ 8/00) [940.53]

8869 Rubin, Susan Goldman. *Searching for Anne Frank: Letters from Amsterdam to Iowa* (5–12). 2003, Abrams $19.95 (978-0-8109-4514-2). A brief penpal exchange between two sisters in Iowa and Anne Frank and her sister serves as the basis for a comparison between life in America and life for Jews in Europe. (Rev: BL 11/1/03; HB 11–12/03; HBG 4/04; SLJ 11/03; VOYA 10/03) [940.5]

8870 Ryan, Cornelius. *The Last Battle* (10–12). 1966, Simon & Schuster paper $16.00 (978-0-684-80329-6). The story of the last three weeks in Berlin before its fall during World War II. [940.54]

8871 Samuel, Wolfgang W. E. *The War of Our Childhood: Memories of World War II* (10–12). 2002, Univ. Press of Mississippi $35.00 (978-1-57806-482-3). German World War II survivors share their wartime experiences as children. (Rev: BL 9/1/02) [940.53]

8872 Sendyk, Helen. *New Dawn: A Triumph of Life After the Holocaust* (10–12). 2002, Syracuse Univ. $29.95 (978-0-8156-0735-9). In this sequel to *The End of Days*, author Helen Sendyk tells how she, her older sister, and her cousin created new lives for themselves in Israel after surviving the horrors of World War II in Poland. (Rev: BL 9/1/02) [940.53]

8873 Shapiro, Stephen, and Tina Forrester. *Hoodwinked: Deception and Resistance* (7–10). Illus. by David Craig. Series: Outwitting the Enemy: Stories from World War II. 2004, Annick paper $14.95 (978-1-55037-832-0). This compelling title explores some of the inventive deceptive strategies that Allied forces employed against the Axis powers. (Rev: BL 1/1–15/05; SLJ 1/05) [940.54]

8874 Shirer, William L. *The Rise and Fall of the Third Reich: A History of Nazi Germany* (9–12). 1990, Simon & Schuster paper $25.00 (978-0-671-72868-7). This is the standard history of the rise of Adolf Hitler, World War II, and the defeat of Germany. [943.086]

8875 Shohei, Ooka. *Taken Captive* (10–12). Trans. by Wayne P. Lammers. 1996, Wiley $32.50 (978-0-471-14285-0). The story of a Japanese soldier who was drafted into the army in 1944 and spent most of the remaining part of the war as a prisoner of the Americans. (Rev: BL 5/15/96; SLJ 2/97) [940.54]

8876 Sides, Hampton. *Ghost Soldiers: The Forgotten Epic Story of World War II's Most Dramatic Mission* (10–12). 2001, Doubleday $24.95 (978-0-385-49564-

6). This is an exciting account of the daring raid on Luzon in January 1945 to rescue the survivors of the infamous Bataan Death March. (Rev: BL 4/1/01) [940.54]

8877 Sloan, Bill. *The Ultimate Battle: Okinawa, 1945 — the Last Epic Struggle of World War II* (10–12). 2007, Simon & Schuster $27.00 (978-0-7432-9246-7). Survivors' accounts add to this examination of the key battle that resulted in huge loss of life. (Rev: BL 9/15/07) [940.54]

8878 Smith, Carl. *Pearl Harbor, 1941: The Day of Infamy* (9–12). 2004, Praeger $35.00 (978-1-84176-390-3). This work is a visually attractive, informative overview of the attack in December 1941. (Rev: BL 3/15/04) [940.54]

8879 Spinelli, Angelo M., and Lewis H. Carlson. *Life Behind Barbed Wire: The Secret World War II Photographs of Prisoner of War Angelo M. Spinelli* (9–12). 2004, Fordham Univ $35.00 (978-0-8232-2305-3). A collection of about 400 photographs that were taken secretly by the author while he was a prisoner in a German camp. (Rev: BL 3/15/04*) [940.54]

8880 Stalcup, Ann. *On the Home Front: Growing up in Wartime England* (6–10). 1998, Shoe String LB $19.50 (978-0-208-02482-4). A vivid first-person account about growing up in a small town in Shropshire during World War II. (Rev: BCCB 9/98; BL 10/15/98; HBG 9/98; SLJ 7/98) [940.54]

8881 Stokesbury, James L. *A Short History of World War II* (9–12). 1980, Morrow paper $15.99 (978-0-688-08587-2). A concise history of the war with coverage of its causes and immediate aftermath. [940.53]

8882 Ten Boom, Corrie, and John Sherrill. *The Hiding Place* (9–12). 1984, Bantam paper $6.99 (978-0-553-25669-7). An account of a Dutch girl growing up in Nazi-occupied Holland and her family's help hiding Jewish people. [940.54]

8883 Tucker, Todd. *The Great Starvation Experiment: The Heroic Men Who Starved So That Millions Could Live* (9–12). 2006, Free Press $26.00 (978-0-7432-7030-4). The fascinating story of 36 conscientious objectors who took part in research at the end of World War II into the effects of lengthy starvation on the human body. (Rev: BL 3/15/06)

8884 Velmans, Loet. *Long Way Back to the River Kwai: Memories of World War II* (10–12). 2003, Arcade $24.95 (978-1-55970-706-0). The Dutch-born author recounts his World War II experiences, including his family's escape from the Netherlands, military service in the Dutch East Indies, and life as a Japanese prisoner of war. (Rev: BL 11/1/03) [940.34]

8885 Wagner, Margaret E., et al. *The Library of Congress World War II Companion* (9–12). 2007, Simon & Schuster $45.00 (978-0-7432-5219-5). Kennedy. Illus. 2007, Simon & Schuster $45.00 (978-0-7432-5219-5). This expansive overview of World War II provides readers and researchers with key facts about the participating nations, details of operations, and profiles of key figures, along with statistics, timelines, photographs, and personal narratives. (Rev: BL 9/15/07) [940.53]

8886 Whitaker, Denis, et al. *Normandy: The Real Story* (10–12). 2004, Presidio paper $15.95 (978-0-345-45907-7). This is a gripping account of the great 1944 invasion campaign with material on problems, mistakes, and heroism. (Rev: BL 5/1/04) [940.54]

8887 Yamazaki, James N., and Louis B. Fleming. *Children of the Atomic Bomb: An American Physician's Memoir of Nagasaki, Hiroshima, and the Marshall Islands* (9–12). 1995, Duke Univ. $27.95 (978-0-8223-1658-9). Yamazaki, a pediatrician and a Nisei, writes this poignant memoir of his journey to Japan to gather firsthand accounts of the attack on Nagasaki. (Rev: BL 8/95) [618.92]

8888 Zargani, Aldo. *For Solo Violin: A Jewish Childhood in Fascist Italy* (10–12). Trans. by Marina Harss. 2002, Paul Dry paper $15.95 (978-0-9679675-3-0). In this poignant memoir, Aldo Zargani, an Italian Jew, tells how he and his family managed to survive Fascist persecution during World War II. (Rev: BL 5/1/02) [858]

8889 Zuckoff, Mitchell. *Lost in Shangri-La: The Epic True Story of a Plane Crash into the Stone Age* (10–12). 2011, HarperCollins $26.99 (978-0-06-198834-9). Tells the incredible story of the passengers who survived a crash in New Guinea in World War II only to find themselves confronting cannibalistic natives. **e** (Rev: SLJ 6/11) [940.54]

Modern World History (1945–)

8890 Antenori, Frank, and Hans Halberstadt. *Roughneck Nine One: The Extraordinary Story of a Special Forces A-Team at War* (9–12). 2006, St. Martin's $24.95 (978-0-312-35332-2). An up-close look at a 2003 battle between U.S. special forces (with Kurdish allies) and Iraqi soldiers. (Rev: BL 5/15/06) [956.7044]

8891 Benson, Sonia G. *Korean War: Almanac and Primary Sources* (6–10). 2001, Gale LB $70.00 (978-0-7876-5691-1). After an almanac section that traces the progress of the war, a selection of primary materials — speeches, memoirs, government documents, and so forth — are presented with introductions that place them in historical context. (Rev: SLJ 5/02) [951.904]

8892 Brzezinski, Matthew. *Red Moon Rising: Sputnik and the Hidden Rivalries That Ignited the Space Age* (9–12). 2007, Times $26.00 (978-0-8050-8147-3). The 1957 launch of the Soviet Union's Sputnik, the first satellite to orbit Earth, spurred the United States into action; the story of the subsequent space race will interest today's teens. (Rev: BL 8/07) [629.4]

8893 Carlisle, Rodney P. *Iraq War* (6–12). Series: America at War. 2007, Facts on File LB $35.00 (978-0-8160-

7129-6). An update of a 2004 title, this straightforward volume covers developments in the war from 2003 to 2006. (Rev: BL 11/1/07) [946.002]

8894 Carroll, Andrew, ed. *Operation Homecoming: Iraq, Afghanistan, and the Home Front, in the Words of U.S. Troops and Their Families* (10–12). 2006, Random House $26.95 (978-1-4000-6562-2). A collection of reflections on the war in the Middle East by soldiers and other Americans directly affected by it. Funded by the National Endowment for the Arts. (Rev: BL 9/1/06) [956]

8895 Feuer, Alan. *Over There: From the Bronx to Baghdad: Two Months in the Life of a Reluctant Reporter* (9–12). 2005, Counterpoint $24.00 (978-1-58243-327-1). A perceptive, personal account by a *New York Times* reporter of the 2003 invasion of Iraq; for mature teens. (Rev: BL 4/1/05) [956.7044]

8896 Gerdes, Louise I., ed. *The Cold War* (6–12). Series: Great Speeches in History. 2003, Gale LB $36.20 (978-0-7377-0869-1); paper $24.95 (978-0-7377-0868-4). Winston Churchill and Che Guevara are among the world leaders whose words are given in this collection that examines the confrontation between East and West. (Rev: BL 5/1/03; SLJ 9/03) [909.82]

8897 Hillstrom, Kevin, and Laurie Collier Hillstrom. *Vietnam War: Almanac* (7–12). Series: UXL Vietnam War Reference Library. 2000, Gale LB $70.00 (978-0-7876-4883-1). An absorbing and comprehensive overview of the causes, conduct, and aftermath of the war that includes interesting sidebars and black-and-white photographs. Also use *Vietnam War: Biographies* and *Vietnam War: Primary Sources* (both 2000). (Rev: BL 3/15/01; SLJ 5/01) [959.704]

8898 Isserman, Maurice. *Korean War. Rev. ed.* (9–12). Series: America at War. 2003, Facts on File $35.00 (978-0-8160-4939-4). A look at the background to this conflict, the fighting that took place, and the aftermath. (Rev: SLJ 2/04) [951.904]

8899 Jordan, June. *Affirmative Acts* (11–12). 1998, Doubleday paper $12.95 (978-0-385-49225-6). Through the 40 poems and essays collected here, Jordan, a poet and professor of African American studies, paints a fascinating portrait of events of the 1990s from the vantage point of a black activist intellectual. (Rev: BL 11/15/98) [305.896]

8900 Koopman, John. *McCoy's Marines: Darkside to Baghdad* (11–12). 2005, Zenith $24.95 (978-0-7603-2088-4). Koopman, a *San Francisco Chronicle* reporter and marine veteran, was embedded with a U.S. Marine Corps battalion during the Iraq War; for mature teens. (Rev: BL 3/1/05) [956.7]

8901 Langley, Andrew. *The Collapse of the Soviet Union: The End of an Empire* (7–12). Series: Snapshots in History. 2006, Compass Point LB $31.93 (978-0-7565-2009-0). This is an informative survey of the events that led to the disintegration of the Soviet empire. (Rev: SLJ 2/07)

8902 Mills, Dan. *Sniper One: On Scope and Under Siege with a Sniper Team in Iraq* (11–12). Illus. 2008, St. Martin's $25.95 (978-031253126-3). A compelling firsthand account of Mills's time in Iraq as a British sniper platoon commander in 2004; for mature readers. e (Rev: BL 9/1/08) [956.7044]

8903 Nakaya, Andrea C., ed. *Iraq* (8–12). Series: Current Controversies. 2004, Gale LB $36.20 (978-0-7377-2210-9); paper $24.95 (978-0-7377-2211-6). Statements by key U.S. figures including President Bush and Colin Powell are included in this survey of opinions about the Iraq war. (Rev: SLJ 12/04; VOYA 6/05) [956]

8904 Parker, Thomas. *Day by Day: The Sixties* (9–12). 1983, Facts on File $214.50 (978-0-87196-648-3). Using a day-by-day chronology, this book, like others in the series, traces the events of a decade, in this case the 1960s. [909.82]

8905 Rieckhoff, Paul. *Chasing Ghosts: A Soldier's Fight for America from Baghdad to Washington* (9–12). 2006, NAL $24.95 (978-0-451-21841-4). The account of a U.S. lieutenant's time in Baghdad and his efforts back home to tell the truth about this unpopular and controversial conflict. (Rev: BL 5/15/06) [956.7044]

8906 Sutherland, James. *The Ten-Year Century: Explaining the First Decade of the New Millennium* (7–10). 2010, Viking $18.99 (978-0-670-01223-7). An engaging overview of key events of the first decade of the 21st century, a time of great innovation and political change. e (Rev: BL 11/15/10; HB 11–12/10; LMC 11–12/10; SLJ 5/11; VOYA 10/10) [973.93]

8907 Tucker, Mike. *Among Warriors in Iraq: True Grit, Special Ops, and Raiding in Mosul and Fallujah* (11–12). 2005, Lyons paper $16.95 (978-1-59228-732-1). A former marine, now a war correspondent, sheds light on the bloody insurgency that followed the campaign to seize control of Iraq; for mature teens. (Rev: BL 5/1/05) [955.7]

8908 Weisskopf, Michael. *Blood Brothers: Among the Soldiers of Ward 57* (11–12). 2006, Henry Holt $25.00 (978-0-8050-7860-2). Ward 57 is the amputee ward of Walter Reed Army hospital, where the author ended up after losing a hand while reporting on the war in Iraq. This account of his experiences there will make the war and its dangers more real to readers. (Rev: BL 8/06) [956.7044]

8909 Winkler, Allan M. *The Cold War: A History in Documents* (10–12). 2000, Oxford $39.95 (978-0-19-512356-2). This excellent collection of primary sources covers the Cold War and attempts to trace the course of U. S. policy through these documents. (Rev: BL 12/15/00; HBG 10/01) [909.8]

8910 Young, Marilyn B., and John J. Fitzgerald. *The Vietnam War: A History in Documents* (6–12). Series: Pages from History. 2002, Oxford $39.95 (978-0-19-512278-7). Primary sources cover the conflict in Vietnam from French involvement through the U.S. withdrawal and include everything from official documents, speeches, and transcripts of White House tapes to North Vietnamese political cartoons and U.S. anti-war posters. (Rev: BCCB 9/02; BL 6/1–15/02; HBG 10/02; SLJ 9/02) [959.704]

Geographical Regions

Africa

General and Miscellaneous

8911 Baroin, Catherine. *Tubu: The Teda and the Daza* (7–12). Series: Heritage Library of African Peoples. 1997, Rosen LB $29.25 (978-0-8239-2000-6). The history and contemporary life of these peoples of Chad, Libya, Niger, and the Sudan are presented in easy-reading text. (Rev: BL 4/15/97) [967.43]

8912 Beckwith, Carol, and Angela Fisher. *Faces of Africa: Thirty Years of Photography* (8–12). 2004, National Geographic $35.00 (978-0-7922-6830-7). Eye-catching photographs document the traditional life of diverse African peoples. (Rev: BL 9/1/04) [305.896]

8913 Caplan, Gerald. *The Betrayal of Africa* (9–12). Series: Groundwork Guides. 2008, Groundwood $18.95 (978-0-88899-824-8); paper $10.00 (978-0-88899-825-5). The author claims the West is to blame for sub-Saharan Africa's troubles, including AIDS, genocides, and famines, and he outlines what will have to change to help the continent's people survive. (Rev: BL 5/15/08) [960]

8914 Davidson, Basil. *The African Slave Trade. Rev. ed.* (10–12). 1988, Little, Brown paper $15.95 (978-0-316-17438-1). This account gives details on the four centuries of the African slave trade, during which millions of people were cruelly forced to leave their homes. (Rev: BL 9/86) [967]

8915 Davidson, Basil. *The Lost Cities of Africa. Rev. ed.* (10–12). 1988, Little, Brown paper $16.95 (978-0-316-17431-2). This volume attempts to reconstruct the history and culture of Africa below the Sahara before the arrival of Europeans. [960]

8916 Fage, J. D., and William Tordoff. *A History of Africa. 4th ed.* (10–12). 2002, Routledge $95.00 (978-0-415-25247-8); paper $28.95 (978-0-415-25248-5). From prehistoric times to the beginning of this century, this is a readable, comprehensive history of Africa. [960]

8917 Follmi, Olivier. *Africa* (9–12). Trans. by Gerald Williams. 2006, Abrams $55.00 (978-0-8109-4832-7). This photographic record of a seven-month journey through Africa includes stunning images of people, animals, and landscapes. (Rev: BL 3/15/07) [960.022]

8918 Habeeb, Mark W. *Africa: Facts and Figures* (7–10). Series: Continent in the Balance: Africa. 2005, Mason Crest LB $21.95 (978-1-59084-817-3). An excellent overview of the continent, including its natural features, climate, cultural diversity, history, and economy. (Rev: BL 4/1/05*) [960]

8919 Laine, Daniel. *African Kings* (10–12). 2000, Ten Speed $40.00 (978-1-58008-224-2). This book features pictures and text about 70 contemporary African monarchs with background material on the history, rituals, and culture of the various tribes. (Rev: BL 11/1/00) [960]

8920 Levitov, Betty. *Africa on Six Wheels: A Semester on Safari* (10–12). 2007, Univ. of Nebraska paper $17.95 (978-0-8032-8054-0). Levitov describes the adventures of a study-abroad group traveling though countries of Africa including Kenya, Tanzania, and Zambia, meeting the local people, reading African literature, and learning Swahili. (Rev: BL 5/1/07) [916.704]

8921 Macintosh, Donald. *Travels in the White Man's Grave: Memoirs from West and Central Africa* (10–12). 2002, Abacus paper $13.95 (978-0-349-11435-4). In this collection of tales from three decades spent in Africa, Scottish-born Macintosh relates various exciting encounters with an assortment of unforgettable humans and deadly wildlife. (Rev: BL 4/15/02) [966.032092]

8922 Murray, Jocelyn, ed. *Cultural Atlas of Africa* (9–12). 1981, Facts on File $45.00 (978-0-87196-558-5).

With hundreds of maps and illustrations plus text, such topics as language, religion, culture, and education are covered for each country. (Rev: BL 9/86) [960]

8923 Nardo, Don. *The European Colonization of Africa* (7–12). Illus. Series: World History. 2010, Morgan Reynolds LB $28.95 (978-159935142-1). This detailed history of imperialism in Africa covers successive European arrivals and their impact on the continent, the slave trade, missionaries, and independence. (Rev: BL 10/1/10)

8924 Reader, John. *Africa* (8–12). Illus. by Michael Lewis. 2001, National Geographic $50.00 (978-0-7922-7681-4). A lavishly illustrated overview of Africa with sections on each of the many ecological divisions, such as savanna, desert, mountains, and coast. (Rev: BL 8/01) [960]

Central and Eastern Africa

8925 Barnes, Virginia Lee, and Janice Boddy, retels. *Aman* (10–12). 1995, Vintage paper $14.00 (978-0-679-76209-6). The candid story of a young Somali woman and the sexual and social taboos of tribal society in her country. (Rev: SLJ 2/96) [967]

8926 Beard, Peter. *Zara's Tales: Perilous Escapades in Equatorial Africa* (8–12). 2004, Knopf $26.95 (978-0-679-42659-2). In this compelling memoir, Beard talks about his many encounters — some life-threatening — with the animals of East Africa. (Rev: BL 10/15/04) [967.70]

8927 Bowden, Rob. *Kenya* (6–10). Series: Countries of the World. 2003, Facts on File $30.00 (978-0-8160-5384-1). This profile of an impoverished nation gives material on physical geography, resources, population, tourism, commerce, and geography. (Rev: BL 2/1/04) [967.62]

8928 Broberg, Catherine. *Kenya in Pictures* (6–10). Series: Visual Geography. 2002, Lerner LB $27.93 (978-0-8225-1957-7). Information on all aspects of life in this African country, including extensive coverage of its history, is accompanied by plenty of photographs and a Web site that offers up-to-date links. (Rev: BL 10/15/02; HBG 3/03; SLJ 12/02) [967]

8929 Burnham, Philip. *Gbaya* (7–12). Series: Heritage Library of African Peoples. 1997, Rosen LB $29.25 (978-0-8239-1995-6). These African people who live in Cameroon, Central African Republic, Congo, and Zaire, are introduced through illustrations and simple text. (Rev: BL 4/15/97) [967]

8930 Edgerton, Robert B. *The Troubled Heart of Africa: A History of the Congo* (10–12). 2002, St. Martin's $25.95 (978-0-312-30486-7). Edgerton chronicles the turbulent history of the Congo from the first European exploration of its interior in the 15th century to the present. (Rev: BL 12/15/02) [967.24]

8931 Fisanick, Christina, ed. *The Rwanda Genocide* (9–12). Series: At Issue in History. 2004, Gale paper $23.70 (978-0-7377-1986-4). The deaths of an estimated 800,000 Rwandans in the mid-1990s are the topic of essays that present different points of view on the causes, the global reaction, and the measures taken to rebuild the country. (Rev: SLJ 12/04) [967]

8932 Gaertner, Ursula. *Elmolo* (7–10). Series: Heritage Library of African Peoples. 1995, Rosen LB $29.25 (978-0-8239-1764-8). Looks at the customs, daily life, and values of the Elmolo tribe in Kenya. (Rev: BL 7/95; SLJ 5/95) [967.62]

8933 Hall, Martin, and Rebecca Stefoff. *Great Zimbabwe: Digging for the Past* (7–10). Series: Digging for the Past. 2006, Oxford $21.95 (978-0-19-515773-4). Traces our knowledge of the ancient city-state that lies in present-day Mozambique, with an emphasis on the archaeological discoveries and discussion of racial preconceptions that blurred understanding. (Rev: BL 6/1–15/06; SLJ 11/06) [968.91]

8934 Holtzman, Jon. *Samburu* (7–10). Series: Heritage Library of African Peoples. 1995, Rosen LB $29.25 (978-0-8239-1759-4). Discusses in detailed but simple text the culture and lifestyle of the Samburu people of Kenya. (Rev: BL 7/95; SLJ 5/95) [967]

8935 Hussein, Ikram. *Teenage Refugees from Somalia Speak Out* (7–12). Series: Teenage Refugees Speak Out. 1997, Rosen LB $27.95 (978-0-8239-2444-8). Teenage refugees from Somalia recount the violent anarchy and acute famine in their country and their journey from Africa to the United States. (Rev: BL 12/15/97; SLJ 12/97) [967]

8936 Ifemesia, Chieka. *Turkana* (7–10). Series: Heritage Library of African Peoples. 1996, Rosen LB $29.25 (978-0-8239-1761-7). Using a simple text and color photographs, this account describes the past and present of the Turkana people, who now live in Ethiopia, Kenya, Sudan, and Uganda. (Rev: BL 2/15/95) [960]

8937 Jackson, Kate. *Mean and Lowly Things: Snakes, Science, and Survival in the Congo* (9–12). 2008, Harvard $27.95 (978-0-674-02974-3). A Canadian herpetologist describes field work in the Congo. (Rev: BL 4/1/08) [597.96096724]

8938 Jansen, Hanna. *Over a Thousand Hills I Walk with You* (7–10). Trans. by Elizabeth D. Crawford. 2006, Carolrhoda $16.95 (978-1-57505-927-3). The heartbreaking story of 8-year-old Jeanne, the only member of her family to survive the Rwandan genocide of 1994, is told by the girl's adoptive mother. (Rev: BL 4/1/06*; SLJ 6/06*) [833]

8939 Kabira, Wanjiku M. *Agikuyu* (7–10). Series: Heritage Library of African Peoples. 1995, Rosen LB $29.25 (978-0-8239-1762-4). Presents social and cultural aspects of the Agikuyu community of Kenya in ways that make them accessible to Western readers. (Rev: BL 7/95; SLJ 6/95) [967]

8940 Koopmans, Andy. *Rwanda* (7–10). Series: Africa. 2005, Mason Crest LB $21.95 (978-1-59084-812-8). Covers the geography, history, politics, government, economy, people, and culture of Rwanda, providing a map, flag, recipes, glossary, timeline, and colorful photographs. (Rev: SLJ 3/05) [967.571]

8941 Lamb, Christina. *House of Stone: The True Story of a Family Divided in War-Torn Zimbabwe* (10–12). 2007, Lawrence Hill $24.95 (978-1-55652-735-7). Zimbabwe's unhappy history is presented through the stories of Aqui, a poor black woman working as a nanny, and Nigel, a wealthy white farmer. (Rev: BL 9/1/07) [968.91051]

8942 MacDonald, Joan Vos. *Tanzania* (7–10). Series: Africa. 2005, Mason Crest LB $21.95 (978-1-59084-813-5). Covers the geography, history, politics, government, economy, people, and culture of Tanzania, providing a map, flag, recipes, glossary, timeline, and colorful photographs. (Rev: SLJ 3/05; VOYA 8/04) [967.8]

8943 Nwaezeigwe, Nwankwo T. *Ngoni* (7–12). Series: Heritage Library of African Peoples. 1997, Rosen LB $29.25 (978-0-8239-2006-8). The history, traditions, and struggle for freedom of this African group in Malawi are laid out in accessible text. (Rev: BL 4/15/97) [968.97]

8944 Ojo, Onukaba A. *Mbuti* (7–10). Series: Heritage Library of African Peoples. 1996, Rosen LB $29.25 (978-0-8239-1998-7). The Mbuti people of Zaire are introduced with details on their environment, history, customs, and present situation. (Rev: BL 2/15/96; SLJ 7/96) [305.896]

8945 Okeke, Chika. *Kongo* (7–12). Series: Heritage Library of African Peoples. 1997, Rosen LB $29.25 (978-0-8239-2001-3). The Kongo people of Angola, Congo, and Zaire in Central Africa are featured in easy-reading text with material on their land, kingdoms, political life, and culture. (Rev: BL 4/15/97) [967]

8946 *Peoples of East Africa* (6–12). Series: Peoples of Africa. 1997, Facts on File $28.00 (978-0-8160-3484-0). This book gives a concise overview of 15 ethnic groups of eastern Africa, with details on history, language, way of life, society, religion, and culture. Included are Falasha, Ganda, Hutus and Tutsis, Masai, Nyoro, Somalis, and Swahili. (Rev: SLJ 10/97) [967]

8947 Roberts, Mary N., and Allen F. Roberts. *Luba* (6–10). Series: Heritage Library of African Peoples. 1997, Rosen LB $29.25 (978-0-8239-2002-0). The Luba people of Zaire are introduced with material on their history, present conditions, and cultural resources. (Rev: BL 9/15/97) [967]

8948 Schnapper, LaDena. *Teenage Refugees from Ethiopia Speak Out* (5–10). Series: Teenage Refugees Speak Out. 1997, Rosen LB $27.95 (978-0-8239-2438-7). Ethiopian teens now living in America tell of the violence, famine, and civil war that drove them from their country and of their reception in America. (Rev: SLJ 2/98) [963]

8949 Scott, Jonathan, and Angela Scott. *Mara-Serengeti: A Photographer's Paradise* (9–12). 2001, Voyageur $39.95 (978-0-86343-398-6). This account contains a superb collection of photographs and drawings plus a running text, all dealing with the complex grassland area known as the Mara-Serengeti ecosystem of Kenya and Tanzania. (Rev: BL 4/1/01) [591.967]

8950 Steidle, Brian. *The Devil Came on Horseback: Bearing Witness to the Genocide in Darfur* (10–12). 2007, Public Affairs $24.95 (978-1-58648-474-3). Steidle arrived unarmed in Darfur as part of an African Union unit monitoring a cease-fire agreement; during his six months there he learned a lot about the horrors taking place and was himself taken hostage. (Rev: BL 4/1/07) [962.404]

8951 Twagilimana, Aimable. *Teenage Refugees from Rwanda Speak Out* (5–10). Series: Teenage Refugees Speak Out. 1997, Rosen LB $27.95 (978-0-8239-2443-1). Teenage refugees from Rwanda describe the warfare between Tutsi and Hutu peoples, the terrible living conditions that forced them to leave their country, and the challenges and difficulties they have experienced in the United States. (Rev: SLJ 2/98) [967]

8952 Wa Wamwere, Koigi. *I Refuse to Die: My Journey for Freedom* (10–12). 2002, Seven Stories $24.95 (978-1-58322-521-9). In this inspiring autobiography, Kenyan human rights activist Koigi wa Wamwere recounts his courageous resistance to the repressive regimes of Jomo Kenyatta and Daniel Arap Moi. (Rev: BL 9/1/02) [967.6227]

8953 Wangari, Esther. *Ameru* (7–10). Series: Heritage Library of African Peoples. 1995, Rosen LB $29.25 (978-0-8239-1766-2). An introduction to the history, traditions, and culture of the Ameru people of Kenya in easy-reading text. (Rev: BL 9/15/95; SLJ 11/95) [967.6]

8954 Zeleza, Tiyambe. *Akamba* (7–10). Series: Heritage Library of African Peoples. 1995, Rosen LB $29.25 (978-0-8239-1768-6). The history, traditions, and fight for freedom of the Akamba people of Kenya are covered in this book with many color illustrations. (Rev: BL 7/95; SLJ 6/95) [960]

8955 Zeleza, Tiyambe. *Mijikenda* (7–10). Series: Heritage Library of African Peoples. 1995, Rosen LB $29.25 (978-0-8239-1767-9). Combines history and anthropology to provide an easy-to-read portrait of the Mijikenda people. (Rev: BL 9/15/95; SLJ 11/95) [967]

North Africa

8956 Azuonye, Chukwuma. *Dogon* (7–10). Series: Heritage Library of African Peoples. 1995, Rosen LB $29.25 (978-0-8239-1976-5). Provides information on the history, culture, and lifestyles of the Dogon people of Mali. (Rev: BL 2/15/96) [966.23]

8957 Benanav, Michael. *Men of Salt: Across the Sahara with the Caravan of White Gold* (11–12). 2006, Lyons $23.95 (978-1-59228-772-7). Benanav writes about his experiences traveling with salt miners who cross the Sahara by camel. (Rev: BL 12/1/05) [916.604]

8958 Childress, Diana. *Omar al-Bashir's Sudan* (10–12). Series: Dictatorships. 2009, Lerner LB $38.60 (978-0-8225-9096-5). Sudan's history and current political situation are addressed clearly in this well-organized volume that includes maps, photographs, and helpful backmatter. (Rev: BL 10/15/09; LMC 11–12/09; SLJ 9/09) [962.404]

8959 Hollyman, Stephenie, and Walter E. A. van Beek. *Dogon: Africa's People of the Cliffs* (10–12). 2001, Abrams $49.50 (978-0-8109-4373-5). This account describes the culture, history, and lifestyles of the Dogon people who live in a remote part of Mali in western Africa. (Rev: BL 5/15/01) [966.23]

Southern Africa

8960 Beck, Roger. *The History of South Africa* (10–12). 2000, Greenwood $51.95 (978-0-313-30730-0). From prehistory through the European invasions and ending with the Mandela years, this is a readable basic guide to South African history. [968]

8961 Beecroft, Simon. *The Release of Nelson Mandela* (6–12). Series: Days that Changed the World. 2004, World Almanac LB $31.00 (978-0-8368-5571-5). The significance of Mandela's release after 27 years of imprisonment is made clear through the explanation of the struggle against apartheid, with discussion of the progress South Africa has made since then. (Rev: BL 4/1/04; SLJ 7/04) [618.1]

8962 Bolaane, Maitseo, and Part T. Mgadla. *Batswana* (6–10). Series: Heritage Library of African Peoples. 1997, Rosen LB $29.25 (978-0-8239-2008-2). This work discusses the history, culture, and present status of the Batswana people of southern Africa. (Rev: BL 1/1–15/98) [968]

8963 Cruden, Alex, and Dedria Bryfonski. *The End of Apartheid* (9–12). Series: Perspectives on Modern World History. 2010, Gale/Greenhaven $38.50 (978-0-7377-4557-3). Articles, speeches, and extracts — combined with maps, charts, and photographs — examine the history of apartheid and the controversies surrounding it; personal narratives add perspective. (Rev: LMC 10/10; SLJ 6/10) [968.06]

8964 Daymond, M. J., et al, ed. *Women Writing Africa: The Southern Region* (10–12). 2002, Feminist $75.00 (978-1-55861-406-2). A collection of varied writings — letters, memoirs, work songs, prison diaries, and poetry — by women from six countries in southern Africa. (Rev: BL 11/1/02) [808.8]

8965 Green, Rebecca L. *Merina* (7–12). Series: Heritage Library of African Peoples. 1997, Rosen LB $29.25 (978-0-8239-1991-8). The history and culture of the Merina people of Madagascar are covered in simple text and many illustrations. (Rev: BL 4/15/97; VOYA 6/97) [969.1]

8966 Harrison, Peter, ed. *History of Southern Africa* (7–12). Series: History of Africa. 2003, Facts on File $30.00 (978-0-8160-5065-9). From prehistory to today, this volume covers in detail the history of southern Africa, detailing in particular European settlement, independence, and apartheid. (Rev: BL 9/15/03; SLJ 5/04) [968]

8967 Lapierre, Dominique. *A Rainbow in the Night: The Tumultuous Birth of South Africa* (10–12). Trans. by Kathryn Spink. 2009, Da Capo $26 (978-030681847-9). This epic overview of South Africa's turbulent history reads like a novel. ∩ ℮ (Rev: BL 12/1/09) [968.]

8968 Mitchell, Peter, ed. *Southern Africa* (8–11). Series: Peoples and Cultures of Africa. 2006, Chelsea House LB $39.00 (978-0-8160-6265-2). A detailed look at the nations of southern Africa (including Madagascar), discussing their culture, history, ethnic groups, religions, languages, and arts and architecture. (Rev: BL 10/15/06) [900]

8969 Njoku, Onwuka N. *Mbundu* (7–12). Series: Heritage Library of African Peoples. 1997, Rosen LB $29.25 (978-0-8239-2004-4). An easy-to-read introduction to the history and contemporary culture of this people of Angola. (Rev: BL 4/15/97) [967.3]

8970 Oluikpe, Benson O. *Swazi* (7–12). Series: Heritage Library of African Peoples. 1997, Rosen LB $29.25 (978-0-8239-2012-9). This accessible book describes the history, traditions, and struggles for freedom of the Swazi people of Swaziland and South Africa. (Rev: BL 4/15/97; SLJ 12/97) [968]

8971 Owens, Mark, and Delia Owens. *Secrets of the Savanna: Twenty-three Years in the African Wilderness Unraveling the Mysteries of Elephants and People* (9–12). 2006, Houghton Mifflin $26.00 (978-0-395-89310-4). A couple works to uplift villagers from poverty while studying Zambia's declining elephant population, noting similarities in the societies of elephants and people. (Rev: BL 4/15/06) [599.67]

8972 Schneider, Elizabeth Ann. *Ndebele* (7–12). Series: Heritage Library of African Peoples. 1997, Rosen LB $29.25 (978-0-8239-2009-9). Topics covered about the Ndebele people of South Africa include environment, history, religion, social organization, politics, and customs. (Rev: BL 4/15/97) [968]

8973 Stone, Judith. *When She Was White: The True Story of a Family Divided by Race* (9–12). 2007, Hyperion $23.95 (978-0-7868-6898-8). To her shock, at the age of 10 in 1966, Sandra Laing was expelled from her white boarding school in South Africa; she had been reclassified as "Coloured" and the community shunned the family. Although she was later ruled to be white, this first decision was to have lasting repercussions on her life. (Rev: BL 3/1/07) [305.48]

8974 Thompson, Leonard Monteath. *A History of South Africa. 3rd ed.* (10–12). 2001, Yale Univ. paper $17.95 (978-0-300-08776-5). An account of South African history that focuses more on the nation's black inhabitants than on the white. [968]

8975 Udechukwu, Ada. *Herero* (7–10). Series: Heritage Library of African Peoples. 1996, Rosen LB $29.25 (978-0-8239-2003-7). In simple text, this book introduces the three Herero subgroups that share a similar language and culture in today's Botswana, Angola, and Namibia, with an emphasis on their political history. (Rev: BL 3/15/96; SLJ 6/96) [968]

8976 Yeats, Charles. *Prisoner of Conscience: One Man's Remarkable Journey from Repression to Freedom* (9–12). 2006, Trafalgar $19.95 (978-1-84604-001-6). The author tells of his imprisonment and spiritual life as an objector to South Africa's apartheid system in the 1980s. (Rev: BL 8/06) [968.06]

West Africa

8977 Azuonye, Chukwuma. *Edo: The Bini People of the Benin Kingdom* (7–10). Series: Heritage Library of African Peoples. 1996, Rosen LB $29.25 (978-0-8239-1985-7). A review of the history, culture, society, and the struggle for freedom of the Bini people, whose empire was part of present-day Nigeria. (Rev: BL 3/15/96) [966.9]

8978 Harmon, Daniel E. *Nigeria: 1880 to the Present: The Struggle, the Tragedy, the Promise* (6–12). 2000, Chelsea LB $35.00 (978-0-7910-5452-9). This survey of Nigerian history is careful to highlight changes and achievements that did not involve European influence; it includes many Royal Geographic Society black-and-white photographs. (Rev: HBG 3/01; SLJ 2/01) [966.9]

8979 Martin, Kathleen. *Kamakwie: Finding Peace, Love and Injustice in Sierra Leone* (9–12). Illus. 2012, Red Deer paper $19.95 (978-08899547-2-4). Canadian journalist Martin spent several weeks in a village in Sierra Leone and describes the aspirations and tragic stories of the people there (tales of child soldiers, rape, violence,

and so forth). (Rev: BL 4/15/12; LMC 10/12; VOYA 6/12) [966.404]

8980 Ndukwe, Pat I. *Fulani* (7–10). Series: Heritage Library of African Peoples. 1995, Rosen LB $29.25 (978-0-8239-1982-6). A description of the history, surroundings, politics, customs, and current conditions of the Fulani people, who live in Cameroon, Mali, and Nigeria. (Rev: BL 2/15/96; SLJ 7/96) [966]

8981 Ogbaa, Kalu. *Igbo* (7–10). Series: Heritage Library of African Peoples. 1995, Rosen LB $29.25 (978-0-8239-1977-2). An introduction to the Igbo people, one of the three most important ethnic groups in Nigeria. (Rev: BL 9/15/95; SLJ 11/95) [966.9]

8982 Reef, Catherine. *This Our Dark Country: The American Settlers of Liberia* (7–12). 2002, Clarion $17.00 (978-0-618-14785-4). This chronological account of Liberia's history makes good use of excerpts from letters and diaries. (Rev: BL 11/15/02; HBG 3/03; SLJ 12/02; VOYA 6/03) [966.62]

8983 Sallah, Tijan M. *Wolof* (7–12). Series: Heritage Library of African Peoples. 1996, Rosen LB $29.25 (978-0-8239-1987-1). Using maps, many color illustrations, and simple text, this book introduces the Wolof people of Senegal and their history, social and political life, customs, religious beliefs, and relations with other peoples in their region. (Rev: BL 3/15/96; SLJ 7/96) [966.3]

8984 Walker, Ida. *Nigeria* (7–10). Series: Africa. 2005, Mason Crest LB $21.95 (978-1-59084-811-1). Covers the geography, history, politics, government, economy, people, and culture of Nigeria, providing a map, flag, recipes, glossary, timeline, and colorful photographs. (Rev: SLJ 3/05) [966.9]

Asia

General and Miscellaneous

8985 Angus, Colin. *Lost in Mongolia: Rafting the World's Last Unchallenged River* (10–12). 2003, Broadway paper $12.95 (978-0-7679-1280-8). Angus details the first successful navigation of Asia's 3,250-mile-long Yenisey River, a thrilling journey that took the author and two companions by raft and kayak from the heart of Mongolia to the Arctic Ocean. (Rev: BL 9/1/03) [796.1]

8986 Des Forges, Roger V., and John S. Major. *The Asian World, 600-1500* (7–12). 2006, Oxford LB $32.95 (978-0-19-517843-2). The authors explore the contributions, culture, empires, and conflicts of China, Japan, India, and Korea over nine centuries, with color photographs, artwork, maps, and quotations. (Rev: SLJ 7/06)

8987 Hanks, Reuel R. *Central Asia: A Global Studies Handbook* (10–12). 2005, ABC-CLIO $55.00 (978-1-85109-656-5). This useful guide combines narrative about the history, geography, culture, and economy of Uzbekistan, Kazakhstan, and Kyrgyzstan with a reference section listing events, organizations, and so forth. (Rev: SLJ 1/06)

8988 Kort, Michael. *Central Asian Republics* (7–12). Series: Nations in Transition. 2003, Facts on File $40.00 (978-0-8160-5074-1). After a history of the region, each of the independent republics is introduced with discussion of the current challenges it faces; these include border disputes, poor environment, poor health care and quality of life, and government corruption. (Rev: SLJ 4/04)

8989 Pascoe, Elaine. *The Pacific Rim: East Asia at the Dawn of a New Century* (7–12). 1999, Twenty-First Century LB $25.90 (978-0-7613-3015-8). Brief historical information and current economic figures are given for Japan, China, Taiwan, the Koreas, Indonesia, Singapore, Malaysia, and the Philippines. (Rev: BL 7/99; SLJ 9/99) [950.4]

8990 Schmidt, Jeremy. *Himalayan Passage: Seven Months in the High Country of Tibet, Nepal, China, India and Pakistan* (9–12). 1991, Mountaineers $22.95 (978-0-89886-262-1). The adventure-filled travels of four experienced mountaineers — on foot, by mountain bike, and in overcrowded buses and trucks — from Tibet to Sikkim. (Rev: BL 9/15/91) [915.49]

China

8991 Fairbank, John King. *The Great Chinese Revolution: 1800-1985* (10–12). 1986, HarperCollins $16.95 (978-0-06-039076-1). This account covers 185 years of Chinese history from the late imperial period to the mid-1980s. [951]

8992 Gay, Kathlyn. *The Aftermath of the Chinese Nationalist Revolution* (7–10). Illus. 2008, Lerner LB $38.60 (978-082257601-3). A well-researched exploration of the Chinese civil turmoil — and eventual transition to communism — after the 1911 Wuchang Rebellion led by Sun Yat-sen. (Rev: BL 10/15/08; LMC 3–4/09; SLJ 3/1/09) [951.04]

8993 Hardy, Grant, and Anne Behnke Kinney. *The Establishment of the Han Empire and Imperial China* (10–12). Series: Greenwood Guides to Historic Events of the Ancient World. 2005, Greenwood LB $46.95 (978-0-313-32588-5). The political, institutional, technological, and social aspects of the Han dynasty are discussed and placed in historical context. (Rev: SLJ 7/05) [951]

8994 Haugen, David M., ed. *China* (8–12). 2006, Gale LB $34.95 (978-0-7377-3389-1); paper $23.70 (978-0-7377-3390-7). China's economic growth, steps toward democracy, military threat, and other important aspects

are discussed in this collection of brief articles that present different perspectives. (Rev: SLJ 8/06)

8995 *Journey into China* (9–12). 1982, National Geographic LB $23.95 (978-0-87044-461-6). A region-by-region description by several travelers of their journeys in China. [915.1]

8996 Ko, Dorothy. *Every Step a Lotus: Shoes for Bound Feet* (10–12). 2002, Univ. of California paper $26.95 (978-0-520-23284-6). An interesting look at the ancient Chinese custom of foot binding, defending the practice as a cultural phenomenon with roots in Chinese history and philosophy. (Rev: BL 3/1/02) [391]

8997 Kort, Michael. *China Under Communism* (9–12). 1995, Millbrook LB $26.40 (978-1-56294-450-6). This detailed history of the Communist movement in China offers opportunities for discussion from both historical and cultural perspectives. (Rev: BL 1/1/95; SLJ 3/95) [951.05]

8998 Langley, Andrew. *The Cultural Revolution: Years of Chaos in China* (6–10). Series: Snapshots in History. 2008, Compass Point LB $24.95 (978-0-7565-3483-7). A look at the events leading up to the violence in China in the 1960s begins this book, which then delves into what happened during the Cultural Revolution and why. (Rev: BL 3/3/08; SLJ 7/08) [951.05]

8999 Mah, Adeline Yen. *China: Land of Dragons and Emperors* (6–12). 2009, Delacorte $17.99 (978-0-385-73748-7); LB $20.99 (978-0-385-90669-2). An engaging history of China from ancient times to the present, with insight into the land's people, traditions, beliefs, and cultures. (Rev: LMC 10/09; SLJ 8/09) [951]

9000 Murowchick, Robert E. *China: Ancient Culture, Modern Land* (9–12). Series: Cradles of Civilization. 1994, Univ. of Oklahoma $39.95 (978-0-8061-2683-8). Follows the development of Chinese cultural history from ancient times to the present, tracing the evolution of religion, philosophy, government, land, and language. (Rev: BL 10/1/94) [951]

9001 Schoppa, R. Keith. *Twentieth Century China: A History in Documents* (9–12). Series: Pages from History. 2004, Oxford LB $39.95 (978-0-19-514745-2). Photographs, reproductions, cartoons, and posters add to the excerpts from primary sources that document the history of China during the 20th century. (Rev: SLJ 4/05) [951]

9002 Slavicek, Louise Chipley. *The Chinese Cultural Revolution* (7–10). Series: Milestones in Modern World History. 2010, Chelsea House $35 (978-1-60413-278-6). With first-person narratives, excerpts from primary documents, and a timeline, this volume tells the story of the political and social upheaval in China from the mid-1960s to the mid-1970s. ℮ (Rev: BL 5/15/10; LMC 8–9/10; SLJ 5/10) [951.05]

9003 Troost, J. Maarten. *Lost on Planet China: The Strange and True Story of One Man's Attempt to Under-*

stand the World's Most Mystifying Nation; or, How He Became Comfortable Eating Live Squid (11–12). 2008, Broadway $22.95 (978-076792200-5). Troost recounts his explorations in China, seeking a suitable place to move his family and finding many interesting social and physical factors to consider. (Rev: BL 7/08) [915.104]

India, Pakistan, and Bangladesh

9004 Brown, Louise. *The Dancing Girls of Lahore: Selling Love and Saving Dreams in Pakistan's Ancient Pleasure District* (11–12). 2005, HarperCollins $23.95 (978-0-06-074042-9). A gritty account of the life of three young girls growing up with their mother, drug-addicted father, and his second wife in the red-light district of Lahore, Pakistan; for mature teens. (Rev: BL 5/15/05) [306.74]

9005 Crompton, Samuel Willard. *Pakistan* (7–12). Series: Modern World Nations. 2002, Chelsea LB $30.00 (978-0-7910-7098-7). An overview of the history, geography, people, politics, and religion of Pakistan, with discussion of current difficulties such as ethnic strife, population problems, and disputes with India. (Rev: SLJ 2/03) [954.91]

9006 Darraj, Susan Muaddi. *The Indian Independence Act of 1947* (8–12). Illus. Series: Milestones in Modern World History. 2011, Chelsea House LB $35 (978-160413496-4). With photographs, timelines, and maps, this volume explains the granting of independence to India and the partitioning of India and Pakistan. **e** (Rev: BL 2/15/12) [954.03]

9007 Eraly, Abraham, and Yasmin Khan. *India* (9–12). Illus. 2008, DK $40.00 (978-075663977-8). The fascinating history of India features beautiful pictures of the land and insightful narratives of its people who have shaped the country. (Rev: BL 9/15/08) [954]

9008 Goodwin, William. *Pakistan* (6–12). Series: Modern Nations of the World. 2002, Gale LB $29.95 (978-1-59018-218-5). An overview of Pakistan's geography, history, culture, and society, with biographical information on key individuals. (Rev: BL 11/15/02; SLJ 1/03) [954.91]

9009 MacDonald, Sarah. *Holy Cow: An Indian Adventure* (10–12). 2004, Broadway paper $12.95 (978-0-7679-1574-8). A lively journey around India in an account that looks at the country's cultures and religions. (Rev: BL 3/15/04) [954]

9010 Sinkler, Adrian. *Pakistan* (9–12). Series: Nations in Transition. 2004, Gale LB $32.45 (978-0-7377-1208-7). Useful for report writers, this profile of Pakistan examines the country's geography, history, people, culture, religion, politics, and government. (Rev: SLJ 3/05) [954.9]

9011 Valliant, Doris. *Bangladesh* (8–12). Series: The Growth and Influence of Islam in the Nations of Asia

and Central Asia. 2005, Mason Crest LB $25.95 (978-1-59084-879-1). A well-illustrated look at Bangladesh and the importance of Islam in the country's history, politics, economy, and foreign relations. (Rev: SLJ 9/05) [954.9]

9012 Viswanath, R. *Teenage Refugees and Immigrants from India Speak Out* (7–12). Series: Teenage Refugees Speak Out. 1997, Rosen LB $27.95 (978-0-8239-2440-0). A description of the ethnic and religious conflicts and economic conditions that have caused the displacement of tens of thousands of Indians, plus the stories of those who came to the United States, told in first-person teenage accounts. (Rev: BL 12/15/97; SLJ 4/98) [954]

Japan

9013 Case, Robert. *Japan* (6–10). Series: Countries of the World. 2003, Facts on File $30.00 (978-0-8160-5381-0). An attractive introduction to Japan that includes material on history, geography, economy, people, and culture. (Rev: BL 1/1–15/04) [952]

9014 Kallen, Stuart A. *Life in Tokyo* (6–10). Series: The Way People Live. 2001, Lucent LB $29.95 (978-1-56006-797-9). After a brief historical introduction, life in present-day Tokyo is featured with material on such topics as daily life, education, entertainment, jobs, food, and culture. (Rev: BL 6/1–15/01; SLJ 6/01) [952]

9015 Steinberger, Aimee Major. *Japan Ai: A Tall Girl's Adventures in Japan* (9–12). Illus. by author. 2008, Go! Comi $16.99 (978-1-933617-83-1). Manga fans will be drawn to this book by the cover and will keep reading when they discover this is an account of a manga-fan's dream tour of Japan. (Rev: BL 4/1/08) [915.2]

Other Asian Countries

9016 Ayub, Awista. *However Tall the Mountain: A Dream, Eight Girls, and a Journey Home* (10–12). 2009, Hyperion $23.99 (978-140132249-6). The story of eight Afghani girls who get an opportunity to play soccer in America and then must return home. (Rev: BL 7/09) [796.334]

9017 Boaz, John, ed. *The U.S. Attack on Afghanistan* (10–12). Series: At Issue in History. 2005, Gale LB $33.70 (978-0-7377-1983-3). Essays present arguments for and against the United States' intervention in Afghanistan after September 11, 2001; a chronology and a foreword provide useful background information. (Rev: BL 9/15/05) [958.104]

9018 Corona, Laurel. *Afghanistan* (6–12). Series: Modern Nations of the World. 2002, Gale LB $29.95 (978-1-59018-217-8). This book covers cultural, geographical, religious, and other aspects of Afghanistan, with discussion of the Taliban and the role of women. (Rev: BL 11/15/02; SLJ 12/02) [958.1]

9019 Einfeld, Jann, ed. *Afghanistan* (9–12). Series: Current Controversies. 2005, Gale LB $36.20 (978-0-7377-2470-7); paper $24.95 (978-0-7377-2471-4). Essays dissect the current political situation in Afghanistan and offer some predictions for the future. (Rev: SLJ 7/05) [958.104]

9020 Emadi, Hafizullah. *Culture and Customs of Afghanistan* (9–12). Series: Culture and Customs of Asia. 2005, Greenwood $51.95 (978-0-313-33089-6). An in-depth look at Afghanistan through history, with an emphasis on social customs and interesting material on family life and the role of women. (Rev: SLJ 1/06) [958.1]

9021 Gritzner, Jeffrey A. *Afghanistan* (7–12). Series: Modern World Nations. 2002, Chelsea LB $30.00 (978-0-7910-6774-1). An overview of the history, geography, people, politics, and religion of Afghanistan, with discussion of the current antiterrorist and rebuilding efforts. (Rev: SLJ 2/03) [958.1]

9022 Guibert, Emmanuel, et al. *The Photographer: Into War-Torn Afghanistan with Doctors Without Borders* (10–12). Illus. 2009, First Second paper $29.95 (978-15964337-5-5). In this graphic-novel presentation, photographer Lefèvre, with artist Guibert, recreates his harrowing journey into Afghanistan in 1986 with the charitable medical organization Médecins sans Frontières and tells the story of his growing awareness of the political forces at play. (Rev: BL 4–5/09*; SLJ 7/09*) [741.5]

9023 Hanson, Jennifer L. *Mongolia* (7–10). Series: Nations in Transition. 2003, Facts on File $40.00 (978-0-8160-5221-9). A thorough review of Mongolia's history, geography, and culture, detailing the difficulties involved in making a transition to democracy. (Rev: SLJ 5/04; VOYA 6/04) [951]

9024 Heidler, Scott. *Women of Courage: Intimate Stories from Afghanistan* (9–12). Photos by Katherine Kiviat. 2007, Gibbs Smith $19.95 (978-1-4236-0253-8). A nurse, a bee keeper, a journalist, a judo champion, and a policewoman — these are only a selection of the 40 women interviewed for this volume of compelling stories of strength and hope in Afghanistan. (Rev: SLJ 1/08) [305.48]

9025 Kamm, Henry. *Dragon Ascending: Vietnam and the Vietnamese* (10–12). 1996, Arcade $24.95 (978-1-55970-306-2). This is a detailed, accurate, personal account of Vietnam, written by a Pulitzer Prize-winning journalist. (Rev: BL 1/1–15/96; SLJ 10/96) [959.7]

9026 Karnow, Stanley. *Vietnam: A History. 2nd rev. and updated ed.* (9–12). 1997, Penguin paper $21.00 (978-0-14-026547-7). Stanley Karnow's insightful history focuses on the Vietnam War and the historical developments that led to the bloody conflict. [959.704]

9027 Kaufman, Murray S. *Reefs and Rain Forests: The Natural Heritage of Malaysian Borneo* (10–12). 2002, Rain Forests $49.95 (978-0-9710655-0-5). The natural beauty of Borneo — home of ancient rain forests and reefs — is captured in this collection of photographs accompanied by informative essays. (Rev: BL 2/1/03) [577.7]

9028 Kizilos, Peter. *Tibet: Disputed Land* (7–10). Series: World in Conflict. 2000, Lerner LB $25.26 (978-0-8225-3563-8). The history of Tibet and its present political divisions are covered in this well-illustrated account. (Rev: BL 10/15/2000; HBG 3/01) [951.1]

9029 Kummer, Patricia K. *North Korea* (7–12). Illus. Series: Enchantment of the World. 2008, Children's Press LB $37.00 (978-0-531-18485-1). Geography, history, economy, religion, sports, and education are all discussed here, along with government oppression, censorship, and the nuclear weapons program; includes numerous maps and photographs. (Rev: BL 8/08) [951.93]

9030 Lankov, Andrei. *North of the DMZ: Essays on Daily Life in North Korea* (9–12). 2007, McFarland paper $39.95 (978-0-7864-2839-7). Articles that appeared in the *Asia Times* and *Korea Times* have been adapted and updated to give a behind-the-scenes view of life in North Korea, with information on schools, families, economics, defectors, and so forth. (Rev: SLJ 8/07) [951.9304]

9031 Mortenson, Greg. *Stones into Schools: Promoting Peace with Books, Not Bombs, in Afghanistan and Pakistan* (10–12). Illus. 2009, Penguin $26.95 (978-067002115-4). Mortenson recounts how the Central Asia Institute braved multiple obstacles to build schools in Afghanistan to promote peace. ⌒ ℮ (Rev: BL 12/1/09) [371.823]

9032 Otfinoski, Steven. *Afghanistan* (7–12). Series: Nations in Transition. 2003, Facts on File $40.00 (978-0-8160-5056-7). A thorough overview of Afghanistan presenting the current political and security problems — including healthcare needs, opium trade, and reliance on foreign funding — as well as material on the country's history, geography, people, culture, and so forth. (Rev: SLJ 4/04; VOYA 6/04) [958.1]

9033 Salter, Christopher. *North Korea* (6–12). 2003, Chelsea LB $30.00 (978-0-7910-7233-2). A thorough and concise overview of North Korea's geography, history, government, politics, economics, language, peoples, and religion, with maps, photographs, and a look at the future. (Rev: BL 9/15/03; HBG 10/03) [951.93]

9034 Sís, Peter. *Tibet: Through the Red Box* (7–12). 1998, Farrar $25.00 (978-0-374-37552-2). Using a journal kept by the author's filmmaker father when he journeyed to Tibet long ago, old tales, and pictures of landscapes and intriguing illustrations inspired by the Tibetan wheel of life, the author writes about the past and present of this land, its culture, and its religion. (Rev: BCCB 12/98; BL 9/15/98; HB 11–12/98; HBG 3/99; SLJ 10/98) [954.96]

9035 Skaine, Rosemarie. *The Women of Afghanistan Under the Taliban* (10–12). 2002, McFarland paper $35.00 (978-0-7864-1090-3). Sociologist Skaine explains in detail how the Taliban's rise to power profoundly altered life for women in Afghanistan. (Rev: BL 3/15/02; VOYA 6/02) [305.4]

9036 Sonneborn, Liz. *The Khmer Rouge* (7–10). Illus. Series: Great Escapes. 2011, Marshall Cavendish LB $34.21 (978-160870474-3). The experiences of journalist Dith Pran introduce this account of the genocide that occurred under the rule of the Khmer Rouge in Cambodia. ℮ (Rev: BLO 3/1/12; LMC 8–9/12) [959.604]

9037 Whitehead, Kim. *Afghanistan* (8–12). Series: The Growth and Influence of Islam in the Nations of Asia and Central Asia. 2005, Mason Crest LB $25.95 (978-1-59084-833-3). A well-illustrated look at Afghanistan and the importance of Islam in the country's history, politics, economy, and foreign relations. (Rev: SLJ 9/05) [958.104]

9038 Zahler, Diane. *Than Shwe's Burma* (9–12). Series: Dictatorships. 2009, Lerner LB $38.60 (978-0-8225-9097-2). With many first-person accounts and quotes from journalists, this riveting, revealing book portrays the devastation, heartbreak, and injustice rampant in Burma under the dictatorship of Than Shwe. (Rev: BL 10/15/09; LMC 11–12/09; SLJ 10/09) [959.105.]

9039 Zwier, Lawrence J. *Sri Lanka: War Torn Island* (8–12). Series: World in Conflict. 1998, Lerner LB $25.26 (978-0-8225-3550-8). The author describes the long political struggle in Sri Lanka. (Rev: BL 4/15/98) [305.8]

Australia and the Pacific Islands

9040 Francia, Luis H. *Eye of the Fish: A Personal Archipelago* (10–12). 2001, Kaya paper $15.95 (978-1-885030-31-3). From his own experiences, background history, and stories collected from others, the author has produced an honest portrait of his country, the Philippines, a nation of more than 7,000 islands. (Rev: BL 3/15/01) [915.9]

9041 Heyerdahl, Thor. *Kon-Tiki: Across the Pacific by Raft* (9–12). Trans. by F. H. Lyon. 1950, Rand McNally paper $5.99 (978-0-671-72652-2). The landmark adventure story about crossing the Pacific in a primitive raft such as the Peruvian natives of the fifth century used. [910.4]

9042 Jones, Phillip. *Boomerang* (10–12). 1997, Ten Speed paper $14.95 (978-0-89815-943-1). A history of the development and use of the boomerang, which has been part of many cultures for more than 10,000 years, focusing on the aboriginal culture of Australia. (Rev: SLJ 6/98) [994]

9043 Morris, Rod, and Alison Ballance. *South Sea Islands: A Natural History* (10–12). 2003, Firefly $35.00 (978-1-55297-609-8). This lushly illustrated book explores the unique natural environments of 14 South Sea islands, including Fiji, Madagascar, Sulawesi, and Hawaii. (Rev: BL 12/1/03) [508.95]

9044 Vail, Martha, and John S. Bowman, eds. *Exploring the Pacific* (6–12). Series: Discovery and Exploration. 2005, Facts on File $40.00 (978-0-8160-5258-5). Exploration in the Pacific, from early Polynesians onward and including such figures as Magellan and Cook, is the focus of this volume that contains clear, informative text plus maps, illustrations, and excerpts from primary sources. (Rev: SLJ 8/05) [973]

Europe

General and Miscellaneous

9045 Blanning, T. C. W. *The Oxford Illustrated History of Modern Europe* (10–12). 1996, Oxford paper $27.99 (978-0-19-285426-1). Eleven chronologically arranged essays examine European culture, economics, industrialization, and politics from the mid-18th century to the closing years of the 20th century. (Rev: BL 4/1/96; SLJ 8/96) [940.2]

9046 Dornberg, John. *Western Europe* (9–12). Series: International Government and Politics. 1996, Oryx paper $49.95 (978-0-89774-943-5). After a general introduction of Western Europe and the formation of the European Union, the author discusses controversial issues such as nationalism, the economy, crime, pollution, and immigration, followed by profiles of the individual countries involved. (Rev: SLJ 9/96) [940]

9047 Stafford, James. *The European Union: Facts and Figures* (8–11). Series: European Union. 2006, Mason Crest LB $21.95 (978-1-4222-0045-2). A useful, information-packed guide to the European Union and its origins and goals. (Rev: BL 4/1/06) [641.242]

Eastern Europe and the Balkans

9048 Black, Eric. *Bosnia: Fractured Region* (9–12). Series: World in Conflict. 1999, Lerner LB $25.26 (978-0-8225-3553-9). In this book about the war in Bosnia, the author presents a clear, detailed, history of Yugoslavia and its neighbors; a careful account of the armed conflicts among Serbs, Croats, and Muslims; and a measured assessment of the future of the region. (Rev: BL 8/99*; SLJ 5/99) [949.6]

9049 Fleming, Thomas. *Montenegro: The Divided Land* (10–12). 2002, Chronicle paper $16.95 (978-0-9619364-9-5). An introduction to the little-known but eventful history of tiny Montenegro. (Rev: BL 7/02) [949.745]

9050 King, David C. *Bosnia and Herzegovina* (7–10). Series: Cultures of the World. 2005, Benchmark LB $37.07 (978-0-7614-1853-5). Explores the geography, history, people, culture, and lifestyles of Bosnia and Herzegovina. (Rev: SLJ 7/05) [949.7]

9051 Nichols, Jeremy, and Emilia Trembicka-Nichols. *Poland* (7–10). Series: Countries of the World. 2005, Facts on File LB $30.00 (978-0-8160-6005-4). History, geography, culture, government, and economy are all covered in this attractive overview of Poland. (Rev: SLJ 1/06) [9.4.3]

9052 Otfinoski, Steven. *The Czech Republic* (7–12). Series: Nations in Transition. 2004, Facts on File $40.00 (978-0-8160-5083-3). An updated edition that adds more recent events to the 1997 text about the history, people, culture, and government of the Czech Republic. (Rev: BL 12/1/04) [943.7105]

9053 Rollyson, Carl S. *Teenage Refugees from Eastern Europe Speak Out* (7–12). Series: Teenage Refugees Speak Out. 1997, Rosen LB $27.95 (978-0-8239-2437-0). Young refugees from Slovakia, Bulgaria, Hungary, Romania, Poland, Yugoslavia, and the former East Germany tell about conditions in their homelands and their receptions in the United States. (Rev: BL 12/15/97) [947]

9054 Sanborne, Mark. *Romania* (9–12). 1996, Facts on File $25.00 (978-0-8160-3089-7). The first half of this book describes the history of Romania, and the second deals with current political and economic conditions and problems. (Rev: VOYA 10/96) [949.8]

9055 Schuman, Michael A. *Bosnia and Herzegovina* (9–12). Series: Nations in Transition. 2003, Facts on File $40.00 (978-0-8160-5052-9). After a section on the area's history through the recent civil war, Schuman looks at the contemporary situation, exploring the economy, culture, education, and way of life in Bosnia and Herzegovina. (Rev: SLJ 5/04) [949.7]

France

9056 Egendorf, Laura K., ed. *The French Revolution* (7–12). Series: Opposing Viewpoints: World History. 2004, Gale LB $37.45 (978-0-7377-1815-7). Questions about the French Revolution, such as the justification for the many executions, are explored in this collection of different points of view about this turning point in French history. (Rev: BL 2/15/04; SLJ 5/04) [944]

9057 Kranz, Nickie. *Teens in France* (7–12). Series: Global Connections. 2006, Compass Point LB $31.93 (978-0-7565-2062-5). Introduces French teens and their schools, family life, hobbies, sports, and so forth, covering both traditional aspects and those that have ar-

rived with new technology and new immigration. (Rev: SLJ 5/07) [305.235]

9058 Powers, Alice Leccese, ed. *France in Mind* (10–12). 2003, Vintage paper $14.00 (978-0-375-71425-2). Both francophiles and literati will delight in this anthology of fiction and nonfiction by English-language writers who spent time in France, among them Charles Dickens, Ernest Hemingway, and Mary McCarthy. (Rev: BL 1/1–15/03) [820.8]

9059 Prosser, Robert. *France* (6–10). Series: Countries of the World. 2003, Facts on File $30.00 (978-0-8160-5380-3). This basic introduction to the land and people of France includes material on economy, culture, and present-day problems. (Rev: BL 1/1–15/04) [944]

9060 Schama, Simon. *Citizens: A Chronicle of the French Revolution* (9–12). 1989, Knopf paper $28.00 (978-0-679-72601-2). A popular, intelligent look at the French Revolution and the key people involved. [944.04]

Germany, Austria, and Switzerland

9061 Bartoletti, Susan Campbell. *Hitler Youth: Growing Up in Hitler's Shadow* (7–10). 2005, Scholastic $19.95 (978-0-439-35379-3). This chilling look at the Hitler Youth movement, which at its peak boasted a membership of roughly 3.5 million boys and girls, includes excerpts from diaries, letters, oral histories, and the author's interviews with former members and resisters. Newbery Honor Book, 2006. (Rev: BL 4/15/05*; SLJ 6/05; VOYA 8/05) [943.086]

9062 Halleck, Elaine, ed. *Living in Nazi Germany* (8–12). Series: Exploring Cultural History. 2004, Gale LB $24.95 (978-0-7377-1732-7). First-person accounts excerpted from other works offer insight into life in Germany under the Nazis, from the point of view of those brutalized and of those who took part in the regime. (Rev: BL 8/04) [943.086]

9063 Larson, Erik. *In the Garden of Beasts: Love, Terror, and an American Family in Hitler's Berlin* (10–12). 2011, Crown $26 (978-030740884-6). The fascinating story of the U.S. ambassador to Berlin in the early 1930s and his and his family's reactions to the activities of the Third Reich. ∩ ℮ (Rev: SLJ 7/11) [921]

Great Britain and Ireland

9064 Bowden, Rob. *United Kingdom* (6–10). Series: Countries of the World. 2003, Facts on File $30.00 (978-0-8160-5383-4). An attractive volume that presents basic material about Great Britain including history, geography, and present social conditions. (Rev: BL 1/1–15/04) [941]

9065 Castor, Helen. *Blood and Roses: One Family's Struggle and Triumph during England's Tumultuous*

Wars of the Roses (9–12). 2006, HarperCollins $25.95 (978-0-00-714808-0). An English family's experiences during the 15th-century Wars of the Roses are revealed through a collection of letters; color photographs and illustrations add to this compelling account. (Rev: SLJ 7/06) [942.04092]

9066 Childress, Diana. *Chaucer's England* (7–12). 2000, Linnet LB $25.00 (978-0-208-02489-3). A fascinating glimpse into the social life, community structure, landscape, and economy of 14th-century England. (Rev: BL 9/15/00; HBG 10/01; SLJ 10/00; VOYA 4/01) [942.03]

9067 Evans, Robert C. *Culture and Society in Shakespeare's Day* (9–12). Illus. Series: Backgrounds to Shakespeare. 2012, Chelsea House LB $40 (978-160413523-7). Attractive and informative, this part of the three-volume series covers daily life in various settings; the religion, education, crime, and medicine of the time; and important historical events. (Rev: BL 10/1/12; SLJ 10/12) [942.05]

9068 Howarth, David Armine. *1066: The Year of the Conquest* (10–12). 1978, Viking paper $14.00 (978-0-14-005850-5). This readable history re-creates the Norman invasion of England in 1066 and the victory of William the Conqueror at the Battle of Hastings. [942.02]

9069 James, Lawrence. *The Rise and Fall of the British Empire* (10–12). 1995, St. Martin's paper $19.95 (978-0-312-16985-5). This is an excellent overview of Britain's rise and decline as a colonial power with particularly good biographical material on key personalities. [909]

9070 Jocelyn, Marthe. *A Home for Foundlings* (7–10). Series: Lord Museum. 2005, Tundra paper $15.95 (978-0-88776-709-8). A fascinating history of London's Foundling Hospital, which was opened in the 18th century to provide a home for babies whose mothers were unable to care for them and did not close until 1953. (Rev: BL 3/1/05; SLJ 6/05) [362.7]

9071 Jones, Becky, and Clare Lewis. *The Bumper Book of London: Fun Facts for All the Family* (5–12). Series: Adventure Walks. 2012, Frances Lincoln paper $19.95 (978-0-7112-3145-0). This attractive volume provides facts and trivia about London's development since Roman times, highlighting notable sites and interesting details about everyday life throughout the ages. (Rev: SLJ 5/1/12) [942.1]

9072 McCourt, Frank. *Angela's Ashes* (10–12). 1996, Scribner $23.00 (978-0-684-87435-7). The harrowing, true story of growing up in extreme poverty in Limerick, Ireland, by a writer whose humor and humanity outshine the terrible conditions he describes. (Rev: SLJ 6/97) [941.5]

9073 McMurtry, Jo. *Understanding Shakespeare's England: A Companion for the American Reader* (9–12).

1989, Archon LB $37.50 (978-0-208-02248-6). This account covers all aspects of Elizabethan life including such topics as marriage customs, women's roles, city and country life, and witches and criminals. [942.05]

9074 Rex, Richard. *The Tudors* (10–12). 2004, Tempus $35.00 (978-0-7524-2588-7). An engaging history of the Tudors and their claim to the British throne. (Rev: BL 8/04) [942.05]

9075 Rosie, George. *Curious Scotland: Tales from a Hidden History* (10–12). 2006, Thomas Dunne $23.95 (978-0-312-35416-9). For trivia buffs and those interested in Scottish history, this is a wide-ranging exploration of all things Scots. (Rev: SLJ 12/06)

9076 Swisher, Clarice. *Victorian England* (7–10). Series: World History. 2000, Lucent LB $32.45 (978-1-56006-323-0). Quotations and period reproductions enhance this interesting survey of the long and eventful reign of Queen Victoria, a time of technological and social innovation and of growing power for Great Britain. (Rev: BL 12/15/00; SLJ 3/01) [942]

9077 Viney, Michael. *Ireland* (10–12). Series: Smithsonian Natural History. 2003, Smithsonian $34.95 (978-1-58834-057-3). This beautifully written volume explores the largely neglected natural history of Ireland. (Rev: BL 3/15/03) [508.415]

9078 Weir, Alison. *The Wars of the Roses* (10–12). 1995, Ballantine paper $14.95 (978-0-345-40433-6). This book covers the civil wars fought in England, mainly between the houses of Lancaster and York, from 1399 through 1471. (Rev: BL 8/95; SLJ 5/96) [942.04]

Italy

9079 Grodin, Elissa D., and Mario M. Cuomo. *C Is for Ciao: An Italy Alphabet* (7–10). Illus. by Marco Ventura. 2009, Sleeping Bear $17.95 (978-158536361-2). Many areas of Italy's culture, history, and language are explored in this alphabet book for older readers. (Rev: BLO 2/9/09) [945]

Russia and Other Former Soviet Republics

9080 Batalden, Stephen K., and Sandra L. Batalden. *The Newly Independent States of Eurasia: Handbook of Former Soviet Republics. 2nd ed.* (7–12). 1997, Oryx paper $59.95 (978-0-89774-940-4). Arranged by geographical region, this volume examines each of the newly formed republics created from the former USSR, with details on their past, their culture, and key problems facing each today. (Rev: SLJ 11/97) [947]

9081 Cartlidge, Cherese. *The Central Asian States* (6–12). Series: Modern Nations of the World: Former Soviet Republics. 2001, Lucent LB $29.95 (978-1-56006-735-1). This well-illustrated introduction to the former Soviet republics of Kazakhstan, Turkmenistan, Uzbekistan, Kyrgyzstan, and Tajikistan presents material on physical features, people, culture, economy, history, and efforts to enter the global market. (Rev: BL 8/01; SLJ 9/01) [958]

9082 Corrigan, Jim. *Kazakhstan* (8–12). Series: The Growth and Influence of Islam in the Nations of Asia and Central Asia. 2005, Mason Crest LB $25.95 (978-1-59084-882-1). A well-illustrated look at Kazakhstan and the importance of Islam in the country's history, politics, economy, and foreign relations. (Rev: SLJ 9/05) [958]

9083 Davenport, John C. *The Bolshevik Revolution* (10–12). Series: Milestones in Modern World History. 2010, Chelsea House $35 (978-1-60413-279-3). Davenport describes the key events and characters of the 1917 revolution and explains its importance for the remainder of the 20th century. (Rev: LMC 8–9/10; SLJ 6/10) [947.084]

9084 Eaton, Katherine B. *Daily Life in the Soviet Union* (11–12). Series: Daily Life Through History. 2004, Greenwood $55.00 (978-0-313-31628-9). Explores what life was like in the Soviet Union, examining such topics as health care, education, economic system, class structure, and the arts. (Rev: SLJ 4/05) [947]

9085 Gay, Kathlyn. *The Aftermath of the Russian Revolution* (8–12). Series: Aftermath of History. 2009, Lerner LB $38.60 (978-0-8225-9092-7). Gay outlines how the Bolshevik revolution and the establishment of communism in Russia would shape the future not only of that country's people, but of world politics as well. (Rev: SLJ 4/1/09)

9086 Gottfried, Ted. *The Road to Communism* (8–12). Illus. by Melanie Reim. 2002, Millbrook LB $28.90 (978-0-7613-2557-4). This first volume on the rise and fall of the Soviet Union traces in depth the developments that led to the establishment of a communist state. The second volume is titled *Stalinist Empire*. (Rev: BL 10/15/02; HBG 3/03; SLJ 11/02) [957]

9087 Harmon, Daniel E. *Kyrgyzstan* (8–12). Series: The Growth and Influence of Islam in the Nations of Asia and Central Asia. 2005, Mason Crest LB $25.95 (978-1-59084-883-8). A well-illustrated look at Kyrgyzstan and the importance of Islam in the country's history, politics, economy, and foreign relations. (Rev: SLJ 9/05)

9088 Lugovskaya, Nina. *I Want to Live: The Diary of a Young Girl in Stalin's Russia* (8–11). Trans. by Andrew Bromfeld. 2007, Houghton Mifflin $17.00 (978-0-618-60575-0). This diary of a teenage girl living in a Soviet gulag is remarkable for its passages (in bold type) that were censored by police who seized it, and also for the fact that its author survived. (Rev: BL 4/15/07; SLJ 8/07) [946.0842]

9089 McCray, Thomas. *Russia and the Former Soviet Republics* (7–10). 2006, Chelsea House LB $30.00 (978-0-7910-8144-0). Examines many aspects of Russia including its geography, economy, history, politics, people, and culture with additional information on some of the surrounding countries that also belonged to the former Soviet Union. (Rev: BL 9/1/06; SLJ 9/06) [947]

9090 Massie, Robert K. *The Romanovs: The Final Chapter* (9–12). 1995, Random House paper $14.95 (978-0-345-40640-8). This book covers the last days of the Romanov family with material on how their remains were identified and on how some relatives survived. [947.08]

9091 Otfinoski, Steven. *The Baltic Republics* (7–10). Series: Nations in Transition. 2004, Facts on File LB $40.00 (978-0-8160-5117-5). Introduces the Baltic republics of Estonia, Latvia, and Lithuania, and the geography, history, people, culture, religious beliefs, and economy of each. (Rev: SLJ 1/05) [947]

9092 Pavlenkov, Victor, and Peter Pappas, eds. *Russia: Yesterday, Today, Tomorrow: Voice of the Young Generation* (8–12). 1997, FC-Izdat paper $12.95 (978-0-9637035-5-2). This is a collection of essays written by Russian high school students who reflect on the past, present, and future of their country. (Rev: BL 2/15/97) [947.08]

9093 Robbins, Gerald. *Azerbaijan* (8–12). Series: The Growth and Influence of Islam in the Nations of Asia and Central Asia. 2005, Mason Crest LB $25.95 (978-1-59084-878-4). A well-illustrated look at Azerbaijan and the importance of Islam in the country's history, politics, economy, and foreign relations. (Rev: SLJ 9/05) [947]

9094 Seierstad, Asne. *The Angel of Grozny: Orphans of a Forgotten War* (11–12). Trans. by Nadia Christensen. 2008, Basic $25.95 (978-0-465-01122-3). Freelance journalist Seierstad provides a gritty, unflinching look at the realities of life in Chechnya and profiles a woman named Hadijat who has provided services for many of the suffering children; for mature readers. (Rev: BL 6/1–15/08) [947.5]

9095 Spilling, Michael. *Estonia* (7–10). Series: Cultures of the World. 1999, Marshall Cavendish LB $37.07 (978-0-7614-0951-9). An overview of this Baltic land that covers basic information and contemporary life and culture. (Rev: HBG 9/99; SLJ 7/99) [947]

9096 Streissguth, Thomas. *Life in Communist Russia* (6–10). Series: The Way People Live. 2001, Lucent LB $29.95 (978-1-56006-378-0). From the 1917 revolution through the collapse of the regime in the 1980s, the history of Communist Russia is told with emphasis on social and economic conditions and everyday life. (Rev: BL 6/1–15/01; SLJ 7/01) [947]

9097 Streissguth, Thomas, ed. *The Rise of the Soviet Union* (7–12). Series: Turning Points in World History.

2002, Gale LB $24.95 (978-0-7377-0928-5). Following an overview of Russian and Soviet history, each of the essays in this anthology explores a different aspect of the rise of Communism and the creation of the Soviet Union. (Rev: BL 6/1–15/02; SLJ 6/02) [947]

9098 Taylor, Peter Lane, and Christos Nicola. *The Secret of Priest's Grotto* (7–10). 2007, Kar-Ben $18.95 (978-1-58013-260-2); paper $8.95 (978-1-58013-261-9). The true story of how 38 members of three Ukrainian Jewish families survived nearly a year hiding from the Nazis in a cave; photographs add impact. Sidney Taylor Book Honor 2008. (Rev: BL 3/1/07; HB 7–8/07; LMC 10/07; SLJ 4/07) [940.53]

9099 Warnes, David. *Chronicle of the Russian Tsars: The Reign by Reign Record of the Rulers of Imperial Russia* (9–12). Series: Chronicle. 1999, Thames & Hudson $29.95 (978-0-500-05093-4). An in-depth look at the czars of Russia and the times in which they ruled, with excerpts from primary sources, extensive maps, and other aids. (Rev: BL 8/99; SLJ 2/00) [947.0099]

9100 Weinberg, Robert, and Laurie Bernstein. *Revolutionary Russia: A History in Documents* (9–12). Illus. Series: Pages from History. 2010, Oxford LB $39.95 (978-019512225-1). This volume provides a generous mix of primary sources — letters, speeches, posters, maps, songs, and so forth. (Rev: BL 9/15/10) [947.084]

Scandinavia, Iceland, and Greenland

9101 Schaffer, David. *Viking Conquests* (7–10). Series: World History. 2002, Gale LB $32.45 (978-1-56006-322-3). Though the Vikings were known mainly for their raids and pillaging, this account also gives details of their lasting contributions to the world. (Rev: BL 8/02) [948]

Spain and Portugal

9102 Skog, Jason. *Teens in Spain* (7–12). Series: Global Connections. 2006, Compass Point LB $31.93 (978-0-7565-2446-3). Introduces Spanish teens and their schools, family life, hobbies, sports, and so forth, covering both traditional aspects and those that have arrived with new technology and new immigration. (Rev: SLJ 5/07) [305.235]

Middle East

General and Miscellaneous

9103 Cohen, Jared. *Children of Jihad: A Young American's Travels among the Youth of the Middle East* (9–12). 2007, Gotham $26.00 (978-1-59240-324-0). Cohen describes his travels through Iran, Lebanon, Syria, and Iraq in 2004 and 2005 and what he learned about the people of the region and their attitudes toward Americans. (Rev: BL 10/1/07) [915.604]

9104 Davenport, John C., ed. *Democracy in the Middle East* (10–12). Series: The World in Focus. 2007, Chelsea House LB $35.00 (978-0-7910-9194-4). For advanced students, this is a useful exploration of the possibility of democracy reigning in the Middle East and the forces that make this unlikely, with discussion of religion and extremism. (Rev: SLJ 1/08)

9105 Einfeld, Jann, ed. *Can Democracy Succeed in the Middle East?* (6–12). Series: At Issue. 2006, Gale LB $28.70 (978-0-7377-3393-8). The title question and many others (can democracy be imposed?) are addressed in this collection of 12 essays. (Rev: SLJ 3/07)

9106 Halliday, Fred. *100 Myths About the Middle East* (9–12). 2005, Univ. of California paper $13.95 (978-0-520-24721-5). Debunks widely held misconceptions about the Middle East and its people. (Rev: BL 8/05) [956.04]

9107 January, Brendan. *The Arab Conquests of the Middle East* (8–11). Series: Pivotal Moments in History. 2009, Lerner LB $38.60 (978-0-8225-8744-6). This volume traces the history of the Arab conquest of the Middle East and parts of Europe, and how the new religion of Islam impacted society in the region. (Rev: SLJ 4/1/09) [956.013]

9108 Worth, Richard. *The Arab-Israeli Conflict* (7–12). Series: Open for Debate. 2006, Benchmark LB $27.95 (978-0-7614-2295-2). Worth gives a balanced overview of this long-running conflict, with historical information, accounts of the key areas of dispute, and explanations of each side's beliefs and goals. (Rev: SLJ 2/07)

Israel and Palestine

9109 Aronson, Marc. *Unsettled: The Problem of Loving Israel* (9–12). 2008, Simon & Schuster $18.99 (978-141691261-3). Anonson blends personal anecdotes and history in this challenging yet engaging and thought-provoking examination of Israel's status and the conflict with Palestine. (Rev: BL 11/15/08; HB 1–2/09; LMC 5–6/09; SLJ 12/08; VOYA 12/08) [956]

9110 Chacham, Remit. *Breaking Ranks: Refusing to Serve in the West Bank and Gaza Strip* (10–12). 2003, Other $25.00 (978-1-59051-043-8). The fascinating story of 52 Israeli army reservists who refused to serve in the occupied Palestinian territories of Gaza and the West Bank and encouraged others to join their action. (Rev: BL 5/15/03) [355.2]

9111 Corrie, Rachel. *Let Me Stand Alone: The Journals of Rachel Corrie* (9–12). 2008, Norton $23.95 (978-0-393-06571-8). The drawings and writings of 23-year-old Rachel Corrie who died standing in front of a bulldozer during a non-violent protest against the Israeli

Army's destruction of Palestinian houses. (Rev: BL 3/1/08) [956.9405]

9112 Greenfeld, Howard. *A Promise Fulfilled: Theodor Herzl, Chaim Weizmann, David Ben-Gurion, and the Creation of the State of Israel* (7–10). 2005, Greenwillow LB $19.89 (978-0-06-051505-8). This story of the creation of the state of Israel focuses on the contributions of three remarkable and very different men. (Rev: BL 4/15/05; SLJ 7/05) [320.54]

9113 Immell, Myra, ed. *The Creation of the State of Israel* (10–12). Series: Perspectives on Modern World History. 2010, Gale/Greenhaven $38.50 (978-0-7377-4556-6). Offering a variety of enlightening perspectives on the state of Israel today, this collection includes many thought-provoking narratives, excerpts, and essays. (Rev: SLJ 3/10)

9114 Katz, Samuel M. *Jerusalem or Death: Palestinian Terrorism* (7–12). Series: Terrorist Dossiers. 2003, Lerner LB $26.60 (978-0-8225-4033-5). This book focuses on the terrorist groups that have been active in Israel and the West Bank. (Rev: BL 3/15/04; HBG 4/04; SLJ 3/04; VOYA 4/04) [956.9]

9115 Marshood, Nabil. *Palestinian Teenage Refugees and Immigrants Speak Out* (7–12). Series: Teenage Refugees Speak Out. 1997, Rosen LB $27.95 (978-0-8239-2442-4). The exodus of Palestinians, many to the United States, and their reasons for leaving their homes are shown through the stories of several teenage immigrants. (Rev: BL 12/15/97) [956.04]

9116 Nusseibeh, Sari. *What Is a Palestinian State Worth?* (11–12). 2011, Harvard $19.95 (978-067404873-7). The president of al-Quds University in Jerusalem examines the relationship between Israel and Palestine, arguing that there can be no two-state solution; for mature readers. (Rev: BL 1/1–15/11) [956.940]

9117 Reich, Bernard. *A Brief History of Israel* (9–12). Series: Brief History. 2004, Facts on File $45.00 (978-0-8160-5118-2); paper $19.95 (978-0-8160-5793-1). Despite its title, this survey of Israeli history is sweeping in character, tracing the country's roots back to biblical times and forward to today's security problems. (Rev: BL 12/1/04) [956.940]

9118 Sacco, Joe. *Footnotes in Gaza* (10–12). Illus. 2010, Henry Holt $29.95 (978-080507347-8). Using vividly imagined graphic novel illustrations, Sacco tells the story of two mass killings that took place in 1950s Gaza and documents the hardships of life in the Gaza Strip. (Rev: BLO 1/1–15/10) [956.04]

9119 Shehadeh, Raja. *Palestinian Walks: Notes on a Vanishing Landscape* (10–12). 2008, Scribner paper $15.00 (978-1-4165-6966-4). This Palestinian lawyer and human-rights advocate discusses how the landscape of his childhood has been irrevocably changed by the disputes between Israel and Palestine. (Rev: BL 4/1/08) [958.95]

9120 Shehadeh, Raja. *When the Birds Stopped Singing: Life in Ramallah Under Siege* (10–12). 2003, Steerforth paper $12.95 (978-1-58642-069-7). The plight of the Palestinians in the West Bank is clearly illustrated in this account covering the events of a single month in Ramallah. (Rev: BL 9/1/03) [956.9405]

9121 Slavicek, Louise Chipley. *The Establishment of the State of Israel* (8–12). Illus. 2011, Chelsea House LB $35 (978-160413917-4). With photographs, timelines, and maps, this volume explains why and how the state of Israel was established. **e** (Rev: BL 2/15/12) [956.74]

9122 Tolan, Sandy. *The Lemon Tree: An Arab, a Jew, and the Heart of the Middle East* (11–12). 2006, Bloomsbury $24.95 (978-1-58234-343-3). The story of a stone house in Ramla, now part of Israel but once owned by Arabs, serves as an illustration of the ongoing Israeli-Palestinian conflict; for mature readers. (Rev: BL 4/1/06) [956.9]

Other Middle East Countries

9123 Asayesh, Gelareh. *Saffron Sky: A Life Between Iran and America* (10–12). 1999, Beacon paper $15.00 (978-0-8070-7211-0). Iran's recent history is covered in this personal account about the author's many trips to and from Iran as a child and young woman. (Rev: BL 10/1/99) [955]

9124 Bodnarchuk, Kari. *Kurdistan: Region Under Siege* (7–10). Series: World in Conflict. 2000, Lerner LB $25.26 (978-0-8225-3556-0). This work gives an unbiased historical picture of this mountainous region of the Middle East and tells of the frequent upheavals that mark its past and present. (Rev: BL 6/1–15/00; HBG 3/01; SLJ 12/00) [955]

9125 Bogdanos, Matthew, and William Patrick. *Thieves of Baghdad: One Marine's Passion for Ancient Civilizations and the Journey to Recover the World's Greatest Stolen Treasures* (9–12). 2005, Bloomsbury $25.95 (978-1-58234-645-8). A riveting, behind-the-scenes look at the U.S. military investigation into the looting of Iraq's national museum in Baghdad following the U.S. invasion. (Rev: BL 11/15/05; SLJ 3/06) [956.704]

9126 Broberg, Catherine. *Saudi Arabia in Pictures* (6–10). Series: Visual Geography. 2002, Lerner LB $27.93 (978-0-8225-1958-4). Full-color photographs complement information on the country's geography, history, government, economy, people, and culture. (Rev: BL 10/15/02; HBG 3/03) [953.8]

9127 Clark, Charles. *Iran* (7–12). Series: Nations in Transition. 2002, Gale LB $32.45 (978-0-7377-1096-0). Iran's internal political upheavals and difficult relationship with the rest of the world are the focus of this thorough and concise volume that includes biographical and cultural features. (Rev: SLJ 1/03) [955]

9128 Egendorf, Laura K., ed. *Iran* (9–12). Series: Opposing Viewpoints. 2006, Gale LB $34.95 (978-0-7377-3417-1). Human rights, women's rights, global security, and nuclear weapons are only a few of the subjects discussed in pro-and-con pairs of essays in this valuable volume. (Rev: SLJ 3/07) [955.05]

9129 Fassihi, Farnaz. *Waiting for an Ordinary Day: The Unraveling of Life in Iraq* (10–12). 2008, PublicAffairs $26.00 (978-158648475-0). Journalist Fassihi interviews a cross-section of middle-class Iraqis for a balanced and honest report about the impact of the war on the Iraqi people. e (Rev: BL 9/1/08) [956.7]

9130 Hiro, Dilip. *The Longest War: The Iran-Iraq Military Conflict* (9–12). 1991, Routledge paper $20.99 (978-0-415-90407-0). A detailed account of the 1980-1988 war between Iran and Iraq. (Rev: BL 2/1/91) [955.05]

9131 Isiorho, Solomon A. *Kuwait* (7–12). Series: Modern World Nations. 2002, Chelsea LB $30.00 (978-0-7910-6781-9). An overview of the history, geography, people, politics, and religion of Kuwait, with discussion of the importance of Islam. Also use *Bahrain* (2002). (Rev: SLJ 2/03) [953.67]

9132 January, Brendan. *The Iranian Revolution* (9–12). 2008, Lerner LB $38.60 (978-0-8225-7521-4). A useful introduction to the causes and effects of the uprising in 1979, this will be helpful to students of contemporary Iran. (Rev: BL 4/15/08; SLJ 5/08) [955.05]

9133 Klaus, Ian. *Elvis Is Titanic* (9–12). 2007, Knopf $24.00 (978-0-307-26456-5). After the first election in Iraq after the U.S. occupation, 26-year-old Rhodes scholar Klaus, inspired by the spirit of volunteerism after 9/11, traveled to Kurdistan to teach American history and English at Salahaddin University in Arbil, where he found a mix of students curious but still suspicious about Americans and their culture that they've learned about only through the media. (Rev: BL 8/07) [370.956]

9134 Levy, Janey. *Iran and the Shia* (8–12). Series: Understanding Iran. 2010, Rosen LB $30.60 (978-1-4358-5282-2). Levy discusses the history of the Shia community in Iran and its current importance in the political and daily life of the nation. (Rev: LMC 1–2/10; SLJ 12/09) [955.05]

9135 Mackey, Sandra. *A Mirror of the Arab World: Lebanon in Conflict* (9–12). 2008, Norton $25.95 (978-0-393-06218-2). Mackey believes that an understanding of the situation in Lebanon is key to understanding the issues facing the region as a whole, and here puts Lebanon under a microscope. (Rev: BL 3/1/08) [956.9204]

9136 Mackintosh-Smith, Tim. *Yemen: Travels in Dictionary Land* (10–12). 2000, Overlook $35.00 (978-1-58567-001-7). This adult account is a fascinating introduction to the history and geography of Yemen by

a renowned traveler and observer. (Rev: BL 1/1–15/00) [915.330453]

9137 Marcovitz, Hal. *Jordan* (7–12). Series: Creation of the Modern Middle East. 2002, Chelsea LB $35.00 (978-0-7910-6507-5). This volume on the history of Jordan, its importance in the Middle East, and its relations with the United States will be useful for report writers. Also use *Syria, Oman,* and *The Kurds* (all 2002). (Rev: LMC 4–5/03; SLJ 2/03) [956.9504]

9138 Maslin, Jamie. *Iranian Rappers and Persian Porn: A Hitchhiker's Adventures in the New Iran* (11–12). Illus. 2009, Skyhorse $24.95 (978-160239791-0). Against his friends' advice, Maslin takes a solo trip into Iran and is surprised by the warm welcome and willingness of the people to share their country and their political opinions with him; for mature readers. (Rev: BL 9/15/09) [955.06]

9139 Miller, Debra A. *Iraq* (6–12). Series: The World's Hot Spots. 2004, Gale LB $31.20 (978-0-7377-1813-3); paper $23.70 (978-0-7377-1814-0). Reprinted essays, speeches, and news articles provide a fascinating overview of Iraq's history and the factors that precipitated the American-led invasion in 2003. (Rev: BL 6/1–15/04; SLJ 8/04) [956.704]

9140 Riverbend. *Baghdad Burning II: More Girl Blog from Iraq* (8–12). 2006, Feminist paper $14.95 (978-1-55861-529-8). This second volume of compiled blogs describes the continuing shortages of water, power, and food; religious and political violence at the hands of Iraqi security forces; repression; and the general chaos that has reigned during the U.S. occupation. (Rev: BL 11/1/06) [956.7044]

9141 Riverbend. *Baghdad Burning: Girl Blog from Iraq* (8–12). 2005, Feminist paper $14.95 (978-1-55861-489-5). A young Iraqi blogger paints a grim picture of life in her country after the 2003 invasion of U.S. and allied forces. (Rev: BL 4/1/05) [956.7]

9142 Schaffer, David, ed. *Iraq* (10–12). Series: The History of Nations. 2003, Gale LB $36.20 (978-0-7377-1660-3). For students researching the history of Mesopotamia and the region that is now Iraq, this collection of scholarly essays and excerpts will be useful. (Rev: SLJ 2/04) [956.7]

9143 Sheehan, Sean. *Lebanon* (5–10). Series: Cultures of the World. 1996, Marshall Cavendish LB $37.07 (978-0-7614-0283-1). A lively, well-written introduction to this war-ravaged country with details on history, economy, culture, religion and foods, including a recipe for a typical dish. (Rev: SLJ 6/97) [569.2]

9144 Sinkler, Adrian. *Iraq* (9–12). Series: Nations in Transition. 2006, Gale LB $32.45 (978-0-7377-3085-2). Covers Iraq's history from 1932 through early 2005. (Rev: SLJ 2/06) [956.7]

9145 South, Coleman. *Jordan* (5–10). Series: Cultures of the World. 1996, Marshall Cavendish LB $37.07

574

(978-0-7614-0287-9). Everyday life in Jordan is the focus of this book that also covers history, religion, culture, geography, festivals, and foods; a single recipe is included. (Rev: SLJ 6/97) [569.5]

9146 Spencer, William. *Iraq: Old Land, New Nation in Conflict* (7–12). 2000, Twenty-First Century LB $23.90 (978-0-7613-1356-4). This account traces the history of Iraq from its Mesopotamian origins to Saddam Hussein's rule prior to the American invasion. (Rev: BL 11/15/00; HBG 3/01; SLJ 12/00) [956.7]

9147 Stewart, Rory. *The Prince of the Marshes: And Other Occupational Hazards of a Year in Iraq* (10–12). 2006, Harcourt $25 (978-0-15-101235-0). Farsi-speaking British diplomat Rory Stewart tells the story of the year he was appointed deputy governor of two provinces in the remote marsh regions of southern Iraq, a time of frustrations but also of building strong relationships within the local Arab society. (Rev: BL 7/06; SLJ 8/06)

North and South America (excluding the United States)

General and Miscellaneous

9148 Haas, Robert B. *Through the Eyes of the Condor: An Aerial Vision of Latin America* (8–12). 2007, National Geographic $50.00 (978-1-4262-0132-5). Haas's camera takes a bird's-eye view of Central and South America, showing the diversity of the landscape in vast panoramas. (Rev: BL 9/15/07) [779.36098]

9149 Long, Cathryn J. *Ancient America* (7–10). Series: World History. 2002, Gale LB $32.45 (978-1-56006-889-1). The story of the hunter-gatherers, agriculturalists, and city dwellers of North and South America from the arrival of the first humans in America to Columbus. (Rev: BL 8/02) [970]

9150 Mann, Charles C. *1491: New Revelations of the Americas Before Columbus* (10–12). 2005, Knopf $30.00 (978-1-4000-4006-3). This eye-opening look at America before the arrival of Europeans finds a world far different from the one depicted in most history books. (Rev: BL 8/05) [970.01]

9151 Morgan, Ted. *Wilderness at Dawn: The Settling of the North American Continent* (9–12). 1993, Simon & Schuster paper $20.00 (978-0-671-88237-2). A historical overview of migration to North America that spans more than 15,000 years — from the arrival of the first human settlers who crossed the Bering landbridge to 18th-century arrivals. [970]

9152 Murphy, Jim. *Gone a-Whaling: The Lure of the Sea and the Hunt for the Great Whale* (7–12). 1998, Clarion $18.00 (978-0-395-69847-1). Diary entries are used to describe American whale hunting and life aboard whaling vessels from the 19th century to the present. (Rev:

BCCB 4/98; BL 3/15/98; HB 5–6/98; SLJ 5/98; VOYA 12/98) [306.3]

9153 O'Neill, Thomas. *Lakes, Peaks, and Prairies: Discovering the United States-Canadian Border* (7–12). 1984, National Geographic LB $12.95 (978-0-87044-483-8). A trip across the continent that reveals much about the diversity of these regions. [973]

9154 Patent, Dorothy Hinshaw. *Treasures of the Spanish Main* (6–10). Series: Frozen in Time. 1999, Marshall Cavendish LB $28.50 (978-0-7614-0786-7). This lavishly illustrated book describes the sinking of Spanish galleons near the Florida Keys in the 1600s and how their excavation has brought us amazing information about life and culture in the New World at that time. (Rev: BL 2/15/00; HBG 10/00; SLJ 3/00) [930]

9155 Smith, Tom. *Discovery of the Americas, 1492-1800* (6–12). Series: Discovery and Exploration. 2005, Facts on File $40.00 (978-0-8160-5262-2). European exploration of the New World is the focus of this volume that contains clear, informative text plus maps, illustrations, and excerpts from primary sources. (Rev: SLJ 8/05) [973]

North America

CANADA

9156 Campbell, Marjorie Wilkins. *The Nor'westers: The Fight for the Fur Trade* (6–12). 2003, Fitzhenry & Whiteside paper $12.95 (978-1-894004-97-8). An absorbing account of the Canadian fur trade in the 19th century, with details of company politics and relations between traders and Native Americans. (Rev: BL 4/1/03) [380.1]

9157 Garrington, Sally. *Canada* (7–10). Series: Countries of the World. 2005, Facts on File LB $30.00 (978-0-8160-6009-2). History, geography, culture, government, and economy are all covered in this attractive overview of Canada. (Rev: SLJ 1/06) [971]

9158 Kizilos, Peter. *Quebec: Province Divided* (7–10). Series: World in Conflict. 2000, Lerner LB $25.26 (978-0-8225-3562-1). The history of the French Canadian province and the separatist movement there. (Rev: BL 10/15/2000; HBG 4/00; VOYA 8/01) [971]

9159 McGrath, Melanie. *The Long Exile: A Tale of Inuit Betrayal and Survival in the High Arctic* (9–12). 2007, Knopf $25.00 (978-1-4000-4047-6). McGrath uses one family's experience to tell the story of Canada's forced relocation, in the 1950s, of Inuit families from their homes in a well-provisioned region to the grim Ellesmere Island 1,200 miles to the north. (Rev: BL 3/1/07) [305.897]

9160 Riendeau, Roger E. *A Brief History of Canada* (9–12). 2000, Facts on File $45.00 (978-0-8160-3157-3). From the Norse discovery to the present day, this history of Canada is enriched with photographs and maps. (Rev: VOYA 4/00) [971]

CENTRAL AMERICA

9161 Foster, Lynn V. *A Brief History of Central America* (9–12). 2000, Facts on File $45.00 (978-0-8160-3962-3). The political, economic, and social history of all the countries in Central America is given, with material on present conditions. [972.8]

9162 Kallen, Stuart A. *The Aftermath of the Sandinista Revolution* (8–12). Series: Aftermath of History. 2009, Lerner LB $38.60 (978-0-8225-9091-0). Kallen outlines how the overthrow of the Nicaraguan government by the Sandinistas in 1979 had an international impact as well as a domestic one, spreading new fears about Communism. (Rev: SLJ 4/1/09) [972.8]

9163 McCullough, David. *The Path Between the Seas: The Creation of the Panama Canal, 1870–1914* (10–12). 1977, Simon & Schuster paper $18.00 (978-0-671-24409-5). A well-told history of the building of the Panama Canal from early attempts to the American completion in 1914. [972.87]

9164 Sheehan, Sean. *Guatemala* (6–10). Series: Cultures of the World. 1998, Marshall Cavendish LB $37.07 (978-0-7614-0812-3). A solid introduction to Guatemala's geography, politics, and culture. (Rev: HBG 9/98; SLJ 2/99) [972.8]

MEXICO

9165 Hadden, Gerry. *Teenage Refugees from Mexico Speak Out* (7–12). Series: Teenage Refugees Speak Out. 1997, Rosen LB $27.95 (978-0-8239-2441-7). Teens who have left Mexico and come to the U.S. to escape economic conditions and political instability tell about their experiences. (Rev: BL 10/15/97; SLJ 1/98) [972]

9166 Stein, R. Conrad. *The Mexican Revolution* (6–12). 2007, Morgan Reynolds LB $27.95 (978-1-59935-051-6). This comprehensive, well-written book covers the Mexican Revolution in detail and does not gloss over the more violent aspects of the conflict (includes maps, photos, reproductions, bibliography, chronology, index, notes and Web sites). (Rev: SLJ 3/08)

9167 Stein, R. Conrad. *The Mexican War of Independence* (6–12). 2007, Morgan Reynolds LB $27.95 (978-1-59935-054-7). Lively text and illustrations will appeal to readers of this volume, which covers three centuries of Spanish rule of Mexico, from 1521-1855 (includes maps, photos, reproductions, bibliography, chronology, index, notes and Web sites). (Rev: SLJ 3/08)

PUERTO RICO, CUBA, AND OTHER CARIBBEAN ISLANDS

9168 Carey, Charles W., Jr, ed. *Castro's Cuba* (7–12). Series: History Firsthand. 2004, Gale LB $36.20 (978-0-7377-1654-2); paper $24.95 (978-0-7377-1655-9). Historical documents, interviews, and newspaper and magazine articles are used in this account of Castro's takeover in Cuba and developments since then. (Rev: SLJ 11/04) [972]

9169 Fernandez, Ronald M. *Puerto Rico Past and Present: An Encyclopedia* (8–12). 1998, Greenwood $86.95 (978-0-313-29822-6). A browsable book that contains biographies of famous Puerto Ricans as well as political terms and groups, buildings, important court decisions, and other information on the island's cultural and historical developments. (Rev: BL 7/97; VOYA 10/98) [972.95]

9170 Fisanick, Christina. *The Bay of Pigs* (6–12). Series: At Issue in History. 2004, Gale paper $23.70 (978-0-7377-1990-1). The failed Bay of Pigs invasion is described in an introductory overview followed by a collection of essays, speeches, and editorials that provide diverse views about the event. (Rev: BL 9/1/04) [972.910]

9171 Harvey, David Alan, and Elizabeth Newhouse. *Cuba* (10–12). 1999, National Geographic $50.00 (978-0-7922-7501-5). Stunning photographs and a brief text introduce the land and people of Cuba. (Rev: BL 1/1–15/00) [972.91]

9172 Sheehan, Sean, and Leslie Jermyn. *Cuba* (7–10). Series: Cultures of the World: Second Edition. 2005, Marshall Cavendish LB $25.95 (978-0-7614-1964-8). A frank, balanced, and readable overview of Cuba's history, geography, economy, culture, and people. (Rev: BL 2/15/06) [972.91]

9173 Worth, Richard. *Puerto Rico in American History* (7–12). Series: From Many Cultures, One History. 2008, Enslow LB $23.95 (978-0-7660-2836-4). An interesting overview of an often-overlooked part of the United States, with an attractive layout. (Rev: BL 4/1/08) [972.95]

South America

9174 Dicks, Brian. *Brazil* (6–10). Series: Countries of the World. 2003, Facts on File $30.00 (978-0-8160-5382-7). A well-illustrated account that covers all important topics including present-day racial friction and economic inequality. (Rev: BL 2/1/04) [949.12]

9175 Fearns, Les, and Daisy Fearns. *Argentina* (7–10). Series: Countries of the World. 2005, Facts on File LB $30.00 (978-0-8160-6008-5). History, geography, culture, government, and economy are all covered in this attractive overview of Argentina. (Rev: SLJ 1/06) [982]

9176 Gorrell, Gena K. *In the Land of the Jaguar: South America and Its People* (6–10). Illus. by Andrej Krystoforski. 2007, Tundra $22.95 (978-0-88776-756-2). A beautiful and informative book that covers all the countries of South America, discussing their geography, animals, and natural resources as well as their people and their customs. (Rev: BL 10/1/07; SLJ 11/07) [980]

9177 Jermyn, Leslie. *Uruguay* (7–10). Series: Cultures of the World. 1998, Marshall Cavendish LB $37.07 (978-0-7614-0873-4). An attractive book that covers all the basic topics relating to Uruguay, plus material on leisure activities, festivals, and food. (Rev: HBG 9/99; SLJ 6/99) [980]

9178 Litteral, Linda L. *Boobies, Iguanas, and Other Critters: Nature's Story in the Galapagos* (6–10). 1994, American Kestrel $23.00 (978-1-883966-01-0). After a historical overview of the Galapagos Islands, this richly illustrated book covers the islands' animals, plants, and geology. (Rev: BL 6/1–15/94; SLJ 9/94) [508.866]

9179 McIntyre, Loren. *The Incredible Incas and Their Timeless Land* (10–12). 1975, National Geographic LB $12.95 (978-0-87044-182-0). An examination of the Incas, their history and culture, and the destruction of their empire by the Spaniards. [985]

9180 Mittermeier, Russell A, et al. *Pantanal: South America's Wetland Jewel* (9–12). Photos by Theo Allofs. 2005, Firefly $35.00 (978-1-55407-090-9). Striking color photographs of landscape and flora and fauna highlight this fascinating profile of South America's Pantanal, a vast wetlands network covering more than 80,000 square miles in the countries of Bolivia, Brazil, and Paraguay. (Rev: BL 10/1/05) [981.72]

9181 Peck, Robert McCracken. *Headhunters and Hummingbirds: An Expedition into Ecuador* (7–10). 1987, Walker LB $14.85 (978-0-8027-6646-5). An account of an ill-fated scientific expedition into the land of the Jívaro Indians in Ecuador. (Rev: SLJ 6/87; VOYA 8/87) [986]

9182 Read, Piers Paul. *Alive: The Story of the Andes Survivors* (9–12). 1979, Avon paper $7.99 (978-0-380-00321-1). The harrowing story of a group of men and women who survive a plane crash in the Andes. [910.4]

Polar Regions

9183 Alexander, Caroline. *The Endurance: Shackleton's Legendary Antarctic Expedition* (10–12). 1998, Knopf $29.95 (978-0-375-40403-0). Drawing on first-person accounts, some previously unpublished, Alexander brings to life Shackleton's ill-fated trans-Antarctic expedition. (Rev: BL 10/15/98) [998]

9184 Anderson, Harry S. *Exploring the Polar Regions. Rev. ed.* (8–11). Series: Discovery and Exploration.

2010, Chelsea House LB $35 (978-1-60413-190-1). An updated edition of Anderson's analytical history of polar exploration that looks at the motivations behind the expeditions as well as the specifics of early and modern ventures into new terrain. (Rev: LMC 8–9/10) [910]

9185 Burch, Ernest S., and Werner Forman. *The Eskimos* (9–12). 1988, Univ. of Oklahoma $19.95 (978-0-8061-2126-0). Color photographs highlight this account of the history, livelihood, and culture of the Eskimo. (Rev: BL 9/1/88) [306]

9186 Counter, S. Allen. *North Pole Legacy: Black, White and Eskimo* (9–12). 2001, Invisible Cities paper $14.95 (978-1-931229-09-8). Supports Peary's claim as first to the North Pole while focusing on Peary's African American partner Matthew Henson — a world-class explorer marginalized by white historians; originally published in 1991. (Rev: BL 5/15/91) [998.2]

9187 Ehrlich, Gretel. *In the Empire of Ice: Encounters in a Changing Landscape* (10–12). 2010, National Geographic $28 (978-142620574-3). Ehrlich draws on her recent National Geographic Expeditions journey into the Arctic to present this dismal assessment of the environmental catastrophes that await us, with portraits of the impact on the peoples of the region. (Rev: BL 4/1/10*) [910.911]

9188 Fiennes, Ranulph. *Race to the Pole: Tragedy, Heroism, and Scott's Antarctic Quest* (8–12). 2004, Hyperion $27.95 (978-1-4013-0047-0). Fiennes, a polar explorer himself, offers an in-depth account of Captain Robert Scott's ill-fated 1911-1912 expedition to the South Pole. (Rev: BL 9/15/04) [919.8]

9189 Griffiths, Tom. *Slicing the Silence: Voyaging to Antarctica* (9–12). 2007, Harvard $29.95 (978-0-674-02633-9). The history of Antarctica is told in an accessible, breezy narrative with many first-person anecdotes. (Rev: BLO 9/25/07) [919.8]

9190 Haas, Robert B. *Through the Eyes of the Vikings: An Aerial Vision of Arctic Lands* (10–12). Illus. 2010, National Geographic $50 (978-142620638-2). This stunning collection of aerial photographs shows the Arctic Circle in all its natural glory. (Rev: BL 9/1–15/10) [910]

9191 Henderson, Bruce. *True North: Peary, Cook, and the Race to the Pole* (8–12). 2005, Norton $24.95 (978-0-393-05791-1). Who got to the North Pole first? Henderson offers evidence for the reader to mull over. (Rev: BL 1/1–15/05) [910]

9192 Legler, Gretchen. *On the Ice: An Intimate Portrait of Life at McMurdo Station, Antarctica* (11–12). 2005, Milkweed paper $15.95 (978-1-57131-282-2). Legler combines a portrait of the spartan life of scientists stationed in Antarctica with an account of her own relationship with a woman named Ruth. (Rev: BL 11/1/05) [919]

9193 Lopez, Barry. *Arctic Dreams: Imagination and Desire in a Northern Landscape* (10–12). 2008, Paw Prints $24.00 (978-1-4352-9614-5). For better readers, this is an account of the history, ecology, and mystique of the arctic region; originally published in 1986. (Rev: BL 1/1/86) [508.98]

9194 Lynch, Wayne. *Planet Arctic: Life at the Top of the World* (9–12). Illus. 2010, Firefly $40 (978-155407632-1). A second volume collecting striking photographs of flora and fauna of the Arctic. (Rev: BL 12/1–15/10) [591.709]

9195 Niven, Jennifer. *Ada Blackjack: A True Story of Survival in the Arctic* (10–12). 2003, Hyperion $24.95 (978-0-7868-6863-6). An ill-fated expedition to the Arctic ends with a sole survivor in this exciting true-life tale. (Rev: BL 10/15/03*) [915.7]

9196 Senungetuk, Vivian, and Paul Tiulana. *A Place for Winter: Paul Tiulana's Story* (7–12). 1988, CIRI Foundation $17.95 (978-0-938227-02-1). The story of a King Island Eskimo boy, his childhood, and his people. (Rev: BL 5/15/88) [917.98]

9197 Wu, Norbert, and Jim Mastro. *Under Antarctic Ice: The Photographs of Norbert Wu* (8–12). 2004, Univ. of California $45.00 (978-0-520-23504-5). Life beneath the ice of Antarctica is brilliantly captured in the photographs of Norbert Wu; with a useful introduction. (Rev: BL 10/15/04) [779]

United States

General History and Geography

9198 Allen, Thomas B., and Charles O. Hyman, eds. *We Americans: Celebrating a Nation, Its People, Its Past* (9–12). 1999, National Geographic $40.00 (978-0-7922-7005-8). Using excellent illustrations and commentary by eminent historians and writers, this is a fine book for browsing America's past and present. (Rev: BL 3/1/00) [973]

9199 Baker, Patricia. *The 1950s* (7–10). Series: Fashions of a Decade. 2007, Chelsea House $35.00 (978-0-8160-6721-3). Pictures and discussion of the fashions of this decade are accompanied by information about the trends and events of the times and how they affected what Americans wore. Also use *The 1940s* (2007). (Rev: BL 4/15/07) [391]

9200 Baxandall, Rosalyn, and Linda Gordon, eds. *America's Working Women: A Documentary History 1600 to the Present* (9–12). 1995, Norton paper $16.95 (978-0-393-31262-1). A chronologically arranged overview of the changing roles and contributions of women. (Rev: BL 3/15/95*) [331.4]

9201 Bennett, William J. *America: The Last Best Hope: From the Age of Discovery to a World at War, Vol. 1* (10–12). 2006, Nelson Current $29.99 (978-1-59555-055-2). Organized chronologically, this is a clear yet informal account of key political and military events in U.S. history, with quotations, anecdotes, and profiles that add flavor. (Rev: SLJ 8/06)

9202 Bockenhauer, Mark H., and Stephen F. Cunha. *Our Fifty States* (4–10). 2004, National Geographic LB $45.90 (978-0-7922-6992-2). Maps of the states are accompanied by basic facts, photographs, and archival reproductions of key historical events; also includes the U.S. territories. (Rev: SLJ 1/05) [973]

9203 Boorstin, Daniel J. *The Americans: The Democratic Experience* (10–12). 1973, Random House paper $19.00 (978-0-394-71011-2). This work chronicles the growth of the democratic spirit in America in the past 100 years. [973]

9204 Bowman, John S. *Facts About the American Wars* (10–12). 1998, H.W. Wilson $115.00 (978-0-8242-0929-2). Military conflicts from the mid-16th-century to the Persian Gulf War of 1991 are covered in detail, with illustrations and maps. [355]

9205 Brokaw, Tom. *An Album of Memories: Personal Histories from the Greatest Generation* (10–12). 2001, Random House $29.95 (978-0-375-50581-2). This is a collection of letters sent to Tom Brokaw by Americans who lived through the Depression and World War II. (Rev: BL 4/1/01) [940.54]

9206 Brokaw, Tom. *The Greatest Generation* (10–12). 1998, Random House paper $24.95 (978-0-375-70569-4). The TV anchorman describes the Americans who came of age during the Great Depression and World War II and created today's America, with stories told by a cross-section of men and woman around the country and divided into eight topics: Ordinary People; Homefront; Heroes; Women in Uniform and Out; Shame; Love, Marriage, and Commitment; Famous People; and the Arena. (Rev: BL 1/1–15/99; SLJ 4/99) [973.9]

9207 Browne, Ray B., and Lawrence A. Kreiser. *The Civil War and Reconstruction* (9–12). Series: American Popular Culture Through History. 2003, Greenwood $59.95 (978-0-313-31325-7). A fascinating exploration of the impact of the Civil War and the ensuing Reconstruction on popular culture in America, looking at topics including fashion, advertising, music, journalism, sports, travel, and transportation. (Rev: SLJ 4/04) [973]

9208 Campbell, Ballard C., ed. *Disasters, Accidents, and Crises in American History: A Reference Guide to the Nation's Most Catastrophic Events* (9–12). Illus. 2008, Facts on File $95 (978-081606603-2). Encompassing about 500 years of events, this book includes chronologically organized, informative accounts of natural disasters, epidemics, accidents, terrorist attacks, and so forth. (Rev: BL 9/15/08; LMC 11–12/08; SLJ 6/08) [363.34]

9209 Carlisle, Rodney P., ed. *The Great Depression and World War II: 1929 to 1949* (9–12). Series: Handbook to Life in America. 2009, Facts on File $50 (978-0-8160-7180-7). Compelling period photographs, maps, charts, and sidebars add impact to this well-researched book exploring the events, social issues, and key figures of the Great Depression and World War II. (Rev: SLJ 1/10)

9210 Collins, Gail. *America's Women: 400 Years of Dolls, Drudges, Helpmates, and Heroines* (10–12). 2003, Morrow $27.95 (978-0-06-018510-7). This ambitious survey of women's role in American history looks at the challenges faced and contributions made. (Rev: BL 9/1/03) [305.4]

9211 Cordingly, David. *Women Sailors and Sailors' Women* (10–12). 2001, Random House $24.95 (978-0-375-50041-1). This book for mature readers covers the lives of women who went to sea (some disguised as men) during the 17th, 18th, and 19th centuries. (Rev: BL 3/1/01) [910.4]

9212 Coster, Patience. *A New Deal for Women, 1938–1960: The Expanding Roles of Women* (6–12). Illus. Series: Cultural History of Women in America. 2011, Chelsea House LB $35 (978-160413934-1). This attractive, accessible volume describes the new opportunities available for women during and after World War II. (Rev: BL 10/1/11; SLJ 10/1/11) [305.40973]

9213 Crump, Donald J., ed. *Exploring America's Scenic Highways* (9–12). 1985, National Geographic $12.95 (978-0-87044-479-1). A celebration of America's colorful highways in words and pictures. [917.3]

9214 Ehlert, Willis J. *America's Heritage: Capitols of the United States* (6–12). 1993, State House paper $10.95 (978-0-9634908-3-4). Provides data on state capitals and capitol buildings, descriptions of architectural details, brief state histories, state symbols, and an extensive bibliography. (Rev: BL 4/15/93) [725]

9215 Evans, Mari-Lynn, et al, ed. *The Appalachians: America's First and Last Frontier* (9–12). 2012, West Virginia University Press paper $24.99 (978-193597896-1). This collection of photographs, essays, and oral histories describes the Appalachian region, which covers thousands of square miles in 13 states. (Rev: BL 3/1/04) [974]

9216 Flamming, Douglas. *African Americans in the West* (9–12). 2009, ABC-CLIO $65 (978-1-59884-002-5). The history of African Americans in the West is the focus of this wide-ranging book that covers everything from Revolutionary-era slavery to the NAACP and urban migration. (Rev: LMC 11–12/09; SLJ 10/09)

9217 Garrington, Sally. *The United States* (6–10). Series: Countries of the World. 2003, Facts on File $30.00 (978-0-8160-5385-8). This basic work supplies an overview of information on the United States with emphasis on present conditions. (Rev: BL 1/1–15/04) [973]

9218 Gay, Kathlyn, and Martin Gay. *After the Shooting Stops: The Aftermath of War* (7–12). 1998, Millbrook LB $24.90 (978-0-7613-3006-6). A look at the political, economic, and social changes that have followed U.S. involvement in various wars. (Rev: BL 8/98; HBG 3/99; SLJ 9/98) [355.00973]

9219 Glackens, Ira. *Did Molly Pitcher Say That? The Men and Women Who Made American History* (9–12). 1989, Writers & Readers $18.95 (978-0-86316-097-4); paper $12.95 (978-0-86316-094-3). An informal view of American history with several amusing and fascinating sidebar features. (Rev: BL 9/15/89) [973]

9220 Gourley, Catherine. *Gibson Girls and Suffragists: Perceptions of Women from 1900 to 1918, Vol. 1* (7–12). Series: Images and Issues of Women in the Twentieth Century. 2007, Twenty-First Century LB $38.60 (978-0-8225-7150-6). With many photographs and reproductions, this volume looks at images and issues relating to women's roles in the early 20th century. Also use *Rosie and Mrs. America: Perceptions of Women in the 1930s and 1940s* (2007). (Rev: SLJ 11/07) [305.4]

9221 Grunwald, Lisa, and Stephen J. Adler, eds. *Women's Letters: America from the Revolutionary War to the Present* (10–12). 2005, Dial $35.00 (978-0-385-33553-9). A fascinating collection of more than 400 letters documenting women's evolving views on everyday life and on key events and issues in American history. (Rev: BL 9/1/05; SLJ 1/06) [305.4]

9222 Harrison, Blake, and Alex Rappaport. *Hip-Hop U.S. History* (9–12). Series: Flocabulary. 2007, Cider Mill paper $16.95 (978-1-933662-35-0). Rap along to U.S. history! Students will have fun while learning important facts with this book and music CD. The time period covered is from Columbus to the civil rights movement. (Rev: BL 1/1–15/07) [973]

9223 Head, Judith. *America's Daughters: 400 Years of American Women* (6–12). 1999, Perspectives paper $16.95 (978-0-9622036-8-8). This overview of the part played by women in American history highlights the work of many who have been unjustly ignored. (Rev: BL 1/1–15/00; SLJ 3/00) [305.4]

9224 Heinemann, Sue. *The New York Public Library Amazing Women in History* (6–10). 1998, Wiley paper $14.95 (978-0-471-19216-9). Using a question-and-answer format, this work supplies hundreds of facts about women in American history, arranged by topics that include activism, sports, recreation, and racial and ethnic groups. (Rev: BL 4/15/98; SLJ 8/98) [973]

9225 Hemming, Heidi, and Julie Hemming Savage. *Women Making America* (6–12). 2009, Clotho $45.95 (978-0-9821271-1-7); paper $28.95 (978-0-9821271-0-0). Women's roles — domestic and professional — throughout American history are the focus of this well-laid out book, which employs numerous biographical sketches, period photographs, and compelling vignettes to engage readers. (Rev: BLO 7/09; SLJ 6/1/09) [900]

9226 Hollinshead, Byron, ed. *I Wish I'd Been There: Twenty Historians Bring to Life Dramatic Events that Changed America* (9–12). 2006, Doubleday $26.95 (978-0-385-51619-8). Prominent scholars provide their interpretations of 20 important events or time periods in American history. (Rev: BL 8/06) [973]

9227 Holsinger, M. Paul, ed. *War and American Popular Culture: A Historical Encyclopedia* (9–12). 1999, Greenwood LB $131.95 (978-0-313-29908-7). Arranged by war periods from colonial days to the present, articles examine how wars have changed U.S. popular culture in the areas of songs, poetry, novels, television, movies, toys, and controversial war memorials. (Rev: BL 4/15/99; SLJ 8/99) [973]

9228 Howarth, W., et al. *America's Wild Woodlands* (9–12). 1985, National Geographic LB $12.95 (978-0-87044-547-7). From the flowering trees of the East to the West's sequoias, this is a description of the wonders of America's forests. [917.3]

9229 Jacoby, Susan. *Freethinkers: A History of American Secularism* (10–12). 2004, Henry Holt $27.50 (978-0-8050-7442-0). This is a history of American freethinkers such as Thomas Jefferson, Walt Whitman, and John F. Kennedy and how they changed American thinking and history. (Rev: BL 4/1/04*) [211]

9230 Kennedy, Caroline, ed. *A Patriot's Handbook: Songs, Poems, Stories, and Speeches Celebrating the Land We Love* (9–12). 2003, Hyperion $24.95 (978-0-7868-6918-3). Compiled by Caroline Kennedy, this anthology of patriotic stories, poems, speeches, and other documents ranges from the lyrics of "The Star-Spangled Banner" to the text of the Supreme Court's decision in Brown *v.* the Board of Education. (Rev: BL 3/1/03) [810]

9231 Kluger, Richard. *Seizing Destiny: How America Grew from Sea to Shining Sea* (9–12). 2007, Knopf $35.00 (978-0-375-41341-4). This is a chronicle of how the territories of the United States were gained from Britain, France, Spain, Mexico, Russia, and native peoples and the role each president played in forming the land that it now encompasses, and how the pioneers and settlers managed to get what they came for, fairly or not. (Rev: BL 8/07) [973]

9232 *Monuments and Historic Places of America* (9–12). Series: Macmillan Profiles. 2000, Macmillan $95.00 (978-0-02-865374-7). Battlefields, churches, homes, forts, and cemeteries are some of the 90 monuments and memorials highlighted in this guide to famous places in the United States. (Rev: BL 5/1/00) [973]

9233 Morris, Richard B. *Basic Documents in American History* (9–12). 1980, Krieger paper $11.50 (978-0-89874-202-2). This collection of important documents in American history covers the years 1620 through the 1960s. [973]

9234 National Geographic Society, ed. *Preserving America's Past* (9–12). 1983, National Geographic LB $12.95 (978-0-87044-420-3). This volume highlights attempts to preserve America's past by restoring buildings, relearning crafts, and similar activities. [973]

9235 Nugent, Walter. *Habits of Empire: A History of American Expansion* (11–12). Illus. 2008, Knopf $28.95 (978-140004292-0). From the Manifest Destiny to early 20th-century Imperialism, this book examines the phenomenon of American expansion and the altruistic philosophies American leaders employed to justify their actions. (Rev: BL 6/1–15/08) [970.01]

9236 Packard, Jerrold M. *American Nightmare: The History of Jim Crow* (10–12). 2002, St. Martin's $24.95 (978-0-312-26122-1). An excellent overview of Jim Crowism from Reconstruction through the passage of the Voting Rights Act in 1965. (Rev: BL 12/15/01) [973]

9237 Panchyk, Richard. *Keys to American History: Understanding Our Most Important Historic Documents* (6–12). Illus. 2009, Chicago Review $24.95 (978-155652716-6); paper $19.95 (978-155652804-0). An anthology of 72 important documents in the history of the United States, from the Mayflower Compact to the Patriot Act. With explanatory notes, facsimiles, and maps. (Rev: BL 5/1/09; SLJ 2/1/09) [973]

9238 Reeves, Thomas C. *Twentieth-Century America: A Brief History* (10–12). 2000, Oxford paper $44.95 (978-0-19-504484-3). A concise history of the United States in the 20th century. [973.9]

9239 Rydell, Robert W. *Fair America: World's Fairs in the United States* (8–12). 2000, Smithsonian $29.95 (978-1-56098-968-4); paper $15.95 (978-1-56098-384-2). This book examines world's fairs held in the United States from 1853 to 1984. [907]

9240 Sedeen, Margaret. *Star-Spangled Banner: Our Nation and Its Flag* (9–12). 1993, National Geographic $37.50 (978-0-87044-944-4). Legends — such as the tale of Betsy Ross — are sorted from fact in this history of the U.S. flag, from Francis Scott Key to the modern controversy about flag desecration. Color photographs. (Rev: BL 10/15/93) [929.9]

9241 Stone, Nathaniel. *On the Water: Discovering America in a Rowboat* (10–12). 2002, Broadway $21.95 (978-0-7679-0841-2). In this engaging memoir/travel book, the author describes his 6,000-mile journey in and around America and the many fascinating people and places he encountered along the way. (Rev: BL 7/02*) [917.304]

9242 Streissguth, Thomas. *Utopian Visionaries* (7–12). 1999, Oliver LB $19.95 (978-1-881508-47-2). This account presents material on attempts to build utopian communities in the U.S. during the 18th and 19th centuries by such visionaries as Ann Lee, a Shaker, and John

Humphrey Noyes, who created the Oneida community. (Rev: BL 12/15/99; HBG 4/00; SLJ 11/99) [321]

9243 Tarrant-Reid, Linda. *Discovering Black America* (7–12). Illus. 2012, Abrams $29.95 (978-0-8109-7098-4). A handsome and thorough overview of more than 400 years of African American history, drawing on diaries, autobiographies, written oral accounts, and interviews. Lexile 1370L (Rev: BL 9/1/12; LMC 3–4/13; SLJ 10/12) [973]

9244 Thompson, Kathleen, and Hilary Mac Austin. *America's Children: Picturing Childhood from Early America to the Present* (10–12). 2002, Norton $39.95 (978-0-393-05182-7). Children's lives at home, at school, and at work are portrayed in narrative, photographs, and extracts from primary sources. (Rev: BL 10/1/02) [305.23]

9245 Torricelli, Robert G., and Andrew Carroll. *In Our Own Words: Extraordinary Speeches of the American Century* (10–12). 1999, Kodansha $28.00 (978-1-56836-291-5). A collection of texts that includes sermons, "fireside chats," eulogies, and other forms of speeches that were delivered throughout the 20th century. (Rev: BL 10/15/99; SLJ 4/00) [815.008]

9246 Uschan, Michael V. *Lynching and Murder in the Deep South* (8–12). Series: Lucent Library of Black History. 2006, Gale LB $28.70 (978-1-59018-845-3). This is a frank discussion of the lynchings and other violence that took place in the South from Reconstruction right up to the 1950s. (Rev: SLJ 4/07) [364.1]

9247 Uschan, Michael V. *The 1940s* (5–10). Series: Cultural History of the United States. 1998, Lucent LB $28.70 (978-1-56510-554-6). Life at home and abroad during World War II dominate this book, which also discusses the Great Depression, the New Deal, events leading up to U.S. participation in the war, the beginnings of the Cold War, the growth of suburban living, and the rise of television, with sidebars on such topics as the Holocaust, the influences of radio, movies, and comics, 1940s slang, and the first computers. (Rev: SLJ 1/99) [973.9]

9248 Whitaker, Jan. *Service and Style: How the American Department Store Fashioned the Middle Class* (9–12). 2006, St. Martin's $35 (978-0-312-32635-7). A history of department stores and their influence on American society. (Rev: SLJ 12/06)

9249 White, Shane, and Graham White. *The Sounds of Slavery: Discovering African American History Through Songs, Sermons, and Speech* (9–12). 2005, Beacon $29.95 (978-0-8070-5026-2). The sounds of everyday life for America's slaves — the spirituals and sermons, field calls and work songs, and the cries of agony — are captured in this volume and the audio CD that accompanies it. (Rev: BL 2/15/05) [973]

9250 Wormser, Richard. *American Childhoods: Three Centuries of Youth at Risk* (7–12). 1996, Walker LB $17.85 (978-0-8027-8427-8). A graphic, realistic picture of childhood and growing up in America from the repressive Puritans to the present day with chapters on work, crime, disease, education, sex, and related topics. (Rev: BL 9/15/96; SLJ 9/96; VOYA 12/96) [305.23]

9251 Wormser, Richard. *Hoboes: Wandering in America, 1870-1940* (6–12). 1994, Walker $17.95 (978-0-8027-8279-3). This account covers the history, rules, literature, songs, and customs of those who rode the rails from the end of the Civil War to the outbreak of World War II. (Rev: BL 6/1–15/94; SLJ 7/94) [305.5]

9252 Worth, Richard. *The Slave Trade in America: Cruel Commerce* (6–12). Series: Slavery in American History. 2004, Enslow LB $26.60 (978-0-7660-2151-8). The slave trade is traced back to its origins in the days of early Romans before a more detailed survey of the American slave trade in the 17th and 18th centuries, with attention to the social and economic aspects. (Rev: SLJ 8/04) [382]

9253 Young, Dwight, and Ira Block. *Saving America's Treasures: National Trust for Historic Preservation* (9–12). 2000, National Geographic $35.00 (978-0-7922-7942-6). This splendid book highlights in text and pictures 43 places, artifacts, and documents that the National Trust has restored and preserved. (Rev: BL 11/1/00) [973]

Historical Periods

NATIVE AMERICANS

9254 Bond, Fred G. *Flatboating on the Yellowstone, 1877* (7–12). 1998, Ward Hill $19.95 (978-1-886747-03-6). A first-person account of the relocation in 1877 of Chief Joseph and other Nez Perce Indians from Oregon to Oklahoma by raft down the Yellowstone and Missouri Rivers, written by their pilot, who documented the trip for the New York Public Library in 1925. (Rev: BL 12/15/98) [973]

9255 Brehm, Victoria, ed. *Star Songs and Water Spirits: A Great Lakes Native Reader* (10–12). Illus. 2010, Ladyslipper paper $27.95 (978-09843340-0-1). This extensive volume collects historical accounts, songs, stories, and poems by the Native American peoples of the Great Lakes past and present. (Rev: BLO 1/1–15/11) [398.208997077]

9256 Bruchac, Joseph. *The Native American Sweat Lodge: History and Legends* (9–12). 1993, Crossing Pr. paper $12.95 (978-0-89594-636-2). Bruchac celebrates the importance of the sweat lodge (lodges or huts heated by steam from water poured on hot stones) in this overview of its history, meaning, and use. Includes 25 traditional Native American poems and stories. (Rev: BL 10/15/93) [391]

9257 Cooper, Michael L. *Indian School: Teaching the White Man's Way* (5–10). 1999, Clarion $18.00 (978-

581

0-395-92084-8). A moving photoessay about Native American children and how they were removed from their homes and uprooted from their culture to attend Indian boarding schools in an effort to "civilize" them. (Rev: BL 12/1/99; HBG 3/00; SLJ 2/00; VOYA 4/00) [370]

9258 Cornell, George L., and Gordon Henry. *Ojibwa* (8–12). Series: North American Indians Today. 2003, Mason Crest LB $22.95 (978-1-59084-673-5). The contemporary status of Ojibwa Indians is emphasized in this volume that covers religion, government, and the arts. (Rev: SLJ 5/04) [973]

9259 Debo, Angie. *A History of the Indians of the United States* (10–12). Series: Civilization of the American Indian. 1970, Univ. of Oklahoma paper $26.95 (978-0-8061-1888-8). This is a historical survey of the Indians of North America with material on the Eskimos and Aleuts of Alaska. [970.004]

9260 Deloria, Vine, Jr. *Custer Died for Your Sins: An Indian Manifesto* (10–12). 1969, Macmillan paper $21.95 (978-0-8061-2129-1). The author tellingly and, at times, shockingly, reconstructs the history of the Native American. [970.004]

9261 *Do All Indians Live in Tipis? Questions and Answers from the National Museum of the American Indian* (8–12). 2007, Smithsonian paper $14.95 (978-0-06-115301-3). With answers to questions posed by the general public, this book aims to set the facts straight about Native American cultures. (Rev: SLJ 3/08)

9262 Dunn, John M. *The Relocation of the North American Indian* (9–12). Series: World History. 2005, Gale LB $31.20 (978-1-59018-656-5). Examines the Native Americans' relationships with the European settlers and later the U.S. government, providing well-written text enhanced with quotations, illustrations, and maps. (Rev: SLJ 5/06*) [970.004]

9263 Durrett, Deanne. *Healers* (8–12). Series: American Indian Lives. 1997, Facts on File $17.95 (978-0-8160-3460-4). This work profiles 12 Native American healers, ranging from the traditional medicine man to modern physicians and nurses. (Rev: VOYA 8/97) [973]

9264 Engels, Mary Tate, ed. *Tales from Wide Ruins: Jean and Bill Cousins, Traders* (10–12). 1996, Texas Tech Univ. $29.95 (978-0-89672-368-9). The Cousinses were traders with Native Americans during the 1930s and 1940s. This book presents the stories they heard and experiences they had involving the past life of Native Americans and other ethnic groups living in the desert of the Southwest. (Rev: SLJ 12/96) [979]

9265 Gibson, Karen Bush. *Native American History for Kids* (6–10). Illus. 2010, Chicago Review paper $16.95 (978-15697628-0-6). With profiles of key individuals and 21 hands-on activities, this is an attractive and accessible survey of Native American life through the centuries. (Rev: BL 7/10; SLJ 2/11) [970.004]

9266 Gilbert, Joan. *The Trail of Tears Across Missouri* (10–12). 1996, Univ. of Missouri paper $11.95 (978-0-8262-1063-0). A simple retelling of the forced exodus of the Cherokee people. [970.004]

9267 Goetzmann, William H. *The First Americans: Photographs from the Library of Congress* (9–12). 1991, Starwood $34.95 (978-0-912347-96-7). This collection of turn-of-the-century commercial photographs of Native Americans illustrates the "sentimental notions about the vanishing American" popular at the time. (Rev: BL 11/15/91) [973.0497]

9268 Hungrywolf, Adolf. *The Tipi: Traditional Native American Shelter* (9–12). 2006, Native Voices paper $17.95 (978-1-57067-174-6). Filled with photographs of various types of tipis, this book features firsthand accounts of how tipis were built, used, decorated, and maintained. (Rev: BL 4/15/06) [970.004]

9269 Josephy, Alvin M, Jr. *The Indian Heritage of America* (10–12). 1991, Houghton Mifflin paper $17.00 (978-0-395-57320-4). This is a fine survey of the cultures and history of the Native Americans of North, Central, and South America. [970.004]

9270 Josephy, Alvin M., Jr., ed. *Lewis and Clark Through Indian Eyes* (10–12). 2006, Knopf $24 (978-1-4000-4267-8). Nine essays by distinguished writers descended from the various Native American tribes that assisted the Lewis and Clark expedition discuss how the expedition's aftermath affected the Indians and their economic and social systems. (Rev: BL 3/15/06; SLJ 8/06)

9271 Katz, Jane B., ed. *We Rode the Wind: Recollections of Native American Life. Rev. ed.* (6–10). 1995, Lerner LB $22.60 (978-0-8225-3154-8). A collection of the autobiographical writings of eight notable Native Americans, among them Charles Eastman and Black Elk, who grew up on the Great Plains. (Rev: BL 2/1/96; SLJ 12/95) [978]

9272 Keoke, Emory Dean, and Kay Marie Porterfield. *Trade, Transportation, and Warfare* (7–10). Series: American Indian Contributions to the World. 2005, Facts on File $35.00 (978-0-8160-5395-7). Native American accomplishments in both North and South America in the realms of transportation, trade, sports, governance, and military strategy are among the aspects highlighted here. (Rev: BL 4/1/05; SLJ 6/05) [970.004]

9273 McIntosh, Kenneth. *Apache* (8–12). Series: North American Indians Today. 2003, Mason Crest LB $22.95 (978-1-59084-664-3). The contemporary status of Apache Indians is emphasized in this volume that covers religion, government, and the arts. (Rev: SLJ 5/04) [973]

9274 McIntosh, Kenneth, and Marsha McIntosh. *Cheyenne* (8–12). Series: North American Indians Today. 2003, Mason Crest LB $22.95 (978-1-59084-666-7). The contemporary status of Cheyenne Indians is emphasized in this volume that covers religion, government, and the arts. Also use *Iroquois* (2003). (Rev: SLJ 5/04) [973]

9275 McMaster, Gerald, and Clifford E. Trafzer, eds. *Native Universe: Voices of Indian America* (9–12). 2004, National Geographic $40.00 (978-0-7922-5994-7). In three main sections — "Our Universe," "Our Peoples," and "Our Lives" — photographs and text document the diversity of Native American culture and history. (Rev: BL 8/04) [970.004]

9276 Marsico, Katie. *The Trail of Tears: The Tragedy of the American Indians* (8–10). Series: Perspectives on. 2009, Marshall Cavendish LB $27.95 (978-0-7614-4029-1). Marsico examines the historical context, heartbreak, and aftermath of the American Cherokee relocation program and provides photographs, illustrations, and engaging sidebars. (Rev: LMC 3–4/10; SLJ 1/10) [973.04]

9277 Nies, Judith. *Native American History: A Chronology of a Culture's Vast Achievements and Their Links to World Events* (6–12). 1997, Ballantine paper $15.00 (978-0-345-39350-0). This chronology of Native North American history and culture from 28,000 B.C. through 1996, using a split-page format to juxtapose simultaneous political, social, religious, and military developments occurring in North America and in other parts of the world. (Rev: SLJ 5/97) [970.003]

9278 Red Shirt, Delphine. *Bead on an Anthill: A Lakota Childhood* (10–12). 1998, Univ. of Nebraska paper $13.95 (978-0-8032-8976-5). The story of a Lakota Indian woman, her childhood on a reservation in South Dakota in the 1960s and 1970s, and her memories of the culture and traditions of her people. (Rev: SLJ 11/98) [909]

9279 Rozema, Vicki. *Voices from the Trail of Tears* (10–12). 2003, John F. Blair paper $11.95 (978-0-89587-271-5). Primary sources, including many first-person accounts, make this an affecting portrait of the government-mandated relocation of the Cherokees. (Rev: BL 4/15/03) [973.04]

9280 Sandoz, Mari. *The Battle of the Little Bighorn* (10–12). 1966, Amereon $20.95 (978-0-89190-879-1). The story of this battle in the war against the Sioux and of the ambitions of General Custer. [973.8]

9281 Sandoz, Mari. *Cheyenne Autumn* (10–12). 1976, Avon paper $4.95 (978-0-380-01094-3). The heartbreaking saga of the Cheyenne Indian trek in 1878 back to their home in Yellowstone. [970.004]

9282 Tehanetorens. *Roots of the Iroquois* (7–10). 2000, Native Voices paper $9.95 (978-1-57067-097-8). A lively, detailed look at the history of the Iroquois Confederation before and after the arrival of European settlers. (Rev: BL 11/15/00) [974.004]

9283 Walker, Paul Robert. *Remember Little Bighorn: Indian, Soldiers, and Scouts Tell Their Stories* (9–12).

2006, National Geographic $17.95 (978-0-7922-5521-5). This is a beautifully designed history of Custer's Last Stand with accounts of the battle from opposing viewpoints; maps, photographs, and archival images aid comprehension. (Rev: BL 6/1–15/06; SLJ 10/06*) [973.8]

9284 Wallace, Anthony F. C. *The Long, Bitter Trail: Andrew Jackson and the Indians* (9–12). 1993, Hill & Wang paper $8.00 (978-0-8090-1552-8). The story of the forced removal of the Cherokees over the Trail of Tears to the Oklahoma Territory in the 1830s. (Rev: BL 7/93; SLJ 12/93) [323.1]

9285 Williams, Jeanne. *Trails of Tears: American Indians Driven from Their Lands* (9–12). 1992, Hendrick-Long $19.95 (978-0-937460-76-4). Details the U.S. government's forced removal of Comanche, Cheyenne, Apache, Navajo, and Cherokee Indians from their native lands. (Rev: BL 6/1/92) [973]

9286 Williams, Maria Shaa Tlaa, ed. *The Alaska Native Reader: History, Culture, Politics* (10–12). Illus. 2009, Duke paper $25.95 (978-08223448-0-3). The history and current status of Alaska's Native peoples are fully explored in this well-researched collection of stories, poems, art, and essays. (Rev: BLO 7/09) [305.89]

DISCOVERY AND EXPLORATION

9287 Cox, Caroline, and Ken Albala. *Opening Up North America, 1497–1800* (6–12). Series: Discovery and Exploration. 2005, Facts on File $40.00 (978-0-8160-5261-5). Chronicles the arrival of Europeans in North America and their progression across the continent, with maps, illustrations, and excerpts from primary sources. (Rev: SLJ 8/05) [973]

9288 Duncan, Dayton, and Ken Burns. *Lewis and Clark: The Journey of the Corps of Discovery* (9–12). 1997, Knopf paper $25.00 (978-0-375-70652-3). A beautifully illustrated companion to a PBS special of the same name, this book chronicles the epic journey from St. Louis through uncharted territory to the Pacific Ocean. (Rev: BL 8/97) [978]

9289 Lepore, Jill. *Encounters in the New World: A History in Documents* (7–12). Series: Pages from History. 1999, Oxford LB $39.95 (978-0-19-510513-1). Documents including letters, journals, and advertisements make relations between Native Americans and European arrivals more real to readers. (Rev: HBG 9/00; SLJ 3/00) [970]

COLONIAL PERIOD AND FRENCH AND INDIAN WARS

9290 Aronson, Marc. *Witch-Hunt: Mysteries of the Salem Witch Trials* (9–12). 2003, Simon & Schuster $18.95 (978-0-689-84864-3). This scholarly yet absorbing study thoughtfully examines the factors that led to the infamous witch trials in late 17th-century Massachusetts. (Rev: BL 11/1/03; HBG 4/04; SLJ 12/03; VOYA 12/03) [133.4]

9291 Boorstin, Daniel J. *The Americans: The Colonial Experience* (10–12). 1958, Random House paper $15.00 (978-0-394-70513-2). This scholarly work about our colonial period traces its history and shows how it gave birth to a distinctive culture. [973.2]

9292 Borneman, Walter R. *The French and Indian War: Deciding the Fate of North America* (10–12). 2006, HarperCollins $27.95 (978-0-06-076184-4). A clear and accessible account of the war and the factions involved, with profiles of key commanders. (Rev: BL 10/15/06) [973.2]

9293 Gray, Edward G. *Colonial America: A History in Documents* (9–12). Series: Pages from History. 2002, Oxford LB $39.95 (978-0-19-513747-7). Excerpts from primary sources — accompanied by reproductions of documents, maps, and works of art — shed light on the lifestyles and important issues of the colonial period. (Rev: BL 2/15/03; SLJ 3/03) [973.2]

9294 Hawke, David Freeman. *Everyday Life in Early America* (9–12). 1988, HarperCollins paper $13.00 (978-0-06-091251-2). A detailed account of what life was like for the average colonists in America. (Rev: BL 12/1/87; SLJ 12/88) [973.2]

9295 Hofstadter, Richard. *America at 1750: A Social Portrait* (10–12). 1971, Knopf paper $11.00 (978-0-394-71795-1). Using a number of sources, this noted historian re-creates life in the colonies in 1750 with material on the slave trade, middle-class life, and the colonists' religious life. [973.2]

9296 Miller, Lee. *Roanoke: Solving the Mystery of the Lost Colony* (10–12). 2001, Arcade $25.95 (978-1-55970-584-4). This interesting book attempts to explain the disappearance of the ill-fated Roanoke colony. [975.6]

9297 Nardo, Don. *The Salem Witch Trials* (9–12). Series: American History. 2007, Gale LB $31.20 (978-1-59018-950-4). Nardo looks at the social tensions that allowed the witch trials to take place. (Rev: SLJ 10/07) [133.4]

9298 O'Connor, George. *Journey into Mohawk Country* (9–12). 2006, Roaring Brook $17.95 (978-1-59643-106-5). O'Connor illustrates entries from the diary of a Dutch trader who traveled through the Indian territories of present-day New York in 1634 hoping to make trade agreements with the Indians. (Rev: BL 10/15/06; LMC 1/07) [917.47]

9299 Purvis, Thomas L. *Colonial America to 1763* (9–12). Series: Almanacs of American Life. 1999, Facts on File $95.00 (978-0-8160-2527-5). This volume covers the big picture and the small details of life in colonial America in chapters on topics that include diet, health, crime, and recreation. (Rev: BL 10/15/99; SLJ 2/00) [973.2]

9300 Steere, Deirdre Clancy, and Amela Baksic. *Colonial America* (6–12). Series: Costume and Fashion Source Books. 2009, Chelsea House $35 (978-1-60413-380-6). This volume looks at the attire of men and women from various different walks of life in Colonial America. (Rev: LMC 11–12/09; SLJ 10/09) [391]

9301 Turner, Glennette Tilley. *Fort Mose: And the Story of the Man Who Built the First Free Black Settlement in Colonial America* (7–10). 2010, Abrams $18.95 (978-0-8109-4056-7). Documenting the first free black settlement in North America and the key role of a slave called Francisco Menendez, Turner provides a thorough look at the culture of the place, which blended African, Native American, and Spanish elements. (Rev: BL 10/15/10*; LMC 1–2/11; SLJ 10/1/10) [975.9]

REVOLUTIONARY PERIOD AND THE YOUNG NATION (1775–1809)

9302 Allison, Robert J., ed. *American Eras: The Revolutionary Era (1754–1783)* (7–12). 1998, Gale $140.00 (978-0-7876-1480-5). A good reference source that opens with an overview of world events during the Revolutionary period, followed by chapters on specific topics such as the arts; business and the economy; law and justice; lifestyles, social trends, and fashions; religion; and sports and recreation. (Rev: BL 3/15/99; SLJ 2/99) [973.3]

9303 Aronson, Marc. *The Real Revolution: The Global Story of American Independence* (9–12). 2005, Clarion $21.00 (978-0-618-18179-7). Was the American Revolution an isolated incident or connected to events elsewhere in the world? A thought-provoking, well-illustrated and well-documented analysis. (Rev: BL 9/15/05; SLJ 10/05*) [973.3]

9304 Bowen, Catherine Drinker. *Miracle at Philadelphia: The Story of the Constitutional Convention, May to September, 1787* (10–12). 1986, Little, Brown paper $8.95 (978-0-316-10398-5). This is considered one of the best accounts of the Constitutional Convention and the people involved. [973.3]

9305 Chadwick, Bruce. *The First American Army: The Remarkable Story of George Washington and the Men Behind America's Fight for Freedom* (10–12). 2005, Sourcebooks $24.95 (978-1-4022-0506-4). Drawing on first-person accounts from letters and journals, Chadwick looks at the American Revolution through the eyes of the boys and men who fought on the front lines. (Rev: BL 11/1/05) [973.3]

9306 Davenport, John. *The American Revolution* (9–12). Series: American History. 2007, Gale LB $31.20 (978-1-59018-939-9). In addition to covering the course of the war, Davenport looks at the human story and the social conflict between the constituencies involved. (Rev: SLJ 10/07) [973.3]

9307 Diouf, Sylviane A. *Growing Up in Slavery* (6–12). 2001, Millbrook LB $25.90 (978-0-7613-1763-0). A compelling account that dispels any myths about happy slave children and describes the hard life on the plantation as well as the atrocious conditions on slave ships. (Rev: BL 3/1/01; HBG 10/01; SLJ 6/01) [380.1]

9308 Ellis, Joseph J. *Founding Brothers: The Revolutionary Generation* (10–12). 2000, Knopf $26.00 (978-0-375-40544-0). Using events in the lives of Founding Fathers including Washington, Hamilton, and Franklin, the author presents six episodes that highlight the character and convictions of each. (Rev: BL 9/15/00) [973.4]

9309 Gaines, Ann Graham. *The Louisiana Purchase in American History* (7–10). Series: In American History. 2000, Enslow LB $26.60 (978-0-7660-1301-8). A well-documented and illustrated account of the 1803 purchase of southern land from the French government. (Rev: BL 1/1–15/00; HBG 9/00) [973.5]

9310 Hibbert, Christopher. *Redcoats and Rebels: The American Revolution Through British Eyes* (10–12). 1990, Norton paper $16.95 (978-0-393-32293-4). Beginning with the Stamp Act of 1765, this account presents the American Revolution from the standpoint of the British. [973.3]

9311 Karapalides, Harry J. *Dates of the American Revolution: Who, What, and Where in the War for Independence* (7–12). 1998, Burd Street paper $19.95 (978-1-57249-106-9). A chronological record tracing the American Revolution from 1760, when King George II inherited the British throne, to George Washington's death in 1799, with an emphasis on military action and commanders. (Rev: SLJ 2/99) [973.3]

9312 Leckie, Robert. *George Washington's War: The Saga of the American Revolution* (9–12). 1992, HarperCollins paper $18.00 (978-0-06-092215-3). A valuable historical overview of the American Revolution from the initial split between Britain and its American colonies to the British surrender at Yorktown, Virginia, on October 19, 1781. [973.3]

9313 McCullough, David. *1776* (8–12). 2005, Simon & Schuster $32.00 (978-0-7432-2671-4). McCullough brings to life the key events of the year 1776 for George Washington and the new young nation. (Rev: SLJ 10/05) [973]

9314 Mitchell, Joseph B. *Decisive Battles of the American Revolution* (9–12). 1985, Fawcett paper $5.99 (978-0-449-30031-2). A re-creation of all the important battles in the Revolution from Lexington to Yorktown. [973.3]

9315 Morton, Joseph C. *The American Revolution* (7–12). Series: Greenwood Guides to Historic Events, 1500-1900. 2003, Greenwood $51.95 (978-0-313-31792-7). A thorough, text-dense overview of the events leading up to the war, the war itself, and its after-

math, with profiles of key individuals. (Rev: SLJ 7/04) [973.3]

9316 Murphy, Jim. *An American Plague: The True and Terrifying Story of the Yellow Fever Epidemic of 1793* (6–12). 2003, Clarion $18.00 (978-0-395-77608-7). Narrative, newspaper articles, and archival prints and photographs combine to tell the dramatic story of the epidemic that hit Philadelphia in the late 18th century. Margaret A. Edwards Award 2010. (Rev: BL 6/1–15/03; HB 7–8/03; HBG 10/03; SLJ 6/03*; VOYA 12/03) [614.5]

9317 Nash, Gary B. *The Forgotten Fifth: African Americans in the Age of Revolution* (9–12). 2006, Harvard $19.95 (978-0-674-02193-8). Based on lectures given by the author at Harvard University in 2004, this book reveals that the treatment of soldier-slaves in the Revolutionary War led to many defections to the British side. (Rev: SLJ 10/06)

9318 Purvis, Thomas L. *Revolutionary America, 1763–1800* (9–12). Series: Almanacs of American Life. 1995, Facts on File $95.00 (978-0-8160-2528-2). Life during revolutionary times in various parts of the country is described under such headings as education, population, health, and religion. (Rev: BL 10/1/95; SLJ 2/96) [973.3]

9319 Raphael, Ray. *A People's History of the American Revolution: How Common People Shaped the Fight for Independence* (10–12). 2001, New Press $25.95 (978-1-56584-653-1). The experiences of ordinary people — farmers, townspeople, Native Americans, African Americans, and women — during the Revolution are told in this readable account. (Rev: BL 3/1/01) [973.3]

9320 Sanders, Nancy I. *America's Black Founders: Revolutionary Heroes and Early Leaders with 21 Activities* (6–10). Series: For Kids. 2010, Chicago Review paper $16.95 (978-15565281-1-8). With activities such as filling a straw mattress, making a stamp, and drawing a political cartoon, this is a lively introduction to the role of African Americans in the early days of the nation, covering well-known figures and ordinary people. (Rev: BL 2/1/10; LMC 3–4/10; SLJ 1/10) [973]

9321 Stokesbury, James L. *A Short History of the American Revolution* (10–12). 1991, Morrow paper $15.95 (978-0-688-12304-8). A concise examination of the factors that led to the American Revolution as well as the war for independence itself. [973.3]

NINETEENTH CENTURY TO THE CIVIL WAR (1809–1861)

9322 Andrews, William L., and Henry Louis Gates, Jr., eds. *Slave Narratives* (9–12). 2000, Library of America $40.00 (978-1-883011-76-5). These 10 narratives — including those by Nat Turner, Frederick Douglass, and Sojourner Truth — paint a vivid picture of the cruelties and injustices of slavery. (Rev: BL 2/15/00) [326]

9323 Baker, Lindsay, and Julie P. Baker, eds. *Till Freedom Cried Out: Memories of Texas Slave Life* (10–12). 1997, Texas A & M Univ. $29.95 (978-0-89096-736-2). Part of the Oklahoma Slave Narrative Project established as part of the WPA, this is a collection of narratives by 32 slaves who were born in Texas and relocated to Oklahoma. (Rev: SLJ 12/97) [973.6]

9324 Berlin, Ira, and Marc Favreau, eds. *Remembering Slavery: African Americans Talk About Their Personal Experiences of Slavery and Emancipation* (10–12). 1998, New Press $49.95 (978-1-56584-425-4). This book and cassette set recaptures the narratives of former slaves as they were first recorded in the 1930s as part of the Federal Writers' Project. These personal recollections convey the harshness, sadism, and brutality of slavery as well as the resilience, survival skills, sense of family, and community among the slaves. (Rev: BL 8/98; SLJ 4/99) [973]

9325 Boorstin, Daniel J. *The Americans: The National Experience* (10–12). 1965, Random House paper $16.00 (978-0-394-70358-9). This work focuses on the years between the Revolution and the Civil War and how this period shaped modern America. [973]

9326 Cloud Tapper, Suzanne. *The Abolition of Slavery: Fighting for a Free America* (7–12). Series: The American Saga. 2006, Enslow LB $31.93 (978-0-7660-2605-6). The history of the abolitionist movement is chronicled in this well-organized book that includes primary source material, photographs, and maps. (Rev: SLJ 7/07) [973.7]

9327 de Ramus, Betty. *Forbidden Fruit: Love Stories from the Underground and Beyond* (9–12). 2005, Atria $25.00 (978-0-7434-8263-9). Drawing on newspaper accounts, oral histories, slave narratives, census data, and unpublished memoirs, De Ramus tells 13 moving stories of love against the backdrop of American slavery. (Rev: BL 2/1/05) [973.7]

9328 DeFord, Deborah H. *Life Under Slavery* (6–12). Series: Slavery in the Americas. 2006, Chelsea House $35 (978-0-8160-6135-8). Middle schoolers studying slavery in the United States will be interested to learn how African blacks adapted their culture and traditions in an effort to survive life as captives. (Rev: SLJ 9/06)

9329 Fradin, Dennis Brindell. *Bound for the North Star: True Stories of Fugitive Slaves* (8–12). 2000, Clarion $21.00 (978-0-395-97017-1). Personal experiences form the basis of these moving profiles that spare no details of the horrors suffered by escaping slaves and the courage of their helpers. (Rev: BL 1/1–15/01*; HB 1–2/01; HBG 3/01; SLJ 11/00*; VOYA 10/01) [973.7]

9330 Geary, Rick. *The Mystery of Mary Rogers* (10–12). Series: Treasury of Victorian Murder. 2001, NBM $15.95 (978-1-56163-274-9). In comic-book format, Geary tells of the 1841 murder of cigar girl Mary Rogers in New York City, a crime that was never solved and

was used as the basis for Edgar Allan Poe's story. (Rev: BL 4/15/01; SLJ 8/01; VOYA 8/01) [364.1]

9331 Griffler, Keith P. *Front Line of Freedom: African Americans and the Forging of the Underground Railroad in the Ohio Valley* (10–12). Series: Ohio River Valley. 2004, Univ. Press of Kentucky $35.00 (978-0-8131-2298-4). Using many first-person narratives, this book details the roles played by African Americans in the operation of the Underground Railroad. (Rev: BL 2/15/04) [973.7]

9332 Heidler, David S., and Jeanne T. Heidler. *The War of 1812* (8–12). Series: Greenwood Guides to Historic Events, 1500-1900. 2002, Greenwood $51.95 (978-0-313-31687-6). This thorough and detailed description of the causes, events, and key figures of the War of 1812 will be useful for report writers. (Rev: BL 10/15/02; SLJ 10/02) [973.5]

9333 Hendrick, George, and Willene Hendrick. *The Creole Mutiny: A Tale of Revolt Aboard a Slave Ship* (10–12). 2003, Ivan R. Dee $24.95 (978-1-56663-493-9). The authors recount how slaves being transported aboard the slave ship *Creole* in the early 1840s revolted, took control of the vessel, and sailed to freedom in the Bahamas. (Rev: BL 2/15/03) [326]

9334 Lord, Walter. *A Time to Stand* (9–12). 1978, Univ. of Nebraska paper $14.95 (978-0-8032-7902-5). A gripping account of the siege and fall of the Alamo. [973.6]

9335 McNeese, Tim. *The Abolitionist Movement: Ending Slavery* (8–12). Series: Reform Movements in American History. 2007, Chelsea House LB $30.00 (978-0-7910-9502-7). An informative survey of the movement and its leaders. (Rev: BL 11/15/07; LMC 4–5/08) [973.7114]

9336 Mancall, Peter C., ed. *American Eras: Westward Expansion (1800–1860)* (8–12). 1999, Gale $140.00 (978-0-7876-1483-6). The period of growth and change in America from the early 19th century up to the Civil War is examined. (Rev: BL 3/15/99; SLJ 8/99) [973.6]

9337 Philbrick, Nathaniel. *The Heart of the Sea: The Tragedy of the Whaleship Essex* (10–12). 2000, Viking $24.95 (978-0-670-89157-3). A fascinating telling of the tragic whaling voyage of the *Essex* from Nantucket in the 1820s that was the inspiration for *Moby Dick*. (Rev: BL 3/1/00*; SLJ 11/00) [910]

9338 Rose, Joel. *New York Sawed in Half* (10–12). 2001, Bloomsbury $19.95 (978-1-58234-098-2). The story of an amazing hoax perpetrated in early 19th-century New York during which people believed that half of Manhattan was sinking because of the weight of its buildings. (Rev: BL 4/15/01) [974.7]

9339 Zeinert, Karen. *The Amistad Slave Revolt and American Abolition* (7–10). 1997, Shoe String LB $21.50 (978-0-208-02438-1); paper $12.95 (978-0-208-02439-8). The dramatic story of Cinque and 52 other slaves onboard the Spanish ship *Amistad* in 1839 and of their historic mutiny and subsequent trial. (Rev: BL 7/97; SLJ 6/97) [326]

9340 Zeinert, Karen. *Tragic Prelude: Bleeding Kansas* (6–10). 2001, Linnet $25.00 (978-0-208-02446-6). An accessible account of the conflict that erupted in Kansas over the question of slavery, with information on individuals including John Brown and Hannah Ropes, a timeline, extracts from primary documents, photographs, and references. (Rev: BL 6/1–15/01; HBG 10/01; SLJ 6/01; VOYA 2/02) [978.1]

CIVIL WAR (1861–1865)

9341 Allen, Thomas B., and Roger MacBride Allen. *Mr. Lincoln's High-Tech War: How the North Used the Telegraph, Railroads, Surveillance Balloons, Ironclads, High-Powered Weapons, and More to Win the Civil War* (6–10). Illus. 2008, National Geographic $18.95 (978-1-4263-0379-1); LB $25.90 (978-1-4263-0380-7). The authors argue that Lincoln's enthusiasm for technology contributed directly to the Union's success in the Civil War. ALA Notable Books 2010. Lexile 1180L (Rev: BL 12/15/08*; LMC 5–6/09; SLJ 2/1/09*; VOYA 2/09) [973.7]

9342 *The American Civil War: A Hands-on History* (10–12). 2006, Hill & Wang $24.00 (978-0-8090-9538-4). This thorough review of the causes, conduct, and outcome of the Civil War includes profiles of key figures, accounts of battles, and thoughtful explanations of the issues. (Rev: BL 6/1–15/06) [973.7]

9343 Bailey, Ronald H. *The Bloodiest Day: The Battle of Antietam* (7–12). 1984, Silver Burdett LB $25.93 (978-0-8094-4741-1). The story of Lee's defeat in the battle that caused terrible losses on both sides. [973.7]

9344 Bailey, Ronald H. *Forward to Richmond* (9–12). 1983, Silver Burdett LB $25.93 (978-0-8094-4721-3). A lavishly illustrated volume that deals with the Peninsula campaign of 1862. Some others in the Time-Life series on the Civil War are *Decoying the Yanks* (1984), *The Fight for Chattanooga* (1985), and *Pursuit to Appomattox* (1989). [973.7]

9345 Barney, William L. *The Civil War and Reconstruction: A Student Companion* (7–12). Series: Oxford Student Companions to American History. 2001, Oxford LB $65.00 (978-0-19-511559-8). An alphabetically arranged series of articles covering all aspects of the Civil War and Reconstruction, illustrated with photographs, maps, and reproductions. (Rev: BL 9/15/01; SLJ 6/01) [973.7]

9346 Bolden, Tonya. *Emancipation Proclamation: Lincoln and the Dawn of Liberty* (6–10). Illus. 2013, Abrams $24.95 (978-141970390-4). Drawing extensively on primary sources, archival photographs, posters and letters, and so forth, this accessible and attractive

volume offers well-written text and detailed captions. (Rev: BL 2/1/13*; HB 7–8/13; SLJ 1/13*) [973.714]

9347 Bowman, John S., ed. *The Civil War Almanac* (9–12). 1986, Newspaper Enterprise Assn. paper $14.95 (978-0-345-35434-1). This book consists chiefly of a detailed chronology of the war plus 133 biographical sketches of key figures. [973.7]

9348 Burgess, Lauren Cook, ed. *An Uncommon Soldier* (9–12). 1994, Minerva Center $25.00 (978-0-9634895-1-7). Letters of a New York farmer's daughter who disguised herself as a man to enlist in the Union Army in 1862 — only the second such published account. (Rev: BL 5/15/94) [973.7]

9349 Catton, Bruce. *A Stillness at Appomattox* (10–12). 1953, Doubleday paper $14.95 (978-0-385-04451-6). One of the best accounts of the Civil War by a leading American historian. [973.7]

9350 *Chancellorsville* (7–12). Series: Voices of the Civil War. 1996, Time-Life $24.95 (978-0-7853-4708-8). A handsome description of this key Civil War battle, featuring regimental histories, letters, diaries, and memoirs. (Rev: BL 1/1–15/97) [973.7]

9351 Colbert, Nancy. *The Firing on Fort Sumter: A Splintered Nation Goes to War* (6–12). 2000, Morgan Reynolds LB $23.95 (978-1-883846-51-0). An intriguing, detailed account, told in lively prose and many photographs, of the incident that began the Civil War. (Rev: BL 10/1/00; HBG 3/01; VOYA 6/01) [973.7]

9352 Davis, Burke. *Sherman's March* (9–12). 1980, Random House paper $14.00 (978-0-394-75763-6). This volume deals with the destructive march of Sherman and his men through Georgia and the Carolinas. [973.7]

9353 Davis, William C. *Death in the Trenches: Grant at Petersburg* (9–12). 1986, Silver Burdett LB $25.93 (978-0-8094-4777-0). This volume of the Time-Life series deals with the Union Army's siege of Petersburg, Virginia. [973.7]

9354 Davis, William C. *First Blood: Fort Sumter to Bull Run* (9–12). 1983, Silver Burdett LB $25.93 (978-0-8094-4705-3). A survey in pictures and text of such early battles of the Civil War as Bull Run and Fort Sumter. Part of the Time-Life series. [973.7]

9355 DeFord, Deborah H. *African Americans during the Civil War* (6–12). Series: Slavery in the Americas. 2006, Chelsea House $35 (978-0-8160-6138-9). The importance of blacks in America during the Civil War — as slaves, civilians, and soldiers — is covered, as is the "National Convention of Colored Men" and the effects that the war had on African Americans' rights. (Rev: SLJ 9/06)

9356 Farwell, Byron. *Ball's Bluff* (9–12). 1990, EPM paper $12.95 (978-0-939009-36-7). A gripping account of the small Civil War battle of Ball's Bluff and its aftermath. (Rev: SLJ 9/90) [973.7]

9357 Geary, Rick. *The Murder of Abraham Lincoln* (9–12). Series: A Treasury of Victorian Murder. 2005, NBM $15.95 (978-1-56163-425-5). Volume seven of the Treasury of Victorian Murder series tackles one of the most infamous crimes of the period: the assassination of President Abraham Lincoln. (Rev: BL 6/1–15/05; SLJ 9/05; VOYA 10/05) [973.709]

9358 Goolrick, William K. *Rebels Resurgent: Fredericksburg to Chancellorsville* (9–12). 1985, Silver Burdett LB $25.93 (978-0-8094-4749-7). In this volume in the Time-Life series, the early southern victories of 1862 and 1863 are reconstructed. [973.7]

9359 Gragg, Rod. *The Civil War Quiz and Fact Book* (9–12). 1985, HarperCollins paper $14.00 (978-0-06-091226-0). Fascinating questions and answers involving little-known facts about the Civil War. (Rev: BL 4/15/85) [973.7]

9360 Horwitz, Tony. *Confederates in the Attic: Dispatches from the Unfinished Civil War* (10–12). 1998, Knopf paper $14.00 (978-0-679-75833-4). This is an exploration by a Pulitzer Prize-winning reporter of why the Civil War continues to fascinate Americans. The author gathered material for a year throughout the Old South, where he visited battlefields and interviewed hundreds of people. (Rev: BL 2/1/98; SLJ 7/98) [973.7]

9361 Howell, Maria L., ed. *The Emancipation Proclamation* (9–12). Series: At Issue in History. 2005, Gale LB $29.95 (978-0-7377-2276-5). A collection of articles that address from different perspectives the text of the proclamation itself and the impact it had on the Civil War and its aftermath. (Rev: SLJ 5/06) [973.7]

9362 Jackson, Donald Dale. *Twenty Million Yankees: The Northern Home Front* (9–12). 1985, Silver Burdett LB $25.93 (978-0-8094-4753-4). This volume in the Time-Life series deals with life in the North during the Civil War. [973.7]

9363 Jarrow, Gail. *Lincoln's Flying Spies* (7–10). Illus. 2010, Boyds Mills $18.95 (978-159078719-9). This volume tells the story of the Union Army's Aeronautics Corps and its fleet of hot-air balloons that helped to spy on the Confederate Army, focusing in particular on the aeronaut Thaddeus Lowe and his contributions. Lexile 1060L (Rev: BL 10/15/10; LMC 1–2/11; SLJ 11/10) [973.7]

9364 Jaynes, Gregory. *The Killing Ground: Wilderness to Cold Harbor* (9–12). 1986, Silver Burdett LB $25.93 (978-0-8094-4769-5). The story of the bloody battles in Virginia early in 1864 are retold in this volume in the Time-Life series. [973.7]

9365 Korn, Jerry. *The Fight for Chattanooga: Chickamauga to Missionary Ridge* (9–12). 1985, Silver Burdett LB $25.93 (978-0-8094-4817-3). In this volume in the Time-Life Civil War series, four battles — Chickam-

auga, Chattanooga, Lookout Mountain, and Missionary Ridge — are highlighted. [973.7]

9366 Logue, Larry M. *To Appomattox and Beyond: The Civil War Soldier in War and Peace* (9–12). 1995, Ivan R. Dee $22.50 (978-1-56663-093-1). Traces Civil War soldiers from the time they enlisted to their discharge and their lives after the war. (Rev: BL 10/15/95) [973.7]

9367 McNeese, Tim. *Civil War Battles* (6–12). Series: Civil War: A Nation Divided. 2009, Chelsea House $35 (978-1-60413-034-8). Bull Run, Shiloh, Antietam, Fredericksburg, Chancellorsville, and Gettysburg are among the battles covered in this volume that looks at real-life stories and the cost of war. (Rev: LMC 11–12/09) [973.73]

9368 McPherson, James M. *Hallowed Ground: A Walk at Gettysburg* (10–12). 2003, Crown $16.00 (978-0-609-61023-7). The Battle of Gettysburg is beautifully chronicled in three chapters, each covering a single day of the three-day conflict. (Rev: BL 3/1/03*; SLJ 8/03) [973.7]

9369 Marten, James A. *Children for the Union: The War Spirit on the Northern Home Front* (9–12). Series: American Childhoods. 2004, Ivan R. Dee $26.00 (978-1-56663-563-9). This volume surveys the lives and living conditions of children growing up in the North during the Civil War. (Rev: BL 4/1/04) [974]

9370 Murphy, Jim. *A Savage Thunder: Antietam and the Bloody Road to Freedom* (6–10). 2009, Simon & Schuster $17.99 (978-0-689-87633-2). The terrible battle of Antietam is chronicled here, with maps, firsthand accounts, and discussion of its importance to the overall war. ♩ (Rev: BL 8/09*; HB 9–10/09; LMC 10/09; SLJ 8/09) [973.7]

9371 Nevin, David. *The Road to Shiloh: Early Battles in the West* (9–12). 1983, Silver Burdett LB $25.93 (978-0-8094-4717-6). This volume of the Time-Life series deals with the early battles in Kentucky and the Battle of Shiloh in 1862. [973.7]

9372 Nevin, David. *Sherman's March: Atlanta to the Sea* (9–12). 1986, Silver Burdett LB $25.93 (978-0-8094-4813-5). A reconstruction of the destructive march through Georgia and the Carolinas by Sherman. Part of the Time-Life Civil War series. [973.7]

9373 Reis, Ronald A. *African Americans and the Civil War* (6–12). Series: Civil War: A Nation Divided. 2009, Chelsea House $35 (978-1-60413-038-6). Free blacks and ex-slaves fought in more than 400 battles but faced prejudice and were underpaid despite their contributions. (Rev: LMC 11–12/09) [973.73]

9374 Sears, Stephen W. *Chancellorsville* (10–12). 1996, Houghton Mifflin paper $18.00 (978-0-395-87744-9). A thorough examination of the course and importance of this Confederate victory. (Rev: BL 10/15/96) [973.7]

9375 Seidman, Rachel Filene. *The Civil War: A History in Documents* (9–12). 2000, Oxford $39.95 (978-0-19-511558-1). These documents, many of which are about the experiences of ordinary people, cover the causes and aftermath of the Civil War as well as the war itself. (Rev: BL 12/15/00; HBG 10/01; SLJ 3/01) [973.7]

9376 Spaulding, Lily May, and John Spaulding, eds. *Civil War Recipes: Recipes from the Pages of Godey's Lady's Book* (9–12). 1999, Univ. Press of Kentucky $19.95 (978-0-8131-2082-9). Recipes for common, everyday meals drawn from 19th-century women's magazines, to which the authors have added interesting historical information such as Confederate and Union army rations, cooking utensils, and food substitutions frequently used by southern cooks. (Rev: SLJ 7/99) [973.7]

9377 *Spies, Scouts, and Raiders: Irregular Operations* (9–12). 1985, Silver Burdett LB $25.93 (978-0-8094-4713-8). This pictorial volume, part of the Time-Life series, presents some of the unusual military operations of the Civil War. [973.7]

9378 Street, James, Jr. *The Struggle for Tennessee: Tupelo to Stones River* (9–12). 1985, Silver Burdett LB $25.93 (978-0-8094-4761-9). This part of the Time-Life series deals with the important areas of Tennessee and Kentucky during the Civil War. [973.7]

9379 Tackach, James, ed. *The Battle of Gettysburg* (8–12). Series: At Issue in History. 2002, Greenhaven paper $18.70 (978-0-7377-0826-4). Excerpts from historical documents and contemporary writings portray events at Gettysburg from both Union and Confederate points of view, with maps, photographs, and other illustrations. (Rev: BL 5/1/02; SLJ 4/02) [973.7]

9380 Tackach, James, ed. *The Civil War* (9–12). Series: Turning Points in World History. 2004, Gale LB $37.45 (978-0-7377-1114-1). The causes, battles, and aftermath of the Civil War are examined in a collection of essays by prominent historians; discussion questions and further readings add to this volume's usefulness. (Rev: SLJ 1/05) [973.7]

9381 Taschek, Karen. *The Civil War* (6–12). Series: Costume and Fashion Source Books. 2009, Chelsea House $35 (978-1-60413-381-3). This volume looks at the attire of men and women from various different walks of life in the years before and during the Civil War, including the uniforms of North and South. (Rev: LMC 11–12/09; SLJ 10/09) [391]

9382 Wagner, Heather Lehr. *Spies in the Civil War* (6–12). Series: Civil War: A Nation Divided. 2009, Chelsea House $35 (978-1-60413-039-3). Wagner tells the stories of the men and women who served as spies during the Civil War, examining their motivations and diverse backgrounds. (Rev: LMC 11–12/09) [973.73]

9383 Wagner, Margaret E. *The American Civil War: 365 Days* (9–12). 2006, Abrams $29.95 (978-0-8109-5847-

0). This book of Civil War images is organized thematically and includes photographs, paintings, drawings, lithographs, and cartoons; descriptive text accompanies each image. (Rev: BL 4/15/06; SLJ 5/06) [973.7022]

9384 Ward, Geoffrey C., et al. *The Civil War: An Illustrated History* (9–12). 1990, Knopf $75.00 (978-0-394-56285-8). A handsome, readable account that was prepared for the television series on the Civil War that aired in 1990. (Rev: BL 8/90; SLJ 3/91) [973.7]

9385 Williams, David. *Bitterly Divided: The South's Inner Civil War* (11–12). Illus. 2008, New Press $27.95 (978-159558108-2). Williams deftly explains that, among other mistakes, the Confederacy defeated itself by pushing secession although the majority of southerners were against it, and by establishing rules of enlistment that favored wealthy planters. (Rev: BL 8/08*) [973.7]

9386 Woodworth, Steven E. *Cultures in Conflict: The American Civil War* (10–12). 2000, Greenwood $55.00 (978-0-313-30651-8). Documents including memoirs, diaries, letters, and photographs illustrate the cultural differences between North and South. (Rev: VOYA 2/01) [973.7]

9387 Zeinert, Karen. *The Lincoln Murder Plot* (6–12). 1999, Shoe String LB $22.50 (978-0-208-02451-0). A detailed, well-documented retelling of the first assassination of a U.S. president and its world-shaking results. (Rev: BL 3/1/99; HB 7–8/99; SLJ 5/99; VOYA 4/99) [973.7]

WESTWARD EXPANSION AND PIONEER LIFE

9388 Bryan, Howard. *Robbers, Rogues and Ruffians: True Tales of the Wild West* (9–12). 1991, Clear Light $22.95 (978-0-940666-04-7). Includes accounts about lesser-known New Mexico Territory desperadoes and pioneers based on period newspaper stories and interviews. (Rev: BL 12/1/91) [978.9]

9389 Dary, David. *Cowboy Culture* (10–12). 1989, Avon paper $14.95 (978-0-7006-0390-9). A 500-year history of the American cowboy. [973]

9390 Dary, David. *The Oregon Trail: An American Saga* (8–12). 2004, Knopf $35.00 (978-0-375-41399-5). A sweeping and very readable history of the Oregon Trail, from its early-19th-century origins through a period of obscurity to its present importance. (Rev: BL 10/15/04) [978]

9391 Flood, Elizabeth Clair, and William Mannis. *Cowgirls: Women of the Wild West* (10–12). 2000, Zon International $45.00 (978-0-939549-18-4). Covering the years 1880 to 1950, this is a lively pictorial history of a rare breed of woman, the American cowgirl. (Rev: BL 6/1–15/00) [978]

9392 Hirschfelder, Arlene B. *Photo Odyssey: Solomon Cavalho's Remarkable Western Adventure, 1853-54* (6–

10). 2000, Clarion $18.00 (978-0-395-89123-0). The story of the last westward journey of John C. Fremont as seen through the eyes of a painter/photographer who was a member of the expedition. (Rev: BCCB 9/00; BL 7/00; HBG 9/00; SLJ 8/00*; VOYA 12/00) [917.8]

9393 Holt, Marilyn Irvin. *Children of the Western Plains: The Nineteenth-Century Experience* (10–12). Series: American Childhoods. 2003, Ivan R. Dee $26.00 (978-1-56663-540-0). Life on the prairie is portrayed through well-researched narrative and the use of period correspondence, diaries, and memoirs. (Rev: BL 10/15/03) [978]

9394 Isserman, Maurice. *Exploring North America, 1800-1900* (6–12). Series: Discovery and Exploration. 2005, Facts on File $40.00 (978-0-8160-5263-9). Clear text and primary sources explain the 19th-century explorations of North America by John Fremont, John Wesley Powell, and others, and put them in historical and social context. (Rev: SLJ 8/05) [973]

9395 Katz, William L. *Black Pioneers: An Untold Story* (7–12). 1999, Simon & Schuster $17.00 (978-0-689-81410-5). The stories of the many determined African Americans who defied prejudice, slavery, and severe legal restrictions such as the Northwest Territory's "Black Laws" to make a new life for themselves in the frontier of pre-Civil War days. (Rev: BL 7/99; HB 7–8/99; HBG 9/99; SLJ 9/99; VOYA 8/99) [977]

9396 Luchetti, Cathy. *Children of the West: Frontier Family Life* (10–12). 2001, Norton $39.95 (978-0-393-04913-8). Using more than 100 photographs plus excerpts from letters, diaries, and other sources, the author re-creates child bearing, child rearing, and childhood in frontier America. (Rev: BL 6/1–15/01) [978]

9397 McEvoy, Anne. *The American West* (6–12). Series: Costume and Fashion Source Books. 2009, Chelsea House $35 (978-1-60413-382-0). This volume looks at the attire of men and women of various different walks of life in the American West, covering explorers, settlers, Native Americans, soldiers, cowboys, and outlaws and lawmen. (Rev: LMC 11–12/09; SLJ 10/09) [391]

9398 McKain, Mark, ed. *Pioneers* (10–12). Series: History Firsthand. 2002, Gale LB $36.20 (978-0-7377-1078-6); paper $24.95 (978-0-7377-1077-9). Original documents cover topics ranging from journey preparations to claiming land to battling nature to create homes and farms in the West. (Rev: BL 12/15/02) [978]

9399 McNeese, Tim. *The Donner Party: A Doomed Journey* (8–10). Series: Milestones in American History. 2009, Chelsea House $35 (978-1-60413-025-6). The author does not shy away from describing exactly what happened to the Donner Party on its trek to California, and places the events in historical context, aiding in understanding of the journey. (Rev: SLJ 8/09) [979.4]

9400 Peavy, Linda, and Ursula Smith. *Frontier Children* (6–12). 1999, Univ. of Oklahoma $24.95 (978-0-8061-

3161-0). This richly illustrated volume full of excerpts from primary sources looks at the lives of children on America's frontier during the 19th century. (Rev: BL 10/1/99; VOYA 12/00) [978]

9401 Peavy, Linda, and Ursula Smith. *Pioneer Women: The Lives of Women on the Frontier* (9–12). 1996, Smithmark paper $24.95 (978-0-8061-3054-5). First-hand accounts and stark black-and-white photographs bring to life the social and physical challenges facing women pioneers in the American West. [305.4]

9402 Peters, Arthur K. *Seven Trails West* (10–12). 1996, Abbeville $39.95 (978-1-55859-782-2). This well-researched work traces the expansion of the American continent from 1804 to 1869 through the development of seven important trails, including the Santa Fe Trail, the Oregon-California Trail, the Pony Express, the Transcontinental Telegraph, and the Transcontinental Railroad, and the trail taken by Lewis and Clark's expedition. (Rev: BL 6/1–15/96; SLJ 12/96) [978]

9403 Rau, Margaret. *The Mail Must Go Through: The Story of the Pony Express* (7–10). Series: America's Moving Frontier. 2005, Morgan Reynolds LB $26.95 (978-1-931798-63-1). A lively account of the exciting — but brief — history of the Pony Express. (Rev: BL 6/1–15/05; SLJ 10/05) [383]

9404 Reinfeld, Fred. *Pony Express* (7–12). 1973, Univ. of Nebraska paper $11.95 (978-0-8032-5786-3). A history of the communication system that linked the East and West and the courageous riders who manned it. [383]

9405 Richards, Colin. *Sheriff Pat Garrett's Last Days* (8–12). 1986, Sunstone paper $8.95 (978-0-86534-079-4). A history of the Wild West drawn into focus by the death of the man who shot Billy the Kid. [978]

9406 Savage, William W. *The Cowboy Hero: His Image in American History and Culture* (10–12). 1987, Univ. of Oklahoma paper $19.95 (978-0-8061-1920-5). A history of the American cowboy with material on how he has been portrayed in the media. [973]

9407 Slatta, Richard W. *Cowboy: The Illustrated History* (9–12). 2006, Sterling $24.95 (978-1-4027-1800-7). Photographs of modern and historic cowboys, plus lots on the lore surrounding these sometimes lone and rugged figures. (Rev: BL 9/1/06) [978]

9408 Stratton, Joanne L. *Pioneer Women: Voices from the Kansas Frontier* (10–12). 1981, Simon & Schuster paper $12.95 (978-0-671-44748-9). This book is based on first-person accounts of almost 800 pioneer women who lived in Kansas between 1854 and 1890. [978.1]

9409 Torr, James D., ed. *The American Frontier* (7–12). Series: Turning Points in World History. 2001, Greenhaven LB $24.95 (978-0-7377-0785-4); paper $37.45 (978-0-7377-0786-1). A collection of essays that explores the opening up of the West, the nature of the pioneer spirit, and the changes this development brought to our history. (Rev: BL 3/15/02) [973.7]

9410 Tunis, Edwin. *Frontier Living* (7–12). 1976, Crowell paper $18.95 (978-1-58574-137-3). Using more than 200 original drawings and a fine text, the author portrays the life, artifacts, and customs of the American frontier. [978]

RECONSTRUCTION TO WORLD WAR I
(1865–1914)

9411 Baker, Julie. *The Bread and Roses Strike of 1912* (6–10). 2007, Morgan Reynolds LB $27.95 (978-1-59935-044-8). Tells the story of the largest textile labor strike in American history, which occurred in Massachusetts in 1912, with profiles of union leaders, photographs of suffering families, and details of the employees' (including children) horrific living and working conditions. (Rev: BL 5/15/07; SLJ 7/07)

9412 Currie, Stephen. *We Have Marched Together: The Working Children's Crusade* (7–12). Series: People's History. 1996, Lerner LB $30.35 (978-0-8225-1733-7). The focus of this book is on child labor in the United States and the protest march from Philadelphia to New York led by Mother Jones in 1903. (Rev: BL 5/1/97; SLJ 7/97) [331.3]

9413 Dudley, William, ed. *Reconstruction* (9–12). Series: At Issue in History. 2003, Gale LB $33.70 (978-0-7377-1356-5); paper $23.70 (978-0-7377-1357-2). Presents the debates that took place over how reconstruction of the infrastructure and institutions of the South should proceed after the Civil War. (Rev: SLJ 1/04) [973]

9414 Ferrell, Claudine L. *Reconstruction* (5–10). Series: Greenwood Guides to Historic Events, 1500-1900. 2003, Greenwood $51.95 (978-0-313-32062-0). Covers key individuals involved in Reconstruction and the speeches, proclamations, and other primary documents that cast light on the events of the time. (Rev: SLJ 6/04) [973.8]

9415 Gourley, Catherine. *Good Girl Work: Factories, Sweatshops, and How Women Changed Their Role in the American Workforce* (7–10). 1999, Millbrook LB $26.90 (978-0-7613-0951-2). This history of the exploitation of female children around the turn of the 20th century includes dramatic, in-depth personal testimonies and first-person accounts from letters, diaries, memoirs, and newspaper interviews. (Rev: BL 5/1/99; SLJ 8/99) [331.3]

9416 Greenwood, Janette Thomas. *The Gilded Age: A History in Documents* (6–12). 2000, Oxford LB $39.95 (978-0-19-510523-0). Documents of all kinds are used to show readers the many changes that took place in American society in the last years of the 19th century. (Rev: BL 10/1/00; HBG 3/01; SLJ 10/00) [973.8]

9417 Haskins, Jim. *Geography of Hope: Black Exodus from the South After Reconstruction* (7–12). 1999, Twenty-First Century LB $31.90 (978-0-7613-0323-7). After information on slavery and the Reconstruction, the author describes the migrations of African Americans to the North, their leaders, and the politics that made life in the South intolerable. (Rev: BL 10/15/99; HBG 4/00; SLJ 11/99; VOYA 6/00) [973]

9418 Marrin, Albert. *Flesh and Blood So Cheap: The Triangle Fire and Its Legacy* (7–10). Illus. 2011, Knopf $19.99 (978-0-375-86889-4). This is a compelling account of the 1911 fire in which 146 workers died, documenting the horrible working conditions in the factory, the fact that the victims were mostly poor Jewish and Italian immigrants, and the fire's legacy in improving workplace safety regulations — in the United States if not around the world. ☊ ℮ (Rev: BL 4/1/11; LMC 10/11*; SLJ 5/11*) [974.7]

9419 Marsico, Katie. *The Triangle Shirtwaist Factory Fire: Its Legacy of Labor Rights* (7–12). Series: Perspectives On. 2009, Marshall Cavendish LB $27.95 (978-0-7614-4027-7). With direct quotations and historical background, this volume offers different perspectives on the 1911 disaster and its causes and consequences. (Rev: LMC 3–4/10; SLJ 2/10) [974.7]

9420 Roosevelt, Theodore. *The Rough Riders* (10–12). 1990, Da Capo paper $16.00 (978-0-306-80405-2). This is a history of the cavalry that fought under the command of Theodore Roosevelt during the Spanish-American War. [973.8]

9421 Ruggiero, Adriane. *American Voices from Reconstruction* (8–11). Series: American Voices. 2006, Marshall Cavendish LB $25.95 (978-0-7614-2168-9). This volume effectively uses primary sources — newspaper accounts, speeches, letters and diary entries, songs, and so forth — to tell the story of Reconstruction, presenting the points of view of key politicians as well as former slaves and slave owners. (Rev: BL 2/1/07) [973.8]

WORLD WAR I

9422 Barnes, Harper. *Never Been a Time: The 1917 Race Riot That Sparked the Civil Rights Movement* (10–12). 2008, Walker $25.99 (978-080271575-3). In this exploration of the 1917 race riots in East St. Louis, IL, a lesser-known event that precipitated the civil rights movement, Barnes provides a strong narrative set atop richly illustrated historical context. ℮ (Rev: BL 7/08; SLJ 8/08) [977.3]

9423 Bausum, Ann. *Unraveling Freedom: The Battle for Democracy on the Home Front During World War I* (8–11). 2010, National Geographic $19.95 (978-1-4263-0702-7); LB $34 (978-1-4263-0703-4). Bausum provides a riveting overview of life in the United States from the sinking of the *Lusitania* to the end of the war, covering the public outrage, the restrictions imposed on free speech and German Americans, the spying, and so forth. (Rev: BL 12/15/10*; SLJ 12/1/10*) [940.3]

BETWEEN THE WARS AND THE GREAT DEPRESSION (1918–1941)

9424 Abdul-Jabbar, Kareem, and Raymond Obstfeld. *On the Shoulders of Giants: My Journey through the Harlem Renaissance* (10–12). 2007, Simon & Schuster $26.00 (978-1-4165-3488-4). Harlem, basketball, jazz, writing — Abdul-Jabbar shares his passion for all of these and the debt he owes to the artists, intellectuals, and athletes of the Harlem Renaissance. ⌒ (Rev: BL 2/1/07) [796.323092]

9425 Bloom, Harold, ed. *The Harlem Renaissance* (9–12). Series: Bloom's Period Studies. 2003, Chelsea House $45.00 (978-0-7910-7679-8). This is a fine history of the Harlem Renaissance, the literary themes explored, and how the phenomenon changed modern African American literature. [810.9]

9426 Blumenthal, Karen. *Six Days in October: The Stock Market Crash of 1929* (7–12). 2002, Simon & Schuster $17.95 (978-0-689-84276-4). An absorbing look at the factors that led to the infamous crash and the fortunes that were lost, with clear definitions of economic concepts and interesting illustrations. (Rev: BL 11/1/02; HB 1–2/03; HBG 3/03; SLJ 10/02; VOYA 12/02) [332.64]

9427 Bragg, Rick. *Ava's Man* (7–12). 2001, Knopf $25.00 (978-0-375-41062-8). Bragg paints a loving portrait of his maternal grandfather, Charlie Bundrum, a simple backwoods man who, with his wife Ava, struggled to raise seven children to adulthood during the lean years of the Great Depression. (Rev: BL 6/1–15/01*; VOYA 4/02) [975]

9428 Brown, Lois. *Encyclopedia of the Harlem Literary Renaissance: The Essential Guide to the Lives and Works of the Harlem Renaissance Writers* (9–12). 2005, Facts on File $65.00 (978-0-8160-4967-7). More than 800 alphabetically arranged entries cover writers and their works, events, educational and other institutions, awards and prizes, and so forth. (Rev: BL 2/15/06; SLJ 2/06) [700]

9429 Burg, David F. *The Great Depression: An Eyewitness History* (9–12). 1996, Facts on File $75.00 (978-0-8160-3095-8). Primary sources help the reader understand what it was like to live during the Great Depression. (Rev: BL 12/15/95; VOYA 4/96) [973.91]

9430 Callan, Jim. *America in the 1930s* (7–10). Series: Decades of American History. 2005, Facts on File $35.00 (978-0-8160-5638-5). Excellent information — especially for report writers — is hampered by poor design. (Rev: BL 1/1–15/06) [973.917]

9431 Cohen, Robert, ed. *Dear Mrs. Roosevelt: Letters from Children of the Great Depression* (9–12). 2002, Univ. of North Carolina paper $20.95 (978-0-8078-

5413-6). Letters written during the Depression reveal the wide-ranging needs of children living in poverty and fear. (Rev: BL 10/15/02) [973.917]

9432 Egan, Timothy. *The Worst Hard Time: The Untold Story of Those Who Survived the Great American Dust Bowl* (10–12). 2006, Houghton Mifflin $28.00 (978-0-618-34697-4). The human toll of the dust storms that ravaged the southern Great Plains in the mid-1930s is brought into vivid focus. (Rev: BL 12/15/05) [978]

9433 Galbraith, John Kenneth. *The Great Crash, 1929* (10–12). 1988, Houghton Mifflin paper $14.00 (978-0-395-85999-5). The economist traces the causes of the stock market crash of 1929 and speculates about the possibility of another one. [338.5]

9434 Geary, Rick. *The Lindbergh Child* (10–12). Illus. Series: Treasury of XXth Century Murder. 2008, NBM $15.95 (978-156163529-0). Well-written and researched, this graphic-novel presentation describes in detail the Lindbergh baby's kidnapping, the ensuing media circus, and the trial and execution of the suspected killer. (Rev: BL 9/1/08; LMC 3–4/09; SLJ 11/08) [921]

9435 Hill, Jeff. *Prohibition* (9–12). Series: Defining Moments. 2005, Omnigraphics $49.00 (978-0-7808-0768-6). A detailed analysis of the years of Prohibition, with a collection of primary sources that shed further light on this period. (Rev: BL 5/1/05; SLJ 10/05) [363.4]

9436 Hintz, Martin. *Farewell, John Barleycorn: Prohibition in the United States* (6–10). Series: People's History. 1996, Lerner LB $25.26 (978-0-8225-1734-4). A well-organized, readable account that traces the history of alcohol use in the United States, covers the 18th Amendment and its effects, and ends with repeal of Prohibition. (Rev: BL 8/96; SLJ 10/96) [363.4]

9437 Kalish, Mildred Armstrong. *Little Heathens: Hard Times and High Spirits on an Iowa Farm during the Great Depression* (10–12). 2007, Bantam $22.00 (978-0-553-80495-9). Readers of this memoir will learn about life on an Iowa farm during the Great Depression — a time of simpler pleasures and tougher chores. ⌒ (Rev: BL 5/1/07) [977.7]

9438 McElvaine, Robert S. *The Great Depression: America, 1929–1941* (10–12). 1984, Times paper $16.00 (978-0-8129-2327-8). This account begins with the presidency of Herbert Hoover and ends with the coming of World War II. [973.91]

9439 Shogan, Robert. *Backlash: The Killing of the New Deal* (10–12). 2006, Ivan R. Dee $26.95 (978-1-56663-674-2). The author examines Roosevelt's standoff with the Supreme Court and Congress after the New Deal was dismantled during the president's second term. (Rev: BL 8/06) [973.917]

9440 Streissguth, Thomas, ed. *The Roaring Twenties: An Eyewitness History* (10–12). 2001, Facts on File $75.00 (978-0-8160-4023-0). A collection of eyewitness accounts that covers the 1920s under such topics as Prohibition, scandals, women's suffrage, prosperity, and the stock market crash of 1929. (Rev: VOYA 2/02) [973.91]

9441 Swisher, Clarice. *Women of the Roaring Twenties* (6–10). Series: Women in History. 2005, Gale LB $22.96 (978-1-59017-363-3). Using primary sources, this readable volume looks at life for women from diverse backgrounds during the turbulent 1920s. (Rev: BL 2/15/06) [305.4]

9442 Watkins, T. H. *The Hungry Years: A Narrative History of the Great Depression in America* (10–12). 1999, Henry Holt paper $17.00 (978-0-8050-6506-0). This book explores the Great Depression through a series of firsthand reports. (Rev: BL 9/15/99) [973.91]

9443 Wintz, Cary D. *Harlem Speaks: A Living History of the Harlem Renaissance* (9–12). 2007, Sourcebooks $29.95 (978-1-4022-0436-4). This lengthy volume introduces the key characters of the Harlem Renaissance in profiles organized by category (literature, music, art, politics) and provides a companion CD with primary audio sources. (Rev: BL 2/1/07; SLJ 11/06) [810.9]

WORLD WAR II

9444 Brinkley, Douglas, ed. *The World War II Memorial: A Grateful Nation Remembers* (8–12). 2004, Smithsonian $39.95 (978-1-58834-210-2). Published in conjunction with the dedication of the World War II Memorial in Washington, D.C., this striking coffee table book is loaded with photos and remembrances of the war and its lasting impact on America. (Rev: BL 9/1/04) [940.54]

9445 Cooper, Michael L. *Fighting for Honor: Japanese Americans and World War II* (6–12). 2000, Clarion $18.00 (978-0-395-91375-8). The experiences of Japanese Americans who were sent to internment camps or faced anti-Asian attacks in their communities are well-documented here. (Rev: BCCB 2/01; BL 1/1–15/01; HB 3–4/01; HBG 10/01; SLJ 3/01) [940.53]

9446 Hillstrom, Laurie Collier. *The Attack on Pearl Harbor* (7–12). Series: Defining Moments. 2009, Omnigraphics $49 (978-0-7808-1069-3). Readers learn why the Japanese attack on Pearl Harbor triggered the U.S. entry into the Second World War; primary documents and biographical information on key figures are included. (Rev: SLJ 8/09; VOYA 10/09) [940.5426]

9447 Homan, Lynn M., and Thomas Reilly. *Black Knights: The Story of the Tuskegee Airmen* (10–12). 2001, Pelican $24.00 (978-1-56554-828-2). This is the story of the social experiment that happened between 1941 and 1948 involving the African American unit known as the Tuskegee Airmen, eventually leading to the desegregation of the armed services. (Rev: BL 2/15/01) [940.5]

9448 Houston, Jeanne Wakatsuki, and James D. Houston. *Farewell to Manzanar* (9–12). 1983, Bantam pa-

per $5.99 (978-0-553-27258-1). The story of the three years that Jeanne Houston, a Japanese American, and her family spent at the Manzanar internment camp during World War II. [940.54]

9449 Moye, J. Todd. *Freedom Flyers: The Airmen of Tuskegee in World War II* (10–12). 2010, Oxford $24.95 (978-019538655-4). Working from more than 800 interviews recorded for the National Park Service's Tuskegee Airmen Oral History Project, the author uses the African American pilots' own words to pen a compelling history of how they battled the enemy abroad and racism at home. (Rev: BL 2/1–15/10) [940.54]

9450 Renner, Elmer, and Kenneth Birks. *Sea of Sharks: A Sailor's World War II Shipwreck Survival Story* (9–12). 2004, Naval Institute $29.95 (978-1-59114-714-5). In this gripping World War II survival story, Renner tells how he and three crewmates survived the sinking of an American minesweeper in the Pacific. (Rev: BL 10/15/04) [940.54]

9451 Schneider, Dorothy, and Carl J. Schneider. *World War II: An Eyewitness History* (9–12). Series: Facts on File Library of American History. 2003, Facts on File $80.00 (978-0-8160-4484-9). Firsthand accounts — letters, speeches, and quotations — illustrate civilian and military life for Americans before and during World War II; maps, profiles of key individuals, and excerpts from significant documents are included. (Rev: SLJ 2/04) [940.53]

9452 Sheinkin, Steve. *Bomb: The Race to Build — and Steal — the World's Most Dangerous Weapon* (5–10). 2012, Roaring Brook/Flash Point $19.99 (978-1-59643-487-5). A compelling account of the race to build the atom bomb, full of espionage, heroism, and eccentric but brilliant characters. Robert F. Sibert Informational Book Award; Newbery Honor Book; Notable Children's Book; YALSA Award for Excellence in Nonfiction for Young Adults. ☊ ℮ Lexile 920L (Rev: BL 9/1/12; HB 11–12/12; SLJ 10/12*; VOYA 10/12) [623.4]

9453 Ward, Geoffrey C., and Ken Burns. *The War: An Intimate History, 1941–1945* (9–12). 2007, Knopf $50.00 (978-0-307-26283-7). The memoirs of nearly 50 Americans, both civilian and military, are presented featuring residents of four hometowns — Sacramento, California; Mobile, Alabama; Luverne, Minnesota; and Watertown, Connecticut — from 1941 to 1945 and is a companion book to PBS's documentary by Burns. (Rev: BL 8/07) [940.53]

POST WORLD WAR II UNITED STATES
(1945–)

9454 Aretha, David. *Freedom Summer* (7–12). Series: The Civil Rights Movement. 2007, Morgan Reynolds LB $27.95 (978-1-59935-059-2). The summer of 1964, when white college students traveled to Mississippi to help blacks register to vote, is the focus of this volume in the Civil Rights Movement series. (Rev: BL 2/1/08; SLJ 3/08) [323.1196]

9455 Beals, Melba Pattillo. *Warriors Don't Cry: A Searing Memoir of the Battle to Integrate Little Rock's Central High* (10–12). 1995, Washington Square $14.00 (978-0-671-86639-6). The author was one of nine African American teenagers chosen to integrate the Little Rock high school in 1957. YALSA Amazing Audiobooks for Young Adults Top Ten 2013. ∩ [323]

9456 Bernstein, Carl, and Bob Woodward. *All the President's Men* (10–12). 1999, Simon & Schuster paper $14.00 (978-0-671-89441-2). The story behind the Watergate scandal that led to Richard Nixon's resignation. [973.924]

9457 Bowers, Rick. *Spies of Mississippi: The True Story of the State-Run Spy Network That Tried to Destroy the Civil Rights Movement* (7–10). 2010, National Geographic LB $26.96 (978-1-4263-0596-2). The alarming story of a spy network established in Mississippi in the mid-1950s to support segregation and work against civil rights. ∩ ℮ (Rev: BL 2/1/10*; HB 3–4/10; LMC 3–4/10; SLJ 2/10) [323.1196]

9458 Ching, Juliet. *The Assassination of Robert F. Kennedy* (6–10). Series: The Library of Political Assassinations. 2002, Rosen LB $27.95 (978-0-8239-3545-1). In addition to discussing the assassination and the events preceding it, the author looks at the rumors of a conspiracy and allegations of incompetence on the part of the Los Angeles police force. (Rev: BL 8/02; SLJ 8/02) [976]

9459 Daniel, Pete. *Lost Revolutions: The South in the 1950s* (10–12). 2000, Univ. of North Carolina $60.00 (978-0-8078-2537-2); paper $25.00 (978-0-8078-4848-7). This portrait of the southern states after World War II contains material on their changing culture, the resistance to integration, the growth of religious fundamentalism, and the evolution of popular music. (Rev: BL 4/1/00) [975.043]

9460 Draper, Allison Stark. *The Assassination of Malcolm X* (6–10). Series: The Library of Political Assassinations. 2002, Rosen LB $27.95 (978-0-8239-3542-0). A description of the assassination and its aftermath is followed by information on Malcolm X's life and beliefs. (Rev: BL 2/15/02; SLJ 7/02) [976.2]

9461 Epstein, Dan. *The 80s: The Decade of Plenty* (7–10). Series: Twentieth Century Pop Culture. 2000, Chelsea LB $22.95 (978-0-7910-6088-9). A mix of popular entertainment and fashion with key news events, all arranged chronologically and accompanied by lots of color photographs. Other books in the series include *The 50s: America Tunes In* and *The 60s: A Decade of Change: The Flintstones to Woodstock.* (Rev: SLJ 6/01) [973.9]

9462 Farber, David, et al. *The Columbia Guide to America in the 1960s* (10–12). 2001, Columbia $80.50

(978-0-231-11372-4). After an excellent overview of the 1960s, this book contains a section on key political, social, and cultural issues and an A-to-Z glossary of people and organizations. (Rev: BL 8/01) [973.923]

9463 Fitzgerald, Brian. *McCarthyism: The Red Scare* (7–12). Series: Snapshots in History. 2006, Compass Point LB $31.93 (978-0-7565-2007-6). This is a clear account of the period of anti-Communism in the United States stirred up by Senator Joseph McCarthy, including the impact on the lives of individuals around the country plus quotations from the Army-McCarthy hearings. (Rev: SLJ 2/07)

9464 Heineman, Kenneth J. *Put Your Bodies Upon the Wheels: Student Revolt in the 1960s* (10–12). Series: American Way. 2001, Ivan R. Dee $26.00 (978-1-56663-351-2). This is a detailed history of the campus-based counterculture of the 1960s and the young people who participated. (Rev: BL 3/1/01) [378.1]

9465 Hill, Laban Carrick. *America Dreaming: How Youth Changed America in the Sixties* (9–12). 2007, Little, Brown $19.99 (978-0-316-00904-1). After introducing American society after World War II, Hill shows the impact teens had on life in the 1960s, using quotations, illustrations, and excerpts from songs and poetry. (Rev: LMC 3/08; SLJ 12/07) [303.48]

9466 MacPherson, Malcolm. *Roberts Ridge: A Story of Courage and Sacrifice on Takur Ghar Mountain, Afghanistan* (11–12). 2005, Delacorte $25.00 (978-0-553-80363-1). The gripping story of Navy SEALs' valiant — and ultimately unsuccessful — attempt to rescue one of their own who was left behind on an Afghani mountaintop; for mature teens. (Rev: BL 9/15/05) [958.104]

9467 Mara, Wil. *Civil Unrest in the 1960s: Riots and Their Aftermath* (8–12). Series: Perspectives On. 2009, Marshall Cavendish LB $27.95 (978-0-7614-4025-3). With excerpts from primary sources and many pertinent sidebars and images, this is a useful survey of the causes, key events, and significance of the civil unrest of the 1960s. (Rev: LMC 3–4/10; SLJ 2/10) [303.6]

9468 Maus, Derek C., ed. *Living Through the Red Scare* (8–12). Series: Living Through the Cold War. 2005, Gale LB $32.45 (978-0-7377-2615-2). This fascinating collection of readings revisits the fear of communism that was rampant in the United States at the beginning of the Cold War. (Rev: SLJ 6/06)

9469 Maus, Derek C., ed. *Living Under the Threat of Nuclear War* (7–10). Series: Living Through the Cold War. 2005, Gale LB $33.70 (978-0-7377-2130-0). This title examines how Americans coped with the ever-present threat of nuclear war during the half-century-long Cold War. (Rev: SLJ 10/05) [973]

9470 Miles, Barry. *Hippie* (11–12). 2004, Sterling $24.95 (978-1-4027-1442-9). For mature readers, this large-format photoessay captures the cultural upheaval of the 1960s. (Rev: BL 8/04) [305.568]

9471 O'Neil, Doris C., ed. *Life: The '60s* (9–12). 1989, Little, Brown $35.00 (978-0-8212-1752-8). An illustrated introduction to the 1960s through 250 photographs and connecting text. (Rev: BL 12/15/89) [973.92]

9472 Pekar, Harvey, and Gary Dumm. *Students for a Democratic Society: A Graphic History* (9–12). 2008, Hill & Wang $22.00 (978-0-8090-9539-1). The story of the 1960s activist organization is told in graphic novel format, with the first section covering the group's history and the second containing stories of individual chapters. (Rev: BL 12/15/07; SLJ 1/08) [973.92]

9473 Roleff, Tamara L., ed. *The Oklahoma City Bombing* (9–12). Series: History Firsthand. 2004, Gale LB $36.20 (978-0-7377-1658-0). Court documents, speeches, letters, and eyewitness accounts tell the story of the bombing from the planning stage through the trial, execution, and building of a memorial. (Rev: SLJ 11/04) [364.16]

9474 Scheibach, Michael. *Atomic Narratives and American Youth: Coming of Age with the Atom, 1945-1955* (10–12). 2003, McFarland paper $35.00 (978-0-7864-1566-3). The varied ways in which government, media, educators, and parents informed young people about the advent and implications of the atom bomb are the focus of this intriguing study. (Rev: BL 9/15/03) [305.235]

9475 Schou, Nicholas. *Orange Sunshine: The Brotherhood of Eternal Love and Its Quest to Spread Peace, Love, and Acid to the World* (11–12). Illus. 2010, St. Martin's $24.99 (978-031255183-4). An in-depth look at a 1960s counterculture group that encouraged the use of LSD and other drugs, considered Timothy Leary a prophet, and eventually devolved into a criminal organization, with interviews of surviving members of the group; for mature readers. (Rev: BL 2/1–15/10) [973]

9476 Schwartz, Richard Alan. *The 1950s* (9–12). Series: Eyewitness History. 2003, Facts on File $80.00 (978-0-8160-4597-6). Each year of the 1950s is described, with coverage of important social, cultural, and political developments. [973.921]

9477 Tracy, Kathleen. *The McCarthy Era* (7–10). Series: Monumental Milestones. 2009, Mitchell Lane LB $29.95 (978-1-58415-694-9). Historic and political factors pertaining to McCarthy's persecution of innocent Americans are the focus of this interesting and informative book. (Rev: SLJ 6/1/09) [973.91]

9478 *Turbulent Years: The 60s* (9–12). Series: Our American Century. 1998, Time-Life $19.99 (978-0-7835-5503-4). Using photographs from *Time* and *Life* magazines, this is a chronicle of the 1960s, including coverage of the Vietnam War, the civil rights movement, the space race, the counterculture, music, sports, and the arts. (Rev: SLJ 5/99) [973.9]

9479 Watson, Bruce. *Freedom Summer: The Savage Season That Made Mississippi Burn and Made America a Democracy* (10–12). 2010, Viking $27.95 (978-

067002170-3). Watson blends the story of the violence of the summer of 1964 with first-person accounts by those who were there, who include Sidney Poitier, Pete Seeger, Stokely Carmichael, and numerous volunteer students. ⌒ ℮ (Rev: BL 5/1–15/10) [323.1196]

9480 Wicker, Tom. *Shooting Star: The Brief Arc of Joe McCarthy* (10–12). 2006, Harcourt $22.00 (978-0-15-101082-0). A very readable and enlightening look back at the McCarthy era of the early 1950s and the Communist witch hunt started by the junior senator from Wisconsin. (Rev: BL 2/15/06) [973.921]

KOREAN, VIETNAM, AND GULF WARS

9481 Al-Windawi, Thura. *Thura's Diary: My Life in Wartime Iraq* (6–12). 2004, Viking $15.99 (978-0-670-05886-0). This diary was kept by a 19-year-old girl in Baghdad from the first bombings to the first days of the occupation by American forces. (Rev: BL 5/15/04; HB 7–8/04; SLJ 7/04) [956]

9482 Atkinson, Rick. *In the Company of Soldiers: A Chronicle of Combat* (10–12). 2004, Henry Holt $25.00 (978-0-8050-7561-8). This account covers two months in the spring of 2003 when the author accompanied U.S. combat units in Iraq. (Rev: SLJ 6/04) [956.7]

9483 Berry, F. Clifton, and Dennis Steele. *United States Army at War: 9/11 Through Iraq* (10–12). 2003, Naval Institute $34.95 (978-1-59114-063-4). From the immediate aftermath of 9/11 through the downfall of the Taliban in Afghanistan and the beginning of the occupation of Iraq, this is the story of the part played by the U.S. Army. (Rev: BL 2/1/04) [973.931]

9484 Boettcher, Thomas D. *Vietnam: The Valor and the Sorrow* (9–12). 1985, Little, Brown paper $21.95 (978-0-316-10081-6). An excellent popular history of the Vietnam War with many black-and-white photographs. (Rev: BL 7/85) [959.73]

9485 Burrows, Larry. *Vietnam* (10–12). 2002, Knopf $50.00 (978-0-375-41102-1). The many faces of the Vietnam War are revisited in this collection of *Life* photographer Burrows's stunning work between 1962 and 1971, when the helicopter on which he was traveling disappeared. (Rev: BL 10/15/02) [959.704]

9486 Caputo, Philip. *10,000 Days of Thunder: A History of the Vietnam War* (7–10). 2005, Simon & Schuster $22.95 (978-0-689-86231-1). In this sweeping overview of the Vietnam War, Caputo traces the fractured country's history from the beginnings of resistance to French colonial rule to the fall of Saigon and also assesses the conflict's enduring impact on Americans. (Rev: BL 10/1/05; SLJ 11/05*; VOYA 10/05) [959.704]

9487 Edelman, Bernard, ed. *Dear America: Letters Home from Vietnam* (9–12). 2002, Norton paper $15.95 (978-0-393-32304-7). This anthology consists of 208 letters, poems, clippings, and diary entries written by

American servicemen in Vietnam. This volume was first published in 1985. [949.704]

9488 FitzGerald, Frances. *Fire in the Lake: The Vietnamese and the Americans in Vietnam* (10–12). 1972, Little, Brown paper $16.95 (978-0-316-15919-7). This work deals with the effects that the American intervention had on Vietnamese social and cultural life. [959.704]

9489 Friedman, Norman. *Desert Victory: The War for Kuwait* (9–12). 1991, Naval Institute $46.95 (978-1-55750-254-4). This book published by the Naval Institute concludes that U.S. strategy in the Persian Gulf War was largely successful but that U.S. intelligence failed to accurately gauge the strength and morale of Iraqi forces. (Rev: BL 10/15/91) [956.704]

9490 Galt, Margot Fortunato. *Stop This War! American Protest of the Conflict in Vietnam* (8–12). Series: People's History. 2000, Lerner LB $26.60 (978-0-8225-1740-5). The author cites her husband, a conscientious objector, among those who protested the war from the early 1960s until its end, and details key events and student and other groups. (Rev: BL 7/00; HBG 9/00; SLJ 8/00) [959.704]

9491 Granfield, Linda. *I Remember Korea: Veterans Tell Their Stories of the Korean War, 1950-53* (6–12). 2003, Clarion $16.00 (978-0-618-17740-0). First-person accounts by American combatants that reveal a wide variety of experiences are accompanied by brief introductory notes, photographs, and a short account of the war itself. (Rev: BCCB 2/04; BL 12/15/03; HBG 4/04; SLJ 2/04) [951.904]

9492 Hastings, Max. *The Korean War* (9–12). 1988, Simon & Schuster paper $15.00 (978-0-671-66834-1). A readable, objective account of the war both in Korea and on the home front. (Rev: BL 10/15/87) [951.8]

9493 Kallen, Stuart A., ed. *Sixties Counterculture* (10–12). Series: History Firsthand. 2001, Greenhaven paper $24.95 (978-0-7377-0406-8). The rise of the so-called counterculture is documented in the writings of some of the period's most prominent figures, including Abbie Hoffman, John Lennon, Malcolm X, and Betty Friedan. (Rev: BL 2/15/01; SLJ 4/01) [973.923]

9494 Kutler, Stanley I. *Encyclopedia of the Vietnam War* (10–12). 1996, Scribner $135.00 (978-0-13-276932-7). This exhaustive examination of the Vietnam War contains more than 550 original articles about the country's history and every aspect of the war. [959.704]

9495 Lansford, Tom, ed. *The War in Iraq* (9–12). Series: Global Viewpoints. 2009, Gale/Greenhaven $36.20 (978-0-7377-4162-9); paper $24.95 (978-0-7377-4163-6). Essays reprinted from a variety of news media provide two opposing viewpoints on the contentious causes of the Iraq War. (Rev: BL 10/15/09; SLJ 10/09) [956.7044]

9496 McCloud, Bill. *What Should We Tell Our Children About Vietnam?* (7–12). 1989, Univ. of Oklahoma paper $16.95 (978-0-8061-3240-2). More than 120 individuals, including the first President Bush and Gary Trudeau, tell what they think young people should know about the war. (Rev: BL 9/15/89) [959.704]

9497 Mills, Randy, and Roxanne Mills. *Unexpected Journey: A Marine Corps Reserve Company in the Korean War* (10–12). 2000, Naval Institute $32.95 (978-1-55750-546-0). This is the story of 240 men, a reserve company of U.S. Marines from Evansville, Indiana, and their fighting record during the Korean War in 1951. (Rev: BL 10/1/00) [951.904]

9498 Pendergast, Tom. *The Vietnam War* (7–10). Series: Defining Moments. 2006, Omnigraphics LB $44.00 (978-0-7808-0954-3). Ten years of the conflict's history are covered in detail and copious background information is provided to help report writers. (Rev: BL 3/15/07) [959.704]

9499 Reich, Dale. *Rockets Like Rain: A Year in Vietnam* (10–12). 2001, Oasis paper $15.95 (978-1-55571-615-8). A readable, profoundly personal account of a native of a tiny Wisconsin town who spent a harrowing year in the army in Vietnam. (Rev: BL 11/15/01) [959.704]

9500 Richie, Jason. *Iraq and the Fall of Saddam Hussein. Rev. ed.* (8–10). 2004, Oliver LB $24.95 (978-1-881508-63-2). This account traces the story of the invasion of Iraq and ends with the capture of Saddam Hussein in December 2003. (Rev: BL 5/1/04; HBG 4/04; SLJ 1/04) [956.7]

9501 Roleff, Tamara L., ed. *The Vietnam War* (10–12). Series: History Firsthand. 2002, Gale LB $36.20 (978-0-7377-0887-5); paper $21.20 (978-0-7377-0886-8). First-person accounts, narratives, and remembrances are used to explore various aspects of the Vietnam War. (Rev: BL 4/15/02) [959.704]

9502 Santoli, Al. *Everything We Had* (10–12). 1982, Ballantine paper $6.99 (978-0-345-32279-1). Interviews with 33 veterans of the Vietnam War on the war and its impact on their lives. (Rev: BL 9/15/89) [959.704]

9503 Sauro, Christy. *The Twins Platoon: An Epic Story of Young Marines at War in Vietnam* (11–12). 2006, Zenith $24.95 (978-0-7603-2387-8). This powerful book follows 150 men from Minnesota on their tours of duty in Vietnam, from basic training to their unwelcome return to the States. (Rev: BL 4/15/06) [959.704]

9504 Stokesbury, James L. *A Short History of the Korean War* (10–12). 1988, Morrow paper $12.00 (978-0-688-09513-0). Solid scholarship and clear writing characterize this fine history of the Korean War and its aftermath. [951.9]

9505 Terry, Wallace, ed. *Bloods: An Oral History of the Vietnam War by Black Veterans* (10–12). 1985, Ballantine paper $6.99 (978-0-345-31197-9). This volume consists of 20 narratives that reveal the experiences and contributions of African American servicemen in the Vietnam War. [959.704]

9506 Van Devanter, Lynda, and Joan A. Furey, eds. *Visions of War, Dreams of Peace: Writings of Women in the Vietnam War* (9–12). 1991, Warner paper $9.95 (978-0-446-39251-8). Recollections of women who served in the Vietnam War. (Rev: BL 5/15/91) [811]

9507 Williams, William Appleman, et al. *America in Vietnam: A Documentary History* (10–12). 1985, Anchor paper $15.95 (978-0-393-30555-5). Original essays and other sources trace America's involvement in Asia and the progress of the Vietnam War from 1963 through 1975. [959.704]

Regions

MIDWEST

9508 Brown, Daniel James. *Under a Flaming Sky: The Great Hinckley Firestorm of 1894* (9–12). 2006, Lyons $22.95 (978-1-59228-863-2). This is the compelling true story of a deadly forest fire in 1894 that claimed the lives of more than 400 Minnesota residents. (Rev: BL 4/15/06*) [977.6]

9509 Dennis, Jerry. *The Living Great Lakes: Exploring North America's Inland Seas* (10–12). 2003, St. Martin's $25.95 (978-0-312-25193-2). In a riveting account that will appeal to ecology-minded teens as well as outdoors lovers, the author talks about his explorations of the Great Lakes and looks at their history. (Rev: BL 2/15/03) [977]

MOUNTAIN AND PLAINS STATES

9510 Forsberg, Michael, et al. *Great Plains: America's Lingering Wild* (10–12). Illus. 2009, Univ. of Chicago $45 (978-022625725-9). With stunning photographs, this sweeping look at the vast and varied area known as the Great Plains juxtaposes the harmony the Native peoples shared with the land and the devastation inflicted by those who later settled there, also describing contemporary efforts to restore the land to its previous grandeur. (Rev: BL 10/15/09) [917.80022]

NORTHEASTERN AND MID-ATLANTIC STATES

9511 Aaseng, Nathan. *The White House* (7–10). Series: Building History. 2000, Lucent LB $32.45 (978-1-56006-708-5). The history of this Washington landmark is given plus material on the presidents and architects who shaped this building through the years. (Rev: BL 9/15/00) [975.3]

9512 Allen, Thomas B. *The Washington Monument: It Stands for All* (8–12). 2000, Discovery $29.95 (978-1-56331-921-1). Full of photographs and drawings plus an interesting text that supplies good background material, this is a handsome guide to one of the capital's most famous landmarks. (Rev: BL 6/1–15/00) [975.3]

9513 Attie, Alice. *Harlem on the Verge* (8–12). 2003, Quantuck Lane $35.00 (978-0-9714548-7-3). After an introductory essay, this book consists of unforgettable color photographs that depict life in Manhattan's Harlem and Spanish Harlem. (Rev: BL 2/15/04*) [974.7]

9514 Berlin, Ira, and Leslie M. Harris, eds. *Slavery in New York* (10–12). 2005, New Press paper $22.50 (978-1-56584-997-6). The little-known history of slavery in New York City is chronicled in this collection of essays by historians specializing in slavery and African American history. (Rev: BL 10/15/05) [974.7]

9515 Bigler, Philip. *Washington in Focus: The Photo History of the Nation's Capital* (9–12). 1988, Vandamere paper $8.95 (978-0-918339-07-2). A history in pictures and text of Washington, D.C., from its beginnings to the building of the Metro and the Vietnam Memorial. (Rev: BL 12/15/88) [975.3]

9516 Conway, Lorie. *Forgotten Ellis Island: The Extraordinary Story of America's Immigrant Hospital* (7–12). Photos by Chris Barnes. 2007, Smithsonian $26.95 (978-0-06-124196-3). The story of the construction and use of the Ellis Island hospital facilities is enhanced by archival photographs and many quotations from doctors and immigrants. (Rev: SLJ 10/07) [362.1109747]

9517 Dunwell, Frances F. *The Hudson: America's River* (9–12). 2008, Columbia Univ. $74.50 (978-0-231-13640-2); paper $29.95 (978-0-231-13641-9). The story of the rise and fall of the Hudson River — and its increasing importance as environmental activists fight to rescue, restore, and protect it. (Rev: BL 4/1/08) [974.7]

9518 Greenlaw, Linda. *The Lobster Chronicles: Life on a Very Small Island* (10–12). 2002, Hyperion $22.95 (978-0-7868-6677-9). Personal anecdotes are interwoven throughout this entertaining snapshot of the Maine lobstering business. (Rev: BL 6/1–15/02) [818]

9519 Korman, Marvin. *In My Father's Bakery: A Bronx Memoir* (10–12). 2003, Red Rock $22.00 (978-0-9714372-4-1). The Bronx of the 1930s and 1940s is brought to life through Korman's memories of growing up in a Jewish family there. (Rev: BL 10/15/03) [974.7]

9520 Locker, Thomas. *In Blue Mountains: An Artist's Return to America's First Wilderness* (6–12). 2000, Bell Pond $18.00 (978-0-88010-471-5). This picture book is a tribute to nature, chronicling the author-artist's return to Kaaterskill Cove in New York State to find inspiration. (Rev: BL 7/00; SLJ 11/00) [974.7]

9521 Myers, Walter Dean. *Harlem* (6–12). 1997, Scholastic paper $16.95 (978-0-590-54340-8). This book is an impressionistic appreciation of Harlem and its culture as seen through the eyes of author Walter Dean Myers and his artist son, Christopher. (Rev: BL 2/15/97; SLJ 2/97; VOYA 10/97) [811]

9522 Rock, Howard B., and Deborah Moore. *Cityscapes: A History of New York in Images* (8–12). 2001, Columbia $80.50 (978-0-231-10624-5). Using fine prints and photographs, this account traces the evolution of Manhattan from a Dutch settlement to the great modern city of massive towers that it is today. (Rev: BL 12/1/01) [974.7]

9523 Traver, Tim. *Sippewissett; or, Life on a Salt Marsh* (10–12). 2006, Chelsea Green $27.50 (978-1-933392-14-1). Traver combines the natural history of the Sippewissett salt marsh in Cape Cod with his own memoirs of spending childhood days there, along with the history of the acclaimed Woods Hole Oceanographic Institute located nearby. (Rev: BL 10/1/06) [508.74]

9524 Weinberg, Jeshajahu, and Rina Elieli Weinberg. *The Holocaust Museum in Washington* (9–12). 1995, Rizzoli $45.00 (978-0-8478-1906-5). Insights are given into the design, plan, and construction of the museum and its exhibits. (Rev: BL 1/1–15/96; SLJ 3/96) [975.3]

PACIFIC STATES

9525 Blessing, Marlene, ed. *A Road of Her Own: Women's Journeys in the West* (10–12). 2002, Fulcrum $24.95 (978-1-55591-307-6). Women's experiences — both physical and spiritual — exploring the American West are the focus of this collection of essays celebrating freedom. (Rev: BL 11/1/02) [917.804]

9526 Bowermaster, Jon. *Aleutian Adventure* (6–12). 2001, National Geographic $17.95 (978-0-7922-7999-0). Beautifully illustrated, this book chronicles a harrowing but ultimately successful kayak expedition among the rugged islands of the Aleutian chain. (Rev: VOYA 8/01) [797.1]

9527 Bruder, Gerry. *Heroes of the Horizon: Flying Adventures of Alaska's Legendary Bush Pilots* (9–12). 1991, Alaska Northwest paper $14.95 (978-0-88240-363-2). Reveals the feats of the last generation of frontier pilots to fly open planes to uncharted Alaskan settlements. (Rev: BL 10/1/91) [629.13]

9528 Krakauer, Jon. *Into the Wild* (9–12). 1996, Villard $22.00 (978-0-679-42850-3). A true story expanded from Krakauer's article about a young man who starved to death in Denali National Park in Alaska. (Rev: BL 12/1/95*) [917.9]

9529 Maharidge, Dale. *Yosemite: A Landscape of Life* (9–12). 1990, Yosemite paper $14.95 (978-0-939666-56-0). An insightful look at the inner workings of the national park. (Rev: BL 1/15/91) [979.4]

9530 Ruth, Maria Mudd. *The Pacific Coast* (7–12). Series: Ecosystems of North America. 2000, Benchmark LB $28.50 (978-0-7614-0935-9). A detailed look at the tides, plants, animals, and ecosystems found along the Pacific Coast from Alaska south to Mexico. (Rev: HBG 3/01; SLJ 4/01) [577.5]

9531 Ryan, Alan, ed. *The Reader's Companion to Alaska* (10–12). 1997, Harcourt paper $17.00 (978-0-15-600368-1). A compilation of writings, many of them first-person accounts, about impressions of Alaska, arranged geographically. (Rev: SLJ 1/98) [979.8]

9532 Salisbury, Gay, and Laney Salisbury. *The Cruelest Miles: The Heroic Story of Dogs and Men in a Race Against an Epidemic* (10–12). 2003, Norton $24.95 (978-0-393-01962-9). A detailed and compelling account of the challenges facing the dogs and humans who undertook the 700-mile expedition to deliver serum to Nome in 1925. (Rev: BL 5/1/03; SLJ 12/03) [614.5]

9533 Ulin, David L., ed. *Writing Los Angeles: A Literary Anthology* (10–12). 2002, Library of America $40.00 (978-1-931082-27-3). The many faces of Los Angeles are brought to life in this anthology of fiction and nonfiction by such diverse writers as F. Scott Fitzgerald, H. L. Mencken, Tom Wolfe, Helen Hunt Jackson, and Truman Capote. (Rev: BL 9/15/02) [810.8]

9534 Walker, Spike, ed. *Alaska: Tales of Adventure from the Last Frontier* (10–12). 2002, St. Martin's paper $14.95 (978-0-312-27562-4). This collection of 31 stories from such well-known writers as Jack London, John Muir, Washington Irving, and Gary Paulsen paints a colorful portrait of life in Alaska, past and present. (Rev: BL 1/1–15/02) [979.8]

SOUTH

9535 Ayers, Harvard, and Jenny Hager, eds. *An Appalachian Tragedy: Air Pollution and Tree Death in the Eastern Forests of North America* (10–12). 1998, Sierra Club $45.00 (978-0-87156-976-9). Forest ecology is highlighted in this beautifully illustrated account of the effects of 40 years of pollution on the Appalachian Mountains. (Rev: SLJ 12/98) [976.1]

9536 Cerulean, Susan, ed. *The Book of the Everglades* (10–12). 2002, Milkweed paper $18.95 (978-1-57131-260-0). Experts assess the threats to the Everglades' biodiversity. (Rev: BL 8/02) [508.75]

SOUTHWEST

9537 Fishbein, Seymour L. *Yellowstone Country: The Enduring Wonder* (9–12). 1989, National Geographic LB $12.95 (978-0-87044-718-1). A profile of the world's oldest national park with particularly good coverage of its flora and fauna. (Rev: BL 11/1/89; SLJ 1/90) [917.87]

9538 Lavender, David. *The Southwest* (10–12). 1984, Univ. of New Mexico paper $19.95 (978-0-8263-0736-1). The history of the entire Southwest is given, with emphasis on New Mexico and Arizona. [979.1]

9539 McCarry, Charles. *The Great Southwest* (7–12). 1980, National Geographic LB $12.95 (978-0-87044-288-9). In pictures and text, descriptions are given of such states as New Mexico, Colorado, and Arizona. [979.1]

9540 Melzer, Richard. *When We Were Young in the West: True Histories of Childhood* (10–12). 2003, Sunstone paper $22.95 (978-0-86534-338-2). This unique history of New Mexico from the viewpoint of children draws on first-person accounts and oral histories to bring alive such memorable events as pioneering wagon train travel and school desegregation. (Rev: BL 6/1–15/03) [978.9]

9541 Pyne, Stephen J. *How the Canyon Became Grand: A Short History* (10–12). 1998, Viking paper $15.00 (978-0-14-028056-2). The Grand Canyon languished in obscurity until the 19th century, when John Wesley Powell sang its praises, spurring its elevation to the national attraction it is today. (Rev: BL 8/98) [979.1]

Philosophy and Religion

Philosophy

9542 Adler, Mortimer J. *How to Think About the Great Ideas from the Great Books of Western Civilization* (10–12). 2000, Open Court paper $24.95 (978-0-8126-9412-3). Basic philosophical questions involving such subjects as evolution, art, law, government, good and evil, and war and peace are introduced in this book that is useful for beginning group discussions. (Rev: BL 5/1/00) [081]

9543 Blackburn, Simon. *Think: A Compelling Introduction to Philosophy* (10–12). 1999, Oxford $27.95 (978-0-19-210024-5). This introduction to philosophy explores questions relating to knowledge, free will, mind, and goodness. (Rev: BL 10/1/99) [100]

9544 Boorstin, Daniel J. *The Seekers: The Story of Man's Continuing Quest to Understand His World* (10–12). 1998, Random House paper $15.00 (978-0-375-70475-8). Historian Boorstin examines the ongoing human search for the meaning and purpose of existence, covering in detail some of the more widely accepted theories put forward by history's great thinkers in both the secular and religious worlds. (Rev: BL 8/98; SLJ 5/99) [909]

9545 Durant, William James. *The Story of Philosophy: The Lives and Opinions of the Great Philosophers. 2nd ed.* (10–12). 1933, Simon & Schuster paper $15.00 (978-0-671-20159-3). A basic history of philosophy

and key thoughts from the ancient Greeks to Dewey. [109]

9546 Holbrook, Kate, et al, ed. *Global Values 101: A Short Course* (10–12). 2006, Beacon paper $14.00 (978-0-8070-0305-3). The interviews in this volume — all originally conducted as part of a Harvard seminar on "Personal Choice and Global Transformation" — explore what individuals can do to help make the world a better place to live. (Rev: BL 1/1–15/06) [170]

9547 Pirsig, Robert M. *Zen and the Art of Motorcycle Maintenance: An Inquiry into Values* (10–12). 1974, HarperCollins $26.00 (978-0-688-00230-5). A number of philosophical musings are presented, all prompted by a motorcycle trip with Pirsig's young son. [191.092]

9548 Russell, Bertrand. *A History of Western Philosophy: And Its Connection with Political and Social Circumstances from the Earliest Times to the Present Day* (10–12). 1945, Simon & Schuster paper $24.00 (978-0-671-20158-6). The author of this overview has stated that his purpose is to show that philosophy is an integral part of everyone's social and political life. [109]

9549 Solomon, Robert C., and Kathleen Marie Higgins. *A Short History of Philosophy* (10–12). 1996, Oxford paper $39.95 (978-0-19-510196-6). This ambitious historical survey of philosophy examines the evolution of human thinking about life's central questions. [109]

World Religions and Holidays

General and Miscellaneous

9550 Aaseng, Rolf E. *A Beginner's Guide to Studying the Bible* (9–12). 1991, Augsburg paper $12.99 (978-0-8066-2571-3). Outlines basic techniques and resources for enriching Bible study. (Rev: BL 4/1/92) [220.07]

9551 Berthrong, John H., and E. Nagai-Berthrong. *Confucianism: A Short Introduction* (10–12). 2000, Oneworld paper $15.95 (978-1-85168-236-2). This work describes the history of Confucianism, its principles, and its impact, particularly on Chinese life. [299]

9552 Braude, Ann. *Women and American Religion* (8–12). Series: Religion in America. 2000, Oxford LB $32.95 (978-0-19-510676-3). Beginning with Native American and Puritan women and continuing to the present, this account traces the many contributions women have made to religion in America. (Rev: BL 3/15/00; HBG 3/01; SLJ 5/00) [200]

9553 Breuilly, Elizabeth. *Religions of the World: The Illustrated Guide to Origins, Beliefs, Traditions and Festivals* (7–12). 1997, Facts on File $29.95 (978-0-8160-3723-0). This well-illustrated work defines religion generally, discusses each of the world's major religions, points out similarities, and links each religion to current events and international politics. (Rev: BL 10/1/97; HBG 3/98; SLJ 2/98) [291]

9554 Cotner, June, ed. *Teen Sunshine Reflections: Words for the Heart and Soul* (6–12). 2002, HarperCollins $15.95 (978-0-06-000525-2); paper $9.95 (978-0-06-000527-6). This anthology of poems and quotations that celebrate spiritual beliefs and appreciation of the world about us includes the works of the well-known (such as Saint Francis, Gandhi, and Anne Frank) and the unknown. (Rev: BL 7/02; HBG 10/02; SLJ 8/02; VOYA 8/02) [082]

9555 Eckel, Malcolm David. *Buddhism* (9–12). Series: Understanding Religions. 2010, Rosen LB $31.95 (978-1-4358-5619-6). Eckels explores the origins, beliefs, scriptures, key figures, festivals, and rituals of Buddhism in this bright and appealing volume. (Rev: LMC 1–2/10)

9556 Engh, Mary Jane. *In the Name of Heaven: 3,000 Years of Religious Persecution* (9–12). 2006, Prometheus $25.00 (978-1-59102-454-5). Examples of religious persecution throughout history are presented in succinct reader-friendly chapters. (Rev: BL 10/1/06) [291]

9557 Ford-Grabowsky, Mary, ed. *Sacred Voices: Essential Women's Wisdom Through the Ages* (10–12). 2002, HarperSanFrancisco $25.95 (978-0-06-251702-9). This impressive anthology documents women's spiritual thinking with selections from such diverse figures as ancient Egypt's Hashepsowe, 8th-century poet Rabia Al-Adawiyya, Sojourner Truth, Emily Dickinson, and Louise Erdrich. (Rev: BL 3/1/02) [200]

9558 Fuller, Cheri, and Ron Luce. *When Teens Pray: Powerful Stories of How God Works* (9–12). 2002, Multnomah paper $9.99 (978-1-57673-970-9). The power of prayer in the lives of young people is explored in this collection of stories, most of which are related by the teens who lived them. (Rev: BL 7/02) [291.4]

9559 Gaskins, Pearl Fuyo. *I Believe In . . .: Christian, Jewish, and Muslim Young People Speak About Their Faiths* (7–10). 2004, Cricket $18.95 (978-0-8126-2713-8). Suitable for browsing, this is a collection of interviews with about 100 young adults from diverse religious backgrounds in the Chicago area. (Rev: BCCB 9/04; BL 10/1/04; HB 7–8/04) [200]

9560 Hartz, Paula. *Baha'i Faith* (6–10). Series: World Religions. 2002, Facts on File $30.00 (978-0-8160-4729-1). A look at the history and beliefs of the Baha'i

Faith and its spread from Persia to the rest of the world. (Rev: HBG 3/03; SLJ 12/02) [297.9]

9561 Head, Tom, ed. *Religion and Education* (9–12). Series: At Issue: Religion. 2005, Gale LB $29.95 (978-0-7377-2743-2); paper $21.20 (978-0-7377-2744-9). Thought-provoking essays and articles explore various aspects of the interplay between religion and education in America, including school prayer and the teaching of evolution. (Rev: BL 10/1/05) [379.2]

9562 Ikeda, Daisaku. *The Way of Youth* (6–12). 2000, Middleway paper $14.95 (978-0-9674697-0-6). The great questions of human behavior — such as the nature of love, friendship, and compassion — are discussed from a Buddhist perspective. (Rev: BL 12/1/00) [294.3]

9563 Lugira, Aloysius. *African Religion* (7–10). Series: World Religions. 1999, Facts on File $30.00 (978-0-8160-3876-3). The author gives a fine overview of the major religious beliefs of the different ethnic groups in Africa plus material on organized religion, witchcraft, and the influence of Western religions on the area. (Rev: BL 1/1–15/00; HBG 4/00; SLJ 1/00) [299]

9564 Mann, Gruinder Singh. *Buddhists, Hindus, and Sikhs in America* (6–12). Series: Religion in American Life. 2002, Oxford $32.95 (978-0-19-512442-2). Photographs, anecdotes, and excerpts from primary sources add appeal to this survey of how three major religions have affected, and been affected by, life in America. (Rev: BL 1/1–15/02; HBG 10/02; SLJ 1/02; VOYA 4/02) [294]

9565 Martin, Joel W. *Native American Religion* (7–12). 1999, Oxford LB $32.95 (978-0-19-511035-7). An overview of historical and contemporary Native American religious beliefs and practices, their importance in daily life, and the conflicts introduced by the Europeans. (Rev: HBG 4/00; SLJ 9/99; VOYA 10/99) [299]

9566 Mayer, Marianna. *Remembering the Prophets of Sacred Scripture* (6–10). 2003, Penguin $16.99 (978-0-8034-2727-3). Old Testament prophets — from Daniel and Moses to Amos and Obadiah — are introduced in this handsome picture book for older readers. (Rev: BL 7/03; SLJ 8/03) [224]

9567 Metcalf, Franz. *Buddha in Your Backpack: Everyday Buddhism for Teens* (7–12). 2002, Ulysses paper $12.95 (978-1-56975-321-7). This humorous and informative guide will satisfy young adults' interest in the spiritual world of Buddhism. (Rev: BL 1/1–15/03; SLJ 2/03; VOYA 2/04) [294.3]

9568 Murphy, Claire Rudolf. *Daughters of the Desert: Stories of Remarkable Women from Christian, Jewish, and Muslim Traditions* (7–10). 2003, SkyLight Paths $19.95 (978-1-893361-72-0). Five authors contributed to these 18 stories, based on the Bible and Koran, of the lives of women including Eve, Esther, Mary Magdalene, Sarah, and Khadiji, the wife of Mohammed. (Rev: BL 10/15/03) [220.9]

9569 Shachtman, Tom. *Rumspringa: To Be or Not to Be Amish* (9–12). 2006, North Point $25 (978-0-86547-687-5). Children of the Old Order Amish are reared with limited freedoms and shielded from worldly ways, but when they reach the age of about 16, they are given rumspringa, the freedom to partake in activities regarded as taboo — drinking, sexual exploration, driving cars — and even live apart from the community for a period after which they make a decision to commit to Amish ways and are baptized and accepted. (Rev: BL 4/1/06; SLJ 8/06)

9570 Stein, Stephen J. *Alternative American Religions* (8–12). Series: Religion in American Life. 2000, Oxford LB $32.95 (978-0-19-511196-5). From Puritan dissenters to cults like Heaven's Gate, this is a look at the alternative religions that have attracted followers in the Americas. (Rev: HBG 9/00; SLJ 4/00; VOYA 12/00) [291.9]

9571 Sweeney, Jon M., ed. *God Within: Our Spiritual Future — As Told by Today's New Adults* (8–12). 2001, SkyLight Paths paper $14.95 (978-1-893361-15-7). Writers in their teens and 20s, who reflect a wide variety of beliefs, present very personal essays on their faiths and their paths to spirituality. (Rev: BL 1/1–15/02) [200]

9572 Taylor, Rodney L. *Confucianism* (9–12). Series: Religions of the World. 2004, Chelsea House LB $35.00 (978-0-7910-7857-0). As well as covering the history and beliefs of Confucianism, this volume looks at the traditions still being practiced today. (Rev: SLJ 9/04) [299]

9573 Tutu, Desmond M., and Mpho A. Tutu. *Made for Goodness: And Why This Makes All the Difference* (10–12). 2010, HarperOne $25.99 (978-006170659-2). Tutu and his daughter, also a minister, address the importance of forgiveness by examining many difficult episodes in South African history, with a special focus on the role of young people. ℮ (Rev: BL 3/1–15/10) [170]

9574 Viswanathan, Ed. *Am I a Hindu?* (9–12). 1992, Halo Books paper $15.95 (978-1-879904-06-4). A comprehensive introduction to Hinduism written in "catechism" form, with questions and answers grouped according to topic. (Rev: BL 10/15/92) [294.5]

9575 Wade, Nicholas. *The Faith Instinct: How Religion Evolved and Why It Endures* (11–12). 2009, Penguin $25.95 (978-159420228-5). In this theoretical exploration of the evolution of religion, the author draws on hard biological evidence, hypothesizing that human civilization is naturally predisposed towards faith. (Rev: BL 11/15/09) [201]

9576 Ward, Elaine. *Old Testament Women* (5–10). Series: Art Revelations. 2004, Enchanted Lion $18.95 (978-1-59270-011-0). Paintings by masters accompany stories about 18 women including Rachel, Ruth, and Bathsheba. (Rev: SLJ 8/04) [224]

9577 Williams, George. *Shinto* (11–12). Series: Religions of the World. 2004, Chelsea House LB $35.00 (978-0-7910-8097-9); paper $15.95 (978-0-7910-8355-0). In this title from the Religions of the World series, author George Williams introduces readers to the history, beliefs, and practices of Shinto, the indigenous religion of Japan. (Rev: SLJ 4/05)

9578 Winston, Diana. *Wide Awake: A Buddhist Guide for Teens* (6–10). 2003, Putnam paper $14.95 (978-0-399-52897-2). In a conversational style, the author introduces the tenets of Buddhism, explains her own beliefs and how she arrived at them, and looks at ways teens can apply Buddhist teachings to their own experiences. (Rev: BL 10/1/03) [294]

Christianity

9579 Bushman, Claudia L., and Richard L. Bushman. *Mormons in America* (10–12). Series: Religion in American Life. 1998, Oxford $32.95 (978-0-19-510677-0). A historical survey of the Church of Jesus Christ of Latter-Day Saints, illustrated with black-and-white photographs. (Rev: BL 10/1/98; HBG 3/99) [289.3]

9580 Carroll, Vincent, and David Shiflett. *Christianity on Trial: The Arguments Against Anti-Religious Bigotry* (10–12). 2001, Encounter paper $14.95 (978-1-893554-15-3). The author looks at all the criticisms aimed at Christianity, such as encouraging slavery, inaction during the Holocaust, hindering science, etc., and tries to refute them. (Rev: BL 10/15/01) [239]

9581 *Christmas in Greece* (5–10). Series: Christmas Around the World. 2000, World Book $19.00 (978-0-7166-0859-2). This account focuses on the religious practices of the Greek Orthodox Church at Christmastime, which begins with a long fasting period. (Rev: BL 9/1/00) [398.2]

9582 Connolly, Sean. *New Testament Miracles* (5–10). Series: Art Revelations. 2004, Enchanted Lion $18.95 (978-1-59270-012-7). Presents brief retellings of 12 miracles performed by Jesus Christ, each illustrated by a well-known painting by an eminent artist, such as Rembrandt, El Greco, and Tintoretto. (Rev: SLJ 8/04) [226.7]

9583 Griffin, Justin. *The Holy Grail: The Legend, the History, the Evidence* (10–12). 2001, McFarland paper $29.95 (978-0-7864-0999-0). Approaching this material as a historian, the author explores theories on the identity of the grail. (Rev: BL 10/1/01) [398]

9584 Kung, Hans. *The Catholic Church: A Short History* (10–12). Trans. by John Bowden. Series: Modern Library Chronicles. 2001, Random House $19.95 (978-0-679-60492-1). As well as presenting an interesting history of the Roman Catholic Church, this account views the church today and recommends democratic reforms. (Rev: BL 4/1/01) [282]

9585 Mornin, Edward, and Lorna Mornin. *Saints: A Visual Guide* (9–12). 2006, Eerdmans paper $20.00 (978-0-8028-3249-8). A useful guide to the saints one may come across in churches, museums, and art. Each entry includes a picture of a representation of the saint and brief information about what the saint is known for. (Rev: BL 4/15/06) [235.2]

9586 Moyers, Bill. *Welcome to Doomsday* (10–12). 2006, New York Review paper $7.95 (978-1-59017-209-4). Moyers provides a critique of the Christian Right's notion of salvation on "doomsday" and how this can be used to justify ignoring issues such as global warming, war, and natural disasters. (Rev: BL 9/15/06) [304.2]

9587 Noll, Mark. *Protestants in America* (7–12). Series: Religion in America. 2000, Oxford $32.95 (978-0-19-511034-0). From the arrival of the Puritans to today, this is a well-organized overview of Protestantism and how it has evolved, changed, and splintered in America. (Rev: BL 10/1/00; HBG 3/01; SLJ 2/01) [280]

9588 Sweeney, Douglas A. *The American Evangelical Story: A History of the Movement* (10–12). 2005, Baker Academic paper $17.99 (978-1-80102-658-1). A readable, informative history of the evangelical movement in America. (Rev: BL 8/05) [277.3]

9589 Wernecke, Herbert H. *Christmas Customs Around the World* (9–12). 1959, Westminster paper $19.95 (978-0-664-24258-9). Using a geographical arrangement, the author describes unusual Christmas traditions around the world. [394.2]

9590 Wills, Garry. *Head and Heart: American Christianities* (10–12). 2007, Penguin $25.95 (978-1-59420-146-2). Wills provides a sweeping survey of Christian beliefs and practice in the United States from the time of the Puritans, distinguishing between reason (head) and passion (heart). (Rev: BL 9/1/07) [277.3]

9591 Zoba, Wendy Murray. *The Beliefnet Guide to Evangelical Christianity* (10–12). 2005, Doubleday paper $9.95 (978-0-385-51452-1). An interesting overview of the essential elements of evangelical Christianity and the major sects existing today and in history. (Rev: BL 5/15/05) [270.8]

Islam

9592 Alkouatli, Chris. *Islam* (9–12). Series: World Religions. 2006, Marshall Cavendish LB $27.95 (978-0-7614-2120-7). The history behind this religion and how it is practiced around the world — with information about Islam in the United States — all presented in a pleasing format. (Rev: BL 2/15/07; SLJ 3/07) [297]

9593 Armstrong, Karen. *Islam: A Short History* (10–12). 2000, Random House $19.95 (978-0-679-64040-0). In addition to presenting a gripping history of this important world religion, the author probes many of its beliefs, including attitudes toward politics. (Rev: BL 8/00*) [297]

9594 Calvert, John. *Islamism: A Documentary and Reference Guide* (10–12). 2007, Greenwood $85.00 (978-0-313-33856-4). Primary sources written by Islamist authors and short informative notes about these sources are included in this collection that contains documents written about jihad, family, women, revolution in Iran, and so forth. (Rev: BL 8/08; LMC 10/08) [320.5]

9595 Carr, Melissa S. *Who Are the Muslims? Where Muslims Live, and How They Are Governed* (9–12). Series: Introducing Islam. 2004, Mason Crest LB $22.95 (978-1-59084-701-5). A look at the widely diverse circumstances — geographic and cultural — in which Muslims live. (Rev: SLJ 10/04) [297]

9596 Egendorf, Laura K., ed. *Islam in America* (7–12). Series: At Issue. 2005, Gale LB $29.95 (978-0-7377-2727-2). Essays cover topics including discrimination against Muslims, the growing popularity of the religion among Hispanic Americans, and the degree of support of terrorism. (Rev: SLJ 2/06) [297]

9597 Esposito, John, ed. *The Oxford History of Islam* (10–12). 1999, Oxford $60.00 (978-0-19-510799-9). Leading scholars contribute material on the history of Islam, its laws, traditions, culture, differences, and contemporary thinking. [297]

9598 Gordon, Matthew S. *Islam. 3rd ed.* (7–10). 2006, Facts on File $30.00 (978-0-8160-6612-4). An overview of the history of Islam, its branches, the Koran, and Islam's place in the modern world. (Rev: SLJ 3/07) [297]

9599 Hafiz, Dilara, et al. *The American Muslim Teenager's Handbook* (7–12). Illus. 2009, Simon & Schuster paper $11.99 (978-141698578-5). Friendly tips for young Muslim Americans on how to stand up to stereotypes and how to discuss their faith are accompanied by facts about the religion that will be useful for all readers. Lexile 1260 (Rev: BL 4/1/09; LMC 10/09; SLJ 4/08) [297.5]

9600 Hassaballa, Hesham A., and Kabir Helminski. *The Beliefnet Guide to Islam* (9–12). Series: Beliefnet. 2006, Doubleday paper $9.95 (978-0-385-51454-5). An excellent overview of Islam, explaining the five pillars of faith and presenting the historical context necessary to a full understanding. (Rev: BL 2/15/06) [297]

9601 Hazleton, Lesley. *After the Prophet: The Epic Story of the Shia-Sunni Split in Islam* (10–12). 2009, Doubleday $27 (978-038552393-6). Carefully extracting events from history and the written word of Islam, Hazelton explains the anguish and upheaval that caused the Shia/Sunni divide that has continued for centuries. **e** (Rev: BL 9/09) [297.8]

9602 Hodges, Rick. *What Muslims Think and How They Live* (9–12). Series: Introducing Islam. 2004, Mason Crest LB $24.95 (978-1-59084-702-2). Muslim opinions on a wide range of topics are based on a Gallup poll. (Rev: SLJ 10/04) [297]

9603 Manji, Irshad. *The Trouble with Islam: A Muslim's Call for Reform in Her Faith* (10–12). 2004, St. Martin's $22.95 (978-0-312-32699-9). A Canadian Muslim woman questions the positions of her religion on such topics as sexism, anti-Semitism, and anti-intellectualism. (Rev: BL 1/1–15/04) [297]

9604 Parfrey, Adam, ed. *Extreme Islam: Anti-American Propaganda of Muslim Fundamentalism* (11–12). 2002, Feral House paper $16.00 (978-0-922915-78-1). Despite sloppy editing, this overview of the rise of anti-American rhetoric and violence offers valuable insights for mature teens. (Rev: BL 3/15/02) [297.09]

9605 Qazwini, Hassan. *American Crescent: A Muslim Cleric on the Power of His Faith, the Struggle against Prejudice, and the Future of Islam and America* (10–12). 2007, Random House $25.95 (978-1-4000-6454-0). Qazwini, an Iraqi who came to the United States in the early 1990s, offers insight into the Muslim faith and emphasizes the need for mutual understanding between Muslims and Americans. (Rev: BL 10/1/07) [297.8]

9606 Siddiqui, Haroon. *Being Muslim* (8–12). Series: Groundwork Guide. 2006, Groundwood $15.95 (978-0-88899-785-2). This is an objective introduction to the Muslim faith and to related topics of current interest including women's rights and terrorist elements. (Rev: BL 12/15/06; LMC 4–5/07; SLJ 2/07) [297]

9607 Whitehead, Kim. *Islamic Fundamentalism* (9–12). Series: Introducing Islam. 2004, Mason Crest LB $22.95 (978-1-59084-703-9). A look at the Islamic fundamentalism that arose in the 20th century, and the varying degrees of radicalism in such countries as Algeria, Indonesia, and Egypt. (Rev: SLJ 10/04) [297]

9608 Wormser, Richard. *American Islam: Growing Up Muslim in America* (7–12). 1994, Walker $16.85 (978-0-8027-8344-8). A portrait of Muslim American youth and their faith. (Rev: BL 12/15/94; SLJ 3/95; VOYA 2/95) [297]

important observances of a lifetime, Jewish rituals are explained. [296.4]

Judaism

9609 Canfield, Jack, et al. *Chicken Soup for the Jewish Soul: Stories to Open the Heart and Rekindle the Spirit* (9–12). 2001, Health Communications $24.00 (978-1-55874-899-6); paper $14.95 (978-1-55874-898-9). A charming book that collects 86 stories that deal with life, being a Jew, love, kindness, the Holocaust, and wisdom. (Rev: BL 10/15/01) [296.7]

9610 Isaacs, Ron. *Ask the Rabbi: The Who, What, Where, Why, and How of Being Jewish* (7–12). 2003, Jossey-Bass paper $22.95 (978-0-7879-6784-0). Questions and answers are divided into thematic chapters and provide information on practices in different denominations. (Rev: BL 10/15/03) [296]

9611 Kushner, Lawrence. *Jewish Spirituality: A Brief Introduction for Christians* (10–12). 2001, Jewish Lights paper $12.95 (978-1-58023-150-3). The author explains the Jewish understanding of creation, the Torah, the commandments of God, and communion with God. (Rev: BL 10/1/01) [296]

9612 Robinson, George. *Essential Judaism: A Complete Guide to Beliefs, Customs and Rituals* (9–12). 2000, Pocket paper $18.00 (978-0-671-03481-8). An introductory account that explains the essentials of Judaism, its beliefs, practices, and customs. (Rev: BL 1/1–15/00) [296]

9613 Trepp, Leo. *The Complete Book of Jewish Observance* (9–12). 1980, Simon & Schuster $25.50 (978-0-671-47197-2). Working from a weekly schedule of the

Religious Cults

9614 Cohen, Daniel. *Cults* (7–10). 1994, Millbrook LB $23.40 (978-1-56294-324-0). This work describes cults throughout American history, including Pilgrims, Quakers, Moonies, and Satanists, and examines their recruiting methods. (Rev: BL 11/1/94; SLJ 2/95; VOYA 2/95) [291.9]

9615 Gaborro, Allen, ed. *Satanism* (9–12). Series: At Issue. 2006, Gale LB $28.70 (978-0-7377-2414-1); paper $19.95 (978-0-7377-2415-8). Eleven essays on Satanism written from different viewpoints are presented in this well-organized volume. (Rev: SLJ 6/07) [133.4]

9616 Guest, Tim. *My Life in Orange: Growing Up with the Guru* (11–12). 2005, Harcourt paper $14.00 (978-0-15-603106-6). British journalist Guest writes about a rootless childhood spent in various communes; for mature readers only. (Rev: BL 12/1/04) [299]

9617 Snow, Robert L. *Deadly Cults: The Crimes of the True Believers* (9–12). 2004, Praeger $62.95 (978-0-275-98052-8). Using sources such as magazines and newspapers, this is a fascinating look at cults and their leaders, including the charismatic Jim Jones and David Koresh. (Rev: BL 3/1/04) [209]

9618 Streissguth, Thomas. *Charismatic Cult Leaders* (7–12). 1995, Oliver LB $19.95 (978-1-881508-18-2). A balanced presentation of a potentially sensational topic. Includes biblical references where appropriate in the discussion of various cults and their leaders. (Rev: BL 8/95; SLJ 5/95) [291]

Society and the Individual

Government and Political Science

General and Miscellaneous

9619 Judson, Karen. *Religion and Government: Should They Mix?* (9–12). Series: Controversy! 2009, Marshall Cavendish $25.95 (978-0-7614-4235-6). A clear discussion of the principles of separation of church and state precedes examples of thinking and practice in American society and throughout the world. (Rev: BL 11/15/09; SLJ 12/09) [322]

9620 Laxer, James. *Democracy* (7–12). Series: Groundwork Guide. 2009, Groundwood $18.95 (978-088899912-2); paper $11.00 (978-088899913-9). Laxer discusses the history, present status, and future of democracy in this clearly written volume. (Rev: BL 7/09; VOYA 2/10) [321.8]

9621 Service, Robert. *Comrades! A History of World Communism* (11–12). 2007, Harvard $35.00 (978-0-674-02530-1). Advanced history students will appreciate this overarching survey of communism. (Rev: BL 4/15/07) [335.4]

United Nations and Other International Organizations

9622 Darraj, Susan Muaddi. *The Universal Declaration of Human Rights* (8–12). Illus. Series: Milestones in Modern World History. 2010, Chelsea House LB $35 (978-160413494-0). An accessible account of the creation of this important document, highlighting the role of Eleanor Roosevelt and introducing other key individuals, as well as the continuing relevance of these rights today. (Rev: BL 5/15/10) [341.4]

9623 Janello, Amy, and Brennon Jones, eds. *A Global Affair: An Inside Look at the United Nations* (9–12).

1995, Jones & Janello $35.00 (978-0-9646322-0-2). A celebration in essay form of the political and humanitarian work of the United Nations. (Rev: BL 9/15/95) [341.23]

9624 Meisler, Stanley. *United Nations: The First Fifty Years* (10–12). 1997, Atlantic Monthly paper $15.00 (978-0-87113-656-5). A look at the successes and failures, the key players, and the organization of this international body, with particular emphasis on its humanitarian and peace-keeping efforts and its role in crises such as Suez and the Six-Day War. [341.23]

International Relations, Peace, and War

9625 Aronson, Marc, and Patty Campbell, eds. *War Is . . . : Soldiers, Survivors, and Storytellers Talk About War* (10–12). 2008, Candlewick $17.99 (978-076363625-8). Offering insight into combat, recruitment, training, and the lasting effects of war on veterans, Aronson and Campbell present a collection of stories, interviews, letters home, and essays stretching from World War II to the present day. (Rev: BL 11/1/08; LMC 3–4/09; SLJ 11/1/08; VOYA 2/09) [810.8]

9626 Barber, Benjamin, and Patrick Watson. *The Struggle for Democracy* (9–12). 1989, Little, Brown $29.95 (978-0-316-08058-3). An examination of the nature of democracy and its problems from the ancient Greeks to the present. (Rev: BL 10/1/89) [321.8]

9627 Bixler, Mark. *The Lost Boys of Sudan: An American Story of the Refugee Experience* (8–12). 2005, Univ. of Georgia $24.95 (978-0-8203-2499-9). Journalist Bixler tracks the progress of four young men — refugees who were part of the so-called Lost Boys of

Sudan — as they adjust to their new lives in America. (Rev: BL 2/1/05) [962.404]

9628 Bradbury, Adrian, and Eric Walters. *When Elephants Fight: The Lives of Children in Conflict in Afghanistan, Bosnia, Sri Lanka, Sudan and Uganda* (6–12). Illus. 2008, Orca $19.95 (978-155143900-6). Each of five chapters provides a haunting, unflinching glimpse into the experience of one child in war — whether as target, child soldier, or collateral damage. ℮ (Rev: BL 10/15/08; LMC 3–4/09; VOYA 4/09) [305.230]

9629 Dalton, David. *Refugees and Asylum Seekers* (7–10). Series: People on the Move. 2005, Heinemann LB $31.36 (978-1-4034-6961-8). A look at the plight of civilians who have been forced from their native lands by war or ethnic cleansing; a poor layout is offset by the personal stories. (Rev: BL 8/05; SLJ 12/05) [305.9]

9630 Davenport, John C., ed. *The American Empire* (9–12). Series: World in Focus. 2007, Chelsea House LB $35.00 (978-0-7910-9195-1). A collection of articles and essays that address the history of U.S. intervention and influence and look at America's present influence in the world through occupation and military force. (Rev: BL 11/1/07) [327.73]

9631 Dunson, Donald H. *Child, Victim, Soldier: The Loss of Innocence in Uganda* (8–12). Illus. 2008, Orbis paper $16.00 (978-157075799-0). The author, a Christian missionary in Uganda, describes the horrors of war and child abuse in that country. (Rev: BL 1/1–15/09) [261.8]

9632 Ellis, Deborah. *Children of War: Voices of Iraqi Refugees* (7–12). Illus. 2009, Groundwood $15.95 (978-088899907-8). Interviews with children who have fled Iraq bring to life the harsh realities of war. Lexile 860L (Rev: BL 3/1/09*; LMC 8–9/09; SLJ 4/1/09; VOYA 6/09) [305.23086]

9633 Ellis, Deborah. *Off to War: Voices of Soldiers' Children* (6–12). Illus. 2008, Groundwood $15.95 (978-088899894-1). Interviews with about 40 children of Canadian and American soldiers deployed in Afghanistan and Iraq reveal pride, anger, and frustration, and a desire for a "normal" life. (Rev: BL 10/15/08; HB 11–12/08; LMC 1–2/09; SLJ 10/1/08; VOYA 12/08) [303.6]

9634 Friedman, Lauri S., ed. *The Middle East* (9–12). Series: Introducing Issues with Opposing Viewpoints. 2007, Gale LB $32.45 (978-0-7377-3575-8). The articles in this collection address the problem of violence and unrest in the Middle East and how — or if — the United States should respond. (Rev: BL 11/1/07; SLJ 11/07) [956.04]

9635 Friedman, Lauri S., ed. *Torture* (7–10). Illus. Series: Introducing Issues with Opposing Viewpoints. 2011, Greenhaven LB $36.82 (978-073775203-8). Presents pro and con arguments on such topics as whether torture is ever justified, what constitutes torture, and what the U.S. position on torture should be. (Rev: BL 12/1/11) [364.6]

9636 Gerdes, Louise I., ed. *Rogue Nations* (6–12). Series: Opposing Viewpoints. 2006, Gale LB $34.95 (978-0-7377-3421-8). What is a "rogue" nation? Iran, North Korea, Pakistan, and the United States are among those mentioned in this provocative pro/con discussion. (Rev: SLJ 3/07) [355]

9637 Gioseffi, Daniela, ed. *Women on War: An International Anthology of Writings from Antiquity to the Present* (10–12). 2003, Feminist paper $19.95 (978-1-55861-409-3). The poems, essays, and eyewitness accounts in this anthology make a passionate case for an end to global violence. (Rev: BL 3/15/03*) [303.6]

9638 Gottfried, Ted. *The Fight for Peace: A History of Antiwar Movements in America* (8–11). Series: People's History. 2005, Twenty-First Century LB $29.90 (978-0-7613-2932-9). Chronicles the history of American protest movements from the Civil War to the present. (Rev: BL 10/1/05; SLJ 11/05) [303.6]

9639 Janeczko, Paul B. *The Dark Game: True Spy Stories* (6–10). 2010, Candlewick $16.99 (978-0-7636-2915-1). Famous spies from the Revolutionary War through the cold war are the focus of this volume that also looks at modern techniques including cryptology and at organizations like the CIA and FBI. (Rev: BL 9/15/10; LMC 11–12/10; SLJ 8/10; VOYA 10/10) [327.73]

9640 Junger, Sebastian. *Fire* (10–12). 2001, Norton $24.95 (978-0-393-01046-6). A collection of 10 essays about people facing life-threatening situations, from war crimes in Kosovo to the hostage crisis in Kashmir. (Rev: BL 9/1/01) [363.378]

9641 Keegan, John. *War and Our World* (10–12). 2001, Vintage paper $10.00 (978-0-375-70520-5). A review of the wars of the 20th century and a look at the underlying causes and actual results of warfare. (Rev: BL 5/15/01) [303.6]

9642 Landau, Elaine. *Big Brother Is Watching: Secret Police and Intelligence Services* (7–12). 1992, Walker LB $15.85 (978-0-8027-8161-1). Describes the activities and methods of intelligence and police services in several Western and former Eastern-bloc nations, including the KGB, the Mossad, the CIA, and Honduran death squads. (Rev: BL 6/1/92; SLJ 8/92) [363.2]

9643 Lewis, Jon E., ed. *The Mammoth Book of War Diaries and Letters* (9–12). Series: Mammoth Book. 1999, Carroll & Graf paper $10.95 (978-0-7867-0589-4). Soldiers' letters and diaries, from the American Revolution through the Gulf War, provide a unique view of the horrors of war. (Rev: BL 12/15/98) [355.02]

9644 Margulies, Phillip. *America's Role in the World* (9–12). Series: Global Issues. 2009, Facts on File $45 (978-0-8160-7611-6). This frank examination of U.S.

foreign policy and how the United States is viewed by other countries in the world provides facts and figures, excerpts from primary sources, information on key organizations, and an annotated bibliography. (Rev: LMC 1–2/10)

9645 Moorehead, Caroline. *Human Cargo: A Journey Among Refugees* (11–12). 2005, Henry Holt $26.00 (978-0-8050-7443-7). After an overview of the plight of 20th-century refugees, the author details individual cases of suffering; for mature teens. (Rev: BL 2/1/05) [305.9]

9646 Moran, Lindsay. *Blowing My Cover: My Life as a CIA Spy and Other Misadventures* (9–12). 2005, Penguin $22.95 (978-0-399-15239-9). Moran writes about the disillusionment she experienced during her five years with the CIA; young readers will particularly enjoy the details of her interviews and early training. (Rev: BL 1/1–15/05) [327.1273]

9647 Ousseimi, Maria. *Caught in the Crossfire: Growing Up in a War Zone* (6–10). 1995, Walker LB $20.85 (978-0-8027-8364-6). Examines the effects of violence on children and how violence changes children's perception of the world. (Rev: BL 9/1/95; SLJ 9/95; VOYA 12/95) [305.23]

9648 Owen, David. *Hidden Secrets: A Complete History of Espionage and the Technology Used to Support It* (10–12). 2002, Firefly paper $24.95 (978-1-55297-564-0). Case studies and a wealth of well-chosen illustrations add to this overview of spying and the tools of the trade. (Rev: BL 4/1/02) [327.12]

9649 Perl, Lila. *Torture* (7–10). Illus. Series: Controversy! 2011, Marshall Cavendish LB $25.95 (978-160870495-8). With a history of torture and examples of contemporary instances in Abu Ghraib and Guantanamo, this volume gives teens material for reports and food for thought. (Rev: BL 5/1/12; SLJ 2/12) [364.6]

9650 Polner, Murray, and Thomas E. Woods, eds. *We Who Dared to Say No to War: American Antiwar Writing from 1812 to Now* (10–12). Illus. 2008, Basic paper $16.95 (978-156858385-3). This is a collection of essays, letters, speeches, and song lyrics that expresses anti-war sentiment. **e** (Rev: BL 9/1/08) [973]

9651 Roy, Arundhati. *War Talk* (10–12). 2003, South End $40.00 (978-0-89608-724-8); paper $12.00 (978-0-89608-723-1). In this collection of political observations, Indian novelist-turned-essayist Arundhati Roy addresses a broad range of timely topics, including the quest for peace in the Middle East, U.S. foreign policy, and the religious conflicts plaguing her homeland. (Rev: BL 4/15/03) [327.1]

9652 Springer, Jane. *Genocide* (9–12). Series: Groundwood Guide. 2006, Groundwood $15.95 (978-0-88899-681-7). A concise survey of mass killings through history, with discussion of their causes and what can be done

to prevent them. (Rev: BL 10/15/06; LMC 4–5/07; SLJ 12/06) [304.6]

9653 Stewart, Sheila, and Joyce Zoldak. *In Defense of Our Country: Survivors of Military Conflict* (6–12). Illus. Series: Survivors — Ordinary People, Extraordinary Circumstances. 2009, Mason Crest LB $24.95 (978-1-4222-0452-8). Wars in Eastern Europe, the Middle East, Africa, and Asia are the focus of this volume that features first-person accounts as well as sidebars with interesting information on nonmilitary aspects of warfare. (Rev: SLJ 9/09) [362.87]

9654 Suvanjieff, Ivan, and Dawn Gifford Engle. *PeaceJam: A Billion Simple Acts of Peace* (5–10). 2008, Puffin paper $16.99 (978-0-14-241234-3). This volume introduces the Nobel Peace laureates who are active in the work of the PeaceJam Foundation and describes their activism along with efforts by young people to support their causes. (Rev: SLJ 5/1/09; VOYA 12/08) [303.6]

9655 Torr, James D., ed. *Americans' Views About War* (11–12). Series: Examining Pop Culture. 2001, Greenhaven LB $36.20 (978-0-7377-0754-0); paper $24.95 (978-0-7377-0753-3). This overview of U.S. attitudes uses excerpts from a wide array of periodicals and primary sources to document America's essential ambivalence on the issue of war. (Rev: BL 10/15/01; SLJ 2/02) [973.9]

9656 Torr, James D., ed. *U.S. Policy Toward Rogue Nations* (9–12). Series: At Issue. 2004, Gale LB $29.95 (978-0-7377-2196-6); paper $21.20 (978-0-7377-2197-3). Authoritative articles that take different perspectives discuss topics including the invasion of Iraq, possible regime change in Syria and Iran, and strategies for dealing with North Korea. (Rev: SLJ 11/04)

9657 van Creveld, Martin. *The Culture of War* (11–12). 2008, Presidio $27.00 (978-034550540-8). An engrossing look at war as part of human society that encourages fighting, decorates the victors, and builds memorials to the fallen. (Rev: BL 8/08) [306.2]

9658 Winckelmann, Thom. *Genocide* (7–12). Series: Man's Inhumanities. 2008, Erickson LB $23.95 (978-160217975-2). For reluctant and struggling readers, this is a simple overview of recent genocides with discussion of the social implications. (Rev: BL 10/15/08; LMC 8–9/09) [364.15]

9659 Woog, Adam. *Military Might and Global Intervention* (7–10). Illus. Series: Controversy! 2011, Marshall Cavendish LB $25.95 (978-160870492-7). This balanced volume gives readers straightforward information on armed and nonmilitary interventions and the pros and cons of such actions. (Rev: BL 5/1/12; SLJ 2/12) [327.1]

United States Government and Institutions

General and Miscellaneous

9660 Anderson, Jodi Lynn, and Daniel Ehrenhaft, et al. *Americapedia: Taking the Dumb out of Freedom* (7–12). Illus. 2011, Walker $24.99 (978-0-8027-9792-6); paper $16.99 (978-0-8027-9-793-3). A breezy, sometimes irreverent and often amusing survey of American government and history that will prompt discussion. (Rev: BL 7/11; LMC 8–9/11; SLJ 8/11; VOYA 4/11) [320.60973]

9661 Kalman, Maira. *And the Pursuit of Happiness* (10–12). 2010, Penguin $29.95 (978-159420267-4). Author/illustrator Kalman collects here her reflections on democracy in America, focusing on key individuals from George Washington to Barack Obama; these pieces were initially published as a blog in the *New York Times*. (Rev: BL 9/1–15/10) [170]

9662 McIntosh, Kenneth, and Marsha McIntosh. *When Religion and Politics Mix: How Matters of Faith Influence Political Policies* (7–10). Series: Religion and Modern Culture. 2006, Mason Crest LB $22.95 (978-1-59084-971-2). Statistics from the 2004 election provide a basis for this overview of Americans' views on religion and politics. (Rev: BL 4/1/06) [201]

9663 Nakaya, Andrea C., ed. *America in the Twenty-first Century* (9–12). Series: Opposing Viewpoints. 2006, Gale LB $34.95 (978-0-7377-2923-8); paper $23.70 (978-0-7377-2924-5). From sustainability to nuclear power to hybrid automobiles to healthcare (and on to many more topics, including foreign policy), this is a wide-ranging collection of conflicting points of view that will be useful for reports and debates and may attract browsers. (Rev: SLJ 7/06)

9664 Roberts, Sam. *Who We Are Now: The Changing Face of America in the Twentyfirst Century* (9–12). 2004, Henry Holt $27.50 (978-0-8050-5555-9); paper $15.00 (978-0-8050-7080-4). *New York Times* reporter Roberts uses data from the 2000 U.S. census to put a face on contemporary America. (Rev: BL 9/1/04) [973.931]

9665 Ventura, Jesse, and Dick Russell. *American Conspiracies: Lies, Lies, and More Dirty Lies That the Government Tells Us* (10–12). 2010, Skyhorse $24.95 (978-160239802-3). Ventura provides interesting and entertaining — although not always objective — analyses of various events in American history where government motivations and actions have come under suspicion. ⋒ (Rev: BL 3/1–15/10) [364.1]

The Constitution

9666 Bartholomew, Paul C., and Joseph F. Menez. *Summaries of Leading Cases on the Constitution* (10–12).

1991, Littlefield Adams paper $21.95 (978-0-8226-3008-1). This volume summarizes the cases involving constitutional law that have come before the Supreme Court. [342]

9667 Biscontini, Tracey Vasil. *Amendment XIII: Abolishing Slavery* (9–12). Series: Constitutional Amendments: Beyond the Bill of Rights. 2009, Gale/Greenhaven $33.70 (978-0-7377-4122-3). Examining the background and historical context of the 13th Amendment, this volume in a recommended series provides a well-researched look at the relevant issues, as well as a discussion of all the court cases that have tested it. (Rev: LMC 10/09)

9668 Boaz, John, ed. *Free Speech* (7–12). Series: Current Controversies. 2006, Gale LB $34.95 (978-0-7377-2204-8); paper $23.70 (978-0-7377-2205-5). Previously published articles involving free speech answer four main questions: "Should Free Speech Be Limited? Is Free Speech Threatened? Does the War on Terror Threaten Free Speech?" and "How Should the Right to Free Speech Apply to Corporations?" (Rev: SLJ 6/06)

9669 Feinberg, Barbara S. *The Articles of Confederation: The First Constitution of the United States* (7–10). 2002, Twenty-First Century LB $24.90 (978-0-7613-2114-9). Feinberg presents the history and text of the constitution that was in force from 1776 to 1787, along with a list of the signers, a timeline, and source notes. (Rev: BL 2/1/02; HBG 10/02; SLJ 3/02) [342.73]

9670 Friedman, Ian C. *Freedom of Speech and the Press* (7–12). Series: American Rights. 2005, Facts on File $35.00 (978-0-8160-5662-0). Issues relating to the freedoms of speech and the press — in the past, present, and future — are explored in this title. (Rev: SLJ 12/05)

9671 Gerberg, Mort. *The U.S. Constitution for Everyone* (8–12). 1987, Putnam paper $7.95 (978-0-399-51305-3). The text of the Constitution and amendments is analyzed with many interesting asides and background information. (Rev: BL 5/1/87) [342.73]

9672 Haynes, Charles C., and Sam Chaltain. *First Freedoms: A Documentary History of the First Amendment Rights in America* (7–12). 2006, Oxford $40.00 (978-0-19-515750-5). A look at the key figures in the struggle for First Amendment rights — John Locke, Thomas Jefferson, Elizabeth Cady Stanton, and John Scopes, among them — and at the topics that raised people's ire. (Rev: SLJ 11/06*)

9673 Head, Tom. *Freedom of Religion* (7–10). Series: American Rights. 2005, Facts on File $35.00 (978-0-8160-5664-4). Examines the significance of freedom of religion as guaranteed by the First Amendment to the Constitution and provides an overview of the role played by religion in America's early history, the Scopes trial, and questions surrounding school prayer. (Rev: BL 10/15/05) [323.44]

9674 Johnson, Terry. *Legal Rights* (7–12). Series: American Rights. 2005, Facts on File $35.00 (978-0-8160-5665-1). A look at the controversial issue of legal rights under the U.S. Constitution, with discussion of government initiatives since September 11, 2001. (Rev: SLJ 12/05)

9675 Monk, Linda R. *The Words We Live By: Your Annotated Guide to the Constitution* (10–12). 2003, Hyperion $23.95 (978-0-7868-6720-2). In easy-to-understand language with plenty of photographs and interesting sidebar features, this is a comprehensive introduction to the U.S. Constitution. (Rev: BL 12/15/02) [342.73]

9676 Morin, Isobel V. *Our Changing Constitution: How and Why We Have Amended It* (9–12). 1998, Millbrook LB $23.90 (978-0-7613-0222-3). After historical background on the U.S. Constitution and the provisions for revising it, each of the amendments is discussed, including the historical events and constitutional and legal arguments surrounding each, how each was passed, and their impact. (Rev: BL 6/1–15/98; VOYA 8/98) [347]

9677 Patrick, John J. *The Bill of Rights: A History in Documents* (9–12). Series: Pages from History. 2002, Oxford LB $39.95 (978-0-19-510354-0). Excerpts from primary sources — accompanied by reproductions of documents, maps, and works of art — shed light on the first 10 amendments to the U.S. Constitution and their historical background and current relevance. (Rev: BL 2/15/03; HBG 10/03; SLJ 3/03) [342.73]

9678 Richie, Donald A. *Our Constitution* (7–12). 2006, Oxford $40 (978-0-19-522385-9). From the reasons for having a constitution to the amendments and their relevance to well-known cases, this is a well-presented overview. (Rev: SLJ 12/06)

9679 Zacharias, Gary, and Jared Zacharias, eds. *The Bill of Rights* (9–12). Series: At Issue in History. 2003, Gale paper $23.70 (978-0-7377-1426-5). After an essay introducing the background to the Constitution, this volume provides correspondence and other primary documents concerning the need for a Bill of Rights plus articles and commentary discussing later developments. (Rev: SLJ 1/04) [342.73]

The Presidency

9680 Aaseng, Nathan. *You Are the President* (7–10). 1994, Oliver LB $19.95 (978-1-881508-10-6). Devotes one chapter each to a crisis faced by eight presidents in the 20th century, among them Theodore Roosevelt, Eisenhower, and Nixon. (Rev: BL 4/1/94; SLJ 7/94; VOYA 8/94) [973.9]

9681 Aaseng, Nathan. *You Are the President II: 1800–1899* (7–10). Series: Great Decisions. 1994, Oliver LB $19.95 (978-1-881508-15-1). This work discusses the powers of the presidency during the 19th century and the major decisions made by presidents during that time. (Rev: BL 11/15/94; SLJ 12/94) [973.5]

9682 Bernstein, Richard B., and Jerome Agel. *The Presidency* (8–12). 1989, Walker LB $13.85 (978-0-8027-6831-5). A basic history of this institution with some biographical information and a final section that explores the advisability of concentrating such power in one office. (Rev: BL 5/1/89; SLJ 1/89; VOYA 4/89) [353.03]

9683 Dallek, Robert, and Terry Golway. *Let Every Nation Know: John F. Kennedy in His Own Words* (9–12). 2006, Sourcebooks $29.95 (978-1-4022-0647-4). A collection of essays on 32 key speeches is accompanied by a CD; organized chronologically, the recordings and commentaries provide insight into Kennedy and his times. (Rev: BL 4/15/06*) [973.922092]

9684 Nelson, W. Dale. *Who Speaks for the President? The White House Press Secretary from Cleveland to Clinton* (10–12). 1998, Syracuse Univ. $29.95 (978-0-8156-0514-0). In 1893, President Grover Cleveland appointed a confidential stenographer. This account traces the evolution of the White House press secretary to what is today, with information on the people, the powers, and the relationships connected with the position. (Rev: BL 6/1–15/98; SLJ 2/99) [324]

9685 Pious, Richard M. *The Presidency of the United States: A Student Companion. 2nd ed.* (10–12). 2001, Oxford LB $65.00 (978-0-19-515006-3). This work covers the political careers of all the presidents up to and including Bill Clinton. [353]

9686 Schlesinger, Arthur M., Jr, ed. *The Election of 2000 and the Administration of George W. Bush* (8–12). Series: Major Presidential Elections and the Administrations That Followed. 2003, Mason Crest LB $24.95 (978-1-59084-365-9). The circumstances of Bush's election and the major events of his administration through 2002 are presented with reference to many primary sources; brief biographical facts about the president and his cabinet are also included. (Rev: HBG 4/04; SLJ 10/03) [324.973]

9687 Thomas, Helen, and Craig Crawford. *Listen Up, Mr. President: Everything You Always Wanted Your President to Know and Do* (10–12). 2009, Scribner $24 (978-143914815-0). Famous journalist Thomas and colleague Crawford offer a history of the American presidency and provide commentary on the intense scrutiny faced by contemporary presidents as well as guidelines for future chief executives. **e** (Rev: BL 10/1/09) [352.23]

9688 Waldman, Michael, comp. *My Fellow Americans: The Most Important Speeches of American Presidents from George Washington to George W. Bush* (7–12). 2003, Sourcebooks paper $45.00 (978-1-4022-0027-4). A collection of more than 40 speeches by 17 presidents, some of which are shown with early drafts; two accompanying CDs contain all the speeches, with the actual voices of presidents starting with Teddy Roosevelt. (Rev: BL 10/15/03; SLJ 10/03*) [352.23]

Federal Government, Its Agencies, and Public Administration

9689 Aaseng, Nathan. *You Are the Senator* (7–10). Series: Great Decisions. 1997, Oliver LB $19.95 (978-1-881508-36-6). This book describes the duties and responsibilities of a U.S. senator and the nature of the decisions that senators make. (Rev: BL 4/15/97; SLJ 8/97; VOYA 8/97) [328.73]

9690 Bernstein, Richard B., and Jerome Agel. *The Congress* (7–12). 1989, Walker LB $13.85 (978-0-8027-6833-9). An introduction to this branch of the government with material arranged chronologically and including some coverage of scandals and decline in prestige. (Rev: BL 5/1/89; SLJ 1/89; VOYA 4/89) [328.73]

9691 Burlingame, Jeff. *Government Entitlements* (7–10). Illus. Series: Controversy! 2011, Marshall Cavendish LB $25.95 (978-160870491-0). Discusses controversial topics such as social security, welfare, workers' compensation, and veterans' benefits. (Rev: BL 5/1/12; VOYA 10/12) [361.60973]

9692 Esherick, Joan. *The FDA and Psychiatric Drugs: How a Drug Is Approved* (6–10). Series: Psychiatric Disorders: Drugs and Psychology for the Mind and Body. 2003, Mason Crest LB $24.95 (978-1-59084-578-3). As well as a clear explanation of the drug approval process, this volume contains information on alternative medicines and an interesting look at how treatment of schizophrenia has advanced over time. (Rev: SLJ 5/04)

9693 Harmon, Daniel E. *The FBI* (7–10). Series: Crime, Justice, and Punishment. 2001, Chelsea LB $30.00 (978-0-7910-4289-2). The highest branch of criminal investigation in the United States is discussed with material on powers, methods, and personnel. (Rev: BL 6/1–15/01; HBG 10/01) [363.2]

9694 *How Congress Works. 3rd ed.* (9–12). 1998, Congressional Quarterly paper $31.00 (978-1-56802-391-5). The inner workings, rules, and procedures of Congress are laid out in a clear and concise manner. [328.73]

9695 Kramer, Mattea. *A People's Guide to the Federal Budget: National Priorities Project* (10–12). 2012, Interlink paper $15.00 (978-1-56656-887-6). Where does the money come from? Where does the money go? These and other questions are answered in this balanced description of the workings of the federal budget, including brief historical details and Obama's 2013 request. (Rev: BL 2012; SLJ 10/12) [352.4]

9696 Remini, Robert V. *The House: The History of the House of Representatives* (11–12). 2006, HarperCollins $34.95 (978-0-06-088434-5). Memorable personalities and dramatic historical episodes dominate this highly readable but lengthy history of the U.S. House of Representatives. (Rev: BL 4/15/06) [973]

9697 Richie, Jason. *Secretaries of State: Making Foreign Policy* (7–10). Series: Cabinet. 2002, Oliver LB $22.95 (978-1-881508-65-6). Succinct profiles of eight secretaries of state, ranging chronologically from John Quincy Adams to James Baker, look at their beliefs and how they influenced the nation's foreign policy. Also recommended in this series is *Secretaries of War, Navy, and Defense: Ensuring National Security* (2002). (Rev: BL 10/15/02; HBG 3/03; SLJ 4/03) [327.73]

State and Municipal Governments and Agencies

9698 Conway, W. Fred. *Firefighting Lore: Strange but True Stories from Firefighting History* (9–12). 1993, Buff House paper $9.95 (978-0-925165-14-5). Written by a former fire chief, this history of firefighting in the United States provides short accounts of famous and lesser-known major fires. (Rev: BL 1/1/94) [363.378]

9699 Gorrell, Gena K. *Catching Fire: The Story of Firefighting* (7–10). 1999, Tundra paper $16.95 (978-0-88776-430-1). This is a history of firefighting, from the bucket brigades of the past to the sophisticated equipment of today, with related information on how fires burn, important fires in history, equipment, firefighting tactics, forms of arson, wildfires, and more. (Rev: BCCB 5/99; BL 6/1–15/99; SLJ 6/99) [363.3]

9700 Ryan, Bernard, Jr. *Serving with Police, Fire, and EMS* (7–12). Series: Community Service for Teens. 1998, Ferguson LB $19.95 (978-0-89434-232-5). This work explains how teens can play an active and productive role in police, fire, and allied community agencies. (Rev: BL 9/15/98; SLJ 2/99) [361.8]

Libraries and Other Educational Institutions

9701 Fortey, Richard. *Dry Storeroom No. 1: The Secret Life of the Natural History Museum* (10–12). Illus. 2008, Knopf $27.50 (978-0-307-26362-9). Paleontologist Fortey describes the different departments of the Natural History Museum in London and tells many interesting stories about hoaxes and accidental discoveries that shed light on the scientists' methods. ℮ (Rev: BL 8/08) [508]

9702 Myron, Vicki, and Bret Witter. *Dewey: The Small-Town Library Cat Who Touched the World* (10–12). 2008, Grand Central $19.99 (978-044640741-0). Both Vicki Myron and Dewey the cat are survivors in this inspiring story about economic struggles, small-town life, and animal-human relationships. ☊ (Rev: BL 8/08*) [636.809]

The Law and the Courts

9703 Aaseng, Nathan. *You Are the Juror* (6–10). 1997, Oliver LB $19.95 (978-1-881508-40-3). The author recreates eight famous criminal trials of the 20th century, including the Lindbergh kidnapping case, the Patty Hearst and O. J. Simpson trials, and the Ford Pinto case, and asks the reader to become a jury member and make a decision. (Rev: SLJ 1/98) [347.73]

9704 Aaseng, Nathan. *You Are the Supreme Court Justice* (7–10). Series: Great Decisions. 1994, Oliver LB $19.95 (978-1-881508-14-4). A description of how the Supreme Court works and the decisions and responsibilities involved in being a Justice. (Rev: BL 11/15/94; SLJ 12/94) [347.73]

9705 Aretha, David. *The Trial of the Scottsboro Boys* (7–12). Series: Civil Rights. 2007, Morgan Reynolds $27.95 (978-1-59935-058-5). A compelling account of what happened to nine young black men in 1930s Alabama. (Rev: BL 11/1/07; SLJ 12/07) [345.761]

9706 Berger, Leslie. *The Grand Jury* (7–12). Series: Crime, Justice, and Punishment. 2000, Chelsea $30.00 (978-0-7910-4290-8). This work traces the history of the grand jury system, outlines procedures at the local and national level, and cites famous grand jury hearings including the Monica Lewinsky case. (Rev: BL 8/00) [345.73]

9707 Bernstein, Richard B., and Jerome Agel. *The Supreme Court* (8–12). 1989, Walker LB $13.85 (978-0-8027-6835-3). An account that gives a history of the Supreme Court, details on landmark cases, and an outline of how it operates today. (Rev: BL 5/1/89; SLJ 1/89; VOYA 4/89) [347]

9708 Campbell, Andrew. *Rights of the Accused* (7–10). Series: Crime, Justice, and Punishment. 2001, Chelsea LB $30.00 (978-0-7910-4303-5). A cleverly written, informative exploration of how and why the judicial system tries to safeguard the rights of accused criminals. (Rev: BL 6/1–15/01; HBG 3/01; SLJ 2/01; VOYA 12/01) [345]

9709 Carrel, Annette. *It's the Law! A Young Person's Guide to Our Legal System* (8–12). 1994, Volcano paper $12.95 (978-1-884244-01-8). The book's goal is voter responsibility through understanding of the laws, how they developed, and how they can be changed. (Rev: BL 2/15/95; VOYA 12/95) [349.73]

9710 Carroll, Jamuna, ed. *Civil Liberties and War* (7–12). Series: Issues on Trial. 2006, Gale LB $34.95 (978-0-7377-2503-2). Jamuna examines the United States' history of restriction of civil liberties during wartime, looking in depth at four instances in the 20th and 21st centuries. (Rev: SLJ 8/06)

9711 Dudley, Mark E. *Gideon v. Wainwright (1963): Right to Counsel* (6–10). Series: Supreme Court Decisions. 1995, Twenty-First Century LB $25.90 (978-0-

8050-3914-6). Reviews how the case was built, argued, and decided, and discusses its impact. (Rev: BL 6/1–15/95; SLJ 8/95) [347.3]

9712 Dudley, Mark E. *United States v. Nixon (1974)* (6–10). Series: Supreme Court Decisions. 1994, Twenty-First Century LB $25.90 (978-0-8050-3658-9). This landmark Supreme Court case concerning the definition of presidential powers is reported on in a step-by-step analysis of the arguments in the Watergate case. (Rev: BL 12/15/94; SLJ 2/95) [342.73]

9713 Dudley, William, ed. *Reproductive Rights* (9–12). Series: Issues on Trial. 2006, Gale LB $34.95 (978-0-7377-2511-7). Supreme Court cases related to reproduction are examined in this collection of essays. (Rev: SLJ 10/06)

9714 Egendorf, Laura K., ed. *The Death Penalty* (7–12). Series: Examining Issues Through Political Cartoons. 2002, Gale paper $21.20 (978-0-7377-1101-1). Egendorf uses cartoons focusing on the death penalty as the basis for a discussion of the controversies surrounding this practice. Also recommended in this series is *Euthanasia* (2002). (Rev: BL 8/02) [364.44]

9715 Friedman, Lauri S. *The Death Penalty* (9–12). Series: Compact Research. 2007, Reference Point LB $24.95 (978-1-60152-008-1). This compact volume provides lots of information for report writers, with illustrations, quotations from primary sources, lists of facts, statistical charts, and brief timelines. (Rev: SLJ 5/07) [364.6]

9716 Friedman, Lauri S., ed. *The Death Penalty* (9–12). Series: Introducing Issues with Opposing Viewpoints. 2005, Gale LB $32.45 (978-0-7377-3341-9). Discusses the issue of the death penalty from various points of view with accompanying photographs, cartoons, fast facts, graphs, and thought-provoking questions. (Rev: SLJ 5/06) [346.6]

9717 Gershman, Gary P. *Death Penalty on Trial: A Handbook with Cases, Laws, and Documents* (10–12). Series: On Trial. 2005, ABC-CLIO $55.00 (978-1-85109-606-0). A balanced and thorough review of the history and current status of the controversial death penalty, with excerpts from key decisions, a glossary, a table of cases, and further reading. (Rev: SLJ 12/05)

9718 Gold, Susan Dudley. *Brown v. Board of Education: Separate But Equal?* (7–12). Series: Supreme Court Milestones. 2004, Benchmark LB $37.07 (978-0-7614-1842-9). An overview of the groundbreaking decision, with information on the key individuals involved and on the legal process itself plus human-interest stories that add depth. (Rev: SLJ 1/05) [344.73]

9719 Gold, Susan Dudley. *The Pentagon Papers: National Security or the Right to Know* (7–12). Series: Supreme Court Milestones. 2004, Benchmark LB $37.07 (978-0-7614-1843-6). An easily understood account of the events surrounding the Pentagon Papers case and the high court's decision that blocked the Nixon administration's efforts to keep the papers secret. (Rev: SLJ 1/05) [342.73]

9720 Gottfried, Ted. *The Death Penalty: Justice or Legalized Murder?* (7–12). 2002, Twenty-First Century LB $24.90 (978-0-7613-2155-2). Gottfried presents an absorbing and balanced examination of the arguments for and against the death penalty, with historical information and details of specific cases. (Rev: BL 3/15/02; HBG 10/02; SLJ 3/02) [364.66]

9721 Gottfried, Ted. *Police Under Fire* (7–12). 1999, Twenty-First Century LB $24.90 (978-0-7613-1313-7). A well-balanced account that gives a history of policing, police culture, pressures on police personnel, corruption, and cases of police brutality. (Rev: BL 12/15/99; HBG 4/00; SLJ 1/00) [363.2]

9722 Grant, Robert, and Joseph Katz. *The Great Trials of the Twenties: The Watershed Decade in America's Courtrooms* (10–12). 1998, Sarpedon $24.95 (978-1-885119-52-0). Ten history-making court cases of the 1920s — including the trial of Sacco and Vanzetti on charges of anarchy and the face-off between Clarence Darrow and William Jennings Bryan — are presented in an absorbing narrative. (Rev: BL 12/15/98) [347]

9723 Harmon, Daniel E. *Defense Lawyers* (7–10). Series: Crime, Justice, and Punishment. 2001, Chelsea LB $30.00 (978-0-7910-4284-7). This introduction to the roles of defense attorney and public defender provides brief profiles of figures including Clarence Darrow and Alan Dershowitz. (Rev: HBG 10/02; SLJ 4/02) [345.73]

9724 Harrison, Maureen, and Steve Gilbert, eds. *Landmark Decisions of the United States Supreme Court II* (9–12). 1992, Excellent Books paper $17.95 (978-0-9628014-2-6). Synopses of far-reaching Supreme Court rulings, including decisions on slavery, women's suffrage, Bible reading in public schools, book banning, and the death penalty. (Rev: BL 1/1/92) [347]

9725 Henderson, Harry, and Stephen A. Flanders, eds. *Capital Punishment. Rev. ed.* (9–12). Series: Library in a Book. 2000, Facts on File $45.00 (978-0-8160-4193-0). This series of readings looks at capital punishment from various viewpoints, including social, political, ethical, and religious perspectives. (Rev: BL 3/1/01) [364.66]

9726 Henningfeld, Diane Andrews, ed. *The Death Penalty* (7–12). Series: Opposing Viewpoints. 2006, Gale LB $34.95 (978-0-7377-2929-0); paper $23.70 (978-0-7377-2930-6). A thought-provoking collection of essays providing many points of view on the use of the death penalty. (Rev: SLJ 9/06)

9727 Herda, D. J. *Furman v. Georgia: The Death Penalty Case* (6–10). Series: Landmark Supreme Court Cases. 1994, Enslow LB $26.60 (978-0-89490-489-9). Summarizes the historical background of this case,

the case itself, and its impact. (Rev: BL 11/15/94; SLJ 11/94) [345.73]

9728 Hogrogian, John. *Miranda v. Arizona: The Rights of the Accused* (9–12). Series: Famous Trials. 1999, Lucent $29.95 (978-1-56006-471-8). This groundbreaking Supreme Court case changed criminal justice in the United States by defining the rights of accused criminals. (Rev: BL 9/15/99; HBG 4/00) [347]

9729 Jacobs, Thomas A. *Teens on Trial: Young People Who Challenged the Law — and Changed Your Life* (8–12). 2000, Free Spirit paper $14.95 (978-1-57542-081-3). Student rights and responsibilities are explored through this examination of 21 cases in which teens participated in the legal process. (Rev: BL 1/1–15/01; SLJ 1/01; VOYA 4/01) [346.7301]

9730 Jacobs, Thomas A. *They Broke the Law, You Be the Judge: True Cases of Teen Crime* (7–12). 2003, Free Spirit paper $15.95 (978-1-57542-134-6). A former juvenile court judge presents 21 real-life cases involving juveniles, gives the reader the sentencing options, and reveals the actual outcome of each case. (Rev: BL 2/1/04; SLJ 1/04) [345.73]

9731 Jarrow, Gail. *The Printer's Trial: The Case of John Peter Zenger and the Fight for a Free Press* (7–10). 2006, Boyds Mills $18.95 (978-1-59078-432-7). Covers the events leading up to and the 1735 trial of John Peter Zenger, a printer from New York who was found not guilty of seditious libel against the British government, establishing freedom of the press. (Rev: BL 10/1/06; LMC 2/07; SLJ 11/06) [345.73]

9732 Johnson, Anne Janette. *The Scopes "Monkey Trial."* (9–12). Series: Defining Moments. 2006, Omnigraphics LB $49.00 (978-0-7808-0955-0). In addition to telling the story of the famous evolution trial, this well-illustrated volume includes biographies of nine key figures and a section of primary sources — newspaper articles, courtroom transcripts, and so forth. (Rev: SLJ 4/07) [345.73]

9733 Koopmans, Andy. *Leopold and Loeb: Teen Killers* (7–12). Series: Famous Trials. 2004, Gale LB $29.95 (978-1-59018-227-7). The story of the famous trial of two privileged boys for the murder of a third, with details of Clarence Darrow's innovative defense strategy. (Rev: SLJ 6/04) [345.73]

9734 Kowalski, Kathiann M. *Lemon v. Kurtzman and the Separation of Church and State Debate* (8–12). Series: Debating Supreme Court Decisions. 2005, Enslow LB $26.60 (978-0-7660-2391-8). This well-documented title examines the Supreme Court's decision in Lemon v. Kurtzman and reviews its impact on the doctrine of separation of church and state. (Rev: SLJ 12/05)

9735 Krygier, Leora. *Juvenile Court: A Judge's Guide for Young Adults and Their Parents* (7–12). 2009, Scarecrow $29.95 (978-081086127-5). Written by a judge in the Los Angeles Superior Court, this book arms teens with advice and practical information about what goes on in juvenile court. **ⓔ** (Rev: BL 3/15/09; SLJ 3/1/09; VOYA 2/09) [345.73]

9736 Lewis, Michelle, ed. *Rights of the Accused* (9–12). Series: Issues on Trial. 2007, Gale LB $34.95 (978-0-7377-2795-1). A discussion of the rights that those accused of crimes have in the United States, with examples of actual cases providing the backdrop for in-depth analysis of the laws relating to criminal cases. (Rev: BL 7/07; SLJ 9/07) [345.73]

9737 McNeese, Tim. *Dred Scott v. Sandford* (7–10). Series: Great Supreme Court Decisions. 2006, Chelsea House LB $30.00 (978-0-7910-9236-1). Illustrations and graphics add interest to this account of the Dred Scott court case and its significance in the nation's division over slavery. (Rev: BL 2/1/07) [342]

9738 Margulies, Phillip, and Maxine Rosaler. *The Devil on Trial: Witches, Anarchists, Atheists, Communists, and Terrorists in America's Courtrooms* (8–12). Illus. 2008, Houghton Mifflin $22.00 (978-061871717-0). The authors examine five key trials in American history: the Salem witch trials, the Haymarket bomb trial, the Scopes monkey trial, the trials of Alger Hiss, and the trials of Zacarias Moussaoui. (Rev: BL 11/15/08; SLJ 9/1/08; VOYA 8/08) [345.73]

9739 Mountjoy, Shane. *Engel v. Vitale: School Prayer and the Establishment Clause* (7–12). Series: Great Supreme Court Decisions. 2006, Chelsea House LB $30.00 (978-0-7910-9241-5). An accessible overview of the ongoing debate about school prayer in the United States. (Rev: SLJ 7/07) [344.73]

9740 Nakaya, Andrea, ed. *The Environment* (7–12). Series: Issues on Trial. 2006, Gale LB $34.95 (978-0-7377-2797-5). Four benchmark court cases illustrate how environmental laws can become forces for social change. (Rev: SLJ 7/06)

9741 Paddock, Lisa. *Facts About the Supreme Court of the United States* (8–12). 1996, H.W. Wilson $105.00 (978-0-8242-0896-7). A one-stop reference source for information about the Supreme Court, from individual justices to the court's history and important cases. (Rev: VOYA 12/96) [347]

9742 Panchyk, Richard. *Our Supreme Court: A History with 14 Activities* (7–10). 2006, Chicago Review paper $17.95 (978-1-55652-607-7). Focusing on the history and development of the Supreme Court and landmark cases handled, this large-format book with effective illustrations includes interviews with attorneys, politicians, and other related figures as well as a variety of activities, a glossary, and useful facts. (Rev: BL 11/1/06; SLJ 3/07) [347.73]

9743 Persico, Deborah A. *New Jersey v. T.L.O.: Drug Searches in Schools* (7–12). Series: Landmark Supreme Court Cases. 1998, Enslow LB $20.95 (978-0-89490-969-6). This Supreme Court case lasted five years and

explored the rights of a student, identified as T.L.O., whose handbag was searched by a school administrator who found marijuana and articles that indicated the student was selling drugs. (Rev: BL 8/98; HBG 9/98; SLJ 8/98; VOYA 2/99) [345.73]

9744 Ramsland, Katherine. *The C.S.I. Effect* (9–12). 2006, Penguin paper $14.00 (978-0-425-21159-5). Examples of actual (the O. J. Simpson case) and fictional (TV episodes of CSI) legal cases are analyzed and forensic and investigative methods of obtaining convictions to crimes are explained. (Rev: BL 9/15/06) [363.25]

9745 Telgen, Diane. *Brown v. Board of Education* (8–12). Series: Defining Moments. 2005, Omnigraphics LB $49.00 (978-0-7808-0775-4). An accessible examination of the landmark Supreme Court decision on school segregation, including many interesting sidebar features and chronicling events before and after the ruling, up to the present day. (Rev: SLJ 12/05*)

9746 Weiner, Mark S. *Black Trials: Citizenship from the Beginnings of Slavery to the End of Caste* (9–12). 2004, Knopf $26.95 (978-0-375-40981-3). Traces the evolution of race relations in America through an examination of 14 court cases that shaped the legal standing of African American citizens. (Rev: BL 10/1/04) [342.7308]

Politics

GENERAL AND MISCELLANEOUS

9747 Boyers, Sara Jane. *Teen Power Politics: Make Yourself Heard* (7–12). 2000, Twenty-First Century LB $24.90 (978-0-7613-1307-6); paper $9.95 (978-0-7613-1391-5). An in-depth and inspiring look at the ways in which teens too young to vote can nonetheless exert their influence. (Rev: BL 11/15/00; HBG 3/01; SLJ 1/01; VOYA 4/01) [323]

9748 Conrad, Jessamyn. *What You Should Know About Politics . . . but Don't* (10–12). 2008, Arcade paper $15.95 (978-155970883-8). Conrad provides a clear and impartial look at politics in the United States, covering a wide range of issues from election procedures and foreign policy to the economy and abortion. (Rev: BL 8/08) [320.60973]

9749 Cox, Vicki. *The History of Third Parties* (7–10). Series: The U.S. Government: How It Works. 2007, Chelsea House LB $30.00 (978-0-7910-9421-1). Third parties have not seen success in the United States; this volume explores the history of third parties and looks at the reasons why they have had trouble attracting voters. (Rev: BL 2/15/08) [324.273]

9750 Luna, Christopher, ed. *Campaign Finance Reform* (10–12). Series: Reference Shelf. 2001, H.W. Wilson paper $50.00 (978-0-8242-0998-8). The essays in this collection cover such topics as corporate influence, soft money, fund-raising, and political action committees, plus other topics relating to money and political campaigns. [324.7]

9751 McCarthy, Timothy Patrick, and John McMillan, eds. *The Radical Reader: A Documentary History of the American Radical Tradition* (10–12). 2003, New Press $65.00 (978-1-56584-827-6); paper $21.95 (978-1-56584-682-1). This comprehensive overview of American radicalism includes more than 200 essays, editorials, and other statements by such notable historic figures as Henry David Thoreau, Frederick Douglass, Sarah Grimke, Emma Goldman, Betty Friedan, Angela Davis, and Cesar Chavez. (Rev: BL 7/03) [303.484]

9752 Morin, Isobel V. *Politics, American Style: Political Parties in American History* (6–12). 1999, Twenty-First Century $24.90 (978-0-7613-1267-3). An engaging account of the history of American political parties, accompanied by political cartoons. (Rev: BL 11/15/99; HBG 4/00; SLJ 1/00) [324.273]

9753 Zinn, Howard, and David Barsamian. *Original Zinn: Conversations on History and Politics* (10–12). 2006, Perennial paper $13.95 (978-0-06-084425-7). This collection of radio interviews and a speech lays out Zinn's opinions on U.S. foreign policy since 9/11; Zinn is a former professor at Boston University and a liberal social activist. (Rev: SLJ 10/06)

ELECTIONS

9754 Cohen, Michael A. *Live from the Campaign Trail: The Greatest Presidential Campaign Speeches of the Twentieth Century and How They Shaped Modern America* (10–12). 2008, Walker paper $16.99 (978-080271697-2). In a comprehensive journey from 1896 to 1992, Cohen presents and interprets some of the most successful and eloquent presidential speeches, providing an interesting cross-section of the evolution of American politics. (Rev: BL 6/1–15/08; SLJ 8/08) [324.97309]

9755 *Declare Yourself: Speak. Connect. Act. Vote* (9–12). 2008, Greenwillow paper $11.99 (978-0-06-147316-6). More than 50 Americans from diverse walks of life — Maya Angelou and Tyra Banks among them — explain why voting is vital. (Rev: BL 8/08) [323]

9756 Espejo, Roman, ed. *Voter Fraud* (10–12). Series: At Issue: American Politics. 2010, Greenhaven LB $30.85 (978-073774693-8); paper $21.85 (9780737746945). Redistricting, voting by mail and computer, and a push to stop voter fraud are all addressed in this interesting volume. (Rev: BL 6/1/11) [324.6]

9757 Haugen, David M., and Susan Musser, eds. *Campaign Finance* (10–12). Series: At Issue: American Politics. 2010, Greenhaven LB $31.80 (978-073774872-7); paper $22.50 (9780737748734). A collection of fascinating articles address the issue of campaign finance, freedom of speech, Internet fund-raising, and other key

topics relating to the American political system. (Rev: BL 6/1/11) [324.7]

9758 Henderson, Harry. *Campaign and Election Reform* (9–12). Series: Library in a Book. 2004, Facts on File $45.00 (978-0-8160-5136-6). From the financing of campaigns to the mechanics of elections, this informative volume examines precedents, existing and potential legal limitations, and the role of interest groups. (Rev: SLJ 6/04) [324.6]

9759 Israel, Fred L. *Student's Atlas of American Presidential Elections 1789 to 1996* (7–12). 1997, Congressional Quarterly $45.00 (978-1-56802-377-9). Each of the 53 presidential elections in U.S. history is described on a page or two, accompanied by maps to illustrate election results. (Rev: BL 11/15/97; SLJ 11/97) [973]

9760 Lansford, Tom, ed. *Voting Rights* (7–12). Series: Opposing Viewpoints. 2008, Gale/Greenhaven $36.20 (978-073774014-1); paper $24.95 (978-073774015-8). Essays by experts address issues relating to voting in the United States and other countries. (Rev: BL 1/1–15/09) [324.6]

The Armed Forces

9761 Aaseng, Nathan. *You Are the General* (7–12). Series: Great Decisions. 1994, Oliver $19.95 (978-1-881508-11-3). This book deals with decisions that have to be made by members of the military, with many examples. (Rev: BL 6/1–15/94) [355]

9762 Axe, David. *Army 101: Inside the ROTC in a Time of War* (10–12). 2007, Univ. of South Carolina $24.95 (978-1-57003-660-6). Prospective soldiers will want to read this survey of Reserve Officers Training Corps culture and training. (Rev: BL 12/15/06) [355.2]

9763 Clancy, Tom, and John Gresham. *Special Forces: A Guided Tour of U.S. Army Special Forces* (10–12). 2001, Berkley paper $16.00 (978-0-425-17268-1). One of several popular military studies, this focuses on the special forces (sometimes known as the Green Berets) and covers recruitment, training, and missions. (Rev: BL 2/1/01) [356]

9764 da Cruz, Daniel. *Boot: The Inside Story of How a Few Good Men Became Today's Marines* (10–12). 1987, St. Martin's paper $6.99 (978-0-312-90060-1). The story of a Marine boot camp platoon from induction to graduation. (Rev: BL 2/15/87) [359.9]

9765 Godson, Susan H. *Serving Proudly: A History of Women in the U.S. Navy* (10–12). 2001, Naval Institute $39.95 (978-1-55750-317-6). This study spans two centuries and covers the role of women in the navy from the front lines to support personnel. (Rev: BL 10/15/01) [359]

9766 Haley, James, ed. *Women in the Military* (9–12). Series: At Issue. 2005, Gale LB $29.95 (978-0-7377-

2298-7); paper $21.20 (978-0-7377-2299-4). Presents differing views about whether women should be involved in combat. (Rev: SLJ 1/05) [355]

9767 McLaurin, Melton A. *The Marines of Montford Point: America's First Black Marines* (10–12). 2007, Univ. of North Carolina $29.95 (978-0-8078-3097-0). The author interviews veterans of the camp in North Carolina where the first African American marines were trained, starting in 1942; the first-person narratives convey the prejudice these recruits faced. (Rev: BL 2/1/07) [359.9]

9768 McNab, Chris. *Protecting the Nation with the U.S. Army* (6–10). Series: Rescue and Prevention: Defending Our Nation. 2003, Mason Crest LB $22.95 (978-1-59084-414-4). This series about the specific roles the various services play in defending U.S. interests at home and abroad also discusses each service's history, structure, equipment, and recent operations. Also use *Protecting the Nation with the U.S. Air Force* and *Protecting the Nation with the U.S. Navy* (2003). (Rev: HBG 4/04; SLJ 7/03) [355]

9769 Sherrow, Victoria. *Women in the Military* (9–12). Series: Point/Counterpoint. 2007, Chelsea House LB $32.95 (978-0-7910-9290-3). Sherrow offers various points of view on the issue of women in the military, with discussion of combat roles, gender segregation, motherhood, the need to expand the military, and so forth. (Rev: BL 9/1/07) [355.0082]

9770 Smith, Larry. *The Few and the Proud: Marine Corps Drill Instructors in Their Own Words* (9–12). 2006, Norton $26.95 (978-0-393-06044-7). A closer look at the Marine trainers who have a reputation for being mean and merciless — and how their techniques for making soldiers have evolved. (Rev: BL 5/1/06) [359.9]

9771 Stewart, Robert. *The Brigade in Review: A Year at the U.S. Naval Academy* (9–12). 1993, Naval Institute $46.95 (978-1-55750-776-1). This illustrated volume covers the Annapolis year, from the introduction of the academy plebes to the senior midshipmen's graduation. (Rev: BL 2/1/94) [359]

9772 Stillwell, Paul, ed. *The Golden Thirteen: Recollections of the First Black Naval Officers* (9–12). 1993, Naval Institute $34.95 (978-1-55750-779-2). Oral histories of African Americans who faced prejudice and overcame limitations to become the first commissioned officers of their race in the U.S. Navy. (Rev: BL 1/15/93) [359]

9773 Stremlow, Mary V. *Coping with Sexism in the Military* (7–12). 1990, Rosen LB $21.95 (978-0-8239-1025-0). An analysis of the military from the perspective of the female recruit that reflects conditions in the late 1980s. (Rev: BL 2/15/91) [355]

9774 *Voices of War: Stories of Service from the Home Front and the Front Lines* (9–12). 2004, National Geographic $30.00 (978-0-7922-7838-2). A close-up look at the horrors of war is provided by this collection of first-person accounts by 60 Americans — men and women, some very young — who served in the major conflicts of the 20th century; a product of the Veterans History Project. (Rev: BL 11/1/04) [355]

9775 Wagner, Viqi, ed. *Military Draft* (9–12). Series: Opposing Viewpoints. 2008, Gale LB $36.20 (978-0-7377-3824-7); paper $24.95 (978-0-7377-3825-4). Should the U.S. armed forces resort to a draft in times of war? What about gay people in the military? These questions and others are addressed in this collection of essays and articles. (Rev: BL 4/15/08) [355.2]

9776 Wiener, Tom. *Forever a Soldier: Unforgettable Stories of Wartime Service* (9–12). 2005, National Geographic $26.00 (978-0-7922-4189-8). Drawn from the Library of Congress's vast Veterans History Project, this collection of firsthand accounts vividly conveys life on the front lines. (Rev: BL 11/1/05) [355]

9777 Wildsmith, Snow. *Joining the United States Air Force: A Handbook* (9–12). Illus. Series: Joining the Military. 2012, McFarland $25 (978-078644758-9). Offers broad and frank advice for young people thinking of joining the military, with a particular focus on the Air Force, its history and career opportunities, and the processes of enlistment and basic training. **e** (Rev: BL 11/15/12*) [358.40023]

9778 Williams, Kayla. *Love My Rifle More Than You: Young and Female in the U.S. Army* (11–12). 2005, Norton $24.95 (978-0-393-06098-0). In this assertive, no-holds-barred memoir, Williams writes about what life was like for a female serving in the male-dominated military in Iraq; for mature teens. (Rev: BL 8/05) [355]

9779 Willis, Clint, ed. *Semper Fi: Stories of the United States Marines from Boot Camp to Battle* (11–12). 2003, Thunder's Mouth paper $17.95 (978-1-56025-504-8). Peacetime and wartime experiences of U.S. Marines have been culled from a variety of well-written sources; the violence in these stories limits the book's use to mature teens. (Rev: BL 10/1/03) [359.9]

Citizenship and Civil Rights

General and Miscellaneous

9780 Andryszewski, Tricia. *Same-Sex Marriage: Moral Wrong or Civil Right?* (7–12). 2008, Lerner LB $38.60 (978-0-8225-7176-6). A balanced look at many aspects of this issue in the United States. The author's discussion is enhanced by quotations from people of all opinions on gay marriage. (Rev: BL 5/1/08; SLJ 6/08) [306.84]

9781 Carroll, Jamuna, ed. *Students' Rights* (9–12). Series: Opposing Viewpoints. 2005, Gale LB $36.20 (978-0-7377-3088-3); paper $24.95 (978-0-7377-3089-0). Essays explore both sides of the continuing debate over student rights regarding such issues as privacy, religion, dress codes, health, a high-quality education, and so forth. (Rev: SLJ 12/05)

9782 D'Souza, Dinesh. *What's So Great About America* (10–12). 2002, Regnery $27.95 (978-0-89526-153-3). D'Souza, a neo-conservative and immigrant from India, discusses some of the accusations leveled at the West and enumerates America's political blessings. (Rev: BL 4/15/02) [973]

9783 Ellis, Richard J. *To the Flag: The Unlikely History of the Pledge of Allegiance* (7–12). 2005, Univ. Press of Kansas $29.95 (978-0-7006-1372-4). Traces the history of the Pledge of Allegiance and the flap over two words — "under God" — that were inserted into the pledge nearly 60 years after it was written. (Rev: BL 3/1/05) [323.6]

Civil and Human Rights

9784 Andryszewski, Tricia. *Same-Sex Marriage: Granting Equal Rights or Damaging the Status of Marriage?* (9–12). Illus. Series: *USA Today*'s Debate: Voices and Perspectives. 2011, Lerner/Twenty-First Century LB $35.93 (978-076136435-1). Drawing on articles from *USA Today,* this title looks at both sides of the same-sex marriage debate. (Rev: BL 9/15/11) [306.84]

9785 Aretha, David. *Montgomery Bus Boycott* (7–10). Illus. Series: Civil Rights Movement. 2008, Morgan Reynolds $28.95 (978-159935020-2). An examination of an important event in the civil rights movement, with letters, photographs, and personal accounts that add impact. (Rev: BL 2/1/09; LMC 5–6/09; SLJ 2/1/09) [323.1196]

9786 Aretha, David. *The Murder of Emmett Till* (7–12). Series: Civil Rights Movement. 2007, Morgan Reynolds LB $27.95 (978-1-59935-057-8). This book explains how the shocking death of Emmett Till sparked outrage around the country and was one factor leading to the civil rights movement. (Rev: BL 12/1/07; SLJ 1/08) [364.1]

9787 Aretha, David. *Selma and the Voting Rights Act* (7–12). Series: Civil Rights. 2007, Morgan Reynolds LB $27.95 (978-1-59935-056-1). This book explains how events in Alabama in the 1960s led to the 1965 Voting Rights Act. (Rev: BL 12/15/07; SLJ 1/08) [324.6]

9788 Baldwin, James. *James Baldwin: Collected Essays* (10–12). 1998, Library of America $35.00 (978-1-883011-52-9). A collection of essays that demonstrate the novelist's support of civil rights. [814]

9789 Bales, Kevin, and Becky Cornell. *Slavery Today* (10–12). Series: Groundwork Guides. 2008, Groundwood $18.95 (978-088899772-2); paper $10.00 (978-088899773-9). The grim reality of slavery today — about 27 million slaves worldwide — and the root causes are examined here; personal stories enhance the text. (Rev: BL 11/15/08; LMC 3–4/09) [306.3]

9790 Bausum, Ann. *With Courage and Cloth: Winning the Fight for a Woman's Right to Vote* (6–12). 2004,

National Geographic $32.90 (978-0-7922-6996-0). A lively, well-illustrated text chronicles the history of the women's suffrage movement in America, focusing in particular on the period between 1913 and 1920 when the more militant National Women's Party, led by Alice Paul, stepped up pressure for women's right to vote. (Rev: BCCB 1/05; BL 10/15/04; SLJ 9/04) [324.6]

9791 Blake, John. *Children of the Movement* (10–12). 2004, Lawrence Hill $24.95 (978-1-55652-537-7). This work looks at the children of civil rights activists such as those of Martin Luther King, Jr., Malcolm X, and Julian Bond, and how the movement affected them. (Rev: BL 5/1/04) [323]

9792 Boerst, William J. *Marching in Birmingham* (7–12). Series: Civil Rights. 2008, Morgan Reynolds LB $27.95 (978-1-59935-055-4). This well-designed volume with firsthand accounts discusses the various efforts to achieve civil rights in Alabama. (Rev: SLJ 3/08)

9793 Bradley, David, and Shelley Fisher Fishkin, eds. *The Encyclopedia of Civil Rights in America* (5–10). 1997, Sharpe Reference $299.00 (978-0-7656-8000-6). This three-volume set contains 683 alphabetically arranged articles that explore the history, meaning, and application of civil rights issues in the United States. (Rev: BL 2/15/98; SLJ 5/98) [323]

9794 Brimner, Larry Dane. *Black and White: The Confrontation Between Reverend Fred L. Shuttlesworth and Eugene "Bull" Connor* (7–12). Illus. 2011, Boyds Mills $16.95 (978-1-59078-766-3). Brimner tells the fascinating story of the tension between two key individuals on opposite sides of the struggle for integration in Birmingham, Alabama. Sibert Honor 2012; ALA Notable Books 2012. (Rev: BL 10/15/11*; LMC 1–2/12; SLJ 11/1/11) [323.1196]

9795 Carson, Clayborne, et al, ed. *The Eyes on the Prize Civil Rights Reader: Documents, Speeches, and Firsthand Accounts from the Black Freedom Struggle, 1954-1990* (9–12). 1991, Penguin paper $18.00 (978-0-14-015403-0). Contains much of the material that is basic to the U.S. civil rights movement, including speeches by Martin Luther King, Jr. and writings by Malcolm X. (Rev: BL 9/15/91) [973]

9796 Cleaver, Eldridge. *Target Zero: A Life in Writing* (11–12). 2006, Palgrave $27.95 (978-1-4039-6237-9). This collection of his writings chronicles Cleaver's transformation from black militant to born-again Christian and champion of the American capitalist system. (Rev: BL 12/15/05) [323]

9797 Collins, Gail. *When Everything Changed: The Amazing Journey of American Women from 1960 to the Present* (9–12). 2009, Little, Brown $27.99 (978-031605954-1). This inspiring account details women's struggle for equality over the past five decades; beginning with the obstacles women faced in the 1950s and drawing parallels with the civil rights movement, it also

addresses the difficulties women currently encounter in balancing their professional and personal lives. (Rev: BL 10/1/09) [305.409]

9798 Crowe, Chris. *Getting Away with Murder: The True Story of the Emmett Till Case* (7–12). 2003, Penguin $18.99 (978-0-8037-2804-2). A gripping and detailed account of the brutal murder of 14-year-old Emmett Till, an African American boy from Chicago who was visiting relatives in Mississippi in 1954, with discussion of the impact of his death and the ensuing trial on the civil rights movement. (Rev: BL 2/15/03; HB 7–8/03; HBG 10/03; SLJ 5/03*) [364.15]

9799 Du Bois, W. E. B. *The Oxford W. E. B. Du Bois Reader* (10–12). 1996, Oxford paper $44.95 (978-0-19-509178-6). This broad-ranging collection of Du Bois's writings offers insights into his thinking about African American leadership, colonialism, communism in America, women's rights, black art and music, and politics. [305.8]

9800 Englebert, Phillis, and Beth Des Chenes, eds. *American Civil Rights: Primary Sources* (7–12). 1999, U.X.L $70.00 (978-0-7876-3170-3). This is a collection of 15 documents relating to the civil rights movement in America, such as speeches, proclamations, and autobiographical texts. (Rev: BL 1/1–15/00; SLJ 5/00; VOYA 4/00) [323.1]

9801 Etzioni, Amitai. *How Patriotic Is the Patriot Act? Freedom Versus Security in the Age of Terrorism* (9–12). 2004, Routledge $25.00 (978-0-415-95047-3). How will the United States balance security concerns and the protection of individual rights? Etzoni tackles practical issues such as ID cards and threats to public health. (Rev: BL 11/15/04) [345.73]

9802 Farrell, Courtney. *Children's Rights* (7–10). Series: Essential Issues. 2010, ABDO LB $32.79 (978-1-60453-952-3). Child labor, child trafficking, child sexual abuse, and child soldiers are all discussed in this volume that also looks specifically at the rights of children in the United States. (Rev: LMC 10/10; SLJ 4/1/10) [305.23086]

9803 Findlen, Barbara, ed. *Listen Up: Voices from the Next Feminist Generation. Rev. ed.* (10–12). 2001, Seal paper $16.95 (978-1-58005-054-8). A lively anthology that contains essays by young feminists that cover many subjects, including race, sexual orientation, and maternity. (Rev: BL 8/01) [305.42]

9804 Fireside, Harvey. *New York Times v. Sullivan: Affirming Freedom of the Press* (6–10). Series: Landmark Supreme Court Cases. 1999, Enslow LB $26.60 (978-0-7660-1085-7). The limits to freedom of the press was the subject of this Supreme Court case that had far-reaching results in the world of journalism. (Rev: BL 8/99) [347.3]

9805 Freedman, Jeri. *Women in the Workplace: Wages, Respect, and Equal Rights* (7–12). Series: A Young

Woman's Guide to Contemporary Issues. 2010, Rosen LB $31.95 (978-1-4358-3541-2). A conversational discussion of the history of women in the workplace, the need for equal opportunity and pay, and the protections available to women today, with chapters on sexual harassment and women in the military. (Rev: LMC 10/10; SLJ 4/1/10) [331.4]

9806 Friedan, Betty. *The Feminine Mystique* (10–12). 2001, Norton paper $14.95 (978-0-393-32257-6). This classic work, first published in 1963, analyzes the roles of women in society since World War II. [305.4]

9807 Frost-Knappman, Elizabeth, and Kathryn Cullen-DuPont. *Women's Suffrage in America: An Eyewitness History. Rev. ed.* (9–12). Series: Eyewitness History. 2005, Facts on File $80.00 (978-0-8160-5693-4). This revised edition adds new images, maps, and letters to the many primary sources that offer insights into the women's suffrage movement. (Rev: SLJ 10/05) [324.6]

9808 Gay, Kathlyn. *Cultural Diversity: Conflicts and Challenges: The Ultimate Teen Guide* (7–12). Series: It Happened to Me. 2003, Scarecrow paper $25.95 (978-0-8108-4805-4). Prejudice, stereotypes, and intolerance are among the topics discussed in this overview of the challenges faced and the possible solutions; teens' personal stories add immediacy. (Rev: SLJ 5/04; VOYA 4/04) [305.8]

9809 George, Charles, ed. *Living through the Civil Rights Movement* (7–12). Series: Living Through the Cold War. 2006, Gale LB $32.45 (978-0-7377-2919-1). Speeches and essays by those who experienced the civil rights movement firsthand lend depth to this overview. (Rev: SLJ 6/07) [323.1196]

9810 Gottfried, Ted. *Homeland Security Versus Constitutional Rights* (8–12). 2003, Millbrook LB $24.90 (978-0-7613-2862-9). Gottfried addresses important questions, both historical and contemporary, in the balancing of safety versus civil liberties. (Rev: BL 11/15/03; HBG 4/04; SLJ 12/03; VOYA 2/04) [303.3]

9811 Gottfried, Ted. *Privacy: Individual Rights v. Social Needs* (8–12). 1994, Millbrook LB $25.90 (978-1-56294-403-2). Discusses debates on privacy in relation to law enforcement, surveillance, abortion, AIDS, and the media. (Rev: BL 9/15/94; SLJ 10/94; VOYA 2/95) [342.73]

9812 Guernsey, JoAnn Bren. *Voices of Feminism: Past, Present, and Future* (7–10). Series: Frontline. 1996, Lerner LB $19.95 (978-0-8225-2626-1). After a 150-year history of feminism, this account covers the complicated issues and concerns surrounding this subject and discusses past and present leaders in the movement. (Rev: BL 9/15/96; SLJ 7/97; VOYA 4/97) [305.42]

9813 Guinier, Lani, and Susan Sturm. *Who's Qualified?* (10–12). 2001, Beacon paper $12.00 (978-0-8070-4335-6). This is an examination of the pros and cons of

affirmative action, with suggestions on how it should be changed. (Rev: BL 6/1–15/01) [331.13]

9814 Hill, Jeff. *Women's Suffrage* (9–12). Series: Defining Moments. 2005, Omnigraphics $49.00 (978-0-7808-0776-1). Covers the history of the movement, with profiles of key figures, excerpts from documents, and a discussion of the impact of passage of the 19th Amendment. (Rev: SLJ 3/06) [305.42]

9815 Hudson, David L., Jr. *Gay Rights* (8–12). Series: Point/Counterpoint. 2004, Chelsea House LB $32.95 (978-0-7910-8094-8). Both sides of the heated debate over gay rights are addressed, including the peripheral issues of military service, rights in the workplace, gay marriage, and adoption rights. (Rev: SLJ 4/05) [305.9]

9816 Jacobs, Thomas A. *What Are My Rights? 95 Questions and Answers About Teens and the Law* (7–12). 1997, Free Spirit paper $14.95 (978-1-57542-028-8). Using a question-and-answer format, this topically arranged manual describes in simple terms concerns relating to teens' rights within the family, at school, and on the job. (Rev: BL 4/1/98; SLJ 4/98; VOYA 6/98) [346.7301]

9817 Joshi, S. T. *In Her Place: A Documentary History of Prejudice Against Women* (9–12). 2006, Prometheus $29.98 (978-1-59102-380-7). Joshi presents primary-source documentation of the antifeminist propaganda that was widely disseminated for generations. (Rev: BL 2/15/06) [305.42]

9818 Kafka, Tina. *Gay Rights* (8–11). 2006, Gale $28.70 (978-1-59018-637-4). A look at the issue of gay rights, with information on historical and contemporary controversies. (Rev: BL 9/15/06; SLJ 1/07) [323.3]

9819 Landau, Elaine. *Your Legal Rights: From Custody Battles to School Searches, the Headline-Making Cases That Affect Your Life* (6–10). 1995, Walker LB $14.85 (978-0-8027-8360-8). A review of advances in protection of the legal rights of children and teenagers. (Rev: BL 5/15/95; SLJ 8/95) [346.7301]

9820 Levinson, Cynthia Y. *We've Got a Job: The 1963 Birmingham Children's March* (6–12). Illus. 2012, Peachtree $19.95 (978-156145627-7). This compelling photo-essay account of the May 1963 march by 4,000 African American students features large black-and-white photographs and draws extensively on primary sources. ALA Notable Books 2013. ∩ Lexile 1020L (Rev: BL 2/1/12*; HB 5–6/12; LMC 8–9/12*; SLJ 5/1/12*) [323.1196]

9821 Lewis, Andrew B. *The Shadows of Youth: The Remarkable Journey of the Civil Rights Generation* (10–12). 2009, Hill & Wang $28 (978-0-8090-8598-9). John Lewis, Julian Bond, and Stokely Carmichael are among the individuals profiled in this account of the formation of the Student Nonviolent Coordinating Committee and its importance in sparking public interest in civil rights. (Rev: BL 10/15/09; SLJ 2/10) [323.1196]

9822 Lucas, Eileen. *Civil Rights: The Long Struggle* (6–10). Series: Issues in Focus. 1996, Enslow LB $20.95 (978-0-89490-729-6). After a discussion of the first 10 amendments to the U.S. Constitution, this account focuses on the civil rights struggles of African Americans. (Rev: BL 9/15/96; SLJ 12/96) [323]

9823 McWhorter, Diane. *Carry Me Home: Birmingham, Alabama: The Climactic Battle of the Civil Rights Revolution* (10–12). 2001, Simon & Schuster paper $17.00 (978-0-7432-1772-9). An exciting account of the people, events, and social background of the struggle for civil rights in Birmingham, Alabama. (Rev: BL 2/15/01) [976.1]

9824 Marantz, Steve. *The Rhythm Boys of Omaha Central: High School Basketball at the '68 Racial Divide* (10–12). Illus. 2011, Univ. of Nebraska paper $17.95 (978-08032343-4-5). Even as the integrated 1967–1968 Omaha Central High School basketball team charged to tournament victory, a visit from segregationist presidential candidate George Wallace ignited racial riots that left the star black player and his coach in jail. (Rev: BL 3/1–15/11) [796.323]

9825 Mayer, Robert H. *The Civil Rights Act of 1964* (6–12). Series: At Issue in History. 2004, Gale LB $33.70 (978-0-7377-2304-5); paper $23.70 (978-0-7377-2305-2). The landmark act is described in an introductory overview followed by a collection of essays, speeches, and editorials that provide diverse views about the legislation and its impact on race relations in the United States. (Rev: BL 9/1/04; SLJ 9/04) [342.73]

9826 Mayer, Robert H. *When the Children Marched: The Birmingham Civil Rights Movement* (6–12). 2008, Enslow LB $25.95 (978-0-7660-2930-9). A moving account of the role young people played in Birmingham, Alabama, during the violent events of the civil rights movement, with photographs, news reports, quotations, a timeline, and so forth. (Rev: BL 6/1–15/08) [323.1196]

9827 Meany, John. *Has the Civil Rights Movement Been Successful?* (7–12). Series: What Do You Think? 2008, Heinemann LB $32.86 (978-1-4329-1675-6). After a history of the civil rights movement, this volume looks at legal reform, discrimination in popular culture, stereotyping, and national security, with a chapter discussing the circumstances revealed by Hurricane Katrina. (Rev: SLJ 1/1/09) [323.0973]

9828 Miller, Calvin Craig. *Backlash: Race Riots in the Jim Crow Era* (8–11). Illus. Series: Civil Rights Movement. 2012, Morgan Reynolds LB $28.95 (978-159935183-4). A survey of the horrific racial violence during the Jim Crow era, with a focus on riots in cities. (Rev: BL 2/1/12; SLJ 6/12) [305.800973]

9829 Monroe, Judy. *The Susan B. Anthony Women's Voting Rights Trial* (6–10). Series: Headline Court Cases. 2002, Enslow LB $26.60 (978-0-7660-1759-7). Monroe explores the fight for women's suffrage and the trial

of Susan B. Anthony for voting illegally in the 1872 election. (Rev: BL 3/15/03; HBG 3/03; SLJ 12/02) [324.6]

9830 Morgan, Bill, and Mary E. Williams, eds. *Howl on Trial: The Battle for Free Expression* (9–12). 2006, City Lights paper $14.95 (978-0-87286-479-5). With essays, correspondence, court transcripts, newspaper accounts, and so forth, this volume traces the reactions to the publication of Allen Ginsberg's *Howl and Other Poems* in 1956; it includes the complete text of the poem and also discusses censorship in general. (Rev: SLJ 2/07)

9831 Morrison, Toni. *Remember: The Journey to School Integration* (5–12). 2004, Houghton Mifflin $18.00 (978-0-618-39740-2). With striking archival photographs and a fictionalized narrative based on historical fact, this fascinating book explores the impact of the American struggle for civil rights on the children who were often at its center. (Rev: BL 4/15/04; SLJ 6/04) [379.2]

9832 Nakaya, Andrea C., ed. *Censorship* (7–12). Series: Opposing Viewpoints. 2005, Gale LB $36.20 (978-0-7377-2925-2); paper $24.95 (978-0-7377-2926-9). This new edition adds thoughtful essays on censorship and free speech as they relate to the press, telemarketing, electronic filtering, spam, and other issues. (Rev: SLJ 9/05) [363.3]

9833 Nakaya, Andrea C., ed. *Civil Liberties* (8–12). Series: Introducing Issues with Opposing Viewpoints. 2005, Gale LB $32.45 (978-0-7377-3387-7). A collection of articles and essays by various authors, all debating issues of civil liberties including the Patriot Act. (Rev: SLJ 5/06) [342.7308]

9834 Nakaya, Andrea C., ed. *Civil Liberties and War* (8–11). Series: Examining Issues Through Political Cartoons. 2005, Gale LB $29.95 (978-0-7377-2517-9). A current hot-button issue — the suspension of civil liberties during wartime — is put into historical perspective in this volume with cartoons dating from the wars as far back as the Civil War. (Rev: BL 2/1/06; SLJ 7/06) [323]

9835 Partridge, Elizabeth. *Marching for Freedom: Walk Together, Children, and Don't You Grow Weary* (6–12). 2009, Viking $19.99 (978-0-670-01189-6). Children and young adults' role in the civil rights movement is the focus of this moving photo-essay that features quotes from personal interviews and detailed photographs. Boston Globe–Horn Book nonfiction winner 2010; ALA Notable Books 2010. ∩ (Rev: BL 8/09*; HB 11–12/09; LMC 11/09; SLJ 10/09; VOYA 10/09) [323.1196]

9836 Pollitt, Katha. *Subject to Debate: Sense and Dissents on Women, Politics, and Culture* (10–12). 2001, Random House paper $12.95 (978-0-679-78343-5). This collection of 80 essays published from 1994 through 2000 deals mainly with the state of feminism and the role that feminism plays in the United States today. (Rev: BL 2/1/01) [814]

9837 Roberts, Terrence. *Simple, Not Easy: Reflections on Community, Social Responsibility, and Tolerance* (10–12). 2010, Parkhurst Brothers $24.95 (978-193516616-0). This collection of stirring and often humorous speeches reveals the philosophy of Roberts, a successful educator and businessman and one of the nine African American students integrated into Central High School in Little Rock, Arkansas, in 1957. (Rev: BL 2/1–15/10) [323]

9838 Sage, Jesse, and Liora Kasten. *Enslaved: True Stories of Modern Day Slavery* (11–12). 2006, Palgrave $24.95 (978-1-4039-7324-5). Hoping to prompt action to curb modern slavery, the authors of this book have collected firsthand stories from people around the globe who were forced to work unpaid and against their will as laborers, house servants, agricultural workers, and sex slaves; for mature teens. (Rev: BL 12/1/06) [306.3]

9839 Sawvel, Patty Jo, ed. *Student Drug Testing* (7–12). Series: Issues That Concern You. 2006, Gale LB $32.45 (978-0-7377-2424-0). Students, educators, journalists, government officials, and a selection of experts present their opinions on the efficacy and ethics of student drug testing. (Rev: SLJ 2/07)

9840 Schulz, William F. *Tainted Legacy: 9/11 and the Ruin of Human Rights* (10–12). 2003, Thunder's Mouth paper $12.95 (978-1-56025-489-8). The author, executive director of Amnesty International, asks tough questions about America's suspension of human rights in the wake of September 11, 2001. (Rev: BL 10/15/03) [323]

9841 Sothern, Billy. *Down in New Orleans: Reflections from a Drowned City* (9–12). 2007, Univ. of California $21.95 (978-0-520-25149-6). This is a testament of some of the lesser known victims of Hurricane Katrina, victims of those in power and their subsequent suspension of rights, such as those abandoned in jails, victims of crimes, those accused of terrorism and held for weeks with no family contact, as well as the author's personal experience of escape. (Rev: BL 8/07) [976.3]

9842 Steele, Philip. *Documenting Slavery and Civil Rights* (6–10). Series: Documenting History. 2010, Rosen LB $26.50 (978-1-4358-9671-0). With many interesting primary source materials — posters, postage stamps, photographs, cartoons, quotations — this slim volume discusses slavery from ancient times and the struggle to achieve civil rights. (Rev: LMC 11–12/10) [306.3]

9843 Steffens, Bradley. *The Free Speech Movement* (9–12). Series: American Social Movements. 2004, Gale LB $36.20 (978-0-7377-1156-1). A good source of balanced opinions on various aspects of free speech and its impact on American life, including Internet filtering. (Rev: SLJ 2/05) [323.44]

9844 Streissguth, Thomas, ed. *Slavery* (10–12). Series: History Firsthand. 2001, Greenhaven $36.20 (978-0-7377-0633-8). This overview of slavery uses primary sources to paint a frank and unrelenting account of the institution's massive emotional and physical toll. (Rev: BL 6/1–15/01) [306.3]

9845 Torr, James D. *The Patriot Act* (7–12). Series: The Lucent Terrorism Library. 2005, Gale LB $29.95 (978-1-59018-774-6). Torr explores the provisions of this controversial piece of legislation and looks at the ongoing criticisms about its threats to privacy and the Fourth Amendment. (Rev: SLJ 3/06) [345.73]

9846 Treanor, Nick, ed. *The Feminist Movement* (10–12). Series: New American Social Movements. 2002, Gale LB $36.20 (978-0-7377-1050-2). This anthology of essays, speeches, and interviews chronicles the strides made by the women's movement from the mid-19th-century suffrage campaigns of Elizabeth Cady Stanton through the present. (Rev: BL 8/02) [305.42]

9847 Turner, Chérie. *Everything You Need to Know About the Riot Grrrl Movement: The Feminism of a New Generation* (6–10). Series: Need to Know Library. 2001, Rosen LB $27.95 (978-0-8239-3400-3). A look at the movement that evolved from a 1970s aggressive punk attitude to a 1990s emphasis on equality and self-esteem. (Rev: SLJ 12/01) [781.66]

9848 Waldstreicher, David. *The Struggle Against Slavery: A History in Documents* (9–12). 2002, Oxford $39.95 (978-0-19-510850-7). This overview of slavery in America draws on primary source documents to chronicle the infamous institution's history from the late 17th century through the end of the Civil War. (Rev: BL 2/15/02; HBG 10/02; SLJ 2/02) [306.3]

9849 Walter, Lynn. *Women's Rights: A Global View* (10–12). Series: World View of Social Issues. 2000, Greenwood $66.95 (978-0-313-30890-1). Using case studies from five continents, this book examines the status of women in the world today. [305.4]

9850 Williams, Juan. *Eyes on the Prize: America's Civil Rights Years, 1954–1965* (9–12). 1986, Viking paper $20.00 (978-0-14-009653-8). Companion to a PBS series, this is a compelling, well-illustrated account of these peak years of civil rights unrest. (Rev: BL 2/15/98) [323.4]

9851 Williams, Mary E. *The Sexual Revolution* (10–12). Series: New American Social Movements. 2002, Gale LB $36.20 (978-0-7377-1052-6); paper $24.95 (978-0-7377-1051-9). From the "free love" movement of the 19th century through the radical changes in sexual mores of the late 20th century, this collection of articles, speeches, and interviews documents America's Sexual Revolution. (Rev: BL 8/02) [306.7]

9852 Williams, Mary E., ed. *Civil Rights* (7–12). Series: Examining Issues Through Political Cartoons. 2002, Gale LB $29.95 (978-0-7377-1100-4). This limited but unusual approach to exploration of the civil rights movement looks at political cartoons in four thematic chapters. (Rev: SLJ 10/02) [323.1]

9853 Wilson, Reginald. *Our Rights: Civil Liberties and the U.S.* (7–12). 1988, Walker $14.85 (978-0-8027-6751-6). A book that explains what civil rights are, how we have these freedoms, and how to protect them. (Rev: SLJ 8/88; VOYA 8/88) [323.4]

Immigration

9854 Allport, Alan. *Immigration Policy* (9–12). Series: Point/Counterpoint. 2005, Chelsea House LB $32.95 (978-0-7910-7923-2). An evenhanded review of hot-button immigration issues, including the challenges posed by widespread illegal immigration and whether the United States should adopt English as its official language. (Rev: BL 8/05; SLJ 9/05) [325.73]

9855 Aykroyd, Clarissa. *Refugees* (8–12). Series: The Changing Face of North America: Immigration Since 1965. 2004, Mason Crest LB $24.95 (978-1-59084-692-6). An overview of the origins of refugees to the United States and Canada, the reasons for their flight from their home countries, and the process they must undergo on arrival. (Rev: SLJ 11/04)

9856 Bacon, David. *Illegal People: How Globalization Creates Migration and Criminalizes Immigrants* (10–12). 2008, Beacon $25.95 (978-080704226-7). Focusing mainly on the United States, Bacon explains why the migration of workers occurs, and advocates for the fair treatment of these laborers. (Rev: BL 9/1/08) [331.6]

9857 Barbour, Scott. *Does Illegal Immigration Harm Society?* (8–12). Series: In Controversy. 2009, ReferencePoint LB $25.95 (978-1-60152-085-2). A timely discussion of immigration issues, answering questions such as "Does Illegal Immigration Harm the American Economy?" and "Does Illegal Immigration Lead to Increased Crime and Terrorism?" (Rev: BL 10/1/09; LMC 1–2/10)

9858 Bausum, Ann. *Denied, Detained, Deported: Stories from the Dark Side of American Immigration* (6–12). Illus. 2009, National Geographic $21.95 (978-142630332-6); LB $32.90 (978-142630333-3). The author discusses cases in which immigrants (Jews, Mexicans, Japanese, and others) have been mistreated by the U.S. government in the past; she also looks at some of today's issues surrounding immigration. Lexile 1170L (Rev: BL 4/15/09; SLJ 5/1/09*) [325.73]

9859 Buchanan, Patrick J. *State of Emergency: The Third World Invasion and Conquest of America* (10–12). 2006, St. Martin's $24.95 (978-0-312-36003-0). Paleoconservative Buchanan argues in this book that immigration is fragmenting America and that the coun-

try is headed toward European-like problems with angry ethnic groups. (Rev: BL 9/1/06) [325.73]

9860 Castaneda, Jorge G. *Ex Mex: From Migrants to Immigrants* (11–12). 2007, New Press $25.95 (978-1-59558-163-1). An examination of the reasons underlying migration from Mexico to the United States and of the economic impact on both countries. (Rev: BL 11/1/07) [973.00468]

9861 Daniels, Roger. *American Immigration: A Student Companion* (6–12). Series: Oxford Student Companions to American History. 2001, Oxford LB $65.00 (978-0-19-511316-7). An alphabetically arranged series of articles covering all aspects of immigration to the United States and the various ethnic groups that have made the journey, illustrated with photographs, maps, and reproductions. (Rev: BL 10/15/01; SLJ 6/01) [304.8]

9862 Daniels, Roger. *Coming to America: A History of Immigration and Ethnicity in American Life. 2nd ed.* (10–12). 2002, Perennial paper $17.95 (978-0-06-050577-6). After a general introduction on immigration, the author discusses various racial and national groups that have migrated to America. [325.73]

9863 Gerdes, Louise I., ed. *Immigration* (10–12). Series: Current Controversies. 2005, Greenhaven $27.96 (978-0-7377-2779-1); paper $18.96 (978-0-7377-2780-7). More than 30 essays cover such topics as illegal immigration, the treatment of immigrants, and the extent of the problem. (Rev: BL 8/05) [325.73]

9864 Haerens, Margaret, ed. *Illegal Immigration* (7–12). Series: Opposing Viewpoints. 2006, Gale LB $34.95 (978-0-7377-3356-3); paper $23.70 (978-0-7377-3357-0). This collection of essays on illegal immigration captures all sides of the issue, allowing readers to form their own opinions. (Rev: SLJ 10/06)

9865 Hay, Jeff, ed. *Immigration* (7–12). Series: Turning Points in World History. 2001, Greenhaven paper $24.95 (978-0-7377-0638-3). In a series of engaging essays, the phenomenon of immigration is explored and how shifting populations have changing world history. (Rev: BL 3/15/02) [325]

9866 Hopkinson, Deborah. *Shutting Out the Sky* (5–12). 2003, Scholastic $17.95 (978-0-439-37590-0). Five personal stories of young immigrants, striking photographs, and excerpts from primary documents form the backbone of this history of immigration to New York City in the late 19th century. (Rev: BL 11/1/03*; HBG 4/04; SLJ 12/03*; VOYA 6/04) [307.76]

9867 Lansford, Tom. *Immigration* (9–12). Series: Global Viewpoints. 2009, Gale/Greenhaven $36.20 (978-0-7377-4158-2). Taking a global view, this balanced book explores the issue of immigration along with its associated issues and implications through clear, concise pro/con discussions. (Rev: LMC 10/09)

9868 McCage, Crystal D. *U.S. Border Control* (9–12). Series: Compact Research. 2008, ReferencePoint LB $25.95 (978-1-60152-052-4). With facts, statistics, and quotations, this volume addresses measures to control American borders. (Rev: SLJ 2/1/09) [363.285]

9869 Meltzer, Milton. *Bound for America: The Story of the European Immigrants* (6–10). Series: Great Journeys. 2001, Benchmark LB $32.79 (978-0-7614-1227-4). An absorbing examination of the reasons for migration within and from Europe in the 19th and early 20th centuries, and of the hardships these travelers suffered. (Rev: BCCB 3/99; HBG 10/02; SLJ 3/02) [325.73]

9870 Miller, Debra A. *Illegal Immigration* (8–12). Series: Compact Research: Current Issues. 2007, Reference Point LB $24.95 (978-1-60152-009-8). Will a guest-worker program work? Do illegal aliens strain social services in the United States? All sides of these questions and many more are examined in this overview. (Rev: BL 4/1/07; LMC 10/07; SLJ 5/07) [304.8]

9871 Miller, Karen, ed. *Immigration* (8–12). Series: Social Issues Firsthand. 2006, Gale LB $28.70 (978-0-7377-2893-4). This compilation of 14 previously published essays gives insight into the experiences of varied immigrants to the United States — from Cuba, Vietnam, Bosnia, and Ethiopia, to name just a few nations — and looks at the difficulties they met in their new country. (Rev: SLJ 6/07) [304.8]

9872 Mills, Nicolaus, ed. *Arguing Immigration: The Debate over the Changing Face of America* (9–12). 1994, Simon & Schuster paper $12.00 (978-0-671-89558-7). Authors such as Toni Morrison discuss immigration, its costs, benefits, and cultural impact. (Rev: BL 9/1/94) [325.73]

9873 Newman, Lori, ed. *What Rights Should Illegal Immigrants Have?* (9–12). Series: At Issue. 2006, Gale LB $28.70 (978-0-7377-3480-5); paper $19.95 (978-0-7377-3481-2). Writers provide different perspectives on various aspects of illegal immigration, including health care and education. (Rev: SLJ 2/07)

9874 Outman, James L., and Lawrence W. Baker. *U.S. Immigration and Migration Primary Sources* (7–10). Series: Immigration and Migration Reference Library. 2004, Gale $70.00 (978-0-7876-7669-8). Primary source documents — including articles, letters, and Supreme Court rulings — chronicle the history of immigration to and migration within America. (Rev: SLJ 2/05) [304.8]

9875 Rangaswamy, Padma. *Indian Americans* (8–12). Series: The New Immigrants. 2006, Chelsea House $27.95 (978-0-7910-8786-2). This volume traces the history of immigration from India to the United States — and of Indians who have been living in Africa, Europe, and the Caribbean. (Rev: LMC 8–9/07; SLJ 3/07) [977.3]

9876 Santos, Edward J. *Everything You Need to Know If You and Your Parents Are New Americans* (7–12). Series: Need to Know Library. 2002, Rosen LB $27.95 (978-0-8239-3547-5). A useful and attractive guide for immigrant teens that gives practical advice on dealing with various facets of American life and emphasizes the possibility of retaining one's heritage while fitting in to a new culture. (Rev: BL 6/1–15/02; SLJ 4/02; VOYA 2/03) [304.8]

9877 Schroeder, Michael J. *Mexican Americans* (6–10). Series: The New Immigrants. 2007, Chelsea House LB $27.95 (978-0-7910-8785-5). A look at the political and social issues surrounding immigrants to the United States from Mexico, with graphics that will improve readers' understanding. (Rev: BL 7/07) [973]

9878 Sherman, Augustus F. *Augustus F. Sherman: Ellis Island Portraits, 1905-1920* (8–12). 2005, Aperture $40.00 (978-1-931788-60-1). Moving photographs taken by an Ellis Island immigration clerk spotlight would-be immigrants — many of them young people — who were held for further interrogation. (Rev: BL 5/15/05) [779.9]

9879 Yans-McLaughlin, Virginia, and Marjorie Lightman. *Ellis Island and the Peopling of America: The Official Guide* (10–12). 1997, New Press paper $19.95 (978-1-56584-364-6). This book chronicles the role of Ellis Island in U.S. history and reviews the waves of immigration to this country and past and present immigration policy, using reproductions of letters, visas, editorials and political cartoons, maps, charts and legal documents to bring the facts to life. (Rev: BL 8/97; SLJ 3/98; VOYA 4/98) [973]

Ethnic Groups and Prejudice

General and Miscellaneous

9880 Asante, Molefi Kete. *Erasing Racism: The Survival of the American Nation* (11–12). 2003, Prometheus $28.98 (978-1-59102-069-1). The legacy of racism is explored in detail in this scholarly study by writer/educator Asante, who offers abundant evidence of the lingering damage caused by racial discrimination. (Rev: BL 2/15/03*) [973]

9881 Barkan, Elliott Robert, ed. *A Nation of Peoples: A Sourcebook on America's Multicultural Heritage* (10–12). 1999, Greenwood $165.00 (978-0-313-29961-2). A group of scholarly essays that covers a number of racial, religious, and ethnic groups. [305.8]

9882 Barone, Michael. *The New Americans: How the Melting Pot Can Work Again* (10–12). 2001, Regnery $27.95 (978-0-89526-202-8). The author compares minority groups today with those at the turn of the last century, such as Irish Americans and African Americans, and finds that there is nothing new about multiculturalism. (Rev: BL 6/1–15/01) [305.9]

9883 Bartoletti, Susan Campbell. *They Called Themselves the K.K.K.: The Birth of an American Terrorist Group* (7–12). 2010, Houghton Mifflin $19 (978-0-618-44033-7). Today's young readers will be fascinated by this account of the rise of the Ku Klux Klan at the end of the Civil War and its continuing presence through much of the 20th century. ALA Notable Books 2011. ∩ (Rev: BL 8/10*; SLJ 8/10) [322.4]

9884 Cole, Carolyn Kozo, and Kathy Kobayashi. *Shades of L.A.: Pictures from Ethnic Family Albums* (7–12). 1996, New Press paper $20.00 (978-1-56584-313-4). A collection of photographs of African American, Mexican American, Asian American, and Native American family life in Los Angeles' ethnic and racial neighborhoods prior to 1965. (Rev: BL 8/96; VOYA 2/97) [979.4]

9885 Ferber, Abby L. *White Man Falling: Race, Gender, and White Supremacy* (11–12). 1998, Rowman & Littlefield $24.95 (978-0-8476-9027-5). Sociologist Ferber dissects the white supremacy movement in America through a thoughtful analysis of the writings and publications of such groups as the National Socialist White People's Party, Ku Klux Klan, and the National Alliance; useful for high school students of history and current events. (Rev: BL 11/15/98) [305.8]

9886 Fountas, Angela Jane, ed. *Waking Up American: Coming of Age Biculturally; First-Generation Women Reflect on Identity* (9–12). 2005, Seal paper $15.95 (978-1-58005-136-1). Young American women of bicultural heritage write candidly about what life is like for those caught between two different worlds. (Rev: BL 9/15/05) [305.48]

9887 Gaskins, Pearl Fuyo, ed. *What Are You? Voices of Mixed-Race Young People* (7–12). 1999, Henry Holt $18.95 (978-0-8050-5968-7). In essays, interviews, and poetry, 45 mixed-race young people ages 14 to 26 talk about themselves and growing up. (Rev: BL 5/15/99; HB 7–8/99; SLJ 7/99; VOYA 10/99) [973]

9888 Grearson, Jessie Carroll, and Lauren B. Smith. *Love in a Global Village: A Celebration of Intercultural Families in the Midwest* (10–12). 2001, Univ. of Iowa paper $19.95 (978-0-87745-740-4). This account examines cross-cultural relationships, such as partners from Iran and Lebanon, and from Germany and Bulgaria. Most of these couples are white but some are black. (Rev: BL 2/15/01) [306.84]

9889 Griffin, John Howard. *Black Like Me. 2nd ed.* (9–12). 1962, Signet paper $7.99 (978-0-451-19203-5). The true story of a white man who blackened his skin to experience firsthand how it felt to be an African American. [305.8]

9890 Haugen, David M., ed. *Interracial Relationships* (7–12). Series: At Issue. 2006, Gale LB $28.70 (978-0-

7377-2390-8); paper $19.95 (978-0-7377-2391-5). Pro and con articles present viewpoints on the degree of acceptance of interracial relationships in various sectors of society. (Rev: SLJ 8/07) [306.84]

9891 Hirschmann, Kris, ed. *Racial Profiling* (9–12). Series: At Issue. 2006, Gale LB $28.70 (978-0-7377-1979-6); paper $19.95 (978-0-7377-1980-2). Writers provide different perspectives on various aspects of racial profiling, including profiling of Muslims. (Rev: SLJ 2/07)

9892 Houze, David. *Twilight People: One Man's Journey to Find His Roots* (10–12). 2006, Univ. of California $24.95 (978-0-520-24398-9). The author discusses his childhood in small-town Mississippi in the 1960s and 1970s and his return to his native South Africa, where racial struggles mirrored what he had seen as a child. (Rev: BL 5/1/06) [916.804]

9893 Jacobs, Bruce. *Race Manners: Navigating the Minefield Between Black and White Americans* (10–12). 1999, Arcade $22.95 (978-1-55970-453-3). This book about interracial relations in America today discusses such topics as dating, everyday social life, stereotyping, and ethnic jokes. (Rev: BL 2/15/99; SLJ 5/99) [305.8]

9894 Kassam, Nadya, ed. *Telling It Like It Is: Young Asian Women Talk* (7–12). 1998, Livewire paper $11.95 (978-0-7043-4941-4). These 22 short, informal essays reveal various attitudes toward sexism and racism as experienced by Hindu and Moslem girls living in Britain whose families are from the Indian subcontinent. (Rev: BL 9/15/98; SLJ 8/98) [305.8914]

9895 O'Hearn, Claudine Chiawei, ed. *Half and Half: Writers on Growing Up Biracial and Bicultural* (7–12). 1998, Pantheon paper $13.00 (978-0-375-70011-8). This work contains 18 personal essays by people who live and work in the U.S., but who, because they are biracial and bicultural, are not sure where they belong. (Rev: BL 9/1/98) [306.84]

9896 St. Stephen's Community House. *It's Not All Black and White: Multiracial Youth Speak Out* (7–12). Illus. 2012, Annick paper $12.95 (978-15545138-0-2). In poems, interviews, essays, and artwork, multiracial young people in Canada discuss racial identity, family ties, stereotypes, assimilation, and so forth. (Rev: BL 12/15/12; LMC 5–6/13; SLJ 3/13) [305.800971]

9897 Stanford, Eleanor, ed. *Interracial America* (7–12). Series: Opposing Viewpoints. 2006, Gale LB $34.95 (978-0-7377-2943-6); paper $23.70 (978-0-7377-2944-3). A useful compilation of essays and excerpts on racial issues such as equal opportunity, interracial families, immigration, and profiling; each chapter includes a bibliography of related articles. (Rev: SLJ 8/06)

9898 Torr, James D., ed. *Race Relations* (10–12). Series: Opposing Viewpoints. 2005, Gale LB $36.20 (978-0-7377-2955-9); paper $24.95 (978-0-7377-2956-6). Essays present both sides of diverse issues including interracial marriage, affirmative action, and reparations for slavery. (Rev: SLJ 11/05) [305.8]

9899 Whittemore, Katharine, and Gerald Marzorati. *Voices in Black and White: Writings on Race in America from Harper's Magazine* (9–12). 1992, Square LB $21.95 (978-1-879957-07-7); paper $14.95 (978-1-879957-06-0). This collection of articles on the American obsession with race includes writings by Mark Twain, William Faulkner, James Baldwin, Shelby Steele, and Jesse Jackson. (Rev: BL 11/15/92) [305.8]

9900 Williams, Mary E., ed. *The White Separatist Movement* (8–12). Series: American Social Movements. 2002, Gale LB $36.20 (978-0-7377-1054-0); paper $24.95 (978-0-7377-1053-3). This collection of essays, speeches, book excerpts, and personal observations looks at groups ranging from the Ku Klux Klan to neo-Nazi skinheads and discusses the reasons why people are attracted to such organizations. (Rev: BL 9/15/02) [305.8]

9901 Young, Mitchell, ed. *Racial Discrimination* (7–12). Series: Issues on Trial. 2006, Gale LB $34.95 (978-0-7377-2787-6). Young has compiled a useful volume of opinions on cases brought before the Supreme Court that involved racial discrimination. (Rev: SLJ 1/07)

African Americans

9902 Anson, Robert Sam. *Best Intentions: The Education and Killing of Edmund Perry* (10–12). 1988, Knopf paper $13.95 (978-0-394-75707-0). An account of the death of a black boy who was a student at a prestigious prep school. (Rev: BL 4/15/87; BR 1–2/88; VOYA 10/87) [305.2]

9903 Astor, Gerald. *The Right to Fight: A History of African Americans in the Military* (11–12). 2001, Da Capo paper $18.50 (978-0-306-81031-2). This overview of the black experience in the American military focuses largely on the period between the end of World War I and the late 1990s, although it also offers a summary of African American service during the Civil War. (Rev: BL 11/15/98*) [355]

9904 Baldwin, James. *The Fire Next Time* (10–12). 1995, Modern Library paper $9.00 (978-0-679-74472-6). This prophesy of things to come concerning race relations is based on the author's feelings about Black Muslims and his religious background. [305.8]

9905 Baldwin, James. *Notes of a Native Son. 3rd ed.* (10–12). 1990, Beacon paper $13.00 (978-0-8070-6431-3). A collection of essays about being black in the United States. [305.8]

9906 Ball, Edward. *Slaves in the Family* (10–12). 1998, Ballantine paper $15.95 (978-0-345-43105-9). A meticulously researched history of the author's family since their arrival in South Carolina in 1698, tracing their role as slave owners and slave traders, including

the author's successful search for several of his distant African American cousins. (Rev: BL 2/15/98; SLJ 6/98) [973]

9907 Carrol, Rebecca. *Sugar in the Raw: Voices of Young Black Girls in America* (10–12). 1997, Crown paper $12.00 (978-0-517-88497-3). This is a collection of 15 monologues by black teenage women about their lives, attitudes, hopes, dreams, frustrations, and experiences. (Rev: BL 12/15/96; SLJ 2/98) [305.8]

9908 Chafe, William, et al, ed. *Remembering Jim Crow: African Americans Tell About Life in the Segregated South* (10–12). 2001, New Press $55.00 (978-1-56584-697-5). The book and accompanying CD give eyewitness accounts of the brutal segregation policies known as Jim Crowism and of the indignities they involved. (Rev: BL 10/1/01) [305.896]

9909 Cleaver, Eldridge. *Soul on Ice* (10–12). 1968, McGraw-Hill paper $13.95 (978-0-385-33379-5). The classic collection of essays for mature readers about a black American and his anger at the state of race relations in the United States. [305.8]

9910 Cole, Harriette, and John Pinderhuges. *Coming Together: Celebrations for African American Families* (4–12). 2003, Hyperion $22.99 (978-0-7868-0753-6). Traditions surrounding celebrations including Christmas, Kwanzaa, and naming ceremonies are covered here, with accompanying crafts, menu suggestions, and activities. (Rev: BL 12/15/03; HBG 4/04; VOYA 2/04) [306.8]

9911 Eaton, Susan. *The Other Boston Busing Story* (10–12). 2001, Yale $17.00 (978-0-300-08765-9). This is a report on the success of busing inner-city black children to white suburban schools since the 1970s and on the personal changes it made in many of the children. (Rev: BL 3/15/01) [379.2]

9912 Ebony, ed. *Ebony Pictorial History of Black America* (7–12). 1971, Johnson $54.95 (978-0-87485-049-9). These three volumes trace African American history from slavery to today's fight for integration and equality. [305.8]

9913 Feelings, Tom. *The Middle Passage: White Ships Black Cargo* (10–12). 1995, Dial paper $75.00 (978-0-8037-1804-3). A powerful visual record and concise narrative of the slave trade that describes life in Africa and horrifying details of slave ships. (Rev: BL 10/15/95; SLJ 2/96) [973]

9914 Garrison, Mary. *Slaves Who Dared: The Stories of Ten African-American Heroes* (7–12). 2002, White Mane LB $19.95 (978-1-57249-272-1). Historical prints and quotations from original texts lend authenticity to these moving accounts of famous and less-well-known men and women who escaped from slavery. (Rev: BL 9/1/02; HBG 3/03; SLJ 7/02) [973]

9915 Genovese, Eugene D. *Roll, Jordan, Roll: The World the Slaves Made* (10–12). 1976, Random House paper $18.00 (978-0-394-71652-7). This is a history of slavery in America that concentrates on the daily life and traditions of slaves. [305.8]

9916 Halberstam, David. *The Children* (10–12). 1998, Random House $29.95 (978-0-679-41561-9); paper $17.95 (978-0-449-00439-5). This prize-winning reporter profiles the eight courageous students who launched the sit-ins in Nashville, Tennessee, in 1960, outlines the moral and political roots of the civil rights movement and the philosophical divisions that developed, assesses the impact of television coverage of the movement, and traces the eight students' later lives and how their experiences affected them as adults. (Rev: BL 1/1–15/98; SLJ 11/98) [370.19]

9917 Haley, Alex. *Roots* (9–12). 2007, Perseus paper $15.95 (978-1-59315-449-3). A thoroughly researched history of the journey of a black American's family from Africa to slavery in the United States, ending with the author's own generation; first published in 1976. [920]

9918 Haley, James, ed. *Reparations for American Slavery* (6–12). Series: At Issue. 2004, Gale LB $29.95 (978-0-7377-1340-4). The arguments for and against the payments or other compensation for the years of slavery to present-day African Americans are the subject of this collection of writings. (Rev: BL 2/15/04) [326]

9919 Hansen, Joyce, and Gary McGowan. *Breaking Ground, Breaking Silence: The Story of New York's African Burial Ground* (8–12). 1998, Henry Holt $19.95 (978-0-8050-5012-7). The graphic story of the finding, in 1991, of the mid-18th-century African Burial Ground in Manhattan and what it reveals about the lives of slaves in New York. (Rev: BL 5/15/98; HBG 10/98; SLJ 5/98; VOYA 8/98) [974.7]

9920 Harris, Laurie Lanzen. *The Great Migration North, 1910–1970* (7–12). Illus. Series: Defining Moments. 2011, Omnigraphics LB $55 (978-078081186-7). This is a detailed yet readable account of the migration of approximately 6 million African Americans to the cities of the North in the 20th century. **e** (Rev: BL 3/15/12*; SLJ 6/12) [307.2]

9921 Holliday, Laurel, ed. *Dreaming in Color, Living in Black and White: Our Own Stories of Growing Up Black in America* (8–12). 2000, Pocket paper $4.99 (978-0-671-04127-4). This is a moving collection of first-person accounts by African Americans who tell of the racism they faced while growing up. (Rev: BL 2/15/00; SLJ 4/00; VOYA 4/00) [305.896]

9922 Horton, James Oliver. *Landmarks of African American History* (8–12). Series: American Landmarks. 2005, Oxford LB $32.95 (978-0-19-514118-4). A tour of 13 historic sites that played a significant role in African American history, with good illustrations and maps. (Rev: SLJ 8/05) [973]

9923 Horton, James Oliver, and Lois E. Horton. *Slavery and the Making of America* (9–12). 2004, Oxford $37.95 (978-0-19-517903-3). Chronicles the history of slavery in America and explores how the legacy of slavery has helped to shape the United States as we know it today, using the stories of well-known and unknown individuals. (Rev: BL 10/1/04; SLJ 2/05) [973]

9924 Hurmence, Belinda. *My Folks Don't Want Me to Talk About Slavery: Twenty-One Oral Histories of Former North Carolina Slaves* (9–12). 1984, Blair paper $6.95 (978-0-89587-039-1). A unique view of slavery as provided by 21 narratives supplied by former slaves. [973]

9925 Hutchinson, Earl Ofari. *Beyond O.J.: Race, Sex, and Class Lessons for America* (9–12). 1996, Middle Passage $12.95 (978-1-881032-12-0). A discussion of the implications of the Simpson case regarding race, class, and sex in America. (Rev: BL 12/15/95) [305.8]

9926 Jacob, Iris. *My Sisters' Voices: Teenage Girls of Color Speak Out* (7–12). 2002, Henry Holt paper $13.00 (978-0-8050-6821-4). Teen girls of color describe their feelings, aspirations, and disappointments in prose and poetry. (Rev: BL 3/1/02; SLJ 10/02; VOYA 12/02) [305.235]

9927 Johnson, Paula. *Inner Lives: Voices of African American Women in Prison* (10–12). 2003, New York Univ. $65.00 (978-0-8147-4254-9). Best suited for mature teens, this fascinating study examines the lives of African American women in prison, offering interviews with incarcerated black women as well as an overview of the justice system that put them behind bars. (Rev: BL 3/15/03) [365]

9928 Kimbro, Dennis. *What Keeps Me Standing: Letters from Black Grandmothers on Peace, Hope, and Inspiration* (10–12). 2003, Doubleday $23.95 (978-0-385-50635-9). This collection of letters, prayers, poems, and scriptures from black grandmothers around the world offers valuable advice for living that will inspire people of all races. (Rev: BL 4/15/03) [305.896]

9929 King, Martin Luther, Jr. *Strength to Love* (10–12). 1985, Fortress paper $17.00 (978-0-8006-1441-6). A collection of sermons against injustice and racism. [151]

9930 King, Martin Luther, Jr. *A Testament of Hope: The Essential Writings of Martin Luther King, Jr.* (9–12). 1986, Harper & Row paper $23.95 (978-0-06-064691-2). This source contains the most important writing of King arranged by such topics as sermons, essays, and interviews. (Rev: SLJ 8/86) [323.1]

9931 McKissack, Patricia C., and Fredrick McKissack. *Black Hands, White Sails: The Story of African-American Whalers* (6–10). 1999, Scholastic paper $17.95 (978-0-590-48313-1). This account of African American involvement in the whaling industry from colonial times through the 19th century also touches on the abolitionist movement, the Underground Railroad, and the Civil War. (Rev: BCCB 11/99; BL 9/1/99; HB 11–12/99; HBG 4/00; VOYA 2/00) [639.2]

9932 Meltzer, Milton. *The Black Americans: A History in Their Own Words, 1619-1983* (7–10). 1984, Crowell paper $12.99 (978-0-06-446055-2). As told through letters, speeches, articles, and other original sources, this is a history of black people in America. [305.8]

9933 Mosley, Walter. *Life Out of Context* (10–12). 2006, Thunder's Mouth $12.95 (978-1-56025-846-9). Mosley calls on young African Americans to take responsibility for their destinies and those of other people of color around the globe. (Rev: BL 12/15/05) [305.8]

9934 Nash, Sunny. *Bigmama Didn't Shop at Woolworth's* (10–12). 1996, Texas A & M Univ. $19.95 (978-0-89096-716-4). A collection of vignettes by an African American woman who remembers growing up in the 1950s in a segregated neighborhood in Bryan, Texas, and the poverty, prejudice, and indignities of the time. (Rev: SLJ 12/96) [323.4]

9935 Oliver, Kitty. *Multicolored Memories of a Black Southern Girl* (10–12). 2001, Univ. Press of Kentucky $35.00 (978-0-8131-2208-3). The author, an African American who came of age in the 1960s, describes the civil and women's rights movements of the time and her participation in them. (Rev: BL 10/1/01) [975.9]

9936 Osborne, Linda Barrett. *Miles to Go for Freedom: Segregation and Civil Rights in the Jim Crow Years* (6–10). Illus. 2012, Abrams $24.95 (978-141970020-0). Drawing on first-person accounts and including many photographs, this companion to *Traveling the Freedom Road* (2009) looks at racial segregation and early civil rights efforts from the 1890s to mid-1950s. (Rev: BL 5/15/12*; LMC 8–9/12; SLJ 1/12) [305.896]

9937 Raboteau, Albert J. *African-American Religion* (9–12). Series: Religion in American Life. 1999, Oxford $32.95 (978-0-19-510680-0). The author explores religious freedom as a basic part of American history and society, traces the influence of black churches in America from colonial times to the present, and examines the contributions of varied religious traditions to African American culture and identity, particularly in the struggle against racism. (Rev: BL 9/15/99; SLJ 8/99) [261.1]

9938 Schomp, Virginia. *Marching Toward Freedom* (6–10). Series: Drama of African-American History. 2008, Marshall Cavendish LB $23.95 (978-0-7614-2643-1). With lots of primary source material, this volume provides a good overview of the struggle for equal rights between the years 1929 and 1954, with profiles of key figures and stories about individuals. (Rev: BLO 6/17/08) [305.896]

9939 Sharp, Anne Wallace. *A Dream Deferred: The Jim Crow Era* (7–10). Series: Lucent Library of Black History. 2005, Gale LB $32.45 (978-1-59018-700-5).

An overview of the impact of the Jim Crow laws that stretched from Reconstruction to the Supreme Court's decision in *Brown* v. *Board of Education* (1954). (Rev: BL 10/15/05) [323.1196]

9940 Sharp, Anne Wallace. *Separate but Equal: The Desegregation of America's Schools* (7–12). Series: Lucent Library of Black History. 2006, Gale LB $28.70 (978-1-59018-953-5). A thorough history of the education of African Americans, complete with interviews of those who experienced first hand the desegregation battles of the 1950s and 1960s. (Rev: SLJ 6/07) [379.2]

9941 Sims, Darryl D., ed. *Sound the Trumpet! Messages to Empower African American Men* (10–12). 2003, Judson paper $14.00 (978-0-8170-1437-7). The unique challenges — both social and spiritual — facing African American men are examined in this collection of sermons by such well-known black clergymen as Otis Moss, Ralph West, Jeremiah Wright Jr., and Charles E. Booth. (Rev: BL 2/15/03) [248.8]

9942 Summers, Barbara, ed. *Open the Unusual Door: True Life Stories of Challenge, Adventure, and Success by Black Americans* (8–11). 2005, Houghton Mifflin paper $7.99 (978-0-618-58531-1). Sixteen successful African Americans write about choices they made that changed the direction of their lives. (Rev: BL 1/1–15/06; SLJ 12/05) [920]

9943 Tackach, James, ed. *Early Black Reformers* (10–12). Series: History Firsthand. 2003, Gale paper $24.95 (978-0-7377-1598-9). This anthology contains the writings and firsthand experiences of African American civil rights advocates before Martin Luther King, Jr. (Rev: BL 6/1–15/03) [973]

9944 Taylor, Yuval, ed. *Growing Up in Slavery: Stories of Young Slaves as Told by Themselves* (9–12). Illus. by Kathleen Judge. 2005, Lawrence Hill $22.95 (978-1-55652-548-3). A searing portrait of slavery and its effects on the enslaved can be found in this collection of first-person accounts written by African Americans who spent the early part of their lives in bondage. (Rev: BL 2/1/05; SLJ 7/05) [306.3]

9945 Van Peebles, Mario. *Panther: A Pictorial History of the Black Panthers and the Story Behind the Film* (8–12). 1995, Newmarket paper $16.95 (978-1-55704-227-9). The first part of this heavily illustrated book recounts the beginnings of the Black Panther Party and its eventual collapse; the second half describes the making of the movie about the party. (Rev: VOYA 2/96) [973]

9946 Wallenfeldt, Jeff, ed. *The Black Experience in America: From Civil Rights to the Present* (8–12). Illus. Series: African American History and Culture. 2010, Rosen LB $45 (978-161530146-1). With a useful timeline and interesting sidebars, this is a broad and informative overview of black influence on American life in the years involved, with profiles of key figures. ℮ (Rev: BL 2/1/11; LMC 5–6/11) [323.1196]

9947 Watkins, Mel, ed. *African American Humor: The Best Black Comedy from Slavery to Today* (10–12). 2002, Lawrence Hill $29.95 (978-1-55652-430-1); paper $18.95 (978-1-55652-431-8). An entertaining overview of African American humor from the time of slavery through the present, with examples of a wide variety of formats. (Rev: BL 7/02) [817.008]

9948 Weaver, Afaa Michael, ed. *These Hands I Know: African-American Writers on Family* (10–12). 2002, Sarabande paper $16.95 (978-1-889330-72-3). A wide-ranging portrait of African American family life is painted in this collection of essays by such well-known writers and poets as Henry Louis Gates, Gwendolyn Brooks, and Alice Walker. (Rev: BL 8/02) [814]

Asian Americans

9949 Galang, M. Evelina. *Her Wild American Self* (10–12). 1996, Coffee House paper $12.95 (978-1-56689-040-3). In a series of essays, the author tells of her life as a Filipino American woman, her cultural background, and her assimilation into American life. (Rev: SLJ 11/96) [304]

9950 Lee, Joann Faung Jean. *Asian Americans in the Twenty-first Century* (10–12). 2008, New Press $24.95 (978-159558152-5). Subtitled *Oral Histories of First-to Fourth-generation Americans from China, Japan, India, Korea, the Philippines, Vietnam, and Laos,* this volume contains nearly 30 interviews with Asian Americans that reveal concerns about cultural choices, assimilation, prejudice, differences between generations, and so forth. (Rev: BL 9/1/08) [920]

9951 Martin, Jennifer C. *The Korean Americans* (10–12). Series: Immigrants in America. 2005, Gale LB $29.95 (978-1-59018-079-2). Examines the pattern of Korean immigration to the United States, assimilation problems, and the contributions of notable Korean Americans. (Rev: BL 8/05) [973]

9952 Nam, Vickie, ed. *Yell-Oh Girls! Emerging Voices Explore Culture, Identity, and Growing up Asian American* (8–12). 2001, HarperCollins paper $13.00 (978-0-06-095944-9). An anthology of fiction and poetry written by Asian American high school and college students, revealing their feelings about topics including heritage, stereotypes, adoption, and interracial dating. (Rev: BL 7/01; SLJ 10/01; VOYA 2/02) [305.235]

9953 Ng, Franklin. *The Taiwanese Americans* (10–12). Series: The New Americans. 1998, Greenwood $55.00 (978-0-313-29762-5). After an introduction to Taiwan, this book describes the immigration of Taiwanese to the United States principally after 1965, their reception here, and their present life and contributions. (Rev: SLJ 11/98) [973]

9954 Oppenheim, Joanne. *Dear Miss Breed: True Stories of the Japanese American Incarceration During World War II and a Librarian Who Made a Difference* (7–10). 2006, Scholastic $22.99 (978-0-439-56992-7). An affecting portrait of a World War II children's librarian and the incarcerated young Japanese Americans who benefited from her commitment to her profession. (Rev: BL 1/1–15/06*; SLJ 3/06; VOYA 2/06) [940.53]

9955 She, Colleen. *Teenage Refugees from China Speak Out* (7–12). Series: In Their Own Voices. 1995, Rosen LB $27.95 (978-0-8239-1847-8). Interviews with native Chinese teenagers who are now living in the United States. (Rev: BL 6/1–15/95; SLJ 5/95) [305.23]

9956 Takaki, Ronald T. *Strangers From a Different Shore: A History of Asian Americans. Rev. ed.* (10–12). 1998, Little, Brown paper $16.95 (978-0-316-83130-7). Chronicles the diverse experiences of different waves of Asian immigrants to the United States, from early 19th-century Chinese workers on the transcontinental railroad to the late 20th-century arrivals from war-torn Southeast Asia. [305.8]

Hispanic Americans

9957 Acuna, Rodolfo F. *U.S. Latino Issues* (10–12). Series: Contemporary American Ethnic Issues. 2003, Greenwood $55.00 (978-0-313-32211-2). Bilingual education, border politics, affirmative action, and services for undocumented immigrants are among the issues addressed here that affect the Latino population in the United States. (Rev: SLJ 6/04) [305.868]

9958 Alvarez, Julia. *Once Upon a Quinceanera* (9–12). 2007, Penguin $23.95 (978-0-670-03873-2). Alvarez, originally from the Dominican Republic and traveling to many American Latino communities, documents the details of the rite of passage for fifteen-year-old girls, known as the quinceanera, typically a grand wedding-type reception complete with limousines, a gown, a young ladies' court of her friends and relatives, photographers, and speeches and she also includes the history of this ritual, stemming from Mayan ceremonies and Spanish balls. (Rev: BL 7/07) [395.2]

9959 Cerar, K. Melissa. *Teenage Refugees from Nicaragua Speak Out* (7–12). Series: In Their Own Voices. 1995, Rosen LB $27.95 (978-0-8239-1849-2). The horror of the contra war, after the corrupt rule of the Somoza family was ended by the Sandinistas, is recalled by Nicaraguan teens who fled their country, leaving their families, to seek refuge in the United States. (Rev: BL 6/1–15/95) [973]

9960 Cofer, Judith Ortiz. *The Year of Our Revolution* (9–12). 1998, Arte Publico $16.95 (978-1-55885-224-2). This collection of stories, poems, and fables explores the experiences of Puerto Rican Americans, focusing in particular on the cultural disconnect between Puerto Rican-born immigrants to the United States and their American-born children. (Rev: BL 7/98; HBG 3/99; VOYA 6/99) [863]

9961 Cofer, Judith Ortiz, ed. *Riding Low on the Streets of Gold* (6–12). 2003, Arte Publico $14.95 (978-1-55885-380-5). Latino writers consider issues close to teen hearts in this collection of fiction, poetry, and memoirs. (Rev: BL 12/1/03; SLJ 6/04) [810]

9962 Cortez, Sarah, ed. *Windows into My World: Latino Youth Write Their Lives* (9–12). 2007, Arte Publico paper $14.95 (978-1-55885-482-6). Short essays by young (and not so young — many are of college age and older) Hispanic Americans reflect typical concerns — friendship, family, death, divorce — with the added dimensions of immigration, a common language and heritage, different hopes and dreams. (Rev: SLJ 5/07) [305.2]

9963 Cuadros, Paul. *A Home on the Field: How One Championship Team Inspires Hope for the Revival of Small Town America* (9–12). 2006, Rayo $22.95 (978-0-06-112027-5). The story of a soccer team made up of Latino immigrant students living in North Carolina that overcame obstacles to make it to a state championship. (Rev: BL 9/1/06) [796.334]

9964 Doak, Robin. *Struggling to Become American: 1899-1940* (5–10). Series: Latino-American History. 2007, Chelsea House LB $35.00 (978-0-8160-6443-4). Doak looks at Latino immigration — especially from Puerto Rico, Cuba, and Mexico — and at the conditions of Hispanic laborers in the United States during World War I and the Great Depression; includes photographs, sidebars, political cartoons, maps, and so forth. (Rev: SLJ 7/07)

9965 Gay, Kathlyn. *Leaving Cuba: From Operation Pedro Pan to Elian* (6–12). 2000, Twenty-First Century LB $22.90 (978-0-7613-1466-0). The plight of young Elian Gonzalez brought attention to Cubans' efforts to escape their oppressive regime and the uncertain welcome they face in the United States. (Rev: BL 3/1/01; HBG 3/01; SLJ 1/01; VOYA 6/01) [362.87]

9966 Molinary, Rosie. *Hijas Americanas: Beauty, Body Image, and Growing Up Latina* (10–12). 2007, Seal paper $15.95 (978-1-58005-189-7). The author and the 80 or so other Latinas she interviewed share their thoughts on everything from body image to sexuality to faith, prejudice, and the portrayal of Latinas in the media. (Rev: BL 4/15/07) [305.235]

Jewish Americans

9967 Alphin, Elaine Marie. *An Unspeakable Crime: The Prosecution and Persecution of Leo Frank* (9–12). 2010, Carolrhoda LB $22.95 (978-0-8225-8944-0). A moving account of the fate of Leo Frank, a Jewish man who was falsely accused of murdering a 13-year-old girl and was lynched by a mob in Atlanta in 1913. Lexile 1210L (Rev: BL 1/1–15/10; LMC 8–9/10; SLJ 3/10) [364.152]

9968 Finkelstein, Norman H. *Forged in Freedom: Shaping the Jewish-American Experience* (6–12). 2002, Jewish Publication Society $19.95 (978-0-8276-0748-4). Text and photographs present an overview of Jews' contributions to the United States, their influence on the culture, and the problems they have faced. (Rev: BL 8/02; HBG 3/03) [973.04]

9969 Schleifer, Jay. *A Student's Guide to Jewish American Genealogy* (7–12). Series: American Family Tree. 1996, Oryx $36.95 (978-0-89774-977-0). An in-depth survey of Jewish history serves as a framework for realistic genealogical information, with plenty of valuable sources cited. (Rev: SLJ 1/97) [973]

Native Americans

9970 Eagle, Adam Fortunate, and Tim Findley. *Heart of the Rock: The Indian Invasion of Alcatraz* (10–12). 2002, Univ. of Oklahoma $29.95 (978-0-8061-3396-6). The 1969 seizure of Alcatraz Island by a small band of Native Americans hoping to call attention to Indian rights is chronicled in this fascinating book. (Rev: BL 3/1/02) [979.4]

9971 Frazier, Ian. *On the Rez* (10–12). 2000, Farrar paper $14.00 (978-0-312-27859-5). The author describes his experiences and the people he met on the Pine Ridge Reservation in South Dakota. (Rev: BL 11/15/99; SLJ 8/00) [970.004]

9972 King, C. Richard. *Media Images and Representations* (11–12). Series: Contemporary Native American Issues. 2005, Chelsea House LB $30 (978-0-7910-7968-3). King explores how Native Americans have been portrayed in television, film, journalism, the Internet, and even sports mascots. (Rev: SLJ 5/06)

9973 Krupat, Arnold, and Brian Swann, eds. *Here First: Autobiographical Essays by Native American Writers* (10–12). 2000, Random House paper $15.95 (978-0-375-75138-7). Twenty-six contemporary Native American writers describe growing up and finding their identity and culture as Native Americans. (Rev: BL 5/15/00) [810]

9974 Moore, MariJo, ed. *Genocide of the Mind: An Anthology of Native American Writing* (10–12). 2003, Thunder's Mouth paper $16.95 (978-1-56025-511-6). This collection of essays by Native American writers, representing more than 25 tribal groups, documents the struggle of native peoples to retain their cultural identity. (Rev: BL 11/1/03) [305.397]

9975 Weitzman, David. *Skywalkers: Mohawk Ironworkers Build the City* (7–10). 2010, Flash Point $19.99 (978-1-59643-162-1). With a dramatic account of a bridge collapse in Quebec in 1907, this volume describes the central role Mohawk men have played in ironwork and bridge and skyscraper construction, discussing the hazards they faced and including primary sources. Lexile 1150L (Rev: BL 10/15/10*; HB

11–12/10; LMC 11–12/10; SLJ 10/1/10; VOYA 8/10) [690.092]

Other Ethnic Groups

9976 Aseel, Maryam Qudrat. *Torn Between Two Cultures: An Afghan-American Woman Speaks Out* (10–12). 2003, Capital $22.95 (978-1-931868-36-5). Aseel writes engagingly about the impact of current events — most notably the terrorist attacks of 9/11 — on the lives of Muslim Americans in the United States. (Rev: BL 4/15/03) [305.48]

9977 Bayoumi, Moustafa. *How Does It Feel to Be a Problem? Being Young and Arab in America* (11–12). 2008, Penguin $24.95 (978-1-59420-176-9). In this compelling book for mature readers, Bayoumi explores the post-9/11 experiences of seven young Arab Americans living in Brooklyn. (Rev: BL 6/1–15/08*) [305.892]

9978 Brockman, Terra Castiglia. *A Student's Guide to Italian American Genealogy* (7–12). Series: American Family Tree. 1996, Oryx $35.00 (978-0-89774-973-2). This book, a guide to searching for Italian American ancestors, contains Web sites, computer programs, addresses, and other sources of information. (Rev: SLJ 10/96) [929]

9979 Cheek, Angie, ed. *The Foxfire 40th Anniversary Book: Faith, Family, and the Land* (9–12). Series: Foxfire. 2006, Doubleday paper $17.95 (978-0-307-27551-6). A collection of folklore, recipes, and wisdom from Appalachia from the nonprofit group Foxfire. (Rev: BL 9/1/06) [975.8]

9980 Fulbeck, Kip. *Part Asian, 100% Hapa* (9–12). 2006, Chronicle paper $19.95 (978-0-8118-4959-3). Portraits of Hawaiians known as "Hapa" (that is, of mixed racial background) are accompanied by their thoughts on the implications of their heritage. (Rev: BL 4/15/06) [305.8]

9981 Hossell, Karen Price. *The Irish Americans* (6–12). Series: Immigrants in America. 2003, Gale LB $29.95 (978-1-56006-752-8). The story of the thousands of Irish people who migrated to America, where they faced discrimination before being assimilated into society and being accepted as true Americans. (Rev: BL 11/15/03) [973]

9982 Katz, William L. *Black Indians: A Hidden Heritage* (7–10). 1986, Macmillan $17.95 (978-0-689-31196-3). A history of the group that represented a mixture of the Indian and black races and its role in opening up the West. (Rev: BL 6/15/86; SLJ 8/86) [970]

9983 Malek, Alia. *A Country Called Amreeka: A Chronicle of America as Lived by Arab-Americans* (10–12). 2009, Free Press $25 (978-141658972-3). Using interviews and background material, the author gives the reader a sense of the experiences of Arab Americans from the early 1960s to the present. ℮ (Rev: BL 9/09) [973]

9984 Paddock, Lisa, and Carl S. Rollyson. *A Student's Guide to Scandinavian American Genealogy* (7–12). Series: American Family Tree. 1996, Oryx $36.95 (978-0-89774-978-7). An introduction to the Scandinavian countries, people, and emigration to America, and information on how to research specific nationalities. (Rev: SLJ 10/96) [929]

9985 Schur, Joan Brodsky. *The Arabs* (8–11). Series: Coming to America. 2005, Gale LB $34.95 (978-0-7377-2148-5). With profiles of several famous Arab Americans (including Ralph Nader and Naomi Shihab Nye), this title uses primary and secondary sources to present an overview of Arab Americans, their reasons for migrating, their social mores, and their adaptation to their new country. (Rev: BL 3/15/05; SLJ 3/05) [973]

9986 Verbrugge, Allen, ed. *Muslims in America* (9–12). Series: Contemporary Issues Companion. 2005, Gale LB $36.20 (978-0-7377-2315-1). A brief history of Muslims in America precedes essays presenting varying viewpoints on topics ranging from bias against Muslims following September 11 to issues facing Muslim women. (Rev: BL 8/05; SLJ 3/05) [305.6]

Forms of Dissent

9987 Katovsky, Bill. *Patriots Act: Voices of Dissent: An Oral History* (9–12). 2006, Lyons $22.95 (978-1-59228-816-8). This collection of interviews with 20 Americans explores the relationship between patriotism and dissent, focusing particularly on how the latter has come to be viewed as disloyal and unpatriotic. (Rev: BL 2/15/06) [320.5]

9988 Schultz, Bud, and Ruth Schultz. *The Price of Dissent: Testimonies to Political Repression in America* (10–12). 2001, Univ. of California paper $29.95 (978-0-520-22402-5). This is an account of three social movements of the 20th century: the labor, civil rights, and antiwar movements with excerpts from about 100 activists including Paul Robeson, Jr., John Lewis, and Abbie Hoffman. (Rev: BL 11/1/01) [325]

Social Concerns and Problems

9989 Andryszewski, Tricia. *The Militia Movement in America: Before and After Oklahoma City* (7–12). 1997, Millbrook LB $24.90 (978-0-7613-0119-6). This work traces the roots of the anti-government militia movement in the United States from the late 1800s to the present, with coverage of events in Ruby Ridge, Waco, Oklahoma City, and elsewhere. (Rev: BL 2/15/97; SLJ 3/97; VOYA 2/98) [320.4]

9990 Atkin, S. Beth. *Gunstories: Life-Changing Experiences with Guns* (7–10). 2006, HarperCollins LB $17.89 (978-0-06-052660-3). In first-person accounts, teenagers write about their very varied experiences with guns. (Rev: BL 1/1–15/06; SLJ 1/06) [363.33]

9991 Bekoff, Marc. *Animals Matter: A Biologist Explains Why We Should Treat Animals with Compassion and Respect* (10–12). 2007, Shambhala paper $14.00 (978-1-59030-522-5). For debates and to spark classroom discussion, this is a thought-provoking, wide-ranging, and balanced exploration of animal rights. (Rev: BL 11/1/07) [179]

9992 Bennetts, Leslie. *The Feminine Mistake: Are We Giving Up Too Much?* (10–12). 2007, Hyperion $24.95 (978-1-4013-0306-8). Should young women concentrate on careers or family? Bennetts looks at the economic realities of forgoing a career. ⌒ (Rev: BL 2/15/07) [331.4]

9993 Berger, Dan, et al, ed. *Letters from Young Activists: Today's Rebels Speak Out* (11–12). 2005, Thunder's Mouth paper $14.95 (978-1-56025-747-9). This collection of essays by young activists addresses a wide array of social issues, including racism, immigration reform, homophobia, sexism, ecology, capital punishment, and peace. (Rev: BL 10/15/05) [322.4]

9994 Cottle, Thomas J. *At Peril: Stories of Injustice* (10–12). 2001, Univ. of Massachusetts $35.00 (978-1-55849-278-3). Through a series of true-life stories, the author presents the cases of people who are "at risk" because of health problems, social and economic status, and other factors, and how this often produces injustice. (Rev: BL 2/15/01) [361.1]

9995 Crooker, Constance Emerson. *Gun Control and Gun Rights* (9–12). Series: Historical Guides to Controversial Issues in America. 2003, Greenwood $57.95 (978-0-313-32174-0). The arguments for and against gun control are clearly laid out, with statistics, quotations, notes, and a bibliography. (Rev: SLJ 2/04) [363.3]

9996 Currid-Halkett, Elizabeth. *Starstruck: The Business of Celebrity* (10–12). 2010, Faber & Faber $26 (978-086547909-8). What makes a celebrity? Currid-Halkett explores why the public is so fascinated by socialites, actors, and other familiar figures. (Rev: BL 10/1–15/10) [306.4]

9997 Desetta, Al, and Sybil Wolin, eds. *The Struggle to Be Strong: True Stories by Teens About Overcoming Tough Times* (6–12). 2000, Free Spirit paper $14.95 (978-1-57542-079-0). Teens talk about problems such as addicted and abusive parents, AIDS, drugs and alcohol, school, health, and so forth. (Rev: SLJ 8/00)

9998 Doeden, Matt. *Gun Control: Preventing Violence of Crushing Constitutional Rights?* (9–12). Illus. Series: USA Today's Debate: Voices and Perspectives. 2011, Lerner/Twenty-First Century LB $35.93 (978-076136433-7). Drawing on articles from *USA Today*, this title looks at both sides of the gun control debate. (Rev: BL 9/15/11) [363.330973]

9999 Ensler, Eve. *Insecure at Last: Losing It in Our Security-Obsessed World* (11–12). 2006, Random House $21.95 (978-1-4000-6334-5). Playwright of *The Vagina Monologues* (1998), Ensler now confronts the world's security obsession in a post-9/11 society, especially threats toward women, and suggests ways to reevaluate our notions of "protection" to regain a sense of true freedom; for mature teens. (Rev: BL 9/15/06) [305.4209]

10000 Gifford, Clive. *Violence on the Screen* (7–10). Series: Voices. 2006, Black Rabbit LB $21.95 (978-1-58340-985-5). Readers are presented with facts, statistics, and opinions about the possible effects of violence in movies and video games and on TV. (Rev: BL 12/15/06) [303.6]

10001 Ginn, Janel, ed. *Do Religious Groups in America Experience Discrimination?* (7–12). Series: At Issue. 2007, Gale LB $28.70 (978-0-7377-3399-0). Many interesting questions are addressed in the articles collected here, including whether feminists discriminate against Islamic women and whether the Episcopal Church discriminates against homosexuals. (Rev: BL 10/1/07) [305.609]

10002 Griffin, Starla. *Girl, 13: A Global Snapshot of Generation e* (6–12). 2005, Hylas paper $22.95 (978-1-59258-112-2). Thirteen-year-olds around the world contributed to this volume, answering questions about their views of the world and writing essays about their lives and aspirations. (Rev: SLJ 2/06)

10003 Haddock, Patricia. *Teens and Gambling: Who Wins?* (7–12). Series: Issues in Focus. 1996, Enslow LB $20.95 (978-0-89490-719-7). The controversial subject of gambling is introduced — its lure, addiction, and problems, particularly as related to teenagers. (Rev: BL 8/96; SLJ 8/96; VOYA 10/96) [363.4]

10004 Herumin, Wendy. *Child Labor Today: A Human Rights Issue* (7–12). Series: Issues in Focus Today. 2007, Enslow LB $23.95 (978-0-7660-2682-7). A look at the often-deplorable working conditions of children around the world, with many photographs and personal stories. (Rev: BL 11/15/07) [331.3]

10005 Homsher, Deborah. *Women and Guns: Politics and the Culture of Firearms in America* (10–12). 2000, M.E. Sharpe $32.95 (978-0-7656-0678-5). This contribution to the pro- and anti-gun debate focuses on women and guns throughout American history and how this adds a new dimension to the controversy. (Rev: BL 12/1/00) [363.3]

10006 Hyde, Margaret O. *Gambling: Winners and Losers* (6–10). 1995, Millbrook LB $23.40 (978-1-56294-532-9). A timely subject gets rather dry treatment in this book that tells of the history, types, and psychology of gambling, with quotations from many case studies. (Rev: BL 12/15/95; SLJ 3/96) [363.4]

10007 Jensen, Carl, ed. *Stories That Changed America: Muckrakers of the 20th Century* (10–12). 2000, Seven Stories $26.95 (978-1-58322-027-6). This is a collection of important exposés from the past century that includes works by Margaret Sanger, Rachel Carson, I. F.

Stone, Edward R. Morrow, Betty Friedan, Malcolm X, Ralph Nader, and Woodward and Bernstein. (Rev: BL 8/00; SLJ 6/01) [070]

10008 Judson, Karen. *Animal Testing* (7–12). 2005, Benchmark LB $25.95 (978-0-7614-1882-5). Covers the history, science, ethics, and new laws relating to experimentation using animals, with sidebars, quotations, and color and black-and-white photographs. (Rev: SLJ 7/06)

10009 Martin, James. *The Meaning of the 21st Century: A Vital Blueprint for Ensuring Our Future* (9–12). 2006, Riverhead $26.95 (978-1-57322-323-2). An overarching look at the issues humans will face in the future — from the environmental to the technological — by the author of 1978's *The Wired Society*. (Rev: BL 8/06) [303.48]

10010 Milite, George A. *Gun Control* (8–12). Series: Compact Research. 2007, Reference Point LB $24.95 (978-1-60152-010-4). This compact volume provides lots of information for report writers, with illustrations, quotations from primary sources, lists of facts, statistical charts, and brief timelines. (Rev: SLJ 5/07) [363.3]

10011 Morrison, Adrian R. *An Odyssey with Animals: A Veterinarian's Reflections on the Animal Rights and Welfare Debate* (10–12). 2009, Oxford $29.95 (978-019537444-5). The case for testing animals in biomedical research, albeit in a humane way, is presented by a leading researcher. (Rev: BL 7/09) [610.72]

10012 Pringle, Laurence. *The Animal Rights Controversy* (7–12). 1989, Harcourt $16.95 (978-0-15-203559-4). A book about the way animals are abused and misused that covers topics such as factory farming, experimentation, and zoos. (Rev: BL 1/15/90; SLJ 5/90; VOYA 4/90) [197]

10013 Roleff, Tamara L., ed. *Gun Control* (9–12). Series: Opposing Viewpoints. 2007, Gale LB $34.95 (978-0-7377-3660-1); paper $23.70 (978-0-7377-3661-8). Both sides of the issue are presented in this Opposing Viewpoints entry, which includes articles, interviews, editorial cartoons, and other materials that address all angles of the debate. (Rev: BL 12/15/07) [344.7305]

10014 Schechter, Harold. *Savage Pastimes: A Cultural History of Violent Entertainment* (9–12). 2005, St. Martin's $24.95 (978-0-312-28276-9). Schechter challenges the idea that today's popular entertainment is more violent than that of the past. (Rev: BL 2/1/05) [303.6]

10015 Senker, Cath. *Privacy and Surveillance* (8–11). Illus. Series: Ethical Debates. 2012, Rosen LB $27.95 (978-144886022-7). This volume takes a balanced look at contemporary surveillance techniques, the reasons for increases in surveillance, and the importance of maintaining individuals' right to privacy. (Rev: BL 5/1/12; SLJ 6/12) [323.44]

10016 Sherman, Aliza. *Working Together Against Violence Against Women* (6–10). Series: Library of Social

Activism. 1996, Rosen LB $27.95 (978-0-8239-2258-1). An examination of violence against women, including date rape, stranger rape, assault, and domestic violence, and of the actions being taken by both government and private agencies; advice on how teenagers can help themselves, a friend, and their communities is also offered. (Rev: SLJ 2/97; VOYA 6/97) [303.6]

10017 Spilsbury, Louise. *Same-Sex Marriage* (8–11). Illus. Series: Ethical Debates. 2012, Rosen LB $27.95 (978-144886020-3). A balanced discussion of the controversies surrounding same-sex marriage, with details of solutions adopted in various places. **e** (Rev: BL 5/1/12; SLJ 6/12) [306.84]

10018 Stallwood, Kim W., ed. *Speaking Out for Animals: True Stories About Real People Who Rescue Animals* (10–12). 2001, Booklight/Lantern paper $18.00 (978-1-930051-34-8). This account describes the work of such activists as Paul McCartney and how they devote part of their lives to helping animals and promoting animal rights. (Rev: BL 7/01) [179]

10019 Streissguth, Thomas. *Hate Crimes* (10–12). Series: Library in a Book. 2003, Facts on File $45.00 (978-0-8160-4879-3). After describing hate crimes and their history, this volume presents easily understood information on legislation and court decisions plus short biographies of important individuals, a glossary, a research guide, and a list of relevant organizations. (Rev: SLJ 2/04) [364.15]

10020 Sugarmann, Josh. *NRA: Money, Firepower and Fear* (9–12). 1991, National $19.95 (978-0-915765-88-1). An in-depth review of the National Rifle Association and the methods it's used to transform a constitutional right into the social nightmare of unregulated possession of weapons. (Rev: BL 12/1/91) [363.3]

10021 Walljasper, Jay. *All That We Share: How to Save the Economy, the Environment, the Internet, Democracy, Our Communities, and Everything Else That Belongs to All of Us* (9–12). Illus. 2011, New Press paper $18.95 (978-15955849-9-1). An interesting exploration of the many ways in which we already share resources, the efficiency of this approach, and possible future developments. **e** (Rev: BL 12/1–15/10) [333.2]

10022 Watkins, Christine. *Child Labor and Sweatshops* (8–12). Series: At Issue. 2010, Greenhaven $31.80 (978-073774874-1); paper $22.50 (978-07377487-5-8). Does child labor harm girls more than boys? This and many other controversies are discussed in this volume that presents opposing viewpoints. (Rev: BL 4/1/11) [331.3]

10023 Weiner, Eric. *The Geography of Bliss: One Grump's Search for the Happiest Places in the World* (9–12). 2008, Twelve $25.99 (978-0-446-58026-7). Are you happy? The answer may depend on where you live, as Weiner discovered during a comparison of wealthy, tranquil, troubled, democratic, and otherwise defined locations. ∩ (Rev: BL 12/1/07) [910.4]

10024 Weisman, Alan. *The World without Us* (9–12). 2007, St. Martin's $24.95 (978-0-312-34729-1). A fascinating survey of how nature would take over if mankind were suddenly to disappear — and of the long-lasting effects of man's presence that nature will not be able to repair. (Rev: BL 4/1/07) [333]

Environmental Issues

General and Miscellaneous

10025 Adair, Rick, ed. *Critical Perspectives on Politics and the Environment* (8–11). Series: Critical Anthologies on Environment and Climate. 2006, Rosen LB $31.95 (978-1-4042-0823-0). A compilation of 16 articles from *Scientific American* that focus on the tension between environmental and political issues, looking in turn at international treaties, domestic regulation, free trade, and current and future problems. (Rev: BL 11/1/06) [333.7]

10026 Alley, Richard. *Earth: The Operators' Manual* (10–12). Illus. 2011, Norton $27.95 (978-039308109-1). Nobel Peace Prize-winner Alley examines the history of humans' use of different kinds of energy, from burning wood to fossil fuels; how we have compromised our environment; and what we can do to save it in the future. (Rev: BL 3/1–15/11) [621.04209]

10027 Anderson, Michael. *The Politics of Saving the Environment* (7–10). Illus. Series: Environment: Ours to Save. 2011, Britannica LB $31.70 (978-161530505-6). This volume provides a history of the environmental movement, discussion of environmental laws, and information on endangered species. (Rev: BL 2/15/12; VOYA 12/11) [337.72]

10028 Andryszewski, Tricia. *The Environment and the Economy: Planting the Seeds for Tomorrow's Growth* (7–12). 1995, Millbrook LB $24.90 (978-1-56294-524-4). Traces the emergence of environment-versus-economy issues. (Rev: BL 12/1/95; SLJ 11/95) [363.7]

10029 Ballesta, Laurent, and Pierre Descamp. *Planet Ocean: Voyage to the Heart of the Marine Realm* (8–12). 2007, National Geographic $40.00 (978-1-4262-0186-8). Full of eye-catching photographs, this ecology-focused volume visits various undersea environments to show just what we may lose to pollution, overfishing, and other threats. (Rev: BLO 11/19/07) [577.7]

10030 Barnes, Peter. *Climate Solutions: A Citizen's Guide* (9–12). 2008, Chelsea Green paper $9.95 (978-1-60358-005-2). Using a question-and-answer format, this is handy guide to global warming, with clear discussion of all important aspects and possible solutions. (Rev: BL 4/1/08) [363.738]

638

10031 Barton, Greg, ed. *American Environmentalism* (9–12). Series: American Social Movements. 2002, Gale LB $36.20 (978-0-7377-1044-1). An excellent historical overview of the American environmental movement, presenting the thoughts of such diverse activists as Ralph Waldo Emerson, Henry David Thoreau, Teddy Roosevelt, and Al Gore. (Rev: BL 9/1/02) [333.7]

10032 Begley, Ed. *Living Like Ed* (8–12). 2008, Clarkson Potter paper $18.00 (978-0-307-39643-3). Begley offers practical tips on adopting a greener way of living, categorizing the changes as "easy," "not-so-big," and "big" and looking separately at the home, transportation, recycling, energy, the garden and kitchen, clothing, and personal care. (Rev: BL 12/1/07) [333.72]

10033 Berne, Emma Carlson. *Global Warming and Climate Change* (8–12). Series: Compact Research. 2007, Reference Point LB $24.95 (978-1-60152-019-7). What are the consequences of global warming? What are the controversies surrounding global warming? These and other questions are discussed from various points of view, with facts, profiles, and illustrations. (Rev: SLJ 1/08)

10034 Bily, Cynthia A. *Global Warming* (8–12). 2006, Gale LB $34.95 (978-0-7377-2935-1); paper $23.70 (978-0-7377-2936-8). Pro and con essays provide diverse viewpoints on the threat of global warming, its causes and effects, and the measures to be taken to combat it. (Rev: SLJ 7/06)

10035 Blatt, Harvey. *America's Environmental Report Card: Are We Making the Grade?* (8–12). 2004, MIT $35.00 (978-0-262-02572-0). From global warming to water pollution, this volume looks at today's burning environmental issues and potential solutions. (Rev: BL 11/1/04) [363.7]

10036 Bowden, Rob. *Building Homes for Tomorrow* (8–12). Series: Development Without Damage. 2010, Smart Apple Media LB $34.25 (978-1-59920-252-5). This is an informative and accessible introduction to the global housing crisis and solutions including sustainable housing, improved energy conservation, and new strategies in urban planning. A companion title explores *Food and Water* (2010). (Rev: LMC 5–6/10; SLJ 11/09) [728.047]

10037 Bowden, Rob. *Earth's Water Crisis* (7–12). Series: What If We Do Nothing? 2007, World Almanac LB $30.60 (978-0-8368-7754-0). Bowden underlines the importance of water in key areas of our lives, presents future scenarios, and asks readers what they would do. (Rev: LMC 11–12/07; SLJ 5/07) [333.91]

10038 Brand, Stewart. *Whole Earth Discipline: An Ecopragmatist Manifesto* (10–12). 2009, Penguin $25.95 (978-067002121-5). Brand, an expert in the environmental field, challenges the usual arguments against nuclear power, cities, and genetic engineering. (Rev: BL 9/15/09) [304.2]

10039 Brower, Michael, and Warren Leon. *The Consumer's Guide to Effective Environmental Choices: Practical Advice from the Union of Concerned Scientists* (9–12). 1999, Three Rivers paper $15.00 (978-0-609-80281-6). The authors present steps people can take to live more ecologically safe and aware lifestyles. (Rev: BL 4/1/99; SLJ 9/99) [363.7]

10040 Brune, Michael. *Coming Clean: Breaking America's Addiction to Oil and Coal* (10–12). 2008, Sierra Club paper $14.95 (978-157805149-6). Brune, of the Rainforest Action Network, uncovers corporate deceit and promotes his quest for clean energy. (Rev: BL 9/1/08) [333.79]

10041 Burdick, Alan. *Out of Eden: An Odyssey of Ecological Invasion* (10–12). 2005, Farrar $25.00 (978-0-374-21973-4); paper $14.00 (978-0-374-53043-3). The disruption caused by animal and plant migrations to new environments — wild camels in Australia, snakes in Hawaii, for example — is the focus of this interesting exploration. (Rev: SLJ 1/06)

10042 Caldicott, Helen. *If You Love This Planet: A Plan to Heal the Earth* (9–12). 1992, Norton paper $13.95 (978-0-393-30835-8). Presents, as a medical metaphor, the diagnosis and tough cure for an ailing planet Earth. (Rev: BL 3/1/92*) [363.7]

10043 Calhoun, Yael. *The Environment in the News* (8–12). Series: Science News Flash. 2007, Chelsea House LB $31.95 (978-0-7910-9253-8). Serious researchers will find this slim volume a useful starting place — it covers various viewpoints on many issues and provides graphs, illustrations, photographs, and resources for further information. (Rev: SLJ 8/07)

10044 Casper, Julie Kerr. *Climate Systems: Interactive Forces of Global Warming* (9–12). 2009, Facts on File $40 (978-0-8160-7260-6). The carbon cycle, atmospheric energy, orbital variations, and ocean currents are among the topics covered in this volume that stresses the urgent need for action against global warming. (Rev: LMC 3–4/10; SLJ 11/09) [863.4]

10045 Chandler, Gary, and Kevin Graham. *Environmental Causes* (5–10). Series: Celebrity Activists. 1997, Twenty-First Century LB $25.90 (978-0-8050-5232-9). This book discusses how entertainers including Robert Redford, Sting, and Chevy Chase and other celebrities such as Al Gore, Ted Turner, and Jerry Greenfield support environmental causes. (Rev: SLJ 1/98) [363.7]

10046 Conaway, James. *Vanishing America: In Pursuit of our Elusive Landscapes* (9–12). 2007, Shoemaker & Hoard $24.95 (978-1-59376-128-8). Conaway (editor of *Preservation* magazine) uses individual instances to underline the ongoing neglect of the natural (and historical) landscape of America. (Rev: BL 10/1/07) [917.3]

10047 Danson, Ted, and Michael D'Orso. *Oceana: Our Endangered Oceans and What We Can Do to Save Them* (10–12). Illus. 2011, Rodale $29.99 (978-160529262-

5). Actor and activist Danson teams up with Pulitzer Prize-nominated author D'Orso to trace Danson's activist roots and provide real-world solutions to the problem of our dying oceans. (Rev: BL 3/1–15/11) [333.95]

10048 Earle, Sylvia A. *The World Is Blue: How Our Fate and the Ocean's Are One* (9–12). Illus. 2009, National Geographic $26 (978-142620541-5). Interspersing scientific data with personal experiences, oceanographer Earle explains the role healthy oceans play in sustaining all life on Earth and details the devastating impact of human activities. (Rev: BL 10/1/09)

10049 Farquharson, Vanessa. *Sleeping Naked Is Green: How an Eco-cynic Unplugged Her Fridge, Sold Her Car, and Found Love in 366 Days* (10–12). 2009, Houghton Mifflin paper $13.95 (978-05470732-8-6). A funny account of Farquharson's efforts to live green for one year. **e** (Rev: BL 4–5/09) [333.72092]

10050 Fishman, Charles. *The Big Thirst: The Secret Life and Turbulent Future of Water* (10–12). 2011, Free Press $26.99 (978-143910207-7). An engrossing analysis of the world's water supply, how it plays a part in poverty and politics, and what will happen in the future as water becomes less and less available. (Rev: BL 3/1–15/11) [333.91]

10051 Flannery, Tim. *We Are the Weather Makers: The History of Climate Change* (7–12). Adapted by Sally M. Walker. 2009, Candlewick $17.99 (978-0-7636-3656-2). This succinct overview of the perils of global warming provides explanations of our scientific understanding of the problem as well as examples of steps we each can take to reduce carbon emissions. (Rev: BL 12/1/09; LMC 11–12/09; SLJ 12/09) [363.73874]

10052 Gonick, Larry, and Alice Outwater. *The Cartoon Guide to the Environment* (10–12). 1996, HarperPerennial paper $16.95 (978-0-06-273274-3). Using cartoons, this sobering account tells how humanity is gradually destroying the earth through heedless misuse of the environment. (Rev: SLJ 9/96) [320.5]

10053 Gore, Al. *Our Choice: A Plan to Solve the Climate Crisis* (10–12). Illus. 2009, Rodale paper $26.99 (978-15948673-4-7). With illuminating diagrams and photographs, Al Gore provides a practical guide to solving the climate change crisis by enlisting the emerging technologies of wind, solar, and geothermal energy. (Rev: BLO 11/15/09*) [363.738]

10054 Gore, Al, and Jane O'Connor. *An Inconvenient Truth* (6–12). 2007, Viking $23.00 (978-0-670-06271-3). The adult companion to the award-winning documentary, adapted for middle- and high-schoolers, will alarm readers and compel them to act. ALA Notable Books 2008. (Rev: BL 4/15/07; HB 5–6/07; SLJ 3/07*) [363.73874]

10055 Haddock, Patricia. *Environmental Time Bomb: Our Threatened Planet* (6–12). Series: Issues in Focus. 2000, Enslow LB $26.60 (978-0-7660-1229-5). Up-to-

date information is given on current dangers to our environment. (Rev: BL 9/15/00; HBG 3/01; SLJ 12/00) [363.7]

10056 Haugen, David M., ed. *Should Drilling Be Permitted in the Arctic National Wildlife Refuge?* (10–12). Series: At Issue: Environment. 2008, Gale/Greenhaven $29.95 (978-073773930-5); paper $23.96 (978-07377393-1-2). This collection of essays examines the environmental implications of drilling for oil in the arctic refuge — a valuable resource for research and debate projects. (Rev: BL 9/1/08) [333.95]

10057 Hawley, Steven. *Recovering a Lost River: Removing Dams, Rewilding Salmon, Revitalizing Communities* (10–12). 2011, Beacon $26.95 (978-080700471-5). A thoughtful examination of the damage dams have caused to our ecosystems, featuring the removal of dams on the Snake River and the impact this would have on both human and wildlife populations. (Rev: BL 3/1–15/11) [333.91]

10058 Horowitz, Joy. *Parts per Million: The Poisoning of Beverly Hills High School* (9–12). 2007, Viking $24.95 (978-0-670-03798-8). One might not associate toxic, cancer-causing elements with a community of the privileged and famous, but cancer has reared its head in Beverly Hills High School where there have been oil wells under the town and there has been little done over the years to protect from exposure. (Rev: BL 7/07) [346.79403]

10059 Hunter, Emily, ed. *The Next Eco Warriors: 20 Young Women and Men Who Are Saving the Planet* (10–12). Illus. 2011, Conari paper $19.95 (978-15732448-6-2). Hunter, daughter of the cofounders of Greenpeace, profiles 22 young people dedicated to spreading ecological awareness through often unconventional and imaginative means. (Rev: BL 3/1–15/11) [333.72]

10060 Isham, Jonathan, and Sissel Waage, eds. *Ignition: What You Can Do to Fight Global Warming and Spark a Movement* (9–12). 2007, Island paper $18.95 (978-1-59726-156-2). For those in a dilemma of wanting to act, but not knowing where to begin to stop or slow global warming, this guide will help, with essays, success stories of activism, and what to avoid. (Rev: BL 7/07) [363.738]

10061 Jensen, Derrick, and Stephanie McMillan. *As the World Burns: 50 Simple Things You Can Do to Stay in Denial* (10–12). 2007, Seven Stories paper $14.95 (978-1-58322-777-0). In punchy graphic novel format, the authors deliver a humorous but eye-opening message about the state of the environment. (Rev: BL 11/15/07; SLJ 5/08) [741.5]

10062 Johnson, Rebecca L. *Investigating Climate Change: Scientists' Search for Answers in a Warming World* (6–10). Illus. Series: Discovery! 2008, Lerner LB $30.60 (978-082256792-9). A compelling historical overview of climate change and its causes is presented in this book full of data, diagrams, photographs, charts, and maps. (Rev: BL 9/1/08; SLJ 1/1/09; VOYA 12/08) [551.6]

10063 Kaye, Cathryn Berger. *Going Blue: A Teen Guide to Saving Our Oceans, Lakes, Rivers, and Wetlands* (6–10). 2010, Free Spirit paper $14.99 (978-1-57542-348-7). Readers learn about the need to protect Earth's water supply in this volume that provides practical tips on water preservation and activism. (Rev: BL 12/1/10; SLJ 12/1/10*) [333.91]

10064 Kidd, J. S., and Renee A. Kidd. *Agricultural Versus Environmental Science: A Green Revolution. Rev. ed* (9–12). Series: Science and Society. 2006, Chelsea House $35 (978-0-8160-5608-8). This revision of 1998's *Shades of Green: The Clash of Agricultural Science and Environmental Science* discusses the "green" contributions of advances in agriculture and the ways in which farming and environmentalism sometimes clash. (Rev: SLJ 9/06)

10065 Kostigen, Thomas M. *You Are Here: The Surprising Link Between What We Do and What That Does to Our Planet* (10–12). 2008, HarperOne $25.95 (978-006158036-9). Kostigen provides detailed examples of how the demands of modern life are currently destroying the planet. ⌒ ℮ (Rev: BL 9/1/08) [363.7]

10066 Kusky, Timothy. *Climate Change: Shifting Glaciers, Deserts, and Climate Belts* (8–12). Series: The Hazardous Earth. 2009, Facts on File $39.50 (978-0-8160-6466-3). The many factors contributing to global warming — both natural and the result of human activities — are covered in this wide-ranging volume. (Rev: SLJ 3/1/09) [551.6]

10067 Lerner, Adrienne. *Climate Change* (9–12). Series: Global Viewpoints. 2009, Gale/Greenhaven $36.20 (978-0-7377-4156-8). Taking a global view, this balanced book explores the issue of climate change along with its associated issues and implications through clear, concise pro/con discussions. (Rev: LMC 10/09)

10068 Lomborg, Bjorn. *Cool It: The Skeptical Environmentalist's Guide to Global Warming* (9–12). 2007, Knopf $21.95 (978-0-307-26692-7). Lomborg argues that poverty and disease are just as important as global warming and criticizes alarmist media coverage; useful fodder for debates. (Rev: BL 9/15/07) [363.738]

10069 London, Mark, and Brian Kelly. *The Last Forest: The Amazon in the Age of Globalization* (10–12). 2007, Random House $25.95 (978-0-679-64305-0). The tension between environmental concerns about the rain forests of the Amazon and the economic needs of the people of the region is the focus of this interesting survey of the ongoing loss of forested land and the impact on the people and wildlife. (Rev: BL 12/1/06) [333.75]

10070 Love, Dennis. *My City Was Gone: The Poisoning of a Small American Town* (10–12). 2006, Morrow $25.95 (978-0-06-058550-1). The sad story of Anniston, Alabama, whose livelihood — the production

of chemicals and chemical weapons — also led to its downfall, through the eyes of three of its citizens. (Rev: BL 8/06) [363.738]

10071 Lynas, Mark. *High Tide: The Truth About Our Climate Crisis* (10–12). 2004, St. Martin's paper $14.00 (978-0-312-30365-5). This is a shocking exposé of the danger of global warming and of the equally shocking energy policies of the second Bush administration. (Rev: BL 5/15/04; SLJ 9/04) [363.7]

10072 Maathai, Wangari. *Replenishing the Earth: Spiritual Values for Healing Ourselves and the World* (10–12). 2010, Doubleday paper $13 (978-03075911-4-2). Nobel Peace Prize winner Maathai deftly combines practical science, religion, and philosophy into a study of how we live with the Earth and its resources. ℮ (Rev: BL 9/1–15/10) [261.8]

10073 McKay, Kim, and Jenny Bonnin. *True Green: 100 Everyday Ways You Can Contribute to a Healthier Planet* (9–12). 2007, National Geographic paper $19.95 (978-1-4262-0113-4). Report writers will find lots of material in this slim volume. (Rev: SLJ 10/07)

10074 McKibben, Bill. *Eaarth: Making a Life on a Tough New Planet* (10–12). 2010, Times $24 (978-080509056-7). Environmentalist McKibben looks back at the effects of global warming and forward at the ways in which mankind can mitigate and reverse some of them. ⌒ ℮ (Rev: BL 12/1/09*) [304.2]

10075 McKibben, Bill, and Phil Aroneanu. *Fight Global Warming Now: The Handbook for Taking Action in Your Community* (9–12). 2007, Henry Holt paper $13.00 (978-0-8050-8704-8). Learn to inspire environmental activism with this practical guide. (Rev: BL 11/15/07) [363.738]

10076 Marcovitz, Hal. *How Serious a Threat Is Climate Change?* (8–11). Illus. Series: In Controversy. 2011, ReferencePoint LB $26.95 (978-1-60152-142-2). What are the potential economic impacts of climate change? How has the world responded to climate change? This volume offers opposing points of view on these and other questions. (Rev: BL 6/1/11; SLJ 9/1/11) [363.738]

10077 Marcovitz, Hal. *Is Offshore Oil Drilling Worth the Risks?* (8–11). Illus. Series: In Controversy. 2011, ReferencePoint LB $26.65 (978-1-60152-143-9). Is America's energy security dependent on offshore oil? Can offshore drilling be made safer? This volume offers opposing points of view on these and other questions. (Rev: BL 6/1/11; SLJ 9/1/11) [363.738]

10078 Miller, Debra A., ed. *Global Warming* (9–12). Series: Current Controversies. 2008, Gale/Greenhaven LB $36.20 (978-0-7377-4070-7); paper $24.95 (978-0-7377-4071-4). A variety of writings from diverse sources present opposing viewpoints on the causes, threats, and potential solutions for global warming. (Rev: SLJ 2/1/09) [363.738]

10079 Mooney, Chris. *Storm World: Hurricanes, Politics, and the Battle over Global Warming* (9–12). 2007, Harcourt $26.00 (978-0-15-101287-9). Mooney takes a clear and balanced look at the question of global warming, what causes it, and what can be done to arrest it. ∩ (Rev: BL 6/1–15/07) [551.6]

10080 Morris, Neil. *Global Warming* (7–12). Series: What If We Do Nothing? 2007, World Almanac LB $30.60 (978-0-8368-7755-7). Morris looks at how we measure climate change, the human and natural causes of these changes, and what we can do to prevent the situation from deteriorating further. (Rev: LMC 11–12/07; SLJ 5/07) [363.738]

10081 Nagle, Jeanne. *Living Green* (10–12). Illus. Series: In the News. 2009, Rosen LB $21.95 (978-143585037-8). Nagle covers why, how, and where people are "living green" and discusses sustainable living as a worldwide movement. (Rev: BL 4/15/09; SLJ 5/1/09) [10. 333.72]

10082 Nagle, Jeanne. *Smart Shopping: Shopping Green* (9–12). Illus. Series: Your Carbon Footprint. 2008, Rosen LB $19.95 (978-140421775-1). This book urges older teens to think about the impact their lifestyle may be having on the environment, and offers suggestions on how to reduce one's carbon footprint and organize for change. (Rev: BL 12/1/08) [640]

10083 Pearce, Fred. *Earth Then and Now: Amazing Images of Our Changing World* (9–12). Illus. 2010, Firefly paper $19.95 (978-15540777-1-7). Pairing photographs of before and after, this is a striking visual chronicle of the impacts on the environment of human activity. (Rev: BL 12/1–15/10) [550]

10084 Pearce, Fred. *With Speed and Violence: Why Scientists Fear Tipping Points in Climate Change* (9–12). 2007, Beacon $24.95 (978-0-8070-8576-9). Environmental journalist Pearce examines the process of global warming, discusses with experts the various manifestations of change (rapid melting of polar ice, rising sea levels, unusual droughts and hurricanes, for example), and looks at fears of inescapable tipping points. (Rev: BL 12/1/06) [551.6]

10085 Petrikin, Jonathan S., ed. *Environmental Justice* (8–12). Series: At Issue. 1995, Greenhaven LB $19.95 (978-0-565-10264-7). A collection of essays exploring whether the wealthy and powerful are risking the health and living conditions of others while protecting their own resources. (Rev: BL 3/15/95) [363.7]

10086 Porter, David L. *Hell on Earth: The Wildfire Pandemic* (10–12). 2008, Forge $24.95 (978-076531380-5). Porter, who lost his home to a fire in 2003, provides a sometimes alarmist examination of the causes and consequences of wildfires. (Rev: BL 7/08) [363.37]

10087 Pregracke, Chad. *From the Bottom Up: One Man's Crusade to Clean America's Rivers* (9–12). 2007, National Geographic $26.00 (978-1-4262-0100-

4). Pregracke, who grew up with the Mississippi as his playground, as a young man was shocked by the amount of trash on its banks and in the water; his efforts to clean up the Mississippi have been so successful that he received the Jefferson Award for Public Service in 2002. (Rev: BL 3/15/07; SLJ 7/07) [363.73]

10088 Rae, Alison. *Oil, Plastics, and Power* (8–12). Series: Development Without Damage. 2010, Smart Apple Media LB $34.25 (978-1-59920-251-8). Oil, gas, nuclear, and alternative sources of power are all covered in this introduction to the environmental damage caused. (Rev: LMC 5–6/10; SLJ 11/09) [333.82]

10089 Rae, Alison. *Trees and Timber Products* (8–12). Series: Development Without Damage. 2010, Smart Apple Media LB $34.25 (978-1-59920-247-1). This is an informative and accessible introduction to the timber industry around the world, discussing deforestation, soil erosion, and pollution as well as opportunities for agroforestry. (Rev: LMC 5–6/10; SLJ 11/09)

10090 Robbins, Ocean, and Sol Solomon. *Choices for Our Future* (7–12). 1994, Book Publg. paper $9.95 (978-1-57067-002-2). The founders of Youth for Environmental Sanity believe that young people can convince other young people to adopt more ecologically responsible lifestyles. This book explains how we can all help. (Rev: BL 3/15/95) [363.7]

10091 Roberts, Callum. *The Unnatural History of the Sea* (9–12). 2007, Island $28.00 (978-1-59726-102-9). The issue examined here is depletion of the ocean's resources through overfishing, its history and viewpoints from a vast array of seafarers from as early as eras when the seas were abundant with animal life. (Rev: BL 8/07) [909]

10092 Rogers, Elizabeth, and Thomas M. Kostigen. *The Green Book: The Everyday Guide to Saving the Planet One Simple Step at a Time* (9–12). 2007, Three Rivers paper $12.95 (978-0-307-38135-4). Divided into sections on home, travel, school, work, shopping, building, and so forth, this book offers practical changes in lifestyle that can make a difference to the future of the planet. (Rev: BL 6/1–15/07) [333.72]

10093 Romm, Joseph. *Hell and High Water: Global Warming — the Solution and the Politics — and What We Should Do* (11–12). 2007, Morrow $24.95 (978-0-06-117212-0). Founder and director of the Center for Energy and Climate Solutions, Romm discusses climate change, stressing that the public has been ill-informed due to the Bush administration's irresponsible policies toward energy and its censorship of global warming threats, and that the technology already exists to reduce greenhouse gases — we just need to put it to work. (Rev: BL 12/1/06) [551]

10094 Rutter, John. *Mining, Minerals, and Metals* (8–12). Series: Development Without Damage. 2010, Smart Apple Media LB $34.25 (978-1-59920-249-5). Rutter reviews how we use coal, iron, and other ores, metals, and minerals and the impact on the environment, before exploring ways to mitigate this. (Rev: LMC 5–6/10; SLJ 11/09) [622.028]

10095 Ryan, Bernard, Jr. *Protecting the Environment* (7–12). Series: Community Service for Teens. 1998, Ferguson LB $19.95 (978-0-89434-228-8). After a general introduction on volunteerism, the author describes how teens can become involved in existing conservation projects and begin their own. (Rev: BL 9/15/98; SLJ 2/99; VOYA 8/99) [363.7]

10096 Safina, Carl. *The View from Lazy Point: A Natural Year in an Unnatural World* (9–12). Illus. 2011, Henry Holt $30 (978-080509040-6). The collision between human abuse of the environment and the lives of a variety of animals is well illustrated here while highlighting the impact on human rights as well. (Rev: BL 12/1–15/10*) [508]

10097 Sivertsen, Linda, and Tosh Sivertsen. *Generation Green: The Ultimate Teen Guide to Living an Eco-Friendly Life* (7–12). 2008, Simon & Schuster paper $9.99 (978-141697242-6). Sivertsen and her 18-year-old son Tosh explore various aspects of green living in this very accessible yet solidly informative guide. (Rev: BLO 10/30/08; SLJ 8/08) [363.73874]

10098 Smith, Rick, et al. *Slow Death by Rubber Duck: The Secret Danger of Everyday Things* (10–12). Illus. 2010, Counterpoint $25 (978-158243567-1). Smith and Lourie present a startlingly grim exposé of the chemicals present in our daily lives — in cookware, carpeting, even pajamas — and the very real and little-known health risks they present. ℮ (Rev: BL 1/1–15/10) [615.9]

10099 Steinman, David. *Safe Trip to Eden: 10 Steps to Save Planet Earth from the Global Warming Meltdown* (9–12). 2007, Thunder's Mouth paper $15.95 (978-1-56025-806-3). In contrast to the many gloomy tomes on global warming, Steinman's guide touts positive, practical steps that will lead to healthier lives for us and for our planet. (Rev: BL 12/1/06) [551]

10100 Stenstrup, Allen. *Forests* (7–12). Illus. Series: Diminishing Resources. 2009, Morgan Reynolds LB $28.95 (978-159935116-2). Direct quotes and hard-hitting facts add drama and appeal to this title discussing the rapid decline of the world's forests, focusing in particular on U.S. forests, deforestation in the Amazon basin, and the disappearing mangroves. (Rev: BL 1/1–15/10) [333.75]

10101 *The Student Environmental Action Guide: By the Student Environmental Action Coalition (SEAC)* (9–12). 1991, EarthWorks paper $4.95 (978-1-879682-04-7). A short manual describing opportunities for recycling in the campus environment and including campus success stories that encourage collective student action. (Rev: BL 10/15/91) [363.7]

10102 Tanaka, Shelley. *Climate Change* (7–10). Series: Groundwood Guide. 2006, Groundwood $15.95 (978-0-88899-783-8). An introduction to the topic for the middle grades that presents possible solutions to the growing problem. (Rev: BL 12/1/06; SLJ 12/06) [363.738]

10103 Taudte, Jeca. *MySpace/OurPlanet* (8–11). Illus. 2008, HarperTeen paper $12.99 (978-00615620-4-4). This engaging guide to eco-savvy, online environmental community OurPlanet provides tips on such compelling, relevant topics as "eco-dating" and green room makeovers via posts from online forums. (Rev: BL 8/08) [363.73874]

10104 Turner, Tom. *Sierra Club: 100 Years of Protecting Nature* (9–12). 1991, Abrams $49.50 (978-0-8109-3820-5). A commemoration of the Sierra Club's founding that provides a history of the organization, its mission, and its accomplishments. (Rev: BL 11/15/91) [333.9516]

10105 Viegas, Jennifer. *Critical Perspectives on Natural Disasters* (9–12). Series: Scientific American Critical Anthologies on Environment and Climate. 2007, Rosen LB $31.95 (978-1-4042-0824-7). Seventeen articles that appeared in *Scientific American* between 1998 and 2005 report on earthquakes, tsunamis, volcanic eruptions, storms, and asteroids; while some articles are quite scientific others will appeal to all readers. (Rev: SLJ 2/07)

10106 Von Ruhland, Catherine. *Living with the Planet: Making a Difference in a Time of Climate Change* (9–12). Illus. 2009, Lion Hudson paper $19.95 (978-0-7459-5255-0). This comprehensive, well-organized volume calls attention to the devastating effects that human consumption continues to have on the global climate and offers examples of climate-related changes occurring throughout the world. (Rev: SLJ 12/09) [363.7]

10107 Waterman, Jonathan. *Running Dry: A Journey from Source to Sea Down the Colorado River* (10–12). 2010, National Geographic $26 (978-142620505-7). Waterman makes a compelling case for saving water as he explores the natural and anthropogenic factors that threaten the Colorado River. ℮ (Rev: BL 5/1/10*) [979.1]

10108 Weinstein, Jay. *The Ethical Gourmet: How to Enjoy Great Food That Is Humanely Raised, Sustainable, Nonendangered, and That Replenishes the Earth* (9–12). 2006, Broadway paper $17.95 (978-0-7679-1834-3). The author explains how to choose foods and products that are Earth-friendly. (Rev: SLJ 9/06)

10109 West, Krista, ed. *Critical Perspectives on Environmental Protection* (9–12). Series: Scientific American Critical Anthologies on Environment and Climate. 2007, Rosen LB $31.95 (978-1-4042-0691-5). Protection of air, water, land, and life is the focus of these 20 articles that appeared in *Scientific American* between

1995 and 2001; while some articles are quite scientific others will appeal to all readers. (Rev: SLJ 2/07)

10110 Weyler, Rex. *Greenpeace: How a Group of Journalists, Ecologists, and Visionaries Changed the World* (9–12). 2004, Rodale $24.95 (978-1-59486-106-2). The fascinating story behind Greenpeace and its brand of highly active activism is told in rich detail by one of its founders. (Rev: BL 10/15/04) [333.72]

10111 Woodward, John, and Jennifer Skancke, eds. *Conserving the Environment* (7–12). Series: Current Controversies. 2006, Gale LB $34.95 (978-0-7377-2476-9); paper $23.70 (978-0-7377-2477-6). Including a review of relevant acts and discussion of various environmentally friendly options (renewable energy, organic farming, fuel-efficient vehicles), this volume explores the seriousness of the problem and what should be done at this point in time. (Rev: SLJ 2/07)

10112 Workman, James G. *Water* (7–12). Illus. Series: Diminishing Resources. 2009, Morgan Reynolds LB $28.95 (978-159935115-5). Discusses everything from the demand for water and regulations that could even out the supply to drought, the benefits and problems associated with water, and the price and availability of bottled water. (Rev: BL 1/1–15/10) [363.6]

10113 Wuerthner, George, and Mollie Matteson, eds. *Welfare Ranching: The Subsidized Destruction of the American West* (10–12). 2002, Island $75.00 (978-1-55963-942-2); paper $45.00 (978-1-55963-943-9). Experts in a variety of fields explore the threats facing public lands in the American West, with effective photography. (Rev: BL 9/15/02) [333.74]

Pollution

10114 Bang, Molly. *Nobody Particular: One Woman's Fight to Save the Bays* (6–12). 2001, Henry Holt $18.00 (978-0-8050-5396-8). Teens will connect to this appealingly presented account about Diane Wilson, who became an environmental activist working to restore the ecology of the bays around her Texas home. (Rev: BCCB 2/01; BL 2/1/01; HB 1–2/01; HBG 10/01; SLJ 1/01; VOYA 4/02) [363.738]

10115 Reed, Jennifer. *Love Canal* (6–12). Series: Great Disasters: Reforms and Ramifications. 2002, Chelsea LB $30.00 (978-0-7910-6742-0). The story of the town that had to be evacuated in the 1970s when hazardous wastes leaked from a disposal site. (Rev: HBG 3/03; SLJ 12/02) [363.738]

10116 Safina, Carl. *A Sea in Flames: The Deepwater Horizon Oil Blowout* (10–12). 2011, Crown $25 (978-030788735-1). Safina offers an in-depth look from all angles at the Deepwater Horizon oil disaster and its short- and long-term effects on the Gulf Coast community, marine life, and politics and "big oil." (Rev: BL 3/1–15/11) [363.738]

10117 Sanna, Emily. *Air Pollution and Health* (7–10). Illus. Series: Health and the Environment. 2008, AlphaHouse LB $29.95 (978-193497035-5). This thought-provoking look at the impact of air pollution on human health discusses such topics as ozone depletion, smog, and acid rain. (Rev: BLO 2/2/09; LMC 3–4/09) [363.739]

10118 Wilson, Diane. *An Unreasonable Woman: A True Story of Shrimpers, Politicos, Polluters, and the Fight for Seadrift, Texas* (10–12). 2005, Chelsea Green $27.50 (978-1-931498-88-3). Diane Wilson, a fourth-generation shrimper and mother of five, recounts her courageous battle to stop a giant plastics company from poisoning the coastal Texas county in which she lives. (Rev: BL 9/1/05) [639]

Waste Management

10119 Dorion, Christiane. *Earth's Garbage Crisis* (7–12). Series: What If We Do Nothing? 2007, World Almanac LB $30.60 (978-0-8368-7753-3). Dorion discusses how and why we create so much garbage and the measures we need to take before this problem swamps us. (Rev: LMC 11–12/07; SLJ 5/07) [363.728]

10120 McVicker, Dee. *Easy Recycling Handbook* (9–12). 1994, Grassroots paper $8.95 (978-0-9638428-5-5). An introduction to recycling methods and waste management, with advice on overcoming limitations posed by time and space. (Rev: BL 3/15/94) [363.7]

10121 Rogers, Heather. *Gone Tomorrow: The Hidden Life of Garbage* (9–12). 2005, New Press $23.95 (978-1-56584-879-5). Sobering answers for all those who wonder what becomes of the vast quantities of household waste in America. (Rev: BL 10/15/05) [363.72]

10122 Young, Mitchell, ed. *Garbage and Recycling* (10–12). Series: Opposing Viewpoints. 2007, Gale $34.95 (978-0-7377-3651-9). A collection of writings on the problems arising from waste disposal in the United States. (Rev: BL 11/1/07) [363.72]

Population Issues

General and Miscellaneous

10123 Carlson, Allan C., and Paul Mero. *The Natural Family: A Manifesto* (9–12). 2007, Spence $27.95 (978-1-890626-70-9). This book defines the concept of family based on human universal experience and suggests a movement toward restoring the family unit in U.S. society that has been in a state of confusion since the 1960s, advocating a family wage, family-friendly tax policies, homeschooling, incentives to homeownership, and more. (Rev: BL 8/07) [306.85]

10124 Currie, Elliott. *The Road to Whatever: Middle-Class Culture and the Crisis of Adolescence* (11–12). 2005, Henry Holt $26.00 (978-0-8050-6763-7). An examination of the growing malaise among white, middle-class adolescents in America; for mature teens. (Rev: BL 1/1–15/05) [305.235]

10125 Haley, John, and Wendy Stein. *The Truth About Abuse* (9–12). Series: The Truth About. 2005, Facts on File $35.00 (978-0-8160-5297-4). Explores various forms of abuse, including domestic violence, bullying, date rape, hazing, and child molestation, offering facts and figures and teens' own stories. (Rev: SLJ 9/05)

10126 Harrison, Kathy. *One Small Boat: The Story of a Little Girl, Lost Then Found* (10–12). 2006, Putnam $23.95 (978-1-58542-465-8). The moving story of a foster child who suffered a severe speech impediment as well as eating disorders. (Rev: BL 3/15/06) [362.73]

10127 Howe, Neil, et al. *Millennials Rising: The Next Great Generation* (10–12). 2000, Random House paper $14.00 (978-0-375-70719-3). A study of the generation born during the Reagan years, and their emerging characteristics, such as a return to conservative family values. (Rev: BL 9/1/00) [305.275]

10128 Kleinfield, Sonny. *His Oldest Friend: The Story of an Unlikely Bond* (9–12). 2005, Henry Holt $24.00 (978-0-8050-7580-9). The story of an unlikely friendship between a 93-year-old nursing home resident and a 20-year-old Hispanic volunteer. (Rev: BL 9/1/05) [305.26]

10129 Lankford, Ronnie D., Jr., ed. *Are America's Wealthy Too Powerful?* (8–12). Series: At Issue. 2010, Greenhaven $31.80 (978-073775087-4); paper $22.50 (978-07377508-8-1). This volume presents pro and con viewpoints on the question of wealth and power in America, looking at Wall Street, the tax system, the roles of celebrities and corporations, philanthropy, and so forth. (Rev: BL 4/1/11) [305.5]

10130 Lorinc, John. *Cities* (7–12). Series: Groundwork Guides. 2008, Groundwood $18.95 (978-088899820-0). A fast-paced, detailed look at urban history and the issues cities face, such as poverty, overcrowding, and transportation. (Rev: BL 12/1/08) [307.76]

10131 Proulx, Brenda, ed. *The Courage to Change: A Teen Survival Guide* (7–12). 2002, Second Story paper $16.95 (978-1-896764-41-2). A thought-provoking compilation of personal stories, poems, and photographs created by teens who participate in Canada's L.O.V.E. (Leave Out ViolencE) program. (Rev: BL 9/1/02; SLJ 7/02; VOYA 8/02) [364.4]

10132 Reef, Catherine. *Alone in the World: Orphans and Orphanages in America* (8–11). 2005, Clarion $18.00 (978-0-618-35670-6). A history of orphanages in America from the early years of the 18th century through their decline in the early 1900s. (Rev: BL 4/1/05; SLJ 6/05; VOYA 10/05) [362.73]

Aging and Death

10133 Gignoux, Jane Hughes. *Some Folk Say: Stories of Life, Death, and Beyond* (6–12). 1998, Foulketale $29.95 (978-0-9667168-0-1). A collection of 38 literary selections on various aspects of death and how people adjust to it, taken from world folklore and such writers as Shakespeare and Walt Whitman. (Rev: BL 2/15/99) [398.27]

10134 Roach, Mary. *Spook: Science Tackles the Afterlife* (10–12). 2005, Norton $24.95 (978-0-393-05962-5). With determination and humor, Roach investigates the possibility of an afterlife. (Rev: BL 9/1/05) [129]

10135 Smith, Olivia J., ed. *Aging in America* (10–12). Series: Reference Shelf. 2000, H.W. Wilson paper $50.00 (978-0-8242-0984-1). The social, economic, and political aspects of aging in the United States are explored in this collection of essays. [362.6]

Crime, Gangs, and Prisons

10136 Adams, Bradley J. *Forensic Anthropology* (9–12). Series: Inside Forensic Science. 2007, Chelsea House LB $30.00 (978-0-7910-9198-2). The medical side of forensic work includes examining and identifying human remains, and this book explains, in language for strong readers, how scientists go about this. (Rev: BL 4/1/07; SLJ 4/07) [614]

10137 Allman, Toney. *The Medical Examiner* (7–10). Series: Crime Scene Investigations. 2006, Gale LB $31.20 (978-1-59018-912-2). A look at the responsibilities, tools, methods, and training of a medical examiner. (Rev: SLJ 9/06)

10138 Anderson, Judith. *People Trafficking* (9–12). Illus. 2011, Black Rabbit/Smart Apple Media $34.25 (978-159920397-3). In double-page spreads with statistics and details of individual cases, this book looks at problems of human trafficking, forced labor, the sex industry and relevant laws around the world. (Rev: BL 10/1/11) [364.15]

10139 Barbour, Scott, ed. *Gangs* (8–12). Series: Introducing Issues with Opposing Viewpoints. 2005, Gale LB $33.70 (978-0-7377-3221-4). Diverse opinions are presented on topics including the reasons why young people join gangs and measures that can be taken to reduce the violence. (Rev: SLJ 1/06) [364.1]

10140 Barton, Chris. *Can I See Your I.D.? True Stories of False Identities* (7–10). Illus. by Paul Hoppe. 2011, Dial $16.99 (978-0-8037-3310-7). With graphic panels and second-person presentations, this volume presents gripping stories of daring impostors throughout history. (Rev: BL 4/15/11; LMC 10/11; SLJ 5/11; VOYA 6/11) [001.9]

10141 Bell, Suzanne. *Fakes and Forgeries* (7–12). Illus. Series: Essentials of Forensic Science. 2008, Facts on

File $35.00 (978-081605514-2). Covering examples of forgery dating from Mesopotamia to the present day, Bell provides a compelling, accessible portrait of the crime, discussing techniques used and methods of detection. (Rev: BL 10/15/08) [363.25]

10142 Bing, Léon. *Do or Die: For the First Time, Members of L.A.'s Most Notorious Teenage Gangs . . . Speak for Themselves* (9–12). 1992, HarperCollins paper $13 (978-0-06-092291-7). Los Angeles gang members describe their incredibly violent world. (Rev: BL 7/91*) [364.3]

10143 Bosco, Antoinette. *Choosing Mercy: A Mother of Murder Victims Pleads to End the Death Penalty* (10–12). 2001, Orbis paper $17.00 (978-1-57075-358-9). A highly personal account by a mother who has had two of her family murdered, this book makes an eloquent plea for an end to capital punishment and for substituting forgiveness. (Rev: BL 3/1/01) [364.66]

10144 Brown, Brooks, and Rob Merritt. *No Easy Answers: The Truth Behind Death at Columbine* (10–12). 2002, Lantern paper $18.95 (978-1-59056-031-0). In this chilling memoir, Brooks Brown, a friend of Columbine High School shooters Dylan Klebold and Eric Harris, tells how he escaped the massacre and searches for explanations for the 1999 tragedy. (Rev: BL 10/15/02) [373.788]

10145 Capote, Truman. *In Cold Blood: A True Account of a Multiple Murder and Its Consequences* (10–12). 1993, Buccaneer paper $13.00 (978-0-679-74558-7). The story of a shocking murder case where a family was killed by two psychotic young men. [364.1]

10146 Chura, David. *I Don't Wish Nobody to Have a Life Like Mine: Tales of Kids in Adult Lockup* (11–12). 2010, Beacon $25.95 (978-080700064-9). This eye-opening true account, written by a teacher who worked with teen convicts in adult prisons, paints a riveting portrait of young men struggling to come to terms with violent home lives, addiction, poverty, and the failure of the juvenile criminal justice system. (Rev: BL 2/1–15/10) [371.93092]

10147 Coppin, Cheryl Branch. *Everything You Need to Know About Healing from Rape Trauma* (7–12). Series: Need to Know Library. 2000, Rosen $27.95 (978-0-8239-3122-4). Emphasizing that rape is about power not sex and that the victim is blameless, the author looks in particular at prevention and recovery. (Rev: SLJ 9/00) [362.883]

10148 Craig, Emily. *Teasing Secrets from the Dead: My Investigations at America's Most Infamous Crime Scenes* (11–12). 2004, Crown $24.95 (978-1-4000-4922-6). Craig describes her work as a forensic anthropologist, imparting technical information and insight into interpersonal relations in the process; for mature readers. (Rev: BL 8/04) [363.25]

10149 Delaney, Lucinda. *A Hunt for Justice: The True Story of a Woman Undercover Wildlife Agent* (9–12). 2006, Lyons $21.95 (978-1-59228-882-3). A real-life thriller in which the author, a longtime agent with the U.S. Fish and Wildlife Service, undertakes an undercover mission to nab a big-time wildlife poacher in Alaska. (Rev: BL 2/15/06) [364.1]

10150 Donohue, Sean, ed. *Gangs: Stories of Survival from the Streets* (10–12). 2002, Thunder's Mouth paper $17.95 (978-1-56025-425-6). This wide-ranging collection of excerpts from works of fiction and nonfiction offers important insights into gangs and the lives of gang members. (Rev: BL 8/02) [364.1]

10151 Dudley, William, and Louise I. Gerdes, eds. *Gangs* (8–12). Series: Opposing Viewpoints. 2005, Gale LB $36.20 (978-0-7377-2234-5); paper $24.95 (978-0-7377-2235-2). A look at the causes of gang behavior and what can be done to combat the alarming increase in violence. (Rev: SLJ 8/05) [364.1]

10152 Dulles, Allen. *Great True Spy Stories* (9–12). 1992, Sales $7.98 (978-0-89009-716-8). This is a collection of thrillers about spy capers that really happened.

10153 Duncan, Lois. *Who Killed My Daughter* (10–12). 1994, Dell paper $7.50 (978-0-440-21342-0). In despair after her college-student daughter was murdered in 1989 and the police came up with no leads, Duncan turned to psychics and a private detective. (Rev: SLJ 8/92) [364]

10154 Espejo, Roman, ed. *Violent Children* (10–12). 2010, Greenhaven LB $30.85 (978-073774446-0); paper $21.85 (9780737744477). Essays present opposing points of view on the causes of youth violence, the impact of violence in media, violence among girls, the role of poverty, and so forth; with statistics and questions for discussion. (Rev: BL 8/10) [303.60835]

10155 Essig, Mark. *Edison and the Electric Chair: A Story of Light and Death* (10–12). 2003, Walker $26.00 (978-0-8027-1406-0). Essig explores the history of electrocution as a means of capital punishment against the backdrop of the battle between Thomas Edison and George Westinghouse over whether AC (Westinghouse) or DC (Edison) would dominate the newly emerging electric power industry. (Rev: BL 9/15/03) [364.66]

10156 Evans, Colin. *Blood on the Table: The Greatest Cases of New York City's Office of the Chief Medical Examiner* (9–12). 2008, Berkley paper $15.00 (978-0-425-21937-9). A highly readable history of the seven Chief Medical Examiners who have led the New York department since 1918. (Rev: BL 3/1/08) [614]

10157 Evans, Wanda, and James Dunn. *Trail of Blood: A Father, a Son and a Tell-Tale Crime Scene* (11–12). 2005, New Horizon $23.95 (978-0-88282-261-7). This gripping whodunit blends the story of a father's six-year quest to find out what happened to his son with an overview of the forensic investigation that solved the case; for mature teens. (Rev: BL 3/1/05) [364]

10158 Fast, Jonathan. *Ceremonial Violence: A Psychological Explanation of School Shootings* (11–12). 2008, Overlook $25.95 (978-159020047-6). Drawing on years of research, this books offers some insight into the common threads that link these teenage killers and the decisions that lead to the violence; for mature readers. (Rev: BL 8/08) [364.1]

10159 Fridell, Ron. *Spying: The Modern World of Espionage* (7–12). 2002, Millbrook LB $24.90 (978-0-7613-1662-6). What spies do, the technology they use, and the politics of espionage are all covered in this concise volume. (Rev: BL 5/1/02; HBG 10/02; SLJ 4/02; VOYA 12/02) [327.1]

10160 Frost, Helen, ed. *Why Darkness Seems So Light: Young People Speak Out About Violence* (9–12). 1998, Grove $10.00 (978-1-877603-58-7). This is a collection of 40 essays by high school students in Allen County, Indiana, who answer the question, "Have you ever been personally affected by violence?" (Rev: VOYA 4/99) [616.85]

10161 Geary, Rick. *The Borden Tragedy: A Memoir of the Infamous Double Murder at Fall River, Mass., 1892* (10–12). 1997, NBM paper $8.95 (978-1-56163-189-6). Using a documentary comic-book format, this is an exciting factual presentation of the Borden murders in Fall River, Massachusetts, adapted from the memoirs of someone who was in Fall River at the time of the crime. (Rev: BL 12/1/97; SLJ 3/98) [973.8]

10162 Gimpel, Diane Marczely. *The Columbine Shootings* (6–10). Illus. Series: Essential Events. 2012, ABDO LB $23.95 (978-161783308-3). Introduces the perpetrators and victims of this 1999 attack and explores the potential causes and ways to prevent future incidents. (Rev: BL 7/12) [373.17]

10163 Hanrahan, Clare, ed. *America's Prisons* (7–12). Series: Opposing Viewpoints. 2006, Gale LB $34.95 (978-0-7377-3344-0); paper $23.70 (978-0-7377-3345-7). This thought-provoking title tackles the thorny issues surrounding America's penal system through a selection of pro and con essays. (Rev: SLJ 9/06)

10164 Harris, Elizabeth Snoke. *Crime Scene Science Fair Projects* (6–10). 2007, Sterling LB $19.95 (978-1-57990-765-5). After an introduction to forensic science and its application, Harris provides projects that teach about fingerprints, lie detection, and so forth. (Rev: SLJ 2/07)

10165 Haugen, David M., and Susan Musser, eds. *Media Violence* (7–12). Series: Opposing Viewpoints. 2008, Gale/Greenhaven $37.40 (978-073774218-3); paper $25.95 (978-073774219-0). Readers explore many aspects of the debate over whether violence in the media encourages violence in society. (Rev: BL 4/1/09) [363.3]

10166 Hinojosa, Maria. *Crews: Gang Members Talk to Maria Hinojosa* (9–12). 1995, Harcourt paper $9.00 (978-0-15-200283-1). A National Public Radio correspondent interviews New York City gang members after a subway stabbing. (Rev: BL 3/15/95; SLJ 4/95*; VOYA 5/95) [302.3]

10167 Hubner, John. *Last Chance in Texas: The Redemption of Criminal Youth* (11–12). 2005, Random House $25.95 (978-0-375-50809-7). Hubner explores an innovative Texas program that is having success in turning juvenile offenders away from a life of crime; for mature teens. (Rev: BL 8/05; SLJ 2/06) [365]

10168 Hutchinson, Earl Ofari. *The Mugging of Black America* (9–12). 1990, American Images paper $8.95 (978-0-913543-21-4). An angry discourse on what defines African Americans as the perpetrators and victims of crime and as the casualties of the criminal justice system. Also offers guidelines for change. (Rev: BL 9/1/91) [305.8]

10169 Innes, Brian. *Fingerprints and Impressions* (7–12). Series: Forensic Evidence. 2007, Sharpe Focus $39.95 (978-0-7656-8114-0). Readers learn about DNA fingerprinting and will gain an understanding of the work of forensic scientists. (Rev: LMC 2/08; SLJ 1/08)

10170 Innes, Brian. *Forensic Science* (8–12). 2003, Mason Crest LB $22.95 (978-1-59084-373-4). A well-illustrated exploration of historic and international crime investigations, with a look at evolving techniques and the importance of evidence in court cases. (Rev: SLJ 6/03) [363.25]

10171 Junger, Sebastian. *A Death in Belmont* (11–12). 2006, Norton $23.95 (978-0-393-05980-9). A fascinating true crime story that also reveals early 1960s politics and race relations, centering on Junger's possible proximity (at the age of one) to the Boston Strangler on the day of a death in Belmont, Massachusetts; for mature teens. (Rev: BL 2/15/06) [364.152]

10172 King, Rachel. *Don't Kill in Our Names: Families of Murder Victims Speak Out Against the Death Penalty* (11–12). 2003, Rutgers $29.95 (978-0-8135-3182-3). This fascinating study looks at families of murder victims who continue to oppose the death penalty; for mature teens. (Rev: BL 2/1/03) [364.66]

10173 Kleid, Neil, and Jake Allen. *Brownsville* (9–12). 2006, NBM $18.95 (978-1-56163-458-3). This profile in graphic novel format of Allie Tannenbaum, a member of Murder Inc., offers an inside look at the world of organized crime and murder for hire. (Rev: BL 3/15/06; SLJ 7/06) [741.5]

10174 Kuklin, Susan. *No Choirboy: Murder, Violence, and Teenagers on Death Row* (10–12). Illus. 2008, Henry Holt $16.95 (978-080507950-0). Drawing on the prisoners' own words, with amplifications by Kuklin and lawyers, this volume addresses the plight of individuals who were sentenced to death while still teenagers and explores the criminal justice system. Best Books for Young Adults 2009. (Rev: BL 9/15/08; HB 7–8/08; SLJ 9/1/08*; VOYA 10/08) [364.66092]

10175 Lewis, Brenda Ralph. *Hostage Rescue with the FBI* (6–10). Series: Rescue and Prevention: Defending Our Nation. 2003, Mason Crest LB $22.95 (978-1-59084-403-8). Famous hostage situations such as the *Achille Lauro* incident are mentioned in this well-illustrated survey of the process of rescuing hostages, negotiating with their takers, and the use of snipers. Also use *Police Crime Prevention* (2003). (Rev: SLJ 7/03) [364.15]

10176 Marcovitz, Hal. *Gangs* (7–10). Series: Essential Issues. 2010, ABDO LB $32.79 (978-1-60453-954-7). "Why do young people join gangs?" "How do communities respond to gangs?" "Is there life after gangs?" These and other questions are answered in this well-organized volume. (Rev: LMC 10/10; SLJ 4/1/10) [364.106]

10177 Mason, Paul. *Frauds and Counterfeits* (6–12). Series: Solve It with Science. 2010, Smart Apple Media LB $34.25 (978-1-59920-329-4). The books in this series explore different ways to catch criminals using crime scene clues. (Rev: LMC 1–2/10)

10178 Nakaya, Andrea C., ed. *Juvenile Crime* (8–12). Series: Opposing Viewpoints. 2005, Gale LB $36.20 (978-0-7377-2945-0); paper $24.95 (978-0-7377-2946-7). A collection of diverse opinions on the causes of juvenile crime and on ways to prevent it, to punish or treat offenders, and to improve the juvenile justice system. (Rev: SLJ 1/06) [364.9]

10179 Owen, David. *Hidden Evidence: 40 True Crimes and How Forensic Science Helped Solve Them* (10–12). 2000, Firefly paper $24.95 (978-1-55209-483-9). Using 40 actual crimes as a focus, this book looks at methods of investigation ranging from those used in ancient China to the latest computerized DNA analysis. (Rev: BL 9/1/00; VOYA 2/01) [363.25]

10180 Owen, David. *Police Lab: How Forensic Science Tracks Down and Convicts Criminals* (6–12). 2002, Firefly $19.95 (978-1-55297-620-3); paper $9.95 (978-1-55297-619-7). The nitty-gritty of forensic science is covered here, with information about the investigations of some well-known crimes and criminals and attention-grabbing photographs, some of them grisly. (Rev: BL 12/15/02; HBG 3/03; SLJ 5/03) [363.25]

10181 Owens, Lois Smith, and Vivian Verdell Gordon. *Think About Prisons and the Criminal Justice System* (6–10). Series: Think. 1991, Walker LB $15.85 (978-0-8027-8121-5); paper $9.95 (978-0-8027-7370-8). Basic information on incarceration, crime and its consequences, the criminal justice system, and the basis for laws. (Rev: BL 6/1/92; SLJ 2/92) [364.973]

10182 Parks, Peggy J. *Gangs* (7–10). Illus. Series: Compact Research: Current Issues. 2010, ReferencePoint LB $26.95 (978-160152114-9). Presents opposing points of view on the nature of gangs, why young people join them, whether they are free to leave gang life, and whether gang violence can be stopped; includes primary source quotes and facts and illustrations plus extensive back matter. (Rev: BL 4/1/11) [364.1]

10183 Platt, Richard. *Forensics* (5–10). Series: Kingfisher Knowledge. 2005, Kingfisher paper $12.95 (978-0-7534-5862-4). This introduction to the use of the forensic sciences in crime investigation is presented in short blocks of text that will make it appealing to reluctant readers. (Rev: SLJ 11/05) [363.2]

10184 Prokos, Anna. *Killer Wallpaper: True Cases of Deadly Poisonings* (5–10). Series: 24/7: Science Behind the Scenes. 2007, Watts LB $25.00 (978-0-531-12061-3); paper $7.95 (978-0-531-15459-5). Prokos uses three real cases to illustrate the work of forensic toxicologists; reluctant readers will enjoy this. (Rev: SLJ 8/07)

10185 Queen, William, and Douglas Century. *Armed and Dangerous: The Hunt for One of America's Most Wanted Criminals* (9–12). 2007, Random House $22.95 (978-1-4000-6577-6). William Queen chronicles his successful apprehension of marijuana grower Mark Stephens who, in 1986 utilized his wilderness survival skills and automatic weapon-making knowledge to avoid capture, but failed to escape due to Queen's matching tracking skills. (Rev: BL 7/07) [364.1]

10186 Rainis, Kenneth G. *Fingerprints: Crime-Solving Science Experiments* (7–12). Series: Forensic Science Projects. 2006, Enslow LB $31.93 (978-0-7660-1960-7). Projects and experiments teach students about collecting evidence, taking notes, and reporting findings as well as the basics of fingerprinting; also use *Hair, Clothing, and Tire Track Evidence* (2006). (Rev: SLJ 7/07) [363.2]

10187 Roleff, Tamara L., ed. *Police Corruption* (6–12). Series: At Issue. 2003, Gale $29.95 (978-0-7377-1172-1); paper $21.20 (978-0-7377-1171-4). This is a thought-provoking exploration of the reasons why corruption can flourish within the law enforcement community. (Rev: BL 4/15/03) [353.4]

10188 Scheffler, Judith A., ed. *Wall Tappings: An International Anthology of Women's Prison Writings, 200 to the Present* (10–12). 2003, Feminist paper $18.95 (978-1-55861-273-0). This stunning collection gives voice to women in prisons around the world, offering more than 30 chronologically arranged selections, starting with a woman's letters from a Roman prison cell in 203 A.D. (Rev: BL 3/15/03) [365]

10189 Schroeder, Andreas. *Thieves!* (5–10). Series: True Stories from the Edge. 2005, Annick $18.95 (978-1-

55037-933-4); paper $8.95 (978-1-55037-932-7). Ten world-class crimes are described in compelling detail. (Rev: SLJ 3/06) [364]

10190 Sekulich, Daniel. *Terror on the Seas: True Tales of Modern-Day Pirates* (10–12). 2009, Thomas Dunne $24.95 (978-0-312-37582-9). Pirates past and present are the topic of this interesting survey that provides information on modern maritime law. (Rev: BL 5/15/09; SLJ 9/09) [910.4]

10191 Silverstein, Herma. *Threads of Evidence: Using Forensic Science to Solve Crimes* (7–12). 1996, Twenty-First Century LB $26.90 (978-0-8050-4370-9). A discussion of the new forensic technology now available to criminologists, such as the use of DNA, blood splatters, fibers, and shell casings, and the role this science has played in solving famous cases. (Rev: BL 12/1/96; SLJ 2/97; VOYA 6/97) [363.2]

10192 Simpson, Colton, and Ann Pearlman. *Inside the Crips: Life Inside L.A.'s Most Notorious Gang* (11–12). 2005, St. Martin's $24.95 (978-0-312-32929-7). Simpson succeeded in extracting himself from the Crips gang, and here reveals what life is like for its members; for mature teens. (Rev: BL 8/05) [364.1]

10193 Smith, Rich. *You Can Get Arrested for That: 2 Guys, 25 Dumb Laws, 1 Absurd American Crime Spree* (9–12). 2006, Three Rivers paper $13.95 (978-0-307-33942-3). Two Brits come to America to break as many silly laws as they can and in the process get to know the country and its citizens. (Rev: BL 8/06) [349.73]

10194 Sparks, Beatrice, ed. *Almost Lost: The True Story of an Anonymous Teenager's Life on the Streets* (9–12). 1996, Avon paper $5.99 (978-0-380-78341-0). This is the story of runaway Sammy, who at 15 was a member of a street gang and who finally returned to his family and began the road to recovery. (Rev: SLJ 7/96; VOYA 10/96) [364.1]

10195 Stefoff, Rebecca. *Criminal Profiling* (7–10). Series: Forensic Science Investigated. 2010, Marshall Cavendish $23.95 (978-076144141-0). After introducing the history and basic principles of forensic sciences, this volume goes on to look at the work of profilers and the kinds of criminals they investigate. (Rev: BL 11/15/10) [363.25]

10196 Swift, Richard. *Gangs* (8–12). Series: Groundwork Guides. 2011, Groundwood $18.95 (978-0-88899-979-5); paper $11 (978-0-88899-978-8). A compact but informative discussion of the forces that motivate young people to join gangs, the prevalence of gangs around the world, and the possibilities for reform. **e** (Rev: BL 5/1/11; LMC 10/11; SLJ 6/11; VOYA 6/11) [364.106]

10197 Webber, Diane. *Do You Read Me? Famous Cases Solved by Handwriting Analysis!* (5–10). Series: 24/7:

Science Behind the Scenes. 2007, Watts LB $25.00 (978-0-531-12066-8); paper $7.95 (978-0-531-15456-4). Webber uses three real cases to illustrate ways in which the study of handwriting can help to solve crimes; reluctant readers will enjoy this. (Rev: SLJ 8/07)

10198 Wilkerson, David. *The Cross and the Switchblade* (9–12). 1987, Jove paper $4.99 (978-0-515-09025-3). A country minister works with the street gangs of New York City. [364.3]

10199 Willis, Laurie, ed. *Hate Crimes* (7–12). Series: Social Issues Firsthand. 2007, Gale LB $28.70 (978-0-7377-2889-7). Hate crimes of various kinds are discussed in the articles and interview excerpts collected here. (Rev: BL 11/1/07) [364.15]

10200 Wright, Cynthia. *Everything You Need to Know About Dealing with Stalking* (7–12). Series: Need to Know Library. 2000, Rosen LB $27.95 (978-0-8239-2841-5). What to do if you're being stalked, as well as where to get help. (Rev: HBG 9/00; SLJ 3/00) [362.88]

10201 Wright, John D. *Fire and Explosives* (7–12). Series: Forensic Evidence. 2007, Sharpe Focus $39.95 (978-0-7656-8117-1). Readers learn about arson and explosives investigation and will gain an understanding of the work of forensic scientists. (Rev: LMC 2/08; SLJ 1/08)

10202 Wright, John D. *Hair and Fibers* (9–12). Series: Forensic Evidence. 2007, M.E. Sharpe LB $35.95 (978-0-7656-8116-4). This volume explains just how hair and fibers can produce evidence to convict someone of a crime, with details of cases, profiles of key individuals, and information on technology and careers. (Rev: BL 2/1/08; SLJ 1/08) [363.25]

10203 Yancey, Diane. *Murder* (7–10). Series: Inside the Crime Lab. 2006, Gale LB $32.45 (978-1-59018-619-0). Readers learn how clues found at a murder scene are analyzed and interpreted to reconstruct what happened; there are references to famous cases, and sidebar features and photographs add interest. (Rev: BL 4/1/06; SLJ 9/06) [363.25]

10204 Yount, Lisa. *Forensic Science: From Fibers to Fingerprints* (9–12). Series: Milestones in Discovery and Invention. 2007, Chelsea House LB $35.00 (978-0-8160-5751-1). Covering the key pioneers and discoveries of forensic science, this is a clear introduction with a timeline, diagrams, and drawings. (Rev: SLJ 4/07) [363.25]

10205 Zehr, Howard. *Transcending: Reflections of Crime Victims* (10–12). 2001, Good Books $29.95 (978-1-56148-337-2); paper $18.95 (978-1-56148-333-4). Using a number of first-person accounts, this book explores the rage, despair, and other emotions experienced by crime victims and their families and the need for restorative justice. (Rev: BL 10/1/01) [362.88]

Poverty, Homelessness, and Hunger

10206 Albeda, Randy, et al. *The War on the Poor: A Defense Manual* (10–12). 1996, New Press paper $10.95 (978-1-56581-262-8). This adult book presents alarming facts and statistics about the status of the poor in the United States near the end of the 20th century. (Rev: VOYA 10/96) [339.4]

10207 Bloom, Jonathan. *American Wasteland: How America Throws Away Nearly Half of Its Food (and What We Can Do About It)* (10–12). 2010, Da Capo $26 (978-073821364-4). The many different ways and reasons that America wastes food are discussed along with the individuals and groups who are trying to remedy this and feed the poor. ℮ (Rev: BL 10/1–15/10) [363.72]

10208 Bolnick, Tina S., and Jamie Pastor Bolnick. *Living at the Edge of the World: A Teenager's Survival in the Tunnels of Grand Central Station* (11–12). 2000, St. Martin's $24.95 (978-0-312-20047-3). The harrowing story of a girl who spent four years as a homeless drug addict and prostitute living in the tunnels of Grand Central Station. (Rev: BL 9/1/00) [362.74]

10209 Erlbach, Arlene. *Everything You Need to Know If Your Family Is on Welfare* (6–10). Series: Need to Know Library. 1997, Rosen LB $27.95 (978-0-8239-2433-2). This book explains the welfare system and details recipients' rights as well as offering tips on how to cope with being on welfare and the social stigma often associated with it. (Rev: SLJ 4/98) [362.5]

10210 Erlbaum, Janice. *Girlbomb: A Halfway Homeless Memoir* (9–12). 2006, Villard $21.95 (978-1-4000-6422-9). In this gritty memoir, Janice Erlbaum writes of her experiences as a teenager navigating the treacherous waters of the social welfare system. (Rev: BL 1/1–15/06; SLJ 7/06) [362.74]

10211 Flood, Nancy Bohac. *Working Together Against World Hunger* (7–12). Series: Library of Social Activism. 1995, Rosen LB $27.95 (978-0-8239-1773-0). A rundown on world hunger, the conditions that cause it, and ways of becoming active in fighting it. (Rev: BL 4/15/95) [363.8]

10212 Haugen, David M., and Matthew J. Box, eds. *Poverty* (8–11). Series: Social Issues Firsthand. 2005, Gale LB $29.95 (978-0-7377-2899-6). Wide-ranging essays present the plight of those living in poverty as well as the thoughts of those who are determined to do something about the problem. (Rev: BL 10/15/05) [362.5]

10213 Khan, Irene. *The Unheard Truth: Poverty and Human Rights* (10–12). Illus. 2009, Norton paper $19.95 (978-03933370-0-6). With particular focus on women's issues, Khan provides meticulous research coupled with real-life examples in this lucid outline of the devastating ways in which poverty hampers basic human rights the world over. (Rev: BL 10/15/09) [330]

10214 LeBlanc, Adrian Nicole. *Random Family: Love, Drugs, Trouble, and Coming of Age in the Bronx* (10–12). 2003, Scribner $25.00 (978-0-684-86387-0). The author spent more than a decade chronicling the lives of two Latinas from the Bronx, producing a revealing profile of life among America's urban poor. (Rev: BL 2/15/03) [305.5]

10215 Lusted, Marcia Amidon. *Poverty* (7–10). Series: Essential Issues. 2010, ABDO LB $32.79 (978-1-60453-957-8). The causes, impact, and stigma of poverty are examined in this volume that also looks at effects including homelessness, lack of education, and lack of health care and at various efforts to alleviate poverty. (Rev: LMC 10/10; SLJ 4/1/10) [363]

10216 Murray, Charles. *In Our Hands: A Plan to Replace the Welfare State* (10–12). 2006, AEI $20.00 (978-0-8447-4223-6). A fascinating proposal for replacing the American system of welfare. (Rev: BL 2/15/06) [361.6]

10217 Parker, Julie. *Everything You Need to Know About Living in a Shelter* (8–12). 1995, Rosen LB $27.95 (978-0-8239-1874-4). A straightforward account that describes life for teens living in shelters, with material on what they can do to control at least some aspects of their lives. (Rev: SLJ 12/95; VOYA 2/96) [362.5]

10218 Roleff, Tamara L., ed. *Inner-City Poverty* (8–12). Series: Contemporary Issues Companion. 2003, Gale LB $36.20 (978-0-7377-0841-7); paper $24.95 (978-0-7377-0840-0). This examination of theories about the causes of urban poverty, the resulting crime and drug use, the impact of the welfare system, and the potential for effective reform provides lots of material for students doing research. (Rev: LMC 4–5/03; SLJ 2/03) [362.5]

10219 Shipler, David K. *The Working Poor: Invisible in America* (10–12). 2004, Knopf $26.00 (978-0-375-40890-8). Using case studies plus statistics, the author has producing a stirring portrait of people who struggle with low-paying jobs and little social assistance to maintain their lives and their families. (Rev: BL 1/1–15/04) [305.5]

10220 Stavsky, Lois, and I. E. Mozeson. *The Place I Call Home: Faces and Voices of Homeless Teens* (8–12). 1990, Shapolsky $14.95 (978-0-944007-81-5). A series of interviews with homeless teens reveals lives of violence, poverty, and drugs. (Rev: BL 11/15/90; SLJ 2/91) [362.7]

10221 Wagner, Viqi, ed. *Poverty* (7–12). Series: Opposing Viewpoints. 2008, Gale/Greenhaven $36.20 (978-0-7377-3747-9); paper $24.95 (978-0-7377-3748-6). This anthology describes the causes of poverty in America and around the world and debates the possible solutions, ranging from migration to government intervention; a revision of the 2003 edition. (Rev: SLJ 2/1/09) [362.5]

10222 Wolny, Philip. *Food Supply Collapse* (7–10). Series: Doomsday Scenarios: Separating Fact from Fiction. 2010, Rosen LB $29.25 (978-1-4358-3563-4). Are we facing food supply doomsday? This volume describes the current situation and the threats that face nations around the world. (Rev: LMC 11–12/10) [363.8]

10223 Yankoski, Mike. *Under the Overpass: A Journey of Faith on the Streets of America* (10–12). 2005, Multnomah paper $11.99 (978-1-59052-402-2). Mike Yankoski, who took a break from college to immerse himself in the world of the homeless, writes movingly about his experiences and the testing of his faith. (Rev: SLJ 7/05) [362.7]

Public Morals

10224 Allison, Jay, and Dan Gediman, eds. *This I Believe: The Personal Philosophies of Remarkable Men and Women* (9–12). 2006, Henry Holt $23.00 (978-0-8050-8087-2). A collection of statements of personal belief that originally aired on National Public Radio. The essays are by people of differing backgrounds and range from humorous to deeply moving. (Rev: BL 9/1/06) [170]

10225 Berne, Emma Carlson. *Online Pornography* (8–12). Series: Opposing Viewpoints. 2007, Gale LB $36.20 (978-0-7377-3657-1); paper $23.70 (978-0-7377-3658-8). Is online pornography harmful to society? Is online pornography a form of free speech? Questions like these are discussed from different points of view. (Rev: SLJ 1/08)

10226 Burns, Kate, ed. *Censorship* (7–12). Series: History of Issues. 2006, Gale LB $34.95 (978-0-7377-2009-9). Primary documents help to illustrate the issues discussed in this pro and con review of censorship throughout American history. (Rev: SLJ 6/07)

10227 Day, Nancy. *Censorship or Freedom of Expression?* (7–12). Series: Pro/Con Issues. 2000, Lerner LB $25.26 (978-0-8225-2628-5). A look at censorship in areas including schools and the arts and entertainment, with discussion of age appropriateness and use of the Internet. (Rev: HBG 3/01; SLJ 1/01) [363.3]

10228 Gold, John C. *Board of Education v. Pico (1982)* (6–10). Series: Supreme Court Decisions. 1994, Twenty-First Century LB $25.90 (978-0-8050-3660-2). A thorough analysis of the Supreme Court case that began in a Long Island school and involved censoring library materials. (Rev: BL 11/15/94; SLJ 1/95) [344.73]

10229 Irons, Peter, ed. *May It Please the Court: Courts, Kids and the Constitution* (10–12). Series: May it Please the Court. 2000, New Press $59.95 (978-1-56584-613-5). This volume, which includes audiotapes, deals with issues involving the constitutional rights of children, such as school prayer, religious clubs, maternity leaves

for teachers, teaching evolution, student newspapers, and censorship. (Rev: BL 9/1/00) [344.73]

10230 Kolbert, Kathryn, and Zak Mettger. *Justice Talking: Leading Advocates Debate Today's Most Controversial Issues — Censoring the Web* (10–12). 2001, New Press $24.95 (978-1-56584-715-6). A debate from National Public Radio on Web censorship is reproduced (with an accompanying CD) with relevant original sources. (Rev: BL 12/1/01) [343.7309]

10231 Nathan, Debbie. *Pornography* (10–12). Series: Groundwork Guide. 2007, Groundwood $15.95 (978-0-88899-766-1). Is pornography truly harmful? Is it demeaning to women? Or is it just another form of protected free speech? The author takes a balanced and frank look at this issue and its history. (Rev: BL 11/1/07) [363.4]

10232 Otfinoski, Steven. *Science Fiction and Fantasy* (9–12). Series: Our Freedom to Read. 2009, Chelsea House LB $40.00 (978-160413032-4). A discussion of science fiction and fantasy books, including *A Wrinkle in Time* and *Fahrenheit 451,* that have been "challenged" and why they have been controversial. (Rev: BL 4/1/09; LMC 8–9/09) [098]

10233 Phelps, Norm. *The Longest Struggle: Animal Advocacy from Pythagoras to PETA* (9–12). 2007, Lantern paper $20.00 (978-1-59056-106-5). Tracing the history of both animal exploitation and advocacy from 600 BCE to the present day, Phelps explores the philosophies of animal rights that evolved into the various animal-rights movements of today, such as RSPCA and PETA. (Rev: BL 8/07) [179]

10234 Ross, Val. *You Can't Read This: Forbidden Books, Lost Writing, Mistranslations and Codes* (7–10). 2006, Tundra $19.95 (978-0-88776-732-6). A survey of censorship of the written word throughout history. (Rev: BL 5/15/06) [028]

Sex Roles

10235 Berg, Barbara J. *Sexism in America: Alive, Well, and Ruining Our Future* (10–12). 2009, Lawrence Hill $24.95 (978-155652776-0). Author Barbara Berg, a women's studies author and expert, cites many examples of why the women's movement has stalled in the 21st century. (Rev: BL 9/09) [305.42]

10236 Douglas, Susan J. *Enlightened Sexism: The Seductive Message that Feminism's Work Is Done* (11–12). 2010, Times $26 (978-080508326-2). This insightful examination into the ways women are negatively portrayed in our supposedly "post-feminist" society draws on examples from popular TV shows and ads, and urges young women to remain active in the fight against such stereotyping. (Rev: BL 2/1–15/10) [302.23082]

10237 Freedman, Estelle B., ed. *The Essential Feminist Reader* (10–12). 2007, Modern Library paper $17.95 (978-0-8129-7460-7). An anthology of feminist writings. (Rev: BL 9/15/07) [305]

10238 Garden, Nancy. *Hear Us Out! Lesbian and Gay Stories of Struggle, Progress and Hope, 1950 to the Present* (9–12). 2007, Farrar $18.00 (978-0-374-31759-1). Moving chronologically through the decades, the author discusses the status of gay rights and social acceptance at each point in time and offers two stories that illustrate typical GLBT (gay, lesbian, bisexual, transgender) experiences. (Rev: BL 5/1/07; HB 9–10/07; SLJ 7/07) [306.76]

10239 Gourley, Catherine. *Flappers and the New American Woman: Perceptions of Women from 1918 through the 1920s* (7–12). Series: Images and Issues of Women in the Twentieth Century. 2007, Lerner LB $38.60 (978-0-8225-6060-9). An interesting chronological examination of the roles women played in this period and how they were portrayed in various media. (Rev: BL 1/1–15/08; LMC 2/08; SLJ 11/07) [305.40973]

10240 Levithan, David, and Billy Merrell, eds. *The Full Spectrum: A New Generation of Writing about Gay, Lesbian, Bisexual, Transgender, Questioning, and Other Identities* (8–11). 2006, Knopf LB $17.99 (978-0-375-93290-8); paper $9.95 (978-0-375-83290-1). Forty essays and other contributions by young people under age 23 reveal their own real-life experiences questioning or establishing their sexual identities. (Rev: BL 5/15/06; HB 7–8/06; SLJ 7/06) [306.76]

10241 Mills, J. Elizabeth. *Expectations for Women: Confronting Stereotypes* (7–12). Series: A Young Woman's Guide to Contemporary Issues. 2010, Rosen LB $31.95 (978-1-4358-3543-6). Growing up too fast, body image, plastic surgery, the need to balance home and work, and aging gracefully are all explored in an easy, conversational manner. (Rev: LMC 10/10; SLJ 4/1/10; VOYA 8/10) [305.235]

Social Action, Social Change, and Futurism

10242 Alsenas, Linas. *Gay America: Struggle for Equality* (7–12). Illus. 2008, Abrams $24.95 (978-081099487-4). Personal accounts of gays and lesbians are interspersed with historical information about their struggles for acceptance in the United States since the Victorian period. Stonewall Honor 2010. Lexile 1340L (Rev: BL 2/1/09; LMC 1–2/09; SLJ 7/08) [306.76]

10243 Coon, Nora E., ed. *It's Your Rite: Girls' Coming-of-Age Stories* (6–12). 2003, Beyond Words paper $9.95 (978-1-58270-074-8). Young authors from around the world describe practical and ceremonial milestones that

mark their coming of age, and the associated worries and joys. (Rev: SLJ 10/03) [305.235]

10244 Cullen-DuPont, Kathryn, ed. *American Women Activists' Writings: An Anthology, 1637–2001* (10–12). 2002, Rowman & Littlefield $35.00 (978-0-8154-1185-7). Sojourner Truth, Elizabeth Cady Stanton, Elizabeth Blackwell, and Amelia Earhart are among the women whose writings are gathered here. (Rev: BL 3/1/02) [305.4]

10245 Gay, Kathlyn. *Volunteering: The Ultimate Teen Guide* (8–12). Series: It Happened to Me. 2004, Scarecrow $32.50 (978-0-8108-4922-8). This guide examines a wide range of volunteering opportunities for teenagers, from working with the elderly or the homeless to tutoring to building houses; real-life stories add interest. (Rev: SLJ 4/05; VOYA 4/05) [361.8]

10246 Goldman, Paula, ed. *Imagining Ourselves: Global Voices from a New Generation of Women* (9–12). 2006, New World Library paper $26.95 (978-1-57731-524-7). Women from diverse walks of life around the world discuss their lives and how they differ from those of their mothers. (Rev: BL 2/15/06; SLJ 8/06) [305.242]

10247 Halpin, Mikki. *It's Your World — If You Don't Like It, Change It: Activism for Teenagers* (7–12). 2004, Simon & Schuster paper $8.99 (978-0-689-87448-2). Covering activism on a wide range of topics — the environment, war, gay rights, women's rights, and so forth — this is a useful guide, providing practical ideas and sensible cautions. (Rev: BL 12/15/04; SLJ 12/04) [305.23]

10248 Karnes, Frances A., and Kristen R. Stephens. *Empowered Girls: A Girl's Guide to Positive Activism, Volunteering, and Philanthropy* (6–12). 2005, Prufrock paper $14.95 (978-1-59363-163-5). A helpful, information-packed guide that will motivate young people to volunteer. (Rev: SLJ 2/06; VOYA 4/06) [361.8]

10249 Kurian, George Thomas, and Graham T. T. Molitor, eds. *The 21st Century* (8–12). 1999, Macmillan $130.00 (978-0-02-864977-1). This book makes predictions for future developments in such areas as abortion, artificial intelligence, crime, extinction, household appliances, sexual behavior, and utopias. (Rev: BL 4/1/99; SLJ 8/99) [133.3]

10250 Lesko, Wendy Schaetzel. *Youth: The 26% Solution* (7–12). 2000, Information U.S.A. paper $14.95 (978-1-878346-47-6). A community action handbook for teens prepared by Project 2000 that provides basic, workable advice, based on the premise that the 26 percent of the population of the United States under the age of 18 can make a difference. (Rev: BL 11/1/98; VOYA 12/98) [361.8]

10251 McGuckin, Frank, ed. *Volunteerism* (10–12). Series: Reference Shelf. 1998, H.W. Wilson paper $50.00 (978-0-8242-0944-5). These articles by a variety of writers explore various facets of volunteering and how individuals can participate. [361.3]

10252 Marcovitz, Hal. *Teens and Volunteerism* (7–10). Series: The Gallup Youth Survey, Major Issues and Trends. 2005, Mason Crest LB $22.95 (978-1-59084-877-7). An attractive volume documenting Gallup findings on teens' attitudes toward various forms of volunteerism including community service, military service, and activism. (Rev: SLJ 1/06) [361.8]

10253 Newkirk, Ingrid E., and Jane Ratcliffe, eds. *One Can Make a Difference: How Simple Actions Can Change the World* (11–12). 2008, Adams Media paper $16.95 (978-159869629-5). A look at more than 50 good deeds that have made a difference. e (Rev: BLO 9/15/08) [363]

10254 Rubel, David. *If I Had a Hammer: Building Homes and Hope with Habitat for Humanity* (6–12). 2009, Candlewick $19.99 (978-0-7636-4701-8). With a foreword by Jimmy Carter, this account of the work of Habitat for Humanity covers everything from the organization's Christian foundation to how it chooses partner families and the various tools and techniques the volunteers use. ⋒ Lexile 1150L (Rev: BL 12/1/09; LMC 1–2/10; SLJ 11/09) [363.5]

10255 Ryan, Bernard, Jr. *Expanding Education and Literacy* (7–12). Series: Community Service for Teens. 1998, Ferguson LB $19.95 (978-0-89434-231-8). This book describes literacy and reading programs in the United States and how teens can participate in them. (Rev: BL 9/15/98; SLJ 11/98) [361.3]

10256 Ryan, Bernard, Jr. *Participating in Government: Opportunities to Volunteer* (7–12). Series: Community Service for Teens. 1998, Ferguson LB $19.95 (978-0-89434-230-1). An upbeat guide that advises teens about how they can volunteer in the areas of government and politics and become involved in their community. Also use *Promoting the Arts and Sciences: Opportunities to Volunteer* (1998). (Rev: SLJ 2/99) [302.14]

10257 Ryan, Bernard, Jr. *Promoting the Arts and Sciences* (7–12). Series: Community Service for Teens. 1998, Ferguson LB $19.95 (978-0-89434-234-9). This work tells how teens can become involved in local agencies that promote the arts and sciences and how their services can make a difference both to the community and to themselves. (Rev: BL 9/15/98; SLJ 2/99) [361.8]

10258 Senker, Cath. *Poverty* (7–12). Series: What If We Do Nothing? 2007, Gareth Stevens LB $22.95 (978-0-8368-7757-1). Individuals can make a difference in fighting poverty, this title suggests, even as it lists discouraging statistics on the pervasiveness of poverty around the globe. (Rev: BL 4/1/07) [363]

10259 Smith, Wendy. *Give a Little: How Your Small Donations Can Transform Our World* (10–12). 2009, Hyperion paper $14.99 (978-14013234-0-0). This accessible guide to philanthropy provides information about various charitable organizations and emphasizes the considerable impact of modest donations. e (Rev: BL 10/15/09) [361.7]

10260 Tisch, Jonathan M., and Karl Weber. *Citizen You: Doing Your Part to Change the World* (10–12). 2010, Crown $24 (978-030758848-7). Tisch calls on young people to move beyond simple volunteerism and into more complex civic engagement by examining present-day examples of philanthropists and the positive changes they're enacting. e (Rev: BL 5/1–15/10) [361.2]

10261 Young, Ralph F. *Dissent in America: Voices That Shaped a Nation* (10–12). 2008, Pearson paper $17.95 (978-0-205-60541-5). Traces the fiery voices of American dissent in writings, speeches, and manifestos from pre-Revolutionary War petitions to Iraq War protests and from social reform to human rights movements. (Rev: BL 3/1/08) [973]

Social Customs and Holidays

10262 Bannatyne, Lesley. *A Halloween How-To: Costumes, Parties, Decorations, and Destinations* (9–12). 2001, Pelican paper $17.95 (978-1-56554-774-2). After a history of Halloween, this book tells you how to have a great Halloween party, how it is celebrated in various cultures, and how to prepare Halloween food. (Rev: BL 7/01) [394.2]

10263 Breuilly, Elizabeth, and Joanne O'Brien. *Festivals of the World: The Illustrated Guide to Celebrations, Customs, Events and Holidays* (6–12). 2002, Checkmark $29.95 (978-0-8160-4481-8). Festivals around the world are organized by religion, with maps, photographs, and interesting sidebar features. (Rev: SLJ 4/03) [394.2]

10264 Denizet-Lewis, Benoit. *American Voyeur: Dispatches from the Far Reaches of Modern Life* (11–12). 2010, Simon & Schuster paper $15 (978-14165391-5-5). Journalist Denizet-Lewis immerses himself in the fringes of American life: from preteen extreme athletes to gay subcultures; first published in magazines such as *Spin* and *Slate,* these 16 articles are suitable for mature readers. e (Rev: BL 12/1/09) [306.70973]

10265 Greene, Meg. *Rest in Peace: A History of American Cemeteries* (8–11). Series: People's History. 2008, Lerner LB $30.60 (978-0-8225-3414-3). American burial traditions are constantly evolving, and this volume looks at everything from early Native American practices to gigantic modern cemeteries, with mentions of ethnic communities and environmentally conscious options along the way. (Rev: BL 3/15/08; SLJ 6/08) [393.09]

10266 Karenga, Maulana. *Kwanzaa: A Celebration of Family, Community and Culture, Special Commemorative Edition* (6–12). 1997, Univ. of Sankore $24.95

(978-0-943412-21-4). This complete book on Kwanzaa explains its African and African American origins, devotes a chapter to each of its seven principles, suggests activities, and gives answers to the most frequently asked questions about this holiday. (Rev: SLJ 10/98) [394.2]

10267 Lopez, Adriana, ed. *Fifteen Candles: 15 Tales of Taffeta, Hairspray, Drunk Uncles, and Other Quinceañera Stories* (8–12). 2007, HarperCollins paper $14.95 (978-0-06-124192-5). Fifteen contributions — some fiction, some nonfiction — describe varied quinceañera experiences. (Rev: BL 6/1–15/07; SLJ 10/07) [395.2]

Terrorism

10268 Abbott, David. *The Twin Towers* (7–10). Illus. Series: A Place in History. 2011, Black Rabbit LB $34.25 (978-184837677-9). Discusses the events of September 11, 2001, exploring the motivation for the attack and the resulting "War on Terror." (Rev: BL 4/1/11) [973.931]

10269 Balkin, Karen F., ed. *The War on Terrorism* (7–12). Series: Opposing Viewpoints. 2004, Gale LB $36.20 (978-0-7377-2336-6); paper $24.95 (978-0-7377-2337-3). The 28 essays in this collection present both sides of the ongoing debate over the Bush administration's measures to combat terrorism. (Rev: SLJ 3/05) [973.9]

10270 Bell, J. Bowyer. *Murder on the Nile: The World Trade Center and Global Terror* (10–12). 2003, Encounter $26.95 (978-1-893554-63-4). This thought-provoking overview of the rising tide of violence by Islamic fundamentalists focuses on Egypt, where a secular government has met resistance. (Rev: BL 12/15/02) [297]

10271 Bergen, Peter L. *Holy War, Inc.: Inside the Secret World of Osama bin Laden* (10–12). 2001, Free Press paper $14.00 (978-0-7432-3495-5). This account, which ends in 2001, gives a history of al-Qaeda, profiles its leaders, and describes the life and ideas of Osama bin Laden. (Rev: BL 11/15/01) [958.1]

10272 Campbell, Geoffrey. *A Vulnerable America* (7–12). Series: Library of Homeland Security. 2004, Gale LB $29.95 (978-1-59018-383-0). This book discusses national security, how the government dealt with terrorist attacks in the past, and how 9/11/01 changed intelligence activities. (Rev: BL 4/15/04; SLJ 5/04) [363.3]

10273 Cart, Michael, ed. *911: The Book of Help* (8–12). 2002, Cricket $17.95 (978-0-8126-2659-9); paper $9.95 (978-0-8126-2676-6). A collection of essays, stories, and poems by well-known writers presented in sections titled "Healing," "Searching for History," "Asking Why? Why? Why?," and "Reacting and Recovering." (Rev: BL 7/02; HB 9–10/02; HBG 3/03; SLJ 9/02*) [818]

10274 Davenport, John C. *Global Extremism and Terrorism* (10–12). Series: The World in Focus. 2007, Chelsea House LB $35.00 (978-0-7910-9279-8). For advanced students, this is a useful exploration of terrorism around the world, looking at its roots and different forms. (Rev: SLJ 1/08)

10275 Dudley, William, ed. *The Attack on America: September 11, 2001* (9–12). Series: At Issue. 2002, Gale LB $29.95 (978-0-7377-1292-6); paper $21.20 (978-0-7377-1293-3). The life-altering effects of the September 11, 2001, terrorist attack are explored in a series of excerpts from materials such as op-ed pieces and speeches that present views from across the political spectrum. (Rev: BL 7/02; SLJ 11/02) [973.931]

10276 Dwyer, Jim, and Kevin Flynn. *102 Minutes: The Untold Story of the Fight to Survive Inside the Twin Towers* (9–12). 2005, Times $26.00 (978-0-8050-7682-0). An unflinching account of the struggle for life within the twin towers of the World Trade Center in the 102 minutes between the impact of the first plane and the collapse of the second tower. (Rev: BL 11/15/04; SLJ 4/05) [974.7]

10277 Friedman, Lauri S. *Terrorist Attacks* (7–12). Series: Compact Research. 2007, Reference Point LB $24.95 (978-1-60152-022-7). Why do people commit terrorist attacks? How can terrorist attacks be prevented? These and other questions are discussed from various points of view, with facts, profiles, and illustrations. (Rev: SLJ 1/08)

10278 Friedman, Lauri S., ed. *What Motivates Suicide Bombers?* (9–12). Series: At Issue. 2005, Gale LB $29.95 (978-0-7377-2320-5); paper $21.20 (978-0-7377-2321-2). This collection of essays looks into the multiplicity of factors that motivate suicide bombers. (Rev: SLJ 4/05) [363.3]

10279 Gaines, Ann. *Terrorism* (7–12). Series: Crime, Justice, and Punishment. 1998, Chelsea LB $30.00 (978-0-7910-4596-1). Beginning with the bombing of Pan Am flight 103 over Lockerbie, Scotland, in 1988, this thorough account discusses terrorism around the world and the groups that are responsible. (Rev: BL 12/15/98; SLJ 3/99) [364.1]

10280 Gerges, Fawaz A. *Journey of the Jihadist: Inside Muslim Militancy* (10–12). 2006, Harcourt $25.00 (978-0-15-101213-8). Based on interviews with high-ranking insiders, this is an insightful, revealing look into radical Islam and the differences among Jihadists. (Rev: BL 4/15/06*) [322.4]

10281 Goodman, Robin, and Andrea Henderson Fahnestock. *The Day Our World Changed: Children's Art of 9/11* (7–12). 2002, Abrams $19.95 (978-0-8109-3544-0). Children's words and art are the main focus of this handsome volume. (Rev: BL 9/15/02) [700]

10282 Gow, Mary. *Attack on America: The Day the Twin Towers Collapsed* (8–12). Series: American Disasters.

2002, Enslow LB $23.93 (978-0-7660-2118-1). This dramatic account of the events of September 11, 2001, includes many survivor and eyewitness accounts. (Rev: BL 9/1/02; HBG 3/03; SLJ 1/03) [973.931]

10283 Gupta, Dipak K. *Who Are the Terrorists?* (8–11). Series: Roots of Terrorism. 2006, Chelsea House $35.00 (978-0-7910-8306-2). This book describes more than 30 terrorist organizations deemed dangerous by the U.S.State Department, providing a balanced account with regard to Islam and looking at the activities of three Nobel Peace Prize winners who were once thought to be terrorists. (Rev: BL 7/06) [303.6]

10284 Halberstam, David. *Firehouse* (10–12). 2002, Hyperion $22.95 (978-1-4013-0005-0). A deeply moving account of how one New York City firehouse came to terms with the devastating loss of 12 of its firemen on September 11, 2001. (Rev: BL 6/1–15/02) [28.9]

10285 Hanson, Victor David. *An Autumn of War: What America Learned from September 11 and the War on Terrorism* (10–12). 2002, Anchor paper $12.00 (978-1-4000-3113-9). In this collection of essays, Hanson dissects the tragic events of September 11, 2001, and examines the causes and responses. (Rev: BL 7/02) [808]

10286 Hendra, Tony, ed. *Brotherhood* (9–12). 2002, American Express $29.95 (978-0-916103-73-6). A handsome tribute to the firefighters who gave their lives in the effort to save people from the Twin Towers on September 11, 2001. (Rev: BL 3/1/02) [363.32]

10287 Heuvel, Katrina vanden, ed. *A Just Response: The Nation on Terrorism, Democracy and September 11, 2001* (10–12). 2002, Thunder's Mouth paper $14.95 (978-1-56025-400-3). In this collection of articles, editorials, and essays, the writers and editors of the *Nation* roundly criticize the Bush administration and the mainstream media for their post-9/11 excesses and sins of omission, respectively. (Rev: BL 4/15/02) [973.931]

10288 Heyden, William, ed. *September 11, 2001: American Writers Respond* (10–12). 2002, Etruscan paper $19.00 (978-0-9718228-0-1). This collection of short stories, essays, and poems offers the reactions of more than 120 writers to the terrorist attacks. (Rev: BL 7/02) [818]

10289 Houle, Michelle E., ed. *Terrorism* (9–12). Series: History of Issues. 2005, Gale LB $36.20 (978-0-7377-1909-3); paper $24.95 (978-0-7377-1910-9). Various forms of terrorism are presented through primary documents and essays that offer historical and cultural context. (Rev: BL 4/1/05) [303.6]

10290 Jacobson, Sid, and Ernie Colon. *The 9/11 Report: A Graphic Adaptation* (9–12). Illus. by authors. 2006, Hill & Wang $30.00 (978-0-8090-5738-2); paper $16.95 (978-0-8090-5739-9). This graphic adaptation reduces the 800-page official report to a manageable size and offers the story of the four planes on foldout pages. (Rev: SLJ 12/06)

10291 Kallen, Stuart A. *National Security* (7–12). Series: Compact Research. 2007, Reference Point LB $24.95 (978-1-60152-020-3). How serious a threat to national security is terrorism? How is the government protecting national security? These and other questions are discussed from various points of view, with facts, profiles, and illustrations. (Rev: SLJ 1/08)

10292 Katz, Samuel M. *Against All Odds: Counterterrorist Hostage Rescues* (6–12). Series: Terrorist Dossiers. 2004, Lerner LB $26.60 (978-0-8225-1567-8). The notable hostage rescues by antiterrorist groups around the world covered here go back to the early 19th century. (Rev: SLJ 4/05; VOYA 6/05) [364.15]

10293 Katz, Samuel M. *At Any Cost: National Liberation Terrorism* (7–12). Series: Terrorist Dossiers. 2004, Lerner LB $26.60 (978-0-8225-0949-3). This is an excellent introduction to the terrorist groups active today whose cause is the liberation of their homelands. (Rev: BL 3/15/04; HBG 4/04; SLJ 3/04; VOYA 4/04) [363.2]

10294 Katz, Samuel M. *Global Counterstrike: International Counterterrorism* (9–12). Series: Terrorist Dossiers. 2004, Lerner LB $26.60 (978-0-8225-1566-1). Discusses various countries' strategies to protect their citizens and infrastructures from terrorist attacks. Also use *U.S. Counterstrike: American Counterterrorism* (2004). (Rev: SLJ 1/05) [364.1]

10295 Katz, Samuel M. *Jihad: Islamic Fundamentalist Terrorism* (7–12). Series: Terrorist Dossiers. 2003, Lerner LB $26.60 (978-0-8225-4031-1). A look at Middle East-based terrorist groups, their histories, and present-day activities. (Rev: BL 3/15/04; HBG 4/04; SLJ 5/04) [303.6]

10296 Katz, Samuel M. *Raging Within: Ideological Terrorism* (7–12). Series: Terrorist Dossiers. 2004, Lerner LB $26.60 (978-0-8225-4032-8). This book examines terrorists whose motivation is based on ideologies and religion. (Rev: BL 3/15/04; HBG 4/04; SLJ 5/04) [363.2]

10297 Keegan, William, and Bart Davis. *Closure: The Untold Story of the Ground Zero Recovery Mission* (11–12). 2006, Simon & Schuster $25.00 (978-0-7432-9186-6). Keegan recounts the harrowing experience of being a first responder to the 2001 terrorist attacks on the World Trade Center, including digging out bodies, notifying grieving families, and losing friends in the tragedy. (Rev: BL 9/1/06) [974.7]

10298 Landau, Elaine. *Suicide Bombers: Foot Soldiers of the Terrorist Movement* (8–11). 2006, Lerner LB $31.93 (978-0-7613-3470-5). Examines suicide bombers, their motivation and reasoning, and how terrorist groups recruit and train them. (Rev: BL 11/1/06; LMC 3/07) [363.325]

10299 Marcovitz, Hal. *Terrorism* (9–12). Series: Great Disasters, Reforms and Ramifications. 2000, Chelsea House $30.00 (978-0-7910-5264-8). The coverage in this volume ends in 2000, but gives background material on such topics as the 1972 Munich Olympics attack, Patty Hearst, and Timothy McVeigh. (Rev: HBG 3/01) [363.3]

10300 Quin, Mary. *Kidnapped in Yemen: One Woman's Amazing Escape from Captivity* (11–12). 2005, Lyons $23.95 (978-1-59228-728-4). In this gripping story of survival, former Xerox executive Mary Quin relives her 1998 kidnapping — along with other tourists — by terrorists in Yemen and her decision to quit her job and find out more about her kidnappers; for mature teens. (Rev: BL 5/15/05) [364.15]

10301 Rees, David. *Get Your War On* (11–12). 2002, Soft Skull paper $9.95 (978-1-887128-76-6). The forthright cynicism of these comic strips exploring the wisdom and conduct of the war on terror is for mature teens only. (Rev: BL 9/15/02) [973.931]

10302 Roleff, Tamara L., ed. *America Under Attack: Primary Sources* (6–12). Series: Lucent Terrorism Library. 2002, Gale LB $29.95 (978-1-59018-216-1). Interviews, speeches, articles, and other items relating to the terrorist attacks of September 11, 2001, are collected in a volume that researchers will find useful. (Rev: BL 11/1/02; SLJ 9/02) [973.931]

10303 Ruschmann, Paul. *The War on Terror* (7–10). Series: Point/Counterpoint. 2005, Chelsea House LB $32.95 (978-0-7910-8091-7). Offers opposing views on terrorism-related topics, including preemptive wars, the suspension of human rights, and anti-terror laws. (Rev: SLJ 9/05)

10304 Shostak, Arthur B., ed. *Trade Towers/War Clouds* (9–12). Series: Defeating Terrorism/Developing Dreams. 2004, Chelsea House LB $31.95 (978-0-7910-7956-0). A look at the impact of the September 11 attacks — and of the subsequent invasion of Iraq — on American society. (Rev: BL 6/1–15/04; SLJ 11/04) [956.7]

10305 Streissguth, Thomas. *International Terrorists* (6–10). Series: Profiles. 1993, Oliver LB $19.95 (978-1-881508-07-6). This book describes the causes of international terrorism, the responsible organizations, and famous incidents. (Rev: BL 10/15/93; SLJ 1/94; VOYA 2/94) [909.82]

10306 Taylor, Robert. *The History of Terrorism* (6–12). Series: Lucent Terrorism Library. 2002, Gale LB $29.95 (978-1-59018-206-2). A chronological look at the history of terrorism around the globe, with discussion of the reasons it has been so widespread and of terrorists' motivation. Also use *Terrorists and Terrorist Groups* (2002). (Rev: BL 11/1/02; SLJ 11/02) [303.6]

10307 Temple-Raston, Dina. *The Jihad Next Door: The Lackawanna Six and Rough Justice in an Age of Terror* (10–12). 2007, Public Affairs $26.00 (978-1-58648-403-3). NPR journalist Temple-Raston investigates what led a group of naive Yemeni American friends from upstate New York to attend an al-Qaeda training camp and later be prosecuted and jailed for terrorism. ⌂ (Rev: BL 9/1/07) [363]

Urban and Rural Life

10308 Dyer, Hadley. *Watch This Space: Designing, Defending and Sharing Public Spaces* (9–12). Illus. by Marc Ngui. 2010, Kids Can $18.95 (978-1-55453-293-3). An interesting and thought-provoking look at a topic that has been neglected at the high-school level. Readers will learn about public spaces and their functions around the world. Dyer presents an interesting survey of the nature of public space, its importance to society, and questions about privacy, urban beautification, and so forth; specific examples and colorful artwork add appeal. (Rev: BL 6/10; LMC 8–9/10; SLJ 5/10) [307.1]

Economics and Business

General and Miscellaneous

10309 Bailey, Diane. *How Markets Work* (7–11). Illus. Series: Real World Economics. 2012, Rosen LB $31.95 (978-144885564-3). This visually appealing offering presents clearly focused, well-written information about how people exchange money, goods, and resources. (Rev: BL 7/12; SLJ 5/1/12) [381]

10310 Folbre, Nancy, and The Center for Popular Economics. *The New Field Guide to the U.S. Economy: A Compact and Irreverent Guide to Economic Life in America* (9–12). 1995, New Press paper $16.95 (978-1-56584-153-6). A compact introduction to the U.S. economy and the factors that affect it, presented in a humorous manner through easy-to-read graphs, illustrations, cartoons, and text divided into chapters on workers, women, people of color, health, environment, and the global economy. (Rev: VOYA 12/96) [330.73]

10311 Furgang, Kathy. *Understanding Economics Indicators: Predicting Future Trends in the Economy* (7–11). Illus. Series: Real World Economics. 2012, Rosen LB $31.95 (978-144885571-1). This visually appealing offering presents clearly focused, well-written information about economists' analysis of key indicators. Also use *Understanding Budget Deficits and the National Debt* (2012). (Rev: BL 7/12) [330.01]

10312 Kamberg, Mary-Lane. *How Business Decisions Are Made* (7–10). Illus. 2012, Rosen LB $31.95 (978-144885565-0). Explores the need for wise decision-making and how such decisions are reached. (Rev: BL 7/12) [658.4]

10313 Klein, Grady, and Yoram Bauman. *The Cartoon Introduction to Economics, Vol. 1: Microeconomics* (10–12). Illus. 2010, Hill & Wang paper $17.95 (978-08090948-1-3). Basic economic concepts are given fresh life in this appealing, comic-style book, where

information is presented by a team of three lab-coated figures with clipboards. (Rev: BL 1/1–15/10) [338.5]

10314 Oleksy, Walter. *Business and Industry* (6–12). Series: Information Revolution. 1996, Facts on File $25.00 (978-0-8160-3075-0). This book describes how companies use Powerbook computers, supercomputers, modems, and videophones to distribute information, increase productivity, and make better business decisions. (Rev: BL 2/15/96; VOYA 6/96) [650]

10315 Waterman, Robert H. *What America Does Right: Learning from Companies That Put People First* (9–12). 1994, Norton $23.00 (978-0-393-03597-1). Examines the successful operations of companies that recognize, understand, and try to meet their employees' needs. (Rev: BL 2/15/94) [658.5]

Economic Systems and Institutions

General and Miscellaneous

10316 Aaseng, Nathan. *You Are the Corporate Executive* (7–10). Series: Great Decisions. 1997, Oliver LB $19.95 (978-1-881508-35-9). This book describes the work of a company's CEO and the nature and consequences of the decisions that CEOs have to make. (Rev: BL 6/1–15/97; SLJ 6/97) [658.4]

10317 Brezina, Corona. *Understanding the Federal Reserve and Monetary Policy* (7–10). Series: Real World Economics. 2012, Rosen LB $31.95 (978-1-4488-5567-4). This volume looks at the history and activities of the Federal Reserve, emphasizing its role during the great recession and the outlook for the future. ℮ (Rev: SLJ 5/1/12) [332.1]

10318 Trahant, LeNora B. *The Success of the Navajo Arts and Crafts Enterprise* (7–10). Series: Success.

1996, Walker LB $16.85 (978-0-8027-8337-0). After a brief history of the Navajo Nation, the author describes how the arts and crafts of the Navajos have prospered under a manufacturing and marketing cooperative. (Rev: BL 5/15/96; SLJ 7/96) [381]

Stock Exchanges

10319 Brennan, Kristine. *The Stock Market Crash of 1929* (8–12). Series: Great Disasters: Reforms and Ramifications. 2000, Chelsea LB $21.95 (978-0-7910-5268-6). This account of the crash and its causes and aftermath looks carefully at the economy of the time and discusses the changes of a similar crash happening today. (Rev: HBG 3/01; SLJ 12/00) [338.5]

Consumerism

10320 Barach, Arnold B. *Famous American Trademarks* (9–12). 1971, Public Affairs paper $9.00 (978-0-8183-0165-0). The origins and history of about 100 trademarks are traced by text and pictures. [341.7]

10321 Lamb, Sharon, and Lyn Mikel Brown. *Packaging Girlhood: Rescuing Our Daughters from Marketers' Schemes* (11–12). 2006, St. Martin's $24.95 (978-0-312-35250-9). Older teens will be interested in this review of the pressures of the media and marketers — including pressures to grow up too fast and to limit their interests. (Rev: BL 9/1/06) [306.3]

10322 Schlosser, Eric. *Fast Food Nation: The Dark Side of the All-American Meal* (10–12). 2001, Houghton Mifflin $26.00 (978-0-395-97789-7). This book examines the growth of the fast-food phenomenon in America and how it has changed the economy, youth culture, and allied industries. (Rev: BL 1/1–15/01; SLJ 4/06) [394.1]

Employment and Jobs

10323 Ching, Jacqueline. *Outsourcing U.S. Jobs* (7–10). Illus. Series: In the News. 2009, Rosen LB $21.95 (978-143585039-2). A helpful resource for students exploring the effects of the global economy on U.S. and foreign workers; includes photographs and diagrams. (Rev: BL 4/15/09) [331.13]

10324 Lutz, Tom. *Doing Nothing: A History of Loafers, Loungers, Slackers, and Bums in America* (10–12). 2006, Farrar $25.00 (978-0-86547-650-9). An enjoyable, interesting chronicle of Americans who avoided

working in the traditional sense and society's reaction to them. (Rev: BL 4/15/06) [174]

Labor Unions and Labor Problems

10325 Blum, Howard. *American Lightning: Terror, Mystery, Movie-Making, and the Crime of the Century* (10–12). 2008, Crown $24.95 (978-030734694-0). A fascinating, detailed account of the investigation into the 1910 *Los Angeles Times* office explosion that brought an ongoing conflict between labor and management to a head. ⌒ℯ (Rev: BL 8/08*) [364.152]

10326 Featherstone, Liza. *Students Against Sweatshops* (10–12). 2002, Verso paper $15.00 (978-1-85984-302-4). Students interested in opposing sweatshop working conditions will find useful information in this slim volume. (Rev: BL 6/1–15/02) [361.2]

10327 Laughlin, Rosemary. *The Ludlow Massacre of 1913-1914* (9–12). Series: American Workers. 2006, Morgan Reynolds LB $26.95 (978-1-931798-86-0). The story of the bitter coal mining strike that culminated in a deadly National Guard attack on a tent city erected by striking workers and their families in Ludlow, Colorado. (Rev: BL 4/1/06; SLJ 9/06) [331.892]

10328 Laughlin, Rosemary. *The Pullman Strike of 1894. Rev. ed.* (7–12). 2006, Morgan Reynolds LB $26.95 (978-1-931798-89-1). A revised edition of this engrossing account of the bitter railroad strike, with good background material on the railroad industry, the planned city of Pullman, the depression of 1893, and the personalities involved, including Eugene Debs; additions include primary source excerpts and recommended Web sites. (Rev: SLJ 5/06)

10329 Skurzynski, Gloria. *Sweat and Blood: A History of U.S. Labor Unions* (7–10). Illus. Series: People's History. 2008, Lerner LB $31.93 (978-082257594-8). Charting the course of workers' rights from Jamestown through industrialization to the present day, Skurzynski provides a detailed, historically grounded survey of the rights, rules, and governance of labor unions in America. (Rev: BL 10/1/08; SLJ 11/1/08) [331.880]

Money and Trade

10330 January, Brendan. *Globalize It!* (8–12). 2003, Millbrook LB $26.90 (978-0-7613-2417-1). The continuing advance of globalization and arguments for and against this phenomenon are thoughtfully examined in this accessible overview. (Rev: BL 1/1–15/04; SLJ 5/04) [337]

Marketing and Advertising

10331 Green, Jen. *Advertising* (8–11). Illus. Series: Ethical Debates. 2012, Rosen LB $27.95 (978-144886018-0). This volume takes a balanced look at the business of advertising in general with a focus on how ads work, the impact on society, and the various checks and controls that are in place. (Rev: BL 5/1/12) [659.1]

10332 Haugen, David M., ed. *How Does Advertising Impact Teen Behavior?* (9–12). Series: At Issue. 2008, Gale/Greenhaven LB $29.95 (978-0-7377-3922-0); paper $23.96 (978-0-7377-3923-7). Diverse articles present varying viewpoints on the connection between advertising and teen behavior. (Rev: SLJ 2/1/09) [659.10]

10333 Reichblum, Charles. *Dr. Knowledge Presents: Strange and Fascinating Facts About Famous Brands* (9–12). 2004, Black Dog & Leventhal paper $9.95 (978-1-57912-356-7). Little-known stories behind some of the food industry's biggest brand names, including Wendy's, Betty Crocker, Spam, Heinz, and Uncle Ben; suitable for browsing but less useful for research. (Rev: SLJ 3/05)

Guidance and Personal Development

Education and Schools

General and Miscellaneous

10334 Anderson, Maggie, and David Hassler, eds. *After the Bell: Contemporary American Prose about School* (10–12). 2007, Univ. of Iowa paper $17.50 (978-1-58729-603-1). Adult authors' thoughts about their school years will resonate with many young people still in that world. (Rev: BL 10/1/07) [810.8]

10335 Ayers, William, et al, ed. *Zero Tolerance: Resisting the Drive for Punishment in Our Schools* (10–12). 2001, Free Press paper $17.95 (978-1-56584-666-1). This series of articles explores zero tolerance in school discipline and finds that it is not only ineffective but also violates basic civil rights. (Rev: BL 12/15/01) [371.5]

10336 Bluestein, Jane, and Eric D. Katz. *High School's Not Forever* (8–12). 2005, Health Communications paper $12.95 (978-0-7573-0256-5). High school students talk about their experiences in high school, covering a range of typical problems plus some of the joys of those years. (Rev: SLJ 1/06) [373.18]

10337 Brown, Oral Lee, and Caille Millner. *The Promise: How One Woman Made Good on Her Extraordinary Pact to Send a Classroom of First Graders to College* (9–12). 2005, Doubleday $22.95 (978-0-385-51147-6). The inspiring story of Oral Lee Brown's adoption of a first-grade class and her success in sending most of them to college. (Rev: BL 2/1/05) [370]

10338 Conroy, Pat. *The Water Is Wide* (10–12). 1972, Houghton Mifflin paper $7.50 (978-0-553-26893-5). This book deals with a white teacher who goes to an island off the coast of South Carolina to teach a group of poor black children. [371.9]

10339 Crew, Rudy, and Thomas Dyja. *Only Connect: The Way to Save Our Schools* (10–12). 2007, Farrar $23.00 (978-0-374-29401-4). High school debaters will appreciate this analysis of the problems in schools today and discussion of potential solutions. (Rev: BL 9/1/07) [371.010973]

10340 Daniels, Peggy, ed. *Zero Tolerance Policies in Schools* (9–12). Illus. Series: Issues That Concern You. 2008, Gale/Greenhaven $33.70 (978-0-7377-4189-6). Articles consider various aspects of zero tolerance policies and the ways in which they impact students, teachers, and schools. (Rev: SLJ 3/1/09) [371.5]

10341 Foote, Donna. *Relentless Pursuit: A Year in the Trenches with Teach for America* (10–12). 2008, Knopf $24.95 (978-0-307-26571-5). This narrative follows four Teach for America recruits in their "relentless pursuit of results" as they struggle through a year at one of the toughest schools in the nation. (Rev: BL 4/15/08) [371.1009794]

10342 Greene, Rebecca. *The Teenagers' Guide to School Outside the Box* (8–12). 2000, Free Spirit paper $15.95 (978-1-57542-087-5). Many learning opportunities are available to teens, including travel, volunteer work, serving as an intern or apprentice, mentoring, and job shadowing. (Rev: BL 2/15/01; SLJ 3/01; VOYA 4/01) [373.2]

10343 Humes, Edward. *School of Dreams: Making the Grade at a Top American High School* (10–12). 2003, Harcourt $25.00 (978-0-15-100703-5). Based on his year-long research at one of the top public high schools in Los Angeles, Humes examines the pressure on students to excel. (Rev: BL 9/1/03) [373.794]

10344 Hurwitz, Sue. *High Performance Through Effective Scheduling* (8–12). Series: Learning-a-Living Library. 1996, Rosen LB $27.95 (978-0-8239-2204-8). This book discusses the basic skill of scheduling time and how it helps students at school, in extracurricular activities, and on the job. (Rev: BL 8/96; SLJ 12/96; VOYA 2/97) [640]

10345 Iversen, Jeremy. *High School Confidential: Secrets of an Undercover Student* (11–12). 2006, Atria $25.00 (978-0-7432-8363-2). The author impersonated a high school student (with the knowledge of the school's administrators) and gained insight into adolescent anguish and preoccupations — alcohol and sex, among them. (Rev: BL 9/1/06) [373.75]

10346 Jacobs, Joanne. *Our School: The Inspiring Story of Two Teachers, One Big Idea, and the School That Beat the Odds* (11–12). 2005, Palgrave $24.95 (978-1-4039-7023-7). The remarkable success story of Downtown College Prep, a San Jose (CA) charter school that has transformed the lives of its mostly Hispanic American student body. (Rev: BL 12/1/05) [371.01]

10347 Kolbert, Kathryn, and Zak Mettger. *Justice Talking: Leading Advocates Debate Today's Most Controversial Issues — School Vouchers* (10–12). 2001, New Press $24.95 (978-1-56584-716-3). The National Public Radio debate on school vouchers is reprinted, with an accompanying CD and primary sources including three key Supreme Court decisions are included. (Rev: BL 12/1/01) [379.1]

10348 Llewellyn, Grace, ed. *Real Lives: Eleven Teenagers Who Don't Go to School Tell Their Own Stories. 2nd ed.* (9–12). 2005, Lowry paper $18.00 (978-0-9629591-2-7). In the first edition of this book, 11 teens explained why they and their families opted for homeschooling; this revision adds interesting details about what these individuals are doing today. (Rev: SLJ 11/05) [370]

10349 Marx, Jeff. *How to Win a High School Election* (9–12). 1999, Jeff Marx paper $14.95 (978-0-9667824-0-0). High school officeholders reveal their strategies for getting elected to student positions. (Rev: BL 9/1/99; SLJ 7/99) [373.159]

10350 Miller, Joe. *Cross-X: A Turbulent, Triumphant Season with an Inner-City Debate Squad* (9–12). 2006, Farrar $26.00 (978-0-374-13194-4). Against tough odds for a school with only one in three freshmen destined to graduate, Kansas City's Central High School debate squad finished in the top ten in the national competition; the team's story reveals the academic gap between rich and poor students. (Rev: BL 10/15/06; SLJ 1/07) [808.5]

10351 Pletka, Bob. *My So-Called Digital Life: 2,000 Teenagers, 300 Cameras, and 30 Days to Document Their World* (9–12). 2005, Santa Monica paper $24.95 (978-1-59580-005-3). The day-to-day lives of typical California high school teens are captured in this collection of students' photos and essays. (Rev: BL 11/15/05; VOYA 2/06) [779]

10352 Williams, Heidi. *Homeschooling* (7–10). Series: At Issue: Education. 2007, Gale LB $29.95 (978-0-7377-3685-4); paper $21.20 (978-0-7377-3686-1). The controversial practice of homeschooling is examined in 13 articles that look at both sides of such questions as

academic worth and the possibility of government involvement. (Rev: BL 3/3/08) [370.04]

Development of Academic Skills

Study Skills

10353 Greenberg, Michael. *Painless Study Techniques* (6–12). Illus. by Michele Earle-Bridges. 2009, Barron's paper $9.99 (978-0-7641-4059-4). Pop culture references will draw students into this guide that teaches skills in all aspects of study organization, including note taking, creating outlines, time management, and effective studying (includes charts and lists of Web sites). (Rev: SLJ 9/09)

Tests and Test Taking

10354 Bardin, Matt, and Susan Fine. *Zen in the Art of the SAT: How to Think, Focus, and Achieve Your Highest Score* (9–12). 2005, Houghton Mifflin paper $7.99 (978-0-618-57488-9). The principles of Zen Buddhism are recommended as an efficient way to reduce anxiety and increase focus when under pressure. (Rev: BL 9/1/05; SLJ 11/05) [378.1]

10355 Cohen, Arianne, and Colleen Kinder, eds. *Confessions of a High School Word Nerd: Increase Your SAT Verbal Score While Laughing Your Gluteus Off* (9–12). 2007, Penguin paper $14.00 (978-0-14-303836-8). Funny essays about topics of interest to teens include highlighted SAT vocabulary words that are defined at the bottom of each page. (Rev: BL 1/1–15/07) [378.1]

10356 Johnson, Ned, and Emily Warner Eskelsen. *Conquering the SAT: How Parents Can Help Teens Overcome the Pressure and Succeed* (10–12). 2007, Palgrave paper $16.95 (978-1-4039-7667-3). Teens will also find useful information in this guide that dissects the college admission test and offers ways to combat under-performance. (Rev: BL 12/1/06) [378.1]

Writing and Speaking Skills

10357 Amberg, Jay, and Mark Larson. *The Creative Writing Handbook* (9–12). 1992, Scott Foresman paper $13.50 (978-0-673-36013-7). A guide to putting effective words on a page. Does not cover marketing techniques. (Rev: BL 3/1/92) [808.02]

10358 Arana, Marie, ed. *The Writing Life: Writers on How They Think and Work* (10–12). 2003, Public Affairs paper $16.00 (978-1-58648-149-0). Some of America's finest writers discuss the writing process — how they get their ideas and what it takes to turn those ideas into books. (Rev: BL 3/15/03) [810.9]

10359 Bauer, Marion Dane. *What's Your Story? A Young Person's Guide to Writing Fiction* (5–10). 1992, Clarion paper $7.95 (978-0-395-57780-6). An award-winning writer gives advice to young authors, including suggestions for planning, writing, and revising. (Rev: BL 4/15/92; SLJ 6/92*) [808.3]

10360 Block, Francesca Lia, and Hillary Carlip. *Zine Scene: The Do-It-Yourself Guide to Zines* (8–12). 1998, Girl paper $14.95 (978-0-9659754-3-8). This is a step-by-step guide to producing one's own magazine, from getting started and writing to layout, production, and marketing. (Rev: VOYA 8/99) [808]

10361 Bodart, Joni Richards. *The World's Best Thin Books: What to Read When Your Book Report Is Due Tomorrow* (6–12). 2000, Scarecrow paper $16.95 (978-1-57886-007-4). For each of the books listed, the author provides background material, themes, characters, and possible book talk or book report ideas. (Rev: BL 1/1–15/00) [028.1]

10362 Brown, Cynthia Stokes. *Like It Was: A Complete Guide to Writing Oral History* (9–12). 1988, Teachers & Writers paper $13.95 (978-0-915924-12-7). A handbook that tells the reader how to conduct an oral history project, from planning it to the final transcription of the interviews. (Rev: BL 2/1/89; SLJ 6/89) [907]

10363 Craig, Steve. *Sports Writing: A Beginner's Guide* (6–12). 2002, Discover Writing paper $15.00 (978-0-9656574-9-5). A fine introduction to writing news and features about sports, to conducting good interviews, and to the training of journalists. (Rev: BL 9/1/02; VOYA 4/03) [070.449]

10364 Detz, Joan. *You Mean I Have to Stand Up and Say Something?* (7–12). 1986, Macmillan LB $13.95 (978-0-689-31221-2). An entertaining guide to effective speaking and overcoming the fear of facing an audience. (Rev: BCCB 2/87; BL 2/87; SLJ 3/87) [808.5]

10365 Estepa, Andrea, and Philip Kay, eds. *Starting with "I": Personal Essays by Teenagers* (7–12). 1997, Persea paper $13.95 (978-0-89255-228-3). This is a collection of 35 brief essays written by teenagers about their families, neighborhoods, race, and culture. (Rev: BL 9/15/97; SLJ 10/97; VOYA 10/97) [305.235]

10366 Fogarty, Mignon. *Grammar Girl Presents the Ultimate Writing Guide for Students* (7–10). Illus. by Erwin Haya. 2011, Henry Holt $19.99 (978-0-8050-8943-1); paper $12.99 (978-0-8050-8-944-8). Covering parts of speech, sentence structure, punctuation, usage, and improving writing in general, this appealing guide includes mnemonics, pop quizzes, and cartoon illustrations. e Lexile 960L (Rev: BL 7/11; LMC 10/11; SLJ 6/11) [428.2]

10367 Friedman, Lauri S. *Oil* (9–12). Illus. Series: Writing the Critical Essay, An Opposing Viewpoints Guide. 2008, Gale/Greenhaven $29.95 (978-0-7377-4038-7). Articles presenting opposing views about petroleum

and alternative fuels are juxtaposed with chapters explaining how to write your own analytical essay — creating an outline, presenting theories and conclusions, using quotations, finding and citing information, and so forth. (Rev: SLJ 1/1/09) [333.8]

10368 Friedman, Lauri S. *Self-Mutilation* (7–10). Illus. Series: Writing the Critical Essay: An Opposing Viewpoints Guide. 2008, Gale/Greenhaven $29.95 (978-073774266-4). After presenting six perspectives on various forms of self-mutilation (including plastic surgery and body art), this volume provides sample essays and exercises that help the student to create thoughtful, well-researched theses. (Rev: BLO 2/17/09) [616.85]

10369 Friedman, Lauri S., ed. *Racism* (7–12). Series: Writing the Critical Essay. 2006, Gale LB $26.20 (978-0-7377-3464-5). Essays on racism that originally appeared in an Opposing Viewpoints volume help students research, draft, and edit effective papers on this topic. (Rev: SLJ 9/06)

10370 Fry, Stephen. *The Ode Less Travelled: Unlocking the Poet Within* (10–12). 2006, Gotham $25.00 (978-1-59240-248-9). An entertaining and accessible guide that emphasizes the importance of knowledge of poetic forms in crafting good poetry. (Rev: BL 8/06) [808.1]

10371 Gaines, Ann Graham. *Don't Steal Copyrighted Stuff!* (5–10). 2008, Enslow LB $28.95 (978-0-7660-2861-6). Students who don't see the harm in cutting and pasting from the Internet will discover that plagiarism can ruin reputations and careers; the story of a writer who got caught brings this truth home, and there are plenty of practical tips on keeping one's work original. (Rev: BL 4/1/08; LMC 3/08) [808]

10372 Hamlett, Christina. *Screenwriting for Teens: The 100 Principles of Screenwriting Every Budding Writer Must Know* (8–12). 2006, Michael Wiese paper $18.95 (978-1-932907-18-6). Practical, friendly advice for screenwriting wannabes. (Rev: SLJ 2/07)

10373 Hart, Jack. *A Writer's Coach: An Editor's Guide to Words That Work* (9–12). 2006, Pantheon $25.00 (978-0-375-42327-7). A straightforward look at what it takes to write well (and quickly) by a veteran journalist. Aspiring writers will find this useful as a source of advice and as a model of efficient writing. (Rev: BL 8/06) [808]

10374 James, Elizabeth, and Carol Barkin. *How to Write a Term Paper* (7–12). 1980, Lothrop paper $3.95 (978-0-688-45025-0). A practical step-by-step approach to report writing that uses many examples. [808]

10375 Janeczko, Paul B., ed. *Seeing the Blue Between: Advice and Inspiration for Young Poets* (7–10). 2002, Candlewick $17.99 (978-0-7636-0881-1). More than 30 poets who write for young people give advice on writing, reading, and simply enjoying poetry, with selected poems and biographical information. (Rev: BL

3/15/02; HB 7–8/02; HBG 10/02; SLJ 5/02; VOYA 6/02) [811]

10376 Kowit, Steve. *In the Palm of Your Hand: The Poet's Portable Workshop* (9–12). 1995, Tilbury House paper $14.95 (978-0-88448-149-2). An informal discussion of the technical demands and creative sources of poetry. (Rev: BL 9/1/95) [808.1]

10377 Ledoux, Denis. *Turning Memories into Memoirs: A Handbook for Writing Lifestories* (9–12). 1993, Soleil paper $19.95 (978-0-9619373-2-4). A step-by-step handbook that encourages individuals to record their oral histories as a legacy for their families. (Rev: BL 3/15/93) [808.06]

10378 Lewis, Norman, and Wilfred Funk. *Thirty Days to a More Powerful Vocabulary* (10–12). 1991, Pocket paper $5.99 (978-0-671-74349-9). This is a proven program for vocabulary building. [413]

10379 Lyon, George Ella. *Where I'm From, Where Poems Come From* (9–12). Illus. by Robert oskins. 1999, Absey paper $13.95 (978-1-888842-12-8). Encouragement for beginning poets is interspersed with the author's memories of her childhood and samples of her poetry. (Rev: BL 9/1/99) [811]

10380 Mlynowski, Sarah, and Farrin Jacobs. *See Jane Write: A Girl's Guide to Writing Chick Lit* (8–12). Illus. by Chuck Gonzalez. 2006, Quirk paper $14.95 (978-1-59474-115-9). Girls who love "chick lit" and who want to take advantage of its popularity will enjoy this practical and readable guide. (Rev: SLJ 9/06)

10381 Mooney, Bill, and David Holt. *The Storyteller's Guide: Storytellers Share Advice for the Classroom, Boardroom, Showroom, Podium, Pulpit and Central Stage* (9–12). 1996, August House paper $23.95 (978-0-87483-482-6). Professional storytellers advise young people on every aspect of storytelling, from selecting the right stories to tell to setting up the location and the actual presentation. (Rev: VOYA 6/97) [808.5]

10382 Myers, Walter Dean. *Just Write: Here's How* (8–12). 2012, HarperCollins $17.99 (978-0-06-220389-2); paper $7.99 (978-0-06-220-390-8). With examples from his own work, Myers offers practical advice on writing both fiction and nonfiction. **e** (Rev: BL 6/12; SLJ 7/12) [808.02]

10383 Prose, Francine. *Reading Like a Writer: A Guide for People Who Love Books and for Those Who Want to Write Them* (9–12). 2006, HarperCollins $23.95 (978-

0-06-077704-3). Aptly named Prose emphasizes the importance of reading for those who want to become writers and explains how and what to read. (Rev: BL 9/1/06; SLJ 8/06) [808]

10384 Sargent, William. *Writing Naturally* (9–12). 2006, Univ. Press of New England $24.95 (978-1-58465-468-1). The author has years of experience writing about science in a way that is interesting and accessible, and this guide will help readers do the same. (Rev: BL 8/06) [508.092]

10385 Shipman, Robert Oliver. *A Pun My Word: A Humorously Enlightened Path to English Usage* (9–12). 1991, Littlefield Adams paper $14.95 (978-0-8226-3011-1). Humorous examples help explain common problems in grammar and word usage. (Rev: BL 7/91) [428]

10386 Sullivan, Helen, and Linda Sernoff. *Research Reports: A Guide for Middle and High School Students* (6–10). 1996, Millbrook LB $24.90 (978-1-56294-694-4). A well-organized, concise book on writing reports that covers each step from selecting a topic to compiling the final bibliography. (Rev: SLJ 9/96) [372.6]

10387 Waldo, Dixie. *Persuasive Speaking* (6–10). 2007, Rosen LB $19.95 (978-1-4042-1028-8). Tips for debaters will also be helpful to teams and individuals who speak in front of groups. (Rev: BL 4/1/07) [808.5]

10388 Williams, Heidi, ed. *Plagiarism* (8–12). Series: Issues That Concern You. 2008, Gale/Greenhaven $33.70 (978-0-7377-4072-1). Twelve essays address the problem of plagiarism from various perspectives, discussing in particular the temptations of new technology and the services available to prevent plagiarism. (Rev: SLJ 2/1/09) [808]

10389 Williams, Mary E. *Global Warming* (7–12). Series: Writing the Critical Essay. 2006, Gale LB $26.20 (978-0-7377-3210-8). Essays on global warming are presented along with questions to encourage students to evaluate their effectiveness; instructions for researching and editing a persuasive essay are included too. (Rev: SLJ 10/06)

10390 Wooldridge, Susan Goldsmith. *Poemcrazy: Freeing Your Life with Words* (6–12). 1996, Clarkson Potter paper $13.00 (978-0-609-80098-0). The author tries to show young people how to free their minds and spirits to write poetry and shares her own poetic experiences and inspirations as well as those of other poets. (Rev: VOYA 12/97) [811]

Academic Guidance

General and Miscellaneous

10391 Lieberman, Susan A. *The Real High School Handbook: How to Survive, Thrive, and Prepare for What's Next* (8–12). 1997, Houghton Mifflin paper $13.00 (978-0-395-79760-0). A book of tips about prospering in high school and making it enjoyable, with material on topics including grade points, testing, course selection, and getting into a college. (Rev: BL 10/15/97) [373.18]

10392 Llewellyn, Grace. *The Teenage Liberation Handbook: How to Quit School and Get a Real Life and Education* (9–12). 1998, Lowry paper $20.00 (978-0-9629591-7-2). This book encourages thoughtful teens to construct their own educational design through independent learning and developing individual ways of satisfying their intellectual curiosity. (Rev: VOYA 12/98) [371.4]

10393 Wissner-Gross, Elizabeth. *What High Schools Don't Tell You: 300+ Secrets to Make Your Kid Irresistible to Colleges by Senior Year* (9–12). 2007, Hudson Street $23.95 (978-1-59463-037-8). Planning ahead for college admission is the focus of this practical resource, as the author has provided more than 300 suggestions based on interviews with teachers, college admissions officers, and parents of nationally recognized high-school students. Part 1 of the book involves the admissions process and how to prepare, starting in 8th grade, while Part 2 provides suggestions for opportunities in specific subject areas. (Rev: BLO 7/17/07) [378.1]

Colleges and Universities

10394 Balaban, Mariah, and Jennifer Shields. *Study Away: The Independent Guide to College Abroad* (10– 12). 2003, Anchor paper $13.95 (978-1-4000-3189-4). English-language higher education opportunities outside the United States are arranged alphabetically by country. (Rev: BL 9/15/03) [370.116]

10395 Berent, Polly. *Getting Ready for College: Everything You Need to Know Before You Go: From Bike Locks to Laundry Baskets, Financial Aid to Health Care* (11–12). 2003, Random House paper $12.95 (978-0-8129-6896-5). This guide focuses not on what it will take to get into college but rather the practical knowledge needed to survive once there, covering such diverse subjects as homesickness, social life, personal finances, and security. (Rev: BL 6/1–15/03) [379.19]

10396 Cohen, Katherine. *Rock Hard Apps: How to Write a Killer College Application* (10–12). 2003, Hyperion paper $16.95 (978-0-7868-6862-9). Cohen offers solid advice about making a positive impression on college applications. (Rev: BL 6/1–15/03) [37.81]

10397 Cohen, Katherine. *The Truth About Getting In: A Top College Advisor Tells You Everything You Need to Know* (9–12). 2002, Hyperion $21.95 (978-0-7868-8747-7). A helpful guide to topics including preparation for admissions tests, writing effective essays, and sources of financial aid. (Rev: BL 3/15/02) [378.1]

10398 *Eye on Apply: Six True Stories of College Admissions* (10–12). 2004, Random House paper $15.95 (978-0-375-76426-4). In their online journal postings, six high school students reveal their college application experiences. (Rev: SLJ 3/05)

10399 Fiske, Edward, and Bruce Hammond. *Fiske Real College Essays that Work* (11–12). 2006, Sourcebooks paper $14.95 (978-1-4022-0164-6). Following a general introduction and tips on essay writing, this volume includes more than 100 essays, which were all accepted and which the authors feel are good examples of the genre; the essays are organized by commonly requested subjects such as a significant experience and personal growth. (Rev: SLJ 11/06)

10400 Fives, Theresa. *Getting Through College Without Going Broke* (9–12). Series: Students Helping Students. 2003, Natavi Guides paper $8.95 (978-1-932204-01-8). This guide offers solid advice to college-bound students about money management and steps they can take to avoid accumulating a mountain of debt. (Rev: BL 4/1/03) [378]

10401 Fox, Gunnar. *Kick Ass in College: A Guerrilla Guide to College Success* (9–12). 2005, Kick Ass Media paper $16.95 (978-0-9762928-2-1). Sound advice for prospective college students, with personal anecdotes and tips on extracurricular activities. (Rev: BL 10/1/05) [378.1]

10402 Hutchin, Megan, et al. *Choose the Right College and Get Accepted!* (10–12). Series: Students Helping Students. 2003, Natavi Guides paper $12.95 (978-0-9719392-9-5). Covering such topics as essays, tests, and campus visits, and financial aid, this helpful guide includes advice from admissions deans and many quotations from college students and recent grads. (Rev: SLJ 2/04) [378]

10403 Israel, Dr. Jerry. *The 75 Biggest Myths about College Admissions: Stand Out from the Pack, Avoid Mistakes and Get into the College of Your Dreams* (9–12). 2008, Sourcebooks paper $12.95 (978-1-4022-0995-6). A former university president debunks myths about college admissions in this accessible and informative guide. (Rev: BLO 6/17/08) [378.1]

10404 Jackson, Katherine. *Leaping from Public High to a Top U* (9–12). Series: Students Helping Students. 2003, Natavi Guides paper $6.95 (978-0-9719392-6-4). Students at some of America's most prestigious universities share their experiences in making the transition from high school and home to the more competitive college setting. (Rev: BL 3/1/03; SLJ 10/03) [378.1]

10405 Kaplan, Ben. *How to Go to College Almost for Free: The Secrets of Winning Scholarship Money. Rev. ed.* (10–12). 2001, HarperResource paper $22.00 (978-0-06-093765-2). This book is filled with useful information on merit awards, scholarships, and other forms of tuition remission. (Rev: BL 8/01; VOYA 4/02) [378.3]

10406 Karo, Aaron. *Ruminations on College Life* (11–12). 2002, Simon & Schuster paper $10.00 (978-0-7434-3293-1). An amusing account of the not-to-be-recommended exploits of a party-loving student. (Rev: BL 8/02) [378.1]

10407 Light, Richard J. *Making the Most of College: Students Speak Their Minds* (10–12). 2001, Harvard $28.50 (978-0-674-00478-8). Though aimed at educators, this volume points out those elements in college life that make it an important experience and makes

suggestions on how to help students make the proper choices. (Rev: BL 2/1/01) [378.1]

10408 Lipsky, David. *Absolutely American: Four Years at West Point* (11–12). 2003, Houghton Mifflin $25.00 (978-0-618-09542-1). This portrait of the U.S. Military Academy follows a class through its four years and offers a glimpse of life after graduation; recommended for mature teens. (Rev: BL 7/03) [355]

10409 Matthews, Arlene. *Getting in Without Freaking Out: The Official College Admissions Guide for Overwhelmed Parents* (10–12). 2006, Three Rivers paper $13.95 (978-1-4000-9841-5). College-bound teens will find this advice salutary. (Rev: BL 1/1–15/06) [378.1]

10410 Metcalf, Linda. *How to Say It to Get into the College of Your Choice: Application, Essay, and Interview Strategies to Get You the Big Envelope* (9–12). 2007, Prentice Hall paper $15.95 (978-0-7352-0420-1). Metcalf offers practical advice for the college-bound. (Rev: SLJ 12/07) [378.1]

10411 *Navigating Your Freshman Year: How to Make the Leap to College Life — and Land on Your Feet* (10–12). Series: Students Helping Students. 2005, Prentice Hall paper $12.95 (978-0-7352-0392-1). Written and edited by current and former college students, this volume offers helpful, if overly upbeat, advice to incoming freshmen. (Rev: BL 6/1–15/05; VOYA 10/05) [378.1]

10412 Rooney, John F., and John F. Reardon. *Preparing for College: Practical Advice for Students and Their Families* (10–12). 2009, Ferguson LB $34.95 (978-0-8160-7377-1); paper $16.95 (978-0-8160-7378-8). With many sidebars, statistics, and Web sites, this comprehensive guide covers numerous aspects of preparing for college, from selecting the right one to how to apply, plus tips on choosing majors and advice for succeeding. (Rev: SLJ 9/09; VOYA 8/09) [378.1]

10413 Rosin, Hanna. *God's Harvard: A Christian College on a Mission to Save America* (10–12). 2007, Harcourt $25.00 (978-0-15-101262-6). Rosin reports on her 18 months exploring the academic and social life at Patrick Henry College, a small private school specializing in educating young evangelical Christians to become elite advocates of a religious life. (Rev: BL 9/1/07; SLJ 1/08) [378.755]

Scholarships and Financial Aid

10414 Kantrowitz, Mark. *FastWeb College Gold: The Step-by-Step Guide to Paying for College* (10–12). 2006, HarperCollins $21.95 (978-0-06-112958-2). A handy guide to meeting the financial requirements of higher education. (Rev: BL 9/15/06) [378.3]

10415 Kaplan, Ben. *The Scholarship Scouting Report: An Insider's Guide to America's Best Scholarships* (11–

12). 2003, HarperResource $23.95 (978-0-06-093654-9). This accessible guide spotlights more than 100 financial awards programs, providing detailed information about entry requirements, application procedures, and the criteria used in judging applicants. (Rev: BL 1/1–15/03) [378.3]

10416 Karnes, Frances A., and Tracy L. Riley. *Competitions for Talented Kids: Win Scholarships, Big Prize Money, and Recognition* (7–10). 2005, Prufrock paper $17.95 (978-1-59363-156-7). More than 140 competitions covering a number of academic subjects, the performing arts, and leadership are listed alphabetically,

with brief advice on entering these contests. (Rev: BL 12/1/05) [371.95]

10417 Minnis, Whitney. *How to Get an Athletic Scholarship: A Student-Athlete's Guide to Collegiate Athletics* (6–12). 1995, ASI paper $12.95 (978-0-9645153-0-7). Basic information on athletic scholarships and the recruitment process, plus tips on training and academic considerations. (Rev: BL 2/1/96) [796]

10418 Wheeler, Dion. *The Sports Scholarships Insider's Guide: Getting Money for College at Any Division* (11–12). 2005, Sourcebooks paper $16.95 (978-1-4022-0376-3). A practical guide to sports scholarships and the recruiting process. (Rev: SLJ 6/05) [378.1]

Careers and Occupational Guidance

General and Miscellaneous

10419 Baldwin, Louis. *Women of Strength* (9–12). 1996, McFarland paper $35.00 (978-0-7864-0250-2). This work contains short biographies of 106 women who have succeeded in traditionally male fields like the military, law, social reform, and religion. (Rev: VOYA 8/97) [331.7]

10420 Figler, Howard. *The Complete Job-Search Handbook: All the Skills You Need to Get Any Job and Have a Good Time Doing It* (9–12). 1995, Henry Holt paper $14.95 (978-0-8050-0537-0). A practical, confidence-inspiring book that offers sound solutions to many job-hunting problems. (Rev: BL 5/15/88; SLJ 11/88) [371.4]

10421 Friedman, Caitlin, and Kimberly Yorio. *The Girl's Guide to Being a Boss (Without Being a Bitch): Valuable Lessons, Smart Suggestions, and True Stories for Succeeding as the Chick-in-Charge* (10–12). 2006, Morgan Road $22.95 (978-0-7679-2284-5). With references to their own experiences as bosses as well as the careers of other successful businesswomen they've interviewed, Friedman and Yorio outline techniques that make a good manager. (Rev: SLJ 8/06)

10422 Lewis, Sydney. *Help Wanted: Tales from the First Job Front* (10–12). 2001, New Press $25.00 (978-1-56584-369-1). This book consists of 25 interviews with young people about their experiences on entering the work force for the first time, including their hopes, disappointments, and fears. (Rev: BL 2/1/01) [331.3]

10423 McGlothlin, Bruce. *High Performance Through Understanding Systems* (7–10). Series: Learning-a-Living Library. 1996, Rosen LB $27.95 (978-0-8239-2210-9). Aimed primarily at youths preparing to enter the world of work directly after graduation, this book explains systems ("any combination of elements that operate together and form a whole") in the family, at school, and at work, and tells how individuals can diagnose problems, predict outcomes, and improve the systems. (Rev: SLJ 3/97) [001.6]

10424 Pedrvola, Cindy, and Debby Hobgood. *How to Get a Job If You Are a Teenager* (9–12). 1998, Alleyside paper $12.95 (978-0-579-50013-2). Using a question-and-answer format, this book covers all the necessary topics relating to job hunting, from résumés, filling out an application, and preparing for an interview to adjusting to the workplace, time management, and work etiquette. (Rev: SLJ 7/98; VOYA 10/98) [650.14]

10425 Reber, Deborah. *In Their Shoes: Extraordinary Women Describe Their Amazing Careers* (8–12). Series: The Real Deal. 2007, Simon & Schuster paper $12.99 (978-1-4169-2578-1). Girls will be inspired to pursue any career they want to after reading these accounts of women and the jobs they love, from sheriff to librarian, and their daily tasks. (Rev: BL 4/1/07; LMC 8–9/07; SLJ 5/07*) [331.4092]

10426 Strazzabosco, Jeanne M. *High Performance Through Dealing with Diversity* (8–12). Series: Learning-a-Living Library. 1996, Rosen LB $27.95 (978-0-8239-2202-4). Through applying attitudes of tolerance and positive feelings, this book prepares students to work with diverse populations in a multicultural workplace. (Rev: BL 8/96) [650.1]

Careers

General and Miscellaneous

10427 *Activism* (7–12). Illus. Series: Careers in Focus. 2011, Ferguson LB $32.95 (978-081608029-8). From environmental activists to lobbyists and elder law attorneys, this is a useful guide to careers in this field and the education and training required. (Rev: BL 12/15/11) [322.4023]

10428 Alagna, Magdalena. *War Correspondents: Life Under Fire* (5–10). Series: Extreme Careers. 2003, Rosen LB $26.50 (978-0-8239-3798-1). The dangers of wartime assignments are emphasized in this volume that also stresses job requirements that include a good education and broad knowledge of world events. (Rev: BL 9/15/03; SLJ 11/03) [808]

10429 *Animal Careers* (9–12). Series: What Can I Do Now? 2010, Ferguson $32.95 (978-0-8160-8075-5). With an overview of the field, descriptions of ten career choices, accounts of a typical day, and details of necessary qualifications and training, this is an attractive and informative volume. (Rev: LMC 11–12/10)

10430 *Archaeology* (7–10). Illus. Series: Careers in Focus. 2010, Ferguson $32.95 (978-081608022-9). Covering 19 professions — from anthropologists, historians, and museum curators to underwater archaeologists and writers and editors — this is a thorough survey of job opportunities in this diverse field. (Rev: BL 4/15/11) [930.1023]

10431 Brezina, Corona. *Jobs in Sustainable Energy* (7–10). Series: Green Careers. 2010, Rosen LB $30.60 (978-1-4358-3569-6). Following an overview of the field, this well-organized book looks at jobs in various sectors (solar, wind, geothermal, and so forth) and explains the necessary education and training and the job prospects and salaries. (Rev: LMC 10/10; SLJ 8/10) [621.042]

10432 *Broadcasting. 2nd ed.* (7–12). Series: Careers in Focus. 2002, Ferguson LB $22.95 (978-0-89434-440-4). Careers in animation, lighting, reporting, editing, and weather forecasting are just a few of those covered in this concise introduction to the world of broadcasting and its educational requirements, employment outlook, and potential salaries. Also use *Fashion* (2002). (Rev: SLJ 7/01) [384.54]

10433 Byers, Ann. *Jobs as Green Builders and Planners* (7–10). Series: Green Careers. 2010, Rosen LB $30.60 (978-1-4358-3566-5). This well-organized book looks at the kinds of jobs available and explains the necessary education and training and the job prospects and salaries. Part of a series that covers other "green" careers in law, tourism, and cleanup of hazardous spills. (Rev: LMC 10/10; SLJ 8/10) [690.023]

10434 Camelo, Wilson. *The U.S. Air Force and Military Careers* (7–10). Series: U.S. Armed Forces and Military Careers. 2006, Enslow LB $23.95 (978-0-7660-2524-0). Traces the history of the U.S. Air Force, its structure, its contributions to U.S. defense and major wars, recent operations, and the various career oppor-

tunities within the organization. (Rev: BL 10/15/06) [358.400973]

10435 *Communication Skills. 2nd ed.* (9–12). Series: Career Skills Library. 2004, Ferguson $25.00 (978-0-8160-5517-3). Examines the importance of communications in the workplace and offers practical advice on public speaking, written communications, and team building; quizzes and problem-solving exercises add interest. (Rev: SLJ 1/05) [384]

10436 *Computers* (9–12). Series: What Can I Do Now. 2007, Ferguson LB $29.95 (978-0-8160-6027-6). Introduces careers that are available for students interested in computer science, such as programmer, network administrator, and Webmaster. (Rev: BL 6/1–15/07) [780.23]

10437 Coon, Nora E. *Teen Dream Jobs: How to Find the Job You Really Want Now!* (8–12). 2004, Beyond Words paper $9.95 (978-1-58270-093-9). Written by a teen, this is a reader-friendly guide that refers teens to online career-choice quizzes, gives advice on job-finding activities, and suggests possible careers and ways to enter them. (Rev: SLJ 6/04)

10438 Devantier, Alecia T., and Carol A. Turkington. *Extraordinary Jobs for Adventurers* (8–12). 2006, Ferguson $35 (978-0-8160-5852-5). Careers for the adventurous are found in fields including logging, vulcanology, and white-water rafting, according to this guide that gives worker profiles. Also use *Extraordinary Jobs for Creative People* and *Extraordinary Jobs in Agriculture and Nature* (both 2006). (Rev: SLJ 1/07)

10439 Donovan, Robert J. *Boxing the Kangaroo: A Reporter's Memoir* (10–12). 2000, Univ. of Missouri $24.95 (978-0-8262-1281-8). This Pulitzer Prize-winning columnist describes the basic elements of a news story and tells how he and other reporters handle these elements in reporting the news and meeting a deadline. (Rev: BL 6/1–15/00) [070]

10440 Dunlop, Reginald. *Come Fly with Me! Your Nineties Guide to Becoming a Flight Attendant* (9–12). 1993, Maxamillian paper $15.95 (978-0-9632749-9-1). Gives specifics on increasing the chances of employment in a competitive field. Provides a tutorial for presenting oneself in the best light. (Rev: BL 6/1–15/93) [387.7]

10441 *Environment. 2nd ed.* (9–12). Series: What Can I Do Now? 2010, Ferguson $32.95 (978-0-8160-8073-1). With an overview of the field, descriptions of ten career choices, accounts of a typical day, and details of necessary qualifications and training, this is an attractive and informative volume. (Rev: LMC 11–12/10)

10442 *Fashion* (5–10). Illus. Series: Discovering Careers. 2011, Ferguson LB $24.95 (978-081608056-4). With information on education and training, earnings potential, and so forth, this volume explores the work of everyone from fashion models and writers to retail sales workers and merchandise displayers. (Rev: BL 5/1/12) [746.9]

10443 Flath, Camden. *Freelance and Technical Writers: Words for Sale* (7–10). Illus. Series: The New Careers for the 21st Century: Find Your Role in the Global Renewal. 2010, Mason Crest $22.95 (978-142222035-1); paper $9.95 (978-14222181-4-3). The ins and outs of being a freelance writer are described in this straightforward guide for students thinking about their place in the future workplace. (Rev: BL 10/1/10) [808]

10444 *Food* (5–10). Illus. Series: Discovering Careers. 2012, Ferguson LB $30 (978-081608057-1). With information on education and training, earnings potential, and so forth, this volume explores the work of everyone involved in the field, from farmers to chefs. (Rev: BL 5/1/12) [647.95023]

10445 Freedman, Samuel G. *Letters to a Young Journalist* (10–12). 2006, Basic Bks $22.95 (978-0-465-02455-1). Freedman, a Columbia University journalism professor and former reporter for the *New York Times*, offers an unflinching appraisal of American journalism over the last several decades. (Rev: BL 3/1/06; SLJ 9/06) [070.4]

10446 Giacobello, John. *Careers in the Fashion Industry* (7–12). Series: Exploring Careers. 1999, Rosen LB $18.95 (978-0-8239-2890-3). This book explains what it takes to get started in a variety of fashion-related careers, and includes tips on writing résumés, interviewing, and so forth. (Rev: SLJ 2/00) [746.9]

10447 Gregory, Michael. *The Career Chronicles: An Insider's Guide to What Jobs Are Really Like — The Good, the Bad, and the Ugly from over 750 Professionals* (10–12). 2008, New World Library paper $15.95 (978-1-57731-573-5). Professionals in a wide range of fields answer survey questions about their jobs, describing the pros and cons and discussing what has pleased and disappointed them. (Rev: SLJ 6/08) [331.702]

10448 Hayhurst, Chris. *Cool Careers Without College for Animal Lovers* (7–12). Series: Cool Careers Without College. 2002, Rosen LB $33.25 (978-0-8239-3500-0). Veterinary technician, groomer, and pet photographer are some of the options explored in this book that gives information on training and on-the-job activities. (Rev: BL 5/15/02; SLJ 7/02) [636]

10449 Heos, Bridget. *A Career as a Hairstylist* (7–12). Illus. Series: Essential Careers. 2010, Rosen LB $30.60 (978-143589474-7). This comprehensive guide to becoming a hairstylist covers everything from training and business plans to ethics and the history of the trade. (Rev: BL 10/1/10; VOYA 2/11) [646.7]

10450 Kenig, Graciela. *Best Careers for Bilingual Latinos: Market Your Fluency in Spanish to Get Ahead on the Job* (10–12). 1999, VGM paper $14.95 (978-0-8442-4541-6). This practical, well-researched handbook based on hundreds of interviews with Latino pro-

fessionals discusses how to market bilingual skills and cope with workplace challenges such as ethnic stereotypes and office politics, and identifies the top fields for bilingual Latinos: health care, financial services, technology, sales and marketing, professional services, and international opportunities. (Rev: SLJ 8/99) [331.6]

10451 Lee, Mary Price. *Opportunities in Animal and Pet Care Careers* (9–12). 1993, VGM $14.95 (978-0-8442-4079-4); paper $11.95 (978-0-8442-4081-7). All aspects of these careers are considered. (Rev: BL 3/15/94; VOYA 6/94) [636]

10452 Longshore, Shirley J. *Office* (10–12). Series: Careers Without College. 1994, Peterson's Guides paper $7.95 (978-0-560-79353-6). This career guide gives details on various positions in the business office that do not require a college degree. (Rev: BL 9/15/94) [651.3]

10453 McAlpine, Margaret. *Working in the Fashion Industry* (6–12). Series: My Future Career. 2005, Gareth Stevens LB $27.00 (978-0-8368-4774-1). Seven careers in the field of fashion are highlighted with plenty of good photographs, explanations of a typical day's activities, and "Good Points and Bad Points." (Rev: SLJ 1/06)

10454 McAlpine, Margaret. *Working in the Food Industry* (6–12). Series: My Future Career. 2005, Gareth Stevens LB $27.00 (978-0-8368-4776-5). Seven careers in the food industry are highlighted with plenty of good photographs, explanations of a typical day's activities, and "Good Points and Bad Points." (Rev: SLJ 1/06)

10455 McAlpine, Margaret. *Working with Animals* (6–10). Series: My Future Career. 2005, Gareth Stevens LB $27.00 (978-0-8368-4240-1). In addition to describing various jobs working with animals, McAlpine discusses the best personality type for each task and provides a detailed breakdown of a typical day. (Rev: SLJ 3/05) [636]

10456 McAlpine, Margaret. *Working with Children* (6–10). Series: My Future Career. 2005, Gareth Stevens LB $27.00 (978-0-8368-4241-8). In addition to describing various jobs working with children, McAlpine discusses the best personality type for each one and provides a detailed breakdown of a typical day. (Rev: SLJ 3/05) [362.7]

10457 Miller, Louise. *Careers for Animal Lovers and Other Zoological Types* (9–12). 1991, VGM paper $9.95 (978-0-8442-8125-4). Information on animal care employment, from pet-sitter to veterinarian. (Rev: BL 6/1/91) [636]

10458 Morem, Susan. *How to Get a Job and Keep It: Career and Life Skills You Need to Succeed.* 2nd ed. (10–12). 2007, Ferguson $34.95 (978-0-8160-6775-6); paper $16.95 (978-0-8160-6776-3). This guide helps the reader to get a job (with advice on resumes, interviews, and so forth) and then, importantly, discusses how to keep it (with information on performance reviews, raises, inter-office relationships, and office politics). (Rev: SLJ 8/07) [650.14]

10459 Morkes, Andrew, et al, ed. *Top 100: The Fastest Growing Careers for the 21st Century. 3rd ed.* (10–12). 2001, Ferguson paper $19.95 (978-0-89434-343-8). The duties, required training, equipment used, and opportunities in a wide range of careers are accompanied by salary ranges and tips for new workers. (Rev: BL 4/1/01; VOYA 8/01) [331.7]

10460 Morkes, Andrew, et al, ed. *25 Jobs That Have It All: High Pay, Fast Growth, Most New Jobs* (10–12). 2001, Ferguson paper $12.95 (978-0-89434-327-8). This career guide spotlights the 25 occupational fields that offer the most job openings, highest pay, and fastest growth. (Rev: VOYA 8/01) [331.7]

10461 *Organization Skills* (8–12). Series: Career Skills Library. 2009, Ferguson $25.95 (978-0-8160-7774-8). Time management, avoiding procrastination, and organization of materials and schedules are emphasized in this easy-to-read book that includes quizzes and exercises. (Rev: LMC 3–4/10) [650.1]

10462 Paquette, Penny Hutchins. *Apprenticeship: The Ultimate Teen Guide* (9–12). Series: It Happened to Me. 2005, Scarecrow $42.00 (978-0-8108-4945-7). A history of apprenticeship is followed by chapters on fields where apprenticeships are common — construction, entertainment, security services, and so forth — and details of what is involved, potential salaries, and outlook for growth; brief real-life stories appear throughout. (Rev: SLJ 2/06)

10463 Pasternak, Ceel, and Linda Thornburg. *Cool Careers for Girls in Air and Space* (6–12). Series: Cool Careers for Girls. 2001, Impact LB $12.95 (978-1-57023-147-6); paper $12.95 (978-1-57023-146-9). This account discusses various careers open to women in the aircraft and space industries with information on qualifications, working conditions, and compensation. (Rev: BL 4/15/01; SLJ 4/01) [629]

10464 Pasternak, Ceel, and Linda Thornburg. *Cool Careers for Girls in Food* (5–10). Series: Cool Careers for Girls. 2000, Impact $19.95 (978-1-57023-127-8); paper $12.95 (978-1-57023-120-9). The 11 women featured in this book are involved in various aspects of the food industry such as cheese making, baking, wine making, selling health food, and cooking for the military. (Rev: SLJ 2/00) [641]

10465 *Preparing for a Career in the Environment* (9–12). 1998, Ferguson $22.95 (978-0-89434-249-3). A variety of environmental careers are introduced, with material on aptitude, education, pay, advancement, and employment outlook. (Rev: SLJ 2/99) [331]

10466 *Professional Ethics and Etiquette. 2nd ed.* (9–12). Series: Career Skills Library. 2004, Ferguson $25.00 (978-0-8160-5523-4). Practical and well-presented advice on how to behave in the business world is

accompanied by quizzes and real-life examples. (Rev: SLJ 1/05) [395]

10467 Reeves, Diane Lindsey, and Gail Karlitz. *Career Ideas for Teens in Architecture and Construction* (8–12). Series: Career Ideas for Teens. 2005, Ferguson $40.00 (978-0-8160-5289-9). In addition to details of education requirements, salaries, and so forth, this attractive guide offers interview tips, advice from "real people," and questionnaires. (Rev: SLJ 2/06)

10468 Reeves, Diane Lindsey, and Gayle Bryan. *Career Ideas for Kids Who Like Travel* (6–10). Series: Career Ideas for Kids. 2001, Checkmark $23.00 (978-0-8160-4325-5); paper $12.95 (978-0-8160-4326-2). A number of careers in the travel industry are presented with coverage of qualifications, training, rewards, and working conditions. (Rev: BL 3/15/02; HBG 10/02) [331.7]

10469 Rosenberg, Aaron. *Cryptologists: Life Making and Breaking Codes* (5–10). Series: Extreme Careers. 2004, Rosen LB $26.50 (978-0-8239-3965-7). After some background material on the history of codes, this volume discusses career opportunities as a cryptologist. (Rev: BL 5/15/04; SLJ 5/90) [410]

10470 Sandler, Ellen. *The TV Writer's Workbook: A Creative Approach to Television Scripts* (11–12). 2007, Bantam paper $15.00 (978-0-385-34050-2). For aspiring screenwriters, this is a helpful guide full of practical advice on writing, interviewing, networking, and navigating the television landscape. (Rev: BL 3/15/07) [808.2]

10471 Scott, Jennifer Power. *Green Career$: You Can Make Money and Save the Planet* (8–12). 2010, Lobster paper $16.95 (978-1-897550-18-2). Students whose interests range from farming to architecture will find that they can use their talents in environmentally friendly ways. (Rev: BL 2/15/10; LMC 8–9/10; SLJ 4/10) [333.72]

10472 Serrin, William, ed. *The Business of Journalism: Ten Leading Reporters and Editors on the Perils and Pitfalls of the Press* (10–12). 2000, New Press paper $16.95 (978-1-56584-581-7). The way modern journalism is conducted is the theme of 10 essays by prominent reporters who also give practical advice for budding journalists. (Rev: BL 6/1–15/00) [071]

10473 Shenk, Ellen. *Outdoor Careers: Exploring Occupations in Outdoor Fields. 2nd ed.* (10–12). 2000, Stackpole paper $18.95 (978-0-8117-2873-7). About 60 careers are examined under eight headings including agriculture and food production, biological sciences, engineering, marine careers, recreation, and indoor careers that also involve the outdoors. (Rev: BL 3/1/00) [331.7]

10474 Taylor, Allan, and James Robert Parish. *Career Opportunities in Writing* (9–12). 2006, Ferguson $49.50 (978-0-8160-5988-1); paper $18.95 (978-0-8160-5989-8). Ninety careers in which writing skills are key, such as reporter, indexer, editor, and lyricist, are comprehensively outlined with information on duties, salary range, advancement opportunities, and so forth. (Rev: SLJ 6/06)

10475 *Teamwork Skills* (7–12). Series: Career Skills Library. 2009, Ferguson $25.95 (978-0-8160-7771-7). The importance of working as a team and solving conflicts are emphasized in this easy-to-read book that includes quizzes and exercises. (Rev: LMC 3–4/10) [658.4022]

10476 *The Teen Vogue Handbook: An Insider's Guide to Careers in Fashion* (7–12). 2009, Penguin paper $24.95 (978-1-59514-261-0). Full of profiles and advice from top fashion-industry movers and shakers, this book provides a practical, authoritative guide to breaking into a career in fashion. (Rev: SLJ 1/10; VOYA 12/09) [746.9]

10477 *Travel and Tourism. 2nd ed.* (9–12). Series: What Can I Do Now? 2010, Ferguson $32.95 (978-0-8160-8078-6). With an overview of the field, descriptions of ten career choices, accounts of a typical day, and details of necessary qualifications and training, this is an attractive and informative volume. (Rev: LMC 11–12/10) [647.94]

10478 Turner, Chérie. *Adventure Tour Guides: Life on Extreme Outdoor Adventures* (5–10). Series: Extreme Careers. 2003, Rosen LB $26.50 (978-0-8239-3793-6). A look at the profession of tour guiding on excursions such as white-water rafting and mountain climbing, with material on qualifications and future possibilities. (Rev: BL 9/15/03) [908]

10479 Vogt, Peter. *Career Opportunities in the Fashion Industry* (7–12). 2002, Facts on File $49.50 (978-0-8160-4616-4). More than 60 jobs in the fashion industry are described with details of daily activities, salary potential, necessary training, and future outlook. (Rev: SLJ 2/03) [746.9]

10480 Weiss, Ann E. *The Glass Ceiling: A Look at Women in the Workforce* (8–12). 1999, Twenty-First Century LB $23.90 (978-0-7613-1365-6). After a brief history of women's place in the world of work, this book focuses on recent changes and new opportunities (and dangers) for women in the workforce. (Rev: BL 6/1–15/99; SLJ 9/99) [331.4]

10481 White, William C., and Donald N. Collins. *Opportunities in Agriculture Careers* (10–12). 1987, VGM $13.95 (978-0-8442-6554-4); paper $10.95 (978-0-8442-6555-1). A guide that covers standard careers plus related ones in transportation, research, and so on. (Rev: BL 6/1/88) [630.203]

10482 Whynott, Douglas. *A Country Practice: Scenes from the Veterinary Life* (7–10). 2004, Farrar $24.00 (978-0-86547-647-9). Covering all aspects of veterinary practice — including finances, staff, and bedside manner — this is an intriguing account of a year in the

life of a veterinarian who treats both domestic pets and farm animals. (Rev: BL 11/1/04) [636.089]

10483 Wilson, Wayne. *Careers in Publishing and Communications* (8–12). Series: Latinos at Work. 2001, Mitchell Lane LB $22.95 (978-1-58415-088-6). This career guide for Latinos explores job opportunities for authors, copy editors, disc jockeys, artists, and agents, and includes personal interviews with successful Hispanic Americans in these fields. (Rev: BL 10/15/01; HBG 3/02) [808]

10484 Zannos, Susan. *Careers in Science and Medicine* (8–12). Series: Latinos at Work. 2001, Mitchell Lane LB $22.95 (978-1-58415-084-8). Descriptions of careers in these fields are accompanied by information on salary and qualifications as well as profiles of Latino men and women who have found success in a variety of career positions. (Rev: BL 10/15/01; HBG 3/02; SLJ 11/01) [502]

10485 Zannos, Susan. *Latino Entrepreneurs* (8–12). Series: Latinos at Work. 2001, Mitchell Lane LB $32.75 (978-1-58415-089-3). This book looks at the many possibilities for self-employment for Hispanics with personal interviews of successful Latinos in a variety of fields. (Rev: BL 3/15/02; HBG 10/02; SLJ 3/02) [650.1]

Arts, Entertainment, and Sports

10486 *Art* (5–10). Illus. Series: Discovering Careers. 2011, Ferguson LB $24.95 (978-081608055-7). With information on education and training, earnings potential, this volume explores the work of everyone involved in the field, from art dealers, teachers, and curators to artists, cartoonists, graphic designers, and so forth. Also use *Movies* (2011). (Rev: BL 5/1/12) [700.23]

10487 *Art* (9–12). Series: Careers in Focus. 2004, Facts on File $22.95 (978-0-8160-5547-0). A look at the wide diversity of career possibilities in the art field — from art and antique dealers to museum curators — with descriptions of duties, salaries, outlook, and so forth. (Rev: BL 7/04; SLJ 11/04) [702]

10488 *Careers in Focus: Film* (9–12). Series: Careers in Focus. 2006, Facts on File $22.95 (978-0-8160-6561-5). This volume contains important information for those interested in a film industry career, including required education, job descriptions, helpful resources, and interviews with professionals. (Rev: BL 6/1–15/06) [791.43023]

10489 Croce, Nicholas. *Cool Careers without College for People Who Love Video Games* (6–12). Series: Cool Careers Without College. 2007, Rosen LB $33.25 (978-1-4042-0747-9). This is a well-organized book with detailed information about the careers available in the field of video games (writing, producing, marketing, for example). (Rev: SLJ 6/07)

10490 Crouch, Tanja L. *100 Careers in the Music Business. 2nd ed.* (10–12). 2008, Barron's paper $16.99 (978-076413914-7). This well-organized volume lists 100 careers in 16 categories and includes the skills that might be needed for each one; it also provides information about music organizations and schools. (Rev: BLO 8/28/08) [780.23]

10491 *Design. 2nd ed.* (7–12). Series: Careers in Focus. 2005, Ferguson $22.95 (978-0-8160-5865-5). Describes careers in the broad field of design — Including architects, fashion designers, exhibit designers, industrial designers, and toy and game designers. (Rev: SLJ 12/05)

10492 Fenjves, Pablo F., and Rocky Lang. *How I Broke into Hollywood: Success Stories from the Trenches* (9–12). 2006, Regan $25.95 (978-0-06-078964-0). Actors, screenwriters, and producers discuss the often roundabout ways they became famous (or at least successful) in movies. (Rev: BL 5/15/06) [791.4302]

10493 *Film* (9–12). Series: What Can I Do Now? 2010, Ferguson $32.95 (978-0-8160-8076-2). With an overview of the field, descriptions of ten career choices, accounts of a typical day, and details of necessary qualifications and training, this is an attractive and informative volume. (Rev: LMC 11–12/10)

10494 *Film* (9–12). Series: Discovering Careers for Your Future. 2005, Facts on File $21.95 (978-0-8160-5569-2). A frank look at the not-always-glamorous film world and the careers available there, with material on education and training, salary ranges, and job outlook. (Rev: BL 3/15/05; SLJ 4/05) [791.43]

10495 Gilbert, George, and Pamela Fehl. *Career Opportunities in Photography* (9–12). 2006, Ferguson $49.50 (978-0-8160-5678-1). A thorough introduction to the career opportunities available for skilled photographers — in medicine, travel, and in commercial and portrait photography in particular. (Rev: SLJ 11/06)

10496 Greenwald, Ted. *Music* (9–12). Series: Careers Without College. 1992, Peterson's Guides paper $7.95 (978-1-56079-219-2). Presents five types of occupations relating to music that may require further education but not a four-year degree. (Rev: BL 2/15/93) [780]

10497 Hofstetter, Adam B. *Cool Careers without College for People Who Love Sports* (6–12). Series: Cool Careers Without College. 2007, Rosen LB $33.25 (978-1-4042-0749-3). Scout, groundskeeper, official scorer, Zamboni driver — these are only a few of the sports careers detailed in this well-organized book. (Rev: SLJ 6/07) [796.023]

10498 Isenberg, Marc, and Rick Rhoads. *The Real Athletes Guide: How to Succeed in Sports, School, and Life* (9–12). 1998, Athlete Network paper $19.95 (978-0-9666764-0-2). This overview examines scholarship opportunities in college athletics and tells how to choose the right college, handle the recruitment process, and prepare for a career. (Rev: BL 12/15/98; SLJ 3/99) [378.1]

10499 Jay, Annie, and Luanne Feik. *Stars in Your Eyes . . . Feet on the Ground: A Practical Guide for Teenage Actors (and Their Parents!)* (7–12). 1999, Theatre Directories paper $16.95 (978-0-933919-42-6). A young actress gives practical advice on how to break into show business, including information on publicity photographs, auditions, managers, agents, publicity packages, résumés, and casting calls. (Rev: BL 6/1–15/99) [792.02]

10500 McAlpine, Margaret. *Working in Film and Television* (6–10). Series: My Future Career. 2005, Gareth Stevens LB $27.00 (978-0-8368-4237-1). In addition to describing various jobs in the film and television world, McAlpine discusses the best personality type for each one and provides a detailed breakdown of a typical day. (Rev: SLJ 3/05) [791.43]

10501 McAlpine, Margaret. *Working in Music and Dance* (6–10). Series: My Future Career. 2005, Gareth Stevens LB $27.00 (978-0-8368-4777-2). Seven careers in the fields of music and dance are highlighted with plenty of good photographs, explanations of a typical day's activities, and "Good Points and Bad Points." (Rev: SLJ 1/06)

10502 Nagle, Jeanne. *Careers in Coaching* (7–12). Series: Careers Library. 2000, Rosen LB $31.95 (978-0-8239-2966-5). This guide to how to become a successful coach covers all aspects of the job. (Rev: SLJ 7/00) [796]

10503 Pasternak, Ceel, and Linda Thornburg. *Cool Careers for Girls in Sports* (5–10). Series: Cool Careers for Girls. 1999, Impact $19.95 (978-1-57023-107-0); paper $12.95 (978-1-57023-104-9). A golf pro, basketball player, ski instructor, sports broadcaster, trainer, sports psychologist, and athletic director are among the 10 women profiled in this overview of careers for women in sports. (Rev: SLJ 7/99; VOYA 8/99) [796]

10504 Peterson, Linda. *Entertainment* (10–12). Series: Careers Without College. 1994, Peterson's Guides paper $7.95 (978-0-560-79352-9). This career guide covers positions in the performing arts and broadcasting. (Rev: BL 9/15/94) [791]

10505 Rosenbaum, Jean, and Mary Prine. *Opportunities in Fitness Careers* (9–12). 1991, VGM $14.95 (978-0-8442-8185-8). Information on educational requirements and income expectations for one of today's fastest-growing industries. (Rev: BL 6/1/91) [613.7]

10506 Salmon, Mark. *Opportunities in Visual Arts Careers* (9–12). 1992, VGM $14.95 (978-0-8442-4031-2). Discusses working for a company, freelance work, teaching art, and art therapy. (Rev: BL 2/15/93) [702.3]

10507 Sommers, Michael A. *Wildlife Photographers: Life Through a Lens* (5–10). Series: Extreme Careers.

2003, Rosen LB $26.50 (978-0-8239-3638-0). A concise explanation of the work of wildlife photographers, the attributes needed, and the training and tenacity required to enter this field. (Rev: BL 9/15/03; SLJ 5/03) [771]

10508 *Sports. 3rd ed.* (9–12). Series: Careers in Focus. 2003, Ferguson LB $22.95 (978-0-8160-5486-2). After a general and historical overview, more than 20 careers are described, covering the nature of the job, educational requirements, rewards, salaries, working conditions, and how to get into the field. (Rev: SLJ 5/04)

10509 Steele, William Paul. *Stay Home and Star! A Step-by-Step Guide to Starting Your Regional Acting Career* (9–12). 1992, Heinemann paper $13.95 (978-0-435-08603-9). Practical advice about acting opportunities on the local level, emphasizing a businesslike approach and the basic requirements for success. (Rev: BL 2/1/92) [792]

10510 Torres, John A., and Susan Zannos. *Careers in the Music Industry* (8–12). Series: Latinos at Work. 2001, Mitchell Lane LB $32.75 (978-1-58415-085-5). Along with personal interviews with Hispanics who did well in the music world, there are descriptions of such related careers as singers, songwriters, managers, and agents. (Rev: BL 3/15/02; HBG 10/02) [780]

10511 Weigant, Chris. *Careers as a Disc Jockey* (8–12). Series: Careers. 1997, Rosen LB $16.95 (978-0-8239-2528-5). This informative book gives many practical tips on how to get started and be successful in radio, with material on making demo tapes, applying for jobs and internships, and working oneself up. There are interviews with eight DJs. Careers in management, sales, technical areas, talk shows, and others are included. (Rev: SLJ 12/97; VOYA 2/98) [384.54]

10512 Wilson, Wayne. *Careers in Entertainment* (8–12). Series: Latinos at Work. 2001, Mitchell Lane LB $32.75 (978-1-58415-083-1). With an emphasis on Hispanic American success stories, this book features careers in film, television, and theater. (Rev: BL 10/15/01; HBG 3/02) [791]

Business

10513 Giles, M. J. *Young Adult's Guide to a Business Career* (8–12). 2004, Business Bks $14.95 (978-0-9723714-3-8). Full of useful tips, this guide describes more than 25 occupations in business and finance, giving details of benefits and drawbacks, salaries, educational requirements, and so forth. (Rev: SLJ 7/04) [331.7]

10514 Healy, Lisa, ed. *My First Year in Book Publishing: Real-World Stories from America's Book Publishing Professionals* (9–12). 1994, Walker $21.95 (978-0-8027-1294-3); paper $11.95 (978-0-8027-7425-5). A guide for those interested in book publishing, including testimony from agents, editors, publicists, and indexers

describing their first year of work. (Rev: BL 9/1/94; VOYA 12/94) [070.5]

10515 Plawin, Paul. *Careers for Travel Buffs and Other Restless Types* (9–12). 1992, VGM paper $9.95 (978-0-8442-8127-8). Covers job descriptions, getting into the business, and future prospects of typical travel careers as well as positions that involve less traveling. (Rev: BL 6/1/92; SLJ 3/92) [331.7]

10516 Ring, Gertrude. *Careers in Finance* (9–12). 1993, VGM $17.95 (978-0-8442-4186-9). A basic guide to careers in the world of finance. (Rev: BL 5/15/93) [332]

10517 Thomason-Carroll, Kristi L. *Young Adult's Guide to Business Communications* (8–12). 2004, Business Bks $14.95 (978-0-9723714-4-5). Full of useful tips, this guide describes the basics required for a job in the business world, including telephone skills, the ability to communicate clearly by letter and e-mail, and proper behavior during meetings. (Rev: SLJ 7/04) [651.7]

Construction and Mechanical Trades

10518 Garvey, Lonny D. *Opportunities in the Machine Trades* (9–12). 1994, VGM $14.95 (978-0-8442-4123-4); paper $11.95 (978-0-8442-4124-1). The machine trades are introduced, with material on a variety of occupations in each. (Rev: BL 8/94) [671]

10519 Paige, Joy. *Cool Careers Without College for People Who Love to Build Things* (7–12). Series: Cool Careers Without College. 2002, Rosen LB $33.25 (978-0-8239-3506-2). Twenty careers in construction are outlined with useful information about salary, future prospects, and training. (Rev: BL 1/1–15/03; SLJ 7/02) [690]

Education and Librarianship

10520 *Careers in Focus: Library and Information Science* (9–12). 2006, Ferguson LB $22.95 (978-0-8160-6562-2). A well-organized look at the careers available in this area, with "Quick Facts" boxes that summarize the requirements for each job. (Rev: SLJ 8/06)

10521 *Education* (9–12). Series: What Can I Do Now? 2010, Ferguson $32.95 (978-0-8160-8079-9). With an overview of the field, descriptions of ten career choices, accounts of a typical day, and details of necessary qualifications and training, this is an attractive and informative volume. (Rev: LMC 11–12/10)

10522 *Education. 2nd ed.* (9–12). Series: Careers in Focus. 2003, Ferguson LB $22.95 (978-0-8160-5485-5). After a general overview and a history of education as an occupation, 20 top careers are described, covering the nature of the job, educational requirements, rewards, salaries, working conditions, and how to get into the field. (Rev: SLJ 5/04)

10523 Fine, Janet. *Opportunities in Teaching* (10–12). 1984, VGM paper $10.95 (978-0-8442-6250-5). Teaching careers at various levels are discussed and questions of suitability explored. [371.7]

10524 Reeves, Diane Lindsey, and Gail Karlitz. *Career Ideas for Teens in Education and Training* (8–12). Series: Career Ideas for Teens. 2005, Ferguson $40.00 (978-0-8160-5295-0). In addition to details of education requirements, salaries, and so forth, this attractive guide offers interview tips, advice from "real people," and questionnaires. (Rev: SLJ 2/06)

10525 Zannos, Susan. *Careers in Education* (8–12). Series: Latinos at Work. 2001, Mitchell Lane LB $22.95 (978-1-58415-081-7). Descriptions of careers in this field are accompanied by information on salary and qualifications as well as profiles of Latino men and women who have found success in a variety of career positions. (Rev: BL 10/15/01; HBG 3/02; SLJ 11/01; VOYA 6/02) [370]

Law, Police, and Other Society-Oriented Careers

10526 Ackerman, Thomas H. *FBI Careers: The Ultimate Guide to Landing a Job as One of America's Finest*. 2nd ed. (9–12). 2005, JIST paper $19.95 (978-1-59357-237-2). Good advice on applying to work at the FBI and descriptions of various positions are accompanied by a history of the organization plus an outline of its structure. (Rev: SLJ 2/06)

10527 Bankston, John. *Careers in Community Service* (8–12). Series: Latinos at Work. 2001, Mitchell Lane LB $32.75 (978-1-58415-082-4). Aimed at Latino youths, this career guide features a multitude of jobs in non-profit agencies, including legal and medical fields, with accompanying stories of success. (Rev: BL 10/15/01; HBG 3/02; SLJ 1/02) [353.001]

10528 Croce, Nicholas. *Detectives: Life Investigating Crimes* (5–10). Series: Extreme Careers. 2003, Rosen LB $26.50 (978-0-8239-3796-7). As well as exploring the exciting side of detective work, this account explains the qualifications and training needed and the techniques that help do this job well. (Rev: BL 9/15/03) [340]

10529 Echaore-McDavid, Susan, and Richard A. McDavid. *Career Opportunities in Forensic Science* (10–12). 2008, Ferguson $49.50 (978-081606156-3); paper $18.95 (978-081606157-0). This text provides a wealth of information about opportunities in forensic science from job descriptions and salaries to education requirements and personalities best suited for specific jobs. (Rev: BLO 9/4/08) [363.25]

10530 Giacobello, John. *Bodyguards: Life Protecting Others* (5–10). Series: Extreme Careers. 2003, Rosen LB $26.50 (978-0-8239-3795-0). This book explores the duties and responsibilities of a bodyguard and in-

cludes information how to stay safe on the job and get ahead in this profession. (Rev: BL 9/15/03; SLJ 11/03) [340]

10531 Hopping, Lorraine Jean. *Investigating a Crime Scene* (7–10). Series: Crime Scene Science. 2007, World Almanac LB $22.95 (978-0-8368-7709-0). A matter-of-fact look at what it is like to examine crime scenes, this should appeal to teens interested in forensic work as a career and to those who just want more of what they see on TV. (Rev: BL 3/15/07) [614]

10532 Murdico, Suzanne J. *Bomb Squad Experts: Life Defusing Explosive Devices* (5–10). Series: Extreme Careers. 2004, Rosen LB $26.50 (978-0-8239-3968-8). A look at the career opportunities in bomb squads, with material on training, salaries, and working conditions. (Rev: BL 5/15/04) [363]

10533 Pasternak, Ceel, and Linda Thornburg. *Cool Careers for Girls in Law* (6–12). Series: Cool Careers for Girls. 2001, Impact LB $19.95 (978-1-57023-160-5); paper $12.95 (978-1-57023-157-5). Ten women who have succeeded in various areas of the legal profession are highlighted, with material on qualifications, salaries, and working conditions. (Rev: BL 4/15/01; SLJ 7/01) [340]

10534 Temple, John. *Deadhouse: Life in a Coroner's Office* (9–12). 2005, Univ. Press of Mississippi $28.00 (978-1-57806-743-5). The experiences of two young interns add to this look at the workings of the Allegheny County Coroner's Office, which serves the city of Pittsburgh and its suburbs. (Rev: BL 4/15/05) [614.1]

10535 Wade, Linda R. *Careers in Law and Politics* (8–12). Series: Latinos at Work. 2001, Mitchell Lane LB $22.95 (978-1-58415-080-0). Along with interviews of successful Hispanic Americans in the fields of law and politics, this book describes such careers as lawyer, law professor, judge, police officer, and state representative. (Rev: BL 3/15/02; HBG 10/02; SLJ 3/02) [340]

10536 Willis, Clint, ed. *Fire Fighters: Stories of Survival from the Front Lines of Firefighting* (10–12). 2002, Thunder's Mouth paper $17.95 (978-1-56025-402-7). First-person accounts, articles, and book excerpts explore the challenges facing fire fighters in both urban and wilderness settings. (Rev: BL 7/02) [628.9]

10537 Wirths, Claudine G. *Choosing a Career in Law Enforcement* (6–10). Series: World of Work. 1996, Rosen LB $17.95 (978-0-8239-2274-1). Careers in law enforcement, such as police officer, security guard, and private investigator, are explored. (Rev: SLJ 3/97) [363]

Medicine and Health

10538 Asher, Dana. *Epidemiologists: Life Tracking Deadly Diseases* (5–10). Series: Extreme Careers. 2003, Rosen LB $26.50 (978-0-8239-3633-5). A concise explanation of the work of epidemiologists, the history of this discipline, and the training required to enter this field, with a case study. (Rev: BL 5/15/03; SLJ 5/03) [614.4]

10539 Curless, Maura. *Fitness* (9–12). Series: Careers Without College. 1992, Peterson's Guides paper $7.95 (978-1-56079-223-9). Career opportunities in the fields of physical fitness and health care are explored in this practical guide. (Rev: BL 2/15/93) [613.7]

10540 Field, Shelly. *Career Opportunities in Health Care. 2nd ed.* (7–12). 2002, Facts on File $49.50 (978-0-8160-4816-8). Information on 80 or so careers is organized in 16 categories, and includes a job profile, salary outlook, and details of necessary education and skills. (Rev: BL 11/1/02; SLJ 1/03) [610.69]

10541 Frederickson, Keville. *Opportunities in Nursing Careers* (9–12). 1989, VGM paper $10.95 (978-0-8442-8636-5). This account describes various kinds of nursing careers, the training and personality necessary, and working conditions. (Rev: VOYA 12/89) [610.73]

10542 *Health Care* (7–12). Series: What Can I Do Now? 2007, Ferguson $29.95 (978-0-8160-6031-3). Following a general introduction to the health care industry, this book describes jobs in the field, education and skill requirements, and salary ranges, and tells students what they can do now, emphasizing volunteer opportunities and internships. (Rev: SLJ 11/07) [610.69]

10543 Reeves, Diane Lindsey, and Gail Karlitz. *Career Ideas for Teens in Health Science* (7–12). Series: Career Ideas for Teens. 2005, Ferguson $40.00 (978-0-8160-5290-5). In addition to details of education requirements, salaries, and so forth, this attractive guide offers interview tips, advice from "real people," and questionnaires. (Rev: SLJ 2/06) [610.69]

10544 Snook, I. Donald, and Leo D'Ozraio. *Opportunities in Health and Medical Careers* (10–12). 1990, VGM $14.95 (978-0-8442-8573-3). This is a fine overview of the many positions available in this expanding field. (Rev: BL 12/15/90) [610]

Science and Engineering

10545 Burnett, Betty. *Math and Science Wizards* (7–12). Series: Cool Careers Without College. 2002, Rosen $33.25 (978-0-8239-3502-4). Jobs in medicine and science that do not require college degrees, such as chemical lab workers, miners, and doctors' helpers, are described with information on salaries, duties, training, and future outlooks. (Rev: BL 5/15/02; SLJ 7/02) [520]

10546 Echaore-Mcdavid, Susan. *Career Opportunities in Science* (9–12). 2003, Facts on File $49.50 (978-0-8160-4905-9). More than 80 careers in the sciences (including those in business and education) are profiled, with material on duties, job titles, salary, job outlook,

education and training, and any special skills or character traits needed. (Rev: SLJ 2/04) [509]

10547 *Meteorology* (7–12). Illus. Series: Careers in Focus. 2011, Ferguson LB $32.95 (978-081608033-5). Careers covered in this useful volume range from broadcast meteorologist to aviation meteorologist, with information about education, opportunities, and salaries. (Rev: BL 12/15/11) [551.5023]

10548 Sullivan, Megan. *All in a Day's Work: Careers Using Science* (9–12). 2006, NSTA paper $15.95 (978-1-933531-07-6). Personal experiences enliven this overview of science-related jobs — among them astronaut, arachnologist, animal nutritionist, and art conservationist. (Rev: SLJ 6/07) [502.3]

10549 Sutherland, Amy. *Kicked, Bitten, and Scratched: Life and Lessons at the World's Premier School for Exotic Animal Trainers* (9–12). 2006, Viking $25.95 (978-0-670-03768-1). A rare glimpse into a top school for animal trainers, where students must undergo rigorous, dangerous, and often distasteful course work in order to land jobs in zoos, film sets, and elsewhere. (Rev: BL 4/15/06) [636.08]

Technical and Industrial Careers

10550 Apel, Melanie Ann. *Careers in Information Technology* (6–12). Series: Exploring Careers. 2000, Rosen LB $18.95 (978-0-8239-2892-7). Testimonials from working professionals add to this survey of opportunities in information technology that gives details on skills required and employment outlook. (Rev: BL 3/15/01; HBG 10/01; SLJ 2/01) [004]

10551 *Computer and Video Game Design* (7–12). Series: Careers in Focus. 2005, Ferguson $22.95 (978-0-8160-5850-1). Describes the tasks of artists and animators, game designers, packaging designers, technical support specialists, and video game testers. (Rev: SLJ 12/05)

10552 Fulton, Michael T. *Exploring Careers in Cyberspace* (7–12). Series: Careers. 1997, Rosen LB $31.95 (978-0-8239-2633-6). A worthwhile source of information on how to prepare oneself to work in cyberspace, the types of jobs available, and the way to make a solid impression. (Rev: BL 6/1–15/98; SLJ 7/98) [004.67802373]

10553 Garcia, Kimberly. *Careers in Technology* (8–12). Series: Latinos at Work. 2001, Mitchell Lane LB $32.75 (978-1-58415-087-9). An easy-to-read guide to careers in computer technology such as Web designers, programmers, and Internet marketing, with particular emphasis on Hispanic success stories in these fields. (Rev: BL 10/15/01; HBG 3/02; SLJ 1/02) [004.6]

10554 Gerardi, Dave, and Peter Suciu. *Careers in the Computer Game Industry* (6–12). Series: Careers in the New Economy. 2005, Rosen LB $31.95 (978-1-4042-0252-8). The authors review a wide array of job opportunities in the computer game industry, including designers, testers, graphic artists, animators, and programmers. (Rev: SLJ 10/05) [331.7]

10555 McAlpine, Margaret. *Working with Computers* (6–10). Series: My Future Career. 2005, Gareth Stevens LB $27.00 (978-0-8368-4242-5). In addition to describing various jobs working with computers, McAlpine discusses the best personality type for each one and provides a detailed breakdown of a typical day. (Rev: SLJ 3/05) [004]

10556 Pasternak, Ceel, and Linda Thornburg. *Cool Careers for Girls in Computers* (7–12). 1999, Impact paper $12.95 (978-1-57023-103-2). This career book for girls features interviews with 10 women in computer-related fields, including a software engineer, sales executive, online specialist, technology trainer, and network administrator. (Rev: SLJ 4/00; VOYA 8/99) [004.6]

10557 Sawyer, Sarah. *Career Building through Podcasting* (7–10). Series: Digital Career Building. 2007, Rosen LB $21.95 (978-1-4042-1944-1). Readers looking into tech careers will enjoy this exploration into how one can make a living podcasting. (Rev: BL 10/15/07; LMC 2/08) [070.5]

10558 Scharnberg, Ken. *Opportunities in Trucking Careers* (9–12). 1992, VGM $14.95 (978-0-8442-8181-0). A thorough discussion of the complexities involved in scheduling and organizing driver, vehicle, client/customer, freight, and destination, as well as salary structures. (Rev: BL 6/1/92) [388.3]

10559 Thornburg, Linda. *Cool Careers for Girls in Cybersecurity and National Safety* (8–11). Series: Cool Careers for Girls. 2004, Impact $21.95 (978-1-57023-209-1). This volume contains 10 case studies of women who have launched careers dealing with the protection of computer networks and the Internet as well as other high-tech areas. (Rev: BL 3/1/04; SLJ 10/04) [331.7]

Personal Finances

Money-Making Ideas

General and Miscellaneous

10560 Bielagus, Peter G. *Quick Cash for Teens: Be Your Own Boss and Make Big Bucks* (7–12). Illus. 2009, Sterling paper $12.95 (978-140276038-9). Bielagus recommends 101 businesses suited for teens and provides step-by-step strategies for success with interesting anecdotes and sample worksheets. (Rev: BL 6/1–15/09) [658.1]

10561 Kravetz, Stacy. *Girl Boss: Running the Show Like the Big Chicks* (7–10). 1999, Girl paper $19.95 (978-0-9659754-2-1). This book gives practical advice and tips for teenage girls who want to start a business of their own. (Rev: VOYA 8/99) [658.1]

10562 Mariotti, Steve. *The Young Entrepreneur's Guide to Starting and Running a Business. 2nd ed.* (9–12). 2000, Times $15.00 (978-0-8129-3306-2). An entertaining and informative resource for business-minded teenagers. (Rev: BL 4/1/00) [658.1141]

Baby-sitting

10563 Bondy, Halley. *Don't Sit on the Baby! The Ultimate Guide to Sane, Skilled, and Safe Babysitting* (6–12). Illus. 2012, Zest paper $12.99 (978-098273223-6). A lighthearted guide full of practical advice, playtime ideas, real-life anecdotes, and tips on getting, keeping, and quitting jobs. (Rev: BL 7/12; LMC 11–12/12; SLJ 2/13) [649]

10564 Chassé, Jill D. *The Babysitter's Survival Guide: Fun Games, Cool Crafts, and How to Be the Best Babysitter in Town* (5–10). Illus. by Jessica Secheret. 2010, Sterling $12.95 (978-1-40274-654-3). With information on how to assess job opportunities, this helpful guide offers plenty of activity ideas, advice for coping with difficult behaviors, and general tips on running a business. (Rev: SLJ 9/1/10) [649]

Money Management

10565 Bellenir, Karen, ed. *Debt Information for Teens: Tips for a Successful Financial Life* (10–12). Series: Teen Finance. 2007, Omnigraphics LB $58.00 (978-0-7808-0989-5). Bellenir provides practical information on managing debt and saving money. (Rev: BL 4/15/08; SLJ 5/08) [332.024]

10566 Bostick, Nan, and Susan M. Freese. *Managing Money* (8–12). Illus. Series: Life Skills Handbooks. 2011, Saddleback Educational paper $16.95 (978-16165165-9-8). Covering spending, banking, credit, and budgeting, this is a useful and practical guide. (Rev: BL 3/1/12) [332.024]

10567 Byers, Ann. *First Apartment Smarts* (8–12). Series: Get Smart With Your Money. 2010, Rosen LB $29.95 (978-1-4358-5272-3). Clearly written and practical, this volume covers planning, budgeting, apartment searching, and moving in, and living smart, asking readers to assess their preparedness frankly. (Rev: BL 10/1/09; LMC 1–2/10)

10568 Deering, Kathryn R. *Savings and Investment Information for Teens: Tips for a Successful Financial Life* (9–12). Series: Teen Finance. 2005, Omnigraphics LB $65.00 (978-0-7808-0781-5). Budgets, bank accounts, investment strategies, and the stock market are all explained in clear language. (Rev: SLJ 1/06) [332]

10569 Deering, Kathryn R., ed. *Cash and Credit Information for Teens* (9–12). Series: Teen Finance. 2005, Omnigraphics LB $65.00 (978-0-7808-0780-8). This title contains a wealth of practical advice to help teenagers make sound decisions on matters of cash management and credit use. (Rev: BL 10/15/05; SLJ 3/06) [332.024]

10570 Fisanick, Christina, ed. *Debt* (8–12). Illus. Series: Opposing Viewpoints. 2010, Gale/Greenhaven LB $38.50 (978-073774202-2); paper $26.75 (9780737742039). A collection of essays and article excerpts explore the reasons underlying individual and government debt from various perspectives. (Rev: BL 5/1/10) [332.024]

10571 Fowles, Debby. *1000 Best Smart Money Secrets for Students* (10–12). 2005, Sourcebooks paper $12.95 (978-1-4022-0548-4). Practical tips for saving, earning, and managing money; aimed at prospective college students. (Rev: SLJ 12/05)

10572 Heath, Julia A. *Decision Making and Budgeting* (9–12). Illus. Series: Personal Finance Essentials. 2012, Facts on File $35 (978-160413986-0). With photographs, sidebars, and quizzes, this volume uses real-world situations to present the importance of making good financial decisions. (Rev: BL 10/1/12; SLJ 4/12) [332.024]

10573 Silver, Don. *The Generation Y Money Book: 99 Smart Ways to Handle Money* (7–12). 2000, Adams-Hall paper $15.95 (978-0-944708-64-4). Sound advice about money management, credit card use, planning for college, savings, and investment. (Rev: VOYA 6/01) [332.024]

10574 Silver, Don. *High School Money Book* (9–12). 2006, Adams-Hall paper $19.95 (978-0-944708-74-3). This useful personal finance guide for teens provides basics on saving and investing as well as repaying college debt. (Rev: SLJ 6/07) [332.02]

10575 Vermond, Kira. *The Secret Life of Money: A Kid's Guide to Cash* (7–10). Illus. by Clayton Hanmer. 2012, Owl $19.95 (978-192697319-7); paper $13.95 (978-19269731-8-0). An engaging introduction to a complex subject, with clear explanations, first-person sidebars, and graphic elements. **e** (Rev: BL 5/1/12; LMC 8–9/12; SLJ 4/12) [332.4]

Health and the Human Body

General and Miscellaneous

10576 Apel, Melanie Ann. *Coping with Stuttering* (6–10). Series: Coping. 2000, Rosen LB $31.95 (978-0-8239-2970-2). Practical advice for stutterers and for listeners is accompanied by information on celebrities who have conquered this problem. (Rev: SLJ 4/00) [616.85]

10577 Carroll, Aaron E., and Rachel C. Vreeman. *Don't Swallow Your Gum! Myths, Half-Truths, and Outright Lies About Your Body and Health* (9–12). 2009, St. Martin's paper $13.95 (978-0-312-53387-8). Accessible, accurate, and entertaining, this conversational book debunks approximately 60 commonly held misconceptions about our bodies and healthful practices. (Rev: SLJ 9/09) [612]

10578 Clegg, Brian. *Upgrade Me: Our Amazing Journey to Human 2.0* (10–12). 2008, St. Martin's $24.95 (978-0-312-37157-9). Clegg discusses the age-old desire of humankind to improve itself physically, and considers the modern pros and cons of this pursuit of perfection, including discussion of such topics as gene therapy, cloning, bionics, and nanotechnology. (Rev: BLO 8/28/08) [599.93]

10579 *The Complete Manual of Fitness and Well-Being* (9–12). 1988, Reader's Digest $34.95 (978-0-88850-154-7). In addition to exercise and diet, this account covers such topics as human growth, body parts, and health. (Rev: BL 5/1/88; SLJ 6/88) [613]

10580 Costello, Patricia. *Female Fitness Stars of TV and the Movies* (7–12). Series: Legends of Health and Fitness. 2000, Mitchell Lane LB $25.70 (978-1-58415-050-3). Cher, Goldie Hawn, and Demi Moore are among the actors profiled here as examples of professionals who put fitness high on their list of priorities. (Rev: SLJ 2/01)

10581 Jukes, Mavis. *The Guy Book: An Owner's Manual* (6–12). 2002, Crown paper $12.95 (978-0-679-89028-7). Jukes takes an appealing, frank-talking approach to sex, health, and hygiene for young men, covering everything from dating and birth control to choosing clothes and slow dancing. (Rev: BL 1/1–15/02; HBG 10/02; SLJ 3/02; VOYA 6/02) [305.235]

10582 Laney, Dawn, ed. *Biomedical Ethics* (9–12). Series: The History of Issues. 2006, Gale LB $34.95 (978-0-7377-2859-0). General ethics for doctors are discussed in historical context along with euthanasia and physician-assisted suicide, reproductive technology and cloning, and eugenics and genetic engineering. (Rev: SLJ 5/07) [174]

10583 Nardo, Don. *Biomedical Ethics* (9–12). Series: Compact Research. 2007, Reference Point LB $24.95 (978-1-60152-013-5). This compact volume provides lots of information for report writers, with illustrations, quotations from primary sources, lists of facts, statistical charts, and brief timelines. (Rev: SLJ 5/07) [575.1]

10584 O'Connor, Anahad. *Always Follow the Elephants: More Surprising Facts and Misleading Myths About Our Health and the World We Live In* (9–12). Illus. 2009, Times paper $14 (978-08050900-0-0). This amusing look at the scientific truths behind many commonly held beliefs concerning healthful behavior separates fact from fiction. ❷ (Rev: BL 10/1/09) [613]

10585 Powell, Phelan. *Trailblazers of Physical Fitness* (7–12). Series: Legends of Health and Fitness. 2000, Mitchell Lane LB $25.70 (978-1-58415-024-4). Jack LaLanne and Richard Simmons are among the individuals profiled here as leading proponents of physical fitness. (Rev: SLJ 2/01)

10586 Rebman, Renee C. *Addictions and Risky Behaviors: Cutting, Bingeing, Snorting, and Other Dangers* (7–12). 2006, Enslow LB $31.93 (978-0-7660-2165-5). The many behaviors associated with addiction —

alcohol, smoking, eating problems, drugs, inhalants, self-mutilation, Internet — are defined and the risks are clearly stated; resources include Web sites and related organizations. (Rev: SLJ 6/06)

10587 Roche, Lorin. *Meditation Made Easy* (10–12). 1998, HarperCollins paper $16.95 (978-0-06-251542-1). An excellent introduction to the art of meditation and its wide array of benefits. (Rev: BL 11/15/98) [158]

10588 Sommers, Annie Leah. *Everything You Need to Know About Looking and Feeling Your Best: A Guide for Girls* (6–12). Series: Need to Know Library. 2000, Rosen LB $27.95 (978-0-8239-3079-1). This book aims to boost girls' self-images as well as their knowledge of health and hygiene. (Rev: HBG 9/00; SLJ 3/00) [613]

10589 Spalding, Frank. *Erasing the Ink: Getting Rid of Your Tattoo* (7–10). Illus. Series: Tattooing. 2011, Rosen LB $30.60 (978-144884615-3). Spalding presents frankly the reasons why a tattoo may be a bad idea — and one you may regret — in this volume in a series that deals with the art of tattooing and what to expect if you set out to get one, and to have one removed. (Rev: BL 9/15/11; SLJ 12/1/11) [617.4]

10590 Villarosa, Linda, ed. *Body and Soul: The Black Women's Guide to Physical Health and Emotional Well-Being* (9–12). 1994, HarperPerennial paper $22.00 (978-0-06-095085-9). Contributors to this straight-from-the-heart guide include black female scientists, academics, healthcare practitioners, and writers. (Rev: BL 11/15/94*) [613]

Aging and Death

10591 Baird, Robert M., and Stuart E. Rosenbaum, eds. *Euthanasia: The Moral Issues* (10–12). 1989, Prometheus paper $23.98 (978-0-87975-555-3). In this collection of 19 essays, euthanasia is explained and the various legal and moral questions surrounding it are explored. (Rev: BL 3/1/90) [179.7]

10592 Colman, Penny. *Corpses, Coffins, and Crypts: A History of Burial* (7–12). 1997, Henry Holt $19.95 (978-0-8050-5066-0). Customs associated with death and burial traditions in various cultures and times are covered in a text enlivened with many photographs. (Rev: BL 11/1/97; HBG 3/98; SLJ 12/97*) [393]

10593 Digiulio, Robert, and Rachel Kranz. *Straight Talk About Death and Dying* (7–12). Series: Straight Talk. 1995, Facts on File $27.45 (978-0-8160-3078-1). Among the topics covered in this book about death and dying are Kubler-Ross's five psychological stages experienced by the dying and various aspects of mourning. (Rev: BL 9/15/95; SLJ 12/95) [155.9]

10594 Fitzgerald, Helen. *The Grieving Teen: A Guide for Teenagers and Their Friends* (9–12). 2000, Simon &

Schuster paper $14.99 (978-0-684-86804-2). This book explains the grieving process for teens and gives advice on how to adjust to the death of a friend or family member. [155.9]

10595 Giddens, Sandra, and Owen Giddens. *Coping with Grieving and Loss* (6–10). 2000, Rosen LB $25.25 (978-0-8239-2894-1). Practical advice about the process of grieving and funerals is accompanied by personal teen stories. (Rev: SLJ 4/00) [155.9]

10596 Gootman, Marilyn E. *When a Friend Dies: A Book for Teens About Grieving and Healing. Rev. ed.* (6–12). 2005, Free Spirit paper $9.95 (978-1-57542-170-4). An updated edition of a guide first published in 1994, this volume offers sound advice and reassurance for teenagers suffering the loss of a friend or peer, including quotes from bereaved teens. (Rev: SLJ 10/05) [155.9]

10597 Grollman, Earl A. *Straight Talk About Death for Teenagers: How to Cope with Losing Someone You Love* (7–12). 1993, Beacon paper $13.00 (978-0-8070-2501-7). Grollman validates the painful feelings teens experience following the death of a loved one, conveying a sense of the grief as well as the need to get on with life. (Rev: BL 4/1/93; SLJ 6/93; VOYA 8/93) [155.9]

10598 Marcovitz, Hal. *Suicide* (7–10). Series: Essential Issues. 2010, ABDO LB $32.79 (978-1-60453-958-5). After a history of suicide this volume looks at risk factors, the contribution of mental disorders, the right to die, and how to prevent these deaths. (Rev: LMC 10/10; SLJ 4/1/10) [362.2]

10599 Medina, John. *The Clock of Ages: Why We Age — How We Age — Winding Back the Clock* (9–12). 1996, Cambridge Univ. paper $34.99 (978-0-521-59456-1). The little-understood process of aging — and the biological factors behind it — are outlined in easy-to-understand language. [612.6]

10600 Myers, Edward. *When Will I Stop Hurting? Teens, Loss, and Grief* (7–12). Illus. by Kelly Adams. Series: It Happened to Me. 2004, Scarecrow $34.50 (978-0-8108-4921-1). Firsthand accounts from teens add to this discussion of the stages of grief and of warning signs that should be monitored. (Rev: SLJ 11/04) [155.9]

10601 O'Connor, Nancy. *Letting Go with Love: The Grieving Process* (9–12). 1985, La Mariposa $24.95 (978-0-9613714-1-8); paper $15.95 (978-0-9613714-0-1). How to cope with the death of a loved one is the subject of this self-help book. [128]

10602 Sharp, Anne Wallace. *The Right to Die* (9–12). Series: Hot Topics. 2009, Gale/Lucent LB $32.45 (978-1-59018-834-7). Euthanasia, assisted suicide, refusing medical treatment, and the withdrawal of life-sustaining treatments are all covered in this volume that also addresses brain death, organ transplants, and cryonics. (Rev: SLJ 1/10) [174]

10603 Strauss, Alix. *Death Becomes Them: Unearthing the Suicides of the Brilliant, the Famous, and the Notorious* (11–12). Illus. 2009, HarperCollins paper $14.99 (978-00617285-6-3). Hitler, Sylvia Plath, Hemingway, Hunter Thompson, and Kurt Cobain are among the individuals featured in this survey of celebrity suicides; for mature readers. (Rev: BL 9/09) [362.28092]

10604 Terkel, Studs. *Will the Circle Be Unbroken? Reflections on Death, Rebirth, and Hunger for a Faith* (10–12). 2001, New Press $25.95 (978-1-56584-692-0). The noted author explores the phenomenon of death, how it occurs, and people's reaction to it, in this account that is also a celebration of life. (Rev: BL 8/01*) [128]

10605 Wolfelt, Alan D. *Healing a Teen's Grieving Heart: 100 Practical Ideas* (6–12). 2001, Companion paper $11.95 (978-1-879651-24-1). Teens who have suffered a loss will find practical reassurance and comfort in the suggestions offered here. (Rev: SLJ 9/01; VOYA 8/01)

Alcohol, Drugs, and Smoking

10606 Alagna, Magdalena. *Everything You Need to Know About the Dangers of Binge Drinking* (6–10). Series: Need to Know Library. 2001, Rosen LB $27.95 (978-0-8239-3289-4). Warnings about the physical and psychological dangers of alcohol are interwoven with fictional examples. (Rev: BL 5/1/02) [362.292]

10607 Anderson, M. A. *Tracey: A Mother's Journal of Teenage Addiction* (9–12). 1988, Black Heron paper $7.95 (978-0-930773-08-3). The harrowing story of one family's fight to save their 14-year-old daughter Tracey from drug addiction. (Rev: VOYA 2/89) [613.8]

10608 Aue, Pamela Willwerth, ed. *Teen Drug Abuse* (8–12). Series: Opposing Viewpoints. 2006, Gale LB $34.95 (978-0-7377-3335-8). Cigarettes, alcohol, marijuana, inhalants, ritalin — they're all discussed in pro and con essays that will be particularly helpful for reports and debates. (Rev: SLJ 3/07) [362.2]

10609 Banfield, Susan. *Inside Recovery: How the Twelve-Step Program Can Work for You* (7–10). Series: Drug Abuse Prevention Library. 1998, Rosen LB $27.95 (978-0-8239-2634-3). A look at the 12-steps to recovery and the many problems one can face going through this program, which has been a successful route for many addicts. (Rev: VOYA 2/99) [613.8]

10610 Barter, James. *Hallucinogens* (8–12). Series: Drug Education Library. 2002, Gale LB $32.45 (978-1-56006-915-7). This absorbing and comprehensive book explains the effects of hallucinogens on the body, traces their use — in ancient rituals, in medical treatments, and as a recreational drug — and looks at the debates over their legalization. Also in this series is *Marijuana*. (Rev: BL 6/1–15/02; SLJ 6/02) [362.29]

10611 Beal, Eileen. *Ritalin: Its Use and Abuse* (7–10). Series: Drug Abuse Prevention Library. 1999, Rosen LB $17.95 (978-0-8239-2775-3). This book explores the drug Ritalin, widely used for attention deficit disorder, and presents the controversies surrounding it. (Rev: BL 5/15/99; VOYA 4/00) [616.85]

10612 Bellenir, Karen, ed. *Tobacco Information for Teens: Health Tips about the Hazards of Using Cigarettes, Smokeless Tobacco, and Other Nicotine Products* (7–12). Series: Teen Health. 2007, Omnigraphics $65.00 (978-0-7808-0976-5). Full of facts and statistics, this book covers types of tobacco, addiction, the impact on health, and ways to stop using the substance. (Rev: SLJ 9/07) [362.2]

10613 Benner, Janet. *Smoking Cigarettes: The Unfiltered Truth — Understanding Why and How to Quit* (9–12). 1987, Joelle paper $10.95 (978-0-942723-12-0). An account that describes the physical effects of smoking on the body and outlines various methods of quitting. (Rev: BL 12/15/87) [613.85]

10614 Berne, Emma Carlson. *Methamphetamine* (7–10). Series: Compact Research: Drugs. 2007, Reference Point LB $24.95 (978-1-60152-004-3). A look at the dangerous drug that is used in rural as well as urban areas in what some are calling an epidemic. Quotations from officials and former users will be useful to report writers. (Rev: BL 4/1/07; LMC 11/07; SLJ 5/07) [362.29]

10615 Bjornlund, Lydia. *Marijuana* (8–12). Illus. Series: Compact Research: Drugs. 2011, ReferencePoint LB $27.95 (978-160152160-6). This volume provides facts and statistics on marijuana and its use and discusses its legalization and the impact on the economy and society. (Rev: BL 2/15/12) [362.29]

10616 Bjornlund, Lydia. *Oxycodone* (8–12). Illus. Series: Compact Research: Drugs. 2011, ReferencePoint LB $27.95 (978-160152161-3). Discusses oxcodone abuse and its effects on health. (Rev: BL 2/15/12) [615]

10617 Bjornlund, Lydia. *Teen Smoking* (9–12). Series: Compact Research: Current Issues. 2010, ReferencePoint $25.95 (978-1-60152-098-2). This book on the causes and consequences of teen smoking includes straightforward factual information as well as compelling graphs, charts, and photos. (Rev: BLO 8/10; SLJ 3/10) [362.29]

10618 Blachford, Stacey, and Kristine Krapp, eds. *Drugs and Controlled Substances: Information for Students* (10–12). 2002, Gale $191.00 (978-0-7876-6264-6). The composition, history, effects, and uses of common drugs — including addictive, illegal, and abused classes of prescription drugs — are covered in this collection of well-written essays. (Rev: SLJ 6/03) [616.86]

10619 Clayton, Lawrence. *Working Together Against Drug Addiction* (6–10). 1996, Rosen LB $27.95 (978-0-8239-2263-5). In addition to discussing drugs and addiction, this work takes an activist approach by providing ways for teens to locate drug and alcohol counselors and programs and ways they can become involved and make a difference. (Rev: SLJ 5/97) [362]

10620 Croft, Jennifer. *Drugs and the Legalization Debate* (6–10). Series: Drug Abuse Prevention Library. 1997, Rosen LB $17.95 (978-0-8239-2509-4). A well-balanced presentation of the pros and cons of legalizing drugs, along with a discussion of drug abuse and penalties and a brief look at how other countries deal with the issue. (Rev: SLJ 5/98) [362.29]

10621 Croft, Jennifer. *PCP: High Risk on the Streets* (7–10). Series: Drug Abuse Prevention Library. 1998, Rosen LB $27.95 (978-0-8239-2774-6). This book provides readers with important information about phencyclidine, or angel dust, the behavior it produces, and its dangers. (Rev: BL 11/15/98; SLJ 12/98) [362.29]

10622 Egendorf, Laura K. *Heroin* (8–10). Series: Compact Research. 2007, Reference Point LB $24.95 (978-1-60152-002-9). This compact volume provides lots of information for report writers, with illustrations, quotations from primary sources, lists of facts, statistical charts, and brief timelines. (Rev: SLJ 5/07) [363.29]

10623 Egendorf, Laura K. *Performance-Enhancing Drugs* (7–10). Series: Compact Research. 2007, Reference Point LB $24.95 (978-1-60152-003-6). A well-organized look at the drugs used to enhance sports performance and the dangers involved. (Rev: LMC 11–12/07; SLJ 9/07) [362.29]

10624 Goldstein, Margaret J. *Legalizing Drugs: Crime Stopper or Social Risk?* (7–10). Series: USA Today's Debate: Voices and Perspectives. 2010, Lerner LB $35.93 (978-0-7613-5116-0). After a history of the war on drugs (since Prohibition), this attractive volume draws on *USA Today* to discuss the effectiveness of this battle and review arguments for and against legalization. (Rev: BL 4/1/10; LMC 10/10; SLJ 6/10) [364.1]

10625 Gottfried, Ted. *The Facts About Alcohol* (7–12). Series: Drugs. 2004, Benchmark LB $37.07 (978-0-7614-1805-4). A history of alcohol use plus discussion of its effects on the body and impact on society. (Rev: SLJ 3/05) [613.8]

10626 Gottfried, Ted, and Lisa Harkrader. *Marijuana* (6–12). Series: Benchmark Rockets. 2010, Marshall Cavendish LB $28.50 (978-0-7614-4351-3). With information about marijuana's history, the ways in which it is consumed, the dangers it poses, the legal problems involved in its use, and some sidebar accounts of teen usage, this title is useful for reports and for young people who have a more personal interest;. (Rev: LMC 3–4/10) [362.29]

10627 Henderson, Elizabeth Connell. *Understanding Addiction* (9–12). Series: Understanding Health and Sickness. 2000, Univ. Press of Mississippi paper $14.00 (978-1-57806-240-9). This work explores the nature of addiction, what causes it, and which are the addictive drugs. (Rev: BL 12/1/00) [362.29]

10628 Hyde, Margaret O. *Drug Wars* (7–12). 1990, Walker LB $12.85 (978-0-8027-6901-5). This account discusses the violence and despair that crack cocaine has brought to America and ways in which its production and distribution can be halted. (Rev: SLJ 6/90; VOYA 6/90) [616.86]

10629 Hyde, Margaret O., and John F. Setaro. *Alcohol 101: An Overview for Teens* (5–10). 1999, Twenty-First Century LB $24.90 (978-0-7613-1274-1). Kinds of alcohol and their effects are described, with material on alcoholism and binge drinking. (Rev: HBG 3/00; SLJ 3/00; VOYA 12/00) [613.8]

10630 Hyde, Margaret O., and John F. Setaro. *Drugs 101: An Overview for Teens* (7–12). 2003, Twenty-First Century LB $25.90 (978-0-7613-2608-3). This well-researched and accessible introduction to the nature of addiction, illicit drugs, and the harmful results of their use features useful photographs, diagrams, and charts. (Rev: BL 5/15/03; HBG 10/03; SLJ 5/03; VOYA 10/03) [362.29]

10631 Hyde, Margaret O., and John K. Setaro. *Smoking 101: An Overview for Teens* (7–12). 2005, Twenty-First Century LB $26.60 (978-0-7613-2835-3). A nonjudgmental account of the physical effects of smoking, with information on tobacco advertising, the kinds of products marketed, and the industry both in the United States and around the world. (Rev: SLJ 1/06) [362.29]

10632 Keegan, Kyle, and Howard Moss. *Chasing the High: A Firsthand Account of One Young Person's Experience with Substance Abuse* (9–12). 2008, Oxford paper $9.95 (978-0-19-531472-4). From stories of dabbling to drug addiction, this part memoir and part reference book contains up-to-date information, details of rehab and recovery approaches, and resource lists. (Rev: BL 3/1/08; SLJ 3/08) [616.86092]

10633 Kittleson, Mark J., ed. *The Truth About Alcohol* (8–12). Series: Truth About. 2004, Facts on File $35.00 (978-0-8160-5298-1). Discusses the effects and dangers of alcohol use, including binge drinking, alcoholism, unsafe sexual behavior, and impaired driving. (Rev: SLJ 4/05) [613.8]

10634 Klosterman, Lorrie. *The Facts about Depressants* (7–12). Series: Drugs. 2005, Benchmark LB $25.95 (978-0-7614-1976-1). A helpful guide to depressants with some basic information about the various kinds on the market, their medical uses, how they are abused, and how they affect the body. (Rev: SLJ 5/06) [362.29]

10635 Kuhn, Cynthia, et al. *Just Say Know: Talking with Kids About Drugs and Alcohol* (10–12). 2002, Norton paper $14.95 (978-0-393-32258-3). Teens will also find value in this accessible overview of the types and threats of specific dangerous drugs. (Rev: BL 1/1–15/02) [649]

10636 Landau, Elaine. *Hooked: Talking About Addiction* (5–10). 1995, Millbrook LB $22.90 (978-1-56294-469-8). This account defines addiction broadly — from use of alcohol and drugs to various forms of compulsive behavior — and gives suggestions for recovery. (Rev: BL 1/1–15/96; SLJ 1/96) [362.29]

10637 Landau, Elaine. *Meth: America's Drug Epidemic* (7–12). 2007, Twenty-First Century LB $30.60 (978-0-8225-6808-7). This cautionary book should scare readers away from methamphetamine by the photos alone and stories of users damaged by the drug serve as additional deterrents; the history of meth use, efforts to stop the current epidemic, and scientific details are also provided. (Rev: BL 10/15/07; SLJ 10/07) [362.29]

10638 Lawton, Sandra Augustyn, ed. *Drug Information for Teens: Health Tips about the Physical and Mental Effects of Substance Abuse. 2nd ed.* (7–12). Series: Teen Health. 2006, Omnigraphics $65 (978-0-7808-0862-1). Updating an earlier edition, this is a comprehensive, well-organized guide to substance abuse — drugs, chemicals, alcohol, and tobacco and including herbal supplements and caffeine and energy drinks — that covers treatment and drug testing as well as places to go to get help. (Rev: SLJ 12/06)

10639 Lee, Mary Price, and Richard S. Lee. *Drugs and Codependency* (6–10). Series: Drug Abuse Prevention Library. 1995, Rosen LB $17.95 (978-0-8239-2065-5). The vulnerability of teens who live in a household where drugs are abused is the focus of this volume. (Rev: BL 9/15/95; SLJ 10/95) [616.869]

10640 Levert, Suzanne. *The Facts about LSD and Other Hallucinogens* (7–12). Series: Drugs. 2005, Benchmark LB $25.95 (978-0-7614-1974-7). A helpful guide to LSD and other hallucinogens, with some history and basic information about the various kinds on the market, their medical uses, how they are abused, and how they affect the body. (Rev: SLJ 5/06) [362.29]

10641 Levert, Suzanne. *The Facts About Steroids* (7–12). Series: Drugs. 2004, Benchmark LB $37.07 (978-0-7614-1808-5). Examines the effects of steroids on users, the health risks, and the laws governing steroid use. (Rev: SLJ 3/05) [362.29]

10642 LeVert, Suzanne, and Jeff Hendricks. *Ecstasy* (6–12). Series: Benchmark Rockets. 2010, Marshall Cavendish LB $28.50 (978-0-7614-4349-0). With information about the history of this drug, the ways in which it is consumed, the dangers it poses, the legal problems involved in its use, and some sidebar accounts of teen usage, this title is useful for reports and for young people who have a more personal interest;. Also use *Steroids* (2010). (Rev: LMC 3–4/10) [362.29]

10643 Lookadoo, Justin. *The Dirt on Drugs: A Dateable Book* (6–10). Series: The Dirt. 2005, Revell paper $9.99 (978-0-8007-5919-3). A former Texas probation officer writes frankly about the dangers of drugs. (Rev: SLJ 7/05) [616.8]

10644 Lyon, Joshua. *Pill Head: The Secret Life of a Painkiller Addict* (10–12). 2009, Hyperion $24.99 (978-1-4013-2298-4). Interviews and statistics add depth to this journalistic look at the startling availability of prescription pills and the devastating effects of addiction. (Rev: SLJ 11/09) [616.86]

10645 McMillan, Daniel. *Teen Smoking: Understanding the Risk* (6–12). Series: Issues in Focus. 1998, Enslow LB $20.95 (978-0-89490-722-7). An interesting, informative account that discusses nicotine addiction, secondhand smoke, health hazards, smoking prevention, and treatments for people who want to stop. (Rev: VOYA 8/98) [362.2]

10646 Marcovitz, Hal. *Should the Drinking Age Be Lowered?* (8–11). Illus. Series: In Controversy. 2011, ReferencePoint LB $26.95 (978-160152144-6). Are teenagers mature enough to drink? Can other countries serve as a model? This book looks at the pros and cons of these and other questions relating to teens and alcohol. (Rev: BL 6/1/11) [362.292]

10647 May, Suellen. *Steroids and Other Performance-Enhancing Drugs* (9–12). Illus. Series: Understanding Drugs. 2011, Chelsea House LB $34.95 (978-160413552-7). Useful for information and reports, this is a good overview of the history of steroids, their effect on the human body, laws regulating them, treatment for addiction, and so forth; part of a series that also covers cocaine and sleep drugs. (Rev: BL 9/15/11) [362.29]

10648 Menhard, Francha Roffe. *The Facts about Amphetamines* (7–12). Series: Drugs. 2005, Benchmark LB $25.95 (978-0-7614-1972-3). This guide gives a brief history of these drugs and basic information about the various kinds on the market, their medical uses, how they are abused, and how they affect the body. (Rev: SLJ 5/06) [362.29]

10649 Menhard, Francha Roffe. *The Facts About Inhalants* (7–12). Series: Drugs. 2004, Benchmark LB $37.07 (978-0-7614-1809-2). Explores the dangers associated with the use of inhalants. (Rev: SLJ 3/05) [362.29]

10650 Menhard, Francha Roffe, and Lisa Harkrader. *Inhalants* (6–12). Series: Benchmark Rockets. 2010, Marshall Cavendish LB $28.50 (978-0-7614-4350-6). With information about inhalants' history, the ways in which they are consumed, the dangers posed, and the legal problems involved, plus some sidebar accounts of teen usage, this title is useful for reports and for young people who have a more personal interest;. (Rev: LMC 3–4/10) [362.29]

10651 Monroe, Judy. *Antidepressants* (7–10). Series: Drug Library. 1997, Enslow LB $26.60 (978-0-89490-848-4). Current information is given about these frequently abused drugs, actual case studies are cited, and discussion questions are provided. (Rev: BL 5/15/97) [616.85]

10652 Monroe, Judy. *Nicotine* (7–10). Series: Drug Library. 1995, Enslow LB $26.60 (978-0-89490-505-6). A concise, easy-to-use look at nicotine, where it is found, its effects, and how to avoid its use. (Rev: BL 7/95; SLJ 9/95) [613.85]

10653 Naff, Clay Farris. *Nicotine and Tobacco* (7–10). Series: Compact Research. 2007, Reference Point LB $24.95 (978-1-60152-006-7). A well-organized look at the use of nicotine and tobacco and the dangers involved. (Rev: LMC 11–12/07; SLJ 9/07) [613.85]

10654 Nakaya, Andrea C. *Marijuana* (8–10). Series: Compact Research. 2007, Reference Point LB $24.95 (978-1-60152-000-5). This compact volume provides lots of information for report writers, with illustrations, quotations from primary sources, lists of facts, statistical charts, and brief timelines. (Rev: SLJ 5/07) [362.29]

10655 Owen, Frank. *No Speed Limit: The Highs and Lows of Meth* (9–12). 2007, St. Martin's $24.95 (978-0-312-35616-3). Methamphetamine (a.k.a. speed) is an addictive drug sometimes used as an unhealthy substitute for sleep and food and always hard to come off of. A bit of its history, statistics of use, and public opinion is covered in this book. (Rev: BL 7/07) [362.29]

10656 Packer, Alex J. *Highs! Over 150 Ways to Feel Really, REALLY Good . . . Without Alcohol or Other Drugs* (6–12). 2000, Free Spirit paper $15.95 (978-1-57542-074-5). Grouped into three areas (serenity, physical improvement, and creativity), the author describes 150 ways teenagers can feel good about themselves. (Rev: BL 11/1/00; SLJ 9/00) [158]

10657 Santamaria, Peggy. *Drugs and Politics* (6–10). Series: Drug Abuse Prevention Library. 1994, Rosen LB $27.95 (978-0-8239-1703-7). A discussion of the influence of drugs on politics, such as in Colombia, where the government is involved with and intimidated by powerful drug interests. (Rev: BL 3/15/95; SLJ 3/95) [363.4]

10658 Shannon, Joyce Brennfleck, ed. *Alcohol Information for Teens: Health Tips About Alcohol and Alcoholism* (7–12). Series: Teen Health. 2005, Omnigraphics $58.00 (978-0-7808-0741-9). Authoritative information about the effects of alcohol on the mind and body and the dangers of alcohol dependency. (Rev: SLJ 7/05) [613.8]

10659 Sherman, Jill. *Drug Trafficking* (7–10). Series: Essential Issues. 2010, ABDO LB $32.79 (978-1-60453-953-0). After a history of drug trafficking this volume looks at the issue from the perspectives of producers, smugglers, dealers, and users and discusses the various approaches to law enforcement. (Rev: LMC 10/10) [363.4]

10660 Sherry, Clifford J. *Drugs and Eating Disorders* (5–10). Series: Drug Abuse Prevention Library. 1994, Rosen LB $17.95 (978-0-8239-1540-8). Shows how diet pills and other weight-loss products can lead to drug abuse and, in some cases, addiction. (Rev: BL 6/1–15/94; SLJ 6/94) [616.85]

10661 Sherry, Clifford J. *Inhalants* (5–10). 1994, Rosen LB $17.95 (978-0-8239-1704-4). A look at inhalants, where they are found, and how they affect the body. (Rev: BL 2/15/95; SLJ 3/95) [362.29]

10662 Shuker, Nancy. *Everything You Need to Know About an Alcoholic Parent. Rev. ed.* (7–12). 1998, Rosen LB $27.95 (978-0-8239-2869-9). After a general discussion of alcoholism, Shuker explains how it changes human relationships and how young people can cope with it. (Rev: BL 1/15/90; VOYA 4/90) [362.29]

10663 Smith, C. Fraser. *Lenny, Lefty, and the Chancellor: The Len Bias Tragedy and the Search for Reform in Big-Time College Basketball* (9–12). 1992, Bancroft paper $12.95 (978-0-9631246-0-9). When a college basketball star died of a drug overdose, school officials attempted to avoid a scandal. (Rev: BL 3/15/92; SLJ 8/92) [796.323]

10664 Strazzabosco-Hayn, Gina. *Drugs and Sleeping Disorders* (7–12). Series: Drug Abuse Prevention Library. 1996, Rosen LB $27.95 (978-0-8239-2144-7). An exploration of sleep disorders and potential problems and dangers of using drugs for sleep. (Rev: SLJ 3/96) [362.2]

10665 Tenaglia-Webster, Maria. *Drugs* (9–12). Series: Global Viewpoints. 2009, Gale/Greenhaven $36.20 (978-0-7377-4152-0). Taking a global view, this balanced book explores the global war on drugs and its associated implications through clear, concise pro/con discussions. (Rev: LMC 10/09)

10666 Van Tuyl, Christine, ed. *Drunk Driving* (7–10). Series: Issues That Concern You. 2006, Gale $32.45 (978-0-7377-3239-9). Article excerpts present various points of view regarding legal drinking ages, blood-alcohol levels, the punishment of offenders, and so forth. (Rev: BL 10/15/06) [363.12]

10667 Webb, Margot. *Drugs and Gangs* (7–12). Series: Drug Abuse Prevention Library. 1996, Rosen LB $17.95 (978-0-8239-2059-4). This book describes the connections between gangs and drugs, in both selling and using, and provides teens with tips on how to avoid these dangers. (Rev: SLJ 3/96; VOYA 6/96) [362.29]

10668 Weir, William. *In the Shadow of the Dope Fiend: America's War on Drugs* (9–12). 1995, Shoe String LB $35.00 (978-0-208-02384-1). A social history of drug use. (Rev: BL 4/1/95; VOYA 12/95) [363.4]

10669 Wilkins, Jessica. *Street Pharma* (6–10). Illus. Series: Dealing with Drugs. 2011, Crabtree LB $30.60 (978-077875512-8). Discusses teens' use of prescription medications and provides breakdowns of types of drugs as well as resources for those seeking treatment. (Rev: BL 4/1/12) [362.29]

10670 Wilkinson, Beth. *Drugs and Depression* (6–12). Series: Drug Abuse Prevention Library. 1994, Rosen LB $27.95 (978-0-8239-3004-3). Some young people turn to drugs to deal with their depression. This book shows the dangers in this approach and offers positive ways of handling depression and places to get assistance. (Rev: BL 6/1–15/94) [616.86]

Bionics and Transplants

10671 McClellan, Marilyn. *Organ and Tissue Transplants: Medical Miracles and Challenges* (7–12). Series: Issues in Focus. 2003, Enslow LB $26.60 (978-0-7660-1943-0). The story of a critically injured teen draws readers into this discussion of transplants of organs and tissues and the ethical issues involved. (Rev: HBG 10/03; SLJ 5/03) [617.9]

10672 Schwartz, Tina P. *Organ Transplants: A Survival Guide for the Entire Family: The Ultimate Teen Guide* (7–12). Series: It Happened to Me. 2005, Scarecrow $36.50 (978-0-8108-4924-2). A clear explanation, in question-and-answer format, of the complex problems relating to medical transplants, with discussion of the hazards and the emotional upheaval to be expected. (Rev: SLJ 10/05) [617.9]

Diseases and Illnesses

10673 Abramovitz, Melissa. *Lou Gehrig's Disease* (7–12). 2006, Gale LB $31.20 (978-1-59018-676-3). Sidebars, diagrams, and photographs help teens understand the causes, symptoms, and diagnosis of ALS, or Lou Gehrig's disease; potential future treatments are also discussed. (Rev: SLJ 7/06)

10674 Ambrose, Marylou. *Investigating Diabetes: Real Facts for Real Lives* (7–10). Series: Investigating Diseases. 2010, Enslow LB $34.60 (978-0-7660-3338-2). Symptoms, diagnosis, treatment, and current research are all covered in this book that also tells the stories of children coping with the disease and provides historical background. (Rev: LMC 10/10) [616.4]

10675 Ambrose, Marylou, and Veronica Deisler. *Investigating Eating Disorders (Anorexia, Bulimia and Binge Eating): Real Facts for Real Lives* (7–10). Series: Investigating Diseases. 2010, Enslow LB $34.60 (978-0-7660-3339-9). Symptoms, diagnosis, treatment, and current research are all covered in this book that also tells the stories of children coping with these problems and provides historical background. (Rev: LMC 10/10) [616.85]

10676 Apel, Melanie Ann. *Cystic Fibrosis: The Ultimate Teen Guide* (9–12). Series: It Happened to Me. 2006, Scarecrow $42.00 (978-0-8108-4821-4). Stories of teenagers with cystic fibrosis will be reassuring to readers with the disease although the realities of the condition are not sugarcoated. (Rev: SLJ 10/06)

10677 Bakewell, Lisa, and Karen Bellenir, eds. *Cancer Information for Teens: Health Tips About Cancer Awareness, Prevention, Diagnosis, and Treatment* (8–12). Series: Teen Health. 2009, Omnigraphics $69 (978-0-7808-1085-3). Provides current information on cancer's warning signs, risk factors, and treatment. (Rev: SLJ 3/10)

10678 Balkin, Karen F., ed. *Food-Borne Illness* (7–12). Series: At Issue. 2004, Gale LB $29.95 (978-0-7377-1334-3); paper $21.20 (978-0-7377-1335-0). A collection of previously published articles that examine the dangers of food-borne illness and what can be done to protect consumers. (Rev: SLJ 4/05) [615.9]

10679 Ballard, Carol. *Explaining Food Allergies* (7–12). Series: Explaining . . . 2010, Smart Apple Media LB $34.25 (978-1-59920-316-4). Well designed and written, these books about common illnesses affecting children include ways to help kids cope with the various conditions (glossary, index). (Rev: BL 10/1/09; LMC 1–2/10)

10680 Bellenir, Karen, ed. *Allergy Information for Teens: Health Tips About Allergic Reactions Such as Anaphylaxis, Respiratory Problems, and Rashes* (7–12). 2006, Omnigraphics $65 (978-0-7808-0799-0). Readers learn about allergy symptoms, tests, treatments, and management strategies with short Q&A sections, diagrams, and sidebars. (Rev: SLJ 7/06)

10681 Bellenir, Karen, ed. *Asthma Information for Teens: Health Tips About Managing Asthma and Related Concerns* (8–12). Series: Teen Health. 2005, Omnigraphics LB $65.00 (978-0-7808-0770-9). Information-packed but readable, this volume covers all aspects of asthma. (Rev: SLJ 9/05) [616.2]

10682 Brill, Marlene Targ. *Tourette Syndrome* (6–12). Series: Twenty-First Century Medical Library. 2002, Millbrook LB $26.90 (978-0-7613-2101-9). This volume provides historical and medical information on the disorder named for neurologist Georges Gilles de la Tourette, presenting the stories of three teenagers who suffer from it. (Rev: BL 3/1/02; HBG 10/02; SLJ 4/02) [375]

10683 Burby, Liza N. *Bulimia Nervosa: The Secret Cycle of Bingeing and Purging* (6–10). Series: Teen Health Library of Eating Disorder Prevention. 1998, Rosen LB $27.95 (978-0-8239-2762-3). Bulimia is an eating disorder characterized by bingeing and purging. This book describes various eating disorders, then focuses on bulimia, its causes, physical and psychological effects, the roles of peer pressure, media images, family relationships, genetics, and treatment and recovery. (Rev: SLJ 1/99) [616.85]

10684 Bush, Jenna. *Ana's Story: A Journey of Hope* (8–11). 2007, HarperCollins $18.99 (978-0-06-137908-6). Bush worked for UNICEF in Latin America and this story highlights the impact of HIV/AIDS in the area, recounting Ana's birth with the disease, the death of both her parents, the struggle to find an accepting home, her eventual success in finding love, and her hope for the future when she gives birth to a disease-free baby. ∩ (Rev: BL 8/07; HB 11–12/07; SLJ 10/07) [362]

10685 Cefrey, Holly. *Coping with Cancer* (6–12). Series: Coping. 2000, Rosen LB $26.50 (978-0-8239-2849-1). As well as discussing how cancer develops in various parts of the body, this book gives self-help advice for anyone who is diagnosed with the disease. (Rev: BL 1/1–15/01; SLJ 12/00) [616.99]

10686 Chamlin, Sarah L. *Living with Skin Conditions* (9–12). Series: Teen's Guides. 2010, Facts on File LB $34.95 (978-081607911-7). With chapters dealing with sun exposure, cuts and burns, stings and rashes, and chronic conditions, this is a useful guide to common skin problems that affect teens and provides accessible and practical advice. (Rev: BLO 8/10) [616.5]

10687 Clarke, Julie M., and Ann Kirby-Payne. *Understanding Weight and Depression* (7–10). Series: Teen Eating Disorder Prevention. 1999, Rosen LB $31.95 (978-0-8239-2994-8). This book discusses the psychological origins of eating disorders such as anorexia and bulimia and suggests ways to develop a healthy self-image. [616.8]

10688 Cunningham, Kevin. *Flu* (9–12). Series: Diseases in History. 2009, Morgan Reynolds LB $28.95 (978-1-59935-105-6). Cunningham explores the history of the flu virus in humans and the likelihood of future pandemics in this comprehensive volume. Lexile 1040 (Rev: BL 10/1/09; SLJ 9/09) [614.5]

10689 Cunningham, Kevin. *HIV/AIDS* (9–12). Series: Diseases in History. 2009, Morgan Reynolds LB $28.95 (978-1-59935-104-9). Cunningham examines the brief history of HIV/AIDS, the treatment and prevention of the virus, and society's reaction to this epidemic. (Rev: SLJ 1/10; VOYA 10/09) [616.97]

10690 Cunningham, Kevin. *Malaria* (9–12). Series: Diseases in History. 2009, Morgan Reynolds LB $28.95 (978-1-59935-103-2). An in-depth look at the history, transmission, treatment, and prevention of this disease. Also use *Plague* (2009). (Rev: SLJ 1/10) [614.532]

10691 Currie-McGhee, Leanne K. *Sexually Transmitted Diseases* (6–12). Illus. Series: Compact Research. 2008, ReferencePoint $25.95 (978-160152045-6). Using a blend of text, diagrams, primary sources, and bullet points this volume delivers sobering information on a variety of STDs, including HPV. (Rev: BL 10/15/08; LMC 8–9/09) [614.5]

10692 Dahl, Ken. *Monsters* (11–12). Illus. 2009, Secret Acres paper $18 (978-09799609-4-9). Giant, intrusive talking herpes sores symbolize the author's feelings of doom and shame in this bitingly funny graphic-novel-style take on the realities of STDs. (Rev: BL 11/15/09) [616.95]

10693 Decker, Janet M. *Mononucleosis* (9–12). Series: Deadly Diseases and Epidemics. 2004, Chelsea House LB $32.95 (978-0-7910-7700-9). Mononucleosis is explored, with material on the virus involved, and its prevention and treatment. [616.9]

10694 DeSalle, Rob, ed. *Epidemic! The World of Infectious Diseases* (10–12). 1999, New Press paper $19.95 (978-1-56584-546-6). In brief essays, specialists discuss such topics as methods of infection, key personnel, important case studies, and prevention techniques. (Rev: BL 9/15/99) [614.4]

10695 Dillon, Erin, ed. *Obesity* (7–12). Series: Issues That Concern You. 2006, Gale LB $32.45 (978-0-7377-2194-2). Colorful photographs underline the importance of this problem being discussed in this helpful volume that presents essays giving different points of view. (Rev: SLJ 2/07)

10696 DiSpezio, Michael. *The Science, Spread, and Therapy of HIV Disease: Everything You Need to Know, but Had No Idea Who to Ask* (9–12). 1997, A T L Pr $26.95 (978-1-882360-20-8); paper $13.95 (978-1-882360-19-2). This comprehensive book in a question-and-answer format addresses both general and specific topics and gives current information on HIV and AIDS. (Rev: BL 2/15/98; SLJ 5/98; VOYA 6/98) [616.97]

10697 Donnelly, Karen. *Coping with Lyme Disease* (6–12). Series: Coping. 2001, Rosen LB $31.95 (978-0-8239-3199-6). This introduction to the symptoms, diagnosis, treatment, and prevention of Lyme disease includes personal stories. (Rev: SLJ 7/01) [616.9]

10698 Drexler, Madeline. *Secret Agents: The Menace of Emerging Infections* (10–12). 2002, National Academy/Joseph Henry $24.95 (978-0-309-07638-8). The dangers of diseases that spread from animals and of an unregulated and ill-equipped public health system are examined in thought-provoking fashion. (Rev: BL 2/15/02) [614.4]

10699 Drisdelle, Rosemary. *Parasites: Tales of Humanity's Most Unwelcome Guests* (10–12). 2010, Univ. of California $27.50 (978-052025938-6). Everything you always wanted to know about the role parasites have played in human history, from the downfall of cities to their role in wartime. (Rev: BLO 1/1–15/11) [757]

10700 Edelson, Edward. *The Immune System* (6–12). Series: 21st Century Health and Wellness. 2000, Chelsea LB $36.00 (978-0-7910-5525-0). A revised edition of Edelson's presentation on the immune system and what happens when it fails to function. (Rev: BL 4/15/00; HBG 9/00; SLJ 6/00) [616.07]

10701 Finer, Kim Renee. *Tuberculosis* (9–12). Series: Deadly Diseases and Epidemics. 2003, Chelsea House

$32.95 (978-0-7910-7309-4). This work discusses the history of tuberculosis (also known as consumption), as well as its causes, symptoms, and treatment. (Rev: HBG 4/04) [616.9]

10702 Frankenberger, Elizabeth. *Food and Love: Dealing with Family Attitudes About Weight* (7–12). Series: Teen Health Library of Eating Disorder Prevention. 1998, Rosen LB $27.95 (978-0-8239-2760-9). This book explores the role the family plays in developing a healthy self-image and affecting a teenager's attitudes toward food. (Rev: VOYA 4/99) [616.85]

10703 Fredericks, Carrie, ed. *Autism* (7–10). Series: Perspectives on Diseases and Disorders. 2008, Gale LB $34.95 (978-0-7377-3869-8). Readers whose lives are affected by autism will be interested in this look at the disorder and its spectrum of symptoms; personal accounts by those with autism and parents of autistic children add to the presentation. (Rev: BL 4/1/08) [616.85]

10704 Frissell, Susan, and Paula Harney. *Eating Disorders and Weight Control* (7–10). 1998, Enslow LB $26.60 (978-0-89490-919-1). This book covers anorexia, bulimia, binge eating disorders, and weight control issues with material on how to cope with them in a healthy, realistic manner. (Rev: BL 4/15/98; HBG 9/98; SLJ 3/98) [616.85]

10705 Gay, Kathlyn, and Sean McGarrahan. *Epilepsy: The Ultimate Teen Guide* (7–12). Series: Ultimate Teen Guide. 2003, Scarecrow LB $32.50 (978-0-8108-4339-4). This informative look at this seizure disease and its impact on typical teen activities (sports, jobs, driving, and so forth) includes the personal experiences of coauthor McGarrahan, who was diagnosed with epilepsy at the age of 16. (Rev: BL 10/15/03; SLJ 10/03) [616]

10706 Goldsmith, Connie. *Battling Malaria: On the Front Lines Against a Global Killer* (8–12). 2010, Lerner LB $37.27 (978-0-8225-8580-0). Goldsmith emphasizes the devastating impact of malaria on nations around the world and provides facts about its transmission, treatment, and methods of control; with personal stories and interesting sidebars. (Rev: LMC 11–12/10; SLJ 11/1/10)

10707 Goldsmith, Connie. *Hepatitis* (7–12). Series: USA Today Health Reports: Diseases and Disorders. 2010, Lerner LB $34.60 (978-0-8225-6787-5). Hepatitis is not sufficiently recognized as a health problem, and this succinct and accessible volume discusses symptoms, transmission, prevention, treatment, and research. (Rev: BL 6/10; LMC 11–12/10) [616.3]

10708 Goldsmith, Connie. *Influenza* (7–12). Series: USA Today Health Reports: Diseases and Disorders. 2010, Lerner LB $34.60 (978-0-7613-5881-7). This succinct and accessible volume discusses symptoms, transmission, prevention, and treatment of influenza as well as outbreaks of bird flu and swine flu. (Rev: BL 6/10; LMC 11–12/10) [616.2]

10709 Goldsmith, Connie. *Invisible Invaders: Dangerous Infectious Diseases* (7–10). Series: Discovery! 2006, Lerner LB $27.93 (978-0-8225-3416-7). This clearly written and well-illustrated book provides information on infectious diseases including SARS, Ebola, mad cow disease, and E.coli. (Rev: BL 5/1/06; SLJ 5/06) [362.196]

10710 Grady, Denise. *Deadly Invaders: Virus Outbreaks around the World, from Marburg Fever to Avian Flu* (7–10). 2006, Kingfisher $16.95 (978-0-7534-5995-9). *New York Times* reporter Grady recalls her trip to Angola during the deadly outbreak of Marburg fever and describes the challenges faced in a community with few basic services; she also discusses other viral diseases including HIV and AIDS, West Nile, avian flu, SARS, and Hantavirus. (Rev: BL 10/1/06; LMC 4–5/07; SLJ 12/06*) [614.5]

10711 Grady, Sean M., and John Tabak. *Biohazards: Humanity's Battle with Infectious Disease* (9–12). 2006, Facts on File $35 (978-0-8160-4687-4). The many ways in which viruses — both new and old — affect life on Earth are discussed in this easy-to-understand illustrated volume, including threats such as bioterrorism, the spread of HIV/AIDS, and the return of smallpox. (Rev: SLJ 6/06)

10712 Grapes, Bryan J., ed. *Sexually Transmitted Diseases* (10–12). Series: Current Controversies. 2001, Greenhaven LB $36.20 (978-0-7377-0687-1); paper $24.95 (978-0-7377-0686-4). Various aspects of sexually transmitted diseases, including prevention and the role of public health agencies, are explored in this collection of essays and articles. [616.95]

10713 Greene, Melissa Fay. *There Is No Me without You: One Woman's Odyssey to Rescue Africa's Children* (9–12). 2006, Bloomsbury $25.95 (978-1-59691-116-1). In Ethiopia, a woman named Haregewoin Teferra takes in abandoned AIDS orphans, quietly trying to make a difference in a continent that has been devastated by the disease. (Rev: BL 8/06) [362.73]

10714 Haerens, Margaret, ed. *Sexually Transmitted Diseases* (10–12). 2006, Gale LB $34.95 (978-0-7377-3333-4). AIDS, abstinence, virginity pledges, the efficacy of government programs — many aspects of the battle against STDs are addressed in this collection of pro/con articles. (Rev: SLJ 3/07) [616.95]

10715 Hardman, Lizabeth. *Plague* (6–10). Series: Diseases and Disorders. 2010, Lucent $32.45 (978-1-4205-0145-2). With real-life examples and many illustrations, this book describes epidemics of plague through the centuries. (Rev: LMC 5–6/10) [616.9232]

10716 Harris, Jacqueline. *Sickle Cell Disease* (6–10). 2001, Twenty-First Century LB $26.90 (978-0-7613-1459-2). After introducing three young victims of this disease, the author describes its symptoms and treatment and traces its history. (Rev: BL 9/15/01; HBG 3/02; SLJ 12/01) [616.1]

10717 Harris, Nancy, ed. *AIDS in Developing Countries* (6–12). Series: At Issue. 2004, Gale LB $29.95 (978-0-7377-1789-1). Through a series of essays that express different points of view, the AIDS situation in countries in Africa, Asia, and South America is explored. (Rev: BL 2/15/04) [616]

10718 Johannsson, Phillip. *Heart Disease* (7–12). Series: Diseases and People. 1998, Enslow LB $20.95 (978-0-7660-1051-2). The causes and types of heart disease are described, along with an overview of current treatments and potential future advances. (Rev: BL 7/98) [616.1]

10719 Kelly, Evelyn B., and Ian Wilker, et al. *Investigating Tuberculosis and Superbugs: Real Facts for Real Lives* (7–10). Illus. Series: Investigating Diseases. 2010, Enslow LB $34.60 (978-076603343-6). A thorough overview of diseases — tuberculosis, malaria, and so forth — that are becoming resistant to today's treatments, with discussion of options for the future. (Rev: BL 12/1/10) [616.9]

10720 Kittleson, Mark J., ed. *The Truth About Eating Disorders* (8–12). Series: Truth About. 2004, Facts on File $35.00 (978-0-8160-5300-1). Causes, diagnosis, and treatment are all covered in this user-friendly guide that looks at emotions along with physical symptoms and does not neglect adolescent males with eating problems. (Rev: SLJ 4/05) [[616.85]

10721 Kittredge, Mary. *The Common Cold* (7–12). Series: 21st Century Health and Wellness. 2000, Chelsea House LB $24.95 (978-0-7910-5985-2). An interesting history of cold cures introduces this overview of the causes, prevention, and treatment of this perennial nuisance. (Rev: BL 11/15/00; HBG 10/01; SLJ 3/01) [616.1]

10722 Kowalski, Kathiann M. *Attack of the Superbugs: The Crisis of Drug-Resistant Diseases* (7–12). 2005, Enslow LB $31.93 (978-0-7660-2400-7). With full-color photographs and diagrams, this book show how viruses and diseases become resistant to drug treatments and mutate, resulting in the return of diseases that were thought extinct. (Rev: SLJ 6/06)

10723 Kuffel, Frances. *Passing for Thin: Losing Half My Weight and Finding My Self* (10–12). 2004, Broadway $24.00 (978-0-7679-1291-4). The author describes how at the age of 42 she took dramatic steps to drop more than half her body weight, only to find she faced another epic struggle to find her identity as a newly thin woman. (Rev: BL 12/1/03; SLJ 3/04) [362.1]

10724 Landau, Elaine. *Alzheimer's Disease: A Forgotten Life* (7–10). Series: Health and Human Disease. 2006, Scholastic LB $26.00 (978-0-531-16755-7). Symptoms, diagnosis, treatment, and prognosis are all covered here, plus a question-and-answer "ask the doctor" feature that adds pertinent information. (Rev: BL 12/1/05; SLJ 1/06) [616.8]

10725 Landau, Elaine. *Food Poisoning and Foodborne Diseases* (7–12). Series: USA Today Health Reports: Diseases and Disorders. 2010, Lerner LB $34.60 (978-0-8225-7290-9). This succinct and accessible volume discusses symptoms, transmission, prevention, and treatment of illnesses caused by contaminated food and water. (Rev: BL 6/10; LMC 11–12/10) [615.9]

10726 Lawton, Sandra Augustyn, ed. *Diabetes Information for Teens: Health Tips about Managing Diabetes and Preventing Related Complications* (9–12). 2006, Omnigraphics $65 (978-0-7808-0811-9). A thorough look at the disease and all its aspects — living with the disease, medical facts, the psychological effects, impact on different ethnic groups, and related health issues. (Rev: SLJ 8/06)

10727 Lawton, Sandra Augustyn, ed. *Eating Disorders Information for Teens: Health Tips About Anorexia, Bulimia, Binge Eating, and Other Eating Disorders* (7–12). Series: Teen Health. 2005, Omnigraphics $65.00 (978-0-7808-0783-9). This title explores all aspects of eating disorders as well as such related topics as body image, nutrition, self-esteem, and athleticism. (Rev: SLJ 12/05; VOYA 4/06)

10728 McMullin, Jordan, ed. *The Black Death* (9–12). Series: Great Disasters. 2003, Gale paper $23.70 (978-0-7377-1499-9). This volume transports readers back to the middle of the 14th century, when a pandemic of plague swept across Europe leaving millions of dead in its wake. (Rev: BL 11/1/03) [614.5]

10729 Marisco, Katie. *HIV/AIDS* (7–10). Series: Essential Issues. 2010, ABDO LB $32.79 (978-1-60453-955-4). After a history of this disease, readers learn about its global impact, the medications available, continuing research, and the misconceptions and prejudices that have contributed to its spread. (Rev: LMC 10/10) [362.196]

10730 Miller, Debra A. *Pandemics* (8–12). Series: Hot Topics. 2006, Gale LB $31.20 (978-1-59018-965-8). A thoughtful exploration of infectious diseases and our ability to prevent and control outbreaks. (Rev: SLJ 4/07) [618.92]

10731 Moe, Barbara. *Coping with Eating Disorders* (7–10). 1999, Rosen $31.95 (978-0-8239-2974-0). Actual case histories are used to explain the characteristics of bulimia, anorexia, and compulsive-eating patterns. Practical coping suggestions are also offered. (Rev: BL 7/91; SLJ 11/91) [616.85]

10732 Moe, Barbara. *Coping with PMS* (7–12). Series: Coping. 1998, Rosen LB $25.25 (978-0-8239-2716-6). Supplemented by personal accounts, this book explains how PMS can be a manageable problem, with material on physiology, diet, lifestyle, attitude, and the relationship between nutrition and PMS control (recipes are included). (Rev: BL 5/15/98; SLJ 5/98) [618.172]

10733 Moe, Barbara. *Coping with Tourette Syndrome and Tic Disorders* (6–10). 2000, Rosen LB $26.50

(978-0-8239-2976-4). Solid information and many case studies are used in this examination of Tourette's syndrome, tic disorders, and related problems with material on how they affect moods, learning, activities, and sleep. (Rev: BL 7/00) [616.8]

10734 Moe, Barbara. *Everything You Need to Know About Migraines and Other Headaches* (7–12). Series: Need to Know Library. 2000, Rosen LB $27.95 (978-0-8239-3291-7). An accessible and thorough exploration of the symptoms, treatment, and prevention of migraines and other headaches. (Rev: HBG 10/01; SLJ 4/01) [616.8]

10735 Moe, Barbara. *Inside Eating Disorder Support Groups* (6–10). Series: Teen Health Library of Eating Disorder Prevention. 1998, Rosen LB $27.95 (978-0-8239-2769-2). After a general discussion of eating disorders and available treatments, this book explains the dynamics of support groups and how they can help teens recover from eating disorders and come to terms with their problems. (Rev: SLJ 1/99) [616.85]

10736 Moehn, Heather. *Everything You Need to Know When Someone You Know Has Leukemia* (5–10). Series: Need to Know Library. 2000, Rosen LB $27.95 (978-0-8239-3121-7). The basic facts about leukemia are covered with material on its various types and treatments, possible causes, and the emotional aspects of the illness. (Rev: SLJ 9/00) [616.99]

10737 Moehn, Heather. *Understanding Eating Disorder Support Groups* (7–12). Series: Teen Eating Disorder Prevention Library. 2000, Rosen LB $31.95 (978-0-8239-2992-4). Extensive information on the diagnosis, symptoms, and treatment of eating disorders precedes discussion of the types of support available; case studies appear throughout. (Rev: HBG 10/01; SLJ 2/01)

10738 Moran, Katherine J. *Diabetes: The Ultimate Teen Guide* (9–12). Illus. by Lisa P. Merriman. Series: It Happened to Me. 2004, Scarecrow $34.50 (978-0-8108-4806-1). Management of diabetes is the main focus of this volume, which covers the basics of the disease and its symptoms, the importance of diet and exercise, and the types of insulin and delivery methods used today. (Rev: SLJ 8/04)

10739 Mukhopadhyay, Tito Rajarshi. *How Can I Talk if My Lips Don't Move? Inside My Autistic Mind* (9–12). 2008, Arcade $25.00 (978-1-55970-859-3). Mukhopadhyay, who is severely autistic but very well-read and a talented writer, describes how he learned to cope with his unusual view of the world. (Rev: BL 12/15/07) [618.92]

10740 Murphy, Jim, and Alison Blank. *Invincible Microbe: Tuberculosis and the Never-Ending Search for a Cure* (6–10). Illus. 2012, Clarion $17.99 (978-0-618-53574-3). With concise text, many images, and interesting anecdotes, this well-researched book traces the history of this devastating infectious disease. Outstanding Science Trade Books for Students K–12. ⊘ Lex-

ile 1200L (Rev: BL 7/12*; LMC 5–6/13; SLJ 7/12*; VOYA 4/12)

10741 Murphy, Wendy. *Asthma* (7–12). Series: Millbrook Medical Library. 1998, Millbrook LB $26.90 (978-0-7613-0364-0). Beginning with the causes of asthma, this book describes what happens during an attack, how the disease is controlled, and various avenues of medical treatment. (Rev: BL 1/1–15/99; HBG 3/99; SLJ 1/99) [616.2]

10742 Murphy, Wendy. *Orphan Diseases: New Hope for Rare Medical Conditions* (7–12). 2002, Millbrook LB $26.90 (978-0-7613-1919-1). Autism, cystic fibrosis, and dwarfism are among the conditions discussed, with information on origin, causes, treatment, and how patients cope with the condition. (Rev: BL 10/15/02; HBG 3/03) [362.1]

10743 Nakaya, Andrea C., ed. *Obesity* (8–12). Series: Opposing Viewpoints. 2005, Gale LB $36.20 (978-0-7377-3233-7). The causes of the soaring rates of obesity are discussed from various viewpoints, as well as who is responsible and what can be done to reduce this health problem. (Rev: SLJ 1/06) [616.3]

10744 Neuwirth, Michael, and Kevin Osborn. *The Scoliosis Sourcebook* (10–12). 2001, NTC paper $16.95 (978-0-7373-0321-6). This book describes the tests that confirm scoliosis, the symptoms, and the medical and surgical treatments available. (Rev: BL 8/01) [616.7]

10745 Newton, David E. *Sick! Diseases and Disorders, Injuries and Infections* (8–12). 1999, U.X.L $247.00 (978-0-7876-3922-8). Arranged alphabetically, this volume covers 140 illnesses, disorders, and injuries with material on symptoms, causes, diagnosis, prevention, and treatment. (Rev: BL 10/1/00) [616]

10746 Nolen, Stephanie. *28 Stories of AIDS in Africa* (10–12). 2007, Walker $24.95 (978-0-8027-1598-2). These affecting stories illustrate how widely HIV/AIDS has impacted the population of Africa. (Rev: BL 5/15/07) [362.196]

10747 Orr, Tamra. *Avian Flu* (9–12). Series: Coping in a Changing World. 2007, Rosen LB $31.95 (978-1-4042-0950-3). Orr discusses the flu epidemic of 1918 and other serious outbreaks before examining avian flu and the threat it poses (less than first believed). (Rev: SLJ 8/07) [614.5]

10748 Orr, Tamra. *When the Mirror Lies: Anorexia, Bulimia, and Other Eating Disorders* (7–12). 2006, Watts LB $30.50 (978-0-531-16791-5); paper $17.95 (978-0-531-17977-2). Case studies help to draw readers into this friendly account of eating disorders and their impact. ⌒ (Rev: SLJ 11/06)

10749 Oshinsky, David M. *Polio: An American Story* (9–12). 2005, Oxford $35.00 (978-0-19-515294-4). The story of the 20th-century marshalling of political and scientific resources to combat the scourge of polio includes material — some not laudatory — on Roosevelt, Salk, and Sabin. (Rev: BL 3/15/05; SLJ 10/05) [614.5]

10750 Ouriou, Katie. *Love Ya Like a Sister: A Story of Friendship* (8–12). 1999, Tundra paper $7.95 (978-0-88776-454-7). After her death from leukemia when only 16 years old, Katie Ouriou's life and thoughts during her last months were reconstructed from journal entries and e-mail correspondence with her many friends. (Rev: SLJ 5/99; VOYA 6/99) [616.95]

10751 Panno, Joseph. *Cancer: The Role of Genes, Lifestyle and Environment* (7–12). Series: The New Biology. 2004, Facts on File $35.00 (978-0-8160-4950-9). In this title from the New Biology series, author Joseph Panno explores the role of genetics, lifestyle choices, and the environment in cancer. (Rev: SLJ 2/05; VOYA 8/04)

10752 Parker, Katrina. *Living with Diabetes* (9–12). Series: Teen's Guides. 2008, Facts on File $34.95 (978-0-8160-7563-8). Both Type 1 and Type 2 diabetes are discussed in this guide, written by a doctor to help teenagers deal with the disease or help others who have it. (Rev: BL 2/15/08) [616.462]

10753 Parks, Peggy J. *Brain Tumors* (7–12). Illus. Series: Compact Research: Diseases and Disorders. 2011, ReferencePoint LB $26.95 (978-160152138-5). Looks at the causes, symptoms, and treatment of these tumors, with lots of graphs, tables, and diagrams. (Rev: BL 10/15/11) [616.99]

10754 Parks, Peggy J. *HPV* (7–12). Illus. Series: Compact Research: Diseases and Disorders. 2008, ReferencePoint LB $25.95 (978-160152070-8). Recent developments in the understanding and prevention of human papillomavirus (HPV) make this an interesting book on a hot health topic. (Rev: BL 4/1/09; SLJ 6/1/09) [362.196]

10755 Parks, Peggy J. *Influenza* (7–12). Illus. Series: Compact Research: Diseases and Disorders. 2010, ReferencePoint LB $26.95 (978-160152118-7). Looks at the causes, treatment, and prevention of influenza and at the danger of epidemics. (Rev: BL 2/1/11) [616.2]

10756 Parks, Peggy J. *Schizophrenia* (7–12). Illus. Series: Compact Research: Diseases and Disorders. 2011, ReferencePoint LB $26.95 (978-160152140-8). Looks at the symptoms and treatment of this disorder, with lots of graphs, tables, and diagrams. (Rev: BL 10/15/11) [616.89]

10757 Peters, Stephanie True. *The Battle Against Polio* (6–10). Series: Epidemic! 2004, Benchmark LB $29.93 (978-0-7614-1635-7). The history of polio, the toll it took on young lives, and the ultimately successful search for a vaccine are related in a compelling presentation. (Rev: BL 12/15/04; SLJ 2/05) [614.54]

10758 Petersen, Christine. *Does Everyone Have ADHD? A Teen's Guide to Diagnosis and Treatment* (9–12). Series: Health and Human Disease. 2006, Watts LB

$30.50 (978-0-531-16794-6). This useful guide surveys the history of our knowledge of attention deficit hyperactivity disorder; lays out the symptoms, diagnosis, causes, and treatment; lists people who have done well even though suffering from the disorder; and provides helpful resource lists. (Rev: LMC 8–9/07; SLJ 3/07) [618.9]

10759 Pierce, John R., and James V. Writer. *Yellow Jack: How Yellow Fever Ravaged America and Walter Reed Discovered Its Deadly Secrets* (9–12). 2005, Wiley $24.95 (978-0-471-47261-2). The fascinating story of the battle against yellow fever — a disease that ravaged the Americas across three centuries. (Rev: BL 4/15/05) [614.5]

10760 Pipher, Mary. *Hunger Pains: The Modern Woman's Tragic Quest for Thinness* (7–12). 1997, Ballantine paper $12.00 (978-0-345-41393-2). This book explains eating disorders, probes into their basic causes, and offers suggestions for help, with separate chapters on bulimia, anorexia, obesity, and diets. (Rev: VOYA 8/97) [616.95]

10761 Rocco, Fiammetta. *The Miraculous Fever Tree: Malaria, Medicine, and the Quest for a Cure That Changed the World* (10–12). 2003, HarperCollins $24.95 (978-0-06-019951-7). A fascinating overview of the importance of quinine in the treatment of malaria and the politics involved in its eventual acceptance. (Rev: BL 8/03) [016.9]

10762 Rocha, Toni L. *Understanding Recovery from Eating Disorders* (6–10). Series: Teen Eating Disorder Prevention Library. 1999, Rosen $31.95 (978-0-8239-2884-2). This book offers first-person accounts of survivors of various types of eating disorders and also offers advice for teens who are in recovery programs. (Rev: BL 10/15/99; HBG 9/00; SLJ 7/00) [616.85]

10763 Sacker, Ira M., and Marc A. Zimmer. *Dying to Be Thin* (9–12). 1987, Warner paper $14.99 (978-0-446-38417-9). This account tells about the onset, symptoms, dangers, and treatment of various eating disorders. (Rev: VOYA 12/87) [613.2]

10764 Saffer, Barbara. *Anthrax* (9–12). Series: Diseases and Disorders. 2004, Gale LB $32.45 (978-1-59018-405-9). The history of anthrax outbreaks, development of vaccines, and potential use as a weapon are all discussed in clear narrative with black-and-white photographs. (Rev: SLJ 10/04) [616.9]

10765 Shmaefsky, Brian. *Syphilis* (9–12). Series: Deadly Diseases and Epidemics. 2003, Chelsea House $32.95 (978-0-7910-7308-7). This book describes the causes of syphilis and its treatment, as well as its symptoms and its place in modern society. (Rev: HBG 4/04) [616.95]

10766 Silverstein, Alvin. *Cancer: Conquering a Deadly Disease* (8–12). Series: Twenty-First Century Medical Library. 2005, Twenty-First Century LB $27.93 (978-0-7613-2833-9). Using case studies to introduce topics,

693

this is a thorough exploration of new developments in the fight against cancer. (Rev: SLJ 3/06)

10767 Silverstein, Alvin. *Mononucleosis* (7–10). Series: Diseases and People. 1994, Enslow LB $20.95 (978-0-89490-466-0). Examines this disease's history, causes, treatment, prevention, and societal response. (Rev: BL 1/15/95; HBG 10/01; SLJ 3/95) [616.9]

10768 Silverstein, Alvin. *Parkinson's Disease* (7–10). Series: Diseases and People. 2001, Enslow LB $26.60 (978-0-7660-1593-7). Parkinson's disease is described, with information on its causes, symptoms. diagnosis, and treatment. (Rev: HBG 3/03) [616.8]

10769 Silverstein, Alvin, and Virginia Silverstein. *The STDs Update* (6–12). Series: Disease Update. 2006, Enslow LB $23.95 (978-0-7660-2484-7). A question-and-answer format and personal accounts of STD infections make this a useful resource. (Rev: SLJ 9/06)

10770 Silverthorne, Elizabeth. *Anorexia and Bulimia* (6–10). Series: Diseases and Disorders. 2010, Lucent $32.45 (978-1-4205-0141-4). With real-life examples and many illustrations, this book describes the causes, diagnosis, and treatment of these eating disorders. (Rev: LMC 5–6/10) [616.85]

10771 Simpson, Carolyn. *Coping with Sleep Disorders* (7–12). Series: Coping. 1995, Rosen LB $31.95 (978-0-8239-2068-6). This book discusses sleeping disorders from snoring to insomnia and offers a wide range of possible solutions. (Rev: SLJ 6/96; VOYA 8/96) [613.7]

10772 Simpson, Carolyn. *Everything You Need to Know About Asthma* (5–10). Series: Need to Know Library. 1998, Rosen LB $27.95 (978-0-8239-2567-4). Vital background information is given about the causes and effects, symptoms, and treatments of asthma. (Rev: SLJ 10/98) [616.2]

10773 Smith, Erica. *Anorexia Nervosa: When Food Is the Enemy* (6–10). Series: Teen Health Library of Eating Disorder Prevention. 1998, Rosen LB $27.95 (978-0-8239-2766-1). The author describes anorexia nervosa and its symptoms and treatment, and discusses what to do if you suspect someone is suffering from the eating disorder. Society's attitudes toward weight and body image and the role of peer pressure, media images, family relationships, and genetics are examined, along with how to deal with these influences. (Rev: SLJ 1/99) [616.85]

10774 Smith, Terry L. *Breast Cancer: Current and Emerging Trends in Detection and Treatment* (6–10). Series: Cancer and Modern Science. 2005, Rosen LB $29.25 (978-1-4042-0386-0). With photographs, diagrams, and sidebar features, this volume offers information on the diagnosis, treatment, and future issues of breast cancer, as well as ways to cope with the disease and survivor stories. (Rev: SLJ 5/06) [616.99]

10775 Sonenklar, Carol. *AIDS* (10–12). Illus. Series: USA Today Health Reports: Diseases and Disorders. 2011, Lerner/Twenty-First Century LB $34.60 (978-082258581-7). Useful for report writers, this volume covers both AIDS and the HIV virus, looks at the impact on the body, treatment, and research, and discusses AIDS' presence around the world and how patients live with the disease. **℮** (Rev: BL 5/1/11; SLJ 6/11) [616.97]

10776 Sparks, Beatrice, ed. *It Happened to Nancy* (7–12). 1994, Avon paper $6.99 (978-0-380-77315-2). In diary format, this is the story of 14-year-old Nancy, who was raped by her boyfriend and infected with the HIV virus. (Rev: BL 6/1–15/94; SLJ 6/94; VOYA 10/94) [362.196]

10777 Stanley, Debbie. *Understanding Anorexia Nervosa* (6–12). Series: Teen Eating Disorder Prevention Library. 1999, Rosen LB $31.95 (978-0-8239-2877-4). Why people get anorexia, how to get help for it, the dangers of this condition, and some of the myths surrounding it are all covered in this volume. (Rev: HBG 9/00; SLJ 2/00) [616.85]

10778 Stanley, Debbie. *Understanding Bulimia Nervosa* (6–10). Series: Teen Eating Disorder Prevention Library. 1999, Rosen $31.95 (978-0-8239-2878-1). A look at this eating disorder, in which a person binges and purges, with material on contributing factors and guidance to help recovery. (Rev: BL 10/15/99; HBG 9/00; SLJ 7/00) [616.85]

10779 Stewart, Gail B. *SARS* (9–12). Series: Diseases and Disorders. 2004, Gale LB $32.45 (978-1-59018-529-2). The story of the SARS outbreak of 2003 and the economic and healthcare implications. (Rev: SLJ 10/04) [616.2]

10780 Stewart, Gail B. *Teens with Cancer* (7–10). Photos by Carl Franzn. Series: The Other America. 2001, Gale LB $29.95 (978-1-56006-884-6). The first-person stories of four young people with life-threatening cancers reveal the hard realities such teens face. (Rev: SLJ 12/01)

10781 Stimola, Aubrey. *Ebola* (7–10). Illus. Series: Epidemics and Society. 2010, Rosen LB $30.60 (978-143589433-4). A brief but informative exploration of this disease, its discovery, the reasons why it is so deadly, and how it is treated. (Rev: BL 12/1/10) [614.57]

10782 Stokes, Mark. *Colon Cancer: Current and Emerging Trends in Detection and Treatment* (6–10). Series: Cancer and Modern Science. 2005, Rosen LB $29.25 (978-1-4042-0387-7). With photographs, diagrams, and sidebar features, this volume offers information on the diagnosis, treatment, and future issues of colon cancer, as well as ways to cope with the disease and survivor stories. Also use *Prostate Cancer* (2005). (Rev: SLJ 5/06)

10783 Stone, Tanya Lee. *Medical Causes* (5–10). Series: Celebrity Activists. 1997, Twenty-First Century LB $25.90 (978-0-8050-5233-6). The contributions of such celebrity activists as Elizabeth Taylor, Elton John, Paul Newman, Jerry Lewis, and Linda Ellerbee to various medical causes are highlighted, with material on each of their causes. (Rev: SLJ 1/98) [616]

10784 Storad, Conrad J. *Inside AIDS: HIV Attacks the Immune System* (8–12). 1998, Lerner LB $27.93 (978-0-8225-2857-9). An unusual book about the HIV virus that tells about the cellular structure of the body, its immune system, and how the virus tricks the host cells into replicating it. (Rev: BL 12/15/98; HBG 3/99; SLJ 1/99) [616.97]

10785 Taylor, Kate, ed. *Going Hungry: Writers on Desire, Self-Denial, and Overcoming Anorexia* (10–12). 2008, Anchor paper $14.95 (978-030727834-0). This volume offers 18 vivid personal accounts of grappling with anorexia. (Rev: BL 8/08) [616.85]

10786 Touchette, Nancy. *The Diabetes Problem Solver: Quick Answers to Your Questions About Treatment and Self-Care* (10–12). 1999, American Diabetes Assn. paper $19.95 (978-1-58040-009-1). A comprehensive and practical manual that covers prevention and treatment of the various symptoms of diabetes. [616.4]

10787 Trillin, Alice Stewart. *Dear Bruno* (9–12). 1996, New Press $12.00 (978-1-56584-057-7). Originally intended as a letter to a friend's son who had cancer, this work is filled with love, compassion, and humor in spite of the grim subject. (Rev: VOYA 10/96) [616.99]

10788 Vogel, Carole G. *Breast Cancer: Questions and Answers for Young Women* (6–12). 2001, Twenty-First Century LB $25.90 (978-0-7613-1855-2). Teen readers will find clear answers to both emotional and physiological questions about breasts, breast development, and breast cancer. (Rev: HBG 10/01; SLJ 5/01; VOYA 8/01) [616.99]

10789 Wagner, Viqi, ed. *AIDS* (9–12). Series: Opposing Viewpoints. 2007, Gale LB $36.20 (978-0-7377-3731-8); paper $24.95 (978-0-7377-3732-5). A thought-provoking collection of differing opinions on how best to treat, control, and prevent this disease. (Rev: BL 4/10/08) [362.196]

10790 Walters, Mark Jerome. *Six Modern Plagues and How We Are Causing Them* (10–12). 2003, Island $22.00 (978-1-55963-992-7). This chilling overview of six outbreaks of disease examines the ways in which ill-advised human actions affect the natural environment. (Rev: BL 9/15/03) [614.4]

10791 Weeldreyer, Laura. *Body Blues: Weight and Depression* (6–12). Series: Teen Health Library of Eating Disorder Prevention. 1998, Rosen LB $27.95 (978-0-8239-2761-6). This book uses case studies of three teenagers who are trying to come to terms with food and their bodies to explore the relationship between weight and depression, and encourages teenagers to learn to accept their bodies rather than aspiring to some media ideal. (Rev: SLJ 2/99) [155.5]

10792 Williams, Mary E., ed. *Epidemics* (9–12). Series: Opposing Viewpoints. 2005, Gale $36.20 (978-0-7377-2282-6); paper $24.95 (978-0-7377-2283-3). Explores various questions surrounding infectious diseases and how best to control their spread. (Rev: SLJ 7/05) [614.4]

10793 Yancey, Diane. *STDs: What You Don't Know Can Hurt You* (6–12). 2002, Millbrook LB $26.90 (978-0-7613-1957-3). The facts on common sexually transmitted diseases are combined with stories of teenagers with STDs, a section on prevention, and tests to help the reader determine his or her risk of becoming infected. (Rev: BL 4/1/02; HBG 10/02; SLJ 5/02) [616.95]

10794 Yancey, Diane. *Tuberculosis* (7–12). Series: Twenty-First Century Medical Library. 2001, Twenty-First Century LB $26.90 (978-0-7613-1624-4). Interesting illustrations and case studies draw the reader into this account of the historical and contemporary incidence of this disease. (Rev: HBG 10/01; SLJ 5/01) [616]

Doctors, Hospitals, and Medicine

10795 Adler, Robert E. *Medical Firsts: From Hippocrates to the Human Genome* (9–12). 2004, Wiley $25.95 (978-0-471-40175-9). A slender but fact-filled volume about the history of medicine starring such luminaries as Hippocrates, Pasteur, Freud, and Alexander Fleming. (Rev: BL 4/15/04) [610]

10796 Billitteri, Thomas J. *Alternative Medicine* (7–10). Series: Twenty-First Century Medical Library. 2001, Twenty-First Century LB $26.90 (978-0-7613-0965-9). This overview of alternative therapies such as hypnosis, acupuncture, and homeopathy balances success stories with solid information on the lack of rigorous scientific investigation and of FDA oversight. (Rev: HBG 3/02; SLJ 12/01; VOYA 4/02) [615.5]

10797 Boleyn-Fitzgerald, Miriam. *Ending and Extending Life* (9–12). Series: Contemporary Issues in Science. 2010, Facts on File $35 (978-0-8160-6205-8). Boleyn-Fitzgerald explores ethical questions raised by medical innovations, looking at specific cases such as Karen Quinlan and Theresa Schiavo, and at the technologies such as ventilators and tube feeding that may improve length but not quality of life. (Rev: LMC 10/10)

10798 Campbell, Andrew. *Cosmetic Surgery* (6–12). Series: Science in the News. 2010, Smart Apple Media LB $34.25 (978-1-59920-322-5). A look at developments in the field of cosmetic surgery and its benefits and pitfalls. (Rev: LMC 1–2/10)

10799 Davis, Sampson. *We Beat the Street: How a Friendship Led to Success* (7–10). 2005, Dutton $16.99 (978-0-525-47407-4). Draper recounts the inspiring story of three young men who grew up in a tough neighborhood of Newark, New Jersey, escaped the mean streets of their childhood, and went on to become doctors. (Rev: BL 4/1/05; SLJ 5/05) [610]

10800 Fleischman, John. *Phineas Gage: A Gruesome But True Story About Brain Science* (7–10). 2002, Houghton Mifflin $16.00 (978-0-618-05252-3). This riveting story of the amiable man whose personality changed when an iron rod shot through his brain presents lots of information on brain science and medical knowledge in the 19th century. (Rev: BL 3/1/02; HB 5–6/02; HBG 10/02; SLJ 3/02; VOYA 6/02) [362.1]

10801 Friedman, Meyer, and Gerald W. Friedland. *Medicine's 10 Greatest Discoveries* (10–12). 1998, Yale Univ. paper $14.95 (978-0-300-08278-4). Arranged chronologically, these 10 discoveries include the circulation of blood, penicillin, and DNA. [610.9]

10802 Goldsmith, Connie. *Superbugs Strike Back: When Antibiotics Fail* (7–10). 2007, Lerner LB $29.27 (978-0-8225-6607-6). Discusses bacteria that have becoming resistant to antibiotics, how antibiotics work, their presence in the food chain, and what can be done to deal with the problem. (Rev: BL 6/1–15/07; SLJ 8/07) [615]

10803 Kelly, Kate. *Early Civilizations: Prehistoric Times to 500 C.E.* (9–12). Series: The History of Medicine. 2009, Facts on File $40 (978-0-8160-7205-7). From Egyptian mummies to Chinese medicine and Hippocrates, this volume explores early beliefs and practices and includes images of instruments used. Also recommended is *The Middle Ages: 500–1450* (2009). (Rev: LMC 3–4/10; SLJ 1/10) [610.938]

10804 Langwith, Jacqueline, ed. *Stem Cells* (10–12). 2007, Delacorte LB $34.95 (978-0-7377-3648-9); paper $23.70 (978-0-7377-3649-6). A collection of articles, essays, and speeches that present different views and opinions on the topic of stem cells. (Rev: BL 8/07) [174.2]

10805 Lawton, Sandra Augustyn, ed. *Complementary and Alternative Medicine Information for Teens: Health Tips about Non-Traditional and Non-Western Medical Practices* (7–12). Series: Teen Health. 2006, Omnigraphics LB $65.00 (978-0-7808-0966-6). The full subtitle of this book tells it all: Health Tips About Non-Traditional and Non-Western Medical Practices Including Information About Acupuncture, Chiropractic Medicine, Dietary and Herbal Supplements, Hypnosis, Massage Therapy, Prayer and Spirituality, Reflexology, Yoga, and More. (Rev: SLJ 5/07) [610]

10806 Lusted, Marcia Amidon. *Cosmetic Surgery* (7–10). Illus. Series: Essential Viewpoints. 2009, ABDO LB $32.79 (978-1-60453-530-3). An informative discussion — drawing on published sources — of the origins, popularity, and pros and cons of cosmetic surgery. (Rev: BL 10/27/09; SLJ 1/10) [617.9]

10807 Marcovitz, Hal. *Health Care* (7–12). Series: Gallup Major Trends and Events. 2007, Mason Crest LB $22.95 (978-1-59084-964-4). A useful, chronological survey of developments in health care over the last century, looking at such topics as polio, AIDS, smoking, and obesity. (Rev: SLJ 10/07) [362.1]

10808 Marzilli, Alan. *Stem Cell Research and Cloning* (9–12). Series: Point/Counterpoint. 2007, Chelsea House LB $32.95 (978-0-7910-9230-9). Students will see both sides of these controversial issues after reading the arguments presented here. Sources are documented and students are directed to resources for additional research. (Rev: BL 2/15/07) [174.2]

10809 Merino, Noel, ed. *Vaccines* (7–10). Illus. Series: Introducing Issues with Opposing Viewpoints. 2011, Greenhaven LB $35.75 (978-073775204-5). Presents pro and con arguments on such topics as vaccines' efficacy, safety, and public health policies. (Rev: BL 12/1/11) [615]

10810 Morley, David. *Healing Our World: Inside Doctors Without Borders* (7–10). 2007, Fitzhenry & Whiteside $18.95 (978-1-55041-565-0). An introduction to the organization that helps the sick around the world, with information on global health problems and what is being done to try to solve them. (Rev: BL 3/1/07; SLJ 5/07) [610]

10811 Sherrow, Victoria. *Medical Imaging* (7–10). Series: Great Inventions. 2007, Marshall Cavendish LB $27.95 (978-0-7614-2231-0). From X-rays to ultrasound to MRI to the future, this is a review of medical imaging and its benefits. (Rev: SLJ 11/07) [616.07]

10812 Sommer, Alfred. *Getting What We Deserve: Health and Medical Care in America* (10–12). 2009, Johns Hopkins $21.95 (978-080189387-2). Dr. Sommer explains that, while modern medical advances have prolonged our lifespans, human behavior and market and economic forces prevent many from benefiting from them. **e** (Rev: BL 12/1/09) [362.1]

10813 Waters, Sophie. *Seeing the Gynecologist* (6–12). Series: Girls' Health. 2007, Rosen LB $19.95 (978-1-4042-1948-9). Girls who don't know what to expect when visiting a gynecologist will be reassured by this straightforward book. (Rev: BL 10/15/07; LMC 2/08) [618.1]

Genetics

10814 Bainbridge, David. *The X in Sex: How the X Chromosome Controls Our Lives* (10–12). 2003, Harvard $22.95 (978-0-674-01028-4). The mystery of sex determination and other aspects of genetic science are explored in detail in this readable study of gender selection and the profound effect it has on our lives. (Rev: BL 2/1/03) [611]

10815 Ballen, Karen Gunnison. *Decoding Our DNA: Craig Venter vs the Human Genome Project* (9–12). Illus. Series: Scientific Rivalries and Scandals. 2012, Lerner/Twenty-First Century LB $33.27 (978-076135489-5). A brief but informative survey of the race to sequence the human genome, best suited to readers with some prior knowledge. (Rev: BL 12/1/12; SLJ 11/1/12) [611]

10816 Cohen, Daniel. *Cloning* (7–10). 1998, Millbrook $22.90 (978-0-7613-0356-5). A balanced examination of the social and ethical concerns raised by the recent cloning of a sheep named Dolly, including the history and scientific background of this area of research and a discussion of genetic engineering. (Rev: SLJ 3/99) [575.1]

10817 Hodge, Russ. *The Molecules of Life: DNA, RNA, and Protein* (9–12). Series: Genetics and Evolution. 2009, Facts on File $39.50 (978-0-8160-6680-3). With many illustrations and clear text, this volume introduces the basics of molecular biology and goes on to discuss DNA and genes and to explain their importance in health, with information on the instruments used in this science. (Rev: LMC 3–4/10) [611]

10818 Hyde, Margaret O., and John F. Setaro. *Medicine's Brave New World: Bioengineering and the New Genetics* (7–12). 2001, Millbrook LB $29.90 (978-0-7613-1706-7). Cloning, stem cell research, and other breakthroughs in genetics are explored in this accessible book that also discusses the ethical issues faced by scientists in this field. (Rev: BL 12/15/01; HBG 10/02; SLJ 12/01; VOYA 2/02) [610]

10819 Innes, Brian. *DNA and Body Evidence* (9–12). Series: Forensic Evidence. 2007, M.E. Sharpe LB $35.95 (978-0-7656-8115-7). The author explains the science of DNA as well as its use in the courtroom, using specific cases as examples. (Rev: BL 10/15/07; LMC 2/08; SLJ 1/08) [614]

10820 Kafka, Tina. *DNA on Trial* (6–12). Series: Overview. 2004, Gale LB $29.95 (978-1-59018-337-3). Stories of DNA's use in solving criminal cases are accompanied by discussion of the technology's potential flaws and of the process involved in DNA testing. (Rev: SLJ 3/05) [614]

10821 Kurpinski, Kyle, and Terry D. Johnson. *How to Defeat Your Own Clone and Other Tips for Surviving the Biotech Revolution* (10–12). 2010, Bantam paper $14 (978-05553857-8-6). This tongue-in-cheek overview examines the science and ethics of cloning. ℮ (Rev: BLO 12/1/09) [660.6]

10822 Marcovitz, Hal. *Gene Therapy Research* (7–12). Illus. Series: Inside Science. 2010, ReferencePoint LB $26.95 (978-160152108-8). From "What is gene thera-

py" to "What is the future of gene therapy?," this is a thorough guide to research in the areas of cloning, stem cells, and methods of delivery of therapy. ℮ (Rev: BL 10/1/10) [615.8]

10823 Marcovitz, Hal. *Genetic Testing* (7–10). Illus. Series: Compact Research: Current Issues. 2010, ReferencePoint LB $26.95 (978-160152115-6). Examines how genetic testing for diseases can have both positive and negative results. (Rev: BL 4/1/11) [616]

10824 Meany, John. *Is Genetic Research a Threat?* (7–12). Series: What Do You Think? 2008, Heinemann LB $32.86 (978-1-4329-1674-9). After an explanation of the nature of genetic research, this volume discusses the topic as it relates to the individual and to society at large, crime and the law, health, and nonhuman life. (Rev: SLJ 1/1/09) [174.957]

10825 Moore, Pete. *Stem Cell Research* (8–11). Illus. Series: Ethical Debates. 2012, Rosen LB $27.95 (978-144886021-0). A balanced review of the nature of stem cells, current and past research, future possibilities, and the ethical questions involved. (Rev: BL 5/1/12) [174.2]

10826 Panno, Joseph. *Stem Cell Research: Medical Applications and Ethical Controversy* (9–12). Series: New Biology. 2004, Facts on File $35.00 (978-0-8160-4949-3). A clear and scientifically detailed look at the potential uses of stem cells, the ethical issues surrounding their use, and the legal practices in the United States and Europe. (Rev: BL 1/1–15/05; SLJ 2/05) [616]

10827 Schwartz, James. *In Pursuit of the Gene: From Darwin to DNA* (11–12). 2008, Harvard $29.95 (978-0-674-02670-4). For advanced students, this is a fascinating survey of the key figures in genetic research and their successes and failures. (Rev: BL 4/1/08) [576.509]

10828 Shannon, Thomas A. *Genetic Engineering: A Documentary History* (10–12). Series: Primary Documents in American History and Contemporary Issues. 1999, Greenwood $65.00 (978-0-313-30457-6). This is a collection of documents that deal with such topics as cloning, ethics, genetically altered food, and the Human Genome Project. [660.6]

10829 Wade, Nicholas. *Before the Dawn: Recovering the Lost History of Our Ancestors* (10–12). 2006, Penguin $24.95 (978-1-59420-079-3). Wade looks at what genetic research is revealing about our prehistoric origins and evolution as a species. (Rev: BL 4/1/06) [599.93]

10830 Walker, Denise. *Inheritance and Evolution* (7–10). Series: Basic Biology. 2006, Smart Apple Media LB $23.95 (978-1-58340-989-3). This is a well-designed introduction to the basics of genetics, inheritance, natural selection, cloning, evolution, and extinction. (Rev: BL 10/15/06) [576]

10831 Yount, Lisa. *Biotechnology and Genetic Engineering. Rev. ed.* (8–12). Series: Library in a Book. 2004, Facts on File $45.00 (978-0-8160-5059-8). An overview of genetic engineering and biotechnology, with chapters on scientific achievements, ethical concerns, court battles, health issues, and scientific problems. (Rev: SLJ 2/05) [303.48]

Grooming, Personal Appearance, and Dress

10832 Bergamotto, Lori. *Skin: The Bare Facts* (6–12). Illus. by Kunkamon Taweenuch. 2009, Zest paper $18.95 (978-0-9800732-5-6). An eye-catching layout adds appeal to this useful guide to skin care, which covers skin types, acne and other problems, makeup, and sunscreens. (Rev: SLJ 5/10; VOYA 4/10) [646.7]

10833 Dawson, Mildred L. *Beauty Lab: How Science Is Changing the Way We Look* (5–10). 1997, Silver Moon $14.95 (978-1-881889-84-7). This work on health and hygiene contains chapters on skin, eyes, teeth, fitness, and hair. (Rev: SLJ 3/97) [613.7]

10834 Espejo, Roman, ed. *The Culture of Beauty* (8–12). Illus. Series: Opposing Viewpoints. 2010, Gale/Greenhaven LB $38.50 (978-073774508-5); paper $26.75 (9780737745092). A collection of essays and article excerpts explore today's standards of beauty from various perspectives, looking at topics such as the advantages of beauty, cosmetics and cosmetic surgery, and the fashion industry. (Rev: BL 5/1/10) [306.4]

10835 Graydon, Shari. *In Your Face: The Culture of Beauty and You* (7–12). 2004, Annick paper $14.95 (978-1-55037-856-6). Graydon offers commonsense advice and reassurance to teenagers who may feel overwhelmed by the seemingly ubiquitous message that beauty is all-important. (Rev: BL 12/15/04; SLJ 3/05) [391.6/3]

10836 Libal, Autumn. *Can I Change the Way I Look? A Teen's Guide to the Health Implications of Cosmetic Surgery, Makeovers, and Beyond* (7–12). Series: The Science of Health. 2005, Mason Crest LB $24.95 (978-1-59804-843-8). Libal clearly lays out the pitfalls of obsessing about body image, as well as the risks involved in piercing, tattooing, eating disorders, cosmetic surgery, and even common cosmetic products. (Rev: SLJ 7/05) [613.4]

10837 Mason, Linda. *Teen Makeup: Looks to Match Your Every Mood* (6–12). 2004, Watson-Guptill paper $16.95 (978-0-8230-2980-8). A photograph-filled how-to guide to the basics of skin care and makeup. (Rev: SLJ 11/04)

10838 Murray, Maggie Pexton. *Changing Styles in Fashion: Who, What, Why* (10–12). 1989, Fairchild $48.00 (978-0-87005-585-0). The world of high fashion past and present is introduced and several modern couturiers are highlighted. (Rev: BL 4/15/89) [746.92]

10839 Warrick, Leanne. *Hair Trix for Cool Chix: The Real Girl's Guide to Great Hair* (6–12). Illus. by Debbie Boon. 2004, Watson-Guptill paper $9.95 (978-0-8230-2179-6). From quizzes and practical tips to step-by-step directions for different styles and accessories, this is a reader-friendly guide to hair care. (Rev: SLJ 7/04) [391.5]

10840 Weiss, Stefanie Iris. *Coping with the Beauty Myth: A Guide for Real Girls* (7–12). Series: Coping. 2002, Rosen LB $31.95 (978-0-8239-3757-8). Readers are urged to ignore unrealistic images presented in the media and to accept their own attributes and deficiencies as well as those of others. (Rev: SLJ 8/00) [155.5]

10841 Wells, Linda. *Allure: Confessions of a Beauty Editor* (9–12). 2006, Bulfinch $24.99 (978-0-8212-5779-1). *Allure* magazine's editor in chief presents step-by-step beauty procedures, enumerates 10 "commandments," and dispels common myths. (Rev: BL 10/15/06) [646.7]

10842 Williams, Heidi, ed. *Body Image* (9–12). Illus. Series: Issues That Concern You. 2008, Gale/Greenhaven $33.70 (978-0-7377-4182-7). Articles consider various aspects of our perceptions of ourselves and the importance of heredity, diet, and media and social forces, along with options such as plastic surgery and weight-loss surgery. (Rev: SLJ 3/1/09) [306.4]

The Human Body

General and Miscellaneous

10843 Ackerman, Jennifer. *Sex Sleep Eat Drink Dream: A Day in the Life of Your Body* (9–12). 2007, Houghton Mifflin $25.00 (978-0-618-18758-4). Ackerman, a science journalist, offers an inside look at bodily processes and healthy living. (Rev: BL 9/1/07) [612]

10844 Bobick, James, and Naomi Balaban. *The Handy Anatomy Answer Book* (9–12). 2008, Visible Ink paper $21.95 (978-1-57859-190-9). Using a question-and-answer format, this volume covers the various body systems. (Rev: BL 12/08; SLJ 8/08) [611]

10845 Brynie, Faith Hickman. *101 Questions About Your Immune System You Felt Defenseless to Answer . . . Until Now* (7–12). 2000, Twenty-First Century $27.90 (978-0-7613-1569-8). A question-and-answer format is used to explain the functioning and vulnerabilities of the immune system. (Rev: BL 6/1–15/00; HBG 9/00; SLJ 9/00; VOYA 4/01) [616.07]

10846 Brynie, Faith Hickman. *101 Questions About Your Skin* (7–12). Illus. by Sharon Lane Holm. Series: 101 Questions. 1999, Twenty-First Century LB $27.90 (978-0-7613-1259-8). This comprehensive, well-illustrated look at the composition, care, and diseases of the skin also includes information on tattooing, the effects of the sun, and aging and will attract both report writers and browsers. (Rev: HBG 4/00; SLJ 11/99) [612.7]

10847 Esherick, Joan. *Balancing Act: A Teen's Guide to Managing Stress* (9–12). Series: The Science of Health: Youth and Well-being. 2005, Mason Crest LB $24.95 (978-1-59084-853-1). A look at the effects of stress on teens, outlining steps that can be taken to cope more effectively with the pressures of everyday life. Also in this series are *Dead on Their Feet: Teen Sleep Deprivation and Its Consequences* and *The Silent Cry: A Teen's Guide to Escaping Self-Injury and Suicide* (both 2005). (Rev: SLJ 6/05)

10848 *Incredible Voyage: Exploring the Human Body* (9–12). 1998, National Geographic $35.00 (978-0-7922-7148-2). Interesting text and outstanding photographs trace human growth, anatomy, and physiology through all stages of life, sick or healthy, with information on many of the innovative, developing breakthroughs that are in the news. (Rev: SLJ 2/99) [612]

10849 Kim, Melissa L. *The Endocrine and Reproductive Systems* (5–10). Series: Human Body Library. 2003, Enslow LB $23.93 (978-0-7660-2020-7). Kim uses a conversational style to introduce detailed facts about these two body systems, with useful graphics and some practical advice. (Rev: BL 4/15/03; HBG 10/03) [612.4]

10850 Macaulay, David. *The Way We Work: Getting to Know the Amazing Human Body* (7–12). Illus. by author. 2008, Houghton Mifflin $35.00 (978-061823378-6). Whimsically illustrated, this book provides a broad, accessible tour of the human body and the myriad complex systems that make it work. Boston Globe–Horn Book Honor 2009; ALA Notable Books 2009. (Rev: BL 10/15/08; HB 9–10/08; LMC 5–6/09; SLJ 10/1/08*; VOYA 1008) [610]

10851 McNally, Robert Aquinas, ed. *Skin Health Information for Teens: Health Tips About Dermatological Concerns and Skin Cancer Risks* (7–12). Series: Teen Health. 2003, Omnigraphics $58.00 (978-0-7808-0446-3). Detailed information is provided on health problems and risks including acne, cosmetics, tanning, tattoos, and piercing. (Rev: SLJ 1/04; VOYA 2/04) [616.5]

10852 Rosen, Marvin. *Sleep and Dreaming* (6–12). Series: Gray Matter. 2005, Chelsea House LB $35.00 (978-0-7910-8639-1). Snoring, sleepwalking, and night terrors are among the topics covered in this survey of our sleep processes and our dreams; Freudian and Jungian theories are also addressed. (Rev: SLJ 3/06) [616]

10853 Walker, Richard. *Firefly Guide to the Human Body* (10–12). 2004, Firefly paper $14.95 (978-1-55297-879-5). Introductory material on the composition of the body is followed by information on each body system and a glossary defining parts of the body, diseases, and medical procedures; a small-format, well-illustrated guide. (Rev: SLJ 6/04; VOYA 6/04) [612]

10854 Weiss, Marisa C., and Isabel Friedman. *Taking Care of Your "Girls": A Breast Health Guide for Girls, Teens, and In-Betweens* (6–12). Illus. 2008, Three Rivers $15.95 (978-030740696-5). Health, beauty, fashion, and personal aspects of breasts and bras are discussed in a conversational tone. e (Rev: BLO 10/7/08) [618.1]

Brain and Nervous System

10855 August, Paul Nordstrom. *Brain Function* (9–12). 1987, Chelsea LB $19.95 (978-0-555-46204-1). An introduction to the nervous system that gives details on the brain and how drugs affect it. (Rev: BL 2/15/88) [612]

10856 Brynie, Faith Hickman. *101 Questions About Sleep and Dreams that Kept You Awake Nights . . . Until Now* (8–11). 2006, Lerner LB $27.93 (978-0-7613-2312-9). This is a sleep information handbook for teens, answering questions about dreaming, stages of sleep, the effect of sleep on the brain and body, and related topics. (Rev: BL 5/15/06) [612.8]

10857 Policoff, Stephen P. *The Dreamer's Companion: A Beginner's Guide to Understanding Dreams and Using Them Creatively* (8–12). 1997, Chicago Review paper $12.95 (978-1-55652-280-2). This book covers mastering the art of lucid dreaming, the causes of dreams, how to analyze them, and how to keep a dream journal. (Rev: BL 5/15/98; SLJ 6/98) [154.63]

10858 Ratey, John J., and Albert M. Galaburda. *A User's Guide to the Brain: Perception, Attention, and the Four Theaters of the Brain* (10–12). 2001, Pantheon paper $14.95 (978-0-375-70107-8). This account introduces the parts of the brain, explains their functions, and gives advice on how to maintain a healthy brain. [612.8]

10859 Saab, Carl Y. *The Spinal Cord* (6–12). Series: Gray Matter. 2005, Chelsea House LB $35.00 (978-0-7910-8511-0). Explores the importance of the spinal cord to the whole nervous system and discusses the impact of disorders and injuries. (Rev: SLJ 3/06)

10860 Vera-Portocarrero, Louis. *Brain Facts* (9–12). Series: Gray Matter. 2007, Chelsea House LB $32.95 (978-0-7910-8956-9). A challenging but highly informative survey of the brain and how it functions. (Rev: BL 5/15/07) [612.8]

Circulatory System

10861 Avraham, Regina. *Circulatory System* (9–12). Series: 21st Century Health and Wellness. 2000, Chelsea House LB $24.95 (978-0-7910-5519-9). The organs of the circulatory system are described, with a discussion of heart problems and their prevention. [612.1]

10862 Silverstein, Alvin, and Virginia Silverstein. *Heart Disease* (8–12). 2006, Twenty-First Century LB $27.93 (978-0-7613-3420-0). This informative and easy-to-understand book explains the causes, treatment, and prevention of heart disease, using true stories as examples and incorporating medical information and photographs. (Rev: SLJ 8/06)

Digestive and Excretory Systems

10863 Magee, Elaine. *Tell Me What to Eat if I Have Irritable Bowel Syndrome* (8–12). 2008, Rosen LB $23.95 (978-140421836-9). This book provides a wealth of information — and debunks some pervasive IBS myths — in an approachable, matter-of-fact manner. (Rev: BL 10/15/08) [616.3]

10864 Monroe, Judy. *Coping with Ulcers, Heartburn, and Stress-Related Stomach Disorders* (7–12). Series: Coping. 2000, Rosen LB $31.95 (978-0-8239-2971-9). Fictional case histories convey lots of information about a variety of uncomfortable stomach conditions, stressing the importance of prevention and early treatment. (Rev: SLJ 6/00) [616.3]

Musculoskeletal System

10865 Brynie, Faith Hickman. *101 Questions About Muscles: To Stretch Your Mind and Flex Your Brain* (7–12). Series: 101 Questions. 2007, Lerner LB $30.60 (978-0-8225-6380-8). Entertaining and interesting, this book uses a question-and-answer format to explore questions of interest to athletes, browsers, and researchers. (Rev: BL 12/1/07; SLJ 6/08) [612.7]

Respiratory System

10866 Whittemore, Susan. *The Respiratory System* (7–12). Series: The Human Body: How It Works. 2009, Chelsea House $35 (978-1-60413-375-2). The functioning of the respiratory system is clearly explained, and there is discussion of diseases affecting it. (Rev: LMC 5–6/10) [612.2]

Senses

10867 Gilbert, Avery. *What the Nose Knows: The Science of Scent in Everyday Life* (10–12). 2008, Crown $23.95 (978-140008234-6). In this surprisingly humorous volume, Gilbert explores the science of smells, from origins to commercial uses. **e** (Rev: BL 7/08; SLJ 2/09) [612.8]

10868 Light, Douglas B. *The Senses* (7–12). Series: The Human Body: How It Works. 2009, Chelsea House $35 (978-1-60413-362-2). Sight, smell, taste, touch, and hearing are all examined here, as well as thirst and hunger, with interesting factboxes and clear illustrations. (Rev: LMC 5–6/10) [612.8]

Hygiene and Physical Fitness

10869 Feuerstein, Georg, and Stephan Bodian, eds. *Living Yoga: A Comprehensive Guide for Daily Life* (9–12). 1993, Putnam paper $16.95 (978-0-87477-729-1). Interviews, essays, and articles on yoga's practices and teachings. (Rev: BL 3/15/93) [181.45]

10870 Finney, Sumukhi. *The Yoga Handbook* (8–12). Illus. 2009, Rosen LB $39.95 (978-143585359-1). For beginners, this is a clear introduction to the physical, mental, and spiritual aspects of yoga, with information on breathing, diet, and meditation plus step-by-step directions for poses. (Rev: BL 4/1/10) [613.7]

10871 Johnson, Marlys. *Understanding Exercise Addiction* (7–12). Series: Teen Eating Disorder Prevention Library. 2000, Rosen LB $31.95 (978-0-8239-2990-0). This book offers teens the opportunity to assess whether attitudes toward exercise, eating, and the human body are normal. (Rev: SLJ 7/00) [616.86]

10872 Kaminker, Laura. *Exercise Addiction: When Fitness Becomes an Obsession* (6–10). Series: Teen Health Library of Eating Disorder Prevention. 1998, Rosen LB $27.95 (978-0-8239-2759-3). Some teens become addicted to exercise and exercise too much for the wrong reasons. This book defines the problem, risks, and causes, describes the symptoms, and tells where to get help and support if needed. (Rev: BL 3/1/89; SLJ 1/99) [613.7]

10873 Kennedy, Denis. *Pilates for Beginners* (10–12). Illus. Series: From Couch to Conditioned: A Beginner's Guide to Getting Fit. 2011, Rosen LB $31.95 (978-144884815-7). Explores the basics of Pilates, with information on the six basic principles and suggestions for 36 exercises of increasing difficulty. (Rev: BL 12/1/11; SLJ 1/12) [613.7]

10874 Vedral, Joyce L. *Toning for Teens: The 20-Minute Workout That Makes You Look Good and Feel Great!* (7–12). 2002, Warner paper $15.95 (978-0-446-67815-5). Three sets of dumbbells and a bench or step are the only items required for this daily workout; nutritional and fitness tips are included. (Rev: SLJ 8/02)

Mental Disorders and Emotional Problems

10875 Allman, Toney. *Autism* (6–10). Series: Diseases and Disorders. 2010, Lucent $32.45 (978-1-4205-0143-8). With real-life examples and many illustrations, this book describes the causes, diagnosis, and treatment of autism and discusses the prospects of finding a cure. (Rev: LMC 5–6/10) [616.8]

10876 Bellenir, Karen, ed. *Mental Health Information for Teens: Health Tips About Mental Wellness and Mental Illness.* 2nd ed. (6–12). Series: Teen Health. 2006, Omnigraphics $58 (978-0-7808-0863-8). A revised edition of this comprehensive and easy-to-use overview of topics relating to mental health — specific disorders, coping mechanisms, treatment, and so forth — with a new emphasis on self-injury and bullying. (Rev: SLJ 12/06)

10877 Bernstein, Jane. *Loving Rachel: A Family's Journey from Grief* (9–12). 1994, Coyne & Chenoweth paper $15.00 (978-0-941038-01-0). A mother's story of how she raised her second daughter who was born with learning disorders. (Rev: BL 5/1/88) [362.3]

10878 Bonnice, Sherry, and Carolyn Hoard. *Drug Therapy and Cognitive Disorders* (6–10). Series: Psychiatric Disorders: Drugs and Psychology for the Mind and Body. 2003, Mason Crest LB $24.95 (978-1-59084-562-2). Diagrams and charts reinforce the easily read text, which includes discussion of the nature of these disorders and how they are treated plus personal anecdotes from one of the authors. (Rev: SLJ 5/04)

10879 Bowman-Kruhm, Mary, and Claudine G. Wirths. *Everything You Need to Know About Learning Disabilities* (6–12). Series: Need to Know Library. 1999, Rosen LB $27.95 (978-0-8239-2956-6). An introduction to learning disabilities and how people cope with them at school and in everyday life, with fictionalized case studies and information on getting help. (Rev: SLJ 1/00; VOYA 4/00) [616.85]

10880 Cobain, Bev. *When Nothing Matters Anymore: A Survival Guide for Depressed Teens* (7–12). 1998, Free Spirit paper $13.95 (978-1-57542-036-3). The author, a psychiatric nurse who works with teens, discusses the types, causes, and warning signs of depression, the dangers of addictions and eating disorders, and the relationship between depression and suicide, and provides information on treatment options and suggestions for developing good mental and physical health. (Rev: SLJ 3/99; VOYA 2/99) [155]

10881 Connelly, Elizabeth Russell. *A World Upside Down and Backwards* (9–12). Series: Encyclopedia of Psychological Disorders. 1998, Chelsea $35.00 (978-0-7910-4894-8). Using brief case studies, this book explores the realities of dyslexia and other learning disorders, with material on the neurological and genetic origins and treatments, as well as examples of how they affect the classroom, family life, and society. Case studies of famous people who have overcome their learning disorder are included. (Rev: BL 4/1/99; SLJ 6/99) [371.91]

10882 Connolly, Sucheta. *Anxiety Disorders* (10–12). Series: Psychological Disorders. 2006, Chelsea House $37.50 (978-0-7910-8543-1). Covers the many different kinds of anxiety disorders — panic attacks, phobias, obsessive-compulsive behavior, and so forth — with information on causes, diagnoses, and treatments. (Rev: BL 10/1/06) [155]

10883 Connors, Paul, ed. *Suicide* (9–12). Series: Current Controversies. 2007, Gale LB $34.95 (978-0-7377-2488-2); paper $23.70 (978-0-7377-2489-9). A collection of essays about the ethics of suicide, including doctor-assisted suicide and suicide bombing. (Rev: BL 1/1–15/08) [179.7]

10884 Corman, Catherine A., and Edward M. Hallowell. *Positively ADD: Real Success Stories to Inspire Your Dreams* (7–10). 2006, Walker $16.95 (978-0-8027-8988-4). Aimed at children with attention deficit disorder, this book includes profiles of successful adults who had ADD beginning in childhood. (Rev: BL 6/1–15/06; LMC 11–12/06; SLJ 9/06) [616.85]

10885 Davis, Brangien. *What's Real, What's Ideal: Overcoming a Negative Body Image* (7–12). Series: Teen Health Library of Eating Disorder Prevention. 1998, Rosen LB $27.95 (978-0-8239-2771-5). Because teenager's bodies are changing so quickly, many become confused about an ideal figure. This book describes why teens develop negative body images and offers suggestions for overcoming self-defeating perceptions. (Rev: VOYA 4/99) [305.23]

10886 Empfield, Maureen, and Nicholas Bakalar. *Understanding Teenage Depression: A Guide to Diagnosis, Treatment, and Management* (10–12). 2001, Henry Holt paper $15.00 (978-0-8050-6761-3). This succinct resource for both parents and teens offers current information on the diagnosis and treatment of teenage depression, with information on both drug and "talk" therapies. (Rev: BL 8/01) [616.85]

10887 Farrell, Courtney. *Mental Disorders* (7–10). Series: Essential Issues. 2010, ABDO LB $32.79 (978-1-60453-956-1). The nature of mental disorders and their impact on society, treatment, and associated stigma are all discussed here along with the role of medical professionals and various key pieces of legislation. (Rev: LMC 10/10; SLJ 4/1/10) [362.2]

10888 Fox, Annie, and Ruth Kirschner. *Too Stressed to Think? A Teen Guide to Staying Sane When Life Makes You Crazy* (7–12). 2005, Free Spirit paper $14.95 (978-1-57542-173-5). A handy review of stress, how to reduce it and how to prevent the external forces that cause it, with tips and various scenarios that illustrate relevant situations. (Rev: SLJ 6/06)

10889 Fynn, Anna. *Mister God, This Is Anna* (10–12). 1985, Ballantine paper $5.99 (978-0-345-32722-2). The haunting story of the life and death of a London waif. [155.4]

10890 Grollman, Earl A., and Max Malikow. *Living When a Young Friend Commits Suicide: Or Even Starts Talking About It* (6–12). 1999, Beacon paper $12.00 (978-0-8070-2503-1). Using simple prose and a compassionate attitude, this book examines suicide from many standpoints and gives good advice on the grieving process. (Rev: BL 11/1/99; SLJ 1/00; VOYA 2/00) [368.28]

10891 Hayden, Torey L. *Ghost Girl: The Story of a Child Who Refused to Talk* (9–12). 1992, HarperCollins paper $7.99 (978-0-380-71681-4). The story of a traumatized 8-year-old who refused to speak and was helped by a caring, committed teacher. (Rev: BL 5/15/91) [362.1]

10892 Hayden, Torey L. *One Child* (10–12). 2002, HarperCollins paper $7.99 (978-0-380-54262-8). The story of an emotionally disturbed 6-year-old girl and the course of her treatment by the author; first published in 1981. [155.4]

10893 Hermes, Patricia. *A Time to Listen: Preventing Youth Suicide* (8–12). 1987, Harcourt $13.95 (978-0-15-288196-2). Through questions and answers plus many case studies, the author explores many aspects of suicidal behavior and its causes. (Rev: BL 4/1/88; SLJ 3/88; VOYA 6/88) [362.2]

10894 Huddle, Lorena, and Jay Schleifer. *Teen Suicide* (7–10). Illus. Series: Teen Mental Health. 2011, Rosen LB $27.95 (978-144884586-6). With information about warning signs of impending suicide, prevention and intervention, and coping with grief, this book will be helpful for report writers and those seeking personal guidance. (Rev: BL 11/15/11) [302.3]

10895 Hyde, Margaret O., and Elizabeth H. Forsyth. *Stress 101: An Overview for Teens* (7–10). Series: Teen Overviews. 2008, Lerner LB $26.60 (978-0-8225-6788-2). A thorough survey of the kinds of stress we suffer, their origins, their impact on our body, and ways to reduce and deal with stress. (Rev: BL 1/1–15/08; SLJ 4/08) [616.9]

10896 Hyman, Bruce M., and Cherry Pedroch. *Obsessive-Compulsive Disorder* (7–10). 2003, Millbrook LB $26.90 (978-0-7613-2758-5). Profiles of teens with OCD introduce a discussion of the condition that will aid understanding and will be useful for teens experiencing anxieties. (Rev: BL 12/15/03; HBG 4/04; SLJ 1/04; VOYA 2/04) [616.85]

10897 Irwin, Cait. *Monochrome Days: A Firsthand Account of One Teenager's Experience with Depression* (8–12). Series: Adolescent Mental Health Initiative. 2007, Oxford Univ $30.00 (978-0-19-531004-7); paper $9.95 (978-0-19-531005-4). Irwin chronicles her own experience with depression — which began in 8th grade and included suicidal thoughts and inpatient treatment — and her co-authors add practical information about symptoms, treatment, and so forth. (Rev: SLJ 7/07) [616.85]

10898 Kaysen, Susanna. *Girl, Interrupted* (10–12). 1994, Vintage paper $12.00 (978-0-679-74604-1). At the age of 18, the author was hospitalized in psychiatry ward for teens; the brief essays in this book describe with perception and wit her own experiences and those of other patients. (Rev: BL 4/1/93) [362]

10899 Kent, Deborah. *Snake Pits, Talking Cures, and Magic Bullets: A History of Mental Illness* (6–12). 2003, Millbrook LB $26.90 (978-0-7613-2704-2). The madhouses of old, shock treatments, psychotherapy, psychoanalysis, and today's effective drug therapies are among the topics discussed in this volume. (Rev: BL 5/1/03; HBG 4/04; SLJ 7/03) [616.89]

10900 Levin, Judith. *Anxiety and Panic Attacks* (7–10). Illus. Series: Teen Mental Health. 2008, Rosen LB $19.95 (978-140421797-3). Teens curious about — or perhaps afflicted by — anxiety disorders will find much practical, comforting advice and information in this helpful guide. (Rev: BL 10/15/08) [616.85]

10901 Levine, Mel. *Keeping a Head in School: A Student's Book About Learning Abilities and Learning Disorders* (8–12). 1990, Educators Publg. paper $24.75 (978-0-8388-2069-8). This account deals with all sorts of learning disorders, how they affect the learning process, and how they can be treated. (Rev: BL 6/15/90) [371.9]

10902 Libal, Autumn. *Runaway Train: Youth with Emotional Disturbance* (7–12). Series: Youth with Special Needs. 2004, Mason Crest LB $24.95 (978-1-59084-732-9). The story of a disturbed high school student who resorts to cutting herself is combined with facts about the causes, symptoms, and treatment of severe emotional disturbance. (Rev: SLJ 12/04)

10903 Marcovitz, Hal. *Bipolar Disorders* (6–10). Illus. Series: Compact Research. 2009, ReferencePoint $25.95 (978-1-60152-066-1). Marcovitz provides a thorough and readable guide to the causes, symptoms, and treatment of bipolar disorders. (Rev: SLJ 6/1/09) [516]

10904 Meisel, Abigail. *Investigating Depression and Bipolar Disorder: Real Facts for Real Lives* (7–10). Series: Investigating Diseases. 2010, Enslow LB $34.60 (978-0-7660-3340-5). Symptoms, diagnosis, treatment, and current research are all covered in this book that also tells the stories of children coping with these problems and provides historical background. (Rev: LMC 10/10) [616.85]

10905 Metcalf, Tom, and Gena Metcalf. *Phobias* (6–10). Series: Perspectives on Diseases and Disorders. 2008, Gale/Greenhaven $34.95 (978-0-7377-4027-1). A collection of articles that discuss the symptoms, causes, and treatment of phobias, with interesting first-person accounts. (Rev: SLJ 2/1/09) [616.85]

10906 Miller, Allen R. *Living with Depression* (6–12). Series: Teen's Guides. 2007, Facts on File LB $34.95 (978-0-8160-6345-1). This guide to recognizing and treating depression will help teenagers with the disease and those who know others who suffer with it. (Rev: BL 10/15/07) [618.92]

10907 Moe, Barbara. *Coping with Mental Illness* (7–10). Series: Coping. 2001, Rosen LB $31.95 (978-0-8239-3205-4). The diagnosis, symptoms, and treatment of major forms of mental illness are discussed, along with the types of professionals who can help. Also use *Schizophrenia* (2001). (Rev: SLJ 8/01) [616.89]

10908 Moehn, Heather. *Social Anxiety* (7–12). 2001, Rosen LB $31.95 (978-0-8239-3363-1). A strong fear of social situations often manifests itself during adolescence, and Moehn combines case studies and coping strategies with an overview of the condition itself and a look at treatment alternatives. (Rev: BL 3/1/02; SLJ 5/02) [616.85]

10909 Mooney, Carla. *Mental Illness Research* (8–11). Illus. Series: Inside Science. 2012, ReferencePoint LB $27.95 (978-160152234-4). Discusses the causes, diagnosis, and treatment of mental disorders, with a focus on future techniques. (Rev: BL 7/12) [362.196]

10910 Mooney, Carla. *Mood Disorders* (7–12). Illus. Series: Compact Research: Diseases and Disorders. 2010, ReferencePoint LB $26.95 (978-160152119-4). Unipolar and bipolar mood disorders are introduced with statistics, primary source quotations, and information on treatment and support. (Rev: BL 2/1/11) [616.85]

10911 Moragne, Wendy. *Depression* (7–12). Series: Medical Library. 2001, Twenty-First Century LB $24.90 (978-0-7613-1774-6). Signs, symptoms, diagnosis, and treatment of depression are introduced clearly and concisely with case histories of seven teenagers. (Rev: BL 5/15/01; HBG 10/01; SLJ 4/01; VOYA 10/01) [616.85]

10912 Nakaya, Andrea C. *ADHD* (7–12). Illus. Series: Compact Research: Diseases and Disorders. 2009, ReferencePoint LB $25.95 (978-160152062-3). A balanced overview of attention deficit hyperactivity disorder and its symptoms and treatment. (Rev: BL 4/1/09; SLJ 6/1/09) [618.92]

10913 Paquette, Penny Hutchins, and Cheryl Gerson Tuttle. *Learning Disabilities: The Ultimate Teen Guide* (7–12). Series: It Happened to Me. 2003, Scarecrow LB $32.50 (978-0-8108-4261-8). Teens suffering from conditions including ADHD and dyslexia will find practical information on these disabilities, success stories, and advice on career and employment choices and strategies. (Rev: SLJ 10/03) [371.9]

10914 Parks, Peggy J. *Alzheimer's Disease* (6–10). Illus. Series: Compact Research: Diseases and Disorders. 2009, ReferencePoint $25.95 (978-1-60152-061-6). This accessible, illustrated book provides a thorough and readable guide to the causes, symptoms, and treatment of Alzheimer's disease. (Rev: SLJ 6/1/09) [616.831]

10915 Parks, Peggy J. *Autism* (7–12). Illus. Series: Compact Research: Diseases and Disorders. 2008, ReferencePoint LB $25.95 (978-160152058-6). "What causes autism?" and "How effective are autism treatments?" are among the questions discussed in this thoughtful and attractive volume. (Rev: BL 4/1/09; LMC 8–9/09) [616.85]

10916 Parks, Peggy J. *Down Syndrome* (7–12). Series: Compact Research. 2009, ReferencePoint $25.95 (978-1-60152-065-4). In this broad overview of Down syndrome, Parks focuses on the genetic causes and ethical considerations surrounding the disorder, also discussing technology that may prevent it in the future. (Rev: SLJ 6/1/09) [362.1]

10917 Parks, Peggy J. *Obsessive-Compulsive Disorder* (7–12). Illus. Series: Compact Research: Diseases and Disorders. 2010, ReferencePoint LB $26.95 (978-160152120-0). The causes and symptoms of OCD are introduced with statistics, primary source quotations, and information on treatment and support. (Rev: BL 2/1/11)

10918 Parks, Peggy J. *Self-Injury Disorder* (7–12). Illus. Series: Compact Research: Diseases and Disorders. 2010, ReferencePoint LB $26.95 (978-160152112-5). The reasons for self-mutilation are introduced with statistics, primary source quotations, and information on treatment and support. (Rev: BL 2/1/11) [618.92]

10919 Peirce, Jeremy. *Attention-Deficit/Hyperactivity Disorder* (9–12). Series: Psychological Disorders. 2008, Chelsea House LB $37.50 (978-0-7910-8541-7). An overview of what this disorder is; how its description, diagnosis, and treatment have changed over the years; and how people cope with it. (Rev: BL 4/15/08) [616.85]

10920 Porterfield, Kay Marie. *Straight Talk About Learning Disabilities* (6–12). 1999, Facts on File $27.45 (978-0-8160-3865-7). Using three fictional case studies, the author discusses various kinds of learning disabilities, their symptoms, methods of diagnosis, and available treatments. (Rev: BL 2/15/00; HBG 4/00; SLJ 2/00; VOYA 4/00) [371.92]

10921 Portner, Jessica. *One in Thirteen: The Silent Epidemic of Teen Suicide* (10–12). 2001, Gryphon House paper $13.00 (978-1-58904-001-4). As well as exploring the reasons why one in 13 U.S. teens attempts suicide, this account focuses on the case histories of three who succeeded. (Rev: BL 4/1/01; SLJ 8/01) [362.28]

10922 Powell, Mark. *Stress Relief: The Ultimate Teen Guide* (7–12). Illus. by Kelly Adams. Series: Ultimate Teen Guide. 2003, Scarecrow LB $32.50 (978-0-8108-4433-9). Typical causes of teen stress — relationships, homework, money, and so forth — are examined and practical suggestions for dealing with them are spelled out. (Rev: BL 10/15/03; SLJ 7/03; VOYA 4/03) [155.5]

10923 Prince-Hughes, Dawn, ed. *Aquamarine Blue 5: Personal Stories of College Students with Autism* (10–12). 2002, Ohio Univ. $32.95 (978-0-8040-1053-5); paper $14.95 (978-0-8040-1054-2). A collection of inspiring personal stories that will give insight to "normal" people. (Rev: BL 11/15/02) [371.94]

10924 Quinn, Patricia O. *Adolescents and ADD: Gaining the Advantage* (6–12). 1996, Magination paper $12.95 (978-0-945354-70-3). As well as citing many case studies, this book on teens and attention deficit disorder provides useful background information plus tips on how to adjust to this condition and how to create a lifestyle that accommodates it. (Rev: BL 1/1–15/96; SLJ 3/96; VOYA 8/96) [371.94]

10925 Rodriguez, Ana Maria. *Autism Spectrum Disorders* (10–12). Illus. Series: USA Today Health Reports: Diseases and Disorders. 2011, Lerner/Twenty-First Century LB $34.60 (978-076135883-1). Useful for report writers, this volume describes autism and the spectrum, along with the causes, diagnosis, treatment, and research being conducted. **e** (Rev: BL 5/1/11; SLJ 6/11) [616.85]

10926 Rogers, Annie G. *The Unsayable: The Hidden Language of Trauma* (11–12). 2006, Random House $25.95 (978-1-4000-6195-2). A former psychiatric patient and trauma victim discusses the use of creative therapies developed by Jacques Lacan to help children recover from abuse and mental illness. (Rev: BL 8/06) [618.92]

10927 Rosenberg, Marsha Sarah. *Coping When a Brother or Sister Is Autistic* (7–12). Series: Coping. 2001, Rosen LB $31.95 (978-0-8239-3194-1). Siblings of autistic children will find facts about the diagnosis and treatment of the disorder, as well as sympathetic, no-nonsense advice on dealing with the pressures of the situation. (Rev: SLJ 9/01) [618.92]

10928 Schutz, Samantha. *I Don't Want to Be Crazy* (9–12). 2006, Scholastic $16.99 (978-0-439-80518-6). This is a moving record, written in verse, of Schutz's struggles with anxiety disorder, which afflicted her through her college years and affected all areas of her life. (Rev: LMC 3/07*; SLJ 1/07)

10929 Scowen, Kate. *My Kind of Sad: What It's Like to Be Young and Depressed* (7–12). Illus. by Jeff Szuc. 2006, Firefly $19.95 (978-1-55037-941-9); paper $10.95 (978-1-55037-940-2). Describes depression and how to tell between normal moods and feelings and what could be harmful; additional information on treatments and medications is included. (Rev: BL 9/15/06; SLJ 2/07) [616.85.5]

10930 Shields, Charles J. *Mental Illness and Its Effects on School and Work Environments* (6–10). Series: Encyclopedia of Psychological Disorders. 2000, Chelsea $35.00 (978-0-7910-5318-8). As well as giving a general introduction to the nature of mental illness, this work discusses how the mentally ill affect American society. (Rev: BL 11/1/00) [616.8]

10931 Shivack, Nadia. *Inside Out: Portrait of an Eating Disorder* (9–12). Illus. by author. 2007, Atheneum

$17.99 (978-068985216-9). The horrors of severe eating disorders are clearly shown in this book that combines a graphic novel format with fact boxes. (Rev: LMC 3/08; SLJ 7/07)

10932 Siana, Jolene. *Go Ask Ogre: Letters from a Death-rock Cutter* (11–12). 2005, Process paper $18.95 (978-0-9760822-1-7). Seventeen-year-old Siana's letters to a punk rocker named Ogre reveal her depression, her self-mutilation, drug and alcohol abuse, and also her creativity; resources for young people suffering similar problems are appended. (Rev: SLJ 1/06) [362.7]

10933 Simpson, Carolyn, and Dwain Simpson. *Coping with Post-Traumatic Stress Disorder* (7–10). Series: Coping. 1997, Rosen LB $25.25 (978-0-8239-2080-8). Post-traumatic stress disorder (PTSD) affects people who have experienced natural disasters, rape, war, or other traumatic events. This book explains the causes and primary signs of PTSD and how it affects family and friends, as well as the victim, and provides useful information on treatment. (Rev: SLJ 10/97) [362]

10934 Snyder, Kurt, et al. *Me, Myself, and Them: A Firsthand Account of One Young Person's Experience with Schizophrenia* (10–12). 2007, Oxford $30.00 (978-0-19-531123-5). This is a compelling account of one person's schizophrenia — its onset, impact, and treatment — but also a valuable guide for others with this problem and their friends and family. (Rev: SLJ 1/08) [616.89]

10935 Stewart, Gail B. *People with Mental Illness* (7–12). Series: The Other America. 2003, Gale LB $29.95 (978-1-59018-237-6). Personal stories of individuals with different conditions show how they cope with daily life and the impact on the families as well as the patients. (Rev: SLJ 6/03) [616.89]

10936 Thakkar, Vatsal. *Depression and Bipolar Disorder* (9–12). Ed. by Christine Collins. Series: Psychological Disorders. 2006, Chelsea House $37.50 (978-079108542-4). Thakkar discusses the causes, symptoms, diagnosis, and treatment of these disorders. (Rev: SLJ 12/06)

10937 Toews, Miriam. *Swing Low* (10–12). 2001, Arcade $23.95 (978-1-55970-587-5). The memoir by a daughter whose father suffered from manic depression and, without suitable treatment, committed suicide. (Rev: BL 12/15/01) [616.89]

10938 Williams, Mary E., ed. *Mental Illness* (9–12). Series: Opposing Viewpoints. 2006, Gale LB $34.95 (978-0-7377-2947-4); paper $23.70 (978-0-7737-2948-1). Pro and con articles present viewpoints on such topics as the prevalence of mental illness, medication, involuntary treatment, illnesses commonly found in young people, and electroconvulsive therapy. (Rev: SLJ 8/07) [362.2]

10939 Zeinert, Karen. *Suicide: Tragic Choice* (6–12). Series: Issues in Focus. 1999, Enslow LB $26.60 (978-

0-7660-1105-2). All aspects of suicide are covered including history, demographic patterns, causes, the grief of survivors, cluster suicide, and assisted suicide. (Rev: BL 12/15/99; HBG 4/00; VOYA 4/00) [362.28]

Nutrition and Diet

10940 Alters, Sandra. *Obesity* (7–12). Series: Introducing Issues with Opposing Viewpoints. 2006, Gale LB $32.45 (978-0-7377-3545-1). Fourteen articles look at the causes and nature of obesity and examine possible ways to deal with this epidemic; fact boxes, charts, photographs, and cartoon strips highlight key points. (Rev: SLJ 4/07) [616.3]

10941 Bellenir, Karen, ed. *Diet Information for Teens: Health Tips About Diet and Nutrition, Including Facts About Nutrients, Dietary Guidelines, Breakfasts, School Lunches, Snacks, Party Food, Weight Control, Eating Disorders, and More* (7–12). 2001, Omnigraphics $48.00 (978-0-7808-0441-8). General nutrition information is amplified by topics of particular interest to teens, such as snacking, school lunches, and eating disorders. (Rev: SLJ 6/01; VOYA 8/01) [613.2]

10942 Bijlefeld, Marjolijn, and Sharon K. Zoumbaris. *Food and You: A Guide to Healthy Habits for Teens* (7–12). 2001, Greenwood $59.95 (978-0-313-31108-6). A comprehensive guide to healthy eating, weight, and exercise that provides lots of information for report writers. (Rev: SLJ 11/01; VOYA 2/02) [613.7]

10943 Brody, Jane E. *Jane Brody's Nutrition Book: A Lifetime Guide to Good Eating for Better Health and Weight Control* (9–12). 1981, Norton $29.95 (978-0-393-01429-7). A straightforward calorie-based diet book that stresses sensible eating habits. [613.2]

10944 Currie-McGhee, Leanne K. *Childhood Obesity* (7–12). Illus. Series: Nutrition and Health. 2012, Gale/Lucent LB $30.95 (978-1-4205-0723-2). With statistics, fact boxes, and anecdotes, this is an informative introduction to the causes and treatment of childhood obesity. (Rev: BL 11/1/12; SLJ 12/12) [618.92]

10945 De Pree, Julia K. *Body Story* (9–12). 2004, Swallow $24.95 (978-0-8040-1063-4); paper $13.95 (978-0-8040-1064-1). A moving memoir of a battle with anorexia; for mature readers with some experience of such disorders. (Rev: BL 6/1–15/04) [362.196]

10946 Drohan, Michele I. *Weight-Loss Programs: Weighing the Risks and Realities* (6–10). Series: Teen Health Library of Eating Disorder Prevention. 1998, Rosen LB $27.95 (978-0-8239-2770-8). This book explores weight-loss programs, sheds light on potential dangers, and discusses safe and sensible approaches to weight loss. (Rev: BL 3/1/99; SLJ 1/99) [616.85]

10947 Favor, Lesli J. *Weighing In: Nutrition and Weight Management* (8–11). Series: Food and Fitness. 2007, Marshall Cavendish LB $25.95 (978-0-7614-2555-7). Information on dieting, healthy weight, general and specialized nutrition, and eating disorders is provided in text, statistics, charts, sidebar features, and photographs. (Rev: BL 1/1–15/08; SLJ 6/08) [613.2]

10948 Fredericks, Carrie. *Obesity* (6–12). Illus. Series: Compact Research: Current Issues. 2008, Reference-Point LB $24.95 (978-160152040-1). This fact-filled volume examines the causes, dangers, and treatment of obesity, including a section on how personal choices influence health. (Rev: BL 8/08) [616.3]

10949 Gay, Kathlyn. *Am I Fat? The Obesity Issue for Teens* (7–12). 2006, Enslow LB $31.93 (978-0-7660-2527-1). Obesity and the health issues associated with it are discussed, as well as strategies for living better and avoiding the wrong dieting decisions that many teens make. (Rev: SLJ 6/06)

10950 Gay, Kathlyn. *The Scoop on What to Eat: What You Should Know About Diet and Nutrition* (6–10). Illus. Series: Issues in Focus Today. 2009, Enslow LB $23.95 (978-076603066-4). A realistic and readable approach to choosing healthy foods, with a chapter on exercise. (Rev: BL 4/15/09; SLJ 10/09) [613.2]

10951 Greene, Bob. *The Get with the Program! Guide to Good Eating* (10–12). 2003, Simon & Schuster $24.00 (978-0-7432-4310-0). Oprah's trainer offers his suggestions for a sensible and healthy weight-loss eating plan. (Rev: BL 12/1/02) [613.2]

10952 Hamilton, Jill, ed. *Vegetarianism* (9–12). Illus. Series: Issues That Concern You. 2008, Gale/Greenhaven $33.70 (978-0-7377-4188-9). Articles consider various aspects of vegetarianism and the ways in which it benefits and limits its adherents, as well as the potential benefits to the environment. (Rev: SLJ 3/1/09) [613.2]

10953 Hillstrom, Kevin. *Food Allergies* (7–12). Illus. Series: Nutrition and Health. 2012, Gale/Lucent LB $30.95 (978-142050720-1). With statistics, fact boxes, and anecdotes, this is an informative introduction to food allergies and their treatment. (Rev: BL 11/1/12; SLJ 12/12) [616.97]

10954 Hillstrom, Kevin. *Genetically Modified Foods* (7–12). Illus. Series: Nutrition and Health. 2012, Gale/Lucent LB $30.95 (978-142050722-5). With statistics, fact boxes, and anecdotes, this is an informative introduction to the rise of GM foods and their benefits and dangers. (Rev: BL 11/1/12; SLJ 12/12) [664]

10955 *The Human Fuel Handbook: Nutrition for Peak Athletic Performance* (9–12). 1988, Health for Life paper $24.95 (978-0-944831-17-5). Written primarily for athletes, this is a no-nonsense guide to top performance through proper diet. (Rev: BL 3/1/89) [613.2]

10956 Hurley, Dan. *Natural Causes: Death, Lies, and Politics in America's Vitamin and Herbal Supplement*

Industry (9–12). 2006, Doubleday $23.95 (978-0-7679-2042-1). In this absorbing account full of compelling examples, Hurley cautions readers against believing claims made by dietary supplement manufacturers and urges us to get our vitamins through eating properly. (Rev: BL 12/1/06) [338.4]

10957 Ingram, Scott. *Want Fries with That? Obesity and the Supersizing of America* (8–11). 2005, Scholastic LB $26.00 (978-0-531-16756-4). Examines the relationship between America's burgeoning fast-food business and the country's obesity epidemic. (Rev: BL 11/15/05; SLJ 1/06) [362.196]

10958 Klimecki, Zachary, and Karen Bellenir, eds. *Diet Information for Teens* (7–12). Illus. Series: Teen Health. 2011, Omnigraphics $62 (978-078081156-0). An updated guide to nutrition and diet, incorporating the new MyPlate Food Guidance System. (Rev: BL 3/1/12) [613.2083]

10959 Lankford, Ronnie D., ed. *Can Diets Be Harmful?* (7–12). Series: At Issue: Health. 2007, Gale LB $28.70 (978-0-7377-3397-6); paper $19.95 (978-0-7377-3398-3). Essays about nutrition and healthy weight tackle such issues as fad diets, eating disorders, and fast food, with some personal stories. (Rev: BL 1/1–15/08) [613.2]

10960 Leon, Warren, et al. *Is Our Food Safe? A Consumer's Guide to Healthy Choices* (10–12). 2002, Crown paper $14.95 (978-0-609-80782-8). This guide to safe and healthy eating offers practical suggestions for minimizing one's chances of contracting foodborne or food-related illnesses. (Rev: BL 7/02) [613.2]

10961 Loonin, Meryl. *Overweight America* (7–12). Series: Hot Topics. 2006, Gale LB $31.20 (978-1-59018-744-9). Covering the reasons why Americans are overweight, the way we eat and think about food. (Rev: SLJ 2/07)

10962 Moe, Barbara. *Understanding Negative Body Image* (6–10). Series: Teen Eating Disorder Prevention Library. 1999, Rosen $31.95 (978-0-8239-2865-1). Our culture stresses body weight and shape, and this book explores the many causes and harmful consequences of a negative body image. (Rev: BL 10/15/99; HBG 9/00; SLJ 1/00; VOYA 2/00) [613.4]

10963 Monroe, Judy. *Understanding Weight-Loss Programs* (6–10). Series: Teen Eating Disorder Prevention Library. 1999, Rosen LB $31.95 (978-0-8239-2866-8). This book discusses good and bad weight loss programs, how to evaluate them, and how to be on guard for bogus products. (Rev: BL 10/15/99; HBG 9/00; SLJ 1/00) [613.7]

10964 Morris, Neil. *Do You Know What's in Your Food?* (6–10). Series: Making Healthy Food Choices. 2006, Heinemann LB $32.86 (978-1-4034-8574-8). Morris challenges teens to look at the questionable components of the foods they eat — bacteria, fat, chemicals,

additives, and so forth. Also use *Food for Sports* (2006). (Rev: SLJ 2/07)

10965 Oz, Daphne. *The Dorm Room Diet: The 8-Step Program for Creating a Healthy Lifestyle Plan That Really Works* (9–12). 2006, Newmarket paper $16.95 (978-1-55704-685-7). Girls on their way to college will find this guide to avoiding the "freshman fifteen" and staying generally healthy helpful and practical. (Rev: BL 9/1/06; SLJ 3/07) [613]

10966 Pierson, Stephanie. *Vegetables Rock! A Complete Guide for Teenage Vegetarians* (7–12). 1999, Bantam paper $13.95 (978-0-553-37924-2). Animal rights and health issues are touched on in this book that describes philosophical and practical aspects of vegetarianism and provides a guide to good foods and balancing nutritional needs. (Rev: BL 3/1/99) [613.2]

10967 Pollan, Michael. *The Omnivore's Dilemma: The Secrets Behind What You Eat* (6–10). Adapted by Richie Chevat. Illus. 2009, Dial $17.99 (978-0-8037-3415-9). For young adults, this condensed version of Pollan's groundbreaking work offers an attractive and accessible take on the importance of choosing your food carefully. (Rev: BL 10/15/09*; HB 11–12/09; LMC 11–12/09; SLJ 10/09) [338.10973.]

10968 Royte, Elizabeth. *Bottlemania: How Water Went on Sale and Why We Bought It* (9–12). 2008, Bloomsbury $24.99 (978-1-59691-371-4). The amazing story of the rise in popularity of bottled water involves cultural, sociological, and health aspects as well as commercial interests and growing concern about the environmental impact. (Rev: SLJ 8/08) [338.4]

10969 Sherman, Roberta Trattner, and Ron A. Thompson. *Bulimia: A Guide for Family and Friends* (9–12). 1997, Jossey-Bass paper $18.95 (978-0-7879-0361-9). A valuable resource for bulimia sufferers and their families, this profile of the eating disorder examines its insidious nature and what can be done to treat it. [616.85]

10970 Simon, Michele. *Appetite for Profit: How the Food Industry Undermines Our Health and How to Fight Back* (9–12). 2006, Nation $14.95 (978-1-56025-932-9). This is an exploration of American beverage and processed food manufacturers' efforts to mislead the public into eating foods that are not healthy — directly contributing to the epidemic of obesity, plus heart disease and diabetes — and of government regulators' willingness to allow this to continue. (Rev: BL 11/1/06) [363.192]

10971 Stare, Frederick J., et al. *Your Guide to Good Nutrition* (9–12). 1991, Prometheus paper $25.98 (978-0-87975-692-5). Professional, no-nonsense answers to basic questions about nutrition, weight control, dietary supplements, and the claims of the health food industry. (Rev: BL 10/1/91; SLJ 12/91) [613.2]

10972 Tattersall, Clare. *Understanding Food and Your Family* (6–10). Series: Teen Eating Disorder Prevention

Library. 1999, Rosen $31.95 (978-0-8239-2860-6). Using many facts and references to case studies, this book describes family dynamics and how eating patterns are developed within the family structure. (Rev: BL 10/15/99; HBG 9/00; SLJ 11/99; VOYA 2/00) [616.85]

10973 Wann, Marilyn. *Fat! So? Because You Don't Have to Apologize for Your Size* (9–12). 1999, Ten Speed paper $15.95 (978-0-89815-995-0). This breezy title filled with facts and humorous anecdotes, aimed largely at oversize women, preaches good health through eating right, exercise, and not worrying about weight. (Rev: SLJ 8/99; VOYA 12/99) [641.1]

10974 Wansink, Brian. *Mindless Eating: Why We Eat More Than We Think* (9–12). 2006, Bantam $25.00 (978-0-553-80434-8). Wansink describes the psychological aspects of overeating and finds devices to train our minds to avoid eating more than we think we are; popular diets are compared in a useful appendix. (Rev: BL 9/15/06) [616.85]

Physical Disabilities and Problems

10975 Cohen, Leah Hager. *Train Go Sorry: Inside a Deaf World* (9–12). 1994, Houghton Mifflin paper $14.00 (978-0-679-76165-5). This work by the grandchild of deaf immigrants covers many aspects of the world of the deaf. (Rev: BL 2/1/94; SLJ 12/94) [371.9]

10976 Deifell, Tony. *Seeing beyond Sight: Photographs by Blind Teenagers* (9–12). 2007, Chronicle $24.95 (978-0-8118-5349-1). Photographs taken by students whose blindness ranges from low vision to no vision illustrate the inventiveness of these young people. (Rev: BL 4/15/07) [779]

10977 Ellison, Brooke, and Jean Ellison. *Miracles Happen: One Mother, One Daughter, One Journey* (9–12). 2002, Hyperion $22.95 (978-0-7868-6770-7). In alternating chapters, Brooke Ellison, the first quadriplegic to graduate from Harvard, and her mother tell their stories. (Rev: BL 12/15/01) [362.4]

10978 Laney, Dawn, ed. *People with Disabilities* (8–12). Series: History of Issues. 2008, Gale/Greenhaven $36.20 (978-0-7377-3972-5). Laney presents articles supporting and opposing issues relating to people with disabilities, addressing such topics as legal rights, education, and new technologies. (Rev: SLJ 2/1/09) [362.40973]

10979 Stark, Clifford D. *Living with Sports Injuries* (9–12). Series: Teen's Guides. 2010, Facts on File LB $34.95 (978-081607848-6). This approachable, well-organized guide offers teens practical advice on the challenges of living with a sports injury. (Rev: BLO 8/10) [617.1]

10980 Stewart, Gail B. *Teens with Disabilities* (8–12). Photos by Carl Franzén. Series: The Other America. 2000, Lucent LB $29.95 (978-1-56006-815-0). The personal — and positive — stories of four teens with physical disabilities show how people with these problems can be accommodated in family and social settings. (Rev: SLJ 3/01)

10981 Thornton, Denise. *Physical Disabilities: The Ultimate Teen Guide* (5–10). Series: It Happened to Me. 2007, Scarecrow $42.00 (978-0-8108-5300-3). In interviews, teens with disabilities describe how they cope at school, with technology and tools, getting around, sports, and so forth. (Rev: SLJ 10/07) [362.40835]

Reproduction and Child Care

10982 Almond, Lucinda, ed. *The Abortion Controversy* (8–12). Series: Current Controversies. 2007, Gale $23.70 (978-0-7377-3273-3). An updated collection of articles expressing many views on abortion and related issues including stem cell research and the rights of activists in general. (Rev: BL 12/1/07) [363.46]

10983 Andryszewski, Tricia. *Abortion: Rights, Options, and Choices* (9–12). Series: Debate. 1996, Millbrook LB $24.90 (978-1-56294-573-2). This book discusses thoroughly Roe v. Wade and its impact, the moral and medical aspects of abortion, and points of view of groups opposed to or supporting the right to abortion. (Rev: BL 4/15/96; SLJ 5/96; VOYA 10/96) [344.73]

10984 Brynie, Faith Hickman. *101 Questions About Reproduction: Or How 1 + 1 = 3 or 4 or More . . . .* (6–10). Illus. by Sharon Lane Holm. 2005, Twenty-First Century LB $27.93 (978-0-7613-2311-2). Information on conception, pregnancy, childbirth, contraception (including a pill for males), abortion, reproductive disorders, and other issues of importance to teens is provided in a question-and-answer format with detailed black-and-white illustrations. (Rev: SLJ 1/06) [612]

10985 Buckingham, Robert W., and Mary P. Derby. *I'm Pregnant, Now What Do I Do?* (10–12). 1997, Prometheus paper $19.98 (978-1-57392-117-6). After a brief discussion of the reproductive process, this candid, helpful book discusses the pros and cons of the three alternatives available to pregnant teens — adoption, abortion, or becoming a parent. (Rev: BL 2/15/97) [306.874]

10986 Byers, Ann. *Teens and Pregnancy: A Hot Issue* (6–12). Series: Hot Issues. 2000, Enslow LB $27.93 (978-0-7660-1365-0). Various aspects of teen pregnancy are discussed, from social factors that put teens at risk to the financial ramifications of single parenthood to ways in which teens can avoid pregnancy. (Rev: HBG 3/01; SLJ 1/01) [306.874]

10987 Coles, Robert. *The Youngest Parents* (8–12). 1997, Norton $27.50 (978-0-393-04082-1). The first two-thirds of this adult book consists of interviews by the author, a child psychiatrist, with teenagers who are or about to be parents, and the last part is a moving photoessay featuring many rural, underprivileged teen parents and their children. (Rev: BL 2/1/97; VOYA 6/98) [306.85]

10988 *Daycare and Diplomas: Teen Mothers Who Stayed in School* (7–12). 2001, Fairview paper $9.95 (978-1-57749-098-2). A group of young women who attend an unusual school that offers childcare relate the difficulties they have experienced in combining parenthood and education. (Rev: BL 5/15/01; VOYA 4/01) [306.874]

10989 DeLoache, Judy, and Alma Gottlieb, eds. *A World of Babies: Imagined Childcare Guides for Seven Societies* (10–12). 2000, Cambridge paper $27.99 (978-0-521-66475-2). From the Puritans of New England to a Muslim village in Turkey, this book outlines in a fictional/factual format how babies are cared for in seven varied cultures. (Rev: BL 5/1/00) [649.1]

10990 Feldt, Gloria. *Behind Every Choice Is a Story* (9–12). 2003, Univ. of North Texas $19.95 (978-1-57441-158-4). Both men and women, including teenagers and teachers, discuss reproductive rights and the value of individual choice. (Rev: BL 3/1/04; VOYA 6/03) [613.9]

10991 Fisanick, Christina, ed. *Childbirth* (8–12). Series: Opposing Viewpoints. 2008, Gale/Greenhaven LB $37.40 (978-0-7377-4196-4); paper $25.95 (978-0-7377-4197-1). A collection of articles showing various points of view on aspects of childbirth practices. (Rev: SLJ 5/1/09) [618.2]

10992 Fontanel, Beatrice, and Claire D'Harcourt. *Babies: History, Art, and Folklore* (10–12). 1998, Abrams $39.95 (978-0-8109-1244-1). This is a lavishly illustrated history about all aspects of child rearing from ancient to modern times — from teething, hygiene, and nutrition to birth instruments, clothing, and toys — placed in a context of changing theories relating to childbirth and child raising over the centuries. (Rev: SLJ 5/98) [305]

10993 Frick, Lisa, ed. *Teen Pregnancy and Parenting* (10–12). Series: Current Controversies. 2006, Gale LB $34.95 (978-0-7377-3295-5). Alternating articles present pro and con views on various aspects of teen pregnancy. (Rev: SLJ 3/07) [306.874]

10994 Gottfried, Ted. *Teen Fathers Today* (8–12). 2001, Twenty-First Century LB $24.90 (978-0-7613-1901-6). Real-life stories add immediacy to this practical guide to the challenges of becoming a father during the teen years. (Rev: HBG 3/02; SLJ 12/01; VOYA 2/02) [306.874]

10995 Heller, Tania. *Pregnant! What Can I Do? A Guide for Teenagers* (6–12). 2002, McFarland $29.95 (978-0-7864-1169-6). Valuable information about pregnancy, abortion, adoption, prenatal care, and parenting is provided in this thoughtful and reassuring volume. (Rev: SLJ 6/02; VOYA 6/02) [306.874/]

10996 Herring, Mark Y. *The Pro-Life/Choice Debate* (9–12). Series: Historical Guides to Controversial Issues in America. 2003, Greenwood $57.95 (978-0-313-31710-1). A wide-ranging overview of abortion and society's past and present attitudes toward it, with details of key court decisions. (Rev: SLJ 2/04) [363.46]

10997 Howard-Barr, Elissa. *The Truth About Sexual Behavior and Unplanned Pregnancy* (10–12). Series: Truth About. 2005, Facts on File $35.00 (978-0-8160-5307-0). A matter-of-fact, balanced, alphabetical discussion of sexual issues, with question-and-answer sections and first-person commentaries. (Rev: BL 9/15/05; SLJ 9/05) [306.7]

10998 Knapp, Lynnette, ed. *The Abortion Controversy* (9–12). Series: Current Controversies. 2001, Greenhaven LB $36.20 (978-0-7377-0334-4); paper $24.95 (978-0-7377-0333-7). Both sides of the divisive abortion debate are well represented in this collection of essays that consider not only the morality of abortion but also specific issues including the use of aborted fetuses for medical research. (Rev: BL 3/1/01) [363.46]

10999 MacDonald, Fiona. *The First "Test-Tube Baby"* (6–12). Series: Days that Changed the World. 2004, World Almanac LB $31.00 (978-0-8368-5567-8); paper $11.95 (978-0-8368-5574-6). The science and ethics of in-vitro fertilization are explored in this overview of the 1978 birth of the world's first "test-tube baby." (Rev: BL 4/1/04; SLJ 7/04) [618.1]

11000 Marzollo, Jean. *Fathers and Babies: How Babies Grow and What They Need from You from Birth to 18 Months* (9–12). 1993, HarperCollins paper $14.95 (978-0-06-096908-0). This practical, illustrated guide describes normal chronological development and offers how-to information on such subjects as making simple toys. (Rev: BL 5/1/93) [306.874]

11001 May, Elaine Tyler. *America and the Pill: A History of Promise, Peril, and Liberation* (10–12). 2010, Basic $25.95 (978-046501152-0). May provides a thorough, apolitical history of "the pill," from its origins in the 1960s to its role today. ℮ (Rev: BL 4/1–15/10)

11002 Naff, Clay Farris, ed. *Reproductive Technology* (9–10). Series: Exploring Science and Medical Discoveries. 2006, Gale LB $34.95 (978-0-7377-2833-0). A survey of various reproductive technologies and the controversies surrounding them. (Rev: BL SLJ 10/06)

11003 Nathanson, Laura Walther. *The Portable Pediatrician for Parents* (9–12). Series: Omnibus. 1994, HarperCollins paper $23.00 (978-0-06-273176-0). Details what to expect at every stage of infancy and toddlerhood and counsels on broader aspects of child rearing as well. (Rev: BL 2/1/94) [618.92]

11004 Parks, Peggy J. *Teenage Sex and Pregnancy* (7–12). Illus. Series: Compact Research: Teenage Problems. 2011, ReferencePoint LB $27.95 (978-160152168-2). Looks at topics ranging from abstinence and contraception to sex education and the consequences of teen pregnancy. (Rev: BL 4/1/12) [306.874]

11005 Powers, Meghan, ed. *The Abortion Rights Movement* (8–11). Series: American Social Movements. 2006, Gale LB $36.20 (978-0-7377-1947-5). This collection of 18 articles, speeches, first-person accounts, and interviews lays out the case for abortion. (Rev: BL 2/15/06) [363.46]

11006 Rosenthal, Beth, ed. *Birth Control* (7–12). Series: Opposing Viewpoints. 2008, Gale/Greenhaven $37.40 (978-073774194-0); paper $25.95 (978-073774195-7). Questions such as "How does birth control affect society?" and "Who should control access to birth control?" are tackled in this collection of articles offering various perspectives. (Rev: BL 4/1/09; SLJ 5/1/09) [363.9]

11007 Sterngass, Jon. *Reproductive Technology* (7–10). Illus. Series: Controversy! 2011, Marshall Cavendish LB $25.95 (978-160870494-1). A balanced discussion of issues relating to reproductive technology such as genetic engineering, abortion, sperm and egg donation, and stem cell research. (Rev: BL 5/1/12; VOYA 10/12) [174.2]

11008 Trapani, Margi. *Listen Up: Teenage Mothers Speak Out* (6–12). Series: Teen Pregnancy Prevention Library. 1997, Rosen LB $23.95 (978-0-8239-2254-3). Young women speak candidly about why they had children at an early age and the impact this has had on their lives. (Rev: BL 6/1–15/97; SLJ 6/97; VOYA 10/97) [306.874]

11009 Trapani, Margi. *Reality Check: Teenage Fathers Speak Out* (7–10). 1997, Rosen LB $23.95 (978-0-8239-2255-0). Case studies of teenage fathers who did not plan on becoming parents are discussed in this book that does not shun the hardships of being a teenage parent. (Rev: BL 6/1–15/97; SLJ 6/97; VOYA 10/97) [306.85]

11010 Wilks, Corinne Morgan, ed. *Dear Diary, I'm Pregnant: Teenagers Talk About Their Pregnancy* (7–12). 1997, Annick paper $9.95 (978-1-55037-440-7). Ten teenage girls talk about how they got pregnant, what they decided to do, and how the pregnancy has changed their lives. (Rev: BL 2/1/98; SLJ 8/97; VOYA 12/97) [306.874]

11011 Zach, Kim K. *Reproductive Technology* (10–12). Series: Great Medical Discoveries. 2004, Gale LB $29.95 (978-1-59018-344-1). This volume explores the options available to infertile couples and the ethical issues associated with current and future technologies. (Rev: SLJ 7/04) [616.6]

11012 Zerucha, Ted. *Human Development* (7–12). Series: The Human Body: How It Works. 2009, Chelsea House $35 (978-1-60413-371-4). Zerucha describes the development of a human being from the initial single cell. (Rev: LMC 5–6/10) [612.64]

Safety and First Aid

11013 Arnold, Caroline. *Coping with Natural Disasters* (7–10). 1988, Walker LB $14.85 (978-0-8027-6717-2). Natural disasters such as earthquakes, hurricanes, and blizzards are discussed, with information on how to react in these emergencies. (Rev: BCCB 6/88; BL 6/15/88; SLJ 6/88; VOYA 10/88) [904]

11014 Auerbach, Paul S. *Medicine for the Outdoors: A Guide to Emergency Medical Procedures and First Aid* (9–12). 1986, Little, Brown $24.95 (978-0-316-05928-2); paper $12.95 (978-0-316-05929-9). A first aid manual for the outdoor person that stresses prevention and safety measures. (Rev: BL 1/15/86) [616.02]

11015 Orndorff, John C., and Suzanne Harper. *Terrorists, Tornados, and Tsunamis: How to Prepare for Life's Danger Zones* (7–12). 2007, Abrams $16.95 (978-0-8109-5767-1). A practical guide to preparing for all kinds of disasters, from storms to Internet predators. (Rev: BL 4/15/07; SLJ 5/07) [613.6]

11016 Wells, Donna K., and Bruce C. Morris. *Live Aware, Not in Fear: The 411 After 9-11 — A Book For Teens* (6–12). 2002, Health Communications paper $9.95 (978-0-7573-0013-4). The authors offer practical advice for teenagers who want to feel safe again, such as preparing escape routes and keeping a survival kit handy. (Rev: BL 5/15/02; VOYA 6/02) [363.3]

Sex Education and Sexual Identity

11017 Ayer, Eleanor H. *It's Okay to Say No: Choosing Sexual Abstinence* (9–12). Series: Teen Pregnancy Prevention Library. 1997, Rosen LB $23.95 (978-0-8239-2250-5). While acknowledging the difficulty of making such a choice, Eleanor Ayer makes the case for sexual abstinence, providing a review of such dangers as unwanted pregnancy and infection with a sexually transmitted disease. (Rev: BL 9/1/97; SLJ 1/98) [306.7]

11018 Baez, John, and Jennifer Howd. *The Gay and Lesbian Guide to College Life* (11–12). 2007, Random House paper $13.95 (978-0-375-76623-7). Gay, lesbian, bisexual, transgendered, and questioning teens will find this matter-of-fact guide helpful. (Rev: BL 9/1/07) [370.193]

11019 Bailey, Jacqui. *Sex, Puberty and All That Stuff: A Guide to Growing Up* (5–10). Illus. by Jan McCafferty. 2004, Barron's paper $12.99 (978-0-7641-2992-6). In this comprehensive volume full of lighthearted illustrations, Bailey covers the wide range of changes that affect young people, emphasizing the individual's right to choose and the need to resist peer pressure. (Rev: SLJ 1/05) [613.9]

11020 Bass, Ellen, and Kate Kaufman. *Free Your Mind: The Book for Gay, Lesbian, and Bisexual Youth — and Their Allies* (10–12). 1996, HarperPerennial paper $16.95 (978-0-06-095104-7). This practical guide for young gay men, lesbians, and bisexuals offers helpful advice on such topics as coming out to family and friends, building a network with other young gays and lesbians, sex, and establishing healthy relationships. [305.23]

11021 Beam, Cris. *Transparent: Love, Family, and Living the T with Transgender Teenagers* (11–12). 2007, Harcourt $25.00 (978-0-15-101196-4). Beam recounts her experiences as a volunteer at a high school for gay and transgender students and the close relationships she developed with some of the young people there, most of them minorities and facing difficult lives even without the added complications of their sexual identities; for mature teens. (Rev: BL 11/15/06) [306.76]

11022 Bell, Ruth. *Changing Bodies, Changing Lives* (9–12). 1998, Times paper $23.00 (978-0-8129-2990-4). A new edition of this ground-breaking, nonjudgmental, explicit book on sex, physical and emotional health, and personal relationships. (Rev: BL 11/1/98) [613.907]

11023 Bily, Cynthia A., ed. *Homosexuality* (7–12). Series: Opposing Viewpoints. 2008, Gale/Greenhaven $37.40 (978-073774214-5); paper $25.95 (978-073774215-2). Questions such as "Should gay men and women serve in the military?" and "Should same-sex couples be allowed to marry?" are tackled in this collection of articles offering various perspectives. (Rev: BL 4/1/09) [306.76]

11024 Brynie, Faith Hickman. *101 Questions About Sex and Sexuality: With Answers for the Curious, Cautious, and Confused* (6–12). Series: 101 Questions. 2003, Twenty-First Century LB $27.90 (978-0-7613-2310-5). Information on abstinence, contraception, sexually transmitted diseases, and other issues of importance to teens is provided in a question-and-answer format with detailed black-and-white illustrations. (Rev: HBG 10/03; SLJ 6/03; VOYA 4/04) [306.7]

11025 Diamond, Shifra N. *Everything You Need to Know About Going to the Gynecologist* (7–12). Series: Need to Know Library. 1999, Rosen LB $27.95 (978-0-8239-2839-2). This book explains what a gynecologist does, when teenage girls should see one, and how to find one. There is helpful information on menstruation, breast self-examinations, treatments for common reproductive problems, contraception, myths, and what to expect from a pelvic examination. (Rev: SLJ 5/99; VOYA 8/99) [612]

11026 Goldstein, Andrew, et al. *When Sex Hurts: A Woman's Guide to Banishing Sexual Pain* (11–12). 2011, Da Capo paper $16 (978-07382139-8-9). Chock full of ob/gyn advice and information on the conditions that can cause women pain while having sex, including bladder infections and skin conditions. (Rev: BLO 1/1–15/11) [618.17]

11027 Gowen, L. Kris. *Making Sexual Decisions: The Ultimate Teen Guide* (7–12). Series: It Happened to Me. 2003, Scarecrow $32.50 (978-0-8108-4647-0). Puberty, safe sex, birth control, and rape are among the topics raised in this volume, which stresses the value of being fully informed about one's options. (Rev: SLJ 11/03) [306.7]

11028 Gravelle, Karen, and Nick Castro. *What's Going on Down There? Answers to Questions Boys Find Hard to Ask* (5–10). Illus. by Robert Leighton. 1998, Walker paper $8.95 (978-0-8027-7540-5). Straightforward information for boys covers such topics as physical changes, sexual intercourse, peer pressure, and pregnancy and birth. (Rev: BL 11/1/98; HB 1–2/99; HBG 3/99; SLJ 12/98) [613]

11029 Hasler, Nikol. *Sex: A Book for Teens: An Uncensored Guide to Your Body, Sex, and Safety* (10–12). Illus. by Michael Capozzola. 2010, Zest paper $16.95 (978-09819733-2-6). This frank, conversational guide to sex takes an at-times comic approach, covering everything from basic anatomy and safe sex guides to fantasies and sex toys. YALSA Quick Picks for Reluctant Young Adult Readers 2011. (Rev: BL 7/10; SLJ 2/1/11; VOYA 8/10) [613.9]

11030 Hoch, Dean, and Nancy Hoch. *The Sex Education Dictionary for Today's Teens and Pre-Teens* (7–12). 1990, Landmark paper $12.95 (978-0-9624209-0-0). A dictionary of 350 words relating to sex, sexuality, and reproduction all given clear, concise definitions. (Rev: BL 8/90) [306.7]

11031 Hyde, Margaret O., and Elizabeth H. Forsyth. *Safe Sex 101* (8–11). 2006, Lerner $26.60 (978-0-8225-3439-6). Straightforward and well-written, this book includes important information for teens on how to protect themselves from STDs and pregnancy, covering contraception as well as abstinence. (Rev: BL 5/1/06; SLJ 6/06) [613.9]

11032 Kamen, Paula. *Her Way: Young Women Remake the Sexual Revolution* (10–12). 2001, New York Univ. $45.00 (978-0-8147-4733-9). More than 100 Generation X women candidly reveal their attitudes on such subjects as sexual abstinence, the feminist movement, AIDS, homosexuality, single life, and marriage. (Rev: BL 12/15/00) [306.7]

11033 Keen, Lisa. *Out Law: What LGBT Youth Should Know about Their Legal Rights* (10–12). Series: Queer Action/Queer Ideas. 2007, Beacon paper $13.00 (978-0-8070-7966-9). Lesbian, gay, bisexual, and transgendered students will find this a useful guide to their rights. (Rev: BL 5/1/07) [342.7308]

11034 Marcovitz, Hal. *Teens and Gay Issues* (7–10). Series: The Gallup Youth Survey, Major Issues and Trends. 2005, Mason Crest LB $22.95 (978-1-59084-873-9). An attractive volume documenting Gallup findings on gay teens' attitudes toward coming out, homophobia, the nature/nurture debate, and gay marriage and adoption. (Rev: SLJ 1/06) [305.9]

11035 Marcus, Eric. *Is It a Choice? Answers to 300 of the Most Frequently Asked Questions About Gays and Lesbians* (9–12). 1993, HarperCollins paper $13.00 (978-0-06-250664-1). A comprehensive primer on homosexuality, answering questions about sex, relationships, discrimination, religion, coming out, AIDS, aging, and many other topics. (Rev: BL 5/1/93) [305.9]

11036 Marcus, Eric. *What If Someone I Know Is Gay? Answers to Questions About What It Means to Be Gay and Lesbian* (7–12). 2007, Simon & Schuster paper $8.99 (978-1-4169-4970-1). This update of the title first published in 2001 uses new terminology and addresses questions that teenagers may have about their own sexuality as well as that of someone they know. (Rev: BL 10/1/07; SLJ 1/08) [306.766]

11037 Moon, Sarah, ed. *The Letter Q: Queer Writers' Notes to Their Younger Selves* (9–12). Illus. 2012, Scholastic $17.99 (978-054539932-6). More than 60 well-known writers who are LGBTQ have contributed letters to their younger selves in this diverse collection suitable for browsing. Lexile 306.76 (Rev: BL 4/15/12*; HB 7–8/12; LMC 10/12; SLJ 5/1/12)

11038 O'Grady, Kathleen, and Paula Wansbrough, eds. *Sweet Secrets: Telling Stories of Menstruation* (6–10). 1997, Second Story paper $9.95 (978-0-929005-33-1). Following an interesting review of attitudes and rituals relating to menstruation in various cultures throughout history, the main body of the book recounts 20 anecdotes about young teens and their first periods, interspersed with boxes providing information on topics including tampons, toxic shock syndrome, and breast examinations. (Rev: VOYA 6/98) [530.8]

11039 Pardes, Bronwen. *Doing It Right: Making Smart, Safe, and Satisfying Choices about Sex* (9–12). 2007, Simon & Schuster paper $14.99 (978-1-4169-1823-3). Teens who are seeking straightforward information on all topics relating to sex — heterosexual and otherwise — will appreciate this frank guide. (Rev: BL 2/1/07; LMC 10/07; SLJ 6/07) [613.9]

11040 Pogany, Susan Browning. *Sex Smart: 501 Reasons to Hold Off on Sex* (8–12). 1998, Fairview paper $14.95 (978-1-57749-043-2). The author uses quotations from teenagers, "Dear Abby," and other sources to explore emotional issues involved in making sexual choices and to argue for abstinence. (Rev: VOYA 4/99) [613.9]

11041 Reed, Rita. *Growing Up Gay: The Sorrows and Joys of Gay and Lesbian Adolescence* (10–12). 1997, Norton paper $19.95 (978-0-393-31659-9). This book concentrates on the lives of two teens, one gay and the other lesbian, and their experiences after they came out. (Rev: VOYA 6/98) [305.9]

11042 Roberts, Tara, ed. *What Your Mama Never Told You: True Stories about Sex and Love* (10–12). 2007, Houghton Mifflin paper $7.99 (978-0-618-64636-4). Sixteen essays by young black women about their first (or most memorable) sexual experiences and discoveries. (Rev: BCCB 5/07; BL 1/1–15/07; SLJ 2/07) [306.7089]

11043 Rooney, Frances, ed. *Hear Me Out: True Stories of Teens Confronting Homophobia* (8–12). 2005, Second Story paper $9.95 (978-1-896764-87-0). Young people who are volunteers in a Toronto organization called T.E.A.C.H. (Teens Educating and Confronting Homophobia) talk about prejudice they've experienced because of their sexual orientation. (Rev: BL 8/05; SLJ 5/05; VOYA 4/05) [306.76]

11044 Singer, Bennett L. *Growing Up Gay: An Anthology for Young People* (10–12). 1993, New Press paper $9.95 (978-1-56584-103-1). Gay and lesbian teens uncertain of their identities will find reassurance in this collection of writings by well-known men and women — James Baldwin, Martina Navratilova, and Rita Mae Brown — who've lived through the experience themselves. [808.8]

11045 White, Joe. *Pure Excitement: A Radical Righteous Approach to Sex, Love, and Dating* (7–12). 1996, Family paper $10.99 (978-1-56179-483-6). Taking a conservative approach, this book, written by a minister and using many conversations with teens, proposes that premarital sex is harmful to young adults. (Rev: VOYA 8/97) [613.9]

Sex Problems
(Abuse, Harassment, etc.)

11046 Chaiet, Donna. *Staying Safe at School* (7–12). Series: Get Prepared Library. 1995, Rosen LB $23.95 (978-0-8239-1864-5). How to stay alert and protect oneself while at school, plus tips for girls on avoiding violent crimes on or near school campuses. (Rev: BL 11/15/95; SLJ 2/96) [613.6]

11047 Feuereisen, Patti, and Caroline Pincus. *Invisible Girls: The Truth About Sexual Abuse* (9–12). 2005, Seal paper $15.95 (978-1-58005-135-4). The author, a psychotherapist, debunks myths about abuse, offers some case studies, and provides suggestions for preventing, reporting, and recovering from incest, rape, and other forms of abuse. (Rev: SLJ 11/05) [362.7]

11048 Gordon, Sherri Mabry. *Beyond Bruises: The Truth About Teens and Abuse* (7–12). Series: Issues in Focus Today. 2009, Enslow LB $31.93 (978-0-7660-3064-0). This book explores the causes and consequences of various forms of abuse through firsthand accounts, photos, and concise sidebars. (Rev: BL 4/15/09; SLJ 10/09) [362.76083]

11049 Layman, Nancy S. *Sexual Harassment in American Secondary Schools: A Legal Guide for Administrators, Teachers, and Students* (9–12). 1994, Contemporary Research paper $18.95 (978-0-935061-52-9). Provides definitions of sexual harassment, examines laws regarding it in secondary schools, and outlines how schools can avoid it or deal with it. (Rev: BL 8/94; VOYA 4/95) [344.73]

11050 Lehman, Carolyn. *Strong at the Heart: How It Feels to Heal from Sexual Abuse* (8–11). 2005, Farrar $16.00 (978-0-374-37282-8). First-person accounts reveal the damage caused by sexual abuse and present strategies for healing. (Rev: BL 9/15/05; SLJ 11/05; VOYA 10/05) [362.76]

11051 McFarland, Rhoda. *Working Together Against Sexual Harassment* (7–12). Series: Library of Social Activism. 1996, Rosen LB $27.95 (978-0-8239-1775-4). Following a review of the history of sexual harassment (of females) and recent scandals, the book emphasizes how teens can combat sexual harassment by responding politically, from fighting for official policies against it at school to organizing chapters of NOW or other organizations. (Rev: SLJ 4/97; VOYA 6/97) [344.73]

11052 Munson, Lulie, and Karen Riskin. *In Their Own Words: A Sexual Abuse Workbook for Teenage Girls* (7–12). 1997, Child Welfare League of America paper $10.95 (978-0-87868-596-7). This manual (for use in therapy situations) helps girls who have been sexually abused work through their problems and plan for the future. (Rev: VOYA 10/97) [382.88]

11053 Reinert, Dale R. *Sexual Abuse and Incest* (7–12). Series: Teen Issues. 1997, Enslow LB $17.95 (978-0-89490-916-0). After a general explanation of what constitutes sexual abuse and incest, this work explains how to identify potential abusive situations and what to do about them. (Rev: BL 12/1/97; HBG 3/98; SLJ 12/97; VOYA 6/98) [362.76]

11054 Wall, Edmund, ed. *Sexual Harassment: Confrontations and Decisions. Rev. ed.* (9–12). Series: Contemporary Issues. 2000, Prometheus paper $22.98 (978-1-57392-830-4). Various aspects of sexual harassment are discussed in this collection of essays, including a thorough examination of the extent of the problem. [305.4]

11055 Warshaw, Robin. *I Never Called It Rape* (10–12). 1994, HarperCollins paper $13.00 (978-0-06-092572-7). Case studies of women who have been raped by friends or acquaintances. (Rev: SLJ 3/89) [364.1]

Human Development and Behavior

General and Miscellaneous

11056 Apter, Terri. *The Myth of Maturity: What Teenagers Need from Parents to Become Adults* (10–12). 2001, Norton $24.95 (978-0-393-04942-8). After interviewing 32 people ages 18 to 32, the author reaches some conclusions about the problems facing this age group after high school. (Rev: BL 5/15/01) [306.874]

11057 Best, Amy. *Prom Night: Youth, Schools, and Popular Culture* (10–12). 2000, Routledge $75.00 (978-0-415-92427-6); paper $19.95 (978-0-415-92428-3). This is an interesting collection of first-person accounts that discuss prom night — the preparations, the event, and the after-prom parties. (Rev: BL 8/00) [394]

11058 Brizendine, Louann. *The Male Brain* (11–12). 2010, Broadway $24.99 (978-076792753-6). This fast-paced, provocative follow-up to the author's *The Female Brain* (2006) draws on the psychiatric clinician's case files to paint a picture of the development of the male brain and the differences between the behavior of men and women. ⌂ (Rev: BL 2/1–15/10) [612.8]

11059 Isaacson, Walter, ed. *Profiles in Leadership: Historians on the Elusive Quality of Greatness* (10–12). 2010, Norton $26.95 (978-039307655-4). "What makes a great leader great?" With profiles of notable Americans by historians, professors, and other commentators, this volume looks at the essential qualities. ⌂ ℯ (Rev: BL 9/1–15/10) [324.2]

11060 Shenk, David. *The Genius in All of Us: Why Everything You've Been Told About Genetics, Talent, and IQ Is Wrong* (10–12). Illus. 2010, Doubleday $26.95 (978-038552365-3). Journalist Shenk makes the case that hard work, parenting, and environment are just as important as genetics in shaping successful lives. ⌂ (Rev: BL 3/1–15/10) [155.2]

11061 Smith, Larry, and Rachel Fershleiser, eds. *I Can't Keep My Own Secrets: Six-Word Memoirs by Teens Famous and Obscure* (6–10). Illus. 2009, HarperTeen paper $8.99 (978-006172684-2). A fascinating and moving collection of more than 600 six-word teen memoirs such as "Born 1992. Unhappy. Adopted 2007. Happy." and "You're the parent, act like one." Includes a subject index. (Rev: BL 7/09; SLJ 8/09) [808]

Psychology and Human Behavior

General and Miscellaneous

11062 Acker, Kerry. *Everything You Need to Know About the Goth Scene* (7–12). 2000, Rosen LB $27.95 (978-0-8239-3223-8). An informative and reliable guide to the origins, fashions, preferences, and behavior associated with the "Goth" movement. (Rev: BL 12/1/00; SLJ 3/01) [306]

11063 Akeret, Robert U. *Photolanguage: How Photos Reveal the Fascinating Stories of Our Lives and Relationships* (10–12). 2000, Norton $29.95 (978-0-393-04968-8). Using many black-and-white images of celebrities and others as examples, psychoanalyst Akeret explains how he "reads" photographs to gain understanding of individuals. (Rev: VOYA 2/01) [770]

11064 Allenbaugh, Kay. *Chocolate for a Teen's Dreams: Heartwarming Stories About Making Your Wishes Come True* (8–12). Series: Chocolate. 2003, Fireside paper $12.00 (978-0-7432-3703-1). A collection of stories by teens and older women about their dreams and desires, and how they came true. (Rev: SLJ 9/03) [305.235]

11065 Balog, Cyn, and Lise Bernier, et al. *Dear Bully: Seventy Authors Tell Their Stories* (7–12). Ed. by Megan Kelley Hall and Carrie Jones. 2011, HarperTeen $17.99 (978-0-06-206098-3). Top children's authors offer stories from the points-of-view of perpetrators, bystanders, and victims in various formats — fiction, poems, letters, and so forth. **e** (Rev: BL 7/11; SLJ 8/11) [302.3]

11066 Baskin, Julia, et al. *The Notebook Girls* (11–12). 2006, Warner $22.95 (978-0-446-57862-2). Produced in journal format, with pasted-in photos, this fascinating volume is the creation of four contemporary teens — classmates at New York City's prestigious Stuyvesant High School — who shared a joint diary and confided in it the interesting aspects of their lives; for mature readers because of discussion of sex, drugs, and alcohol. (Rev: BL 3/15/06; SLJ 6/06) [305.235]

11067 Carlson, Dale, and Hannah Carlson. *Where's Your Head? Teenage Psychology* (8–12). 1998, Bick paper $14.95 (978-1-884158-19-3). This book explores in readable format the basic elements of psychological thought concerning personality, influences on beliefs and behavior, the stages of adolescence, and mental illness. (Rev: VOYA 8/98) [150]

11068 Freud, Sigmund. *The Basic Writings of Sigmund Freud* (10–12). Trans. by A. A. Brill. 1995, Modern Library $24.95 (978-0-679-60166-1). This is a reprint of all the major books and articles by Freud, including *The Interpretation of Dreams* and *Totem and Taboo*. [150.19]

11069 Gardner, Robert, and Barbara Gardner Conklin. *Health Science Projects About Psychology* (7–12). 2002, Enslow LB $26.60 (978-0-7660-1439-8). Interesting activities that illustrate psychological concepts are extended by suggestions for further investigation. (Rev: HBG 10/02; SLJ 7/02) [150]

11070 Goldwasser, Amy, ed. *Red: The Next Generation of Writers — Teenage Girls — on What Fires Up Their Lives Today* (10–12). 2007, Hudson Street $21.95 (978-1-59463-040-8). Teen girls write about what concerns them most in chapters on the body and beauty, family, friendship, love and sex, leisure time and work, the media and pop culture, and global problems. (Rev: BL 11/1/07) [814.6]

11071 Gonzales, Laurence. *Deep Survival: Who Lives, Who Dies, and Why* (10–12). 2003, Norton $25.95 (978-0-393-05276-3). True stories draw readers into this study of the factors — physiological, psychological, and spiritual — that have helped many to survive close brushes with death. (Rev: BL 9/1/03) [613.6]

11072 Headley, Maria Dahvana. *The Year of Yes* (10–12). 2006, Hyperion $22.95 (978-1-4013-0230-6). In this engaging dating memoir, Headley tells how her decision to relax her standards finally led her to Mr. Right. (Rev: BL 1/1–15/06) [306.81]

11073 Hernández, Roger K. *Teens and Relationships* (7–10). Series: The Gallup Youth Survey, Major Issues

and Trends. 2005, Mason Crest LB $22.95 (978-1-59084-875-3). An attractive volume documenting Gallup findings on teens' attitudes toward parents, divorce, blended families, friendship, and dating the opposite sex. (Rev: SLJ 1/06)

11074 Howe, Florence, and Jean Casella, eds. *Almost Touching the Skies: Women's Coming of Age Stories* (10–12). 2000, Feminist paper $15.95 (978-1-55861-234-1). This collection of fiction and nonfiction written in the past 120 years by 22 authors contains various viewpoints and perspectives on women's coming of age. (Rev: BL 5/1/00; VOYA 8/01) [813]

11075 Jarvis, Cheryl. *The Necklace: Thirteen Women and the Experiment That Transformed Their Lives* (11–12). Illus. 2008, Ballantine $24.00 (978-0-345-50071-7). This is a true account of the experiences of an unlikely club that is formed when a group of women jointly buy an expensive necklace. ∩ **e** (Rev: BL 8/08) [302.3]

11076 Louv, Richard. *The Nature Principle: Human Restoration and the End of Nature-Deficit Disorder* (11–12). 2011, Algonquin $24.95 (978-156512581-0). Louv lays out his latest findings, culled from sources as varied as medical research and poetry, to argue that reconnecting in a meaningful way with nature can help our minds as well as our bodies, and strengthen our human connections. (Rev: BL 3/1–15/11) [155.4]

11077 Musgrave, Susan, ed. *Nerves Out Loud: Critical Moments in the Lives of Seven Teen Girls* (8–12). 2001, Annick $19.95 (978-1-55037-693-7); paper $9.95 (978-1-55037-692-0). Seven adult women look back at events and problems that absorbed them as teenagers. (Rev: BL 10/1/01; HBG 3/02; SLJ 10/01; VOYA 2/02) [305.235]

11078 Musgrave, Susan, ed. *Perfectly Secret: The Hidden Lives of Seven Teen Girls* (10–12). 2004, Annick $18.95 (978-1-55037-865-8); paper $8.95 (978-1-55037-864-1). Seven women tell frank, autobiographical stories of dreadful secrets — about abuse, adultery, rape, self-mutilation, and alcoholism — that they kept when they were teens. (Rev: SLJ 12/04)

11079 Nikkah, John. *Our Boys Speak: Adolescent Boys Write About Their Inner Lives* (10–12). 2000, St. Martin's paper $12.95 (978-0-312-26280-8). This collection of essays, journal entries, letters, stories, and poems by teenagers deals with their feelings, relationships, families, and concerns. (Rev: BL 7/00) [305.2]

11080 O'Halloran, Barbara Collopy. *Creature Comforts: People and Their Security Objects* (6–12). Illus. by Betty Udesen. 2002, Houghton Mifflin $17.00 (978-0-618-11864-9). First-person accounts, accompanied by photographs, explain why objects such as "blankies" prove invaluable to both children and adults. (Rev: BL 5/1/02; HBG 10/02; SLJ 3/02) [155.4]

11081 Oliver, Neil. *Amazing Tales for Making Men out of Boys* (10–12). Illus. 2009, Morrow $25.99 (978-006176613-8). The author has collected true tales of bravery, persistence, and toughness from the warriors of Sparta to explorer Captain Scott to the soldiers who fought in Normandy and so forth. ℮ (Rev: BL 4–5/09) [170.81]

11082 Quartz, Steven R., and Terrence J. Sejnowski. *Liars, Lovers, and Heroes: What the New Brain Science Reveals About How We Become Who We Are* (10–12). 2002, Morrow $26.95 (978-0-688-16218-4). "Cultural biology" is the focus of this thought-provoking and accessible exploration of what makes us who we are. (Rev: BL 10/1/02) [612.8]

11083 Ridley, Matt. *Nature via Nurture: Genes, Experience, and What Makes Us Human* (10–12). 2003, HarperCollins $25.95 (978-0-06-000678-5). A wide-ranging and thought-provoking discussion of the age-old question of nature versus nurture. (Rev: BL 3/15/03) [155.7]

11084 Salerno, Steve. *SHAM: How the Self-Help Movement Made America Helpless* (9–12). 2005, Crown $24.95 (978-1-4000-5409-1). An indictment of the self-help industry and its leading lights, among them Suze Orman, Drs. Laura and Phil, Tony Robbins, Marianne Williamson, and John Gray. (Rev: BL 6/1–15/05) [155.2]

11085 Slater, Lauren. *Blue Beyond Blue: Extraordinary Tales for Ordinary Dilemmas* (11–12). 2005, Norton $23.95 (978-0-393-05959-5). Slater, a psychologist, explores the use of narrative psychotherapy as a way to help patients gain greater insight into their problems; the 16 original fairy tales included are symbol-filled stories of love, addiction, and so forth; for mature readers. (Rev: BL 6/1–15/05) [823]

11086 Spilsbury, Louise. *Together As a Team!* (6–10). Series: Life Skills. 2008, Heinemann LB $32.86 (978-1-4329-1363-2). With practical tips and quizzes at the ends of chapters, this volume discusses the benefits of teamwork and how to achieve it. (Rev: SLJ 3/1/09)

11087 Tannen, Deborah. *You Were Always Mom's Favorite! Sisters in Conversation Throughout Their Lives* (11–12). 2009, Random House $26 (978-140006632-2). Through interviews and her own experience, Tannen studies the connections and bonds between sisters and the lasting effects these bonds can have. ⌒ (Rev: BL 9/09) [306.875]

Emotions and Emotional Behavior

11088 Spilsbury, Louise. *Cool That Anger!* (6–10). Series: Life Skills. 2008, Heinemann LB $32.86 (978-1-4329-1365-6). With tips on handling anger and quizzes at the ends of chapters, this volume discusses the causes of anger and physical reactions to it. (Rev: SLJ 3/1/09)

Ethics and Moral Behavior

11089 Altman, Linda J. *Bioethics: Who Lives, Who Dies, and Who Decides* (7–12). Series: Issues in Focus Today. 2007, Enslow LB $23.95 (978-0-7660-2546-2). Both sides of moral issues in bioethics (such as cloning, abortion, and organ transplants) are presented fairly. (Rev: BL 3/15/07; SLJ 8/07) [174]

11090 Canfield, Jack, and Mark Victor Hansen. *Chicken Soup for the Teenage Soul II: 101 More Stories of Life, Love and Learning* (7–12). 1998, Health Communications $24.00 (978-1-55874-615-2); paper $14.95 (978-1-55874-616-9). A new collection of personal stories from teens that supply inspiration and guidance. (Rev: BL 11/1/98; HBG 3/99) [158.1]

11091 Dimauro, Laurie, and George Pérez, eds. *Ethics* (9–12). Series: Opposing Viewpoints. 2006, Gale LB $34.95 (978-0-7377-3319-8); paper $23.70 (978-0-7377-3320-4). The importance of ethical behavior is discussed from different perspectives and focusing on areas including biomedical engineering and corporate actions; many quotations are included. (Rev: SLJ 2/07)

Etiquette and Manners

11092 Hoving, Walter. *Tiffany's Table Manners for Teenagers* (7–12). 1989, Random House $17.00 (978-0-394-82877-0). A practical guide to good table manners. (Rev: SLJ 6/89) [395]

11093 Packer, Alex J. *How Rude! The Teenagers' Guide to Good Manners, Proper Behavior, and Not Grossing People Out* (6–12). 1997, Free Spirit paper $19.95 (978-1-57542-024-0). A candid, often humorous guide to good manners for teenagers that stresses common sense and covers situations ranging from inline skating to computer hacking. (Rev: BL 2/1/98; SLJ 2/98; VOYA 6/98) [395.1]

Intelligence and Thinking

11094 Quart, Alissa. *Hothouse Kids: The Dilemma of the Gifted Child* (9–12). 2006, Penguin $24.95 (978-1-59420-095-3). Are gifted children pushed too hard? The author of this book (a former gifted child herself) looks at the industry that has grown up around putting pressure on bright children. (Rev: BL 8/06) [305.9]

Personal Guidance

11095 Allenbaugh, Kay. *Chocolate for a Teen's Heart* (9–12). 2001, Simon & Schuster paper $12.00 (978-0-7432-1380-6). Fifty-five original stories of first love, heartbreak, friendship, and loss are included in this collection of inspirational tales. (Rev: BL 6/1–15/01) [152.4]

11096 Allenbaugh, Kay. *Chocolate for a Teen's Soul: Life-Changing Stories for Young Women About Growing Wise and Growing Strong* (6–12). 2000, Simon & Schuster $12.00 (978-0-684-87081-6). Inspiring essays explore a wide array of issues, including first love, disabilities, beauty pageants, friendship, first jobs, and family relations. (Rev: VOYA 4/01) [152.4]

11097 Asgedom, Mawi. *The Code: The Five Secrets of Teen Success* (7–12). 2003, Little, Brown paper $9.99 (978-0-316-73689-3). Asgedom, a motivational speaker who was a refugee before coming to the United States and later attending Harvard, advises teens on strategies for success. (Rev: HBG 4/04; SLJ 11/03; VOYA 12/03)

11098 Bachel, Beverly K. *What Do You Really Want? How to Set a Goal and Go for It!* (6–12). 2001, Free Spirit paper $12.95 (978-1-57542-085-1). Bachel lays out ways to define and achieve goals, supported by quotations from teens who have tried them; reproducible forms are included. (Rev: BL 5/15/01; VOYA 8/01) [153.8]

11099 Bezdecheck, Bethany. *Relationships: 21st-Century Roles* (9–12). Series: A Young Woman's Guide to Contemporary Issues. 2010, Rosen LB $31.95 (978-1-4358-3540-5). A conversational discussion of ways to ensure good relationships with relatives, friends, and boys, with a chapter on being your own best friend. (Rev: LMC 10/10; SLJ 4/1/10; VOYA 8/10)

11100 Blatt, Jessica. *The Teen Girl's Gotta-Have-It Guide to Boys: From Getting Them to Getting Over Them* (6–10). Illus. by Cynthia Frenette. 2007, Watson-Guptill paper $8.95 (978-0-8230-1725-6). Complete with self-quizzes, this is an entertaining, well-written guide for girls about dating and relationships. (Rev: SLJ 7/07)

11101 Blatt, Jessica. *The Teen Girl's Gotta-Have-It Guide to Embarrassing Moments: How to Survive Life's Cringe-Worthy Situations!* (6–10). Illus. by Cynthia Frenette. 2007, Watson-Guptill paper $8.95 (978-0-8230-1724-9). This is a lighthearted book that teaches girls how to overcome embarrassing situations with grace and humor. (Rev: SLJ 7/07)

11102 Bolden, Tonya, ed. *33 Things Every Girl Should Know: Stories, Songs, Poems and Smart Talk by 33 Extraordinary Women* (6–12). 1998, Crown paper $13.00 (978-0-517-70936-8). A collection of highly readable pieces by well-known and successful women on the difficult transition from childhood to adulthood. (Rev: BL 5/15/98; HBG 9/98; SLJ 5/98) [810.8092827]

11103 Bradley, Michael J. *Yes, Your Parents Are Crazy! A Teen Survival Guide* (9–12). Illus. by Randy Glasbergen. 2004, Harbor paper $14.95 (978-0-936197-48-7). Dealing with parents is the focus of this teen-friendly book full of case histories of the challenges young people face and advice on tackling societal inconsistencies. (Rev: SLJ 12/04; VOYA 2/05)

11104 Bridgers, Jay. *Everything You Need to Know About Having an Addictive Personality* (7–12). Series: Need to Know Library. 1998, Rosen LB $27.95 (978-0-8239-2777-7). The author examines the social, psychological, and biochemical aspects of an "addictive personality," explains why some people are more susceptible to addiction than others, and offers sound advice on how teens can cope with addiction. (Rev: SLJ 1/99) [157]

11105 Brown, Bobbi, and Annemarie Iverson. *Bobbi Brown Teenage Beauty: Everything You Need to Look Pretty, Natural, Sexy and Awesome* (8–12). 2000, Cliff St $25.00 (978-0-06-019636-3). As well as supplying beauty tips, this book stresses the importance of diet and exercise. (Rev: SLJ 12/00) [646.7]

11106 Burningham, Sarah O'Leary. *Boyology: A Crash Course in All Things Boy* (7–12). Illus. by Keri Smith. 2009, Chronicle paper $12.99 (978-0-8118-6436-7). This chatty, approachable book provides guidance on everything from making the boy friend–boyfriend transition to kissing and setting sexual boundaries. (Rev: SLJ 6/1/09; VOYA 4/10) [306.7]

11107 Burton, Bonnie. *Girls Against Girls: Why We Are Mean to Each Other and How We Can Change* (7–10). Illus. 2009, Zest paper $12.95 (978-097901736-0). The author calls on "mean girls" and their targets to understand why girls can be cruel and what can be done about it. Lexile 860L (Rev: BL 2/15/09; SLJ 5/1/09; VOYA 4/09) [300]

11108 Camron, Roxanne. *60 Clues About Guys: A Guide to Feelings, Flirting, and Falling in Like* (6–10). Illus. by Ariane Elsammak. Series: 60 Clues About. 2002, Lunchbox paper $8.95 (978-0-9678285-5-8). For girls, this is a how-to manual for coping with relationships with the opposite sex, with a personal dating diary at the end. (Rev: SLJ 7/02)

11109 Canfield, Jack, and Mark Victor Hansen, comps. *Chicken Soup for the Teenage Soul — The Real Deal: School: Cliques, Classes, Clubs and More* (7–12). Series: Chicken Soup for the Soul. 2005, Health Communications paper $14.95 (978-0-7573-0255-8). Written for teenagers by teenagers, this collection of essays addresses many problems that confront high school students today. (Rev: SLJ 11/05) [158]

11110 Canfield, Jack, ed. *Chicken Soup for the Christian Teenage Soul: Stories of Faith, Love, Inspiration and Hope* (6–12). 2003, Health Communications paper $14.95 (978-0-7573-0095-0). Stories, poems, and cartoons of particular relevance to teens are grouped in thematic chapters. (Rev: BL 10/1/03) [242]

11111 Carlson, Dale. *Talk: To Yourself, to Others, to Parents, Teachers, Bosses, to Sisters and Brothers, to Your Best Friend, to People You Don't Like, to the Universe* (9–12). Illus. by Carol Nicklaus. 2006, Bick paper $14.95 (978-1-884158-32-2). This guide shows teens how to improve their communication skills and connect better with the people in their lives, even those they don't like. (Rev: SLJ 8/06)

11112 Carlson, Richard. *Don't Sweat the Small Stuff for Teens: Simple Ways to Keep Your Cool in Stressful Times* (9–12). 2000, Hyperion paper $11.95 (978-0-7868-8597-8). Motivational writer Richard Carlson offers solid advice on ways to reduce stress and appreciate life. (Rev: BL 12/1/00) [158.1]

11113 Chopra, Deepak. *Fire in the Heart: A Spiritual Guide for Teens* (8–12). 2004, Simon & Schuster $14.95 (978-0-689-86216-8). In this book of spiritual advice for teens, the author uses the device of having a wise old man named Baba give self-help information. (Rev: BL 5/15/04; SLJ 8/04) [204]

11114 Chopra, Deepak. *Teens Ask Deepak: All the Right Questions* (7–10). 2006, Simon & Schuster $12.95 (978-0-689-86218-2). The popular spiritual guru turns his attention to teenage concerns — friendship, success, health, religion, and so forth. (Rev: BL 1/1–15/06; SLJ 1/06) [616]

11115 Choron, Sandra, and Harry Choron. *The Book of Lists for Teens* (7–12). 2002, Houghton Mifflin paper $13.95 (978-0-618-17907-7). More than 300 lists cover a wide range of topics of interest to teens, such as music videos, sports, eating disorders, substance abuse, and bullying. (Rev: SLJ 1/03; VOYA 4/03) [031.02]

11116 Corriveau, Danielle, ed. *Trail Mix: Stories of Youth Overcoming Adversity* (7–12). 2001, Corvo Communications $14.95 (978-0-9702366-0-9). Fourteen teens tell inspiring first-person stories about hard times and the value of spending time in an outdoor program. (Rev: BL 12/1/01; SLJ 1/02) [158.1]

11117 Covey, Sean. *The 6 Most Important Decisions You'll Ever Make: A Guide for Teens* (8–12). 2006, Fireside paper $15.95 (978-0-7432-6504-1). Advice on education, friendship, family, dating and sex, avoiding addiction, and nurturing healthy self-esteem is presented in lively text with lots of graphics, charts, cartoons, and so forth. (Rev: SLJ 2/07)

11118 Dentemaro, Christine, and Rachel Kranz. *Straight Talk About Student Life* (6–10). Series: Straight Talk. 1993, Facts on File $27.45 (978-0-8160-2735-4). This book explores problems that students are likely to experience, including communication with teachers and other students, parental pressures, homework, and developing a healthy social life. (Rev: BL 9/1/93) [373.18]

11119 Desetta, Al. *The Courage to Be Yourself: True Stories by Teens About Cliques, Conflicts, and Overcoming Peer Pressure* (8–11). 2005, Free Spirit paper $13.99 (978-1-57542-185-8). Teens from a wide variety of backgrounds offer personal accounts of how they overcame adversities such as bullying, cliques, prejudice, and peer pressure. (Rev: BL 2/1/06; SLJ 6/06; VOYA 4/06) [305.235]

11120 DeVenzio, Dick. *Smart Moves: How to Succeed in School, Sports, Career, and Life* (10–12). 1989, Prometheus paper $22.98 (978-0-87975-546-1). A compendium of practical advice on such topics as how to do well at school, make and keep friends, and succeed in career goals. [155.5]

11121 Devillers, Julia. *GirlWise: How to Be Confident, Capable, Cool, and in Control* (8–12). 2002, Prima paper $12.95 (978-0-7615-6363-1). Topics covered in this accessible volume of advice from experts range from fashion and diet to car repair and doing laundry. (Rev: SLJ 12/02) [646.7]

11122 Doeden, Matt. *Conflict Resolution Smarts: How to Communicate, Negotiate, Compromise, and More* (8–12). Illus. Series: USA Today Teen Wise Guides. 2012, Lerner/Twenty-First Century LB $31.93 (978-076137020-8). This accessible guide offers strategies for dealing with conflict and learning how to listen and negotiate. (Rev: BL 4/1/12) [303.6]

11123 Drew, Naomi. *The Kids' Guide to Working Out Conflicts: How to Keep Cool, Stay Safe, and Get Along* (6–10). Illus. by Chris Sharp. 2004, Free Spirit paper $13.95 (978-1-57542-150-6). Misunderstandings, teasing, bullying, and sexual harassment are all discussed in this guide that includes scenarios and offers strategies for improving self-control plus many quotations from middle school students. (Rev: SLJ 9/04) [303.6]

11124 Drill, Esther. *Deal with It! A Whole New Approach to Your Body, Brain and Life as a Gurl* (8–12). 1999, Pocket paper $15.00 (978-0-671-04157-1). Much of the flavor of the popular Gurl.com site is duplicated in this eye-catching book full of frank information about sex, adolescent development and behavior, and succeeding in life. (Rev: BL 10/1/99) [305.235]

11125 Ellis, Deborah. *We Want You to Know: Kids Talk About Bullying* (6–10). Illus. 2010, Coteau $21.95 (978-155050417-0). Teens describe their experiences as victims, witnesses, and perpetrators of bullying. (Rev: BL 9/1/10; LMC 5–6/11; SLJ 9/10; VOYA 12/10) [302.3]

11126 Ensler, Eve. *I Am an Emotional Creature: The Secret Life of Girls Around the World* (11–12). 2010, Villard $20 (978-140006104-4). While explicit themes and language are found in the entries throughout this book, the message to young women that they can be strong and powerful is authentic and empowering. **e** (Rev: BL 2/1–15/10) [155.43]

11127 Espeland, Pamela. *Life Lists for Teens: Tips, Steps, Hints, and How-tos for Growing Up, Getting Along, Learning, and Having Fun* (8–12). 2003, Free Spirit paper $11.95 (978-1-57542-125-4). Lists of suggestions, tips, and resources cover all topics of interest to teens — health, school, homework, safety, bullying, pregnancy, abuse, and so forth. (Rev: LMC 11–12/03; SLJ 5/03; VOYA 6/03) [646.7]

11128 Flaherty, Somer. *The Book of Styling: An Insider's Guide to Creating Your Own Look* (8–12). Illus. 2012, Zest $16.99 (978-098273224-3). An accessible guide to identifying your body type and face shape, plus closet-organization tips and the basics of building a wardrobe. (Rev: BL 12/1/12; SLJ 10/12) [746.9]

11129 Ford, Amanda. *Be True to Yourself: A Daily Guide for Teenage Girls* (6–12). 2001, Conari paper $17.95 (978-1-57324-189-2). Drawing on her own experiences, Amanda Ford offers daily inspirational nuggets of wisdom for girls making the difficult passage to womanhood. (Rev: VOYA 6/01) [158.1]

11130 Fox, Annie. *Can You Relate? Real-World Advice for Teens on Guys, Girls, Growing Up, and Getting Along* (6–12). 2000, Free Spirit paper $15.95 (978-1-57542-066-0). This guidance book tells teens how to form relationships with family, peers, and girl or boy friends, with material on how to understand oneself. (Rev: BL 4/15/00; SLJ 7/00) [305.235]

11131 Galbraith, Judy, and Jim Delisle. *The Gifted Teen Survival Guide: Smart, Sharp, and Ready For (Almost) Anything* (8–11). 2011, Free Spirit $15.99 (978-157542381-4). With quizzes, stories, and quotations from gifted teens, this is a helpful guide for gifted teens who may feel distant from their peers. (Rev: BL 11/1/11; SLJ 1/12; VOYA 2/12) [155.5087]

11132 Gibbon, Andy. *Make College Yours: How to Leave Home, Make Your Place, and Build Relationships for Success* (9–12). 2003, Preston paper $17.95 (978-0-9740986-0-9). Homesickness, roommates, long-distance relationships, dating, and drinking are covered in this guide to the social aspects of moving on from high school to college. (Rev: SLJ 3/04)

11133 *Girlsource: A Book by and for Young Women About Relationships, Rights, Futures, Bodies, Minds, and Souls* (10–12). 2003, Ten Speed paper $12.95 (978-1-58008-555-7). Solid advice for teens on social, mental, and physical well-being, with checklists, quizzes, and quotations from teens. (Rev: SLJ 2/04; VOYA 2/04)

11134 Goldstein, Mark A., and Myrna Chandler Goldstein. *Boys to Men: Staying Healthy Through the Teen Years* (7–12). 2000, Greenwood $59.95 (978-0-313-30966-3). This book is divided into three age groups between 12 and 21, and for each there are descriptions of changes that occur and how to adjust to them. (Rev: SLJ 6/01; VOYA 4/01) [613]

11135 Hantman, Clea. *30 Days to Finding and Keeping Sassy Sidekicks and BFFs: A Friendship Field Guide* (7–10). 2009, Delacorte paper $7.99 (978-038573623-7). An upbeat approach to making lifelong friends, with practical tips and activities that will make the effort easier. (Rev: BL 7/09; VOYA 4/09) [158.2]

11136 Harlan, Judith. *Girl Talk: Staying Strong, Feeling Good, Sticking Together* (6–10). 1977, Walker pa-

per $8.95 (978-0-8027-7524-5). A breezy, lighthearted guide to approaching everyday problems faced by adolescent girls, with practical tips on how to solve them. (Rev: BL 12/1/97; VOYA 2/98) [305.23]

11137 Harris-Johnson, Debrah. *The African-American Teenagers' Guide to Personal Growth, Health, Safety, Sex and Survival: Living and Learning in the 21st Century* (6–12). 2000, Amber paper $19.95 (978-0-9655064-4-1). This guide for young African Americans growing up in America today covers such topics as family structure, friendships, sexual orientation, work, and spirituality. (Rev: BL 2/15/00; VOYA 6/02) [646.7]

11138 Hugel, Bob. *I Did It Without Thinking: True Stories About Impulsive Decisions That Changed Lives* (6–10). Series: Scholastic Choices. 2008, Watts LB $27 (978-0-531-13868-7); paper $8.95 (978-0-531-20526-6). Teens share their own stories of impulsive behavior and how the results changed their lives. (Rev: SLJ 10/1/08; VOYA 12/08)

11139 Jacobs, Tom. *Teen Cyberbullying Investigated: Where Do Your Rights End and Consequences Begin?* (7–12). 2010, Free Spirit paper $15.99 (978-1-57542-339-5). Jacobs encourages teens to think critically and consider every situation from the perspective of victim, bystander, and perpetrator. (Rev: BL 3/1/10; SLJ 3/10; VOYA 8/10) [345.73]

11140 Jakes, T. D. *Mama Made the Difference: Life Lessons My Mother Taught Me* (9–12). 2006, Putnam $19.95 (978-0-399-15363-1). This inspirational book contains essays by Jakes and others recalling the loving, often profound wisdom mothers communicate to their children about life; this volume will appeal particularly to Christian teens. (Rev: BL 4/15/06) [248.8]

11141 Judson, Karen. *Resolving Conflicts: How to Get Along When You Don't Get Along* (6–12). Series: Issues in Focus Today. 2005, Enslow LB $31.93 (978-0-7660-2359-8). "Dealing with Difficult People" and "Turning Conflict into Collaboration" are two of the chapters in this thorough volume that also covers bullying and gives historical examples of effective conflict resolution. (Rev: SLJ 5/06) [303.6]

11142 Kaywell, Joan F., ed. *Dear Author: Letters of Hope* (8–11). 2007, Philomel $14.99 (978-0-399-23705-8). A collection of letters to YA authors from teens, many with serious problems. Readers with problems of their own will find reassurance and some good advice. (Rev: BCCB 6/07; BL 2/15/07; SLJ 5/07) [028.5]

11143 Kimball, Gayle. *The Teen Trip: The Complete Resource Guide* (9–12). 1997, Equality paper $16.95 (978-0-938795-26-1). Comments by 1,500 teenagers via the Internet are the highlight of this book about the teen experience, from abortion and yeast infection to self-esteem and peer pressure. (Rev: SLJ 6/97) [305.23]

11144 Kirberger, Kimberly. *On Relationships: A Book for Teenagers* (7–12). Series: Teen Love. 1999, Health

Communications paper $14.95 (978-1-55874-734-0). Letters, stories, and poems tackle problems that arise in romantic relationships. (Rev: BL 10/15/99; SLJ 1/00) [306.7]

11145 Kirberger, Kimberly, and Colin Mortensen. *On Friendship: A Book for Teenagers* (6–10). Series: Teen Love. 2000, Health Communications paper $12.95 (978-1-55874-815-6). This comforting overview of the meaning of friendship features writings by teenagers. (Rev: BL 1/1–15/01; SLJ 4/01) [302.3]

11146 Kirberger, Kimberly, ed. *No Body's Perfect: Stories by Teens About Body Image, Self-Acceptance, and the Search for Identity* (7–12). 2003, Scholastic paper $12.95 (978-0-439-42638-1). Mostly written by girls, these stories are intended to help teens grapple with problems of identity and image. (Rev: SLJ 6/03; VOYA 4/03)

11147 Kreiner, Anna. *Creating Your Own Support System* (7–10). Series: Need to Know Library. 1996, Rosen LB $27.95 (978-0-8239-2215-4). An easy-to-read account that teaches how to create a support system of friends, neighbors, relatives, clergy members, and teachers, if support is not available at home. (Rev: SLJ 1/97) [305.23]

11148 Lawson, Dorie McCullough. *Posterity: Letters of Great Americans to Their Children* (9–12). 2004, Doubleday $24.95 (978-0-385-50330-3). Letters — from individuals who have made a significant contribution to the United States — offering advice to the next generation are collected in this thought-provoking volume. (Rev: SLJ 7/04) [973]

11149 Lound, Karen. *Girl Power in the Family: A Book About Girls, Their Rights, and Their Voice* (5–10). Series: Girl Power. 2000, Lerner LB $30.35 (978-0-8225-2692-6). A book that explores the problems of growing up female today with material on gender roles, biases, and relationships. (Rev: HBG 10/00; SLJ 6/00) [303.6]

11150 McCune, Bunny, and Deb Traunstein. *Girls to Women: Sharing Our Stories* (7–10). 1998, Celestial Arts paper $14.95 (978-0-89087-881-1). Arranged under thematic chapters that deal with self-esteem, friendships, menstruation, sexuality, and mother-daughter relations, this collection of essays, stories, and poems explores various aspects of being young and female. (Rev: SLJ 4/99) [305.23]

11151 McFarland, Rhoda. *Coping Through Assertiveness* (9–12). 1986, Rosen $12.95 (978-0-8239-0680-2). The author explains the difference between assertiveness and aggressive behavior and, among other things, how to say "no." (Rev: BL 1/15/87; SLJ 1/87) [158.1]

11152 Morgenstern, Julie, and Jessi Morgenstern- Colon. *Organizing from the Inside Out for Teens: The Foolproof System for Organizing Your Room, Your Time, and Your Life* (7–12). 2002, Henry Holt paper $15.00 (978-0-8050-6470-4). Strategies for managing the time,

space, and responsibilities of typical teens are presented in this practical manual. (Rev: BL 1/1–15/03) [646.7]

11153 Morgenstern, Mindy. *The Real Rules for Girls* (8–12). 2000, Girl $14.95 (978-0-9659754-5-2). Advice on life, love, friends, and more is presented in an attractive, conversational way. (Rev: SLJ 3/00; VOYA 4/00)

11154 Morrison, Betsy S., and Ruth Ann Ruiz. *Self-Esteem* (7–10). Illus. Series: Teen Mental Health. 2011, Rosen LB $27.95 (978-144884587-3). With information about building self-confidence and setting goals, this book will be helpful for report writers and those seeking personal guidance. (Rev: BL 11/15/11; LMC 5–6/12) [155.5]

11155 Musgrave, Susan, ed. *You Be Me: Friendship in the Lives of Teen Girls* (7–12). 2002, Annick $18.95 (978-1-55037-739-2); paper $7.95 (978-1-55037-738-5). Stories of girls' experiences show the sometimes difficult realities of teenage friendships. (Rev: BL 12/15/02; HBG 3/03; SLJ 1/03; VOYA 12/02) [305.235]

11156 Noel, Carol. *Get It? Got It? Good! A Guide for Teenagers* (7–12). 1996, Serious Business paper $7.95 (978-0-9649479-0-0). A teen self-help guide that discusses such topics as self-esteem, sex, health, relations with others, goals, and violence. (Rev: BL 6/1–15/96) [361.8]

11157 O'Reilly, Bill, and Charles Flowers. *The O'Reilly Factor for Kids: A Survival Guide for America's Family* (9–12). 2004, HarperCollins $22.95 (978-0-06-054424-9). Controversial talk show host Bill O'Reilly serves up advice for today's teenagers. (Rev: BL 8/04; SLJ 11/04) [646.7]

11158 Packard, Gwen K. *Coping When a Parent Goes Back to Work* (8–12). Series: Coping. 1995, Rosen LB $31.95 (978-0-8239-1698-6). Gives children whose parents return to work tips on adapting to the new situation. Includes real-life examples. (Rev: BL 7/95) [306.874]

11159 Piquemal, Michel, and Melissa Daly. *When Life Stinks: How to Deal with Your Bad Moods, Blues, and Depression* (6–10). Illus. by Olivier Tossan. Series: Sunscreen. 2004, Abrams paper $9.95 (978-0-8109-4932-4). Sensible advice for adolescents suffering from normal anxieties and frustrations and for those who need to recognize that their problems are more deep-seated and professional help is necessary. (Rev: SLJ 4/05) [616.85]

11160 Quindlen, Anna. *Being Perfect* (11–12). 2005, Random House $12.95 (978-0-375-50549-2). Quindlen urges readers to steer clear of the "perfection trap." (Rev: SLJ 6/05)

11161 Ricciotti, Hope, and Monique Doyle Spencer. *The Real Life Body Book: A Young Woman's Complete Guide to Health and Wellness* (11–12). Illus. 2010, Celestial Arts paper $22 (978-15876135-7-9). This conversational book covers everything from acne to tattoo care to rape, with "Real Life Facts" and checklists. **e** (Rev: BLO 5/1–15/10) [613]

11162 Rutledge, Jill Zimmerman. *Dealing with the Stuff That Makes Life Tough: The 10 Things That Stress Girls Out and How to Cope with Them* (8–10). 2003, Contemporary paper $15.95 (978-0-07-142326-7). Body image, boys, homosexuality, smoking and drinking, divorce — these and other sources of stress are addressed with sensible advice and helpful anecdotes. (Rev: SLJ 1/04)

11163 Ryan, Peter. *Online Bullying* (7–10). Illus. 2011, Rosen LB $27.95 (978-144884588-0). With information about bullies and their victims — and the laws governing such behavior, this book will be helpful for report writers and those seeking personal guidance. (Rev: BL 11/15/11) [302.3]

11164 Savage, Dan, and Terry Miller, eds. *It Gets Better: Coming Out, Overcoming Bullying, and Creating a Life Worth Living* (9–12). 2011, Dutton $21.95 (978-0-525-95233-6). A collection of essays, stories, and testimonials written by celebrities, political leaders, and others designed to show LGBT youth that life will get better. ∩ **e** (Rev: BLO 4/27/2011; SLJ 5/11) [306.76]

11165 Schwager, Tina, and Michele Schuerger. *The Right Moves: A Girl's Guide to Getting Fit and Feeling Good* (6–12). 1998, Free Spirit paper $15.95 (978-1-57542-035-6). Topics including self-esteem, diet, and exercise are covered in this upbeat guide for girls that promotes a positive, healthy lifestyle. (Rev: BL 1/1–15/99; SLJ 1/99*; VOYA 8/99) [613.7]

11166 Shipp, Josh. *The Teen's Guide to World Domination: Advice on Life, Liberty, and the Pursuit of Awesomeness* (8–11). Illus. 2010, St. Martin's paper $14.99 (978-03126415-4-2). Motivational speaker Shipp offers thought-provoking advice for teens seeking to boost their self-esteem, to deal with crises at home and at school, and generally to succeed. (Rev: BL 8/10; VOYA 10/10) [646.7]

11167 Simmons, Rachel. *Odd Girl Speaks Out: Girls Write About Bullies, Cliques, Popularity, and Jealousy* (10–12). 2004, Harcourt paper $13.00 (978-0-15-602815-8). First-person accounts from teens — victims, perpetrators, and bystanders — are blended with the author's comments on aggression and other typical adolescent problems. (Rev: BL 12/15/03) [305.23]

11168 Steinem, Gloria. *Revolution from Within: A Book of Self-Esteem* (9–12). 1992, Little, Brown paper $14.95 (978-0-316-81247-4). Drawing on her own personal experiences and those of others, outspoken feminist Gloria Steinem suggests ways in which women can build self-esteem. [155.2]

11169 Stepp, Laura Sessions. *Unhooked: How Young Women Pursue Sex, Delay Love, and Lose at Both* (11–12). 2007, Riverhead $24.95 (978-1-59448-938-9). Just what does the current phrase "hooking up" mean, and when it denotes casual encounters rather than long-term dating, is it a healthy phenomenon? This book offers thought-provoking material and good advice for mature teenage girls. ∩ (Rev: BL 2/15/07) [306.73]

11170 Stillman, Sarah. *Soul Searching: A Girl's Guide to Finding Herself* (7–12). 2012, Simon & Schuster $17.99 (978-1-5827-0342-8); paper $9.99 (978-1-5827-0303-9). An updated edition of the guide that covers everything relating to self-improvement and now includes cyberbullying, sexting, social media, and healthy eating. **e** (Rev: LMC 8–9/12; SLJ 3/12; VOYA 12/11) [158.0835]

11171 Tarshis, Thomas Paul. *Living with Peer Pressure and Bullying* (6–12). Series: Teen's Guides. 2010, Facts on File LB $34.95 (978-143813074-3). "What is peer pressure?" "Who are your friends, really?" This practical guide answers these and other questions relating to problems facing many teens. **e** (Rev: BLO 8/10; SLJ 9/10) [303.3]

11172 Taylor, Julie. *The Girls' Guide to Friends* (7–12). 2002, Three Rivers paper $12.00 (978-0-609-80857-3). A lighthearted look at getting and keeping friends, with quizzes and other entertaining features. (Rev: BL 12/15/02) [158.2]

11173 Taylor, Sally. *On My Own: The Ultimate How-to Guide for Young Adults* (11–12). 2002, Silly Goose paper $34.95 (978-0-9711500-0-3). A comprehensive and practical guide to living independently, covering everything from budgeting and sharing with a roommate to the importance of charity and citizenship. (Rev: BL 1/1–15/03) [646.700842]

11174 Tym, Kate, and Penny Worms. *Coping with Your Emotions: A Guide to Taking Control of Your Life* (6–10). Series: Get Real. 2004, Raintree LB $29.93 (978-1-4109-0575-8). The magazine-style layout, case studies, quizzes, photos, and advice will draw teens to this discussion of issues including depression, peer pressure, love interests, schoolwork, and teacher conflicts. Also use *School Survival: A Guide to Taking Control of Your Life* (2004). (Rev: SLJ 3/05) [646]

11175 Van Buren, Abigail. *The Best of Dear Abby* (10–12). 1989, Andrews McMeel paper $9.95 (978-0-8362-6241-4). This is a collection of the best of the advice columns written by this popular counselor. [361.3]

11176 Weinstein, Bruce. *Is It Still Cheating if I Don't Get Caught?* (8–12). Illus. by Harriet Russell. 2009, Flash Point paper $9.95 (978-159643306-9). The author gives readers five "life principles" to help guide them in making ethical decisions: "Do no harm," "Make things better," "Respect others," "Be fair," and "Be loving." He then gives examples of times when teens may have to make tough decisions. Lexile 1080L (Rev: BL 4/1/09; LMC 10/09; SLJ 4/1/09; VOYA 6/09) [300]

11177 Wesson, Carolyn McLenahan. *Teen Troubles* (7–12). 1988, Walker $17.95 (978-0-8027-1011-6); paper

$11.95 (978-0-8027-7310-4). A candid, sometimes humorous self-help book on teenage problems and how to face them. (Rev: VOYA 12/88) [155.5]

11178 White, Lee, and Mary Ditson. *The Teenage Human Body Operator's Manual* (6–10). 1999, Northwest Media paper $9.95 (978-1-892194-01-5). Using an appealing layout and cartoon illustrations, this is an overview of teenagers' physical and psychological needs, touching on hygiene, nutrition, disease, pregnancy and birth control, and mental health. (Rev: SLJ 11/98) [305.23]

11179 Willis, Teresa Ann. *It's All Good! Daily Affirmations for Teens* (10–12). 1999, Emp! Emp! Press/The Human Race Works paper $20.76 (978-0-9667677-0-4). A daily calendar of quotations and positive, life-affirming messages from celebrities. (Rev: VOYA 2/00)

11180 Winik, Marion. *Rules for the Unruly: Living the Unconventional Life* (10–12). 2001, Simon & Schuster paper $12.00 (978-0-7432-1603-6). This powerful account tells frank stories of dealing with challenges including drug addiction and unwanted pregnancy. (Rev: BL 3/15/01) [170]

11181 Winkler, Kathleen. *Bullying: How to Deal with Taunting, Teasing, and Tormenting* (6–10). Series: Issues in Focus Today. 2005, Enslow $31.93 (978-0-7660-2355-0). Including a chapter on girls who bully, this is an accessible look at the problem that draws on discussions with both teens and professionals. (Rev: SLJ 12/05)

11182 Wirths, Claudine G., and Mary Bowman- Kruhm. *Coping with Confrontations and Encounters with the Police* (7–12). Series: Coping. 1997, Rosen LB $31.95 (978-0-8239-2431-8). This book gives teens essential and realistic information that will help them deal successfully with police encounters and minimize potential risks. (Rev: SLJ 4/98; VOYA 2/98) [364.3]

11183 Wolfelt, Alan D. *Healing Your Grieving Heart for Teens: 100 Practical Ideas* (6–12). 2001, Companion paper $11.95 (978-1-879651-23-4). The author, a teacher and grief counselor, offers 100 practical tips on accepting and dealing with grief and provides tasks that will help teens identify their needs. (Rev: BL 3/15/01; SLJ 9/01; VOYA 8/01)

11184 Youngs, Bettie B., and Jennifer Leigh Youngs, eds. *More Taste Berries for Teens: A Second Collection of Inspirational Short Stories Encouragement on Life, Love, Friendship and Tough Issues* (6–12). Series: Taste Berries for Teens. 2000, Health Communications paper $12.95 (978-1-55874-813-2). Written almost exclusively by teens, the inspiring stories and essays in this collection touch on such varied issues of teen concern as love and relationships, family relations, friendship, deciding on a career, and getting into college. (Rev: VOYA 2/01)

11185 Zimbardo, Philip G. *Shyness* (10–12). 1990, Addison-Wesley paper $16.00 (978-0-201-55018-4). What causes shyness and how to relieve this anxiety are explored in this volume. [152.4]

Social Groups

Family and Family Problems

11186 Brondino, Jeanne. *Raising Each Other* (7–12). 1988, Hunter House paper $8.95 (978-0-89793-044-4). This book, written and illustrated by a high school class, is about parent-teen relationships, problems, and solutions. (Rev: SLJ 1/89; VOYA 4/89) [306.1]

11187 Buscemi, Karen. *Split in Two: Keeping It Together When Your Parents Live Apart* (7–12). Illus. by Corinne Mucha. 2009, Zest paper $14.95 (978-098007321-8). For children of divorce, this is a practical guide to creating your own living space in both houses, synchronizing schedules, packing and hauling, and negotiating with two sets of adults. (Rev: BL 7/09; VOYA 8/09) [300]

11188 Desetta, Al, ed. *The Heart Knows Something Different: Teenage Voices from the Foster Care System* (9–12). 1996, Persea paper $13.95 (978-0-89255-218-4). Divided into four parts, the 57 essays in this book, written by teens who were foster children, tell about individual situations leading to foster-care placement, living in foster homes, self-awareness, and hopes of the future. (Rev: BL 5/15/96; SLJ 6/96; VOYA 8/96) [362.7]

11189 Eidse, Faith, and Nina Sichel, eds. *Unrooted Childhoods: Memoirs of Growing Up Global* (10–12). 2004, Nicholas Brealey paper $23.95 (978-1-85788-338-1). The essays in this collection — all written by men and women who lived the nomadic life as children — will resonate with teens faced with being uprooted. (Rev: BL 12/15/03) [306]

11190 Fakhrid-Deen, Tina. *Let's Get This Straight: The Ultimate Handbook for Youth with LGBTQ Parents* (5–10). 2010, Seal $15.95 (978-1-58005-333-4). This insightful book discusses the various challenges children with LGBTQ parents will face and offers excerpts from interviews, questionnaires, and a good list of resources. (Rev: SLJ 3/1/11) [306.8]

11191 Fields, Julianna. *Foster Families* (6–12). Illus. Series: The Changing Face of Modern Families. 2009, Mason Crest $22.95 (978-142221497-8). Fields explores the history of foster care and the reasons why children end up in foster homes, with real-life examples and discussion of potential problems. Also use *Gay and Lesbian Parents, Kids Growing Up Without a Home, Multiracial Families,* and *Teen Parents* (all 2009). (Rev: LMC 5–6/10; SLJ 2/10) [306.874]

11192 Flaming, Allen, and Kate Scowen, eds. *My Crazy Life: How I Survived My Family* (8–12). 2002, Annick paper $9.95 (978-1-55037-732-3). Ten teen narratives describe how each managed to deal with family problems such as abuse, addiction, AIDS, divorce, and homosexuality. (Rev: BL 9/1/02; HBG 10/02; SLJ 7/02) [306.87]

11193 Ford, Judy, and Amanda Ford. *Between Mother and Daughter: A Teenager and Her Mom Share the Secrets of a Strong Relationship* (6–12). 1999, Conari paper $14.95 (978-1-57324-164-9). Alternate chapters written by mother and daughter reveal the power of communication. (Rev: BL 8/99; VOYA 2/00) [306.874]

11194 Gravelle, Karen, and Susan Fischer. *Where Are My Birth Parents? A Guide for Teenage Adoptees* (7–12). 1993, Walker LB $15.85 (978-0-8027-8258-8). Includes firsthand experiences of young people who searched for their birth families with varied success. (Rev: BL 9/1/93; SLJ 7/93; VOYA 10/93) [362.7]

11195 Haugen, David M., and Matthew J. Box, eds. *Adoption* (8–12). Series: Social Issues Firsthand. 2005, Gale LB $29.95 (978-0-7377-2881-1). Personal accounts from adoptees, birth parents, and adoptive parents give moving perspectives on the process of adoption; gay parents, transracial adoptions, custody battles, and the search for adoptees and birth parents are all covered. (Rev: SLJ 2/06) [362.7]

11196 Havrilesky, Heather. *Disaster Preparedness* (10–12). 2010, Riverhead $25.95 (978-159448768-2). The disaster movies popular in the 1970s prepared Havrilesky for various catastrophes, but she was not so well-armed against everyday grief and personal problems; a funny and poignant memoir. ⋒ (Rev: BL 10/1–15/10) [921]

11197 Hull, Lise. *Tracing Your Family History: The Complete Guide to Locating Your Ancestors and Finding Out Where You Came From* (9–12). 2006, Reader's Digest $26.95 (978-0-7621-0573-1). New and veteran genealogical researchers will be well served by this comprehensive guide organized in five sections with sidebars, photographs, an international resource directory, and a listing of genealogy software. (Rev: SLJ 7/06) [929]

11198 Huston, Perdita. *Families as We Are: Conversations from Around the World* (10–12). 2001, Feminist $25.95 (978-1-55861-250-1). Multigenerational families in 11 countries including Thailand, China, Egypt, Brazil, and the United States were asked how changes in such areas as human rights and economics were affecting them. (Rev: BL 7/01) [306.85]

11199 Hyde, Margaret O. *Know About Abuse* (7–12). Series: Know About. 1992, Walker LB $14.85 (978-0-8027-8177-2). Provides facts on child abuse, reasons, symptoms, examples, and solutions, covering a wide range of abuse, from obvious to subtle. (Rev: BL 11/1/92; SLJ 9/92) [362.7]

11200 Kaminker, Laura. *Everything You Need to Know About Being Adopted* (7–12). Series: Need to Know Library. 1999, Rosen $27.95 (978-0-8239-2834-7). As well as the legal aspects of adoption, this account explores the problems young people may face when they are adopted. [362.7]

11201 Kempe, C. Henry, and Ray E. Helfer, eds. *The Battered Child.* 4th ed. (10–12). 1987, National Center for the Prevention of Child Abuse $37.00 (978-0-318-14670-6). The causes, treatment, and prevention of child abuse are covered in this sympathetic account. [362.7]

11202 Lerner, Alicia. *Marriage* (9–12). Series: Global Viewpoints. 2009, Gale/Greenhaven $36.20 (978-0-7377-4160-5). Taking a global view, this balanced book explores various marriage customs and variations from generally recognized norms. (Rev: LMC 10/09)

11203 Lipper, Joanna. *Growing Up Fast* (10–12). 2003, St. Martin's $25.00 (978-0-312-42222-6). The lives and interests of six teen mothers are revealed in this volume that draws on taped interviews. (Rev: BL 9/15/03; VOYA 6/04) [306.874]

11204 Meyer, Don, ed. *The Sibling Slam Book: What It's Really Like to Have a Brother or Sister with Special Needs* (7–12). 2005, Woodbine paper $15.95 (978-1-890627-52-2). Young people with special-needs siblings share their hopes, joys, fears, frustrations, and triumphs in this slam book. (Rev: SLJ 6/05)

11205 Mufson, Susan, and Rachel Kranz. *Straight Talk About Child Abuse* (7–12). Series: Straight Talk. 1991, Facts on File $27.45 (978-0-8160-2376-9). Beginning with a general discussion of child abuse, this book describes the common signs of physical, emotional, and sexual abuse, gives some case studies, and offers some solutions. (Rev: BL 4/1/91; SLJ 3/91) [362.7]

11206 Musgrave, Susan, ed. *Certain Things About My Mother: Daughters Speak* (10–12). 2003, Annick $18.95 (978-1-55037-813-9); paper $7.95 (978-1-55037-812-2). Seven adult daughters write about their memories — some good, some bad — of their relationships with their mothers as teens. (Rev: SLJ 3/04; VOYA 2/04) [306.874]

11207 Plummer, William. *Wishing My Father Well: A Memoir of Fathers, Sons, and Fly-Fishing* (10–12). 2000, Overlook $21.95 (978-1-58567-031-4). A moving account that explores a father-son relationship by using the father's fishing journals as jumping-off point. (Rev: BL 6/1–15/00) [306.874]

11208 Presma, Frances, and Paula Edelson. *Straight Talk About Today's Families* (9–12). 1999, Facts on File $27.45 (978-0-8160-3905-0). This work discusses different types of families, the challenges of being a part of a family, and ways to deal with family-related problems. [306.8]

11209 Ryan, Elizabeth A. *Straight Talk About Parents* (7–12). 1989, Facts on File $27.45 (978-0-8160-1526-9). A self-help manual to help teens sort out their feelings about parents. (Rev: BL 8/89; SLJ 9/89; VOYA 2/90) [306.8]

11210 Simpson, Carolyn. *Everything You Need to Know About Living with a Grandparent or Other Relatives* (8–12). 1995, Rosen LB $27.95 (978-0-8239-1872-0). This book explores the various situations that may cause teenagers to move in with grandparents, how to adjust, ways to maintain privacy, and the emotions involved on both sides. (Rev: VOYA 2/96) [306]

11211 Slade, Suzanne. *Adopted: The Ultimate Teen Guide. #20* (9–12). Illus. by Christopher Papile and Mary Sandage. Photos by Chris Washburn. Series: It Happened to Me. 2007, Scarecrow $45.00 (978-0-8108-5774-2). This is a comprehensive and sensitive guide to all aspects of adoption, and will be of particular help to young adults who are searching for their birth parents. (Rev: SLJ 11/07) [362.73409]

11212 Stefoff, Rebecca. *Marriage* (9–12). Series: Open for Debate. 2006, Benchmark LB $27.95 (978-0-7614-2299-0). After a history of marriage, Stefoff looks at divorce, same-sex unions, and other relevant contemporary questions, providing arguments on both sides of each issue plus facts and figures. (Rev: SLJ 4/07)

11213 Trenka, Jane Jeong. *The Language of Blood* (10–12). 2003, Minnesota Historical Soc $23.95 (978-0-87351-466-8). Korean-born Trenka, adopted at a young age by a Minnesota couple, describes her search for her cultural identity. (Rev: BL 9/15/03) [977.6]

11214 Trueit, Trudi. *Surviving Divorce* (7–10). Series: Scholastic Choices. 2006, Scholastic LB $22.50 (978-0-531-12368-3). Personal stories add to the facts and quizzes in this book and will reassure readers whose parents are divorcing. (Rev: BL 1/1–15/07) [306.89]

11215 Weiss, Ann E. *Adoptions Today: Questions and Controversy* (7–12). 2001, Twenty-First Century LB $24.90 (978-0-7613-1914-6). This comprehensive and informative overview covers such topics as international adoptions, adoption by unconventional couples, open adoption, and privacy. (Rev: BL 12/15/01; HBG 3/02; VOYA 12/01) [362.73]

11216 Williams, Mary E., ed. *Adoption* (7–12). Series: Opposing Viewpoints. 2006, Gale LB $34.95 (978-0-7377-3301-3). Essays present both sides of various topics relating to adoption: gay adoptions, international adoptions, transracial adoptions, protection of identity, and so forth. (Rev: SLJ 11/06)

11217 Winchester, Elizabeth Siris. *Sisters and Brothers: The Ultimate Guide to Understanding Your Siblings and Yourself* (6–10). Series: Scholastic Choices. 2008, Watts LB $27 (978-0-531-13870-0); paper $8.95 (978-0-531-20528-0). Teens share stories about coping with siblings, including topics such as birth order, step and foster siblings, and being an only child. (Rev: SLJ 10/1/08)

Youth Groups

11218 Cryan, Rosemarie, et al. *A Resource Book for Senior Girl Scouts* (9–12). 1995, Girl Scouts of the USA paper $9.95 (978-0-88441-284-7). Details on scouting and its goals and awards are accompanied by information on careers, college admission, health and wellness, and other topics of interest.

11219 Mechling, Jay. *On My Honor: Boy Scouts and the Making of American Youth* (9–12). 2001, Univ. of Chicago $30.00 (978-0-226-51704-9). After comparing Scouting in the 1900s with issues of today, the author follows a troop through a summer camp experience and discusses concerns including girls, God, and gays. (Rev: BL 10/1/01) [369.43]

11220 Slayton, Elaine Doremus. *Empowering Teens: A Guide to Developing a Community Based Youth Organization* (10–12). 2000, CROYA $19.95 (978-0-615-11164-3). This book, a blueprint for good teen programming, is a case study on how one community offered teens a safe place to grow and be a force in the community. (Rev: BL 10/15/00) [362.7]

11221 Townley, Alvin. *Spirit of Adventure: Eagle Scouts and the Making of America's Future* (9–12). 2009, Thomas Dunne $24.95 (978-0-312-37898-1). Townley reviews the principles and history of scouting and provides a collection of anecdotes about the contributions and achievements of Eagle Scouts. (Rev: SLJ 12/09) [369.4]

Physical and Applied Sciences

General and Miscellaneous

11222 Amato, Ivan. *Super Vision: A New View of Nature* (10–12). 2003, Abrams $40.00 (978-0-8109-4545-6). From a close-up view of a rose petal's texture to the budding of a deadly virus, this stunning collection of photographs demonstrates scientists' advances in such technologies as spectroscopy; the accompanying text gives technical explanations. (Rev: BL 12/1/03) [502.2]

11223 Bjornlund, Lydia. *Natural Disaster Research* (8–11). Illus. Series: Inside Science. 2012, ReferencePoint LB $27.95 (978-160152236-8). With many quotations and interesting sidebars, this visually appealing book presents an overview of research into tsunamis, earthquakes, volcanic eruptions, tornadoes, floods, and hurricanes. (Rev: BL 7/12) [363.34]

11224 Brockman, John, ed. *The Next Fifty Years: Science in the First Half of the Twenty-first Century* (10–12). 2002, Random House paper $14.00 (978-0-375-71342-2). Twenty-five essays by scientists offer interesting speculation on the likely direction of scientific research over the next half century. (Rev: BL 3/15/02) [501.12]

11225 Bryson, Bill. *A Short History of Nearly Everything* (10–12). 2003, Broadway $26.00 (978-0-7679-0817-7). Bryson proves his versatility with this easy-to-read introduction to such basic scientific subjects as the atom, cells, light, and the origin of human life. (Rev: BL 4/15/03) [001]

11226 Carlson, Dale. *In and Out of Your Mind: Teen Science: Human Bites* (8–12). Illus. by Carol Nicklaus. 2002, Bick paper $14.95 (978-1-884158-27-8). Teens with a curious, contemplative nature will find food for thought in this look at the wonders of science, humankind, and the universe that touches on topics including evolution, environmental concerns, and medicine. (Rev: SLJ 9/02) [500]

11227 Chown, Marcus. *The Matchbox That Ate a Forty-Ton Truck: What Everyday Things Tell Us About the Universe* (10–12). 2010, Farrar $25 (978-086547922-

7). Astronomer Chown emphasizes that simple observations of the world around us can teach us much about scientific principles and about our planet. ℮ (Rev: BL 4/1–15/10) [500]

11228 Dawkins, Richard, and Tim Folger, eds. *The Best American Science and Nature Writing, 2003* (10–12). 2003, Houghton Mifflin paper $13.00 (978-0-618-17892-6). This 2003 collection reflects the current preoccupation with defense and security concerns but also includes more cheerful pieces such as those celebrating author Rachel Carson and a mother's determination to succeed in the male-dominated field of science. (Rev: BL 10/15/03) [500]

11229 Fisher, Len. *How to Dunk a Doughnut: The Science of Everyday Life* (10–12). 2003, Arcade $23.95 (978-1-55970-680-3). Fun and facts abound in this appealing book that explores science's all-pervasive influence on our lives, including such routine tasks as dunking a doughnut or catching a ball. (Rev: BL 10/15/03) [502]

11230 Gawande, Atul, and Jesse Cohen, eds. *The Best American Science Writing, 2006* (9–12). 2006, HarperCollins paper $13.95 (978-0-06-072644-7). A collection of "cool" essays from popular magazines, accessible to and enjoyable for the layperson who enjoys reading about science and its social implications. (Rev: BL 9/1/06) [500]

11231 Gould, Stephen Jay. *The Richness of Life: The Essential Stephen Jay Gould* (10–12). 2007, Norton $35.00 (978-0-393-06498-8). A collection of the well-known science writer's essays and speeches, including autobiographical pieces, profiles of scientists, and thoughtful discussions of evolution and other topics. (Rev: SLJ 6/07) [508]

11232 Gribbin, John, and Mary Gribbin. *Almost Everyone's Guide to Science: The Universe, Life and Everything* (10–12). 1999, Yale Univ. paper $11.95 (978-0-

300-08460-3). This is a general history of science, with a special focus on biography and theory. (Rev: BL 9/1/99) [500]

11233 Hakim, Joy. *The Story of Science: Newton at the Center* (7–10). Series: Smithsonian's Story of Science. 2005, Smithsonian $24.95 (978-1-58834-161-7). In the second volume of the series, Hakim introduces readers to the discoveries of Copernicus, Galileo, Newton, and others. (Rev: BL 12/1/05; SLJ 12/05*; VOYA 2/05) [590]

11234 Halpern, Paul. *What's Science Ever Done for Us? What the Simpsons Can Teach Us about Physics, Robots, Life, and the Universe* (9–12). 2007, Wiley paper $14.95 (978-0-470-11460-5). The humor of the cartoon family of the Simpsons is key in illustrating scientific explanations and discussions on various mind-expanding topics, using actual TV episodes as sounding off points, this book is a fun look at science. (Rev: BL 7/07) [500]

11235 Horvitz, Leslie Alan. *Eureka! Scientific Breakthroughs that Changed the World* (9–12). 2002, Wiley $32.50 (978-0-471-40276-3). Twelve scientific discoveries and their discoverers are highlighted, such as Einstein and relativity, Fleming and penicillin, Darwin and evolution, and Watson and Crick and the double helix. [509]

11236 Kolata, Gina, ed. *The Best American Science Writing, 2007* (9–12). 2007, Ecco paper $14.95 (978-0-06-134577-7). Originally seen in mainstream publications such as *Harper's, Esquire,* and the *New Yorker,* this is the 2007 annual selection of 20 of the best pieces of American science writing on such subjects as diagnosing Alzheimer's disease, environmental predictions, movie science, and the teaching of evolution. (Rev: BL 8/07) [500]

11237 Kurtis, Bill. *New Explorers* (10–12). 1995, WTTW Chicago paper $28.95 (978-0-9647457-0-4). The frontiers of today's scientific research are divided into four categories — medical advances, great mysteries, amazing creatures, and fragile earth. Topics range from superconductors, endangered species, and care of newborn babies to the history of dinosaurs, pollution, and rain forests. (Rev: SLJ 4/96) [500]

11238 Leland, John. *Aliens in the Backyard: Plant and Animal Imports into America* (9–12). 2005, Univ. of South Carolina $29.95 (978-1-57003-582-1). Non-indigenous species' good and bad effects on North America's environment are documented in this engaging look at history and science. (Rev: BL 8/05) [578.6]

11239 Lightman, Alan. *The Discoveries: Great Breakthroughs in 20th Century Science* (10–12). 2005, Pantheon $32.50 (978-0-375-42168-6). From a century of revolutionary scientific discoveries, Lightman singles out 25 breakthrough achievements in such diverse disciplines as cosmology, molecular biology, and medi-

cine and introduces the original documentation. (Rev: BL 10/15/05) [509]

11240 Lightman, Alan, ed. *The Best American Science Writing, 2005* (10–12). 2005, HarperPerennial paper $13.95 (978-0-06-072642-3). Twenty-seven articles cover a wide array of science-related topics, including bioterrorism, life on Mars, bumblebees, human genome study, and the delicate relationship between humans and nature. (Rev: BL 9/1/05) [500]

11241 McGrayne, Sharon Bertsch. *Blue Genes and Polyester Plants: 365 More Surprising Scientific Facts, Breakthroughs and Discoveries* (8–12). 1997, Wiley paper $16.95 (978-0-471-14575-2). A compendium of strange and unusual facts from various branches of science. [500]

11242 Ouellette, Jennifer. *The Physics of the Buffyverse* (9–12). 2006, Penguin paper $15.00 (978-0-14-303862-7). Science writer Ouellette looks at the science in *Buffy the Vampire Slayer* and its *Angel* spin-off, explaining the basics of vampire physiology, robotics, and artificial intelligence in chapters with titles such as "Conductivity Unbecoming: The Shocking Truth About Electromagnetism" and "Rough Magic: Spellbound by the Laws of Thermodynamics." (Rev: BL 12/15/06) [530]

11243 Piel, Gerard. *The Age of Science: What Scientists Learned in the Twentieth Century* (10–12). 2001, Basic $40.00 (978-0-465-05755-9). Using a clear text and dozens of illustrations, the author has provided an excellent survey of 100 years of science with coverage of such areas as motion, gravitation, light, the anatomy of a cell, evolution, subatomic particles, and the Big Bang. (Rev: BL 10/15/01) [509.04]

11244 Pinker, Steven, and Tim Folger, eds. *The Best American Science and Nature Writing, 2004* (10–12). 2004, Houghton Mifflin paper $14.00 (978-0-618-24698-4). An eclectic collection of science articles compiled from popular and specialized periodicals. (Rev: BL 10/1/04) [500]

11245 Roberts, Royston M. *Serendipity: Accidental Discoveries in Science* (9–12). 1989, Wiley paper $17.95 (978-0-471-60203-3). An entertaining collection of anecdotes concerning the unusual circumstances surrounding some scientific discoveries. (Rev: SLJ 11/89) [500]

11246 *Scientific American's Ask the Experts: Intrepid Travels Through the Perplexing and Amazing World of Science* (10–12). 2003, HarperResource paper $14.95 (978-0-06-052336-7). For science students and trivia fanatics, this is an excellent compilation of facts and figures, arranged in an easy-to-follow question-and-answer format. (Rev: BL 10/1/03) [500]

11247 Sides, Hampton, ed. *Why Moths Hate Thomas Edison and Other Inquiries into the Odd Nature of Nature* (9–12). 2001, Norton paper $13.95 (978-0-393-32150-0). This collection of columns from *Outside* magazine covers all sorts of nature questions, such as what causes Arctic mirages and why men have nipples. (Rev: BL 8/01) [508]

11248 Spangenburg, Ray, and Diane Kit Moser. *The Birth of Science: Ancient Times to 1699. Rev. ed.* (6–10). Series: The History of Science. 2004, Facts on File $40.00 (978-0-8160-4851-9). A survey of the development of scientific knowledge from ancient times through the seventeenth century, with brief profiles of major scientists plus discussion of discoveries that didn't pan out. Also use *The Rise of Reason: 1700–1799, The Age of Synthesis: 1800–1895, Modern Science: 1896–1945,* and *Science Frontiers: 1946 to the Present* (all 2004). (Rev: SLJ 12/04) [509]

11249 Sussman, Art. *Dr. Art's Guide to Science: Connecting Atoms, Galaxies, and Everything in Between* (6–12). 2006, Jossey-Bass $22.95 (978-0-7879-8326-0). The author makes understanding science fun, using colorful illustrations, chapter overviews, activities, Web links to experiments, a "Glindex" (combining glossary and index), and "Stop & Think" pages. (Rev: SLJ 6/06)

11250 Thomas, Lewis. *The Lives of a Cell: Notes of a Biology Watcher* (10–12). 1974, Viking paper $14.00 (978-0-14-004743-1). The 29 short essays in this collection deal with a variety of scientific subjects including insect behavior, the cell, and intelligent life in outer space. [570.1]

11251 True, Alianor, ed. *Wildfire* (10–12). 2001, Island paper $17.95 (978-1-55963-907-1). A collection of stories and legends about fires and their consequences,

beginning with Native American folklore and continuing with contributions from Twain, Thoreau, and other great writers. (Rev: BL 7/01) [577.2]

11252 Weiner, Jonathan, and Tim Folger, eds. *The Best American Science and Nature Writing, 2005* (9–12). Series: Best American. 2005, Houghton Mifflin $27.50 (978-0-618-27341-6); paper $14.00 (978-0-618-27343-0). Twenty-five essays look at aspects of science and nature that are important to our technological, social, and political lives today. (Rev: BL 10/15/05) [500]

11253 *Why Don't Penguins' Feet Freeze? And 114 Other Questions* (9–12). 2007, Free Press paper $14.00 (978-1-4165-4146-2). Scientific facts are smoothly conveyed in this entertaining collection of "Last Words" columns from *New Scientist* magazine, mostly answering everyday questions such as "why does slicing onions make us cry?" (Rev: BL 5/1/07) [500]

11254 Young, Michael, ed. *The Scientific Revolution* (10–12). Series: Turning Points in World History. 2005, Gale LB $37.45 (978-0-7377-2987-0). A look at the roots and achievements of the "scientific revolution," covering such major figures as Copernicus, Galileo, Kepler, Boyle, and Newton. (Rev: BL 1/1–15/06) [509]

11255 Zotti, Ed. *Know It All! Everything They Should Have Told You in School but Didn't* (9–12). 1993, Ballantine paper $9.00 (978-0-345-36232-2). Zotti provides no-nonsense, sometimes amusing, answers to questions about animals, weather, space, time, and many other subjects. (Rev: BL 7/93) [031]

Experiments and Projects

11256 Brown, Robert J. *333 Science Tricks and Experiments* (7–12). 1984, McGraw-Hill $15.95 (978-0-8306-0825-6). Basic scientific principles are demonstrated in experiments and projects. (Rev: BL 4/1/89) [507]

11257 Downie, Neil. *Vacuum Bazookas, Electric Rainbow Jelly, and 27 Other Saturday Science Projects* (9–12). Illus. by Jim Wilkinson. 2001, Princeton paper $24.95 (978-0-691-00986-5). This book outlines several science projects that involve creating strange constructions to prove physical principles behind technology. (Rev: BL 12/1/01) [507.8]

11258 Dutton, Judy. *Science Fair Season: Twelve Kids, a Robot Named Scorch . . . and What It Takes to Win* (10–12). 2011, Hyperion $24.99 (978-1-4013-2379-0). Profiles teens who have succeeded in the Intel International Science and Engineering Fair (ISEF), which, apart from inspiring really innovative projects, carries a top prize of $50,000. (Rev: BL 3/1–15/11; SLJ 9/11) [507.8]

11259 Iritz, Maxine Haren. *Blue-Ribbon Science Fair Projects* (7–12). 1991, McGraw-Hill paper $9.95 (978-0-07-157629-1). A variety of science fair projects for the novice are presented, with charts, graphs, photographs, and a chapter on choosing a topic. (Rev: BL 9/15/91) [507.8]

11260 Iritz, Maxine Haren. *Science Fair: Developing a Successful and Fun Project* (8–12). 1987, TAB $16.95 (978-0-8306-0936-9). A thorough step-by-step introduction to doing a science project. (Rev: BL 4/15/88) [507]

11261 Johnson, George. *The Ten Most Beautiful Experiments* (9–12). 2008, Knopf $22.00 (978-1-4000-4101-5). Johnson explores ten experiments chosen for their beauty and simplicity — What is motion? What is light? How does blood circulate? What is air made of? — and provides details of the early testers and their successes and failures. (Rev: BL 3/15/08; SLJ 5/08) [507]

11262 Rainis, Kenneth G. *Blood and DNA Evidence: Crime-Solving Science Experiments* (8–11). Series: Forensic Science Projects. 2006, Enslow LB $23.95 (978-0-7660-1958-4). Contains accounts of real-life crime cases and challenges the reader with step-by-step forensic science experiments to solve the case just as real detectives do. (Rev: BL 10/15/06; SLJ 5/07) [363.25]

11263 Rathjen, Don, et al. *Square Wheels and Other Easy-to-Build, Hands-on Science Activities* (9–12). Series: Exploratorium Science Snackbook. 2002, Exploratorium paper $19.95 (978-0-943451-55-8). Step-by-step instructions are provided for 31 projects that demonstrate basic scientific principles, plus interesting factual tidbits and discussions. (Rev: BL 4/1/02) [507]

11264 Rosner, Marc Alan. *Science Fair Success Using the Internet* (8–12). Series: Science Fair Success. 1999, Enslow LB $26.60 (978-0-7660-1172-4). As well as an explanation of how to use Internet resources, this book explains how the Internet can enhance science projects. [507.8]

11265 VanCleave, Janice. *Janice VanCleave's A+ Projects in Chemistry: Winning Experiments for Science Fairs and Extra Credit* (6–10). 1993, Wiley paper $12.95 (978-0-471-58630-2). Thirty experiments that investigate such topics as calories, acids, and electrolytes, among others. (Rev: BL 12/1/95; SLJ 4/94) [930]

11266 Vickers, Tanya M. *Teen Science Fair Sourcebook: Winning School Science Fairs and National Competitions* (6–10). Illus. 2009, Enslow LB $25.95 (978-076602711-4). In chapters such as "The Research Plan and the Scientific Method," "The Rules: Safety, Originality, and Consent," and "The Project Notebook: A Scientist's Cookbook," Vickers lays out the various stages of project creation and provides useful tips. (Rev: BL 7/09; LMC 10/09) [507.8]

Astronomy and Space Science

General and Miscellaneous

11267 Banqueri, Eduardo. *The Night Sky* (6–10). Series: Field Guides. 2007, Enchanted Lion LB $16.95 (978-1-59270-066-0). An informative introduction to the night sky and how best to view it. (Rev: BL 5/15/07; LMC 11/07; SLJ 9/07) [523.80]

11268 Barnes-Svarney, Patricia, and Michael R. Porcellino. *Through the Telescope: A Guide for the Amateur Astronomer. Rev. ed.* (10–12). 2000, McGraw-Hill paper $19.95 (978-0-07-134804-1). As well as describing telescopes, this work shows how to use them to observe the planets, moon, stars, and other objects. [522]

11269 Berry, Richard. *Discover the Stars* (9–12). 1987, Crown paper $12.95 (978-0-517-56529-2). A beginner's guide to exploring stars, planets, and the moon with hints on how to use a telescope. (Rev: SLJ 4/88; VOYA 4/88) [523]

11270 Brunier, Serge, and Anne-Marie Lagrange. *Great Observatories of the World* (9–12). 2005, Firefly $59.95 (978-1-55407-055-8). A dramatic photographic tour of the great astronomical observatories of the world and outer space, with discussion of the technology and the value of the research done there. (Rev: BL 9/1/05) [522.1]

11271 Carlson, Shawn, ed. *Scientific American: The Amateur Astronomer* (10–12). 2001, Wiley paper $17.95 (978-0-471-38282-9). This collection of articles on astronomy from *Scientific American* covers such topics as building a telescope, observing the moon, planets, and stars, and the composition and behavior of our sun. (Rev: BL 12/1/00) [520]

11272 Couper, Heather, and Nigel Henbest. *The History of Astronomy* (8–12). 2007, Firefly $59.95 (978-1-55407-325-2). From Stonehenge and other ancient monuments forward, this attractive volume documents man's interest in the skies and the scientific advances in studying them. (Rev: BL 12/1/07) [520]

11273 Dorminey, Bruce G. *Distant Wanderers: The Search for Planets Beyond the Solar System* (10–12). 2001, Springer-Verlag $29.95 (978-0-387-95074-7). This is an enjoyable account concerning the search for planets outside our solar system (more than 60 have already been located) and the complex techniques used in this study. (Rev: BL 12/1/01) [523]

11274 Dyson, Marianne J. *Space and Astronomy: Decade by Decade* (9–12). Series: Twentieth-Century Science. 2007, Facts on File LB $49.50 (978-0-8160-5536-4). Twentieth-century scientific discoveries in the areas of space and astronomy are examined decade by decade in this well-written and attractive book. (Rev: SLJ 3/08)

11275 Hope, Terry. *Spacecam: Photographing the Final Frontier from Apollo to Hubble* (6–12). 2005, Fitzhenry & Whiteside $24.99 (978-0-7153-2164-5). Images captured from space — many never before published — offer fantastic views of Earth and beyond. (Rev: BL 12/15/05) [778.35]

11276 Impey, Chris. *The Living Cosmos* (9–12). 2007, Random House $27.95 (978-1-4000-6506-6). Is there anyone or anything out there? In this well-illustrated, accessible volume, Impey explains the basic requirements for life and looks at the possible locations. (Rev: BL 12/1/07) [576.8]

11277 Levy, David H. *Deep Sky Objects: The Best and Brightest from Four Decades of Comet Chasing* (9–12). 2005, Prometheus paper $21.98 (978-1-59102-361-6). A fascinating guide, organized by distance from earth and full of interesting personal and historical anecdotes, to the objects that may be confused with comets. (Rev: BL 11/15/05) [523.8]

11278 Levy, David H., and Wendee Wallach-Levy. *Cosmic Discoveries: The Wonder of Astronomy* (10–12).

2001, Prometheus $28.98 (978-1-57392-931-8). For advanced science students, the 24 pieces in this collection explore various aspects of astronomy, past and present, and the perseverance of astronomers. (Rev: BL 9/15/01) [520]

11279 McAleer, Neil. *The Cosmic Mind-Boggling Book* (9–12). 1982, Warner paper $11.95 (978-0-446-39046-0). A fascinating collection of unusual facts about the planets, stars, and universe. [523]

11280 Miller, Ron. *Extrasolar Planets* (7–12). Series: Worlds Beyond. 2002, Millbrook LB $25.90 (978-0-7613-2354-9). A handsome and accessible overview of the planets in our solar system and elsewhere in the universe that includes historical information, biographies of scientists, basic concepts, and many attention-grabbing illustrations. (Rev: BL 2/15/02; HBG 10/02; SLJ 3/02) [523]

11281 Mitchell, Mark G. *Seeing Stars: The McDonald Observatory and Its Astronomers* (6–10). 1997, Sunbelt Media $17.95 (978-1-57168-117-1). This is a history of the famous observatory operated by the University of Texas in Austin, with material on the equipment used and the day-to-day operation. (Rev: HBG 9/98; SLJ 5/98) [523]

11282 Moore, Patrick. *Guide to Stars and Planets. Rev. ed.* (9–12). 2005, Firefly paper $19.95 (978-1-55407-053-4). An excellent guide that provides the basics of identifying celestial bodies, maps of constellations, and categories that can be viewed using binoculars and small telescopes. (Rev: BL 9/15/05) [523]

11283 Moore, Patrick. *Stargazing: Astronomy Without a Telescope. 2nd ed.* (9–12). 2001, Cambridge Univ. paper $31.99 (978-0-521-79445-9). This guide to the night sky using only the naked eye identifies constellations, planets, comets, and meteors. [523]

11284 Plait, Philip. *Death from the Skies! These Are the Ways the World Will End . . .* (10–12). Illus. 2008, Viking $24.95 (978-067001997-7). Expert Philip Plait describes how Earth could be destroyed by a variety of cosmic disasters, the likelihood of that happening, and what we should be doing to prevent such a catastrophe; a fascinating book full of astronomical facts. (Rev: BL 9/1/08) [520]

11285 Raymo, Chet. *An Intimate Look at the Night Sky* (10–12). 2001, Walker $25.00 (978-0-8027-1369-8). Though this is not a field guide, the author supplies lots of astronomical information about the heavens, including the stars, planets, and comets, in a personal and engaging manner. (Rev: BL 5/1/01) [520]

11286 Sagan, Carl. *Cosmos* (9–12). 1980, Random House paper $7.99 (978-0-345-33135-9). A chronological account of how and what we have learned about our universe. [520]

11287 Savage, Marshall T. *The Millennial Project: Colonizing the Galaxy — in 8 Easy Steps* (9–12). 1993, Empyrean LB $24.95 (978-0-9633914-8-3); paper $18.95 (978-0-9633914-9-0). An eight-step program, from colonies in the sea through orbiting colonies. (Rev: BL 1/15/93*) [629.47]

11288 Schaaf, Fred. *The 50 Best Sights in Astronomy and How to See Them: Observing Eclipses, Bright Comets, Meteor Showers, and Other Celestial Wonders* (9–12). 2007, Wiley $19.95 (978-0-471-69657-5). This is an enthusiastic view of the 50 most awe-inspiring views to be caught of the night sky, such as comets, the Andromeda Galaxy, a supernova, Neptune, and much more, and how these phenomena can affect our planet. (Rev: BL 7/07) [520]

11289 Shapiro, Robert. *Planetary Dreams: The Quest to Discover Life Beyond Earth* (9–12). 1999, Wiley $27.95 (978-0-471-17936-8). An engaging look at man's curiosity about this subject, from antiquity to the present day and from many points of view. (Rev: BL 4/99; SLJ 2/00) [576.8]

11290 Snow, Theodore P. *The Cosmic Cycle* (9–12). 1985, Darwin $14.95 (978-0-87850-041-3). A fine introduction to astronomy complete with 34 excellent color plates. (Rev: SLJ 3/86) [523]

11291 Steel, Duncan. *Eclipse: The Celestial Phenomenon That Changed the Course of History* (9–12). 2001, Joseph Henry $24.95 (978-0-309-07438-4). This work surveys all types of eclipses although the focus is on the solar variety and includes material on famous eclipses. (Rev: BL 10/15/01) [523.78]

11292 Stott, Carole, and Clint Twist. *1001 Facts About Space* (7–12). Series: Backpack Books. 2002, DK paper $8.99 (978-0-7894-8450-5). A handy-sized overview full of illustrations that presents useful facts about the universe, galaxies, stars, solar system, and planets as well as pulsars, space history, and stellar classification. (Rev: BL 3/15/02) [590]

11293 Taschek, Karen. *Death Stars, Weird Galaxies, and a Quasar-Spangled Universe: The Discoveries of the Very Large Array Telescope* (7–10). 2006, Univ. of New Mexico $17.95 (978-0-8263-3211-0). Compelling images of space captured from New Mexico's VLA (Very Large Array) telescope are combined with readable descriptions of recent discoveries in astronomy and an overview of the problems that still plague astronomers. (Rev: BL 5/1/06; SLJ 7/06) [522]

11294 Tyson, Neil deGrasse. *Death by Black Hole and Other Cosmic Quandaries* (11–12). 2007, Norton $24.95 (978-0-393-06224-3). Essayist and astrophysicist at the American Museum of Natural History, Tyson covers a multitude of subjects regarding the cosmos: the results of falling in a black hole, how the earth could end, the accuracy of the movie industry's interpretation of skies, and the history of astronomic discoveries. (Rev: BL 12/1/06) [523.8]

11295 Tyson, Neil deGrasse. *Universe Down to Earth* (9–12). 1994, Columbia Univ. $75.50 (978-0-231-07560-2). Translates the fundamental meaning of various scientific models of the cosmos into language comprehensible to the general reader. (Rev: BL 5/1/94) [523.1]

11296 Zimmerman, Robert. *The Universe in a Mirror: The Saga of the Hubble Space Telescope and the Visionaries Who Built It* (10–12). Illus. 2008, Princeton $29.95 (978-069113297-6). This engrossing read chronicles the design and execution of the Hubble space telescope, from its rocky start to the triumph of the deep-space images it eventually transmitted. (Rev: BL 6/1–15/08*) [629.435]

Astronautics and Space Exploration

11297 Barbree, Jay. *Live from Cape Canaveral: Covering the Space Race, from Sputnik to Today* (8–12). 2007, Smithsonian $26.95 (978-0-06-123392-0). Journalist Barbree offers a behind-the-scenes look at the great events and personalities of space flight, from 1957 onward. (Rev: BL 9/1/07) [629.450973]

11298 Belfiore, Michael. *Rocketeers: How a Visionary Band of Business Leaders, Engineers, and Pilots Is Boldly Privatizing Space* (9–12). 2007, Smithsonian $26.95 (978-0-06-114902-3). In 2004 when Scaled Composites put the first astronaut in space without the help of a government agency, the commercial space was begun. This book explores several companies in their endeavors to make space rides available to civilians for profit. (Rev: BL 8/07) [338.0919]

11299 Carlisle, Rodney P. *Exploring Space* (6–10). Series: Discovery and Exploration. 2004, Facts on File $40.00 (978-0-8160-5265-3). The motivations for exploring space are examined in clear, informative text plus photographs, illustrations, and excerpts from primary sources. (Rev: SLJ 12/04) [629.5]

11300 Collins, Martin. *After Sputnik: 50 Years of the Space Age* (8–12). 2007, HarperCollins $35.00 (978-0-06-089781-9). With photographs accompanied by essays, this volume uses approximately 200 artifacts — John Glenn's space suit and a lunar rover, for example — to tell the story of the first 50 years of space exploration. (Rev: SLJ 7/07) [629.409]

11301 Comins, Neil F. *The Hazards of Space Travel: A Tourist's Guide* (9–12). 2007, Villard $19.95 (978-1-4000-6597-4). A look at the hazards of space tourism — from mechanical problems and motion sickness to volcanic eruptions, lack of water, and radiation — with fictitious entries from a space traveler's diary. (Rev: BL 4/1/07; SLJ 6/07) [629.4]

11302 D'Antonio, Michael. *A Ball, a Dog, and a Monkey: 1957 — the Space Race Begins* (9–12). 2007,

Simon & Schuster $26.00 (978-0-7432-9431-7). The forerunners of spacecraft as we now know it, satellites such as Sputnik were sent into orbit by rockets and gadgets crafted quickly and crudely by the superpowers in the hopes of being first in space; the atmosphere of this frantic time (1957-1958) in space flight's birth is also well covered in this fascinating book. (Rev: BL 8/07) [629.43]

11303 Duggins, Pat. *Final Countdown: NASA and the End of the Space Shuttle Program* (8–12). 2007, Univ. Press of Florida $24.95 (978-0-8130-3146-0). Duggins tells the story of the space shuttle from initial inception to the planning of the final missions, with information on shuttle astronauts and on the two shuttle disasters. (Rev: BL 9/1/07) [629.45]

11304 Fischer, Daniel. *Mission Jupiter: The Spectacular Journey of the Galileo Space Probe* (10–12). 2001, Springer-Verlag $32.00 (978-0-387-98764-4). For advanced science students, this is an account, with pictures, of the successful spacecraft *Galileo,* its mission to Jupiter, and what it found out. (Rev: BL 5/15/01) [629.43]

11305 Jones, Chris. *Too Far from Home: A Story of Life and Death in Space* (9–12). 2007, Doubleday $24.95 (978-0-385-51465-1). Readers learn all about flying in the space shuttle and life aboard the International Space Station, as well as the harrowing experience of the crew stranded on the space station after the *Columbia* disaster. ⋒ (Rev: BL 3/1/07) [629.45]

11306 Kraemer, Robert S. *Beyond the Moon: A Golden Age of Planetary Exploration, 1971-1978* (9–12). 2000, Smithsonian $34.95 (978-1-56098-954-7). This volume traces the space probes launched by NASA, including journeys to Mars, the other planets, and the asteroid belt. [629.43]

11307 Mari, Christopher, ed. *Space Exploration* (9–12). Series: Reference Shelf. 1999, H.W. Wilson paper $50.00 (978-0-8242-0963-6). A collection of articles that explores past, present, and possible future developments in space exploration, and how knowledge of space has changed human lives. [629]

11308 Miller, Ron. *Satellites* (7–10). Series: Space Innovations. 2007, Lerner LB $31.93 (978-0-8225-7154-4). How do satellites get up there? Which country was the first to launch one? What do they do? Do they ever fall back to Earth? This well-designed book answers these questions and more, providing lots of relevant history. (Rev: BL 12/1/07) [629.44]

11309 Morton, Oliver. *Mapping Mars: Science, Imagination, and the Birth of a World* (10–12). 2002, St. Martin's $30.00 (978-0-312-24551-1). An interesting look at how the physical realities of Mars differ markedly from the images projected by earlier earthbound astronomers. (Rev: BL 7/02) [523.43]

11310 Neal, Valerie, et al. *Spaceflight: A Smithsonian Guide* (9–12). Series: Smithsonian Guide. 1995, Macmillan $18.00 (978-0-02-860007-9). The history of space flight beginning with Sputnik, with photographs of missions, launches, landings, and designs. (Rev: BL 6/1–15/95) [629.4]

11311 Nelson, Craig. *Rocket Men: The Epic Story of the First Men on the Moon* (9–12). Illus. 2009, Viking $27.95 (978-067002103-1). This is a detailed account of the scientific and political reasons behind Apollo 11, the many people involved with the project, and the innumerable steps taken to ensure the success of the mission. ∩ ℮ (Rev: BL 4–5/09*) [629.45]

11312 Parks, Peggy J. *Space Research* (8–11). Illus. Series: Inside Science. 2010, ReferencePoint LB $26.95 (978-160152111-8). A slim but informative overview of the kinds of research being conducted in space, the challenges of living and working in space, and the importance of this work for mankind as a whole. (Rev: BL 12/1/10) [500.5]

11313 Pyle, Rod. *Destination Moon: The Apollo Missions in the Astronauts' Own Words* (9–12). 2005, HarperCollins $24.95 (978-0-06-087349-3). With photographs and dialogue from the astronauts themselves, Pyle chronicles the story of the Apollo space program. (Rev: BL 11/15/05) [629.45]

11314 Reynolds, David West. *Kennedy Space Center: Gateway to Space* (9–12). 2006, Firefly $40.00 (978-1-55407-039-8). Full of illustrations, this book looks at the history of the Space Center, at key individuals involved (such as Wernher von Braun), and — in some detail — at the act of launching a rocket and how this has evolved. (Rev: BL 10/15/06) [629.47]

11315 Roach, Mary. *Packing for Mars: The Curious Science of Life in the Void* (10–12). Illus. 2010, Norton $25.95 (978-039306847-4). Covering everything from weightlessness-induced motion sickness to hygiene and toilet procedures, Roach applies her zeal for science and novel experiences to this intriguing book. ∩ ℮ (Rev: BL 7/10) [629.45]

11316 Sparrow, Giles. *Space Flight: The Complete Story from Sputnik to Shuttle — and Beyond* (9–12). 2007, DK $40.00 (978-0-7566-2858-1). The history of space travel is introduced in this attractive volume illustrated with more than 800 photographs and diagrams, chronicling how the technology has evolved and the role the visionaries and scientists played in its development. (Rev: BLO 7/17/07) [629.41]

11317 Thimmesh, Catherine. *Team Moon: How 400,000 People Landed Apollo 11 on the Moon* (5–10). 2006, Houghton Mifflin $19.95 (978-0-618-50757-3). A breathless account of all the behind-the-scenes work that went into the Apollo space program, with plenty of photographs. Sibert Medal 2007. (Rev: SLJ 6/06) [629.45]

11318 Voit, Mark. *Hubble Space Telescope: New Views of the Universe* (8–12). 2000, Abrams paper $19.95 (978-0-8109-2923-4). With an accompanying text, this book includes more than 100 photographs taken by the Hubble Space Telescope. (Rev: SLJ 4/01) [520]

11319 Walsh, Patrick J. *Echoes Among the Stars: A Short History of the U.S. Space Program* (10–12). 2000, M.E. Sharpe $31.95 (978-0-7656-0537-5). This is a history of manned space flight, from the early successes of the Mercury and Gemini missions to the beginning of the 21st century. [629.4]

Comets, Meteors, and Asteroids

11320 Bevan, Alex, and John de Laeter. *Meteorites: A Journey Through Space and Time* (10–12). 2002, Smithsonian $35.95 (978-1-58834-021-4). Richly illustrated, this overview of meteorites focuses on the information they can reveal about their origins and the history of space. (Rev: BL 5/1/02) [523.5]

11321 Burnham, Robert. *Great Comets* (9–12). 2000, Cambridge Univ. paper $47.00 (978-0-521-64600-0). Various comets are identified and described, including Hyakutake in 1996 and Hale-Bopp in 1997. (Rev: BL 12/1/99) [523.6]

11322 Koppes, Steven N. *Killer Rocks from Outer Space: Asteroids, Comets, and Meteorites* (7–10). 2003, Lerner LB $27.93 (978-0-8225-2861-6). Koppes examines the science and history of planetary impacts by asteroids, comets, and meteorites and looks at steps being taken to protect the Earth from such impacts in the future. (Rev: BL 1/1–15/04; SLJ 3/04) [523.5]

11323 Levy, David H. *Comets: Creators and Destroyers* (9–12). 1998, Simon & Schuster paper $12.00 (978-0-684-85255-3). Levy explores the life cycle of a comet and examines theories about comets' potential benefits and dangers. (Rev: BL 5/1/98) [523.6]

11324 Miller, Ron. *Asteroids, Comets, and Meteors* (7–10). Series: Worlds Beyond. 2005, Twenty-First Century LB $27.93 (978-0-7613-2363-1). Using color photographs, vivid paintings, and helpful diagrams, this title introduces readers to asteroids, comets, and meteors. (Rev: SLJ 12/05)

11325 Nardo, Don. *Asteroids and Comets* (7–10). Illus. Series: Extreme Threats. 2009, Morgan Reynolds LB $28.95 (978-159935121-6). With chapters including "The Day the Sky Exploded," "Giant Impacts and Mass Extinctions," and "Recent Strikes and Near Misses," this book discusses past collisions with Earth and the likelihood of future disasters. (Rev: BL 4/1/10; VOYA 12/09) [523.44]

11326 Peebles, Curtis. *Asteroids* (10–12). 2000, Smithsonian $29.95 (978-1-56098-389-7). As revealed in this book, the study of these small celestial wanderers has led scientists to rethink the structure of the solar system and the history of the earth. (Rev: BL 10/15/00*) [523.44]

11327 Smith, Caroline, et al. *Meteorites* (10–12). Illus. 2009, Firefly $24.95 (978-155407515-7). A thorough and heavily illustrated overview of meteorites and their significance from London's Natural History Museum. (Rev: BL 12/1/09) [523.51]

Earth and the Moon

11328 Hockey, Thomas A. *The Book of the Moon* (10–12). 1986, Prentice Hall $19.95 (978-0-13-079971-5). Although mainly about the moon, this book also furnishes information on space exploration and astronomy. (Rev: BL 10/15/86) [523.3]

11329 Johnson, Kirk R., and Richard K. Stucky. *Prehistoric Journey* (10–12). 1995, Rinehart paper $19.95 (978-1-57098-145-6). A chronology of the evolution of life on Earth from its creation 4.6 billion years ago to the present. (Rev: SLJ 5/96; VOYA 8/97) [575]

11330 Mackenzie, Dana. *The Big Splat; or, How Our Moon Came to Be* (10–12). 2003, Wiley $33.95 (978-0-471-15057-2). More than just an exploration of conflicting theories about the moon's origin, this fascinating study also examines the historical evolution of human perceptions of the moon. (Rev: BL 4/15/03) [523.3]

Stars

11331 Kaler, James B. *The Hundred Greatest Stars* (10–12). 2002, Copernicus/Springer-Verlag $32.50 (978-0-387-95436-3). This personal selection of the top 100 stars, with a brief description and accompanying image of each, will be useful for reports. (Rev: BL 8/02) [523.8]

11332 Kerrod, Robin. *The Star Guide: Learn How to Read the Night Sky Star by Star. 2nd ed.* (8–12). 2005, Wiley $29.95 (978-0-471-70617-5). This guide to identifying heavenly bodies is well organized for novices and includes a removable sky map. (Rev: BL 4/15/05) [523.8]

11333 VanCleave, Janice. *Janice VanCleave's Constellations for Every Kid: Easy Activities That Make Learning Science Fun* (8–12). 1997, Wiley paper $12.95 (978-0-471-15979-7). An excellent guide to the heavens, with each chapter presenting a different constellation with concise facts, new concepts, simple activities, and solutions to problems. (Rev: BL 12/1/97; HBG 3/98; SLJ 10/97) [523.8]

Sun and the Solar System

11334 Bone, Neil. *Mars Observer's Guide* (10–12). 2003, Firefly paper $14.95 (978-1-55297-802-3). This guide intended for amateur astronomers will also prove invaluable to report writers. (Rev: BL 5/1/03) [523.43]

11335 Cattermole, Peter. *Mars: The Story of the Red Planet* (9–12). 1992, Chapman & Hall paper $59.95 (978-0-412-44140-0). A detailed, technical look at the scientific study of Mars, filled with photographs, graphs, and charts. (Rev: BL 10/1/92) [523.43]

11336 Clark, Stuart. *The Sun Kings: The Unexpected Tragedy of Richard Carrington and the Tale of How Modern Astronomy Began* (11–12). 2007, Princeton $24.95 (978-0-691-12660-9). Advanced science students will enjoy this accessible account of 19th-century scientific controversy about the nature of the sun, and the story of Richard Carrington, who failed to make a career in astronomy despite his scientific discoveries. (Rev: BL 4/15/07) [520]

11337 Corfield, Richard. *Lives of the Planets: A Natural History of the Solar System* (9–12). 2007, Basic $30.00 (978-0-465-01403-3). Corfield enthusiastically presents a comprehensive discussion of our knowledge of the members of the solar system: the history of ancient discoveries and the wealth of information we now have, due to the most recent technological probes. (Rev: BL 7/07) [523.2]

11338 Harrington, Philip S. *Eclipse! The What, Where, When, Why, and How Guide to Watching Solar and Lunar Eclipses* (9–12). 1997, Wiley paper $19.95 (978-0-471-12795-6). An explanation of lunar and solar eclipses, with advice on how best to view and photograph them. [523.7]

11339 Hartmann, William K. *A Traveler's Guide to Mars* (10–12). 2003, Workman paper $18.95 (978-0-7611-2606-5). The history, geography, geology, and topography are covered in detail, with photographs, digital images, and interesting sidebar features. (Rev: BL 8/03; SLJ 12/03) [919.9]

11340 Lorenz, Ralph, and Jacqueline Mitton. *Titan Unveiled: Saturn's Mysterious Moon Explored* (10–12). 2008, Princeton $29.95 (978-0-691-12587-9). The discoveries on Saturn's moon will fascinate science students, particularly those interested in astronomy and astrophysics. (Rev: BL 4/15/08) [523.2]

11341 McNab, David, and James Younger. *The Planets* (9–12). 1999, Yale Univ. $45.00 (978-0-300-08044-5). Illustrated with space-age photographs, this book introduces and compares the planets. (Rev: BL 9/1/99; SLJ 6/00) [523]

11342 Miller, Ron. *Mars* (7–10). Series: Worlds Beyond. 2005, Twenty-First Century LB $27.93 (978-0-7613-2362-4). Introduces readers to the planet Mars in a blend of easy-to-understand narrative and colorful space photos. (Rev: SLJ 12/05)

11343 Raeburn, Paul. *Mars: Uncovering the Secrets of the Red Planet* (9–12). 1998, National Geographic $40.00 (978-0-7922-7373-8). With magnificent illustrations ranging from superpanoramas to technical drawings, this book describes the findings of the Mars Pathfinder expedition and the work of the rover named Sojourner. (Rev: BL 8/98; SLJ 4/99) [523.2]

11344 Sheehan, William, and Stephen James O'Meara. *Mars: The Lure of the Red Planet* (10–12). 2001, Prometheus $28.98 (978-1-57392-900-4). From Kepler to today, here is the story of the endless fascination people have had for the planet Mars and what we have found out about it. (Rev: BL 3/15/01) [523.43]

11345 Sobel, Dava. *The Planets* (10–12). 2005, Viking $24.95 (978-0-670-03446-8). Science, culture, mythology, and astrology are all blended in this interesting survey of the planets of our solar system. (Rev: BL 8/05; SLJ 2/06) [523.2]

11346 Spence, Pam. *Sun Observer's Guide* (7–12). 2004, Firefly paper $14.95 (978-1-55297-941-9). A useful guide to the sun and the equipment that ensures safe observation of it. (Rev: BL 11/1/04) [522]

11347 Weintraub, David A. *Is Pluto a Planet? A Historical Journey through the Solar System* (11–12). 2007, Princeton $27.95 (978-0-691-12348-6). In August 2006 Pluto was stripped of its planet status by the International Astronomical Union, giving Weintraub, an astronomy professor, cause to explore this declaration by defining what a planet is and looking at the planetary discoveries of the past. (Rev: BL 12/1/06) [523.2]

Universe

11348 Comins, Neil F. *Heavenly Errors: Misconceptions About the Real Nature of the Universe* (10–12). 2001, Columbia $27.95 (978-0-231-11644-2). Drawing on material he garnered from his college students, the author describes many common scientific misconceptions in astronomy and sets the record straight. (Rev: BL 7/01) [520]

11349 Hawking, Stephen. *A Brief History of Time* (10–12). 1998, Bantam $27.95 (978-0-553-10953-5); paper $16.95 (978-0-553-38016-3). This revised edition of Hawking's classic offers an updated overview of what scientists have learned about the natural order of the universe and the questions that remain to be answered. [523.1]

11350 Hawking, Stephen. *The Universe in a Nutshell* (10–12). 2001, Bantam $35.00 (978-0-553-80202-3). For advanced students, this renowned scientist explains the basic laws of physics beginning with a brief history of the concept of relativity. (Rev: BL 12/1/01; SLJ 5/02) [530.12]

11351 Hawking, Stephen, and Leonard Mlodinow. *A Briefer History of Time* (9–12). 2005, Bantam $25.00 (978-0-553-80436-2). More concise and accessible than the classic *A Brief History of Time* (1988), this explanation of the concept of a dynamic cosmos makes excellent reading, especially for physics students. (Rev: BL 7/05) [523.1]

11352 Laidler, Keith J. *The Harmonious Universe: The Beauty and Unity of Scientific Understanding* (10–12). 2004, Prometheus $29.98 (978-1-59102-187-2). This overview of material relating to the universe focuses on understanding the atom and discovering facts about mass. (Rev: BL 5/15/04) [500]

11353 Miller, Ron. *Stars and Galaxies* (7–10). Series: Worlds Beyond. 2005, Twenty-First Century LB $27.93 (978-0-7613-3466-8). A comprehensive overview of the universe, discussing theories and facts about neighboring stars and distant galaxies alike, with wonderful NASA photos mixed with original art. (Rev: BL 12/1/05; SLJ 12/05) [523.8]

11354 Perricone, Mike. *The Big Bang* (6–12). Series: Science Foundations. 2009, Chelsea House $35 (978-1-60413-015-7). This volume covers the pioneering work of Hubble and other key scientists before discussing what we now know about the origins of the universe and the implications of the Big Bang. (Rev: LMC 11–12/09) [523.1]

11355 Villard, Ray, and Lynette Cook. *Infinite Worlds: An Illustrated Voyage to Planets Beyond Our Sun* (8–12). 2005, Univ. of California $39.95 (978-0-520-23710-0). Using known data, the author and illustrator speculate about the likely appearance of planets in other solar systems. (Rev: BL 6/1–15/05) [523.21]

Biological Sciences

General and Miscellaneous

11356 Bakalar, Nicholas. *Where the Germs Are: A Scientific Safari* (10–12). 2003, Wiley $24.95 (978-0-471-15589-8). A fascinating exploration of the hidden world of germs, the threats they pose, and the everyday places we are most likely to encounter bad ones. (Rev: BL 2/1/03) [616.014]

11357 Bowler, Peter J. *The Norton History of the Environmental Sciences* (9–12). 1993, Norton $35.00 (978-0-393-03535-3). Historical highlights and development of the environmental sciences. (Rev: BL 7/93) [363.7]

11358 Brooks, Bruce. *The Red Wasteland* (6–10). 1995, Henry Holt $15.95 (978-0-8050-4495-9). A fine anthology of essays, stories, poems, and book excerpts by some of the best nature writers, who raise themes and questions about crucial issues relating to the environment. (Rev: BL 8/98; HBG 3/99; SLJ 6/98; VOYA 8/98) [808]

11359 Dillard, Annie. *Pilgrim at Tinker Creek* (10–12). 1974, Harper & Row paper $13.95 (978-0-06-095302-7). A wonderful nature study book that records the seasons at Tinker Creek in Virginia. [818]

11360 Duensing, Edward, and A. B. Millmoss. *Backyard and Beyond: A Guide for Discovering the Outdoors* (9–12). 1992, Fulcrum paper $19.95 (978-1-55591-071-6). Descriptions of various animals, plants, and insects, with tips on how to observe and track them. (Rev: BL 3/15/92) [508.2]

11361 Ensminger, Peter A. *Life Under the Sun* (10–12). 2001, Yale $30.00 (978-0-300-08804-5). This science book about sunlight explains the relationship between Earth's creatures and the Sun. (Rev: BL 3/1/01) [571.4]

11362 Foster, Steven, and Roger A. Caras. *A Field Guide to Venomous Animals and Poisonous Plants: North America, North of Mexico* (9–12). 1994, Houghton Mifflin paper $21.00 (978-0-395-93608-5). About 90 venomous animals and about 250 plants are described in the field guide. [578.6]

11363 Glavin, Terry. *The Sixth Extinction: Journey Among the Lost and Left Behind* (9–12). 2007, St. Martin's $24.95 (978-0-312-36231-7). Glavin looks at extinction in new wide-ranging terms — the loss of animal species, of fruits and vegetables, and of languages, art forms, and even scenery — in this well-written and compelling book. (Rev: BL 1/1–15/07) [598.17]

11364 Hamilton, Gary. *Super Species: The Creatures That Will Dominate the Planet* (9–12). Illus. 2010, Firefly $35 (978-155407630-7). An interesting discussion of 20 successful invasive species, the threats they pose, and the surprising ways in which they may actually benefit the environment. (Rev: BL 12/1–15/10) [577]

11365 Haupt, Lyanda Lynn. *Pilgrim on the Great Bird Continent: The Importance of Everything and Other Lessons from Darwin's Lost Notebooks* (10–12). 2006, Little, Brown $24.95 (978-0-316-83664-7). For students interested in Darwin and nature, this is an interesting observation of his voyage of discovery. (Rev: BL 3/1/06) [508]

11366 Lawlor, Elizabeth P. *Discover Nature at Sundown: Things to Know and Things to Do* (9–12). 1995, Stackpole paper $14.95 (978-0-8117-2527-9). Sensory awareness for nature lovers to track and observe creatures at night. (Rev: BL 2/15/95) [591.5]

11367 McLeish, Todd. *Golden Wings and Hairy Toes: Encounters with New England's Most Imperiled Wildlife* (9–12). 2007, Univ. Press of New England $26.00 (978-1-58465-626-5). McLeish accompanies scientists on expeditions to look at examples of 14 endangered species (plant and animal) in New England. (Rev: BL 9/1/07) [574.529]

11368 Murray, John A., ed. *Nature's New Voices* (9–12). 1992, Fulcrum paper $15.95 (978-1-55591-117-1). Personal literary observations on natural history by a contemporary generation of nature essayists. (Rev: BL 10/1/92) [508.73]

11369 O'Brien, Stephen J. *Tears of the Cheetah and Other Tales from the Genetic Frontier* (10–12). 2003, St. Martin's $25.95 (978-0-312-27286-9). Advanced students will enjoy these stories of research into the genetic makeup of animal species including the lion, panda, and humpback whale. (Rev: BL 9/1/03) [591.3]

11370 Quinn, John R. *Wildlife Survivors: The Flora and Fauna of Tomorrow* (9–12). 1994, TAB $21.95 (978-0-8306-4346-2); paper $12.95 (978-0-8306-4345-5). A serious study that explores the concept that plants and animals will continue to survive despite the encroachment of human civilization. (Rev: BL 3/1/94) [574.5]

11371 Raham, R. Gary. *Dinosaurs in the Garden: An Evolutionary Guide to Backyard Biology* (6–10). 1988, Plexus $22.95 (978-0-937548-10-3). The author uses common creatures to explain how they fit into the scheme of nature and overall patterns of evolution. (Rev: BL 12/1/88) [575]

11372 Trauth, Joy, and Aldemaro Romero, eds. *Adventures in the Wild: Tales from Biologists of the Natural State* (10–12). 2008, Univ. of Arkansas paper $19.95 (978-1-55728-872-1). Interesting stories of biological research will draw students in and inform them about scientific work in the field. (Rev: BL 4/15/08) [570.72]

11373 VanCleave, Janice. *Janice VanCleave's A+ Projects in Biology: Winning Experiments for Science Fairs and Extra Credit* (6–10). 1993, Wiley paper $12.95 (978-0-471-58628-9). Offers a variety of experiments in botany, zoology, and the human body. (Rev: BL 1/15/94; SLJ 11/93) [574]

11374 Walker, Pam, and Elaine Wood. *Ecosystem Science Fair Projects Using Worms, Leaves, Crickets, and Other Stuff* (6–12). Series: Biology! Best Science Projects. 2005, Enslow LB $26.60 (978-0-7660-2367-3). Biology science projects are clearly presented with background information necessary to full understanding of the underlying principles. (Rev: SLJ 7/05) [570]

Botany

General and Miscellaneous

11375 Lincoff, Gary. *The Audubon Society Field Guide to North American Mushrooms* (7–12). 1981, Knopf $19.95 (978-0-394-51992-0). More than 700 species are introduced and pictured in color photographs. [589.2]

Foods, Farms, and Ranches

GENERAL AND MISCELLANEOUS

11376 *Bound for Glory: America in Color, 1939–43* (8–12). 2004, Abrams $35.00 (978-0-8109-4348-3). American farm life during the late 1930s and early 1940s is beautifully captured in these color photographs taken under the auspices of the Farm Security Administration, best known for earlier black-and-white collections. (Rev: BL 6/1–15/04) [779]

11377 Carlip, Hillary. *A la Cart: The Secret Lives of Grocery Shoppers* (9–12). 2008, Virgin $17.95 (978-1-905264-17-9). The lost shopping lists of 26 strangers and the imagined lives behind the lists form the narrative for this funny one-of-a-kind book. (Rev: BL 3/15/08) [818]

11378 Damerow, Gail, ed. *Barnyard in Your Backyard: A Beginner's Guide to Raising Chickens, Ducks, Geese, Rabbits, Goats, Sheep, and Cows* (10–12). 2002, Storey paper $24.95 (978-1-58017-456-5). A practical, friendly, and fact-filled guide to the care and feeding of farm animals. (Rev: BL 12/15/02) [636]

11379 Dunn-Georgiou, Elisha. *Everything You Need to Know About Organic Foods* (6–10). Series: Need to Know Library. 2002, Rosen LB $27.95 (978-0-8239-3551-2). An examination of the techniques that produce organic foods and the benefits of eating foods that are free of certain additives. (Rev: BL 5/1/02; SLJ 6/02) [641.3]

11380 Foer, Jonathan Safran. *Eating Animals* (11–12). 2009, Little, Brown $25.99 (978-031606990-8). Foer takes a hard, critical look at the practice of factory farming (including fish), supplying copious detail about the miserable lives of feedlot animals along the way; for mature readers. ◯ ℮ (Rev: BL 11/15/09*) [641.3]

11381 Freedman, Jeri. *Genetically Modified Food: How Biotechnology Is Changing What We Eat* (7–12). 2009, Rosen LB $29.95 (978-1-4358-5025-5). This balanced, thorough book provides insight into the history, challenges, issues, and risks of genetic modification of the foods we eat. (Rev: LMC 10/09) [363.1]

11382 Friend, Catherine. *Hit by a Farm: How I Learned to Stop Worrying and Love the Barn* (11–12). 2006, Marlowe & Co. paper $14.95 (978-1-56924-298-8). Friend writes about what she learns — about farming and about life — when she and her partner, Melissa, buy 53 acres in Minnesota. (Rev: BL 4/15/06) [630.9776]

11383 Gay, Kathlyn. *Food: The New Gold* (8–12). Illus. 2012, Lerner/Twenty-First Century LB $31.93 (978-0-7613-4607-4). From global hunger and food distribution to trends in farming, the impact of climate change, genetic modification of plants and animals, food safety, and food policy, this informative book provides clear text and interesting sidebars. (Rev: BL 12/1/12*; LMC 5–6/13; SLJ 9/12) [338.1]

11384 Goldstein, Myrna Chandler, and Mark A. Goldstein. *Controversies in Food and Nutrition* (9–12). Series: Contemporary Controversies. 2002, Greenwood $51.95 (978-0-313-31787-3). Such controversial topics as diets, vegetarianism, food irradiation, vitamin supplements, and genetic modification are discussed from differing points of view. (Rev: BL 5/1/03) [641.3]

11385 Hamilton, Lisa M. *Deeply Rooted: Unconventional Farmers in the Age of Agribusiness* (10–12). 2009, Counterpoint $25 (978-159376180-6). Hamilton presents farmers and ranchers who believe in doing what is best for the land and its people by eschewing big business farming practices. **e** (Rev: BL 4–5/09) [338.10973]

11386 Hayhurst, Chris. *Everything You Need to Know About Food Additives* (6–10). Series: Need to Know Library. 2002, Rosen LB $27.95 (978-0-8239-3548-2). An examination of the kinds of additives used in foods, their benefits and disadvantages, and the alternatives available to people seeking a healthier diet. (Rev: BL 5/1/02) [664]

11387 Henderson, Elizabeth, and Robyn Van En. *Sharing the Harvest: A Citizen's Guide to Community-Supported Agriculture. Rev. ed* (9–12). 2008, Chelsea House $35.00 (978-1-933392-10-3). This is a new edition of the guide to locally grown food, with advice for growers and consumers alike. (Rev: BL 3/15/08) [334]

11388 Igoe, Robert S. *Dictionary of Food Ingredients* (10–12). 1989, Van Nostrand paper $39.95 (978-0-442-31927-4). A dictionary of the approximately 1,000 food ingredients approved by the Food and Drug Administration. [664]

11389 Montgomery, M. R. *A Cow's Life: The Surprising History of Cattle and How the Black Angus Came to Be Home on the Range* (9–12). 2004, Walker $25.00 (978-0-8027-1414-5). An entertaining evolutionary history of domesticated cattle. (Rev: BL 10/15/04) [636.2]

11390 Niman, Bill. *The Niman Ranch Cookbook: From Farm to Table with America's Finest Meats* (9–12). 2005, Ten Speed $35.00 (978-1-58008-520-5). For readers interested in humane animal treatment and high-quality food, this is a fascinating account of modern farming practices. (Rev: BL 10/15/05) [641.3]

11391 Pelczar, Rita, ed. *Homegrown Harvest: A Season-by-Season Guide to a Sustainable Kitchen Garden* (9–12). Illus. 2010, Mitchell Beazley $32.50 (978-184533560-1). A thorough and practical guide suitable for beginners and experts alike. (Rev: BLO 12/1–15/10) [635]

11392 Rosenblum, Mort. *Chocolate: A Bittersweet Saga of Dark and Light* (9–12). 2005, Farrar $24.00 (978-0-86547-635-6). For an in-depth report, this volume offers history, statistics, important characters, and debate. (Rev: BL 2/1/05) [641.3]

11393 Satin, Morton. *Food Alert! The Ultimate Sourcebook for Food Safety* (10–12). 1999, Facts on File $38.50 (978-0-8160-3935-7); paper $14.95 (978-0-8160-3936-4). This book discusses types of food, food production and processing, and the problems that can arise. (Rev: BL 7/99) [615.9]

11394 Singer, Peter, and Jim Mason. *The Way We Eat: Why Our Food Choices Matter* (10–12). 2006, Rodale $25.95 (978-1-57954-889-6). A look at the food processing and distribution industries and how they end up disconnecting us from our sources of nutrition. The authors strongly advocate vegetarianism as being easier on animals, people, and the economy. (Rev: BL 5/15/06) [178]

11395 Smith, Jeremy N. *Growing a Garden City* (10–12). Illus. 2010, Skyhorse $24.95 (978-161608108-9). The lengthy subtitle *How Farmers, First Graders, Counselors, Troubled Teens, Foodies, A Homeless Shelter Chef, Single Mothers, and More Are Transforming Themselves and Their Neighborhoods Through the Intersection of Local Agriculture and Community — and How You Can, Too* describes this profile of food programs in Missoula, Montana. **e** (Rev: BL 9/1–15/10) [635.09786]

11396 Tannahill, Reay. *Food in History. Rev. ed.* (9–12). 1989, Crown paper $16.00 (978-0-517-88404-1). From prehistoric times to the present, this is the history of food and how it has changed the course of human development. [641.3]

VEGETABLES

11397 Letcher, Andy. *Shroom: A Cultural History of the Magic Mushroom* (10–12). 2007, Ecco $25.95 (978-0-06-082828-8). A straightforward history of the use of psychedelic mushrooms and their periods of popularity. (Rev: BL 1/1–15/07) [394.1]

11398 Weaver, William Woys. *100 Vegetables and Where They Come From* (9–12). 2000, Algonquin $18.95 (978-1-56512-238-3). The author highlights 100 vegetables, describes their characteristics, and tells about the origin of each. (Rev: BL 11/15/00) [635.9]

Forestry and Trees

11399 Bjornlund, Lydia. *Deforestation* (7–12). Series: Compact Research. 2009, ReferencePoint LB $25.95 (978-1-60152-075-3). Answering questions including "What Are the Consequences of Deforestation?," Bjornlund describes how the world's forests are being destroyed and discusses sustainable solutions for the future. (Rev: LMC 1–2/10)

11400 Little, Elbert L. *The Audubon Society Field Guide to North American Trees: Eastern Region* (7–12). 1980, Knopf $19.95 (978-0-394-50760-6). This volume describes through text and pictures of leaves, needles, and so on, the trees found east of the Rocky Mountains. [582.16]

11401 Little, Elbert L. *The Audubon Society Field Guide to North American Trees: Western Region* (7–12). 1980, Knopf $19.95 (978-0-394-50761-3). Trees west of the Rockies are identified and pictured in photographs and drawings. [582.16]

11402 Logan, William Bryant. *Oak: The Frame of Civilization* (9–12). 2005, Norton $24.95 (978-0-393-04773-8). An attractive and accessible history of the oak and its many contributions to human civilization. (Rev: BL 5/1/05) [634.7]

11403 Pakenham, Thomas. *Remarkable Trees of the World* (10–12). 2002, Norton $49.95 (978-0-393-04911-4). Tall, short, long-lived, revered — trees with "strong personality" are the focus of this absorbing narrative accompanied by eye-catching photographs. (Rev: BL 11/1/02; SLJ 4/03) [582.16]

11404 Petrides, George A. *A Field Guide to Trees and Shrubs* (7–12). 1973, Houghton Mifflin paper $19.00 (978-0-395-35370-7). A total of 646 varieties found in northern United States and southern Canada are described and illustrated. [582.1]

11405 Preston, Richard. *The Wild Trees: A Story of Passion and Daring* (9–12). 2007, Random House $25.95 (978-1-4000-6489-2). The fascinating story of dangerous but rewarding research done in the canopies (hundreds of feet above the ground) of redwood forests and the discovery of endangered redwood groves that were previously unknown. ∩ (Rev: BL 2/15/07) [585]

11406 Rodd, Tony, and Jennifer Stackhouse. *Trees: A Visual Guide* (10–12). Illus. 2008, Univ. of California $29.95 (978-052025650-7). This beautifully illustrated guide looks at trees' form and function, diversity and design, their importance in the ecosystem, and the ways in which we use them. (Rev: BL 9/15/08) [582.16]

11407 Tudge, Colin. *The Tree: A Natural History of What Trees Are, How They Live, and Why They Matter* (9–12). 2006, Crown $27.95 (978-1-4000-5036-9). We may take trees for granted but they are one of our most important natural resources, says the author, providing us with wood, food, medicine, shade, oxygen, and beauty. (Rev: BL 9/1/06) [582.16]

11408 Walker, Laurence C. *Forests: A Naturalist's Guide to Woodland Trees* (9–12). 1997, Univ. of Texas paper $24.95 (978-0-292-79112-1). This overview of forest ecology examines many different species of trees and how they are affected by such variables as climate and soil type. [582.16]

11409 Wells, Diana. *Lives of the Trees: An Uncommon History* (9–12). Illus. 2009, Algonquin $19.95 (978-156512491-2). In this illustrated album with brief and informative essays, Wells introduces 100 varieties of trees and offers insight into their cultural, historical, and environmental value. (Rev: BL 11/15/09) [398.24]

11410 Whitman, Ann H., and Jane Friedman, eds. *Familiar Trees of North America: Eastern Region* (8–12). 1986, Knopf paper $9.00 (978-0-394-74851-1). As well as pictures and descriptions, this guide supplies historical information, habitats, and uses for 80 trees commonly found in the eastern parts of North America. [582.16]

11411 Whitman, Ann H., and Jane Friedman, eds. *Familiar Trees of North America: Western Region* (8–12). 1986, Knopf paper $9.00 (978-0-394-74852-8). This pocket guide covers 80 trees found commonly in the western United States. [582.16]

Plants and Flowers

11412 Angier, Bradford. *Field Guide to Medicinal Wild Plants* (10–12). 1978, Stackpole paper $19.95 (978-0-8117-2076-2). With many color illustrations the author introduces more than 100 wild medicinal plants, many of them originally used by primitive tribes. [581.6]

11413 Hershey, David R. *Plant Biology Science Projects* (9–12). Series: Best Science Projects for Young Adults. 1995, Wiley paper $16.95 (978-0-471-04983-8). This book supplies good step-by-step instructions for experiments and projects involving plants. (Rev: SLJ 4/95) [580.7]

11414 Kesseler, Rob, and Madeline Harley. *Pollen: The Hidden Sexuality of Flowers* (9–12). 2006, Firefly $60.00 (978-1-55407-219-4). Illustrated with photographs, illustrations, and electron microscopy images, this is a beautiful guide — created by an internationally recognized scientist and an artist, both associated with London's Royal Botanic Gardens — to the nature of pollen, the journey it must make to fertilize plants, and its impact on our lives. (Rev: BL 12/1/06) [571.8]

11415 Peterson, Roger Tory, and Margaret McKenny. *A Field Guide to Wildflowers of Northeastern and North-Central North America: A Visual Approach Arranged by Color, Form, and Detail* (9–12). 1968, Houghton Mifflin paper $19.00 (978-0-395-91172-3). Nearly 1,300 species are discussed and pictured in this invaluable guide. [582.13]

11416 Silverstein, Alvin. *Plants* (7–10). Series: Kingdoms of Life. 1996, Twenty-First Century LB $25.90 (978-0-8050-3519-3). The classification system of plants is explained, from simple plants through ferns and on to flowering plants. (Rev: BL 6/1–15/96; SLJ 7/96) [581]

11417 Spellenberg, Richard. *Familiar Flowers of North America: Eastern Region* (8–12). 1986, Knopf paper $9.00 (978-0-394-74843-6). Photographs, diagrams, and descriptions are found in this guide to 80 wildflowers found in the eastern regions of North America. Also use *Familiar Flowers of North America: Western Region*. [582.13]

11418 Stuppy, Wolfgang, and Madeline Harley. *The Bizarre and Incredible World of Plants* (9–12). Ed. by Alexandra Papadakis. Illus. by Rob Kesseler. 2009, Firefly $29.95 (978-155407533-1). Illustrated with beautiful electron microscopy images, this is a handsome guide to the diversity of plants. (Rev: BL 12/1/09) [580]

Seeds

11419 Kesseler, Rob, and Wolfgang Stuppy. *Seeds: Time Capsules of Life* (9–12). 2006, Firefly $60.00 (978-1-55407-221-7). The amazing journeys of seeds — which can entail thousands of miles and hundreds of years before germination — and their evolution are shown in beautiful artwork and electron photomicroscopy in this guide that also discusses the importance of seed conservation. (Rev: BL 12/1/06) [581.4]

Zoology

General and Miscellaneous

11420 Conniff, Richard. *Swimming with Piranhas at Feeding Time: My Life Doing Dumb Stuff with Animals* (10–12). 2009, Norton $25.95 (978-039306893-1). Conniff provides amusing and interesting anecdotes from his international travels through the animal kingdom. (Rev: BL 4–5/09) [590]

11421 Greek, C. Ray, and Jean Swingle Greek. *Sacred Cows and Golden Geese: The Human Cost of Experiments on Animals* (10–12). 2000, Continuum $29.95 (978-0-8264-1226-3). This book opposes experimentation with animals, offering evidence that it is not only cruel but also ineffective. (Rev: BL 5/15/00) [179]

11422 Laufer, Peter. *Forbidden Creatures: Inside the World of Animal Smuggling and Exotic Pets* (10–12). 2010, Lyons $19.95 (978-159921926-4). Journalist Laufer provides a haunting glimpse into the criminal world of exotic animal smuggling, and the often catastrophic effects of escaped exotics outside their native habitat. (Rev: BLO 6/1–15/10) [364.1]

11423 *Mammal Anatomy: An Illustrated Guide* (8–12). 2010, Marshall Cavendish LB $99.80 (978-0-7614-7882-9). This detailed yet accessible volume (a repackaging of an earlier multivolume set) examines the anatomy and physiology of mammals including chimpanzees, dolphins, elephants, giraffes, gray whales, grizzly bears, kangaroos, lions, manatees, seals, squirrels, wolves, and zebras. (Rev: BLO 1/21/10; LMC 1–2/10) [571.3]

11424 Mills, Guy, and Martin Harvey. *African Predators* (9–12). 2001, Smithsonian $39.95 (978-1-56098-096-4). This handsome book profiles such African predatory animals as cheetahs, lions, leopards, and hyenas. (Rev: BL 12/1/01) [599.7]

11425 Noyes, Deborah. *One Kingdom: Our Lives with Animals* (7–10). 2006, Houghton $18.00 (978-0-618-49914-4). The bond between humans and animals is the topic of this thoughtful photo-essay that looks in particular at zoos and conservation. (Rev: BL 10/15/06; HB 9–10/06; LMC 10/06; SLJ 11/06) [590]

11426 Peterson, Brenda. *Build Me an Ark: A Life with Animals* (10–12). 2001, Norton $25.95 (978-0-393-05014-1). This book describes the important role that wild animals have played in the life of the author, particularly in the western states and Hawaii. (Rev: BL 1/1–15/01) [599]

11427 Wells, Ken, ed. *Herd on the Street: Animal Stories from the Wall Street Journal* (10–12). 2003, Free Press paper $14.00 (978-0-7432-5420-5). This delightful collection of more than 50 animal stories from the pages of the *Wall Street Journal* touches on a wide variety of subjects, including a $1.9 million veterinary hospital for hedgehogs and the dangers of canoeing among hippos. (Rev: BL 11/1/03) [590]

11428 Williams, Erin E., and Margo DeMello. *Why Animals Matter: The Case for Animal Protection* (10–12). 2007, Prometheus paper $20.00 (978-1-59102-523-8). Debaters will find lots of material here as the authors discuss the meat industry, hunting, the textile industry, animal experimentation, and the pet and entertainment industries. (Rev: BL 5/15/07) [179.3]

11429 Wolfe, Art. *The Living Wild* (9–12). 2000, Wildlands $55.00 (978-0-9675918-0-3). As well as a series of essays about animals, this splendid book contains beautiful photographs showing various creatures in their natural habitats. (Rev: BL 10/15/00) [590]

Amphibians and Reptiles

GENERAL AND MISCELLANEOUS

11430 Behler, John, and F. W. King. *The Audubon Society Field Guide to North American Reptiles and Amphibians* (9–12). 1979, Knopf $19.00 (978-0-394-50824-5). This comprehensive account covers reptiles and amphibians found in continental United States, Canada, and Hawaii. [597.6]

11431 Crump, Marty. *Amphibians, Reptiles, and Their Conservation* (6–12). 2002, Linnet LB $25.00 (978-0-208-02511-1). After describing these animals and giving the pertinent scientific information, the author describes the challenges to their survival and what can be done to save them. (Rev: BL 12/1/02; HBG 3/03; SLJ 1/03; VOYA 6/03) [597.9]

11432 Gibbons, Whit. *Their Blood Runs Cold: Adventures with Reptiles and Amphibians* (7–12). 1983, Univ. of Alabama paper $15.95 (978-0-8173-0133-0).

An informal guide, geographically arranged, to snakes, crocodiles, turtles, salamanders, and toads. [597.6]

11433 Means, D. Bruce. *Stalking the Plumed Serpent and Other Adventures in Herpetology* (10–12). Illus. 2008, Pineapple $19.95 (978-1-56164-433-9). Respected herpetologist Means shares his adventures in the field and explains the curious habits and anatomy of many different kinds of reptiles and amphibians. (Rev: BL 8/08) [597.9]

FROGS AND TOADS

11434 Behler, John, and Deborah Behler. *Frogs: A Chorus of Colors* (9–12). 2005, Sterling $19.95 (978-1-4027-2814-3). An attractive and informative introduction to the diverse world of frogs, created to accompany a traveling exhibit. (Rev: BL 11/1/05) [597.89]

11435 Beltz, Ellin. *Frogs: Inside Their Remarkable World* (9–12). 2005, Firefly $34.95 (978-1-55297-869-6). A bright and thorough introduction to frogs and the threats they face today, with information on frogs in literature and some interesting frog facts. (Rev: BL 1/1–15/06) [597.8]

SNAKES AND LIZARDS

11436 Coates, Jennifer. *Lizards* (7–12). Illus. Series: Our Best Friends. 2009, Eldorado Ink LB $26.95 (978-193290431-4). An in-depth review of the benefits and responsibilities of owning a lizard, covering choosing the best lizard, potential health problems, and how to make an attractive terrarium. (Rev: BL 6/1–15/09) [639.3]

11437 Gaywood, Martin, and Ian Spellerberg. *Snakes* (6–12). Series: WorldLife Library. 1999, Voyageur paper $16.95 (978-0-89658-449-5). Facts about snakes and their ability to adapt to their environment are accompanied by discussion of their relationship with humans and eye-catching full-color photographs. (Rev: SLJ 4/00) [597.96]

11438 Greene, Harry W. *Snakes: The Evolution of Mystery in Nature* (10–12). 1997, Univ. of California $60.00 (978-0-520-20014-2). With unusual photographs and a lucid text, this is a tribute to snakes, their beauty, unique characteristics, history, and place in the environment. (Rev: BL 5/1/97; SLJ 12/97) [597.96]

11439 Mattison, Chris. *The Encyclopedia of Snakes* (10–12). 1995, Facts on File $35.00 (978-0-8160-3072-9). This book can be used for both browsing and research, because it offers interesting facts about all aspects of reptile life in an attractive text, with many colorful photographs. (Rev: BL 8/95; SLJ 2/96) [597.96]

11440 O'Shea, Mark. *Boas and Pythons of the World* (9–12). 2007, Princeton $29.95 (978-0-691-13100-9). Covering the continents in turn, O'Shea looks at the pythons and boas of all sizes and abilities, using con-

cise text and excellent photographs. (Rev: BL 4/15/07) [597.967]

11441 Rubio, Manny. *Rattlesnake: Portrait of a Predator* (9–12). 1998, Smithsonian $49.95 (978-1-56098-808-3). With 250 color photographs and detailed text, this book describes the origin, habitats, physiology, and anatomy of the rattlesnake and chronicles a history of people's different relationships with it, from commercial exploitation to snake-handling religious sects. (Rev: BL 12/1/98; SLJ 4/99) [597.96]

TORTOISES AND TURTLES

11442 Franklin, Carl J. *Turtles: An Extraordinary Natural History 200 Million Years in the Making* (9–12). Illus. by David C. Killpack. 2007, MBI $35.00 (978-0-7603-2981-8). Full of information for researchers, this is a thorough and well-illustrated survey of turtles and the many species found all over the world. (Rev: BL 9/1/07) [597.92]

11443 Nicholls, Henry. *Lonesome George: The Life and Loves of a Conservation Icon* (9–12). 2006, Macmillan $24.95 (978-1-4039-4576-1). The sad tale of Lonesome George, the last known Galapagos giant tortoise, is a good introduction to the importance of conservation. (Rev: BL 4/1/06) [597.9]

11444 Ripple, Jeff. *Sea Turtles* (10–12). Series: World Life Library. 1996, Voyageur paper $16.95 (978-0-89658-315-3). Using more than 50 color photographs, this book introduces the sea turtle and its distribution, behavior, anatomy, history, and characteristics, plus information on current conservation techniques and future trends. (Rev: SLJ 5/97) [597.92]

11445 Safina, Carl. *Voyage of the Turtle: In Pursuit of the Earth's Last Dinosaur* (9–12). 2006, Henry Holt $27.50 (978-0-8050-7891-6). A look at leatherback, loggerhead, and green turtles, from their egg-laying habits to the dangers they face. Stories of people whose lives are connected to turtles enhance readers' understanding and enjoyment. (Rev: BL 5/15/06; SLJ 11/06) [597.92]

11446 Spotila, James R. *Sea Turtles: A Complete Guide to Their Biology, Behavior, and Conservation* (9–12). 2004, Johns Hopkins paper $25.95 (978-0-8018-8007-0). The need for conservation is a strong theme in this detailed but accessible guide to sea turtles. (Rev: BL 12/1/04) [597.92]

11447 Witherington, Blair. *Sea Turtles: An Extraordinary Natural History of Some Uncommon Turtles* (9–12). 2006, MBI $29.95 (978-0-7603-2644-2). Biologist Witherington presents the results of 20 years of studying the seven species of sea turtles in this well-illustrated volume that covers the turtles; physiology, anatomy, life cycle, and natural history; it also provides information on their intriguing nesting ritual and birth and on conservation. (Rev: BL 11/1/06) [597.928]

Animal Behavior

GENERAL AND MISCELLANEOUS

11448 Balcombe, Jonathan. *Pleasurable Kingdom: Animals and the Nature of Feeling Good* (9–12). 2006, Macmillan $24.95 (978-1-4039-8601-6). Do animals feel pleasure? It's an important question involving animal welfare, and Balcombe looks at the research to answer it. (Rev: BL 5/1/06) [591.5]

11449 Bekoff, Marc. *The Emotional Lives of Animals: A Leading Scientist Explores Animal Joy, Sorrow, and Empathy and Why They Matter* (10–12). 2007, New World $23.95 (978-1-57731-502-5). Interesting anecdotes add to the accessible text in this survey of animal emotions or "cognitive ethology." (Rev: BL 2/1/07) [591.51]

11450 Berger, Joel. *The Better to Eat You With: Fear in the Animal World* (10–12). Illus. 2008, Univ. of Chicago $29.00 (978-022604363-0). Joel Berger examines whether or not animals' survival instincts will resurface when natural predators that have been gone for many years are returned to the environment. **e** (Rev: BL 9/15/08) [591.5]

11451 Brown, Augustus. *Why Pandas Do Handstands: And Other Curious Truths about Animals* (9–12). 2006, Free Press $15.95 (978-1-4165-3190-6). An entertaining book full of fun facts and curiosities (such as the title question) about all sorts of animals, including their intelligence, tool use, warfare, coexistence, anatomy, and so forth. (Rev: BL 10/1/06) [591.5]

11452 Crump, Marty, and Alan Crump. *Headless Males Make Great Lovers and Other Unusual Natural Histories* (9–12). 2005, Univ. of Chicago $25.00 (978-0-226-12199-4). Bizarre behavior within the animal kingdom is showcased by field biologist Marty Crump in this richly illustrated volume. (Rev: BL 11/1/05) [590]

11453 Gould, James R., and Carol Grant Gould. *Animal Architects: Building and the Evolution of Intelligence* (11–12). 2007, Basic $26.95 (978-0-465-02782-8). Animals' abilities to build complex — and often beautiful — structures are shown here, with discussion of their motives, techniques, materials, and inventiveness. (Rev: BL 3/15/07) [591.5]

11454 Halliday, Tim, ed. *Animal Behavior* (9–12). 1994, Univ. of Oklahoma $24.95 (978-0-8061-2647-0). A basic book on how animals are born, live, and die. Contains its share of cuddly creatures but does not shy away from portraying (with photographs) their place in the food chain. (Rev: BL 5/1/94) [591.51]

11455 Lorenz, Konrad. *On Aggression* (10–12). Trans. by Marjorie Kerr Wilson. 1966, Harcourt paper $17.00 (978-0-15-668741-6). The author examines aggression in animals and humans and describes both positive and negative aspects of this emotion. [152.4]

11456 Schutt, Bill. *Dark Banquet: Blood and the Curious Lives of Blood-Feeding Creatures* (11–12). Illus. 2008, Harmony $25.95 (978-030738112-5). Vampire bats, chiggers, ticks, bedbugs, and the history and importance of blood are discussed informally in this scientifically correct and accessible book. (Rev: BL 8/08) [591.5]

11457 Smith, Lewis. *Why the Cheetah Cheats and Other Mysteries of the Natural World* (10–12). Illus. 2009, Firefly paper $29.95 (978-15540753-4-8). Smith recounts multiple incidents of animal responses to natural and man-made encroachments on their environments in lively text with eye-catching photographs. (Rev: BL 12/1/09) [590]

11458 Stevens, Kathy. *Where the Blind Horse Sings* (9–12). 2007, Sterling $22.95 (978-1-60239-055-3). This is a moving story of the Catskill Animal Sanctuary, where troubled animals have found humans they can trust. (Rev: BL 4/15/07) [630]

COMMUNICATION

11459 Reynolds, Bonnie Jones, and Dawn E. Hayman. *If Only They Could Talk: The Miracles of Spring Farm* (10–12). 2005, Pocket paper $14.00 (978-0-7434-6486-4). The story of New York's Spring Farm and its groundbreaking research into communications between species. (Rev: BL 10/15/05) [636.08]

HOMES

11460 Hansell, Mike. *Built by Animals: The Natural History of Animal Architecture* (10–12). 2007, Oxford $29.95 (978-0-19-920556-1). Do animals build their structures purely by instinct? Hansell explores the amazing buildings created by termites, wasps, beavers, and other animals, looking for similarities and for clues to the architects' processes. (Rev: BL 11/1/07) [591.564]

11461 MacNamara, Peggy, and John Bates. *Architecture by Birds and Insects: A Natural Art* (10–12). Illus. 2008, Univ. of Chicago $25.00 (978-022650097-3). The study of birds' and insects' nests and burrows is shown to have relevance to human architecture in this dynamic fusion of art and science. (Rev: BLO 7/30/08) [598.156]

MIGRATION

11462 Wilcove, David S. *No Way Home: The Decline of the World's Greatest Animal Migrations* (10–12). 2007, Island $24.95 (978-1-55963-685-9). The upheavals that migrating animals and birds are facing around the world is the focus of this well-written book that also looks at the hows and whys of the migratory process. (Rev: BL 11/1/07*) [591.56]

REPRODUCTION AND BABIES

11463 Senson, Pat. *Nasty, Brutish and Short: The Quirks and Quarks Guide to Animal Sex and Other Weird Behavior* (10–12). 2010, McClelland & Stewart paper $18.95 (978-07710796-8-9). Tales of the weird and wacky sexual habits of fish and animals across the globe, gleaned from Canadian radio interviews of experts. ℮ (Rev: BLO 1/1–15/11)

TRACKS

11464 Murie, Olaus J. *A Field Guide to Animal Tracks. 2nd ed.* (7–12). 1996, Houghton Mifflin paper $8.95 (978-0-395-58297-8). This important volume in the Peterson Field Guide series first appeared in 1954 and now has become a classic in the area of identifying animal tracks and droppings. [591.5]

Animal Species

GENERAL AND MISCELLANEOUS

11465 Alden, Peter. *Peterson First Guide to Mammals of North America* (8–12). 1988, Houghton Mifflin paper $5.95 (978-0-395-91181-5). An uncluttered basic guide to mammal identification with many illustrations and useful background material. (Rev: BL 5/15/87) [599]

11466 Anderson, Sydney, ed. *Simon and Schuster's Guide to Mammals* (9–12). 1984, Simon & Schuster paper $17.00 (978-0-671-42805-1). This guide, originally published in Italy, introduces the orders of mammals and highlights 426 species. [599]

11467 Attenborough, David. *The Life of Mammals* (10–12). 2003, Princeton $29.95 (978-0-691-11324-1). In this richly illustrated companion to the Discovery Channel documentary series of the same name, Attenborough examines in detail the diverse world of mammals. (Rev: BL 4/15/03) [599]

11468 Carson, Mary Kay. *The Bat Scientists* (7–10). Photos by Tom Uhlman. Series: Scientists in the Field. 2010, Houghton Mifflin $18.99 (978-0-547-19956-6). A fascinating photo-filled overview of bats, the environmental challenges they face, and the ways in which scientists study them. ALA Notable Books 2011. (Rev: BL 10/15/10*; SLJ 11/1/10) [599.4]

11469 Davis, Susan E., and Margo DeMello. *Stories Rabbits Tell: A Natural and Cultural History of a Misunderstood Creature* (10–12). 2003, Lantern paper $20.00 (978-1-59056-044-0). A lively look at rabbits and their roles in the wild, as pets, and in fantasy and folklore. (Rev: BL 9/1/03) [636.932]

11470 Fenton, M. Brock. *Just Bats* (7–12). 1983, Univ. of Toronto paper $15.95 (978-0-8020-6464-6). An introduction to this frequently misunderstood and very useful flying rodent. [599.4]

11471 Gibson, Graeme. *The Bedside Book of Beasts: A Wildlife Miscellany* (10–12). Illus. 2009, Doubleday $35 (978-038552459-9). This eye-catching compendium of images and text ranging from folklore and poetry to the writings of naturalists explores the relationship between humans and the larger predatory beasts. (Rev: BL 10/15/09) [591.5]

11472 Graves, Russell A. *The Prairie Dog: Sentinel of the Plains* (9–12). 2001, Texas Tech Univ. $39.95 (978-0-89672-456-3); paper $19.95 (978-0-89672-455-6). This beautifully illustrated book transports readers to the world of prairie dogs, exploring their social structure and the important role they once played in the ecosystem of America's Great Plains. (Rev: BL 1/1–15/02) [599.37]

11473 Harris, Tim, ed. *Invertebrates* (9–12). Illus. Series: Facts at Your Fingertips: Endangered Animals. 2011, Black Rabbit LB $35.65 (978-193633333-2). Introduces a variety of invertebrates and their general characteristics, with a focus on those that are endangered and the nature of the threats. (Rev: BL 2/15/12) [592.168]

11474 Hyde, Dayton O. *All the Wild Horses: Preserving the Spirit and Beauty of the World's Wild Horses* (9–12). 2006, Voyageur $40.00 (978-0-7603-2590-2). With photographs by Rita and Charles Summers, Hyde presents a fascinating look at wild horse herds — in France's Camargue and Virginia's Chincoteague Island, for example — and describes his own wild horse sanctuary. (Rev: BL 11/1/06) [599.665]

11475 Irwin, Robert. *Camel* (10–12). Illus. 2010, Reaktion paper $19.95 (978-18618964-9-0). In addition to covering camels' physiology and characteristics, this well-illustrated book looks at their history, place in literature and art, relationship with humans, and modern uses; with tips on riding them and eating their meat. (Rev: BLO 1/1–15/11) [599.6362]

11476 Joubert, Beverly. *Relentless Enemies: Lions and Buffalo* (9–12). 2006, National Geographic $40.00 (978-1-4262-0004-5). The predator/prey relationship between the lions and buffalo in Botswana's Okavango Delta is the subject of this fascinating book. (Rev: BL 11/15/06) [599.757096883]

11477 Langton, Jerry. *Rat: How the World's Most Notorious Rodent Clawed Its Way to the Top* (9–12). 2007, St. Martin's $21.95 (978-0-312-36384-0). Everything you want to know about rats — their history, their ubiquity, how they harm humans, and how they can help humans — plus some gross stories you could probably do without. (Rev: BL 5/1/07) [599.35]

11478 Mares, Michael A. *A Desert Calling: Life in a Forbidding Landscape* (10–12). 2002, Harvard $29.95 (978-0-674-00747-5). Field biologist Mares transports readers to the deserts of the world to introduce them to the wide array of animal life that flourishes there and to reveal the joys of doing research in the field. (Rev: BL 4/1/02) [599.1754]

11479 Masson, Jeffrey Moussaieff. *Altruistic Armadillos, Zenlike Zebras: A Menagerie of 100 Favorite Animals* (9–12). 2006, Ballantine $27.95 (978-0-345-47881-8). In short essays, author Masson lovingly celebrates his 100 favorite animals — octopi, sturgeon, okapis, and chickens among them — combining facts with his own views about them and why he finds them the most fascinating. (Rev: BL 11/1/06) [590]

11480 Rath, Sara. *The Complete Pig: An Entertaining History of Pigs* (9–12). 2000, Voyageur $29.95 (978-0-89658-435-8). An entertaining, informative book about pigs, their diversity, history, behavior, and folklore. (Rev: BL 6/1–15/00) [636.4]

11481 Ross, Mark C., and David Reesor. *Predator: Life and Death in the African Bush* (7–12). 2007, Abrams $35.00 (978-0-8109-9301-3). Lions, cheetahs, hyenas, crocodiles, and leopards are shown in various activities in their native habitats, with accompanying text that discusses their daily lives, anatomy, behavior, and so forth. (Rev: BL 9/15/07) [599.7096]

11482 Rue, Leonard Lee. *Beavers* (9–12). 2002, Voyageur paper $16.95 (978-0-89658-548-5). A beautifully illustrated introduction to the beaver, its amazing building abilities, and its relationship with humans. (Rev: BL 5/1/02) [599.37]

11483 Stillman, Deanne. *Mustang: The Saga of the Wild Horse in the American West* (9–12). 2008, Houghton Mifflin $25.00 (978-0-618-45445-7). Tough little Mustang horses are icons of the American West and the author traces their sometimes controversial story from the 1500s to the present day. (Rev: BL 4/15/08) [599.665]

APE FAMILY

11484 Fossey, Dian. *Gorillas in the Mist* (9–12). 1983, Houghton Mifflin paper $15.00 (978-0-618-08360-2). This account covers 15 years in the author's life when she lived with the mountain gorillas in their natural habitat. (Rev: SLJ 12/83) [599.8]

11485 Swindler, Daris Ray. *Introduction to the Primates* (10–12). 1998, Univ. of Washington paper $22.00 (978-0-295-97704-1). Traces the evolutionary history of monkeys and apes and looks at their anatomy, diet and habitat, and behavior. [599.8]

11486 Waal, Frans de. *My Family Album: Thirty Years of Primate Photography* (10–12). 2003, Univ. of California $34.95 (978-0-520-23615-8). De Waal's passion for primates shows in these stunning photographs, which are accompanied by sound scientific details. (Rev: BL 10/1/03) [779]

BEARS

11487 Breiter, Matthias. *Bears: A Year in the Life* (9–12). 2005, Firefly $34.95 (978-1-55407-077-0). Traces the lives of black, grizzly, and polar bears through a year, with cubs maturing and learning to hunt and socialize. (Rev: BL 9/15/05) [599.78]

11488 Craighead, Frank C, Jr. *Track of the Grizzly* (10–12). 1979, Sierra Club paper $16.00 (978-0-87156-322-4). This introduction to the grizzly bear is the result of a 13-year study in Yellowstone National Park. [599.74]

11489 Ellis, Richard. *On Thin Ice: The Changing World of the Polar Bear* (10–12). 2009, Knopf $27.95 (978-030727059-7). A thorough history of the polar bear and its habitat and life cycle, with discussion of its importance to Inuits and the potentially devastating impact of climate change on its survival. (Rev: BL 10/15/09*) [599.786]

11490 Fergus, Charles. *Bears* (10–12). 2005, Stackpole $19.95 (978-0-8117-3251-2). Introduces readers to the three major bear species — black, grizzly, and polar — of North America, examining physical characteristics, social behavior, feeding behavior, habitat, hibernation, territoriality, and relations with humans. (Rev: BL 9/15/05) [599.78]

11491 Lawter, William Clifford. *Smokey Bear 20252: A Biography* (9–12). 1994, Lindsay Smith $26.95 (978-0-9640017-0-1). Outlines the history of Smokey Bear (a real bear, rescued from a forest fire and sent to the National Zoo), the famous poster, and the uniforms worn by the nation's forest service. (Rev: BL 5/1/94) [363.377]

11492 Lourie, Peter. *The Polar Bear Scientists* (7–10). Illus. Series: Scientists in the Field. 2012, Houghton Mifflin $18.99 (978-054728305-0). Lourie provides a fascinating look at the work of scientists studying Alaskan polar bears and the threats to their survival. ℮ (Rev: BL 4/15/12; HB 3–4/12; LMC 8–9/12; SLJ 3/12) [599.786]

11493 Milse, Thorsten. *Little Polar Bears* (7–12). 2006, Prestel $45.00 (978-3-7658-1586-7). As newly born polar bear cubs frolic and explore their surroundings in Hudson Bay, Manitoba, photographer Milse captures their every move amid a vast landscape, following the journey with their mother from birthing den to hunting grounds. (Rev: BL 11/15/06) [779.9599786]

11494 Ovsyanikov, Nikita. *Polar Bears* (10–12). Series: World Life Library. 1998, Voyageur paper $16.95 (978-0-89658-358-0). This absorbing and well-illustrated volume examines in detail the life of polar bears. (Rev: BL 12/15/98) [599.786]

11495 Rosing, Norbert. *The World of the Polar Bear* (9–12). 2006, Firefly $45.00 (978-1-55407-155-5). Photographer Rosing captures the activities of the largest of the land-based carnivores as their lives fluctuate between land and ice according to the changing seasons on Hudson Bay. (Rev: BL 10/1/06) [599.786]

11496 Schullery, Paul, ed. *Mark of the Bear* (10–12). 1996, Sierra Club $30.00 (978-0-87156-903-5). Ten naturalists describe their encounters with bears, with more than half the book devoted to full-page, full-color photographs. (Rev: BL 12/1/96; SLJ 1/97) [599.74]

11497 Turbak, Gary. *Grizzly Bears* (6–10). Series: World Life Library. 1997, Voyageur paper $14.95 (978-0-89658-334-4). High-quality photographs and concise, readable text are used to introduce the grizzly bear's life cycle, origin, habits, anatomy, and future. (Rev: SLJ 10/97) [599.74]

CATS (LIONS, TIGERS, ETC.)

11498 Adamson, Joy. *Born Free: A Lioness of Two Worlds* (7–12). 1987, Pantheon $11.95 (978-0-679-56141-5). First published in 1960, this is an account of a young lioness growing up in captivity in Kenya. [599.74]

11499 Bekoff, Marc, and Cara Blessley Lowe, eds. *Listening to Cougar* (10–12). 2007, Univ. Press of Colorado $24.95 (978-0-87081-894-3). Stories of personal encounters with cougars — interwoven with discussion of the animals' importance in the ecosystem and in Native American legend — make compelling reading. (Rev: BL 11/15/07) [599.75]

11500 Bertram, Brian. *Lions* (10–12). Series: World Life Library. 1998, Voyageur paper $16.95 (978-0-89658-399-3). This absorbing and well-illustrated volume examines in detail the life of lions. (Rev: BL 12/15/98) [599.757]

11501 Caputo, Philip. *Ghosts of Tsavo: Stalking the Mystery Lions of East Africa* (10–12). 2002, Geographic/Adventure $27.00 (978-0-7922-6362-3). Pulitzer Prize–winning novelist Caputo recounts encounters with the big cats and other dangerous wildlife of Kenya's Tsavo region. (Rev: BL 5/1/02) [599.757]

11502 Gamble, Cyndi. *Leopards: Natural History and Conservation* (7–10). Photos by Rodney Griffiths. Series: WorldLife Library. 2004, Voyageur paper $12.95 (978-0-89658-656-7). Introduces readers to the three leopard species of the world, their habitats, and the threats they face. (Rev: SLJ 4/05) [599.74]

11503 Mangelsen, Thomas D., and Cara Shea Blessley. *Spirit of the Rockies: The Mountain Lions of Jackson Hole* (9–12). 2000, Images of Nature $19.95 (978-1-890310-19-6). Beautiful photographs and an interesting text highlight this story of a mother mountain lion and her three cubs during the winter of 1999 in Wyoming. (Rev: BL 5/15/00) [599.75]

11504 Seidensticker, John, and Susan Lumpkin. *Cats: Smithsonian Answer Book* (8–12). 2004, Smithsonian paper $24.95 (978-1-58834-126-6). From the char-

acteristics of the common tabby to the exotic puma, researchers and browsers will find a wealth of information in this book, which is arranged in question-and-answer format and includes many color photographs. (Rev: BL 10/1/04) [599.75]

11505 Siedensticker, John. *Tigers* (10–12). Series: World Life Library. 1996, Voyageur paper $19.95 (978-0-89658-295-8). The distribution, anatomy, behavior, history, and endangered status of the tiger are discussed in this book that contains more than 50 stunning color photographs. (Rev: SLJ 5/97) [599.74]

11506 Sinha, Vivek R. *The Vanishing Tiger* (8–12). 2004, Trafalgar $29.95 (978-1-84065-441-7). A wonderful photographic record of an expedition to locate and photograph India's massive Bengal tiger. (Rev: BL 3/1/04) [599.7]

COYOTES, FOXES, AND WOLVES

11507 Askani, Tanja. *Kinship with the Wolf: The Amazing Story of the Woman Who Lives with Wolves* (9–12). 2006, Inner Traditions paper $19.95 (978-1-59477-130-9). A long-time falconer, Askani became interested in wolves when she was given a three-day-old wolf pup; here she tells the story of that pup and of her experiences with subsequent wolves that learned to trust humans. (Rev: BL 11/1/06) [599.773]

11508 Leslie, Robert Franklin. *In the Shadow of a Rainbow* (10–12). 1986, Norton paper $9.95 (978-0-393-30392-6). The story of an unusual friendship between man and wolf. [599.74]

11509 Lopez, Barry. *Of Wolves and Men* (9–12). 1978, Macmillan paper $18.00 (978-0-684-16322-2). An account that contrasts the wolf of folklore with the true nature of this caring social creature. [599.74]

11510 McAllister, Ian. *The Last Wild Wolves: Ghosts of the Rain Forest* (7–12). 2007, Univ. of California $39.95 (978-0-520-25473-2). Beautiful photographs document the lives of wolves living on the Pacific Coast. (Rev: BL 12/15/07) [599.77309711]

11511 Smith, Douglas W., and Gary Ferguson. *Decade of the Wolf: Returning the Wild to Yellowstone* (9–12). 2005, Lyons $23.95 (978-1-59228-700-0). Smith describes the ultimately successful reintroduction of wolves to the wild in Yellowstone National Park. (Rev: BL 4/15/05) [599.773]

11512 Steinhart, Peter. *The Company of Wolves* (9–12). 1995, Knopf paper $14.00 (978-0-679-74387-3). As well as exploring the habits and behavior of wolves, this volume gives a great deal of information on the relationship between wolves and humans. [599.77]

DEER FAMILY

11513 Cox, Daniel, and John Ozoga. *Whitetail Country* (8–12). 1988, Willow Creek $39.00 (978-0-932558-43-

5). Wonderful photographs complement this account of the life and living habits of the deer. [599.73]

11514 Heuer, Karsten. *Being Caribou: Five Months on Foot with an Arctic Herd* (9–12). 2005, Mountaineers $24.95 (978-1-59485-010-3). Heuer describes how he and his wife following the annual migration of a vast caribou herd to and from calving grounds in the Arctic National Wildlife Refuge — a refuge threatened by development. (Rev: BL 12/15/05) [599.65]

ELEPHANTS

11515 Groning, Karl, and Martin Saller. *Elephants: A Cultural and Natural History* (8–12). 1999, Konemann $15.33 (978-3-8290-1752-7). Both the scientific and mythological aspects of elephants are covered, with material on behavior, anatomy, and habitats. (Rev: BL 6/1–15/99; SLJ 5/00) [599.67]

11516 O'Connell, Caitlin. *The Elephant's Secret Sense: The Hidden Life of the Wild Herds of Africa* (9–12). 2007, Free Press $24.00 (978-0-7432-8441-7). Can elephants hear with their feet? The answer apparently is yes; this investigation of elephants' abilities is a good example of scientific investigation. (Rev: BL 2/1/07) [591.51]

11517 Poole, Joyce. *Elephants* (9–12). Series: World Life Library. 1997, Voyageur paper $14.95 (978-0-89658-357-3). This slim volume examines the natural history of elephants — both African and Asian — and the growing threat they face as humans invade more of their habitat. [599.67]

PANDAS

11518 Schaller, George B. *The Last Panda* (9–12). 1993, Univ. of Chicago $24.95 (978-0-226-73628-0). A noted field biologist recounts his experiences researching the giant panda in the wilds of China. (Rev: BL 3/15/93) [599.74]

Birds

GENERAL AND MISCELLANEOUS

11519 Attenborough, David. *The Life of Birds* (9–12). 1998, Princeton $29.95 (978-0-691-01633-7). In this book, a companion piece to the PBS series of the same name, Attenborough explores the human fascination with birds and their lives. (Rev: BL 12/1/98) [598.15]

11520 Blechman, Andrew D. *Pigeons: The Fascinating Saga of the World's Most Revered and Reviled Bird* (9–12). 2006, Grove $23.00 (978-0-8021-1834-9). Breeding, history, myths, racing, and showing are among the topics covered in this comprehensive and informative look at pigeons. (Rev: BL 10/1/06; SLJ 2/07) [598.6]

11521 Brown, Stephen, ed. *Arctic Wings: Birds of the Arctic National Wildlife Refuge* (9–12). 2006, Moun-

taineers $39.95 (978-0-89886-975-0); paper $27.95 (978-0-89886-976-7). Birds from all over the world converge on the Arctic refuge each summer; this book features many of them in color photographs and discusses their behavior in this special habitat. (Rev: BL 4/15/06) [598.09]

11522 Burger, Joanna. *Birds: A Visual Guide* (9–12). 2006, Firefly $29.95 (978-1-55407-177-7). All aspects of the lives of birds — anatomy and intelligence through their relationships with the human world — are covered by this author who specializes in bird behavior; maps show distribution and migration. (Rev: BL 9/15/06) [598]

11523 Dunne, Pete. *Pete Dunne on Bird Watching: The How-to, Where-to, and When-to of Birding* (10–12). 2003, Houghton Mifflin paper $12.00 (978-0-395-90686-6). Both veteran and novice bird watchers will find value in this guide, which is loaded with advice on proper equipment and techniques, as well as tips for homeowners who would like to attract birds. (Rev: BL 3/15/03) [598]

11524 Ehrlich, Paul R., et al. *The Birder's Handbook: A Field Guide to the Natural History of North American Birds* (9–12). 1988, Simon & Schuster paper $18.00 (978-0-671-65989-9). An extremely comprehensive guide to the 646 birds native to North America. (Rev: BL 10/1/88) [598.297]

11525 Farrand, John. *How to Identify Birds* (10–12). 1987, McGraw-Hill paper $17.95 (978-0-07-019975-0). A noted bird watcher tells how to identify birds by such characteristics as size, habitat, and voice. For more specific information see the author's *Eastern Birds* and *Western Birds* (both 1987). (Rev: BL 11/15/87) [598]

11526 Gibson, Graeme. *The Bedside Book of Birds: An Avian Miscellany* (9–12). 2005, Doubleday $29.95 (978-0-385-51483-5). Gibson, a Canadian novelist and avid birder, has compiled a rich selection of works touching on the relationship between humans and birds. (Rev: BL 10/15/05) [598]

11527 Hoose, Phillip. *Moonbird: A Year on the Wind with the Great Survivor B95* (7–12). Illus. 2012, Farrar $21.99 (978-0-374-30468-3). The remarkable migration of a single rufa red knot — an endangered species that winters in Argentina and breeds in the Canadian Arctic — is chronicled here. ∩ Lexile 1150L (Rev: BL 6/12*; HB 7–8/12; LMC 11–12/12; SLJ 10/12*; VOYA 8/12) [598.072]

11528 Montgomery, Sy. *Birdology: Lessons Learned from a Pack of Hens, a Peck of Pigeons, Cantankerous Crows, Fierce Falcons, Hip Hop Parrots, Baby Hummingbirds, and One Murderously Big Cassowary* (10–12). Illus. 2010, Free Press $25 (978-141656984-8). Nature junkie Montgomery describes memorable encounters with birds large and small, providing smart, compelling insights into their behavior and the threats they face. (Rev: BL 3/1–15/10) [598]

11529 Peterson, Roger Tory. *All Things Reconsidered: My Birding Adventures* (9–12). 2006, Houghton Mifflin $30.00 (978-0-618-75862-3). This is a collection of personal narratives by the well-known field guide author and columnist about his worldwide birding adventures. (Rev: BL 10/1/06) [598.072]

11530 Peterson, Roger Tory, and Virginia Marie Peterson. *A Field Guide to the Birds of Eastern and Central North America. 5th ed.* (8–12). 2002, Houghton Mifflin $30.00 (978-0-395-74047-7). This book identifies birds found east of the Rockies with both verbal and pictorial descriptions. [598]

11531 Savage, Candace. *Crows: Encounters with the Wise Guys of the Avian World* (9–12). 2007, Greystone paper $16.95 (978-1-55365-286-1). A fascinating look at crows and their amazing abilities, reviewing their roles in myth and legend. (Rev: BL 10/15/07) [598.8]

11532 Sibley, David. *The Sibley Field Guide to Birds of Western North America* (9–12). 2003, Knopf paper $19.95 (978-0-679-45121-1). This is a reliable, attractive guide to the 703 bird species found west of the Rockies. [598]

11533 Sibley, David. *The Sibley Guide to Birds* (9–12). 2000, Knopf paper $35.00 (978-0-679-45122-8). Each of 810 species is described in pictures and detailed text, with identification tips. [598]

11534 Stokes, Donald, and Lillian Stokes. *The Bird Feeder Book: An Easy Guide to Attracting, Identifying, and Understanding Your Feeder Birds* (8–12). 1987, Little, Brown paper $12.95 (978-0-316-81733-2). A manual that describes, with color photographs, 72 backyard birds, plus tips on how to attract and feed them. (Rev: BL 2/1/88) [598]

11535 Stokes, Donald, and Lillian Stokes. *The Complete Birdhouse Book: The Easy Guide to Attracting Nesting Birds* (9–12). 1990, Little, Brown paper $13.00 (978-0-316-81714-1). Plans for various birdhouses are given plus instructions on how to build them. (Rev: BL 9/15/90) [598]

11536 Stuart, Chris, and Tilde Stuart. *Birds of Africa: From Seabirds to Seed-Eaters* (10–12). 2000, MIT $32.00 (978-0-262-19430-3). A well-illustrated account that offers good basic information about the many species of African birds, their habitats, and their characteristics. (Rev: BL 3/1/00*; SLJ 11/00) [598]

11537 Stutchbury, Bridget. *Silence of the Songbirds: How We Are Losing the World's Songbirds and What We Can Do to Save Them* (9–12). 2007, HarperCollins $24.95 (978-0-8027-1609-5). Stutchbury documents the shocking loss of songbirds in North America and looks at ways we can help them to survive. (Rev: BL 4/1/07) [598.8]

11538 Tudge, Colin. *The Bird: A Natural History of Who Birds Are, Where They Came From, and How They Live* (10–12). Illus. 2009, Crown $30 (978-030734204-1).

This illustrated guide focuses on birds: their unique physical adaptations, their classification, their life cycle, and their interactions with humans. (Rev: BL 11/15/09)

11539 Watkins, Peter, and Jonathan Stockland. *Winged Wonders: A Celebration of Birds in Human History* (9–12). 2007, BlueBridge $22.00 (978-1-933346-07-6). Quotations, legends, poems, songs, folk tales, and trivia about birds are illustrated with line drawings and bolstered by information on U.S. state birds, bird songs, and famous bird illustrators. (Rev: BL 9/1/07) [598]

BEHAVIOR

11540 Chu, Miyoko. *Songbird Journeys: Four Seasons in the Lives of Migratory Birds* (9–12). 2006, Walker $23.00 (978-0-8027-1468-8). Ornithologist Chu follows songbirds from their winter territory in the American tropics to their spring and summer homes as far north as Canada and then back south again as the weather turns cooler. (Rev: BL 2/1/06) [598.252]

11541 Elphick, Jonathan, ed. *Atlas of Bird Migration: Tracing the Great Journeys of the World's Birds* (8–12). 2007, Firefly $35.00 (978-1-55407-248-4). This handsome atlas presents the latest research into migration and the impact of climate change, with breeding/migration calendars, fact boxes on species, and much more for the bird watcher and researcher. (Rev: SLJ 6/07) [598.156]

11542 Leveille, Jean. *Birds in Love: The Secret Courting and Mating Rituals of Extraordinary Birds* (8–12). 2007, Voyageur $20.00 (978-0-7603-2807-1). Essays and photographs reveal a lot about the behavior of bird couples and bird families. (Rev: BL 12/15/07) [598.156]

11543 Read, Marie. *Secret Lives of Common Birds: Enjoying Bird Behavior Through the Seasons* (8–12). 2005, Houghton Mifflin paper $14.95 (978-0-618-55872-8). Beautiful photographs and season-by-season discussion of bird behavior make this satisfying both for browsers and report writers. (Rev: BL 12/15/05) [598.15]

EAGLES, HAWKS, AND OTHER BIRDS OF PREY

11544 Heintzelman, Donald S. *Hawks and Owls of Eastern North America* (10–12). 2004, Rutgers $29.95 (978-0-8135-3350-6). More than 30 species of eagles, hawks, and owls are profiled in this comprehensive guide. (Rev: BL 12/1/03) [598.9]

11545 Moir, John. *Return of the Condor: The Race to Save Our Largest Bird from Extinction* (9–12). 2006, Lyons $24.95 (978-1-59228-949-3). The rescue of the California condor from extinction is the focus of this success story involving the controversial program of breeding in captivity. (Rev: BL 10/1/06) [598.9]

11546 Snyder, Noel, and Helen Snyder. *Raptors of North America* (8–12). 2006, MBI $50.00 (978-0-7603-2582-7). Equally suitable for reference and browsing, this book contains a wealth of information about the more than 50 species of North America's birds of prey. (Rev: BL 11/1/06) [598.9097]

11547 Winn, Marie. *Red-Tails in Love: A Wildlife Drama in Central Park* (10–12). 1998, Pantheon paper $13.00 (978-0-679-75846-4). A true-life adventure involving a group of bird watchers in Central Park and the mating of a pair of red-tail hawks on the 12th-floor facade of a nearby apartment building. (Rev: BL 2/1/98; SLJ 8/98) [598.9]

OWLS

11548 Berger, Cynthia, and Amelia Hansen. *Owls* (9–12). Series: Wild Guide. 2005, Stackpole paper $19.95 (978-0-8117-3213-0). Introduces the members of the owl family, examining their physical characteristics, behavior, habitat, diet, and life cycle. (Rev: BL 8/05) [598.9]

PENGUINS

11549 Love, John. *Penguins* (9–12). Series: World Life Library. 1997, Voyageur paper $16.95 (978-0-89658-339-9). This book uses color photographs to introduce penguins, their anatomy, habits, food, mating rituals, and social life. (Rev: SLJ 1/98) [598]

11550 Lynch, Wayne. *Penguins of the World . 2nd ed.* (9–12). 2007, Firefly $34.95 (978-1-55407-334-4); paper $24.95 (978-1-55407-274-3). For browsers and researchers alike, this is a rewarding examination of penguins and their lives. (Rev: BL 10/15/07) [598.441]

Environmental Protection and Endangered Species

11551 Adams, Douglas, and Mark Carwardine. *Last Chance to See* (10–12). 1992, Ballantine paper $10.00 (978-0-345-37198-0). The noted science fiction writer examines the plight of many of the earth's endangered species. (Rev: BL 12/1/90) [591.52]

11552 Andryszewski, Tricia. *Mass Extinction: Examining the Current Crisis* (9–12). Series: Discovery. 2008, Lerner LB $30.60 (978-0-8225-7523-8). Two-thirds of the earth's species could disappear in the near future, the author asserts and goes on to examine the reasons why, and what, if anything, can be done to stop this; color photographs and sidebar features balance the dense text. (Rev: BL 3/15/08) [576.8]

11553 Claggett, Hilary D. *Wildlife Conservation* (10–12). Series: Reference Shelf. 1997, H.W. Wilson paper $50.00 (978-0-8242-0915-5). Reprinted articles consider the threat to various wildlife species, what is being

done to address those threats, and why it's important to save these animals from extinction. [639.9]

11554 Clover, Charles. *The End of the Line: How Over-fishing Is Changing the World and What We Eat* (9–12). 2006, New Press $26.95 (978-1-59558-109-9). An environmental journalist provides facts, figures, and useful information regarding ecologically destructive and even illegal fishing practices of the world, along with lists of fish to avoid and fish we should choose to eat. (Rev: BL 10/1/06) [333.95]

11555 DeNapoli, Dyan. *The Great Penguin Rescue: The Inspiring True Story of the World's Largest Live Animal Rescue* (10–12). 2010, Free Press $26 (978-143914817-4). DeNapoli recounts her experiences as a first responder in efforts to rescue a huge number of penguins when an oil tanker sank in the ocean near Cape Town, South Africa, in 2000. (Rev: BL 10/1–15/10) [639.9]

11556 Dewdney, A. K. *Hungry Hollow: The Story of a Natural Place* (10–12). 1998, Springer-Verlag $26.00 (978-0-387-98415-5). This detailed tale of flora and fauna in an area near the author's home in the eastern United States provides an accessible introduction to ecological concepts and concerns. (Rev: BL 12/1/98) [508.74]

11557 Dinerstein, Eric. *Tigerland and Other Unintended Science Destinations* (10–12). 2005, Island $25.95 (978-1-55963-578-3). The chief scientist for the World Wildlife Fund writes about his wildlife expeditions to far-flung corners of the globe. (Rev: BL 9/15/05) [590.92]

11558 Ehrlich, Paul R., et al. *Birds in Jeopardy: The Imperiled and Extinct Birds of the United States and Canada, Including Hawaii and Puerto Rico* (9–12). 1992, Stanford Univ. paper $22.95 (978-0-8047-1981-0). Lists the endangered and extinct birds of North America, with information on nesting, food, and breeding. (Rev: BL 2/1/92) [333.95]

11559 Flannery, Tim, and Peter Schouten. *A Gap in Nature: Discovering the World's Extinct Animals* (9–12). 2001, Grove $34.95 (978-0-87113-797-5). In words and illustrations, this book describes the process of extinction and introduces 103 species that have become extinct between 1500 and 1999. (Rev: BL 10/1/01) [591.68]

11560 Franke, Mary Ann. *To Save the Wild Bison: Life on the Edge in Yellowstone* (9–12). 2005, Univ. of Oklahoma $29.95 (978-0-8061-3683-7). The bison of Yellowstone, the last true bison in the nation, are threatened by cattle farmers who fear contamination. (Rev: BL 9/15/05) [333.95]

11561 Grossman, Elizabeth. *Watershed: The Undamming of America* (10–12). 2002, Counterpoint $27.00 (978-1-58243-108-6). The movement to remove dams and return rivers to their natural courses and ecology is the focus of this interesting study. (Rev: BL 7/02) [333.91]

11562 Grosz, Terry. *Defending Our Wildlife Heritage: The Life and Times of a Special Agent* (9–12). 2001, Johnson paper $18.00 (978-1-55566-316-2). This is a memoir of a former conservation officer and his years defending the nation's natural resources and wildlife. (Rev: BL 11/15/01) [363.28]

11563 Heller, Peter. *The Whale Warriors: The Battle at the Bottom of the World to Save the Planet's Largest Mammals* (9–12). 2007, Free Press $25.00 (978-1-4165-3246-0). The riveting sea adventures of the radical environmental group the Sea Shepherd Conservation Society, led by former Greenpeace member Paul Watson and responsible for the sinking and ramming of illegal whaling ships, are chronicled here in an eyewitness account as they encounter the Japanese whaling fleet in Antarctica. (Rev: BL 8/07) [599.5]

11564 Hill, Julia Butterfly. *One Makes the Difference: Inspiring Actions that Change Our World* (10–12). 2002, HarperSanFrancisco paper $15.95 (978-0-06-251756-2). An environmental activist offers tips on behaving in a pro-environment manner, gives examples of individual actions that have had good results, and provides lists of facts, organizations, and resources. (Rev: BL 4/1/02) [333.7]

11565 Jacobsen, Rowan. *The Living Shore: Rediscovering a Lost World* (10–12). Illus. 2009, Bloomsbury $20 (978-159691684-5). Using the Olympia oyster beds of British Columbia as a springboard, Jacobsen explains how people and the natural world can coexist. **e** (Rev: BL 9/09) [639.9]

11566 McClung, Robert M. *Last of the Wild: Vanished and Vanishing Giants of the Animal World* (8–12). 1997, Shoe String LB $27.50 (978-0-208-02452-7). Moving from continent to continent, this account gives historical and geographical background material on 60 animal species that have already disappeared or are currently in extreme danger of extinction. (Rev: BL 7/97; HBG 3/98; SLJ 11/97; VOYA 10/97) [591.51]

11567 McLeish, Todd. *Basking with Humpbacks: Tracking Threatened Marine Life in New England Waters* (10–12). Illus. 2009, Univ. Press of New England $26.95 (978-158465676-0). In 11 fascinating essays based on interviews, McLeish writes vividly about the residents of New England's coastal waters — from humpback whales to horseshoe crabs to leatherback turtles — and the ways in which their habitats are compromised. (Rev: BLO 9/09) [78.680974]

11568 Nelson, Gaylord, et al. *Beyond Earth Day: Fulfilling the Promise* (10–12). 2002, Univ. of Wisconsin $26.95 (978-0-299-18040-9). The founder of Earth Day and other environmentalists voice their concerns about the continuing toll on our natural resources. (Rev: BL 10/15/02) [333.7]

11569 Newbold, Heather, ed. *Life Stories: World-Renowned Scientists Reflect on Their Lives and the Future of Life on Earth* (10–12). 2000, Univ. of California paper $17.95 (978-0-520-21896-3). Sixteen important scientists write about their lives, share their views on life on earth, and explain their commitment to conservation. (Rev: BL 4/1/00; SLJ 10/00) [363.7]

11570 Novacek, Michael, ed. *The Biodiversity Crisis: Losing What Counts* (10–12). 2000, New Press paper $19.95 (978-1-56584-570-1). A visually attractive book that discusses what species are going extinct, what has caused the extinction of species, and how we can slow the rate of extinction. (Rev: BL 4/1/00) [333.95]

11571 Rothman, Hal K. *Saving the Planet: The American Response to the Environment in the Twentieth Century* (10–12). 2000, Ivan R. Dee $24.95 (978-1-56663-288-1). This lucid, mature account traces the evolution of American environmentalism with emphasis on its relationship to economics and technology. (Rev: BL 4/1/00) [333.7]

11572 Tait, Malcom. *Going, Going, Gone? Animals and Plants on the Brink of Extinction and How You Can Help* (9–12). 2007, Sterling $17.95 (978-1-84525-027-0). A happy reminder that people are in fact working to save endangered species, this is a collection of 100 efforts that are under way, with information on how to help. (Rev: BL 3/1/07) [578.68]

11573 Waldau, Paul. *Animal Rights: What Everyone Needs to Know* (9–12). Series: What Everyone Needs to Know. 2011, Oxford paper $16.95 (978-01997399-6-7). This is a thought-provoking and thorough exploration of the subject of animal rights, covering history, culture, philosophy, activism, and the nature of the animals themselves. (Rev: BL 12/1–15/10) [179]

11574 Wilson, Edward O. *The Creation: A Meeting of Science and Religion* (9–12). 2006, Norton $21.95 (978-0-393-06217-5). The author charges that religion has not done enough to protect creation and calls for scientists and people of faith to join forces to stop the degradation of the environment. (Rev: BL 8/06) [333]

Insects and Arachnids

GENERAL AND MISCELLANEOUS

11575 Attenborough, David. *Life in the Undergrowth* (9–12). 2006, Princeton $29.95 (978-0-691-12703-3). In this companion volume to the Animal Planet TV series of the same name, Attenborough offers a close-up look at the world of invertebrates, including insects and spiders. (Rev: BL 2/15/06) [595.7]

11576 Berger, Cynthia. *Dragonflies* (9–12). Series: Wild Guides. 2004, Stackpole paper $19.95 (978-0-8117-2971-0). After an overview of dragonflies and damselflies and an examination of a year in their lives, this well-illustrated book discusses species identification, behavior, anatomy, hunting, and mating. (Rev: BL 2/15/04) [595.7]

11577 *Discovery Channel Insects and Spiders: An Explore Your World Handbook* (8–12). 2000, Discovery paper $14.95 (978-1-56331-841-2). About 160 insects and spiders are identified in text and pictures, with material on their anatomy, behavior, evolution, and the possibility of keeping them as pets. [595.7]

11578 Dourlot, Sonia. *Insect Museum* (9–12). Illus. 2009, Firefly $39.95 (978-155407483-9). This lavishly illustrated compendium of insects and spiders will delight (or horrify) the eye and spur further research. (Rev: BL 12/1/09) [595.7]

11579 Holldobler, Bert, and Edward O. Wilson. *The Leafcutter Ants: Civilization by Instinct* (10–12). 2010, Norton paper $19.95 (978-03933386-8-3). Leafcutter ants and their fascinating society are thoroughly examined in this title that makes the case that these ant colonies are virtual superorganisms. (Rev: BL 10/1–15/10) [595.79]

11580 Milne, Lorus, and Margery Milne. *The Audubon Society Field Guide to North American Insects and Spiders* (7–12). 1980, Knopf $19.95 (978-0-394-50763-7). An extensive use of color photographs makes this a fine guide for identifying insects. [595.7]

11581 Moffett, Mark W. *Adventures Among Ants: A Global Safari with a Cast of Trillions* (10–12). Illus. 2010, Univ. of California $29.95 (978-052026199-0). A world-traveling entomologist examines ants and their environments in this volume that includes excellent close-up photos of his subjects at work. (Rev: BLO 1/1–15/11) [595.796]

11582 Purser, Bruce. *Jungle Bugs: Masters of Camouflage and Mimicry* (10–12). 2003, Firefly paper $19.95 (978-1-55297-663-0). Beautiful photographs illustrate two strategies of survival for jungle insects. (Rev: BL 8/03) [595.7]

11583 Stewart, Amy. *Wicked Bugs: The Louse That Conquered Napoleon's Army and Other Diabolical Insects* (10–12). Illus. 2011, Algonquin $18.95 (978-156512960-3). Stewart provides an overview of our relationship with bugs of all kinds, from the annoying to the deadly, in this fascinating, often funny book full of intriguing illustrations. (Rev: BL 3/1–15/11) [632]

11584 Turpin, Tom. *Flies in the Face of Fashion, Mites Make Right, and Other Bugdacious Tales* (9–12). 2006, Purdue Univ. paper $14.95 (978-1-55753-417-0). A collection of did-you-know style stories that reveal little-known facts about insects — and about how humans have used and interacted with insects through the ages. (Rev: BL 5/1/06) [595.7]

11585 Waldbauer, Gilbert. *Insights from Insects: What Bad Bugs Can Teach Us* (8–12). 2005, Prometheus paper $20.98 (978-1-59102-277-0). Friend or foe? Waldbauer profiles 20 insects that most humans consider

pests and their roles in the natural world. (Rev: BL 3/15/05) [632]

11586 Waldbauer, Gilbert. *A Walk Around the Pond: Insects in and over the Water* (9–12). 2006, Harvard $22.95 (978-0-674-02211-9). A highly readable and fascinating look at the multitudes of insects living in and near water; contains a useful bibliography. (Rev: BL 4/15/06) [595.7]

11587 Wangberg, James K. *Do Bees Sneeze? And Other Questions Kids Ask About Insects* (7–10). 1997, Fulcrum paper $18.95 (978-1-55591-963-4). Full, interesting answers to more than 200 questions about insects on such subjects as physical characteristics, anatomical features, locomotion, behavior, habitat, and human health and safety. (Rev: BL 1/1–15/98; SLJ 4/98) [595.7]

11588 Wangberg, James K. *Six-Legged Sex: The Erotic Lives of Bugs* (9–12). Illus. by Marjorie Leggitt. 2001, Fulcrum paper $17.95 (978-1-55591-292-5). The sex life of insects is popularized in this whimsical but accurate account of mating behavior in the bug world. (Rev: BL 9/15/01) [595.7]

BEES AND WASPS

11589 Pundyk, Grace. *The Honey Trail: In Pursuit of Liquid Gold and Vanishing Bees* (10–12). 2010, St. Martin's $25.99 (978-031262981-6). All about honey, the bees that produce it, the resulting commerce around the world, and the myriad uses for this "liquid gold." e (Rev: BLO 1/1–15/11) [638.16]

11590 Seeley, Thomas D. *Honeybee Democracy* (10–12). 2010, Princeton $29.95 (978-069114721-5). This highly readable book describes bees' behavior and includes an in-depth look at the research process. e (Rev: BLO 1/1–15/11) [595.79]

BUTTERFLIES, MOTHS, AND CATERPILLARS

11591 Baran, Myriam, and Gilles Martin. *Butterflies of the World* (9–12). Trans. by Simon Jones. 2006, Abrams $35.00 (978-0-8109-5953-8). Beautiful photographs bring readers extra-close to butterflies and their habits and habitats, and the text adds plenty of pertinent details. (Rev: BL 8/06) [595.78]

11592 Burris, Judy, and Wayne Richards. *The Life Cycles of Butterflies: From Egg to Maturity, a Visual Guide to 23 Common Garden Butterflies* (9–12). 2006, Storey $26.95 (978-1-58017-618-7); paper $16.95 (978-1-58017-617-0). This guide to butterflies, full of photographs as well as explanations of the stages of butterfly life, is useful for reports and attractive for browsing. (Rev: BL 5/1/06) [595.78]

11593 Majerus, Michael. *Moths* (10–12). 2002, HarperCollins $60.00 (978-0-00-220141-4). A thorough and comprehensive survey of the mysterious world of moths. (Rev: BL 11/15/02) [595.78]

11594 Marent, Thomas, and Ben Morgan. *Butterfly* (10–12). Illus. by author. 2008, DK $30.00 (978-0-7566-3340-0). Details of butterfly life, such as egg-laying, feeding, migration, and metamorphosis, are described through clearly written captions in this beautifully photographed book. (Rev: BLO 6/16/08) [595.78]

11595 Pyle, Robert Michael. *The Audubon Society Field Guide to North American Butterflies* (7–12). 1981, Knopf $19.95 (978-0-394-51914-2). An introduction to more than 600 species of butterflies in about 1,000 color photographs and text. [595.7]

11596 Schappert, Phil. *The Last Monarch Butterfly: Conserving the Monarch Butterfly in a Brave New World* (8–12). 2004, Firefly paper $19.95 (978-1-55297-969-3). The fascinating story of the monarch butterfly and its incredible migrations is told with an emphasis on the threats it faces. (Rev: BL 12/15/04) [595.78]

SPIDERS AND SCORPIONS

11597 Hillyard, Paul. *The Private Life of Spiders* (9–12). 2008, Princeton $29.95 (978-0-691-13552-6). The life of the spider is no longer quite so private in this lush look at spider ecology; includes lifestyles, fascinating facts, and close-up photographs. (Rev: BL 3/1/08) [595.44]

Marine and Freshwater Life

GENERAL AND MISCELLANEOUS

11598 *America's Seashore Wonderlands* (9–12). 1985, National Geographic $12.95 (978-0-87044-543-9). Beginning with the northwest coast and ending with New England, this is an illustrated tour of our seashores. (Rev: BL 5/1/86) [574.5]

11599 Cousteau, Jacques, and Susan Schiefelbein. *The Human, the Orchid, and the Octopus: Exploring and Conserving Our Natural World* (9–12). 2007, Bloomsbury $25.95 (978-1-59691-417-9). Cousteau finished this extraordinary account the year before he died, chronicling his experiences in the marine world and how his observations confirmed the fact that we could lose this fascinating realm necessary to our survival if we continue our irresponsibility toward it. (Rev: BL 7/07) [333.95]

11600 Ellis, Richard. *Singing Whales, Flying Squid, and Swimming Cucumbers: The Discovery of Marine Life* (10–12). 2006, Lyons $24.95 (978-1-59228-842-7). Ellis, a marine researcher at the American Museum of Natural History, chronicles some of the most exciting discoveries of marine life and looks at potential future exploitation. (Rev: BL 1/1–15/06) [578.77]

11601 Kurlansky, Mark. *The Big Oyster: History on the Half Shell* (9–12). 2006, Ballantine $23.95 (978-0-345-47638-8). The oyster's popularity in early America and the fall in their availability due to pollution are covered in this tribute to the luscious mollusk. ⌒ (Rev: BL 10/1/05; SLJ 6/06) [641.6]

11602 Meinkoth, Norman A. *The Audubon Society Field Guide to North American Seashore Creatures* (7–12). 1981, Knopf $19.95 (978-0-394-51993-7). This is a guide to such invertebrates as sponges, corals, urchins, and anemones. [592]

11603 Molyneaux, Paul. *Swimming in Circles: Aquaculture and the Death of Wild Oceans* (10–12). 2007, Thunder's Mouth paper $15.95 (978-1-56025-756-1). A depressing account of the state of aquaculture and the dangers it poses to wild fish. (Rev: BL 1/1–15/07) [639]

11604 O'Neill, Michael Patrick. *Wild Waters Photo Journal* (6–12). 2010, Batfish Books $29.95 (978-0-9728653-6-4). A wonderful collection of color photographs and brief descriptions of marine life in ecosystems as varied as Komodo National Park, Bali, the Palm Beach coral reefs, and the Everglades. (Rev: LMC 11–12/10; SLJ 8/10) [591.77]

11605 Rehder, Harold A. *The Audubon Society Field Guide to North American Seashells* (7–12). 1981, Knopf $19.95 (978-0-394-51913-5). Seven hundred of the most common seashells from our coasts are pictured in color photographs and described in the text. [594]

11606 Wallace, David Rains. *Neptune's Ark: From Ichthyosaurs to Orcas* (10–12). 2007, Univ. of California $27.50 (978-0-520-24322-4). The West Coast of California is the focus of this exploration of marine evolution that includes interesting anecdotes and cautions about the future. (Rev: BL 4/15/07) [560]

11607 Waller, Geoffrey. *SeaLife: A Complete Guide to the Marine Environment* (8–12). 1996, Smithsonian $55.00 (978-1-56098-633-1). A comprehensive reference to marine biology, including profiles of more than 600 species of marine animals, this guide is written in easy-to-understand language and includes numerous illustrations and maps. [591.7]

CORALS AND JELLYFISH

11608 Love, Rosaleen. *Reefscape: Reflections on the Great Barrier Reef* (10–12). 2001, Joseph Henry $24.95 (978-0-309-07260-1). General information is given about coral reefs, with in-depth material on the Great Barrier Reef of Australia. [508]

11609 Walker, Pam, and Elaine Wood. *The Coral Reef* (8–11). Series: Life in the Seas. 2005, Facts on File $35.00 (978-0-8160-5703-0). An excellent introduction to the world's coral reefs, looking at how they were formed, the creatures that thrive within them, and the threats they face. (Rev: BL 1/1–15/06) [5/8.77]

FISHES

11610 Behnke, Robert J., and Joseph R. Tomelleri. *Trout and Salmon of North America* (10–12). 2002, Free Press $40.00 (978-0-7432-2220-4). A detailed but highly readable guide to the Salmonidae family, which includes such popular fish as the salmon, trout, white-fish, grayling, and char. (Rev: BL 9/15/02) [597.5]

11611 Eschmeyer, William N., and Earl S. Herald. *A Field Guide to Pacific Coast Fishes* (7–12). 1983, Houghton Mifflin $20.00 (978-0-618-00212-2). In this volume in the Peterson Field Guide series, about 500 fish are described and illustrated. [597]

11612 Filisky, Michael. *Peterson First Guide to Fishes of North America* (7–12). 1989, Houghton Mifflin paper $4.95 (978-0-393-91179-4). This is a concise version of the parent Peterson guide that gives basic material on common fish but with less detail. (Rev: BL 6/1/89) [597]

11613 Greenberg, Paul. *Four Fish: The Future of the Last Wild Food* (10–12). 2010, Penguin $25.95 (978-159420256-8). Greenberg examines the sorry state of the world's fisheries by focusing on four fish — tuna, cod, sea bass, and salmon — and the natural and anthropogenic pressures on their habitat. (Rev: BL 7/10) [338.372]

11614 Page, Lawrence M., and Brooks M. Burr. *A Field Guide to Freshwater Fishes: North America North of Mexico* (9–12). Series: Peterson Field Guides. 1991, Houghton Mifflin paper $19.00 (978-0-395-91091-7). This richly illustrated handbook identifies the nearly 800 species of freshwater fishes found in the United States and Canada. [597]

11615 Reebs, Stephan. *Fish Behavior: In the Aquarium and in the Wild* (9–12). 2001, Cornell paper $19.95 (978-0-8014-8772-9). This primer on fish behavior explains how they find food, avoid predators, relate to other fish, mate, and raise young. (Rev: BL 12/1/01) [597.15]

11616 Scales, Helen. *Poseidon's Steed: The Story of Seahorses, from Myth to Reality* (10–12). Illus. 2009, Gotham $20 (978-159240474-2). Sea horses and their importance in cultures around the world and throughout history are examined in fascinating detail. (Rev: BLO 7/09) [597]

11617 Schweid, Richard. *Consider the Eel* (8–12). 2002, Univ. of North Carolina $24.95 (978-0-8078-2693-5). A fascinating profile of the eel, with information on its history, life cycle, importance as a food product, and appearances in folklore, along with a selection of eel recipes. (Rev: BL 3/15/02) [597]

SHARKS

11618 Capuzzo, Michael. *Close to Shore: The Terrifying Shark Attacks of 1916* (7–12). 2003, Crown $16.95 (978-0-375-82231-5). Photographs and newspaper clippings enhance this true story of a shark's brief and dangerous detour into a New Jersey creek in 1916. (Rev: BL 5/15/03; HBG 10/03; SLJ 4/03) [597.3]

11619 Pope, Joyce. *1001 Facts About Sharks* (7–12). Series: Backpack Books. 2002, DK paper $8.99 (978-0-7894-8449-9). More than 550 photographs are used to present basic facts about sharks, their anatomy, habits, and varieties. (Rev: BL 3/15/02) [597]

11620 Reader's Digest, ed. *Sharks: Silent Hunters of the Deep* (8–12). 1987, Reader's Digest $19.95 (978-0-86438-014-2). This handsomely illustrated account describes the ways of sharks, gives material on famous encounters, and identifies all 344 species. (Rev: BL 5/15/87; SLJ 1/88; VOYA 8/87) [597]

11621 Springer, Victor G., and Joy P. Gold. *Sharks in Question: The Smithsonian Answer Book* (9–12). 1989, Smithsonian paper $24.95 (978-0-87474-877-2). Using a question-and-answer format plus stunning photographs, the authors tell all and explode myths about this sea creature. (Rev: BL 6/1/89; SLJ 8/89) [597]

11622 Willis, Clint, ed. *Shark: Stories of Life and Death from the World's Most Dangerous Waters* (10–12). 2002, Thunder's Mouth paper $17.95 (978-1-56025-397-6). Essays, short stories, and excerpts from fiction and nonfiction books discuss sharks and describe a variety of shark experiences. (Rev: BL 6/1–15/02) [597.3]

WHALES, DOLPHINS, AND OTHER SEA MAMMALS

11623 Brower, Kenneth. *Freeing Keiko: The Journey of a Killer Whale from Free Willy to the Wild* (10–12). 2005, Gotham $26.00 (978-1-59250-147-2). The true, controversial story of Keiko the whale, the model for the central character in the film *Free Willy*. (Rev: BL 11/15/05) [599.5]

11624 Calambokidis, John, and Gretchen Steiger. *Blue Whales* (9–12). Series: World Life Library. 1997, Voyageur paper $16.95 (978-0-89658-338-2). An oversize book with color photographs and text that explores the evolution, anatomy, and habits of the blue whale and the impact of whaling. (Rev: SLJ 1/98) [599.5]

11625 Chadwick, Douglas H. *The Grandest of Lives: Eye to Eye with Whales* (8–12). Illus. by author. 2006, Sierra Club $24.95 (978-1-57805-126-7). Chadwick followed scientists on their whale observations as he compiled this compelling overview of five species and their behavior, intelligence, and the threats they face. (Rev: BL 6/1–15/06) [599.5]

11626 Clapham, Phil. *Humpback Whales* (10–12). Series: World Life Library. 1996, Voyageur paper $16.95 (978-0-89658-296-5). Over 50 full-color photographs enhance this introduction to the anatomy, behavior, characteristics, history, and present status of the humpback whale. (Rev: SLJ 5/97) [599.5]

11627 Darling, Jim. *Gray Whales* (6–12). Series: World Life Library. 1999, Voyageur paper $16.95 (978-0-89658-447-1). Physiology, behavior, habitat, migration, and relations with humans are all discussed in this volume that contains lots of full-color photographs. (Rev: SLJ 4/00) [599.5]

11628 Dudzinski, Kathleen, and Toni Frohoff. *Dolphin Mysteries: Unlocking the Secrets of Communication* (10–12). Illus. 2008, Yale $30.00 (978-030012112-4). This book is set apart by its informal first-person accounts of dolphin interactions and what has been learned about these creatures. **e** (Rev: BL 9/15/08) [599.53]

11629 Ellis, Richard. *The Book of Whales* (9–12). 1980, Knopf paper $35.00 (978-0-394-73371-5). A beautifully illustrated book that describes how whales evolved, various species, and their behavior. [599.5]

11630 Gordon, Jonathan. *Sperm Whales* (10–12). Series: World Life Library. 1998, Voyageur paper $16.95 (978-0-89658-398-6). This absorbing and well-illustrated volume examines in detail the life of sperm whales. (Rev: BL 12/15/98) [599.5]

11631 Harrison, Richard, and M. M. Bryden, eds. *Whales, Dolphins and Porpoises* (9–12). 1988, Facts on File $35.00 (978-0-8160-1977-9). A handsome oversize volume with lucid text and copious illustrations. (Rev: BL 1/1/89) [599.5]

11632 Lord, Nancy. *Beluga Days: Tracking a White Whale's Truths* (10–12). 2004, Counterpoint $25.00 (978-1-58243-151-2). When the population of the beluga whales began to decline, the author decided to investigate. This account is not only about whales but also about the making of an environmentalist. (Rev: BL 1/1–15/04) [599.5]

11633 Payne, Roger. *Among Whales* (9–12). 1995, Macmillan $24.00 (978-0-02-595245-4). An introduction to the anatomy, habits, and characteristics of whales by one of the world's leading marine mammal experts. (Rev: BL 4/15/95*) [599.5]

11634 Reeps, Roger L., and Robert K. Bonde. *The Florida Manatee: Biology and Conservation* (9–12). 2006, Univ. Press of Florida $24.95 (978-0-8130-2949-8). Those strange-looking "sea cows" are the subject of this fascinating book, which covers everything from the creatures' evolutionary history to conservation efforts. (Rev: BL 5/1/06) [599.55]

11635 Rothenberg, David. *Thousand Mile Song: Whale Music in a Sea of Sound* (10–12). 2008, Basic Bks $27.50 (978-0-465-07128-9). A fascinating and thought-provoking celebration of whales and the music they make, with discussion of research into whales and their place in legend and myth; includes a CD of whale songs. (Rev: BL 4/1/08) [599.5]

11636 Simmonds, Mark. *Whales and Dolphins of the World* (8–12). 2005, MIT $29.95 (978-0-262-19519-

5). This photo-filled volume introduces readers to the cetaceans — whales, dolphins, and porpoises — and to their relationship with humans. (Rev: BL 3/15/05) [599.5]

Microscopes, Microbiology, and Biotechnology

11637 Aldridge, Susan. *Cloning* (7–10). Illus. Series: Cutting-Edge Science. 2010, Black Rabbit LB $34.25 (978-184898326-7). After introducing the basics of cloning and the story of Dolly the sheep, this volume looks in turn at the structure of cells, cloning and DNA, the history and current status of cloning, cloning in plants and animals, the ethics of cloning and various challenges to the practice, and the future of cloning. (Rev: BL 12/1/10; LMC 5–6/11) [571.8]

11638 Rainis, Kenneth G. *Cell and Microbe Science Fair Projects Using Microscopes, Mold, and More* (6–12). Series: Biology! Best Science Projects. 2005, Enslow LB $26.60 (978-0-7660-2369-7). This introduction to the study of cells and microbes contains step-by-step instructions for a number of related experiments and projects. (Rev: SLJ 9/05) [578]

11639 Stefoff, Rebecca. *Microscopes and Telescopes* (7–10). Series: Great Inventions. 2007, Marshall Cavendish LB $27.95 (978-0-7614-2230-3). From early spectacles through the invention of refractors and reflectors to space telescopes and on into the future, this history of microscopes and telescopes offers lots of hard scientific information. (Rev: SLJ 11/07) [502.8]

11640 Zimmer, Carl. *Microcosm: E. Coli and the New Science of Life* (11–12). 2008, Pantheon $25.95 (978-0-375-42430-4). An unexpectedly fascinating story of the E. coli bacteria's role in genetic research, metabolism, and biotechnology products such as artificial insulin; for advanced students of biology. (Rev: BL 4/1/08) [579.3]

Pets

GENERAL AND MISCELLANEOUS

11641 Albrecht, Kat. *The Lost Pet Chronicles: Adventures of a K-9 Cop Turned Pet Detective* (8–12). 2004, Bloomsbury $23.95 (978-1-58234-379-2). This is a memoir of a former police officer who has become a pet detective and a solver of such crimes as dognapping. (Rev: BL 3/1/04) [363.28]

11642 Becker, Marty, and Danelle Morton. *The Healing Power of Pets: Harnessing the Amazing Ability of Pets to Make and Keep People Healthy* (9–12). 2002, Hyperion $22.95 (978-0-7868-6808-7). A thoughtful and readable study of the unexpected benefits humans can derive from having a pet in their home. (Rev: BL 1/1–15/02) [158]

11643 Birmelin, Immanuel, and Annette Wolter. *The New Parakeet Handbook* (9–12). 1986, Barron's paper $9.95 (978-0-8120-2985-7). A manual on selecting and caring for parakeets, also known as budgerigars. (Rev: BL 5/15/86) [636.6]

11644 Katz, Jon. *Soul of a Dog: Reflections on the Spirits of the Animals of Bedlam Farm* (10–12). 2009, Villard $24 (978-1-4000-6629-2). Katz describes his relationships with the various animals on his farm and discusses their inner lives. (Rev: BL 7/09; SLJ 11/09) [636]

11645 *Petspeak: You're Closer Than You Think to a Great Relationship with Your Dog or Cat!* (9–12). 2000, Rodale $29.95 (978-1-57954-337-2); paper $16.95 (978-1-57954-077-7). This huge, attractive book, based on a PBS television series, explains pet behavior and tells how to get along with your cat or dog. (Rev: BL 9/15/00) [636.088]

11646 Sullivant, Holly J. *Hamsters* (7–12). Illus. Series: Our Best Friends. 2009, Eldorado Ink LB $26.95 (978-193290430-7). Everything you need to know about caring for a pet hamster, with interesting sidebars and eye-catching images. (Rev: BL 6/1–15/09) [636.935]

11647 Tarte, Bob. *Fowl Weather* (9–12). 2007, Algonquin $23.95 (978-1-56512-502-5). The Tartes lead a hectic family life leavened by the joys of the animals — ducks, geese, hens, cats, and rabbits, among them — that surround them. (Rev: BL 1/1–15/07) [636.088]

11648 Taylor, Michael. *Pot Bellied Pigs as a Family Pet* (9–12). 1993, TFH $35.95 (978-0-86622-081-1). Includes what to feed pot-bellies, how they are related to other swine, and legal restrictions on ownership. (Rev: BL 4/15/93) [636.4]

CATS

11649 Brown, Philip. *Uncle Whiskers* (9–12). 1980, Warner paper $2.95 (978-0-446-87108-2). The true story of a remarkable cat that was crippled in an accident. [636.8]

11650 Denny, D. Michael. *How to Get a Cat to Sit in Your Lap: Confessions of an Unconventional Cat Person* (9–12). 1995, Andiron paper $9.95 (978-0-9645799-0-3). Based on 30 years of living with cats, the author humorously tells of cat evolution, anatomy, behavior, naming, hunting, eating, and more. (Rev: BL 6/1–15/95) [636.8]

11651 Gerstenfeld, Sheldon L. *The Cat Care Book: All You Need to Know to Keep Your Cat Healthy and Happy. Rev. ed.* (8–12). 1989, Addison-Wesley paper $17.50 (978-0-201-09569-2). Tips on how to choose a cat and detailed information on taking care of cats as pets. (Rev: BL 9/15/89) [636.8]

11652 Herriot, James. *James Herriot's Cat Stories* (9–12). 1994, St. Martin's $17.95 (978-0-312-11342-1). A

small collection of cat tales, ranging from the informative and scientific to the humorous and poignant. (Rev: BL 7/94) [636.8]

11653 Morris, Desmond. *Catwatching* (8–12). 1987, Crown paper $8.95 (978-0-517-88053-1). Using a question-and-answer approach, the author explores many facets of cat behavior. (Rev: BL 4/1/87) [636.8]

11654 Zistel, Era. *A Gathering of Cats* (9–12). 1993, J. N. Townsend paper $11.95 (978-1-880158-00-5). Zistel tells the stories of various members of her pride of cats. (Rev: BL 11/1/93) [636.8]

DOGS

11655 American Kennel Club. *The Complete Dog Book. 19th ed.* (7–12). 1998, Book House $32.95 (978-0-87605-148-1). The standard manual for dog owners and guide to every AKC-recognized breed. (Rev: BL 6/15/85) [636.7]

11656 Bain, Terry. *You Are a Dog (Life Through the Eyes of Man's Best Friend)* (8–12). 2004, Harmony $16.00 (978-1-4000-5242-4). A humorous dog's-eye view of the world. (Rev: SLJ 1/05) [636.7]

11657 Bauer, Nona Kilgore. *Dog Heroes of September 11th: A Tribute to America's Search and Rescue Dogs* (9–12). 2006, Kennel Club $29.95 (978-1-59378-999-2). An oversize celebration of dogs' contributions to the search-and-rescue efforts on September 11. (Rev: SLJ 1/07)

11658 Bolan, Sandra. *Caring for Your Mutt* (7–12). Series: Our Best Friend. 2008, Eldorado Ink LB $25.95 (978-1-932904-20-8). Readers who own mixed-breed (and no-breed) dogs will enjoy this book, which gives information on basic care and explains that mutts are sometimes puzzling and often pleasant surprises. (Rev: BL 4/1/08) [636.7]

11659 Choron, Sandra, and Harry Choron. *Planet Dog: A Doglopedia* (9–12). 2005, Houghton Mifflin paper $14.95 (978-0-618-51752-7). From practical tips to historical trivia, this is an attractive resource for dog lovers. (Rev: SLJ 6/06)

11660 Coppinger, Raymond, and Lorna Coppinger. *Dogs: A Startling New Understanding of Canine Origin, Behavior, and Evolution* (9–12). 2001, Scribner $26.00 (978-0-684-85530-1). This book about our oldest domestic animal describes its evolution and how and why different breeds came about. (Rev: BL 3/1/01) [636.7]

11661 Davis, Caroline. *Essential Dog: The Ultimate Guide to Owning a Happy and Healthy Pet* (9–12). Illus. by author. 2006, Reader's Digest $26.95 (978-0-7621-0669-1). Want a puppy? This guide provides everything the prospective dog owner needs to know — breeds, care, training, and so forth — with photographs. (Rev: BL 6/1–15/06) [636.7]

11662 Dye, Dan, and Mark Beckloff. *Amazing Gracie: A Dog's Tale* (9–12). 2000, Workman $18.95 (978-0-7611-1938-8). This amazing story tells how a deaf and partially blind Great Dane inspired her owners to create a chain of specialty dog bakeries. (Rev: BL 10/15/00) [636.73]

11663 Fennell, Jan. *The Dog Listener: Learn How to Communicate with Your Dog for Willing Cooperation* (8–12). 2004, HarperResource paper $16.95 (978-0-06-008946-7). This comprehensive guide tells how one can peacefully coexist with one's dog and how successful training can be accomplished without violent behavior. (Rev: BL 1/1–15/04) [636.7]

11664 Fogle, Bruce. *Dog: The Definitive Guide for Dog Owners* (9–12). Illus. 2010, Firefly $39.95 (978-155407779-3); paper $29.95 (978-15540770-0-7). This comprehensive guide to dog selection, care, training, health, and so forth, with discussion of dogs' relationships with humans through history. (Rev: BL 12/1–15/10*) [646.7]

11665 Forbes, Harrison. *Dog Talk: Lessons Learned from a Life with Dogs* (10–12). 2008, St. Martin's $24.95 (978-031237873-8). Drawing on his wealth of experience as a police dog trainer, Forbes discusses his theories of dog behavior and explains how time spent observing a dog's reactions throughout the day will aid in training. (Rev: BL 8/08) [636.7]

11666 Foster, Ken. *The Dogs Who Found Me: What I've Learned from Pets Who Were Left Behind* (9–12). 2006, Lyons paper $12.95 (978-1-59228-749-9). In this touching memoir, Foster writes about his relationships with a number of abandoned dogs that he took in over the years. (Rev: BL 2/1/06) [636.7]

11667 Gerstenfeld, Sheldon L. *The Dog Care Book: All You Need to Know to Keep Your Dog Healthy and Happy. Rev. ed.* (8–12). 1989, Addison-Wesley paper $17.00 (978-0-201-09667-5). Tips on selecting a dog plus extensive material on care and feeding. (Rev: BL 9/15/89) [636.7]

11668 Grogan, John. *Marley and Me: Life and Love with the World's Worst Dog* (9–12). 2005, Morrow $21.95 (978-0-06-081708-4). Grogan tells how a Labrador retriever named Marley taught him important lessons about love and generally enriched his life. (Rev: BL 10/1/05) [636.752]

11669 Hampl, Patricia. *The Nature of Dogs* (7–12). Illus. by Mary Ludington. 2007, Simon & Schuster $35.00 (978-1-4165-4287-2). Beautiful photographs accompany well-written informative text about various breeds of dogs. (Rev: BL 9/15/07) [636.7]

11670 Hawkins, Barrie. *Tea and Dog Biscuits: Our First Topsy-Turvy Year Fostering Orphan Dogs* (10–12). 2010, Chicago Review paper $14.95 (978-15697634-1-4). A touching account of a man and his wife who foster abandoned, neglected, and abused dogs and rehabilitate

them before matching them to new owners. (Rev: BLO 1/1–15/11) [636.7]

11671 Katz, Jon. *A Good Dog: The Story of Orson, Who Changed My Life* (9–12). 2006, Villard $21.95 (978-1-4000-6189-1). The author writes about his meaningful relationship with Orson, his sheep dog and friend. (Rev: BL 9/1/06) [636.737]

11672 Katz, Jon. *Izzy and Lenore: Two Dogs, an Unexpected Journey, and Me* (10–12). 2008, Villard $24.00 (978-1-4000-6630-8). An emotional story of a trainer and his two newly rescued dogs who have a talent for bringing comfort to the sick and dying. ∩ (Rev: BL 8/08) [636.737]

11673 Kerasote, Ted. *Merle's Door: Lessons from a Freethinking Dog* (9–12). 2007, Harcourt $25.00 (978-0-15-101270-1). Merle, a Lab mix with an independent mind, found his life more rewarding when a dog door gave him a new measure of freedom; this touching and thoughtful story will appeal to fans of *Marley and Me*. (Rev: BL 6/1–15/07) [636]

11674 Koontz, Dean. *A Big Little Life: A Memoir of a Joyful Dog* (10–12). Illus. 2009, Hyperion $24.99 (978-140132352-3). This well-written account of the life of a beloved golden retriever explores deeper philosophical questions about animal intelligence and the deep connection between humans and pets. ∩ ℮ (Rev: BL 7/09) [636.752]

11675 McTague, Tracey. *City Puppy: Finding, Training, and Loving Your Urban Dog* (10–12). 2010, Overlook paper $16.95 (978-15902026-0-9). A helpful guide to the selection and training of a dog suitable for limited living space and an urban environment. (Rev: BLO 1/1–15/11) [636]

11676 Murphy, Claire Rudolf, and Jane G. Haigh. *Gold Rush Dogs* (6–12). 2001, Alaska Northwest $16.95 (978-0-88240-534-6). Nine dogs that played important roles in the Yukon are profiled here with many sidebars that provide background historical detail. (Rev: BL 9/1/01; SLJ 9/01) [636.7]

11677 Page, Jake. *Dogs: A Natural History* (6–12). 2007, Smithsonian $24.95 (978-0-06-113259-9). Owner of six dogs, Page shares his extensive knowledge of doggy history, behavior, breeds, and relationship with humans. (Rev: BL 9/1/07) [636.7]

11678 Paulsen, Gary. *My Life in Dog Years* (5–10). 1998, Delacorte $15.95 (978-0-385-32570-7). The famous novelist tells about eight wonderful dogs that he has known and loved over the years. (Rev: BCCB 3/98; BL 1/1–15/98; SLJ 3/98; VOYA 4/98) [636.7]

11679 Rogers, Tammie. *4-H Guide to Dog Training and Dog Tricks* (5–12). 2010, Voyageur paper $18.99 (978-0-7603-3629-8). Learn how to train your dog to master the basics and then move on to competition skills and even emptying the dryer! (Rev: SLJ 5/10) [636.7]

11680 Schuler, Elizabeth M. *Simon and Schuster's Guide to Dogs* (9–12). 1980, Simon & Schuster paper $14.00 (978-0-671-25527-5). A handbook that gives information on 324 breeds. [636.7]

11681 Scott, Traer. *Street Dogs* (9–12). 2007, Merrell $22.95 (978-1-85894-408-1). Moving photographs illustrate the plight of dogs living on the streets in this followup to *ShelterDogs* (2006). (Rev: BL 12/15/07) [636.700222]

11682 Siegal, Mordecai, and Matthew Margolis. *GRRR! The Complete Guide to Understanding and Preventing Aggressive Behavior* (10–12). 2000, Little, Brown $23.95 (978-0-316-79022-2). This introduction to dog behavior and training emphasizes aggressive behavior, its causes, and its cures. (Rev: BL 3/1/00) [636.7]

11683 Smith, Ernie. *Warm Hearts and Cold Noses: A Common Sense Guide to Understanding the Family Dog* (9–12). 1987, Sunstone paper $10.95 (978-0-86534-109-8). A pet-care manual that covers topics such as feeding, housebreaking, and leash training. [636.7]

11684 Trout, Nick. *Love Is the Best Medicine: What Two Dogs Taught One Veterinarian About Hope, Humility, and Everyday Miracles* (10–12). 2010, Broadway $23.99 (978-076793197-7). Two very different dogs — an abandoned cocker spaniel and a spoiled miniature pincher — intersect in the ER of a Boston animal hospital in this book that looks at the relationships between people and their pets. ∩ (Rev: BL 2/1–15/10) [636.7]

11685 Winn, Steven. *Come Back, Como: Winning the Heart of a Reluctant Dog* (9–12). 2009, HarperCollins $23.99 (978-006180259-1). *San Francisco Chronicle* columnist Steve Winn's humorous and poignant memoir recounts his efforts to acclimate Como, the cantankerous canine his family rescued from a shelter, to family life. (Rev: BLO 10/15/09) [636.70887]

HORSES

11686 Bowles, Melanie Sue. *Hoof Prints: More Stories from Proud Spirit* (9–12). 2008, Pineapple $18.95 (978-1-56164-412-4). Proud Spirit is a sanctuary for abused and abandoned horses. (Rev: BL 3/15/08) [636.1]

11687 Budd, Jackie. *Seasons of the Horse: A Practical Guide to Year-Round Equine Care* (5–12). 2007, T.F.H. $29.95 (978-0-7938-0611-9). Well-organized and visually pleasing, this book provides a complete guide to caring for a horse, including nutrition and exercise. (Rev: SLJ 3/08)

11688 Chapple, Judy. *Your Horse: A Step-by-Step Guide to Horse Ownership* (10–12). 1984, Garden Way paper $16.95 (978-0-88266-353-1). Starting with how to choose a horse, this guide supplies all kinds of information on caring for and training horses. [636.1]

11689 Kelley, Brent. *The Horse Doctor Is In: A Kentucky Veterinarian's Guide to Horse Health, Care, Disease Prevention and Treatment* (10–12). 2002, Storey paper $19.95 (978-1-58017-460-2). Case studies and anecdotes add to the appeal of this accessible and fact-filled guide. (Rev: BL 11/15/02) [636.1]

11690 Korda, Margaret, and Michael Korda. *Horse Housekeeping: Everything You Need to Know to Keep a Horse at Home* (9–12). 2005, HarperCollins $26.95 (978-0-06-057308-9). You *can* keep a horse in your own backyard — given certain space and other strictures — is the message of this practical guide. (Rev: BL 11/1/05) [798.2]

11691 Roberts, Monty. *The Horses in My Life* (10–12). 2005, Trafalgar $29.95 (978-1-57076-323-6). The author of *The Man Who Listens to Horses* writes about the most memorable horses in his lengthy career. (Rev: BL 9/1/05) [636.1]

11692 Roberts, Monty. *The Man Who Listens to Horses* (10–12). 1997, Random House $23.00 (978-0-679-45689-6). The story of how the author, a child rodeo star, overcame abuse, rejection, and ridicule to become trainer of Queen Elizabeth II's horses, what he has learned about horses and their ways, and his unique, nonviolent methods of training. (Rev: SLJ 5/98) [636.1]

11693 Stromberg, Tony. *Spirit Horses* (8–12). 2005, New World Library $40.00 (978-1-57731-499-8). A photographic celebration of horses in a large-format album, accompanied by quotes from diverse sources. (Rev: BL 11/1/05) [636.1]

Zoos, Aquariums, and Animal Care

11694 Alderton, David. *Firefly Encyclopedia of the Vivarium: Keeping Amphibians, Reptiles, and Insects, Spiders and Other Invertebrates in Terraria, Aquaterraria, and Aquaria* (9–12). 2007, Firefly $39.95 (978-1-55407-300-9). A thorough guide to the maintenance of indoor environments for live amphibians, reptiles, and invertebrates, with color photographs. (Rev: BL 3/1/08) [639.39]

11695 Anthony, Lawrence, and Graham Spence. *Babylon's Ark: The Incredible Wartime Rescue of the Baghdad Zoo* (9–12). 2007, St. Martin's $23.95 (978-0-312-35832-7). Animals always suffer in wartime and those in the Baghdad Zoo during and after the American invasion were no exception; this book describes efforts to keep them alive and healthy. (Rev: BL 2/1/07) [303.485]

11696 Axelrod, Herbert R, et al. *Dr. Axelrod's Mini-Atlas of Freshwater Aquarium Fishes* (10–12). 1987, TFH $49.95 (978-0-86622-385-0). This large volume not only identifies freshwater aquarium fish but also covers setting up and maintaining an aquarium. (Rev: BL 12/1/87) [639]

11697 Balliet, Gay L. *Lions and Tigers and Mares . . . Oh My!* (8–12). 2004, RDR paper $17.95 (978-1-57143-105-9). In humorous, appealing text, the wife of a Pennsylvania veterinarian sheds new light on the day-to-day challenges facing a vet who treats large and exotic animals. (Rev: BL 9/15/04) [636.089]

11698 Brightwell, Chris R. *The Nano-Reef Handbook: The Ultimate Guide to Reef Systems under 15 Gallons* (9–12). 2006, T.F.H $26.95 (978-0-7938-0572-3). From water quality to filters, lighting, and selecting of appropriate invertebrates and fish, this is an informative guide to small marine aquaria. (Rev: SLJ 1/07)

11699 Brown, Bradford B. *While You're Here, Doc: Farmyard Adventures of a Maine Veterinarian* (8–12). 2006, Tilbury House paper $15.00 (978-0-88448-279-6). Entertaining stories about life as a veterinarian in rural Maine. (Rev: BL 3/15/06) [636.0]

11700 Fisher, Lester E. *Dr. Fisher's Life on the Ark: Green Alligators, Bushman, and Other "Hare-Raising Tales" from America's Most Popular Zoo and Around the World* (9–12). 2004, Racom $26.95 (978-0-9704515-6-9). The longtime director of Chicago's Lincoln Park Zoo recalls some of the more memorable experiences from his years with the zoo and his foreign expedition. (Rev: BL 9/1/04) [590.73]

11701 Glen, Samantha. *Best Friends: The True Story of the World's Most Beloved Animal Sanctuary* (9–12). 2001, Kensington paper $15.00 (978-1-57566-735-5). This is the heart-warming story of the Best Friends Animal Sanctuary in Angel Canyon, Utah, and how friends pooled their money to buy 3,000 acres of desert scrubland to rescue homeless animals. (Rev: BL 2/15/01) [636]

11702 Jensen, Derrick. *Thought to Exist in the Wild: Awakening from the Nightmare of Zoos* (9–12). 2007, No Voice Unheard paper $19.95 (978-0-9728387-1-9). Zoos are presented in a very negative light through passionate text and moving photographs. (Rev: BL 5/1/07) [590.092]

11703 Mee, Benjamin. *We Bought a Zoo: The Amazing True Story of a Young Family, a Broken Down Zoo, and the 200 Wild Animals That Changed Their Lives Forever* (10–12). 2008, Weinstein $24.95 (978-160286048-3). An appealing account of how Mee and his family bought a rundown zoo full of exotic animals in southwest England and their adventures bringing the operation back to viability. (Rev: BL 9/15/08) [590.73]

11704 Scanlon, Edward J. *Animal Patients: 50 Years in the Life of an Animal Doctor* (10–12). 2000, Camino paper $14.95 (978-0-940159-65-5). This is an entertaining, informative look at the life of a big-city veterinarian, his practice, and his patients. (Rev: BL 8/00) [636.089]

Chemistry

General and Miscellaneous

11705 Cobb, Allan B. *Earth Chemistry* (8–12). Illus. Series: Essential Chemistry. 2009, Chelsea House $35 (978-0-7910-9677-2). Colorful illustrations and informative sidebars punctuate this comprehensive book on the chemical interactions between the four spheres — the atmosphere, hydrosphere, lithosphere, and biosphere — of the Earth. (Rev: SLJ 5/1/09)

11706 Goodstein, Madeline. *Plastics and Polymers Science Fair Projects: Using Hair Gel, Soda Bottles, and Slimy Stuff* (7–12). Series: Chemistry! Best Science Projects. 2004, Enslow LB $26.60 (978-0-7660-2123-5). Introduced by a discussion of the concept of polymers and a model of a hydrocarbon chain, subsequent projects build on this knowledge. (Rev: SLJ 7/04) [507]

11707 Green, Dan. *The Elements* (7–10). Illus. Series: Discover More. 2012, Scholastic $15.99 (978-054533019-0). A visually attractive survey of the periodic table, this volume also comes with a downloadable ebook supplement. (Rev: BL 4/1/12; SLJ 4/12) [546]

11708 Greenberg, Arthur. *A Chemical History Tour: Picturing Chemistry from Alchemy to Modern Molecular Science* (10–12). 2000, Wiley $94.95 (978-0-471-35408-6). Using all sorts of illustrations and a clear text, this is a history of chemistry from earliest times to today. [540.9]

11709 Kean, Sam. *The Disappearing Spoon and Other True Tales of Madness, Love, and the History of the World from the Periodic Table of the Elements* (10–12). 2010, Little, Brown $24.99 (978-031605164-4). A fascinating collection of stories about the scientists who contributed to the creation of the periodic table. ⌒ (Rev: BL 7/10) [546]

11710 Lew, Kristi. *Acids and Bases* (8–12). Illus. Series: Essential Chemistry. 2009, Chelsea House $35 (978-0-7910-9783-0). Colorful illustrations and informative sidebars punctuate this comprehensive book on acids and bases and their importance. (Rev: SLJ 5/1/09)

11711 Miller, Ron. *The Elements: What You Really Want to Know* (7–12). Illus. by author. 2005, Twenty-First Century LB $29.27 (978-0-7613-2794-3). After historical information and profiles of key scientists, Miller provides information on each element in order of atomic number. (Rev: SLJ 3/06) [540]

11712 Newton, David. *Chemistry of the Environment* (9–12). Series: New Chemistry. 2007, Facts on File $35.00 (978-0-8160-5273-8). This look at how chemistry and the environment are interrelated in the areas of air pollution, water pollution, the atmosphere, and solid waste disposal will interest students in both fields, especially those with a strong knowledge of chemistry. (Rev: BL 10/15/07) [628.5]

11713 Roston, Eric. *The Carbon Age: How Life's Core Element Has Become Civilization's Greatest Threat* (10–12). 2008, Walker $25.99 (978-0-8027-1557-9). Science journalist Roston provides a compelling glimpse into the life of a carbon atom by examining its structure, properties, and many uses — and pitfalls — for humans. ℮ (Rev: BL 6/1–15/08) [577.144]

Geology and Geography

Earth and Geology

11714 Gardner, Robert. *Planet Earth Science Fair Projects Using the Moon, Stars, Beach Balls, Frisbees, and Other Far-Out Stuff* (6–12). Series: Earth Science! Best Science Projects. 2005, Enslow LB $26.60 (978-0-7660-2362-8). Earth science projects are clearly presented with background information necessary to give full understanding of the underlying principles. (Rev: SLJ 7/05) [551]

11715 Gerdes, Louise I., ed. *Intelligent Design versus Evolution* (9–12). Series: At Issue. 2007, Gale LB $29.95 (978-0-7377-3679-3); paper $21.20 (978-0-7377-3680-9). Readers gain a thorough understanding of both sides of this argument. (Rev: BL 4/10/08) [231.7]

11716 Hehner, Barbara Embury. *Blue Planet* (7–12). Series: Wide World. 1992, Harcourt $17.95 (978-0-15-200423-1). An examination of the interdependent systems that make up our planet, including plate tectonics, volcanoes, weather, satellites, and the ozone layer. (Rev: BL 11/15/92; SLJ 10/92) [508]

11717 Luhr, James F., ed. *Earth: The Definitive Visual Guide to Our Planet* (10–12). 2003, DK $50.00 (978-0-7894-9643-0). This richly illustrated and comprehensive guide traces the origins and evolution of the planet in both text and graphics and provides a wealth of information about the atmosphere, tectonic plates and earthquakes, glaciers, all varieties of physical characteristics, and more. (Rev: BL 12/1/03; VOYA 4/04) [550]

11718 Macdougall, Doug. *Frozen Earth: The Once and Future Story of Ice Ages* (10–12). 2004, Univ. of California $45.00 (978-0-520-23922-7). A fascinating presentation that combines information on ice ages — and the author's belief that the earth is currently cooling —

with biographies of key scientists and the importance of geology in general. (Rev: BL 9/15/04) [551.7]

11719 Mathez, Edmond A., and James D. Webster. *The Earth Machine: The Science of a Dynamic Planet* (10–12). 2004, Columbia $39.95 (978-0-231-12578-9). The story of geology and such phenomena as plate tectonics and how this information has explained such natural wonders as the Grand Canyon, the Alps, and the Hawaiian Islands. (Rev: BL 4/1/04) [550]

11720 Meissner, Rolf. *The Little Book of Planet Earth* (10–12). 2002, Copernicus/Springer-Verlag $20.00 (978-0-387-95258-1). A clear and concise natural history of the earth that discusses geology in general along with its many specialties — seismology, mineralogy, and so forth; suitable for advanced students. (Rev: BL 4/15/02) [550]

11721 O'Neill, Catherine. *Natural Wonders of North America* (7–12). 1984, National Geographic LB $12.50 (978-0-87044-519-4). Excellent color photographs complement the text and maps that describe such natural wonders as tundra regions, volcanoes, glaciers, and the Badlands of South Dakota. [557]

11722 Poynter, Jane. *The Human Experiment: Two Years and Twenty Minutes Inside Biosphere 2* (9–12). 2006, Thunder's Mouth $26.95 (978-1-56025-775-2). What went on among the eight participants in the Biosphere experiment was almost more significant than the ecological findings, according to the author, who was one of the brave humans in the experiment. (Rev: BL 9/1/06) [551.9]

11723 VanCleave, Janice. *Janice VanCleave's A+ Projects in Earth Science: Winning Experiments for Science Fairs and Extra Credit* (5–10). 1999, Wiley paper $12.95 (978-0-471-17770-8). Thirty projects varying in complexity are included in this exploration of topography, minerals, atmospheric composition, the ocean floor, and erosion. (Rev: BL 12/1/98; SLJ 6/99) [550]

Earthquakes and Volcanoes

11724 Christian, Spencer, and Antonia Felix. *Shake, Rattle and Roll: The World's Most Amazing Natural Forces* (6–10). Series: Spencer Christian's World of Wonders. 1997, Wiley paper $13.95 (978-0-471-15291-0). This book supplies good information and suitable projects involving earthquakes and volcanoes, with material on topics including plate tectonics, seismic waves, geysers, and hot springs. (Rev: SLJ 6/98) [551.2]

11725 Clarkson, Peter. *Volcanoes* (8–12). Series: World Life Library. 2000, Voyageur paper $16.95 (978-0-89658-502-7). Illustrated with color photographs and diagrams, this account gives general information about volcanoes and presents a tour of the world's most famous ones. [551.2]

11726 Erickson, Jon. *Volcanoes and Earthquakes* (10–12). 1988, TAB $22.95 (978-0-8306-1942-9); paper $15.95 (978-0-8306-2842-1). In addition to general information on volcanoes and earthquakes the author gives a valuable introduction to plate tectonics and how planets were formed. (Rev: BL 1/1/89) [551.2]

11727 Winchester, Simon. *Krakatoa: The Day the World Exploded: August 27, 1883* (10–12). 2003, HarperCollins $25.95 (978-0-06-621285-2). This detailed yet absorbing examination of the 1883 explosion of the volcanic island of Krakatoa explores both the local and global impact. (Rev: BL 2/1/03*; SLJ 10/03) [551.21]

Physical Geography

General and Miscellaneous

11728 Bass, Rick. *The Wild Marsh: Four Seasons at Home in Montana* (10–12). 2009, Houghton Mifflin $26 (978-054705516-9). Nature writer Rick Bass takes the reader on a 12-month exploration of the seasonal beauty of Yaak Valley, Montana. **e** (Rev: BL 4–5/09) [508.786]

11729 Erickson, Jon. *An Introduction to Fossils and Minerals: Seeking Clues to the Earth's Past* (9–12). 1992, Facts on File LB $26.95 (978-0-8160-2587-9). An overview of how rocks, fossils, and minerals have moved naturally over the ages and how they can provide information to the earth's history. (Rev: BL 4/15/92) [560]

11730 Heinrichs, Ann. *Continents* (10–12). Series: Real World Math: Geography. 2010, Cherry Lake LB $27.07 (978-1-60279-490-0). Clearly written and filled with bright photographs, the volumes in this series provide lessons in science, geography and mathematics, making for an interdisciplinary learning experience. Also use *Islands* and *Oceans* (both 2010). (Rev: LMC 1–2/10)

11731 Moore, Peter D. *Tundra* (6–10). Illus. by Richard Garratt. 2006, Chelsea House $39.50 (978-0-8160-5325-4). This interesting volume discusses not only the geography, geology, ecosystem, and biodiversity of tundras around the world but also history related to the tundra, uses of the tundra, and the future of the tundra in terms of climate change and conservation. (Rev: SLJ 12/06)

11732 Taylor, Michael Ray. *Caves: Exploring Hidden Realms* (9–12). 2001, National Geographic $35.00 (978-0-7922-7904-4). This visually attractive book discusses the nature and history of caves, the life they support, and spelunkers and their tools, looking at sites in Greenland, the Yucatan, and the United States. (Rev: BL 6/1–15/01) [796.52]

Deserts

11733 Allaby, Michael. *Deserts* (6–10). Illus. by Richard Garratt. Series: Biomes of the Earth. 2006, Chelsea House $39.50 (978-0-8160-5320-9). This interesting volume discusses not only the geography, geology, climates, and flora and fauna of deserts around the world but also history related to deserts, desert exploration, desert industries (oil, solar energy, minerals, and tourism), threats to deserts, and efforts to manage deserts. (Rev: LMC 1/07; SLJ 12/06)

Forests and Rain Forests

11734 Allaby, Michael. *Tropical Forests* (9–12). Illus. by Richard Garratt. Series: Biomes of the Earth. 2006, Chelsea House $39.50 (978-0-8160-5322-3). This informative book on tropical forests and their flora, fauna, peoples, and environmental problems comes complete with illustrations, maps, photographs, glossary, and lists of recommended books and Web sites. (Rev: BL 7/06) [577.34]

11735 Lewington, Anna. *Atlas of the Rain Forests* (6–12). 1997, Raintree $22.98 (978-0-8172-4756-0). Enhanced by maps and photographs, this work contains information on the plant and animal life found in rain forests, the cultures of the people who live in them, and how these environments are changed by economic development. (Rev: BL 5/15/97; SLJ 8/97) [574.5]

11736 Lowman, Margaret D, et al. *It's a Jungle Up There: More Tales from the Treetops* (9–12). 2006, Yale $30.00 (978-0-300-10863-7). In addition to interesting descriptions of the rain forest canopy and the threats to its health, Lowman and her sons recount family adventures in wilderness areas around the globe. (Rev: BL 3/15/06) [509]

11737 McLeish, Ewan. *Rain Forest Destruction* (7–12). Series: What If We Do Nothing? 2007, World Almanac LB $30.60 (978-0-8368-7758-8). McLeish looks at the causes and potentially catastrophic results of deforestation in the rain forests and discusses what we can do to stop the destruction. (Rev: LMC 11–12/07; SLJ 5/07) [578.734]

11738 Oldfield, Sara. *Rainforest* (10–12). 2003, MIT $32.95 (978-0-262-15106-1). This clearly written overview of rain forests and the incredible diversity of plant and animal life found there will be especially useful for report writers. (Rev: BL 7/03) [578.734]

Mountains

11739 Collier, Michael. *Over the Mountains: An Aerial View of Geology* (9–12). Photos by Michael Collier. Series: An Aerial View of Geology. 2007, Mikaya $29.95 (978-1-931414-18-0). Collier uses strikingly beautiful photography to illustrate geological principles. (Rev: SLJ 6/07) [557]

Ponds, Rivers, and Lakes

11740 Beck, Gregor Gilpin. *Watersheds: A Practical Handbook for Healthy Water* (7–12). 1999, Firefly $19.95 (978-1-55037-330-1). This account highlights the importance of water in our lives, with special attention to pollution, flooding, and other environmental problems. (Rev: BL 9/1/99) [333.73]

11741 Palmer, Tim. *Rivers of America* (9–12). 2006, Abrams $40.00 (978-0-8109-5485-4). Photographs by conservationist Palmer show breathtaking views of American rivers, seemingly untouched, while his commentary on the need to protect these rivers in a nation where nearly half are polluted provides a contrasting reality. (Rev: BL 10/15/06) [551.48]

Prairies and Grasslands

11742 Coenraads, Robert R. *Rocks and Fossils: A Visual Guide* (9–12). 2005, Firefly $29.95 (978-1-55407-068-

8). Full of illustrations and photographs, this is an excellent overview of rocks, fossils, and geologic processes that will serve as a good resource for report writers. (Rev: BL 9/1/05) [552]

Rocks, Minerals, and Soil

11743 Chesterman, Charles W., and Kurt E. Lowe. *The Audubon Society Field Guide to North American Rocks and Minerals* (7–12). 1978, Knopf $19.95 (978-0-394-50269-4). A basic guide that includes color illustrations of nearly 800 rocks and minerals. [549]

11744 Finlay, Victoria. *Jewels: A Secret History* (9–12). 2006, Ballantine $25.95 (978-0-345-46694-5). Finlay travels the world to learn the lore behind all sorts of precious gems, and tells some fascinating stories about the lengths to which people will go to obtain them. (Rev: BL 8/06) [553.8]

11745 Oldershaw, Cally. *Firefly Guide to Gems* (10–12). 2004, Firefly paper $14.95 (978-1-55297-814-6). This small-format, well-illustrated guide to gemstones starts with background material and proceeds to a listing of gems by chemical composition. (Rev: SLJ 6/04; VOYA 6/04) [553.8]

11746 Pough, Frederick H. *A Field Guide to Rocks and Minerals. 4th ed.* (7–12). 1976, Houghton Mifflin paper $20.00 (978-0-395-91096-2). This volume in the Peterson Field Guide series gives photographs and identifying information on 270 rocks and minerals. [549]

11747 Vernon, Ron. *Beneath Our Feet: The Rocks of Planet Earth* (10–12). 2000, Cambridge $55.00 (978-0-521-79030-7). This effectively illustrated volume discusses various kinds of rocks, how they are shaped, rock formations, and how natural forces such as earthquakes and water can change the face of the earth. (Rev: BL 12/1/00) [552]

Mathematics

General and Miscellaneous

11748 Diacu, Florin. *Megadisasters: The Science of Predicting the Next Catastrophe* (10–12). Illus. 2009, Princeton $24.95 (978-069113350-8). Diacu explains very simply how multiple disasters — from earthquakes to hurricanes to market crashes — can be predicted by mathematicians who hope to avoid them or at least to mitigate their effects. (Rev: BL 12/1/09) [904]

11749 du Sautoy, Marcus. *Symmetry: A Journey into the Patterns of Nature* (9–12). 2008, HarperCollins $25.95 (978-0-06-078940-4). We thought symmetry was just about balance, but it's much more than that as the author deftly engages readers in the intellectual pleasures of pure mathematics. (Rev: BL 3/1/08) [515]

11750 Frederick, Shane. *Football: The Math of the Game* (6–10). Illus. Series: Sports Math. 2011, Capstone LB $22.99 (978-142966567-4); paper $7.95 (9781429673198). Shows how important a role math plays in the game of football, giving clear examples and appealing illustrations. (Rev: BL 10/1/11) [796.332]

11751 Hodges, Andrew. *One to Nine: The Inner Life of Numbers* (10–12). 2008, Norton $23.95 (978-0-393-06641-8). Written with clarity and intelligence, this surprising look at numbers one through nine will disarm even those who dislike math. (Rev: BL 4/1/08) [513.2]

11752 Huff, Darrell. *How to Lie with Statistics* (10–12). 1954, Norton paper $3.95 (978-0-393-09426-8). A now-classic account of how numbers can be manipulated to produce desired results. [519.5]

11753 Jacobs, Harold R. *Mathematics, A Human Endeavor: A Book for Those Who Think They Don't Like the Subject. 3rd ed.* (10–12). 1994, W. H. Freeman $79.40 (978-0-7167-2426-1). An overview of mathematics that delves into its history and many applications. [510]

11754 Kogelman, Stanley, and Joseph Warren. *Mind over Math* (10–12). 1978, McGraw-Hill paper $10.95 (978-0-07-035281-0). Based on the authors' many workshops, this is a course on how to overcome math anxiety. [510]

11755 Niederman, Derrick, and David Boyum. *What the Numbers Say: A Field Guide to Mastering Our Numerical World* (10–12). 2003, Broadway $24.95 (978-0-7679-0098-0). An entertaining attempt to demystify and popularize mathematics, this volume recommends that readers regard figures and statistics offered by others with a healthy degree of skepticism. (Rev: BL 5/15/03) [001]

11756 Schwartz, David M. *G Is for Googol: A Math Alphabet Book* (6–10). 1998, Tricycle $15.95 (978-1-883672-58-4). A humorous romp through mathematical terms and concepts using an alphabetical approach and cartoon illustrations. (Rev: BL 10/15/98; HBG 3/99; SLJ 11/98) [510]

11757 Tattersall, Graham. *Geekspeak: How Life + Mathematics = Happiness* (10–12). 2008, HarperCollins $19.95 (978-0-06-162924-2). By using mathematical formulas in an engaging and accessible manner that will appeal to independent thinkers, Tattersall answers twenty-six different questions about the world around us; the real-world nature of the topics will appeal to teens. ℮ (Rev: BL 8/08; SLJ 11/08) [510]

11758 Zaslavsky, Claudia. *Fear of Math: How to Get Over It and Get On with Your Life* (9–12). 1994, Rutgers paper $21.95 (978-0-8135-2099-5). This book gives many ideas on how to conquer math phobia and enjoy this field of knowledge. (Rev: BL 6/1–15/94) [510.7]

763

Algebra, Numbers, and Number Systems

11759 McKellar, Danica. *Hot X: Algebra Exposed* (10–12). 2010, Penguin $26.95 (978-159463070-5). Part tutorial, part girl-talk, McKellar's book provides an appealing tool for mathematically challenged young women to gain confidence and skills while having plenty of fun. (Rev: BL 7/10) [512]

11760 Wingard-Nelson, Rebecca. *Algebra Word Problems* (6–10). Series: Math Busters Word Problems. 2010, Enslow LB $27.93 (978-0-7660-3367-2). A step-by-step guide to understanding basic algebra concepts and how they can be applied in real-life situations. Also use *Fraction and Decimal Word Problems* (2010). (Rev: LMC 11–12/10) [512.0076]

Mathematical Games and Puzzles

11761 Tahan, Malba. *The Man Who Counted: A Collection of Mathematical Adventures* (9–12). 1993, Norton paper $14.95 (978-0-393-30934-8). Regales readers with delightful mathematical adventures featuring beautiful princesses, viziers, sultans, and Tahan himself. (Rev: BL 2/15/93*) [793.7]

Meteorology

General and Miscellaneous

11762 Allaby, Michael. *Fog, Smog and Poisoned Rain* (7–12). Illus. by Richard Garratt. Series: Dangerous Weather. 2003, Facts on File $40.00 (978-0-8160-4789-5). Natural sources of pollution such as volcanoes are included in this survey of dangerous weather phenomena. (Rev: SLJ 10/03) [363.739]

11763 Cox, John D. *Climate Crash: Abrupt Climate Change and What It Means for Our Future* (10–12). 2005, Joseph Henry $27.95 (978-0-309-09312-5). In easy-to-understand language, science/environment journalist Cox outlines the history of research into sudden climate change and explores how such changes might affect the future, cautioning that it may be too early to assess the impact of greenhouse gases. (Rev: BL 5/15/05) [551.79]

11764 de Villiers, Marq. *Windswept: The Story of Wind and Weather* (10–12). 2006, Walker $25.00 (978-0-8027-1469-5). An interesting discussion of our understanding of wind over time, touching on ancient myths about winds, the discovery of the jet stream, and specific windstorms of note. (Rev: BL 3/15/06; SLJ 10/06) [551.51]

11765 Harper, Kristine C. *Weather and Climate: Decade by Decade* (10–12). Series: Twentieth-Century Science. 2007, Facts on File LB $49.50 (978-0-8160-5535-7). Harper provides a chronological look at developments on the weather front from 1900 to 2000, with a timeline of key events and profiles of important individuals. (Rev: BL 8/07; SLJ 8/07) [551.509]

Air

11766 Walker, Gabrielle. *An Ocean of Air: Why the Wind Blows and Other Mysteries of the Atmosphere* (9–12). 2007, Harcourt $25.00 (978-0-15-101124-7). Scientists and their discoveries regarding air and the atmosphere are featured in this informative guide to the properties and functions of the air that sustains and shields us. (Rev: BL 7/07) [551.509]

Storms

11767 Allaby, Michael. *Blizzards* (9–12). Series: Dangerous Weather. 1997, Facts on File $35.00 (978-0-8160-3518-2). As well as defining blizzards and discussing the climatic conditions that cause them, this volume looks at the areas most susceptible to blizzards, and what can be done to minimize the threat posed by winter hazards. [551.55]

11768 Allaby, Michael. *Tornadoes* (7–12). Series: Dangerous Weather. 1997, Facts on File $35.00 (978-0-8160-3517-5). This excellent book on tornadoes describes how they begin, their structure, travel patterns, interiors, historic tornadoes, and when and where tornadoes occur. (Rev: SLJ 4/98) [551.55]

11769 Cerveny, Randy. *Freaks of the Storm: From Flying Cows to Stealing Thunder* (8–12). 2006, Thunder's Mouth paper $16.95 (978-1-56025-801-8). Cerveny chronicles bizarre weather phenomena — from fish falling from the sky to chickens plucked bare by hurricane winds — and extremes of heat, cold, rainfall, and so forth. (Rev: BL 12/1/05) [551.5]

11770 De Hahn, Tracee. *The Blizzard of 1888* (7–12). Series: Great Disasters: Reforms and Ramifications. 2000, Chelsea $21.95 (978-0-7910-5787-2). Exciting illustrations and eyewitness accounts enhance this exploration of the impact of this famous blizzard and of the changes in infrastructure and services that resulted from it. (Rev: BL 4/15/01; HBG 10/01; SLJ 6/01) [974.7]

11771 Dudley, William, ed. *Hurricane Katrina* (6–10). Series: At Issue. 2006, Gale LB $28.70 (978-0-7377-3551-2). An examination of the governmental, social, and natural forces that affected the victims of Hurricane Katrina and the city of New Orleans, this collection of articles will help students to see that there were many differing opinions on what action to take. (Rev: SLJ 9/06)

11772 Emanuel, Kerry. *Divine Wind: The History and Science of Hurricanes* (11–12). 2005, Oxford $55.00 (978-0-19-514941-8). Advanced students will appreciate this comprehensive discussion of the science of hurricanes and the references to relevant art and literature. (Rev: BL 12/1/05) [551.55]

11773 Erickson, Jon. *Violent Storms* (10–12). 1988, TAB $24.95 (978-0-8306-9042-8); paper $16.95 (978-0-8306-2942-8). In addition to a description of the nature and causes of storms, the author gives a general introduction to weather and such topics as the greenhouse effect and acid rain. (Rev: BL 1/1/89; VOYA 4/89) [551.5]

11774 Horne, Jed. *Breach of Faith: Hurricane Katrina and the Near Death of a Great American City* (9–12). 2006, Random House $25.95 (978-1-4000-6552-3). A moving portrait of the suffering caused by Katrina and the unfair distribution of immediate and follow-up assistance, health care, and other basic needs. (Rev: BL 7/06) [976.3]

11775 Junger, Sebastian. *The Perfect Storm* (10–12). 1997, Norton $23.95 (978-0-393-04016-6). This bestselling book re-creates the last few hours of the swordfishing vessel *Andrea Gail* as it heads into "the perfect storm" and tragedy. (Rev: SLJ 11/97) [904]

11776 Larson, Erik. *Isaac's Storm: A Man, a Time, and the Deadliest Hurricane in History* (10–12). 1999, Crown $25.00 (978-0-609-60233-1). This wide-ranging account of the 1900 hurricane that devastated Galveston, Texas, focuses on the disaster's personal impact on the head of the local office of the fledgling U.S. Weather Bureau. (Rev: BL 6/1–15/99; SLJ 3/00; VOYA 2/00)

11777 Palser, Barb. *Hurricane Katrina: Aftermath of Disaster* (7–10). Series: Snapshots in History. 2006, Compass Point LB $31.93 (978-0-7565-2101-1). An interesting yet detailed look at how Katrina affected

residents of New Orleans, and at the rescue and restoration efforts that followed the storm. (Rev: BL 12/1/06) [976]

11778 Rose, Chris. *1 Dead in Attic: After Katrina* (9–12). 2007, Simon & Schuster paper $15.00 (978-1-4165-5298-7). The Pulitzer prize-winning columnist of the *Times-Picayune* offers a collection of essays covering a year and a half after Hurricane Katrina, including his own experiences, even his decline into depression. (Rev: BL 8/07) [976.3]

11779 Sheets, Bob, and Jack Williams. *Hurricane Watch: Forecasting the Deadliest Storms on Earth* (10–12). 2001, Random House paper $15.00 (978-0-375-70390-4). A fascinating account of storm watchers and the most severe storms in history from the time of Columbus through the terrible onslaught on Florida in 1992. (Rev: BL 7/01; SLJ 1/02) [551.55]

11780 Timmer, Reed, and Andrew Tilin. *Into the Storm: Violent Tornadoes, Killer Hurricanes, and Death-Defying Adventures in Extreme Weather* (10–12). 2010, Dutton $26.95 (978-052595193-3). The Discovery Channel's host of *Storm Chasers* recounts his most harrowing adventures and provides a brief history of storm chasing. (Rev: BL 10/1–15/10) [551]

11781 Treaster, Joseph B. *Hurricane Force: In the Path of America's Deadliest Storms* (7–10). Series: New York Times Book. 2007, Kingfisher $16.95 (978-0-7534-3086-3). A reporter for the *New York Times* who witnessed firsthand the devastation wrought by Hurricane Katrina discusses that storm and hurricanes in general; with photographs and other visuals. (Rev: BL 3/1/07; SLJ 5/07) [551.55]

Water

11782 Ball, Philip. *Life's Matrix: A Biography of Water* (10–12). 2000, Farrar paper $21.95 (978-0-520-23008-8). This book describes the past and present contributions of water to world civilization, and also explains its properties and uses. (Rev: BL 5/15/00) [553.7]

11783 de Villiers, Marq. *Water: The Fate of Our Most Precious Resource* (10–12). 2000, Houghton Mifflin paper $16.00 (978-0-618-12744-3). As well as describing the history, folklore, and politics of water, this account gives details on the worsening water situation worldwide and efforts to avoid an international crisis. (Rev: SLJ 4/06) [333.91]

11784 Kandel, Robert. *Water from Heaven: The Story of Water from the Big Bang to the Rise of Civilization, and Beyond* (10–12). 2003, Columbia $27.95 (978-0-231-12244-3). This well-researched study looks at the origins of fresh water, the water cycle, and the formidable threats to the world's fresh water supplies today. (Rev: BL 12/1/02) [551.46]

Weather

11785 Burt, Christopher C. *Extreme Weather: A Guide and Record Book* (8–12). 2004, Norton paper $24.95 (978-0-393-32658-1). An overview of weather at its worst, this richly illustrated volume contains a wealth of meteorological data on extreme events, including heat, drought, cold, floods, thunderstorms, windstorms, tornadoes, and fog. (Rev: SLJ 2/05) [551.6]

11786 Dickinson, Terence. *Exploring the Sky by Day: The Equinox Guide to Weather and the Atmosphere* (7–10). 1988, Camden House paper $9.95 (978-0-920656-71-6). A book about weather that explores such subjects as types of clouds and kinds of precipitation. (Rev: BL 3/1/89; SLJ 1/89) [551.6]

11787 Lee, Laura. *Blame It on the Rain: How the Weather Has Changed History* (10–12). 2006, HarperCollins paper $13.95 (978-0-06-083982-6). A wide-ranging and entertaining review of how weather has affected important events over time, this is suitable for browsers. (Rev: BL 7/1/06; SLJ 11/06)

11788 Libbrecht, Kenneth, and Patricia Rasmussen. *The Snowflake: Winter's Secret Beauty* (10–12). 2003, Voyageur $20.00 (978-0-89658-630-7). Stunning photographs are combined with a clear explanation of the science behind the formation of ice crystals. (Rev: BL 12/1/03) [551.57]

11789 Ramsey, Dan. *Weather Forecasting: A Young Meteorologist's Guide* (8–12). 1990, TAB $19.95 (978-0-8306-8338-3); paper $10.95 (978-0-8306-3338-8). A detailed and often technical examination of the techniques of weather forecasting with many tables, charts, and diagrams. (Rev: BL 10/15/90) [551.6]

11790 Reynolds, Ross. *Guide to Weather: A Practical Guide to Observing, Measuring and Understanding the Weather* (10–12). 2005, Firefly paper $19.95 (978-1-55407-110-4). A detailed yet easy-to-understand guide to the atmospheric forces that create weather. (Rev: BL 9/15/05) [551.6]

11791 Robinson, Kim Stanley. *Fifty Degrees Below* (9–12). 2005, Bantam $25.00 (978-0-553-80312-9). In this sequel to *Forty Signs of Rain* (2004), weather catastrophes attributable to global warming include the stalling of the Gulf Stream, frigid temperatures along the East Coast, and flooding. (Rev: SLJ 3/06)

11792 Upgren, Arthur R., and Jurgen Stock. *Weather: How It Works and Why It Matters* (9–12). 2000, Perseus paper $18.00 (978-0-7382-0521-2). After describing factors that affect the weather and the causes of seasonal changes, this account discusses current threats such as global warming and ozone depletion. [551.5]

11793 Williams, Jack. *The Weather Book. 2nd ed.* (9–12). 1997, Vintage paper $20.00 (978-0-679-77665-9). Featuring easy-to-follow color graphics from *USA Today,* this handy guide explores a wide range of weather-related topics, including computer forecasting, basic changes in weather patterns, cold fronts, heat waves, tornadoes, blizzards, hurricanes, and droughts. [551.6]

Oceanography

General and Miscellaneous

11794 Burns, Loree Griffin. *Tracking Trash: Flotsam, Jetsam, and the Science of Ocean Motion* (7–10). Series: Scientists in the Field. 2007, Houghton Mifflin $18.00 (978-0-618-58131-3). Trash in the ocean can help scientists study currents as well as posing a threat to animals and ecosystems, according to this attractive book. Boston Globe–Horn Book Honor 2007; ALA Notable Books 2008. (Rev: BCCB 5/07; BL 4/1/07; HB 3–4/07; LMC 11/07; SLJ 3/07*) [551.46]

11795 Carson, Rachel. *The Sea Around Us* (10–12). 1989, Oxford paper $19.99 (978-0-19-506997-6). A classic introduction to oceans with material on how they were formed, currents and tides, volcanic islands, and life in the sea. [551.46]

11796 Day, Trevor. *Oceans. Rev. ed.* (9–12). Illus. by Richard Garratt. Series: Ecosystem. 2007, Facts on File $70.00 (978-0-8160-5932-4). Understandable explanations of ocean-related phenomena are provided in this detail-rich overview. (Rev: SLJ 3/08)

11797 Desonie, Dana. *Oceans: How We Use the Seas* (8–12). Series: Our Fragile Planet. 2007, Chelsea House LB $35.00 (978-0-8160-6216-4). An overview of oceanography with an emphasis on environmental protection and a no-frills format. (Rev: BL 10/15/07; SLJ 4/08) [551.46]

11798 Dinwiddie, Robert. *Ocean: The World's Last Wilderness Revealed* (7–12). 2006, DK $50.00 (978-0-7566-2205-3). With many eye-catching images and lots of information on the ocean environment (tides, waves, shallow seas, polar seas, and so forth) and the life found therein, this well-designed volume is useful both for browsers and researchers. (Rev: BL 11/15/06) [551.46]

11799 Erickson, Jon. *The Mysterious Oceans* (9–12). 1988, TAB paper $15.95 (978-0-8306-9342-9). After discussing how oceans were formed, the author explores such topics as deep sea life, waves, food resources, and pollution. (Rev: VOYA 2/89) [551.46]

11800 Friedman, Lauri S., ed. *Oceans* (7–10). Illus. Series: Introducing Issues with Opposing Viewpoints. 2011, Greenhaven LB $36.82 (978-073775200-7). Presents pro and con arguments on such topics as how our oceans are changing, the threats they face, and the measures that can be taken to protect them. (Rev: BL 12/1/11) [551.46]

11801 Hutchinson, Stephen, and Lawrence E. Hawkins. *Oceans: A Visual Guide* (8–12). 2005, Firefly $29.95 (978-1-55407-069-5). With dramatic photographs and highly readable text, oceanographers Hutchinson and Hawkins introduce readers to the oceans of the world and the qualities that clearly distinguish one from the other. (Rev: BL 10/15/05; VOYA 4/06) [551.46]

11802 Prager, Ellen. *Chasing Science at Sea: Racing Hurricanes, Stalking Sharks, and Living Undersea with Ocean Experts* (11–12). Illus. 2008, Univ. of Chicago $22.50 (978-022667870-2). Exciting and informative, this book, which spotlights various marine scientists who describe their fieldwork and discoveries, will be useful for students considering careers in this field. (Rev: BL 9/1/08) [551.46]

11803 Ulanski, Stan. *The Gulf Stream: Tiny Plankton, Giant Bluefin, and the Amazing Story of the Powerful River in the Atlantic* (10–12). Illus. 2008, Univ. of North Carolina $28.00 (978-0-8078-3217-2). A clear and very interesting explanation of the nature of the Gulf Stream and its importance today and throughout history. (Rev: BL 8/08) [551.46]

11804 Weber, Michael, and Judith Gradwohl. *The Wealth of Oceans* (9–12). 1995, Norton $25.00 (978-0-393-03764-7). New discoveries in marine ecology are discussed with regard to the stresses imposed by human societies. (Rev: BL 4/1/95) [333.71]

Underwater Exploration and Sea Disasters

11805 Krauss, Erich. *Wave of Destruction: The Stories of Four Families and History's Deadliest Tsunami* (11–12). 2005, Rodale $24.95 (978-1-59486-378-3). The enormity of the disaster caused by the December 2004 Indian Ocean tsunami is revealed in this look at how the catastrophe affected four families in the path of the deadly wave; for mature readers. (Rev: BL 12/1/05) [959.304]

11806 Kusky, Timothy. *Tsunamis: Giant Waves from the Sea* (8–11). Series: Hazardous Earth. 2008, Facts on File $39.50 (978-0-8160-6464-9). Kusky explains the causes and behavior of these destructive waves, describes some particularly tragic occurrences, and looks at efforts to give people advance warning. (Rev: BL 4/1/08) [551.46]

Physics

General and Miscellaneous

11807 Barnett, Lincoln. *The Universe of Dr. Einstein* (8–12). 1980, Amereon $18.95 (978-0-8488-0146-5). A lucid explanation of Einstein's theory of relativity and how it has changed our ideas of the universe. [530.1]

11808 Bortz, Fred. *The Quark* (7–10). Series: The Library of Subatomic Particles. 2004, Rosen LB $27.95 (978-0-8239-4533-7). Suitable for reluctant readers, this is a clear explanation of the quark, featuring large text and many color illustrations. Also recommended in this series are *The Proton*, *The Photon*, and *The Electron* (all 2004). (Rev: SLJ 10/04)

11809 Clegg, Brian. *The God Effect: Quantum Entanglement, Science's Strangest Phenomenon* (10–12). 2006, St. Martin's $24.95 (978-0-312-34341-5). For students with some knowledge of physics, this is a fascinating introduction to the concept of quantum entanglement and its possible uses in new technologies. (Rev: SLJ 10/06)

11810 Darling, David. *Teleportation: The Impossible Leap* (10–12). 2005, Wiley $24.95 (978-0-471-47095-3). Is teleportation in our future? Darling reviews the theories behind it and the experiments now being undertaken. (Rev: BL 5/1/05) [537.5]

11811 Falk, Dan. *Universe on a T-Shirt: The Quest for the Theory of Everything* (10–12). 2004, Arcade $24.95 (978-1-55970-707-7). An accessible, sometimes humorous history of physics from the Greeks through Newton and Einstein to today's complex thinking including string theory. (Rev: BL 1/1–15/04; SLJ 10/04) [530.14]

11812 Field, Andrea R., ed. *The Science of Physics* (7–10). Illus. Series: Introduction to Physics. 2012, Britannica LB $31.70 (978-161530676-3). Straightforward and clearly written text accompanies appealing graph-ics in this guide to the basic principles of physics. Also in this series: *Electricity, Energy,* and *Electronics* (all 2012). (Rev: BL 8/12) [530]

11813 Fleisher, Paul. *Liquids and Gases: Principles of Fluid Mechanics* (6–12). Series: Secrets of the Universe. 2001, Lerner LB $25.26 (978-0-8225-2988-0). Archimedes's principle, Pascal's law, and Bernoulli's principle are among the topics covered in this volume adapted from an adult title. (Rev: HBG 3/02; SLJ 12/01) [532]

11814 Fleisher, Paul. *Matter and Energy: Principles of Matter and Thermodynamics* (7–12). Series: Secrets of the Universe. 2001, Lerner LB $25.26 (978-0-8225-2986-6). The periodic tables and the basic principles of thermodynamics and matter are explained in conversational language with clear diagrams and simple experiments. (Rev: BL 8/01; HBG 3/02; SLJ 1/02) [530.11]

11815 Gardner, Robert. *Easy Genius Science Projects with Light: Great Experiments and Ideas* (6–10). Illus. Series: Easy Genius Science Projects. 2008, Enslow LB $23.95 (978-076602926-2). Gardner provides fascinating physics experiments and mind-benders in this approachable, well-organized book. (Rev: BL 10/15/08) [537.078]

11816 Greene, Brian. *The Fabric of the Cosmos: Space, Time, and the Texture of Reality* (10–12). 2004, Knopf $28.95 (978-0-375-41288-2). Using simple imagery to illustrate complicated points, the author explains new conceptions of space and time in this book for better physics students. (Rev: BL 2/15/04*) [523.1]

11817 Hakim, Joy. *Einstein Adds a New Dimension* (7–12). Series: Story of Science. 2007, Smithsonian $27.95 (978-1-58834-162-4). Not just about Einstein, this book also covers the giants upon whose shoulders Einstein stood and the many other factors in history and society that led to quantum theory; readable and compelling. (Rev: BL 12/1/07; SLJ 12/07) [509]

11818 Jargodzki, Christopher, and Franklin Potter. *Mad About Physics: Braintwisters, Paradoxes, and Curiosities* (10–12). 2000, Wiley paper $16.95 (978-0-471-56961-9). Using a question-and-answer format, this book deals with 397 questions, from the sublime to the ridiculous, about physics. (Rev: BL 11/15/00) [530]

11819 Kakalios, James. *The Amazing Story of Quantum Mechanics: A Math-Free Exploration of the Science That Made Our World* (10–12). Illus. 2010, Gotham $26 (978-159240479-7). Kakalios explains quantum mechanics using popular science fiction comic-book characters. ℮ (Rev: BL 10/1–15/10) [530.12]

11820 Karam, P. Andrew, and Ben P. Stein. *Radioactivity* (6–12). Series: Science Foundations. 2009, Chelsea House $35 (978-1-60413-016-4). Providing an overview of radiation and its characteristics, this volume looks at its uses in warfare, medicine, and other areas. (Rev: LMC 11–12/09) [539.2]

11821 Langone, John. *Theories for Everything: An Illustrated History of Science from Numbers to String Theory* (9–12). 2006, National Geographic $40.00 (978-0-7922-3912-3). This well-illustrated volume full of timelines, biographies, and sidebars informs readers about science as a discipline — about its history, about the difference between suppositions and theories, and so forth. (Rev: BL 12/1/06) [509]

11822 Muller, Richard A. *The Instant Physicist: An Illustrated Guide* (10–12). Illus. by Joey Manfre. 2010, Norton $16.95 (978-039307826-8). Physics prof Muller offers humorous and understandable explanations of various aspects of physics, from the greenhouse effect to the relative toxicity of plutonium to the alleged alien spacecraft crash in Roswell, New Mexico, all accompanied by amusing illustrations. (Rev: BL 11/1–15/10) [530]

11823 Orzel, Chad. *How to Teach Physics to Your Dog* (10–12). Illus. 2009, Scribner $24 (978-141657228-2). Orzel uses the unique (and humorous) approach of explaining physics principles to his dog to make the discipline approachable for all audiences. ℮ (Rev: BL 12/1/09) [530.12]

11824 Ouellette, Jennifer. *Black Bodies and Quantum Cats: Tales from the Annals of Physics* (11–12). 2005, Penguin paper $15.00 (978-0-14-303603-6). In this collection of 50 articles, Ouellette examines a wide array of physics principles from the layperson's viewpoint. (Rev: BL 11/1/05) [530]

11825 Randall, Lisa. *Warped Passages: Unraveling the Mysteries of the Universe's Hidden Dimensions* (10–12). 2005, Ecco $27.95 (978-0-06-053108-9). Randall explains recent findings in cosmology, particle physics, string theory, and super symmetry using easy-to-understand analogies. (Rev: BL 9/1/05) [530]

11826 Rigden, John S. *Einstein, 1905: The Standard of Greatness* (10–12). 2005, Harvard $21.95 (978-0-674-

01544-9). Physics professor Rigden helps readers to understand the science behind five key documents that Albert Einstein published in 1905. (Rev: BL 12/1/04; SLJ 7/05) [530.11]

11827 Smolin, Lee. *The Trouble with Physics: The Rise of String Theory, the Fall of a Science, and What Comes Next* (11–12). 2006, Houghton Mifflin $26.00 (978-0-618-55105-7). Theoretical physicist Smolin explores the rise and fall of string theory and other theories in physics and science in general and speculates about the future of scientific advances. (Rev: BL 9/15/06) [530.14]

11828 Sonneborn, Liz. *Forces in Nature: Understanding Gravitational, Electrical, and Magnetic Force* (7–12). Series: Library of Physics. 2005, Rosen LB $26.50 (978-1-4042-0332-7). Explores a wide variety of forces, including gravitational, electrical, magnetic, and electromagnetic, using clear narrative with diagrams and photographs. (Rev: SLJ 12/05)

11829 Stwertka, Albert. *The World of Atoms and Quarks* (7–12). Series: Scientific American Sourcebooks. 1995, Twenty-First Century LB $28.90 (978-0-8050-3533-9). Using profiles of important scientists, this work traces humankind's quest for an understanding of matter and its building blocks. (Rev: BL 12/1/95; SLJ 2/96) [539.7]

11830 Toomey, David. *The New Time Travelers: A Journey to the Frontiers of Physics* (9–12). 2007, Norton $25.95 (978-0-393-06013-3). Tapping into the theories of time travel stemming from the studies of such scientists as Kip Thorne, Albert Einstein, John Wheeler, Stephen Hawking, Frank Tipler, and Igor Novikov, Toomey, along with recent team of theoretical physicists from Cal Tech, explores the possibilities and variables looking at black holes, cosmic strings, parallel universes, and other phenomenon. (Rev: BL 7/07) [530.11]

11831 Wilczek, Frank. *The Lightness of Being: Mass, Ether, and the Unification of Forces* (11–12). 2008, Basic $26.95 (978-0-465-00321-1). This accessible book explains the nature of mass and gravity, quarks and gluons. ℮ (Rev: BL 8/08) [539.7]

11832 Willett, Edward. *The Basics of Quantum Physics: Understanding the Photoelectric Effect and Line Spectra* (7–12). Series: Library of Physics. 2005, Rosen LB $26.50 (978-1-4042-0334-1). Examines the nature of light and the atom, key elements in the study of quantum physics, using clear narrative with diagrams and photographs. (Rev: SLJ 12/05)

Energy and Motion

General and Miscellaneous

11833 Crosby, Alfred W. *Children of the Sun: A History of Humanity's Unappeasable Appetite for Energy* (10–12). 2006, Norton $23.95 (978-0-393-05935-9). An overview of humankind's historical demands for energy and the outlook for the future. (Rev: BL 1/1–15/06) [333.79]

11834 Doeden, Matt. *Green Energy: Crucial Gains or Economic Strains?* (7–10). Series: USA Today's Debate: Voices and Perspectives. 2010, Lerner LB $35.93 (978-0-7613-5112-2). After a history of energy and a discussion of global warming, this attractive volume that draws on *USA Today* looks at nuclear, solar, and wind power as well as biomass and biofuel, and electric cars, hybrids, and fuel cells. (Rev: LMC 10/10; SLJ 6/10) [163.25]

11835 Fredericks, Carrie, ed. *Natural Gas* (9–12). Series: Fueling the Future. 2006, Gale LB $34.95 (978-0-7377-3578-7). After an account of how natural gas is formed, this volume looks at its impact on the environment and its potential to solve America's energy problems, providing charts, color photographs, and fast facts. (Rev: SLJ 5/07) [553.2]

11836 Fredericks, Carrie, ed. *Water* (9–12). Series: Fueling the Future. 2006, Gale LB $34.95 (978-0-7377-3593-2). After a history of water's use to generate energy, this volume looks at the impact on the environment and at hydroelectricity's potential to solve America's energy problems, providing charts, color photographs, and fast facts. (Rev: SLJ 5/07)

11837 Friedman, Lauri S., ed. *Energy Alternatives* (7–10). Illus. Series: Introducing Issues with Opposing Viewpoints. 2011, Greenhaven $36.82 (978-073775198-7). Presents pro and con arguments on such topics as the remaining oil reserves, climate change, the benefits and shortfalls of renewables, nuclear energy, and passenger cars of the future. (Rev: BL 12/1/11) [333.79]

11838 Gardner, Timothy. *Oil* (7–12). Illus. Series: Diminishing Resources. 2009, Morgan Reynolds LB $28.95 (978-159935117-9). Direct quotes and hard-hitting facts add drama and appeal to this title discussing America's dependence on oil, efforts to find alternative fuels, pollution problems, and relationship with the Middle East. (Rev: BL 1/1–15/10; VOYA 6/10) [333.8]

11839 Goodell, Jeff. *Big Coal: The Dirty Secret behind America's Energy Future* (10–12). 2006, Houghton Mifflin $25.95 (978-0-618-31940-4). An exposé of the industry America depends on for its power, with a realistic examination of the environmental harm it causes and how this can be remedied. (Rev: BL 5/1/06) [333.793]

11840 Kallen, Stuart A. *Hydrogen Power* (9–12). Illus. Series: Compact Research: Energy and the Environment. 2009, ReferencePoint $25.95 (978-160152073-9). Answering such questions as "Can Hydrogen Vehicles Reduce Dependence on Fossil Fuels?" and "How Will Hydrogen Use Impact Global Warming?," this useful volume draws on primary sources and provides sections of facts and illustrations. (Rev: BL 2/15/10; LMC 1–2/10) [665.8]

11841 Kallen, Stuart A. *World Energy Crisis* (8–12). Series: Compact Research. 2007, Reference Point LB $24.95 (978-1-60152-011-1). This compact volume provides lots of information for report writers, with illustrations, quotations from primary sources, lists of facts, statistical charts, and brief timelines. (Rev: SLJ 5/07) [333.79]

11842 Kaufman, Allan. *Exploring Solar Energy: Principles and Projects* (9–12). 1989, Prakken paper $8.95 (978-0-911168-60-0). An account that explains the three aspects of solar energy and gives eight projects of varying difficulty and sophistication. [621.47]

11843 Margonelli, Lisa. *Oil on the Brain: Adventures from the Pump to the Pipeline* (9–12). 2007, Doubleday $26.00 (978-0-385-51145-2). The author takes a worldwide tour of petroleum, looking at the many stages of its production, from harvest to delivery to the consumer and at the many other processes affected by the industry. (Rev: BL 11/1/06) [338.2]

11844 Marrin, Albert. *Black Gold: The Story of Oil in Our Lives* (7–12). Illus. 2012, Knopf $19.99 (978-037586673-9); LB $22.99 (978-037596673-6). A thought-provoking overview of oil deposits through history and our increasing dependence on them even as they dwindle. Outstanding Science Trade Books for Students K–12. ℮ Lexile 1070L (Rev: BLO 7/12; HB 5–6/12; LMC 10/12; SLJ 4/12) [553.2]

11845 Mooney, Carla. *What Is the Future of Biofuels?* (7–10). Illus. Series: Future of Renewable Energy. 2012, ReferencePoint $27.95 (978-160152272-6). Presenting opposing viewpoints, this volume looks at various questions relating to biofuels: are they affordable; do they impact the environment; can they replace fossil fuels; and should the government be involved in biofuel development. (Rev: BL 2/15/13; LMC 5–6/13) [662]

11846 Morris, Neil. *Biomass Power* (7–12). 2010, Smart Apple Media LB $34.25 (978-1-59920-337-9). A look at the technology of biomass power, with discussion of economic and environmental factors. Also use *The Energy Mix, Fossil Fuels, Geothermal Power, Nuclear Power, Solar Power, Water Power,* and *Wind Power* (all 2010). (Rev: LMC 1–2/10) [333.95]

11847 Naff, Clay Farris, ed. *Solar Power* (9–12). Series: Fueling the Future. 2006, Gale LB $34.95 (978-0-7377-3565-9). After a history of solar power, this volume looks at its impact on the environment and potential to solve America's energy problems, providing charts, color photographs, and fast facts. (Rev: SLJ 5/07)

11848 Nakaya, Andrea C. *Energy Alternatives* (8–12). Series: Compact Research. 2007, Reference Point LB $24.95 (978-1-60152-017-3). What alternative energy sources should be pursued? Can alternative energy be used for transportation? These and other questions are discussed from various points of view, with facts, profiles, and illustrations. (Rev: SLJ 1/08)

11849 Passero, Barbara, ed. *Energy Alternatives* (9–12). Series: Opposing Viewpoints. 2006, Gale LB $34.95 (978-0-7377-3350-1). In chapters that offer juxtaposed opposing viewpoints, Passero looks at the following questions: "Are Alternative Energy Sources Necessary?"; "Is Nuclear Power a Viable Energy Alternative?"; "What Renewable Energy Sources Should Be Developed?"; and "Should Alternatives to Fossil Fuels Be Pursued?" (Rev: SLJ 4/07) [333.79]

11850 Smil, Vaclav. *Energies: An Illustrated Guide to the Biosphere and Civilization* (11–12). 1998, MIT $50.00 (978-0-262-19410-5). An information-packed survey of energy sources and the various means humans have used to tap into that power; for advanced science students. (Rev: BL 12/1/98) [531]

11851 Tabak, John. *Coal and Oil* (10–12). Illus. Series: Energy and the Environment. 2009, Facts on File $40 (978-081607083-1). Tabak provides thorough information on each fuel's history, use, associated dangers, and so forth in this fact-filled volume. (Rev: BL 2/15/09) [333.8]

11852 Viegas, Jennifer. *Kinetic and Potential Energy: Understanding Changes Within Physical Systems* (7–12). Series: Library of Physics. 2005, Rosen LB $26.50 (978-1-4042-0333-4). Examines the distinction between potential and kinetic energy, as well as momentum, mechanical energy, and the laws of energy, using clear narrative with diagrams and photographs. (Rev: SLJ 12/05)

Nuclear Energy

11853 Alexievich, Svetlana. *Voices from Chernobyl* (9–12). Trans. by Keith Gessen. 2005, Dalkey Archive $22.95 (978-1-56478-401-8). First-person accounts make this a shocking and vivid portrait of the human costs of the 1986 nuclear catastrophe. (Rev: BL 5/15/05) [363.17]

11854 Bortz, Fred. *Meltdown! The Nuclear Disaster in Japan and Our Energy Future* (7–10). Illus. 2012, Lerner/Twenty-First Century $31.93 (978-076138660-5). Tells the story of the March 2011 earthquake in Japan and the disastrous impact on the Fukushima nuclear plant, and includes discussion of alternative sources of energy. (Rev: BL 2/1/12; LMC 10/12; SLJ 5/1/12; VOYA 6/12) [363.17]

11855 Cravens, Gwyneth. *Power to Save the World: The Truth about Nuclear Energy* (9–12). 2007, Knopf $27.95 (978-0-307-26656-9). Science journalist Cravens here provides a thorough (and favorable) evaluation of nuclear power as an alternative to petroleum, with a caveat about the still-unsolved problem of the resulting waste. (Rev: BL 10/1/07) [333.792]

11856 Daley, Michael J. *Nuclear Power: Promise or Peril?* (7–12). Series: Pro/Con Issues. 1997, Lerner LB $30.35 (978-0-8225-2611-7). This book examines conflicting opinions about nuclear power, the possibility of nuclear accidents, the demand for energy, and the problems involving storage of nuclear waste. (Rev: BL 11/1/97; SLJ 12/97) [333.792]

11857 Lusted, Marcia Amidon, and Greg Lusted. *A Nuclear Power Plant* (8–12). Series: Building History. 2005, Gale LB $32.45 (978-1-59018-392-2). Explores the history of nuclear power generation and considers the arguments for and against the construction of more nuclear power plants in the United States and elsewhere. (Rev: SLJ 6/05) [333.792]

11858 Metcalf, Tom, and Gena Metcalf, eds. *Nuclear Power* (9–12). Series: Fueling the Future. 2006, Gale LB $34.95 (978-0-7377-3587-1). After a history of nuclear power, this volume looks at its impact on the environment and potential to solve America's energy problems, providing charts, color photographs, and fast facts. (Rev: SLJ 5/07)

11859 Nelson, David Erik. *Chernobyl* (9–12). Series: Perspectives on Modern World History. 2010, Gale/Greenhaven $38.50 (978-0-7377-4555-9). Nelson pulls together articles from secondary sources that discuss the historical background of the disaster, the impact on population and environment, and the relative safety of nuclear energy; personal accounts are also included. (Rev: BL 4/1/10; LMC 10/10; SLJ 4/10) [621.48]

Light, Color, and Laser Science

11860 Kirkland, Kyle. *Light and Optics* (8–12). Series: Physics in Our World. 2007, Facts on File $35.00 (978-0-8160-6114-3). A good explanation of the physics of light is followed by a look at real-world examples and applications of light put to use. (Rev: BL 4/15/07) [535]

Magnetism and Electricity

11861 Fara, Patricia. *An Entertainment for Angels: Electricity in the Enlightenment* (10–12). 2003, Columbia $22.50 (978-0-231-13148-3). Fara tells the story of electricity's discovery, in the process setting the record straight on the importance of Benjamin Franklin's kite-flying exploits. (Rev: BL 11/15/03) [306.4]

11862 Fleisher, Paul. *Waves: Principles of Light, Electricity, and Magnetism* (6–12). Series: Secrets of the Universe. 2001, Lerner LB $25.26 (978-0-8225-2987-3). Optics, electric current, and electromagnetism are among the topics covered in this volume adapted from an adult title. (Rev: HBG 3/02; SLJ 12/01) [539.2]

Sound

11863 Kosko, Bart. *Noise* (9–12). 2006, Viking $24.95 (978-0-670-03495-6). Not just the physics of noise but also its social and psychological effects and significances are well covered in this engaging book from the author of *Fuzzy Thinking* (1993). (Rev: BL 9/1/06) [534]

Technology and Engineering

General Works and Miscellaneous Industries

11864 Angelo, Joseph A. *Rockets* (9–12). Series: Frontiers in Space. 2007, Facts on File $39.50 (978-0-8160-5771-9). Examines the history of rockets from ancient China to the present, how they are used for military purposes and space exploration, the science of how they're made, and how they've impacted history and our present lives. (Rev: BL 10/15/06) [621.43]

11865 Benford, Gregory, et al. *The Wonderful Future That Never Was: Flying Cars, Mail Delivery by Parachute, and Other Predictions from the Past* (10–12). 2010, Sterling $24.95 (978-158816822-1). A fascinating and sometimes hilarious look at the predictions of past generations, including hovercraft cars and aluminum clothing, drawn from the archives of *Popular Mechanics*. (Rev: BL 9/1–15/10) [609]

11866 Brockman, John, ed. *This Will Change Everything: Ideas That Will Shape the Future* (10–12). 2010, HarperPerennial paper $14.99 (978-00618996-7-6). Scientists and authors offer their predictions of the technological developments that will radically change the world in their lifetimes. ⓔ (Rev: BL 12/1/09) [500.01]

11867 Broderick, Damien. *The Spike: How Our Lives Are Being Transformed by Rapidly Advancing Technologies* (10–12). 2001, Tor $24.95 (978-0-312-87781-1). The author makes predictions about future advances in technology such as artificial intelligence, and how society's adjustments to these advances can be painless. (Rev: BL 2/15/01) [303.48]

11868 *CDs, Super Glue, and Salsa Series 2: How Everyday Products Are Made* (5–10). 1996, Gale LB $126.00 (978-0-7876-0870-5). This two-volume set tells how 30 everyday products are made, including air bags, bungee cords, contact lenses, ketchup, pencils, soda bottles, and umbrellas. (Rev: SLJ 8/97) [658.5]

11869 Challoner, Jack, ed. *1001 Inventions That Changed the World* (10–12). Illus. 2009, Barron's $35 (978-076416136-0). An interesting and useful although incomplete look at inventions that have shaped how we live, ranging from stone tools to the locomotive and the World Wide Web. (Rev: BLO 4–5/09) [600]

11870 Crompton, Samuel Willard. *The Printing Press* (7–10). Series: Transforming Power of Technology. 2003, Chelsea House LB $30.00 (978-0-7910-7451-0). This interesting volume explores the impact of the invention of the printing press on literacy and general social and economic conditions. (Rev: SLJ 6/04)

11871 Forbes, Peter. *The Gecko's Foot: Bioinspiration: Engineering New Materials from Nature* (10–12). 2006, Norton $24.95 (978-0-393-06223-6). This informative book explores the new science of nanotechnology as it applies to mimicking the innovative biological structures of animals and plants. (Rev: BL 4/15/06) [620.0042]

11872 George, Charles, and Linda George. *Biotech Research* (10–12). Illus. Series: Inside Science. 2011, ReferencePoint LB $27.95 (978-160152176-7). A lucid and thought-provoking overview of the use of biotechnology in foods and agriculture, medicine, and industry, with discussion of the benefits and risks of genetic engineering. (Rev: BL 12/1/11; SLJ 1/12; VOYA 12/12) [660.6]

11873 Gurstelle, William. *Adventures from the Technology Underground: Catapults, Pulsejets, Rail Guns, Flamethrowers, Tesla Coils, Air Cannons, and the Garage Warriors Who Love Them* (10–12). 2006, Clarkson Potter $25.00 (978-1-4000-5028-4). A fascinating tour of technology for teens entranced by such notions as flying cars and fighting robots. (Rev: BL 1/1–15/06) [608]

11874 Hambling, David. *Weapons Grade: How Modern Warfare Gave Birth to Our High-Tech World* (10–12). 2005, Carroll & Graf $25.00 (978-0-7867-1476-6). An interesting look at how military technologies developed during World War II and the Cold War have been transformed to meet civilian needs. (Rev: BL 3/15/05) [338.47]

11875 Harrison, Ian. *The Book of Inventions* (8–12). 2004, National Geographic $30.00 (978-0-7922-8296-9). A photo-filled review of some eclectic and entertaining inventions, including sliced bread and the lava lamp. (Rev: BL 12/1/04) [609]

11876 Hohn, Donovan. *Moby-Duck: The True Story of 28,000 Bath Toys Lost at Sea and of the Beachcombers, Oceanographers, Environmentalists, and Fools, Including the Author, Who Went in Search of Them* (9–12). 2011, Viking $27.95 (978-067002219-9). Hohn's investigation of 28,000 rubber ducks that fell from a container ship in 1992 leads him to fascinating facts about oceanography, weather, shipping, and trade and industry. ⌒ ℯ (Rev: BL 12/1–15/10*) [551.46]

11877 Kaku, Michio. *Physics of the Impossible: A Scientific Exploration into the World of Phasers, Force Fields, Teleportation, and Time Travel* (9–12). 2008, Doubleday $26.95 (978-0-385-52069-0). String theorist Michio Kaku imagines a variety of theoretically possible but logistically improbable sf gadgets. (Rev: BL 3/15/08) [530]

11878 Klein, Maury. *The Power Makers: Steam, Electricity, and the Men Who Invented Modern America* (10–12). 2008, Bloomsbury $29.95 (978-159691412-4). Klein explores the inventors behind the names everyone knows — Edison, Fulton, Morse — and provides a compelling chronological glimpse into the American Industrial Revolution and era of innovation. (Rev: BL 6/1–15/08) [609.73]

11879 Laxer, James. *Oil* (7–10). 2008, Groundwood $18.95 (978-0-88899-815-6); paper $10.00 (978-0-88899-816-3). An illuminating overview of the oil industry, with information on major oil companies, the industry's history, and its impact on the environment and politics. (Rev: BL 6/1–15/08) [333.8]

11880 Levy, Matthys, and Richard Panchyk. *Engineering the City* (6–12). 2000, Chicago Review $14.95 (978-1-55652-419-6). There are many curriculum connections in this book that includes information and activities relating to electricity, garbage, transportation, and other urban infrastructure issues. (Rev: BL 2/15/01) [624]

11881 Macaulay, David, and Neil Ardley. *The New Way Things Work* (6–12). 1998, Houghton Mifflin $35.00 (978-0-395-93847-8). With an emphasis on visual cutaways, this revision of a fascinating 1988 introduction to modern machines now includes more material on computers. (Rev: BL 12/1/98; HBG 9/99; SLJ 12/98) [600]

11882 MacFarlane, Alan, and Gerry Martin. *Glass: A World History* (10–12). 2002, Univ. of Chicago $27.50 (978-0-226-50028-7). The history of glassmaking — and its importance in many areas of our lives — is explored in detail in this fascinating study. (Rev: BL 10/15/02) [666]

11883 Marsden, Ben. *Watt's Perfect Engine: Steam and the Age of Invention* (10–12). 2004, Columbia Univ. $24.00 (978-0-231-13172-8). The story of the Scotsman James Watt and his contribution to the development of the steam engine. (Rev: BL 3/1/04) [621.1]

11884 Parkyn, Neil, ed. *The Seventy Wonders of the Modern World: 1,500 Years of Extraordinary Feats of Engineering and Construction* (10–12). 2002, Thames & Hudson $40.00 (978-0-500-51047-6). Architectural and engineering wonders from around the world are introduced with photographs and technical, historical, and cultural details. (Rev: BL 12/1/02; SLJ 5/03) [720]

11885 Ryles, Briony, and Derek Hall, eds. *Medieval Period and the Renaissance* (9–12). Series: Curriculum Connections: Technology Through the Ages. 2010, Black Rabbit LB $39.95 (978-1-933834-84-9). An attractive survey of the technological innovations during the Middle Ages and Renaissance, stretching from the abacus and early water systems to paper, clocks and watches, guns, printing, and so forth. Also by these authors are *The Ages of Steam and Electricity, The Early 20th Century,* and *The Modern World* (all 2010). (Rev: BL 3/1/10; LMC 8–9/10) [609]

11886 Ryles, Briony, and Derek Hall, eds. *The Scientific Revolution* (9–12). Series: Curriculum Connections: Technology Through the Ages. 2010, Black Rabbit LB $39.95 (978-1-933834-85-6). From the time of Galileo through the invention of the barometer and navigation instruments, locks and keys, the steam engine, and electricity, this attractive volume introduces many fascinating innovations and innovators. (Rev: LMC 8–9/10) [609.03]

11887 Sargent, Ted. *The Dance of Molecules: How Nanotechnology Is Changing Our Lives* (11–12). 2006, Thunder's Mouth $25.00 (978-1-56025-809-4). Sargent explores the fascinating field of nanotechnology and offers a glimpse at how this type of molecular-level engineering is likely to shape the future of life on Earth. (Rev: BL 12/1/05) [620]

11888 Sobey, Ed. *A Field Guide to Roadside Technology* (9–12). 2006, Chicago Review paper $14.95 (978-1-55652-609-1). A fascinating look at all those devices, big and small, that are sprinkled across our landscape in chapters including "Highways and Roadways," "Bridges," "Industrial Sites, Buildings, and Things Attached to Buildings," and "Fields and Streams." (Rev: SLJ 9/06)

11889 Sutton, Caroline, and Duncan M. Anderson. *How Do They Do That?* (10–12). 1982, Morrow paper $11.95 (978-0-688-01111-6). An explanation is given for a variety of present-day achievements. [600]

11890 Vare, Ethlie Ann, and Greg Ptacek. *Patently Female: From AZT to TV Dinners, Stories of Women Inventors and Their Breakthrough Ideas* (9–12). 2001, Wiley $32.50 (978-0-471-02334-0). An enjoyable survey of women as inventors which includes the women behind Liquid Paper, the windshield wiper, and the first computer language. (Rev: BL 12/1/01) [609]

11891 Vare, Ethlie Ann, and Greg Ptacek. *Women Inventors and Their Discoveries* (6–10). 1993, Oliver LB $19.95 (978-1-881508-06-9). A review of women who are known in the world of industry and technology for their unusual inventions. (Rev: BL 10/15/93; SLJ 1/94; VOYA 2/94) [609.2]

11892 Woodford, Chris. *Cool Stuff and How It Works* (8–12). 2005, DK $24.99 (978-0-7566-1465-2). The inner workings of products ranging from the digital camera to the microwave oven are explained in clear text with lots of bright, often high-tech illustrations. (Rev: BL 12/1/05) [600]

Building and Construction

11893 Hawkes, Nigel. *Structures: The Way Things Are Built* (9–12). 1990, Macmillan $39.95 (978-0-02-549105-2). An illustrated look at some of the marvels of civil engineering throughout the world. (Rev: BL 1/15/91) [624.09]

11894 Jackson, Tom, ed. *Buildings and Structures* (7–10). Illus. Series: Facts at Your Fingertips: Invention and Technology. 2012, Black Rabbit LB $35.65 (978-193633341-7). A fascinating introduction to structural engineering and design and the various elements that must be taken into consideration, with a timeline of developments and profiles of key characters including Gustav Eiffel and Frank Lloyd Wright. (Rev: BL 10/1/12) [690]

11895 Korres, Manolis. *The Stones of the Parthenon* (7–12). Trans. by D. Turner. 2001, Getty paper $14.95 (978-0-89236-607-1). The construction of the Parthenon is described in text and detailed drawings in this small-format book, which includes notes, a glossary, and a bibliography. (Rev: BL 2/1/01) [622]

11896 Macaulay, David. *Building Big* (7–12). 2000, Houghton Mifflin $30.00 (978-0-395-96331-9). This companion book to a set of videos explains the problems posed by ambitious construction projects such as tunnels, bridges, dams, domes, and skyscrapers. (Rev: BL 12/15/00*; HB 1–2/01; HBG 3/01; SLJ 11/00; VOYA 4/01) [720]

11897 Macaulay, David. *Underground* (5–10). Illus. by author. 1983, Houghton Mifflin $19.00 (978-0-395-24739-6); paper $9.95 (978-0-395-34065-3). An exploration in text and detailed drawings of the intricate network of systems under city streets. [624]

11898 Priwer, Shana, and Cynthia Phillips. *Bridges and Spans* (9–12). Illus. Series: Frameworks. 2009, Sharpe Focus $39.95 (978-0-7656-8120-1). This well-designed book focuses on the art and science of bridge design and looks at some of the better-known bridge failures. (Rev: SLJ 6/1/09) [624]

11899 Roberts, Russell. *Building the Panama Canal* (7–10). Series: Monumental Milestones. 2009, Mitchell Lane LB $29.95 (978-1-58415-692-5). Both interesting and informative, this book focuses on the historic and technological factors relevant to the construction of the Panama Canal. (Rev: SLJ 6/1/09) [386.44]

11900 Tobin, James. *Great Projects: The Epic Story of the Building of America, from the Taming of the Mississippi to the Invention of the Internet* (10–12). 2001, Free Press $40.00 (978-0-7432-1064-5). Eight great engineering feats, such as the Hoover Dam, and their creators are highlighted in this book about America's greatest construction projects. (Rev: BL 9/1/01) [609.73]

Clothing, Textiles, and Jewelry

11901 Behnke, Alison. *The Little Black Dress and Zoot Suits: Depression and Wartime Fashions from the 1930s to the 1950s* (7–10). Illus. Series: Dressing a Nation: The History of U.S. Fashion. 2011, Lerner/Twenty-First Century LB $31.93 (978-076135892-3). This visually appealing offering offers readers a glimpse into the innovative realm of fashion in America in the 1930s through 1950s. e (Rev: BL 10/1/11; LMC 1–2/12) [391.00973]

11902 Bell, Alison. *Fearless Fashion* (6–10). 2005, Lobster paper $14.95 (978-1-894222-86-0). From preppy to punk to goth to boho, this volume analyzes seven hot fashion trends, looks at trends in history, and gives tips on developing one's own style. (Rev: SLJ 3/05) [391]

11903 MacFarlane, Katherine. *The Jeweler's Art* (7–12). Series: Eye on Art. 2007, Gale LB $32.45 (978-1-59018-984-9). This book reviews the history of jewelry from ancient times through the Renaissance, Baroque and Rococo periods to the Victorians and Edwardians and contemporary styles and techniques. (Rev: LMC 2/08; SLJ 12/07) [739.27]

11904 Stalder, Erika. *Fashion 101: A Crash Course in Clothing* (9–12). Illus. by Ariel Krietzman. 2008, Zest paper $17.95 (978-0-9790173-4-6). A good choice for reluctant readers, this collection presents information on the history of various types of women's clothing, looks at the influence celebrities have on fashion, and gives tips on making and wearing outfits. (Rev: BL 6/1–15/08) [391.6]

11905 Sullivan, James. *Jeans: A Cultural History of an American Icon* (9–12). 2006, Gotham $26.00 (978-1-

59240-214-4). Who doesn't own at least one pair of jeans? This item of clothing is both (nearly) universal and meaningful, as this history, complete with photographs, reveals. (Rev: BL 5/15/06) [687]

11906 Zoellner, Tom. *The Heartless Stone: A Journey Through the World of Diamonds, Deceit, and Desire* (10–12). 2006, St. Martin's $24.95 (978-0-312-33969-2). A fascinating account of the mining, marketing, and mystery of diamonds, which the author claims are responsible for all sorts of exploitation. (Rev: BL 6/1–15/06; SLJ 9/06)

Computers, Automation, and the Internet

11907 Baker, Stephen. *The Numerati* (10–12). 2008, Houghton Mifflin $26.00 (978-061878460-8). Here is an insightful look into the field of data mining — collecting the traces that we leave behind when we use technology such as cell phones and online services. ⌒ e (Rev: BL 9/1/08) [303.48]

11908 Benford, Gregory, and Elisabeth Malartre. *Beyond Human: Living with Robots and Cyborgs* (10–12). 2007, Forge $24.95 (978-0-7653-1082-8). Where will our use of robotics lead? The authors look at surgical, domestic, and other applications of the future. (Rev: BL 10/1/07) [303.48]

11909 Billings, Charlene W. *Supercomputers: Shaping the Future* (7–12). Series: Science Sourcebooks. 1995, Facts on File $25.00 (978-0-8160-3096-5). A history of the silicon revolution — focusing on the megamachines that are the most powerful computers in the world. (Rev: BL 10/15/95; SLJ 4/96; VOYA 4/96) [004.1]

11910 Billings, Charlene W., and Sean M. Grady. *Supercomputers: Charting the Future of Cybernetics. Rev. ed.* (8–12). Series: Science and Technology in Focus. 2004, Facts on File $35.00 (978-0-8160-4730-7). This revised and expanded edition covers the history of computing devices from ancient clay tablets onward and looks forward to the future potential of optical and quantum computers. (Rev: SLJ 6/04) [004.1]

11911 Blascovich, Jim, and Jeremy Bailenson. *Infinite Reality: Avatars, Eternal Life, New Worlds, and the Dawn of the Virtual Revolution* (11–12). Illus. 2011, Morrow $27.99 (978-006180950-7). A fascinating, insightful look into the future of virtual reality technology and how it may affect our lives, from entertainment to education and medicine and beyond. (Rev: BL 3/1–15/11) [303.48]

11912 Burns, Michael. *Digital Fantasy Painting: A Step-by-Step Guide to Creating Visionary Art on Your Computer* (7–12). 2002, Watson-Guptill paper $24.95 (978-0-8230-1574-0). Eye-catching illustrations make

this an attractive volume for browsing as well as for use as a manual of graphic design. (Rev: SLJ 3/03; VOYA 2/03) [760]

11913 Cate, Fred H. *The Internet and the First Amendment: Schools and Sexually Explicit Expression* (10–12). 1998, Phi Delta Kappa Educ. Foundation paper $12.00 (978-0-87367-398-3). A discussion of the complex questions surrounding children's access to the Internet and of the legal issues that come into play. (Rev: SLJ 10/98) [342]

11914 German, Dave. *Dave Gorman's Googlewhack! Adventure* (8–12). 2004, Overlook $24.95 (978-1-58567-614-9). Gorman, a British stand-up comic, writes about his global quest to find googlewhacks — two-word Google search queries that yield a single, solitary hit — in the process of which he successfully put off writing a contracted novel. (Rev: BL 9/15/04) [910.4]

11915 Godin, Seth. *The Big Red Fez: How to Make Any Web Site Better* (10–12). 2002, Fireside paper $11.00 (978-0-7432-2790-2). This slim but information-packed volume offers sound and entertaining advice on jazzing up Web sites — mainly for entrepreneurs but full of tips for teens. (Rev: BL 1/1–15/02) [005.7]

11916 Gordon, Sherri Mabry. *Downloading Copyrighted Stuff from the Internet: Stealing or Fair Use?* (7–10). Series: Issues in Focus Today. 2005, Enslow LB $31.93 (978-0-7660-2164-8). In concise, accessible text, Gordon defines fair use and copyright and examines issues involving downloading of text, music, games, and so forth. (Rev: BL 11/1/05; SLJ 11/05) [346.730]

11917 Gutkind, Lee. *Almost Human: Making Robots Think* (10–12). 2007, Norton $25.95 (978-0-393-05867-3). Teens interested in technology will enjoy this account of the work done at Carnegie Mellon's Robotics Institute, where scientists and graduate students engage in research in an atmosphere of cooperation and competition. (Rev: BL 3/15/07) [629.8]

11918 Hally, Mike. *Electronic Brains: Stories from the Dawn of the Computer Age* (10–12). 2005, Joseph Henry $27.95 (978-0-309-09630-0). The birth of the computer age and the questions surrounding its parentage are explored in this fascinating volume that chronicles the achievements of computer pioneers in the United States, United Kingdom, Australia, and Soviet Union. (Rev: BL 10/15/05) [004]

11919 Henderson, Harry. *Computer Viruses* (9–12). 2005, Gale LB $28.70 (978-1-59018-102-7). The origins, nature, and destructive power of computer viruses are discussed here along with the motives of hackers and the impact and cost of virus attacks. (Rev: SLJ 8/06)

11920 Herumin, Wendy. *Censorship on the Internet: From Filters to Freedom of Speech* (5–12). Series: Issues in Focus. 2004, Enslow LB $26.60 (978-0-7660-

1946-1). A look at the various ways we restrict the free exchange of information over the Internet and the pros and cons of doing so. (Rev: SLJ 4/04) [303.48]

11921 Kling, Andrew A. *Web 2.0* (7–10). Illus. Series: Technology 360. 2011, Gale/Lucent LB $33.45 (978-142050171-1). A clear discussion of the history of the Internet, the development of Web 2.0, and some of the groundbreaking sites; useful for report writers. (Rev: BL 11/1/11) [006.7]

11922 Lindsay, Dave. *Dave's Quick 'n' Easy Web Pages 2: A Guide to Creating Multi-page Web Sites* (6–10). Illus. by Sean Lindsay. 2004, Erin paper $11.95 (978-0-9690609-9-4). Readers with little prior knowledge will learn such techniques as creating frames and cascading style sheets as this straightforward title introduces concepts clearly with graphics and advice boxes. (Rev: SLJ 11/04) [005.7]

11923 McGonigal, Jane. *Reality Is Broken: Why Games Make Us Better and How They Can Change the World* (9–12). 2011, Penguin $26.95 (978-159420285-8). McGonigal posits that playing computer games is not a waste of time but can improve problem solving abilities and inspire hard work, collaboration, and happiness. ♫ (Rev: BL 12/1–15/10) [306.4]

11924 McQuade, Samuel C., and Sarah E. Gentry, et al. *Internet Addiction and Online Gaming* (7–12). Illus. Series: Cybersafety. 2012, Chelsea House LB $39.95 (978-160413696-8). This volume examines the dangers of excessive use of social computing, online shopping, and Internet gambling. Also use *Living with the Internet* (2012). (Rev: BL 9/15/12) [616.85]

11925 Maushart, Susan. *The Winter of Our Disconnect: How Three Totally Wired Teenagers (and a Mother Who Slept with Her iPhone) Pulled the Plug on Their Technology and Lived to Tell the Tale* (9–12). 2011, Tarcher paper $16.95 (978-15854285-5-7). One family's six-month hiatus from all electronic gadgetry is chronicled in this funny, intelligent title. ℮ (Rev: BL 12/1–15/10) [303.48]

11926 Menhard, Francha Roffe. *Internet Issues: Pirates, Censors, and Cybersquatters* (6–12). Series: Issues in Focus. 2001, Enslow LB $26.60 (978-0-7660-1687-3). Menhard's effective overview of problems concerning filtering, copyright, privacy, and piracy uses clear examples, many of which involve young people. (Rev: BL 2/1/02; HBG 10/02; SLJ 2/02) [384.3]

11927 Mooney, Carla. *Online Predators* (6–12). Illus. Series: Issues in the Digital Age. 2011, ReferencePoint LB $27.95 (978-160152193-4). Scary case studies add interest to this guide to the kinds of dangers that lurk online. (Rev: BL 10/1/11) [004.67]

11928 Naughton, John. *A Brief History of the Future: From Radio Days to Internet Years in a Lifetime* (10–12). 2000, Overlook $26.95 (978-1-58567-032-1). In this readable narrative, the author traces the history of

the Internet and explains its importance in the study of technology. (Rev: BL 7/00; SLJ 6/01) [621.382]

11929 Owen, Trevor, and Ronald Owston. *The Learning Highway: The Student's Guide to the Internet* (9–12). 1997, Key Porter paper $19.95 (978-1-55013-905-1). This well-written work explains how students can use the Internet to enhance classroom learning, with extensive material on connecting and searching and chapters detailing projects done on the Internet by different schools, plus exercises and programs at the back of the book. (Rev: SLJ 8/98; VOYA 8/98) [004.6]

11930 Parks, Peggy J. *Online Addiction* (7–12). Illus. Series: Cybersafety. 2012, ReferencePoint LB $27.95 (978-160152270-2). Is online addiction real? Can people get addicted to social networking? With primary source quotes, facts, and illustrations, Parks addresses these and other questions. (Rev: BL 10/1/12; LMC 5–6/13; SLJ 11/1/12) [616.85]

11931 Parks, Peggy J. *Online Social Networking* (7–10). Series: Compact Research: Current Issues. 2011, ReferencePoint LB $26.95 (978-160152116-3). With primary source quotes plus "Facts and Illustrations" this book examines how online social networking affects human interaction, associated dangers and potential addiction, and whether more regulation is necessary. (Rev: BL 4/1/11) [006.7]

11932 Pearce, Q. L. *Artificial Intelligence* (7–10). Illus. Series: Technology 360. 2011, Gale/Lucent LB $34.62 (978-142050384-5). A clear discussion of the history, future, and ethical issues surrounding artificial intelligence, with a chapter on robots, a timeline, and "Bits & Bytes" statistics. (Rev: BL 11/1/11) [006.3]

11933 Plotkin, Robert. *Computer Ethics* (9–12). Illus. Series: Computers, Internet, and Society. 2011, Facts on File LB $45 (978-081607755-7). A thought-provoking discussion of the ethics of privacy, computer security, virtual worlds, storing and saving of data, and so forth, with mentions of cyberbullying and WikiLeaks. Also recommended: *Computers and Creativity* and *Computers in Science and Mathematics* (both 2011). (Rev: BL 12/1/11; LMC 8–9/12*) [004]

11934 Reid, T. R. *The Chip: How Two Americans Invented the Microchip and Launched a Revolution. Rev. ed.* (10–12). 2001, Random House paper $13.95 (978-0-375-75828-7). The book gives a history of electronics and then focuses on the invention of the microchip by rivals Jack Kilby and Robert Noyce. (Rev: BL 9/1/01) [621.381]

11935 Rothman, Kevin F. *Coping with Dangers on the Internet: Staying Safe On-Line* (7–12). Series: Coping. 2001, Rosen LB $31.95 (978-0-8239-3201-6). Readers will find practical advice on safe use of Web sites, e-mail, chat rooms, newsgroups, and so forth, with a useful list of acronyms and emoticons. (Rev: SLJ 8/01) [025.04]

11936 Ryan, Ken. *Computer Anxiety? Instant Relief!* (9–12). 1991, Castle Mountain paper $9.95 (978-1-879925-05-2). Using subtle humor, this work attempts to simplify an intimidating subject for novice users, with definitions of computer terms and illustrations of difficult concepts. (Rev: BL 9/1/91) [004]

11937 Sandler, Corey. *Living with the Internet and On-line Dangers* (6–10). Series: Teen's Guides. 2010, Facts on File LB $34.95 (978-143812971-6). A practical guide to safe use of the Internet, covering such topics as social networking, shopping, scams, file sharing, text messaging, wireless security, and protecting one's identity. e (Rev: BLO 8/10; SLJ 9/10) [004.67]

11938 Selfridge, Benjamin, and Peter Selfridge. *A Kid's Guide to Creating Web Pages for Home and School* (5–10). 2004, Chicago Review paper $19.95 (978-1-56976-180-9). Simple instructions on creating Web pages using HTML are accompanied by helpful illustrations and sample finished pages. (Rev: SLJ 2/05) [005.7]

11939 Vacca, John, and Mary E. Vacca. *Identity Theft* (7–12). Illus. Series: Cybersafety. 2012, Chelsea House LB $39.95 (978-160413700-2). "Types and Methods of Identity Theft," "Minimizing Risk," and "Protecting Identity Information" are three of the chapters in this useful volume. (Rev: BL 9/15/12) [332.024]

11940 Weber, Sandra. *The Internet* (7–10). Series: Transforming Power of Technology. 2003, Chelsea House LB $30.00 (978-0-7910-7449-7). A look at the influence of the Internet on areas ranging from the economy to society to health care and at the implications for schools and libraries. (Rev: SLJ 6/04) [004.6]

Electronics

11941 Chaplin, Heather, and Aaron Ruby. *SmartBomb: Inside the $25 Billion Videogame Explosion* (10–12). 2005, Algonquin $24.95 (978-1-56512-346-5). The birth and development of the video game industry are presented in a riveting text that profiles key figures and clearly explains their importance. (Rev: BL 9/15/05; SLJ 4/06) [338.4]

11942 Grob, Bernard. *Basic Electronics. 6th ed.* (10–12). 1988, McGraw-Hill $95.48 (978-0-07-025119-9). An introduction to the principles of electronics and their applications in radio, television, and other industrial areas. [621.38]

Telecommunications

11943 Hillstrom, Laurie Collier. *Global Positioning Systems* (7–10). Illus. Series: Technology 360. 2011, Gale/Lucent LB $33.45 (978-142050325-8). A clear discussion of the history and importance of these satellites, with a timeline, and "Bits & Bytes" statistics. (Rev: BL 11/1/11) [910.285]

11944 Kling, Andrew A. *Cell Phones* (8–12). Series: Technology 360. 2009, Lucent $32.45 (978-1-4205-0164-3). An attractive and informative look at cell phone technology with a glossary and lists of material for further research. e (Rev: LMC 8–9/10; SLJ 1/1/11) [621.3845]

11945 Larson, Erik. *Thunderstruck* (10–12). 2006, Crown $25.95 (978-1-4000-8066-3). A detailed explanation of the how and why of Marconi's invention of wireless communication comes together with a true crime story that hinges on the use of a radiotelegraph to nab a murderer. ⌂ (Rev: BL 7/06*; SLJ 10/06)

11946 Szumski, Bonnie, and Jill Karson. *Are Cell Phones Dangerous?* (7–10). Illus. Series: Controversy. 2012, ReferencePoint LB $27.95 (978-160152232-0). After a history of cell phone technology, this volume looks at potential risks ranging from a decline in male fertility to texting while driving. (Rev: BL 10/15/12) [615.9]

Television, Motion Pictures, Radio, and Recording

11947 Hampe, Barry. *Making Documentary Films and Reality Videos* (10–12). 1997, Henry Holt paper $17.95 (978-0-8050-4451-5). A handy, practical manual for aspiring filmmakers on all aspects of film production, from arriving at an idea to distribution of the final product. (Rev: BL 1/1–15/97; SLJ 3/98) [791]

11948 Harris, Bob. *Prisoner of Trebekistan: A Decade in Jeopardy* (9–12). 2006, Crown $23.95 (978-0-307-33956-0). A *Jeopardy!* champion, Harris reveals his secrets to conquering the game show (he memorized a lot of trivia) and gives readers a look into the world of host Alex Trebek. (Rev: BL 9/1/06) [791.45]

11949 Hart, Christopher. *How to Draw Animation* (10–12). 1997, Watson-Guptill paper $? (978-0-8230-2365-3). This is a simple, step-by-step guide to cartooning and creating animation. [741.5]

Transportation

General and Miscellaneous

11950 Davidson, Janet F., and Michael S. Sweeney. *On the Move: Transportation and the American Story* (10–12). 2003, National Geographic $35.00 (978-0-7922-5140-8). In addition to exploring the various forms of transportation that have moved Americans and their goods, this well-illustrated volume also looks at the impact on society of improved freedom of movement. (Rev: BL 12/1/03) [388]

11951 *Go! The Whole World of Transportation* (5–10). Illus. 2006, DK $26.99 (978-0-7566-2224-4). This wide-ranging, visually fascinating journey through the world of transportation touches on everything from buses and ferries to speedboats and fighter jets. (Rev: SLJ 2/07*) [388]

11952 McPhee, John. *Uncommon Carriers* (9–12). 2006, Farrar $24.00 (978-0-374-28039-0). A fascinating look at the workers who drive the trucks, trains and ships responsible for conveying the many necessities of modern life, and at the calculations and maneuvers they must perform. (Rev: BL 4/15/06; SLJ 9/06) [388]

11953 Welsch, Roger. *From Tinkering to Torquing: A Beginner's Guide to Tractors and Tools* (9–12). 2005, MBI $21.95 (978-0-7603-2082-2). In this one-of-a-kind guide, Welsch blends advice for collectors and restorers of antique tractors with plenty of folksy anecdotes. (Rev: BL 12/15/05) [631.3]

Airplanes, Aeronautics, and Ballooning

11954 Abrams, Michael. *Birdmen, Batmen and Skyfliers: Wingsuits and the Pioneers Who Flew in Them, Fell in Them, and Perfected Them* (9–12). 2006, Harmony $23.95 (978-1-4000-5491-6). The *very* early days of aviation, when inventors tested animal-like wings in their attempts to take to the skies (often with disastrous results), are examined in this book. (Rev: BL 5/1/06) [629.1]

11955 Blatner, David. *The Flying Book: Everything You've Ever Wondered About Flying on Airplanes* (10–12). 2003, Walker $22.00 (978-0-8027-1378-0). This eminently readable book covers not just the science and technology of air travel but also contains fascinating facts about the human side of flight. (Rev: BL 4/1/03) [387.7]

11956 Bryan, C. D. B. *The National Air and Space Museum* (10–12). 1988, Abrams $75.00 (978-0-8109-1380-6). A history of aeronautics and the airplane as reflected in the collection of the National Air and Space Museum. (Rev: BL 12/15/88) [629.13]

11957 Chiles, James R. *The God Machine: From Boomerangs to Black Hawks; The Story of the Helicopter* (10–12). 2007, Bantam $25.00 (978-0-553-80447-8). A fascinating history of the helicopter and its hazy origins and uses over time. (Rev: BL 11/1/07) [629.133]

11958 Crouch, Tom D., and Peter Jakab. *The Wright Brothers and the Invention of the Aerial Age* (10–12). 2003, National Geographic $35.00 (978-0-7922-6985-4). This riveting chronicle of the Wright brothers' lives

and their lifelong quest for flight is enriched by 100 archival photographs. (Rev: BL 5/1/03) [629.13]

11959 Dick, Ron, and Dan Patterson. *Aviation Century: The Golden Age* (9–12). Series: Aviation Century. 2004, Firefly $39.95 (978-1-55046-409-2). Chronicles the history of aviation from 1919 to 1939, profiling some of the period's best-known aviators, including Amelia Earhart, Charles Lindbergh, Billy Mitchell, and Eddie Rickenbacker. Also use *Aviation Century: World War II* (2004). (Rev: BL 12/1/04) [940.54]

11960 Edgerton, Clyde. *Solo: My Adventures in the Air* (10–12). 2005, Algonquin $23.95 (978-1-56512-426-4). Novelist Clyde Edgerton writes engagingly of his lifelong love of planes and flying, and the service that earned him a Distinguished Flying Cross during the Vietnam War. (Rev: BL 9/1/05) [629.130]

11961 Friedrich, Belinda. *The Explosion of TWA Flight 800* (8–10). Series: Great Disasters: Reforms and Ramifications. 2001, Chelsea LB $30.00 (978-0-7910-6325-5). An account of this tragedy over Long Island in 1996, detailing the recovery efforts, the investigation, and the many theories about the cause of the disaster. (Rev: HBG 10/02; SLJ 5/02) [363.12]

11962 Gitlin, Martin. *The Hudson Plane Landing* (7–10). Illus. Series: Essential Events. 2012, ABDO LB $23.95 (978-161783309-0). This concise account of pilot Sullenberger's successful landing on the Hudson River in 2009, saving the lives of 150 passengers, includes information on "Sully" himself and on the dangers birds pose to aircraft. (Rev: BL 7/12; SLJ 6/12) [363.12]

11963 Olsen, W. Scott. *Hard Air: Adventures from the Edge of Flying* (10–12). 2008, Univ. of Nebraska paper $19.95 (978-0-8032-1144-5). This exciting narrative describes four kinds of dangerous peacetime flying — flying dog teams into the Arctic for rescue, helicopter air-ambulance work, hurricane hunting, and aerial firefighting. (Rev: BL 3/15/08) [629.132]

11964 Ryan, Craig. *The Pre-Astronauts: Manned Ballooning on the Threshold of Space* (9–12). 1995, Naval Institute $34.95 (978-1-55750-732-7). A chronicle of the achievements of people involved in the dangerous, manned balloon programs after World War II. (Rev: BL 5/1/95) [629.13]

11965 Sutter, Joe, and Jay Spender. *747: Creating the World's First Jumbo Jet and Other Adventures from a Life in Aviation* (9–12). 2006, HarperCollins $26.95 (978-0-06-088241-9). Readers will be fascinated to learn of the politics, pressure, economics, and engineering behind the famous Boeing aircraft. (Rev: BL 5/1/06) [629.13]

Automobiles and Trucks

11966 Edmonston, Phil, and Maureen Sawa. *Car Smarts: Hot Tips for the Car Crazy* (7–10). Illus. by Gordon Sauve. 2003, Tundra paper $15.95 (978-0-88776-646-6). Attractive and lively, this is a large-format compendium of facts and advice about cars — their history, how they work, and their purchase and maintenance. (Rev: BL 4/1/04; SLJ 7/04; VOYA 10/04) [629.222]

11967 Gravelle, Karen. *The Driving Book* (9–12). Illus. by Helen Flook. 2005, Walker $16.95 (978-0-8027-8933-4); paper $9.95 (978-0-8027-7706-5). An excellent resource for new drivers, this straightforward guide addresses a wide range of important topics, including auto maintenance, driving in bad weather, road rage, the effects of legal and illegal drugs on driving ability, and what to do in an emergency. (Rev: BL 3/1/05; SLJ 5/05; VOYA 8/05) [629.28]

11968 *In the Driver's Seat: A Girl's Guide to Her First Car* (8–11). 2009, Zest paper $14.995 (978-09800732-4-9). From choosing your car to learning about maintenance, insurance, and troubleshooting problems and dealing with auto mechanics, this is a useful and eye-catching guide. Lexile 1360L (Rev: BLO 2/1/10; VOYA 6/10) [380]

11969 Italia, Bob. *Great Auto Makers and Their Cars* (6–10). Series: Profiles. 1993, Oliver LB $19.95 (978-1-881508-08-3). This is a history of automobiles with coverage of famous cars and biographies of famous engineers and automakers. (Rev: BL 10/15/93; SLJ 11/93) [629.2]

11970 Nakaya, Andrea C., ed. *Cars in America* (7–12). Series: Opposing Viewpoints. 2006, Gale LB $34.95 (978-0-7377-3307-5); paper $23.70 (978-0-7377-3308-2). Opposing points of view are offered on everything from seatbelt laws to SUVs to urban sprawl. (Rev: SLJ 12/06)

11971 Sikorsky, Robert. *From Bumper to Bumper: Robert Sikorsky's Automotive Tips* (9–12). 1991, TAB $16.95 (978-0-8306-2134-7). Practical advice on automobile maintenance, driving techniques, buying tips, and motoring information. (Rev: BL 11/1/91) [629.28]

Cycles

11972 Davidson, Jean. *Jean Davidson's Harley-Davidson Family Album: 100 Years of the World's Greatest Motorcycle in Rare Photos* (9–12). 2003, Voyageur $19.95 (978-0-89658-629-1). An eye-catching and informative review of the first 100 years of the Harley-Davidson company. (Rev: BL 2/15/03) [629.227]

11973 Wilson, Hugo. *Motorcycle Owner's Manual* (10–12). 1997, DK paper $10.00 (978-0-7894-1615-5). In addition to basic maintenance, this manual covers some more challenging tasks. [629.28]

Railroads

11974 Ambrose, Stephen E. *Nothing Like It in the World: The Men Who Built the Transcontinental Railroad, 1863-1869* (10–12). 2000, Simon & Schuster $28.00 (978-0-684-84609-5). From the surveyors and engineers to the Chinese and Irish laborers, this is the story of the men who built the transcontinental railroad and of their mighty accomplishment. (Rev: BL 7/00) [385]

11975 Murphy, Jim. *Across America on an Emigrant Train* (6–12). 1993, Clarion $18.00 (978-0-395-63390-8). A cross-country train trip by Robert Louis Stevenson in 1879 is the backdrop for information on the history of railroads. (Rev: BCCB 1/94; BL 12/1/93*; SLJ 12/93*) [625.2]

11976 Sandler, Martin W. *The Secret Subway: The Fascinating Tale of an Amazing Feat of Engineering* (6–12). Illus. 2009, National Geographic $17.95 (978-142630462-0); LB $26.90 (978-142630463-7). Sandler tells the compelling story of engineer Alfred Beach who in the late 1860s hoped to build an air-powered subway system in New York City without the knowledge of Tammany Hall boss William Tweed. (Rev: BL 6/1–15/09; LMC 8–9/09) [388.4]

Ships and Boats

11977 Butler, Daniel Allen. *Unsinkable: The Full Story of the RMS Titanic* (8–12). 1998, Stackpole $21.95 (978-0-8117-1814-1). First-person accounts add to the tension of this narrative. (Rev: BL 5/1/98) [910.4]

11978 Davie, Michael. *Titanic: The Death and Life of a Legend* (10–12). 1987, Knopf $19.95 (978-0-317-58565-0). A re-creation of the sinking of the *Titanic* that highlights the mysteries surrounding it that have not yet been solved. (Rev: BL 6/1/87) [363.1]

11979 Geller, Judith B. *Titanic: Women and Children First: Poignant Accounts of Those Caught Up in the World's Worst Maritime Disaster* (11–12). 1998, Norton $35.00 (978-0-393-04666-3). The horrors of the sinking of the *Titanic* are brought to life in this collection of firsthand accounts from women and children who were aboard, accompanied by postcards, brochures, and other materials. (Rev: BL 11/15/98) [910]

11980 Kurson, Robert. *Shadow Divers: The True Adventure of Two Americans Who Risked Everything to Solve One of the Last Mysteries of World War II* (9–12). 2004, Random House $26.95 (978-0-375-50858-5). This compelling story of two divers' discovery of the wreckage of a German U-boat in deep ocean waters off New Jersey contains fascinating details of their dangerous explorations. (Rev: SLJ 2/05) [940.54]

11981 McPherson, Stephanie Sammartino. *Iceberg, Right Ahead! The Tragedy of the Titanic* (6–10). Illus. 2011, Lerner/Twenty-First Century LB $33.26 (978-

076136756-7). This is a compelling account of the disaster, giving information on the ship itself, newspaper and primary source accounts, and details of regulations and explorations that followed. ALA Notable Books 2013. **e** (Rev: BL 12/15/11; HB 3–4/12; LMC 3–4/12; SLJ 11/1/11*; VOYA 12/11) [910.9163]

11982 Paine, Lincoln P. *Ships of Discovery and Exploration* (9–12). 2000, Houghton Mifflin paper $21.95 (978-0-395-98415-4). This work introduces in text and pictures 125 ships that have played important roles in exploration and science. [910.4]

11983 *Simple Courage: A True Story of Peril on the Sea* (10–12). 2006, Random House $24.95 (978-1-4000-6524-0). An exciting story of a ship full of passengers that came near to foundering in a violent storm in 1951. (Rev: BL 6/1–15/06) [910.9163]

11984 Walker, Spike. *On the Edge of Survival: A Shipwreck, a Raging Storm, and the Harrowing Alaskan Rescue That Became a Legend* (10–12). Illus. 2010, St. Martin's $24.99 (978-031228634-7). Perfect for those who love man-against-nature survival stories, this book provides a tense, fast-paced account of the Coast Guard rescue of a ship-wrecked crew in the frigid waters of Alaska in 2004, including interviews with rescuers and survivors. ⋂ **e** (Rev: BL 9/1–15/10)

Weapons, Submarines, and the Armed Forces

11985 Caldicott, Helen. *The New Nuclear Danger: George W. Bush's Military-Industrial Complex* (10–12). 2002, New Press paper $16.95 (978-1-56584-740-8). A disturbing overview of the U.S. nuclear weapons program and weapons manufacturers' tireless lobbying for an expansion of a program that, the author argues, would prove largely ineffective against America's terrorist enemies. (Rev: BL 3/15/02) [627.1]

11986 Durant, Michael J. *The Night Stalkers: Top-Secret Missions of the U.S. Army's Special Operations Aviation Regiment* (9–12). 2007, Putnam $25.95 (978-0-399-15392-1). A compelling account of the exploits of the elite "Night Stalkers" unit — known for night operations using stealth helicopters — told by veterans of the regiment and full of action scenes. (Rev: BL 12/1/06) [355.3]

11987 Ermey, R. Lee. *Mail Call* (8–12). 2005, Hyperion paper $17.95 (978-1-4013-0779-0). History Channel personality offers facts and figures about military weaponry, modern warfare, and other military trivia. (Rev: BL 12/15/04) [355.009]

11988 Friedman, Lauri S. *Nuclear Weapons and Security* (8–12). Series: Compact Research. 2007, Reference Point LB $24.95 (978-1-60152-021-0). Is the United

States likely to be attacked with nuclear weapons? Could the world survive a nuclear war? These and other questions are discussed from various points of view, with facts, profiles, and illustrations. (Rev: SLJ 1/08)

11989 Graham, Ian. *Military Technology* (7–10). Illus. Series: New Technology. 2008, Smart Apple Media LB $22.95 (978-159920165-8). Unmanned spy planes, body armor, lasers, robots, and many other kinds of high-tech military equipment are examined in this accessible volume that includes many illustrations and thought-provoking ("What's Next?") sidebars. (Rev: BL 10/15/08; LMC 5–6/09) [355]

11990 Gurstelle, William. *The Art of the Catapult: Build Greek Ballistae, Roman Onagers, English Trebuchets, and More Ancient Artillery* (5–12). 2004, Chicago Review paper $14.95 (978-1-55652-526-1). Information on history, physics, and military tactics, plus step-by-step instructions for the construction of 10 working catapults. (Rev: SLJ 11/04) [623.4]

11991 Halberstadt, Hans. *Trigger Men: Shadow Team, Spiderman, the Magnificent Bastards, and the American Combat Sniper* (10–12). 2008, St. Martin's $25.95 (978-0-312-35456-5). A serious military title on the training and mind set of snipers and how they improve infantry effectiveness and reduce civilian casualties in urban areas. The sniper's role in modern combat is the focus of this serious military title that also looks at the general work of the infantry. (Rev: BL 3/1/08) [956.7044]

11992 Jackson, Robert. *Warships: Inside and Out* (9–12). Illus. Series: Weapons of War. 2012, Rosen LB $39.95 (978-144885981-8). Looking at classic ships (1859–1949) and modern ships (1950–present), this book offers detailed illustrations and diagrams and lots of information suitable for enthusiasts and researchers. (Rev: BLO 3/15/12) [623.82509]

11993 Keith, Don. *Final Patrol: True Stories of World War II Submarines* (9–12). 2006, NAL paper $15.00 (978-0-451-21951-0). The stories of 18 World War II submarines (one German, the rest U.S.) that have been restored and are now open to the public. (Rev: BL 9/1/06) [940.54]

11994 Landau, Elaine. *The New Nuclear Reality* (6–12). 2000, Twenty-First Century LB $22.90 (978-0-7613-1555-1). This account chronicles the post-war growth of countries that have nuclear arms including Russia, North Korea, Pakistan, and India. (Rev: BL 7/00; HBG 9/00; SLJ 9/00) [327.1]

11995 Lefkowitz, Arthur. *Bushnell's Submarine: The Best Kept Secret of the American Revolution* (7–10). 2006, Scholastic $16.99 (978-0-439-74352-5). The little-known story of the *Turtle*, America's first submarine, which was launched during the closing days of the American Revolution. (Rev: BL 2/15/06; SLJ 4/06) [973.3]

11996 Light, Michael. *100 Suns: 1945–1962* (10–12). 2003, Knopf $45.00 (978-1-4000-4113-8). The awesome power of a nuclear explosion is conveyed in this collection of photographs — both black-and-white and color — of above-ground atom bomb tests. (Rev: BL 10/1/03*) [355.8]

11997 Marcovitz, Hal. *Biological and Chemical Warfare* (7–10). Series: Essential Issues. 2010, ABDO LB $32.79 (978-1-60453-951-6). The characteristics of biological, chemical, and radiological substances are explained here and there is discussion of their use as weapons and measures that can be taken to guard against this. (Rev: BL 10/1/10; LMC 10/10; SLJ 4/1/10) [358.3]

11998 Merino, Noel, ed. *U.S. Military Deployment* (9–12). Illus. Series: At Issue. 2011, Greenhaven LB $31.80 (978-073775373-8); paper $22.50 (9780737754117). This volume takes a balanced look at a controversial issue, collecting 14 previously published essays that present various points of view. (Rev: BL 4/1/11) [355.4.]

11999 Regan, Paul, ed. *Weapon: A Visual History of Arms and Armor* (8–12). 2006, DK $40.00 (978-0-7566-2210-7). In the usual DK style, the history of handheld weapons is displayed with silhouetted images and captions, covering everything from the most primitive — such as a rock — to the automatic guns of today. (Rev: BL 11/1/06) [623.4]

12000 Richie, Jason. *Weapons: Designing the Tools of War* (5–10). 2000, Oliver LB $21.95 (978-1-881508-60-1). Using separate chapters for different categories of weapons — for example, submarines, battleships, and tanks — this is a history of the development of weaponry from 300 B.C. to today. (Rev: BL 5/1/00; HBG 10/00; SLJ 8/00) [623]

12001 Streissguth, Thomas. *Nuclear Weapons: More Countries, More Threats* (6–12). Series: Issues in Focus. 2000, Enslow LB $26.60 (978-0-7660-1248-6). An overview of nuclear weapons, who controls the technology to produce them, and the efforts to control this threat to human survival. (Rev: BL 9/15/00; HBG 3/01) [355.02]

12002 Torr, James D., ed. *Weapons of Mass Destruction* (7–10). Series: Opposing Viewpoints. 2004, Gale LB $36.20 (978-0-7377-2250-5); paper $24.95 (978-0-7377-2251-2). Terrorist attacks using nuclear or biological weapons, the threat from "rogue" nations, U.S. policies regarding its own weapons of mass destruction, and national defense are all discussed in essays introduced by focus questions. (Rev: SLJ 4/05) [355.02]

12003 Walker, Sally M. *Secrets of a Civil War Submarine: Solving the Mysteries of the H. L. Hunley* (7–10). 2005, Carolrhoda $18.95 (978-1-57505-830-6). Walker chronicles the story of the Confederate submarine *H. L. Hunley* from its design and construction through its successful attack on the *USS Housatonic* in 1864 to its discovery on the bottom of Charleston Harbor in 1995. Sibert Medal, 2006. (Rev: BL 4/15/05*; SLJ 5/05) [973.7]

12004 *Weapons: An International Encyclopedia from 5000 B.C. to 2000 A.D.* (9–12). 1991, St. Martin's paper $21.95 (978-0-312-03950-9). From the clubs of cavemen to nuclear weapons, this account describes them all in pictures and text. [623.4]

Recreation and Sports

Crafts, Hobbies, and Pastimes

General and Miscellaneous

12005 Bell, Alison. *Let's Party!* (6–10). Illus. by Kun-Sung Chung. Series: What's Your Style? 2005, Lobster paper $14.95 (978-1-894222-99-0). Eight theme parties are suggested, complete with invitations, decorations, food, music, and so forth; particularly useful may be the tips on keeping parents at bay and dealing with crashers. (Rev: SLJ 3/06) [793.2]

12006 Brown, Rachel. *The Weaving, Spinning, and Dyeing Book. Rev. ed.* (10–12). 1983, Knopf paper $40.00 (978-0-394-71595-7). Various kinds of weaving techniques and patterns are introduced through 50 different projects. [746.1]

12007 Browning, Marie. *Metal Crafting Workshop* (9–12). 2006, Sterling $24.95 (978-1-4027-2450-3). An informative guide for those interested in metal crafts and those looking to enhance other crafts (scrapbooking, collage, and jewelry, for example) with well-explained techniques and inspiring projects. (Rev: BL 11/1/06) [745.56]

12008 Cherry, Raymond. *Leathercrafting: Procedures and Projects. 5th ed.* (9–12). 1979, Glencoe paper $15.18 (978-0-02-672700-6). A how-to book that explains the basics of leather work with many sample projects. [745.53]

12009 Dooley, Sean. *The Big Twitch: One Man, One Continent, a Race against Time — a True Story about Birdwatching* (9–12). 2006, Allen & Unwin paper $16.95 (978-1-74114-528-1). Who knew that bird watching could be so funny? Dooley tries to break the Australian record of 700 bird sightings in 365 days, fully aware that his quest makes no rational sense. (Rev: BL 9/1/06) [598]

12010 Ellington, Elisabeth, and Jane Freimiller. *A Year of Reading: A Month-by-Month Guide to Classics and Crowd-Pleasers for You and Your Book Group* (10–12). 2002, Sourcebooks paper $14.95 (978-1-57071-935-6). Five diverse titles are suggested for each month, with discussion questions and related information. (Rev: BL 10/15/02) [011]

12011 Genat, Robert. *Lowriders* (9–12). 2001, MBI paper $14.95 (978-0-7603-0962-9). Custom engineered and colorfully detailed lowriders, aptly named for their lack of clearance from chassis to the street, are represented here in this overview in both Spanish and English, with colorful photographs and explanations on the transformations from ordinary street vehicles. (Rev: BLO 7/11/07) [629.2872]

12012 Hennessy, Alena. *Alter This!* (8–12). 2007, Sterling $14.95 (978-1-57990-948-2). Books can be craft material! This unusual book encourages teens to use books to create art or practical objects — hardbacks can be purses or clocks, for example, or words can be cut out to create poetry or stories. (Rev: BL 12/15/07; SLJ 9/07) [745.593]

12013 Jans, Martin. *Stage Make-Up Techniques* (9–12). 1993, Players paper $24.00 (978-0-88734-621-7). A primer of basic makeup techniques, including children's makeup, with detailed illustrations of all aspects of the craft. (Rev: BL 11/1/92) [792]

12014 Jennings, Lynette. *Have Fun with Your Room: 28 Cool Projects for Teens* (6–10). 2001, Simon & Schuster paper $12.00 (978-0-689-82585-9). The author offers a number of affordable ways to decorate bedrooms, with suggestions for walls, windows, headboards, bulletin boards, and so forth. (Rev: SLJ 11/01)

12015 Marsh, Don. *Calligraphy* (9–12). Series: First Steps. 1996, North Light $18.99 (978-0-89134-666-1). This introduction to the art of calligraphy offers an easy-to-understand, step-by-step guide to the basic strokes, as well as such simple projects for beginners as invitations and greeting cards. [745.6]

12016 Miller, Jill. *Fabrics and Florals: 100+ Ideas for "Dressing Up" Your Pages!* (9–12). 2005, Watson-Guptill paper $14.95 (978-0-8230-1637-2). Miller presents many ideas for giving scrapbooks a personal touch. (Rev: BL 12/15/05) [745.593]

12017 Murillo, Kathy Cano. *The Crafty Diva's Lifestyle Makeover: Awesome Ideas to Spice Up Your Life!* (5–12). Illus. by Carrie Wheeler. 2005, Watson-Guptill paper $12.95 (978-0-8230-1008-0). The Crafty Diva is back with this collection of easy-to-follow instructions for 50 projects that cover everything from room makeovers to fashion accessories. (Rev: SLJ 9/05)

12018 Ralston, Birgitta. *Snow Play: How to Make Forts and Slides and Winter Campfires, Plus the Coolest Loch Ness Monster and 23 Other Brrrilliant Projects in the Snow* (4–12). Photos by Vegard Fimland. 2010, Artisan $14.95 (978-1-57965-405-4). Ralston presents a variety of compelling snow projects, ranging from small ornaments to an LED-illuminated birthday cake to a snow cave. (Rev: SLJ 4/11) [796.9]

12019 *Reader's Digest Crafts and Hobbies* (9–12). 1979, Reader's Digest $27.95 (978-0-89577-063-9). Information on 37 popular crafts including leatherwork, jewelry making, and bookbinding. [745.5]

12020 Shannon, George W., and Pat Torlen. *The Stained Glass Home: Projects and Patterns* (8–12). 2007, Sterling $24.95 (978-1-895569-59-9). Two talented stained glass artists provide 23 projects, each one complete with patterns, directions, materials lists, and photographs, suitable for beginners as well as experienced crafters. (Rev: BL 12/15/06) [748.5]

12021 Taylor, Terry. *Altered Art: Techniques for Creating Altered Books, Boxes, Cards and More* (8–12). 2004, Lark $19.95 (978-1-57990-550-7). Terry Taylor provides a fascinating introduction into the world of altered art. (Rev: BL 12/15/04; SLJ 4/05)

12022 Weaver, Janice, and Frieda Wishinsky. *It's Your Room: A Decorating Guide for Real Kids* (6–10). Illus. by Claudia Dávila. 2006, Tundra paper $14.95 (978-0-88776-711-1). A step-by-step guide to room decoration, with tips on practical things like creating a budget and storage organization. (Rev: SLJ 6/06)

12023 Winters, Eleanor. *1-2-3 Calligraphy* (7–10). 2006, Sterling $14.95 (978-1-4027-1839-7). A companion to the author's *Calligraphy for Kids* (2004), this instructional book helps beginners gather the correct tools, learn different styles of calligraphy, and choose projects to practice their art. (Rev: BL 12/15/06; SLJ 1/07) [745.6]

12024 *Working with Metal* (10–12). 1990, Silver Burdett LB $20.60 (978-0-8094-7388-5). With many illustrations and clear text, this volume covers the basic terms, tools, and practices in metalworking. Part of Time-Life's Home Repair and Improvement series. [684]

American Historical Crafts

12025 Anderson, Maxine. *Great Civil War Projects You Can Build Yourself* (7–10). 2005, Nomad paper $16.95 (978-0-9749344-1-9). Craft projects explore various aspects of life on the Civil War battlefield and home front — making cornbread, a pinhole camera, a rag doll, and so forth. (Rev: BL 11/1/05; SLJ 11/05) [745.5]

12026 Worick, Jennifer. *The Prairie Girl's Guide to Life: How to Sew a Sampler Quilt and 49 Other Pioneer Projects for the Modern Girl* (9–12). 2007, Taunton $14.95 (978-1-56158-986-9). Learn to make poultices and calling cards, to cure meat, or to make soap with this handy guide to pioneer life. (Rev: SLJ 2/08) [745.5]

Clay Modeling and Ceramics

12027 Belcher, Judy. *Polymer Clay Creative Traditions: Techniques and Projects Inspired by the Fine and Decorative Arts* (8–12). 2006, Watson-Guptill paper $21.95 (978-0-8230-4065-0). Step-by-step instructions for more than 30 items that can be crafted from polymer clay. (Rev: BL 12/15/05) [745.57]

Cooking

12028 Amari, Suad. *Cooking the Lebanese Way. Rev. ed.* (5–10). Series: Easy Menu Ethnic Cookbooks. 2003, Lerner LB $25.26 (978-0-8225-4116-5). Revised to include low-fat and vegetarian foods, this introduction to Lebanese cooking contains about 40 recipes, clearly explained and well-illustrated. (Rev: BL 9/15/02; HBG 3/03) [641.5]

12029 Baggett, Nancy. *The All-American Cookie Book* (9–12). 2001, Houghton Mifflin $35.00 (978-0-395-91537-0). Recipe by recipe, the author traces the history of cookies and how they developed into such amazing varieties. (Rev: BL 10/15/01; SLJ 6/02) [641.8]

12030 Barnard, Tanya, and Sarah Kramer. *How It All Vegan! Irresistible Recipes for an Animal-Free Diet* (10–12). 2000, Arsenal Pulp paper $15.95 (978-1-55152-067-4). The vegan regime, which avoids all animal products, is described, with plenty of nutritious, mouth-watering recipes. (Rev: BL 2/15/00) [641.5]

12031 Behnke, Alison, and Ehramjian Vartkes. *Cooking the Middle Eastern Way* (7–10). Series: Easy Ethnic Menu Cookbooks. 2005, Lerner LB $25.26 (978-0-8225-1238-7). An introduction to the basics of Middle

East cooking plus a number of authentic recipes from the region. (Rev: BL 5/15/05) [641.5956]

12032 *Better Homes and Gardens New Cook Book. 11th ed.* (9–12). 1996, Bantam paper $7.99 (978-0-553-57795-2). A fine basic cookbook with easy-to-follow instructions and ample illustrations. (Rev: BL 11/1/89) [641.5]

12033 *Betty Crocker's Great Chicken Recipes* (9–12). 1993, Prentice Hall paper $8.00 (978-0-671-84689-3). Contains more than 100 recipes, color photographs, food ideas, boxed tips, and practical hints. (Rev: BL 3/1/93) [641.6]

12034 *Betty Crocker's Holiday Baking* (9–12). 1993, Prentice Hall paper $8.00 (978-0-671-86961-8). More than 100 simple recipes for the holiday season, including nutritional information for classic and revamped favorites. Color photographs and sidebar tips make directions easy to follow. (Rev: BL 10/1/93) [641.7]

12035 *Betty Crocker's Low-Calorie Cooking* (9–12). 1993, Prentice Hall paper $8.00 (978-0-671-84690-9). Contains more than 100 recipes, color photographs, food ideas, boxed tips, and practical hints. (Rev: BL 3/1/93) [641.5]

12036 *Betty Crocker's Quick Dinners: In 30 Minutes or Less* (9–12). 1993, Prentice Hall paper $8.00 (978-0-671-84692-3). Contains more than 100 recipes, color photographs, food ideas, boxed tips, and practical hints. (Rev: BL 3/1/93) [641.5]

12037 *Betty Crocker's Soups and Stews* (9–12). 1993, Prentice Hall paper $8.00 (978-0-671-86960-1). More than 100 soups and stews are presented, with color photographs, sidebar explanations and tips, and nutritional information. (Rev: BL 10/1/93) [641.5]

12038 Bisignano, Alphonse. *Cooking the Italian Way. Rev. ed.* (5–10). Series: Easy Menu Ethnic Cookbooks. 2001, Lerner $25.26 (978-0-8225-4113-4); paper $7.95 (978-0-8225-4161-5). A revised edition that now includes vegetarian and low-fat recipes as well as an expanded introductory section on the country, the people, and the culture. (Rev: HBG 3/02; SLJ 9/01) [641]

12039 Brill, "Wildman" Steve. *The Wild Vegetarian Cookbook* (10–12). 2002, Harvard Common $29.95 (978-1-55832-214-1). A selection of appetizing vegetarian recipes that use wild foods such as violets, cow parsnips, and sassafras as key ingredients. (Rev: BL 6/1–15/02) [641.5]

12040 Burros, Marian. *Cooking for Comfort: More Than 100 Wonderful Recipes That Are as Satisfying to Cook as They Are to Eat* (10–12). 2003, Simon & Schuster $24.00 (978-0-7432-3681-2). An appetizing collection of memorable comfort food recipes. (Rev: BL 5/15/03) [641.5]

12041 Caldicott, Chris, and Carolyn Caldicott. *World Food Cafe: Global Vegetarian Cooking* (10–12). 1999,

Bay $28.00 (978-1-57959-060-4). For vegetarians and readers looking for international recipes, this adult vegetarian cookbook features recipes collected by the authors while they traveled worldwide for 10 years. (Rev: BL 1/1–15/00) [641.5]

12042 Campbell, Regina. *Regina's International Vegetarian Favorites* (10–12). 2003, Berkley paper $18.95 (978-0-557-88410-0). Campbell draws on traditional recipes from countries around the world to add new interest to vegetarian cooking. (Rev: BL 9/15/03) [641.5]

12043 Carle, Megan, and Jill Carle. *Teens Cook: How to Cook What You Want to Eat* (7–12). 2004, Ten Speed paper $19.95 (978-1-58008-584-7). A witty and practical cookbook that introduces varied recipes used by teenage siblings Megan and Jill Carle. (Rev: SLJ 10/04; VOYA 12/04) [641]

12044 Child, Julia. *The Way to Cook* (9–12). 1989, Knopf $65.00 (978-0-394-53264-6); paper $39.95 (978-0-679-74765-9). Although this is part recipe book, it is more a guide to cooking methods and useful tips. [641.5]

12045 Chung, Okwha, and Judy Monroe. *Cooking the Korean Way. Rev. ed.* (5–10). Series: Easy Menu Ethnic Cookbooks. 2003, Lerner LB $25.26 (978-0-8225-4115-8). Tempting recipes and a brief look at where they come from. (Rev: BL 8/88; HBG 3/03; SLJ 9/88) [641.59519]

12046 Cornell, Kari. *Holiday Cooking Around the World. Rev. ed.* (5–10). Series: Easy Menu Ethnic Cookbooks. 2002, Lerner LB $25.26 (978-0-8225-4128-8); paper $7.95 (978-0-8225-4159-2). Beginning cooks will appreciate the clear instructions and varied options in this appealing book that includes cultural and social information. (Rev: BL 1/1–15/02; HBG 10/02; SLJ 5/02) [641.5]

12047 Coronado, Rosa. *Cooking the Mexican Way. Rev. ed.* (5–10). Series: Easy Menu Ethnic Cookbooks. 2002, Lerner LB $25.26 (978-0-8225-4117-2). Recipes organized by type of meal are preceded by a section that covers the geography, culture, and festivals and by information on equipment, ingredients, and eating customs. Other titles in this series include *Cooking the East African Way* and *Cooking the Spanish Way* (both 2001). (Rev: HBG 3/02; SLJ 2/02) [641]

12048 Cox, Beverly, and Martin Jacobs. *Spirit of the Harvest: North American Indian Cooking* (9–12). 1991, Tabori & Chang $35.00 (978-1-55670-186-3). Native American experts have helped the authors with recipes of various North American tribes, adapted for modern kitchens and substituting readily available ingredients when required. (Rev: BL 9/15/91) [641.59]

12049 Damerow, Gail. *Ice Cream! The Whole Scoop* (9–12). 1991, Glenbridge Publg $26.95 (978-0-944435-09-0). This collection of recipes is also a thorough survey of all types of frozen desserts and includes technical information on ingredients, techniques, and special equipment. (Rev: BL 9/1/91) [641.8]

12050 DeBorde, Rob. *Fish on a First-Name Basis: How Fish Is Caught, Bought, Cleaned, Cooked, and Eaten* (10–12). 2006, St. Martin's $24.95 (978-0-312-34220-3). A basic cookbook-cum-useful reference tool, this volume by a writer for the Food Network's *Good Eats* show is easy to digest. (Rev: BL 3/1/06) [641.6]

12051 Delmar, Charles. *The Essential Cook* (9–12). 1989, Hill House $24.95 (978-0-929694-00-9). An excellent handbook on food preparation that includes such subjects as methods of cooking, equipment needed, and shopping tips. (Rev: SLJ 7/89) [641.5]

12052 Dunnington, Rose. *Bake It Up! Desserts, Breads, Entire Meals and More* (6–12). Photos by Steven Mann. 2007, Sterling $9.95 (978-1-57990-778-5). Mouthwatering recipes are presented in an appealing and straightforward manner. Also use *Super Sandwiches: Wrap 'em, Stack 'em, Stuff 'em* (2007). (Rev: SLJ 2/07)

12053 Geiskopf-Hadler, Susann, and Mindy Toomay. *The Complete Vegan Cookbook: Over 200 Tantalizing Recipes, Plus Plenty of Kitchen Wisdom for Beginners and Experienced Cooks* (9–12). 2001, Prima Health paper $19.95 (978-0-7615-2951-4). For both the novice and the seasoned cook, this is a fine collection of vegan recipes. [641.5]

12054 Greenwald, Michelle. *The Magical Melting Pot: The All-Family Cookbook That Celebrates America's Diversity* (7–12). 2003, Cherry $29.95 (978-0-9717565-0-2). Chefs from ethnic restaurants around the country contribute favorite recipes and cultural explanations. (Rev: SLJ 11/03)

12055 Hall, Dede. *The Starving Students' Vegetarian Cookbook: Over 150 Recipes for Quick, Cheap, and Delicious Meals* (9–12). 2001, Warner paper $11.95 (978-0-446-67675-5). This book offers vegetarian recipes that provide good food at reasonable prices with minimal fuss and equipment. (Rev: BL 6/1–15/01) [641.5]

12056 Hansen, Barbara. *Mexican Cookery* (9–12). 1988, Price Stern Sloan paper $14.95 (978-0-89586-589-2). Easily followed recipes and many illustrations highlight this guide to the food of many different regions of Mexico. [641.5]

12057 Hargittai, Magdolna. *Cooking the Hungarian Way. Rev. ed.* (5–10). Series: Easy Menu Ethnic Cookbooks. 2002, Lerner LB $25.26 (978-0-8225-4132-5). After an introduction to Hungary and its cuisine, there are about 40 clearly presented recipes from appetizers through desserts. (Rev: BL 9/15/02; HBG 3/03) [641.5]

12058 Harris, Jessica. *The Africa Cookbook: Taste of a Continent* (9–12). 1998, Simon & Schuster $25.00 (978-0-684-80275-6). Representative recipes from many African countries are accompanied by information on the cultures and the peoples. (Rev: BL 12/15/98) [641.596]

12059 Harrison, Supenn, and Judy Monroe. *Cooking the Thai Way. Rev. ed.* (5–10). Series: Easy Menu Ethnic Cookbooks. 2002, Lerner LB $25.26 (978-0-8225-4124-0); paper $7.95 (978-0-8225-0608-9). The country of Thailand is introduced followed by general information on its foods and several easy-to-follow recipes. (Rev: BL 9/15/02) [641.5]

12060 Herbst, Sharon Tyler. *The Food Lover's Tiptionary* (9–12). 1994, Morrow paper $16.00 (978-0-688-12146-4). Tips on buying, storing, cooking, preparing, and serving food and drink. (Rev: BL 3/15/94) [641.3]

12061 Hess, Susan. *Bi-Lingual American Cooking / Cocina Americana Bilingue: English and Spanish Family Recipes in Side-by-Side Translations / Ingles y Espanol Recetas de Familias con su Traduccion de Lado a Lado* (10–12). 2002, Meta $19.95 (978-0-9714051-2-7). Basic traditional North American and Mexican recipes are displayed side by side in both English and Spanish. (Rev: BL 6/1–15/02) [641.5]

12062 Hill, Barbara W. *Cooking the English Way. Rev. ed.* (5–10). Series: Easy Menu Ethnic Cookbooks. 2002, Lerner LB $25.26 (978-0-8225-4105-9). The land and people of England are briefly introduced followed by material on their favorite dishes and easy-to-follow recipes. (Rev: BL 9/15/02) [641.5]

12063 Lemlin, Jeanne. *Quick Vegetarian Pleasures* (9–12). 1992, HarperCollins paper $18.00 (978-0-06-096911-0). Tasty, easy-to-prepare meatless recipes ranging from appetizers to entrees. (Rev: BL 3/1/92) [641.5]

12064 Locricchio, Matthew. *The Cooking of France* (7–12). Series: Superchef. 2002, Marshall Cavendish $29.93 (978-0-7614-1216-8). Recipes are accompanied by details on technique and equipment and by information about the country's traditions and festivals. Also use *The Cooking of Mexico* (2002). (Rev: BL 12/15/02; HBG 3/03; SLJ 2/03) [641.5944]

12065 Locricchio, Matthew. *The Cooking of Italy* (7–12). Series: Superchef. 2002, Marshall Cavendish LB $29.93 (978-0-7614-1215-1). The different regional cuisines of Italy are described and a number of traditional recipes clearly outlined and colorfully illustrated. (Rev: BL 3/15/03; HBG 3/03; SLJ 4/03) [641]

12066 Luard, Elisabeth. *The Latin American Kitchen: A Book of Essential Ingredients with Over 200 Authentic Recipes* (10–12). 2006, Kyle paper $19.95 (978-1-904920-46-5). Luard introduces all the ingredients used in the cuisine of Latin America and provides recipes that use each. (Rev: BL 2/1/07) [641.5]

12067 Montgomery, Bertha Vining, and Constance Nabwire. *Cooking the West African Way. Rev. ed.* (5–10). Series: Easy Menu Ethnic Cookbooks. 2002, Lerner LB $25.26 (978-0-8225-4163-9). An appealing introduction to West African cuisine, with information on the land, people, and culture, and several low-fat and vegetarian recipes. (Rev: HBG 10/02; SLJ 5/02) [641.5966]

12068 Opie, Fredrick Douglass. *Hog and Hominy: Soul Food from Africa to America* (10–12). Illus. 2008, Columbia Univ. $24.95 (978-023114638-8). A historical look at African American cooking, this book reveals information about the origins of familiar recipes. (Rev: BL 9/1/08) [641.5]

12069 Parnell, Helga. *Cooking the German Way. Rev. ed.* (5–10). Series: Easy Menu Ethnic Cookbooks. 1988, Lerner LB $25.26 (978-0-8225-4107-3). Includes such treats as Black Forest torte and apple cake. (Rev: BL 8/88) [641.5943]

12070 Parnell, Helga. *Cooking the South American Way. Rev. ed.* (5–10). Series: Easy Menu Ethnic Cookbooks. 2002, Lerner LB $25.26 (978-0-8225-4121-9). The continent of South America is introduced followed by about 40 clearly presented recipes from several countries. (Rev: BL 9/15/02; HBG 3/03) [641.5]

12071 Paul, Anthea. *Girlosophy: Real Girls Eat* (8–12). 2006, Allen & Unwin paper $19.95 (978-1-74114-142-9). This colorful cookbook and healthy eating guide takes a holistic approach, giving suggestions on nurturing both the mind and body. (Rev: SLJ 6/06)

12072 Peters, Colette. *Colette's Cakes: The Art of Cake Decorating* (9–12). 1991, Little, Brown $27.50 (978-0-316-70205-8). A guide to creative cake design and decorating, not just a cake cookbook, with step-by-step instructions for assembling elaborate baked desserts. (Rev: BL 9/1/91) [641.8]

12073 Plotkin, Gregory, and Rita Plotkin. *Cooking the Russian Way. Rev. ed.* (5–10). Series: Easy Menu Ethnic Cookbooks. 2002, Lerner LB $25.26 (978-0-8225-4120-2). Included along with history and information are such recipes as Russian honey spice cake. (Rev: BL 10/15/86) [641.5947]

12074 Roden, Nadia. *Granita Magic* (10–12). 2003, Artisan $15.00 (978-1-57965-223-4). Roden celebrates the universal summertime appeal of the granita — a confection of finely crushed ice blended with such diverse ingredients as fruit, berries, vegetables, alcohol, and spices. (Rev: BL 9/15/03) [641.863]

12075 Samuelsson, Marcus. *The Soul of a New Cuisine: A Discovery of the Foods and Flavors of Africa* (9–12). 2006, Wiley $40.00 (978-0-7645-6911-1). Photographs of people and places in Africa are interspersed with the recipes in this cookbook by the chef of New York's Aquavit restaurant. (Rev: BL 9/1/06) [641.59]

12076 Schwartz, Joan. *Macaroni and Cheese: 52 Recipes, from Simple to Sublime* (10–12). 2001, Villard paper $15.95 (978-0-375-75700-6). This book includes enough variations on the basic macaroni and cheese recipe to have a different dish each week for a year. (Rev: BL 10/15/01) [641.8]

12077 Segan, Francine. *Shakespeare's Kitchen: Renaissance Recipes for the Contemporary Cook* (10–12). 2003, Random House $35.00 (978-0-375-50917-9). A food historian introduces readers to the delights of Elizabethan England's cuisine with period recipes updated for today's cooks. (Rev: BL 10/15/03) [641.5945]

12078 Shaw, Maura D., and Synda Altschuler Byrne. *Foods from Mother Earth* (6–10). 1994, Shawangunk paper $9.95 (978-1-885482-02-0). A vegetarian cookbook in which most of the recipes can be prepared in three or four easy steps. (Rev: BL 1/15/95; SLJ 2/95) [641.5]

12079 This, Hervé. *Kitchen Mysteries: Revealing the Science of Cooking* (9–12). Trans. by Jody Gladding. 2007, Columbia Univ. $22.95 (978-0-231-14170-3). The author has a knack for explaining the chemistry and physics of cooking in a manner that is clear and interesting, explaining basic techniques and answering common questions. (Rev: BL 11/1/07) [645]

12080 Webb, Lois Sinaiko, and Lindsay Grace Roten. *The Multicultural Cookbook for Students: Updated and Revised* (10–12). 2009, Greenwood paper $85 (978-1-313-37560-6). Organized in seven regions, this cookbook introduces each country with basic information on the culture and typical ingredients and provides at least two recipes; a revised and expanded edition of the book published in 1993. (Rev: LMC 3–4/10; SLJ 3/10) [641.59]

12081 Wedman, Betty. *Quick and Easy Diabetic Menus: More Than 150 Delicious Recipes for Breakfast, Lunch, Dinner, and Snacks* (9–12). 1993, Contemporary paper $16.95 (978-0-8092-3853-8). These recipes are useful for both diabetics and anyone watching his or her weight. (Rev: BL 7/93) [641.5]

12082 Whitman, Sylvia. *What's Cooking? The History of American Food* (7–10). 2001, Lerner LB $22.60 (978-0-8225-1732-0). An absorbing account of how American nutrition and tastes have changed over the years, with discussion of methods of food preparation and preservation, the impact of outside forces such as transportation and war, the use of pesticides, and the advent of fast food. (Rev: BCCB 7–8/01; BL 8/01; HBG 10/01; SLJ 7/01; VOYA 8/01) [394.1]

12083 Wilkinson, Wendy, and Donna Lee. *Morgan Freeman and Friends: Caribbean Cooking for a Cause* (9–12). 2006, Rodale $35.00 (978-1-59486-424-7). To benefit the Grenada Relief Fund for the victims of Hurricane Ivan (in 2004), celebrities give their take on Caribbean delights and local cooks provide accompanying recipes. (Rev: BL 12/15/06) [641.5]

12084 Wolke, Robert L. *What Einstein Told His Cook: Further Adventures in Kitchen Science, Vol. 2* (8–12). 2005, Norton $25.95 (978-0-393-05963-2). Frequently asked culinary questions are answered in this collection of essays on food and food preparation. (Rev: BL 3/15/05) [641.5]

12085 Woods, Sylvia, and Christopher Styler. *Sylvia's Soul Food: Recipes from Harlem's World-Famous Restaurant* (9–12). 1992, Hearst $21.95 (978-0-688-10012-4). A Harlem restaurateur and her chef present more than 100 recipes from her kitchen, all representative of African American culture. (Rev: BL 10/15/92) [641.59]

12086 Yan, Martin. *Martin Yan's Invitation to Chinese Cooking* (10–12). 2000, Bay paper $24.95 (978-1-57959-504-3). A fine introduction to Chinese cooking by a celebrity chef. (Rev: BL 4/15/00) [641.5951]

Costume and Jewelry Making, Dress, and Fashion

12087 Aveline, Erick, and Joyce Chargueraud. *Temporary Tattoos* (6–12). 2001, Firefly LB $19.95 (978-1-55209-609-3); paper $9.95 (978-1-55209-601-7). A book of body art designs that provides plenty of practical tips and guidance on the use of cosmetics. (Rev: BL 11/15/01; HBG 3/02; SLJ 11/01; VOYA 4/02) [391.65]

12088 Baskett, Mickey. *Jazzy Jeans* (8–12). 2007, Sterling $24.95 (978-1-4027-3513-4). How to jazz up your jeans with appliqués, embroidery, painting, and so forth. (Rev: BL 1/1–15/07) [746.4]

12089 Bateman, Sharon. *Findings and Finishings: A Beadwork How-to-Book* (9–12). Series: Beadwork How-To. 2003, Interweave paper $21.95 (978-1-931499-40-8). Projects ranging from simple earrings to complex pieces are presented in clear images and text along with a brief history of jewelry and discussion of tools and materials. (Rev: SLJ 4/04) [745.58]

12090 Blakeney, Faith, and Justina Blakeney. *99 Ways to Cut, Sew and Deck Out Your Denim* (9–12). Photos by Kira Lillie. 2007, Potter $19.95 (978-0-307-35170-8). A wide range of projects — from appliqués and bags to skirts and pants — vary in degree of difficulty. (Rev: SLJ 6/07) [646]

12091 Campbell, Jean, ed. *The Art of Beaded Beads: Exploring Design, Color and Technique* (8–12). 2006, Sterling $24.95 (978-1-57990-825-6). Learn to make projects using beaded beads — beads made out of other seed beads using a variety of knots and stitches; detailed instructions are accompanied by color photographs. (Rev: BL 11/1/06) [745.58]

12092 Carnegy, Vicky. *Fashions of a Decade: The 1980s* (7–12). Series: Fashions of a Decade. 1990, Facts on File $25.00 (978-0-8160-2471-1). This elegantly illustrated volume traces styles and trends in fashion for this decade, linking them to social and political developments. There are volumes in this set for each decade from the 1920s to the 1990s. (Rev: BL 2/15/91; SLJ 5/91) [391]

12093 Chermay-Debray, Isabelle. *Polymer Clay Beaded Jewellery: 35 Beautiful Designs* (10–12). 2009, Search paper $13.95 (978-1-84448-400-3). The process of making jewelry and accessories from polymer clay is presented through detailed descriptions and color photographs. (Rev: SLJ 11/09) [745.5]

12094 *CosmoGirl! Make It Yourself: 50 Fun and Funky Projects* (9–12). 2007, Sterling LB $7.95 (978-1-58816-624-1). Teens can have fun making their own jewelry, clothing, and accessories with the help of this attractively designed book. (Rev: SLJ 3/08)

12095 Haab, Sherri. *Designer Style Handbags: Techniques and Projects for Unique, Fun, and Elegant Designs from Classic to Retro* (7–12). Photos by Dan Haab. 2005, Watson-Guptill paper $19.95 (978-0-8230-1288-6). Projects suitable for every skill level are accompanied by advice on choosing materials and include bags made from objects such as cigar boxes and candy tins as well as a variety of fabrics and yarns. (Rev: SLJ 1/06; VOYA 12/05) [646.4]

12096 Hantman, Clea. *I Wanna Make My Own Clothes* (7–12). Illus. by Azadeh Houshyar. 2006, Simon & Schuster paper $9.99 (978-0-689-87462-8). Nearly 50 sewing projects are featured in this guide to making your own unique apparel, including black-and-white illustrations and ideas to spark creativity. (Rev: SLJ 6/06)

12097 Haxell, Kate. *Customizing Cool Clothes: From Dull to Divine in 30 Projects* (8–12). 2006, Interweave paper $21.95 (978-1-59668-015-9). With the help of photographs and easy-to-follow instructions, this guide shows you how to get creative and embellish your bland wardrobe. (Rev: BL 11/15/06) [746]

12098 Hunnisett, Jean. *Period Costume for Stage and Screen: Patterns for Women's Dress, 1500-1800* (9–12). 1991, Players $59.00 (978-0-88734-610-1). A discussion of historic costume plus over 20 patterns are given. (Rev: BL 3/1/87) [791.43]

12099 Jackson, Sheila. *Costumes for the Stage: A Complete Handbook for Every Type of Play* (9–12). 1988, New Amsterdam paper $14.95 (978-0-941533-36-2). A manual for junior and senior high students on creating costumes for their productions. [792]

12100 LaFerla, Jane. *Make Your Own Great Earrings: Beads, Wire, Polymer Clay, Fabric, Found Objects* (10–12). 1998, Lark $24.95 (978-1-57990-031-1). Thirty-one artists present 45 different projects for making quality earrings, with simple directions, full-color photographs, and a history of earring making. (Rev: SLJ 10/98) [745.594]

12101 Litherland, Janet, and Sue McAnally. *Broadway Costumes on a Budget: Big Time Ideas for Amateur Producers* (7–12). 1996, Meriwether paper $15.95 (978-1-56608-021-7). Information about period costumes is given in this helpful manual with instructions for making costumes for nearly 100 Broadway plays and musicals. (Rev: BL 12/1/96) [792.6]

12102 Mokona, and Clamp. *Okimono Kimono* (10–12). Illus. by Clamp. 2010, Dark Horse paper $12.99 (978-15958245-6-1). A celebration of the kimono by manga author and kimono designer Mokona. (Rev: BL 9/1–15/10) [391.00952]

12103 O'Donnol, Shirley Miles. *American Costume, 1915–1970: A Source Book for the Stage Costumer* (9–12). 1982, Indiana Univ. paper $19.95 (978-0-253-20543-8). A nicely illustrated guide to 20th-century fashion that emphasizes women's clothes. [792]

12104 O'Keeffe, Linda. *Shoes: A Celebration of Pumps, Sandals, Slippers and More* (10–12). 1996, Workman paper $13.95 (978-0-7611-0114-7). Divided by types of shoe, such as sandals and boots, this is an illustrated history of footwear and famous shoe designers, filled with quotations about shoes from celebrities, ordinary people, designers, and historical figures, quips, and historical oddities. (Rev: SLJ 4/97) [646]

12105 Rogge, Hannah. *Hardwear: Jewelry from a Toolbox* (9–12). 2006, Tabori & Chang $18.95 (978-1-58479-480-6). Instructions for making edgy, industrial-looking jewelry, with illustrations, photographs, and a list of sources for materials. The cool design of the book itself adds to the appeal. (Rev: SLJ 10/06)

12106 Taylor, Carol. *Creative Bead Jewelry* (9–12). 1995, Sterling paper $18.95 (978-0-8069-1306-3). This book, with 70 examples from 38 bead artists, is guaranteed to send one off to the nearest bead emporium. (Rev: BL 11/15/95) [745.594]

12107 Warrick, Leanne. *Style Trix for Cool Chix: Your One-Stop Guide to Finding the Perfect Look* (7–10). Illus. by Debbie Boon. Photos by Shona Wood. 2005, Watson-Guptill paper $9.95 (978-0-8230-4940-0). A useful collection of tips on shopping, color coordination, closet organization, accessories, and finding clothes that fit. (Rev: SLJ 8/05; VOYA 8/05) [391]

12108 Webber, Carmen, and Carmia Marshall. *Chic Sweats: 22 Ways to Transform and Restyle Your Sweatshirts* (9–12). Illus. 2009, St. Martin's paper $21.95 (978-0-312-37861-5). This how-to book offers suggestions for repurposing the common sweatshirt as garments ranging from hoodies to dresses, and contains detailed instructions with illustrations. (Rev: SLJ 12/09) [746.9]

Dolls and Other Toys

12109 Aronzo, Aranzi. *Cute Dolls* (6–10). Trans. by Rui Munakata. Series: Let's Make Cute Stuff. 2007, Vertical paper $14.95 (978-1-932234-78-7). A compact guide to

making rag dolls that will appeal to manga fans. (Rev: BL 12/15/07) [745.59]

12110 Sobey, Ed, and Woody Sobey. *The Way Toys Work: The Science Behind the Magic 8 Ball, Etch a Sketch, Boomerang, and More* (9–12). 2008, Chicago Review paper $14.95 (978-1-55652-745-6). The ultimate toy story, this selection focuses on 50 classic toys including yo-yos, potato guns, and slinkies; each toy gets a brief history and a "look under the hood" in photographs and mechanical drawings. (Rev: BL 4/1/08; SLJ 6/08) [688.7]

12111 Stone, Tanya Lee. *The Good, the Bad, and the Barbie: A Doll's History and Her Impact on Us* (7–10). Illus. 2010, Viking $19.99 (978-067001187-2). Stone tells a fascinating story of a controversial doll and her evolution. Lexile 1120L (Rev: BL 11/15/10*; HB 11–12/10; SLJ 10/1/10*) [688.7]

Drawing and Painting

12112 Abel, Jessica, and Matt Madden. *Drawing Words and Writing Pictures — Making Comics: Manga, Graphic Novels, and Beyond* (9–12). Illus. 2008, First Second paper $29.95 (978-159643131-7). Abel and Madden provide skill-building exercises and inspiring activities in this accessible, well-written how-to. (Rev: BL 6/1–15/08) [741.5]

12113 Bartges, Dan. *Color Is Everything: Master the Use of Color in Oils, Acrylics or Watercolors* (9–12). 2008, Oaklea paper $14.99 (978-1-892538-36-9). This is a practical and accessible guide to using color and achieving pleasing, balanced color schemes, with lots of examples by a variety of painters. (Rev: SLJ 8/08)

12114 Bohl, Al. *Guide to Cartooning* (6–12). 1997, Pelican paper $14.95 (978-1-56554-177-1). Though actually a textbook, this work is a splendid guide to the history of cartooning as well as a practical guide to all the basics. (Rev: BL 9/15/97) [741.5]

12115 Chiarello, Mark, and Todd Klein. *The DC Comics Guide to Coloring and Lettering Comics* (9–12). 2004, Watson-Guptill paper $19.95 (978-0-8230-1030-1). Step-by-step instructions for comic book coloring and lettering are accompanied by a look at their evolution. (Rev: BL 2/1/05) [741.5]

12116 Clinch, Moira. *The Watercolor Painter's Pocket Palette: Instant, Practical Visual Guidance on Mixing and Matching Watercolors to Suit All Subjects* (9–12). 1991, North Light $17.99 (978-0-89134-401-8). A guide to mixing watercolors. (Rev: BL 1/1/92) [751.422]

12117 Dean, Selina. *Drawing Manga* (9–12). 2007, HarperCollins paper $14.95 (978-0-00-723178-2). In addition to offering tips on drawing manga, this book provides a good introduction to manga themes and character types. (Rev: SLJ 3/08) [741.5]

12118 Gordon, Louise. *How to Draw the Human Figure: An Anatomical Approach* (7–10). 1979, Penguin paper $18.00 (978-0-14-046477-1). This is both a short course on anatomy and a fine manual on how to draw the human body. [743]

12119 Graves, Douglas R. *Drawing Portraits* (10–12). 1974, Watson-Guptill paper $14.95 (978-0-8230-1431-6). An excellent guide to portraiture that covers such topics as posing positions, lighting, and drawing faces and hands. [743]

12120 Hart, Christopher. *Drawing on the Funny Side of the Brain* (7–12). 1998, Watson-Guptill paper $19.95 (978-0-8230-1381-4). This book describes how to create single and multipanel comic strips, with tips on joke writing, pacing, framing, color, and dialogue. (Rev: BL 7/98) [741.5]

12121 Hart, Christopher. *How to Draw Comic Book Heroes and Villains* (10–12). 1995, Watson-Guptill paper $18.95 (978-0-8230-2245-8). An excellent how-to book for older teens, with numerous sketches to demonstrate how to draw, costume, and equip comic book heroes, heroines, and villains. (Rev: BL 1/1–15/96) [741.5]

12122 Janson, Klaus. *The DC Comics Guide to Penciling Comics* (7–12). 2002, Watson-Guptill paper $19.95 (978-0-8230-1028-8). This practical guide for budding comics creators also contains lots of material for comics fans. (Rev: BL 5/1/02) [741.5]

12123 Jennings, Simon. *The New Artist's Manual: The Complete Guide to Painting and Drawing Materials and Techniques* (9–12). 2005, Chronicle paper $29.95 (978-0-8118-5124-4). A comprehensive guide providing advice on everything from setting up a studio and selecting materials and equipment to the best techniques for various media, with lots of color photographs and step-by-step examples. (Rev: SLJ 3/06) [751]

12124 Johnson, Cathy. *Painting Watercolors* (9–12). 1995, North Light paper $18.99 (978-0-89134-616-6). A book for beginners. (Rev: BL 9/15/95) [751.42]

12125 Lee, Stan, and John Buscema. *How to Draw Comics the Marvel Way* (9–12). 1984, Simon & Schuster paper $15.00 (978-0-671-53077-8). Step-by-step instructions are given for drawing cartoons like the Hulk and the Thing. [741.5]

12126 McCloud, Scott. *Making Comics: Storytelling Secrets of Comics, Manga, and Graphic Novels* (9–12). 2006, HarperCollins $22.95 (978-0-06-078094-4). Comic book and graphic novel lovers will enjoy the advice given in this book as well as its format — it is in the form of a comic itself. (Rev: BL 9/1/06; SLJ 12/06) [741.5]

12127 Miller, Steve, and Bryan Baugh. *Scared! How to Draw Fantastic Horror Comic Characters* (9–12).

2004, Watson-Guptill paper $19.95 (978-0-8230-1664-8). A clear how-to guide, with historical information and profiles of successful practitioners. (Rev: BL 2/1/05) [741.5]

12128 Nagatomo, Haruno. *Draw Your Own Manga: Beyond the Basics* (7–12). Trans. from Japanese by Françoise White. Illus. by author. 2005, Kodansha paper $19.95 (978-4-7700-2304-9). Written and illustrated by Japanese manga artists, this is an entertaining yet professional guide to drawing in this style. (Rev: SLJ 9/05; VOYA 12/04) [741.5]

12129 Nicolaides, Kimon. *The Natural Way to Draw: A Working Plan for Art Study* (9–12). 1990, Houghton Mifflin paper $16.00 (978-0-395-53007-8). Using illustrations from both old masters and students, this book demonstrates drawing basics. [741.2]

12130 Okum, David. *Manga Madness* (7–12). 2004, North Light paper $19.99 (978-1-58180-534-5). This is an excellent guide for would-be cartoonists and *manga* fans with step-by-step directions on how to produce your own art. (Rev: BL 3/15/04) [741.5]

12131 Peffer, Jessica. *DragonArt: How to Draw Fantastic Dragons and Fantasy Creatures* (5–12). Illus. by author. 2005, Impact paper $19.99 (978-1-58180-657-1). Beautiful creatures from the author's imagination fill the pages of this well-written book and will inspire young artists to develop their own fantasy style. (Rev: SLJ 5/06) [743]

12132 Petrie, Ferdinand, and John Shaw. *The Big Book of Painting Nature in Watercolor* (9–12). 1990, Watson-Guptill paper $29.95 (978-0-8230-0499-7). This book contains 135 separate lessons on techniques of painting subjects from nature using watercolors. (Rev: BL 9/1/90) [751.42]

12133 Sarnoff, Bob. *Cartoons and Comics: Ideas and Techniques* (9–12). 1988, Davis $18.95 (978-0-87192-202-1). A basic handbook with plenty of examples to help the novice. (Rev: BL 3/15/89) [741.5]

12134 Scott, Damian, and Kris Ex. *How to Draw Hip Hop* (7–12). 2006, Watson-Guptill paper $19.95 (978-0-8230-1446-0). This guide to drawing bright graffiti-style art with a manga flavor includes lots of back-and-forth between the authors, revealing a passion for hip-hop culture. (Rev: SLJ 7/06)

12135 Self, Caroline, and Susan Self. *Chinese Brush Painting: A Hands-on Introduction to the Traditional Art* (6–12). 2007, Tuttle $16.95 (978-0-8048-3877-1). An attractive introduction to Chinese calligraphy and brush painting, with history as well as step-by-step instructions. (Rev: BL 12/15/07) [751.4]

12136 Sheppard, Joseph. *Realistic Figure Drawing* (9–12). 1991, North Light paper $21.99 (978-0-89134-374-5). A guide to using different materials and approaches to capture figures in rest and in motion. (Rev: BL 5/15/91; SLJ 10/91) [751]

Gardening

12137 Klindienst, Patricia. *The Earth Knows My Name: Food, Culture, and Sustainability in the Gardens of Ethnic Americans* (8–12). 2006, Beacon $26.95 (978-0-8070-8562-2). A tour of 15 American gardens that represent the culture and ethnicity of their immigrant designers. (Rev: BL 4/1/06) [635.09]

12138 Rich, Libby. *Odyssey Book of Houseplants* (9–12). 1990, Plant Odyssey paper $19.95 (978-0-9625702-0-9). A guide to the characteristics and care of 150 different houseplants. (Rev: BL 3/15/90) [635.965]

12139 Smith, Miranda. *Your Backyard Herb Garden: A Gardener's Guide to Growing over 50 Herbs Plus How to Use Them in Cooking, Crafts, Companion Planting, and More* (9–12). 1997, Rodale paper $16.95 (978-0-87596-994-7). Both gardeners and cooks will find a useful resource in Miranda Smith's guide to growing and using more than 70 kinds of herbs. [635]

Home Repair

12140 Time-Life Books, ed. *The Home Workshop* (10–12). 1989, Silver Burdett LB $23.27 (978-0-8094-6281-0). A basic guide to setting up and maintaining a practical home workshop. This is part of a 36-volume set from Time-Life Books called the Home Repair and Improvement series that covers all sorts of projects from kitchens and bathrooms to porches and patios. [684]

Masks and Mask Making

12141 Sivin, Carole. *Maskmaking* (9–12). 1987, Davis $25.95 (978-0-87192-178-9). A history of maskmaking plus the techniques and materials needed to create your own. (Rev: BL 3/1/87) [731.75]

12142 Smith, Dick. *Dick Smith's Do-It-Yourself Monster Make-Up Handbook* (9–12). 1985, Imagine paper $9.95 (978-0-911137-02-6). An Academy Award-winning makeup artist tells how to create several monster disguises and supplies photographs of the finished products. (Rev: BL 11/1/85) [792.027]

Paper Crafts

12143 Grummer, Arnold E. *Trash-to-Treasure Papermaking* (10–12). 2011, Storey $16.95 (978-1-60342-547-6). This is a useful guide to papermaking, with a variety of creative ideas that progress in difficulty. (Rev: SLJ 6/11) [676]

12144 Smith, Esther K. *How to Make Books: Fold, Cut and Stitch Your Way to a One-of-a-Kind Book* (9–12). Illus. by Lindsay Stadig. Photos by David Michael Zimmerman. 2007, Potter Craft $25.00 (978-0-307-35336-8). This volume offers step-by-step instructions for a number of book projects. (Rev: SLJ 2/08) [686.3]

Photography, Video, and Film Making

12145 Bidner, Jenni. *The Kids' Guide to Digital Photography: How to Shoot, Save, Play with and Print Your Digital Photos* (7–10). 2004, Sterling $14.95 (978-1-57990-604-7). A user-friendly guide to digital photography and the transfer of the results to the Web and other applications. (Rev: BL 1/1–15/05; SLJ 5/05) [775]

12146 Gaines, Thom. *Digital Photo Madness! 50 Weird and Wacky Things to Do with Your Digital Camera* (7–10). 2006, Sterling paper $9.95 (978-1-57990-624-5). The fun part of digital photography is altering the images, and this guide explains how, after first covering the basics. (Rev: BL 12/15/06; SLJ 8/06) [773]

12147 Levy, Edmond. *Making a Winning Short: How to Write, Direct, Edit, and Produce a Short Film* (9–12). 1994, Henry Holt paper $15.95 (978-0-8050-2680-1). Gives advice and instructions on the creation of short films. (Rev: BL 10/1/94) [791]

12148 Schaefer, John P. *Basic Techniques of Photography* (9–12). 1992, Little, Brown $50.00 (978-0-8212-1801-3). An introduction to photography, with information on techniques, film development, and equipment. (Rev: BL 2/15/92) [771]

12149 Shulman, Mark, and Hazlitt Krog. *Attack of the Killer Video Book, Take 2: Tips and Tricks for Young Directors* (6–10). Illus. by Martha Newbigging. 2012, Annick $24.95 (978-155451367-3); paper $14.95 (978-155451366-6). A revised edition that brings up to date (well, to early 2012) the key techniques and resources used in film creation. (Rev: BLO 7/12) [778.59]

Sewing and Other Needle Crafts

12150 Barnden, Betty. *Very Easy Crazy Patchwork* (7–12). 2007, Reader's Digest $24.95 (978-0-7621-0671-4); paper $19.95 (978-0-7621-0672-1). From a potholder to an evening purse or even a quilt, this book shows how to make attractive patchwork projects using hand techniques and sewing machines. (Rev: SLJ 5/07) [746.46]

12151 Bayard, Marie-Noelle, and Charlie Abad. *Sewing: Techniques and Patterns* (9–12). 2007, Sterling $24.95 (978-1-4027-3771-8). This handy guide to sewing offers introductory material on fabrics and stitches, a wide range of projects grouped by technique, and a helpful reference section. (Rev: BL 3/1/07) [646.2]

12152 Brack, Heather, and Shannon Okey. *Felt Frenzy: 26 Projects for All Forms of Felting* (8–12). 2007, Interweave paper $21.95 (978-1-59668-009-8). For beginners and experts, this book contains projects creating purses, scarves, hats, and so forth through felting. (Rev: SLJ 7/07) [746]

12153 Brant, Sharon. *Finishing Techniques for Hand Knitters: Give Your Knitting That Professional Look* (9–12). 2007, Trafalgar $24.95 (978-1-57076-336-6). Knitters who have mastered the basics will enjoy this guide to finishing more complex pieces; includes patterns and clear photographs. (Rev: BL 12/15/06) [746.43]

12154 Carron, Cathy. *Hip Knit Hats: 40 Fabulous Designs* (9–12). 2005, Sterling $24.95 (978-1-57990-644-3). Step-by-step instructions for knitting 40 fashionable hats; most patterns require double-pointed needles. (Rev: BL 12/15/05) [746.43]

12155 Doherty, Elisabeth A. *Amigurumi! Super Happy Crochet Cute* (8–12). 2007, Sterling paper $14.95 (978-1-60059-017-7). Doherty provides patterns and clear instructions for 14 crocheted or knitted doll projects. (Rev: BL 9/15/07) [746.43]

12156 Eckman, Edie. *The Crochet Answer Book: Solutions to Every Problem You'll Ever Face, Answers to Every Question You'll Ever Ask* (7–12). 2005, Storey paper $12.95 (978-1-58017-598-2). For novice crocheters, this is a well-organized and comprehensive guide. (Rev: BL 12/15/05) [746.43]

12157 Ham, Catherine. *Knitting: 20 Simple and Stylish Wearables for Beginners* (10–12). 2003, Lark paper $14.95 (978-1-57990-351-0). Ideal for would-be or novice knitters, this richly illustrated introduction is loaded with simply written, step-by-step instructions. (Rev: BL 6/1–15/03) [746.43]

12158 Hantman, Clea. *I Wanna Re-Do My Room* (7–12). Illus. by Azadeh Houshyar. 2006, Simon & Schuster paper $9.99 (978-0-689-87463-5). More than 50 projects are featured in this guide to room decoration, such as wall décor, box adornment, pillows, curtains, furniture, and storage ideas; illustrated with black-and-white photographs. (Rev: SLJ 6/06)

12159 Ivarsson, Anna-Stina Linden. *Second-Time Cool: The Art of Chopping Up a Sweater* (7–10). Trans. by Maria Lundin. 2005, Annick $24.95 (978-1-55037-911-2); paper $12.95 (978-1-55037-910-5). Adventurous clothes recycling for the ambitious teen with too much old wool lying around. (Rev: BL 1/1–15/06; SLJ 1/06) [646.4]

12160 Mably, Brandon. *Brilliant Knits: 25 Contemporary Designs* (10–12). 2001, Taunton $24.95 (978-1-56158-511-3). This book features 25 designs for the experienced knitter. (Rev: BL 11/1/01) [746.4]

12161 Marston, Gwen, and Joe Cunningham. *Quilting with Style: Principles for Great Pattern Design* (9–12). 1993, American Quilter's Society $24.95 (978-0-89145-814-2). Methods of planning the cable, fan, and feather of a quilt are described, with more than 75 color photographs of traditional quilts and traceable, full-size figures. (Rev: BL 11/1/93) [746.9]

12162 Percival, Kris. *Speed Knitting: 24 Quick and Easy Projects* (8–12). 2006, Chronicle paper $19.95 (978-0-8118-5245-6). Beginners will appreciate these simple projects that can be quickly accomplished. (Rev: BL 11/15/06) [746.32]

12163 Radcliffe, Margaret. *The Knitting Answer Book* (8–12). 2005, Storey paper $12.95 (978-1-58017-599-9). This well-organized volume introduces newcomers to knitting and also provides expert guidance for long-time knitters. (Rev: BL 12/15/05) [746.43]

12164 *Singer: The Complete Photo Guide to Sewing* (9–12). 1999, Creative Pub. Int $24.95 (978-0-86573-173-8). As well as the techniques of sewing, this manual covers such topics as patterns, fabrics, and home decorating. [646.2]

12165 Stoller, Debbie. *Son of Stitch 'n Bitch: 45 Projects to Knit and Crochet for Men* (9–12). Series: Stitch 'n Bitch. 2007, Workman paper $15.95 (978-0-7611-4617-9). Socks, scarves, sweaters, and gloves are among the projects — the majority involving knitting — included in this volume. (Rev: BL 12/15/07) [677.028]

12166 Taylor, Kathleen. *Knit One, Felt Too* (9–12). 2003, Storey paper $18.95 (978-1-58017-497-8). Twenty-five projects are described in which, after initial knitting, the product is crafted into a different shape through purposeful shrinking. (Rev: BL 1/1–15/04; SLJ 5/04) [746.48]

12167 Werker, Kim. *Crochet Me: Designs to Fuel the Crochet Revolution* (8–12). 2007, Interweave paper $21.95 (978-1-59668-044-9). Not for beginners, this is a collection of crochet designs with information on designers and technical aspects. (Rev: BL 12/15/07) [746.43]

12168 Worrall, Jocelyn. *Simple Gifts to Stitch: 30 Elegant and Easy Projects* (8–12). 2007, Potter paper $19.95 (978-0-307-34756-5). Provides easy-to-follow patterns for scarves, bags, hats, aprons, pillows, and so forth. (Rev: SLJ 8/07) [746]

12169 Zent, Sheila. *Sew Teen: Make Your Own Cool Clothes* (9–12). 2006, Sterling $17.95 (978-1-931543-90-3). For teenagers who want to go a little further with their sewing, this book features 21 projects that require a sewing machine, basic skill, and the desire to create something special. (Rev: BL 12/15/06; SLJ 10/06) [646.2]

12170 Zieman, Nancy, and Robbie Fanning. *The Busy Woman's Sewing Book. Rev. ed.* (9–12). 1988, Open Chain paper $9.95 (978-0-932086-03-7). Sewing basics are covered in a time-efficient mode. Well-illustrated. (Rev: BL 5/1/88) [646.2]

Stamp, Coin, and Other Types of Collecting

12171 Mackay, James. *The Guinness Book of Stamps, Facts and Feats* (7–12). 1989, Guinness $34.95 (978-0-85112-351-6). All sorts of curiosities about postage stamps such as the most valuable, the largest, and so on. (Rev: BL 4/15/89) [769.56]

12172 *The Postal Service Guide to U.S. Stamps* (7–12). 1988, U.S. Postal Service $5.00 (978-0-9604756-8-1). A well-illustrated history of U.S. postage stamps. [769.56]

Woodworking and Carpentry

12173 Jackson, Albert, et al. *The Complete Manual of Woodworking* (9–12). 1989, Knopf paper $25.00 (978-0-679-76611-7). Such topics as choosing materials, types of tools, sawing, gluing, and finishing are covered in this fine introduction to woodworking. [684]

12174 Miller, Wilbur R., et al. *Woodworking* (9–12). 1978, Glencoe paper $9.33 (978-0-02-672800-3). A guide that covers basic tools, techniques, and materials in woodworking. [684]

12175 Tangerman, Elmer J. *Whittling and Woodcarving* (9–12). 1936, Dover paper $12.95 (978-0-486-20965-4). This is a beginner's guide to these ancient crafts. [684]

12176 *Working with Wood* (9–12). 1979, Silver Burdett LB $20.60 (978-0-8094-2427-6). Basic woodworking skills, tools, and techniques are introduced in this volume from the Time-Life Home Repair and Improvement series. [694]

Jokes, Puzzles, Riddles, and Word Games

12177 Fisher, Adrian. *The Amazing Book of Mazes* (9–12). 2006, Abrams $28.95 (978-0-8109-4311-7). With the help of photographs, diagrams, and text, Fisher explores the history and design principles of mazes, with examples of Renaissance hedges, labyrinth paths, and two-dimensional mazes both past and present. (Rev: BL 11/1/06) [793.73]

12178 Salny, Abbie, and Burke Lewis Frumkes. *The Mensa Think Smart Book* (9–12). 1986, HarperCollins paper $10.00 (978-0-06-091255-0). A collection of word games, puzzles, and quizzes that are mind benders. (Rev: BL 4/1/86) [153]

12179 Sloane, Paul, and Des MacHale. *Challenging Lateral Thinking Puzzles* (9–12). 1993, Sterling paper $6.95 (978-0-8069-8671-5). More than 90 brainteasers, with clues leading the reader through a "lateral thinking" mode. (Rev: BL 5/1/93) [793.73]

Mysteries, Curiosities, and Controversial Subjects

12180 Aaronovitch, David. *Voodoo Histories: The Role of the Conspiracy Theory in Shaping Modern History* (10–12). 2010, Riverhead $26.95 (978-159448895-5). Aaronovitch explores conspiracy theories and why they survive and thrive. ⌒ ℮ (Rev: BL 2/1–15/10) [909.08]

12181 Aaseng, Nathan. *The Bermuda Triangle* (7–10). Series: Mystery Library. 2001, Lucent LB $27.45 (978-1-56006-769-6). Using a variety of sources, this book explores the past and present of this controversial phenomenon. (Rev: BL 9/15/01) [001.9]

12182 Amberstone, Ruth Ann, and Wald Amberstone. *Tarot Tips: 78 Practical Techniques to Enhance Your Tarot Reading Skills* (10–12). Series: Special Topics in Tarot. 2003, Llewellyn paper $14.95 (978-0-7387-0216-2). A light introduction to tarot cards and their interpretation that includes practical tips that will be of use to novice and advanced practitioners. (Rev: SLJ 5/04) [133.3]

12183 Boese, Alex. *Hippo Eats Dwarf: A Field Guide to Hoaxes and Other B.S.* (9–12). 2006, Harcourt paper $14.00 (978-0-15-603083-0). Phony celebrities, advertising disguised as news, and fraudulent sales pitches are only a few examples of the misinformation featured in this follow-up to *The Museum of Hoaxes* (2002). (Rev: BL 2/1/06) [001.9]

12184 Buckingham, Jane. *What's Next: The Experts' Guide: Predictions from 50 of America's Most Compelling People* (9–12). 2008, HarperCollins $24.95 (978-0-06-088535-9). For those interested in others' views of the future, this is a wide-ranging and thought-provoking collection of opinions. (Rev: BL 12/15/07) [973.93]

12185 Charpak, Georges, and Henri Broch. *Debunked! ESP, Telekinesis, and Other Pseudoscience* (9–12). Trans. by Bart K. Holland. 2004, Johns Hopkins $27.50 (978-0-8018-7867-1). This is an examination of many kinds of paranormal phenomena, like astrology, by a master debunker. (Rev: BL 4/1/04) [130]

12186 Craig, Roy. *UFOs: An Insider's View of the Official Quest for Evidence* (9–12). 1995, Univ. of North Texas paper $19.95 (978-0-929398-94-5). The controversial investigation of UFOs in the late 1960s is reviewed by a chemist and field investigator who was there. (Rev: BL 10/1/95) [001.9]

12187 Crawford, Saffi, and Geraldine Sullivan. *The Power of Birthdays, Stars and Numbers* (9–12). 1998, Ballantine paper $24.95 (978-0-345-41819-7). This introduction to astrology not only explains the effects of planets on personality, but also describes each day in the calendar in terms of the zodiac and numerology. ℮ (Rev: SLJ 4/99) [133.5]

12188 D'Epiro, Peter, and Mary Desmond Pinkowish. *What Are the Seven Wonders of the World? And 100 Other Great Cultural Lists — Fully Explicated* (9–12). 1998, Doubleday paper $14.95 (978-0-385-49062-7). A treasure trove of cultural trivia, this almanac-like collection contains lists of numerically organized miscellany ranging from the identities of the Three Furies and Four Horsemen of the Apocalypse to Egypt's 10 plagues and the 14 points of Woodrow Wilson's plan for world peace. (Rev: BL 12/1/98) [031]

12189 Dinsdale, Tim. *Loch Ness Monster. 4th ed.* (9–12). 1982, Routledge paper $7.95 (978-0-7100-9022-5). An account of the search for Nessie, the monster that supposedly lives in this picturesque lake in the Scottish Highlands. [001.9]

12190 Dugan, Ellen. *Elements of Witchcraft: Natural Magick for Teens* (8–12). 2003, Llewellyn paper $14.94 (978-1-73870-393-7). A practicing witch introduces teens to the basics of witchcraft, with tips on proper casting of spells and a discussion of ethical concerns. (Rev: BL 6/1–15/03) [133.4]

12191 *Exploring the Unexplained: The World's Greatest Marvels, Mysteries and Myths* (9–12). 2006, Time $24.95 (978-1-933405-16-2). Mysteries of science, religion, the animal world, the ancient world, the unknown beyond — it's all here, and students will enjoy sharing the amazing tales with their friends. (Rev: BL 12/1/06) [001.94]

12192 Feldman, David. *Why Do Clocks Run Clockwise? And Other Imponderables: Mysteries of Everyday Life* (8–12). 1987, Harper & Row paper $12.95 (978-0-06-091515-5). Questions about everyday occurrences and objects, like "Why do nurses wear white?" are answered in this book of curiosities. [031.02]

12193 Fulghum, Hunter S. *Don't Try This at Home: How to Win a Sumo Match, Catch a Great White Shark, Start an Independent Nation and Other Extraordinary Feats (for Ordinary People)* (9–12). 2002, Broadway paper $12.95 (978-0-7679-1159-7). This hilarious, offbeat guide provides step-by-step instructions for such daring feats as breaking into Fort Knox and smuggling secret documents. (Rev: BL 9/15/02; VOYA 4/03) [904]

12194 Gardner, Martin. *On the Wild Side: The Big Bang, ESP, the Beast 666, Levitation, Rain Making, Trance-Channeling, Seances and Ghosts, and More* (9–12). 1992, Prometheus $34.98 (978-0-87975-713-7). A collection of articles that examine, expose, and debunk many offbeat scientific theories, cults, and beliefs. (Rev: BL 2/15/92) [500]

12195 Genge, N. E. *The Book of Shadows: The Unofficial Charmed Companion* (7–12). 2000, Three Rivers $14.00 (978-0-609-80652-4). A guide to some of the basic tenets of witchcraft that form the basis for *Charmed*, the popular TV series about teen witches. (Rev: SLJ 2/01; VOYA 6/01)

12196 Gibson, Marley, and Dave Schrader, et al. *The Other Side: A Teen's Guide to Ghost Hunting and the Paranormal* (7–10). Illus. 2009, Graphia paper $10.99 (978-0-547-25829-4). This concise, often witty guide doesn't glamorize ghost-hunting — the authors stress that it's a hobby, not a career — but it does contain much in the way of practical advice for teens interested in paranormal investigation. (Rev: SLJ 3/10; VOYA 2/10)

12197 Goodwin, Simon, and John Gribbin. *XTL: Extraterrestrial Life and How to Find It* (10–12). 2002, Cassell $29.95 (978-0-304-35897-7). In this thought-provoking overview of the search for life elsewhere, the authors examine recent research and discoveries. (Rev: BL 6/1–15/02) [523.1]

12198 Gray, Amy. *How to Be a Vampire: A Fangs-on Guide for the Newly Undead* (7–12). Illus. by Scott Erwert. 2009, Candlewick $14.99 (978-0-7636-4915-9). The ultimate guide to all things vampire, covering feeding, etiquette, fashion, pets, dating mortals, and so forth. Lexile 1070L (Rev: SLJ 1/10; VOYA 4/10) [398.4]

12199 Holt, David, retel. *The Exploding Toilet: Modern Urban Legends* (7–12). Retold by Bill Mooney. Illus.

by Kevin Pope. 2004, August House $16.95 (978-0-87483-754-4); paper $6.95 (978-0-87483-715-5). Amazing, often funny, shocking stories, many of which have appeared on the Internet. (Rev: SLJ 8/04) [398.2]

12200 Jack, Albert. *Loch Ness Monsters and Raining Frogs: The World's Most Puzzling Mysteries Solved* (9–12). Illus. 2009, Random House paper $15 (978-0-8129-8005-9). This highly readable collection of short essays addresses a variety of popular mysteries from the past two centuries. (Rev: SLJ 8/09) [001.94]

12201 Johnson, Julie Tallard. *Teen Psychic: Exploring Your Intuitive Spiritual Powers* (8–12). 2003, Inner Traditions paper $14.95 (978-0-89281-094-9). An introduction to investigating and developing one's intuitive powers, with quizzes, exercises, mediations, and many personal stories from teens. (Rev: BL 1/1–15/04; VOYA 4/04) [131]

12202 Kallen, Stuart A. *Communication with the Dead* (7–12). Series: The Library of Ghosts and Hauntings. 2010, ReferencePoint LB $31.19 (978-1-60152-089-0). Well-written and filled with sources and documentation, this book allows students to examine claims of the paranormal in a straightforward, scholarly way. (Rev: LMC 1–2/10)

12203 Kallen, Stuart A. *Witches* (7–10). Series: Mystery Library. 2000, Lucent LB $29.95 (978-1-56006-688-0). A history of witchcraft precedes discussion of the beliefs and rituals of today's Wiccans. (Rev: BL 9/1/00; HBG 3/01; SLJ 9/00) [133.4]

12204 Knowles, Elizabeth. *What They Didn't Say: A Book of Misquotations* (9–12). 2006, Oxford $19.95 (978-0-19-920359-8). A chatty and informal survey of things people didn't say, this makes for entertaining browsing and can be used for reference. (Rev: SLJ 1/07)

12205 Maberry, Jonathan, and David F. Kramer. *They Bite: Endless Cravings of Supernatural Predators* (10–12). Illus. 2009, Citadel paper $16.95 (978-08065282-0-5). This book explains the genesis of werewolves, zombies, and other monsters and compares the old folktales with modern interpretations. (Rev: BL 9/09) [398.21]

12206 Moseley, James W., and Karl T. Pflock. *Shockingly Close to the Truth: Confessions of a Grave-Robbing Ufologist* (10–12). 2002, Prometheus $27.98 (978-1-57392-991-2). The dubious antics of many UFO believers are revealed in this entertaining read. (Rev: BL 2/15/02; SLJ 9/02) [001.942]

12207 Myers, Arthur. *The Ghostly Register* (9–12). 1986, Contemporary paper $18.95 (978-0-8092-5081-3). A guide to 64 houses that are reputedly haunted. (Rev: SLJ 3/87) [133.1]

12208 Netzley, Patricia D. *Haunted Houses* (7–10). Series: Mystery Library. 2000, Lucent LB $29.95 (978-1-56006-685-9). A balanced account that examines specific cases of hauntings and discusses such topics as ghosts, poltergeists, seances, and mediums. (Rev: BL 9/1/00; HBG 3/01; SLJ 9/00; VOYA 4/01) [133.1]

12209 Nickell, Joe. *The Mystery Chronicles: More Real-Life X-Files* (9–12). 2004, Univ. Press of Kentucky $29.95 (978-0-8131-2318-9). This compilation of 41 reports investigates a number of paranormal phenomena like the Amityville horror. (Rev: BL 3/15/04) [001.94]

12210 Nickell, Joe. *Real-Life X-Files: Investigating the Paranormal* (9–12). 2001, Univ. Press of Kentucky $29.95 (978-0-8131-2210-6). With excellent background research, the author debunks such paranormal phenomena as crop circles, stigmata, and spiritualist mediums. (Rev: BL 10/15/01) [133]

12211 Nickell, Joe, and John F. Fischer. *Secrets of the Supernatural: Investigating the World's Occult Mysteries* (9–12). 1988, Prometheus $41.98 (978-0-87975-461-7). The scientific investigation of 10 supernatural occurrences. (Rev: BL 9/1/88) [133]

12212 Olmsted, Larry. *Getting into Guinness: One Man's Longest, Fastest, Highest Journey Inside the World's Most Famous Record Book* (10–12). 2008, HarperCollins $24.95 (978-0-06-137348-0). Guinness world-record holder Olmsted tells fascinating stories about incredible records and offers advice on selecting a feat to perform; many of the records are serious, but a large percentage are totally wacky. (Rev: BL 8/08) [030]

12213 O'Neill, Catherine. *Amazing Mysteries of the World* (7–12). 1983, National Geographic LB $12.50 (978-0-87044-502-6). UFOs, Bigfoot, and Easter Island are only three of the many mysteries explored. [001.9]

12214 Pickover, Clifford A. *Dreaming the Future: The Fantastic Story of Prediction* (9–12). 2001, Prometheus $32.98 (978-1-57392-895-3). This book looks at various forms of fortunetelling, such as tarot cards and the zodiac, and introduces great soothsayers of history, including Nostradamus. (Rev: BL 3/1/01) [133.3]

12215 Regan, Sally. *The Vampire Book: The Legends, the Lore, the Allure* (7–12). 2009, DK $19.99 (978-0-7566-5551-8). Regan surveys the various myths and stories that exist about vampires and similar beings around the world and throughout history, with details of vampires in literature and on the screen; with eye-catching illustrations. (Rev: LMC 1–2/10; SLJ 12/09) [398.21]

12216 Reis, Ronald A. *Easter Island* (8–12). Illus. Series: Lost Worlds and Mysterious Civilizations. 2011, Chelsea House LB $39.95 (978-160413972-3). A thorough overview of what we know about the mysteries of Easter Island. (Rev: BL 4/1/12; SLJ 5/1/12) [996.1]

12217 Robson, David. *Encounters with Vampires* (7–10). Illus. Series: Vampire Library. 2010, ReferencePoint LB $26.95 (978-160152133-0). A compelling survey of vampire tales from around the world, covering both

legend and real incidents. ℮ Lexile 1130L (Rev: BL 10/1/10; LMC 3–4/11) [398]

12218 Roeper, Richard. *Debunked! Conspiracy Theories, Urban Legends, and Evil Plots of the 21st Century* (9–12). 2008, Chicago Review $19.95 (978-155652707-4). Roeper debunks myths surrounding recent events ranging from the collapse of the Twin Towers to the death of Princess Diana in this irreverent and often humorous book. (Rev: BL 6/1–15/08) [364.10973]

12219 Schott, Ben. *Schott's Original Miscellany* (9–12). 2003, Bloomsbury $14.95 (978-1-58234-349-5). A wonderful source of trivia that is great for browsers and also has a useful index. (Rev: SLJ 1/04) [030]

12220 Selzer, Adam. *Your Neighborhood Gives Me the Creeps: True Tales of an Accidental Ghost Hunter* (9–12). 2009, Llewellyn paper $15.95 (978-07387155-7-5). He says he's a skeptic, but the author gives ghost tours in the Chicago area and shares some of his favorite eerie stories. (Rev: BLO 7/09) [133.1]

12221 Shaw, Maria. *Maria Shaw's Book of Love: Horoscopes, Palmistry, Numbers, Candles, Gemstones and Colors* (8–12). 2005, Llewellyn paper $14.95 (978-0-7387-0545-3). A lighthearted guide to unscientific methods of predicting the course of true love. (Rev: SLJ 2/05) [133.3]

12222 Shuker, Karl P. N. *Mysteries of Planet Earth: An Encyclopedia of the Inexplicable* (6–12). 1999, Carlton $22.95 (978-1-85868-802-2). A well-illustrated exploration of unusual — and mostly unexplained — phenomena including the Loch Ness monster, the Shroud of Turin, green polar bears, pea-soup fog, and the dodo bird. (Rev: VOYA 4/00) [001.94]

12223 Steiger, Brad. *Real Vampires, Night Stalkers, and Creatures from the Darkside* (10–12). 2009, Gale/Visible Ink paper $24.95 (978-1-57859-255-5). Steiger draws on news articles, historical accounts, and first-person interviews to provide a history of vampirism and includes thirty tales of real vampires. (Rev: LMC 3–4/10; SLJ 4/10) [133.4]

12224 Valentino, Serena. *How to Be a Zombie: The Essential Guide for Anyone Who Craves Brains* (7–10). Illus. by Scott Erwert. 2010, Candlewick $14.99 (978-076364934-0). This tongue-in-cheek title offers up everything from "Decor for the Decaying" to makeup and behavioral advice for young zombie wannabes. (Rev: BL 8/10; VOYA 4/11) [398]

12225 Van Praagh, James. *Looking Beyond: A Teen's Guide to the Spiritual World* (8–12). 2003, Simon & Schuster paper $12.00 (978-0-7432-2942-5). Psychic Van Praagh tells teens what his contacts with the spirit world have taught him about the meaning of life and what we can do to make the most of it. (Rev: BL 1/1–15/04) [133.9]

12226 Wand, Kelly, ed. *Ape-Men: Fact or Fiction?* (6–12). 2005, Gale LB $29.95 (978-0-7377-1892-8). This volume consists of ten essays about large, legendary apelike creatures (known variously as Bigfoot, Sasquatch, and Yeti) sighted from the Himalayas to North America; half of the essays refute their existence and the others conversely offer proof. (Rev: SLJ 6/06)

12227 Windham, Kathryn Tucker. *Jeffrey Introduces 13 More Southern Ghosts* (7–10). 1978, Univ. of Alabama paper $13.95 (978-0-8173-0381-5). A total of 13 ghosts tell their weird stories. [133]

12228 Wolf, Leonard. *Dracula: The Connoisseur's Guide* (9–12). 1997, Broadway paper $16.00 (978-0-553-06907-5). This book is filled with fascinating vampire lore and discussion of vampire fiction stemming from Bram Stoker's 19th-century novel and the Dracula movies. (Rev: SLJ 6/98) [001.9]

Sports and Games

General and Miscellaneous

12229 Aaseng, Nathan. *The Locker Room Mirror: How Sports Reflect Society* (7–10). 1993, Walker LB $15.85 (978-0-8027-8218-2). Aaseng argues that problems in professional sports today — cheating, drug abuse, violence, commercialization, discrimination — are reflections of society at large. (Rev: BL 6/1–15/93; SLJ 5/93) [306.4]

12230 Allred, Alexandra Powe. *Atta Girl! A Celebration of Women in Sports* (9–12). 2003, Wish $16.95 (978-1-930546-61-5). This is a history of women in sports with material on those women who fought for equality. (Rev: BL 3/1/04; VOYA 6/03) [796]

12231 Aymar, Brandt. *Men in Sports: Great Sports Stories of All Time From the Greek Olympic Games to the American World Series* (9–12). 1994, Crown paper $25.00 (978-0-517-88395-2). Arranged alphabetically, this volume contains almost 50 sporting entries that include nonfiction, fiction, and sports reporting. [796]

12232 Berkow, Ira. *The Minority Quarterback and Other Lives in Sports* (10–12). 2002, Ivan R. Dee $26.00 (978-1-56663-422-9). This collection of inspiring sports stories spotlights athletes' triumphs over such diverse challenges as racial discrimination, physical disability, and hearing loss. (Rev: BL 2/1/02*) [796]

12233 Birkemoe, Karen. *Strike a Pose: The Planet Girl Guide to Yoga* (5–10). Illus. by Heather Collett. Series: Planet Girl. 2007, Kids Can paper $12.95 (978-155337004-8). This is a practical, easy-going guide to yoga poses, breathing, meditation, and uses in sports. (Rev: SLJ 8/07) [613.7]

12234 Blumenthal, Karen. *Let Me Play: The Story of Title IX: The Law That Changed the Future of Girls in America* (6–10). 2005, Simon & Schuster $17.95 (978-0-689-85957-1). Personal anecdotes, political cartoons, and profiles of female athletes add to the story of the 1972 passage of Title IX, which bans sex discrimination in U.S. schools. (Rev: BL 7/05; SLJ 7/05*) [796]

12235 Borden, Fred, and Jay Elias. *Bowling: Knowledge Is the Key* (9–12). 1987, Bowling Concepts paper $19.95 (978-0-9619177-0-8). A straightforward instructional program that is simple to follow and thorough. (Rev: BL 6/15/87) [794.6]

12236 Brenkus, John. *The Perfection Point: Sport Science Predicts the Fastest Man, the Highest Jump, and the Limits of Athletic Performance* (10–12). 2010, HarperCollins $26.99 (978-006184545-1). How fast can a human run? What's the longest someone can hold his breath? This fascinating volume answers these and many other questions about our expanding sports abilities. ℮ (Rev: BL 9/1–15/10) [612.044]

12237 *Cheerleading: From Tryouts to Championships* (10–12). 2007, Universe paper $29.95 (978-0-7893-1565-6). A guide to competitive cheerleading, stressing attitude and fitness. (Rev: SLJ 12/07) [791.6]

12238 Ching, Jacqueline. *Adventure Racing* (7–10). Series: Ultra Sports. 2002, Rosen LB $26.50 (978-0-8239-3555-0). This is a fine introduction to this new, outdoor, multidiscipline sport that involves biking, paddling, and climbing plus survival skills and outdoor savvy. (Rev: BL 9/1/02) [796.5]

12239 Douglass, Kara. *Becoming an Ironman: First Encounters with the Ultimate Endurance Event* (9–12). 2001, Breakaway $23.00 (978-1-891369-24-7). This work surveys the history of the Ironman triathlon, which involves swimming, bike riding, and running a marathon in one event. [796]

12240 Duncan, Joyce D., ed. *Sport in American Culture: From Ali to X-Games* (9–12). 2004, ABC-CLIO $95.00 (978-1-57607-024-6). Four hundred entries explore the cultural impact of sports on American society, covering such topics as sports apparel, scandals, civil rights issues, children's issues, and sports in literature, film, and humor. (Rev: BL 3/15/05; SLJ 6/05) [306.4]

12241 Fair, Erik. *Right Stuff for New Hang Glider Pilots* (9–12). 1987, Publitec Editions paper $9.95 (978-0-913581-00-1). A collection of articles by Fair exploring many topics relating to hang gliding. (Rev: BL 4/1/87) [797.5]

12242 Finnigan, Dave. *The Joy of Juggling* (9–12). 1993, Jugglebug paper $6.50 (978-0-9615521-3-8). Describes and provides illustrations for 25 juggling routines, discusses plagiarism of others' acts, and gives performance tips for various audiences. (Rev: BL 12/15/93) [793.8]

12243 Fleder, Rob, ed. *Fifty Years of Great Writing: Sports Illustrated, 1954–2004* (10–12). 2003, Sports Illustrated $25.95 (978-1-932273-06-9). A collection of excellent sports articles that appeared in America's premier sports magazine. (Rev: BL 11/1/03*) [070.449790]

12244 Hastings, Penny. *Sports for Her: A Reference Guide for Teenage Girls* (7–12). 1999, Greenwood $57.95 (978-0-313-30551-1). The basics of many individual sports are covered, with tips on playing sports in general for the young female athlete. (Rev: SLJ 7/00; VOYA 6/00) [796]

12245 Hinkson, Jim. *Lacrosse Fundamentals* (9–12). 1993, Firefly paper $15.95 (978-1-895629-11-8). Tips and techniques for stick selection, cradling, grip, catching, passing, offense and defense, shooting, face-offs, and goal-tending. (Rev: BL 11/15/93) [796.34]

12246 Hunter, Nick. *Money in Sports* (7–10). Illus. Series: Ethics of Sports. 2012, Heinemann $34 (978-143295977-7); paper $9 (978-14329598-2-1). Hunter reviews the history of sports before focusing on money's role in today's competitions. (Rev: BL 4/1/12*) [338.47796]

12247 Judson, Karen. *Sports and Money: It's a Sellout!* (7–12). Series: Issues in Focus. 1995, Enslow LB $20.95 (978-0-89490-622-0). A straightforward presentation that uses first-person accounts concerning the financial side of being in the sports business. (Rev: BL 11/15/95; SLJ 6/96) [796.0619]

12248 Krantz, Les. *Not Till the Fat Lady Sings: The Most Dramatic Sports Finishes of All Time* (9–12). 2003, Triumph $29.95 (978-1-57243-558-2). The details of 50 dramatic last-minute finishes are accompanied by video footage on DVD. (Rev: BL 11/15/03) [796]

12249 Lamovsky, Jesse, and Matthew Rosetti. *The Worst of Sports: Chumps, Cheats, and Chokers from the Games We Love* (8–12). 2007, Ballantine paper $13.95 (978-0-345-49891-5). Reluctant readers and sports fans will be drawn to this irreverent compilation of sorry facts about various sports. (Rev: BL 9/1/07; SLJ 12/07) [796.02]

12250 Li, WenFang. *Extreme Sports* (7–10). Illus. Series: Getting the Edge: Conditioning, Injuries, and Legal and Illicit Drugs. 2010, Mason Crest LB $24.95 (978-142221729-0). Mental and physical preparation are a focus of this book that also covers injuries, nutrition and supplements, and the dangers of performance-enhancing drugs. (Rev: BL 12/15/10) [796.04]

12251 Luby, Thia. *Yoga for Teens: How to Improve Your Fitness, Confidence, Appearance, and Health — and Have Fun Doing It* (6–12). 2000, Clear Light $14.95 (978-1-57416-032-1). The benefits of yoga, particularly in the teen years, are presented with eye-catching photographs and clear instructions for achieving the poses. (Rev: SLJ 5/00) [613.7]

12252 Maraniss, David, and Glenn Stout, eds. *The Best American Sports Writing, 2007* (10–12). 2007, Houghton Mifflin $28.00 (978-0-618-75115-0). The 2007 edition in this long-running series features the best of sports journalism of the previous year, covering a wide variety of sports and achievements. (Rev: BL 10/1/07) [796]

12253 Mayne, Kenny. *An Incomplete and Inaccurate History of Sport* (9–12). 2008, Crown $24.95 (978-0-307-39615-0). A tongue-in-cheek ramble through all things sports from snowball fights to football by an ESPN sports anchorman. (Rev: BL 3/1/08) [818]

12254 Morris, Neil. *Should Substance-Abusing Athletes Be Banned for Life?* (7–12). Series: What Do You Think? 2008, Heinemann LB $32.86 (978-1-4329-1676-3). After a discussion of the use of drugs in sports, this volume discusses drug tests, penalties for abuse, and so forth; it includes a case study that looks at the Tour de France. (Rev: SLJ 1/1/09) [362.29]

12255 Musiker, Liz Hartman. *The Smart Girl's Guide to Sports: A Hip Handbook for Women Who Don't Know a Slam Dunk from a Grand Slam* (9–12). 2005, Hudson Street $19.95 (978-1-59463-011-8). A helpful guide to sports rules, legend, lingo, and traditions. (Rev: BL 9/1/05) [796]

12256 Neil, Randy L., and Elaine Hart. *The All-New Official Cheerleader's Handbook* (9–12). 1986, Simon & Schuster paper $14.95 (978-0-671-61210-8). This guide covers cheerleading from basic movements to complex stunts. [791]

12257 Nelson, Mariah Burton. *The Stronger Women Get, the More Men Love Football: Sexism and the American Culture of Sports* (9–12). 1994, Harcourt $22.95 (978-0-15-181393-3). A hard-hitting account asserting that women are better athletes than men and capable of competing with men. (Rev: BL 5/15/94) [796]

12258 Paulsen, Gary. *Winterdance: The Fine Madness of Running the Iditarod* (9–12). 1994, Harcourt $26.00 (978-0-15-126227-4). This survival adventure describes the author's experiences running with his dog team in the 1,180-mile Alaskan Iditarod race. (Rev: BL 2/15/94; VOYA 10/94) [798.8]

12259 Quirk, Charles F., ed. *Sports and the Law: Major League Cases* (10–12). Series: American Law and Society. 1996, Garland $61.00 (978-0-8153-0220-9). Fifty essays explore legal cases involving such controversies as the rights and responsibilities of coaches, franchise owners moving their teams from one city to another, and access to locker rooms by female journalists. (Rev: SLJ 10/96) [796]

12260 Savage, Jeff. *A Sure Thing? Sports and Gambling* (7–12). Series: Sports Issues. 1996, Lerner LB $28.75 (978-0-8225-3303-0). After a brief history of gambling, this book looks at the many forms of gambling available today, from church bingo games to horse racing to Las Vegas casinos, with a focus on the connection between gambling and sports and emphasis on the dangers of gambling addiction. (Rev: BL 7/97; HBG 3/98; SLJ 11/97) [796]

12261 Scheppler, Bill. *The Ironman Triathlon* (7–10). 2002, Rosen LB $26.50 (978-0-8239-3556-7). Scheppler provides tips on training body and mind for the challenge of these races that combine running, swimming, and biking. (Rev: BL 9/1/02; VOYA 8/02) [796.42]

12262 Schwartz, Ellen. *I Love Yoga: A Guide for Kids and Teens* (5–12). Illus. by Ben Hodson. 2003, Tundra paper $9.95 (978-0-88776-598-8). Illustrated instructions for 18 basic poses are accompanied by breathing and relaxation exercises, discussion of the benefits of yoga, and a description of the different types of yoga practiced around the world. (Rev: SLJ 12/03; VOYA 10/03) [613.7]

12263 Schwarzenegger, Arnold. *Arnold's Bodybuilding for Men* (10–12). 1981, Simon & Schuster paper $16.00 (978-0-671-53163-8). A guide to exercise and weight lifting that stresses a total fitness program. [613.7]

12264 Shannon, Joyce Brennfleck, ed. *Sports Injuries Information for Teens: Health Tips About Sports Injuries and Injury Prevention* (8–12). Series: Teen Health. 2003, Omnigraphics $58.00 (978-0-7808-0447-0). Basic information on sports injuries and treatment is provided in separate sections on such topics as emergency treatment, common injuries affecting teens, rehabilitation and physical therapy, injury prevention, and sports nutrition. (Rev: SLJ 7/04; VOYA 10/04) [617.1]

12265 Sokolove, Michael. *Warrior Girls: Protecting Our Daughters Against the Injury Epidemic in Women's Sports* (10–12). 2008, Simon & Schuster $25.00 (978-074329755-4). Sokolove discusses the physiology and psychology of injury in women's sports, and the sometimes-high cost of an athlete's quest for perfection. e (Rev: BL 6/1–15/08) [796.083]

12266 St. John, Allen. *Made to Be Broken: The 50 Greatest Records and Streaks in Sports* (9–12). 2006, Triumph $29.95 (978-1-57243-857-6). A compilation of 50 of the greatest sports' broken record statistics not only includes the numbers, but also the interviews, photographs, sidebars, and a companion DVD showing the events as they happened. (Rev: BL 7/07) [796]

12267 Stark, Peter, and Steven M. Krauzer. *Winter Adventure: A Complete Guide to Winter Sports* (8–12). Series: Trailside Guide. 1995, Norton $17.95 (978-0-393-31400-7). This is a complete guide to winter sports including sledding, dogsledding, curling, ice skating, and cross-country skiing with additional material on organizations, safety tips, and information sources. [796.9]

12268 Steiner, Andy. *Girl Power on the Playing Field: A Book About Girls, Their Goals, and Their Struggles* (5–10). Series: Girl Power. 2000, Lerner LB $30.35 (978-0-8225-2690-2). This book explains women's roles in sports with good personal guidance for young girls on participation and goals. (Rev: HBG 10/00; SLJ 6/00) [796]

12269 Summers, Kit. *Juggling with Finesse* (9–12). 1987, Finesse paper $19.95 (978-0-938981-00-8). Simple instructions, profusely illustrated, on how to juggle a variety of objects. (Rev: BL 10/1/87) [793.8]

12270 Urick, Dave. *Sports Illustrated Lacrosse: Fundamentals for Winning. Rev. ed.* (9–12). Series: Sports Illustrated Winner's Circle. 1991, Sports Illustrated paper $12.95 (978-1-56800-071-8). This guide to the fundamentals of lacrosse covers rules game, skills, equipment, and strategy. [796.34]

12271 Vizard, Frank, ed. *Why a Curveball Curves: The Incredible Science of Sports* (9–12). 2008, Hearst $19.95 (978-1-58816-475-9). This title throws readers a pleasant curve as they discover the intimate relationship between physics and a variety of popular sports. (Rev: BL 4/1/08) [613.7]

12272 Willker, Joshua D. G. *Everything You Need to Know About the Dangers of Sports Gambling* (5–10). Series: Need to Know Library. 2000, Rosen LB $27.95 (978-0-8239-3229-0). This brief, well-written book surveys the world of gambling on sports, its legal and illegal aspects, and how it has ruined the careers of many fine athletes. (Rev: BL 1/1–15/01) [796]

12273 Woods, Karl Morrow. *The Sports Success Book: The Athlete's Guide to Sports Achievement* (9–12). 1985, Copperfield $17.95 (978-0-933857-00-1); paper $12.95 (978-0-933857-01-8). A guide to becoming a successful athlete from junior high through the Olympics to the pros. (Rev: BL 10/15/85; SLJ 4/86; VOYA 12/85) [796]

Automobile Racing

12274 Gifford, Clive. *Racing: The Ultimate Motorsports Encyclopedia* (6–12). 2006, Kingfisher $19.95 (978-0-7534-6040-5). Racing of all sorts — from motorbikes to stock cars, rally cars, and Formula One — is covered in this well-illustrated volume that also profiles 60 famous drivers. (Rev: SLJ 5/07) [796.72092]

12275 Golenbock, Peter. *American Zoom: Stock Car Racing — from the Dirt Tracks to Daytona* (9–12). 1993, Macmillan $23.00 (978-0-02-544615-1). Presents the history of the sport from the mouths of drivers, mechanics, crew chiefs, and promoters. (Rev: BL 9/15/93*) [796.7]

12276 Latford, Bob. *A Celebration of 50 Years of NASCAR: Half a Century of High-Speed Drama* (9–12). 1999, Carlton $24.95 (978-1-85868-796-4). A decade-by-decade history of the past 50 years of auto racing, with profiles of top drivers. [796.72]

12277 Leslie-Pelecky, Diandra. *The Physics of NASCAR: How to Make Steel + Gas + Rubber = Speed* (9–12). 2008, Dutton $25.95 (978-0-525-95053-0). This volume provides NASCAR fans with painless physics lessons. (Rev: BL 3/1/08) [796.7201]

12278 McCarthy, Todd. *Fast Women: The Legendary Ladies of Racing* (10–12). 2007, Miramax $23.95 (978-1-4013-5202-8). A look at the many women who raced cars from the late 19th century to the 1950s. (Rev: BL 5/1/07) [796.72]

12279 Menzer, Joe. *The Wildest Ride: A History of NASCAR (or, How a Bunch of Good Ol' Boys Built a Billion-Dollar Industry Out of Wrecking Cars)* (9–12). 2001, Simon & Schuster paper $14.00 (978-0-7432-2625-7). A highly entertaining history of NASCAR from the founding France family to the present. (Rev: BL 7/01) [796.72]

12280 Thompson, Neal. *Driving with the Devil: Southern Moonshine, Detroit Wheels, and the Birth of NASCAR* (9–12). 2006, Crown $25.00 (978-1-4000-8225-4). Even diehard NASCAR fans may be unaware that the sport's origins are connected to bootlegging, and they will enjoy this account of its earliest days. (Rev: BL 9/1/06) [796.720975]

Baseball

12281 Adair, Robert Kemp. *The Physics of Baseball.* 2nd ed. (10–12). 1994, HarperPerennial paper $12.00 (978-0-06-095047-7). A fascinating account that links science to the moves, plays, and maneuvers of baseball. [796.357]

12282 Asinof, Eliot. *Eight Men Out* (9–12). 1981, Holtzman $24.95 (978-0-941372-00-8); paper $14.00 (978-0-8050-0346-8). The story of a shameful incident in baseball history when eight Chicago White Sox players in 1919 were bribed into losing the World Series. [796.357]

12283 Bissinger, Buzz. *Three Nights in August: Strategy, Heartbreak, and Joy Inside the Heart of a Manager* (8–12). 2005, Houghton Mifflin $25.00 (978-0-618-40544-2). Bissinger dissects a three-game August 2003 series between baseball's St. Louis Cardinals and Chicago Cubs. (Rev: BL 3/1/05) [796.357]

12284 Boxerman, Burton A., and Benita W. Boxerman. *Jews and Baseball: Volume 1, Entering the American Mainstream, 1871-1948* (9–12). 2006, McFarland $39.95 (978-0-7864-2828-1). A history of Jewish participation in baseball up to the late 1940s, with material on players, owners, managers, umpires, sportswriters, and others. (Rev: SLJ 4/07) [796.357]

12285 Carroll, Will. *The Juice: The Real Story of Baseball's Drug Problems* (9–12). 2005, Ivan R. Dee $24.95 (978-1-56663-668-1). Carroll, a columnist for the online Baseball Prospectus, dissects the growing controversy over the use of performance enhancing drugs by professional baseball players. (Rev: SLJ 11/05)

12286 Castle, George. *Throwbacks: Old-School Baseball Players of Today's Game* (10–12). 2003, Brassey's $26.95 (978-1-57488-453-1). Castle's profiles current players who, he believes, embody the best of the qualities esteemed in baseball players of old. (Rev: BL 7/03) [796.357]

12287 Dawidoff, Nicholas. *Baseball: A Literary Anthology* (9–12). 2002, Library of America $35.00 (978-1-931082-09-9). Well-known writers including Damon Runyon, Ring Lardner, James Thurber, and Jacques Barzun are included in this anthology of writings about baseball. (Rev: BL 2/15/02) [810.8]

12288 Dickson, Paul. *The Hidden Language of Baseball: How Signs and Sign Stealing Have Influenced the Course of Our National Pastime* (10–12). 2003, Walker $22.00 (978-0-8027-1392-6). A fascinating study of the mysterious world of baseball signs — the signals by which a team's players communicate with each other — and their impact on the game's development. (Rev: BL 5/15/03) [796.357]

12289 Dixon, Phil, and Patrick J. Hannigan. *The Negro Baseball Leagues: A Photographic History* (9–12). 1992, Amereon $39.95 (978-0-8488-0425-1). Celebrates the defunct Negro Baseball Leagues with anecdotes, newspaper accounts, and hundreds of photographs. (Rev: BL 10/1/92) [796.357]

12290 Forker, Dom. *Baseball Brain Teasers* (7–12). 1986, Sterling paper $6.95 (978-0-8069-6284-9). A baseball trivia book in which baseball situations are described and questions are asked about them. (Rev: SLJ 12/86) [796.357]

12291 Hample, Zack. *The Baseball: Stunts, Scandals, and Secrets Beneath the Stitches* (10–12). Illus. 2011, Vintage paper $14.95 (978-03074754-5-9). Hample, a veteran collector of baseballs — many of them caught during games — shares personal anecdotes, tidbits about famous catches, tips on the best ways to catch a foul ball, and much more in this rousing tribute to the baseball. (Rev: BL 3/1–15/11) [796.357]

12292 Hample, Zack. *Watching Baseball Smarter: A Professional Fan's Guide for Beginners, Semi-Experts, and Deeply Serious Geeks* (8–12). 2007, Vintage paper $13.95 (978-0-307-28032-9). A guide to all aspects of baseball, from management to technique to trivia. (Rev: BL 2/1/07) [796.357]

12293 Irvin, Monte, and Phil Pepe. *Few and Chosen: Defining Negro League Greatness* (10–12). 2007, Triumph $25.95 (978-1-57243-855-2). Irvin, a former Negro League star, and his coauthor look at the players and other key personnel of the Negro Leagues and name the best players for each position in a team. (Rev: BL 2/1/07) [796.357]

12294 Kreidler, Mark. *Six Good Innings: How One Small Town Became a Little League Giant* (10–12). 2008, HarperCollins $25.95 (978-006147357-9). Sportswriter Kreidler offers a detailed yet compelling story about a hardworking team and the supportive parents and town that helped them achieve so much. ℮ (Rev: BL 9/1/08*) [796.357]

12295 Lewis, Michael. *Moneyball: The Art of Winning an Unfair Game* (10–12). 2003, Norton $24.95 (978-0-393-05765-2). In this fascinating study of Major League Baseball's Oakland Athletics, the author explores the ways in which a smaller team can use its wits to compete with the larger clubs for which money is no object. (Rev: BL 6/1–15/03) [796.357]

12296 McGuire, Mark, and Michael Sean Gormley. *The 100 Greatest Baseball Players of the 20th Century Ranked* (8–12). 2000, McFarland $30.00 (978-0-7864-0914-3). Using a variety of measuring techniques, the 100 greatest baseball players are ranked by importance. [796.357]

12297 Roeper, Richard. *Sox and the City: A Fan's Love Affair with the White Sox from the Heartbreak of '67 to the Wizards of Oz* (10–12). 2006, Chicago Review $19.95 (978-1-55652-650-3). Full of interesting anecdotes and trivia, this is the story of a fan's lasting devotion to a mostly losing team. (Rev: SLJ 8/06)

12298 Rubin, Adam. *Pedro, Carlos, and Omar: A Season in the Big Apple with "Los Mets"* (9–12). 2006, Lyons $22.95 (978-1-59228-875-5). Rubin explores Omar Minaya's first season as general manager of the New York Mets. (Rev: BL 3/15/06) [796.357]

12299 Schenin, Richard. *Field of Screams: The Dark Underside of America's National Pastime* (9–12). 1994, Norton paper $14.95 (978-0-393-31138-9). A chronologically arranged collection of items from the "underside" of baseball history. (Rev: BL 3/15/94) [796.357]

12300 Schmidt, Mike, and Rob Ellis. *The Mike Schmidt Study: Hitting Theory, Skills and Techniques* (9–12). 1994, McGriff & Bell $22.95 (978-0-9634609-1-2); paper $18.95 (978-0-9634609-2-9). Designed to help coaches teach Little Leaguers how to hit, Schmidt explains the three major systems and the mental aspects involved. (Rev: BL 12/15/93) [796.35726]

12301 Simmons, Bill. *Now I Can Die in Peace: How ESPN's Sports Guy Found Salvation, with a Little Help from Buckner, Pedro, Shawshank and the 2004 Red Sox* (11–12). 2005, Hyperion $24.95 (978-1-933060-05-7). The long and winding Red Sox road to a championship season in 2004 is described with humor and lots of authentically strong language; for mature teens. [796.357]

12302 Skipper, John C. *Umpires: Classic Baseball Stories from the Men Who Made the Calls* (8–12). 1997, McFarland paper $29.95 (978-0-7864-0364-6). Great, memorable moments in the careers of 19 umpires. (Rev: VOYA 12/97) [796.323]

12303 Stewart, John. *The Baseball Clinic: Skills and Drills for Better Baseball: A Handbook for Players and Coaches* (6–10). 1999, Burford paper $12.95 (978-1-58080-073-0). Written by a major league scout, this book contains useful tips for young baseball players in the areas of pitching, fielding, hitting, base running, and catching. (Rev: SLJ 7/99) [796.357]

12304 Stout, Glenn, and Richard A. Johnson. *The Cubs: The Complete Story of Chicago Cubs Baseball* (9–12). 2007, Houghton Mifflin $40.00 (978-0-618-59500-6). The Cubs have maintained a loyal fan base despite their poor performance on the field since the early 20th century; this is a chronological survey of the team that once won three succeeding National League pennants. (Rev: BL 9/1/07) [796.357]

12305 Vecsey, George. *Baseball: A History of America's Favorite Game* (9–12). 2006, Modern Library $21.95 (978-0-679-64338-8). A good general introduction to the sport, written by a *New York Times* sports columnist. (Rev: BL 8/06) [796.357]

12306 Ward, Geoffrey C., and Ken Burns. *Baseball: An Illustrated History* (9–12). 1994, Knopf $60.00 (978-0-679-40459-0). A history of the game, published in conjunction with a PBS documentary, with essays, facts, and more than 500 photographs. (Rev: BL 7/94*) [796.357]

Basketball

12307 Austin, Dan. *True Fans: A Basketball Odyssey* (9–12). 2005, Lyons $19.95 (978-1-59228-779-6). A bicycle road trip across the United States with basketball as a purpose (the Basketball Hall of Fame in Springfield, Massachusetts) and a unifying theme. (Rev: BL 9/1/05) [796.323]

12308 Becker, Lisa Liberty. *Net Prospect: The Courting Process of Women's College Basketball Recruiting* (10–12). 2002, Wish paper $16.95 (978-1-930546-56-1). Useful information for high school girl basketball players who expect to make the leap to college ball. (Rev: BL 6/1–15/02) [796.323]

12309 Blais, Madeleine. *In These Girls, Hope Is Muscle* (9–12). 2008, Paw Prints $22.95 (978-1-4395-0485-7). Covers the championship season of a girls' high school basketball team; originally published in 1995. (Rev: BL 12/1/94; SLJ 11/95; VOYA 5/95) [797.323]

12310 D'Orso, Michael. *Eagle Blue: A Team, a Tribe, and a High School Basketball Season in Arctic Alaska* (9–12). 2006, Bloomsbury $23.95 (978-1-58234-623-6). D'Orso follows the fortunes of a successful high school basketball team in an isolated Alaska town over the course of the 2004-2005 season. (Rev: BL 3/1/06) [796.323]

12311 Einhorn, Eddie, and Ron Rapoport. *How March Became Madness: How The NCAA Tournament Became the Greatest Sporting Event in America* (9–12). 2006, Triumph $27.95 (978-1-57243-809-5). America is mad about March Madness — a yearly college basketball tournament that pits unlikely teams against one another — and fans will enjoy this account of how it came about and its major players. (Rev: BL 9/1/06) [796.323]

12312 Joravsky, Ben. *Hoop Dreams: A True Story of Hardship and Triumph* (8–12). 1995, Turner paper $13.95 (978-0-06-097689-7). Based on the movie documentary, this book explores the dream on inner-city kids to play in the NBA. [796.323]

12313 Klein, Leigh, and Matt Masiero, eds. *My Favorite Moves: Shooting Like the Stars* (6–12). Series: Five Star Basketball. 2003, Wish paper $12.95 (978-1-930546-58-5). Best for readers already familiar with the game, this drill book includes advice from five professional women players. Also use *My Favorite Moves: Making the Big Plays* (2003). (Rev: SLJ 1/04) [796.323]

12314 Lazenby, Roland. *The Show: The Inside Story of the Spectacular Los Angeles Lakers in the Words of Those Who Lived It* (8–12). 2006, McGraw-Hill $27.95 (978-0-07-143034-0). This excellent volume traces the NBA team's fortunes from its inauspicious beginnings in Minneapolis in the early 1950s through its most recent string of championships. (Rev: BL 11/15/05) [796.323]

12315 Lieberman-Cline, Nancy, and Robin Roberts. *Basketball for Women* (7–12). 1995, Kinetics paper $19.95 (978-0-87322-610-3). After a brief history of women's basketball, Lieberman-Cline, who has played in college, Olympics, and professional women's basketball, discusses the commitment required of a serious basketball player, how to formulate a plan for skill development, the recruitment process, and other concerns, and devotes seven chapters to more than 100 drill exercises. (Rev: VOYA 6/96) [796.323]

12316 Merlino, Doug. *The Hustle: One Team and Ten Lives in Black and White* (9–12). Illus. 2011, Bloomsbury $26 (978-160819215-1). Ten years afterward, a member of a Seattle basketball team that mixed privileged white kids with poor black ones revisits the lives of the others, who range from a hedge fund manager and a prosecutor to a victim of murder. ⌒ **e** (Rev: BL 12/1–15/10) [796.323]

12317 O'Connor, Ian. *The Jump: Sebastian Telfair and the High Stakes Business of High School Ball* (9–12). 2005, Rodale $23.95 (978-1-59486-107-9). The harrowing journey of Sebastian Telfair from the high school basketball court to the heady atmosphere of the NBA, a story that shines a poor light on many. (Rev: BL 3/1/05) [796.323]

12318 Palmer, Chris. *Streetball: All the Ballers, Moves, Slams, and Shine* (8–12). 2004, Harper Resource paper $16.95 (978-0-06-072444-3). A celebration of urban playground basketball and the talented young people who enjoy it. (Rev: BL 11/15/04) [796.323]

12319 Peavy, Linda, and Ursula Smith. *Full-Court Quest: The Girls from Fort Shaw Indian School, Basketball Champions of the World* (10–12). Illus. 2008, Univ. of Oklahoma $29.95 (978-080613973-9). Written by two well-known historians, this is an interesting and lively account of the Native American girls' basketball team that won the title of World Champions in 1904. (Rev: BL 9/1/08; SLJ 1/09) [796.323]

12320 Shirley, Paul. *Can I Keep My Jersey? 11 Teams, 6 Years, 5 Countries, and My So-Called Career as a Professional Basketball Player* (9–12). 2007, Villard $23.95 (978-0-345-49136-7). Shirley recounts with humor his travels and experiences as a pro hoops player. (Rev: BL 5/1/07) [796.323]

12321 Simmons, Bill. *The Book of Basketball: The NBA According to the Sports Guy* (10–12). Illus. 2009, Ballantine $30 (978-034551176-8). ESPN commentator Simmons looks back on the history of the NBA and chronicles his own personal fandom with a funny, self-deprecating tone. (Rev: BL 11/15/09) [796.323]

12322 Swidey, Neil. *The Assist: Hoops, Hope, and the Game of Their Lives* (9–12). 2008, Public Affairs $26.00 (978-1-58648-469-9). Coach Jack O'Brien of

Charlestown High School in Boston has great success in using basketball not only to win successive state championships but also to send players from deprived backgrounds on to college. (Rev: BL 11/15/07; SLJ 2/08) [796.323]

12323 Thomas, Rob. *They Cleared the Lane: The NBA's Black Pioneers* (10–12). 2002, Univ. of Nebraska $29.95 (978-0-8032-4437-5). A historical overview of the integration of professional basketball. (Rev: BL 3/15/02) [796.323]

12324 Weatherspoon, Teresa. *Teresa Weatherspoon's Basketball for Girls* (6–10). 1999, Wiley paper $15.95 (978-0-471-31784-5). This manual, by the famous basketball star and Olympic gold medalist, gives wonderful, practical information about playing the game and becoming a healthy, happy athlete. (Rev: BL 7/99; SLJ 8/99) [796.323]

12325 Yancey, Diane. *Basketball* (5–10). Series: Science Behind Sports. 2011, Gale/Lucent LB $33.45 (978-1-4205-0293-0). This volume looks at all aspects of the sport, focusing in particular on the physics involved and the mental attitude required for success. e (Rev: SLJ 9/1/11) [796.3]

Bicycling, Motorcycling, etc.

12326 Burke, Edmund R., and Ed Pavelka. *The Complete Book of Long-Distance Cycling: Build the Strength, Skills, and Confidence to Ride as Far as You Want* (10–12). 2000, Rodale paper $19.95 (978-1-57954-199-6). This well-organized book covers the basics — training, equipment, and safety — plus other topics relating to biking, such as nutrition and bike technology. (Rev: BL 9/1/00) [613.7]

12327 Gibb, Evelyn McDaniel. *Two Wheels North: Bicycling the West Coast in 1909* (10–12). 2000, Oregon State Univ. $15.95 (978-0-87071-485-6). The true story of the 1,000 mile, 54-day bicycle trip the author's father took from Santa Rosa, California, to Seattle in 1909. (Rev: BL 11/15/00) [917.904]

12328 Oliver, Peter. *Bicycling: Touring and Mountain Bike Basics* (9–12). Series: Trailside Guide. 1995, Norton $18.95 (978-0-393-31337-6). This mountain bike manual covers topics like equipment, clothing, safety, techniques, maintenance, and organizations. [796.6]

12329 Pavelka, Ed. *Bicycling Magazine's Basic Maintenance and Repair: Simple Techniques to Make Your Bike Ride Better and Last Longer* (8–12). 1999, Rodale paper $9.99 (978-1-57954-170-5). This book clearly explains how to maintain and repair a bicycle so it remains in tip-top condition. [629.28]

12330 Robinson, Rocky. *Flat Out: The Race for the Motorcycle World Land Speed Record* (9–12). 2007,

Motorbooks $25.95 (978-0-7603-3163-7). This is a story of a determined effort to win the world land speed record, which paid off eventually in 2006 (at 342.797 miles per hour) but only held for two days. (Rev: BL 8/07) [796.75]

12331 Sidwells, Chris. *Complete Bike Book* (8–12). 2005, DK paper $17.95 (978-0-7566-1427-0). History, technology, training, and maintenance are all covered in this volume for all levels of riders that also includes a stunning section of color photographs. (Rev: BL 9/1/05) [796.6]

12332 Turner, Chérie. *Marathon Cycling* (7–10). Series: Ultra Sports. 2002, Rosen LB $26.50 (978-0-8239-3553-6). Long-distance cycling competitions are described with material on tips and tricks, safety, gear, and racing events. (Rev: BL 9/1/02; SLJ 9/02) [796.6]

Boxing and Wrestling

12333 Douglas, Bobby. *Take It to the Mat* (9–12). 1993, Sigler paper $15.95 (978-0-9635812-0-4). U.S. Olympic wrestler/coach Douglas presents an introductory guide to competitive wrestling, with photographs of holds and escapes, as well as diet guidelines. (Rev: BL 9/15/93) [796.8]

12334 Heenan, Bobby, and Steve Anderson. *Bobby the Brain: Wrestling's Bad Boy Tells All* (10–12). 2002, Triumph $19.95 (978-1-57243-465-3). Longtime professional wrestler Bobby "Bobby the Brain" Heenan muses entertaining on his career, his personal life, and the world of wrestling. (Rev: BL 9/1/02) [796.812]

12335 Jarman, Tom, and Reid Hanley. *Wrestling for Beginners* (7–12). 1983, Contemporary paper $15.95 (978-0-8092-5656-3). From a history of wrestling, this book moves on to skills, strategies, moves, and holds. [796.8]

12336 Kreidler, Mark. *Four Days to Glory: Wrestling with the Soul of the American Heartland* (9–12). 2007, HarperCollins $24.95 (978-0-06-082318-4). For wrestling and other sports fans, this is a detailed story of two dedicated Iowa competitors who are vying for multiple state titles. (Rev: BL 12/15/06; SLJ 5/07) [796.81]

Camping, Hiking, Backpacking, and Mountaineering

12337 Berger, Karen. *Hiking and Backpacking: A Complete Guide* (8–12). Series: Trailside Guide. 1995, Norton paper $18.95 (978-0-393-31334-5). A complete guide to outdoor hiking and backpacking with material on techniques, equipment, safety, camping, and related topics. [796.51]

12338 Bonatti, Walter. *The Mountains of My Life* (10–12). Trans. by Robert Marshall. 2001, Random House paper $14.95 (978-0-375-75640-5). What mountain climbing has meant to this Italian mountaineer and his part in the conquest of K2, the world's second-highest mountain, in 1954 are the subjects of this adventure-filled memoir. (Rev: BL 2/15/01) [796.5]

12339 Boukreev, Anatoli. *Above the Clouds: The Diaries of a High-Altitude Mountaineer* (9–12). 2001, St. Martin's $27.95 (978-0-312-26970-8). The diary of the mountaineer who disappeared in a Himalayan avalanche in 1997 and his career scaling mountains of peaks 8,000 meters and more. (Rev: BL 10/1/01) [796.52]

12340 Brunelle, Lynn. *Camp Out! The Ultimate Kids' Guide* (5–12). Illus. by Brian Biggs and Elara Tanguy. 2007, Workman paper $11.95 (978-0-7611-4122-8). This volume is packed with information about camping out, covering equipment, planning, and skills, and offering games, activities, recipes, nature tips, and so forth. (Rev: SLJ 2/08)

12341 Cook, Charles. *The Essential Guide to Hiking in the United States* (9–12). 1991, Michael Kesend paper $19.95 (978-0-935576-41-2). Contains information on such hiking essentials as shoes, clothing, safety, and the best areas for hiking and the trails in each state. (Rev: BL 12/1/91) [996.5]

12342 Krakauer, Jon. *Into Thin Air: A Personal Account of the Mt. Everest Disaster* (10–12). 1997, Villard $24.95 (978-0-679-45752-7). A history of Mount Everest expeditions is intertwined with the disastrous expedition the author was a part of, during which five members were killed by a hurricane-strength blizzard. (Rev: BL 4/1/97; SLJ 11/97) [796.5]

12343 Manning, Harvey. *Backpacking One Step at a Time*. Rev. ed. (9–12). 1986, Random House paper $15.00 (978-0-394-72939-8). In addition to information on equipment and techniques, this book tells how to get the most enjoyment possible out of backpacking. (Rev: SLJ 9/86; VOYA 8/86) [796.5]

12344 Mellor, Don. *American Rock: Region, Rock, and Culture in American Rock Climbing* (9–12). 2001, Countryman $27.95 (978-0-88150-428-6). Written by a veteran rock climber and guide, this book on rock climbing is "not about conquering the mountain, it's about becoming part of the mountain." (Rev: BL 9/1/01) [796,52]

12345 Purnell, Karl H. *A Mountain Too Far: A Father's Search for Meaning in the Climbing Death of His Son* (9–12). 2001, New Horizon $24.95 (978-0-88282-204-4). Torn with grief over the death of his son in a climbing accident, a father takes up mountaineering and ac-

complishes what his son perished trying to do. (Rev: BL 4/1/01) [796.52]

12346 Venables, Stephen. *Voices from the Mountains: 40 True-Life Stories of Unforgettable Adventure, Drama, and Human Endurance* (8–12). 2006, Reader's Digest $26.95 (978-0-7621-0810-7). Eye-catching photographs add to these tales of mountain climbing, stories of determination and courage ranging from 1889 to 2005. (Rev: BL 2/1/07; SLJ 3/07) [796.552]

12347 Viesturs, Ed, and David Roberts. *No Shortcuts to the Top: Climbing the World's 14 Highest Peaks* (9–12). 2006, Broadway $23.95 (978-0-7679-2470-2). The world's fourteen highest peaks — in Nepal, Pakistan, and Tibet — are the author's passion and challenge, and in this book he describes the danger, thrill, and exhilaration of climbing them. (Rev: BL 9/1/06) [796.323]

12348 Willis, Clint, ed. *Climb: Stories of Survival from Rock, Snow, and Ice* (10–12). 2000, Thunder's Mouth paper $16.95 (978-1-56025-250-4). This collection of true survival stories explores the phenomenon of risk-taking in outdoor sports like mountain climbing and the motivation behind getting involved in these activities. (Rev: BL 2/15/00) [796.52]

Chess, Checkers, and Other Board and Card Games

12349 Frey, Richard. *According to Hoyle* (9–12). 1985, Fawcett paper $5.99 (978-0-449-21112-0). This handbook supplies instructions, rules, and regulations for over 200 games. [795.4]

12350 Gibson, Walter B. *Hoyle's Modern Encyclopedia of Card Games: Rules of All the Basic Games and Popular Variations* (10–12). 1974, Dolphin Books paper $12.95 (978-0-385-07680-7). The master of "according to Hoyle" fame describes a number of card games including poker and solitaire. [795.4]

12351 Sheinwold, Alfred. *101 Best Family Card Games* (5–12). 1993, Sterling paper $5.95 (978-0-8069-8635-7). A book filled with games enjoyed by many age groups. (Rev: BL 2/15/93) [795.4]

12352 Shenk, David. *The Immortal Game: A History of Chess; or, How 32 Carved Pieces on a Board Illuminated Our Understanding of War, Art, Science, and the Human Brain* (9–12). 2006, Doubleday $26.00 (978-0-385-51010-3). Can the game of chess ever be truly mastered? The author discusses the game from all angles and intersperses an analysis of an 1851 match that has been called "the immortal game." (Rev: BL 9/1/06) [794.109]

Fishing and Hunting

12353 Capstick, Peter Hathaway. *Sands of Silence* (9–12). 1991, St. Martin's $35.00 (978-0-312-06459-4). The author muses on life and death in the wild in this story of elephant hunting near the edge of the African Kalahari desert, with an in-depth report on the lives of the region's natives. (Rev: BL 10/15/91) [799.2]

12354 Mason, Bill. *Sports Illustrated Fly Fishing: Learn from a Master. Rev. ed.* (8–12). 1994, Sports Illustrated paper $14.95 (978-1-56800-033-6). Equipment and techniques are emphasized in this illustrated introduction to fly fishing. [799.1]

Football

12355 Anastasia, Phil. *Broken Wing, Broken Promise: A Season Inside the Philadelphia Eagles* (9–12). 1993, Camino $18.00 (978-0-940159-20-4). Reporter Anastasia chronicles the Eagles' 1992 season, including Jerome Brown's death, mistrust of coach Kotite, and the division of team loyalty between two quarterbacks. (Rev: BL 10/1/93) [796.332]

12356 Anderson, Lars. *Carlisle vs. Army: Jim Thorpe, Dwight Eisenhower, Pop Warner, and the Forgotten Story of Football's Greatest Battle* (8–12). 2007, Random House $24.95 (978-1-4000-6600-1). In 1912, the Carlisle Indian School football team, led by Jim Thorpe and coached by Pop Warner, played against the Army team, led by Dwight D. Eisenhower; the story of this exciting game is retold in historical context, with background on Thorpe's achievements, the rules of the Indian School, and other details. (Rev: BL 9/1/07) [796.332]

12357 Billick, Brian, and Michael MacCambridge. *More Than a Game: The Glorious Present — and the Uncertain Future — of the NFL* (10–12). 2009, Scribner $26 (978-143910918-2). Billick, former coach of the Baltimore Ravens, covers the many aspects of coaching in a straightforward style and with reference to the methods of many other NFL coaches. (Rev: BL 9/09) [796.332.]

12358 Borowski, Greg. *First and Long: A Black School, a White School and Their Season of Dreams* (9–12). 2004, Badger $25.00 (978-1-932542-02-8). The story of how a white suburban school and a black Catholic city school joined forces in 2001 to form a joint football team. (Rev: BL 2/15/04) [796.332]

12359 Brown, Scott, and Sam Carchidi. *Miracle in the Making: The Adam Taliaferro Story* (9–12). 2001, Triumph paper $16.95 (978-1-57243-422-6). When he was severely injured in a football game and told he would never walk again, Adam Taliaferro and his medical team accomplished a miracle — not only did he walk again, he played football again. (Rev: BL 9/1/01) [362.4]

12360 Dent, Jim. *Twelve Mighty Orphans* (9–12). 2007, Thomas Dunne $24.95 (978-0-312-30872-8). This is an inspiring story of a depression-era Texas high-school football team made up of low-weight orphan players (hence their name, the "Mighty Mites") with little resources other than an innovative coach, Rusty Russell, who led them to three state semifinal games and a championship game. (Rev: BL 7/07) [796.332]

12361 Drape, Joe. *Our Boys: A Perfect Season on the Plains with the Smith Center Redmen* (10–12). 2009, Times $25 (978-080508890-8). Drape tells the story of a Kansas high school football team's amazing successes. (Rev: BL 9/09) [796.33]

12362 Emmanuel, Greg. *The 100-Yard War: Inside the 100-Year-Old Michigan-Ohio State Football Rivalry* (9–12). 2004, Wiley $32.50 (978-0-471-67552-5). Emmanuel explores the football rivalry between Ohio State University and the University of Michigan, still going strong after more than a century. (Rev: BL 9/1/04) [790.332]

12363 Fatsis, Stefan. *A Few Seconds of Panic: A 5-Foot-8, 170-Pound, 43-Year-Old Sportswriter Plays in the NFL* (9–12). 2008, Penguin $25.95 (978-1-59420-178-3). Though out of shape and older than most players, sportswriter Fatsis tries out for the Denver Broncos in this entertaining, behind-the-scenes experiment in participatory journalism. ∩ (Rev: BL 6/1–15/08) [070.44]

12364 Freedman, Lew. *Thunder on the Tundra: Football Above the Arctic Circle* (9–12). Illus. 2008, Alaska Northwest paper $14.95 (978-088240742-5). Despite many obstacles, a high school superintendent of a remote Alaskan town starts a football program with the hope of lowering teenage substance abuse and keeping the kids in school. (Rev: BL 9/1/08; SLJ 11/1/08) [796.332]

12365 Hopkins, Theron. *The 80-Yard Run: A Twenty-Week, Coast-to-Coast Quest for the Heart of High School Football* (10–12). 2008, Skyhorse $24.95 (978-160239284-7). Hopkins taught high school English and coached football before embarking on a journey across America to get the inside story about high school football programs. (Rev: BL 9/1/08) [796.332]

12366 Jennings, Jay. *Carry the Rock: Race, Football, and the Soul of an American City* (10–12). Illus. 2010, Rodale $25.99 (978-160529637-1). Football and civil rights are interwoven in this account of the 2007 football season at Central High School in Little Rock, Arkansas, where desegregation was a hot issue 50 years earlier. ℯ (Rev: BL 9/1–15/10) [796.332]

12367 Longman, Jere. *The Hurricanes: One High School Team's Homecoming after Katrina* (10–12). 2008, PublicAffairs $26.00 (978-158648673-0). South

Plaquemines High School and its Hurricanes football team emerge from the wreckage caused by Katrina with a strong spirit and the ability to inspire. **e** (Rev: BL 9/1/08; SLJ 11/08) [796.332]

12368 McDonnell, Chris, ed. *The Football Game I'll Never Forget: 100 NFL Stars' Stories* (8–12). 2004, Firefly paper $24.95 (978-1-55297-850-4). One hundred football stars talk about the games they remember. (Rev: BL 9/1/04; VOYA 4/05) [796.332]

12369 Mooney, Chuck. *The Recruiting Survival Guide* (10–12). 1991, Twenty-First Century paper $9.95 (978-0-9630239-0-2). A former college ball player explains how recruiters work and the pitfalls and rewards that await the targeted athlete. (Rev: BL 4/15/92) [796.33]

12370 Price, Christopher. *The Blueprint: How the New England Patriots Beat the System to Create the Last Great NFL Superpower* (8–12). 2007, St. Martin's $24.95 (978-0-312-36838-8). This is a compelling history of the Patriots with lots of behind-the-scenes information and interesting anecdotes. (Rev: BL 9/1/07) [796.332]

12371 Whittingham, Richard. *What Bears They Were: Chicago Bears Greats Talk About Their Teams, Their Coaches, and the Times of Their Lives* (10–12). 2002, Triumph $27.95 (978-1-57243-482-0). A fascinating collection of memories and anecdotes about this famous team, its founder-coach George Halas, and stars, including Dick Butkus and Mike Singletary. (Rev: BL 9/1/02) [796.332]

Golf

12372 Hogan, Ben. *Power Golf* (10–12). 1990, Pocket paper $6.50 (978-0-671-72905-9). Expert advice for people already familiar with the basics of golf. [796.352]

12373 McDaniel, Pete. *Uneven Lies: The Heroic Story of African-Americans in Golf* (9–12). 2001, American Golfer $50.00 (978-1-888531-36-7). An attractively illustrated volume that traces the roles played by African Americans in the history of golf, including the story of George Grant who invented the golf tee. (Rev: BL 2/15/01) [796.353]

12374 Sampson, Curt. *Chasing Tiger* (10–12). 2002, Simon & Schuster $26.00 (978-0-7432-4212-7). Tiger Woods's championship season in 2001 is seen largely through the eyes of the golfer's rivals. (Rev: BL 6/1–15/02) [796.352]

12375 Stout, Glenn, ed. *Chasing Tiger: A Tiger Woods Reader* (9–12). 2002, Da Capo paper $15.00 (978-0-306-81124-1). This collection of original newspaper and magazine articles chronicles Woods's dazzling career from 1991 to 2001. (Rev: BL 4/15/02) [796.357]

Gymnastics

12376 McIntosh, J. S. *Gymnastics* (7–10). Illus. Series: Getting the Edge: Conditioning, Injuries, and Legal and Illicit Drugs. 2010, Mason Crest LB $24.95 (978-142221734-4). Mental and physical preparation are a focus of this book that also covers injuries, nutrition and supplements, and the dangers of performance-enhancing drugs. (Rev: BL 12/15/10) [796.44]

12377 Schwartz, Heather E. *Gymnastics* (7–10). Illus. Series: Science Behind Sports. 2011, Gale/Lucent LB $33.45 (978-142050277-0). After a history of gymnastics, this useful book looks at training and conditioning, explores basic scientific principles involved in gymnastics movements, discusses injuries and diet and exercise, and introduces the importance of competitors' psychological approach. (Rev: BL 10/1/11; SLJ 9/1/11) [796.4]

Hockey

12378 Dunn, Tricia, et al. *Gold Medal Ice Hockey for Women and Girls* (9–12). 1999, National Bk. Network $15.95 (978-1-886284-37-1). This fine book on ice hockey for women includes material on rules, equipment, skills, and the fun of the game. [796.962]

12379 Hornby, Lance, ed. *Hockey Dynasties: Blue Lines and Bloodlines* (10–12). 2003, Firefly $40.00 (978-1-55297-676-0). Action photographs supplement this fascinating study of hockey's first families, including the Bentleys, Espositos, Howes, Hulls, Richards, and Sutters. (Rev: BL 2/1/03) [796.962]

12380 McDonnell, Chris, ed. *The Game I'll Never Forget: 100 Hockey Stars' Stories* (10–12). 2002, Firefly paper $24.95 (978-1-55297-604-3). Excellent for browsing, this is a collection of hockey memories. (Rev: BL 9/15/02) [796.962]

12381 McKinley, Michael. *Hockey: A People's History* (9–12). 2006, McClelland & Stewart $45.00 (978-0-7710-5769-4). Focusing on Canadian hockey, this is a well-illustrated companion to a Canadian TV series on the sport and goes into its history and development before discussing the most popular teams of today. (Rev: BL 9/1/06) [796.96]

12382 Vanderhoof, Gabrielle. *Hockey* (7–10). Illus. Series: Getting the Edge: Conditioning, Injuries, and Legal and Illicit Drugs. 2010, Mason Crest LB $24.95 (978-142221735-1). Mental and physical preparation are a focus of this book that also covers injuries, nutrition and supplements, and the dangers of performance-enhancing drugs. (Rev: BL 12/15/10) [796.355]

12383 Wolfe, Bernie, and Mitch Henkin. *How to Watch Ice Hockey* (9–12). 1985, National paper $9.95 (978-0-915765-09-6). All of the rules of a hockey match are carefully explained plus a description of each position and the kinds of action one can expect at a typical game. (Rev: BL 12/15/85) [796.96]

Horse Racing and Horsemanship

12384 Best, David Grant. *Portrait of a Racetrack: A Behind the Scenes Look at a Racetrack Community* (9–12). 1992, Best Editions paper $24.95 (978-0-9634241-0-5). A black-and-white photoessay featuring the horses, jockeys, grooms, and trainers at a Seattle racetrack. (Rev: BL 12/1/92*) [798.4]

12385 Hillenbrand, Laura. *Seabiscuit: An American Legend* (10–12). 2001, Random House $24.95 (978-0-375-50291-0). This highly acclaimed book, not only tells the rags-to-riches story of this great racehorse but also highlights the lives of those people connected with him. (Rev: BL 1/1–15/01; SLJ 11/01) [798.4]

12386 Moates, Tom. *Discovering Natural Horsemanship: A Beginner's Odyssey* (9–12). 2006, Lyons $24.95 (978-1-59228-950-9). Communicating and empathizing with a horse is the "Better Way" to train these graceful animals, according to the author. (Rev: BL 9/1/06) [798.2]

Ice Skating

12387 Jackson, Jon, and James Pereira. *On Edge: Backroom Dealing, Cocktail Scheming, Triple Axels, and How Top Skaters Get Screwed* (11–12). 2006, Thunder's Mouth $25.00 (978-1-56025-804-9). For mature skaters and fans of skating, this is a rare behind-the-scenes look at the many problems associated with this popular sport. (Rev: BL 12/15/05) [796.91]

In-Line Skating

12388 Werner, Doug. *In-Line Skater's Start-Up: A Beginner's Guide to In-Line Skating and Roller Hockey* (6–12). 1995, Tracks paper $9.95 (978-1-884654-04-6). Using many black-and-white photographs, this book is both a guide to inline skating basics for beginners and an introduction to the growing sport of roller hockey. (Rev: BL 2/1/96) [796.2]

Martial Arts

12389 Konzak, Burt. *Samurai Spirit: Ancient Wisdom for Modern Life* (6–12). 2002, Tundra paper $8.95 (978-0-88776-611-4). Martial arts are the focus of this combination of traditional tales, historical and cultural information, and advice from the author, a teacher of martial arts. (Rev: SLJ 6/03) [813]

12390 Pawlett, Ray. *The Karate Handbook* (7–12). Series: Martial Arts. 2008, Rosen LB $29.95 (978-1-4042-1394-4). The basics about karate as well as its history and philosophy, accompanied by many helpful photographs. (Rev: BL 4/1/08) [796.815]

12391 Tegner, Bruce. *Bruce Tegner's Complete Book of Jujitsu* (7–12). 1978, Thor paper $14.00 (978-0-87407-027-9). A master in the martial arts introduces this ancient Japanese form of self-defense and gives basic information on stances and routines. [796.8]

12392 Tegner, Bruce. *Bruce Tegner's Complete Book of Self-Defense* (7–12). 1975, Thor paper $14.00 (978-0-87407-030-9). A basic primer on ways to defend oneself including hand blows and restraints. [796.8]

12393 Tegner, Bruce. *Karate: Beginner to Black Belt* (7–12). 1982, Thor paper $14.00 (978-0-87407-040-8). Techniques for both the novice and the experienced practitioner are explained in this account that stresses safety and fitness. [796.8]

12394 Tegner, Bruce, and Alice McGrath. *Self-Defense and Assault Prevention for Girls and Women* (7–12). 1977, Thor paper $10.00 (978-0-87407-026-2). Various defensive and offensive techniques are introduced in situations where they would be appropriate. [796.8]

12395 Tegner, Bruce, and Alice McGrath. *Solo Forms of Karate, Tai Chi, Aikido and Kung Fu* (9–12). 1981, Thor paper $10.00 (978-0-87407-034-7). Routines are described in copious pictures plus text that emphasize exercise and good training. [796.8]

Olympic Games

12396 Coffey, Wayne. *The Boys of Winter: The Untold Story of a Coach, a Dream, and the 1980 U.S. Olympic Hockey Team* (8–12). 2005, Crown $23.95 (978-1-4000-4765-9). In this inspiring look back at the 1980 Winter Olympics victory of the U.S. men's hockey team, sportswriter Coffey introduces readers to the players and coach who pulled off this miracle on ice. (Rev: BL 11/15/04; SLJ 5/05) [796.962]

12397 Wallechinsky, David. *The Complete Book of the Winter Olympics* (9–12). 2001, Overlook $25.95 (978-1-58567-195-3); paper $15.95 (978-1-58567-185-4).

This account provides information and statistics for every one of the winter Olympic games from 1924 on. [796.98]

Running and Jogging

12398 Barrios, Dagny Scott. *Runner's World Complete Guide to Trail Running* (10–12). 2003, Rodale paper $19.95 (978-1-57954-466-9). This comprehensive guide to the sport of trail running is loaded with solid information about gear, training, and technique. (Rev: BL 4/1/03) [796.42]

12399 Brant, John. *Duel in the Sun: Alberto Salazar, Dick Beardsley, and America's Greatest Marathon* (9–12). 2006, Rodale $22.95 (978-1-59486-262-5). The story of the exciting 1982 Boston Marathon and the fates of the two runners who finished within seconds of each other. (Rev: BL 2/15/06) [796.42]

12400 Hayhurst, Chris. *Ultra Marathon Running* (7–10). Series: Ultra Sports. 2002, Rosen LB $26.50 (978-0-8239-3557-4). This work looks at different long running races, the athletes that engage in this sport, and the mind-boggling distances they run. (Rev: BL 9/1/02; SLJ 9/02) [796.4]

12401 Lear, Chris. *Sub 4:00: Alan Webb and the Quest for the Fastest Mile* (10–12). 2003, Rodale $22.95 (978-1-57954-746-2). This is an absorbing account that follows University of Michigan distance runners — led by Alan Webb, high school record holder for the mile — through a complete season. (Rev: BL 8/03) [796.42]

12402 Robbins, Liz. *A Race Like No Other: 26.2 Miles Through the Streets of New York* (10–12). 2008, HarperCollins $24.95 (978-006137313-8). This inside look at the New York Marathon covers the top runners, details of the course, and the many people who work behind the scenes. e (Rev: BL 9/15/08*) [796.42]

12403 Taylor, Russell. *The Looniness of the Long Distance Runner: An Unfit Londoner's Attempt to Run the New York City Marathon from Scratch* (10–12). 2002, Carlton $22.50 (978-1-85868-568-7). In hilarious detail, British journalist Taylor tells the story of his foray into the world of marathon running. (Rev: BL 10/1/02) [796]

Sailing, Boating, and Canoeing

12404 Adkins, Jan. *The Craft of Sail* (10–12). 1973, Walker paper $10.95 (978-0-8027-7214-5). A respected manual on small-boat craftsmanship. [797.1]

12405 Goodman, Di, and Ian Brodie. *Learning to Sail: The Annapolis Sailing School Guide for All Ages* (9–12). 1994, Marine paper $12.95 (978-0-07-024014-8). Provides instruction for novices on how to begin recreational sailing, including nautical jargon, safety tips, and helpful drawings. (Rev: BL 7/94) [797.1]

12406 Grant, Gordon. *Canoeing* (9–12). Series: Trailside Guide. 1997, Norton $18.95 (978-0-393-31489-2). Both beginners and advanced canoeists will find useful advice in this guide, which covers essential equipment, basic paddling strokes, safety tips, and guidelines for navigating moving water and white water. [797.1]

12407 Krauzer, Steven M. *Kayaking: Whitewater and Touring Basics* (9–12). Series: Trailside Guide. 1995, Norton $18.95 (978-0-393-31336-9). This illustrated guide to kayaking covers equipment, techniques, information sources, and safety tips. [797.1]

12408 Ray, Slim. *The Canoe Handbook: Techniques for Mastering the Sport of Canoeing* (9–12). 1992, Stackpole paper $18.95 (978-0-8117-3032-7). A handbook covering canoeing fundamentals, including paddling techniques, styles, maneuvers, design, and equipment. (Rev: BL 2/15/92) [797.1]

12409 Wurdinger, Scott, and Leslie Rapparlie. *Kayaking* (7–10). Series: Adventure Sports. 2006, Creative Education LB $21.95 (978-1-58341-397-5). Outlines the history of kayaking as well as the different types of boats, equipment used, the techniques and skills involved, competitions, and the dangers of the sport. (Rev: BL 10/15/06; SLJ 12/06) [797.122]

Skateboarding

12410 Badillo, Steve, and Doug Werner. *Skateboarding: Book of Tricks* (7–12). 2003, Tracks paper $12.95 (978-1-884654-19-0). Basic and advanced moves are well illustrated in black-and-white photographs although Badillo is shown without protective gear. (Rev: SLJ 5/04) [796.2]

12411 Badillo, Steve, and Doug Werner. *Skateboarding: Legendary Tricks* (9–12). Photos by Gavin Badillo. 2008, Tracks paper $12.95 (978-1-884654-30-5). In addition to descriptions (with photographs) of various skateboarding feats, this book includes the history of the trick and information on its inventor. (Rev: SLJ 7/08) [796.2]

12412 Goodfellow, Evan. *Skateboarding: Ramp Tricks* (9–12). Photos by Tadashi Yamaoda. 2006, Tracks paper $12.95 (978-1-884654-26-8). Exciting and impressive ramp tricks are explained, with photographs for clarity. Readers will also learn a little about the history and stars of the sport. (Rev: SLJ 10/06)

12413 Stutt, Ryan. *The Skateboarding Field Manual* (7–12). 2009, Firefly $29.95 (978-1-55407-467-9); paper $19.95 (978-1-55407-362-7). Stutt focuses on various skateboarding tricks and skills in this irreverent, nicely illustrated book; safety warnings are included, but are not prominent. (Rev: SLJ 6/1/09) [796.22]

Skiing and Snowboarding

12414 Cazeneuve, Brian. *Cross-Country Skiing: A Complete Guide* (8–12). Series: Trailside Guide. 1995, Norton $18.95 (978-0-393-31335-2). An illustrated manual that covers equipment, techniques, clothing, safety and other topics relating to cross-country skiing. [796.93]

12415 Kleh, Cindy. *Snowboarding Skills: The Back-to-Basics Essentials for All Levels* (7–12). 2002, Annick paper $16.95 (978-1-55297-626-5). Tips from an expert, with photographs and a glossary, make this a hip title for enthusiasts. (Rev: BL 12/15/02; SLJ 1/03) [796.9]

12416 Masoff, Joy. *Snowboard!* (9–12). Series: Extreme Sports. 2002, National Geographic paper $8.95 (978-0-7922-6740-9). An excellent overview of the increasingly popular winter sport of snowboarding, covering equipment, boarding techniques, and training tips. (Rev: BL 3/15/02) [796.93]

12417 Pollack, Pamela. *Ski!* (9–12). Series: Extreme Sports. 2002, National Geographic paper $8.95 (978-0-7922-6738-6). Ideal for teens, this is an excellent introduction to the popular sport of skiing, covering such basics as equipment, techniques, and advice on getting in shape for the slopes. (Rev: BL 3/15/02) [796.93]

12418 Schwartz, Heather E. *Snowboarding* (5–10). Series: Science Behind Sports. 2011, Gale/Lucent LB $33.45 (978-1-4205-0322-7). After reviewing the history of snowboarding, this book discusses training and other preparations, glides and turns, jumps and rails, and aerial moves before looking at psychological aspects. **e** (Rev: SLJ 9/1/11) [796.9]

12419 Stiefer, Sandy. *Marathon Skiing* (7–10). Series: Ultra Sports. 2002, Rosen LB $26.50 (978-0-8239-3554-3). This work describes the sport of marathon skiing — cross-country skiing pushed to its limits. (Rev: BL 9/1/02) [796.95]

12420 Werner, Doug, and Jim Waide. *Snowboarder's Start-Up: A Beginner's Guide to Snowboarding. Rev. ed.* (9–12). 1999, Tracks paper $9.95 (978-1-884654-11-4). An appealing introduction to snowboarding, with information on equipment, clothing, and basic techniques. (Rev: BL 12/15/98) [796.9]

Soccer

12421 Bauer, Gerhard. *Soccer Techniques, Tactics and Teamwork* (9–12). 1993, Sterling paper $14.95 (978-0-8069-8730-9). Basic soccer training and skill development, with color photographs. (Rev: BL 7/93*) [796.344]

12422 Buxton, Ted. *Soccer Skills: For Young Players* (6–12). 2000, Firefly paper $14.95 (978-1-55209-329-0). A practical guide to training and technique that will be useful for beginners and advanced players. (Rev: SLJ 10/00; VOYA 12/00) [796.344]

12423 Gifford, Clive. *The Kingfisher Soccer Encyclopedia* (6–10). 2006, Kingfisher $19.95 (978-0-7534-5928-7). Covers all aspects of the sport, including basic rules, skills, legends, famous games, and winning teams. (Rev: SLJ 5/06) [796.334]

12424 Hamm, Mia, and Aaron Heifetz. *Go for the Goal: A Champion's Guide to Winning in Soccer and Life* (9–12). 1999, HarperCollins paper $12.95 (978-0-06-093159-9). Using anecdotes and pictures, basic soccer skills and techniques are explained. [796.334]

12425 Herbst, Dan. *Sports Illustrated Soccer: The Complete Player* (7–12). 1988, Sports Illustrated for Kids paper $9.95 (978-1-56800-038-1). Basic and advanced skills are explained plus a variety of game strategies. [796.334]

12426 Luongo, Albert M. *Soccer Drills: Skill-Builders for Field Control* (9–12). 2000, McFarland paper $29.95 (978-0-7864-0682-1). This book offers a systematic plan to strengthen one's soccer game from beginning skills to advanced. (Rev: VOYA 6/00) [796.334]

12427 Radnedge, Keir, and Mark Bushell. *The Treasures of the World Cup* (7–12). 2006, Trafalgar $50.00 (978-1-84442-321-7). A scrapbook-like collection of all kinds of goodies connected to the World Cup soccer competitions dating from 1930 to 2002. Stickers, letters, posters, tickets and other souvenirs will thrill soccer fans. (Rev: BL 8/06) [796.334668]

Surfing, Water Skiing, and Other Water Sports

12428 Brems, Marianne. *The Fit Swimmer: 120 Workouts and Training Tips* (9–12). 1984, Contemporary paper $12.95 (978-0-8092-5454-5). For a person who has chosen swimming as a way of keeping fit, this book describes 120 workouts. [797.2]

12429 Gabbard, Andrea. *Girl in the Curl: A Century of Women in Surfing* (10–12). 2000, Seal paper $29.95

(978-1-58005-048-7). This eye-catching overview of women surfers spotlights achievements and looks at inequities in the world of professional surfing. (Rev: VOYA 12/01) [797.3]

12430 Grubb, Jake, et al. *The New Sailboard Book* (9–12). 1990, Norton paper $16.95 (978-0-393-30682-8). This guide to a fast-growing sport contains information on equipment, basic techniques, and types of competitions. (Rev: BL 5/1/85) [797.124]

12431 Manley, Claudia B. *Ultra Swimming* (7–10). Series: Ultra Sports. 2002, Rosen LB $26.50 (978-0-8239-3558-1). An introduction to the history of this demanding new sport that gives tips on improving performance, maintaining safety, and training both body and mind for the challenges. (Rev: BL 9/1/02) [797.2]

12432 Werner, Doug. *Surfer's Start-Up: A Beginner's Guide to Surfing. 2nd ed.* (7–12). 1999, Tracks paper $11.95 (978-1-884654-12-1). A new edition of this standard instructional guide that covers basic instruction, surfing gear, safety, etiquette, and history. (Rev: SLJ 9/99) [797]

Tennis and Other Racquet Games

12433 Boga, Steve. *Badminton* (9–12). 1996, Stackpole paper $10.00 (978-0-8117-2487-6). Designed for backyard badminton players, this guide explores badminton's history and rules and provides easy-to-follow guidance on such key elements as footwork, racket grip, and strategies for use in singles, doubles, and mixed-doubles play. [796.34]

12434 Jennings, Jay, ed. *Tennis and the Meaning of Life: A Literary Anthology of the Game* (9–12). 1995, Breakaway $24.00 (978-1-55821-378-4). A collection of tennis-related stories and poetry by well-known writers. (Rev: BL 5/15/95) [808.8]

12435 MacCurdy, Doug, and Shawn Tully. *Sports Illustrated Tennis: Strokes for Success! Rev. ed.* (8–12). 1994, Sports Illustrated paper $12.95 (978-1-56800-006-0). Using many illustrations, this volume covers topics like rules, equipment, techniques, and competitions. [796.342]

12436 Sherrow, Victoria. *Tennis* (6–12). Series: History of Sports. 2003, Gale LB $29.95 (978-1-56006-959-1). The origins and evolution of the game are followed by information on recreational and competitive tennis and on outstanding players. (Rev: SLJ 9/03) [796.342]

12437 Turner, Ed, and Woody Clouse. *Winning Racquetball: Skills, Drills, and Strategies* (9–12). 1995, Human Kinetics paper $19.95 (978-0-87322-721-6). This handbook on racquetball includes drills to develop recommended shots, strategies, and tips on conditioning. (Rev: BL 12/1/95) [796.34]

Video Games

12438 Frederick, Shane. *Gamers Unite! The Video Game Revolution* (6–10). Illus. Series: Pop Culture Revolutions. 2010, Compass Point LB $31.99 (978-0-7565-4244-3). Looks at the history of video games, starting with Pong, and discusses the growth in their popularity of issues of violence and ratings. (Rev: SLJ 5/10) [794.8]

Author Index

Authors are arranged alphabetically by last name. Authors' and joint authors' names are followed by book titles — which are also arranged alphabetically — and the text entry number. Book titles may refer to those that appear as a main entry or as an internal entry mentioned in the text. Fiction titles are indicated by (F) following the entry number.

Aamodt, Donald. *A Name to Conjure With*, 2287(F)
Aaron, Henry. *I Had a Hammer*, 7951
Aaron, Rachel. *The Spirit Eater*, 2288(F)
Spirit Rebellion, 2289(F)
The Spirit Thief, 2290(F)
Aaronovitch, David. *Voodoo Histories*, 12180
Aaseng, Nathan. *The Bermuda Triangle* , 12181
Business Builders in Broadcasting, 7801
The Locker Room Mirror, 12229
The White House, 9511
You Are the Corporate Executive, 10316
You Are the General, 9761
You Are the Juror, 9703
You Are the President, 9680
You Are the President II, 9681
You Are the Senator, 9689
You Are the Supreme Court Justice, 9704
Aaseng, Rolf E. *A Beginner's Guide to Studying the Bible*, 9550
Abad, Charlie. *Sewing*, 12151
Abadzis, Nick. *Boy Toy*, 1296(F)
Laika, 3212(F)
Abbey, Lynn. *Sanctuary*, 2291(F)
Unicorn and Dragon, 2292(F)
Abbey, Lynn (ed.). *Turning Points*, 2293(F)
Abbotson, Susan C. W. *Student Companion to Arthur Miller*, 7052
Abbott, David. *The Twin Towers*, 10268
Abbott, Ellen Jensen. *Watersmeet*, 2294(F)
Abbott, Stacey (ed.). *Reading Angel*, 8594
Abdel-Fattah, Randa. *Does My Head Look Big in This?*, 782(F)
Ten Things I Hate About Me, 783(F)

Abdul-Jabbar, Kareem. *Black Profiles in Courage*, 7563
On the Shoulders of Giants, 9424
Abel, Jessica. *Drawing Words and Writing Pictures — Making Comics*, 12112
La Perdida, 3213(F)
Life Sucks, 3214(F)
Abelove, Joan. *Go and Come Back*, 2195(F)
Abi-Ezzi, Nathalie. *A Girl Made of Dust*, 3950(F)
Abirached, Zeina. *A Game for Swallows*, 3215(F)
Abouet, Marguerite. *Aya*, 3216(F)
Aya, 3217(F)
Aya of Yop City, 3217(F)
Abraham, Daniel. *A Betrayal in Winter*, 2295(F)
Abrahams, Peter. *Down the Rabbit Hole*, 4996(F)
Into the Dark, 4997(F)
Reality Check, 4998(F)
Up All Night, 6315(F)
Abrahams, Roger D. (ed.). *African Folktales*, 6788
Abramovitz, Melissa. *Lou Gehrig's Disease*, 10673
Abrams, Amir. *Crazy Love*, 1489(F)
Abrams, Dennis. *Hamid Karzai*, 8077
Hillary Rodham Clinton, 7713
Nicolas Sarkozy, 8129
Rachael Ray, 7934
Abrams, Michael. *Birdmen, Batmen and Skyfliers*, 11954
Abu-Jaber, Diana. *Crescent*, 5520(F)
Acampora, Paul. *Defining Dulcie*, 4902(F)
Achebe, Chinua. *Collected Poems*, 6762
Things Fall Apart, 3839(F)
Acheson, Alison. *House*, 3218(F)
Aciman, André. *Baby*, 963(F)
Acito, Marc. *How I Paid for Co*, 1490(F)

Acker, Kerry. *Dorothea Lange*, 7273
Everything You Need to Know About the Goth Scene, 11062
Nina Simone, 7552
Ackerman, Diane. *The Zookeeper's Wife*, 8804
Ackerman, Jane. *Louis Pasteur and the Founding of Microbiology*, 7900
Ackerman, Jennifer. *Sex Sleep Eat Drink Dream*, 10843
Ackerman, Thomas H. *FBI Careers*, 10526
Ackermann, Joan. *In the Space Left Behind*, 964(F)
Ackley, Amy. *Sign Language*, 230(F)
Ackroyd, Peter. *The Canterbury Tales*, 182(F)
Acosta, Belinda. *Sisters, Strangers, and Starting Over*, 784(F)
Acosta, Marta. *Dark Companion*, 4573(F)
Acuna, Rodolfo F. *U.S. Latino Issues*, 9957
Adair, Gene. *Alfred Hitchcock*, 7509
Adair, Rick (ed.). *Critical Perspectives on Politics and the Environment*, 10025
Adair, Robert Kemp. *The Physics of Baseball. 2nd ed.* , 12281
Adamowicz, Adam, et al. *New Recruits, Vol. 1*, 8417
Adams, Amanda. *A Mermaid's Tale*, 6776
Adams, Ansel. *Ansel Adams*, 8460
Adams, Bradley J. *Forensic Anthropology*, 10136
Adams, Douglas. *Last Chance to See*, 11551
The Long Dark Tea-Time of the Soul, 5842(F)
The Salmon of Doubt, 5843(F)
Adams, John Joseph (ed.). *By Blood We Live*, 4574(F)
Seeds of Change, 5844(F)

Aspin, Diana. *Ordinary Miracles*, 6321(F)

Asprin, Robert. *Dragons Wild*, 2325(F)
No Phule Like an Old Phule, 5866(F)

Astor, Gerald. *The Right to Fight*, 9903

Atangan, Patrick. *The Yellow Jar*, 3237(F)

Atkin, S. Beth. *Gunstories*, 9990

Atkins, Catherine. *The File on Angelyn Stark*, 247(F)

Atkins, Charles. *Mother's Milk*, 5011(F)

Atkinson, Rick. *In the Company of Soldiers*, 9482

Atlema, Martha. *A Time to Choose*, 4463(F)

Atta, Sefi. *Everything Good Will Come*, 3841(F)
News from Home, 6322(F)

Attebery, Brian (ed.). *The Norton Book of Science Fiction*, 6064(F)
The Norton Book of Science Fiction, 1960–1990, 6063(F)

Attenberg, Jami. *Instant Love*, 5528(F)

Attenborough, David. *Life in the Undergrowth*, 11575
The Life of Birds, 11519
The Life of Mammals, 11467

Attie, Alice. *Harlem on the Verge*, 9513

Atwan, Robert (ed.). *The Best American Essays, 2000*, 6886
The Best American Essays, 2003, 6881
The Best American Essays, 2004, 6891
The Best American Essays, 2005, 6893
The Best American Essays, 2006, 6902

Atwater-Rhodes, Amelia. *Hawksong*, 2326(F)
Persistence of Memory, 4581(F)
Poison Tree, 2327(F)
Token of Darkness, 4582(F)

Atwood, Margaret. *Cat's Eye*, 1501(F)
The Handmaid's Tale, 5867(F)
Oryx and Crake, 5868(F)
The Tent, 6323(F)
The Year of the Flood, 5868(F)

Aubert, Rosemary. *Free Reign*, 5012(F)

Auchincloss, Louis. *Theodore Roosevelt*, 7694

Auden, W. H. *Auden*, 6639

Audubon, John James. *The Audubon Reader*, 7244

Aue, Pamela Willwerth (ed.). *Teen Drug Abuse*, 10608

Auerbach, Paul S. *Medicine for the Outdoors*, 11014

Augarde, Steve. *Celandine*, 2328(F)
Celandine, 2329(F)
The Various, 2329(F)
Winter Wood, 2329(F)
X-Isle, 2330(F)

Augenbraum, Harold (ed.). *Growing Up Latino*, 796(F)

August, Paul Nordstrom. *Brain Function*, 10855

Auriemma, Geno. *Geno*, 7972

Auslander, Joseph. *The Winged Horse*, 7017

Austen, Jane. *Sense and Sensibility*, 3238(F)

Auster, Paul. *Auggie Wren's Christmas Story*, 248(F)

Austerlitz, Saul. *Another Fine Mess*, 7216

Austin, Dan. *True Fans*, 12307

Austin, Hilary Mac. *America's Children*, 9244

Avasthi, Swati. *Split*, 973(F)

Aveline, Erick. *Temporary Tattoos*, 12087

Averett, Edward. *The Rhyming Season*, 6259(F)

Avi. *The Man Who Was Poe*, 2331(F)

Avraham, Regina. *Circulatory System*, 10861

Axe, David. *Army 101*, 9762

Axelrod, Alan. *Patton*, 7749

Axelrod, Herbert R, et al. *Dr. Axelrod's Mini-Atlas of Freshwater Aquarium Fishes*, 11696

Axelrod, Toby. *Hans and Sophie Scholl*, 8131

Axelrod-Contrada, Joan. *Women Who Led Nations*, 8034

Ayarbe, Heidi. *Compulsion*, 1302(F)
Freeze Frame, 249(F)
Wanted, 5013(F)

Ayer, Eleanor H. *It's Okay to Say No*, 11017

Ayers, Harvard (ed.). *An Appalachian Tragedy*, 9535

Ayers, William, et al (ed.). *Zero Tolerance*, 10335

Aykroyd, Clarissa. *Julia Alvarez*, 7304
Refugees, 9855
Savage Satire, 7423

Aymar, Brandt. *Men in Sports*, 12231

Ayub, Awista. *However Tall the Mountain*, 9016

Azuonye, Chukwuma. *Dogon*, 8956
Edo, 8977

Azzarello, Brian, et al. *For Tomorrow, Vol. 2*, 3239(F)

Babcock, Joe. *The Tragedy of Miss Geneva Flowers*, 1502(F)

Babinski, Tony. *Cirque du Soleil*, 8546

Babra, Neil. *Hamlet*, 3240(F)

Baca, Jimmy Santiago. *A Glass of Water*, 797(F)

Bach, Richard. *Jonathan Livingston Seagull*, 2332(F)

Bachel, Beverly K. *What Do You Really Want? How to Set a Goal and Go for It!*, 11098

Bacigalupi, Paolo. *The Drowned Cities*, 2333(F)
Ship Breaker, 2333(F)
Ship Breaker, 5869(F)

The Windup Girl, 5870(F)

Bacon, Charlotte. *Split Estate*, 974(F)

Bacon, David. *Illegal People*, 9856

Bacon, Tony. *The Ultimate Guitar Book*, 8537

Bacus, K. C. *Calamity Jayne*, 5014(F)

Bacus, Kathleen. *Calamity Jayne Rides Again*, 5015(F)

Badcott, Nicholas. *Pocket Timeline of Islamic Civilizations*, 8662

Badillo, Steve. *Skateboarding*, 12410
Skateboarding, 12411

Badoe, Adwoa. *Between Sisters*, 3842(F)

Baer, Marianna. *Frost*, 4583(F)

Baez, Annecy. *My Daughter's Eyes and Other Stories*, 798(F)

Baez, John. *The Gay and Lesbian Guide to College Life*, 11018

Baggett, Jennifer, et al. *The Lost Girls*, 8157

Baggett, Nancy. *The All-American Cookie Book*, 12029

Baiev, Khassan, et al. *The Oath*, 8174

Bail, Paul. *John Saul*, 6966

Bailenson, Jeremy. *Infinite Reality*, 11911

Bailey, Diane. *How Markets Work*, 10309

Bailey, Elisabeth Tova. *The Sound of a Wild Snail Eating*, 8175

Bailey, Em. *Shift*, 250(F)

Bailey Hutchinson, Kay. *Leading Ladies*, 7568

Bailey, Jacqui. *Sex, Puberty and All That Stuff*, 11019

Bailey, Ronald H. *The Bloodiest Day*, 9343
Forward to Richmond, 9344

Bailey, Roz. *Postcards from Last Summer*, 251(F)

Bailey-Williams, Nicole. *A Little Piece of Sky*, 799(F)

Baillie, Liz. *My Brain Hurts, Vol. 1*, 3241(F)

Bain, Terry. *You Are a Dog (Life Through the Eyes of Man's Best Friend)*, 11656

Bainbridge, David. *The X in Sex*, 10814

Baird, Robert M. (ed.). *Euthanasia*, 10591

Bajoria, Paul. *The God of Mischief*, 3958(F)

Bakalar, Nicholas. *Understanding Teenage Depression*, 10886
Where the Germs Are, 11356

Baker, Calvin. *Dominion*, 4201(F)

Baker, Charles F. *Ancient Egyptians*, 8035
Ancient Greeks, 8728
Ancient Romans, 8742

Baker, E. D. *The Wide-Awake Princess*, 2334(F)

Baker, Julie. *The Bread and Roses Strike of 1912*, 9411

Baker, Julie P. (ed.). *Till Freedom Cried Out*, 9323

Dryer, Matt (ed.). *Hellboy*, 3223(F)

D'Souza, Dinesh. *What's So Great About America*, 9782

Du Bois, W. E. B. *The Oxford W. E. B. Du Bois Reader*, 9799

Du Maurier, Daphne. *Echoes from the Macabre*, 4639(F)
  Jamaica Inn, 4001(F)
  My Cousin Rachel, 4002(F)
  Rebecca, 5127(F)

du Sautoy, Marcus. *Symmetry*, 11749

Duane, Diane. *The Book of Night with Moon*, 2575(F)
  Omnitopia Dawn, 5969(F)
  A Wizard Alone, 2576(F)

Duberstein, John. *A Velvet Revolution*, 8108

Dubis, Michael. *The Hangman*, 4480(F)

DuBois, Andrew (ed.). *The Anthology of Rap*, 8490

DuBois, Michelle. *The Complete Jacob Lawrence*, 8466

Dudley, David L. *Caleb's Wars*, 4481(F)

Dudley, Mark E. *Gideon v. Wainwright (1963)*, 9711
  United States v. Nixon (1974), 9712

Dudley, William (ed.). *The Attack on America*, 10275
  Gangs, 10151
  Hurricane Katrina, 11771
  Reconstruction, 9413
  Reproductive Rights, 9713

Dudzinski, Kathleen. *Dolphin Mysteries*, 11628

Duensing, Edward. *Backyard and Beyond*, 11360

Duey, Kathleen. *Skin Hunger*, 2577(F)

Duffy, Carol Ann. *Mrs. Scrooge*, 6644

Duffy, Michael. *The Preacher and the Presidents*, 7775

Dufresne, John. *Deep in the Shade of Paradise*, 5586(F)

Dugan, Ellen. *Elements of Witchcraft*, 12190

Dugard, Jaycee. *A Stolen Life*, 8225

Duggins, Pat. *Final Countdown*, 11303

Duggleby, John. *Uh Huh! The Story of Ray Charles*, 7484

Duiker, William J. *Ho Chi Minh*, 8074

Dulles, Allen. *Great True Spy Stories*, 10152

Dumas, Alexandre. *The Count of Monte Cristo*, 167(F)
  The Man in the Iron Mask, 168(F)
  The Man in the Iron Mask, 3315(F)
  The Three Musketeers, 169(F)

Dumas, Firoozeh. *Laughing Without an Accent*, 8226

Dumas, Margaret. *Speak Now*, 5128(F)

Dumm, Gary. *Students for a Democratic Society*, 9472

Dunant, Sarah. *Fatlands*, 5129(F)

Dunbar, Paul Laurence. *The Complete Poems of Paul Laurence Dunbar*, 6682

In His Own Voice, 6683

Duncan, Dave. *The Alchemist's Code*, 2578(F)

Duncan, Dayton. *Lewis and Clark*, 9288

Duncan, Joyce D. (ed.). *Sport in American Culture*, 12240

Duncan, Lois. *Daughters of Eve*, 5130(F)
  Down a Dark Hall, 5131(F)
  Killing Mr. Griffin, 5132(F)
  Locked in Time, 4640(F)
  Stranger with My Face, 4641(F)
  Summer of Fear, 4642(F)
  The Third Eye, 5133(F)
  The Twisted Window, 5134(F)
  Who Killed My Daughter, 10153

Dungy, Camille T. (ed.). *Black Nature*, 6684

Dunker, Kristina. *Summer Storm*, 5135(F)

Dunkle, Clare B. *The House of Dead Maids*, 4643(F)
  In the Coils of the Snake, 2579(F)

Dunkleberger, Amy. *A Student's Guide to Arthur Miller*, 7057

Dunlap, Susanne. *Anastasia's Secret*, 4003(F)
  The Musician's Daughter, 4004(F)

Dunlop, Reginald. *Come Fly with Me! Your Nineties Guide to Becoming a Flight Attendant*, 10440

Dunn, Danielle. *A Teen's Guide to Getting Published*, 7091

Dunn, James. *Trail of Blood*, 10157

Dunn, Jane. *Elizabeth and Mary*, 8038

Dunn, Jessica. *A Teen's Guide to Getting Published*, 7091

Dunn, John M. *The Relocation of the North American Indian*, 9262

Dunn, Susan. *George Washington*, 7701

Dunn, Tricia, et al. *Gold Medal Ice Hockey for Women and Girls*, 12378

Dunn, Wendy. *Famous Hispanic Americans*, 7585

Dunn-Georgiou, Elisha. *Everything You Need to Know About Organic Foods*, 11379

Dunne, Pete. *Pete Dunne on Bird Watching*, 11523

Dunning, John Harris. *Salem Brownstone*, 3316(F)

Dunnington, Rose. *Bake It Up! Desserts, Breads, Entire Meals and More*, 12052
  Super Sandwiches: Wrap 'em, Stack 'em, Stuff 'em, 12052

Dunson, Donald H. *Child, Victim, Soldier*, 9631

Dunwell, Frances F. *The Hudson*, 9517

DuPont, Kathryn Cullen-. *Women's Suffrage in America*, 9807

DuPrau, Jeanne. *Car Trouble*, 376(F)

Durant, Michael J. *The Night Stalkers*, 11986

Durant, William James. *The Story of Philosophy*, 9545

Durham, M. Gigi. *The Lolita Effect*, 7127

Durrett, Deanne. *Healers*, 9263

Durrow, Heidi W. *The Girl Who Fell from the Sky*, 1058(F)

Durschmied, Erik. *Blood of Revolution*, 8672

Durst, Sarah Beth. *Drink, Slay, Love*, 4644(F)
  Enchanted Ivy, 2580(F)
  Ice, 2581(F)
  Vessel, 2582(F)

Duskis, Neil. *Barlowe's Guide to Fantasy*, 6935

Dutton, Judy. *Science Fair Season*, 11258

Dutton, Monte. *True to the Roots*, 8498

Dwyer, Jim. *102 Minutes*, 10276

Dyan, Sheldon. *The Crazy Things Girls Do for Love*, 5587(F)

Dye, Dan. *Amazing Gracie*, 11662

Dyer, Davis (ed.). *The Reader's Companion to the American Presidency*, 7569

Dyer, Hadley. *Watch This Space*, 10308

Dygard, Thomas J. *Second Stringer*, 6274(F)

Dyja, Thomas. *The Moon in Our Hands*, 5136(F)
  Only Connect, 10339

Dysart, Joshua. *Neil Young's Greendale*, 3317(F)

Dyson, Marianne J. *Space and Astronomy*, 11274

Eagle, Adam Fortunate. *Heart of the Rock*, 9970

Earle, Sylvia A. *The World Is Blue*, 10048

Earley, Tony. *Jim the Boy*, 4367(F)

Earls, Irene. *Young Musicians in World History*, 7225

Earls, Nick. *After Summer*, 5588(F)
  48 Shades of Brown, 1651(F)

Easton, Kelly. *Aftershock*, 32(F)
  Hiroshima Dreams, 823(F)
  To Be Mona, 377(F)
  White Magic, 378(F)

Eaton, Katherine B. *Daily Life in the Soviet Union*, 9084

Eaton, Susan. *The Other Boston Busing Story*, 9911

Ebadi, Shirin. *Iran Awakening*, 8227

Eberstadt, Fernanda. *Rat*, 4005(F)

Ebisch, Glen. *Ghosts from the Past*, 5137(F)

Ebony (ed.). *Ebony Pictorial History of Black America*, 9912

Echaore-McDavid, Susan. *Career Opportunities in Forensic Science*, 10529
  Career Opportunities in Science, 10546

Echevarria, Alex. *Sweet 15*, 785(F)

Echlin, Kim. *Inanna*, 6840

Echo-Hawk, Roger C. *Battlefields and Burial Grounds*, 8654

Echo-Hawk, Walter R. *Battlefields and Burial Grounds*, 8654

Echols, Jennifer. *Major Crush*, 5589(F)

Eck, Matthew. *The Farther Shore*, 4570(F)

Eckel, Malcolm David. *Buddhism*, 9555

Eckman, Edie. *The Crochet Answer Book*, 12156

Eddings, David. *The Belgariad, Vol. I*, 2583(F)

Guardians of the West, 2584(F)

Edelman, Bernard (ed.). *Dear America*, 9487

Edelson, Edward. *Gregor Mendel*, 7889

The Immune System, 10700

Edelson, Paula. *Straight Talk About Today's Families*, 11208

Edey, Maitland Armstrong. *Lucy*, 8639

Edge, Laura B. *Andrew Carnegie*, 7920

Edgerton, Clyde. *Solo*, 11960

Edgerton, Leslie H. (ed.). *Monday's Meal*, 4645(F)

Edgerton, Robert B. *The Troubled Heart of Africa*, 8930

Edghill, Rosemary. *Dead Reckoning*, 4746(F)

Paying the Piper at the Gates of Dawn, 6356(F)

Edginton, Ian. *The Great Game*, 3319(F)

H. G. Wells' The War of the Worlds, 3318(F)

The Picture of Dorian Gray, 199(F)

Edmonds, Walter D. *Tales My Father Never Told*, 7342

Edmonston, Phil. *Car Smarts*, 11966

Edwards, David H. *The World Don't Owe Me Nothing*, 7497

Edwards, Grace. *If I Should Die*, 5138(F)

Edwards, Johanna. *The Next Big Thing*, 1347(F)

Edwardson, Debby Dahl. *My Name Is Not Easy*, 4408(F)

Ee, Susan. *Angelfall*, 4646(F)

Efaw, Amy. *After*, 379(F)

Effinger, George Alec. *Budayeen Nights*, 5970(F)

Egan, Jennifer. *The Keep*, 4647(F)

Egan, Timothy. *The Worst Hard Time*, 9432

Egendorf, Laura K. *Heroin*, 10622

Performance-Enhancing Drugs, 10623

Egendorf, Laura K. (ed.). *The Death Penalty*, 9714

The French Revolution, 9056

Iran, 9128

Islam in America, 9596

Eggers, Dave. *What Is the What*, 2214(F)

Eggers, Dave (ed.). *The Best American Nonrequired Reading, 2002*, 6878

The Best American Nonrequired Reading, 2005, 6879

Ehlert, Willis J. *America's Heritage*, 9214

Ehrenberg, Pamela. *Ethan, Suspended*, 380(F)

Tillmon County Fire, 381(F)

Ehrenhaft, Daniel. *Dirty Laundry*, 5139(F)

Drawing a Blank, 5140(F)

Friend Is Not a Verb, 382(F)

Ehrenhaft, Daniel (ed.). *21 Proms*, 1856(F)

Ehrenhaft, Daniel, et al. *Americapedia*, 9660

Ehrlich, Gretel. *In the Empire of Ice*, 9187

John Muir, 7893

Ehrlich, Paul R, et al. *The Birder's Handbook*, 11524

Birds in Jeopardy, 11558

Eichengreen, Lucille. *From Ashes to Life*, 8228

Eickhoff, Diane. *Revolutionary Heart*, 7633

Eidse, Faith (ed.). *Unrooted Childhoods*, 11189

Eidus, Janice. *The War of the Rosens*, 4409(F)

Eig, Jonathan. *Opening Day*, 7966

Einfeld, Jann (ed.). *Afghanistan*, 9019

Can Democracy Succeed in the Middle East?, 9105

Einhorn, Eddie. *How March Became Madness*, 12311

Eire, Carlos. *Learning to Die in Miami*, 8229

Waiting for Snow in Havana, 8229

Eisen, Adrienne. *Making Scenes*, 1652(F)

Eisenberg, John. *My Guy Barbaro*, 8026

Eisner, Will. *The Best of the Spirit*, 3320(F)

Fagin the Jew, 3321(F)

Will Eisner's The Spirit Archives, Vol. 12, 3322(F)

Will Eisner's The Spirit Archives, Vol. 17, 3323(F)

Will Eisner's The Spirit Archives, Vol. 19, 3324(F)

El Rassi, Toufic. *Arab in America*, 3325(F)

Elderkin, Susan. *The Voices*, 1653(F)

Eldred, Tim. *Grease Monkey*, 3326(F)

Eldredge, Niles. *Charles Darwin and the Mystery of Mysteries*, 7846

Darwin, 7845

Eleveld, Mark (ed.). *The Spoken Word Revolution Redux*, 6589

Elgin, Kathy. *Elizabethan England*, 8755

The Medieval World, 8756

Elias, Jay. *Bowling*, 12235

Eliot, T. S. *The Complete Poems and Plays, 1909–1950*, 6645

Eliot, 6646

Old Possum's Book of Practical Cats, 6647

Elish, Dan. *Screenplays*, 7128

Elkeles, Simone. *How to Ruin a Summer Vacation*, 1059(F)

How to Ruin My Teenage Life, 383(F)

How to Ruin Your Boyfriend's Reputation, 384(F)

Leaving Paradise, 1654(F)

Rules of Attraction, 5590(F)

Ellabbad, Mohieddin. *The Illustrator's Notebook*, 7263

Ellington, Elisabeth. *A Year of Reading*, 12010

Elliot, Jessie. *Girls Dinner Club*, 1655(F)

Elliott, L. M. *Annie, Between the States*, 4254(F)

Elliott, Patricia. *Ambergate*, 2585(F)

The Pale Assassin, 4006(F)

Elliott, Stephen. *A Life Without Consequences*, 1656(F)

Elliott, Stephen (ed.). *Politically Inspired*, 6357(F)

Ellis, Deborah. *Bifocal*, 2215(F)

Children of War, 9632

Lunch with Lenin and Other Stories, 6358(F)

Off to War, 9633

We Want You to Know, 11125

Ellis, Helen. *What Curiosity Kills*, 2586(F)

Ellis, Jamellah. *That Faith, That Trust, That Love*, 385(F)

Ellis, Joseph J. *American Sphinx*, 7666

Founding Brothers, 9308

His Excellency, 7702

Ellis, Richard. *The Book of Whales*, 11629

On Thin Ice, 11489

Singing Whales, Flying Squid, and Swimming Cucumbers, 11600

Ellis, Richard J. *To the Flag*, 9783

Ellis, Rob. *The Mike Schmidt Study*, 12300

Ellis, Roger. *The Complete Audition Book for Young Actors*, 8547

Ellis, Roger (ed.). *Audition Monologs for Student Actors*, 6501

Audition Monologs for Student Actors II, 6500

International Plays for Young Audiences, 6502

More Scenes and Monologs from the Best New Plays, 6503

Ellis, Sherry (ed.). *Now Write! Screenwriting*, 7129

Ellis, Warren, et al. *Ocean*, 3327(F)

Ellison, Brooke. *Miracles Happen*, 10977

Ellison, James W. *Finding Forrester*, 824(F)

Ellison, Jean. *Miracles Happen*, 10977

Fleming, Tom. *The Complete Guitar Course*, 8539

Fletcher, Christine. *Tallulah Falls*, 1674(F)

Fletcher, Joann. *Exploring the Life, Myth, and Art of Ancient Egypt*, 8717

Fletcher, Marty. *J. Robert Oppenheimer*, 7898

Fletcher, Ralph. *One O'Clock Chop*, 398(F)

Fletcher, Susan. *Eve Green*, 1067(F)
Oystercatchers, 1068(F)

Flewelling, Lynn. *The Bone Doll's Twin*, 2608(F)
Hidden Warrior, 2609(F)

Flexner, James Thomas. *Washington, the Indispensable Man*, 7703

Flinn, Alex. *Beastly*, 2610(F)
Bewitching, 2611(F)
Breathing Underwater, 1675(F)
Diva, 399(F)
A Kiss in Time, 2612(F)
Nothing to Lose, 1069(F)

Flint, Eric. *Boundary*, 5982(F)
Fortune's Stroke, 2613(F)
The Wizard of Karres, 6050(F)

Flood, Bo. *Pacific Island Legends*, 6798

Flood, Elizabeth Clair. *Cowgirls*, 9391

Flood, Nancy Bo. *No-Name Baby*, 4371(F)

Flood, Nancy Bohac. *Working Together Against World Hunger*, 10211

Florescu, Radu R. N. *Dracula*, 8139

Flowers, Charles. *The O'Reilly Factor for Kids*, 11157

Flynn, Kevin. *102 Minutes*, 10276

Flynn, Leonie (ed.). *The Ultimate Teen Book Guide*, 6930

Flynn, Michael. *Falling Stars*, 5983(F)

Flynn, Pat. *Alex Jackson*, 6277(F)
Out of His League, 6278(F)

Flynn, Raymond. *John Paul II*, 8116

Foer, Jonathan Safran. *Eating Animals*, 11380
Extremely Loud and Incredibly Close, 1676(F)

Fogarty, Mignon. *Grammar Girl Presents the Ultimate Writing Guide for Students*, 10366

Fogelin, Adrian. *The Real Question*, 400(F)

Fogle, Bruce. *Dog*, 11664

Folbre, Nancy. *The New Field Guide to the U.S. Economy*, 10310

Foley, Gaelen. *Lord of Fire*, 5602(F)

Foley, John. *Hoops of Steel*, 6279(F)
A Mighty Wall, 401(F)

Folger, Tim (ed.). *The Best American Science and Nature Writing, 2003*, 11228
The Best American Science and Nature Writing, 2004, 11244
The Best American Science and Nature Writing, 2005, 11252

Follain, John. *Jackal*, 8143

Follmi, Olivier. *Africa*, 8917

Fontanel, Beatrice. *Babies*, 10992

Foon, Dennis. *The Dirt Eaters*, 2614(F)
Double or Nothing, 1677(F)

Foote, Donna. *Relentless Pursuit*, 10341

Forbes, Harrison. *Dog Talk*, 11665

Forbes, Kathryn. *Mama's Bank Account*, 1070(F)

Forbes, Peter. *The Gecko's Foot*, 11871

Ford, Amanda. *Be True to Yourself*, 11129
Between Mother and Daughter, 11193

Ford, G. M. *Cast in Stone*, 5155(F)

Ford, Jeffrey. *The Empire of Ice Cream*, 6364(F)
The Shadow Year, 402(F)

Ford, John C. *The Morgue and Me*, 5156(F)

Ford, John R. *Twelfth Night*, 7040

Ford, Judy. *Between Mother and Daughter*, 11193

Ford, Michael Thomas. *Suicide Notes*, 1678(F)

Ford-Grabowsky, Mary (ed.). *Sacred Voices*, 9557

Forester, C. S. *The African Queen*, 33(F)
Mr. Midshipman Hornblower, 4008(F)

Forker, Dom. *Baseball Brain Teasers*, 12290

Forman, Gayle. *If I Stay*, 403(F)
Just One Day, 5603(F)

Forman, Jack Jacob. *Presenting Paul Zindel*, 7452

Forman, Werner. *The Eskimos*, 9185

Forrester, Tina. *Hoodwinked*, 8873

Forsberg, Michael, et al. *Great Plains*, 9510

Forster, E. M. *A Room with a View*, 4009(F)

Forster, Gwynne. *If You Walked in My Shoes*, 1071(F)

Forsyth, Elizabeth H. *Safe Sex 101*, 11031
Stress 101, 10895

Forsyth, Frederick. *The Day of the Jackal*, 34(F)
The Devil's Alternative, 35(F)
The Dogs of War, 36(F)
The Fist of God, 37(F)
The Odessa File, 38(F)

Fortey, Richard. *Dry Storeroom No. 1*, 9701

Fortier, Anne. *Juliet*, 5604(F)

Foss, Clive. *Fidel Castro*, 8144

Fossey, Dian. *Gorillas in the Mist*, 11484
No One Loved Gorillas More, 7863

Foster, Alan Dean. *Splinter of the Mind's Eye*, 5984(F)

Foster, Ken. *The Dogs Who Found Me*, 11666

Foster, Lynn V. *A Brief History of Central America*, 9161

Foster, Richard J. *Mark Spitz*, 8027

Foster, Sharon Ewell. *Abraham's Well*, 4186(F)

Foster, Steven. *A Field Guide to Venomous Animals and Poisonous Plants*, 11362

Fountas, Angela Jane (ed.). *Waking Up American*, 9886

Fowler, Therese. *Exposure*, 1679(F)
Souvenir, 5605(F)

Fowles, Debby. *1000 Best Smart Money Secrets for Students*, 10571

Fox, Andrew. *Bride of the Fat White Vampire*, 4653(F)

Fox, Annie. *Can You Relate? Real-World Advice for Teens on Guys, Girls, Growing Up, and Getting Along*, 11130
Too Stressed to Think? A Teen Guide to Staying Sane When Life Makes You Crazy, 10888

Fox, Carol. *In Times of War*, 6365(F)

Fox, Gunnar. *Kick Ass in College*, 10401

Fox, Janet. *Forgiven*, 5157(F)

Fox, Margalit. *Talking Hands*, 7076

Foxlee, Karen. *The Anatomy of Wings*, 3891(F)

Frader, Laura L. *The Industrial Revolution*, 8778

Fradin, Dennis Brindell. *Bound for the North Star*, 9329
Ida B. Wells, 7641
The Power of One, 7608

Fradin, Judith Bloom. *Ida B. Wells*, 7641
The Power of One, 7608

Frame, Ronald. *The Lantern Bearers*, 1680(F)

Francia, Luis H. *Eye of the Fish*, 9040

Francis, Barbara. *Other People's Words*, 7093

Francis, Brian. *Fruit*, 1681(F)

Francis, Melissa. *Bite Me!*, 2615(F)

Franco, Betsy. *Metamorphosis*, 404(F)

Franco, Betsy (ed.). *Things I Have to Tell You*, 1682(F)

Frank, Anne. *The Diary of a Young Girl*, 8103

Frank, E. R. *America*, 1354(F)

Frank, Hillary. *Better Than Running at Night*, 405(F)
I Can't Tell You, 1683(F)

Frank, Lucy. *Will You Be My Brussels Sprout?*, 5606(F)

Frank, Richard B. *MacArthur*, 7738

Franke, Mary Ann. *To Save the Wild Bison*, 11560

Frankenberger, Elizabeth. *Food and Love*, 10702

Franklin, Carl J. *Turtles*, 11442

Franklin, Emily. *The Other Half of Me*, 1072(F)
Tessa Masterson Will Go to Prom, 406(F)

Franzen, Jonathan. *The Discomfort Zone*, 7350

Gaus, P. L. *Clouds Without Rain*, 5166(F)

Gaustad, Edwin S. *Benjamin Franklin*, 7718

Gavin, Jamila. *See No Evil*, 5167(F)

Gawande, Atul (ed.). *The Best American Science Writing, 2006*, 11230

Gay, Kathlyn. *After the Shooting Stops*, 9218

　The Aftermath of the Chinese Nationalist Revolution, 8992

　The Aftermath of the Russian Revolution, 9085

　Am I Fat? The Obesity Issue for Teens, 10949

　Cultural Diversity, 9808

　Epilepsy, 10705

　Food, 11383

　Leaving Cuba, 9965

　The Scoop on What to Eat, 10950

　Volunteering, 10245

Gay, Martin. *After the Shooting Stops*, 9218

Gayle, Mike. *Dinner for Two*, 1082(F)

　My Legendary Girlfriend, 1701(F)

Gaywood, Martin. *Snakes*, 11437

Gealt, Adelheid M. *Art of the Western World*, 8437

Gear, Kathleen O'Neal. *The Visitant*, 5168(F)

Gear, W. Michael. *The Visitant*, 5168(F)

Geary, Rick. *The Borden Tragedy*, 10161

　The Case of Madeleine Smith, 3349(F)

　Cravan, 8215

　J. Edgar Hoover, 7726

　The Lindbergh Child, 9434

　The Murder of Abraham Lincoln, 9357

　The Mystery of Mary Rogers, 9330

　The Saga of the Bloody Benders, 3350(F)

Gébler, Carlo. *The Bull Raid*, 2636(F)

Gediman, Dan (ed.). *This I Believe*, 10224

Gee, Maurice. *Salt*, 2637(F)

Geerling, Marjetta. *Fancy White Trash*, 4924(F)

Geisel, Theodor Seuss. *The Early Works of Dr. Seuss, Vol. 1*, 8425

Geiskopf-Hadler, Susann. *The Complete Vegan Cookbook*, 12053

Gelabert, Dorcas. *Chronicle of Jewish History*, 8698

Gelder, Gordon Van (ed.). *In Lands That Never Were*, 2638(F)

Geller, Judith B. *Titanic*, 11979

Gelletly, LeeAnne. *Gift of Imagination*, 7330

Gellis, Roberta. *This Scepter'd Isle*, 2818(F)

Genat, Robert. *Lowriders*, 12011

Genet, Jean. *The Maids and Deathwatch*, 6547

Genge, N. E. *The Book of Shadows*, 12195

Genovese, Eugene D. *Roll, Jordan, Roll*, 9915

Gentry, Sarah E, et al. *Internet Addiction and Online Gaming*, 11924

　Living with the Internet, 11924

George, Charles. *Biotech Research*, 11872

　Maya Civilization, 8708

George, Charles (ed.). *Living through the Civil Rights Movement*, 9809

George, Elizabeth. *The Edge of Nowhere*, 5169(F)

George, Jessica Day. *Princess of the Midnight Ball*, 2639(F)

　Sun and Moon, Ice and Snow, 2640(F)

George, Linda. *Biotech Research*, 11872

　Maya Civilization, 8708

George, Madeleine. *The Difference between You and Me*, 1702(F)

　Looks, 418(F)

George, Nelson. *Thriller*, 7511(F)

George-Warren, Holly. *The Road to Woodstock*, 8512

Gerard, Carolyn Forcheand Philip (ed.). *Writing Creative Nonfiction*, 7109

Gerardi, Dave. *Careers in the Computer Game Industry*, 10554

Geras, Adele. *Ithaka*, 6854(F)

　Pictures of the Night, 5612(F)

　The Tower Room, 5613(F)

Gerber, Linda. *Death by Bikini*, 5170(F)

　Death by Bikini, 5171(F)

　Death by Denim, 5171(F)

　Death by Latte, 5171(F)

Gerber, Michael. *Freshman*, 4925(F)

Gerber, Philip. *Robert Frost*, 7059

Gerberg, Mort. *The U.S. Constitution for Everyone*, 9671

Gerdes, Louise I. (ed.). *The Cold War*, 8896

　Gangs, 10151

　Immigration, 9863

　Intelligent Design versus Evolution, 11715

　Rogue Nations, 9636

Gerges, Fawaz A. *Journey of the Jihadist*, 10280

German, Dave. *Dave Gorman's Googlewhack! Adventure*, 11914

Gerrold, David. *Blood and Fire*, 5986(F)

　Chess with a Dragon, 5987(F)

　Child of Earth, 5988(F)

Gershman, Gary P. *Death Penalty on Trial*, 9717

Gerstenfeld, Sheldon L. *The Cat Care Book*, 11651

　The Dog Care Book, 11667

Gervay, Susanne. *Butterflies*, 1703(F)

Getzinger, Donna. *Antonio Vivaldi and the Baroque Tradition*, 7466

　George Frideric Handel and Music for Voices, 7462

　Johann Sebastian Bach and the Art of Baroque Music, 7453

Geus, Mireille. *Piggy*, 1360(F)

Gevinson, Tavi (ed.). *Rookie Yearbook One*, 7095

Geyer, Georgie Anne. *Guerrilla Prince*, 8145

Ghahramani, Zarah. *My Life as a Traitor*, 8238

Ghislain, Gary. *How I Stole Johnny Depp's Alien Girlfriend*, 5989(F)

Giacobello, John. *Bodyguards*, 10530

　Careers in the Fashion Industry, 10446

Giallongo, Zack. *Broxo*, 3351(F)

Giardino, Vittorio. *A Jew in Communist Prague*, 4012(F)

Gibb, Evelyn McDaniel. *Two Wheels North*, 12327

Gibbon, Andy. *Make College Yours*, 11132

Gibbons, Dave. *Thunderbolt Jaxon*, 3352(F)

Gibbons, Kaye. *On the Occasion of My Last Afternoon*, 4257(F)

Gibbons, Whit. *Their Blood Runs Cold*, 11432

Gibbs, Nancy. *The Preacher and the Presidents*, 7775

Giblin, James Cross. *Charles A. Lindbergh*, 7197

　The Rise and Fall of Senator Joe McCarthy, 7743

　Secrets of the Sphinx, 8718

Gibran, Kahlil. *The Prophet*, 6687

Gibsen, Cole. *Katana*, 2641(F)

Gibson, Donald B. *The Red Badge of Courage*, 6981

Gibson, Graeme. *The Bedside Book of Beasts*, 11471

　The Bedside Book of Birds, 11526

Gibson, Karen Bush. *Native American History for Kids*, 9265

Gibson, Marley. *The Awakening*, 4658(F)

　The Other Side, 12196

Gibson, Phil. *Natural Selection*, 8637

Gibson, Tanya Egan. *How to Buy a Love of Reading*, 1704(F)

Gibson, Terri R. *Natural Selection*, 8637

Gibson, Walter B. *Hoyle's Modern Encyclopedia of Card Games*, 12350

Gibson, William. *Neuromancer*, 5990(F)

Giddens, Owen. *Coping with Grieving and Loss*, 10595

Giddens, Sandra. *Coping with Grieving and Loss*, 10595

Gideon, Melanie. *Pucker*, 5991(F)

Gidwitz, Adam. *In a Glass Grimmly*, 4926(F)

Gould, Carol Grant. *Animal Architects*, 11453

Gould, James R. *Animal Architects*, 11453

Gould, Lewis L. *American First Ladies*, 7575

Gould, Sasha. *Cross My Heart*, 4017(F)

Gould, Stephen Jay. *The Richness of Life*, 11231

Gould, Steven. *Reflex*, 5996(F)
7th Sigma, 5997(F)
Wild Side, 5998(F)

Gourley, Catherine. *Beryl Markham*, 7199
Flappers and the New American Woman, 10239
Gibson Girls and Suffragists, 9220
Good Girl Work, 9415
The Horrors of Andersonville, 4259(F)
Rosie and Mrs. America: Perceptions of Women in the 1930s and 1940s, 9220

Gourley, Susan. *The Keepers of Sulbreth*, 2656(F)

Govenar, Alan. *Untold Glory*, 7576

Gow, Mary. *Attack on America*, 10282

Gowen, L. Kris. *Making Sexual Decisions*, 11027

Gower, Iris. *Bomber's Moon*, 4490(F)

Goyer, Tricia. *Night Song*, 4491(F)
The Swiss Courier, 4492(F)

Grab, Daphne. *Alive and Well in Prague, New York*, 1715(F)

Grabenstein, Chris. *Mad Mouse*, 5183(F)

Graber, Janet. *Resistance*, 4493(F)

Grabien, Deborah. *New-Slain Knight*, 4665(F)

Grace, Amanda. *But I Love Him*, 1716(F)
In Too Deep, 426(F)

Grace, C. L. *The Merchant of Death*, 5184(F)

Gradwohl, Judith. *The Wealth of Oceans*, 11804

Grady, Denise. *Deadly Invaders*, 10710

Grady, Sean M. *Biohazards*, 10711
Supercomputers, 11910

Graff, Henry. *Grover Cleveland*, 7650

Grafton, Sue. *G Is for Gumshoe*, 5185(F)
M Is for Malice, 5186(F)
P Is for Peril, 5187(F)

Gragg, Rod. *The Civil War Quiz and Fact Book*, 9359

Graham, Hilary Weisman. *Reunited*, 427(F)

Graham, Ian. *Military Technology*, 11989

Graham, Kevin. *Environmental Causes*, 10045
Ralph Nader, 7745

Graham, Kristen (ed.). *The Great Monologues from the Women's Project*, 6559

Graham, Robin Lee. *Dove*, 7189

Grahame-Smith, Seth. *Abraham Lincoln*, 4666(F)
Pride and Prejudice and Zombies, 4667(F)

Granfield, Linda. *I Remember Korea*, 9491

Grange, Michael. *Basketball's Greatest Stars*, 7942

Grant, Alan. *Holiday Hell*, 3353(F)

Grant, Donna. *Far from the Tree*, 1046(F)

Grant, Gavin J. (ed.). *Steampunk! An Anthology of Fantastically Rich and Strange Stories*, 2849(F)

Grant, Gordon. *Canoeing*, 12406

Grant, Helen. *The Glass Demon*, 5188(F)
The Vanishing of Katharina Linden, 5189(F)

Grant, John (ed.). *The Encyclopedia of Fantasy*, 6936

Grant, K. M. *Blue Flame*, 2657(F)
Blue Flame, 3816(F)
How the Hangman Lost His Heart, 4018(F)
White Heat, 2657(F)

Grant, Michael. *BZRK*, 5999(F)
Eve and Adam, 6001(F)
Fear, 6000(F)
Myths of the Greeks and Romans, 6855

Grant, Mira. *Deadline*, 4668(F)

Grant, Robert. *The Great Trials of the Twenties*, 9722

Grant, Sara. *Dark Parties*, 6002(F)

Grant, Steven. *Hamlet*, 3623(F)

Grant, Vicki. *B Negative*, 1087(F)
Comeback, 1088(F)
Dead-End Job, 1717(F)
Quid Pro Quo, 5190(F)

Grapes, Bryan J. (ed.). *Sexually Transmitted Diseases*, 10712

Grattan-Dominguez, Alejandro. *Breaking Even*, 1718(F)

Gratz, Alan. *Samurai Shortstop*, 3897(F)
Something Rotten, 5191(F)

Gravelle, Karen. *The Driving Book*, 11967
What's Going on Down There? Answers to Questions Boys Find Hard to Ask, 11028
Where Are My Birth Parents? A Guide for Teenage Adoptees, 11194

Graves, Douglas R. *Drawing Portraits*, 12119

Graves, Robert. *I, Claudius*, 3790(F)

Graves, Russell A. *The Prairie Dog*, 11472

Gray, Amy. *How to Be a Vampire*, 12198(F)
Spygirl, 8242

Gray, Anne. *Rites of the Healer*, 2658(F)

Gray, Charlotte. *Reluctant Genius*, 7829

Gray, Claudia. *Balthazar*, 4669(F)
Evernight, 2659(F)
Evernight, 4670(F)
Fateful, 2660(F)
Hourglass, 2661(F)
Spellcaster, 2662(F)
Stargazer, 4670(F)

Gray, Edward G. *Colonial America*, 9293

Gray, Frances Clayton. *Born to Win*, 8007

Gray, Justin. *Superman Returns*, 3637(F)

Gray, Keith. *Ostrich Boys*, 4019(F)

Graydon, Shari. *In Your Face*, 10835

Grayson, Devin. *Shay's Story*, 3728(F)

Grayson, Gabriel. *Talking with Your Hands, Listening with Your Eyes*, 7070

Grearson, Jessie Carroll. *Love in a Global Village*, 9888

Greek, C. Ray. *Sacred Cows and Golden Geese*, 11421

Greek, Jean Swingle. *Sacred Cows and Golden Geese*, 11421

Green, Dan. *The Elements*, 11707

Green, Jen. *Advertising*, 10331

Green, John. *An Abundance of Katherines*, 1719(F)
The Fault in Our Stars, 1364(F)
Looking for Alaska, 1720(F)
Paper Towns, 5192(F)
Will Grayson, Will Grayson, 1721(F)

Green, Julia. *Hunter's Heart*, 1722(F)

Green, Rebecca L. *Merina*, 8965

Green, Simon R. *The Man with the Golden Torc*, 4671(F)

Green, Timothy. *Twilight Boy*, 5193(F)

Greenberg, Arielle (ed.). *Starting Today*, 6761

Greenberg, Arthur. *A Chemical History Tour*, 11708

Greenberg, David. *Calvin Coolidge*, 7652

Greenberg, Jan. *Andy Warhol, Prince of Pop*, 7298
Runaway Girl, 7246

Greenberg, Jan (ed.). *Heart to Heart*, 6594
Side by Side, 6595

Greenberg, Keith Elliot. *December 8, 1980*, 7524

Greenberg, Martin H. (ed.). *The Best Alternate History Stories of the 20th Century*, 6209(F)
The Best Military Science Fiction of the 20th Century, 6210(F)
Catfantastic, 6123(F)
Civil War Women II, 4260(F)
Fantasy Gone Wrong, 2663(F)
Future Americas, 6015(F)
Heroes in Training, 6373(F)
Hitchcock in Prime Time, 5346(F)
Man vs. Machine, 6374(F)
Pandora's Closet, 6442(F)

Sci-Fi Private Eye, 6220(F)
Sisters of the Night, 4674(F)
Greenberg, Michael. *Painless Study Techniques*, 10353
Greenberg, Morrie. *Survival in the Square*, 7986
Greenberg, Paul. *Four Fish*, 11613
Greene, Bette. *Summer of My German Soldier*, 4494(F)
Greene, Bob. *The Get with the Program! Guide to Good Eating*, 10951
Greene, Brenda, et al. *America's Girl*, 8017
Greene, Brian. *The Fabric of the Cosmos*, 11816
Icarus at the Edge of Time, 428(F)
Greene, Constance C. *Monday I Love You*, 1723(F)
Greene, Harry W. *Snakes*, 11438
Greene, Jennifer. *Sparkle*, 429(F)
Greene, Meg. *Jane Goodall*, 7873
Rest in Peace, 10265
Greene, Melissa Fay. *There Is No Me without You*, 10713
Greene, Michele Dominguez. *Chasing the Jaguar*, 5194(F)
Greene, Rebecca. *The Teenagers' Guide to School Outside the Box*, 10342
Greenfeld, Howard. *A Promise Fulfilled*, 9112
Greenfield, Jacquie. *Colorado Pride*, 5618(F)
Greenfield, Robert. *Exile on Main Street*, 7548
Greenlaw, Lavinia. *The Importance of Music to Girls*, 8243
Greenlaw, Linda. *The Lobster Chronicles*, 9518
Greenman, Catherine. *Hooked*, 1724(F)
Greenwald, Andy. *Nothing Feels Good*, 8505
Greenwald, Michelle. *The Magical Melting Pot*, 12054
Greenwald, Ted. *Music*, 10496
Greenway, Alice. *White Ghost Girls*, 1725(F)
Greenwood, Janette Thomas. *The Gilded Age*, 9416
Gregory, Michael. *The Career Chronicles*, 10447
Gregory, Philippa. *Changeling*, 3817(F)
Gregson, Julia. *Band of Angels*, 4020(F)
Greif, Jean-Jacques. *The Fighter*, 4495(F)
Greitens, Eric. *The Warrior's Heart*, 8244
Grenville, Kate. *The Secret River*, 3898(F)
Gresham, John. *Special Forces*, 9763
Grey, Christopher. *Leonardo's Shadow*, 3818(F)
Grey, Zane. *Riders of the Purple Sage*, 4298(F)

The Wolf Tracker and Other Animal Tales, 153(F)
Gribbin, John. *Almost Everyone's Guide to Science*, 11232
XTL, 12197
Gribbin, Mary. *Almost Everyone's Guide to Science*, 11232
Griffin, Adele. *All You Never Wanted*, 1089(F)
The Julian Game, 430(F)
My Almost Epic Summer, 1726(F)
Where I Want to Be, 1365(F)
Griffin, Bethany. *Masque of the Red Death*, 4672(F)
Griffin, Jason. *My Name Is Jason. Mine Too*, 6730
Griffin, John Howard. *Black Like Me. 2nd ed.* , 9889
Griffin, Justin. *The Holy Grail*, 9583
Griffin, Molly Beth. *Silhouette of a Sparrow*, 4375(F)
Griffin, Paul. *Burning Blue*, 5195(F)
The Orange Houses, 431(F)
Ten Mile River, 2221(F)
Griffin, Starla. *Girl, 13*, 10002
Griffiths, Tom. *Slicing the Silence*, 9189
Griffler, Keith P. *Front Line of Freedom*, 9331
Griggs, Vanessa Davis. *Practicing What You Preach*, 5619(F)
Ray of Hope, 1090(F)
Griggs, Winnie. *Whatever It Takes*, 5620(F)
Grimberg, Tina. *Out of Line*, 8245
Grimes, Nikki. *Bronx Masquerade*, 1727(F)
Grimsley, Jim. *The Ordinary*, 2664(F)
Grisham, John. *The Client*, 5196(F)
A Painted House, 1728(F)
The Pelican Brief, 5197(F)
The Street Lawyer, 5198(F)
Gritzner, Jeffrey A. *Afghanistan*, 9021
Grob, Bernard. *Basic Electronics. 6th ed.* , 11942
Grodin, Elissa D. *C Is for Ciao*, 9079
Grogan, John. *The Longest Trip Home*, 7360
Marley and Me, 11668
Grollman, Earl A. *Living When a Young Friend Commits Suicide*, 10890
Straight Talk About Death for Teenagers, 10597
Groneman, William. *David Crockett*, 7771
Groning, Karl. *Elephants*, 11515
Gross, Andrew. *Judge and Jury*, 5368(F)
Gross, Milt. *He Done Her Wrong*, 3359(F)
Gross, Peter. *Chosen*, 3499(F)
Tommy Taylor and the Bogus Identity, 3275(F)
Gross, Philip. *The Lastling*, 46(F)
Grossman, Elizabeth. *Watershed*, 11561

Grossman, Lev. *The Magician King*, 2665(F)
The Magicians, 2665(F)
Grossman, Nancy. *A World Away*, 432(F)
Grosz, Terry. *Defending Our Wildlife Heritage*, 11562
Grubb, Jake, et al. *The New Sailboard Book*, 12430
Gruen, Sara. *Ape House*, 433(F)
Riding Lessons, 1091(F)
Grummer, Arnold E. *Trash-to-Treasure Papermaking*, 12143
Gruner, Jessica. *The Lost Days*, 5405(F)
The Lost Days, 5406(F)
Stranger and Stranger, 5406(F)
Grunwald, Lisa (ed.). *Women's Letters*, 9221
Gruver, Edward. *Koufax*, 7959
Gueldenpfennig, Sonia. *Women in Space Who Changed the World*, 7171
Guene, Faiza. *Kiffe Kiffe Tomorrow*, 4021(F)
Gueraseva, Stacy. *Def Jam, Inc*, 8506
Guernsey, JoAnn Bren. *Voices of Feminism*, 9812
Guerrero, Eddie. *Cheating Death, Stealing Life*, 8020
Guest, Jacqueline. *Racing Fear*, 6282(F)
War Games, 2222(F)
Guest, Judith. *Ordinary People*, 1092(F)
Guest, Tim. *My Life in Orange*, 9616
Guibert, Emmanuel. *The Professor's Daughter*, 3618(F)
Guibert, Emmanuel, et al. *The Photographer*, 9022
Guidry, Jeff. *An Eagle Named Freedom*, 8246
Guinier, Lani. *Who's Qualified?*, 9813
Gunderson, Jessica. *Gothic Art*, 8456
Gunesekera, Romesh. *Reef*, 3899(F)
Guo, Xiaolu. *Twenty Fragments of a Ravenous Youth*, 3900(F)
Gupta, Dipak K. *Who Are the Terrorists?*, 10283
Guralnick, Peter. *Careless Love*, 7542
Last Train to Memphis, 7543
Gurdon, Martin. *Travels with My Chicken*, 8247
Gurr, Andrew. *Rebuilding Shakespeare's Globe*, 7041
Gurstelle, William. *Adventures from the Technology Underground*, 11873
The Art of the Catapult, 11990
Gurtler, Janet. *If I Tell*, 1093(F)
I'm Not Her, 1729(F)
Who I Kissed, 434(F)
Guterson, David. *Snow Falling on Cedars*, 4412(F)
Guthrie, Woody. *Bound for Glory*, 7459
Gutkind, Lee. *Almost Human*, 11917
Guy, Rosa. *The Friends*, 836(F)

The Music of Summer, 837(F)

Gwin, Minrose. *The Queen of Palmyra*, 4413(F)

Gwynn, R. S. (ed.). *The Art of the Short Story*, 6371(F)

Ha, Thu-Huong. *Hail Caesar*, 1730(F)

Haab, Sherri. *Designer Style Handbags*, 12095

Haas, Robert B. *Through the Eyes of the Condor*, 9148

Through the Eyes of the Vikings, 9190

Habeeb, Mark W. *Africa*, 8918

Habel, Lia. *Dearly, Departed*, 2666(F)

Haber, Melissa Glenn. *The Pluto Project*, 435(F)

Habila, Helon. *Measuring Time*, 3848(F)

Waiting for an Angel, 3849(F)

Hadden, Gerry. *Teenage Refugees from Mexico Speak Out*, 9165

Haddix, Margaret Peterson. *Found*, 6003(F)

Just Ella, 1731(F)

Haddock, Patricia. *Environmental Time Bomb*, 10055

Teens and Gambling, 10003

Haerens, Margaret (ed.). *Illegal Immigration*, 9864

Sexually Transmitted Diseases, 10714

Hafiz, Dilara, et al. *The American Muslim Teenager's Handbook*, 9599

Hager, Jenny (ed.). *An Appalachian Tragedy*, 9535

Hager, Tom. *Linus Pauling and the Chemistry of Life*, 7902

Haggard, H. Rider. *King Solomon's Mines*, 47(F)

Hague, Michael. *In the Small*, 3360(F)

Hahn, Daniel (ed.). *The Ultimate Teen Book Guide*, 6930

Hahn, Mary Downing. *Look for Me by Moonlight*, 4673(F)

Mister Death's Blue-Eyed Girls, 5199(F)

The Wind Blows Backward, 5621(F)

Haig, Matt. *The Dead Fathers Club*, 5200(F)

Haigh, Jane G. *Gold Rush Dogs*, 11676

Gold Rush Women, 7175

Haigh, Jennifer. *Baker Towers*, 4414(F)

The Condition, 1094(F)

Haines, Kathryn Miller. *The Girl Is Murder*, 5201(F)

Haines, Tim. *Walking with Dinosaurs*, 8626

Hakim, Joy. *Einstein Adds a New Dimension*, 11817

The Story of Science, 11233

Halaby, Laila. *West of the Jordan*, 2223(F)

Halam, Ann. *Snakehead*, 6856

Halberstadt, Hans. *Roughneck Nine One*, 8890

Trigger Men, 11991

Halberstam, David. *The Children*, 9916

Firehouse, 10284

The Teammates, 7943

Haldeman, Joe. *Marsbound*, 6004(F)

Tool of the Trade, 48(F)

Halder, Baby. *A Life Less Ordinary*, 8248

Hale, Janet Campbell. *The Owl's Song*, 838(F)

Hale, Marian. *The Goodbye Season*, 4334(F)

Hale, Shannon. *Book of a Thousand Days*, 2667(F)

Enna Burning, 2668(F)

Enna Burning, 2671(F)

Forest Born, 2669(F)

The Goose Girl, 2670(F)

The Goose Girl, 2671(F)

River Secrets, 2671(F)

Hale, Stephanie. *The Alpha Bet*, 1732(F)

Haley, Alex. *The Autobiography of Malcolm X*, 7632

Roots, 9917

Haley, James (ed.). *Reparations for American Slavery*, 9918

Women in the Military, 9766

Haley, John. *The Truth About Abuse*, 10125

Haley, Matt. *Superman Returns*, 3552(F)

Hall, Barbara. *Dixie Storms*, 1095(F)

The Noah Confessions, 1096(F)

Tempo Change, 436(F)

Hall, Dede. *The Starving Students' Vegetarian Cookbook*, 12055

Hall, Derek (ed.). *The Ages of Steam and Electricity*, 11885

The Early 20th Century, 11885

Medieval Period and the Renaissance, 11885

The Modern World, 11885

Philosophy, Invention, and Engineering, 7810

The Scientific Revolution, 11886

Hall, James N. *The Bounty Trilogy*, 111(F)

Hall, John. *Is He or Isn't He?*, 5622(F)

Hall, Lynn. *Ride a Dark Horse*, 5202(F)

Hall, Martin. *Great Zimbabwe*, 8933

Hall, Rachel Howzell. *A Quiet Storm*, 1366(F)

Hall, Sarah. *The Electric Michelangelo*, 1733(F)

Halleck, Elaine (ed.). *Living in Nazi Germany*, 9062

Halliburton, Warren J. (ed.). *Historic Speeches of African Americans*, 6914

Halliday, Fred. *100 Myths About the Middle East*, 9106

Halliday, Gemma. *Deadly Cool*, 5203(F)

Deadly Cool, 5204(F)

Social Suicide, 5204(F)

Halliday, Tim (ed.). *Animal Behavior*, 11454

Halline, Allan G. (ed.). *Six Modern American Plays*, 6560

Hallowell, Edward M. *Positively ADD*, 10884

Hally, Mike. *Electronic Brains*, 11918

Halperin, David. *Journal of a UFO Investigator*, 437(F)

Halperin, Michael. *Jacob's Rescue*, 4479(F)

Halpern, Charna, et al. *Truth in Comedy*, 8609

Halpern, Julie. *Don't Stop Now*, 438(F)

Get Well Soon, 439(F)

Get Well Soon, 1367(F)

Have a Nice Day, 439(F)

Into the Wild Nerd Yonder, 1734(F)

Halpern, Paul. *What's Science Ever Done for Us? What the Simpsons Can Teach Us about Physics, Robots, Life, and the Universe*, 11234

Halpin, Brendan. *Donorboy*, 1097(F)

Forever Changes, 1368(F)

How Ya Like Me Now, 1735(F)

Shutout, 6283(F)

Tessa Masterson Will Go to Prom, 406(F)

Halpin, Mikki. *It's Your World — If You Don't Like It, Change It*, 10247

Ham, Catherine. *Knitting*, 12157

Hamamura, John Hideyo. *Color of the Sea*, 4496(F)

Hambling, David. *Weapons Grade*, 11874

Hambly, Barbara. *Renfield*, 2672(F)

Hambly, Barbara (ed.). *Sisters of the Night*, 4674(F)

Hamen, Susan E. *How to Analyze the Films of the Coen Brothers*, 8563

Hamill, Dorothy. *A Skating Life*, 8003

Hamilton, Dorothy. *Mythology*, 6842

Hamilton, Edith. *The Greek Way*, 8729

The Roman Way, 8744

Hamilton, Gary. *Super Species*, 11364

Hamilton, Harriet. *Ribbons of the Sun*, 4153(F)

Hamilton, Hugo. *The Harbor Boys*, 7363

Hamilton, Jane. *When Madeline Was Young*, 1098(F)

Hamilton, Jill (ed.). *Vegetarianism*, 10952

Hamilton, Julia. *Other People's Rules*, 839(F)

Hamilton, Kersten. *Tyger Tyger*, 2673(F)

Hamilton, Kiki. *The Faerie Ring*, 2674(F)

Hamilton, Leni. *Clara Barton*, 7761

Hamilton, Lisa M. *Deeply Rooted*, 11385

Hamilton, Martha. *How and Why Stories*, 6769

Hamilton, Rick. *A Midsummer Night's Dream*, 7043

Highwater, Jamake. *Legend Days*, 4189(F)
Higson, Charlie. *The Dead*, 54(F)
The Enemy, 54(F)
The Enemy, 55(F)
The Fear, 55(F)
Higuri, You. *Angel's Coffin*, 3365(F)
Hijuelos, Oscar. *Dark Dude*, 850(F)
Hilderbrand, Elin. *The Love Season*, 1109(F)
Hill, Barbara W. *Cooking the English Way. Rev. ed.*, 12062
Hill, C. J. *Slayers*, 2701(F)
Hill, Christine M. *Gwendolyn Brooks*, 7316
Hill, Ernest. *Cry Me a River*, 1110(F)
Hill, Frank Ernest. *The Winged Horse*, 7017
Hill, Jeff. *Prohibition*, 9435
Women's Suffrage, 9814
Hill, Jeff (ed.). *The Holocaust*, 8848
Hill, Julia Butterfly. *One Makes the Difference*, 11564
Hill, Laban Carrick. *America Dreaming*, 9465
Casa Azul, 2702(F)
Hill, Pamela Smith. *The Last Grail Keeper*, 2703(F)
Hill, Selma. *Bunny*, 6599
Hill, Stuart. *Blade of Fire*, 2704(F)
The Cry of the Icemark, 2705(F)
Hill, Will. *Department 19*, 6021(F)
The Rising, 4690(F)
Hill, William. *The Vampire Hunters*, 5222(F)
Hillenbrand, Laura. *Seabiscuit*, 12385
Hillerman, Tony. *The Best American Mystery Stories of the Century*, 5223(F)
The Best of the West, 6380(F)
Finding Moon, 4554(F)
People of Darkness, 5224(F)
Talking God, 5225(F)
Hillerman, Tony (ed.). *The Mysterious West*, 5226(F)
Hillesum, Etty. *Etty Hillesum*, 8849
Hillman, Laura. *I Will Plant You a Lilac Tree*, 8850
Hillman, Robert. *My Life as a Traitor*, 8238
Hills, Lia. *The Beginner's Guide to Living*, 1756(F)
Hillstrom, Kevin. *Food Allergies*, 10953
Genetically Modified Foods, 10954
Vietnam War, 8897
Vietnam War: Biographies, 8897
Vietnam War: Primary Sources, 8897
Hillstrom, Laurie Collier. *The Attack on Pearl Harbor*, 9446
Global Positioning Systems, 11943
Vietnam War, 8897
Vietnam War: Biographies, 8897
Vietnam War: Primary Sources, 8897
Hillyard, Paul. *The Private Life of Spiders*, 11597

Hilton, David E. *Kings of Colorado*, 4417(F)
Hilton, James. *Good-bye Mr. Chips*, 4031(F)
Random Harvest, 5638(F)
Hindle, Lee J. *Dragon Fall*, 2706(F)
Hinds, Gareth. *King Lear*, 3366(F)
The Merchant of Venice, 3367(F)
The Odyssey, 3368(F)
Hinds, Kathryn. *Everyday Life in the Renaissance*, 8760
Everyday Life in the Roman Empire, 8745
Hine, David. *Spider-Man Noir*, 3369(F)
Hines, Jim C. *Goblin War*, 2707(F)
Hines, Jim C. (ed.). *Heroes in Training*, 6373(F)
Hines, T. L. *Waking Lazarus*, 4691(F)
Hinkson, Jim. *Lacrosse Fundamentals*, 12245
Hinman, Bonnie. *A Stranger in My Own House*, 7619
Tony Blair. Rev. ed., 8091
Hino, Matsuri. *Captive Hearts, Vol. 2*, 3370(F)
Hinojosa, Maria. *Crews*, 10166
Hinton, Nigel. *The Road from Home*, 4032(F)
Hinton, S. E. *The Outsiders*, 56(F)
Rumble Fish, 57(F)
Taming the Star Runner, 1111(F)
Tex, 58(F)
That Was Then, This Is Now, 59(F)
Hintz, Martin. *Farewell, John Barleycorn*, 9436
Hinwood, Christine. *The Returning*, 2708(F)
Hiro, Dilip. *The Longest War*, 9130
Hirsch, James S. *Hurricane*, 7984
Hirsch, Jeff. *The Eleventh Plague*, 6022(F)
Hirschfelder, Arlene B. *Photo Odyssey*, 9392
Hirschmann, Kris (ed.). *Racial Profiling*, 9891
Hirshenson, Janet. *A Star Is Found*, 8566
Hirshey, Gerri. *Nowhere to Run*, 8508
Hirsi Ali, Ayaan. *Infidel*, 8253
Hitchcock, Susan Tyler. *Karen Horney*, 7877
Hitchens, Christopher. *Thomas Jefferson*, 7667
Hite, Sid. *I'm Exploding Now*, 1757(F)
Hitler, Adolf. *Mein Kampf*, 8111
Ho, Minfong. *Rice Without Rain*, 2227(F)
Hoag, Tami. *Deeper Than the Dead*, 5227(F)
Hoard, Carolyn. *Drug Therapy and Cognitive Disorders*, 10878
Hoban, Russell. *Soonchild*, 2709(F)
Hobb, Robin. *Dragon Haven*, 2710(F)
Dragon Keeper, 2711(F)
Hobbs, Valerie. *Anything but Ordinary*, 5639(F)

Get It While It's Hot. Or Not, 1758(F)
Letting Go of Bobby James, Or How I Found My Self of Steam, 1759(F)
Hobbs, Will. *The Big Wander*, 60(F)
Far North, 61(F)
Leaving Protection, 62(F)
The Maze, 63(F)
Wild Man Island, 64(F)
Hobgood, Debby. *How to Get a Job If You Are a Teenager*, 10424
Hoch, Dean. *The Sex Education Dictionary for Today's Teens and Pre-Teens*, 11030
Hoch, Nancy. *The Sex Education Dictionary for Today's Teens and Pre-Teens*, 11030
Hockenberry, John. *Moving Violations*, 8255
Hockensmith, Steve. *Dawn of the Dreadfuls*, 4692(F)
Pride and Prejudice and Zombies, 4692(F)
Hockey, Thomas A. *The Book of the Moon*, 11328
Hocking, Amanda. *Ascend*, 2712(F)
Switched, 2713(F)
Torn, 2714(F)
Hodge, Deborah. *Rescuing the Children*, 8851
Hodge, Russ. *The Molecules of Life*, 10817
Hodges, Andrew. *One to Nine*, 11751
Hodges, Rick. *What Muslims Think and How They Live*, 9602
Hodkin, Michelle. *The Evolution of Mara Dyer*, 5640(F)
The Unbecoming of Mara Dyer, 5640(F)
The Unbecoming of Mara Dyer, 5641(F)
Hoekstra, Molly. *Upstream*, 1374(F)
Hoeye, Michael. *Time to Smell the Roses*, 2715(F)
Hoffman, Alice. *At Risk*, 1112(F)
Green Angel, 2716(F)
Green Witch, 2716(F)
Incantation, 851(F)
The Red Garden, 2717(F)
The Third Angel, 5642(F)
Hoffman, Eva. *The Secret*, 6023(F)
Hoffman, Mary. *David*, 3791(F)
The Falconer's Knot, 4033(F)
Stravaganza, 2718(F)
Hoffman, Nina Kiriki. *Spirits That Walk in Shadow*, 4693(F)
Hoffman, William. *Tidewater Blood*, 5228(F)
Hoffmann, Kerry Cohen. *Easy*, 1760(F)
Hofstadter, Richard. *America at 1750*, 9295
Hofstetter, Adam B. *Cool Careers without College for People Who Love Sports*, 10497
Hogan, Ben. *Power Golf*, 12372

Katz, Eric D. *High School's Not Forever*, 10336

Katz, Jane B. (ed.). *We Rode the Wind*, 9271

Katz, Jeff. *Blue and Gold*, 3402(F)

Katz, Jon. *A Good Dog*, 11671
Izzy and Lenore, 11672
Soul of a Dog, 11644

Katz, Joseph. *The Great Trials of the Twenties*, 9722

Katz, Samuel M. *Against All Odds*, 10292
At Any Cost, 10293
Global Counterstrike, 10294
Jerusalem or Death, 9114
Jihad, 10295
Raging Within, 10296
U.S. Counterstrike: American Counterterrorism, 10294

Katz, William L. *Black Indians*, 9982
Black Pioneers, 9395

Kauffman, Bill. *Forgotten Founder, Drunken Prophet*, 7787

Kaufman, Allan. *Exploring Solar Energy*, 11842

Kaufman, Jennifer. *A Version of the Truth*, 5662(F)

Kaufman, Kate. *Free Your Mind*, 11020

Kaufman, Michael T. *1968*, 8788

Kaufman, Moises, et al. *The Laramie Project*, 7063

Kaufman, Murray S. *Reefs and Rain Forests*, 9027

Kawamura, Mika. *Panic X Panic, Vol. 1*, 3417(F)

Kay, Glenn. *Disaster Movies*, 8568

Kay, Guy Gavriel. *Ysabel*, 2768(F)

Kay, Philip (ed.). *Starting with "I"*, 10365

Kaye, Amy. *The Real Deal*, 498(F)

Kaye, Cathryn Berger. *Going Blue*, 10063

Kaye, Harvey J. *Thomas Paine*, 7748

Kaye, Marilyn. *Demon Chick*, 2769(F)

Kaysen, Susanna. *Girl, Interrupted*, 10898

Kaywell, Joan F. (ed.). *Dear Author*, 11142

Kazimiroff, Theodore L. *The Last Algonquin*, 8378

Kean, Roger Michael. *Pirates*, 8685

Kean, Sam. *The Disappearing Spoon and Other True Tales of Madness, Love, and the History of the World from the Periodic Table of the Elements*, 11709

Kearney, Meg. *The Girl in the Mirror: A Novel in Poems and Journal Entries*, 1131(F)
The Secret of Me, 1131(F)
The Secret of Me, 1132(F)

Kearney, Paul. *The Mark of Ran*, 2770(F)

Keat, Nawuth. *Alive in the Killing Fields*, 8275

Keatman, Martin. *King Arthur*, 6813

Keaton, Kelly. *A Beautiful Evil*, 2771(F)

Keats, John. *Poems*, 6652

Keegan, John. *War and Our World*, 9641

Keegan, Kyle. *Chasing the High*, 10632

Keegan, William. *Closure*, 10297

Keen, Lisa. *Out Law*, 11033

Keene, Michael L. *After the Vote Was Won*, 7564

Kehoe, Stasia Ward. *Audition*, 1810(F)

Kehret, Peg. *Encore! More Winning Monologs for Young Actors*, 6514
Tell It Like It Is, 6515

Keiler, Allan. *Marian Anderson*, 7468

Keillor, Garrison. *Leaving Home*, 6883

Keillor, Garrison (ed.). *Good Poems*, 6606

Keith, Don. *Final Patrol*, 11993

Keith, Lois. *A Different Life*, 1390(F)

Kelleher, Victor. *Del-Del*, 4714(F)

Keller, Bill. *Tree Shaker*, 8057

Keller, Emily. *Frances Perkins*, 7752

Keller, Helen. *The Story of My Life*, 7781

Kellerman, Aliza. *Prism*, 6040(F)

Kellerman, Faye. *Prism*, 6040(F)

Kelley, Aimee (ed.). *Isn't It Romantic*, 6706

Kelley, Ann. *Lost Girls*, 72(F)

Kelley, Brent. *The Horse Doctor Is In*, 11689

Kelley, William. *The Sweet Summer*, 863(F)

Kelly, Brian. *The Last Forest*, 10069

Kelly, Evelyn B. *Investigating Tuberculosis and Superbugs*, 10719

Kelly, James Patrick. *Burn*, 6041(F)
The Wreck of the Godspeed and Other Stories, 6042(F)

Kelly, James Patrick (ed.). *Feeling Very Strange*, 6386(F)

Kelly, Joe. *Four Eyes, Vol. 1*, 3418(F)
Godfall, 3421(F)
I Kill Giants, 3419(F)
Justice League Elite, Vol. 1, 3420(F)

Kelly, Kate. *Early Civilizations:*, 10803
The Middle Ages: 500–1450, 10803

Kelly, Lauren. *Blood Mask*, 5253(F)

Kelly, Richard. *Lewis Carroll*, 6955

Kelly, Ronald. *Hell Hollow*, 4715(F)

Kelly, Tara. *Amplified*, 499(F)

Kelsey, Harry. *Sir Francis Drake*, 7184

Keltner, Kim Wong. *Buddha Baby*, 864(F)

Kemal, Yasher. *Memed, My Hawk*, 2233(F)

Kemmerer, Brigid. *Storm*, 4716(F)

Kemp, Kenny. *I Hated Heaven*, 2772(F)

Kempe, C. Henry (ed.). *The Battered Child. 4th ed.*, 11201

Kendall, Martha. *Alive in the Killing Fields*, 8275

Kendrick, Beth. *Fashionably Late*, 5663(F)

Keneally, Thomas. *Schindler's List*, 4504(F)

Kenig, Graciela. *Best Careers for Bilingual Latinos*, 10450

Kenneally, Miranda. *Stealing Parker*, 5664(F)

Kennedy, Caroline. *Profiles in Courage for our Time*, 7581

Kennedy, Caroline (ed.). *A Patriot's Handbook*, 9230

Kennedy, Cate. *The World Beneath*, 1133(F)

Kennedy, Denis. *Pilates for Beginners*, 10873

Kennedy, George (ed.). *What Good Is Journalism? How Reporters and Editors Are Saving America's Way of Life*, 7098

Kennedy, James. *The Order of Odd-Fish*, 2773(F)

Kennedy, Joanne. *One Fine Cowboy*, 5665(F)

Kennedy, John. *Word Stems*, 7079

Kennedy, John F. *Profiles in Courage. Memorial Ed. (*, 7582

Kennedy, William. *Ironweed*, 4380(F)

Kennen, Ally. *Beast*, 1811(F)

Kenner, Julie. *Demon Ex Machina*, 5254(F)
Demons Are Forever, 2774(F)

Kenschaft, Lori. *Lydia Maria Child*, 7612

Kent, Deborah. *Snake Pits, Talking Cures, and Magic Bullets*, 10899

Kent, Kathleen. *The Wolves of Andover*, 4206(F)

Kenyon, Kay. *Maximum Ice*, 6043(F)

Kenyon, Nate. *Sparrow Rock*, 4717(F)

Keoke, Emory Dean. *Trade, Transportation, and Warfare*, 9272

Kephart, Beth. *Dangerous Neighbors*, 4337(F)
House of Dance, 1134(F)
Nothing but Ghosts, 5255(F)
Small Damages, 500(F)
Undercover, 501(F)
You Are My Only, 1135(F)

Keplinger, Kody. *A Midsummer's Nightmare*, 502(F)

Kerasote, Ted. *Merle's Door*, 11673

Kerman, Piper. *Orange Is the New Black*, 8276

Kerner, Charlotte. *Blueprint*, 2775(F)

Kerney, Kelly. *Born Again*, 503(F)

Kerouac, Jack. *Book of Sketches, 1952–54*, 6884

Kerouac-Parker, Frankie Edith. *You'll Be Okay*, 7382

Kerr, Jean. *Please Don't Eat the Daisies*, 6885

Kerr, Katharine. *Darkspell*, 2776(F)
The Fire Dragon, 2777(F)

Kerr, M. E. *Deliver Us from Evie*, 504(F)
Fell, 5256(F)

Kisseloff, Jeff. *Generation on Fire*, 7583

Kitanidis, Phoebe. *Glimmer*, 2786(F)
Whisper, 2787(F)

Kittle, Katrina. *Reasons to Be Happy*, 510(F)

Kittleson, Mark J. (ed.). *The Truth About Alcohol*, 10633
The Truth About Eating Disorders, 10720

Kittredge, Mary. *The Common Cold*, 10721

Kiyouoki, Satoko. *Shoulder-A-Coffin Kuro, Vol. 2*, 3433(F)

Kizer, Amber. *Meridian*, 2788(F)
Meridian, 2789(F)
One Butt Cheek at a Time, 1822(F)
Seven Kinds of Ordinary Catastrophes, 1822(F)
Wildcat Fireflies, 2789(F)

Kizilos, Peter. *Quebec*, 9158
Tibet, 9028

Klasky, Mindy. *The Girl's Guide to Witchcraft*, 5669(F)

Klass, David. *Danger Zone*, 6286(F)
Dark Angel, 511(F)
Firestorm, 6046(F)
Home of the Braves, 1823(F)

Klaus, Ian. *Elvis Is Titanic*, 9133

Klause, Annette Curtis. *Blood and Chocolate*, 4736(F)
Freaks, 2790(F)
The Silver Kiss, 4737(F)

Klauss, Lucas. *Everything You Need to Survive the Apocalypse*, 1824(F)

Klavan, Andrew. *If We Survive*, 77(F)

Kleh, Cindy. *Snowboarding Skills*, 12415

Kleid, Neil. *Brownsville*, 10173

Klein, Grady. *The Cartoon Introduction to Economics, Vol. 1*, 10313
The Red Menace, 3434(F)
The Snodgrass Conspiracy, 3435(F)

Klein, Leigh (ed.). *My Favorite Moves*, 12313
My Favorite Moves: Making the Big Plays, 12313

Klein, Lisa. *Cate of the Lost Colony*, 5670(F)
Lady Macbeth's Daughter, 4046(F)
Ophelia, 194(F)
Two Girls of Gettysburg, 4267(F)

Klein, Maury. *The Power Makers*, 11878

Klein, Norma. *Breaking Up*, 1139(F)
Going Backwards, 1140(F)

Klein, Stephanie. *Moose*, 8277

Klein, Todd. *The DC Comics Guide to Coloring and Lettering Comics*, 12115

Kleinfield, Sonny. *His Oldest Friend*, 10128

Klimecki, Zachary (ed.). *Diet Information for Teens*, 10958

Klindienst, Patricia. *The Earth Knows My Name*, 12137

Kling, Andrew A. *Cell Phones*, 11944
Web 2.0, 11921

Klosterman, Lorrie. *The Facts about Depressants*, 10634

Kluger, Richard. *Seizing Destiny*, 9231

Kluger, Steve. *My Most Excellent Year*, 512(F)

Knaak, Richard A. *Dragon Hunt*, 3436(F)

Knapp, Lynnette (ed.). *The Abortion Controversy*, 10998

Knauf, Charles. *The Eternals*, 3437(F)

Knauf, Daniel. *The Eternals*, 3437(F)

Kneale, Matthew. *When We Were Romans*, 1141(F)

Kneece, Mark. *Death's-Head Revisited*, 3613(F)

Knight, Arthur Winfield. *Johnnie D*, 4382(F)

Knight, Dominic. *Disco Boy*, 3916(F)

Knight, Judson. *Middle Ages*, 8761
Middle Ages, 8762
Middle Ages: Biographies, 8761

Knight, Karsten. *Wildfire*, 4738(F)

Knobel, Beth. *Heat and Light*, 7159

Knoll, John. *Creating the Worlds of Star Wars*, 8570

Knowles, Elizabeth. *What They Didn't Say*, 12204

Knowles, Jo. *Jumping Off Swings*, 1825(F)
Lessons from a Dead Girl, 1392(F)

Knowles, John. *Peace Breaks Out*, 1826(F)

Knox, Bernard (ed.). *The Norton Book of Classical Literature*, 6933

Knox, Elizabeth. *Dreamhunter*, 2791(F)
Dreamquake, 2792(F)

Knudson, R. R. *Just Another Love Story*, 5671(F)

Knudson, R. R. (ed.). *American Sports Poems*, 6705

Knutsson, Catherine. *Shadows Cast by Stars*, 2793(F)

Ko, Dorothy. *Every Step a Lotus*, 8996

Kobayashi, Jin. *School Rumble, Vol. 1*, 3438(F)

Kobayashi, Kathy. *Shades of L.A.*, 9884

Koenig, David. *Mouse Under Glass*, 8571

Koertge, Ron. *The Arizona Kid*, 1827(F)
Boy Girl Boy, 1828(F)
Deadville, 513(F)
Lies, Knives, and Girls in Red Dresses, 2794(F)
Now Playing, 5672(F)
Stoner and Spaz, 1393(F)
Stoner and Spaz, 5672(F)
Strays, 1142(F)
Where the Kissing Never Stops, 4938(F)

Koestler-Grack, Rachel A. *Marie Curie*, 7840
Michelle Kwan, 8004

Kogelman, Stanley. *Mind over Math*, 11754

Kogler, Jennifer Ann. *The Death Catchers*, 2795(F)

Kogler, Jennifer Anne. *Ruby Tuesday*, 1143(F)

Kohler, Dean Ellis. *Rock 'n' Roll Soldier*, 8278

Koja, Kathe. *The Blue Mirror*, 5673(F)
Buddha Boy, 1829(F)
Going Under, 1144(F)
Headlong, 1830(F)
Kissing the Bee, 1831(F)
Straydog, 1832(F)

Kokie, E. M. *Personal Effects*, 514(F)

Kolata, Gina (ed.). *The Best American Science Writing, 2007*, 11236

Kolbert, Kathryn. *Justice Talking*, 10230
Justice Talking, 10347

Kolosov, Jacqueline. *The Red Queen's Daughter*, 2796(F)
A Sweet Disorder, 4047(F)

Konigsberg, Bill. *Out of the Pocket*, 515(F)

Konstam, Angus. *Pirates*, 8685
Scourge of the Seas, 8684

Kontis, Alethea. *Enchanted*, 2797(F)

Konzak, Burt. *Samurai Spirit*, 12389

Koolish, Lynda. *African American Writers*, 7227

Koontz, Dean. *A Big Little Life*, 11674
Breathless, 6047(F)
Brother Odd, 4739(F)
The Darkest Evening of the Year, 5260(F)
The Face, 5261(F)
Fear Nothing, 5262(F)
Forever Odd, 4740(F)
The Husband, 5263(F)
Life Expectancy, 4741(F)
Odd Thomas, 4740(F)
Odd Thomas, 4742(F)
Prodigal Son, 4743(F)
Velocity, 5264(F)

Koopman, John. *McCoy's Marines*, 8900

Koopmans, Andy. *Filmmakers*, 7228
Leopold and Loeb, 9733
Rwanda, 8940

Kopelman, Jay. *From Baghdad to America*, 8279
From Baghdad, with Love, 8279

Koppes, Steven N. *Killer Rocks from Outer Space*, 11322

Kor, Eva Mozes. *Surviving the Angel of Death*, 8280

Korda, Margaret. *Horse Housekeeping*, 11690

Korda, Michael. *Horse Housekeeping*, 11690

Kordi, Gohar. *An Iranian Odyssey*, 8080

Koren, Brittany A. (ed.). *Fantasy Gone Wrong*, 2663(F)

Korman, Gordon. *Don't Care High*, 4939(F)

MacCullough, Carolyn. *Always a Witch*, 2869(F)
Drawing the Ocean, 1160(F)
Once a Witch, 2869(F)
Once a Witch, 2870(F)
Stealing Henry, 1161(F)
McCullough, Colleen. *The Song of Troy*, 3794(F)
The Thorn Birds, 3919(F)
McCullough, David. *John Adams*, 7645
The Path Between the Seas, 9163
1776, 9313
Truman, 7699
McCullough, Frances (ed.). *Earth, Air, Fire, and Water. Rev. ed.*, 6608
Love Is Like a Lion's Tooth, 6609
McCullough, Kathy. *Don't Expect Magic*, 554(F)
McCullough, L. E. *Anyone Can Produce Plays with Kids*, 8613
Plays of America from American Folklore for Young Actors, 6564
McCullough, L. E. (ed.). *111 Shakespeare Monologues for Teens*, 6488
McCullough, Noah. *The Essential Book of Presidential Trivia*, 7584
McCune, Bunny. *Girls to Women*, 11150
MacCurdy, Doug. *Sports Illustrated Tennis*, 12435
McDaniel, Lurlene. *Angel of Hope*, 3851(F)
Baby Alicia Is Dying, 2245(F)
Breathless, 1404(F)
Don't Die, My Love, 5693(F)
How Do I Love Thee? Three Stories, 1405(F)
Prey, 1884(F)
Saving Jessica, 1406(F)
Telling Christina Goodbye, 1885(F)
McDaniel, Pete. *Uneven Lies*, 12373
McDavid, Richard A. *Career Opportunities in Forensic Science*, 10529
McDermid, Val. *The Grave Tattoo*, 5303(F)
McDermott, Alice. *After This*, 4430(F)
McDevitt, Jack. *Time Travelers Never Die*, 6097(F)
McDonald, Abby. *The Anti-Prom*, 555(F)
Getting Over Garrett Delaney, 5694(F)
Sophomore Switch, 556(F)
MacDonald, Ann-Marie. *The Way the Crow Flies*, 557(F)
McDonald, Brix. *Riding on the Wind*, 4306(F)
MacDonald, Caroline. *Hostilities*, 4757(F)
Speaking to Miranda, 1886(F)
MacDonald, Fiona. *The First "Test-Tube Baby"*, 10999
MacDonald, Gina. *James Clavell*, 6991
McDonald, Ian. *Planesrunner*, 6098(F)

McDonald, Janet. *Brother Hood*, 887(F)
Harlem Hustle, 1887(F)
Off-Color, 1162(F)
Spellbound, 1163(F)
MacDonald, Joan Vos. *Tanzania*, 8942
McDonald, John. *Macbeth*, 3621(F)
McDonald, Joyce. *Swallowing Stones*, 1888(F)
MacDonald, Margaret Read. *Ghost Stories from the Pacific Northwest*, 6834
Three Minute Tales, 6772
McDonald, Sandra. *Diana Comet and Other Improbable Stories*, 2871(F)
MacDonald, Sarah. *Holy Cow*, 9009
McDonald, Steven E. *Waystation*, 6099(F)
MacDonald, Warren. *A Test of Will*, 8295
McDonell, Nick. *Twelve*, 1889(F)
McDonnell, Chris (ed.). *The Football Game I'll Never Forget*, 12368
The Game I'll Never Forget, 12380
McDonnell, Margot. *Torn to Pieces*, 5304(F)
McDougall, Chros. *Kurt Cobain*, 7489
Macdougall, Doug. *Frozen Earth*, 11718
McDowell, Michael. *Candles Burning*, 4735(F)
McEachern, Shelagh. *Mr. Perfect*, 5695(F)
Macela, Ann. *Wild Magic*, 2872(F)
McElvaine, Robert S. *The Great Depression*, 9438
McEnroe, Patrick. *Hardcourt Confidential*, 8008
MacEnulty, Pat. *Picara*, 4431(F)
McEvoy, Anne. *The American West*, 9397
The 1920s and 1930s, 8789
McEwan, Ian. *Atonement*, 1164(F)
McEwen, Christian (ed.). *Jo's Girls*, 6405(F)
McFann, Jane. *Deathtrap and Dinosaur*, 4949(F)
McFarland, Rhoda. *Coping Through Assertiveness*, 11151
Working Together Against Sexual Harassment, 11051
MacFarlane, Alan. *Glass*, 11882
MacFarlane, Katherine. *The Jeweler's Art*, 11903
McFerrin, Linda Watanabe. *Namako*, 3920(F)
McGann, Oisín. *The Gods and Their Machines*, 2873(F)
McGarrahan, Sean. *Epilepsy*, 10705
McGarrity, Michael. *Tularosa*, 5305(F)
McGarry, Katie. *Pushing the Limits*, 5696(F)
McGearhart, Susea. *Red Sky in Mourning*, 8172
McGee, Julie L. *David C. Driskell*, 7262

McGee, Marni. *The Ancient Near Eastern World*, 8725
The Ancient Roman World, 8748
McGhee, Alison. *Falling Boy*, 558(F)
McGlothlin, Bruce. *High Performance Through Understanding Systems*, 10423
McGonigal, Jane. *Reality Is Broken*, 11923
McGovern, Cammie. *Eye Contact*, 5306(F)
McGowan, Anthony. *Jack Tumor*, 4950(F)
The Knife that Killed Me, 4065(F)
MacGowan, Christopher (ed.). *Poetry for Young People*, 7066
McGowan, Gary. *Breaking Ground, Breaking Silence*, 9919
McGown, Jill. *Unlucky for Some*, 5307(F)
McGrath, Alice. *Self-Defense and Assault Prevention for Girls and Women*, 12394
Solo Forms of Karate, Tai Chi, Aikido and Kung Fu, 12395
McGrath, Marci. *Twitter*, 7820
McGrath, Melanie. *The Long Exile*, 9159
McGrayne, Sharon Bertsch. *Blue Genes and Polyester Plants*, 11241
McGuckin, Frank (ed.). *Volunteerism*, 10251
McGuigan, Mary Ann. *Morning in a Different Place*, 4432(F)
McGuire, Mark. *The 100 Greatest Baseball Players of the 20th Century Ranked*, 12296
MacHale, D. J. *The Light*, 4758(F)
MacHale, Des. *Challenging Lateral Thinking Puzzles*, 12179
Macht, Norman L. *Roberto Alomar*, 7953
McInerney, Monica. *The Alphabet Sisters*, 1165(F)
McIntire, Suzanne (ed.). *The American Heritage Book of Great American Speeches for Young People*, 6916
Macintosh, Donald. *Travels in the White Man's Grave*, 8921
McIntosh, J. S. *Gymnastics*, 12376
McIntosh, Kenneth. *Apache*, 9273
Cheyenne, 9274
Iroquois, 9274
When Religion and Politics Mix, 9662
McIntosh, Marsha. *Cheyenne*, 9274
Iroquois, 9274
When Religion and Politics Mix, 9662
McIntyre, Loren. *The Incredible Incas and Their Timeless Land*, 9179
McIver, Stuart B. *Death in the Everglades*, 7768
Mack, Karen. *A Version of the Truth*, 5662(F)
Mack, Tracy. *Birdland*, 1166(F)
McKain, Mark (ed.). *Pioneers*, 9398

Marz, Ron. *Crisis of Faith*, 3484(F)
Heaven and Earth, 3485(F)
Marzilli, Alan. *Stem Cell Research and Cloning*, 10808
Marzollo, Jean. *Fathers and Babies*, 11000
Marzorati, Gerald. *Voices in Black and White*, 9899
Mash, Robert. *How to Keep Dinosaurs*. Rev. ed., 6890
Mashima, Hiro. *Fairy Tail, Vol. 1*, 3486(F)
Masiero, Matt (ed.). *My Favorite Moves*, 12313
My Favorite Moves: Making the Big Plays, 12313
Maslin, Jamie. *Iranian Rappers and Persian Porn*, 9138
Masoff, Joy. *Snowboard!*, 12416
Mason, Antony. *A History of Western Art*, 8444
In the Time of Michelangelo, 8445
In the Time of Renoir: The Impressionist Era, 8445
Mason, Bill. *Sports Illustrated Fly Fishing*, 12354
Mason, Bobbie Ann. *In Country*, 1908(F)
Mason, Francis. *101 Stories of the Great Ballets*, 8549
Mason, Jim. *The Way We Eat*, 11394
Mason, Linda. *Teen Makeup*, 10837
Mason, Paul. *Frauds and Counterfeits*, 10177
Mason, Phil. *How George Washington Fleeced the Nation*, 8689
Mason, Sarah. *Party Girl*, 5705(F)
Playing James, 5706(F)
Mass, Wendy. *Heaven Looks a Lot like the Mall*, 578(F)
Massey, Misty. *Mad Kestrel*, 2919(F)
Massey, Sujata. *Shimura Trouble*, 5324(F)
Massie, Robert K. *Peter the Great*, 8125
The Romanovs, 9090
Masson, Jeffrey Moussaieff. *Altruistic Armadillos, Zenlike Zebras*, 11479
Masson, Sophie. *The Madman of Venice*, 4071(F)
Masters, Jarvis Jay. *That Bird Has My Wings*, 8301
Masterton, Graham. *Blind Panic*, 4773(F)
Mastro, Jim. *Under Antarctic Ice*, 9197
Masur, Louis P. *The Soiling of Old Glory*, 8430
Matar, Hisham. *In the Country of Men*, 3853(F)
Matas, Carol. *Past Crimes*, 5325(F)
Matheson, Richard. *Duel*, 6409(F)
Nightmare at 20,000 Feet, 4774(F)
Mathews, Dan. *Committed*, 8302
Mathews, Eddie. *Eddie Mathews and the National Pastime*, 7963
Mathez, Edmond A. *The Earth Machine*, 11719

Mathis, Sharon. *Teacup Full of Roses*, 1410(F)
Matlock, Curtiss Ann. *Little Town, Great Big Life*, 579(F)
Matson, Morgan. *Second Chance Summer*, 580(F)
Matsumoto, Taiyo. *Gogo Monster*, 3487(F)
Mattawa, Khaled (ed.). *Dinarzad's Children*, 861(F)
Matteson, Mollie (ed.). *Welfare Ranching*, 10113
Matthee, Dalene. *Fiela's Child*, 3854(F)
Matthews, Arlene. *Getting in Without Freaking Out*, 10409
Matthews, Kezi. *Scorpio's Child*, 4435(F)
Matthews, L. S. *The Outcasts*, 4775(F)
Matthews, Phoebe. *Switchstance*, 1909(F)
Matthews, Tom. *Like We Care*, 2247(F)
Mattison, Chris. *The Encyclopedia of Snakes*, 11439
Matyszak, Philip. *Legionary*, 8747
Maude, Rachel. *Poseur*, 581(F)
Maupassant, Guy de. *The Best Short Stories of Guy de Maupassant*, 172(F)
Maus, Derek C. (ed.). *Living Through the Red Scare*, 9468
Living Under the Threat of Nuclear War, 9469
Mauser, Pat Rhoads. *Love Is for the Dogs*, 5707(F)
Maushart, Susan. *The Winter of Our Disconnect*, 11925(F)
Maxwell, Katie. *They Wear What Under Their Kilts?*, 4956(F)
May, Elaine Tyler. *America and the Pill*, 11001
May, Suellen. *Steroids and Other Performance-Enhancing Drugs*, 10647
May-Treanor, Misty. *Misty*, 8024
Mayer, Marianna. *Remembering the Prophets of Sacred Scripture*, 9566
Mayer, Melody. *Friends with Benefits*, 1910(F)
Mayer, Robert H. *The Civil Rights Act of 1964*, 9825
When the Children Marched, 9826
Mayhew, Margaret. *The Little Ship*, 4072(F)
Maynard, Jeff. *Wings of Ice*, 7212
Maynard, Joyce. *Labor Day*, 582(F)
Mayne, Kenny. *An Incomplete and Inaccurate History of Sport*, 12253
Mayor, Mireya. *Pink Boots and a Machete*, 8303
Mazer, Anne (ed.). *Going Where I'm Coming From*, 7230
A Walk in My World, 6410(F)
Working Days, 1911(F)
Mazer, Harry. *Bright Days, Stupid Nights*, 1915(F)
The Girl of His Dreams, 1912(F)

Heroes Don't Run, 4511(F)
Hey, Kid! Does She Love Me?, 1913(F)
I Love You, Stupid!, 1914(F)
The Last Mission, 4512(F)
Somebody, Please Tell Me Who I Am, 1411(F)
Mazer, Norma Fox. *After the Rain*, 1174(F)
Bright Days, Stupid Nights, 1915(F)
Downtown, 1175(F)
The Missing Girl, 5326(F)
Missing Pieces, 1176(F)
Meaney, Flynn. *The Boy Recession*, 5708(F)
Means, D. Bruce. *Stalking the Plumed Serpent and Other Adventures in Herpetology*, 11433
Meany, John. *Has the Civil Rights Movement Been Successful?*, 9827
Is Genetic Research a Threat?, 10824
Mechling, Jay. *On My Honor*, 11219
Mechling, Lauren. *All Q, No A*, 583(F)
Foreign Exposure, 584(F)
The Rise and Fall of a 10th Grade Social Climber, 1916(F)
Mechner, Jordan. *Prince of Persia*, 3489(F)
Solomon's Thieves, 3488(F)
Medawar, Mardi O. *Witch of the Palo Duro*, 4193(F)
Medeiros, Teresa. *Fairest of Them All*, 3826(F)
Medina, John. *The Clock of Ages*, 10599
Medina, Nico. *The Straight Road to Kylie*, 1917(F)
Medley, Linda. *Castle Waiting*, 3490(F)
Mee, Benjamin. *We Bought a Zoo*, 11703
Meehl, Brian. *Suck It Up*, 4957(F)
You Don't Know About Me, 585(F)
Meekings, Sam. *Under Fishbone Clouds*, 3925(F)
Mehan, Uppinder (ed.). *So Long Been Dreaming*, 6025(F)
Meimu. *Ju-On, Vol. 2*, 3628(F)
Meinkoth, Norman A. *The Audubon Society Field Guide to North American Seashore Creatures*, 11602
Meisel, Abigail. *Investigating Depression and Bipolar Disorder*, 10904
Meisler, Stanley. *Kofi Annan*, 8048
United Nations, 9624
Meissner, Rolf. *The Little Book of Planet Earth*, 11720
Meister, Ellen. *The Smart One*, 586(F)
Mekler, Eva. *Sunrise Shows Late*, 5709(F)
Meldrum, Christina. *Madapple*, 4776(F)
Melling, O. R. *The Book of Dreams*, 2920(F)
The Light-Bearer's Daughter, 2921(F)

The Summer King, 2922(F)

Melling, Orla. *The Druid's Tune*, 2923(F)

Mellom, Robin. *Ditched*, 587(F)

Mellor, Don. *American Rock*, 12344

Mellor, Ronald. *The Ancient Roman World*, 8748

The World in Ancient Times, 8712

Melnikoff, Pamela. *Prisoner in Time*, 4513(F)

Meltzer, Brad. *The Tenth Justice*, 97(F)

Meltzer, Milton. *The Black Americans*, 9932

Bound for America, 9869

Carl Sandburg, 7413

Edgar Allan Poe, 7405

Emily Dickinson, 7338

Henry David Thoreau, 7426

Herman Melville, 7394

Nathaniel Hawthorne, 7367

Walt Whitman, 7439

Willa Cather, 7320

Meltzer, Milton (ed.). *Frederick Douglass*, 7617

Hour of Freedom, 6715

Melville, Herman. *Moby Dick*, 3491(F)

Melzer, Richard. *When We Were Young in the West*, 9540

Meminger, Neesha. *Shine, Coconut Moon*, 896(F)

Menand, Louis (ed.). *The Best American Essays, 2004*, 6891

Mendell, David. *Obama*, 7685

Mendle, Jane. *Better Off Famous?*, 588(F)

Menez, Joseph F. *Summaries of Leading Cases on the Constitution*, 9666

Menhard, Francha Roffe. *The Facts about Amphetamines*, 10648

The Facts About Inhalants, 10649

Inhalants, 10650

Internet Issues, 11926

Meno, Joe. *Bluebirds Used to Croon in the Choir*, 6411(F)

The Boy Detective Fails, 2924(F)

Hairstyles of the Damned, 1918(F)

Menzer, Joe. *The Wildest Ride*, 12279

Mercado, Nancy E. (ed.). *Every Man for Himself*, 6412(F)

Mercier, Cathryn M. *Presenting Avi*, 7310

Merino, Noel (ed.). *U.S. Military Deployment*, 11998

Vaccines, 10809

Meriwether, Louise. *Daddy Was a Number Runner*, 897(F)

Fragments of the Ark, 4268(F)

Merlino, Doug. *The Hustle*, 12316

Mero, Paul. *The Natural Family*, 10123

Merrell, Billy. *Talking in the Dark*, 6611

Merrell, Billy (ed.). *The Full Spectrum*, 10240

Merritt, Rob. *No Easy Answers*, 10144

Mertz, Stephen. *Night Wind*, 4777(F)

Merullo, Roland. *The Talk-Funny Girl*, 1919(F)

Messinger, Jonathan. *Hiding Out*, 6413(F)

Messner-Loebs, William. *Epicurus the Sage*, 3492(F)

Metcalf, Franz. *Buddha in Your Backpack*, 9567

Metcalf, Gena. *Phobias*, 10905

Metcalf, Gena (ed.). *Nuclear Power*, 11858

Metcalf, Linda. *How to Say It to Get into the College of Your Choice*, 10410

Metcalf, Tom. *Phobias*, 10905

Metcalf, Tom (ed.). *Nuclear Power*, 11858

Metselaar, Menno. *Anne Frank*, 8106

Mettger, Zak. *Justice Talking*, 10230

Justice Talking, 10347

Metzger, Barbara. *The Hourglass*, 5710(F)

Meyer, Adam. *The Last Domino*, 2248(F)

Meyer, Carolyn. *Cleopatra Confesses*, 3778(F)

Duchessina, 4073(F)

In Mozart's Shadow, 4074(F)

Loving Will Shakespeare, 4075(F)

The True Adventures of Charley Darwin, 4076(F)

Where the Broken Heart Still Beats, 4309(F)

Meyer, Don (ed.). *The Sibling Slam Book*, 11204

Meyer, John (ed.). *Friends and Family*, 6918

Love and Relationships, 6919

Teen Ink 2: More Voices, More Visions, 6920

Meyer, L. A. *In the Belly of the Bloodhound*, 98(F)

The Mark of the Golden Dragon, 99(F)

Mississippi Jack, 100(F)

Rapture of the Deep, 101(F)

Under the Jolly Roger, 102(F)

The Wake of the Lorelei Lee, 103(F)

Meyer, Marissa. *Cinder*, 6105(F)

Scarlet, 6106(F)

Meyer, Stephanie H. (ed.). *Friends and Family*, 6918

Love and Relationships, 6919

Teen Ink 2: More Voices, More Visions, 6920

Meyer, Stephenie. *Breaking Dawn*, 2925(F)

Eclipse, 4778(F)

Eclipse, 4780(F)

The Host, 6107(F)

New Moon, 4779(F)

The Short Second Life of Bree Tanner, 4780(F)

Twilight, 4781(F)

Meyers, Karen. *Colonialism and the Revolutionary Period, Beginnings to 1800*, 6993

Contemporary American Literature, 1945 to Present, 6998

Realism and Regionalism, 1860– 1910, 6990

Romanticism and Transcendentalism, 1800–1860, 6989

Meyers, Odette. *Doors to Madame Marie*, 8860

Mgadla, Part T. *Batswana*, 8962

Mi Young Hur, Angela. *The Queens of K-Town*, 898(F)

Michaelis, Antonia. *Dragons of Darkness*, 2926(F)

Tiger Moon, 2927(F)

Michaels, Barbara. *Shattered Silk*, 5327(F)

Stitches in Time, 5328(F)

Michaels, Fern. *Plain Jane*, 5329(F)

Michaels, Jamie. *Kiss My Book*, 589(F)

Michaels, Kasey. *Becket's Last Stand*, 5711(F)

Beware of Virtuous Women, 5712(F)

Bowled Over, 5330(F)

The Dangerous Debutante, 5713(F)

A Gentleman by Any Other Name, 5714(F)

High Heels and Homicide, 5331(F)

The Kissing Game, 5715(F)

Maggie by the Book, 5716(F)

Maggie Needs an Alibi, 5332(F)

A Reckless Beauty, 4077(F)

The Return of the Prodigal, 2928(F)

This Can't Be Love, 5717(F)

Michaels, Rune. *Fix Me*, 590(F)

Genesis Alpha, 5333(F)

Michener, James A. *The Bridges at Toko-Ri*, 4561(F)

Legacy, 2249(F)

Tales of the South Pacific, 4514(F)

Micklem, Sarah. *Firethorn*, 2929(F)

Wildfire, 2929(F)

Mieville, China. *Railsea*, 2930(F)

Perdido Street Station, 2931(F)

Mignola, Mike. *B.P.R.D.*, 3494(F)

Baltimore, 4782(F)

The Black Flame, 3495(F)

Strange Places, 3493(F)

Mignola, Mike, et al. *The Black Goddess*, 3496(F)

The Dead, 3497(F)

The Soul of Venice and Other Stories, 3498(F)

Mikaelsen, Ben. *Tree Girl*, 4164(F)

Mikkelsen, Einar. *Two Against the Ice*, 7202

Miklowitz, Gloria D. *After the Bomb*, 104(F)

Camouflage, 105(F)

Masada, 3779(F)

The War Between the Classes, 899(F)

Mikolaycak, Charles. *Orpheus*, 6860

Miles, Barry. *Hippie*, 9470

Miles, Bernard. *Favorite Tales from Shakespeare*, 6537

Miles, Elizabeth. *Fury*, 2932(F)

Miles, Jackie Lee. *All That's True*, 1177(F)

Moriarty, Jaclyn. *A Corner of White*, 2947(F)

The Murder of Bindy Mackenzie, 597(F)

The Spell Book of Listen Taylor, 1184(F)

The Year of Secret Assignments, 1929(F)

Moriarty, Laura. *The Center of Everything*, 1930(F)

The Rest of Her Life, 598(F)

Morin, Isobel V. *Our Changing Constitution*, 9676

Politics, American Style, 9752

Women of the U.S. Congress, 7587

Women Who Reformed Politics, 7588

Morkes, Andrew, et al (ed.). *Top 100*, 10459

25 Jobs That Have It All, 10460

Morley, David. *Healing Our World*, 10810

Mornin, Edward. *Saints*, 9585

Mornin, Lorna. *Saints*, 9585

Morpurgo, Michael. *Beowulf*, 6811

Private Peaceful, 4457(F)

Morressy, John. *The Juggler*, 3827(F)

Morrill, Lauren. *Meant to Be*, 5721(F)

Morris, Bruce C. *Live Aware, Not in Fear*, 11016

Morris, Deborah. *Teens 911*, 106(F)

Morris, Desmond. *Catwatching*, 11653

Morris, Gilbert. *Toward the Sunrising*, 4343(F)

Morris, Ian Macgregor. *Themistocles*, 8136

Morris, Jeannie. *Brian Piccolo*, 7996

Morris, Jim. *The Oldest Rookie*, 7965

Morris, JoAnne Prichard. *Barefootin'*, 7609

Morris, Keith Lee. *The Dart League King*, 599(F)

Morris, Lynn. *Toward the Sunrising*, 4343(F)

Morris, Mark (ed.). *Cinema Macabre*, 8579

Morris, Mary McGarry. *Light from a Distant Star*, 600(F)

Morris, Neil. *Biomass Power*, 11846

Do You Know What's in Your Food?, 10964

The Energy Mix, 11846

Food for Sports, 10964

Fossil Fuels, 11846

Geothermal Power, 11846

Global Warming, 10080

Should Substance-Abusing Athletes Be Banned for Life?, 12254

Morris, Richard B. *Basic Documents in American History*, 9233

Morris, Rod. *South Sea Islands*, 9043

Morris, Winifred. *Liar*, 1931(F)

Morrison, Adrian R. *An Odyssey with Animal*, 10011

Morrison, Betsy S. *Self-Esteem*, 11154

Morrison, Grant. *Kid Eternity*, 3517(F)

Neil Gaiman's Neverwhere, 3273(F)

Seven Soldiers of Victory, Vol. 3, 3515(F)

Vimanarama, 3516(F)

WE3, 3518(F)

Morrison, Grant, et al. *Deus ex Machina*, 7141

Seven Soldiers of Victory, Vol. 1, 3519(F)

Seven Soldiers of Victory, Vol. 2, 3520(F)

Morrison, Toni. *Beloved*, 4344(F)

Remember, 9831

Morrissey, Donna. *Kit's Law*, 4166(F)

Morrow, James (ed.). *Nebula Awards 26*, 6110(F)

Nebula Awards 27, 6111(F)

Morrow, John (ed.). *Streetwise*, 7222

Morse, Tim. *Classic Rock Stories*, 8517

Mortensen, Colin. *On Friendship*, 11145

Mortenson, Greg. *Stones into Schools*, 9031

Three Cups of Tea, 8309

Mortimer, Sean. *Hawk*, 8021

Morton, Danelle. *The Healing Power of Pets*, 11642

Morton, Joseph C. *The American Revolution*, 9315

Morton, Oliver. *Mapping Mars*, 11309

Morvan, Jean David. *Wake, Vol. 6/7*, 3521(F)

Wake, 3522(F)

Morwood, Peter. *Star Trek*, 6112(F)

Mosby, Rebekah Presson (ed.). *Poetry Speaks Expanded*, 6620

Moseley, James W. *Shockingly Close to the Truth*, 12206

Moser, Diane Kit. *The Age of Synthesis: 1800–1895*, 11248

Barbara McClintock, 7887

The Birth of Science, 11248

Modern Science: 1896–1945, 11248

The Rise of Reason: 1700–1799, 11248

Moser, Laura. *All Q, No A*, 583(F)

Foreign Exposure, 584(F)

Playground, 392(F)

The Rise and Fall of a 10th Grade Social Climber, 1916(F)

Moses, Shelia P. *I, Dred Scott*, 4233(F)

Mosier, John. *Grant*, 7656

Moskowitz, Hannah. *Break*, 1416(F)

Gone, Gone, Gone, 1932(F)

Invincible Summer, 1185(F)

Mosley, Walter. *Fortunate Son*, 901(F)

Life Out of Context, 9933

Moss, Howard. *Chasing the High*, 10632

Moss, Leonard. *Arthur Miller*, 7067

Moss, Marissa. *A Soldier's Secret*, 4271(F)

Mosse, Kate. *The Winter Ghosts*, 4078(F)

Moulton, Courtney Allison. *Wings of the Wicked*, 2948(F)

Mountjoy, Shane. *Engel v. Vitale*, 9739

Mourlevat, Jean-Claude. *Winter's End*, 2949(F)

Mowat, Farley. *Woman in the Mists*, 7864

Mowll, Joshua. *Operation Red Jericho*, 3523(F)

Operation Typhoon Shore, 107(F)

Mowry, Jess. *Babylon Boyz*, 1417(F)

Moye, J. Todd. *Freedom Flyers*, 9449

Moyer, Kermit. *The Chester Chronicles*, 1933(F)

Moyers, Bill. *Welcome to Doomsday*, 9586

Mozeson, I. E. *The Place I Call Home*, 10220

Mucci, Michael. *Dracula*, 3524(F)

Mucha, Corinne. *Freshman*, 3525(F)

Muckenhoupt, Margaret. *Dorothea Dix*, 7613

Mueller, Melinda. *What the Ice Gets*, 7068

Mufson, Susan. *Straight Talk About Child Abuse*, 11205

Mukherjee, Bharati. *Desirable Daughters*, 601(F)

Mukhopadhyay, Tito Rajarshi. *How Can I Talk if My Lips Don't Move? Inside My Autistic Mind*, 10739

Mullane, Deirdre. *Crossing the Danger Water*, 902(F)

Mullany, Janet. *Jane and the Damned*, 4787(F)

Muller, Melissa. *Anne Frank*, 8107

Muller, Richard A. *The Instant Physicist*, 11822

Mullin, Caryl Cude. *Rough Magic*, 2950(F)

Mullin, Mike. *Ashen Winter*, 6113(F)

Ashfall, 108(F)

Ashfall, 6113(F)

Mullin, Rita Thievon. *Thomas Jefferson*, 7668

Munson, Lulie. *In Their Own Words*, 11052

Munson, Sam. *The November Criminals*, 1934(F)

Murakami, Maki. *Kanpai! Vol. 1*, 3526(F)

Murdico, Suzanne J. *Bomb Squad Experts*, 10532

Murdoch, Emily. *If You Find Me*, 1186(F)

Murdoch, Patricia. *Exposure*, 1935(F)

Murdock, Catherine Gilbert. *Front and Center*, 1936(F)

The Off Season, 1937(F)

Princess Ben, 2951(F)

Wisdom's Kiss, 5722(F)

Murguia, Alejandro. *This War Called Love*, 903(F)

Murie, Olaus J. *A Field Guide to Animal Tracks. 2nd ed.*, 11464

Murillo, Kathy Cano. *The Crafty Diva's Lifestyle Makeover*, 12017

Murowchick, Robert E. *China*, 9000

Murphy, Bill. *In a Time of War*, 8160

886

Parker, Julie. *Everything You Need to Know About Living in a Shelter*, 10217

Parker, Katrina. *Living with Diabetes*, 10752

Parker, Linda Busby. *Seven Laurels*, 918(F)

Parker, Robert B. *Chasing the Bear*, 5364(F)

Parker, Thomas. *Day by Day*, 8904

Parkhouse, Steve. *The Milkman Murders*, 3277(F)

Parkhurst, Carolyn. *Lost and Found*, 4962(F)

Parkin, Joe. *A Dog in a Hat*, 8025

Parks, Adele. *Larger Than Life*, 4963(F)

Parks, Deborah. *Nature's Machines*, 7880

Parks, Gordon. *The Learning Tree*, 919(F)

Parks, Peggy J. *Alzheimer's Disease*, 10914

Autism, 10915

Brain Tumors, 10753

Down Syndrome, 10916

Gangs, 10182

HPV, 10754

Influenza, 10755

Obsessive-Compulsive Disorder, 10917

Online Addiction, 11930

Online Social Networking, 11931

Schizophrenia, 10756

Self-Injury Disorder, 10918

Space Research, 11312

Teenage Sex and Pregnancy, 11004

Parks, Richard. *The Long Look*, 2986(F)

Parks, Rosa. *Rosa Parks*, 7634

Parkyn, Neil (ed.). *The Seventy Wonders of the Modern World*, 11884

Parnell, Helga. *Cooking the German Way. Rev. ed.*, 12069

Cooking the South American Way. Rev. ed., 12070

Parnham, I. J. *Miss Dempsey's School for Gunslingers*, 4314(F)

Parra, Nancy J. *The Bettin' Kind*, 5736(F)

The Lovin' Kind, 5737(F)

Loving Lana, 5738(F)

The Marryin' Kind, 5739(F)

A Wanted Man, 5740(F)

Parton, Sarah. *Cleisthenes*, 8096

Partridge, Elizabeth. *John Lennon*, 7526

Marching for Freedom, 9835

This Land Was Made for You and Me, 7460

Pasachoff, Naomi. *Ernest Rutherford*, 7904

Pascal, Francine. *Fearless FBI*, 5365(F)

The Ruling Class, 1970(F)

Pascal, Janet B. *Arthur Conan Doyle*, 7341

Jacob Riis, 7410

Paschen, Elise (ed.). *Poetry Speaks Expanded*, 6620

Pascoe, Elaine. *The Pacific Rim*, 8989

Pasko, Martin. *Superman Returns*, 3552(F)

Passero, Barbara (ed.). *Energy Alternatives*, 11849

Pasternak, Boris Leonidovich, et al. *Doctor Zhivago*, 4090(F)

Pasternak, Ceel. *Cool Careers for Girls in Air and Space*, 10463

Cool Careers for Girls in Computers, 10556

Cool Careers for Girls in Food, 10464

Cool Careers for Girls in Law, 10533

Cool Careers for Girls in Sports, 10503

Patent, Dorothy Hinshaw. *Treasures of the Spanish Main*, 9154

Paterson, Katherine. *Come Sing, Jimmy Jo*, 1196(F)

Jacob Have I Loved, 1197(F)

Lyddie, 4235(F)

Patmore, Chris. *Moviemaking Course*, 8582

Patneaude, David. *Epitaph Road*, 6133(F)

Thin Wood Walls, 4517(F)

Patrick, Cat. *Forgotten*, 5366(F)

Revived, 5367(F)

Patrick, John J. *The Bill of Rights*, 9677

Patrick, William. *Thieves of Baghdad*, 9125

Patterson, Charles. *From Buchenwald to Carnegie Hall*, 8835

Patterson, Dan. *Aviation Century*, 11959

Aviation Century: World War II, 11959

Patterson, James. *Beach Road*, 5370(F)

Judge and Jury, 5368(F)

Maximum Ride, 2987(F)

Maximum Ride, Vol. 1, 3553(F)

Med Head, 8231

10th Anniversary, 5369(F)

Patterson, Janci. *Chasing the Skip*, 1198(F)

Pattillo, Beth. *Mr. Darcy Broke My Heart*, 632(F)

Patton, Fiona. *The Golden Sword*, 2988(F)

Pattou, Edith. *East*, 2989(F)

Paul, Anthea. *Girlosophy*, 12071

Paul, Dominique. *The Possibility of Fireflies*, 1199(F)

Pauley, Kimberly. *Cat Girl's Day Off*, 2990(F)

Sucks to Be Me, 2991(F)

Paulsen, Gary. *Canyons*, 113(F)

Harris and Me, 4964(F)

The Island, 1971(F)

My Life in Dog Years, 11678

Nightjohn, 4236(F)

Popcorn Days and Buttermilk Nights, 1972(F)

The River, 114(F)

Sentries, 2256(F)

Sisters / Hermanas, 1973(F)

Winterdance, 12258

Pausewang, Gudrun. *Traitor*, 4518(F)

Pavelka, Ed. *Bicycling Magazine's Basic Maintenance and Repair*, 12329

The Complete Book of Long-Distance Cycling, 12326

Pavlenkov, Victor (ed.). *Russia*, 9092

Pavlik, John V. *Journalism and New Media*, 7145

Pawlak, Mark, et al (ed.). *Bullseye*, 6434(F)

Shooting the Rat, 6621

Pawlett, Ray. *The Karate Handbook*, 12390

Payne, Ann Kirby-. *Understanding Weight and Depression*, 10687

Payne, C. D. *Revolting Youth*, 4965(F)

Payne, Lucille. *The Seventeenth Child*, 8326

Payne, Roger. *Among Whales*, 11633

Pazira, Nelofer. *A Bed of Red Flowers*, 8327

Peacock, Kathleen. *Hemlock*, 2992(F)

Peacock, Shane. *Eye of the Crow*, 5371(F)

Vanishing Girl, 5372(F)

Pearce, Fred. *Earth Then and Now*, 10083

With Speed and Violence, 10084

Pearce, Jackson. *As You Wish*, 2993(F)

Fathomless, 2994(F)

Purity, 633(F)

Sisters Red, 4801(F)

Pearce, Q. L. *Artificial Intelligence*, 11932

Pearlman, Ann. *Inside the Crips*, 10192

Pearlman, Jeff. *Love Me, Hate Me*, 7954

Pearson, Joanna. *Rites and Wrongs of Janice Wills*, 5741(F)

Pearson, Mary E. *The Adoration of Jenna Fox*, 6134(F)

The Adoration of Jenna Fox, 6135(F)

The Fox Inheritance, 6135(F)

The Miles Between, 1974(F)

A Room on Lorelei Street, 1200(F)

Pearson, Michael. *Shohola Falls*, 1975(F)

Pearson, Susan. *Charles Darwin and the Mystery of Mysteries*, 7846

Pease, Donald E. *Theodor Seuss Geisel*, 7356

Peavy, Linda. *Frontier Children*, 9400

Full-Court Quest, 12319

Pioneer Women, 9401

Peck, Dale. *The Drift House*, 2995(F)

The Lost Cities, 2996(F)

Sprout, 1976(F)

Peck, Richard. *Bed and Breakfast*, 1977(F)

Father Figure, 1201(F)

A Long Way from Chicago, 4966(F)
Past Perfect, Present Tense, 6435(F)
Remembering the Good Times,
1427(F)
The River Between Us, 4275(F)
A Year Down Yonder, 4967(F)
Peck, Robert McCracken. *Headhunters
and Hummingbirds*, 9181
Pedersen, Laura. *Beginner's Luck*,
1978(F)
Beginners Luck, 1202(F)
The Big Shuffle, 1202(F)
Heart's Desire, 1202(F)
Pedroch, Cherry. *Obsessive-
Compulsive Disorder*, 10896
Pedrosa, Cyril. *Three Shadows*,
3554(F)
Pedrvola, Cindy. *How to Get a Job If
You Are a Teenager*, 10424
Peebles, Curtis. *Asteroids*, 11326
Peet, Mal. *Exposure*, 6296(F)
Keeper, 6297(F)
Life, 4091(F)
The Penalty, 6298(F)
Tamar, 4519(F)
Peeters, Benoit. *The Invisible Frontier,
Vol. 1*, 3607(F)
Peffer, Jessica. *DragonArt*, 12131
Peirce, Jeremy. *Attention-Deficit/
Hyperactivity Disorder*, 10919
Pekar, Harvey. *The Quitter*, 7404
Students for a Democratic Society,
9472
Pelczar, Rita (ed.). *Homegrown
Harvest*, 11391
Pella, Judith. *Mark of the Cross*,
5742(F)
Pellegrino, Marge. *Journey of Dreams*,
920(F)
Peloquin, Lili. *The Innocents*, 5373(F)
Pelosi, Nancy. *Know Your Power*, 7751
Pendergast, Tom. *The Vietnam War*,
9498
Pendergrass, Tess. *Dark of the Moon*,
5374(F)
Pendleton, Thomas. *Mason*, 4802(F)
Penhallow, David. *Concrete to Canvas*,
8409
Penman, Sharon Kay. *The Queen's
Man*, 5375(F)
Pennac, Daniel. *The Rights of the
Reader*, 7113
Pennell, Melissa McFarland. *Student
Companion to Edith Wharton*,
6995
Penzler, Otto (ed.). *Uncertain Endings*,
5376(F)
The Vampire Archives, 6436(F)
Pepe, Phil. *Few and Chosen*, 12293
Percival, Kris. *Speed Knitting*, 12162
Pereira, James. *On Edge*, 12387
Perera, Anna. *The Glass Collector*,
4092(F)
Guantanamo Boy, 2257(F)
Perez, Ashley Hope. *The Knife and the
Butterfly*, 2258(F)

Pérez, George. *Wonder Woman*,
3555(F)
Pérez, George (ed.). *Ethics*, 11091
Perez, Marlene. *Dead Is a State of
Mind*, 4803(F)
Dead Is the New Black, 4803(F)
Perker, M. K. *Cairo*, 3744(F)
Perkins, James A. (ed.). *Brother
Enemy*, 6770
Perkins, Mitali. *Extreme American
Makeover*, 634(F)
Secret Keeper, 921(F)
White House Rules, 635(F)
Perkins, Stephanie. *Anna and the
French Kiss*, 5743(F)
Lola and the Boy Next Door, 5744(F)
Perl, Erica S. *Vintage Veronica*,
5745(F)
Perl, Lila. *Torture*, 9649
Perrault, Charles. *Cinderella*, 6812
Perret, Patti. *The Faces of Science
Fiction*, 6996
Perricone, Mike. *The Big Bang*, 11354
Perrin, Kayla. *We'll Never Tell*,
5377(F)
Perrotta, Tom. *Joe College*, 1979(F)
Perry, Anne. *Brunswick Gardens*,
5378(F)
Perry, Dal. *Chris Bunch's The
Gangster Conspiracy*, 6136(F)
Perry, James M. *Arrogant Armies*, 8693
Perry, Kate. *Project Date*, 4968(F)
Perry, Mark. *A Dress for Mona*, 6551
Perry, Steve. *Chris Bunch's The
Gangster Conspiracy*, 6136(F)
Death Star, 6143(F)
Persico, Deborah A. *New Jersey v.
T.L.O.*, 9743
Pessl, Marisha. *Special Topics in
Calamity Physics*, 5379(F)
Peterfreund, Diana. *For Darkness
Shows the Stars*, 6137(F)
Rampant, 2997(F)
Secret Society Girl, 636(F)
Peters, Arthur K. *Seven Trails West*,
9402
Peters, Colette. *Colette's Cakes*, 12072
Peters, Elizabeth. *Crocodile on the
Sandbank*, 5380(F)
Peters, Ellis. *The Holy Thief*, 5381(F)
Peters, Julie Anne. *By the Time You
Read This, I'll Be Dead*, 1428(F)
grl2grl, 1980(F)
It's Our Prom (So Deal with It),
1981(F)
*She Loves You, She Loves You Not
. . .*, 5746(F)
Peters, Kimberly Joy. *Painting Caitlyn*,
637(F)
Peters, Margaret. *The Ebony Book of
Black Achievement*, 7590
Peters, Stephanie True. *The Battle
Against Polio*, 10757
Petersen, Christine. *Does Everyone
Have ADHD? A Teen's Guide to
Diagnosis and Treatment*, 10758

Petersen, David. *Mouse Guard*,
3556(F)
Peterson, Brenda. *Build Me an Ark*,
11426
I Want to Be Left Behind, 8328
Peterson, Linda. *Entertainment*, 10504
Peterson, Lois. *Disconnect*, 1982(F)
Peterson, Roger Tory. *All Things
Reconsidered*, 11529
*A Field Guide to the Birds of Eastern
and Central North America. 5th
ed.*, 11530
*A Field Guide to Wildflowers of
Northeastern and North-Central
North America*, 11415
Peterson, Todd. *Tony Hawk*, 8022
Peterson, Tracie. *Controlling Interests*,
5747(F)
Embers of Love, 5748(F)
A Promise to Believe In, 5749(F)
Tidings of Peace, 4520(F)
Peterson, Virginia Marie. *A Field
Guide to the Birds of Eastern and
Central North America. 5th ed.*,
11530
Petrides, George A. *A Field Guide to
Trees and Shrubs*, 11404
Petrie, Ferdinand. *The Big Book of
Painting Nature in Watercolor*,
12132
Petrikin, Jonathan S. (ed.).
Environmental Justice, 10085
Petrucha, Stefan. *Breaking Down*,
3430(F)
Ripper, 5382(F)
Split, 1983(F)
Teen, Inc., 115(F)
Petterson, Per. *Out Stealing Horses*,
1203(F)
Pettit, Marilyn (ed.). *Romeo and Juliet*,
7046
Peyton, K. M. *Darkling*, 157(F)
Pfaff, Daniel W. *Joseph Pulitzer II and
the Post-Dispatch*, 7933
Pfeffer, Susan Beth. *Blood Wounds*,
1204(F)
The Dead and the Gone, 116(F)
Life as We Knew It, 6138(F)
Pflock, Karl T. *Shockingly Close to the
Truth*, 12206
Phelps, Norm. *The Longest Struggle*,
10233
Phibbs, Cheryl Fisher (ed.). *Pioneers of
Human Rights*, 8040
Philbrick, Nathaniel. *The Heart of the
Sea*, 9337
Philbrick, Rodman. *Freak the Mighty*,
1984(F)
Philip, Neil. *Mythology of the World*,
6845
Philip, Neil (ed.). *The Great Mystery*,
6825
War and the Pity of War, 6622
Phillips, Carlene. *Mary Queen of Scots*,
8121
Phillips, Carly. *Sealed with a Kiss*,
5383(F)

Reasoner, James. *Antietam*, 4276(F)

Reaver, Chap. *A Little Bit Dead*, 5404(F)

Reaves, Michael. *Death Star*, 6143(F)

Reavill, Gil. *Antarctica 2041*, 8371

Reber, Deborah. *In Their Shoes*, 10425

Rebman, Renee C. *Addictions and Risky Behaviors*, 10586

The Sistine Chapel, 8459

Rebolledo, Tey Diana (ed.). *Infinite Divisions*, 923(F)

Red Shirt, Delphine. *Bead on an Anthill*, 9278

Reddi, Rishi. *Karma and Other Stories*, 924(F)

Rediker, Marcus. *The Slave Ship*, 8781

Redmond, J. B. *Assassin's Apprentice*, 3153(F)

Redsand, Anna S. *Viktor Frankl*, 7866

Reebs, Stephan. *Fish Behavior*, 11615

Reed, Amy. *Clean*, 1435(F)

Reed, Arthea J. S. *Norma Fox Mazer*, 6999

Reed, Don C. *The Kraken*, 2001(F)

Reed, Gary. *Mary Shelley's Frankenstein*, 3579(F)

Reed, Jennifer. *Love Canal*, 10115

Reed, M. K. *Americus*, 3580(F)

Reed, Rita. *Growing Up Gay*, 11041

Reed, Robert. *Marrow*, 6144(F)

Reed, Tucker, et al. *Amber House*, 4784(F)

Reef, Catherine. *Alone in the World*, 10132

E. E. Cummings, 7326

Ernest Hemingway, 7369

John Steinbeck, 7422

Sigmund Freud, 7870

This Our Dark Country, 8982

Walt Whitman, 7440

Reeps, Roger L. *The Florida Manatee*, 11634

Rees, Celia. *The Fool's Girl*, 4098(F)

Pirates!, 120(F)

Sorceress, 4194(F)

Sovay, 4099(F)

This Is Not Forgiveness, 2266(F)

The Wish House, 2002(F)

Rees, David. *Get Your War On*, 10301

Rees, Douglas. *Smoking Mirror*, 3932(F)

Rees, Elizabeth M. *The Wedding*, 4100(F)

Reese, James. *The Strange Case of Doctor Jekyll and Mademoiselle Odile*, 4816(F)

Reesor, David. *Predator*, 11481

Reeve, Christopher. *Still Me*, 7545

Reeve, Philip. *A Darkling Plain*, 3023(F)

Here Lies Arthur, 3830(F)

Infernal Devices, 6145(F)

Reeves, Amy Carol. *Ripper*, 4101(F)

Reeves, Diane Lindsey. *Career Ideas for Kids Who Like Travel*, 10468

Career Ideas for Teens in Architecture and Construction, 10467

Career Ideas for Teens in Education and Training, 10524

Career Ideas for Teens in Health Science, 10543

Reeves, Richard. *A Force of Nature*, 7905

Reeves, Thomas C. *Twentieth-Century America*, 9238

Regan, Paul (ed.). *Weapon*, 11999

Regan, Sally. *The Vampire Book*, 12215

Reger, Rob. *The Lost Days*, 5405(F)

The Lost Days, 5406(F)

Stranger and Stranger, 5406(F)

Reger, Rob, et al. *Emily the Strange*, 3581(F)

Rehder, Harold A. *The Audubon Society Field Guide to North American Seashells*, 11605

Reich, Bernard. *A Brief History of Israel*, 9117

Reich, Dale. *Rockets Like Rain*, 9499

Reich, Howard. *The First and Final Nightmare of Sonia Reich*, 8864

Reich, Susanna. *Painting the Wild Frontier*, 7251

Reichblum, Charles. *Dr. Knowledge Presents*, 10333

Reichl, Ruth. *Tender at the Bone*, 8333

Reid, Howard. *The Rise and Fall of Alexandria*, 8726

Reid, Kim. *No Place Safe*, 8334

Reid, Kimberly. *Creeping with the Enemy*, 5407(F)

My Own Worst Frenemy, 2003(F)

Reid, P. Carey. *Swimming in the Starry River*, 1436(F)

Reid, Suzanne Elizabeth. *Presenting Cynthia Voigt*, 7000

Presenting Young Adult Science Fiction, 6940

Reid, T. R. *The Chip*, 11934

Reiken, Frederick. *Day for Night*, 5408(F)

Reilly, Matthew. *The 6 Sacred Stones*, 3024(F)

Reilly, Thomas. *Black Knights*, 9447

Reinert, Dale R. *Sexual Abuse and Incest*, 11053

Reinfeld, Fred. *Pony Express*, 9404

Reinhard, Johan. *The Ice Maiden*, 8713

Reinhardt, Dana. *Harmless*, 2004(F)

How to Build a House, 5762(F)

The Things a Brother Knows, 1212(F)

Reino, Joseph. *Stephen King*, 7001

Reis, Ronald A. *African Americans and the Civil War*, 9373

Easter Island, 12216

Reisen, Harriet. *Louisa May Alcott*, 7302

Reisfeld, Randi. *Starlet*, 655(F)

Reiss, Johanna. *The Upstairs Room*, 8335

Reiss, Kathryn. *Pale Phoenix*, 3025(F)

Rej, Bent. *The Rolling Stones in the Beginning*, 7549

Relin, David Oliver. *Three Cups of Tea*, 8309

Remarque, Erich Maria. *All Quiet on the Western Front*, 173(F)

Remini, Robert V. *Andrew Jackson*, 7662

The House, 9696

John Quincy Adams, 7647

Joseph Smith, 7793

Remini, Robert V. (ed.). *Fellow Citizens*, 6921

Renault, Mary. *The King Must Die*, 3799(F)

Renn, Diana. *Tokyo Heist*, 5409(F)

Renner, Elmer. *Sea of Sharks*, 9450

Rennison, Louise. *A Midsummer Tights Dream*, 4970(F)

Startled by His Furry Shorts, 4971(F)

Then He Ate My Boy Entrancers, 4972(F)

Withering Tights, 4973(F)

Rense, Paige (ed.). *Architectural Digest*, 8411

Resau, Laura. *The Indigo Notebook*, 656(F)

The Indigo Notebook, 5763(F)

The Queen of Water, 4170(F)

Red Glass, 657(F)

The Ruby Notebook, 5763(F)

Reston, James, Jr. *Fragile Innocence*, 8336

Rettig, Liz. *My Desperate Love Diary*, 658(F)

Revis, Beth. *Across the Universe*, 6146(F)

Across the Universe, 6147(F)

A Million Suns, 6146(F)

A Million Suns, 6147(F)

Shades of Earth, 6147(F)

Rewald, John. *Cezanne*, 7252

Rex, Richard. *The Tudors*, 9074

Reynolds, Abigail. *Mr. Darcy's Obsession*, 4102(F)

Reynolds, Bonnie Jones. *If Only They Could Talk*, 11459

Reynolds, Clay. *Monuments*, 2005(F)

Reynolds, David. *Summits*, 8792

Reynolds, David S. *John Brown, Abolitionist*, 7610

Reynolds, David West. *Kennedy Space Center*, 11314

Reynolds, Jason. *My Name Is Jason. Mine Too*, 6730

Reynolds, Marilyn. *Baby Help*, 1213(F)

Beyond Dreams, 2006(F)

But What About Me?, 2007(F)

Detour for Emmy, 2008(F)

If You Loved Me, 2009(F)

Love Rules, 659(F)

Shut Up!, 1214(F)

Telling, 2010(F)

Too Soon for Jeff, 2011(F)

Reynolds, Mike. *How to Analyze the Films of Spike Lee*, 8583

898

The Search, 5771(F)

Tribute, 5419(F)

Roberts, Nora, et al. *Once Upon a Rose*, 3031(F)

Roberts, Robin. *Basketball for Women*, 12315

Roberts, Royston M. *Serendipity*, 11245

Roberts, Russell. *Building the Panama Canal*, 11899

The Life and Times of Nostradamus, 8124

Roberts, Sam. *Who We Are Now*, 9664

Roberts, Tara (ed.). *What Your Mama Never Told You*, 11042

Roberts, Terrence. *Simple, Not Easy*, 9837

Roberts, Willo Davis. *Undercurrents*, 5420(F)

Robertshaw, Peter. *The Early Human World*, 8645

Every Bone Tells a Story, 8655

Robertson, Brian. *Little Blues Book*, 8522

Robertson, James I. *Robert E. Lee*, 7737

Robertson, R. Garcia y. *White Rose*, 4104(F)

Robertson, Ray. *Moody Food*, 4441(F)

Robinson, Alex. *Too Cool to Be Forgotten*, 3582(F)

Robinson, Andrew. *Einstein*, 7852

Robinson, C. E. *Everyday Life in Ancient Greece*, 8733

Robinson, C. Kelly. *No More Mr. Nice Guy*, 5772(F)

Robinson, George. *Essential Judaism*, 9612

Robinson, Holly. *The Gerbil Farmer's Daughter*, 8339

Robinson, James. *The Starman Omnibus 1*, 3583(F)

Robinson, Kim Stanley. *Fifty Degrees Below*, 11791

Robinson, Lynda S. *Eater of Souls*, 5421(F)

Murder at the Feast of Rejoicing, 5422(F)

Robinson, Rocky. *Flat Out*, 12330

Robinson, Shannon. *Cubism*, 8448

Robinson, Spider. *God Is an Iron and Other Stories*, 6152(F)

Robison, Mary. *Tell Me*, 6443(F)

Robson, Claire (ed.). *Outside Rules*, 6444(F)

Robson, David. *The Black Arts Movement*, 8406

Encounters with Vampires, 12217

Rocco, Fiammetta. *The Miraculous Fever Tree*, 10761

Rocha, Toni L. *Understanding Recovery from Eating Disorders*, 10762

Roche, Lorcan. *The Companion*, 2017(F)

Roche, Lorin. *Meditation Made Easy*, 10587

Rochelle, Warren. *The Wild Boy*, 3032(F)

Rochman, Hazel (ed.). *Leaving Home*, 122(F)

Somehow Tenderness Survives, 2267(F)

Rock, Howard B. *Cityscapes*, 9522

Rock, Peter. *The Bewildered*, 4819(F)

Rodd, Tony. *Trees*, 11406

Roden, Nadia. *Granita Magic*, 12074

Rodi, Rob. *Crossovers*, 3584(F)

Rodman, Sean. *Infiltration*, 123(F)

Rodrigues, Carmen. *34 Pieces of You*, 666(F)

Rodriguez, Ana Maria. *Autism Spectrum Disorders*, 10925

Rodriguez, Gaby. *The Pregnancy Project*, 8340

Rodriguez, Jason (ed.). *Postcards*, 6445(F)

Rodriguez, Luis J. *My Nature Is Hunger*, 6731

Rodriguez, Pedro. *Chilling Tales of Horror*, 4820(F)

Rodriguez, Robert. *Frank Miller's Sin City*, 8575

Great Hispanic-Americans, 7593

Roecker, Laura. *The Lies That Bind*, 5423(F)

Roecker, Lisa. *The Lies That Bind*, 5423(F)

Roeper, Richard. *Debunked! Conspiracy Theories, Urban Legends, and Evil Plots of the 21st Century*, 12218

Sox and the City, 12297

Roesch, Mattox. *Sometimes We're Always Real Same-Same*, 667(F)

Roessel, David (ed.). *Poetry for Young People*, 6732

Rogers, Annie G. *The Unsayable*, 10926

Rogers, Elizabeth. *The Green Book*, 10092

Rogers, Heather. *Gone Tomorrow*, 10121

Rogers, Mark E. *Samurai Cat Goes to the Movies*, 3033(F)

Rogers, Tammie. *4-H Guide to Dog Training and Dog Tricks*, 11679

Rogge, Hannah. *Hardwear*, 12105

Rohmer, Harriet. *Heroes of the Environment*, 7817

Rol, Ruud van der. *Anne Frank*, 8106

Roleff, Tamara L. (ed.). *America Under Attack*, 10302

Gun Control, 10013

The Holocaust, 8866

Inner-City Poverty, 10218

The Oklahoma City Bombing, 9473

Police Corruption, 10187

The Vietnam War, 9501

Rolling Stone (ed.). *Harrison*, 7504

Rollins, James. *Amazonia*, 5424(F)

Rollins, Prentis. *The Making of a Graphic Novel*, 7149

Rollyson, Carl S. *A Student's Guide to Scandinavian American Genealogy*, 9984

Teenage Refugees from Eastern Europe Speak Out, 9053

Romain, Joseph. *The Mystery of the Wagner Whacker*, 6301(F)

Roman, Dave. *Agnes Quill*, 3585(F)

Romero, Aldemaro (ed.). *Adventures in the Wild*, 11372

Romm, Joseph. *Hell and High Water*, 10093

Rooke, Constance (ed.). *Writing Life*, 7101

Rooney, Andrew A. *A Few Minutes with Andy Rooney*, 6898

Rooney, Anne. *The 1950s and 1960s*, 8793

Rooney, Frances (ed.). *Hear Me Out*, 11043

Rooney, John F. *Preparing for College*, 10412

Roosevelt, Elliott. *Murder and the First Lady*, 5425(F)

Murder in the Oval Office, 5426(F)

The White House Pantry Murder, 5427(F)

Roosevelt, Theodore. *The Rough Riders*, 9420

Theodore Roosevelt's History of the United States, 6922

Rosaler, Maxine. *The Devil on Trial*, 9738

Rosati, Gina. *Auracle*, 4821(F)

Rose, Chris. *1 Dead in Attic*, 11778

Rose, Elisabeth. *Instant Family*, 5773(F)

Outback Hero, 5774(F)

Rose, Joel. *New York Sawed in Half*, 9338

Rose, Malcolm. *Final Lap*, 5428(F)

Rose, Michael. *Disaster Movies*, 8568

Rose, Phyllis (ed.). *The Norton Book of Women's Lives*, 7167

Rose, Tricia. *Black Noise*, 8523

Roseman, Janet Lynn. *Dance Masters*, 8555

Rosen, Christine. *My Fundamentalist Education*, 8341

Rosen, Marvin. *Sleep and Dreaming*, 10852

Rosen, Michael. *Shakespeare's Romeo and Juliet*, 6540

Rosen, R. D. *A Buffalo in the House*, 8342

Rosen, Renee. *Every Crooked Pot*, 2018(F)

Rosen, Roger (ed.). *Border Crossings*, 2268(F)

Coming of Age, 2019(F)

East-West, 6923

On Heroes and the Heroic, 6446(F)

Teenage Soldiers, Adult Wars, 6447(F)

Rosenbaum, Jean. *Opportunities in Fitness Careers*, 10505

Sirvaitis, Karen. *Danica Patrick*, 7949

Sís, Peter. *Tibet*, 9034
The Wall, 7421

Sites, Kevin. *In the Hot Zone*, 7155

Sitiki. *The Odyssey of an African Slave*, 7792

Sitomer, Alan Lawrence. *Hip-Hop High School*, 694(F)
Homeboyz, 2273(F)

Sittenfeld, Curtis. *American Wife*, 695(F)

Sivertsen, Linda. *Generation Green*, 10097

Sivertsen, Tosh. *Generation Green*, 10097

Sivin, Carole. *Maskmaking*, 12141

Sizer, Paul. *B. P. M*, 3638(F)

Sjoholm, Barbara (ed.). *Steady as She Goes*, 8163

Skaine, Rosemarie. *The Women of Afghanistan Under the Taliban*, 9035

Skancke, Jennifer (ed.). *Conserving the Environment*, 10111

Skelton, Renee. *Forecast Earth*, 7871

Skinner, Jeffrey (ed.). *Passing the Word*, 7103

Skinner, Jose. *Flight and Other Stories*, 938(F)

Skipper, John C. *Umpires*, 12302

Skog, Jason. *Teens in Spain*, 9102

Skovron, Jon. *Misfit*, 4848(F)
Struts and Frets, 2071(F)

Skurzynski, Gloria. *The Revolt*, 6179(F)
Sweat and Blood, 10329

Slack, Charles. *Noble Obsession*, 7924

Slade, Arthur. *The Hunchback Assignments*, 3084(F)
Megiddo's Shadow, 4460(F)

Slade, Suzanne. *Adopted*, 11211

Slaight, Craig (ed.). *Great Monologues for Young Actors*, 6525
Great Scenes for Young Actors from the Stage, 6526
Multicultural Monologues for Young Actors, 6527
Multicultural Scenes for Young Actors, 6528
New Plays from A.C.T.'s Young Conservatory, 6569
New Plays from A.C.T.'s Young Conservatory, Vol. II, 6570
Short Plays for Young Actors, 6529

Slate, Barbara. *You Can Do a Graphic Novel*, 7115

Slater, Adam. *Hunted*, 3085(F)
Skinned, 4849(F)

Slater, Lauren. *Blue Beyond Blue*, 11085

Slater, Lauren (ed.). *The Best American Essays, 2006*, 6902

Slater, Susan. *Thunderbird*, 5456(F)

Slatta, Richard W. *Cowboy*, 9407

Slavicek, Louise Chipley. *The Chinese Cultural Revolution*, 9002
Daniel Inouye, 7727

The Establishment of the State of Israel, 9121
Mother Teresa, 8086

Slawenski, Kenneth. *J. D. Salinger*, 7412

Slayton, Elaine Doremus. *Empowering Teens*, 11220

Sleator, William. *The Boy Who Reversed Himself*, 6180(F)
House of Stairs, 6181(F)
Interstellar Pig, 6182(F)
Oddballs, 4981(F)
Parasite Pig, 6183(F)
Singularity, 6184(F)
Test, 2274(F)

Slezak, Ellen. *All These Girls*, 1244(F)

Sloan, Bill. *The Ultimate Battle*, 8877

Sloan, Brian. *Tale of Two Summers*, 2072(F)

Sloan, Holly Goldberg. *I'll Be There*, 1245(F)

Sloan, Kay. *The Patron Saint of Red Chevys*, 5457(F)

Sloane, Paul. *Challenging Lateral Thinking Puzzles*, 12179

Slovo, Gillian. *Red Dust*, 3862(F)

Slowik, Theresa J. *America's Art*, 8469

Small, David. *Stitches*, 8356

Smart, Jamie. *Ubu Bubu*, 3639(F)

Smay, David (ed.). *Bubblegum Music Is the Naked Truth*, 8496

Smibert, Angie. *Memento Nora*, 6185(F)

Smil, Vaclav. *Energies*, 11850

Smiley, Jane. *Charles Dickens*, 7336
The Man Who Invented the Computer, 7828

Smiley, Jane, et al (ed.). *Best New American Voices, 2006*, 6461(F)

Smiley, Tavis. *What I Know for Sure*, 7553

Smith, Andrew. *Ghost Medicine*, 696(F)
In the Path of Falling Objects, 4566(F)
The Marbury Lens, 3086(F)
Passenger, 3086(F)
Stick, 697(F)

Smith, Anna Deavere. *Letters to a Young Artist*, 8407

Smith, Anne Warren. *Sister in the Shadow*, 1246(F)

Smith, Betty. *Joy in the Morning*, 2073(F)
A Tree Grows in Brooklyn, 4352(F)

Smith, Bonnie G. *Imperialism*, 8699

Smith, Brian. *The Stuff of Legend, Vol. 1*, 3576(F)

Smith, C. Fraser. *Lenny, Lefty, and the Chancellor*, 10663

Smith, Cameron M. *The Top 10 Myths About Evolution*, 8648

Smith, Carl. *Pearl Harbor, 1941*, 8878

Smith, Caroline, et al. *Meteorites*, 11327

Smith, Chris. *Twitter*, 7820

Smith, Cotton. *Dark Trail to Dodge*, 128(F)

Smith, Cynthia Leitich. *Diabolical*, 4851(F)
Eternal, 4852(F)
Tantalize, 4852(F)
Tantalize, 4853(F)
Tantalize, 4854(F)

Smith, D. James. *My Brother's Passion*, 2074(F)

Smith, Danny. *Lost Hero*, 8141

Smith, David James. *Young Mandela*, 8061

Smith, Dick. *Dick Smith's Do-It-Yourself Monster Make-Up Handbook*, 12142

Smith, Dodie. *I Capture the Castle*, 4113(F)

Smith, Donald B. *Chief Buffalo Child Long Lance*, 7785

Smith, Douglas W. *Decade of the Wolf*, 11511

Smith, Edwin R. *Blue Star Highway*, 4982(F)

Smith, Emily Wing. *Back When You Were Easier to Love*, 5790(F)

Smith, Erica. *Anorexia Nervosa*, 10773

Smith, Ernie. *Warm Hearts and Cold Noses*, 11683

Smith, Esther K. *How to Make Books*, 12144

Smith, Helaine L. *Masterpieces of Classic Greek Drama*, 7031

Smith, Jean Edward. *Grant*, 7658

Smith, Jeff. *The Art of Bone*, 3640(F)
Bone, 3641(F)
Bone, 3644(F)
Old Man's Cave, 3642(F)
Shazam! The Monster Society of Evil, 3643(F)

Smith, Jennifer E. *The Statistical Probability of Love at First Sight*, 5791(F)
You Are Here, 2075(F)

Smith, Jeremy. *The Fairer Sex*, 3673(F)

Smith, Jeremy N. *Growing a Garden City*, 11395

Smith, Kirsten. *The Geography of Girlhood*, 2076(F)

Smith, L. J. *The Initiation and the Captive, Part 1*, 3087(F)

Smith, Larry. *The Few and the Proud*, 9770

Smith, Larry (ed.). *I Can't Keep My Own Secrets*, 11061

Smith, Lauren B. *Love in a Global Village*, 9888

Smith, Lewis. *Why the Cheetah Cheats and Other Mysteries of the Natural World*, 11457

Smith, Marisa (ed.). *The Actor's Book of Movie Monologues*, 8590
Seattle Children's Theatre, 6571
Showtime's Act One Festival, 6530

Smith, Michael Marshall. *The Servants*, 4114(F)

Steiner, Andy. *Girl Power on the Playing Field*, 12268
Steiner, Barbara. *Dreamstalker*, 5472(F)
Spring Break, 5473(F)
Steinhart, Peter. *The Company of Wolves*, 11512
Steinman, David. *Safe Trip to Eden*, 10099
Steinmetz, Karen. *The Mourning Wars*, 4212(F)
Stemple, Heidi E. Y. *Bad Girls*, 8165
Stenstrup, Allen. *Forests*, 10100
Stepakoff, Jeffrey. *Fireworks over Toccoa*, 5803(F)
Stepanek, Mattie J. T. *Hope Through Heartsongs*, 6744
Stephens, Kristen R. *Empowered Girls*, 10248
Stephenson, Lynda. *Dancing with Elvis*, 4445(F)
Stepp, Laura Sessions. *Unhooked*, 11169
Stepto, Michele (ed.). *African-American Voices*, 940(F)
Stering, Shirley. *My Name Is Seepeetza*, 941(F)
Stern, Gerald. *What I Can't Bear Losing*, 6745
Sterngass, Jon. *Reproductive Technology*, 11007
Stetter, Cornelius. *The Secret Medicine of the Pharaohs*, 8727
Stevens, Chambers. *Sensational Scenes for Teens*, 8615
Stevens, Joann. *In Goode Faith*, 7723
Stevens, Kathy. *Where the Blind Horse Sings*, 11458
Stevens, Marcus. *Useful Girl*, 942(F)
Stevenson, Robert Louis. *The Black Arrow*, 195(F)
Dr. Jekyll and Mr. Hyde, 196(F)
The Strange Case of Dr. Jekyll and Mr. Hyde, 197(F)
Stevenson, Robin. *Escape Velocity*, 1252(F)
Inferno, 2088(F)
Out of Order, 2089(F)
A Thousand Shades of Blue, 1253(F)
Stevermer, Caroline. *The Grand Tour*, 3192(F)
The Mislaid Magician or Ten Years After, 3192(F)
Sorcery and Cecelia, 3192(F)
Sorcery and Cecelia or the Enchanted Chocolate Pot, 3193(F)
Stewart, Amy. *Wicked Bugs*, 11583
Stewart, Bridgett. *No Matter What*, 7795
Stewart, Dave. *DC*, 3295(F)
Stewart, Elizabeth. *The Lynching of Louie Sam*, 4353(F)
Stewart, Gail B. *People with Mental Illness*, 10935
Saddam Hussein, 8075
SARS, 10779

Teens with Cancer, 10780
Teens with Disabilities, 10980
Stewart, Jeffrey C. (ed.). *Paul Robeson*, 7546
Stewart, John. *The Baseball Clinic*, 12303
Stewart, Jon, et al. *Earth (The Book)*, 6904
Stewart, Mary. *Mary Stewart's Merlin Trilogy*, 3097(F)
Stewart, Robert. *The Brigade in Review*, 9771
Mysteries of History, 8701
Stewart, Rory. *The Prince of the Marshes*, 9147
Stewart, Sally. *Appointment in Venice*, 5804(F)
Stewart, Sean. *Cathy's Ring*, 3098(F)
Dark Rendezvous, 6193(F)
Perfect Circle, 5474(F)
Stewart, Sheila. *In Defense of Our Country*, 9653
Stewart, Shelley. *The Road South*, 7556
Stiebing, William H. *Uncovering the Past*, 8659
Stiefer, Sandy. *Marathon Skiing*, 12419
Stiefvater, Maggie. *Forever*, 3099(F)
Lament, 3100(F)
Linger, 3101(F)
The Raven Boys, 3102(F)
The Scorpio Races, 3103(F)
Shiver, 3101(F)
Shiver, 4863(F)
Stillman, Deanne. *Mustang*, 11483
Stillman, Sarah. *Soul Searching: A Girl's Guide to Finding Herself*, 11170
Stillwell, Paul (ed.). *The Golden Thirteen*, 9772
Stimola, Aubrey. *Ebola*, 10781
Stinson, Loretta. *Little Green*, 2090(F)
Stinson, Susan. *Fat Girl Dances with Rocks*, 2091(F)
Stirling, S. M. *Ice, Iron and Gold*, 6464(F)
A Meeting at Corvallis, 3104(F)
On the Oceans of Eternity, 3105(F)
The Sky People, 6194(F)
Stivers, Valerie. *Blood Is the New Black*, 4864(F)
Stock, Jurgen. *Weather*, 11792
Stockland, Jonathan. *Winged Wonders*, 11539
Stohl, Margaret. *Beautiful Creatures*, 2631(F)
Beautiful Creatures, 2632(F)
Beautiful Darkness, 2632(F)
Stoker, Bram. *Dracula*, 198(F)
Dracula, 3655(F)
Stokes, Donald. *The Bird Feeder Book*, 11534
The Complete Birdhouse Book, 11535
Stokes, Lillian. *The Bird Feeder Book*, 11534
The Complete Birdhouse Book, 11535

Stokes, Mark. *Colon Cancer*, 10782
Prostate Cancer, 10782
Stokesbury, James L. *A Short History of the American Revolution*, 9321
A Short History of the Korean War, 9504
A Short History of World War I, 8800
A Short History of World War II, 8881
Stokoe, James. *Wonton Soup*, 3656(F)
Stolar, Daniel. *The Middle of the Night*, 6465(F)
Stolarz, Laurie Faria. *Project 17*, 4865(F)
Stoller, Debbie. *Son of Stitch 'n Bitch*, 12165
Stolz, Joelle. *The Shadows of Ghadames*, 3863(F)
Stone, Brad. *Gearheads*, 8604
Stone, Heather Duffy. *This Is What I Want to Tell You*, 2092(F)
Stone, Irving. *Love Is Eternal*, 4282(F)
Lust for Life, 4117(F)
Stone, Judith. *When She Was White*, 8973
Stone, Nathaniel. *On the Water*, 9241
Stone, Norman. *World War One*, 8801
Stone, Tamara Ireland. *Time Between Us*, 3106(F)
Stone, Tanya Lee. *Abraham Lincoln*, 7680
Ella Fitzgerald, 7500
The Good, the Bad, and the Barbie, 12111
Medical Causes, 10783
Stoppard, Tom. *Rosencrantz and Guildenstern Are Dead*, 6541
Storad, Conrad J. *Inside AIDS*, 10784
Stork, Francisco X. *Behind the Eyes*, 2093(F)
Irises, 1254(F)
Last Summer of the Death Warriors, 709(F)
Marcelo in the Real World, 1452(F)
Storr, Robert, et al. *Art 21*, 8472
Storrie, Paul D. *Made for Each Other*, 3657(F)
Stott, Carole. *1001 Facts About Space*, 11292
Stout, Glenn. *The Cubs*, 12304
DiMaggio, 7958
Stout, Glenn (ed.). *The Best American Sports Writing, 2007*, 12252
Chasing Tiger, 12375
Stover, Leon. *Robert A. Heinlein*, 7006
Stover, Lois T. *Presenting Phyllis Reynolds Naylor*, 7007
Stowe, Harriet Beecher. *The Annotated Uncle Tom's Cabin*, 7008
Uncle Tom's Cabin, 218(F)
Strachan, Mari. *The Earth Hums in B Flat*, 5475(F)
Strahan, Jonathan (ed.). *The Locus Awards*, 5904(F)
The Starry Rift, 6195(F)
Under My Hat, 3108(F)
Wings of Fire, 3107(F)

Trumbo, Dalton. *Johnny Got his Gun*, 2280(F)

Truss, Lynne. *Eats, Shoots and Leaves*, 7084

Trussoni, Danielle. *Falling Through the Earth*, 8377

Trzebinski, Errol. *The Lives of Beryl Markham*, 7200

Tschinag, Galsan. *The Blue Sky*, 3946(F)

Tsuda, Masami. *Castle of Dreams*, 3690(F)

Tsukiji, Toshihiko. *Maburaho, Vol. 1*, 3691(F)

Tsukiyama, Gail. *The Street of a Thousand Blossoms*, 4533(F)

Tuaolo, Esera. *Alone in the Trenches*, 7998

Tucci, Billy. *Shi*, 3692(F)

Tuchman, Barbara Wertheim. *A Distant Mirror*, 8771
The Guns of August, 8802
The Proud Tower, 8795
The Zimmermann Telegram. New ed, 8803

Tucker, Mike. *Among Warriors in Iraq*, 8907

Tucker, Todd. *The Great Starvation Experiment*, 8883
Over and Under, 4447(F)

Tudge, Colin. *The Bird*, 11538
The Tree, 11407

Tullson, Diane. *Blue Highway*, 2115(F)
Edge, 2116(F)
Riley Park, 1464(F)
Zero, 1465(F)

Tully, Shawn. *Sports Illustrated Tennis*, 12435

Tunis, Edwin. *Frontier Living*, 9410

Turbak, Gary. *Grizzly Bears*, 11497

Turkington, Carol A. *Extraordinary Jobs for Adventurers*, 10438
Extraordinary Jobs for Creative People, 10438
Extraordinary Jobs in Agriculture and Nature, 10438

Turnbull, Ann. *Forged in the Fire*, 4127(F)

Turner, Ann W. *Grass Songs*, 6752
A Lion's Hunger, 6753

Turner, Chérie. *Adventure Tour Guides*, 10478
Everything You Need to Know About the Riot Grrrl Movement, 9847
Marathon Cycling, 12332

Turner, Ed. *Winning Racquetball*, 12437

Turner, Glennette Tilley. *Fort Mose*, 9301

Turner, James. *I, Librarian*, 3693(F)

Turner, Joan Frances. *Dust*, 4871(F)

Turner, Michael. *Godfall*, 3421(F)

Turner, Nancy E. *Sarah's Quilt*, 4319(F)

Turner, Nathan Hale. *The Road South*, 7556

Turner, Tom. *Sierra Club*, 10104

Turpin, Tom. *Flies in the Face of Fashion, Mites Make Right, and Other Bugdacious Tales*, 11584

Turtledove, Harry. *The Disunited States of America*, 3142(F)
The Great War, 6207(F)
Hitler's War, 3148(F)
Hitler's War, 3143(F)
In at the Death, 3144(F)
In High Places, 3145(F)
Liberating Atlantis, 3146(F)
Opening Atlantis, 3147(F)
The Valley-Westside War, 6208(F)
West and East, 3148(F)

Turtledove, Harry (ed.). *The Best Alternate History Stories of the 20th Century*, 6209(F)
The Best Military Science Fiction of the 20th Century, 6210(F)

Tuttle, Cheryl Gerson. *Learning Disabilities*, 10913

Tutu, Desmond M. *Made for Goodness*, 9573

Tutu, Mpho A. *Made for Goodness*, 9573

Twagilimana, Aimable. *Teenage Refugees from Rwanda Speak Out*, 8951

Twain, Mark. *The Adventures of Huckleberry Finn*, 219(F)
The Complete Short Stories of Mark Twain, 220(F)
A Connecticut Yankee in King Arthur's Court, 221(F)
How Nancy Jackson Married Kate Wilson and Other Tales of Rebellious Girls and Daring Young Women, 222(F)
The Innocents Abroad and Roughing It, 6906
Life on the Mississippi, 6907
A Murder, a Mystery, and a Marriage, 223(F)
The Prince and the Pauper, 224(F)
Pudd'nhead Wilson, 225(F)
Roughing It, 6908
Tom Sawyer Abroad [and] Tom Sawyer, Detective, 226(F)

Twist, Clint. *1001 Facts About Space*, 11292

Twomey, Cathleen. *Beachmont Letters*, 4534(F)

Tyler, Anne. *Digging to America*, 2281(F)
Dinner at the Homesick Restaurant, 1267(F)

Tym, Kate. *Coping with Your Emotions*, 11174

Type-Moon. *Fate/Stay Night*, 3694(F)

Tyson, Neil deGrasse. *Death by Black Hole and Other Cosmic Quandaries*, 11294
Universe Down to Earth, 11295

Tyszka, Alberto Barrera. *Hugo Chavez*, 8147

Udechukwu, Ada. *Herero*, 8975

Ueda, Miwa. *Papillon, Vol. 1*, 3695(F)
Peach Girl, 3696(F)

Uhlig, Richard. *Last Dance at the Frosty Queen*, 2117(F)

Ulanski, Stan. *The Gulf Stream*, 11803

Ulin, David L. (ed.). *Writing Los Angeles*, 9533

Ulinich, Anya. *Petropolis*, 735(F)

Umrigar, Thrity. *First Darling of the Morning*, 8379

Underdahl, S. T. *The Other Sister*, 1268(F)

Unferth, Deb Olin. *Revolution*, 8380

Ungar, Harlow G. *Teachers and Educators*, 7602

Unger, Lisa. *Fragile*, 5487(F)

Updale, Eleanor. *Montmorency and the Assassins*, 5488(F)
Montmorency's Revenge, 5489(F)

Updike, John. *Gertrude and Claudius*, 4128(F)
Terrorist, 2282(F)

Upgren, Arthur R. *Weather*, 11792

Uppal, Priscila. *The Divine Economy of Salvation*, 2118(F)

Urasawa, Naoki, et al. *Pluto, Vol. 1*, 3697(F)

Ure, Jean. *Plague*, 6211(F)

Urick, Dave. *Sports Illustrated Lacrosse*, 12270

Uris, Leon. *Exodus*, 4129(F)
Mila 18, 4535(F)

Urrea, Luis Alberto. *Mr. Mendoza's Paintbrush*, 3698(F)

Urushibara, Yuki. *Mushishi, Vol. 1*, 3699(F)

Uschan, Michael V. *Che Guevara, Revolutionary*, 8152
Lynching and Murder in the Deep South, 9246
The 1940s, 9247

Usher, Kerry. *Heroes, Gods and Emperors from Roman Mythology*, 6863

Vacca, John. *Identity Theft*, 11939

Vacca, Mary E. *Identity Theft*, 11939

Vail, Martha (ed.). *Exploring the Pacific*, 9044

Vail, Rachel. *Gorgeous*, 2119(F)
If We Kiss, 2120(F)
Lucky, 2121(F)
You, Maybe, 2122(F)

Valdes-Rodriguez, Alisa. *Haters*, 736(F)

Valentine, Jenny. *Broken Soup*, 1269(F)
Me, the Missing, and the Dead, 5490(F)

Valentino, Jim (ed.). *Fractured Fables*, 3700(F)

Valentino, Serena. *How to Be a Zombie*, 12224

Valliant, Doris. *Bangladesh*, 9011

Van Beirs, Pat. *A Sword in Her Hand*, 4130(F)

Vogel, Steve. *The Pentagon*, 8412

Vogt, Peter. *Career Opportunities in the Fashion Industry*, 10479

Vogts, Deborah. *Seeds of Summer*, 5825(F)

Voigt, Cynthia. *Glass Mountain*, 5826(F)

The Wings of a Falcon, 3157(F)

Voit, Mark. *Hubble Space Telescope*, 11318

Vollmar, Rob. *Bluesman*, 3713(F)

Volponi, Paul. *Black and White*, 2134(F)

Crossing Lines, 2135(F)

The Final Four, 6306(F)

The Hand You're Dealt, 743(F)

Homestretch, 2136(F)

Hurricane Song, 139(F)

Rikers High, 2137(F)

Rooftop, 947(F)

Voltaire, Francois M. *The Portable Voltaire*, 178(F)

Von Ruhland, Catherine. *Living with the Planet*, 10106

Von Sholly, Pete. *Dead But Not Out! Pete Von Sholly's Morbid 2*, 3714(F)

Pete Von Sholly's Morbid, 3715(F)

Von Ziegesar, Cecily. *Because I'm Worth It*, 2138(F)

Gossip Girl, 744(F)

Nothing Can Keep Us Together, 2139(F)

Only in Your Dreams, 745(F)

Vonnegut, Kurt. *Cat's Cradle*, 6215(F)

Conversations with Kurt Vonnegut, 7435

Slaughterhouse-Five, 3158(F)

While Mortals Sleep, 6473(F)

Voorhoeve, Anne C. *My Family for the War*, 4538(F)

vos Savant, Marilyn. *The Art of Spelling*, 7085

Vreeman, Rachel C. *Don't Swallow Your Gum! Myths, Half-Truths, and Outright Lies About Your Body and Health*, 10577

Vrettos, Adrienne Maria. *Sight*, 5495(F)

Skin, 746(F)

Wa Wamwere, Koigi. *I Refuse to Die*, 8952

Waage, Sissel (ed.). *Ignition*, 10060

Waal, Frans de. *My Family Album*, 11486

Wada, Shinji. *Crown*, 3716(F)

Wade, Linda R. *Careers in Law and Politics*, 10535

Wade, Nicholas. *Before the Dawn*, 10829

The Faith Instinct, 9575

The Science Times Book of Language and Linguistics, 7086

Wadsworth, Ginger. *John Muir*, 7894

Wager, Walter. *Kelly's People*, 5496(F)

Wagner, Heather Lehr. *Jane Austen*, 7309

Rigoberta Menchú Tum, 8155

Spies in the Civil War, 9382

Wagner, Margaret E. *The American Civil War*, 9383

Wagner, Margaret E, et al. *The Library of Congress World War II Companion*, 8885

Wagner, Matt. *Batman and the Monster Men 1*, 3717(F)

Wagner, Viqi (ed.). *AIDS*, 10789

Military Draft, 9775

Poverty, 10221

Wagoner, Mary S. *Agatha Christie*, 6962

Wahl, Mats. *The Invisible*, 5497(F)

Waid, Mark. *Absolute Kingdom Come*, 3721(F)

Daredevil, Vol. 1, 3718(F)

Legion of Super-Heroes, 3719(F)

Ruse, 3720(F)

Waide, Jim. *Snowboarder's Start-Up*, 12420

Waite, Judy. *Forbidden*, 747(F)

Shopaholic, 1467(F)

Wald, Elijah. *Escaping the Delta*, 7513

Riding with Strangers, 8385

Waldau, Paul. *Animal Rights*, 11573

Waldbauer, Gilbert. *Insights from Insects*, 11585

A Walk Around the Pond, 11586

Waldman, Michael, comp. *My Fellow Americans*, 9688

Waldo, Dixie. *Persuasive Speaking*, 10387

Waldo, Donna Lee. *Sacajawea*, 7207

Waldorf, Heather. *Grist*, 1274(F)

Tripping, 1468(F)

Waldrop, Howard. *Other Worlds, Better Lives*, 6216(F)

Waldstreicher, David. *The Struggle Against Slavery*, 9848

Walker, Alice. *The Color Purple*, 1469(F)

Walker, Brian F. *Black Boy White School*, 948(F)

Walker, Denise. *Inheritance and Evolution*, 10830

Walker, Gabrielle. *An Ocean of Air*, 11766

Walker, Ida. *Nigeria*, 8984

Walker, Jerald. *Street Shadows*, 8386

Walker, Laurence C. *Forests*, 11408

Walker, Melissa. *Small Town Sinners*, 2140(F)

Walker, Pam. *The Coral Reef*, 11609

Ecosystem Science Fair Projects Using Worms, Leaves, Crickets, and Other Stuff, 11374

Walker, Paul R. *The Method*, 2141(F)

Walker, Paul Robert. *Remember Little Bighorn*, 9283

Walker, Richard. *Firefly Guide to the Human Body*, 10853

Walker, Sally M. *Secrets of a Civil War Submarine*, 12003

Written in Bone, 8650

Walker, Spike. *On the Edge of Survival*, 11984

Walker, Spike (ed.). *Alaska*, 9534

Wall, Edmund (ed.). *Sexual Harassment*, 11054

Wallace, Anthony F. C. *The Long, Bitter Trail*, 9284

Wallace, Daniel. *Star Wars*, 8593

Wallace, David Foster (ed.). *The Best American Essays, 2007*, 6909

Wallace, David Rains. *Neptune's Ark*, 11606

Wallace, Karen. *The Unrivalled Spangles*, 4132(F)

Wallace, Lew. *Ben Hur*, 179(F)

Wallace, Maurice. *Langston Hughes*, 7374

Wallace, Mike. *Heat and Light*, 7159

Wallace, Rich. *Losing Is Not an Option*, 2142(F)

One Good Punch, 2143(F)

Perpetual Check, 1275(F)

Wallace, Sean (ed.). *Horror*, 4593(F)

Wallach-Levy, Wendee. *Cosmic Discoveries*, 11278

Wallechinsky, David. *The Complete Book of the Winter Olympics*, 12397

Wallenda, Delilah. *The Last of the Wallendas*, 7557

Wallenfeldt, Jeff (ed.). *The Black Experience in America*, 9946

Wallenfels, Stephen. *POD*, 6217(F)

Waller, Geoffrey. *SeaLife*, 11607

Waller, Maureen. *Sovereign Ladies*, 8046

Wallington, Aury. *Pop!*, 748(F)

Walljasper, Jay. *All That We Share*, 10021

Walls, Jeannette. *Half Broke Horses*, 749(F)

Walsh, Jill Paton. *Grace*, 4133(F)

Walsh, Patrick J. *Echoes Among the Stars*, 11319

Walter, Chip. *Thumbs, Toes, and Tears and Other Traits That Make Us Human*, 8651

Walter, Lynn. *Women's Rights*, 9849

Walters, Eric. *Bifocal*, 2215(F)

Sketches, 2144(F)

Stuffed, 750(F)

When Elephants Fight, 9628

Walters, Mark Jerome. *Six Modern Plagues and How We Are Causing Them*, 10790

Waltman, Kevin. *Learning the Game*, 6307(F)

Nowhere Fast, 2145(F)

Walton, Anthony (ed.). *The Vintage Book of African American Poetry*, 6695

Walton, Jo. *Among Others*, 3159(F)

Farthing, 5498(F)

Farthing, 5499(F)

Ha'penny, 5499(F)

Wand, Kelly (ed.). *Ape-Men*, 12226

Williams, David. *Bitterly Divided*, 9385

Williams, Erin E. *Why Animals Matter*, 11428

Williams, George. *Shinto*, 9577

Williams, Heidi. *Homeschooling*, 10352

Williams, Heidi (ed.). *Body Image*, 10842

Plagiarism, 10388

Williams, Jack. *Hurricane Watch*, 11779

The Weather Book. 2nd ed. , 11793

Williams, Jeanne. *Trails of Tears*, 9285

Williams, Juan. *Eyes on the Prize*, 9850

Thurgood Marshall, 7741

Williams, Kathryn. *Pizza, Love, and Other Stuff That Made Me Famous*, 5829(F)

Williams, Katie. *The Space Between Trees*, 5512(F)

Williams, Kayla. *Love My Rifle More Than You*, 9778

Williams, Liz. *The Ghost Sister*, 6241(F)

Williams, Lori Aurelia. *Shayla's Double Brown Baby Blues*, 2164(F)

When Kambia Elaine Flew in from Neptune, 2165(F)

Williams, Margaret. *Haverstraw*, 2166(F)

Williams, Maria Shaa Tlaa (ed.). *The Alaska Native Reader*, 9286

Williams, Mary E. *Global Warming*, 10389

The Sexual Revolution, 9851

Williams, Mary E. (ed.). *Adoption*, 11216

Civil Rights, 9852

Epidemics, 10792

Howl on Trial, 9830

Mental Illness, 10938

The White Separatist Movement, 9900

Williams, Michael. *The Genuine Half-Moon Kid*, 142(F)

Now Is the Time for Running, 3869(F)

Williams, Pat. *How to Be Like Mike*, 7978

Williams, Rita. *If the Creek Don't Rise*, 8392

Williams, Rob. *Star Wars Rebellion*, 3735(F)

Williams, Saul. *The Dead Emcee Scrolls*, 6757

Williams, Sean. *The Resurrected Man*, 6242(F)

Williams, Sheila (ed.). *Asimov's Science Fiction Magazine*, 6480(F)

A Woman's Liberation, 6246(F)

Williams, Stanley Tookie. *Blue Rage, Black Redemption*, 7799

Williams, Suzanne Morgan. *Bull Rider*, 1284(F)

Williams, Tennessee. *The Glass Menagerie*, 6577

Williams, William Appleman, et al. *America in Vietnam*, 9507

Williams-Garcia, Rita. *Jumped*, 2162(F)

Williamson, Debrah. *Paper Hearts*, 1285(F)

Singing with the Top Down, 762(F)

Williamson, Jack. *The Black Sun*, 6243(F)

Willig, Lauren. *The Betrayal of the Blood Lily*, 5830(F)

The Deception of the Emerald Ring, 5831(F)

The Mischief of the Mistletoe, 5832(F)

The Orchid Affair, 5833(F)

Willingham, Bill. *Arabian Nights (and Days)*, 3737(F)

The Dark Ages, 3184(F)

The Good Prince, 3738(F)

1001 Nights of Snowfall, 3739(F)

Peter and Max, 3183(F)

Robin, 3736(F)

Wolves, 3740(F)

Willingham, Bill, et al. *Fables*, 3741(F)

Fables, 3742(F)

Fables, 3743(F)

Willis, Clint (ed.). *Climb*, 12348

Fire Fighters, 10536

Semper Fi, 9779

Shark, 11622

Willis, Connie. *Blackout*, 6244(F)

Impossible Things, 6245(F)

Willis, Connie (ed.). *A Woman's Liberation*, 6246(F)

Willis, Laurie (ed.). *Hate Crimes*, 10199

Willis, Teresa Ann. *It's All Good! Daily Affirmations for Teens*, 11179

Willker, Joshua D. G. *Everything You Need to Know About the Dangers of Sports Gambling*, 12272

Willman, Chris. *Rednecks and Bluenecks*, 8533

Wills, Garry. *Head and Heart*, 9590

James Madison, 7682

Wilson, August. *Jitney*, 6578

Joe Turner's Come and Gone, 6579

The Piano Lesson, 6580

Wilson, Budge. *Before Green Gables*, 1286(F)

Sharla, 2167(F)

Wilson, Daniel H. *Robopocalypse*, 6247(F)

Wilson, Dawn. *Saint Jude*, 1477(F)

Wilson, Derek. *Charlemagne*, 8095

Wilson, Diane. *An Unreasonable Woman*, 10118

Wilson, Diane Lee. *Black Storm Comin'*, 4248(F)

Firehorse, 4361(F)

Wilson, Edward O. *Anthill*, 2283(F)

The Creation, 11574

The Leafcutter Ants, 11579

Wilson, F. Paul. *Masque*, 6248(F)

Wilson, G. Willow. *The Butterfly Mosque*, 8393

Cairo, 3744(F)

Wilson, Hugo. *Motorcycle Owner's Manual*, 11973

Wilson, Jacqueline. *Kiss*, 2168(F)

Wilson, John. *And in the Morning*, 4462(F)

Death on the River, 4284(F)

Wilson, Kevin. *Tunneling to the Center of the Earth*, 6481(F)

Wilson, Martin. *What They Always Tell Us*, 2169(F)

Wilson, N. D. *The Dragon's Tooth*, 3185(F)

The Drowned Vault, 3185(F)

Wilson, Reginald. *Our Rights*, 9853

Wilson, Susan. *One Good Dog*, 163(F)

Wilson, Wayne. *Careers in Entertainment*, 10512

Careers in Publishing and Communications, 10483

Wimsley, Jim. *Dream Boy*, 2170(F)

Winchester, Elizabeth Siris. *Sisters and Brothers*, 11217

Winchester, Simon. *Krakatoa*, 11727

The Professor and the Madman, 7087

Winckelmann, Thom. *Genocide*, 9658

Windham, Kathryn Tucker. *Jeffrey Introduces 13 More Southern Ghosts*, 12227

Windle, J. M. *Veiled Freedom*, 5513(F)

Windling, Terri (ed.). *After*, 5955(F)

The Beastly Bride, 2528(F)

Black Thorn, White Rose, 2529(F)

The Coyote Road, 6351(F)

The Green Man, 6352(F)

Swan Sister, 2530(F)

Windsor-Smith, Barry. *The Freebooters*, 3745(F)

Wingard-Nelson, Rebecca. *Algebra Word Problems*, 11760

Fraction and Decimal Word Problems, 11760

Wingate, Lisa. *Drenched in Light*, 1478(F)

The Language of Sycamores, 1287(F)

Never Say Never, 763(F)

Over the Moon at the Big Lizard Diner, 5834(F)

Tending Roses, 1288(F)

Winick, Judd. *Outsiders*, 3746(F)

Pedro and Me, 3747(F)

Winik, Marion. *Rules for the Unruly*, 11180

Winkler, Allan M. *The Cold War*, 8909

Winkler, Kathleen. *Bullying*, 11181

Winn, Marie. *Red-Tails in Love*, 11547

Winn, Steven. *Come Back, Como*, 11685

Winnacker, Susanne. *The Other Life. Bk. 1*, 4890(F)

Winslow, Emily. *The Whole World*, 5514(F)

Winston, Diana. *Wide Awake*, 9578

Title Index

This index contains both main entry and internal titles cited in the entries. References are to entry numbers, not page numbers. All fiction titles are indicated by (F), following the entry number.

963

Sea Turtles: A Complete Guide to Their Biology, Behavior, and Conservation, 11446

Sea Turtles: An Extraordinary Natural History of Some Uncommon Turtles, 11447

The Sea-Wolf, 212(F)

The Sea Wolves, 43(F)

Seabiscuit: An American Legend, 12385

The Seadragon's Daughter, 3141(F)

Seagull Bay, 5809(F)

Sealed with a Kiss, 5383(F)

SeaLife: A Complete Guide to the Marine Environment, 11607

The Search, 5771(F)

Search and Destroy, 4556(F)

Search for Safety, 526(F)

The Search for the Red Dragon, 2978(F)

Searching for Anne Frank: Letters from Amsterdam to Iowa, 8869

Searching for David's Heart: A Christmas Story, 1304(F)

Searching for Dragons, 3190(F)

The Season, 5700(F)

Season of Ice, 1152(F)

The Season of Risks, 4699(F)

Seasons of the Horse: A Practical Guide to Year-Round Equine Care, 11687

Seattle Children's Theatre: Six Plays for Young Audiences, 6571

Seattle Ghost Story, 4637(F)

Second Chance Summer, 580(F)

Second Death, 3211(F)

Second Lives: A Novel of the Gilded Age, 4321(F)

Second Skin: Appearances Can Be Deceiving, 3187(F)

Second Stringer, 6274(F)

The Second Summoning: The Keeper's Chronicles #2, 2731(F)

Second-Time Cool: The Art of Chopping Up a Sweater, 12159

The Second Virginity of Suzy Green, 1737(F)

Second Wave, 2866(F)

Secondhand World, 900(F)

Seconds Away, 5092(F)

The Secret, 6023(F)

Secret Agents: The Menace of Emerging Infections, 10698

A Secret Atlas, 3095(F)

The Secret Between Us, 5119(F)

The Secret Clan: Abducted Heiress, 4107(F)

Secret Daughter: A Mixed-Race Daughter and the Mother Who Gave Her Away, 8216

The Secret Diary of Adrian Mole, Age Thirteen and Three Quarters, 4987(F)

Secret Father, 5068(F)

The Secret History of Fantasy, 2360(F)

The Secret Hour, 4882(F)

Secret Keeper, 921(F)

Secret Letters, 5437(F)

The Secret Life of Bees, 4424(F)

The Secret Life of Money: A Kid's Guide to Cash, 10575

The Secret Life of Prince Charming, 286(F)

The Secret Life of Sparrow Delaney, 4676(F)

Secret Lives of Common Birds: Enjoying Bird Behavior Through the Seasons, 11543

The Secret Lives of Dresses, 5697(F)

The Secret Medicine of the Pharaohs: Ancient Egyptian Healing, 8727

The Secret of Laurel Oaks, 4822(F)

The Secret of Life, 6081(F)

The Secret of Me (Kearney), 1131(F); (Kearney), 1132(F)

The Secret of Priest's Grotto, 9098

Secret of the Swamp Thing, 3723(F)

The Secret of Two Brothers, 847(F)

The Secret of Whispering Springs, 4657(F)

The Secret Rites of Social Butterflies, 2191(F)

The Secret River, 3898(F)

Secret Sacrament, 2760(F)

Secret Sins, 4503(F)

The Secret Sisterhood of Heartbreakers, 754(F)

Secret Society Girl, 636(F)

The Secret Subway: The Fascinating Tale of an Amazing Feat of Engineering, 11976

The Secret to Lying, 1923(F)

The Secret Twin, 5359(F)

A Secret Word, 1968(F)

The Secret Year, 467(F)

Secretaries of State: Making Foreign Policy, 9697

Secretaries of War, Navy, and Defense: Ensuring National Security, 9697

Secrets, 5583(F)

Secrets in the Fire, 3852(F)

Secrets in the Shadows: The Art and Life of Gene Colan, 7255

Secrets of a Civil War Submarine: Solving the Mysteries of the H. L. Hunley, 12003

Secrets of My Hollywood Life: On Location, 291(F)

Secrets of My Suburban Life, 252(F)

The Secrets of Peaches, 238(F)

Secrets of Powerful Women: Leading Change for a New Generation, 7603

Secrets of the Hollywood Girls Club, 573(F)

Secrets of the Savanna: Twenty-three Years in the African Wilderness Unraveling the Mysteries of Elephants and People, 8971

Secrets of the Sphinx, 8718

Secrets of the Supernatural: Investigating the World's Occult Mysteries, 12211

See Jane Write: A Girl's Guide to Writing Chick Lit, 10380

See No Evil, 5167(F)

See Rock City, 7772

See You Down the Road, 1282(F)

Seeds: Time Capsules of Life, 11419

Seeds of Change, 5844(F)

Seeds of Summer, 5825(F)

Seeing beyond Sight: Photographs by Blind Teenagers, 10976

Seeing Stars, 979(F)

Seeing Stars: The McDonald Observatory and Its Astronomers, 11281

Seeing the Blue Between: Advice and Inspiration for Young Poets, 10375

Seeing the Gynecologist, 10813

Seek, 397(F)

The Seekers: The Story of Man's Continuing Quest to Understand His World, 9544

Seemed Like a Good Idea at the Time: A Memoir, 7358

Seize the Storm, 5062(F)

Seizing Destiny: How America Grew from Sea to Shining Sea, 9231

Selected Poems (Dove), 6681; (Sandburg), 6738

The Selected Poems of Nikki Giovanni (1968-1995), 6691

The Selection, 5930(F)

Self-Defense and Assault Prevention for Girls and Women, 12394

Self-Esteem, 11154

Self-Injury Disorder, 10918

Self-Mutilation, 10368

Self-Reliance: The Story of Ralph Waldo Emerson, 7344

Sellout, 2160(F)

Selma and the Voting Rights Act, 9787

Semper Fi: Stories of the United States Marines from Boot Camp to Battle, 9779

Senator: A Profile of Bill Bradley in the U.S. Senate, 7711

The Senator's Other Daughter, 5542(F)

Send, 1531(F)

Send Me a Sign, 1445(F)

Sengoku: Nights, Vol. 1, 3447(F)

Sensational Scenes for Teens: The Scene Studyguide for Teen Actors!, 8615

Sensational Scientists: The Journeys and Discoveries of 24 Men and Women of Science, 7819

Sensational TV: Trash or Journalism?, 7125

Sense and Sensibility, 3238(F)

Sense and Sensibility and Sea Monsters, 4891(F)

A Sense of the World: How a Blind Man Became History's Greatest Traveler, 8258

The Senses, 10868

Sensitive, 4893(F)

Sentries, 2256(F)

Separate but Equal: The Desegregation of America's Schools, 9940

September 11, 2001: American Writers Respond, 10288

September Fair, 5288(F)

The September Sisters, 5063(F)

Serafina's Stories, 4179(F)

Seraphina, 2687(F)

Serendipity: Accidental Discoveries in Science, 11245

Serendipity Market, 2401(F)

Serious Girls, 2102(F)

The Universal Declaration of Human Rights, 9622

Universe Down to Earth, 11295

The Universe in a Mirror: The Saga of the Hubble Space Telescope and the Visionaries Who Built It, 11296

The Universe in a Nutshell, 11350

The Universe of Dr. Einstein, 11807

Universe on a T-Shirt: The Quest for the Theory of Everything, 11811

The Unknowns, 5064(F)

Unlikely Pairs: Fun with Famous Works of Art, 8433

The Unlikely Romance of Kate Bjorkman, 5753(F)

Unlucky for Some: A Novel of Suspense, 5307(F)

The Unnatural History of the Sea, 10091

Unraveling Freedom: The Battle for Democracy on the Home Front During World War I, 9423

Unraveling Isobel, 327(F)

An Unreasonable Woman: A True Story of Shrimpers, Politicos, Polluters, and the Fight for Seadrift, Texas, 10118

The Unresolved, 4359(F)

The Unrivalled Spangles, 4132(F)

Unrooted Childhoods: Memoirs of Growing Up Global, 11189

The Unsayable: The Hidden Language of Trauma, 10926

Unseen Academicals, 3011(F)

Unseen Companion, 2255(F)

Unsettled: The Problem of Loving Israel, 9109

Unsettling America: An Anthology of Contemporary Multicultural Poetry, 6688

Unsinkable: The Full Story of the RMS Titanic, 11977

The Unsinkable Molly Malone, 239(F)

An Unspeakable Crime: The Prosecution and Persecution of Leo Frank, 9967

Unspoken, 4603(F)

The Unspoken, 4651(F)

An Unsuitable Job for a Woman, 5242(F)

An Untamed Land, 4318(F)

Unthinkable Thoughts of Jacob Green, 997(F)

Until I Die, 3004(F)

Untold Glory, 7576

UnWholly, 6174(F)

Up Against It, 6075(F)

Up All Night: A Short Story Collection, 6315(F)

Up Close: Oprah Winfrey, 7558

Up from Slavery: An Autobiography by Booker T. Washington, 7640

Upgrade Me: Our Amazing Journey to Human 2.0, 10578

Uppity Women of the New World, 8687

The Upstairs Room, 8335

Upstream, 1860(F)

Upstream: A Novel, 1374(F)

Uruguay, 9177

Usagi Yojimbo: Glimpses of Death, Vol. 20, 3599(F)

Usagi Yojimbo: Travels with Jotaro, Vol. 18, 3600(F)

Usagi Yojimbo, Vol. 24: Return of the Black Soul, 3598(F)

Useful Fools, 4172(F)

Useful Girl, 942(F)

User Friendly, 2653(F)

A User's Guide to the Brain: Perception, Attention, and the Four Theaters of the Brain, 10858

Uses for Boys, 2043(F)

Utopian Visionaries, 9242

The V Club, 1546(F)

Vacations from Hell, 4602(F)

Vaccines, 10809

Vaclav and Lena, 715(F)

Vacuum Bazookas, Electric Rainbow Jelly, and 27 Other Saturday Science Projects, 11257

Valiant: A Modern Tale of Faerie, 2391(F)

The Valley-Westside War, 6208(F)

Vampire Academy, 4606(F)

The Vampire Archives: The Most Complete Volume of Vampire Tales Ever Published, 6436(F)

The Vampire Book: The Legends, the Lore, the Allure, 12215

The Vampire Brat and Other Tales of Supernatural Law, 3455(F)

The Vampire Hunters, 5222(F)

Vampire Loves, 3617(F)

Vampireville, 4830(F)

Van Gogh, 7294

Van Gogh: The Passionate Eye, 7293

Vandal, 1243(F)

Vanish, 2762(F)

Vanishing America: In Pursuit of our Elusive Landscapes, 10046

The Vanishing Game, 5344(F)

Vanishing Girl, 5372(F)

The Vanishing of Katharina Linden, 5189(F)

The Vanishing Point (Hawes), 4025(F); (Sharratt), 5447(F)

The Vanishing Tiger, 11506

Variant, 6234(F)

The Various, 2329(F)

Various Positions, 2042(F)

The Vast Fields of Ordinary, 1566(F)

The Vault, 5289(F)

Vegan Virgin Valentine, 1893(F)

Vegetables Rock! A Complete Guide for Teenage Vegetarians, 10966

Vegetarianism, 10952

Veiled Alliances, 3229(F)

Veiled Freedom, 5513(F)

Velocity, 5264(F)

Velvet, 4037(F)

A Velvet Revolution: Vaclav Havel and the Fall of Communism, 8108

Velveteen, 2906(F)

Vendetta, 2736(F)

Venus, 5890(F)

Venus Envy, 5698(F)

Vera Wang, 7939

Veracity, 5911(F)

A Version of the Truth, 5662(F)

Very Easy Crazy Patchwork, 12150

Very Far Away from Anywhere Else, 1845(F)

Very LeFreak, 316(F)

Vessel, 2582(F)

Victim Rights, 5301(F)

Victoria Woodhull: Fearless Feminist, 7643

Victoria Woodhull: Free Spirit for Women's Rights, 7642

Victorian England, 9076

The Victorian Novel, 6948

Victory, 3393(F)

Vidalia in Paris, 752(F)

Vietnam, 9485

Vietnam: A History. 2nd rev. and updated ed. , 9026

Vietnam: The Valor and the Sorrow, 9484

The Vietnam War (Pendergast), 9498; (Roleff), 9501

The Vietnam War: A History in Documents, 8910

Vietnam War: Almanac, 8897

Vietnam War: Biographies, 8897

Vietnam War: Primary Sources, 8897

The View from a Kite, 1380(F)

The View from Garden City, 3965(F)

The View from Here, 854(F)

The View from Lazy Point: A Natural Year in an Unnatural World, 10096

View from the Imperium, 6124(F)

Viking Conquests, 9101

Viktor Frankl: A Life Worth Living, 7866

Villeggiatura: A Trilogy Condensed, 6548

Vimanarama, 3516(F)

Vincent van Gogh (Schapiro), 7295; (Whiting), 7296

The Vintage Book of African American Poetry, 6695

The Vintage Book of American Women Writers, 7005

The Vintage Guide to Classical Music, 8483

Vintage Hughes, 6702

Vintage Reading: From Plato to Bradbury, a Personal Tour of Some of the World's Best Books, 6931

Vintage Veronica, 5745(F)

The Vinyl Princess, 646(F)

Viola in Reel Life (Trigiani), 732(F); (Trigiani), 733(F)

Viola in the Spotlight, 733(F)

Violence in William Golding's Lord of the Flies, 6972

Violence on the Screen, 10000

Violent Children, 10154

Violent Storms, 11773

Violet and Claire, 1526(F)

Violins of Autumn, 4508(F)

The Virgin Widow, 4084(F)

Virginia Hamilton: Speeches, Essays, and Conversations, 7364

Virginia Woolf (Caws), 7446; (Mills), 7447

The Virginia Woolf Reader, 6910

The Virginian, 4323(F)

Subject/Grade Level Index

All entries are listed by subject and then according to grade level suitability (see the key at the foot of pages for grade level designations). Subjects are arranged alphabetically and subject heads may be subdivided into nonfiction (e.g., "Africa") and fiction (e.g. "Africa — Fiction"). References to entries are by entry number, not page number.

A

Aaron, Hank
S–Adult: 7952

Aaron, Henry
JS: 7951

Abandoned children — Fiction
J: 1176
JS: 985

Abdul-Jabbar, Kareem
S: 9424

Abolitionists
JS: 9335

Abolitionists — Biography
J: 7614
JS: 7610, 7617, 7626, 7638
S: 7615–16

Aborigines — Fiction
JS: 5235

Aborigines — Folklore
J: 6799

Abortion
JS: 10982–83, 10996, 10998, 11005
S: 8331, 10985

Abortion — Fiction
JS: 1562, 1837
S: 1794

Abuse
JS: 11048

Abuse — Fiction
JS: 247, 662, 1107, 1115, 1716

Academic guidance
JS: 10391, 10393, 10401

Academy of Motion Picture Arts and Sciences
JS: 8581

Acadia — Fiction
J: 4159

Accidents
J: 11854
JS: 9208

Accidents — Fiction
J: 2044
JS: 1413, 1691, 1703, 1921, 5119, 5385
S: 403

Achebe, Chinua — Criticism
JS: 7015

Acting
J: 8615
JS: 6487, 6508, 6518–19, 6523, 7240, 8547, 8609, 8612

Acting — Biography
J: 7503, 7519, 7539, 7544
JS: 7501, 7536, 7538, 7545
S: 7241, 7241, 7490, 7499, 7546
S–Adult: 8203

Acting — Careers
JS: 10509

Acting — Fiction
J: 289, 322–23, 781, 878
JS: 291, 324, 685, 1865, 2141, 5317
S–Adult: 5315

Activism
J: 9654, 10045, 10783
JS: 9472, 10247
S: 9464, 9988, 9993, 10261

Activism — Careers
JS: 10427

Activism — Fiction
J: 2254
JS: 2250

Adams, Arthur
JS: 7242

Adams, John
J: 7646
JS: 7644
S: 7645

Adams, John Quincy
S: 7647

Adams, Samuel
JS: 7709

Adaptation (biology)
JS: 11370

Addictions
J: 10636
JS: 10586, 10627, 11104, 11104

Adoption
JS: 11194–95, 11200, 11211, 11215–16
S: 10985, 11213

Adoption — Biography
JS: 8304

Adoption — Fiction
See also Foster care
J: 634, 952, 984, 1113, 1128, 1132, 1156, 2182, 4551
JS: 1039, 1131, 1218, 1268, 1294–95, 1963, 2213, 2281, 6003
S: 617
S–Adult: 255

Adultery — Fiction
JS: 454

Adventure stories — Fiction
See also Mystery stories — Fiction; Sea stories — Fiction; Survival stories — Fiction
IJ: 4926
J: 1–2, 18–19, 24–25, 28, 43, 60, 64, 67–68–69, 87, 90, 92, 113–14–15, 121, 125, 128, 130, 132, 137–38, 140–41–42, 191, 435, 981, 3671, 3771, 3806, 3827, 3878, 3892, 4029, 4187, 4303, 4305, 5231, 5441, 6141
JS: 3–4–5–6, 12, 16–17, 29, 39–40–41–42, 44, 46, 49, 51, 61–62–63, 66, 70, 74, 77, 89, 91, 93–94–95–96, 99–00–01, 103, 107, 111–12, 122–23, 129, 136, 144, 147, 169, 175–76–77, 211–12, 219, 226, 331, 551, 1016, 1972, 2023, 2736, 3024,

Aging
JS: 10599
S: 10135

Aging — Fiction
JS: 199
S: 3338

Agriculture
See also Farms and farm life
JS: 10064, 11390
S–Adult: 8700

Agriculture — Careers
S: 10481

Ahmadinejad, Mahmoud
JS: 8065

AIDS
See also HIV (virus)
J: 10729
JS: 10684, 10689, 10696, 10713, 10717, 10776, 10784, 10789
S: 10746, 10775

AIDS — Fiction
J: 1450, 2245
JS: 1813, 2114, 2213, 3747, 3864
S: 1112
S–Adult: 2077

Air
JS: 11766

Air Force (U.S.)
J: 10434
JS: 9777
S: 9447

Air Force (U.S.) — Biography
JS: 7744

Air Force (U.S.) — Careers
J: 10434

Air Force (U.S.) — Fiction
S: 863

Air pollution
J: 10117
JS: 11762

Airplane accidents
J: 11961–62
JS: 9182
S–Adult: 8889

Airplane accidents — Fiction
J: 25, 1448

Airplane pilots
JS: 7570, 9527

Airplane pilots — Biography
J: 7199
JS: 7168, 7181, 7187–88, 7194–95–96–97, 7916–17
S: 7186, 7200, 11960

Airplane pilots — Careers
JS: 10463

Airplane pilots — Fiction
J: 4531

Airplanes
JS: 11959

S: 11963

Airplanes — Fiction
JS: 4561

Akamba (African people)
J: 8954

Akbar, Said Hyder
JS: 8168

Akeley, Carl
S–Adult: 7825

Al Qaeda
S: 10271

Al-Haytham, Ibn
JS: 7826

Alabama
JS: 9792

Alabama — Fiction
JS: 918, 2025, 2169, 4365
S–Adult: 2283

Alamo (TX)
JS: 9334

Alaska
JS: 7175, 8254, 9526–27–28, 12310
S: 9531–32, 9534
S–Adult: 9286, 11984, 12364

Alaska — Fiction
J: 64, 269, 4408
JS: 62, 1860
S: 50, 1804, 2255, 5454
S–Adult: 667, 5626

Albany (NY) — Fiction
S: 4380

Alcatraz Island
S: 9970

Alchemy — Fiction
JS: 3051, 4800

Alcohol and alcohol abuse
J: 10606, 10609, 10619, 10629, 10629
JS: 1878, 10625, 10633, 10638, 10646, 10656, 10658, 10662
S: 8377, 10932

Alcohol and alcohol abuse — Biography
S–Adult: 8211

Alcohol and alcohol abuse — Fiction
J: 893, 1006, 1051, 1075, 1121, 1670
JS: 780, 909, 982, 1080, 1115, 1158, 1200, 1320, 1403, 1420, 1435, 1447, 1557, 1751, 2033, 2087, 2115
S: 1042, 1255, 1782
S–Adult: 1239

Alcott, Louisa May
JS: 7302

Alexander the Great
JS: 8090, 8736

Alexander the Great — Fiction
JS: 3784

Alexandria (Egypt)
J: 8722
JS: 8726

Alfred, King of England — Fiction
JS: 3810

Algebra
J: 11760
S–Adult: 11759

Algeria — Fiction
JS: 3615

Algonquin Indians
S: 8378

Ali, Muhammad
J: 7983
JS: 7982

Ali, Nujood
S–Adult: 8169

Aliens — Fiction
JS: 3375, 5944
S: 4725

Allergies
JS: 10680

Alligators and crocodiles — Fiction
JS: 1811

Allison, Peter
JS: 8170

Almanacs
JS: 12188

Alomar, Roberto
J: 7953

Alonso, Alicia
J: 7467

Alphabet books
J: 9079

Alphabets
JS: 7096

Alternate histories
JS: 5498

Alternative medicine
J: 10796
JS: 10805

Alvarez, Julia
J: 7304
S: 7303

Alzheimer's disease
J: 10724, 10914

Alzheimer's disease — Fiction
JS: 1140
S: 989

Amazon
JS: 7918

Amazon jungle — Fiction
JS: 3

Ambition — Fiction
J: 462

America
JS: 9155
S: 9150

American literature
JS: 6989–90, 6993, 6998

American Sign Language
JS: 7070

Ameru (African people)
J: 8953

Amigurumi
JS: 12155

Amish
JS: 9569

Amish — Fiction
JS: 432, 1538, 1617, 2285
S: 876, 5166
S–Adult: 543

Amistad (ship) — Poetry
S–Adult: 6759

Amistad mutiny
J: 9339
JS: 8557

Amnesia — Fiction
J: 1471, 1488, 5405
JS: 86, 5295
S: 5638

Amphetamines
JS: 10648

Amphibians
JS: 11430–31–32, 11694
S–Adult: 11433

Amputation
S: 8908

Amputees — Fiction
J: 460, 1305

Amundsen, Roald
S–Adult: 7173

**Amyotrophic lateral sclerosis —
Fiction**
J: 1439

Anasazi Indians — Fiction
J: 4185

Anastasia (Romanov)
JS: 8128

Anastasia (Romanov) — Fiction
JS: 4003

Ancient history
J: 8723
JS: 8658, 8707, 8709, 8711–12, 8714,
8717, 8733, 10803
S: 8706

Anderson, Laurie Halse
JS: 6982

Anderson, Marian
JS: 7468

Andersonville Prison
JS: 4259

Andersonville Prison — Fiction
S: 4266

Andoe, Joe
S: 7243

Angel dust (drug)
J: 10621

Angelou, Maya
J: 7307
JS: 7306
S: 6912
S–Adult: 7305

Angels — Fiction
J: 2678, 2789, 2887, 3054
JS: 1451, 3167
S: 2700, 3073
S–Adult: 4942

Anger
J: 11088
S–Adult: 8398

Anger — Fiction
JS: 1327

Anglo-Saxons — Fiction
JS: 3810

Angola
J: 8975
JS: 8945, 8969

Animal behavior
S–Adult: 11457, 11463

Animal experimentation
S–Adult: 10011

Animal Farm — Criticism
JS: 6959

Animal rescue
S–Adult: 11555

Animal rescue — Fiction
JS: 5260

Animal rights
JS: 10008, 10012, 10233, 10233,
11573
S: 8302, 9991, 10018, 11428
S–Adult: 10011

Animal rights — Fiction
S–Adult: 433

Animal smuggling
S–Adult: 11422

Animal trainers — Careers
JS: 10549

Animals
See also Endangered species; Pets; specific types or species, as Mammals
JS: 6874, 9180, 11238, 11362, 11424,
11429, 11448, 11451, 11458, 11464,
11479, 11481
S: 11426–27, 11459
S–Adult: 7317, 11420, 11457, 11471,
11644

Animals — Behavior
JS: 11451–52, 11454, 11507
S: 11453, 11455, 11459–60

Animals — Care
JS: 11701

Animals — Care — Careers
J: 10455
JS: 10451, 10457

Animals — Communication
JS: 11516

Animals — Emotions
S: 11449

Animals — Experimentation
S: 11421

Animals — Fiction
JS: 211, 2976
S: 153, 1091, 3901

Animals — Folklore
JS: 6826

Animals — Habitats
S: 11478, 11557

Animals — Homes
S: 11460

Animals — Migration
S: 11462

Animation (motion pictures)
JS: 8564, 8592
S: 8571, 11949

**Animation (motion pictures) —
Biography**
J: 7561–62
JS: 7291

Annan, Kofi
S: 8048

Anniston, Alabama
S: 10070

Anniversaries — Fiction
S–Adult: 579

Anorexia nervosa
See also Eating disorders
J: 10704, 10731, 10770, 10773
JS: 10760, 10777, 10945
S–Adult: 10785

Anorexia nervosa — Fiction
J: 1438, 1458
JS: 746, 1298–99–00, 1374, 1431,
1465
S: 1398, 1807

Antarctica
See also Arctic; Polar regions
JS: 7209, 9188–89, 9197
S: 9183, 9192
S–Adult: 8371

Antarctica — Fiction
J: 87, 5266
JS: 3469
S: 4178

Antarctica — Poetry
S: 7068

Anthologies
JS: 6365, 6397, 11236
S: 6343, 6587, 6683, 6875, 6878, 6911,

8964, 9533, 9637, 11228
S–Adult: 6366, 6925, 7005

Anthologies — Poetry
JS: 6677

Anthony, Susan B.
J: 7571, 7606, 9829

Anthrax
JS: 10764

Anthropology
JS: 8644–45
S: 8639, 8642, 8651

Anthropology — Biography
J: 7883, 7888
JS: 7882

Anthropology — Fiction
J: 2195

Anti-Semitism
J: 8833

Anti-Semitism — Fiction
J: 4088, 4396, 5252
JS: 4487

Antibiotics
J: 10802

Antidepressants (drugs)
J: 10651

Antietam, Battle of
J: 9370

Antietam, Battle of — Fiction
S: 4270, 4276

Antiwar movements
S: 9988

Antoinette, Marie
S: 8120

Ants
S–Adult: 11579, 11581

Ants — Fiction
S–Adult: 2283

Anxiety
J: 10900
JS: 10908, 10928
S: 10882

Anxiety — Fiction
JS: 1572

Apache Indians
JS: 9273
S: 7722

Apache Indians — Fiction
J: 4181, 4187
JS: 4192, 4369

Apartheid
JS: 8963, 8973, 8976

Apartheid — Biography
JS: 8057, 8064
S: 8056
S–Adult: 8055

Apartheid — Fiction
J: 6422

JS: 3847
S: 3862

Apes
See also individual species, e.g. Chimpanzees
S: 11486

Apes — Fiction
JS: 5888

Apollo (space mission)
J: 11317
JS: 11311, 11313

Apollo 11 **(spacecraft)**
J: 11317

Appalachia
JS: 9215, 9979
S: 9535

Appalachia — Fiction
JS: 381, 4342

Appelt, Kathi
JS: 8171

Apple Computer — Biography
J: 7927

Apprentices
JS: 10462

Aquaculture
S: 11603

Aquariums
JS: 11698
S: 11696

Arab Americans
JS: 9985
S: 9977
S–Adult: 9983

Arab Americans — Fiction
JS: 861, 3325
S: 1658, 2199, 2223
S–Adult: 961

Arab Americans — Poetry
JS: 6669

Arab-Israeli conflict
S–Adult: 9116, 9118

Arab-Israeli conflict — Biography
J: 8176
S–Adult: 8076

Arab-Israeli conflict — Fiction
S–Adult: 4040

Arab-Israeli relations
See also Israeli-Arab relations
JS: 9108

Arabs
JS: 9106

Arabs — Biography
JS: 8066

Arabs — Fiction
JS: 4044
S: 2223

Arafat, Yasir
JS: 8066

Archaeology
J: 8636, 8654, 8657, 9154, 12003
JS: 8650, 8658–59, 8663
S: 6887, 8653

Archaeology — Biography
S–Adult: 8656

Archaeology — Careers
J: 10430

Archaeology — Fiction
S: 109, 5168

Archimedes
J: 7827

Archimedes — Fiction
JS: 3789

Architecture
See also Building and construction
J: 8410, 8415, 8746, 11894
JS: 8411, 8413, 11896
S: 8416, 11884

Architecture — Biography
J: 7254, 7265, 7280
JS: 7299–00

Architecture — Careers
JS: 10467

Arctic
See also Antarctica; Polar regions
JS: 9194
S: 9193
S–Adult: 7212, 9187, 9190

Arctic — Biography
S: 7202, 8272

Arctic — Fiction
J: 5444
S: 126

Arctic National Wildlife Refuge
JS: 11521
S: 10056

Argentina
J: 9175

Argentina — Fiction
JS: 4176

Ariadne (Greek mythology) — Fiction
J: 2347

Aristide, Jean-Bertrand — Fiction
JS: 4173

Arizona
S: 9538

Arizona — Fiction
S–Adult: 749

Arkansas — Fiction
S: 1728
S–Adult: 5550

Armed forces (U.S.)
JS: 9761, 9774–75, 11987

S: 9762, 11991

Armed forces (U.S.) — Biography
J: 7755
JS: 7749, 8230
S: 7756

Armed forces (U.S.) — Women
JS: 9766, 9773
S: 9778

Armenia — Fiction
JS: 3957

Armstrong, Lance
JS: 8015
S–Adult: 8016

Armstrong, Louis
S: 7469

Army (U.S.)
J: 9768
JS: 11986, 12356
S: 9483, 9763

Army (U.S.) — Biography
JS: 7738

Army (U.S.) — Fiction
JS: 4530

Arnold, Benedict
J: 7710

Arranged marriages — Fiction
JS: 347, 1774, 4100
S: 3513
S–Adult: 388

Arson — Fiction
J: 1250
JS: 381, 4727

Art
See also Drawing and painting; Museums; and names of individuals, e.g., Van Gogh, Vincent
J: 6594, 7072, 8444–45, 8456, 9582
JS: 3280, 3640, 6397, 6806, 6812, 7226, 8405, 8408, 8421, 8423, 8426, 8432, 8435–36–37–38, 8440, 8443, 8451–52–53–54, 8457–58, 8461, 8468–69, 8473, 8720, 9520, 11903, 11912, 12123
S: 8400, 8409, 8439, 8441, 8449, 8455, 8471–72, 8472

Art — Beatles (musical group)
JS: 8434

Art — Biography
J: 7263, 7277, 7285–86–87, 7294
JS: 7217, 7226, 7242, 7245–46, 7248–49–50–51, 7253, 7256–57, 7262, 7266–67–68, 7281, 7283–84, 7293, 7296, 7298, 7311, 7355
S: 7222, 7243, 7252, 7260, 7275, 7282, 7295, 7301, 8466
S–Adult: 7269, 7272, 8356

Art — Careers
J: 10486
JS: 8407, 10487, 10506

Art — Fiction
J: 239, 3818, 4025
JS: 752, 2132, 3302, 3932, 3991, 4100, 5097
S: 689, 2002, 4117, 5253
S–Adult: 3383

Art — Poetry
JS: 6595

Art (U.S.)
JS: 8469

Art appreciation
JS: 8421, 8426, 8433, 8436, 8443, 8457
S: 8462

Art Institute of Chicago
JS: 8452

Art thefts — Fiction
JS: 752

Arthur, Chester A.
S: 7648

Arthur, King
J: 6819
JS: 6810, 6813–14–15

Arthur, King — Criticism
S: 6946

Arthur, King — Fiction
J: 2703, 3825, 3830
JS: 2407, 2532, 3097, 3176, 3178, 3196, 3835, 3838, 4131
S: 2830, 3177, 3824, 4139
S–Adult: 2811

Artificial insemination — Fiction
JS: 1097

Artificial intelligence
J: 11932

Artificial intelligence — Fiction
S–Adult: 310

Arts
JS: 6901

As You Like It **— Adaptations**
J: 3622

Ashe, Arthur
JS: 8006

Asia
See also specific countries, e.g., China
JS: 6923, 8073, 8986, 8989
S: 8985

Asia — Folklore
JS: 6792–93

Asia — Mythology
JS: 6792

Asian Americans
See also specific groups, e.g., Japanese Americans
JS: 6923, 9952, 9955
S: 6969, 9956
S–Adult: 9950

Asian Americans — Biography
J: 7937, 7939, 8005

JS: 7486

Asian Americans — Fiction
JS: 811, 844, 958, 4564
S: 960

Asperger's syndrome — Fiction
JS: 1308, 1452
S–Adult: 639

Assassinations — Fiction
J: 5440
JS: 34, 5160

Assassinations (U.S.)
J: 9458, 9460

Assertiveness
JS: 11151

Assisted suicide — Fiction
J: 387, 1404

Associated Press
JS: 7120

Asteroids
J: 11322, 11324
S: 11326

Asthma
J: 10772
JS: 10681, 10741

Asthma — Fiction
J: 5637
S: 1624

Astrology
JS: 12185, 12187, 12221

Astronauts — Biography
J: 7171, 7177, 7206
JS: 7170, 7878–79

Astronomy
J: 7802, 11267, 11281, 11293, 11322
JS: 11269–70, 11272, 11274, 11277, 11279–80, 11282–83, 11286, 11288, 11290, 11292, 11295, 11318, 11332
S: 7906, 11271, 11273, 11278, 11285, 11294, 11334, 11336, 11348
S–Adult: 11284

Astronomy — Biography
J: 7802, 7823, 7872, 7875
JS: 7837

Astronomy — Experiments and projects
JS: 11333

Astrophysics
S: 11294

Atalanta (Greek mythology)
JS: 6862

Atanasoff, John V
S–Adult: 7828

Athletes
JS: 7945

Atlanta (GA) — Fiction
JS: 886

Atlases
J: 8618

S: 8616, 8620

Atmosphere
J: 11786
JS: 11766

Atomic bomb
J: 9452

Atomic bomb
J: 8859
JS: 8818, 8827, 8856, 8887
S: 8846, 9474, 11996

Atomic bomb — Biography
J: 7898
JS: 7861, 8083

Atoms
JS: 11829

Attention deficit hyperactivity disorder
J: 10884
JS: 10758, 10912, 10919, 10924

Attention deficit hyperactivity disorder — Fiction
J: 6282

Audubon, John James
JS: 7244

Aung San Suu Kyi
JS: 8067

Aunts — Fiction
JS: 482

Auriemma, Geno
JS: 7972

Austen, Cassandra — Fiction
S–Adult: 4094

Austen, Jane
J: 7309
JS: 6950, 7308

Austen, Jane — Criticism
S: 6945, 6954

Austen, Jane — Fiction
JS: 3969
S: 3952, 5019–20
S–Adult: 632, 4094, 4102, 4787, 5733, 5788, 6475

Australia
S: 8089, 9042

Australia — Fiction
J: 67, 69, 92, 782–83, 1020, 1105, 1737, 1754, 1886, 2541, 3892, 3905, 3924, 3930, 4757, 5290, 5574
JS: 82, 91, 93–94–95–96, 144, 279, 544, 597, 1184, 1187, 1597, 1703, 1753, 1871, 1929, 2827, 2915–16, 3285, 3884, 3891, 3898, 3903–04, 3923, 3941, 4714, 4947, 5235, 5555, 6345
S: 972, 1165, 1651, 3901, 3919, 5117, 5588
S–Adult: 3916, 5617, 5774

Australia — Folklore
JS: 6798

Austria — Biography
JS: 7866

Austria — Fiction
JS: 4004
S: 3365

Authors
J: 7223
JS: 6988, 6996, 7101, 7332, 7365, 7379, 7415, 7450
S: 6895, 6969, 7103, 7112, 9973
S–Adult: 7005

Authors — Biography
J: 7220, 7307, 7309–10, 7321, 7324–25, 7330, 7333–34, 7344, 7347, 7362, 7371, 7378, 7385, 7389, 7391, 7397, 7399, 7406, 7411, 7413, 7418, 7421, 7430, 7436, 7448, 7612
JS: 6988, 7213–14, 7219, 7221, 7227, 7230, 7238, 7302, 7306, 7308, 7318, 7320, 7328–29, 7332, 7340–41–42–43, 7349, 7351, 7353, 7355, 7364, 7368–69–70, 7373–74, 7380, 7383, 7387–88, 7390, 7393–94–95, 7403–04–05, 7407, 7410, 7415–16, 7420, 7422–23, 7426–27–28–29, 7431, 7433–34, 7440, 7443, 7445, 7447, 7449, 7747, 8124, 8197, 11975
S: 7233, 7235, 7237, 7303, 7313, 7319, 7322–23, 7335–36, 7339, 7348, 7350, 7357–58, 7372, 7375–76–77, 7381, 7384, 7408, 7417, 7419, 7424–25, 7432, 7435, 7438, 7444, 7446
S–Adult: 6987, 7305, 7331, 7356, 7360, 7386, 7409, 8205, 8356, 8379, 8386

Authors — Careers
JS: 10474

Authors — Criticism
JS: 6983

Authors — Fiction
JS: 306, 3963, 4152, 5286, 5330
S–Adult: 4335

Authorship — Fiction
JS: 280

Autism
J: 10703, 10875
JS: 10739, 10915, 10927
S: 10923, 10925

Autism — Biography
S: 8374

Autism — Fiction
J: 1360
JS: 480, 1242, 5306
S: 3679–80

Autobiography
J: 11061
JS: 7553
S: 7163

Autobiography — Criticism
JS: 6932

Automobile accidents — Fiction
J: 1885

JS: 1301, 1418, 1425, 1654, 1801, 2087, 5515

Automobile driving
JS: 11971

Automobile racing
JS: 12274–75–76–77, 12279–80
S: 12278

Automobile racing — Biography
J: 7949
S–Adult: 7950

Automobile racing — Fiction
J: 6276, 6282
JS: 5547, 6258, 6284, 6288, 6310, 6312

Automobile travel — Fiction
J: 657, 4902, 5790
JS: 262, 427, 438, 489, 509, 524, 585, 1005, 1307, 2075, 5572
S: 559, 762, 771

Automobiles
J: 11966, 11969
JS: 11967–68, 11970–71, 11971, 12011

Automobiles — Fiction
JS: 4720

Avant-garde movement
S: 8400

Avi (author)
J: 7310

Avian flu
JS: 10747

Aviation
JS: 11954, 11959, 11965
S: 11955, 11958, 11960

Aviation — Biography
JS: 7172

Avignon — Fiction
S: 3808

Ayers, Nathaniel
JS: 8173

Azerbaijan
JS: 9093

Aztecs — Fiction
J: 4162
JS: 4161

B

Babies — Fiction
J: 1563

Babylon 5 **(television series)**
JS: 8597

Babysitting
IJ: 10564
JS: 10563

JS = Junior High/Senior High; S = Senior High; S–Adult = Senior High/Adult

JS = Junior High/Senior High; S = Senior High; S–Adult = Senior High/Adult

JS: 421, 6340

Behr, Hans-Georg
JS: 8182

Beiderbecke, Bix
JS: 7479

Beirut (Lebanon) — Fiction
JS: 3215

Belgian Congo — Fiction
S: 3850

Bell, Alexander Graham
JS: 7829–30

Bell, Margaret.
S: 8183

Bellil, Samira
S–Adult: 8184

Beluga whales
S: 11632

Belushi, John
JS: 7480

Ben-Atar, Roma Nutkiewicz
JS: 8185

Ben-Gurion, David
J: 9112

Bennet, Elizabeth (fictitious character) — Fiction
JS: 4085
S–Adult: 4667

Beowulf
S: 6641

Beowulf **— Adaptations**
J: 6811
JS: 6816

Berg, Mary
S: 8186

Berland-Hyatt, Felicia
JS: 8813

Berlin (Germany)
S: 8870

Berlin Airlift
JS: 8820

Bermuda Triangle
J: 12181

Bernstein, Harry
JS: 8187

Bernstein, Leonard
JS: 7456–57
S: 7455

Best Friends Animal Sanctuary (UT)
JS: 11701

Bettis, Jerome
JS: 7987

Beverly Hills (CA)
JS: 10058

Bezos, Jeff
JS: 7918

Bible
J: 9568, 9576, 9582
JS: 9550

Bible — Fiction
JS: 3781, 4016
S: 3787

Biculturalism
JS: 9886, 9894–95

Bicycle racing
J: 12332

Bicycle racing — Biography
JS: 8015
S–Adult: 8016, 8025

Bicycles
JS: 12307, 12328–29, 12331
S: 12326, 12326–27

Bicycles — Biography
JS: 8029
S: 8364

Big Bang theory
JS: 11354

Big cats
See individual species, e.g., Lions

Bigamy — Fiction
S–Adult: 1130

Bill of Rights (U.S.)
J: 9673
JS: 9670, 9677, 9679

Billy the Kid
JS: 7763

Billy the Kid — Fiction
S: 4296

Bin Laden, Osama
S: 10271

Binding of feet
S: 8996

Bini (African people)
J: 8977

Biochemistry
JS: 10817

Bioethics
JS: 11089

Biofuels
J: 11845

Biography
See under specific occupations, e.g., Acting — Biography; specific sports, e.g., Baseball — Biography; and cultural groups, e.g, African Americans — Biography
JS: 7162
S: 7581

Biography — Collective
J: 7164, 7171, 7174, 7224, 7801, 7817, 8041, 8043
JS: 7168, 7214, 7593–94, 7605, 7803, 7807, 7810, 7814, 7820, 7942, 7947, 8044, 8667
S: 7233

S–Adult: 7216, 7564, 7591

Biology
J: 11371, 11492
S: 11329, 11361, 11372, 11569

Biology — Biography
JS: 7821
S: 7831

Biology — Experiments and projects
J: 11373
JS: 11374

Biomedical ethics
JS: 10582–83

Biosphere 2
JS: 11722

Biotechnology
JS: 10831
S: 11872

Bioterrorism — Fiction
JS: 5453

Bipolar disorder
J: 10904
S: 10937

Bipolar disorder — Fiction
JS: 377, 1477, 1674

Biracial families — Fiction
S–Adult: 1058

Bird watching
JS: 11529, 12009
S: 11547

Birdhouses
JS: 11535

Birds
JS: 7244, 11519, 11521–22, 11524, 11526, 11529–30, 11532–33–34–35, 11537, 11539–40–41–42–43, 11558
S: 11461, 11523, 11525, 11536
S–Adult: 8246, 11528, 11538

Birds — Fiction
JS: 11526

Birds — Folklore
JS: 11526

Birds — Migration
JS: 11527

Birds of prey
JS: 11546

Birds of prey — Fiction
J: 321

Birmingham (AL)
JS: 9826
S: 9823

Birth control
JS: 11006
S–Adult: 11001

Birthdays — Fiction
J: 494

Birthmarks — Fiction
JS: 1372

Bisexuality
JS: 11037
S: 11018, 11020

Bisexuality — Fiction
JS: 2037

Bisland, Elizabeth
JS: 7765

Bison
JS: 8342, 11560

Bitton-Jackson, Livia
JS: 8188

Black Arts movement
JS: 8406

Black Death
J: 10715
JS: 8752, 8774

Black Death — Fiction
JS: 3814
S: 3819

Black Muslims — Biography
JS: 7632
S: 7631

Black Panthers
JS: 9945
S: 9796

Black Panthers — Fiction
J: 889, 4434

Blacks
JS: 8192

Blacks — Fiction
JS: 805, 4173

Blackwell, Unita
JS: 7609

Blair, Tony
J: 8091

Blake, William
JS: 7311

Blanco, Jodee
S: 8189

Bledsoe, Lucy Jane
JS: 7178

Blind
JS: 10976

Blind — Biography
JS: 7782, 8080, 8282
S: 7780, 8283

Blind — Fiction
J: 566, 1330, 5218
JS: 1222
S: 1389
S–Adult: 6167

Blind and deaf — Fiction
JS: 1412

Blizzard of 1888
JS: 11770

Blizzards
JS: 11767

Blizzards — Fiction
JS: 4390

Blogs — Fiction
J: 276, 1048, 1961, 1995
JS: 314, 448, 2209, 3274

Bloodsucking animals
S–Adult: 11456

Blue whales
JS: 11624

Blues (music)
JS: 8484
S: 8522, 8524

Blues (music) — Biography
JS: 7512, 7515
S: 7513

The Bluest Eye — **Criticism**
JS: 6976

Blume, Judy — Criticism
JS: 6994, 7013

Bly, Nellie
J: 7223, 7764
JS: 7765

Bly, Nellie — Fiction
S–Adult: 5296

Board of Education v. Pico
J: 10228

Body decoration
JS: 12087

Body image
J: 10962
JS: 10836, 10842

Body image — Fiction
JS: 6381

Bodybuilding — Biography
JS: 8018

Bodybuilding — Fiction
J: 5671

Bodyguards — Careers
J: 10530

Bogues, Tyrone "Muggsy"
JS: 7973

Bomb squads — Careers
J: 10532

Bombings (U.S.)
S–Adult: 10325

Bonaparte, Napoleon
J: 8123

Bonds, Barry
JS: 7954

Bonhoeffer, Dietrich
JS: 8190

Bonner, John Tyler
S: 7831

Bonobos
S–Adult: 8396

Bonobos — Fiction
JS: 3861

Book clubs — Fiction
JS: 679

Book making
JS: 7111
S: 7106

Book reports
JS: 10361

Book talks
JS: 10361

Books and reading
See also Alphabet books; Comic books
JS: 6930, 7113, 12012
S: 6875, 12010
S–Adult: 7107

Books and reading — Fiction
J: 407
JS: 679, 2967, 5893
S: 1745
S–Adult: 568

Bookstores — Fiction
JS: 4437

Boomerangs
S: 9042

Boone, Daniel
JS: 7766

Booth, John Wilkes
JS: 7767

Booth, John Wilkes — Fiction
S–Adult: 3290

Borden, Lizzie
S: 10161

Border control
JS: 9868

Borneo
S: 9027

Bosnia
J: 9050
JS: 9048, 9055

Bosnia — Fiction
S: 3595

Boston (MA)
S: 9911

Boston (MA) — Fiction
J: 4361

Boston Red Sox (baseball team) — Biography
JS: 7943

Botany
JS: 11414, 11419

Botswana
J: 8962, 8975
JS: 11476

Botswana — Biography
JS: 8170

Botswana — Fiction
JS: 3844

Bottled water
JS: 10968

Bourgeois, Louise
JS: 7246

Bourke-White, Margaret
JS: 7247

Bowling
JS: 12235

Boxing — Biography
J: 7983, 7986
JS: 7982
S: 7984–85

Boxing — Fiction
J: 878
JS: 877, 879, 2035, 2061, 6314
S: 863

Boy Scouts
JS: 11219
S–Adult: 11221

Boycotts — Fiction
JS: 750

Boyfriends — Fiction
JS: 5622

Boyle, Brian
S–Adult: 8191

Boyle, Robert
JS: 7832

Bradley, Bill
J: 7711

Bradley, Guy
S: 7768

Bradstreet, Anne Dudley
S: 7312

Brady, Tom
S: 7988

Brain and nervous system
J: 10800
JS: 8479, 10855, 10860, 10865
S: 10858
S–Adult: 11058

Brain damage — Fiction
JS: 1411, 1466, 2244

Brain tumors
JS: 10753

Braithwaite, E. R.
JS: 8192

Braque, Georges
JS: 7248

Bray, Rosemary
S: 7313

Brazil
J: 9174

Bread and Roses Strike
J: 9411

Breast cancer
J: 10774
JS: 10788

Breast cancer — Fiction
S: 595

Breasts
JS: 10854

Breazeal, Cynthia
J: 7833

Brennan, Christine
JS: 7314

Bridge (game) — Fiction
JS: 1222

Bridges
J: 9975
JS: 11898

Brill, Leigh
S–Adult: 8193

Brin, Sergey
J: 7812
JS: 7818

Broadcasting
JS: 8603

Broadcasting — Biography
J: 7801
JS: 7553
S: 7424, 7481, 7491, 7556

Broadcasting — Careers
JS: 10432

Broadway — Fiction
JS: 498

Brokaw, Tom
S: 7481

Brontë family
JS: 7315

Brontë family — Fiction
J: 4643

Bronte, Charlotte
JS: 6949
S: 6944

Bronx (NY) — Biography
S: 9519
S–Adult: 8346

Bronx (NY) — Fiction
J: 2160
JS: 994

Brooklyn (NY)
S: 9977

Brooklyn (NY) — Fiction
J: 733, 4429
JS: 4336, 4352
S: 1655
S–Adult: 715, 3242

Brooks, Gwendolyn
J: 7316
S: 6666

Brotherhood of Eternal Love
S–Adult: 9475

Brothers — Fiction
J: 458, 2194, 2389
JS: 514, 1245, 2128
S: 686, 1777

Brothers and sisters
S: 1608

Brothers and sisters — Fiction
J: 411, 703, 917, 990, 1017, 1101,
1199, 1243, 4010, 4429, 4550, 4569,
5099, 5333, 6276
JS: 335, 498, 511, 668, 725, 1005,
1125, 1144, 1190, 1212, 1275, 1686,
1725, 2169, 4423, 5126, 5140, 5326
S: 299, 1106, 1165, 1182, 1207, 1220,
1236, 1255, 1304, 1366, 1433, 1505,
1841, 2030, 2063, 4393, 4566, 5687

Brown v. Board of Education
JS: 9718, 9745

Brown, John
JS: 7610

Brown, John — Fiction
JS: 4239

Brown, Rita Mae
S–Adult: 7317

Browning, Robert
JS: 6649

Brownsworth, Claire
JS: 7179

Broyard, Bliss
JS: 8194

Bryson, Bill
JS: 7318

Buck, Pearl S. — Criticism
S: 6979

Buckley, Bryan
S–Adult: 8196

Buckley, Kristen
JS: 8197

Buddhism
J: 9578
JS: 9562, 9564, 9567
S–Adult: 8069

Buddhism — Biography
S–Adult: 8070

Buddhism — Fiction
S: 3906

Budget (U.S.)
S: 9695

Buffett, Warren
JS: 7919

***Buffy the Vampire Slayer* (TV series)**
JS: 11242
S: 8605

Buford, Bill
JS: 8198

Building and construction
See also Architecture

10507, 10528, 10530, 10537–38,
10555, 10557
JS: 8407, 9777, 10426–27, 10429,
10432, 10435–36–37–38, 10441,
10448–49, 10453–54, 10462–63,
10466–67, 10471, 10474, 10476–77,
10479, 10483–84–85, 10487–88–89,
10491, 10493–94–95, 10497, 10499,
10501–02, 10508, 10510–11–12–13,
10517, 10519–20–21–22, 10524–
25–26–27, 10533, 10535, 10540,
10542–43, 10545–46–47–48–49–50–
51–52–53–54, 10556
S: 10422, 10445, 10447, 10458–59–60,
10470, 10523, 10544
S–Adult: 10490, 10529, 11684

Careers — Fiction
JS: 546

Careers — Hispanic Americans
S: 10450

Careers — Women
JS: 10419, 10425
S: 10421

Caribbean Islands — Cookbooks
JS: 12083

Caribbean Islands — Fiction
JS: 987, 1100, 4154

Caribou
JS: 11514

Carjacking — Fiction
J: 5218

Carlos the Jackal
S: 8143

Carnegie, Andrew
J: 7920

Carpentry
JS: 12173

Carrington, Richard
S: 11336

Carroll, Lewis
S: 7319

Carroll, Lewis — Criticism
JS: 6955

Carroll, Lewis — Fiction
S–Adult: 3967

Carson, Kit
S: 7769

Carson, Rachel
J: 7834

Carter, Rubin "Hurricane"
S: 7984

Carthage — Biography
J: 8052

Cartoons and cartooning
JS: 7133, 7270, 9834, 12114, 12117,
12120, 12125, 12130, 12133
S: 4928, 7160

**Cartoons and cartooning —
Biography**
J: 7561–62
JS: 7266, 7271, 7276, 7290–91, 7297

Carver, George Washington
S: 7835

Casting (motion pictures)
JS: 8566

Castles
S: 8758

Castles — Fiction
J: 4908

Castro, Fidel
JS: 9168
S: 8144–45

Catapults
J: 11990

Cather, Willa
JS: 7320

Catherine de' Medici — Fiction
JS: 4073

Catherine the Great
JS: 8094
S: 8093

Catholicism
JS: 6545
S: 9584

Catholicism — Biography
S: 7899
S–Adult: 7360

Catholicism — Fiction
S: 2118

Catlin, George
JS: 7251

Cats
See also individual species of big cats,
e.g., Lions
JS: 6888, 8453, 11504, 11645,
11649–50–51–52–53–54

Cats — Fiction
J: 3116, 3300
JS: 150, 2363, 2732, 2952, 3033, 3616,
6123
S: 5046, 5182

Cats — Folklore
JS: 6778

Cats — Poetry
J: 6734
JS: 6647

Cattle
JS: 11389

**Caulfield, Holden (fictitious
character) — Fiction**
S–Adult: 1376

Cavalho, Solomon
J: 9392

Cavalry (U.S.)
S: 9420

Caves
JS: 11732

Caves — Fiction
JS: 133

Celebrities
JS: 7240

Celebrities — Biography
S: 8345

Celebrities — Fiction
JS: 714
S: 507

Celebrity
S–Adult: 9996, 10603

Celebrity — Fiction
J: 289–90, 718, 2182, 4929
JS: 263, 314, 350, 573, 588, 655, 710
S–Adult: 4931, 4983, 10603

Cell phones
J: 11946
JS: 11944

Cell phones — Fiction
J: 1982

Cells (human body)
JS: 11638

Celts — Fiction
S: 2552

Celts — Mythology
JS: 6841, 6843

Cemeteries
JS: 10265

Censorship
J: 10228, 10234, 11920
JS: 7387, 9668, 9830, 9832, 10226–27,
10232
S: 10230, 10230

Censorship — Fiction
J: 2226, 3580
JS: 1699

Census (U.S.)
JS: 9664

Central African Republic
JS: 8929

Central America
JS: 9161

Central America — Biography
S–Adult: 8380

Central America — Fiction
S: 468, 2249

Central America — Mythology
JS: 6839

Central Asia
JS: 8988

**Central Intelligence Agency
(U.S.)**
JS: 9642, 9646

Cerebral palsy
JS: 8325

Cerebral palsy — Fiction
J: 1266, 1463
JS: 1387, 1393, 1462, 5672

Cézanne, Paul
S: 7252

Chad
JS: 8911

Chad — Biography
S: 8376

Chagall, Marc
JS: 7253

Chai, May-Lee
S: 8204

Challenger (space shuttle)
S: 354

Chancellorsville, Battle of
JS: 9350
S: 9374

Chaplin, Charlie
J: 7482
S: 7483

Characters in literature — Fiction
S: 2794

Charities
S–Adult: 10259

Charities — Fiction
S: 775

Charlemagne
S: 8095

Charles, Bryan
S–Adult: 8205

Charles, Ray
JS: 7484–85

Chaucer, Geoffrey — Adaptations
S–Adult: 182

Chaucer, Geoffrey — Criticism
S: 7018

Chavez, Cesar
J: 7611

Chavez, Hugo
JS: 8146, 8148
S: 8147

Chavez, Jesus
S: 7985

Cheating — Fiction
J: 1844
JS: 6308

Chechnya
S: 8174, 9094

Cheerleading
JS: 12256
S: 12237

Cheerleading — Fiction
J: 2053
JS: 2054, 5807

Chekhov, Anton — Criticism
S: 6928

Chemical elements
J: 11707

Chemistry
See also Environmental chemistry
JS: 11705, 11710, 11712, 11829
S: 11708

Chemistry — Biography
JS: 7832, 7902

Chemistry — Experiments and projects
J: 11265

Chernobyl nuclear disaster
JS: 11853, 11859

Cherokee Indians
J: 9276
S: 9266, 9279

Cherokee Indians — Fiction
S: 1821

Cherry-Garrard, Apsley — Fiction
S: 4178

Chess
J: 410
JS: 1275, 12352

Cheyenne Indians
JS: 9274
S: 9281

Chicago (IL) — Fiction
JS: 4438, 6400
S: 815, 953, 1009, 1918, 4351, 4422

Chicago White Sox (baseball team)
S: 12297

Chicanos — Poetry
S: 6741

Chickens
JS: 8247

Chief Joseph (Nez Perce Indian)
JS: 9254

Child abuse
JS: 8390, 10125, 11199, 11205
S: 8350, 10889, 10892, 11201

Child abuse — Fiction
J: 827, 1279, 1603, 2146, 4183
JS: 112, 309, 670, 1015, 1271, 1377, 1476, 1487, 1623, 2108
S: 1009, 1071, 1373, 1967
S–Adult: 1919

Child care
JS: 11000, 11003
S: 10989, 10992

Child care — Careers
J: 10456

Child care — Fiction
JS: 1910

Child labor
J: 9415
JS: 4153, 6055, 9412, 10004, 10022

Child soldiers
S: 8688

Child soldiers — Biography
S: 8179

Child soldiers — Fiction
JS: 3865

Child, Lydia Maria
J: 7612

Childbirth
JS: 10991

Childbirth — Poetry
S: 6630

Childhood
S: 9396, 10229

Childhood — Fiction
JS: 798

Children — Poetry
J: 6698
JS: 6655
S: 6630

Children — United States
JS: 9250, 9431
S: 9244

Children of celebrities — Fiction
JS: 2050

Children's literature
J: 7072
JS: 7013

Children's literature — Biography
J: 7220, 7406

Children's rights
J: 9802, 9819

Chile — Fiction
JS: 2250

Chilean Americans — Fiction
JS: 2250

Chimpanzees — Fiction
J: 628

Chin, Staceyann
S–Adult: 8206

China
J: 8266, 8397, 8715, 8992, 8998, 9002
JS: 7351, 8265, 8994–95, 8997, 8999–00–01, 11518
S: 8991, 8993, 8996, 9003

China — Biography
J: 7517, 8397
JS: 7979, 8291
S: 7516, 8235

China — Fiction
J: 4525
JS: 3005, 3470, 3523, 3627, 3875, 3877, 3880–81, 3910, 3949, 6794
S: 22, 3761, 3882, 3900, 3927–28,

3933, 3937, 3940, 3948
S–Adult: 3888, 3917

China — Folklore
J: 6797
S: 6796

China — Poetry
J: 6771

China-Japan War — Fiction
JS: 3875

Chinese Americans
JS: 9955
S: 3758

Chinese Americans —
Biography
J: 7274, 7280, 7529, 8004
S: 8204

Chinese Americans — Fiction
JS: 453, 532, 871, 910, 4378
S: 864, 944, 1290, 4329
S–Adult: 956

Chinese Canadians — Fiction
J: 957, 6483

Chinn, May
JS: 7836

Chinn, May — Fiction
JS: 7836

Chippewa Indians — Fiction
J: 1579

Chivalry, Age of
S: 6817

Cho, Margaret
JS: 7486

Chocolate
JS: 11392

Chocolate — Biography
JS: 7926

The Chocolate War **— Criticism**
JS: 6972

Choctaw Indians — Fiction
S: 4292

Choctaw Indians — Folklore
JS: 6827

Choi, Annie
JS: 8207

Chol, Beny Ngor
S–Adult: 8158

Chong, Gordon H.
J: 7254

Choo, Jimmy
J: 7921

Choquette, Sonia
S: 8208

Choreography — Biography
JS: 7470, 7492
S: 8555

Chorn-Pond, Arn — Fiction
JS: 3918

Christian life
S: 10223, 10413

Christian life — Fiction
J: 777, 1530, 1954
JS: 77, 342, 503, 585, 1013, 1260, 1520–21, 1599, 1632, 1896, 2140, 4636, 5095
S: 479, 1739
S–Adult: 1090, 1663, 2239, 4335, 4348, 4373, 5215, 5565, 5619, 5631, 5748, 5779, 5783, 5793, 5806

Christian rock (music)
JS: 8488

Christianity
JS: 8341, 9585
S: 9580, 9586, 9590–91

Christianity — Fiction
J: 3786
JS: 1424, 1626, 1824
S: 1442, 2676, 4317, 4520

Christianity (U.S.) — Biography
J: 7579

Christie, Agatha — Criticism
JS: 6962

Christmas
J: 9581
JS: 8541, 9589
S: 6338, 6657

Christmas — Fiction
JS: 231, 248, 317
S: 6467
S–Adult: 345

Christmas — Poetry
JS: 6644

A Christmas Carol **— Criticism**
S: 6952

The Chronicles of Narnia **—**
Criticism
S: 6943

Church and state
JS: 9734

Circulatory system
JS: 10861

Circuses
JS: 8546

Circuses — Biography
JS: 7557, 7559
S: 7560

Circuses — Fiction
J: 4132, 4364
JS: 89
S: 2045, 2100

Cities and city life
See also Urban planning; names of specific cities, e.g., New York (NY)
J: 11897
JS: 6877, 8702, 10130, 10218, 11880

Cities and city life — Fiction
J: 2277
JS: 728, 5390, 6476

S: 1707, 1777
S–Adult: 345

Citizenship (U.S.)
JS: 9987

Civil liberties
JS: 9674, 9710, 9810, 9987

Civil rights
See also names of specific civil rights leaders, e.g., Du Bois, W. E. B.; and specific civil rights, e.g., Human rights; Women's rights
J: 9457, 9708, 9711, 9785, 9793, 9804, 9819, 9822, 9831, 9842, 9936
JS: 9454, 9467, 9705, 9743, 9786–87, 9792, 9795, 9798, 9800–01, 9809, 9811, 9816, 9818, 9820, 9825–26–27–28, 9833–34–35, 9850, 9852–53, 9901
S: 9236, 9422, 9455, 9791, 9796, 9799, 9806, 9823, 9836, 9892, 9916, 9929, 9934, 9988, 11033
S–Adult: 9479, 9821, 9837, 12366

Civil rights — Biography
J: 7612, 7618, 7623, 7627, 7630, 7634, 7636–37
JS: 7578, 7580, 7600, 7607–08, 7619, 7625, 7629, 7632, 7770, 8058
S: 7546, 7567, 7620, 7624, 7631, 7712, 9935, 9943

Civil rights — Fiction
J: 889, 4415, 4434
JS: 822, 918, 4402, 4419
S: 894, 4424, 5457

Civil War (Spain) — Fiction
S: 4027

Civil War (U.S.)
See also specific battles, e.g., Antietam, Battle of; and names of specific individuals, e.g., Lincoln, Abraham
J: 9341, 9363, 9370, 12003, 12025
JS: 4259, 9207, 9343–44–45, 9347, 9350–51–52–53–54–55–56, 9358–59, 9361–62, 9364–65–66–67, 9369, 9371–72–73, 9375–76–77–78, 9380–81–82–83–84, 9387
S: 8471, 9342, 9349, 9360, 9386
S–Adult: 9385

Civil War (U.S.) — Biography
J: 7728, 7736–37, 7761
JS: 7656–57, 7767, 7797
S: 7658, 7729, 7735, 7753, 7762

Civil War (U.S.) — Fiction
J: 4252–53, 4255, 4260, 4265, 4267, 4278–79, 4284
JS: 208, 4249, 4251, 4254, 4261–62, 4268–69, 4271, 4273, 4275, 4280, 4283
S: 4250, 4256–57–58, 4264, 4266, 4270, 4274, 4276, 4281–82
S–Adult: 3146

Civil War (U.S.) — Poetry
JS: 6713

Civil War (U.S.) — Women
JS: 9348

JS = Junior High/Senior High; S = Senior High; S–Adult = Senior High/Adult

J: 10045
JS: 10042, 11443, 11562, 11572
S: 10052
S–Adult: 11565

Conservation — Biography
J: 7805, 7834
JS: 7813, 7894
S: 7893, 7895

Conspiracies
JS: 12218
S–Adult: 12180

Conspiracy theories
S–Adult: 9665

Constellations
JS: 11333

Constitution (U.S.)
J: 9669, 9673
JS: 9667, 9671–72, 9674, 9676, 9678, 9834
S: 9304, 9666, 9675
S–Adult: 7787

Constitutional Convention, 1787
S: 9304

Consumer credit
JS: 10570

Consumer protection — Biography
JS: 7745

Consumerism
JS: 11377
S: 10321, 11394

Consumerism — Fiction
J: 718
JS: 1952, 5506

Conway, Jill Ker
S: 8089

Cook, Captain James
JS: 7182

Cook, Frederick
JS: 9191

Cook, Paul
S–Adult: 8211

Cookbooks
J: 12078
JS: 12029, 12032–33–34–35–36–37, 12043–44, 12048–49, 12051–52–53–54, 12063, 12071–72, 12079, 12081, 12085
S: 12040, 12050, 12061, 12074, 12076–77, 12080

Cookbooks — Africa
JS: 12058, 12075

Cookbooks — Caribbean Islands
JS: 12083

Cookbooks — Chinese
S: 12086

Cookbooks — Civil War (U.S.)
JS: 9376

Cookbooks — Ethnic
J: 12028, 12031, 12038, 12045–46–47, 12057, 12059, 12062, 12067, 12069–70, 12073
JS: 12056, 12065
S: 12086

Cookbooks — France
JS: 12064

Cookbooks — Latin America
S: 12066

Cookbooks — Vegan
S: 12030

Cookbooks — Vegetarian
JS: 12055
S: 12039, 12041–42

Cookies
JS: 12029

Cooking
JS: 12044, 12060, 12084, 12139

Cooking — Biography
JS: 8198
S: 8251, 8333

Cooking — Fiction
J: 1630
JS: 270

Cooks — Biography
J: 7934

Coolidge, Calvin
JS: 7652

Cooper, Helene
JS: 8212

Cooperation
J: 11086

Cooperation — Fiction
JS: 270

Copernicus
JS: 7837

Copyright
J: 11916

Coral reefs
JS: 11609
S: 11608

Cormier, Robert
S: 7323

Cormier, Robert — Criticism
JS: 6972, 6974

Cornwall (England) — Fiction
JS: 4665
S–Adult: 5648

Coroner's office
JS: 10534

Corporations
J: 10316
JS: 10315

Corporations — Fiction
JS: 4905

Corsica (France) — Fiction
JS: 2736

Coryat, Sonja Heinze
S: 8213

Cosby, Bill
S: 7490

Cosmetic surgery
J: 10806

Cosmetics
JS: 10837

Coste, Chris
JS: 7956

Costumes and costume making
JS: 12098–99, 12101, 12103

Cougars
JS: 11503
S: 11499

Country life — Fiction
J: 1715

Country music
S: 8533

Country music — Biography
JS: 7494

Country music — Fiction
JS: 712
S–Adult: 5656

Courage
S–Adult: 11081

Courlander, Harold
J: 7324

Courtroom trials
See also Witchcraft trials
J: 9703, 9711–12, 9727, 9731, 10228
JS: 9705, 9729, 9733, 9738, 9743, 9967

Courts (U.S.)
JS: 9706, 9709, 9730, 9746
S: 9722

Cousins — Fiction
JS: 875, 3884, 4433

Cowboys
JS: 9407
S: 9389, 9406

Cowboys — Fiction
J: 128
JS: 30, 4299, 4312, 6346

Cowgirls
S: 9391

Cox, Lynne
JS: 8214

Crack cocaine
JS: 10628

Crafts
J: 12014, 12017, 12025
JS: 12007, 12012, 12016, 12019–20–21, 12026–27, 12091, 12094–95, 12097, 12144, 12150, 12155, 12158

Crane, Stephen — Criticism
JS: 6941
S: 6973

Cravan, Arthur
S: 8215

Crazy Horse (Sioux chief)
JS: 7715

Creationism
J: 8649

Creative writing
J: 7099
JS: 7105

Creative writing — Fiction
J: 5007

Crichton, Michael — Criticism
S: 7011

Crick, Francis
JS: 7838

Crime and criminals
J: 9708, 10181, 10189
JS: 9125, 9730, 9736, 10166,
10168, 10173, 10178, 10185, 10187,
10198–99–00
S: 8391, 9330, 10145, 10150, 10157,
10161, 10171, 10179, 10188, 10205

Crime and criminals — Biography
JS: 8395
S: 7596, 8215
S–Adult: 8292

Crime and criminals — Fiction
J: 1051, 2051, 4401, 5153, 5492
JS: 23, 319, 420, 779, 904, 1270, 1282,
1497, 1580, 2134, 2219, 2221, 3375,
5341, 5343, 6307
S: 119, 1314, 4382, 5368

Crime laboratories
S: 10179

Crimean War — Fiction
S–Adult: 4020

Criminal justice
J: 10181
JS: 9709, 9730, 9744, 10149, 10168,
10820
S: 9927, 10171

Criminal justice — Fiction
JS: 5004

Crippen, Hawley Harvey
S: 11945

Crocheting
JS: 12156, 12165, 12167

Crockett, Davy
S: 7771

Cromwell, Oliver
J: 8750
S: 8097

Cronkite, Walter
S: 7491

Cross-country skiing
J: 12419
JS: 12414

Cross, June
JS: 8216

Crows
JS: 11531

Crusades
JS: 8753
S: 8767
S–Adult: 8769

Crusades — Fiction
J: 3822, 3833

Crutcher, Chris
J: 7325

Cryptograms and cryptography — Careers
J: 10469

Crystal, David
JS: 8217

Cuba
J: 9172
JS: 9168, 9170
S: 9171

Cuba — Biography
J: 7392, 7467, 8142, 8150–51
JS: 8149, 8152
S: 8144–45

Cuba — Fiction
J: 7, 835
JS: 4148, 4152, 4482

Cuba — Poetry
JS: 6768

Cuban Americans
JS: 9965
S–Adult: 8229

Cuban Americans — Biography
S: 8236

Cuban Americans — Fiction
J: 835, 914, 5537
JS: 821, 850, 929

Cubism
JS: 8448

Cults
J: 9614
JS: 9617–18

Cults — Biography
S: 9616
S–Adult: 8373

Cults — Fiction
J: 419, 1695, 5511
JS: 242, 257, 337, 719, 747

Cultural Revolution (China)
J: 8266, 8397, 8998

Cultural Revolution (China) — Fiction
S: 3882, 3940

Culture
JS: 12240
S: 9470

Cummings, E. E.
JS: 7326

Curie family
J: 7839

Curie, Marie
J: 7840–41, 7843
S: 7842

Curiosities and wonders
JS: 12191–92, 12194, 12200–01,
12209, 12213, 12222

Custer, George Armstrong
S: 9280

Custer, George Armstrong — Fiction
S: 4287

Cyberbullying
JS: 11139

Cyclones — Fiction
S–Adult: 5417

Cyrano de Bergerac — Fiction
J: 4063

Cystic fibrosis
JS: 10676

Cystic fibrosis — Fiction
JS: 1368

Czech Republic
JS: 9052

Czechoslovakia — Biography
J: 7421
JS: 8108

D

d'Aboville, Gerard
JS: 7183

D'Angelo, Pascal
JS: 7327

da Vinci, Leonardo
JS: 8458

da Vinci, Leonardo — Fiction
JS: 5725

Dahl, Roald
JS: 7328–29
S–Adult: 7331

Dahl, Roald — Biography
J: 7330

Dalai Lama
JS: 8068
S–Adult: 8069–70

Dali, Salvador
JS: 7256–57

JS: 1192, 1229, 1319, 1346, 1367, 1477, 1486, 3941, 4568
S: 1224, 1384

Desegregation
JS: 9940

Desegregation — Fiction
JS: 822

Deserts
J: 11733
S: 11478

Design — Careers
JS: 10491

Desserts
JS: 12049, 12072

Devil — Fiction
J: 4660

Dewey (cat)
S–Adult: 9702

Diabetes
J: 10674
JS: 10726, 10738, 10752
S: 10786

Diabetes — Cookbooks
JS: 12081

Diabetes — Fiction
JS: 1371

Diagnostic imaging
J: 10811

Diakite, Baba Wague
J: 7333

Diamonds
JS: 8474
S: 11906

Diana, Princess of Wales
J: 8098

Diaries
JS: 8787, 9088, 9481, 9643
S: 8186, 8347, 8556, 11066

Diaries — Fiction
J: 404, 1249, 1639, 1665, 1902, 2062, 2085, 3986, 4158, 4911–12–13, 4971–72
JS: 351, 658, 737–38, 1078, 1757, 2014, 3987, 4113, 4462, 4914, 4987, 6071
S: 595, 1596, 3995, 4319

Dickens, Charles
J: 7334
S: 6952, 7335–36

Dickens, Charles — Criticism
JS: 6953
S: 6956

Dickens, Charles — Fiction
S: 5361

Dickinson, Emily
JS: 7055, 7337–38

Dickinson, Emily — Criticism
S: 7058

Dickinson, Emily — Fiction
JS: 1312

Dictators
JS: 9038

Dictionaries
S: 7087

Diderot, Denis
JS: 8099

Diet and nutrition
J: 10660, 10704, 10946
JS: 10760, 10941, 10943, 10947, 10957–58–59, 10961, 10974, 11165

Diet and nutrition — Fiction
JS: 1454, 1871

Digestive system
JS: 10864

Dillinger, John — Fiction
S: 4382

DiMaggio, Joe
S: 7957–58

Dinesen, Isak
JS: 7340
S: 7339

Dinosaurs
J: 8622, 8628–29, 11371
JS: 6890, 8624, 8626–27, 8630
S: 8625

Dinosaurs — Fiction
JS: 5950

Disabilities
J: 10981

Disabilities — Biography
JS: 8262

Disabilities — Fiction
J: 1305, 1690
JS: 730, 1316, 1353, 4399
S: 558, 3384
S–Adult: 1475

Disaster preparedness
JS: 11016

Disasters
See also Natural disasters
JS: 10105
S: 9586, 9640

Disasters — Fiction
JS: 4359

Disasters (U.S.)
JS: 9208

Disc jockeys — Careers
JS: 10511

Discovery and exploration
JS: 8703, 9184

Discrimination
JS: 10001
S: 9976

Diseases and illness
See also specific diseases, e.g., Cancer
J: 10709–10, 10719, 10783

JS: 10679, 10711, 10722, 10742, 10745, 10747, 10769, 10792
S: 10694, 10698, 10744, 10790
S–Adult: 8175

Diseases and illness — Fiction
J: 1174, 1405
JS: 1324, 1350, 1424, 1436, 4423, 5547
S: 1329, 5424
S–Adult: 1137

Disfigurement — Fiction
JS: 1809
S: 395

Disney, Walt
JS: 7258–59

Disney, Walt — Criticism
S: 8571

Ditko, Steve
JS: 7261
S: 7260

Divorce
J: 11214
JS: 11187

Divorce — Fiction
J: 569, 1077, 1139, 1657, 1909, 5568
JS: 360, 362, 576, 988, 1050, 1063, 1525, 1992, 2109
S: 1760
S–Adult: 640, 996

Dix, Dorothea
JS: 7613

Dixie Chicks
JS: 7494

DNA
JS: 10815, 10819–20, 11262
S: 7867, 8633

DNA — Biography
JS: 7838

Doctors — Biography
J: 10799
JS: 7913, 8343

Doctors — Fiction
JS: 5551
S: 1618, 4090, 4315, 4343, 5098

Doctors Without Borders
J: 10810

Dodd, William E.
S–Adult: 9063

Dogon (African people)
J: 8956
S: 8959

Dogs
See also Service dogs
J: 11678–79
JS: 8279, 11645, 11655–56–57–58–59–60–61–62–63–64, 11666–67–68–69, 11671, 11673, 11676–77, 11680–81, 11683, 11685
S: 11682, 11682

S: 134, 6035
S–Adult: 490, 2601, 3427

E

E-zines
JS: 7095

E. coli bacteria
S: 11640

Eagles
S: 11544

Earhart, Amelia
JS: 7187–88
S: 7186

Earhart, Amelia — Fiction
S–Adult: 4392

Earth
JS: 11275, 11716
S: 11329

Earth science
JS: 11705
S: 11717, 11717

Earth science — Experiments and projects
J: 11723
JS: 11714

Earthquakes
J: 11724
S: 11726

Earthquakes — Fiction
S–Adult: 367

East Germany — Fiction
J: 1955

East Indian Americans
JS: 9875

East Indian Americans — Fiction
JS: 496
S–Adult: 1947

East St. Louis (IL) race riot
S: 9422

Easter Island
JS: 12216

Eastern Europe
JS: 9053

Eating disorders
See also specific disorders, e.g., Anorexia nervosa
J: 10660, 10675, 10683, 10687, 10704, 10731, 10735, 10762, 10773
JS: 10702, 10720, 10727, 10737, 10748, 10760, 10763, 10777, 10791, 10931
S: 10126

Eating disorders — Fiction
J: 418
JS: 279, 1298, 3734

S: 1049, 1398, 1652

Ebadi, Shirin
S: 8227

Ebola
J: 10781

Eccentricity — Fiction
S: 369

Eclipses
JS: 11291, 11338

Ecology and environment
See also Conservation; Pollution
J: 10027, 10045, 10063, 11358, 11834, 11845
JS: 8661, 9530, 9663, 9740, 10024–25, 10028–29, 10031–32, 10034–35–36–37, 10039, 10042–43, 10046, 10048, 10054–55, 10060, 10064, 10073, 10075, 10080, 10082–83, 10085, 10085, 10087–88–89–90–91–92, 10094–95–96–97, 10100–01, 10103–04, 10104, 10108–09–10–11–12, 10114, 10119, 10121, 10471, 10751, 10968, 11357, 11370, 11399, 11405, 11537, 11554, 11562–63, 11574, 11585, 11712, 11722, 11737, 11797, 11838, 11876
S: 9536, 10041, 10052, 10056, 10061, 10071, 10081, 10113, 10790, 11556, 11564, 11568–69, 11571, 11571, 11603, 11632, 11851
S–Adult: 8371, 9187, 10026, 10038, 10040, 10047, 10049–50, 10053, 10057, 10059, 10065, 10072, 10074, 10098, 10106–07, 10116, 11489, 11565, 11613

Ecology and environment — Biography
J: 7805, 7817
JS: 7813, 8054
S: 7768, 7893, 7895
S–Adult: 8303

Ecology and environment — Careers
JS: 10465

Ecology and environment — Fiction
J: 321, 5971
JS: 1952, 2203, 2209, 2212, 2252, 2366, 2877, 3481, 6046, 11791
S: 660, 2230, 5433–34–35
S–Adult: 5043

Economics and business
J: 10312, 10323
JS: 8994, 10309–10–11, 10314–15, 10330, 10517, 10562
S–Adult: 10313

Economics and business — Biography
JS: 7804, 7816, 7932
S: 7925

Economics and business — Careers
J: 10316

JS: 10513, 10516

Ecoterrorism — Fiction
JS: 2225

Ecstasy
JS: 10642

Ecuador
J: 9181

Ecuador — Fiction
J: 656
JS: 4170
S: 683

Eden, Garden of — Fiction
JS: 2301

Ederle, Gertrude
JS: 8017

Edison, Thomas Alva
S: 7848–49

Edmonds, Emma — Fiction
JS: 4271

Edmonds, Walter D.
JS: 7342

Edmondson, William — Poetry
JS: 6743

Education
J: 12234
JS: 9133, 9561, 10342, 10392
S: 8647, 10341, 10346, 10413

Education — Biography
J: 7602

Education — Careers
JS: 10522, 10524–25

Education — Fiction
JS: 357, 5662

Edwards, Honeyboy
S: 7497

Eels
JS: 11617

Efficiency experts — Biography
JS: 8159

Egypt
J: 8415, 8716, 8723, 8723, 8723
JS: 8035, 8063, 8414, 8718–19–20–21, 8727
S: 10270
S–Adult: 8656

Egypt — Biography
J: 8050
JS: 8035, 8051, 8062
S–Adult: 8393

Egypt — Fiction
J: 5732
JS: 3778, 5076, 5097
S: 3774, 3777, 3965, 5380, 5421–22
S–Adult: 5116

Egypt — Poetry
S: 7016

Eichengreen, Lucille
JS: 8228

F

2962–63–64, 2966–67–68–69, 2972,
2976–77–78, 2980–81–82–83–84–85,
2992, 2994–95–96–97, 3001–02,
3004–05–06, 3015–16, 3018,
3020–21–22, 3024, 3026–27, 3029,
3033–34, 3036, 3038–39–40–41–42,
3044–45–46–47, 3049–50–51–52,
3056, 3058, 3060, 3062, 3064–65–66,
3068–69–70, 3080, 3083, 3090–91,
3093–94, 3096–97–98, 3100,
3102–03–04, 3106, 3109–10–11–12–
13, 3115, 3117–18–19, 3121–22–23,
3125, 3128, 3130–31–32–33–34–35,
3139, 3141–42, 3144, 3147, 3150,
3153, 3156–57, 3159, 3163–64,
3168, 3171–72, 3175–76, 3178,
3185–86–87–88–89, 3195–96–97,
3200–01–02–03, 3205–06, 3208,
3211, 3220, 3235, 3247, 3260, 3269,
3284, 3289, 3297–98, 3302, 3314,
3316, 3335, 3370, 3375, 3388–89,
3409, 3422, 3432–33, 3446–47, 3449,
3468, 3471, 3482, 3486, 3495, 3504,
3515–16, 3545, 3556–57–58, 3599,
3641, 3675, 3685, 3694, 3706, 3716,
3744–45, 3754, 3759, 4601, 4624,
4657, 4722, 4923, 4969, 4984, 5047,
5248, 5580, 5686, 5948, 5991, 6016,
6085, 6096, 6110–11, 6165, 6188,
6301, 6339, 6350, 6352, 6373, 6375,
6388, 6406, 6442, 6484
S: 229, 2291–92–93, 2309, 2312–13,
2315–16–17, 2332, 2337, 2346, 2370,
2377, 2385, 2399, 2408, 2412, 2418,
2433, 2458, 2469, 2475, 2478–79,
2489, 2493, 2496, 2505–06–07,
2528, 2540, 2543, 2545, 2547–48,
2552, 2566, 2568, 2571, 2583–84,
2596, 2608–09, 2613, 2630, 2643,
2645–46, 2648–49, 2664, 2676, 2681,
2683, 2698, 2700, 2720, 2728, 2753,
2755–56, 2759, 2766, 2768, 2772,
2776–77–78, 2780–81, 2784, 2800,
2802, 2805–06, 2809, 2812, 2814–
15–16, 2818, 2824, 2830, 2840–41,
2846, 2859, 2894, 2903, 2906,
2910–11, 2917, 2931, 2944, 2948,
2953–54, 2959–60, 2988, 3013–14,
3030–31–32, 3043, 3072–73, 3078,
3086, 3089, 3095, 3105, 3120, 3140,
3145, 3155, 3158, 3161–62, 3165,
3169, 3177, 3193–94, 3204, 3252,
3273, 3282, 3328, 3352, 3372, 3382,
3425, 3458, 3493, 3505, 3509, 3607,
3654, 3665, 3686, 3788, 4608, 4877,
5121, 5152, 5755, 5904, 5908, 6025,
6354, 6356, 6409, 6467
S–Adult: 2288–89–90, 2335–36, 2360,
2380, 2421, 2424, 2428, 2459, 2476,
2531, 2542, 2574, 2656, 2665, 2684,
2710–11, 2811, 2817, 2825, 2857,
2868, 2871–72, 2874, 2901, 2918,
2929, 2970–71, 2986, 3011, 3028,
3061, 3088, 3146, 3148, 3151, 3166,
3179, 3183–84, 3461, 3533, 3639

Fantasy — History and criticism
JS: 6935, 6992, 6996
S: 6936, 6938, 6942

Faraday, Michael
JS: 7857–58

Farley, Chris
S: 7499

Farm animals
S: 11378

Farms and farm life
See also Rural life
JS: 11376, 11953
S: 11382
S–Adult: 11385

**Farms and farm life —
Biography**
J: 7611

Farms and farm life — Fiction
J: 1931, 1937, 4325
JS: 1287, 1628, 4318, 6311
S: 2166, 2170, 4295, 5668

Farnsworth, Philo
JS: 7860
S: 7859

Farrakhan, Louis
JS: 7621

Fashion
J: 9199, 11901–02, 12107
JS: 11128, 12092, 12096–97

Fashion — Biography
J: 7921, 7937, 7939
JS: 7930

Fashion — Careers
J: 10442
JS: 10432, 10446, 10453, 10476,
10479

Fashion — Fiction
J: 297, 363, 820, 2371
JS: 495, 581, 3339
S: 5360, 5663

Fast food industry — Biography
S: 10322

Fate — Fiction
JS: 668

Fathers
JS: 8210, 11000

Fathers — Fiction
JS: 286, 443, 1038, 1082

Fathers and daughters
JS: 8171

Fathers and daughters — Fiction
JS: 275, 436, 1033, 4360, 5608

Fathers and sons
JS: 8349
S: 1470, 9547, 11207

Fathers and sons — Fiction
J: 269, 400, 964, 5452, 6335
JS: 313, 966, 1129, 1145, 1262, 3611,
4416, 6264
S: 800, 1054, 1237, 1676
S–Adult: 1149, 4165

Favre, Brett
S–Adult: 7990

**Federal Bureau of Investigation
(U.S.) — Biography**
JS: 7725

**Federal Bureau of Investigation
(U.S.)**
J: 9693
S: 7726

**Federal Bureau of Investigation
(U.S.) — Careers**
JS: 10526

**Federal Bureau of Investigation
(U.S.) — Fiction**
JS: 5365
S–Adult: 5106

Federal Reserve banks
J: 10317

Feig, Paul
S: 7345

Felting
JS: 12152

**Female circumcision —
Biography**
S: 8053

Female circumcision — Fiction
JS: 2206

Feminism
J: 9812, 9847
JS: 9817
S: 9803, 9806, 9836, 9846, 9999,
10237
S–Adult: 10236

Feminism — Fiction
J: 778

Fencing — Fiction
J: 3762
JS: 4385

Fermi, Enrico
JS: 7861

Festivals
JS: 10263

Feudalism
JS: 8754

Feynman, Richard
J: 7862

Fiction — Criticism
JS: 7002
S: 6947–48, 6964

Fiction — Writing
J: 10359
JS: 10357

1500s — Fiction
JS: 4125

15th century
JS: 8770
S: 8771

15th century — Fiction
J: 4028, 4118

Fighter pilots — Fiction
JS: 3415

Figure skating
S: 12387

Filar, Marian
S: 8835

Filipino Americans
S: 9949

Filipino Americans — Fiction
JS: 808

Film criticism
JS: 8563

Finance — Careers
JS: 10516

Finances (personal)
JS: 10400, 10573

Fire — Fiction
J: 2880

Fire fighters
JS: 9698–99
S: 10284, 10286, 10536

Fire fighters — Fiction
S: 3541

Fires
JS: 9698
S: 11251

Fires — Fiction
J: 24

First aid
JS: 11015

First aid manuals
JS: 11014

First Amendment
S: 11913

First Daughters — Fiction
J: 288

First Ladies (U.S.) — Biography
J: 7689, 7713
JS: 7681

First Ladies (U.S.) — Fiction
S: 695, 5425–26–27

Fish
JS: 11611–12, 11614–15
S: 11610, 11696, 12050
S–Adult: 11613

Fish and Wildlife Service (U.S.) — Fiction
S: 5467

Fishing
JS: 10091, 11554, 12354
S: 9518, 11207, 11603

Fishing — Fiction
JS: 51, 62, 3574

Fist-fighting — Fiction
JS: 623

Fitness
S: 10951

Fitzgerald, Ella
J: 7500

Fitzgerald, F. Scott
J: 7347
S: 7348

Fitzgerald, F. Scott — Fiction
S: 4394

Flags (U.S.)
JS: 9240

Fleischman, Sid
JS: 7349

Fleming, Edward
JS: 8230

Flight — Fiction
JS: 5414

Flight attendants — Careers
JS: 10440

Florida — Fiction
J: 1201
JS: 4405, 4449, 4982, 5236, 5259

Flowers
JS: 11414–15, 11417

Flu epidemic of 1918 — Fiction
J: 4334

Fluid mechanics
JS: 11813

Fly fishing
JS: 12354

Fly fishing — Fiction
S: 595

Flying — Fiction
JS: 4941, 6389

Fog
JS: 11762

Folk art
JS: 8467

Folk art — Biography
JS: 7267

Folk music
JS: 8545
S: 8542, 8542

Folk music — Biography
JS: 7496

Folklore
See also Mythology, and specific topics,
e.g., Animals — Folklore
J: 6769, 7324
JS: 6329, 6418, 6763, 6772, 6774,
6777–78, 6787–88, 6798, 6801, 6804,
6814, 6827, 9979
S: 3237, 6776, 6779, 6795, 6808, 6824

Folklore — Africa
JS: 6790–91

Folklore — African American
JS: 6820
S: 7377

Folklore — Asia
JS: 6792

Folklore — Celtic
JS: 6838

Folklore — England
J: 6811
JS: 6816

Folklore — History and criticism
S: 6942

Folklore — Jewish
JS: 6818

Folklore — Mesopotamia
JS: 6840

Folklore — Native American
JS: 3304
S–Adult: 9255

Folklore — United States
J: 6835
JS: 6564
S: 6831, 6834

Food
J: 10222, 10464, 11386, 12082
JS: 8690, 10036, 10108, 10971, 11384,
11387, 11396, 12084
S: 10960, 11388, 11393
S–Adult: 8700, 10207, 11380

Food — Biography
JS: 8233, 8321

Food — Careers
J: 10444

Food — Fiction
S: 3656

Food allergy — Biography
JS: 8180

Food and Drug Administration (U.S.)
J: 9692

Food industry
JS: 10970
S: 10322, 11393, 11393–94

Food industry — Careers
J: 10464
JS: 10454

Food poisoning
JS: 10678, 10725
S: 10960

Food supply
JS: 11383
S: 10960

Football
J: 11750
JS: 6555, 12355–56, 12358, 12362–63,
12370
S: 12369, 12371
S–Adult: 12321, 12357, 12361,
12364–65–66–67

JS = Junior High/Senior High; S = Senior High; S–Adult = Senior High/Adult

Friendship — Fiction

J: 244, 253, 290, 308, 341, 358, 380, 413, 418, 435, 520, 537, 618, 626, 698, 703, 732, 761, 778, 813, 836, 847, 1325, 1382, 1404, 1427, 1467, 1488, 1542, 1544, 1636, 1642, 1684–85, 1697, 1726, 1742, 1762, 1779–80, 1786, 1796, 1833, 1842, 1845, 1849, 1909, 1915, 1946, 1948, 2059, 2064, 2094, 2119–20–21, 2168, 2172, 2191, 2284, 2544, 3149, 4415, 4425, 4921, 4946, 4964, 5616, 5660, 6282–83, 6291, 6300

JS: 133, 236–37–38, 249–50, 258, 272, 279, 301, 326, 330, 349, 366, 377–78, 391, 393, 427, 429–30, 438, 448, 452, 461, 489, 512, 518, 524, 531, 539, 541, 550, 552, 567, 572, 591, 597, 612, 619, 643, 677, 685, 688, 690, 696, 705, 709, 711, 756, 767, 769, 802, 887, 970, 977, 1179, 1322, 1324, 1338, 1361, 1381, 1390, 1495, 1521, 1541, 1559, 1577, 1594, 1610, 1622, 1634, 1641, 1643–44, 1674, 1683, 1687, 1691, 1719–20, 1734, 1736, 1750, 1758–59, 1767, 1770, 1805, 1828, 1830–31, 1838–39, 1865–66, 1896, 1898, 1901, 1905, 1910, 1944, 1958, 1962, 1966, 1974, 1989–90, 2028, 2032, 2035, 2038, 2060, 2089, 2112, 2132, 2134, 2145, 2173, 2286, 3280, 3627, 3855, 3870, 3954, 3981, 4019, 4034, 4106, 4381, 4397, 4432, 4445, 4472, 4565, 4705, 4839, 4924, 4934, 5044, 5279, 5448, 5562, 5745, 5784, 6264

S: 241, 251, 415, 471, 507–08, 596, 683, 748, 757, 894, 1154, 1235, 1490, 1526, 1532, 1558, 1607, 1616, 1648, 1655, 1738, 1881, 1918, 1945, 1968, 1977, 2046, 2072, 3355, 3909, 3937, 3940, 4072, 4486, 5449, 6280

S–Adult: 477, 715, 753, 1475, 2098, 4348

Friendship — Poetry

JS: 6730

Fritz, Jean

JS: 7351

Frogs and toads

JS: 11434–35

Frontier life (U.S.)

J: 9392, 9399

JS: 3350, 9388, 9395, 9397, 9400–01, 9404–05, 9409–10, 12026

S: 8183, 9389, 9393, 9396, 9398, 9402, 9406, 9408

Frontier life (U.S.) — Biography

J: 7169, 7174

JS: 7763, 7766, 8343

S: 7714, 7769, 7771

Frontier life (U.S.) — Fiction

J: 128, 529, 4290, 4303, 4305–06, 4311

JS: 79, 206–07, 4247, 4285, 4288–89, 4293–94, 4297–98–99–00, 4307–08, 4312, 4314, 4316, 4318, 4320

S: 202–03, 4250, 4286, 4292, 4296, 4301–02, 4315, 4319, 4323, 5113

S–Adult: 4313, 4322, 5749

Frontier life (U.S.) — Poetry

JS: 6752

Frost, Robert

J: 7352

Frost, Robert — Criticism

S: 7059

Fry, Varian

JS: 7773

Fugitives — Fiction

J: 1938

Fulani (African people)

J: 8980

Fung, Inez

J: 7871

Fur trade

JS: 9156

Furiya, Linda

JS: 8233

Furman v. Georgia

J: 9727

Fussell, Samuel Wilson

JS: 8018

Future

S: 6882, 11867

Future — Fiction

J: 4843

JS: 3091, 5893

G

Galapagos Islands

J: 9178

JS: 11443

Galapagos Islands Biosphere Reserve

J: 9178

Galileo

J: 7872

JS: 6545

Galileo (spacecraft)

S: 11304

Gallagher, Hugh

S: 7774

Gallagher, Tim

S: 8234

Gambling

J: 10006, 12272

JS: 10003, 12260

Gambling — Fiction

J: 446, 1143

JS: 631, 1028, 1677, 1876, 5013

S: 1516

Game shows — Fiction

JS: 391

Games

J: 12351

Games — Fiction

JS: 676

Gandhi, Indira

JS: 8071

Gandhi, Mahatma

S: 8072

Gangs

J: 10176, 10182

JS: 10139, 10142, 10151, 10166, 10194, 10196, 10198, 10667

S: 10150, 10192

Gangs — Biography

JS: 8267

S: 7799

Gangs — Fiction

J: 56–57, 505, 1650, 2123, 2277, 2284

JS: 464, 527, 603, 954, 1363, 1500, 1620, 4438

S: 417, 2093, 2258, 4065, 5928

Gantos, Jack

JS: 7353

Gao, Anhua

S: 8235

Garbage

JS: 10119–20–21

S: 10122

Garbage collectors — Fiction

JS: 4092

Garcia Marquez, Gabriel

S: 7354

García-López, José Luis

JS: 7264

Garcia, Luis M.

S: 8236

Gardens and gardening

JS: 8680, 11391, 12137–38–39

Gardner, Rulon

JS: 8019

Garner, Eleanor

JS: 8237

Garrett, Pat — Fiction

S: 4296

Garvey, Marcus

J: 7623, 7623, 7623

JS: 7625, 7625, 7625

S: 7624

Gases

JS: 11813

Gates, Bill

J: 7922

Gates, Bill and Melinda

J: 7923

Gauguin, Paul — Fiction

JS: 3932

Gay and lesbian parents
IJ: 11190
JS: 11191

**Gay and lesbian parents —
Fiction**
JS: 1097

Gay and lesbian students
JS: 5622

Gay men — Fiction
JS: 1932, 1981

Gay men and lesbians
JS: 6325, 10242, 11023, 11037, 11043,
11164
S: 11021, 11041

**Gay men and lesbians —
Biography**
S: 7998, 8181, 8241, 8289

Gay men and lesbians — Fiction
J: 672, 951, 951, 1742, 1762, 1843,
2129, 2129, 11034
JS: 366, 406, 476, 491, 515, 531, 536,
585, 659, 697, 821, 1081, 1375, 1518,
1536, 1566, 1602, 1625, 1686, 1699,
1699, 1702, 1721, 1743, 1816, 1816,
1819, 1827, 1878, 1901, 1917, 1980,
1981, 1990, 1997, 2027–29, 2031,
2037–40, 2055, 2086, 2088, 2091,
2091, 2099, 2099, 2112, 2114, 2169,
2173, 2237, 2253, 2855, 2945, 4375,
4397, 4536, 4536, 4924, 5622, 5681,
5746, 6266, 6266, 6325, 6325, 10238,
10240, 11035, 11035, 11035–36, 11043
S: 504, 734, 1290, 1358, 1358,
1442, 1490, 1502, 1565, 1631, 1651,
1680–81, 1678, 1712–13, 1739, 1807,
1857, 1976, 2030, 2069, 2072, 2081,
2170, 2170, 2180, 2183, 3241, 4903,
9192, 11018, 11020, 11020, 11033,
11041, 11044
S–Adult: 232, 640, 2077

Gay men and lesbians — Plays
S: 7063

Gay men and lesbians — Poetry
JS: 6625

Gay rights
JS: 9815, 9818, 10238, 10242
S: 11033

Gbaya (African people)
JS: 8929

Geeks — Fiction
JS: 548, 6330

Gehry, Frank
J: 7265

Geisel, Theodor Seuss
JS: 7355
S: 8425
S–Adult: 7356

Geisha — Fiction
S: 3895

Gems
S: 11745

Gene therapy
JS: 10822

Genealogy
JS: 9978, 9984, 11197

Genealogy — Biography
S: 8372

Generals (U.S.) — Biography
J: 7750
JS: 7605
S–Adult: 7662

Genetic engineering
J: 10816
JS: 10818, 10824, 10831
S: 10828

Genetic engineering — Fiction
J: 5333
JS: 5505, 5950
S–Adult: 5179

Genetic screening
J: 10823

Genetically modified foods
JS: 10954, 11381

Genetics
J: 10816, 10830
JS: 10751, 10831
S: 8652, 10814, 10827–28–29, 11082,
11369
S–Adult: 11060

Genetics — Biography
JS: 7868, 7886–87
S: 7867

Genetics — Fiction
JS: 5321
S: 5302

Genghis Khan
JS: 8073

Genocide
J: 8938
JS: 9652, 9658

Genocide — Fiction
JS: 3843, 3957
S: 3653

Geography
J: 8704
JS: 8661, 8678, 8691, 9231
S: 7876, 11730

Geology
JS: 11716, 11721, 11729, 11739
S: 11718–19–20

**Geology — Experiments and
projects**
J: 11723

Gerbils
S–Adult: 8339

Germany
J: 9061
JS: 8811, 8847, 8874, 9062
S: 8111–12

Germany — Biography
JS: 8190
S: 8110, 8113

Germany — Cookbooks
J: 12069

Germany — Fiction
J: 1955, 4522
JS: 4051, 4081, 4465, 4472
S: 173, 5709
S–Adult: 3973, 5189

Germs
S: 11356

Geronimo
S: 7722

Geronimo — Fiction
J: 4181

Gettysburg, Battle of
JS: 9379
S: 9368

Gettysburg, Battle of — Fiction
J: 4267

Ghahramani, Zarah
S: 8238

Ghana — Biography
S: 8048

Ghana — Fiction
J: 510
JS: 3842
S–Adult: 999

Ghost stories
S: 6834

Ghosts
J: 12208, 12227
JS: 12220

Ghosts — Fiction
J: 327, 353, 1954, 2318, 2653, 3025,
3404, 4338, 4582, 4607, 4610, 4652,
4658, 4676, 4689, 4768, 4794, 4822,
4856, 4858, 4860, 4865, 5229, 5397
JS: 371, 1160, 2396, 3258, 3364,
4124, 4578, 4598, 4620, 4624, 4629,
4657, 4665, 4683, 4706, 4710, 4747,
4763, 4767, 4784, 4804, 4847, 4850,
4886–87, 4897, 5240, 5339, 5474,
5519, 5642
S: 2894, 3628, 4296, 4576, 4616, 4637,
4681, 4785, 5200, 5769
S–Adult: 2958, 4078, 4649, 5137

Giant pandas
JS: 11518

Giants — Fiction
S–Adult: 3428

Gibson, Althea
JS: 8007

Gideon v. Wainwright
J: 9711

Gifted teenagers
JS: 11131

Gilbreth family
JS: 8159

Gildiner, Catherine
S–Adult: 8239

Gilman, Susan Jane
S: 7357

Ginsberg, Allen
JS: 9830

Girl Scouts
JS: 11218

Girls — Fiction
J: 494, 1763–64
JS: 1586
S: 1508

Glass making
JS: 8473
S: 11882

Global positioning systems
J: 11943

Global warming
J: 10102
JS: 10030, 10033–34, 10044, 10060, 10068, 10076, 10078–79–80, 10084, 10099, 10389, 11792
S: 9586, 10071, 10093, 11763
S–Adult: 10074

Global warming — Fiction
J: 2382–83

Globe Theatre (London)
JS: 7041

Gnomes
S: 6782

Goblins — Fiction
J: 2673

Goh, Chan Hon
JS: 7502

Gold Rush (Alaska and Yukon)
JS: 7175, 11676

Goldberg, Whoopi
J: 7503

Golding, William — Criticism
JS: 6972

Goldsworthy, Anna
S–Adult: 8240

Golf
JS: 12373, 12375
S: 12372, 12374

Golf — Biography
J: 8023
JS: 8031

Golf — Fiction
J: 1157

Gómez de Avellaneda y Arteaga, Gertrudis — Fiction
JS: 4152

González, Rigoberto
S: 8241

Goodall, Jane
JS: 7873–74

Goode, W. Wilson
JS: 7723

Goodwillie, David
S: 7358

Goodyear, Charles
S: 7924

Google (company)
JS: 7818

Gore, Ariel
S: 7359

Gorillas
JS: 11484
S: 7863–64

Gossip — Fiction
JS: 350, 1741

Goths
JS: 11062

Government and politics
JS: 9467, 9619
S–Adult: 9665

Government and politics — Biography
J: 8042
JS: 7733, 7752

Government and politics — Careers
JS: 10535

Government and politics — China
JS: 8994

Government and politics — Fiction
JS: 425, 5124, 5349
S: 2201, 5658

Government and politics (U.S.)
See also House of Representatives (U.S.); Senate (U.S.)
J: 8906, 9662, 9681, 9689, 9697
JS: 9231, 9630, 9660, 9663
S: 9201, 9201, 9753–54, 9756–57, 10287
S–Adult: 7787–88, 9687, 9748

Government and politics (U.S.) — Biography
J: 7713
JS: 7739, 7743, 7751
S: 7574

Graffiti
JS: 8424

Graffiti — Fiction
J: 5574

Graham, Billy
JS: 7775

Graham, Robin Lee
JS: 7189

Grammar
JS: 7074, 7084, 10385
S: 7083

Grand Canyon
S: 9541

Grand Central Station (NY)
S: 10208

Grandfathers — Fiction
J: 702, 1134, 1157
JS: 1021, 1805, 5294
S: 5314

Grandmothers — Fiction
J: 823, 1258, 4967
JS: 910
S–Adult: 1090

Grandparents
JS: 11210

Grandparents — Fiction
JS: 1100, 1140

Grant, Ulysses S.
JS: 7656–57
S: 7658

The Grapes of Wrath —
Criticism
S: 7014

Graphic art
S: 8464

Graphic art — Fiction
S: 1817

Graphic novels
J: 3621–22–23
JS: 3619, 3624, 7105, 7115, 7149, 12112, 12117
S: 8428, 8575

Graphic novels — Biography
JS: 7249

Graphic novels — Fiction
J: 180, 3231–32, 3254, 3300, 3351, 3360, 3366, 3377, 3381, 3385, 3387, 3392–93, 3404, 3407, 3417, 3436, 3448, 3459, 3472–73–74, 3488, 3491, 3508, 3514, 3525, 3540, 3540, 3543, 3543, 3579–80, 3584–85, 3597, 3603, 3606, 3613, 3642, 3657, 3662, 3671, 3728, 3755, 3762, 4820
JS: 199, 201, 213, 217, 496, 3212, 3214–15, 3220–21, 3224–25, 3227–28–29–30, 3233, 3235–36, 3238–39–40, 3244–45, 3247–48–49, 3253, 3258, 3260–61–62–63–64, 3267–68–69–70, 3274, 3276, 3279–80–81, 3283–84–85–86, 3288–89, 3292–93–94, 3296–97–98, 3301–02, 3307–08–09, 3311–12, 3314, 3316, 3318–19, 3322, 3324–25–26–27, 3329, 3333, 3335, 3339–40–41–42–43–44, 3347, 3350, 3359, 3363, 3367, 3370, 3375, 3378, 3380, 3388–89–90, 3397, 3399–00–01, 3405–06, 3408, 3410–11, 3414–15–16, 3418–19, 3422, 3424, 3426, 3429–30–31–32, 3432–33–34, 3438–39–40–41, 3443–44–45, 3447, 3449–50, 3453,

3457, 3464–65, 3467–68–69–70–71, 3476, 3480, 3482–83–84–85–86, 3489–90, 3494–95, 3497–98, 3500, 3502, 3504, 3507, 3510, 3515–16, 3520–21–22–23–24, 3526–27–28–29, 3532, 3534–35–36, 3536, 3538–39, 3542, 3545, 3548, 3552, 3554–55–56–57–58–59–60–61–62, 3564–65–66, 3570, 3573–74, 3581, 3586–87, 3596, 3598–99–00, 3602, 3608–09–10–11, 3615–16, 3618, 3620, 3625, 3627, 3629–30–31, 3633, 3636–37, 3640, 3643–44, 3647–48–49, 3652, 3655, 3659–60, 3666–67–68–69–70, 3672, 3675–76, 3678, 3682–83–84–85, 3687–88–89, 3691–92–93–94–95–96, 3698–99–00–01, 3706, 3709, 3716–17–18, 3720–21–22–23–24–25–26–27, 3730–31–32, 3734–35–36–37–38–39, 3744–45, 3747–48–49, 3753–54, 3756–57, 3759, 3763–64, 3766, 3766, 4854, 12128, 12130
S: 3213, 3216, 3218–19, 3219, 3223, 3226, 3234, 3237, 3241, 3243, 3246, 3250–51–52, 3255, 3259, 3271–72–73, 3277–78, 3282, 3287, 3303, 3313, 3321, 3328, 3330–31–32, 3334, 3336–37–38, 3346, 3348, 3352–53, 3355–56, 3361–62, 3365, 3369, 3372–73, 3379, 3382, 3384, 3386, 3394, 3396, 3412–13, 3425, 3435, 3451–52, 3454–55, 3458, 3463, 3466, 3477–78–79, 3492–93, 3499, 3501, 3505, 3509, 3511–12–13, 3518, 3531, 3537, 3541, 3544, 3547, 3549–50–51, 3563, 3567–68–69, 3572, 3582, 3592, 3594–95, 3601, 3604–05, 3607, 3612, 3614, 3617, 3628, 3634, 3638, 3645, 3653–54, 3656, 3658, 3663, 3665, 3673, 3677, 3679–80, 3697, 3702–03–04–05, 3707–08, 3713, 3715, 3729, 3733, 3740–41–42–43, 3746, 3750–51–52, 3758, 3761, 3765, 5878
S–Adult: 3217, 3242, 3257, 3265, 3275, 3299, 3306, 3317, 3374, 3376, 3383, 3395, 3403, 3427–28, 3456, 3460–61, 3475, 3487, 3503, 3506, 3533, 3571, 3576, 3583, 3635, 3639, 3711, 3760

Graphic novels — Mythology
JS: 3368

Grave robbing — Fiction
JS: 1145

Gravity
JS: 7897

Gray, Amy
S: 8242

Great Barrier Reef
S: 11608

Great Britain
J: 9064
S: 9069

Great Britain — Biography
J: 7911, 8091
JS: 7185, 8046
S: 8097, 8138

Great Britain — Fiction
See also England, Scotland
J: 2750
JS: 3811, 3977, 4126
S: 1631, 4082
S–Adult: 3635, 4022, 4649, 5355

Great Depression
JS: 9209, 9426–27, 9429, 9431, 12360
S: 8213, 9205, 9433, 9437–38, 9442

Great Depression — Fiction
J: 4364, 4967
JS: 897, 4367, 4369, 4376, 4379, 4381, 4386–87, 4475
S: 919, 1227, 4368, 4380, 4382, 4393

Great Depression — Poetry
JS: 6736

Great Expectations **— Criticism**
JS: 6953

Great Lakes
S: 9509

Great Plains
S–Adult: 9510

Great Zimbabwe
J: 8933

Greece
J: 8096, 8133, 8136, 8731–32, 8737–38, 8738, 8738, 9581
JS: 3756, 6933, 7031, 8730, 8733–34
S: 6550, 6601, 8729, 8729, 8735

Greece — Biography
JS: 8090, 8728

Greece — Fiction
J: 2348, 3798
JS: 3789, 3795, 5562
S: 3788, 3799

Greece — Mythology
J: 6848
JS: 3181, 3368, 3626, 6842, 6846–47, 6849–50–51–52–53, 6855–56, 6859–60
S: 3492, 6854, 6858

Greece — Mythology — Fiction
JS: 2618

Green Day (musical group)
JS: 8528

Greene, Nathanael
S: 7724

Greenland
JS: 8028

Greenland — Fiction
JS: 29

Greenlaw, Lavinia
S: 8243

Greenpeace
JS: 10110

Greitens, Eric
JS: 8244

Grief
JS: 10596, 10600, 11183

Grief — Biography
JS: 8249, 8384

Grief — Fiction
J: 32, 230, 888, 1017, 1061, 1142, 1250, 1423, 1439, 1443, 2094, 2284, 5607
JS: 467, 509, 513–14, 525, 1131, 1147, 1189, 1269, 1295, 1300, 1312, 1346, 1408, 1418, 1457, 1484, 1575, 1599, 1756, 1860, 1867, 2131, 2163, 3008, 3891, 5255, 5782
S: 303, 1676, 1964
S–Adult: 477, 1177, 3999, 4078

Grimberg, Tina
JS: 8245

Grimke, Angelina
JS: 7626

Grizzly bears
J: 11497
S: 11488

Grogan, John
S–Adult: 7360

Grooming
J: 10833

Group homes — Fiction
J: 1833

Growing up
See also Coming of age
JS: 1682, 11077
S: 7398, 11079
S–Adult: 8330

Growing up — Biography
JS: 8207
S–Adult: 11196

Growing up — Fiction
J: 733, 1928
JS: 112, 280, 362, 580, 1148, 1497, 1524, 1573, 1727, 1787, 1924, 1985, 2026, 2050, 2083, 2145, 2176, 6333, 6421
S: 734, 1235, 1822

Guadeloupe — Fiction
J: 3231

Guam — Fiction
J: 1114

Guantanamo Bay — Fiction
JS: 2257

Guardian angels — Fiction
JS: 2419

Guatemala
J: 9164

Guatemala — Biography
JS: 8153–54–55

Guatemala — Fiction
J: 920, 2205
JS: 4164

Guenevere, Queen — Fiction
J: 3825

Guerrero, Eddie
JS: 8020

Guevara, Che
J: 8150–51
JS: 8149, 8152

Guide dogs — Fiction
J: 566

Guidry, Jeff
S–Adult: 8246

Guilt — Fiction
JS: 615, 1418, 1447, 1921, 5119

Guitars
JS: 8537–38–39

Guitars — Biography
S: 7550

Gulf Stream
S–Adult: 11803

Gulf War (1991)
JS: 9489

Gulf War (1991) — Biography
J: 7755

Gulf Wars
S: 9483

Gun control
J: 9990
JS: 9995, 9998, 10010, 10013, 10020
S: 10005

Guns
J: 9990
S: 10005

Guns — Biography
JS: 10185

Guns — Fiction
J: 1888
JS: 1722, 1921, 2236

Gurdon, Martin
JS: 8247

Guthrie, Woody
J: 7461
JS: 7460
S: 7459

Guy, Rosa
JS: 7361

Gwyn, Nell — Fiction
S: 4036

Gymnastics
J: 12376–77

Gymnastics — Biography
JS: 8000–01

Gymnastics — Fiction
S: 6263

Gynecology
JS: 10813, 11025

Gypsies
S: 4477

H

Habitat for Humanity
JS: 10254

Hackers (computers)
JS: 11919

Hackers (computers) — Fiction
JS: 751

Haiku
J: 6603

Hairdressing
JS: 10449

Haiti — Fiction
JS: 4173
S: 4150, 4160

Haitian Americans — Fiction
J: 827, 946

Halder, Baby
S: 8248

Haley, Alex
J: 7362

Hall, Glenn
S: 8002

Halloween
JS: 10262

Halloween — Fiction
J: 4872
JS: 4601

Hallucinogenic drugs
JS: 10610, 10640

Hamer, Fannie Lou
J: 7627

Hamill, Dorothy
S: 8003

Hamilton, Hugo
S: 7363

Hamilton, Virginia
JS: 7364

Hamlet — **Adaptations**
J: 3623
JS: 3240

Hamlet (**play**)
S: 4128

Hamlet (**play**) — **Fiction**
JS: 194, 574, 653, 5599

Hammel, Heidi
J: 7875

Hamsters
JS: 11646

Hancock, Bill
JS: 8249

Handbags
JS: 12095

Handel, George Frideric
J: 7462

Hang gliding
JS: 12241

Hannibal
J: 8052

Hansberry, Lorraine
JS: 7365–66

Hanukkah — Fiction
J: 936

Happiness
JS: 10023

Harding, Warren G.
S: 7659

Hardy, Thomas — Criticism
S: 6947

Harems — Biography
S–Adult: 8285

Hargreaves, Alice Liddell — Fiction
S–Adult: 3967

Harlem (NY)
JS: 7361, 8383, 9513, 9521
S: 6324, 6871

Harlem (NY) — Fiction
J: 836, 905, 908, 4389
JS: 605, 879, 897, 904, 907, 4437, 6293
S: 5138

Harlem (NY) — Poetry
J: 6718

Harlem Renaissance
JS: 9425, 9428, 9443
S: 6331, 6398, 9424

Harlem Renaissance — Biography
JS: 7379

Harlem Renaissance — Fiction
JS: 7836

Harper, Martha Matilda
S: 7925

Harper's Ferry Raid — Fiction
JS: 4239

Harrison, Benjamin
JS: 7660

Harrison, George
S: 7504

Harrison, John
S: 7876

Haskins, Don
S: 7974

Hastings, Battle of
S: 9068

Hate groups and hate crimes
JS: 9900, 10199
S: 10019

JS = Junior High/Senior High; S = Senior High; S–Adult = Senior High/Adult

Hip-hop — Poetry
JS: 6757
S: 6673

Hippies — Fiction
JS: 1791

Hiroshima (Japan)
J: 8859
JS: 8083, 8818, 8827, 8856, 8887
S: 8846

Hirsi Ali, Ayaan
S: 8253

Hispanic American literature
JS: 798
S: 6368
S–Adult: 6925

Hispanic Americans
J: 9964
JS: 391, 9958–59, 9961, 9963
S: 6903, 9957, 9966

**Hispanic Americans —
Biography**
J: 7547, 7585, 7611, 7962, 7970, 8023
JS: 7214, 7593, 9962
S: 7303, 7730
S–Adult: 8346

Hispanic Americans — Careers
JS: 10483–84–85, 10510, 10512,
10525, 10527, 10535, 10553
S: 10450

Hispanic Americans — Fiction
J: 846–47, 855, 884, 895, 2129, 2179,
2208, 5537
JS: 527, 790, 796, 807, 812, 818, 848,
882, 923, 927, 932, 1996, 2080, 2279,
9961
S: 687, 734, 791–92–93, 815, 881, 903,
938, 2648, 6486

Hispanic Americans — Folklore
JS: 6821

Hispanic Americans — Plays
JS: 6573

Hispanic Americans — Poetry
JS: 923, 6667, 6717, 6742, 9961
S: 6697

Historic sites
JS: 9232

Historic sites (U.S.)
JS: 9922

Historical films
JS: 7143

Historical television programs
JS: 7143

History
See specific countries and continents
  and time periods, e.g., Ancient his-
  tory; Elizabethan England; 1920s
JS: 8663, 8676, 8690, 8784
S: 6868, 8681, 8687
S–Adult: 6904

History (U.S.)
JS: 9208, 9237
S: 3658, 9235

Hit-and-run accidents — Fiction
J: 5351
JS: 1129, 5385

Hitchcock, Alfred
J: 7509

Hitchhiking
JS: 8385

Hitler Youth
JS: 8847

Hitler, Adolf
JS: 8874
S: 8110–11–12–13, 8870

HIV (virus)
J: 7892, 10729
JS: 10689, 10696, 10784
S: 10746, 10775

Ho Chi Minh
S: 8074

Hoaxes
JS: 12183
S: 9338

Hobbes, Anne
JS: 8254

Hoboken (NJ) — Fiction
JS: 261

Hockenberry, John
JS: 8255

Hockey
JS: 12378

Holidays
JS: 10263

Holidays — Cookbooks
JS: 12034

Holidays — Fiction
J: 5719

Holloway, Monica
S: 8256

Holloway, Natalee
S: 8257

Hollywood — Fiction
J: 289
JS: 291
S: 4410
S–Adult: 295, 356

Holman, James
S: 8258

**Holmes, Sherlock (fictitious
character) — Fiction**
J: 5270, 5371

Holocaust
J: 8807, 8833, 8868, 9098
JS: 6549, 8161, 8381, 8806, 8811,
8814, 8816, 8819, 8828–29, 8836–37,
8840, 8842–43, 8848, 8850, 8858,
8863, 8865, 8882, 9524

S: 4477, 8830, 8834, 8841, 8849, 8855,
8860, 8862, 8866
S–Adult: 8817

Holocaust — Biography
J: 8102, 8104, 8280, 8335
JS: 7773, 7866, 8103, 8105–06–07,
8130, 8140–41, 8185, 8188, 8228,
8261, 8813, 8845
S: 8186, 8195, 8273, 8835, 8864

Holocaust — Fiction
J: 3613, 4088, 4468, 4470, 4479, 4485,
4488–89, 4513, 4515, 4522, 4540–41
JS: 1614, 3363, 3444, 4411, 4471,
4482, 4484, 4491, 4505, 4516, 4521,
4528, 4542, 4546–47, 5533
S: 4053, 4480, 4483, 4495, 4500, 4504,
4527, 4535

**Holocaust Museum
(Washington, DC)**
JS: 9524

Holy Grail
S: 9583

Holy Grail — Fiction
JS: 3532

**Homeland Security, Department
of**
JS: 10272

Homeless people
JS: 10217, 10217, 10220
S: 10208, 10223

Homeless people — Biography
JS: 8173
S–Adult: 8310

Homeless people — Fiction
J: 239, 1035, 2144
JS: 242, 352, 650, 674, 994, 1543,
1747, 2096, 2221, 3573, 4153, 4336
S: 1306, 1540, 5016, 5198
S–Adult: 2133

Homeschooling
J: 10352
JS: 10348

Hominids
S: 8646

Homophobia — Plays
S: 7063

Honesty — Fiction
J: 1548
JS: 426, 1570, 2004, 2143, 2826

Honey
S–Adult: 11589

Honeybees
S–Adult: 11590

Hong Kong — Fiction
JS: 1725, 5173, 5570

Hoover, J. Edgar
JS: 7725
S: 7726

Hope — Fiction
JS: 1455

Hope diamond
JS: 8474

Horney, Karen
JS: 7877

Horror stories
JS: 6939, 8579
S: 6966

Horror stories — Fiction
J: 2446, 4627–28, 4673, 4689, 4758, 4764, 4790, 4802, 4806, 4820, 4830, 4834, 4844, 4849, 4865–66, 4872, 4890, 4901
JS: 55, 196–97, 213, 2706, 3096, 3524, 3561, 3633, 3655, 3660, 3685, 3725, 4584, 4588, 4591, 4593, 4615, 4622–23, 4634–35, 4639, 4646, 4650–51, 4654, 4664, 4672, 4697–98, 4714, 4719–20, 4726, 4730, 4733, 4737, 4751, 4755, 4763, 4766, 4788, 4797, 4805, 4808, 4824–25–26–27, 4831–32, 4835, 4880, 4884, 4900, 5954, 6350, 6384, 6427
S: 198, 3218, 3226, 3277, 3337, 3477, 3645, 3715, 4585, 4605, 4608, 4611, 4614, 4645, 4648, 4656, 4662–63, 4681, 4708–09, 4718, 4721, 4724–25, 4728, 4731–32, 4749–50, 4774, 4777, 4798, 4807, 4813, 4817, 4819, 4829, 4838, 4855, 4859, 4878, 6354, 6409
S–Adult: 3357, 4626, 4666, 4700, 4711, 4715, 4717, 4729, 4754, 4773, 4812, 4828, 4845, 4867–68, 4891, 5188

Horse racing
JS: 12384
S: 12385

Horse racing — Fiction
JS: 4386

Horseback riding
JS: 12386

Horseback riding — Fiction
J: 307
JS: 491

Horses
J: 11687
JS: 8026, 8435, 11474, 11483, 11686, 11690, 11693
S: 11688–89, 11691–92, 11692
S–Adult: 8338

Horses — Fiction
J: 60, 311, 4303, 4361, 5202
JS: 82, 151, 156–57, 160, 3784
S: 4163
S–Adult: 4417, 5665

Hospice care
S–Adult: 11672

Hostages
J: 10175
JS: 10292

Hot rods
JS: 12011

Hotels — Fiction
J: 483

JS: 484

Hotlines — Fiction
JS: 1485

House of Representatives (U.S.)
S: 9696

Houseplants
JS: 12138

Houses
JS: 8411

Houston (TX) — Fiction
JS: 1879, 2165

Houston, Whitney
J: 7510

Howard, Catherine — Fiction
JS: 4055, 4060

Hubble space telescope
JS: 11318
S: 11296

Hübener, Helmuth — Fiction
JS: 4464

Hudson River
JS: 9517

Hughes, Langston
JS: 7373–74
S: 6702, 6980

Human beings
S: 8646

Human body
See also specific parts and systems, e.g., Circulatory system
J: 12118
JS: 10843–44, 10848, 10850
S: 8651, 10853

Human development and behavior
JS: 11067

Human embryos — Fiction
S–Adult: 640

Human evolution
S–Adult: 10578

Human Genome Project
JS: 10815

Human rights
See also civil rights
J: 10303
JS: 9622, 9841
S: 9840
S–Adult: 10213

Human rights — Biography
JS: 8040, 8060, 8067, 8153–54–55, 8190

Human rights — Fiction
S: 6319

Human trafficking
JS: 2234, 10138

Human trafficking — Fiction
JS: 2263

Human-animal relations
J: 11425
JS: 11647
S–Adult: 7317, 11644

Humanitarians — Biography
JS: 8086, 8088, 8141

Humor
JS: 6866, 6890, 6924, 7144, 11914, 12009, 12193, 12249
S: 6868, 6879, 6896, 7130, 7346, 8260, 8289, 8449, 9947, 10061, 10301
S–Adult: 6889, 6904

Humor — Fiction
IJ: 4926
J: 244, 635, 692, 1768, 1949, 4866, 4902, 4908–09–10, 4912–13, 4919, 4921, 4929–30, 4932, 4939–40, 4944–45–46, 4952–53–54, 4959–60, 4964, 4966–67, 4970–71–72–73–74, 4977–78–79, 4988, 4992, 5707
JS: 14, 219, 240, 259, 429, 512, 540, 562, 587, 737–38, 1571, 1645, 1666, 1803, 2108, 2321, 3033, 3307, 3423, 3648, 4062, 4095, 4314, 4653, 4748, 4905–06–07, 4914–15, 4920, 4922–23, 4933, 4935, 4941, 4947, 4949, 4956, 4968–69, 4975–76, 4981–82, 4984, 4986–87, 4989–90–91, 4993–94, 5015, 5317, 5330, 5518, 5584, 5609, 5645, 5839, 5842, 5866
S: 364, 553, 1123, 1880, 2177, 3511, 4772, 4903–04, 4916–17–18, 4925, 4937–38, 4943, 4948, 4955, 4958, 4961, 4963, 4965, 4985, 4999, 5003, 5014, 5072, 5271, 5593, 5614, 5679, 5705, 5716
S–Adult: 542, 586, 3011, 3376, 3503, 4590, 4783, 4931, 4936, 4942, 4951, 4983, 5964

Humpback whales
S: 11626

Hungarian Americans — Fiction
S: 1807

Hungary — Biography
S: 8274

Hungary — Cookbooks
J: 12057

Hungary — Fiction
JS: 4141, 4471, 4505

Hunger
JS: 10211

Hunter-Gault, Charlayne
JS: 8259

Hunter, Clementine
JS: 7267

Hunters and hunting
JS: 12353

Hunters and hunting — Fiction
J: 1379

Hurricane Katrina
J: 11771, 11777, 11781
JS: 8465, 8468, 9841, 11774, 11778

S–Adult: 8306, 12367

Hurricane Katrina — Biography
JS: 7948

Hurricane Katrina — Fiction
J: 243
JS: 139, 1483

Hurricanes
JS: 8697
S: 11772, 11776

Hurricanes
S: 11779

Hurston, Zora Neale
J: 7378
JS: 7379–80
S: 7375–76–77

**Hurston, Zora Neale —
Criticism**
S–Adult: 6987

Hussein, Saddam
J: 9500
JS: 8075

Hussein, Saddam — Fiction
JS: 37

Hydroelectricity
JS: 11836

Hydrogen (energy source)
JS: 11840

Hygiene
J: 10833, 11178
JS: 10588

Hypochondria — Fiction
JS: 2014

I

**Icarus (mythological character)
— Fiction**
S–Adult: 428

Ice ages
J: 8634
S: 11718

Ice ages — Fiction
S: 3768

Ice cream
JS: 12049

Ice hockey
J: 12382
JS: 12381, 12383, 12396
S: 12379–80

Ice hockey — Biography
S: 8002

Ice hockey — Fiction
JS: 6281, 6290
S: 6280

Ice skating — Biography
J: 8004

S: 8003

Ice skating — Fiction
J: 501
JS: 312, 624

Iceland
JS: 8028

Iceland — Fiction
J: 3081

Identity (psychology) — Fiction
J: 634, 1983
JS: 851, 1072, 1162, 1706, 5056
S: 3241

Identity theft
JS: 11939

Iditarod Sled Dog Race (AK)
JS: 12258

Igbo (African people)
J: 8981

Illegal aliens
JS: 9870
S–Adult: 9856

Illegal aliens — Fiction
J: 1973, 2202, 2208
JS: 564, 2279
S: 431
S–Adult: 2220

Illiteracy — Fiction
J: 374

Imaginary languages
JS: 8560

Immigration
J: 4010, 9869
JS: 9632, 9865, 9867
S: 8299, 9862

Immigration — Biography
S–Adult: 8300

Immigration — Fiction
J: 957, 4032, 4143, 4532
JS: 1500, 2268, 3669
S: 935, 2235

**Immigration (Canada) —
Fiction**
S: 803

**Immigration (Germany) —
Fiction**
S–Adult: 3973

Immigration (U.S.)
J: 9866, 9877
JS: 8935, 9012, 9115, 9151, 9165,
9516, 9627, 9854, 9858, 9861, 9864,
9868, 9870–72, 9875–76, 9963–64,
9874, 9981, 9878
S: 8359, 9859–60, 9863, 9879, 9951,
9953
S–Adult: 8229

Immigration (U.S.) — Biography
JS: 8188
S: 8236, 8313
S–Adult: 8367

Immigration (U.S.) — Fiction
J: 835, 846, 883, 920, 2202, 4345,
4354–55, 4510, 4932
JS: 49, 669, 809, 817, 880, 921, 929,
4378
S: 788, 788, 4246
S–Adult: 867

Immigration (U.S.) — Illegal
JS: 9873

Immortality — Fiction
JS: 3098

Immune system
JS: 10700, 10845

Imperialism
JS: 8699

Imperialism (U.S.)
S: 9235

Imposters
J: 10140

Impressionism (art)
S: 8455

Improvisation (theater)
JS: 8607, 8609, 8614

Incas
JS: 8713
S: 9179

Incest
JS: 11053

Incest — Fiction
JS: 1030, 1527, 2264, 5711
S: 440, 1255

India
JS: 9006, 9012
S: 8072, 9009
S–Adult: 9007

India — Biography
JS: 8071, 8086, 8088, 8304
S: 8248, 8382
S–Adult: 8379

India — Fiction
J: 3878, 3947
JS: 88, 2927, 3874, 3887, 3890, 3912,
3938–39, 4618, 4899
S: 192, 2272, 3871–72, 3896, 3906,
3944
S–Adult: 1126, 1947, 3299, 3886,
3929, 5830

**Indian (Asian) Americans —
Fiction**
J: 820, 896
JS: 849, 921
S: 868, 924
S–Adult: 367, 3299

Indian (Asian) students
S–Adult: 1126

Indiana — Fiction
S: 5114

Indians (Asians) — Fiction
S: 892

Indians of Central America
JS: 8552

Indians of Central America — Fiction
J: 2205

Indians of North America — Biography
S: 8378

Indians of North America — Fiction
J: 2205

Indians of South America
J: 9181
S: 9179, 9269

Individualism — Fiction
J: 1902
JS: 496
S: 2265

Indonesia — Biography
S: 8281

Industrial Revolution
J: 8779, 9415
JS: 8776
S: 8778

Industry — Biography
J: 7920
S: 7924

Infanticide — Fiction
JS: 379

Inferno — Adaptations
JS: 164

Infertility
S: 11011

Influenza
JS: 10688, 10708, 10755

Influenza — Fiction
JS: 6093

Influenza epidemic, 1918 — Fiction
J: 4338

Information technology — Careers
JS: 10436

Inhalants
J: 10661
JS: 10649–50

Inheritance — Fiction
S–Adult: 1265

Injuries
JS: 10745

Inline skating
JS: 12388

Inouye, Daniel K.
J: 7727

Insects
J: 11587
JS: 11575, 11577–78, 11580, 11584–85–86, 11588

S: 11461, 11582
S–Adult: 11579, 11583

Insects — Drawing and painting — Biography
S: 7891

Insects — Fiction
JS: 4615

Insomnia — Fiction
S–Adult: 5234

Integration — Fiction
S: 4406

Intelligence
JS: 11094
S–Adult: 11060

Intelligence service
JS: 9642

Intelligent design
JS: 8638, 11715

Interculturalism
S: 9888

Interior decoration
J: 12022
JS: 12158

International relations
JS: 9656, 10330

International relations (U.S.)
JS: 9634

International Space Station
JS: 11305

Internet
J: 11916, 11920, 11931, 11937, 11940
JS: 11264, 11914, 11924–25–26–27, 11929, 11933, 11935, 11939
S: 11913, 11928

Internet — Biography
J: 7812
JS: 7818

Internet — Fiction
JS: 245, 676, 1944

Internet addiction
JS: 11930

Internships — Fiction
JS: 2013

Interpersonal relations — Fiction
J: 376
JS: 548, 1873
S: 745

Interracial dating
JS: 9890

Interracial dating — Fiction
J: 5838
JS: 741
S: 5723

Interracial families — Fiction
S: 901

Interracial marriage
JS: 9890

Interracial marriage — Fiction
J: 1579

Intersex children
S–Adult: 2171

Interstellar travel — Fiction
S–Adult: 428

Inuit
JS: 9159, 9185, 9196

Inuit — Fiction
J: 130, 4340
JS: 162

Invasive species
JS: 11364

Inventors and inventions
See also Scientists; and specific inventions, e.g., Telephones
J: 11870, 11891
JS: 8707, 11875, 11881, 11890
S: 11873
S–Adult: 11865, 11869

Inventors and inventions — Biography
JS: 7720, 7809, 7811, 7829–30, 7858, 7909, 7916–17
S: 7848–49, 7924

Invertebrates
JS: 11473, 11575, 11602

Invisibility — Fiction
JS: 6231

Iran
JS: 6551, 9127–28, 9130, 9132, 9134
S: 9123
S–Adult: 9138

Iran — Biography
JS: 8065, 8078, 8080, 8085, 8226
S: 8166, 8227, 8238, 8311, 8348
S–Adult: 8219

Iran — Fiction
J: 869
JS: 3934, 4080
S: 3990
S–Adult: 4109

Iran-Iraq War
JS: 9130

Iran-Iraq War — Fiction
JS: 2264

Iranian Americans — Fiction
JS: 2264
S–Adult: 388

Iraq
J: 9500
JS: 8890, 8903, 9125, 9130, 9133, 9139, 9141, 9144, 9146, 9489
S: 9142

Iraq — Biography
JS: 8075

Iraq — Fiction
J: 869
JS: 37
S: 5520

JS = Junior High/Senior High; S = Senior High; S–Adult = Senior High/Adult

S–Adult: 4041

Iraq War
JS: 7094, 9495, 9632, 11695
S–Adult: 8902, 9129

Iraq War — Biography
S: 9147
S–Adult: 8196

Iraq War — Fiction
JS: 514, 1789, 2244, 3953, 5781
S: 3702
S–Adult: 442

Iraq War — Memoirs
JS: 8357

Ireland
S: 9077

Ireland — Biography
S: 7363, 9072

Ireland — Fiction
J: 1688, 2376, 2863, 2923, 3126, 4093, 4136–37
JS: 371, 2125, 2921–22, 3978, 4000, 4056, 4124
S: 3976, 4059, 5770
S–Adult: 3951, 3992, 5208, 5357

Ireland — Folklore
S: 6808

Ireland — Mythology — Fiction
JS: 2636

Irish — Fiction
S–Adult: 2017

Irish Americans
JS: 9981

Irish Americans — Fiction
JS: 4273

Irish potato famine — Fiction
J: 4093

Iron
JS: 10094

Iroquois Indians
J: 9282

Irritable colon
JS: 10863

Islam
JS: 8405, 8442, 8662, 9011, 9037, 9082, 9087, 9093, 9107, 9134, 9592, 9595–96, 9599–00, 9602, 9606–07–08, 10295
S: 9593, 9597, 9603–04–05, 10270, 10280
S–Adult: 9594, 9601

Islam — Biography
S–Adult: 8393

Islam — Fiction
JS: 859, 1136
S: 2240

Islamic art
JS: 8442

Islands — Fiction
J: 137, 1971
JS: 44
S: 6215

Israel
J: 9112
JS: 9106, 9109, 9111, 9117, 9121
S: 8698, 9113, 9119

Israel — Biography
JS: 8081, 8399

Israel — Fiction
J: 1059, 3786
JS: 2232, 4044, 4054, 4129
S: 4053, 4097, 4123

Israeli-Arab relations
See also Arab-Israeli relations
S: 9110, 9120, 9122

Israeli-Arab relations — Fiction
JS: 2286, 4571

Italian Americans
JS: 9978

Italian Americans — Biography
JS: 7327, 7861, 8332
S–Adult: 8203

Italian Americans — Fiction
J: 4345
JS: 5645

Italy
J: 9079
JS: 6548, 8454
S: 8122, 8888

Italy — Biography
S: 8119

Italy — Cookbooks
J: 12038
JS: 12065

Italy — Fiction
J: 307, 3055, 3966, 3982, 4025, 4096, 4118
JS: 441, 2097, 4906, 4933
S: 4009, 4030, 4111, 5643
S–Adult: 5180

Italy — Folklore
JS: 6805

Ivory Coast — Fiction
S: 3216
S–Adult: 3217

Iwo Jima, Battle of
JS: 8867

J

Jack the Ripper — Fiction
S: 4101

Jackson, Andrew
J: 7663
JS: 9284
S: 7664

S–Adult: 7662

Jackson, Michael
S–Adult: 7511

Jackson, Stonewall
J: 7728
S: 7729

Jacobs, A. J.
S: 8260

Jacobs, Jane
JS: 7778

Jacobsen, Ruth
JS: 8261

Jamaica — Biography
J: 7532
JS: 7534
S–Adult: 7533, 8206

Jamaica — Fiction
JS: 987
S: 4146

James, LeBron
JS: 7976
S–Adult: 7975

Jamestown (VA) — Fiction
JS: 4202

Jane Eyre — **Adaptations**
J: 180

Janitors — Fiction
J: 4902

Japan
J: 8859, 9013–14, 11854
JS: 9015
S: 8875

Japan — Biography
JS: 7964
S: 8323

Japan — Fiction
J: 3385, 3907, 6466
JS: 2721, 3467, 3483, 3599–00, 3683, 3696, 3897, 3902, 4533, 5000
S: 3885, 3889, 3895, 3915, 3920, 4999, 5319

Japan — Folklore
S: 3237

Japan — Mythology
S: 6836

Japanese — Fiction
JS: 4237

Japanese Americans
J: 9954
JS: 9445, 9448

Japanese Americans — Biography
J: 7727
JS: 7279, 8233, 8360

Japanese Americans — Fiction
J: 823, 853, 899, 3385, 4517
JS: 4423, 4476
S: 852, 1122, 4412, 4496

Jaramillo, Mari-Luci
S: 7730

Java — Fiction
JS: 3945

Jazz
JS: 8503, 8514–15, 8526, 8529
S: 8531
S–Adult: 8516

Jazz — Biography
JS: 7479
S: 7469

Jealousy — Fiction
JS: 637

Jeans
JS: 11905

Jefferson, Thomas
J: 7668, 7670
JS: 7667, 7669
S: 7665–66

Jefferson, Thomas — Fiction
J: 4219
JS: 4224

Jemison, Mae
JS: 7878

Jenifer, Trevon
JS: 8262

Jenkins, Missy
JS: 8263

Jenkins, Peter
S: 7191

Jensen, K. Thor
S: 8264

Jerusalem — Fiction
S: 4123

Jesus Christ — Fiction
JS: 3782
S: 179

Jewelry
JS: 8474, 11744, 11903
S–Adult: 12093

Jewelry making
JS: 12094, 12105–06
S: 12100, 12100

Jewish Americans
JS: 9968–69

Jewish Americans — Fiction
J: 4512
JS: 926, 4336
S: 997

Jewish holy days
JS: 9613

Jewish holy days — Fiction
J: 936

Jews
J: 8851, 8868
JS: 6553, 8811, 8819, 8865, 9609, 9969, 12284
S: 4012, 8698, 8830, 8834, 8841, 8855,

8862, 8866, 8888

Jews — Biography
JS: 7404, 7420, 8161, 8187
S: 8298, 8366

Jews — Fiction
J: 383, 671, 2238, 3448, 3779, 3786, 4143, 4354–55, 4396, 4470, 4479, 4512–13, 4515, 4522, 4525, 4532
JS: 265, 384, 454, 629, 802, 804, 875, 931, 1018, 1956, 3857, 4129, 4140–41, 4482, 4505–06, 4538, 4976, 5533, 6316
S: 735, 3321, 3808, 4057, 4072, 4483, 4504, 6457
S–Adult: 535, 996, 4041

Jews — Folklore
JS: 6783, 6818

Jiang Lu, Shu
JS: 8265

Jiang, Ji-li
J: 8266

Jim Crow laws
S: 9236, 9908

Joan of Arc
JS: 8114

Job hunting
JS: 10420, 10424

Jobs, Steve
J: 7927–28

John Paul II, Pope
J: 8115, 8117
S: 8116

Johnson, Lyndon B.
JS: 7672
S: 7671

Johnson, Robert
JS: 7512
S: 7513

Johnstown Flood — Fiction
JS: 4347

Jones, Caroline
J: 7929

Jones, Diana Wynne
JS: 7097

Jones, John Paul
J: 7731

Jones, Marion
S–Adult: 8009

Jones, Mother
JS: 9412

Jones, Thomas D.
JS: 7879

Joplin, Janis
JS: 7514

Joplin, Scott
JS: 7463

Jordan (country)
J: 9145
JS: 9137

Jordan, Michael
J: 7977
S: 7978

Joseph (Nez Perce chief)
JS: 7732

Journalism
J: 7125, 7125
JS: 7098, 7119–20–21, 7121, 7123, 7140, 7314, 8601, 8784, 12363
S: 7117, 7131, 7145–46, 7148, 7152–53–54–55, 8495, 10007, 10439, 10445, 11427, 12243
S–Adult: 7159

Journalism — Biography
J: 7223, 7764
JS: 7236, 7314, 7765, 7777, 7933, 8255
S: 7398, 7425, 7931
S–Adult: 7414, 7791

Journalism — Careers
J: 10428
S: 10472

Journalism — Fiction
J: 584, 1915
JS: 1264, 6298

Journals
J: 7263
JS: 10377

Journals — Fiction
J: 3000
JS: 4474

Joyner-Kersee, Jackie
J: 8010

Judaism
JS: 9609–10, 9612–13
S: 9611

Judge, Oney — Fiction
JS: 4223

Juette, Melvin
JS: 8267

Juggling
JS: 12242, 12269

Jujitsu
JS: 12391

Julius Caesar **— Adaptations**
JS: 3619

Jundi, Sami al
S–Adult: 8076

Junger, Sebastian
S–Adult: 8268

Jupiter (planet)
S: 11304

Jury system
J: 9703
JS: 9706

Justice
J: 9708

Justice — Folklore
JS: 6777

Juvenile court
JS: 9735

Juvenile delinquents
S–Adult: 10146

Juvenile delinquents — Fiction
J: 56–57–58–59, 1833, 1941
JS: 124, 1111, 1714, 2095
S–Adult: 4417

Juvenile detention — Fiction
JS: 1776

K

K2 (mountain)
S: 12338

Kafka, Franz
S: 7381

Kahlo, Frida — Fiction
J: 2702

Kahlo, Frida — Poetry
JS: 7268

Kamara, Mariatu
JS: 8269

Kambalu, Samson
S–Adult: 7269

Kane, Bob
JS: 7270

Kang, Hyok
S: 8270

Kann, Wendy
S: 8271

Kansas
J: 9340
S: 9408

Kansas — Fiction
S: 2117

Kantner, Seth
S: 8272

Karate
JS: 12390, 12393

Karenina, Anna — Fiction
S–Adult: 6249

Karpel, Nini
S: 8273

Karzai, Hamid
JS: 8077

Katin, Miriam
S: 8274

Kayaks and kayaking
J: 12409
JS: 9526, 12407

Kayaks and kayaking — Fiction
JS: 143

Kaysen, Susanna
S: 10898

Kazakhstan
JS: 9081–82
S: 8987

Keat, Nawuth
JS: 8275

Keller, Helen
J: 7779
JS: 7781–82, 7782
S: 7780

Keller, Helen — Fiction
JS: 1412

Kennedy Space Center
JS: 11314

Kennedy, John F.
J: 7673–74
JS: 9683

Kennedy, Robert F.
J: 9458
JS: 7733

Kentucky — Fiction
J: 758

Kenya
J: 8927–28, 8932, 8934, 8936, 8939, 8953–54–55
S: 11501

Kenya — Biography
J: 8288
JS: 7340, 8054, 8926
S: 8952

Kenya — Fiction
JS: 3855

Kerman, Piper
S–Adult: 8276

Kerouac, Jack
S: 7382

Kerouac-Parker, Edie
S: 7382

Kerr, M. E. — Criticism
JS: 7383

Kerry, John
J: 7734

Khamenei, Ali
JS: 8078

Khmer Rouge
J: 9036

Kidnapping
S: 10300
S–Adult: 9434

Kidnapping — Biography
S–Adult: 8225

Kidnapping — Fiction
J: 329, 1036, 1984, 2876, 5042, 5132, 5134, 5194, 6181
JS: 98, 313, 603, 654, 675, 1135, 5095, 5172, 5233, 5278, 5321, 5326, 5402, 5443

S: 2049, 2198, 3733, 5009, 5263
S–Adult: 5250, 5281

Kidney failure — Fiction
J: 1406

Kim Jong II
JS: 8079

Kimonos
S–Adult: 12102

Kindertransport
J: 8851

King Arthur — Fiction
J: 3092

King, B. B.
JS: 7515

King, Coretta Scott
JS: 7629

King, Ginevra — Fiction
S: 4394

King Lear **— Adaptations**
J: 3366

King Lear **— History and Criticism**
JS: 7051

King, Martin Luther, Jr.
J: 7630

King, Stephen
J: 7385
JS: 7012
S: 7384

King, Stephen — Criticism
JS: 7001–02

Kings and queens — Biography
JS: 8046

Kings and queens — Fiction
JS: 3812

Kingsley, Anna Madgigine Jai
S: 7783

Kiowa Indians — Fiction
S: 4193

Kirby, Jack
JS: 7271
S–Adult: 7272

Kirn, Walter
S–Adult: 7386

Kissing — Fiction
J: 6337

Kleckley, Elizabeth
J: 7784

Klein, Stephanie
S–Adult: 8277

Klezmer music — Fiction
S: 3614

Knights
S: 8666, 8757

Knights — Fiction
J: 3822, 5027

JS = Junior High/Senior High; S = Senior High; S–Adult = Senior High/Adult

Knights Templar — Fiction
J: 3488, 4617

Knitting
JS: 12153–54, 12162–63, 12165–66
S: 12157, 12157, 12160

Knitting — Fiction
J: 1849
JS: 475

Koehl, Mimi
J: 7880

Kohler, Dean Ellis
JS: 8278

Kongo (African people)
JS: 8945

Kopelman, Jay
JS: 8279

Kor, Eva Mozes
J: 8280

Koran — Women
J: 9568

Kordi, Gobar
JS: 8080

Korea — Fiction
J: 3883
S: 3379, 3936
S–Adult: 3914

Korean Americans
S: 9951

Korean Americans — Biography
JS: 8207

Korean Americans — Fiction
J: 959
JS: 608, 873, 898, 900, 909, 4564
S: 874, 2074, 3425

Korean War
J: 8891
JS: 8898, 9491–92
S: 6770, 9497, 9504

Korean War — Biography
J: 8036

Korean War — Fiction
JS: 4561
S: 4558

Korman, Marvin
S: 9519

Korn, Fadumo
S: 8053

Koufax, Sandy
JS: 7959

Ku Klux Klan
J: 7118
JS: 9883

Ku Klux Klan — Fiction
JS: 4377

Kübler-Ross, Elisabeth
JS: 7881

Kuegler, Sabine
S: 8281

Kurdistan
J: 9124
JS: 9133

Kurds — Fiction
J: 869

Kuusisto, Stephen
JS: 8282
S: 8283

Kuwait
JS: 9131, 9489

Kwan, Michelle
J: 8004

Kwanzaa
JS: 10266

Kyrgyzstan
JS: 9081, 9087
S: 8987

L

L'Engle, Madeleine
JS: 7387

Labor camps — Fiction
S: 2275

Labor movements
J: 9411

Labor movements — Biography
J: 7611, 7635

Labor problems — Fiction
JS: 933, 4447

Labor unions
J: 10329
JS: 10327–28
S: 9988
S–Adult: 10325

Labor unions — Biography
JS: 7597

Labyrinths
JS: 12177

Lacrosse
JS: 12245, 12270

Lady of the Lake — Fiction
J: 3092

Lakota Indians
S: 9278

Lambke, Bryan
JS: 8284

Landmines — Fiction
J: 2218

Lang, Lang
J: 7517
S: 7516

Lange, Dorothea
JS: 7273

Langstaff, John
JS: 7518

Language
JS: 7073
S: 7079, 7086

Language — Biography
JS: 8217

Languages
S–Adult: 7078

Lantz, Walter
J: 7561

Laos — Fiction
JS: 5104
S–Adult: 5105

Lapland — Fiction
S: 1272

Las Vegas (NV) — Fiction
S: 1516

Lasky, Kathryn
JS: 7388

Lasseter, John
J: 7562

Latifah, Queen
J: 7519

Latin America
JS: 9148

Latin America — Cookbooks
S: 12066

Latinos — Fiction
JS: 1534

Latvia
J: 9091

Lauren, Jillian
S–Adult: 8285

Lauren, Ralph
JS: 7930

Law
JS: 9709, 9736, 10533, 10535
S: 8527

Law — Humor
JS: 10193

Law (U.S.)
JS: 9710

Law enforcement
JS: 9744

Law enforcement — Biography
JS: 10185

Law enforcement — Careers
J: 10528, 10537

Law enforcement — Fiction
JS: 5518

Lawrence, Candida
S: 8286

Lawrence, Jacob
S: 8466

Lawrence, Sarahlee
S–Adult: 8287

Lawyers
J: 9723

Lawyers — Fiction
JS: 3963
S: 5198

Laziness
S: 10324

Leach, Terry
JS: 7960

Leadership
S–Adult: 11059

Leakey family
J: 7883

Leakey, Louis and Mary
JS: 7882

Learning disabilities
JS: 10877, 10879, 10881, 10901, 10913, 10920

Learning disabilities — Fiction
J: 1984

Leather work
JS: 12008

Lebanon
J: 9143
JS: 9135

Lebanon — Cookbooks
J: 12028

Lebanon — Fiction
S–Adult: 3950

Led Zeppelin (musical group)
JS: 7520

Lee, Bruce
JS: 7521

Lee, Harper
J: 7389
JS: 7390

Lee, Robert E.
J: 7736–37
S: 7735

Lee, Spike
J: 7522

Lee, Spike — Criticism
JS: 8583

Lefevre, Didier
S–Adult: 9022

Legal system
JS: 9674

Leiber, Jerry
S–Adult: 7229

Lekuton, Joseph Lemasolai
J: 8288

Leleux, Robert
S: 8289

Lenape Indians — Fiction
S: 5212

Lenin, Vladimir Ilich
J: 8118

Lennon, John
JS: 7526–27
S: 7525
S–Adult: 7523–24

Leonardo da Vinci — Fiction
J: 3818

Leopards
J: 11502

Lerner, Gerda
S: 8290

Lesbians
See Gay men and lesbians

Letter writing
JS: 8853, 11142

Letter writing — Fiction
J: 2085
JS: 1367, 1683, 4534, 9431, 9643, 11148

Letters — Fiction
J: 486
S–Adult: 4509

Leukemia
J: 10736
JS: 8294, 10750

Leukemia — Biography
JS: 8083

Leukemia — Fiction
J: 1379
JS: 240, 1293, 1342, 1350, 1445
S: 1207, 1329
S–Adult: 1376

Levi-Montalcini, Rita
JS: 7884

Levitation
JS: 7234

Lewis and Clark Expedition
JS: 9288
S: 7192, 9270

Lewis and Clark Expedition — Fiction
J: 4291
JS: 4324
S: 4197

Lewis, Meriwether
JS: 7193
S: 7192

Lewis, Sinclair — Criticism
S: 6970

Li, Moying
JS: 8291

Libby Prison — Fiction
S: 4258

Liberia
JS: 8982

Liberia — Biography
JS: 8212

Liberia — Fiction
JS: 3870

Libraries and librarians
J: 9954, 10228
JS: 8224

Libraries and librarians — Careers
JS: 10520

Libraries and librarians — Fiction
See also Books and reading
S–Adult: 568

Libya
JS: 8911

Libya — Fiction
J: 3863
S: 3853

Lies and lying — Fiction
JS: 5629

Life (periodical)
JS: 8429

Light (physics)
JS: 11860

Lighthouses — Fiction
JS: 4133

Lightning — Fiction
S–Adult: 2185

Lin, Maya
J: 7274

Lincoln, Abraham
J: 7678, 7680
JS: 7675–76–77, 9357, 9387
S: 7679

Lincoln, Abraham — Fiction
J: 4279
JS: 4272, 4272
S: 4282
S–Adult: 3290, 4666

Lincoln, Abraham and Mary Todd
JS: 7681

Lincoln, Mary Todd
J: 7784

Lindbergh, Anne Morrow
JS: 7194

Lindbergh, Charles A.
JS: 7195–96–97
S–Adult: 9434

Lindbergh, Charles A. — Fiction
S: 4524

Linguistics
JS: 7076

JS = Junior High/Senior High; S = Senior High; S–Adult = Senior High/Adult

Lions
JS: 11476, 11498
S: 11500–01

Lions — Fiction
S: 3702

Lipsyte, Robert — Criticism
JS: 6975

Liquids
JS: 11813

Literacy programs
JS: 10255

Literary agents — Fiction
S: 5174

Literary characters — Fiction
JS: 4261, 4923

Literature — Anthologies
JS: 6434

Literature — History and criticism
J: 7347
JS: 6939, 6950–51, 6997, 7012, 7055, 7057
S: 6931, 6980

Lithuania
J: 9091

Little Bighorn, Battle of
JS: 9283
S: 9280

Little Women **— Fiction**
JS: 4249

Lizards
JS: 11436

Loch Ness monster
JS: 12189

Logic — Fiction
JS: 5272

London (England)
J: 9070–71
JS: 6951

London (England) — Fiction
J: 584, 1708, 2361, 3964, 4026, 4037, 4103, 5178
JS: 556, 572, 1500, 2189, 3009, 4042, 4095, 4115, 5265, 5502, 5642
S: 892, 1977, 2540, 2814, 3273, 4101, 4961
S–Adult: 2197, 2958

London, Jack
J: 7391

London, Jack — Criticism
JS: 7009

Loneliness — Fiction
S: 395

Long Island (NY) — Fiction
JS: 1812

Long Lance, Chief Buffalo Child
S: 7785

Long Tack Sam
JS: 7528

Longboat, Tom
JS: 8011

Lopez, Nancy
J: 8023

Lord of the Flies **— Criticism**
JS: 6972

The Lord of the Rings **— Criticism**
S: 6958

Lord's Resistance Army
JS: 9631

Los Angeles (CA)
JS: 9884
S: 9533

Los Angeles (CA) — Fiction
J: 24, 1862, 3508, 5194
JS: 326, 355, 684, 1023
S: 1783, 5663

Los Angeles Lakers (basketball team)
JS: 12314

Loss
JS: 10605

Loss — Fiction
IJ: 2104
J: 616
JS: 974, 1592, 4043
S: 1551

Lou Gehrig's disease
JS: 10673

Lou Gehrig's disease — Fiction
J: 387

Louisiana Purchase
J: 9309

Louisville (KY) — Fiction
S–Adult: 4403

Louvre — Fiction
JS: 3302

Love
JS: 6919, 11144

Love — Fiction
J: 253, 2085, 3173, 4063
JS: 538, 606, 1158, 1300, 1364, 1848, 2266, 2501, 2838, 5682, 5776, 8853
S: 519, 521, 1604, 1841, 2021, 2959–60, 3234, 4097, 4156
S–Adult: 273, 300, 1153, 3916, 3929, 4102, 4745, 5788, 5803, 5827

Love — Poetry
J: 6612
JS: 6593, 6600, 6609, 6753
S: 6706

Lowe, Thaddeus
J: 9363

Lowriders
JS: 12011

LSD (drug)
JS: 10640

Luba (African people)
J: 8947

Lucas, Frank
S–Adult: 8292

Lucas, Jack H.
JS: 7786

Lukas, Christopher
S–Adult: 8293

Lund, Eric
JS: 8294

Lying — Fiction
JS: 370

Lyme disease
JS: 10697

Lymphoma — Fiction
JS: 1381

Lynchings
JS: 9246, 9967

Lynchings — Fiction
JS: 4353, 4426
S: 4420

M

Ma, Yo-Yo
J: 7529

Maathai, Wangari
JS: 8054

Macaroni — Cookbooks
S: 12076

MacArthur, Douglas
JS: 7738

Macbeth **— Adaptations**
J: 3621

Macbeth, King of Scotland — Fiction
JS: 4046

Macbeth **(play)**
J: 6536

Macbeth **(play) — Fiction**
JS: 3985

Macdonald, Warren
JS: 8295

Machiavelli, Niccolò
S: 8119

Machines and machinery
JS: 11881

Machines and machinery — Careers
JS: 10518

Madagascar
JS: 8965

JS = Junior High/Senior High; S = Senior High; S–Adult = Senior High/Adult

Madison, James
S: 7682

Madonna (singer)
JS: 7530–31

Mafia — Fiction
J: 4429
S: 119, 3478, 5368

Magazines
J: 7108
JS: 7157, 10360
S: 7124

Magellan, Ferdinand
JS: 7198

Magic and magicians
JS: 12190
S: 3493

Magic and magicians — Biography
JS: 7234, 7528

Magic and magicians — Fiction
J: 2302–03–04, 2349, 2389, 2404, 2411, 2483, 2519, 2567, 2572, 2577, 3000, 3037, 4242, 4811
JS: 378, 754, 2287, 2400, 2416, 2442, 2449, 2452, 2484, 2488, 2494, 2827, 3041, 3051, 3113, 3118, 3691, 3757, 4984
S: 2755, 5249, 5669
S–Adult: 2476, 2918

Magical realism — Fiction
JS: 565

Magnetism
JS: 11862

Mai, Mukhtar
S: 8296

Maine
JS: 11699
S: 9518

Maine — Fiction
JS: 1152, 4349

Makeup (stage)
JS: 12013, 12142

Malaria
JS: 10690, 10706

Malarkey, Don
JS: 8297

Malawi
JS: 8943

Malawi — Biography
S–Adult: 7269

Malaysia — Biography
J: 7921

Malaysia — Fiction
JS: 3261

Malcolm X
J: 9460
JS: 7632
S: 7631

Mali
J: 8956, 8980
S: 8957, 8959

Mali — Biography
J: 7333

Mammals
J: 8634
JS: 11423, 11465–66
S: 11467

Mammoths
S: 8623

Manatees
JS: 11634

Mandan Indians — Fiction
JS: 4195

Mandela, Nelson
JS: 8057–58, 8060, 8961
S: 8056, 8059
S–Adult: 8055, 8061

Manga
JS: 3661, 7137

Manic depression
J: 10903
JS: 10936
S: 10937

Manitoba — Fiction
J: 2167

Manjiro — Fiction
JS: 4237

Mann, Reva
S: 8298

Manning, Peyton
J: 7991

Mantle, Mickey
S: 7961

Manufacturing
J: 11868

Manzano, Juan Francisco
J: 7392

Manzoor, Sarfraz
S: 8299

Maori (people) — Fiction
JS: 930, 2693

Maori (people) — Folklore
JS: 6800

Mapplethorpe, Robert
S–Adult: 7554

Maps and globes
J: 8618–19
JS: 8702
S: 7876
S–Adult: 8617

Maps and globes — Biography
J: 7890

Mara-Serengeti (Africa)
JS: 8949

Marathon (race)
J: 12400
JS: 12399
S: 12403

Marching bands
JS: 8477

Marconi, Guglielmo
S: 11945

Maric, Vesna
S–Adult: 8300

Marijuana
J: 10654
JS: 10610, 10615, 10626

Marijuana — Fiction
S: 664

Marine animals
See also specific species, e.g., Sharks
JS: 11604, 11607
S: 11606

Marine biology
JS: 10029, 10091, 11599, 11609, 11798
S: 11600

Marine biology — Biography
JS: 8317

Marine Corps (U.S.)
JS: 9770
S: 9764, 9767, 9779

Marketing
JS: 8247

Markham, Beryl
J: 7199
S: 7200

Marley, Bob
J: 7532
JS: 7534, 8504
S–Adult: 7533

Marriage
JS: 6876, 11202, 11212

Marriage — Fiction
JS: 1894, 2073

Mars (planet)
J: 11342
JS: 11335, 11343
S: 11309, 11334, 11339, 11344

Mars (planet) — Fiction
S: 5894

Mars Pathfinder mission
JS: 11343

Marshall Plan
JS: 8695

Marshall, George C.
JS: 7739

Marshall, Kerry James
S: 7275

Marshall, Thurgood
JS: 7740
S: 7741

Martial arts
JS: 12389, 12391–92–93–94–95

Martial arts — Biography
JS: 7521

Martial arts — Fiction
JS: 1000, 3470, 5685
S: 417

Martians — Fiction
JS: 6233

Martin, Jesse
JS: 7201

Martin, Luther
S–Adult: 7787

Martinez, Pedro
J: 7962

Mary Magdalene — Fiction
JS: 3772

Mary, Queen of Scots
J: 8121
S: 8038

Mary, Queen of Scots — Fiction
J: 4039
S: 4144

Maryland — Fiction
J: 1197

Masada — Fiction
J: 3779

**Masai (African people) —
Biography**
J: 8288

Masks and mask making
JS: 12141–42

Mass media
JS: 7098, 7156, 10332
S: 7122, 7127, 7145, 7152, 7152, 8598,
9972, 10287

Massachusetts
J: 8750
S: 10171

Massachusetts — Fiction
J: 4231
JS: 4235

Masters, Jarvis Jay
S–Adult: 8301

Mathematics
See also specific branches, e.g., Algebra
J: 11750, 11756
JS: 11758, 11761
S: 11751, 11753–54–55
S–Adult: 11748, 11757, 11759

Mathematics — Biography
J: 7806, 7827, 7856, 7872, 7911
JS: 7822, 7853, 7912
S: 7899

Mathematics — Careers
JS: 10545

Mathematics — Fiction
J: 5064

JS: 1719, 4436
S: 1794

Mathews, Dan
S: 8302

Mathews, Eddie
JS: 7963

Matisse, Henri
JS: 8423

Matsui, Hideki
JS: 7964

Matter (physics)
JS: 11814

Mauretania (ship)
S: 5003

May-Treanor, Misty
S–Adult: 8024

Mayan Indians
J: 8708
JS: 8710

Mayan Indians — Fiction
J: 2205, 5194
S: 5458

Mayer, Maria Goeppert
JS: 7885

Mayor, Mireya
S–Adult: 8303

Mayors — Fiction
JS: 726

Maze puzzles
JS: 12177

Mazer, Norma Fox — Criticism
JS: 6999

Mbundu (African people)
JS: 8969

Mbuti (African people)
J: 8944

McCain, John
JS: 7742

McCandless, Chris
JS: 9528

McCarthy, Joseph
J: 9477
JS: 7743, 9463
S: 9480

McCarthyism
JS: 9468

McCartney, Paul
S–Adult: 7535

McCartney, Paul — Criticism
JS: 8521

McCay, Winsor
JS: 7276

McClintock, Barbara
JS: 7886

McCourt, Frank
JS: 7393

McDaniel, Hattie
JS: 7536

McEnroe, Patrick
S–Adult: 8008

McKinley, William
S: 7683

McKoy, Millie and Christine
S: 7537

Mead, Margaret
J: 7888

Meaning (philosophy) — Fiction
JS: 722

Meat
JS: 11390

Medea (play) — Criticism
JS: 7029

Medecins sans Frontieres
S–Adult: 9022

Media
JS: 10165
S–Adult: 9687

Medical ethics
S: 10591

Medicinal plants
S: 11412

Medicine
See also Disease and illnesses; Doctors
J: 10783, 10800, 10810–11
JS: 8727, 9263, 10577, 10584, 10795,
10797, 10803, 10805
S: 10761, 10801
S–Adult: 10812

Medicine — Biography
JS: 7877, 7881

Medicine — Careers
J: 10799
JS: 10484, 10545
S: 10544

Medicine — Fiction
JS: 4126

Meditation
S: 10587

Mediterranean Sea — Fiction
JS: 35

Meir, Golda
JS: 8081

Melville, Herman
JS: 7394

Memoirs
J: 7263, 8142, 8176, 8280, 8363, 8388,
8397
JS: 3301, 3528, 6611, 7178, 7201,
7211, 7244, 7314, 7393, 7404, 7443,
7879, 7932, 7956, 7981, 7999, 8001,
8026, 8168, 8171, 8180, 8185,
8187–88, 8197, 8199, 8201–02, 8207,
8210, 8212, 8214, 8217, 8224, 8226,
8232–33, 8244–45, 8247, 8249,
8252, 8259, 8263, 8265, 8269, 8275,

8278–79, 8284, 8291, 8295, 8297, 8305, 8308–09, 8316–17, 8320–21, 8332, 8337, 8340–41, 8349, 8351, 8357, 8370, 8383–84, 8387, 8390, 8399, 8787, 8845, 8850, 8926, 9646, 10210, 10337, 10945, 11077, 11666, 11668, 11697, 11699–00
S: 3567, 6349, 6353, 7191, 7237, 7243, 7322, 7345–46, 7350, 7354, 7357–58–59, 7363, 7396, 7398, 7402, 7424, 7556, 7974, 7998, 8163, 8166, 8172, 8177, 8179, 8181, 8183, 8189, 8195, 8204, 8209, 8213, 8220, 8227, 8234, 8236, 8238, 8242–43, 8248, 8256–57, 8260, 8264, 8270–71–72–73–74, 8281, 8286, 8289–90, 8296, 8298–99, 8302, 8311–12, 8319, 8327, 8331, 8334, 8347–48, 8350, 8353–54, 8358–59, 8361–62, 8365–66, 8375–76–77, 8382, 8391, 8556, 8835, 8871, 8884, 8921, 9147, 9437, 9518–19, 9523, 9616, 9778, 10118, 10144, 10300, 10723, 11213, 11960
S–Adult: 7360, 7386, 7409, 7414, 7508, 7554, 8049, 8076, 8157–58, 8164, 8167, 8169, 8175, 8178, 8191, 8193, 8203, 8205, 8219, 8221–22, 8225, 8229, 8239–40, 8246, 8276–77, 8285, 8292, 8300–01, 8303, 8310, 8314–15, 8322, 8328, 8330, 8338–39, 8346, 8352, 8356, 8367–68–69, 8373, 8379–80, 8386, 8389, 8393–94, 8398, 11196

Memory — Fiction
JS: 5366

Menchu, Rigoberta
JS: 8153–54–55

Mendel, Gregor
J: 7889

Mendelssohn, Fanny
JS: 7464

Mennonites — Fiction
JS: 1538

Menstruation
J: 11038

Menstruation — Fiction
JS: 1356

Mental disabilities
JS: 10978

Mental disabilities — Fiction
J: 4341, 4675

Mental health
JS: 10876

Mental illness
See also specific disorders, e.g., Schizophrenia
J: 10878, 10887, 10907, 10930, 10930
JS: 5403, 10881, 10899, 10909–10, 10935, 10938
S: 10892, 10898, 10926

Mental illness — Fiction
J: 287, 1159, 1343, 1365, 1370, 1422, 1696, 5134

JS: 250, 439, 740, 1002, 1245, 1321, 1334–35, 1338, 1341, 1355, 1386, 1429–30, 1473, 1485, 1927, 2743, 5337
S: 1086, 1315, 1366, 1391, 1414
S–Adult: 3571

Mental illness — Poetry
JS: 6626

Mental problems
JS: 10877, 11204

Mental problems — Fiction
JS: 1352, 1480

Mercator, Gerardus
J: 7890

**The Merchant of Venice —
Adaptations**
JS: 3367

Merian, Maria Sibylla
S: 7891

Merina (African people)
JS: 8965

**Merlin (legendary character) —
Fiction**
J: 2352–53

**Mermaids and mermen —
Fiction**
J: 2889, 3007
JS: 3797

**Mermaids and mermen —
Folklore**
JS: 6775
S: 6776

Mesopotamia
JS: 8724–25

Mesopotamia — Folklore
JS: 6840

Metalwork
JS: 12007
S: 12024

Meteorites
S: 11320
S–Adult: 11327

Meteorology
J: 11324
S: 11718, 11765

Meteorology — Biography
JS: 7914

Meteorology — Careers
JS: 10547

Meteors
J: 11325

Methamphetamine (speed)
J: 10614
JS: 10637, 10655, 10655

**Methamphetamine (speed) —
Fiction**
JS: 1483, 2228
S: 2229

Mexican Americans
J: 9877

**Mexican Americans —
Biography**
S: 7985, 8241

Mexican Americans — Fiction
J: 787, 847, 855, 885, 1441, 2129, 2136, 5267, 6463
JS: 49, 551, 603, 688, 786, 807, 810, 856, 882, 923, 1316, 1718, 1787, 1793, 2034, 6360
S: 708, 928, 2093
S–Adult: 784, 797

Mexican Americans — Folklore
JS: 6821

Mexican Americans — Poetry
JS: 6731

Mexican literature
S: 6368

Mexico
JS: 9165–66–67

Mexico — Biography
J: 7285–86–87

Mexico — Cookbooks
J: 12047
JS: 12056

Mexico — Fiction
J: 604, 657, 846, 4162, 4168
JS: 1045, 1251, 4153
S: 826, 3213, 4163

Mexico — Folklore
JS: 6837

Meyer, Stephenie
JS: 7395

Michaux, Lewis H. — Fiction
JS: 4437

Michelangelo
J: 8459

Michelangelo — Fiction
JS: 3791

Michigan — Fiction
JS: 643, 1797
S: 6415

Microchips
S: 11934

Microscopes and microbiology
J: 11639
JS: 7900, 11638

**Microscopes and microbiology
— Biography**
JS: 7901

**Microscopes and microbiology
— Experiments and projects**
JS: 11638

Middle Ages
J: 8761, 8766
JS: 8752–53–54, 8759, 8762, 8765, 8772–73–74, 10803, 11885

JS = Junior High/Senior High; S = Senior High; S–Adult = Senior High/Adult

S: 8666, 8751, 8758, 8764, 8767, 8771

Middle Ages — Biography
JS: 8100
S: 8095, 8101

Middle Ages — Fiction
J: 2750, 3377, 3806–07, 3815–16, 3822, 3827, 3831–32–33, 3836, 4096, 4130
JS: 2515, 3803, 3811–12–13–14, 3817, 3820–21, 3823, 3828–29, 3834, 4081, 5184, 5381
S: 3808, 3826, 5676
S–Adult: 5082–83

Middle Ages — Poetry
S: 6640

Middle East
JS: 8662, 9103, 9105–06–07, 9135, 9634
S: 9104

Middle East — Biography
JS: 8066

Middle East — Fiction
JS: 1136, 4007
S: 4527

Middle East — Folklore
S: 6795

Middle East — Poetry
JS: 6773

A Midsummer Night's Dream — **Adaptations**
JS: 3230

A Midsummer Night's Dream — **Criticism**
JS: 7043

Midwest (U.S.)
S: 6900

Midwest (U.S.) — Fiction
JS: 225, 995, 1972, 4297
S: 203, 919

Midwives — Fiction
JS: 3813

Migrant workers
S: 943
S–Adult: 9856

Migrant workers — Fiction
J: 855, 1001
JS: 856, 1787

Mijikenda (African people)
J: 8955

Mikkelsen, Einar
S: 7202

Military Academy (West Point)
S: 10408

Military cadets — Fiction
JS: 1560

Military deployment (U.S.)
JS: 11998

Military history
JS: 8667
S: 9903

Military occupation — Fiction
J: 5785

Military policy
JS: 9761

Militia movement (U.S.)
JS: 9989

Militia movement (U.S.) — **Fiction**
J: 105

Miller, Adam David
S: 7396

Miller, Arthur
J: 7397
JS: 7057

Miller, Arthur — Criticism
JS: 7052
S: 7067

Miller, Shannon
JS: 8000

Mills, Dan
S–Adult: 8902

Mime
JS: 8611

Mind control — Fiction
JS: 21

Mines and mining — Fiction
JS: 268
S: 4414, 4451

Ming, Yao
JS: 7979

Minik
J: 4340

Minnesota
JS: 9508

Minnesota — Fiction
S: 1713

Minotaur (Greek mythology) — **Fiction**
J: 2347

Miracles — Fiction
JS: 773, 1031

Miranda rights
JS: 9728

Miro, Asha
JS: 8304

Misinformation
JS: 12183

Missiles — Fiction
S: 5940

Missing persons
S: 8257

Missing persons — Fiction
J: 533, 777

JS: 1104, 755, 5063, 5140, 5161, 5259, 5278, 5390, 5480, 5881, 6298
S: 998, 5016, 5356
S–Adult: 1987, 5017, 5189, 5487

Missionaries — Fiction
J: 3851
S: 202, 1619, 3850

Mississippi River
JS: 10087
S: 6907

Mississippi River — Fiction
JS: 219, 5048
S: 4327

Mississippi (state) — Fiction
J: 946
S: 854, 4332, 4406
S–Adult: 4413

Missoula (MT)
S–Adult: 11395

Missouri (state) — Fiction
JS: 4261, 4395
S: 4374

Mitchell, Billy
JS: 7744

Moby Dick — Fiction
JS: 2406

Modeling (fashion) — Fiction
JS: 347, 451, 481, 1939

Modern art — Fiction
JS: 5053

Moehringer, J. R.
S: 7398

Mohawk Indians
J: 9975

Mohawk Indians — Fiction
J: 4183

Molecular biology
JS: 10817

Monaque, Mathilde
JS: 8305

Monarch butterfly
JS: 11596

Monasteries — Fiction
JS: 5381

Monet, Claude
J: 7277

Monetary policy (U.S.)
J: 10317

Money
J: 10575

Money management
JS: 10400
S: 10565

Money-making ideas
J: 10561
JS: 10560

JS = Junior High/Senior High; S = Senior High; S–Adult = Senior High/Adult

Mongolia
J: 9023

Mongolia — Biography
S–Adult: 8221

Mongolia — Fiction
JS: 3946

Monologues
JS: 6488, 6490–91–92–93–94,
6497–98, 6500, 6503–04, 6514–15–16,
6524–25, 6527, 6559, 6574, 8590
S: 6510, 7027

Mononucleosis
J: 10767
JS: 10693

Monroe, James
JS: 7684

Monroe, Marilyn
J: 7539
JS: 7538

Monsters
See also Fantasy; Folklore; Mythology;
Supernatural
JS: 12142, 12189

Monsters — Fiction
J: 3579
JS: 2706
S: 4743

Montagnier, Luc
J: 7892

Montana
S: 4295
S–Adult: 11728

Montana — Fiction
JS: 131, 1625
S: 4558, 5400

Montana-Leblanc, Phyllis
S–Adult: 8306

Montenegro
S: 9049

Montgomery bus boycott
J: 9785

Monuments
J: 8410

Moody, Anne
S: 8307

Moon
S: 11328, 11330

Moon — Fiction
JS: 5112, 6229
S: 5162, 6012

Moore, Wes
JS: 8308

Morals
JS: 10224

More, Sir Thomas — Plays
JS: 6532

Mormons
S: 9579

Mormons — Biography
S: 7793

Mormons — Fiction
J: 5790
JS: 652, 1115
S–Adult: 4234

Morocco — Fiction
S: 2235

Morris, Gouverneur
S–Adult: 7788

Morris, Jim
JS: 7965

Morrison, Toni
J: 7399
JS: 7400

Morrison, Toni — Criticism
JS: 6976

Mortenson, Greg
JS: 8309

Moses (Bible) — Fiction
S: 3787

Mosques
JS: 8413

Motherhood
S: 6897

Motherhood — Poetry
JS: 6591

Mothers
JS: 11140

Mothers — Fiction
JS: 1155, 3981

Mothers and daughters
JS: 8216, 11193
S: 11206

**Mothers and daughters —
Fiction**
J: 322–23, 407, 766, 1019, 1171, 1199,
1507, 6417
JS: 324, 399, 577, 1010, 1033, 1057,
1148, 1162, 1403, 1468, 1709, 4399,
5304, 5317, 6403
S: 344, 1042, 1067, 1170, 1234, 1540

Mothers and sons — Fiction
J: 1258
JS: 1078

Motion (physics)
J: 7896

Motion pictures
J: 7128, 8567, 8572, 8577, 8580
JS: 3714, 8557–58, 8561–62, 8564–65,
8568, 8573, 8579, 8581–82, 8584–85–
86, 8588, 8590–91, 9945, 10372, 12147
S: 8559, 8569–70, 8575, 8578, 8587,
8589, 11947
S–Adult: 7216, 8576

Motion pictures — Biography
J: 7224, 7228, 7482, 7509, 7522, 7547
JS: 7258–59, 7521
S: 7483

Motion pictures — Careers
J: 8567, 8577, 10486, 10500
JS: 8566, 8584, 10488, 10492, 10494

Motion pictures — Criticism
JS: 8583

Motion pictures — Fiction
JS: 1770, 3281

Motorcycles
JS: 11972, 12274, 12330
S: 11973

Mount Everest
S: 12342

Mountain and rock climbing
JS: 12339, 12344, 12344–45–46–47
S: 12338, 12342, 12348

**Mountain and rock climbing —
Biography**
JS: 7190, 7211, 8295, 8309

**Mountain and rock climbing —
Fiction**
J: 401
JS: 129

Mountain bikes
JS: 12328

Mountain life — Fiction
J: 1474

Mountain lions
JS: 11503

Mountains
JS: 11739

Moving
S: 11189

Moving — Fiction
J: 327, 411, 1201, 1715, 1859, 1891,
1982, 2085, 2151, 2544, 4175, 4902
JS: 252, 334, 360, 378, 670, 1011,
1050, 1515, 1740, 2089, 2110, 4079,
5021, 5093, 5367
S: 1042
S–Adult: 999

Mozambique — Fiction
S: 3852

Mozart, Nannerl — Fiction
JS: 4074

Mozart, Wolfgang Amadeus
JS: 6552, 7465

Mubarak, Hosni
JS: 8062

Muckraking
S: 10007

Muir, John
JS: 7894
S: 7893, 7895

Multiculturalism
JS: 10426
S: 9882, 9888

Multiculturalism — Fiction
JS: 831

Multiple sclerosis — Fiction
J: 1446

Mummies
JS: 8713

Muppets
JS: 7507

Murder
J: 10203
JS: 3350, 9967
S: 10153, 10171, 11945

Murder — Biography
J: 7796
S: 8334

Murder — Fiction
J: 1191, 1613, 3473, 4856, 5170, 5495
JS: 445, 615, 1204, 1420, 1464, 1581, 1706, 1797, 2022, 2253, 3008, 3349, 3961, 4134, 4407, 4650, 5004–05, 5021, 5060, 5090, 5191, 5199, 5214, 5243, 5245, 5325, 5340, 5502, 5512
S: 575, 1231, 1551, 3452, 3594, 3713, 3915, 4101, 4174, 4404, 4443, 5143, 5264, 5360, 5370, 5415, 5457
S–Adult: 600, 639, 1934, 3973, 4715, 5227, 5277, 5503

Murray, Liz
S–Adult: 8310

Muscular dystrophy — Fiction
S–Adult: 2017

Musculoskeletal system
JS: 10865

Museums
JS: 8420, 8426, 9125
S–Adult: 9701

Museums (U.S.)
JS: 9524

Mushrooms
JS: 11375

Mushrooms, hallucogenic
S: 11397

Music
J: 8480–81
JS: 8476, 8479, 8482–83, 8488, 8499, 8511–12
S: 8299, 8475, 8478, 8496, 8498, 8510, 8513
S–Adult: 8500, 10490

Music — Biography
J: 7461, 7478, 7517, 7529
JS: 7225, 7456–57–58, 7460, 7484–85, 8173
S: 7218, 7455, 7459, 7488, 7497, 7516, 7550, 8243
S–Adult: 8240

Music — Careers
JS: 10496, 10501, 10510

Music — Fiction
J: 618, 663, 978, 2113, 3982
JS: 261, 361, 436, 469, 524, 577, 646, 1021, 1361, 1529, 1705, 1953, 2071, 4004, 4665, 6288

S: 716, 3638

Music — Poetry
JS: 6746

Music appreciation
JS: 8515

Musicals
JS: 8536

Musicals — Fiction
JS: 770

Muslim Americans
JS: 9599, 9986
S: 9976

Muslim Americans — Fiction
J: 862

Muslims — Biography
JS: 7826
S: 8253

Muslims — Fiction
J: 782–83, 934, 2215, 4103
JS: 347, 842, 2278, 3457
S–Adult: 4041

Mussolini, Benito
S: 8122

Muybridge, Eadweard
S: 7278

Myanmar (Burma) — Biography
JS: 8067

Myers, Walter Dean — Criticism
JS: 6968

Myron, Vicki
S–Adult: 9702

MySpace.com
JS: 10103

Mystery stories — Fiction
J: 121, 311, 423, 626, 774, 2331, 2491, 2715, 2990, 3000, 3907, 3958, 4071, 4803, 4862, 4996–97, 5007, 5027, 5031, 5041, 5055, 5059, 5062, 5064–65–66, 5070, 5099, 5118, 5130–31–32, 5134, 5144, 5146, 5148, 5167, 5171, 5178, 5190, 5193–94, 5201–02, 5211, 5213, 5219, 5229, 5231, 5252, 5266–67–68, 5270, 5283, 5290, 5290, 5310, 5316, 5351–52, 5354, 5359, 5371–72–73, 5382, 5384, 5387, 5397, 5405, 5409, 5420, 5423, 5429, 5432, 5438, 5442, 5444, 5450, 5452, 5473, 5479, 5488–89, 5495, 5510, 5700
JS: 42, 185–86–87–88–89–90, 216, 225–26, 402, 597, 740, 755, 786, 1348, 2308, 2378, 2564, 2741, 2743, 2763, 2952, 2973, 3227, 3268, 3285, 3343, 3548, 3722, 3904, 3963, 4004, 4033, 4294, 4400, 4476, 4638, 4657, 4771, 4795, 4933, 4998, 5000–01–02, 5004, 5015, 5024–25, 5033–34, 5044–45, 5047–48, 5050–51–52–53, 5058, 5060, 5063, 5069, 5071, 5073–74–75–76–77–78–79–80, 5084–85–86–87–88, 5091–92–93, 5097, 5104, 5107, 5110,

5115, 5119–20, 5123, 5127, 5129, 5139–40–41–42, 5145, 5147, 5149, 5156, 5158, 5160–61, 5163, 5169, 5173, 5176–77, 5184, 5191–92, 5195–96–97, 5204–05–06, 5214, 5216–17, 5221–22–23, 5226, 5230, 5235–36–37, 5241, 5243, 5245, 5247–48, 5255–56–57, 5259–60, 5265, 5269, 5272, 5274–75–76, 5278, 5280, 5286, 5293–94–95, 5297–98–99–00–01, 5303–04, 5306–07–08–09, 5311, 5323, 5325, 5328, 5330, 5338–39–40–41, 5344, 5348–49–50, 5353, 5363, 5374, 5374, 5379, 5381, 5383, 5385–86, 5388–89–90–91, 5399, 5403–04, 5407, 5414, 5416, 5419, 5428, 5437, 5439, 5443, 5446–47–48, 5451, 5453, 5455, 5461–62–63–64–65–66, 5472, 5474, 5477–78, 5480, 5486, 5490, 5497–98, 5500–01, 5504–05–06, 5515–16–17–18–19, 5677, 5685, 5789, 6066, 6220, 6254, 6441
S: 50, 97, 183, 223, 553, 601, 839, 2183, 2645, 3463, 3512, 3604–05, 3673, 3697, 3801, 4015, 4193, 4443, 4877, 4999, 5003, 5006, 5009–10, 5012, 5014, 5016, 5018–19–20, 5026, 5028–29–30, 5035, 5037–38, 5046, 5049, 5054, 5057, 5061, 5081, 5094, 5096, 5098, 5100–01–02–03, 5109, 5111, 5113–14, 5117, 5121–22, 5128, 5135–36, 5138, 5143, 5151–52, 5155, 5162, 5166, 5168, 5174, 5182–83, 5185–86–87, 5198, 5200, 5212, 5220, 5224–25, 5228, 5238, 5242, 5246, 5249, 5251, 5253, 5258, 5261–62–63–64, 5284, 5287, 5289, 5292, 5302, 5305, 5314, 5318–19, 5322, 5324, 5327, 5329, 5331–32, 5334–35, 5342, 5345–46, 5356, 5358, 5360–61–62, 5368, 5370, 5375–76–77–78, 5380, 5393–94–95, 5398, 5400, 5410–11–12, 5418, 5421–22, 5424–25–26–27, 5431, 5433–34–35–36, 5445, 5449, 5454, 5456–57, 5460, 5467–68, 5470, 5481–82–83–84–85, 5491, 5494, 5507, 5593, 5644, 5716, 5768, 5811, 5858, 6242, 9330
S–Adult: 586, 4577, 4696, 4931, 5008, 5011, 5017, 5022–23, 5039–40, 5082–83, 5105–06, 5116, 5137, 5150, 5154, 5159, 5175, 5180–81, 5188–89, 5208–09–10, 5227, 5239, 5244, 5250, 5285, 5288, 5291, 5296, 5315, 5347, 5355, 5357, 5369, 5401, 5408, 5430, 5493, 5503, 5514, 5626, 5830

Mythology
JS: 6839, 6841–42, 6845–46–47
S: 6854, 6938

Mythology — Asia
JS: 6792

Mythology — Celts
JS: 6843

Mythology — Classical
J: 2975
JS: 3626, 6849, 6851, 6853, 6855

Mythology — Fiction
J: 2348, 3796
JS: 3795, 6442

Mythology — Greece
J: 2975, 6848, 6857
JS: 2564, 3368, 3797, 6856, 6859–60–61
S: 3492, 3799, 6858

Mythology — Ireland — Fiction
JS: 2636

Mythology — Japan
S: 6836

Mythology — Rome
JS: 6863

Mythology — Scandinavia
J: 3114

Mythology — Scandinavia — Fiction
S: 2683

N

Nader, Ralph
JS: 7745

Nagasaki, Japan
JS: 8887

Namibia
J: 8975

Namibia — Fiction
JS: 41

Nannies — Fiction
JS: 246, 532
S–Adult: 1926, 4951

Nanotechnology
S: 11871, 11887

Nantucket (MA) — Fiction
S: 1109

Napoleonic Wars
JS: 8783

Napoleonic Wars — Fiction
JS: 2928, 4077
S: 3983

Narrangansett Indians — Fiction
S: 4286

NASA
JS: 11303, 11306

NASCAR
JS: 12276–77, 12279–80

Nash, Ogden
S: 7401

Nashville (TN)
S: 9916

Nation of Islam — Biography
JS: 7621

National Air and Space Museum (U.S.)
S: 11956

National Football League
JS: 12368

National parks (U.S.)
JS: 8460, 8694

National Rifle Association
JS: 10020

National security
JS: 10291

National Storytelling Festival
JS: 6329, 6418

National Trust
JS: 9253

Native Americans
See also Inuit; and specific Indian tribes, e.g., Cherokee Indians
J: 8640, 8654, 9149, 9257, 9257, 9272, 9282, 9982
JS: 8014, 8463, 8552, 8552, 9254, 9256, 9261–62–63, 9267–68, 9275, 9277, 9284–85, 9289, 9298, 9565, 12356
S: 789, 9259–60, 9264, 9269–70, 9278, 9280–81, 9970–71–72–73–74
S–Adult: 9255, 9286, 12319

Native Americans — Biography
See also Nez Perce Indians — Biography
J: 9271
JS: 7238, 7715, 7732, 7759, 8011, 8013
S: 7207, 7233, 7722, 7754, 7758, 7776, 7785
S–Adult: 8012, 8369

Native Americans — Cookbooks
JS: 12048

Native Americans — Fiction
J: 60, 113, 878, 913, 941, 957, 1492, 1579, 4185, 4187, 4189, 4198, 4212, 4303, 4408, 6275
JS: 16, 207, 336, 877, 1554, 2366, 4167, 4180, 4182, 4184, 4186, 4190–91, 4194–95, 4227, 4309, 5399, 5404
S: 789, 819, 838, 942, 3412, 4193, 4196, 4287, 4292, 5094, 5168, 5456, 5485
S–Adult: 825

Native Americans — Folklore
J: 6829
JS: 3304, 4182, 6822, 6825–26, 6828, 9256
S: 6823–24, 6830
S–Adult: 9255

Native Americans — Poetry
S: 6723, 6830

Natural disasters
J: 11013
JS: 8697, 9841, 11223
S: 11727
S–Adult: 11748

Natural disasters — Fiction
J: 6138
JS: 4347

Natural gas
JS: 11835

Natural history
JS: 11368, 11798
S: 9523, 11231, 11365

Naturalists — Biography
JS: 7873–74, 7894
S: 7891

Nature
JS: 6877, 7288, 9520, 10024, 11252, 11741
S: 11222
S–Adult: 11076

Nature — Poetry
S–Adult: 6684

Nature conservation — Fiction
S–Adult: 2283

Nature study
J: 11358
JS: 11360, 11366, 11599
S: 6905, 11359, 11365, 11426

Navajo Arts and Crafts Enterprise (NACE)
J: 10318

Navajo Indians
J: 10318

Navajo Indians — Fiction
J: 60, 5193
JS: 4188, 4191
S: 5224–25, 5485

Naval Academy (U.S.)
JS: 9771

Navy (U.S.)
JS: 8852
S: 9466, 9765

Navy (U.S.) — African Americans
JS: 9772

Navy (U.S.) — Biography
J: 7731

Navy SEALS — Biography
JS: 8244, 8387

Naylor, Phyllis Reynolds — Criticism
JS: 7007

Nazi Germany
S–Adult: 9063

Nazi Germany — Biography
JS: 8109
S: 8111

Nazis and Nazism
J: 9061
JS: 8786, 9062
S: 8112

JS = Junior High/Senior High; S = Senior High; S–Adult = Senior High/Adult

1960s
JS: 8793, 9465, 9467, 9472
S: 6343
S–Adult: 8520, 9475

1960s — Fiction
J: 835, 889, 4408, 4450
JS: 1933, 4788
S: 1083
S–Adult: 437, 795, 4413, 4417

1968
JS: 8788

1970s — Fiction
S: 2074
S–Adult: 4431

1980s
JS: 8794

1980s — Biography
S–Adult: 8314

1980s — Fiction
J: 3448
JS: 301, 4442
S: 2063
S–Adult: 2077

1990s
JS: 8794

1990s — Fiction
JS: 4438
S: 1667

19th century — Fiction
J: 3972, 4310
JS: 3960, 4085, 4337, 5667
S: 4244

Ninjas — Fiction
JS: 2820, 3293

Nissel, Angela
JS: 7789

Niven, Jennifer
S–Adult: 8314

Nixon, Richard M.
J: 9712
S: 9456

Noah's Ark — Fiction
J: 3776

Nobel Prize
JS: 8673

Nobel Prize — Biography
JS: 7814, 7885–86

Noguchi, Isamu
JS: 7279

Noise
JS: 11863

Nonconformists — Biography
JS: 7589

Normandy invasion
S: 8886

Norris, Michele
S–Adult: 8315

North America
See also Canada, Mexico, United States
JS: 9231, 9287, 9394, 11721

North Carolina — Biography
S: 7772

North Carolina — Fiction
JS: 1628, 4350, 4367, 4920

North Korea
JS: 9029–30, 9033

North Korea — Biography
JS: 8079
S: 8270

North Pole
JS: 9186, 9191

Northern Ireland — Fiction
S: 4067

Norton, Trevor
JS: 8317

Norway
JS: 8838

Norway — Fiction
JS: 1203

Norwegian Americans — Fiction
J: 1070
JS: 4318

Nova Scotia — Fiction
J: 4157

Nuclear accidents — Fiction
JS: 35

Nuclear energy
J: 11854
JS: 11855–56–57–58
S: 8286

Nuclear physics
JS: 11829

Nuclear power plants
JS: 11859

Nuclear war — Fiction
J: 1746
JS: 104, 2256

Nuclear waste — Fiction
J: 5266

Nuclear weapons
JS: 8887, 11988, 11994, 12001
S: 11985

Nunez, Tommy
J: 7980

Nuremberg trials
S: 8812

Nurses — Careers
JS: 10541

Nurses — Fiction
JS: 4453, 4568
S–Adult: 4020

Nursing homes
JS: 10128

Nursing homes — Fiction
JS: 1248

Nutrition and diet
J: 10950, 10964, 10967
JS: 10579, 10863, 10942–43, 10947,
10955–56, 10958, 10965, 10970–71,
10973–74, 11381, 12071
S: 10951

Nye, Naomi Shihab
S: 8318

O

O'Connor, Larry
S: 8319

O'Connor, Sandra Day
J: 7746

O'Dell, Carol D.
JS: 8320

O'Neill, Molly
JS: 8321

Oakley, Annie
JS: 7540

Obama, Barack
S: 7685
S–Adult: 6761

Obesity
JS: 10695, 10743, 10940, 10944,
10948–49, 10957, 10961, 10970
S: 10723

Obesity — Fiction
J: 1323, 1382, 1906, 2101
JS: 1361, 1396, 2091, 2126, 2587
S: 1965

Observatories
J: 11281
JS: 11270

Obsessive-compulsive disorder
J: 341, 10896
JS: 10917
S: 8177

**Obsessive-compulsive disorder
— Biography**
J: 8231

**Obsessive-compulsive disorder
— Fiction**
J: 1317, 1369
JS: 315, 1005, 1348, 1403
S: 1302

Occult — Fiction
S–Adult: 5254

Occupational guidance
JS: 10424
S: 10422

**Occupations and work —
Fiction**
IJ: 267

JS = Junior High/Senior High; S = Senior High; S–Adult = Senior High/Adult

P

Pachen, Ani
S: 8324

Pacific Coast (U.S.)
JS: 9530

Pacific Islands
S: 9043

Pacific Islands — Folklore
JS: 6798

Pacific Ocean
JS: 8861, 9044

Pacific Rim
JS: 8989

Page, Larry
J: 7812
JS: 7818

Paine, Thomas
J: 7748
JS: 7747

Pakistan
JS: 8309, 9005, 9008, 9010
S: 9004
S–Adult: 9031

Pakistan — Biography
S: 8296
S–Adult: 8167

Pakistan — Fiction
J: 3931
JS: 3942–43
S: 1234

Pakistani Americans — Fiction
J: 635, 862
S–Adult: 2251

Paleontology
J: 8622
JS: 8621, 8624, 8631
S: 8625

Paleontology — Fiction
J: 3769
JS: 5834

Palestine
JS: 9111, 9115
S: 9119–20

Palestine — Biography
J: 8176
JS: 8066
S–Adult: 8076

Palestine — Fiction
J: 4088
JS: 3979
S: 4527

Palestinian Americans
S: 8318

Panama Canal
J: 11899
S: 9163

Panama Canal — Fiction
S: 4156

Panic attacks
J: 10900
JS: 10928

Panther (motion picture)
JS: 9945

Panthers
S: 11499

Paper crafts
S–Adult: 12143

Papillomavirus
JS: 10754

Parakeets
JS: 11643

Paralysis — Fiction
JS: 1301

Paranormal phenomena
JS: 12185, 12209–10, 12225

Paranormal phenomena — Fiction
S: 3278

Parasites (biology)
S–Adult: 10699

Parenting
JS: 10987

Parents
JS: 11209

Parents — Fiction
J: 1065, 1533
JS: 1002, 1022
S: 4938

Paris (France) — Fiction
JS: 752, 4021

Parker, Bonnie
S: 7596

Parker, Cynthia Ann — Fiction
JS: 4309

Parkin, Joe
S–Adult: 8025

Parkinson's disease
J: 10768

Parks, Rosa
J: 7634

Parodies — Fiction
JS: 3430

Parthenon (Greece)
J: 8737
JS: 11895

Parties
J: 12005

Parties — Fiction
JS: 1854

Pascal, Blaise
S: 7899

Passover — Fiction
JS: 4546

Pasteur, Louis
JS: 7900–01

Paterno, Joe
JS: 7995

Patrick, Danica
J: 7949

Patriot Act (U.S.)
JS: 9845

Patriotism
JS: 9987

Patton, George S.
J: 7750
JS: 7749

Patton, Larry
JS: 8325

Pauling, Linus
JS: 7902

Paulsen, Gary — Criticism
JS: 7003

Payne, Lucille M. W.
JS: 8326

Pazira, Nelofer
S: 8327

PCP (drug)
J: 10621

Peace
J: 9654

Peace — Poetry
JS: 6633

Peace Corps — Biography
S–Adult: 8221

Peace movements
JS: 9638

Peace movements — Fiction
J: 2242

Pearl Harbor
JS: 8878, 9446

Peary, Robert E.
JS: 9191

Peary, Robert E. — Fiction
J: 4340

Peer pressure
JS: 11119, 11171

Peer pressure — Fiction
S: 2118

Pei, I. M.
J: 7280

Pekar, Harvey
JS: 7404

Pelosi, Nancy
JS: 7751

Penguins
JS: 11549–50

JS = Junior High/Senior High; S = Senior High; S–Adult = Senior High/Adult

7016–17, 7020, 7022–23, 7028, 7048, 7060–61, 7064, 7312, 9637, 10370
S–Adult: 6672, 6684, 6692, 6739, 6759, 6761

Poetry — Biography
J: 7304, 7316, 7352, 7392
JS: 6701, 7311, 7326–27, 7337–38, 7439–40, 7451
S: 7215, 7312, 7396, 7401–02, 7835

Poetry — Criticism
JS: 6620

Poetry — Fiction
J: 829
JS: 1727, 2157

Poets laureate (U.S.)
S–Adult: 6739

Poison
J: 10184
JS: 10058

Poker — Fiction
JS: 743, 6376

Poland
J: 9051

Poland — Biography
JS: 8161

Poland — Fiction
J: 4032, 4088, 4143, 4479, 4515
JS: 4066
S: 4500

Polar bears
J: 11492
JS: 11493, 11495
S: 11494
S–Adult: 11489

Polar regions
JS: 9184
S: 9193

Police
JS: 9721, 9721, 10187, 11182
S: 6740

Police — Biography
JS: 8199

Police — Fiction
J: 1613

Polio
J: 10757
JS: 10749

Polio — Biography
S: 7774

Polio — Fiction
J: 4418

Political activism — Biography
JS: 8044
S: 7583

Political activism — Fiction
JS: 1702

Political parties (U.S.)
J: 9749
JS: 9752

Politics
JS: 9747
S: 8533, 9750, 9782

Polk, James K.
S: 7687

Pollen
JS: 11414

Pollution
See also Air pollution; Water pollution
JS: 10039, 10042, 10055, 10090, 10101, 10114–15
S: 9535, 10070, 10118
S–Adult: 10098

Pollution — Fiction
JS: 1178, 2850

Polo, Marco
J: 7203
S: 7204

Polygamy — Fiction
J: 5511
S–Adult: 4234

Pompeii (Italy) — Fiction
J: 3775

Pony Express
J: 9403
JS: 9404

Pony Express — Fiction
J: 4248, 4306

Poole, Eric
S–Adult: 8330

Pop culture — United States
JS: 6901

Popes — Biography
J: 8117
S: 8116

Popular culture
J: 9461
JS: 8401, 8603, 8630, 9207
S: 8559, 9655

Popular music
S: 8496, 8505, 8527

Popular music — Biography
JS: 7531

Popular music — Criticism
JS: 8501

Popularity
JS: 8232

Popularity — Fiction
J: 353, 363, 449, 492, 672, 717, 758, 2121, 2191, 6291, 6313
JS: 250, 284, 416, 591, 611, 711, 1487, 1545, 1734, 1923, 2052, 3187

Population
S: 10127

Pornography
JS: 10225
S: 10231

Porpoises
JS: 11631, 11636

Portrait painting
S: 12119

Portraits
JS: 8432

Portraits — Fiction
JS: 199

Post-traumatic stress disorder
J: 10933

Post-traumatic stress disorder — Biography
S: 8864

Post-traumatic stress disorder — Fiction
J: 1415, 4418

Postpartum depression — Fiction
S–Adult: 294

Pot-bellied pigs
JS: 11648

Poverty
J: 10209, 10215
JS: 9251, 10212, 10218, 10221, 10258
S: 9072, 10206, 10214, 10216, 10219, 10223
S–Adult: 10213

Poverty — Fiction
J: 1001, 1292, 3930, 4334
JS: 464, 769, 933, 994, 1064, 1289, 1289, 1417, 2231, 3874, 4042, 4142, 4235, 4352
S: 2180, 2276

Powell, Colin
J: 7755
S: 7756

Prado, Edgar
JS: 8026

Prague (Czech Republic)
S: 4012

Prairie dogs
JS: 11472

Prayers
JS: 9558

Predictions
JS: 10249, 12184, 12214

Pregnancy
JS: 8340, 11004, 11010
S: 10985, 11180

Pregnancy — Fiction
J: 1007, 1563, 1662, 4371
JS: 349, 379, 500, 576, 682, 764, 1173, 1295, 1509, 1586, 1661, 1724, 1755, 1758, 1766, 1825, 1837, 1960, 2067, 2103, 2105, 4428, 6067
S: 1083, 1419, 4750, 4963
S–Adult: 359

Prehistoric life
J: 9149

Prehistoric life — Fiction
J: 3769–70
JS: 3049
S: 3120, 3768

Prejudice
JS: 9808, 11043, 11119
S: 9902, 9934

Prejudice — Fiction
J: 899, 2044, 2136, 2238, 4345, 4425, 4517, 5838
JS: 536, 659, 741, 802, 833, 851, 858, 873, 945, 985, 2246, 2453, 3091, 3696
S: 209, 803, 1225, 1607

Premenstrual syndrome
JS: 10732

Presidents (France) — Biography
J: 8129

Presidents (U.S.)
J: 7646, 7678, 7734, 9680–81
JS: 7566, 7573, 7575, 9682–83, 9686, 9688, 9759
S: 7565, 9685, 9754
S–Adult: 6921–22, 9661, 9687

Presidents (U.S.) — Biography
J: 7663, 7668, 7670, 7673–74, 7680, 7688, 7691, 7693, 7704, 7706–07–08
JS: 7566, 7584, 7644, 7649, 7651–52, 7655–56–57, 7660, 7667, 7669, 7672, 7675–76–77, 7681, 7684, 7690, 7695–96, 7698–99–00, 7702
S: 7569, 7645, 7647–48, 7650, 7653–54, 7658–59, 7661, 7664–65–66, 7671, 7679, 7682–83, 7685, 7687, 7692, 7694, 7701, 7703
S–Adult: 7662, 7686, 7697, 7705

Presidents (U.S.) — Fiction
J: 288, 635, 1280–81
JS: 759

Presley, Elvis
JS: 7543
S: 7542

Presley, Elvis — Fiction
J: 893

Press, Eyal
S: 8331

Pride and Prejudice — Criticism
S: 6954

Pride and Prejudice (novel)
S: 5727

Pride and Prejudice (novel) — Criticism
S: 6945

Priests — Fiction
JS: 476, 550

Primates
S: 11485

Primatology — Fiction
S–Adult: 5179

Primitive peoples
JS: 8644

Prince Edward Island — Fiction
JS: 1053, 1286

Princesses — Fiction
J: 2334, 2483, 2612, 2639, 2670, 4130, 4911, 4913
JS: 27, 2452, 3828, 3838, 4914

Printing
JS: 7111

Printing press
J: 11870

Prison — Biography
S–Adult: 8301

Prisoners of war
JS: 8879

Prisons
J: 10181
JS: 10163
S: 8375, 10167, 10188
S–Adult: 10146

Prisons — Biography
S–Adult: 8276

Prisons — Fiction
J: 1669, 4039, 4168
JS: 167, 1999, 2137, 3205, 4467
S: 1110, 2255

Privacy
JS: 9811, 10015

Private detectives — Biography
S: 8242

Prohibition (U.S.)
J: 9436
JS: 9435

Prohibition (U.S.) — Fiction
J: 5282

Proms (high school) — Fiction
JS: 406, 555, 587, 1981

Prophecies
JS: 12214

Prophets (Bible)
J: 9566

Prosopagnosia
S–Adult: 8352

Prosser, Gabriel — Fiction
JS: 4213

Prostate cancer
J: 10782

Prostitution
S: 9004

Prostitution — Fiction
J: 1973
JS: 88, 1205, 1552, 1846
S: 1765, 2198, 3287, 4443

Protestantism
JS: 9587

Protests and demonstrations
S: 7583

Protests and demonstrations — Biography
JS: 7798

Proust, Marcel
S: 3572

Psychiatry — Biography
JS: 7866

Psychiatry — Fiction
J: 5148
JS: 1864
S: 1608

Psychic abilities — Biography
S: 8208

Psychic abilities — Fiction
J: 4676, 4702, 4862
JS: 609–10, 2787, 3163, 4530, 4703, 5169
S: 736

Psychoanalysis
JS: 7870
S: 11068

Psychoanalysis — Biography
S: 7869

Psychology
JS: 11067, 11069
S: 11063, 11068, 11083, 11085

Psychology — Biography
JS: 7877

Psychotherapy — Fiction
JS: 2033

Puberty
J: 11019, 11019, 11028
S: 11074

Public service — Careers
JS: 10527

Public spaces
JS: 10308

Public speaking
J: 10387
JS: 10364, 10435

Publishing
J: 7108
JS: 7157

Publishing — Biography
JS: 7777

Publishing — Careers
JS: 10514

Publishing — Fiction
S: 5122

Pueblo Indians
J: 6829
JS: 6828

Pueblo Indians — Fiction
JS: 4179

Puerto Ricans
JS: 9960

JS = Junior High/Senior High; S = Senior High; S–Adult = Senior High/Adult

Puerto Ricans — Biography
JS: 8383
S–Adult: 7955

Puerto Ricans — Fiction
J: 785, 816, 917
JS: 1271

Puerto Rico
JS: 9169, 9173

Puerto Rico — Fiction
JS: 818, 915

Pulitzer, Joseph, II
JS: 7933

Pullman strike (1894)
JS: 10328

Pullman, Philip
J: 7406
S: 6963

Punctuation
JS: 7084

Punk rock — Fiction
S: 1918

Puns
JS: 10385

Puppeteers — Biography
JS: 7507

Puppets and marionettes
JS: 8606

Puppets and marionettes — Fiction
JS: 2498

Puritans
J: 8750

Putin, Vladimir
J: 8127
S: 8126

Puzzles
JS: 12178–79

Pyramids
JS: 8414

Q

Quadriplegics
JS: 10977

Quakers — Fiction
J: 1062
JS: 4283

Quantum physics
S: 11809

Quantum theory
S–Adult: 11819

Quebec (province)
J: 9158

Quebec (province) — Fiction
S: 1225

Quilts and quilting
JS: 12161

Quilts and quilting — Fiction
J: 4211
JS: 5328

Quinceañera (coming-of-age ritual)
JS: 9958, 10267

Quinceañera (coming-of-age ritual) — Fiction
J: 785, 787, 914
S–Adult: 784

Quotations
J: 7102
JS: 12204

R

Rabbits
S: 11469

Rabbits — Fiction
JS: 2296–97

Rabies — Fiction
JS: 4384

Raccoons
JS: 8316

Race
JS: 8660

Race horses — Fiction
S–Adult: 2133

Race relations
J: 9938–39
JS: 9746, 9795, 9825, 9889, 9897, 12316, 12358
S: 9893, 9898, 9904

Race relations — Biography
S: 7974

Race relations — Fiction
J: 380, 1852
JS: 649, 937, 3855, 4363, 4423, 4432, 4445, 4449
S: 4422
S–Adult: 4403

Race relations (U.S.)
JS: 9897

Race riots
JS: 9828
S: 9422

Racial prejudice
S: 8350

Racial prejudice — Fiction
JS: 5004

Racial profiling
JS: 9891

Racially mixed people
JS: 9887, 9895–96, 9980

S: 9892

Racially mixed people — Biography
JS: 7789, 8194, 8216, 8332
S: 8204

Racially mixed people — Fiction
J: 888, 912, 1852, 4248
JS: 1093, 1162, 1635, 3890, 4273, 6439
S: 1792

Racism
JS: 6985, 8660, 9808, 9899, 9901, 9921, 9925, 9930, 10369
S: 6867, 9880, 9885, 9893, 9908
S–Adult: 9449

Racism — Biography
JS: 8029

Racism — Fiction
J: 893, 946, 951, 2215, 2226, 4253, 4388
JS: 456, 833, 843, 866, 955, 1534, 1614, 2068, 2134, 4275, 4358, 4372, 4377, 4407, 4426, 4448
S: 209, 218, 665, 870, 939, 4326, 4368, 5036, 5136, 5689

Racism — Poetry
JS: 6676

Racquetball
JS: 12437

Radiation
JS: 11820

Radicalism
S: 9751

Radio
JS: 8599

Radio — Careers
JS: 10511

Radio — Fiction
JS: 572

Radioactivity
JS: 11820

Ragusa, Kym
JS: 8332

Railroads and trains
JS: 10328, 11975
S: 11974

Railroads and trains — Fiction
JS: 5079

Rain forests
JS: 11734–35–36–37
S: 9027, 10069, 11738

Rain forests — Fiction
J: 1105
S: 5424

Rainmaking — Fiction
S: 71

Raleigh, Sir Walter
J: 7205

JS = Junior High/Senior High; S = Senior High; S–Adult = Senior High/Adult

Ramadan — Fiction
J: 934

Ranches and ranch life — Fiction
JS: 160, 1111
S: 5543, 5569

Rand, Ayn
JS: 7407

Randolph, A. Philip
J: 7635

Rap music
JS: 8485, 8493, 8507, 8519, 8523, 8525
S: 8492, 8506
S–Adult: 8490

Rap music — Biography
J: 7519
JS: 7472, 7498, 7551

Rap music — Fiction
JS: 1887, 2189

Rape
JS: 10147
S: 11055

Rape — Biography
S–Adult: 8184

Rape — Fiction
J: 1339, 1499, 2059, 6291
JS: 549, 872, 1496, 5126
S: 1071, 1206, 1875

Rats
JS: 11477

Rattlesnakes
JS: 11441

Rawlings, Marjorie Kinnan
S: 7408

Ray, Rachael
J: 7934

Reagan, Ronald
J: 7688

Real estate development — Fiction
S–Adult: 5649

Realism
JS: 6990

Reality television
S–Adult: 8600

Reality television — Fiction
J: 78, 290, 297, 5099, 6240
JS: 326, 498, 561, 1029, 1347
S: 4962

Ream, Vinnie — Fiction
J: 4279

Reconstruction (U.S.)
J: 9414
JS: 9207, 9345, 9413, 9416, 9421

Reconstruction (U.S.) — Fiction
JS: 4277
S: 4327, 4343

Recycling
J: 12159
JS: 10101, 10120
S: 10122

***The Red Badge of Courage* (novel) — Criticism**
S: 6981

Red Cross — Biography
J: 7761
S: 7762

Red knot
JS: 11527

Red Shirt, Delphine
S: 9278

Reefs
S: 9027

Reeve, Christopher
J: 7544
JS: 7545

Reform school — Fiction
J: 505
S: 2093

Refugees
J: 8851, 9629
JS: 8843, 9165, 9627, 9632, 9855, 9955, 9959
S: 9645

Refugees — Biography
JS: 8275
S: 8220, 8253
S–Adult: 8158

Refugees — Fiction
J: 706, 869, 920, 4456, 4470
JS: 916, 2207, 2211, 2216, 2279, 3922
S: 2214, 2270, 4053, 5709
S–Adult: 2197

Reggae music
JS: 8504
S: 8491

Reggae music — Biography
J: 7532
JS: 7534
S–Adult: 7533

Regionalism
JS: 6990

Reichl, Ruth
S: 8333

Reid, Kim
S: 8334

Reincarnation — Fiction
J: 3173, 5283
JS: 2933–34
S–Adult: 273, 1331

Reiss, Johanna
J: 8335

Relationships — Fiction
JS: 1736, 6326

Relativity (physics)
JS: 11807

S: 7854, 11350

Religion
J: 9559, 9563, 9662, 9673
JS: 9550, 9552, 9552–53, 9553–54–55–56, 9558, 9561, 9564, 9570–71, 9619, 9937, 10001
S: 8647, 9544, 9557, 9588, 9588
S–Adult: 9575

Religion — Biography
S–Adult: 8069, 8328

Religion — Fiction
J: 621, 1769, 1815, 2151, 4930, 6459
JS: 661, 1031, 1774
S: 385, 648, 894, 1584, 1795, 2111, 3499
S–Adult: 530

Religion — Poetry
JS: 6632

Religious cults — Fiction
S–Adult: 1919

Religious life
S–Adult: 9573

Rembrandt van Rijn
JS: 7284

Rembrandt van Rijn — Fiction
JS: 3991

Renaissance
J: 8445, 8760
JS: 8454, 11885
S: 8768

Renaissance — Biography
S: 8119

Renaissance — Fiction
J: 3966, 4025
JS: 4033, 5725
S: 4111

Renewable energy
J: 10431, 10433

Report writing
J: 10368, 10386

Reproduction
J: 10849, 10984, 11007
JS: 11002, 11012
S: 11011

Reproductive rights
JS: 9713, 10990

Reptiles
See also Alligators and crocodiles
JS: 11430–31–32, 11694
S–Adult: 11433

Reptiles — Fiction
JS: 728

Resistance movement (World War II) — Fiction
J: 4493

Respiratory system
JS: 10866

Responsibility — Fiction
J: 4927

Reston, Hillary
JS: 8336

Restorative justice
S: 10205

Resurrection — Fiction
S: 5978

Revenge — Fiction
JS: 709, 5207
S: 1964

Revolutionaries — Biography
J: 8150

Revolutionary period (U.S.)
JS: 9302–03, 9312, 9318
S: 7592, 9304

Revolutionary period (U.S.) — Biography
J: 7717–18
JS: 7644, 7709, 7719
S: 7592, 7716, 7721, 7724, 9308
S–Adult: 7591

Revolutionary period (U.S.) — Fiction
J: 4221, 4225

Revolutionary War (U.S.)
J: 8782, 11995
JS: 9306, 9311, 9313–14–15, 9317
S: 9305, 9310, 9319, 9321

Revolutionary War (U.S.) — Biography
J: 7710, 7731, 7748
JS: 7604
S: 7574
S–Adult: 7790

Revolutionary War (U.S.) — Fiction
J: 4215
JS: 3608, 4220
S: 4217, 4222

Revolutions
See also specific revolutions, e.g., French Revolution; Industrial Revolution
J: 8992
S: 8672

Revolutions — Fiction
JS: 27, 77

Rhode Island — Fiction
J: 5282

Rhodes-Courter, Ashley
JS: 8337

Rhythm and blues (music)
JS: 8485

Rice, Anne
S–Adult: 7409

Richard III, King of England — Fiction
S: 5483

Richards, Susan
S–Adult: 8338

Richter, Charles
S: 7903

Ride, Sally
J: 7206

Right to die
JS: 10602

Riis, Jacob
JS: 7410

Rikers Island (NY) — Fiction
JS: 2137

Rio de Janeiro — Fiction
JS: 464

Riordan, Rick
J: 7411

Riot Grrrl movement
J: 9847

Riots — Fiction
JS: 4273

Ritalin (drug)
J: 10611

Rivera, Diego
J: 7285–86–87

Rivers
S: 8985, 11561

Rivers (U.S.)
JS: 11741

Rizal, Jose
JS: 8082

Road trips — Fiction
JS: 443

Roanoke Colony
S: 9296

Roanoke Colony — Fiction
J: 5670

Robbers and robbery — Fiction
JS: 283

Roberts, Monty
S: 11691–92

Roberts, Terrence
S–Adult: 9837

Robeson, Paul
S: 7546

Robin Hood
JS: 6809

Robin Hood — Fiction
J: 3805–06
JS: 3837, 4011

Robinson, Holly
S–Adult: 8339

Robinson, Jackie
JS: 7966–67

Robots
S: 8604, 11908, 11917

Robots — Fiction
J: 6027

JS: 343, 3701, 5428
S: 5862, 5884

Rock music
J: 8509, 8518
JS: 7240, 8486–87, 8489, 8497, 8511
S: 7495, 8502, 8517
S–Adult: 8520

Rock music — Biography
J: 7489, 7506
JS: 7473–74–75–76–77, 7487, 7520, 7526–27, 7530, 7541, 7543, 7549, 7555, 8528
S: 7488, 7504–05, 7525, 7548, 8530
S–Adult: 7523–24, 7535

Rock music — Criticism
JS: 8521

Rock music — Fiction
J: 382
JS: 284, 499, 629, 1385, 1600, 2128, 3467, 5605
S: 522, 704, 2241, 4441, 6451
S–Adult: 7511

Rockefeller, John D.
JS: 7935

Rockets
JS: 11298, 11302, 11314, 11864

Rocks and minerals
JS: 10094, 11729, 11742–43, 11746
S: 11747

Rodeos — Fiction
J: 1284
S: 5579

Rodriguez, Robert
J: 7547

Roller hockey
JS: 12388

Rolling Stones (musical group)
JS: 7549
S: 7548

Roman Empire
JS: 6933, 8743

Roman Empire — Biography
JS: 8742, 8749

Roman Empire — Fiction
JS: 3802
S: 174, 179
S–Adult: 5116

Romance
JS: 5528, 5743
S: 5689, 5698

Romance — Fiction
J: 239, 281, 328, 398, 692, 1139, 1259, 1405, 1474, 1564, 1582, 1642, 1650, 1754, 1786, 2079, 2120, 2508, 2572, 2597, 2667, 2699, 2729, 2843, 2886, 2993, 3597, 3905, 4028, 4071, 4149, 4159, 4226, 4265, 4290, 4469, 4610, 4803, 4821, 4893, 4909, 4944–45, 4977, 5170, 5526, 5530, 5537–38, 5571, 5587, 5601, 5606–07, 5611, 5630, 5630, 5647, 5655, 5660, 5670,

5700, 5707, 5719, 5732, 5741, 5750,
5753, 5785, 5787, 5790, 5794, 5797,
5805, 5816, 5821, 5829, 5835, 5838,
5841, 5930, 6766
JS: 39, 65, 131, 257, 317, 362, 368,
396, 497, 571, 609–10, 646, 724, 837,
907, 1350, 1506, 1536, 1552, 1591,
1595, 1601, 1615, 1634, 1700, 1733,
1748–49, 1798, 1805, 1898, 1903,
1913, 1913–14, 1929, 1994, 2007,
2009, 2050, 2092, 2105, 2147, 2227,
2269, 2381, 2396, 2439, 2534, 2598,
2660, 2762, 2803, 2845, 3096, 3106,
3167, 3238, 3339, 3378, 3438, 3575,
3684, 3691, 3811, 3875, 3969, 3971,
3993, 4054, 4066, 4077, 4100, 4104,
4115, 4122, 4127, 4191, 4229, 4289,
4312, 4320, 4333, 4369, 4383, 4436,
4473, 4624, 4670, 4704, 4707, 4713,
4770, 4781, 4886, 4896, 4907, 4949,
4968, 5015, 5341, 5521–22–23, 5533,
5535–36, 5540–41–42, 5547, 5549,
5551, 5553–54–55, 5557–58–59, 5562–
63–64, 5566, 5570, 5572, 5576–77,
5580–81, 5583–84–85, 5589, 5591,
5594–95, 5600, 5603, 5605, 5608–09,
5612–13, 5621, 5624–25, 5629,
5633–34, 5639–40–41–42, 5645, 5650,
5662, 5664, 5667, 5673, 5675, 5681,
5686, 5692–93–94–95–96–97, 5702,
5708, 5711–12–13, 5713, 5717–18,
5725, 5729–30–31, 5735, 5739, 5742,
5744–45, 5757–58, 5760, 5762–63–
64–65, 5775, 5775, 5780–81–82, 5789,
5791, 5795, 5798, 5807, 5810, 5819,
5823, 5826, 5828, 5834, 5839–40,
6130, 6137, 6257
S: 299, 303, 405, 440, 466, 468,
680, 1041, 1547, 1655, 1730, 1880,
1998, 2016, 2170, 2475, 2664, 2894,
3030–31, 3072–73, 3466, 3531,
3612, 3808, 3826, 3896, 3970, 3984,
4027, 4107, 4116, 4150, 4230, 4232,
4304, 4317, 4356, 4374, 4394, 4454,
4904, 4963, 5014, 5061, 5089, 5113,
5121, 5251, 5329, 5335, 5342, 5362,
5481–82, 5520, 5524–25, 5529, 5531,
5534, 5543–44, 5548, 5556, 5567,
5569, 5573, 5575, 5579, 5586, 5588,
5590, 5593, 5596–97–98, 5602,
5610, 5614, 5620, 5632, 5636, 5638,
5643–44, 5646, 5652, 5654, 5657–58,
5663, 5668–69, 5674, 5676, 5678–79,
5683, 5687–88, 5690, 5701, 5704–
05–06, 5709–10, 5714–15–16, 5720,
5723–24, 5726–27–28, 5736–37–38,
5740, 5747, 5751–52, 5755–56, 5759,
5766, 5768–69–70, 5772, 5786, 5792,
5796, 5799–00–01–02, 5804, 5808,
5811–12–13, 5815, 5817, 5822, 5824,
5831, 5836, 5858, 5906
S–Adult: 264, 433, 543, 632, 723,
763, 2872, 4013, 4206, 4891, 5083,
5175, 5527, 5545–46, 5550, 5552,
5561, 5565, 5604, 5615, 5617–18–19,
5626–27–28, 5631, 5635, 5648–49,
5651, 5656, 5665, 5680, 5684, 5691,
5703, 5733–34, 5748–49, 5754, 5761,
5767, 5771, 5773–74, 5777–78–79,

5783, 5793, 5806, 5814, 5818, 5825,
5830, 5832, 5837, 6101

Romance — Poetry
JS: 6753

Romania
JS: 9054

Romania — Biography
JS: 8139

Romanov family (Russia)
JS: 9090

Romanticism
JS: 6989

Rome
J: 8745–46, 8748
JS: 8741
S: 166, 8744, 8744
S–Adult: 8747

Rome — Biography
JS: 8092

Rome — Fiction
JS: 3997
S: 1141, 3790, 3792–93, 3801, 5436
S–Adult: 3800

Rome — Mythology
JS: 6855, 6863

Romeo and Juliet (play)
J: 6535
JS: 6539
S: 6534

Romeo and Juliet (play) —
Adaptations
JS: 3620

Romeo and Juliet (play) —
Criticism
JS: 7036, 7044, 7046

Romeo and Juliet (play) —
Fiction
J: 3055

Romeo and Juliet (play) —
Adaptations
J: 6540

Romero, Oscar
S–Adult: 8156

Roosevelt, Eleanor
J: 7689

Roosevelt, Eleanor — Fiction
S: 5425–26–27

Roosevelt, Franklin D.
J: 7691, 7693
JS: 7690
S: 7692, 9439

Roosevelt, Theodore
JS: 7695–96
S: 7694, 9420
S–Adult: 6922

Rosen, Christine
JS: 8341

Rosenberg, Isaac
JS: 6586

Ross, Betsy
S–Adult: 7790

Rowell, Galen
JS: 7288

Rowland, Mary Canaga
JS: 8343

Royalty
See also Kings and queens

Royalty — Fiction
J: 4029
JS: 20, 224

Rumors — Fiction
JS: 426

Rumspringa (coming-of-age rite)
JS: 9569

Runaways
JS: 10194

Runaways — Fiction
J: 1088, 1842, 2136, 3964
JS: 351, 538, 544, 675, 697, 954, 1055,
1069, 1218, 1673, 1920, 2108, 2206,
3667, 5240
S: 701, 1012, 1433, 1624, 1656, 2100,
3988
S–Adult: 2090

Running and jogging
J: 12400
JS: 12399
S: 12398, 12401, 12403
S–Adult: 12402

**Running and jogging —
Biography**
JS: 8011

Runyan, Brent
JS: 8344

Rural life
See also Farms and farm life
JS: 9979
S: 9437

Rural life — Fiction
JS: 6285
S–Adult: 2717

Russia
J: 9096
JS: 9090, 9092, 9099–00
S: 8093, 8174, 9083

Russia — Biography
J: 8127
JS: 7429, 8094, 8128
S: 8125–26

Russia — Cookbooks
J: 12073

Russia — Fiction
J: 125, 2417
JS: 1218, 4003, 4034, 4523
S: 735, 935, 3313, 4090, 4529, 6472
S–Adult: 6249

Russia — Folklore
JS: 6801

Russian Americans — Fiction
J: 794
S: 935, 6472

Russian Revolution
JS: 9085
S: 9083

Russian Revolution — Biography
J: 8118

Russian Revolution — Fiction
S: 4090

Rustin, Bayard
J: 7636

Ruth, Babe
JS: 7968–69

Rutherford, Ernest
JS: 7904
S: 7905

Rwanda
J: 8938, 8940, 8951
JS: 8931
S: 7863

Rwanda — Fiction
JS: 3843
S: 3653

Ryan, Donald P.
S–Adult: 8656

S

Saberi, Roxana
S–Adult: 7791

Sacagawea
S: 7207

Sacagawea — Fiction
J: 4291
S: 4197

Safety
J: 11013
JS: 11015–16

Safety — Fiction
JS: 106

Safety education
JS: 11046

Sagan, Carl
S: 7906

Sailboarding
JS: 12430

Saints
JS: 9585

Saints — Biography
JS: 8114

Salem (MA)
JS: 9290

Salinger, J. D.
JS: 7412

Salome — Fiction
JS: 4016

Salsitz, Norman
JS: 8161

Salt
S: 8686, 8957

Sam, Louie — Fiction
JS: 4353

Samburu (African people)
J: 8934

Same-sex marriage
JS: 9780, 9784, 10017

Samuels, Allison
S: 8345

Samurai — Fiction
JS: 5, 2721, 3485, 3897, 3902
S: 3885

San Antonio (TX)
S: 8318

San Antonio (TX) — Fiction
JS: 848

San Francisco (CA) — Fiction
J: 5157
JS: 1601, 4339, 5480
S: 4329, 5128

San Francisco earthquake (1906) — Fiction
J: 5157

Sanchez, Ivan
S–Adult: 8346

Sandburg, Carl
J: 7413

Sandell, Laurie
S–Adult: 7414

Santa Claus — Fiction
JS: 3307

Santana, Carlos
S: 7550

Sarkozy, Nicolas
J: 8129

SARS
JS: 10779

Sartor, Margaret
S: 8347

Sasaki, Sadako
JS: 8083

Saskatchewan — Fiction
JS: 4169

Sasquatch
JS: 12226

Satanism
JS: 9615

Satellites
J: 11308
JS: 11302

Satire — Fiction
S–Adult: 535

Satrapi, Marjane
S: 8166, 8348

Saturn (planet)
S: 11340

Saudi Arabia
J: 9126

Saudi Arabia — Fiction
JS: 3954
S–Adult: 5150

Saul, John — Criticism
S: 6966

Sayers, Gale
JS: 7997

Scandinavia — Fiction
JS: 4108

Scandinavia — Folklore
JS: 6804

Scandinavia — Mythology
JS: 6842

Scandinavia — Mythology — Fiction
S: 2683, 3043

Scandinavian Americans
JS: 9984

The Scarlet Letter (novel) — **Criticism**
S: 6967

Schaffer, Dylan and Alfred Alan
JS: 8349

Scheeres, Julia
S: 8350

Schindler, Oskar
JS: 8130

Schizophrenia
J: 10907
JS: 10756
S: 10934

Schizophrenia — Fiction
J: 1336, 1362, 1383, 1461
JS: 1276, 1355, 1386, 1444

Scholarships
J: 10416
JS: 10417

Scholarships — Fiction
JS: 1546

Scholastic Aptitude Tests (SATs)
JS: 10355
S: 10356

Scholastic Aptitude Tests (SATs) — Fiction
JS: 408, 707

JS = Junior High/Senior High; S = Senior High; S–Adult = Senior High/Adult

Service dogs — Biography
S–Adult: 8193

1700s — Fiction
J: 4212

1770s — Fiction
J: 4157

7th century — Fiction
JS: 3780

Sewing
JS: 12096, 12150–51, 12161, 12164, 12168–69–70

Sex
S: 11169

Sex — Fiction
J: 1737, 1785, 1949, 2094, 5630
JS: 619, 1825, 1907, 1914, 2042, 2141, 2175, 4914–15, 5563
S: 559, 700, 1567, 1760, 1782, 1792, 1847, 2016, 2066, 2187, 5654

Sex education
J: 11028, 11178
JS: 10581, 10990, 11017, 11022, 11024–25, 11027, 11030–31, 11039–40, 11045
S: 11029
S–Adult: 11026

Sex roles
JS: 11043
S: 10814
S–Adult: 10236

Sex roles — Fiction
JS: 1899, 3942
S: 1349

Sex scandals — Fiction
S–Adult: 305, 691

Sexism
JS: 9773, 12257

Sexism (U.S.)
S–Adult: 10235

Sexual abstinence — Fiction
JS: 1546

Sexual abuse
JS: 11047, 11050, 11052–53

Sexual abuse — Fiction
J: 1056, 1085, 1441, 1474, 2010
JS: 968, 1015, 1018, 1107, 1214, 1283, 1363, 1392, 1407, 1568, 1997, 2127
S: 487, 557, 1296, 1328, 1354, 1432, 1658, 2049, 2170
S–Adult: 1664, 4005

Sexual behavior
JS: 11017
S: 9851, 10997

Sexual behavior — Fiction
S: 748

Sexual discrimination
JS: 12257

Sexual harassment
JS: 11049, 11051, 11054

Sexual orientation
JS: 10240

Sexual orientation — Fiction
JS: 1767, 2174
S: 266, 1578

Sexuality — Fiction
S: 1523

Sexually transmitted diseases
JS: 10691, 10769, 10793, 11017
S: 10712, 10714
S–Adult: 10692

Sey, Jennifer
JS: 8001

Shackleton, Sir Ernest
J: 7208
JS: 7209
S: 7068, 9183

Shakespeare, William
JS: 6538–39, 7036, 7042, 7046, 7051, 7416, 9073
S: 6534
S–Adult: 7107

Shakespeare, William — Adaptations
J: 3621–22–23, 6535
JS: 3619

Shakespeare, William — Criticism
J: 6537
JS: 7043–44–45, 7049–50
S: 7035, 7038, 7047

Shakespeare, William — Fiction
J: 4089
JS: 441, 4024, 4052, 4075, 4098
S: 2728, 4015

Shakespeare, William — History and criticism
S: 7039

Shakespeare, William — Plays — Criticism
S: 7037

Shakespeare, William — Plays — Fiction
JS: 5599

Shakespeare, William — Poetry
JS: 6656
S: 7048

Shakespeare, William — Theater
JS: 7041

Shakur, Tupac
JS: 7551

Shamans — Fiction
J: 3947

Shape shifting — Fiction
JS: 2586, 3034

Sharks
JS: 11618–19–20–21
S: 11622

Sharks — Fiction
JS: 146

Sharpton, Al
JS: 7757

Sheba, Queen of
JS: 8084

Sheep — Fiction
J: 2861

Sheff, Nic
S: 8353–54

Shelley, Mary Wollstonecraft
J: 7418
S: 7417, 7419

Shelley, Mary Wollstonecraft — Fiction
S: 3968

Shepard, Matthew — Fiction
JS: 2253

Sherlock Holmes — Fiction
JS: 185, 3227

Shining Path (guerrilla group) — Fiction
S: 4172

Shinto (religion)
S: 9577

Ships and boats
See also Warships; Titanic (ship)
JS: 9450, 11982, 12405
S: 7876, 8172, 9241, 12404

Ships and boats — Fiction
J: 4510
JS: 1621, 4365
S: 4543

Shipwrecks
JS: 8777, 11980
S: 11978, 11983

Shipwrecks — Fiction
J: 137, 3892
JS: 4133
S: 126

Shoes
S: 12104

Shootings — Fiction
JS: 249

Shoplifting — Fiction
JS: 450, 642

Shopping — Fiction
J: 1467

Shopping malls — Fiction
J: 1660

Short stories — Criticism
S: 6928

Short stories — Fiction
J: 829, 855, 936, 1587–88, 2124, 2627, 2734, 2748, 2880, 3170, 3199, 4260, 4757, 4768, 4791, 4796, 4872, 4966, 5719, 5927, 6335, 6367, 6391, 6417, 6422–23, 6425, 6435, 6455–56, 6458,

JS = Junior High/Senior High; S = Senior High; S–Adult = Senior High/Adult

JS: 8780, 9249, 9252, 9317, 9326–27–28–29, 9335, 9355, 9361, 9914, 9918, 9924
S: 8781, 9331, 9789, 9844

Slavery — 20th century
S: 9838

Slavery — Biography
J: 7599, 7784
JS: 7622
S–Adult: 7792

Slavery — Fiction
J: 1852
JS: 4154, 4213
S: 4155

Slavery — Poetry
S–Adult: 6759

Slavery (U.S.)
JS: 9307, 9848, 9923
S: 9333, 9514

Slavery (U.S.) — Biography
JS: 7610, 7797
S: 7639, 7783

Slavery (U.S.) — Fiction
J: 120, 4215, 4219, 4226, 4241–42, 4794
JS: 830, 2835, 3828, 3857, 4148, 4186, 4201, 4223–24, 4228, 4233, 4236, 4238, 4245, 4268, 4277, 4358, 9322
S: 218, 806, 4146, 4243, 4257, 4263, 4344, 8914, 9323–24, 9906, 9913, 9915

Slavery (U.S.) — Memoirs
JS: 9944

Slavery (U.S.) — Poetry
JS: 6721

Sled dogs
JS: 12258

Sled dogs — Fiction
JS: 963

Sleep
JS: 10847, 10852, 10856–57

Sleep disorders
JS: 10771

Sleep disorders — Fiction
JS: 5459

Sleepwalking — Fiction
JS: 4650

Slowinski, Joseph
S: 7907

Slugs — Fiction
JS: 5987

Small, David
S–Adult: 8356

Smallpox — Fiction
JS: 4307

Smell (sense)
S: 10867

Smiley, Tavis
JS: 7553

Smith Center (KS)
S–Adult: 12361

Smith, Joseph
S: 7793

Smith, Patti
S–Adult: 7554

Smith, Venture — Poetry
JS: 7794

Smithson, Ryan
JS: 8357

Smokey Bear
JS: 11491

Smoking
J: 10652–53
JS: 10612–13, 10617, 10631, 10645

Snails as pets
S–Adult: 8175

Snakes
JS: 8937, 11437, 11440–41
S: 11438–39

Sneden, Robert Knox
S: 8471

Snipers
S: 11991
S–Adult: 8902

Snow
IJ: 12018
S: 11788

Snowboarding
IJ: 12418
JS: 12415–16, 12420

Snowboarding — Fiction
JS: 453

Snowmen
IJ: 12018

Soccer
J: 12423
JS: 9963, 12421–22, 12424–25–26–27
S–Adult: 9016

Soccer — Fiction
J: 1528, 6275, 6283, 6291
JS: 452, 725, 916, 1256, 1823, 3006, 3869, 6296–97–98
S: 1847

Social action
JS: 10211, 10250
S: 8665, 9464, 10018, 11220
S–Adult: 10253, 10260

Social change
JS: 10246

Social life and customs (U.S.)
S–Adult: 10264

Social networks
S–Adult: 11075

Social problems
JS: 10002, 10009
S: 9993–94, 10124, 10229, 11032, 11056, 11198, 11220

Social problems — Fiction
S: 4009

Social problems (U.S.)
JS: 10123

Social work — Biography
JS: 7613

Social work — Fiction
S–Adult: 5628

Sociology — Modern
S: 10127

Socrates
S: 8132

Soffee, Anne Thomas
S: 8358

Softball — Fiction
J: 663

Sojourner (Mars rover)
JS: 11343

Solar eclipses
JS: 11291

Solar energy
JS: 11842

Solar power
JS: 11847

Solar system
See also names of specific bodies, e.g., Mars (planet)
J: 11342
JS: 11337
S: 11345, 11347

Soldiers
JS: 9769
S–Adult: 8747

Soldiers — Biography
JS: 8039
S–Adult: 8160

Soldiers — Fiction
JS: 4054

Solon
J: 8133

Soloway, Elaine
S: 8359

Somali Americans — Fiction
JS: 916

Somalia
JS: 8935
S: 8925

Somalia — Biography
S: 8053

Somalia — Fiction
J: 4103
JS: 2211

Sone, Monica
JS: 8360

Songs
J: 8543–44
JS: 8541

Sontag Family
S: 8361

Sororities — Fiction
JS: 4622
S: 5377

Sosa, Sammy
J: 7970

Soul music
JS: 8508

Sound
JS: 11863

Soups
JS: 12037

South (U.S.)
JS: 9364, 9372, 9378, 9427
S: 8307, 9459

South (U.S.) — Fiction
JS: 872, 945, 4328, 4767
S: 218, 3013

South Africa
JS: 8961, 8963, 8970, 8972–73, 8976
S: 6506, 8059, 8960, 8974, 9892
S–Adult: 8967, 9573

South Africa — Biography
JS: 8057–58, 8060, 8064, 8961
S: 8056, 8059
S–Adult: 8055, 8061

South Africa — Fiction
J: 142, 6422
JS: 325, 737–38, 2210, 2267, 3847, 3854
S: 3846, 3858, 3862
S–Adult: 2239

South America
J: 9176
JS: 9180

South America — Cookbooks
J: 12070

South America — Fiction
S: 229

South America — Mythology
JS: 6839

South Carolina
S: 10338

South Carolina — Fiction
S: 457, 939, 1103

South Dakota
S: 8204, 9278

South Korea
S: 8375

South Korea — Cookbooks
J: 12045

Southeast Asia — Fiction
JS: 331

Southwest (U.S.)
JS: 9334, 9539
S: 9264, 9538

Southwest (U.S.) — Fiction
S: 5485

Soviet Republics
J: 9089

Soviet Union
JS: 8901, 9086, 9088, 9097
S: 9084

Soviet Union — Biography
J: 8118
JS: 8134, 8245
S: 8135

Soviet Union — Fiction
S: 2275

Space and time
JS: 11275
S: 11349, 11816

Space and time — Fiction
JS: 3111, 5944

Space colonies
JS: 11287

Space colonies — Fiction
JS: 5863, 6254

Space exploration
J: 11299, 11317
JS: 8892, 11274, 11287, 11289, 11297, 11300–01, 11306–07, 11310, 11313, 11335, 11337
S: 11304, 11319, 11328
S–Adult: 11315

Space exploration — Biography
JS: 7172

Space exploration — Careers
JS: 10463

Space exploration — Fiction
JS: 3212, 5982

Space fiction — Fiction
JS: 6067

Space race
JS: 11302

Space research
JS: 11312

Space shuttles
JS: 11303, 11305

Space stations — Fiction
S: 6065

Space travel
JS: 11298, 11314, 11316, 11316
S: 11319

Space travel — Fiction
JS: 5941
S: 354, 5935

Spain
J: 9154
JS: 9102

Spain — Biography
JS: 7256, 7281, 7283

Spain — Fiction
J: 3833

JS: 500
S: 2235, 3204, 4027, 4057

Spanish Armada — Fiction
J: 3975

Spanish Harlem (NY)
JS: 9513

Spanish Inquisition — Fiction
JS: 4140
S: 4057

Spanish language — Poetry
J: 6698
JS: 6667

Spanish Main
J: 9154

Spanish-American War
S: 9420

Speaking skills
JS: 11111

Special education — Fiction
JS: 1316

Spector, Phil
JS: 7555

Speech disorders — Fiction
S: 772

Speeches
JS: 6899, 6914, 6916, 8896, 9683, 9688
S: 9245, 9754
S–Adult: 6921–22

Speed skating — Biography
J: 8005

Spelling
S: 7085

Spelling bees — Fiction
JS: 848

Spencer (IA)
S–Adult: 9702

Spenser (fictitious character) — Fiction
J: 5364

Sphinx
JS: 8718

Spiders
JS: 11575, 11577, 11580, 11597

Spies and spying
J: 9639
JS: 9382, 9642, 10152, 10159
S: 9648

Spies and spying — Biography
JS: 9646

Spies and spying — Fiction
J: 125, 435, 1861, 5469
JS: 48, 89, 3269, 5160, 5163, 5221, 5232, 5312–13, 5459, 5499, 5833
S: 5271, 5273, 5314

Spilsbury, Sir Bernard
JS: 7908

JS = Junior High/Senior High; S = Senior High; S–Adult = Senior High/Adult

Spinal cord
JS: 10859

Spiritualism — Fiction
J: 4037
JS: 4240

Spitz, Mark
S–Adult: 8027

Sports
See also Extreme sports; individual sports, e.g., Baseball
J: 12229, 12229, 12229, 12234, 12246, 12268, 12272
JS: 7945, 8032–33, 10417, 10498, 12230–31, 12240, 12244, 12247–48–49, 12253–54–55, 12257, 12266, 12266–67, 12267, 12271, 12273, 12362
S: 10418, 12232, 12243, 12252, 12259, 12259, 12265, 12369
S–Adult: 12236

Sports — Biography
See also under specific sports, e.g., Baseball — Biography
JS: 7947, 8013, 8020, 8030, 8032–33
S: 7941
S–Adult: 8009, 8012, 8191

Sports — Careers
J: 10503
JS: 10497–98, 10502, 10508

Sports — Poetry
JS: 6705

Sports injuries
JS: 10979, 12264

Sports nutrition
J: 10964

Sports stories — Fiction
J: 1266, 2142
JS: 339, 6266, 6289
S: 819

Sri Lanka
JS: 9039

Sri Lanka — Biography
S–Adult: 8178

Sri Lanka — Fiction
JS: 2055, 3899, 5828
S: 2230

St. John, Lauren
S: 8362

St. Louis Post-Dispatch **(newspaper)**
JS: 7933

Stained glass
JS: 12020

Stalin, Joseph
JS: 8134
S: 8135

Stalkers — Fiction
J: 717

Stalking
JS: 10200

Stalking — Fiction
S: 1489

Stamps
JS: 12171–72

Standardized testing — Fiction
J: 2274

Stanton, Elizabeth Cady
J: 7571, 7637

Star Wars **(TV and motion picture series)**
J: 8574
JS: 2516, 6080, 6143, 6189, 6193, 8558, 8560, 8588, 8593

Starks, John
JS: 7981

Stars
J: 11353
JS: 11269, 11282, 11288, 11332–33
S: 11331

Starvation
JS: 8883

States (U.S.)
JS: 9214

Statistics
S: 11752

Stealing — Fiction
J: 545
JS: 2003

Steam engines
S: 11883

Steinbeck, John
JS: 7422

Steinbeck, John — Criticism
JS: 7004
S: 7014

Steinem, Gloria
JS: 11168

Steiner, Matthew
J: 8363

Stem cells
JS: 10808, 10825–26
S: 10804

Stepfamilies — Fiction
J: 244, 287, 327, 4278, 4673, 5420, 6764
S: 409, 1074
S–Adult: 3571

Stepfathers — Fiction
J: 1441

Stepmothers — Fiction
J: 278

Stepsisters — Fiction
JS: 3138

Stereotypes
JS: 10241

Steroids (drugs)
JS: 10641, 10647

Steroids (drugs) — Fiction
JS: 643, 6264, 6270, 6289

Stevenson, Robert Louis
JS: 3565, 6961, 11975

Stevenson, Robert Louis — Criticism
S: 6957

Stewart, Bridgett
JS: 7795

Stewart, Martha
J: 7936

Stewart, Shelley
S: 7556

Stine, R. L. — Criticism
JS: 6986

Stock car racing — Fiction
JS: 6308

Stock markets — Crash of 1929
JS: 9426, 10319
S: 9433

Stoller, Mike
S–Adult: 7229

Stone, Biz
JS: 7820

Stories without words — Fiction
JS: 3669, 3701

Storm chasers
S–Adult: 11780

Storms
S: 11773, 11775, 11779
S–Adult: 11780

Storytelling
JS: 6772, 10381
S: 6823

Storytelling — Fiction
J: 2401
JS: 2927, 4179
S: 683
S–Adult: 367

Stress (mental state)
J: 10895
JS: 10847, 10888, 10922, 11112

Strickland, Bill
S: 8364

Stringer, Lee
S: 8365

Student movements
JS: 9781
S: 8665

Student movements — Fiction
S–Adult: 535

Student rights
JS: 9743

Student-teacher relationships — Fiction
S: 1884

Students — Fiction
JS: 5272

Students for a Democratic Society
JS: 9472

Study abroad
S: 8920

Study skills
JS: 10353, 10374, 10393

Stuttering
J: 10576

Suberman, Stella
S: 8366

Submarines
J: 11995, 12003
JS: 11993

Suburban life
JS: 6885

Subways
J: 11897
JS: 11976

Subways — Fiction
J: 1943

Sudan
J: 8936
JS: 8911, 9627
S: 8950, 8958

Sudan — Biography
S: 8220
S–Adult: 8158

Sudan — Fiction
JS: 2216

Sui, Anna
J: 7937

Suicide
J: 10598, 10894
JS: 8344, 10847, 10883, 10890, 10893, 10939
S: 8177, 10921, 10937
S–Adult: 8293, 10603

Suicide — Fiction
J: 965, 1114, 1259, 1345, 1427, 1439, 2146
JS: 277, 1026, 1078, 1283, 1307, 1311, 1337, 1351, 1361, 1363, 1378, 1428, 1459, 1466, 1629, 1711, 1750, 1838–39, 1962, 2089, 2125, 2924, 5172, 5621
S: 1067, 1074, 1297, 1357, 1414, 1678, 3251

Suicide bombers
JS: 10278

Sukrungruang, Ira
S–Adult: 8367

Sullivan, Annie
JS: 7782

Summer camp — Fiction
J: 292

Summer employment — Fiction
J: 2619

Summer schools — Fiction
J: 328

Summit meetings
S: 8792

Sun
JS: 11346

Sundquist, Josh
S–Adult: 8368

Sunlight
S: 11361

Supercomputers
JS: 11909

Superheroes
JS: 3292, 3308, 3345, 3431, 3643

Superheroes — Fiction
J: 3459
JS: 2945, 3239, 3249, 3270, 3324, 3397, 3399–00, 3402, 3406, 3437, 3439, 3464, 3500, 3510, 3520, 3530, 3545, 3552, 3555, 3566, 3586, 3636–37, 3693, 3718, 3721, 3723, 3736, 3748, 5850
S: 3369, 3478, 3703–04
S–Adult: 3306, 3403, 3583, 5493

Superman (fictitious character)
J: 7118

Supernatural
JS: 12202
S–Adult: 12205

Supernatural — Fiction
J: 2555–56, 2675, 2834, 2965, 3116, 3417, 3585, 4575, 4586, 4597, 4617, 4640–41–42–43, 4655, 4659, 4675, 4738, 4757, 4765, 4768, 4775, 4792–93, 4796, 4803, 4806, 4821, 4842, 4846, 4861, 4882–83, 4889, 4893, 5067, 5316, 5611
JS: 215, 265, 2387, 2456, 2534–35, 2599, 2744, 2782, 3188, 3497, 3527, 3548, 3596, 3664, 3699, 3978, 4069, 4573, 4579–80, 4583–84, 4587, 4602–03, 4613, 4621, 4633, 4661, 4671, 4674, 4680, 4684–85, 4687, 4691, 4693–94, 4701, 4704–05, 4707, 4713, 4722–23, 4727, 4733, 4735, 4741, 4744, 4751–52, 4755, 4760, 4763, 4770, 4776, 4781–82, 4789, 4795, 4797, 4804, 4809, 4818, 4836, 4841, 4864, 4870, 4874, 4876, 4879, 4884, 4888, 4892, 4894–95–96–97–98, 5001, 5455, 5541, 6350, 12211
S: 2790, 2823, 3223, 3454, 3537, 3715, 4576, 4592, 4637, 4647, 4678, 4716, 4725, 4734, 4739–40, 4742, 4753, 4761, 4772, 4833, 5575, 6452
S–Adult: 2531, 2825, 4577, 4762, 4823

Supernaw, Susan
S–Adult: 8369

Supreme Court (U.S.)
J: 8649, 9704, 9742, 9804, 10228
JS: 9707, 9710, 9718–19, 9724, 9728, 9734, 9739, 9741, 9745
S: 9666

Supreme Court (U.S.) — Biography
J: 7746, 7760
JS: 7740
S: 7741

Supreme Court (U.S.) — Fiction
JS: 5197

Surfing
JS: 12432
S: 12429

Surfing — Fiction
JS: 6260, 6303
S: 1154

Surrealism
JS: 7257

Surrogate parents — Fiction
J: 1007

Surveillance
JS: 9642

Survival
JS: 45, 8777, 9182, 9450
S: 9195, 11071, 12348

Survival — Biography
JS: 8295

Survival — Fiction
J: 7, 52, 114, 117, 132, 137, 981, 3926, 4890, 5857, 6206, 6221
JS: 9–10, 14, 42, 53, 61, 72, 75–76, 79, 84, 88, 104, 108, 116, 338, 714, 5396, 5820, 5949, 5951, 6211, 6250
S: 11, 126, 134, 4256, 4566
S–Adult: 11984

Suspense fiction
S: 4829

Sustainable living
S–Adult: 10049

Swados, Elizabeth
JS: 8370

Swan, Robert
S–Adult: 8371

Swazi (African people)
JS: 8970

Swaziland
JS: 8970

Sweatshops
JS: 10022

Swift, Jonathan
JS: 7423

Swimming
J: 12431
JS: 8214, 12428

Swimming — Biography
JS: 8017
S–Adult: 8027

JS = Junior High/Senior High; S = Senior High; S–Adult = Senior High/Adult

Teenagers — Problems — Fiction
J: 1692
S: 3568

Teenagers — Romance
JS: 11144
S: 1975

Teenagers — Sexuality — Fiction
JS: 4433

Teenagers — Suicide
S: 10921

Teenagers — Violence
JS: 10160

Teenagers — Violence — Fiction
JS: 1615, 4043

Teenagers — Workers — Fiction
JS: 1911

Telepathy — Fiction
JS: 155, 5336

Telephones — Biography
JS: 7829–30

Telescopes
J: 11293, 11639
JS: 11270, 11318
S: 11268

Television
J: 1815
JS: 8597
S: 8604

Television — Biography
JS: 7558, 7860
S: 7859

Television — Careers
J: 10500

Television — Careers — Fiction
JS: 1736

Television — Criticism
JS: 8603
S: 8598, 8605

Television — Fiction
JS: 254, 926, 5086

Television — Journalism
J: 7125

Television — Production
S: 11947

Television — Programs
JS: 8595–96, 8601, 11948
S: 8594, 8602

The Tempest **— Fiction**
JS: 3131

The Tempest **(play) — Adaptations**
JS: 3624

Tennessee — Fiction
J: 1482
S: 4326

Tennis
JS: 7944, 12434–35–36

Tennis — Biography
JS: 8006–07, 8031
S–Adult: 8008

Tennis — Fiction
J: 6300
JS: 1063

Teresa, Mother
JS: 8086–87–88

Terezin (concentration camp)
J: 8868

Terkel, Studs
S: 7424

Terrorism
See also Cyberterrorism; Ecoterrorism; September 11, 2001
J: 7090, 10268, 10303, 10305
JS: 9114, 9114, 9636, 9801, 9810, 9833, 9989, 10269, 10272–73, 10275–76–77, 10279, 10281–82–83, 10289, 10291–92–93–94–95–96, 10298–99, 10302, 10304, 10306, 11016
S: 9017, 9604, 10270–71, 10274, 10280, 10287, 10300–01, 10307

Terrorism — Biography
S: 8047, 8143

Terrorism — Fiction
J: 2215, 2260, 4846
JS: 20, 29, 2232, 2257, 2266, 4000, 4571, 5125, 5173, 5232, 5392
S: 2199, 2230, 2282, 5165, 5496

Tesla, Nikola
JS: 7909

Test tube babies
JS: 10999

Tests and test taking
JS: 10354
S: 10356

Texas
JS: 9334
S: 10167, 11776

Texas — Fiction
J: 132, 233, 1017, 1900, 1973
JS: 832, 1718, 4445, 5353, 6278, 6360
S: 1182, 2005, 4246
S–Adult: 723, 763

Texas — Poetry
JS: 6703

Thai Americans — Biography
S–Adult: 8367

Thailand — Cookbooks
J: 12059

Thailand — Fiction
JS: 2227

Than Shwe
JS: 9038

Thanksgiving
S: 6338

Theater
JS: 8608, 8610, 8613
S: 7027

Theater — Careers
JS: 8608

Theater — Fiction
S: 1806

Theft — Fiction
JS: 5032

Themistocles
J: 8136

Theresienstadt (concentration camp)
S–Adult: 8817

Thermodynamics
JS: 11814

Theseus (Greek mythology) — Fiction
J: 2347

Things Fall Apart **— Criticism**
JS: 7015

Third World
JS: 8679

13th Amendment
JS: 9667

13th century — Fiction
JS: 3809

Thomas, Cullen
S: 8375

Thompson, Hunter S.
S: 7425

Thoreau, Henry David
JS: 7426–27–28

Thoreau, Henry David — Fiction
JS: 719

Thorpe, Jim
JS: 8013–14, 12356
S–Adult: 8012

Tibet
J: 9028
JS: 8990, 9034

Tibet — Biography
JS: 8068
S: 8324
S–Adult: 8070

Tibet — Fiction
S: 3948

Tigers
JS: 11506, 11506
S: 11505

Till, Emmett
J: 7796
JS: 6722, 9786, 9798

Timbuktu
S: 8957

Timbuktu — Fiction
JS: 74

Time and clocks
S: 11816

Time management
JS: 10344, 10461

Time travel
J: 2508, 2923, 3025, 4513, 5571, 6049, 6141
JS: 221, 2524, 2807, 4546, 5005, 6011, 6122, 6232, 11830
S: 2552, 2960, 5704, 6010

Time travel — Fiction
See also Fantasy; Science fiction
J: 2642, 2694, 2729, 2737, 2938, 2979, 3055
JS: 416, 1430, 2515, 2538, 2935, 2985, 2996, 3186, 3293, 3618, 4104, 5839, 5952, 6003, 6169, 6198
S: 2664, 3105
S–Adult: 5691, 6097, 6244, 6251

Timm, Bruce
JS: 7291

Tissue transplants — Fiction
S: 1304

Tipis
JS: 9268

***Titanic* (ship)**
J: 11981
JS: 11977
S: 11978–79

***Titanic* (ship) — Fiction**
JS: 4135, 4362
S: 5445

Tobacco
J: 10653
JS: 10612, 10617, 10638

Tobacco — Fiction
S: 3582

Toingar, N. Esaie
S: 8376

Tokyo
J: 9014

Tolerance — Fiction
J: 2294

Tolkien, J. R. R. — Criticism
JS: 6960
S: 6958

Tolstoy, Leo
JS: 7429

Tomboys
S: 6405

Toms River (NJ)
S–Adult: 12294

Tornadoes
JS: 11768

Tornadoes — Fiction
JS: 780, 1513

Toronto (ON) — Fiction
J: 1895

Torture
J: 9635, 9649

Torture — Fiction
JS: 5508

Tour guides — Careers
J: 10478

Tourette's syndrome
J: 10733
JS: 10682

Tourette's syndrome — Biography
J: 8231

Toxic waste — Fiction
JS: 1178

Toys
JS: 12110

Toys — Fiction
JS: 6399

Track and field
S: 12401

Track and field — Biography
J: 8010
JS: 8014

Track and field — Fiction
JS: 258, 1912

Tractors
JS: 11953

Trade
JS: 10330
S: 8686

Trademarks
JS: 10320

Traffic accidents — Biography
S–Adult: 8191

Traffic signs and signals
JS: 11888

Trail of Tears
J: 9276
JS: 9284–85
S: 9266

Tramps (U.S.)
JS: 9251

Tranquilizing drugs
JS: 10634

Transcendentalism
JS: 6989

Transgender people
JS: 11037
S: 11021

Transgender people — FIction
JS: 348, 1326, 1808, 2135

Transplants
JS: 10671

Transportation
J: 11951
JS: 11952
S: 11950

Transvestism — Fiction
JS: 1309

Traumas
JS: 10891

Travel
JS: 6913, 7178, 8385, 8683, 10023, 11914
S: 7204, 8264, 8312, 8692, 8957

Travel — Biography
S: 7191, 8258
S–Adult: 8157

Travel — Careers
J: 10468
JS: 10515

Travel — Fiction
J: 376
JS: 485, 541, 1372
S: 3988, 6892

Treasure hunt (game) — Fiction
JS: 317

***Treasure Island* — Criticism**
JS: 6961

Trees
JS: 11400–01–02, 11404, 11407, 11409–10–11
S: 11403
S–Adult: 11406

Trenka, Jane Jeong
S: 11213

Trials
J: 9804, 9829
JS: 9786, 9798

Trials — Fiction
JS: 607, 843, 4209
S: 171, 3862, 4412

Triangle Shirtwaist Factory fire
J: 9418
JS: 9419

Triangle Shirtwaist Factory fire — Fiction
J: 4330

Triathlons
J: 12261
JS: 12239

Triathlons — Fiction
JS: 6266

Trivia
JS: 12188, 12219

Trivia — Biography
JS: 7584

Trojan War
S: 8735

JS = Junior High/Senior High; S = Senior High; S–Adult = Senior High/Adult

Trojan War — Fiction
JS: 3625
S: 3794

Troy (Turkey)
JS: 3626

Trucks and trucking — Careers
JS: 10558

Trucks and trucking — Fiction
S: 3656

Trujillo, Rafael — Fiction
JS: 4145

Truman, Harry S
JS: 7698–99
S–Adult: 7697

Trussoni, Danielle
S: 8377

Truth, Sojourner
JS: 7638

Tsunamis
JS: 8697, 11806
S: 11805

Tsunamis — Fiction
J: 117

Tuaolo, Esera
S: 7998

Tuberculosis
J: 10740
JS: 10701, 10794

Tuberculosis — Fiction
J: 4147
JS: 1380

Tubman, Harriet
S: 7639

Tubu (African people)
JS: 8911

Tundras
J: 11731

Turing, Alan
J: 7910–11
JS: 7912

Turkana (African people)
J: 8936

Turkey
JS: 8739

Turkey — Fiction
JS: 3957
S: 2233, 2240

Turkmenistan
JS: 9081

Turner, Nat — Fiction
S: 4243

Turtles and tortoises
JS: 11442–43, 11445
S: 11444

Tuscany (Italy) — Fiction
JS: 5608

Tuskegee Airmen
S: 9447
S–Adult: 9449

Tutankhamen, King
JS: 8719–20

Tutu, Desmond
JS: 8064

TWA Flight 800 (disaster)
J: 11961

Twain, Mark
J: 7430
JS: 7431, 7433–34
S: 7432

Twain, Mark — Criticism
S: 6984

12th century — Fiction
JS: 2955

Twelfth Night
S: 7040

20th century
J: 9469
JS: 8785, 8791
S: 8899, 9206, 9238, 9245, 11239
S–Adult: 8790

21st century
J: 8906
JS: 10249, 12184

Twins — Fiction
J: 651, 2936, 3071, 4641, 5359, 6049
JS: 348, 764, 1160, 1293, 1922, 2075,
2092, 3285, 4119, 4337, 4841, 4899,
5233, 5336, 5500, 5820, 6094, 6184
S: 1049, 1108, 3848, 4393
S–Adult: 2958

Two Trees, Joe
S: 8378

Tyrants — Biography
J: 8043

U

UFOs
JS: 12186
S: 12206

UFOs — Fiction
S–Adult: 437

Uganda
J: 8936
JS: 9631

Uganda — Fiction
J: 3851
JS: 3856

Ukrainian Americans — Fiction
JS: 962

Ulmann, Doris
JS: 7292

Umbrell, Colby
S–Adult: 8196

Umpires (baseball)
JS: 12302

Umrigar, Thrity N.
S–Adult: 8379

Uncle Tom's Cabin — Criticism
S: 7008

Uncles — Fiction
JS: 623

Underground Railroad
JS: 4238, 9329
S: 7639, 9331

Underground Railroad — Biography
JS: 7628

Underground Railroad — Fiction
J: 4226, 4241

Underwater exploration
JS: 11599, 11980

Underwater exploration — Fiction
JS: 177

Unemployment
JS: 9251

Unferth, Deb Olin
S–Adult: 8380

Unicorns
S–Adult: 6844

Unicorns — Fiction
JS: 2358, 2393, 2997

United Kingdom
S: 9074

United Kingdom — Biography
J: 8098

United Kingdom — Fiction
JS: 3780, 5320

United Nations
JS: 9622–23
S: 9624

United Nations — Biography
S: 8048

United States
J: 8618, 9217, 9224, 9681
JS: 7582, 9153, 9198, 9198, 9202,
9212–13, 9215, 9218–19, 9222–23,
9226–27–28, 9230, 9232, 9232–33–34,
9237, 9250, 9253, 9289, 9471, 10132,
10226, 11238, 11376
S: 7080, 9203–04, 9221, 9241, 9325,
10324

United States — Biography
JS: 7572, 7595

United States — Fiction
S: 4218

JS = Junior High/Senior High; S = Senior High; S–Adult = Senior High/Adult

Veterinarians — Fiction
J: 4361
S: 4110

Victoria, Queen of England
J: 9076
S: 8138

Victoria, Queen of England — Fiction
JS: 4064

Victorian Age
J: 9076
JS: 8776
S: 6948

Victorian Age — Fiction
J: 2572, 3964, 4026, 4037
JS: 3961, 3971, 4095, 4142, 5275, 6454
S: 3962, 5361

Video games
J: 12438
S: 11941

Video games — Careers
JS: 10489, 10551, 10554

Video games — Fiction
J: 5333
S: 2620

Video recordings
J: 12149

Viesturs, Ed
JS: 7211

Vietnam
J: 9498
JS: 9026
S: 9025

Vietnam — Biography
S: 8074

Vietnam — Fiction
JS: 3913

Vietnam Veterans Memorial
J: 7274

Vietnam War
J: 9486, 9498
JS: 8278, 8897, 8910, 9026, 9467, 9484, 9487, 9490, 9496, 9506, 9719
S: 9485, 9488, 9494, 9499, 9501–02–03, 9505, 9507

Vietnam War — Biography
JS: 7742
S: 11960

Vietnam War — Fiction
J: 3893, 4551, 4556, 4569, 5007
JS: 1908, 3440, 4552, 4554, 4559–60, 4562, 4565, 4568
S: 2074, 4549, 4557, 4563
S–Adult: 4553, 4567

Vietnamese Americans
JS: 7992

Vietnamese Americans — Biography
J: 8363

S: 8313

Vietnamese Americans — Fiction
JS: 832–33

Vikings
J: 9101
JS: 8705

Vikings — Fiction
J: 3771
JS: 3773, 3783, 3810–11
S: 3412

Vincent, Erin
JS: 8384

Violence
J: 10000, 10016
JS: 10014, 10125, 10131, 10160, 10165–66
S: 6747, 10154

Violence — Biography
JS: 8201–02

Violence — Fiction
J: 1191, 2273, 2284
JS: 518, 973, 1037, 1675, 1798, 2217, 2219, 2236, 3329
S: 1303, 1332, 4172

Violins — Fiction
JS: 577

Virginity — Fiction
S: 2015

Virtual reality
S–Adult: 11911

Virtual reality — Fiction
J: 5936
S: 2620

Viruses
J: 10710
JS: 10722

Viruses (computer)
JS: 11919

Visions — Fiction
J: 4702

Vitamins
JS: 10956

Vivaldi, Antonio
J: 7466

Vivariums
JS: 11694

Vlad III, Prince of Wallachia
JS: 8139

Vocabulary
JS: 1016
S: 10378

Vocational guidance
JS: 10420, 10440, 10451, 10457, 10461, 10475, 10496, 10505–06, 10509, 10514–15–16, 10518, 10539, 10541, 10558
S: 10481, 10523, 10544

Voigt, Cynthia — Criticism
JS: 7000

Volcanoes
J: 11724
JS: 8697, 11725
S: 11726–27

Volcanoes — Fiction
JS: 176

Volleyball — Biography
S–Adult: 8024

Volunteerism
J: 10252
JS: 9700, 10095, 10245, 10248, 10250, 10254–55–56–57
S: 10251

Volunteerism — Fiction
J: 1665, 2245

Vonnegut, Kurt
S: 7435

Voodooism — Fiction
J: 4866

Voting
JS: 9760

Voting rights
J: 9829

Voting Rights Act
JS: 9787

Voyages and travels
S: 8668

W

Wa Wamwere, Koigi
S: 8952

Wakeman, Sarah Rosetta
JS: 9348

Wales
S: 6542, 6657, 8758

Wales — Biography
JS: 7328

Wales — Fiction
JS: 3809, 4058
S: 1067, 5302
S–Adult: 4068, 5475

Walker, Jerald
S–Adult: 8386

Walker, Madam C. J.
JS: 7938

Walker, Mary
JS: 7913

Wallenberg, Raoul
JS: 8140–41

Wallenda, Delilah
JS: 7557

Wang, Vera
J: 7939

War
See also specific battles and wars, e.g.,
Antietam, Battle of; World War II
J: 6915, 8782, 9629, 9647, 9659
JS: 6365, 8680, 8787, 8890, 9218,
9227, 9628, 9631, 9633, 9643, 9653,
9776, 9834
S: 3334, 8693, 9625, 9637, 9640–41,
9651, 9655
S–Adult: 9650, 9657

War — Biography
JS: 8039
S: 8376

War — Fiction
J: 3926, 4435
JS: 21, 96, 1212, 2266, 2916, 3147,
3865, 3911, 4034, 4091, 4530, 4570,
4991, 6365
S: 2271, 2280, 3356, 3935
S–Adult: 3950

War — Poetry
J: 6610
JS: 6365, 6622, 6633

War games — Fiction
JS: 73

War of 1812
JS: 9332

War of 1812 — Fiction
JS: 4229

War of the Roses — Fiction
JS: 4104

War widows — Fiction
S–Adult: 1153

Warhol, Andy
JS: 7298

Warren, Earl
J: 7760

Wars of the Roses
S: 9078

Wars of the Roses — Fiction
JS: 195

Warships
JS: 11992

Wasdin, Howard E.
JS: 8387

Washington (DC)
JS: 9515

Washington (DC) — Fiction
S: 5327
S–Adult: 1240

Washington (state) — Fiction
S: 4412

Washington Monument (DC)
JS: 9512

Washington, Booker T.
JS: 7640

Washington, DC
JS: 9444

Washington, DC — Fiction
JS: 425

Washington, George
J: 7704, 7706–07
JS: 7702, 9313
S: 7701, 7703
S–Adult: 7705

Washington, George — Fiction
J: 4225
S: 4207

Washington, John
JS: 7797

Waste (economics)
S–Adult: 10207

Waste recycling
JS: 10119, 10121

Water
J: 10063
JS: 10036–37, 10112, 10968, 11740
S: 11782–83
S–Adult: 10050

Water conservation
S–Adult: 10107

Water cycle
S: 11784

Water pollution
JS: 11741
S: 11783

Water supply
S: 11784

Watercolor painting
JS: 12116, 12124, 12132

Watergate affair
J: 9712
S: 9456

Watt, James
S: 11883

Wealth
JS: 10129

Wealth — Fiction
J: 545
JS: 275, 4980
S: 285, 1089

Weapons
J: 11989, 12000
JS: 11987, 11999, 12004

Weapons — Fiction
S: 6215

Weapons of mass destruction
J: 11997, 12002

Weather
J: 11786
JS: 11769, 11785, 11789, 11791,
11791–92, 11792–93, 11793, 11793
S: 11773, 11787, 11790

Weatherman (organization)
JS: 7798

Weaving
S: 12006

Weddings — Fiction
JS: 5560
S: 4937

Wegener, Alfred
JS: 7914

Weight lifting
S: 12263

Weight loss — Biography
S–Adult: 8277

Weight problems
J: 10946, 10962–63, 10972

Weight problems — Fiction
J: 1723, 1892
JS: 539, 1347, 1399, 1472, 1969

Weight-loss programs
J: 10946, 10963

Weinstein, Lauren
J: 8388

Weisskopf, Michael
S: 8908

Weizmann, Chaim
J: 9112

Welfare (U.S.)
J: 10209
JS: 10210
S: 10216

Wells, Ida B.
J: 7223, 7641

Wells, Jeff
S–Adult: 8389

Werewolves — Fiction
J: 43, 2555–56, 2742, 4631, 4786, 4834
JS: 2512, 2514, 2992, 3101, 4599,
4636, 4736, 4801, 4854, 4863, 6163
S–Adult: 4677, 4745

West (U.S.)
J: 9982
JS: 6380, 8252, 9371, 9388, 9404–05,
11401
S: 9402, 9406, 9525

West (U.S.) — Fiction
JS: 12, 15, 131, 696, 4298, 6380
S: 13, 4287, 4323, 6372

West (U.S.) — Poetry
JS: 6752

West Africa — Fiction
JS: 74

**West Indian Americans —
Fiction**
JS: 865

West Virginia — Fiction
JS: 630, 2181
S–Adult: 1663

Westerns — Fiction
J: 128, 4290
JS: 12, 4289, 4293, 5404
S: 3645, 5813
S–Adult: 5818

Wetlands
JS: 9180

Wexler, Nancy
J: 7915

Whales
JS: 8214, 11624–25, 11627, 11629, 11631, 11633, 11636
S: 11623, 11626, 11630, 11632, 11635

Whaling
J: 9931
JS: 9152, 11563
S: 9337

Whaling — Fiction
J: 3491

Wharton, Edith
J: 7436

Wharton, Edith — Criticism
S: 6995

Wheatley, Phillis
JS: 7437

Whedon, Joss
S: 7438

Wheelchair basketball — Biography
JS: 8267

Wheelchairs — Fiction
S: 3909

White House (Washington, DC)
J: 9511

White House press secretary
S: 9684

White-water rafting — Fiction
JS: 2023

White, Shane
JS: 8390

Whitfield, Simon
JS: 8030

Whitman, Walt
JS: 6756, 7439–40

Whitman, Walt — Fiction
S: 340

Whitman, Walt — Poetry
JS: 6710

Whittling
JS: 12175

Wiccans — Fiction
S: 5410–11–12

Wild horses
JS: 11474

Wild West shows — Biography
JS: 7540

Wilder, Laura Ingalls
JS: 7441

Wildfires
S: 10086

Wildfires — Fiction
JS: 564

Wildflowers
JS: 11415, 11417

Wildlife conservation
JS: 10149, 11517, 11563
S: 11553, 11557

Wildlife photography
JS: 11493, 11495

Wildlife photography — Careers
J: 10507

Wildlife rehabilitation — Biography
S–Adult: 8246

Wildlife rescue — Fiction
JS: 1029

Wilkerson, Cathy
JS: 7798

Wilkins, Hubert
S–Adult: 7212

William the Conqueror
S: 9068

Williams, Evan
JS: 7820

Williams, Rita
JS: 8392

Williams, Stanley Tookie
S: 7799

Williams, Ted
JS: 7971

Williams, Tennessee
JS: 7442

Williams, William Carlos
JS: 7066

Wilson, August — Criticism
S: 7054

Wilson, G. Willow
S–Adult: 8393

Wilson, Woodrow
J: 7708

Wind
S: 11764

Winfrey, Oprah
JS: 7558

Winter — Fiction
J: 3012

Winter sports — Fiction
JS: 333

Winthrop, John
J: 8750

Wishes — Fiction
J: 3054
JS: 2442

Wit and humor
JS: 6864, 6869, 6876, 6883, 6898, 6906
S: 6887, 6907–08

Wit and humor — Fiction
JS: 6870

Wit and humor — Poetry
JS: 6719–20

Witchcraft
J: 12203
JS: 12190, 12195
S: 6565

Witchcraft — Fiction
J: 2576, 2576, 3190–91, 4642
JS: 2837, 3225, 4194, 4209, 4816

Witchcraft — Folklore
JS: 6837

Witchcraft trials
JS: 9290, 9297

Witchcraft trials — Fiction
JS: 4204, 4209
S: 4203

Witches — Fiction
J: 2404, 3012, 3087, 4689, 4959
JS: 2598, 2611, 2719, 3009, 3050, 3093, 3108, 3225, 4625
S–Adult: 2825, 4632

Witness protection program — Fiction
JS: 5584

Wizards — Fiction
J: 2349, 3192
JS: 2484
S: 3458

Wolfe, Swain
JS: 7443

Wolff, Mishna
S–Adult: 8394

Wolff, Tobias
S: 7444

Wolof (African people)
JS: 8983

Wolves
JS: 11507, 11509–10–11–12
S: 11508

Wolves — Fiction
JS: 148, 162, 3109

Women
J: 9224, 9441
JS: 9200, 9212, 9220, 9223, 9225, 10239, 10241, 10246
S: 6897, 8687, 8964, 9210–11, 9557, 10188
S–Adult: 10235, 12319

Women — Abuse
S: 9999

JS = Junior High/Senior High; S = Senior High; S–Adult = Senior High/Adult

Women — Afghanistan
JS: 9024

Women — Armed forces
JS: 8399

Women — Artists
S: 8439

Women — Authors
JS: 7213, 7332, 7361, 7379, 7415,
7437, 7441
S–Adult: 7005

Women — Automobile racing
S: 12278

Women — Aviators
J: 7199
S: 7186, 7200

Women — Biography
J: 7171, 7174, 7206, 7274, 7304,
7307, 7309, 7316, 7321, 7371, 7378,
7389, 7399, 7418, 7436, 7493, 7500,
7503, 7510, 7519, 7539, 7587, 7606,
7612, 7627, 7634, 7637, 7643, 7713,
7764, 7784, 7833–34, 7840–41, 7843,
7871, 7875, 7880, 7915, 7929, 7934,
7936–37, 7939, 7949, 8004, 8023,
8034, 8098, 8165
JS: 7166–67, 7181, 7187–88, 7194,
7219, 7221, 7246–47, 7268, 7302,
7306, 7308, 7314, 7320, 7337, 7340,
7364, 7366, 7380, 7383, 7388, 7390,
7395, 7407, 7464, 7502, 7514, 7536,
7540, 7552, 7558, 7568, 7580, 7588,
7594, 7607, 7609, 7613, 7626, 7629,
7642, 7751–52, 7765, 7770, 7778,
7781, 7798, 7813, 7821–22, 7824,
7868, 7873–74, 7877–78, 7881,
7884–85–86, 7913, 7945, 7947, 8001,
8007, 8017, 8032–33, 8037, 8051,
8054, 8067, 8071, 8081, 8086, 8088,
8100, 8106, 8153–54–55, 8197, 8212,
8226, 8237, 8259, 8269, 8305, 8326
S: 7303, 7313, 7339, 7375–76, 7417,
7419, 7592, 7639, 7842, 7863–64,
7867, 8038, 8089, 8093, 8101, 8163,
8186, 8209, 8238, 8248, 8253, 8298,
8361
S–Adult: 6987, 7305, 7409, 7790–91,
8009, 8024, 8167, 8169, 8184, 8206,
8276–77, 8287, 8328, 8369, 8379

Women — Biography — Fiction
JS: 7836

Women — Business
JS: 7938
S: 7925

Women — Careers
J: 10503
JS: 10463, 10480, 10533, 10556
S: 9992, 10421

Women — Fiction
J: 4096, 4531
JS: 347, 4152, 5662, 6341
S: 3841, 3965, 5867
S–Adult: 295, 749, 4335, 6392

Women — Mathematicians
J: 7806

Women — Military careers
JS: 9506, 9773

Women — Pioneers
S: 9408

Women — Poetry
JS: 6691

Women — Poets
JS: 6600, 6680–81
S: 6726

Women — Politicians
J: 8042
JS: 7588, 7601

Women — Scientists
J: 7806

Women — Sea stories
S: 9211

Women — Self-defense
JS: 12394

Women — Sex roles
S: 6405

Women — Social attitudes
S: 11032

Women — Sports
J: 12268, 12324
JS: 12315
S: 12265, 12429

Women — 20th century
JS: 7167

Women — Workers
JS: 9200, 10419, 10480

Women (U.S.)
JS: 9223
S: 9210, 9221

Women authors
S: 6926

Women executives (U.S.)
S–Adult: 7603

Women in the military
JS: 9769

Women physicians — Fiction
S–Adult: 4171

Women's rights
J: 9812, 9829
JS: 9790, 9814, 9817, 11005
S: 8053, 9035, 9803, 9846, 9849,
10244
J: 7571
JS: 9797, 9805

Women's rights — Biography
J: 7606, 7637, 7641, 7643
JS: 7626, 7642
S: 7633, 8296, 9935
S–Adult: 7564

Women's rights — Fiction
J: 3863, 4158
JS: 3938

Women's suffrage
JS: 9807

Women's suffrage — Fiction
JS: 4346

Women's suffrage — Poetry
JS: 6767

Woodcarving
JS: 12175

Woodhull, Victoria
J: 7643
JS: 7642

Woods, Tiger
JS: 12375
S: 12374

Woods, Vanessa
S–Adult: 8396

Woodstock festival (1969)
JS: 8512
S–Adult: 8500

Woodwork and woodworking
JS: 12174, 12176

Woodworking
JS: 12173

Woolf, Virginia
JS: 7445, 7447
S: 7446

Words
S: 7086

Wordsworth, William
J: 6642

Workers and laboring classes
S: 10326, 10422

Working mothers
JS: 11158

Workshops
S: 12140

World Cup
JS: 12427

World history
J: 8682
JS: 8664, 8770, 8785, 11886
S: 8616, 8620, 8671, 8677, 8792
S–Adult: 8674, 8689, 8700

World records
S–Adult: 12212

World Trade Center
JS: 10276, 10286

World War I
J: 8797, 8799
JS: 8800, 9423
S: 8795–96, 8798, 8802–03
S–Adult: 8801

World War I — Fiction
J: 4456, 4461
JS: 4115, 4452–53, 4457–58–59–60,
4462
S: 173, 4454, 5638, 6207
S–Adult: 4455

JS = Junior High/Senior High; S = Senior High; S–Adult = Senior High/Adult

World War I — Poetry
JS: 6586

World War II
See also Holocaust
J: 8807, 8831–32, 8868–69, 8873,
8880, 9247, 9452, 9954
JS: 8381, 8786, 8804–05, 8808–09–10,
8814, 8818–19, 8821, 8826, 8836–
37–38–39–40, 8847, 8852–53–54,
8856–57, 8865, 8867, 8874, 8878–79,
8881–82–83, 8885, 8887, 9209,
9445–46, 9448, 9450–51, 9453,
11959, 11993
S: 4480, 8122, 8366, 8812, 8815,
8822–23–24–25, 8830, 8834, 8841,
8844, 8846, 8849, 8855, 8860–61,
8866, 8870–71, 8875–76–77, 8884,
8886, 8888, 9205, 9447
S–Adult: 4041, 8889, 9449

World War II — Biography
J: 7750, 8137, 8335
JS: 7738–39, 7749, 7786, 8131, 8182,
8185, 8228, 8237, 8250, 8297, 8813
S: 8110, 8113, 8273–74, 8872
S–Adult: 8222

World War II — Fiction
J: 1861, 3391–92–93, 3883, 4088,
4418, 4469, 4478–79, 4497, 4501,
4510–11–12, 4515, 4517–18, 4522,
4525, 4531–32
JS: 149, 152, 1585, 1812, 2261, 3429,
3444, 3873, 4381, 4463–67, 4471,
4473–76, 4481, 4487, 4503, 4505–08,
4514, 4519, 4523, 4526, 4533–34,
4536, 4538–39, 4545, 4547, 5702, 6360
S: 4393, 4483, 4486, 4494, 4496,
4498–99–00, 4502, 4504, 4520, 4524,
4527, 4529, 4535, 4543–44
S–Adult: 3143, 3383, 4490, 4492,
4509, 4537, 5803, 5806, 6244

World War II Memorial
JS: 9444

World Wide Web
J: 11921–22, 11938
JS: 11935
S: 11915

World's Fairs
JS: 9239, 9239

Wrestling
JS: 12333, 12335–36

Wrestling — Biography
JS: 8019–20, 8262
S: 12334

Wrestling — Fiction
J: 1258, 3508
JS: 6292

Wright, Frank Lloyd
JS: 7299–00

Wright, Richard
J: 7448
JS: 7449–50

Wright, Wilbur and Orville
JS: 7916–17

S: 11958

Writers — Biography
JS: 7412

Writing
J: 7088, 7090, 7099, 7128, 10359,
10366, 10375, 10386
JS: 6371, 6397, 7096–97, 7100–01,
7110, 7119, 7230, 10357, 10360,
10363, 10369, 10373–74, 10376–77,
10380, 10382–83–84, 10389
S: 6867, 7083, 7103, 7109, 7109, 7112,
7117, 7384, 10358, 10370
S–Adult: 7092

Writing — Careers
JS: 7091, 7110, 10363, 10474, 10483
S: 10470

Writing — Fiction
J: 4988
JS: 824
S: 2178

Writing — Poetry
JS: 10390

Wyeth, Andrew
S: 7301

Wyoming — Fiction
J: 4306
JS: 974, 4312
S–Adult: 5665

Y

Yachting — Biography
S–Adult: 8162

Yana Indians — Fiction
JS: 5404

Yeats, William Butler
J: 6642
JS: 7451

Yellow fever
JS: 9316, 10759

Yellow fever — Fiction
J: 4216

Yellowstone National Park
JS: 9537, 11511, 11560
S: 11488

Yemen
S: 9136

Yemen — Biography
S–Adult: 8169

Yemeni Americans
S: 10307

Yep, Laurence — Criticism
JS: 6983

Yeti
JS: 12226

Yetis — Fiction
JS: 46

Yoast, Bill
JS: 7999

Yoga
J: 12233, 12262
JS: 10869–70, 12251

Yorkshire
JS: 7315

Yosemite National Park
JS: 9529

**Young adult literature —
Biography**
JS: 7332, 7415

**Young adult literature —
Criticism**
JS: 6974–75, 6978, 7361, 7383, 7452

**Young adult literature —
History and criticism**
JS: 7000, 7003, 7007

Young, Charles
S: 7800

Yu, Chun
J: 8397

Yugoslavia — Fiction
JS: 4112

Yukon
JS: 7175

Z

Zaharias, Babe Didrikson
JS: 8031–32–33

Zailckas, Koren
S–Adult: 8398

Zaire
J: 8944, 8947
JS: 8929, 8945

Zambia
JS: 8971

Zamora, Pedro
JS: 3747

Zenatti, Valérie
JS: 8399

Zenger, John Peter
J: 9731

Zero tolerance policies
JS: 10340
S: 10335

Zimbabwe
S: 8362, 8941

Zimbabwe — Biography
S: 8271

Zimbabwe — Fiction
J: 5976
JS: 3859, 3869
S–Adult: 3860

JS = Junior High/Senior High; S = Senior High; S–Adult = Senior High/Adult

About the Author

CATHERINE BARR is the coauthor of other volumes in the Best Books series (*Best Books for Children* and *Best Books for High School Readers*) and of *Popular Series Fiction for K–6 Readers, Popular Series Fiction for Middle School and Teen Readers,* and *High/Low Handbook: Best Books and Web Sites for Reluctant Teen Readers*, 4th Edition.